Neu

Preiswert

Zuverlässig

Dieses neue Taschenbuch ist ein ganz außergewöhnliches Wörterbuch. Sein Inhalt basiert auf den zweisprachigen Wörterbüchern des Verlages Langenscheidt — des bedeutendsten Verlages auf diesem Gebiet. Es enthält über 40 000 Stichwörter, gibt die Aussprache in beiden Teilen in Internationaler Lautschrift und besitzt besondere Anhänge für Eigennamen, Abkürzungen und Maße und Gewichte.

Neu und einzigartig ist die Fülle der grammatischen Informationen: Mehr als 15 000 deutsche Substantive und Verben haben Angaben zur Deklination und Konjugation. Über die unregelmäßigen Verben in beiden Sprachen gibt der Hauptteil und der Anhang zuverlässig Auskunft.

Dieses Wörterbuch ist somit ein modernes und handliches Nachschlagewerk für jeden, der in seinem Beruf, beim Lernen oder Lehren mit der englischen und deutschen Sprache zu tun hat.

LANGENSCHEIDTS

DEUTSCH-ENGLISCHES
ENGLISCH-DEUTSCHES

WÖRTERBUCH

Beide Teile in einem Band

Bearbeitet und herausgegeben

von der

LANGENSCHEIDT-REDAKTION

PUBLISHED BY POCKET BOOKS NEW YORK

LANGENSCHEIDT'S
GERMAN-ENGLISH
ENGLISH-GERMAN
DICTIONARY

Two Volumes in One

Edited by
THE LANGENSCHEIDT
EDITORIAL STAFF

PUBLISHED BY POCKET BOOKS NEW YORK

POCKET BOOKS, a Simon & Schuster division of GULF & WESTERN CORPORATION
1230 Avenue of the Americas, New York, N.Y. 10020

This Pocket Books edition may not be sold in Germany, Switzerland or Austria.

Copyright 1952, © 1969, 1970 by Langenscheidt KG, Berlin and Munich, Germany.

Published by arrangement with Langenscheidt KG, Publishers, Berlin and Munich, Germany

ISBN: 0-671-83568-8

First Pocket Books printing March, 1953

25   24   23   22   21   20

POCKET and colophon are trademarks of Simon & Schuster.

Printed in the U.S.A.

Preface

For over 100 years Langenscheidt's bilingual dictionaries have been an essential tool of the language student. For several decades Langenscheidt's German-English dictionaries have been used in all walks of life as well as in schools.

However, languages are in a constant process of change. To bring you abreast of these changes Langenscheidt has compiled this entirely new dictionary. Many new words which have entered the German and English languages in the last few years have been included in the vocabulary: e.g., Mondfähre, Mehrwertsteuer, Einwegflasche, Antirakete; lunar probe, heart transplant, non-violence.

Langenscheidt's German-English Dictionary contains another new and long desired feature for the English-speaking user: it provides clear answers to questions of declension and conjugation in over 15,000 German noun and verb entries (see pp. 7 to 8).

The phonetic transcription of the German and English headwords follows the principles laid down by the International Phonetic Association (IPA).

In addition to the vocabulary this Dictionary contains special quick-reference sections of proper names — up-to-date with names like Wankel, Mössbauer, Henze —, abbreviations and weights and measures.

Designed for the widest possible variety of uses, this Dictionary, with its more than 40,000 entries in all, will be of great value to students, teachers, and tourists as well as in home and office libraries.

Contents

Arrangement of the Dictionary and Guide for the User

1. Arrangement. Strict alphabetical order has been maintained throughout this Dictionary. The irregular plural forms of English nouns as well as the principal parts (infinitive, preterite, and past participle) of the irregular English and German verbs have also been given in their proper alphabetical order; e.g. *man - men; bite - bit - bitten; beißen - biß - gebissen.*

2. Pronunciation. Pronunciation is given in square brackets by means of the symbols of the International Phonetic Association. No transcription of compounds is given if the parts appear as separate headwords. The German suffixes as given on page 12 are not transcribed unless they are parts of catchwords.

3. Explanatory additions have been printed in italics; e.g. *abstract Inhalt kurz zs.-fassen; Abbau pulling down (of structure); abbauen pull down (structure); durchsichtig glass, etc.*: transparent.

4. Subject Labels. The field of knowledge from which a headword or some of its meanings are taken is, where possible, indicated by figurative or abbreviated labels or by other labels written out in full. A figurative or abbreviated label placed immediately after a headword applies to all translations. Any label preceding an individual translation refers to this only. In Part I, any abbreviated label with a colon applies to all following translations. An F placed before a German illustrative phrase or its English equivalent indicates that the phrase in question is colloquial usage. An F: placed before a German phrase applies to that phrase and its translation(s). Figurative labels have always, other labels sometimes, been placed between illustrative phrases and their translations.

5. Translations of similar meanings have been subdivided by **commas,** the various senses by **semicolons.**

6. American spelling has been given in the following ways: *theat|re, Am. -er, defen|ce, Am. -se; council(l)or, hono(u)r, judg(e)ment; plough, Am. plow.*

7. Grammatical References in Part I. Parts of speech (adjective, verb, etc.) have been indicated throughout. Entries have been subdivided by Arabic numerals to distinguish the various parts of speech.

I. Nouns. The inflectional forms (*genitive singular / nominative plural*) follow immediately after the indication of gender. No forms are given for compounds if the parts appear as separate headwords.

The horizontal stroke replaces that part of the word which remains unchanged in the inflexion: *Affe m (-n/-n); Affäre f (-/-n).*

The sign ⁼ indicates that an Umlaut appears in the inflected form in question: *Blatt n (-[e]s/⁼er).*

II. Verbs. Verbs have been treated in the following ways:

a) *bändigen v/t. (ge-, h):* The past participle of this verb is formed by means of the prefix ge- and the auxiliary verb *haben: er hat gebändigt.*

b) *abfassen v/t. (sep., -ge-, h):* In conjugation the prefix *ab* must be separated from the primary verb *fassen: er faßt ab; er hat abgefaßt.*

c) *verderben v/i. (irr., no -ge-, sein):* irr. following the verb refers the reader to the list of irregular German verbs in the appendix (p. 573) for the principal parts of this particular verb: *es verdarb; es ist verdorben.*

d) *abfallen v/i. (irr. fallen, sep., -ge-, sein):* A reference such as *irr. fallen* indicates that the compound verb *abfallen* is conjugated exactly like the primary verb *fallen* as given in the list of irregular verbs: *er fiel ab; er ist abgefallen.*

e) *sieden v/t. and v/i. ([irr.,] ge-, h):* The square brackets indicate that *sieden* can be treated as a regular or irregular verb: *er siedete or sott; er hat gesiedet or er hat gesotten.*

III. Prepositions. Prepositions governing a headword are given in both languages. The grammatical construction following a German preposition is indicated only if the preposition governs two different cases. If a German preposition applies to all translations it is given only with the first whereas its English equivalents are given after each translation: *schützen* ... protect (*gegen*, *vor dat*. against, from), defend (against, from), guard (against, from); shelter (from).

IV. Subdivision. Entries have been subdivided by Arabic numerals
  a) to distinguish the various parts of speech: *laut* 1. *adj*. ...; 2. *adv*. ...; 3. *prp*. ...; 4. ⌔ *m* ...;
  b) to distinguish between the transitive and intransitive meanings of a verb if these differ in their translations;
  c) to show that in case of change of meaning a noun or verb may be differently inflected or conjugated: *Bau m* 1. (-[e]s/*no pl*.) ...; 2. (-[e]s/-*ten* ...; 3. (-[e]s/-*e*) ...; *schwimmen v/i.* (*irr.*, ge-) 1. (sein) ...; 2. (h) ...

If grammatical indications come

before the subdivision they refer to all translations following: *Alte* (-*n*/-*n*) 1. *m* ...; 2. *f* ...; *humpeln v/i.* (ge-) 1. (sein) ...; 2. (h) ...

8. Grammatical References in Part II. Parts of speech (adjective, verb, etc.) have been indicated only in cases of doubt. Entries have been subdivided by Arabic numerals to distinguish the various parts of speech.

  a) (⌔*ally*) after an English adjective means that the adverb is formed by affixing ...ally: *automatic* (⌔*ally*) = *automatically*.

  b) *irr.* following a verb refers the reader to the list of irregular English verbs in the appendix (p. 575) for the principal parts of this particular verb. A reference such as *irr. fall* indicates that the compound verb, e.g. *befall*, is conjugated exactly like the primary verb *fall*.

Symbols and Abbreviations Used in This Dictionary

1. Symbols

The swung dash or tilde (~ ⌔, ~ ⌔) serves as a mark of repetition within an entry. The tilde in bold type (⌔) represents either the complete word at the beginning of the entry or the unchanged part of that word which is followed by a vertical line (|). The simple tilde (~) represents: a) the headword immediately preceding, which itself may contain a tilde in bold type; b) in phonetic transcrip-

tion, any part of the preceding transcription that remains unchanged.

When the initial letter changes from small to capital or vice versa, the usual tilde is replaced by ⌔ or ⌔.

Examples: *abandon* [ə'bændən], ⌔*ment* [⌔nmənt = ə'bændənmənt]; *certi|ficate*, ⌔*fication*, ⌔*fy*, ⌔*tude*. *Drama*, ⌔*tiker*, ⌔*tisch*; *Haus|flur*; ⌔*frau*; *fassen: sich kurz* ⌔.

□ after an English adjective means that an adverb may be formed regularly from it by adding ...ly, or by changing ...*le* into ...*ly*, or ...*y* into ...*ily*; e.g.: *rich* □ = *richly*; *acceptable* □ = *acceptably*; *happy* □ = *happily*.

F *familiar*, familiär; *colloquial usage*, Umgangssprache.

P *low colloquialism*, populär, Sprache des Volkes.

V *vulgar*, vulgär.

† *archaic*, veraltet.

⚹ *rare, little used*, selten.

⫛ *scientific term*, wissenschaftlich.

⚘ *botany*, Botanik.

⊕ *engineering*, Technik; *handicraft*, Handwerk.

⚒ *mining*, Bergbau.

⚔ *military term*, militärisch.

⚓ *nautical term*, Schiffahrt.

† *commercial term*, Handelswesen.

⛭ *railway, railroad*, Eisenbahn.

✈ *aviation*, Flugwesen.

✉ *postal affairs*, Postwesen.

♪ *musical term*, Musik.
△ *architecture*, Architektur.
⚡ *electrical engineering*, Elektrotechnik.
⚖ *legal term*, Rechtswissenschaft.

⅄ *mathematics*, Mathematik.
↗ *farming*, Landwirtschaft.
♎ *chemistry*, Chemie.
⚕ *medicine*, Medizin.

2. Abbreviations

a. *also*, auch.
abbr. *abbreviation*, Abkürzung.
acc. *accusative (case)*, Akkusativ.
adj. *adjective*, Adjektiv.
adv. *adverb*, Adverb.
allg. *commonly*, allgemein.
Am. *American English*, amerikanisches Englisch.
anat. *anatomy*, Anatomie.
appr. *approximately*, etwa.
art. *article*, Artikel.
ast. *astronomy*, Astronomie.
attr. *attributively*, attributiv.

biol. *biology*, Biologie.
Brt. *British English*, britisches Englisch.
b.s. *bad sense*, in schlechtem Sinne.
bsd. *especially*, besonders.

cj. *conjunction*, Konjunktion.
co. *comic(al)*, scherzhaft.
coll. *collectively*, als Sammelwort.
comp. *comparative*, Komparativ.
contp. *contemptuously*, verächtlich.

dat. *dative (case)*, Dativ.
dem. *demonstrative*, Demonstrativ...

ea. *one another, each other*, einander.
eccl. *ecclesiastical*, kirchlich.
e-e, e-e, e-e a(n), eine.
e-m, e-m, e-m to a(n), einem.
e-n, e-n, e-n a(n), einen.
engS. *more strictly taken*, in engerem Sinne.
e-r, e-r, e-r of a(n), to a(n), einer.
e-s, e-s, e-s of a(n), eines.
esp. *especially*, besonders.
et., et., et. *something*, etwas.
etc. *et cetera, and so on*, und so weiter.

f *feminine*, weiblich.
fig. *figuratively*, bildlich.
frz. *French*, französisch.

gen. *genitive (case)*, Genitiv.
geogr. *geography*, Geographie.
geol. *geology*, Geologie.
geom. *geometry*, Geometrie.
ger. *gerund*, Gerundium.
Ggs. *antonym*, Gegensatz.
gr. *grammar*, Grammatik.

h *have*, haben.
hist. *history*, Geschichte.
hunt. *hunting*, Jagdwesen.

ichth. *ichthyology*, Ichthyologie.
impers. *impersonal*, unpersönlich.
indef. *indefinite*, Indefinit...
inf. *infinitive (mood)*, Infinitiv.
int. *interjection*, Interjektion.
interr. *interrogative*, Interrogativ...
iro. *ironically*, ironisch.
irr. *irregular*, unregelmäßig.

j., j., j. *someone*, jemand.
j-m, j-m, j-m to s.o. jemandem.
j-n, j-n, j-n someone, jemanden.
j-s, j-s, j-s, someone's, jemandes.

konkr. *concretely*, konkret.

ling. *linguistics*, Linguistik.
lit. *literary*, nur in der Schriftsprache vorkommend.

m *masculine*, männlich.
m-e, m-e, m-e my, meine.
m-r *of my, to my*, meiner.
metall. *metallurgy*, Metallurgie.
meteor. *meteorology*, Meteorologie.
min. *mineralogy*, Mineralogie.
mot. *motoring*, Kraftfahrwesen.
mount. *mountaineering*, Bergsteigerei.
mst *mostly, usually*, meistens.
myth. *mythology*, Mythologie.

n *neuter*, sächlich.
nom. *nominative (case)*, Nominativ.
npr. *proper name*, Eigenname.

od. *or*, oder.
opt. *optics*, Optik.

orn.	*ornithology*, Ornithologie.
o.s.	*oneself*, sich.
P.,	*person*, Person.
p.	*person*, Person.
paint.	*painting*, Malerei.
parl.	*parliamentary term*, parlamentarischer Ausdruck.
pass.	*passive voice*, Passiv.
pers.	*personal*, Personal...
pharm.	*pharmacy*, Pharmazie.
phls.	*philosophy*, Philosophie.
phot.	*photography*, Photographie.
phys.	*physics*, Physik.
physiol.	*physiology*, Physiologie.
pl.	*plural*, Plural.
poet.	*poetry*, Dichtung.
pol.	*politics*, Politik.
poss.	*possessive*, Possessiv...
p.p.	*past participle*, Partizip Perfekt.
p.pr.	*present participle*, Partizip Präsens.
pred.	*predicative*, prädikativ.
pres.	*present*, Präsens.
pret.	*preterit(e)*, Präteritum.
pron.	*pronoun*, Pronomen.
prov.	*provincialism*, Provinzialismus.
prp.	*preposition*, Präposition.
psych.	*psychology*, Psychologie.
refl.	*reflexive*, reflexiv.
rel.	*relative*, Relativ...
rhet.	*rhetoric*, Rhetorik.
S., S.	*thing*, Sache.
s.	*see*, *refer to*, siehe.
schott.	*Scotch*, schottisch.
s-e, s-e,	*s-e his*, *one's*, seine.
sep.	*separable*, abtrennbar.
sg.	*singular*, Singular.

sl.	*slang*, Slang.
s-m, s-m, s-m	*to his, to his, to one's*, seinem.
s-n, s-n, s-n	*his, one's*, seinen.
s.o., s.o., s.o.	*someone*, jemand(en).
s-r, s-r, s-r	*of his, of one's, to his, to one's*, seiner.
s-s, s-s, s-s	*of his, of one's*, seines.
s.th., s.th., s.th.	*something*, etwas.
subj.	*subjunctive (mood)*, Konjunktiv.
sup.	*superlative*, Superlativ.
surv.	*surveying*, Landvermessung.
tel.	*telegraphy*, Telegraphie.
teleph.	*telephony*, Fernsprechwesen.
thea.	*theat|re, Am. -er*, Theater.
typ.	*typography*, Typographie.
u., u.	*and*, und.
univ.	*university*, Hochschulwesen, Studentensprache.
v/aux.	*auxiliary verb*, Hilfsverb.
vb.	*verb*, Verb.
vet.	*veterinary medicine*, Veterinärmedizin.
vgl.	*confer*, vergleiche.
v/i.	*verb intransitive*, intransitives Verb.
v/refl.	*verb reflexive*, reflexives Verb.
v/t.	*verb transitive*, transitives Verb.
weitS.	*more widely taken*, in weiterem Sinne.
z.B.	*for example*, zum Beispiel.
zo.	*zoology*, Zoologie.
zs.	*together*, zusammen.
Zssg(n).	*compound word(s)*, Zusammensetzung(en).

Guide to Pronunciation
for the German-English Part

The length of vowels is indicated by [ː] following the vowel symbol, the stress by [ˈ] preceding the stressed syllable. The glottal stop [ˀ] is the forced stop between one word or syllable and a following one beginning with a vowel, as in *unentbehrlich* [unˀɛntˈbeːrlɪç].

A. Vowels

[a] as in French *carte*: *Mann* [man].

[aː] as in *father*: *Wagen* [ˈvaːgən].

[e] as in *bed*: *Edikt* [eˈdɪkt].

[eː] resembles the sound in *day*: *Weg* [veːk].

[ə] unstressed e as in *ago*: *Bitte* [ˈbitə].

[ɛ] as in *fair*: *männlich* [ˈmɛnlɪç], *Geld* [gɛlt].

[ɛː] same sound but long: *zählen* [ˈtsɛːlən].

[i] as in *it*: *Wind* [vɪnt].

[iː] as in *meet*: *hier* [hiːr].

[ɔ] as in *long*: *Ort* [ɔrt].

[ɔː] same sound but long as in *draw*: *Komfort* [kɔmˈfɔːr].

[o] as in *molest*: *Moral* [moˈraːl].

[oː] resembles the English sound in *go* [gou] but without the [u]: *Boot* [boːt].

[øː] as in French *feu*. The sound may be acquired by saying [e] through closely rounded lips: *schön* [ʃøːn].

[ø] same sound but short: *Ökonomie* [økonoˈmiː].

[œ] as in French *neuf*. The sound resembles the English vowel in *her*. Lips, however, must be well rounded as for [ɔ]: *öffnen* [ˈœfnən].

[u] as in *book*: *Mutter* [ˈmutər].

[uː] as in *boot*: *Uhr* [uːr].

[y] almost like the French u as in *sur*. It may be acquired by saying [i] through fairly closely rounded lips: *Glück* [glyk].

[yː] same sound but long: *führen* [ˈfyːrən].

B. Diphthongs

[aɪ] as in *like*: *Mai* [maɪ].
[au] as in *mouse*: *Maus* [maus].

[ɔʏ] as in *boy*: *Beute* [ˈbɔʏtə], *Läufer* [ˈlɔʏfər].

C. Consonants

[b] as in *better*: *besser* [ˈbɛsər].

[d] as in *dance*: *du* [duː].

[f] as in *find*: *finden* [ˈfɪndən], *Vater* [ˈfaːtər], *Philosoph* [filoˈzoːf].

[g] as in *gold*: *Gold* [gɔlt], *Geld* [gɛlt].

[ʒ] as in *measure*: *Genie* [ʒeˈniː], *Journalist* [ʒurnaˈlɪst].

[h] as in *house* but not aspirated: *Haus* [haus].

[ç] an approximation to this sound may be acquired by assuming the mouth-configuration for [i] and emitting a strong current of breath: *Licht* [lɪçt], *Mönch* [mœnç], *lustig* [ˈlustɪç].

[x] as in Scotch *loch*. Whereas [ç] is pronounced at the front of the mouth, [x] is pronounced in the throat: *Loch* [lɔx].

[j] as in *year*: *ja* [jaː].

[k] as in *kick*: *keck* [kɛk], *Tag* [taːk], *Chronist* [kroˈnɪst], *Café* [kaˈfeː].

[l] as in *lump*. Pronounced like English initial "clear l": *lassen* [ˈlasən].

[m] as in *mouse*: *Maus* [maus].

[n] as in *not*: *nein* [naɪn].

[ŋ] as in *sing*, *drink*: *singen* [ˈzɪŋən], *trinken* [ˈtrɪŋkən].

[p] as in *pass*: *Paß* [pas], *Weib* [vaɪp], *obgleich* [ɔpˈglaɪç].

[r] as in *rot*. There are two pronunciations: the frontal or lingual r and the uvular r (the latter unknown in England): *rot* [ro:t].

[s] as in *miss*. Unvoiced when final, doubled, or next a voiceless consonant: *Glas* [glɑːs], *Masse* ['masə], *Mast* [mast], *naß* [nas].

[z] as in *zero*. S voiced when initial in a word or syllable: *Sohn* [zo:n], *Rose* ['ro:zə].

[ʃ] as in *ship*: *Schiff* [ʃif], *Charme* [ʃarm], *Spiel* [ʃpiːl], *Stein* [ʃtain].

[t] as in *tea*: *Tee* [te:], *Thron* [tro:n], *Stadt* [ʃtat], *Bad* [bɑːt], *Findling* ['fintliŋ], *Wind* [vint].

[v] as in *vast*: *Vase* ['vɑːzə], *Winter* ['vintər].

[ă, ĕ, ŏ] are nasalized vowels. Examples: *Ensemble* [ă'să:bəl], *Terrain* [tɛ'rɛ̃:], *Bonbon* [bŏ'bŏ:].

List of Suffixes

often given without phonetic transcription

-bar	[-bɑːr]		-ist	[-ist]
-chen	[-çən]		-keit	[-kait]
-d	[-t]		-lich	[-liç]
-de	[-də]		-ling	[-liŋ]
-ei	[-ai]		-losigkeit	[-lo:ziçkait]
-en	[-ən]		-nis	[-nis]
-end	[-ənt]		-sal	[-zɑːl]
-er	[-ər]		-sam	[-zɑːm]
-haft	[-haft]		-schaft	[-ʃaft]
-heit	[-hait]		-sieren	[-zi:rən]
-ie	[-iː]		-ste	[-stə]
-ieren	[-iːrən]		-tät	[-tɛːt]
-ig	[-iç]		-tum	[-tuːm]
-ik	[-ik]		-ung	[-uŋ]
-in	[-in]		-ungs-	[-uŋs-]
-isch	[-iʃ]			

Erläuterung der phonetischen Umschrift im englisch-deutschen Teil

A. Vokale und Diphthonge

[ɑ:] reines langes a, wie in Vater, kam, Schwan: *far* [fɑ:], *father* ['fɑ:ðə].

[ʌ] kommt im Deutschen nicht vor. Kurzes dunkles a, bei dem die Lippen nicht gerundet sind. Vorn und offen gebildet: *butter* ['bʌtə], *come* [kʌm], *colour* ['kʌlə], *blood* [blʌd], *flourish* ['flʌriʃ], *twopence* ['tʌpəns].

[æ] heller, ziemlich offener, nicht zu kurzer Laut. Raum zwischen Zunge und Gaumen noch größer als bei ä in Ähre: *fat* [fæt], *man* [mæn].

[ɛə] nicht zu offenes halblanges ä; im Englischen also vor r, das als ein dem ä nachhallendes ə erscheint: *bare* [bɛə], *pair* [pɛə], *there* [ðɛə].

[ai] Bestandteile: helles, zwischen ɑ und æ liegendes a und schwächeres offenes i. Die Zunge hebt sich halbwegs zur i-Stellung: *I* [ai], *lie* [lai], *dry* [drai].

[au] Bestandteile: helles, zwischen ɑ und æ liegendes a und schwächeres offenes u: *house* [haus], *now* [nau].

[ei] halboffenes e, nach i auslautend, indem die Zunge sich halbwegs zur i-Stellung hebt: *date* [deit], *play* [plei], *obey* [ə'bei].

[e] halboffenes kurzes e, etwas geschlossener als das e in Bett: *bed* [bed], *less* [les].

[ə] flüchtiger Gleitlaut, ähnlich dem deutschen flüchtig gesprochenen e in Gelage: *about* [ə'baut], *butter* ['bʌtə], *nation* ['neiʃən], *connect* [kə'nekt].

[i:] langes i wie in lieb, Bibel, aber etwas offener einsetzend als im Deutschen; wird in Südengland doppellautig gesprochen, indem sich die Zunge allmählich zur i-Stellung hebt: *scene* [si:n], *sea* [si:], *feet* [fi:t], *ceiling* ['si:liŋ].

[i] kurzes offenes i wie in bin, mit: *big* [big], *city* ['siti].

[iə] halblanges i mit nachhallendem ə: *here* [hiə], *hear* [hiə], *inferior* [in'fiəriə].

[ou] halboffenes langes o, in schwaches u auslautend; leichte Rundung der Lippen, kein Heben der Zunge: *note* [nout], *boat* [bout], *below* [bi'lou].

[ɔ:] offener langer, zwischen a und o schwebender Laut: *fall* [fɔ:l], *nought* [nɔ:t], *or* [ɔ:], *before* [bi'fɔ:].

[ɔ] offener kurzer, zwischen a und o schwebender Laut, offener als das o in Motto: *god* [gɔd], *not* [nɔt], *wash* [wɔʃ], *hobby* ['hɔbi].

[ə:] im Deutschen fehlender Laut; offenes langes ö, etwa wie gedehnt gesprochenes ö in öffnen, Mörder; kein Vorstülpen oder Runden der Lippen, kein Heben der Zunge: *word* [wə:d], *girl* [gə:l], *learn* [lə:n], *murmur* ['mə:mə].

[ɔi] Bestandteile: offenes o und schwächeres offenes i. Die Zunge hebt sich halbwegs zur i-Stellung: *voice* [vɔis], *boy* [bɔi], *annoy* [ə'nɔi].

[u:] langes u wie in Buch, doch ohne Lippenrundung; vielfach diphthongisch als halboffenes langes u mit nachhallendem geschlossenen u: *fool* [fu:l], *shoe* [ʃu:], *you* [ju:], *rule* [ru:l], *canoe* [kə'nu:].

[uə] halboffenes halblanges u mit nachhallendem ə: *poor* [puə], *sure* [ʃuə], *allure* [ə'ljuə].

[u] flüchtiges u: *put* [put], *look* [luk], *full* [ful].

Die **Länge** eines Vokals wird durch [:] bezeichnet, z.B. *ask* [ɑ:sk], *astir* [ə'stə:].

Vereinzelt werden auch die folgenden französischen Nasallaute gebraucht: [ɑ̃] wie in frz. *blanc*, [ɔ̃] wie in frz. *bonbon* und [ɛ̃] wie in frz. *vin*.

B. Konsonanten

[r] nur vor Vokalen gesprochen. Völlig verschieden vom deutschen Zungenspitzen- oder Zäpfchen-r. Die Zungenspitze bildet mit der oberen Zahnwulst eine Enge, durch die der Ausatmungsstrom mit Stimmton hindurchgetrieben wird, ohne den Laut zu rollen. Am Ende eines Wortes wird r nur bei Bindung mit dem Anlautvokal des folgenden Wortes gesprochen: *rose* [rouz], *pride* [praid], *there is* [ðɛər'iz].

[ʒ] stimmhaftes sch, wie g in Genie, j in Journal: *azure* ['æʒə], *jazz* [dʒæz], *jeep* [dʒi:p], *large* [lɑ:dʒ].

[ʃ] stimmloses sch, wie im Deutschen Schnee, rasch: *shake* [ʃeik], *washing* ['wɔʃiŋ], *lash* [læʃ].

[θ] im Deutschen nicht vorhandener stimmloser Lispellaut; durch Anlegen der Zunge an die oberen Schneidezähne hervorgebracht: *thin* [θin], *path* [pɑ:θ], *method* ['meθəd].

[ð] derselbe Laut wie θ, nur stimmhaft, d.h. mit Stimmton: *there* [ðɛə], *breathe* [bri:ð], *father* ['fɑ:ðə].

[s] stimmloser Zischlaut, entsprechend dem deutschen ß in Spaß, reißen: *see* [si:], *hats* [hæts], *decide* [di'said].

[z] stimmhafter Zischlaut wie im Deutschen sausen: *zeal* [zi:l], *rise* [raiz], *horizon* [hə'raizn].

[ŋ] wird wie der deutsche Nasenlaut in fangen, singen gebildet: *ring* [riŋ], *singer* ['siŋə].

[ŋk] derselbe Laut mit nachfolgendem k wie im Deutschen senken, Wink: *ink* [iŋk], *tinker* ['tiŋkə].

[w] flüchtiges, mit Lippe an Lippe gesprochenes w, aus der Mundstellung für u: gebildet: *will* [wil], *swear* [swɛə], *queen* [kwi:n].

[f] stimmloser Lippenlaut wie im Deutschen flott, Pfeife: *fat* [fæt], *tough* [tʌf], *effort* ['efət].

[v] stimmhafter Lippenlaut wie im Deutschen Vase, Ventil: *vein* [vein], *velvet* ['velvit].

[j] flüchtiger zwischen j und i schwebender Laut: *onion* ['ʌnjən], *yes* [jes], *filial* ['filjəl].

Die Betonung der englischen Wörter wird durch das Zeichen ['] vor der zu betonenden Silbe angegeben, z.B. *onion* ['ʌnjən]. Sind zwei Silben eines Wortes mit Tonzeichen versehen, so sind beide gleichmäßig zu betonen, z.B. *unsound* ['ʌn'saund].

Um Raum zu sparen, werden die Endung -ed* und das Plural-s** der englischen Stichwörter hier im Vorwort einmal mit Lautschrift gegeben, erscheinen dann aber im Wörterverzeichnis ohne Lautschrift, sofern keine Ausnahmen vorliegen.

* [-d] nach Vokalen und stimmhaften Konsonanten; [-t] nach stimmlosen Konsonanten; [-id] nach auslautendem d und t.

** [-z] nach Vokalen und stimmhaften Konsonanten; [-s] nach stimmlosen Konsonanten.

Numerals

Cardinal Numbers

0 null *nought, zero, cipher*	51 einundfünfzig *fifty-one*
1 eins *one*	60 sechzig *sixty*
2 zwei *two*	61 einundsechzig *sixty-one*
3 drei *three*	70 siebzig *seventy*
4 vier *four*	71 einundsiebzig *seventy-one*
5 fünf *five*	80 achtzig *eighty*
6 sechs *six*	81 einundachtzig *eighty-one*
7 sieben *seven*	90 neunzig *ninety*
8 acht *eight*	91 einundneunzig *ninety-one*
9 neun *nine*	100 hundert *a* or *one hundred*
10 zehn *ten*	101 hundert(und)eins *a hundred and one*
11 elf *eleven*	200 zweihundert *two hundred*
12 zwölf *twelve*	300 dreihundert *three hundred*
13 dreizehn *thirteen*	572 fünfhundert(und)zweiund- siebzig *five hundred and seventy-two*
14 vierzehn *fourteen*	1000 tausend *a* or *one thousand*
15 fünfzehn *fifteen*	1972 neunzehnhundertzweiund- siebzig *nineteen hundred and seventy-two*
16 sechzehn *sixteen*	500 000 fünfhunderttausend *five hundred thousand*
17 siebzehn *seventeen*	1 000 000 eine Million *a* or *one million*
18 achtzehn *eighteen*	2 000 000 zwei Millionen *two million*
19 neunzehn *nineteen*	1 000 000 000 eine Milliarde *a* or *one milliard (Am. billion)*
20 zwanzig *twenty*	
21 einundzwanzig *twenty-one*	
22 zweiundzwanzig *twenty-two*	
23 dreiundzwanzig *twenty-three*	
30 dreißig *thirty*	
31 einunddreißig *thirty-one*	
40 vierzig *forty*	
41 einundvierzig *forty-one*	
50 fünfzig *fifty*	

Ordinal Numbers

1. erste *first (1st)*	16. sechzehnte *sixteenth*
2. zweite *second (2nd)*	17. siebzehnte *seventeenth*
3. dritte *third (3rd)*	18. achtzehnte *eighteenth*
4. vierte *fourth (4th)*	19. neunzehnte *nineteenth*
5. fünfte *fifth (5th), etc.*	20. zwanzigste *twentieth*
6. sechste *sixth*	21. einundzwanzigste *twenty-first*
7. siebente *seventh*	22. zweiundzwanzigste *twenty- second*
8. achte *eighth*	23. dreiundzwanzigste *twenty- third*
9. neunte *ninth*	30. dreißigste *thirtieth*
10. zehnte *tenth*	31. einunddreißigste *thirty-first*
11. elfte *eleventh*	40. vierzigste *fortieth*
12. zwölfte *twelfth*	41. einundvierzigste *forty-first*
13. dreizehnte *thirteenth*	50. fünfzigste *fiftieth*
14. vierzehnte *fourteenth*	
15. fünfzehnte *fifteenth*	

51. einundfünfzigste *fifty-first*	**300.** dreihundertste *three hundredth*
60. sechzigste *sixtieth*	**572.** fünfhundert(und)zweiund-
61. einundsechzigste *sixty-first*	siebzigste *five hundred and*
70. siebzigste *seventieth*	*seventy-second*
71. einundsiebzigste *seventy-first*	**1000.** tausendste *(one) thousandth*
80. achtzigste *eightieth*	**1970.** neunzehnhundert(und)sieb-
81. einundachtzigste *eighty-first*	zigste *nineteen hundred and*
90. neunzigste *ninetieth*	*seventieth*
100. hundertste *(one) hundredth*	**500000.** fünfhunderttausendste *five*
101. hundert(und)erste *(one) hundred*	*hundred thousandth*
and first	**1000000.** millionste *(one) millionth*
200. zweihundertste *two hundredth*	**2000000.** zweimillionste *two millionth*

Fractional Numbers and other Numerical Values

$^1/_2$ halb *one or a half*

$^1/_2$ eine halbe Meile *half a mile*

$1^1/_2$ anderthalb *or* eineinhalb *one and a half*

$2^1/_2$ zweieinhalb *two and a half*

$^1/_3$ ein Drittel *one or a third*

$^2/_3$ zwei Drittel *two thirds*

$^1/_4$ ein Viertel *one fourth, one or a quarter*

$^3/_4$ drei Viertel *three fourths, three quarters*

$1^1/_4$ ein und eine viertel Stunde *one hour and a quarter*

$^1/_5$ ein Fünftel *one or a fifth*

$3^4/_5$ drei vier Fünftel *three and four fifths*

0,4 null Komma vier *point four (.4)*

2,5 zwei Komma fünf *two point five (2.5)*

einfach *single*
  zweifach *double, twofold*
  dreifach *threefold, treble, triple*
  vierfach *fourfold, quadruple*
  fünffach *fivefold, quintuple*

einmal *once*
  zweimal *twice*
  drei-, vier-, fünfmal *three or four or five times*
  zweimal soviel(e) *twice as much or many*

erstens, zweitens, drittens *first(ly), secondly, thirdly; in the first or second or third place*

$2 \times 3 = 6$ zwei mal drei ist sechs, zwei multipliziert mit drei ist sechs *twice three are or make six, two multiplied by three are or make six*

$7 + 8 = 15$ sieben plus acht ist fünfzehn *seven plus eight are fifteen*

$10 - 3 = 7$ zehn minus drei ist sieben *ten minus three are seven*

$20 : 5 = 4$ zwanzig (dividiert) durch fünf ist vier *twenty divided by five make four*

PART I

GERMAN-ENGLISH
DICTIONARY

A

Aal *ichth.* [a:l] *m* (-[e]s/-e) eel; **'≗-glatt** *adj.* (as) slippery as an eel.

Aas [a:s] *n* **1.** (-es/≗-e) carrion, carcass; **2.** *fig.* (-es/Äser) beast; **'≗geier** *orn. m* vulture.

ab [ap] **1.** *prp.* (*dat.*): ~ *Brüssel* from Brussels onwards; ~ *Fabrik, Lager* etc. ♰ *ex* works, warehouse, etc.; **2.** *prp.* (*dat.*, ϝ *acc.*): ~ *erstem* or *ersten März* from March 1st, on and after March 1st; **3.** ♰ *prp.* (*gen.*) less; ~ *Unkosten* less charges; **4.** *adv. time*: *von jetzt* ~ from now on, in future; ~ *und zu* from time to time, now and then; *von da* ~ from that time forward; *space*: *thea.* exit, *pl.* exeunt; *von da* ~ from there (on).

abänder|n ['ap⁹-] *v/t.* (*sep.*, -ge-, h) alter, modify; *parl.* amend; **'≗ung** *f* alteration, modification; *parl.* amendment (*to bill*, etc.); **'≗ungs-antrag** *parl. m* amendment.

abarbeiten ['ap⁹-] *v/t.* (*sep.*, -ge-, h) work off (*debt*); *sich* ~ drudge, toil.

Abart ['ap⁹-] *f* variety.

'Abbau *m* **1.** (-[e]s/*no pl.*) pulling down, demolition (*of structure*); dismantling (*of machine*, etc.); dismissal, discharge (*of personnel*); reduction (*of staff, prices*, etc.); cut (*of prices*, etc.); **2.** ⚒ (-[e]s/-e) working, exploitation; **'≗en** *v/t.* (*sep.*, -ge-, h) pull or take down, demolish (*structure*); dismantle (*machine*, etc.); dismiss, discharge (*personnel*); reduce (*staff, prices*, etc.); cut (*prices*, etc.); ⚒ work, exploit.

'ab|beißen *v/t.* (*irr. beißen, sep.*, -ge-, h) bite off; **'≗bekommen** *v/t.* (*irr. kommen, sep.*, *no* -ge-, h) get off; *s-n Teil* or *et.* ~ get one's share; *et.* ~ be hurt, get hurt.

abberuf|en *v/t.* (*irr. rufen, sep.*, *no* -ge-, h) recall; **'≗ung** *f* recall.

'ab|bestellen *v/t.* (*sep.*, *no* -ge-, h) countermand, cancel one's order for (*goods*, etc.); cancel one's subscription to, discontinue (*newspaper*, etc.); **'≗biegen** *v/i.* (*irr. biegen, sep.*, -ge-, *sein*) *p.* turn off; *road*: turn off, bend; *nach rechts* (*links*) ~ turn right (left); *von e-r Straße* ~ turn off a road.

'Abbild *n* likeness; image; **≗en** ['≗dən] *v/t.* (*sep.*, -ge-, h) figure, represent; *sie ist auf der ersten Seite abgebildet* her picture is on the front page; **~ung** ['≗duŋ] *f* picture, illustration.

'abbinden *v/t.* (*irr. binden, sep.*,

-ge-, h) untie, unbind, remove; ✂ ligate, tie up.

'Abbitte *f* apology; ~ *leisten* or *tun* make one's apology (*bei j-m wegen et.* to s.o. for s.th.); **≗n** *v/t.* (*irr. bitten, sep.*, -ge-, h): *j-m et.* ~ apologize to s.o. for s.th.

'ab|blasen *v/t.* (*irr. blasen, sep.*, -ge-, h) blow off (*dust*, etc.); call off (*strike*, etc.), cancel; ⚔ break off (*attack*); **'≗blättern** *v/i.* (*sep.*, -ge-, *sein*) *paint*, etc.: scale, peel (off); ⚘ *skin*: desquamate; ⚘ shed the leaves; **'≗blenden** (*sep.*, -ge-, h) **1.** *v/t.* screen (*light*); *mot.* dim, dip (*headlights*); **2.** *v/i. mot.* dim or dip the headlights; *phot.* stop down; **'≗blitzen** ϝ *v/i.* (*sep.*, -ge-, *sein*) meet with a rebuff; ~ *lassen* snub; **'≗brausen** (*sep.*, -ge-) **1.** *v/refl.* (h) have a shower(-bath), douche; **2.** ϝ *v/i.* (*sein*) rush off; **'≗brechen** (*irr. brechen, sep.*, -ge-) **1.** *v/t.* (h) break off (*a. fig.*); pull down, demolish (*building*, etc.); strike (*tent*); *fig.* stop; *das Lager* ~ break up camp, strike tents; **2.** *v/i.* (*sein*) break off; **3.** *fig. v/i.* (h) stop; **'≗bremsen** *v/t.* and *v/i.* (*sep.*, -ge-, h) slow down; brake; **'≗brennen** (*irr. brennen, sep.*, -ge-) **1.** *v/t.* (h) burn down (*building*, etc.); let or set off (*firework*); **2.** *v/i.* (*sein*) burn away or down; *s. abgebrannt*; **'≗bringen** *v/t.* (*irr. bringen, sep.*, -ge-, h) get off; *j-n* ~ *von* argue s.o. out of; dissuade s.o. from; **'≗bröckeln** *v/i.* (*sep.*, -ge-, *sein*) crumble (*a.* ♰).

'Abbruch *m* pulling down, demolition (*of building*, etc.); rupture (*of relations*); breaking off (*of negotiations*, etc.); *fig.* damage, injury; *j-m* ~ *tun* damage s.o.

'ab|brühen *v/t.* (*sep.*, -ge-, h) scald; *s. abgebrüht*; **'≗bürsten** *v/t.* (*sep.*, -ge-, h) brush off (*dirt*, etc.); brush (*coat*, etc.); **'≗büßen** *v/t.* (*sep.*, -ge-, h) expiate, atone for (*sin*, etc.); serve (*sentence*).   [bet.]

Abc [a:be'tse:] *n* (-/-) ABC, alpha-

'abdank|en *v/i.* (*sep.*, -ge-, h) resign; *ruler*: abdicate; **'≗ung** *f* (-/-en) resignation, abdication.

'ab|decken *v/t.* (*sep.*, -ge-, h) uncover; untile (*roof*); unroof (*building*); clear (*table*); cover; **'≗dichten** *v/t.* (*sep.*, -ge-, h) make tight; seal up (*window*, etc.); ⊕ pack (*gland*, etc.); **'≗dienen** *v/t.* (*sep.*, -ge-, h): *s-e Zeit* ~ ⚔ serve one's time; **'≗drängen** *v/t.* (*sep.*, -ge-, h) push aside; **'≗drehen** (*sep.*, -ge-, h)

1. v/t. twist off (*wire*); turn off (*water*, *gas*, *etc.*); ✗ switch off (*light*); **2.** ⚓, ✗ v/i. change one's course; '**∼drosseln** mot. v/t. (*sep.*, *-ge-*, *h*) throttle.

'**Abdruck** *m* (*-[e]s/⸗e*) impression, print, mark; cast; '**Sen** v/t. (*sep.*, *-ge-*, *h*) print; publish (*article*).

'**abdrücken** (*sep.*, *-ge-*, *h*) **1.** v/t. fire (*gun, etc.*); F hug or squeeze affectionately; *sich* ∼ leave an impression or a mark; **2.** v/i. pull the trigger.

Abend ['a:bənt] *m* (*-s/-e*) evening; *am* ∼ in the evening, at night; *heute abend* tonight; *morgen* (*gestern*) *abend* tomorrow (last) night; *s.* *essen*; '**∼anzug** *m* evening dress; '**∼blatt** *n* evening paper; '**∼brot** *n* supper, dinner; '**∼dämmerung** *f* (evening) twilight, dusk; '**∼essen** *n* *s.* Abendbrot; '**∼gesellschaft** *f* evening party; '**∼kasse** *thea.* *f* box-office; '**∼kleid** *n* evening dress or gown; '**∼land** *n* (*-[e]s/no pl.*) *the* Occident; Sländisch *adj.* ['∼lendiʃ] western, occidental; '**∼mahl** *eccl. n* (*-[e]s/-e*) *the* (Holy) Communion, *the* Lord's Supper; '**∼rot** *n* evening or sunset glow. [evening.\]

abends *adv.* ['a:bənts] in the '**Abend|schule** *f* evening school, night-school; '**∼sonne** *f* setting sun; '**∼toilette** *f* evening dress; '**∼wind** *m* evening breeze; '**∼zeitung** *f* evening paper.

Abenteu|er ['a:bəntɔyər] *n* (*-s/-*) adventure; '**Serlich** *adj.* adventurous; *fig.*: strange; wild, fantastic; **∼rer** ['∼ɔyrər] *m* (*-s/-*) adventurer.

aber ['a:bər] **1.** *adv.* again; *Tausende und* ∼ *Tausende* thousands upon thousands; **2.** *cj.* but; *oder* ∼ otherwise, (or) else; **3.** *int.*: ∼! now then!; ∼, ∼! come, come!; ∼ *nein!* no!, on the contrary!; **4.** 2 *n* (*-s/-*) but.

'**Aber|glaube** *m* superstition; 2-**gläubisch** *adj.* ['∼ɡlɔybiʃ] superstitious.

aberkenn|en ['ap⁹-] v/t. (*irr. kennen*, *sep.*, *no -ge-*, *h*): *j-m et.* ∼ deprive s.o. of s.th. (*a.* ⚖); dispossess s.o. of s.th.; '2ung *f* (*-/-en*) deprivation (*a.* ⚖); dispossession.

aber|malig *adj.* ['a:bərma:liç] repeated; **∼mals** *adv.* ['∼s] again, once more.

ab|ernten ['ap⁹-] v/t. (*sep.*, *-ge-*, *h*) reap, harvest; **∼essen** ['ap⁹-] (*irr. essen*, *sep.*, *-ge-*, *h*) **1.** v/t. clear (*plate*); **2.** v/i. finish eating; '**∼fahren** (*irr. fahren*, *sep.*, *-ge-*) **1.** v/i. (*sein*) leave (*nach* for), depart (for), start (for); set out or off (for); **2.** v/t. (*h*) carry or cart away (*load*).

'**Abfahrt** *f* departure (*nach* for), start (for); setting out or off (for); *skiing*: downhill run; '**∼sbahnsteig**

m departure platform; '**∼slauf** *m* *skiing*: downhill race; '**∼ssignal** *n* starting-signal; '**∼szeit** *f* time of departure; ⚓ *a.* time of sailing.

'**Abfall** *m* defection (*von* from), falling away (from); *esp. pol.* secession (from); *eccl.* apostasy (from); *often* Abfälle *pl.* waste, refuse, rubbish, *Am. a.* garbage; ⊕ clippings *pl.*, shavings *pl.*; *at butcher's*: offal; '**∼eimer** *m* dust-bin, *Am.* ash can; '**Sen** v/i. (*irr. fallen*, *sep.*, *-ge-*, *sein*) *leaves, etc.*: fall (off); *ground, etc.*: slope (down); *fig.* fall away (*von* from); *esp. pol.* secede (from); *eccl.* apostatize (from); ∼ *gegen* come off badly by comparison with, be inferior to; '**∼erzeugnis** *n* waste product; by-product.

'**abfällig** *adj.* *judgement, etc.*: adverse, unfavo(u)rable; *remark*: disparaging, depreciatory.

'**Abfallprodukt** *n* by-product; waste product.

'**ab|fangen** v/t. (*irr. fangen*, *sep.*, *-ge-*, *h*) catch; snatch (*ball, etc.*); intercept (*letter, etc.*); ⚓, ✗ prop; ✗ check (*attack*); ✗ flatten out; *mot.*, ✗ right; '**∼färben** v/i. (*sep.*, *-ge-*, *h*): *der Pullover färbt ab* the colo(u)r of the pull-over runs (*auf acc.* on); ∼ *auf* (*acc.*) influence, affect.

'**abfass|en** v/t. (*sep.*, *-ge-*, *h*) compose, write, pen; catch (*thief, etc.*); '2ung *f* composition; wording.

'**ab|faulen** v/i. (*sep.*, *-ge-*, *sein*) rot off; '**∼fegen** v/t. (*sep.*, *-ge-*, *h*) sweep off; '**∼feilen** v/t. (*sep.*, *-ge-*, *h*) file off.

abfertig|en ['apfertiɡən] v/t. (*sep.*, *-ge-*, *h*) dispatch (*a.* ⚓); *customs*: clear; serve, attend to (*customer*); *j-n kurz* ∼ snub s.o.; '2ung *f* (*-/-en*) dispatch; *customs*: clearance; *schroffe* ∼ snub. [(off), discharge.\]

'**abfeuern** v/t. (*sep.*, *-ge-*, *h*) fire\

'**abfind|en** v/t. (*irr. finden*, *sep.*, *-ge-*, *h*) satisfy, pay off (*creditor*); compensate; *sich mit et.* ∼ resign o.s. to s.th.; put up with s.th.; '2ung *f* (*-/-en*) settlement; satisfaction; compensation; '2ung(ssumme) *f* indemnity, compensation.

'**ab|flachen** v/t. *and* v/refl. (*sep.*, *-ge-*, *h*) flatten; '**∼flauen** v/i. (*sep.*, *-ge-*, *sein*) *wind, etc.*: abate; *interest, etc.*: flag; ✝ *business*: slacken; '**∼fliegen** v/i. (*irr. fliegen*, *sep.*, *-ge-*, *sein*) leave by plane; ✗ take off, start; '**∼fließen** v/i. (*irr. fließen*, *sep.*, *-ge-*, *sein*) drain or flow off or away. [parture.\]

'**Abflug** ✗ *m* take-off, start, de-\

'**Abfluß** *m* flowing or draining off or away; discharge (*a.* ⚕); drain (*a. fig.*); sink; outlet (*of lake, etc.*).

'**abfordern** v/t. (*sep.*, *-ge-*, *h*): *j-m et.* ∼ demand s.th. of or from s.o.

Abfuhr ['apfuːr] *f* (-/-en) removal; *fig.* rebuff.

'abführ|en (*sep.*, -ge-, *h*) **1.** *v/t.* lead off *or* away; march (*prisoner*) off; pay over (*money*) (*an acc.* to); **2.** ✗ *v/i.* purge (the bowels), loosen the bowels; **~end** ✗ *adj.* purgative, aperient, laxative; **'~mittel** ✗ *n* purgative, aperient, laxative.

'abfüllen *v/t.* (*sep.*, -ge-, *h*) decant; *in Flaschen ~* bottle; *Bier in Fässer ~* rack casks with beer.

'Abgabe *f sports*: pass; casting (*of one's vote*); sale (*of shares, etc.*); *mst ~n pl.* taxes *pl.*; rates *pl.*, *Am.* local taxes *pl.*; duties *pl.*; **'~frei** *adj.* tax-free; duty-free; **'~npflichtig** *adj.* taxable; dutiable; liable to tax *or* duty.

'Abgang *m* departure; start; *thea.* exit (*a. fig.*); retirement (*from a job*); loss, wastage; deficiency (*in weight, etc.*); ✗ discharge; ✗ miscarriage; *nach ~ von der Schule* after leaving school.

'abgängig *adj.* missing.

'Abgangszeugnis *n* (school-)leaving certificate, *Am. a.* diploma.

'Abgas *n* waste gas; *esp. mot.* exhaust gas.   [toil-worn, worn-out.)

abgearbeitet *adj.* ['apgə'arbaitət])

abgeben *v/t.* (*irr. geben*, *sep.*, -ge-, *h*) leave (*bei, an dat.* at); hand in (*paper, etc.*); deposit, leave (*luggage*); cast (*one's vote*); *sports*: pass (*ball, etc.*); sell, dispose of (*goods*); give off (*heat, etc.*); *e-e Erklärung ~* make a statement; *s-e Meinung ~* express one's opinion (*über acc.* on); *j-m et. ~ von et.* give s.o. some of s.th.; *e-n guten Gelehrten ~* make a good scholar; *sich ~* mit occupy o.s. with s.th.; *sie gibt sich gern mit Kindern ab* she loves to be among children.

'abge|brannt *adj.* burnt down; F *fig.* hard up, *sl.* broke; **~brüht** *fig. adj.* ['~bryːt] hardened, callous; **'~droschen** *adj.* trite, hackneyed; **~feimt** *adj.* ['~faimt] cunning, crafty; **'~griffen** *adj.* worn; *book*: well-thumbed; **~härtet** *adj.* ['~hertet] hardened (*gegen* to), inured (to); **~härmt** *adj.* ['~hermt] careworn.

'abgehen (*irr. gehen*, *sep.*, -ge-) **1.** *v/i.* (*sein*) go off *or* away; leave, start, depart; *letter, etc.*: be dispatched; *post:* go; *thea.* make one's exit; *side-road:* branch off; *goods:* sell; *button, etc.*: come off; *stain, etc.*: come out; ✗ be discharged; (*von e-m Amt*) ~ give up a post; retire; *von der Schule ~* leave school; *~ von* digress from (*main subject*); deviate from (*rule*); alter, change (*one's opinion*); relinquish (*plan, etc.*); *diese Eigenschaft geht ihm ab* he lacks this quality; *gut ~* end well, pass off well; *hiervon geht or gehen*

... ab ✟ less, minus; **2.** *v/t.* (*h*) measure by steps; patrol.

abge|hetzt *adj.* ['apgəhetst] harassed; exhausted; run down; breathless; **~kartet** F *adj.* ['~kartət]: *~e Sache* prearranged affair, put-up job; **'~legen** *adj.* remote, distant; secluded; out-of-the-way; **~macht** *adj.* ['~maxt]: *~! it's a bargain or deal!;* **~magert** *adj.* ['~maːgərt] emaciated; **~neigt** *adj.* ['~naikt] disinclined (*dat.* for *s.th.;* *zu tun* to do), averse (*to;* *from doing*), unwilling (*zu tun* to do); **~nutzt** *adj.* ['~nutst] worn-out.

Abgeordnete ['apgə'ɔrdnətə] *m, f* (-n/-n) deputy, delegate; *in Germany:* member of the Bundestag *or* Landtag; *Brt.* Member of Parliament, *Am.* Representative.

'abgerissen *fig. adj.* ragged; shabby; *style, speech:* abrupt, broken.

'Abgesandte *m, f* (-n/-n) envoy; emissary; ambassador.

'abgeschieden *fig. adj.* isolated; secluded, retired; **'~heit** *f* (-/-en) seclusion; retirement.

'abgeschlossen *adj.* flat: self-contained; *training, etc.:* complete.

abgeschmackt *adj.* ['apgəʃmakt] tasteless; tactless; **'~heit** *f* (-/-en) tastelessness; tactlessness.

'abgesehen *adj.:* *~ von* apart from, *Am. a.* aside from.

abge|spannt *fig. adj.* ['apgəʃpant] exhausted, tired, run down; **'~standen** *adj.* stale, flat; **'~storben** *adj.* numb; dead; **~stumpft** *adj.* ['~ʃtumpft] blunt(ed); *fig.* indifferent (*gegen* to); **'~tragen** *adj.* worn-out; threadbare, shabby.

'abgewöhnen *v/t.* (*sep.*, -ge-, *h*): *j-m et. ~* break *or* cure s.o. of s.th.; *sich das Rauchen ~* give up smoking.

abgezehrt *adj.* ['apgətseːrt] emaciated, wasted.

'abgießen *v/t.* (*irr. gießen*, *sep.*, -ge-, *h*) pour off; ⚗ decant; ⊕ cast.

'Abglanz *m* reflection (*a. fig.*).

'abgleiten *v/i.* (*irr. gleiten*, *sep.*, -ge-, *sein*) slip off; slide off; glide)

'Abgott *m* idol.   [off.)

abgöttisch *adv.* ['apgœtiʃ]: *j-n ~ lieben* idolize *or* worship s.o.; dote (up)on s.o.

'ab|grasen *v/t.* (*sep.*, -ge-, *h*) graze; *fig.* scour; **'~grenzen** *v/t.* (*sep.*, -ge-, *h*) mark off, delimit; demarcate (*a. fig.*); *fig.* define.

'Abgrund *m* abyss; precipice; chasm, gulf; *am Rande des ~s* on the brink of disaster.

'Abguß *m* cast.

'ab|hacken *v/t.* (*sep.*, -ge-, *h*) chop *or* cut off; **'~haken** *fig. v/t.* (*sep.*, -ge-, *h*) tick *or* check off; **'~halten** *v/t.* (*irr. halten*, *sep.*, -ge-, *h*) hold (*meeting, examination, etc.*); keep out (*rain*); *j-n von der Arbeit ~* keep s.o. from his work; *j-n davon* ~ *et. zu tun* keep *or* restrain s.o. from doing s.th.; *et. von j-m* ~ keep s.th. away from s.o.; '**~handeln** *v/t.* (*sep.*, *-ge-*, *h*) discuss, treat; *j-m et.* ~ bargain s.th. out of s.o.

abhanden *adv.* ['ap'handən]: ~ *kommen* get lost.

'**Abhandlung** *f* treatise (*über acc.* [*up*]*on*), dissertation ([*up*]*on*, *concerning*); essay.

'**Abhang** *m* slope, incline; declivity.

'**abhängen** 1. *v/t.* (*sep.*, *-ge-*, *h*) take down (*picture*, *etc.*); 🙼 uncouple; 2. *v/i.* (*irr.* hängen, *sep.*, *-ge-*, *h*): ~ *von* depend (*up*)*on*.

abhängig *adj.* ['apheŋiç]: ~ *von* dependent (*up*)*on*; '**2keit** *f* (*-/no pl.*) dependence (*von* [*up*]*on*).

ab|härmen ['aphɛrmən] *v/refl.* (*sep.*, *-ge-*, *h*) pine away (*über acc.* at); '**~härten** *v/t.* (*sep.*, *-ge-*, *h*) harden (*gegen* to), inure (to); *sich* ~ harden o.s. (*gegen* to), inure o.s. (to); '**~hauen** (*irr.* hauen, *sep.*, *-ge-*) 1. *v/t.* (*h*) cut *or* chop off; 2. F *v/i.* (*sein*) be off; *hau ab!* sl. beat it!, scram!; '**~häuten** *v/t.* (*sep.*, *-ge-*, *h*) skin, flay; '**~heben** (*irr.* heben, *sep.*, *-ge-*, *h*) 1. *v/t.* lift *or* take off; *teleph.* lift (*receiver*); (*with*)draw (*money*); *sich* ~ *von* stand out against; *fig. a.* contrast with; 2. *v/i.* cut (the cards); *teleph.* lift the receiver; '**~heilen** *v/i.* (*sep.*, *-ge-*, *sein*) heal (up); '**~helfen** *v/i.* (*irr.* helfen, *sep.*, *-ge-*, *h*): *e-m Übel* ~ cure *or* redress an evil; *dem ist nicht abzuhelfen* there is nothing to be done about it; '**~hetzen** *v/refl.* (*sep.*, *-ge-*, *h*) tire o.s. out; rush, hurry.

'**Abhilfe** *f* remedy, redress, relief; ~ *schaffen* take remedial measures.

'**abhobeln** *v/t.* (*sep.*, *-ge-*, *h*) plane (away, down).

abhold *adj.* ['apholt] averse (*dat.* to *s.th.*); ill-disposed (*towards s.o.*).

'**ab|holen** *v/t.* (*sep.*, *-ge-*, *h*) fetch; call for, come for; *j-n von der Bahn* ~ go to meet s.o. at the station; '**~holzen** *v/t.* (*sep.*, *-ge-*, *h*) fell, cut down (*trees*); deforest; '**~horchen** 🐾 *v/t.* (*sep.*, *-ge-*, *h*) auscultate, sound; '**~hören** *v/t.* (*sep.*, *-ge-*, *h*) listen in to, intercept (*telephone conversation*); *e-n Schüler* ~ hear a pupil's lesson.

Abitur [abi'tu:r] *n* (*-s/*🐾*-e*) school-leaving examination (*qualifying for university entrance*).

'**ab|jagen** *v/t.* (*sep.*, *-ge-*, *h*): *j-m et.* ~ recover s.th. from s.o.; '**~kanzeln** F *v/t.* (*sep.*, *-ge-*, *h*) reprimand, F tell *s.o.* off; '**~kaufen** *v/t.* (*sep.*, *-ge-*, *h*): *j-m et.* ~ buy *or* purchase s.th. from s.o.

Abkehr *fig.* ['apke:r] *f* (*-/no pl.*) estrangement (*von* from); withdrawal (from); '**2en** *v/t.* (*sep.*, *-ge-*, *h*) sweep off; *sich* ~ *von* turn away from; *fig.*: take no further interest in; become estranged from; withdraw from.

'**ab|klingen** *v/i.* (*irr.* klingen, *sep.*, *-ge-*, *sein*) fade away; *pain, etc.*: die down; *pain, illness*: ease off; '**~klopfen** (*sep.*, *-ge-*, *h*) 1. *v/t.* knock (*dust, etc.*) off; dust (*coat, etc.*); 🐾 sound, percuss; 2. *v/i. conductor*: stop the orchestra; '**~knicken** *v/t.* (*sep.*, *-ge-*, *h*) snap *or* break off; bend off; '**~knöpfen** *v/t.* (*sep.*, *-ge-*, *h*) unbutton; F *j-m Geld* ~ get money out of s.o.; '**~kochen** (*sep.*, *-ge-*, *h*) 1. *v/t.* boil; scald (*milk*); 2. *v/i.* cook in the open air (*a.* ✕); '**~kommandieren** ✕ *v/t.* (*sep.*, *no -ge-*, *h*) detach, detail; second (*officer*).

Abkomme ['apkɔmə] *m* (*-n/-n*) descendant.

'**abkommen** 1. *v/i.* (*irr.* kommen, *sep.*, *-ge-*, *sein*) come away, get away *or* off; *von e-r Ansicht* ~ change one's opinion; *von e-m Thema* ~ digress from a topic; *vom Wege* ~ lose one's way; 2. 2 *n* (*-s/-*) agreement.

abkömm|lich *adj.* ['apkœmliç] dispensable; available; *er ist nicht* ~ he cannot be spared; **2ling** ['~liŋ] *m* (*-s/-e*) descendant.

'**ab|koppeln** *v/t.* (*sep.*, *-ge-*, *h*) uncouple; '**~kratzen** (*sep.*, *-ge-*) 1. *v/t.* (*h*) scrape off; 2. *sl. v/i.* (*sein*) kick the bucket; '**~kühlen** *v/t.* (*sep.*, *-ge-*, *h*) cool; refrigerate; *sich* ~ cool down (*a. fig.*).

Abkunft ['apkunft] *f* (*-/*✎*e*) descent; origin, extraction; birth.

'**abkürz|en** *v/t.* (*sep.*, *-ge-*, *h*) shorten; abbreviate (*word, story, etc.*); *den Weg* ~ take a short cut; '**2ung** *f* (*-/-en*) abridgement; abbreviation; short cut.

'**abladen** *v/t.* (*irr.* laden, *sep.*, *-ge-*, *h*) unload; dump (*rubbish, etc.*).

'**Ablage** *f* place of deposit; filing tray; files *pl.*; cloak-room.

'**ab|lagern** (*sep.*, *-ge-*) 1. *v/t.* (*h*) season (*wood, wine*); age (*wine*); *sich* ~ settle; be deposited; 2. *v/i.* (*sein*) *wood, wine*: season; *wine*: age; '**~lassen** (*irr.* lassen, *sep.*, *-ge-*, *h*) 1. *v/t.* let (*liquid*) run off; let off (*steam*); drain (*pond, etc.*); 2. *v/i.* leave off (*von et.* [*doing*] s.th.).

'**Ablauf** *m* running off; outlet, drain; *sports*: start; *fig.* expiration, end; *nach* ~ *von* at the end of; '**2en** (*irr.* laufen, *sep.*, *-ge-*) 1. *v/i.* (*sein*) run off; drain off; *period of time*: expire; † *bill of exchange*: fall due; *clock, etc.*: run down; *thread, film*: unwind; *spool*: run out; *gut* ~ end well; 2. v/t. (h) wear out (shoes); scour (region, etc.); sich die Beine ~ run one's legs off; s. Rang.

'**Ableben** n (-s) no pl.) death, decease (esp. ⚕z), ⚕z demise.

'**ab|lecken** v/t. (sep., -ge-, h) lick (off); '**~legen** (sep., -ge-, h) 1. v/t. take off (garments); leave off (garments); give up, break o.s. of (habit); file (documents, letters, etc.); make (confession, vow); take (oath, examination); Zeugnis ~ bear witness (für to; von of); s. Rechenschaft; 2. v/i. take off one's (hat and) coat.

'**Ableger** ⚘ m (-s/-) layer, shoot.

'**ablehn|en** (sep., -ge-, h) 1. v/t. decline, refuse; reject (doctrine, candidate, etc.); turn down (proposal, etc.); 2. v/i. decline; dankend ~ decline with thanks; '**~end** adj. negative; '**2ung** f (-/-en) refusal; rejection.

ableit|en v/t. (sep., -ge-, h) divert (river, etc.); drain off or away (water, etc.); gr., ⚓, fig. derive (aus, von from); fig. infer (from); '**2ung** f diversion; drainage; gr., ⚓ derivation (a. fig.).

'**ab|lenken** v/t. (sep., -ge-, h) turn aside; divert (suspicion, etc.) (von from); phys., etc.: deflect (rays, etc.); j-n von der Arbeit ~ distract s.o. from his work; '**~lesen** v/t. (irr. lesen, sep., -ge-, h) read (speech, etc.); read (off) (values from instruments); '**~leugnen** v/t. (sep., -ge-, h) deny, disavow, disown.

'**abliefer|n** v/t. (sep., -ge-, h) deliver; hand over; surrender; '**2ung** f delivery.

'**ablöschen** v/t. (sep., -ge-, h) blot (up) (ink); ⊕ temper (steel).

'**ablös|en** v/t. (sep., -ge-, h) detach; take off; ✗, etc.: relieve; supersede (predecessor in office); discharge (debt); redeem (obligation); sich ~ come (off); fig. alternate, take turns; '**2ung** f detachment; ✗, etc.: relief; fig. supersession; discharge; redemption.

'**abmach|en** v/t. (sep., -ge-, h) remove, detach; fig. settle, arrange (business, etc.); agree (up)on (price, etc.); '**2ung** f (-/-en) arrangement, settlement; agreement.

'**abmager|n** v/i. (sep., -ge-, sein) lose flesh; grow lean or thin; '**2ung** f (-/-en) emaciation.

'**ab|mähen** v/t. (sep., -ge-, h) mow (off); '**~malen** v/t. (sep., -ge-, h) copy.

'**Abmarsch** m start; ✗ marching off; '**2ieren** v/i. (sep., no -ge-, sein) start; ✗ march off.

'**abmeld|en** v/t. (sep., -ge-, h): j-n von der Schule ~ give notice of the withdrawal of a pupil (from school); sich polizeilich ~ give notice to the police of one's departure (from

town, etc.); '**2ung** f notice of withdrawal; notice of departure.

'**abmess|en** v/t. (irr. messen, sep., -ge-, h) measure; '**2ung** f (-/-en) measurement.

'**ab|montieren** v/t. (sep., no -ge-, h) disassemble; dismantle, strip (machinery); remove (tyre, etc.); '**~mühen** v/refl. (sep., -ge-, h) drudge, toil; '**~nagen** v/t. (sep., -ge-, h) gnaw off; pick (bone).

Abnahme ['apnɑːmə] f (-/⚘-n) taking off; removal; ⚕ amputation; ✝ taking delivery; ✝ purchase; ✝ sale; ⊕ acceptance (of machine, etc.); administering (of oath); decrease, diminution; loss (of weight).

'**abnehm|en** (irr. nehmen, sep., -ge-, h) 1. v/t. take off; remove; teleph. lift (receiver); ⚕ amputate; gather (fruit); ⊕ accept (machine, etc.); j-m et. ~ take s.th. from s.o.; ✝ a. buy or purchase s.th. from s.o.; j-m zuviel ~ overcharge s.o.; 2. v/i. decrease, diminish; decline; lose weight; moon: wane; storm: abate; days: grow shorter; '**2er** ✝ m (-s/-) buyer; customer; consumer.

'**Abneigung** f aversion (gegen to); disinclination (to); dislike (to, of, for); antipathy (against, to).

abnorm adj. [ap'nɔrm] abnormal; anomalous; exceptional; ⚓'**tät** f (-/-en) abnormality; anomaly.

'**abnötigen** v/t. (sep., -ge-, h): j-m et. ~ extort s.th. from s.o.

'**ab|nutzen** v/t. and v/refl. (sep., -ge-, h), '**~nützen** v/t. and v/refl. (sep., -ge-, h) wear out; '**2nutzung** f, '**2nützung** f (-/-en) wear (and tear).

Abonn|ement [abɔn(ə)'mãː] n (-s/ -s) subscription (auf acc. to); '**~ent** [,'nɛnt] m (-en/-en) subscriber; **2ieren** [,'niːrən] v/t. (no -ge-, h) subscribe to (newspaper); **2iert** adj. [,'niːrt]: ~ sein auf (acc.) take in (newspaper, etc.).

abordn|en ['ap⁹-] v/t. (sep., -ge-, h) depute, delegate, Am. a. deputize; '**2ung** f delegation, deputation.

Abort [a'bɔrt] m (-[e]s/-e) lavatory, toilet.

'**ab|passen** v/t. (sep., -ge-, h) fit, adjust; watch for, wait for (s.o., opportunity); waylay s.o.; '**~pflücken** v/t. (sep., -ge-, h) pick, pluck (off), gather; '**~plagen** v/refl. (sep., -ge-, h) toil; '**~platzen** v/i. (sep., -ge-, sein) burst off; fly off; '**~prallen** v/i. (sep., -ge-, sein) rebound, bounce (off); ricochet; '**~putzen** v/t. (sep., -ge-, h) clean (off, up); wipe off; polish; '**~raten** v/i. (irr. raten, sep., -ge-, h): j-m ~ von dissuade s.o. from, advise s.o. against; '**~räumen** v/t. (sep., -ge-, h) clear (away); '**~reagieren** v/t. (sep., no -ge-, h) work off (one's anger, etc.); sich ~ F a. let off steam.

'**abrechn|en** (*sep.*, -ge-, *h*) **1.** *v/t.* deduct; settle (*account*); **2.** *v/i.*: mit *j-m* ~ settle with s.o.; *fig.* settle (accounts) with s.o., F get even with s.o.; '2ung *f* settlement (of accounts); deduction, discount.

'**Abrede** *f*: in ~ stellen deny *or* question *s.th.*

'**abreib|en** *v/t.* (*irr.* reiben, *sep.*, -ge-, *h*) rub off; rub down (*body*); polish; '2ung *f* rub-down; F *fig.* beating.

'**Abreise** *f* departure (*nach* for); '2n *v/i.* (*sep.*, -ge-, *sein*) depart (*nach* for), leave (for), start (for), set out (for).

'**abreiß|en** (*irr.* reißen, *sep.*, -ge-) **1.** *v/t.* (*h*) tear *or* pull off; pull down (*building*); *s.* abgerissen; **2.** *v/i.* (*sein*) break off; *button, etc.*: come off; '2kalender *m* tear-off calendar.

'**ab|richten** *v/t.* (*sep.*, -ge-, *h*) train (*animal*), break (*horse*) (in); '~riegeln** *v/t.* (*sep.*, -ge-, *h*) bolt, bar (*door*); block (*road*).

'**Abriß** *m* draft; summary, abstract; (brief) outlines *pl.*; brief survey.

'**ab|rollen** (*sep.*, -ge-) *v/t.* (*h*) and *v/i.* (*sein*) unroll; uncoil; unwind, unreel; roll off; '~rücken** (*sep.*, -ge-) **1.** *v/t.* (*h*) move off *or* away (*von* from), remove; **2.** ✕ *v/i.* (*sein*) march off, withdraw.

'**Abruf** *m* call; recall; *auf* ~ ☝ on call; '2en *v/t.* (*irr.* rufen, *sep.*, -ge-, *h*) call off (a. ☝), call away; recall; ☝ call out.

'**ab|runden** *v/t.* (*sep.*, -ge-, *h*) round (off); '~rupfen** *v/t.* (*sep.*, -ge-, *h*) pluck off.

abrupt *adj.* [ap'rupt] abrupt.

'**abrüst|en** ✕ *v/i.* (*sep.*, -ge-, *h*) disarm; '2ung ✕ *f* disarmament.

'**abrutschen** *v/i.* (*sep.*, -ge-, *sein*) slip off, glide down; ✇ skid.

'**Absage** *f* cancellation; refusal; '2n (*sep.*, -ge-) **1.** *v/t.* cancel, call off; refuse; recall (*invitation*); **2.** *v/i. guest*: decline; *j-m* ~ cancel one's appointment with s.o.

'**absägen** *v/t.* (*sep.*, -ge-, *h*) saw off; F *fig.* sack *s.o.*

'**Absatz** *m* stop, pause; *typ.* paragraph; ☝ sale; heel (*of shoe*); landing (*of stairs*); '2fähig ☝ *adj.* saleable, marketable; '~markt** ☝ *m* market, outlet; '~möglichkeit** ☝ *f* opening, outlet.

'**abschaben** *v/t.* (*sep.*, -ge-, *h*) scrape off.

'**abschaff|en** *v/t.* (*sep.*, -ge-, *h*) abolish; abrogate (*law*); dismiss (*servants*); '2ung *f* (-/-en) abolition; abrogation; dismissal.

'**ab|schälen** *v/t.* (*sep.*, -ge-, *h*) peel (off), pare; bark (*tree*); '~schalten** *v/t.* (*sep.*, -ge-, *h*) switch off, turn off *or* out; ✂ disconnect.

'**abschätz|en** *v/t.* (*sep.*, -ge-, *h*) esti-

mate; value; assess; '2ung *f* valuation; estimate; assessment.

'**Abschaum** *m* (-[e]s/*no pl.*) scum; *fig. a.* dregs *pl.*

'**Abscheu** *m* (-[e]s/*no pl.*) horror (*vor dat.* of), abhorrence (of); loathing (of); disgust (for).

'**abscheuern** *v/t.* (*sep.*, -ge-, *h*) scour (off); wear out; chafe, abrade.

abscheulich *adj.* [ap'ʃɔylɪç] abominable, detestable, horrid; 2keit *f* (-/-en) detestableness; atrocity.

'**ab|schicken** *v/t.* (*sep.*, -ge-, *h*) send off, dispatch; ☝ post, *esp. Am.* mail; '~schieben** *v/t.* (*irr.* schieben, *sep.*, -ge-, *h*) push *or* shove off.

Abschied ['apʃiːt] *m* (-[e]s/✎-e) departure; parting; leave-taking, farewell; dismissal, ✕ discharge; ~ nehmen take leave (*von* of), bid farewell (to); *j-m den* ~ geben dismiss s.o., ✕ discharge s.o.; *s-n* ~ nehmen resign, retire; '~sfeier** *f* farewell party; '~sgesuch** *n* resignation.

'**ab|schießen** *v/t.* (*irr.* schießen, *sep.*, -ge-, *h*) shoot off; shoot, discharge, fire (off) (*fire-arm*); launch (*rocket*); kill, shoot; (shoot *or* bring) down (*aircraft*); *s.* Vogel; '~schinden** *v/refl.* (*irr.* schinden, *sep.*, -ge-, *h*) toil and moil, slave, drudge; '~schirmen** *v/t.* (*sep.*, -ge-, *h*) shield (*gegen* from); screen (from), screen off (from); '~schlachten** *v/t.* (*sep.*, -ge-, *h*) slaughter, butcher.

'**Abschlag** ☝ *m* reduction (*in price*); *auf* ~ on account; 2en ['~ɡən] *v/t.* (*irr.* schlagen, *sep.*, -ge-, *h*) knock off, beat off, strike off; cut off (*head*); refuse (*request*); repel (*attack*).

abschlägig *adj.* ['apʃlɛːɡɪç] negative; ~e Antwort refusal, denial.

'**Abschlagszahlung** *f* payment on account; instal(l)ment.

'**abschleifen** *v/t.* (*irr.* schleifen, *sep.*, -ge-, *h*) grind off; *fig.* refine, polish.

'**Abschlepp|dienst** *mot. m* towing service, *Am. a.* wrecking service; '2en *v/t.* (*sep.*, -ge-, *h*) drag off; *mot.* tow off.

'**abschließen** (*irr.* schließen, *sep.*, -ge-, *h*) **1.** *v/t.* lock (up); ⊕ seal (up); conclude (*letter, etc.*); settle (*account*); balance (*the books*); effect (*insurance*); contract (*loan*); *fig.* seclude, isolate; *e-n Handel* ~ strike a bargain; *sich* ~ seclude o.s.; **2.** *v/i.* conclude; '~d **1.** *adj.* concluding; final; **2.** *adv.* in conclusion.

'**Abschluß** *m* settlement; conclusion; ⊕ seal; '~prüfung** *f* final examination, finals *pl.*, *Am. a.* graduation; '~zeugnis** *n* leaving certificate; diploma.

'**ab|schmeicheln** *v/t.* (*sep.*, -ge-, *h*): *j-m et.* ~ coax s.th. out of s.o.; '~schmelzen** (*irr.* schmelzen, *sep.*,

-e°) v/t. (h) and v/i. (sein) melt
(off); ⊕ fuse; '~schmieren ⊕ v/t.
(sep., -ge-, h) lubricate, grease; '~
schnallen v/t. (sep., -ge-, h) un-
buckle; take off (ski, etc.); '~
schneiden (irr. schneiden, sep.,
-ge-, h) 1. v/t. cut (off); slice off;
den Weg ~ take a short cut; j-m das
Wort ~ cut s.o. short; 2. v/i.: gut ~
come out or off well.

'Abschnitt m ᚷ segment; ✝ coupon; typ. section, paragraph; counterfoil, Am. a. stub (of cheque, etc.);
stage (of journey); phase (of development); period (of time).

'ab|schöpfen v/t. (sep., -ge-, h)
skim (off); '~schrauben v/t. (sep.,
-ge-, h) unscrew, screw off.

'abschrecken v/t. (sep., -ge-, h)
deter (von from); scare away; '~d
adj. deterrent; repulsive, forbid-
ding.

'abschreib|en (irr. schreiben, sep.,
-ge-, h) 1. v/t. copy; write off (debt,
etc.); plagiarize; in school: crib;
2. v/i. send a refusal; '2er m copy-
ist; plagiarist; '2ung ✝ f (-/-en)
depreciation.

'abschreiten v/t. (irr. schreiten,
sep., -ge-, h) pace (off); e-e Ehren-
wache ~ inspect a guard of hono(u)r.

'Abschrift f copy, duplicate.

'abschürf|en v/t. (sep., -ge-, h)
graze, abrade (skin); '2ung f (-/-en)
abrasion.

'Abschuß m discharge (of fire-arm);
launching (of rocket); hunt. shooting; shooting down, downing (of
aircraft); '~rampe f launching
platform.

abschüssig adj. ['apʃysiç] sloping;
steep.

'ab|schütteln v/t. (sep., -ge-, h)
shake off (a. fig.); fig. get rid of;
'~schwächen v/t. (sep., -ge-, h)
weaken, lessen, diminish; '~schwei-
fen v/i. (sep., -ge-, sein) deviate; fig.
digress; '~schwenken v/i. (sep.,
-ge-, sein) swerve; ✗ wheel;
'~schwören v/i. (irr. schwören,
sep., -ge-, h) abjure; forswear;
'~segeln v/i. (sep., -ge-, sein) set
sail, sail away.

abseh|bar adj. ['apze:baːr]: in ~er
Zeit in the not-too-distant future;
'~en (irr. sehen, sep., -ge-, h) 1. v/t.
(fore)see; j-m et. ~ learn s.th. by
observing s.o.; es abgesehen haben
auf (acc.) have an eye on, be aiming
at; 2. v/i.: ~ von refrain from; disregard.

abseits ['apzaɪts] 1. adv. aside,
apart; football, etc.: off side; 2. prp.
(gen.) aside from; off (the road).

'absend|en v/t. ([irr. senden], sep.,
-ge-, h) send off, dispatch; ✉
post, esp. Am. mail; '2er ⚭ m
sender.

'absengen v/t. (sep., -ge-, h) singe off.

'Absenker ⚭ m (-s/-) layer, shoot.

'absetz|en (sep., -ge-, h) 1. v/t. set
or put down, deposit; deduct (sum);
take off (hat); remove, dismiss
(official); depose, dethrone (king);
drop, put down (passenger); ✝ sell
(goods); typ. set up (in type); thea.:
ein Stück ~ take off a play; 2. v/i.
break off, stop, pause; '2ung f
(-/-en) deposition; removal, dismissal.

'Absicht f (-/-en) intention, purpose,
design; '2lich 1. adj. intentional;
2. adv. on purpose.

'absitzen (irr. sitzen, sep., -ge-)
1. v/i. (sein) rider: dismount; 2. v/t.
(h) serve (sentence), F do (time).

absolut adj. [apzo'luːt] absolute.

absolvieren [apzɔl'viːrən] v/t. (no
-ge-, h) absolve; complete (studies);
get through, graduate from (school).

'absonder|n v/t. (sep., -ge-, h)
separate; ⚕ secrete; sich ~ withdraw; '2ung f (-/-en) separation; ⚕
secretion.

ab|sorbieren [apzɔr'biːrən] v/t. (no
-ge-, h) absorb; '~speisen fig. v/t.
(sep., -ge-, h) put s.o. off.

abspenstig adj. ['apʃpɛnstiç]: ~
machen entice away (von from).

'absperr|en v/t. (sep., -ge-, h) lock;
shut off; bar (way); block (road);
turn off (gas, etc.); '2hahn m stop-
cock.

'ab|spielen v/t. (sep., -ge-, h) play
(record, etc.); play back (tape recording); sich ~ happen, take place;
'~sprechen v/t. (irr. sprechen, sep.,
-ge-, h) deny; arrange, agree;
'~springen v/i. (irr. springen, sep.,
-ge-, sein) jump down or off; ✈
jump, bale out, (Am. only) bail out;
rebound.

'Absprung m jump; sports: take-
off.

'abspülen v/t. (sep., -ge-, h) wash
up; rinse.

'abstamm|en v/i. (sep., -ge-, sein)
be descended; gr. be derived (both:
von from); '2ung f (-/-en) descent;
gr. derivation.

'Abstand m distance; interval; ✝
compensation, indemnification; ~
nehmen von desist from.

ab|statten v/t. (sep.,
-ge-, h): e-n Besuch ~ pay a visit;
Dank ~ return or render thanks;
'~stauben v/t. (sep., -ge-, h) dust.

'abstech|en (irr. stechen, sep., -ge-,
h) 1. v/t. cut (sods); stick (pig, sheep,
etc.); stab (animal); 2. v/i. contrast
(von with); '2er m (-s/-) excursion,
trip; detour.

'ab|stecken v/t. (sep., -ge-, h) unpin,
undo; fit, pin (dress); surv. mark
out; '~stehen v/i. (irr. stehen, sep.,
-ge-, h) stand off; stick out, pro-
trude; s. abgestanden; '~steigen
v/i. (irr. steigen, sep., -ge-, sein)

descend; alight (von from) (*carriage*); get off, dismount (from) (*horse*); put up (*in dat.* at) (*hotel*); **~stellen** v/t. (*sep., -ge-, h*) put down; stop, turn off (*gas, etc.*); park (*car*); *fig.* put an end to *s.th.*; **~stempeln** v/t. (*sep., -ge-, h*) stamp; **~sterben** v/i. (*irr. sterben, sep., -ge-, sein*) die off; *limb:* mortify.

Abstieg ['apʃtiːk] *m* (*-[e]s/-e*) descent; *fig.* decline.

'abstimm|en (*sep., -ge-, h*) **1.** v/i. vote; **2.** v/t. tune in (*radio*); *fig.:* harmonize; time; ✝ balance (*books*); **'Qung** *f* voting; vote; tuning.

Abstinenzler [apstiˈnɛntslər] *m* (*-s/-*) teetotal(l)er.

'abstoppen (*sep., -ge-, h*) **1.** v/t. stop; slow down; *sports:* clock, time; **2.** v/i. stop.

'abstoßen v/t. (*irr. stoßen, sep., -ge-, h*) knock off; push off; clear off (*goods*); *fig.* repel; *sich die Hörner ~* sow one's wild oats; **'~d** *fig. adj.* repulsive.

abstrakt *adj.* [apˈstrakt] abstract.

'ab|streichen v/t. (*irr. streichen, sep., -ge-, h*) take *or* wipe off; **'~streifen** v/t. (*sep., -ge-, h*) strip off; take *or* pull off (*glove, etc.*); slip off (*dress*); wipe (*shoes*); **'~streiten** v/t. (*irr. streiten, sep., -ge-, h*) contest, dispute; deny.

'Abstrich *m* deduction, cut; ✄ swab.

'ab|stufen v/t. (*sep., -ge-, h*) graduate; gradate; **'~stumpfen** (*sep., -ge-*) **1.** v/t. (*h*) blunt; *fig.* dull (*mind*); **2.** *fig.* v/i. (*sein*) become dull.

'Absturz *m* fall; ✈ crash.

'ab|stürzen v/i. (*sep., -ge-, sein*) fall down; ✈ crash; **'~suchen** v/t. (*sep., -ge-, h*) search (*nach* for); scour *or* comb (*area*) (for).

absurd *adj.* [apˈzurt] absurd, preposterous.

Abszeß ✄ [apsˈtsɛs] *m* (*Abszesses/Abszesse*) abscess.

Abt [apt] *m* (*-[e]s/‖e*) abbot.

'abtakeln ✈ v/t. (*sep., -ge-, h*) unrig, dismantle, strip.

Abtei [apˈtaɪ] *f* (*-/-en*) abbey.

Ab|'teil ⚞ *n* compartment; **'Qteilen** v/t. (*sep., -ge-, h*) divide; ⚞ partition off; **'~teilung** *f* division; **~'teilung** *f* department; ward (*of hospital*); compartment; ✕ detachment; **~'teilungsleiter** *m* head of a department.

'abtelegraphieren v/i. (*sep., no -ge-, h*) cancel a visit, *etc.* by telegram.

Äbtissin [ɛpˈtisin] *f* (*-/-nen*) abbess.

'ab|töten v/t. (*sep., -ge-, h*) destroy, kill (*bacteria, etc.*); **'~tragen** v/t. (*irr. tragen, sep., -ge-, h*) carry off; pull down (*building*); wear out (*garment*); pay (*debt*).

abträglich *adj.* ['aptrɛːklɪç] injurious, detrimental.

'abtreib|en (*irr. treiben, sep., -ge-*) **1.** v/t. (*h*) drive away *or* off; *ein Kind ~* procure abortion; **2.** ⚓, ✕ v/i. (*sein*) drift off; **'Qung** *f* (*-/-en*) abortion.

'abtrennen v/t. (*sep., -ge-, h*) detach; separate; sever (*limbs, etc.*); take (*trimmings*) off (*dress*).

'abtret|en (*irr. treten, sep., -ge-*) **1.** v/t. (*h*) wear down (*heels*); wear out (*steps, etc.*); *fig.* cede, transfer; **2.** v/i. (*sein*) retire, withdraw; resign; *thea.* make one's exit; **'Qer** *m* (*-s/-*) doormat; **'Qung** *f* (*-/-en*) cession, transfer.

'ab|trocknen (*sep., -ge-*) **1.** v/t. (*h*) dry (up); wipe (dry); *sich ~* dry oneself, rub oneself down; **2.** v/i. (*sein*) dry up, become dry; **'~tropfen** v/i. (*sep., -ge-, sein*) *liquid:* drip; *dishes, vegetables:* drain.

abtrünnig *adj.* ['aptrʏnɪç] unfaithful, disloyal; *eccl.* apostate; **Qe** ['~gə] *m* (*-n/-n*) deserter; *eccl.* apostate.

'ab|tun v/t. (*irr. tun, sep., -ge-, h*) *fig.:* dispose of; dismiss; **~urteilen** ['apᵍ-] v/t. (*sep., -ge-, h*) pass sentence on *s.o.*; **'~wägen** v/t. (*[irr. wägen,] sep., -ge-, h*) weigh (out); *fig.* consider carefully; **'~wälzen** v/t. (*sep., -ge-, h*) roll away; *fig.* shift; **'~wandeln** v/t. (*sep., -ge-, h*) vary, modify; **'~wandern** v/i. (*sep., -ge-, sein*) wander away; migrate (*von* from).

'Abwandlung *f* modification, variation.

'abwarten (*sep., -ge-, h*) **1.** v/t. wait for, await; *s-e Zeit ~* bide one's time; **2.** v/i. wait.

abwärts *adv.* ['apvɛrts] down, downward(s).

'abwaschen v/t. (*irr. waschen, sep., -ge-, h*) wash (off, away); bathe; sponge off; wash up (*dishes, etc.*).

'abwechseln (*sep., -ge-, h*) **1.** v/t. vary; alternate; **2.** v/i. vary; alternate; *mit j-m ~* take turns; **'~d** *adj.* alternate.

'Abwechs(e)lung *f* (*-/-en*) change; alternation; variation; diversion; *zur ~* for a change.

'Abweg *m: auf ~e geraten* go astray; **Qig** *adj.* ['~gɪç] erroneous, wrong.

'Abwehr *f* defen|ce, *Am.* -se; warding off (*of thrust, etc.*); **'~dienst** ✕ *m* counter-espionage service; **'Qen** v/t. (*sep., -ge-, h*) ward off; avert; repulse; repel, ward off (*attack, enemy*).

'abweich|en v/i. (*irr. weichen, sep., -ge-, sein*) deviate (*von* from), swerve (from); differ (from); *compass-needle:* deviate; **'Qung** *f* (*-/-en*) deviation; difference; deflexion, (*Am. only*) deflection.

'abweiden v/t. (*sep., -ge-, h*) graze.

'abweis|en v/t. (*irr. weisen, sep., -ge-, h*) refuse, reject; repel (*a.* ✕);

rebuff; '∼end adj. unfriendly, cool; '2ung f refusal, rejection; repulse (a. ⚔.); rebuff.

'ab|wenden v/t. ([irr. wenden,] sep., -ge-, h) turn away; avert (disaster, etc.); parry (thrust); sich ∼ turn away (von from); '∼werfen v/t. (irr. werfen, sep., -ge-, h) throw off; 🌣 drop (bombs); shed, cast (skin, etc.); shed (leaves); yield (profit).

'abwert|en v/t. (sep., -ge-, h) devaluate; '2ung f devaluation.

abwesen|d adj. ['apve:zənt] absent; '2heit f (-/⚓ -en) absence.

'ab|wickeln v/t. (sep., -ge-, h) unwind, unreel, wind off; transact (business); '∼wiegen v/t. (irr. wiegen, sep., -ge-, h) weigh (out) (goods); '∼wischen v/t. (sep., -ge-, h) wipe (off); '∼würgen v/t. (sep., -ge-, h) strangle, throttle, choke; mot. stall; '∼zahlen v/t. (sep., -ge-, h) pay off; pay by instal(l)ments; '∼zählen v/t. (sep., -ge-, h) count (out, over).

'Abzahlung f instal(l)ment, payment on account; '∼sgeschäft n hire-purchase.

'abzapfen v/t. (sep., -ge-, h) tap, draw off.

'Abzehrung f (-/-en) wasting away, emaciation; 🕮 consumption.

'Abzeichen n badge; 🕮 marking.

'ab|zeichnen v/t. (sep., -ge-, h) copy, draw; mark off; initial; tick off; sich ∼ gegen stand out against; '∼ziehen (irr. ziehen, sep., -ge-) 1. v/t. (h) take off, remove; 𝒜 subtract; strip (bed); bottle (wine); phot. print (film); typ. pull (proof); take out (key); das Fell ∼ skin (animal); 2. v/i. (sein) go away; 🌣 march off; smoke: escape; thunderstorm, clouds: move on.

'Abzug m departure; 🌣 withdrawal, retreat; ⊕ drain; outlet; deduction (of sum); phot. print; typ. proof (-sheet).

abzüglich prp. (gen.) ['aptsy:kliç] less, minus, deducting.

'Abzugsrohr n waste-pipe.

abzweig|en ['aptsvaɪgən] (sep., -ge-) 1. v/t. (h) branch; divert (money); sich ∼ branch off; 2. v/i. (sein) branch off; '2ung f (-/-en) branch; road-junction.

ach int. [ax] oh!, ah!, alas!; ∼ so! oh, I see!

Achse ['aksə] f (-/-n) axis; ⊕: axle; shaft; axle(-tree) (of carriage); auf der ∼ on the move.

Achsel ['aksəl] f (-/-n) shoulder; die ∼n zucken shrug one's shoulders; '∼höhle f armpit.

acht¹ [axt] 1. adj. eight; in ∼ Tagen today week, this day week; vor ∼ Tagen a week ago; 2. ♀ f (-/-en) (figure) eight.

Acht² [∼] f (-/no pl.) ban, outlawry; attention; außer acht lassen dis-

regard; sich in acht nehmen be careful; be on one's guard (vor j-m or et. against s.o. or s.th.); look out (for s.o. or s.th.).

'achtbar adj. respectable.

'achte adj. eighth; ♀1 ['∼əl] n (-s/-) eighth (part).

'achten (ge-, h) 1. v/t. respect, esteem; regard; 2. v/i.: ∼ auf (acc.) pay attention to; achte auf meine Worte mark or mind my words; darauf ∼, daß see to it that, take care that.

ächten ['ɛçtən] v/t. (ge-, h) outlaw, proscribe; ban.

'Achter m (-s/-) rowing: eight.

achtfach adj. ['axtfax] eightfold.

'achtgeben v/i. (irr. geben, sep., -ge-, h) be careful; pay attention (auf acc. to); take care (of); gib acht! look or watch out!, be careful!

'achtlos adj. inattentive, careless, heedless.

Acht'stundentag m eight-hour day.

'Achtung f (-/no pl.) attention; respect, esteem, regard; ∼! look out!, ⚔ attention!; ∼ Stufe! mind the step!; 2svoll adj. respectful.

'achtzehn adj. eighteen; ∼te adj. ['∼tə] eighteenth.

achtzig adj. ['axtsiç] eighty; '∼ste adj. eightieth.

ächzen ['ɛçtsən] v/i. (ge-, h) groan, moan.

Acker ['akər] m (-s/¨) field; '2bau m agriculture; farming; '2bautreibend adj. agricultural, farming; '∼geräte n/pl. farm implements pl.; '∼land n arable land; '2n v/t. and v/i. (ge-, h) plough, till, Am. plow.

addi|eren [a'di:rən] v/t. (no -ge-, h) add (up); 2tion [adi'tsjo:n] f (-/-en) addition, adding up.

Adel ['a:dəl] m (-s/no pl.) nobility, aristocracy; '2ig adj. noble; '2n v/t. (ge-, h) ennoble (a. fig.); Brt.: knight, raise to the peerage; '∼sstand m nobility; aristocracy; Brt. peerage.

Ader ['a:dər] f (-/-n) 🕮, wood, etc.: vein; anat.: vein; artery; zur ∼ lassen bleed.

adieu int. [a'djø:] good-bye, farewell, adieu, F cheerio.

Adjektiv gr. ['atjɛkti:f] n (-s/-e) adjective.

Adler orn. ['a:dlər] m (-s/-) eagle; '∼nase f aquiline nose.

adlig adj. ['a:dliç] noble; 2e ['∼gə] m (-n/-n) nobleman, peer.

Admiral ⚓ [atmi'ra:l] m (-s/-e, ¨e) admiral.

adopt|ieren [adɔp'ti:rən] v/t. (no -ge-, h) adopt; 2ivkind [∼'ti:f-] n adopted child.

Adressat [adrɛ'sa:t] m (-en/-en) addressee; consignee (of goods).

Adreßbuch [a'drɛs-] n directory.

Adress|e [a'drɛsə] f (-/-n) address; direction; per ~ care of (abbr. c/o); **2ieren** [~'si:rən] v/t. (no -ge-, h) address, direct; ✝ consign; falsch ~ misdirect.

adrett adj. [a'drɛt] smart, neat.

Adverb gr. [at'vɛrp] n (-s/-ien) adverb.

Affäre [a'fɛ:rə] f (-/-n) (love) affair; matter, business, incident.

Affe zo. ['afə] m (-n/-n) ape; monkey.

Affekt [a'fɛkt] m (-[e]s/-e) emotion; passion; **2iert** adj. [~'ti:rt] affected.

'affig F adj. foppish; affected; silly.

Afrikan|er [afri'ka:nər] m (-s/-) African; **2isch** adj. African.

After anat. ['aftər] m (-s/-) anus.

Agent [a'gɛnt] m (-en/-en) agent; broker; pol. (secret) agent; **~ur** [~'tu:r] f (-/-en) agency.

aggressiv adj. [agrɛ'si:f] aggressive.

Agio ✝ ['a:ʒio] n (-s/no pl.) agio, premium.

Agitator [agi'ta:tər] m (-s/-en) agitator. [brooch.]

Agraffe [a'grafə] f (-/-n) clasp;]

agrarisch adj. [a'gra:riʃ] agrarian.

Ägypt|er [ɛ:'gyptər] m (-s/-) Egyptian; **2isch** adj. Egyptian.

ah int. [a:] ah!

aha int. [a'ha] aha!, I see!

Ahle ['a:lə] f (-/-n) awl, pricker; punch.

Ahn [a:n] m (-[e]s, -en/-en) ancestor; **~en** pl. a. forefathers pl.

ähneln ['ɛ:nəln] v/i. (ge-, h) be like, resemble.

ahnen ['a:nən] v/t. (ge-, h) have a presentiment of or that; suspect; divine.

ähnlich adj. ['ɛ:nliç] like, resembling; similar (dat. to); iro.: das sieht ihm ~ that's just like him; **'2keit** f (-/-en) likeness, resemblance; similarity.

Ahnung [a:nuŋ] f (-/-en) presentiment; foreboding; notion, idea; **'2slos** adj. unsuspecting; **'2svoll** adj. full of misgivings.

Ahorn ♀ ['a:hɔrn] m (-s/-e) maple (-tree).

Ähre ♀ ['ɛ:rə] f (-/-n) ear, head; spike; **~n lesen** glean.

Akademi|e [akadə'mi:] f (-/-n) academy, society; **~ker** [~'de:mikər] m (-s/-) university man, esp. Am. university graduate; **2sch** adj. [~'de:miʃ] academic.

Akazie ♀ [a'ka:tsjə] f (-/-n) acacia.

akklimatisieren [aklimati'zi:rən] v/t. and v/refl. (no -ge-, h) acclimatize, Am. acclimate.

Akkord [a'kɔrt] m (-[e]s/-e) ♪ chord; ✝: contract; agreement; composition; im ~ ✝ by the piece or job; **~arbeit** f piece-work; **~arbeiter** m piece-worker; **~lohn** m piece-wages pl.

akkredit|ieren [akredi'ti:rən] v/t. (no -ge-, h) accredit (bei to); **2iv** [~'ti:f] n (-s/-e) credentials pl.; ✝ letter of credit.

Akku F ⊕ ['aku] m (-s/-s), **~mulator** ⊕ [~mu'la:tɔr] m (-s/-en) accumulator, (storage-)battery.

Akkusativ gr. ['akuzati:f] m (-s/-e) accusative (case). [acrobat.]

Akrobat [akro'ba:t] m (-en/-en)]

Akt [akt] m (-[e]s/-e) act(ion), deed; thea. act; paint. nude.

Akte ['aktə] f (-/-en) document, deed; file; **~n** pl. records pl., papers pl.; deeds pl., documents pl.; files pl.; zu den ~n to be filed; zu den ~n legen file; **'~ndeckel** m folder; **'~nmappe** f, **'~ntasche** f portfolio; briefcase; **'~nzeichen** n reference or file number.

Aktie ✝ ['aktsjə] f (-/-n) share, Am. stock; ~n besitzen hold shares, Am. hold stock; **~nbesitz** m shareholdings pl., Am. stockholdings pl.; **'~ngesellschaft** f appr. joint-stock company, Am. (stock) corporation; **'~nkapital** n share-capital, Am. capital stock.

Aktion [ak'tsjo:n] f (-/-en) action; activity; pol., etc.: campaign, drive; ✗ operation; **~är** [~'nɛ:r] m (-s/-e) shareholder, Am. stockholder.

aktiv adj. [ak'ti:f] active.

Aktiv|a ✝ [ak'ti:va] n/pl. assets pl.; **~posten** [~'ti:f-] m asset (a. fig.).

aktuell adj. [aktu'ɛl] current, present-day, up-to-date, topical.

Akustik [a'kustik] f (-/no pl.) acoustics sg., pl.; **2isch** adj. acoustic.

akut adj. [a'ku:t] acute.

Akzent [ak'tsɛnt] m (-[e]s/-e) accent; stress; **2uieren** [~u'i:rən] v/t. (no -ge-, h) accent(uate); stress.

Akzept ✝ [ak'tsɛpt] n (-[e]s/-e) acceptance; **~ant** [~'tant] m (-en/-en) acceptor; **2ieren** [~'ti:rən] v/t. (no -ge-, h) accept.

Alarm [a'larm] m (-[e]s/-e) alarm; ~ blasen or schlagen ✗ sound or give the alarm; **~bereitschaft** f: in ~ sein stand by; **2ieren** [~'mi:rən] v/t. (no -ge-, h) alarm.

Alaun ♠ [a'laun] m (-[e]s/-e) alum.

albern adj. ['albərn] silly, foolish.

Album ['album] n (-s/Alben) album.

Alge ♀ ['algə] f (-/-n) alga, seaweed.

Algebra ♠ ['algebra] f (-/no pl.) algebra.

Alibi ✝ ['a:libi] n (-s/-s) alibi.

Alimente ✝ [ali'mɛntə] pl. alimony.

Alkohol ['alkohol] m (-s/-e) alcohol; **'2frei** adj. non-alcoholic, esp. Am. soft; **~es Restaurant** temperance restaurant; **~iker** [~'ho:likər] m (-s/-) alcoholic; **2isch** adj. [~'ho:liʃ] alcoholic; **'~schmuggler** m liquor-smuggler, Am. bootlegger; **'~verbot** n prohibition; **'~vergiftung** f alcoholic poisoning.

all¹ [al] 1. *pron.* all; ～e everybody; ～es in ～em on the whole; vor ～em first of all; 2. *adj.* all; every, each; any; ～e beide both of them; auf ～e Fälle in any case, at all events; ～e Tage every day; ～e zwei Minuten every two minutes.

All² [～] n (-s/no pl.) the universe.

'alle F *adj.* all gone; ～ werden come to an end; supplies, etc.: run out.

Allee [a'le:] f (-/-n) avenue; (tree-lined) walk.

allein [a'laɪn] 1. *adj.* alone; single; unassisted; 2. *adv.* alone; only; 3. *cj.* yet, only, but, however; ℒberechtigung f exclusive right; ℒbesitz m exclusive possession; ℒherrscher m absolute monarch, autocrat; dictator; ～ig *adj.* only, exclusive, sole; ℒsein n loneliness, solitariness; solitude; ～stehend *adj. p.*: alone in the world; single; building, etc.: isolated, detached; ℒverkauf m exclusive sale; monopoly; ℒvertreter m sole representative or agent; ℒvertrieb m sole distributors pl.

allemal *adv.* ['alə'ma:l] always; ein für ～ once (and) for all.

'allen'falls *adv.* if need be; possibly, perhaps; at best.

allenthalben † *adv.* ['alənt'halbən] everywhere.

'aller|'best *adj.* best ... of all, very best; ～dings *adv.* ['～'dɪŋs] indeed; to be sure; ～l certainly!, Am. F sure!; '～'erst 1. *adj.* first ... of all, very first; foremost; 2. *adv.*: zu ～ first of all.

Allergie ♂ [aler'gi:] f (-/-n) allergy.

'aller|'hand *adj.* of all kinds or sorts; F das ist ja ～! F I say!; sl. that's the limit!; '℥'heiligen n (-/no pl.) All Saints' Day; ～lei *adj.* ['～'laɪ] of all kinds or sorts; '℥'lei n (-s/-s) medley; '～'letzt 1. *adj.* last of all, very last; latest (news, fashion, etc.); 2. *adv.*: zu ～ last of all; '～'liebst 1. *adj.* dearest of all; (most) lovely; 2. *adv.*: am ～en best of all; '～'meist 1. *adj.* most; 2. *adv.*: am ～en mostly; chiefly; '～'nächst *adj.* very next; '～'neu(e)st *adj.* the very latest; '℥'seelen n (-/no pl.) All Souls' Day; '～'seits *adv.* on all sides; universally; '～'wenigst *adv.*: am ～en least of all.

'alle|'samt *adv.* one and all, all together; '～'zeit *adv.* always, at all times, for ever.

'all|'gegenwärtig *adj.* omnipresent, ubiquitous; '～ge'mein 1. *adj.* general; common; universal; 2. *adv.*: im ～en in general, generally; '℥ge'meinheit f (-/no pl.) generality; universality; general public; '℥'heilmittel n panacea, cure-all (both a. fig.).

Allianz [ali'ants] f (-/-en) alliance.

alli'ier|en v/refl. (no -ge-, h) ally o.s. (mit to, with); ℒte m (-n/-n) ally.

'all|'jährlich 1. *adj.* annual; 2. *adv.* annually, every year; '℥macht f (-/no pl.) omnipotence; ～'mächtig *adj.* omnipotent, almighty; ～mählich [～'mɛ:liç] 1. *adj.* gradual; 2. *adv.* gradually, by degrees.

Allopathie ♂ [alopa'ti:] f allopathy.

all|'seitig *adj.* ['alzaɪtɪç] universal; all-round; '℥strom ∮ m (-[e]s/no pl.) alternating current/direct current (abbr. A.C./D.C.); '℥tag m workday; week-day; fig. everyday life, daily routine; ～'täglich *adj.* daily; fig. common, trivial; '℥tagsleben n (-s/no pl.) everyday life; '～'wissend *adj.* omniscient; '℥'wissenheit f (-/no pl.) omniscience; '～'wöchentlich *adj.* weekly; '～zu *adv.* (much) too; '～zu'viel *adv.* too much.

Alm [alm] f (-/-en) Alpine pasture, alp.

Almosen ['almo:zən] n (-s/-) alms; ～ pl. alms pl., charity.

Alp|druck ['alp-] m (-[e]s/～e), '～drücken n (-s/no pl.) nightmare.

Alpen ['alpən] pl. Alps pl.

Alphabet [alfa'be:t] n (-[e]s/-e), ℒisch *adj.* alphabetic(al).

'Alptraum m nightmare.

als cj. [als] than; as, like; (in one's capacity) as; but, except; temporal: after, when; as; ～ ob as if, as though; so viel ～ as much as; er ist zu dumm, ～ daß er es verstehen könnte he is too stupid to understand it; ～'bald *adv.* immediately; '～'dann *adv.* then.

also ['alzo:] 1. *adv.* thus, so; 2. *cj.* therefore, so, consequently; (na ～! there you are!

alt¹ *adj.* [alt] old; aged; ancient, antique; stale; second-hand.

Alt² ♪ [～] m (-s/-e) alto, contralto.

Altar [al'ta:r] m (-[e]s/～e) altar.

Alteisen ['alt?-] n scrap-iron.

'Alte (-n/-n) 1. m old man; F: der ～ the governor; hist.: die ～n pl. the ancients pl.; 2. f old woman.

Alter n (-s/-) age; old age; seniority; er ist in meinem ～ he is my age; von mittlerem ～ middle-aged.

älter *adj.* ['eltər] older; senior; der ～e Bruder the elder brother.

altern ['altərn] v/i. (ge-, h, sein) grow old, age.

Alternative [alterna'ti:və] f (-/-n) alternative; keine ～ haben have no choice.

'Alters|grenze f age-limit; retirement age; '～heim n old people's home; '～rente f old-age pension; '℥schwach *adj.* decrepit; senile; '～schwäche f decrepitude; '～versorgung f old-age pension.

Altertum ['altərtu:m] *n* 1. (-*s/no pl.*) antiquity; 2. (-*s/ᵁer*) *mst* Altertümer *pl.* antiquities *pl.*

altertümlich *adj.* ['altərty:mliç] ancient, antique, archaic.

'Altertums|forscher *m* arch(a)eologist; **'ᵁkunde** *f* arch(a)eology.

ältest *adj.* ['ɛltəst] oldest; eldest (*sister, etc.*); earliest (*recollections*); **'Ǫe m** (-*n/-n*) elder; senior; *mein* ᵁr my eldest (son).

Altistin *♪* [al'tistin] *f* (-/-*nen*) alto-singer, contralto-singer.

'altklug *adj.* precocious, forward.

ältlich *adj.* ['ɛltliç] elderly, oldish.

'Alt|material *n* junk, scrap; salvage; **ᵁmeister** *m* doyen, dean, F Grand Old Man (*a. sports*); *sports*: ex-champion; **'Ǫmodisch** *adj.* old-fashioned; **'ᵁpapier** *n* waste paper; **'ᵁphiloge** *m* classical philologist *or* scholar; **'ᵁstadt** *f* old town *or* city; **'ᵁwarenhändler** *m* second-hand dealer; **ᵁ'weibersommer** *m* Indian summer; gossamer.

Aluminium ⌕̂ₘ [alu'mi:njum] *n* (-*s/no pl.*) aluminium, *Am.* aluminum.

am *prp.* [am] = an dem.

Amateur [ama'tø:r] *m* (-*s/-e*) amateur.

Amboß ['ambɔs] *m* (Ambosses/Ambosse) anvil.

ambulan|t ⚕ *adj.* [ambu'lant]: ᵁ Behandelter out-patient; **Ǫz** [ᵁts] *f* (-/-*en*) ambulance.

Ameise *zo.* ['a:maizə] *f* (-/-*n*) ant; **'ᵁnhaufen** *m* ant-hill.

Amerikan|er [ameri'ka:nər] *m* (-*s/-*), **ᵁerin** *f* (-/-*nen*) American; **Ǫisch** *adj.* American.

Amme ['amə] *f* (-/-*n*) (wet-)nurse.

Amnestie [amnɛs'ti:] *f* (-/-*n*) amnesty, general pardon.

Amor ['a:mɔr] *m* (-*s/no pl.*) Cupid.

Amortis|ation [amɔrtiza'tsjo:n] *f* (-/-*en*) amortization, redemption; **Ǫieren** [ᵁ'zi:rən] *v/t.* (*no -ge-, h*) amortize, redeem; pay off.

Ampel ['ampəl] *f* (-/-*n*) hanging lamp; traffic light.

Amphibie *zo.* [am'fi:bjə] *f* (-/-*n*) amphibian.

Ampulle [am'pulə] *f* (-/-*n*) ampoule.

Amput|ation [amputa'tsjo:n] *f* (-/-*en*) amputation; **Ǫieren** ⚕ [ᵁ'ti:rən] *v/t.* (*no -ge-, h*) amputate; **ᵁierte** *m* (-*n/-n*) amputee.

Amsel *orn.* ['amzəl] *f* (-/-*n*) blackbird.

Amt [amt] *n* (-[*e*]*s/ᵁer*) office; post; charge; office, board; official duty, function; (telephone) exchange; **Ǫieren** [ᵁ'ti:rən] *v/i.* (*no -ge-, h*) hold office; officiate; **'Ǫlich** *adj.* official; **'ᵁmann** *m* district administrator; *hist.* bailiff.

'Amts|arzt *m* medical officer of

health; **ᵁbefugnis** *f* competence, authority; **'ᵁbereich** *m*, **'ᵁbezirk** *m* jurisdiction; **'ᵁblatt** *n* gazette; **'ᵁeid** *m* oath of office; **ᵁeinführung** *f* inauguration; **'ᵁführung** *f* administration; **ᵁgeheimnis** *n* official secret; **'ᵁgericht** *n* appr. district court; **'ᵁgeschäfte** *pl.* official duties *pl.*; **'ᵁgewalt** *f* (official) authority; **'ᵁhandlung** *f* official act; **'ᵁniederlegung** *f* (-/-ᵁ-*en*) resignation; **'ᵁrichter** *m* appr. district court judge; **'ᵁsiegel** *n* official seal; **'ᵁvorsteher** *m* head official.

Amulett [amu'lɛt] *n* (-[*e*]*s/-e*) amulet, charm.

amüs|ant *adj.* [amy'zant] amusing, entertaining; **ᵁieren** [ᵁ'zi:rən] *v/t.* (*no -ge-, h*) amuse, entertain; *sich* ᵁ amuse *or* enjoy o.s., have a good time.

an [an] 1. *prp.* (*dat.*) at; on, upon; in; against; to; by, near, close to; ᵁ der Themse on the Thames; ᵁ der Wand on *or* against the wall; es ist ᵁ dir zu inf. it is up to you to *inf.*; am Leben alive; am 1. März on March 1st; am Morgen in the morning; 2. *prp.* (*acc.*) to; on; to; at; against; about; bis ᵁ as far as, up to; 3. *adv.* on; von heute ᵁ from this day forth, from today; von nun *or* jetzt ᵁ from now on.

analog *adj.* [ana'lo:k] analogous (*dat. or zu* to, with).

Analphabet [an⁽ʔ⁾alfa'be:t] *m* (-*en*/ -*en*) illiterate (person).

Analys|e [ana'ly:zə] *f* (-/-*n*) analysis; **Ǫieren** [ᵁ'zi:rən] *v/t.* (*no -ge-, h*) analy|se, *Am.* -ze.

Anämie ⚕ [anɛ'mi:] *f* (-/-*n*) an(a)emia.

Ananas ['ananas] *f* (-/-, -*se*) pineapple.

Anarchie [anar'çi:] *f* (-/-*n*) anarchy.

Anatom|ie [anato'mi:] *f* (-/*no pl.*) anatomy; **Ǫisch** *adj.* [ᵁ'to:miʃ] anatomical.

'anbahnen *v/t.* (*sep., -ge-, h*) pave the way for, initiate; open up; *sich* ᵁ be ᵁopening up.

'Anbau *m* 1. ✗ (-[*e*]*s/no pl.*) cultivation; 2. Δ (-[*e*]*s/-ten*) outbuilding, annex, extension, addition; **'Ǫen** *v/t.* (*sep., -ge-, h*) ✗ cultivate, grow; Δ add (*an acc.* to); **'ᵁfläche** ✗ *f* arable land.

'anbehalten *v/t.* (*irr. halten, sep., -ge-, h*) keep (*garment, etc.*) on.

an'bei † *adv.* enclosed.

'an|beißen (*irr. beißen, sep., -ge-, h*) 1. *v/t.* bite into; 2. *v/i. fish:* bite; **ᵁbellen** *v/t.* (*sep., -ge-, h*) bark at; **ᵁberaumen** ['ᵁbəraumən] *v/t.* (*sep., no -ge-, h*) appoint, fix; **ᵁbeten** *v/t.* (*sep., -ge-, h*) adore, worship.

'Anbetracht *m: in* ᵁ considering, in consideration of.

'anbetteln v/t. (sep., -ge-, h) beg from, solicit alms of.

'Anbetung f (-/~-en) worship, adoration; ₂swürdig adj. adorable.

'an|bieten v/t. (irr. bieten, sep., -ge-, h) offer; '~binden v/t. (irr. binden, sep., -ge-, h) bind, tie (up); ~ an (dat., acc.) tie to; s. angebunden; '~blasen v/t. (irr. blasen, sep., -ge-, h) blow at or (up)on.

'Anblick m look; view; sight, aspect; ₂en v/t. (sep., -ge-, h) look at; glance at; view; eye.

'an|blinzeln v/t. (sep., -ge-, h) wink at; '~brechen (irr. brechen, sep., -ge-) 1. v/t. (h) break into (provisions, etc.); open (bottle, etc.); 2. v/i. (sein) begin; day: break, dawn; '~brennen (irr. brennen, sep., -ge-) 1. v/t. (h) set on fire; light (cigar, etc.); 2. v/i. (sein) catch fire; burn; '~bringen v/t. (irr. bringen, sep., -ge-, h) bring; fix (an dat. to), attach (to); place; ₮ dispose of (goods); lodge (complaint); s. angebracht.

'Anbruch m (-[e]s/no pl.) beginning; break (of day).

'anbrüllen v/t. (sep., -ge-, h) roar at.

Andacht ['andaxt] f (-/-en) devotion(s pl.); prayers pl.

andächtig adj. ['andεçtiç] devout.

'andauern v/i. (sep., -ge-, h) last, continue, go on.

'Andenken n (-s/-) memory, remembrance; keepsake, souvenir; zum ~ an (acc.) in memory of.

ander adj. ['andər] other; different; next; opposite; am ~en Tag (on) the next day; e-n Tag um den ~en every other day; ein ~er Freund another friend; nichts ~es nothing else.

andererseits adv. ['andərər'zaɪts] on the other hand.

ändern ['εndərn] v/t. (ge-, h) alter; change; ich kann es nicht ~ I can't help it; sich ~ alter; change.

'andern|falls adv. otherwise, else.

anders adv. ['andərs] otherwise; differently (als from); else; j. ~ somebody else; ich kann nicht ~, ich muß weinen I cannot help crying; ~ werden change.

'ander'seits adv. s. andererseits.

'anders'wo adv. elsewhere.

anderthalb adj. ['andərt'halp] one and a half.

'Änderung f (-/-en) change, alteration.

ander|wärts adv. ['andər'vεrts] elsewhere; '~weitig 1. adj. other; 2. adv. otherwise.

'andeut|en v/t. (sep., -ge-, h) indicate; hint; intimate; imply; suggest; ₂ung f intimation; hint; suggestion.

'Andrang m rush; ⚕ congestion.

andre adj. ['andrə] s. andere.

'andrehen v/t. (sep., -ge-, h) turn on (gas, etc.); ⚡ switch on (light).

'androh|en v/t. (sep., -ge-, h): j-m et. ~ threaten s.o. with s.th.; ₂ung f threat.

aneignen ['an⁹-] v/refl. (sep., -ge-, h) appropriate; acquire; adopt; seize; usurp.

aneinander adv. [an⁹aɪ'nandər] together; ~geraten v/i. (irr. raten, sep., no -ge-, sein) clash (mit with).

anekeln ['an⁹-] v/t. (sep., -ge-, h) disgust, sicken.

Anerbieten ['an⁹-] n (-s/-) offer.

anerkannt adj. ['an⁹-] acknowledged, recognized.

anerkenn|en ['an⁹-] v/t. (irr. kennen, sep., no -ge-, h) acknowledge (als as), recognize; appreciate; own (child); hono(u)r (bill); ₂ung f (-/-en) acknowledgement; recognition; appreciation.

'anfahr|en (irr. fahren, sep., -ge-) 1. v/i. (sein) start; ⚓ descend; angefahren kommen drive up; 2. v/t. (h) run into; carry, convey; j-n ~ let fly at s.o.; ₂t f approach; drive.

'Anfall ⚕ m fit, attack; ₂en (irr. fallen, sep., -ge-) 1. v/t. (h) attack; assail; 2. v/i. (sein) accumulate; money: accrue.

anfällig adj. ['anfεliç] susceptible (für to); prone to (diseases, etc.).

'Anfang m beginning, start, commencement; ~ Mai at the beginning of May; early in May; ₂en v/t. and v/i. (irr. fangen, sep., -ge-, h) begin, start, commence.

Anfäng|er ['anfεŋər] m (-s/-) beginner; ₂lich 1. adj. initial; 2. adv. in the beginning.

anfangs adv. ['anfaŋs] in the beginning; ₂buchstabe m initial (letter); großer ~ capital letter; ₂gründe ['~gryndə] m/pl. elements pl.

'anfassen (sep., -ge-, h) 1. v/t. seize; touch; handle; 2. v/i. lend a hand.

anfecht|bar adj. ['anfεçtbaːr] contestable; '~en v/t. (irr. fechten, sep., -ge-, h) contest, dispute; ₰ avoid (contract); ₂ung f (-/-en) contestation; ₰ avoidance; fig. temptation.

an|fertigen ['anfεrtigən] v/t. (sep., -ge-, h) make, manufacture; '~feuchten v/t. (sep., -ge-, h) moisten, wet, damp; '~feuern v/t. (sep., -ge-, h) fire, heat; sports: cheer; fig. encourage; '~flehen v/t. (sep., -ge-, h) implore; '~fliegen ✈ v/t. (irr. fliegen, sep., -ge-, h) approach, head for (airport, etc.); ₂flug m ✈ approach (flight); fig. touch, tinge.

'anforder|n v/t. (sep., -ge-, h) demand; request; claim; ₂ung f demand; request; claim.

'Anfrage f inquiry; ₂n v/i. (sep., -ge-, h) ask (bei j-m s.o.); inquire (bei j-m nach et. of s.o. about s.th.).

an|freunden ['anfrɔyndən] *v/refl.* (*sep.*, -ge-, h): sich ~ mit make friends with; '~frieren *v/i.* (*irr.* frieren, *sep.*, -ge-, sein) freeze on (an *dat.* or *acc.* to); '~fügen *v/t.* (*sep.*, -ge-, h) join, attach (an *acc.* to); '~fühlen *v/t.* (*sep.*, -ge-, h) feel, touch; sich ~ feel.

Anfuhr ['anfu:r] *f* (-/-en) conveyance, carriage.

'**anführ|en** *v/t.* (*sep.*, -ge-, h) lead; allege; ✗ command; quote, cite (*authority, passage, etc.*); dupe, fool, trick; '2er *m* (ring)leader; '2ungszeichen *n/pl.* quotation marks *pl.*, inverted commas *pl.*

'**Angabe** *f* declaration; statement; instruction; F *fig.* bragging, showing off.

'**angeb|en** (*irr.* geben, *sep.*, -ge-, h) **1.** *v/t.* declare; state; specify; allege; give (*name, reason*); † quote(*prices*); denounce, inform against; **2.** *v/i.* cards: deal first; F *fig.* brag, show off, Am. blow; '2er *m* (-s/-) informer; F braggart, Am. blowhard; ~lich *adj.* ['~pliç] supposed; pretended, alleged.

'**angeboren** *adj.* innate, inborn; ✗ congenital.

'**Angebot** *n* offer (a. †); *at auction sale:* bid; † supply.

'**ange|bracht** *adj.* appropriate, suitable; well-timed; '~bunden *adj.:* kurz ~ sein be short (gegen with).

'**angehen** (*irr.* gehen, *sep.*, -ge-) **1.** *v/i.* (sein) begin; meat, etc.: go bad, go off; es geht an it will do; **2.** *v/t.* (h): j-n ~ concern s.o.; das geht dich nichts an that is no business of yours.

'**angehör|en** *v/i.* (*sep.*, no -ge-, h) belong to; 2ige ['~iga] *m, f* (-/-n): seine ~n *pl.* his relations *pl.*; die nächsten ~n *pl.* the next of kin.

Angeklagte ♈ ['angəkla:ktə] *m, f* (-n/-n) the accused; prisoner (at the bar); defendant.

Angel ['aŋəl] *f* (-/-n) hinge; fishing-tackle, fishing-rod.

'**angelegen** *adj.:* sich et. ~ sein lassen make s.th. one's business; '2heit *f* business, concern, affair, matter.

Angel|gerät *n* fishing-tackle; '2n (-ge-, h) **1.** *v/i.* fish (nach for), angle (for) (both a. *fig.*); ~ in fish (river, etc.); **2.** *v/t.* fish (trout); '~punkt *fig. m* pivot.

Angel|sachse *m* Anglo-Saxon; '2sächsisch *adj.* Anglo-Saxon.

'**Angelschnur** *f* fishing-line.

'**ange|messen** *adj.* suitable, appropriate; reasonable; adequate; '~nehm *adj.* pleasant, agreeable, pleasing; sehr ~! glad or pleased to meet you; ~regt *adj.* ['~re:kt] stimulated; *discussion:* animated, lively; '~sehen *adj.* respected, esteemed.

'**Angesicht** *n* (-[e]s/-er, -e) face, countenance; von ~ zu ~ face to face; '2s *prp.* (gen.) in view of.

angestammt *adj.* ['angəʃtamt] hereditary, innate.

Angestellte ['angəʃtɛltə] *m, f* (-n/-n) employee; die ~n *pl.* the staff.

'**ange|trunken** *adj.* tipsy; ~wandt *adj.* ['~vant] applied; ~wiesen *adj.:* ~ sein auf (*acc.*) be dependent or thrown (up)on.

'**angewöhnen** *v/t.* (*sep.*, -ge-, h): j-m et. ~ accustom s.o. to s.th.; sich et. ~ get into the habit of s.th.; take to (*smoking*).

'**Angewohnheit** *f* custom, habit.

Angina ♈ [aŋ'gi:na] *f* (-/Anginen) angina; tonsillitis.

'**angleichen** *v/t.* (*irr.* gleichen, *sep.*, -ge-, h) assimilate (an *acc.* to, with), adjust (to); sich ~ an (*acc.*) assimilate to or with, adjust or adapt o.s. to.

Angler ['aŋlər] *m* (-s/-) angler.

'**angliedern** *v/t.* (*sep.*, -ge-, h) join; annex; affiliate.

Anglist [aŋ'glist] *m* (-en/-en) professor or student of English, Angli(ci)st.

'**angreif|en** *v/t.* (*irr.* greifen, *sep.*, -ge-, h) touch; draw upon (*capital, provisions*); attack; affect (*health, material*); 🜊 corrode; exhaust; '2er *m* (-s/-) aggressor, assailant.

'**angrenzend** *adj.* adjacent; adjoining.

'**Angriff** *m* attack, assault; in ~ nehmen set about; '~skrieg *m* offensive war; '2slustig *adj.* aggressive.

Angst [aŋst] *f* (-/⁔e) fear; anxiety; anguish; ich habe ~ I am afraid (vor *dat.* of); '~hase *m* coward.

ängstigen ['ɛŋstigən] *v/t.* (ge-, h) frighten, alarm; sich ~ be afraid (vor *dat.* of); be alarmed (um about).

ängstlich *adj.* ['ɛŋstliç] uneasy, nervous; anxious; afraid; scrupulous; timid; '2keit *f* (-/no *pl.*) anxiety; scrupulousness; timidity.

'**an|haben** *v/t.* (*irr.* haben, *sep.*, -ge-, h) have (*garment*) on; das kann mir nichts ~ that can't do me any harm; '~haften *v/i.* (*sep.*, -ge-, h) stick, adhere (dat. to); '~haken *v/t.* (*sep.*, -ge-, h) hook on; tick (off), Am. check (off) (*name, item*).

'**anhalten** (*irr.* halten, *sep.*, -ge-, h) **1.** *v/t.* stop; j-n ~ zu et. keep s.o. to s.th.; den Atem ~ hold one's breath; **2.** *v/i.* continue, last; stop; um ein Mädchen ~ propose to a girl; '~d *adj.* continuous; persevering.

'**Anhaltspunkt** *m* clue.

'**Anhang** *m* appendix, supplement (to book, etc.); followers *pl.*, adherents *pl.*

'**anhäng|en** (*sep.*, -ge-, h) **1.** hang on; affix, attach, join; add; couple (on) (*coach, vehicle*); **2.** *v/i.*

(*irr. hängen*) adhere to; '**⊆er** *m* (-s/-) adherent, follower; pendant (*of necklace, etc.*); label, tag; trailer (*behind car, etc.*).

anhänglich *adj.* ['anhɛŋlɪç] devoted, attached; '**⊆keit** *f* (-/no *pl.*) devotion, attachment.

Anhängsel ['anhɛŋzəl] *n* (-s/-) appendage.

'**anhauchen** *v/t.* (*sep.*, -ge-, *h*) breathe on; blow (*fingers*).

'**anhäuf|en** *v/t. and v/refl.* (*sep.*, -ge-, *h*) pile up, accumulate; '**⊆ung** *f* accumulation.

'**an|heben** *v/t.* (*irr. heben, sep.*, -ge-, *h*) lift, raise; '**⊆heften** *v/t.* (*sep.*, -ge-, *h*) fasten (*an acc.* to); stitch (to).

an'heim|fallen *v/i.* (*irr. fallen, sep.*, -ge-, *sein*): j-m ∼ fall to s.o.; **⊆stellen** *v/t.* (*sep.*, -ge-, *h*): j-m et. ∼ leave s.th. to s.o.

'**Anhieb** *m*: auf ∼ at the first go.

'**Anhöhe** *f* rise, elevation, hill.

'**anhören** *v/t.* (*sep.*, -ge-, *h*) listen to; *sich* ∼ sound.

Anilin ⚗ [ani'li:n] *n* (-s/no *pl.*) anilin(e).

'**ankämpfen** *v/i.* (*sep.*, -ge-, *h*): ∼ *gegen* struggle against.

'**Ankauf** *m* purchase.

Anker ⚓ ['aŋkər] *m* (-s/-) anchor; *vor* ∼ *gehen* cast anchor; '**⊆kette** ⚓ *f* cable; '**⊆n** *v/t. and v/i.* (*sep.*, -ge-, *h*) anchor; '**⊆uhr** *f* lever watch.

'**anketten** *v/t.* (*sep.*, -ge-, *h*) chain (*an dat. or acc.* to).

'**Anklage** *f* accusation, charge; ⚖ *a.* indictment; '**⊆n** *v/t.* (*sep.*, -ge-, *h*) accuse (*gen. or wegen* of), charge (with); ⚖ *a.* indict (for).

'**Ankläger** *m* accuser; *öffentlicher* ∼ ⚖ public prosecutor, *Am.* district attorney.

'**anklammern** *v/t.* (*sep.*, -ge-, *h*) clip *s.th.* on; *sich* ∼ cling (*an dat. or acc.* to).

'**Anklang** *m*: ∼ *an* (*acc.*) suggestion of; ∼ *finden* meet with approval.

'**an|kleben** *v/t.* (*sep.*, -ge-, *h*) stick on (*an dat. or acc.* to); glue on (to); paste on (to); gum on (to); '**⊆kleiden** *v/t.* (*sep.*, -ge-, *h*) dress; *sich* ∼ dress (o.s.); '**⊆klopfen** *v/i.* (*sep.*, -ge-, *h*) knock (*an acc.* at); '**⊆knipsen** ⚡ *v/t.* (*sep.*, -ge-, *h*) turn or switch on; '**⊆knüpfen** (*sep.*, -ge-, *h*) **1.** *v/t.* tie (*an dat. or acc.* to); *fig.* begin; *Verbindungen* ∼ form connexions *or* (*Am. only*) connections; **2.** *v/i.* refer (*an acc.* to); '**⊆kommen** *v/i.* (*irr. kommen, sep.*, -ge-, *sein*) arrive; ∼ *auf* (*acc.*) depend (up)on; *es darauf* ∼ *lassen* run the risk, risk it; *darauf kommt es an* that is the point; *es kommt nicht darauf an* it does not matter.

Ankömmling ['ankœmlɪŋ] *m* (-s/-e) new-comer, new arrival.

'**ankündig|en** *v/t.* (*sep.*, -ge-, *h*) announce; advertise; '**⊆ung** *f* announcement; advertisement.

Ankunft ['ankunft] *f* (-/no *pl.*) arrival.

'**an|kurbeln** *v/t.* (*sep.*, -ge-, *h*) *mot.* crank up; *die Wirtschaft* ∼ F boost the economy; '**⊆lächeln** *v/t.* (*sep.*, -ge-, *h*), '**⊆lachen** *v/t.* (*sep.*, -ge-, *h*) smile at.

'**Anlage** *f* construction; installation; ⊕ plant; grounds *pl.*, park; plan, arrangement, layout; enclosure (*to letter*); ⚵ investment; talent; predisposition, tendency; *öffentliche* ∼ *pl.* public gardens *pl.*; '**⊆kapital** ⚵ *n* invested capital.

'**anlangen** (*sep.*, -ge-) **1.** *v/i.* (*sein*) arrive at; **2.** *v/t.* (*h*) F touch; concern; *was mich anlangt* as far as I am concerned, (speaking) for myself.

Anlaß ['anlas] *m* (*Anlasses/Anlässe*) occasion; *ohne allen* ∼ without any reason.

'**anlass|en** *v/t.* (*irr. lassen, sep.*, -ge-, *h*) F leave *or* keep (*garment, etc.*) on; leave (*light, etc.*) on; ⊕ start, set going; *sich gut* ∼ promise well; '**⊆er** *mot. m* (-s/-) starter.

anläßlich *prp.* (*gen.*) ['anleslɪç] on the occasion of.

'**Anlauf** *m* start, run; '**⊆en** (*irr. laufen, sep.*, -ge-) **1.** *v/i.* (*sein*) run up; start; tarnish, (grow) dim; ∼ *gegen* run against; **2.** ⚓ *v/t.* (*h*) call *or* touch at (*port*).

'**an|legen** (*sep.*, -ge-, *h*) **1.** *v/t.* put (*an acc.* to, against); lay out (*garden*); invest (*money*); level (*gun*); put on (*garment*); found (*town*); ⚡ apply (*dressing*); lay in (*provisions*); *Feuer* ∼ *an* (*acc.*) set fire to; **2.** *v/i.* ⚓: land; moor; ∼ *auf* (*acc.*) aim at; '**⊆lehnen** *v/t.* (*sep.*, -ge-, *h*) lean (*an acc.* against); leave *or* set (*door*) ajar; *sich* ∼ *an* (*acc.*) lean against *or* on.

Anleihe ['anlaɪə] *f* (-/-n) loan.

'**anleit|en** *v/t.* (*sep.*, -ge-, *h*) guide (*zu* to); instruct (*in dat.* in); '**⊆ung** *f* guidance, instruction; guide.

'**Anliegen** *n* (-s/-) desire, request.

'**an|locken** *v/t.* (*sep.*, -ge-, *h*) allure, entice; decoy; '**⊆machen** *v/t.* (*sep.*, -ge-, *h*) fasten (*an acc.* to), fix (to); make, light (*fire*); ⚡ switch on (*light*); dress (*salad*); '**⊆malen** *v/t.* (*sep.*, -ge-, *h*) paint.

'**Anmarsch** *m* approach.

anmaß|en ['anmasən] *v/refl.* (*sep.*, -ge-, *h*) arrogate *s.th.* to o.s.; assume (*right*); presume; '**⊆end** *adj.* arrogant; '**⊆ung** *f* (-/-en) arrogance, presumption.

'**anmeld|en** *v/t.* (*sep.*, -ge-, *h*) announce, notify; *sich* ∼ *bei* make an appointment with; '**⊆ung** *f* announcement, notification.

'anmerk|en v/t. (sep., -ge-, h) mark; note down; j-m et. ~ observe or perceive s.th. in s.o.; **'2ung** f (-/-en) remark; note; annotation; comment.

'anmessen v/t. (irr. messen, sep., -ge-, h): j-m e-n Anzug ~ measure s.o. for a suit; s. angemessen.

'Anmut f (-/no pl.) grace, charm, loveliness; **'2ig** adj. charming, graceful, lovely.

'an|nageln v/t. (sep., -ge-, h) nail on (an acc. to); **'~nähen** v/t. (sep., -ge-, h) sew on (an acc. to).

annäher|nd adj. ['anneːərnt] approximate; **'2ung** f (-/-en) approach.

Annahme ['annaːmə] f (-/-n) acceptance; receiving-office; fig. assumption, supposition.

'annehm|bar adj. acceptable; price: reasonable; **'~en** (irr. nehmen, sep., -ge-, h) **1.** v/t. accept, take; fig.: suppose, take it, Am. guess; assume; contract (habit); adopt (child); parl. pass (bill); sich (gen.) ~ attend to s.th.; befriend s.o.; **2.** v/i. accept; **'2lichkeit** f (-/-en) amenity, agreeableness.

Annexion [anek'sjoːn] f (-/-en) annexation.

Annonce [a'nõːsə] f (-/-n) advertisement. [mous.)

anonym adj. [ano'nyːm] anony-)

anordn|en ['anʔ-] v/t. (sep., -ge-, h) order; arrange; direct; **'2ung** f arrangement; direction; order.

'anpacken v/t. (sep., -ge-, h) seize, grasp; fig. tackle.

'anpass|en v/t. (sep., -ge-, h) fit, adapt, suit; adjust; try or fit (garment) on; sich ~ adapt o.s. (dat. to); **'2ung** f (-/-en) adaptation; **'~ungsfähig** adj. adaptable.

'anpflanz|en v/t. (sep., -ge-, h) cultivate, plant; **'2ung** f cultivation; plantation.

Anprall ['anpral] m (-[e]s/⚓-e) impact; **'2en** v/i. (sep., -ge-, sein) strike (an acc. against).

'anpreisen v/t. (irr. preisen, sep., -ge-, h) commend, praise; boost, push.

'Anprobe f try-on, fitting.

'an|probieren v/t. (sep., no -ge-, h) try or fit on; **'~raten** v/t. (irr. raten, sep., -ge-, h) advise; **'~rechnen** v/t. (sep., -ge-, h) charge; hoch ~ value highly.

'Anrecht n right, title, claim (auf acc. to).

'Anrede f address; **'2n** v/t. (sep., -ge-, h) address, speak to.

'anreg|en v/t. (sep., -ge-, h) stimulate; suggest; **'~end** adj. stimulative, stimulating; suggestive; **'2ung** f stimulation; suggestion.

'Anreiz m incentive; **'2en** v/t. (sep., -ge-, h) stimulate; incite.

'an|rennen v/i. (irr. rennen, sep., -ge-, sein): ~ gegen run against; angerannt kommen come running; **'~richten** v/t. (sep., -ge-, h) prepare, dress (food, salad); cause, do (damage).

anrüchig adj. ['anryçiç] disreputable.

'anrücken v/i. (sep., -ge-, sein) approach.

'Anruf m call (a. teleph.); **'2en** v/t. (irr. rufen, sep., -ge-, h) call (zum Zeugen to witness); teleph. ring up, F phone, Am. call up; hail (ship); invoke (God, etc.); appeal to (s.o.'s help).

'anrühren v/t. (sep., -ge-, h) touch; mix.

'Ansage f announcement; **'2n** v/t. (sep., -ge-, h) announce; **'~r** m (-s/-) announcer; compère, Am. master of ceremonies.

'ansammeln v/t. (sep., -ge-, h) collect, gather; accumulate, amass; sich ~ collect, gather; accumulate.

ansässig adj. ['anzɛsiç] resident.

'Ansatz m start.

'an|schaffen v/t. (sep., -ge-, h) procure, provide; purchase; sich et. ~ provide or supply o.s. with s.th.; **'~schalten** ⚡ v/t. (sep., -ge-, h) connect; switch on (light).

'anschau|en v/t. (sep., -ge-, h) look at, view; **'~lich** adj. clear, vivid; graphic.

'Anschauung f (-/-en) view; perception; conception; intuition; contemplation; **'~smaterial** n illustrative material; **'~sunterricht** ['anʃauuŋsʔ-] m visual instruction; object-lessons pl.; **'~svermögen** n intuitive faculty.

'Anschein m (-[e]s/no pl.) appearance; **'2end** adj. apparent, seeming.

'an|schicken v/refl. (sep., -ge-, h): sich ~ et. zu tun get ready for s.th.; prepare for s.th.; set about doing s.th.; **'~schirren** ['~ʃirən] v/t. (sep., -ge-, h) harness.

'Anschlag m ⊕ stop, catch; ♪ touch; notice; placard, poster, bill; estimate; calculation; plot; e-n ~ auf j-n verüben make an attempt on s.o.'s life; **'~brett** ['~k-] n noticeboard, Am. bulletin board; **2en** ['~gən] (irr. schlagen, sep., -ge-, h) **1.** v/t. strike (an dat. or acc. against), knock (against); post up (bill); ♪ touch; level (gun); estimate, rate; **2.** v/i. strike (an acc. against), knock (against); dog: bark; ⚔ take (effect); food: agree (bei with); **~säule** ['~k-] f advertising pillar; **~zettel** ['~k-] m notice; placard, poster, bill.

anschließen v/t. (irr. schließen, sep., -ge-, h) fix with a lock; join, attach, annex; ⊕, ⚡ connect; sich j-m ~ join s.o.; sich e-r Meinung ~

anschließend *adj.* adjacent (*an acc.* to); subsequent (to).

'Anschluß *m* joining; 🚂, ⚡, *teleph.*, *gas*, *etc.*: connexion, (*Am. only*) connection; ~ *haben an* (*acc.*) 🚂, *boat*: connect with; 📞 run in connexion with; ~ *finden* make friends (*an acc.* with), F pal up (with); *teleph.*: ~ *bekommen* get through; **'~dose** ⚡ *f* (wall) socket; **'~zug** 🚂 *m* connecting train, connexion.

'an|schmiegen *v/refl.* (*sep.*, -ge-, h): *sich ~ an* (*acc.*) nestle to; **'~schmieren** *v/t.* (*sep.*, -ge-, h) (be)smear, grease; F *fig.* cheat; **'~schnallen** *v/t.* (*sep.*, -ge-, h) buckle on; *bitte ~! 🔒* fasten seat-belts, please!; **'~schnauzen** F *v/t.* (*sep.*, -ge-, h) snap at, blow *s.o.* up, *Am. a.* bawl *s.o.* out; **'~schneiden** *v/t.* (*irr.* schneiden, *sep.*, -ge-, h) cut; broach (*subject*).

'Anschnitt *m* first cut or slice.

'an|schrauben *v/t.* (*sep.*, -ge-, h) screw on (*an dat.* or *acc.* to); **'~schreiben** *v/t.* (*irr.* schreiben, *sep.*, -ge-, h) write down; *sports*, *games*: score; *et. ~ lassen* have s.th. charged to one's account; buy s.th. on credit; **'~schreien** *v/t.* (*irr.* schreien, *sep.*, -ge-, h) shout at.

'Anschrift *f* address.

an|schuldigen ['anʃuldigən] *v/t.* (*sep.*, -ge-, h) accuse, incriminate; **'~schwärzen** *v/t.* (*sep.*, -ge-, h) blacken; *fig. a.* defame.

'anschwell|en (*irr.* schwellen, *sep.*, -ge-) **1.** *v/i.* (sein) swell; increase, rise; **2.** *v/t.* (h) swell; **'2ung** *f* swelling.

anschwemm|en ['anʃvɛmən] *v/t.* (*sep.*, -ge-, h) wash ashore; *geol.* deposit (*alluvium*); **'2ung** *f* (-/-en) wash; *geol.* alluvial deposits *pl.*, alluvium.

'ansehen 1. *v/t.* (*irr.* sehen, *sep.*, -ge-, h) (take a) look at; view; regard, consider (*als*); *et. mit ~* witness s.th.; ~ *für* take for; *man sieht ihm sein Alter nicht an* he does not look his age; **2.** 2 *n* (-s/*no pl.*) authority, prestige; respect; F appearance, aspect.

ansehnlich *adj.* ['anze:nlic̦] considerable; good-looking.

'an|seilen *mount.* *v/t. and v/refl.* (*sep.*, -ge-, h) rope; **'~sengen** *v/t.* (*sep.*, -ge-, h) singe; **'~setzen** (*sep.*, -ge-, h) **1.** *v/t.* put (*an acc.* to); add (to); fix, appoint (*date*); rate; fix, quote (*prices*); charge; put forth (*leaves, etc.*); put on (*flesh*); put (*food*) on (to boil); *Rost ~* rust; **2.** *v/i.* try; start; get ready.

'Ansicht *f* (-/-en) sight, view; *fig.* view, opinion; *meiner ~ nach* in my opinion; *zur ~* 🕯 on approval; **'~s-(post)karte** *f* picture postcard; **'~ssache** *f* matter of opinion.

'ansied|eln *v/t. and v/refl.* (*sep.*, -ge-, h) settle; **'2ler** *m* settler; **'2lung** *f* settlement.

'Ansinnen *n* (-s/-) request, demand.

'anspann|en *v/t.* (*sep.*, -ge-, h) stretch; put or harness (*horses, etc.*) to the carriage, *etc.*; *fig.* strain, exert; **'2ung** *fig. f* strain, exertion.

anspeien *v/t.* (*irr.* speien, *sep.*, -ge-, h) spit (up)on or at.

'anspiel|en *v/i.* (*sep.*, -ge-, h) *cards*: lead; *sports*: lead off; *football*: kick off; ~ *auf* (*acc.*) allude to, hint at; **'2ung** *f* (-/-en) allusion, hint.

'anspitzen *v/t.* (*sep.*, -ge-, h) point, sharpen.

'Ansporn *m* (-[e]s/🔨 -e) spur; **'2en** *v/t.* (*sep.*, -ge-, h) spur *s.o.* on.

'Ansprache *f* address, speech; *e-e ~ halten* deliver an address.

'ansprechen *v/t.* (*irr.* sprechen, *sep.*, -ge-, h) speak to, address; appeal to; **'~d** *adj.* appealing.

'an|springen (*irr.* springen, *sep.*, -ge-) **1.** *v/i.* (sein) *engine*: start; **2.** *v/t.* (h) jump (up)on, leap at; **'~spritzen** *v/t.* (*sep.*, -ge-, h) splash (*j-n mit* s.th. on *s.o.*); (be-) sprinkle.

'Anspruch *m* claim (*a. 🔨*) (*auf acc.* to), pretension (to); 🔨 title (to); ~ *haben auf* (*acc.*) be entitled to; *in ~ nehmen* claim *s.th.*; *Zeit in ~ nehmen* take up time; **'~slos** *adj.* unpretentious; unassuming; **'~svoll** *adj.* pretentious.

'an|spülen *v/t.* (*sep.*, -ge-, h) *s.* anschwemmen; **'~stacheln** *v/t.* (*sep.*, -ge-, h) goad (on).

Anstalt ['anʃtalt] *f* (-/-en) establishment, institution; *~en treffen zu* make arrangements for.

'Anstand *m* **1.** ~ [-[e]s/-e] *hunt.* stand; objection; **2.** (-[e]s/🔨-e) good manners *pl.*; decency, propriety.

anständig *adj.* ['anʃtɛndic̦] decent; respectable; *price*: fair, handsome; **'2keit** *f* (-/🔨-en) decency.

'Anstands|gefühl *n* sense of propriety; tact; **'~los** *adv.* unhesitatingly.

'anstarren *v/t.* (*sep.*, -ge-, h) stare or gaze at.

anstatt *prp.* (*gen.*) *and cj.* [an'ʃtat] instead of.

'anstaunen *v/t.* (*sep.*, -ge-, h) gaze at *s.o.* or *s.th.* in wonder.

'ansteck|en *v/t.* (*sep.*, -ge-, h) pin on; put on (*ring*); 🔥 infect; set on fire; kindle (*fire*); light (*candle, etc.*); **'~end** *adj.* infectious; contagious; *fig. a.* catching; **'2ung** 🔥 *f* (-/-en) infection; contagion.

'an|stehen *v/i.* (*irr.* stehen, *sep.*, -ge-, h) queue up (*nach* for), *Am.* stand in line (for); **'~steigen** *v/i.* (*irr.* steigen, *sep.*, -ge-, sein) ground: rise, ascend; *fig.* increase.

'anstell|en *v/t.* (*sep.*, -ge-, h) engage, employ, hire; make (*ex-*

periments); draw (*comparison*); turn on (*light, etc.*); manage; *sich ~* queue up (*nach* for), *Am.* line up (for); *sich dumm ~* set about *s.th.* stupidly; '**~ig** *adj.* handy, skil(l)ful; '**2ung** *f* place, position, job; employment.

Anstieg ['an∫tiːk] *m* (-[e]s/-e) ascent.
'**anstift|en** *v/t.* (*sep., -ge-, h*) instigate; '**2er** *m* instigator; '**2ung** *f* instigation.
'**anstimmen** *v/t.* (*sep., -ge-, h*) strike up (*tune*).
'**Anstoß** *m football*: kick-off; *fig.* impulse; offen|ce, *Am. -se*; *~ erregen* give offence (*bei* to); *~ nehmen an (dat.*) take offence at; *~ geben zu* et. start s.th., initiate s.th.; '**2en** (*irr. stoßen, sep., -ge-*) 1. *v/t.* (*h*) push, knock (*acc. or an* against); nudge; 2. *v/i.* (*sein*) knock (*an acc.* against); border (on, upon); adjoin; 3. *v/i.* (*h*): *mit der Zunge ~* lisp; *auf j-s Gesundheit ~* drink (to) s.o.'s health; '**2end** *adj.* adjoining.
anstößig *adj.* ['an∫tøːsiç] shocking.
'**an|strahlen** *v/t.* (*sep., -ge-, h*) illuminate; floodlight (*building, etc.*); *fig.* beam at *s.o.*; '**~streben** *v/t.* (*sep., -ge-, h*) aim at, aspire to, strive for.
'**anstreich|en** *v/t.* (*irr. streichen, sep., -ge-, h*) paint; whitewash; mark; underline (*mistake*); '**2er** *m* (-s/-) house-painter; decorator.
anstreng|en ['an∫trεŋən] *v/t.* (*sep., -ge-, h*) exert; try (*eyes*); fatigue; *Prozeß ~* bring an action (*gegen j-n* against s.o.); *sich ~* exert o.s.; '**~end** *adj.* strenuous; trying (*für* to); '**2ung** *f* (-/-en) exertion, strain, effort.
'**Anstrich** *m* paint, colo(u)r; coat (-ing); *fig.*: tinge; air.
'**Ansturm** *m* assault; onset; *~ auf (acc.*) rush for; † run on (*bank*).
'**anstürmen** *v/i.* (*sep., -ge-, sein*) storm, rush.
'**Anteil** *m* share, portion; *~ nehmen an (dat.*) take an interest in; sympathize with; '**~nahme** ['~naːmə] *f* (-/*no pl.*) sympathy; interest; '**~schein** † *m* share-certificate.
Antenne [an'tεnə] *f* (-/-n) aerial.
Antialkoholiker [anti⁹alko'hoːlikər, '~] *m* (-s/-) teetotaller.
antik *adj.* [an'tiːk] antique.
Antilope *zo.* [anti'loːpə] *f* (-/-n) antelope.
Antipathie [antipa'tiː] *f* (-/-n) antipathy.
'**antippen** F *v/t.* (*sep., -ge-, h*) tap.
Antiquar [anti'kvaːr] *m* (-s/-e) second-hand bookseller; '**~iat** [~ar-'jaːt] *n* (-[e]s/-e) second-hand bookshop; **2isch** *adj. and adv.* [~'kvaːri∫] second-hand.
Antiquitäten [antikvi'tεːtən] *f/pl.* antiques *pl.*

'**Anti-Rakete** *f* anti-ballistic missile.
antiseptisch 🞰 *adj.* [anti'zεpti∫] antiseptic.
Antlitz ['antlits] *n* (-es/🞰 -e) face, countenance.
Antrag ['antraːk] *m* (-[e]s/⁼e) offer, proposal, application, request; *parl.* motion; *~ stellen auf (acc.*) make an application for; *parl.* put a motion for; '**~steller** *m* (-s/-) applicant; *parl.* mover; ⚖ᵗˢ petitioner.
'**an|treffen** *v/t.* (*irr. treffen, sep., -ge-, h*) meet with, find; '**~treiben** (*irr. treiben, sep., -ge-*) 1. *v/i.* (*sein*) drift ashore; 2. *v/t.* (*h*) drive (on); *fig.* impel; '**~treten** (*irr. treten, sep., -ge-*) 1. *v/t.* (*h*) enter upon (*office*); take up (*position*); set out on (*journey*); enter upon take possession of (*inheritance*); 2. *v/i.* (*sein*) take one's place; ✗ fall in.
'**Antrieb** *m* motive, impulse; ⊕ drive, propulsion.
'**Antritt** *m* (-[e]s/🞰 -e) entrance (*into office*); taking up (*of position*); setting out (*on journey*); entering into possession (*of inheritance*).
'**antun** *v/t.* (*irr. tun, sep., -ge-, h*): *j-m* et. *~* do s.th. to s.o.; *sich* et. *~* lay hands on o.s.
'**Antwort** *f* (-/-en) answer, reply (*auf acc.* to); '**2en** (*ge-, h*) 1. *v/i.* answer (*j-m* s.o.), reply (*j-m* to s.o.; *both: auf acc.* to); 2. *v/t.* answer (*auf acc.* to), reply (to); '**~schein** *m* (international) reply coupon.
'**an|vertrauen** *v/t.* (*sep., no -ge-, h*): *j-m* et. *~* (en)trust s.o. with s.th., entrust s.th. to s.o.; confide s.th. to s.o.; '**~wachsen** *v/i.* (*irr. wachsen, sep., -ge-, sein*) take root; *fig.* increase; *~ an (acc.*) grow on to.
Anwalt ['anvalt] *m* (-[e]s/⁼e) lawyer; solicitor, *Am.* attorney; counsel; barrister, *Am.* counsel(l)or; *fig.* advocate.
'**Anwandlung** *f* fit; impulse.
'**Anwärter** *m* candidate, aspirant; expectant.
Anwartschaft ['anvart∫aft] *f* (-/-en) expectancy; candidacy; prospect (*auf acc.* of).
'**anweis|en** *v/t.* (*irr. weisen, sep., -ge-, h*) assign; instruct; direct; *s. angewiesen*; '**2ung** *f* assignment; instruction; direction; †: cheque, *Am.* check; draft; *s. Postanweisung.*
'**anwend|en** *v/t.* (*[irr. wenden,] sep., -ge-, h*) employ, use; apply (*auf acc.* to); *s. angewandt*; '**2ung** *f* application.
'**anwerben** *v/t.* (*irr. werben, sep., -ge-, h*) ✗ enlist, enrol(l); engage.
'**Anwesen** *n* estate; property.
'**anwesen|d** *adj.* present; '**2heit** *f* (-/*no pl.*) presence.
'**Anzahl** *f* (-/*no pl.*) number; quantity.

'**anzahl|en** v/t. (sep., -ge-, h) pay on account; pay a deposit; '2**ung** f (first) instal(l)ment; deposit.

'**anzapfen** v/t. (sep., -ge-, h) tap.

'**Anzeichen** n symptom; sign.

Anzeige ['antsaɪgə] f (-/-n) notice, announcement; ✝ advice; advertisement; ⚡ information; '2**n** v/t. (sep., -ge-, h) announce, notify; ✝ advise; advertise; indicate; ⊕ instrument: indicate, show; thermometer: read (degrees); j-n ~ denounce s.o., inform against s.o.

'**anziehen** (irr. ziehen, sep., -ge-, h) 1. v/t. draw, pull; draw (rein); tighten (screw); put on (garment); dress; fig. attract; 2. v/i. draw; prices: rise; '**~d** adj. attractive, interesting.

'**Anziehung** f attraction; '**~skraft** f attractive power; attraction.

'**Anzug** m 1. (-[e]s/-̈e) dress; suit; 2. (-[e]s/no pl.): im ~ sein storm: be gathering; danger: be impending.

anzüglich adj. ['antsy:kliç] personal; '2**keit** f (-/-en) personality.

'**anzünden** v/t. (sep., -ge-, h) light, kindle; strike (match); set (building) on fire.

apathisch adj. [a'pɑ:tiʃ] apathetic.

Apfel ['apfəl] m (-s/-̈) apple; '**~mus** n apple-sauce; '**~sine** [~'zi:nə] f (-/-n) orange; '**~wein** m cider.

Apostel [a'pɔstəl] m (-s/-) apostle.

Apostroph [apo'stro:f] m (-s/-e) apostrophe.

Apotheke [apo'te:kə] f (-/-n) chemist's shop, pharmacy, Am. drug-store; **~r** m (-s/-) chemist, Am. druggist, pharmacist.

Apparat [apa'rɑ:t] m (-[e]s/-e) apparatus; device; teleph.: am ~l speaking!; teleph.: am ~ bleiben hold the line.

Appell [a'pɛl] m (-s/-e) ✗: roll-call; inspection; parade; fig. appeal (an acc. to); 2**ieren** [~'li:rən] v/i. (no -ge-, h) appeal (an acc. to).

Appetit [ape'ti:t] m (-[e]s/-e) appetite; 2**lich** adj. appetizing, savo(u)ry, dainty.

Applaus [a'plaus] m (-es/✗ -e) applause.

Aprikose [apri'ko:zə] f (-/-n) apricot.

April [a'pril] m (-[s]/-e) April.

Aquarell [akva'rɛl] n (-s/-e) water-colo(u)r (painting), aquarelle.

Aquarium [a'kvɑ:rium] n (-s/ Aquarien) aquarium.

Äquator [ɛ'kvɑ:tɔr] m (-s/✗ -en) equator.

Ära ['ɛ:ra] f (-/✗ Ären) era.

Arab|er ['arabər] m (-s/-) Arab; 2**isch** adj. [a'rɑ:biʃ] Arabian, Arab(ic).

Arbeit ['arbaɪt] f (-/-en) work; labo(u)r, toil; employment; job;

task; paper; workmanship; bei der ~ at work; sich an die ~ machen, an die ~ gehen set to work; (keine) ~ haben be in (out of) work; die ~ niederlegen stop work, down tools; '2**en** (ge-, h) 1. v/i. work; labo(u)r, toil; 2. v/t. work; make.

'**Arbeiter** m (-s/-) worker; workman, labo(u)rer, hand; '**~in** f (-/-nen) female worker; working woman, workwoman; '**~klasse** f working class(es pl.); '**~partei** f Labo(u)r Party; '**~schaft** f (-/-en), '**~stand** m working class(es pl.), labo(u)r.

'**Arbeit|geber** m (-s/-), '**~geberin** f (-/-nen) employer; '**~nehmer** m (-s/-), '**~nehmerin** f (-/-nen) employee.

'**arbeitsam** adj. industrious.

'**Arbeits|amt** n labo(u)r exchange; '**~anzug** m overall; '**~beschaffung** f (-/-en) provision of work; '**~bescheinigung** f certificate of employment; '**~einkommen** n earned income; '2**fähig** adj. able to work; '**~gericht** n labo(u)r or industrial court; '**~kleidung** f working clothes pl.; '**~kraft** f working power; worker, hand; Arbeitskräfte pl. a. labo(u)r; '**~leistung** f efficiency; power (of engine); output (of factory); '**~lohn** m wages pl., pay; '2**los** adj. out of work, unemployed; '**~lose** m (-n/-n): die ~n pl. the unemployed pl.; '**~losenunterstützung** f unemployment benefit; ~ beziehen F be on the dole; '**~losigkeit** f (-/no pl.) unemployment; '**~markt** m labo(u)r market; '**~minister** m Minister of Labour, Am. Secretary of Labor; '**~nachweis(stelle** f) m employment registry office, Am. labor registry office; '**~niederlegung** f (-/-en) strike, Am. F a. walkout; '**~pause** f break, intermission; '**~platz** m place of work; job; '**~raum** m work-room; '2**scheu** adj. work-shy; '**~scheu** f aversion to work; '**~schutzgesetz** n protective labo(u)r law; '**~tag** m working day, work-day; '2**unfähig** adj. incapable of working; disabled; '**~weise** f practice, method of working; '**~willige** m (-n/-n) non-striker; '**~zeit** f working time; working hours pl.; '**~zeug** n tools pl.; '**~zimmer** n workroom; study.

Archäo|loge [arçɛo'lo:gə] m (-n/-n) arch(a)eologist; '**~logie** [~o'gi:] f (-/no pl.) arch(a)eology.

Arche ['arçə] f (-/-n) ark.

Architekt [arçi'tɛkt] m (-en/-en) architect; **~ur** [~'tu:r] f (-/-en) architecture.

Archiv [ar'çi:f] n (-s/-e) archives pl.; record office.

Areal [are'a:l] n (-s/-e) area.

Arena [a're:na] *f* (-/Arenen) arena; bullring; (circus-)ring.

arg *adj.* [ark] bad; wicked; gross.

Ärger ['ɛrgər] *m* (-s/no pl.) vexation, annoyance; anger; **'Qlich** *adj.* vexed, F mad, angry (auf, über acc. at s.th., with s.o.); annoying, vexatious; '**Qn** *v/t.* (ge-, h) annoy, vex, irritate, fret; bother; sich ~ feel angry or vexed (über acc. at, about s.th.; with s.o.); **~nis** *n* (-ses/-se) scandal, offen|ce, Am. -se.

'Arg|list *f* (-/no pl.) cunning, craft (-iness); **Qlistig** *adj.* crafty, cunning; **Qlos** *adj.* guileless, artless, unsuspecting; **~wohn** ['~vo:n] *m* (-[e]s/no pl.) suspicion; **Qwöhnen** ['~vø:nən] *v/t.* (ge-, h) suspect; **Qwöhnisch** *adj.* suspicious.

Arie ♪ ['a:rjə] *f* (-/-n) aria.

Aristokrat [aristo'kra:t] *m* (-en/-en), **~in** *f* (-/-nen) aristocrat; **~ie** [~kra-'ti:] *f* (-/-nen) aristocracy.

Arkade [ar'ka:də] *f* (-/-n) arcade.

arm¹ *adj.* [arm] poor.

Arm² [~] *m* (-[e]s/-e) arm; branch (of river, etc.); F: j-n auf den ~ nehmen pull s.o.'s leg.

Armaturenbrett [arma'tu:rənbrɛt] *n* instrument board, dash-board.

'Arm|band *n* bracelet; **~banduhr** ['armbant⁹-] *f* wrist watch; '**~bruch** *m* fracture of the arm.

Armee [ar'me:] *f* (-/-n) army.

Ärmel ['ɛrməl] *m* (-s/-) sleeve; '**~kanal** *m* the (English) Channel.

'Armen|haus *n* alms-house, Brt. a. workhouse; '**~pflege** *f* poor relief; '**~pfleger** *m* guardian of the poor; welfare officer; '**~unterstützung** *f* poor relief.

ärmlich *adj.* ['ɛrmliç] s. armselig.

'armselig *adj.* poor; wretched; miserable; shabby; paltry.

Armut ['armu:t] *f* (-/no pl.) poverty.

Aroma [a'ro:ma] *n* (-s/Aromen, Aromata, -s) aroma, flavo(u)r; fragrance.

Arrest [a'rɛst] *m* (-es/-e) arrest; confinement; seizure (of goods); detention (of pupil, etc.); ~ bekommen be kept in.

Art [a:rt] *f* (-/-en) kind, sort; ♀, zo. species; manner, way; nature; manners pl.; breed, race (of animals); auf die(se) ~ in this way; 'Qen *v/i.* (ge-, sein): ~ nach take after. [artery.\

Arterie anat. [ar'te:rjə] *f* (-/-n)\

artig *adj.* ['a:rtiç] good, well-behaved; civil, polite; '**Qkeit** *f* (-/-en) good behavio(u)r; politeness; civility, a. civilities pl.

Artikel [ar'ti:kəl] *m* (-s/-) article; commodity.

Artillerie [artilə'ri:] *f* (-/-n) artillery.

Artist [ar'tist] *m* (-en/-en), **~in** *f* (-/-nen) circus performer.

Arznei [arts'naɪ] *f* (-/-en) medicine, F physic; **~kunde** *f* (-/no pl.) pharmaceutics; **~mittel** *n* medicine, drug.

Arzt [a:rtst] *m* (-es/⁼e) doctor, medical man; physician.

Ärztin ['ɛ:rtstin] *f* (-/-nen) woman or lady doctor.

ärztlich *adj.* ['ɛ:rtstliç] medical.

As [as] *n* (-ses/-se) ace.

Asche ['aʃə] *f* (-/-n) ash(es pl.); '**~nbahn** *f* sports: cinder-track, mot. dirt-track; '**~nbecher** *m* ash-tray; **~nbrödel** ['~nbrø:dəl] *n* (-s/no pl.), **~nputtel** ['~nputəl] *n* 1. (-s/no pl.) Cinderella; 2. (-s/-) drudge.

Ascher'mittwoch *m* Ash Wednesday.

'asch'grau *adj.* ash-grey, ashy, Am. ash-gray.

äsen hunt. ['ɛ:zən] *v/i.* (ge-, h) graze, browse.

Asiat [az'ja:t] *m* (-en/-en), **~in** *f* (-/-nen) Asiatic, Asian; **Qisch** *adj.* Asiatic, Asian.

Asket [as'ke:t] *m* (-en/-en) ascetic.

Asphalt [as'falt] *m* (-[e]s/-e) asphalt; **Qieren** [~'ti:rən] *v/t.* (no -ge-, h) asphalt.

aß [a:s] pret. of essen.

Assistent [asis'tɛnt] *m* (-en/-en), **~in** *f* (-/-nen) assistant.

Ast [ast] *m* (-es/⁼e) branch, bough; knot (in timber); '**~loch** *n* knot-hole.

Astro|naut [astro'naut] *m* (-en/-en) astronaut; **~nom** [~'no:m] *m* (-en/-en) astronomer.

Asyl [a'zy:l] *n* (-s/-e) asylum; fig. sanctuary.

Atelier [atə'lje:] *n* (-s/-s) studio.

Atem ['a:təm] *m* (-s/no pl.) breath; außer ~ out of breath; '**Qlos** *adj.* breathless; '**~not** ♀ *f* difficulty in breathing; '**~pause** *f* breathing-space; '**~zug** *m* breath, respiration.

Äther ['ɛ:tər] *m* 1. (-s/no pl.) ether; 2. ♪ (-s/-) ether; **Qisch** *adj.* [ɛ'tɛ:riʃ] ethereal, etheric.

Athlet [at'le:t] *m* (-en/-en), **~in** *f* (-/-nen) athlete; **~ik** *f* (-/no pl.) athletics mst sg.; **Qisch** *adj.* athletic.

atlantisch *adj.* [at'lantiʃ] Atlantic.

Atlas ['atlas] *m* 1. geogr. (-/no pl.) Atlas; 2. (-, -ses/-se, Atlanten) maps: atlas; 3. (-, -ses/-se) textiles: satin.

atmen ['a:tmən] *v/i. and v/t.* (ge-, h) breathe.

Atmosphär|e [atmo'sfɛ:rə] *f* (-/-n) atmosphere; **Qisch** *adj.* atmospheric.

'Atmung *f* (-/-en) breathing, respiration.

Atom [a'to:m] *n* (-s/-e) atom; **Qar** *adj.* [ato'ma:r] atomic; **~bombe** *f* atomic bomb, atom-bomb, A-bomb; **~energie** *f* atomic or nuclear energy; **~forschung** *f* atomic or nuclear research; **~kern** *m* atomic nucleus; **~kraftwerk** *n* nuclear power station; ~meiler *m* atomic pile, nuclear reactor; ~physiker *m* atomic physicist; ~reaktor *m* nuclear reactor, atomic pile; ~versuch *m* atomic test; ~waffe *f* atomic or nuclear weapon; ~wissenschaftler *m* atomic scientist; ~zeitalter *n* atomic age.

Attent|at [aten'tɑːt] *n* (-[e]s/-e) (attempted) assassination; *fig.* outrage; ~**äter** [~ɛːtər] *m* (-s/-) assailant, assassin.

Attest [a'test] *n* (-es/-e) certificate; 2**ieren** [~'tiːrən] *v/t.* (no -ge-, h) attest, certify.

Attraktion [atrak'tsjoːn] *f* (-/-en) attraction.

Attrappe [a'trapə] *f* (-/-n) dummy.

Attribut [atri'buːt] *n* (-[e]s/-e) attribute; *gr.* attributive.

ätz|en ['etsən] *v/t.* (ge-, h) corrode; ⚕ cauterize; etch (*metal plate*); ~**end** *adj.* corrosive; caustic (*a. fig.*); 2**ung** *f* (-/-en) corrosion; ⚕ cauterization; etching.

au *int.* [au] oh!; ouch!

auch *cj.* [aux] also, too, likewise; even; ~ *nicht* neither, nor; *wo* ~ (*immer*) wher(eso)ever; *ist es* ~ *wahr?* is it really true?

Audienz [audi'ents] *f* (-/-en) audience, hearing.

auf [auf] **1.** *prp.* (*dat.*) (up)on; in; at; of; by; ~ *dem Tisch* (up)on the table; ~ *dem Markt* in the market; ~ *der Universität* at the university; ~ *e-m Ball* at a ball; **2.** *prp.* (*acc.*) on; in; at; to; towards (*a.* ~ ... *zu*); up; ~ *deutsch* in German; ~ *e-e Entfernung von* at a range of; ~ *die Post etc.* gehen to the post-office, *etc.*; ~ *ein Pfund gehen 20 Schilling* 20 shillings go to a pound; *es geht* ~ *neun* it is getting on to nine; ~ ... *hin* on the strength of; **3.** *adv.* up(wards); ~ *und ab gehen* walk up and down *or* to and fro; **4.** *cj.*: ~ *daß* (in order) that; ~ *daß nicht* that not, lest; **5.** *int.*: ~*l* up!

auf|arbeiten ['auf⁹-] *v/t.* (*sep.*, -ge-, h) work off (*arrears of work*); furbish up; F do up (*garments*); ~**atmen** ['auf⁹-] *v/i.* (*sep.*, -ge-, h) breathe again.

'**Aufbau** *m* (-[e]s/*no pl.*) building up; construction (*of play*, *etc.*); F *esp. Am.* setup (*of organization*); *mot.* body (*of car*, *etc.*); 2**en** *v/t.* (*sep.*, -ge-, h) erect, build up; construct.

'**auf|bauschen** *v/t.* (*sep.*, -ge-, h) puff out; *fig.* exaggerate; ~**beißen** *v/t.* (*irr.* beißen, *sep.*, -ge-, h) crack; ~**bekommen** *v/t.* (*irr.* kommen, *sep.*, *no* -ge-, h) get open (*door*); be given (*a task*); ~**bessern** *v/t.* (*sep.*, -ge-, h) raise (*salary*); ~**bewahren** *v/t.* (*sep.*, *no* -ge-, h) keep; preserve;

~**bieten** *v/t.* (*irr.* bieten, *sep.*, -ge-, h) summon; exert; ✕ raise; '~**binden** *v/t.* (*irr.* binden, *sep.*, -ge-, h) untie; '~**bleiben** *v/i.* (*irr.* bleiben, *sep.*, -ge-, sein) sit up; door, *etc.*: remain open; '~**blenden** (*sep.*, -ge-, h) **1.** *mot.* *v/i.* turn up the headlights; **2.** *v/t.* fade in (*scene*); '~**blicken** *v/i.* (*sep.*, -ge-, h) look up; raise one's eyes; '~**blitzen** *v/i.* (*sep.*, -ge-, h, sein) flash (up); '~**blühen** *v/i.* (*sep.*, -ge-, sein) bloom; flourish.

'**aufbrausen** *fig. v/i.* (*sep.*, -ge-, sein) fly into a passion; '~**d** *adj.* hot-tempered.

'**auf|brechen** (*irr.* brechen, *sep.*, -ge-) **1.** *v/t.* (h) break open; force open; **2.** *v/i.* (sein) burst open; set out (*nach* for); '~**bringen** *v/t.* (*irr.* bringen, *sep.*, -ge-, h) raise (*money, troops*); capture (*ship*); rouse *or* irritate *s.o.*

'**Aufbruch** *m* departure, start.

'**auf|bügeln** *v/t.* (*sep.*, -ge-, h) iron; '~**bürden** *v/t.* (*sep.*, -ge-, h): *j-m et.* ~ impose s.th. on s.o.; '~**decken** *v/t.* (*sep.*, -ge-, h) uncover; spread (*cloth*); *fig.* disclose; '~**drängen** *v/t.* (*sep.*, -ge-, h) force, obtrude (*j-m* [up]on s.o.); '~**drehen** *v/t.* (*sep.*, -ge-, h) turn on (*gas*, *etc.*).

'**aufdringlich** *adj.* obtrusive.

'**Aufdruck** *m* (-[e]s/-e) imprint; surcharge.

'**aufdrücken** *v/t.* (*sep.*, -ge-, h) impress.

aufeinander *adv.* [auf⁹aı'nandər] one after *or* upon another; 2**folge** *f* succession; 2**folgend** *adj.* successive.

Aufenthalt ['aufenthalt] *m* (-[e]s/-e) stay; residence; delay; 🚇 stop; '~s-genehmigung *f* residence permit.

auferlegen ['auf⁹erleːgən] *v/t.* (*sep.*, *no* -ge-, h) impose (*j-m* on s.o.).

aufersteh|en ['auf⁹erʃteːən] *v/i.* (*irr.* stehen, *sep.*, *no* -ge-, sein) rise (from the dead); 2**ung** *f* (-/-en) resurrection.

auf|essen ['auf⁹-] *v/t.* (*irr.* essen, *sep.*, -ge-, h) eat up; '~**fahren** *v/i.* (*irr.* fahren, *sep.*, -ge-, sein) ascend; start up; *fig.* fly out; ⚓ run aground; *mot.* drive *or* run (*auf acc.* against, into).

'**Auffahrt** *f* ascent; driving up; approach; drive, *Am.* driveway; '~**srampe** *f* ramp.

'**auf|fallen** *v/i.* (*irr.* fallen, *sep.*, -ge-, sein) be conspicuous; *j-m* ~ strike s.o.; '~**fallend** *adj.*, '~**fällig** *adj.* striking; conspicuous; flashy.

'**auffangen** *v/t.* (*irr.* fangen, *sep.*, -ge-, h) catch (up); parry (*thrust*).

'**auffass|en** *v/t.* (*sep.*, -ge-, h) conceive; comprehend; interpret; 2**ung** *f* conception; interpretation; grasp.

'auffinden v/t. (irr. finden, sep., -ge-, h) find, trace, discover, locate.

'aufforder|n v/t. (sep., -ge-, h) ask, invite; call (up)on; esp. ⚖ summon; 'ₐung f invitation; esp. ⚖ summons.

'auffrischen (sep., -ge-) 1. v/t. (h) freshen up, touch up; brush up (knowledge); revive; 2. v/i. (sein) wind: freshen.

'aufführ|en v/t. (sep., -ge-, h) thea. represent, perform, act; enumerate; enter (in list); einzeln ~ specify, Am. itemize; sich ~ behave; 'ₐung f thea. performance; enumeration; entry; specification; conduct.

'Aufgabe f task; problem; school: homework; posting, Am. mailing (of letter); booking, Am. checking (of luggage); resignation (from office); abandonment; giving up (business); es sich zur ~ machen make it one's business.

'Aufgang m ascent; ast. rising; staircase.

'aufgeben (irr. geben, sep., -ge-, h) 1. v/t. give up, abandon; resign from (office); insert (advertisement); post, Am. mail (letter); book (luggage), Am. check (baggage); hand in, send (telegram); ✝ give (order); set, Am. assign (homework); set (riddle); 2. v/i. give up or in.

'Aufgebot n public notice; ⚔ levy; fig. array; banns pl. (of marriage).

'aufgehen v/i. (irr. gehen, sep., -ge-, sein) open; Ⱥ leave no remainder; sewing: come apart; paste, star, curtain: rise; seed: come up; ~ in (dat.) be merged in; fig. be devoted to (work); in Flammen ~ go up in flames.

aufgeklärt adj. ['aufgəklɛːrt] enlightened; 'ₐheit f (-/no pl.) enlightenment.

'Aufgeld ✝ n agio, premium.

aufge|legt adj. ['aufgəleːkt] disposed (zu for); in the mood (zu inf. for ger., to inf.); gut (schlecht) ~ in a good (bad) humo(u)r; '~schlossen fig. adj. open-minded; ~weckt fig. adj. ['~vɛkt] bright.

'auf|gießen v/t. (irr. gießen, sep., -ge-, h) pour (on); make (tea); '~greifen v/t. (irr. greifen, sep., -ge-, h) snatch up, fig. take up;}

'Aufguß m infusion.   [seize.]

'auf|haben (irr. haben, sep., -ge-, h) 1. v/t. have on (hat); have open (door); have to do (task); 2. F v/i.: das Geschäft hat auf the shop is open; '~haken v/t. (sep., -ge-, h) unhook; '~halten v/t. (irr. halten, sep., -ge-, h) keep open; stop, detain, delay; hold up (traffic); sich ~ stay; sich ~ bei dwell on; sich ~ mit spend one's time on; '~hängen v/t. (irr. hängen, sep., -ge-, h) hang (up); ⊕ suspend.

'aufheb|en v/t. (irr. heben, sep., -ge-, h) lift (up), raise; pick up; raise (siege); keep, preserve; cancel, annul, abolish; break off (engagement); break up (meeting); sich ~ neutralize; die Tafel ~ rise from the table; gut aufgehoben sein be well looked after; viel Aufhebens machen make a fuss (von about); 'ₐung f (-/-en) raising; abolition; annulment; breaking up.

'auf|heitern v/t. (sep., -ge-, h) cheer up; sich ~ weather: clear up; face: brighten; '~hellen v/t. and v/refl. (sep., -ge-, h) brighten.

'aufhetz|en v/t. (sep., -ge-, h) incite, instigate s.o.; 'ₐung f (-/-en) instigation, incitement.

'auf|holen (sep., -ge-, h) 1. v/t. make up (for); ⚓ haul up; 2. v/i. gain (gegen on); pull up (to); '~hören v/i. (sep., -ge-, h) cease, stop; Am. quit (all: zu tun doing); F: da hört (sich) doch alles auf! that's the limit!, Am. that beats everything!; '~kaufen v/t. (sep., -ge-, h) buy up.

'aufklär|en v/t. (sep., -ge-, h) clear up; enlighten (über acc. on); ⚔ reconnoit|re, Am. -er; sich ~ clear up; 'ₐung f enlightenment; ⚔ reconnaissance.

'auf|kleben v/t. (sep., -ge-, h) paste on, stick on, affix on; '~klinken v/t. (sep., -ge-, h) unlatch; '~knöpfen v/t. (sep., -ge-, h) unbutton.

'aufkommen 1. v/i. (irr. kommen, sep., -ge-, sein) rise; recover (from illness); come up; come into fashion or use; thought: arise; ~ für et. answer for s.th.; ~ gegen prevail against s.o.; 2. ⚔ n (-s/no pl.) rise; recovery.

'auf|krempeln ['aufkrɛmpəln] v/t. (sep., -ge-, h) turn up, roll up; tuck up; '~lachen v/i. (sep., -ge-, h) burst out laughing; '~laden v/t. (irr. laden, sep., -ge-, h) load; ⚡ charge.

'Auflage f edition (of book); circulation (of newspaper); ⊕ support.

'auf|lassen v/t. (irr. lassen, sep., -ge-, h) F leave open (door, etc.); F keep on (hat); ⚖ cede; '~lauern v/i. (sep., -ge-, h): j-m ~ lie in wait for s.o.

'Auflauf m concourse; riot; dish: soufflé; 'ₐen v/i. (irr. laufen, sep., -ge-, sein) interest: accrue; ⚓ run aground.

'auflegen (sep., -ge-, h) 1. v/t. put on, lay on; apply (auf acc. to); print, publish (book); teleph. hang up; 2. teleph. v/i. ring off.

'auflehn|en v/t. (sep., -ge-, h) lean (on); sich ~ lean (on); fig. rebel, revolt (gegen against); 'ₐung f (-/-en) rebellion.

'**auf|lesen** v/t. (irr. lesen, sep., -ge-, h) gather, pick up; '**~leuchten** v/i. (sep., -ge-, h) flash (up); '**~liegen** v/i. (irr. liegen, sep., -ge-, h) lie (auf dat. on).

'**auflös|bar** adj. (dis)soluble; '**~en** v/t. (sep., -ge-, h) undo (knot); break up (meeting); dissolve (salt, etc.; marriage, business, Parliament, etc.); solve (Å, riddle); disintegrate; fig. aufgelöst upset; '**Qung** f (dis-)solution; disintegration.

'**aufmach|en** v/t. (sep., -ge-, h) open; undo (dress, parcel); put up (umbrella); make up, get up; sich ~ wind: rise; set out (nach acc. for); make for; die Tür ~ answer the door; '**Qung** f (-/-en) make-up, get-up.

'**aufmarschieren** v/i. (sep., no -ge-, sein) form into line; ~ lassen ✕ deploy.

'**aufmerksam** adj. attentive (gegen to); j-n ~ machen auf (acc.) call s.o.'s attention to; '**Qkeit** f (-/-en) attention; token.

'**aufmuntern** v/t. (sep., -ge-, h) rouse; encourage; cheer up.

Aufnahme ['aufnɑːmə] f (-/-n) taking up (of work); reception; admission; phot.: taking; photograph, shot; shooting (of a film); '**Qfähig** adj. capable of absorbing; mind: receptive (für of); '**~gebühr** f admission fee; '**~gerät** n phot. camera; recorder; '**~prüfung** f entrance examination.

'**aufnehmen** v/t. (irr. nehmen, sep., -ge-, h) take up; pick up; take s.o. in; take down (dictation, etc.); take s.th. in (mentally); receive (guests); admit; raise, borrow (money); draw up, record; shoot (film); phot. take (picture); gut (übel) ~ take well (ill); es ~ mit be a match for.

aufopfer|n ['auf⁹-] v/t. (sep., -ge-, h) sacrifice; '**Qung** f sacrifice.

'**auf|passen** v/i. (sep., -ge-, h) attend (auf acc. to); watch; at school: be attentive; look out; ~ auf (acc.) take care of; '**~platzen** v/i. (sep., -ge-, sein) burst (open); '**~polieren** v/t. (sep., no -ge-, h) polish up; '**~prallen** v/i. (sep., -ge-, sein): auf den Boden ~ strike the ground; '**~pumpen** v/t. (sep., -ge-, h) blow up (tyre, etc.); '**~raffen** v/t. (sep., -ge-, h) snatch up; sich ~ rouse o.s. (zu for); muster up one's energy; '**~räumen** (sep., -ge-, h) 1. v/t. put in order; tidy (up), Am. straighten up; clear away; 2. v/i. tidy up; ~ mit do away with.

'**aufrecht** adj. and adv. upright (a. fig.), erect; '**~erhalten** v/t. (irr. halten, sep., no -ge-, h) maintain, uphold; '**Qerhaltung** f (-/no pl.) maintenance.

'**aufreg|en** v/t. (sep., -ge-, h) stir up, excite; sich ~ get excited or upset (über acc. about); aufgeregt excited; upset; '**Qung** f excitement, agitation.

'**auf|reiben** v/t. (irr. reiben, sep., -ge-, h) chafe (skin, etc.); fig.: destroy; exhaust, wear s.o. out; '**~reißen** (irr. reißen, sep., -ge-) 1. v/t. (h) rip or tear up or open; fling open (door); open (eyes) wide; 2. v/i. (sein) split open, burst.

'**aufreiz|en** v/t. (sep., -ge-, h) incite, stir up; '**~end** adj. provocative; '**Qung** f instigation.

'**aufrichten** v/t. (sep., -ge-, h) set up, erect; sich ~ stand up; straighten; sit up (in bed).

'**aufrichtig** adj. sincere, candid; '**Qkeit** f sincerity, cando(u)r.

'**aufriegeln** v/t. (sep., -ge-, h) unbolt.

Aufriß △ m elevation.

'**aufrollen** v/t. and v/refl. (sep., -ge-, h) roll up; unroll.

'**Aufruf** m call, summons; '**Qen** v/t. (irr. rufen, sep., -ge-, h) call up; call on s.o.

Aufruhr ['aufruːr] m (-[e]s/-e) uproar, tumult; riot, rebellion.

'**aufrühr|en** v/t. (sep., -ge-, h) stir up; revive; fig. rake up; '**Qer** m (-s/-) rebel; '**~erisch** adj. rebellious.

Aufrüstung ✕ f (re)armament.

'**auf|rütteln** v/t. (sep., -ge-, h) shake up; rouse; '**~sagen** v/t. (sep., -ge-, h) say, repeat; recite.

aufsässig adj. ['aufzɛsiç] rebellious.

'**Aufsatz** m essay; composition; ⊕ top.

'**auf|saugen** v/t. (sep., -ge-, h) suck up; ∻ absorb; '**~scheuchen** v/t. (sep., -ge-, h) scare (away); disturb; rouse; '**~scheuern** v/t. (sep., -ge-, h) scour; ⊰ chafe; '**~schichten** v/t. (sep., -ge-, h) pile up; '**~schieben** v/t. (irr. schieben, sep., -ge-, h) slide open; fig.: put off; defer, postpone; adjourn.

'**Aufschlag** m striking; impact; additional or extra charge; facing (on coat), lapel (of coat); cuff (on sleeve); turn-up (on trousers); tennis: service; '**Qen** ['~gən] (irr. schlagen, sep., -ge-) 1. v/t. (h) open; turn up (sleeve, etc.); take up (abode); pitch (tent); raise (prices); cut (one's knee) open; 2. v/i. (sein) strike, hit; ⧓ rise, go up (in price); tennis: serve.

'**auf|schließen** v/t. (irr. schließen, sep., -ge-, h) unlock, open; '**~schlitzen** v/t. (sep., -ge-, h) slit or rip open.

'**Aufschluß** fig. m information.

'**auf|schnallen** v/t. (sep., -ge-, h) unbuckle; '**~schnappen** (sep., -ge-) 1. v/t. (h) snatch; fig. pick up; 2. v/i. (sein) snap open; '**~schnei-**

den (*irr.* schneiden, *sep.*, -ge-, h)
1. *v/t.* cut open; cut up (*meat*);
2. *fig.* *v/i.* brag, boast.

'Aufschnitt *m* (slices *pl.* of) cold
meat, *Am.* cold cuts *pl.*

'auf|schnüren *v/t.* (*sep.*, -ge-, h)
untie; unlace; **'~schrauben** *v/t.*
(*sep.*, -ge-, h) screw (*auf acc.* on);
unscrew; **'~schrecken** (*sep.*, -ge-)
1. *v/t.* (h) startle; **2.** *v/i.* (*irr.*
schrecken, sein) start (up).

'Aufschrei *m* shriek, scream; *fig.*
outcry.

'auf|schreiben *v/t.* (*irr.* schreiben,
sep., -ge-, h) write down; **'~
schreien** *v/i.* (*irr.* schreien, *sep.*,
-ge-, h) cry out, scream.

'Aufschrift *f* inscription; address,
direction (*on letter*); label.

'Aufschub *m* deferment; delay;
adjournment; respite.

'auf|schürfen *v/t.* (*sep.*, -ge-, h)
graze (*skin*); **'~schwingen** *v/refl.*
(*irr.* schwingen, *sep.*, -ge-, h) soar,
rise; *sich zu et.* ~ bring o.s. to do
s.th.

'Aufschwung *m* *fig.* rise, *Am.* up-
swing; ✝ boom.

'aufsehen 1. *v/i.* (*irr.* sehen, *sep.*,
-ge-, h) look up; **2.** ⌾ *n* (-s/*no pl.*)
sensation; ~ *erregen* cause a sensation; **'~erregend** *adj.* sensational.

'Aufseher *m* overseer; inspector.

'aufsetzen (*sep.*, -ge-, h) **1.** *v/t.* set
up; put on (*hat*, *countenance*); draw
up (*document*); *sich* ~ sit up; **2.** ✈
v/i. touch down.

'Aufsicht *f* (-/-en) inspection, supervision; *store*: shopwalker, *Am.* floor-
walker; **'~behörde** *f* board of control; **'~srat** *m* board of directors.

'auf|sitzen *v/i.* (*irr.* sitzen, *sep.*,
-ge-, h) rider: mount; **'~spannen**
v/t. (*sep.*, -ge-, h) stretch; put up
(*umbrella*); spread (*sails*); **'~sparen**
v/t. (*sep.*, -ge-, h) save; *fig.* reserve;
'~speichern *v/t.* (*sep.*, -ge-, h)
store up; **'~sperren** *v/t.* (*sep.*, -ge-,
h) open wide; **'~spielen** (*sep.*, -ge-,
h) **1.** *v/t.* and *v/i.* strike up; **2.** *v/refl.*
show off; *sich* ~ *als* set up for; **'~
spießen** *v/t.* (*sep.*, -ge-, h) pierce;
with horns: gore; run through;
spear; **'~springen** *v/i.* (*irr.* springen, *sep.*, -ge-, sein) jump up; *door*:
fly open; crack; *skin*: chap; **'~spü-
ren** *v/t.* (*sep.*, -ge-, h) hunt up;
track down; **'~stacheln** *fig.* *v/t.*
(*sep.*, -ge-, h) goad; incite, instigate;
'~stampfen *v/t.* (*sep.*, -ge-, h)
stamp (one's foot).

'Aufstand *m* insurrection; rebellion;
uprising, revolt.

aufständisch *adj.* ['aufſtendiſ] rebellious; **'⌾e** *m* (-n/-n) insurgent,
rebel.

'auf|stapeln *v/t.* (*sep.*, -ge-, h) pile
up; ✝ store (up); **'~stechen** *v/t.*
(*irr.* stechen, *sep.*, -ge-, h) puncture;

prick open; ⚕ lance; **'~stecken** *v/t.*
(*sep.*, -ge-, h) pin up; put up (*hair*);
'~stehen *v/i.* (*irr.* stehen, *sep.*, -ge-)
1. (sein) stand up; rise, get up; revolt; **2.** F (h) stand open; **'~steigen**
v/i. (*irr.* steigen, *sep.*, -ge-, sein) rise,
ascend; ✈ take off; *rider*: mount.

'aufstell|en *v/t.* (*sep.*, -ge-, h) set
up, put up; ⚔ draw up; post (*sen-
tries*); make (*assertion*); set (*example*); erect (*column*); set (*trap*);
nominate (*candidate*); draw up
(*bill*); lay down (*rule*); make out
(*list*); set up, establish (*record*);
'⌾ung *f* putting up; drawing up;
erection; nomination; ✝ statement;
list.

Aufstieg ['aufſti:k] *m* (-[e]s/-e)
ascent, *Am. a.* ascension; *fig.* rise.

'auf|stöbern *fig.* *v/t.* (*sep.*, -ge-, h)
hunt up; **'~stoßen** (*irr.* stoßen, *sep.*,
-ge-) **1.** *v/t.* (h) push open; ~ *auf*
(*acc.*) knock against; **2.** *v/i.* (h, sein)
of food: rise, repeat; belch; **'~strei-
chen** *v/t.* (*irr.* streichen, *sep.*, -ge-,
h) spread (*butter*).

'Aufstrich *m* spread (*for bread*).

'auf|stützen *v/t.* (*sep.*, -ge-, h) prop
up, support s.th.; *sich* ~ *auf* (*acc.*)
lean on; **'~suchen** *v/t.* (*sep.*, -ge-, h)
visit (*places*); go to see *s.o.*, look
s.o. up.

'Auftakt *m* ♪ upbeat; *fig.* prelude,
preliminaries *pl.*

'auf|tauchen *v/i.* (*sep.*, -ge-, sein)
emerge, appear, turn up; **'~tauen**
(*sep.*, -ge-) **1.** *v/t.* (h) thaw; **2.** *v/i.*
(sein) thaw (*a. fig.*); **'~teilen** *v/t.*
(*sep.*, -ge-, h) divide (up), share.

Auftrag ['auftra:k] *m* (-[e]s/✸e)
commission; instruction; mission;
⚖ mandate; ✝ order; **2en** ['~gən]
v/t. (*irr.* tragen, *sep.*, -ge-, h) serve
(up) (*meal*); lay on (*paint*); wear
out (*dress*); *j-m* et. ~ charge *s.o.*
with s.th.; **~geber** ['~k-] *m* (-s/-)
employer; customer; principal; **~s-
erteilung** ['~ksǝertailuŋ] *f* (-/-en)
placing of an order.

'auf|treffen *v/i.* (*irr.* treffen, *sep.*,
-ge-, sein) strike, hit; **'~treiben** *v/t.*
(*irr.* treiben, *sep.*, -ge-, h) hunt up;
raise (*money*); **'~trennen** *v/t.* (*sep.*,
-ge-, h) rip; unstitch (*seam*).

'auftreten 1. *v/i.* (*irr.* treten, *sep.*,
-ge-, sein) tread; *thea.*, *witness*, *etc.*:
appear (*als* as); behave, act; *diffi-
culties*: arise; **2.** ⌾ *n* (-s/*no pl.*) appearance; occurrence (*of events*);
behavio(u)r.

'Auftrieb *m* *phys.* and *fig.* buoyancy; ✈ lift; *fig.* impetus.

'Auftritt *m* *thea.* scene (*a. fig.*);
appearance (*of actor*).

'auf|trumpfen *fig.* *v/i.* (*sep.*, -ge-, h)
put one's foot down; **'~tun** *v/t.* (*irr.*
tun, *sep.*, -ge-, h) open; *sich* ~ open;
chasm: yawn; *society*: form; **'~tür-
men** *v/t.* (*sep.*, -ge-, h) pile *or* heap

up; *sich* ~ tower up; pile up; *diffi-culties*: accumulate; '~**wachen** *v/i.* (*sep.*, *-ge-*, *sein*) awake, wake up; '~**wachsen** *v/i.* (*irr. wachsen, sep.*, *-ge-*, *sein*) grow up.

'**Aufwallung** *f* ebullition, surge.

Aufwand ['aufvant] *m* (-[e]s/*no pl.*) expense, expenditure (*an dat.* of); pomp; splendid *or* great display (*of words, etc.*).

'**aufwärmen** *v/t.* (*sep.*, *-ge-*, *h*) warm up.

'**Aufwarte|frau** *f* charwoman, *Am. a.* cleaning woman; '2n *v/i.* (*sep.*, *-ge-*, *h*) wait (up)on *s.o.*, attend on *s.o.*; wait (at table).

aufwärts *adv.* ['aufverts] upward(s).

'**Aufwartung** *f* attendance; visit; *j-m s-e* ~ *machen* pay one's respects to s.o., call on s.o.

'**aufwasch|en** *v/t.* (*irr. waschen, sep.*, *-ge-*, *h*) wash up; '2**wasser** *n* dish-water.

'**auf|wecken** *v/t.* (*sep.*, *-ge-*, *h*) awake(n), wake (up); '~**weichen** (*sep.*, *-ge-*) **1.** *v/t.* (*h*) soften; soak; **2.** *v/i.* (*sein*) soften, become soft; '~**weisen** *v/t.* (*irr. weisen, sep.*, *-ge-*, *h*) show, exhibit; produce; '~**wenden** *v/t.* (*[irr. wenden,] sep.*, *-ge-*, *h*) spend; *Mühe* ~ take pains; '~**werfen** *v/t.* (*irr. werfen, sep.*, *-ge-*, *h*) raise (*a. question*).

'**aufwert|en** *v/t.* (*sep.*, *-ge-*, *h*) revalorize; revalue; '2**ung** *f* revalorization; revaluation.

'**aufwickeln** *v/t. and v/refl.* (*sep.*, *-ge-*, *h*) wind up, roll up.

'**aufwiegel|n** ['aufvi:gəln] *v/t.* (*sep.*, *-ge-*, *h*) stir up, incite, instigate; '2**ung** *f* (-/-*en*) instigation.

'**aufwiegen** *fig.* *v/t.* (*irr. wiegen, sep.*, *-ge-*, *h*) make up for.

Aufwiegler ['aufvi:glər] *m* (-*s*/-) agitator; instigator.

'**aufwirbeln** (*sep.*, *-ge-*) **1.** *v/t.* (*h*) whirl up; raise (*dust*); *fig. viel Staub* ~ create a sensation; **2.** *v/i.* (*sein*) whirl up.

'**aufwisch|en** *v/t.* (*sep.*, *-ge-*, *h*) wipe up; '2**lappen** *m* floor-cloth.

'**aufwühlen** *v/t.* (*sep.*, *-ge-*, *h*) turn up; *fig.* stir.

'**aufzähl|en** *v/t.* (*sep.*, *-ge-*, *h*) count up; *fig.* enumerate, *Am. a.* call off; specify, *Am.* itemize; '2**ung** *f* (-/-*en*) enumeration; specification.

'**auf|zäumen** *v/t.* (*sep.*, *-ge-*, *h*) bridle; '~**zehren** *v/t.* (*sep.*, *-ge-*, *h*) consume.

'**aufzeichn|en** *v/t.* (*sep.*, *-ge-*, *h*) draw; note down; record; '2**ung** *f* note; record.

'**auf|zeigen** *v/t.* (*sep.*, *-ge-*, *h*) demonstrate; point out (*mistakes, etc.*); disclose; '~**ziehen** (*irr. zie-hen, sep.*, *-ge-*) **1.** *v/t.* (*h*) draw *or* pull up (*pull*) open; hoist (*flag*); bring up (*child*); mount (*picture*);

wind (up) (*clock, etc.*); *j-n* ~ tease s.o., pull s.o.'s leg; *Saiten auf e-e Violine* ~ string a violin; **2.** *v/i.* (*sein*) ✕ draw up; *storm*: approach.

'**Aufzucht** *f* rearing, breeding.

'**Aufzug** *m* ⊕ hoist; lift, *Am.* elevator; *thea.* act; attire; show.

'**aufzwingen** *v/t.* (*irr. zwingen, sep.*, *-ge-*, *h*): *j-m et.* ~ force s.th. upon s.o.

Augapfel ['auk?-] *m* eyeball.

Auge ['augə] *n* (-*s*/-*n*) eye; sight; ♀ bud; *in meinen* ~*n* in my view; *im* ~ *behalten* keep an eye on; keep in mind; *aus den* ~*n verlieren* lose sight of; *ein* ~ *zudrücken* turn a blind eye (*bei* to); *ins* ~ *fallen* strike the eye; *große* ~*n machen* open one's eyes wide; *unter vier* ~*n* face to face, privately; *kein* ~ *zutun* not to get a wink of sleep.

'**Augen|arzt** *m* oculist, eye-doctor; '~**blick** *m* moment, instant; '2**blicklich** **1.** *adj.* instantaneous; momentary; present; **2.** *adv.* instant(aneous)ly; at present; '~**braue** *f* eyebrow; '~**entzündung** ♀ *f* inflammation of the eye; '~**heilkunde** *f* ophthalmology; '~**klinik** *f* ophthalmic hospital; '~**leiden** ♀ *n* eye-complaint; '~**licht** *n* eyesight; '~**lid** *n* eyelid; '~**maß** *n*: *ein gutes* ~ a sure eye; *nach dem* ~ by eye; '~**merk** ['~merk] *n* (-[e]s/*no pl.*): *sein* ~ *richten auf* (*acc.*) turn one's attention to; have *s.th.* in view; '~**schein** *m* appearance; *in* ~ *nehmen* examine, view, inspect; '2**scheinlich** *adj.* evident; '~**wasser** *n* eyewash, eye-lotion; '~**wimper** *f* eyelash; '~**zeuge** *m* eyewitness.

August [au'gust] *m* (-[e]s, - /-*e*) August.

Auktion [auk'tsjo:n] *f* (-/-*en*) auction; ~**ator** [~o'na:tor] *m* (-*s*/-*en*) auctioneer.

Aula ['aula] *f* (-/*Aulen*, -*s*) (assembly) hall, *Am.* auditorium.

aus [aus] **1.** *prp.* (*dat.*) out of; from; of; by; for; in; ~ *Achtung* out of respect; ~ *London kommen* come from London; ~ *diesem Grunde* for this reason; ~ *Ihrem Brief ersehe ich* I see from your letter; **2.** *adv.* out; over; *die Schule ist* ~ school is over; F: *von mir* ~ for all I care; *auf et.* ~ *sein* be keen on it.; *es ist* ~ *mit ihm* it is all over with him; *das Spiel ist* ~! the game is up!; *er weiß weder ein noch* ~ he is at his wit's end; *on instruments, etc.*: *an* — ~ on — off.

ausarbeit|en ['aus?-] *v/t.* (*sep.*, *-ge-*, *h*) work out; elaborate; '2**ung** *f* (-/-*en*) working-out; elaboration; composition.

aus|arten ['aus?-] *v/i.* (*sep.*, *-ge-*, *sein*) degenerate; get out of hand; ~**atmen** ['aus?-] (*sep.*, *-ge-*, *h*)

1. v/i. breathe out; **2.** v/t. breathe out; exhale (*vapour*, *etc.*); '**~baggern** v/t. (*sep.*, *-ge-*, h) dredge (*river*, *etc.*); excavate (*ground*).

'**Ausbau** m (-[e]s/-ten) extension; completion; development; '**2en** v/t. (*sep.*, *-ge-*, h) develop; extend; finish, complete; ⊕ dismantle (*engine*).

'**ausbedingen** v/t. (*irr.* bedingen, *sep.*, *no -ge-*, h) stipulate.

'**ausbesser|n** v/t. (*sep.*, *-ge-*, h) mend, repair, Am. F a. fix; '**2ung** f repair, mending.

'**Ausbeut|e** f (-/%-n) gain, profit; yield; ⚒ output; '**2en** v/t. (*sep.*, *-ge-*, h) exploit; sweat (*workers*); '**~ung** f (-/-en) exploitation.

'**ausbild|en** v/t. (*sep.*, *-ge-*, h) form, develop; train; instruct, educate; ⚔ drill; '**2ung** f development; training; instruction; education; ⚔ drill.

'**ausbitten** v/t. (*irr.* bitten, *sep.*, *-ge-*, h): sich et. ~ request s.th.; insist on s.th.

'**ausbleiben 1.** v/i. (*irr.* bleiben, *sep.*, *-ge-*, sein) stay away, fail to appear; **2.** 2 n (-s/*no pl.*) non-arrival, non-appearance; absence.

'**Ausblick** m outlook (*auf acc.* over, on), view (of), prospect (of); *fig.* outlook (on).

'**aus|bohren** v/t. (*sep.*, *-ge-*, h) bore, drill; '**~brechen** (*irr.* brechen, *sep.*, *-ge-*) **1.** v/t. (h) break out; vomit; **2.** v/i. (sein) break out; *fig.* burst out (*laughing*, *etc.*).

'**ausbreit|en** v/t. (*sep.*, *-ge-*, h) spread (out); stretch (out) (*arms*, *wings*); display; sich ~ spread; '**2ung** f (-/%-en) spreading.

'**ausbrennen** (*irr.* brennen, *sep.*, *-ge-*) **1.** v/t. (h) burn out; ⚕ cauterize; **2.** v/i. (sein) burn out.

'**Ausbruch** m outbreak; eruption (*of volcano*); escape (*from prison*); outburst (*of emotion*).

'**aus|brüten** v/t. (*sep.*, *-ge-*, h) hatch (a. *fig.*); '**~bürgern** v/t. (*sep.*, *-ge-*, h) denationalize, expatriate.

'**Ausdauer** f perseverance; **2nd** *adj.* persevering; ♃ perennial.

'**ausdehn|en** v/t. and v/refl. (*sep.*, *-ge-*, h) extend (*auf acc.* to); expand; stretch; '**2ung** f expansion; extension; extent.

'**aus|denken** v/t. (*irr.* denken, *sep.*, *-ge-*, h) think s.th. out, Am. a. think s.th. up, contrive, devise, invent; imagine; '**~dörren** v/t. (*sep.*, *-ge-*, h) dry up; parch; '**~drehen** v/t. (*sep.*, *-ge-*, h) turn off (*radio*, *gas*); ⚡ turn out, switch off (*light*).

'**Ausdruck** m **1.** (-[e]s/*no pl.*) expression; **2.** (-[e]s/⁺e) expression; term.

'**ausdrück|en** v/t. (*sep.*, *-ge-*, h) press, squeeze (out); stub out (*cig-*

arette); *fig.* express; '**~lich** *adj.* express, explicit.

'**ausdrucks|los** *adj.* inexpressive, expressionless; blank; '**~voll** *adj.* expressive; '**2weise** f mode of expression; style.

'**Ausdünstung** f (-/-en) exhalation; perspiration; odo(u)r, smell.

auseinander *adv.* [aus⁹ar'nandər] asunder, apart; separate(d); **~brin gen** v/t. (*irr.* bringen, *sep.*, *-ge-*, h) separate, sever; **~gehen** v/i. (*irr.* gehen, *sep.*, *-ge-*, sein) meeting, *crowd*: break up; *opinions*: differ; *friends*: part; *crowd*: disperse; *roads*: diverge; **~nehmen** v/t. (*irr.* nehmen, *sep.*, *-ge-*, h) take apart or to pieces; ⊕ disassemble, dismantle; **~setzen** *fig.* v/t. (*sep.*, *-ge-*, h) explain; sich mit j-m ~ ⁺ compound with s.o.; argue with s.o.; have it out with s.o.; sich mit e-m Problem ~ get down to a problem; come to grips with a problem; **2setzung** f (-/-en) explanation; discussion; settlement (*with creditors*, *etc.*); kriegerische ~ armed conflict.

auserlesen *adj.* ['aus⁹-] exquisite, choice; select(ed).

auswählen ['aus⁹-] v/t. (*sep.*, *no -ge-*, h) select, choose.

'**ausfahr|en** (*irr.* fahren, *sep.*, *-ge-*) **1.** v/i. (sein) drive out, go for a drive; ⚓ leave (*port*); **2.** v/t. (h) take (*baby*) out (*in pram*); take s.o. for a drive; rut (*road*); ⚓ lower (*undercarriage*); '**2t** f drive; excursion; way out, exit (*of garage*, *etc.*); gateway; departure.

'**Ausfall** m falling out; ✝: loss; deficit; '**2en** v/i. (*irr.* fallen, *sep.*, *-ge-*, sein) fall out; not to take place; turn out, prove; ~ lassen drop; cancel; die Schule fällt aus there is no school; '**2end** *adj.* offensive, insulting.

'**aus|fasern** v/i. (*sep.*, *-ge-*, sein) ravel out, fray; '**~fegen** v/t. (*sep.*, *-ge-*, h) sweep (out).

ausfertig|en ['ausfɛrtigən] v/t. (*sep.*, *-ge-*, h) draw up (*document*); make out (*bill*, *etc.*); issue (*passport*); '**2ung** f (-/-en) drawing up; issue; draft; copy; in doppelter ~ in duplicate. [*chen* find out; discover.]

ausfindig *adj.* ['ausfindiç]: ~ ma-]

'**Ausflucht** f (-/⁺e) excuse, evasion, shift, subterfuge.

'**Ausflug** m trip, excursion, outing.

Ausflügler ['ausfly:klər] m (-s/-) excursionist, tripper, tourist.

'**Ausfluß** m flowing out; discharge (a. ⚕); outlet, outfall.

'**aus|fragen** v/t. (*sep.*, *-ge-*, h) interrogate, Am. a. quiz; sound; '**~fran sen** v/i. (*sep.*, *-ge-*, sein) fray.

Ausfuhr ✝ ['ausfu:r] f (-/-en) export(ation); **~artikel** ✝ m export (article).

'ausführ|bar *adj.* practicable; † exportable; '~en *v/t.* (*sep.*, -ge-, *h*) execute, carry out, perform, *Am. a.* fill; † export; explain; *j-n* ~ take s.o. out.

'Ausfuhr|genehmigung *f* export permit; '~handel *m* export trade.

'ausführlich 1. *adj.* detailed; comprehensive; circumstantial; 2. *adv.* in detail, at (some) length; '2keit *f* (-/no *pl.*) minuteness of detail; particularity; comprehensiveness; copiousness.

'Ausführung *f* execution, performance; workmanship; type, make; explanation; '~sbestimmungen † *f/pl.* export regulations *pl.*

'Ausfuhr|verbot *n* embargo on exports; '~waren *f/pl.* exports *pl.*; '~zoll *m* export duty.

'ausfüllen *v/t.* (*sep.*, -ge-, *h*) fill out *or* up; fill in, complete (*form*); *Am.* fill out (*blank*).

'Ausgabe *f* distribution; edition (*of book*); expense, expenditure; issue (*of shares, etc.*); issuing office.

'Ausgang *m* going out; exit; way out; outlet; end; result; '~skapital † *n* original capital; '~spunkt *m* starting-position; '~stellung *f* starting-position.

'ausgeben *v/t.* (*irr. geben, sep.*, -ge-, *h*) give out; spend (*money*); issue (*shares, etc.*); *sich* ~ *für* pass o.s. off for, pretend to be.

ausge|beult *adj.* ['ausɡəbɔylt] baggy; ~bombt *adj.* ['~bɔmpt] bombed out; ~dehnt *adj.* ['~de:nt] expansive, vast, extensive; ~dient *adj.* ['~di:nt] worn out; superannuated; retired, pensioned off; ~er *Soldat* ex-serviceman, veteran; '~fallen *fig. adj.* odd, queer, unusual.

'ausgehen *v/i.* (*irr. gehen, sep.*, -ge-, *sein*) go out; take a walk; end; *colour:* fade; *hair:* fall out; *money, provisions:* run out; *uns gehen die Vorräte aus* we run out of provisions; *darauf* ~ aim at; *gut etc.* ~ turn out well, *etc.*; *leer* ~ come away empty-handed; *von et.* ~ start from s.th.

'ausge|lassen *fig. adj.* frolicsome, boisterous; '~nommen *prp.* 1. (*acc.*) except (for); 2. (*nom.*): *Anwesende* ~ present company excepted; ~prägt *adj.* ['~prɛːkt] marked, pronounced; ~rechnet *fig. adv.* ['~rɛçnət] just; ~ *er* he of all people; ~ *heute* today of all days; '~schlossen *fig. adj.* impossible.

'ausgestalten *v/t.* (*sep.*, *no* -ge-, *h*) arrange (*celebration*); *et. zu et.* ~ develop *or* turn s.th. into s.th.

ausge|sucht *fig. adj.* ['ausɡəzu:xt] exquisite, choice; '~wachsen *adj.* full-grown; ~zeichnet *fig. adj.* ['~tsaiçnət] excellent.

ausgiebig *adj.* ['ausɡi:biç] abundant, plentiful; *meal:* substantial.

'ausgießen *v/t.* (*irr. gießen, sep.*, -ge-, *h*) pour out.

Ausgleich ['ausɡlaiç] *m* (-[e]s/-e) compromise; compensation; † settlement; *sports:* equalization (*of score*); *tennis:* deuce (*score of 40 all*); '2en *v/t.* (*irr. gleichen, sep.*, -ge-, *h*) equalize; compensate (*loss*); † balance.

'aus|gleiten *v/i.* (*irr. gleiten, sep.*, -ge-, *sein*) slip, slide; '~graben *v/t.* (*irr. graben, sep.*, -ge-, *h*) dig out *or* up (*a. fig.*); excavate; exhume (*body*).

Ausguck ⊕ ['ausɡuk] *m* (-[e]s/-e) look-out.

'Ausguß *m* sink; '~eimer *m* slop-pail.

'aus|haken *v/t.* (*sep.*, -ge-, *h*) unhook; '~halten (*irr. halten, sep.*, -ge-, *h*) 1. *v/t.* endure, bear, stand; ♪ sustain (*note*); 2. *v/i.* hold out; last; ~händigen ['~hɛndiɡən] *v/t.* (*sep.*, -ge-, *h*) deliver up, hand over, surrender.

'Aushang *m* notice, placard, poster.

'aushänge|n 1. *v/t.* (*sep.*, -ge-, *h*) hang *or* put out; unhinge (*door*); 2. *v/i.* (*irr. hängen, sep.*, -ge-, *h*) have been hung *or* put out; '2-schild *n* signboard.

aus|harren ['ausharən] *v/i.* (*sep.*, -ge-, *h*) persevere; hold out; '~hauchen *v/t.* (*sep.*, -ge-, *h*) breathe out, exhale; '~heben *v/t.* (*irr. heben, sep.*, -ge-, *h*) dig (*trench*); unhinge (*door*); recruit, levy (*soldiers*); excavate (*earth*); rob (*nest*); clean out, raid (*nest of criminals*); '~helfen *v/i.* (*irr. helfen, sep.*, -ge-, *h*) help out.

'Aushilf|e *f* (temporary) help *or* assistance; *sie hat e-e* ~ she has s.o. to help out; '2sweise *adv.* as a makeshift; temporarily.

'aushöhl|en *v/t.* (*sep.*, -ge-, *h*) hollow out; '2ung *f* hollow.

'aus|holen (*sep.*, -ge-, *h*) 1. *v/i.* raise one's hand (*as if to strike*); *weit* ~ go far back (*in narrating s.th.*); 2. *v/t.* sound, pump *s.o.*; '~horchen *v/t.* (*sep.*, -ge-, *h*) sound, pump *s.o.*; '~hungern *v/t.* (*sep.*, -ge-, *h*) starve (out); '~husten *v/t.* (*sep.*, -ge-, *h*) cough up; '~kennen *v/refl.* (*irr. kennen, sep.*, -ge-, *h*) know one's way (*about place*); be well versed, be at home (*in subject*); *er kennt sich aus* he knows what's what; '~kleiden *v/t.* (*sep.*, -ge-, *h*) undress; ⊕ line, coat; *sich* ~ undress; '~klopfen *v/t.* (*sep.*, -ge-, *h*) beat (out); dust (*garment*); knock out (*pipe*); ~klügeln ['~kly:ɡəln] *v/t.* (*sep.*, -ge-, *h*) work *s.th.* out; contrive; puzzle *s.th.* out.

'auskommen 1. *v/i.* (*irr. kommen, sep.*, -ge-, *sein*) get out; escape; ~

mit manage with *s.th.*; get on with *s.o.*; ~ *ohne* do without; *mit dem Geld* ~ make both ends meet; 2. ♀ *n* (-*s*/*no pl.*) competence, competency.

'**auskundschaften** *v/t.* (*sep.*, -ge-, *h*) explore; ✗ reconnoit|re, *Am.* -er, scout.

Auskunft ['auskunft] *f* (-/⸚e) information; inquiry office, inquiries *pl.*, *Am.* information desk; '**~stelle** *f* inquiry office, inquiries *pl.*, *Am.* information bureau.

'**aus**|**lachen** *v/t.* (*sep.*, -ge-, *h*) laugh at, deride; '**~laden** *v/t.* (*irr. laden*, *sep.*, -ge-, *h*) unload; discharge (*cargo from ship*); cancel *s.o.'s* invitation, put off (*guest*).

'**Auslage** *f* display, show (*of goods*); *in der* ~ in the (shop) window; ~*n pl.* expenses *pl.*

'**Ausland** *n* (-[e]s/*no pl.*): *das* ~ foreign countries *pl.*; *ins* ~, *im* ~ abroad.

Ausländ|**er** ['auslɛndər] *m* (-*s*/-), '**~erin** *f* (-/-nen) foreigner; alien; '**2isch** *adj.* foreign; ♀, *zo.* exotic.

'**Auslandskorrespondent** *m* foreign correspondent.

'**auslass**|**en** *v/t.* (*irr. lassen*, *sep.*, -ge-, *h*) let out (*water*); melt (down) (*butter*); render down (*fat*); let out (*garment*); let down (*hem*); leave out, omit (*word*); cut *s.th.* out; miss *or* cut out (*meal*); miss (*dance*); *s-n Zorn an j-m* ~ vent one's anger on *s.o.*; *sich* ~ *über* (*acc.*) say *s.th.* about; express one's opinion about; '**2ung** *f* (-/-en) omission; remark, utterance; '**2ungszeichen** *gr. n* apostrophe.

'**aus**|**laufen** *v/i.* (*irr. laufen*, *sep.*, -ge-, *sein*) run *or* leak out (*aus et.* of *s.th.*); leak; end (*in s.th.*); *machine*: run down; ♧ (set) sail; '**~leeren** *v/t.* (*sep.*, -ge-, *h*) empty; ⚕ evacuate (*bowels*).

'**ausleg**|**en** *v/t.* (*sep.*, -ge-, *h*) lay out; display (*goods*); explain, interpret; advance (*money*); '**2ung** *f* (-/-en) explanation, interpretation.

'**aus**|**leihen** *v/t.* (*irr. leihen*, *sep.*, -ge-, *h*) lend (out), *esp. Am.* loan; '**~lernen** *v/i.* (*sep.*, -ge-, *h*) finish one's apprenticeship; *man lernt nie aus* we live and learn.

'**Auslese** *f* choice, selection; *fig.* pick; '**2n** *v/t.* (*irr. lesen*, *sep.*, -ge-, *h*) pick out, select; finish reading (*book*).

'**ausliefer**|**n** *v/t.* (*sep.*, -ge-, *h*) hand *or* turn over, deliver (up); extradite (*criminal*); *ausgeliefert sein* (*dat.*) be at the mercy of; '**2ung** *f* delivery; extradition.

'**aus**|**liegen** *v/i.* (*irr. liegen*, *sep.*, -ge-, *h*) be displayed, be on show; '**~löschen** *v/t.* (*sep.*, -ge-, *h*) put out, switch off (*light*); extinguish (*fire*) (*a. fig.*); efface (*word*); wipe

out, erase; '**~losen** *v/t.* (*sep.*, -ge-, *h*) draw (lots) for.

'**auslös**|**en** *v/t.* (*sep.*, -ge-, *h*) ⊕ release; redeem, ransom (*prisoner*); redeem (*from pawn*); *fig.* cause, start; arouse (*applause*); '**2er** *m* (-*s*/-) ⊕ release, *esp. phot.* trigger.

'**aus**|**lüften** *v/t.* (*sep.*, -ge-, *h*) air, ventilate; '**~machen** *v/t.* (*sep.*, -ge-, *h*) make out, sight, spot; *sum:* amount to; constitute, make up; put out (*fire*); ⚡ turn out, switch off (*light*); agree on, arrange; settle; *es macht nichts aus* it does not matter; *würde es Ihnen et.* ~, *wenn ...?* would you mind (*ger.*) ...?; '**~malen** *v/t.* (*sep.*, -ge-, *h*) paint; *sich et.* ~ picture *s.th.* to *o.s.*, imagine *s.th.*

'**Ausmaß** *n* dimension(s *pl.*), measurement(s *pl.*); *fig.* extent.

aus|**mergeln** ['ausmɛrgəln] *v/t.* (*sep.*, -ge-, *h*) emaciate; exhaust; '**~merzen** ['~mɛrtsən] *v/t.* (*sep.*, -ge-, *h*) eliminate; eradicate; '**~messen** *v/t.* (*irr. messen*, *sep.*, -ge-, *h*) measure.

Ausnahm|**e** ['ausnɑːmə] *f* (-/-n) exception; '**2sweise** *adv.* by way of exception; exceptionally.

'**ausnehmen** *v/t.* (*irr. nehmen*, *sep.*, -ge-, *h*) take out; draw (*fowl*); F fleece *s.o.*; *fig.* except, exempt; '**~d** 1. *adj.* exceptional; 2. *adv.* exceedingly.

'**aus**|**nutzen** *v/t.* (*sep.*, -ge-, *h*) utilize; take advantage of; *esp.* ♘, ✗ exploit; '**~packen** (*sep.*, -ge-, *h*) 1. *v/t.* unpack; 2. F *fig. v/i.* speak one's mind; '**~pfeifen** *thea. v/t.* (*irr. pfeifen*, *sep.*, -ge-, *h*) hiss; '**~plaudern** *v/t.* (*sep.*, -ge-, *h*) blab *or* let out; '**~polstern** *v/t.* (*sep.*, -ge-, *h*) stuff, pad; wad; '**~probieren** *v/t.* (*sep.*, *no* -ge-, *h*) try, test.

Auspuff *mot.* ['auspuf] *m* (-[e]s/-e) exhaust; '**~gas** *mot. n* exhaust gas; '**~rohr** *mot. n* exhaust-pipe; '**~topf** *mot. m* silencer, *Am.* muffler.

'**aus**|**putzen** *v/t.* (*sep.*, -ge-, *h*) clean; '**~quartieren** *v/t.* (*sep.*, *no* -ge-, *h*) dislodge; ✗ billet out; '**~radieren** *v/t.* (*sep.*, *no* -ge-, *h*) erase; '**~rangieren** *v/t.* (*sep.*, *no* -ge-, *h*) discard; '**~rauben** *v/t.* (*sep.*, -ge-, *h*) rob; ransack; '**~räumen** *v/t.* (*sep.*, -ge-, *h*) empty, clear (out); remove (*furniture*); '**~rechnen** *v/t.* (*sep.*, -ge-, *h*) calculate, compute; reckon (out), *Am.* figure out *or* up (*all a. fig.*).

'**Ausrede** *f* excuse, evasion, subterfuge; '**2n** (*sep.*, -ge-, *h*) 1. *v/i.* finish speaking; ~ *lassen* hear *s.o.* out; 2. *v/t.*: *j-m et.* ~ dissuade *s.o.* from *s.th.*

'**ausreichen** *v/i.* (*sep.*, -ge-, *h*) suffice; '**~d** *adj.* sufficient.

'**Ausreise** *f* departure; ♧ voyage out.

'ausreiß|en (irr. reißen, sep., -ge-) 1 .v/t. (h) pull or tear out; 2. v/i. (sein) run away; 'Ler m runaway.

aus|renken ['ausrɛŋkən] v/t. (sep., -ge-, h) dislocate; '~richten v/t. (sep., -ge-, h) straighten; ✗ dress; adjust; deliver (message); do, effect; accomplish; obtain; arrange (feast); richte ihr e-n Gruß von mir aus! remember me to her!; ~rotten ['~rɔtən] v/t. (sep., -ge-, h) root out; fig. extirpate, exterminate.

'Ausruf m cry; exclamation; 'Len (irr. rufen, sep., -ge-,h) 1. v/i. cry out, exclaim; 2. v/t. proclaim; '~e-zeichen n exclamation mark, Am. a. exclamation point; '~ung f (-/-en) proclamation; '~ungszeichen n s. Ausrufezeichen.   [-ge-, h) rest.\
'ausruhen v/i., v/t. and v/refl. (sep.,\
'ausrüst|en v/t. (sep., -ge-, h) fit out; equip; 'Lung f outfit, equipment, fittings pl.   [disseminate.\
'aussäen v/t. (sep., -ge-, h) sow; fig.\
'Aussage f statement; declaration; ᵗⅉₜ evidence; gr. predicate; 'Ln (sep., -ge-, h) 1. v/t. state, declare; ᵗⅉₜ depose; 2. ᵗⅉₜ v/i. give evidence.

'Aussatz ℱ m (-es/no pl.) leprosy.

'aus|saugen v/t. (sep., -ge-, h) suck (out); fig. exhaust (land); '~schalten v/t. (sep., -ge-, h) eliminate; ⚡ cut out, switch off, turn off or out (light).

Ausschank ['ausʃaŋk] m (-[e]s/⁼e) retail (of alcoholic drinks); public house, F pub.

'Ausschau f (-/no pl.): ~ halten nach be on the look-out for, watch for.

'ausscheid|en (irr. scheiden, sep., -ge-) 1. v/t. (h) separate; 🜍 ♒ ♃, physiol. eliminate; 🜊 secrete; 2. v/i. (sein) retire; withdraw; sports: drop out; 'Lung f separation; elimination (a. sports); 🜊 secretion.

'aus|schiffen v/t. and v/refl. (sep., -ge-, h) disembark; '~schimpfen v/t. (sep., -ge-, h) scold, tell s.o. off, berate; ~schirren ['~ʃirən] v/t. (sep.,-ge-,h) unharness; '~schlach-ten v/t. (sep., -ge-, h) cut up; cannibalize (car, etc.); fig. exploit, make the most of; '~schlafen (irr. schlafen, sep., -ge-) 1. v/i. sleep one's fill; 2. v/t. sleep off (effects of drink, etc.).

'Ausschlag m 🜊 eruption, rash; deflexion (of pointer); den ~ geben settle it; 2en ['~gən] (irr. schlagen, sep., -ge-) 1. v/t. (h) knock or beat out; line; refuse, decline; 2. v/i. (h) horse: kick; pointer: deflect; 🜄 bud; '2gebend adj. ['~k-] decisive.

'ausschließ|en v/t. (irr. schließen, sep., -ge-, h) shut or lock out; fig.: exclude; expel; sports: disqualify; '~lich adj. exclusive.

'Ausschluß m exclusion; expulsion; sports: disqualification.

'ausschmücken v/t. (sep., -ge-, h) adorn, decorate; fig. embellish.

'Ausschnitt m cut; décolleté, (low) neck (of dress); cutting, Am. clipping (from newspaper); fig. part, section.

'ausschreib|en v/t. (irr. schreiben, sep., -ge-, h) write out; copy; write out (word) in full; make out (invoice); announce; advertise; '2ung f (-/-en) announcement; advertisement.

'ausschreit|en (irr. schreiten, sep., -ge-) 1. v/i. (sein) step out, take long strides; 2. v/t. (h) pace (room), measure by steps; '2ung f (-/-en) excess; ~en pl. riots pl.

'Ausschuß m refuse, waste, rubbish; committee, board.

'aus|schütteln v/t. (sep., -ge-, h) shake out; '~schütten v/t. (sep., -ge-, h) pour out; spill; ✝ distribute (dividend); j-m sein Herz ~ pour out one's heart to s.o.; '~schwär-men v/i. (sep., -ge-, sein) swarm out; ~ (lassen) ✗ extend, deploy.

'ausschweif|end adj. dissolute; '2ung f (-/-en) debauchery, excess.

'ausschwitzen v/t. (sep., -ge-, h) exude.

'aussehen 1. v/i. (irr. sehen, sep., -ge-, h) look; wie sieht er aus? what does he look like?; es sieht nach Regen aus it looks like rain; 2. 2 n (-s/ no pl.) look(s pl.), appearance.

außen adv. ['ausən] (on the) outside; von ~ her from (the) outside; nach ~ (hin) outward(s); '2auf-nahme f film: outdoor shot; '2bordmotor m outboard motor.

'aussenden v/t. ([irr. senden,] sep., -ge-, h) send out.

'Außen|hafen m outport; '~handel m foreign trade; '~minister m foreign minister; Foreign Secretary, Am. Secretary of State; '~ministerium n foreign ministry; Foreign Office, Am. State Department; '~politik f foreign policy; '2politisch adj. of or referring to foreign affairs; '~seite f outside, surface; '~seiter m (-s/-) outsider; ~stände ✝ ['~ʃtɛndə] pl. outstanding debts pl., Am. accounts pl. receivable; '~welt f outer or outside world.

außer ['ausər] 1. prp. (dat.) out of; beside(s), Am. aside from; except; ~ sich sein be beside o.s. (vor Freude with joy); 2. cj.: ~ daß except that; ~ wenn unless; '~dem cj. besides, moreover.

äußere ['ɔysərə] 1. adj. exterior, outer, external, outward; 2. 2 n (Äußer[e]n/no pl.) exterior, outside, outward appearance.

'außer|gewöhnlich adj. extraordinary; exceptional; '⁓halb **1.** *prp.* (*gen.*) outside, out of; beyond; **2.** *adv.* on the outside.

äußerlich *adj.* ['ɔysərlïç] external, outward; '⁓keit *f* (-/-en) superficiality; formality.

äußern ['ɔysərn] *v/t.* (ge-, h) utter, express; advance; *sich ⁓ matter*: manifest itself; *p.* express o.s.

'**außer|ordentlich** *adj.* extraordinary.

äußerst ['ɔysərst] **1.** *adj.* outermost; *fig.* utmost, extreme; **2.** *adv.* extremely, highly.

außerstande *adj.* [ausər'ʃtandə] unable, not in a position.

'**Äußerung** *f* (-/-en) utterance, remark.

'**aussetz|en** (*sep.*, -ge-, h) **1.** *v/t.* set *or* put out; lower (*boat*); promise (*reward*); settle (*pension*); bequeath; expose (*child*); expose (*dat.* to); *et. ⁓ an* (*dat.*) find fault with; **2.** *v/i.* intermit; fail; *activity*: stop; suspend; *mot.* misfire; '⁓ung *f* (-/-en) exposure (*of child, to weather, etc.*) (*a.* 🕮).

'**Aussicht** *f* (-/-en) view (*auf acc.* of); *fig.* prospect (of), chance (of); *in ⁓ haben* have in prospect; '⁓slos *adj.* hopeless, desperate; '⁓sreich *adj.* promising, full of promise.

aussöhn|en ['ausˀzøːnən] *v/t.* (*sep.*, -ge-, h) reconcile *s.o.* (*mit* to *s.th.*, *with s.o.*); *sich ⁓* reconcile o.s. (to *s.th.*, *with s.o.*); '⁓ung *f* (-/-en) reconciliation.

'**aussondern** *v/t.* (*sep.*, -ge-, h) single out; separate.

'**aus|spannen** (*sep.*, -ge-, h) **1.** *v/t.* stretch, extend; F *fig.* steal (*s.o.'s girl friend*); unharness (*draught animal*); **2.** *fig.* *v/i.* (take a) rest, relax; '⁓speien *v/t. and v/i.* (*irr.* speien, sep., -ge-, h) spit out.

'**aussperr|en** *v/t.* (*sep.*, -ge-, h) shut out; lock out (*workmen*); '⁓ung *f* (-/-en) lock-out.

'**aus|spielen** (*sep.*, -ge-, h) **1.** *v/t.* play (*card*); **2.** *v/i.* at cards: lead; *er hat ausgespielt* he is done for; '⁓spionieren *v/t.* (*sep.*, *no* -ge-, h) spy out. [cent; discussion.\
'**Aussprache** *f* pronunciation, ac-]

'**aussprechen** (*irr.* sprechen, sep., -ge-, h) **1.** *v/t.* pronounce, express; *sich ⁓ für* (*gegen*) declare o.s. for (against); **2.** *v/i.* finish speaking.

'**Ausspruch** *m* utterance; saying; remark.

'**aus|spucken** *v/i. and v/t.* (*sep.*, -ge-, h) spit out; '⁓spülen *v/t.* (*sep.*, -ge-, h) rinse.

'**Ausstand** *m* strike, *Am.* F *a.* walk-out; *in den ⁓ treten* go on strike, *Am.* F *a.* walk out.

ausstatt|en ['ausʃtatən] *v/t.* (*sep.*, -ge-, h) fit out, equip; furnish; supply (*mit* with); give a dowry to (*daughter*); get up (*book*); '⁓ung *f* (-/-en) outfit, equipment; furniture; supply; dowry; get-up (*of book*).

'**aus|stechen** *v/t.* (*irr.* stechen, sep., -ge-, h) cut out (*a. fig.*); put out (*eye*); '⁓stehen (*irr.* stehen, sep., -ge-, h) **1.** *v/i.* payments: be outstanding; **2.** *v/t.* endure, bear; '⁓steigen *v/i.* (*irr.* steigen, sep., -ge-, sein) get out *or* off, alight.

'**ausstell|en** *v/t.* (*sep.*, -ge-, h) exhibit; make out (*invoice*); issue (*document*); draw (*bill*); '⁓er *m* (-s/-) exhibitor; drawer; '⁓ung *f* exhibition, show; '⁓ungsraum *m* show-room.

'**aussterben** *v/i.* (*irr.* sterben, sep., -ge-, sein) die out; become extinct.

'**Aussteuer** *f* trousseau, dowry.

'**ausstopfen** *v/t.* (*sep.*, -ge-, h) stuff; wad, pad.

'**ausstoß|en** *v/t.* (*irr.* stoßen, sep., -ge-, h) thrust out, eject; expel; utter (*cry*); heave (*sigh*); ✂ cashier; '⁓ung *f* (-/-en) expulsion.

'**aus|strahlen** *v/t. and v/i.* (*sep.*, -ge-, h) radiate; '⁓strecken *v/t.* (*sep.*, -ge-, h) stretch (out); '⁓streichen *v/t.* (*irr.* streichen, sep., -ge-, h) strike out; smooth (down); '⁓streuen *v/t.* (*sep.*, -ge-, h) scatter; spread (*rumours*); '⁓strömen (*sep.*, -ge-) **1.** *v/i.* (*sein*) stream out; *gas, light*: emanate; *gas, steam*: escape; **2.** *v/t.* (h) pour (out); '⁓suchen *v/t.* (*sep.*, -ge-, h) choose, select.

'**Austausch** *m* exchange; '⁓bar *adj.* exchangeable; '⁓en *v/t.* (*sep.*, -ge-, h) exchange.

'**austeil|en** *v/t.* (*sep.*, -ge-, h) distribute; deal out (*blows*); '⁓ung *f* distribution.

Auster *zo.* ['austər] *f* (-/-n) oyster.

'**austragen** *v/t.* (*irr.* tragen, sep., -ge-, h) deliver (*letters, etc.*); hold (*contest*).

Austral|ier [au'straːliər] *m* (-s/-) Australian; ⁓isch *adj.* Australian.

'**austreib|en** *v/t.* (*irr.* treiben, sep., -ge-, h) drive out; expel; '⁓ung *f* (-/-en) expulsion.

'**aus|treten** (*irr.* treten, sep., -ge-) **1.** *v/t.* (h) tread *or* stamp out; wear out (*shoes*); wear down (*steps*); **2.** *v/i.* (sein) emerge, come out; *river*: overflow its banks; retire (*aus* from); F ease o.s.; *⁓ aus* leave (*society, etc.*); '⁓trinken (*irr.* trinken, sep., -ge-, h) **1.** *v/t.* drink up; empty, drain; **2.** *v/i.* finish drinking; '⁓tritt *m* leaving; retirement; '⁓trocknen (*sep.*, -ge-) **1.** *v/t.* (h) dry up; drain (*land*); parch (*throat, earth*); **2.** *v/i.* (sein) dry up.

ausüb|en ['ausˀ-] *v/t.* (*sep.*, -ge-, h) exercise; practi|se, *Am.* -ce (*profession*); exert (*influence*); '⁓ung *f* practice; exercise.

'Ausverkauf ✝ *m* selling off *or* out (*of stock*); sale; '²t ✝, *thea. adj.* sold out; *theatre notice:* 'full house'.

'Auswahl *f* choice; selection; ✝ assortment. [choose, select.\
'auswählen *v/t.* (*sep.*, -ge-, *h*)\
'Auswander|er *m* emigrant; '²n *v/i.* (*sep.*, -ge-, *sein*) emigrate; '~ung *f* emigration.

auswärt|ig *adj.* ['ausvertiç] out-of-town; non-resident; foreign; *das Auswärtige Amt s. Außenministerium*; ~s *adv.* ['~s] outward(s); out of doors; out of town; abroad; ~ *essen* dine out.

'auswechseln 1. *v/t.* (*sep.*, -ge-, *h*) exchange; change; replace; 2. ♀ *n* (-*s/no pl.*) exchange; replacement.

'Ausweg *m* way out (*a. fig.*); outlet; *fig.* expedient.

'ausweichen *v/i.* (*irr. weichen, sep.*, -ge-, *sein*) make way (for); *fig.* evade, avoid; '~d *adj.* evasive.

Ausweis ['ausvaɪs] *m* (-*es/-e*) (bank) return; identity card, *Am.* identification (card); ²en ['~zən] *v/t.* (*irr. weisen, sep.*, -ge-, *h*) turn out, expel; evict; deport; show, prove; *sich* ~ prove one's identity; '~papiere *n/pl.* identity papers *pl.*; ~ung ['~zuŋ] *f* expulsion; '~ungsbefehl *m* expulsion order.

'ausweiten *v/t. and v/refl.* (*sep.*, -ge-, *h*) widen, stretch, expand.

'auswendig 1. *adj.* outward, outside; 2. *adv.* outwardly, outside; *fig.* by heart.

'aus|werfen *v/t.* (*irr. werfen, sep.*, -ge-, *h*) throw out, cast; eject; ⚕ expectorate; allow (*sum of money*); '~werten *v/t.* (*sep.*, -ge-, *h*) evaluate; analyze, interpret; utilize, exploit; '~wickeln *v/t.* (*sep.*, -ge-, *h*) unwrap; '~wiegen *v/t.* (*irr. wiegen, sep.*, -ge-, *h*) weigh out; '~wirken *v/refl.* (*sep.*, -ge-, *h*) take effect, operate; *sich* ~ *auf* (*acc.*) affect; '²wirkung *f* effect; '~wischen *v/t.* (*sep.*, -ge-, *h*) wipe out, efface; '~wringen *v/t.* (*irr. wringen, sep.*, -ge-, *h*) wring out.

'Auswuchs *m* excrescence, outgrowth (*a. fig.*), protuberance.

'Auswurf *m* ⚕ expectoration; *fig.* refuse, dregs *pl.*

'aus|zahlen *v/t.* (*sep.*, -ge-, *h*) pay out; pay *s.o.* off; '~zählen *v/t.* (*sep.*, -ge-, *h*) count out.

'Auszahlung *f* payment.

'Auszehrung *f* (-/-en) consumption.

'auszeichn|en *v/t.* (*sep.*, -ge-, *h*) mark (out); *fig.* distinguish (*sich o.s.*); '²ung *f* marking; distinction; hono(u)r; decoration.

'auszieh|en (*irr. ziehen, sep.*, -ge-) 1. *v/t.* (*h*) draw out, extract; take off (*garment*); *sich* ~ undress; 2. *v/i.* (*sein*) set out; move (out), remove, move house; '²platte *f* leaf (*of table*).

'Auszug *m* departure; ♀ marching out; removal; extract, excerpt (*from book*); summary; ✝ statement (of account). [tic, genuine.\
authentisch *adj.* [aʊ'tentiʃ] authen-\
Auto ['auto] *n* (-*s/-s*) (motor-)car, *Am. a.* automobile; ~ *fahren* drive, motor; '~bahn *f* motorway, autobahn; ~biogra'phie *f* autobiography; ~bus ['~bus] *m* (-*ses/-se*) (motor-)bus; (motor) coach; '~bushaltestelle *f* bus stop; ~didakt [~di'dakt] *m* (-*en/-en*) autodidact, self-taught person; '~droschke *f* taxi(-cab), *Am.* cab; '~fahrer *m* motorist; ~'gramm *n* autograph; ~'grammjäger *m* autograph hunter; '~händler *m* car dealer; '~kino *n* drive-in cinema; ~krat [~'kra:t] *m* (-*en/-en*) autocrat; ~kratie [~a-'ti:] *f* (-/-en) autocracy; ~mat [~'ma:t] *m* (-*en/-en*) automaton; slot-machine, vending machine; ~'matenrestaurant *n* self-service restaurant, *Am.* automat; ~mation ⊕ [~ma'tsjo:n] *f* (-/no pl.) automation; ²'matisch *adj.* automatic; '~mechaniker *m* car mechanic; ~mobil [~mo'bi:l] *n* (-*s/-e*) *s.* Auto; ²nom *adj.* [~'no:m] autonomous; ~nomie [~o'mi:] *f* (-/-n) autonomy. Autor ['autor] *m* (-*s/-en*) author. 'Autoreparaturwerkstatt *f* car repair shop, garage. [thor(ess).\
Autorin [aʊ'to:rin] *f* (-/-nen) au-\
autori|sieren [autori'zi:rən] *v/t.* (*no* -ge-, *h*) authorize; ~tär *adj.* [~'tɛ:r] authoritarian; ²'tät *f* (-/-en) authority.

'Auto|straße *f* motor-road; '~vermietung *f* (-/-en) car hire service.

avisieren ✝ [avi'zi:rən] *v/t.* (*no* -ge-, *h*) advise.

Axt [akst] *f* (-/⁺e) ax(e).

Azetylen [atsety'le:n] *n* (-*s/no pl.*) acetylene. [²n *adj.* azure.\
Azur ['atsu:r] *m* (-*s/no pl.*) azure;\

B

Bach [bax] *m* (-[*e*]*s/⁺e*) brook, *Am. a.* run. [port.\
Backbord ⚓ ['bak-] *n* (-[*e*]*s/-e*)\
Backe ['bakə] *f* (-/-n) cheek.
backen ['bakən] (*irr.*, ge-, *h*) 1.

v/t. bake; fry; dry (*fruit*); 2. *v/i.* bake; fry.

'Backen|bart *m* (side-)whiskers *pl.*, *Am. a.* sideburns *pl.*; '~zahn *m* molar (tooth), grinder.

Bäcker ['bɛkər] m (-s/-) baker; ~ei [~'raɪ] f (-/-en) baker's (shop), bakery.

'**Back|fisch** m fried fish; fig. girl in her teens, teenager, Am. a. bobby soxer; '~obst n dried fruit; '~pflaume f prune; '~pulver n baking-powder; '~stein m brick; '~ware f baker's ware.

Bad [baːt] n (-[e]s/~er) bath; in river, etc.: a. bathe; s. Badeort; ein ~ nehmen take or have a bath.

Bade|anstalt ['baːdəʔ-] f (public swimming) baths pl.; '~anzug m bathing-costume, bathing-suit; '~hose f bathing-drawers pl., (bathing) trunks pl.; '~kappe f bathing-cap; '~kur f spa treatment; '~mantel m bathing-gown, Am. bathrobe; '~meister m bath attendant; swimming-instructor; '2n (ge-, h) 1. v/t. bath (baby, etc.); bathe (eyes, etc.); 2. v/i. bath, tub; have or take a bath; in river, etc.: bathe; ~ gehen go swimming; '~ofen m geyser, boiler, Am. a. water heater; '~ort m watering-place; spa; seaside resort; '~salz n bath-salt; '~strand m bathing-beach; '~tuch n bath-towel; '~wanne f bath-tub; '~zimmer n bathroom.

Bagatell|e [baga'tɛlə] f (-/-n) trifle, trifling matter, bagatelle; 2i'sieren v/t. (no -ge-, h) minimize (the importance of), Am. a. play down.

Bagger ['bagər] m (-s/-) excavator; dredge(r); '2n v/i. and v/t. (ge-, h) excavate; dredge.

Bahn [baːn] f (-/-en) course; path; ⚏ railway, Am. railroad; mot. lane; trajectory (of bullet, etc.); ast. orbit; sports: track, course, lane; skating: rink; bowling: alley; '2brechend adj. pioneer(ing), epoch-making; art: avant-gardist; '~damm m railway embankment, Am. railroad embankment; '2en v/t. (ge-, h) clear, open (up) (way); den Weg ~ prepare or pave the way (dat. for); sich e-n Weg ~ force or work or elbow one's way; '~hof m (railway-) station, Am. (railroad-)station; '~linie f railway-line, Am. railroad line; '~steig m platform; '~steigkarte f platform ticket; '~übergang m level crossing, Am. grade crossing.

Bahre ['baːrə] f (-/-n) stretcher, litter; bier.

Bai [baɪ] f (-/-en) bay; creek.

Baisse ✝ ['bɛːs(ə)] f (-/-n) depression (on the market); fall (in prices); auf ~ spekulieren ✝ bear, speculate for a fall, Am. sell short; '~spekulant m bear.

Bajonett ⚔ [bajo'nɛt] n (-[e]s/-e) bayonet; das ~ aufpflanzen fix the bayonet.

Bake ['baːkə] f (-/-n) ⚓ beacon; ⚏ warning-sign.

Bakterie [bak'teːrjə] f (-/-n) bacterium, microbe, germ.

bald adv. [balt] soon; shortly; before long; F almost, nearly; early; so ~ als möglich as soon as possible; ~ hier, ~ dort now here, now there; '~ig adj. ['~dɪç] speedy; ~e Antwort ✝ early reply.

Baldrian ['baldriaːn] m (-s/-e) valerian.

Balg [balk] 1. m (-[e]s/~e) skin; body (of doll); bellows pl.; 2. F m, n (-[e]s/~er) brat, urchin; 2en ['balgən] v/refl. (ge-, h) scuffle (um for), wrestle (for).

Balken ['balkən] m (-s/-) beam; rafter.

Balkon [bal'kõ; ~'koːn] m (-s/-s; -s/-e) balcony; thea. dress circle, Am. balcony; ~tür f French window.

Ball [bal] m (-[e]s/~e) ball; geogr., ast. a. globe; ball, dance; auf dem ~ at the ball.

Ballade [ba'laːdə] f (-/-n) ballad.

Ballast ['balast] m (-es/~-e) ballast; fig. burden, impediment; dead weight.

'**ballen**[1] v/t. (ge-, h) (form into a) ball; clench (fist); sich ~ (form into a) ball; cluster.

'**Ballen**[2] m (-s/-) bale; anat. ball; ~ Papier ten reams pl.

Ballett [ba'lɛt] n (-[e]s/-e) ballet; ~änzer [ba'lɛttɛntsər] m (-s/-) ballet-dancer.

ball|förmig adj. ['balfœrmɪç] ball-shaped, globular; '2kleid n ball-dress.

Ballon [ba'lõː; ~'oːn] m (-s/-s; -s/-s, -e) balloon.

'**Ball|saal** m ball-room; '~spiel n ball-game, game of ball.

Balsam ['balzaːm] m (-s/-e) balsam, balm (a. fig.); 2ieren [~a'miːrən] v/t. (no -ge-, h) embalm.

Balz [balts] f (-/-en) mating season; display (by cock-bird).

Bambus ['bambus] m (-ses/-se) bamboo; '~rohr n bamboo, cane.

banal adj. [ba'naːl] commonplace, banal, trite; trivial; 2ität [~ali'tɛːt] f (-/-en) banality; commonplace; triviality.

Banane [ba'naːnə] f (-/-n) banana; ~nstecker ⚡ m banana plug.

Band [bant] 1. m (-[e]s/~e) volume; 2. n (-[e]s/~er) band; ribbon; tape; anat. ligament; 3. fig. n (-[e]s/-e) bond, tie; 4. 2 pret. of binden.

Bandag|e [ban'daːʒə] f (-/-n) bandage; 2ieren [~a'ʒiːrən] v/t. (no -ge-, h) (apply a) bandage.

Bande ['bandə] f (-/-n) billiards: cushion; fig. gang, band.

bändigen ['bɛndigən] v/t. (ge-, h)

tame; break in (*horse*); subdue (*a. fig.*); *fig.* restrain: master.

Bandit [ban'di:t] *m* (-en/-en) bandit.

'Band|maß *n* tape measure; '~säge *f* band-saw; '~scheibe *anat. f* intervertebral disc; '~wurm *zo. m* tapeworm.

bang *adj.* [baŋ], ~e *adj.* ['~ə] anxious (*um* about), uneasy (about), concerned (for); *mir ist* ~ I am afraid (*vor dat.* of); *j-m* **bange machen** frighten *or* scare s.o.; '~en *v/i.* (ge-, h) be anxious *or* worried (*um* about).

Bank [baŋk] *f* 1. (-/~e) bench; *school*: desk; F *durch die* ~ without exception, all through; *auf die lange* ~ *schieben* put off, postpone; *shelve*; 2. ✝ (-/-en) bank; *Geld auf der* ~ money in the bank; '~anweisung *f* cheque, *Am.* check; '~ausweis *m* bank return *or* statement; '~beamte *m* bank clerk *or* official; '~einlage *f* deposit.

Bankett [baŋ'ket] *n* (-[e]s/-e) banquet.

'Bank|geheimnis *n* banker's duty of secrecy; '~geschäft ✝ *n* bank (-ing) transaction, banking operation; '~haus *n* bank(ing-house).

Bankier [baŋk'je:] *m* (-s/-s) banker.

'Bank|konto *n* bank(ing) account; '~note *f* (bank) note, *Am.* (bank) bill.

bankrott [baŋ'krɔt] 1. *adj.* bankrupt; 2. ⚥ *m* (-[e]s/-e) bankruptcy, insolvency, failure; ~ *machen* fail, go *or* become bankrupt.

'Bankwesen *n* banking.

Bann [ban] *m* (-[e]s/-e) ban; *fig.* spell; *eccl.* excommunication; '⚥en *v/t.* (ge-, h) banish (*a. fig.*); exorcize (*devil*); avert (*danger*); *eccl.* excommunicate; spellbind.

Banner ['banər] *n* (-s/-) banner (*a. fig.*); standard; '~träger *m* standard-bearer.

'Bann|fluch *m* anathema; '~meile *f* precincts *pl.*; ⚥ *area around government buildings within which processions and meetings are prohibited.*

bar[1] [ba:r] 1. *adj.*: e-r *Sache* ~ destitute *or* devoid of s.th.; ~es *Geld* ready money, cash; ~er *Unsinn* sheer nonsense; 2. *adv.*: ~ *bezahlen* pay in cash, pay money down.

Bar[2] [~] *f* (-/-s) bar; night-club.

Bär [bɛ:r] *m* (-en/-en) bear; *j-m* e-n ~en *aufbinden* hoax s.o.

Baracke [ba'rakə] *f* (-/-n) barrack; ~nlager *n* hutment.

Barbar [bar'ba:r] *m* (-en/-en) barbarian; ~ei [~a'raɪ] *f* (-/-en) barbarism; barbarity; ⚥isch ['~ba:rɪʃ] *adj.* barbarian; barbarous; *art, taste*: barbaric.

'Bar|bestand *m* cash in hand; '~betrag *m* amount in cash.

'Bärenzwinger *m* bear-pit.

barfuß *adj. and adv.* ['ba:r-], ~füßig *adj. and adv.* ['~fy:sɪç] barefoot.

barg [bark] *pret.* of **bergen**.

'Bar|geld *n* cash, ready money; '⚥geldlos *adj.* cashless; ~er *Zahlungsverkehr* cashless money transfers *pl.*; ⚥häuptig *adj. and adv.* ['~hɔyptɪç] bare-headed, uncovered.

Bariton ⚥ ['ba:ritɔn] *m* (-s/-e) baritone. [launch.\]

Barkasse ⚓ [bar'kasə] *f* (-/-n)

barmherzig *adj.* [barm'hɛrtsɪç] merciful, charitable; *der* ~e *Samariter* the good Samaritan; ⚥e *Schwester* Sister of Mercy *or* Charity; ⚥keit *f* (-/-en) mercy, charity.

Barometer [baro'-] *n* barometer.

Baron [ba'ro:n] *m* (-s/-e) baron; ~in *f* (-/-nen) baroness.

Barre ['barə] *f* (-/-n) bar.

Barren ['barən] *m* (-s/-) *metall.* bar, ingot, bullion; *gymnastics*: parallel bars *pl.*

Barriere [bar'je:rə] *f* (-/-n) barrier.

Barrikade [bari'ka:də] *f* (-/-n) barricade; ~n *errichten* raise barricades.

barsch *adj.* [barʃ] rude, gruff, rough.

'Bar|schaft *f* (-/-en) ready money, cash; '~scheck ✝ *m* open cheque, *Am.* open check.

barst [barst] *pret.* of **bersten**.

Bart [ba:rt] *m* (-[e]s/~e) beard; bit (*of key*); *sich* e-n ~ *wachsen lassen* grow a beard.

bärtig *adj.* ['bɛ:rtɪç] bearded.

'bartlos *adj.* beardless.

'Barzahlung *f* cash payment; *nur gegen* ~ ✝ terms strictly cash.

Basis ['ba:zɪs] *f* (-/*Basen*) base; *fig.* basis.

Baß ♩ [bas] *m* (*Basses/Bässe*) bass; '~geige *f* bass-viol.

Bassist [ba'sɪst] *m* (-en/-en) bass (singer).

Bast [bast] *m* (-es/-e) bast; velvet (*on antlers*).

Bastard ['bastart] *m* (-[e]s/-e) bastard; half-breed; *zo.*, ♀ hybrid.

bast|eln ['bastəln] (ge-, h) 1. *v/t.* build, F rig up; 2. *v/i.* build; '⚥ler *m* (-s/-) amateur craftsman, do-it-yourself man.

bat [ba:t] *pret.* of **bitten**.

Bataillon [batal'jo:n] *n* (-s/-e) battalion.

Batist [ba'tɪst] *m* (-[e]s/-e) cambric.

Batterie ✕, ⚡ [bata'ri:] *f* (-/-n) battery.

Bau [bau] *m* 1. (-[e]s/*no pl.*) building, construction; build, frame; 2. (-[e]s/-ten) building, edifice; 3. (-[e]s/-e) burrow, den (*a. fig.*), earth.

'Bau|arbeiter *m* workman in the building trade; '~art *f* architecture, style; method of construction; *mot.* type, model.

Bauch [baʊx] m (-[e]s/ᵘe) anat. abdomen, belly; paunch; *ship*: bottom; 'ᵉig adj. big-bellied, bulgy; 'ᵕlandung f belly landing; 'ᵕredner m ventriloquist; 'ᵕschmerzen m/pl., 'ᵕweh n (-s/no pl.) belly-ache, stomach-ache.

bauen ['baʊən] (ge-; h) 1. v/t. build, construct; erect, raise; build, make (*nest*); make (*violin, etc.*); 2. v/i. build; ~ auf (*acc.*) trust (in); rely or count or depend on.

Bauer ['baʊər] 1. m (-n, -s/-n) farmer; peasant, countryman; *chess*: pawn; 2. n, m (-s/-) (bird-)cage.

Bäuerin ['bɔʏərɪn] f (-/-nen) farmer's wife; peasant woman.

Bauerlaubnis ['baʊ-]f building permit.

bäuerlich adj. ['bɔʏərlɪç] rural, rustic.

Bauern|fänger contp. ['baʊərnfeŋər] m (-s/-) trickster, confidence man; 'ᵕhaus n farm-house; 'ᵕhof m farm.

'**bau|fällig** adj. out of repair, dilapidated; 'ᵉgerüst n scaffold (-ing); 'ᵉhandwerker m craftsman in the building trade; 'ᵉherr m owner; 'ᵉholz n timber, Am. lumber; 'ᵉjahr n year of construction; ~ 1969 1969 model or make; 'ᵉkasten m box of bricks; 'ᵉkunst f architecture.

'**baulich** adj. architectural; structural; in gutem ᵕen Zustand in good repair.

Baum [baʊm] m (-[e]s/ᵘe) tree.

'**Baumeister** m architect.

baumeln ['baʊməln] v/i. (ge-, h) dangle, swing; mit den Beinen ~ dangle or swing one's legs.

'**Baum|schere** f (eine a pair of) pruning-shears pl.; 'ᵕschule f nursery (of young trees); 'ᵕstamm m trunk; 'ᵕwolle f cotton; 'ᵉwollen adj. (made of) cotton.

'**Bau|plan** m architect's or building plan; 'ᵕplatz m building plot or site, Am. location; 'ᵕpolizei f Board of Surveyors.

Bausch [baʊʃ] m (-es/-e, ᵘe) pad; bolster; wad; in ~ und Bogen altogether, wholesale, in the lump; 'ᵉen v/t. (ge-, h) swell; sich ~ bulge, swell out, billow (out).

'**Bau|stein** m brick, building stone; building block; fig. element; 'ᵕstelle f building site; 'ᵕstil m (architectural) style; 'ᵕstoff m building material; 'ᵕunternehmer m building contractor; 'ᵕzaun m hoarding.

Bay|er ['baɪər] m (-n/-n) Bavarian; 'ᵉ(e)risch adj. Bavarian.

Bazill|enträger ♂ [ba'tsɪlən-] m (germ-)carrier; ᵕus [ᵕʊs] m (-/Bazillen) bacillus, germ.

beabsichtigen [bə'apzɪçtɪgən] v/t.

(no -ge-, h) intend, mean, propose (zu tun to do, doing).

be'acht|en v/t. (no -ge-, h) pay attention to; notice; observe; ᵕenswert adj. noteworthy, remarkable; ᵕlich adj. remarkable; considerable; ᵉung f attention; consideration; notice; observance.

Beamte [bə'amtə] m (-n/-n) official, officer, Am. a. officeholder; functionary; Civil Servant.

be'ängstigend adj. alarming, disquieting.

beanspruch|en [bə'anʃpruxən] v/t. (no -ge-, h) claim, demand; require (efforts, time, space, etc.); ⊕ stress; ᵉung f (-/-en) claim; demand (gen. on); ⊕ stress, strain.

beanstand|en [bə'anʃtandən] v/t. (no -ge-, h) object to; ᵉung f (-/-en) objection (gen. to).

beantragen [bə'antraːgən] v/t. (no -ge-, h) apply for; ⚖ parl. move, make a motion; propose.

be'antwort|en v/t. (no -ge-, h) answer (a. fig.), reply to; ᵉung f (-/-en) answer, reply; in ~ (gen.) in answer or reply to.

be'arbeit|en v/t. (no -ge-, h) work; ⚒ till; dress (leather); hew (stone); process; ⚒ treat; ⚖ be in charge of (case); edit, revise (book); adapt (nach from); esp. ♪ arrange; j-n ~ work on s.o.; batter s.o.; ᵉung f (-/-en) working; revision (of book); thea. adaptation; esp. ♪ arrangement; processing; ⚒ treatment.

be'argwöhnen v/t. (no -ge-, h) suspect, be suspicious of.

beaufsichtig|en [bə'aʊfzɪçtɪgən] v/t. (no -ge-, h) inspect, superintend, supervise, control; look after (child); ᵉung f (-/-en) inspection, supervision, control.

be'auftrag|en v/t. (no -ge-, h) commission (zu inf. to inf.), charge (mit with); ᵉte [ᵕktə] m (-n/-n) commissioner; representative; deputy; proxy.

be'bauen v/t. (no -ge-, h) ⚘ build on; ⚒ cultivate.

beben ['beːbən] v/i. (ge-, h) shake (vor dat. with), tremble (with); shiver (with); earth: quake.

Becher ['bɛçər] m (-s/-) cup (a. fig.).

Becken ['bɛkən] n (-s/-) basin, Am. a. bowl; ♪ cymbal(s pl.); anat. pelvis.

bedacht adj. [bə'daxt]: ~ sein auf (acc.) look after, be concerned about, be careful or mindful of; darauf ~ sein zu inf. be anxious to inf.

bedächtig adj. [bə'dɛçtɪç] deliberate.

bedang [bə'daŋ] pret. of bedingen.

be'danken v/refl. (no -ge-, h): sich bei j-m für et. ~ thank s.o. for s.th.

Bedarf [bə'darf] *m* (-[e]s/*no pl.*) need (*an dat.* of), want (of); ✝ demand (for); ~sartikel [bə'darfs⁹-] *m/pl.* necessaries *pl.*, requisites *pl.*

bedauerlich *adj.* [bə'dauərliç] regrettable, deplorable.

be'dauern 1. *v/t.* (*no -ge-*, *h*) feel or be sorry for *s.o.*; pity *s.o.*; regret, deplore *s.th.*; **2.** ♀ *n* (-s/*no pl.*) regret; pity; ~swert *adj.* pitiable, deplorable.

be'deck|en *v/t.* (*no -ge-*, *h*) cover; ✕ escort; ⚓ convoy; ~t *adj.* sky: overcast; ♀ung *f* cover(ing); ✕ escort; ⚓ convoy.

be'denken 1. *v/t.* (*irr.* denken, *no -ge-*, *h*) consider; think *s.th.* over; *j-n in s-m Testament* ~ remember *s.o.* in one's will; **2.** ♀ *n* (-s/-) consideration; objection; hesitation; scruple; ~los *adj.* unscrupulous.

be'denklich *adj.* doubtful; *character:* a. dubious; *situation, etc.:* dangerous, critical; delicate; risky.

Be'denkzeit *f* time for reflection; *ich gebe dir e-e Stunde* ~ I give you one hour to think it over.

be'deut|en *v/t.* (*no -ge-*, *h*) mean, signify; stand for; ~end *adj.* important, prominent; *sum, etc.* considerable; ~sam *adj.* significant.

Be'deutung *f* meaning, significance; importance; ♀slos *adj.* insignificant; meaningless; ♀svoll *adj.* significant; ~swandel *ling.* *m* semantic change.

be'dien|en (*no -ge-*, *h*) **1.** *v/t.* serve; wait on; ⊕ operate, work (*machine*); ✕ serve (*gun*); answer (*telephone*); *sich* ~ *at table:* help o.s.; **2.** *v/i.* serve; wait (at table); *cards:* follow suit; ♀ung *f* (-/-en) service, *esp.* ✝ attendance; *in restaurant, etc.:* service; waiter, waitress; shop assistant(s *pl.*).

beding|en [bə'diŋən] *v/t.* ([*irr.*,] *no -ge-*, *h*) condition; stipulate; require; cause; imply; ~t *adj.* conditional (*durch* on); restricted; *~ sein durch* be conditioned by; ♀ung *f* (-/-en) condition; stipulation; ~en *pl.* ✝ terms *pl.*; ~ungslos *adj.* unconditional.

be'dräng|en *v/t.* (*no -ge-*, *h*) press hard, beset; ♀nis *f* (-/-se) distress.

be'droh|en *v/t.* (*no -ge-*, *h*) threaten; menace; ~lich *adj.* threatening; ♀ung *f* threat, menace (*gen.* to).

be'drück|en *v/t.* (*no -ge-*, *h*) oppress; depress; deject; ♀ung *f* (-/-en) oppression; depression; dejection.

bedungen [bə'duŋən] *p.p.* of bedingen.

be'dürf|en *v/i.* (*irr.* dürfen, *no -ge-*, *h*): *e-r Sache* ~ need or want or require *s.th.*; ♀nis *n* (-ses/-se) need, want, requirement; *sein* ~ *verrichten* relieve o.s. or nature; ♀nisan-

stalt [bə'dyrfnis⁹-] *f* public convenience, *Am.* comfort station; ~tig *adj.* needy, poor, indigent.

be'ehren *v/t.* (*no -ge-*, *h*) hono(u)r, favo(u)r; *ich beehre mich zu inf.* I have the hono(u)r to *inf.*

be'eilen *v/refl.* (*no -ge-*, *h*) hasten, hurry, make haste, *Am.* F *a.* hustle.

beeindrucken [bə'aindrukən] *v/t.* (*no -ge-*, *h*) impress, make an impression on.

beeinfluss|en [bə'ainflussən] *v/t.* (*no -ge-*, *h*) influence; affect; *parl.* lobby; ♀ung *f* (-/-en) influence; *parl.* lobbying.

beeinträchtig|en [bə'aintreçtigən] *v/t.* (*no -ge-*, *h*) impair, injure, affect (adversely); ♀ung *f* (-/-en) impairment (*gen.* of); injury (to).

be'end|en *v/t.* (*no -ge-*, *h*), ~igen [~igən] *v/t.* (*no -ge-*, *h*) (bring to an) end, finish, terminate; ♀igung [~iguŋ] *f* (-/-en) ending, termination.

beengt *adj.* [bə'ɛŋkt] *space:* narrow, confined, cramped; *sich* ~ *fühlen* feel cramped (for room); feel oppressed or uneasy.

be'erben *v/t.* (*no -ge-*, *h*): *j-n* ~ be *s.o.'s* heir.

beerdig|en [bə'e:rdigən] *v/t.* (*no -ge-*, *h*) bury; ♀ung *f* (-/-en) burial, funeral.

Beere ['be:rə] *f* (-/-n) berry.

Beet ✓ [be:t] *n* (-[e]s/-e) bed.

befähig|en [bə'fɛ:igən] *v/t.* (*no -ge-*, *h*) enable (*zu inf.* to *inf.*); qualify (*für*, *zu* for); ~t *adj.* (~çt] (cap)able; ♀ung *f* (-/-en) qualification; capacity.

befahl [bə'fa:l] *pret.* of befehlen.

befahr|bar *adj.* [bə'fa:rba:r] passable, practicable, trafficable; ⚓ navigable; ~en *v/t.* (*irr.* fahren, *no -ge-*, *h*) drive or travel on; ⚓ navigate (*river*).

be'fallen *v/t.* (*irr.* fallen, *no -ge-*, *h*) attack; befall; *disease:* a. strike; *fear:* seize.

be'fangen *adj.* embarrassed; self-conscious; prejudiced (*a.* ♃); ♃ bias(s)ed; ♀heit *f* (-/*no pl.*) embarrassment; self-consciousness; ♃ bias, prejudice.

be'fassen *v/refl.* (*no -ge-*, *h*): *sich* ~ *mit* occupy o.s. with; engage in; attend to; deal with.

Befehl [bə'fe:l] *m* (-[e]s/-e) command (*über acc.* of); order; ♀en (*irr.*, *no -ge-*, *h*) **1.** *v/t.* command; order; **2.** *v/i.* command; ♀igen ✕ [~igən] *v/t.* (*no -ge-*, *h*) command.

Be'fehlshaber *m* (-s/-) commander(-in-chief); ♀isch *adj.* imperious.

be'festig|en *v/t.* (*no -ge-*, *h*) fasten (*an dat.* to), fix (to), attach (to); ✕ fortify, *fig.* strengthen; ♀ung *f* (-/-en) fixing, fastening; ✕ fortification; *fig.* strengthening.

be'feuchten v/t. (no -ge-, h) moisten, damp; wet.

be'finden 1. v/refl. (irr. finden, no -ge-, h) be; **2.** 2 n (-s/no pl.) (state of) health.

be'flaggen v/t. (no -ge-, h) flag.

be'flecken v/t. (no -ge-, h) spot, stain (a. fig.); fig. sully.

beflissen adj. [bə'flisən] studious; 2heit f (-/no pl.) studiousness, assiduity.

befohlen [bə'fo:lən] p.p. of befehlen.

be'folg|en v/t. (no -ge-, h) follow, take (advice); obey (rule); adhere to (principle); 2ung f (-/%-en) observance (of); adherence (to).

be'förder|n v/t. (no -ge-, h) convey, carry; haul (goods), transport; forward; ✝ ship (a. ♻); promote (to be) (a. ✗); 2ung f conveyance, transport(ation), forwarding; promotion; 2ungsmittel n (means of) transport, Am. (means of) transportation.

be'fragen v/t. (no -ge-, h) question, interview; interrogate.

be'frei|en v/t. (no -ge-, h) (set) free (von from); liberate (nation, mind, etc.) (from); rescue (captive) (from); exempt s.o. (from); deliver s.o. (aus, von from); 2er m liberator; 2ung f (-/-en) liberation. deliverance; exemption.

Befremden [bə'fremdən] n (-s/ no pl.) surprise.

befreund|en [bə'frɔyndən] v/refl. (no -ge-, h): sich mit j-m ~ make friends with s.o.; sich mit et. ~ get used to s.th., reconcile o.s. to s.th.; ~et adj. friendly; on friendly terms; ~ sein be friends.

befriedig|en [bə'fri:digən] v/t. (no -ge-, h) satisfy; appease (hunger); meet (expectations, demand); pay off (creditor); 2end adj. satisfactory; 2ung f (-/-en) satisfaction.

be'fristen v/t. (no -ge-, h) set a time-limit.

be'frucht|en v/t. (no -ge-, h) fertilize; fructify; fecundate; impregnate; 2ung f (-/-en) fertilization; fructification; fecundation; impregnation.

Befug|nis [bə'fu:knis] f (-/-se) authority, warrant; esp. ⚖ competence; 2t adj. authorized; competent.

be'fühlen v/t. (no -ge-, h) feel; touch, handle, finger.

Be'fund m (-[e]s/-e) result; finding(s pl.); ⚕ diagnosis.

be'fürcht|en v/t. (no -ge-, h) fear, apprehend; suspect; 2ung f (-/-en) fear, apprehension, suspicion.

befürworten [bə'fy:rvɔrtən] v/t. (no -ge-, h) plead for, advocate.

begab|t [bə'ga:pt] gifted, talented; 2ung [~buŋ] f (-/-en) gift, talent(s pl.).

begann [bə'gan] pret. of beginnen.

be'geben v/t. (irr. geben, no -ge-, h) ✝ negotiate (bill of exchange); sich ~ happen; sich ~ nach go to, make for; sich in Gefahr ~ expose o.s. to danger.

begegn|en [bə'ge:gnən] v/i. (no -ge-, sein) meet s.o. or s.th., meet with; incident: happen to; anticipate, prevent; 2ung f (-/-en) meeting.

be'gehen v/t. (irr. gehen, no -ge-, h) walk (on); inspect; celebrate (birthday, etc.); commit (crime); make (mistake); ein Unrecht ~ do wrong.

begehr|en [bə'ge:rən] v/t. (no -ge-, h) demand, require; desire, crave (for); long for; ~lich adj. desirous, covetous.

begeister|n [bə'gaistərn] v/t. (no -ge-, h) inspire, fill with enthusiasm; sich ~ für feel enthusiastic about; 2ung f (-/no pl.) enthusiasm, inspiration.

Be'gier f, ~de [~də] f (-/-n) desire (nach for), appetite (for); concupiscence; 2ig adj. eager (auf acc. for, auf acc. for; zu inf. to inf.), desirous (nach of; zu inf. to inf.), anxious (zu inf. to inf.).

be'gießen v/t. (irr. gießen, no -ge-, h) water; baste (roasting meat); F wet (bargain).

Beginn [bə'gin] m (-[e]s/no pl.) beginning, start, commencement; origin; 2en v/t. and v/i. (irr. no -ge-, h) begin, start, commence.

beglaubig|en [bə'glaubigən] v/t. (no -ge-, h) attest, certify; legalize, authenticate; 2ung f (-/-en) attestation, certification; legalization; 2ungsschreiben n credentials pl.

be'gleichen ✝ v/t. (irr. gleichen, no -ge-, h) pay, settle (bill, debt).

be'gleit|en v/t. (no -ge-, h) accompany (a. ♪ auf dat. on), escort; attend (a. fig.); see (s.o. home, etc.); 2er m (-s/-) companion, attendant; escort; ♪ accompanist; 2erschei-nung f attendant symptom; 2-schreiben n covering letter; 2ung f (-/-en) company; attendants pl., retinue (of sovereign, etc.); esp. ✗ escort; ♻, ✗ convoy; ♪ accompaniment.

be'glückwünschen v/t. (no -ge-, h) congratulate (zu on).

begnadig|en [bə'gna:digən] v/t. (no -ge-, h) pardon; pol. amnesty; 2ung f (-/-en) pardon; pol. amnesty.

begnügen [bə'gny:gən] v/refl. (no -ge-, h): sich ~ mit content o.s. with, be satisfied with.

begonnen [bə'gɔnən] p.p. of beginnen.

be'graben v/t. (irr. graben, no -ge-, h) bury (a. fig.); inter.

Begräbnis [bə'grɛ:pnis] n (-ses/-se) burial; funeral, obsequies pl.

begradigen [bə'grɑːdigən] *v/t. (no -ge-, h)* straighten *(road, frontier, etc.).*

be'greif|en *v/t. (irr. greifen, no -ge-, h)* comprehend, understand; **~lich** *adj.* comprehensible.

be'grenz|en *v/t. (no -ge-, h)* bound, border; *fig.* limit; **2theit** *f (-/-en)* limitation *(of knowledge);* narrowness *(of mind);* **2ung** *f (-/-en)* boundary; bound, limit, limitation.

Be'griff *m* idea, notion, conception; comprehension; *im ~ sein zu inf.* be about *or* going to *inf.*

be'gründ|en *v/t. (no -ge-, h)* establish, found; give reasons for, substantiate *(claim, charge);* **2ung** *f* establishment, foundation; *fig.* substantiation *(of claim or charge);* reason.

be'grüß|en *v/t. (no -ge-, h)* greet, welcome; salute; **2ung** *f (-/-en)* greeting, welcome; salutation.

begünstig|en [bə'gynstigən] *v/t. (no -ge-, h)* favo(u)r; encourage; patronize; **2ung** *(-/-en) f* favo(u)r; encouragement; patronage.

begutachten [bə'guːtʔ-] *v/t. (no -ge-, h)* give an opinion on; examine; *~ lassen* obtain expert opinion on, submit *s.th.* to an expert.

begütert *adj.* [bə'gyːtərt] wealthy, well-to-do.

be'haart *adj.* hairy.

behäbig *adj.* [bə'hɛːbiç] phlegmatic, comfort-loving; *figure:* portly.

be'haftet *adj.* afflicted *(with disease, etc.).*

behag|en [bə'hɑːgən] **1.** *v/i. (no -ge-, h)* please *or* suit *s.o.;* **2.** *♀ n (-s/no pl.)* comfort, ease; **~lich** *adj.* [-k-] comfortable; cosy, snug.

be'halten *v/t. (irr. halten, no -ge-, h)* re¹tain; keep *(für sich* to o.s.); remember.

Behälter [bə'hɛltər] *m (-s/-)* container, receptacle; box; *for liquid:* reservoir; *for oil, etc.:* tank.

be'hand|eln *v/t. (no -ge-, h)* treat; deal with *(a. subject);* ⊕ process; *✦* treat; dress *(wound);* **2lung** *f* treatment; handling; ⊕ processing.

be'hängen *v/t. (no -ge-, h)* hang, drape *(mit with); sich ~ mit* cover *or* load o.s. with *(jewellery).*

beharr|en [bə'harən] *v/i. (no -ge-, h)* persist *(auf dat.* in); **~lich** *adj.* persistent; **2lichkeit** *f (-/no pl.)* persistence.

be'hauen *v/t. (no -ge-, h)* hew; trim *(wood).*

behaupt|en [bə'hauptən] *v/t. (no -ge-, h)* assert; maintain; **2ung** *f (-/-en)* assertion; statement.

Behausung [bə'hauzuŋ] *f (-/-en)* habitation; lodging.

Be'helf *m (-[e]s/-e)* expedient, (make)shift; *s.* Notbehelf; **2en** *v/refl. (irr. helfen, no -ge-, h):* sich

~ mit make shift with; *sich ~ ohne* do without; **~sheim** *n* temporary home.

behend *adj.* [bə'hɛnt], **~e** *adj.* [-də] nimble, agile; smart; **2igkeit** [-d-] *f (-/no pl.)* nimbleness, agility; smartness.   [lodge, shelter.)

be'herbergen *v/t. (no -ge-, h)}*

be'herrsch|en *v/t. (no -ge-, h)* rule (over), govern; command *(situation, etc.);* have command of *(language); sich ~* control o.s.; **2er** *m* ruler *(gen.* over, of); **2ung** *f (-/-en)* command, control.

beherzigen [bə'hɛrtsigən] *v/t. (no -ge-, h)* take to heart, (bear in) mind.

be'hexen *v/t. (no -ge-, h)* bewitch.

be'hilflich *adj.: j-m ~ sein* help s.o. *(bei* in).

be'hindern *v/t. (no -ge-, h)* hinder, hamper, impede; handicap; obstruct *(a. traffic, etc.).*

Behörde [bə'høːrdə] *f (-/-n)* authority, *mst* authorities *pl.;* board; council.

be'hüten *v/t. (no -ge-, h)* guard, preserve *(vor dat.* from).

behutsam *adj.* [bə'huːtzɑːm] cautious, careful; **2keit** *f (-/no pl.)* caution.

bei *prp. (dat.) ~ bai] address: ~ Schmidt* care of *(abbr.* c/o) Schmidt; *~m Buchhändler* at the bookseller's; *~ uns* with us; *~ der Hand nehmen* take by the hand; *ich habe kein Geld ~ mir* I have no money about *or* on me; *~ der Kirche* near the church; *~ guter Gesundheit* in good health; *wie es ~ Schiller heißt* as Schiller says; *die Schlacht ~ Waterloo* the Battle of Waterloo; *~ e-m Glase Wein* over a glass of wine; *~ alledem* for all that; *Stunden nehmen ~* take lessons from *or* with; *~ günstigem Wetter* weather permitting.

'beibehalten *v/t. (irr. halten, sep., no -ge-, h)* keep up, retain.

'Beiblatt *n* supplement *(zu* to).

'beibringen *v/t. (irr. bringen, sep., -ge-, h)* bring forward; produce *(witness, etc.); j-m et. ~* impart *(news, etc.)* to s.o.; teach s.o. *s.th.;* inflict *(defeat, wound, etc.)* on s.o.

Beichte ['baiçtə] *f (-/-n)* confession; **2n** *v/t. and v/i. (ge-, h)* confess.

beide *adj.* [baidə] both; *nur wir ~* just the two of us; *in ~n Fällen* in either case.

beider|lei *adj.* ['baidərlai] of both kinds; *~ Geschlechts* of either sex; **'~seitig 1.** *adj.* on both sides; mutual; **2.** *adv.* mutually; **'~seits 1.** *prp.* on both sides *(gen.* of); **2.** *adv.* mutually.

'Beifahrer *m (-s/-)* (front-seat) passenger; assistant driver; *motor racing:* co-driver.

'**Beifall** m (-[e]s/no pl.) approbation; applause; cheers pl.

'**beifällig** adj. approving; favo(u)r-able.

'**Beifallsruf** m acclaim; ~e pl. cheers pl.

'**beifügen** v/t. (sep., -ge-, h) add; enclose.

'**Beigeschmack** m (-[e]s/no pl.) slight flavo(u)r; smack (of) (a. fig.).

'**Beihilfe** f aid; allowance; for study: grant; for project: subsidy; ⊥⊥ aid-ing and abetting; j-m ~ leisten ⊥⊥ aid and abet s.o.

'**beikommen** v/i. (irr. kommen, sep., -ge-, sein) get at.

Beil [baɪl] n (-[e]s/-e) hatchet; chopper; cleaver; ax(e).

'**Beilage** f supplement (to news-paper); F trimming~ pl. (of meal); vegetables pl.

beiläufig adj. ['baɪləyfɪç] casual; incidental.

'**beileg|en** v/t. (sep., -ge-, h) add (dat. to); enclose; settle (dispute); '2ung f (-/-en) settlement.

Beileid ['baɪlaɪt] n condolence; j-m sein ~ bezeigen condole with s.o. (zu on, upon).

'**beiliegen** v/i. (irr. liegen, sep., -ge-, h) be enclosed (dat. with).

'**beimessen** v/t. (irr. messen, sep., -ge-, h) attribute (dat. to), ascribe (to); attach (importance) (to).

'**beimisch|en** v/t. (sep., -ge-, h): e-r Sache et. ~ mix s.th. with s.th.; '2ung f admixture.

Bein [baɪn] n (-[e]s/-e) leg; bone.

'**beinah(e)** adv. almost, nearly.

'**Beiname** m appellation; nickname.

'**Beinbruch** m fracture of the leg.

beiordnen ['baɪ?-] v/t. (sep., -ge-, h) adjoin; co-ordinate (a. gr.).

'**beipflichten** v/i. (sep., -ge-, h) agree with s.o.; assent to s.th.

'**Beirat** m (-[e]s/⸚e) adviser, coun-sel(l)or; advisory board.

be'irren v/t. (no -ge-, h) confuse.

beisammen adv. [baɪ'zamən] to-gether.

'**Beisein** n presence; im ~ (gen.) or von in the presence of s.o., in s.o.'s presence.

bei'seite adv. aside ,apart; Spaß ~! joking apart!

'**beisetz|en** v/t. (sep., -ge-, h) bury, inter; '2ung f (-/-en) burial, fu-neral.

'**Beisitzer** ⊥⊥ m (-s/-) assessor; asso-ciate judge; member (of committee).

'**Beispiel** n example, instance; zum ~ for example or instance; '2haft adj. exemplary; '2los adj. unprece-dented, unparalleled; unheard of.

beißen ['baɪsən] (irr., ge-, h) **1.** v/t. bite; fleas, etc.: bite, sting; **2.** v/i. bite (auf acc. on; in acc. into); fleas, etc.: bite, sting; smoke: bite; burn (in dat. in); pepper, etc.: bite,

burn (auf dat. on); ~d adj. biting, pungent (both a. fig.); pepper, etc.: hot.

'**Beistand** m assistance.

'**beistehen** v/i. (irr. stehen, sep., -ge-, h): j-m ~ stand by or assist or help s.o.

'**beisteuern** v/t. and v/i. (sep., -ge-, h) contribute (zu to).

Beitrag ['baɪtra:k] m (-[e]s/⸚e) con-tribution; share; subscription, Am. dues pl.; article (in newspaper, etc.).

'**bei|treten** v/i. (irr. treten, sep., -ge-, sein) join (political party, etc.); '2tritt m joining.

'**Beiwagen** m side-car (of motor-cycle); trailer (of tram).

'**Beiwerk** n accessories pl.

'**beiwohnen** v/i. (sep., -ge-, h) assist or be present at, attend.

bei'zeiten adv. early; in good time.

beizen ['baɪtsən] v/t. (ge-, h) cor-rode; metall. pickle; bate (hides); stain (wood); ⚕ cauterize; hunt. hawk.

bejahen [bə'ja:ən] v/t. (no -ge-, h) answer in the affirmative, affirm; ~d adj. affirmative.

be'jahrt adj. aged.

Bejahung f (-/-en) affirmation, af-firmative answer; fig. acceptance.

be'jammern s. beklagen.

be'kämpfen v/t. (no -ge-, h) fight (against), combat; fig. oppose.

bekannt [bə'kant] known (dat. to); j-n mit j-m ~ machen introduce s.o. to s.o.; 2e m, f (-n/-n) acquaint-ance, mst friend; ~lich adv. as you know; ~machen v/t. (sep., -ge-, h) make known; 2machung f (-/-en) publication; public notice; 2schaft f (-/-en) acquaintance.

be'kehr|en v/t. (no -ge-, h) convert; 2te m, f (-n/-n) convert; 2ung f (-/-en) conversion (zu to).

be'kenn|en v/t. (irr. kennen, no -ge-, h) admit; confess; sich schuldig ~ ⊥⊥ plead guilty; sich ~ zu declare o.s. for; profess s.th.; 2tnis n (-ses/-se) confession; creed.

be'klagen v/t. (no -ge-, h) lament, deplore; sich ~ complain (über acc. of, about); ~swert adj. deplorable, pitiable.

Beklagte [bə'kla:ktə] m, f (-n/-n) civil case: defendant, the accused.

be'klatschen v/t. (no -ge-, h) ap-plaud, clap.

be'kleben v/t. (no -ge-, h) glue or stick s.th. on s.th.; mit Etiketten ~ label s.th.; mit Papier ~ paste s.th. up with paper; e-e Mauer mit Pla-katen ~ paste (up) posters on a wall.

bekleckern F [bə'klɛkərn] v/t. (no -ge-, h) stain (garment); sich ~ soil one's clothes.

be'klecksen v/t. (no -ge-. h) stain, daub; blot.

be'kleid|en v/t. (no -ge-, h) clothe, dress; hold, fill (office, etc.); ~ mit invest with; 2ung f clothing, clothes pl.

be'klemm|en v/t. (no -ge-, h) oppress; 2ung f (-/-en) oppression; anguish, anxiety.

be'kommen (irr. kommen, no -ge-) 1. v/t. (h) get, receive; obtain; get, catch (illness); have (baby); catch (train, etc.); Zähne ~ teethe, cut one's teeth; 2. v/i. (sein): j-m (gut) ~ agree with s.o.; j-m nicht or schlecht ~ disagree with s.o.

bekömmlich adj. [bə'kœmliç] wholesome (dat. to).

bekostig|en [bə'kœstigən] v/t. (no -ge-, h) board, feed; 2ung f (-/-en) board(ing).

be'kräftig|en v/t. (no -ge-, h) confirm; 2ung f (-/-en) confirmation.

be'kränzen v/t. (no -ge-, h) wreathe; festoon.

be'kritteln v/t. (no -ge-, h) carp at, criticize.

be'kümmern v/t. (no -ge-, h) afflict, grieve; trouble; s. kümmern.

be'laden v/t. (irr. laden, no -ge-, h) load; fig. burden.

Belag [bə'la:k] m (-[e]s/¨e) covering; ⊕ coat(ing); surface (of road); foil (of mirror); ✗ fur (on tongue); (slices of) ham, etc. (on bread); filling (of roll).

Belager|er [bə'la:gərər] m (-s/-) besieger; 2n v/t. (no -ge-, h) besiege, beleaguer; ~ung f siege.

Belang [bə'laŋ] m (-[e]s/-e) importance; ~e pl. interests pl.; 2en v/t. (no -ge-, h) concern; ⅈⅉ sue; 2los adj. unimportant; ~losigkeit f (-/-en) insignificance.

be'lasten v/t. (no -ge-, h) load; fig. burden; ⅈⅉ incriminate; mortgage (estate, etc.); j-s Konto (mit e-r Summe) ~ ♱ charge or debit s.o.'s account (with a sum).

belästig|en [bə'lɛstigən] v/t. (no -ge-, h) molest; trouble; bother; 2ung f molestation; trouble.

Be'lastung f (-/-en) load (a. ≠, ⊕); fig. burden; ♱ debit; encumbrance; ⅈⅉ incrimination; erbliche ~ hereditary taint; ~szeuge ⅈⅉ m witness for the prosecution.

be'laufen v/refl. (irr. laufen, no -ge-, h): sich ~ auf (acc.) amount to.

be'lauschen v/t. (no -ge-, h) overhear, eavesdrop on s.o.

be'leb|en fig. v/t. (no -ge-, h) enliven, animate; stimulate; ~t adj. street: busy, crowded; stock exchange: brisk; conversation: lively, animated.

Beleg [bə'le:k] m (-[e]s/-e) proof; ⅈⅉ (supporting) evidence; document; voucher; 2en [~gən] v/t. (no -ge-, h) cover; reserve (seat, etc.); prove, verify; univ. enrol(l) or register for,

Am. a. sign up for (course of lectures, term); ein Brötchen mit et. ~ put s.th. on a roll, fill a roll with s.th.; ~schaft f (-/-en) personnel, staff; labo(u)r force; ~stelle f reference; 2t adj. engaged, occupied; hotel, etc.: full; voice: thick, husky; tongue: coated, furred; ~es Brot (open) sandwich.

be'lehr|en v/t. (no -ge-, h) instruct, inform; sich ~ lassen take advice; ~end adj. instructive; 2ung f (-/-en) instruction; information; advice.

beleibt adj. [bə'laɪpt] corpulent, stout, bulky, portly.

beleidig|en [bə'laɪdigən] v/t. (no -ge-, h) offend (s.o.; ear, eye, etc.); insult; ~end adj. offensive; insulting; 2ung f (-/-en) offen|ce, Am. -se; insult.

be'lesen adj. well-read.

be'leucht|en v/t. (no -ge-, h) light (up), illuminate (a. fig.); fig. shed or throw light on; 2ung f (-/-en) light(ing); illumination; 2ungskörper m lighting appliance.

be'licht|en phot. v/t. (no -ge-, h) expose; 2ung phot. f exposure.

Be'lieb|en n (-s/no pl.) will, choice; nach ~ at will; es steht in Ihrem ~ I leave it to you; 2ig 1. adj. any; jeder ~e anyone; 2. adv. at pleasure; ~ viele as many as you like; 2t adj. [~pt] popular (bei with); ~theit f (-/no pl.) popularity.

be'liefer|n v/t. (no -ge-, h) supply, furnish (mit with); 2ung f (-/no pl.) supply.

bellen ['bɛlən] v/i. (ge-, h) bark.

belobigen [bə'lo:bigən] v/t. (no -ge-, h) commend, praise.

be'lohn|en v/t. (no -ge-, h) reward; recompense; 2ung f (-/-en) reward; recompense.

be'lügen v/t. (irr. lügen, no -ge-, h): j-n ~ lie to s.o.

belustig|en [bə'lustigən] v/t. (no -ge-, h) amuse, entertain; sich ~ amuse o.s.; 2ung f (-/-en) amusement, entertainment.

bemächtigen [bə'mɛçtigən] v/refl. (no -ge-, h): sich e-r Sache ~ take hold of s.th., seize s.th.; sich e-r Person ~ lay hands on s.o., seize s.o.

be'malen v/t. (no -ge-, h) cover with paint; paint; daub.

bemängeln [bə'mɛŋəln] v/t. (no -ge-, h) find fault with, cavil at.

be'mannen v/t. (no -ge-, h) man.

be'merk|bar adj. perceptible; ~en v/t. (no -ge-, h) notice, perceive; remark, mention; ~enswert adj. remarkable (wegen for); 2ung f (-/-en) remark.

bemitleiden [bə'mitlaidən] v/t. (no -ge-, h) pity, commiserate (with); ~swert adj. pitiable.

be'müh|en v/t. (no -ge-, h) trouble (j-n in or wegen et. s.o. about s.th.);

sich ~ trouble o.s.; endeavo(u)r; *sich um e-e Stelle* ~ apply for a position; 2ung *f* (-/-en) trouble; endeavo(u)r, effort.

be'nachbart *adj.* neighbo(u)ring; adjoining, adjacent (to).

benachrichtig|en [bə'naːxriçtigən] *v/t.* (*no* -ge-, *h*) inform, notify; † advise; 2ung *f* (-/-en) information; notification; † advice.

benachteilig|en [bə'naːxtailigən] *v/t.* (*no* -ge-, *h*) place *s.o.* at a disadvantage, discriminate against *s.o.*; handicap; *sich benachteiligt fühlen* feel handicapped *or* at a disadvantage; *sich benachteiligt fühlen* feel handicapped *or* at a disadvantage; 2ung *f* (-/-en) disadvantage; discrimination; handicap.

be'nehmen 1. *v/refl.* (*irr. nehmen, no* -ge-, *h*) behave (o.s.); 2. 2 *n* (-*s*/*no pl.*) behavio(u)r, conduct.

be'neiden *v/t.* (*no* -ge-, *h*) envy (*j-n um et.* s.o. s.th.); ~**swert** *adj.* enviable.

be'nennen *v/t.* (*irr. nennen, no* -ge-, *h*) name. [rascal, urchin.)

Bengel ['beŋəl] *m* (-*s*/-) (little))

benommen *adj.* [bə'nɔmən] bemused, dazed, stunned; ~ *sein* be in a daze.

be'nötigen *v/t.* (*no* -ge-, *h*) need, require, want.

be'nutz|en *v/t.* (*no* -ge-, *h*) use (*a. patent, etc.*); make use of; avail o.s. of (*opportunity*); take (*tram, etc.*); 2ung *f* use.

Benzin [ben'tsiːn] *n* (-*s*/-*e*) ⚗ benzine; *mot.* petrol, F juice, *Am.* gasoline, F gas; ~**motor** *m* petrol engine, *Am.* gasoline engine; *s.* Tank.

beobacht|en [bə'oːbaxtən] *v/t.* (*no* -ge-, *h*) observe; watch; *police:* shadow; 2er *m* (-*s*/-) observer; 2ung *f* (-/-en) observation.

beordern [bə'ɔrdərn] *v/t.* (*no* -ge-, *h*) order, command.

be'packen *v/t.* (*no* -ge-, *h*) load (*mit* with). [(mit with).)

be'pflanzen *v/t.* (*no* -ge-, *h*) plant)

bequem *adj.* [bə'kveːm] convenient; comfortable; *p.:* easy-going; lazy; ~en *v/refl.* (*no* -ge-, *h*): *sich* ~ *zu* condescend to; consent to; 2lichkeit *f* (-/-en) convenience; comfort, ease; indolence.

be'rat|en (*irr. raten, no* -ge-, *h*) 1. *v/t.* advise *s.o.*; consider, debate, discuss *s.th.*; *sich* ~ confer (*mit j-m* with s.o.; *über et. on or* about s.th.); 2. *v/i.* confer; *über et.* ~ consider, debate, discuss s.th., confer on *or* about s.th.; 2er *m* (-*s*/-) adviser, counsel(l)or; consultant; 2schlagen (*no* -ge-, *h*) 1. *v/i. s.* beraten 2; 2. *v/refl.* confer (*mit j-m* with s.o.; *über et. on or* about s.th.); 2ung *f* (-/-en) advice; debate; consultation; conference; 2ungsstelle *f* advisory bureau.

be'raub|en *v/t.* (*no* -ge-, *h*) rob, deprive (*gen.* of); 2ung *f* (-/-en) robbery, deprivation.

be'rauschen *v/t.* (*no* -ge-, *h*) intoxicate (*a. fig.*).

be'rechn|en *v/t.* (*no* -ge-, *h*) calculate; † charge (*zu* at); ~**end** *adj.* calculating, selfish; 2ung *f* calculation.

berechtig|en [bə'reçtigən] *v/t.* (*no* -ge-, *h*) *j-n* ~ *zu* entitle s.o. to; authorize s.o. to; ~t *adj.* [~çt] entitled (*zu* to); qualified (to); *claim:* legitimate; 2ung *f* (-/-en) title (*zu* to); authorization.

be'red|en *v/t.* (*no* -ge-, *h*) talk *s.th.* over; persuade *s.o.*; gossip about *s.o.*; 2samkeit [~tzaːmkait] *f* (-/*no pl.*) eloquence; ~t *adj.* [~t] eloquent (*a. fig.*).

Be'reich *m, n* (-[e]s/-e) area; reach; *fig.* scope, sphere; science, *etc.*: field, province; 2ern *v/t.* (*no* -ge-, *h*) enrich; *sich* ~ enrich o.s.; ~**erung** *f* (-/-en) enrichment.

be'reif|en *v/t.* (*no* -ge-, *h*) hoop (*barrel*); tyre, (*Am. only*) tire (*wheel*); 2ung *f* (-/-en) (set of) tyres *pl.*, (*Am. only*) (set of) tires *pl.*

be'reisen *v/t.* (*no* -ge-, *h*) tour (in), travel (over); *commercial traveller:* cover (*district*).

bereit *adj.* [bə'rait] ready, prepared; ~en *v/t.* (*no* -ge-, *h*) prepare; give (*joy, trouble, etc.*); ~s *adv.* already; 2schaft *f* (-/-en) readiness; *police:* squad; ~stellen *v/t.* (*sep.*, -ge-, *h*) place *s.th.* ready; provide; 2ung *f* (-/-en) preparation; ~**willig** *adj.* ready, willing; 2willigkeit *f* (-/*no pl.*) readiness, willingness.

be'reuen *v/t.* (*no* -ge-, *h*) repent (of); regret, rue.

Berg [berk] *m* (-[e]s/-e) mountain; hill; ~e *pl. von* F heaps *pl.* of, piles *pl.* of; *über den* ~ *sein* be out of the wood, *Am.* be out of the woods; *über alle* ~e off and away; *die Haare standen ihm zu* ~e his hair stood on end; 2'ab *adv.* downhill (*a. fig.*); 2'an *adv. s.* bergauf; '~**arbeiter** *m* miner; 2'auf *adv.* uphill (*a. fig.*); '~**bahn** 🚟 *f* mountain railway; '~**bau** *m* (-[e]s/*pl.*) mining.

bergen ['bergən] *v/t.* (*irr.*, ge-, *h*) save; rescue *s.o.*; ⚓ salvage, salve.

bergig *adj.* ['bergiç] mountainous, hilly.

'Berg|kette *f* mountain chain *or* range; '~**mann** ⚒ *m* (-[e]s/Bergleute) miner; '~**predigt** *f* (-/*no pl.*) *the* Sermon on the Mount; '~**recht** *n* mining laws *pl.*; '~**rennen** *mot. n* mountain race; '~**rücken** *m* ridge; '~**rutsch** *m* landslide, landslip; '~**spitze** *f* mountain peak; '~**steiger** *m* (-*s*/-) mountaineer; '~**sturz** *m s.* Bergrutsch.

'Bergung f (-/-en) ⚓ salvage; rescue; ~arbeiten ['bɛrguŋˀ-] f/pl. salvage operations pl.; rescue work.

'Bergwerk n mine; ~saktien ['bɛrkvɛrksˀ-] f/pl. mining shares pl.

Bericht [bə'rɪçt] m (-[e]s/-e) report (über acc. on); account (of); 2en (no -ge-, h) 1. v/t. report; j-m et. ~ inform s.o. of s.th.; tell s.o. about s.th.; 2. v/i. report (über acc. on); journalist: a. cover (über et. s.th.); ~erstatter m (-s/-) reporter; correspondent; ~erstattung f reporting; report(s pl.).

berichtig|en [bə'rɪçtɪgən] v/t. (no -ge-, h) correct (s.o.; error, mistake, etc.); put right (mistake); emend (corrupt text); ✝ settle (claim, debt, etc.); 2ung f (-/-en) correction; emendation; settlement.

be'riechen v/t. (irr. riechen, no -ge-, h) smell or sniff at.

Berliner [bɛr'liːnər] 1. m (-s/-) Berliner; 2. adj. (of) Berlin.

Bernstein ['bɛrnʃtain] m amber; schwarzer ~ jet.

bersten ['bɛrstən] v/i. (irr., ge-, sein) burst (fig. vor dat. with).

berüchtigt [bə'rʏçtɪçt] notorious (wegen for), ill-famed.

berücksichtig|en [bə'rʏkzɪçtɪgən] v/t. (no -ge-, h) take s.th. into consideration, pay regard to s.th.; consider s.o.; 2ung f (-/-en) consideration; regard.

Beruf [bə'ruːf] m (-[e]s/-e) calling; profession; vocation; trade; occupation; 2en 1. v/t. (irr. rufen, no -ge-, h): j-n zu e-m Amt ~ appoint s.o. to an office; sich auf j-n ~ refer to s.o.; 2. adj. competent; qualified; 2lich adj. professional; vocational.

Be'rufs|ausbildung f vocational or professional training; ~beratung f vocational guidance; ~kleidung f work clothes pl.; ~krankheit f occupational disease; ~schule f vocational school; ~spieler m sports: professional (player); 2tätig adj. working; ~tätige [~gə] pl. working people pl.

Be'rufung f (-/-en) appointment (zu to); ✝✝ appeal (bei dat. to); reference (auf acc. to); ~sgericht n court of appeal.

be'ruhen v/i. (no -ge-, h): ~ auf (dat.) rest or be based on; et. auf sich ~ lassen let a matter rest.

beruhig|en [bə'ruːɪgən] v/t. (no -ge-, h) quiet, calm; soothe; sich ~ calm down; 2ung f (-/-en) calming (down); soothing; comfort; 2ungsmittel 🕮 n sedative.

berühmt adj. [bə'ryːmt] famous (wegen for); celebrated; 2heit f (-/-en) fame, renown; famous or celebrated person, celebrity; person of note.

be'rühr|en v/t. (no -ge-, h) touch (a. fig.); touch (up)on (subject); 2ung f (-/-en) contact; touch; in ~ kommen mit come into contact with.

be'sag|en v/t. (no -ge-, h) say; mean, signify; ~t adj. [~kt] (afore-) said; above(-mentioned).

besänftigen [bə'zɛnftɪgən] v/t. (no -ge-, h) appease, calm, soothe.

Be'satz m (-es/ᵉe) trimming; braid.

Be'satzung f ⚔ occupation troops pl.; ⚔ garrison; ⚓, ✈ crew; ~smacht ⚔ f occupying power.

be'schädig|en v/t. (no -ge-, h) damage, injure; 2ung f damage, injury (gen. to).

be'schaffen 1. v/t. (no -ge-, h) procure; provide; raise (money); 2. adj.: gut (schlecht) ~ sein be in good (bad) condition or state; 2heit f (-/-en) state, condition; properties pl.

beschäftig|en [bə'ʃɛftɪgən] v/t. (no -ge-, h) employ, occupy; keep busy; sich ~ occupy or busy o.s.; 2ung f (-/-en) employment; occupation.

be'schäm|en v/t. (no -ge-, h) (put to) shame, make s.o. feel ashamed; ~end adj. shameful; humiliating; ~t adj. ashamed (über acc. of); 2ung f (-/-en) shame; humiliation.

beschatten [bə'ʃatən] v/t. (no -ge-, h) shade; fig. shadow s.o., Am. sl. tail s.o.

be'schau|en v/t. (no -ge-, h) look at, view; examine, inspect (goods, etc.); ~lich adj. contemplative, meditative.

Bescheid [bə'ʃait] m (-[e]s/-e) answer; ✝✝ decision; information (über acc. on, about); ~ geben let s.o. know; ~ bekommen be informed or notified; ~ hinterlassen leave word (bei with, at); ~ wissen be informed, know, F be in the know.

bescheiden adj. [bə'ʃaidən] modest, unassuming; 2heit f (-/no pl.) modesty.

bescheinig|en [bə'ʃainɪgən] v/i. (no -ge-, h) certify, attest; den Empfang ~ acknowledge receipt; es wird hiermit bescheinigt, daß this is to certify that; 2ung f (-/-en) certification, attestation; certificate; receipt; acknowledgement.

be'schenken v/t. (no -ge-, h): j-n ~ make s.o. a present; j-n mit et. ~ present s.o. with s.th.; j-n reichlich ~ shower s.o. with gifts.

be'scher|en v/t. (no -ge-, h): j-n ~ give s.o. presents (esp. for Christmas); 2ung f (-/-en) presentation of gifts; F fig. mess.

be'schieß|en v/t. (irr. schießen, no -ge-, h) fire or shoot at or on; bombard (a. phys.), shell; 2ung f (-/-en) bombardment.

be'schimpf|en v/t. (no -ge-, h) abuse, insult; call s.o. names; 2ung f (-/-en) abuse; insult, affront.

be'schirmen v/t. (no -ge-, h) shelter, shield, guard, protect (vor dat. from); defend (against).

be'schlafen v/t. (irr. schlafen, no -ge-, h): et. ~ sleep on a matter, take counsel of one's pillow.

Be'schlag m ⊕ metal fitting(s pl.); furnishing(s pl.) (of door, etc.); shoe (of wheel, etc.); (horse)shoe; ⚡ seizure, confiscation; in ~ nehmen, mit ~ belegen seize; ⚖ seize, attach (real estate, salary, etc.); confiscate (goods, etc.); monopolize s.o.'s attention.

be'schlagen 1. v/t. (irr. schlagen, no -ge-, h) cover (mit with); ⊕ fit, mount; shoe (horse); hobnail (shoe); 2. v/i. (irr. schlagen, no -ge-, h) window, wall, etc.: steam up; mirror, etc.: cloud or film over; 3. adj. windows, etc.: steamed-up; fig. well versed (auf, in dat. in).

Beschlagnahme [bə'ʃlɑːknɑːmə] f (-/-n) seizure; confiscation (of contraband goods, etc.); ⚖ sequestration, distraint (of property); ✕ requisition (of houses, etc.); embargo, detention (of ship); ⚓n v/t. (no -ge-, h) seize; attach (real estate); confiscate; ⚖ sequestrate, distrain upon (property); ✕ requisition; ⚓ embargo.

beschleunig|en [bə'ʃlɔynigən] v/t. (no -ge-, h) mot. accelerate; hasten, speed up; s-e Schritte ~ quicken one's steps; 2ung f (-/-en) acceleration.

be'schließen v/t. (irr. schließen, no -ge-, h) end, close, wind up; resolve, decide.

Be'schluß m decision, resolution, Am. a. resolve; ⚖ decree; 2fähig adj.: ~ sein form or have a quorum; ~fassung f (passing of a) resolution.

be'schmieren v/t. (no -ge-, h) (be)smear (with grease, etc.).

be'schmutzen v/t. (no -ge-, h) soil (a. fig.), dirty; bespatter.

be'schneiden v/t. (irr. schneiden, no -ge-, h) clip, cut; lop (tree); trim, clip (hair, hedge, etc.); dress (vinestock, etc.); fig. cut down, curtail, F slash.

beschönig|en [bə'ʃøːnigən] v/t. (no -ge-, h) gloss over, palliate; 2ung f (-/-en) gloss, palliation.

beschränk|en [bə'ʃrɛŋkən] v/t. (no -ge-, h) confine, limit, restrict, Am. a. curb; sich ~ auf (acc.) confine o.s. to; ~t fig. adj. of limited intelligence; 2ung f (-/-en) limitation, restriction.

be'schreib|en v/t. (irr. schreiben, no -ge-, h) write on (piece of paper, etc.), cover with writing; describe, give a description of; 2ung f (-/-en) description; account.

be'schrift|en v/t. (no -ge-, h) inscribe; letter; 2ung f (-/-en) inscription; lettering.

beschuldig|en [bə'ʃuldigən] v/t. (no -ge-, h) accuse (gen. of [doing] s.th.), esp. ⚖ charge (with); 2te [~ktə] m, f (-n/-n) the accused; 2ung f (-/-en) accusation, charge.

Be'schuß m (Beschusses/no pl.) bombardment.

be'schütz|en v/t. (no -ge-, h) protect, shelter, guard (vor dat. from); 2er m (-s/-) protector; 2ung f (-/-en) protection.

be'schwatzen v/t. (no -ge-, h) talk s.o. into (doing) s.th., coax s.o. into (doing s.th.).

Beschwerde [bə'ʃveːrdə] f (-/-n) trouble; ⚕ complaint; complaint (über acc. about); ⚖ objection (gegen to); ~buch n complaints book.

beschwer|en [bə'ʃveːrən] v/t. (no -ge-, h) burden (a. fig.); weight (loose sheets, etc.); lie heavy on (stomach); weigh on (mind, etc.); sich ~ complain (über acc. about, of; bei to); ~lich adj. troublesome.

beschwichtigen [bə'ʃvIçtigən] v/t. (no -ge-, h) appease, calm (down), soothe.

be'schwindeln v/t. (no -ge-, h) tell a fib or lie; cheat, F diddle (um out of).

be'schwipst F adj. tipsy.

be'schwör|en v/t. (irr. schwören, no -ge-, h) take an oath on s.th.; implore or entreat s.o.; conjure (up), invoke (spirit); 2ung f (-/-en) conjuration.

be'seelen v/t. (no -ge-, h) animate, inspire.

be'sehen v/t. (irr. sehen, no -ge-, h) look at; inspect; sich et. ~ look at s.th.; inspect s.th.

beseitig|en [bə'zaitigən] v/t. (no -ge-, h) remove, do away with; 2ung f (-/-en) removal.

Besen ['beːzən] m (-s/-) broom; ~stiel m broomstick.

besessen adj. [bə'zɛsən] obsessed, possessed (von by, with); wie ~ like mad; 2e m, f (-n/-n) demoniac.

be'setz|en v/t. (no -ge-, h) occupy (seat, table, etc.); fill (post, etc.); man (orchestra); thea. cast (play); ✕ occupy; trim (dress, etc.); set (crown with jewels, etc.); ~t adj. engaged, occupied; seat: taken; F bus, etc.: full up; hotel: full; teleph. engaged, Am. busy; 2ung f (-/-en) thea. cast; ✕ occupation.

besichtig|en [bə'ziçtigən] v/t. (no -ge-, h) view, look over; inspect (a. ✕); visit; 2ung f (-/-en) sightseeing; visit (gen. to); inspection (a. ✕).

be'sied|eln v/t. (no -ge-, h) colonize, settle; populate; 2lung f (-/-en) colonization, settlement.

be'siegeln v/t. (no -ge-, h) seal (a. fig.).

be'siegen v/t. (no -ge-, h) conquer; defeat, beat (a. sports).

be'sinn|en v/refl. (irr. sinnen, no -ge-, h) reflect, consider; sich ~ auf (acc.) remember, think of; ~lich adj. reflective, contemplative.

Be'sinnung f (-/no pl.) reflection; consideration; consciousness; (wieder) zur ~ kommen recover consciousness; fig. come to one's senses; 2slos adj. unconscious.

Be'sitz m possession; in ~ nehmen, ~ ergreifen von take possession of; 2anzeigend gr. adj. possessive; 2en v/t. (irr. sitzen, no -ge-, h) possess; ~er m (-s/-) possessor, owner, proprietor; den ~ wechseln change hands; ~ergreifung f taking possession (von of), occupation; ~tum n (-s/=er), ~ung f (-/-en) possession; property; estate.

be'sohlen v/t. (no -ge-, h) sole.

besold|en [bə'zɔldən] v/t. (no -ge-, h) pay a salary to (civil servant, etc.); pay (soldier); 2ung f (-/-en) pay; salary.

be'sonder adj. [bə'zɔndər] particular, special; peculiar; separate; 2heit f (-/-en) particularity; peculiarity; ~s adv. especially, particularly; chiefly, mainly; separately.

besonnen adj. [bə'zɔnən] sensible, considerate, level-headed; prudent; discreet; 2heit f (-/no pl.) considerateness; prudence; discretion; presence of mind.

be'sorg|en v/t. (no -ge-, h) get (j-m et. s.o. s.th.), procure (s.th. for s.o.); do, manage; 2nis [~knis] f (-/-se) apprehension, fear, anxiety, concern (über acc. about, at); ~niserregend adj. alarming; ~t adj. [~kt] uneasy (um about); worried (about), concerned (about); anxious (um for, about); 2ung f (-/-en) procurement; management; errand; ~en machen go shopping.

be'sprech|en v/t. (irr. sprechen, no -ge-, h) discuss, talk s.th. over; arrange; review (book, etc.); sich ~ mit confer with (über acc. about); 2ung f (-/-en) discussion; review; conference.

be'spritzen v/t. (no -ge-, h) splash, (be)spatter.

besser ['bɛsər] 1. adj. better; superior; 2. adv. better; '~n v/t. (ge-, h) make) better, improve; reform; sich ~ get or become better, improve; change for the better; mend one's ways; '2ung f (-/-en) improvement; change for the better; reform (of character); & improvement, recovery; gute ~! I wish you a speedy recovery!

est [bɛst] 1. adj. best; der erste ~e (just) anybody; ~en Dank thank

you very much; sich von s-r ~en Seite zeigen be on one's best behavio(u)r; 2. adv. best; am ~en best; aufs ~e, ~ens in the best way possible; zum ~en geben recite (poem), tell (story), oblige with (song); j-n zum ~en haben or halten make fun of s.o., F pull s.o.'s leg; ich danke ~ens! thank you very much!

Be'stand m (continued) existence; continuance; stock; † stock-intrade; † cash in hand; ~ haben be lasting, last.

be'ständig adj. constant, steady; lasting; continual; weather: settled; 2keit f (-/-en) constancy, steadiness; continuance.

Bestand|saufnahme † [bə-'ʃtants?-] f stock-taking, Am. inventory; ~teil m component, constituent; element., ingredient; part.

be'stärken v/t. (no -ge-, h) confirm, strengthen, encourage (in dat. in).

bestätig|en [bə'ʃtɛːtigən] v/t. confirm (a. ‡‡ verdict, † order); attest; verify (statement, etc.); ratify (law, treaty); † acknowledge (receipt); 2ung f (-/-en) confirmation; attestation; verification; ratification; acknowledgement.

bestatt|en [bə'ʃtatən] v/t. (no -ge-, h) bury, inter; 2ung f (-/-en) burial, interment; funeral; 2ungsinstitut [bə'ʃtatuŋs?-] n undertakers pl.

'Beste 1. n (-n/no pl.) the best (thing); zu deinem ~n in your interest; zum ~n der Armen for the benefit of the poor; das ~ daraus machen make the best of it; 2. m, f (-n/-n): er ist der ~ in s-r Klasse he is the best in his class.

Besteck [bə'ʃtɛk] n (-[e]s/-e) ⚕ (case or set of) surgical instruments pl.; (single set of) knife, fork and spoon; (complete set of) cutlery, Am. a. flatware.

be'stehen 1. v/t. (irr. stehen, no -ge-, h) come off victorious in (combat, etc.); have (adventure); stand, undergo (well) (test, trial); pass (test, examination); 2. v/i. (irr. stehen, no -ge-, h) be, exist; continue, last; ~ auf (dat.) insist (up)on; ~ aus consist of; 3. 2 n (-s/no pl.) existence; continuance; passing.

be'stehlen v/t. (irr. stehlen, no -ge-, h) steal from, rob.

be'steig|en v/t. (irr. steigen, no -ge-, h) climb (up) (mountain, tree, etc.); mount (horse, bicycle, etc.); ascend (throne); get into or on, board (bus, train, plane); 2ung f ascent; accession (to throne).

be'stell|en v/t. (no -ge-, h) order; † a. place an order for; subscribe to (newspaper, etc.); book, reserve (room, seat, etc.); make an appointment with s.o.; send for (taxi, etc.); cultivate, till (soil, etc.); give (mes-

sage, greetings); *j-n zu sich* ~ send for s.o.; 2ung *f* order; subscription (to); booking, *esp. Am.* reservation; ✗ cultivation; message.

'besten'falls *adv.* at (the) best.

be'steuer|n *v/t.* (*no -ge-, h*) tax; 2ung *f* taxation.

besti|alisch *adj.* [best'jɑːliʃ] bestial; brutal; inhuman; *weather, etc.:* F beastly; 2e [´ˌjə] *f* (*-/-n*) beast; *fig.* brute, beast, inhuman person.

be'stimmen (*no -ge-, h*) **1.** *v/t.* determine, decide; fix (*date, place, price, etc.*); appoint (*date, time, place, etc.*); prescribe; define (*species, word, etc.*); *j-n für or zu et.* ~ designate *or* intend s.o. for s.th.; **2.** *v/t.:* ~ *über* (*acc.*) dispose of.

be'stimmt 1. *adj. voice, manner, etc.:* decided, determined, firm; *time, etc.:* appointed, fixed; *point, number, etc.:* certain; *answer, etc.:* positive; *tone, answer, intention, idea:* definite (*a. gr.*); ~ *nach* ⚓ ✈ bound for; **2.** *adv.* certainly, surely; 2heit *f* (*-/-en*) determination, firmness; certainty.

Be'stimmung *f* determination; destination (*of s.o. for the church, etc.*); designation, appointment (*of s.o. as successor, etc.*); definition; ⚖ provision (*in document*); (*amtliche*) ~en *pl.* (official) regulations *pl.*; ~sort [bə´ʃtimuŋ²-] *m* destination.

be'straf|en *v/t.* (*no -ge-, h*) punish (*wegen, für* for; *mit* with); 2ung *f* (*-/-en*) punishment.

be'strahl|en *v/t.* (*no -ge-, h*) irradiate (*a.* ✗); 2ung *f* irradiation; ✗ ray treatment, radiotherapy.

Be'streb|en *n* (*-s/no pl.*), ~ung *f* (*-/-en*) effort, endeavo(u)r.

be'streichen *v/t.* (*irr. streichen, no -ge-, h*) coat, cover; spread; *mit Butter* ~ butter.

be'streiten *v/t.* (*irr. streiten, no -ge-, h*) contest, dispute, challenge (*point, right, etc.*); deny (*facts, guilt, etc.*); defray (*expenses, etc.*); fill (*programme*).

be'streuen *v/t.* (*no -ge-, h*) strew, sprinkle (*mit* with); *mit Mehl* ~ flour; *mit Zucker* ~ sugar.

be'stürmen *v/t.* (*no -ge-, h*) storm, assail (*a. fig.*); pester, plague (*s.o. with questions, etc.*).

be'stürz|t *adj.* dismayed, struck with consternation (*über acc.* at); 2ung *f* (*-/-en*) consternation, dismay.

Besuch [bə´zuːx] *m* (*-[e]s/-e*) visit (*gen., bei, in dat.* to); call (*bei* on; *in dat.* at); attendance (*gen.* at) (*lecture, church, etc.*); visitor(s *pl.*), company; 2en *v/t.* (*no -ge-, h*) visit; call on, go to see; attend (*school, etc.*); frequent; ~er *m* visitor, caller; ~szeit *f* visiting hours *pl.*

be'tasten *v/t.* (*no -ge-, h*) touch, feel, finger; ✗ palpate.

betätigen [bə´tɛːtigən] *v/t.* (*no -ge-, h*) ⊕ operate (*machine, etc.*); put on, apply (*brake*); *sich* ~ *als* act *or* work as; *sich politisch* ~ dabble in politics.

betäub|en [bə´tɔybən] *v/t.* (*no -ge-, h*) stun (*a. fig.*), daze (*by blow, noise, etc.*); deafen (*by noise, etc.*); slaughtering: stun (*animal*); ✗ an(a)esthetize; 2ung *f* (*-/-en*) an(a)esthetization; ✗ an(a)esthesia; *fig.* stupefaction; 2ungsmittel ✗ *n* narcotic, an(a)esthetic.

beteilig|en [bə´tailigən] *v/t.* (*no -ge-, h*): *j-n* ~ give s.o. a share (*an dat.* in); *sich* ~ take part (*an dat., bei* in), participate (*a.* ⚖) (in); 2te [~çtə] *m, f* (*-n/-n*) person *or* party concerned; 2ung *f* (*-/-en*) participation (*a.* ⚖, ✟), partnership; share, interest (*a.* ✟).

beten ['beːtən] *v/i.* (*ge-, h*) pray (*um* for), say one's prayers; *at table:* say grace

be'teuer|n *v/t.* (*no -ge-, h*) protest (*one's innocence*); swear (*to s.th.; that*); 2ung *f* protestation; solemn declaration.

be'titeln *v/t.* (*no -ge-, h*) entitle (*book, etc.*); style (*s.o. 'baron', etc.*).

Beton ⊕ [be´tõ; be´toːn] *m* (*-s/-s; -s/-e*) concrete.

be'tonen *v/t.* (*no -ge-, h*) stress; *fig. a.* emphasize.

betonieren [beto´niːrən] *v/t.* (*no -ge-, h*) concrete.

Be'tonung *f* (*-/-en*) stress; emphasis.

betör|en [bə´tøːrən] *v/t.* (*no -ge-, h*) dazzle; infatuate, bewitch; 2ung *f* (*-/-en*) infatuation.

Betracht [bə´traxt] *m* (*-[e]s/no pl.*): *in* ~ *ziehen* take into consideration; (*nicht*) *in* ~ *kommen* (not to) come into question; 2en *v/t.* (*no -ge-, h*) view; contemplate; *fig. a.* consider.

beträchtlich *adj.* [bə´trɛçtliç] considerable.

Be'trachtung *f* (*-/-en*) view; contemplation; consideration.

Betrag [bə´traːk] *m* (*-[e]s/-⁀e*) amount, sum; 2en [~gən] *v/t.* **1.** *v/t.* (*irr. tragen, no -ge-, h*) amount to; **2.** *v/refl.* (*irr. tragen, no -ge-, h*) behave (*o.s.*); **3.** 2 *n* (*-s/no pl.*) behavio(u)r, conduct.

be'trauen *v/t.* (*no -ge-, h*): *j-n mit et.* ~ entrust *or* charge s.o. with s.th.

be'trauern *v/t.* (*no -ge-, h*) mourn (for, over).

Betreff [bə´trɛf] *m* (*-[e]s/-e*) *at head of letter:* reference; 2en *v/t.* (*irr. treffen, no -ge-, h*) befall; refer to; concern; *was ... betrifft* as for, as to; 2end *adj.* concerning; *das* ~*e Geschäft* the business referred to or in question; 2s *prp.* (*gen.*) concerning; as to.

be'treiben 1. v/t. (irr. treiben, no -ge-, h) carry on (business, etc.); pursue (one's studies); operate (railway line, etc.); 2. ♀ n (-s/no pl.): auf ~ von at or by s.o.'s instigation.

be'treten 1. v/t. (irr. treten, no -ge-, h) step on; enter (room, etc.); 2. adj. embarrassed, abashed.

betreu|en [bə'trɔyən] v/t. (no -ge-, h) look after; attend to; care for; ♀ung f (-/no pl.) care (gen. of, for).

Betrieb [bə'tri:p] m (-[e]s/-e) working, running, esp. Am. operation; business, firm, enterprise; plant, works sg.; workshop, Am. a. shop; fig. bustle; in ~ working; ♀sam adj. active; industrious.

Be'triebs|anleitung f operating instructions pl.; ~ausflug m firm's outing; ~ferien pl. (firm's, works) holiday; ~führer m s. Betriebsleiter; ~kapital n working capital; ~kosten pl. working expenses pl., Am. operating costs pl.; ~leiter m (works) manager, superintendent; ~leitung f management; ~material n working materials pl.; 🚃 rolling stock; ~rat m works council; ♀sicher adj. safe to operate; foolproof; ~störung f breakdown; ~unfall m industrial accident, accident while at work.

be'trinken v/refl. (irr. trinken, no -ge-, h) get drunk.

betroffen adj. [bə'trɔfən] afflicted (von by), stricken (with); fig. disconcerted.

be'trüben v/t. (no -ge-, h) grieve, afflict.

Be'trug m cheat(ing); fraud (a. 🏛); deceit.

be'trüg|en v/t. (irr. trügen, no -ge-, h) deceive; cheat (a. at games); defraud; F skin; ♀er m (-s/-) cheat, deceiver, impostor, confidence man, swindler, trickster; ~erisch adj. deceitful, fraudulent.

be'trunken adj. drunken; pred. drunk; ♀e m (-n/-n) drunk(en man).

Bett [bɛt] n (-[e]s/-en) bed; '~bezug m plumeau case; '~decke f blanket; bedspread, coverlet.

Bettel|brief ['bɛtəl-] m begging letter; ~ei [~'laɪ] f (-/-en) begging, mendicancy; '♀n v/i. (ge-, h) beg (um for); ~ gehen go begging; '~stab m: an den ~ bringen reduce to beggary.

'Bett|gestell n bedstead; ♀lägerig adj. ['~lɛ:gəriç] bedridden, confined to bed, Am. a. bedfast; '~laken n sheet.

Bettler ['bɛtlər] m (-s/-) beggar, Am. sl. panhandler.

'Bett|überzug m plumeau case; ~uch ['bɛttu:x] n sheet; '~vorleger m bedside rug; '~wäsche f bedlinen; '~zeug n bedding.

be'tupfen v/t. (no -ge-, h) dab.

beug|en ['bɔygən] v/t. (ge-, h) bend, bow; fig. humble, break (pride); gr. inflect (word), decline (noun, adjective); sich ~ bend (vor dat. to), bow (to); '♀ung f (-/-en) bending; gr. inflection, declension.

Beule ['bɔylə] f (-/-n) bump, swelling; boil; on metal, etc.: dent.

beunruhig|en [bə'unru:igən] v/t. (no -ge-, h) disturb, trouble, disquiet, alarm; sich ~ über (acc.) be uneasy about, worry about; ♀ung f (-/no pl.) disturbance; alarm; uneasiness.

beurkund|en [bə'u:rkundən] v/t. (no -ge-, h) attest, certify, authenticate; ♀ung f (-/-en) attestation, certification, authentication.

beurlaub|en [bə'u:rlaubən] v/t. (no -ge-, h) give or grant s.o. leave (of absence); give s.o. time off; suspend (civil servant, etc.); ♀ung f (-/-en) leave (of absence); suspension.

beurteil|en [bə'urtaɪlən] v/t. (no -ge-, h) judge (nach by); ♀ung f (-/-en) judg(e)ment.

Beute ['bɔytə] f (-/no pl.) booty, spoil(s pl.); loot; prey; hunt. bag; fig. prey, victim (gen. to).

Beutel ['bɔytəl] m (-s/-) bag; purse; pouch.

'Beutezug m plundering expedition.

bevölker|n [bə'fœlkərn] v/t. (no -ge-, h) people, populate; ♀ung f (-/-en) population.

bevollmächtig|en [bə'fɔlmɛçtigən] v/t. (no -ge-, h) authorize, empower; ♀te [~çtə] m,f (-n/-n) authorized person or agent, deputy; pol. plenipotentiary; ♀ung f (-/-en) authorization.

be'vor cj. before.

bevormund|en fig. [bə'fo:rmundən] v/t. (no -ge-, h) patronize, keep in tutelage; ♀ung fig. f (-/-en) patronizing, tutelage.

be'vorstehen v/i. (irr. stehen, sep., -ge-, h) be approaching, be near; crisis, etc.: be imminent; j-m ~ be in store for s.o., await s.o.; ~d adj. approaching; imminent.

bevorzug|en [bə'fo:rtsu:gən] v/t. (no -ge-, h) prefer; favo(u)r; 🏛 privilege; ♀ung f (-/-en) preference.

be'wach|en v/t. (no -ge-, h) guard, watch; ♀ung f (-/-en) guard; escort.

bewaffn|en [bə'vafnən] v/t. (no -ge-, h) arm; ♀ung f (-/-en) armament; arms pl.

be'wahren v/t. (no -ge-, h) keep, preserve (mst fig.: secret, silence, etc.).

be'währen v/refl. (no -ge-, h) stand the test, prove a success; sich ~ als prove o.s. (as a good teacher, etc.); sich ~ in prove o.s. efficient in (one's profession, etc.); sich nicht ~ prove a failure.

be'wahrheiten v/refl. (no -ge-, h) prove (to be) true; prophecy, etc.: come true.

be'währt adj. friend, etc.: tried; solicitor, etc.: experienced; friendship, etc.: long-standing; remedy, etc.: proved, proven.

Be'währung f ɪ̞ɪ̞ probation; in Zeiten der ~ in times of trial; s. bewähren; ~sfrist ɪ̞ɪ̞ f probation.

bewaldet adj. [bə'valdət] wooded, woody, Am. a. timbered.

bewältigen [bə'vɛltigən] v/t. (no -ge-, h) overcome (obstacle); master (difficulty); accomplish (task).

be'wandert adj. (well) versed (in dat. in), proficient (in); in e-m Fach gut ~ sein have a thorough knowledge of a subject.

be'wässer|n v/t. (no -ge-, h) water (garden, lawn, etc.); irrigate (land, etc.); ℒung f (-/-en) watering; irrigation.

bewegen[1] [bə've:gən] v/t. (irr., no -ge-, h): j-n ~ zu induce or get s.o. to.

beweg|en[2] [~] v/t. and v/refl. (no -ge-, h) move, stir; ℒgrund [~k-] m motive (gen., for); ~lich adj. [~k-] movable, p., mind, etc.: agile, versatile; active; ℒlichkeit [~k-] f (-/no pl.) mobility; agility, versatility; ~t adj. [~kt] sea: rough, heavy; fig. moved, touched; voice: choked, trembling; life: eventful; times, etc.: stirring, stormy; ℒung f (-/-en) movement; motion (a. phys.); fig. emotion; in ~ setzen set going or in motion; ~ungslos adj. motionless, immobile.

be'weinen v/t. (no -ge-, h) weep or cry over; lament (for, over).

Beweis [bə'vais] m (-es/-e) proof (für of); ~(e pl.) evidence (esp. ɪ̞ɪ̞); ℒen [~zən] v/t. (irr. weisen, no -ge-, h) prove; show (interest, etc.); ~führung f argumentation; ~grund m argument; ~material n evidence; ~stück n (piece of) evidence; ɪ̞ɪ̞ exhibit. [leave it at that.]

be'wenden vb.: es dabei ~ lassen]

be'werb|en v/refl. (irr. werben, no -ge-, h): sich ~ um apply for, Am. run for; stand for; compete for (prize); court (woman); ℒer m (-s/-) applicant (um for); candidate; competitor; suitor; ℒung f application; candidature; competition; courtship; ℒungsschreiben n (letter of) application.

bewerkstelligen [bə'vɛrkʃtɛligən] v/t. (no -ge-, h) manage, effect, bring about.

be'wert|en v/t. (no -ge-, h) value (auf acc. at; nach by); ℒung f valuation.

bewillig|en [bə'viligən] v/t. (no -ge-, h) grant, allow; ℒung f (-/-en) grant, allowance.

be'wirken v/t. (no -ge-, h) cause; bring about, effect.

be'wirt|en v/t. (no -ge-, h) entertain; ~schaften v/t. (no -ge-, h) farm (land); ✍ cultivate (field); manage (farm, etc.); ration (food, etc.); control (foreign exchange, etc.); ℒung f (-/-en) entertainment; hospitality.

bewog [bə'vo:k] pret. of bewegen[1]; ~en [bə'vo:gən] p.p. of bewegen[1].

be'wohn|en v/t. (no -ge-, h) inhabit, live in; occupy; ℒer m (-s/-) inhabitant; occupant.

bewölk|en [bə'vœlkən] v/refl. (no -ge-, h) sky: cloud up or over; brow: cloud over, darken; ~t adj. sky: clouded, cloudy, overcast; brow: clouded, darkened; ℒung f (-/no pl.) clouds pl.

be'wunder|n v/t. (no -ge-, h) admire (wegen for); ~nswert adj. admirable; ℒung f (-/-en) admiration.

bewußt adj. [bə'vust] deliberate, intentional; sich e-r Sache ~ sein be conscious or aware of s.th.; die ~e Sache the matter in question; ~los adj. unconscious; ℒsein n (-s/no pl.) consciousness.

be'zahl|en (no -ge-, h) 1. v/t. pay; pay for (s.th. purchased); pay off, settle (debt); 2. v/i. pay (für for); ℒung f payment; settlement.

be'zähmen v/t. (no -ge-, h) tame (animal); restrain (one's anger, etc.); sich ~ control or restrain o.s.

be'zauber|n v/t. (no -ge-, h) bewitch, enchant (a. fig.); fig. charm, fascinate; ℒung f (-/-en) enchantment, spell; fascination.

be'zeichn|en v/t. (no -ge-, h) mark; describe (als as), call; ~end adj. characteristic, typical (für of); ℒung f indication (of direction, etc.); mark, sign, symbol; name, designation, denomination.

be'zeugen v/t. (no -ge-, h) ɪ̞ɪ̞ testify to, bear witness to (both a. fig.); attest.

be'zieh|en v/t. (irr. ziehen, no -ge-, h) cover (upholstered furniture, etc.); put cover on (cushion, etc.); move into (flat, etc.); enter (university); draw (salary, pension, etc.); get, be supplied with (goods); take in (newspaper, etc.); sich ~ sky: cloud over; sich ~ auf (acc.) refer to; ℒer m (-s/-) subscriber (gen. to).

Be'ziehung f relation (zu et. to sth.; zu j-m with s.o.); connexion, (Am. only) connection (zu with); in dieser ~ in this respect; ℒsweise adv. respectively; or rather.

Bezirk [bə'tsirk] m (-[e]s/-e) district, Am. a. precinct; s. Wahlbezirk.

Bezogene † [bə'tso:gənə] m (-n/-n) drawee.

Bezug [bə'tsu:k] m cover(ing), case; purchase (of goods); subscription (*to newspaper*); *in* ~ *auf* (*acc.*) with regard *or* reference to, as to; ~ *nehmen auf* (*acc.*) refer to, make reference to.

bezüglich [bə'tsy:kliç] **1.** *adj.* relative, relating (*both: auf acc.* to); **2.** *prp.* (*gen.*) regarding, concerning.

Be'zugsbedingungen † *f/pl.* terms *pl.* of delivery.

be'zwecken *v/t.* (*no -ge-, h*) aim at; ~ *mit* intend by.

be'zweifeln *v/t.* (*no -ge-, h*) doubt, question.

be'zwing|en *v/t.* (*irr. zwingen, no -ge-, h*) conquer (*fortress, mountain, etc.*); overcome, master (*feeling, difficulty, etc.*); *sich* ~ keep o.s. under control, restrain o.s.; **2ung** *f* (*-/-en*) conquest; mastering.

Bibel ['bi:bəl] *f* (*-/-n*) Bible.

Biber *zo.* ['bi:bər] *m* (*-s/-*) beaver.

Bibliothek [biblio'te:k] *f* (*-/-en*) library; ~**ar** [~e'ka:r] *m* (*-s/-e*) librarian.

biblisch *adj.* ['bi:bliʃ] biblical, scriptural; ~*e Geschichte* Scripture.

bieder *adj.* ['bi:dər] honest, upright, worthy (*a. iro.*); simple-minded; **'2keit** *f* (*-/no pl.*) honesty, uprightness; simple-mindedness.

bieg|en ['bi:gən] (*irr., ge-*) **1.** *v/t.* (*h*) bend; **2.** *v/refl.* (*h*) bend; *sich vor Lachen* ~ double up with laughter; **3.** *v/i.* (*sein*): *um e-e Ecke* ~ turn (round) a corner; ~**sam** *adj.* ['bi:kza:m] *wire, etc.*: flexible; *body*: lithe, supple; pliant (*a. fig.*); **'2samkeit** *f* (*-/no pl.*) flexibility; suppleness; pliability; **'2ung** *f* (*-/-en*) bend, wind (*of road, river*); curve (*of road, arch*).

Biene *zo.* ['bi:nə] *f* (*-/-n*) bee; '~**nkönigin** *f* queen bee; '~**nkorb** *m* (bee)hive; '~**nschwarm** *m* swarm of bees; '~**nstock** *m* (bee)hive; '~**nzucht** *f* bee-keeping; '~**nzüchter** *m* bee-keeper.

Bier [bi:r] *n* (*-[e]s/-e*) beer; *helles* ~ pale beer, ale; *dunkles* ~ dark beer; *stout, porter; ~ vom Faß* beer on draught; '~**brauer** *m* brewer; '~**brauerei** *f* brewery; '~**garten** *m* beer-garden; '~**krug** *m* beer-mug, *Am.* stein.

Biest [bi:st] *n* (*-es/-er*) beast, brute.

bieten ['bi:tən] (*irr., ge-, h*) **1.** *v/t.* offer; † *at auction sale*: bid; *sich* ~ *opportunity, etc.*: offer itself, arise, occur; **2.** † *v/i. at auction sale*: bid.

Bigamie [biga'mi:] *f* (*-/-n*) bigamy.

Bilanz [bi'lants] *f* (*-/-en*) balance; balance-sheet, *Am. a.* statement; *fig.* result, outcome; *die* ~ *ziehen* strike a balance; *fig.* take stock (*of one's life, etc.*).

Bild [bilt] *n* (*-[e]s/-er*) picture; image; illustration; portrait; *fig.* idea, notion; '~**bericht** *m press:* picture story.

bilden ['bildən] *v/t.* (*ge-, h*) form; shape; *fig.:* educate, train (*s.o., mind, etc.*); develop (*mind, etc.*); form, be, constitute (*obstacle, etc.*); *sich* ~ form; *fig.* educate o.s., improve one's mind; *sich e-e Meinung* ~ form an opinion.

Bilder|buch ['bildər-] *n* picture-book; '~**galerie** *f* picture-gallery; '~**rätsel** *n* rebus.

'Bild|fläche *f:* F *auf der* ~ *erscheinen* appear on the scene; F *von der* ~ *verschwinden* disappear (from the scene); '~**funk** *m* radio picture transmission; television; '~**hauer** *m* (*-s/-*) sculptor; '~**hauerei** [~'rai] *f* (*-/-en*) sculpture; '**2lich** *adj.* pictorial; *word, etc.:* figurative; '~**nis** *n* (*-ses/-se*) portrait; '~**röhre** *f* picture *or* television tube; '~**säule** *f* statue; '~**schirm** *m* (television) screen; '**2schön** *adj.* most beautiful; '~**seite** *f* face, head (*of coin*); '~**streifen** *m* picture *or* film strip; '~**telegraphie** *f* (*-/no pl.*) phototelegraphy.

'Bildung *f* (*-/-en*) forming, formation (*both a. gr.: of plural, etc.*); constitution (*of committee, etc.*); education; culture; (good) breeding. [*sg.*: billiard-table.)

Billard ['biljart] *n* (*-s/-e*) billiards

billig *adj.* ['biliç] just, equitable; fair; *price:* reasonable, moderate; *goods:* cheap, inexpensive; *recht und* ~ right and proper; ~**en** ['~gən] *v/t.* (*ge-, h*) approve of, *Am. a.* approbate; **2keit** *f* (*-/no pl.*) justness, equity; fairness; reasonableness, moderateness; **2ung** ['~guŋ] *f* (*-/*~-en) approval, sanction.

Binde ['bində] *f* (*-/-n*) band; tie; ♀ bandage; (arm-)sling; *s. Damenbinde;* '~**gewebe** *anat. n* connective tissue; '~**glied** *n* connecting link; '~**haut** *anat. f* conjunctiva; '~**hautentzündung** ♀ *f* conjunctivitis; '**2n** (*irr., ge-, h*) **1.** *v/t.* bind, tie (*an acc.* to); bind (*book, etc.*); make (*broom, wreath, etc.*); knot (*tie*); *sich* ~ bind *or* commit *or* engage o.s.; **2.** *v/i.* bind; unite; ⊕ *cement, etc.:* set, harden; '~**strich** *m* hyphen; '~**wort** *gr. n* (*-[e]s/~er*) conjunction.

Bindfaden ['bint-] *m* string; pack-thread.

'Bindung *f* (*-/-en*) binding (*a. of ski*); ♪ slur, tie, ligature; *fig.* commitment (*a. pol.*); engagement; ~**en** *pl.* bonds *pl.*, ties *pl.*

binnen *prp.* (*dat., a. gen.*) ['binən] within; ~ *kurzem* before long.

'Binnen|gewässer *n* inland water; '~**hafen** *m* close port; '~**handel** *m* domestic *or* home trade, *Am.* domestic commerce; '~**land** *n* inland, interior; '~**verkehr** *m* inland traffic *or* transport.

Binse ♧ ['binzə] f (-/-n) rush; F: *in die ~n gehen* go to pot; '~nwahrheit f, '~nweisheit f truism.

Biochemie [bioçe'mi:] f (-/no pl.) biochemistry.

Biograph|ie [biogra'fi:] f (-/-n) biography; ℨisch adj. [~'gra:fiʃ] biographic(al).

Biolog|ie [biolo'gi:] f (-/no pl.) biology; ℨisch adj. [~'lo:giʃ] biological.

Birke ♧ ['birkə] f (-/-n) birch(-tree).

Birne ['birnə] f (-/-n) ♀ pear; ⚡ (electric) bulb; *fig. sl.* nob, *Am.* bean.

bis [bis] **1.** *prp.* (*acc.*) *space:* to, as far as; *time:* till, until, by; *zwei ~ drei* two or three, two to three; *~ auf weiteres* until further orders, for the meantime; *~ vier zählen* count up to four; *alle ~ auf drei* all but *or* except three; **2.** *cj.* till, until.

Bisamratte zo. ['bi:zam-] f muskrat.

Bischof ['biʃɔf] m (-s/⁻e) bishop.

bischöflich adj. ['biʃøfliç] episcopal.

bisher adv. [bis'he:r] hitherto, up to now, so far; '~ig adj. until now; hitherto existing; former.

Biß [bis] **1.** m (Bisses/Bisse) bite; **2.** ℨ pret. of beißen.

bißchen ['bisçən] **1.** adj.: ein ~ a little, a (little) bit of; **2.** adv.: ein ~ a little (bit).

Bissen ['bisən] m (-s/-) mouthful, morsel; bite.

'**bissig** adj. biting (a. fig.); remark: cutting; Achtung, ~er Hund! beware of the dog!

Bistum ['bistu:m] n (-s/⁻er) bishopric, diocese.

bisweilen adv. [bis'vailən] sometimes, at times, now and then.

Bitte ['bitə] f (-/-n) request (um for); entreaty; auf j-s ~ (hin) at s.o.'s request.

'**bitten** (*irr.*, ge-, h) **1.** v/t.: j-n um et. ~ ask *or* beg s.o. for s.th.; j-n um Entschuldigung ~ beg s.o.'s pardon; dürfte ich Sie um Feuer ~? may I trouble you for a light?; bitte please; (wie) bitte? (I beg your) pardon?; bitte! offering s.th.: (please,) help yourself, (please,) do take some *or* one; danke (schön) — bitte (sehr)! thank you — not at all, you're welcome, don't mention it, F that's all right; **2.** v/i.: um et. ~ ask *or* beg for s.th.

bitter adj. ['bitər] bitter (a. fig.); *frost:* sharp; 'ℨkeit f (-/-en) bitterness; *fig. a.* acrimony; '~lich adv. bitterly.

'**Bitt|gang** eccl. m procession; '~schrift f petition; '~steller m (-s/-) petitioner.

bläh|en ['blɛ:ən] (ge-, h) **1.** v/t. inflate, distend, swell out; belly (out),

swell out (sails); sich ~ sails: belly (out), swell out; skirt: balloon out; **2.** ⚕ v/i. cause flatulence; '~end adj. flatulent; 'ℨung ℬ f (-/-en) flatulence, F wind.

Blam|age [bla'ma:ʒə] f (-/-n) disgrace, shame; ℨieren [~'mi:rən] v/t. (no -ge-, h) make a fool of s.o., disgrace; sich ~ make a fool of o.s.

blank adj. [blaŋk] shining, shiny, bright; polished; F fig. broke.

blanko † ['blaŋko] **1.** adj. form, etc.: blank, not filled in; in blank; **2.** adv.: ~ verkaufen stock exchange: sell short; 'ℨscheck m blank cheque, Am. blank check; 'ℨunterschrift f blank signature; 'ℨvollmacht f full power of attorney, carte blanche.

Bläschen ♂ ['blɛ:sçən] n (-s/-) vesicle, small blister.

Blase ['bla:zə] f (-/-n) bubble; blister (a. ♂); anat. bladder; bleb (in glass); ⊕ flaw; '~balg m (ein a pair of) bellows pl.; 'ℨn (irr., ge-, h) **1.** v/t. blow; blow, sound; play (wind-instrument); **2.** v/i. blow.

Blas|instrument ♪ ['bla:s-] n wind-instrument; '~kapelle f brass band.

blaß adj. [blas] pale (vor dat. with); ~ werden turn pale; keine blasse Ahnung not the faintest idea.

Blässe ['blɛsə] f (-/no pl.) paleness.

Blatt [blat] n (-[e]s/⁻er) leaf (of book, ♀); petal (of flower); leaf, sheet (of paper); ♪ sheet; blade (of oar, saw, airscrew, etc.); sheet (of metal); cards: hand; (news)paper.

Blattern ♂ ['blatərn] pl. smallpox.

blättern ['blɛtərn] v/i. (ge-, h): in e-m Buch ~ leaf through a book, thumb a book.

'**Blatternarb|e** f pock-mark; 'ℨig adj. pock-marked.

'**Blätterteig** m puff paste.

'**Blatt|gold** n gold-leaf, gold-foil; '~laus zo. f plant-louse; '~pflanze f foliage plant.

blau [blau] **1.** adj. blue; F fig. drunk, tight, boozy; ~er Fleck bruise; ~es Auge black eye; mit e-m ~en Auge davonkommen get off cheaply; **2.** ℨ n (-s/no pl.) blue (colo[u]r); Fahrt ins ~e mystery tour. [blue.]

bläuen ['blɔyən] v/t. (ge-, h) (dye)

'**blaugrau** adj. bluish grey; 'ℨjacke ⚓ f bluejacket, sailor.

'**bläulich** adj. bluish.

'**Blausäure** ♠ f (-/no pl.) hydrocyanic or prussic acid.

Blech [blɛç] n (-[e]s/-e) sheet metal; metal sheet, plate; F fig. balderdash, rubbish, Am. sl. ♣ baloney; '~büchse f tin, Am. can; 'ℨern adj. (of) tin; sound: brassy; sound, voice: tinny; '~musik f brass-band music; '~waren f/pl. tinware.

Blei [blai] n (-[e]s/-e) **1.** n lead; **2.** F n, m (lead) pencil.

bleiben ['blaɪbən] *v/i. (irr., ge-, sein)* remain, stay; be left; *ruhig ~* keep calm; *~ bei* keep to *s.th.*, stick to *s.th.*; *bitte bleiben Sie am Apparat teleph.* hold the line, please; '**~d** *adj.* lasting, permanent; '**~lassen** *v/t. (irr. lassen, sep., no -ge-, h)* leave *s.th.* alone; *laß das bleiben!* don't do it!; leave it alone!; stop that *(noise, etc.)!*

bleich *adj.* [blaɪç] pale *(vor dat.* with); '**~en** *(ge-)* 1. *v/t. (h)* make pale; bleach; blanch; 2. *v/i. (irr., sein)* bleach; lose colo(u)r, fade; '**~süchtig** *adj.* chlorotic, greensick.

'**bleiern** *adj.* (of) lead, leaden *(a. fig.)*.

'**Blei|rohr** *n* lead pipe; '**~soldat** *m* tin soldier; '**~stift** *m* (lead) pencil; '**~stifthülse** *f* pencil cap; '**~stiftspitzer** *m (-s/-)* pencil-sharpener; '**~vergiftung** *f* lead-poisoning.

Blend|e ['blɛndə] *f (-/-n) phot.* diaphragm, stop; ⚠ blind *or* sham window; '**~en** *(ge-, h)* 1. *v/t.* blind; dazzle *(both a. fig.)*; 2. *v/i.* light: dazzle the eyes; **~laterne** ['blɛnt-] *f* dark lantern.

blich [blɪç] *pret.* of bleichen 2.

Blick [blɪk] *m (-[e]s/-e)* glance, look; view *(auf acc.* of); *auf den ersten ~* at first sight; *ein böser ~* an evil *or* angry look; '**~en** *v/i. (ge-, h)* look, glance *(auf acc., nach* at); '**~fang** *m* eye-catcher.

blieb [bli:p] *pret.* of bleiben.

blies [bli:s] *pret.* of blasen.

blind *adj.* [blɪnt] blind *(a. fig.:* gegen, für to; *vor dat.* with); *metal:* dull, tarnished; *window:* opaque *(with age, dirt)*; *mirror:* clouded, dull; *cartridge:* blank; *~er Alarm* false alarm; *~er Passagier* stowaway; *auf e-m Auge ~* blind in one eye.

'**Blinddarm** *anat. m* blind gut; appendix; '**~entzündung** *f* appendicitis.

Blinde ['blɪndə] *(-n/-n)* 1. *m* blind man; 2. *f* blind woman; **~nanstalt** ['blɪndən⁹-] *f* institute for the blind; '**~nheim** *n* home for the blind; '**~nhund** *m* guide dog, *Am. a.* seeing-eye dog; '**~nschrift** *f* braille.

'**blind|fliegen** 🛩 *(irr. fliegen, sep., -ge-) v/t. (h) and v/i. (sein)* fly blind *or* on instruments; '**⁹flug** 🛩 *m* blind flying *or* flight; '**⁹gänger** *m* 🛩 blind shell, dud; F *fig.* washout; '**⁹heit** *f (-/no pl.)* blindness; **~lings** *adv.* ['~lɪŋs] blindly; at random; '**⁹schleiche** *zo. f (-/-n)* slow-worm, blind-worm; '**~schreiben** *v/t. and v/i. (irr. schreiben, sep., -ge-, h)* touch-type.

blink|en ['blɪŋkən] *v/i. (ge-, h)* star, light: twinkle; *metal, leather, glass, etc.:* shine; signal (with lamps),

flash; '**⁹er** *mot. m (-s/-)* flashing indicator; '**⁹feuer** *n* flashing light.

blinzeln ['blɪntsəln] *v/i. (ge-, h)* blink *(at light, etc.)*; wink.

Blitz [blɪts] *m (-es/-e)* lightning; '**~ableiter** *m (-s/-)* lightning-conductor; '**⁹en** *v/i. (ge-, h)* flash; *es blitzt* it is lightening; '**~gespräch** *teleph. n* special priority call; '**~licht** *phot. n* flash-light; '**⁹schnell** *adv.* with lightning speed; '**~strahl** *m* flash of lightning.

Block [blɔk] *m* 1. *(-[e]s/⁔e)* block; slab *(of cooking chocolate)*; block, log *(of wood)*; ingot *(of metal)*; *parl., pol.*, ✝ bloc; 2. *(-[e]s/⁔e, -s)* block *(of houses)*; pad, block *(of paper)*; **~ade** ✗, ⚓ [**~**'ka:də] *f (-/-n)* blockade; **~adebrecher** *m (-s/-)* blockade-runner; '**~haus** *n* log cabin; **⁹ieren** [**~**'ki:rən] *(no -ge-, h) v/t.* block (up); lock *(wheel)*; 2. *v/i.* brakes, *etc.*: jam.

blöd *adj.* [bløːt], **~e** *adj.* ['**~**də] imbecile; stupid, dull; silly; '**⁹heit** *f (-/-en)* imbecility; stupidity, dullness; silliness; '**⁹sinn** *m* imbecility; rubbish, nonsense; '**~sinnig** *adj.* imbecile; idiotic, stupid, foolish.

blöken ['bløːkən] *v/i. (ge-, h) sheep, calf:* bleat.

blond *adj.* [blɔnt] blond, fair (-haired).

bloß [bloːs] 1. *adj.* bare, naked; mere; *~e Worte* mere words; *mit dem ~en Auge wahrnehmbar* visible to the naked eye; 2. *adv.* only, merely, simply, just.

Blöße ['bløːsə] *f (-/-n)* bareness, nakedness; *fig.* weak point *or* spot; *sich e-e ~ geben* give o.s. away; lay o.s. open to attack; *keine ~ bieten* be invulnerable.

'**bloß|legen** *v/t. (sep., -ge-, h)* lay bare, expose; '**~stellen** *v/t. (sep., -ge-, h)* expose, compromise, unmask; *sich ~* compromise o.s.

blühen ['blyːən] *v/i. (ge-, h)* blossom, flower, bloom; *fig.* flourish, thrive, prosper; ✝ boom.

Blume ['bluːmə] *f (-/-n)* flower; *wine:* bouquet; *beer:* froth.

'**Blumen|beet** *n* flower-bed; '**~blatt** *n* petal; '**~händler** *m* florist; '**~strauß** *m* bouquet *or* bunch of flowers; '**~topf** *m* flowerpot; '**~zucht** *f* floriculture.

Bluse ['bluːzə] *f (-/-n)* blouse.

Blut [bluːt] *n (-[e]s/no pl.)* blood; *~ vergießen* shed blood; *böses ~ machen* breed bad blood; '**~andrang** ⚕ *m* congestion; '**⁹arm** *adj.* bloodless, an(a)emic; '**~armut** ⚕ *f* an(a)emia; '**⁹bad** *n* carnage, massacre; '**~bank** ⚕ *f* blood bank; '**~blase** *f* blood blister; '**~druck** *m* blood pressure; '**⁹dürstig** *adj.* ['~dyrstɪç] bloodthirsty.

Blüte ['blyːtə] *f (-/-n)* blossom,

bloom, flower; *esp. fig.* flower; prime, heyday (*of life*).

Blutegel ['blu:t⁹e:gəl] *m* (-s/-) leech.

'bluten *v/i.* (ge-, h) bleed (*aus* from); *aus der Nase* ~ bleed at the nose.

Bluterguß ♣ ['blu:t⁹-] *m* effusion of blood.

'Blütezeit *f* flowering period *or* time; *fig. a.* prime, heyday.

'Blut|gefäß *anat. n* blood-vessel; **~gerinnsel** ♣ ['~gərinzəl] *n* (-s/-) clot of blood; **'~gruppe** *f* blood group; **'~hund** *zo. m* bloodhound; **'blutig** *adj.* bloody, blood-stained; *es ist mein ~er Ernst* I am dead serious; *~er Anfänger* mere beginner, F greenhorn.

Blut|körperchen ['blu:tkœrpərçən] *n* (-s/-) blood corpuscle; **'~kreis-lauf** *m* (blood) circulation; **'~lache** *f* pool of blood; **'2leer** *adj.*, **'2los** *adj.* bloodless; **'~probe** *f* blood test; **'~rache** *f* blood feud *or* revenge *or* vengeance, vendetta; **'2-'rot** *adj.* blood-red; crimson; **2rün-stig** *adj.* ['~rynstiç] bloodthirsty; bloody; **'~schande** *f* incest; **'~spender** *m* blood-donor; **'2stillend** *adj.* blood-sta(u)nching; **'~sturz** ♣ *m* h(a)emorrhage; **'2sverwandt** *adj.* related by blood (*mit* to); **'~s-verwandtschaft** *f* blood-relation-ship, consanguinity; **'~übertra-gung** *f* blood-transfusion; **'~ung** *f* (-/-en) bleeding, h(a)emorrhage; **'2unterlaufen** *adj.* eye: blood-shot; **'~vergießen** *n* bloodshed; **'~vergiftung** *f* blood-poisoning.

Bö [bø] *f* (-/-en) gust, squall.

Bock [bɔk] *m* (-[e]s/⁼e) deer, hare, *rabbit:* buck; he-goat, F billy-goat; *sheep:* ram; *gymnastics:* buck; *e-n ~ schießen* commit a blunder, *sl.* commit a bloomer; *den ~ zum Gärtner machen* set the fox to keep the geese; **'2en** *v/i.* (ge-, h) *horse:* buck; *child:* sulk; *p.* be obstinate *or* refractory; *mot.* move jerkily, *Am.* F *a.* buck; **'2ig** *adj.* stubborn, obstinate, pigheaded; **'~sprung** *m* leap-frog; *gymnastics:* vault over the buck; *Bocksprünge machen* caper, cut capers.

Boden ['bo:dən] *m* (-s/⁼) ground; ♪ soil; bottom; floor; loft; **'~kam-mer** *f* garret, attic; **'2los** *adj.* bottomless; *fig.* enormous; un-heard-of; **'~personal** ✈ *n* ground personnel *or* staff, *Am.* ground crew; **'~reform** *f* land reform; **'~satz** *m* grounds *pl.*, sediment; **~schätze** ['~fɛtsə] *m/pl.* mineral resources *pl.*; **'2ständig** *adj.* native, indigenous.

bog [bo:k] *pret. of* biegen.

Bogen ['bo:gən] *m* (-s/-, ⁼) bow, bend, curve; ⌒ arc; ⌂ arch; *ski-ing:* turn; *skating:* curve; sheet (*of*

paper); **'2förmig** *adj.* arched; **'~gang** ⌂ *m* arcade; **'~lampe** ⚡ *f* arc-lamp; **'~schütze** *m* archer, bowman.

Bohle ['bo:lə] *f* (-/-n) thick plank, board.

Bohne ['bo:nə] *f* (-/-n) bean; *grüne ~n pl.* French beans *pl.*, *Am.* string beans *pl.*; *weiße ~n pl.* haricot beans *pl.*; F *blaue ~n pl.* bullets *pl.*; **'~n-stange** *f* beanpole (*a.* F *fig.*).

bohnern ['bo:nərn] *v/t.* (ge-, h) polish (*floor*, *etc.*), (bees)wax (*floor*).

bohr|en ['bo:rən] (ge-, h) **1.** *v/t.* bore, drill (*hole*); sink, bore (*well*, *shaft*); bore, cut, drive (*tunnel*, *etc.*); **2.** *v/i.* drill (*a. dentistry*); bore; **'2er** ⊕ *m* (-s/-) borer, drill.

'böig *adj.* squally, gusty; ✈ bumpy.

Boje ['bo:jə] *f* (-/-n) buoy.

Bollwerk ⚔ ['bɔlvɛrk] *n* bastion, bulwark (*a. fig.*).

Bolzen ⊕ ['bɔltsən] *m* (-s/-) bolt.

Bombard|ement [bɔmbardə'mã:] *n* (-s/-s) bombardment; bombing; shelling; **2ieren** [~'di:rən] *v/t.* (no -ge-, h) bomb; shell; bombard (*a. fig.*).

Bombe ['bɔmbə] *f* (-/-n) bomb; *fig.* bomb-shell; **'2nsicher** *adj.* bomb-proof; F *fig.* dead sure; **'~nschaden** *m* bomb damage; **'~r** ✈ ✈ *m* (-s/-) bomber.

Bon ✝ [bõ:] *m* (-s/-s) coupon; vouch-er; credit note.

Bonbon [bõ'bõ:] *m*, *n* (-s/-s) sweet (-meat), bon-bon, F goody, *Am.* candy.

Bonze F ['bɔntsə] *m* (-n/-n) bigwig, *Am. a.* big shot.

Boot [bo:t] *n* (-[e]s/-e) boat; **'~shaus** *n* boat-house; **'~smann** *m* (-[e]s/ *Bootsleute*) boatswain.

Bord [bɔrt] (-[e]s/-e) **1.** *n* shelf; **2.** ⚓, ✈ *m:* an ~ on board, aboard (*ship, aircraft, etc.*); *über* ~ over-board; *von* ~ *gehen* go ashore; **'~funker** ⚓, ✈ *m* wireless *or* radio operator; **'~stein** *m* kerb, *Am.* curb.

borgen ['bɔrgən] *v/t.* (ge-, h) borrow (*von, bei* from, of); lend, *Am. a.* loan (*j-m et. s.th.* to s.o.).

Borke ['bɔrkə] *f* (-/-n) bark (*of tree*).

borniert *adj.* [bɔr'ni:rt] narrow-minded, of restricted intelligence.

Borsalbe ['bo:r-] *f* boracic oint-ment.

Börse ['bœrzə] *f* (-/-n) purse; ✝ stock exchange; stock-market; money-market; **'~nbericht** *m* mar-ket report; **'2nfähig** *adj.* stock: negotiable on the stock exchange; **'~nkurs** *m* quotation; **'~nmakler** *m* stock-broker; **'~nnotierung** *f* (official, stock exchange) quota-tion; **'~npapiere** *n/pl.* listed secu-rities *pl.*; **'~nspekulant** *m* stock-jobber; **'~nzeitung** *f* financial newspaper.

Borst|e ['bɔrstə] f (-/-n) bristle (of hog or brush, etc.); **ʼ2ig** adj. bristly.

Borte ['bɔrtə] f (-/-n) border (of carpet, etc.); braid, lace.

'bösartig adj. malicious, vicious; ʒ malignant; **ʼ2keit** f (-/-en) viciousness; ʒ malignity.

Böschung ['bœʃʊŋ] f (-/-en) slope; embankment (of railway); bank (of river).

böse ['bøːzə] 1. adj. bad, evil, wicked; malevolent, spiteful; angry (über acc. at, about; auf j-n with s.o.); er meint es nicht ~ he means no harm; 2. 2 n (-n/no pl.) evil; **2wicht** ['~vɪçt] n (-[e]s/-er, -e) villain, rascal.

bos|haft adj. ['boːshaft] wicked; spiteful; malicious; **ʼ2heit** f (-/-en) wickedness; malice; spite.

'böswillig adj. malevolent; ~e Absicht ⚖ malice prepense; ~es Verlassen ⚖ wilful desertion; **ʼ2keit** f (-/-en) malevolence.

bot [boːt] pret. of bieten.

Botan|ik [bo'taːnik] f (-/no pl.) botany; **~iker** m (-s/-) botanist; **2isch** adj. botanical.

Bote ['boːtə] m (-n/-n) messenger; **~ngang** m errand; Botengänge machen run errands.

'Botschaft f (-/-en) message; pol. embassy; **~er** m (-s/-) ambassador; in British Commonwealth countries: High Commissioner.

Bottich ['bɔtiç] m (-[e]s/-e) tub; wash-tub; brewing: tun. vat.

Bouillon [bu'ljõː] f (-/-s) beef tea.

Bowle ['boːlə] f (-/-n) vessel: bowl; cold drink consisting of fruit, hock and champagne or soda-water: appr. punch.

box|en ['bɔksən] 1. v/i. (ge-, h) box; 2. v/t. (ge-, h) punch s.o.; 3. 2 n (-s/no pl.) boxing; pugilism; **ʼ2er** m (-s/-) boxer; pugilist; **ʼ2handschuh** m boxing-glove; **ʼ2kampf** m boxing-match, bout, fight; **ʼ2sport** m boxing.

Boykott [bɔy'kɔt] (-[e]s/-e) boycott; **2ieren** [~'tiːrən] v/t. (no -ge-, h) boycott.

brach [braːx] 1. pret. of brechen. 2. ~ adv. fallow; uncultivated (both a. fig.).

brachte ['braxtə] pret. of bringen.

Branche † ['brãːʃə] f (-/-n) line (of business), trade; branch.

Brand [brant] m (-[e]s/~e) burning; fire, blaze; ♂ gangrene; ♀ blight, smut, mildew; **ʼ~blase** f blister; **ʼ~bombe** f incendiary bomb; **2en** ['~dən] v/i. (ge-, h) surge (a. fig.), break (an acc., gegen against); **ʼ~fleck** m burn; **2ig** adj. ['~diç] ♀, ♂ blighted, smutted; ♂ gangrenous; **ʼ~mal** n brand; fig. stigma, blemish; **ʼ2marken** v/t. (ge-, h) brand (animal); fig. brand

or stigmatize s.o.; **ʼ~mauer** f fire (-proof) wall; **ʼ~schaden** m damage caused by or loss suffered by fire; **ʼ2schatzen** v/t. (ge-, h) lay (town) under contribution; sack, pillage; **ʼ~stätte** f, **ʼ~stelle** f scene of fire; **ʼ~stifter** m incendiary, Am. F a. firebug; **ʼ~stiftung** f arson; **~ung** ['~dʊŋ] f (-/-en) surf, surge, breakers pl.; **ʼ~wache** f fire-watch; **ʼ~wunde** f burn; scald; **ʼ~zeichen** n brand.

brannte ['brantə] pret. of brennen.

Branntwein ['brantvaɪn] m brandy, spirits pl.; whisk(e)y; gin; **ʼ~brennerei** f distillery.

braten ['braːtən] 1. v/t. (irr., ge-, h) in oven: roast; grill; in frying-pan: fry; bake (apple); am Spieß ~ roast on a spit, barbecue; 2. v/i. (irr., ge-, h) roast; grill; fry; in der Sonne ~ p. roast or grill in the sun; 3. 2 m (-s/-) roast (meat); joint; **ʼ2fett** n dripping; **ʼ2soße** f gravy.

'Brat|fisch m fried fish; **ʼ~hering** m grilled herring; **ʼ~huhn** n roast chicken; **ʼ~kartoffeln** pl. fried potatoes pl.; **ʼ~ofen** m (kitchen) oven; **ʼ~pfanne** f frying-pan, Am. a. skillet; **ʼ~röhre** f s. Bratofen.

Brauch [braux] m (-[e]s/~e) custom, usage; use, habit; practice; **ʼ2bar** adj. p., thing: useful; p. capable, able; thing: serviceable; **ʼ2en** (h) 1. v/t. (ge-, h) want; require; take (time); use; 2. v/aux. (no -ge-): du brauchst es nur zu sagen you only have to say so; er hätte nicht zu kommen ~ he need not have come; **ʼ~tum** n (-[e]s/~er) custom; tradition; folklore.

Braue ['braʊə] f (-/-n) eyebrow.

brau|en ['braʊən] v/t. (ge-, h) brew; **ʼ2er** m (-s/-) brewer; **2erei** [~'raɪ] f (-/-en) brewery; **ʼ2haus** n brewery.

braun adj. [braun] brown; horse: bay; ~ werden get a tan (on one's skin).

Bräune ['brɔʏnə] f (-/no pl.) brown colo(u)r; (sun) tan; **ʼ2n** (ge-, h) 1. v/t. make or dye brown; sun: tan; 2. v/i. tan.

'Braunkohle f brown coal, lignite.

'bräunlich adj. brownish.

Brause ['braʊzə] f (-/-n) rose, sprinkling-nozzle (of watering can); s. Brausebad; s. Brauselimonade; **ʼ~bad** n shower(-bath); **ʼ~limonade** f fizzy lemonade; **ʼ2n** v/i. (ge-, h) wind, water, etc.: roar; rush; have a shower(-bath); **ʼ~pulver** n effervescent powder.

Braut [braut] f (-/~e) fiancée; on wedding-day: bride; **ʼ~führer** m best man.

Bräutigam ['brɔʏtigam] m (-s/-e) fiancé; on wedding-day: bridegroom, Am. a. groom.

'Braut|jungfer f bridesmaid; **ʼ~**

kleid n wedding-dress; '**~kranz** m bridal wreath; '**~leute** pl., '**~paar** n engaged couple; on wedding-day: bride and bridegroom; '**~schleier** m bridal veil.

brav adj. [brɑːf] honest, upright; good, well-behaved; brave.

bravo int. ['brɑːvo] bravo!, well done!

Bravour [bra'vuːr] f (-/no pl.) bravery, courage; brilliance.

Brecheisen ['brɛçʔ-] n crowbar; (burglar's) jemmy, Am. a. jimmy.

'**brechen** (irr., ge-) 1. v/t. (h) break; pluck (flower); refract (ray, etc.); fold (sheet of paper); quarry (stone); vomit; die Ehe ~ commit adultery; sich ~ break (one's leg, etc.); opt. be refracted; 2. v/i. (h) break; vomit; mit j-m ~ break with s.o.; 3. v/i. (sein) break, get broken; bones: break, fracture.

'**Brech|mittel** ♉ n emetic; F fig. sickener; '**~reiz** m nausea; '**~stange** f crowbar, Am. a. pry; '**~ung** opt. f (-/-en) refraction.

Brei [brai] m (-[e]s/-e) paste; pulp; mash; pap (for babies); made of oatmeal: porridge; (rice, etc.) pudding; '**2ig** adj. pasty; pulpy; pappy.

breit adj. [brait] broad, wide; zehn Meter ~ ten metres wide; ~e Schichten der Bevölkerung large sections of or the bulk of the population; '**~beinig** 1. adj. with legs wide apart; 2. adv.: ~ gehen straddle.

Breite ['braitə] f (-/-n) breadth, width; ast., geogr. latitude; '**2n** v/t. (ge-, h) spread; '**~ngrad** m degree of latitude; '**~nkreis** m parallel (of latitude).

'**breit|machen** v/refl. (sep., -ge-, h) spread o.s.; take up room; '**~schlagen** v/t. (irr. schlagen, sep., -ge-, h): F j-n ~ persuade s.o.; F j-n zu et. ~ talk s.o. into (doing) s.th.; '**2seite** ⚓ f broadside.

Bremse ['brɛmzə] f (-/-n) zo. gadfly; horse-fly; ⊕ brake; '**2n** (ge-, h) v/i. brake, put on the brakes; slow down; 2. v/t. brake, put on the brakes to; slow down; fig. curb.

'**Brems|klotz** m brake-block; ⚡ wheel chock; '**~pedal** n brake pedal; '**~vorrichtung** f brake-mechanism; '**~weg** m braking distance.

brenn|bar adj. ['brɛnbaːr] combustible, burnable; '**2dauer** f burning time; '**~en** (irr., ge-, h) 1. v/t. burn; distil(l) (brandy); roast (coffee); bake (brick, etc.); 2. v/i. burn; be ablaze, be on fire; wound, eye: smart, burn; nettle: sting; vor Ungeduld ~ burn with impatience; F darauf ~ zu inf. be burning to inf.; es brennt! fire!

'**Brenn|er** m (-s/-) p. distiller; fixture: burner; '**~essel** ['brɛnnɛsəl] f

stinging nettle; '**~glas** n burning glass; '**~holz** n firewood; '**~material** n fuel; '**~öl** n lamp-oil; fuel-oil; '**~punkt** m focus, focal point; in den ~ rücken bring into focus (a. fig.); im ~ des Interesses stehen be the focus of interest; '**~schere** f curling-tongs pl.; '**~spiritus** m methylated spirit; '**~stoff** m combustible; mot. fuel.

brenzlig ['brɛntsliç] 1. adj. burnt; matter: dangerous; situation: precarious; ~er Geruch burnt smell, smell of burning; 2. adv.: es riecht ~ it smells of burning.

Bresche ['brɛʃə] f (-/-n) breach (a. fig.), gap; in die ~ springen help s.o. out of a dilemma.

Brett [brɛt] n (-[e]s/-er) board; plank; shelf; spring-board; '**~spiel** n game played on a board.

Brezel ['breːtsəl] f (-/-n) pretzel.

Brief [briːf] m (-[e]s/-e) letter; '**~aufschrift** f address (on a letter); '**~beschwerer** m (-s/-) paperweight; '**~bogen** m sheet of notepaper; '**~geheimnis** n secrecy of correspondence; '**~karte** f correspondence card (with envelope); '**~kasten** m letter-box; pillar-box; Am. mailbox; '**2lich** adj. and adv. by letter, in writing; '**~marke** f (postage) stamp; '**~markensammlung** f stamp-collection; '**~öffner** m letter-opener; '**~ordner** m letterfile; '**~papier** n notepaper; '**~porto** n postage; '**~post** f mail, post; '**~tasche** f wallet, Am. a. billfold; '**~taube** f carrier pigeon, homing pigeon, homer; '**~träger** m postman, Am. mailman; '**~umschlag** m envelope; '**~waage** f letterbalance; '**~wechsel** m correspondence; '**~zensur** f postal censorship.

briet [briːt] pret. of braten.

Brikett [bri'kɛt] n (-[e]s/-s) briquet (-te).

Brillant [bril'jant] 1. m (-en/-en) brilliant, cut diamond; 2. ♀ adj. brilliant; '**~ring** m diamond ring.

Brille ['brilə] f (-/-n) (eine a pair of) glasses pl. or spectacles pl.; goggles pl.; lavatory seat; '**~nfutteral** n spectacle-case; '**~nträger** m person who wears glasses.

bringen ['briŋən] v/t. (irr., ge-, h) bring; take; see (s.o. home, etc.); put (in order); make (sacrifice); yield (interest); an den Mann ~ dispose of, get rid of; j-n dazu ~ et. zu tun make or get s.o. to do s.th.; et. mit sich ~ involve s.th.; j-n um et. ~ deprive s.o. of s.th.; j-n zum Lachen ~ make s.o. laugh.

Brise ['briːzə] f (-/-n) breeze.

Brit|e ['britə] m (-n/-n) Briton, Am. a. Britisher; die ~n pl. the British pl.; '**2isch** adj. British.

bröckeln ['brœkəln] v/i. (ge-, h) crumble; become brittle.

Brocken ['brɔkən] 1. m (-s/-) piece; lump (of earth or stone, etc.); morsel (of food); F ein harter ~ a hard nut; 2. ♀ v/t. (ge-, h): Brot in die Suppe ~ break bread into soup.

brodeln ['bro:dəln] v/i. (ge-, h) bubble, simmer.

Brombeer|e ['brɔm-] f blackberry; '~strauch m blackberry bush.

Bronch|ialkatarrh ♫ [brɔnçi'a:l-katar] m bronchial catarrh; '~ien anat. f/pl. bronchi(a) pl.; '~itis ♫ [~'çitis] f (-/Bronchitiden) bronchitis.

Bronze ['brõːsə] f (-/-n) bronze; '~medaille f bronze medal.

Brosche ['brɔʃə] f (-/-n) brooch.

broschier|en [brɔ'ʃiːrən] v/t. (no -ge-, h) sew, stitch (book); ~t adj. book: paper-backed, paper-bound; fabric: figured.

Broschüre [brɔ'ʃyːrə] f (-/-n) booklet; brochure; pamphlet.

Brot [broːt] n (-[e]s/-e) bread; loaf; sein ~ verdienen earn one's living; '~aufstrich m spread.

Brötchen ['brøːtçən] n (-s/-) roll.

'Brot|korb m: j-m den ~ höher hängen put s.o. on short allowance; '♀los fig. adj. unemployed; unprofitable; '~rinde f crust; '~schneidemaschine f bread-cutter; '~schnitte f slice of bread; '~studium n utilitarian study; '~teig m bread dough.

Bruch [brux] m (-[e]s/~e) break(ing); breach; ♫ fracture (of bones); ♫ hernia; crack; fold (in paper); crease (in cloth); split (in silk); Ⓐ fraction; breach (of promise); violation (of oath, etc.); violation, infringement (of law, etc.); '~band ♫ n truss.

brüchig adj. ['bryçiç] fragile; brittle, voice: cracked.

'Bruch|landung ♯ f crash-landing; '~rechnung f fractional arithmetic, F fractions pl.; '~strich Ⓐ m fraction bar; '~stück n fragment (a. fig.); '~teil m fraction; im ~ e-r Sekunde in a split second; '~zahl f fraction(al) number.

Brücke ['brykə] f (-/-n) bridge; carpet: rug; sports: bridge; e-e ~ schlagen über (acc.) build or throw a bridge across, bridge (river); '~nkopf ✕ m bridge-head; '~npfeiler m pier (of bridge).

Bruder ['bruːdər] m (-s/~) brother; eccl. (lay) brother, friar; '~krieg m fratricidal or civil war; '~kuß m fraternal kiss.

brüderlich ['bryːdərliç] 1. adj. brotherly, fraternal; 2. adv.: ~ teilen share and share alike; '2keit f (-/no pl.) brotherliness, fraternity.

Brüh|e ['bryːə] f (-/-n) broth; stock;

beef tea; F dirty water; drink: F dishwater; '♀heiß adj. scalding hot; '~würfel m beef cube.

brüllen ['brylən] v/i. (ge-, h) roar; bellow; cattle: low; bull: bellow; vor Lachen ~ roar with laughter; ~des Gelächter roar of laughter.

brumm|en ['brumən] v/i. (ge-, h) p. speak in a deep voice, mumble; growl (a. fig.); insect: buzz; engine: buzz, boom; fig. grumble, Am. grouch; mir brummt der Schädel my head is buzzing; '2bär fig. m grumbler, growler, Am. F grouch; '2er m (-s/-) bluebottle; dung-beetle; '~ig adj. grumbling, Am. F grouchy.

brünett adj. [bry'nɛt] woman: brunette.

Brunft hunt. [brunft] f (-/~e) rut; '~zeit f rutting season.

Brunnen ['brunən] m (-s/-) well; spring; fountain (a. fig.); e-n ~ graben sink a well; '~wasser n pump-water, well-water.

Brunst [brunst] f (-/~e) zo. rut (of male animal), heat (of female animal); lust, sexual desire.

brünstig adj. ['brynstiç] zo. rutting, in heat; lustful.

Brust [brust] f (-/~e) chest, anat. thorax; breast; (woman's) breast(s pl.), bosom; aus voller ~ at the top of one's voice, lustily; '~bild n half-length portrait.

brüsten ['brystən] v/refl. (ge-, h) boast, brag.

'Brust|fell anat. n pleura; '~fell-entzündung ♫ f pleurisy; '~kasten m, '~korb m chest, anat. thorax; '~schwimmen n (-s/no pl.) breast-stroke.

Brüstung ['brystuŋ] f (-/-en) balustrade, parapet.

'Brustwarze anat. f nipple.

Brut [bruːt] f (-/-en) brooding, sitting; brood; hatch; fry, spawn (of fish); fig. F brood, (bad) lot.

brutal adj. [bru'taːl] brutal; 2ität [~ali'tɛːt] f (-/-en) brutality.

Brutapparat zo. ['bruːt?-] m incubator.

brüten ['bryːtən] v/i. (ge-, h) brood, sit (on egg); incubate; ~ über (dat.) brood over.

'Brutkasten ♫ m incubator.

brutto † adv. ['bruto] gross; '2ge-wicht n gross weight; '2register-tonne f gross register ton; '2ver-dienst m gross earnings pl.

Bube ['buːbə] m (-n/-n) boy, lad; knave, rogue; cards: knave, jack; '~nstreich m, '~nstück n boyish prank; knavish trick.

Buch [buːx] n (-[e]s/~er) book; volume; '~binder m (book-)binder; '~drucker m printer; '~druckerei [~'rai] f printing; printing-office, Am. print shop.

Buche ❦ ['buːxə] f (-/-n) beech.

buchen ['buːxən] v/t. (ge-, h) book, reserve (passage, flight, etc.); book-keeping: book (item, sum), enter (transaction) in the books; et. als Erfolg ~ count s.th. as a success.

Bücher|abschluß † ['byːçər-] m closing of or balancing of books; '~brett n bookshelf; ~ei [~'raɪ] f (-/-en) library; '~freund m book-lover, bibliophil(e); '~revisor † m (-s/-en) auditor; accountant; '~schrank m bookcase; '~wurm m bookworm.

'Buch|fink orn. m chaffinch; '~halter m (-s/-) book-keeper; '~haltung f book-keeping; '~handel m book-trade; '~händler m bookseller; '~handlung f bookshop, Am. bookstore.

Büchse ['byksə] f (-/-n) box, case; tin, Am. can; rifle; '~nfleisch n tinned meat, Am. canned meat; '~nöffner ['byksənˀ-] m tin-opener, Am. can opener.

Buchstab|e ['buːxʃtaːbə] m (-n/-n) letter, character; typ. type; Ωieren [~a'biːrən] v/t. (no -ge-, h) spell.

buchstäblich ['buːxʃtɛːplɪç] 1. adj. literal; 2. adv. literally; word for word.

Bucht [buxt] f (-/-en) bay; bight; creek, inlet.

'Buchung f (-/-en) booking, reservation; book-keeping: entry.

Buckel ['bukəl] 1. m (-s/-) hump, hunch; humpback, hunchback; boss, stud, knob; 2. f (-/-n) boss, stud, knob.

'buckelig adj. s. bucklig.

bücken ['bykən] v/refl. (ge-, h) bend (down), stoop.

bucklig adj. ['buklɪç] humpbacked, hunchbacked.

Bückling ['byklɪŋ] m (-s/-e) bloater, red herring; fig. bow.

Bude ['buːdə] f (-/-n) stall, booth; hut, cabin, Am. shack; F: place; den; (student's, etc.) digs pl.

Budget [by'dʒeː] n (-s/-s) budget.

Büfett [by'feː; by'fɛt] n (-[e]s/-s; -[e]s/-e) sideboard, buffet; buffet, bar, Am. a. counter; kaltes ~ buffet supper or lunch.

Büffel ['byfəl] m (-s/-) zo. buffalo; F fig. lout, blockhead.

Bug [buːk] m (-[e]s/-e) ⊕ bow; ⚓ nose; fold; (sharp) crease.

Bügel ['byːgəl] m (-s/-) bow (of spectacles, etc.); handle (of handbag, etc.); coat-hanger; stirrup; '~brett n ironing-board; '~eisen n (flat-) iron; '~falte f crease; Ωn v/t. (ge-, h) iron (shirt, etc.), press (suit, skirt, etc.).

Bühne ['byːnə] f (-/-n) platform (a. ⊕); scaffold; thea. stage; fig.: die ~ the stage; die politische ~ the political scene; ~nanweisungen ['byː-

nən?-] f/pl. stage directions pl.; '~nbild n scene(ry); décor; stage design; '~ndichter m playwright, dramatist; '~nlaufbahn f stage career; '~nstück n stage play.

buk [buːk] pret. of backen.

Bull|auge ⚓ ['bul-] n porthole, bull's eye; '~dogge zo. f bulldog.

Bulle ['bulə] 1. zo. m (-n/-n) bull; 2. eccl. f (-/-n) bull.

Bummel F ['buməl] m (-s/-) stroll; spree, pub-crawl, sl. binge; ~ei [~'laɪ] f (-/-en) dawdling; negligence; Ωn v/i. (ge-) 1. (sein) stroll, saunter; pub-crawl; 2. (h) dawdle (on way, at work), waste time; '~streik m go-slow (strike), Am. slowdown; '~zug m slow train, Am. way train.

Bummler ['bumlər] m (-s/-) saunterer, stroller; loafer, Am. F a. bum; dawdler.

Bund [bunt] 1. m (-[e]s/⁺e) pol. union, federation, confederacy; (waist-, neck-, wrist)band; 2. n (-[e]s/-e) bundle (of faggots); bundle, truss (of hay or straw); bunch (of radishes, etc.).

Bündel ['byndəl] n (-s/-) bundle, bunch; Ωn v/t. (ge-, h) make into a bundle, bundle up.

Bundes|bahn ['bundəs-] f Federal Railway(s pl.); '~bank f Federal Bank; '~genosse m ally; '~gerichtshof m Federal Supreme Court; '~kanzler m Federal Chancellor; '~ministerium n Federal Ministry; '~post f Federal Postal Administration; '~präsident m President of the Federal Republic; '~rat m Bundesrat, Upper House of German Parliament; '~republik f Federal Republic; '~staat m federal state; confederation; '~tag m Bundestag, Lower House of German Parliament.

bündig adj. ['byndɪç] style, speech: concise, to the point, terse.

Bündnis ['byntnɪs] n (-ses/-se) alliance; agreement.

Bunker ['bunkər] m (-s/-) ⚒, coal, fuel, etc.: bunker; bin; air-raid shelter; ⚓ bunker, pill-box; ⚓ (submarine) pen.

bunt adj. [bunt] (multi-)colo(u)red, colo(u)rful; motley; bird, flower, etc.: variegated; bright, gay; fig. mixed, motley; full of variety; 'Ωdruck m colo(u)r-print(ing); 'Ωstift m colo(u)red pencil, crayon.

Bürde ['byrdə] f (-/-n) burden (a. fig.: für j-n to so.), load.

Burg [burk] f (-/-en) castle; fortress; citadel (a. fig.).

Bürge ⚖ ['byrgə] m (-n/-n) guarantor, security, surety; bailsman; sponsor; Ωn v/i. (ge-, h): für j-n ~ stand guarantee or surety or security for s.o., Am. a. bond s.o.; stand bail for s.o.; vouch or answer for s.o.; sponsor s.o.; für et. ~ stand security for s.th. guarantee s.th.; vouch or answer for s.th.

Bürger ['byrgər] m (-s/-) citizen; townsman; '~krieg m civil war.

'**bürgerlich** adj. civic, civil; ~e Küche plain cooking; Verlust der ~en Ehrenrechte loss of civil rights; Bürgerliches Gesetzbuch German Civil Code; '2e m (-n/-n) commoner.

'**Bürger|meister** m mayor; in Germany: a. burgomaster; in Scotland: provost; '~recht n civic rights pl.; citizenship; '~schaft f (-/-en) citizens pl.; '~steig m pavement, Am. sidewalk; '~wehr f militia.

Bürgschaft ['byrkʃaft] f (-/-en) security; bail; guarantee.

Büro [by'ro:] n (-s/-s) office; ~angestellte m, f (-n/-n) clerk; ~arbeit f office-work; ~klammer f paper-clip; ~krat [~o'kra:t] m (-en/-en) bureaucrat; ~kratie [~o-kra'ti:] f (-/-en) bureaucracy; red tape; 2kratisch adj. [~o'kra:tiʃ] bureaucratic; ~stunden f/pl. office hours pl.; ~vorsteher m head or senior clerk.

Bursch [burʃ] m (-en/-en), ~e ['~ə] m (-n/-n) boy, lad, youth; F chap, Am. a. guy; ein übler ~ a bad lot, F a bad egg.

burschikos adj. [burʃi'ko:s] free and easy; esp. girl: boyish, unaffected, hearty.

Bürste ['byrstə] f (-/-n) brush; '2n v/t. (ge-, h) brush.

Busch [buʃ] m (-es/ᵘe) bush, shrub.

Büschel ['byʃəl] n (-s/-) bunch;

tuft, handful (of hair); wisp (of straw or hair).

'**Busch|holz** n brushwood, underwood; '2ig adj. hair, eyebrows, etc.: bushy, shaggy; covered with bushes or scrub, bushy; '~messer n bush-knife; machete; '~neger m maroon; '~werk n bushes pl., shrubbery, Am. a. brush.

Busen ['bu:zən] m (-s/-) bosom, breast (esp. of woman); fig. bosom, heart; geog. bay, gulf; '~freund m bosom friend.

Bussard orn. ['busart] m (-[e]s/-e) buzzard.

Buße ['bu:sə] f (-/-n) atonement (for sins), penance; repentance; satisfaction; fine; ~ tun do penance.

büßen ['by:sən] (ge-, h) 1. v/t. expiate, atone for (sin, crime); er mußte es mit s-m Leben ~ he paid for it with his life; das sollst du mir ~! you'll pay for that!; 2. v/i. atone, pay (für for).

'**Büßer** m (-s/-) penitent.

'**buß|fertig** adj. penitent, repentant, contrite; '2fertigkeit f (-/no pl.) repentance, contrition; '2tag m day of repentance; Buß- und Bettag day of prayer and repentance.

Büste ['by:stə] f (-/-n) bust; '~n-halter m (-s/-) brassière, F bra.

Büttenpapier ['bytən-] n hand-made paper.

Butter ['butər] f (-/no pl.) butter; '~blume ♀ f buttercup; '~brot n (slice or piece of) bread and butter; F: für ein ~ for a song; '~brotpapier n greaseproof paper; '~dose f butter-dish; '~faß n butter-churn; '~milch f buttermilk; '2n v/i. (ge-, h) churn.

C

Café [ka'fe:] n (-s/-s) café, coffee-house.

Cape [ke:p] n (-s/-s) cape.

Cell|ist ♪ [tʃe'list] m (-en/-en) violoncellist, (')cellist; ~o ♪ ['~o] n (-s/-s, Celli) violoncello, (')cello.

Celsius ['tsɛlzius]: 5 Grad ~ (abbr. 5° C) five degrees centigrade.

Chaiselongue [ʃɛz(ə)'lõ:] f (-/-n, -s) chaise longue, lounge, couch.

Champagner [ʃam'panjər] m (-s/-) champagne.

Champignon ♀ ['ʃampinjõ] m (-s/-s) champignon, (common) mushroom.

Chance ['ʃã:s(ə)] f (-/-n) chance; keine ~ haben not to stand a chance; sich eine ~ entgehen lassen miss a chance or an opportunity; die ~n sind gleich the chances or odds are even.

Chaos ['ka:ɔs] n (-/no pl.) chaos.

Charakter [ka'raktər] m (-s/-e) character; nature; 2bild n character (sketch); ~darsteller thea. m character actor; ~fehler m fault in s.o.'s character; 2fest adj. of firm or strong character; 2i'sieren v/t. (no -ge-, h) characterize, describe (als acc. as); ~i'sierung f (-/-en), ~istik [~'ristik] f (-/-en) characterization; 2istisch adj. [~'ristiʃ] characteristic or typical (für of); 2lich adj. of or concerning (the) character; 2los adj. characterless, without (strength of) character, spineless; ~rolle thea. f character role; ~zug m characteristic, feature, trait.

charm|ant adj. [ʃar'mant] charming, winning; 2e [ʃarm] m (-s/no pl.) charm ,grace.

Chassis [ʃa'si:] n (-/-) mot., radio: frame, chassis.

Chauffeur [ʃɔ'føːr] m (-s/-e) chauffeur, driver.

Chaussee [ʃo'se:] f (-/-n) highway, (high) road.

Chauvinismus [ʃovi'nismus] m (-/ no pl.) jingoism; chauvinism.

Chef [ʃef] m (-s/-s) head, chief; ✝ principal, F boss; senior partner.

Chem|ie [çe'mi:] f (-/no pl.) chemistry; **~iefaser** f chemical fib|re, Am. -er; **~ikalien** [~i'kɑːljən] f/pl. chemicals pl.; **~iker** ['çeːmikər] m (-s/-) (analytical) chemist; **2isch** adj. ['çeːmiʃ] chemical.

Chiffre ['ʃifər] f (-/-n) number; cipher; in advertisement: box number; **2ieren** [ʃi'friːrən] v/t. (no -ge-, h) cipher, code (message, etc.); write in code or cipher.

Chines|e [çi'neːzə] m (-n/-n) Chinese, contp. Chinaman; **2isch** adj. Chinese.

Chinin 🜍 [çi'niːn] n (-s/no pl.) quinine.

Chirurg [çi'rurk] m (-en/-en) surgeon; **~ie** [~'giː] f (-/-n) surgery; **2isch** adj. [~giʃ] surgical.

Chlor 🜍 [kloːr] n (-s/no pl.) chlorine; **2en** v/t. (ge-, h) chlorinate (water); **~kalk** 🜍 m chloride of lime.

Chloroform 🜍 [kloro'fɔrm] n (-/no pl.) chloroform; **2ieren** 🜿 [~'miː-rən] v/t. (no -ge-, h) chloroform.

Cholera 🜿 ['koːləra] f (-/no pl.) cholera.

cholerisch adj. [ko'leːriʃ] choleric, irascible.

Chor [koːr] m 1. 🜨 a. n (-[e]s/-e, ᵘe) chancel, choir; (organ-)loft; 2. (-[e]s/ᵘe) in drama: chorus; singers: choir, chorus; piece of music: chorus; **~al** [ko'rɑːl] m (-s/ᵘe) choral(e); hymn; **~gesang** m choral singing, chorus; **~sänger** m member of a choir; chorister.

Christ [krist] m (-en/-en) Christian; **~baum** m Christmas-tree; **~enheit** f (-/no pl.): die ~ Christendom; **~entum** n (-s/no pl.) Christianity; **~kind** n (-[e]s/no pl.) Christ-child, Infant Jesus; **2lich** adj. Christian.

Chrom [kroːm] n (-s/no pl.) metal: chromium; pigment: chrome.

chromatisch ♪, opt. adj. [kro'mɑːtiʃ] chromatic.

Chronik ['kroːnik] f (-/-en) chronicle.

chronisch adj. ['kroːniʃ] disease: chronic (a. fig.).

Chronist [kro'nist] m (-en/-en) chronicler.

chronologisch adj. [krono'loːgiʃ] chronological.

circa adv. ['tsirka] about, approximately.

Clique ['klikə] f (-/-n) clique, set, group, coterie; **~nwirtschaft** f (-/no pl.) cliquism.

Conférencier [kõferɑ̃'sjeː] m (-s/-s) compère, Am. master of ceremonies.

Couch [kautʃ] f (-/-s) couch.

Coupé [ku'peː] n (-s/-s) mot. coupé; 🜨 🚃 compartment.

Couplet [ku'pleː] n (-s/-s) comic or music-hall song.

Coupon [ku'põ:] m (-s/-s) coupon; dividend-warrant; counterfoil.

Courtage ✝ [kur'tɑːʒə] f (-/-n) brokerage.

Cousin [ku'zɛ̃] m (-s/-s), **~e** [~i:nə] f (-/-n) cousin.

Creme [kreːm, kreːm] f (-/-s) cream (a. fig.: only sg.).

Cut [kœt, kat] m (-s/-s), **~away** ['kœtəve:, 'katave:] m (-s/-s) cutaway (coat), morning coat.

D

da [dɑː] 1. adv. space: there; ~ wo where; hier und ~ here and there; ~ bin ich here I am; ~ haben wir's! there we are!; von ~ an from there; time: ~ erst only then, not till then; von ~ an from that time (on), since then; hier und ~ now and then or again; 2. cj. time: as, when, while; nun, ~ du es einmal gesagt hast now (that) you have mentioned it; causal: as, since, because; ~ ich krank war, konnte ich nicht kommen as or since I was ill I couldn't come.

dabei adv. [da'baɪ, when emphatic: 'dɑːbaɪ] near (at hand), by; about, going (zu inf. to inf.), on the point

(of ger.); besides; nevertheless, yet, for all that; was ist schon ~? what does it matter?; lassen wir es ~ let's leave it at that; ~ bleiben stick to one's point, persist in it.

da'bei|bleiben v/i. (irr. bleiben, sep., -ge-, sein) stay with it or them; **~sein** v/i. (irr. sein, sep., -ge-, sein) be present or there; **~stehen** v/i. (irr. stehen, sep., -ge-, h) stand by or near.

'dableiben v/i. (irr. bleiben, sep., -ge-, sein) stay, remain.

da capo adv. [dɑ'kɑːpo] at opera, etc.: encore.

Dach [dax] n (-[e]s/ᵘer) roof; fig. shelter; **~antenne** f roof aerial;

'⁓decker m (-s/-) roofer; tiler; slater; '⁓fenster n skylight; dormer window; '⁓garten m roofgarden; '⁓gesellschaft † f holding company; '⁓kammer f attic, garret; '⁓pappe f roofing felt; '⁓rinne f gutter, eaves pl.

dachte ['daxtə] pret. of denken.

Dachs zo. [daks] m (-es/-e) badger; '⁓bau m (-[e]s/-e) badger's earth.

'Dach|sparren m rafter; '⁓stube f attic, garret; '⁓stuhl m roof framework; '⁓ziegel m (roofing) tile.

dadurch [da'durç, when emphatic: 'da:durç] 1. adv. for this reason, in this manner or way, thus; by it or that; 2. cj.: ⁓, daß owing to (the fact that), because; by ger.

dafür adv. [da'fy:r, when emphatic: 'da:fy:r] for it or that; instead (of it); in return (for it), in exchange; ⁓ sein be in favo(u)r of it; ⁓ sein zu inf. be for ger., be in favo(u)r of ger.; er kann nichts ⁓ it is not his fault; ⁓ sorgen, daß see to it that.

Da'fürhalten n (-s/no pl.): nach meinem ⁓ in my opinion.

dagegen [da'ge:gən, when emphatic: 'da:ge:gən] 1. adv. against it or that; in comparison with it, compared to it; ⁓ sein be against it, be opposed to it; ich habe nichts ⁓ I have no objection (to it); 2. cj. on the other hand, however.

daheim adv. [da'haɪm] at home.

daher [da'he:r, when emphatic: 'da:he:r] 1. adv. from there; prefixed to verbs of motion: along; fig. from this, hence; ⁓ kam es, daß thus it happened; that; 2. cj. therefore; that is (the reason) why.

dahin [da'hin, when emphatic: 'da:hin] there, to that place; gone, past; prefixed to verbs of motion: along; j-n ⁓ bringen, daß induce s.o. to inf.; m-e Meinung geht ⁓, daß my opinion is that.

da'hingestellt adj.: es ⁓ sein lassen (,ob) leave it undecided (whether).

dahinter adv. [da'hintər, when emphatic: 'da:hintər] behind it or that, at the back of it; es steckt nichts ⁓ there is nothing in it.

da'hinterkommen v/i. (irr. kommen, sep., -ge-, sein) find out about it.

damalig adj. ['da:ma:lɪç] then, of that time; der ⁓e Besitzer the then owner; '⁓s adv. then, at that time.

Damast m ['da'mast] m (-es/-e) damask.

Dame ['da:mə] f (-/-n) lady; dancing, etc.: partner; cards, chess: queen; s. Damespiel; '⁓brett n draught-board, Am. checkerboard.

'Damen|binde f (woman's) sanitary towel, Am. sanitary napkin; '⁓doppel n tennis: women's doubles pl.; '⁓einzel n tennis: women's

singles pl.; '⁓haft adj. ladylike; '⁓konfektion f ladies' ready-made clothes pl.; '⁓mannschaft f sports: women's team; '⁓schneider m ladies' tailor, dressmaker.

'Damespiel n (game of) draughts pl., Am. (game of) checkers pl.

damit 1. adv. [da'mit, when emphatic: 'da:mit] with it or that; therewith, herewith; by it or that; was will er ⁓ sagen? what does he mean by it?; wie steht es ⁓? how about it?; ⁓ einverstanden sein agree to it; 2. cj. (in order) that, in order to inf.; so (that); ⁓ nicht lest, (so as) to avoid that; for fear that (all with subjunctive).

dämlich F adj. ['dɛ:mlɪç] silly, asinine.

Damm [dam] m (-[e]s/⁓e) dam; dike, dyke; 🚇 embankment; embankment, Am. levee (of river); roadway; fig. barrier; '⁓bruch m bursting of a dam or dike.

dämmer|ig adj. ['dɛmərɪç] dusky; 'Licht n twilight; '⁓n v/i. (ge-, h) dawn (a. fig.: F j-m on s.o.); grow dark or dusky; 'Lung f (-/-en) twilight, dusk; in the morning: dawn.

Dämon ['dɛ:mɔn] m (-s/-en) demon; Lisch adj. [dɛ'mo:nɪʃ] demoniac(al).

Dampf [dampf] m (-[e]s/⁓e) steam; vapo(u)r; '⁓bad n vapo(u)r-bath; '⁓boot n steamboat; 'Len v/i. (ge-, h) steam.

dämpfen ['dɛmpfən] v/t. (ge-, h) deaden (pain, noise, force of blow); muffle (bell, drum, oar); damp (sound, oscillation, fig. enthusiasm); ♩ mute (stringed instrument); soften (colour, light); attenuate (wave); steam (cloth, food); stew (meat, fruit); fig. suppress, curb (emotion).

'Dampfer m (-s/-) steamer, steamship.

'Dämpfer m (-s/-) damper (a. ♩ of piano); ♩ mute (for violin, etc.).

'Dampf|heizung f steam-heating; '⁓kessel m (steam-)boiler; '⁓maschine f steam-engine; '⁓schiff n steamer, steamship; '⁓walze f steam-roller.

danach adv. [da'na:x, when emphatic: 'da:na:x] after it or that; afterwards; subsequently; accordingly; ich fragte ihn ⁓ I asked him about it; iro. er sieht ganz ⁓ aus he looks very much like it.

Däne ['dɛ:nə] m (-n/-n) Dane.

daneben adv. [da'ne:bən, when emphatic: 'da:ne:bən] next to it or that, beside it or that; besides, moreover; beside the mark.

da'nebengehen F v/i. (irr. gehen, sep., -ge-, sein) bullet, etc.: miss the target or mark; remark, etc.: miss one's effect, F misfire.

daniederliegen [da'ni:dər-] v/i.

(*irr. liegen*, *sep.*, *-ge-*, *h*) be laid up (*an dat.* with); *trade*: be depressed.

dänisch *adj.* ['dɛːniʃ] Danish.

Dank [daŋk] 1. *m* (-[e]s/*no pl.*) thanks *pl.*, gratitude; reward; *j-m* ~ *sagen* thank s.o.; *Gott sei* ~*l* thank God!; 2. ♀ *prp.* (*dat.*) owing *or* thanks to; '♀**bar** *adj.* thankful, grateful (*j-m* to s.o.; *für* for); profitable; '~**barkeit** *f* (-/*no pl.*) gratitude; '♀**en** *v/i.* (*ge-*, *h*) thank (*j-m für* s.t. s.o. for s.th.); *danke* (*schön*)*l* thank you (very much)!; *danke* thank you; |*nein*, *danke* no, thank you; *nichts zu* ~ don't mention it; '♀**enswert** *adj. thing*: one can be grateful for; *efforts*, etc.: kind; *task*, etc.: rewarding, worth-while; '~**gebet** *n* thanksgiving (prayer); '~**schreiben** *n* letter of thanks.

dann *adv.* [dan] then; ~ *und wann* (every) now and then.

daran *adv.* [da'ran, *when emphatic*: 'daːran] at (*or* by, in, on, to) it *or* that; *sich* ~ *festhalten* hold on tight to it; ~ *festhalten* stick to it; *nahe* ~ *sein zu inf.* be on the point *or* verge of *ger.*

da'rangehen *v/i.* (*irr. gehen*, *sep.*, *-ge-*, *sein*) set to work; set about *ger.*

darauf *adv.* [da'rauf, *when emphatic*: 'daːrauf] *space*: on (top of) it *or* that; *time*: thereupon, after it *or* that; *am Tage* ~ the day after, the next *or* following day; *zwei Jahre* ~ two years later; ~ *kommt es an* that's what matters; ~**hin** *adv.* [darauf'hin, *when emphatic*: 'daːraufhin] thereupon.

daraus *adv.* [da'raus, *when emphatic*: 'daːraus] out of it *or* that, from it *or* that; ~ *folgt* hence it follows; *was ist* ~ *geworden?* what has become of it?; *ich mache mir nichts* ~ I don't care *or* mind (about it).

darben ['darbən] *v/i.* (*ge-*, *h*) suffer want; starve.

darbiet|en ['daːr-] *v/t.* (*irr. bieten*, *sep.*, *-ge-*, *h*) offer, present; perform; '♀**ung** *f* (-/-en) *thea.*, etc.: performance.

'darbringen *v/t.* (*irr. bringen*, *sep.*, *-ge-*, *h*) offer; make (*sacrifice*).

darein *adv.* [da'rain, *when emphatic*: 'daːrain] into it *or* that, therein.

da'rein|finden *v/refl.* (*irr. finden*, *sep.*, *-ge-*, *h*) put up with it; ~**mischen** *v/refl.* (*sep.*, *-ge-*, *h*) interfere (with it); ~**reden** *v/i.* (*sep.*, *-ge-*, *h*) interrupt; *fig.* interfere.

darin *adv.* [da'rin, *when emphatic*: 'daːrin] in it *or* that; therein; *es war nichts* ~ there was nothing in it *or* them.

darleg|en ['daːr-] *v/t.* (*sep.*, *-ge-*, *h*)

lay open, expose, disclose; show; explain; demonstrate; point out; '♀**ung** *f* (-/-en) exposition; explanation; statement.

Darlehen ['daːrleːən] *n* (-s/-) loan.

Darm [darm] *m* (-[e]s/=e) gut, *anat.* intestine; (sausage-)skin; *Därme pl.* intestines *pl.*, bowels *pl.*

'darstell|en *v/t.* (*sep.*, *-ge-*, *h*) represent; show, depict; delineate; describe; *actor*: interpret (*character*, *part*), represent (*character*); *graphic arts*: graph, plot (*curve*, etc.); '♀**er** *thea. m* (-s/-) interpreter (*of a part*); actor; '♀**ung** *f* representation; *thea.* performance.

'dartun *v/t.* (*irr. tun*, *sep.*, *-ge-*, *h*) prove; demonstrate; set forth.

darüber *adv.* [da'ryːbər, *when emphatic*: 'daːryːbər] over it *or* that; across it; in the meantime; ~ *werden Jahre vergehen* it will take years; *wir sind* ~ *hinweg* we are over it; *ein Buch* ~ *schreiben* write a book about it.

darum [da'rum, *when emphatic*: 'daːrum] 1. *adv.* around it *or* that; *er kümmert sich nicht* ~ he does not care; *es handelt sich* ~ *zu inf.* the point is to *inf.*; 2. *cj.* therefore, for that reason, ~ *ist er nicht gekommen* that's (the reason) why he hasn't come.

darunter *adv.* [da'runtər, *when emphatic*: 'daːruntər] under it *or* that; beneath it; among them; less; *zwei Jahre und* ~ two years and under; *was verstehst du* ~? what do you understand by it?

das [das] *s. der*.

dasein ['daː-] 1. *v/i.* (*irr. sein*, *sep.*, *-ge-*, *sein*) be there *or* present; exist; 2. ♀ *n* (-s/*no pl.*) existence; life; being.

daß *cj.* [das] that; ~ *nicht* less; *es sei denn*, ~ unless; *ohne* ~ without *ger.*; *nicht* ~ *ich wüßte* not that I know of.

'dastehen *v/i.* (*irr. stehen*, *sep.*, *-ge-*, *h*) stand (there).

Daten ['daːtən] *pl.* data *pl.* (*a.* ⊕), facts *pl.*; particulars *pl.*; '~**verarbeitung** *f* (-/-en) data processing.

datieren [da'tiːrən] *v/t. and v/i.* (*no* *-ge-*, *h*) date. [(case).]

Dativ *gr.* ['daːtiːf] *m* (-s/-e) dative/

Dattel ['datəl] *f* (-/-n) date.

Datum ['daːtum] *n* (-s/*Daten*) date.

Dauer ['dauər] *f* (-/*no pl.*) length, duration; continuance; *auf die* ~ in the long run; *für die* ~ *von* for a period *or* term of; *von* ~ *sein* last well; '♀**haft** *adj.* peace, etc.: lasting; *material*, etc.: durable; *colour*, *dye*: fast; '~**karte** *f* season ticket, *Am.* commutation ticket; '~**lauf** *m* jog-trot; endurance-run; '♀**n** *v/i.* (*ge-*, *h*) continue, last; take (*time*); '~**welle** *f* permanent wave, *F* perm.

Daumen ['daumən] *m* (-s/-) thumb;
j-m den ~ *halten* keep one's fingers
crossed (for s.o.); '**~abdruck** *m*
(-[e]s/~e) thumb-print.

Daune ['daunə] *f* (-/-n): ~(*n pl.*)
down; '**~ndecke** *f* eiderdown
(quilt).

davon *adv.* [da'fɔn, *when emphatic*:
'da:fɔn] of it *or* that; thereof; from
it *or* that; off, away; *was habe ich*
~? what do I get from it?; *das
kommt* ~*l* it serves you right!

da'von|kommen *v/i.* (*irr. kommen,
sep.,* -ge-, *sein*) escape, get off;
~laufen *v/i.* (*irr. laufen, sep.,* -ge-,
sein) run away.

davor *adv.* [da'fo:r, *when emphatic*:
'da:fo:r] *space*: before it *or* that, in
front of it *or* that; *er fürchtet sich* ~
he is afraid of it.

dazu *adv.* [da'tsu:, *when emphatic*:
'da:tsu:] to it *or* that; for it *or* that;
for that purpose; in addition to
that; *noch* ~ at that; ~ *gehört Zeit*
it requires time.

da'zu|gehörig *adj.* belonging to it;
~kommen *v/i.* (*irr. kommen, sep.,*
-ge-, *sein*) appear (on the scene);
find time.

dazwischen *adv.* [da'tsviʃən] between (them), in between; **~kom-
men** *v/i.* (*irr. kommen, sep.,* -ge-,
sein) *thing*: intervene, happen.

Debatt|e [de'batə] *f* (-/-n) debate;
2ieren [~'ti:rən] (*no* -ge-, *h*) **1.** *v/t.*
discuss; debate; **2.** *v/i.* debate
(*über acc.* on).

Debüt [de'by:] *n* (-s/-s) first appearance, début.

dechiffrieren [deʃi'fri:rən] *v/t.* (*no*
-ge-, *h*) decipher, decode.

Deck ⚓ [dɛk] *n* (-[e]s/-s, ⚓-e)
deck; '**~adresse** *f* cover (address);
'**~bett** *n* feather bed.

Decke ['dɛkə] *f* (-/-n) cover(ing);
blanket; (travel[l]ing) rug; ceiling;
'**~l** *m* (-s/-) lid, cover (*of box or pot,
etc.*); lid (*of piano*); (book-)cover;
'**2n** (ge-, *h*) **1.** *v/t.* cover; *den Tisch*
~ lay the table; **2.** *v/i. paint*: cover.

'**Deck|mantel** *m* cloak, mask, dis-
guise; '**~name** *m* assumed name,
pseudonym; '**~ung** *f* (-/-en) cover;
security.

defekt [de'fɛkt] **1.** *adj.* defective,
faulty; **2.** 2 *m* (-[e]s/-e) defect,
fault.

defin|ieren [defi'ni:rən] *v/t.* (*no*
-ge-, *h*) define; **2ition** [~i'tsjo:n] *f*
(-/-en) definition; **~itiv** [~i'ti:f]
definite; definitive.

Defizit ✝ ['de:fitsit] *n* (-s/-e) deficit, deficiency.

Degen ['de:gən] *m* (-s/-) sword;
fencing: épée.

degradieren [degra'di:rən] *v/t.* (*no*
-ge-, *h*) degrade, *Am. a.* demote.

dehn|bar *adj.* ['de:nba:r] extensi-
ble; elastic; *metal*: ductile; *notion*:

etc.: vague; '**~en** *v/t.* (ge-, *h*) extend; stretch; '**2ung** *f* (-/-en) extension; stretch(ing).

Deich [daiç] *m* (-[e]s/-e) dike, dyke.

Deichsel ['daiksəl] *f* (-/-) pole,
shaft.

dein *poss. pron.* [dain] your; *der (die,
das)* ~*e* yours; *ich bin* ~ I am yours;
die Deinen pl. your family; **~er-
seits** *adv.* ['~ər'zaits] for *or* on your
part; '**~esgleichen** *pron.* your like,
your (own) kind, F the like(s) of
you.

Dekan *eccl. and univ.* [de'ka:n] *m*
(-s/-e) dean.

Deklam|ation [deklama'tsjo:n] *f*
(-/-en) declamation; reciting; **2ie-
ren** [~'mi:rən] *v/t. and v/i.* (*no* -ge-,
h) recite; declaim.

Deklin|ation *gr.* [deklina'tsjo:n] *f*
(-/-en) declension; **2ieren** *gr.* [~
'ni:rən] *v/t.* (*no* -ge-, *h*) decline.

Dekor|ateur [dekora'tø:r] *m* (-s/-e)
decorator; window-dresser; *thea.*
scene-painter; **~ation** [~'tsjo:n] *f*
(-/-en) decoration; (window-)dress-
ing; *thea.* scenery; **2ieren** [~'ri:rən]
v/t. (*no* -ge-, *h*) decorate; dress
(*window*).

Dekret [de'kre:t] *n* (-[e]s/-e) decree.

delikat *adj.* [deli'ka:t] delicate (*a.
fig.*); delicious; *fig.* ticklish; **2esse**
[~a'tɛsə] *f* (-/-n) delicacy; dainty.

Delphin *zo.* [dɛl'fi:n] *m* (-s/-e) dolphin.

Dement|i [de'menti] *n* (-s/-s) (for-
mal) denial; **2ieren** [~'ti:rən] *v/t.* (*no*
-ge-, *h*) deny, give a (formal) denial
of.

'**dem|entsprechend** *adv.*, '**~gemäß**
adv. correspondingly, accordingly;
'**~nach** *adv.* therefore, hence; accordingly; '**~nächst** *adv.* soon,
shortly, before long.

demobili|sier|en (*no* -ge-, *h*) **1.** *v/t.*
demobilize; disarm; **2.** *v/i.* disarm;
2ung *f* (-/-en) demobilization.

Demokrat [demo'kra:t] *m* (-en/-en)
democrat; **~ie** [~a'ti:] *f* (-/-n) de-
mocracy; **2isch** *adj.* [~'kra:tiʃ]
democratic.

demolieren [demo'li:rən] *v/t.* (*no*
-ge-, *h*) demolish.

Demonstr|ation [demɔnstra'tsjo:n]
f (-/-en) demonstration; **2ieren**
[~'stri:rən] *v/t. and v/i.* (*no* -ge-, *h*)
demonstrate.

Demont|age [demɔn'ta:ʒə] *f* (-/-n)
disassembly; dismantling; **2ieren**
[~'ti:rən] *v/t.* (*no* -ge-, *h*) disassemble; dismantle.

Demut ['de:mu:t] *f* (-/*no pl.*) humility, humbleness.

demütig *adj.* ['de:my:tiç] humble;
~en [~gən] *v/t.* (ge-, *h*) humble,
humiliate.

denk|bar ['dɛŋkba:r] **1.** *adj.* con-
ceivable; thinkable, imaginable;
2. *adv.:* ~ *einfach* most simple;

'**.en** (*irr.*, ge-, *h*) 1. *v/i.* think; ~ *an* (*acc.*) think of; remember; ~ *über* (*acc.*) think about; *j-m zu* ~ *geben* set s.o. thinking; 2. *v/t.* think; *sich et.* ~ imagine *or* fancy s.th.; *das habe ich mir gedacht* I thought as much; '2mal *n* monument; memorial; '2schrift *f* memorandum; memoir; '2stein *m* memorial stone; '~würdig *adj.* memorable; '2zettel *fig. m* lesson.

denn [dɛn] 1. *cj.* for; *mehr ~ je* more than ever; 2. *adv.* then; *es sei ~*, *daß* unless, except; *wieso ~?* how so.

dennoch *cj.* ['dɛnnɔx] yet, still, nevertheless; though.

Denunz|iant [denun'tsjant] *m* (-en/ -en) informer; **~iation** [~tsjoˈn] *f* (-/-en) denunciation; **2ieren** [~ˈtsiː- rən] *v/t.* (*no* -ge-, *h*) inform against, denounce.

Depesche [deˈpɛʃə] *f* (-/-n) dispatch; telegram, F wire; wireless.

deponieren [depoˈniːrən] *v/t.* (*no* -ge-, *h*) deposit.

Depositen † [depoˈziːtən] *pl.* deposits *pl.*; **2bank** *f* deposit bank.

der [deːr], **die** [diː], **das** [das] 1. *art.* the; 2. *dem. pron.* that, this; he, she, it; *die pl.* these, those, they, them; 3. *rel. pron.* who, which, that.

'**der'artig** *adj.* such, of such a kind of this *or* that kind.

derb *adj.* [dɛrp] *cloth*: coarse, rough; *shoes*, etc.: stout, strong; *ore*, etc.: massive; *p.*: sturdy; rough; *food*: coarse; *p.*, *manners*: rough, coarse; *way of speaking*: blunt, unrefined; *joke*: crude; *humour*: broad.

der'gleichen *adj.* such, of that kind; *used as a noun*: the like, such a thing; *und* ~ and the like; *nichts* ~ nothing of the kind.

der- ['deːrˈjeːnigə], '**die-**, '**dasjenige** *dem. pron.* he *who*, she *who*, that *which*; *diejenigen pl.* those *who*, those *which*.

der- [deːrˈzɛlbə], **die-**, **das'selbe** *dem. pron.* the same; he, she, it.

Desert|eur [dezɛrˈtøːr] *m* (-s/-e) deserter; **2ieren** [~ˈtiːrən] *v/i.* (*no* -ge-, *sein*) desert.

desgleichen [dɛsˈglaɪçən] 1. *dem. pron.* such a thing; 2. *adv.* likewise.

deshalb ['dɛshalp] 1. *cj.* for this *or* that reason; therefore; 2. *adv.*: *ich tat es nur* ~, *weil* I did it only because.

desinfizieren [dɛsˀinfiˈtsiːrən] *v/t.* (*no* -ge-, *h*) disinfect.

Despot [dɛsˈpoːt] *m* (-en/-en) despot; **2isch** *adj.* despotic.

destillieren [dɛstiˈliːrən] *v/t.* (*no* -ge-, *h*) distil.

desto *adv.* ['dɛsto] (all, so much) the; ~ *besser* all the better; ~ *erstaunter* (all) the more astonished.

deswegen *cj. and adv.* ['dɛsˈveːgən] *s.* deshalb.

Detail [deˈtaɪ] *n* (-s/-s) detail.

Detektiv [detɛkˈtiːf] *m* (-s/-e) detective.

deuten ['dɔʏtən] (ge-, *h*) 1. *v/t.* interpret; read (*stars*, *dream*, etc.); 2. *v/i.*: ~ *auf* (*acc.*) point at.

'**deutlich** *adj.* clear, distinct, plain.

deutsch *adj.* [dɔʏtʃ] German; '2e *m*, *f* (-n/-n) German.

'**Deutung** *f* (-/-en) interpretation, explanation.

Devise [deˈviːzə] *f* (-/-n) motto; **~n** *pl.* † foreign exchange *or* currency.

Dezember [deˈtsɛmbər] *m* (-[s]/-) December.

dezent *adj.* [deˈtsɛnt] *attire*, etc.: decent, modest; *literature*, etc.: decent; *behaviour*: decent, proper; *music*, *colour*: soft, restrained; *lighting*, etc.: subdued.

Dezernat [detsɛrˈnaːt] *n* (-[e]s/-e) (administrative) department.

dezimal *adj.* [detsiˈmaːl] decimal; **2bruch** *m* decimal fraction; **2stelle** *f* decimal place.

dezi'mieren *v/t.* (*no* -ge-, *h*) decimate; *fig. a.* reduce (drastically).

Diadem [diaˈdeːm] *n* (-s/-e) diadem.

Diagnose [diaˈgnoːzə] *f* (-/-n) diagnosis.

diagonal *adj.* [diagoˈnaːl] diagonal; **2e** *f* (-/-n) diagonal.

Dialekt [diaˈlɛkt] *m* (-[e]s/-e) dialect; **2isch** *adj.* dialectal.

Dialog [diaˈloːk] *m* (-[e]s/-e) dialogue, *Am. a.* dialog.

Diamant [diaˈmant] *m* (-en/-en) diamond.

Diät [diˈɛːt] *f* (-/*no pl.*) diet; *diät leben* live on a diet. [yourself.]

dich *pers. pron.* [diç] you; ~ (*selbst*)

dicht [diçt] 1. *adj.* *fog*, *rain*, etc.: dense; *fog*, *forest*, *hair*: thick; *eyebrows*: bushy, thick; *crowd*: thick, dense; *shoe*, etc.: (water)tight; 2. *adv.*: ~ *an* (*dat.*) *or bei* close to.

'**dichten[1]** *v/t.* (ge-, *h*) make tight.

'**dicht|en[2]** (ge-, *h*) 1. *v/t.* compose, write; 2. *v/i.* compose *or* write poetry; '2er *m* (-s/-) poet; author; '~erisch *adj.* poetic(al); '2kunst *f* poetry.

'**Dichtung[1]** ⊕ *f* (-/-en) seal(ing).

'**Dichtung[2]** *f* (-/-en) poetry; fiction; poem, poetic work.

dick *adj.* [dik] *wall*, *material*, etc.: thick; *book*: thick, bulky; *p.* fat, stout; '2e *f* (-/-n) thickness; bulkiness; *p.* fatness, stoutness; '2flüssig *adj. p.* thick-skinned; '~flüssig *adj.* thick; viscid, viscous, syrupy; 2**icht** ['~içt] *n* (-[e]s/-e) thicket; '2kopf *m* stubborn person, F pig-headed person; **~leibig** *adj.* ['~laɪbiç] corpulent; *fig.* bulky.

die [diː] *s.* der.

Dieb [diːp] *m* (-[e]s/-e) thief, *Am. F a.* crook; **~erei** [diːbəˈraɪ] *f* (-/-en) thieving, thievery.

Diebes|bande ['diːbəs-] *f* band of thieves; '**~gut** *n* stolen goods *pl.*

dieb|isch *adj.* ['diːbiʃ] thievish; *fig.* malicious; **2stahl** ['diːp-] *m* (-[e]s/ ~e) theft, ⚡ *mst* larceny.

Diele ['diːlə] *f* (-/-n) board, plank; hall, *Am. a.* hallway.

dienen ['diːnən] *v/i.* (ge-, *h*) serve (*j-m* s.o.; *als* as; *zu* for; *dazu, zu inf.* to *inf.*); *womit kann ich ~?* what can I do for you?

'**Diener** *m* (-s/-) (man-, domestic) servant; *fig.* bow (*vor dat.* to); '**~in** *f* (-/-nen) (woman-)servant; maid; '**~schaft** *f* (-/-en) servants *pl.*

'**dienlich** *adj.* useful, convenient; expedient, suitable.

Dienst [diːnst] *m* (-es/-e) service; duty; employment; *~ haben* be on duty; *im (außer) ~* on (off) duty.

Dienstag ['diːnstaːk] *m* (-[e]s/-e) Tuesday.

'**Dienst|alter** *n* seniority, length of service; '**2bar** *adj.* subject (*j-m* to s.o.); subservient (to); '**~bote** *m* domestic (servant), *Am.* help; '**2eifrig** *adj.* (over-)eager (in one's duty); '**2frei** *adj.* off duty; *~er Tag* day off; '**~herr** *m* master; employer; '**~leistung** *f* service; '**2lich** *adj.* official; '**~mädchen** *n* maid, *Am.* help; '**~mann** *m* (street-)porter; '**~stunden** *f/pl.* office hours *pl.*; '**2tauglich** *adj.* fit for service *or* duty; **2tuend** *adj.* ['~tuːənt] on duty; '**2untauglich** *adj.* unfit for service *or* duty; '**~weg** *m* official channels *pl.*; '**~wohnung** *f* official residence.

dies [diːs], **~er** ['diːzər], **~e** ['diːzə], **~es** ['diːzəs] *adj. and dem. pron.* this; *diese pl.* these; *dieser Tage* one of these days; *used as a noun:* this one; he, she, it; *diese pl.* they.

Dieselmotor ['diːzəl-] *m* Diesel engine.

dies|jährig *adj.* ['diːsjɛːriç] of this year, this year's; '**~mal** *adv.* this time; for (this) once; **~seits** ['~zaɪts] **1.** *adv.* on this side; **2.** *prp.* (*gen.*) on this side of.

Dietrich ['diːtriç] *m* (-s/-e) skeleton key; picklock.

Differenz [difə'rɛnts] *f* (-/-en) difference; disagreement.

Diktat [dik'taːt] *n* (-[e]s/-e) dictation; *nach ~* at *or* from dictation; **~or** [~ɔr] *m* (-s/-en) dictator; **2orisch** *adj.* [~a'toːriʃ] dictatorial; **~ur** [~a'tuːr] *f* (-/-en) dictatorship.

dik'tieren *v/t. and v/i.* (no -ge-, *h*) dictate.

Dilettant [dile'tant] *m* (-en/-en) dilettante, dabbler; amateur.

Ding [diŋ] *n* (-[e]s/-e) thing; *guter ~e* in good spirits; *vor allen ~en* first of all, above all.

Diphtherie 💊 [diftə'riː] *f* (-/-n) diphtheria.

Diplom [di'ploːm] *n* (-[e]s/-e) diploma, certificate.

Diplomat [diplo'maːt] *m* (-en/-en) diplomat; diplomatist; **~ie** [~a'tiː] *f* (-/no *pl.*) diplomacy; **2isch** *adj.* [~'maːtiʃ] diplomatic (*a. fig.*).

dir *pers. pron.* [diːr] (to) you.

direkt [di'rɛkt] **1.** *adj.* direct; **~er Wagen** 🚂 through carriage, *Am.* through car; **2.** *adv.* direct(ly); **2ion** [~'tsjoːn] *f* (-/-en) direction; management; board of directors; **2or** [di'rɛktɔr] *m* (-s/-en) director; manager; headmaster, *Am.* principal; **2orin** [~'toːrin] *f* (-/-nen) headmistress, *Am.* principal; **2rice** [~'triːs(ə)] *f* (-/-n) directress; manageress.

Dirig|ent [diri'gɛnt] *m* (-en/-en) conductor; **2ieren** 🎵 [~'giːrən] *v/t. and v/i.* (no -ge-, *h*) conduct.

Dirne ['dirnə] *f* (-/-n) prostitute.

Disharmon|ie 🎵 [disharmo'niː] *f* (-/-n) disharmony, dissonance (*both a. fig.*); **2isch** *adj.* [~'moːniʃ] discordant, dissonant.

Diskont 💰 [dis'kɔnt] *m* (-s/-e) discount; **2ieren** [~'tiːrən] *v/t.* (no -ge-, *h*) discount.

diskret *adj.* [dis'kreːt] discreet; **2ion** [~e'tsjoːn] *f* (-/no *pl.*) discretion.

Disku|ssion [disku'sjoːn] *f* (-/-en) discussion, debate; **2'tieren** (no -ge-, *h*) **1.** *v/t.* discuss, debate; **2.** *v/i.: ~ über* (*acc.*) have a discussion about, debate (up)on.

dispo|nieren [dispo'niːrən] *v/i.* (no -ge-, *h*) make arrangements; plan ahead; dispose (*über acc.* of); **2si-tion** [~zi'tsjoːn] *f* (-/-en) disposition; arrangement; disposal.

Distanz [di'stants] *f* (-/-en) distance (*a. fig.*); **2ieren** [~'tsiːrən] *v/refl.* (no -ge-, *h*): *sich ~ von* dis(as)sociate o.s. from.

Distel 🌿 ['distəl] *f* (-/-n) thistle.

Distrikt [di'strikt] *m* (-[e]s/-e) district; region; area.

Disziplin [distsi'pliːn] *f* (-/-en) discipline.

Divid|ende 💰 [divi'dendə] *f* (-/-n) dividend; **2ieren** [~'diːrən] *v/t.* (no -ge-, *h*) divide (*durch* by).

Diwan ['diːvaːn] *m* (-s/-e) divan.

doch [dɔx] **1.** *cj.* but, though; however, yet; **2.** *adv. in answer to negative question:* yes; *bist du noch nicht fertig? — ~!* aren't you ready yet? — yes, I am; *also ~!* I knew it!, I was right after all!; *komm ~ herein!* do come in!; *nicht ~!* don't!

Docht [dɔxt] *m* (-[e]s/-e) wick.

Dock ⚓ [dɔk] *n* (-[e]s/-s) dock.

Dogge *zo.* ['dɔgə] *f* (-/-n) Great Dane.

Dohle *orn.* ['doːlə] *f* (-/-n) (jack)daw.

Doktor ['dɔktɔr] *m* (-s/-en) doctor.

Dokument [doku'mɛnt] *n* (-[e]s/-e)

document; 초초 instrument; ~arfilm [~'ta:r-] *m* documentary (film).

Dolch [dɔlç] *m* (-[e]s/-e) dagger; poniard; '~stoß *m* dagger-thrust.

Dollar ['dɔlar] *m* (-s/-s) dollar.

dolmetsch|en ['dɔlmetʃən] *v/i. and v/t.* (ge-, h) interpret; '2er *m* (-s/-) interpreter.

Dom [do:m] *m* (-[e]s/-e) cathedral.

Domäne [do'mɛːnə] *f* (-/-n) domain (*a. fig.*); province.

Domino ['do:mino] (-s/-s) **1.** *m* domino; **2.** *n* (game of) dominoes *pl.*

Donner ['dɔnər] *m* (-s/-) thunder; '2n *v/i.* (ge-, h) thunder (*a. fig.*); '~schlag *m* thunderclap (*a. fig.*); '~stag *m* Thursday; '~wetter *n* thunderstorm; F *fig.* telling off; F: ~! my word!, by Jove!; F zum ~! F confound it!, *sl.* damn it!

Doppel ['dɔpəl] *n* (-s/-) duplicate; *tennis, etc.*: double, *Am.* doubles *pl.*; '~bett *n* double bed; '~decker *m* (-s/-) biplane; double-decker (bus); '~ehe *f* bigamy; ~gänger ['~gɛnər] *m* (-s/-) double; '~punkt *m* colon; '~sinn *m* double meaning, ambiguity; '2sinnig *adj.* ambiguous, equivocal; '~stecker *ɇ m* two-way adapter; '2t **1.** *adj.* double; **2.** *adv.* doubly; twice; '~zentner *m* quintal; 2züngig *adj.* ['~tsyŋɪç] two-faced.

Dorf [dɔrf] *n* (-[e]s/=er) village; '~bewohner *m* villager.

Dorn [dɔrn] *m* **1.** (-[e]s/-en) thorn (*a. fig.*), prickle, spine; *j-m ein ~ im Auge sein* be a thorn in s.o.'s flesh or side; **2.** (-[e]s/-e) tongue (*of buckle*); spike (*of running-shoe, etc.*); ⊕ punch; '2ig *adj.* thorny (*a. fig.*).

dörr|en ['dœrən] *v/t.* (ge-, h) dry; '2fleisch *n* dried meat; '2gemüse *n* dried vegetables *pl.*; '2obst *n* dried fruit.

Dorsch *ichth.* [dɔrʃ] *m* (-es/-e) cod(fish).

dort *adv.* [dɔrt] there; over there; '~her *adv.* from there; '~hin *adv.* there, to that place; '~ig *adj.* there, in or of that place.

Dose ['do:zə] *f* (-/-n) box; tin, *Am.* can; ~nöffner ['do:zən?-] *m* (-s/-) tin-opener, *Am.* can opener.

Dosis ['do:zis] *f* (-/Dosen) dose (*a. fig.*).

dotieren [do'ti:rən] *v/t.* (no -ge-, h) endow.

Dotter ['dɔtər] *m, n* (-s/-) yolk.

Dozent [do'tsɛnt] *m* (-en/-en) (university) lecturer, *Am.* assistant professor.

Drache ['draxə] *m* (-n/-n) dragon; '~n *m* (-s/-) kite; *fig.* termagant, shrew, battle-axe.

Dragoner [dra'go:nər] *m* (-s/-) ✗ dragoon (*a. fig.*).

Draht [dra:t] *m* (-[e]s/=e) wire; '2en

v/t. (ge-, h) telegraph, wire; '~geflecht *n* (-[e]s/-e) wire netting; '~hindernis ✗ *n* wire entanglement; '2ig *adj. p.* wiry; '2los *adj.* wireless; '~seilbahn *f* funicular (railway); '~stift *m* wire tack; '~zieher F *fig. m* (-s/-) wire-puller.

drall *adj.* [dral] *girl, legs, etc.*: plump; *woman*: buxom.

Drama ['dra:ma] *n* (-s/Dramen) drama; ~tiker [dra'ma:tikər] *m* (-s/-) dramatist; 2tisch *adj.* [dra-'ma:tiʃ] dramatic.

dran F *adv.* [dran] *s. daran; er ist gut (übel)* ~ he's well (badly) off; *ich bin* ~ it's my turn.

Drang [draŋ] **1.** *m* (-[e]s/✗ -e) pressure, rush; *fig.* urge; **2.** 2 *pret. of dringen.*

drängen ['drɛŋən] (ge-, h) **1.** *v/t.* press (*a. fig.*), push; *fig.* urge; *creditor:* dun; *sich* ~ crowd, throng; **2.** *v/i.* press, be pressing or urgent.

drangsalieren [draŋza'li:rən] *v/t.* (no -ge-, h) harass, vex, plague.

drastisch *adj.* ['drastiʃ] drastic.

drauf F *adv.* [drauf] *s. darauf;* ~ *und dran sein zu inf.* be on the point of *ger.*; 2gänger ['~gɛŋər] *m* (-s/-) dare-devil, *Am. sl. a.* go-getter.

draus F *adv.* [draus] *s. daraus.*

draußen F *adv.* ['drausən] outside; out of doors; abroad; out at sea.

drechs|eln ['drɛksəln] *v/t.* (ge-, h) turn (*wood, etc.*); 2ler ['~slər] *m* (-s/-) turner.

Dreck F [drɛk] *m* (-[e]s/*no pl.*) dirt; mud; filth (*a. fig.*); *fig.* trash; F ~ *am Stecken haben* not to have a clean slate; F *das geht dich einen* ~ *an* that's none of your business; '2ig *adj.* dirty; filthy.

Dreh|bank ['dre:-] *f* (-/=e) (turning-) lathe; '2bar *adj.* revolving, rotating; '~bleistift *m* propelling pencil; '~buch *n* scenario, script; '~bühne *thea. f* revolving stage; '2en (ge-, h) turn; shoot (*film*); roll (*cigarette*); *es dreht sich darum zu inf.* it is a matter of *ger.*; *sich* ~ turn; '~kreuz *n* turnstile; '~orgel *f* barrel-organ; '~punkt *m* ⊕ centre of rotation, *Am.* center of rotation, pivot (*a. fig.*); '~strom *ɇ m* three-phase current; '~stuhl *m* swivel-chair; '~tür *f* revolving door; '~ung *f* (-/-en) turn; rotation.

drei *adj.* [drai] three; '~beinig *adj.* three-legged; '2eck *n* triangle; '~eckig *adj.* triangular; '~erlei *adj.* ['~ər'lai] of three kinds or sorts; '~fach *adj.* ['~fax] threefold, treble, triple; '~farbig *adj.* three-col-o(u)r(ed); '2fuß *m* tripod; '~jährig *adj.* ['~jɛːrɪç] three-year-old; trien-nial; '~mal *adv.* three or repeated three times; three; 2'meilenzone ⊕, 초초 *f* three-mile limit; '2rad *n* tricycle;

'**„seitig** adj. three-sided; trilateral; '**„silbig** adj. trisyllabic.

dreißig ['draɪsɪç] thirty; '**„ste** adj. thirtieth.

dreist adj. [draɪst] bold, audacious; cheeky, saucy; **Qigkeit** f (-/-en) boldness, audacity; cheek, sauciness.

'**drei|stimmig** ♪ adj. for or in three-voices; '**„tägig** adj. ['„tɛːgɪç] three-day; '**„teilig** adj. in three parts, tripartite; '**„zehn(te)** adj. thirteen(th).

dresch|en ['drɛʃən] v/t. and v/i. (irr., ge-, h) thresh; thrash; '**Qflegel** m flail; '**Qmaschine** f threshing-machine.

dressieren [drɛˈsiːrən] v/t. (no -ge-, h) train; break in (horse).

drillen ⚔, ✍ ['drɪlən] v/t. (ge-, h) drill.

Drillinge ['drɪlɪŋə] m/pl. triplets pl.

drin F adv. [drɪn] s. darin.

dringen ['drɪŋən] v/i. (irr., ge-) 1. (sein): ~ durch force one's way through s.th., penetrate or pierce s.th.; ~ aus break forth from s.th.; noise: come from; ~ in (acc.) penetrate into; in j-n ~ urge or press s.o.; an die Öffentlichkeit ~ get abroad; 2. (h): ~ auf (acc.) insist on, press for; '**„d** adj. urgent, pressing; suspicion: strong.

'**dringlich** adj. urgent, pressing; '**Qkeit** f (-/no pl.) urgency.

drinnen adv. ['drɪnən] inside; indoors.

dritt|e adj. ['drɪtə] third; '**Qel** n (-s/-) third; '**„ens** adv. thirdly; '**„letzt** adj. last but two.

Drog|e ['droːgə] f (-/-n) drug; **„erie** [drogəˈriː] f (-/-n) chemist's (shop), Am. drugstore; **„ist** [droˈgɪst] m (-en/-en) (retail pharmaceutical) chemist.

drohen ['droːən] v/i. (ge-, h) threaten, menace.

Drohne ['droːnə] f (-/-n) zo. drone (a. fig.).

dröhnen ['drøːnən] v/i. (ge-, h) voice, etc.: resound; cannon, drum, etc.: roar; voice, cannon: boom.

Drohung ['droːuŋ] f (-/-en) threat, menace.

drollig adj. ['drɔlɪç] amusing, quaint, comical.

Dromedar zo. [dromeˈdaːr] n (-s/-e) dromedary.

drosch [drɔʃ] pret. of dreschen.

Droschke ['drɔʃkə] f (-/-n) taxi (-cab), Am. a. cab, hack; **„nkutscher** m cabman, driver, Am. a. hackman.

Drossel orn. ['drɔsəl] f (-/-n) thrush; '**Qn** ⊕ v/t. (ge-, h) throttle.

drüben adv. ['dryːbən] over there, yonder.

drüber F adv. ['dryːbər] s. darüber.

Druck [druk] m 1. (-[e]s/e) pres-

---

sure; squeeze (of hand, etc.); 2. typ. (-[e]s/-e) print(ing); '**„bogen** m printed sheet; '**„buchstabe** m block letter.

drucken ['drukən] v/t. (ge-, h) print; ~ lassen have s.th. printed, publish.

drücken ['drykən] (ge-, h) 1. v/t. press; squeeze (hand, etc.); force down (prices, wages, etc.); lower (record); press, push (button, etc.); F sich ~ vor (dat.) or von shirk (work, etc.); 2. v/i. shoe: pinch.

'**Drucker** m (-s/-) printer.

'**Drücker** m (-s/-) door-handle; trigger.

Drucker|ei [drukəˈraɪ] f (-/-en) printing office, Am. printery, print shop; '**„schwärze** f printer's or printing-ink.

'**Druck|fehler** m misprint; '**„fehlerverzeichnis** n errata pl.; '**Qfertig** adj. ready for press; '**„kammer** f pressurized cabin; '**„knopf** m patent fastener, snap-fastener; ⚡ push-button; '**„luft** f compressed air; '**„pumpe** f pressure pump; '**„sache** (n pl.) & f printed matter, Am. a. second-class or third-class matter; '**„schrift** f block letters; publication; '**„taste** f press key.

drum F adv., cj. [drum] s. darum.

drunter F adv. ['druntər] s. darunter.

Drüse anat. ['dryːzə] f (-/-n) gland.

du pers. pron. [duː] you.

Dublette [duˈblɛtə] f (-/-n) duplicate.

ducken ['dukən] v/refl. (ge-, h) duck, crouch; fig. cringe (vor dat. to, before).

Dudelsack ♪ ['duːdəl-] m bagpipes pl.

Duell [duˈɛl] n (-s/-e) duel; **Qieren** [dueˈliːrən] v/refl. (no -ge-, h) (fight a) duel (mit with).

Duett ♪ [duˈɛt] n (-[e]s/-e) duet.

Duft [duft] m (-[e]s/e) scent, fragrance, perfume; '**Qen** v/i. (ge-, h) smell, have a scent, be fragrant; '**Qend** adj. fragrant; '**Qig** adj. dainty, fragrant.

duld|en ['duldən] (ge-, h) 1. v/t. bear, stand, endure, suffer (pain, grief, etc.); tolerate, put up with; 2. v/i. suffer; '**„sam** adj. ['„t-] tolerant; '**Qsamkeit** f (-/no pl.) tolerance; **Qung** ['„duŋ] f (-/-en) toleration; sufferance.

dumm adj. [dum] stupid, dull, Am. F dumb; '**Qheit** f (-/-en) stupidity, dullness; stupid or foolish action; '**Qkopf** m fool, blockhead, Am. sl. a. dumbbell.

dumpf adj. [dumpf] smell, air, etc.: musty, fusty; atmosphere: stuffy, heavy; sound, sensation, etc.: dull; '**Qig** adj. cellar, etc.: damp, musty.

Düne ['dyːnə] f (-/-n) dune, sandhill.

Dung [duŋ] m (-[e]s/no pl.) dung, manure.

dünge|n ['dyŋən] v/t. (ge-, h) dung, manure; fertilize; '2r m (-s/-) s. Dung; fertilizer.

dunkel ['duŋkəl] 1. adj. dark; dim; fig. obscure; idea, etc.: dim, faint, vague; 2. 2 n (-s/no pl.) s. Dunkelheit.

Dünkel ['dyŋkəl] m (-s/no pl.) conceit, arrogance; '2haft adj. conceited, arrogant.

'**Dunkel|heit** f (-/no pl.) darkness (a. fig.); fig. obscurity; '~kammer phot. f dark-room; '2n v/i. (ge-, h) grow dark, darken.

dünn adj. [dyn] paper, material, voice, etc.: thin; hair, population, etc.: thin, sparse; liquid: thin, watery; air: rare(fied).

Dunst [dunst] m (-es/=e) vapo(u)r; haze, mist; fume.

dünsten ['dynstən] (ge-, h) 1. v/t. steam (fish, etc.); stew (fruit, etc.); 2. v/i. steam.

'**dunstig** adj. vaporous; hazy.

Duplikat [dupli'ka:t] n (-[e]s/-e) duplicate.

Dur ♪ [du:r] n (-/-) major.

durch [durç] 1. prp. (acc.) through; 2. adv.: die ganze Nacht ~ all night long; ~ und ~ through and through; thoroughly.

durcharbeiten ['durç?-] (sep., -ge-, h) 1. v/t. study thoroughly; sich ~ durch work through (book, etc.); 2. v/i. work without a break.

durch'aus adv. through and through; thoroughly; by all means; absolutely, quite; ~ nicht not at all, by no means.

'**durch|biegen** v/t. (irr. biegen, sep., -ge-, h) bend; deflect (beam, etc.); sich ~ beam, etc.: deflect, sag; '~blättern v/t. (sep., -ge-, h) glance or skim through (book, etc.), Am. thumb through, skim; '2blick m: ~ auf (acc.) view through to, vista over, view of; '~blicken v/i. (sep. -ge-, h) look through; ~ lassen, daß give to understand that.

durch|'bluten v/t. (no -ge-, h) supply with blood; ~'bohren v/t. (no -ge-, h) pierce, perforate; mit Blicken ~ look daggers at s.o.

'**durch|braten** v/t. (irr. braten, sep., -ge-, h) roast thoroughly; ~brechen (irr. brechen) 1. ['~brɛçən] v/i. (sep., -ge-, sein) break through or apart; 2. ['~] v/t. (sep., -ge-, h) break apart or in two; 3. [~'brɛçən] v/t. (no -ge-, h) break through, breach; run (blockade); crash (sound barrier); '~brennen v/i. (irr. brennen, sep., -ge-, sein) ∮ fuse; blow; F fig. run away; woman: elope; '~bringen v/t. (irr. bringen, sep., -ge-, h) bring or get through; dissipate, squander (money); '2bruch m ✂ break-

through; rupture; breach; fig. ultimate success.

durch'denken v/t. (irr. denken, no -ge-, h) think s.th. over thoroughly.

'**durch|drängen** v/refl. (sep., -ge-, h) force or push one's way through; ~dringen (irr. dringen) 1. ['~driŋən] v/i. (sep., -ge-, sein) penetrate (through); win acceptance (mit for) (proposal); 2. [~'driŋən] v/t. (no -ge-, h) penetrate, pierce; water, smell, etc.: permeate.

durcheinander [durç?aı'nandər] 1. adv. in confusion or disorder; pell-mell; 2. 2 n (-s/-) muddle, mess, confusion; ~bringen v/t. (irr. bringen, sep., -ge-, h) confuse s.o.; fig. mix (things) up; ~werfen v/t. (irr. werfen, sep., -ge-, h) throw into disorder; fig. mix up.

durchfahr|en (irr. fahren) 1. ['~fa:-rən] v/i. (sep., -ge-, sein) go or pass or drive through; 2. [~'fa:rən] v/t. (no -ge-, h) go or pass or travel or drive through; traverse (tract of country, etc.); '2t f passage (through); gate(way); ~ verboten! no thoroughfare!

'**Durchfall** m ✍ diarrh(o)ea; F fig. failure, Am. a. flunk; 2en (irr. fallen) 1. ['~falən] v/i. (sep., -ge-, sein) fall through; fail, F get ploughed (in examination); thea. be a failure, sl. be a flop; ~ lassen reject, F plough; 2. [~'falən] v/t. (no -ge-, h) fall or drop through (space).

'**durch|fechten** v/t. (irr. fechten, sep., -ge-, h) fight or see s.th. through; '~finden v/refl. (irr. finden, sep., -ge-, h) find one's way (through).

durch|'flechten v/t. (irr. flechten, no -ge-, h) interweave, intertwine; ~'forschen v/t. (no -ge-, h) search through, investigate; explore (region, etc.).

'**Durchfuhr** † f (-/-en) transit.

durchführ|bar adj. ['durçfy:rba:r] practicable, feasible, workable; '2en v/t. (sep., -ge-, h) lead or take through or across; fig. carry out or through; realize; '2ungsbestimmung f (implementing) regulation.

'**Durchgang** m passage; † transit; sports: run; '~sverkehr m through traffic; † transit traffic; '~szoll m transit duty.

'**durchgebraten** adj. well done.

'**durchgehen** (irr. gehen, sep., -ge-) 1. v/i. (sein) go or walk through; bill: pass, be carried; run away or off; abscond; woman: elope; horse: bolt; 2. v/t. (sein) go through (street, etc.); 3. v/t. (h, sein) go or look or read through (work, book, etc.); '~d 1. adj. continuous; ~er Zug through train; 2. adv. generally; throughout.

durch'geistigt adj. spiritual.

'**durch|greifen** v/i. (irr. greifen,

sep., -ge-, *h*) put one's hand through; *fig.* take drastic measures or steps; '**~greifend** *adj.* drastic; radical, sweeping; '**~halten** (*irr. halten, sep.*, -ge-, *h*) keep up (*pace, etc.*); 2. *v/i.* hold out; '**~hauen** *v/t.* (*irr. hauen, sep.*, -ge-, *h*) cut or chop through; *fig.* give *s.o.* a good hiding; '**~helfen** *v/i.* (*irr. helfen, sep.*, -ge-, *h*) help through (*a. fig.*); '**~kämpfen** *v/t.* (*sep.*, -ge-, *h*) fight out; sich **~** fight one's way through; '**~kneten** *v/t.* (*sep.*, -ge-, *h*) knead or work thoroughly; '**~kommen** *v/i.* (*irr. kommen, sep.*, -ge-, *sein*) come or get or pass through; *sick person:* pull through; *in examination:* pass.

durch'kreuzen *v/t.* (*no* -ge-, *h*) cross, foil, thwart (*plan, etc.*).

Durch'laß ['durçlas] *m* (*Durchlasses/Durchlässe*) passage; '**Qlassen** *v/t.* (*irr. lassen, sep.*, -ge-, *h*) let pass, allow to pass, let through; *Wasser* **~** leak; '**Qlässig** *adj.* pervious (to), permeable (to); leaky.

durchlaufen (*irr. laufen*) 1. ['~laufən] *v/i.* (*sep.*, -ge-, *sein*) run or pass through; 2. ['~] *v/t.* (*sep.*, -ge-, *h*) wear out (*shoes, etc.*); 3. [~'laufən] *v/t.* (*no* -ge-, *h*) pass through (*stages, departments, etc.*); *sports:* cover (*distance*).

durch'leben *v/t.* (*no* -ge-, *h*) go or live through.

'**durchlesen** *v/t.* (*irr. lesen, sep.*, -ge-, *h*) read through.

durchleuchten (*h*) 1. ['~lɔyçtən] *v/i.* (*sep.*, -ge-) shine through; 2. [~'lɔyçtən] *v/t.* (*no* -ge-) 💀 X-ray; *fig.* investigate.

durchlöchern [durç'lœçərn] *v/t.* (*no* -ge-, *h*) perforate, make holes into *s.th.*

'**durchmachen** *v/t.* (*sep.*, -ge-, *h*) go through (*difficult times, etc.*); undergo (*suffering*).

'**Durchmarsch** *m* march(ing) through.

'**Durchmesser** *m* (-s/-) diameter.

durch'nässen *v/t.* (*no* -ge-, *h*) wet through, soak, drench.

'**durchnehmen** *v/t.* (*irr. nehmen, sep.*, -ge-, *h*) go through or over (*subject*); '**~pausen** *v/t.* (*sep.*, -ge-, *h*) trace, calk (*design, etc.*).

durchqueren [durç'kve:rən] *v/t.* (*no* -ge-, *h*) cross, traverse.

'**durchrechnen** *v/t.* (*sep.*, -ge-, *h*) (re)calculate, check; '**Qreise** *f* journey or way through; '**~reisen** 1. ['~raizən] *v/i.* (*sep.*, -ge-, *sein*) travel or pass through; 2. [~'raizən] *v/t.* (*no* -ge-, *h*) travel over or through or across; '**Qreisende** *m, f* (-n/-n) person travel(l)ing through, *Am. a.* transient; 💀 through passenger; '**~reißen** (*irr. reißen, sep.*, -ge-) 1. *v/i.* (*sein*) tear, break; 2. *v/t.* (*h*) tear

asunder, tear in two; **~schauen** (*h*) 1. ['~fauən] *v/i.* and *v/t.* (*sep.*, -ge-) look through; 2. *fig.* [~'fauən] *v/t.* (*no* -ge-) see through.

'**durchscheinen** *v/i.* (*irr. scheinen, sep.*, -ge-, *h*) shine through; '**~d** *adj.* translucent; transparent.

'**durchscheuern** *v/t.* (*sep.*, -ge-, *h*) rub through; **~schießen** (*irr. schießen*) 1. ['~fi:sən] *v/i.* (*sep.*, -ge-, *h*) shoot through; 2. ['~] *v/i.* (*sep.*, -ge-, *sein*) *water:* shoot or race through; 3. [~'fi:sən] *v/t.* (*no* -ge-, *h*) shoot *s.th.* through; *typ.* space out (*lines*); interleave (*book*).

'**Durchschlag** *m* colander, strainer; carbon copy; **Qen** (*irr. schlagen*) 1. ['~fla:gən] *v/t.* (*sep.*, -ge-, *h*) break or pass through; strain (*peas, etc.*); *sich* **~** get along, make one's way; 2. ['~] *v/i.* (*sep.*, -ge-, *h*) *typ.* come through; take or have effect; 3. [~'fla:gən] *v/t.* (*no* -ge-, *h*) pierce; *bullet:* penetrate; '**Qend** *adj.* effective, telling; **~papier** ['~k-] *n* copying paper.

durchschneiden *v/t.* (*irr. schneiden, h*) 1. ['~fnaidən] (*sep.*, -ge-) cut through; 2. [~'fnaidən] (*no* -ge-) cut through, cut in two.

'**Durchschnitt** *m* cutting through; ⊕ section, profile; 📐 intersection; *fig.* average; *im* **~** on an average; '**Qlich** 1. *adj.* average; normal; 2. *adv.* on an average; normally; '**~swert** *m* average value.

'**durchsehen** (*irr. sehen, sep.*, -ge-, *h*) 1. *v/i.* see or look through; 2. *v/t.* see or look through *s.th.*; look *s.th.* over, go over *s.th.*; '**~seihen** *v/t.* (*sep.*, -ge-, *h*) filter, strain; **~setzen** *v/t.* (*h*) 1. ['~zetsən] (*sep.*, -ge-) put (*plan, etc.*) through; force through; *seinen Kopf* **~** have one's way; *sich* **~** *opinion, etc.*: gain acceptance; 2. [~'zetsən] (*no* -ge-) intersperse.

'**Durchsicht** *f* looking through or over; examination; correction; *typ.* reading; '**Qig** *adj.* glass, water, etc.: transparent; *fig.* clear, lucid; '**~igkeit** *f* (-/no pl.) transparency; *fig.* clarity, lucidity.

'**durchsickern** *v/i.* (*sep.*, -ge-, *sein*) seep or ooze through; *news, etc.*: leak out; **~sieben** *v/t.* (*h*) 1. ['~zi:bən] (*sep.*, -ge-) sieve, sift; bolt (*flour*); 2. [~'zi:bən] (*no* -ge-) riddle (*with bullets*); '**~sprechen** *v/t.* (*irr. sprechen, sep.*, -ge-, *h*) discuss, talk over; **~stechen** *v/t.* (*irr. stechen, h*) 1. ['~fteçən] (*sep.*, -ge-) stick (*needle, etc.*) through *s.th.*; stick through *s.th.*; 2. [~'fteçən] (*no* -ge-) pierce; cut through (*dike, etc.*); '**~stecken** *v/t.* (*sep.*, -ge-, *h*) pass or stick through.

'**Durchstich** *m* cut(ting).

durch'stöbern *v/t.* (*no* -ge-, *h*) ransack (*room, pockets, etc.*); rummage through (*drawers, papers, etc.*).

'durchstreichen *v/t.* (*irr. streichen, sep., -ge-. h*) strike *or* cross out, cancel.

durch'streifen *v/t.* (*no -ge-, h*) roam *or* wander through *or* over *or* across.

durch'such|en *v/t.* (*no -ge-, h*) search (*a.* 🕱); **2ung** *f* (*-/-en*) search.

durchtrieben *adj.* ['durç'tri:bən] cunning, artful; **2heit** *f* (*-/no pl.*) cunning, artfulness.

durch'wachen *v/t.* (*no -ge-, h*) pass (*the night*) waking.

durch'wachsen *adj.* bacon: streaky.

durchwandern 1. ['⁓vandərn] *v/i.* (*sep., -ge-, sein*) walk *or* pass through; **2.** [⁓'vandərn] *v/t.* (*no -ge-, h*) walk *or* pass through (*place, area, etc.*).

durch'weben *v/t.* (*no -ge-, h*) interweave; *fig. a.* intersperse.

durchweg *adv.* ['durçvɛk] throughout, without exception.

durch'weich|en 1. ['⁓vaiçən] *v/i.* (*sep., -ge-, sein*) soak; **2.** [⁓'vaiçən] *v/t.* (*no -ge-, h*) soak, drench; '⁓**winden** *v/refl.* (*irr. winden, sep., -ge-, h*) worm *or* thread one's way through; ⁓**wühlen** (*h*) **1.** *fig.* ['⁓vy:lən] *v/refl.* (*sep., -ge-*) work one's way through; **2.** [⁓'vy:lən] *v/t.* (*no -ge-*) rummage; '⁓**zählen** *v/t.* (*sep., -ge-, h*) count; ⁓**ziehen** (*irr. ziehen*) **1.** ['⁓tsi:ən] *v/i.* (*sep., -ge-, sein*) pass *or* go *or* come *or* march through; **2.** ['⁓] *v/t.* (*sep., -ge-, h*) pull (*thread, etc.*) through; **3.** [⁓'tsi:ən] *v/t.* (*no -ge-, h*) go *or* travel through; *scent, etc.*: fill, pervade (*room, etc.*).

durch'zucken *v/t.* (*no -ge-, h*) flash through.

'Durchzug *m* passage through; draught, *Am.* draft.

'durchzwängen *v/refl.* (*sep., -ge-, h*) squeeze o.s. through.

dürfen ['dyrfən] (*irr., h*) **1.** *v/i.* (*ge-*): *ich darf* (*nicht*) I am (not) allowed to; **2.** *v/aux.* (*no -ge-*): *ich darf inf.* I am permitted *or* allowed to *inf.*; I may *inf.*; *du darfst nicht inf.* you must not *inf.*; *iro.*: *wenn ich bitten darf* if you please.

durfte ['durftə] *pret. of* dürfen.

dürftig *adj.* ['dyrftiç] poor; scanty.

dürr *adj.* [dyr] *wood, leaves, etc.*: dry; *land*: barren, arid; *p.* gaunt, lean, skinny; **2e** *f* (*-/-n*) dryness; barrenness; leanness.

Durst [durst] *m* (*-es/no pl.*) thirst (*nach* for); ⁓ **haben** be thirsty.

dürsten ['dyrstən] *v/i.* (*ge-, h*): ⁓ *nach* thirst for.

'durstig *adj.* thirsty (*nach* for).

Dusche ['duʃə] *f* (*-/-n*) shower (-bath); **2n** *v/refl. and v/i.* (*ge-, h*) have a shower(-bath).

Düse ['dy:zə] *f* (*-/-n*) ⊕ nozzle; 🛦 jet; ⁓**nantrieb** ['⁓nⁱ-] *m* jet propulsion; *mit* ⁓ jet-propelled; '⁓**nflugzeug** *n* jet(-propelled) aircraft, F jet; ⁓**njäger** 🛦 *m* jet fighter.

düster *adj.* ['dy:stər] dark, gloomy (*both a. fig.*); *light*: dim; *fig.*: sad; depressing; '**2heit** *f* (*-/no pl.*), '**2keit** *f* (*-/no pl.*) gloom(iness).

Dutzend ['dutsənt] *n* (*-s/-e*) dozen; *ein* ⁓ *Eier* a dozen eggs; ⁓*e von Leuten* dozens of people; '**2weise** *adv.* by the dozen, in dozens.

Dynam|ik [dy'na:mik] *f* (*-/no pl.*) dynamics; **2isch** *adj.* dynamic(al).

Dynamit [dyna'mi:t] *n* (*-s/no pl.*) dynamite.

Dynamo [dy'na:mo] *m* (*-s/-s*), ⁓**maschine** *f* dynamo, generator.

D-Zug ['de:tsu:k] *m* express train.

E

Ebbe ['ɛbə] *f* (*-/-n*) ebb(-tide); low tide; **2n** *v/i.* (*ge-, sein*) ebb.

eben ['e:bən] **1.** *adj.* even; plain, level; 🛦 plane; *zu* ⁓*er Erde* on the ground floor, *Am.* on the first floor; **2.** *adv.* exactly; just; ⁓ *erst* just now; '**2bild** *n* image, likeness; ⁓**bürtig** *adj.* ['⁓byrtiç] of equal birth; *j-m* ⁓ *sein* be a match for s.o., be s.o.'s equal; '⁓**da** *adv.*, '⁓**da'selbst** *adv.* at the very (same) place, just there; *quoting books*: ibidem (*abbr.* ib., ibid.); '⁓**der**, '⁓**die**, '⁓**das** *dem. pron.* = '⁓**derselbe**, '⁓**die'selbe**, '⁓**das'selbe** *dem. pron.* the very (same); '⁓

des'wegen *adv.* for that very reason.

Ebene ['e:bənə] *f* (*-/-n*) plain; 🛦 plane; *fig.* level.

'eben|erdig *adj. and adv.* at street level; on the ground floor, *Am.* on the first floor; '⁓**falls** *adv.* likewise; '**2holz** *n* ebony; '⁓**maß** *n* symmetry; harmony; regularity (*of features*); '⁓**mäßig** *adj.* symmetrical; harmonious; regular; '⁓**so** *adv.* just so; just as ...; likewise; '⁓**sosehr** *adv.*, '⁓**soviel** *adv.* just as much; '⁓**sowenig** *adv.* just as little *or* few (*pl.*), no more.

Eber *zo.* ['e:bər] *m* (-s/-) boar; '**~esche** ♀ *f* mountain-ash.

ebnen ['e:bnən] *v/t.* (ge-, *h*) level; *fig.* smooth.

Echo ['eço] *n* (-s/-s) echo.

echt *adj.* [eçt] genuine; true; pure; real; *colour:* fast; *document:* authentic; '**~heit** *f* (-/*no pl.*) genuineness; purity; reality; fastness; authenticity.

Eck [ɛk] *n* (-[e]s/-e) *s.* **Ecke;** '**~ball** *m sports:* corner-kick; '**~e** *f* (-/-n) corner; edge; *fig.* angular; *fig.* awkward; '**~platz** *m* corner-seat; '**~stein** *m* corner-stone; '**~zahn** *m* canine tooth.

edel *adj.* ['e:dəl] noble; *min.* precious; *organs of the body:* vital; '**~denkend** *adj.* noble-minded; '2**mann** *m* nobleman; '2**mut** *m* generosity; '**~mütig** *adj.* ['~my:tiç] noble-minded, generous; '2**stein** *m* precious stone; gem.

Edikt [e'dikt] *n* (-[e]s/-e) edict.

Efeu ♀ ['e:fɔy] *m* (-s/*no pl.*) ivy.

Effekt [e'fɛkt] *m* (-[e]s/-e) effect; **~en** *pl.* effects *pl.*; ♱: securities *pl.*; stocks *pl.*; **~enhandel** *m* dealing in stocks; **~hascherei** [~haʃə'raɪ] *f* (-/-en) claptrap; 2**iv** *adj.* [~'ti:v] effective; 2**uieren** [~u'i:rən] *v/t.* (*no -ge-, h*) effect; execute, *Am. a.* fill; 2**voll** *adj.* effective, striking.

egal *adj.* [e'ga:l] equal; *F* all the same.

Egge ['egə] *f* (-/-n) harrow; '2**n** *v/t.* (ge-, *h*) harrow.

Egois|mus [ego'ismus] *m* (-/*Egoismen*) ego(t)ism; **~t** *m* (-en/-en) ego(t)ist; 2**tisch** *adj.* selfish, ego(t)istic(al).

ehe[1] *cj.* ['e:ə] before.

Ehe[2] [~.] *f* (-/-n) marriage; matrimony; '**~anbahnung** *f* (-/-en) matrimonial agency; '**~brecher** *m* (-s/-) adulterer; '**~brecherin** *f* (-/-nen) adulteress; '2**brecherisch** *adj.* adulterous; '**~bruch** *m* adultery; '**~frau** *f* wife; '**~gatte** *m,* '**~gattin** *f* spouse; '**~leute** *pl.* married people *pl.*; '2**lich** *adj.* conjugal; *child:* legitimate; '**~losigkeit** *f* (-/*no pl.*) celibacy; single life.

ehemal|ig *adj.* ['e:əma:liç] former, ex-...; old; '**~s** *adv.* formerly.

'**Ehe|mann** *m* husband; '**~paar** *n* married couple.

'**eher** *adv.* sooner; rather; more likely; *je* **~,** *desto besser* the sooner the better.

'**Ehering** *m* wedding ring.

ehern *adj.* ['e:ərn] brazen, of brass.

'**Ehe|scheidung** *f* divorce; '**~schließung** *f* (-/-en) (contraction of) marriage; '**~stand** *m* (-[e]s/*no pl.*) married state, matrimony; '**~stifter** *m,* '**~stifterin** *f* (-/-nen) matchmaker; '**~vermittlung** *f s.* Eheanbahnung; '**~versprechen** *n* promise of mar-

riage; '**~vertrag** *m* marriage contract.

Ehrabschneider ['e:r⁹apʃnaɪdər] *m* (-s/-) slanderer.

'**ehrbar** *adj.* hono(u)rable, respectable; modest; '2**keit** *f* (-/*no pl.*) respectability; modesty.

Ehre ['e:rə] *f* (-/-n) hono(u)r; *zu* **~n** (*gen.*) in hono(u)r of; **~n** *v/t.* (ge-, *h*) hono(u)r; esteem.

'**ehren|amtlich** *adj.* honorary; '2**bürger** *m* honorary citizen; '2**doktor** *m* honorary doctor; '2**erklärung** *f* (full) apology; '2**gast** *m* guest of hono(u)r; '2**gericht** *n* court of hono(u)r; '**~haft** *adj.* hono(u)rable; '2**kodex** *m* code of hono(u)r; 2**legion** ['~legio:n] *f* (-/*no pl.*) Legion of Hono(u)r; '2**mann** *m* man of hono(u)r; '2**mitglied** *n* honorary member; '2**platz** *m* place of hono(u)r; '**~recht** *n: bürgerliche* **~e** *pl.* civil rights *pl.*; '2**rettung** *f* rehabilitation; '**~rührig** *adj.* defamatory; '2**sache** *f* affair of hono(u)r; point of hono(u)r; '**~voll** *adj.* hono(u)rable; '**~wert** *adj.* hono(u)rable; '2**wort** *n* (-[e]s/-e) word of hono(u)r.

ehr|erbietig *adj.* ['e:r⁹ɛrbi:tiç] respectful; 2**erbietung** *f* (-/-en) reverence; 2**furcht** *f* (-/*no pl.*) respect; awe; '**~furchtgebietend** *adj.* aweinspiring, awesome; **~fürchtig** *adj.* ['~fyrçtiç] respectful; '2**gefühl** *n* (-[e]s/*no pl.*) sense of hono(u)r; 2**geiz** *m* ambition; '**~geizig** *adj.* ambitious.

'**ehrlich** *adj.* honest; *commerce, game:* fair; *opinion:* candid; **~** *währt am längsten* honesty is the best policy; '2**keit** *f* (-/*no pl.*) honesty; fairness.

'**ehrlos** *adj.* dishono(u)rable, infamous; '2**igkeit** *f* (-/-en) dishonesty, infamy.

'**ehr|sam** *adj. s.* ehrbar; '2**ung** *f* (-/-en) hono(u)r (conferred on *s.o.*); '**~vergessen** *adj.* dishono(u)rable, infamous; '2**verlust** ♱♱ *m* (-es/*no pl.*) loss of civil rights; '**~würdig** *adj.* venerable, reverend.

ei[1] *int.* [aɪ] ah!, indeed!

Ei[2] [~.] *n* (-[e]s/-er) egg; *physiol.* ovum.

Eibe ♀ ['aɪbə] *f* (-/-n) yew(-tree).

Eiche ♀ ['aɪçə] *f* (-/-n) oak(-tree); **~l** ['~.] *f* (-/-n) ♀ acorn; *cards:* club; '**~häher** *orn.* ['~he:ər] *m* (-s/-) jay.

eichen[1] ['aɪçən] *v/t.* (ge-, *h*) ga(u)ge.

eichen[2] *adj.* [~.] oaken, of oak.

Eich|hörnchen *zo.* ['aɪçhœrnçən] *n* (-s/-) squirrel; '**~maß** *n* standard.

Eid [aɪt] *m* (-es/-e) oath; '2**brüchig** *adj.:* **~** *werden* break one's oath.

Eidechse *zo.* ['aɪdɛksə] *f* (-/-n) lizard.

eidesstattlich ♱♱ *adj.* ['~] in lieu of (an) oath; **~e** *Erklärung* statutory declaration.

'eidlich 1. *adj.* sworn; **2.** *adv.* on oath.

'Eidotter *m, n* yolk.

'Eier|kuchen *m* omelet(te), pancake; **⊾schale** *f* egg-shell; **⊾stock** *anat. m* ovary; **⊾uhr** *f* egg-timer.

Eifer ['aɪfər] *m* (-s/*no pl.*) zeal; eagerness; ardo(u)r; **⊾er** *m* (-s/-) zealot; **'⊾sucht** *f* (-/*no pl.*) jealousy; **'⊇süchtig** *adj.* jealous (*auf acc.* of).

eifrig *adj.* ['aɪfriç] zealous, eager; ardent.

eigen *adj.* ['aɪgən] own; particular; strange, odd; *in compounds*: ...-owned; peculiar (*dat.* to); **'⊇art** *f* peculiarity; **'⊾artig** *adj.* peculiar; singular; **⊇brötler** ['⊾brøːtlər] *m* (-s/-) odd *or* eccentric person, crank; **'⊇gewicht** *n* dead weight; **⊾händig** *adj. and adv.* ['⊾hɛndiç] with one's own hands; **'⊇heim** *n* house of one's own; homestead; **'⊇heit** *f* (-/-en) peculiarity; oddity; *of language*: idiom; **'⊇liebe** *f* self-love; **'⊇lob** *n* self-praise; **'⊾mächtig** *adj.* arbitrary; **'⊇name** *m* proper name; **⊾nützig** *adj.* ['⊾nytsiç] self-interested, selfish; **'⊾s** *adv.* expressly, specially; on purpose.

'Eigenschaft *f* (-/-en) quality (*of s.o.*); property (*of s.th.*); *in s-r ⊾ als* in his capacity as; **'⊾swort** *gr. n* (-[e]s/*⊾er*) adjective.

'Eigensinn *m* (-[e]s/*no pl.*) obstinacy; **⊇ig** *adj.* wil(l)ful, obstinate.

'eigentlich 1. *adj.* proper; actual; true, real; **2.** *adv.* properly (speaking).

'Eigentum *n* (-s/*⊾er*) property.

Eigentüm|er ['aɪgənty:mər] *m* (-s/-) owner, proprietor; **⊇lich** *adj.* peculiar; odd; **'⊾lichkeit** *f* (-/-en) peculiarity.

'Eigentums|recht *n* ownership; copyright; **'⊾wohnung** *f* freehold flat.

'eigenwillig *adj.* self-willed; *fig.* individual.

eign|en ['aɪgnən] *v/refl.* (ge-, h): *sich ⊾ für* be suited for; **'⊇ung** *f* (-/-en) aptitude, suitability.

'Eil|bote *☜ m* express messenger; *durch ⊾n* by special delivery; **'⊾brief** *☜ m* express letter, *Am.* special delivery letter.

Eile ['aɪlə] *f* (-/*no pl.*) haste, speed; hurry; **'⊇n** *v/i.* (ge-, sein) hasten, make haste; hurry; *letter, affair:* be urgent; **⊇nds** *adv.* ['⊾ts] quickly, speedily.

'Eil|fracht *f*, **'⊾gut** *n* express goods *pl., Am.* fast freight; **⊇ig** *adj.* hasty, speedy; urgent; *es ⊾ haben* be in a hurry.

Eimer ['aɪmər] *m* (-s/-) bucket, pail.

ein [aɪn] **1.** *adj.* one; **2.** *indef. art.* a, an.

einander *adv.* [aɪ'nandər] one another; each other.

ein|arbeiten ['aɪnʔ-] *v/t.* (sep., -ge-, h): *j-n ⊾ in* (*acc.*) make s.o. acquainted with; **⊾armig** *adj.* ['aɪnʔ-] one-armed; **⊾äschern** ['aɪnʔɛʃərn] *v/t.* (sep., -ge-, h) burn to ashes; cremate (*dead body*); **'⊇äscherung** *f* (-/-en) cremation; **⊾atmen** ['aɪnʔ-] *v/t.* (sep., -ge-, h) breathe, inhale; **⊾äugig** *adj.* ['aɪnʔɔygiç] one-eyed.

'Einbahnstraße *f* one-way street.

'einbalsamieren *v/t.* (sep., *no* -ge-, h) embalm.

'Einband *m* (-[e]s/*⊾e*) binding; cover.

'ein|bauen *v/t.* (sep., -ge-, h) build in; install (*engine, etc.*); **⊾behalten** *v/t.* (irr. halten, sep., no -ge-, h) detain; **⊾berufen** *v/t.* (irr. rufen, sep., no -ge-, h) convene; ✕ call up, *Am.* induct.

'einbett|en *v/t.* (sep., -ge-, h) embed; **'⊇zimmer** *n* single(-bedded) room.

'einbild|en *v/refl.* (sep., -ge-, h) fancy, imagine; **'⊇ung** *f* imagination, fancy; conceit.

'einbinden *v/t.* (irr. binden, sep., -ge-, h) bind (*books*).

'Einblick *m* insight (*in acc.* into).

'einbrechen *v/t.* (irr. brechen, sep., -ge-) **1.** *v/t.* (h) break open; **2.** *v/i.* (sein) break in; *of night, etc.*: set in; *⊾ in* (*acc.*) break into (*house*).

'Einbrecher *m at night*: burglar; *by day*: housebreaker.

'Einbruch *m* ✕ invasion; housebreaking, burglary; *bei ⊾ der Nacht* at nightfall; **'⊾(s)diebstahl** *m* house-breaking, burglary.

einbürger|n ['aɪnbyrgərn] *v/t.* (sep., -ge-, h) naturalize; **'⊇ung** *f* (-/-en) naturalization.

'Ein|buße *f* loss; **'⊇büßen** *v/t.* (sep., -ge-, h) lose, forfeit.

ein|dämmen ['aɪndɛmən] *v/t.* (sep., -ge-, h) dam (up); embank (*river*); *fig.* check; **'⊾deutig** *adj.* unequivocal; clear, plain.

'eindring|en *v/i.* (irr. dringen, sep., -ge-, sein) enter; penetrate; intrude; *⊾ in* (*acc.*) penetrate (into); force one's way into; invade (*country*); **'⊾lich** *adj.* urgent; **⊇ling** ['⊾liŋ] *m* (-s/-e) intruder; invader.

'Eindruck *m* (-[e]s/*⊾e*) impression.

'ein|drücken *v/t.* (sep., -ge-, h) press in; crush (in) (*hat*); break (*pane*); **'⊾drucksvoll** *adj.* impressive; **⊾engen** ['aɪnʔ-] *v/t.* (sep., -ge-, h) narrow; *fig.* limit.

ein|er¹ ['aɪnər], **'⊾e**, **'⊾(e)s** *indef. pron.* one.

Einer² [⊾] *m* (-s/-) *⅍* unit, digit; *rowing*: single sculler, skiff.

einerlei ['aɪnər'laɪ] **1.** *adj.* of the same kind; immaterial; *es ist mir ⊾* it is all the same to me; **2.** *⊇ n* (-s/*no pl.*) sameness; monotony; humdrum (*of one's existence*).

einerseits adv. ['aɪnər'zaɪts] on the one hand.

einfach adj. ['aɪnfax] simple; single; plain; *meal:* frugal; *ticket:* single, Am. one-way; '2heit f (-/no pl.) simplicity.

einfädeln ['aɪnfɛːdəln] v/t. (sep., -ge-, h) thread; fig. start, set on foot; contrive.

'Einfahrt f entrance, entry.

'Einfall m ⚔ invasion; idea, inspiration; '2en v/i. (irr. fallen, sep., -ge-, sein) fall in, collapse; break in (on a conversation), interrupt, cut short; chime in; ♪ join in; invade; j-m ~ occur to s.o.

Ein|falt ['aɪnfalt] f (-/no pl.) simplicity; silliness; '2fältig adj. ['~fɛltiç] simple; silly; '~faltspinsel m simpleton, Am. F sucker.

'ein|farbig adj. one-colo(u)red, unicolo(u)red; plain; '~fassen v/t. (sep., -ge-, h) border; set (precious stone); '2fassung f border; setting; '~fetten v/t. (sep., -ge-, h) grease; oil; '~finden v/refl. (irr. finden, sep., -ge-, h) appear; arrive; '~flechten fig. v/t. (irr. flechten, sep.,-ge-, h) put in, insert; '~fließen v/i. (irr. fließen, sep., -ge-, sein) flow in; ~ in (acc.) flow into; ~ lassen mention in passing; '~flößen v/t. (sep., -ge-, h) infuse.

'Einfluß m influx; fig. influence; '2reich adj. influential.

ein|förmig adj. ['aɪnfœrmiç] uniform; monotonous; '~frieden ['~friːdən] v/t. (sep., -ge-, h) fence, enclose; '2friedung f (-/-en) enclosure; '~frieren v/i. (irr. frieren, sep., -ge-) 1. v/i. (sein) freeze (in); 2. v/t. (h) freeze (food); '~fügen v/t. (sep., -ge-, h) put in; fig. insert; sich ~ fit in.

Einfuhr ✝ ['aɪnfuːr] f (-/-en) import(ation); '~bestimmungen f/pl. import regulations pl.

'einführen v/t. (sep., -ge-, h) ✝ import; introduce (s.o., custom); insert; initiate; install (s.o. in an office).

'Einfuhrwaren ✝ f/pl. imports pl.

'Eingabe f petition; application.

'Eingang m entrance; entry; arrival (of goods); nach ~ on receipt; '~sbuch ✝ n book of entries.

'eingeben v/t. (irr. geben, sep., -ge-, h) give, administer (medicine) (dat. to); prompt, suggest (to).

'einge|bildet adj. imaginary; conceited (auf acc. of); '~boren adj. native; '2borene m, f (-n/-n) native.

Eingebung ['aɪngeːbuŋ] f (-/-en) suggestion; inspiration.

'einge|denk adj. ['aɪngədeŋk] mindful (gen. of of); '~fallen adj. eyes, cheeks: sunken, hollow; emaciated; '~fleischt fig. adj. ['~gəflaɪʃt] in-

veterate; confirmed; '~er Junggeselle confirmed bachelor.

'eingehen (irr. gehen, sep., -ge-) 1. v/i. (sein) mail, goods: come in, arrive; ⚔, animal: die; cease (to exist); material: shrink; ~ auf (acc.) agree to; enter into; 2. v/t. (h, sein) enter into (relationship); contract (marriage); ein Risiko ~ run a risk, esp. Am. take a chance; e-n Vergleich ~ come to terms; Verbindlichkeiten ~ incur liabilities; e-e Wette ~ make a bet; eingegangene Gelder n/pl. receipts pl.; '~d adj. detailed; thorough; examination: close.

Eingemachte ['aɪngəmaxtə] n (-n/ no pl.) preserves pl.; pickles pl.

'eingemeinden v/t. (sep., no -ge-, h) incorporate (dat. into).

'einge|nommen adj. partial (für to); prejudiced (gegen against); von sich ~ conceited; '2sandt ✱ n (-s/-s) letter to the editor; '~schnappt F fig. adj. ['~gəʃnapt] offended, touchy; '~sessen adj. long-established; '2ständnis n confession, avowal; '~stehen v/t. (irr. stehen, sep., no -ge-, h) confess, avow.

Eingeweide anat. ['aɪngəvaɪdə] pl. viscera pl.; intestines pl.; bowels pl.; esp. of animals: entrails pl.

'einge|wöhnen v/refl. (sep., no -ge-, h) accustom o.s. (in acc. to); acclimatize o.s., Am. acclimate o.s. (to); get used (to).

eingewurzelt adj. ['~gəvurtsəlt] deep-rooted, inveterate.

'eingießen v/t. (irr. gießen, sep., -ge-, h) pour in or out.

eingleisig adj. ['aɪnglaɪziç] single-track.

'ein|graben v/t. (irr. graben, sep., -ge-, h) dig in; bury; engrave; sich ~ ⚔ dig o.s. in, entrench o.s.; fig. engrave itself (on one's memory); '~gravieren v/t. (sep., no -ge-, h) engrave.

'eingreifen 1. v/i. (irr. greifen, sep., -ge-, h) intervene; ~ in (acc.) interfere with; encroach on (s.o.'s rights); in die Debatte ~ join in the debate; 2. ⚙ n (-s/no pl.) intervention.

'Eingriff m fig. encroachment; ⚙ operation.

'einhaken v/t. (sep., -ge-, h) fasten; sich bei j-m ~ take s.o.'s arm.

'Einhalt m (-[e]s/no pl.): ~ gebieten (dat.) put a stop to; '2en (irr. halten, sep., -ge-, h) 1. v/t. observe, keep; 2. v/i. stop, leave off (zu tun doing).

'ein|hängen ([irr. hängen,] sep.,-ge-, h) 1. v/t. hang in; hang up, replace (receiver); sich bei j-m ~ take s.o.'s arm, link arms with s.o.; 2. teleph. v/i. hang up; '~heften v/t. (sep., -ge-, h) sew or stitch in.

'einheimisch adj. native (in dat.

to), indigenous (to) (*a.* ♀); ✗ endemic; *product:* home-grown; '**2e** *m, f* (-n/-n) native; resident.

'**Einheit** *f* (-/-en) unity; oneness; ♈, *phys.*, ✗ unit; '**2lich** *adj.* uniform; '**~spreis** *m* standard price.

'**einheizen** (*sep.*, -ge-, h) **1.** *v/i.* make a fire; **2.** *v/t.* heat (*stove*).

einhellig *adj.* ['aɪnhɛlɪç] unanimous.

'**einholen** (*sep.*, -ge-, h) **1.** *v/t.* catch up with, overtake; make up for (*lost time*); make (*inquiries*); take (*order*); seek (*advice*); ask for (*permission*); buy; **2.** *v/i.*: ~ gehen go shopping.

'**Einhorn** *zo. n* unicorn.

'**einhüllen** *v/t.* (*sep.*, -ge-, h) wrap (up *or* in); envelop.

einig *adj.* ['aɪnɪç] united; ~ sein agree; nicht ~ sein differ (*über acc.* about); **~e** *indef. pron.* ['~gə] several; some; **~en** ['~ɪgən] *v/t.* (*ge-*, h) unite; sich ~ come to terms; **~ermaßen** *adv.* ['~gərˈmaːsən] in some measure; somewhat; **~es** *indef. pron.* ['~gəs] some(thing); '**2keit** *f* (-/no pl.) unity; concord; **2ung** ['~g-] *f* (-/-en) union; agreement.

ein|impfen ['aɪn?-] *v/t.* (*sep.*, -ge-, h) ✗ inoculate (*a. fig.*); '**~jagen** *v/t.* (*sep.*, -ge-, h): j-m Furcht ~ scare s.o.

einjährig *adj.* ['aɪnjɛːrɪç] one-year-old; *esp.* ♀ annual; *animal:* yearling.

'**ein|kalkulieren** *v/t.* (*sep.*, no -ge-, h) take into account, allow for; '**~kassieren** *v/t.* (*sep.*, no -ge-, h) cash; collect.

'**Einkauf** *m* purchase; Einkäufe machen s. einkaufen 2; '**2en** (*sep.*, -ge-, h) **1.** *v/t.* buy, purchase; **2.** *v/i.* make purchases, go shopping.

'**Einkäufer** *m* buyer.

'**Einkaufs|netz** *n* string bag; '**~preis** ♈ *m* purchase price; '**~tasche** *f* shopping-bag.

'**ein|kehren** *v/i.* (*sep.*, -ge-, sein) put up *or* stop (at an inn); '**~kerben** *v/t.* (*sep.*, -ge-, h) notch; '**~kerkern** *v/t.* (*sep.*, -ge-, h) imprison; '**~klagen** *v/t.* (*sep.*, -ge-, h) sue for; '**~klammern** *v/t.* (*sep.*, -ge-, h) *typ.* bracket; put in brackets.

'**Einklang** *m* unison; harmony.

'**ein|kleiden** *v/t.* (*sep.*, -ge-, h) clothe; fit out; '**~klemmen** *v/t.* (*sep.*, -ge-, h) squeeze (in); jam; '**~klinken** (*sep.*, -ge-) **1.** *v/t.* (h) latch; **2.** *v/i.* (sein) latch; engage; '**~knicken** (*sep.*, -ge-) *v/t.* (h) and *v/i.* (sein) bend in, break; '**~kochen** (*sep.*, ge-) **1.** *v/t.* (h) preserve; **2.** *v/i.* (sein) boil down *or* away.

'**Einkommen** *n* (-s/-) income, revenue; '**~steuer** *f* income-tax.

'**einkreisen** *v/t.* (*sep.*, -ge-, h) encircle.

Einkünfte ['aɪnkynftə] *pl.* income, revenue.

'**einlad|en** *v/t.* (*irr.* laden, *sep.*, -ge-, h) load (in) (*goods*); *fig.* invite; '**2ung** *f* invitation.

'**Einlage** *f* enclosure (*in letter*); ♈ investment; deposit (*of money*); *gambling:* stake; inserted piece; ✗ arch-support; temporary filling (*of tooth*); '**2rn** ♈ *v/t.* (*sep.*, -ge-, h) store (up).

Einlaß ['aɪnlas] *m* (Einlasses/Einlässe) admission, admittance.

'**einlassen** *v/t.* (*irr.* lassen, *sep.*, -ge-, h) let in, admit; ~ in (*acc.*) ⊕ imbed in; sich ~ in *or* auf (*both acc.*) engage in, enter into.

'**ein|laufen** *v/i.* (*irr.* laufen, *sep.*, -ge-, sein) come in, arrive; *ship:* enter; *material:* shrink; '**~leben** *v/refl.* (*sep.*, -ge-, h) accustom o.s. (*in acc.* to).

'**einlege|n** *v/t.* (*sep.*, -ge-, h) lay *or* put in; insert; ⊕ inlay; deposit (*money*); pickle; preserve (*fruit*); Berufung ~ lodge an appeal (*bei* to); Ehre ~ mit gain hono(u)r *or* credit by; '**2sohle** *f* insole, sock.

'**einleit|en** *v/t.* (*sep.*, -ge-, h) start; introduce; '**~end** *adj.* introductory; '**2ung** *f* introduction.

'**ein|lenken** *fig. v/i.* (*sep.*, -ge-, h) come round; '**~leuchten** *v/i.* (*sep.*, -ge-, h) be evident *or* obvious; '**~liefern** *v/t.* (*sep.*, -ge-, h) deliver (up); *in ein Krankenhaus* ~ take to a hospital, *Am.* hospitalize; '**~lösen** *v/t.* (*sep.*, -ge-, h) ransom (*prisoner*); redeem (*pledge*); ♈ hono(u)r (*bill*); cash (*cheque*); ♈ meet (*bill*); '**~machen** *v/t.* (*sep.*, -ge-, h) preserve (*fruit*); tin, *Am.* can.

'**einmal** *adv.* once; one day; *auf* ~ all at once; es war ~ once (upon a time) there was; *nicht* ~ not even; '**2eins** *n* (-/-) multiplication table; '**~ig** *adj.* single; unique.

'**Einmarsch** *m* marching in, entry; '**2ieren** *v/i.* (*sep.*, no -ge-, sein) march in, enter.

'**ein|mengen** *v/refl.* (*sep.*, -ge-, h), '**~mischen** *v/refl.* (*sep.*, -ge-, h) meddle, interfere (*in acc.* with), *esp. Am. sl.* butt in.

'**Einmündung** *f* junction (*of roads*); mouth (*of river*).

einmütig *adj.* ['aɪnmyːtɪç] unanimous; '**2keit** *f* (-/no pl.) unanimity.

Einnahme ['aɪnnɑːmə] *f* (-/-n) ✗ taking, capture; *mst* **~n** *pl.* takings *pl.*, receipts *pl.*

'**einnehmen** *v/t.* (*irr.* nehmen, *sep.*, -ge-, h) take (*meal, position*, ✗); ♈ take (*money*); ♈ earn, make (*money*); take up, occupy (*room*); *fig.* captivate; '**~d** *adj.* taking, engaging, captivating.

'**einnicken** *v/i.* (*sep.*, -ge-, sein) doze *or* drop off.

Einöde ['aɪnˀ-] f desert, solitude.
ein|ordnen ['aɪnˀ-] v/t. (sep., -ge-, h) arrange in proper order; classify; file (letters, etc.); **~packen** v/t. (sep., -ge-, h) pack up; wrap up; **~pferchen** v/t. (sep., -ge-, h) pen in; fig. crowd, cram; **~pflanzen** v/t. (sep., -ge-, h) plant; fig. implant; **~pökeln** v/t. (sep., -ge-, h) pickle, salt; **~prägen** v/t. (sep., -ge-, h) imprint; impress; sich ~ imprint itself; commit s.th. to one's memory; **~quartieren** v/t. (sep., no -ge-, h) quarter, billet; **~rahmen** v/t. (sep., -ge-, h) frame; **~räumen** fig. v/t. (sep., -ge-, h) grant, concede; **~rechnen** v/t. (sep., -ge-, h) comprise, include; **~reden** (sep., -ge-, h) 1. v/t.: j-m ~ persuade or talk s.o. into (doing) s.th.; 2. v/i.: auf j-n ~ talk insistently to s.o.; **~reichen** v/t. (sep., -ge-, h) hand in, send in, present; **~reihen** v/t. (sep., -ge-, h) insert (unter acc. in); class (with); place (among); sich ~ take one's place.
einreihig adj. ['aɪnraɪç] jacket: single-breasted.
'Einreise f entry; **~erlaubnis** f, **~genehmigung** f entry permit.
'ein|reißen (irr. reißen, sep., -ge-) 1. v/t. (h) tear; pull down (building); 2. v/i. (sein) tear; abuse, etc.: spread; **~renken** ['~rɛŋkən] v/t. (sep., -ge-, h) ✗ set; fig. set right.
'einricht|en v/t. (sep. -ge-, h) establish; equip; arrange; set up (shop); furnish (flat); es ~ manage; sich ~ establish o.s., settle down; economize; sich ~ auf (acc.) prepare for; **'2ung** f establishment; arrangement, esp. Am. setup; equipment; furniture; fittings pl. (of shop); institution.
'ein|rollen v/t. (sep., -ge-, h) roll up or in; sich ~ roll up; curl up; **'~rosten** v/i. (sep., -ge-, sein) rust; screw, etc.: rust in; **'~rücken** (sep., -ge-) 1. v/i. (sein) enter, march in; ✗ join the army; 2. v/t. (h) insert (advertisement in a paper); typ. indent (line, word, etc.); **'~rühren** v/t. (sep., -ge-, h) stir (in).
eins adj. [aɪns] one.
'einsam adj. lonely, solitary; **'2keit** f (-/✎ -en) loneliness, solitude.
'einsammeln v/t. (sep., -ge-, h) gather; collect.
'Einsatz m inset; insertion (of piece of material); gambling: stake, pool; ♪ striking in, entry; employment; engagement (a. ✗); ✗ action, operation; unter ~ s-s Lebens at the risk of one's life.
'ein|saugen v/t. (sep., -ge-, h) suck in; fig. imbibe; **'~schalten** v/t. (sep., -ge-, h) insert; ∮ switch or turn on; den ersten Gang ~ mot. go into first or bottom gear; sich ~

intervene; **~schärfen** v/t. (sep., -ge-, h) inculcate (dat. upon); **~schätzen** v/t. (sep., -ge-, h) assess, appraise, estimate (auf acc. at); value (a. fig.); **~schenken** v/t. (sep., -ge-, h) pour in or out; **~schicken** v/t. (sep., -ge-, h) send in; **~schieben** v/t. (irr. schieben, sep., -ge-, h) insert; **~schiffen** v/t. and v/refl. (sep., -ge-, h) embark; **2schiffung** f (-/-en) embarkation; **~schlafen** v/i. (irr. schlafen, sep., -ge-, sein) fall asleep; **~schläfern** ['~ʃlɛːfərn] v/t. (sep., -ge-, h) lull to sleep; ✗ narcotize.
'Einschlag m striking (of lightning); impact (of missile); fig. touch; **'2en** (irr. schlagen, sep., -ge-, h) 1. v/t. drive in (nail); break (in); smash (in); wrap up; take (road); tuck in (hem, etc.); enter upon (career); 2. v/i. shake hands; lightning, missile: strike; fig. be a success; nicht ~ fail; (wie e-e Bombe) ~ cause a sensation; auf j-n ~ belabour s.o.
einschlägig adj. ['aɪnʃlɛːgɪç] relevant, pertinent.
'Einschlagpapier n wrapping-paper.
'ein|schleichen v/refl. (irr. schleichen, sep., -ge-, h) creep or sneak in; **~schleppen** v/t. (sep., -ge-, h) ⚓ tow in; import (disease); **~schleusen** fig. v/t. (sep., -ge-, h) channel or let in; **~schließen** v/t. (irr. schließen, sep., -ge-, h) lock in or up; enclose; ✗ surround, encircle; fig. include; **~schließlich** prp. (gen.) inclusive of; including, comprising; **~schmeicheln** v/refl. (sep., -ge-, h) ingratiate o.s. (bei with); **~schmeichelnd** adj. insinuating; **~schmuggeln** v/t. (sep., -ge-, h) smuggle in; **~schnappen** v/i. (sep., -ge-, sein) catch; fig. s. eingeschnappt; **~schneidend** fig. adj. incisive, drastic.
'Einschnitt m cut, incision; notch.
'ein|schnüren v/t. (sep., -ge-, h) lace (up); **~schränken** ['~ʃrɛŋkən] v/t. (sep., -ge-, h) restrict, confine; reduce (expenses); sich ~ economize; **2schränkung** f (-/-en) restriction; reduction.
'Einschreibe|brief m registered letter; **'2n** v/t. (irr. schreiben, sep., -ge-, h) enter; book; enrol(l); ✗ enlist, enrol(l); ✉ register; ~ lassen have registered; sich ~ enter one's name.
'einschreiten 1. fig. v/i. (irr. schreiten, sep., -ge-, sein) step in, interpose, intervene; take action (gegen against); 2. 2 n (-s/no pl.) intervention.
'ein|schrumpfen v/i. (sep., -ge-, sein) shrink; **~schüchtern** v/t. (sep., -ge-, h) intimidate; bully; **'2schüchterung** f (-/-en) intim-

idation; '~schulen v/t. (sep., -ge-, h) put to school.

'Einschuß m bullet-hole; ✝ invested capital.

'ein|segnen v/t. (sep., -ge-, h) consecrate; confirm (children); '2segnung f consecration; confirmation.

'einsehen 1. v/t. (irr. sehen, sep., -ge-, h) look into; fig.: see, comprehend; realize; 2. 2 n (-s/no pl.): ein ~ haben show consideration.

'einseifen v/t. (sep., -ge-, h) soap; lather (beard); F fig. humbug (s.o.).

einseitig adj. ['aɪnzaɪtɪç] one-sided; ⚔, pol., ⚖ unilateral.

'einsend|en v/t. ([irr. senden], sep., -ge-, h) send in; '2er m (-s/-) sender; contributor (to a paper).

'einsetz|en (sep., -ge-, h) 1. v/t. set or put in; stake (money); insert; institute; instal(l), appoint (s.o.); fig. use, employ; risk (one's life); sich ~ für stand up for; 2. v/i. fever, flood, weather: set in; ♪ strike in; '2ung f (-/-en) insertion; appointment, installation.

'Einsicht f (-/-en) inspection; fig. insight, understanding; judiciousness; '2ig adj. judicious; sensible.

'einsickern v/i. (sep., -ge-, sein) soak in; infiltrate.

'Einsiedler m hermit.

einsilbig adj. ['aɪnzilbɪç] monosyllabic; fig. taciturn; '2keit f (-/no pl.) taciturnity.

'einsinken v/i. (irr. sinken, sep., -ge-, sein) sink (in).

Einspänn|er ['aɪnʃpɛnər] m (-s/-) one-horse carriage; '2ig adj. one-horse.

'ein|sparen v/t. (sep., -ge-, h) save, economize; '~sperren v/t. (sep., -ge-, h) imprison; lock up, confine; '~springen v/i. (irr. springen, sep., -ge-, sein) ⊕ catch; fig. step in, help out; für j-n ~ substitute for s.o.; '~spritzen v/t. (sep., -ge-, h) inject; '2spritzung f (-/-en) injection.

'Einspruch m objection, protest, veto; appeal; '~srecht n veto.

'einspurig adj. single-track.

einst adv. [aɪnst] once; one or some day.

'Einstand m entry; tennis: deuce.

'ein|stecken v/t. (sep., -ge-, h) put in; pocket; plug in; '~steigen v/i. (irr. steigen, sep., -ge-, sein) get in; ~l ⊕ take your seats!, Am. all aboard!

'einstell|en v/t. (sep., -ge-, h) put in; ⚔ enrol(l), enlist, Am. muster in; engage, employ, Am. a. hire; give up; stop, cease, Am. a. quit (payment, etc.); adjust (mechanism) (auf acc. to); tune in (radio) (to); opt., focus (on) (a. fig.); die Arbeit ~ cease working; strike, Am. a. walk out; sich ~ appear; sich ~ auf (acc.) be

prepared for; adapt o.s. to; '2ung f ⚔ enlistment; engagement; adjustment; focus; (mental) attitude, mentality.

'einstimm|en ♪ v/i. (sep., -ge-, h) join in; '~ig adj. unanimous; '2igkeit f (-/no pl.) unanimity.

einstöckig adj. ['aɪnʃtœkɪç] one-storied.

'ein|streuen fig. v/t. (sep., -ge-, h) intersperse; '~studieren v/t. (sep., no -ge-, h) study; thea. rehearse; '~stürmen v/i. (sep., -ge-, sein): auf j-n ~ rush at s.o.; '2sturz m falling in, collapse; '~stürzen v/i. (sep., -ge-, sein) fall in, collapse.

einst'weilen adv. ['aɪnst'vaɪlən] for the present; in the meantime; '~weilig adj. temporary.

'ein|tauschen v/t. (sep., -ge-, h) exchange (gegen for); '~teilen v/t. (sep., -ge-, h) divide (in acc. into); classify; '~teilig adj. one-piece; '2teilung f division; classification.

eintönig adj. ['aɪntø:nɪç] monotonous; '2keit f (-/⚔, -en) monotony.

'Eintopf(gericht n) m hot-pot; stew.

'Eintracht f (-/no pl.) harmony, concord.

einträchtig adj. ['aɪntrɛçtɪç] harmonious.

'ein|tragen v/t. (irr. tragen, sep., -ge-, h) enter; register; bring in, yield (profit); sich ~ in (acc.) sign.

einträglich adj. ['aɪntrɛ:klɪç] profitable.

'Eintragung f (-/-en) entry; registration.

'ein|treffen v/i. (irr. treffen, sep., -ge-, sein) arrive; happen; come true; '~treiben v/t. (irr. treiben, sep., -ge-, h) drive in or home; collect (debts, taxes); '~treten (irr. treten, sep., -ge-) 1. v/i. (sein) enter; occur, happen, take place; ~ für stand up for; ~ in (acc.) enter into (rights); enter upon (possession); enter (room); join (the army, etc.); 2. v/t. (h) kick in (door); sich et. ~ run s.th. into one's foot.

'Eintritt m entry, entrance; admittance; beginning, setting-in (of winter, etc.); ~ frei! admission free!; ~ verboten! no admittance!; '~sgeld n entrance or admission fee; sports: gate money; '~skarte f admission ticket.

'ein|trocknen v/i. (sep., -ge-, sein) dry (up); '~trüben v/refl. (sep., -ge-, h) become cloudy or overcast; '~üben ['aɪn⁹-] v/t. (sep., -ge-, h) practi|se, Am. -ce s.th.; train s.o.

einver|leiben ['aɪnfɛrlaɪbən] v/t. ([sep.]) no -ge-, h) incorporate (dat. in); annex (to); F sich et. ~ eat or drink s.th.; '2nehmen n (-s/no pl.) agreement, understanding; in gutem ~ on friendly terms; '~standen *adj.:* ~ *sein* agree; '2ständnis *n* agreement.

'Einwand *m* (-[e]s/=e) objection (*gegen* to).

'Einwander|er *m* immigrant; '2n *v/i.* (*sep.*, -ge-, *sein*) immigrate; '~ung *f* immigration.

'einwandfrei *adj.* unobjectionable; perfect; faultless; *alibi:* sound.

einwärts *adv.* ['aɪnvɛrts] inward(s).

'Einwegflasche *f* one-way bottle, non-return bottle.

'einweih|en *v/t.* (*sep.*, -ge-, *h*) *eccl.* consecrate; inaugurate; ~ *in* (*acc.*) initiate *s.o.* into; '~ung *f* (*-/-en*) consecration; inauguration; initiation.

'einwend|en *v/t.* ([*irr.* wenden,] *sep.*, -ge-, *h*) object; '2ung *f* objection.

'einwerfen (*irr.* werfen, *sep.*, -ge-, *h*) 1. *v/t.* throw in (*a. fig.*); smash, break (*window-pane*); post, *Am.* mail (*letter*); interject (*remark*); 2. *v/i.* football: throw in.

'einwickel|n *v/t.* (*sep.*, -ge-, *h*) wrap (up), envelop; '2papier *n* wrapping-paper.

'einwillig|en ['aɪnvɪligən] *v/i.* (*sep.*, -ge-, *h*) consent, agree (*in acc.* to); '2ung *f* (*-/-en*) consent, agreement.

'einwirk|en *v/i.* (*sep.*, -ge-, *h*): ~ *auf* (*acc.*) act (up)on; influence; effect; '2ung *f* influence; effect.

Einwohner *f* ['aɪnvo:nər] *m* (-s/-), '~in *f* (*-/-nen*) inhabitant, resident.

'Einwurf *m* throwing in; *football:* throw-in; *fig.* objection; slit (*for letters, etc.*); slot (*for coins*).

'Einzahl *gr. f* (-/~-en) singular (number); '2en *v/t.* (*sep.*, -ge-, *h*) pay in; '~ung *f* payment; deposit (*at bank*).

einzäunen ['aɪntsɔynən] *v/t.* (*sep.*, -ge-, *h*) fence in.

Einzel ['aɪntsəl] *n* (-s/-) *tennis:* single, *Am.* singles pl.; '~gänger ['~gɛŋər] *m* (-s/-) outsider; F lone wolf; '~handel ✝ *m* retail trade; '~händler ✝ *m* retailer, retail dealer; '~heit *f* (*-/-en*) detail, item; ~en *pl.* particulars *pl.*, details *pl.*; '2n 1. *adj.* single; particular; individual; separate; *of shoes, etc.:* odd; *im* ~en *in* detail; 2. *adv.:* ~ *angeben or aufführen* specify, *esp. Am.* itemize; '~ne *m* (*-n/-n*) *the* individual; '~verkauf *m* retail sale; '~wesen *n* individual.

'einziehen (*irr.* ziehen, *sep.*, -ge-) 1. *v/t.* (*h*) draw in; *esp.* ⊕ retract; ✗ call up, *Am.* draft, induct; ⚖ seize, confiscate; make (*inquiries*) (*über acc.* on, about); 2. *v/i.* (*sein*) enter; move in; *liquid:* soak in; ~ *in* (*acc.*) move into (*flat, etc.*).

einzig *adj.* ['aɪntsɪç] only; single; sole; unique; '~artig *adj.* unique, singular.

'Einzug *m* entry, entrance; moving in.

'einzwängen *v/t.* (*sep.*, -ge-, *h*) squeeze, jam.

Eis [aɪs] *n* (-es/*no pl.*) ice; ice-cream; '~bahn *f* skating-rink; '~bär zo. *m* polar bear; '~bein *n* pickled pork shank; '~berg *m* iceberg; '~decke *f* sheet of ice; '~diele *f* ice-cream parlo(u)r.

Eisen ['aɪzən] *n* (-s/-) iron.

'Eisenbahn *f* railway, *Am.* railroad; *mit der* ~ by rail, by train; '~er *m* (-s/-) railwayman; '~fahrt *f* railway journey; '~knotenpunkt *m* (railway) junction; '~unglück *n* railway accident; '~wagen *m* railway carriage, *Am.* railroad car; coach.

'Eisen|blech *n* sheet-iron; '~erz *n* iron-ore; '~gießerei *f* iron-foundry; '2haltig *adj.* ferruginous; '~hütte *f* ironworks *sg., pl.*; '~waren *f/pl.* ironmongery, *esp. Am.* hardware; '~warenhändler *m* ironmonger, *esp. Am.* hardware dealer.

eisern *adj.* ['aɪzərn] iron, of iron.

'Eis|gang *m* breaking up of the ice; ice-drift; '2gekühlt *adj.* ['~gəky:lt] iced; '2grau *adj.* hoary; '~hockey *n* ice-hockey; '2ig *adj.* ['aɪzɪç] icy; '2kalt *adj.* icy (cold); '~kunstlauf *m* figure-skating; '~lauf *m*, '~laufen *n* (-s/*no pl.*) skating; skate; '~läufer *m* skater; '~meer *n* polar sea; '~schnellauf *m* speed-skating; '~scholle *f* ice-floe; '~schrank *m s.* Kühlschrank; '~vogel *orn. m* kingfisher; '~zapfen *m* icicle; '~zeit *geol. f* ice-age.

eitel *adj.* ['aɪtəl] vain (*auf acc.* of); conceited; mere; '2keit *f* (*-/-en*) vanity.

Eiter 🦠 ['aɪtər] *m* (-s/*no pl.*) matter, pus; '~beule *f* abscess; '2ig *adj.* purulent; '2n 🦠 *v/i.* (ge-, *h*) fester, suppurate; '~ung 🦠 *f* (*-/-en*) suppuration.

eitrig *adj.* ['aɪtrɪç] purulent.

'Eiweiß *n* (-es/-e) white of egg; 🦠 albumen; '2haltig 🦠 *adj.* albuminous.

'Eizelle *f* egg-cell, ovum.

Ekel ['e:kəl] 1. *m* (-s/*no pl.*) disgust (*vor dat.* at), loathing; aversion; 🦠 nausea; 2. F *n* (-s/-) nasty person; '2erregend *adj.* nauseating, sickening; '2haft *adj.*, '2ig *adj.* revolting; *fig.* disgusting; '2n *v/refl.* (ge-, *h*): *sich* ~ be nauseated (*vor dat.* at); *fig.* be *or* feel disgusted (at).

eklig *adj.* ['e:klɪç] *s.* ekelhaft.

elasti|sch *adj.* [e'lastɪʃ] elastic; 2zität [~tsi'tɛ:t] *f* (-/*no pl.*) elasticity.

Elch *zo.* [ɛlç] *m* (-[e]s/-e) elk; moose.

Elefant *zo.* [ele'fant] *m* (-en/-en) elephant.

elegan|t *adj.* [ele'gant] elegant; smart; **♀z** [⌐ts] *f* (-/*no pl.*) elegance.
elektrifizier|en [elɛktrifi'tsiːrən] *v/t.* (*no* -ge-, *h*) electrify; **♀ung** *f* (-/-en) electrification.
Elektri|ker [e'lɛktrikər] *m* (-s/-) electrician; **♀sch** *adj.* electric(al); **♀sieren** [⌐'ziːrən] *v/t.* (*no* -ge-, *h*) electrify.
Elektrizität [elɛktritsi'tɛːt] *f* (-/*no pl.*) electricity; **♀sgesellschaft** *f* electricity supply company; **♀s-werk** *n* (electric) power station, power-house, *Am.* power plant.
Elektrode [elɛk'troːdə] *f* (-/-n) electrode.
Elektro|gerät [e'lɛktro-] *n* electric appliance; **♀lyse** [⌐'lyːzə] *f* (-/-n) electrolysis.
Elektron *⚡* [e'lɛktrɔn] *n* (-s/-en) electron; **♀engehirn** [⌐'troːnən-] *n* electronic brain; **♀ik** [⌐'troːnik] *f* (-/*no pl.*) electronics *sg.*
Elektro'technik *f* electrical engineering; **♀er** *m* electrical engineer.
Element [ele'mɛnt] *n* (-[e]s/-e) element.
elementar *adj.* [elemen'taːr] elementary; **♀schule** elementary *or* primary school, *Am.* grade school.
Elend ['eːlɛnt] **1.** *n* (-[e]s/*no pl.*) misery; need, distress; **2.** **♀** *adj.* miserable, wretched; needy, distressed; **'♀sviertel** *n* slums *pl.*
elf¹ [ɛlf] **1.** *adj.* eleven; **2.** **♀** *f* (-/-en) eleven (*a. sports*).
Elf² [⌐] *m* (-en/-en), **♀e** ['ɛlfə] *f* (-/-n) elf, fairy.
'Elfenbein *n* (-[e]s/♀-e) ivory; **'♀ern** *adj.* ivory.
Elf'meter *m football:* penalty kick; **♀marke** *f* penalty spot.
'elfte *adj.* eleventh.
Elite [e'liːtə] *f* (-/-n) élite.
'Ellbogen *anat. m* (-s/-) elbow.
Elle ['ɛlə] *f* (-/-n) yard; *anat.* ulna.
Elster *orn.* ['ɛlstər] *f* (-/-n) magpie.
elter|lich *adj.* ['ɛltərliç] parental; **'♀n** *pl.* parents *pl.*; **'♀nlos** *adj.* parentless, orphaned; **'♀nteil** *m* parent.   [(-/-n) enamel.|
Email [e'maːj] *n* (-s/-s), **♀le** [⌐] *f|*
Emanzipation [emantsipa'tsjoːn] *f* (-/-en) emancipation.
Embargo [ɛm'bargo] *n* (-s/-s) embargo.
Embolie *⚕* [ɛmbo'liː] *f* (-/-n) embolism.
Embryo *biol.* ['ɛmbryo] *m* (-s/-s, -nen) embryo.
Emigrant [emi'grant] *m* (-en/-en) emigrant.
empfahl [ɛm'pfaːl] *pret. of empfehlen.*
Empfang [ɛm'pfaŋ] *m* (-[e]s/♀e) reception; *fig.*; receipt (*of s.th.*); *nach or bei* ♀ on receipt; **'♀en** *v/t.* (*irr. fangen, no* -ge-, *h*) receive; welcome; conceive (*child*).

Empfänger [ɛm'pfɛŋər] *m* (-s/-) receiver, recipient; payee (*of money*); addressee (*of letter*); **♀** consignee (*of goods*).
em'pfänglich *adj.* susceptible (*für* to); **♀keit** *f* (-/*no pl.*) susceptibility.
Em'pfangs|dame *f* receptionist; **♀gerät** *n* receiver, receiving set; **♀schein** *m* receipt; **♀zimmer** *n* reception-room.
empfehl|en [ɛm'pfeːlən] *v/t.* (*irr.*, *no* -ge-, *h*) recommend; commend; **♀** *Sie mich* (*dat.*) please remember me to; **♀enswert** *adj.* (re)commendable; **♀ung** *f* (-/-en) recommendation; compliments *pl.*
empfinden [ɛm'pfindən] *v/t.* (*irr. finden, no* -ge-, *h*) feel; perceive.
empfindlich *adj.* [ɛm'pfintliç] sensitive (*a. phot.*, *⚡*) (*für, gegen* to); *pred. a.* susceptible (*gegen* to); delicate; tender; *p.:* touchy, sensitive; *cold:* severe; *pain, loss, etc.:* grievous; *pain:* acute; **♀keit** *f* (-/-en) sensitivity; sensibility; touchiness; delicacy.
empfindsam *adj.* [ɛm'pfintzaːm] sensitive; sentimental; **♀keit** *f* (-/-en) sensitiveness; sentimentality.
Empfindung [ɛm'pfinduŋ] *f* (-/-en) perception; sensation; sentiment; **♀slos** *adj.* insensible; *esp. fig.* unfeeling; **♀svermögen** *n* faculty of perception.
empfohlen [ɛm'pfoːlən] *p.p. of empfehlen.*
empor *adv.* [ɛm'poːr] up, up-wards.
empören [ɛm'pøːrən] *v/t.* (*no* -ge-, *h*) incense; shock; *sich* ♀ revolt (*a. fig.*), rebel; grow furious (*über acc.* at); *empört* indignant, shocked (*both: über acc.* at).
em'por|kommen *v/i.* (*irr. kommen, sep.*, -ge-, *sein*) rise (in the world); **♀kömmling** [⌐kœmliŋ] *m* (-s/-e) upstart; **♀ragen** *v/i.* (*sep.*, -ge-, *h*) tower, rise; **♀steigen** *v/i.* (*irr. steigen, sep.*, -ge-, *sein*) rise, ascend.
Em'pörung *f* (-/-en) rebellion, revolt; indignation.
emsig *adj.* ['ɛmziç] busy, industrious, diligent; **♀keit** *f* (-/*no pl.*) busyness, industry, diligence.
Ende ['ɛndə] *n* (-s/-n) end; *am* ♀ at *or* in the end; after all; eventually; *zu* ♀ *gehen* end; expire; run short; **'♀n** *v/i.* (ge-, *h*) end; cease, finish.
end|gültig *adj.* ['ɛntgyltiç] final, definitive; **'♀lich** *adv.* finally, at last; **♀los** *adj.* ['⌐loːs] endless; **'♀punkt** *m* final point; **'♀runde** *f sports:* final; **'♀station** *f* terminus, *Am.* terminal; **'♀summe** *f* (sum) total.
Endung *ling.* ['ɛnduŋ] *f* (-/-en) ending, termination.
Endzweck ['ɛnt-] *m* ultimate object.

Energie [enɛr'gi:] f (-/-n) energy;
2los adj. lacking (in) energy.

e'nergisch adj. vigorous; energetic.

eng adj. [eŋ] narrow; *clothes*: tight;
close; intimate; *im ~eren Sinne*
strictly speaking.

engagieren [ãga'ʒi:rən] v/t. (no
-ge-, h) engage, Am. a. hire.

Enge ['eŋə] f (-/-n) narrowness; fig.
straits pl.

Engel ['eŋəl] m (-s/-) angel.

'engherzig adj. ungenerous, petty.

Engländer ['eŋlɛndər] m (-s/-)
Englishman; *die ~ pl.* the English
pl.; '*~in* f (-/-nen) Englishwoman.

englisch adj. ['eŋliʃ] English;
British.

'Engpaß m defile, narrow pass, Am.
a. notch; fig. bottle-neck.

en gros † adv. [ã'gro:] wholesale.

En'groshandel † m wholesale
trade.

'engstirnig adj. narrow-minded.

Enkel ['eŋkəl] m (-s/-) grandchild;
grandson; '*~in* f (-/-nen) grand-
daughter.

enorm adj. [e'nɔrm] enormous; F
fig. tremendous.

Ensemble thea., ♪ [ã'sã:bəl] n
(-s/-s) ensemble; company.

entart|en [ɛnt'ɑ:rtən] v/i. (no -ge-,
sein) degenerate; **2ung** f (-/-en)
degeneration.

entbehr|en [ɛnt'be:rən] v/t. (no
-ge-, h) lack; miss, want; do without; *~lich* adj. dispensable; superfluous; **2ung** f (-/-en) want, privation.

ent'bind|en (irr. binden, no -ge-, h)
1. v/t. dispense, release (von from);
deliver (of a child); 2. v/i. be confined; **2ung** f dispensation, release;
delivery; **2ungsheim** n maternity
hospital.

ent'blöß|en v/t. (no -ge-, h) bare,
strip; uncover (head); *~t adj.* bare.

ent'deck|en v/t. (no -ge-, h) dis-
cover; detect; disclose; *~er m* (-s/-)
discoverer; **2ung** f discovery.

Ente ['ɛntə] f (-/-n) orn. duck; false
report: F canard, hoax.

ent'ehr|en v/t. (no -ge-, h) dis-
hono(u)r; **2ung** f degradation; rape.

ent'eign|en v/t. (no -ge-, h) ex-
propriate; dispossess; **2ung** f ex-
propriation; dispossession.

ent'erben v/t. (no -ge-, h) disinherit.

entern ['ɛntərn] v/t. (ge-, h) board,
grapple (ship).

ent|'fachen v/t. (no -ge-, h) kindle;
fig. a. rouse (passions); *~'fallen v/i.*
(irr. fallen, no -ge-, sein): j-m ~
escape s.o.; fig. slip s.o.'s memory;
auf j-n ~ fall to s.o.'s share; s. weg-
fallen; *~'falten v/t.* (no -ge-, h)
unfold; fig.: develop; display; sich ~
unfold; fig. develop (zu into).

ent'fern|en v/t. (no -ge-, h) remove;
sich ~ withdraw; *~t adj.* distant,

remote (both a. fig.); **2ung** f (-/-en)
removal; distance; range; **2ungs-
messer** phot. m (-s/-) range-finder.

ent'flammen (no -ge-) v/t. (h) and
v/i. (sein) inflame; *~'fliehen v/i.*
(irr. fliehen, no -ge-, sein) flee,
escape (aus or dat. from); *~'frem-
den* v/t. (no -ge-, h) estrange,
alienate (j-m from s.o.).

ent'führ|en v/t. (no -ge-, h) abduct,
kidnap; run away with; **2er** m
abductor, kidnap(p)er; **2ung** f ab-
duction, kidnap(p)ing.

ent'gegen 1. prp. (dat.) in opposition
to, contrary to; against; 2. adv.
towards; *~gehen v/i.* (irr. gehen,
sep., -ge-, sein) go to meet; *~ge-
setzt* adj. opposite; fig. contrary;
~halten v/t. (irr. halten, sep., -ge-,
h) hold out; fig. object; *~kommen*
v/i. (irr. kommen, sep., -ge-, sein)
come to meet; fig. meet s.o.('s
wishes) halfway; **2kommen** n
(-s/no pl.) obligingness; *~kommend*
adj. obliging; *~nehmen* v/t. (irr.
nehmen, sep., -ge-, h) accept,
receive; *~sehen v/i.* (dat.) (irr.
sehen, sep., -ge-, h) await; look forward to; *~setzen* v/t. (sep., -ge-, h)
oppose; *~stehen v/i.* (irr. stehen,
sep., -ge-, h) be opposed (dat. to);
~strecken v/t. (sep., -ge-, h) hold
or stretch out (dat. to); *~treten v/i.*
(dat.) (irr. treten, sep., -ge-, sein)
step up to s.o.; oppose; face (danger).

entgegn|en [ɛnt'ge:gnən] v/t. (no
-ge-, h) reply; return; retort; **2ung**
f (-/-en) reply; retort.

ent'gehen v/i. (irr. gehen, no -ge-,
sein) escape.

entgeistert adj. [ɛnt'gaɪstərt] a-
ghast, thunderstruck, flabbergasted.

Entgelt [ɛnt'gɛlt] n (-[e]s/no pl.)
recompense; **2en** v/t. (irr. gelten,
no -ge-, h) atone or suffer or pay for.

entgleis|en [ɛnt'glaɪzən] v/i. (no
-ge-, sein) run off the rails, be
derailed; fig. (make a) slip; **2ung** f
(-/-en) derailment; fig. slip.

ent'gleiten v/i. (irr. gleiten, no -ge-,
sein) slip (dat. from).

ent'halt|en v/t. (irr. halten, no
-ge-, h) contain, hold; include;
sich ~ (gen.) abstain or refrain from;
~sam adj. abstinent; **2samkeit** f
(-/no pl.) abstinence; **2ung** f
abstention.

ent'haupten v/t. (no -ge-, h) behead,
decapitate.

ent'hüll|en v/t. (no -ge-, h) un-
cover; unveil; fig. reveal, disclose;
2ung f (-/-en) uncovering; unveil-
ing; fig. revelation, disclosure.

Enthusias|mus [ɛntuzi'asmus] m
(-/no pl.) enthusiasm; *~t m* (-en/-en)
enthusiast; film, sports: F fan;
2tisch adj. enthusiastic.

ent'kleiden v/t. and v/refl. (no -ge-,
h) undress.

ent'kommen 1. *v/i.* (*irr.* kommen, *no* -ge-, sein) escape (j-m s.o.; aus from), get away *or* off; **2.** 2 *n* (-s/no pl.) escape.

entkräft|en [ɛnt'krɛftən] *v/t.* (*no* -ge-, h) weaken, debilitate; *fig.* refute; 2ung *f* (-/-en) weakening; debility; *fig.* refutation.

ent'lad|en *v/t.* (*irr.* laden, *no* -ge-, h) unload; ⚡ discharge; explode; *sich ~ esp.* ⚡ discharge; *gun:* go off; *anger:* vent itself; 2ung *f* unloading; *esp.* ⚡ discharge; explosion.

ent'lang 1. *prp.* (*dat.*; *acc.*) along; **2.** *adv.* along; er geht die Straße ~ he goes along the street.

ent'larven *v/t.* (*no* -ge-, h) unmask; *fig. a.* expose.

ent'lass|en *v/t.* (*irr.* lassen, *no* -ge-, h) dismiss, discharge; F give *s.o.* the sack, Am. a. fire; 2ung *f* (-/-en) dismissal, discharge; 2ungsgesuch *n* resignation.

ent'lasten *v/t.* (*no* -ge-, h) unburden; ⚖ exonerate, clear (*from suspicion*).

Ent'lastung *f* (-/-en) relief; discharge; exoneration; ~sstraße *f* by-pass (road); ~szeuge *m* witness for the defen|ce, Am. ~se.

ent'|laufen *v/i.* (*irr.* laufen, *no* -ge-, sein) run away (dat. from); ~'ledigen [~'le:dɪgən] *v/refl.* (gen.) (*no* -ge-, h): rid o.s. of s.th., get rid of s.th.; acquit o.s. of (duty); execute (orders); ~'leeren *v/t.* (*no* -ge-, h) empty. [of-the-way.]

ent'legen *adj.* remote, distant, out-

ent'|lehnen *v/t.* (*no* -ge-, h) borrow (dat. or aus from); ~'locken *v/t.* (*no* -ge-, h) draw, elicit (dat. from); ~'lohnen *v/t.* (*no* -ge-, h) pay (off); ~'lüften *v/t.* (*no* -ge-, h) ventilate; ~militarisieren [~militari'zi:rən] *v/t.* (*no* -ge-, h) demilitarize; ~mutigen [~'mu:tigən] *v/t.* (*no* -ge-, h) discourage; ~'nehmen *v/t.* (*irr.* nehmen, *no* -ge- h) take (dat. from); ~ aus (with)draw from; *fig.* gather or learn from; ~'rätseln *v/t.* (*no* -ge-, h) unriddle; ~'reißen *v/t.* (*irr.* reißen, *no* -ge-, h) snatch away (dat. from); ~'richten *v/t.* (*no* -ge-, h) pay; ~'rinnen *v/i.* (*irr.* rinnen, *no* -ge-, sein) escape (dat. from); ~'rollen *v/t.* (*no* -ge-, h) unroll; ~'rücken *v/t.* (*no* -ge-, h) remove (dat. from), carry off or away; ~'rückt *adj.* entranced; lost in thought.

ent'rüst|en *v/t.* (*no* -ge-, h) fill with indignation; *sich ~* become angry or indignant (über acc. at s.th., with s.o.); ~et *adj.* indignant (über acc. at s.th., with s.o.); 2ung *f* indignation.

ent'sag|en *v/i.* (*no* -ge-, h) renounce, resign; 2ung *f* (-/-en) renunciation, resignation.

ent'schädig|en *v/t.* (*no* -ge-, h) indemnify, compensate; 2ung *f* indemnification, indemnity; compensation.

ent'scheid|en (*irr.* scheiden, *no* -ge-, h) **1.** *v/t.* decide; *sich ~* question, etc.: be decided; *p.:* decide (für for; gegen against; über acc. on); come to a decision; **2.** *v/i.* decide; ~end *adj.* decisive; crucial; 2ung *f* decision.

entschieden *adj.* [ɛnt'ʃi:dən] decided; determined, resolute; 2heit *f* (-/no pl.) determination.

ent'schließen *v/refl.* (*irr.* schließen, *no* -ge-, h) resolve, decide, determine (zu on s.th.; zu inf. to inf.), make up one's mind (zu inf. to inf.).

ent'schlossen *adj.* resolute, determined; 2heit *f* (-/no pl.) resoluteness.

ent'schlüpfen *v/i.* (*no* -ge-, sein) escape, slip (dat. from).

Ent'schluß *m* resolution, resolve, decision, determination.

entschuldig|en [ɛnt'ʃuldɪgən] *v/t.* (*no* -ge-, h) excuse; *sich ~* apologize (bei to; für for); sich ~ lassen beg to be excused; 2ung *f* (-/-en) excuse; apology; ich bitte (Sie) um ~ I beg your pardon.

ent'senden *v/t.* (*irr.* senden, *no* -ge-, h) send off, dispatch; delegate, depute.

ent'setz|en 1. *v/t.* (*no* -ge-, h) dismiss (from a position); ✗ relieve; frighten; *sich ~* be terrified or shocked (über acc. at); **2.** 2 *n* (-/no pl.) horror, fright; ~lich *adj.* horrible, dreadful, terrible, shocking.

ent'sinnen *v/refl.* (gen.) (*irr.* sinnen, *no* -ge-, h) remember or recall *s.o.*, s.th.

ent'spann|en *v/t.* (*no* -ge-, h) relax; unbend; *sich ~* relax; *political situation:* ease; 2ung *f* relaxation; *pol.* détente.

ent'sprech|en *v/i.* (*irr.* sprechen, *no* -ge-, h) answer (description, etc.); correspond to; meet (demand); ~end *adj.* corresponding; appropriate; 2ung *f* (-/-en) equivalent.

ent'springen *v/i.* (*irr.* springen, *no* -ge-, sein) escape (dat. from); *river:* rise, Am. head; s. entstehen.

ent'stammen *v/i.* (*no* -ge-, sein) be descended from; come from or of, originate from.

ent'steh|en *v/i.* (*irr.* stehen, *no* -ge-, sein) arise, originate (both: aus from); 2ung *f* (-/-en) origin.

ent'stell|en *v/t.* (*no* -ge-, h) disfigure; deface, deform; distort; 2ung *f* disfigurement; distortion, misrepresentation.

ent'täusch|en *v/t.* (*no* -ge-, h) disappoint; 2ung *f* disappointment.

ent'thronen *v/t.* (*no* -ge-, h) dethrone.

entvölker|n [ɛnt'fœlkərn] *v/t.* (*no*

-ge-, h) depopulate; 2ung f (-/-en) depopulation.

ent'wachsen v/i. (irr. wachsen, no -ge-, sein) outgrow.

entwaffn|en [ent'vafnən] v/t. (no -ge-, h) disarm; 2ung f (-/-en) disarmament.

ent'warnen v/i. (no -ge-, h) civil defence: sound the all-clear (signal).

ent'wässer|n v/t. (no -ge-, h) drain; 2ung f (-/-en) drainage; ⚕ dehydration.

ent'weder cj.: ~ ... oder either ... or.

ent|'weichen v/i. (irr. weichen, no -ge-, sein) escape (aus from); ~'weihen v/t. (no -ge-, h) desecrate, profane; ~'wenden v/t. (no -ge-, h) pilfer, purloin (j-m et. s.th. from s.o.); ~'werfen v/t. (irr. werfen, no -ge-, h) draft, draw up (document); design; sketch, trace out, outline; plan.

ent'wert|en v/t. (no -ge-, h) depreciate, devaluate; cancel (stamp); 2ung f depreciation, devaluation; cancellation.

ent'wickeln v/t. (no -ge-, h) develop (a. phot.); evolve; sich ~ develop.

Entwicklung [ent'viklun] f (-/-en) development; evolution; ~shilfe f development aid.

ent|'wirren v/t. (no -ge-, h) disentangle, unravel; ~'wischen v/i. (no -ge-, sein) slip away, escape (j-m [from] s.o.; aus from); j-m ~ give s.o. the slip; ~'wöhnen [~'vø:nən] v/t. (no -ge-, h) wean.

Ent'wurf m sketch; design; plan; draft.

ent|'wurzeln v/t. (no -ge-, h) uproot; ~'ziehen v/t. (irr. ziehen, no -ge-, h) deprive (j-m et. s.o. of s.th.); withdraw (dat. from); sich ~ avoid, elude; evade (responsibility); ~'ziffern v/t. (no -ge-, h) decipher, make out; tel. decode.

ent'zück|en 1. v/t. (no -ge-, h) charm, delight; 2. 2 n (-s/no pl.) delight, rapture(s pl.), transport(s pl.).

ent'zückend adj. delightful; charming.

Ent'zug m (-[e]s/no pl.) withdrawal; cancellation (of licence); deprivation.

entzünd|bar adj. [ent'tsyntba:r] (in)flammable; ~en v/t. (no -ge-, h) inflame (a. ⚕), kindle; sich ~ catch fire; ⚕ become inflamed; 2ung f ⚕ inflammation.

ent'zwei adv. asunder, in two, to pieces; ~en v/t. (no -ge-, h) disunite, set at variance; sich ~ quarrel, fall out (both: mit with); ~gehen v/i. (irr. gehen, sep., -ge-, sein) break, go to pieces; 2ung f (-/-en) disunion.

Enzian ⚘ ['ɛntsja:n] m (-s/-e) gentian.

Enzyklopädie [ɛntsyklopɛ'di:] f (-/-n) (en)cyclop(a)edia.

Epidemie ⚕ [epide'mi:] f (-/-n) epidemic (disease).

Epilog [epi'lo:k] m (-s/-e) epilog(ue).

episch adj. ['e:pɪʃ] epic.

Episode [epi'zo:də] f (-/-n) episode.

Epoche [e'pɔxə] f (-/-n) epoch.

Epos ['e:pɔs] n (-/Epen) epic (poem).

er pers. pron. [e:r] he.

erachten [ɛr'-] 1. v/t. (no -ge-, h) consider, think, deem; 2. 2 n (-s/no pl.) opinion; m-s ~s in my opinion.

erbarmen [ɛr'barmən] 1. v/refl. (gen.) (no -ge-, h) pity or commiserate s.o.; 2. 2 n (-s/no pl.) pity, compassion, commiseration; mercy; ~swert adj. pitiable.

erbärmlich adj. [ɛr'bɛrmlɪç] pitiful, pitiable; miserable; behaviour: mean.

er'barmungslos adj. pitiless, merciless, relentless.

er'bau|en v/t. (no -ge-, h) build (up), construct, raise; fig. edify; 2er m (-s/-) builder; constructor; ~lich adj. edifying; 2ung fig. f (-/-en) edification, Am. uplift.

Erbe ['ɛrbə] 1. m (-n/-n) heir; 2. n (-s/no pl.) inheritance, heritage.

er'beben v/i. (no -ge-, sein) tremble, shake, quake.

'erben v/t. (ge-, h) inherit.

er'beuten v/t. (no -ge-, h) capture.

er'bieten v/refl. (irr. bieten, no -ge-, h) offer, volunteer.

'Erbin f (-/-nen) heiress.

er'bitten v/t. (irr. bitten, no -ge-, h) beg or ask for, request, solicit.

er'bitter|n v/t. (no -ge-, h) embitter, exasperate; 2ung f (-/⚓ -en) bitterness, exasperation.

Erbkrankheit ⚕ ['ɛrp-] f hereditary disease.

erblassen [ɛr'blasən] v/i. (no -ge-, sein) grow or turn pale, lose colo(u)r.

Erblasser ⚖ [ɛr'blasər] m (-s/-) testator; ~in f (-/-nen) testatrix.

er'bleichen v/i. (no -ge-, sein) s. erblassen.

erblich adj. ['ɛrplɪç] hereditary; 2keit physiol. f (-/no pl.) heredity.

er'blicken v/t. (no -ge-, h) perceive, see; catch sight of.

erblind|en [ɛr'blɪndən] v/i. (no -ge-, sein) grow blind; 2ung f (-/-en) loss of sight.

er'brechen 1. v/t. (irr. brechen, no -ge-, h) break or force open; vomit; sich ~ vomit; 2. 2 n (-s/no pl.) vomiting.

Erbschaft ['ɛrpʃaft] f (-/-en) inheritance, heritage.

Erbse ⚘ ['ɛrpsə] f (-/-n) pea; ~nbrei m pease-pudding, Am. pea purée; ~nsuppe f pea-soup.

Erb|stück ['ɛrp-] n heirloom; ~sünde f original sin; ~teil n (portion of an) inheritance.

Erd|arbeiter ['e:rt-] *m* digger, navvy; **'_ball** *m* globe; **'_beben** *n* (-s/-) earthquake; **'_beere ♀** *f* strawberry; **'_boden** *m* earth; ground, soil; **_e** ['e:rdə] *f* (-/°\, -n) earth; ground; soil; world; **'ℒen ♀** *v/t.* (ge-, *h*) earth, ground.

er'denklich *adj.* imaginable.

Erdgeschoß ['e:rt-] *n* ground-floor, *Am.* first floor.

er'dicht|en *v/t.* (no -ge-, *h*) invent, feign; **_et** *adj.* fictitious.

erdig *adj.* ['e:rdiç] earthy.

Erd|karte ['e:rt-] *f* map of the earth; **'_kreis** *m* earth, world; **'_kugel** *f* globe; **'_kunde** *f* geography; **'_leitung ⚡** *f* earth-connexion, earth-wire, *Am.* ground wire; **'_nuß** *f* peanut; **'_öl** *n* mineral oil, petroleum.

er'dolchen *v/t.* (no -ge-, *h*) stab (with a dagger).

Erdreich ['e:rt-] *n* ground, earth.

er'dreisten *v/refl.* (no -ge-, *h*) dare, presume.

er'drosseln *v/t.* (no-ge-, *h*) strangle, throttle.

er'drücken *v/t.* (no -ge-, *h*) squeeze *or* crush to death; **_d** *fig. adj.* overwhelming.

Erd|rutsch ['e:rt-] *m* landslip; landslide (*a. pol.*); **'_schicht** *f* layer of earth, stratum; **'_teil** *m* part of the world; *geogr.* continent.

er'dulden *v/t.* (no -ge-, *h*) suffer, endure.

er'eifern *v/refl.* (no -ge-, *h*) get excited, fly into a passion.

er'eignen *v/refl.* (no -ge-, *h*) happen, come to pass, occur.

Ereignis [ɛr'aiknis] *n* (-ses/-se) event, occurrence; **ℒreich** *adj.* eventful.

Eremit [ere'mi:t] *m* (-en/-en) hermit, anchorite.

ererbt *adj.* [ɛr'ɛrpt] inherited.

er'fahr|en 1. *v/t.* (*irr. fahren, no* -ge-, *h*) learn; hear; experience; **2.** *adj.* experienced, expert, skil(l)-ful; **ℒung** *f* (-/-en) experience; practice; skill.

er'fassen *v/t.* (no -ge-, *h*) grasp (*a. fig.*), seize, catch; cover; register, record.

er'find|en *v/t.* (*irr. finden, no* -ge-, *h*) invent; **ℒer** *m* inventor; **_erisch** *adj.* inventive; **ℒung** *f* (-/-en) invention.

Erfolg [ɛr'fɔlk] *m* (-[e]s/-e) success; result; **ℒen** [_gən] *v/i.* (no -ge-, *sein*) ensue; follow; happen; **ℒlos** *adj.* [_k-] unsuccessful; vain; **ℒreich** *adj.* [_k-] successful.

er'forder|lich *adj.* necessary, required; **_n** *v/t.* (no -ge-, *h*) require, demand; **ℒnis** *n* (-ses/-se) requirement, demand, exigence, exigency.

er'forsch|en *v/t.* (no -ge-, *h*) inquire into, investigate; explore

(*country*); **ℒer** *m* investigator; explorer; **ℒung** *f* investigation; exploration.

er'freu|en *v/t.* (no -ge-, *h*) please; delight; gratify; rejoice; *sich e-r Sache* **_** enjoy s.th.; **_lich** *adj.* delightful, pleasing, pleasant, gratifying.

er'frier|en *v/i.* (*irr. frieren, no* -ge-, *sein*) freeze to death; **ℒung** *f* (-/-en) frost-bite.

er'frisch|en *v/t.* (no -ge-, *h*) refresh; **ℒung** *f* (-/-en) refreshment.

er'froren *adj.* limb: frost-bitten.

er'füll|en *v/t.* (no -ge-, *h*) fill; *fig.* fulfil(l); perform (*mission*); comply with (*s.o.'s wishes*); meet (*requirements*); **ℒung** *f* fulfil(l)ment; performance; compliance; **ℒungsort ✝, ⚖** [ɛr'fʏluŋs°-] *m* place of performance (*of contract*).

ergänz|en [ɛr'gɛntsən] *v/t.* (no -ge-, *h*) complete, complement; supplement; replenish (*stores, etc.*); **_end** *adj.* complementary, supplementary; **ℒung** *f* (-/-en) completion; supplement; replenishment; *gr.* complement; **ℒungsband** *m* (-[e]s/°e) supplementary volume.

er'geben 1. *v/t.* (*irr. geben, no* -ge-, *h*) yield, give; prove; *sich* **_** surrender; *difficulties:* arise; devote o.s. to *s.th.*; *sich* **_** *aus* result from; *sich* **_** *in* (*acc.*) resign o.s. to; **2.** *adj.* devoted (*dat.* to); **_st** *adv.* respectfully; **ℒheit** *f* (-/*no pl.*) devotion.

Ergeb|nis [ɛr'ge:pnis] *n* (-ses/-se) result, outcome; *sports:* score; **_ung** [_buŋ] *f* (-/-en) resignation; ⚔ surrender.

er'gehen *v/i.* (*irr. gehen, no* -ge-, *sein*) be issued; **_** *lassen* issue, publish; *über sich* **_** *lassen* suffer, submit to; *wie ist es ihm ergangen?* how did he come off?; *sich* **_** *in* (*dat.*) indulge in.

ergiebig *adj.* [ɛr'gi:biç] productive, rich.

er'gießen *v/refl.* (*irr. gießen, no* -ge-, *h*) flow (*in acc.* into; *über acc.* over).

er'götz|en 1. *v/t.* (no -ge-, *h*) delight; *sich* **_** *an* (*dat.*) delight in; **2.** ℒ *n* (-s/*no pl.*) delight; **_lich** *adj.* delightful.

er'greif|en *v/t.* (*irr. greifen, no* -ge-, *h*) seize; grasp; take (*possession, s.o.'s part, measures, etc.*); take to (*flight*); take up (*profession, pen, arms*); *fig.* move, affect, touch; **ℒung** *f* (-/°\, -en) seizure.

Er'griffenheit *f* (-/*no pl.*) emotion.

er'gründen *v/t.* (no -ge-, *h*) fathom; *fig.* penetrate, get to the bottom of.

Er'guß *m* outpouring; effusion.

er'haben *adj.* elevated; *fig.* exalted, sublime; **_** *sein über* (*acc.*) be above; **ℒheit** *f* (-/°\, -en) elevation; *fig.* sublimity.

er'halt|en 1. v/t. (irr. halten, no -ge-, h) get; obtain; receive; preserve, keep; support, maintain; sich ~ von subsist on; 2. adj.: gut ~ in good repair or condition; 2ung f preservation; maintenance.

erhältlich adj. [ɛr'hɛltlɪç] obtainable.

er|'hängen v/t. (no -ge-, h) hang; ~härten v/t. (no -ge-, h) harden; fig. confirm; ~haschen v/t. (no -ge-, h) snatch, catch.

er'heb|en v/t. (irr. heben, no -ge-, h) lift, raise; elevate; exalt; levy, raise, collect (taxes, etc.); Klage ~ bring an action; sich ~ rise; question, etc.; arise; ~end fig. adj. elevating; ~lich adj. [~p-] considerable; 2ung f [~bun] f (-/-en) elevation; levy (of taxes); revolt; rising ground.

er|'heitern v/t. (no -ge-, h) cheer up, amuse; ~hellen v/t. (no -ge-, h) light up; fig. clear up; ~hitzen v/t. (no -ge-, h) heat; sich ~ get or grow hot; ~hoffen v/t. (no -ge-, h) hope for.

er'höh|en v/t. (no -ge-, h) raise; increase; 2ung f (-/-en) elevation; rise (in prices, wages); advance (in prices); increase.

er'hol|en v/refl. (no -ge-, h) recover; (take a) rest, relax; 2ung f (-/-en) recovery; recreation; relaxation; 2ungsurlaub [ɛr'ho:luns?-] m holiday, Am. vacation; recreation leave; ⚕ convalescent leave, sickleave.   [(request).\

er'hören v/t. (no-ge-, h) hear; grant\

erinner|n [ɛr'ɪnərn] v/t. (no -ge-, h): j-n ~ an (acc.) remind s.o. of; sich ~ (gen.), sich ~ an (acc.) remember s.o. or s.th., recollect s.th.; 2ung f (-/-en) remembrance; recollection; reminder; ~en pl. reminiscences pl.

er'kalten v/i. (no -ge-, sein) cool down (a. fig.), get cold.

erkält|en [ɛr'kɛltən] v/refl. (no -ge-, h): sich (sehr) ~ catch (a bad) cold; 2ung f (-/-en) cold.

er'kennen v/t. (irr. kennen, no -ge-, h) recognize (an dat. by); perceive, discern; realize.

er'kenntlich adj. perceptible; sich ~ zeigen show one's appreciation; 2keit f (-/-en) gratitude; appreciation.

Er'kenntnis 1. f perception; realization; 2. ⚖ n (-ses/-se) decision, sentence, finding.

Erker ['ɛrkər] m (-s/-) bay; '~fenster n bay-window.

er'klär|en v/t. (no -ge-, h) explain; account for; declare, state; sich ~ declare (für for; gegen against); ~lich adj. explainable, explicable; ~t adj. professed, declared; 2ung f explanation; declaration.

er'klingen v/i. (irr. klingen, no -ge-, sein) (re)sound, ring (out).

erkoren adj. [ɛr'ko:rən] (s)elect, chosen.

er'krank|en v/i. (no -ge-, sein) fall ill, be taken ill (an dat. of, with); become affected; 2ung f (-/-en) illness, sickness, falling ill.

er|'kühnen v/refl. (no -ge-, h) venture, presume, make bold (zu inf. to inf.); ~'kunden v/t. (no -ge-, h) explore; ✗ reconnoit|re, Am. -er.

erkundig|en [ɛr'kundɪgən] v/refl. (no -ge-, h) inquire (über acc. after; nach after or for s.o.; about s.th.); 2ung f (-/-en) inquiry.

er|'lahmen fig. v/i. (no -ge-, sein) grow weary, tire; slacken; interest: wane, flag; ~'langen v/t. (no -ge-, h) obtain, get.

Er|laß [ɛr'las] m (Erlasses/Erlasse) dispensation, exemption; remission (of debt, penalty, etc.); edict, decree; 2'lassen v/t. (irr. lassen, no -ge-, h) remit (debt, penalty, etc.); dispense (j-m et. s.o. from s.th.); issue (decree); enact (law).

erlauben [ɛr'laubən] v/t. (no -ge-, h) allow, permit; sich et. ~ indulge in s.th.; sich ~ zu inf. ✝ beg to inf.

Erlaubnis [ɛr'laupnɪs] f (-/no pl.) permission; authority; ~schein m permit.

er'läuter|n v/t. (no -ge-, h) explain, illustrate; comment (up)on; 2ung f explanation, illustration; comment.

Erle ⚕ ['ɛrlə] f (-/-n) alder.

er'leb|en v/t. (no -ge-, h) (live to) see; experience; go through; 2nis [~pnɪs] n (-ses/-se) experience; adventure.

erledig|en [ɛr'le:dɪgən] v/t. (no -ge-, h) dispatch; execute; settle (matter); ~t adj. [~çt] finished, settled; fig.: played out; F done for; F: du bist für mich ~ I am through with you; 2ung [~gun] f (-/-% -en) dispatch; settlement.

er'leichter|n v/t. (no -ge-, h) lighten (burden); fig.: make easy, facilitate; relieve; 2ung f (-/-en) ease; relief; facilitation; ~en pl. facilities pl.

er|'leiden v/t. (irr. leiden, no -ge-, h) suffer, endure; sustain (damage, loss); ~'lernen v/t. (no -ge-, h) learn, acquire.

er'leucht|en v/t. (no -ge-, h) illuminate; fig. enlighten; 2ung f (-/-en) illumination; fig. enlightenment.

er'liegen v/i. (irr. liegen, no -ge-, sein) succumb (dat. to).

erlogen adj. [ɛr'lo:gən] false, untrue.

Erlös [ɛr'lø:s] m (-es/-e) proceeds pl.

erlosch|en [ɛr'lɔʃ] pret. of erlöschen; ~en 1. p.p. of erlöschen; 2. adj. extinct.

er'löschen v/i. (irr., no -ge-, sein) go out; fig. become extinct; contract: expire.

er'lös|en v/t. (no -ge-, h) redeem;

deliver; 2er *m* (-s/-) redeemer, deliverer; *eccl.* Redeemer, Saviour; 2ung *f* redemption; deliverance.

ermächtig|en [ɛr'mɛçtigən] *v/t.* (no -ge-, h) authorize; 2ung *f* (-/-en) authorization; authority; warrant.

er'mahn|en *v/t.* (no -ge-, h) admonish; 2ung *f* admonition.

er'mangel|n *v/i.* (no -ge-, h) be wanting (*gen.* in); 2ung *f* (-/no pl.): in ~ (*gen.*) in default of, for want of, failing.

er'mäßig|en *v/t.* (no -ge-, h) abate, reduce, cut (down); 2ung *f* (-/-en) abatement, reduction.

er'matt|en (no -ge-) 1. *v/t.* (h) fatigue, tire, exhaust; 2. *v/i.* (sein) tire, grow weary; *fig.* slacken; 2ung *f* (-/%, -en) fatigue, exhaustion.

er'messen 1. *v/t.* (*irr.* messen, no -ge-, h) judge; 2. 2 *n* (-s/no pl.) judg(e)ment; discretion.

er'mitt|eln *v/t.* (no -ge-, h) ascertain, find out; ♯ investigate; 2(e)lung [~(ə)luŋ] *f* (-/-en) ascertainment; inquiry; ♯ investigation.

er'möglichen *v/t.* (no -ge-, h) render *or* make possible.

er'mord|en *v/t.* (no -ge-, h) murder; assassinate; 2ung *f* (-/-en) murder; assassination.

er'müd|en (no -ge-) 1. *v/t.* (h) tire, fatigue; 2. *v/i.* (sein) tire, get tired *or* fatigued; 2ung *f* (-/%, -en) fatigue, tiredness.

er'munter|n *v/t.* (no -ge-, h) rouse, encourage; animate; 2ung *f* (-/-en) encouragement, animation.

ermutig|en [ɛr'muːtigən] *v/t.* (no -ge-, h) encourage; 2ung *f* (-/-en) encouragement.

er'nähr|en *v/t.* (no -ge-, h) nourish, feed; support; 2er *m* (-s/-) breadwinner, supporter; 2ung *f* (-/%, -en) nourishment; support; *physiol.* nutrition.

er'nenn|en *v/t.* (*irr.* nennen, no -ge-, h) nominate, appoint; 2ung *f* nomination, appointment.

er'neu|ern *v/t.* (no -ge-, h) renew, renovate; revive; 2erung *f* renewal, renovation; revival; ~t *adv.* once more.

erniedrig|en [ɛr'niːdrigən] *v/t.* (no -ge-, h) degrade; humiliate, humble; 2ung *f* (-/-en) degradation; humiliation.

Ernst [ɛrnst] 1. *m* (-es/no pl.) seriousness; earnest(ness); gravity; *im* ~ in earnest; 2. 2 *adj.* = '2haft *adj.*, '2lich *adj.* serious, earnest; grave.

Ernte ['ɛrntə] *f* (-/-n) harvest; crop; ~'dankfest *n* harvest festival; '2n *v/t.* (ge-, h) harvest, gather (in), reap (*a. fig.*).

er'nüchter|n *v/t.* (no -ge-, h) (make) sober; *fig.* disillusion; 2ung *f* (-/-en) sobering; *fig.* disillusionment.

Er'ober|er *m* (-s/-) conqueror; 2n *v/t.* (no -ge-, h) conquer; ~ung *f* (-/-en) conquest.

er'öffn|en *v/t.* (no -ge-, h) open; inaugurate; disclose (*j-m et. s.th. to s.o.*); notify; 2ung *f* opening; inauguration; disclosure.

erörter|n [ɛr'œrtərn] *v/t.* (no -ge-, h) discuss; 2ung *f* (-/-en) discussion.

Erpel *orn.* ['ɛrpəl] *m* (-s/-) drake.

erpicht *adj.* [ɛr'piçt]: ~ auf (*acc.*) bent *or* intent *or* set *or* keen on.

er'press|en *v/t.* (no -ge-, h) extort (*von* from); blackmail; 2er *m* (-s/-), 2erin *f* (-/-nen) extort(ion)er; blackmailer; 2ung *f* (-/-en) extortion; blackmail.

er'proben *v/t.* (no -ge-, h) try, test.

erquick|en [ɛr'kvikən] *v/t.* (no -ge-, h) refresh; 2ung *f* (-/-en) refreshment.

er|'raten *v/t.* (*irr.* raten, no -ge-, h) guess, find out; ~'rechnen *v/t.* (no -ge-, h) calculate, compute, work out.

erreg|bar *adj.* [ɛr'reːkbaːr] excitable; ~en [~gən] *v/t.* (no -ge-, h) excite; cause; 2er [~gər] *m* (-s/-) exciter (*a. ∉*); ♯ germ, virus; 2ung [~guŋ] *f* excitation; excitement.

er'reich|bar *adj.* attainable; within reach *or* call; ~en *v/t.* (no -ge-, h) reach; *fig.* achieve, attain; catch (*train*); come up to (*certain standard*).

er'rett|en *v/t.* (no -ge-, h) rescue; 2ung *f* rescue.

er'richt|en *v/t.* (no -ge-, h) set up, erect; establish; 2ung *f* erection; establishment.

er|'ringen *v/t.* (*irr.* ringen, no -ge-, h) gain, obtain; achieve (*success*); ~'röten *v/i.* (no -ge-, sein) blush.

Errungenschaft [ɛr'ruŋənʃaft] *f* (-/-en) acquisition; achievement.

Er'satz *m* (-es/no pl.) replacement; substitute; compensation; amends *sg.*, damages *pl.*; indemnification; *s.* Ersatzmann, Ersatzmittel; ~ leisten make amends; ~mann *m* substitute; ~mine *f* refill (*for pencil*); ~mittel *n* substitute, surrogate; ~reifen *mot. m* spare tyre, (*Am. only*) spare tire; ~teil ⊕ *n*, *m* spare (part).

er'schaff|en *v/t.* (*irr.* schaffen, no -ge-, h) create; 2ung *f* (-/no pl.) creation.

er'schallen *v/i.* ([*irr.* schallen,] no -ge-, sein) (re)sound; ring.

er'schein|en 1. *v/i.* (*irr.* scheinen, no -ge-, sein) appear; 2. 2 *n* (-s/no pl.) appearance; 2ung *f* (-/-en) appearance; apparition; vision.

er|'schießen *v/t.* (*irr.* schießen, no -ge-, h) shoot (dead); ~'schlaffen *v/i.* (no -ge-, sein) tire; relax; *fig.* languish, slacken; ~'schlagen *v/t.* (*irr.* schlagen, no -ge-, h) kill; slay;

~'schließen v/t. (irr. schließen, no -ge-, h) open; open up (new market); develop (district).

er'schöpf|en v/t. (no -ge-, h) exhaust; 2ung f exhaustion.

erschrak [ɛr'ʃraːk] pret. of erschrecken 2.

er'schrecken 1. v/t. (no -ge-, h) frighten, scare; 2. v/i. (irr., no -ge-, sein) be frightened (über acc. at); ~d adj. alarming, startling.

erschrocken [ɛr'ʃrɔkən] 1. p.p. of erschrecken 2; 2. adj. frightened, terrified.

erschütter|n [ɛr'ʃytərn] v/t. (no -ge-, h) shake; fig. shock, move; 2ung f (-/-en) shock; fig. emotion; ⚕ concussion; ⊕ percussion.

er'schweren v/t. (no -ge-, h) make more difficult; aggravate.

er'schwing|en v/t. (irr. schwingen, no -ge-, h) afford; ~lich adj. within s.o.'s means; prices: reasonable.

er'seh|en v/t. (irr. sehen, no -ge-, h) see, learn, gather (all: aus from); ~'sehnen v/t. (no -ge-, h) long for; ~'setzen v/t. (no -ge-, h) repair; make up for, compensate (for); replace; refund.

er'sichtlich adj. evident, obvious.

er'sinnen v/t. (irr. sinnen, no -ge-, h) contrive, devise.

er'spar|en v/t. (no -ge-, h) save; j-m et. ~ spare s.o. s.th.; 2nis f (-/-se) saving.

er'sprießlich adj. useful, beneficial.

erst [ɛːrst] 1. adj.: der (die, das) ~e the first; 2. adv. first; at first; only; not ... till or until.

er'starr|en v/i. (no -ge-, sein) stiffen; solidify; congeal; set; grow numb; fig. blood: run cold; ~t adj. benumbed; 2ung f (-/-en) numbness; solidification; congealment; setting.

erstatt|en [ɛr'ʃtatən] v/t. (no -ge-, h) restore; s. ersetzen; Bericht ~ (make a) report; 2ung f (-/-en) restitution.

'Erstaufführung f thea. first night or performance, premiere; film: a. first run.

er'staun|en 1. v/i. (no -ge-, sein) be astonished (über acc. at); 2. v/t. (no -ge-, h) astonish; 3. 2 n astonishment; in ~ setzen astonish; ~lich adj. astonishing, amazing.

er'stechen v/t. (irr. stechen, no -ge-, h) stab.

er'steig|en v/t. (irr. steigen, no -ge-, h) ascend, climb; 2ung f ascent.

erstens adv. ['eːrstəns] first, firstly.

er'stick|en (no -ge-) v/t. (h) and v/i. (sein) choke, suffocate; stifle; 2ung f (-/-en) suffocation. [rate, F A 1.)

'erstklassig adj. first-class, first-)

er'streben v/t. (no -ge-, h) strive after or for; ~swert adj. desirable.

er'strecken v/refl. (no -ge-, h) extend; sich ~ über (acc.) cover.

er'suchen 1. v/t. (no -ge-, h) request; 2. 2 n (-s/-) request.

er'tappen v/t. (no -ge-, h) catch, surprise; s. frisch; ~'tönen v/i. (no -ge-, sein) (re)sound.

Ertrag [ɛr'traːk] m (-[e]s/⁼e) produce, yield; proceeds pl., returns pl.; ✗ output; 2en [~gən] v/t. (irr. tragen, no -ge-, h) bear, endure; suffer; stand.

erträglich adj. [ɛr'trɛːkliç] tolerable.

er'tränken v/t. (no -ge-, h) drown; ~'trinken v/i. (irr. trinken, no -ge-, sein) be drowned, drown; ~'übrigen [ɛr'yːbrigən] v/t. (no -ge-, h) save; spare (time); sich ~ be unnecessary; ~'wachen v/i. (no -ge-, sein) awake, wake up.

er'wachsen 1. v/i. (irr. wachsen, no -ge-, sein) arise (aus from); 2. adj. grown-up, adult; 2e m, f (-n/-n) grown-up, adult.

er'wäg|en v/t. (irr. wägen, no -ge-, h) consider, think s.th. over; 2ung f (-/-en) consideration.

er'wählen v/t. (no -ge-, h) choose, elect.

er'wähn|en v/t. (no -ge-, h) mention; 2ung f (-/-en) mention.

er'wärmen v/t. (no -ge-, h) warm, heat; sich ~ warm (up).

er'wart|en v/t. (no -ge-, h) await, wait for; fig. expect; 2ung f expectation.

er'weck|en v/t. (no -ge-, h) wake, rouse; fig. awake; cause (fear); arouse (suspicion); ~'wehren v/refl. (gen.) (no -ge-, h) keep or ward off; ~'weichen v/t. (no -ge-, h) soften; fig. move; ~'weisen v/t. (irr. weisen, no -ge-, h) prove; show (respect); render (service); do, pay (honour); do (favour).

er'weiter|n v/t. and v/refl. (no -ge-, h) expand, enlarge, extend, widen; 2ung f (-/-en) expansion, enlargement, extension.

Erwerb [ɛr'vɛrp] m (-[e]s/-e) acquisition; living; earnings pl.; business; 2en [~bən] v/t. (irr. werben, no -ge-, h) acquire; gain; earn.

erwerbs|los adj. [ɛr'vɛrpsloːs] unemployed; ~tätig adj. (gainfully) employed; ~unfähig adj. [ɛr-'vɛrps?-] incapable of earning one's living; 2zweig m line of business.

Erwerbung [ɛr'vɛrbuŋ] f acquisition.

erwider|n [ɛr'viːdərn] v/t. (no -ge-, h) return; answer, reply; retort; 2ung f (-/-en) return; answer, reply.

er'wischen v/t. (no -ge-, h) catch, trap, get hold of.

er'wünscht adj. desired; desirable; welcome.

er'würgen v/t. (no -ge-, h) strangle, throttle.

Erz ⚔ [eːrts] *n* (-es/-e) ore; *poet.* brass.

er'zähl|en *v/t.* (*no* -ge-, *h*) tell; relate; narrate; **2er** *m*, **2erin** *f* (-/-nen) narrator; writer; **2ung** *f* narration; (short) story, narrative.

'Erz|bischof *eccl.* *m* archbishop; **'~bistum** *eccl.* *n* archbishopric; **'~engel** *eccl.* *m* archangel.

er'zeug|en *v/t.* (*no* -ge-, *h*) beget; produce; make, manufacture; **2er** *m* (-s/-) father (*of child*); ⚘ producer; **2nis** *n* produce; production; ⊕ product; **2ung** *f* production.

'Erz|feind *m* arch-enemy; **'~herzog** *m* archduke; **'~herzogin** *f* archduchess; **'~herzogtum** *n* archduchy.

er'ziehe|n *v/t.* (*irr.* ziehen, *no* -ge-, *h*) bring up, rear, raise; educate; **2r** *m* (-s/-) educator; teacher, tutor; **2rin** *f* (-/-nen) teacher; governess; **~risch** *adj.* educational, pedagogic (-al).

Er'ziehung *f* (-/~ -en) upbringing; breeding; education; **~sanstalt** [ɛr'tsiːʊŋs?-] *f* reformatory, approved school; **~swesen** *n* (-s/*no pl.*) educational matters *pl. or* system.

er|'zielen *v/t.* (*no* -ge-, *h*) obtain; realize (*price*); achieve (*success*); *sports:* score (*points, goal*); **~'zür-nen** *v/t.* (*no* -ge-, *h*) make angry, irritate, enrage; **~'zwingen** *v/t.* (*irr.* zwingen, *no* -ge-, *h*) (en)force; compel; extort (*von* from).

es *pers. pron.* [ɛs] 1. *pers.:* it, he, she; *wo ist das Buch?* — ~ *ist auf dem Tisch* where is the book? — it is on the table; *das Mädchen blieb stehen, als* ~ *seine Mutter sah* the girl stopped when she saw her mother; 2. *impers.:* it; ~ *gibt* there is, there are; ~ *ist kalt* it is cold; ~ *klopft* there is a knock at the door.

Esche ♣ [ˈɛʃə] *f* (-/-n) ash(-tree).

Esel *zo.* [ˈeːzəl] *m* (-s/-) donkey; *esp. fig.* ass; **~ei** [~'laɪ] *f* (-/-en) stupidity, stupid thing, folly; **'~s-brücke** *f* *at school:* crib, *Am.* pony; **~sohr** [ˈeːzəls?-] *n* dog's ear (*of book*).

Eskorte [ɛsˈkɔrtə] *f* (-/-n) ⚔ escort; ⚓ convoy.

Espe ♣ [ˈɛspə] *f* (-/-n) asp(en).

'eßbar *adj.* eatable, edible.

Esse [ˈɛsə] *f* (-/-n) chimney.

essen [ˈɛsən] 1. *v/i.* (*irr.*, ge-, *h*) eat; *zu Mittag* ~ (have) lunch; dine, have dinner; *zu Abend* ~ dine, have dinner; *esp. late at night:* sup, have supper; *auswärts* ~ eat or dine out; 2. *v/t.* (*irr.*, ge-, *h*) eat; et. *zu Mittag etc.* ~ have s.th. for lunch, *etc.*; 3. **2** *n* (-s/-) eating; food; meal; dish; *midday meal:* lunch, dinner; *evening meal:* dinner; *last meal of the day:* supper; **'2szeit** *f* lunch-time; dinner-time; supper-time.

Essenz [ɛˈsɛnts] *f* (-/-en) essence.

Essig [ˈɛsiç] *m* (-s/-e) vinegar; **'~gurke** *f* pickled cucumber, gherkin.

'Eß|löffel *m* soup-spoon; **'~nische** *f* dining alcove, *Am.* dinette; **'~tisch** *m* dining-table; **'~waren** *f/pl.* eatables *pl.*, victuals *pl.*, food; **'~zim-mer** *n* dining-room.

etablieren [eta'bliːrən] *v/t.* (*no* -ge-, *h*) establish, set up.

Etage [e'taːʒə] *f* (-/-n) floor, stor(e)y; **~nwohnung** *f* flat, *Am. a.* apartment.

Etappe [e'tapə] *f* (-/-n) ⚔ base; *fig.* stage, leg.

Etat [e'taː] *m* (-s/-s) budget, *parl.* the Estimates *pl.*; **~sjahr** *n* fiscal year. [*or sg.*]

Ethik [ˈeːtik] *f* (-/~ -en) ethics *pl.*]

Etikett [eti'kɛt] *n* (-[e]s/-e, -s) label, ticket; tag; *gummed:* Am. a. sticker; **~e** *f* (-/-n) etiquette; **2ieren** [~'tiː-rən] *v/t.* (*no* -ge-, *h*) label.

etliche *indef. pron.* [ˈɛtliçə] some, several.

Etui [e'tviː] *n* (-s/-s) case.

etwa *adv.* [ˈɛtva] perhaps, by chance; about, *Am. a.* around; **~ig** *adj.* [ˈ~iç] possible, eventual.

etwas [ˈɛtvas] 1. *indef. pron.* something; anything; 2. *adj.* some; any; 3. *adv.* somewhat; *4.* **2** *n* (-/-): *das gewisse* ~ that certain something.

euch *pers. pron.* [ɔʏç] you; ~ (*selbst*) yourselves.

euer *poss. pron.* [ˈɔʏər] your; *der* (*die, das*) eu(e)re yours.

Eule *orn.* [ˈɔʏlə] *f* (-/-n) owl; **~n** *nach Athen tragen* carry coals to Newcastle.

euresgleichen *pron.* [ˈɔʏrəs'glaɪçən] people like you, F the likes of you.

Europä|er [ɔʏro'pɛːər] *m* (-s/-) European; **2isch** *adj.* European.

Euter [ˈɔʏtər] *n* (-s/-) udder.

evakuieren [evaku'iːrən] *v/t.* (*no* -ge-, *h*) evacuate.

evangeli|sch *adj.* [evan'geːliʃ] evangelic(al); Protestant; **2um** [~jum] *n* (-s/*Evangelien*) gospel.

eventuell [eventu'ɛl] 1. *adj.* possible; 2. *adv.* possibly, perhaps.

ewig *adj.* [ˈeːviç] eternal; everlasting; perpetual; *auf* ~ for ever; **2keit** *f* (-/-en) eternity; F: *seit e-r* ~ for ages.

exakt *adj.* [ɛ'ksakt] exact; **2heit** *f* (-/-en) exactitude, exactness; accuracy.

Exam|en [ɛ'ksaːmən] *n* (-s/-, *Exa-mina*) examination, F exam; **2inie-ren** [~ami'niːrən] *v/t.* (*no* -ge-, *h*) examine.

Exekutive [ɛksəku'tiːvə] *f* (-/*no pl.*) executive power.

Exempel [ɛ'ksɛmpəl] *n* (-s/-) example, instance.

Exemplar [ɛksɛm'plaːr] n (-s/-e) specimen; copy (of book).

exerzier|en ⚔ [ɛkser'tsiːrən] v/i. and v/t. (no -ge-, h) drill; ⚔platz ⚔ m drill-ground, parade-ground.

Exil [ɛ'ksiːl] n (-s/-e) exile.

Existenz [ɛksis'tɛnts] f (-/-en) existence; living, livelihood; ~minimum n subsistence minimum.

exis'tieren v/i. (no -ge-, h) exist; subsist.

exotisch adj. [ɛ'ksoːtiʃ] exotic.

exped|ieren [ɛkspe'diːrən] v/t. (no -ge-, h) dispatch; ⚔ition [~i'tsjoːn] f (-/-en) dispatch, forwarding; expedition; † dispatch or forwarding office.

Experiment [ɛksperi'mɛnt] n (-[e]s/-e) experiment; ⚔ieren [~'tiːrən] v/i. (no -ge-, h) experiment.

explo|dieren [ɛksplo'diːrən] v/i. (no -ge-, sein) explode, burst; ⚔sion [~'zjoːn] f (-/-en) explosion; ~siv adj. [~'ziːf] explosive.

Export [ɛks'pɔrt] m (-[e]s/-e) export(ation); ⚔ieren [~'tiːrən] v/t. (no -ge-, h) export.

extra adj. ['ɛkstra] extra; special; ⚔blatt n extra edition (of newspaper), Am. extra.

Extrakt [ɛks'trakt] m (-[e]s/-e) extract.

Extrem [ɛks'treːm] 1. n (-s/-e) extreme; 2. ⚔ adj. extreme.

Exzellenz [ɛkstsɛ'lɛnts] f (-/-en) Excellency.

exzentrisch adj. [ɛks'tsɛntriʃ] eccentric.

Exzeß [ɛks'tsɛs] m (Exzesses/Exzesse) excess.

F

Fabel ['faːbəl] f (-/-n) fable (a. fig.); plot (of story, book, etc.); ⚔haft adj. fabulous; marvellous; ⚔n v/i. (ge-, h) tell (tall) stories.

Fabrik [fa'briːk] f (-/-en) factory, works sg., pl., mill; ~ant [~i'kant] m (-en/-en) factory-owner, mill-owner; manufacturer; ~arbeit f factory work; s. Fabrikware; ~arbeiter m factory worker or hand; ~at [~i'kaːt] n (-[e]s/-e) make; product; ~ationsfehler [~a'tsjoːns-] m flaw; ~besitzer m factory-owner; ~marke f trade mark; ~stadt f factory or industrial town; ~ware f manufactured article; ~zeichen n s. Fabrikmarke.

Fach [fax] n (-[e]s/⁻er) section, compartment, shelf (of bookcase, cupboard, etc.); pigeon-hole (in desk); drawer; fig. subject; s. Fachgebiet; ~arbeiter m skilled worker; ~arzt m specialist (für in); ~ausbildung f professional training; ~ausdruck m technical term.

fächeln ['fɛçəln] v/t. (ge-, h) fan s.o.

Fächer ['fɛçər] m (-s/-) fan; ⚔förmig adj. ['~fœrmiç] fan-shaped.

Fach|gebiet n branch, field, province; ⚔kenntnisse f/pl. specialized knowledge; ~kreis m: in ~ among experts; ⚔kundig adj. competent, expert; ⚔literatur f specialized literature; ~mann m expert; ⚔männisch adj. ['~mɛniʃ] expert; ~schule f technical school; ~werk △ n framework.

Fackel ['fakəl] f (-/-n) torch; ⚔n F v/i. (ge-, h) hesitate, F shilly-shally; ~zug m torchlight procession.

fad adj. [faːt], ~e adj. ['faːdə] food: insipid, tasteless; stale; p. dull, boring.

Faden ['faːdən] m (-s/⁻) thread (a. fig.); fig.: an e-m ~ hängen hang by a thread; ~nudeln f/pl. vermicelli pl.; ⚔scheinig adj. ['~ʃainiç] threadbare; excuse, etc.: flimsy, thin.

fähig adj. ['fɛːiç] capable (zu inf. of ger.; gen. of); able (to inf.); ⚔keit f (-/-en) (cap)ability; talent, faculty.

fahl adj. [faːl] pale, pallid; colour: faded; complexion: leaden, livid.

fahnd|en ['faːndən] v/i. (ge-, h): nach j-m ~ search for s.o.; ⚔ung f (-/-en) search.

Fahne ['faːnə] f (-/-n) flag; standard; banner; ⚔, ⚔, fig. colo(u)rs pl.; typ. galley-proof.

'Fahnen|eid m oath of allegiance; ~flucht f desertion; ⚔flüchtig adj.: ~ werden desert (the colo[u]rs); ~stange f flagstaff, Am. a. flagpole.

'Fahr|bahn f, ~damm m roadway.

Fähre ['fɛːrə] f (-/-n) ferry(-boat).

fahren ['faːrən] (irr., ge-) 1. v/i. (sein) driver, vehicle, etc.: drive, go, travel; cyclist: ride, cycle; ⚔ sail; mot. motor; mit der Eisenbahn ~ go by train or rail; spazieren ~ go for or take a drive; mit der Hand ~ über (acc.) pass one's hand over; ~ lassen let go or slip; gut (schlecht) ~ bei do or fare well (badly) at or with; er ist gut dabei gefahren he did very well out of it; 2. v/t. (h) carry, convey; drive (car, train, etc.); ride (bicycle, etc.).

'Fahrer m (-s/-) driver; '~flucht f (-/no pl.) hit-and-run offence, Am. hit-and-run offense.

'**Fahr|gast** *m* passenger; *in taxi*: fare; '**~geld** *n* fare; '**~gelegenheit** *f* transport facilities *pl.*; '**~gestell** *n mot.* chassis; ✈ undercarriage, landing gear; '**~karte** *f* ticket; '**~kartenschalter** *m* booking-office, *Am.* ticket office; '**⒉lässig** *adj.* careless, negligent; '**~lässigkeit** *f* (-/**~**-en) carelessness, negligence; '**~lehrer** *mot. m* driving instructor; '**~plan** *m* timetable, *Am. a.* schedule; '**⒉planmäßig 1.** *adj.* regular, *Am.* scheduled; **2.** *adv.* on time, *Am. a.* on schedule; '**~preis** *m* fare; '**~rad** *n* bicycle, F bike; '**~schein** *m* ticket; '**~schule** *mot. f* driving school, school of motoring; '**~stuhl** *m* lift, *Am.* elevator; '**~stuhlführer** *m* lift-boy, lift-man, *Am.* elevator operator; '**~stunde** *mot. f* driving lesson.

Fahrt [fɑːrt] *f* (-/-en) ride, drive; journey, voyage, passage; trip; ~ *ins Blaue* mystery tour; *in voller* ~ (at) full speed.

Fährte ['fɛːrtə] *f* (-/-n) track (*a. fig.*); *auf der falschen* ~ *sein* be on the wrong track.

'**Fahr|vorschrift** *f* rule of the road; '**~wasser** *n* ⚓ navigable water; *fig.* track; '**~weg** *m* roadway; '**~zeug** *n* vehicle; ⚓ vessel.

Fakt|or ['faktɔr] *m* (-s/-en) factor; **~otum** [**~**'toːtum] *n* (-s/-s, Faktoten) factotum; **~ur** † [**~**'tuːr] *f* (-/-en), **~ura** † [**~**'tuːra] *f* (-/Fakturen) invoice.

Fakultät *univ.* [fakul'tɛːt] *f* (-/-en) faculty.

Falke *orn.* ['falkə] *m* (-n/-n) hawk, falcon.

Fall [fal] *m* (-[e]s/**ᵘ**e) fall (*of body, stronghold, city, etc.*); *gr.*, ✶ ﹩ case; *gesetzt den* ~ suppose; *auf alle Fälle* at all events; *auf jeden* ~ in any case, at any rate; *auf keinen* ~ on no account, in no case.

Falle ['falə] *f* (-/-n) trap (*a. fig.*); pitfall (*a. fig.*); *e-e* ~ *stellen* set a trap (*j-m* for s.o.).

fallen ['falən] **1.** *v/i.* (*irr.*, ge-, sein) fall, drop; ✗ be killed in action; *shot*: be heard; *flood water*: subside; *auf j-n* ~ *suspicion, etc.*: fall on s.o.; ~ *lassen* drop (*plate, etc.*). **2.** ⒉ *n* (-s/*no pl.*) fall(ing).

fällen ['fɛlən] *v/t.* (ge-, h) fell, cut down (*tree*); ✗ lower (*bayonet*); ﹩ pass (*judgement*), give (*decision*).

'**fallenlassen** *v/t.* (*irr. lassen, sep., no -ge-, h*) drop (*plan, claim, etc.*).

fällig *adj.* ['fɛliç] due; payable; '**⒉keit** *f* (-/**~**-en) maturity; '**⒉keitstermin** *m* date of maturity.

'**Fall|obst** *n* windfall; **~reep** ⚓ ['**~**reːp] *n* (-[e]s/-e) gangway.

falls *cj.* [fals] if; in the event of *ger.*; in case.

'**Fall|schirm** *m* parachute; '**~**

'**~schirmspringer** *m* parachutist; '**~strick** *m* snare; '**~tür** *f* trap door.

falsch [falʃ] **1.** *adj.* false; wrong; *bank-note, etc.*: counterfeit; *money*: base; *bill of exchange, etc.*: forged; *p.* deceitful; **2.** *adv.*: ~ *gehen* *watch*: go wrong; ~ *verbunden* *teleph.* sorry, wrong number.

fälsch|en ['fɛlʃən] *v/t.* (ge-, h) falsify; forge, fake (*document, etc.*); counterfeit (*bank-note, coin, etc.*); fake (*calculations, etc.*); tamper with (*financial account*); adulterate (*food, wine*); '**⒉er** *m* (-s/-) forger, faker; adulterator.

'**Falsch|geld** *n* counterfeit *or* bad *or* base money; '**~heit** *f* (-/-en) falseness, falsity; duplicity, deceitfulness; '**~meldung** *f* false report; '**~münzer** *m* (-s/-) coiner; '**~münzerwerkstatt** *f* coiner's den; '**⒉spielen** *v/i.* (*sep., -ge-, h*) cheat (at cards); '**~spieler** *m* cardsharper.

'**Fälschung** *f* (-/-en) forgery; falsification; fake; adulteration.

Falt|boot ['falt-] *n* folding canoe, *Am.* foldboat, faltboat; **~e** ['**~**ə] *f* (-/-n) fold; pleat (*in skirt, etc.*); crease (*in trousers*); wrinkle (*on face*); '**⒉en** *v/t.* (ge-, h) fold; clasp or join (*one's hands*); '**⒉ig** *adj.* folded; pleated; wrinkled.

Falz [falts] *m* (-es/-e) fold; rabbet (*for woodworking, etc.*); bookbinding: guard; '**⒉en** *v/t.* (ge-, h) fold; rabbet.

familiär *adj.* [famil'jɛːr] familiar; informal.

Familie [fa'miːljə] *f* (-/-n) family (*a. zo.*, ♀).

Fa'milien|angelegenheit *f* family affair; **~anschluß** *m*: ~ *haben* live as one of the family; **~nachrichten** *f/pl. in newspaper*: birth, marriage, and death announcements *pl.*; **~name** *m* family name, surname, *Am. a.* last name; **~stand** *m* marital status.

Fanati|ker [fa'nɑːtikər] *m* (-s/-) fanatic; **⒉sch** *adj.* fanatic(al).

Fanatismus [fana'tismus] *m* (-/*no pl.*) fanaticism.

fand [fant] *pret. of finden.*

Fanfare [fan'fɑːrə] *f* (-/-n) fanfare, flourish (of trumpets).

Fang [faŋ] *m* (-[e]s/**ᵘ**e) capture, catch(ing); *hunt.* bag; '**⒉en** *v/t.* (*irr.* ge-, h) catch (*animal, ball, thief, etc.*); '**~zahn** *m* fang (*of dog, wolf, etc.*); tusk (*of boar*).

Farb|band ['farp-] *n* (typewriter) ribbon; **~e** ['**~**bə] *f* (-/-n) colo(u)r; paint; dye; complexion; *cards*: suit; **⒉echt** *adj.* ['farp⁹-] colo(u)r-fast.

färben ['fɛrbən] *v/t.* (ge-, h) colo(u)r (*glass, food, etc.*); dye (*material, hair, Easter eggs, etc.*); tint (*hair,*

paper, glass); stain (*wood, fabrics, glass,* etc.); *sich ~* take on *or* assume a colo(u)r; *sich rot ~* turn *or* go red.
'farben|blind *adj.* colo(u)r-blind; **'2druck** *m* (-[e]s/-e) colo(u)r print; **'~prächtig** *adj.* splendidly col-o(u)rful.
Färber ['fɛrbər] *m* (-s/-) dyer.
Farb|fernsehen ['farp-] *n* colo(u)r television; **'~film** *m* colo(u)r film; **2ig** *adj.* ['~biç] colo(u)red; *glass*: tinted, stained; *fig.* colo(u)rful; **2los** *adj.* ['~p-] colo(u)rless; **'~pho-tographie** *f* colo(u)r photography; **'~stift** *m* colo(u)red pencil; **'~stoff** *m* colo(u)ring matter; **'~ton** *m* tone; shade, tint.
Färbung ['fɛrbuŋ] *f* (-/-en) colo(u)r-ing (*a. fig.*); shade (*a. fig.*).
Farnkraut ⚘ ['farnkraut] *n* fern.
Fasan *orn.* [fa'zɑːn] *m* (-[e]s/-e[n]) pheasant.
Fasching ['faʃiŋ] *m* (-s/-e, -s) carni-val.
Fasel|ei [fɑːzə'laɪ] *f* (-/-en) driv-elling, waffling; twaddle; **'2n** *v/i.* (ge-, h) blather; F waffle.
Faser ['fɑːzər] *f* (-/-n) anat., ⚘, *fig.* fib|re, *Am.* -er; *cotton, wool,* etc.: staple; **'2ig** *adj.* fibrous; **'2n** *v/i.* (ge-, h) *wool*: shed fine hairs.
Faß [fas] *n* (*Fasses/Fässer*) cask, barrel; tub; vat; **'~bier** *n* draught beer.
Fassade △ [fa'sɑːdə] *f* (-/-n) façade, front (*a. fig.*); **~nkletterer** *m* (-s/-) cat burglar.
fassen ['fasən] (ge-, h) **1.** *v/t.* seize, take hold of; catch, apprehend (*criminal*); hold; *s. einfassen; fig.* grasp, understand, believe; pluck up (*courage*); form (*plan*); make (*decision*); *sich ~* compose o.s.; *sich kurz ~* be brief; **2.** *v/i.: ~ nach* reach for.   [ceivable.\
'faßlich *adj.* comprehensible, con-]
'Fassung *f* (-/-en) setting (*of jewels*); ⚡ socket; *fig.:* composure; draft (-ing); wording, version; *die ~ verlieren* lose one's self-control; *aus der ~ bringen* disconcert; **'~s-kraft** *f* (powers of) comprehension, mental capacity; **'~svermögen** *n* (holding) capacity; *fig. s. Fassungs-kraft.*
fast *adv.* [fast] almost, nearly; *~ nichts* next to nothing; *~ nie* hardly ever.
fasten ['fastən] *v/i.* (ge-, h) fast; abstain from food and drink; **'2zeit** *f* Lent.
'Fast|nacht *f* (-/no pl.) Shrovetide; carnival; **'~tag** *m* fast-day.
fatal *adj.* [fa'tɑːl] *situation,* etc.: awkward; *business,* etc.: unfortu-nate; *mistake,* etc.: fatal.
fauchen ['fauxən] *v/i.* (ge-, h) *cat,* etc.: spit; F *p.* spit (*with anger*); *locomotive,* etc.: hiss.

faul *adj.* [faul] *fruit,* etc.: rotten, bad; *fish, meat:* putrid, bad; *fig.* lazy, indolent, idle; fishy; **~e** *Aus-rede* lame excuse; **'~en** *v/i.* (ge-, h) rot, go bad, putrefy.
faulenze|n ['faulɛntsən] *v/i.* (ge-, h) idle; laze, loaf; **'2r** *m* (-s/-) idler, sluggard, F lazy-bones.
'Faul|heit *f* (-/no pl.) idleness, laziness; **'2ig** *adj.* putrid.
Fäulnis ['fɔʏlnis] *f* (-/no pl.) rotten-ness; putrefaction; decay.
'Faul|pelz *m s.* Faulenzer; **'~tier** *n* zo. sloth (*a. fig.*).
Faust [faust] *f* (-/-e) fist; *auf eigene ~* on one's own initiative; **'~hand-schuh** *m* mitt(en); **'~schlag** *m* blow with the fist, punch, *Am.* F *a.* slug.
Favorit [favo'riːt] *m* (-en/-en) favo(u)rite.
Faxe ['faksə] *f* (-/-n): *~n machen* (play the) fool; *~n schneiden* pull *or* make faces.
Fazit ['fɑːtsit] *n* (-s/-e, -s) result, upshot; total; *das ~ ziehen* sum *or* total up.
Februar ['feːbruɑːr] *m* (-[s]/-e) February.
fecht|en ['fɛçtən] *v/i.* (*irr.,* ge-, h) fight; *fenc.* fence; **'2er** *m* (-s/-) fencer.
Feder ['feːdər] *f* (-/-n) feather; (*ornamental*) plume; pen; ⊕ spring; **'~bett** *n* feather bed; **'~busch** *m* tuft of feathers; plume; **'~gewicht** *n boxing,* etc.: featherweight; **'~hal-ter** *m* (-s/-) penholder; **'~kiel** *m* quill; **'~kraft** *f* elasticity, resilience; **'~krieg** *m* paper war; literary con-troversy; **'2leicht** *adj.* (as) light as a feather; **'~lesen** *n* (-s/no pl.): *nicht viel ~s machen mit* make short work of; **'~messer** *n* penknife; **'2n** *v/i.* (ge-, h) be elastic; **'2nd** *adj.* springy, elastic; **'~strich** *m* stroke of the pen; **'~vieh** *n* poultry; **'~zeichnung** *f* pen-and-ink draw-ing.
Fee [feː] *f* (-/-n) fairy.
Fegefeuer ['feːgə-] *n* purgatory.
fegen ['feːgən] *v/t.* (ge-, h) sweep; clean.
Fehde ['feːdə] *f* (-/-n) feud; private war; *in ~ liegen* be at feud; F be at daggers drawn.
Fehl [feːl] *m: ohne ~* without fault *or* blemish; **'~betrag** *m* deficit, deficiency.
fehlen ['feːlən] *v/i.* (ge-, h) be absent; be missing *or* lacking; do wrong; *es fehlt ihm an* (*dat.*) he lacks; *was fehlt Ihnen?* what is the matter with you?; *weit gefehlt!* far off the mark!
Fehler ['feːlər] *m* (-s/-) mistake, error, F slip; fault; ⊕ defect, flaw; **'2frei** *adj.,* **'2los** *adj.* faultless, perfect; ⊕ flawless; **'2haft** *adj.* faulty; defective; incorrect.
'Fehl|geburt *f* miscarriage, abor-

tion; '2gehen v/i. (irr. gehen, sep., -ge-, sein) go wrong; 'griff fig. m mistake, blunder; 'schlag fig. m failure; '2schlagen fig. v/i. (irr. schlagen, sep., -ge-, sein) fail, miscarry; 'schuß m miss; '2treten v/i. (irr. treten, sep., -ge-, sein) make a false step; 'tritt m false step; slip; fig. slip, fault; 'urteil ꝑⁿ n error of judg(e)ment; 'zündung mot. f misfire, backfire.

Feier ['faɪər] f (-/-n) ceremony; celebration; festival; festivity; 'abend m finishing or closing time; ~ machen finish, F knock off; '2lich adj. promise, oath, etc.: solemn; act: ceremonial; 'lichkeit f (-/-en) solemnity; ceremony; '2n (ge-, h) 1. v/t. hold (celebration); celebrate, observe (feast, etc.); 2. v/i. celebrate; rest (from work), make holiday; 'tag m holiday; festive day.

feig adj. [faɪk] cowardly.

feige¹ adj. ['faɪgə] cowardly.

Feige² [⁀] f (-/-n) fig; 'nbaum ♀ m fig-tree; 'nblatt n fig-leaf.

Feig|heit ['faɪkhaɪt] f (-/no pl.) cowardice, cowardliness; 'ling ['klɪŋ] m (-s/-e) coward.

feil adj. [faɪl] for sale, to be sold; fig. venal; 'bieten v/t. (irr. bieten, sep., -ge-, h) offer for sale.

Feile ['faɪlə] f (-/-n) file; '2n (ge-, h) 1. v/t. file (a. fig.); fig. polish; 2. v/i.: ~ an (dat.) file (at); fig. finish (up).

feilschen ['faɪlʃən] v/i. (ge-, h) bargain (um for), haggle (for, about), Am. a. dicker (about).

fein adj. [faɪn] fine; material, etc.: high-grade; wine, etc.: choice; fabric, etc.: delicate, dainty; manners: polished; p. polite; distinction: subtle.

Feind [faɪnt] m (-[e]s/-e) enemy (a. ⨉); '2lich adj. hostile, inimical; 'schaft f (-/-en) enmity; animosity; hostility; '2selig adj. hostile (gegen to); 'seligkeit f (-/-en) hostility; malevolence.

'fein|fühlend adj., 'fühlig adj. sensitive; '2gefühl n sensitiveness; delicacy; '2gehalt m (monetary) standard; '2heit f (-/-en) fineness, delicacy, daintiness; politeness; elegance; '2kost f high-class groceries pl., Am. delicatessen; '2mechanik f precision mechanics; '2schmecker m (-s/-) gourmet, epicure; 'sinnig adj. subtle.

feist adj. [faɪst] fat, stout.

Feld [fɛlt] n (-[e]s/-er) field (a. ⨉, ⚔, sports); ground; soil; plain; chess: square; ⚞, ⊕ panel, compartment; ins ~ ziehen take the field; 'arbeit f agricultural work; 'bett n camp-bed; 'blume f wild flower; 'dienst ⨉ m field service; 'flasche f water-bottle;

'frucht f fruit of the field; 'geschrei n war-cry, battle-cry; 'herr m general; 'kessel m camp-kettle; 'lazarett ⨉ n field-hospital; 'lerche orn. f skylark; 'marschall m Field Marshal; '2marschmäßig ⨉ adj. in full marching order; 'maus zo. f field-mouse; 'messer m (land) surveyor; 'post ⨉ f army postal service; 'schlacht ⨉ f battle; 'stecher m (-s/-) (ein a pair of) field-glasses pl.; 'stuhl m camp-stool; 'webel ['ve:bəl] m (-s/-) sergeant; 'weg m (field) path; 'zeichen ⨉ n standard; 'zug m ⨉ campaign (a. fig.), (military) expedition; Am. fig. a. drive.

Felge ['fɛlgə] f (-/-n) felloe (of cart-wheel); rim (of car wheel, etc.).

Fell [fɛl] n (-[e]s/-e) skin, pelt, fur (of dead animal); coat (of cat, etc.); fleece (of sheep).

Fels [fɛls] m (-en/-en), ~en ['zən] m (-s/-) rock; ~block ['fɛls-] m rock; boulder; '2ig adj. ['zɪç] rocky.

Fenchel ♀ ['fɛnçəl] m (-s/no pl.) fennel.

Fenster ['fɛnstər] n (-s/-) window; 'brett n window-sill; 'flügel m casement (of casement window); sash (of sash window); 'kreuz n cross-bar(s pl.); 'laden m shutter; 'rahmen m window-frame; 'riegel m window-fastener; 'scheibe f (window-)pane; 'sims m, n window-sill.

Ferien ['fe:rjən] pl. holiday(s pl.), esp. Am. vacation; leave, Am. a. furlough; parl. recess; ꝑꝓ vacation, recess; 'kolonie f children's holiday camp.

Ferkel ['fɛrkəl] n (-s/-) young pig; contp. p. pig.

fern [fɛrn] 1. adj. far (off), distant; remote; 2. adv. far (away); von ~ from a distance.

'Fernamt teleph. n trunk exchange, Am. long-distance exchange.

'fernbleiben 1. v/i. (irr. bleiben, sep., -ge-, sein) remain or stay away (dat. from); 2. 2 n (-s/no pl.) absence (from school, etc.); absenteeism (from work).

Fern|e ['fɛrnə] f (-/-n) distance; remoteness; aus der ~ from or at a distance; '2er 1. adj. farther; fig.: further; future; 2. adv. further (-more), in addition, also; ~ liefen ... also ran ...; 'flug ⨉ m long-distance flight; '2gelenkt adj. ['gəlɛŋkt] missile: guided; aircraft, etc.: remote-control(l)ed; 'gespräch teleph. n trunk call, Am. long-distance call; '2gesteuert adj. s. ferngelenkt; 'glas n binoculars pl.; '2halten v/t. and v/refl. (irr. halten, sep., -ge-, h) keep away (von from); 'heizung f district heating; 'la-

ster F *mot.* *m* long-distance lorry, *Am.* long haul truck; '**~lenkung** *f* (-/-en) remote control; '**2liegen** *v/i.* (*irr.* liegen, *sep.*, *-ge-*, h): es liegt mir fern *zu* inf. I am far from *ger.*; '**~rohr** *n* telescope; '**~schreiber** *m* teleprinter, *Am.* teletypewriter; '**~sehen 1.** *n* (-s/no *pl.*) television; **2.** **2** *v/i.* (*irr.* sehen, *sep.*, *-ge-*, h) watch television; '**~seher** *m* television set; *p.* television viewer, televiewer; '**~sehsendung** *f* television broadcast, telecast; '**~sicht** *f* visual range.

'**Fernsprech|amt** *n* telephone exchange, *Am. a.* central; '**~anschluß** *m* telephone connection; '**~er** *m* telephone; '**~leitung** *f* telephone line; '**~zelle** *f* telephone box.

'**fern|stehen** *v/i.* (*irr.* stehen, *sep.*, *-ge-*, h) have no real (point of) contact (*dat.* with); '**2steuerung** *f* *s.* Fernlenkung; '**2unterricht** *m* correspondence course *or* tuition; '**2verkehr** *m* long-distance traffic.

Ferse ['fɛrzə] *f* (-/-n) heel.

fertig *adj.* ['fɛrtiç] ready; *article, etc.*: finished; *clothing*: ready-made; mit et. **~** werden get s.th. finished; mit et. **~** sein have finished s.th.; '**~bringen** *v/t.* (*irr.* bringen, *sep.*, *-ge-*, h) bring about; manage; '**2keit** *f* (-/-en) dexterity; skill; fluency (*in the spoken language*); '**~machen** *v/t.* (*sep.*, *-ge-*, h) finish, complete; get *s.th.* ready; *fig.* finish, settle *s.o.'s* hash; *sich* **~** get ready; '**2stellung** *f* completion; '**2waren** *f/pl.* finished goods *pl.* or products *pl.*

fesch F *adj.* [fɛʃ] *hat, dress, etc.*: smart, stylish, chic; dashing.

Fessel ['fɛsəl] *f* (-/-n) chain, fetter, shackle; *vet.* fetlock; *fig.* bond, fetter, tie; '**~ballon** *m* captive balloon; '**2n** *v/t.* (*ge-*, h) chain, fetter, shackle; *j-n* **~** hold *or* arrest *s.o.'s* attention; fascinate *s.o.*

fest [fɛst] **1.** *adj.* firm; solid; fixed; fast; *principle*: firm, strong; *sleep*: sound; *fabric*: close; **2.** **2** *n* (-es/-e) festival, celebration; holiday; *eccl.* feast; '**~binden** *v/t.* (*irr.* binden, *sep.*, *-ge-*, h) fasten, tie (*an dat.* to); '**2essen** *n* banquet, feast; '**~fahren** *v/refl.* (*irr.* fahren, *sep.*, *-ge-*, h) get stuck; *fig.* reach a deadlock; '**2halle** *f* (festival) hall; '**~halten** (*irr.* halten, *sep.*, *-ge-*, h) **1.** *v/i.* hold fast *or* tight; **~** *an* (*dat.*) adhere *or* keep to; **2.** *v/t.* hold on to; hold tight; *sich* **~** *an* (*dat.*) hold on to; '**~igen** ['~igən] *v/t.* (*ge-*, h) consolidate (*one's position, etc.*); strengthen (*friendship, etc.*); stabilize (*currency*); '**2igkeit** ['~ç-] *f* (-/no *pl.*) firmness; solidity; '**~land** *n* mainland, continent; '**~legen** *v/t.* (*sep.*, *-ge-*, h) fix, set; *sich auf* et. **~**

commit o.s. to s.th.; '**~lich** *adj.* meal, day, *etc.*: festive; *reception etc.*: ceremonial; '**2lichkeit** *f* (-/-en) festivity; festive character; '**~machen** (*sep.*, *-ge-*, h) **1.** *v/t.* fix, fasten, attach (*an dat.* to); **ᛐ** moor; **2.** **ᛐ** *v/i.* moor; put ashore; '**2mahl** *n* banquet, feast; '**2nahme** ['~naːmə] *f* (-/-n) arrest; '**~nehmen** *v/t.* (*irr.* nehmen, *sep.*, *-ge-*, h) arrest, take into custody; '**2rede** *f* speech of the day; '**~setzen** *v/t.* (*sep.*, *-ge-*, h) fix, set; *sich* **~** *dust, etc.*: become ingrained; *p.* settle (down); '**2spiel** *n* festival; '**~stehen** *v/i.* (*irr.* stehen, *sep.*, *-ge-*, h) stand firm; *fact*: be certain; '**~stehend** *adj.* fixed, stationary; *fact*: established; '**~stellen** *v/t.* (*sep.*, *-ge-*, h) establish (*fact, identity, etc.*); ascertain, find out (*fact, s.o.'s whereabouts, etc.*); state; see, perceive (*fact, etc.*); '**2stellung** *f* establishment; ascertainment; statement; '**2tag** *m* festive day; festival, holiday; *eccl.* feast; '**2ung** **ᛐ** *f* (-/-en) fortress; '**2zug** *m* festive procession.

fett [fɛt] **1.** *adj.* fat; fleshy; *voice*: oily; *land, area.*: rich; **2.** **2** *n* (-[e]s/-e) fat; grease (*a.* ⊕); '**2druck** *typ.* *m* bold type; '**2fleck** *m* grease-spot; '**~ig** *adj.* hair, skin, *etc.*: greasy, oily; *fingers, etc.*: greasy; *substance*: fatty.

Fetzen ['fɛtsən] *m* (-s/-) shred, rag, *Am. a.* frazzle; scrap (*of paper*); in **~** in rags.

feucht *adj.* [fɔyçt] *climate, air, etc.*: damp, moist; *air, zone, etc.*: humid; '**2igkeit** *f* (-/no *pl.*) moisture (*of substance*); dampness (*of place, etc.*); humidity (*of atmosphere, etc.*).

Feuer ['fɔyər] *n* (-s/-) fire; light; *fig.* ardo(u)r; **~** *fangen* catch fire; *fig.* fall for (*girl*); '**~alarm** *m* fire alarm; '**2beständig** *adj.* fire-proof, fire-resistant; '**~bestattung** *f* cremation; '**~eifer** *m* ardo(u)r; '**2fest** *adj.* *s.* feuerbeständig; '**2gefährlich** *adj.* inflammable; '**~haken** *m* poker; '**~löscher** *m* (-s/-) fire extinguisher; '**~melder** *m* (-s/-) fire-alarm; '**2n** (*ge-*, h) **1.** *v/i.* **X** *fig.* shoot, fire (*auf acc.* at, on); **2.** F *fig.* *v/t.* hurl; '**~probe** *fig.* *f* crucial test; '**2rot** *adj.* fiery (red), (as) red as fire; '**~sbrunst** *f* conflagration; '**~schiff** **ᛐ** *n* lightship; '**~schutz** *m* fire prevention; **X** covering fire; '**~sgefahr** *f* danger *or* risk of fire; '**2speiend** *adj.*: **~** *er Berg* volcano; '**~spritze** *f* fire engine; '**~stein** *m* flint; '**~versicherung** *f* fire insurance (company); '**~wache** *f* fire station, *Am. a.* firehouse; '**~wehr** *f* fire-brigade, *Am. a.* fire department; '**~wehrmann** *m* fireman; '**~werk** *n* (display of) fireworks *pl.*; '**~werkskörper** *m* firework; '**~**

zange f (e-e a pair of) firetongs pl.; '~zeug n lighter.

feurig adj. ['fɔʏriç] fiery (a. fig.); fig. ardent.

Fiasko [fi'asko] n (-s/-s) (complete) failure, fiasco; sl. flop.

Fibel ['fi:bəl] f (-/-n) spelling-book, primer.

Fichte ♀ ['fiçtə] f (-/-n) spruce; '~nnadel f pine-needle.

fidel adj. [fi'de:l] cheerful, merry, jolly, Am. F a. chipper.

Fieber ['fi:bər] n (-s/-) temperature, fever; ~ haben have or run a temperature; '~anfall m attack or bout of fever; '2haft adj. feverish (a. fig.); febrile; '2krank adj. ill with fever; '~mittel n febrifuge; '2n v/i. (ge-, h) have or run a temperature; ~ nach crave or long for; '~schauer m chill, shivers pl.; '~tabelle f temperature-chart; '~thermometer n clinical thermometer.

fiel [fi:l] pret. of fallen.

Figur [fi'gu:r] f (-/-en) figure; chess: chessman, piece.

figürlich adj. [fi'gy:rliç] meaning, etc.: figurative.

Filet [fi'le:] n (-s/-s) fillet (of beef, pork, etc.).

Filiale [fi'ja:lə] f (-/-n) branch.

Filigran(arbeit f) [fili'gra:n(ʔ-)] n (-s/-e) filigree.

Film [film] m (-[e]s/-e) film, thin coating (of oil, wax, etc.); phot. film; film, (moving) picture, Am. a. motion picture, F movie; e-n ~ einlegen phot. load a camera; '~atelier n film studio; '~aufnahme f filming, shooting (of a film); film (of sporting event, etc.); '2en v/i. (ge-, h) 1. v/t. film, shoot (scene, etc.); 2. v/i. film; make a film; '~gesellschaft f film company, Am. motion-picture company; '~kamera f film camera, Am. motion-picture camera; '~regisseur m film director; '~reklame f screen advertising; '~schauspieler m film or screen actor, Am. F movie actor; '~spule f (film) reel; '~streifen m film strip; '~theater n cinema, Am. motion-picture or F movie theater; '~verleih m (-[e]s/-e) film distributors pl.; '~vorführer m projectionist; '~vorstellung f cinema performance, Am. F movie performance.

Filter ['filtər] (-s/-) 1. m (coffee-, etc.) filter; 2. ⊕ n filter; '2n v/t. (ge-, h) filter (water, air, etc.); filtrate (water, impurities, etc.); strain (liquid); '~zigarette f filter-tipped cigarette.

Filz [filts] m (-es/-e) felt; fig. F skinflint; '2ig adj. felt-like; of felt; fig. F niggardly, stingy; '~laus f crab louse.

Finanz|amt [fi'nants²amt] n (inland) revenue office, office of the Inspector of Taxes; ~en f/pl. finances pl.; 2iell adj. [~'tsjel] financial; 2ieren [~'tsi:rən] v/t. (no -ge-, h) finance (scheme, etc.); sponsor (radio programme, etc.); ~lage f financial position; ~mann m financier; ~minister m minister of finance; Chancellor of the Exchequer, Am. Secretary of the Treasury; ~ministerium n ministry of finance; Exchequer, Am. Treasury Department; ~wesen n (-s/no pl.) finances pl.; financial matters pl.

Findelkind ['findəl-] n foundling.

finden ['findən] (irr., ge-, h) 1. v/t. find; discover, come across; find, think, consider; wie ~ Sie ...? how do you like ...?; sich ~ thing: be found; 2. v/i.: ~ zu find one's way to.

'Finder m (-s/-) finder; '~lohn m finder's reward.

'findig adj. resourceful, ingenious.

Findling ['fintlɪŋ] m (-s/-e) foundling; geol. erratic block, boulder.

fing [fiŋ] pret. of fangen.

Finger ['fiŋər] m (-s/-) finger; sich die ~ verbrennen burn one's fingers; er rührte keinen ~ he lifted no finger; '~abdruck m fingerprint; '~fertigkeit f manual skill; '~hut m thimble; ♀ foxglove; '2n v/i. (ge-, h): ~ nach fumble for; '~spitze f finger-tip; '~spitzengefühl fig. n sure instinct; '~übung ♪ f finger exercise; ~zeig ['~tsaɪk] m (-[e]s/-e) hint, F pointer.

Fink orn. [fiŋk] m (-en/-en) finch.

finster adj. ['finstər] night, etc.: dark; shadows, wood, etc.: sombre; night, room, etc.: gloomy, murky; person, nature: sullen; thought, etc.: sinister, sombre, gloomy; '2nis f (-/no pl.) darkness, gloom.

Finte ['fintə] f (-/-n) feint; fig. a. ruse, trick.

Firma ✝ ['firma] f (-/Firmen) firm, business, company.

firmen eccl. ['firmən] v/t. (ge-, h) confirm.

'Firmen|inhaber m owner of a firm; '~wert m goodwill.

Firn [firn] m (-[e]s/-e) firn, névé.

First △ [first] m (-es/-e) ridge; '~ziegel m ridge tile.

Fisch [fiʃ] m (-es/-e) fish; '~dampfer m trawler; '2en v/t. and v/i. (ge-, h) fish; '~er m (-s/-) fisherman; '~erboot n fishing-boat; '~erdorf n fishing-village; '~erei [~'raɪ] f (-/-en) fishery; fishing; '~fang m fishing; '~geruch m fishy smell; '~gräte f fish-bone; '~grätenmuster n herring-bone pattern; '~händler m fishmonger, Am. fish dealer; '2ig adj. fishy; '~laich m spawn; '~leim m fish-glue; '~mehl n fish-meal; '~schuppe f scale; '~tran m train-oil; '~vergiftung

⚓ f fish-poisoning; '⚓zucht f pisci-
culture, fish-hatching; '⚓zug m
catch, haul, draught (of fish).

fiskalisch adj. [fis'kɑːliʃ] fiscal,
governmental.

Fiskus ['fiskus] m (-/⚓ -se, Fisken)
Exchequer, esp. Am. Treasury;
government.

Fistel ⚓ ['fistəl] f (-/-n) fistual;
'⚓stimme ♪ f falsetto.

Fittich ['fitiç] m (-[e]s/-e) poet. wing;
j-n unter s-e ⚓e nehmen take s.o.
under one's wing.

fix adj. [fiks] salary, price, etc.:
fixed; quick, clever, smart; e-e ⚓e
Idee an obsession; ein ⚓er Junge a
smart fellow; '⚓ierbad phot. [fi-
'ksiːrbɑːt] n fixing bath; '⚓ieren
[fi'ksiːrən] v/t. (no -ge-, h) fix (a.
phot.); fix one's eyes (up)on, stare
at s.o.; '⚓stern ast. m fixed star;
'⚓um n (-s/Fixa) fixed or basic
salary.

flach adj. [flax] roof, etc.: flat;
ground, etc.: flat, level, even; water,
plate, fig.: shallow; ♭ plane.

Fläche ['flɛçə] f (-/-n) surface, fig.:
plane; sheet (of water, snow, etc.);
geom. area; tract, expanse (of land,
etc.); '⚓ninhalt ♭ ['flɛçən⚓-] m
(surface) area; '⚓nmaß n square or
surface measure.

'Flach|land n plain, flat country;
'⚓rennen n turf: flat race.

Flachs ⚓ [flaks] m (-es/no pl.) flax.

flackern ['flakərn] v/i. (ge-, h) light,
flame, eyes, etc.: flicker, wave;
voice: quaver, shake.

Flagge ⚓ ['flagə] f (-/-n) flag,
colo(u)rs pl.; '⚓n v/i. (ge-, h) fly or
hoist a flag; signal (with flags).

Flak ⚓ [flak] f (-/-, -s) anti-aircraft
gun; anti-aircraft artillery.

Flamme ['flamə] f (-/-n) flame;
blaze; '⚓nmeer n sea of flames;
'⚓nwerfer ⚓ m (-s/-) flame-
thrower.

Flanell [fla'nɛl] m (-s/-e) flannel;
'⚓anzug m flannel suit; '⚓hose f
flannel trousers pl., flannels pl.

Flank|e ['flaŋkə] f (-/-n) flank (a.
△, ⚓, mount.); side; '⚓ieren
[⚓'kiːrən] v/t. (no -ge-, h) flank.

Flasche ['flaʃə] f (-/-n) bottle; flask.

'Flaschen|bier n bottled beer; '⚓-
hals m neck of a bottle; '⚓öffner
m (-s/-) bottle-opener; '⚓zug ⊕ m
block and tackle.

flatter|haft adj. ['flatərhaft] girl,
etc.: fickle, flighty; mind: fickle,
volatile; '⚓n v/i. (ge-) 1. (h, sein)
bird, butterfly, etc.: flutter (about);
bird, bat, etc.: flit (about); 2. (h)
hair, flag, garment, etc.: stream,
fly; mot. wheel: shimmy, wobble;
car steering: judder; 3. (sein): auf
den Boden ⚓ flutter to the ground.

flau adj. [flau] weak, feeble, faint;
sentiment, reaction, etc.: lukewarm;

drink: stale; colour: pale, dull; ✝
market, business, etc.: dull, slack;
⚓e Zeit slack period.

Flaum [flaum] m (-[e]s/no pl.)
down, fluff; fuzz.

Flau|s [flaus] m (-es/-e), ⚓sch [⚓ʃ] m
(-es/-e) tuft (of wool, etc.); napped
coating.

Flausen F ['flauzən] f/pl. whims pl.,
fancies pl.; (funny) ideas pl.; F fibs
pl.; j-m ⚓ in den Kopf setzen put
funny ideas into s.o.'s head; j-m ⚓
vormachen tell s.o. fibs.

Flaute ['flautə] f (-/-n) ♭ dead
calm; esp. ✝ dullness, slack period.

Flecht|e ['flɛçtə] f (-/-n) braid, plait
(of hair); ♀ lichen; ⚓ herpes; '⚓en
v/t. (irr., ge-, h) braid, plait (hair,
ribbon, etc.); weave (basket, wreath,
etc.); wreath (flowers); twist (rope,
etc.); '⚓werk n wickerwork.

Fleck [flɛk] m (-[e]s/-e, -en) 1. mark
(of dirt, grease, etc.; zo.); spot (of
grease, grime, etc.); smear (of oil,
blood, etc.); stain (of wine, coffee,
etc.); blot (of ink); place, spot; fig.
blemish, spot, stain; 2. patch (of
material); bootmaking: heel-piece;
'⚓en m (-s/-) s. Fleck 1; '⚓en m
(market-)town, townlet; '⚓enwas-
ser n spot or stain remover; '⚓fie-
ber ⚓ n (epidemic) typhus; '⚓ig
adj. spotted; stained.

Fledermaus zo. ['fleːdər-] f bat.

Flegel ['fleːgəl] m (-s/-) flail; fig.
lout, boor; '⚓ei [⚓'lai] f (-/-en) rudeness; loutishness; '⚓haft adj. rude-
ill-mannered; loutish; '⚓jahre pl.
awkward age.

flehen ['fleːən] 1. v/i. (ge-, h) entreat, implore (zu j-m s.o.; um et.
s.th.); 2. ⚓ n (-s/no pl.) supplication;
imploration, entreaty.

Fleisch [flaiʃ] n (-es/no pl.) flesh;
meat; ♀ pulp; '⚓brühe f meat-
broth; beef tea; '⚓er m (-s/-)
butcher; ⚓erei [⚓'rai] f (-/-en)
butcher's (shop), Am. butcher
shop; '⚓extrakt m meat extract;
'⚓fressend adj. carnivorous; '⚓-
hackmaschine f mincing machine,
mincer, Am. meat grinder; '⚓ig adj.
fleshy; ♀ pulpy; '⚓konserven f/pl.
tinned or potted meat, Am. canned
meat; '⚓kost f meat (food); '⚓lich
adj. desires, etc.: carnal, fleshly;
'⚓los adj. meatless; '⚓pastete f
meat pie, Am. a. potpie; '⚓speise f
meat dish; '⚓vergiftung f meat or
ptomaine poisoning; '⚓ware f meat
(product); '⚓wolf m s. Fleischhack-
maschine.

Fleiß [flais] m (-es/no pl.) diligence,
industry; '⚓ig adj. diligent, industrious, hard-working.

fletschen ['flɛtʃən] v/t. (ge-, h): die
Zähne ⚓ animal: bare its teeth; p.
bare one's teeth.

Flicken ['flikən] 1. m (-s/-) patch;

2. ♀ v/t. (ge-, h) patch (dress, tyre, etc.); repair (shoe, roof, etc.); cobble (shoe).

'Flick|schneider m jobbing tailor; **~schuster** m cobbler; **~werk** n (-[e]s/no pl.) patchwork.

Flieder ♀ ['fliːdər] m (-s/-) lilac.

Fliege ['fliːgə] f (-/-n) zo. fly; bow-tie.

'fliegen 1. v/i. (irr., ge-, sein) fly; go by air; **2.** v/t. (irr., ge-, h) fly, pilot (aircraft, etc.); convey (goods, etc.) by air; **3.** ♀ n (-s/no pl.) flying; ✈ a. aviation.

Fliegen|fänger ['fliːgənfɛŋər] m (-s/-) fly-paper; **~fenster** n fly-screen; **~gewicht** n boxing, etc.: flyweight; **~klappe** f fly-flap, Am. fly swatter; **~pilz** ♀ m fly agaric.

'Flieger m (-s/-) flyer; ✈ airman, aviator; pilot; F plane, bomber; cycling: sprinter; **~abwehr** ✕ f anti-aircraft defen|ce, Am. -se; **~alarm** ✕ m air-raid alarm or warning; **~bombe** ✕ f aircraft bomb; **~offizier** ✕ m air-force officer.

flieh|en ['fliːən] (irr., ge-, sein) **1.** v/i. (sein) flee (vor dat. from), run away from; **2.** v/t. (h) flee, avoid, keep away from; **~kraft** phys. f centrifugal force. [(floor-)tile.\

Fliese ['fliːzə] f (-/-n) (wall-)tile.\

Fließ|band ['fliːs-] n (-[e]s/uer) conveyor-belt; assembly-line; **~en** v/i. (irr., ge-, sein) river, traffic, etc.: flow; tap-water, etc.: run; **~end 1.** adj. water: running; traffic: moving; speech, etc.: fluent; **2.** adv.: ~ lesen (sprechen) read (speak) fluently; **~papier** n blotting-paper.

Flimmer ['flimər] m (-s/-) glimmer, glitter; **~n** v/i. (ge-, h) glimmer, glitter; television, film: flicker; es flimmert mir vor den Augen everything is dancing in front of my eyes.

flink adj. [fliŋk] quick, nimble, brisk.

Flinte ['flintə] f (-/-n) shotgun; die ~ ins Korn werfen throw up the sponge.

Flirt [flœrt] m (-es/-s) flirtation; **~en** v/i. (ge-, h) flirt (mit with).

Flitter ['flitər] m (-s/-) tinsel (a. fig.), spangle; **~kram** m cheap finery; **~wochen** pl. honeymoon.

flitzen F ['flitsən] v/i. (ge-, sein) whisk, scamper; dash (off, etc.).

flocht [flɔxt] pret. of flechten.

Flock|e ['flɔkə] f (-/-n) flake (of snow, soap, etc.); flock (of wool); **~ig** adj. fluffy, flaky.

flog [floːk] pret. of fliegen.

floh¹ [floː] pret. of fliehen.

Floh² [floː] m (-[e]s/ue) flea.

Flor [floːr] m (-s/-e) bloom, blossom; fig. bloom, prime; gauze; crêpe, crape.

Florett fenc. [floˈrɛt] n (-[e]s/-e) foil.

florieren [floˈriːrən] v/i. (no -ge-, h)

business, etc.: flourish, prosper, thrive.

Floskel ['flɔskəl] f (-/-n) flourish; empty phrase.

floß¹ [flɔs] pret. of fließen.

Floß² [floːs] n (-es/ue) raft, float.

Flosse ['flɔsə] f (-/-n) fin; flipper (of penguin, etc.).

flöß|en ['fløːsən] v/t. (ge-, h) raft, float (timber, etc.); **~er** m (-s/-) rafter, raftsman.

Flöte ♪ ['fløːtə] f (-/-n) flute; **~n** (ge-, h) **1.** v/i. (play the) flute; **2.** v/t. play on the flute.

flott adj. [flɔt] ⚓ floating, afloat; pace, etc.: quick, brisk; music, etc.: gay, lively; dress, etc.: smart, stylish; car, etc.: sporty, racy; dancer, etc.: excellent.

Flotte ['flɔtə] f (-/-n) ⚓ fleet; ✕ navy; **~nstützpunkt** ✕ m naval base.

Flotille ⚓ [flɔˈtiljə] f (-/-n) flotilla.

Flöz geol. ↗ [fløːts] n (-es/-e) seam; layer, stratum.

Fluch [fluːx] m (-[e]s/ue) curse, malediction; eccl. anathema; curse, swear-word; **~en** v/i. (ge-, h) swear, curse.

Flucht [fluxt] f (-/-en) flight (vor dat. from); escape (aus dat. from); line (of windows, etc.); suite (of rooms); flight (of stairs).

flücht|en ['flyçtən] (ge-) v/i. (sein) and v/refl. (h) flee (nach, zu to); run away; escape; **~ig** adj. fugitive (a. fig.); thought, etc.: fleeting; fame, etc.: transient; p. careless; superficial; ↗ volatile; **~ling** ['~liŋ] m (-s/-e) fugitive; pol. refugee; **~lingslager** n refugee camp.

Flug [fluːk] m (-[e]s/ue) flight; im **~(e)** rapidly; quickly; **~abwehrrakete** f anti-aircraft missile; **~bahn** f trajectory of (rocket, etc.); ✈ flight path; **~ball** m tennis, etc.: volley; **~blatt** n handbill, leaflet, Am. a. flier; **~boot** ✈ n flying-boat; **~dienst** ✈ m air service.

Flügel ['flyːgəl] m (-s/-) wing (a. △, ✈, ✕); blade, vane (of propeller, etc.); ✕ Fensterflügel, Türflügel, Lungenflügel; sail (of windmill, etc.); ♪ grand piano; **~fenster** △ n casement-window; **~lahm** adj. broken-winged; **~mann** ✕ m marker; flank man; **~tür** △ f folding door.

Fluggast ['fluːk-] m (air) passenger.

flügge adj. ['flygə] fledged; ~ werden fledge; fig. begin to stand on one's own feet.

'Flug|hafen m airport; **~linie** f ✈ air route; airline; **~platz** m airfield, aerodrome, Am. a. airdrome; airport; **~sand** geol. m wind-blown sand; **~schrift** f pamphlet; **~sicherung** f air traffic control; **~sport** m sporting aviation; **~wesen** n aviation, aeronautics.

'**Flugzeug** *n* aircraft, aeroplane, F plane, *Am. a.* airplane; '~**bau** *m* aircraft construction; '~**führer** *m* pilot; '~**halle** *f* hangar; '~**rumpf** *m* fuselage, body; '~**träger** *m* aircraft carrier, *Am. sl.* flattop; '~**unglück** *n* air crash *or* disaster.

Flunder *ichth.* ['flundər] *f* (-/-n) flounder.

Flunker|ei F [fluŋkə'raɪ] *f* (-/-en) petty lying, F fib(bing); '2n *v/i.* (ge-, h) F fib, tell fibs.

fluoreszieren [fluores'tsi:rən] *v/i.* (*no -ge-, h*) fluoresce.

Flur [flu:r] **1.** *f* (-/-en) field, meadow; *poet.* lea; **2.** *m* (-[e]s/-e) (entrance-)hall.

Fluß [flus] *m* (*Flusses/Flüsse*) river, stream; flow(ing); *fig.* fluency, flux; 2'**abwärts** *adv.* downriver, downstream; 2'**aufwärts** *adv.* upriver, upstream; '~**bett** *n* river bed.

flüssig *adj.* ['flysiç] fluid, liquid; *metal:* molten, melted; † *money, capital, etc.:* available, in hand; *style:* fluent, flowing; '2**keit** *f* (-/-en) fluid, liquid; fluidity, liquidity; availability; fluency.

'**Fluß|lauf** *m* course of a river; '~**mündung** *f* mouth of a river; '~**pferd** *zo.* *n* hippopotamus; '~**schiffahrt** *f* river navigation *or* traffic.

flüstern ['flystərn] *v/i. and v/t.* (ge-, h) whisper.

Flut [flu:t] *f* (-/-en) flood; high tide, (flood-)tide; *fig.* flood, torrent, deluge; '2en (ge-) **1.** *v/i.* (sein) water, crowd, *etc.*: flood, surge (*über acc.* over); **2.** *v/t.* (h) flood (*dock, etc.*); '~**welle** *f* tidal wave.

focht [fɔxt] *pret. of* fechten.

Fohlen *zo.* ['fo:lən] **1.** *n* (-s/-) foal; *male:* colt; *female:* filly; **2.** 2 *v/i.* (ge-, h) foal.

Folge ['fɔlgə] *f* (-/-n) sequence, succession (*of events*); instalment, part (*of radio series, etc.*); consequence, result; series; set, suit; future; ~n *pl.* aftermath.

'**folgen** *v/i.* (dat.) (ge-, sein) follow; succeed (*j-m s.o.*; *auf acc.* to); follow, ensue (*aus* from); obey (*j-m s.o.*); ~**dermaßen** *adv.* ['~dərmaːsən] as follows; '~**schwer** *adj.* of grave consequence, grave.

'**folgerichtig** *adj.* logical; consistent.

folger|n ['fɔlgərn] *v/t.* (ge-, h) infer, conclude, deduce (*aus* from); '2**ung** *f* (-/-en) inference, conclusion, deduction.

'**folgewidrig** *adj.* illogical; inconsistent.

folglich *cj.* ['fɔlkliç] therefore, consequently.

folgsam *adj.* ['fɔlkzaːm] obedient; '2**keit** *f* (-/*no pl.*) obedience.

Folie ['fo:ljə] *f* (-/-n) foil.

Folter ['fɔltər] *f* (-/-n) torture; *auf die ~ spannen* put to the rack; *fig.* F *a.* keep on tenterhooks; '2n *v/t.* (ge-, h) torture, torment; '~**qual** *f* torture, *fig. a.* torment.

Fonds † [fõ:] *m* (-/-) fund (*a. fig.*); funds *pl.*

Fontäne [fɔn'tɛ:nə] *f* (-/-n) fountain.

foppen ['fɔpən] *v/t.* (ge-, h) tease, F pull s.o.'s leg; hoax, fool.

forcieren [fɔr'si:rən] *v/t.* (*no -ge-, h*) force (up).

'**Förder|band** *n* (-[e]s/~er) conveyor-belt; '2**lich** *adj.* conducive (*dat.* to), promotive (of); '~**korb** ⚒ *m* cage.

fordern ['fɔrdərn] *v/t.* (ge-, h) demand; claim (*compensation, etc.*); ask (*price, etc.*); challenge (*to duel*).

fördern ['fœrdərn] *v/t.* (ge-, h) further, advance, promote; ⚒ haul; raise (*coal, etc.*); *zutage* ~ reveal, bring to light.

'**Forderung** *f* (-/-en) demand; claim; charge; challenge.

'**Förderung** *f* (-/-en) furtherance, advancement, promotion; ⚒ haulage; output. [trout.]

Forelle *ichth.* [fo'rɛlə] *f* (-/-n)|

Form [fɔrm] *f* (-/-en) form; figure, shape; model; ⊕ mo(u)ld; *sports:* form, condition; 2**al** *adj.* [~'maːl] formal; ~**alität** [~ali'tɛ:t] *f* (-/-en) formality; ~**at** [~'maːt] *n* (-[e]s/-e) size; *von* ~ of distinction; ~**el** ['~əl] *f* (-/-n) formula; 2**ell** *adj.* [~'mɛl] formal; '2**en** *v/t.* (ge-, h) form (*object, character, etc.*); shape, fashion (*wood, metal, etc.*); mo(u)ld (*clay, character, etc.*); '~**enlehre** *gr.* f accidence; '~**fehler** *m* informality; ½ flaw; 2**ieren** [~'mi:rən] *v/t.* (*no -ge-, h*) form; draw up, line up; *sich* ~ line up.

förmlich *adj.* ['fœrmliç] formal; ceremonious; '2**keit** *f* (-/-en) formality; ceremoniousness.

'**formlos** *adj.* formless, shapeless; *fig.* informal.

Formular [fɔrmu'laːr] *n* (-s/-e) form, *Am. a.* blank.

formu'lieren *v/t.* (*no -ge-, h*) formulate (*question, etc.*); word, phrase (*question, contract, etc.*).

forsch *adj.* [fɔrʃ] vigorous, energetic; smart, dashing.

forsch|en ['fɔrʃən] *v/i.* (ge-, h): ~ *nach* (dat.) search for *or* after; ~ *in* (dat.) search (through); '2**er** *m* (-s/-) researcher, research worker.

'**Forschung** *f* (-/-en) research (work); '~**sreise** *f* (exploring) expedition; '~**sreisende** *m* explorer.

Forst [fɔrst] *m* (-es/-e[n]) forest; '~**aufseher** *m* (forest-)keeper, gamekeeper.

Förster ['fœrstər] *m* (-s/-) forester; ranger.

'Forst|haus *n* forester's house; '~revier *n* forest district; '~wesen *n*, '~wirtschaft *f* forestry.

Fort¹ ⚔ [fo:r] *n* (-s/-s) fort.

fort² *adv*. [fɔrt] away, gone; on; gone, lost; *in e-m* ~ continuously; *und so* ~ and so on *or* forth; *s. a.* weg.

'fort|bestehen *v/i*. (*irr. stehen*, *sep*., *no* -ge-, *h*) continue, persist; '~bewegen *v/t*. (*sep*., *no* -ge-, *h*) move (on, away); *sich* ~ move, walk; '2dauer *f* continuance; '~dauern *v/i*. (*sep*., -ge-, *h*) continue, last; '~fahren *v/i*. (*irr. fahren*, *sep*., -ge-) 1. (*sein*) depart, leave; drive off; 2. (*h*) continue, keep on (*et. zu tun* doing s.th.); '~führen *v/t*. (*sep*., -ge-, *h*) continue, carry on; 2gang *m* departure, leaving; continuance; '~gehen *v/i*. (*irr. gehen*, *sep*., -ge-, *sein*) go (away), leave; '~geschritten *adj*. advanced; '2kommen *n* (-s/*no pl.*) progress; '~laufend *adj*. consecutive, continuous; '~pflanzen *v/t*. (*sep*., -ge-, *h*) propagate; *sich* ~ *biol*. propagate, reproduce; *phys*., *disease*, *rumour*: be propagated; '2pflanzung *f* propagation; reproduction; '~reißen *v/t*. (*irr. reißen*, *sep*., -ge-, *h*) avalanche, *etc*.: sweep *or* carry away; '~schaffen *v/t*. (*sep*., -ge-, *h*) get *or* take away, remove; '~schreiten *v/i*. (*irr. schreiten*, *sep*., -ge-, *sein*) advance, proceed, progress; '~schreitend *adj*. progressive; '2schritt *m* progress; '~schrittlich *adj*. progressive; '~setzen *v/t*. (*sep*., -ge-, *h*) continue, pursue; '2setzung *f* (-/-en) continuation, pursuit; ~ *folgt* to be continued; '~während 1. *adj*. continual, continuous; perpetual; 2. *adv*. constantly, always.

Forum ['fo:rum] *n* (-s/*Foren, Fora* *and* -s) forum.

Foto... ['fo:to-] *s*. Photo...

Foyer [foa'je:] *n* (-s/-s) *thea*. foyer, *Am. and parl*. lobby; *hotel*: foyer, lounge.

Fracht [fraxt] *f* (-/-en) goods *pl*.; ⚓ carriage, freight; ⚓, 🚂 freight (-age), cargo; '~brief *m* 🚂 consignment note, *Am*., ⚓ bill of lading; '~dampfer *m* cargo steamer, freighter; '~er *m* (-s/-) freighter; '2frei *adj*. carriage *or* freight paid; '~führer *m* carrier, *Am. a*. teamster; '~geld *n* carriage charges *pl*., 🚂, ⚓, *Am*. freight; '~gut *n* goods *pl*., freight; '~stück *n* package.

Frack [frak] *m* (-[e]s/⸚e, -s) dress coat, tail-coat, F tails; '~anzug *m* dress-suit.

Frag|e ['fra:gə] *f* (-/-n) question; *gr*., *reth*. interrogation; problem, point; *e-e* ~ *stellen* ask a question; *in* ~ *stellen* question; '~ebogen *m* questionnaire; form; '2en (ge-, *h*)

1. *v/t*. ask; question; *es fragt sich, ob* it is doubtful whether; 2. *v/i*. ask; '~er *m* (-s/-) questioner; '~ewort *gr. n* (-[e]s/⸚er) interrogative; '~ezeichen *n* question-mark, point of interrogation, *Am. mst* interrogation point; 2lich *adj*. ['fra:k-] doubtful, uncertain; in question; 2los *adv*. ['fra:k-] undoubtedly, unquestionably.

Fragment [frag'ment] *n* (-[e]s/-e) fragment.

fragwürdig *adj*. ['fra:k-] doubtful, dubious, questionable.

Fraktion *parl*. [frak'tsjo:n] *f* (-/-en) (parliamentary) group.

frank|ieren [fraŋ'ki:rən] *v/t*. (*no* -ge-, *h*) prepay, stamp; ~o *adv*. ['~o] free; post(age) paid; *parcel*: carriage paid.

Franse ['franzə] *f* (-/-n) fringe.

Franz|ose [fran'tso:zə] *m* (-n/-n) Frenchman; *die* ~*n pl*. the French *pl*.; ~ösin [~ø:zin] *f* (-/-nen) Frenchwoman; 2ösisch *adj*. [~ø:ziʃ] French.

fräs|en ⊕ ['frɛ:zən] *v/t*. (ge-, *h*) mill; 2maschine ['frɛ:s-] *f* milling-machine.

Fraß [fra:s] 1. *m* (-es/-e) *sl*. grub; 2. *pret*. *of* fressen.

Fratze ['fratsə] *f* (-/-n) grimace, F face; ~*n schneiden* make grimaces.

Frau [frau] *f* (-/-en) woman; lady; wife; ~ X Mrs X.

'Frauen|arzt *m* gyn(a)ecologist; '~klinik *f* hospital for women; '~rechte *n/pl*. women's rights *pl*.; '~stimmrecht *pol. n* women's suffrage; '~zimmer *mst contp. n* female, woman.

Fräulein ['frɔylaɪn] *n* (-s/-, F -s) young lady; teacher; shop-assistant; waitress; ~ X Miss X.

'fraulich *adj*. womanly.

frech *adj*. [frɛç] impudent, insolent, F saucy, cheeky, *Am*. F *a*. sassy, *sl*. fresh; *lie*, *etc*.: brazen; *thief*, *etc*.: bold, daring; '2heit *f* (-/-en) impudence, insolence; F sauciness, cheek; boldness.

frei *adj*. [fraɪ] free (*von* from, of); *position*: vacant; *field*: open; *parcel*: carriage-paid; *journalist*, *etc*.: freelance; liberal; candid, frank; licentious; ~ *Haus* † franco domicile; *im Freien* in the open air.

'Frei|bad *n* open-air bath; '~beuter ['~bɔytər] *m* (-s/-) freebooter; '2bleibend † *adj*. price, *etc*.: subject to alteration; *offer*: conditional; '~brief *m* charter; *fig*. warrant; '~denker *m* (-s/-) freethinker.

Freier ['fraɪər] *m* (-s/-) suitor.

'Frei|exemplar *n* free *or* presentation copy; '~frau *f* baroness; '~gabe *f* release; '2geben (*irr. geben*, *sep*., -ge-, *h*) 1. *v/t*. release; give *(s.o. an hour, etc.)* off; 2. *v/i.*: j-n ~ give s.o. time off; '2gebig *adj.* generous, liberal; '~gebigkeit *f* (-/-en) generosity, liberality; '~gepäck *n* free luggage; '2haben *v/i.* *(irr. haben, sep., -ge-, h)* have a holiday; have a day off; '~hafen *m* free port; '2halten *v/t.* *(irr. halten, sep., -ge-, h)* keep free *or* clear; *in restaurant, etc.*: treat; '~handel *m* free trade.

'Freiheit *f* (-/-en) liberty; freedom; *dichterische* ~ poetic licence, *Am.* poetic license.

'Frei|herr *m* baron; '~karte *f* free *(thea. a.* complimentary) ticket; '2lassen *v/t.* *(irr. lassen, sep., -ge-, h)* release, set free *or* at liberty; *gegen Kaution* ~ ⚖ release on bail; '~lassung *f* (-/-en) release; '~lauf *m* free-wheel.

'freilich *adv.* indeed, certainly, of course; admittedly.

'Frei|lichtbühne *f* open-air stage *or* theat|re, *Am.* -er; '2machen *v/t.* *(sep., -ge-, h)* ✉ prepay, stamp *(letter, etc.)*; *sich* ~ undress, take one's clothes off; '~marke *f* stamp; '~maurer *m* freemason; ~maurerei [~'raɪ] *f* (-/no *pl.*) freemasonry; '~mut *m* frankness; 2mütig *adj.* ['~my:tiç] frank; '2schaffend *adj.*: ~er *Künstler* free-lance artist; ~schärler ✕ ['~ʃɛːrlər] *m* (-s/-) volunteer, irregular; '~schein *m* licen|ce, *Am.* -se; '2sinnig *adj.* liberal; '2sprechen *v/t.* *(irr. sprechen, sep., -ge-, h) esp. eccl.* absolve *(von* from); ⚖ acquit (of); release *(apprentice)* from his articles; '~sprechung *f* (-/-en) *esp. eccl.* absolution; release from articles; = '~spruch ⚖ *m* acquittal; '~staat *pol. m* free state; '2stehen *v/i.* *(irr. stehen, sep., -ge-, h)* house, *etc.*: stand empty; *es steht Ihnen frei zu inf.* you are free *or* at liberty to *inf.*; '2stellen *v/t.* *(sep., -ge-, h)*: j-n ~ exempt s.o. *(von* from) *(a.* ✕); j-m et. ~ leave s.th. open to s.o.; '~stoß *m* football: free kick; '~tag *m* Friday; '~tod *m* suicide; '2tragend ⚠ *adj.* cantilever; '~treppe *f* outdoor staircase; '2willig 1. *adj.* voluntary; 2. *adv. a.* of one's own free will; '~willige ['~vɪligə] *m* (-n/-n) volunteer; '~zeit *f* free *or* spare *or* leisure time; '2zügig *adj.* ['~tsy:giç] free to move; '~zügigkeit *f* (-/no *pl.*) freedom of movement.

fremd *adj.* [fremt] strange; foreign; alien; extraneous; '~artig *adj.* strange; exotic.

Fremde ['fremdə] 1. *f* (-/no *pl.*) distant *or* foreign parts; *in der* ~ far away from home, abroad; 2. *m, f* (-/-n) stranger; foreigner; '~buch *n* visitors' book; '~nführer *m* guide, cicerone; '~nheim *n*

---

boarding house; '~nindustrie ['fremdən?-] *f* tourist industry; '~nlegion ✕ *f* Foreign Legion; '~nverkehr *m* tourism, tourist traffic; '~nzimmer *n* spare (bed-) room; *tourism*: room.

'Fremd|herrschaft *f* fofeign rule; '~körper 🡒 *m* foreign body; 2ländisch *adj.* ['~lendiʃ] foreign, exotic; '~sprache *f* foreign language; '2sprachig *adj.*, '2sprachlich *adj.* foreign-language; '~wort *n* (-[e]s/̈er) foreign word.

Frequenz *phys.* [fre'kvɛnts] *f* (-/-en) frequency.

fressen ['fresən] 1. *v/t.* *(irr., ge-, h)* eat; *beast of prey*: devour; F *p.* devour, gorge; 2. *v/i.* *(irr., ge-, h)* eat; F *p.* gorge; 3. ♀ *n* (-s/no *pl.*) feed, food.

'Freß|gier *f* voracity, gluttony; '~napf *m* feeding dish.

Freude ['frɔydə] *f* (-/-n) joy, gladness; delight; pleasure; ~ *haben an (dat.)* find *or* take pleasure in.

'Freuden|botschaft *f* glad tidings *pl.*; '~fest *n* happy occasion; '~feuer *n* bonfire; '~geschrei *n* shouts *pl.* of joy; '~tag *m* day of rejoicing, red-letter day; '~taumel *m* transports *pl.* of joy.

'freud|estrahlend *adj.* radiant with joy; '~ig *adj.* joyful; happy; ~es *Ereignis* happy event; '~los *adj.* ['frɔytloːs] joyless, cheerless.

freuen ['frɔyən] *v/t.* *(ge-, h)*: *es freut mich, daß* I am glad *or* pleased *(that)*; *sich* ~ *über (acc.)* be pleased about *or* with, be glad about; *sich* ~ *auf (acc.)* look forward to.

Freund [frɔynt] *m* (-es/-e) (boy-) friend; ~in ['~dɪn] *f* (-/-nen) (girl-) friend; '2lich *adj.* friendly, kind, nice; cheerful, bright; *climate*: mild; '~lichkeit *f* (-/-en) friendliness, kindness; '~schaft *f* (-/-en) friendship; ~ *schließen* make friends *(mit* with); '2schaftlich *adj.* friendly.

Frevel ['freːfəl] *m* (-s/-) outrage *(an dat., gegen* on), crime (against); '2haft *adj.* wicked, outrageous; impious; '2n *v/i.* *(ge-, h)* commit a crime *or* outrage *(gegen* against).

Frevler ['freːflər] *m* (-s/-) evil-doer, offender; blasphemer.

Friede(n) ['friːdə(n)] *m (Friedens/ Frieden)* peace; *im Frieden* in peacetime; *laß mich in Frieden!* leave me alone!

'Friedens|bruch *m* violation of (the) peace; '~stifter *m* peacemaker; '~störer *m* (-s/-) disturber of the peace; '~verhandlungen *f/pl.* peace negotiations *pl.*; '~vertrag *m* peace treaty.

fried|fertig *adj.* ['friːt-] peaceable, peace-loving; '2hof *m* cemetery, graveyard; churchyard; '~lich *adj.*

s. *friedfertig*; peaceful; '~liebend *adj.* peace-loving.

frieren ['fri:rən] *v/i.* (*irr.*, ge-) **1.** (sein) *liquid*: freeze, become frozen; *river*, *etc.*: freeze (over, up); *window-pane*, *etc.*: freeze over; **2.** (h) be *or* feel cold; *mich friert or ich friere an den Füßen* my feet are cold.

Fries △ [fri:s] *m* (-es/-e) frieze.

frisch [friʃ] **1.** *adj.* food, *flowers*, *etc.*: fresh; *egg*: new-laid; *linen*, *etc.*: clean; *auf ~er Tat ertappen* catch red-handed; **2.** *adv.*: ~ *gestrichen!* wet paint!, *Am.* fresh paint!; 2e ['~ə] *f* (-/no *pl.*) freshness.

Friseu|r [fri'zø:r] *m* (-s/-e) hair-dresser; (*men's*) barber; ~**se** [~zə] *f* (-/-n) (woman) hairdresser.

fri'sier|en *v/t.* (no -ge-, h): *j-n* ~ do *or* dress s.o.'s hair; F: *einen Wagen* ~ *mot.* tune up *or* soup up *or* hot up a car; *sich* ~ do one's hair; 2**kommode** *f* dressing-table; 2**salon** *m* hairdressing saloon; 2**tisch** *m* s. *Frisierkommode*.

Frist [frist] *f* (-/-en) (fixed *or* limited) period of time; time allowed; term; ⅌ prescribed time; ⅌, ✝ respite, grace; '2**en** *v/t.* (ge-, h): *sein Dasein* ~ scrape along, scrape a living.

Frisur [fri'zu:r] *f* (-/-en) hair-style, hair-do, coiffure.

frivol *adj.* [fri'vo:l] frivolous, flippant; 2**ität** [~oli'tɛ:t] *f* (-/-en) frivolity, flippancy.

froh *adj.* [fro:] joyful, glad; cheerful; happy; gay (a. *colour*).

fröhlich *adj.* ['frø:liç] gay, merry, cheerful, happy, *Am.* F a. chipper; '2**keit** *f* (-/~ -en) gaiety, cheerfulness; merriment.

froh|'locken *v/i.* (no -ge-, h) shout for joy, be jubilant; exult (*über acc.* at, in); gloat (over); '2**sinn** *m* (-[e]s/no *pl.*) gaiety, cheerfulness.

fromm *adj.* [frɔm] p. pious, religious; *life*, *etc.*: godly; *prayer*, *etc.*: devout; *horse*, *etc.*: docile; ~*e Lüge* white lie; ~*er Wunsch* wishful thinking, idle wish.

Frömmelei [frœmə'laɪ] *f* (-/-en) affected piety, bigotry.

'**Frömmigkeit** *f* (-/-en) piety, religiousness; godliness; devoutness.

Fron [fro:n] *f* (-/-en), '~**arbeit** *f*, '~**dienst** *hist. m* forced *or* compulsory labo(u)r *or* service; *fig.* drudgery.

frönen ['frø:nən] *v/i.* (dat.) (ge-, h) indulge in; be a slave to.

Front [frɔnt] *f* (-/-en) △ front, façade, face; ✕ front (line); line; *pol.*, ✝, *etc.*: front.

fror [fro:r] *pret.* of *frieren.*

Frosch *zo.* [frɔʃ] *m* (-es/~e) frog; '~**perspektive** *f* worm's-eye view.

Frost [frɔst] *m* (-es/~e) frost; chill; '~**beule** *f* chilblain.

frösteln ['frœstəln] *v/i.* (ge-, h) feel chilly, shiver (with cold).

'**frostig** *adj.* frosty (a. *fig.*); *fig.* cold, frigid, icy.

'**Frost|salbe** ⚕ *f* chilblain ointment; '~**schaden** *m* frost damage; '~**schutzmittel** *mot. n* anti-freezing mixture; '~**wetter** *n* frosty weather.

frottier|en [frɔ'ti:rən] *v/t.* (no -ge-, h) rub; 2(**hand**)**tuch** *n* Turkish towel.

Frucht [fruxt] *f* (-/~e) ⚘ fruit (a. *fig.*); corn; crop; *fig.* reward, result; '2**bar** *adj.* fruitful (*esp. fig.*); fertile (a. *biol.*); '~**barkeit** *f* (-/no *pl.*) fruitfulness; fertility; '2**bringend** *adj.* fruit-bearing; *fig.* fruitful; '2**en** *fig. v/i.* (ge-, h) be of use; '~**knoten** ⚘ *m* ovary; '2**los** *adj.* fruitless; *fig. a.* ineffective.

früh [fry:] **1.** *adj.* early; *am ~en Morgen* in the early morning; *~es Aufstehen* early rising; *~e Anzeichen* early symptoms; *~er former*; **2.** *adv.* in the morning; ~ *aufstehen* rise early; *heute* ~ this morning; *morgen* ~ tomorrow morning; *~er* earlier; formerly, in former times; *~estens* at the earliest; '2**aufsteher** *m* (-s/-) early riser, F early bird; '2**e** *f* (-/no *pl.*): *in aller* ~ very early in the morning; '2**geburt** *f* premature birth; premature baby *or* animal; '2**gottesdienst** *m* early service; '2**jahr** *n*, 2**ling** ['~liŋ] *m* (-s/-e) spring; '~**morgens** *adv.* early in the morning; '~**reif** *fig. adj.* precocious; '2**sport** *m* early morning exercises; '2**stück** *n* breakfast; '~**stücken** (ge-, h) **1.** *v/i.* (have) breakfast; **2.** *v/t.* have *s.th.* for breakfast; '2**zug** ⚅ *m* early train.

Fuchs [fuks] *m* (-es/~e) *zo.* fox (a. *fig.*); *horse*: sorrel.

Füchsin *zo.* ['fyksin] *f* (-/-nen) she-fox, vixen.

'**Fuchs|jagd** *f* fox-hunt(ing); '~**pelz** *m* fox-fur; '2**rot** *adj.* foxy-red, sorrel; '~**schwanz** *m* foxtail; ⊕ pad-saw; ⚘ amarant(h); '2**teufels-wild** F *adj.* mad with rage, F hopping mad.

fuchteln ['fuxtəln] *v/i.* (ge-, h): ~ *mit* (dat.) wave (*one's hands*) about.

Fuder ['fu:dər] *n* (-s/-) cart-load; tun (*of wine*). [f *fugue*.]

Fuge ['fu:gə] *f* (-/-n) ⊕ joint; seam;)

füg|en ['fy:gən] *v/refl.* (ge-, h) submit, give in, yield (dat., *in acc.* to); comply (with); ~**sam** *adj.* ['fy:k-] (com)pliant; manageable.

fühl|bar *adj.* ['fy:lba:r] tangible, palpable; *fig.* sensible, noticeable; '~**en** (ge-, h) **1.** *v/t.* feel; be aware of; *sich glücklich* ~ feel happy; **2.** *v/i.*: *mit j-m* ~ feel for *or* sympathize with s.o.; '2**er** *m* (-s/-) feeler

(a. fig.); '2ung f (-/-en) touch, contact (a. ⚡); ~ haben be in touch (mit with); ~ verlieren lose touch.
fuhr [fu:r] pret. of fahren.
Fuhre ['fu:rə] f (-/-n) cart-load.
führen ['fy:rən] (ge-, h) 1. v/t. lead, guide (blind person, etc.); show (zu dat. to); wield (paint-brush, etc.); ✗ command (regiment, etc.); have, bear (title, etc.); carry on (conversation, etc.); conduct (campaign, etc.); ✝ run (shop, etc.); deal in (goods); lead (life); keep (diary, etc.); ⚖ try (case); wage (war) (mit, gegen against); ~ durch show round; sich ~ conduct o.s., behave (o.s.); 2. v/i. path, etc.: lead, run, go (nach, zu to); sports, etc.: (hold the) lead, be ahead; ~ zu lead to, result in; '~d adj. leading, prominent, Am. a. banner.
'Führer m (-s/-) leader (a. pol., sports); guide(-book); '~raum 🖃 m cockpit; '~schein mot. m driving licence, Am. driver's license; '~sitz m mot. driver's seat, 🖃 pilot's seat; '~stand 🖴 m (driver's) cab.
'Fuhr|geld n, '~lohn m cartage, carriage; '~mann m (-[e]s/=er, Fuhrleute) carter, carrier, wag(g)oner; driver; '~park m fleet (of lorries), Am. fleet (of trucks).
'Führung f (-/-en) leadership; conduct, management; guidance; conduct, behavio(u)r; sports, etc.: lead; '~szeugnis n certificate of good conduct.
'Fuhr|unternehmer m carrier, haulage contractor, Am. a. trucker, teamster; '~werk n (horse-drawn) vehicle; cart, wag(g)on.
Fülle ['fylə] f (-/no pl.) fullness (a. fig.); corpulence, plumpness, stoutness; fig. wealth, abundance, profusion.
füllen¹ ['fylən] v/t. (ge-, h) fill (a. tooth); stuff (cushion, poultry, etc.).
Füllen² zo. [~] n (-s/-) foal; male: colt; female: filly.
'Füll|er F m (-s/-), '~feder(halter m) f fountain-pen; '~horn n horn of plenty; '~ung f (-/-en) filling; panel (of door, etc.).
Fund [funt] m (-[e]s/-e) finding, discovery; find.
Fundament [funda'ment] n (-[e]s/-e) ⚛ foundation; fig. basis.
'Fund|büro n lost-property office; '~gegenstand m object found; '~grube fig. f rich source, mine.
fünf adj. [fynf] five; '2eck n pentagon; ~fach adj. ['~fax] fivefold, quintuple; '2kampf m sports: pentathlon; 2linge ['~liŋə] m/pl. quintuplets pl.; '~te adj. fifth; '2tel n (-s/-) fifth; '~tens adv. fifthly, in the fifth place; '~zehn(te) adj. fifteen(th); ~zig adj. ['~tsiç] fifty; '~zigste adj. fiftieth.

fungieren [fuŋ'gi:rən] v/i. (no -ge-, h): ~ als officiate or act as.
Funk [fuŋk] m (-s/no pl.) radio, wireless; '~anlage f radio or wireless installation or equipment; '~bastler m do-it-yourself radio ham; '~bild n photo-radiogram.
Funke ['fuŋkə] m (-ns/-n) spark; fig. a. glimmer.
'funkeln v/i. (ge-, h) sparkle, glitter; star: twinkle, sparkle.
'Funken¹ esp. fig. m (-s/-) s. Funke.
'funken² v/t. (ge-, h) radio, wireless, broadcast.
'Funk|er m (-s/-) radio or wireless operator; '~gerät n radio (communication) set; '~spruch m radio or wireless message; '~station f radio or wireless station; '~stille f radio or wireless silence; '~streifenwagen m radio patrol car.
Funktion [fuŋk'tsjo:n] f (-/-en) function; '~är [~tsjo'nɛ:r] m (-s/-e) functionary, official; 2ieren [~o-'ni:rən] v/i. (no -ge-, h) function, work.
'Funk|turm m radio or wireless tower; '~verkehr m radio or wireless communication; '~wagen m radio car; '~wesen n (-s/no pl.) radio communication.
für prp. (acc.) [fy:r] for; in exchange or return for; in favo(u)r of; in s.o.'s place; Schritt ~ Schritt step by step; Tag ~ Tag day after day; ich ~ meine Person ... as for me, I ...; das Für und Wider the pros and cons pl.
'Fürbitte f intercession.
Furche ['furçə] f (-/-n) furrow (a. in face); rut; ⊕ groove; '2n v/t. (ge-, h) furrow (a. face); ⊕ groove.
Furcht [furçt] f (-/no pl.) fear, dread; aus ~ vor for fear of; '2bar adj. awful, terrible, dreadful.
fürchten ['fyrçtən] (ge-, h) 1. v/t. fear, dread; sich ~ vor (dat.) be afraid or scared of; 2. v/i.: ~ um fear for.
'fürchterlich adj. s. furchtbar.
'furcht|los adj. fearless; '2losigkeit f (-/no pl.) fearlessness; '~sam adj. timid, timorous; '2samkeit f (-/no pl.) timidity.
Furie fig. ['fu:rjə] f (-/-n) fury.
Furnier ⊕ [fur'ni:r] n (-s/-e) veneer; 2en v/t. (no -ge-, h) veneer.
'Für|sorge f care; öffentliche ~ public welfare work; '~sorgeamt n welfare department; '~sorgeerziehung f corrective training for juvenile delinquents; '~sorger m (-s/-) social or welfare worker; '2sorglich adj. considerate, thoughtful, solicitous; '~sprache f intercession (für for, bei with); '~sprecher m intercessor.
Fürst [fyrst] m (-en/-en) prince; sovereign; '~enhaus n dynasty;

'**∼enstand** m prince's rank; '**∼entum** n (-s/∼er) principality; '**∼lich 1.** adj. princely (a. fig.), royal; fig. magnificent, sumptuous; **2.** adv.: ∼ leben live like a lord or king; '**∼lichkeiten** f/pl. royalties pl.

Furt [furt] f (-/-en) ford.

Furunkel ⚕ [fu'ruŋkəl] m (-s/-) boil, furuncle.

'**Fürwort** gr. n (-[e]s/∼er) pronoun.

Fusel F ['fuːzəl] m (-s/-) low-quality spirits, F rotgut.

Fusion ✝ [fu'zjoːn] f (-/-en) merger, amalgamation.

Fuß [fuːs] m (-es/∼e) foot; ∼ fassen find a foothold; fig. become established; auf gutem (schlechtem) ∼ stehen mit be on good (bad) terms with; zu ∼ on foot; zu ∼ gehen walk; gut zu ∼ sein be a good walker; '**∼abstreifer** m (-s/-) door-scraper, door-mat; '**∼angel** f mantrap; '**∼ball** m (association) football, F and Am. soccer; '**∼ballspieler** m football player, footballer; '**∼bank** f footstool; '**∼bekleidung** f footwear, footgear; '**∼boden** m floor (-ing); '**∼bodenbelag** m floor covering; '**∼bremse** mot. f foot-brake;

'**∼en** v/i. (ge-, h): ∼ auf (dat.) be based or founded on; **∼gänger** ['∼gɛŋər] m (-s/-) pedestrian; '**∼gelenk** anat. n ankle joint; '**∼note** f footnote; '**∼pfad** m footpath; '**∼sack** m foot-muff; '**∼sohle** anat. f sole of the foot; '**∼soldat** ✗ m footsoldier, infantryman; '**∼spur** f footprint; track; **∼stapfe** ['∼ʃtapfə] f (-/-n) footprint, fig. a. footstep; '**∼steig** m footpath; '**∼tritt** m kick; '**∼wanderung** f walking tour, hike; '**∼weg** m footpath.

Futter ['futər] n **1.** (-s/no pl.) food, sl. grub, Am. F a. chow; feed, fodder; **2.** (-s/-) lining; △ casing.

Futteral [futə'raːl] n (-s/-e) case (for spectacles, etc.); cover (of umbrella); sheath (of knife).

'**Futtermittel** n feeding stuff.

füttern ['fytərn] v/t. (ge-, h) feed; line (dress, etc.); △ case.

'**Futter|napf** m feeding bowl or dish; '**∼neid** fig. m (professional) jealousy; '**∼stoff** m lining (material).

'**Fütterung** f (-/-en) feeding; lining; △ casing.

Futur gr. [fu'tuːr] n (-s/-e) future (tense).

G

gab [gaːp] pret. of geben.

Gabe ['gaːbə] f (-/-n) gift, present; alms; donation; ✍ dose; talent.

Gabel ['gaːbəl] f (-/-n) fork; '**∼n** v/refl. (ge-, h) fork, bifurcate; '**∼ung** f (-/-en) bifurcation.

gackern ['gakərn] v/i. (ge-, h) cackle.

gaffen ['gafən] v/i. (ge-, h) gape; stare.

Gage ['gaːʒə] f (-/-n) salary, pay.

gähnen ['gɛːnən] **1.** v/i. (ge-, h) yawn; **2.** ♀ n (-s/no pl.) yawning.

Gala ['gaːla] f (-/no pl.) gala; in ∼ in full dress.

galant adj. [ga'lant] gallant; courteous; ♀erie [∼ə'riː] f (-/-n) gallantry; courtesy.

Galeere ⚓ [ga'leːrə] f (-/-n) galley.

Galerie [galə'riː] f (-/-n) gallery.

Galgen ['galgən] m (-s/-) gallows, gibbet; '**∼frist** f respite; '**∼gesicht** n gallows-look, hangdog look; '**∼humor** m grim humo(u)r; '**∼strick** m, '**∼vogel** m gallows-bird, hangdog.

Galle anat. ['galə] f (-/-n) bile (of person); gall (of animal) (a. fig.); '**∼nblase** anat. f gall-bladder; '**∼nleiden** ✍ n bilious complaint; '**∼nstein** ⚕ m gall-stone, bile-stone.

Gallert ['galərt] n (-[e]s/-e), **∼e** [ga'lertə] f (-/-n) gelatine, jelly.

'**gallig** fig. adj. bilious.

Galopp [ga'lɔp] m (-s/-s, -e) gallop; canter; ♀ieren [∼'piːrən] v/i. (no -ge-, sein) gallop; canter.

galt [galt] pret. of gelten.

galvani|sch adj. [gal'vaːniʃ] galvanic; **∼sieren** [∼ani'-] v/t. (no -ge-, h) galvanize.

Gang¹ [gaŋ] m (-[e]s/∼e) walk; s. Gangart; fig. motion; running; working (of machine); errand; way; course (of events, of a meal, etc.); passage(-way); alley; corridor, gallery; in vehicle, between seats: gangway, esp. Am. aisle; 🚢 corridor, Am. aisle; fencing: pass; anat. duct; mot. gear; erster (zweiter, dritter, vierter) ∼ low or bottom (second, third, top) gear; in ∼ bringen or setzen set going or in motion, Am. operate; in ∼ kommen get going, get started; im ∼ sein be in motion; ⊕ be working or running; fig. be in progress; in vollem ∼ in full swing.

gang² adj. [∼]: ∼ und gäbe customary, traditional.

'**Gang|art** f gait, walk (of person); pace (of horse); '**∼bar** adj. road: practicable, passable; money: current; ✝ goods: marketable; s. gängig.

Gängelband ['gɛŋəl-] n leading-strings *pl.*; *am ~ führen* keep in leading-strings, lead by the nose.

gängig *adj.* ['gɛnɪç] *money:* current; ✝ *goods:* marketable; **~er** *Ausdruck* current word or phrase.

Gans *orn.* [gans] *f* (-/⸚e) goose.

Gänse|blümchen ⚘ ['gɛnzəbly:mçən] *n* (-s/-) daisy; '**~braten** *m* roast goose; '**~feder** *f* goose-quill; '**~füßchen** ['~fy:sçən] *n/pl.* quotation marks *pl.*, inverted commas *pl.*; '**~haut** *f* goose-skin; *fig. a.* goose-flesh, *Am. a.* goose pimples *pl.*; '**~klein** *n* (-s/*no pl.*) (goose-)giblets *pl.*; '**~marsch** *m* single *or* Indian file; **~rich** *orn.* ['~rɪç] *m* (-s/-e) gander; '**~schmalz** *n* goose-grease.

ganz [gants] 1. *adj.* all; entire, whole; complete, total, full; *den ~en Tag* all day (long); 2. *adv.* quite; entirely, *etc.* (s. 1.); very; ~ *Auge (Ohr)* all eyes (ears); ~ *und gar* wholly, totally; ~ *und gar nicht* not at all; *im ~en* on the whole, generally; *in all ~en* in the lump; '**2e** *n* (-n/*no pl.*) whole; totality; *aufs ~ gehen* go all out, *esp. Am. sl.* go the whole hog.

gänzlich *adj.* ['gɛntslɪç] complete, total, entire.

'**Ganztagsbeschäftigung** *f* full-time job *or* employment.

gar [ga:r] 1. *adj. food:* done; 2. *adv.* quite, very; even; ~ *nicht* not at all.

Garage [ga'ra:ʒə] *f* (-/-n) garage.

Garantie [garan'ti:] *f* (-/-n) guarantee, warranty, ⟨🇹🇹⟩ guaranty; **2ren** *v/t.* (*no* -ge-, *h*) guarantee, warrant.

Garbe ['garbə] *f* (-/-n) sheaf.

Garde ['gardə] *f* (-/-n) guard.

Garderobe [gardə'ro:bə] *f* (-/-n) wardrobe, cloakroom, *Am.* check-room; *thea.* dressing-room; '**~nfrau** *f* cloak-room attendant, *Am.* hat-check girl; '**~nmarke** *f* check; '**~nschrank** *m* wardrobe; '**~nständer** *m* coat-stand, hat-stand, hall-stand.

Garderobiere [gardəro'bjɛːrə] *f* (-/-n) *s. Garderobenfrau; thea.* wardrobe mistress.

Gardine [gar'di:nə] *f* (-/-n) curtain.

gär|en ['gɛːrən] *v/i.* (*irr.*, ge-, *h, sein*) ferment; '**2mittel** *n* ferment.

Garn [garn] *n* (-[e]s/-e) yarn; thread; cotton; net; *j-m ins ~ gehen* fall into s.o.'s snare.

Garnele *zo.* [gar'ne:lə] *f* (-/-n) shrimp.

garnieren [gar'ni:rən] *v/t.* (*no* -ge-, *h*) trim; garnish (*esp. a dish*).

Garnison ⚔ [garni'zo:n] *f* (-/-en) garrison, post.

Garnitur [garni'tu:r] *f* (-/-en) trimming; ⊕ fittings *pl.*; set.

garstig *adj.* ['garstɪç] nasty, bad; ugly.

Gärstoff *m* ferment.

Garten ['gartən] *m* (-s/⸚) garden; '**~anlage** *f* gardens *pl.*, park; '**~ar-**

beit *f* gardening; '**~bau** *m* horticulture; '**~erde** *f* (garden-)mo(u)ld; '**~fest** *n* garden-party, *Am. a.* lawn party; '**~geräte** *n/pl.* gardening-tools *pl.*; '**~stadt** *f* garden city.

Gärtner ['gɛrtnər] *m* (-s/-) gardener; **~ei** [~'raɪ] *f* (-/-en) gardening, horticulture; nursery; '**~in** *f* (-/-nen) gardener.

Gärung ['gɛːruŋ] *f* (-/-en) fermentation.

Gas [ga:s] *n* (-es/-e) gas; ~ *geben mot.* open the throttle, *Am.* step on the gas; '**~anstalt** *f* gas-works, *Am. a.* gas plant; '**~behälter** *m* gasometer, *Am.* gas tank *or* container; '**~beleuchtung** *f* gaslight; '**~brenner** *m* gas-burner; 2**förmig** *adj.* ['~fœrmɪç] gaseous; '**~hahn** *m* gas-tap; '**~herd** *m* gas-stove, *Am.* gas range; '**~leitung** *f* gas-mains *pl.*; '**~messer** *m* (-s/-) gas-meter; '**~ofen** *m* gas-oven; '**~pedal** *mot. n* accelerator (pedal), *Am.* gas pedal.

Gasse ['gasə] *f* (-/-n) lane, by-street, alley(-way); '**~nhauer** *m* (-s/-) street ballad, popular song; '**~n-junge** *m* street arab.

Gast [gast] *m* (-es/⸚e) guest; visitor; customer (*of public house, etc.*); *thea.:* guest (artist); guest star; '**~arbeiter** *m* foreign worker; '**~bett** *n* spare bed.

Gäste|buch ['gɛstə-] *n* visitors' book; '**~zimmer** *n* guest-room; spare (bed)room; *s. Gaststube.*

'**gast|freundlich** *adj.* hospitable; '2**freundschaft** *f* hospitality; '2**geber** *m* (-s/-) host; '2**geberin** *f* (-/-nen) hostess; '2**haus** *n,* '2**hof** *m* restaurant; inn, hotel; '2**hörer** *univ. m* guest student, *Am. a.* auditor.

gastieren *thea.* [gas'ti:rən] *v/i.* (*no* -ge-, *h*) appear as a guest.

'**gast|lich** *adj.* hospitable; '2**mahl** *n* feast, banquet; '2**recht** *n* right of *or* to hospitality; '2**rolle** *thea. f* guest part; starring part *or* role; '2**spiel** *thea. n* guest appearance *or* performance; starring (performance); '2**stätte** *f* restaurant; '2**stube** *f* taproom; restaurant; '2**wirt** *m* innkeeper, landlord; '2**wirtin** *f* innkeeper, landlady; '2**wirtschaft** *f* inn, public house, restaurant; '2**zimmer** *n s. Gästezimmer.*

'**Gas|uhr** *f* gas-meter; '**~werk** *n s. Gasanstalt.*

Gatte ['gatə] *m* (-n/-n) husband; spouse, consort.

Gatter ['gatər] *n* (-s/-) lattice; railing, grating.

'**Gattin** *f* (-/-nen) wife; spouse, consort.

Gattung ['gatuŋ] *f* (-/-en) kind; sort; type; species; genus.

gaukeln ['gaukəln] *v/i.* (ge-, *h*) juggle; *birds, etc.:* flutter.

Gaul [gavl] m (-[e]s/ⁿe) (old) nag.

Gaumen anat. ['gaumən] m (-s/-) palate.

Gauner ['gaunər] m (-s/-) scoundrel, swindler, sharper, sl. crook; ~ei [~'rai] f (-/-en) swindling, cheating, trickery.

Gaze ['gɑːzə] f (-/-n) gauze.

Gazelle zo. [ga'tsɛlə] f (-/-n) gazelle.

Geächtete [gə'ɛçtətə] m, f (-n/-n) outlaw.

Gebäck [gə'bɛk] n (-[e]s/-e) baker's goods pl.; pastry; fancy cakes pl.

ge'backen p.p. of backen.

Gebälk [gə'bɛlk] n (-[e]s/no pl.) framework, timber-work; beams pl.

gebar [gə'baːr] pret. of gebären.

Gebärde [gə'bɛːrdə] f (-/-n) gesture; ~n v/refl. (no -ge-, h) conduct o.s., behave; ~nspiel n (-[e]s/no pl.) gesticulation; dumb show, pantomime; ~nsprache f language of gestures.

Gebaren [gə'baːrən] n (-s/no pl.) conduct, deportment, behavio(u)r.

gebären [gə'bɛːrən] v/t. (irr., no -ge-, h) bear, bring forth (a. fig.); give birth to.

Ge|bäude [gə'bɔydə] n (-s/-) building, edifice, structure; ~bell [~'bɛl] n (-[e]s/no pl.) barking.

geben ['geːbən] v/t. (irr., ge-, h) give (j-m et. s.o. s.th.); present (s.o. with s.th.); put; yield s.th.; deal (cards); pledge (one's word); von sich ~ emit; utter (words); bring up, vomit (food); et. (nichts) ~ auf (acc.) set (no) great store by; sich geschlagen ~ give in; sich zufrieden ~ content o.s. (mit with); sich zu erkennen ~ make o.s. known; es gibt there is, there are; was gibt es? what is the matter?; thea.: gegeben werden be on.

Gebet [gə'beːt] n (-[e]s/-e) prayer.

ge'beten p.p. of bitten.

Gebiet [gə'biːt] n (-[e]s/-e) territory; district; region; area; fig.: field; province; sphere.

ge'biet|en (irr. bieten, no -ge-, h) 1. v/t. order, command; 2. v/i. rule; ~er m (-s/-) master, lord, governor; ~erin f (-/-nen) mistress; ~erisch adj. imperious; commanding.

Gebilde [gə'bildə] n (-s/-) form, shape; structure; 2t adj. educated; cultured, cultivated.

Gebirg|e [gə'birgə] n (-s/-) mountains pl.; mountain chain or range; 2ig adj. mountainous; ~sbewohner m mountaineer; ~szug m mountain range.

Ge'biß n (Gebisses/Gebisse) (set of) teeth; (set of) artificial or false teeth, denture; harness: bit.

ge|'bissen p.p. of beißen; ~'blasen p.p. of blasen; ~'blichen p.p. of bleichen 2; ~blieben [~'bliːbən] p.p. of bleiben; ~blümt adj.

[~'blyːmt] pattern, design: flowered; material: sprigged; ~'bogen 1. p.p. of biegen; 2. adj. bent, curved; ~boren [~'boːrən] 1. p.p. of gebären; 2. adj. born; ein ~er Deutscher German by birth; ~e Schmidt née Smith.

ge'borgen 1. p.p. of bergen; 2. adj. safe, sheltered; 2heit f (-/no pl.) safety, security.

geborsten [gə'bɔrstən] p.p. of bersten.

Ge'bot n (-[e]s/-e) order; command; bid(ding), offer; eccl.: die Zehn ~e pl. the Ten Commandments pl.; 2en p.p. of bieten.

ge|bracht [gə'braxt] p.p. of bringen; ~brannt [~'brant] p.p. of brennen; ~'braten p.p. of braten.

Ge'brauch m 1. (-[e]s/no pl.) use; ⚕ application; 2. (-[e]s/ⁿe) usage, practice; custom; 2en v/t. (no -ge-, h) use, employ; 2t adj. clothes, etc.: second-hand.

gebräuchlich adj. [gə'brɔyçliç] in use; usual, customary.

Ge'brauchs|anweisung f directions pl. or instructions pl. for use; ~artikel m commodity, necessary, requisite; personal article; 2fertig adj. ready for use; coffee, etc.: instant; ~muster ✝ n sample; registered design.

Ge'braucht|wagen mot. m used car; ~waren f/pl. second-hand articles pl.

Ge'brechen n (-s/-) defect, infirmity; affliction.

ge'brechlich adj. fragile; p.: frail, weak; infirm; 2keit f (-/-en) fragility; infirmity.

gebrochen [gə'brɔxən] p.p. of brechen.

Ge|brüder [gə'bryːdər] pl. brothers pl.; ~brüll [~'bryl] n (-[e]s/no pl.) roaring; lowing (of cattle).

Gebühr [gə'byːr] f (-/-en) due; duty; charge; rate; fee; ~en pl. fee(s pl.); dues pl.; 2en v/i. (no -ge-, h) be due (dat. to); sich ~ be proper or fitting; 2end adj. due; becoming; proper; 2enfrei adj. free of charge; 2enpflichtig adj. liable to charges, chargeable.

gebunden [gə'bundən] 1. p.p. of binden; 2. adj. bound.

Geburt [gə'buːrt] f (-/-en) birth; ~enkontrolle f, ~enregelung f birth-control; ~enziffer f birth-rate.

gebürtig adj. [gə'byrtiç]: ~ aus native of.

Ge'burts|anzeige f announcement of birth; ~fehler m congenital defect; ~helfer m obstetrician; ~hilfe f obstetrics, midwifery; ~jahr n year of birth; ~land n native country; ~ort m birth-place; ~schein m birth certificate;

birthday; **~urkunde** f birth certificate.

Gebüsch [gə'byʃ] n (-es/-e) bushes pl., undergrowth, thicket.

gedacht [gə'daxt] p.p. of denken.

Gedächtnis [gə'dɛçtnis] n (-ses/-se) memory; remembrance, recollection; **im ~ behalten** keep in mind; **zum ~** (gen.) in memory of; **~feier** f commemoration.

Gedanke [gə'daŋkə] m (-ns/-n) thought; idea; **in ~n** (versunken or verloren) absorbed in thought; **sich ~n machen über** (acc.) worry about.

Ge'danken|gang m train of thought; **~leser** m, **~leserin** f (-/-nen) thought-reader; **Qlos** adj. thoughtless; **~strich** m dash; **Qvoll** adj. thoughtful, pensive.

Ge|därm [gə'dɛrm] n (-[e]s/-e) mst pl. entrails pl., bowels pl., intestines pl.; **~deck** [‿'dɛk] n (-[e]s/-e) cover; menu; **ein ~ auflegen** lay a place.

gedeihen [gə'daɪən] 1. v/i. (irr., no -ge-, sein) thrive, prosper; 2. Q n (-s/no pl.) thriving, prosperity.

ge'denken v/i.(gen.) (irr. denken, no -ge-, h) think of; remember, recollect; commemorate; mention; **~ zu inf.** intend to inf.; 2. Q n (-s/no pl.) memory, remembrance (an acc. of).

Ge'denk|feier f commemoration; **~stein** m memorial stone; **~tafel** f commemorative or memorial tablet.

Ge'dicht n (-[e]s/-e) poem.

gediegen [gə'di:gən] solid; pure; Qheit f (-/no pl.) solidity; purity.

gedieh [gə'di:] pret. of gedeihen; **~en** p.p. of gedeihen.

Gedräng|e [gə'drɛŋə] n (-s/no pl.) crowd, throng; Qt adj. crowded, packed, crammed; style: concise.

ge'droschen [gə'drɔʃən] p.p. of dreschen; **~'drückt** fig. adj. depressed; **~'drungen** [‿'druŋən] 1. p.p. of dringen; 2. adj. compact, squat, stocky, thickset.

Geduld [gə'dult] f (-/no pl.) patience; Qen [‿dən] v/refl. (no -ge-, h) have patience; Qig adj. [‿diç] patient.

ge|dunsen adj. [gə'dunzən] bloated; **~durft** [‿'durft] p.p. of dürfen 1; **~ehrt** adj. [‿'e:rt] hono(u)red; correspondence: **Sehr ~er Herr N.!** Dear Sir, Dear Mr N.; **~eignet** adj. [‿'aɪgnət] fit (für, zu, als for s.th.); suitable (to, for); qualified (for).

Gefahr [gə'fa:r] f (-/-en) danger, peril; risk; **auf eigene ~** at one's own risk; **~ laufen zu inf.** run the risk of ger.

gefährden [gə'fɛːrdən] v/t. (no -ge-, h) endanger; risk.

ge'fahren p.p. of fahren.

gefährlich adj. [gə'fɛːrliç] dangerous.

ge'fahrlos adj. without risk, safe.

Gefährt|e [gə'fɛːrtə] m (-en/-en), **~in** f (-/-nen) companion, fellow.

Gefälle [gə'fɛlə] n (-s/-) fall, slope, incline, descent, gradient, esp. Am. a. grade; fall (of river, etc.).

Ge'fallen 1. m (-s/-) favo(u)r; 2. n (-s/no pl.): **~ finden an** (dat.) take (a) pleasure in, take a fancy to or for; 3. Q v/i. (irr. fallen, no -ge-, h) please (j-m s.o.); **er gefällt mir** I like him; **sich et. ~ lassen** put up with s.th.; 4. Q p.p. of fallen.

gefällig adj. [gə'fɛliç] pleasing, agreeable; p.: complaisant, obliging; kind; Qkeit f (-/~-en) complaisance, kindness; favo(u)r; **~st** adv. (if you) please.

ge'fangen 1. p.p. of fangen; 2. adj. captive, imprisoned; Qe m (-n/-n), f (-n/-n) prisoner, captive; Qenlager n prison(ers') camp; Qnahme f (-/no pl.) capture; seizure, arrest; **~nehmen** v/t. (irr. nehmen, sep., -ge-, h) take prisoner; fig. captivate; Qschaft f (-/no pl.) captivity, imprisonment; **~setzen** v/t. (sep., -ge-, h) put in prison.

Gefängnis [gə'fɛŋnis] n (-ses/-se) prison, jail, gaol, Am. a. penitentiary; **~direktor** m governor, warden; **~strafe** f (sentence or term of) imprisonment; **~wärter** m warder, gaoler, jailer, (prison) guard.

Gefäß [gə'fɛːs] n (-es/-e) vessel.

gefaßt adj. [gə'fast] composed; **~ auf** (acc.) prepared for.

Ge|fecht [gə'fɛçt] n (-[e]s/-e) engagement; combat, fight; action; **~fieder** [‿'fiːdər] n (-s/-) plumage, feathers pl.

ge|'fleckt adj. spotted; **~flochten** [‿'flɔxtən] p.p. of flechten; **~flogen** [‿'floːgən] p.p. of fliegen; **~flohen** [‿'floːən] p.p. of fliehen; **~flossen** [‿'flɔsən] p.p. of fließen.

Ge|'flügel n (-s/no pl.) fowl; poultry; **~flüster** [‿'flystər] n (-s/no pl.) whisper(ing).

gefochten [gə'fɔxtən] p.p. of fechten.

Ge'folg|e n (-s/no pl.) retinue, train, followers pl.; attendants pl.; **~schaft** [‿kʃaft] f (-/-en) followers pl.

gefräßig adj. [gə'frɛːsiç] greedy, voracious, Qkeit f (-/no pl.) greediness, gluttony, voracity.

ge'fressen p.p. of fressen.

ge'frier|en v/i. (irr. frieren, no -ge-, sein) congeal, freeze; Qfleisch n frozen meat; Qpunkt m freezing-point; Qschutz(mittel n) m antifreeze.

gefroren [gə'froːrən] p.p. of frieren; Qe [‿ə] n (-n/no pl.) ice-cream.

Gefüge [gə'fyːgə] n (-s/-) structure; texture.

ge'fügig adj. pliant; 2keit f (-/no pl.) pliancy.

Gefühl [gə'fy:l] n (-[e]s/-e) feeling; touch; sense (für of); sensation; 2los adj. unfeeling, insensible (gegen to); 2sbetont adj. emotional; 2voll adj. (full of) feeling; tender; sentimental.

ge|funden [gə'fundən] p.p. of finden; ~gangen [~'gaŋən] p.p. of gehen.

ge'geben p.p. of geben; ~enfalls adv. in that case; if necessary.

gegen prp. (acc.) ['ge:gən] space, time: towards; against, 🚂 versus; about, Am. around; by; compared with; (in exchange) for; remedy: for; freundlich sein ~ be kind to (-wards); ~ bar for cash.

'Gegen|angriff m counter-attack; '~antrag m counter-motion; '~antwort f rejoinder; '~befehl m counter-order; '~beschuldigung f countercharge; '~besuch m return visit; '~bewegung f counter-movement; '~beweis m counter-evidence.

Gegend ['ge:gənt] f (-/-en) region; area.

'Gegen|dienst m return service, service in return; '~druck m counter-pressure; fig. reaction; 2ei'nander adv. against one another or each other; '~erklärung f counter-statement; '~forderung f counter-claim; '~frage f counter-question; '~geschenk n return present; '~gewicht n counterbalance, counterpoise; '~gift 🜍 n antidote; '~kandidat m rival candidate; '~klage f countercharge; '~leistung f return (service), equivalent; ~lichtaufnahme phot. ['gə:gən-lɪçt?-] f back-lighted shot; '~liebe f requited love; keine ~ finden meet with no sympathy or enthusiasm; '~maßnahme f counter-measure; '~mittel n remedy (gegen for), antidote (against, for); '~partei f opposite party; '~probe f checktest; '~satz m contrast; opposition; im ~ zu in contrast to or with, in opposition to; 2sätzlich adj. ['~zetslɪç] contrary, opposite; '~seite f opposite side; 2seitig adj. mutual, reciprocal; '~seitigkeit f (-/no pl.) auf ~ assurance: mutual; auf ~ beruhen be mutual; '~spieler m games, sports: opponent; antagonist; '~spionage f counter-espionage; '~stand m object; subject, topic; '~strömung f counter-current; '~stück n counterpart; match; '~teil n contrary, reverse; im ~ on the contrary; '2teilig adj. contrary, opposite; 2'über 1. adv. opposite; 2. prp. (dat.) opposite (to); to (-wards); as against; face to face with; ~'über n (-s/-) vis-à-vis;

2'überstehen v/i. (irr. stehen, sep?, -ge-, h) (dat.) be faced with, face; ~'überstellung esp. ⚖ f confrontation; '~vorschlag m counterproposal; ~wart ['~vart] f (-/no pl.) presence; present time; gr. present tense; 2wärtig adj. ['~vertiç] 1. aa present; actual; 2. adv. at present; '~wehr f defen|ce, Am. -se; resistance; '~wert m equivalent; '~wind m contrary wind, head wind; '~wirkung f counter-effect, reaction; 2zeichnen v/t. (sep., -ge-, countersign; '~zug m counter-move (a. fig.); 🚂 corresponding train.

ge|gessen [gə'gesən] p.p. of esse. ~glichen [~'gliçən] p.p. of gle chen; ~'gliedert adj. articulat jointed; ~glitten [~'glitən] p.p. gleiten; ~glommen [~'glomə p.p. of glimmen.

Gegner ['ge:gnər] m (-s/-) adve sary, opponent; '~schaft f (-/-e opposition.

ge|golten [gə'gɔltən] p.p. of gelte ~goren [~'go:rən] p.p. of gäre ~gossen [~'gɔsən] p.p. of gieße ~graben p.p. of graben; ~griffe [~'grifən] p.p. of greifen; ~ha [~'ha:pt] p.p. of haben.

Gehalt [gə'halt] 1. m (-[e]s/-e) co tents pl.; capacity; merit; 2. (-[e]s/=er) salary; 2en p.p. of h ten; 2los adj. [~'lo:s] adj. empty; ~empfänger [gə'halts?-] m salari employee or worker; ~serhöhu [gə'halts?-] f rise (in salary), A raise; 2voll adj. rich; substanti wine: racy.

gehangen [gə'haŋən] p.p. of hä gen 1.

gehässig adj. [gə'hesiç] maliciou spiteful; 2keit f (-/-en) mali spitefulness.

ge'hauen p.p. of hauen.

Ge|häuse [gə'hɔyzə] n (-s/-) ca box; cabinet; shell; core (of app etc.); ~hege [~'he:gə] n (-s/-) ε closure.

geheim adj. [gə'haɪm] secret; dienst m secret service.

Ge'heimnis n (-ses/-se) secr mystery; ~krämer m myste monger; 2voll adj. mysterious.

Ge'heim|polizei f secret police; polizist m detective; plain-cloth man; ~schrift f cipher; tel. co ge'heißen p.p. of heißen.

gehen ['ge:ən] v/i. (irr., ge-, ge go; walk; leave; machine: work; clock, watch: go; merchand sell; wind: blow; paste: rise; geht es Ihnen? how are you (gett on)?; das geht nicht that won't in sich ~ repent; wieviel Pfennig auf e-e Mark? how many pfenn go to a mark?; das Fenster ge nach Norden the window faces looks north; es geht nichts ü *(acc.)* there is nothing like; *wenn es nach mir ginge* if I had my way.

Geheul [gə'hɔʏl] *n* (-[e]s/*no pl.*) howling.

Ge'hilf|e *m* (-n/-n), **~in** *f* (-/-nen) assistant; *fig.* helpmate.

Ge'hirn *n* (-[e]s/-e) brain(s *pl.*); **~erschütterung** *f* concussion (of the brain); **~schlag** *m* cerebral apoplexy.

gehoben [gə'ho:bən] **1.** *p.p. of* heben; **2.** *adj. speech, style:* elevated; **~e** *Stimmung* elated mood.

Gehöft [gə'hø:ft] *n* (-[e]s/-e) farm (-stead).

geholfen [gə'hɔlfən] *p.p. of* helfen.

Gehölz [gə'hœlts] *n* (-es/-e) wood, coppice, copse.

Gehör [gə'hø:r] *n* (-[e]s/*no pl.*) hearing; ear; *nach dem ~* by ear; *j-m ~ schenken* lend an ear to s.o.; *sich ~ verschaffen* make o.s. heard.

ge'horchen *v/i.* (*no* -ge-, h) obey (*j-m* s.o.).

ge'hör|en *v/i.* (*no* -ge-, h) belong (*dat. or zu* to); *es gehört sich* it is proper *or* fit *or* right *or* suitable; *das gehört nicht hierher* that's not to the point; **~ig 1.** *adj.* belonging (*dat. or zu* to); fit, proper, right; due; F good; **2.** *adv.* duly; F thoroughly.

gehorsam [gə'ho:rza:m] **1.** *adj.* obedient; **2.** **2** *m* (-s/*no pl.*) obedience.

'Geh|steig *m*, **'~weg** *m* pavement, *Am.* sidewalk; **'~werk** ⊕ *n* clockwork, works *pl.*

Geier *orn.* ['gaɪər] *m* (-s/-) vulture.

Geige ♪ ['gaɪgə] *f* (-/-n) violin, F fiddle; *(auf der) ~ spielen* play (on) the violin; **'~nbogen** ♪ *m* (violin-) bow; **'~nkasten** ♪ *m* violin-case; **'~r** ♪ *m* (-s/-), **'~rin** ♪ *f* (-/-nen) violinist.

'Geigerzähler *phys. m* Geiger counter.

geil *adj.* [gaɪl] lascivious, wanton; luxuriant.

Geisel ['gaɪzəl] *f* (-/-n) hostage.

Geiß *zo.* [gaɪs] *f* (-/-en) (she-, nanny-)goat; **'~blatt** ♀ *n* (-[e]s/*no pl.*) honeysuckle, woodbine; **'~bock** *zo. m* he-goat, billy-goat.

Geißel ['gaɪsəl] *f* (-/-n) whip, lash; *fig.* scourge; **'2n** *v/t.* (ge-, h) whip, lash; *fig.* castigate.

Geist [gaɪst] *m* (-es/-er) spirit; mind, intellect; wit; ghost; sprite; **'Geister|erscheinung** *f* apparition; **'2haft** *adj.* ghostly.

'geistes|abwesend *adj.* absent-minded; **'2arbeiter** *m* brainworker, white-collar worker; **'2blitz** *m* brain-wave, flash of genius; **'2gabe** *f* talent; **'2gegenwart** *f* presence of mind; **'~gegenwärtig** *adj.* alert; quick-witted; **'~gestört** *adj.* mentally disturbed; **'~krank**

adj. insane, mentally ill; **'2krankheit** *f* insanity, mental illness; **'~schwach** *adj.* feeble-minded, imbecile; **'~verwandt** *adj.* congenial; **'2wissenschaften** *f/pl. the* Arts *pl., the* Humanities *pl.*; **'2zustand** *m* state of mind.

'geistig *adj.* intellectual, mental; spiritual; **~e** *Getränke n/pl.* spirits *pl.*

'geistlich *adj.* spiritual; clerical; sacred; **'2e** *m* (-n/-n) clergyman; minister; **'2keit** *f* (-/*no pl.*) clergy.

'geist|los *adj.* spiritless; dull; stupid; **'~reich** *adj.*, **'~voll** *adj.* ingenious, spirited.

Geiz [gaɪts] *m* (-es/*no pl.*) avarice; **'~hals** *m* miser, niggard; **'2ig** *adj.* avaricious, stingy, mean.

Gejammer [gə'jamər] *n* (-s/*no pl.*) lamentation(s *pl.*), wailing.

gekannt [gə'kant] *p.p. of* kennen.

Geklapper [gə'klapər] *n* (-s/*no pl.*) rattling.

Geklirr [gə'klir] *n* (-[e]s/*no pl.*), **~e** [~ə] *n* (-s/*no pl.*) clashing, clanking.

ge|klungen [~'kluŋən] *p.p. of* klingen; **~'kniffen** *p.p. of* kneifen; **~'kommen** *p.p. of* kommen; **~konnt** [~'kɔnt] *p.p. of* können 1, 2.

Ge|kreisch [gə'kraɪʃ] *n* (-es/*no pl.*) screaming, screams *pl.*; shrieking; **~kritzel** ['kritsəl] *n* (-s/*no pl.*) scrawl(ing), scribbling, scribble.

ge|krochen [gə'krɔxən] *p.p. of* kriechen; **~künstelt** ['~kynstəlt] affected.

Gelächter [gə'lɛçtər] *n* (-s/-) laughter.

ge'laden *p.p. of* laden.

Ge'lage *n* (-s/-) feast; drinking-bout.

Gelände [gə'lɛndə] *n* (-s/-) ground; terrain; country; area; **2gängig** *mot. adj.* cross-country; **~lauf** *m sports:* cross-country race *or* run.

Geländer [gə'lɛndər] *n* (-s/-) railing, balustrade; banisters *pl.*

ge'lang *pret. of* gelingen.

ge'langen *v/i.* (*no* -ge-, sein): *~ an* (*acc.*) *or in* (*acc.*) arrive at, get *or* come to; *~ zu* attain (to), gain.

ge'lassen 1. *p.p. of* lassen; **2.** *adj.* calm, composed.

Gelatine [ʒela'ti:nə] *f* (-/*no pl.*) gelatin(e).

ge|'laufen *p.p. of* laufen; **~läufig** *adj.* [~'lɔʏfɪç] current; fluent, easy; *tongue:* voluble; familiar; **~launt** *adj.* [~'laʊnt] in a (*good, etc.*) humo(u)r *or Am.* mood.

Geläut [gə'lɔʏt] *n* (-[e]s/-e), **~e** [~ə] *n* (-s/-) ringing (*of bells*); chimes *pl.* (*of church bells*).

gelb *adj.* [gɛlp] yellow; **'~lich** *adj.* yellowish; **'2sucht** ♂ *f* (-/*no pl.*) jaundice.

Geld [gɛlt] *n* (-[e]s/-er) money; *im*

~ schwimmen be rolling in money; zu ~ machen turn into cash; '~angelegenheit f money-matter; '~anlage f investment; '~ausgabe f expense; '~beutel m purse; '~entwertung f devaluation of the currency; '~erwerb m money-making; '~geber m (-s/-) financial backer, investor; '~geschäfte n/pl. money transactions pl.; '♀gierig adj. greedy for money, avaricious; '~mittel n/pl. funds pl., resources pl.; '~schein m bank-note, Am. bill; '~schrank m strong-box, safe; '~sendung f remittance; '~strafe f fine; '~stück n coin; '~tasche f money-bag; notecase, Am. billfold; '~überhang m surplus money; '~umlauf m circulation of money; '~umsatz m turnover (of money); '~verlegenheit f pecuniary embarrassment; '~wechsel m exchange of money; '~wert m (-[e]s/no pl.) value of money, money value.

Gelee [ʒə'le:] n, m (-s/-s) jelly.

ge'legen 1. p.p. of liegen; **2.** adj. situated, Am. a. located; convenient, opportune; ♀heit f (-/-en) occasion; opportunity; chance; facility; bei ~ on occasion.

Ge'legenheits|arbeit f casual or odd job, Am. a. chore; ~arbeiter m casual labo(u)rer, odd-job man; ~kauf m bargain.

ge'legentlich 1. adj. occasional; **2.** prp. (gen.) on the occasion of.

ge'lehr|ig adj. docile; ♀igkeit f (-/no pl.) docility; ♀samkeit f (-/no pl.) learning; ~t adj. [~t] learned; ♀te [~ə] m (-n/-n) learned man, scholar.

Geleise [gə'laɪzə] n (-s/-) rut, track; 🚂 rails pl., line, esp. Am. tracks pl.

Geleit [gə'laɪt] n (-[e]s/-e) escort; attendance; j-m das ~ geben accompany s.o.; ♀en v/t. (no -ge-, h) accompany, conduct; escort; ~zug ⚓ m convoy.

Gelenk anat., ⊕, ♀ [gə'lɛŋk] n (-[e]s/-e) joint; ♀ig adj. pliable, supple.

ge'lernt adj. worker: skilled; trained; ~lesen p.p. of lesen.

Geliebte [gə'li:ptə] (-n/-n) **1.** m lover; **2.** f mistress, sweetheart.

geliehen [gə'li:ən] p.p. of leihen.

ge'linde 1. adj. soft, smooth; gentle; **2.** adv.: gelinde gesagt to put it mildly, to say the least.

gelingen [gə'lɪŋən] **1.** v/i. (irr., no -ge-, sein) succeed; es gelingt mir zu inf. I succeed in ger.; **2.** ♀ n (-s/no pl.) success.

ge'litten p.p. of leiden.

gellen ['gɛlən] (ge- h) **1.** v/i. shrill; yell; of ears: ring, tingle; **2.** v/t. shrill; yell; '~d adj. shrill, piercing.

ge'loben v/t. (no -ge-, h) vow, promise.

Gelöbnis [gə'lø:pnis] n (-ses/-se) promise, pledge; vow.

ge'logen p.p. of lügen.

gelt|en ['gɛltən] (irr., ge-, h) **1.** v/t. be worth; **2.** v/i. be of value; be valid; go; count; money: be current; maxim, etc.: hold (good or true); et. ~ have credit or influence; j-m ~ concern s.o.; ~ für or als pass for, be reputed or thought or supposed to be; ~ für apply to; ~ lassen let pass, allow; ~d machen maintain, assert; s-n Einfluß bei j-m ~d machen bring one's influence to bear on s.o.; das gilt nicht that is not fair; that does not count; es galt unser Leben our life was at stake; '♀ung f (-/-🔹 -en) validity; value; currency; authority (of person); zur ~ kommen tell; take effect; show; '♀ungsbedürfnis n desire to show off. [ise; vow.]

Gelübde [gə'lypdə] n (-s/-) prom-

gelungen [gə'luŋən] **1.** p.p. of gelingen; **2.** adj. successful; amusing, funny; F: das ist ja ~! that beats everything!

gemächlich adj. [gə'mɛ:çliç] comfortable, easy; ♀keit f (-/no pl.) ease, comfort.

Gemahl [gə'ma:l] m (-[e]s/-e) consort; husband.

ge'mahlen p.p. of mahlen.

Gemälde [gə'mɛ:ldə] n (-s/-) painting, picture; ~galerie f picture-gallery.

gemäß prp. (dat.) [gə'mɛ:s] according to; ~igt adj. moderate; temperate (a. geogr.).

gemein adj. [gə'maɪn] common; general; low, vulgar, mean, coarse; et. ~ haben mit have s.th. in common with.

Gemeinde [gə'maɪndə] f (-/-n) community; parish; municipality; eccl. congregation; ~bezirk m district; municipality; ~rat m municipal council; ~steuer f rate, Am. local tax; ~vorstand m district council.

ge'mein|gefährlich adj. dangerous to the public; ~er Mensch public danger, Am. public enemy; ♀heit f (-/-en) vulgarity; meanness; mean trick; ~nützig adj. of public utility; ♀platz m commonplace; ~sam adj. common; joint; mutual; ♀schaft f (-/-en) community; intercourse; ~schaftlich adj. s. gemeinsam; ♀schaftsarbeit [gə'maɪnʃafts?-] f team-work; ~sinn m (-[e]s/no pl.) public spirit; ~verständlich adj. popular; ♀wesen n community; ♀wohl n public welfare.

Ge'menge n (-s/-) mixture.

ge'messen 1. p.p. of messen; **2.** adj. measured; formal; grave.

Gemetzel [gə'mɛtsəl] n (-s/-) slaughter, massacre.

gemieden [gə'mi:dən] *p.p. of* **meiden**.

Gemisch [gə'miʃ] *n* (-es/-e) mixture; ⚗ compound, composition.

ge|mocht [gə'mɔxt] *p.p. of* **mögen**; **~molken** [gə'mɔlkən] *p.p. of* **melken**.

Gemse *zo.* ['gɛmzə] *f* (-/-n) chamois.

Gemurmel [gə'murməl] *n* (-s/*no pl.*) murmur(ing).

Gemüse [gə'my:zə] *n* (-s/-) vegetable(s *pl.*); greens *pl.*; **~anbau** *m* vegetable gardening, *Am.* truck farming; **~garten** *m* kitchen garden; **~händler** *m* greengrocer.

gemußt [gə'must] *p.p. of* **müssen 1.**

Gemüt [gə'my:t] *n* (-[e]s/-er) mind; feeling; soul; heart; disposition; temper; ℒlich *adj.* good-natured; genial; comfortable, snug, cosy, cozy; **~lichkeit** *f* (-/*no pl.*) snugness, cosiness; easy-going; genial temper.

Ge'müts|art *f* disposition, nature, temper, character; **~bewegung** *f* emotion; ℒkrank *adj.* emotionally disturbed; melancholic; depressed; **~krankheit** *f* mental disorder; melancholy; **~ruhe** *f* composure; **~verfassung** *f*, **~zustand** *m* state of mind, humo(u)r.

ge'mütvoll *adj.* emotional; full of feeling.

genannt [gə'nant] *p.p. of* **nennen**.

genas [gə'nɑ:s] *pret. of* **genesen**.

genau *adj.* [gə'nau] exact, accurate; precise; strict; *es* ~ *nehmen* (*mit*) be particular (about); ℒeres full particulars *pl.*; ℒigkeit *f* (-/-en) accuracy, exactness; precision; strictness.

genehm *adj.* [gə'ne:m] agreeable, convenient; **~igen** [~igən] *v/t.* (*no -ge-, h*) grant; approve (of); ℒigung *f* (-/-en) grant; approval; licen|ce, *Am.* -se; permit; permission; consent.

geneigt *adj.* [gə'naıkt] well disposed (*j-m* towards *s.o.*); inclined (*zu* to).

General ✗ [genə'rɑ:l] *m* (-s/-e, *e*) general; **~bevollmächtigte** *m* chief representative *or* agent; **~direktor** *m* general manager, managing director; **~'feldmarschall** ✗ *m* field-marshal; **~intendant** *thea. m* (artistic) director; **~konsul** *m* consul-general; **~konsulat** *n* consulate-general; **~leutnant** ✗ *m* lieutenant-general; **~major** ✗ *m* major-general; **~probe** *thea. f* dress rehearsal; **~stab** ✗ *m* general staff; **~stabskarte** ✗ *f* ordnance (survey) map, *Am.* strategic map; **~streik** *m* general strike; **~versammlung** *f* general meeting; **~vertreter** *m* general agent; **~vollmacht** *f* full power of attorney.

Generation [genərɑ'tsjo:n] *f* (-/-en) generation.

generell *adj.* [genə'rɛl] general.

genes|en [gə'ne:zən] **1.** *v/i.* (*no -ge-, sein*) recover (*von* from); **2.** *p.p. of* **1**; ℒende *m, f* (-n/-n) convalescent; ℒung *f* (-/*no pl.* -en) recovery.

genial *adj.* [gen'jɑ:l] highly gifted, ingenious; ℒität [~ali'tɛ:t] *f* (-/*no pl.*) genius.

Genick [gə'nik] *n* (-[e]s/-e) nape (of the neck), (back of the) neck.

Genie [ʒe'ni:] *n* (-s/-s) genius.

ge'nieren *v/t.* (*no -ge-, h*) trouble, bother; *sich* ~ feel *or* be embarrassed *or* shy; be self-conscious.

genießen [gə'ni:sən] *v/t.* (*irr.*, *no -ge-, h*) enjoy; eat; drink; et. ~ take some food *or* refreshments; *j-s Vertrauen* ~ be in *s.o.'s* confidence.

Genitiv *gr.* ['ge:niti:f] *m* (-s/-e) genitive (case); possessive (case).

ge|nommen [gə'nɔmən] *p.p. of* **nehmen**; **~normt** *adj.* standardized; **~noß** [~'nɔs] *pret. of* **genießen**.

Genoss|e [gə'nɔsə] *m* (-n/-n) companion, mate; comrade (*a. pol.*); ℒen *p.p. of* **genießen**; **~enschaft** *f* (-/-en) company, association; co(-)operative (society); **~in** *f* (-/-nen) (female) companion; comrade (*a. pol.*).

genug *adj.* [gə'nu:k] enough, sufficient.

Genüg|e [gə'ny:gə] *f* (-/*no pl.*); *zur* ~ enough, sufficiently; ℒen *v/i.* (*no -ge-, h*) be enough, suffice; *das genügt* that will do; *j-m* ~ satisfy *s.o.*; ℒend *adj.* sufficient; ℒsam *adj.* [~.k-] easily satisfied, frugal; **~samkeit** [~.k-] *f* (-/*no pl.*) modesty; frugality.

Genugtuung [gə'nu:ktu:uŋ] *f* (-/-en) satisfaction. (gender.)

Genus *gr.* ['ge:nus] *n* (-/Genera)

Genuß [gə'nus] *m* (Genusses/Genüsse) enjoyment; pleasure; use; consumption; taking (*of food*); *fig.* treat; **~mittel** *n* semi-luxury; **~sucht** *f* (-/*no pl.*) thirst for pleasure; ℒsüchtig *adj.* pleasure-seeking.

Geo|graph [geo'grɑ:f] *m* (-en/-en) geographer; **~graphie** [~a'fi:] *f* (-/*no pl.*) geography; ℒgraphisch *adj.* [~'grɑ:fiʃ] geographic(al); **~loge** [~'lo:gə] *m* (-n/-n) geologist; **~logie** [~'lo:gi:] *f* (-/*no pl.*) geology; ℒlogisch *adj.* [~'lo:giʃ] geologic(al); **~metrie** [~me'tri:] *f* (-/-en) geometry; ℒmetrisch *adj.* [~'me:triʃ] geometric(al).

Gepäck [gə'pɛk] *n* (-[e]s/*no pl.*) luggage, ✗ *or Am.* baggage; **~annahme** *f* luggage (registration) counter, *Am.* baggage (registration) counter; **~aufbewahrung** *f* (-/-en) left-luggage office, *Am.* checkroom; **~ausgabe** *f* luggage delivery office, *Am.* baggage room; **~netz** *n* luggage-rack, *Am.* baggage rack; **~schein** *m* luggage-ticket, *Am.* baggage check; **~träger** *m* porter, *Am. a.* redcap *on bicycle*: carrier; **~wagen** *m* luggage van, *Am.* baggage car.

ge|pfiffen [gə'pfıfən] *p.p. of* pfeifen; **~pflegt** [.'pfle:kt] *appearance*: well-groomed; *hands, garden, etc.*: well cared-for; *garden, etc.*: well-kept.

Gepflogenheit [gə'pflo:gənhaıt] *f* (-/-en) habit; custom; usage.

Ge|plapper [gə'plapər] *n* (-s/no pl.) babbling, chattering; **~plauder** [~'plaudər] *n* (-s/no pl.) chatting, small talk; **~polter** [.'poltər] *n* (-s/no pl.) rumble; **~präge** [.'pre:gə] *n* (-s/-) impression; stamp (*a. fig.*).

ge|priesen [gə'pri:zən] *p.p. of* preisen; **~quollen** [.'kvolən] *p.p. of* quellen.

gerade [gə'ra:də] **1.** *adj.* straight (*a. fig.*); *number, etc.*: even; direct; *bearing*: upright, erect; **2.** *adv.* just; er schrieb ~ he was (just) writing; nun ~ now more than ever; ~ an dem Tage on that very day; **3.** ♀ *f* (-/-n) ♈ straight line; straight(*ofrace-course*); linke(rechte) ~ boxing: straight left (right); **~'aus** *adv.* straight on or ahead; **~he'raus** *adv.* frankly; **~nwegs** *adv.* [.nve:ks] directly; **~stehen** *v/i.* (irr. stehen, sep., -ge-, h) stand erect; ~ für answer for *s.th.*; **~wegs** *adv.* [.ve:ks] straight, directly; **~'zu** *adv.* straight; almost; downright.

ge'rannt *p.p. of* rennen.

Gerassel [gə'rasəl] *n* (-s/no pl.) clanking; rattling.

Gerät [gə're:t] *n* (-[e]s/-e) tool, implement, utensil; ⊕ gear; teleph., radio: set; apparatus; equipment; elektrisches ~ electric(al) appliance.

ge'raten 1. *v/i.* (irr. raten, no -ge-, sein) come or fall or get (an acc. by, upon; auf acc. on, upon; in acc. in, into); (gut) ~ succeed, turn out well; in Brand ~ catch fire; ins Stocken ~ come to a standstill; in Vergessenheit ~ fall or sink into oblivion; in Zorn ~ fly into a passion; **2.** *p.p. of* raten.

Gerate'wohl *n*: aufs ~ at random.

geräumig *adj.* [gə'rɔymıç] spacious.

Geräusch [gə'rɔyʃ] *n* (-es/-e) noise; **2los** *adj.* noiseless; **2voll** *adj.* noisy.

gerb|en ['gɛrbən] *v/t.* (ge-, h) tan; **2er** *m* (-s/-) tanner; **2erei** [.'raı] *f* (-/-en) tannery.

ge'recht *adj.* just; righteous; ~ werden (dat.) do justice to; be fair to; meet; please *s.o.*; fulfil (requirements); **2igkeit** *f* (-/no pl.) justice; righteousness; j-m ~ widerfahren lassen do s.o. justice.

Ge'rede *n* (-s/no pl.) talk; gossip; rumo(u)r.

ge'reizt *adj.* irritable, irritated; **2heit** *f* (-/no pl.) irritation.

ge'reuen *v/t.* (no -ge-, h): es gereut mich I repent (of) it, I am sorry for it.

Gericht [gə'rıçt] *n* (-[e]s/-e) dish, course; *s.* Gerichtshof; mst rhet. and fig. tribunal; **2lich** *adj.* judicial, legal.

Ge'richts|barkeit *f* (-/-en) jurisdiction; **~bezirk** *m* jurisdiction; **~diener** *m* (court) usher; **~gebäude** *n* court-house; **~hof** *m* law-court, court of justice; **~kosten** *pl.* (law-)costs *pl.*; **~saal** *m* court-room; **~schreiber** *m* clerk (of the court); **~stand** *m* (legal) domicile; venue; **~tag** *m* court-day; **~verfahren** *n* legal proceedings *pl.*, lawsuit; **~verhandlung** *f* (court) hearing; trial; **~vollzieher** *m* (-s/-) (court-)bailiff.

gerieben [gə'ri:bən] *p.p. of* reiben.

gering *adj.* [gə'rıŋ] little, small; trifling, slight; mean, low; poor; inferior; **~achten** *v/t.* (sep., -ge-, h) think little of; disregard; **~er** *adj.* inferior. less, minor; **~fügig** *adj.* insignificant, trifling, slight; **~schätzen** *v/t.* (sep., -ge-, h) *s.* geringachten; **~schätzig** *adj.* disdainful, contemptuous, slighting; **2schätzung** *f* (-/no pl.) disdain; disregard; **~st** *adj.* least; nicht im ~en not in the least.

ge'rinnen *v/i.* (irr. rinnen, no -ge-, sein) curdle (*a. fig.*); congeal; coagulate. clot.

Ge'rippe *n* (-s/-) skeleton (*a. fig.*); ⊕ framework.

ge|rissen [gə'rısən] **1.** *p.p. of* reißen; **2.** *fig. adj.* cunning, crafty, smart; **~ritten** [.'rıtən] *p.p. of* reiten.

germanis|ch *adj.* [gɛr'ma:nıʃ] Germanic, Teutonic; **2t** [.a'nıst] *m* (-en/-en) Germanist, German scholar; student of German.

gern(e) *adv.* ['gɛrn(ə)] willingly, gladly; ~ haben or mögen be fond of, like; er singt ~ he is fond of singing, he likes to sing.

ge'rochen *p.p. of* riechen.

Geröll [gə'rœl] *n* (-[e]s/-e) boulders *pl.*

geronnen [gə'rɔnən] *p.p. of* rinnen.

Gerste ♀ ['gɛrstə] *f* (-/-n) barley; **~nkorn** *n* barleycorn; ♈ sty(e).

Gerte ['gɛrtə] *f* (-/-n) switch, twig.

Geruch [gə'rux] *m* (-[e]s/~e) smell, odo(u)r; scent; fig. reputation; **2los** *adj.* odo(u)rless, scentless; **~ssinn** *m* (-[e]s/ no pl.) sense of smell.

Gerücht [gə'rʏçt] *n* (-[e]s/-e) rumo(u)r.

ge'ruchtilgend *adj.*: ~es Mittel deodorant.

ge'rufen *p.p. of* rufen.

ge'ruhen *v/i.* (no -ge-, h) deign, condescend, be pleased.

Gerümpel [gə'rympəl] *n* (-s/*no pl.*) lumber, junk.

Gerundium *gr.* [gə'rundjum] *n* (-s/Gerundien) gerund.

gerungen [gə'ruŋən] *p.p. of ringen.*

Gerüst [gə'ryst] *n* (-[e]s/-e) scaffold(ing); stage; trestle.

ge'salzen *p.p. of salzen.*

gesamt *adj.* [gə'zamt] whole, entire, total, all; 2ausgabe *f* complete edition; 2betrag *m* sum total; ~deutsch *adj.* all-German.

gesandt [gə'zant] *p.p. of senden;* 2e [~ə] *m* (-n/-n) envoy; 2schaft *f* (-/-en) legation.

Ge'sang *m* (-[e]s/=e) singing; song; ~buch *eccl. n* hymn-book; ~lehrer *m* singing-teacher; ~verein *m* choral society, *Am.* glee club.

Gesäß *anat.* [gə'zɛːs] *n* (-es/-e) seat, buttocks *pl.*, posterior, F bottom, behind.

ge'schaffen *p.p. of schaffen 1.*

Geschäft [gə'ʃɛft] *n* (-[e]s/-e) business; transaction; affair; occupation; shop, *Am.* store; 2ig *adj.* busy, active; 2igkeit *f* (-/*no pl.*) activity; 2lich **1.** *adj.* business ...; commercial; **2.** *adv.* on business.

Ge'schäfts|bericht *m* business report; ~brief *m* business letter; ~frau *f* business woman; ~freund *m* business friend, correspondent; ~führer *m* manager; ~haus *n* business firm; office building; ~inhaber *m* owner *or* holder of a business; shopkeeper; ~jahr *n* financial *or* business year, *Am.* fiscal year; ~lage *f* business situation; ~leute *pl.* businessmen *pl.*; ~mann *m* businessman; 2mäßig *adj.* business-like; 2ordnung *f* standing orders *pl.*; rules *pl.* (of procedure); ~papiere *n/pl.* commercial papers *pl.*; ~partner *m* (business) partner; ~räume *m/pl.* business premises *pl.*; ~reise *f* business trip; ~reisende *m* commercial travel(l)er, *Am.* travel(l)ing salesman; ~schluß *m* closing-time; *nach ~ a.* after business hours; ~stelle *f* office; ~träger *m pol.* chargé d'affaires; ✝ agent, representative; 2tüchtig *adj.* efficient, smart; ~unternehmen *n* business enterprise; ~verbindung *f* business connexion *or* connection; ~viertel *n* business cent|re, *Am.* -er; *Am.* -er; downtown; shopping cent|re, *Am.* -er; ~zeit *f* office hours *pl.*, business hours *pl.*; ~zimmer *n* office, bureau; ~zweig *m* branch (of business), line (of business).

geschah [gə'ʃɑː] *pret. of geschehen.*

geschehen [gə'ʃeːən] **1.** *v/i.* (*irr.*, *no* -ge-, *sein*) happen, occur, take place; be done; *es geschieht ihm recht* it serves him right; **2.** *p.p. of*

1; 3. 2 *n* (-s/-) events *pl.*, happenings *pl.*

gescheit *adj.* [gə'ʃaɪt] clever, intelligent, bright.

Geschenk [gə'ʃɛŋk] *n* (-[e]s/-e) present, gift; ~packung *f* gift-box.

Geschicht|e [gə'ʃɪçtə] *f* **1.** (-/-) story; tale; *fig.* affair; **2.** (-/*no pl.*) history; tale; 2lich *adj.* historical; ~forscher *m*, ~sschreiber *m* historian.

Ge'schick *n* **1.** (-[e]s/-e) fate; destiny; **2.** (-[e]s/*no pl.*) = ~lichkeit *f* (-/-en) skill; dexterity; aptitude; 2t *adj.* skil(l)ful; dexterous; apt; clever.

ge|schieden [gə'ʃiːdən] *p.p. of scheiden;* ~schienen [~'ʃiːnən] *p.p. of scheinen.*

Geschirr [gə'ʃɪr] *n* (-[e]s/-e) vessel; dishes *pl.*; china; earthenware, crockery; service; *horse:* harness.

ge'schlafen *p.p. of schlafen;* ~'schlagen *p.p. of schlagen.*

Ge'schlecht *n* (-[e]s/-er) sex; kind; species; race; family; generation; *gr.* gender; 2lich *adj.* sexual.

Ge'schlechts|krankheit 𝔰 *f* venereal disease; ~reife *f* puberty; ~teile *anat. n/pl.* genitals *pl.*; ~trieb *m* sexual instinct *or* urge; ~verkehr *m* (-[e]s/*no pl.*) sexual intercourse; ~wort *gr. n* (-[e]s/=er) article.

ge|schlichen [gə'ʃlɪçən] *p.p. of schleichen;* ~schliffen [~'ʃlɪfən] **1.** *p.p. of schleifen;* **2.** *adj. jewel:* cut; *fig.* polished; ~schlossen [~'ʃlɔsən] **1.** *p.p. of schließen;* **2.** *adj. formation:* close; collective; ~e *Gesellschaft* private party; ~schlungen [~'ʃluŋən] *p.p. of schlingen.*

Geschmack [gə'ʃmak] *m* (-[e]s/=e, *co.* =er) taste (*a. fig.*); flavo(u)r; *finden an* (*dat.*) take a fancy to; 2los *adj.* tasteless; *pred. fig.* in bad taste; ~(s)sache *f* matter of taste; 2voll *adj.* tasteful; *pred. fig.* in good taste.

ge|schmeidig *adj.* [gə'ʃmaɪdɪç] supple, pliant; ~schmissen [~'ʃmɪsən] *p.p. of schmeißen;* ~schmolzen [~'ʃmɔltsən] *p.p. of schmelzen.*

Geschnatter [gə'ʃnatər] *n* (-s/*no pl.*) cackling (*of geese*); chatter(ing) (*of girls, etc.*).

ge|schnitten [gə'ʃnɪtən] *p.p. of schneiden;* ~schoben [~'ʃoːbən] *p.p. of schieben;* ~scholten [~'ʃɔltən] *p.p. of schelten.*

Geschöpf [gə'ʃœpf] *n* (-[e]s/-e) creature.

ge'schoren *p.p. of scheren.*

Geschoß [gə'ʃɔs] *n* (Geschosses/Geschosse) projectile; missile; stor(e)y, floor.

geschossen [gə'ʃɔsən] *p.p. of schießen.*

Ge'schrei n (-[e]s/no pl.) cries pl.; shouting; fig. noise, fuss.

ge|schrieben [gə'ʃriːbən] p.p. of schreiben; **~schrie(e)n** [~'ʃriː(ə)n] p.p. of schreien; **~schritten** [~'ʃritən] p.p. of schreiten; **~schunden** [~'ʃundən] p.p. of schinden.

Geschütz ✗ [gə'ʃyts] n (-es/-e) gun, cannon; ordnance.

Geschwader ✗ [gə'ʃvaːdər] n (-s/-) ⚓ squadron; ✈ wing, Am. group.

Geschwätz [gə'ʃvets] n (-es/no pl.) idle talk; gossip; **2ig** adj. talkative.

geschweige cj. [gə'ʃvaɪgə]: **~** (denn) not to mention; let alone, much less.

geschwiegen [gə'ʃviːgən] p.p. of schweigen.

geschwind adj. [gə'ʃvint] fast, quick, swift; **2igkeit** [~diçkaɪt] f (-/-en) quickness; speed, pace; phys. velocity; rate; mit e-r ~ von ... at the rate of ...; **2igkeitsbegrenzung** f speed limit.

Geschwister [gə'ʃvistər] n (-s/-): ~ pl. brother(s pl.) and sister(s pl.).

ge|schwollen [gə'ʃvɔlən] **1.** p.p. of schwellen; **2.** adj. language: bombastic, pompous; **~schwommen** [~'ʃvɔmən] p.p. of schwimmen.

geschworen [gə'ʃvoːrən] p.p. of schwören; **2e** [~ə] m, f (-n/-n) juror; die **~n** pl. the jury; **2engericht** n jury.

Geschwulst ✚ [gə'ʃvulst] f (-/⁓e) swelling; tumo(u)r.

ge|schwunden [gə'ʃvundən] p.p. of schwinden; **~schwungen** [~'ʃvuŋən] p.p. of schwingen.

Geschwür ✚ [gə'ʃvyːr] n (-[e]s/-e) abscess, ulcer.

ge'sehen p.p. of sehen.

Gesell ✎ [gə'zel] ✎, **~e** [~ə] m (-n/-n) companion, fellow; ⊕ journeyman; **2en** v/refl. (no -ge-, h) associate, come together; sich zu j-m **~** join s.o.; **2ig** adj. social; sociable.

Ge'sellschaft f (-/-en) society; company (a. ✝); party; j-m **~** leisten keep s.o. company; **~er** m (-s/-) companion; ✝ partner; **~erin** f (-/-nen) (lady) companion; ✝ partner; **2lich** adj. social.

Ge'sellschafts|dame f (lady) companion; **~reise** f party tour; **~spiel** n party or round game; **~tanz** m ball-room dance.

gesessen [gə'zesən] p.p. of sitzen.

Gesetz [gə'zets] n (-es/-e) law; statute; **~buch** n code; statute-book; **~entwurf** m bill; **~eskraft** f legal force; **~essammlung** f code; **2gebend** adj. legislative; **~geber** m (-s/-) legislator; **2gebung** f (-/-en) legislation; **2lich 1.** adj. lawful, legal; **2.** adv.: **~** geschützt patented, registered; **2los** adj. lawless; **2mäßig** adj. legal; lawful.

ge'setzt 1. adj. sedate, staid; sober;

mature; **2.** cj.: **~** den Fall, (daß) ... suppose or supposing (that) ...

ge'setzwidrig adj. unlawful, illegal.

Ge'sicht n (-[e]s/-er) face; countenance; fig. character; zu **~** bekommen catch sight or a glimpse of; set eyes on.

Ge'sichts|ausdruck m (facial) expression; **~farbe** f complexion; **~kreis** m horizon; **~punkt** m point of view, viewpoint, aspect, esp. Am. angle; **~zug** m mst Gesichtszüge pl. feature(s pl.), lineament(s pl.).

Ge'sims n ledge.

Gesinde [gə'zində] n (-s/-) (domestic) servants pl.; **~l** [~l] n (-s/no pl.) rabble, mob.

ge'sinn|t adj. in compounds: ...-minded; wohl **~** well disposed (j-m towards s.o.); **2ung** f (-/-en) mind; conviction; sentiment(s pl.); opinions pl.

gesinnungs|los adj. [gə'zinuŋsloːs] unprincipled; **~treu** adj. loyal; **2wechsel** m change of opinion; esp. pol. volte-face.

ge|sittet adj. [gə'zitət] civilized; well-bred, well-mannered; **~'soffen** p.p. of saufen; **~sogen** [~'zoːgən] p.p. of saugen; **~sonnen** [~'zɔnən] **1.** p.p. of sinnen; **2.** adj. minded, disposed; **~sotten** [~'zɔtən] p.p. of sieden; **~spalten** p.p. of spalten.

Ge'spann n (-[e]s/-e) team, Am. a. span; oxen: yoke; fig. pair, couple.

ge'spannt adj. tense (a. fig.); rope: tight, taut; fig. intent; attention: close; relations: strained; **~** sein auf (acc.) be anxious for; auf **~em** Fuß on bad terms; **2heit** f (-/no pl.) tenseness, tension.

Gespenst [gə'ʃpenst] n (-es/-er) ghost, spect|re, Am. -er; **2isch** adj. ghostly.

Ge'spiel|e m (-n/-n), **~in** f (-/-nen) playmate.

gespien [gə'ʃpiːn] p.p. of speien.

Gespinst [gə'ʃpinst] n (-es/-e) web, tissue (both a. fig.); spun yarn.

gesponnen [gə'ʃpɔnən] p.p. of spinnen.

Gespött [gə'ʃpœt] n (-[e]s/no pl.) mockery, derision, ridicule; zum **~** der Leute werden become a laughing-stock.

Gespräch [gə'ʃprɛːç] n (-[e]s/-e) talk; conversation; teleph. call; dialogue; **2ig** adj. talkative.

ge|sprochen [gə'ʃprɔxən] p.p. of sprechen; **~'sprossen** p.p. of sprießen; **~sprungen** [~'ʃpruŋən] p.p. of springen.

Gestalt [gə'ʃtalt] f (-/-en) form, figure, shape; stature; **2en** v/t. and v/refl. (no -ge-, h) form, shape; **~ung** f (-/-en) formation; arrangement, organization.

gestanden [gə'ʃtandən] p.p. of stehen.

ge'ständ|ig *adj.*: ~ *sein* confess; ~nis [~t-] *n* (-ses/-se) confession.

Ge'stank *m* (-[e]s/*no pl.*) stench.

gestatten [gə'ʃtatən] *v/t.* (*no -ge-, h*) allow, permit.

Geste ['gɛstə] *f* (-/-n) gesture.

ge'stehen (*irr.* stehen, *no -ge-, h*) 1. *v/t.* confess, avow; 2. *v/i.* confess.

Ge|'stein [~ʃtaɪn] *n* (-[e]s/-e) rock, stone; ~stell [~ʃtɛl] *n* (-[e]s/-e) stand, rack, shelf; frame; trestle, horse.

gestern *adv.* ['gɛstərn] yesterday; ~ abend last night.

gestiegen [gə'ʃtiːgən] *p.p. of* steigen.

Ge'stirn *n* (-[e]s/-e) star; *astr.* constellation; 2t *adj.* starry.

ge|stoben [gə'ʃtoːbən] *p.p. of* stieben; ~stochen [~ʃtɔxən] *p.p. of* stechen; ~stohlen [~ʃtoːlən] *p.p. of* stehlen; ~storben [~ʃtɔrbən] *p.p. of* sterben; ~stoßen [~ʃtoːsən] *p.p. of* stoßen; ~strichen [~ʃtrɪçən] *p.p. of* streichen.

gestrig *adj.* ['gɛstrɪç] of yesterday, yesterday's ...

ge'stritten *p.p. of* streiten.

Gestrüpp [gə'ʃtryp] *n* (-[e]s/-e) brushwood; undergrowth.

gestunken [gə'ʃtuŋkən] *p.p. of* stinken.

Gestüt [gə'ʃtyːt] *n* (-[e]s/-e) stud farm; *horses kept for breeding, etc.*: stud.

Gesuch *n* (-[e]s/-e) application, request; petition; 2t *adj.* wanted; sought-after; *politeness*: studied.

gesund *adj.* [gə'zunt] sound, healthy; salubrious; wholesome (*a. fig.*); ~er Menschenverstand common sense; ~en [~dən] *v/i.* (*no -ge-, sein*) recover.

Ge'sundheit *f* (-/*no pl.*) health (-iness); wholesomeness (*a. fig.*); *auf j-s* ~ *trinken* drink (to) s.o.'s health; 2lich *adj.* sanitary; ~ *geht es ihm gut* he is in good health.

Ge'sundheits|amt *n* Public Health Department; ~pflege *f* hygiene; public health service; 2schädlich *adj.* injurious to health, unhealthy, unwholesome; ~wesen *n* Public Health; ~zustand *m* state of health, physical condition.

ge|sungen [gə'zuŋən] *p.p. of* singen; ~sunken [~'zuŋkən] *p.p. of* sinken; ~tan [~'taːn] *p.p. of* tun.

Getöse [gə'tøːzə] *n* (-s/*no pl.*) din, noise.

ge'tragen 1. *p.p. of* tragen; 2. *adj.* solemn.

Getränk [gə'trɛŋk] *n* (-[e]s/-e) drink, beverage.

ge'trauen *v/refl.* (*no -ge-, h*) dare, venture.

Getreide [gə'traɪdə] *n* (-s/-) corn, *esp. Am.* grain; cereals *pl.*; ~(an)bau *m* corn-growing, *esp. Am.* grain growing; ~pflanze *f* cereal plant;

~speicher *m* granary, grain silo, *Am.* elevator.

ge'treten *p.p. of* treten.

ge'treu(lich) *adj.* faithful, loyal; true.

Getriebe [gə'triːbə] *n* (-s/-) bustle; ⊕ gear(ing); ⊕ drive.

ge|trieben [gə'triːbən] *p.p. of* treiben; ~troffen [~'trɔfən] *p.p. of* treffen; ~trogen [~'troːgən] *p.p. of* trügen.

ge'trost *adv.* confidently.

ge'trunken *p.p. of* trinken.

Ge|tue [gə'tuːə] *n* (-s/*no pl.*) fuss; ~tümmel [~'tyməl] *n* (-s/-) turmoil; ~viert [~'fiːrt] *n* (-[e]s/-e) square.

Gewächs [gə'vɛks] *n* (-es/-e) growth (*a. 🎇*); plant; vintage; ~haus *n* greenhouse, hothouse, conservatory.

gel'wachsen 1. *p.p. of* wachsen; 2. *adj.*: *j-m* ~ *sein* be a match for s.o.; *e-r Sache* ~ *sein* be equal to s.th.; *sich der Lage* ~ *zeigen* rise to the occasion; ~wagt *adj.* [~'vaːkt] risky; bold; ~wählt *adj.* [~'vɛːlt] *style*: refined; ~'wahr *adj.*: ~ *werden* (*acc. or gen.*) perceive *s.th.*; become aware of *s.th.*; ~ *werden, daß* become aware that.

Gewähr [gə'vɛːr] *f* (-/*no pl.*) guarantee, warrant, security; 2en *v/t.* (*no -ge-, h*) grant, allow; give, yield; afford; *j-n* ~ *lassen* let s.o. have his way; leave s.o. alone; 2leisten *v/t.* (*no -ge-, h*) guarantee.

Ge'wahrsam *m* (-s/-e) custody, safe keeping.

Ge'währsmann *m* informant, source.

Gewalt [gə'valt] *f* (-/-en) power; authority; control; force, violence; *höhere* ~ act of God; *mit* ~ by force; ~herrschaft *f* despotism, tyranny; 2ig *adj.* powerful, mighty; vehement; vast; ~maßnahme *f* violent measure; 2sam 1. *adj.* violent; 2. *adv.* a. forcibly; ~ *öffnen* force open; open by force; ~tat *f* act of violence; 2tätig *adj.* violent.

Gewand [gə'vant] *n* (-[e]s/ʉer) garment; robe; *esp. eccl.* vestment.

ge'wandt 1. *p.p. of* wenden 2; 2. *adj.* agile, nimble, dexterous, adroit; clever; 2heit *f* (-/*no pl.*) agility, nimbleness; adroitness, dexterity; cleverness.

ge'wann *pret. of* gewinnen.

Gewäsch F [gə'vɛʃ] *n* (-es/*no pl.*) twaddle, nonsense.

ge'waschen *p.p. of* waschen.

Gewässer [gə'vɛsər] *n* (-s/-) water(s *pl.*).

Gewebe [gə'veːbə] *n* (-s/-) tissue (*a. anat. and fig.*); fabric, web; texture.

Ge'wehr *n* gun; rifle; ~kolben *m* (rifle-)butt; ~lauf *m* (rifle-, gun-) barrel.

Geweih [gə'vaɪ] n (-[e]s/-e) horns pl., head, antlers pl.

Gewerbe [gə'verbə] n (-s/-) trade, business; industry; ~freiheit f freedom of trade; ~schein m trade licen|ce, Am. -se; ~schule f technical school; ~steuer f trade tax; 2treibend adj. carrying on a business, engaged in trade; ~treibende m (-n/-n) tradesman.

gewerb|lich adj. [gə'verplɪç] commercial, industrial; ~smäßig adj. professional.

Ge'werkschaft f (-/-en) trade(s) union, Am. labor union; ~ler m (-s/-) trade(s)-unionist; 2lich adj. trade-union; ~sbund m Trade Union Congress, Am. Federation of Labor.

ge|wesen [gə've:zən] p.p. of sein; ~wichen [~'vɪçən] p.p. of weichen.

Gewicht [gə'vɪçt] n (-[e]s/-e) weight, Am. F a. heft; e-r Sache ~ beimessen attach importance to s.th.; ~ haben carry weight (bei dat. with); ~ legen auf et. lay stress on s.th.; ins ~ fallen be of great weight, count, matter; 2ig adj. weighty (a. fig.).

ge|wiesen [gə'vi:zən] p.p. of weisen; ~willt adj. [~'vɪlt] willing.

Ge|wimmel [gə'vɪməl] n (-s/no pl.) swarm; throng; ~winde ⊕ [~'vɪndə] n (-s/-) thread.

Gewinn [gə'vɪn] m (-[e]s/-e) gain; † gains pl.; profit; lottery ticket: prize; game: winnings pl.; ~anteil m dividend; ~beteiligung f profit-sharing; 2bringend adj. profitable; 2en (irr., no -ge-, h) 1. v/t. win; gain; get; 2. v/i. win; gain; fig. improve; 2end adj. manner, smile: winning, engaging; ~er m (-s/-) winner.

Ge'wirr n (-[e]s/-e) tangle, entanglement; streets: maze; voices: confusion.

gewiß [gə'vɪs] 1. adj. certain; ein gewisser Herr N. a certain Mr. N., one Mr. N.; 2. adv.: ~! certainly!, to be sure!, Am. sure!

Ge'wissen n (-s/-) conscience; 2haft adj. conscientious; 2los adj. unscrupulous; ~sbisse m/pl. remorse, pangs pl. of conscience; ~sfrage f question of conscience.

gewissermaßen adv. [gəvɪsər-'ma:sən] to a certain extent.

Ge'wißheit f (-/-en) certainty; certitude.

Gewitter [gə'vɪtər] n (-s/-) (thunder)storm; 2n v/i. (no -ge-, h): es gewittert there is a thunderstorm; ~regen m thunder-shower; ~wolke f thundercloud.

ge|woben [gə'vo:bən] p.p. of weben; ~wogen¹ 1. p.p. of wägen and wiegen¹; 2. adj. (dat.) well or kindly disposed towards, favo(u)rably inclined towards.

gewöhnen [gə'vø:nən] v/t. (no -ge-, h) accustom, get used (an acc. to).

Gewohnheit [gə'vo:nhaɪt] f (-/-en) habit; custom; 2smäßig adj. habitual.

ge'wöhnlich adj. common; ordinary; usual, customary; habitual; common, vulgar.

ge'wohnt adj. customary, habitual; (es) ~ sein zu inf. be accustomed or used to inf.

Gewölbe [gə'vœlbə] n (-s/-) vault.

ge|wonnen [gə'vɔnən] p.p. of gewinnen; ~worben [~'vɔrbən] p.p. of werben; ~worden [~'vɔrdən] p.p. of werden; ~worfen [~'vɔrfən] p.p. of werfen; ~wrungen [~'vruŋən] p.p. of wringen.

Gewühl [gə'vy:l] n (-[e]s/no pl.) bustle; milling crowd.

gewunden [gə'wundən] 1. p.p. of winden; 2. adj. twisted; winding.

Gewürz [gə'vyrts] n (-es/-e) spice; condiment; ~nelke ♀ f clove.

ge'wußt p.p. of wissen.

Ge|'zeit f: mst ~en pl. tide(s pl.); ~'zeter n (-s/no pl.) (shrill) clamo(u)r.

ge|'ziert adj. affected; ~zogen [~'tso:gən] p.p. of ziehen.

Gezwitscher [gə'tsvɪtʃər] n (-s/no pl.) chirping, twitter(ing).

gezwungen [gə'tsvuŋən] 1. p.p. of zwingen; 2. adj. forced, constrained.

Gicht ♫ [gɪçt] f (-/no pl.) gout; 2isch ♫ adj. gouty; ~knoten m gouty knot.

Giebel ['gi:bəl] m (-s/-) gable(-end).

Gier [gi:r] f (-/no pl.) greed(iness) (nach for); 2ig adj. greedy (nach for, of).

'Gießbach m torrent.

gieß|en ['gi:sən] (irr., ge-, h) 1. v/t. pour; ⊕ cast, found; water (flowers); 2. v/i.: es gießt it is pouring (with rain); 2er m (-s/-) founder; 2erei [~'raɪ] f (-/-en) foundry; 2kanne f watering-can or -pot.

Gift [gɪft] n (-[e]s/-e) poison; venom (esp. of animals) (a. fig.); malice, spite; 2ig adj. poisonous; venomous; malicious, spiteful; '~schlange f venomous or poisonous snake; '~zahn m poison-fang.

Gigant [gi'gant] m (-en/-en) giant.

Gimpel orn. ['gɪmpəl] m (-s/-) bullfinch.

ging [gɪŋ] pret. of gehen.

Gipfel ['gɪpfəl] m (-s/-) summit, top; peak; '~konferenz pol. f summit meeting or conference; '2n v/i. (ge-, h) culminate.

Gips [gɪps] m (-es/-e) min. gypsum; ⊕ plaster (of Paris); '~abdruck m, '~abguß m plaster cast; '2en v/t. (ge-, h) plaster; '~verband ♫ m plaster (of Paris) dressing.

Giraffe zo. [gi'rafə] f (-/-n) giraffe.

girieren ♱ [ʒi'riːrən] v/t. (no -ge-, h) endorse, indorse (bill of exchange).
Girlande [gir'landə] f (-/-n) garland.
Giro ♱ ['ʒiːro] n (-s/-s) endorsement; indorsement; '~bank f clearing-bank; '~konto n current account.
girren ['girən] v/i. (ge-, h) coo.
Gischt [giʃt] m (-es/% -e) and f (-/% -en) foam, froth; spray; spindrift.
Gitarre ♪ [gi'tarə] f (-/-n) guitar.
Gitter ['gitər] n (-s/-) grating; lattice; trellis; railing; '~bett n crib; '~fenster n lattice-window.
Glacéhandschuh [gla'seː-] m kid glove.
Glanz [glants] m (-es/no pl.) brightness; lust|re, Am. -er; brilliancy; splendo(u)r.
glänzen ['glɛntsən] v/i. (ge-, h) glitter, shine; '~d adj. bright, brilliant; fig. splendid.
'Glanz|leistung f brilliant achievement or performance; '~papier n glazed paper; '~punkt m highlight; '~zeit f golden age, heyday.
Glas [glaːs] n (-es/~er) glass; ~er ['~zər] m (-s/-) glazier.
gläsern adj. ['glɛːzərn] of glass; fig. glassy.
'Glas|glocke f (glass) shade or cover; globe; bell-glass; '~hütte f glassworks sg., pl.
glasieren [gla'ziːrən] v/t. (no -ge-, h) glaze; ice, frost (cake).
glasig adj. ['glaːziç] glassy, vitreous.
'Glasscheibe f pane of glass.
Glasur [gla'zuːr] f (-/-en) glaze, glazing; enamel; icing, frosting (on cakes).
glatt [glat] 1. adj. smooth (a. fig.); even; lie, etc.: flat, downright; road, etc.: slippery; 2. adv. smoothly; evenly; ~ anliegen fit closely or tightly; ~ rasiert clean-shaven; et. ~ ableugnen deny s.th. flatly.
Glätte ['glɛtə] f (-/-n) smoothness; road, etc.: slipperiness.
'Glatteis n glazed frost, icy glaze, Am. glaze; F: j-n aufs ~ führen lead s.o. up the garden path.
'glätten v/t. (ge-, h) smooth.
Glatze ['glatsə] f (-/-n) bald head.
Glaube ['glaubə] m (-ns/% -n) faith, belief (an acc. in); '~n (ge-, h) 1. v/t. believe; think, suppose, Am. a. guess; 2. v/i. believe (j-m s.o.; an acc. in).
'Glaubens|bekenntnis n creed, profession or confession of faith; '~lehre f, '~satz m dogma, doctrine.
glaubhaft adj. ['glaup-] credible; plausible; authentic.
gläubig adj. ['glɔybiç] believing, faithful; 2e [~gə] m, f (-n/-n)

believer; 2er ♱ ['~gər] m (-s/-) creditor.
glaubwürdig adj. ['glaup-] credible.
gleich [glaiç] 1. adj. equal (an dat. in); the same; like; even, level; in ~er Weise likewise; zur ~en Zeit at the same time; es ist mir ~ it's all the same to me; das ~e the same; as much; er ist nicht (mehr) der ~e he is not the same man; 2. adv. alike, equally; immediately, presently, directly, at once; just; es ist ~ acht (Uhr) it is close on or nearly eight (o'clock); '~altrig adj. ['~altriç] (of) the same age; '~artig adj. homogeneous; similar; uniform; '~bedeutend adj. synonymous; equivalent (to); tantamount (mit to); '~berechtigt adj. having equal rights; '~bleibend adj. constant, steady; '~en v/i. (irr., ge-, h) equal; resemble.
'gleich|falls adv. also, likewise; ~förmig adj. ['~fœrmiç] uniform; '~gesinnt adj. like-minded; '2gewicht n balance (a. fig.); equilibrium, equipoise; pol.: ~ der Kräfte balance of power; '~gültig adj. indifferent (gegen to); es ist mir ~ I don't care; ~ was du tust no matter what you do; '2gültigkeit f indifference; '2heit f (-/-en) equality; likeness; '2klang m unison; consonance, harmony; '~kommen v/i. (irr. kommen, sep., -ge-, sein): e-r Sache ~ amount to s.th.; j-m ~ equal s.o.; '~laufend adj. parallel; '~lautend adj. consonant; identical; '~machen v/t. (sep., -ge-, h) make equal (dat. to), equalize (to or with); '2maß n regularity; evenness; fig. equilibrium; '~mäßig adj. equal; regular; constant; even; '2mut m equanimity; '~mütig adj. even-tempered; calm; '~namig adj. ['~naːmiç] of the same name; '2nis n (-ses/-se) parable; rhet. simile; '~sam adv. as it were, so to speak; '~schalten v/t. (sep., -ge-, h) ⊕ synchronize; pol. co-ordinate, unify; '~seitig adj. equilateral; '~setzen v/t. (sep., -ge-, h) equate (dat. or mit with); '~stehen v/i. (irr. stehen, sep., -ge-, h) be equal; '~stellen v/t. (sep., -ge-, h) equalize, equate (dat. with); put s.o. on an equal footing (with); '2stellung f equalization, equation; '2strom ⚡ m direct current; '2ung ⚕ f (-/-en) equation; '~wertig adj. equivalent, of the same value, of equal value; '~zeitig adj. simultaneous; synchronous; contemporary.
Gleis [glais] n (-es/-e) s. Geleise.
gleiten ['glaitən] v/i. (irr., ge-, sein) glide, slide.
'Gleit|flug m gliding flight, glide, ⚔ volplane; '~schutzreifen m

non-skid tyre, (*Am. only*) non-skid tire; '**~schutz(vorrichtung** *f*) *m* anti-skid device.

Gletscher ['glɛtʃər] *m* (-s/-) glacier; '**~spalte** *f* crevasse.

glich [gliç] *pret. of* gleichen.

Glied [gli:t] *n* (-[e]s/-er) *anat.* limb; member (*a. anat.*); link; ✗ rank, file; '**~ern** ['·ʤərn] *v/t.* (ge-, *h*) joint, articulate; arrange; divide (*in acc.* into); '**~erung** *f* (-/-en) articulation; arrangement; division; formation; **~maßen** ['·tma:sən] *pl.* limbs *pl.*, extremities *pl.*

glimmen ['glimən] *v/i.* ((*irr.*,] ge-, *h*) *fire:* smo(u)lder (*a. fig.*); glimmer; glow.

glimpflich ['glimpfliç] **1.** *adj.* lenient, mild; **2.** *adv.*: ~ davon-kommen get off lightly.

glitschig *adj.* ['glitʃiç] slippery.

glitt [glit] *pret. of* gleiten.

glitzern ['glitsərn] *v/i.* (ge-, *h*) glitter, glisten.

Globus ['glo:bus] *m* (-, -ses/Globen, Globusse) globe.

Glocke ['glɔkə] *f* (-/-n) bell; shade; (glass) cover.

'**Glocken|schlag** *m* stroke of the clock; '**~spiel** *n* chime(s *pl.*); '**~stuhl** *m* bell-cage; '**~turm** *m* bell tower, belfry.

Glöckner ['glœknər] *m* (-s/-) bell-ringer.

glomm [glɔm] *pret. of* glimmen.

Glorie ['glo:rjə] *f* (-/-n) glory; '**~schein** *fig.* *m* halo, aureola.

glorreich *adj.* ['glo:r-] glorious.

glotzen F ['glɔtsən] *v/i.* (ge-, *h*) stare.

Glück [glyk] *n* (-[e]s/*no pl.*) fortune; good luck; happiness, bliss, felicity; prosperity; *auf gut* ~ on the off chance; ~ *haben* be lucky, succeed; *das* ~ *haben zu inf.* have the good fortune to *inf.*; *j-m* ~ *wünschen* congratulate s.o. (*zu* on); *viel* ~*!* good luck!; *zum* ~ fortunately; **2bringend** *adj.* lucky.

Glucke *orn.* ['glukə] *f* (-/-n) sitting hen. [gen.]

'**glücken** *v/i.* (ge-, *sein*) s. gelin-]

gluckern ['glukərn] *v/i.* (ge-, *h*) *water, etc.*: gurgle.

'**glücklich** *adj.* fortunate; happy; lucky; '**~erweise** *adv.* fortunately.

'**Glücksbringer** *m* (-s/-) mascot.

glück'selig *adj.* blissful, blessed, happy.

glucksen ['gluksən] *v/i.* (ge-, *h*) gurgle.

'**Glücks|fall** *m* lucky chance, stroke of (good) luck; '**~göttin** *f* Fortune; '**~kind** *n* lucky person; '**~pfennig** *m* lucky penny; '**~pilz** *m* lucky person; '**~spiel** *n* game of chance; *fig.* gamble; '**~stern** *m* lucky star; '**~tag** *m* happy *or* lucky day, red-letter day.

'**glück|strahlend** *adj.* radiant(ly happy); '**2wunsch** *m* congratulation, good wishes *pl.*; compliments *pl.*; ~ *zum Geburtstag* many happy returns (of the day).

Glüh|birne ⚡ ['gly:-] *f* (electric-light) bulb; '**2en** *v/i.* (ge-, *h*) glow; '**2end** *adj.* glowing; *iron:* red-hot; *coal:* live; *fig.* ardent, fervid; '**2(end)'heiß** *adj.* burning hot; '**~lampe** *f* incandescent lamp; '**~wein** *m* mulled wine; **~würmchen** *zo.* ['·vyrmçən] *n* (-s/-) glow-worm.

Glut [glu:t] *f* (-/-en) heat, glow (*a. fig.*); glowing fire, embers *pl.*; *fig.* ardo(u)r.

Gnade ['gna:də] *f* (-/-n) grace; favo(u)r; mercy; clemency; pardon; ✗ quarter.

'**Gnaden|akt** *m* act of grace; '**~brot** *n* (-[e]s/*no pl.*) bread of charity; '**~frist** *f* reprieve; '**~gesuch** *n* petition for mercy.

gnädig *adj.* ['gnɛ:diç] gracious; merciful; *address:* 2e Frau Madam.

Gnom [gno:m] *m* (-en/-en) gnome, goblin.

Gobelin [gobə'lɛ̃:] *m* (-s/-s) Gobelin tapestry.

Gold [gɔlt] *n* (-[e]s/*no pl.*) gold; '**~barren** *m* gold bar, gold ingot, bullion; '**~borte** *f* gold lace; 2en *adj.* ['·dən] gold; *fig.* golden; '**~feder** *f* gold nib; '**~fisch** *m* goldfish; '2**gelb** *adj.* golden-(yellow); '**~gräber** ['·grɛ:bər] *m* (-s/-) gold-digger; '**~grube** *f* gold-mine; '2**haltig** *adj.* gold-bearing, containing gold; 2ig *fig.* *adj.* ['·diç] sweet, lovely, *Am.* F *a.* cute; '**~mine** *f* gold-mine; '**~münze** *f* gold coin; '**~schmied** *m* goldsmith; '**~schnitt** *m* gilt edge; *mit* ~ gilt-edged; '**~stück** *n* gold coin; '**~waage** *f* gold-balance; '**~währung** *f* gold standard.

Golf[1] *geogr.* [gɔlf] *m* (-[e]s/-e) gulf.

Golf[2] [~] *n* (-s/*no pl.*) golf; '**~platz** *m* golf-course, (golf-)links *pl.*; '**~schläger** *m* golf-club; '**~spiel** *n* golf; '**~spieler** *m* golfer.

Gondel ['gɔndəl] *f* (-/-n) gondola; ✗ *mst* car.

gönnen ['gœnən] *v/t.* (ge-, *h*): *j-m et.* ~ allow *or* grant *or* not to grudge s.o. s.th.

'**Gönner** *m* (-s/-) patron; *Am. a.* sponsor; '2**haft** *adj.* patronizing.

gor [go:r] *pret. of* gären.

Gorilla *zo.* [go'rila] *m* (-s/-s) gorilla.

goß [gɔs] *pret. of* gießen.

Gosse ['gɔsə] *f* (-/-n) gutter (*a. fig.*).

Gott [gɔt] *m* (-es, ⚓ -s/-er) God; god, deity; '2**ergeben** *adj.* resigned (to the will of God).

'**Gottes|dienst** *eccl.* *m* (divine) service; '2**fürchtig** *adj.* godfearing; '**~haus** *n* church, chapel; '**~läste-**

rer *m* (-s/-) blasphemer; '**~läste-
rung** *f* blasphemy.

'**Gottheit** *f* (-/-en) deity, divinity.

Göttin ['gœtin] *f* (-/-nen) goddess.

göttlich *adj.* ['gœtliç] divine.

gott'lob *int.* thank God *or* goodness!; '**~los** *adj.* godless; impious;
F *fig. deed:* unholy, wicked; '**Qver-
trauen** *n* trust in God.

Götze ['gœtsə] *m* (-n/-n) idol;
'**~nbild** *n* idol; '**~ndienst** *m* idolatry.

Gouvern|ante [guvɛr'nantə] *f* (-/-n)
governess; **~eur** [~'nøːr] *m* (-s/-e)
governor.

Grab [graːp] *n* (-[e]s/**~**er) grave,
tomb, sepulchre, *Am.* -er.

Graben ['graːbən] 1. *m* (-s/**~**) ditch;
✕ trench; 2. ♀ *v/t.* (*irr.*, ge-, *h*)
dig; *animal:* burrow.

Grab|gewölbe ['graːp-] *n* vault,
tomb; '**~mal** *n* monument; tomb,
sepulch|re, *Am.* -er; '**~rede** *f* funeral
sermon; funeral oration *or* address;
'**~schrift** *f* epitaph; '**~stätte** *f*
burial-place; grave, tomb; '**~stein**
m tombstone; gravestone.

Grad [graːt] *m* (-[e]s/-e) degree;
grade, rank; *15 ~ Kälte* 15 degrees
below zero; '**~einteilung** *f* graduation; '**~messer** *m* (-s/-) graduated
scale, graduator; *fig.* criterion;
'**~netz** *n map:* grid.

Graf [graːf] *m* (-en/-en) *in Britain:*
earl; count.

Gräfin ['grɛːfin] *f* (-/-nen) countess.

'**Grafschaft** *f* (-/-en) county.

Gram [graːm] 1. *m* (-[e]s/*no pl.*)
grief, sorrow; 2. ♀ *adj.: j-m ~
sein* bear s.o. ill will *or* a grudge.

grämen ['grɛːmən] *v/t.* (ge-, *h*)
grieve; *sich ~* grieve (*über acc.* at,
for, over).

Gramm [gram] *n* (-s/-e) gramme,
Am. gram.

Grammati|k [gra'matik] *f* (-/-en)
grammar; **Qsch** *adj.* grammatical.

Granat *min.* [gra'naːt] *m* (-[e]s/-e)
garnet; **~e** ✕ *f* (-/-n) shell; grenade;
'**~splitter** ✕ *m* shell-splinter;
'**~trichter** ✕ *m* shell-crater; **~wer-
fer** ✕ *m* (-s/-) mortar.

Granit *min.* [gra'niːt] *m* (-s/-e)
granite.

Granne ♀ ['granə] *f* (-/-n) awn,
beard.

Graphi|k ['graːfik] *f* (-/-en) graphic
arts *pl.*; **Qsch** *adj.* graphic(al).

Graphit *min.* [gra'fiːt] *m* (-s/-e)
graphite.

Gras ♀ [graːs] *n* (-es/**~**er) grass;
Qbewachsen *adj.* ['~bəvaksən]
grass-grown, grassy; **Qen** ['~zən]
v/i. (ge-, *h*) graze; '**~halm** *m* blade
of grass; '**~narbe** *f* turf, sod;
'**~platz** *m* grass-plot, green.

grassieren [gra'siːrən] *v/i.* (*no -ge-*,
h) rage, prevail.

gräßlich *adj.* ['grɛsliç] horrible;
hideous, atrocious.

Grassteppe ['graːs-] *f* prairie,
savanna(h).

Grat [graːt] *m* (-[e]s/-e) edge, ridge.

Gräte ['grɛːtə] *f* (-/-n) (fish-)bone.

Gratifikation [gratifika'tsjoːn] *f*
(-/-en) gratuity, bonus.

gratis *adv.* ['graːtis] gratis, free of
charge.

Gratul|ant [gratu'lant] *m* (-en/-en)
congratulator; **~ation** [~'tsjoːn] *f*
(-/-en) congratulation; **Qieren** [~
'liːrən] *v/i.* (*no -ge-*, *h*) congratulate
(*j-m zu et. s.o. on s.th.*); *j-m zum
Geburtstag ~* wish s.o. many happy
returns (of the day).

grau *adj.* [grau] grey, *esp. Am.* gray.

'**grauen**[1] *v/i.* (ge-, *h*) *day:* dawn.

'**grauen**[2] 1. *v/i.* (ge-, *h*): *mir graut
vor* (*dat.*) I shudder at, I dread;
2. 2 *n* (-s/*no pl.*) horror (*vor dat.* of);
'**~erregend** *adj.*, '**~haft** *adj.*, '**~voll**
adj. horrible, dreadful.

gräulich *adj.* ['grɔyliç] greyish, *esp.
Am.* grayish.

Graupe ['graupə] *f* (-/-n) (peeled)
barley, pot-barley; '**~ln** 1. *f/pl.*
sleet; 2. 2 *v/i.* (ge-, *h*) sleet.

'**grausam** *adj.* cruel; '**Qkeit** *f* (-/-en)
cruelty.

grausen ['grauzən] 1. *v/i.* (ge-, *h*)
s. grauen[2]; 2. 2 *n* (-s/*no pl.*)
horror (*vor dat.* of).

'**grausig** *adj.* horrible. [graver.]

Graveur [gra'vøːr] *m* (-s/-e) en-]

gravieren [gra'viːrən] *v/t.* (*no -ge-*,
h) engrave; **~d** *fig. adj.* aggravating.

gravitätisch *adj.* [gravi'tɛːtiʃ] grave;
dignified; solemn; stately.

Grazie ['graːtsjə] *f* (-/-n) grace(ful-
ness).

graziös *adj.* [gra'tsjøːs] graceful.

greifen ['graifən] (*irr.*, ge-, *h*) 1. *v/t.*
seize, grasp, catch hold of; ♪ touch
(*string*); 2. *v/i.*: *an den Hut ~* touch
one's hat; **~** *nach* grasp *or* snatch
at; *um sich ~* spread; *j-m unter die
Arme ~* give s.o. a helping hand;
zu strengen Mitteln ~ resort to
severe measures; *zu den Waffen ~*
take up arms.

Greis [grais] *m* (-es/-e) old man;
Qenhaft *adj.* ['~zən-] senile (*a. ✻*);
'**~in** ['~zin] *f* (-/-nen) old woman.

grell *adj.* [grɛl] *light:* glaring;
colour: loud; *sound:* shrill.

Grenze ['grɛntsə] *f* (-/-n) limit;
territory: boundary; *state:* frontier, borders *pl.*; *e-e ~ ziehen* draw
the line; '**Qn** *v/i.* (ge-, *h*): *~ an* (*acc.*)
border on (*a. fig.*); *fig.* verge on;
'**Qnlos** *adj.* boundless.

'**Grenz|fall** *m* border-line case;
'**~land** *n* borderland; '**~linie** *f*
boundary *or* border line; '**~schutz**
m frontier *or* border protection;
frontier *or* border guard; '**~stein** *m*
boundary stone; '**~übergang** *m*
frontier *or* border crossing(-point).

Greuel ['grɔyəl] *m* (-s/-) horror;

abomination; atrocity; **'~tat** f atrocity.

Griech|e ['griːçə] m (-n/-n) Greek; **'2isch** adj. Greek; △, features: Grecian.

griesgrämig adj. ['griːsɡrɛːmiç] morose, sullen.

Grieß [griːs] m (-es/-e) gravel (a. ✻), grit; semolina; **'~brei** m semolina pudding.

Griff [ɡrɪf] 1. m (-[e]s/-e) grip, grasp, hold; ♪ touch; handle (of knife, etc.); hilt (of sword); 2. 2 pret. of greifen.

Grille ['ɡrɪlə] f (-/-n) zo. cricket; fig. whim, fancy; **'2nhaft** adj. whimsical.

Grimasse [ɡriˈmasə] f (-/-n) grimace; **~n schneiden** pull faces.

Grimm [ɡrɪm] m (-[e]s/no pl.) fury, rage; **'2ig** adj. furious, fierce, grim.

Grind [ɡrɪnt] m (-[e]s/-e) scab, scurf.

grinsen ['ɡrɪnzən] 1. v/i. (ge-, h) grin (über acc. at); sneer (at); 2. 2 n (-s/no pl.) grin; sneer.

Grippe ✻ ['ɡrɪpə] f (-/-n) influenza, F flu(e), grippe.

grob adj. [ɡrɔp] coarse; gross; rude; work, skin: rough; **'2heit** f (-/-en) coarseness; grossness; rudeness; **~en** pl. rude things pl.

grölen F ['ɡrøːlən] v/t. and v/i. (ge-, h) bawl.

Groll [ɡrɔl] m (-[e]s/no pl.) grudge, ill will; **'2en** v/i. (ge-, h) thunder: rumble; j-m **~** bear s.o. ill will or a grudge.

Gros¹ ✝ [ɡrɔs] n (-ses/-se) gross. **Gros²** [ɡroː] n (-/-) main body.

Groschen ['ɡrɔʃən] m (-s/-) penny.

groß adj. [ɡroːs] great; large; big; figure: tall; huge; fig. great, grand; heat: intense; cold: severe; loss: heavy; **die 2en** pl. the grown-ups pl.; **im ~en** wholesale, on a large scale; **im ~en (und) ganzen** on the whole; **~er Buchstabe** capital (letter); **das ~e Los** the first prize; **ich bin kein ~er Tänzer** I am not much of a dancer; **'~artig** adj. great, grand, sublime; first-rate; **'2aufnahme** f film: close-up.

Größe ['ɡrøːsə] f (-/-n) size; largeness; height, tallness; quantity (esp. Å); importance: greatness; p. celebrity; thea. star.

'Großeltern pl. grandparents pl. **'großenteils** adv. to a great or large extent, largely.

'Größenwahn m megalomania.

'Groß|grundbesitz m large landed property; **'~handel** ✝ m wholesale trade; **'~handelspreis** ✝ m wholesale price; **'~händler** ✝ m wholesale dealer, wholesaler; **'~handlung** ✝ f wholesale business; **'~herzog** m grand duke; **'~industrielle** m big industrialist.

Grossist [ɡrɔˈsɪst] m (-en/-en) Großhändler.

groß|jährig adj. ['ɡroːsjɛːriç] of age; **~ werden** come of age; **'2jährigkei** f (-/no pl.) majority, full (legal) age; **'2kaufmann** m wholesale mer chant; **'2kraftwerk** ⚡ n super power station; **'2macht** f grea power; **'2maul** n braggart; **'2mu** f (-/no pl.) generosity; **~müti** adj. ['~myːtiç] magnanimous, gen erous; **'2mutter** f grandmother **'2neffe** m great-nephew, grand nephew; **'2nichte** f great-niece grand-niece; **'2onkel** m great uncle, grand-uncle; **'2schreibun** f (-/-en) use of capital letters; capi talization; **'~sprecherisch** adj boastful; **~spurig** adj. arrogant **'2stadt** f large town or city; **'~ städtisch** adj. of or in a large tow or city; **'2tante** f great-aunt, grand aunt.

größtenteils adv. ['ɡrøːstəntaɪls mostly, chiefly, mainly.

'groß|tun v/i. (irr. tun, sep., -ge-, h swagger, boast; **sich mit et. ~ boas** or brag of or about s.th.; **'2vater** n grandfather; **'2verdiener** m (-s/ big earner; **'2wild** n big game; **'~ ziehen** v/t. (irr. ziehen, sep., -ge-, h bring up (child); rear, raise (child animal); **~zügig** adj. ['~tsyːɡiç liberal; generous; broad-minded planning: a. on a large scale.

grotesk adj. [ɡroˈtɛsk] grotesque. **Grotte** ['ɡrɔtə] f (-/-n) grotto. **grub** [ɡruːp] pret. of graben. **Grübchen** ['ɡryːpçən] n (-s/ dimple.

Grube ['ɡruːbə] f (-/-n) pit; ✻ mine, pit.

Grübel|ei [ɡryːbəˈlaɪ] f (-/-en brooding, musing, meditation; **'2** ['~ln] v/i. (ge-, h) muse, meditate ponder (all: über acc. on, over) Am. F a. mull (over).

'Gruben|arbeiter ✻ m miner; **'2 gas** ✻ n fire-damp; **'~lampe** ✻ miner's lamp.

Gruft [ɡruft] f (-/⁻e) tomb, vaul **grün** [ɡryːn] 1. adj. green; **~er He ring** fresh herring; **~er Junge** green horn; **~ und blau schlagen** beat s.o black and blue; **vom ~en Tisch au** armchair (strategy, etc.); 2. 2 (-s/no pl.) green; verdure.

Grund [ɡrunt] m (-[e]s/⁻e) ground soil; bottom (a. fig.); land, estate foundation; fig.: motive; reason argument; **von ~ auf** thoroughly **fundamentally**; **'~ausbildung** ✕ basic instruction; ✕ basic (mili tary) training; **'~bedeutung** f basi or original meaning; **'~bedingun** f basic or fundamental condition **'~begriff** m fundamental or basi idea; **~e** pl. principles pl.; rudi ments pl.; **'~besitz** m land(ed prop erty]; '~besitzer *m* landowner; '~buch *n* land register.

gründ|en ['gryndən] *v/t.* (ge-, h) establish; ✝ promote; *sich ~ auf* (*acc.*) be based *or* founded on; '2er *m* (-s/-) founder; ✝ promoter.

'grund|'falsch *adj.* fundamentally wrong; '2farbe *f* ground-colo(u)r; *opt.* primary colo(u)r; '2fläche *f* base; area (*of room, etc.*); '2gebühr *f* basic rate *or* fee; flat rate; '2gedanke *m* basic *or* fundamental idea; '2gesetz *n* fundamental law; ʒᵗᶻ *appr.* constitution; '2kapital ✝ *n* capital (fund); '2lage *f* foundation, basis; '~legend *adj.* fundamental, basic.

gründlich *adj.* ['gryntliç] thorough; *knowledge*: profound.

'Grund|linie *f* base-line; '2los *adj.* bottomless; *fig.*: groundless; unfounded; '~mauer *f* foundation-wall. [Thursday.]

Grün'donnerstag *eccl. m* Maundy⏉

'Grund|regel *f* fundamental rule; '~riß *m* △ ground-plan; outline; compendium; '~satz *m* principle; 2sätzlich ['~zetsliç] 1. *adj.* fundamental; 2. *adv.* in principle; on principle; '~schule *f* elementary *or* primary school; '~stein *m* △ foundation-stone; *fig.* corner-stone; '~steuer *f* land-tax; '~stock *m* basis, foundation; '~stoff *m* element; '~strich *m* down-stroke; '~stück *n* plot (of land); ʒᵗᶻ (real) estate; premises *pl.*; '~stücksmakler *m* real estate agent, *Am.* realtor; '~ton *m* ♪ keynote; ground shade.

'Gründung *f* (-/-en) foundation, establishment.

'grund|ver'schieden *adj.* entirely different; '2wasser *geol. n* (under-)ground water; '2zahl *gr. f* cardinal number; '2zug *m* main feature, characteristic.

'grünlich *adj.* greenish.

'Grün|schnabel *fig. m* greenhorn; whipper-snapper; '~span *m* (-[e]s/*no pl.*) verdigris.

grunzen ['gruntsən] *v/i. and v/t.* (ge-, h) grunt.

Grupp|e ['grupə] *f* (-/-n) group; ✗ section, *Am.* squad; 2ieren [~'pi:rən] *v/t.* (*no* -ge-, h) group, arrange in groups; *sich ~* form groups.

Gruselgeschichte ['gru:zəl-] *f* tale of horror, spine-chilling story *or* tale, F creepy story *or* tale.

Gruß [gru:s] *m* (-es/⸚e) salutation; greeting; *esp.* ✗, ⚓ salute; *mst* Grüße *pl.* regards *pl.*; respects *pl.*, compliments *pl.*

grüßen ['gry:sən] *v/t.* (ge-, h) greet, *esp.* ✗ salute; hail; *~ Sie ihn von mir* remember me to him; *j-n ~ lassen* send one's compliments *or* regards to s.o.

9*

Grütze ['grytsə] *f* (-/-n) grits *pl.*, groats *pl.*

guck|en ['gukən] *v/i.* (ge-, h) look; peep, peer; '2loch *n* peep- *or* spyhole.

Guerilla ✗ [ge'ril(j)a] *f* (-/-s) guer(r)illa war.

gültig *adj.* ['gyltiç] valid; effective, in force; legal; *coin*: current; *ticket*: available; '2keit *f* (-/*no pl.*) validity; currency (*of money*); availability (*of ticket*).

Gummi ['gumi] *n, m* (-s/-s) gum; (india-)rubber; '~ball *m* rubber ball; '~band *n* elastic (band); rubber band; '~baum ♀ *m* gum-tree; (india-)rubber tree.

gum'mieren *v/t.* (*no* -ge-, h) gum.

'Gummi|handschuh *m* rubber glove; '~knüppel *m* truncheon, *Am.* club; '~schuhe *m/pl.* rubber shoes *pl.*, *Am.* rubbers *pl.*; '~sohle *f* rubber sole; '~stiefel *m* wellington (boot), *Am.* rubber boot; '~zug *m* elastic; elastic webbing.

Gunst [gunst] *f* (-/*no pl.*) favo(u)r, goodwill; *zu ~en* (*gen.*) in favo(u)r of.

günst|ig *adj.* ['gynstiç] favo(u)rable; *omen*: propitious; *im ~sten Fall* at best; *zu ~en Bedingungen* ✝ on easy terms; '2ling ['~liŋ] *m* (-s/-e) favo(u)rite.

Gurgel ['gurgəl] *f* (-/-n): *j-m an die ~ springen* leap *or* fly at s.o.'s throat; '2n *v/i.* (ge-, h) ❧ gargle; gurgle.

Gurke ['gurkə] *f* (-/-n) cucumber; *pickled*: gherkin.

gurren ['gurən] *v/i.* (ge-, h) coo.

Gurt [gurt] *m* (-[e]s/-e) girdle; *harness*: girth; strap; belt.

Gürtel ['gyrtəl] *m* (-s/-) belt; girdle; *geogr.* zone.

Guß [gus] *m* (Gusses/Güsse) ⊕ founding, casting; *typ.* fount, *Am.* font; *rain*: downpour, shower; '~eisen *n* cast iron; '2eisern *adj.* cast-iron; '2stahl *m* cast steel.

gut[1] [gu:t] 1. *adj.* good; *~e Worte* fair words; *~es Wetter* fine weather; *~er Dinge or ~en Mutes sein* be of good cheer; *~e Miene zum bösen Spiel machen* grin and bear it; *~ so!* good!, well done!; *~ werden* get well, heal; *fig.* turn out well; *ganz ~* not bad; *schon ~!* never mind!, all right!; *sei so ~ und ...* (will you) be so kind as to *inf.*; *auf ~ deutsch* in plain German; *j-m ~ sein* love *or* like s.o.; 2. *adv.* well; *ein ~ gehendes Geschäft* a flourishing business; *du hast ~ lachen* it's easy *or* very well for you to laugh; *es ~ haben* be lucky; be well off.

Gut[2] [~] *n* (-[e]s/⸚er) possession, property; (landed) estate; ✝ goods *pl.*

'Gut|achten n (-s/-) (expert) opinion; '~achter m (-s/-) expert; consultant; '2artig adj. good-natured; ℳ benign; ~dünken ['~dynkən] n (-s/no pl.): nach ~ at discretion or pleasure.

Gute 1. n (-n/no pl.) the good; ~s tun do good; 2. m, f (-n/-n): die ~n pl. the good pl.

Güte ['gy:tə] f (-/no pl.) goodness, kindness; † class, quality; in ~ amicably; F: meine ~l good gracious!; haben Sie die ~ zu inf. be so kind as to inf.

'Güter|abfertigung f dispatch of goods; = '~annahme f goods office, Am. freight office; '~bahnhof m goods station, Am. freight depot or yard; '~gemeinschaft ₰₰ f community of property; '~trennung ₰₰ f separation of property; '~verkehr m goods traffic, Am. freight traffic; '~wagen m (goods) wag(g)on, Am. freight car; offener ~ (goods) truck; geschlossener ~ (goods) van, Am. boxcar; '~zug m goods train, Am. freight train.

'gut|gelaunt adj. good-humo(u)red; '~gläubig adj. acting or done in good faith; s. leichtgläubig; '~haben v/t. (irr. haben, sep., -ge-, h) have credit for [sum of money); '2~haben † n credit (balance); '~heißen v/t. (irr. heißen, sep., -ge-, h)

approve (of); '~herzig adj. good-natured, kind-hearted.

'gütig adj. good, kind(ly).

'gütlich adv.: sich ~ einigen settle s.th. amicably; sich ~ tun an (dat.) regale o.s. on.

'gut|machen v/t. (sep., -ge-, h) make up for, compensate, repair; ~mütig adj. ['~my:tiç] good-natured; '2mütigkeit f (-/℈ -en) good nature.

'Gutsbesitzer m landowner; owner of an estate.

'Gut|schein m credit note, coupon; voucher; '2schreiben v/t. (irr. schreiben, sep., -ge-, h): j-m e-n Betrag ~ put a sum to s.o.'s credit; '~schrift † f credit(ing).

'Guts|haus n farm-house; manor house; '~herr m lord of the manor; landowner; '~hof m farmyard; estate, farm; '~verwalter m (landlord's) manager or steward.

'gutwillig adj. willing; obliging.

Gymnasi|albildung ['gymna'zja:l-] f classical education; ~ast [~ast] m (-en/-en) appr. grammar-school boy; ~um [~'na:zjum] n (-s/Gymnasien) appr. grammar-school.

Gymnasti|k [gym'nastik] f (-/no pl.) gymnastics pl.; 2sch adj. gymnastic.

Gynäkologe ℳ [gynɛ:ko'lo:gə] m (-n/-n) gyn(a)ecologist.

H

Haar [ha:r] n (-[e]s/-e) hair; sich die ~e kämmen comb one's hair; sich die ~e schneiden lassen have one's hair cut; aufs ~ to a hair; um ein ~ by a hair's breadth; '~ausfall m loss of hair; '~bürste f hairbrush; '2en v/i. and v/refl. (ge-, h) lose or shed one's hairs; '~esbreite f: um ~ by a hair's breadth; '2fein adj. (as) fine as a hair; fig. subtle; '~gefäß anat. n capillary (vessel); '2e'nau adj. exact to a hair; '2ig adj. hairy; in compounds: ...-haired; '2klein adv. to the last detail; '~klemme f hair grip, Am. bobby pin; '~nadel f hairpin; '~nadelkurve f hairpin bend; '~netz n hair-net; '~öl n hair-oil; '2scharf 1. adj. very sharp; fig. very precise; 2. adv. by a hair's breadth; '~schneidemaschine f (e-e a pair of) (hair) clippers pl.; '~schneider m barber, (men's) hairdresser; '~schnitt m haircut; '~schwund m loss of hair; '~spalte'rei f (-/-en) hair-splitting; '2sträubend adj. hair-raising, horrifying; '~tracht f hair-style, coiffure; '~wäsche f hair-wash,

shampoo; '~wasser n hair-lotion; '~wuchs m growth of the hair; '~wuchsmittel n hair-restorer.

Habe ['ha:bə] f (-/no pl.) property; belongings pl.

haben ['ha:bən] 1. v/t. (irr., ge-, h) have; F fig.: sich ~ (make a) fuss; etwas (nichts) auf sich ~ be of (no) consequence; unter sich ~ be in control of, command; zu ~ † goods: obtainable, to be had; da ~ wir's f there we are!; 2. 2 † n (-s/-) credit (side).

Habgier ['ha:p-] f avarice, covetousness; '2ig adj. avaricious, covetous.

habhaft adj. ['ha:phaft]: ~ werden (gen.) get hold of; catch, apprehend.

Habicht orn. ['ha:biçt] m (-[e]s/-e) (gos)hawk.

Hab|seligkeiten ['ha:p-] f/pl. property, belongings pl.; '~sucht f s. Habgier; '2süchtig adj. s. habgierig.

Hacke ['hakən] f (-/-n) ♂ hoe, mattock; (pick)axe; heel.

Hacken ['hakən] 1. m (-s/-) heel; die ~ zusammenschlagen ✕ click one's heels; 2. 2 v/t. (ge-, h) ♂

hack (*soil*); mince (*meat*); chop (*wood*).

'**Hackfleisch** *n* minced meat, *Am.* ground meat.

Häcksel ['hɛksəl] *n, m* (-s/no *pl.*) chaff, chopped straw.

Hader ['hɑːdər] *m* (-s/no *pl.*) dispute, quarrel; discord; '**₂n** *v/i.* (ge-, *h*) quarrel (*mit* with).

Hafen ['hɑːfən] *m* (-s/ᵘ) harbo(u)r; port; '**₂anlagen** *f/pl.* docks *pl.*; '**₂arbeiter** *m* docker, *Am. a.* longshoreman; '**₂damm** *m* jetty; pier; '**₂stadt** *f* seaport.

Hafer ['hɑːfər] *m* (-s/-) oats *pl.*; '**₂brei** *m* (oatmeal) porridge; '**₂flocken** *f/pl.* porridge oats *pl.*; '**₂grütze** *f* groats *pl.*, grits *pl.*; '**₂schleim** *m* gruel.

Haft 🏛 [haft] *f* (-/no *pl.*) custody; detention, confinement; '**₂bar** *adj.* responsible, 🏛 liable (*für* for); '**₂befehl** *m* warrant of arrest; '**₂en** *v/i.* (ge-, *h*) stick, adhere (*an dat.* to); ~ *für* 🏛 answer for, be liable for.

Häftling ['hɛftliŋ] *m* (-s/-e) prisoner.

'**Haftpflicht** 🏛 *f* liability; '**₂ig** *adj.* liable (*für* for); '**₂versicherung** *f* third-party insurance.

'**Haftung** *f* (-/-en) responsibility, 🏛 liability; *mit beschränkter* ~ limited.

Hagel ['hɑːgəl] *m* (-s/-) hail; *fig. a.* shower, volley; '**₂korn** *n* hailstone; '**₂n** *v/i.* (ge-, *h*) hail (*a. fig.*); '**₂schauer** *m* shower of hail, (brief) hailstorm.

hager *adj.* ['hɑːgər] lean, gaunt; scraggy, lank.

Hahn [hɑːn] *m* **1.** *orn.* (-[e]s/ᵘe) cock; rooster; **2.** ⊕ (-[e]s/ᵘe, -en) (stop)cock, tap, *Am. a.* faucet; '**₂enkampf** *m* cock-fight; '**₂enschrei** *m* cock-crow.

Hai *ichth.* [haɪ] *m* (-[e]s/-e), '**₂fisch** *m* shark.

Hain *poet.* [haɪn] *m* (-[e]s/-e) grove; wood.

häkel|n ['hɛːkəln] *v/t. and v/i.* (ge-, *h*) crochet; '**₂nadel** *f* crochet needle *or* hook.

Haken ['hɑːkən] **1.** *m* (-s/-) hook (*a. boxing*); peg; *fig.* snag, catch; **2.** ₂ *v/i.* (ge-, *h*) get stuck, jam.

'**hakig** *adj.* hooked.

halb [halp] **1.** *adj.* half; *eine ₂e Stunde* half an hour, a half-hour; *eine ₂e Flasche Wein* a half-bottle of wine; *ein ₂es Jahr* half a year; *₂e Note J* minim, *Am. a.* half note; *₂er Ton J* semitone, *Am. a.* half tone; **2.** *adv.* half; ~ *voll* half full; ~ *soviel* half as much; *es schlug* ~ it struck the half-hour.

'**halb|amtlich** *adj.* semi-official; '**₂bruder** *m* half-brother; '**₂dunkel** *n* semi-darkness; dusk, twilight; '**₂er** *prp.* (*gen.*) ['halbər] on account of; for the sake of; '**₂fabri**-

kat ⊕ *n* semi-finished product; '**₂gar** *adj.* underdone, *Am. a.* rare; '**₂gott** *m* demigod; '**₂heit** *f* (-/-en) half-measure.

halbieren [hal'biːrən] *v/t.* (no -ge-, *h*) halve, divide in half; 🏛 bisect.

'**Halb|insel** *f* peninsula; '**₂jahr** *n* half-year, six months *pl.*; '**₂jährig** *adj.* ['₂jɛːriç] half-year, six months; of six months; '**₂jährlich** **1.** *adj.* half-yearly; **2.** *adv. a.* twice a year; '**₂kreis** *m* semicircle; '**₂kugel** *f* hemisphere; '**₂laut** **1.** *adj.* low, subdued; **2.** *adv.* in an undertone; '**₂mast** *adv.* (at) half-mast, *Am. a.* (at) half-staff; '**₂messer** ⚕ *m* (-s/-) radius; '**₂mond** *m* half-moon, crescent; '**₂part** *adv.*: ~ *machen* go halves, F go fifty-fifty; '**₂schuh** *m* (low) shoe; '**₂schwester** *f* half-sister; '**₂tagsbeschäftigung** *f* part-time job *or* employment; '**₂tot** *adj.* half-dead; ₂wegs *adv.* ['₂veːks] half-way; *fig.* to some extent, tolerably; '**₂welt** *f* demi-monde; ₂wüchsig *adj.* ['₂vyːksiç] adolescent, *Am. a.* teen-age; '**₂zeit** *f* *sports:* half(-time).

Halde ['haldə] *f* (-/-n) slope; ⚒ dump.

half [half] *pret. of* helfen.

Hälfte ['hɛlftə] *f* (-/-n) half, 🏛 moiety; *die* ~ *von* half of.

Halfter ['halftər] *m, n* (-s/-) halter.

Halle ['halə] *f* (-/-n) hall; *hotel:* lounge; *tennis:* covered court; ✈ hangar.

hallen ['halən] *v/i.* (ge-, *h*) (re)sound, ring, (re-)echo.

'**Hallen|bad** *n* indoor swimming-bath, *Am. a.* natatorium; '**₂sport** *m* indoor sports *pl.*

hallo [ha'loː] **1.** *int.* hallo!, hello!, hullo!; **2.** ₂ *fig. n* (-s/-s) hullabaloo.

Halm ⚘ [halm] *m* (-[e]s/-e) blade; stem, stalk; straw.

Hals [hals] *m* (-es/ᵘe) neck; throat; ~ *über Kopf* head over heels; *auf dem ₂e haben* have on one's back, be saddled with; *sich den ~ verrenken* crane one's neck; '**₂abschneider** *fig. m* extortioner, F shark; '**₂band** *n* necklace; collar (*for dog, etc.*); '**₂entzündung** ⚕ *f* sore throat; '**₂kette** *f* necklace; string; chain; '**₂kragen** *m* collar; '**₂schmerzen** *m/pl.*: ~ *haben* have a sore throat; '**₂starrig** *adj.* stubborn, obstinate; '**₂tuch** *n* neckerchief; scarf; '**₂weite** *f* neck size.

Halt [halt] *m* (-[e]s/-e) hold; foothold, handhold; support (*a. fig.*); *fig.*: stability; security; mainstay.

halt 1. *int.* stop!; ✗ halt!; **2.** F *adv.* just; *das ist so* ~ so that's the way it is.

'**haltbar** *adj. material, etc.*: durable, lasting; *colour:* fast; *fig. theory, etc.*: tenable.

'**halten** (*irr.*, ge-, *h*) **1.** *v/t.* hold (*fort,*

position, water, etc.); maintain (*position, level, etc.*); keep (*promise, order, animal, etc.*); make, deliver (*speech*); give, deliver (*lecture*); take in (*newspaper*); ~ *für* regard as, take to be; take for; es ~ *mit* side with; be fond of; *kurz*~ keep *s.o.* short; *viel* (*wenig*) ~ *von* think highly (little) of; *sich* ~ hold out; last; *food:* keep; *sich gerade* ~ hold o.s. straight; *sich gut* ~ *in examination, etc.:* do well; *p.* be well preserved; *sich* ~ *an* (*acc.*) adhere or keep to; **2.** *v/i.* stop, halt; *ice:* bear; *rope, etc.:* stand the strain; ~ *zu* stick to or by; ~ *auf* (*acc.*) set store by, value; *auf sich* ~ pay attention to one's appearance; have self-respect.

'Halte|punkt *m* ⚑, *etc.*: wayside stop, halt; *shooting:* point of aim; *phys.* critical point; '~r *m* (*-s/-*) keeper; *a.* owner; *devices:* ... holder; '~stelle *f* stop; ⚑ station, stop; '~signal ⚑ *n* stop signal.

halt|los *adj.* ['haltlo:s] *p.* unsteady, unstable; *theory, etc.:* baseless, without foundation; '~machen *v/i.* (*sep., -ge-, h*) stop, halt; *vor nichts* ~ stick or stop; at nothing; '~ung *f* (*-/-en*) deportment, carriage; pose; *fig.* attitude (*gegenüber* towards); self-control; *stock exchange:* tone.

hämisch *adj.* ['hɛːmiʃ] spiteful, malicious.

Hammel ['haməl] *m* (*-s/-,* ⁼) wether; '~fleisch *n* mutton; '~keule *f* leg of mutton; '~rippchen *n* (*-s/-*) mutton chop.

Hammer ['hamər] *m* (*-s/*⁼) hammer; (*auctioneer's*) gavel; *unter den* ~ *kommen* come under the hammer.

hämmern ['hɛmərn] (*ge-, h*) **1.** *v/t.* hammer; **2.** *v/i.* hammer (*a. an dat.* at *door, etc.*); hammer away (*auf dat.* at *piano*); *heart, etc.:* throb (violently), pound.

Hämorrhoiden ⚕ [hɛːmɔrɔˈiːdən] *f/pl.* h(a)emorrhoids *pl.*, piles *pl.*

Hampelmann ['hampəlman] *m* jumping-jack; *fig.* (mere) puppet.

Hamster *zo.* ['hamstər] *m* (*-s/-*) hamster; '2n *v/t. and v/i.* (*ge-, h*) hoard.

Hand [hant] *f* (*-/*⁼e) hand; *j-m die* ~ *geben* shake hands with s.o.; *an* ~ (*gen.*) or *von* with the help or aid of; *aus erster* ~ first-hand, at first hand; *bei der* ~, *zur* ~ at hand; ~ *und Fuß haben* be sound, hold water; *seine* ~ *im Spiele haben* have a finger in the pie; '~arbeit *f* manual labo(u)r or work; (*handi*)craft; needlework; '~arbeiter *m* manual labo(u)rer; '~bibliothek *f* reference library; '~breit **1.** *f* (*-/-*) hand's breadth; **2.** ♀ *adj.* a hand's breadth across; '~bremse *mot. f* hand-brake; '~buch *n* manual, handbook.

Hände|druck ['hɛndə-] *m* (*-[e]s/*⁼e)

handshake; '~klatschen *n* (*-s/no pl.*) (hand-)clapping; applause.

Handel ['handəl] *m* **1.** (*-s/no pl.*) commerce; trade; business; market; traffic; transaction, deal, bargain; **2.** (*-s/*⁼): *Händel pl.* quarrels *pl.*, contention; '2n *v/i.* (*ge-, h*) act, take action; ✝ trade (*mit with s.o.,* in *goods*), deal (in *goods*); bargain (*um for*), haggle (*over*); ~ *von treat of,* deal with; *es handelt sich um it* concerns, it is a matter of.

'Handels|abkommen *n* trade agreement; '~bank *f* commercial bank; '2einig *adj.:* ~ *werden* come to terms; '~genossenschaft *f* traders' co-operative association; '~gericht *n* commercial court; '~gesellschaft *f* (trading) company; '~haus *n* business house, firm; '~kammer *f* Chamber of Commerce; '~marine *f* mercantile marine; '~minister *m* minister of commerce; President of the Board of Trade, *Am.* Secretary of Commerce; '~ministerium *n* ministry of commerce; Board of Trade, *Am.* Department of Commerce; '~reisende *m* commercial traveller, *Am.* traveling salesman, F drummer; '~schiff *n* merchantman; '~schiffahrt *f* merchant shipping; '~schule *f* commercial school; '~stadt *f* commercial town; '2üblich *adj.* customary in trade; '~vertrag *m* commercial treaty, trade agreement.

'handeltreibend *adj.* trading.

'Hand|feger *m* (*-s/-*) hand-brush; '~fertigkeit *f* manual skill; '2fest *adj.* sturdy, strong; *fig.* well-founded, sound; '~feuerwaffen *f/pl.* small arms *pl.*; '~fläche *f* flat of the hand, palm; '2gearbeitet *adj.* hand-made; '~geld *n* earnest money; ⚔ bounty; '~gelenk *anat. n* wrist; '~gemenge *n* scuffle, mêlée; '~gepäck *n* hand luggage, *Am.* hand baggage; '~granate ⚔ *f* hand-grenade; '2greiflich *adj.* violent; *fig.* tangible, palpable; ~ *werden* turn violent, *Am. a.* get tough; '~griff *m* grasp; handle, grip; *fig.* manipulation; '~habe *fig. f* handle; '2haben *v/t.* (*ge-, h*) handle, manage; operate (*machine, etc.*); administer (*law*); '~karren *m* hand-cart; '~koffer *m* suitcase, *Am. a.* valise; '~kuß *m* kiss on the hand; '~langer *m* (*-s/-*) hodman, handy man; *fig.* dog's-body, henchman.

Händler ['hɛndlər] *m* (*-s/-*) dealer, trader.

'handlich *adj.* handy; manageable.

Handlung ['handluŋ] *f* (*-/-en*) act, action; deed; *thea.* action, plot; ✝ shop, *Am.* store.

'Handlungs|bevollmächtigte *m* proxy; '~gehilfe *m* clerk; shop-assistant, *Am.* salesclerk; '**~reisen-de** *m s.* Handelsreisende; '**~weise** *f* conduct; way of acting.

'**Hand|rücken** *m* back of the hand; '**~schelle** *f* handcuff, manacle; '**~schlag** *m* handshake; '**~schrei-ben** *n* autograph letter; '**~schrift** *f* handwriting; manuscript; '**2-schriftlich 1.** *adj.* hand-written; **2.** *adv.* in one's own handwriting; '**~schuh** *m* glove; '**~streich** ✕ *m* surprise attack, coup de main; *im ~ nehmen* take by surprise; '**~tasche** *f* handbag, *Am. a.* purse; '**~tuch** *n* towel; '**~voll** *f* (-/-) handful; '**~wa-gen** *m* hand-cart; '**~werk** *n* (handi)craft, trade; '**~werker** *m* (-s/-) (handi)craftsman, artisan; workman; '**~werkzeug** *n* (kit of) tools *pl.*; '**~wurzel** *anat. f* wrist; '**~zeichnung** *f* drawing.

Hanf ♀ [hanf] *m* (-[e]s/*no pl.*) hemp.

Hang [haŋ] *m* (-[e]s/-e) slope, incline, declivity; hillside; *fig.* inclination, propensity (*zu* for; *zu inf. to inf.*); tendency (to).

Hänge|boden ['hɛŋə-] *m* hanging-loft; '**~brücke** △ *f* suspension bridge; '**~lampe** *f* hanging lamp; '**~matte** *f* hammock.

hängen ['hɛŋən] **1.** *v/i.* (*irr.*, ge-, h) hang, be suspended; adhere, stick, cling (*an dat.* to); *~ an (dat.)* be attached *or* devoted to; **2.** *v/t.* (ge-, h) hang, suspend; '**~bleiben** *v/i.* (*irr. bleiben, sep.*, -ge-, sein) get caught (up) (*an dat.* on, in); *fig.* stick (in the memory).

hänseln ['hɛnzəln] *v/t.* (ge-, h) tease (*wegen* about), F rag.

Hansestadt ['hanzə-] *f* Hanseatic town.

Hanswurst [hans'-] *m* (-es/-e, F ∞e) merry andrew; Punch; *fig. contp.* clown, buffoon.

Hantel ['hantəl] *f* (-/-n) dumb-bell.

hantieren [han'tiːrən] *v/i.* (*no* -ge-, h) be busy (*mit* with); work (*an dat.* on).

Happen ['hapən] *m* (-s/-) morsel, mouthful, bite; snack.

Harfe ♪ ['harfə] *f* (-/-n) harp.

Harke ♪ ['harkə] *f* (-/-n) rake; '**2n** *v/t. and v/i.* (ge-, h) rake.

harmlos *adj.* ['harmloːs] harmless, innocuous; inoffensive.

Harmon|ie [harmo'niː] *f* (-/-n) harmony (*a.* ♪); **2ieren** *v/i.* (*no* -ge-, h) harmonize (*mit* with); *fig. a.* be in tune (with); '**~ika** ♪ [~'moː-nika] *f* (-/-s, Harmoniken) accordion; mouth-organ; **2isch** *adj.* [~'moːniʃ] harmonious.

Harn [harn] *m* (-[e]s/-e) urine; '**~blase** *anat. f* (urinary) bladder; '**2en** *v/i.* (ge-, h) pass water, urinate.

Harnisch ['harniʃ] *m* (-es/-e) armo(u)r; *in ~ geraten* be up in arms (*über acc.* about).

'**Harnröhre** *anat. f* urethra.

Harpun|e [har'puːnə] *f* (-/-n) harpoon; **2ieren** [~u'niːrən] *v/t.* (*no* -ge-, h) harpoon.

hart [hart] **1.** *adj.* hard; *fig. a.* harsh; heavy, severe; **2.** *adv.* hard; *~ arbeiten* work hard.

Härte ['hɛrtə] *f* (-/-n) hardness; *fig. a.* hardship; severity; '**2n** (ge-, h) **1.** *v/t.* harden (*metal*); temper (*steel*); case-harden (*iron, steel*); **2.** *v/i. and v/refl.* harden, become *or* grow hard; *steel:* temper.

'**Hart|geld** *n* coin(s *pl.*), specie; '**~gummi** *n* hard rubber; ♥ ebon-ite, vulcanite; '**2herzig** *adj.* hard-hearted; **2köpfig** *adj.* ['~kœpfiç] stubborn, headstrong; **2näckig** *adj.* ['~nɛkiç] *p.* obstinate, obdurate; *effort:* dogged, tenacious; ☞ *ail-ment:* refractory.

Harz [haːrts] *n* (-es/-e) resin; ♪ rosin; *mot.* gum; '**2ig** *adj.* resinous.

Hasardspiel [ha'zart-] *n* game of chance; *fig.* gamble.

haschen ['haʃən] (ge-, h) **1.** *v/t.* catch (hold of), snatch; *sich ~ children:* play tag; **2.** *v/i.: ~ nach* snatch at; *fig.* strain after (*effect*), fish for (*compliments*).

Hase ['haːzə] *m* (-n/-n) *zo.* hare; *ein alter ~* an old hand, an old-timer.

Haselnuß ♀ ['haːzəlnus] *f* hazel-nut.

'**Hasen|braten** *m* roast hare; '**~fuß** F *fig. m* coward, F funk; '**~panier** F *n: das ~ ergreifen* take to one's heels; '**~scharte** ☞ *f* hare-lip.

Haß [has] *m* (Hasses/*no pl.*) hatred.

'**hassen** *v/t.* (ge-, h) hate.

häßlich *adj.* ['hɛslic] ugly; *fig. a.* nasty, unpleasant.

Hast [hast] *f* (-/*no pl.*) hurry, haste; rush; *in wilder ~* in frantic haste; '**2en** *v/i.* (ge-, sein) hurry, hasten; rush; '**2ig** *adj.* hasty, hurried.

hätscheln ['hɛːtʃəln] *v/t.* (ge-, h) caress, fondle, pet; pamper, coddle.

hatte ['hatə] *pret. of* haben.

Haube ['haubə] *f* (-/-n) bonnet (*a.* ⊕, *mot.*); cap; *orn.* crest, tuft; *mot. Am. a.* hood.

Haubitze ✕ [hau'bitsə] *f* (-/-n) howitzer.

Hauch [haux] *m* (-[e]s/↖-e) breath; *fig.:* waft, whiff (*of perfume, etc.*); touch, tinge (*of irony, etc.*); '**2en** (ge-, h) **1.** *v/i.* breathe; **2.** *v/t.* breathe, whisper; *gr.* aspirate.

Haue ['hauə] *f* (-/-n) ♪ hoe, mat-tock; pick; F hiding, spanking; '**2n** (*irr.*, ge-, h) **1.** *v/t.* hew (*coal, stone*); cut up (*meat*); chop (*wood*); cut (*hole, steps, etc.*); beat (*child*); *sich ~* have a fight; **2.** *v/i.: ~ nach* cut at, strike out at.

Haufen ['haufən] *m* (-s/-) heap, pile (*both* F *a. fig.*); *fig.* crowd.

häufen ['hɔyfən] *v/t.* (ge-, h) heap

(up), pile (up); accumulate; *sich* ~ pile up, accumulate; *fig.* become more frequent, increase.

'**häufig** *adj.* frequent; '**Qkeit** *f* (-/*no pl.*) frequency.

'**Häufung** *fig. f* (-/-en) increase, *fig.* accumulation.

Haupt [haupt] *n* (-[e]s/*-*er) head; *fig.* chief, head, leader; '~**altar** *m* high altar; '~**anschluß** *teleph. m* subscriber's main station; '~**bahnhof** 🚊 *m* main *or* central station; '~**beruf** *m* full-time occupation; '~**buch** ✝ *n* ledger; '~**darsteller** *thea. m* leading actor; '~**fach** *univ. n* main *or* principal subject, *Am. a.* major; '~**film** *m* feature (film); '~**geschäft** *n* main transaction; main shop; '~**geschäftsstelle** *f* head *or* central office; '~**gewinn** *m* first prize; '~**grund** *m* main reason; ~**handelsartikel** ✝ ['haupthandəls?-] *m* staple.

Häuptling ['hɔyptliŋ] *m* (-s/-e) chief(tain).

'**Haupt|linie** 🚊 *f* main *or* trunk line; '~**mann** ✕ *m* (-[e]s/*Haupt-leute*) captain; '~**merkmal** *n* characteristic feature; '~**postamt** *n* general post office, *Am.* main post office; '~**punkt** *m* main *or* cardinal point; '~**quartier** *n* headquarters *sg. or pl.*; '~**rolle** *thea. f* lead(ing part); '~**sache** *f* main thing *or* point; '**Qsächlich** *adj.* main, chief, principal; '~**satz** *gr. m* main clause; '~**stadt** *f* capital; '**Qstädtisch** *adj.* metropolitan; '~**straße** *f* main street; major road; '~**treffer** *m* first prize, jackpot; '~**verkehrsstraße** *f* main road; arterial road; '~**verkehrsstunden** *f/pl.*, '~**verkehrszeit** *f* rush hour(s *pl.*), peak hour(s *pl.*); '~**versammlung** *f* general meeting; '~**wort** *gr. n* (-[e]s/*-*er) substantive, noun.

Haus [haus] *n* (-es/*-*er) house; building; home, family, household; dynasty; ✝ (business) house, firm; *parl.* House; *nach* ~ home; *zu* ~ at home, F in; '~**angestellte** *f* (-n/-n) (house-)maid; '~**apotheke** *f* (household) medicine-chest; '~**arbeit** *f* housework; '~**arrest** *m* house arrest; '~**arzt** *m* family doctor; '~**aufgaben** *f/pl.* homework, F prep; '**Qbacken** *fig. adj.* homely; '~**bar** *f* cocktail cabinet; '~**bedarf** *m* household requirements *pl.*; '~**besitzer** *m* (house-)owner; '~**diener** *m* (man-)servant; *hotel:* porter, boots *sg.*

hausen ['hauzən] *v/i.* (ge-, h) live; play *or* work havoc (*in a place*).

'**Haus|flur** *m* (entrance-)hall, *esp. Am.* hallway; '~**frau** *f* housewife; '~**halt** *m* household; '**Qhalten** *v/i.* (*irr.* halten, *sep.*, -ge-, h) be economical (*mit* with), economize (on);

'~**hälterin** ['~hɛltərin] *f* (-/-nen) housekeeper; '~**halt(s)plan** *parl. m* budget; '~**haltung** *f* housekeeping; household, family; '~**haltwaren** *f/pl.* household articles *pl.*; '~**herr** *m* master of the family; landlord.

hausier|en [hau'ziːrən] *v/i.* (*no -ge-, h*) hawk, peddle (*mit et.* s.th.); ~ *gehen* be a hawker *or* pedlar; **Qer** *m* (-s/-) hawker, pedlar.

'**Haus|kleid** *n* house dress; '~**knecht** *m* boots; '~**lehrer** *m* private tutor.

häuslich *adj.* ['hɔyslic] ·domestic; domesticated; '**Qkeit** *f* (-/*no pl.*) domesticity; family life; home.

'**Haus|mädchen** *n* (house-)maid; '~**mannskost** *f* plain fare; '~**meister** *m* caretaker; janitor; '~**mittel** *n* popular medicine; '~**ordnung** *f* rules *pl.* of the house; '~**rat** *m* household effects *pl.*; '~**recht** *n* domestic authority; '~**sammlung** *f* house-to-house collection; '~**schlüssel** *m* latchkey; front-door key; '~**schuh** *m* slipper.

Hauss|e ✝ ['hoːs(ə)] *f* (-/-n) rise, boom; ~**ier** [hos'jeː] *m* (-s/-s) speculator for a rise, bull.

'**Haus|stand** *m* household; *e-n* ~ *gründen* set up house; '~**suchung** 🚔 *f* house search, domiciliary visit, *Am. a.* house check; '~**tier** *n* domestic animal; '~**tür** *f* front door; '~**verwalter** *m* steward; '~**wirt** *m* landlord; '~**wirtin** *f* (-/-nen) landlady.

Haut [haut] *f* (-/*-*e) skin; hide; film; *bis auf die* ~ to the skin; *aus der* ~ *fahren* jump out of one's skin; F *e-e ehrliche* ~ an honest soul; '~**abschürfung** *f* skin abrasion; '~**arzt** *m* dermatologist; '~**ausschlag** *m* rash; **Qeng** *adj.* garment: skin-tight; '~**farbe** *f* complexion.

Hautgout [o'gu] *m* (-s/*no pl.*) high taste.

häutig *adj.* ['hɔytic] membranous; covered with skin.

'**Haut|krankheit** *f* skin disease; '~**pflege** *f* care of the skin; '~**schere** *f* (e-e a pair of) cuticle scissors *pl.*

Havarie ⚓ [hava'riː] *f* (-/-n) average.

H-Bombe ✕ ['haː-] *f* H-bomb.

he *int.* [heː] hi!, hi there!; I say!

Hebamme ['heːpˀamə] *f* midwife.

Hebe|baum ['heːbə-] *m* lever (for raising heavy objects); '~**bühne** *mot. f* lifting ramp; '~**eisen** *n* crowbar; '~**kran** *m* lifting crane.

Hebel ⊕ ['heːbəl] *m* (-s/-) lever; '~**arm** *m* lever arm.

heben ['heːbən] *v/t.* (*irr.*, ge-, h) lift (*a. sports*), raise (*a. fig.*); heave (*heavy load*); hoist; recover (*treas-*

ure); raise (*sunken ship*); *fig.* promote, improve, increase; *sich ~* rise, go up.

Hecht *ichth.* [hɛçt] *m* (-[e]s/-e) pike.

Heck [hɛk] *n* (-[e]s/-e, -s) ⚓ stern; *mot.* rear; ⚓ tail.

Hecke ['hɛkə] *f* (-/-n) ⚘ hedge; *zo.* brood, hatch; '*2n v/t. and v/i.* (ge-, h) breed, hatch; '**~nrose** ⚘ *f* dog-rose. [hallo!\

heda *int.* ['he:da:] hi (there)!,\

Heer [he:r] *n* (-[e]s/-e) ✕ army; *fig. a.* host; '**~esdienst** *m* military service; '**~esmacht** *f* military force(s *pl.*); '**~eszug** *m* military expedition; '**~führer** *m* general; '**~lager** *n* (army) camp; '**~schar** *f* army, host; '**~straße** *f* military road; highway; '**~zug** *m s. Heereszug.*

Hefe ['he:fə] *f* (-/-n) yeast; barm.

Heft [hɛft] *n* (-[e]s/-e) dagger, etc.: haft; *knife:* handle; *fig.* reins *pl.*; exercise book; *periodical, etc.:* issue, number.

'**heft|en** *v/t.* (ge-, h) fasten, fix (*an acc.* on to); affix, attach (to); pin on (to); tack, baste (*seam, etc.*); stitch, sew (*book*); '**2faden** *m* basting thread.

'**heftig** *adj. storm, anger, quarrel, etc.:* violent, fierce; *rain, etc.:* heavy; *pain, etc.:* severe; *speech, desire, etc.:* vehement, passionate; *p.* irascible; '**2keit** *f* (-/-n) violence, fierceness; severity; vehemence; irascibility.

'**Heft|klammer** *f* paper-clip; '**~pflaster** *n* sticking plaster.

hegen ['he:gən] *v/t.* (ge-, h) preserve (*game*); nurse, tend (*plants*); have, entertain (*feelings*); harbo(u)r (*fears, suspicions, etc.*).

Hehler ⚖ ['he:lər] *m* (-s/-) receiver (of stolen goods); **~ei** [~'raɪ] *f* (-/-en) receiving (of stolen goods).

Heide ['haɪdə] **1.** *m* (-n/-n) heathen; **2.** *f* (-/-n) heath(-land); = '**~kraut** ⚘ *n* heather; '**~land** *n* heath(-land).

'**Heiden|geld** F *n* pots *pl.* of money; '**~lärm** F *m* hullabaloo; '**~spaß** F *m* capital fun; '**~tum** *n* (-s/no *pl.*) heathenism. [(-ish).\

heidnisch *adj.* ['haɪdnɪʃ] heathen\

heikel *adj.* ['haɪkəl] *p.* fastidious, particular; *problem, etc.:* delicate, awkward.

heil [haɪl] **1.** *adj. p.* safe, unhurt; whole, sound; **2.** 2 *n* (-[e]s/no *pl.*) welfare, benefit; *eccl.* salvation; **3.** *int.* hail!

Heiland *eccl.* ['haɪlant] *m* (-[e]s/-e) Saviour, Redeemer.

'**Heil|anstalt** *f* sanatorium, *Am. a.* sanitarium; '**~bad** *n* medicinal bath; spa; '**2bar** *adj.* curable; '**2en** (ge-) **1.** *v/t.* (h) cure, heal; *~ von* cure *s.o.* of; **2.** *v/i.* (sein) heal (up); '**~gehilfe** *m* male nurse.

heilig *adj.* ['haɪlɪç] holy; sacred; solemn; 2er *Abend* Christmas Eve; 2e ['~gə] *m, f* (-n/-n) saint; '**~en** ['~gən] *v/t.* (ge-, h) sanctify (*a. fig.*), hallow; '**2keit** *f* (-/no *pl.*) holiness; sacredness, sanctity; '**~sprechen** *v/t.* (*irr. sprechen, sep., -ge-, h*) canonize; '**2sprechung** *f* (-/-en) canonization; '**2tum** *n* (-[e]s/⁼er) sanctuary; sacred relic; '**2ung** ['~guŋ] *f* (-/-en) sanctification (*a. fig.*), hallowing.

'**Heil|kraft** *f* healing *or* curative power; '**2kräftig** *adj.* healing, curative; '**~kunde** *f* medical science; '**2los** *fig. adj. confusion:* utter, great; '**~mittel** *n* remedy, medicament; '**~praktiker** *m* non-medical practitioner; '**~quelle** *f* medicinal spring; '**2sam** *adj.* curative; *fig.* salutary. [Army.\

Heilsarmee ['haɪls?-] *f* Salvation\

'**Heil|ung** *f* (-/-en) cure, healing, successful treatment; '**~verfahren** *n* therapy.

heim [haɪm] **1.** *adv.* home; **2.** 2 *n* (-[e]s/-e) home; hostel; '**2arbeit** *f* homework, outwork.

Heimat ['haɪma:t] *f* (-/⁼-en) home; own country; native land; '**~land** *n* own country; native land; '**2lich** *adj.* native; '**2los** *adj.* homeless; '**~ort** *m* home town *or* village; '**~vertriebene** *m* expellee.

Heimchen *zo.* ['haɪmçən] *n* (-s/-) cricket.

'**heimisch** *adj. trade, industry, etc.:* home, local, domestic; ⚘, *zo., etc.:* native, indigenous; *~ werden* settle down; become established; *sich ~ fühlen* feel at home.

Heim|kehr ['haɪmke:r] *f* (-/no *pl.*) return (home), homecoming; '**2kehren** *v/i.* (*sep., -ge-, sein*); '**2kommen** *v/i.* (*irr. kommen, sep., -ge-, sein*) return home.

'**heimlich** *adj. plan, feeling, etc.:* secret; *meeting, organization, etc.:* clandestine; *glance, movement, etc.:* stealthy, furtive.

'**Heim|reise** *f* homeward journey; '**2suchen** *v/t.* (*sep., -ge-, h*) *disaster, etc.:* afflict, strike; *ghost:* haunt; *God:* visit, punish; '**~tücke** *f* underhand malice, treachery; '**2tückisch** *adj.* malicious, treacherous, insidious; **2wärts** *adv.* ['~verts] homeward(s); '**~weg** *m* way home; '**~weh** *n* homesickness, nostalgia; *~ haben* be homesick.

Heirat ['haɪra:t] *f* (-/-en) marriage; '**2en** (ge-, h) **1.** *v/t.* marry; **2.** *v/i.* marry, get married.

'**Heirats|antrag** *m* offer *or* proposal of marriage; '**2fähig** *adj.* marriageable; '**~kandidat** *m* possible marriage partner; '**~schwindler** *m* marriage impostor; '**~vermittler** *m* matrimonial agent.

heiser adj. ['haɪzər] hoarse; husky; '**2keit** f (-/no pl.) hoarseness; huskiness.

heiß adj. [haɪs] hot; fig. a. passionate, ardent; mir ist ~ I am or feel hot.

heißen ['haɪsən] (irr., ge-, h) 1. v/t.: e-n Lügner ~ call s.o. a liar; willkommen ~ welcome; 2. v/i. be called; mean; wie ~ Sie? what is your name?; was heißt das auf englisch? what's that in English?

heiter adj. ['haɪtər] day, weather: bright; sky: bright, clear; p., etc.: cheerful, gay; serene; '**2keit** f (-/no pl.) brightness; cheerfulness, gaiety; serenity.

heiz|en ['haɪtsən] (ge-, h) 1. v/t. heat (room, etc.); light (stove); fire (boiler); 2. v/i. stove, etc.: give out heat; turn on the heating; mit Kohlen ~ burn coal; '**2er** m (-s/-) stoker, fireman; '**2kissen** n electric heating pad; '**2körper** m central heating: radiator; ∮ heating element; '**2material** n fuel; '**2ung** f (-/-en) heating.

Held [hɛlt] m (-en/-en) hero.

'**Helden|gedicht** n epic (poem); '**2haft** adj. heroic, valiant; '**.mut** m heroism, valo(u)r; **2mütig** adj. ['.my:tɪç] heroic; '**.tat** f heroic or valiant deed; '**.tod** m hero's death; '**.tum** n (-[e]s/no pl.) heroism.

helfen ['hɛlfən] v/i. (dat.) (irr., ge-, h) help, assist, aid; ~ gegen be good for; sich nicht zu ~ wissen be helpless.

'**Helfer** m (-s/-) helper, assistant; '**.shelfer** m accomplice.

hell adj. [hɛl] sound, voice, light, etc.: clear; light, flame, etc.: bright; hair: fair; colour: light; ale: pale; '**.blau** adj. light-blue; '**.blond** adj. very fair; '**.hörig** adj. p. quick of hearing; fig. perceptive; △ poorly sound-proofed; '**2seher** m clairvoyant.

Helm [hɛlm] m ([-e]s/-e) ✗ helmet; △ dome, cupola; ⚓ helm; '**.busch** m plume.

Hemd [hɛmt] n (-[e]s/-en) shirt; vest; '**.bluse** f shirt-blouse, Am. shirtwaist.   [hemisphere.)

Hemisphäre [he:mi'sfɛ:rə] f (-/-n)

hemm|en ['hɛmən] v/t. (ge-, h) check, stop (movement, etc.); stem (stream, flow of liquid); hamper (free movement, activity); be a hindrance to; psych.: gehemmt sein be inhibited; '**2nis** n (-ses/-se) hindrance, impediment; '**2schuh** m slipper; fig. hindrance, F drag (für acc. on); '**2ung** f (-/-en) stoppage, check; psych.: inhibition.

Hengst zo. [hɛŋst] m (-es/-e) stallion.

Henkel ['hɛŋkəl] m (-s/-) handle, ear.

Henker ['hɛŋkər] m (-s/-) hangman, executioner; F: zum ~! hang it (all)!

Henne zo. ['hɛnə] f (-/-n) hen.

her adv. [he:r] here; hither; es ist schon ein Jahr ~, daß ... or seit ... it is a year since ...; wie lange ist es ~, seit ... how long is it since ...; hinter (dat.) ~ sein be after; ~ damit! out with it!

herab adv. [hɛ'rap] down, downward; **.lassen** v/t. (irr. lassen, sep., -ge-, h) let down, lower; fig. sich ~ condescend; **.lassend** adj. condescending; **.setzen** v/t. (sep., -ge-, h) take down; fig. belittle, disparage s.o.; ∮ reduce, lower, cut (price, etc.); **2setzung** fig. f (-/-en) reduction; disparagement; **.steigen** v/i. (irr. steigen, sep., -ge-, sein) climb down, descend; **.würdigen** v/t. (sep., -ge-, h) degrade, belittle, abase.

heran adv. [hɛ'ran] close, near; up; nur ~! come on!; sep., -ge-, h) train, educate (zu as s.th., to be s.th.); **.kommen** v/i. (irr. kommen, sep., -ge-, sein) come or draw near; approach; ~ an (acc.) come up to s.o.; measure up to; ~ wachsen v/i. (irr. wachsen, sep., -ge-, sein) grow (up) (zu into).

herauf adv. [hɛ'rauf] up(wards), up here; upstairs; **.beschwören** v/t. (irr. schwören, sep., no -ge-, h) evoke, call up, conjure up (spirit, etc.); fig. a. bring about, provoke, give rise to (war, etc.); **.steigen** v/i. (irr. steigen, sep., -ge-, sein) climb up (here), ascend; **.ziehen** (irr. ziehen, sep., -ge-) 1. v/t. (h) pull or hitch up (trousers, etc.); 2. v/i. (sein) cloud, etc.: come up.

heraus adv. [hɛ'raus] out, out here; zum Fenster ~ out of the window; ~ mit der Sprache! speak out!; **.bekommen** v/t. (irr. kommen, sep., no -ge-, h) get out; get (money) back; fig. find out; **.bringen** v/t. (irr. bringen, sep., -ge-, h) bring or get out; thea. stage; **.finden** v/t. (irr. finden, sep., -ge-, h) find out; fig. a. discover; **2forderer** m (-s/-) challenger; **.fordern** v/t. (sep., -ge-, h) challenge (to a fight); provoke; **2forderung** f (-/-en) challenge; provocation; **.geben** v/t. (irr. geben, sep., -ge-, h) 1. v/t. surrender; hand over; restore; edit (periodical, etc.); publish (book, etc.); issue (regulations, etc.); 2. v/i. give change (auf acc. for); **2geber** m (-s/-) editor; publisher; **.kommen** v/i. (irr. kommen, sep., -ge-, sein) come out; fig. a. appear, be published; **.nehmen** v/t. (irr. nehmen, sep., -ge-, h) take out; sich viel ~ take liberties; **.putzen** v/t. (sep., -ge-, h) dress up; sich ~ dress (o.s.)

up; ~reden v/refl. (sep., -ge-, h) talk one's way out; ~stellen v/t. (sep., -ge-, h) put out; fig. emphasize, set forth; sich ~ emerge, turn out; ~strecken v/t. (sep., -ge-, h) stretch out; put out; ~streichen v/t. (irr. streichen, sep., -ge-, h) cross out, delete (word, etc.); fig. extol, praise; ~winden fig. v/refl. (irr. winden, sep., -ge-, h) extricate o.s. (aus from).

herb adj. [herp] fruit, flavour, etc.: tart; wine, etc.: dry; features, etc.: austere; criticism, etc.: harsh; disappointment, etc.: bitter.

herbei adv. [her'baɪ] here; ~I come here!; ~eilen [her'baɪ⁹-] v/i. (sep., -ge-, sein) come hurrying; ~führen fig. v/t. (sep., -ge-, h) cause, bring about, give rise to; ~schaffen v/t. (sep., -ge-, h) bring along; procure.

Herberge ['herbergə] f (-/-n) shelter, lodging; inn.

'Herbheit f (-/no pl.) tartness; dryness; fig.: austerity; harshness, bitterness.

Herbst [herpst] m (-[e]s/-e) autumn, Am. a. fall.

Herd [he:rt] m (-[e]s/-e) hearth, fireplace; stove; fig. seat, focus.

Herde ['he:rdə] f (-/-n) herd (of cattle, pigs, etc.) (contp. a. fig.); flock (of sheep, geese, etc.).

herein adv. [hε'raɪn] in (here); ~I come in!; ~brechen fig. v/i. (irr. brechen, sep., -ge-, sein) night: fall; ~ über (acc.) misfortune, etc.: befall; ~fallen fig. v/i. (irr. fallen, sep., -ge-, sein) be taken in.

'her|fallen v/i. (irr. fallen, sep., -ge-, sein): ~ über (acc.) attack (a. fig.), fall upon; F fig. pull to pieces; '2gang m course of events, details pl.; '~geben v/t. (irr. geben, sep., -ge-, h) give up, part with, return; yield; sich ~ zu lend o.s. to; '~gebracht fig. adj. traditional; customary; '~halten v/t. (irr. halten, sep., -ge-, h) 1. v/t. hold out; 2. v/i.: ~ müssen be the one to pay or suffer (für for).

Hering ichth. ['he:rɪŋ] m (-s/-e) herring.

'her|kommen v/i. (irr. kommen, sep., -ge-, sein) come or get here; come or draw near; ~ von come from; fig. a. be due to, be caused by; '~kömmlich adj. ['~kœmlɪç] traditional; customary; 2kunft ['~kunft] f (-/no pl.) origin; birth, descent; '~leiten v/t. (sep., -ge-, h) lead here; fig. derive (von from); '2leitung fig. f derivation.

Herold ['he:rɔlt] m (-[e]s/-e) herald.

Herr [her] m (-n, ⚔-en/-en) lord, master; eccl. the Lord; gentleman; ~ Maier Mr Maier; mein ~ Sir; m-e ~en gentlemen; ~ der Situation master of the situation.

'Herren|bekleidung f men's cloth-

ing; '~einzel n tennis: men's singles pl.; '~haus n manor-house; 2-los adj. ['~lo:s] ownerless; '~reiter m sports: gentleman-jockey; '~schneider m men's tailor; '~zimmer n study; smoking-room.

herrichten ['he:r-] v/t. (sep., -ge-, h) arrange, prepare.

'herrisch adj. imperious, overbearing; voice, etc.: commanding, peremptory.

'herrlich adj. excellent, glorious, magnificent, splendid; '2keit f (-/-en) glory, splendo(u)r.

'Herrschaft f (-/-en) rule, dominion (über acc. of); fig. mastery; master and mistress; m-e ~en! ladies and gentlemen!; 2lich adj. belonging to a master or landlord; fig. high-class, elegant.

herrsch|en ['herʃən] v/i. (ge-, h) rule (über acc. over); monarch: reign (over); govern; fig. prevail, be; '2er m (-s/-) ruler; sovereign, monarch; '2sucht f thirst for power; '~süchtig adj. thirsting for power; imperious.

'her|rühren v/i. (sep., -ge-, h): ~ von come from, originate with; '~sagen v/t. (sep., -ge-, h) recite; say (prayer); '~stammen v/i. (sep., -ge-, h): ~ von or aus be descended from; come from; be derived from; '~stellen v/t. (sep., -ge-, h) place here; ✝ make, manufacture, produce; '2stellung f (-/-en) manufacture, production.

herüber adv. [hε'ry:bər] over (here), across.

herum adv. [hε'rum] (a)round; about; ~führen v/t. (sep., -ge-, h) show (a)round; ~ in (dat.) show over; ~lungern v/i. (sep., -ge-, h) loaf or loiter or hang about; ~reichen v/t. (sep., -ge-, h) pass or hand round; ~sprechen v/refl. (irr. sprechen, sep., -ge-, h) get about, spread; ~treiben v/refl. (irr. treiben, sep., -ge-, h) F gad or knock about.

herunter adv. [hε'runtər] down (here); downstairs; von oben ~ down from above; ~bringen v/t. (irr. bringen, sep., -ge-, h) bring down; fig. a. lower, reduce; ~kommen v/i. (irr. kommen, sep., -ge-, sein) come down(stairs); fig.: come down in the world; deteriorate; ~machen v/t. (sep., -ge-, h) take down; turn (collar, etc.) down; fig. give s.o. a dressing-down; fig. pull to pieces; ~reißen v/t. (irr. reißen, sep., -ge-, h) pull or tear down; fig. pull to pieces; ~sein F fig. v/i. (irr. sein, sep., -ge-, h) be low in health; ~wirtschaften v/t. (sep., -ge-, h) run down.

hervor adv. [hεr'fo:r] forth, out; ~bringen v/t. (irr. bringen, sep.,

-ge-, h) bring out, produce (a. fig.); yield (fruit); fig. utter (word); ~gehen v/i. (irr. gehen, sep., -ge-, sein) p. come (aus from); come off (victorious) (from); fact, etc.: emerge (from); be clear or apparent (from); ~heben fig. v/t. (irr. heben, sep., -ge-, h) stress, emphasize; give prominence to; ~holen v/t. (sep., -ge-, h) produce; ~ragen v/i. (sep., -ge-, h) project (über acc. over); fig. tower (above); ~ragend adj. projecting, prominent; fig. outstanding, excellent; ~rufen v/t. (irr. rufen, sep., -ge-, h) thea. call for; fig. arouse, evoke; ~stechend fig. adj. outstanding; striking; conspicuous.

Herz [herts] n (-ens/-en) anat. heart (a. fig.); cards: hearts pl.; fig. courage, spirit; sich ein ~ fassen take heart; mit ganzem ~en whole-heartedly; sich et. zu ~en nehmen take s.th. to heart; es nicht übers ~ bringen zu inf. not to have the heart to inf.; '~anfall m heart attack.

'**Herzens|brecher** m (-s/-) lady-killer; '~lust f: nach ~ to one's heart's content; '~wunsch m heart's desire.

'**herz|ergreifend** fig. adj. heart-moving; '2fehler ⚕ m cardiac defect; '2gegend anat. f cardiac region; '~haft adj. hearty, good; '~ig adj. lovely, Am. a. cute; 2infarkt ⚕ ['~'infarkt] m (-[e]s/-e) cardiac infarction; '2klopfen ⚕ n (-s/no pl.) palpitation; '~krank adj. having heart trouble; '~lich 1. adj. heartfelt; cordial, hearty; ~es Beileid sincere sympathy; 2. adv.: ~ gern with pleasure; '~los adj. heartless; unfeeling.

Herzog ['hɛrtso:k] m (-[e]s/~e, -e) duke; '~in f (-/-nen) duchess; '~tum n (-[e]s/~er) dukedom; duchy.

'**Herz|schlag** m heartbeat; ⚕ heart failure; '~schwäche ⚕ f cardiac insufficiency; '~verpflanzung ⚕ f heart transplant; '2zerreißend adj. heart-rending.

Hetz|e ['hɛtsə] f (-/-n) hurry, rush; instigation (gegen acc. against); baiting (of); '2en (ge-) 1. v/t. (h) course (hare); bait (bear, etc.); hound: hunt, chase (animal); fig. hurry, rush; sich ~ hurry, rush; e-n Hund auf j-n ~ set a dog at s.o.; 2. v/i. (h) fig.: cause discord; agitate (gegen against); 3. fig. v/i. (sein) hurry, rush; '~er fig. m (-s/-) instigator; agitator; '2erisch adj. virulent, inflammatory; '~jagd f hunt(ing); fig.: virulent campaign; rush, hurry; '~presse f yellow press.

Heu [hɔy] n (-[e]s/no pl.) hay; '~boden m hayloft.

Heuchel|ei [hɔyçə'laɪ] f (-/-en) hypocrisy; '2n (ge-, h) 1. v/t. sim-

ulate, feign, affect; 2. v/i. feign, dissemble; play the hypocrite.

'**Heuchler** m (-s/-) hypocrite; '2isch adj. hypocritical.

heuer ['hɔyər] 1. adv. this year; 2. 2 ⚓ f (-/-n) pay, wages pl.; '~n v/t. (ge-, h) hire; ⚓ engage, sign on (crew), charter (ship).

heulen ['hɔylən] v/i. (ge-, h) wind, etc.: howl; storm, wind, etc.: roar; siren: wail; F p. howl, cry.

'**Heu|schnupfen** ⚕ m hay-fever; ~schrecke zo. ['~ʃrɛkə] f (-/-n) grasshopper, locust.

heut|e ['hɔytə] today; ~ abend this evening, tonight; ~ früh, ~ morgen this morning; ~ in acht Tagen today or this day week; ~ vor acht Tagen a week ago today; '~ig adj. this day's, today's; present; ~zutage adv. ['hɔyttsuːtaːgə] nowadays, these days.

Hexe ['hɛksə] f (-/-n) witch, sorceress; fig.: hell-cat; hag; '2n v/i. (ge-, h) practice witchcraft; F fig. work miracles; '~nkessel fig. m inferno; '~nmeister m wizard, sorcerer; '~nschuß ⚕ m lumbago; ~rei [~'raɪ] f (-/-en) witchcraft, sorcery, magic.

Hieb [hiːp] 1. m (-[e]s/-e) blow, stroke; lash, cut (of whip, etc.); a. punch (with fist); fenc. cut; ~e pl. hiding, thrashing; 2. 2 pret. of hauen.

hielt [hiːlt] pret. of halten.

hier adv. [hiːr] here; in this place; ~! present!; ~ entlang! this way!

hier|an adv. ['hiːran, when emphatic 'hiːran] at or by or in or on or to it or this; ~auf adv. ['hiːraʊf, when emphatic 'hiːraʊf] on it or this; after this or that, then; ~aus adv. ['hiːraʊs, when emphatic 'hiːraʊs] from or out of it or this; ~bei adv. ['hiːrbaɪ, when emphatic 'hiːrbaɪ] here; in this case, in connection with this; ~durch adv. ['hiːr'durç, when emphatic 'hiːrdurç] through here; by this, hereby; ~für adv. ['hiːrfyːr, when emphatic 'hiːrfyːr] for it or this; ~her adv. ['hiːrheːr, when emphatic 'hiːrheːr] here, hither; bis ~ as far as here; ~in adv. ['hiːrin, when emphatic 'hiːrin] in it or this; in here; ~mit adv. ['hiːr'mit, when emphatic 'hiːrmit] with it or this, herewith; ~nach adv. ['hiːrnaːx, when emphatic 'hiːrnaːx] after it or this; according to this; ~über adv. ['hiːry:bər, when emphatic 'hiːry:bər] over it or this; over here; on this (subject); ~unter adv. ['hiːruntər, when emphatic 'hiːruntər] under it or this; among these; by this or that; ~von adv. ['hiːrfɔn, when emphatic 'hiːrfɔn] of or from it or this; ~zu adv. ['hiːrtsuː, when emphatic 'hiːrtsuː]

with it *or* this; (in addition) to this.

hiesig *adj.* ['hi:ziç] of *or* in this place *or* town, local.

hieß [hi:s] *pret. of* heißen.

Hilfe ['hilfə] *f* (-/-n) help; aid, assistance; succour; relief (für to); ∼! help!; mit ∼ von with the help *or* aid of; '∼ruf *m* shout *or* cry for help.

'hilf|los *adj.* helpless; '∼reich *adj.* helpful.

'Hilfs|aktion *f* relief measures *pl.*; '∼arbeiter *m* unskilled worker *or* labo(u)rer; 'Ջbedürftig *adj.* needy, indigent; '∼lehrer *m* assistant teacher; '∼mittel *n* aid; device; remedy; expedient; '∼motor *m*: Fahrrad mit ∼ motor-assisted bicycle; '∼quelle *f* resource; '∼schule *f* elementary school for backward children; '∼werk *n* relief organization. [berry.)

Himbeere ♀ ['himbe:rə] *f* rasp-)

Himmel ['himəl] *m* (-s/-) sky, heavens *pl.*; *eccl.*, *fig.* heaven; '∼bett *n* tester-bed; 'Ջblau *adj.* sky-blue; '∼fahrt *eccl.* ascension (of Christ); Ascension-day; 'Ջschreiend *adj.* crying.

'Himmels|gegend *f* region of the sky; cardinal point; '∼körper *m* celestial body; '∼richtung *f* point of the compass, cardinal point; direction; '∼strich *m* region, climate zone.

'himmlisch *adj.* celestial, heavenly.

hin *adv.* [hin] there; gone, lost; ∼ und her to and fro, *Am.* back and forth; ∼ und wieder now and again *or* then; ∼ und zurück there and back.

hinab *adv.* [hi'nap] down; ∼steigen *v/i.* (*irr.* steigen, *sep.*, -ge-, sein) climb down, descend.

hinarbeiten ['hin'-] *v/i.* (*sep.*, -ge-, h): ∼ auf (*acc.*) work for *or* towards.

hinauf *adv.* [hi'nauf] up (there); upstairs; ∼gehen *v/i.* (*irr.* gehen, *sep.*, -ge-, sein) go up(stairs); *prices, wages, etc.*: go up, rise; ∼steigen *v/i.* (*irr.* steigen, *sep.*, -ge-, sein) climb up, ascend.

hinaus *adv.* [hi'naus] out; ∼ mit euch! out with you!; auf (viele) Jahre ∼ for (many) years (to come); ∼gehen *v/i.* (*irr.* gehen, *sep.*, -ge-, sein) go *or* walk out; ∼ über (*acc.*) go beyond, exceed; ∼ auf (*acc.*) *window, etc.*: look out on, overlook; *intention, etc.*: drive *or* aim at; ∼laufen *v/i.* (*irr.* laufen, *sep.*, -ge-, sein) run *or* rush out; ∼ auf (*acc.*) come *or* amount to; ∼schieben *fig.* *v/t.* (*irr.* schieben, *sep.*, -ge-, h) put off, postpone, defer; ∼werfen *v/t.* (*irr.* werfen, *sep.*, -ge-, h) throw out (*aus* of); turn *or* throw *or* F chuck *s.o.* out.

'Hin|blick *m*: im ∼ auf (*acc.*) in view of, with regard to; 'Ջbringen *v/t.* (*irr.* bringen, *sep.*, -ge-, h) take there; while away, pass (*time*).

hinder|lich *adj.* ['hindərliç] hindering, impeding; j-m ∼ sein be in s.o.'s way; '∼n *v/t.* (ge-, h) hinder, hamper (*bei*, *in dat.* in); ∼ an (*dat.*) prevent from; 'Ջnis *n* (-ses/-se) hindrance; *sports*: obstacle; turf, *etc.*: fence; 'Ջnisrennen *n* obstacle-race.

hin'durch *adv.* through; all through, throughout; across.

hinein *adv.* [hi'nain] in; ∼ mit dir! in you go!; ∼gehen *v/i.* (*irr.* gehen, *sep.*, -ge-, sein) go in; ∼ in (*acc.*) go into; *in den Topf gehen ... hinein* the pot holds *or* takes ...

'Hin|fahrt *f* journey *or* way there; 'Ջfallen *v/i.* (*irr.* fallen, *sep.*, -ge-, sein) fall (down); 'Ջfällig *adj.* *p.* frail; *regulation, etc.*: invalid; ∼ machen invalidate, render invalid.

hing [hiŋ] *pret. of* hängen 1.

'Hin|gabe *f* devotion (*an acc.* to); 'Ջgeben *v/t.* (*irr.* geben, *sep.*, -ge-, h) give up *or* away; sich ∼ (*dat.*) give o.s. to; devote o.s. to; '∼gebung *f* (-/-en) devotion; 'Ջgehen *v/i.* (*irr.* gehen, *sep.*, -ge-, sein) go *or* walk there; go (zu to); *path, etc.*: lead there; lead (zu *to a place*); 'Ջhalten *v/t.* (*irr.* halten, *sep.*, -ge-, h) hold out (*object, etc.*); put *s.o.* off.

hinken ['hiŋkən] *v/i.* (ge-) **1.** (h) limp (*auf dem rechten Fuß* with one's right leg), have a limp; **2.** (sein) limp (along).

'hin|länglich *adj.* sufficient, adequate; '∼legen *v/t.* (*sep.*, -ge-, h) lay *or* put down; sich ∼ lie down; '∼nehmen *v/t.* (*irr.* nehmen, *sep.*, -ge-, h) accept, take; put up with; '∼raffen *v/t.* (*sep.*, -ge-, h) *death, etc.*: snatch *s.o.* away, carry *s.o.* off; '∼reichen (*sep.*, -ge-, h) **1.** *v/t.* reach *or* stretch *or* hold out (*dat.* to); **2.** *v/i.* suffice; '∼reißen *fig.* *v/t.* (*irr.* reißen, *sep.*, -ge-, h) carry away; enrapture, ravish; '∼reißend *adj.* ravishing, captivating; '∼richten *v/t.* (*sep.*, -ge-, h) execute, put to death; 'Ջrichtung *f* execution; '∼setzen *v/t.* (*sep.*, -ge-, h) set *or* put down; sich ∼ sit down; 'Ջsicht *f* regard, respect; in ∼ auf (*acc.*) = '∼sichtlich *prp.* (*gen.*) with regard to, as to, concerning; '∼stellen *v/t.* (*sep.*, -ge-, h) place; put; put down; *et.* ∼ *als* represent s.th. as; make s.th. appear (as).

hintan|setzen [hint'an-] *v/t.* (*sep.*, -ge-, h) set aside; Ջsetzung *f* (-/-en) setting aside; ∼stellen *v/t.* (*sep.*, -ge-, h) set aside; Ջstellung *f* (-/-en) setting aside.

hinten *adv.* ['hintən] behind, at the

back; in the background; in the rear.

hinter *prp.* ['hɪntər] **1.** (*dat.*) behind, *Am. a.* back of; ~ sich lassen outdistance; **2.** (*acc.*) behind; '2bein *n* hind leg; '2bliebenen *pl.* [.'bliːbənən] *the* bereaved *pl.*; surviving dependants *pl.*; ~'bringen *v/t.* (*irr.* bringen, *no* -ge-, h); j-m et. ~ inform s.o. of s.th. (secretly); ~ei'nander *adv.* one after the other; in succession; '2gedanke *m* ulterior motive; ~'gehen *v/t.* (*irr.* gehen, *no* -ge-, h) deceive, F doublecross; ~'gehung *f* (-/-en) deception; '2grund *m* background (*a. fig.*); '2halt *m* ambush; ~hältiç *adj.* ['.heltiç] insidious; underhand; '2haus *n* back *or* rear building; ~'her *adv.* behind; afterwards; '2hof *m* backyard; '2kopf *m* back of the head; ~'lassen *v/t.* (*irr.* lassen, *no* -ge-, h) leave (behind); '2lassenschaft *f* (-/-en) property (left), estate; ~'lassen *v/t.* (*no* -ge-, h) deposit, lodge (*bei* with); '2legung *f* (-/-en) deposit(ion); '2list *f* deceit; craftiness; insidiousness; ~'listig *adj.* deceitful; crafty; insidious; '2mann *m* ⚔ rear-rank man; *fig.*: ✝ subsequent endorser; *pol.* backer; wire-puller; instigator; '2n F *m* (-s/-) backside, behind, bottom; '2rad *n* rear wheel; ~rücks *adv.* ['.ryks] from behind; *fig.* behind his, *etc.* back; '2seite *f* back; '2teil *n* back (part); rear (part); F *s. Hintern;* ~'treiben *v/t.* (*irr.* treiben, *no* -ge-, h) thwart, frustrate; '2treppe *f* backstairs *pl.*; '2tür *f* back door; ~'ziehen ⚖ *v/t.* (*irr.* ziehen, *no* -ge-, h) evade (*tax, duty, etc.*); '2ziehung *f* evasion.

hinüber *adv.* [hɪ'nyːbər] over (there); across.

Hin- und 'Rückfahrt *f* journey there and back, *Am.* round trip.

hinunter *adv.* [hɪ'nʊntər] down (there); downstairs; ~schlucken *v/t.* (*sep.*, -ge-, h) swallow (down); *fig.* swallow.

'Hinweg[1] *m* way there *or* out.

hinweg[2] *adv.* [hɪn'vɛk] away, off; ~gehen *v/i.* (*irr.* gehen, *sep.*, -gesein): ~ über (*acc.*) go *or* walk over *or* across; *fig.* pass over, ignore; ~kommen *v/i.* (*irr.* kommen, *sep.*, -ge-, sein): ~ über (*acc.*) get over (*a. fig.*); ~sehen *v/i.* (*irr.* sehen, *sep.*, -ge-, h): ~ über (*acc.*) see *or* look over; *fig.* overlook, shut one's eyes to; ~setzen *v/refl.* (*sep.*, -ge-, h): sich ~ über (*acc.*) ignore, disregard, make light of.

Hin|weis ['hɪnvaɪs] *m* (-es/-e) reference (*auf acc.* to); hint (at); indication (of); '2weisen (*irr.* weisen, *sep.*, -ge-, h) **1.** *v/t.*: j-n ~ *auf* (*acc.*) draw *or* call s.o.'s attention to; **2.** *v/i.*: ~

auf (*acc.*) point at *or* to, indicate (*a. fig.*); *fig.*: point out; hint at; '2werfen *v/t.* (*irr.* werfen, *sep.*, -ge-, h) throw down; *fig.*: dash off (*sketch, etc.*); say s.th. casually; '2wirken *v/i.* (*sep.*, -ge-, h): ~ auf (*acc.*) work towards; use one's influence to; '2ziehen (*irr.* ziehen, *sep.*, -ge-) **1.** *fig. v/t.* (h) attract *or* draw there; with *space:* extend (*bis zu* to), stretch (to); *time:* drag on; **2.** *v/i.* (sein) go *or* move there; '2zielen *fig. v/i.* (*sep.*, -ge-, h): ~ auf (*acc.*) aim *or* drive at.

hin'zu *adv.* there; near; in addition; ~fügen *v/t.* (*sep.*, -ge-, h) add (zu to) (*a. fig.*); 2fügung *f* (-/-en) addition; ~kommen *v/i.* (*irr.* kommen, *sep.*, -ge-, sein) come up (zu to); supervene; be added; es kommt (noch) hinzu, daß add to this that, (and) moreover; ~rechnen *v/t.* (*sep.*, -ge-, h) add (zu to), include (in, among); ~setzen *v/t.* (*sep.*, -ge-, h) *s.* hinzufügen; ~treten *v/i.* (*irr.* treten, *sep.*, -ge-, sein) *s.* hinzukommen; join; ~ziehen *v/t.* (*irr.* ziehen, *sep.*, -ge-, h) call in (*doctor, etc.*).

Hirn [hɪrn] *n* (-[e]s/-e) *anat.* brain; *fig.* brains *pl.*, mind; '~gespinst *n* figment of the mind, chimera; '2los *fig. adj.* brainless, senseless; '~schale *anat.* f brain-pan, cranium; '~schlag ⚕ *m* apoplexy; '2verbrannt *adj.* crazy, F crack-brained, cracky.

Hirsch *zo.* [hɪrʃ] *m* (-es/-e) *species:* deer; stag, hart; '~geweih *n* (stag's) antlers *pl.*; '~kuh *f* hind; '~leder *n* buckskin, deerskin.

Hirse ♀ ['hɪrzə] *f* (-/-n) millet.

Hirt [hɪrt] *m* (-en/-en), ~e ['.ə] *m* (-n/-n) herdsman; shepherd.

hissen ['hɪsən] *v/t.* (ge-, h) hoist, raise (*flag*); ⚓ a. trice up (*sail*).

Histori|ker [hɪ'stoːrikər] *m* (-s/-) historian; 2sch *adj.* historic(al).

Hitz|e ['hɪtsə] *f* (-/*no pl.*) heat; '2ebeständig *adj.* heat-resistant, heat-proof; '~ewelle *f* heat-wave, hot spell; '2ig *adj. p.* hot-tempered, hot-headed; *discussion:* heated; '~kopf *m* hothead; '~schlag ⚕ *m* heat-stroke.

hob [hoːp] *pret. of* heben.

Hobel ⊕ ['hoːbəl] *m* (-s/-) plane; ~bank *f* carpenter's bench; '2n *v/t.* (ge-, h) plane.

hoch [hoːx] **1.** *adj.* high; *church spire, tree, etc.:* tall; *position, etc.:* high, important; *guest, etc.:* distinguished; *punishment, etc.:* heavy, severe; *age:* great, old; hohe See open sea, high seas *pl.*; **2.** *adv.:* ~ leben ...! long live ...! **3.** ♈ *n* (-s/-s) cheer; toast; *meteorology:* high (-pressure area).

'hoch|achten *v/t.* (*sep.*, -ge-, h) esteem highly; '2achtung *f* high esteem *or* respect; '~achtungsvoll 1. *adj.* (most) respectful; 2. *adv. correspondence*: yours faithfully *or* sincerely, *esp. Am.* yours truly; '2adel *m* greater *or* higher nobility; '2amt *eccl. n* high mass; '2antenne *f* overhead aerial; '2bahn *f* elevated *or* overhead railway, *Am.* elevated railroad; '2betrieb *m* intense activity, rush; '2burg *fig. f* stronghold; '~deutsch *adj.* High *or* standard German; '2druck *m* high pressure (*a. fig.*); *mit* ~ *arbeiten* work at high pressure; 2ebene *f* plateau, tableland; '~fahrend *adj.* highhanded, arrogant; '~fein *adj.* superfine; 2form *f*: *in* ~ in top form; '2frequenz *≠ f* high frequency; '2gebirge *n* high mountains *pl.*; '2genuß *m* great enjoyment; '2glanz *m* high polish; '2haus *n* multi-stor(e)y building, skyscraper; '~herzig *adj.* noble-minded; generous; '2herzigkeit *f* (-/-en) noble-mindedness, generosity; '2konjunktur *† f* boom, business prosperity; '2land *n* upland (*s pl.*), highlands *pl.*; '2mut *m* arrogance, haughtiness; ~mütig *adj.* ['~my:tiç] arrogant, haughty; ~näsig F *adj.* ['~nɛ:ziç] stuck-up; '2ofen ⊕ *m* blast-furnace; '~rot *adj.* bright red; '2saison *f* peak season, height of the season; '~schätzen *v/t.* (*sep.,-ge-, h*) esteem highly; '2schule *f* university; academy; '2seefischerei *f* deep-sea fishing; '2sommer *m* midsummer; '2spannung *≠ f* high tension *or* voltage; '2sprung *m sports:* high jump.

höchst [hø:çst] 1. *adj.* highest; *fig. a.*: supreme; extreme; 2. *adv.* highly, most, extremely.

Hochstap|elei [ho:xʃtɑːpəˈlaɪ] *f* (-/-en) swindling; '~ler *m* (-s/-) confidence man, swindler.

höchstens *adv.* ['hø:çstəns] at (the) most, at best.

'**Höchst|form** *f sports:* top form; '~geschwindigkeit *f* maximum speed; speed limit; '~leistung *f sports:* record (performance); ⊕ maximum output (*of machine, etc.*); '~lohn *m* maximum wages *pl.*; '~maß *n* maximum; '~preis *m* maximum price.

'**hoch|trabend** *fig. adj.* high-flown; pompous; '2verrat *m* high treason; '2wald *m* high forest; '2wasser *n* high tide *or* water; flood; '~wertig *adj.* high-grade, high-class; '2wild *n* big game; '2wohlgeboren *m* (-s/-) Right Hono(u)rable.

Hochzeit ['hɔxtsaɪt] *f* (-/-en) wedding; marriage; '2lich *adj.* bridal, nuptial; '~sgeschenk *n* wedding present; '~sreise *f* honeymoon (trip).

Hocke ['hɔkə] *f* (-/-n) *gymnastics:* squat-vault; *skiing:* crouch; '2n *v/i.* (*ge-, h*) squat, crouch; '~r *m* (-s/-) stool.

Höcker ['hœkər] *m* (-s/-) *surface, etc.*: bump; *camel, etc.*: hump; *p.* hump, hunch; '2ig *adj. animal:* humped; *p.* humpbacked, hunch-backed; *surface, etc.*: bumpy, rough, uneven.

Hode *anat.* ['ho:də] *m* (-n/-n), *f* (-/-n), '~n *anat. m* (-s/-) testicle.

Hof [ho:f] *m* (-[e]s/⸗e) court(yard); farm; *king, etc.*: court; *ast.* halo; *j-m den* ~ *machen* court s.o.; '~dame *f* lady-in-waiting; '2fähig *adj.* presentable at court.

Hoffart ['hɔfart] *f* (-/*no pl.*) arrogance, haughtiness; pride.

hoffen ['hɔfən] (*ge-, h*) 1. *v/i.* hope (*auf acc.* for); trust (in); 2. *v/t.*: *das Beste* ~ hope for the best; '~t-lich *adv.* it is to be hoped that, I hope, let's hope.

Hoffnung ['hɔfnuŋ] *f* (-/-en) hope (*auf acc.* for, of); *in der* ~ *zu inf.* in the hope of *ger.*, hoping to *inf.*; *s-e* ~ *setzen auf* (*acc.*) pin one's hopes on; '2slos *adj.* hopeless; '2svoll *adj.* hopeful; promising.

'**Hofhund** *m* watch-dog.

höfisch *adj.* ['hø:fiʃ] courtly.

höflich *adj.* ['hø:fliç] polite, civil, courteous (*gegen* to); '2keit *f* (-/-en) politeness, civility, courtesy.

'**Hofstaat** *m* royal *or* princely household; suite, retinue.

Höhe ['hø:ə] *f* (-/-n) height; ✈, ⚗, *ast., geogr.* altitude; hill; peak; amount (*of bill, etc.*); size (*of sum, fine, etc.*); level (*of price, etc.*); severity (*of punishment, etc.*); *♪* pitch; *in gleicher* ~ *mit* on a level with; *auf der* ~ *sein* be up to the mark; *in die* ~ up(wards).

Hoheit ['ho:haɪt] *f* (-/-en) *pol.* sovereignty; *title:* Highness; '~s-gebiet *n* (sovereign) territory; '~s-gewässer *n/pl.* territorial waters *pl.*; '~szeichen *n* national emblem.

'**Höhen|kurort** *m* high-altitude health resort; '~luft *f* mountain air; '~sonne *f* mountain sun; *🔆* ultra-violet lamp; '~steuer *⚗ m* elevator; '~zug *m* mountain range.

'**Höhepunkt** *m* highest point; *ast., fig.* culmination, zenith; *fig. a.*: climax; summit, peak.

hohl *adj.* [ho:l] hollow (*a. fig.*); *cheeks, etc.*: sunken; *hand:* cupped; *sound:* hollow, dull.

Höhle ['hø:lə] *f* (-/-n) cave, cavern; den, lair (*of bear, lion, etc.*) (*both a. fig.*); hole, burrow (*of fox, rabbit, etc.*); hollow; cavity.

'**Hohl|maß** *n* dry measure; '~raum *m* hollow, cavity; '~spiegel *m* concave mirror.

Höhlung ['høːluŋ] f (-/-en) excavation; hollow, cavity.

'**Hohlweg** m defile.

Hohn [hoːn] m (-[e]s/no pl.) scorn, disdain; derision.

höhnen ['høːnən] v/i. (ge-, h) sneer, jeer, mock, scoff (über acc. at).

'**Hohngelächter** n scornful or derisive laughter.

'**höhnisch** adj. scornful; sneering, derisive.

Höker ['høːkər] m (-s/-) hawker, huckster; 2n v/i. (ge-, h) huckster, hawk about.

holen ['hoːlən] v/t. (ge-, h) fetch; go for; a. ~ lassen send for; draw (breath); sich e-e Krankheit ~ catch a disease; sich bei j-m Rat ~ seek s.o.'s advice.

Holländer ['hɔlɛndər] m (-s/-) Dutchman.

Hölle ['hœlə] f (-/⸗-n) hell.

'**Höllen|angst** fig. f: e-e ~ haben be in a mortal fright or F blue funk; '~lärm F m infernal noise; '~maschine f infernal machine, time bomb; '~pein F fig. f torment of hell.

'**höllisch** adj. hellish, infernal (both a. fig.).

holper|ig adj. ['hɔlpəriç] surface, road, etc.: bumpy, rough, uneven; vehicle, etc.: jolty, jerky; verse, style, etc.: rough, jerky; '~n (ge-) 1. v/i. (sein) vehicle: jolt, bump; 2. v/i. (h) vehicle: jolt, bump; be jolty or bumpy.

Holunder ♀ [hoˈlundər] m (-s/-) elder.

Holz [hɔlts] n (-es/⸗er) wood; timber, Am. lumber; '~bau ⚒ m wooden structure; '~bildhauer m woodcarver; '~blasinstrument ♪ n woodwind instrument; '~boden m wood(en) floor; wood-loft.

hölzern adj. ['hœltsərn] wooden; fig. a. clumsy, awkward.

'**Holz|fäller** m (-s/-) woodcutter, woodman, Am. a. lumberjack, logger; '~hacker m (-s/-) woodchopper, woodcutter, Am. lumberjack; '~händler m wood or timber merchant, Am. lumberman; '~haus n wooden house, Am. frame house; '2ig adj. woody; '~kohle f charcoal; '~platz m wood or timber yard, Am. lumberyard; '~schnitt m woodcut, wood-engraving; '~schnitzer m wood-carver; '~schuh m wooden shoe, clog; '~stoß m pile or stack of wood; stake; '~weg m: auf dem ~ sein be on the wrong track; '~wolle f wood-wool; fine wood shavings pl., Am. a. excelsior.

Homöopath ⚕ [homøoˈpaːt] m (-en/-en) hom(o)eopath(ist); ~ie [~aˈtiː] f (-/no pl.) hom(o)eopathy; 2isch adj. [~ˈpaːtiʃ] hom(o)eopathic.

Honig ['hoːniç] m (-s/-e) honey; '~kuchen m honey-cake; gingerbread; '2süß adj. honey-sweet, honeyed (a. fig.); '~wabe f honeycomb.

Honor|ar [honoˈraːr] n (-s/-e) fee; royalties pl.; salary; ~atioren [~aˈtsjoːrən] pl. notabilities pl.; 2ieren [~ˈriːrən] v/t. (no -ge-, h) fee, pay a fee to; ✝ hono(u)r, meet (bill of exchange).

Hopfen ['hɔpfən] m (-s/-) ♀ hop; brewing: hops pl.

hops|a int. ['hɔpsa] (wh)oops!; upsadaisy!; '~en F v/i. (ge-, sein) hop, jump.

hörbar adj. ['høːrbaːr] audible.

horch|en ['hɔrçən] v/i. (ge-, h) listen (auf acc. to); eavesdrop; 2er m (-s/-) eavesdropper.

Horde ['hɔrdə] f (-/-n) horde, gang.

hör|en ['høːrən] (ge-, h) 1. v/t. hear; listen (in) to (radio); attend (lecture, etc.); hear, learn; 2. v/i. hear (von dat. from); listen; ~ auf (acc.) listen to; schwer ~ be hard of hearing; ~ Sie mal! look here!; I say!; '2er m (-s/-) hearer; radio: listener(-in); univ. student; teleph. receiver; '2erschaft f (-/-en) audience; '2gerät n hearing aid; '2ig adj.: j-m ~ sein be enslaved to s.o.; '2igkeit f (-/no pl.) subjection.

Horizont [horiˈtsɔnt] m (-[e]s/-e) horizon; skyline; s-n ~ erweitern broaden one's mind; das geht über meinen ~ that's beyond me; 2al adj. [~ˈtaːl] horizontal.

Hormon [hɔrˈmoːn] n (-s/-e) hormone.

Horn [hɔrn] n 1. (-[e]s/⸗er) horn (of bull); ♪, mot., etc.: horn; ✕ bugle; peak; 2. (-[e]s/-e) horn, horny matter; '~haut f horny skin; anat. cornea (on eye).

Hornisse zo. [hɔrˈnisə] f (-/-n) hornet.

Hornist ♪ [hɔrˈnist] m (-en/-en) horn-player; ✕ bugler.

Horoskop [horoˈskoːp] n (-s/-e) horoscope; j-m das ~ stellen cast s.o.'s horoscope.

'**Hör|rohr** n ear-trumpet; ✍ stethoscope; '~saal m lecture-hall; '~spiel n radio play; '~weite f: in ~ within earshot.

Hose ['hoːzə] f (-/-n) (e-e a pair of) trousers pl. or Am. pants pl.; slacks pl.

'**Hosen|klappe** f flap; ~latz [~lats] m (-es/⸗e) flap; fly; '~tasche f trouser-pocket; '~träger m: (ein Paar) ~ pl. (a pair of) braces pl. or Am. suspenders pl.

Hospital [hɔspiˈtaːl] n (-s/-e, ⸗er) hospital.

Hostie eccl. ['hɔstjə] f (-/-n) host, consecrated or holy wafer.

Hotel [hoˈtɛl] n (-s/-s) hotel; ~besitzer m hotel owner or proprietor;

~gewerbe *n* hotel industry; ~ier [~'je:] *m* (-s/-s) hotel-keeper.

Hub ⊕ [hu:p] *m* (-[e]s/ᵘe) *mot.* stroke (*of piston*); lift (*of valve, etc.*); '~raum *mot. m* capacity.

hübsch *adj.* [hypʃ] pretty, nice; good-looking, handsome; attractive.

'Hubschrauber ✈ *m* (-s/-) helicopter.

Huf [hu:f] *m* (-[e]s/-e) hoof; '~eisen *n* horseshoe; '~schlag *m* hoof-beat; (horse's) kick; '~schmied *m* farrier.

Hüft|e *anat.* ['hyftə] *f* (-/-n) hip; *esp. zo.* haunch; '~gelenk *n* hip-joint; '~gürtel *m* girdle; suspender belt, *Am.* garter belt.

Hügel ['hy:gəl] *m* (-s/-) hill(ock); '2ig *adj.* hilly.

Huhn *orn.* [hu:n] *n* (-[e]s/ᵘer) fowl, chicken; hen; *junges* ~ chicken.

Hühnchen ['hy:nçən] *n* (-s/-) chicken; *ein* ~ *zu rupfen haben* have a bone to pick (*mit* with).

Hühner|auge ✽ ['hy:nər-] *n* corn; '~ei *n* hen's egg; '~hof *m* poultry-yard, *Am.* chicken yard; '~hund *zo. m* pointer, setter; '~leiter *f* chicken-ladder.

Huld [hult] *f* (-/no *pl.*) grace, favo(u)r; 2igen ['~digən] *v/i.* (*dat.*) (ge-, h) pay homage to (*sovereign, lady, etc.*); indulge in (*vice, etc.*); '~igung *f* (-/-en) homage; '2reich *adj.*, '2voll *adj.* gracious.

Hülle ['hylə] *f* (-/-n) cover(ing), wrapper; *letter, balloon, etc.*: envelope; *book, etc.*: jacket; *umbrella, etc.*: sheath; '2n *v/t.* (ge-, h) wrap, cover, envelope (*a. fig.*); *sich in Schweigen* ~ wrap o.s. in silence.

Hülse ['hylzə] *f* (-/-n) legume, pod (*of leguminous plant*); husk, hull (*of rice, etc.*); skin (*of pea, etc.*); ✕ case; '~nfrucht *f* legume(n); leguminous plant; '~nfrüchte *f/pl.* pulse.

human *adj.* [hu'ma:n] humane; 2i-tät [~ani'tɛ:t] *f* (-/no *pl.*) humanity.

Hummel *zo.* ['huməl] *f* (-/-n) bumble-bee.

Hummer *zo.* ['humər] *m* (-s/-) lobster.

Humor [hu'mo:r] *m* (-s/✕-e) humo(u)r; ~ist [~o'rist] *m* (-en/-en) humorist; 2istisch *adj.* [~o'ristiʃ] humorous.

humpeln ['humpəln] *v/i.* (ge-) 1. (sein) hobble (along), limp (along); 2. (h) (have a) limp, walk with a limp.

Hund [hunt] *m* (-[e]s/-e) *zo.* dog; ✕ tub; *ast.* dog, canis; *auf den* ~ *kommen* go to the dogs.

'Hunde|hütte *f* dog-kennel, *Am. a.* doghouse; '~kuchen *m* dog-biscuit; '~leine *f* (dog-)lead *or* leash; '~peitsche *f* dog-whip.

hundert ['hundərt] 1. *adj.* a *or* one

hundred; 2. 2 *n* (-s/-e) hundred; *fünf vom* ~ five per cent; *zu* ~*en* by hundreds; '~fach *adj.*, '~fältig *adj.* hundredfold; 2'jahrfeier *f* centenary, *Am. a.* centennial; ~jährig *adj.* ['~jɛ:rɪç] centenary, a hundred years old; '~st *adj.* hundredth.

'Hunde|sperre *f* muzzling-order; '~steuer *f* dog tax.

Hündi|n *zo.* ['hyndɪn] *f* (-/-nen) bitch, she-dog; '2sch *adj.* doggish; *fig.* servile, cringing.

'hunds|ge'mein F *adj.* dirty, mean, scurvy; '~mise'rabel F *adj.* rotten, wretched, lousy; '2tage *m/pl.* dog-days *pl.*

Hüne ['hy:nə] *m* (-n/-n) giant.

Hunger ['huŋər] *m* (-s/no *pl.*) hunger (*fig. nach* for); ~ *bekommen* get hungry; ~ *haben* be *or* feel hungry; '~kur *f* starvation cure; '~leider F *m* (-s/-) starveling, poor devil; '~lohn *m* starvation wages *pl.*; '2n *v/i.* (ge-, h) hunger (*fig. nach* after, for); go without food; ~ *lassen* starve *s.o.*; '~snot *f* famine; '~streik *m* hunger-strike; '~tod *m* death from starvation; '~tuch *n*: *am* ~ *nagen* have nothing to bite.

'hungrig *adj.* hungry (*fig. nach* for).

Hupe *mot.* ['hu:pə] *f* (-/-n) horn, hooter; klaxon; '2n *v/i.* (ge-, h) sound one's horn, hoot.

hüpfen ['hypfən] *v/i.* (ge-, sein) hip, skip; gambol, frisk (about).

Hürde ['hyrdə] *f* (-/-n) hurdle; fold, pen; '~nrennen *n* hurdle-race.

Hure ['hu:rə] *f* (-/-n) whore, prostitute.

hurtig *adj.* ['hurtɪç] quick, swift; agile, nimble.

Husar ✕ [hu'za:r] *m* (-en/-en) hussar.

husch *int.* [huʃ] in *or* like a flash; shoo!; '~en *v/i.* (ge-, sein) slip, dart; *small animal*: scurry, scamper; *bat, etc.*: flit.

hüsteln ['hy:stəln] 1. *v/i.* (ge-, h) cough slightly; 2. 2 *n* (-s/no *pl.*) slight cough.

husten ['hu:stən] 1. *v/i.* (ge-, h) cough; 2. 2 *m* (-s/✕-) cough.

Hut [hu:t] 1. *m* (-[e]s/ᵘe) hat; *den* ~ *abnehmen* take off one's hat; ~ *ab vor* (*dat.*)! hats off to ...!; 2. *f* (-/no *pl.*) care, charge; guard; *auf der* ~ *sein* be on one's guard (*vor dat.* against).

hüte|n ['hy:tən] *v/t.* (ge-, h) guard, protect, keep watch over; keep (*secret*); tend (*sheep, etc.*); *das Bett* ~ be confined to (one's) bed; *sich* ~ *vor* (*dat.*) beware of; '2r *m* (-s/-) keeper, guardian; herdsman.

'Hut|futter *n* hat-lining; '~krempe *f* hat-brim; '~macher *m* (-s/-) hatter; '~nadel *f* hat-pin.

Hütte ['hytə] *f* (-/-n) hut; cottage, cabin; ⊕ metallurgical plant; *mount.*

refuge; '~nwesen ⊕ *n* metallurgy, metallurgical engineering.
Hyäne *zo.* [hy'ɛ:nə] *f* (-/-n) hy(a)ena.
Hyazinthe ♀ [hya'tsintə] *f* (-/-n) hyacinth. [hydrant.]
Hydrant [hy'drant] *m* (-en/-en)
Hydraulik *phys.* [hy'draʊlik] *f* (-/*no pl.*) hydraulics *pl.*; ♀**sch** *adj.* hydraulic.
Hygiene [hy'gje:nə] *f* (-/*no pl.*) hygiene; ♀**isch** *adj.* hygienic(al).
Hymne ['hymnə] *f* (-/-n) hymn.
Hypnose [hyp'no:zə] *f* (-/-n) hypnosis; ♀**tisieren** [~oti'zi:rən] *v/t. and v/i. (no -ge-, h)* hypnotize.

Hypochonder [hypo'xɔndər] *m* (-s/-) hypochondriac; ♀**risch** *adj.* hypochondriac.
Hypotenuse ♫ [hypote'nu:zə] *f* (-/-n) hypotenuse.
Hypothek [hypo'te:k] *f* (-/-en) mortgage; e-e ~ *aufnehmen* raise a mortgage; ♀**arisch** *adj.* [~e'ka:riʃ]: ~*e Belastung* mortgage.
Hypothese [hypo'te:zə] *f* (-/-n) hypothesis; ♀**tisch** *adj.* hypothetical.
Hysterie *psych.* [hyste'ri:] *f* (-/-n) hysteria; ♀**isch** *psych. adj.* [~'te:riʃ] hysterical.

I

ich [iç] 1. *pers. pron.* I; 2. ♀ *n* (-[s]/ -[s]) self; *psych. the* ego.
Ideal [ide'a:l] 1. *n* (-s/-e) ideal; 2. ♀ *adj.* ideal; ♀**isieren** [~ali'zi:rən] *v/t. (no -ge-, h)* idealize; ~**ismus** [~a'lismus] *m* (-/*Idealismus*) idealism; ~**ist** [~a'list] *m* (-en/-en) idealist.
Idee [i'de:] *f* (-/-n) idea, notion.
identifizieren [identifi'tsi:rən] *v/t. (no -ge-, h)* identify; *sich* ~ identify o.s.; ~**sch** *adj.* [i'dentiʃ] identical; ♀**tät** [~'tɛ:t] *f* (-/*no pl.*) identity.
Ideologie [ideolo'gi:] *f* (-/-n) ideology; ♀**isch** *adj.* [~'lo:giʃ] ideological.
Idiot [idi'o:t] *m* (-en/-en) idiot; ~**ie** [~o'ti:] *f* (-/-n) idiocy; ♀**isch** *adj.* [~'o:tiʃ] idiotic.
Idol [i'do:l] *n* (-s/-e) idol.
Igel *zo.* ['i:gəl] *m* (-s/-) hedgehog.
Ignorant [igno'rant] *m* (-en/-en) ignorant person, ignoramus; ~**anz** [~ts] *f* (-/*no pl.*) ignorance; ♀**ieren** *v/t. (no -ge-, h)* ignore, take no notice of.
ihm *pers. pron.* [i:m] *p.* (to) him; *thing:* (to) it.
ihn *pers. pron.* [i:n] *p.* him; *thing:* it.
ihnen *pers. pron.* (to) them; *Ihnen sg. and pl.* (to) you.
ihr [i:r] 1. *pers. pron.:* (*2nd pl. nom.*) you; (*3rd pl. dat.*) (to) her; 2. *poss. pron.:* her; their; *Ihr sg. and pl.* your; *der (die, das)* ~*e* hers; theirs; *der (die, das) Ihre sg. and pl.* yours; ~**erseits** ['~ɔr'zaits] *adv.* on her part; on their part; *Ihrerseits sg. and pl.* on your part; '~**es'gleichen** *pron.* (of) her *or* their kind, her *or* their equal; *Ihresgleichen sg.* (of) your kind, your equal; *pl.* (of) your kind, your equals; '~**et'wegen** *adv.* for her *or* their sake, on her *or* their account; *Ihretwegen sg. or pl.* for your sake, on your account; '~**etwillen** *adv.:* um ~ *s. ihretwegen;*

~**ige** *poss. pron.* ['~igə]: *der (die, das)* ~ hers; theirs; *der (die, das) Ihrige* yours.
illegitim *adj.* [ilegi'ti:m] illegitimate.
illusorisch *adj.* [ilu'zo:riʃ] illusory, deceptive.
illustrieren [ilu'stri:rən] *v/t. (no -ge-, h)* illustrate.
Iltis *zo.* ['iltis] *m* (-ses/-se) fitchew, polecat.
im *prp.* [im] = *in dem.*
imaginär *adj.* [imagi'nɛ:r] imaginary.
'**Imbiß** *m* light meal, snack; '~**stube** *f* snack bar.
Imker ['imkər] *m* (-s/-) bee-master, bee-keeper.
immatrikulieren [imatriku'li:rən] *v/t. (no -ge-, h)* matriculate, enrol(l); *sich* ~ *lassen* matriculate, enrol(l).
immer *adv.* ['imər] always; ~ *mehr* more and more; ~ *wieder* again and again; *für* ~ for ever, for good; '♀**grün** ♀ *n* (-s/-e) evergreen; '~'**hin** *adv.* still, yet; '~'**zu** *adv.* always, continually.
Immobilien [imo'bi:ljən] *pl.* immovables *pl.*, real estate; ~**händler** *m s. Grundstücksmakler.*
immun *adj.* [i'mu:n] immune (*gegen* against, from); ♀**ität** [~uni'tɛ:t] *f* (-/*no pl.*) immunity.
Imperativ *gr.* ['imperati:f] *m* (-s/-e) imperative (mood).
Imperfekt *gr.* ['imperfɛkt] *n* (-s/-e) imperfect (tense), past tense.
Imperialismus [imperia'lismus] *m* (-/*no pl.*) imperialism; ~**t** *m* (-en/-en) imperialist; ♀**tisch** *adj.* imperialistic.
impertinent *adj.* [imperti'nɛnt] impertinent, insolent.
impfen ⚕ ['impfən] *v/t.* (ge-, h) vaccinate; inoculate; '♀**schein** *m* certificate of vaccination *or* inoculation; '♀**stoff** ⚕ *m* vaccine,

serum; '**Qung** *f* (-/-en) vaccination; inoculation.

imponieren [impo'ni:rən] *v/i.* (*no* -ge-, *h*): *j-m* ~ impress s.o.

Import ✝ [im'port] *m* (-[e]s/-e) import(ation); **~eur** ✝ [~'tø:r] *m* (-s/-e) importer; **Qieren** [~'ti:rən] *v/t.* (*no* -ge-, *h*) import.

imposant *adj.* [impo'zant] imposing, impressive.

imprägnieren [imprɛ'gni:rən] *v/t.* (*no* -ge-, *h*) impregnate; (water-)proof (*raincoat, etc.*).

improvisieren [improvi'zi:rən] *v/t. and v/i.* (*no* -ge-, *h*) improvise.

Im'puls *m* (-es/-e) impuls; **Qiv** *adj.* [~'zi:f] impulsive. [be able.]

imstande *adj.* [im'ʃtandə]: ~ *sein*

in *prp.* (*dat.*; *acc.*) [in] **1.** *place*: in, at; within; into, in; *with names of important towns*: in, ʒɢ at, of; *with names of villages and less important towns*: at; *im Hause* in the house, indoors, in; *im ersten Stock* on the first floor; ~ *der Schule* (*im Theater*) at school (the theat[re, *Am.* -er); ~ *die Schule* (~*s Theater*) to school (the theat[re, *Am.* -er); ~ *England* in England; *waren Sie schon einmal in England?* have you ever been to England?; **2.** *time*: in, at; during; within; ~ *drei Tagen* (with)in three days; *heute ~ vierzehn Tagen* today fortnight; *im Jahre 1960* in 1960; *im Februar* in February; *im Frühling* in (the) spring; ~ *der Nacht* at night; ~ *letzter Zeit* lately, of late, recently; **3.** *mode*: ~ *großer Eile* in great haste; ~ *Frieden leben* live at peace; ~ *Reichweite* within reach; **4.** *condition, state*: *im Alter von fünfzehn Jahren* at (the age of) fifteen; ~ *Behandlung* under treatment.

'**Inbegriff** *m* (quint)essence; embodiment, incarnation; paragon; '**Qen** *adj.* included, inclusive (of).

'**Inbrunst** *f* (-/*no pl.*) ardo(u)r, fervo(u)r.

'**inbrünstig** *adj.* ardent, fervent.

in'dem *cj.* whilst, while; by (*ger.*); ~ *er mich ansah, sagte er* looking at me he said.

Inder ['indər] *m* (-s/-) Indian.

in'des(sen) **1.** *adv.* meanwhile; **2.** *cj.* while; however.

Indianer [in'dja:nər] *m* (-s/-) (American *or* Red) Indian.

Indikativ *gr.* ['indikati:f] *m* (-s/-e) indicative (mood).

'**indirekt** *adj.* indirect.

'**indisch** *adj.* ['indiʃ] Indian.

'**indiskret** *adj.* indiscreet; **Qion** [~e'tsjo:n] *f* (-/-en) indiscretion.

indiskutabel *adj.* ['indiskuta:bəl] out of the question.

individu|ell *adj.* [individu'ɛl] individual; **Qum** [~'vi:duum] *n* (-s/ *Individuen*) individual.

10*

Indizienbeweis ʒɢ [in'di:tsjən-] *m* circumstantial evidence.

Indoss|ament ✝ [indɔsa'mɛnt] *n* (-s/-e) endorsement, indorsement; **Qieren** ✝ [~'si:rən] *v/t.* (*no* -ge-, *h*) indorse, endorse.

Industrialisierung [industriali'zi:-ruŋ] *f* (-/-en) industrialization.

Industrie [indus'tri:] *f* (-/-n) industry; **~anlage** *f* industrial plant; **~arbeiter** *m* industrial worker; **~ausstellung** *f* industrial exhibition; **~erzeugnis** *n* industrial product; **~gebiet** *n* industrial district *or* area; **Qll** *adj.* [~i'ɛl] industrial; **~lle** [~i'ɛlə] *m* (-n/-n) industrialist; **~staat** *m* industrial country.

ineinander *adv.* [in²aɪ'nandər] into one another; **~greifen** ⊕ *v/i.* (*irr.* greifen, *sep.,* -ge-, *h*) gear into one another, interlock.

infam *adj.* [in'fa:m] infamous.

Infanter|ie ✕ [infantə'ri:] *f* (-/-n) infantry; **~ist** ✕ *m* (-en/-en) infantryman.

Infektion 𝒮 [infɛk'tsjo:n] *f* (-/-en) infection; **~skrankheit** 𝒮 *f* infectious disease.

Infinitiv *gr.* ['infiniti:f] *m* (-s/-e) infinitive (mood).

infizieren [infi'tsi:rən] *v/t.* (*no* -ge-, *h*) infect. [flation.]

Inflation [infla'tsjo:n] *f* (-/-en) in-

in'folge *prp.* (*gen.*) in consequence of, owing *or* due to; **~'dessen** *adv.* consequently.

Inform|ation [informa'tsjo:n] *f* (-/-en) information; **Qieren** [~'mi:rən] *v/t.* (*no* -ge-, *h*) inform; *falsch* ~ misinform.

Ingenieur [inʒe'njø:r] *m* (-s/-e) engineer.

Ingwer ['iŋvər] *m* (-s/*no pl.*) ginger.

Inhaber ['inha:bər] *m* (-s/-) owner, proprietor (*of business or shop*); occupant (*of flat*); keeper (*of shop*); holder (*of office, share, etc.*); bearer (*of cheque, etc.*).

'**Inhalt** *m* (-[e]s/-e) contents *pl.* (*of bottle, book, etc.*); tenor (*of speech*); *geom.* volume; capacity (*of vessel*).

'**Inhalts|angabe** *f* summary; '**Qlos** *adj.* empty, devoid of substance; '**Qreich** *adj.* full of meaning; *life*: rich, full; '**~verzeichnis** *n on parcel*: list of contents; *in book*: table of contents.

Initiative [initsja'ti:və] *f* (-/*no pl.*) initiative; *die* ~ *ergreifen* take the initiative.

Inkasso ✝ [in'kaso] *n* (-s/-s, *Inkassi*) collection.

'**inkonsequen|t** *adj.* inconsistent; '**Qz** [~ts] *f* (-/-en) inconsistency.

In'krafttreten *n* (-s/*no pl.*) coming into force, taking effect (*of new law, etc.*).

'**Inland** *n* (-[e]s/*no pl.*) home (country); inland.

inländisch adj. ['inlɛndiʃ] native; inland; home; domestic; *product*: home-made.

Inlett ['inlet] n (-[e]s/-e) bedtick.

in'mitten prp. (gen.) in the midst of, amid(st).

'inne|haben v/t. (irr. haben, sep., -ge-, h) possess, hold (*office, record, etc.*); occupy (*flat*); '~halten v/i. (irr. halten, sep., -ge-, h) stop, pause.

innen adv. ['inən] inside, within; indoors; nach ~ inwards.

'Innen|architekt m interior decorator; '~ausstattung f interior decoration, fittings pl., furnishing; '~minister m minister of the interior; Home Secretary, Am. Secretary of the Interior; '~ministerium n ministry of the interior; Home Office, Am. Department of the Interior; '~politik f domestic policy; '~seite f inner side, inside; '~stadt f city, Am. downtown.

inner adj. ['inər] interior; inner; ⚓, pol. internal; '2e n (-n/no pl.) interior; Minister(ium) des Innern s. Innenminister(ium); 2eien [~'raiən] f/pl. offal(s pl.); '~halb 1. prp. (gen.) within; 2. adv. within, inside; '~lich adv. inwardly; esp. ⚓ internally.

innig adj. ['iniç] intimate, close; affectionate.

Innung ['inuŋ] f (-/-en) guild, corporation.

inoffiziell adj. ['in⁹-] unofficial.

ins prp. [ins] = in das.

Insasse ['inzasə] m (-n/-n) inmate, occupant, passenger (*of car*).

'Inschrift f inscription; legend (*on coin, etc.*).

Insekt zo. [in'zekt] n (-[e]s/-en) insect.

Insel ['inzəl] f (-/-n) island; '~bewohner m islander.

Inser|at [inzə'ra:t] n (-[e]s/-e) advertisement, F ad; 2ieren [~'ri:rən] v/t. and v/i. (no -ge-, h) advertise.

insge|'heim adv. secretly; ~'samt adv. altogether.

in'sofern cj. so far; ~ als in so far as.

insolvent † adj. ['inzɔlvɛnt] insolvent.

Inspek|tion [inspɛk'tsjo:n] f (-/-en) inspection; ~or [in'spɛktɔr] m (-s/-en) inspector; surveyor; overseer.

inspirieren [inspi'ri:rən] v/t. (no -ge-, h) inspire.

inspizieren [inspi'tsi:rən] v/t. (no -ge-, h) inspect (*troops, etc.*); examine (*goods*); survey (*buildings*).

Install|ateur [instala'tø:r] m (-s/-e) plumber; (gas- or electrical) fitter; 2ieren [~'li:rən] v/t. (no -ge-, h) install.

instand adv. [in'ʃtant]: ~ halten keep in good order; keep up; ⊕

maintain; ~ setzen repair; 2haltung f maintenance; upkeep.

'inständig adv.: j-n ~ bitten implore or beseech s.o.

Instanz [in'stants] f (-/-en) authority; ⚖ instance; ~enweg ⚖ m stages of appeal; auf dem ~ through the prescribed channels.

Instinkt [in'stiŋkt] m (-[e]s/-e) instinct; 2iv adv. [~'ti:f] instinctively.

Institut [insti'tu:t] n (-[e]s/-e) institute.

Instrument [instru'mɛnt] n (-[e]s/-e) instrument.

inszenier|en esp. thea. [instse'ni:rən] v/t. (no -ge-, h) (put on the) stage; 2ung thea. f (-/-en) staging, production.

Integr|ation [integra'tsjo:n] f (-/-en) integration; 2ieren [~'gri:rən] v/t. (no -ge-, h) integrate.

intellektuell adj. [intelektu'ɛl] intellectual, highbrow; 2e m (-n/-n) intellectual, highbrow.

intelligen|t adj. [inteli'gɛnt] intelligent; 2z [~ts] f (-/-en) intelligence.

Intendant thea. [inten'dant] m (-en/-en) director.

intensiv adj. [inten'zi:f] intensive; intense.

interess|ant adj. [intere'sant] interesting; 2e [~'resə] n (-s/-n) interest (an dat., für in); 2engebiet [~'re-sən-] n field of interest; 2engemeinschaft [~'resən-] f community of interests; combine, pool, trust; 2ent [~'sɛnt] m (-en/-en) interested person or party; † prospective buyer, esp. Am. prospect; 2ieren [~'si:rən] v/t. (no -ge-, h) interest (für in); sich ~ für take an interest in.

intern adj. [in'tern] internal; 2at [~'na:t] n (-[e]s/-e) boarding-school.

international adj. [internatsjo'na:l] international.

inter|'nieren v/t. (no -ge-, h) intern; 2'nierung f (-/-en) internment; 2'nist ⚓ m (-en/-en) internal specialist, Am. internist.

inter|pretieren [interpre'ti:rən] v/t. (no -ge-, h) interpret; 2punktion [~puŋk'tsjo:n] f (-/-en) punctuation; 2vall [~'val] n (-s/-e) interval; 2venieren [~ve'ni:rən] v/i. (no -ge-, h) intervene; 2'zonenhandel m interzonal trade; 2'zonenverkehr m interzonal traffic.

intim adj. [in'ti:m] intimate (*mit* with); 2ität [~imi'tɛ:t] f (-/-en) intimacy.

'intoleran|t adj. intolerant; 2z ['~ts] f (-/-en) intolerance.

intransitiv gr. adj. ['intranziti:f] intransitive.

I.:trig|e [in'tri:gə] f (-/-n) intrigue, scheme, plot; 2ieren [~i'gi:rən] v/t. (no -ge-, h) intrigue, scheme, plot.

Invalid|e [inva'li:də] *m* (-n/-n) invalid; disabled person; **~enrente** *f* disability pension; **~ität** [~idi-'tɛːt] *f* (-/no pl.) disablement, disability.

Inventar [inven'taːr] *n* (-s/-e) inventory, stock.

Inventur ✝ [inven'tuːr] *f* (-/-en) stock-taking; **~ machen** take stock.

invest|ieren ✝ [inves'tiːrən] *v/t.* (no -ge-, *h*) invest; **⑨ition** ✝ [~i'tsjoːn] *f* (-/-en) investment.

inwie'fern *cj.* to what extent; in what way *or* respect; **~'weit** *cj.* how far, to what extent.

in'zwischen *adv.* in the meantime, meanwhile.

Ion *phys.* [i'oːn] *n* (-s/-en) ion.

ird|en *adj.* ['irdən] earthen; **~isch** *adj.* earthly; worldly; mortal.

Ire ['iːrə] *m* (-n/-n) Irishman; **die ~n** *pl.* the Irish *pl.*

irgend *adv.* ['irgənt] *in compounds:* some; any (*a. negative and in questions*); wenn ich ~ kann if I possibly can; **'~'ein(e)** *indef. pron. and adj.* some(one); any(one); **'~'einer** *indef. pron. s.* irgend jemand; **'~'ein(e)s** *indef. pron.* some; any; **~ etwas** *indef. pron.* something; anything; **~ jemand** *indef. pron.* someone; anyone; **'~'wann** *adv.* some time (*or* other); **'~'wie** *adv.* somehow; anyhow; **'~'wo** *adv.* somewhere; anywhere; **'~wo'her** *adv.* from somewhere; from anywhere; **'~wo'hin** *adv.* somewhere; anywhere.

'irisch *adj.* Irish.

Iron|ie [iro'niː] *f* (-/-n) irony; **⑨isch** *adj.* [i'roːnif] ironic(al).

irre ['irə] **1.** *adj.* confused; ✚ insane; mad; **2.** ⑨ *f* (-/no pl.): in die **~ gehen** go astray; **3.** ⑨ *m, f* (-n/-n) lunatic; mental patient; **wie ein ~r** like a madman; **~führen** *v/t.* (*sep.*, -ge-, *h*) lead astray; *fig.* mislead; **'~gehen** *v/i.* (*irr.* gehen, *sep.*, -ge-, *sein*) go astray, stray; lose one's way; **'~machen** *v/t.* (*sep.*, -ge-, *h*) puzzle, bewilder; perplex; confuse;

'~n 1. *v/i.* (ge-, *h*) err; wander; **2.** *v/refl.* (ge-, *h*) be mistaken (*in dat.* in *s.o.*, about *s.th.*); be wrong.

'Irren|anstalt ✚ *f* lunatic asylum, mental home *or* hospital; **'~arzt** *m* alienist, mental specialist; **'~haus** ✚ *n s.* Irrenanstalt.

'irrereden *v/i.* (*sep.*, -ge-, *h*) rave.

'Irr|fahrt *f* wandering; Odyssey; **'~garten** *m* labyrinth, maze; **'~glaube** *m* erroneous belief; false doctrine, heterodoxy; heresy; **'⑨gläubig** *adj.* heterodox; heretical; **'⑨ig** *adj.* erroneous, mistaken, false, wrong.

irritieren [iri'tiːrən] *v/t.* (no -ge-, *h*) irritate, annoy; confuse.

'Irr|lehre *f* false doctrine, heterodoxy; heresy; **'~licht** *n* will-o'-the-wisp, jack-o'-lantern; **'~sinn** *m* insanity; madness; **'⑨sinnig** *adj.* insane; mad; *fig.*: fantastic; terrible; **'~sinnige** *m, f* (-n/-n) *s.* irre 3; **'~tum** *m* (-s/⁼er) error, mistake; im ~ sein be mistaken; **⑨tümlich** ['~tyːmliç] **1.** *adj.* erroneous; **2.** *adv.* = **'⑨tümlicherweise** *adv.* by mistake; mistakenly, erroneously; **'~wisch** *m s.* Irrlicht; *p.* flibbertigibbet.

Ischias ✚ ['ifias] *f*, F *a.*: *n, m* (-/no pl.) sciatica.

Islam ['islam, is'laːm] *m* (-s/no pl.) Islam.

Isländ|er ['iːslɛndər] *m* (-s/-) Icelander; **'⑨isch** *adj.* Icelandic.

Isolator ⚡ [izo'laːtɔr] *m* (-s/-en) insulator.

Isolier|band ⚡ [izo'liːr-] *n* insulating tape; **⑨en** *v/t.* (no -ge-, *h*) isolate; **~masse** ⚡ *f* insulating compound; **~schicht** ⚡ *f* insulating layer; **~ung** *f* (-/-en) isolation (*a. ✚*); ✚ quarantine; ⚡ insulation.

Isotop ⚛, *phys.* [izo'toːp] *n* (-s/-e) isotope.

Israeli [isra'eːli] *m* (-s/-s) Israeli.

Italien|er [ital'jeːnər] *m* (-s/-) Italian; **⑨isch** *adj.* Italian.

I-Tüpfelchen *fig.* ['iːtypfəlçən] *n* (-s/-): bis aufs ~ to a T.

J

ja [jaː] **1.** *adv.* yes; ⚓, *parl.* aye, *Am. parl. a.* yea; ~ doch, ~ freilich yes, indeed; to be sure; *da ist er ~l* well, there he is!; *ich sagte es Ihnen ~* I told you so; *tut es ~ nicht!* don't you dare do it!; *vergessen Sie es ~ nicht!* be sure not to forget it!; **2.** *cj.*: ~ sogar, ~ selbst nay (even); *wenn ~* if so; *er ist ~ mein Freund* why, he is my friend; **3.** *int.*: ~, weißt du

denn nicht, daß why, don't you know that.

Jacht ⚓ [jaxt] *f* (-/-en) yacht; **'~klub** *m* yacht-club.

Jacke ['jakə] *f* (-/-n) jacket.

Jackett [ʒa'kɛt] *n* (-s/-e, -s) jacket.

Jagd [jaːkt] *f* (-/-en) hunt(ing); *with a gun:* shoot(ing); chase; *s.* Jagdrevier; *auf* (dat.) ~ *gehen* go hunting or shooting, *Am. a.* be gunning; ~ *machen auf* (acc.) hunt after *or* for;

'~aufseher m gamekeeper, Am. game warden; '~bomber ✗ m (-s/-) fighter-bomber; '~büchse f sporting rifle; '~flinte f sporting gun; fowling-piece; '~flugzeug ✗ n fighter (aircraft); '~geschwader ✗ n fighter wing, Am. fighter group; '~gesellschaft f hunting or shooting party; '~haus n shooting-box or -lodge, hunting-box or -lodge; '~hund m hound; '~hütte f shooting-box, hunting-box; '~pächter m game-tenant; '~rennen n steeplechase; '~revier n hunting-ground, shoot; '~schein m shooting licen|ce, Am. -se; '~schloß n hunting seat; '~tasche f game-bag.

jagen ['ja:gən] (ge-, h) 1. v/i. go hunting or shooting, hunt; shoot; rush, dash; 2. v/t. hunt; chase; aus dem Hause~ turn s.o. out (of doors).

Jäger ['je:gər] m (-s/-) hunter, huntsman, sportsman; ✗ rifleman; '~latein F fig. n huntsmen's yarn, tall stories pl. [jaguar.\

Jaguar ['ja:gua:r] m (-s/-e)\

jäh adj. [je:] sudden, abrupt; precipitous, steep.

Jahr [ja:r] n (-[e]s/-e) year; ein halbes ~ half a year, six months pl.; einmal im ~e once a year; im ~e 1900 in 1900; mit 18 ~en, im Alter von 18 ~en at (the age of) eighteen; letztes ~ last year; das ganze ~ hindurch or über all the year round; 2'aus adv.: ~, jahrein year in, year out; year after year; '~buch n yearbook, annual; '~ein adv. s. jahraus.

'jahrelang 1. adv. for years; 2. adj.: ~e Erfahrung (many) years of experience.

jähren ['je:rən] v/refl. (ge-, h): es jährt sich heute, daß ... it is a year ago today that ..., it is a year today since ...

'Jahres|abonnement n annual subscription (to magazine, etc.); thea. yearly season ticket; '~abschluß m annual statement of accounts; '~anfang m beginning of the year; zum ~ die besten Wünsche! best wishes for the New Year; '~bericht m annual report; '~einkommen n annual or yearly income; '~ende n end of the year; '~gehalt n annual salary; '~tag m anniversary; '~wechsel m turn of the year; '~zahl f date, year; '~zeit f season, time of the year.

'Jahrgang m volume, year (of periodical, etc.); p. age-group; univ., school: year, class; wine: vintage.

Jahr'hundert n (-s/-e) century; ~feier f centenary, Am. centennial; ~wende f turn of the century.

jährig adj. ['je:riç] one-year-old.

jährlich ['je:rliç] 1. adj. annual, yearly; 2. adv. every year; yearly, once a year.

'Jahr|markt m fair; ~tausend n (-s/-e) millennium; ~tausendfeier f millenary; ~zehnt n (-[e]s/-e) decade.

'Jähzorn m violent (fit of) temper; irascibility; '2ig adj. hot-tempered; irascible.

Jalousie [ʒalu'zi:] f (-/-n) (Venetian) blind, Am. a. window shade.

Jammer ['jamər] m (-s/no pl.) lamentation; misery; es ist ein ~ it is a pity.

jämmerlich adj. ['jemərliç] miserable, wretched; piteous; pitiable (esp. contp.).

jammer|n ['jamərn] v/i. (ge-, h) lament (nach, um for; über acc. over); moan; wail, whine; '2schade adj.: es ist ~ it is a thousand pities, it is a great shame.

Januar ['janua:r] m (-[s]/-e) January.

Japan|er [ja'pa:nər] m (-s/-) Japanese; die ~ pl. the Japanese pl.; 2isch adj. Japanese.

Jargon [ʒar'gõ] m (-s/-s) jargon, cant, slang.

Jasmin ♀ [jas'mi:n] m (-s/-e) jasmin(e), jessamin(e).

'Jastimme parl. f aye, Am. a. yea.

jäten ['je:tən] v/t. (ge-, h) weed.

Jauche ['jauxə] f (-/-n) ♪ liquid manure; sewage.

jauchzen ['jauxtsən] v/i. (ge-, h) exult, rejoice, cheer; vor Freude ~ shout for joy.

jawohl adv. [ja'vo:l] yes; yes, indeed; yes, certainly; that's right; ✗, etc.: yes, Sir!

'Jawort n consent; j-m das ~ geben accept s.o.'s proposal (of marriage).

je [je:] 1. adv. ever, at any time; always; ohne ihn ~ gesehen zu haben without ever having seen him; seit eh und ~ since time immemorial, always; distributive with numerals: ~ zwei two at a time, two each, two by two, by or in twos; sie bekamen ~ zwei Äpfel they received two apples each; für ~ zehn Wörter for every ten words; in Schachteln mit or zu ~ zehn Stück verpackt packed in boxes of ten; 2. cj.: ~ nach Größe according to or depending on size; ~ nachdem it depends; ~ nachdem, was er für richtig hält according as he thinks fit; ~ nachdem, wie er sich fühlt depending on how he feels; ~ mehr, desto besser the more the better; ~ länger, ~ lieber the longer the better; 3. prp.: die Birnen kosten e-e Mark ~ Pfund the pears cost one mark a pound; s. pro.

jede|(r, -s) indef. pron. ['je:də(r, -s)] every; any; of a group: each; of two persons: either; jeder, who-ever; jeden zweiten Tag every other day; '~n'falls adv. at all events, in any case; '**~rmann** *indef. pron.* everyone, everybody; '**~r'zeit** *adv.* always, at any time; '**~s'mal** *adv.* each *or* every time; **~ wenn** whenever.

jedoch *cj.* [je'dɔx] however, yet, nevertheless.

'**jeher** *adv.*: *von or seit* **~** at all times, always, from time immemorial.

jemals *adv.* ['je:ma:ls] ever, at any time.

jemand *indef. pron.* ['je:mant] someone, somebody; *with questions and negations*: anyone, anybody.

jene(r, -s) *dem. pron.* ['je:nə(r, -s)] that (one); *jene pl.* those *pl.*

jenseitig *adj.* ['jɛnzaitiç] opposite.

'**jenseits 1.** *prp.* (gen.) on the other side of, beyond, across; **2.** *adv.* on the other side, beyond; **3.** ♀ *n* (-/no *pl.*) the other *or* next world, the world to come, *the* beyond.

jetzig *adj.* ['jɛtsiç] present, existing; *prices, etc.*: current.

jetzt *adv.* [jɛtst] now, at present; *bis* **~** until now; so far; *eben* **~** just now; *erst* **~** only now; *für* **~** for the present; *gleich* **~** at once, right away; *noch* **~** even now; *von* **~** *an* from now on.

jeweilig *adj.* ['je:vailiç] respective; **~s** *adv.* ['**~**s] respectively, at a time; from time to time (*esp.* ♂).

Joch [jɔx] *n* (-[e]s/-e) yoke; *in mountains*: col, pass, saddle; ⚠ bay; '**~bein** *anat. n* cheek-bone.

Jockei ['dʒɔkeɪ] *m* (-s/-s) jockey.

Jod ♒ [jo:t] *n* (-[e]s/no *pl.*) iodine.

jodeln ['jo:dəln] *v/i.* (ge-, h) yodel.

Johanni [jo'hani] *n* (-/no *pl.*), **~s** [**~**s] *n* (-/no *pl.*) Midsummer day; **~s-beere** *f* currant; *rote* **~** red currant; **~stag** *m eccl.* St John's day; Midsummer day.

johlen ['jo:lən] *v/i.* (ge-, h) bawl, yell, howl.

Jolle ⚓ ['jɔlə] *f* (-/-n) jolly-boat, yawl, dinghy.

Jongleur [ʒõ'glø:r] *m* (-s/-e) juggler; **~ieren** *v/t. and v/i.* (no -ge-, h) juggle.

Journal [ʒur'na:l] *n* (-s/-e) journal; newspaper; magazine; diary; ⚓ log-book; '**~ist** [**~**a'list] *m* (-en/-en) journalist, *Am. a.* newspaperman.

Jubel ['ju:bəl] *m* (-s/no *pl.*) jubilation, exultation, rejoicing; cheering; '♀n *v/i.* (ge-, h) jubilate; exult, rejoice (*über acc.* at).

Jubilar [jubi'la:r] *m* (-s/-e) person celebrating his jubilee, *etc.*; **~äum** [**~**'ɛ:um] *n* (-s/ *Jubiläen*) jubilee.

Juchten ['juxtən] *m*, *n* (-s/no *pl.*), '**~leder** *n* Russia (leather).

jucken ['jukən] (ge-, h) **1.** *v/i.* itch; **2.** *v/t.* irritate, (make) itch; F *sich* **~** scratch (o.s.).

Jude ['ju:də] *m* (-n/-n) Jew; '♀n-**feindlich** *adj.* anti-Semitic; '**~n-**

tum *n* (-s/no *pl.*) Judaism; '**~nver-folgung** *f* persecution of Jews, Jew-baiting; pogrom.

Jüd|in ['jy:din] *f* (-/-nen) Jewess; ♀isch *adj.* Jewish.

Jugend ['ju:gənt] *f* (-/no *pl.*) youth; '**~amt** *n* youth welfare department; '**~buch** *n* book for the young; '**~freund** *m* friend of one's youth; school-friend; '**~fürsorge** *f* youth welfare; '**~gericht** *n* juvenile court; '**~herberge** *f* youth hostel; '**~jahre** *n/pl.* early years, youth; '**~krimi-nalität** *f* juvenile delinquency; '♀-**lich** *adj.* youthful, juvenile, young; '**~liche** *m, f* (-n/-n) young person; juvenile; young man, youth; young girl; teen-ager; '**~liebe** *f* early *or* first love, calf-love, *Am. a.* puppy love; old sweetheart *or* flame; '**~schriften** *f/pl.* books for the young; '**~schutz** *m* protection of children and young people; '**~streich** *m* youthful prank; '**~werk** *n* early work (*of author*); **~e** *f.a.* juvenilia *pl.*; '**~zeit** *f* (time *or* days of) youth.

Jugoslav|e [ju:go'sla:və] *m* (-en/-en) Jugoslav, Yugoslav; ♀isch *adj.* Jugoslav, Yugoslav.

Juli ['ju:li] *m* (-[s]/-s) July.

jung *adj.* [juŋ] young; youthful; *peas*: green; *beer, wine*: new; **~es** *Gemüse* young *or* early vegetables *pl.*; F *fig.* young people, small fry.

'**Junge 1.** *m* (-n/-n) boy, youngster; lad; fellow, chap, *Am.* guy; *cards*: knave, jack; **2.** *n* (-n/-n) young; puppy (*of dog*); kitten (*of cat*); calf (*of cow, elephant, etc.*); cub (*of beast of prey*); **~** *werfen* bring forth young; *ein* **~** *s* a young one; ♀**nhaft** *adj.* boyish; '**~nstreich** *m* boyish prank *or* trick.

jünger ['jyŋər] **1.** *adj.* younger, junior; *er ist drei Jahre* **~** *als ich* he is my junior by three years, he is three years younger than I; **2.** ♀ *m* (-s/-) disciple.

Jungfer ['juŋfər] *f* (-/-n): *alte* **~** old maid *or* spinster.

'**Jungfern|fahrt** ⚓ *f* maiden voyage *or* trip; '**~flug** 🦅 *m* maiden flight; '**~rede** *f* maiden speech.

'**Jung|frau** *f* maid(en), virgin; ♀**-fräulich** *adj.* ['**~**frɔyliç] virginal; *fig.* virgin; '**~fräulichkeit** *f* (-/no *pl.*) virginity, maidenhood; '**~ge-selle** *m* bachelor; '**~gesellenstand** *m* bachelorhood; '**~gesellin** *f* (-/-nen) bachelor girl.

Jüngling ['jyŋliŋ] *m* (-s/-e) youth, young man.

jüngst [jyŋst] **1.** *adj.* youngest; *time*: (most) recent, latest; *das* ♀*e Ge-richt, der* ♀*e Tag* Last Judg(e)ment, Day of Judg(e)ment; **2.** *adv.* recently, lately.

'**jungverheiratet** *adj.* newly married; ♀*en pl. the* newlyweds *pl.*

Juni ['ju:ni] m (-[s]/-s) June; **~käfer** zo. m cockchafer, June-bug.

junior ['ju:njɔr] 1. adj. junior; 2. ♀ m (-s/-en) junior (a. sports).

Jura ['ju:ra] n/pl.: ~ studieren read or study law.

Jurist [ju'rist] m (-en/-en) lawyer; law-student; ♀isch adj. legal.

Jury [ʒy'ri:] f (-/-s) jury.

justier|en ⊕ [jus'ti:rən] v/t. (no -ge-, h) adjust; ♀ung ⊕ f (-/-en) adjustment.

Justiz [ju'sti:ts] f (-/no pl.) (administration of) justice; **~beamte** m judicial officer; **~gebäude** n courthouse; **~inspektor** m judicial officer; **~irrtum** m judicial error; **~minister** m minister of justice; Lord Chancellor, Am. Attorney General; **~ministerium** n ministry of justice; Am. Department of Justice; **~mord** m judicial murder.

Juwel [ju've:l] m, n (-s/-en) jewel, gem; **~en** pl. jewel(le)ry; **~ier** [~e'li:r] m (-s/-e) jewel(l)er.

Jux F [juks] m (-es/-e) (practical) joke, fun, spree, lark; prank.

K

(Compare also C and Z)

Kabel ['kɑ:bəl] n (-s/-) cable.

Kabeljau ichth. ['kɑ:bəljau] m (-s/-e, -s) cod(fish).

'kabeln v/t. and v/i. (ge-, h) cable.

Kabine [ka'bi:nə] f (-/-n) cabin; at hairdresser's, etc.: cubicle; cage (of lift).

Kabinett pol. [kabi'net] n (-s/-e) cabinet, government.

Kabriolett [kabrio'let] n (-s/-e) cabriolet, convertible.

Kachel ['kaxəl] f (-/-n) (Dutch or glazed) tile; **~ofen** m tiled stove.

Kadaver [ka'dɑ:vər] m (-s/-) carcass.

Kadett [ka'det] m (-en/-en) cadet.

Käfer zo. ['kɛ:fər] m (-s/-) beetle, chafer.

Kaffee ['kafe, ka'fe:] m (-s/-s) coffee; (')**~bohne** ♀ f coffee-bean; (')**~kanne** f coffee-pot; (')**~mühle** f coffee-mill or -grinder; (')**~satz** m coffee-grounds pl.; (')**~tasse** f coffee-cup.

Käfig ['kɛ:fiç] m (-s/-e) cage (a. fig.).

kahl adj. [kɑ:l] p. bald; tree, etc.: bare; landscape, etc.: barren, bleak; rock, etc.: naked; ♀kopf m baldhead, baldpate; **~köpfig** adj. ['kœpfiç] bald(-headed).

Kahn [kɑ:n] m (-[e]s/♂e) boat; riverbarge; ~ fahren go boating; **~fahren** n (-s/no pl.) boating.

Kai [kai] m (-s/-e, -s) quay, wharf.

Kaiser ['kaizər] m (-s/-) emperor; **~krone** f imperial crown; ♀lich adj. imperial; **~reich** n, **~tum** n (-[e]s/♂er) empire; **~würde** f imperial status.

Kajüte ♣ [ka'jy:tə] f (-/-n) cabin.

Kakao [ka'kɑ:o] m (-s/-s) cocoa; ♀ a. cacao.

Kakt|ee ♀ [kak'te:(ə)] f (-/-n), **~us** ♀ ['~us] m (-/Kakteen, F Kaktusse) cactus.

Kalauer ['kɑ:lauər] m (-s/-) stale joke; pun.

Kalb zo. [kalp] n (-[e]s/♂er) calf; ♀en ['~bən] v/i. (ge-, h) calve; **~fell** n calfskin; **~fleisch** n veal; **~leder** n calf(-leather).

'Kalbs|braten m roast veal; **~keule** f leg of veal; ~ s. Kalbleder; **~nierenbraten** m loin of veal.

Kalender [ka'lendər] m (-s/-) calendar; almanac; **~block** m dateblock; **~jahr** n calendar year; **~uhr** f calendar watch or clock.

Kali ♠ ['kɑ:li] n (-s/-s) potash.

Kaliber [ka'li:bər] n (-s/-) calib|re, Am. -er (a. fig.), bore (of firearm).

Kalk [kalk] m (-[e]s/-e) lime; geol. limestone; **~brenner** m limeburner; ♀en v/t. (ge-, h) whitewash (wall, etc.); ♠ lime (field); ♀ig adj. limy; **~ofen** m limekiln; **~stein** m limestone; **~steinbruch** m limestone quarry.

Kalorie [kalo'ri:] f (-/-n) calorie.

kalt adj. [kalt] climate, meal, sweat, etc.: cold; p., manner, etc.: cold, chilly, frigid; mir ist ~ I am cold; **~e** Küche cold dishes pl. or meat, etc.; j-m die **~e** Schulter zeigen give s.o. the cold shoulder; **~blütig** adj. ['~bly:tiç] cold-blooded (a. fig.).

Kälte ['keltə] f (-/no pl.) cold; chill; coldness, chilliness (both a. fig.); vor ~ zittern shiver with cold; fünf Grad ~ five degrees below zero; **~grad** m degree below zero; **~welle** f cold spell.

'kalt|stellen fig. v/t. (sep., -ge-, h) shelve, reduce to impotence; ♀**welle** f cold wave.

kam [kɑ:m] pret. of kommen.

Kamel zo. [ka'me:l] n (-[e]s/-e) camel; **~haar** n textiles: camel hair.

Kamera phot. ['kaməra] f (-/-s) camera.

Kamerad [kamə'raːt] *m* (-en/-en) comrade; companion; mate, F pal, chum; **~schaft** *f* (-/-en) comradeship, companionship; **2schaftlich** *adj.* comradely, companionable.

Kamille ♀ [ka'milə] *f* (-/-n) camomile; **~ntee** *m* camomile tea.

Kamin [ka'miːn] *m* (-s/-e) chimney (*a. mount.*); fireplace, fireside; **~sims** *m*, *n* mantelpiece; **~vorleger** *m* hearth-rug; **~vorsetzer** *m* (-s/-) fender.

Kamm [kam] *m* (-[e]s/⸗e) comb; crest (*of bird or wave*); crest, ridge (*of mountain*).

kämmen ['kɛmən] *v/t.* (ge-, *h*) comb; *sich* (*die Haare*) **~** comb one's hair.

Kammer ['kamər] *f* (-/-n) (small) room; closet; *pol.* chamber; board; ⸗⸗ division (*of court*); **~diener** *m* valet; **~frau** *f* lady's maid; **~gericht** ⸗⸗ *n* supreme court; **~herr** *m* chamberlain; **~jäger** *m* vermin exterminator; **~musik** *f* chamber music; **~zofe** *f* chambermaid.

'Kamm|garn *n* worsted (yarn); **~rad** ⊕ *n* cogwheel.

Kampagne [kam'panjə] *f* (-/-n) campaign.

Kampf [kampf] *m* (-[e]s/⸗e) combat, fight (*a. fig.*); struggle (*a. fig.*); battle (*a. fig.*); *fig.* conflict; *sports*: contest, match; *boxing*: fight, bout; **~bahn** *f sports*: stadium, arena; **2bereit** *adj.* ready for battle.

kämpfen ['kɛmpfən] *v/i.* (ge-, *h*) fight (*gegen* against; *mit* with; *um* for) (*a. fig.*); struggle (*a. fig.*); *fig.* contend, wrestle (*mit* with).

Kampfer ['kampfər] *m* (-s/*no pl.*) camphor.

Kämpfer ['kɛmpfər] *m* (-s/-) fighter (*a. fig.*); ⚔ combatant, warrior.

'Kampf|flugzeug *n* tactical aircraft; **~geist** *m* fighting spirit; **~platz** *m* battlefield; *fig., sports*: arena; **~preis** *m sports*: prize; ✝ cut-throat price; **~richter** *m* referee, judge, umpire; **'2unfähig** *adj.* disabled.

kampieren [kam'piːrən] *v/i.* (*no* -ge-, *h*) camp.

Kanal [ka'naːl] *m* (-s/⸗e) canal; channel (*a.* ⊕, *fig.*); *geogr. the* Channel; sewer, drain; **~isation** [~aliza'tsjoːn] *f* (-/-en) *river*: canalization; *town, etc.*: sewerage; drainage; **2isieren** [~ali'ziːrən] *v/t.* (*no* -ge-, *h*) canalize; sewer.

Kanarienvogel *orn.* [ka'naːrjən-] *m* canary(-bird).

Kandare [kan'daːrə] *f* (-/-n) curb (-bit).

Kandid|at [kandi'daːt] *m* (-en/-en) candidate; applicant; **~atur** [~a'tuːr] *f* (-/-en) candidature, candidacy; **2ieren** [~'diːrən] *v/i.* (*no* -ge-, *h*) be a candidate (*für* for);

~ *für* apply for, stand for, *Am.* run for (*office, etc.*).

Känguruh *zo.* ['kɛŋguruː] *n* (-s/-s) kangaroo.

Kaninchen *zo.* [ka'niːnçən] *n* (-s/-) rabbit; **~bau** *m* rabbit-burrow.

Kanister [ka'nistər] *m* (-s/-) can.

Kanne ['kanə] *f* (-/-n) milk, etc.: jug; coffee, tea: pot; oil, milk: can; **~gießer** F *fig. m* political wiseacre.

Kannibal|e [kani'baːlə] *m* (-n/-n) cannibal; **2isch** *adj.* cannibal.

kannte ['kantə] *pret. of* kennen.

Kanon ♪ ['kaːnɔn] *m* (-s/-s) canon.

Kanon|ade ⚔ [kano'naːdə] *f* (-/-n) cannonade; **~e** [~'noːnə] *f* (-/-n) ⚔ cannon, gun; F *fig.*: big shot; *esp. sports*: ace, crack.

Ka'nonen|boot ⚔ *n* gunboat; **~donner** *m* boom of cannon; **~futter** *fig. n* cannon-fodder; **~kugel** *f* cannon-ball; **~rohr** *n* gun barrel.

Kanonier ⚔ [kano'niːr] *m* (-s/-e) gunner.

Kant|e ['kantə] *f* (-/-n) edge; brim; **~en** *m* (-s/-) end of loaf; **2en** *v/t.* (ge-, *h*) square (*stone, etc.*); set on edge; tilt; edge (*skis*); **2ig** *adj.* angular, edged; square(d).

Kantine [kan'tiːnə] *f* (-/-n) canteen.

Kanu ['kaːnu] *n* (-s/-s) canoe.

Kanüle ⚕ [ka'nyːlə] *f* (-/-n) tubule, cannula.

Kanzel ['kantsəl] *f* (-/-n) *eccl.* pulpit; ✈ cockpit; ⚔ (gun-)turret.; **~redner** *m* preacher.

Kanzlei [kants'lai] *f* (-/-en) office.

'Kanzler *m* (-s/-) chancellor.

Kap *geogr.* [kap] *n* (-s/-s) headland.

Kapazität [kapatsi'tɛːt] *f* (-/-en) capacity; *fig.* authority.

Kapell|e [ka'pɛlə] *f* (-/-n) *eccl.* chapel; ♪ band; **~meister** *m* band-leader, conductor.

kaper|n ⚓ ['kaːpərn] *v/t.* (ge-, *h*) capture, seize; **2schiff** *n* privateer.

kapieren F [ka'piːrən] *v/t.* (*no* -ge-, *h*) grasp, get.

Kapital [kapi'taːl] **1.** *n* (-s/-e, -ien) capital, stock, funds *pl.*; **~** *und* Zinsen principal and interest; **2.** ♀ *adj.* capital; **~anlage** *f* investment; **~flucht** *f* flight of capital; **~gesellschaft** *f* joint-stock company; **2isieren** [~ali'ziːrən] *v/t.* (*no* -ge-, *h*) capitalize; **~ismus** [~a'lismus] *m* (-/*no pl.*) capitalism; **~ist** [~a'list] *m* (-en/-en) capitalist; **~markt** [~'taːl-] *m* capital market; **~verbrechen** *n* capital crime.

Kapitän [kapi'tɛːn] *m* (-s/-e) captain; **~** *zur* See naval captain; **~leutnant** *m* (senior) lieutenant.

Kapitel [ka'pitəl] *n* (-s/-) chapter (*a. fig.*).

Kapitul|ation ⚔ [kapitula'tsjoːn] *f* (-/-en) capitulation, surrender; **2ieren** [~'liːrən] *v/i.* (*no* -ge-, *h*) capitulate, surrender.

Kaplan *eccl.* [ka'plɑːn] *m* (-s/ᵘe) chaplain.

Kappe ['kapə] *f* (-/-n) cap; hood (*a.* ⊕); bonnet; **~n** *v/t.* (ge-, h) cut (*cable*); lop, top (*tree*).

Kapriole [kapri'oːlə] *f* (-/-n) equitation: capriole; *fig.*: caper; prank.

Kapsel ['kapsəl] *f* (-/-n) case, box; ♀, ♂, *anat.*, *etc.*: capsule.

kaputt *adj.* [ka'put] broken; *elevator*, *etc.*: out of order; *fruit*, *etc.*: spoilt; *p.*: ruined; tired out, F fagged out; **~gehen** *v/i.* (irr. gehen, *sep.*, -ge-, sein) break, go to pieces; spoil.

Kapuze [ka'puːtsə] *f* (-/-n) hood; *eccl.* cowl.

Karabiner [kara'biːnər] *m* (-s/-) carbine.

Karaffe [ka'rafə] *f* (-/-n) carafe (*for wine or water*); decanter (*for liqueur*, *etc.*).

Karambol|age [karambo'lɑːʒə] *f* (-/-n) collision, crash; *billiards*: cannon, *Am. a.* carom; **2ieren** *v/i.* (no -ge-, sein) cannon, *Am. a.* carom; F *fig.* collide.

Karat [ka'rɑːt] *n* (-[e]s/-e) carat.

Karawane [kara'vɑːnə] *f* (-/-n) caravan.

Karbid [kar'biːt] *n* (-[e]s/-e) carbide.

Kardinal *eccl.* [kardi'nɑːl] *m* (-s/ᵘe) cardinal.

Karfreitag *eccl.* [kɑr'-] *m* Good Friday.

karg *adj.* [kark] *soil*: meagre; *vegetation*: scant, sparse; *meal*: scanty, meagre, frugal; **~en** ['~gən] *v/i.* (ge-, h): **~ mit** be sparing of.

kärglich *adj.* ['kɛrkliç] scanty, meagre; poor.

kariert *adj.* [ka'riːrt] check(ed), chequered, *Am.* checkered.

Karik|atur [karika'tuːr] *f* (-/-en) caricature, cartoon; **2ieren** [~'kiːrən] *v/t.* (no -ge-, h) caricature, cartoon.

karmesin *adj.* [karme'ziːn] crimson.

Karneval ['karnəval] *m* (-s/-e, -s) Shrovetide, carnival.

Karo ['kɑːro] *n* (-s/-s) square, check; *cards*: diamonds *pl.*

Karosserie *mot.* [karosə'riː] *f* (-/-n) body.

Karotte ♀ [ka'rɔtə] *f* (-/-n) carrot.

Karpfen *ichth.* ['karpfən] *m* (-s/-) carp.

Karre ['karə] *f* (-/-n) cart; wheelbarrow.

Karriere [kar'jeːrə] *f* (-/-n) (successful) career.

Karte ['kartə] *f* (-/-n) card; postcard; map; chart; ticket; menu, bill of fare; list.

Kartei [kar'tai] *f* (-/-en) card-index; **~karte** *f* index-card, filing-card; **~schrank** *m* filing cabinet.

Kartell † [kar'tel] *n* (-s/-e) cartel.

'Karten|brief *m* letter-card; **'~haus** *n* ⊕ chart-house; *fig.* house of cards; **'~legerin** *f* (-/-nen) fortuneteller from the cards; **'~spiel** *n* card-playing; card-game.

Kartoffel [kar'tɔfəl] *f* (-/-n) potato, F spud; **~brei** *m* mashed potatoes *pl.*; **~käfer** *m* Colorado *or* potato beetle, *Am. a.* potato bug; **~schalen** *f/pl.* potato peelings *pl.*

Karton [kar'tõː, kar'tɔːn] *m* (-s/-s, -e) cardboard, pasteboard; cardboard box, carton. [*Kartei.*]

Kartothek [karto'teːk] *f* (-/-en) *s.*]

Karussell [karu'sɛl] *n* (-s/-s, -e) roundabout, merry-go-round, *Am. a.* car(r)ousel.

Karwoche *eccl.* ['kɑr-] *f* Holy *or* Passion Week.

Käse ['kɛːzə] *m* (-s/-) cheese.

Kasern|e ⚔ [ka'zɛrnə] *f* (-/-n) barracks *pl.*; **~enhof** *m* barrack-yard *or* -square; **2ieren** [~'niːrən] *v/t.* (no -ge-, h) quarter in barracks, barrack.

käsig *adj.* cheesy; *complexion*: pale, pasty.

Kasino [ka'ziːno] *n* (-s/-s) casino, club(-house); (officers') mess.

Kasperle ['kaspərlə] *n*, *m* (-s/-) Punch; **~theater** *n* Punch and Judy show.

Kasse ['kasə] *f* (-/-n) cash-box; till (*in shop*, *etc.*); cash-desk, pay-desk (*in bank*, *etc.*); pay-office (*in firm*); *thea.*, *etc.*: box-office, booking-office; cash; **bei ~** in cash.

'Kassen|abschluß † *m* balancing of the cash (accounts); **'~anweisung** *f* disbursement voucher; **'~bestand** *m* cash in hand; **'~bote** *m* bank messenger; **'~buch** *n* cash book; **'~erfolg** *m* *thea.*, *etc.*: box-office success; **'~patient** ♂ *m* panel patient; **'~schalter** *m* *bank*, *etc.*: teller's counter.

Kasserolle [kasə'rɔlə] *f* (-/-n) stewpan, casserole.

Kassette [ka'setə] *f* (-/-n) box (*for money*, *etc.*); casket (*for jewels*, *etc.*); slip-case (*for books*); *phot.* plateholder.

kassiere|n [ka'siːrən] (no -ge-, h) **1.** *v/i.* waiter, *etc.*: take the money (für for); **2.** *v/t.* take (*sum of money*); collect (*contributions*, *etc.*); annul; ⅔ quash (*verdict*); **2r** *m* (-s/-) cashier; *bank*: *a.* teller; collector.

Kastanie ♀ [ka'stɑːnjə] *f* (-/-n) chestnut.

Kasten ['kastən] *m* (-s/ᵘ, ⚓) box; chest (*for tools*, *etc.*); case (*for violin*, *etc.*); bin (*for bread*, *etc.*).

Kasus *gr.* ['kɑːsus] *m* (-/-) case.

Katalog [kata'loːk] *m* (-[e]s/-e) catalogue, *Am. a.* catalog; **2isieren** [~ogi'ziːrən] *v/t.* (no -ge-, h) catalogue, *Am. a.* catalog.

Katarrh ♂ [ka'tar] *m* (-s/-e) (common) cold, catarrh.

katastroph|al *adj.* [katastro'fɑːl] catastrophic, disastrous; **2e** [~'stroːfə] *f* (-/-*n*) catastrophe, disaster.
Katechismus *eccl.* [kate'çismus] *m* (-/*Katechismen*) catechism.
Katego|rie [katego'riː] *f* (-/-*n*) category; **2risch** *adj.* [~'goːriʃ] categorical.
Kater ['kɑːtər] *m* (-*s*/-) *zo.* male cat, tom-cat; *fig. s. Katzenjammer.*
Katheder [ka'teːdər] *n, m* (-*s*/-) lecturing-desk.
Kathedrale [kate'drɑːlə] *f* (-/-*n*) cathedral.
Katholi|k [kato'liːk] *m* (-*en*/-*en*) (Roman) Catholic; **2sch** *adj.* [~'toːliʃ] (Roman) Catholic.
Kattun [ka'tuːn] *m* (-*s*/-*e*) calico; cotton cloth *or* fabric; chintz.
Katze *zo.* ['katsə] *f* (-/-*n*) cat; '**~njammer** F *fig. m* hangover, morning-after feeling.
Kauderwelsch ['kaudərvɛlʃ] *n* (-[*s*]/*no pl.*) gibberish, F double Dutch; '**2en** *v/i.* (ge-, *h*) gibber, F talk double Dutch.
kauen ['kauən] *v/t. and v/i.* (ge-, *h*) chew.
kauern ['kauərn] (ge-, *h*) **1.** *v/i.* crouch; squat; **2.** *v/refl.* crouch (down); squat (down); duck (down).
Kauf [kauf] *m* (-[*e*]*s*/*ˮe*) purchase; bargain, F good buy; acquisition; purchasing, buying; '**~brief** *m* deed of purchase; '**2en** *v/t.* (ge-, *h*) buy, purchase; acquire (by purchase); *sich et.* ~ buy o.s. s.th., buy s.th. for o.s.
Käufer ['kɔʏfər] *m* (-*s*/-) buyer, purchaser; customer.
'**Kauf|haus** *n* department store; '**~laden** *m* shop, *Am. a.* store.
käuflich ['kɔʏfliç] **1.** *adj.* for sale; purchasable; *fig.* open to bribery, bribable; venal; **2.** *adv.*: ~ *erwerben* (acquire by) purchase; ~ *überlassen* transfer by way of sale.
'**Kauf|mann** *m* (-[*e*]*s*/*Kaufleute*) businessman; merchant; trader, dealer, shopkeeper; *Am. a.* storekeeper; **2männisch** *adj.* ['~mɛniʃ] commercial, mercantile; '**~vertrag** *m* contract of sale.
'**Kaugummi** *m* chewing-gum.
kaum *adv.* [kaum] hardly, scarcely, barely; ~ *glaublich* hard to believe.
'**Kautabak** *m* chewing-tobacco.
Kaution [kau'tsjoːn] *f* (-/-*en*) security, surety; ⚖ *mst* bail.
Kautschuk ['kautʃuk] *m* (-*s*/-*e*) caoutchouc, pure rubber.
Kavalier [kava'liːr] *m* (-*s*/-*e*) gentleman; beau, admirer.
Kavallerie ⚔ [kavalə'riː] *f* (-/-*n*) cavalry, horse.
Kaviar ['kɑːviar] *m* (-*s*/-*e*) caviar(e).
keck *adj.* [kɛk] bold; impudent, saucy, cheeky; '**2heit** *f* (-/-*en*) boldness; impudence, sauciness, cheekiness.

Kegel ['keːgəl] *m* (-*s*/-) *games*: skittle, pin; *esp.* ⅍, ⊕ cone; ~ *schieben s. kegeln*; '**~bahn** *f* skittle, alley, *Am.* bowling alley; **2förmig** *adj.* ['~fœrmiç] conic(al), coniform; tapering; '**2n** *v/i.* (ge-, *h*) play (at) skittles *or* ninepins, *Am.* bowl.
Kegler ['keːglər] *m* (-*s*/-) skittle-player, *Am.* bowler.
Kehl|e ['keːlə] *f* (-/-*n*) throat; '**~kopf** *anat. m* larynx.
Kehre ['keːrə] *f* (-/-*n*) (sharp) bend, turn; '**2n** *v/t.* (ge-, *h*) sweep, brush; turn (*nach oben* upwards); *j-m den Rücken* ~ turn one's back on s.o.
Kehricht ['keːriçt] *m, n* (-[*e*]*s*/*no pl.*) sweepings *pl.*, rubbish.
'**Kehrseite** *f* wrong side, reverse; *esp. fig.* seamy side.
'**kehrtmachen** *v/i.* (*sep.*, -ge-, *h*) turn on one's heel; ⚔ turn *or* face about.
keifen ['kaɪfən] *v/i.* (ge-, *h*) scold, chide.
Keil [kaɪl] *m* (-[*e*]*s*/-*e*) wedge; gore, gusset; '**~e** F *f* (-/*no pl.*) thrashing, hiding; '**~er** *zo. m* (-*s*/-) wild-boar; **~erei** F [~'raɪ] *f* (-/-*en*) row, scrap; **2förmig** *adj.* ['~fœrmiç] wedge-shaped, cuneiform; '**~kissen** *n* wedge-shaped bolster; '**~schrift** *f* cuneiform characters *pl.*
Keim [kaɪm] *m* (-[*e*]*s*/-*e*) ♀, *biol.* germ; ♀: seed-plant; shoot; sprout; *fig.* seeds *pl.*, germ, bud; '**2en** *v/i.* (ge-, *h*) *seeds, etc.*: germinate; *seeds, plants, potatoes, etc.*: sprout; *fig.* b(o)urgeon; '**2frei** *adj.* sterilized, sterile; '**~träger** ⚕ *m* (germ-)carrier; '**~zelle** *f* germ-cell.
kein *indef. pron.* [kaɪn] *as adj.*: ~(e) no, not any; ~ *anderer als* none other but; *as noun*: ~*er*, ~*e*, ~(*e*)*s* none, no one, nobody; ~*er von beiden* neither (of the two); ~*er von uns* none of us; '**~es'falls** *adv.*, **~eswegs** *adv.* ['~'veːks] by no means, not at all; '**~mal** *adv.* not once, not a single time.
Keks [keːks] *m, n* (-, -*es*/-, -*e*) biscuit, *Am.* cookie; cracker.
Kelch [kɛlç] *m* (-[*e*]*s*/-*e*) cup, goblet; *eccl.* chalice, communion-cup; ♀ calyx.
Kelle ['kɛlə] *f* (-/-*n*) scoop; ladle; *tool*: trowel.
Keller ['kɛlər] *m* (-*s*/-) cellar; basement; **~ei** [~'raɪ] *f* (-/-*en*) wine-vault; '**~geschoß** *n* basement; '**~meister** *m* cellarman.
Kellner ['kɛlnər] *m* (-*s*/-) waiter; '**~in** *f* (-/-*nen*) waitress.
Kelter ['kɛltər] *f* (-/-*n*) winepress; '**2n** *v/t.* (ge-, *h*) press.
kenn|en ['kɛnən] *v/t.* (*irr.*, ge-, *h*) know, be acquainted with; have knowledge of *s.th.*; '**~enlernen** *v/t.* (*sep.*, -ge-, *h*) get *or* come to know;

make s.o.'s acquaintance, meet s.o.; **'2er** m (-s/-) expert; connoisseur; **'~tlich** adj. recognizable (an dat. by); ~ machen mark; label; **'2tnis** f (-/-se) knowledge; ~ nehmen von take not(ic)e of; **'2zeichen** n mark, sign; mot. registration (number), Am. license number; fig. hallmark, criterion; **'~zeichnen** v/t. (ge-, h) mark, characterize.

kentern ✛ ['kɛntərn] v/i. (ge-, sein) capsize, keel over, turn turtle.

Kerbe ['kɛrbə] f (-/-n) notch, nick; slot; **'2n** v/t. (ge-, h) notch, nick, indent.

Kerker ['kɛrkər] m (-s/-) gaol, jail, prison; **'~meister** m gaoler, jailer.

Kerl F [kɛrl] m (-s, ~ -es/-e, F -s) man; fellow, F chap, bloke, esp. Am. guy.

Kern [kɛrn] m (-[e]s/-e) kernel (of nut, etc.); stone, Am. pit (of cherry, etc.); pip (of orange, apple, etc.); core (of the earth); phys. nucleus; fig. core, heart, crux; Kern... s. a. Atom...; **'~energie** f nuclear energy; **'~forschung** f nuclear research; **'~gehäuse** n core; **'2ge'sund** adj. thoroughly healthy, F as sound as a bell; **'2ig** adj. full of pips; fig.: pithy; solid; **'~punkt** m central or crucial point; **'~spaltung** f nuclear fission.

Kerze ['kɛrtsə] f (-/-n) candle; **'~n-licht** n candle-light; **'~nstärke** f candle-power.

keß F adj. [kɛs] pert, jaunty; smart.

Kessel ['kɛsəl] m (-s/-) kettle (-drum); boiler; hollow.

Kette ['kɛtə] f (-/-n) chain; range (of mountains, etc.); necklace; **'2n** v/t. (ge-, h) chain (an acc. to).

'Ketten|hund m watch-dog; **'~raucher** m chain-smoker; **'~reaktion** f chain reaction.

Ketzer ['kɛtsər] m (-s/-) heretic; **~ei** [~'raɪ] f (-/-en) heresy; **2isch** adj. heretical.

keuch|en ['kɔyçən] v/i. (ge-, h) pant, gasp; **'2husten** ✍ m (w)hooping cough.

Keule ['kɔylə] f (-/-n) club; leg (of mutton, pork, etc.).

keusch adj. [kɔyʃ] chaste, pure; **'2heit** f (-/no pl.) chastity, purity.

kichern ['kiçərn] v/i. (ge-, h) giggle, titter.

Kiebitz ['ki:bits] m (-es/-e) orn. pe(e)wit; F fig. kibitzer; **'2en** F fig. v/i. (ge-, h) kibitz.

Kiefer ['ki:fər] 1. anat. m (-s/-) jaw(-bone); 2. ♀ f (-/-n) pine.

Kiel [ki:l] m (-[e]s/-e) ✛ keel; quill; **'~raum** m bilge, hold; **'~wasser** n wake (a. fig.).

Kieme zo. ['ki:mə] f (-/-n) gill.

Kies [ki:s] m (-es/-e) gravel; sl. fig. dough; **~el** ['~zəl] m (-s/-) pebble, flint; **'~weg** m gravel-walk.

Kilo ['ki:lo] n (-s/-[s]), **~gramm** [kilo'gram] n kilogram(me); **~hertz** [~'hɛrts] n (-/no pl.) kilocycle per second; **~meter** m kilomet|re, Am. -er; **~watt** n kilowatt.

Kimme ['kimə] f (-/-n) notch.

Kind [kint] n (-[e]s/-er) child; baby. **'Kinder|arzt** m p(a)ediatrician; **~ei** [~'raɪ] f (-/-en) childishness; childish trick; trifle; **'~frau** f nurse; **'~fräulein** n governess; **'~funk** m children's program(me); **'~garten** m kindergarten, nursery school; **'~lähmung** ✍ f infantile paralysis, polio(myelitis); **'2leicht** adj. very easy or simple, F as easy as winking or as ABC; **'~lied** n children's song; **2los** adj. childless; **'~mädchen** n nurse(maid); **'~spiel** n children's game; ein ~ s. kinderleicht; **'~stube** f nursery; fig. manners pl., upbringing; **'~wagen** m perambulator, F pram, Am. baby carriage; **'~zeit** f childhood; **'~zimmer** n children's room.

'Kindes|alter n childhood, infancy; **'~beine** n/pl.: von ~ an from childhood, from a very early age; **'~kind** n grandchild.

'Kind|heit f (-/no pl.) childhood; **2isch** adj. ['~diʃ] childish; **'2lich** adj. childlike.

Kinn anat. [kin] n (-[e]s/-e) chin; **'~backe** f, **'~backen** m (-s/-) jaw (-bone); **'~haken** m boxing: hook to the chin; uppercut; **'~lade** f jaw(-bone).

Kino ['ki:no] n (-s/-s) cinema, F the pictures pl., Am. motion-picture theater, F the movies pl., Am. ~ ins ~ gehen go to the cinema or F pictures, Am. F go to the movies; **'~besucher** m cinema-goer, Am. F moviegoer; **'~vorstellung** f cinema-show, Am. motion-picture show.

Kippe F ['kipə] f (-/-n) stub, fag-end, Am. a. butt; auf der ~ stehen or sein hang in the balance; **'2n** (ge-) 1. v/i. (sein) tip (over), topple (over), tilt (over); 2. v/t. (h) tilt, tip over or up.

Kirche ['kirçə] f (-/-n) church.

'Kirchen|älteste m (-n/-n) churchwarden, elder; **'~buch** n parochial register; **'~diener** m sacristan, sexton; **'~gemeinde** f parish; **'~jahr** n ecclesiastical year; **'~lied** n hymn; **'~musik** f sacred music; **'~schiff** ⚠ n nave; **'~steuer** f church-rate; **'~stuhl** m pew; **'~vorsteher** m churchwarden.

'Kirch|gang m church-going; **~gänger** [~'gɛŋər] m (-s/-) churchgoer; **'~hof** m churchyard; **'2lich** adj. ecclesiastical; **'~spiel** n parish; **'~turm** m steeple; **~weih** ['~vaɪ] f (-/-en) parish fair.

Kirsche ['kirʃə] f (-/-n) cherry.

Kissen ['kisən] n (-s/-) cushion; pillow; bolster, pad.

Kiste ['kistə] f (-/-n) box, chest; crate.

Kitsch [kitʃ] m (-es/no pl.) trash, rubbish; '2ig adj. shoddy, trashy.

Kitt [kit] m (-[e]s/-e) cement; putty.

Kittel ['kitəl] m (-s/-) overall; smock, frock.

'kitten v/t. (ge-, h) cement; putt.

kitz|eln ['kitsəln] (ge-, h) 1. v/t. tickle; 2. v/i.: meine Nase kitzelt my nose is tickling; '~lig adj. ticklish (a. fig.).

Kladde ['kladə] f (-/-n) rough note-book, waste-book.

klaffen ['klafən] v/i. (ge-, h) gape, yawn.

kläffen ['klɛfən] v/i. (ge-, h) yap, yelp.

klagbar tꜩ adj. ['kla:kba:r] matter, etc.: actionable; debt, etc.: suable.

Klage ['kla:gə] f (-/-n) complaint; lament; tꜩ action, suit; '2n (ge-, h) 1. v/i. complain (über acc. of, about; bei to); lament; tꜩ take legal action (gegen against); 2. v/t.: j-m et. ~ complain to s.o. of or about s.th.

Kläger tꜩ ['klɛ:gər] m (-s/-) plaintiff; complainant.

kläglich adj. ['klɛ:gliç] pitiful, piteous, pitiable; cries, etc.: plaintive; condition: wretched, lamentable; performance, result, etc.: miserable, poor; failure, etc.: lamentable, miserable.

klamm [klam] 1. adj. hands, etc.: numb or stiff with cold, clammy; 2. 2 f (-/-en) ravine, gorge, canyon.

Klammer ['klamər] f (-/-n) ⊕ clamp, cramp; (paper-)clip; gr., typ., 𝔸 bracket, parenthesis; '2n (ge-, h) 1. v/t. clip together; 2. close (wound) with clips; sich ~ an (acc.) cling to (a. fig.); 2. v/i. boxing: clinch.

Klang [klaŋ] 1. m (-[e]s/⸗e) sound, tone (of voice, instrument, etc.); tone (of radio, etc.); clink (of glasses, etc.); ringing (of bells, etc.); timbre; 2. 2 pret. of klingen; '~fülle f sonority; '2los adj. toneless; '2voll adj. sonorous.

Klappe ['klapə] f (-/-n) flap; flap, drop leaf (of table, etc.); shoulder strap (of uniform, etc.); tailboard (of lorry, etc.); ⊕, ♀, anat. valve; ♪ key; F fig.: bed; trap; '2n (ge-, h) 1. v/t.: nach oben ~ tip up; nach unten ~ lower, put down; 2. v/i. clap, flap; fig. come off well, work out fine, Am. sl. a. click.

Klapper ['klapər] f (-/-n) rattle; '2ig adj. vehicle, etc.: rattly, ramshackle; furniture: rickety; person, horse, etc.: decrepit; '~kasten F m wretched piano; rattletrap; '2n v/i. (ge-, h) clatter, rattle (mit et. s.th.); er klapperte vor Kälte mit den Zäh-

nen his teeth were chattering with cold; '~schlange zo. f rattlesnake, Am. a. rattler.

'Klapp|kamera phot. f folding camera; '~messer n clasp-knife, jack-knife; '~sitz m tip-up or flap seat; '~stuhl m folding chair; '~tisch m folding table, Am. a. gate-leg(ged) table; '~ult f (klappult] n folding desk.

Klaps [klaps] m (-es/-e) smack, slap; '2en v/t. (ge-, h) smack, slap.

klar adj. [kla:r] clear; bright; transparent, limpid; pure; fig.: clear, distinct; plain; evident, obvious; sich ~ sein über (acc.) be clear about; ~en Kopf bewahren keep a clear head.

klären ['klɛ:rən] v/t. (ge-, h) clarify; fig. clarify, clear up, elucidate.

'klar|legen v/t. (sep., -ge-, h), '~stellen v/t. (sep., -ge-, h) clear up.

'Klärung f (-/-en) clarification; fig. a. elucidation.

Klasse ['klasə] f (-/-n) class, category; school: class, form, Am. a. grade; (social) class.

'Klassen|arbeit f (test) paper; '2bewußt adj. class-conscious; '~bewußtsein n class-consciousness; '~buch n class-book; '~haß m class-hatred; '~kamerad m classmate; '~kampf m class-war(fare); '~zimmer n classroom, schoolroom.

klassifizier|en [klasifi'tsi:rən] v/t. (no -ge-, h) classify; 2ung f (-/-en) classification.

Klass|iker ['klasikər] m (-s/-) classic; '2isch adj. classic(al).

klatsch [klatʃ] 1. int. smack!, slap!; 2. 2 m (-es/-e) smack, slap; F fig.: gossip; scandal; 2base f ['~ba:zə] f (-/-n) gossip; '2e f (-/-n) fly-flap; '~en (ge-, h) 1. v/t. fling, hurl; Beifall ~ clap, applaud (j-m s.o.) 2. v/i. splash; applaud, clap; F fig. gossip; '~haft adj. gossiping, gossipy; '2maul F n s. Klatschbase; '~naß F adj. soaking wet.

Klaue ['klauə] f (-/-n) claw; paw; fig. clutch.

Klause ['klauzə] f (-/-n) hermitage; cell.

Klausel tꜩ ['klauzəl] f (-/-n) clause; proviso; stipulation.

Klaviatur ♪ [klavja'tu:r] f (-/-en) keyboard, keys pl.

Klavier ♪ [kla'vi:r] n (-s/-e) piano (-forte); '~konzert n piano concert or recital; '~lehrer m piano teacher; '~sessel m music-stool; '~stimmer m (-s/-) piano-tuner; '~stunde f piano-lesson.

kleb|en ['kle:bən] (ge-, h) 1. v/t. glue, paste, stick; 2. v/i. stick, adhere (an dat. to); '~end adj. adhesive; '2epflaster n adhesive or sticking plaster; '~rig adj. adhesive, sticky; '2stoff m adhesive; glue.

Klecks [klɛks] m (-es/-e) blot (of ink); mark (of dirt, grease, paint, etc.); spot (of grease, paint, etc.); stain (of wine, coffee, etc.); '2en (ge-) 1. v/i. (h) make a mark or spot or stain; 2. v/i. (sein) ink, etc.: drip (down); 3. v/t. (h): et. auf et. ~ splash or spill s.th. on s.th.

Klee ⚕ [kle:] m (-s/no pl.) clover, trefoil.

Kleid [klaɪt] n (-[e]s/-er) garment; dress, frock; gown; ~er pl. clothes pl.; 2en ['~dən] v/t. (ge-, h) dress, clothe; sich ~ dress (o.s.); j-n gut ~ suit or become s.o.

Kleider|ablage ['klaɪdər-] f cloakroom, Am. a. checkroom; '~bügel m coat-hanger; '~bürste f clothesbrush; '~haken m clothes-peg; '~schrank m wardrobe; '~ständer m hat and coat stand; '~stoff m dress material.

'kleidsam adj. becoming.

Kleidung ['klaɪduŋ] f (-/-en) clothes pl., clothing; dress; '~sstück n piece or article of clothing; garment.

Kleie ['klaɪə] f (-/-n) bran.

klein [klaɪn] 1. adj. little (only attr.), small; fig. a. trifling, petty; 2. adv.: ~ schreiben write with a small (initial) letter; ~ anfangen start in a small or modest way; 3. noun: von ~ auf from an early age; '2auto n baby or small car; '2bahn f narrow-ga(u)ge railway; '2bildkamera f miniature camera; '2geld n (small) change; '~gläubig adj. of little faith; '2handel ✝ m retail trade; '2händler m retailer; '2heit f (-/no pl.) smallness, small size; '2holz n firewood, matchwood, kindling.

'Kleinigkeit f (-/-en) trifle, triviality; '~skrämer m pettifogger.

'Klein|kind n infant; '2laut adj. subdued; '2lich adj. paltry; pedantic, fussy; '~mut m pusillanimity, despondency; 2mütig adj. ['~my:tiç] pusillanimous; despondent; '2schneiden v/t. (irr. schneiden, sep., -ge-, h) cut into small pieces; '~staat m small or minor state; '~stadt f small town; '~städter m small-town dweller, Am. a. small-towner; '2städtisch adj. small-town, provincial; '~vieh n small livestock.

Kleister ['klaɪstər] m (-s/-) paste; '2n v/t. (ge-, h) paste.

Klemm|e ['klɛmə] f (-/-n) ⊕ clamp; ⚡ terminal; F in der ~ sitzen be in a cleft stick, F be in a jam; '2en v/t. (ge-, h) jam, squeeze, pinch; '~er m (-s/-) pince-nez; '~schraube ⊕ f set screw.

Klempner ['klɛmpnər] m (-s/-) tinman, tin-smith, Am. a. tinner; plumber.

Klerus ['kle:rus] m (-/no pl.) clergy.

Klette ['klɛtə] f (-/-n) ⚕ bur(r); fig. a. leech.

Kletter|er ['klɛtərər] m (-s/-) climber; '2n v/i. (ge-, sein) climb, clamber (auf e-n Baum [up] a tree); '~pflanze f climber, creeper.

Klient [kli'ɛnt] m (-en/-en) client.

Klima ['kli:ma] n (-s/-s, -te) climate; fig. a. atmosphere; '~anlage f air-conditioning plant; 2tisch adj. ['~ma:tiʃ] climatic.

klimpern ['klɪmpərn] v/i. (ge-, h) jingle, chink (mit et. s.th.); F strum or tinkle away (auf acc. on, at piano, guitar).

Klinge ['klɪŋə] f (-/-n) blade.

Klingel ['klɪŋəl] f (-/-n) bell, handbell; '~knopf m bell-push; '2n v/i. (ge-, h) ring (the bell); doorbell, etc.: ring; es klingelt the doorbell is ringing; '~zug m bell-pull.

klingen ['klɪŋən] v/i. (irr., ge-, h) sound; bell, metal, etc.: ring; glasses, etc.: clink; musical instrument: speak.

Klini|k ['kli:nik] f (-/-en) nursing home; private hospital; clinic(al hospital); '2sch adj. clinical.

Klinke ['klɪŋkə] f (-/-n) latch; (door-)handle.

Klippe ['klɪpə] f (-/-n) cliff; reef; crag; rocky ledge; fig. rock, hurdle.

klirren ['klɪrən] v/i. (ge-, h) windowpane, chain, etc.: rattle; chain, swords, etc.: clank, jangle; keys, spurs, etc.: jingle; glasses, etc.: clink, chink; pots, etc.: clatter; ~ mit rattle; jingle.

Klistier ✍ [kli'sti:r] n (-s/-e) enema.

Kloake [klo'a:kə] f (-/-n) sewer, cesspool (a. fig.).

Klob|en ['klo:bən] m (-s/-) ⊕ pulley, block; log; '2ig adj. clumsy (a. fig.).

klopfen ['klɔpfən] (ge-, h) 1. v/i. heart, pulse: beat, throb; knock (at door, etc.); tap (on shoulder); pat (on cheek); es klopft there's a knock at the door; 2. v/t. knock, drive (nail, etc.).

Klöppel ['klœpəl] m (-s/-) clapper (of bell); lacemaking: bobbin; beetle; '~spitze f pillow-lace, bone-lace.

Klops [klɔps] m (-es/-e) meat ball.

Klosett [klo'zɛt] n (-s/-e, -s) lavatory, (water-)closet, W.C., toilet; '~papier n toilet-paper.

Kloß [klo:s] m (-es/⸚e) earth, clay, etc.: clod, lump; cookery: dumpling.

Kloster ['klo:stər] n (-s/⸚) cloister; monastery; convent, nunnery; '~bruder m friar; '~frau f nun; '~gelübde n monastic vow.

Klotz [klɔts] m (-es/⸚e) block, log (a. fig.).

Klub [klup] m (-s/-s) club; '~kamerad m clubmate; '~sessel m lounge-chair.

Kluft [kluft] f 1. (-/⸚e) gap (a. fig.),

crack; cleft; gulf, chasm (*both a. fig.*); 2. F (-/-en) outfit, F togs *pl.*; uniform.

klug *adj.* [klu:k] clever; wise, intelligent, sensible; prudent; shrewd; cunning; **'2heit** *f* (-/*no pl.*) cleverness; intelligence; prudence; shrewdness; good sense.

Klump|en ['klumpǝn] *m* (-s/-) lump (*of earth, dough, etc.*); clod (*of earth, etc.*); nugget (*of gold, etc.*); heap; **'⁓fuß** *m* club-foot; **'2ig** *adj.* lumpy; cloddish.

knabbern ['knabǝrn] (ge-, h) 1. *v/t.* nibble, gnaw; 2. *v/i.* nibble, gnaw (*an dat.* at).

Knabe ['kna:bǝ] *m* (-n/-n) boy; lad; F *alter* ⁓ F old chap.

'Knaben|alter *n* boyhood; **'⁓chor** *m* boys' choir; **'2haft** *adj.* boyish.

Knack [knak] *m* (-[e]s/-e) crack, snap, click; **'2en** (ge-, h) 1. *v/i. wood:* crack; *fire:* crackle; click; 2. *v/t.* crack (*nut, etc.*); F crack open (*safe*); *e-e harte Nuß zu ⁓ haben* have a hard nut to crack; **⁓s** [⁓s] *m* (-es/-e) *s.* Knack; F *fig.* defect; **'2sen** *v/i.* (ge-, h) *s.* knacken 1.

Knall [knal] *m* (-[e]s/-e) crack, bang (*of shot*); bang (*of explosion*); crack (*of rifle or whip*); report (*of gun*); detonation, explosion, report; **'⁓bonbon** *m, n* cracker; **'⁓effekt** *fig. m* sensation; **'2en** *v/i.* (ge-, h) rifle, *whip:* crack; *fireworks, door, etc.:* bang; *gun:* fire; *cork, etc.:* pop; *explosive, etc.:* detonate.

knapp *adj.* [knap] *clothes:* tight, close-fitting; *rations, etc.:* scanty, scarce; *style, etc.:* concise; lead, *victory, etc.:* narrow; *majority, etc.:* bare; *mit ⁓er Not entrinnen* have a narrow escape; ⁓ *werden* run short; **'2e** **⁓** *m* (-n/-n) miner; **'⁓halten** *v/t.* (irr. halten, sep., -ge-, h) keep *s.o.* short; **'2heit** *f* (-/*no pl.*) scarcity, shortage; conciseness; **'⁓schaft** ⚒ *f* (-/-en) miners' society.

Knarre ['knarǝ] *f* (-/-n) rattle; F rifle, gun; **'2n** *v/i.* (ge-, h) creak; *voice:* grate.

knattern ['knatǝrn] *v/i.* (ge-, h) crackle; *machine-gun, etc.:* rattle; *mot.* roar.

Knäuel ['knɔɔʏǝl] *m, n* (-s/-) clew, ball; *fig.* bunch, cluster.

Knauf [knauf] *m* (-[e]s/ᵘe) knob, pommel (*of sword*).

Knauser ['knauzǝr] *m* (-s/-) niggard, miser, skinflint; **⁓ei** [⁓'rai] *f* (-/-en) niggardliness, miserliness; **'2ig** *adj.* niggardly, stingy; **'2n** *v/i.* (ge-, h) be stingy.

Knebel ['kne:bǝl] *m* (-s/-) gag; **'2n** *v/t.* (ge-, h) gag; *fig.* muzzle (*press*).

Knecht [knɛçt] *m* (-[e]s/-e) servant; farm-labo(u)rer, farm-hand; slave; **'2en** *v/t.* (ge-, h) enslave; tyrannize;

subjugate; **'⁓schaft** *f* (-/*no pl.*) servitude, slavery.

kneif|en ['knaifǝn] (*irr.*, ge-, h) 1. *v/t.* pinch, nip; 2. *v/i.* pinch; F *fig.* back out, *Am.* F *a.* crawfish; **'2er** *m* (-s/-) pince-nez; **'2zange** *f* (e-e a pair of) pincers *pl.* or nippers *pl.*

Kneipe ['knaipǝ] *f* (-/-n) public house, tavern, F pub, *Am. a.* saloon; **'2n** *v/i.* (ge-, h) carouse, tipple, F booze; **⁓rei** *f* (-/-en) drinking-bout, carousal.

kneten ['kne:tǝn] *v/t.* (ge-, h) knead (*dough, etc.*); ⚕ *a.* massage (*limb, etc.*).

Knick [knik] *m* (-[e]s/-e) *wall, etc.:* crack; *paper, etc.:* fold, crease; *path, etc.:* bend; **'2en** *v/t.* (ge-, h) fold, crease; bend; break.

Knicker F ['knikǝr] *m* (-s/-) *s.* Knauser.

Knicks [kniks] *m* (-es/-e) curts(e)y; *e-n* ⁓ *machen* = **'2en** *v/i.* (ge-, h) (drop a) curts(e)y (*vor dat.* to).

Knie [kni:] *n* (-s/-) knee; **'2fällig** *adv.* on one's knees; **'⁓kehle** *anat.* *f* hollow of the knee; **'2n** *v/i.* (ge-, h) kneel, be on one's knees; **'⁓scheibe** *anat.* *f* knee-cap, knee-pan; **'⁓strumpf** *m* knee-length sock.

Kniff [knif] 1. *m* (-[e]s/-e) crease, fold; *fig.* trick, knack; 2. *2 pret. of* kneifen; **2(e)lig** *adj.* ['⁓(ǝ)liç] tricky; intricate.

knipsen ['knipsǝn] (ge-, h) 1. *v/t.* clip, punch (*ticket, etc.*); F *phot.* take a snapshot of, snap; 2. F *phot. v/i.* take snapshots.

Knirps [knirps] *m* (-es/-e) little man; little chap, F nipper; **'2ig** *adj.* very small.

knirschen ['knirʃǝn] *v/i.* (ge-, h) *gravel, snow, etc.:* crunch, grind; *teeth, etc.:* grate; *mit den Zähnen* ⁓ grind or gnash one's teeth.

knistern ['knistǝrn] *v/i.* (ge-, h) *woodfire, etc.:* crackle; *dry leaves, silk, etc.:* rustle.

knitter|frei *adj.* ['knitǝr-] crease-resistant; **'2n** *v/t.* and *v/i.* (ge-, h) crease, wrinkle.

Knoblauch ⚘ ['kno:plaux] *m* (-[e]s/*no pl.*) garlic.

Knöchel *anat.* ['knœçǝl] *m* (-s/-) knuckle; ankle.

Knoch|en *anat.* ['knɔxǝn] *m* (-s/-) bone; **'⁓enbruch** *m* fracture (*of a bone*); **'2ig** *adj.* bony.

Knödel ['knø:dǝl] *m* (-s/-) dumpling.

Knolle ⚘ ['knɔlǝ] *f* (-/-n) tuber; bulb.

Knopf [knɔpf] *m* (-[e]s/ᵘe) button.

knöpfen ['knœpfǝn] *v/t.* (ge-, h) button.

'Knopfloch *n* buttonhole.

Knorpel ['knɔrpǝl] *m* (-s/-) cartilage, gristle.

Knorr|en ['knɔrǝn] *m* (-s/-) knot,

knag, gnarl; '₂ig *adj.* gnarled, knotty.

Knospe ₰ ['knɔspə] *f* (-/-n) bud; '₂n *v/i.* (ge-, *h*) (be in) bud.

Knot|en ['knoːtən] **1.** *m* (-s/-) knot (*a. fig.*, ⚓.); **2.** ₂ *v/t.* (ge-, *h*) knot; '₂enpunkt *m* 🚂 junction; intersection; '₂ig *adj.* knotty.

Knuff F [knuf] *m* (-[e]s/¤e) poke, cuff, nudge; '₂en F *v/t.* (ge-, *h*) poke, cuff, nudge.

knülle|n ['knylən] *v/t.* and *v/i.* (ge-, *h*) crease, crumple; '₂r F *m* (-s/-) hit.

knüpfen ['knypfən] *v/t.* (ge-, *h*) make, tie (*knot*, etc.); make (*net*); knot (*carpet*, etc.); tie (*shoe-lace*, etc.); strike up (*friendship*, etc.); attach (*condition*, etc.) (an acc. to).

Knüppel ['knypəl] *m* (-s/-) cudgel.

knurren ['knurən] *v/i.* (ge-, *h*) growl, snarl; *fig.* grumble (*über acc.* at, over, about); *stomach:* rumble.

knusp(e)rig *adj.* ['knusp(ə)riç] crisp, crunchy.

Knute ['knuːtə] *f* (-/-n) knout.

Knüttel ['knytəl] *m* (-s/-) cudgel.

Kobold ['koːbɔlt] *m* (-[e]s/-e) (hob)goblin, imp.

Koch [kɔx] *m* (-[e]s/¤e) cook; '₂buch *n* cookery-book, *Am.* cookbook; '₂en (ge-, *h*) **1.** *v/t.* boil (*water, egg, fish*, etc.); cook (*meat, vegetables*, etc.) (*by boiling*); make (*coffee, tea*, etc.); **2.** *v/i. water,* etc.: boil (*a. fig.*); do the cooking; be a (*good,* etc.) cook; '₂er *m* (-s/-) cooker.

Köcher ['kœçər] *m* (-s/-) quiver.

Koch|kiste *f* haybox; '₂löffel *m* wooden spoon; '₂nische *f* kitchenette; '₂salz *n* common salt; '₂topf *m* pot, saucepan.

Köder ['køːdər] *m* (-s/-) bait (*a. fig.*); lure (*a. fig.*); '₂n *v/t.* (ge-, *h*) bait; lure; *fig. a.* decoy.

Kodex ['koːdɛks] *m* (-es, -/-e, *Kodizes*) code.

Koffer ['kɔfər] *m* (-s/-) (suit)case; trunk; '₂radio *n* portable radio (set).

Kognak ['kɔnjak] *m* (-s/-s, ₰ -e) French brandy, cognac.

Kohl ₰ [koːl] *m* (-[e]s/-e) cabbage.

Kohle ₰ ['koːlə] *f* (-/-n) coal; charcoal; ⚡ carbon; *wie auf (glühenden) ₂n sitzen* be on tenterhooks.

'Kohlen|bergwerk *n* coal-mine, coal-pit, colliery; '₂eimer *m* coalscuttle; '₂händler *m* coal-merchant; '₂kasten *m* coal-box; '₂revier ⚒ *n* coal-district; '₂säure 🧪 *f* carbonic acid; '₂stoff 🧪 *m* carbon.

'Kohle|papier *n* carbon paper; '₂zeichnung *f* charcoal-drawing; **'Kohl|kopf** ₰ *m* (head of) cabbage; '₂rübe ₰ *f* Swedish turnip.

Koje ⚓ ['koːjə] *f* (-/-n) berth, bunk.

Kokain [koka'iːn] *n* (-s/*no pl.*) cocaine, *sl.* coke, snow.

kokett *adj.* [ko'kɛt] coquettish; ₂erie [₂ə'riː] *f* (-/-n) coquetry, coquettishness; ₂ieren [₂'tiːrən] *v/i.* (*no* -ge-, *h*) coquet, flirt (*mit* with; *a. fig.*).

Kokosnuß ₰ ['koːkɔs-] *f* coconut.

Koks [koːks] *m* (-es/-e) coke.

Kolben ['kɔlbən] *m* (-s/-) butt (*of rifle*); ⊕ piston; '₂stange *f* piston-rod.

Kolchose [kɔl'çoːzə] *f* (-/-n) collective farm, kolkhoz.

Kolleg *univ.* [kɔ'leːk] *n* (-s/-s, -ien) course of lectures; ₂e [₂gə] *m* (-n/-n) colleague; ₂ium [₂'gjum] *n* (-s/*Kollegien*) council, board; teaching staff.

Kollekt|e *eccl.* [kɔ'lɛktə] *f* (-/-n) collection; ₂ion ✝ [₂'tsjoːn] *f* (-/-n) collection, range.

Koller ['kɔlər] *m* (-s/-) *vet.* staggers *pl.*; F *fig.* rage, tantrum; '₂n *v/i.* **1.** (*h*) *turkey-cock:* gobble; *pigeon:* coo; *bowels:* rumble; *vet.* have the staggers; **2.** (*sein*) *ball, tears,* etc.: roll.

kolli|dieren [kɔli'diːrən] *v/i.* (*no* -ge-, *sein*) collide; *fig.* clash; ₂sion [₂'zjoːn] *f* (-/-en) collision; *fig.* clash, conflict.

Kölnischwasser ['kœlniʃ-] *n* eau-de-Cologne.

Kolonialwaren [kolo'njaːl-] *f/pl.* groceries *pl.*; ₂händler *m* grocer; ₂handlung *f* grocer's (shop), *Am.* grocery.

Kolon|ie [kolo'niː] *f* (-/-n) colony; ₂isieren [₂i'ziːrən] *v/t.* (*no* -ge-, *h*) colonize.

Kolonne [ko'lɔnə] *f* (-/-n) column; convoy; gang (*of workers,* etc.).

kolorieren [kolo'riːrən] *v/t.* (*no* -ge-, *h*) colo(u)r.

Kolo|ß [ko'lɔs] *m* (*Kolosses/Kolosse*) colossus; ₂ssal *adj.* [₂'saːl] colossal, huge (*both a. fig.*).

Kombin|ation [kɔmbina'tsjoːn] *f* (-/-en) combination; overall; 🧥 flying-suit; *football,* etc.: combined attack; ₂ieren [₂'niːrən] *v/i.* (*no* -ge-, *h*) **1.** *v/t.* combine; **2.** *v/i.* reason, deduce; *football,* etc.: combine, move.

Kombüse ⚓ [kɔm'byːzə] *f* (-/-n) galley, caboose.

Komet *ast.* [ko'meːt] *m* (-en/-en) comet.

Komfort [kɔm'foːr] *m* (-s/*no pl.*) comfort; ₂abel *adj.* [₂r'taːbəl] comfortable.

Komik ['koːmik] *f* (-/*no pl.*) humo(u)r, fun(niness); '₂er *m* (-s/-) comic actor, comedian.

komisch *adj.* ['koːmiʃ] comic(al), funny; *fig.* funny, odd, queer.

Komitee [komi'teː] *n* (-s/-s) committee.

Kommand|ant ✕ [kɔman'dant] *m* (-en/-en), **~eur** ✕ [~'døːr] *m* (-s/-e) commander, commanding officer; **2ieren** [~'diːrən] (*no* -ge-, *h*) **1.** *v/i.* order, command, be in command; **2.** *v/t.* ✕ command, be in command of; order; **~itgesellschaft** † [~'dit-] *f* limited partnership; **~o** [~'mando] *n* (-s/-s) ✕ command, order; order(s *pl.*), directive(s *pl.*); ✕ detachment; **~obrücke** ♣ *f* navigating bridge.

kommen ['kɔmən] *v/i.* (*irr.*, ge-, sein) come; arrive; **~** *lassen* send for *s.o.*, order *s.th.*; *et.* **~** *sehen* foresee; *an die Reihe* **~** it is one's turn; **~** *auf* (*acc.*) think of, hit upon; remember; *zu dem Schluß* **~**, *daß* decide that; *hinter et.* **~** find s.th. out; *um et.* **~** lose s.th.; *zu et.* **~** come by s.th.; *wieder zu sich* **~** come round *or* to; *wie* **~** *Sie dazu!* how dare you!

Komment|ar [kɔmɛn'taːr] *m* (-s/-e) commentary, comment; **~ator** [~tɔr] *m* (-s/-en) commentator; **2ieren** [~'tiːrən] *v/t.* (*no* -ge-, *h*) comment on.

Kommissar [kɔmi'saːr] *m* (-s/-e) commissioner; superintendent; *pol.* commissar.

Kommißbrot F [kɔ'mis-] *n* army *or* ration bread, *Am. a.* G.I. bread.

Kommission [kɔmi'sjoːn] *f* (-/-en) commission (*a.* †); committee; **~är** † [~o'nɛːr] *m* (-s/-e) commission agent.

Kommode [kɔ'moːdə] *f* (-/-n) chest of drawers, *Am.* bureau.

Kommunis|mus *pol.* [kɔmu'nismus] *m* (-/*no* d.) communism; **~t** *m* (-en/-en) communist; **2tisch** *adj.* communist(ic).

Komöd|iant [kɔmø'djant] *m* (-en/-en) comedian; *fig.* play-actor; **~ie** [~'møːdjə] *f* (-/-n) comedy; **~** *spielen* play-act.

Kompagnon † [kɔmpan'jõ] *m* (-s/-s) (business-)partner, associate.

Kompanie ✕ [kɔmpa'niː] *f* (-/-n) company.

Kompaß ['kɔmpas] *m* (Kompasses/Kompasse) compass.

kompetent *adj.* [kɔm'pletɛnt] competent.

komplett *adj.* [kɔm'plɛt] complete.

Komplex [kɔm'plɛks] *m* (-es/-e) complex (*a. psych.*); block (*of houses*).

Kompliment [kɔmpli'mɛnt] *n* (-[e]s/-e) compliment.

Komplize [kɔm'pliːtsə] *m* (-n/-n) accomplice.

komplizier|en [kɔmpli'tsiːrən] *v/t.* (*no* -ge-, *h*) complicate; **~t** *adj.* machine, *etc.*: complicated; *argument, situation, etc.*: complex; **~er Bruch** ♣ compound fracture.

Komplott [kɔm'plɔt] *n* (-[e]s/-e) plot, conspiracy.

kompo|nieren ♪ [kɔmpo'niːrən] *v/t. and v/i.* (*no* -ge-, *h*) compose; **2nist** *m* (-en/-en) composer; **2sition** [~zi'tsjoːn] *f* (-/-en) composition.

Kompott [kɔm'pɔt] *n* (-[e]s/-e) compote, stewed fruit, *Am. a.* sauce.

komprimieren [kɔmpri'miːrən] *v/t.* (*no* -ge-, *h*) compress.

Kompromi|ß [kɔmpro'mis] *m* (Kompromisses/Kompromisse) compromise; **2ßlos** *adj.* uncompromising; **2ttieren** [~'tiːrən] *v/t.* (*no* -ge-, *h*) compromise.

Kondens|ator [kɔndɛn'zaːtɔr] *m* (-s/-en) ∮ capacitor, condenser (*a.* ♯); **2ieren** [~'ziːrən] *v/t.* (*no* -ge-, *h*) condense.

Kondens|milch [kɔn'dɛns-] *f* evaporated milk; **~streifen** ✕ *m* condensation *or* vapo(u)r trail; **~wasser** *n* water of condensation.

Konditor [kɔn'diːtɔr] *m* (-s/-en) confectioner, pastry-cook; **~ei** [~ito'raɪ] *f* (-/-en) confectionery, confectioner's (shop); **~eiwaren** *f/pl.* confectionery.

Konfekt [kɔn'fɛkt] *n* (-[e]s/-e) sweets *pl.*, sweetmeat, *Am. a.* soft candy; chocolates *pl.*

Konfektion [kɔnfɛk'tsjoːn] *f* (-/-en) (manufacture of) ready-made clothing; **~sanzug** [kɔnfɛk'tsjoːns-] *m* ready-made suit; **~sgeschäft** *n* ready-made clothes shop.

Konfer|enz [kɔnfe'rɛnts] *f* (-/-en) conference; **2ieren** [~'riːrən] *v/i.* (*no* -ge-, *h*) confer (*über acc.* on).

Konfession [kɔnfɛ'sjoːn] *f* (-/-en) confession, creed; denomination; **2ell** *adj.* [~o'nɛl] confessional, denominational; **~sschule** [~'sjoːns-] *f* denominational school.

Konfirm|and *eccl.* [kɔnfir'mant] *m* (-en/-en) candidate for confirmation, confirmee; **~ation** [~'tsjoːn] *f* (-/-en) confirmation; **2ieren** [~'miːrən] *v/t.* (*no* -ge-, *h*) confirm.

konfiszieren ♯♯ [kɔnfis'tsiːrən] *v/t.* (*no* -ge-, *h*) confiscate, seize.

Konfitüre [kɔnfi'tyːrə] *f* (-/-n) preserve(s *pl.*), (whole-fruit) jam.

Konflikt [kɔn'flikt] *m* (-[e]s/-e) conflict.

konform *adv.* [kɔn'fɔrm]: **~** *gehen* *mit* agree *or* concur with.

konfrontieren [kɔnfrɔn'tiːrən] *v/t.* (*no* -ge-, *h*) confront (*mit* with).

konfus *adj.* [kɔn'fuːs] *p.*, *a. ideas*: muddled; *p.* muddle-headed.

Kongreß [kɔn'grɛs] *m* (Kongresses/Kongresse) congress; *Am. parl. Congress*; **~halle** *f* congress hall.

König ['køːniç] *m* (-s/-e) king; **2lich** *adj.* [~k-] royal; regal; **~reich** ['~k-] *n* kingdom; **~swürde** ['~ks-] *f* royal dignity, kingship; **'~tum** *n* (-s/*~er*) monarchy; kingship.

Konjug|ation *gr.* [kɔnjuga'tsjoːn] *f*

(-/-en); 2ieren [~'gi:rən] v/t. (no -ge-, h) conjugate.

Konjunkt|iv gr. ['kɔnjuŋktiːf] m (-s/-e) subjunctive (mood); ~ur ✝ [~'tuːr] f (-/-en) trade or business cycle; economic or business situation.

konkret adj. [kɔn'kreːt] concrete.

Konkurrent [kɔnku'rent] m (-en/ -en) competitor, rival.

Konkurrenz [kɔnku'rents] f (-/-en) competition; competitors pl., rivals pl.; sports: event; 2fähig adj. able to compete; competitive; ~geschäft n rival business or firm; ~kampf m competition.

konkur'rieren v/i. (no -ge-, h) compete (mit with; um for).

Konkurs ✝, 🕮 [kɔn'kurs] m (-es/-e) bankruptcy, insolvency, failure; ~ anmelden file a petition in bankruptcy; in ~ gehen or geraten become insolvent, go bankrupt; ~er-klärung 🕮 f declaration of insolvency; ~masse 🕮 f bankrupt's estate; ~verfahren 🕮 n bankruptcy proceedings pl.; ~verwalter 🕮 m trustee in bankruptcy; liquidator.

können ['kœnən] 1. v/i. (irr., ge-, h): ich kann nicht I can't, I am not able to; 2. v/t. (irr., ge-, h) know, understand; e-e Sprache ~ know a language, have command of a language; 3. v/aux. (irr., no -ge-, h) be able to inf., be capable of ger.; be allowed or permitted to inf.; es kann sein it may be; du kannst hingehen you may go there; er kann schwimmen he can swim, he knows how to swim; 4. 2 n (-s/no pl.) ability; skill; proficiency.

Konnossement ✝ [kɔnɔsə'ment] n (-[e]s/-e) bill of lading.

konnte ['kɔntə] pret. of können.

konsequen|t adj. [kɔnze'kvent] consistent; 2z [~ts] f (-/-en) consistency; consequence; die ~en ziehen do the only thing one can.

konservativ adj. [kɔnzerva'tiːf] conservative.

Konserven [kɔn'zervən] f/pl. tinned or Am. canned foods pl.; ~büchse f, ~dose f tin, Am. can; ~fabrik f tinning factory, esp. Am. cannery.

konservieren [kɔnzer'viːrən] v/t. (no -ge-, h) preserve.

Konsonant gr. [kɔnzo'nant] m (-en/ -en) consonant.

Konsortium ✝ [kɔn'zɔrtsjum] n (-s/Konsortien) syndicate.

konstruieren [kɔnstru'iːrən] v/t. (no -ge-, h) gr. construe; ⊕: construct; design.

Konstruk|teur ⊕ [kɔnstruk'tøːr] m (-s/-e) designer; ~tion ⊕ [~'tsjoːn] f (-/-en) construction; ~tionsfehler ⊕ m constructional defect.

Konsul pol. ['kɔnzul] m (-s/-n) con-

---

sul; ~at pol. [~'laːt] n (-[e]s/-e) consulate; 2'tieren v/t. (no -ge-, h) consult, seek s.o.'s advice.

Konsum [kɔn'zuːm] m 1. (-s/no pl.) consumption; 2. (-s/-s) co-operative shop, Am. co-operative store, F co-op; 3. (-s/no pl.) consumers' co-operative society, F co-op; ~ent [~u'ment] m (-en/-en) consumer; 2ieren [~u'miːrən] v/t. (no -ge-, h) consume; ~verein m s. Konsum 3.

Kontakt [kɔn'takt] m (-[e]s/-e) contact (a. ⚡); in ~ stehen mit be in contact or touch with.

Kontinent ['kɔntinent] m (-[e]s/-e) continent.

Kontingent [kɔntiŋ'gent] n (-[e]s/ -e) 💥 contingent, quota (a. ✝).

Konto ✝ ['kɔnto] n (-s/Konten, Kontos, Konti) account; '~auszug ✝ m statement of account; ~korrent-konto ✝ [~kɔ'rent-] n current account.

Kontor [kɔn'toːr] n (-s/-e) office; ~ist [~o'rist] m (-en/-en) clerk.

Kontrast [kɔn'trast] m (-es/-e) contrast.

Kontroll|e [kɔn'trɔlə] f (-/-n) control; supervision; check; 2ieren [~'liːrən] v/t. (no -ge-, h) control; supervise; check.

Kontroverse [kɔntro'verzə] f (-/-n) controversy.

konventionell adj. [kɔnventsjo'nel] conventional.

Konversation [kɔnverza'tsjoːn] f (-/-en) conversation; ~slexikon n encyclop(a)edia.

Konzentr|ation [kɔntsentra'tsjoːn] f (-/-en) concentration; 2ieren [~-'triːrən] v/t. (no -ge-, h) concentrate, focus (attention, etc.) (auf acc. on); sich ~ concentrate (auf acc. on).

Konzern ✝ [kɔn'tsern] m (-s/-e) combine, group.

Konzert ♪ [kɔn'tsert] n (-[e]s/-e) concert; recital; concerto; ~saal ♪ m concert-hall.

Konzession [kɔntse'sjoːn] f (-/-en) concession; licen|ce, Am. -se; 2ieren [~o'niːrən] v/t. (no -ge-, h) license.

Kopf [kɔpf] m (-[e]s/=e) head; top; brains pl.; pipe: bowl; ein fähiger ~ a clever fellow; ~ hoch! chin up!; j-m über den ~ wachsen outgrow s.o.; fig. get beyond s.o.; '~arbeit f brain-work; '~bahnhof 🚉 m terminus, Am. terminal; '~bedeck-kung f headgear, headwear.

köpfen ['kœpfən] v/t. (ge-, h) behead, decapitate; football: head (ball).

'Kopf|ende n head; '~hörer m headphone, headset; '~kissen n pillow; 2los adj. headless; fig. confused; '~nicken n (-s/no pl.) nod; '~rechnen n (-s/no pl.) mental arithmetic; '~salat m cabbage-lettuce;

'**schmerzen** m/pl. headache; '**sprung** m header; '**tuch** n scarf; ♀**über** adv. head first, headlong; '**weh** n (-[e]s/-e) s. Kopfschmerzen; '**zerbrechen** n (-s/no pl.): j-m ~ machen puzzle s.o.

Kopie [ko'pi:] f(-/-n) copy; duplicate; phot., film: print; '**rstift** m indelible pencil.

Koppel ['kɔpəl] 1. f (-/-n) hounds: couple; horses: string; paddock; 2. ⚥ n (-s/-) belt; ♀n v/t. (ge-, h) couple (a. ⊕, ♪).

Koralle [ko'ralə] f (-/-n) coral; **nfischer** m coral-fisher.

Korb [kɔrp] m (-[e]s/⁼e) basket; fig. refusal; Hahn im ~ cock of the walk; '**möbel** n/pl. wicker furniture.

Kordel ['kɔrdəl] f (-/-n) string, twine; cord.

Korinthe [ko'rintə] f (-/-n) currant.

Kork [kɔrk] m (-[e]s/-e), '**en** m (-s/-) cork; '**(en)zieher** m (-s/-) corkscrew.

Korn [kɔrn] 1. n (-[e]s/⁼er) seed; grain; 2. n (-[e]s/-e) corn, cereals pl.; 3. n (-[e]s/⁖-e) front sight; 4. F m (-[e]s/-) (German) corn whisky.

körnig adj. ['kœrniç] granular; in compounds: ...-grained.

Körper ['kœrpər] m (-s/-) body (a. phys., ♁); ♯ solid; '**bau** m build, physique; ♀**behindert** adj. ['..bə-hindərt] (physically) disabled, handicapped; '**beschaffenheit** f constitution, physique; '**fülle** f corpulence; '**geruch** m body-odo(u)r; '**größe** f stature; '**kraft** f physical strength; ♀**lich** adj. physical; corporal; bodily; '**pflege** f care of the body, hygiene; '**schaft** f (-/-en) body; ♯♯ body (corporate), corporation; '**verletzung** ♯♯ f bodily harm, physical injury.

korrekt adj. [kɔ'rɛkt] correct; ♀or [..ɔr] m (-s/-en) (proof-)reader; ♀ur [..'tu:r] f (-/-en) correction; ♀urbogen m proof-sheet.

Korrespond|ent [kɔrɛspɔn'dɛnt] m (-en/-en) correspondent; **enz** [..ts] f (-/-en) correspondence; ♀ieren [..'di:rən] v/i. (no -ge-, h) correspond (mit with).

korrigieren [kɔri'gi:rən] v/t. (no -ge-, h) correct.

Korsett [kɔr'zɛt] n (-[e]s/-e, -s) corset, stays pl.

Kosename ['ko:zə-] m pet name.

Kosmetik [kɔs'me:tik] f (-/no pl.) beauty culture; **erin** f (-/-nen) beautician, cosmetician.

Kost [kɔst] f (-/no pl.) food, fare; board; diet; '♀**bar** adj. present, etc.: costly, expensive; health, time, etc.: valuable; mineral, etc.: precious.

'**kosten**[1] v/t. (ge-, h) taste, try, sample.

'**Kosten**[2] 1. pl. cost(s pl.); expense(s pl.), charges pl.; auf ~ (gen.) at the expense of; 2. ♀ v/t. (ge-, h) cost; take, require (time, etc.); '**anschlag** m estimate, tender; '♀**frei** 1. adj. free; 2. adv. free of charge; '♀**los** s. kostenfrei.

Kost|gänger ['kɔstgɛŋər] m (-s/-) boarder; '**geld** n board-wages pl.

köstlich adj. ['kœstliç] delicious.

'**Kost|probe** f taste, sample (a. fig.); ♀**spielig** adj. ['..ʃpi:liç] expensive, costly.

Kostüm [kɔs'ty:m] n (-s/-e) costume, dress; suit; '**fest** n fancy-dress ball.

Kot [ko:t] m (-[e]s/no pl.) mud, mire; excrement.

Kotelett [kɔt(ə)'lɛt] n (-[e]s/-s, ⚥ -e) pork, veal, lamb: cutlet; pork, veal, mutton: chop; **en** pl. sidewhiskers pl., Am. a. sideburns pl.

'**Kot|flügel** mot. m mudguard, Am. a. fender; '♀**ig** adj. muddy, miry.

Krabbe zo. ['krabə] f (-/-n) shrimp; crab.

krabbeln ['krabəln] v/i. (ge-, sein) crawl.

Krach [krax] m (-[e]s/-e, -s) crack, crash (a. ↑); quarrel, sl. bust-up; F row; ~ machen kick up a row; '♀en v/i. (ge-) 1. (h) thunder: crash; cannon: roar, thunder; 2. (sein) crash (a. ↑), smash.

krächzen ['krɛçtsən] v/t. and v/i. (ge-, h) croak.

Kraft [kraft] 1. f (-/⁼e) strength; force (a. ⚥); power (a. ♪, ⊕); energy; vigo(u)r; efficacy; in ~ sein (setzen, treten) be in (put into, come into) operation or force; außer ~ setzen repeal, abolish (law); 2. ♀ prp. (gen.) by virtue of; '**anlage** ⚡ f power plant; '**brühe** f beef tea; '**fahrer** m driver, motorist; '**fahrzeug** n motor vehicle.

kräftig adj. ['krɛftiç] strong (a. fig.), powerful; fig. nutritious, rich; **en** ['..gən] (ge-, h) 1. v/t. strengthen; 2. v/i. give strength.

'**kraft|los** adj. powerless; feeble; weak; '♀**probe** f trial of strength; '♀**rad** n motor cycle; '♀**stoff** mot. m fuel; '**voll** adj. powerful (a. fig.); '♀**wagen** m motor vehicle; '♀**werk** ⚡ n power station.

Kragen ['kra:gən] m (-s/-) collar; '**knopf** m collar-stud, Am. collar button.

Krähe orn. ['krɛ:ə] f (-/-n) crow; '♀n v/i. (ge-, h) crow.

Kralle ['kralə] f (-/-n) claw (a. fig.); talon, clutch.

Kram [kra:m] m (-[e]s/no pl.) stuff, odds and ends pl.; fig. affairs pl., business.

Krämer ['krɛ:mər] m (-s/-) shopkeeper.

Krampf ⚥ [krampf] m (-[e]s/⸚e) cramp; spasm, convulsion; '⸚ader ⚥ f varicose vein; 'Qhaft adj. ⚥ spasmodic, convulsive; laugh: forced.

Kran ⊕ [krɑːn] m (-[e]s/⸚e, -e) crane.

krank adj. [kraŋk] sick; organ, etc.: diseased; ⸚ sein p. be ill, esp. Am. be sick; animal: be sick or ill; ⸚ werden p. fall ill or esp. Am. sick; animal: fall sick; 'Qe m, f (-n/-n) sick person, patient, invalid.

kränkeln ['krɛŋkəln] v/i. (ge-, h) be sickly, be in poor health.

'kranken fig. v/i. (ge-, h) suffer (an dat. from).

kränken ['krɛŋkən] v/t. (ge-, h) offend, injure; wound or hurt s.o.'s feelings; sich ⸚ feel hurt (über acc. at, about).

'Kranken|bett n sick-bed; '⸚geld n sick-benefit; '⸚haus n hospital; '⸚kasse f health insurance (fund); '⸚kost f invalid diet; '⸚lager n s. Krankenbett; '⸚pflege f nursing; '⸚pfleger m male nurse; '⸚schein m medical certificate; '⸚schwester f (sick-)nurse; '⸚versicherung f health or sickness insurance; '⸚wagen m ambulance; '⸚zimmer n sick-room.

'krank|haft adj. morbid, pathological; 'Qheit f (-/-en) illness, sickness; disease.

'Krankheits|erreger ⚥ m pathogenic agent; '⸚erscheinung f symptom (a. fig.).

'kränklich adj. sickly, ailing.

'Kränkung f (-/-en) insult, offen|ce, Am. -se.

Kranz [krants] m (-es/⸚e) wreath; garland.

Kränzchen fig. ['krɛntsçən] n (-s/-) tea-party, F hen-party.

kraß adj. [kras] crass, gross.

kratzen ['kratsən] (ge-, h) 1. v/i. scratch; 2. v/t. scratch; sich ⸚ scratch (o.s.).

kraulen ['kraʊlən] (ge-) 1. v/t. (h) scratch gently; 2. v/i. (sein) sports: crawl.

kraus adj. [kraʊs] curly, curled; crisp; frizzy; die Stirn ⸚ ziehen knit one's brow; 'Qe f (-/-n) ruff(le), frill.

kräuseln ['krɔʏzəln] v/t. (ge-, h) curl; crimp (hair, etc.); pucker (lips); sich ⸚ hair: curl; waves, etc.: ruffle; smoke: curl or wreath up.

Kraut ⚘ [kraʊt] n 1. (-[e]s/⸚er) plant; herb; 2. (-[e]s/no pl.) tops pl.; cabbage; weed.

Krawall [kra'val] m (-[e]s/-e) riot; shindy, F row, sl. rumpus.

Krawatte [kra'vatə] f (-/-n) (neck-)tie.

Kreatur [krea'tuːr] f (-/-en) creature.

Krebs [kreːps] m (-es/-e) zo. crayfish, Am. a. crawfish; ast. Cancer, Crab; ⚥ cancer; ⸚e pl. ⚕ returns pl.

Kredit ⚥ [kre'diːt] m (-[e]s/-e) credit; auf ⸚ on credit; Qfähig ⚥ adj. credit-worthy.

Kreide ['kraɪdə] f (-/-n) chalk; paint. crayon.

Kreis [kraɪs] m (-es/-e) circle (a.fig.); ast. orbit; ⚡ circuit; district, Am. county; fig.: sphere, field; range.

kreischen ['kraɪʃən] (ge-, h) 1. v/i. screech, scream; squeal, shriek; circular saw, etc.: grate (on the ear); 2. v/t. shriek, screech (insult, etc.).

Kreisel ['kraɪzəl] m (-s/-) (whipping-)top; '⸚kompaß m gyro-compass.

kreisen ['kraɪzən] v/i. (ge-, h) (move in a) circle; revolve, rotate; ⚡, bird: circle; bird: wheel; blood, money: circulate.

kreis|förmig adj. ['kraɪsfœrmiç] circular; 'Qlauf m physiol., money, etc.: circulation; business, trade: cycle; 'Qlaufstörungen ⚥ f/pl. circulatory trouble; '⸚rund adj. circular; 'Qsäge ⊕ f circular saw, Am. a. buzz saw; 'Qverkehr m roundabout (traffic).

Krempe ['krɛmpə] f (-/-n) brim (of hat).

Krempel F ['krɛmpəl] m (-s/no pl.) rubbish, stuff, lumber.

krepieren [kre'piːrən] v/i. (no -ge-, sein) shell: burst, explode; sl. kick the bucket, peg or snuff out; animal: die, perish.

Krepp [krɛp] m (-s/-s, -e) crêpe; crape; '⸚apier ['krɛppapiːr] n crêpe paper; '⸚sohle f crêpe(-rubber) sole.

Kreuz [krɔʏts] 1. n (-es/-e) cross (a. fig.); crucifix; anat. small of the back; ⚥ sacral region; cards: club(s pl.); ♪ sharp; zu ⸚(e) kriechen eat humble pie; 2. ♀ adv.: ⸚ und quer in all directions; criss-cross.

'kreuzen (ge-, h) 1. v/t. cross, fold (arms, etc.); ♀, zo. cross(-breed), hybridize; sich ⸚ roads: cross, intersect; plans, etc.: clash; 2. ⚓ v/i. cruise.

'Kreuzer ⚓ m (-s/-) cruiser.

'Kreuz|fahrer hist. m crusader; '⸚fahrt f hist. crusade; ⚓ cruise; '⸚feuer n ⚔ cross-fire (a. fig.); Qigen ['⸚igən] v/t. (ge-, h) crucify; ⸚igung ['⸚igʊŋ] f (-/-en) crucifixion; '⸚otter zo. f common viper; '⸚ritter hist. m knight of the Cross; '⸚schmerzen m/pl. back ache; '⸚spinne zo. f garden- or cross-spider; '⸚ung f (-/-en) ⚥, roads, etc.: crossing, intersection; roads: crossroads; ♀, zo. cross-breeding, hybridization; '⸚verhör ⚖ n cross-examination; ins ⸚ nehmen cross-examine; '⊋weise *adv.* crosswise, crossways; '⊸worträtsel *n* crossword (puzzle); '⊸zug *hist. m* crusade.

kriech|en ['kri:çən] *v/i. (irr., ge-, sein)* creep, crawl; *fig.* cringe (*vor dat.* to, before); '⊋er *contp. m (-s/-)* toady; ⊋erei *contp.* [⊸'raɪ] *f (-/-en)* toadyism.

Krieg [kri:k] *m (-[e]s/-e)* war; *im* ⊸ at war; *s.* führen.

kriegen F ['kri:gən] *v/t. (ge-, h)* catch, seize; get.

Krieg|er ['kri:gər] *m (-s/-)* warrior; '⊸erdenkmal *n* war memorial; '⊋erisch *adj.* warlike; militant; '⊋führend *adj.* belligerent; '⊸führung *f* warfare.

'Kriegs|beil *fig. n: das* ⊸ *begraben* bury the hatchet; ⊋beschädigt *adj.* ['⊸bəʃəːdiçt] war-disabled; '⊸beschädigte *m (-n/-n)* disabled ex-serviceman; '⊸dienst ⚔ *m* war service; '⊸dienstverweigerer ⚔ *m (-s/-)* conscientious objector; '⊸erklärung *f* declaration of war; '⊸flotte *f* naval force; '⊸gefangene *m* prisoner of war; '⊸gefangenschaft ⚔ *f* captivity; *fig.* climax, culmination. n court martial; '⊸gewinner ['⊸gəvinlər] *m (-s/-)* war profiteer; '⊸hafen *m* naval port; '⊸kamerad *m* wartime comrade; '⊸list *f* stratagem; '⊸macht *f* military forces *pl.*; '⊸minister *hist. m* minister of war; Secretary of State for War, *Am.* Secretary of War; '⊸ministerium *hist. n* ministry of war; War Office, *Am.* War Department; '⊸rat *m* council of war; '⊸schauplatz ⚔ *m* theat|re *or Am.* -er of war; '⊸schiff *n* warship; '⊸schule *f* military academy; '⊸teilnehmer *m* combatant; ex-serviceman, *Am.* veteran; '⊸treiber *m (-s/-)* warmonger; '⊸verbrecher *m* war criminal; '⊸zug *m* (military) expedition, campaign.

Kriminal|beamte [krimi'naːl-] *m* criminal investigator, *Am.* plainclothes man; ⊸film *m* crime film; thriller; ⊸polizei *f* criminal investigation department; ⊸roman *m* detective *or* crime novel, thriller, *sl.* whodun(n)it.

kriminell *adj.* [krimi'nɛl] criminal; ⊋e *m (-n/-n)* criminal.

Krippe ['kripə] *f (-/-n)* crib, manger; crèche.

Krise ['kri:zə] *f (-/-n)* crisis.

Kristall [kris'tal] 1. *m (-s/-e)* crystal; 2. *n (-s/no pl.)* crystal(-glass); ⊋isieren [⊸i'zi:rən] *v/i. and v/refl. (no -ge-, h)* crystallize.

Kriti|k [kri'ti:k] *f (-/-en)* criticism; ♩, *thea.*, *etc.*: review, critique; F *unter aller* ⊸ beneath contempt; ⊸ *üben an (dat.) s.* kritisieren; ⊸ker ['kri:tikər] *m (-s/-)* critic; *books*: re-

viewer; ⊋sch *adj.* ['kri:tiʃ] critical *(gegenüber* of); ⊋sieren [kriti'zi:rən] *v/t. (no -ge-, h)* criticize; review *(book)*.

kritt|eln ['kritəln] *v/t. (ge-, h)* find fault *(an dat.* with), cavil (at); ⊋ler ['⊸lər] *m (-s/-)* fault-finder, caviller.

Kritzel|ei [kritsə'laɪ] *f (-/-en)* scrawl(ing), scribble, scribbling; '⊋n *v/t. and v/i. (ge-, h)* scrawl, scribble.

kroch [krɔx] *pret. of* kriechen.

Krokodil *zo.* [kroko'di:l] *n (-s/-e)* crocodile.

Krone ['kro:nə] *f (-/-n)* crown; coronet *(of duke, earl, etc.).*

krönen ['krø:nən] *v/t. (ge-, h)* crown *(zum König* king) *(a.fig.).*

'Kron|leuchter *m* chandelier; lust|re, *Am.* -er; electrolier; '⊸prinz *m* crown prince; '⊸prinzessin *f* crown princess.

'Krönung *f (-/-en)* coronation, crowning; *fig.* climax, culmination.

'Kronzeuge ♩ *m* chief witness; King's evidence, *Am.* State's evidence.

Kropf ♩ [krɔpf] goit|re, *Am.* -er.

Kröte *zo.* ['krø:tə] *f (-/-n)* toad.

Krücke ['krykə] *f (-/-n)* crutch.

Krug [kru:k] *m (-[e]s/-e)* jug, pitcher; jar; mug; tankard.

Krume ['kru:mə] *f (-/-n)* crumb; ⊸ topsoil.

Krümel ['kry:məl] *m (-s/-)* small crumb; ⊋n *v/t. and v/i. (ge-, h)* crumble.

krumm *adj.* [krum] *p.* bent, stooping; *limb, nose, etc.*: crooked; *spine*: curved; *deal, business, etc.*: crooked; '⊸beinig *adj.* bandy- *or* bow-legged.

krümmen ['krymən] *v/t. (ge-, h)* bend *(arm, back, etc.)*; crook *(finger, etc.)*; curve *(metal sheet, etc.)*; *sich* ⊸ *person, snake, etc.*: writhe; *worm, etc.*: wriggle; *sich vor Schmerzen* ⊸ writhe with pain; *sich vor Lachen* ⊸ be convulsed with laughter.

'Krümmung *f (-/-en)* road, *etc.*: bend; *arch, road, etc.*: curve; *river, path, etc.*: turn, wind, meander; *earth's surface, spine, etc.*: curvature.

Krüppel ['krypəl] *m (-s/-)* cripple.

Kruste ['krustə] *f (-/-n)* crust.

Kübel ['ky:bəl] *m (-s/-)* tub; pail, bucket.

Kubik|meter [ku'bi:k-] *n, m* cubic met|re, *Am.* -er; ⊸wurzel Ⅹ *f* cube root.

Küche ['kyçə] *f (-/-n)* kitchen; cuisine, cookery; *s.* kalt.

Kuchen ['ku:xən] *m (-s/-)* cake, flan; pastry.

'Küchen|geschirr *n*, '⊸geschirr *n* kitchen utensils *pl.*; '⊸herd *m* (kitchen-)range; cooker, stove; '⊸schrank *m* kitchen cupboard *or* cabinet; '~zettel *m* bill of fare, menu.

Kuckuck *orn.* ['kukuk] *m* (-s/-e) cuckoo.

Kufe ['ku:fə] *f* (-/-n) ≋ skid; *sleigh, etc.*: runner.

Küfer ['ky:fər] *m* (-s/-) cooper; cellarman.

Kugel ['ku:gəl] *f* (-/-n) ball; ✕ bullet; ♪, *geogr.* sphere; *sports*: shot, weight; 2förmig *adj.* ['~fœrmiç] spherical, ball-shaped, globular; '~gelenk ⊕, *anat. n* ball-and-socket joint; '~lager ⊕ *n* ball-bearing; '2n (ge-) 1. *v/i.* (sein) *ball, etc.*: roll; 2. *v/t.* (h) roll (*ball, etc.*); *sich ~ children, etc.*: roll about; F double up (vor with *laughter*); '~schreiber *m* ball-(point)-pen; '~stoßen *n* (-s/*no pl.*) *sports*: putting the shot or weight.

Kuh *zo.* [ku:] *f* (-/⁀e) cow.

kühl *adj.* [ky:l] cool (*a. fig.*); '2anlage *f* cold-storage plant; '2e *f* (-/*no pl.*) cool(ness); '~en *v/t.* (ge-, h) cool (*wine, wound, etc.*); chill (*wine, etc.*); '2er *mot. m* (-s/-) radiator; '2raum *m* cold-storage chamber; '2schrank *m* refrigerator, F fridge.

kühn *adj.* [ky:n] bold (*a. fig.*), daring; audacious.

'**Kuhstall** *m* cow-house, byre, *Am. a.* cow barn.

Küken *orn.* ['ky:kən] *n* (-s/-) chick.

kulant ✝ *adj.* [ku'lant] firm, *etc.*: accommodating, obliging; *price, terms, etc.*: fair, easy.

Kulisse [ku'lisə] *f* (-/-n) *thea.* wing, side-scene; *fig.* front; *~n pl. a.* scenery; *hinter den ~n* behind the scenes.

Kult [kult] *m* (-[e]s/-e) cult, worship.

kultivieren [kulti'vi:rən] *v/t.* (*no* -ge-, h) cultivate (*a. fig.*).

Kultur [kul'tu:r] *f* (-/-en) ⚓ cultivation; *fig.*: culture; civilization; 2ell *adj.* ['~u'rel] cultural; '~film [~'tu:r-] *m* educational film; '~geschichte *f* history of civilization; '~volk *n* civilized people.

Kultus ['kultus] *m* (-/Kulte) *s.* Kult; '~minister *m* minister of education and cultural affairs; '~ministerium *n* ministry of education and cultural affairs.

Kummer ['kumər] *m* (-s/*no pl.*) grief, sorrow; trouble, worry.

kümmer|lich *adj.* ['kymərliç] *life, etc.*: miserable, wretched; *conditions, etc.*: pitiful, pitiable; *result, etc.*: poor; *resources*: scanty; '~n *v/t.* (ge-, h): *es kümmert mich* I bother, I worry; *sich ~ um* look after, take care of; see to; meddle with.

'**kummervoll** *adj.* sorrowful.

Kump|an F [kum'pa:n] *m* (-s/-e) companion; F mate, chum, *Am.* F *a.*

buddy; ~el ['~pəl] *m* (-s/-, F -s) ✕ pitman, collier; F work-mate; F *s. Kumpan.*

Kunde ['kundə] 1. *m* (-n/-n) customer, client; 2. *f* (-/-n) knowledge.

Kundgebung ['kunt-] *f* (-/-en) manifestation; *pol.* rally.

kündig|en ['kyndigən] (ge-, h) 1. *v/i.*: *j-m ~* give s.o. notice; 2. *v/t.* ✝ call in (*capital*); ⚖ cancel (*contract*); *pol.* denounce (*treaty*); '2ung *f* (-/-en) notice; ✝ calling in; ⚖ cancellation; *pol.* denunciation.

'**Kundschaft** *f* (-/-en) customers *pl.*, clients *pl.*; custom, clientele; '~er ✕ *m* (-s/-) scout; spy.

künftig ['kynftiç] 1. *adj. event, years, etc.*: future; *event, programme, etc.*: coming; *life, world, etc.*: next; 2. *adv.* in future, from now on.

Kunst [kunst] *f* (-/⁀e) art; skill; '~akademie *f* academy of arts; '~ausstellung *f* art exhibition; '~druck *m* art print(ing); '~dünger *m* artificial manure, fertilizer; '2fertig *adj.* skilful, skilled; '~fertigkeit *f* artistic skill; '~gegenstand *m* objet d'art; '2gerecht *adj.* skilful; professional; expert; '~geschichte *f* history of art; '~gewerbe *n* arts and crafts *pl.*; applied arts *pl.*; '~glied *n* artificial limb; '~griff *m* trick, dodge; artifice, knack; '~händler *m* art-dealer; '~kenner *m* connoisseur of or in art; '~leder *n* imitation or artificial leather.

Künstler ['kynstlər] *m* (-s/-) artist; ♪, *thea.* performer; '2isch *adj.* artistic.

künstlich *adj.* ['kynstliç] *eye, flower, light, etc.*: artificial; *teeth, hair, etc.*: false; *fibres, dyes, etc.*: synthetic.

'**Kunst|liebhaber** *m* art-lover; '~maler *m* artist, painter; '~reiter *m* equestrian; circus-rider; '~schätze ['~fetsə] *m/pl.* art treasures *pl.*; '~seide *f* artificial silk, rayon; '~stück *n* feat, trick, F stunt; '~tischler *m* cabinet-maker; '~verlag *m* art publishers *pl.*; '2voll *adj.* artistic, elaborate; '~werk *n* work of art.

kunterbunt F *fig. adj.* ['kuntər-] higgledy-piggledy.

Kupfer ['kupfər] *n* (-s/*no pl.*) copper; '~geld *n* copper coins *pl.*, F coppers *pl.*; '2n *adj.* (of) copper; '2rot *adj.* copper-colo(u)red; '~stich *m* copper-plate engraving.

Kupon [ku'põ:] *m* (-s/-s) *s.* Coupon.

Kuppe ['kupə] *f* (-/-n) rounded hill-top; *nail*: head.

Kuppel △ ['kupəl] *f* (-/-n) dome, cupola; '~ei *f* [~'laı] *f* (-/-en) procuring; '2n (ge-, h) 1. *v/t. s. koppeln*; 2. *mot. v/i.* declutch.

Kuppl|er ['kuplər] *m* (-s/-) pimp, procurer; '~ung *f* (-/-en) ⊕ coupling (*a.* 🚃); *mot.* clutch.

Kur [ku:r] *f* (-/-en) course of treatment, cure.

Kür [ky:r] *f* (-/-en) *sports*: s. *Kürlauf*; voluntary exercise.

Kuratorium [kura'to:rium] *n* (-s/ *Kuratorien*) board of trustees.

Kurbel ⊕ ['kurbəl] *f* (-/-n) crank, winch, handle; '2n (ge-, *h*) 1. *v/t.* shoot (*film*); *in die Höhe* ~ winch up (*load, etc.*); wind up (*car window, etc.*); 2. *v/i.* crank.

Kürbis ♀ ['kyrbis] *m* (-ses/-se) pumpkin.

'**Kur|gast** *m* visitor to *or* patient at a health resort *or* spa; '~haus *n* spa hotel.

Kurier [ku'ri:r] *m* (-s/-e) courier, express (messenger).

kurieren ⚗ [ku'ri:rən] *v/t.* (no -ge-, *h*) cure.

kurios *adj.* [kur'jo:s] curious, odd, strange, queer. [skating.]

'**Kürlauf** *m* *sports*: free (roller)]

'**Kur|ort** *m* health resort; spa; '~pfuscher *m* quack (doctor); ~pfusche'rei *f* (-/-en) quackery.

Kurs [kurs] *m* (-es/-e) ♣ currency; ✝ rate, price; ⚓ *and fig.* course; course, class; '~bericht ✝ *m* market-report; '~buch 🚂 *n* railway guide, *Am.* railroad guide.

Kürschner ['kyrʃnər] *m* (-s/-) furrier.

kursieren [kur'zi:rən] *v/i.* (no -ge-, *h*) *money, etc.*: circulate, be in circulation; *rumour, etc.*: circulate, be afloat, go about.

Kursivschrift *typ.* [kur'zi:f-] *f* italics *pl.*

Kursus ['kurzus] *m* (-/*Kurse*) course, class.

'**Kurs|verlust** ✝ *m* loss on the stock exchange; '~wert ✝ *m* market value; '~zettel ✝ *m* stock exchange list.

Kurve ['kurvə] *f* (-/-n) curve; *road, etc.*: a. bend, turn.

kurz [kurts] 1. *adj. space*: short; *time, etc.*: short, brief; ~ *und bündig* brief, concise; ~e *Hose* shorts *pl.*; *mit* ~en *Worten* with a few words; *den kürzeren ziehen* get the worst of it; 2. *adv.* in short; ~ *angebunden sein* be curt or sharp; ~ *und gut* in short, in a word; ~ *vor London* short of London; *sich* ~ *fassen* be brief *or* concise; *in* ~em before long, shortly; *vor* ~em a short time ago; *zu* ~ *kommen* come off badly, get a raw deal; *um es* ~ *zu sagen* to cut a long story short; '2arbeit ✝ *f* short-time work; '2arbeiter ✝ *m* short-time worker; ~atmig *adj.* ['~ʔa:t-miç] short-winded.

Kürze ['kyrtsə] *f* (-/no *pl.*). shortness; brevity; *in* ~ shortly, before long; '2n *v/t.* (ge-, *h*) shorten (*dress, etc.*) (*um by*); abridge, condense (*book, etc.*); cut, reduce (*expenses, etc.*).

'**kurz|er'hand** *adv.* without hesitation; on the spot; '2film *m* short (film); '2form *f* shortened form; '~fristig *adj.* short-term; ✝ *bill, etc.*: short-dated; '2geschichte *f* (short) short story; ~lebig *adj.* ['~'le:biç] short-lived; '2nachrichten *f/pl.* news summary.

kürzlich *adv.* ['kyrtsliç] lately, recently, not long ago.

'**Kurz|schluß** ⚡ *m* short circuit, F short; '~schrift *f* shorthand, stenography; '2sichtig *adj.* short-sighted, near-sighted; 2'um *adv.* in short, in a word.

'**Kürzung** *f* (-/-en) shortening (*of dress, etc.*); abridg(e)ment, condensation (*of book, etc.*); cut, reduction (*of expenses, etc.*).

'**Kurz|waren** *f/pl.* haberdashery, *Am.* dry goods *pl.*, notions *pl.*; '~weil *f* (-/no *pl.*) amusement, entertainment; '2weilig *adj.* amusing, entertaining; '~welle ⚡ *f* short wave; *radio*: short-wave band.

Kusine [ku'zi:nə] *f* (-/-n) s. *Cousine*.

Kuß [kus] *m* (*Kusses/Küsse*) kiss; '2echt *adj.* kiss-proof.

küssen ['kysən] *v/t. and v/i.* (ge-, *h*) kiss.

'**kußfest** *adj.* s. *kußecht*.

Küste ['kystə] *f* (-/-n) coast; shore.

'**Küsten|bewohner** *m* inhabitant of a coastal region; '~fischerei *f* inshore fishery *or* fishing; '~gebiet *n* coastal area *or* region; '~schiffahrt *f* coastal shipping.

Küster *eccl.* ['kystər] *m* (-s/-) verger, sexton, sacristan.

Kutsch|bock ['kutʃ-] *m* coach-box; '~e *f* (-/-n) carriage, coach; '~enschlag *m* carriage-door, coach-door; '~er *m* (-s/-) coachman; 2ieren [~'tʃi:rən] (no -ge-) 1. *v/t.* (*h*) drive *s.o.* in a coach; 2. *v/i.* (*h*) (drive a) coach; 3. *v/i.* (*sein*) (drive *or* ride in a) coach.

Kutte ['kutə] *f* (-/-n) cowl.

Kutter ⚓ ['kutər] *m* (-s/-) cutter.

Kuvert [ku'vɛrt] *n* (-[e]s/-e; -s/-s) envelope; *at table*: cover.

Kux ⚒ [kuks] *m* (-es/-e) mining share.

L

Lab zo. [lɑːp] n (-[e]s/-e) rennet.
labil adj. [la'biːl] unstable (a. ⊕, ⚕); phys., ⚓ labile.
Labor [la'boːr] n (-s/-s, -e) s. **Laboratorium**; **∼ant** [labo'rant] m (-en/-en) laboratory assistant; **∼atorium** [labora'toːrjum] n (-s/ Laboratorien) laboratory; **∼ieren** [∼o'riːrən] v/i. (no -ge-, h): **∼** an (dat.) labo(u)r under, suffer from.
Labyrinth [laby'rint] n (-[e]s/-e) labyrinth, maze.
Lache ['laxə] f (-/-n) pool, puddle.
lächeln ['lɛçəln] **1.** v/i. (ge-, h) smile (über acc. at); höhnisch **∼** sneer (über acc. at); **2.** ⚲ n (-s/no pl.) smile; höhnisches **∼** sneer.
lachen ['laxən] **1.** v/i. (ge-, h) laugh (über acc. at); **2.** ⚲ n (-s/no pl.) laugh(ter).
lächerlich adj. ['lɛçərliç] ridiculous, laughable, ludicrous; absurd; derisory, scoffing; **∼ machen** ridicule; **sich ∼ machen** make a fool of o.s.
Lachs ichth. [laks] m (-es/-e) salmon.
Lack [lak] m (-[e]s/-e) (gum-)lac, varnish; lacquer, enamel; **∼ieren** [la'kiːrən] v/t. (no -ge-, h) lacquer, varnish; enamel; **∼leder** n patent leather; **∼schuhe** m/pl. patent leather shoes pl., F patents pl.
Lade|fähigkeit ['lɑːdə-] f loading capacity; **∼fläche** f loading area; **∼hemmung** ⚔ f jam, stoppage; **∼linie** ⚓ f load-line.
laden[1] ['lɑːdən] v/t. (irr., ge-, h) load; load (gun), charge (a. ⚡); freight, ship; ⚖ cite, summon; invite, ask (guest).
Laden[2] [∼] m (-s/⁼) shop, Am. store; shutter; **∼besitzer** m s. Ladeninhaber; **∼dieb** m shop-lifter; **∼diebstahl** m shop-lifting; **∼hüter** m drug on the market; **∼inhaber** m shopkeeper, Am. storekeeper; **∼kasse** f till; **∼preis** m selling-price, retail price; **∼schild** n shopsign; **∼schluß** m closing time; nach **∼** after hours; **∼tisch** m counter.
'Lade|platz m loading-place; **'∼rampe** f loading platform or ramp; **'∼raum** m loading space; ⚓ hold; **'∼schein** ⚓ m bill of lading.
'Ladung f (-/-en) loading; load, freight; ⚓ cargo; ⚡ charge (a. of gun); ⚖ summons.
lag [lɑːk] pret. of liegen.
Lage ['lɑːgə] f (-/-n) situation, position; site, location (of building); state, condition; attitude; geol. layer, stratum; round (of beer, etc.); in der **∼** sein zu inf. be able to inf., be in a position to inf.; versetzen

Sie sich in meine **∼** put yourself in my place.
Lager ['lɑːgər] n (-s/-) couch, bed; den, lair (of wild animals); geol. deposit; ⊕ bearing; warehouse, storehouse, depot; store, stock (⭱ pl. a. Läger); ✕, etc.: camp, encampment; auf **∼** ✝ on hand, in stock; **'∼buch** n stock-book; **'∼feuer** n camp-fire; **'∼geld** n storage; **'∼haus** n warehouse; **'∼n** (ge-, h) **1.** v/i. lie down, rest; ✕ (en)camp; ✝ be stored; **2.** v/t. lay down; ✕ (en)camp; ✝ store, warehouse; **sich ∼** lie down, rest; **'∼platz** m ✝ depot; resting-place; ✕, etc.: camp-site; **'∼raum** m store-room; **'∼ung** f (-/-en) storage (of goods).
Lagune [la'guːnə] f (-/-n) lagoon.
lahm adj. [lɑːm] lame; **'∼en** v/i. (ge-, h) be lame.
lähmen ['lɛːmən] v/t. (ge-, h) (make) lame; paraly|se, Am. -ze (a. fig.).
'lahmlegen v/t. (sep., -ge-, h) paraly|se, Am. -ze; obstruct.
'Lähmung ⚕ f (-/-en) paralysis.
Laib [laɪp] m (-[e]s/-e) loaf.
Laich [laɪç] m (-[e]s/-e) spawn; **'∼en** v/i. (ge-, h) spawn.
Laie ['laɪə] m (-n/-n) layman; amateur; **'∼nbühne** f amateur theat|re, Am. -er.
Lakai [la'kaɪ] m (-en/-en) lackey (a. fig.), footman.
Lake ['lɑːkə] f (-/-n) brine, pickle.
Laken ['lɑːkən] n (-s/-) sheet.
lallen ['lalən] v/i. and v/t. (ge-, h) stammer; babble.
Lamelle [la'melə] f (-/-n) lamella, lamina; ♀ gill (of mushrooms).
lamentieren [lamen'tiːrən] v/i. (no -ge-, h) lament (um for; über acc. over).
Lamm zo. [lam] n (-[e]s/⁼er) lamb; **'∼fell** n lambskin; **'⚲fromm** adj. (as) gentle or (as) meek as a lamb.
Lampe ['lampə] f (-/-n) lamp.
'Lampen|fieber n stage fright; **'∼licht** n lamplight; **'∼schirm** m lamp-shade.
Lampion [lã'pjoː] m, n (-s/-s) Chinese lantern.
Land [lant] n (-[e]s/⁼er, poet. -e) land; country; territory; ground, soil; an **∼** gehen go ashore; auf dem **∼e** in the country; aufs **∼** gehen go into the country; außer **∼es** gehen go abroad; zu **∼e** by land; **'∼arbeiter** m farm-hand; **'∼besitz** m landed property; ⚖ real estate; **'∼besitzer** m landowner, landed proprietor; **'∼bevölkerung** f rural population.
Lande|bahn ✈ ['landə-] f runway; **'∼deck** ✈ n flight-deck.

land'einwärts *adv.* upcountry, inland.

landen ['landən] (ge-) **1.** *v/i.* (sein) land; **2.** *v/t.* (h) ⚓ disembark (*troups*); ⚓ land, set down (*troups*).

'Landenge *f* neck of land, isthmus.

Landeplatz ⚓ ['landə-] *m* landing-field.

Ländereien [lɛndə'raɪən] *pl.* landed property, lands *pl.*, estates *pl.*

Länderspiel ['lɛndər-] *n sports:* international match.

Landes|grenze ['landəs-] *f* frontier, boundary; '**~innere** *n* interior, inland, upcountry; '**~kirche** *f* national church; *Brt.* Established Church; '**~regierung** *f* government; *in Germany:* Land government; '**~sprache** *f* native language, vernacular; '**²üblich** *adj.* customary; '**~verrat** *m* treason; '**~verräter** *m* traitor to his country; '**~verteidigung** *f* national defen|ce, *Am.* -se.

'Land|flucht *f* rural exodus; '**~friedensbruch** ⚖ *m* breach of the public peace; '**~gericht** *n appr.* district court; '**~gewinnung** *f* (-/-en) reclamation of land; '**~gut** *n* country-seat, estate; '**~haus** *n* country-house, cottage; '**~karte** *f* map; '**~kreis** *m* rural district; '**²läufig** *adj.* ['~lɔyfɪç] customary, current, common.

ländlich *adj.* ['lɛntlɪç] rural, rustic.

'Land|maschinen *f/pl.* agricultural or farm equipment; '**~partie** *f* picnic, outing, excursion into the country; '**~plage** *iro. f* nuisance; '**~rat** *m* (-[e]s/≠e) *appr.* district president; '**~ratte** ⚓ *f* landlubber; '**~recht** *n* common law; '**~regen** *m* persistent rain.

'Landschaft *f* (-/-en) province, district, region; countryside, scenery; *esp. paint.* landscape; '**²lich** *adj.* provincial; scenic (*beauty, etc.*).

'Landsmann *m* (-[e]s/Landsleute) (fellow-)countryman, compatriot; *was sind Sie für ein ~?* what's your native country?

'Land|straße *f* highway, high road; '**~streicher** *m* (-s/-) vagabond, tramp, *Am.* -sl. hobo; '**~streitkräfte** *f/pl.* land forces *pl., the* Army; ground forces *pl.*; '**~strich** *m* tract of land, region; '**~tag** *m* Landtag, Land parliament.

Landung ['landuŋ] *f* (-/-en) ✈ landing; disembarkation; arrival; '**~sbrücke** ⚓ *f floating:* landing-stage; pier; '**~ssteg** ⚓ *m* gangway, gang-plank.

'Land|vermesser *m* (-s/-) surveyor; '**~vermessung** *f* land-surveying; **²wärts** *adv.* ['~vɛrts] landward(s); '**~weg** *m:* *auf dem ~e* by land; '**~wirt** *m* farmer, agriculturist; '**~wirtschaft** *f* agriculture, farming; '**²wirtschaftlich** *adj.* agri-

cultural; '**~e Maschinen** *f/pl. s. Landmaschinen*; '**~zunge** *f* spit.

lang [laŋ] **1.** *adj.* long; *p.* tall; *er machte ein ~es Gesicht* his face fell; **2.** *adv.* long; *e-e Woche ~* for a week; *über kurz oder ~* sooner or later; '**~(e)** *anhaltend* continuous; '**~(e)** *entbehrt* long-missed; '**~(e)** *ersehnt* long-wished-for; *das ist schon ~(e) her* that was a long time ago; *~ und breit* at (full or great) length; *noch ~(e) nicht* not for a long time yet; *far from ger.*; *wie ~e lernen Sie schon Englisch?* how long have you been learning English?; **~atmig** *adj.* ['~ɑːtmɪç] long-winded; '**~e** *adv. s. lang 2.*

Länge ['lɛŋə] *f* (-/-n) length; tallness; *geogr., ast.* longitude; *der ~ nach* (at) full length, lengthwise.

langen ['laŋən] *v/i.* (ge-, h) suffice, be enough; *~ nach* reach for.

'Längen|grad *m* degree of longitude; '**~maß** *n* linear measure.

'länger 1. *adj.* longer; '**~e Zeit** (for) some time; **2.** *adv.* longer; *ich kann es nicht ~ ertragen* I cannot bear it any longer; *je ~, je lieber* the longer the better.

'Langeweile *f* (-, Langenweile/no pl.) boredom, tediousness, ennui.

'lang|fristig *adj.* long-term; '**~jährig** *adj.* of long standing; '**~e Erfahrung** (many) years of experience; '**²lauf** *m skiing:* cross-country run or race.

'länglich *adj.* longish, oblong.

'Langmut *f* (-/no pl.) patience, forbearance.

längs [lɛŋs] **1.** *prp.* (*gen., dat.*) along(side of); *~ der Küste fahren* ⚓ (sail along the) coast; **2.** *adv.* lengthwise; '**²achse** *f* longitudinal axis.

'lang|sam *adj.* slow; **²schläfer** ['~ʃlɛːfər] *m* (-s/-) late riser, lie-abed; '**²spielplatte** *f* long-playing record.

längst *adv.* [lɛŋst] long ago *or* since; *ich weiß es ~* I have known it for a long time; '**~ens** *adv.* at the longest; at the latest; at the most.

'lang|stielig *adj.* long-handled; ⚘ long-stemmed, long-stalked; '**²streckenlauf** *m* long-distance run or race; '**²weile** *f* (-, Langenweile/no pl.) *s. Langeweile*; '**~weilen** *v/t.* (ge-, h) bore; *sich ~* be bored; '**~weilig** *adj.* tedious, boring, dull; '**~e Person** bore; '**²welle** *f ≴* long wave; *radio:* long wave band; '**~wierig** *adj.* ['~viːrɪç] protracted, lengthy; **≴** lingering.

Lanze ['lantsə] *f* (-/-n) spear, lance.

Lappalie [la'pɑːljə] *f* (-/-n) trifle.

Lapp|en ['lapən] *m* (-s/-) patch; rag; duster; (dish- *or* floor-)cloth; *anat.,* ⚘ lobe; '**²ig** *adj.* flabby.

läppisch *adj.* ['lɛpɪʃ] foolish, silly.

Lärche ♀ ['lɛrçə] f (-/-n) larch.

Lärm [lɛrm] m (-[e]s/no pl.) noise; din; ~ schlagen give the alarm; ~ schlagen give the noise; '♀end adj. noisy.

Larve ['larfə] f (-/-n) mask; face (often iro.); zo. larva, grub.

las [laːs] pret. of lesen.

lasch F adj. [laʃ] limp, lax.

Lasche ['laʃə] f (-/-n) strap; tongue (of shoe).

lassen ['lasən] (irr., h) 1. v/t. (ge-) let; leave; laß das! don't!; laß das Weinen! stop crying!; ich kann es nicht ~ I cannot help (doing) it; sein Leben ~ für sacrifice one's life for; 2. v/i. (ge-): von et.~ desist from s.th., renounce s.th.; do without s.th.; 3. v/aux. (no -ge-) allow, permit, let; make, cause; drucken ~ have s. th. printed; gehen ~ let s.o. go; ich habe ihn dieses Buch lesen ~ I have made him read this book; von sich hören ~ send word; er läßt sich nichts sagen he won't take advice; es läßt sich nicht leugnen there is no denying (the fact).

lässig adj. ['lɛsiç] indolent, idle; sluggish; careless.

Last [last] f (-/-en) load; burden; weight; cargo, freight; fig. weight, charge, trouble; zu ~en von ♀ to the debit of; j-m zur ~ fallen be a burden to s.o.; j-m et. zur ~ legen lay s.th. at s.o.'s door or to s.o.'s charge; '~auto n s. Lastkraftwagen.

'lasten v/i. (ge-, h): ~ auf (dat.) weigh or press (up)on; '~aufzug m goods lift, Am. freight elevator.

Laster ['lastər] n (-s/-) vice.

Lästerer ['lɛstərər] m (-s/-) slanderer, backbiter.

'lasterhaft adj. vicious; corrupt.

Läster|maul ['lɛstər-] n s. Lästerer; '♀n v/i. (ge-, h) slander, calumniate, defame; abuse; '~ung f (-/-en) slander, calumny.

lästig adj. ['lɛstiç] troublesome; annoying; uncomfortable, inconvenient.

'Last|kahn m barge, lighter; '~kraftwagen m lorry, Am. truck; '~schrift ♀ f debit; '~tier n pack animal; '~wagen m s. Lastkraftwagen.

Latein [la'taɪn] n (-s/no pl.) Latin; ♀isch adj. Latin.

Laterne [la'tɛrnə] f (-/-n) lantern; street-lamp; ~npfahl m lamp-post.

latschen ['laːtʃən] v/i. (ge-, sein) shuffle (along).

Latte ['latə] f (-/-n) pale; lath; sports: bar; '~nkiste f crate; '~nverschlag m latticed partition; '~nzaun m paling, Am. picket fence.

Lätzchen ['lɛtsçən] n (-s/-) bib, feeder.

lau adj. [lau] tepid, lukewarm (a. fig.).

Laub [laup] n (-[e]s/no pl.) foliage, leaves pl.; '~baum m deciduous tree.

Laube ['laubə] f (-/-n) arbo(u)r, bower; '~ngang m arcade.

'Laub|frosch zo. m tree-frog; '~säge f fret-saw.

Lauch ♀ [laux] m (-[e]s/-e) leek.

Lauer ['lauər] f (-/no pl.): auf der ~ liegen or sein lie in wait or ambush, be on the look-out; '♀n v/i. (ge-, h) lurk (auf acc. for); ~ auf (acc.) watch for; '♀nd adj. louring, lowering.

Lauf [lauf] m (-[e]s/⸚e) run(ning); sports: a. run, heat; race; current (of water); course; barrel (of gun); ♪ run; im ~ der Zeit in (the) course of time; '~bahn f career; '~bursche m errand-boy, office-boy; '~disziplin f sports: running event.

'laufen (irr., ge-) 1. v/i. (sein) run; walk; flow; time: pass, go by, elapse; leak; die Dinge ~ lassen let things slide; j-n ~ lassen let s.o. go; 2. v/t. (sein, h) run; walk; '~d adj. running; current; regular; ~en Monats ♀ instant; auf dem ~en sein be up to date, be fully informed.

Läufer ['lɔyfər] m (-s/-) runner (a. carpet); chess: bishop; football: half-back.

'Lauf|masche f ladder, Am. a. run; '~paß F m sack, sl. walking papers pl.; '~planke ⚓ f gang-board, gang-plank; '~schritt m: im ~ running; '~steg m footbridge; ⚓ gangway.

Lauge ['laugə] f (-/-n) lye.

Laun|e ['launə] f (-/-n) humo(u)r; mood; temper; caprice, fancy, whim; guter ~ in (high) spirits; '♀enhaft adj. capricious; '♀isch adj. moody; wayward.

Laus zo. [laus] f (-/⸚e) louse; ~bub ['~buːp] m (-en/-en) young scamp, F young devil, rascal.

lausch|en ['lauʃən] v/i. (ge-, h) listen; eavesdrop; '~ig adj. snug, cosy; peaceful.

laut [laut] 1. adj. loud (a. fig.); noisy; 2. adv. aloud, loud(ly); (sprechen Sie) ~er! speak up!, Am. louder!; 3. prp. (gen., dat.) according to; ♀ as per; 4. ♀ m (-[e]s/-e) sound; '♀e ♪ f (-/-n) lute; '~en v/i. (ge-, h) sound; words, etc.: run; read; ~ auf (acc.) passport, etc.: be issued to.

läuten ['lɔytən] (ge-, h) 1. v/i. ring; toll; es läutet the bell is ringing; 2. v/t. ring; toll.

'lauter adj. pure; clear; genuine; sincere; mere, nothing but, only.

läuter|n ['lɔytərn] v/t. (ge-, h) purify; ⊕ cleanse; refine; '♀ung f (-/-en) purification; refining.

'laut|los adj. noiseless; mute; silent; silence: hushed; '2schrift f phonetic transcription; '2sprecher m loud-speaker; '2stärke f sound intensity; radio: (sound-)volume; 2stärkeregler ['‿re:glər] m (-s/-) volume control.

'lauwarm adj. tepid, lukewarm.

Lava geol. ['la:va] f (-/Laven) lava.

Lavendel ♀ [la'vɛndəl] m (-s/-) lavender.

lavieren [la'vi:rən] v/i. (no -ge-, h, sein) ♣ tack (a. fig.).

Lawine [la'vi:nə] f (-/-n) avalanche.

lax adj. [laks] lax, loose; morals: a. easy.

Lazarett [latsa'rɛt] n (-[e]s/-e) (military) hospital.

leben¹ ['le:bən] (ge-, h) 1. v/i. live; be alive; ‿ Sie wohl! good-bye!, farewell!; j-n hochleben lassen cheer s.o.; at table: drink s.o.'s health; von et. ‿ live on s.th.; hier lebt es sich gut it is pleasant living here; 2. v/t. live (one's life).

Leben² [‿] n (-s/-) life; stir, animation, bustle; am ‿ bleiben remain alive, survive; am ‿ erhalten keep alive; ein neues ‿ beginnen turn over a new leaf; ins ‿ rufen call into being; sein ‿ aufs Spiel setzen risk one's life; sein ‿ lang all one's life; ums ‿ kommen lose one's life; perish.

lebendig adj. [le'bɛndiç] living; pred.: alive; quick; lively.

'Lebens|alter n age; '‿anschauung f outlook on life; '‿art f manners pl., behavio(u)r; '‿auffassung f philosophy of life; '‿bedingungen f/pl. living conditions pl.; '‿beschreibung f life, biography; '‿dauer f span of life; ⊕ durability; '2echt adj. true to life; '‿erfahrung f experience of life; '2fähig adj. ⚕ and fig. viable; '‿gefahr f danger of life; ‿! danger (of death)!; unter ‿ at the risk of one's life; '2gefährlich adj. dangerous (to life), perilous; '‿gefährte m life's companion; '‿größe f lifesize; in ‿ at full length; '‿kraft f vital power, vigo(u)r, vitality; '2länglich adj. for life, lifelong; '‿lauf m course of life; personal record, curriculum vitae; '2lustig adj. gay, merry; '‿mittel pl. food (-stuffs pl.), provisions pl., groceries pl.; '2müde adj. weary or tired of life; '2notwendig adj. vital, essential; '‿retter m life-saver, rescuer; '‿standard m standard of living; '‿unterhalt m livelihood; s-n ‿ verdienen earn one's living; '‿versicherung f life-insurance; '‿wandel m life, (moral) conduct; '‿weise f mode of living, habits pl.; gesunde ‿ regimen; '‿weisheit f worldly wisdom; '2wichtig adj. vital, essential; ‿e Organe pl. vitals

pl.; '‿zeichen n sign of life; '‿zeit f lifetime; auf ‿ for life.

Leber anat. ['le:bər] f (-/-n) liver; '‿fleck m mole; '2krank adj., '2leidend adj. suffering from a liver-complaint; '‿tran m cod-liver oil; '‿wurst f liver-sausage, Am. liverwurst.

'Lebewesen n living being, creature.

Lebe'wohl n (-[e]s/-e, -s) farewell.

leb|haft adj. ['le:phaft] lively; vivid; spirited; interest: keen; traffic: busy; '2kuchen m gingerbread; '‿los adj. lifeless; '2zeiten pl.: zu s-n ‿ in his lifetime.

lechzen ['lɛçtsən] v/i. (ge-, h): ‿ nach languish or yearn or pant for.

Leck [lɛk] 1. n (-[e]s/-s) leak; 2. 2 adj. leaky; ‿ werden ♣ spring a leak.

lecken ['lɛkən] (ge-, h) 1. v/t. lick; 2. v/i. lick; leak.

lecker adj. ['lɛkər] dainty; delicious; '2bissen m dainty, delicacy.

Leder ['le:dər] n (-s/-) leather; in ‿ gebunden leather-bound; '2n adj. leathern, of leather.

ledig adj. ['le:diç] single, unmarried; child: illegitimate; '‿lich adv. ['‿k-] solely, merely.

Lee ♣ [le:] f (-/no pl.) lee (side).

leer [le:r] 1. adj. empty; vacant; void; vain; blank; 2. adv.: ‿ laufen ⊕ idle; '2e f (-/no pl.) emptiness, void (a. fig.); phys. vacuum; '‿en v/t. (ge-, h) empty; clear (out); pour out; '2gut ⚕ n empties pl.; '2lauf m ⊕ idling; mot. neutral gear; fig. waste of energy; '2stehend adj. flat: empty, unoccupied, vacant.

legal adj. [le'ga:l] legal, lawful.

Legat [le'ga:t] 1. m (-en/-en) legate; 2. ⚖ n (-[e]s/-e) legacy.

legen ['le:gən] (ge-, h) 1. v/t. lay; place, put; sich ‿ wind, etc.: calm down, abate; cease; Wert ‿ auf (acc.) attach importance to; 2. v/i. hen: lay.

Legende [le'gɛndə] f (-/-n) legend.

legieren [le'gi:rən] v/t. (no -ge-, h) ⊕ alloy; cookery: thicken (mit with).

Legislative [le:gisla'ti:və] f (-/-n) legislative body or power.

legitim adj. [legi'ti:m] legitimate; ‿ieren [‿i'mi:rən] v/t. (no -ge-, h) legitimate; authorize; sich ‿ prove one's identity.

Lehm [le:m] m (-[e]s/-e) loam; mud; '2ig adj. loamy.

Lehn|e ['le:nə] f (-/-n) support; arm, back (of chair); '2en (ge-, h) 1. v/i. lean (an dat. against); 2. v/t. lean, rest (an acc., gegen against); sich ‿ an (acc.) lean against; sich ‿ auf (acc.) rest or support o.s. (up-) on; sich aus dem Fenster ‿ lean out of the window; '‿sessel m, '‿stuhl m armchair, easy chair.

Lehrbuch ['le:r-] n textbook.
Lehre ['le:rə] f (-/-n) rule, precept; doctrine; system; science; theory; lesson, warning; moral (of fable); instruction, tuition; ⊕ ga(u)ge; ⊕ pattern; in der ~ sein be apprenticed (bei to); in die ~ geben apprentice, article (both: bei, zu to); '2n v/t. (ge-, h) teach, instruct; show.
'**Lehrer** m (-s/-) teacher; master, instructor; '~in f (-/-nen) (lady) teacher; (school)mistress; '~kollegium n staff (of teachers).
'**Lehr|fach** n subject; '~film m instructional film; '~gang m course (of instruction); '~geld n premium; '~herr m master, sl. boss; '~jahre n/pl. (years pl. of) apprenticeship; '~junge m s. Lehrling; '~körper m teaching staff; univ. professoriate, faculty; '~kraft f teacher; professor; '~ling m (-s/-e) apprentice; '~mädchen n girl apprentice; '~meister m master; '~methode f method of teaching; '~plan m curriculum, syllabus; '2reich adj. instructive; '~satz m ₰ theorem; doctrine; eccl. dogma; '~stoff m subject-matter, subject(s pl.); '~stuhl m professorship; '~vertrag m articles pl. of apprenticeship, indenture(s pl.); '~zeit f apprenticeship.
Leib [laɪp] m (-[e]s/-er) body; belly, anat. abdomen; womb; bei lebendigem ~ alive; mit ~ und Seele body and soul; sich j-n vom ~e halten keep s.o. at arm's length; '~arzt m physician in ordinary, personal physician; '~chen n (-s/-) bodice.
Leibeigen|e ['laɪpˀaɪɡənə] m (-n/-n) bond(s)man, serf; '~schaft f (-/no pl.) bondage, serfdom.
Leibes|erziehung ['laɪbəs-] f physical training; '~frucht f f(o)etus; '~kraft f: aus Leibeskräften pl. with all one's might; '~übung f bodily or physical exercise.
'**Leib|garde** f body-guard; '~gericht n favo(u)rite dish; 2haftig adj. [~'haftiç]: der ~e Teufel the devil incarnate; '2lich adj. bodily, corpor(e)al; '~rente f life-annuity; '~schmerzen m/pl. stomach-ache, belly-ache, ₰ colic; '~wache f body-guard; '~wäsche f underwear.
Leiche ['laɪçə] f (-/-n) (dead) body, corpse.
Leichen|beschauer ₰ ['laɪçənbəʃaʊər] m (-s/-) appr. coroner; '~bestatter m (-s/-) undertaker, Am. a. mortician; '~bittermiene F f woebegone look or countenance; '2blaß adj. deadly pale; '~halle f mortuary; '~schau ₰ f appr. (coroner's) inquest; '~schauhaus n morgue; '~tuch n (-[e]s/ˇer) shroud; '~verbrennung f cremation; '~wagen m hearse.

Leichnam ['laɪçnɑːm] m (-[e]s/-e) s. Leiche.
leicht [laɪçt] 1. adj. light; easy; slight; tobacco: mild; 2. adv.: es ~ nehmen take it easy; '2athlet m athlete; '2athletik f athletics pl., Am. track and field events pl.; '~fertig adj. light(-minded); careless; frivolous, flippant; '2fertigkeit f levity; carelessness; frivolity, flippancy; '2gewicht n boxing: lightweight; '~gläubig adj. credulous; '~hin adv. lightly, casually; 2igkeit ['~iç-] f (-/-en) lightness; ease, facility; '~lebig adj. easy-going; '2metall n light metal; '2sinn m (-[e]s/no pl.) frivolity, levity; carelessness; '~sinnig adj. light-minded, frivolous; careless; '~verdaulich adj. easy to digest; '~verständlich adj. easy to understand.
leid [laɪt] 1. adv.: es tut mir ~ I am sorry (um for), I regret; 2. 2 n (-[e]s/no pl.) injury, harm; wrong; grief, sorrow; ~en ['~dən] (irr., ge-, h) 1. v/i. suffer (an dat. from); 2. v/t.: (nicht) ~ können (dis)like; 2en ['~dən] n (-s/-) suffering; ₰ complaint; '~end ₰ adj. ['~dənt] ailing.
'**Leidenschaft** f (-/-en) passion; '2lich adj. passionate; ardent; vehement; '2slos adj. dispassionate.
'**Leidens|gefährte** m, '~gefährtin f fellow-sufferer.
leid|er adv. ['laɪdər] unfortunately; int. alas!; ~ muß ich inf. I'm (so) sorry to inf.; ich muß ~ gehen I am afraid I have to go; '~ig adj. disagreeable; '~lich adj. ['laɪt-] tolerable; fairly well; 2tragende ['laɪt-] m, f (-n/-n) mourner; er ist der ~ dabei he is the one who suffers for it; 2wesen ['laɪt-] n (-s/no pl.): zu meinem ~ to my regret.
Leier ♪ ['laɪər] f (-/-n) lyre; '~kasten m barrel-organ; '~kastenmann m organ-grinder.
Leih|bibliothek ['laɪ-] f, '~bücherei f lending or circulating library, Am. a. rental library; '2en v/t. (irr., ge-, h) lend; borrow (von from); '~gebühr f lending fee(s pl.); '~haus n pawnshop, Am. a. loan office; '2weise adv. as a loan.
Leim [laɪm] m (-[e]s/-e) glue; F aus dem ~ gehen get out of joint; F auf den ~ gehen fall for it, fall into the trap; '2en v/t. (ge-, h) glue; size.
Lein ♀ [laɪn] m (-[e]s/-e) flax.
Leine ['laɪnə] f (-/-n) line, cord; (dog-)lead, leash.
leinen ['laɪnən] 1. adj. (of) linen; 2. 2 n (-s/-) linen; in ~ gebunden cloth-bound; '2schuh m canvas shoe.
'**Lein|öl** n linseed-oil; '~samen m linseed; '~wand f (-/no pl.) linen (cloth); paint. canvas; film: screen.

leise adj. ['laɪzə] low, soft; gentle; slight, faint; ~r stellen turn down (radio).

Leiste ['laɪstə] f (-/-n) border, ledge; △ fillet; anat. groin.

leisten ['laɪstən] 1. v/t. (ge-, h) do; perform; fulfil(l); take (oath); render (service); ich kann mir das ~ I can afford it; 2. ♀ ⊕ m (-s/-) last; boot-tree, Am. a. shoetree; '2bruch ♂ m inguinal hernia.

'**Leistung** f (-/-en) performance; achievement; work(manship); result(s pl.); ⊕ capacity; output (of factory); benefit (of insurance company); '2sfähig adj. productive; efficient, ⊕ a. powerful; '~sfähigkeit f efficiency; ⊕ productivity; ⊕ capacity, producing-power.

Leit|artikel ['laɪt-] m leading article, leader, editorial; '~bild n image; example.

leiten ['laɪtən] v/t. (ge-, h) lead, guide; conduct (a. phys., ♪); fig. direct, run, manage, operate; preside over (meeting); '~d adj. leading; phys. conductive; ~e Stellung key position.

'**Leiter** 1. m (-s/-) leader; conductor (a. phys., ♪); guide; manager; 2. f (-/-n) ladder; '~in f (-/-nen) leader; conductress, guide; manageress; '~wagen m rack-wag(g)on.

'**Leit|faden** m manual, textbook, guide; '~motiv ♪ n leit-motiv; '~spruch m motto; '~tier n leader; '~ung f (-/-en) lead(ing), conducting, guidance; management, direction, administration, Am. a. operation; phys. conduction; ⚡ lead; circuit; tel. line; mains pl. (for gas, water, etc.); pipeline; die ~ ist besetzt teleph. the line is engaged or Am. busy.

'**Leitungs|draht** m conducting wire, conductor; '~rohr n conduit(-pipe); main (for gas, water, etc.); '~wasser n (-s/ꞏ) tap water.

'**Leitwerk** ✈ n tail unit or group, empennage.

Lekt|ion [lɛk'tsjoːn] f (-/-en) lesson; '~or ['lɛktɔr] m (-s/-en) lecturer; reader; '~üre [~'tyːrə] f 1. (-/no pl.) reading; 2. (-/-n) books pl.

Lende anat. ['lɛndə] f (-/-n) loin(s pl.).

lenk|bar adj. ['lɛŋkbaːr] guidable, manageable, tractable, docile; ⊕ steerable, dirigible; '~en v/t. (ge-, h) direct, guide; turn; rule; govern; drive (car); ♿ steer; Aufmerksamkeit ~ auf (acc.) draw attention to; '2rad mot. n steering wheel; '2-säule mot. f steering column; '2-stange f handle-bar (of bicycle); '2ung mot. f (-/-en) steering-gear.

Lenz [lɛnts] m (-es/-e) spring.

Leopard zo. [leo'part] m (-en/-en) leopard.

Lepra ♂ ['leːpra] f (-/no pl.) leprosy.

Lerche orn. ['lɛrçə] f (-/-n) lark.

lern|begierig adj. ['lɛrn-] eager to learn, studious; '~en v/t. and v/i. (ge-, h) learn; study.

Lese ['leːzə] f (-/-n) gathering; s. Weinlese; '~buch n reader; '~lampe f reading-lamp.

lesen ['leːzən] (irr., ge-, h) 1. v/t. read; ⚘ gather; Messe ~ eccl. say mass; 2. v/i. read; univ. (give a) lecture (über acc. on); '~swert adj. worth reading.

'**Leser** m (-s/-), '~in f (-/-nen) reader; ⚘ gatherer; vintager; '2lich adj. legible; '~zuschrift f letter to the editor.

'**Lesezeichen** n book-mark.

'**Lesung** parl. f (-/-en) reading.

letzt adj. [lɛtst] last; final; ultimate; ~e Nachrichten pl. latest news pl.; ~e Hand anlegen put the finishing touches (an acc. to); das ~e the last thing; der ~ere the latter; der (die, das) Letzte the last (one); zu guter Letzt last but not least; finally; '~ens adv., '~hin adv. lately, of late; '~lich adv. s. letztens; finally; ultimately.⎬

Leucht|e ['lɔyçtə] f (-/-n) (fig. shining) light, lamp (a. fig.), luminary (a. fig., esp. p.); '2en v/i. (ge-, h) (give) light, shine (forth); beam, gleam; '~en n (-s/no pl.) shining, light, luminosity; '2end adj. shining, bright; luminous; brilliant (a. fig.); '~er m (-s/-) candlestick; s. Kronleuchter; '~feuer n ♣, ✈, etc.: beacon(-light), flare (light); '~käfer zo. m glow-worm; '~kugel ✕ f Very light; flare; '~turm m lighthouse; '2ziffer f luminous figure.

leugnen ['lɔygnən] v/t. (ge-, h) deny; disavow; contest.

Leukämie ♂ [lɔykɛ'miː] f (-/-n) leuk(a)emia.

Leumund ['lɔymunt] m (-[e]s/no pl.) reputation, repute; character; '~szeugnis ⚖ n character reference.

Leute ['lɔytə] pl. people pl.; persons pl.; ✕, pol. men pl.; workers: hands pl.; F folks pl.; domestics pl., servants pl.

Leutnant ✕ ['lɔytnant] m (-s/-s, ⚓ -e) second lieutenant.

leutselig adj. ['lɔytzeːliç] affable.

Lexikon ['lɛksikɔn] n (-s/Lexika, Lexiken) dictionary; encyclop(a)edia.

Libelle zo. [li'bɛlə] f (-/-n) dragonfly.

liberal adj. [libe'raːl] liberal.

Licht [liçt] 1. n (-[e]s/-er) light; brightness; lamp; candle; hunt. eye; ~ machen ⚡ switch or turn on the light(s pl.); das ~ der Welt erblicken see the light, be born; 2. 2 adj. light, bright; clear; ~er Augenblick ♂ lucid interval; '~anlage f lighting plant; '**~bild** n photo (-graph); '**~bildervortrag** m slide lecture; '**~blick** fig. m bright spot; '**~bogen** ⚡ m arc; '**2durchlässig** adj. translucent; '**2echt** adj. fast (to light), unfading; '**2empfindlich** adj. sensitive to light, phot. sensitive; **~ machen** sensitize.

'**lichten** v/t. (ge-, h) clear (forest); **den Anker ~ ⚓** weigh anchor; **sich ~** hair, crowd: thin.

lichterloh adv. ['liçtər'lo:] blazing, in full blaze.

'**Licht**|**geschwindigkeit** f speed of light; '**~hof** m glass-roofed court; patio; halo (a. phot.); '**~leitung** f lighting mains pl.; '**~maschine** mot. f dynamo, generator; '**~pause** f blueprint; '**~quelle** f light source, source of light; '**~reklame** f neon sign; '**~schacht** m well; '**~schalter** m (light) switch; '**~schein** m gleam of light; '**2scheu** adj. shunning the light; '**~signal** n light or luminous signal; '**~spieltheater** n s. Filmtheater, Kino; '**~strahl** m ray or beam of light (a. fig.); '**2undurchlässig** adj. opaque.

'**Lichtung** f (-/-en) clearing, opening, glade.

'**Lichtzelle** f s. Photozelle.

Lid [li:t] n (-[e]s/-er) eyelid.

lieb adj. [li:p] dear; nice, kind; child: good; in letters: **~er Herr N.** dear Mr N.; **~er Himmel!** good Heavens!, dear me!; **es ist mir ~, daß** I am glad that; '**2chen** n (-s/-) sweetheart.

Liebe ['li:bə] f (-/no pl.) love (zu of, for); **aus ~** for love; **aus ~ zu** for the love of; '**2n** (ge-, h) **1.** v/t. love; be in love with; be fond of, like; **2.** v/i. (be in) love; '**~nde** m, f (-n/-n): **die ~n** pl. the lovers pl.

'**liebens**|**wert** adj. lovable; charming; '**~würdig** adj. lovable, amiable; **das ist sehr ~ von Ihnen** that is very kind of you; '**2würdigkeit** f (-/-en) amiability, kindness.

'**lieber 1.** adj. dearer; **2.** adv. rather, sooner; **~ haben** prefer, like better.

'**Liebes**|**brief** m love-letter; '**~dienst** m favo(u)r, kindness; good turn; '**~erklärung** f: **e-e ~ machen** declare one's love; '**~heirat** f love-match; '**~kummer** m lover's grief; '**~paar** n (courting) couple, lovers pl.; '**~verhältnis** n love-affair.

'**liebevoll** adj. loving, affectionate.

lieb|**gewinnen** ['li:p-] v/t. (irr. gewinnen, sep., no -ge-, h) get or grow fond of; '**~haben** v/t. (irr. haben, sep., -ge-, h) love, be fond of; '**2haber** m (-s/-) lover; beau; fig. amateur; **2haberei** f [~'rai] f (-/-en) hobby; '**2haberpreis** m fancy price; '**2haberwert** m sentimental value; '**~kosen** v/t. (no -ge-, h) caress, fondle; '**2kosung** f (-/-en) caress;

'**~lich** adj. lovely, charming, delightful.

Liebling ['li:pliŋ] m (-s/-e) darling; favo(u)rite; esp. animals: pet; esp. form of address: darling, esp. Am. honey; '**~sbeschäftigung** f favo(u)rite occupation, hobby.

lieb|**los** adj. ['li:p-] unkind; careless; '**2schaft** f (-/-en) (love-)affair; '**2ste** m, f (-n/-n) sweetheart; darling.

Lied [li:t] n (-[e]s/-er) song; tune.

liederlich adj. ['li:dərliç] slovenly, disorderly; careless; loose, dissolute.

lief [li:f] pret. of laufen.

Lieferant [li:fə'rant] m (-en/-en) supplier, purveyor; caterer.

Liefer|**auto** ['li:fər-] n s. Lieferwagen; '**2bar** adj. to be delivered; available; '**~bedingungen** f/pl. terms pl. of delivery; '**~frist** f term of delivery; '**2n** v/t. (ge-, h) deliver; **j-m et. ~** furnish or supply s.o. with s.th.; '**~schein** m delivery note; '**~ung** f (-/-en) delivery; supply; consignment; instal(l)ment (of book); '**~ungsbedingungen** f/pl. s. Lieferbedingungen; '**~wagen** m deliveryvan, Am. delivery wagon.

Liege ['li:gə] f (-/-n) couch; bedchair.

liegen ['li:gən] v/i. (irr., ge-, h) lie; house, etc.: be (situated); room: face; **an wem liegt es?** whose fault is it? **es liegt an** or **bei ihm zu** inf. it is for him to inf.; **es liegt daran, daß** the reason for it is that; **es liegt mir daran zu** inf. I am anxious to inf.; **es liegt mir nichts daran** it does not matter or it is of no consequence to me; '**~bleiben** v/i. (irr. bleiben, sep., -ge-, sein) stay in bed; break down (on the road, a. mot., etc.); work, etc.: stand over; fall behind; ✝ goods: remain on hand; '**~lassen** v/t. (irr. lassen, sep., [-ge-,] h) leave; leave behind; leave alone; leave off (work); **j-n links ~** ignore s.o., give s.o. the cold shoulder; '**2schaften** f/pl. real estate.

'**Liege**|**stuhl** m deck-chair; '**~wagen** 🚃 m couchette coach.

lieh [li:] pret. of leihen.

ließ [li:s] pret. of lassen.

Lift [lift] m (-[e]s/-e, -s) lift, Am. elevator.

Liga ['li:ga] f (-/Ligen) league.

Likör [li'kø:r] m (-s/-e) liqueur, cordial.

lila adj. ['li:la] lilac.

Lilie 🌿 ['li:ljə] f (-/-n) lily.

Limonade [limo'na:də] f (-/-n) soft drink, fruit-juice; lemonade.

Limousine mot. [limu'zi:nə] f (-/-n) limousine, saloon car, Am. sedan.

lind adj. [lint] soft, gentle; mild.

Linde 🌿 ['lində] f (-/-n) lime(-tree), linden(-tree).

linder|n ['lindərn] *v/t.* (ge-, h) soften; mitigate; alleviate, soothe; allay, ease (*pain*); '2**ung** *f* (-/⁓-en) softening; mitigation; alleviation; easing.

Lineal [line'ɑːl] *n* (-s/-e) ruler.

Linie ['liːnjə] *f* (-/-n) line; '⁓**papier** *n* ruled paper; '⁓**richter** *m sports:* linesman; '2**ntreu** *pol. adj.*: ⁓ **sein** follow the party line.

lin(i)ieren [li'niːrən; lini'iːrən] *v/t.* (no -ge-, h) rule, line.

link *adj.* ['liŋk] left; ⁓**e** *Seite* left (-hand) side, left; *of cloth:* wrong side; '2**e** *f* (-n/-n) *the* left (hand); *pol. the* Left (Wing); *boxing: the* left; '⁓**isch** *adj.* awkward, clumsy.

links *adv.* on *or* to the left; 2**händer** ['⁓hɛndər] *m* (-s/-) left-hander, *Am. a.* southpaw.

Linse ['linzə] *f* (-/-n) ♧ lentil; *opt.* lens.

Lippe ['lipə] *f* (-/-n) lip; '⁓**nstift** *m* lipstick.

liquidieren [likvi'diːrən] *v/t.* (no -ge-, h) liquidate (*a. pol.*); wind up (*business company*); charge (*fee*).

lispeln ['lispəln] *v/i. and v/t.* (ge-, h) lisp; whisper.

List [list] *f* (-/-en) cunning, craft; artifice, ruse, trick; stratagem.

Liste ['listə] *f* (-/-n) list, roll.

listig *adj.* cunning, crafty, sly.

Liter ['liːtər] *n, m* (-s/-) lit|re, *Am.* -er.

literarisch *adj.* [lite'rɑːriʃ] literary.

Literatur [litera'tuːr] *f* (-/-en) literature; ⁓**beilage** *f* literary supplement (*in newspaper*); ⁓**geschichte** *f* history of literature; ⁓**verzeichnis** *n* bibliography.

litt [lit] *pret. of* leiden.

Litze ['litsə] *f* (-/-n) lace, cord, braid; ∮ strand(ed wire).

Livree [li'vreː] *f* (-/-n) livery.

Lizenz [li'tsɛnts] *f* (-/-en) licen|ce, *Am.* -se; ⁓**inhaber** *m* licensee.

Lob [loːp] *n* (-[e]s/no pl.) praise; commendation; 2**en** ['loːbən] *v/t.* (ge-, h) praise; 2**enswert** *adj.* ['loːbəns-] praise-worthy, laudable; ⁓**gesang** ['loːp-] *m* hymn, song of praise; ⁓**hudelei** [loːphuːdə'lai] *f* (-/-en) adulation, base flattery.

löblich *adj.* ['løːpliç] *s.* lobenswert.

Lobrede ['loːp-] *f* eulogy, panegyric.

Loch [lɔx] *n* (-[e]s/⁓er) hole; 2**en** *v/t.* (ge-, h) perforate, pierce; punch (*ticket, etc.*); ⁓**er** *m* (-s/-) punch, perforator; '⁓**karte** *f* punch(ed) card.

Locke ['lɔkə] *f* (-/-n) curl, ringlet.

locken[1] *v/t. and v/refl.* (ge-, h) curl.

locken[2] *v/t.* (ge-, h) *hunt.:* bait; decoy (*a. fig.*); *fig.* allure, entice.

Locken|kopf *m* curly head; ⁓**wickler** ['⁓viklər] *m* (-s/-) curler, roller.

locker *adj.* ['lɔkər] loose; slack; '⁓

v/t. (ge-, h) loosen; slacken; relax (*grip*); break up (*soil*); *sich* ⁓ loosen, (be)come loose; give way; *fig.* relax.

'**lockig** *adj.* curly.

'**Lock|mittel** *n s.* Köder; '⁓**vogel** *m* decoy (*a. fig.*); *Am. a.* stool pigeon (*a. fig.*).

lodern ['loːdərn] *v/i.* (ge-, h) flare, blaze.

Löffel ['lœfəl] *m* (-s/-) spoon; ladle; '2**n** *v/t.* (ge-, h) spoon up; ladle out; '⁓**voll** *m* (-/-) spoonful.

log [loːk] *pret. of* lügen.

Loge ['loːʒə] *f* (-/-n) *thea.* box; *freemasonry:* lodge; '⁓**nschließer** *thea.* *m* (-s/-) box-keeper.

logieren [lo'ʒiːrən] *v/i.* (no -ge-, h) lodge, stay, *Am. a.* room (*all:* bei with; *in dat.* at).

logisch *adj.* ['loːgiʃ] logical; '⁓**erweise** *adv.* logically.

Lohn [loːn] *m* (-[e]s/⁓e) wages *pl.*, pay(ment); hire; *fig.* reward; '⁓**büro** *n* pay-office; '⁓**empfänger** *m* wage-earner; '2**en** *v/t.* (ge-, h) compensate, reward; *sich* ⁓ pay; *es lohnt sich zu inf.* it is worth while *ger.*, it pays to *inf.*; '2**end** *adj.* paying; advantageous; *fig.* rewarding; '⁓**erhöhung** *f* increase in wages, rise, *Am.* raise; '⁓**forderung** *f* demand for higher wages; '⁓**steuer** *f* tax on wages *or* salary; '⁓**stopp** *m* (-s/no pl.) wage freeze; '⁓**tarif** *m* wage rate; '⁓**tüte** *f* pay envelope.

lokal [lo'kɑːl] 1. *adj.* local; 2. 2 *n* (-[e]s/-e) locality, place; restaurant; public house, F pub, F local, *Am.* saloon.

Lokomotiv|e [lokomo'tiːvə] *f* (-/-n) (railway) engine, locomotive; ⁓**führer** [⁓'tiːf-] *m* engine-driver, *Am.* engineer.

Lorbeer ♧ ['lɔrbeːr] *m* (-s/-en) laurel, bay.

Lore ['loːrə] *f* (-/-n) lorry, truck.

Los[1] [loːs] *n* (-es/-e) lot; lottery ticket; *fig.* fate, destiny, lot; *das Große* ⁓ ziehen win the first prize, *Am. sl.* hit the jackpot; *durchs* ⁓ *entscheiden* decide by lot.

los[2] [⁓] 1. *pred. adj.* loose; free; *was ist* ⁓? what is the matter?, F what's up?, *Am.* F what's cooking?; ⁓ *sein* be rid of; 2. *int.:* ⁓! go (on *or* ahead)!

losarbeiten ['loːsʔ-] *v/i.* (*sep.*, -ge-, h) start work(ing).

lösbar *adj.* ['løːsbɑːr] soluble, ♧ *a.* solvable.

'**los|binden** *v/t.* (*irr.* binden, *sep.*, -ge-, h) untie, loosen; '⁓**brechen** (*irr.* brechen, *sep.*, -ge-) 1. *v/t.* (h) break off; 2. *v/i.* (sein) break *or* burst out.

Lösch|blatt ['lœʃ-] *n* blotting-paper; '2**en** *v/t.* (ge-, h) extinguish, put out (*fire, light*); blot out (*writing*);

erase (*tape recording*); cancel (*debt*); quench (*thirst*); slake (*lime*); ⚓ unload; **~er** *m* (-s/-) blotter; **~papier** *n* blotting-paper.
lose *adj.* ['lo:zə] loose.
'Lösegeld *n* ransom.
losen ['lo:zən] *v/i.* (ge-, h) cast *or* draw lots (*um* for).
lösen ['lø:zən] *v/t.* (ge-, h) loosen, untie; buy, book (*ticket*); solve (*task, doubt, etc.*); break off (*engagement*); annul (*agreement, etc.*); ⚗ dissolve; *ein Schuß löste sich* the gun went off.
'los|fahren *v/i.* (*irr. fahren, sep.,* -ge-, *sein*) depart, drive off; **~gehen** *v/i.* (*irr. gehen, sep.,* -ge-, *sein*) go *or* be off; come off, get loose; *gun:* go off; begin, start; F *auf j-n ~* fly at s.o.; **~haken** *v/t.* (*sep.,* -ge-, h) unhook; **~kaufen** *v/t.* (*sep.,* -ge-, h) ransom, redeem; **~ketten** *v/t.* (*sep.,* -ge-, h) unchain; **~kommen** *v/i.* (*irr. kommen, sep.,* -ge-, *sein*) get loose *or* free; **~lachen** *v/i.* (*sep.,* -ge-, h) laugh out; **~lassen** *v/t.* (*irr. lassen, sep.,* -ge-, h) let go; release.
löslich ⚗ *adj.* ['lø:sliç] soluble.
'los|lösen *v/t.* (*sep.,* -ge-, h) loosen, detach; sever; **~machen** *v/t.* (*sep.,* -ge-, h) unfasten, loosen; *sich ~* disengage (o.s.) (*von* from); **~reißen** *v/t.* (*irr. reißen, sep.,* -ge-, h) tear off; *sich ~* break away, *esp. fig.* tear o.s. away (*both: von* from); **~sagen** *v/refl.* (*sep.,* -ge-, h): *sich ~ von* renounce; **~schlagen** (*irr. schlagen, sep.,* -ge-, h) 1. *v/t.* knock off; 2. *v/i.* open the attack; *auf j-n ~* attack s.o.; **~schnallen** *v/t.* (*sep.,* -ge-, h) unbuckle; **~schrauben** *v/t.* (*sep.,* -ge-, h) unscrew, screw off; **~sprechen** *v/t.* (*irr. sprechen, sep.,* -ge-, h) absolve (*von* of, from); acquit (*of*); free (*from, of*); **~stürzen** *v/i.* (*sep.,* -ge-, *sein*): *~ auf* (*acc.*) rush at.
Losung ['lo:zuŋ] *f* 1. (-/-en) ✗ password, watchword; *fig.* slogan; 2. *hunt.* (-/*no pl.*) droppings *pl.,* dung.
Lösung ['lø:zuŋ] *f* (-/-en) solution; **~smittel** *n* solvent.
'los|werden *v/t.* (*irr. werden, sep.,* -ge-, *sein*) get rid of, dispose of; **~ziehen** *v/i.* (*irr. ziehen, sep.,* -ge-, *sein*) set out, take off, march away.
Lot [lo:t] *n* (-[e]s/-e) plumb(-line), plummet.
löten ['lø:tən] *v/t.* (ge-, h) solder.
Lotse ⚓ ['lo:tsə] *m* (-n/-n) pilot; **'~n** *v/t.* (ge-, h) ⚓ pilot (*a. fig.*).
Lotterie [lɔtə'ri:] *f* (-/-n) lottery; **~gewinn** *m* prize; **~los** *n* lottery ticket.
Lotto ['lɔto] *n* (-s/-s) numbers pool, lotto.
Löwe ᴢᴼ. ['lø:və] *m* (-n/-n) lion.

'Löwen|anteil F *m* lion's share; **'~maul** ♚ *n* (-[e]s/*no pl.*) snapdragon; **'~zahn** ♚ *m* (-[e]s/*no pl.*) dandelion.
'Löwin ᴢᴼ. *f* (-/-nen) lioness.
loyal *adj.* [loa'ja:l] loyal.
Luchs ᴢᴼ. [luks] *m* (-es/-e) lynx.
Lücke ['lykə] *f* (-/-n) gap; blank; void (*a. fig.*); **'~nbüßer** *m* stopgap; **'~nhaft** *adj.* full of gaps; *fig.* defective, incomplete; **'~nlos** *adj.* without a gap; *fig.*: unbroken; complete; **~er Beweis** close argument.
lud [lu:t] *pret. of* laden.
Luft [luft] *f* (-/̈e) air; breeze; breath; *frische ~ schöpfen* take the air; *an die ~ gehen* go for an airing; *aus der ~ gegriffen* (totally) unfounded, fantastic; *es liegt et. in der ~* there is s.th. in the wind; *in die ~ fliegen* be blown up, explode; *in die ~ gehen* explode, *sl.* blow one's top; *in die ~ sprengen* blow up; F *j-n an die ~ setzen* turn s.o. out, *Am. sl.* give s.o. the air; *sich or s-n Gefühlen ~ machen* give vent to one's feelings.
'Luft|alarm *m* air-raid alarm; **'~angriff** *m* air raid; **'~aufnahme** *f* aerial photograph; **'~ballon** *m* (air-)balloon; **'~bild** *n* aerial photograph, airview; **'~blase** *f* air-bubble; **'~brücke** *f* air-bridge; *for supplies, etc.*: air-lift.
Lüftchen ['lyftçən] *n* (-s/-) gentle breeze.
'luft|dicht *adj.* air-tight; **'²druck** *phys. m* (-[e]s/*no pl.*) atmospheric *or* air pressure; **'²druckbremse** ⊕ *f* air-brake; **'~durchlässig** *adj.* permeable to air.
lüften ['lyftən] (ge-, h) 1. *v/i.* air; 2. *v/t.* air; raise (*hat*); lift (*veil*); disclose (*secret*).
'Luft|fahrt *f* aviation, aeronautics; **'~feuchtigkeit** *f* atmospheric humidity; **'²gekühlt** ⊕ *adj.* air-cooled; **'~hoheit** *f* air sovereignty; **'²ig** *adj.* airy; breezy; flimsy; **'~kissen** *n* air-cushion; **'~klappe** *f* air-valve; **'~korridor** *m* air corridor; **'~krankheit** *f* airsickness; **'~krieg** *m* aerial warfare; **'~kurort** *m* climatic health resort; **'~landetruppen** *f/pl.* airborne troops *pl.*; **'²leer** *adj.* void of air, evacuated; **~er Raum** vacuum; **'~linie** *f* air line, bee-line; **'~loch** *n* ✗ airpocket; vent(-hole); **'~post** *f* air mail; **'~pumpe** *f* air-pump; **'~raum** *m* airspace; **'~röhre** *anat. f* windpipe, trachea; **'~schacht** *m* air-shaft; **'~schaukel** *f* swing-boat; **'~schiff** *n* airship; **'~schloß** *n* castle in the air *or* in Spain; **'~schutz** *m* air-raid protection; **'~schutzkeller** *m* air-raid shelter; **'~sprünge** ['~ʃpryŋə] *m/pl.*: *~ machen* cut capers *pl.*; gambol; **'~stützpunkt** ✗ *m* air base.

'**Lüftung** f (-/-en) airing; ventilation.

'**Luft|veränderung** f change of air; '~**verkehr** m air-traffic; '~**verkehrsgesellschaft** f air transport company, airway, Am. airline; '~**verteidigung** ✕ f air defen|ce, Am. -se; '~**waffe** ✕ f air force; '~**weg** m airway; auf dem ~ by air; '~**zug** m draught, Am. draft.

Lüge ['ly:gə] f (-/-n) lie, falsehood; j-n ~n strafen give the lie to s.o.

'**lügen** v/i. (irr., ge-, h) (tell a) lie; '~**haft** adj. lying, mendacious; untrue, false.

'**Lügner** ['ly:gnər] m (-s/-), '~**in** f (-/-nen) liar; '**2isch** adj. s. lügenhaft.

Luke ['lu:kə] f (-/-n) dormer- or garret-window; hatch.

Lümmel ['lyməl] m (-s/-) lout, boor; saucy fellow; '**2n** v/refl. (ge-, h) loll, lounge, sprawl.

Lump [lump] m (-en/-en) ragamuffin, beggar; cad, Am. sl. rat, heel; scoundrel.

'**Lumpen 1.** m (-s/-) rag; **2. 2** vb.: sich nicht ~ lassen come down handsomely; '~**pack** n rabble, riffraff; '~**sammler** m rag-picker.

'**lumpig** adj. ragged; fig.: shabby, paltry; mean.

Lunge ['luŋə] f (-/-n) anat. lungs pl.; of animals: a. lights pl.

'**Lungen|entzündung** ✚ f pneumonia; '~**flügel** anat. m lung; '**2krank** ✚ adj. suffering from consumption, consumptive; '~**kranke** ✚ m, f consumptive (patient); '~**krankheit** ✚ f lung-disease; '~**schwindsucht** ✚ f (pulmonary) consumption.

lungern ['luŋərn] v/i. (ge-, h) s. herumlungern.

Lupe ['lu:pə] f (-/-n) magnifying-glass; unter die ~ nehmen scrutinize, take a good look at.

Lust [lust] f (-/- e) pleasure, delight; desire; lust; ~ haben zu inf. have a mind to inf., feel like ger.; haben Sie ~ auszugehen? would you like to go out?

lüstern adj. ['lystərn] desirous (nach of), greedy (of, for); lewd, lascivious, lecherous.

'**lustig** adj. merry, gay; jolly, cheerful; amusing, funny; sich ~ machen über (acc.) make fun of; '**2keit** f (-/no pl.) gaiety, mirth; jollity, cheerfulness; fun.

Lüstling ['lystliŋ] m (-s/-e) voluptuary, libertine.

'**lust|los** adj. dull, spiritless; ✝ flat; '**2mord** m rape and murder; '**2spiel** n comedy.

lutschen ['lutʃən] v/i. and v/t. (ge-, h) suck.

Luv ⚓ [lu:f] f (-/no pl.) luff, windward.

luxuriös adj. [luksu'rjø:s] luxurious.

Luxus ['luksus] m (-/no pl.) luxury (a. fig.); '~**artikel** m luxury; '~**ausgabe** f de luxe edition (of books); '~**ware** f luxury (article); fancy goods pl.

Lymph|drüse anat. ['lymf-] f lymphatic gland; '~**e** f (-/-n) lymph; ✚ vaccine; '~**gefäß** anat. n lymphatic vessel.

lynchen ['lynçən] v/t. (ge-, h) lynch.

Lyrik ['ly:rik] f (-/no pl.) lyric verses pl., lyrics pl.; '~**er** m (-s/-) lyric poet.

'**lyrisch** adj. lyric; lyrical (a. fig.).

M

Maat ⚓ [ma:t] m (-[e]s/-e[n]) (ship's) mate.

Mache F ['maxə] f (-/no pl.) make-believe, window-dressing, sl. eyewash; et. in der ~ haben have s.th. in hand.

machen ['maxən] (ge-, h) **1.** v/t. make; do; produce, manufacture; give (appetite, etc.); sit for, undergo (examination); come or amount to; make (happy, etc.); was macht das (aus)? what does that matter?; das macht nichts! never mind!, that's (quite) all right!; da(gegen) kann man nichts ~ that cannot be helped; ich mache mir nichts daraus I don't care about it; mach, daß du fortkommst! off with you!; j-n ~ lassen, was er will let s.o. do as he pleases; sich ~ an (acc.) go or set

about; sich et. ~ lassen have s.th. made; **2.** F v/i.: na, mach schon! hurry up!; '**2schaften** f/pl. machinations pl.

Macht [maxt] f (-/- e) power; might; authority; control (über acc. of); an der ~ pol. in power; '~**befugnis** f authority, power; '~**haber** pol. m (-s/-) ruler.

mächtig adj. ['meçtiç] powerful (a. fig.); mighty; immense, huge; ~ sein (gen.) be master of s.th.; have command of (language).

'**Macht|kampf** m struggle for power; '**2los** adj. powerless; '~**politik** f power politics sg., pol.; policy of the strong hand; '~**spruch** m authoritative decision; '**2voll** adj. powerful (a. fig.); '~**vollkommenheit** f authority; '~**wort** n (-[e]s/-e) word of command; *ein ~ sprechen* put one's foot down.

'Machwerk *n* concoction, F put-up job; *elendes ~* bungling work.

Mädchen ['mɛːtçən] *n* (-s/-) girl; maid(-servant); *~ für alles* maid of all work; *fig. a.* jack of all trades; **'Shaft** *adj.* girlish; **'..name** *m* girl's name; maiden name; **'..schule** *f* girls' school.

Made *zo.* ['maːdə] *f* (-/-n) maggot, mite; *fruit:* worm.

Mädel ['mɛːdəl] *n* (-s/-, F -s) girl, lass(ie).

madig *adj.* ['maːdiç] maggoty, full of mites; *fruit:* wormeaten.

Magazin [maga'tsiːn] *n* (-s/-e) store, warehouse; ✗ *in rifle, periodical:* magazine.

Magd [maːkt] *f* (-/⁼e) maid(-servant).

Magen ['maːgən] *m* (-s/⁼, a. -) stomach, F tummy; *animals:* maw; **'..beschwerden** *f/pl.* stomach *or* gastric trouble, indigestion; **'..bitter** *m* (-s/-) bitters *pl.*; **'..geschwür** ⚕ *n* gastric ulcer; **'..krampf** *m* stomach cramp; **'..krebs** ⚕ *m* stomach cancer; **'..leiden** *n* gastric complaint; **'..säure** *f* gastric acid.

mager *adj.* ['maːgər] meag|re, *Am.* -er (*a. fig.*); *p., animal, meat:* lean, *Am. a.* scrawny; **'Smilch** *f* skim milk.

Magie [ma'giː] *f* (-/no *pl.*) magic; **~r** ['maːgjər] *m* (-s/-) magician.

magisch *adj.* ['maːgiʃ] magic(al).

Magistrat [magis'traːt] *m* (-[e]s/-e) municipal *or* town council.

Magnet [ma'gneːt] *m* (-[e]s-, -en/ -e[n]) magnet (*a. fig.*); lodestone; **Sisch** *adj.* magnetic; **Sisieren** [..eti'ziːrən] *v/t.* (no -ge-, h) magnetize; **..nadel** [..'gneːt-] *f* magnetic needle.

Mahagoni [maha'goːni] *n* (-s/no *pl.*) mahogany (wood).

mähen ['mɛːən] *v/t.* (ge-, h) cut, mow, reap.

Mahl [maːl] *n* (-[e]s/⁼er, -e) meal, repast.

'mahlen (*irr.*, ge-, h) 1. *v/t.* grind, mill; 2. *v/i. tyres:* spin.

'Mahlzeit *f s.* Mahl; F feed.

Mähne ['mɛːnə] *f* (-/-n) mane.

mahn|en ['maːnən] *v/t.* (ge-, h) remind, admonish (*both: an acc.* of); *j-n wegen e-r Schuld ~* press s.o. for payment, dun s.o.; **'Smal** *n* (-[e]s/-e) memorial; **'Sung** *f* (-/-en) admonition; ✝ reminder, dunning; **'Szettel** *m* reminder.

Mai [mai] *m* (-[e]s, -/-e) May; **'..baum** *m* maypole; **..glöckchen** ⚘ ['..glœkçən] *n* (-s/-) lily of the valley; **'..käfer** *zo. m* cockchafer, may-beetle, may-bug.

Mais ⚘ [mais] *m* (-es/-e) maize, Indian corn, *Am.* corn.

Majestät [maje'stɛːt] *f* (-/-en) majesty; **Sisch** *adj.* majestic; **~s-beleidigung** *f* lese-majesty.

Major ✗ [ma'joːr] *m* (-s/-e) major.

Makel ['maːkəl] *m* (-s/-) stain, spot; *fig. a.* blemish, fault; **'Slos** *adj.* stainless, spotless; *fig. a.* unblemished, faultless, immaculate.

mäkeln F ['mɛːkəln] *v/i.* (ge-, h) find fault (*an dat.* with), carp (at), F pick (at).

Makler ✝ ['maːklər] *m* (-s/-) broker; **'..gebühr** ✝ *f* brokerage.

Makulatur ⊕ [makula'tuːr] *f* (-/-en) waste paper.

Mal¹ [maːl] *n* (-[e]s/-e, ⁼er) mark, sign; *sports:* start(ing-point), goal; spot, stain; mole.

Mal² [~] 1. *n* (-[e]s/-e) time; *für dieses ~* this time; *zum ersten ~* for the first time; *mit e-m ~e* all at once, all of a sudden; 2. ⚣ *adv.* times, multiplied by; *drei ~ fünf ist fünfzehn* three times five is *or* are fifteen; F *s. einmal.*

'malen *v/t.* (ge-, h) paint; portray.

'Maler *m* (-s/-) painter; artist; **..ei** [..'rai] *f* (-/-en) painting; **Sisch** *adj.* pictorial, painting; *fig.* picturesque.

'Malkasten *m* paint-box.

'malnehmen ⚣ *v/t.* (*irr. nehmen, sep.,* -ge-, h) multiply (*mit* by).

Malz [malts] *n* (-es/no *pl.*) malt; **'..bier** *n* malt beer.

Mama [ma'maː, F 'mama] *f* (-/-s) mamma, mammy, F ma, *Am.* F a. mummy, mom.

man *indef. pron.* [man] one, you, we; they, people; *~ sagte mir* I was told. [manager.]

Manager ['mɛnidʒər] *m* (-s/-))

manch [manç], **'..er**, **'..e**, **'..es** *adj. and indef. pron.* many a; *~ e pl.* some, several; **'..erlei** *adj.* [''..ər'lai] diverse, different; all sorts of, ... of several sorts; *auf ~ Art* in various ways; *used as a noun:* many *or* various things; **'..mal** *adv.* sometimes, at times.

Mandant ⚖ [man'dant] *m* (-en/-en) client.

Mandarine ⚘ [manda'riːnə] *f* (-/-n) tangerine.

Mandat [man'daːt] *n* (-[e]s/-e) authorization; ⚖ brief; *pol.* mandate; *parl.* seat.

Mandel ['mandəl] *f* (-/-n) ⚘ almond; *anat.* tonsil; **'..baum** ⚘ *m* almond-tree; **'..entzündung** ⚕ *f* tonsillitis.

Manege [ma'nɛːʒə] *f* (-/-n) (circus-) ring, manège.

Mangel¹ ['maŋəl] *m* 1. (-s/no *pl.*) want, lack, deficiency; shortage; penury; *aus ~ an* for want of; *~ leiden an* (*dat.*) be in want of; 2. (-s/⁼) defect, shortcoming.

Mangel² [~] *f* (-/-n) mangle; calender.

'**mangelhaft** adj. defective; deficient; unsatisfactory; '2igkeit f (-/no pl.) defectiveness; deficiency.

'**mangeln**[1] v/i. (ge-, h): es mangelt an Brot there is a lack or shortage of bread, bread is lacking or wanting; es mangelt ihm an (dat.) he is in need of or short of or wanting in, he wants or lacks.

'**mangeln**[2] v/t. (ge-, h) mangle (clothes, etc.); ⊕ calender (cloth, paper).

'**mangels** prp. (gen.) for lack or want of; esp. ⅌ in default of.

'**Mangelware** f scarce commodity; goods pl. in short supply.

Manie [ma'ni:] f (-/-n) mania.

Manier [ma'ni:r] f (-/-en) manner; 2lich adj. well-behaved; polite, mannerly.

Manifest [mani'fɛst] n (-es/-e) [manifesto.]

Mann [man] m (-[e]s/⸚er) man; husband.

'**mannbar** adj. marriageable; '2-keit f (-/no pl.) puberty, manhood.

Männchen ['mɛnçən] n (-s/-) little man; zo. male; birds: cock.

'**Mannes|alter** n virile age, manhood; '~kraft f virility.

mannig|fach adj. ['maniç-], '~faltig adj. manifold, various, diverse; '2faltigkeit f (-/no pl.) manifoldness, variety, diversity.

männlich adj. ['mɛnliç] male; gr. masculine; fig. manly; '2keit f (-/no pl.) manhood, virility.

'**Mannschaft** f (-/-en) (body of) men; ♣ crew; sports: team, side; '~sführer m sports: captain; '~sgeist m (-es/no pl.) sports: team spirit.

Manöv|er [ma'nø:vər] n (-s/-) manœuvre, Am. maneuver; 2rieren [~'vri:rən] v/i. (no -ge-, h) manœuvre, Am. maneuver.

Mansarde [man'zardə] f (-/-n) attic, garret; ~nfenster n dormer-window.

mansche|n F ['manʃən] (ge-, h) 1. v/t. mix, work; 2. v/i. dabble (in dat. in); 2'rei F f (-/-en) mixing, F mess; dabbling.

Manschette [man'ʃɛtə] f (-/-n) cuff; ~nknopf m cuff-link.

Mantel ['mantəl] m (-s/⸚) coat; overcoat, greatcoat; cloak, mantle (both a. fig.); ⊕ case, jacket; (outer) cover (of tyre).

Manuskript [manu'skript] n (-[e]s/-e) manuscript; typ. copy.

Mappe ['mapə] f (-/-n) portfolio, brief-case; folder; s. a. Schreibmappe, Schulmappe.

Märchen ['mɛ:rçən] n (-s/-) fairy-tale; fig. (cock-and-bull) story, fib; '~buch n book of fairy-tales; '2haft adj. fabulous (a. fig.).

Marder zo. ['mardər] m (-s/-) marten.

12*

Marine [ma'ri:nə] f (-/-n) marine; ⚔ navy, naval forces pl.; ~minister m minister of naval affairs; First Lord of the Admiralty, Am. Secretary of the Navy; ~ministerium n ministry of naval affairs; the Admiralty, Am. Department of the Navy.

marinieren [mari'ni:rən] v/t. (no -ge-, h) pickle, marinade.

Marionette [mario'nɛtə] f (-/-n) puppet, marionette; ~ntheater n puppet-show.

Mark [mark] 1. f (-/-) coin: mark; 2. n (-[e]s/no pl.) anat. marrow; ♀ pith; fig. core.

markant adj. [mar'kant] characteristic; striking; (well-)marked.

Marke ['markə] f (-/-n) mark, sign, token; ⚙, etc.: stamp; ⚓ brand, trade-mark; coupon; ~nartikel ⚓ m branded or proprietary article.

mar'kier|en (no -ge-, h) 1. v/t. mark (a. sports); brand (cattle, goods, etc.); 2. F fig. v/i. put it on; 2ung f (-/-en) mark(ing).

'**markig** adj. marrowy; fig. pithy.

Markise [mar'ki:zə] f (-/-n) blind, (window-)awning.

'**Markstein** m boundary-stone, landmark (a. fig.).

Markt [markt] m (-[e]s/⸚e) market; s. Marktplatz; fair; auf den ~ bringen ⚓ put on the market; '~flecken m small market-town; '~platz m market-place; '~schreier m (-s/-) quack; puffer.

Marmelade [marmə'la:də] f (-/-n) jam; marmalade (made of oranges).

Marmor ['marmər] m (-s/-e) marble; 2ieren [~o'ri:rən] v/t. (no -ge-, h) marble, vein, grain; 2n adj. ['~ɔrn] (of) marble; [whim, caprice.]

Marotte [ma'rɔtə] f (-/-n) fancy,]

Marsch [marʃ] 1. m (-es/⸚e) march (a. ♩); 2. f (-/-en) marsh, fen.

Marschall ['marʃal] m (-s/⸚e) marshal.

'**Marsch|befehl** ⚔ m marching orders pl.; 2ieren [~'ʃi:rən] v/i. (no -ge-, sein) march; '~land n marshy land.

Marter ['martər] f (-/-n) torment, torture; '2n v/t. (ge-, h) torment, torture; '~pfahl m stake.

Märtyrer ['mɛrtyrər] m (-s/-) martyr; '~tod m martyr's death; '~tum n (-s/no pl.) martyrdom.

Marx|ismus pol. [mar'ksismus] m (-/no pl.) Marxism; ~t pol. m (-en/-en) Marxian, Marxist; 2tisch pol. adj. Marxian, Marxist.

März [mɛrts] m (-[e]s/-e) March.

Marzipan [martsi'pa:n] n, ⚙ m (-s/-e) marzipan, marchpane.

Masche ['maʃə] f (-/-n) mesh; knitting: stitch; F fig. trick, line; '2n-fest adj. ladder-proof, Am. runproof.

Maschine [ma'ʃi:nə] *f* (-/-n) machine; engine.

maschinell *adj.* [maʃi'nɛl] mechanical; ~e *Bearbeitung* machining.

Ma'schinen|bau ⊕ *m* (-[e]s/*no pl.*) mechanical engineering; ~**gewehr** ✗ *n* machine-gun; ♀**mäßig** *adj.* mechanical; automatic; ~**pistole** ✗ *f* sub-machine-gun; ~**schaden** *m* engine trouble; ~**schlosser** *m* (engine) fitter; ~**schreiberin** *f* (-/-nen) typist; ~**schrift** *f* typescript.

Maschin|erie [maʃinə'ri:] *f* (-/-n) machinery; ~**ist** [~'nist] *m* (-en/-en) machinist.

Masern ✗ ['ma:zərn] *pl.* measles *pl.*

Mask|e ['maskə] *f* (-/-n) mask (*a. fig.*); ~**enball** *m* fancy-dress or masked ball; ~**erade** [~'ra:də] *f* (-/-n) masquerade; ♀**ieren** [~'ki:rən] *v/t.* (*no* -ge-, *h*) mask; *sich* ~ put on a mask; dress o.s. up (*als* as).

Maß [ma:s] **1.** *n* (-es/-e) measure; proportion; *fig.* moderation; ~e *pl. und Gewichte pl.* weights and measures *pl.*; ~e *pl.* room, *etc.*: measurements *pl.*; **2.** ♀ *f* (-/[-e]) *appr.* quart (*of beer*); **3.** ♀ *pret. of* messen.

Massage [ma'sɑ:ʒə] *f* (-/-n) massage.

'Maßanzug *m* tailor-made or bespoke suit, *Am. a.* custom(-made) suit.

Masse ['masə] *f* (-/-n) mass; bulk; substance; multitude; crowd; ⊕ assets *pl.*, estate; *die breite* ~ the rank and file; F *e-e* ~ a lot of, F lots *pl. or* heaps *pl.* of.

'Maßeinheit *f* measuring unit.

'Massen|flucht *f* stampede; ~**grab** *n* common grave; ~**güter** ✝ [~'gy:tər] *n/pl.* bulk goods *pl.*; ♀**haft** *adj.* abundant; ~**produktion** ✝ *f* mass production); ~**versammlung** *f* mass meeting, *Am. a.* rally; ♀**weise** *adv.* in masses, in large numbers.

Masseu|r [ma'sø:r] *m* (-s/-e) masseur; ~**se** [~zə] *f* (-/-n) masseuse.

'maß|gebend *adj.* standard; authoritative, decisive; *board*: competent; *circles*: influential, leading; ~**halten** *v/i.* (*irr. halten, sep., -ge-, h*) keep within limits, be moderate.

mas'sieren *v/t.* (*no* -ge-, *h*) massage, knead.

'massig *adj.* massy, bulky; solid.

mäßig *adj.* ['mɛ:siç] moderate; *food, etc.*: frugal; ✝ *price*: moderate, reasonable; *result, etc.*: poor; ~**en** ['~gən] *v/t.* (*ge-, h*) moderate; *sich* ~ moderate or restrain o.s.; ♀**ung** *f* (-/-en) moderation; restraint.

massiv [ma'si:f] **1.** *adj.* massive, solid; **2.** ♀ *geol. n* (-s/-e) massif.

'Maß|krug *m* beer-mug, *Am. a.* stein; ♀**los** *adj.* immoderate; boundless; exorbitant, excessive;

extravagant; ~**nahme** ['~na:mə] *f* (-/-n) measure, step, action; ♀**regeln** *v/t.* (*ge-, h*) reprimand; inflict disciplinary punishment on; '~**schneider** *m* bespoke or *Am.* custom tailor; '~**stab** *m* measure, rule(r); *maps, etc.*: scale; *fig.* yardstick, standard; ♀**voll** *adj.* moderate.

Mast¹ ⊕ [mast] *m* (-es/-e[n]) mast.

Mast² ✗ [~] *f* (-/-en) fattening; mast, food; ~**darm** *anat. m* rectum.

mästen ['mɛstən] *v/t.* (*ge-, h*) fatten, feed; stuff (*geese, etc.*).

'Mastkorb ⊕ *m* mast-head, crows-nest.

Material [mater'jɑ:l] *n* (-s/-ien) material; substance; stock, stores *pl.*; *fig.*: material, information; evidence; ~**ismus** *phls.* [~a'lismus] *m* (-/*no pl.*) materialism; ~**ist** [~a'list] *m* (-en/-en) materialist; ♀**istisch** *adj.* [~a'listiʃ] materialistic.

Materie [ma'te:rjə] *f* (-/-n) matter (*a. fig.*), stuff; *fig.* subject; ♀**ll** *adj.* [~er'jɛl] material.

Mathemati|k [matema'ti:k] *f* (-/*no pl.*) mathematics *sg.*; ~**ker** [~'ma:tikər] *m* (-s/-) mathematician; ♀**sch** *adj.* [~'ma:tiʃ] mathematical.

Matinee *thea.* [mati'ne:] *f* (-/-n) morning performance.

Matratze [ma'tratsə] *f* (-/-n) mattress.

Matrone [ma'tro:nə] *f* (-/-n) matron; ♀**nhaft** *adj.* matronly.

Matrose ⊕ [ma'tro:zə] *m* (-n/-n) sailor, seaman.

Matsch [matʃ] *m* (-es/*no pl.*), ~**e** F ['~ə] *f* (-/*no pl.*) pulp, squash; mud, slush; ♀**ig** *adj.* pulpy, squashy; muddy, slushy.

matt *adj.* [mat] faint, feeble; *voice, etc.*: faint; *eye, colour, etc.*: dim; *colour, light,* ✝ *stock exchange, style, etc.*: dull; *metal*: tarnished; *gold, etc.*: dead, dull; *chess*: mated; ♀ *bulb*: non-glare; ~ *geschliffen glass*: ground, frosted, matted; ~ *setzen at chess*: (check)mate *s.o.*

Matte ['matə] *f* (-/-n) mat.

'Mattigkeit *f* (-/*no pl.*) exhaustion, feebleness; faintness.

'Mattscheibe *f* *phot.* focus(s)ing screen; *television*: screen.

Mauer ['mauər] *f* (-/-n) wall; ~**blümchen** *fig.* ['~bly:mçən] *n* (-s/-) wall-flower; ♀**n** *v/t.* (*ge-, h*) **1.** *v/i.* make a wall, lay bricks; **2.** *v/t.* build (in stone or brick); '~**stein** *m* brick; '~**werk** *n* masonry, brickwork.

Maul [maul] *n* (-[e]s/*⁀er*) mouth; *sl.*: *halt's* ~! shut up!; ♀**en** F *v/i.* (*ge-, h*) sulk, pout; '~**esel** *zo. m* mule, hinny; '~**held** F *m* braggart; '~**korb** *m* muzzle; '~**schelle** F *f* box on the ear; '~**tier** *zo. n* mule;

~wurf *zo. m* mole; **'~wurfshügel** *m* molehill.

Maurer ['maurər] *m* (-s/-) bricklayer, mason; **'~meister** *m* master mason; **'~polier** *m* bricklayers' foreman.

Maus *zo.* [maus] *f* (-/⁻e) mouse; **~efalle** ['~zə-] *f* mousetrap; **♀en** ['~zən] (ge-, h) 1. *v/i.* catch mice; 2. F *v/t.* pinch, pilfer, F swipe.

Mauser ['mauzər] *f* (-/no *pl.*) mo(u)lt(ing); *in der* ~ *sein* be mo(u)lting; **'♀n** *v/refl.* (ge-, h) mo(u)lt.

Maximum ['maksimum] *n* (-s/Maxima) maximum.

Mayonnaise [majo'nɛːzə] *f* (-/-n) mayonnaise.

Mechani|k [me'çaːnik] *f* 1. (-/no *pl.*) mechanics *mst sg.*; 2. ⊕ (-/-en) mechanism; **~ker** *m* (-s/-) mechanic; **♀sch** *adj.* mechanical; **♀sieren** [~ani'ziːrən] *v/t.* (no -ge-, h) mechanize; **~smus** ⊕ [~a'nismus] *m* (-/Mechanismen) mechanism; *clock, watch, etc.*: works *pl.*

meckern ['mɛkərn] *v/i.* (ge-, h) bleat; *fig.* grumble (*über acc.* over, at, about), carp (at); nag (at); *sl.* grouse, *Am. sl.* gripe.

Medaill|e [me'daljə] *f* (-/-n) medal; **~on** [~'jõː] *n* (-s/-s) medallion; locket.

Medikament [medika'mɛnt] *n* (-[e]s/-e) medicament, medicine.

Medizin [medi'tsiːn] *f* 1. (-/no *pl.*) (science of) medicine; 2. (-/-en) medicine, F physic; **~er** *m* (-s/-) medical man; medical student; **♀isch** *adj.* medical; medicinal.

Meer [meːr] *n* (-[e]s/-e) sea (*a. fig.*), ocean; **'~busen** *m* gulf, bay; **'~enge** *f* strait(s *pl.*); **'~esspiegel** *m* sea level; **'~rettich** ♀ *m* horse-radish; **'~schweinchen** *n* guinea-pig.

Mehl [meːl] *n* (-[e]s/-e) flour; meal; **'~brei** *m* pap; **'♀ig** *adj.* floury, mealy, farinaceous; **'~speise** *f* sweet dish, pudding; **'~suppe** *f* gruel.

mehr [meːr] 1. *adj.* more; *er hat ~ Geld als ich* he has (got) more money than I; 2. *adv.* more; *nicht ~* no more, no longer, not any longer; *ich habe nichts ~* I have nothing left; **'♀arbeit** *f* additional work; overtime; **'~ausgaben** *f/pl.* additional expenditure; **'♀betrag** *m* surplus; **'~deutig** *adj.* ambiguous; **'♀einnahme(n** *pl.*) *f* additional receipts *pl.*; **'~en** *v/t.* (ge-, h) augment, increase; *sich ~* multiply, grow; **'~ere** *adj.* and *indef. pron.* several, some; **'~fach** 1. *adj.* manifold, repeated; 2. *adv.* repeatedly, several times; **'♀gebot** *n* higher bid; **'♀heit** *f* (-/-en) majority, plurality; **'♀kosten** *pl.* additional expense; **'~malig** *adj.* repeated, reiterated;

~mals *adv.* ['~maːls] several times, repeatedly; **'~sprachig** *adj.* polyglot; **'~stimmig** ♪ *adj.*: *~er Gesang* part-song; **'♀verbrauch** *m* excess consumption; **'♀wertsteuer** ✝ *f* (-/no *pl.*) value-added tax; **'♀zahl** *f* majority; *gr.* plural (form); *die ~* (*gen.*) most of.

meiden ['maidən] *v/t.* (irr., ge-, h) avoid, shun, keep away from.

Meile ['mailə] *f* (-/-n) mile; **'~nstein** *m* milestone.

mein *poss. pron.* [main] my; *der* (*die, das*) *~e* my; *die* ♀*en pl.* my family, F my people *or* folks *pl.*; *ich habe das ~e getan* I have done all I can; *~e Damen und Herren!* Ladies and Gentlemen!

Meineid ✝ ['main⁻] *m* perjury; **'♀ig** *adj.* perjured.

meinen ['mainən] *v/t.* (ge-, h) think, believe, be of (the) opinion, *Am. a.* reckon, guess; say; mean; *wie ~ Sie das?* what do you mean by that?; *~ Sie das ernst?* do you (really) mean it?; *es gut ~* mean well.

meinetwegen *adv.* ['main⁻t-] for my sake; on my behalf; because of me, on my account; for all I care; I don't mind *or* care.

'Meinung *f* (-/-en) opinion (*über acc., von* about, of); *die öffentliche ~* (the) public opinion; *meiner ~ nach* in my opinion, to my mind; *j-m* (*gehörig*) *die ~ sagen* give s.o. a piece of one's mind; **'~saustausch** ['mainuŋs⁻] *m* exchange of views (*über acc.* on); **'~sverschiedenheit** *f* difference of opinion (*über acc.* on); disagreement.

Meise *orn.* ['maizə] *f* (-/-n) titmouse.

Meißel ['maisəl] *m* (-s/-) chisel; **'♀n** *v/t. and v/i.* (ge-, h) chisel; carve.

meist [maist] 1. *adj.* most; *die ~en Leute* most people; *die ~e Zeit* most of one's time; 2. *adv.*: *s. meistens*; *am ~en* most (of all); **'♀bietende** ['~biːtəndə] *m* (-n/-n) highest bidder; **'~ens** *adv.* ['~əns], **'~en'teils** *adv.* mostly, in most cases; usually.

Meister ['maistər] *m* (-s/-) master, *sl.* boss; *sports:* champion; **'♀haft** 1. *adj.* masterly; 2. *adv.* in a masterly manner *or* way; **'♀n** *v/t.* (ge-, h) master; **'~schaft** *f* 1. (-/no *pl.*) mastery; 2. (-/-en) *sports:* championship, title; **'~stück** *n*, **'~werk** *n* masterpiece.

'Meistgebot *n* highest bid, best offer.

Melancholie [melaŋko'liː] *f* (-/-n) melancholy; **♀isch** *adj.* [~'koːlif] melancholy; **~ sein** F have the blues.

Melde|amt ['mɛldə-] *n* registration office; **'~liste** *f sports:* list of entries; **'♀n** *v/t.* (ge-, h) announce; *j-m et. ~* inform s.o. of s.th.; *officially:* notify s.th. to s.o.; *j-n ~*

enter s.o.'s name (für, zu for); sich
~ report o.s. (bei to); school, etc.:
put up one's hand; answer the telephone; enter (one's name) (für, zu
for examination, etc.); sich ~ zu
apply for; sich auf ein Inserat ~
answer an advertisement.

'**Meldung** f (-/-en) information, advice; announcement; report; registration; application; sports: entry.

melke|n ['mɛlkən] v/t. (irr., ge-, h)
milk; '2**r** m (-s/-) milker.

Melod|ie ♩ [melo'di:] f (-/-n) mel-
ody; tune, air; 2**isch** adj. [~'lo:diʃ]
melodious, tuneful.

Melone [me'lo:nə] f (-/-n) ♦ melon;
F bowler(-hat), Am. derby.

Membran [mɛm'brɑ:n] f (-/-en),
~**e** f (-/-n) membrane; teleph. a.
diaphragm.

Memme F ['mɛmə] f (-/-n) coward;
poltroon.

Memoiren [memo'ɑ:rən] pl. mem-
oirs pl.

Menagerie [menaʒə'ri:] f (-/-n)
menagerie.

Menge ['mɛŋə] f (-/-n) quantity;
amount; multitude; crowd; in
großer ~ in abundance; persons,
animals: in crowds; e-e ~ Geld
plenty of money, F lots pl. of
money; e-e ~ Bücher a great many
books; '2**n** v/t. (ge-, h) mix, blend;
sich ~ mix (unter acc. with), mingle
(with); sich ~ in (acc.) meddle or
interfere with.

Mensch [mɛnʃ] m (-en/-en) human
being; man; person, individual; die
~**en** pl. people pl., the world, mankind; kein ~ nobody.

'**Menschen|affe** zo. m anthropoid
ape; '~**alter** n generation, age; '~
feind m misanthropist; '2**feindlich**
adj. misanthropic; '~**fresser** m
(-s/-) cannibal, man-eater; '~
freund m philanthropist; '2**freundlich** adj. philanthropic; '~
gedenken n (-s/no pl.): seit ~ from
time immemorial, within the memory of man; '~**geschlecht** n human
race, mankind; '~**haß** m misan-
thropy; '~**kenner** m judge of men
or human nature; '~**kenntnis** f
knowledge of human nature; '~
leben n human life; '2**leer** adj.
deserted; '~**liebe** f philanthropy;
'~**menge** f crowd (of people),
throng; '2**möglich** adj. humanly
possible; '~**raub** m kidnap(p)ing;
'~**rechte** n/pl. human rights pl.;
'2**scheu** adj. unsociable, shy; '~
seele f: keine ~ not a living soul;
'~**verstand** m human understanding; gesunder ~ common sense, F
horse sense; '~**würde** f dignity of
man.

'**Menschheit** f (-/no pl.) human
race, mankind.

'**menschlich** adj. human; fig. hu-

mane; '2**keit** f (-/no pl.) human
nature; humanity, humaneness.

Mentalität [mɛntali'tɛ:t] f (-/-en)
mentality.

merk|bar adj. ['mɛrkbɑ:r] s. merk-
lich; 2**blatt** n leaflet, instructional
pamphlet; 2**buch** n notebook; '~**en**
(ge-, h) 1. v/i.: ~ auf (acc.) pay
attention to, listen to; 2. v/t. notice,
perceive; find out, discover; sich
et. ~ remember s.th.; bear s.th. in
mind; '~**lich** adj. noticeable, perceptible; 2**mal** n (-[e]s/-e) mark,
sign; characteristic, feature.

'**merkwürdig** adj. noteworthy, re-
markable; strange, odd, curious;
~**erweise** adv. ['~gər] strange to
say, strangely enough; '2**keit** f
(-/-en) remarkableness; curiosity;
peculiarity.

meßbar adj. ['mɛsbɑ:r] measurable.

Messe ['mɛsə] f (-/-n) ♱ fair; eccl.
mass; ⨯, ⚓ mess.

messen ['mɛsən] v/t. (irr., ge-, h)
measure; ⚓ sound; sich mit j-m ~
compete with s.o.; sich nicht mit
j-m ~ können be no match for s.o.;
gemessen an (dat.) measured
against, compared with.

Messer ['mɛsər] n (-s/-) knife; ⚔
scalpel; bis aufs ~ to the knife; auf
des ~s Schneide on a razor-edge or
razor's edge; '~**griff** m knife-
handle; '~**held** m stabber; '~**klinge**
f knife-blade; '~**schmied** m cutler;
'~**schneide** f knife-edge; '~**stecher**
m (-s/-) stabber; '~**stecherei** [~ʃtɛ-
çə'raɪ] f (-/-en) knifing, knife-
battle; '~**stich** m stab with a knife.

Messing ['mɛsiŋ] n (-s/no pl.) brass;
'~**blech** n sheet-brass.

'**Meß|instrument** n measuring in-
strument; '~**latte** f surveyor's rod;
'~**tisch** m surveyor's or plane table.

Metall [me'tal] n (-s/-e) metal; ~**arbeiter** m metal worker; 2**en** adj.
(of) metal, metallic; ~**geld** n coin(s
pl.), specie; ~**glanz** m metallic
lust|re, Am. -er; 2**haltig** adj.
metalliferous; ~**industrie** f metallurgical industry; ~**waren** f/pl.
hardware.

Meteor ast. [mete'o:r] m (-s/-e)
meteor; ~**ologe** [~oro'lo:gə] m
(-n/-n) meteorologist; ~**ologie**
[~orolo'gi:] f (-/no pl.) meteorology.

Meter ['me:tər] n, m (-s/-) met|re,
Am. -er; '~**maß** n tape-measure.

Method|e [me'to:də] f (-/-n) meth-
od; ⊕ a. technique; 2**isch** adj.
methodical.

Metropole [metro'po:lə] f (-/-n))
metropolis.

Metzel|ei [mɛtsə'laɪ] f (-/-en)
slaughter, massacre; '2**n** v/t.
(ge-, h) butcher, slaughter, massacre.

Metzger ['mɛtsgər] m (-s/-) butcher;
~**ei** [~'raɪ] f (-/-en) butcher's (shop).

Meuchel|mord ['mɔʏçəl-] m assas-
sination; '~**mörder** m assassin.

Meute ['mɔytə] f (-/-n) pack of hounds; fig. gang; ~**rei** [~'raɪ] f (-/-en) mutiny; '~**rer** m (-s/-) mutineer; '**2risch** adj. mutinous; '**2rn** v/i. (ge-, h) mutiny (gegen against).

mich pers. pron. [mɪç] me; ~ (selbst) myself.

mied [mi:t] pret. of meiden.

Mieder ['mi:dər] n (-s/-) bodice; corset; '~**waren** f/pl. corsetry.

Miene ['mi:nə] f (-/-n) countenance, air; feature; gute ~ zum bösen Spiel machen grin and bear it; ~ machen zu inf. offer or threaten to inf.

mies F adj. [mi:s] miserable, poor; out of sorts, seedy.

Miet|**e** ['mi:tə] f (-/-n) rent; hire; zur ~ wohnen live in lodgings, be a tenant; '**2en** v/t. (ge-, h) rent (land, building, etc.); hire (horse, etc.); (take on) lease (land, etc.); ⚓, ✈; charter; '~**er** m (-s/-) tenant; lodger, Am. a. roomer; ♫ lessee; '**2frei** adj. rent-free; '~**shaus** n block of flats, Am. apartment house; '~**vertrag** m tenancy agreement; lease; '~**wohnung** f lodgings pl., flat, Am. apartment.

Migräne ♫ [mi'grɛːnə] f (-/-n) migraine, megrim; sick headache.

Mikrophon [mikro'fo:n] n (-s/-e) microphone, F mike.

Mikroskop [mikro'sko:p] n (-s/-e) microscope; **2isch** adj. microscopic(al).

Milbe zo. ['mɪlbə] f (-/-n) mite.

Milch [mɪlç] f (-/no pl.) milk; milt, soft roe (of fish); '~**bar** f milk-bar; '~**bart** fig. m stripling; '~**brötchen** n (French) roll; '~**gesicht** n baby face; '~**glas** n frosted glass; '**2ig** adj. milky; '~**kanne** f milk-can; '~**kuh** f milk cow (a. fig.); '~**mädchen** F n milkmaid, dairymaid; '~**mann** F m milkman, dairyman; '~**pulver** n milk-powder; '~**reis** m rice-milk; '~**straße** ast. f Milky Way, Galaxy; '~**wirtschaft** f dairy-farm(ing); '~**zahn** m milktooth.

mild [mɪlt] 1. adj. weather, punishment, etc.: mild; air, weather, light, etc.: soft; wine, etc.: mellow, smooth; reprimand, etc.: gentle; 2. adv.: et. ~ beurteilen take a lenient view of s. th.

milde ['mɪldə] 1. adj. s. mild 1; 2. adv.: ~ gesagt to put it mildly; 3. ♀ f (-/no pl.) mildness; softness; smoothness; gentleness.

milder|**n** ['mɪldərn] v/t. (ge-, h) soften, mitigate; soothe, alleviate (pain, etc.); ~de Umstände ♫ extenuating circumstances; '**2ung** f (-/-en) softening, mitigation; alleviation.

mild|**herzig** adj. charitable; '**2herzigkeit** f (-/no pl.) charitableness;

'~**tätig** adj. charitable; '**2tätigkeit** f charity.

Milieu [mil'jøː] n (-s/-s) surroundings pl., environment; class, circles pl.; local colo(u)r.

Militär [mili'tɛːr] 1. n (-s/no pl.) military, armed forces pl.; army; 2. m (-s/-s) military man, soldier; ~**attaché** [~ataʃe:] m (-s/-s) military attaché; ~**dienst** m military service; **2isch** adj. military; ~**musik** f military music; ~**regierung** f military government; ~**zeit** f (-/no pl.) term of military service.

Miliz ✕ [mi'li:ts] f (-/-en) militia; ~**soldat** ✕ m militiaman.

Milliarde [mil'jardə] f (-/-n) thousand millions, milliard, Am. billion.

Millimeter [mili'~] n, m millimet|re, Am. -er.

Million [mil'jo:n] f (-/-en) million; ~**är** [~o'nɛːr] m (-s/-e) millionaire.

Milz anat. [mɪlts] f (-/-en) spleen, milt.

minder ['mɪndər] 1. adv. less; nicht ~ no less, likewise; 2. adj. less(er); smaller; minor; inferior; '~**begabt** adj. less gifted; ~**bemittelt** adj. ['~bəmɪtəlt] of moderate means; '**2betrag** m deficit, shortage; '**2einnahme** f shortfall in receipts; '**2gewicht** n short weight; '**2heit** f (-/-en) minority; ~**jährig** adj. ['~jɛːrɪç] under age, minor; '**2jährigkeit** f (-/no pl.) minority; '~**n** v/t. and v/refl. (ge-, h) diminish, lessen, decrease; '**2ung** f (-/-en) decrease, diminution; '~**wertig** adj. inferior, of inferior quality; '**2wertigkeit** f (-/no pl.) inferiority; † inferior quality; '**2wertigkeitskomplex** m inferiority complex.

mindest adj. ['mɪndəst] least; slightest; minimum; nicht die ~e Aussicht not the slightest chance; nicht im ~en not in the least, by no means; zum ~en at least; '~**alter** n minimum age; '**2anforderungen** f/pl. minumum requirements pl.; '**2betrag** m lowest amount; '**2einkommen** n minimum income; '~**ens** adv. at least; '**2gebot** n lowest bid; '**2lohn** m minimum wage; '**2maß** n minimum; auf ein ~ herabsetzen minimize; '**2preis** m minimum price.

Mine ['mi:nə] f (-/-n) ✕, ✕, ⚓ mine; pencil: lead; ball-point-pen: refill.

Mineral [minə'ra:l] n (-s/-e, -ien) mineral; **2isch** adj. mineral; ~**ogie** [~alo'gi:] f (-/no pl.) mineralogy; ~**wasser** n (-s/ᴗ) mineral water.

Miniatur [minia'tu:r] f (-/-en) miniature; ~**gemälde** n miniature.

Minirock ['mini-] m miniskirt.

Minister [mi'nɪstər] m (-s/-) minister; Secretary (of State), Am. Sec-

retary; ~ium [~'te:rjum] n (-s/Mi-
nisterien) ministry; Office, Am.
Department; ~präsident m prime
minister, premier; in Germany, etc.:
minister president; ~rat m (-[e]s/~e)
cabinet council.

minus adv. ['mi:nus] minus, less,
deducting.

Minute [mi'nu:tə] f (-/-n) minute;
~nzeiger m minute-hand.

mir pers. pron. [mi:r] (to) me.

Misch|ehe ['miʃ?-] f mixed mar-
riage; intermarriage; '2en v/t. (ge-,
h) mix, mingle; blend (coffee, tobacco, etc.); alloy (metal); shuffle
(cards); sich ~ in (acc.) interfere in;
join in (conversation); sich ~ unter
(acc.) mix or mingle with (the
crowd); ~ling ['~lin] m (-s/-e) half-
breed, half-caste; ♀, zo. hybrid;
~masch F ['~maʃ] m (-es/-e) hotchpotch, jumble; '~ung f (-/-en)
mixture; blend; alloy.

miß|achten [mis'-] v/t. (no -ge-, h)
disregard, ignore, neglect; slight,
despise; '2achtung f disregard,
neglect; '~behagen 1. v/i. (no -ge-,
h) displease; '2~ 2. n discomfort,
uneasiness; '2bildung f malforma-
tion, deformity; ~'billigen v/t. (no
-ge-, h) disapprove (of); '2billi-
gung f disapproval; '2brauch m
abuse; misuse; ~'brauchen v/t.
(no -ge-, h) abuse; misuse; ~
bräuchlich adj. ['~brɔyçliç] abusive; improper; ~'deuten v/t. (no
-ge-, h) misinterpret; '2deutung f
misinterpretation.

missen ['misən] v/t. (ge-, h) miss;
do without, dispense with.

'Miß|erfolg m failure, fiasco; '~
ernte f bad harvest, crop failure.

Misse|tat ['misə-] f misdeed; crime;
'~täter m evil-doer, offender;
criminal.

miß|'fallen v/i. (irr. fallen, no -ge-,
h): j-m ~ displease s.o.; '2fallen
n (-s/no pl.) displeasure, dislike;
'~fällig 1. adj. displeasing; shocking; disparaging; 2. adv.: sich ~
äußern über (acc.) speak ill of; '2ge-
burt f monster, freak (of nature),
deformity; '2geschick n bad luck,
misfortune; mishap; ~gestimmt
fig. adj. ['~gəʃtimt] s. mißmutig;
~'glücken v/i. (no -ge-, sein) fail;
~'gönnen v/t. (no -ge-, h): j-m et. ~
envy or grudge s.o. s.th.; '2griff m
mistake, blunder; '2gunst f envy,
jealousy; '~günstig adj. envious,
jealous; ~'handeln v/t. (no -ge-, h)
ill-treat; maul, sl. manhandle;
2'handlung f ill-treatment; maul-
ing, sl. manhandling; ẕ̓ẕ̓ assault
and battery; '2heirat f misalliance;
'~hellig adj. dissonant, dissentient;
'2helligkeit f (-/-en) dissonance,
dissension, discord.

Mission [mis'jo:n] f (-/-en) mission

(a. pol. and fig.); ~ar [~o'na:r] m
(-s/-e) missionary.

'Miß|klang m dissonance, discord
(both a. fig.); '~kredit fig. m
(-[e]s/no pl.) discredit; in ~ bringen
bring discredit upon s.o.

miß|'lang pret. of mißlingen; '~
lich adj. awkward; unpleasant;
~liebig adj. ['~li:biç] unpopular;
~lingen [~'liŋən] v/i. (irr., no
-ge-, sein) fail; '2lingen n (-s/no
pl.) failure; '2mut m ill humo(u)r;
discontent; '~mutig adj. ill-
humo(u)red; discontented; ~'raten
1. v/i. (irr. raten, no -ge-, sein)
fail; turn out badly; 2. adj. way-
ward; ill-bred; '2stand m nuisance;
grievance; '2stimmung f ill
humo(u)r; '2ton m (-[e]s/~e) dissonance, discord (both a. fig.); ~'trau-
en v/i. (no -ge-, h): j-m ~ distrust
or mistrust s.o.; '2trauen n (-s/no
pl.) distrust, mistrust; '~trauisch
adj. distrustful; suspicious; '2ver-
gnügen n (-s/no pl.) displeasure;
'~vergnügt adj. displeased; discontented; '2verhältnis n dispropor-
tion; incongruity; '2verständnis
n misunderstanding; dissension;
'~verstehen v/t. (irr. stehen, no
-ge-, h) misunderstand, mistake
(intention, etc.); '2wirtschaft f maladministration, mismanagement.

Mist [mist] m (-es/-e) dung, manure;
dirt; F fig. trash, rubbish; '~beet n
hotbed.

Mistel ♀ ['mistəl] f (-/-n) mistletoe.

'Mist|gabel f dung-fork; '~haufen
m dung-hill.

mit [mit] 1. prp. (dat.) with; ~ 20
Jahren at (the age of) twenty; ~ e-m
Schlage at a blow; ~ Gewalt by
force; ~ der Bahn by train; 2. adv.
also, too; ~ dabeisein be there too,
be (one) of the party.

Mit|arbeiter ['mit?-] m co-worker;
writing, art, etc.: collaborator;
colleague; newspaper, etc.: contrib-
utor (an dat. to); '2benutzen v/t.
(sep., no -ge-, h) use jointly or in
common; '~besitzer m joint owner;
'~bestimmungsrecht n right of
co-determination; '~bewerber m
competitor; '~bewohner m co-
inhabitant, fellow-lodger; '2brin-
gen v/t. (irr. bringen, sep., -ge-, h)
bring along (with one); '~bringsel
['~brinzəl] n (-s/-) little present;
'~bürger m fellow-citizen; 2ein-
ander adv. [mit?ai'nandər] together, jointly; with each other,
with one another; '~empfinden
['mit?-] n (-s/no pl.) sympathy;
~erbe ['mit?-] m co-heir; '~esser ♂
['mit?-] m (-s/-) blackhead; '2fah-
ren v/i. (irr. fahren, sep., -ge-, sein):
mit j-m ~ drive or go with s.o.; j-n
~ lassen give s.o. a lift; '2fühlen

v/i. (sep., -ge-, h) sympathize (mit with); 'Ꝍgeben v/t. (irr. geben, sep., -ge-, h) give along (dat. with); '₂gefühl n sympathy; 'Ꝍgehen v/i. (irr. gehen, sep., -ge-, sein): mit j-m ~ go with s.o.; '₂gift f (-/-ei) dowry, marriage portion.

'Mitglied n member; '₂erversammlung f general meeting; '₂erzahl f membership; '₂sbeitrag m subscription; '₂schaft f (-/no pl.) membership.

mit|'hin adv. consequently, therefore; ₂inhaber ['mit'-] m co-partner; '₂kämpfer m fellow-combatant; '₂kommen v/i. (irr. kommen, sep., -ge-, sein) come along (mit with); fig. be able to follow; '₂läufer pol. m nominal member; contp. trimmer.

'Mitleid n (-[e]s/no pl.) compassion, pity; sympathy; aus ~ out of pity; ~ haben mit have or take pity on; '₂enschaft f (-/no pl.): in ~ ziehen affect; implicate, involve; damage; '₂ig adj. compassionate, pitiful; ₂(s)los adj. ['₂t-] pitiless, merciless; ₂(s)voll adj. ['₂t-] pitiful, compassionate.

'mit|machen (sep., -ge-, h) 1. v/i. make one of the party; 2. v/t. take part in, participate in; follow, go with (fashion); go through (hardships); '₂mensch m fellow creature; '₂nehmen v/t. (irr. nehmen, sep., -ge-, h) take along (with one); fig. exhaust, wear out; j-n (im Auto) ~ give s.o. a lift; '₂nichten adv. [~'niçtn] by no means, not at all; '₂rechnen v/t. (sep., -ge-, h) include (in the account); nicht ~ leave out of account; nicht mitgerechnet not counting; '₂reden (sep., -ge-, h) 1. v/i. join in the conversation; 2. v/t.: ein Wort or Wörtchen mitzureden haben have a say (bei in); '₂reißen v/t. (irr. reißen, sep., -ge-, h) tear or drag along; fig. sweep along.

'Mitschuld f complicity (an dat. in); '₂ig adj. accessary (an dat. to crime); '₂ige m accessary, accomplice.

'Mitschüler m schoolfellow.

'mitspiel|en (sep., -ge-, h) 1. v/i. play (bei with); sports: be on the team; thea. appear, star (in a play); join in a game; matter: be involved; j-m arg or übel ~ play s.o. a nasty trick; 2. fig. v/t. join in (game); '₂er m partner.

'Mittag m midday, noon; heute ₂ at noon today; zu ~ essen lunch, dine; '₂essen n lunch(eon), dinner; '₂s adv. at noon.

'Mittags|pause f lunch hour; '~ruhe f midday rest; '₂schlaf m, '₂schläfchen n after-dinner nap, siesta; '₂stunde f noon; '₂tisch

fig. m lunch, dinner; '₂zeit f noon-tide; lunch-time, dinner-time.

Mitte ['mitə] f (-/-n) middle; cent|re, Am. -er; die goldene ~ the golden or happy mean; aus unserer ~ from among us; ~ Juli in the middle of July; ~ Dreißig in the middle of one's thirties.

'mitteil|en v/t. (sep., -ge-, h): j-m et. ~ communicate s.th. to s.o.; impart s.th. to s.o.; inform s.o. of s.th.; make s.th. known to s.o.; '₂sam adj. communicative; '₂ung f (-/-en) communication; information; communiqué.

Mittel ['mitəl] n (-s/-) means sg., way; remedy (gegen for); average; ₳ mean; phys. medium; ~ pl. a. means pl., funds pl., money; ~ pl. und Wege ways and means pl.; '₂alter n Middle Ages pl.; '₂alterlich adj. medi(a)eval; '₂bar adj. mediate, indirect; '₂ding n: ein ~ zwischen ... und ... something between ... and ...; '₂finger m middle finger; '₂gebirge n highlands pl.; '₂groß adj. of medium height; medium-sized; '₂läufer m sports: centre half back, Am. center half back; '₂los adj. without means, destitute; '₂mäßig adj. middling; mediocre; '₂mäßigkeit f (-/no pl.) mediocrity; '₂punkt m cent|re, Am. -er; fig. a. focus; '₂s prp. (gen.) by (means of), through; '₂schule f intermediate school, Am. high school; '₂smann m (-[e]s/⁓er, Mittelsleute) mediator, go-between; '₂stand m middle classes pl.; '₂stürmer m sports: centre forward, Am. center forward; '₂weg fig. m middle course; '₂wort gr. n (-[e]s/⁓er) participle.

mitten adv. ['mitən]: ~ in or an or auf or unter (acc.; dat.) in the midst or middle of; ~ entzwei right in two; ~ im Winter in the depth of winter; ~ in der Nacht in the middle or dead of night; ~ ins Herz right into the heart; ~'drin F adv. right in the middle; ~'durch F adv. right through or across.

Mitter|nacht ['mitər-] f midnight; um ~ at midnight; ₂nächtig adj. ['₂neçtiç], ₂nächtlich adj. midnight.

Mittler ['mitlər] 1. m (-s/-) mediator, intercessor; 2. ₂ adj. middle, central; average, medium; '₂weile adv. meanwhile, (in the) meantime.

Mittwoch ['mitvɔx] m (-[e]s/-e) Wednesday; '₂s adv. on Wednesday(s), every Wednesday.

mit|'unter adv. now and then, sometimes; '₂verantwortlich adj. jointly responsible; ₂welt f (-/no pl.): die ~ our, etc. contemporaries pl.

'mitwirk|en v/i. (sep., -ge-, h) co-operate (bei in), contribute (to), take part (in); **'2ende** m (-n/-n) thea. performer, actor, player (a. ♩); die ~n pl. the cast; **'2ung** f (-/no pl.) co(-)operation, contribution.

'Mitwisser m (-s/-) confidant; ⚊ accessary. [rechnen.|

'mitzählen v/t. (sep.,-ge-,h) s. mit-|

Mix|becher ['miks-] m (cocktail-) shaker; **'2en** v/t. (ge-, h) mix; **~tur** [~'tu:r] f (-/-en) mixture.

Möbel ['mø:bəl] n (-s/-) piece of furniture; ~ pl. furniture; **'~händler** m furniture-dealer; **'~spediteur** m furniture-remover; **'~stück** n piece of furniture; **'~tischler** m cabinet-maker; **'~wagen** m pantechnicon, Am. furniture truck.

mobil adj. [mo'bi:l] ⚔ mobile; F active, nimble; ~ machen ⚔ mobilize; **2iar** [~il'ja:r] n (-s/-e) furniture; movables pl.; **~isieren** [~ili-'zi:rən] v/t. (no -ge-, h) ⚔ mobilize; ✝ realize (property, etc.); **2machung** ⚔ [mo'bi:lmaxuŋ] f (-/-en) mobilization.

möblieren [mø'bli:rən] v/t. (no -ge-, h) furnish; möbliertes Zimmer furnished room, F bed-sitter.

mochte ['mɔxtə] pret. of mögen.

Mode ['mo:də] f (-/-n) fashion, vogue; use, custom; die neueste ~ the latest fashion; in ~ in fashion or vogue; aus der ~ kommen grow or go out of fashion; die ~ bestimmen set the fashion; **'~artikel** m/pl. fancy goods pl., novelties pl.; **'~farbe** f fashionable colo(u)r.

Modell [mo'dɛl] n (-s/-e) ⊕, fashion, paint.: model; pattern, design; ⊕ mo(u)ld; j-m ~ stehen paint. pose for s.o.; **2eisenbahn** f model railway; **2ieren** [~'li:rən] v/t. (no -ge-, h) model, mo(u)ld, fashion.

'Moden|schau f dress parade, fashion-show; **'~zeitung** f fashion magazine.

Moder ['mo:dər] m (-s/no pl.) must, putrefaction; **'~geruch** m musty smell; **'2ig** adj. musty, putrid.

modern[1] ['mo:dərn] v/i. (ge-, h) putrefy, rot, decay.

modern[2] adj. [mo'dɛrn] modern; progressive; up-to-date; fashionable; **~isieren** [~i'zi:rən] v/t. (no -ge-, h) modernize, bring up to date.

'Mode|salon m fashion house; **'~schmuck** m costume jewel(le)ry; **'~waren** f/pl. fancy goods pl.; **'~zeichner** m fashion-designer.

modifizieren [modifi'tsi:rən] v/t. (no -ge-, h) modify.

modisch adj. ['mo:diʃ] fashionable, stylish. [liner.|

Modistin [mo'distin] f (-/-nen) mil-|

Mogel|ei F [mo:gə'lai] f (-/-en) cheat; **'2n** F v/i. (ge-, h) cheat.

mögen ['mø:gən] (irr., h) 1. v/i. (ge-) be willing; ich mag nicht I don't like to; 2. v/t. (ge-) want, wish; like, be fond of; nicht ~ dislike; not to be keen on (food, etc.); lieber ~ like better, prefer; 3. v/aux. (no -ge-) may, might; ich möchte wissen I should like to know; ich möchte lieber gehen I would rather go; das mag (wohl) sein that's (well) possible; wo er auch sein mag wherever he may be; mag er sagen, was er will let him say what he likes.

möglich ['mø:kliç] 1. adj. possible; practicable, feasible; market, criminal, etc.: potential; alle ~en all sorts of; alles ~e all sorts of things; sein ~stes tun do one's utmost or level best; nicht ~! you don't say (so)!; so bald etc. wie ~ = 2. adv.:~st bald etc. as soon, etc., as possible; **'~er'weise** adv. possibly, if possible; perhaps; **'2keit** f (-/-en) possibility; chance; nach ~ if possible.

Mohammedan|er [mohame'da:-nər] m (-s/-) Muslim, Moslem, Mohammedan; **2isch** adj. Muslim, Moslem, Mohammedan.

Mohn ♥ [mo:n] m (-[e]s/-e) poppy.

Möhre ♥ ['mø:rə] f (-/-n) carrot.

Mohrrübe ♥ ['mo:r-] f carrot.

Molch zo. [mɔlç] m (-[e]s/-e) salamander; newt.

Mole ⚓ [mo:lə] f (-/-n) mole, jetty.

molk [mɔlk] pret. of melken.

Molkerei [mɔlkə'rai] f (-/-en) dairy; **~produkte** n/pl. dairy products pl.

Moll ♩ [mɔl] n (-/-) minor (key).

mollig F adj. ['mɔliç] snug, cosy; plump, rounded.

Moment [mo'mɛnt] (-[e]s/-e) 1. m moment, instant; im ~ at the moment; 2. n ⊕ motive; fact(or); ⊕ momentum; ⊕ impulse (a. fig.); **2an** [~'ta:n] 1. adj. momentary; 2. adv. at the moment, for the time being; **~aufnahme** phot. f snapshot, instantaneous photograph.

Monarch [mo'narç] m (-en/-en) monarch; **~ie** [~'çi:] f (-/-n) monarchy.

Monat ['mo:nat] m (-[e]s/-e) month; **2elang** 1. adj. lasting for months; 2. adv. for months; **2lich** 1. adj. monthly; 2. adv. monthly, a month.

Mönch [mœnç] m (-[e]s/-e) monk, friar.

'Mönchs|kloster n monastery; **'~kutte** f (monk's) frock; **'~leben** n monastic life; **'~orden** m monastic order; **'~zelle** f monk's cell.

Mond [mo:nt] m (-[e]s/-e) moon; hinter dem ~ leben be behind the times; **'~fähre** f lunar module; **'~finsternis** f lunar eclipse; **'2lich** adj. moonlit; **'~schein** m (-[e]s/no pl.) moonlight; **'~sichel** f crescent; **'2süchtig** adj. moonstruck.

Mono|log [mono'lo:k] m (-s/-e)

monologue, *Am. a.* monolog;
soliloquy; **∼pol ✝** *n* (-s/-e) monopoly; **2polisieren** [∼oli'zi:rən] *v/t.*
(no -ge-, *h*) monopolize; **2'ton** *m*
monotonous; **∼tonie** [∼to'ni:] *f*
(-/-n) monotony.

Monstrum ['mɔnstrum] *n* (-s/*Monstren, Monstra*) monster.

Montag ['mo:n-] *m* Monday; **2s**
adv. on Monday(s), every Monday.

Montage ⊕ [mɔn'ta:ʒə] *f* (-/-n)
mounting, fitting; setting up; assemblage, assembly.

Montan|industrie [mɔn'ta:n-] *f*
coal and steel industries *pl.*; **∼union**
f European Coal and Steel Community.

Mont|eur [mɔn'tø:r] *m* (-s/-e) ⊕
fitter, assembler; *esp. mot.*,
mechanic; **∼euranzug** *m* overall;
2ieren [∼'ti:rən] *v/t.* (no -ge-, *h*)
mount, fit; set up; assemble; **∼ur**
✕ [∼'tu:r] *f* (-/-en) regimentals *pl.*

Moor [mo:r] *n* (-[e]s/-e) bog; swamp;
'**∼bad** *n* mud-bath; '**2ig** *adj.* boggy,
marshy.

Moos ♀ [mo:s] *n* (-es/-e) moss; '**2ig**
adj. mossy.

Moped *mot.* ['mo:pεt] *n* (-s/-s)
moped.

Mops *zo.* [mɔps] *m* (-es/ᵘe) pug;
'**2en** *v/t.* (ge-, *h*) F pilfer, pinch; *sl.*:
sich ∼ be bored stiff.

Moral [mo'ra:l] *f* (-/∼ -en) morality; morals *pl.*; moral; ✕, *etc.*:
morale; **2isch** *adj.* moral; **2isieren**
[∼ali'zi:rən] *v/i.* (no -ge-, *h*) moralize.

Morast [mo'rast] *m* (-es/-e, ᵘe)
slough, morass; *s. Moor*; mire, mud;
2ig *adj.* marshy; muddy, miry.

Mord [mɔrt] *m* (-[e]s/-e) murder
(*an dat.* of); *e-n ∼ begehen* commit
murder; '**∼anschlag** *m* murderous
assault; **2en** ['∼dən] *v/i.* (ge-, *h*)
commit murder(s).

Mörder ['mœrdər] *m* (-s/-) murderer; **2isch** *adj.* murderous;
climate, etc.: deadly; ✝ *competition*:
cut-throat.

'**Mord|gier** *f* lust of murder, bloodthirstiness; '**2gierig** *adj.* bloodthirsty; '**∼kommission** *f* homicide
squad; '**∼prozeß** ⚖ *m* murder trial.

'**Mords|angst** F *f* blue funk, *sl.*
mortal fear; '**∼glück** F *n* stupendous
luck; '**∼kerl** F *m* devil of a fellow;
'**∼spek'takel** F *m* hullabaloo.

Morgen ['mɔrgən] 1. *m* (-s/-) morning; *measure*: acre; *am ∼ s. morgens*;
2. ♀ *adv.* tomorrow; *∼ früh (abend)*
tomorrow morning (evening *or*
night); *∼ in acht Tagen* tomorrow
week; '**∼ausgabe** *f* morning edition; '**∼blatt** *n* morning paper;
'**∼dämmerung** *f* dawn, daybreak;
'**∼gebet** *n* morning prayer; '**∼gymnastik** *f* morning exercises *pl.*;
'**∼land** *n* (-[e]s/*no pl.*) Orient, East;

'**∼rock** *m* peignoir, dressing-gown,
wrapper (*for woman*); '**∼röte** *f*
dawn; '**2s** *adv.* in the morning; '**∼zeitung** *f* morning paper.

'**morgig** *adj.* of tomorrow.

Morphium *pharm.* ['mɔrfium] *n*
(-s/*no pl.*) morphia, morphine.

morsch *adj.* [mɔrʃ] rotten, decayed;
brittle.

Mörser ['mœrzər] *m* (-s/-) mortar
(*a.* ✕).

Mörtel ['mœrtəl] *m* (-s/-) mortar.

Mosaik [moza'i:k] *n* (-s/-en) mosaic;
∼fußboden *m* mosaic *or* tessellated
pavement.

Moschee [mɔ'ʃe:] *f* (-/-n) mosque.

Moschus ['mɔʃus] *m* (-/*no pl.*) musk.

Moskito *zo.* [mɔs'ki:to] *m* (-s/-s)
mosquito; **∼netz** *n* mosquito-net.

Moslem ['mɔslεm] *m* (-s/-s) Muslim, Moslem.

Most [mɔst] *m* (-es/-e) must, grapejuice; *of apples*: cider; *of pears*:
perry.

Mostrich ['mɔstriç] *m* (-[e]s/*no pl.*)
mustard.

Motiv [mo'ti:f] *n* (-s/-e) motive,
reason; *paint.*, ♪ motif; **2ieren**
[∼i'vi:rən] *v/t.* (no -ge-, *h*) motivate.

Motor ['mo:tɔr] *m* (-s/-en) engine,
esp. ⚡ motor; '**∼boot** *n* motor boat;
'**∼defekt** *m* engine *or* ⚡ motor
trouble; '**∼haube** *f* bonnet, *Am.*
hood; **2isieren** [motori'zi:rən] *v/t.*
(no -ge-, *h*) motorize; **∼isierung**
[motori'zi:ruŋ] *f* (-/*no pl.*) motorization; '**∼rad** *n* motor (bi)cycle;
'**∼radfahrer** *m* motor cyclist; '**∼roller** *m* (motor) scooter; '**∼sport** *m*
motoring.

Motte *zo.* ['mɔtə] *f* (-/-n) moth.

'**Motten|kugel** *f* moth-ball; '**2sicher** *adj.* mothproof; '**2zerfressen**
adj. moth-eaten.

Motto ['mɔto] *n* (-s/-s) motto.

Möwe *orn.* ['mø:və] *f* (-/-n) sea-gull,
(sea-)mew.

Mücke *zo.* ['mykə] *f* (-/-n) midge,
gnat, mosquito; *aus e-r ∼ e-n Elefanten machen* make a mountain
out of a molehill; '**∼nstich** *m* gnatbite.

Mucker ['mukər] *m* (-s/-) bigot,
hypocrite.

müd|e *adj.* ['my:də] tired, weary;
e-r Sache ∼ sein be weary *or* tired
of s.th.; '**2igkeit** *f* (-/*no pl.*) tiredness, weariness.

Muff [muf] *m* 1. (-[e]s/-e) muff;
2. (-[e]s/*no pl.*) mo(u)ldy *or* musty
smell; '**∼e** ⊕ *f* (-/-n) sleeve, socket;
'**2eln** F *v/i.* (ge-, *h*) munch; mumble; '**2ig** *adj.* smell, *etc.*: musty,
fusty; *air*: close; *fig.* sulky, sullen.

Mühe ['my:ə] *f* (-/-n) trouble, pains
pl.; *(nicht) der ∼ wert* (not) worth
while; *j-m ∼ machen* give s.o.
trouble; *sich ∼ geben* take pains
(*mit* over, with *s.th.*); '**2los** *adj.*

effortless, easy; '2n v/refl. (ge-, h) take pains, work hard; '2voll adj. troublesome, hard; laborious.

Mühle ['my:lə] f (-/-n) mill.

'Müh|sal f (-/-e) toil, trouble; hardship; '2sam, '2selig 1. adj. toilsome, troublesome; difficult; 2. adv. laboriously; with difficulty.

Mulatte [mu'latə] m (-n/-n) mulatto.

Mulde ['muldə] f (-/-n) trough; depression, hollow.

Mull [mul] m (-[e]s/-e) mull.

Müll [myl] m (-[e]s/no pl.) dust, rubbish, refuse, Am. a. garbage; '~abfuhr f removal of refuse; '~eimer m dust-bin, Am. garbage can.

Müller ['mylər] m (-s/-) miller.

'Müll|fahrer m dust-man, Am. garbage collector; '~haufen m dust-heap; '~kasten m s. Mülleimer; '~kutscher m s. Müllfahrer; '~wagen m dust-cart, Am. garbage cart.

Multipli|kation Å [multiplika-'tsjo:n] f (-/-en) multiplication; 2zieren Å [~'tsi:rən] v/t. (no -ge-, h) multiply (mit by).

Mumie ['mu:mjə] f (-/-n) mummy.

Mumps ℱ [mumps] m, ℱ f (-/no pl.) mumps.

Mund [munt] m (-[e]s/-er) mouth; den ~ halten hold one's tongue; den ~ voll nehmen talk big; sich den ~ verbrennen put one's foot in it; nicht auf den ~ gefallen sein have a ready or glib tongue; j-m über den ~ fahren cut s.o. short; '~art f dialect; '2artlich adj. dialectal.

Mündel ['myndəl] m, n (-s/-), girl: a. f (-/-n) ward, pupil; '2sicher adj.: ~e Papiere n/pl. ✝ gilt-edged securities pl.

münden ['myndən] v/i. (ge-, h): ~ in (acc.) river, etc.: fall or flow into; street, etc.: run into.

'mund|faul adj. too lazy to speak; '~gerecht adj. palatable (a. fig.); '2harmonika ♪ f mouth-organ; '2höhle anat. f oral cavity.

mündig ✠ adj. ['myndiç] of age; ~ werden come of age; '2keit f (-/no pl.) majority.

mündlich ['myntliç] 1. adj. oral, verbal; 2. adv. a. by word of mouth.

'Mund|pflege f oral hygiene; '~raub ✠ m theft of comestibles; '~stück n mouthpiece (of musical instrument, etc.); tip (of cigarette); '2tot adj.: ~ machen silence or gag s.o.

'Mündung f (-/-en) mouth; a. estuary (of river); muzzle (of fire-arms).

'Mund|vorrat m provisions pl., victuals pl.; '~wasser n (-s/-) mouth-wash, gargle; '~werk ℱ fig. n: ein gutes ~ haben have the gift of the gab.

Munition [muni'tsjo:n] f (-/-en) ammunition.

munkeln ℱ ['muŋkəln] (ge-, h) 1. v/i. whisper; 2. v/t. whisper, rumo(u)r; man munkelt there is a rumo(u)r afloat. [lively; merry.]

munter adj. ['muntər] awake; fig.:)

Münz|e ['myntsə] f (-/-n) coin; (small) change; medal; mint; für bare ~ nehmen take at face value; j-m et. mit gleicher ~ heimzahlen pay s.o. back in his own coin; '~einheit f (monetary) unit, standard of currency; '2en v/t. (ge-, h) coin, mint; gemünzt sein auf (acc.) be meant for, be aimed at; '~fernsprecher teleph. m coin-box telephone; '~fuß m standard (of coinage); '~wesen n monetary system.

mürbe adj. ['myrbə] tender; pastry, etc.: crisp, short; meat: well-cooked; material: brittle; ℱ fig. worn-out, demoralized; ℱ j-n ~ machen break s.o.'s resistance; ℱ ~ werden give in.

Murmel ['murməl] f (-/-n) marble; '2n v/t. and v/i. (ge-, h) mumble, murmur; '~tier zo. n marmot.

murren ['murən] v/i. (ge-, h) grumble, ℱ grouch (both: über acc. at, over, about).

mürrisch adj. ['myriʃ] surly, sullen.

Mus [mu:s] n (-es/-e) pap; stewed fruit.

Muschel ['muʃəl] f (-/-n) zo.: mussel; shell, conch; teleph. ear-piece.

Museum [mu'ze:um] n (-s/Museen) museum.

Musik [mu'zi:k] f (-/no pl.) music; ~alienhandlung [~i'ka:ljən-] f music-shop; 2alisch adj. [~i'ka:-liʃ] musical; ~ant [~i'kant] m (-en/-en) musician; ~automat m juke-box; ~er ['mu:zikər] m (-s/-) musician; bandsman; ~instrument n musical instrument; ~lehrer m music-master; ~stunde f music-lesson; ~truhe f radiogram(ophone), Am. radio-phonograph.

musizieren [muzi'tsi:rən] v/i. (no -ge-, h) make or have music.

Muskat ♀ [mus'ka:t] m (-[e]s/-e) nutmeg; ~nuß ♀ f nutmeg.

Muskel ['muskəl] m (-s/-n) muscle; '~kater ℱ m stiffness and soreness, Am. a. charley horse; '~kraft f muscular strength; '~zerrung ✠ f pulled muscle.

Muskul|atur [muskula'tu:r] f (-/-en) muscular system, muscles pl.; 2ös adj. [~'lø:s] muscular, brawny.

Muß [mus] n (-/no pl.) necessity; es ist ein ~ it is a must.

Muße ['mu:sə] f (-/no pl.) leisure; spare time; mit ~ at one's leisure.

Musselin [musə'li:n] m (-s/-e) muslin.

müssen ['mysən] (irr., h) 1. v/i. (ge-): ich muß I must; 2. v/aux. (no -ge-): ich muß I must, I have to;

I am obliged or compelled or forced to; I am bound to; *ich habe gehen ~* I had to go; *ich müßte (eigentlich) wissen* I ought to know.

müßig *adj.* ['my:siç] idle; superfluous; useless; '2gang *m* idleness, laziness; 2gänger ['~gɛŋər] *m* (-s/-) idler, loafer; lazy-bones.

mußte ['mustə] *pret. of* müssen.

Muster ['mustər] *n* (-s/-) model; example, paragon; design, pattern; specimen; sample; '~betrieb *m* model factory or ✱ farm; '~gatte *m* model husband; 2gültig, 2haft 1. *adj.* model, exemplary, perfect; 2. *adv.*: *sich ~ benehmen* be on one's best behavio(u)r; '~kollektion ♱ *f* range of samples; '2n *v/t.* (ge-, h) examine; eye; ✗ inspect, review; figure, pattern (*fabric, etc.*); '~schutz *m* protection of patterns and designs; '~ung *f* (-/-en) examination; ✗ review; pattern (*of fabric, etc.*); '~werk *n* standard work.

Mut [mu:t] *m* (-[e]s/*no pl.*) courage; spirit; pluck; *~ fassen* pluck up courage, summon one's courage; *den ~ sinken lassen* lose courage or heart; *guten ~(e)s sein* be of good cheer; '2ig *adj.* courageous; plucky; '2los *adj.* discouraged; despondent; '~losigkeit *f* (-/*no pl.*) discouragement; despondency; 2maßen ['~ma:sən] *v/t.* (ge-, h) suppose, guess, surmise; '2maßlich *adj.* presumable; supposed; *heir:* presumptive; '~maßung *f* (-/-en) supposition, surmise; *bloße ~en pl.* guesswork.

Mutter ['mutər] *f* 1. (-/-) mother; 2. ⊕ (-/-n) nut; '~brust *f* mother's breast; '~leib *m* womb.

mütterlich *adj.* ['mytərliç] motherly; maternal; ~erseits *adv.* ['~ər-'zarts] on or from one's mother's side; *uncle, etc.:* maternal.

'**Mutter|liebe** *f* motherly love; '2los *adj.* motherless; '~mal *n* birth-mark, mole; '~milch *f* mother's milk; '~schaft *f* (-/*no pl.*) maternity, motherhood; '2seelen-al'lein *adj.* all or utterly alone; ~söhnchen ['~zø:nçən] *n* (-s/-) milksop, *sl.* sissy; '~sprache *f* mother tongue; '~witz *m* (-es/*no pl.*) mother wit.

'**Mutwill|e** *m* wantonness; mischievousness; '2ig *adj.* wanton; mischievous; wilful.

Mütze ['mytsə] *f* (-/-n) cap.

Myrrhe ['myrə] *f* (-/-n) myrrh.

Myrte ⚘ ['myrtə] *f* (-/-n) myrtle.

mysteri|ös *adj.* [myster'jø:s] mysterious; 2um [~'te:rjum] *n* (-s/ *Mysterien*) mystery.

Mystifi|kation [mystifika'tsjo:n] *f* (-/-en) mystification; 2zieren [~'tsi:rən] *v/t.* (*no* -ge-, h) mystify.

Mysti|k ['mystik] *f* (-/*no pl.*) mysticism; 2ker *adj.* mystic(al).

Myth|e ['my:tə] *f* (-/-n) myth; '2isch *adj.* mythic; *esp. fig.* mythical; ~ologie [mytolo'gi:] *f* (-/-n) mythology; 2ologisch *adj.* [myto-'lo:giʃ] mythological; ~os ['~ɔs] *m* (-/*Mythen*), ~us ['~us] *m* (-/*Mythen*) myth.

N

na *int.* [na] now!, then!, well!, *Am. a.* hey!

Nabe ['na:bə] *f* (-/-n) hub.

Nabel *anat.* ['na:bəl] *m* (-s/-) navel.

nach [na:x] 1. *prp.* (*dat.*) direction, striving: after; to(wards), for (*a. ~ ... hin or zu*); succession: after; *time:* after, past; *manner, measure, example:* according to; *~ Gewicht* by weight; *~ deutschem Geld in* German money; *e-r ~ dem andern* one by one; *fünf Minuten ~ eins* five minutes past one; 2. *adv.* after; *~ und ~* little by little, gradually; *wie vor* now as before, still.

nachahm|en ['na:x'aːmən] *v/t.* (*sep.*, -ge-, h) imitate, copy; counterfeit; '~ens'wert *adj.* worthy of imitation, exemplary; '2er *m* (-s/-) imitator; '2ung *f* (-/-en) imitation; copy; counterfeit, fake.

Nachbar ['naxba:r] *m* (-n, -s/-n), '~in *f* (-/-nen) neighbo(u)r; '~-

schaft *f* (-/-en) neighbo(u)rhood, vicinity.

'**Nachbehandlung** ⚕ *f* after-treatment.

'**nachbestell|en** *v/t.* (*sep.*, *no* -ge-, h) repeat one's order for *s.th.*; '2ung *f* repeat (order).

'**nachbeten** *v/t.* (*sep.*, -ge-, h) echo.

'**Nachbildung** *f* copy, imitation; replica; dummy.

'**nachblicken** *v/i.* (*sep.*, -ge-, h) look after.

nachdem *cj.* [na:x'de:m] after, when; *je ~ according as.*

'**nachdenk|en** *v/i.* (*irr. denken, sep.,* -ge-, h) think (*über acc.* over, about); reflect, meditate (*über acc.* on); '2en *n* (-s/*no pl.*) reflection, meditation; musing; '~lich *adj.* meditative, reflecting; pensive.

'**Nachdichtung** *f* free version.

'**Nachdruck** *m* 1. (-[e]s/*no pl.*) stress, emphasis; 2. *typ.* (-[e]s/-e)

reprint; *unlawfully*: piracy, pirated edition; '⸤en v/t. (sep., -ge-, h) reprint; *unlawfully*: pirate.
nachdrücklich ['naːxdrykliç] 1. *adj.* emphatic, energetic; forcible; positive; 2. *adv.*: ~ betonen emphasize.
nacheifern ['naːxʔ-] v/i. (sep., -ge-, h) emulate *s.o.*
nacheinander adv. [naːxʔaɪˈnandər] one after another, successively; by *or* in turns.
nachempfinden ['naːxʔ-] v/t. (irr. empfinden, sep., no -ge-, h) s. nachfühlen.
nacherzähl|en ['naːxʔ-] v/t. (sep., no -ge-, h) repeat; retell; dem Englischen nacherzählt adapted from the English; '⸤ung ['naːxʔ-] f repetition; story retold, reproduction.
'**Nachfolge** f succession; '⸤n v/i. (sep., -ge-, sein) follow *s.o.*; j-m im Amt ~ succeed s.o. in his office; '⸤r m (-s/-) follower; successor.
'**nachforsch|en** v/i. (sep., -ge-, h) investigate; search for; '⸤ung f investigation, inquiry, search.
'**Nachfrage** f inquiry; ✝ demand; '⸤n v/i. (sep., -ge-, h) inquire (nach after).
'**nach|fühlen** v/t. (sep., -ge-, h): es j-m ~ feel *or* sympathize with s.o.; '⸤füllen v/t. (sep., -ge-, h) fill up, refill; '⸤geben v/i. (irr. geben, sep., -ge-, h) give way (dat. to); fig. give in, yield (to); '⸤gebühr ✝ f surcharge; '⸤gehen v/i. (irr. gehen, sep., -ge-, sein) follow (s.o., business, trade, etc.); pursue (pleasure); attend to (business); investigate s.th.; watch: be slow; '⸤geschmack m (-[e]s/no pl.) after-taste.
nachgiebig adj. ['naːxgiːbiç] elastic, flexible; fig. a. yielding, compliant; '⸤keit f (-/-en) flexibility; compliance.
'**nachgrübeln** v/i. (sep., -ge-, h) ponder, brood (both: über acc. over), muse (on).
nachhaltig adj. ['naːxhaltiç] lasting, enduring.
nach'her adv. afterwards; then; bis ~! see you later!, so long!
'**Nachhilfe** f help, assistance; '⸤lehrer m coach, private tutor; '⸤unterricht m private lesson(s pl.), coaching.
'**nach|holen** v/t. (sep., -ge-, h) make up for, make good; '⸤hut ⚔ f (-/-en) rear(-guard); die ~ bilden bring up the rear (a. fig.); '⸤jagen v/i. (sep., -ge-, sein) chase *or* pursue s.o.; '⸤klingen v/i. (irr. klingen, sep., -ge-, h) resound, echo.
'**Nachkomme** m (-n/-n) descendant; ~n pl. esp. ⁂ issue; '⸤n v/i. (irr. kommen, sep., -ge-, sein) follow; come later; obey (order); meet (liabilities); '⸤nschaft f (-/-en) descendants pl., esp. ⁂ issue.

'**Nachkriegs...** post-war.
Nachlaß ['naːxlas] m (Nachlasses/Nachlasse, Nachlässe) ✝ reduction, discount; assets pl., estate, inheritance (of deceased).
'**nachlassen** (irr. lassen, sep., -ge-, h) 1. v/t. reduce (price); 2. v/i. deteriorate; slacken, relax; diminish; pain, rain, etc.: abate; storm: calm down; strength: wane; interest: flag.
'**nachlässig** adj. careless, negligent.
'**nach|laufen** v/i. (irr. laufen, sep., -ge-, sein) run (dat. after); '⸤lesen v/t. (irr. lesen, sep., -ge-, h) in book: look up; ✎ glean; '⸤liefern v/t. (sep., -ge-, h) deliver subsequently; repeat delivery of; '⸤lösen v/t. (sep., -ge-, h): e-e Fahrkarte ~ take a supplementary ticket; buy a ticket en route; '⸤machen v/t. (sep., -ge-, h) imitate (j-m et. s.o. in s.th.); copy; counterfeit, forge; '⸤messen v/t. (irr. messen, sep., -ge-, h) measure again.
'**Nachmittag** m afternoon; '⸤s adv. in the afternoon; '⸤svorstellung thea. f matinée.
Nach|nahme ['naːxnaːmə] f (-/-) cash on delivery, Am. collect on delivery; per ~ schicken send C.O.D.; '⸤name m surname, last name; '⸤porto ⊠ n surcharge.
'**nach|prüfen** v/t. (sep., -ge-, h) verify; check; '⸤rechnen v/t. (sep., -ge-, h) reckon over again; check (bill).
'**Nachrede** f: üble ~ defamation (of character); oral: slander, written: libel; '⸤n v/t. (sep., -ge-, h): j-m Übles ~ slander s.o.
Nachricht ['naːxriçt] f (-/-en) news; message; report; information, notice; ~ geben s. benachrichtigen; '⸤enagentur f news agency; '⸤endienst m news service; ⚔ intelligence service; '⸤ensprecher m newscaster; '⸤enwesen n (-s/no pl.) communications pl.
'**nachrücken** v/i. (sep., -ge-, sein) move along.
'**Nach|ruf** m obituary (notice); '⸤ruhm m posthumous fame.
'**nachsagen** v/t. (sep., -ge-, h) repeat; man sagt ihm nach, daß he is said to inf.
'**Nachsaison** f dead *or* off season.
'**nachschicken** v/t. (sep., -ge-, h) s. nachsenden.
'**nachschlage|n** v/t. (irr. schlagen, sep., -ge-, h) consult (book); look up (word); '⸤werk n reference-book.
'**Nach|schlüssel** m skeleton key; '⸤schrift f in letter: postscript; '⸤schub ⚔ m supplies pl.; '⸤schubweg ⚔ m supply line.
'**nach|sehen** (irr. sehen, sep., -ge-, h) 1. v/i. look after; ~, ob (go and) see whether; 2. v/t. look after; examine,

inspect; check; overhaul (*machine*); *s. nachschlagen*; *j-m et.* ~ indulge s.o. in s.th.; '~**senden** v/t. (*irr. senden,*] *sep.*, -ge-, *h*) send after; send on, forward (*letter*) (*j-m* to s.o.).

Nachsicht *f* indulgence; '2**ig** *adj.*, '2**svoll** *adj.* indulgent, forbearing.

Nachsilbe *gr. f* suffix.

nach|sinnen v/i. (*irr. sinnen, sep.*, -ge-, *h*) muse, meditate (*über acc.* [up]on); '~**sitzen** v/i. (*irr. sitzen, sep.*, -ge-, *h*) *pupil:* be kept in.

Nach|sommer *m* St. Martin's summer, *esp. Am.* Indian summer; '~**speise** *f* dessert; '~**spiel** *fig. n* sequel.

nach|spionieren v/i. (*sep., no -ge-, h*) spy (*dat.* on); '~**sprechen** v/i. *and* v/t. (*irr. sprechen, sep.*, -ge-, *h*) repeat; '~**spülen** v/t. (*sep.*, -ge-, *h*) rinse; '~**spüren** v/i. (*sep.*, -ge-, *h*) (*dat.*) track, trace.

nächst [nɛːçst] 1. *adj.* succession, time: next; *distance, relation:* nearest; 2. *prp.* (*dat.*) next to, next after; '2**beste** *m, f, n* (-n/-n): der (die) ~ anyone; *das* ~ anything; *er fragte den* ~*n* he asked the next person he met.

nachstehen v/i. (*irr. stehen, sep.*, -ge-, *h*): *j-m in nichts* ~ be in no way inferior to s.o.

nachstell|en (*sep.*, -ge-, *h*) 1. v/t. place behind; put back (*watch*); ⊕ adjust (*screw, etc.*); 2. v/i.: *j-m* ~ be after s.o.; '2**ung** *fig. f* persecution.

Nächstenliebe *f* charity.

'**nächstens** *adv.* shortly, (very) soon, before long.

'**nach|streben** v/i. (*sep.*, -ge-, *h*) *s. nacheifern*; '~**suchen** v/i. (*sep.*, -ge-, *h*): ~ *um* apply for, seek.

Nacht [naxt] *f* (-/⁻e) night; *bei* ~, *des* ~*s* at night; '~**arbeit** *f* nightwork; '~**asyl** *n* night-shelter; '~**ausgabe** *f* night edition (*of newspaper*); '~**dienst** *m* night-duty.

Nachteil *m* disadvantage, drawback; *im* ~ *sein* be at a disadvantage; '2**ig** *adj.* disadvantageous.

'**Nacht|essen** *n* supper; '~**falter** *zo. m* (-s/-) moth; '~**gebet** *n* evening prayer; '~**geschirr** *n* chamberpot; '~**hemd** *n* night-gown, *Am. a.* night robe; *for men:* nightshirt.

Nachtigall *orn.* ['naxtigal] *f* (-/-en) nightingale.

'**Nachtisch** *m* (-es/*no pl.*) sweet, dessert.

'**Nachtlager** *n* (*a*) lodging for the night; bed.

'**nächtlich** *adj.* ['nɛçtliç] nightly, nocturnal.

Nacht|lokal *n* night-club; '~**mahl** *n* supper; '~**portier** *m* night-porter; '~**quartier** *n* night-quarters *pl.*

Nachtrag ['naːxtraːk] *m* (-[e]s/⁻e) supplement; '2**en** v/t. (*irr. tragen, sep.*, -ge-, *h*) carry (*j-m et.* s.th. after s.o.); add; † post up (*ledger*); *j-m et.* ~ bear s.o. a grudge; '2**end** *adj.* unforgiving, resentful.

nachträglich *adj.* ['naːxtrɛːkliç] additional; subsequent.

nachts *adv.* [naxts] at *or* by night.

'**Nacht|schicht** *f* night-shift; '2**schlafend** *adj.*: *zu* ~*er Zeit* in the middle of the night; '~**schwärmer** *fig. m* night-reveller; '~**tisch** *m* bedside table; '~**topf** *m* chamberpot; '~**vorstellung** *thea. f* night performance; '~**wache** *f* nightwatch; '~**wächter** *m* (night-) watchman; '~**wandler** ['~vandlər] *m* (-s/-) sleep-walker; '~**zeug** *n* night-things *pl.*

'**nachwachsen** v/i. (*irr. wachsen, sep.*, -ge-, *sein*) grow again.

'**Nachwahl** *parl. f* by-election.

Nachweis ['naːxvais] *m* (-es/-e) proof, evidence; '2**bar** *adj.* demonstrable; traceable; 2**en** ['~zən] v/t. (*irr. weisen, sep.*, -ge-, *h*) point out, show; trace; prove; '2**lich** *adj. s. nachweisbar.*

'**Nach|welt** *f* posterity; '~**wirkung** *f* after-effect; consequences *pl.*; aftermath; '~**wort** *n* (-[e]s/-e) epilog(ue); '~**wuchs** *m* (-[e]s/*no pl.*) rising generation.

'**nach|zahlen** v/t. (*sep.*, -ge-, *h*) pay in addition; '~**zählen** v/t. (*sep.*, -ge-, *h*) count over (again), check; '2**zahlung** *f* additional payment.

Nachzügler ['naːxtsyːglər] *m* (-s/-) straggler, late-comer.

Nacken ['nakən] *m* (-s/-) nape (of the neck), neck.

nackt *adj.* [nakt] naked, nude; bare (*a. fig.*); *young birds:* unfledged; *truth:* plain.

Nadel ['naːdəl] *f* (-/-n) needle; pin; brooch; '~**arbeit** *f* needlework; '~**baum** ♀ *m* conifer(ous tree); '~**stich** *m* prick; stitch; *fig.* pinprick.

Nagel ['naːgəl] *m* (-s/⁻) *anat.*, ⊕ nail; *of wood:* peg; spike; stud; *die Arbeit brennt mir auf den Nägeln* it's a rush job; '~**haut** *f* cuticle; '~**lack** *m* nail varnish; '2**n** v/t. (*ge-*, *h*) nail (*an or auf acc.* to); '~**necessaire** ['~nesesɛːr] *n* (-s/-s) manicure-case; '2**neu** F *adj.* bran(d)-new; '~**pflege** *f* manicure.

nage|n ['naːgən] (*ge-*, *h*) 1. v/i. gnaw; ~ *an* (*dat.*) gnaw at; pick (*bone*); 2. v/t. gnaw; '2**tier** *zo. n* rodent, gnawer.

nah *adj.* [naː] near, close (*bei* to); nearby; *danger:* imminent.

Näharbeit ['nɛːʔ-] *f* needlework, sewing.

'**Nahaufnahme** *f film:* close-up.

nahe *adj.* ['naːə] *s. nah.*

Nähe ['nɛːə] f (-/no pl.) nearness, proximity; vicinity; *in der ~* close by.

'**nahe|gehen** v/i. (irr. gehen, sep., -ge-, sein) (dat.) affect, grieve; '**~kommen** v/i. (irr. kommen, sep., -ge-, sein) (dat.) approach; get at (truth); '**~legen** v/t. (sep., -ge-, h) suggest; '**~liegen** v/i. (irr. liegen, sep., -ge-, h) suggest itself, be obvious.

nahen ['naːən] 1. v/i. (ge-, sein) approach; 2. v/refl. (ge-, h) approach (j-m s.o.).

nähen ['nɛːən] v/t. and v/i. (ge-, h) sew, stitch.

näher adj. ['nɛːər] nearer, closer; road: shorter; das Nähere (further) particulars pl. or details pl.

'**Näherin** f (-/-nen) seamstress.

'**nähern** v/t. (ge-, h) approach (dat. to); sich ~ approach (j-m s.o.).

'**nahe'zu** adv. nearly, almost.

'**Nähgarn** n (sewing-)cotton.

'**Nahkampf** ✕ m close combat.

nahm [naːm] pret. of nehmen.

'**Näh|maschine** f sewing-machine; '**~nadel** f (sewing-)needle.

nähren ['nɛːrən] v/t. (ge-, h) nourish (a. fig.), feed; nurse (child); sich ~ von live or feed on.

nahrhaft adj. ['naːrhaft] nutritious, nourishing.

'**Nahrung** f (-/no pl.) food, nourishment, nutriment.

'**Nahrungs|aufnahme** f intake of food; '**~mittel** n/pl. food(-stuff), victuals pl.

'**Nährwert** m nutritive value.

Naht [naːt] f (-/ᵉe) seam; ✚ suture.

'**Nahverkehr** m local traffic.

'**Nähzeug** n sewing-kit.

naiv adj. [na'iːf] naïve, naive, simple; ◊ität [naivi'tɛːt] f (-/no pl.) naïveté, naivety, simplicity.

Name ['naːmə] m (-ns/-n) name; im ~n (gen.) on behalf of; dem ~n nach nominal(ly), in name only; dem ~n nach kennen know by name; die Dinge beim rechten ~n nennen call a spade a spade; darf ich um Ihren ~n bitten? may I ask your name?

'**namen|los** adj. nameless, anonymous; fig. unutterable; '**~s 1.** adv. named, by the name of, called; **2.** prp. (gen.) in the name of.

'**Namens|tag** m name-day; '**~vetter** m namesake; '**~zug** m signature.

namentlich ['naːməntliç] **1.** adj. nominal; **2.** adv. by name; especially, in particular.

'**namhaft** adj. notable; considerable; ~ machen name.

nämlich ['nɛːmliç] **1.** adj. the same; **2.** adv. namely, that is (to say).

nannte ['nantə] pret. of nennen.

Napf [napf] m (-[e]s/ᵘe) bowl, basin.

Narb|e ['narbə] f (-/-n) scar; '◊ig adj. scarred; leather: grained.

Narko|se ✚ [nar'koːzə] f (-/-n) narcosis; ◊tisieren [~oti'ziːrən] v/t. (no -ge-, h) narcotize.

Narr [nar] m (-en/-en) fool; jester; zum ~en halten = '◊en v/t. (ge-, h) make a fool of, fool.

'**Narren|haus** F n madhouse; '**~kappe** f fool's-cap; ◊sicher adj. foolproof.

'**Narrheit** f (-/-en) folly.

Närrin ['nerin] f (-/-nen) fool, foolish woman.

'**närrisch** adj. foolish, silly; odd.

Narzisse ⚘ [nar'tsisə] f (-/-n) narcissus; gelbe ~ daffodil.

nasal adj. [na'zaːl] nasal; ~e Sprechweise twang.

nasch|en ['naʃən] (ge-, h) **1.** v/i. nibble (an dat. at); gern ~ have a sweet tooth; **2.** v/t. nibble; eat s.th. on the sly; ◊erei [~'raɪən] f/pl. dainties pl., sweets pl.; '**~haft** adj. fond of dainties or sweets.

Nase ['naːzə] f (-/-n) nose; die ~ rümpfen turn up one's nose (über acc. at).

näseln ['nɛːzəln] v/i. (ge-, h) speak through the nose, nasalize; snuffle.

'**Nasen|bluten** n (-s/no pl.) nosebleeding; '**~loch** n nostril; '**~spitze** f tip of the nose.

naseweis adj. ['naːzəvaɪs] pert, saucy.

nasführen ['naːs-] v/t. (ge-, h) fool, dupe.

Nashorn zo. ['naːs-] n rhinoceros.

naß adj. [nas] wet; damp, moist.

Nässe ['nɛsə] f (-/no pl.) wet(ness); moisture; ♒ humidity; '◊n (ge-, h) **1.** v/t. wet; moisten; **2.** ✚ v/i. discharge.

'**naßkalt** adj. damp and cold, raw.

Nation [na'tsjoːn] f (-/-en) nation.

national adj. [natsjo'naːl] national; ◊hymne f national anthem; ◊ismus [~a'lismus] m (-/Nationalismen) nationalism; ◊ität [~ali'tɛːt] f (-/-en) nationality; ◊mannschaft f national team.

Natter ['natər] f (-/-n) zo. adder, viper; fig. serpent.

Natur [na'tuːr] f **1.** (-/no pl.) nature; **2.** (-/-en) constitution; temper(ament), disposition, nature; von ~ by nature.

Naturalien [natu'raːljən] pl. natural produce sg.; in ~ in kind.

naturalisieren [naturali'ziːrən] v/t. (no -ge-, h) naturalize.

Naturalismus [natura'lismus] m (-/no pl.) naturalism.

Naturanlage [na'tuːr-ᵍ-] f (natural) disposition.

Naturell [natu'rel] n (-s/-e) natural disposition, nature, temper.

Na'tur|ereignis n, **~erscheinung** f phenomenon; **~forscher** m naturalist, scientist; 2gemäß *adj.* natural; ~geschichte *f* natural history; ~gesetz *n* law of nature, natural law; 2getreu *adj.* true to nature; life-like; ~kunde *f* (natural) science.

natürlich [na'ty:rlic] 1. *adj.* natural; genuine; innate; unaffected; 2. *adv.* naturally, of course.

Na'tur|produkte *n/pl.* natural products *pl.* or produce *sg.*; ~schutz *m* wild-life conservation; ~schutzgebiet *n*, ~schutzpark *m* national park, wild-life (p)reserve; ~trieb *m* instinct; ~wissenschaft *f* (natural) science; ~wissenschaftler *m* (natural) scientist.

Nebel ['ne:bəl] *m* (-s/-) fog; mist; haze; smoke; 2haft *fig. adj.* nebulous, hazy, dim; ~horn *n* fog-horn.

neben *prp.* (*dat.*; *acc.*) ['ne:bən] beside, by (the side of); near to; against, compared with; apart *or Am. a.* aside from, besides.

neben|'an *adv.* next door; close by; 2anschluß *teleph.* ['ne:bən?-] *m* extension(line); 2arbeit['ne:bən?-] *f* extra work; 2ausgaben ['ne:bən?-] *f/pl.* incidental expenses *pl.*, extras *pl.*; 2ausgang ['ne:bən?-] *m* side-exit, side-door; 2bedeutung *f* secondary meaning, connotation; ~'bei *adv.* by the way; besides; 2beruf *m* side-line; ~beruflich *adv.* as a side-line; in one's spare time; 2beschäftigung *f s.* Nebenberuf; 2buhler ['~bu:lər] *m* (-s/-) rival; ~ei'nander *adv.* side by side; ~ bestehen co-exist; 2eingang ['ne:bən?-] *m* side-entrance; 2einkünfte ['ne:bən?-] *pl.*, 2einnahmen ['ne:bən?-] *f/pl.* casual emoluments *pl.*, extra income; 2erscheinung ['ne:bən?-] *f* accompaniment; 2fach *n* subsidiary subject, *Am.* minor (subject); 2fluß *m* tributary (river); 2gebäude *n* annex(e); outhouse; 2geräusch *n radio:* atmospherics *pl.*, interference, jamming; 2gleis 🚋 *n* siding, side-track; 2handlung *thea. f* underplot; 2haus *n* adjoining house; ~'her *adv.*, ~'hin *adv.* by his or her side; *s. nebenbei;* 2kläger 🚋 *m* co-plaintiff; 2kosten *pl.* extras *pl.*; 2mann *m* person next to one; 2produkt *n* by-product; 2rolle *f* minor part (*a. thea.*); 2sache *f* minor matter, side issue; ~sächlich *adj.* subordinate, incidental, unimportant; 2satz *gr. m* subordinate clause; ~stehend *adj.* in the margin; 2stelle *f* branch; agency; *teleph.* extension; 2straße *f* bystreet, by-road; 2strecke 🚋 *f* branch line; 2tisch *m* next table; 2tür *f* side-door; 2verdienst *m* extra or extra earnings *pl.*; 2zimmer *n* adjoining room.

neblig *adj.* foggy, misty, hazy.

nebst *prp.* (*dat.*) [ne:pst] together with, besides; including.

neck|en ['nɛkən] *v/t.* (ge-, *h*) tease, banter, *sl.* kid; 2erei ['~raɪ] *f* (-/-en) teasing, banter; ~isch *adj.* playful; droll, funny.

Neffe ['nɛfə] *m* (-n/-n) nephew.

negativ [nega'ti:f] 1. *adj.* negative; 2. 2 *n* (-s/-e) negative.

Neger ['ne:gər] *m* (-s/-) negro; '~in *f* (-/-nen) negress.

nehmen ['ne:mən] *v/t.* (*irr.*, ge-, *h*) take; receive; charge (*money*); zu sich ~ take, have (*meal*); j-m et. ~ take s.th. from s.o.; ein Ende ~ come to an end; es sich nicht ~ lassen zu *inf.* insist upon *ger.*; streng genommen strictly speaking.

Neid [naɪt] *m* (-[e]s/no *pl.*) envy; 2en ['naɪdən] *v/t.* (ge-, *h*): j-m et. ~ envy s.o. s.th.; ~er ['~dər] *m* (-s/-) envious person; ~hammel *F* ['naɪt-] *m* dog in the manger; 2isch *adj.* ['~diʃ] envious (auf *acc.* of); 2los *adj.* ['naɪt-] ungrudging.

Neige ['naɪgə] *f* (-/-n) decline; *barrel:* dregs *pl.*; *glass:* heeltap; zur ~ gehen (be on the) decline; *esp.* 🌑 run short; 2n ['~gən] (ge-, *h*) 1. *v/t.* and *v/refl.* bend, incline; 2. *v/i.*: er neigt zu Übertreibungen he is given to exaggeration.

Neigung *f* (-/-en) inclination (*a. fig.*); slope, incline.

nein *adv.* [naɪn] no.

Nektar ['nɛktɑ:r] *m* (-s/no *pl.*) nectar.

Nelke 🌱 ['nɛlkə] *f* (-/-n) carnation, pink; *spice:* clove.

nennen ['nɛnən] *v/t.* (*irr.*, ge-, *h*) name; call; term; mention; nominate (*candidate*); *sports:* enter (für for); sich ... ~ be called ...; ~swert *adj.* worth mentioning.

Nenn|er 🔀 *m* (-s/-) denominator; ~ung *f* (-/-en) naming; mentioning; nomination (*of candidates*); *sports:* entry; ~wert *m* nominal or face value; zum ~ 🌑 at par.

Neon 🔀 ['ne:ɔn] *n* (-s/no *pl.*) neon; ~röhre *f* neon tube.

Nerv [nɛrf] *m* (-s/-en) nerve; j-m auf die ~en fallen or gehen get on s.o.'s nerves.

Nerven|arzt *m* neurologist; 2aufreibend *adj.* trying; ~heilanstalt *f* mental hospital; ~kitzel *m* (-s/no *pl.*) thrill, sensation; 2krank *adj.* neurotic; 2leidend *adj.* neuropathic, neurotic; ~schwäche *f* nervous debility; 2stärkend *adj.* tonic; ~system *n* nervous system; ~zusammenbruch *m* nervous breakdown.

nerv|ig *adj.* ['nɛrviç] sinewy; ~ös *adj.* [~'vø:s] nervous; 2osität [~ozi-'tɛ:t] *f* (-/no *pl.*) nervousness.

Nerz *zo.* [nɛrts] *m* (-es/-e) mink.

Nessel ♀ ['nɛsəl] *f* (-/-n) nettle.

Nest [nɛst] *n* (-es/-er) nest; F *fig.* bed; F *fig.* hick *or* one-horse town.

nett *adj.* [nɛt] nice; neat, pretty, *Am. a.* cute; pleasant; kind.

netto ✝ *adv.* ['nɛto] net, clear.

Netz [nɛts] *n* (-es/-e) net; *fig.* network; '**~anschluß** ⚡ *m* mains connection, power supply; '**~haut** *anat. f* retina; '**~spannung** ⚡ *f* mains voltage.

neu *adj.* [nɔy] new; fresh; recent; modern; **~ere Sprachen** modern languages; **~este Nachrichten** latest news; **von ~em** anew, afresh; **ein ~es Leben beginnen** turn over a new leaf; **was gibt es Neues?** what is the news?, *Am.* what is new?

'**Neu|anschaffung** *f* (-/-en) recent acquisition; '**Ջartig** *adj.* novel; '**~auflage** *typ. f,* '**~ausgabe** *typ. f* new edition; reprint; '**~bau** *m* (-[e]s/-ten) new building; '**Ջbearbeitet** *adj.* revised; '**~e** *m* (-n/-n) new man; new-comer; novice; '**Ջentdeckt** *adj.* recently discovered.

neuer|dings *adv.* ['nɔyɔr'diŋs] of late, recently; '**Ջer** *m* (-s/-) innovator.

Neuerscheinung ['nɔy°-] *f* new book *or* publication.

'**Neuerung** *f* (-/-en) innovation.

'**neu|geboren** *adj.* new-born; '**~gestalten** *v/t.* (*sep.,* -ge-, h) reorganize; '**Ջgestaltung** *f* reorganization; '**Ջgier** *f,* '**Ջgierde** ['~də] *f* (-/no pl.) curiosity, inquisitiveness; '**~gierig** *adj.* curious (*auf acc.* about, of), inquisitive, *sl.* nos(e)y; **ich bin ~, ob** I wonder whether *or* if; '**Ջheit** *f* (-/-en) newness, freshness; novelty.

'**Neuigkeit** *f* (-/-en) (**e-e** a piece of) news.

'**Neu|jahr** *n* New Year('s Day); '**~land** *n* (-[e]s/no pl.): **~ erschließen** break fresh ground (*a. fig.*); '**Ջlich** *adv.* the other day, recently; '**~ling** *m* (-s/-e) novice; *contp.* greenhorn; '**Ջmodisch** *adj.* fashionable; '**~mond** *m* (-[e]s/no pl.) new moon.

neun *adj.* [nɔyn] nine; '**~te** *adj.* ninth; '**Ջtel** *n* (-s/-) ninth part; '**~tens** *adv.* ninthly; '**~zehn** *adj.* nineteen; '**~zehnte** *adj.* nineteenth; **~zig** *adj.* ['~tsiç] ninety; '**~zigste** *adj.* ninetieth.

'**Neu|philologe** *m* student *or* teacher of modern languages; '**~regelung** *f* reorganization, rearrangement.

neutr|al *adj.* [nɔy'trɑːl] neutral; **Ջalität** [~ali'tɛːt] *f* (-/no pl.) neutrality; '**Ջum** *gr.* ['nɔytrʊm] *n* (-s/Neutra, Neutren) neuter.

'**neu|vermählt** *adj.* newly married; **die Ջen** *pl.* the newly-weds *pl.*; '**Ջwahl** *parl. f* new election; '**~wertig** *adj.* as good as new; '**Ջzeit** *f* (-/no pl.) modern times *pl.*

---

nicht *adv.* [niçt] not; *auch* **~ nor; ~ anziehend** unattractive; **~ besser** no better; **~ bevollmächtigt** non-commissioned; **~ einlösbar** ✝ inconvertible; **~ erscheinen** fail to attend.

'**Nicht|achtung** *f* disregard; '**Ջamtlich** *adj.* unofficial; '**~angriffspakt** *pol. m* non-aggression pact; '**~annahme** *f* non-acceptance; '**~befolgung** *f* non-observance.

Nichte ['niçtə] *f* (-/-n) niece.

'**nichtig** *adj.* null, void; invalid; vain, futile; **für ~ erklären** declare null and void, annul; '**Ջkeit** *f* (-/-en) ⚖ nullity; vanity, futility.

'**Nichtraucher** *m* non-smoker.

nichts [niçts] **1.** *indef. pron.* nothing, naught, not anything; **2.** **Ջ** *n* (-/no pl.) nothing(ness); *fig.*: nonentity; void; '**~ahnend** *adj.* unsuspecting; **~destoweniger** *adv.* nevertheless; **~nutzig** *adj.* ['~nutsiç] good-for-nothing, worthless; '**~sagend** *adj.* insignificant; **Ջtuer** ['~tuːɔr] *m* (-s/-) idler; '**~würdig** *adj.* vile, base, infamous.

'**Nicht|vorhandensein** *n* absence; lack; '**~wissen** *n* ignorance.

nick|en ['nikən] *v/i.* (ge-, h) nod; bow; '**Ջerchen** F *n* (-s/-): **ein ~ machen** take a nap, have one's forty winks.

nie *adv.* [niː] never, at no time.

nieder ['niːdər] **1.** *adj.* low; base, mean, vulgar; *value, rank:* inferior; **2.** *adv.* down.

'**Nieder|gang** *m* decline; '**Ջgedrückt** *adj.* dejected, downcast; '**Ջgehen** *v/i.* (*irr. gehen,* sep., -ge-, sein) go down; ✈ descend; *storm:* break; '**Ջgeschlagen** *adj.* dejected, downcast; '**Ջhauen** *v/t.* (*irr. hauen,* sep., -ge-, h) cut down; '**Ջkommen** *v/i.* (*irr. kommen,* sep., -ge-, sein) be confined; be delivered (**mit** of); '**~kunft** ['~kʊnft] *f* (-/⁓e) confinement, delivery; '**~lage** *f* defeat; ✝ warehouse; branch; '**Ջlassen** *v/t.* (*irr. lassen,* sep., -ge-, h) let down; **sich ~** settle (down); *bird:* alight; sit down; establish o.s.; settle (*in dat.* at); '**~lassung** *f* (-/-en) establishment; settlement; branch, agency; '**Ջlegen** *v/t.* (sep., -ge-, h) lay *or* put down; resign (*position*); retire from (*business*); abdicate; **die Arbeit ~** (go on) strike, down tools, *Am.* F *a.* walk out; **sich ~** lie down, go to bed; '**Ջmachen** *v/t.* (*sep.,* -ge-, h) cut down; massacre; '**~schlag** *m* ✈ precipitate; sediment; precipitation (*of rain, etc.*); *radioactive:* fall-out; *boxing:* knock-down, knock-out; '**Ջschlagen** *v/t.* (*irr. schlagen,* sep., -ge-, h) knock down; *boxing: a.* floor; cast down (*eyes*); suppress; put down, crush (*rebellion*); ⚖ quash; **sich ~**

~ precipitate; **~schmettern** *fig.* *v/t.* (*sep.*, -ge-, h) crush; **~setzen** *v/t.* (*sep.*, -ge-, h) set *or* put down; *sich* ~ sit down; *birds*: perch, alight; **~strecken** *v/t.* (*sep.*, -ge-, h) lay low, strike to the ground, floor; **~trächtig** *adj.* base, mean; F beastly; **~ung** *f* (-/-en) lowlands *pl.*

niedlich *adj.* ['ni:tliç] neat, nice, pretty, *Am. a.* cute.

Niednagel ['ni:t-] *m* agnail, hangnail.

niedrig *adj.* ['ni:driç] low (*a. fig.*); moderate; *fig.* mean, base.

niemals *adv.* ['ni:ma:ls] never, at no time.

niemand *indef. pron.* ['ni:mant] nobody, no one, none; **~sland** *n* (-[e]s/*no pl.*) no man's land.

Niere ['ni:rə] *f* (-/-n) kidney; **~n-braten** *m* loin of veal.

niesel|n F ['ni:zəln] *v/i.* (ge-, h) drizzle; **~regen** F *m* drizzle.

niesen ['ni:zən] *v/i.* (ge-, h) sneeze.

Niet ⊕ [ni:t] *m* (-[e]s/-e) rivet; **~e** *f* (-/-n) *lottery*: blank; F *fig.* washout; **~en** ⊕ *v/t.* (ge-, h) rivet.

Nilpferd *zo.* ['ni:l-] *n* hippopotamus.

nimmer *adv.* ['nimər] never; **~mehr** *adv.* nevermore; **~satt** *m* (-, -[e]s/-e) glutton; **~'wiedersehen** F *n*: *auf* ~ never to meet again; *er verschwand auf* ~ he left for good. [*dat.* at).\

nippen ['nipən] *v/i.* (ge-, h) sip (*an*)

Nipp|es ['nipəs] *pl.*, **~sachen** *pl.* (k)nick-(k)nacks *pl.*

nirgend|s *adv.* ['nirgənts], **~(s)'wo** *adv.* nowhere.

Nische ['ni:ʃə] *f* (-/-n) niche, recess.

nisten ['nistən] *v/i.* (ge-, h) nest.

Niveau [ni'vo:] *n* (-s/-s) level; *fig. a.* standard.

nivellieren [nive'li:rən] *v/t.* (*no* -ge-, h) level, grade.

Nixe ['niksə] *f* (-/-n) water-nymph, mermaid.

noch [nɔx] **1.** *adv.* still; yet; ~ *ein* another, one more; ~ *einmal* once more *or* again; ~ *etwas* something more; ~ *etwas?* anything else?; ~ *heute* this very day; ~ *immer* still; ~ *nicht* not yet; ~ *nie* never before; ~ *so* ever so; ~ *im 19. Jahrhundert* as late as the 19th century; *es wird* ~ *2 Jahre dauern* it will take two more *or* another two years; **2.** *cj.*: *s. weder;* **~malig** *adj.* ['~ma:liç] repeated; **~mals** *adv.* ['~ma:ls] once more *or* again.

Nomad|e [no'ma:də] *m* (-n/-n) nomad; **~isch** *adj.* nomadic.

Nominativ *gr.* ['no:minati:f] *m* (-s/-e) nominative (case).

nominieren [nomi'ni:rən] *v/t.* (*no* -ge-, h) nominate.

Nonne ['nɔnə] *f* (-/-n) nun; **~n-kloster** *n* nunnery, convent.

Nord *geogr.* [nɔrt], **~en** ['~dən] *m* (-s/*no pl.*) north; **~isch** *adj.* ['~diʃ] northern.

nördlich *adj.* ['nœrtliç] northern, northerly.

'Nord|licht *n* northern lights *pl.*; **~'ost(en** *m*) north-east; **~pol** *m* North Pole; **~wärts** *adv.* ['~verts] northward(s), north; **~'west(en** *m*) north-west.

nörg|eln ['nœrgəln] *v/i.* (ge-, h) nag, carp (*an dat.* at); grumble; **2ler** ['~lər] *m* (-s/-) faultfinder, grumbler.

Norm [nɔrm] *f* (-/-en) standard; rule; norm.

normal *adj.* [nɔr'ma:l] normal; regular; *measure, weight, time*: standard; **~isieren** [~ali'zi:rən] *v/refl.* (*no* -ge-, h) return to normal.

'norm|en *v/t.* (ge-, h), **~ieren** [~'mi:rən] *v/t.* (*no* -ge-, h) standardize.

Not [no:t] *f* (-/-̈e) need, want; necessity; difficulty, trouble; misery; danger, emergency, distress (*a.* ⚓); ~ *leiden* suffer privations; *in* ~ *geraten* become destitute, get into trouble; *in* ~ *sein* to be in trouble; *zur* ~ at a pinch; *es tut not, daß* it is necessary that.

Notar [no'ta:r] *m* (-s/-e) (public) notary.

'Not|ausgang *m* emergency exit; **~behelf** *m* makeshift, expedient, stopgap; **~bremse** *f* emergency brake; **~brücke** *f* temporary bridge; **~durft** ['~durft] *f* (-/*no pl.*): *s-e* ~ *verrichten* relieve o.s.; **2dürf-tig** *adj.* scanty, poor; temporary.

Note ['no:tə] *f* (-/-n) note (*a.* ♩); *pol.* note, memorandum; *school*: mark.

'Noten|bank † *f* bank of issue; **~schlüssel** ♪ *m* clef; **~system** ♪ *n* staff.

'Not|fall *m* case of need, emergency; **2falls** *adv.* if necessary; **2gedrungen** *adv.* of necessity, needs.

notier|en [no'ti:rən] *v/t.* (*no* -ge-, h) make a note of, note (down); † quote; **2ung** † *f* (-/-en) quotation.

nötig ['nø:tiç] *adj.* necessary; ~ *haben* need; **~en** ['~gən] *v/t.* (ge-, h) force, oblige, compel; press, urge (*guest*); **~en'falls** *adv.* if necessary; **2ung** *f* (-/-en) compulsion; pressing; ⚖ intimidation.

Notiz [no'ti:ts] *f* (-/-en) notice, note, memorandum; ~ *nehmen von* take notice of; pay attention to; *keine* ~ *nehmen von* ignore; *sich* ~*en ma-chen* take notes; **~block** *m* pad, *Am. a.* scratch pad; **~buch** *n* notebook.

'Not|lage *f* distress; emergency; **2landen** ✈ *v/i.* (-ge-, sein) make a forced *or* emergency landing; '~landung ⚔ *f* forced *or* emergency landing; '2leidend *adj.* needy, destitute; distressed; '~lösung *f* expedient; '~lüge *f* white lie.

notorisch *adj.* [no'to:riʃ] notorious.

'Not|ruf *teleph. m* emergency call; '~signal *n* emergency *or* distress signal; '~sitz *mot. m* dick(e)y(-seat), *Am. a.* rumble seat; '~stand *m* emergency; '~standsarbeiten *f/pl.* relief works *pl.*; '~standsgebiet *n* distressed area; '~standsgesetze *n/pl.* emergency laws *pl.*; '~verband *m* first-aid dressing; '~verordnung *f* emergency decree; '~wehr *f* self-defen|ce, *Am.* -se; '2wendig *adj.* necessary; '~wendigkeit *f* (-/-en) necessity; '~zucht *f* (-/no pl.) rape.

Novelle [no'vɛlə] *f* (-/-n) short story, novella; *parl.* amendment.

November [no'vɛmbər] *m* (-[s]/-) November.

Nu [nu:] *m* (-/no pl.): im ~ in no time.

Nuance [ny'ã:sə] *f* (-/-n) shade.

nüchtern *adj.* ['nyçtərn] empty, fasting; sober (*a. fig.*); matter-of-fact; *writings:* jejune; prosaic; cool; plain; '2heit *f* (-/no pl.) sobriety; *fig.* soberness.

Nudel ['nu:dəl] *f* (-/-n) noodle.

null [nul] 1. *adj.* null; nil; *tennis:* love; ~ und nichtig null and void; 2. 2 *f* (-/-en) nought, cipher (*a. fig.*); zero; '2punkt *m* zero.

numerieren [numə'ri:rən] *v/t.* (no -ge-, h) number; *numerierter Platz* reserved seat.

Nummer ['numər] *f* (-/-n) number

(*a. newspaper, thea.*); size (*of shoes, etc.*); *thea.* turn; *sports:* event; '~nschild *mot. n* number-plate.

nun [nu:n] 1. *adv.* now, at present; then; ~? well?; ~ *also* well then; 2. *int.* now then!; '~mehr *adv.* now.

nur *adv.* [nu:r] only; (nothing) but; merely; ~ noch only.

Nuß [nus] *f* (-/Nüsse) nut; '~kern *m* kernel; '~knacker *m* (-s/-) nutcracker; '~schale *f* nutshell.

Nüstern ['ny:stərn] *f/pl.* nostrils *pl.*

nutz *adj.* [nuts] *s.* nütze; '2anwendung *f* practical application; '~bar *adj.* useful; '~bringend *adj.* profitable.

nütze *adj.* ['nytsə] useful; *zu nichts* ~ *sein* be of no use, be good for nothing.

Nutzen ['nutsən] 1. *m* (-s/-) use; profit, gain; advantage; utility; 2. 2 *v/i.* and *v/t.* (ge-, h) *s.* nützen.

nützen ['nytsən] (ge-, h) 1. *v/i.:* zu et. ~ be of use *or* useful for s.th.; *j-m* ~ serve s.o.; es nützt nichts zu *inf.* it is no use *ger.*; 2. *v/t.* use, make use of; put to account; avail o.s. of, seize (*opportunity*).

'Nutz|holz *n* timber; '~leistung *f* capacity.

nützlich *adj.* ['nytsliç] useful, of use; advantageous.

'nutz|los *adj.* useless; 2nießer ['~ni:sər] *m* (-s/-) usufructuary; '2nießung *f* (-/-en) usufruct.

'Nutzung *f* (-/-en) using; utilization.

Nylon ['naɪlɔn] *n* (-s/no pl.) nylon; ~strümpfe ['~ʃtrympfə] *m/pl.* nylons *pl.*, nylon stockings *pl.*

Nymphe ['nymfə] *f* (-/-n) nymph.

O

o *int.* [o:] oh!, ah!; ~ weh! alas!, oh dear (me)!

Oase [o'a:zə] *f* (-/-n) oasis.

ob *cj.* [ɔp] whether, if; als ~ as if, as though.

Obacht ['o:baxt] *f* (-/no pl.): ~ geben auf (*acc.*) pay attention to, take care of, heed.

Obdach ['ɔpdax] *n* (-[e]s/no pl.) shelter, lodging; '2los *adj.* unsheltered, homeless; '~lose *m, f* (-n/-n) homeless person; '~losenasyl *n* casual ward.

Obdu|ktion [ɔpduk'tsjo:n] *f* (-/-en) post-mortem (examination), autopsy; 2zieren ⚔ [~'tsi:rən] *v/t.* (no -ge-, h) perform an autopsy on.

oben *adv.* ['o:bən] above; *mountain:* at the top; *house:* upstairs; on the surface; von ~ from above; von ~ bis unten from top to bottom;

von ~ herab behandeln treat haughtily; '~an *adv.* at the top; '~auf *adv.* on the top; on the surface; ~drein *adv.* ['~'draɪn] into the bargain, at that; ~erwähnt *adj.* ['o:bən''ɛrve:nt], '~genannt *adj.* above-mentioned, aforesaid; '~hin *adv.* superficially, perfunctorily.

ober ['o:bər] 1. *adj.* upper, higher; *fig. a.* superior; 2. 2 *m* (-s/-) (head) waiter; *German cards:* queen.

Ober|arm ['o:bərˀ-] *m* upper arm; ~arzt ['o:bərˀ-] *m* head physician; ~aufseher ['o:bərˀ-] *m* superintendent; ~aufsicht ['o:bərˀ-] *f* superintendence; '~befehl *m* supreme command; '~befehlshaber ⚔ *m* commander-in-chief; '~bekleidung *f* outer garments *pl.*, outer wear; '~bürgermeister *m* chief burgomaster; Lord Mayor;

'⸾deck ⚓ n upper deck; '⸾fläche f surface; ²flächlich adj. ['⸾fleçliç] superficial; fig. a. shallow; '²halb prp. (gen.) above; '⸾hand fig. f: die ~ gewinnen über (acc.) get the upper hand of; '⸾haupt n head, chief; '⸾haus Brt. parl. n House of Lords; '⸾hemd n shirt; '⸾herrschaft f supremacy.

'Oberin f (-/-nen) eccl. Mother Superior; at hospital: matron.

ober|irdisch adj. ['o:bər²-] overground, above ground; ≠ overhead; '²kellner m head waiter; '²kiefer anat. m upper jaw; '²körper m upper part of the body; '²land n upland; '²lauf m upper course (of river); '²leder n upper; '²leitung f chief management; ≠ overhead wires pl.; '²leutnant ✕ m (Am. first) lieutenant; '²licht n skylight; '²lippe f upper lip; '²schenkel m thigh; '²schule f secondary school, Am. a. high school.

'oberst 1. adj. uppermost, topmost, top; highest (a. fig.); fig. chief, principal; rank, etc.: supreme; 2. ♀ ✕ m (-en, -s/-en, -e) colonel. 'Ober|staatsanwalt ⚖ m chief public prosecutor; '⸾stimme ♪ f treble, soprano.

'Oberst'leutnant ✕ m lieutenant-colonel.

'Ober|tasse f cup; '⸾wasser fig. n: ~ bekommen get the upper hand.

obgleich cj. [ɔp'glaiç] (al)though.

'Obhut f (-/no pl.) care, guard; protection; custody; in (seine) ~ nehmen take care or charge of.

obig adj. ['o:biç] above(-mentioned), aforesaid.

Objekt [ɔp'jɛkt] n (-[e]s/-e) object (a. gr.); project; ♥ a. transaction.

objektiv [ɔpjɛk'ti:f] 1. adj. objective; impartial, detached; actual, practical; 2. ♀ n (-s/-e) object-glass, objective; phot. lens; ²ität [⸾ivi-'tɛ:t] f (-/no pl.) objectivity; impartiality.

obligat adj. [obli'ga:t] obligatory; indispensable; inevitable; ²ion ♦ [⸾a'tsjo:n] f (-/-en) bond, debenture; ⸾orisch adj. [⸾a'to:riʃ] obligatory (für on), compulsory, mandatory.

'Obmann m chairman; ⚖ foreman (of jury); umpire; ♦ shop-steward, spokesman.

Oboe ♪ [o'bo:ə] f (-/-n) oboe, hautboy.

Obrigkeit ['o:briçkait] f (-/-en) the authorities pl.; government; '²lich adj. magisterial, official; '⸾sstaat m authoritarian state.

ob'schon cj. (al)though.

Observatorium ast. [ɔpzɛrva'to:r-jum] n (-s/Observatorien) observatory.

Obst [o:pst] n (-es/no pl.) fruit;

'⸾bau m fruit-culture, fruit-growing; '⸾baum m fruit-tree; '⸾ernte f fruit-gathering; fruit-crop; '⸾garten m orchard; '⸾händler m fruiterer, Am. fruitseller; '⸾züchter m fruiter, fruit-grower.

obszön adj. [ɔps'tsø:n] obscene, filthy.

ob'wohl cj. (al)though.

Ochse zo. ['ɔksə] m (-n/-n) ox; bullock; '⸾nfleisch n beef.

öde ['ø:də] 1. adj. deserted, desolate; waste; fig. dull, tedious; 2. ♀ f (-/-n) desert, solitude; fig. dullness, tedium.

oder cj. ['o:dər] or.

Ofen ['o:fən] m (-s/=) stove; oven; kiln; furnace; '⸾heizung f heating by stove; '⸾rohr n stove-pipe.

offen adj. ['ɔfən] open (a. fig.); position: vacant; hostility: overt; fig. frank, outspoken.

'offen'bar 1. adj. obvious, evident, apparent; 2. adv. a. it seems that; ⸾en [ɔfən'-] v/t. (no -ge-, h) reveal, disclose; manifest; sich j-m ~ open one's heart to s.o.; ²ung [ɔfən'-] f (-/-en) manifestation; revelation; ²ungseid ⚖ [ɔfən'ba:runs²-] m oath of manifestation.

'Offenheit fig. f (-/no pl.) openness, frankness.

'offen|herzig adj. open-hearted, sincere; frank; '⸾kundig adj. public; notorious; '⸾sichtlich adj. manifest, evident, obvious.

offensiv adj. [ɔfɛn'zi:f] offensive; ²e [⸾və] f (-/-n) offensive.

'offenstehen v/i. (irr. stehen, sep., -ge-, h) stand open; ♦ bill: be outstanding; fig. be open (j-m to s.o.); es steht ihm offen zu inf. he is free or at liberty to inf.

öffentlich ['œfəntliç] 1. adj. public; ⸾es Ärgernis public nuisance; ⸾er Dienst Civil Service; 2. adv. publicly, in public; ~ auftreten make a public appearance; '²keit f (-/no pl.) publicity; the public; in aller ~ in public.

offerieren [ɔfə'ri:rən] v/t. (no -ge-, h) offer.

Offerte [ɔ'fɛrtə] f (-/-n) offer; tender.

offiziell adj. [ɔfi'tsjɛl] official.

Offizier ✕ [ɔfi'tsi:r] m (-s/-e) (commissioned) officer; ⸾skorps ✕ [⸾sko:r] n (-/-) body of officers, the officers pl.; ⸾smesse f ✕ officers' mess; ⚓ a. wardroom.

offiziös adj. [ɔfi'tsjø:s] officious, semi-official.

öffn|en ['œfnən] v/t. (ge-, h) open; a. uncork (bottle); ⚕ dissect (body); sich ~ open; '²er m (-s/-) opener; '²ung f (-/-en) opening, aperture; '²ungszeiten f/pl. hours pl. of opening, business hours pl.

oft adv. [ɔft] often, frequently;

öfters adv. ['œftərs] s. oft.
'oftmal|ig adj. frequent, repeated; '~s adv. s. oft.
oh int. [o:] o(h)!
ohne ['o:nə] 1. prp. (acc.) without; 2. cj.: ~ daß, ~ zu inf. without ger.; ~'dies adv. anyhow, anyway; ~'glei-chen adv. unequal(l)ed, matchless; ~'hin adv. s. ohnedies.
'Ohn|macht f (-/-en) powerlessness; impotence; ☆ faint, unconscious-ness; in ~ fallen faint, swoon; ~machtsanfall ☆ ['o:nmaxts⁹-] m fainting fit, swoon; '☆mächtig adj. powerless; impotent; ☆ uncon-scious; ~ werden faint, swoon.
Ohr [o:r] n (-[e]s/-en) ear; fig. a. hearing; ein ~ haben für have an ear for; ganz ~ sein be all ears; F j-n übers ~ hauen cheat s.o., sl. do s.o. (in the eye); bis über die ~en up to the ears or eyes.
Öhr [ø:r] n (-[e]s/-e) eye (of needle).
'Ohren|arzt m aurist, ear specialist; '☆betäubend adj. deafening; '~lei-den n ear-complaint; '~schmalz n ear-wax; '~schmaus m treat for the ears; '~schmerzen m/pl. ear-ache; '~zeuge m ear-witness.
'Ohr|feige f box on the ear(s), slap in the face (a. fig.); '☆feigen v/t. (ge-, h): j-n ~ box s.o.'s ear, slap s.o.'s face; '~läppchen ['~lɛpçən] n (-s/-) lobe of ear; '~ring m ear-ring.
Ökonom|ie [økono'mi:] f (-/-n) economy; ☆isch adj. [~'no:miʃ] economical.
Oktav [ɔk'ta:f] n (-s/-e) octavo; ~e ♩ [~və] f (-/-n) octave.
Oktober [ɔk'to:bər] m (-[s]/-) October.
Okul|ar opt. [oku'la:r] n (-s/-e) eye-piece, ocular; ☆ieren ♪ v/t. (no -ge-, h) inoculate, graft.
Öl [ø:l] n (-[e]s/-e) oil; ~ ins Feuer gießen add fuel to the flames; ~ auf die Wogen gießen pour oil on the (troubled) waters; '~baum ♀ m olive-tree; '~berg eccl. m (-[e]s/no pl.) Mount of Olives; '☆en v/t. (ge-, h) oil; ⊕ a. lubricate; '~farbe f oil-colo(u)r, oil-paint; '~gemälde n oil-painting; '~heizung f oil heating; '☆ig adj. oily (a. fig.).
Oliv|e ♀ [o'li:və] f (-/-n) olive; ~enbaum ♀ m olive-tree; ☆grün adj. olive(-green).
Öl|male'rei f oil-painting; '~quelle f oil-spring, gusher; oil-well; '~ung f (-/-en) oiling; ⊕ a. lubrication; Letzte ~ eccl. extreme unction.
Olympi|ade [olymp'ja:də] f (-/-n) Olympiad; a. Olympic Games pl.; ☆sch adj. [o'lympiʃ] Olympic; Olym-pische Spiele pl. Olympic Games pl.
'Ölzweig m olive-branch.
Omelett [ɔm(ə)'lɛt] n (-[e]s/-e, -s), ~e [~'lɛt] f (-/-n) omelet(te).

Om|en ['o:mən] n (-s/-, Omina) omen, augury; ☆inös adj. [omi'nø:s] ominous.
Omnibus ['ɔmnibus] m (-ses/-se) (omni)bus; (motor-)coach; '~halte-stelle f bus-stop.
Onkel ['ɔŋkəl] m (-s/-, F -s) uncle.
Oper ['o:pər] f (-/-n) ♩ opera; opera-house.
Operat|eur [opəra'tø:r] m (-s/-e) operator; ☆ surgeon; ☆ion ♀ ⚔ [~'tsjo:n] f (-/-en) operation; ~ions-saal ☆ m operating room, Am. surgery; ☆iv ☆ adj. [~'ti:f] operative.
Operette ♩ [opə'rɛtə] f (-/-n) operetta.
operieren [opə'ri:rən] (no -ge-, h) 1. v/t.: j-n ~ ☆ operate (up)on s.o. (wegen for); 2. ⚔, ⚒ v/i. operate; sich ~ lassen ☆ undergo an opera-tion.
'Opern|glas n, ~gucker F ['~gukər] m (-s/-) opera-glass(es pl.); '~haus n opera-house; '~sänger m opera-singer, operatic singer; '~text m libretto, book (of an opera).
Opfer ['ɔpfər] n (-s/-) sacrifice; offering; victim (a. fig.); ein ~ brin-gen make a sacrifice; j-m zum ~ fallen be victimized by s.o.; '~gabe f offering; '☆n (ge-, h) 1. v/t. sacri-fice; immolate; sich für et. ~ sacri-fice o.s. for s.th.; 2. v/i. (make a) sacrifice (dat. to); '~stätte f place of sacrifice; '~tod m sacrifice of one's life; '~ung f (-/-en) sacrificing, sacrifice; immolation.
Opium ['o:pjum] n (-s/no pl.) opium.
opponieren [ɔpo'ni:rən] v/i. (no -ge-, h) be opposed (gegen to), resist.
Opposition [ɔpozi'tsjo:n] f (-/-en) opposition (a. parl.); ~sführer parl. m opposition leader; ~spartei parl. f opposition party.
Optik ['ɔptik] f (-/☆-en) optics; phot. lens system; fig. aspect; '~er m (-s/-) optician.
Optim|ismus [ɔpti'mismus] m (-/no pl.) optimism; ☆ist m (-en/-en) optimist; ☆istisch adj. optimis-tic.
'optisch adj. optic(al); ~e Täu-schung optical illusion.
Orakel [o'ra:kəl] n (-s/-) oracle; ☆haft adj. oracular; ☆n v/i. (no -ge-, h) speak oracularly; ~spruch m oracle.
Orange [o'rãːʒə] f (-/-n) orange; ☆farben adj. orange(-colo[u]red); ~nbaum ♀ m orange-tree.
Oratorium ♩ [ora'to:rjum] n (-s/ Oratorien) oratorio.
Orchester ♩ [ɔr'kɛstər] n (-s/-) orchestra.
Orchidee ♀ [ɔrçi'de:ə] f (-/-n) orchid.

Orden ['ɔrdən] m (-s/-) order (a. eccl.); order, medal, decoration.

'Ordens|band n ribbon (of an order); **'∼bruder** eccl. m brother, friar; **'∼gelübde** eccl. n monastic vow; **'∼schwester** eccl. f sister, nun; **'∼verleihung** f conferring (of) an order.

ordentlich adj. ['ɔrdentliç] tidy; orderly; proper; regular; respectable; good, sound; **∼er** Professor univ. professor in ordinary.

ordinär adj. [ɔrdi'nɛːr] common, vulgar, low.

ordn|en ['ɔrdnən] v/t. (ge-, h) put in order; arrange, fix (up); settle (a. ✝ liabilities); **'2er** m (-s/-) at festival, etc.: steward; for papers, etc.: file.

'Ordnung f (-/-en) order; arrangement; system; rules pl., regulations pl.; class; in ∼ bringen put in order.

'ordnungs|gemäß, **'∼mäßig 1.** adj. orderly, regular; 2. adv. duly; **'2ruf** parl. m call to order; **'2strafe** f disciplinary penalty; fine; **'∼widrig** adj. contrary to order, irregular; **'2zahl** f ordinal number.

Ordonnanz ✗ [ɔrdɔ'nants] f (-/-en) orderly.

Organ [ɔr'gaːn] n (-s/-e) organ.

Organisat|ion [ɔrganiza'tsjoːn] f (-/-en) organization; **∼ionstalent** n organizing ability; **∼or** [∼'zaːtɔr] m (-s/-en) organizer; **2orisch** adj. [∼a'toːriʃ] organizational, organizing.

or'ganisch adj. organic.

organi'sieren v/t. (no -ge-, h) organize; sl. scrounge; (nicht) organisiert(er Arbeiter) (non-)unionist.

Organismus [ɔrga'nismus] m (-/Organismen) organism; ✿ a. system.

Organist ♪ [ɔrga'nist] m (-en/-en) organist.

Orgel ♪ ['ɔrgəl] f (-/-n) organ, Am. a. pipe organ; **'∼bauer** m organbuilder; **'∼pfeife** f organ-pipe; **'∼spieler** ♪ m organist.

Orgie ['ɔrgjə] f (-/-n) orgy.

Oriental|e [orien'taːlə] m (-n/-n) oriental; **2isch** adj. oriental.

orientier|en [orien'tiːrən] v/t. (no -ge-, h) inform, instruct; sich ∼ orient(ate) o.s. (a. fig.); inform o.s. (über acc. of); gut orientiert sein über (acc.) be well informed about, be familiar with; **2ung** f (-/-en) orientation; fig. a. information; die ∼ verlieren lose one's bearings.

Origin|al [origi'naːl] 1. n (-s/-e) original; 2. 2 adj. original; **∼alität** [∼ali'tɛːt] f (-/-en) originality; **2ell** adj. [∼'nɛl] original; design, etc.: ingenious.

Orkan [ɔr'kaːn] m (-[e]s/-e) hur-

ricane; typhoon; **2artig** adj. storm: violent; applause: thunderous, frenzied.

Ornat [ɔr'naːt] m (-[e]s/-e) robe(s pl.), vestment.

Ort [ɔrt] m (-[e]s/-e) place; site; spot, point; locality; place, village, town; ∼ der Handlung thea. scene (of action); an ∼ und Stelle on the spot; höher(e)n ∼(e)s at higher quarters; **2en** v/t. (ge-, h) locate.

ortho|dox adj. [ɔrto'dɔks] orthodox; **2graphie** [∼gra'fiː] f (-/-n) orthography; **∼graphisch** adj. [∼'graːfiʃ] orthographic(al); **2päde** ✿ [∼'pɛːdə] m (-n/-n) orthop(a)edist; **2pädie** ✿ [∼pɛ'diː] f (-/no pl.) orthop(a)edics, orthop(a)edy; **∼pädisch** adj. [∼'pɛːdiʃ] orthop(a)edic.

örtlich adj. ['œrtliç] local; ✿ a. topical; **'2keit** f (-/-en) locality.

'Orts|angabe f statement of place; **'2ansässig** adj. resident, local; **∼ansässige** ['∼gə] m (-n/-n) resident; **'∼beschreibung** f topography; **'∼besichtigung** f local inspection.

'Ortschaft f (-/-en) place, village.

'Orts|gespräch teleph. n local call; **'∼kenntnis** f knowledge of a place; **'2kundig** adj. familiar with the locality; **'∼name** m place-name; **'∼verkehr** m local traffic; **'∼zeit** f local time.

Öse ['øːzə] f (-/-n) eye, loop; eyelet (of shoe).

Ost geogr. [ɔst] east; **'∼en** m (-s/no pl.) east; the East; der Ferne (Nahe) ∼ the Far (Near) East.

ostentativ adj. [ɔstenta'tiːf] ostentatious.

Oster|ei ['oːstər∼] n Easter egg; **'∼fest** n Easter; **'∼hase** m Easter bunny or rabbit; **'∼lamm** n paschal lamb; **'∼n** n (-/-) Easter.

Österreich|er ['øːstəraiçər] m (-s/-) Austrian; **2isch** adj. Austrian.

östlich ['œstliç] 1. adj. eastern; wind, etc.: easterly; 2. adv.: ∼ von east of.

ost|wärts adv. ['ɔstverts] eastward(s); **'2wind** m east(erly) wind.

Otter zo. ['ɔtər] 1. m (-s/-) otter; 2. f (-/-n) adder, viper.

Ouvertüre ♪ [uver'tyːrə] f (-/-n) overture.

oval [o'vaːl] 1. adj. oval; 2. 2 n (-s/-e) oval.

Ovation [ova'tsjoːn] f (-/-en) ovation; j-m ∼en bereiten give s.o. ovations.

Oxyd ✿ [ɔ'ksyːt] n (-[e]s/-e) oxide; **2ieren** [∼y'diːrən] (no -ge-) 1. v/t. (h) oxidize; 2. v/i. (sein) oxidize.

Ozean ['oːtseaːn] m (-s/-e) ocean.

P

Paar [pɑːr] **1.** n (-[e]s/-e) pair; couple; **2.** ♀ adj.: ein ~ a few, some; j-m ein ~ Zeilen schreiben drop s.o. a few lines; '♀**en** v/t. (ge-, h) pair, couple; mate (animals); sich ~ (form a) pair; animals: mate; fig. join, unite; '~**lauf** m sports: pair-skating; '~**läufer** m sports: pair-skater; '♀**mal** adv.: ein ~ several or a few times; '~**ung** f (-/-en) coupling; mating, copulation; fig. union; '♀**weise** adv. in pairs or couples, by twos.

Pacht [paxt] f (-/-en) lease, tenure, tenancy; money payment: rent; '♀**en** v/t. (ge-, h) (take on) lease; rent.

Pächter [ˈpɛçtər] m (-s/-), '~**in** f (-/-nen) lessee, lease-holder; tenant.

'**Pacht|ertrag** m rental; '~**geld** n rent; '~**gut** n farm; '~**vertrag** m lease; '♀**weise** adv. on lease.

Pack [pak] **1.** m (-[e]s/-e, ⁻e) s. Packen²; **2.** n (-[e]s/no pl.) rabble.

Päckchen [ˈpɛkçən] n (-s/-) small parcel, Am. a. package; ein ~ Zigaretten a pack(et) of cigarettes.

packen¹ [ˈpakən] (ge-, h) **1.** v/t. pack (up); seize, grip, grasp, clutch; collar; fig. grip, thrill; F pack dich! F clear out!, sl. beat it!; **2.** v/i. pack (up); **3.** ♀ n (-s/no pl.) packing.

Packen² [~] m (-s/-) pack(et), parcel; bale.

'**Packer** m (-s/-) packer; ~**ei** [~ˈraɪ] f **1.** (-/-en) packing-room; **2.** (-/no pl.) packing.

'**Pack|esel** fig. m drudge; '~**material** n packing materials pl.; '~**papier** n packing-paper, brown paper; '~**pferd** n pack-horse; '~**ung** f (-/-en) pack(age), packet; ♀ pack; e-e ~ Zigaretten a pack(et) of cigarettes; '~**wagen** m s. Gepäckwagen.

Pädagog|e [pɛdaˈgoːgə] m (-n/-n) pedagog(ue), education(al)ist; ~**ik** f (-/no pl.) pedagogics, pedagogy; ♀**isch** adj. pedagogic(al).

Paddel [ˈpadəl] n (-s/-) paddle; '~**boot** n canoe; '♀**n** v/i. (ge-, h, sein) paddle, canoe.

Page [ˈpɑːʒə] m (-n/-n) page.

pah int. [pɑː] pah!, pooh!, pshaw!

Paket [paˈkeːt] n (-[e]s/-e) parcel, packet, package; ~**annahme** ♀ f parcel counter; ~**karte** ♀ f dispatch-note; '~**post** f parcel post; ~**zustellung** ♀ f parcel delivery.

Pakt [pakt] m (-[e]s/-e) pact; agreement; treaty.

Palast [paˈlast] m (-es/⁻e) palace.

Palm|e ♀ [ˈpalmə] f (-/-n) palm (-tree); '~**öl** n palm-oil; ~'**sonntag** eccl. m Palm Sunday.

panieren [paˈniːrən] v/t. (no -ge-, h) crumb.

Pani|k [ˈpɑːnik] f (-/-en) panic; stampede; '♀**sch** adj. panic; von ~**em Schrecken** erfaßt panic-stricken.

Panne [ˈpanə] f (-/-n) breakdown, mot. a. engine trouble; tyres: puncture; fig. blunder.

panschen [ˈpanʃən] (ge-, h) **1.** v/i. splash (about); **2.** v/t. adulterate (wine, etc.).

Panther zo. [ˈpantər] m (-s/-) panther.

Pantine [panˈtiːnə] f (-/-n) clog.

Pantoffel [panˈtɔfəl] m (-s/-n, F -) slipper; unter dem ~ stehen be henpecked; ~**held** F m henpecked husband.

pantschen [ˈpantʃən] v/i. and v/t. (ge-, h) s. panschen.

Panzer [ˈpantsər] m (-s/-) armo(u)r; ⚔ tank; zo. shell; '~**abwehr** ⚔ f anti-tank defen(s)ce, Am. -se; '~**glas** n bullet-proof glass; '~**hemd** n coat of mail; '~**kreuzer** ⚔ m armo(u)red cruiser; '♀**n** v/t. (ge-, h) armo(u)r; '~**platte** f armo(u)r-plate; '~**schiff** ⚔ n ironclad; '~**schrank** m safe; '~**ung** f (-/-en) armo(u)r-plating; '~**wagen** m armo(u)red car; ⚔ tank.

Papa [paˈpɑː, F ˈpapa] m (-s/-s) papa, F pa, dad(dy), Am. a. pop.

Papagei orn. [papaˈgaɪ] m (-[e]s, -en/-e[n]) parrot.

Papier [paˈpiːr] n (-s/-e) paper; ~**e** pl. papers pl., documents pl.; papers pl., identity card; ein Bogen ~ a sheet of paper; ♀**en** adj. (of) paper; fig. dull; ~**fabrik** f paper-mill; ~**geld** n (-[e]s/no pl.) paper-money; banknotes pl., Am. bills pl.; ~**korb** m waste-paper-basket; ~**schnitzel** F n or m/pl. scraps pl. of paper; ~**tüte** f paper-bag; ~**waren** f/pl. stationery.

'**Papp|band** m (-[e]s/⁻e) paperback; '~**deckel** m pasteboard, cardboard.

Pappe [ˈpapə] f (-/-n) pasteboard, cardboard.

Pappel ♀ [ˈpapəl] f (-/-n) poplar.

päppeln F [ˈpɛpəln] v/t. (ge-, h) feed (with pap).

papp|en F [ˈpapən] (ge-, h) **1.** v/t. paste; **2.** v/i. stick; '♀**ig** adj. sticky; '♀**karton** m, '♀**schachtel** f cardboard box, carton.

Papst [pɑːpst] m (-es/⁻e) pope.

päpstlich adj. [ˈpeːpstliç] papal.

'**Papsttum** n (-s/no pl.) papacy.

Parade [paˈrɑːdə] f (-/-n) parade; ⚔ review; fencing: parry.

Paradies [paraˈdiːs] n (-es/-e) paradise; ♀**isch** fig. adj. [~ˈdiːziʃ] heavenly, delightful.

paradox adj. [paraˈdɔks] paradoxical.

Paragraph [para'grɑ:f] *m* (-en, -s/-en) article, section; paragraph; section-mark.

parallel *adj.* [para'le:l] parallel; **2e** *f* (-/-n) parallel.

Paralys|e 𝒮 [para'ly:zə] *f* (-/-n) paralysis; **2ieren** 𝒮 [~y'zi:rən] *v/t.* (*no* -ge-, *h*) paralyse.

Parasit [para'zi:t] *m* (-en/-en) parasite.

Parenthese [paren'te:zə] *f* (-/-n) parenthesis.

Parforcejagd [par'fɔrs-] *f* hunt (-ing) on horseback (with hounds), *after hares:* coursing.

Parfüm [par'fy:m] *n* (-s/-e, -s) perfume, scent; **~erie** [~ymə'ri:] *f* (-/-n) perfumery; **2ieren** [~y'mi:rən] *v/t.* (*no* -ge-, *h*) perfume, scent.

pari † *adv.* ['pɑ:ri] par; *al* ~ at par.

parieren [pa'ri:rən] (*no* -ge-, *h*) 1. *v/t. fencing:* parry (*a. fig.*); pull up (*horse*); 2. *v/i.* obey (*j-m s.o.*).

Park [park] *m* (-s/-s, -e) park; **~anlage** *f* park; **~aufseher** *m* park-keeper; **2en** (ge-, *h*) 1. *v/i.* park; ~ *verboten!* no parking!; 2. *v/t.* park.

Parkett [par'kɛt] *n* (-[e]s/-e) parquet; *thea.* (orchestra) stalls *pl., esp. Am.* orchestra or parquet.

'Park|gebühr *f* parking-fee; **~licht** *n* parking light; **~platz** *m* (car-) park, parking lot; **~uhr** *mot.* *f* parking meter.

Parlament [parla'ment] *n* (-[e]s/-e) parliament; **2arisch** *adj.* [~'tɑ:riʃ] parliamentary.

Parodie [paro'di:] *f* (-/-n) parody; **2ren** *v/t.* (*no* -ge-, *h*) parody.

Parole [pa'ro:lə] *f* (-/-n) ✕ password, watchword; *fig.* slogan.

Partei [par'tai] *f* (-/-en) party (*a. pol.*); *j-s* ~ *ergreifen* take s.o.'s part, side with s.o.; **~apparat** *pol.* *m* party machinery; **~gänger** [~gɛŋər] *m* (-s/-) partisan; **2isch** *adj.*, **2lich** *adj.* partial (*für* to); prejudiced (*gegen* against); **2los** *pol. adj.* independent; **~mitglied** *pol. n* party member; **~programm** *pol. n* platform; **~tag** *pol. m* convention; **~zugehörigkeit** *pol. f* party membership.

Parterre [par'tɛr] *n* (-s/-s) ground floor, *Am.* first floor; *thea.:* pit, *Am.* parterre, *Am.* parquet circle.

Partie [par'ti:] *f* (-/-n) † parcel, lot; outing, excursion; *cards, etc.:* game; ♪ part; *marriage:* match.

Partitur ♪ [parti'tu:r] *f* (-/-en) score.

Partizip *gr.* [parti'tsi:p] *n* (-s/-ien) participle.

Partner ['partnər] *m* (-s/-), **~in** *f* (-/-nen) partner; *film: a.* co-star; **~schaft** *f* (-/-en) partnership.

Parzelle [par'tsɛlə] *f* (-/-n) plot, lot, allotment.

Paß [pas] *m* (*Passes/Pässe*) pass;

passage; *football, etc.:* pass; passport.

Passage [pa'sɑ:ʒə] *f* (-/-n) passage; arcade.

Passagier [pasa'ʒi:r] *m* (-s/-e) passenger, *in taxis: a.* fare; **~flugzeug** *n* air liner.

Passah ['pasa] *n* (-s/*no pl.*), **~fest** *n* Passover.

Passant [pa'sant] *m* (-en/-en), **~in** *f* (-/-nen) passer-by.

'Paßbild *n* passport photo(graph).

passen ['pasən] (ge-, *h*) 1. *v/i.* fit (*j-m s.o.; auf, acc. or für or zu et. s.th.*); suit (*j-m s.o.*), be convenient; *cards, football:* pass; ~ *zu* go with, match (with); 2. *v/refl.* be fit or proper; **~d** *adj.* fit, suitable; convenient (*für* for).

passier|bar *adj.* [pa'si:rbɑ:r] passable, practicable; **~en** (*no* -ge-) 1. *v/i.* (*sein*) happen; 2. *v/t.* (*h*) pass (over or through); **2schein** *m* pass, permit.

Passion [pa'sjo:n] *f* (-/-en) passion; hobby; *eccl.* Passion.

passiv ['pasi:f] 1. *adj.* passive; 2. **2** *gr.* *n* (-s/⁕, -e) passive (voice); **2a** † [pa'si:va] *pl.* liabilities *pl.*

Paste ['pastə] *f* (-/-n) paste.

Pastell [pa'stel] *n* (-[e]s/-e) pastel.

Pastete [pa'ste:tə] *f* (-/-n) pie; **~n-bäcker** *m* pastry-cook.

Pate ['pɑ:tə] 1. *m* (-n/-n) godfather; godchild; 2. *f* (-/-n) godmother; **~nkind** *n* godchild; **~nschaft** *f* (-/-en) sponsorship.

Patent [pa'tent] *n* (-[e]s/-e) patent; ✕ commission; *ein* ~ *anmelden* apply for a patent; **~amt** *n* Patent Office; **~anwalt** *m* patent agent; **2ieren** [~'ti:rən] *v/t.* (*no* -ge-, *h*) patent; *et.* ~ *lassen* take out a patent for s.th.; **~inhaber** *m* patentee; **~urkunde** *f* letters patent.

Patient [pa'tsjent] *m* (-en/-en), **~in** *f* (-/-nen) patient.

Patin ['pɑ:tin] *f* (-/-nen) godmother.

Patriot [patri'o:t] *m* (-en/-en), **~in** *f* (-/-nen) patriot.

Patron [pa'tro:n] *m* (-s/-e) patron, protector, *contp.* fellow, bloke, customer; **~at** [~o'nɑ:t] *n* (-[e]s/-e) patronage; **~e** [pa'tro:nə] *f* (-/-n) cartridge, *Am. a.* shell.

Patrouill|e ✕ [pa'truljə] *f* (-/-n) patrol; **2ieren** ✕ [~'ji:rən] *v/i.* (*no* -ge-, *h*) patrol.

Patsch|e F *fig.* ['patʃə] *f* (-/*no pl.*): *in der* ~ *sitzen* be in a fix or scrape; **2en** F (ge-) 1. *v/i.* (*h, sein*) splash; 2. *v/t.* (*h*) slap; **2'naß** *adj.* dripping wet, drenched.

patzig F *adj.* ['patsiç] snappish.

Pauke ♪ ['paukə] *f* (-/-n) kettle-drum; **2n** F *v/i. and v/t.* (ge-, *h*) *school:* cram.

Pauschal|e [pau'ʃa:lə] *f* (-/-n), **~summe** *f* lump sum.

Pause ['pauzə] f (-/-n) pause, stop, interval; *school:* break, *Am.* recess; *thea.* interval, *Am.* intermission; ♩ rest; *drawing:* tracing; '⁀n v/t. (ge-, h) trace; '⁀nlos adj. uninterrupted, incessant; '⁀nzeichen n *wireless:* interval signal.

pau'sieren v/i. (no -ge-, h) pause.

Pavian zo. ['pɑːviɑːn] m (-s/-e) baboon.

Pavillon ['paviljõ] m (-s/-s) pavilion.

Pazifist [patsi'fist] m (-en/-en) pacif(ic)ist.

Pech [pɛç] n 1. (-[e]s /-e) pitch; **2.** F *fig.* (-[e]s/no pl.) bad luck; '⁀strähne F f run of bad luck; '⁀vogel F m unlucky fellow.

pedantisch adj. [pe'dantiʃ] pedantic; punctilious, meticulous.

Pegel ['peːgəl] m (-s/-) water-ga(u)ge.

peilen ['paɪlən] v/t. (ge-, h) sound (*depth*); take the bearings of (*coast*).

Pein [paɪn] f (-/no pl.) torment, torture, anguish; ⁀igen ['paɪgən] v/t. (ge-, h) torment; ⁀iger ['paɪgər] m (-s/-) tormentor.

'peinlich adj. painful, embarrassing; particular, scrupulous, meticulous.

Peitsche ['paɪtʃə] f (-/-n) whip; '⁀n v/t. (ge-, h) whip; '⁀nhieb m lash.

Pelikan orn. ['peːlikɑːn] m (-s/-e) pelican.

Pell|e ['pɛlə] f (-/-n) skin, peel; '⁀en v/t. (ge-, h) skin, peel; '⁀kartoffeln f/pl. potatoes pl. (boiled) in their jackets or skins.

Pelz [pɛlts] m (-es/-e) fur; *garment:* mst furs pl.; '⁀gefüttert adj. fur-lined; '⁀händler m furrier; '⁀handschuh m furred glove; '⁀ig adj. furry; ⚕ *tongue:* furred; '⁀mantel m fur coat; '⁀stiefel m fur-lined boot; '⁀tiere n/pl. fur-covered animals pl.

Pendel ['pɛndəl] n (-s/-) pendulum; '⁀n v/i. (ge-, h) oscillate, swing; 🚋 shuttle, *Am.* commute; '⁀tür f swing-door; '⁀verkehr 🚋 m shuttle service.

Pension [pã'sjõː, pɛn'zjoːn] f (-/-en) (old-age) pension, retired pay; board; boarding-house; ⁀är [⁀o-'nɛːr] m (-s/-e) (old-age) pensioner; boarder; ⁀at [⁀o'nɑːt] n (-[e]s/-e) boarding-school; ⁀ieren [⁀o'niːrən] v/t. (no -ge-, h) pension (off); sich ⁀ lassen retire; ⁀sgast m boarder.

Pensum ['pɛnzum] n (-s/Pensen, Pensa) task, lesson.

perfekt 1. adj. [pɛr'fɛkt] perfect; *agreement:* settled; 2. ⁀ gr. ['⁀] n (-[e]s/-e) perfect (tense).

Pergament [pɛrga'mɛnt] n (-[e]s/-e) parchment.

Period|e [per'joːdə] f (-/-n) period; ⚕ periods pl.; ⁀isch adj. periodic (-al).

Peripherie [perife'riː] f (-/-n)

circumference; outskirts pl. (of *town*).

Perle ['pɛrlə] f (-/-n) pearl; *of glass:* bead; '⁀n v/i. (ge-, h) sparkle; '⁀nkette f pearl necklace; '⁀nschnur f string of pearls or beads.

'Perl|muschel zo. f pearl-oyster; ⁀mutt ['⁀mut] n (-s/no pl.), '⁀mutter f (-/no pl.) mother-of-pearl.

Person [pɛr'zoːn] f (-/-en) person; *thea.* character.

Personal [pɛrzo'nɑːl] n (-s/no pl.) staff, personnel; ⁀abteilung f personnel office; '⁀angaben f/pl. personal data pl.; ⁀ausweis m identity card; '⁀chef m personnel officer or manager or director; ⁀ien [⁀jən] pl. particulars pl., personal data pl.; ⁀pronomen gr. n personal pronoun.

Per'sonen|verzeichnis n list of persons; *thea.* dramatis personae pl.; ⁀wagen m 🚋 (passenger-)carriage or *Am.* car, coach; *mot.* (motor-)car; ⁀zug 🚋 m passenger train.

personifizieren [pɛrzonifi'tsiːrən] v/t. (no -ge-, h) personify.

persönlich adj. [pɛr'zøːnliç] personal; *opinion, letter:* a. private; ⁀keit f (-/-en) personality; personage.

Perücke [pe'rykə] f (-/-n) wig.

Pest ⚕ [pɛst] f (-/no pl.) plague.

Petersilie ♧ [petər'ziːljə] f (-/-n) parsley.

Petroleum [pe'troːleum] n (-s/no pl.) petroleum; *for lighting, etc.:* paraffin, esp. *Am.* kerosene.

Pfad [pfɑːt] m (-[e]s/-e) path, track; '⁀finder m boy scout; '⁀finderin f (-/-nen) girl guide, *Am.* girl scout.

Pfahl [pfɑːl] m (-[e]s/⁀e) stake, pale, pile.

Pfand [pfant] n (-[e]s/⁀er) pledge; ♟ deposit, security; *real estate:* mortgage; *game:* forfeit; '⁀brief ♟ m debenture (bond).

pfänden ♟ ['pfɛndən] v/t. (ge-, h) seize *s.th.*; distrain upon *s.o.* or *s.th.*

'Pfand|haus n s. *Leihhaus;* '⁀leiher m (-s/-) pawnbroker; '⁀schein m pawn-ticket.

'Pfändung ♟ f (-/-en) seizure; distraint.

Pfann|e f ['pfanə] f (-/-n) pan; '⁀kuchen m pancake.

Pfarr|bezirk ['pfar-] m parish; '⁀er m (-s/-) parson; *Church of England:* rector, vicar; *dissenters:* minister; '⁀gemeinde f parish; '⁀haus n parsonage; *Church of England:* rectory, vicarage; '⁀kirche f parish church; '⁀stelle f (church) living.

Pfau orn. [pfau] m (-[e]s/-en) peacock.

Pfeffer ['pfɛfər] m (-s/-) pepper; '⁀gurke f gherkin; '⁀ig adj. peppery; '⁀kuchen m gingerbread;

~minze ♀ ['~mintsə] f (-/no pl.) peppermint; '~minzplätzchen n peppermint; '♀n v/t. (ge-, h) pepper; '~streuer m (-s/-) pepperbox, pepper-castor, pepper-caster.

Pfeife ['pfaifə] f (-/-n) whistle; ✂ fife; pipe (of organ, etc.); (tobacco-) pipe; '♀n (irr., ge-, h) 1. v/i. whistle (dat. to, for); radio: howl; pipe; 2. v/t. whistle; pipe; '~nkopf m pipe-bowl.

Pfeil [pfail] m (-[e]s/-e) arrow.

Pfeiler ['pfailər] m (-s/-) pillar (a. fig.); pier (of bridge, etc.).

'pfeil|'schnell adj. (as) swift as an arrow; '♀spitze f arrow-head.

Pfennig ['pfeniç] m (-[e]s/-e) coin: pfennig; fig. penny, farthing.

Pferch [pfɛrç] m (-[e]s/-e) fold, pen; '♀en v/t. (ge-, h) fold, pen; fig. cram.

Pferd zo. [pfe:rt] n (-[e]s/-e) horse; zu ~e on horseback.

Pferde|geschirr ['pfe:rdə-] n harness; '~koppel f (-/-n) paddock, Am. a. corral; '~rennen n horse-race; '~schwanz m horse's tail; hair-style: pony-tail; '~stall m stable; '~stärke ⊕ f horsepower.

pfiff[1] [pfif] pret. of pfeifen.

Pfiff[2] m (-[e]s/-e) whistle; fig. trick; '♀ig adj. cunning, artful.

Pfingst|en eccl. ['pfiŋstən] n (-/-), '~fest eccl. n Whitsun(tide); '~montag eccl. m Whit Monday; '~rose ♀ f peony; '~sonntag eccl. m Whit Sunday.

Pfirsich ['pfirziç] m (-[e]s/-e) peach.

Pflanze ['pflantsə] f (-/-n) plant; '♀n v/t. (ge-, h) plant, set; pot; '~enfaser f vegetable fib|re, Am. -er; '~enfett n vegetable fat; '♀en-fressend adj. herbivorous; '~er m (-s/-) planter; '~ung f (-/-en) plantation.

Pflaster ['pflastər] n (-s/-) ✶ plaster; road: pavement; '~er m (-s/-) paver, pavio(u)r; '♀n v/t. (ge-, h) ✶ plaster; pave (road); '~stein m paving-stone; cobble.

Pflaume ['pflaumə] f (-/-n) plum; dried: prune.

Pflege ['pfle:gə] f (-/-n) care; nursing; cultivation (of art, garden, etc.); ⊕ maintenance; in ~ geben put out (child) to nurse; in ~ nehmen take charge of; '♀bedürftig adj. needing care; '~befohlene ['~bəfo:lənə] m, f (-n/-n) charge; '~eltern pl. foster-parents pl.; '~heim ♀ n nursing home; '~kind n foster-child; '♀n (ge-, h) 1. v/t. take care of; attend (to); foster (child); ✶ nurse; maintain; cultivate (art, garden); 2. v/i.: ~ zu inf. be accustomed or used or wont to inf., be in the habit of ger.; sie pflegte zu sagen she used to say; '~r m (-s/-) fosterer; ✶ male nurse;

trustee; ⚖ guardian, curator; '~rin f (-/-nen) nurse.

Pflicht [pfliçt] f (-/-en) duty (gegen to); obligation; '♀bewußt adj. conscious of one's duty; '♀eifrig adj. zealous; '~erfüllung f performance of one's duty; '~fach n school, univ.: compulsory subject; '~gefühl n sense of duty; '♀gemäß adj. dutiful; '♀getreu adj. dutiful, loyal; '♀schuldig adj. in duty bound; '♀vergessen adj. undutiful, disloyal; '~verteidiger ⚖ m assigned counsel.

Pflock [pflɔk] m (-[e]s/⁓e) plug, peg.

pflücken ['pflʏkən] v/t. (ge-, h) pick, gather, pluck.

Pflug [pflu:k] m (-[e]s/⁓e) plough, Am. plow.

pflügen ['pfly:gən] v/t. and v/i. (ge-, h) plough, Am. plow.

Pforte ['pfɔrtə] f (-/-n) gate, door.

Pförtner ['pfœrtnər] m (-s/-) gate-keeper, door-keeper, porter, janitor.

Pfosten ['pfɔstən] m (-s/-) post.

Pfote ['pfo:tə] f (-/-n) paw.

Pfropf [pfrɔpf] m (-[e]s/-e) s. Pfropfen.

'**Pfropfen** 1. m (-s/-) stopper; cork; plug; ✶ clot (of blood); 2. ♀ v/t. (ge-, h) stopper; cork; fig. cram; ✿ graft.

Pfründe eccl. ['pfrʏndə] f (-/-n) prebend; benefice, (church) living.

Pfuhl [pfu:l] m (-[e]s/-e) pool, puddle; fig. sink, slough.

pfui int. [pfui] fie!, for shame!

Pfund [pfunt] n (-[e]s/-e) pound; ♀ig F adj. ['~diç] great, Am. swell; '♀weise adv. by the pound.

pfusch|en F ['pfuʃən] (ge-, h) 1. v/i. bungle; 2. v/t. bungle, botch; ♀erei F ['~rai] f (-/-en) bungle, botch.

Pfütze ['pfʏtsə] f (-/-n) puddle, pool.

Phänomen [fɛno'me:n] n (-s/-e) phenomenon; '♀al adj. [~e'na:l] phenomenal.

Phantasie [fanta'zi:] f (-/-n) imagination, fancy; vision; ♪ fantasia; ♀ren (no -ge-, h) 1. v/i. dream; ramble; ✶ be delirious or raving; ♪ improvise; 2. v/t. dream; ♪ improvise.

Phantast [fan'tast] m (-en/-en) visionary, dreamer; ♀isch adj. fantastic; F great, terrific.

Phase ['fa:zə] f (-/-n) phase (a. ⚡), stage.

Philanthrop [filan'tro:p] m (-en/-en) philanthropist.

Philolog|e [filo'lo:gə] m (-n/-n), ~in f (-/-nen) philologist; ~ie [~o'gi:] f (-/-n) philology.

Philosoph [filo'zo:f] m (-en/-en) philosopher; ~ie [~o'fi:] f (-/-n) philosophy; ♀ieren [~o'zo:fy] phil.] philosoph-ical.

Phlegma ['flɛgma] n (-s/no pl.) phlegm; **2tisch** adj. [~'ma:tiʃ] phlegmatic.

phonetisch adj. [fo'ne:tiʃ] phonetic.

Phosphor ᴧ̃ ['fɔsfɔr] m (-s/no pl.) phosphorus.

Photo F ['fo:to] **1.** n (-s/-s) photo; **2.** m (-s/-s) = '~apparat m camera.

Photograph [foto'gra:f] m (-en/-en) photographer; **~ie** [~a'fi:] f **1.** (-/-n) photograph, F: photo, picture; **2.** (-/no pl.) as an art: photography; **2ieren** [~a'fi:rən] (no -ge-, h) **1.** v/t. photograph; take a picture of; sich ~ lassen have one's photo(graph) taken; **2.** v/i. photograph; **2isch** adj. [~'gra:fiʃ] photographic.

Photo|ko'pie f photostat; **~ko'piergerät** n photostat; '~zelle f photo-electric cell.

Phrase ['fra:zə] f (-/-n) phrase.

Physik [fy'zi:k] f (-/no pl.) physics sg.; **2alisch** adj. [~i'ka:liʃ] physical; **~er** ['fy:zikər] m (-s/-) physicist.

physisch adj. ['fy:ziʃ] physical.

Pian|ist [pia'nist] m (-en/-en) pianist; **~o** [pi'a:no] n (-s/-s) piano.

Picke ⊕ ['pikə] f (-/-n) pick(axe).

Pickel ['pikəl] m (-s/-) ᵱ pimple; ⊕ pick(axe); ice-pick; '2ig adj. pimpled, pimply.

picken ['pikən] v/i. and v/t. (ge-, h) pick, peck.

picklig adj. ['pikliç] s. pickelig.

Picknick ['piknik] n (-s/-e, -s) picnic.

piekfein F adj. ['pi:k'-] smart, tip-top, slap-up.

piep(s)en ['pi:p(s)ən] v/i. (ge-, h) cheep, chirp, peep; squeak.

Pietät [pie'tɛ:t] f (-/no pl.) reverence; piety; **2los** adj. irreverent; **2voll** adj. reverent.

Pik [pi:k] **1.** m (-s/-e, -s) peak; **2.** F m (-s/-e): e-n ~ auf j-n haben bear s.o. a grudge; **3.** n (-s/-s) cards: spade(s pl.).

pikant adj. [pi'kant] piquant, spicy (both a. fig.); das Pikante the piquancy.

Pike ['pi:kə] f (-/-n) pike; von der ~ auf dienen rise from the ranks.

Pilger ['pilgər] m (-s/-) pilgrim; '~fahrt f pilgrimage; '2n v/i. (ge-, sein) go on or make a pilgrimage; wander.

Pille ['pilə] f (-/-n) pill.

Pilot [pi'lo:t] m (-en/-en) pilot.

Pilz ⚇ [pilts] m (-es/-e) fungus, edible: mushroom, inedible: toad-stool.

pimp(e)lig F adj. ['pimp(ə)liç] sickly; effeminate.

Pinguin orn. ['piŋgui:n] m (-s/-e) penguin.

Pinsel ['pinzəl] m (-s/-) brush; F fig. simpleton; '2n v/t. and v/i. (ge-, h) paint; daub; '~strich m stroke of the brush.

Pinzette [pin'tsɛtə] f (-/-n) (e-e a pair of) tweezers pl.

Pionier [pio'ni:r] m (-s/-e) pioneer, Am. a. trail blazer; ⚒ engineer.

Pirat [pi'ra:t] m (-en/-en) pirate.

Pirsch hunt. [pirʃ] f (-/no pl.) deer-stalking, Am. a. still hunt.

Piste ['pistə] f (-/-n) skiing, etc.: course; ✈ runway.

Pistole [pis'to:lə] f (-/-n) pistol, Am. F a. gun, rod; **~ntasche** f holster.

placieren [pla'si:rən] v/t. (no -ge-, h) place; sich ~ sports: be placed (second, etc.).

Plackerei F [plakə'raɪ] f (-/-en) drudgery.

plädieren [plɛ'di:rən] v/i. (no -ge-, h) plead (für for).

Plädoyer ᴢ̃ᵗ [plɛdoa'je:] n (-s/-s) pleading.

Plage ['pla:gə] f (-/-n) trouble, nuisance, F plague; torment; '2n v/t. (ge-, h) torment; trouble, bother; F plague; sich ~ toil, drudge.

Plagiat [plag'ja:t] n (-[e]s/-e) plagiarism; ein ~ begehen plagiarize.

Plakat [pla'ka:t] n (-[e]s/-e) poster, placard, bill; '~säule f advertisement pillar.

Plakette [pla'kɛtə] f (-/-n) plaque.

Plan [pla:n] m (-[e]s/~e) plan; design, intention; scheme.

Plane ['pla:nə] f (-/-n) awning, tilt.

'planen v/t. (ge-, h) plan; scheme.

Planet [pla'ne:t] m (-en/-en) planet.

planieren ⊕ [pla'ni:rən] v/t. (no -ge-, h) level.

Planke ['plaŋkə] f (-/-n) plank, board.

plänkeln ['plɛŋkəln] v/i. (ge-, h) skirmish (a. fig.).

'plan|los 1. adj. planless, aimless, desultory; **2.** adv. at random; '~mäßig **1.** adj. systematic, planned; **2.** adv. as planned.

planschen ['planʃən] v/i. (ge-, h) splash, paddle.

Plantage [plan'ta:ʒə] f (-/-n) plantation.

Plapper|maul F ['plapər-] n chatterbox; '2n F v/i. (ge-, h) chatter, prattle, babble.

plärren ['plɛrən] v/i. and v/t. (ge-, h) blubber; bawl.

Plasti|k [plastik] **1.** f (-/no pl.) plastic art; **2.** f (-/-en) sculpture; ᵱ plastic; **3.** ⊕ n (-s/-s) plastic; '2sch adj. plastic; three-dimensional.

Platin [pla'ti:n] n (-s/no pl.) platinum.

plätschern ['plɛtʃərn] v/i. (ge-, h) dabble, splash; water: ripple, murmur.

platt adj. [plat] flat, level, even; fig. trivial, commonplace, trite; F fig. flabbergasted.

Plättbrett ['plɛt-] n ironing-board.

Platte ['platə] *f* (-/-n) plate; dish; sheet (*of metal, etc.*); flag, slab (*of stone*); *mountain*: ledge; top (*of table*); tray, salver; disc, record; F *fig.* bald pate; *kalte* ～ cold meat.

plätten ['plɛtən] *v/t.* (ge-, h) iron.

'**Platten|spieler** *m* record-player; '～**teller** *m* turn-table.

'**Platt|form** *f* platform; '～**fuß** *m* ⚕ flat-foot; F *mot.* flat; '～**heit** *fig.* *f* (-/-en) triviality; commonplace, platitude, *Am. sl. a.* bromide.

Platz [plats] *m* (-es/-e) place; spot, *Am. a.* point; room, space; site; seat; square; *round*: circus; *sports*: ground; *tennis*: court; ～ *behalten* remain seated; ～ *machen* make way or room (*dat.* for); ～ *nehmen* take a seat, sit down, *Am. a.* have a seat; *ist hier noch* ～*?* is this seat taken or engaged or occupied?; *den dritten* ～ *belegen sports*: be placed third, come in third; '～**anweiserin** *f* (-/-nen) usherette.

Plätzchen ['plɛtsçən] *n* (-s/-) snug place; spot; biscuit, *Am.* cookie.

'**platzen** *v/i.* (ge-, sein) burst; explode; crack, split.

'**Platz|patrone** *f* blank cartridge; '～**regen** *m* downpour.

Plauder|ei [plaudə'raɪ] *f* (-/-en) chat; talk; small talk; '**2n** *v/i.* (ge-, h) (have a) chat (*mit* with), talk (to); chatter.

plauz *int.* [plauts] bang!

Pleite F ['plaɪtə] **1.** *f* (-/-n) smash; *fig.* failure; **2.** ⚙ F *adj.* (dead) broke, *Am. sl.* bust.

Plissee [pli'se:] *n* (-s/-s) pleating; ～**rock** *m* pleated skirt.

Plombe ['plɔmbə] *f* (-/-n) (lead) seal; stopping, filling (*of tooth*); **2ieren** [～'bi:rən] *v/t.* (no -ge-, h) seal; stop, fill (*tooth*).

plötzlich *adj.* ['plœtslıç] sudden.

plump *adj.* [plump] clumsy; ～**s** *int.* plump, plop; '～**sen** *v/i.* (ge-, sein) plump, plop, flop.

Plunder F ['plundər] *m* (-s/*no pl.*) lumber, rubbish, junk.

plündern ['plyndərn] (ge-, h) **1.** *v/t.* plunder, pillage, loot, sack; **2.** *v/i.* plunder, loot.

Plural *gr.* ['plu:ra:l] *m* (-s/-e) plural (number).

plus *adv.* [plus] plus.

Plusquamperfekt *gr.* ['pluskvamperfɛkt] *n* (-s/-e) pluperfect (tense), past perfect.

Pöbel ['pø:bəl] *m* (-s/*no pl.*) mob, rabble; '**2haft** *adj.* low, vulgar.

pochen ['pɔxən] *v/i.* (ge-, h) knock, rap, tap; *heart*: beat, throb, thump; *auf sein Recht* ～ stand on one's rights.

Pocke ⚕ ['pɔkə] *f* (-/-n) pock; '～**n** ⚕ *pl.* smallpox; '**2nnarbig** *adj.* pock-marked.

Podest [po'dɛst] *n, m* (-es/-e) pedestal (*a. fig.*).

Podium ['po:dium] *n* (-s/*Podien*) podium, platform, stage.

Poesie [poe'zi:] *f* (-/-n) poetry.

Poet [po'e:t] *m* (-en/-en) poet; **2isch** *adj.* poetic(al).

Pointe [po'ɛ̃:tə] *f* (-/-n) point.

Pokal [po'ka:l] *m* (-s/-e) goblet; *sports*: cup; ～**endspiel** *n sports*: cup final; ～**spiel** *n football*: cup-tie.

Pökel|fleisch ['pø:kəl-] *n* salted meat; '**2n** *v/t.* (ge-, h) pickle, salt.

Pol [po:l] *m* (-s/-e) pole; ⚡ *a.* terminal; **2ar** *adj.* [po'la:r] polar (*a.* ⚡).

Pole ['po:lə] *m* (-n/-n) Pole.

Polemi|k [po'le:mik] *f* (-/-en) polemic(s *pl.*); **2sch** *adj.* polemic (-al); **2sieren** [～emi'zi:rən] *v/i.* (*no* -ge-, h) polemize.

Police [po'li:s(ə)] *f* (-/-n) policy.

Polier ⊕ [po'li:r] *m* (-s/-e) foreman; **2en** *v/t.* (*no* -ge-, h) polish, burnish; furbish.

Politi|k [poli'ti:k] *f* (-/⚡ -en) policy; politics *sg., pl.*; ～**ker** [po'li:tikər] *m* (-s/-) politician; statesman; **2sch** *adj.* [po'li:tiʃ] political; **2sieren** [～iti'zi:rən] *v/i.* (*no* -ge-, h) talk politics.

Politur [poli'tu:r] *f* (-/-en) polish; lust|re, *Am.* -er, finish.

Polizei [poli'tsaɪ] *f* (-/⚡ -en) police; ～**beamte** *m* police officer; ～**knüppel** *m* truncheon, *Am.* club; ～**kommissar** *m* inspector; **2lich** *adj.* (of *or* by the) police; ～**präsident** *m* president of police; *Brt.* Chief Constable, *Am.* Chief of Police; ～**präsidium** *n* police headquarters *pl.*; ～**revier** *n* police-station; police precinct; ～**schutz** *m*: *unter* ～ under police guard; ～**streife** *f* police patrol; police squad; ～**stunde** *f* (-/*no pl.*) closing-time; ～**verordnung** *f* police regulation(s *pl.*); ～**wache** *f* police-station.

Polizist [poli'tsıst] *m* (-en/-en) policeman, constable, *sl.* bobby, cop; ～**in** *f* (-/-nen) policewoman.

polnisch *adj.* ['pɔlnıʃ] Polish.

Polster ['pɔlstər] *n* (-s/-) pad; cushion; bolster; *s. Polsterung*; '～**möbel** *n/pl.* upholstered furniture; upholstery; '**2n** *v/t.* (ge-, h) upholster, stuff; pad, wad; '～**sessel** *m*, '～**stuhl** *m* upholstered chair; '～**ung** *f* (-/-en) padding, stuffing; upholstery.

poltern ['pɔltərn] *v/i.* (ge-, h) make a row; rumble; *p.* bluster.

Polytechnikum [poly'tɛçnikum] *n* (-s/*Polytechnika, Polytechniken*) polytechnic (school).

Pommes frites [pɔm'frit] *pl.* chips *pl., Am.* French fried potatoes *pl.*

Pomp [pɔmp] *m* (-[e]s/*no pl.*) pomp, splendo(u)r; **2haft** *adj.*, **2ös** *adj.* [～'pø:s] pompous, splendid.

Pony ['pɔni] **1.** *zo. n* (-s/-s) pony; **2.** *m* (-s/-s) *hairstyle:* bang, fringe.

popul|är *adj.* [popu'lɛːr] popular; **~arität** [~ari'tɛːt] *f* (-/*no pl.*) popularity.

Por|e ['poːrə] *f* (-/-n) pore; **~ös** *adj.* [po'røːs] porous; permeable.

Portemonnaie [pɔrtmɔ'nɛː] *n* (-s/-s) purse.

Portier [pɔr'tjeː] *m* (-s/-s) *s.* Pförtner.

Portion [pɔr'tsjoːn] *f* (-/-en) portion, share; ✕ ration; helping, serving; zwei ~en Kaffee coffee for two.

Porto ['pɔrto] *n* (-s/-s, Porti) postage; **²frei** *adj.* post-free; prepaid, *esp. Am.* postpaid; **²pflichtig** *adj.* subject to postage.

Porträt [pɔr'trɛː; ~t] *n* (-s/-s; -[e]s/-e) portrait, likeness; **²ieren** [~ɛ'tiːrən] *v/t.* (no -ge-, *h*) portray.

Portugies|e [pɔrtu'giːzə] *m* (-n/-n) Portuguese; die ~n *pl.* the Portuguese *pl.*; **²isch** *adj.* Portuguese.

Porzellan [pɔrtsɛ'laːn] *n* (-s/-e) porcelain, china.

Posaune [po'zaunə] *f* (-/-n) ♪ trombone; *fig.* trumpet.

Pose ['poːzə] *f* (-/-n) pose, attitude; *fig. a.* air.

Position [pozi'tsjoːn] *f* (-/-en) position; social standing; ♱ station.

positiv *adj.* ['poːziti:f] positive.

Positur [pozi'tuːr] *f* (-/-en) posture; sich in ~ setzen strike an attitude.

Posse *thea.* ['pɔsə] *f* (-/-n) farce.

'Possen *m* (-s/-) trick, prank; **²haft** *adj.* farcical, comical; **'~reißer** *m* (-s/-) buffoon, clown.

possessiv *gr. adj.* ['pɔsɛsiːf] possessive.

pos'sierlich *adj.* droll, funny.

Post [pɔst] *f* (-/-en) post, *Am.* mail; mail, letters *pl.*; post office; mit der ersten ~ by the first delivery; **'~amt** *n* post office; **'~anschrift** *f* mailing address; **'~anweisung** *f* postal order; **'~beamte** *m* postoffice clerk; **'~bote** *m* postman, *Am.* mailman; **'~dampfer** *m* packet-boat.

Posten ['pɔstən] *m* (-s/-) post, place, station; job; ✕ sentry, sentinel; item; entry; *goods:* lot, parcel.

'Postfach *n* post-office box.

pos'tieren *v/t.* (no -ge-, *h*) post, station, place; sich ~ station o.s.

'Post|karte *f* postcard, *with printed postage stamp: Am. a.* postal card; **'~kutsche** *f* stage-coach; **²lagernd** *adj.* to be (kept until) called for, poste restante, *Am.* (in care of) general delivery; **'~leitzahl** *f* postcode; **'~minister** *m* minister of post; *Brt. and Am.* Postmaster General; **'~paket** *n* postal parcel; **'~schalter** *m* (post-office) window; **'~scheck** *m* postal cheque, *Am.* postal check; **'~schließfach** *n*

post-office box; **'~sparbuch** *n* post-office savings-book; **'~stempel** *m* postmark; **²wendend** *adv.* by return of post; **'~wertzeichen** *n* (postage) stamp; **'~zug** 🚂 *m* mail-train.

Pracht [praxt] *f* (-/✎ -en, ✎e) splendo(u)r, magnificence; luxury.

prächtig *adj.* ['prɛçtiç] splendid, magnificent; gorgeous; grand.

'prachtvoll *adj. s.* prächtig.

Prädikat [predi'kaːt] *n* (-[e]s/-e) *gr.* predicate; *school, etc.:* mark.

prägen ['prɛːgən] *v/t.* (ge-, *h*) stamp; coin (*word, coin*).

prahlen ['praːlən] *v/i.* (ge-, *h*) brag, boast (*mit of*); ~ mit show off *s.th.*

'Prahler *m* (-s/-) boaster, braggart; **~ei** [~'rai] *f* (-/-en) boasting, bragging; **²isch** *adj.* boastful; ostentatious.

Prakti|kant [prakti'kant] *m* (-en/-en) probationer; **'~ker** *m* (-s/-) practical man; expert; **~kum** ['~kum] *n* (-s/Praktika, Praktiken) practical course; **²sch** *adj.* practical; useful, handy; ~er Arzt general practitioner; **²zieren** ✍, ❧ [~'tsiːrən] *v/i.* (no -ge-, *h*) practi|se, *Am.* -ce medicine or the law. [prelate.\]

Prälat *eccl.* [prɛ'laːt] *m* (-en/-en)\

Praline [pra'liːnə] *f* (-/-n): ~n *pl.* chocolates *pl.*

prall *adj.* [pral] tight; plump; *sun:* blazing; **'~en** *v/i.* (ge-, sein) bounce or bound (*auf acc., gegen* against).

Prämi|e ['prɛːmjə] *f* (-/-n) 🏦 premium; prize; bonus; **²(i)eren** [prɛ'miːrən, premi'iːrən] *v/t.* (no -ge-, *h*) award a prize to.

prang|en ['praŋən] *v/i.* (ge-, *h*) shine, make a show; **²er** *m* (-s/-) pillory.

Pranke ['praŋkə] *f* (-/-n) paw.

pränumerando *adv.* [prɛːnumɛ'rando] beforehand, in advance.

Präpa|rat [prɛpa'raːt] *n* (-[e]s/-e) preparation; *microscopy:* slide; **²'rieren** *v/t.* (no -ge-, *h*) prepare.

Präposition *gr.* [prepozi'tsjoːn] *f* (-/-en) preposition.

Prärie [prɛ'riː] *f* (-/-n) prairie.

Präsens *gr.* ['prɛːzɛns] *n* (-/Präsentia, Präsenzien) present (tense).

Präsi|dent [prezi'dent] *m* (-en/-en) president; chairman; **²'dieren** *v/i.* (no -ge-, *h*) preside (*über acc.* over); be in the chair; **~dium** [~'ziːdjum] *n* (-s/Präsidien) presidency, chair.

prasseln ['prasəln] *v/i.* (ge-, *h*) *fire:* crackle; *rain:* patter.

prassen ['prasən] *v/i.* (ge-, *h*) feast, carouse.

Präteritum *gr.* [prɛ'teːritum] *n* (-s/Präterita) preterite (tense); past tense.

Praxis ['praksis] *f* **1.** (-/*no pl.*) practice; **2.** (-/Praxen) practice (of doctor or lawyer).

Präzedenzfall [prɛtse'dɛnts-] *m* precedent; ⚖ *a.* case-law.

präzis *adj.* [prɛ'tsi:s], **~e** *adj.* [~zə] precise.

predig|en ['pre:digən] *v/i. and v/t.* (ge-, h) preach; **~er** *m* (-s/-) preacher; clergyman; **2t** ['~diçt] *f* (-/-en) sermon (*a. fig.*); *fig.* lecture.

Preis [praɪs] *m* (-es/-e) price; cost; *competition:* prize; award; reward; praise; *um jeden* ~ at any price *or* cost; **'~ausschreiben** *n* (-s/-) competition.

preisen ['praɪzən] *v/t.* (*irr.*, ge-, h) praise.

'Preis|erhöhung *f* rise *or* increase in price(s); **'~gabe** *f* abandonment; revelation (*of secret*); **'2geben** *v/t.* (*irr.* geben, sep., -ge-, h) abandon; reveal, give away (*secret*); disclose, expose; **'2gekrönt** *adj.* prize-winning, prize (*novel, etc.*); **'~gericht** *n* jury; **'~lage** *f* range of prices; **'~liste** *f* price-list; **'~nachlaß** *m* price cut; discount; **'~richter** *m* judge, umpire; **'~schießen** *n* (-s/-) shooting competition; **'~stopp** *m* (-s/*no pl.*) price freeze; **'~träger** *m* prize-winner; **'2wert** *adj.:* ~ *sein* be a bargain.

prell|en ['prɛlən] *v/t.* (ge-, h) *fig.* cheat, defraud (*um of*); *sich et.* ~ ★ contuse *or* bruise s.th.; **'2ung** 🕮 *f* (-/-en) contusion.

Premier|e *thea.* [prəm'je:rə] *f* (-/-n) première, first night; **~minister** [~'je:-] *m* prime minister.

Presse ['prɛsə] *f* **1.** (-/-n) ⊕, *typ.* press; squeezer; **2.** (-/*no pl.*) *newspapers generally:* the press; **'~amt** *n* public relations office; **'~freiheit** *f* freedom of the press; **'~meldung** *f* news item; **'2n** *v/t.* (ge-, h) press; squeeze; **'~photograph** *m* press-photographer; **'~vertreter** *m* reporter; public relations officer.

Preßluft ['prɛs-] *f* (-/*no pl.*) compressed air.

Prestige [prɛs'ti:ʒə] *n* (-s/*no pl.*) prestige; ~ *verlieren a.* lose face.

Preuß|e ['prɔʏsə] *m* (-n/-n) Prussian; **'2isch** *adj.* Prussian.

prickeln ['prikəln] *v/i.* (ge-, h) prick(le), tickle; itch; *fingers:* tingle.

Priem [pri:m] *m* (-[e]s/-e) quid.

pries [pri:s] *pret. of* preisen.

Priester ['pri:stər] *m* (-s/-) priest; **'~in** *f* (-/-nen) priestess; **'2lich** *adj.* priestly, sacerdotal; **'~rock** *m* cassock.

prim|a F *adj.* ['pri:ma] first-rate, F A 1; ♥ *a.* prime; F swell; **'~är** *adj.* [pri'mɛ:r] primary.

Primel ♧ ['pri:məl] *f* (-/-n) primrose.

Prinz [prints] *m* (-en/-en) prince; **~essin** [~'tsesin] *f* (-/-nen) princess; **'~gemahl** *m* prince consort.

Prinzip [prin'tsi:p] *n* (-s/-ien)

principle; *aus* ~ on principle; *im* ~ in principle, basically.

Priorität [priori'tɛ:t] *f* **1.** (-/-en) priority; **2.** (-/*no pl.*) *time:* priority.

Prise ['pri:zə] *f* (-/-n) ⚓ prize; e-e ~ a pinch of (*salt, snuff*).

Prisma ['prisma] *n* (-s/Prismen) prism.

Pritsche ['pritʃə] *f* (-/-n) bat; plank-bed.

privat *adj.* [pri'va:t] private; **2adresse** *f* home address; **2mann** *m* (-[e]s/Privatmänner, Privatleute) private person *or* gentleman; **2patient** ♂ *m* paying patient; **2person** *f* private person; **2schule** *f* private school.

Privileg [privi'le:k] *n* (-[e]s/-ien, -e) privilege.

pro *prp.* [pro:] per; ~ *Jahr* per annum; ~ *Kopf* per head; ~ *Stück* a piece.

Probe ['pro:bə] *f* (-/-n) experiment; trial, test; *metall.* assay; sample; specimen; proof; probation; check; *thea.* rehearsal; audition; *auf* ~ on probation, on trial; *auf die* ~ *stellen* (put to the) test; **'~abzug** *typ., phot. m* proof; **'~exemplar** *n* specimen copy; **'~fahrt** *f* ⚓ trial trip; *mot.* trial run; **'~flug** *m* test *or* trial flight; **'2n** *v/t.* (ge-, h) exercise; *thea.* rehearse; **'~nummer** *f* specimen copy *or* number; **'~seite** *typ. f* specimen page; **'~sendung** *f* goods on approval; **'2weise** *adv.* on trial; *p. a.* on probation; **'~zeit** *f* time of probation.

probieren [pro'bi:rən] *v/t.* (*no* -ge-, h) try, test; taste (*food.*)

Problem [pro'ble:m] *n* (-s/-e) problem; **2atisch** *adj.* [~e'ma:tiʃ] problematic(al).

Produkt [pro'dukt] *n* (-[e]s/-e) product (*a.* ♣); ✐ produce; result; **~ion** [~'tsjo:n] *f* (-/-en) production; output; ♂ (~'ti:f] productive.

Produz|ent [produ'tsɛnt] *m* (-en/-en) producer; **2ieren** [~'tsi:rən] *v/t.* (*no* -ge-, h) produce; *sich* ~ perform; *contp.* show off.

professionell *adj.* [profesio'nɛl] professional, by trade.

Profess|or [pro'fɛsɔr] *m* (-s/-en) professor; **~ur** [~'su:r] *f* (-/-en) professorship, chair.

Profi ['pro:fi] *m* (-s/-s) *sports:* professional, F pro.   [*on tyre:* tread.\]

Profil [pro'fi:l] *n* (-s/-e) profile;/

Profit [pro'fi:t] *m* (-[e]s/-e) profit; **2ieren** [~i'ti:rən] *v/i.* (*no* -ge-, h) profit (*von* by).

Prognose [pro'gno:zə] *f* (-/-n) ♂ prognosis; *meteor.* forecast.

Programm [pro'gram] *n* (-s/-e) program(me); *politisches* ~ political program(me), *Am.* platform.

Projektion [projɛk'tsjo:n] *f* (-/-en) projection; **~sapparat** [projɛk-'tsjo:ns⁹-] *m* projector.

proklamieren [prokla'mi:rən] *v/t.* (*no -ge-, h*) proclaim.

Prokur|a ✝ [pro'ku:ra] *f* (*-/Prokuren*) procuration; **~ist** [~ku'rist] *m* (*-en/-en*) confidential clerk.

Proletari|er [prole'ta:rjər] *m* (*-s/-*) proletarian; **2sch** *adj.* proletarian.

Prolog [pro'lo:k] *m* (*-[e]s/-e*) prolog(ue).

prominen|t *adj.* [promi'nent] prominent; **2z** [~ts] *f* (*-/no pl.*) notables *pl.*, celebrities *pl.*; high society.

Promo|tion *univ.* [promo'tsjo:n] *f* (*-/-en*) graduation; **2vieren** [~'vi:rən] *v/i.* (*no -ge-, h*) graduate (*an dat.* from), take one's degree.

Pronomen *gr.* [pro'no:mən] *n* (*-s/-, Pronomina*) pronoun.

Propeller [pro'pɛlər] *m* (*-s/-*) ⚓, ✈ (screw-)propeller, screw; ✈ airscrew.

Prophe|t [pro'fe:t] *m* (*-en/-en*) prophet; **2tisch** *adj.* prophetic; **2zeien** [~e'tsaiən] *v/t.* (*no -ge-, h*) prophesy; predict, foretell; **~'zeiung** *f* (*-/-en*) prophecy; prediction.

Proportion [propɔr'tsjo:n] *f* (*-/-en*) proportion.

Prosa ['pro:za] *f* (*-/no pl.*) prose.

prosit *int.* ['pro:zit] your health!, here's to you!, cheers!

Prospekt [pro'spɛkt] *m* (*-[e]s/-e*) prospectus; brochure, leaflet, folder.

prost *int.* [pro:st] *s. prosit.*

Prostituierte [prostitu'i:rtə] *f* (*-n/-n*) prostitute.

Protest [pro'tɛst] *m* (*-es/-e*) protest; **~ einlegen** *or* **erheben gegen** (enter a) protest against.

Protestant *eccl.* [protes'tant] *m* (*-en/-en*) Protestant; **2isch** *adj.* Protestant.

protes'tieren *v/i.* (*no -ge-, h*): **gegen et. ~** protest against s.th., object to s.th.

Prothese 🦷 [pro'te:zə] *f* (*-/-n*) pro(s)thesis; *dentistry:* a. denture; artificial limb.

Protokoll [proto'kɔl] *n* (*-s/-e*) record, minutes *pl.* (*of meeting*); *diplomacy:* protocol; **das ~ aufnehmen** take down the minutes; **das ~ führen** keep the minutes; **zu ~ geben** ⚖️ depose, state in evidence; **zu ~ nehmen** take down, record; **2ieren** [~'li:rən] (*no -ge-, h*) 1. *v/t.* record, take down (on record); 2. *v/i.* keep the minutes.

Protz *contp.* [prɔts] *m* (*-en, -es/ -e[n]*) braggart, F show-off; **2en** *v/i.* (*ge-, h*) show off (*mit dat.* with); **2ig** *adj.* ostentatious, showy.

Proviant [pro'vjant] *m* (*-s/✎-e*) provisions *pl.*, victuals *pl.*

Provinz [pro'vints] *f* (*-/-en*) province; *fig. the* provinces *pl.*; **2ial** *adj.* [~'tsja:l], **2iell** *adj.* [~'tsjɛl] provincial.

Provis|ion ✝ [provi'zjo:n] *f* (*-/-en*) commission; **2orisch** *adj.* [~'zo:riʃ] provisional, temporary.

provozieren [provo'tsi:rən] *v/t.* (*no -ge-, h*) provoke.

Prozent [pro'tsent] *n* (*-[e]s/-e*) per cent; **~satz** *m* percentage; proportion; **2ual** *adj.* [~u'a:l] percental; **~er Anteil** percentage.

Prozeß [pro'tsɛs] *m* (*Prozesses/Prozesse*) process; ⚖️: action, lawsuit; trial; (legal) proceedings *pl.*; **e-n ~ gewinnen** win one's case; **e-n ~ gegen j-n anstrengen** bring an action against s.o., sue s.o.; **j-m den ~ machen** try s.o., put s.o. on trial; **kurzen ~ machen** *mit* make short work of.

prozessieren [protsɛ'si:rən] *v/i.* (*no -ge-, h*): **mit j-m ~** go to law against s.o., have the law of s.o.

Prozession [protsɛ'sjo:n] *f* (*-/-en*) procession.

prüde *adj.* ['pry:də] prudish.

prüf|en ['pry:fən] *v/t.* (*ge-, h*) examine; try, test; quiz; check, verify; **'~end** *adj.* *look:* searching, scrutinizing; **2er** *m* (*-s/-*) examiner; **2ling** *m* (*-s/-e*) examinee; **2stein** *fig. m* touchstone; **2ung** *f* (*-/-en*) examination; *school, etc.:* a. F exam; test; quiz; verification, checking, check-up; **e-e ~ machen** go in for *or* sit for *or* take an examination.

'Prüfungs|arbeit *f*, **'~aufgabe** *f* examination-paper; **'~ausschuß** *m*, **'~kommission** *f* board of examiners.

Prügel ['pry:gəl] 1. *m* (*-s/-*) cudgel, club, stick; 2. F *fig. pl.* beating, thrashing; **~ei** F [~'lai] *f* (*-/-en*) fight, row; **'~knabe** *m* scapegoat; **'2n** F *v/t.* (*ge-, h*) cudgel, flog; beat (up), thrash; **sich ~** (have a) fight.

Prunk [pruŋk] *m* (*-[e]s/no pl.*) splendo(u)r; pomp, show; **'2en** *v/i.* (*ge-, h*) make a show (*mit* of), show off (*mit et. s.th.*); **'2voll** *adj.* splendid, gorgeous.

Psalm *eccl.* [psalm] *m* (*-s/-en*) psalm.

Pseudonym [psɔydo'ny:m] *n* (*-s/-e*) pseudonym.

pst *int.* [pst] hush!

Psychi|ater [psyçi'a:tər] *m* (*-s/-*) psychiatrist, alienist; **2sch** *adj.* ['psy:çiʃ] psychic(al).

Psycho|analyse [psyço'ana'ly:zə] *f* (*-/no pl.*) psychoanalysis; **~analytiker** [~'tikər] *m* (*-s/-*) psycho-analist; **~loge** [~'lo:gə] *m* (*-n/-n*) psychologist; **~se** [~'ço:zə] *f* (*-/-n*) psychosis; panic.

Pubertät [puber'tɛːt] *f* (*-/no pl.*) puberty.

Publikum ['pu:blikum] *n* (*-s/no pl.*) *the* public; audience; spectators *pl.*, crowd; readers *pl.*

publiz|ieren [publi'tsi:rən] *v/t.* (*no*

-ge-, *h*) publish; **⸨ist** *m* (-en/-en) publicist; journalist.

Pudding ['pudiŋ] *m* (-s/-e, -s) cream.

Pudel *zo.* ['pu:dəl] *m* (-s/-) poodle; **'⸨naß** F *adj.* dripping wet, drenched.

Puder ['pu:dər] *m* (-s/-) powder; **'⸍dose** *f* powder-box; compact; **'⸨n** *v/t.* (ge-, *h*) powder; *sich* ~ powder o.s. *or* one's face; **'⸍quaste** *f* powder-puff; **'⸍zucker** *m* powdered sugar.

Puff F [puf] *m* (-[e]s/⸍e, -e) poke, nudge; **⸨en** (ge-, *h*) 1. F *v/t.* nudge; 2. *v/i.* pop; **'⸍er** *m* (-s/-) buffer.

Pullover [pu'lo:vər] *m* (-s/-) pullover, sweater.

Puls *m* [puls] (-es/-e) pulse; **'⸍ader** *anat. f* artery; **⸨ieren** [⸍zi:rən] *v/i.* (no -ge-, *h*) pulsate, throb; **'⸍schlag** *m* pulsation.

Pult [pult] *n* (-[e]s/-e) desk.

Pulv|er ['pulfər] *n* (-s/-) powder; gunpowder; F fig. cash, sl. brass, dough; **⸨erig** *adj.* powdery; **⸨eri-sieren** [⸍vəri'zi:rən] *v/t.* (no -ge-, *h*) pulverize; **⸨rig** *adj.* ['⸍friç] powdery.

Pump F [pump] *m* (-[e]s/-e): *auf* ~ on tick; **⸨e** *f* (-/-n) pump; **'⸨en** (ge-, *h*) 1. *v/i.* pump; 2. *v/t.* pump; F *fig.*: give *s.th.* on tick; borrow (*et. von j-m* s.th. from s.o.).

Punkt [puŋkt] *m* (-[e]s/-e) point (*a. fig.*); dot; *typ., gr.* full stop, period; spot, place; *fig.* item; article, clause (*of agreement*); *der springende* ~ the point; *toter* ~ deadlock, dead end; *wunder* ~ tender subject, sore point; ~ *zehn Uhr* on the stroke of ten, at 10 (o'clock) sharp; *in vielen* ⸍en on many points, in many respects; *nach* ⸍en *siegen sports*: win on points; **⸨ieren** [⸍'ti:rən] *v/t.* (no -ge-, *h*) dot, point; *g* puncture, tap; *drawing, painting*: stipple.

pünktlich *adj.* ['pyŋktliç] punctual; ~ *sein* be on time; **'⸨keit** *f* (-/no *pl.*) punctuality.

Punsch [punʃ] *m* (-es/-e) punch.

Pupille *anat.* [pu'pilə] *f* (-/-n) pupil.

Puppe ['pupə] *f* (-/-n) doll (*a. fig.*); puppet (*a. fig.*); *tailoring*: dummy; *zo.* chrysalis, pupa; **'⸍nspiel** *n* puppet-show; **'⸍nstube** *f* doll's room; **'⸍nwagen** *m* doll's pram, *Am.* doll carriage *or* buggy.

pur *adj.* [pu:r] pure, sheer.

Püree [py're:] *n* (-s/-s) purée, mash.

Purpur ['purpur] *m* (-s/no *pl.*) purple; **'⸨farben** *adj.*, **'⸨n** *adj.*, **⸨rot** *adj.* purple.

Purzel|baum ['purtsəl-] *m* somersault; *e-n* ~ *schlagen* turn a somersault; **'⸨n** *v/i.* (ge-, *sein*) tumble.

Puste F ['pu:stə] *f* (-/no *pl.*) breath; *ihm ging die* ~ *aus* he got out of breath.

Pustel *g* ['pustəl] *f* (-/-n) pustule, pimple.

pusten ['pu:stən] *v/i.* (ge-, *h*) puff, pant; blow.

Pute *orn.* ['pu:tə] *f* (-/-n) turkey (-hen); **'⸍r** *orn. m* (-s/-) turkey (-cock); **'⸨r'rot** *adj.* (as) red as a turkey-cock.

Putsch [putʃ] *m* (-es/-e) putsch, insurrection; riot; **'⸨en** *v/i.* (ge-, *h*) revolt, riot.

Putz [puts] *m* (-es/-e) *on garments*: finery; ornaments *pl.*; trimming; ⚭ roughcast, plaster; **'⸨en** *v/t.* (ge-, *h*) clean, cleanse; polish, wipe; adorn; snuff (*candle*); polish, *Am.* shine (*shoes*); *sich* ~ smarten *or* dress o.s. up; *sich die Nase* ~ blow *or* wipe one's nose; *sich die Zähne* ~ brush one's teeth; **'⸍frau** *f* charwoman, *Am. a.* scrubwoman; **'⸨ig** *adj.* droll, funny; **'⸍lappen** *m* cleaning rag; **'⸍zeug** *n* cleaning utensils *pl.*

Pyjama [pi'dʒa:ma] *m* (-s/-s) (*ein a suit of*) pyjamas *pl. or Am.* pajamas *pl.*

Pyramide [pyra'mi:də] *f* (-/-n) pyramid (*a.* ⚭); ⚔ stack (*of rifles*); **⸨nförmig** *adj.* [⸍nfœrmiç] pyramidal.

Q

Quacksalber ['kvakzalbər] *m* (-s/-) quack (doctor); **⸍ei** F [⸍'rai] *f* (-/-en) quackery; **'⸨n** *v/i.* (ge-, *h*) (play the) quack.

Quadrat [kva'dra:t] *n* (-[e]s/-e) square; *2 Fuß im* ~ 2 feet square; *ins* ~ *erheben* square; **⸨isch** *adj.* square; ⚖ *equation*: quadratic; **⸍meile** *f* square mile; **⸍meter** *n, m* square met|re, *Am.* -er; **⸍wurzel** ⚖ *f* square root; **⸍zahl** ⚖ *f* square number.

quaken ['kva:kən] *v/i.* (ge-, *h*) duck: quack; *frog*: croak.

quäken ['kvɛ:kən] *v/i.* (ge-, *h*) squeak.

Quäker ['kvɛ:kər] *m* (-s/-) Quaker, member of the Society of Friends.

Qual [kva:l] *f* (-/-en) pain; torment; agony.

quälen ['kvɛ:lən] *v/t.* (ge-, *h*) torment (*a. fig.*); torture; agonize; *fig.* bother, pester; *sich* ~ toil, drudge.

Qualifikation [kvalifika'tsjoːn] *f* (-/-en) qualification.

qualifizieren [kvalifi'tsiːrən] *v/t. and v/refl.* (no -ge-, h) qualify (*zu* for).

Qualit|ät [kvali'tɛːt] *f* (-/-en) quality; **ℒ**ativ [ˌˋa'tiːf] **1.** *adj.* qualitative; **2.** *adv.* as to quality.

Quali'täts|arbeit *f* work of high quality; **ˌstahl** *m* high-grade steel; **ˌware** *f* high-grade *or* quality goods *pl.*

Qualm [kvalm] *m* (-[e]s/*no pl.*) dense smoke; fumes *pl.*; vapo(u)r, steam; **'ℒen** (ge-, h) **1.** *v/i.* smoke, give out vapo(u)r *or* fumes; F *p.* smoke heavily; **2.** F *v/t.* puff (away) at (*cigar, pipe, etc.*); **'ℒig** *adj.* smoky.

'qualvoll *adj.* very painful; *pain:* excruciating; *fig.* agonizing, harrowing.

Quantit|ät [kvanti'tɛːt] *f* (-/-en) quantity; **ℒ**ativ [ˌˋa'tiːf] **1.** *adj.* quantitative; **2.** *adv.* as to quantity.

Quantum ['kvantum] *n* (-s/Quanten) quantity, amount; quantum (*a. phys.*).

Quarantäne [karan'tɛːnə] *f* (-/-n) quarantine; *in* ˌ *legen* (put in) quarantine; [curd(s *pl.*).\

Quark [kvark] *m* (-[e]s/*no pl.*))

Quartal [kvar'taːl] *n* (-s/-e) quarter (of a year); *univ.* term.

Quartett [kvar'tɛt] *n* (-[e]s/-e) *f* quartet(te); *cards:* four.

Quartier [kvar'tiːr] *n* (-s/-e) accommodation; ✕ quarters *pl.*, billet.

Quaste ['kvastə] *f* (-/-n) tassel; (powder-)puff.

Quatsch F [kvatʃ] *m* (-es/*no pl.*) nonsense, fudge, *sl.* bosh, rot, *Am. sl. a.* baloney; **'ℒen** F *v/i.* (ge-, h) twaddle, blether, *sl.* talk rot; (have a) chat; **'ˌkopf** F *m* twaddler.

Quecksilber ['kvɛk-] *n* mercury, quicksilver.

Quelle ['kvɛlə] *f*(-/-n) spring, source (*a. fig.*); *oil:* well; *fig.* fountain, origin; **'ℒn** *v/i.* (*irr.*, ge-, *sein*) gush, well; **ˌnangabe** ['kvɛlən?-] *f*

mention of sources used; **'ˌnforschung** *f* original research.

Quengel|ei F [kvɛŋə'laɪ] *f* (-/-en) grumbling, whining; nagging; **'ℒn** F *v/i.* (ge-, h) grumble, whine; nag.

quer *adv.* [kveːr] crossways, crosswise; F *fig.* wrong; F ˌ *gehen* go wrong; ˌ *über* (*acc.*) across.

'Quer|e *f* (-/*no pl.*): *der* ˌ *nach* crossways, crosswise; F *j-m in die* ˌ *kommen* cross s.o.'s path; *fig.* thwart s.o.'s plans; **'ˌfrage** *f* cross-question; **'ˌkopf** *fig. m* wrong-headed fellow; **'ℒschießen** F *v/i.* (*irr.* schießen, sep., -ge-, h) try to foil s.o.'s plans; **'ˌschiff** 🜊 *n* transept; **'ˌschläger** ✕ *m* ricochet; **'ˌschnitt** *m* cross-section (*a. fig.*); **'ˌstraße** *f* cross-road; *zweite* ˌ *rechts* second turning to the right; **ˌtreiber** *m* (-s/-) schemer; **ˌtrei-be'rei** *f* (-/-en) intriguing, machination.

Querulant [kveru'lant] *m* (-en/-en) querulous person, grumbler, *Am. sl. a.* griper.

quetsch|en ['kvɛtʃən] *v/t.* (ge-, h) squeeze; 🜏 bruise, contuse; *sich den Finger* ˌ jam one's finger; **'ℒung** 🜏 *f* (-/-en), **'ℒwunde** 🜏 *f* bruise, contusion.

quick *adj.* [kvik] lively, brisk.

quieken ['kviːkən] *v/i.* (ge-, h) squeak, squeal.

quietsch|en ['kviːtʃən] *v/i.* (ge-, h) squeak, squeal; *door-hinge, etc.:* creak, squeak; *brakes, etc.:* screech; **'ˌver'gnügt** F *adj.* (as) jolly as a sandboy.

Quirl [kvirl] *m* (-[e]s/-e) twirling-stick; **'ℒen** *v/t.* (ge-, h) twirl.

quitt *adj.* [kvit]: ˌ *sein mit j-m* be quits *or* even with s.o.; *jetzt sind wir* ˌ that leaves us even; **ˌieren** [ˌˋtiːrən] *v/t.* (no -ge-, h) receipt (*bill, etc.*); quit, abandon (*post, etc.*); **'ℒung** *f* (-/-en) receipt; *fig.* answer; *gegen* ˌ against receipt.

quoll [kvɔl] *pret. of* quellen.

Quot|e ['kvoːtə] *f* (-/-n) quota, share, portion; **ˌient** A͟ [kvo'tsjɛnt] *m* (-en/-en) quotient.

R

Rabatt 🕂 [ra'bat] *m* (-[e]s/-e) discount, rebate.

Rabe *orn.* ['raːbə] *m* (-n/-n) raven; **'ℒn'schwarz** F *adj.* raven, jet-black.

rabiat *adj.* [ra'bjaːt] rabid, violent.

Rache ['raxə] *f* (-/*no pl.*) revenge, vengeance; retaliation.

Rachen *anat.* ['raxən] *m* (-s/-) throat, pharynx; jaws *pl.*

rächen ['rɛçən] *v/t.* (ge-, h) avenge,

revenge; *sich* ˌ *an* (*dat.*) revenge o.s. *or* be revenged on.

'Rachen|höhle *anat. f* pharynx; **'ˌkatarrh** 🜏 *m* cold in the throat.

'rach|gierig *adj.*, **'ˌsüchtig** *adj.* revengeful, vindictive.

Rad [raːt] *n* (-[e]s/ˮer) wheel; (bi)cycle, F bike; (*ein*) ˌ *schlagen peacock:* spread its tail; *sports:* turn cart-wheels; *unter die Räder* *kommen* go to the dogs; '**~achse** *f* axle(-tree).

Radar ['rɑːdɑːr, ra'dɑːr] *m, n* (-s/-s) radar.

Radau F [ra'dau] *m* (-s/*no pl.*) row, racket, hubbub.

radebrechen ['rɑːdə-] *v/t.* (ge-, h) speak (*language*) badly, murder (*language*).

radeln ['rɑːdəln] *v/i.* (ge-, sein) cycle, pedal, F bike.

Rädelsführer ['rɛːdəls-] *m* ringleader.

Räderwerk ⊕ ['rɛːdər-] *n* gearing.

'**rad|fahren** *v/i.* (*irr. fahren, sep., -ge-, sein*) cycle, (ride a) bicycle, pedal, F bike; '**2fahrer** *m* cyclist, *Am. a.* cycler *or* wheelman.

radier|en [ra'diːrən] *v/t.* (*no -ge-, h*) rub out, erase; *art*: etch; **2gummi** *m* (india-)rubber, *esp. Am.* eraser; **2messer** *n* eraser; **2ung** *f* (-/-en) etching.

Radieschen ♧ [ra'diːsçən] *n* (-s/-) (red) radish.

radikal *adj.* [radi'kɑːl] radical.

Radio ['rɑːdjo] *n* (-s/-s) radio, wireless; *im ~* on the radio, on the air; **2aktiv** *phys. adj.* [radjoak'tiːf] radio(-)active; **~er** *Niederschlag* fall-out; '**~apparat** *m* radio *or* wireless (set).

Radium ⚛ ['rɑːdjum] *n* (-s/*no pl.*) radium.

Radius ⚕ ['rɑːdjus] *m* (-/Radien) radius.

'**Rad|kappe** *f* hub cap; '**~kranz** *m* rim; '**~rennbahn** *f* cycling track; '**~rennen** *n* cycle race; '**~sport** *m* cycling; '**~spur** *f* rut, track.

raffen ['rafən] *v/t.* (ge-, h) snatch up; gather (*dress*).

raffiniert *adj.* [rafi'niːrt] refined; *fig.* clever, cunning.

ragen ['rɑːgən] *v/i.* (ge-, h) tower, loom.

Ragout [ra'guː] *n* (-s/-s) ragout, stew, hash.

Rahe ⚓ ['rɑːə] *f* (-/-n) yard.

Rahm [rɑːm] *m* (-[e]s/*no pl.*) cream.

Rahmen ['rɑːmən] 1. *m* (-s/-) frame; *fig.*: frame, background, setting; scope; *aus dem ~ fallen* be out of place; 2. ⚑ *v/t.* (ge-, h) frame.

Rakete [ra'keːtə] *f* (-/-n) rocket; *e-e ~ abfeuern or starten* launch a rocket; *dreistufige ~* three-stage rocket; **~nantrieb** [ra'keːtən'-] *m* rocket propulsion; *mit ~* rocket-propelled; **~nflugzeug** *n* rocket (-propelled) plane; **~ntriebwerk** *n* propulsion unit.

Ramm|bär ⊕ ['ram-] *m*, '**~bock** *m*, '**~e** *f* (-/-n) ram(mer); '**2en** *v/t.* (ge-, h) ram.

Rampe ['rampə] *f* (-/-n) ramp, ascent; '**~nlicht** *n* footlights *pl.*; *fig.* limelight.

Ramsch [ramʃ] *m* (-es/♧ -e) junk,

14*

trash; *im ~ kaufen* buy in the lump; '**~verkauf** *m* jumble-sale; '**~ware** *f* job lot.

Rand [rant] *m* (-[e]s/**~er**) edge, brink (*a. fig.*); *fig.* verge; border; brim (*of hat, cup, etc.*); rim (*of plate, etc.*); margin (*of book, etc.*); lip (*of wound*); *Ränder pl. under the eyes*: rings *pl.*, circles *pl.*; *vor Freude außer ~ und Band geraten* be beside o.s. with joy; *er kommt damit nicht zu ~e* he can't manage it; '**~bemerkung** *f* marginal note; *fig.* comment.

rang[1] [ran] *pret. of ringen*.

Rang[2] [~] *m* (-[e]s/**~e**) rank, order; ✗ rank; position; *thea.* tier; *erster ~ thea.* dress-circle, *Am.* first balcony; *zweiter ~ thea.* upper circle, *Am.* second balcony; *ersten ~es* first-class, first-rate; *j-m den ~ ablaufen* get the start *or* better of s.o.

Range ['raŋə] *m* (-n/-n), *f* (-/-n) rascal; romp.

rangieren [rɑ̃'ʒiːrən] (*no -ge-, h*) 1. ⚑ *v/t.* shunt, *Am. a.* switch; 2. *fig. v/i.* rank.

'**Rang|liste** *f* sports, *etc.*: ranking list; ✗ army-list, navy *or* air-force list; '**~ordnung** *f* order of precedence.

Ranke ♧ ['raŋkə] *f* (-/-n) tendril; runner.

Ränke ['rɛŋkə] *m/pl.* intrigues *pl.*

'**ranken** *v/refl.* (ge-, h) creep, climb.

rann [ran] *pret. of rinnen*.

rannte ['rantə] *pret. of rennen*.

Ranzen ['rantsən] *m* (-s/-) knapsack; satchel.

ranzig *adj.* ['rantsiç] rancid, rank.

Rappe *zo.* ['rapə] *m* (-n/-n) black horse.

rar *adj.* [rɑːr] rare, scarce.

Rarität [rari'tɛːt] *f* (-/-en) rarity; curiosity, curio.

rasch *adj.* [raʃ] quick, swift, brisk; hasty; prompt.

rascheln ['raʃəln] *v/i.* (ge-, h) rustle.

rasen[1] ['rɑːzən] *v/i.* (ge-) 1. (h) rage, storm; rave; 2. (sein) race, speed; '**~d** *adj.* raving; frenzied; *speed*: tearing; *pains*: agonizing; *headache*: splitting; *j-n ~ machen* drive s.o. mad.

Rasen[2] [~] *m* (-s/-) grass; lawn; turf; '**~platz** *m* lawn, grass-plot.

Raserei F [rɑːzə'rai] *f* (-/-en) rage, fury, frenzy, madness; F *mot.* scorching; *j-n zur ~ bringen* drive s.o. mad.

Rasier|apparat [ra'ziːr-] *m* (safety) razor; *sich ~ (lassen* get a) shave; **~klinge** *f* razor-blade; **~messer** *n* razor; **~pinsel** *m* shaving-brush; **~seife** *f* shaving-soap; **~wasser** *n* after-shave lotion; **~zeug** *n* shaving kit.

Rasse ['rasə] *f* (-/-n) race; *zo.* breed.

rasseln ['rasəln] *v/i.* (ge-, h) rattle.

'Rassen|frage f (-/no pl.) racial issue; ~kampf m race conflict; ~problem n racial issue; ~schranke f colo(u)r bar; ~trennung f (-/no pl.) racial segregation; ~unruhen f/pl. race riots pl.

'rasserein adj. thoroughbred, purebred.

'rassig adj. thoroughbred; fig. racy.

Rast [rast] f (-/-en) rest, repose; break, pause; '2en v/i. (ge-, h) rest, repose; '2los adj. restless; '~platz m resting-place; mot. picnic area.

Rat [ra:t] m 1. (-[e]s/no pl.) advice, counsel; suggestion; fig. way out; zu ~e ziehen consult; j-n um ~ fragen ask s.o.'s advice; 2. (-[e]s/~e) council, board; council(l)or, alderman.

Rate ['ra:tə] f (-/-n) instal(l)ment (a. ✝); auf ~n ✝ on hire-purchase.

'raten (irr., ge-, h) 1. v/i. advise, counsel (j-m zu inf. s.o. to inf.); 2. v/t. guess, divine.

'raten|weise adv. by instal(l)ments; '2zahlung ✝ f payment by instal(l)ments.

'Rat|geber m (-s/-) adviser, counsel(l)or; '~haus n town hall, Am. a. city hall.

ratifizieren [ratifi'tsi:rən] v/t. (no -ge-, h) ratify.

Ration [ra'tsjo:n] f (-/-en) ration, allowance; 2ell adj. [~o'nɛl] rational; efficient; economical; 2ieren [~o'ni:rən] v/t. (no -ge-, h) ration.

'rat|los adj. puzzled, perplexed, at a loss; '~sam adj. advisable; expedient; '2schlag m (piece of) advice, counsel.

Rätsel ['rɛ:tsəl] n (-s/-) riddle, puzzle; enigma, mystery; '2haft adj. puzzling; enigmatic(al), mysterious.

Ratte zo. ['ratə] f (-/-n) rat.

rattern ['ratərn] v/i. (ge-, h, sein) rattle, clatter.

Raub [raup] m (-[e]s/no pl.) robbery; kidnap(p)ing; piracy (of intellectual property); booty, spoils pl.; '~bau m (-[e]s/no pl.): ~ treiben ⚷ exhaust the land; ⚒ rob a mine; ~ treiben mit undermine (one's health); '2en ['~bən] v/t. (ge-, h) rob, take by force, steal; kidnap; j-m et. ~ rob or deprive s.o. of s.th.

Räuber ['rɔybər] m (-s/-) robber; '~bande f gang of robbers; '2isch adj. rapacious, predatory.

'Raub|fisch icht. m fish of prey; '~gier f rapacity; '2gierig adj. rapacious; '~mord m murder with robbery; '~mörder m murderer and robber; '~tier zo. n beast of prey; '~überfall m hold-up, armed robbery; '~vogel orn. m bird of prey; '~zug m raid.

Rauch [raux] m (-[e]s/no pl.) smoke; fume; '2en (ge-, h) 1. v/i. smoke;

fume; p. (have a) smoke; 2. v/t. smoke (cigarette); '~er m (-s/-) smoker; s. Raucherabteil.

Räucheraal ['rɔyçər?-] m smoked eel.

Raucherabteil 🚃 ['rauxər?-] n smoking-car(riage), smoking-compartment, smoker.

'Räucher|hering m red or smoked herring, kipper; '2n (ge-, h) 1. v/t. smoke, cure (meat, fish); 2. v/i. burn incense.

'Rauch|fahne f trail of smoke; '~fang m chimney, flue; '~fleisch n smoked meat; '2ig adj. smoky; '~tabak m tobacco; '~waren f/pl. tobacco products pl.; furs pl.; '~zimmer n smoking-room.

Räude ['rɔydə] f (-/-n) mange, scab; '2ig adj. mangy, scabby.

Rauf|bold contp. ['raufbɔlt] m (-[e]s/-e) brawler, rowdy, Am. sl. tough; '2en (ge-, h) 1. v/t. pluck, pull; sich die Haare ~ tear one's hair; 2. v/i. fight, scuffle; ~erei [~ə'raɪ] f (-/-en) fight, scuffle.

rauh adj. [rau] rough; rugged; weather: inclement, raw; voice: hoarse; fig.: harsh; coarse, rude; F: in ~en Mengen galore; '2reif m (-[e]s/no pl.) hoar-frost, poet. rime.

Raum [raum] m (-[e]s/~e) room, space; expanse; area; room; premises pl.; '~anzug m space suit.

räumen ['rɔymən] v/t. (ge-, h) remove, clear (away); leave, give up, esp. ✕ evacuate; vacate (flat).

'Raum|fahrt f astronautics; '~flug m space flight; '~inhalt m volume, capacity; '~kapsel f capsule.

räumlich adj. ['rɔymlɪç] relating to space, of space, spatial.

'Raum|meter n, m cubic met|re, Am. -er; '~schiff n space craft or ship; '~sonde f space probe; '~station f space station.

'Räumung f (-/-en) clearing, removal; esp. ✕ clearance; vacating (of flat), by force: eviction; ✕ evacuation (of town); '~sverkauf ✝ m clearance sale.

raunen ['raunən] (ge-, h) 1. v/i. whisper, murmur; 2. v/t. whisper, murmur; man raunt rumo(u)r has it.

Raupe zo. ['raupə] f (-/-n) caterpillar; '~nschlepper ⊕ m caterpillar tractor.

raus int. [raus] get out!, sl. beat it!, scram!

Rausch [rauʃ] m (-es/~e) intoxication, drunkenness; fig. frenzy, transport(s pl.); e-n ~ haben be drunk; '2en v/i. (ge-) 1. (h) leaves, rain, silk: rustle; water, wind: rush; surf: roar; applause: thunder; 2. (sein) movement: sweep; '~gift n narcotic (drug), F dope.

räuspern ['rɔyspərn] v/refl. (ge-, h) clear one's throat.

Razzia ['ratsja] f (-/Razzien) raid, round-up.

reagieren [rea'giːrən] v/i. (no -ge-, h) react (auf acc. [up]on; to); fig. and ⊕ a. respond (to).

Reaktion [reak'tsjoːn] f (-/-en) reaction (a. pol.); fig. a. response (auf acc. to); **~är** [~o'nɛːr] 1. m (-s/-e) reactionary; 2. ♀ adj. reactionary.

Reaktor phys. [re'aktɔr] m (-s/-en) (nuclear) reactor, atomic pile.

real adj. [re'aːl] real; concrete; **~isieren** [reali'ziːrən] v/t. (no -ge-, h) realize; **♀ismus** [rea'lismus] m (-/no pl.) realism; **~istisch** adj. [rea'listiʃ] realistic; **♀ität** [reali'tɛːt] f (-/-en) reality; **♀schule** f non-classical secondary school.

Rebe ♀ ['reːbə] f (-/-n) vine.

Rebell [re'bɛl] m (-en/-en) rebel; **♀ieren** [~'liːrən] v/i. (no -ge-, h) rebel, revolt, rise; **♀isch** adj. rebellious.

Reb|huhn orn. ['reːp-] n partridge; **~laus** zo. ['reːp-] f vine-fretter, phylloxera; **~stock** ♀ ['reːp-] m vine.

Rechen ['rɛçən] m (-s/-) rake; grid.

Rechen|aufgabe ['rɛçən-] f sum, (arithmetical) problem; **~fehler** m arithmetical error, miscalculation; **~maschine** f calculating-machine; **~schaft** f (-/no pl.): ~ ablegen give or render an account (über acc. of), account or answer (for); zur ~ziehen call to account (wegen for); **~schieber** ♀ m slide-rule.

rechne|n ['rɛçnən] (ge-, h) 1. v/t. reckon, calculate; estimate, value; charge; ~ zu rank with or among(st); 2. v/i. count; ~ auf (acc.) or mit count or reckon or rely (up)on; **~risch** adj. arithmetical.

'Rechnung f (-/-en) calculation, sum, reckoning; account, bill; invoice (of goods); in restaurant: bill, Am. check; score; auf ~ on account; ~ legen render an account (über acc. of); e-r Sache ~ tragen make allowance for s.th.; es geht auf meine ~ in restaurants: it is my treat, Am. F this is on me; **'~sprüfer** m auditor.

recht¹ [rɛçt] 1. adj. right; real; legitimate; right, correct; zur ~en Zeit in due time, at the right moment; ein ~er Narr a regular fool; mir ist es ~ I don't mind; ~ haben be right; j-m ~ geben agree with s.o.; 2. adv. right(ly), well; very; rather; really; correctly; ganz ~! quite (so)!; es geschieht ihm ~ it serves him right; ~ gern gladly, with pleasure; ~ gut quite good or well; ich weiß nicht ~ I wonder.

Recht² [~] n (-[e]s/-e) right (auf

acc. to), title (to), claim (on), interest (in); privilege; power, authority; ♂♂ law; justice; ~ sprechen administer justice; mit ~ justly.

'Rechte f (-n/-n) right hand; boxing: right; pol. the Right.

Rechteck ['rɛçt?-] n (-[e]s/-e) rectangle; **♀ig** adj. rectangular.

recht|fertigen ['rɛçtfɛrtigən] v/t. (ge-, h) justify; defend, vindicate; **♀fertigung** f (-/-en) justification; vindication, defen[c]e, Am. -se; **~gläubig** adj. orthodox; **~haberisch** adj. ['~haːbəriʃ] dogmatic; **~lich** adj. legal, lawful, legitimate; honest, righteous; **~los** adj. without rights; outlawed; **♀losigkeit** f (-/no pl.) outlawry; **~mäßig** adj. legal, lawful, legitimate; **♀mäßigkeit** f (-/no pl.) legality, legitimacy.

rechts adv. [rɛçts] on or to the right (hand).

'Rechts|anspruch m legal right or claim (auf acc. on, to), title (to); **~anwalt** m lawyer, solicitor; barrister, Am. attorney (at law); **~außen** m (-/-) football: outside right; **~beistand** m legal adviser, counsel.

'recht|schaffen 1. adj. honest, righteous; 2. adv. thoroughly, downright, F awfully; **♀schreibung** f (-/-en) orthography, spelling.

'Rechts|fall m case, cause; **~frage** f question of law; issue of law; **~gelehrte** m jurist, lawyer; **♀gültig** adj. s. rechtskräftig; **~kraft** f (-/no pl.) legal force or validity; **♀kräftig** adj. valid, legal; judgement: final; **~kurve** f right-hand bend; **~lage** f legal position or status; **~mittel** n legal remedy; **~nachfolger** m assign, assignee; **~person** f legal personality; **~pflege** f administration of justice, judicature.

'Rechtsprechung f (-/-en) jurisdiction.

'Rechts|schutz m legal protection; **~spruch** m legal decision; judg(e)-ment; sentence; verdict (of jury); **~steuerung** mot. f (-/-en) right-hand drive; **~streit** m action, lawsuit; **~verfahren** n (legal) proceedings pl.; **~verkehr** mot. m right-hand traffic; **~verletzung** f infringement; **~vertreter** m s. Rechtsbeistand; **~weg** m: den ~ beschreiten take legal action, go to law; unter Ausschluß des ~es eliminating legal proceedings; **♀widrig** adj. illegal, unlawful; **~wissenschaft** f jurisprudence.

'recht|wink(e)lig adj. right-angled; **~zeitig** adj. punctual; opportune; 2. adv. in (due) time, punctually, Am. on time.

Reck [rɛk] n (-[e]s/-e) sports: horizontal bar.

recken ['rɛkən] v/t. (ge-, h) stretch; sich ~ stretch o.s.

Redakt|eur [redak'tøːr] m (-s/-e) editor; ~ion [~'tsjoːn] f (-/-en) editorship; editing, wording; editorial staff, editors pl.; editor's or editorial office; 2ionell adj. [~tsjo'nel] editorial.

Rede ['reːdə] f (-/-n) speech; oration; language; talk, conversation; discourse; direkte ~ gr. direct speech; indirekte ~ gr. reported or indirect speech; e-e ~ halten make or deliver a speech; zur ~ stellen call to account (wegen for); davon ist nicht die ~ that is not the point; davon kann keine ~ sein that's out of the question; es ist nicht der ~ wert it is not worth speaking of; 2gewandt adj. eloquent; '~kunst f rhetoric; '2n (ge-, h) 1. v/t. speak; talk; 2. v/i. speak (mit to); talk (to), chat (with); discuss (über et. s.th.); sie läßt nicht mit sich ~ she won't listen to reason.

Redensart ['reːdəns?-] f phrase, expression; idiom; proverb, saying.

redigieren [redi'giːrən] v/t. (no -ge-, h) edit; revise.

redlich ['reːtlɪç] 1. adj. honest, upright; sincere; 2. adv.: sich ~ bemühen take great pains.

Redner ['reːdnər] m (-s/-) speaker; orator; '~bühne f platform; '2isch adj. oratorical, rhetorical; '~pult n speaker's desk.

redselig adj. ['reːtzeːlɪç] talkative.

reduzieren [redu'tsiːrən] v/t. (no -ge-, h) reduce (auf acc. to).

Reede ⚓ ['reːdə] f (-/-n) roads pl., roadstead; '~r m (-s/-) shipowner; ~'rei f (-/-en) shipping company or firm.

reell [re'ɛl] 1. adj. respectable, honest; business firm: solid; goods: good; offer: real; 2. adv.: ~ bedient werden get good value for one's money.

Refer|at [refe'raːt] n (-[e]s/-e) report; lecture; paper; ein ~ halten esp. univ. read a paper; ~endar [~ɛn'daːr] m (-s/-e) ⚖ junior lawyer; at school: junior teacher; ~ent [~'rɛnt] m (-en/-en) reporter, speaker; ~enz [~'rɛnts] f (-/-en) reference; 2ieren [~'riːrən] v/i. (no -ge-, h) report (über acc. [up]on); (give a) lecture (on); esp. univ. read a paper (on).

reflektieren [reflɛk'tiːrən] (no -ge-, h) 1. phys. v/t. reflect; 2. v/i. reflect (über acc. [up]on); ~ auf (acc.) † think of buying; be interested in.

Reflex [re'flɛks] m (-es/-e) phys. reflection or reflexion; ⚕ reflex (action); 2iv gr. adj. [~'ksiːf] reflexive.

Reform [re'fɔrm] f (-/-en) reform; ~er m (-s/-) reformer; 2ieren [~'miːrən] v/t. (no -ge-, h) reform.

Refrain [rə'frɛː] m (-s/-s) refrain, chorus, burden.

Regal [re'gaːl] n (-s/-e) shelf.

rege adj. ['reːgə] active, brisk, lively; busy.

Regel ['reːgəl] f (-/-n) rule; regulation; standard; physiol. menstruation, menses pl.; in der ~ as a rule; '2los adj. irregular; disorderly; '2mäßig adj. regular; '2n v/t. (ge-, h) regulate, control; arrange, settle; put in order; '2recht adj. regular; '~ung f (-/-en) regulation, control; arrangement, settlement; '2widrig adj. contrary to the rules, irregular; abnormal; sports: foul.

regen[1] ['reːgən] v/t. and v/refl. (ge-, h) move, stir.

Regen[2] [~] m (-s/-) rain; vom ~ in die Traufe kommen jump out of the frying-pan into the fire, get from bad to worse; '2arm adj. dry; '~bogen m rainbow; '~bogenhaut anat. f iris; '2dicht adj. rain-proof; '~guß m downpour; '~mantel m waterproof, raincoat, mac(k)intosh, F mac; '2reich adj. rainy; '~schauer m shower (of rain); '~schirm m umbrella; '~tag m rainy day; '~tropfen m raindrop; '~wasser n rain-water; '~wetter n rainy weather; '~wolke f rain-cloud; '~wurm zo. m earthworm, Am. a. angleworm; '~zeit f rainy season.

Regie [re'ʒiː] f (-/-n) management; thea., film: direction; unter der ~ von directed by.

regier|en [re'giːrən] (no -ge-, h) 1. v/i. reign; 2. v/t. govern (a. gr.); rule; 2ung f (-/-en) government, Am. administration; reign.

Re'gierungs|antritt m accession (to the throne); ~beamte m government official; Brt. Civil Servant; ~bezirk m administrative district; ~gebäude n government offices pl.

Regiment [regi'mɛnt] n 1. (-[e]s/-e) government, rule; 2. ⚔ (-[e]s/-er) regiment.

Regisseur [reʒi'søːr] m (-s/-e) thea. stage manager, director; film: director.

Regist|er [re'gɪstər] n (-s/-) register (a. ♪), record; index; ~ratur [~ra'tuːr] f (-/-en) registry; registration.

registrier|en [regis'triːrən] v/t. (no -ge-, h) register, record; 2kasse f cash register.

reglos adj. ['reːkloːs] motionless.

regne|n ['reːgnən] v/i. (ge-, h) rain; es regnet in Strömen it is pouring with rain; '~risch adj. rainy.

Regreß ⚖, † [re'grɛs] m (Regresses/Regresse) recourse; 2pflichtig ⚖, † adj. liable to recourse.

regulär adj. [regu'lɛːr] regular.

regulier|bar adj. [regu'li:rba:r] adjustable, controllable; **~en** v/t. (no -ge-, h) regulate, adjust; control.

Regung ['re:guŋ] f (-/-en) movement, motion; emotion; impulse; **'2slos** adj. motionless.

Reh zo. [re:] n (-[e]s/-e) deer, roe; female: doe.

rehabilitieren [rehabili'ti:rən] v/t. (no -ge-, h) rehabilitate.

'Reh|bock zo. m roebuck; **'2braun** adj., **'2farben** adj. fawn-colo(u)red; **~geiß** zo. f doe; **'~kalb** zo. n, **~kitz** zo. ['~kits] n (-es/-e) fawn.

Reib|e ['raibə] f (-/-n), **~eisen** ['raip?-] n grater.

reib|en ['raibən] (irr., ge-, h) 1. v/i. rub (an dat. [up]on); 2. v/t. rub, grate; pulverize; wund ~ chafe, gall; **2erei** F fig. [~'rai] f (-/-en) (constant) friction; **'2ung** f (-/-en) friction; **'~ungslos** adj. frictionless; fig. smooth.

reich1 adj. [raiç] rich (an dat. in); wealthy; ample, abundant, copious.

Reich2 [~] n (-es/-e) empire; kingdom (of animals, vegetables, minerals); pomp., rhet., fig. realm.

reichen ['raiçən] (ge-, h) 1. v/t. offer; serve (food); j-m et. ~ hand or pass s.th. to s.o.; sich die Hände ~ join hands; 2. v/i. reach; extend; suffice; das reicht! that will do!

reich|haltig adj. ['raiçhaltiç] rich; abundant, copious; **'~lich** 1. adj. ample, abundant, copious, plentiful; ~ Zeit plenty of time; 2. F adv. rather, fairly, F pretty, plenty; **'2tum** m (-s/≈er) riches pl.; wealth (an dat. of).

'Reichweite f reach; ✗ range; in ~ within reach, near at hand.

reif1 adj. [raif] ripe; mature.

Reif2 [~] m (-[e]s/no pl.) white or hoar-frost, poet. rime.

'Reife f (-/no pl.) ripeness, maturity.

'reifen1 v/i. (ge-) 1. (sein) ripen, mature; 2. (h): es hat gereift there is a white or hoar-frost.

'Reifen2 m (-s/-) hoop; ring; tyre, (Am. only) tire; as ornament: circlet; ~ wechseln mot. change tyres; **'~panne** mot. f puncture, Am. a. blowout.

'Reife|prüfung f s. Abitur; **'~zeugnis** n s. Abschlußzeugnis.

'reiflich adj. mature, careful.

Reihe ['raiə] f (-/-n) row; line; rank; series; number; thea. row, tier; der ~ nach by turns; ich bin an der ~ it is my turn.

'Reihen|folge f succession, sequence; alphabetische ~ alphabetical order; **'~haus** n terrace-house, Am. row house; **'2weise** adv. in rows.

Reiher orn. ['raiər] m (-s/-) heron.

Reim [raim] m (-[e]s/-e) rhyme; **'2en** (ge-, h) 1. v/i. rhyme; 2. v/refl. rhyme (auf acc. with).

rein adj. [rain] pure; clean; clear; **~e** Wahrheit plain truth; **'2ertrag** m net proceeds pl.; **'2fall** F m letdown; **'2gewicht** n net weight; **'2gewinn** m net profit; **'2heit** f (-/no pl.) purity; cleanness.

'reinig|en v/t. (ge-, h) clean(se); fig. purify; **'2ung** f (-/-en) clean(s)ing; fig. purification; cleaners pl.; chemische ~ dry cleaning; **'2ungs-mittel** n detergent, cleanser.

'rein|lich adj. clean; cleanly; neat, tidy; **'2machefrau** f charwoman; **'~rassig** adj. pedigree, thoroughbred, esp. Am. purebred; **'2schrift** f fair copy.

Reis1 ♀ [rais] m (-es/-e) rice.

Reis2 ♀ [~] n (-es/-er) twig, sprig.

Reise ['raizə] f (-/-en) journey, ⚓, ✈ voyage; travel; tour; trip; passage; **~büro** n travel agency or bureau; **~decke** f travel(l)ing-rug; **'2fertig** adj. ready to start; **'~führer** m guide(-book); **'~gepäck** n luggage, Am. baggage; **'~gesellschaft** f tourist party; **'~kosten** pl. travel(l)ing-expenses pl.; **'~leiter** m courier; **'2n** v/i. (ge-, sein) travel, journey; ~ nach go to; ins Ausland ~ go abroad; **'~nde** m, f (-n/-n) (✝ commercial) travel(l)er; in trains: passenger; for pleasure: tourist; **~necessaire** ['~nesese:r] n (-s/-s) dressing-case; **'~paß** m passport; **'~scheck** m traveller's cheque, Am. traveler's check; **'~schreibmaschine** f portable typewriter; **'~tasche** f travel(l)ing-bag, Am. grip(sack).

Reisig ['raiziç] n (-s/no pl.) brushwood.

Reißbrett ['rais-] n drawing-board.

reißen ['raisən] 1. v/t. (irr., ge-, h) tear; pull; an sich ~ seize; sich ~ scratch o.s. (an dat. with); sich ~ um scramble for; 2. v/i. (irr., ge-, sein) break; burst; split; tear; mir riß die Geduld I lost (all) patience; 3. 2 F ✗ n (-s/no pl.) rheumatism; **'~d** adj. rapid; animal: rapacious; pain: acute; ~en Absatz finden sell like hot cakes.

'Reiß|er F m (-s/-) draw, box-office success; thriller; **'~feder** f drawing-pen; **'~leine** f rip-cord; **'~nagel** m s. Reißzwecke; **'~schiene** f (T-)square; **'~verschluß** m zip-fastener, zipper, Am. a. slide fastener; **'~zeug** n drawing instruments pl.; **'~zwecke** f drawing-pin, Am. thumbtack.

Reit|anzug ['rait-] m riding-dress; **'~bahn** f riding-school, manège; riding-track; **'2en** (irr., ge-) 1. v/i. (sein) ride, go on horseback; 2. v/t. (h) ride; **'~er** m (-s/-) rider, horseman; ✗, police: trooper; filing: tab; **~e'rei** f (-/-er) cavalry; **'~erin** f (-/-nen) horsewoman; **'~gerte** f riding-whip; '**~hose** f (riding-) breeches pl.; '**~knecht** m groom; '**~kunst** f horsemanship; '**~lehrer** m riding master; '**~peitsche** f riding-whip; '**~pferd** zo. n riding-horse, saddle-horse; '**~schule** f riding-school; '**~stiefel** m/pl. riding-boots pl.; '**~weg** m bridle-path.

Reiz [raɪts] m (-es/-e) irritation; charm, attraction; allurement; '**2-bar** adj. sensitive; irritable, excitable, Am. sore; '**2en** (ge-, h) **1.** v/t. irritate (a. ⚕); excite; provoke; nettle; stimulate, rouse; entice, (al)lure, tempt, charm, attract; **2.** v/i. cards: bid; '**2end** adj. charming, attractive; Am. cute; lovely; '**2los** adj. unattractive; '**~mittel** n stimulus; ⚕ stimulant; '**~ung** f (-/-en) irritation; provocation; '**2-voll** adj. charming, attractive.

rekeln F ['reːkəln] v/refl. (ge-, h) loll, lounge, sprawl.

Reklamation [reklamaˈtsjoːn] f (-/-en) claim; complaint, protest.

Reklame [reˈklaːmə] f (-/-en) advertising; advertisement, F ad; publicity; ~ machen advertise; ~ machen für et. advertise s.th.

rekla'mieren (no -ge-, h) **1.** v/t. (re)claim; **2.** v/i. complain (wegen about).

Rekonvaleszen|t [rekɔnvalɛsˈtsɛnt] m (-en/-en), **~tin** f (-/-nen) convalescent; **~z** [~ts] f (-/no pl.) convalescence.

Rekord [reˈkɔrt] m (-[e]s/-e) sports, etc.: record.

Rekrut ✗ [reˈkruːt] m (-en/-en) recruit; **2ieren** ✗ [~uˈtiːrən] v/t. (no -ge-, h) recruit.

Rektor ['rɛktɔr] m (-s/-en) headmaster, rector, Am. principal; univ. chancellor, rector, Am. president.

relativ adj. [relaˈtiːf] relative.

Relief [relˈjɛf] n (-s/-s, -e) relief.

Religi|on [reliˈgjoːn] f (-/-en) religion; **2ös** adj. [~ˈøːs] religious; pious, devout; **~osität** [~oziˈtɛːt] f (-/no pl.) religiousness; piety.

Reling ⚓ ['reːlɪŋ] f (-/-s, -e) rail.

Reliquie [reˈliːkvjə] f (-/-n) relic.

Ren zo. [rɛn; reːn] n (-s/-s; -s/-e) reindeer.

Renn|bahn ['rɛn-] f racecourse, Am. race track, horse-racing: a. the turf; mot. speedway; '**~boot** n racing boat, racer.

rennen ['rɛnən] **1.** v/i. (irr., ge-, sein) run; race; **2.** v/t. (irr., ge-, h): j-n zu Boden ~ run s.o. down; **3.** 2 n (-s/-) run(ning); race; heat.

'**Renn|fahrer** m mot. racing driver, racer; racing cyclist; '**~läufer** m ski racer; '**~mannschaft** f racecrew; '**~pferd** zo. n racehorse, racer; '**~rad** n racing bicycle, racer; '**~sport** m racing; horse-racing: a. the turf; '**~stall** m racing stable;

'**~strecke** f racecourse, Am. race track; mot. speedway; distance (to be run); '**~wagen** m racing car, racer.

renommiert adj. [renɔˈmiːrt] famous, noted (wegen for).

renovieren [renoˈviːrən] v/t. (no -ge-, h) renovate, repair; redecorate (interior of house).

rent|abel adj. [rɛnˈtaːbəl] profitable, paying; **2e** f (-/-n) income, revenue; annuity; (old-age) pension; rent; **2enempfänger** ['rɛntən?-] m s. Rentner; rentier.

Rentier zo. ['rɛn-] n s. Ren.

rentieren [rɛnˈtiːrən] v/refl. (no -ge-, h) pay.

Rentner ['rɛntnər] m (-s/-) (old-age) pensioner.

Reparatur [reparaˈtuːr] f (-/-en) repair; **~werkstatt** f repair-shop; mot. a. garage, service station.

repa'rieren v/t. (no -ge-, h) repair, Am. fix.

Report|age [repɔrˈtaːʒə] f (-/-n) reporting, commentary, coverage; **~er** [reˈpɔrtər] m (-s/-) reporter.

Repräsent|ant [reprɛzɛnˈtant] m (-en/-en) representative; **~antenhaus** Am. parl. n House of Representatives; **2ieren** (no -ge-, h) **1.** v/t. represent; **2.** v/i. cut a fine figure.

Repressalie [reprɛˈsaːljə] f (-/-n) reprisal.

reproduzieren [reproduˈtsiːrən] v/t. (no -ge-, h) reproduce.

Reptil zo. [rɛpˈtiːl] n (-s/-ien, ✿-e) reptile.

Republik [repuˈbliːk] f (-/-en) republic; **~aner** pol. [~iˈkaːnər] m (-s/-) republican; **2anisch** adj. [~iˈkaːnɪʃ] republican.

Reserve [reˈzɛrvə] f (-/-n) reserve; **~rad** mot. n spare wheel.

reser'vier|en v/t. (no -ge-, h) reserve; ~ lassen book (seat, etc.); **~t** adj. reserved (a. fig.).

Resid|enz [reziˈdɛnts] f (-/-en) residence; **2ieren** v/i. (no -ge-, h) reside.

resignieren [reziˈɡniːrən] v/i. (no -ge-, h) resign.

Respekt [reˈspɛkt] m (-[e]s/no pl.) respect; **2ieren** [~ˈtiːrən] v/t. (no -ge-, h) respect; **2los** adj. irreverent, disrespectful; **2voll** adj. respectful.

Ressort [rɛˈsoːr] n (-s/-s) department; province.

Rest [rɛst] m (-es/-e, ✝ -er) rest, remainder; residue (a. ⚕); esp. ✝ remnant (of cloth); leftover (of food); das gab ihm den ~ that finished him (off).

Restaurant [rɛstoˈrãː] n (-s/-s) restaurant.

'**Rest|bestand** m remnant; '**~betrag** m remainder, balance; '**2lich** adj. remaining; '**2los** adv. completely; entirely; '**~zahlung** *f* payment of balance; final payment.

Resultat [rezul'ta:t] *n* (-[e]s/-e) result, outcome; *sports*: score.

retten ['rɛtən] *v/t.* (ge-, *h*) save; deliver, rescue.

Rettich ♀ ['rɛtiç] *m* (-s/-e) radish.

'**Rettung** *f* (-/-en) rescue; deliverance; escape.

'**Rettungs|boot** *n* lifeboat; '**~gürtel** *m* lifebelt; '**2los** *adj.* irretrievable, past help *or* hope, beyond recovery; '**~mannschaft** *f* rescue party; '**~ring** *m* life-buoy.

Reu|e ['rɔʏə] *f* (-/*no pl.*) repentance (*über acc.* of), remorse (at); '**2en** *v/t.* (ge-, *h*): *et. reut mich* I repent (of) s.th.; '**2evoll** *adj.* repentant; 2(müt)ig *adj.* ['~(mʏt)iç] repentant.

Revanche [re'vã:ʃ(ə)] *f* (-/-n) revenge; **~spiel** *n* return match.

revan'chieren *v/refl.* (no -ge-, *h*) take *or* have one's revenge (*an dat.* on); return (*für et.* s.th.).

Revers 1. [re'veːr] *m, n* (-/-) lapel (*of coat*); **2.** [re'vɛrs] *n* (-es/-e) declaration; ♈ bond.

revidieren [revi'diːrən] *v/t.* (no -ge-, *h*) revise; check; ♈ audit.

Revier [re'viːr] *n* (-s/-e) district, quarter; *s. Jagdrevier.*

Revision [revi'zjoːn] *f* (-/-en) revision (*a. typ.*); ♈ audit; ♈ appeal; **~ einlegen** ♈ lodge an appeal.

Revolt|e [re'vɔltə] *f* (-/-n) revolt, uprising; **2ieren** [~'tiːrən] *v/i.* (no -ge-, *h*) revolt, rise (in revolt).

Revolution [revolu'tsjoːn] *f* (-/-en) revolution; **~är** [~o'nɛːr] **1.** *m* (-s/-e) revolutionary; **2.** 2 *adj.* revolutionary.

Revolver [re'vɔlvər] *m* (-s/-) revolver, *Am.* F a. gun.

Revue [rə'vyː] *f* (-/-n) review; *thea.* revue, (musical) show; **~ passieren lassen** pass in review.

Rezens|ent [retsen'zɛnt] *m* (-en/-en) critic, reviewer; **2ieren** *v/t.* (no -ge-, *h*) review, criticize; **~ion** [~'zjoːn] *f* (-/-en) review, critique.

Rezept [re'tsɛpt] *n* (-[e]s/-e) ♈ prescription; *cooking*: recipe (*a. fig.*).

Rhabarber ♀ [ra'barbər] *m* (-s/*no pl.*) rhubarb.

rhetorisch adj. [re'toːriʃ] rhetorical.

rheumati|sch ♈ *adj.* [rɔʏ'maːtiʃ] rheumatic; **2smus** ♈ [~a'tismus] *m* (-/*Rheumatismen*) rheumatism.

rhythm|isch *adj.* ['rʏtmiʃ] rhythmic(al); **2us** [~us] *m* (-/*Rhythmen*) rhythm.

richten ['riçtən] *v/t.* (ge-, *h*) set right, arrange, adjust; level, point (*gun*) (*auf acc.* at); direct (*gegen* at); ♈ judge; execute; *zugrunde* ~ ruin, destroy; *in die Höhe* ~ raise, lift up; *sich* ~ *nach* conform to, act according to; take one's bearings from;

gr. agree with; depend on; *price*: be determined by; *ich richte mich nach Ihnen* I leave it to you.

'**Richter** *m* (-s/-) judge; '**2lich** *adj.* judicial; '**~spruch** *m* judg(e)ment, sentence.

'**richtig 1.** *adj.* right, correct, accurate; proper; true; just; *ein* ~*er Londoner* a regular cockney; **2.** *adv.*: ~ *gehen clock*: go right; '**2keit** *f* (-/*no pl.*) correctness; accuracy; justness; '**~stellen** *v/t.* (*sep.*, -ge-, *h*) put *or* set right, rectify.

'**Richt|linien** *f/pl.* (general) directions *pl.*, rules *pl.*; '**~preis** ♈ *m* standard price; '**~schnur** *f* ⊕ plumb-line; *fig.* rule (of conduct), guiding principle.

'**Richtung** *f* (-/-en) direction; course, way; *fig.* line; **~sanzeiger** *mot.* ['riçtuŋs?-] *m* (-s/-) flashing indicator, trafficator; '**2weisend** *adj.* directive, leading, guiding.

'**Richtwaage** ⊕ *f* level.

rieb [riːp] *pret. of reiben.*

riechen ['riːçən] (*irr.*, ge-, *h*) **1.** *v/i.* smell (*nach* of; *an dat.* at); sniff (*an dat.* at); **2.** *v/t.* smell; sniff.

rief [riːf] *pret. of rufen.*

riefeln ⊕ ['riːfəln] *v/t.* (ge-, *h*) flute, groove.

Riegel ['riːgəl] *m* (-s/-) bar, bolt; bar, cake (*of soap*); bar (*of chocolate*).

Riemen ['riːmən] *m* (-s/-) strap, thong; belt; ♈ oar.

Ries [riːs] *n* (-es/-e) ream.

Riese ['riːzə] *m* (-n/-n) giant.

rieseln ['riːzəln] *v/i.* (ge-) **1.** (*sein*) *small stream*: purl, ripple; trickle; **2.** (*h*): *es rieselt* it drizzles.

ries|engroß *adj.* ['riːzən'-], '**~enhaft** *adj.*, '**~ig** *adj.* gigantic, huge; '**2in** *f* (-/-en) giantess.

riet [riːt] *pret. of raten.*

Riff [rif] *n* (-[e]s/-e) reef.

Rille ['rilə] *f* (-/-n) groove; ⊕ *a.* flute.

Rimesse ♈ [ri'mɛsə] *f* (-/-n) remittance.

Rind *zo.* [rint] *n* (-[e]s/-er) ox; cow; neat; ~*er pl.* (horned) cattle *pl.*; *zwanzig* ~*er* twenty head of cattle.

Rinde ['rində] *f* (-/-n) ♀ bark; rind (*of fruit, bacon, cheese*); crust (*of bread*).

'**Rinder|braten** *m* roast beef; '**~herde** *f* herd of cattle; '**~hirt** *m* cowherd, *Am.* cowboy.

'**Rind|fleisch** *n* beef; '**~(s)leder** *n* neat's-leather, cow-hide; '**~vieh** *n* (horned) cattle *pl.*, neat *pl.*

Ring [riŋ] *m* (-[e]s/-e) ring; circle; link (*of chain*); ♈ ring, pool, trust, *Am.* F combine; '**~bahn** *f* circular railway.

ringeln ['riŋəln] *v/refl.* (ge-, *h*) curl, coil; '**2natter** *zo.* *f* ringsnake.

ring|en ['riŋən] (*irr.*, *ge-*, *h*) **1.** *v/i.* wrestle; struggle (*um* for); *nach Atem* ~ gasp (for breath); **2.** *v/t.* wring (*hands*, *washing*); **'2er** *m* (*-s/-*) wrestler.

ring|förmig *adj.* ['riŋfœrmiç] annular, ring-like; **'2kampf** *m* *sports*: wrestling(-match); **'2richter** *m* *boxing*: referee.

rings *adv.* [riŋs] around; **'~he'rum** *adv.*, **'~'um** *adv.*, **~um'her** *adv.* round about, all (a)round.

Rinn|e ['rinə] *f* (*-/-n*) groove, channel; gutter (*of roof or street*); gully; **'2en** *v/i.* (*irr.*, *ge-*, *sein*) run, flow; drip; leak; **~sal** ['..za:l] *n* (*-[e]s/-e*) watercourse, streamlet; **'~stein** *m* gutter; sink (*of kitchen unit*).

Rippe ['ripə] *f* (*-/-n*) rib; ⚓ groin; bar (*of chocolate*); **'2n** *v/t.* (*ge-*, *h*) rib; **'~nfell** *anat.* *n* pleura; **'~nfellentzündung** ⚕ *f* pleurisy; **'~nstoß** *m* dig in the ribs; nudge.

Risiko ['ri:ziko] *n* (*-s/-s*, *Risiken*) risk; *ein* ~ *eingehen* take a risk.

risk|ant *adj.* [ris'kant] risky; **~ieren** *v/t.* (*no -ge-*, *h*) risk.

Riß [ris] **1.** *m* (*Risses/Risse*) rent, tear; split (*a. fig.*); crack; *in skin*: chap; scratch; ⊕ draft, plan; *fig.* rupture; **2.** *2 pret. of reißen.*

rissig *adj.* ['risiç] full of rents; *skin*, *etc.*: chappy; ~ *werden* crack.

Rist [rist] *m* (*-es/-e*) instep; back of the hand; wrist.

Ritt [rit] **1.** *m* (*-[e]s/-e*) ride; **2.** *2 pret. of reiten.*

'Ritter *m* (*-s/-*) knight; *zum* ~ *schlagen* knight; **'~gut** *n* manor; **'2lich** *adj.* knightly, chivalrous; **'~lichkeit** *f* (*-/-en*) gallantry, chivalry.

rittlings *adv.* ['ritliŋs] astride (*auf e-m Pferd* a horse).

Ritz [rits] *m* (*-es/-e*) crack, chink; scratch; **'~e** *f* (*-/-n*) crack, chink; fissure; **'2en** *v/t.* (*ge-*, *h*) scratch; cut.

Rival|e [ri'va:lə] *m* (*-n/-n*), **~in** *f* (*-/-nen*) rival; **2isieren** [..ali'zi:rən] *v/i.* (*no -ge-*, *h*) rival (*mit j-m* s.o.); **~ität** [..ali'tɛ:t] *f* (*-/-en*) rivalry.

Rizinusöl ['ri:tsinus?-] *n* (*-[e]s/no pl.*) castor oil.

Robbe *zo.* ['rɔbə] *f* (*-/-n*) seal.

Robe ['ro:bə] *f* (*-/-n*) gown; robe.

Roboter ['rɔbɔtər] *m* (*-s/-*) robot.

robust *adj.* [ro'bust] robust, sturdy, vigorous.

roch [rɔx] *pret. of riechen.*

röcheln ['rœçəln] *v/i.* (*ge-*, *h*) **1.** rattle; **2.** *v/t.* gasp out (*words*).

Rock [rɔk] *m* (*-[e]s/-e*) skirt; coat, jacket; **'~schoß** *m* coat-tail.

Rodel|bahn ['ro:dəl-] *f* toboggan-run; **'2n** *v/i.* (*ge-*, *h*, *sein*) toboggan, *Am. a.* coast; **'~schlitten** *m* sled(ge), toboggan.

roden ['ro:dən] *v/t.* (*ge-*, *h*) clear (*land*); root up, stub (*roots*).

Rogen *ichth.* ['ro:gən] *m* (*-s/-*) roe, spawn.

Roggen ♀ ['rɔgən] *m* (*-s/-*) rye.

roh *adj.* [ro:] raw; *fig.*: rough, rude; cruel, brutal; *oil, metal*: crude; **'2bau** *m* (*-[e]s/-ten*) rough brickwork; **'2eisen** *n* pig-iron.

Roheit ['ro:hait] *f* (*-/-en*) rawness; roughness (*a. fig.*); *fig.*: rudeness; brutality.

'Roh|ling *m* (*-s/-e*) brute, ruffian; **'~material** *n* raw material; **'~produkt** *n* raw product.

Rohr [ro:r] *n* (*-[e]s/-e*) tube, pipe; duct; ♀: reed; cane.

Röhre ['rø:rə] *f* (*-/-n*) tube, pipe; duct; *radio*: valve, *Am.* (electron) tube.

'Rohr|leger *m* (*-s/-*) pipe fitter, plumber; **'~leitung** *f* plumbing; pipeline; **'~post** *f* pneumatic dispatch *or* tube; **'~stock** *m* cane; **'~zucker** *m* cane-sugar.

'Rohstoff *m* raw material.

Rolladen ['rɔlla:dən] *m* (*-s/-*, *-*) rolling shutter.

'Rollbahn ✈ *f* taxiway, taxi-strip.

'Rolle ['rɔlə] *f* (*-/-n*) roll; roller; coil (*of rope, etc.*); pulley; *beneath furniture*: cast|or, *-er*; mangle; *thea.* part, role; *fig.* figure; ~ *Garn* reel of cotton, *Am.* spool of thread; *das spielt keine* ~ that doesn't matter, it makes no difference; *Geld spielt keine* ~ money (is) no object; *aus der* ~ *fallen* forget o.s.

'rollen (*ge-*) **1.** *v/i.* (*sein*) roll; ✈ taxi; **2.** *v/t.* (*h*) roll; wheel; mangle (*laundry*).

'Rollenbesetzung *thea.* *f* cast.

'Roller *m* (*-s/-*) *children's toy*: scooter; *mot.* (motor) scooter.

'Roll|feld ✈ *n* man œuvring area, *Am.* maneuvering area; **'~film** *phot.* *m* roll film; **'~kragen** *m* turtle neck; **'~schrank** *m* rollfronted cabinet; **'~schuh** *m* rollerskate; **'~schuhbahn** *f* roller-skating rink; **'~stuhl** *m* wheel chair; **'~treppe** *f* escalator; **'~wagen** *m* lorry, truck.

Roman [ro'mɑ:n] *m* (*-s/-e*) novel, (work of) fiction; *novel of adventure and fig.*: romance; **~ist** [..a'nist] *m* (*-en/-en*) Romance scholar *or* student; **~schriftsteller** *m* novelist.

Romanti|k [ro'mantik] *f* (*-/no pl.*) romanticism; **2sch** *adj.* romantic.

Röm|er ['rø:mər] *m* (*-s/-*) Roman; **'2isch** *adj.* Roman.

röntgen ['rœntgən] *v/t.* (*ge-*, *h*) X-ray; **'2aufnahme** *f*, **'2bild** *n* X-ray; **'2strahlen** *m/pl.* X-rays *pl.*

rosa *adj.* ['ro:za] pink.

Rose ['ro:zə] *f* (*-/-n*) ♀ rose; ⚕ erysipelas.

'Rosen|kohl ♀ *m* Brussels sprouts *pl.*; **'~kranz** *eccl.* *m* rosary; **'2rot**

adj. rose-colo(u)red, rosy; '~**stock** ♀ *m* (-[e]s/~e) rose-bush.

'**rosig** *adj.* rosy (*a. fig.*), rose-colo(u)red, roseate.

Rosine [ro'zi:nə] *f* (-/-n) raisin.

Roß *zo.* [rɔs] *n* (Rosses/Rosse, F *Rösser*) horse, *poet.* steed; '~**haar** *n* horsehair.

Rost [rɔst] *m* 1. (-es/*no pl.*) rust; 2. (-es/-e) grate; gridiron; grill; '~**braten** *m* roast joint.

'**rosten** *v/i.* (ge-, *h*, sein) rust.

rösten ['rø:stən] *v/t.* (ge-, *h*) roast, grill; toast (*bread*); fry (*potatoes*).

'**Rost|fleck** *m* rust-stain; *in cloth:* iron-mo(u)ld; '~**frei** *adj.* rustless, rustproof; *esp. steel:* stainless; '2**ig** *adj.* rusty, corroded.

rot [ro:t] 1. *adj.* red; 2. 2 *n* (-s/-, F -s) red.

Rotationsmaschine *typ.* [rota-'tsjo:ns-] *f* rotary printing machine.

'**rot|backig** *adj.* ruddy; '~**blond** *adj.* sandy.

Röte ['rø:tə] *f* (-/*no pl.*) redness, red (colo[u]r); blush; '2**n** *v/t.* (ge-, *h*) redden; paint *or* dye red; *sich* ~ redden; flush, blush.

'**rot|gelb** *adj.* reddish yellow; '~**glühend** *adj.* red-hot; '2**haut** *f* red-skin.

rotieren [ro'ti:rən] *v/i.* (*no* -ge-, *h*) rotate, revolve.

Rot|käppchen ['ro:tkɛpçən] *n* (-s/-) Little Red Riding Hood; '~**kehlchen** *orn. n* (-s/-) robin (redbreast).

rötlich ['rø:tlɪç] *adj.* reddish.

'**Rot|stift** *m* red crayon *or* pencil; '~**tanne** ♀ *f* spruce (fir).

Rotte ['rɔtə] *f* (-/-n) band, gang.

'**Rot|wein** *m* red wine; claret; '~**wild** *zo. n* red deer.

Rouleau [ru'lo:] *n* (-s/-s) *s.* Rollladen; blind, *Am.* (window) shade.

Route ['ru:tə] *f* (-/-n) route.

Routine [ru'ti:nə] *f* (-/*no pl.*) routine, practice.

Rübe ♀ ['ry:bə] *f* (-/-n) beet; *weiße* ~ (Swedish) turnip, *Am. a.* rutabaga; *rote* ~ red beet, beet(root); *gelbe* ~ carrot.

Rubin [ru'bi:n] *m* (-s/-e) ruby.

ruch|bar *adj.* ['ru:xba:r]: ~ *werden* become known, get about *or* abroad; '~**los** *adj.* wicked, profligate.

Ruck [rʊk] *m* (-[e]s/-e) jerk, *Am.* F yank; jolt (*of vehicle*).

Rück|antwort ['ryk♀-] *f* reply; *Postkarte mit* ~ reply postcard; *mit bezahlter* ~ *telegram*: reply paid; '2**bezüglich** *gr. adj.* reflexive; '~**blick** *m* retrospect(ive view) (*auf acc.* at); reminiscences *pl.*

rücken[1] ['rykən] (ge-) 1. *v/t.* (*h*) move, shift; 2. *v/i.* (sein) move; *näher* ~ near, approach.

Rücken[2] [~] *m* (-s/-) back; ridge (*of mountain*); '~**deckung** *fig. f* backing, support; '~**lehne** *f* back

(*of chair, etc.*); '~**mark** *anat. n* spinal cord; '~**schmerzen** *m/pl.* pain in the back, back ache; '~**schwimmen** *n* (-s/*no pl.*) back-stroke swimming; '~**wind** *m* following *or* tail wind; '~**wirbel** *anat. m* dorsal vertebra.

Rück|erstattung ['ryk♀-] *f* restitution; refund (*of money*), reimbursement (*of expenses*); '~**fahrkarte** *f* return (ticket), *Am. a.* round-trip ticket; '~**fahrt** *f* return journey *or* voyage; *auf der* ~ on the way back; '~**fall** *m* relapse; '2**fällig** *adj.:* ~ *werden* relapse; '~**flug** *m* return flight; '~**frage** *f* further inquiry; '~**gabe** *f* return, restitution; '~**gang** *fig. m* retrogression; ✝ recession, decline; '2**gängig** *adj.* retrograde; ~ *machen* cancel; '~**grat** *anat. n* (-[e]s/-e) spine, backbone (*both a. fig.*); '~**halt** *m* support; '2**haltlos** *adj.* unreserved, frank; '~**hand** *f* (-/*no pl.*) *tennis:* backhand (stroke); '~**kauf** *m* repurchase; '~**kehr** f ['~ke:r] *f* (-/*no pl.*) return; '~**kopp(e)lung** ♀ *f* (-/-en) feed-back; '~**lage** *f* reserve(s *pl.*); savings *pl.*; '2**läufig** *fig. adj.* ['~lɔyfɪç] retrograde; '~**licht** *mot. n* tail-light, tail-lamp, rear-light; '2**lings** *adv.* backwards; from behind; '~**marsch** *m* march back *or* home; retreat; '~**porto** ♀ *n* return postage; '~**reise** *f* return journey, journey back *or* home.

'**Rucksack** *m* knapsack, ruck-sack.

'**Rück|schlag** *m* backstroke; *fig.* set-back; '~**schluß** *m* conclusion, inference; '~**schritt** *fig. m* retrogression, set-back; *pol.* reaction; '~**seite** *f* back, reverse; *a.* tail (*of coin*); '~**sendung** *f* return; '~**sicht** *f* respect, regard, consideration (*auf j-n* for s.o.); '2**sichtslos** *adj.* inconsiderate (*gegen* of), regardless (of); ruthless; reckless; *~es Fahren mot.* reckless driving; '2**sichtsvoll** *adj.* regardful (*gegen* of); considerate, thoughtful; '~**sitz** *mot. m* back-seat; '~**spiegel** *mot. m* rear-view mirror; '~**spiel** *n sports*: return match; '~**sprache** *f* consultation; ~ *nehmen mit* consult (*lawyer*), consult with (*fellow workers*); *nach* ~ *mit* on consultation with; '~**stand** *m* arrears *pl.*; backlog; ✝ residue; *im* ~ *sein mit* be in arrears *or* behind with; '2**ständig** *fig. adj.* old-fashioned, backward; *~e Miete* arrears of rent; '~**stoß** *m* recoil; kick (*of gun*); '~**strahler** *m* (-s/-) rear reflector, cat's eye; '~**tritt** *m* withdrawal, retreat; resignation; '~**trittbremse** *f* back-pedal brake, *Am.* coaster brake; '~**versicherung** *f* reinsurance; 2**wärts** *adv.* ['~verts] back, backward(s); '~**wärtsgang** *mot. m* reverse (gear); '**~weg** *m* way back, return.

'**ruckweise** *adv.* by jerks.

'**rück|wirkend** *adj.* reacting; ⚖️, *etc.*: retroactive, retrospective; '**2-wirkung** *f* reaction; '**2zahlung** *f* repayment; '**2zug** *m* retreat.

Rüde ['ry:də] **1.** *zo. m* (-*n*/-*n*) male dog *or* fox *or* wolf; large hound; **2.** ⚤ *adj.* rude, coarse, brutal.

Rudel ['ru:dəl] *n* (-*s*/-) troop; pack (*of wolves*); herd (*of deer*).

Ruder ['ru:dər] *n* (-*s*/-) oar; rudder (*a.* ✕); helm; '**~boot** *n* row(ing)-boat; '**~er** *m* (-*s*/-) rower, oarsman; '**fahrt** *f* row; '**2n** (*ge*-) **1.** *v/i.* (*h*, *sein*) row; **2.** *v/t.* (*h*) row; '**~regatta** ['~regata] *f* (-/*Ruderregatten*) boat race, regatta; '**~sport** *m* rowing.

Ruf [ru:f] *m* (-[*e*]*s*/-*e*) call; cry, shout; summons, *univ.* call; reputation, repute; fame; standing, credit; '**2en** (*irr., ge*-, *h*) **1.** *v/i.* call; cry, shout; **2.** *v/t.* call; **~** *lassen* send for.

'**Ruf|name** *m* Christian *or* first name; '**~nummer** *f* telephone number; '**~weite** *f* (-/*no pl.*): *in* ~ within call *or* earshot.

Rüge ['ry:gə] *f* (-/-*n*) rebuke, censure, reprimand; '**2n** *v/t.* (*ge*-, *h*) rebuke, censure, blame.

Ruhe ['ru:ə] *f* (-/*no pl.*) rest, repose; sleep; quiet, calm; tranquillity; silence; peace; composure; *sich zur* ~ *setzen* retire; ~*!* quiet!, silence!; *immer mit der* ~*!* take it easy!; *lassen Sie mich in* ~*!* let me alone!; '**2bedürftig** *adj.*: ~ *sein* want *or* need rest; '**~gehalt** *n* pension; '**~los** *adj.* restless; '**2n** *v/i.* (*ge*-, *h*) rest, repose; sleep; *laß die Vergangenheit* ~*!* let bygones be bygones!; '**~pause** *f* pause; lull; '**~platz** *m* resting-place; '**~stand** *m* (-[*e*]*s*/*no pl.*) retirement; *im* ~ retired; *in den* ~ *treten* retire; *in den* ~ *versetzen* superannuate, pension off, retire; '**~stätte** *f*: *letzte* ~ last resting-place; '**~störer** *m* (-*s*/-) disturber of the peace, peacebreaker; '**~störung** *f* disturbance (of the peace), disorderly behavio(u)r, riot.

'**ruhig** *adj.* quiet; *mind, water*: tranquil, calm; silent; ⊕ smooth.

Ruhm [ru:m] *m* (-[*e*]*s*/*no pl.*) glory; fame, renown.

rühm|en ['ry:mən] *v/t.* (*ge*-, *h*) praise, glorify; *sich e-r Sache* ~ boast of s.th.; '**~lich** *adj.* glorious, laudable.

'**ruhm|los** *adj.* inglorious; '**~reich** *adj.* glorious.

Ruhr ‡ [ru:r] *f* (-/*no pl.*) dysentery.

Rühr|ei ['ry:r?-] *n* scrambled egg; '**2en** (*ge*-, *h*) **1.** *v/t.* stir, move; *fig.* touch, move, affect; *sich* ~ stir, move, bustle; **2.** *v/i.*: *an et.* ~ touch s.th.; *wir wollen nicht daran* ~ let sleeping dogs lie; '**2end**

adj. touching, moving; '**2ig** *adj.* active, busy; enterprising; nimble; '**2selig** *adj.* sentimental; '**~ung** *f* (-/*no pl.*) emotion, feeling.

Ruin [ru'i:n] *m* (-*s*/*no pl.*) ruin; decay; ~*e f* (-/-*n*) ruin(s *pl.*); *fig.* ruin, wreck; 2*ieren* [rui'ni:rən] *v/t.* (*no -ge-*, *h*) ruin; destroy, wreck; spoil; *sich* ~ ruin o.s.

rülpsen ['rylpsən] *v/i.* (*ge-*, *h*) belch.

Rumän|e [ru'mɛ:nə] *m* (-*n*/-*n*) Ro(u)manian; 2*isch adj.* Ro(u)manian.

Rummel F ['ruməl] *m* (-*s*/*no pl.*) hurly-burly, row; bustle; revel; *in publicity*: F ballyhoo; '**~platz** *m* fun fair, amusement park.

rumoren [ru'mo:rən] *v/i.* (*no -ge-*, *h*) make a noise *or* row; *bowels*: rumble.

Rumpel|kammer F ['rumpəl-] *f* lumber-room; '**2n** F *v/i.* (*ge-*, *h*, *sein*) rumble.

Rumpf [rumpf] *m* (-[*e*]*s*/⁀*e*) *anat.* trunk, body; torso (*of statue*); ⚓ hull, frame, body; ✈ fuselage, body.

rümpfen ['rympfən] *v/t.* (*ge-*, *h*): *die Nase* ~ turn up one's nose, sniff (*über acc.* at).

rund [runt] **1.** *adj.* round (*a. fig.*); circular; **2.** *adv.* about; '**2blick** *m* panorama, view all (a)round; 2*e* ['rundə] *f* (-/-*n*) round; *sports*: lap; *boxing*: round; round, patrol; beat (*of policeman*); *in der or die* ~ (a)round; '**~en** ['~dən] *v/refl.* (*ge-*, *h*) (grow) round; '**2fahrt** *f* drive round (*town, etc.*); *s. Rundreise*; '**2flug** *m* circuit (*über of*); '**2frage** *f* inquiry, poll.

'**Rundfunk** *m* broadcast(ing); broadcasting service; broadcasting company; radio, wireless; *im* ~ over the wireless, on the radio *or* air; '**~anstalt** *f* broadcasting company; '**~ansager** *m* (radio) announcer; '**~gerät** *n* radio *or* wireless set; '**~gesellschaft** *f* broadcasting company; '**~hörer** *m* listener(-in); ~ *pl. a.* (radio) audience; '**~programm** *n* broadcast *or* radio program(me); '**~sender** *m* broadcast transmitter; broadcasting *or* radio station; '**~sendung** *f* broadcast; '**~sprecher** *m* broadcaster, broadcast speaker, (radio) announcer; '**~station** *f* broadcasting *or* radio station; '**~übertragung** *f* radio transmission, broadcast(ing); broadcast (*of programme*).

'**Rund|gang** *m* tour, round, circuit; '**~gesang** *m* glee, catch; '**2he'raus** *adv.* in plain words, frankly, plainly; '**2he'rum** *adv.* round about, all (a)round; '**2lich** *adj.* round(ish); rotund, plump; '**~reise** *f* circular tour *or* trip, sight-seeing trip, *Am. a.* round trip; '**~schau** *f* panorama, *newspaper*: review; '~schreiben *n* circular (letter); '~weg *adv.* flatly, plainly.

Runz|el ['runtsəl] *f* (-/-n) wrinkle; '~elig *adj.* wrinkled; '~eln *v/t.* (ge-, h) wrinkle; *die Stirn* ~ knit one's brows, frown; '~lig *adj.* wrinkled.

Rüpel ['ry:pəl] *m* (-s/-) boor, lout; '~haft *adj.* coarse, boorish, rude.

rupfen ['rupfən] *v/t.* (ge-, h) pull up or out, pick; pluck (*fowl*) (*a. fig.*).

ruppig *adj.* ['rupiç] ragged, shabby; *fig.* rude.

Rüsche ['ry:ʃə] *f* (-/-n) ruffle, frill.

Ruß [ru:s] *m* (-es/no pl.) soot.

Russe ['rusə] *m* (-n/-n) Russian.

Rüssel ['rysəl] *m* (-s/-) trunk (*of elefant*); snout (*of pig*).

'ruß|en *v/i.* (ge-, h) smoke; '~ig *adj.* sooty.

'russisch *adj.* Russian.

rüsten ['rystən] (ge-, h) 1. *v/t. and v/refl.* prepare, get ready (*zu for*); 2. *esp.* ✗ *v/i.* arm.

rüstig *adj.* ['rystiç] vigorous, strong; '~keit *f* (-/no pl.) vigo(u)r.

'Rüstung *f* (-/-en) preparations *pl.*; ✗ arming, armament; armo(u)r; ~sindustrie ['rystuŋʔ-] *f* armament industry.

'Rüstzeug *n* (set of) tools *pl.*, implements *pl.*; *fig.* equipment.

Rute ['ru:tə] *f* (-/-n) rod; switch; *fox's tail*: brush.

Rutsch [rutʃ] *m* (-es/-e) (land)slide; F short trip; '~bahn *f*, '~e *f* (-/-n) slide, chute; '~en *v/i.* (ge-, sein) glide, slide; slip; *vehicle*: skid; '~ig *adj.* slippery.

rütteln ['rytəln] (ge-, h) 1. *v/t.* shake, jog; jolt; 2. *v/i.* shake, jog; *car*: jolt; *an der Tür* ~ rattle at the door; *daran ist nicht zu* ~ that's a fact.

S

Saal [za:l] *m* (-[e]s/Säle) hall.

Saat ✗ [za:t] *f* (-/-en) sowing; standing or growing crops *pl.*; seed (*a. fig.*); '~feld ✗ *n* cornfield; '~gut ✗ *n* (-[e]s/no pl.) seeds *pl.*; '~kartoffel ✗ *f* seed-potato.

Sabbat ['zabat] *m* (-s/-e) Sabbath.

sabbern F ['zabərn] *v/i.* (ge-, h) slaver, slobber, *Am. a.* drool; twaddle, *Am. sl. a.* drool.

Säbel ['zɛ:bəl] *m* (-s/-) sab|re, *Am.* -er; *mit dem* ~ *rasseln pol.* rattle the sabre; '~beine *n/pl.* bandy legs *pl.*; '~beinig *adj.* bandy-legged; '~hieb *m* sabre-cut; '~n F *fig. v/t.* (ge-, h) hack.

Sabot|age [zabo'ta:ʒə] *f* (-/-n) sabotage; '~eur [~ø:r] *m* (-s/-e) saboteur; '~ieren *v/t.* (no -ge-, h) sabotage.

Sach|bearbeiter ['zax-] *m* (-s/-) official in charge; *social work*: case worker; '~beschädigung *f* damage to property; '~dienlich *adj.* relevant, pertinent; useful, helpful.

'Sache *f* (-/-n) thing; affair, matter, concern; ⟨⟩⟨⟩ case; point; issue; ~n *pl.* things *pl.*; *beschlossene* ~ foregone conclusion; *e-e* ~ *für sich* a matter apart; (*nicht*) *zur* ~ *gehörig* (ir)relevant, *pred. a.* to (off) the point; *bei der* ~ *bleiben* stick to the point; *gemeinsame* ~ *machen mit* make common cause with.

'sach|gemäß *adj.* appropriate, proper; '~kenntnis *f* expert knowledge; '~kundig *adj. s.* sachverständig; '~lage *f* state of affairs, situation; '~lich 1. *adj.* relevant,

pertinent, *pred. a.* to the point; matter-of-fact, business-like; unbias(s)ed; objective; 2. *adv.*: ~ *einwandfrei od.* richtig factually correct.

sächlich *gr. adj.* ['zɛçliç] neuter.

'Sachlichkeit *f* (-/no pl.) objectivity; impartiality; matter-of-factness.

'Sach|register *n* (subject) index; '~schaden *m* damage to property.

Sachse ['zaksə] *m* (-n/-n) Saxon.

sächsisch *adj.* ['zɛksiʃ] Saxon.

sacht *adj.* [zaxt] soft, gentle; slow.

Sach|verhalt ['zaxfɛrhalt] *m* (-[e]s/-e) facts *pl.* (of the case); '~verständig *adj.* expert; '~verständige *m* (-n/-n) expert, authority; ⟨⟩⟨⟩ expert witness; '~wert *m* real value.

Sack [zak] *m* (-[e]s/ᵘe) sack; bag; *mit* ~ *und Pack* with bag and baggage; '~gasse *f* blind alley, cul-de-sac, impasse (*a. fig.*), *Am. a.* dead end (*a. fig.*); *fig.* deadlock; '~leinwand *f* sackcloth.

Sadis|mus [za'dismus] *m* (-/no pl.) sadism; '~t *m* (-en/-en) sadist; '~tisch *adj.* sadistic.

säen ['zɛ:ən] *v/t. and v/i.* (ge-, h) sow (*a. fig.*).

Saffian ['zafja:n] *m* (-s/no pl.) morocco.

Saft [zaft] *m* (-[e]s/ᵘe) juice (*of vegetables or fruits*); sap (*of plants*) (*a. fig.*); '~ig *adj. fruits, etc.*: juicy; *meadow, etc.*: lush; *plants*: sappy (*a. fig.*); *joke, etc.*: spicy, coarse; '~los *adj.* juiceless; sapless (*a. fig.*).

Sage ['za:gə] *f* (-/-n) legend, myth; *die* ~ *geht* the story goes.

Säge ['zɛːɡə] f (-/-n) saw; '~blatt n saw-blade; '~bock m saw-horse, Am. a. sawbuck; '~fisch ichth. m sawfish; '~mehl n sawdust.

sagen ['zaːɡən] (ge-, h) **1.** v/t. say; j-m et. ~ tell s.o. s.th., say s.th. to s.o.; j-m ~ lassen, daß send s.o. word that; er läßt sich nichts ~ he will not listen to reason; das hat nichts zu ~ that doesn't matter; j-m gute Nacht ~ bid s.o. good night; **2.** v/i. say; es ist nicht zu ~ it is incredible or fantastic; wenn ich so ~ darf if I may express myself in these terms; sage und schreibe believe it or not; no less than, as much as.

'**sägen** v/t. and v/i. (ge-, h) saw.

'**sagenhaft** adj. legendary, mythical; F fig. fabulous, incredible.

Säge|späne ['zɛːɡəʃpɛːnə] m/pl. sawdust; '~werk n sawmill.

sah [zaː] pret. of sehen.

Sahne ['zaːnə] f (-/no pl.) cream.

Saison [zɛˈzõ] f (-/-s) season; 2**bedingt** adj. seasonal.

Saite ['zaɪtə] f (-/-n) string, chord (a. fig.); ~**ninstrument** ['zaɪtnʔ-] n stringed instrument.

Sakko ['zako] m, n (-s/-s) lounge coat; '~anzug m lounge suit.

Sakristei [zakrɪsˈtaɪ] f (-/-en) sacristy, vestry.

Salat [zaˈlaːt] m (-[e]s/-e) salad; 2 lettuce.

Salb|e ['zalbə] f (-/-n) ointment; 2**en** v/t. (ge-, h) rub with ointment; anoint; '~ung f (-/-en) anointing, unction (a. fig.); 2**ungsvoll** fig. adj. unctuous.

saldieren † [zalˈdiːrən] v/t. (no -ge-, h) balance, settle.

Saldo † ['zaldo] m (-s/Salden, Saldos, Saldi) balance; den ~ ziehen strike the balance; '~vortrag † m balance carried down.

Saline [zaˈliːnə] f (-/-n) salt-pit, salt-works.

Salmiak 🜊 [zalˈmjak] m, n (-s/no pl.) sal-ammoniac, ammonium chloride; ~**geist** m (-es/no pl.) liquid ammonia.

Salon [zaˈlõː] m (-s/-s) drawing-room, Am. a. parlor; 🜊 saloon; 2**fähig** adj. presentable; ~**löwe** fig. m lady's man, carpet-knight; ~**wagen** 🜊 m salooncar, saloon carriage, Am. parlor car.

Salpeter 🜊 [zalˈpeːtər] m (-s/no pl.) saltpetre; ~**säure** Am. -er; nit|re, Am. -er.

Salto ['zalto] m (-s/-s, Salti) somersault; ~ mortale break-neck leap; e-n ~ schlagen turn a somersault.

Salut [zaˈluːt] m (-[e]s/-e) salute; ~ schießen fire a salute; 2**ieren** [~uˈtiːrən] v/i. (no -ge-, h) (stand at the) salute.

Salve ['zalvə] f (-/-n) volley; 🜊 broadside; salute.

Salz [zalts] n (-es/-e) salt; '~berg-werk n salt-mine; '2en v/t. [(irr.,] ge-, h) salt; '~faß n, '~fäßchen ['~fɛsçən] n (-s/-) salt-cellar; '~gurke f pickled cucumber; '2**haltig** adj. saline, saliferous; '~hering m pickled herring; 2**ig** adj. salt(y); s. salzhaltig; '~säure 🜊 f hydro-chloric or muriatic acid; '~wasser n (-s/=) salt water, brine; '~werk n salt-works, saltern.

Same ['zaːmə] m (-ns/-n), '~n m (-s/-) 🜊 seed (a. fig.); biol. sperm, semen; '~nkorn 🜊 n grain of seed.

Sammel|büchse ['zaməl-] f collecting-box; '~lager n collecting point; refugees, etc.: assembly camp; 2**n** (ge-, h) **1.** v/t. gather; collect (stamps, etc.); sich ~ gather; fig.: concentrate; compose o.s.; **2.** v/i. collect money (für for); '~platz m meeting-place, place of appointment; ✗, 🜊 rendezvous.

Samml|er ['zamlər] m (-s/-) collector; '~ung f **1.** (-/-en) collection; **2.** fig. (-/no pl.) composure; concentration.

Samstag ['zamstaːk] m Saturday.

samt[1] [zamt] **1.** adv.: ~ und sonders one and all; **2.** prp. (dat.) together or along with.

Samt[2] [zamt] m (-[e]s/-e) velvet.

sämtlich ['zɛmtlɪç] **1.** adj. all (together); complete; **2.** adv. all (together or of them).

Sanatorium [zanaˈtoːrjum] n (-s/Sanatorien) sanatorium, Am. a. sanitarium.

Sand [zant] m (-[e]s/-e) sand; j-m ~ in die Augen streuen throw dust into s.o.'s eyes; im ~e verlaufen end in smoke, come to nothing.

Sandale [zanˈdaːlə] f (-/-n) sandal.

'**Sand|bahn** f sports: dirt-track; '~bank f sandbank; '~boden m sandy soil; '~grube f sand-pit; 2**ig** ['~dɪç] sandy; '~korn n grain of sand; '~mann fig. m (-[e]s/no pl.) sandman, dustman; '~papier n sandpaper; '~sack m sand-bag; '~stein m sandstone.

sandte ['zantə] pret. of senden.

'**Sand|torte** f Madeira cake; '~uhr f sand-glass; '~wüste f sandy desert.

sanft adj. [zanft] soft; gentle, mild; smooth; slope, death, etc.: easy; ~er Zwang non-violent coercion; mit ~er Stimme softly, gently; ~**mütig** adj. ['~myːtɪç] gentle, mild; meek.

sang [zaŋ] pret. of singen.

Sänger ['zɛŋər] m (-s/-) singer.

Sanguini|ker [zaŋguˈiːnikər] m (-s/-) sanguine person; 2**sch** adj. sanguine.

sanier|en [zaˈniːrən] v/t. (no -ge-, h) improve the sanitary conditions of; esp. †: reorganize; readjust; 2**ung** f (-/-en) sanitation; esp. †: reorganization; readjustment.

sanitär *adj.* [zaniˈtɛːr] sanitary.

Sanität|er [zaniˈtɛːtər] *m* (-s/-) ambulance man; ✕ medical orderly.

sank [zaŋk] *pret. of sinken.*

Sankt [zaŋkt] Saint, St.

sann [zan] *pret. of sinnen.*

Sard|elle *ichth.* [zarˈdɛlə] *f* (-/-n) anchovy; ⸗ine *ichth.* [⸗iːnə] *f* (-/-n) sardine.

Sarg [zark] *m* (-[e]s/ᵘe) coffin, *Am. a.* casket; ⸗deckel *m* coffin-lid.

Sarkas|mus [zarˈkasmus] *m* (-/⸗, Sarkasmen) sarcasm; ⸗tisch *adj.* [⸗tiʃ] sarcastic.

saß [zaːs] *pret. of sitzen.*

Satan [ˈzɑːtan] *m* (-s/-e) Satan; *fig.* devil; ⸗isch *fig. adj.* [zaˈtɑːniʃ] satanic.

Satellit *ast.,pol.* [zatɛˈliːt] *m* (-en/-en) satellite; ⸗enstaat *pol. m* satellite state.

Satin [saˈtɛ̃ː] *m* (-s/-s) satin; sateen.

Satir|e [zaˈtiːrə] *f* (-/-n) satire; ⸗iker [⸗ikər] *m* (-s/-) satirist; ⸗isch *adj.* satiric(al).

satt [zat] *adj.* [zat] satisfied, satiated, full; *colour:* deep, rich; *sich* ⸗ *essen* eat one's fill; *ich bin* ⸗ I have had enough; F *et.* ⸗ *haben* be tired *or* sick of s.th., *sl.* be fed up with s.th.

Sattel [ˈzatəl] *m* (-s/ᵘ) saddle; ⸗gurt *m* girth; ⸗n *v/t.* (ge-, h) saddle.

'Sattheit *f* (-/no *pl.*) satiety, fullness; richness, intensity (*of colours*).

sättigen ['zɛtigən] (ge-, h) 1. *v/t.* satisfy, satiate; ⸗, *phys.* saturate; 2. *v/i. food:* be substantial; ⸗ung *f* (-/-en) satiation; ⸗, *fig.* saturation.

Sattler [ˈzatlər] *m* (-s/-) saddler; ⸗ei [⸗ˈraɪ] *f* (-/-en) saddlery.

'sattsam *adv.* sufficiently.

Satz [zats] *m* (-es/ᵘe) *gr.* sentence, clause; *phls.* maxim; ⅋ proposition, theorem; ♪ movement; *tennis, etc.:* set; *typ.* setting, composition; sediment, dregs *pl.*, grounds *pl.*; rate (*of prices, etc.*); set (*of stamps, tools, etc.*); leap, bound.

'Satzung *f* (-/-en) statute, by-law; ⸗sgemäß *adj.* statutory.

'Satzzeichen *gr. n* punctuation mark.

Sau [zau] *f* 1. (-/ᵘe) *zo.* sow; *fig. contp.* filthy swine; 2. *hunt.* (-/-en) wild sow.

sauber *adj.* [ˈzaubər] clean; neat (*a. fig.*), tidy; *attitude:* decent; *iro.* fine, nice; 'Skeit *f* (-/no *pl.*) clean(li)ness; tidiness, neatness, decency (*of attitude*).

säuber|n [ˈzɔybərn] *v/t.* (ge-, h) clean(se); tidy, clean up (*room, etc.*); clear (*von* of); purge (of, from) (*a. fig., pol.*); 'Sungsaktion *pol. f* purge.

sauer [ˈzauər] 1. *adj.* sour (*a. fig.*), acid (*a.* ⸗); *cucumber:* pickled; *task, etc.:* hard, painful; *fig.* morose,

surly; 2. *adv.:* ⸗ *reagieren auf et.* take s.th. in bad part.

säuer|lich *adj.* [ˈzɔyərliç] sourish, acidulous; ⸗n *v/t.* (ge-, h) (make) sour, acidify (*a.* ⸗); leaven (*dough*).

'Sauer|stoff ⸗ *m* (-[e]s/no *pl.*) oxygen; ⸗teig *m* leaven.

saufen [ˈzaufən] *v/t. and v/i.* (irr., ge-, h) *animals:* drink; F *p. sl.* soak, lush.

Säufer F [ˈzɔyfər] *m* (-s/-) sot, *sl.* soak.

saugen [ˈzaugən] (irr., ge-, h) 1. *v/i.* suck (*an et. s.th.*); 2. *v/t.* suck.

säuge|n [ˈzɔygən] *v/t.* (ge-, h) suckle, nurse; 'Stier *n* mammal.

Säugling [ˈzɔyklɪŋ] *m* (-s/-e) baby, suckling; ⸗sheim *n* baby-farm, baby-nursery.

'Saug|papier *n* absorbent paper; ⸗pumpe *f* suction-pump; ⸗wirkung *f* suction-effect.

Säule [ˈzɔylə] *f* (-/-n) △, *anat.* column (*a. of smoke, mercury, etc.*); pillar, support (*both a. fig.*); ⸗ngang *m* colonnade; ⸗nhalle *f* pillared hall; portico.

Saum [zaum] *m* (-[e]s/ᵘe) seam, hem; border, edge.

säum|en [ˈzɔymən] *v/t.* (ge-, h) hem; border, edge; *die Straßen* ⸗ line the streets; '⸗ig *adj. payer:* dilatory.

'Saum|pfad *m* mule-track; '⸗tier *n* sumpter-mule.

Säure [ˈzɔyrə] *f* (-/-n) sourness; acidity (*a.* ⸗ *of stomach*); ⸗ acid.

Saure'gurkenzeit *f* silly *or* slack season.

säuseln [ˈzɔyzəln] (ge-, h) 1. *v/i. leaves, wind:* rustle, whisper; 2. *v/t. p.* say airily, purr.

sausen [ˈzauzən] *v/i.* (ge-) 1. (sein) F rush, dash; *bullet, etc.:* whiz(z), whistle; 2. (h) *wind:* whistle, sough.

'Saustall *m* pigsty; F *fig. a.* horrid mess.

Saxophon ♪ [zaksoˈfoːn] *n* (-s/-e) saxophone.

Schab|e [ˈʃɑːbə] *f* (-/-n) *zo.* cockroach; ⊕ *s. Schabeisen;* ⸗efleisch *n* scraped meat; ⸗eisen ⊕ *n* scraper, shaving-tool; ⸗emesser ⊕ *n* scraping-knife; 'Sen *v/t.* (ge-, h) scrape (*a.* ⊕); grate, rasp; scratch; ⸗er ⊕ *m* (-s/-) scraper.

Schabernack [ˈʃɑːbərnak] *m* (-[e]s/-e) practical joke, hoax, prank.

schäbig *adj.* [ˈʃɛːbiç] shabby (*a. fig.*), F seedy, *Am.* F *a.* dowdy, tacky; *fig.* mean.

Schablone [ʃaˈbloːnə] *f* (-/-n) model, pattern; stencil; *fig.:* routine; cliché; 2haft *adj.*, 2nmäßig *adj.* according to pattern; *fig.:* mechanical; *attr. a.* routine.

Schach [ʃax] *n* (-s/-s) chess; ⸗! check!; ⸗ *und matt!* checkmate!;

in or im ~ *halten* keep *s.o.* in check; '~**brett** *n* chessboard.

schachern ['ʃaxərn] *v/i.* (ge-, h) haggle (*um* about, over), chaffer (about, over), *Am. a.* dicker; ~ *mit* barter (away).

'**Schach|feld** *n* square; '~**figur** *f* chess-man, piece; *fig.* pawn; '2-'**matt** *adj.* (check)mated; *fig.* tired out, worn out; '~**spiel** *n* game of chess. [*a.* pit.]

Schacht [ʃaxt] *m* (-[e]s/⸚e) shaft; ⚒

Schachtel ['ʃaxtəl] *f* (-/-n) box; F *alte* ~ old frump.

'**Schachzug** *m* move (at chess); *geschickter* ~ clever move (*a. fig.*).

schade *pred. adj.* ['ʃaːdə]: *es ist* ~ it is a pity; *wie* ~! what a pity!; *zu* ~ *für* too good for.

Schädel ['ʃɛːdəl] *m* (-s/-) skull; cranium; '~**bruch** ⚕ *m* fracture of the skull.

schaden ['ʃaːdən] 1. *v/i.* (ge-, h) damage, injure, harm, hurt (*j-m s.o.*); be detrimental (to *s.o.*); *das schadet nichts* it does not matter, never mind; 2. 2 *m* (-s/⸚) damage (*an dat.* to); injury, harm; infirmity; hurt; loss; '~**ersatz** *m* indemnification, compensation; damages *pl.*; ~ *verlangen* claim damages; ~ *leisten* pay damages; *auf* ~ *(ver)klagen* ⚖ sue for damages; '2**freude** *f* malicious enjoyment of others' misfortunes, schadenfreude; '~**froh** *adj.* rejoicing over others' misfortunes.

schadhaft *adj.* ['ʃaːthaft] damaged; defective, faulty; *building, etc.*: dilapidated; *pipe, etc.*: leaking; *tooth, etc.*: decayed.

schädig|en ['ʃɛːdigən] *v/t.* (ge-, h) damage, impair; wrong, harm; '2**ung** *f* (-/-en) damage (*gen.* to), impairment (of); prejudice (to).

schädli|ch *adj.* ['ʃɛːtliç] harmful, injurious; noxious; detrimental, prejudicial; 2**ng** *m* ['~ŋ] *m* (-s/-e) zo. pest; ⚘ destructive weed; noxious person; ~*e pl.* ⚰ *a.* vermin.

schadlos *adj.* ['ʃaːtloːs]: *sich* ~ *halten* recoup *or* idemnify o.s. (*für* for).

Schaf [ʃaːf] *n* (-[e]s/-e) zo. sheep; *fig.* simpleton; '~**bock** zo. *m* ram.

Schäfer ['ʃɛːfər] *m* (-s/-) shepherd; '~**hund** *m* sheep-dog; Alsatian (wolf-hound).

Schaffell ['ʃaːf⁹-] *n* sheepskin.

schaffen ['ʃafən] 1. *v/t.* (*irr.,* ge-, h) create, produce; 2. *v/t.* (ge-, h) convey, carry, move; take, bring; cope with, manage; 3. *v/i.* (ge-, h) be busy, work.

Schaffner ['ʃafnər] *m* (-s/-) ⚏ guard, *Am.* conductor; *tram, bus*: conductor.

'**Schafhirt** *m* shepherd.

Schafot [ʃaˈfɔt] *n* (-[e]s/-e) scaffold.

'**Schaf|pelz** *m* sheepskin coat; '~**stall** *m* fold.

Schaft [ʃaft] *m* (-[e]s/⸚e) shaft (*of lance, column, etc.*); stick (*of flag*); stock (*of rifle*); shank (*of tool, key, etc.*); leg (*of boot*); '~**stiefel** *m* high boot; ~ *pl. a.* Wellingtons *pl.*

'**Schaf|wolle** *f* sheep's wool; '~**zucht** *f* sheep-breeding, sheep-farming.

schäkern ['ʃɛːkərn] *v/i.* (ge-, h) jest, joke; flirt.

schal[1] *adj.* [ʃaːl] insipid; stale; *fig. a.* flat.

Schal[2] [~] *m* (-s/-e, -s) scarf, muffler; comforter.

Schale ['ʃaːlə] *f* (-/-n) bowl; ⊕ scale (*of scales*); shell (*of eggs, nuts, etc.*); peel, skin (*of fruit*); shell, crust (*of tortoise*); paring, peeling; F: *sich in* ~ *werfen* doll o.s. up.

schälen ['ʃɛːlən] *v/t.* (ge-, h) remove the peel *or* skin from; pare, peel (*fruit, potatoes, etc.*); *sich* ~ *skin*: peel *or* come off.

Schalk [ʃalk] *m* (-[e]s/-e, ⸚e) rogue, wag; '2**haft** *adj.* roguish, waggish.

Schall [ʃal] *m* (-[e]s/-e, ⸚e) sound; '~**dämpfer** *m* sound absorber; *mot.* silencer, *Am.* muffler; silencer (*on fire-arms*); '2**dicht** *adj.* sound-proof; '2**en** *v/i.* (*[irr.,]* ge-, h) sound; ring, peal; '2**end** *adj.*: ~*es Gelächter* roars *pl. or* a peal of laughter; '~**mauer** *f* sound barrier; '~**platte** *f* record, disc, disk; '~**welle** *f* sound-wave.

schalt [ʃalt] *pret. of* schelten.

'**Schaltbrett** ⚡ *n* switchboard.

'**schalten** ['ʃaltən] (ge-, h) 1. *v/i.* ⚡ switch; *mot.* change *or* shift gears; direct, rule; 2. *v/t.* ⊕ actuate; operate, control.

'**Schalter** *m* (-s/-) ⚏, *theatre, etc.*: booking-office; ✉, *bank, etc.*: counter; ⚡ switch; ⊕, *mot.* controller.

'**Schalt|hebel** *m mot.* gear lever; ⊕, ⚙ control lever; ⚡ switch lever; '~**jahr** *n* leap-year; '~**tafel** ⚡ *f* switchboard, control panel; '~**tag** *m* intercalary day.

Scham [ʃaːm] *f* (-/*no pl.*) shame; bashfulness, modesty; *anat.* privy parts *pl.,* genitals *pl.*

schämen ['ʃɛːmən] *v/refl.* (ge-, h) be *or* feel ashamed (*gen. or wegen* of).

'**Scham|gefühl** *n* sense of shame; '2**haft** *adj.* bashful, modest; '~**haftigkeit** *f* (-/*no pl.*) bashfulness, modesty; '2**los** *adj.* shameless; impudent; '~**losigkeit** *f* (-/-*en*) shamelessness; impudence; '2**rot** *adj.* blushing; ~ *werden* blush; '~**röte** *f* blush; '~**teile** *anat. m/pl.* privy parts *pl.,* genitals *pl.*

Schande ['ʃandə] *f* (-/⚖-n) shame, disgrace.

schänden ['ʃɛndən] *v/t.* (ge-, h)

dishono(u)r, disgrace; desecrate, profane; rape, violate; disfigure.

Schandfleck fig. ['ʃant-] m blot, stain; eyesore.

schändlich adj. ['ʃɛntliç] shameful, disgraceful, infamous; **'ˌkeit** f (-/-en) infamy.

'Schandtat f infamous act(ion).

'Schändung f (-/-en) dishono(u)r-ing; profanation, desecration; rape, violation; disfigurement.

Schanze ['ʃantsə] f (-/-n) ✕ en-trenchment; ⚓ quarter-deck; sports: ski-jump; **'ˌn** v/i. (ge-, h) throw up entrenchments, entrench.

Schar [ʃaːr] f (-/-en) troop, band; geese, etc.: flock; ✗ ploughshare, Am. plowshare; **'ˌen** v/t. (ge-, h) assemble, collect; sich ˌ a. flock (um round).

scharf [ʃarf] 1. adj. sharp; edge: keen; voice, sound: piercing, shrill; smell, taste: pungent; pepper, etc.: hot; sight, hearing, intelligence, etc.: keen; answer, etc.: cutting; ✕ am-munition: live; ˌ sein auf (acc.) be very keen on; 2. adv.: ˌ ansehen look sharply at; ˌ reiten ride hard; **'ˌblick** fig. m (-[e]s/no pl.) clear-sightedness.

Schärfe ['ʃɛrfə] f (-/-n) sharpness, keenness; pungency; **'ˌn** v/t. (ge-, h) put an edge on, sharpen; strengthen (memory); sharpen (sight, hearing, etc.).

'Scharf|macher fig. m (-s/-) fire-brand, agitator; **'ˌrichter** m ex-ecutioner; **'ˌschütze** ✕ m sharp-shooter, sniper; **'ˌsichtig** adj. sharp-sighted; fig. clear-sighted; **'ˌsinn** m (-[e]s/no pl.) sagacity; acumen; **'ˌsinnig** adj. sharp-witted, shrewd; sagacious.

Scharlach ['ʃarlax] m 1. (-s/-e) scarlet; 2. ❧ (-s/no pl.) scarlet fever; **'ˌrot** adj. scarlet.

Scharlatan ['ʃarlatan] m (-s/-e) charlatan, quack (doctor); mounte-bank.

Scharmützel [ʃar'mytsəl] n (-s/-) skirmish.

Scharnier ⊕ [ʃar'niːr] n (-s/-e) hinge, joint.

Schärpe ['ʃɛrpə] f (-/-n) sash.

scharren ['ʃarən] (ge-, h) 1. v/i. scrape (mit den Füßen one's feet); hen, etc.: scratch; horse: paw; 2. v/t. horse: paw (ground).

Schart|e ['ʃartə] f (-/-n) notch, nick; mountains: gap, Am. notch; e-e ˌ auswetzen repair a fault; wipe out a disgrace; **'ˌig** adj. jagged, notchy.

Schatten ['ʃatən] m (-s/-) shadow (a. fig.); shade (a. paint.); **'ˌbild** n silhouette; **'ˌhaft** adj. shadowy; **'ˌkabinett** pol. n shadow cabinet; **'ˌriß** m silhouette; **'ˌseite** f shady side; fig. seamy side.

schattier|en [ʃa'tiːrən] v/t. (no -ge-, h) shade, tint; **ˌung** f (-/-en) shading; shade (a. fig.), tint.

'schattig adj. shady.

Schatz [ʃats] m (-es/ˌe) treasure; fig. sweetheart, darling; **'ˌamt** † n Exchequer, Am. Treasury (Department); **'ˌanweisung** † f Treasury Bond, Am. a. Treasury Note.

schätzen ['ʃɛtsən] v/t. (ge-, h) esti-mate; value (auf acc. at); price (at); rate; appreciate; esteem; sich glück-lich ˌ zu inf. be delighted to inf.; **'ˌswert** adj. estimable.

'Schatz|kammer f treasury; **'ˌmeister** m treasurer.

'Schätzung f 1. (-/-en) estimate, valuation; rating; 2. (-/no pl.) ap-preciation, estimation; esteem.

'Schatzwechsel † m Treasury Bill.

Schau [ʃau] f (-/-en) inspection; show, exhibition; zur ˌ stellen exhibit, display.

Schauder ['ʃaudər] m (-s/-) shud-der(ing), shiver, tremor; fig. horror, terror; **'ˌhaft** adj. horrible, dread-ful; F fig. a. awful; **'ˌn** v/i. (ge-, h) shudder, shiver (both: vor dat. at).

schauen ['ʃauən] v/i. (ge-, h) look (auf acc. at).

Schauer ['ʃauər] m (-s/-) rain, etc.: shower (a. fig.); shudder(ing), shiver; attack, fit; thrill; **'ˌlich** adj. dreadful, horrible; **'ˌn** v/i. (ge-, h) s. schaudern; **'ˌroman** m penny dreadful, thriller.

Schaufel ['ʃaufəl] f (-/-n) shovel; dust-pan; **'ˌn** v/t. and v/i. (ge-, h) shovel.

'Schaufenster n shop window, Am. a. show-window; **'ˌbummel** m: e-n ˌ machen go window-shopping; **'ˌdekoration** f window-dressing; **'ˌeinbruch** m smash-and-grab raid.

Schaukel ['ʃaukəl] f (-/-n) swing; **'ˌn** (ge-, h) 1. v/i. swing; ship, etc.: rock; 2. v/t. rock (baby, etc.); **'ˌpferd** n rocking-horse; **'ˌstuhl** m rocking-chair, Am. a. rocker.

Schaum [ʃaum] m (-[e]s/ˌe) foam; beer, etc.: froth, head; soap: lather; **'ˌbad** n bubble bath.

schäumen ['ʃɔymən] v/i. (ge-, h) foam, froth; lather; wine, etc.: sparkle.

'Schaum|gummi n, m foam rub-ber; **'ˌig** adj. foamy, frothy; **'ˌwein** m sparkling wine.

'Schau|platz m scene (of action), theat|re, Am. -er; **'ˌprozeß** ⚖ m show trial.

schaurig adj. ['ʃauriç] horrible, horrid.

'Schau|spiel n spectacle; thea. play; **'ˌspieler** m actor, player; **'ˌspiel-haus** n playhouse, theat|re, Am. -er; **'ˌspielkunst** f (-/no pl.) dramatic art, *the* drama; '~steller *m* (-s/-) showman.

Scheck † [ʃɛk] *m* (-s/-s) cheque, *Am.* check; '~buch *n*, '~heft *n* cheque-book, *Am.* checkbook.

'scheckig *adj.* spotted; *horse:* pie-bald.

scheel [ʃe:l] **1.** *adj.* squint-eyed, cross-eyed; *fig.* jealous, envious; **2.** *adv.*: j-n ~ ansehen look askance at s.o.

Scheffel ['ʃɛfəl] *m* (-s/-) bushel; '2n *v/t.* (ge-, h) amass (*money, etc.*).

Scheibe ['ʃaibə] *f* (-/-n) disk, disc (*a. of sun, moon*); *esp. ast.* orb; slice (*of bread, etc.*); pane (*of window*); *shooting:* target; '~nhonig *m* honey in combs; '~nwischer *mot. m* (-s/-) wind-screen wiper, *Am.* windshield wiper.

Scheide ['ʃaidə] *f* (-/-n) sword, *etc.*: sheath, scabbard; border, boundary; '~münze *f* small coin; '2n (*irr.,* ge-) **1.** *v/t.* (h) separate; 🜍 analyse; ♂ divorce; *sich* ~ *lassen von* ♂ divorce (*one's husband or wife*); **2.** *v/i.* (sein) depart; part (*von* with); *aus dem Dienst* ~ retire from service; *aus dem Leben* ~ depart from this life; '~wand *f* partition; '~weg *fig. m* cross-roads *sg.*

'Scheidung *f* (-/-en) separation; ♂ divorce; ~sgrund ♂ *m* ground for divorce; '~sklage ♂ *f* divorce-suit; *die* ~ *einreichen* file a petition for divorce.

Schein [ʃain] *m* **1.** (-[e]s/*no pl.*) shine; *sun, lamp, etc.*: light; *fire:* blaze; *fig.* appearance; **2.** (-[e]s/-e) certificate; receipt; bill; (bank-)note; '2bar *adj.* seeming, apparent; '2en (*irr.,* ge-, h) shine; *fig.* seem, appear, look; '~grund *m* pretext, preten|ce, *Am.* -se; '2heilig *adj.* sanctimonious, hypocritical; '~tod ♂ *m* suspended animation; '2tot *adj.* in a state of suspended animation; '~werfer *m* (-s/-) reflector, projector; ✕, ⚓, ✈ searchlight; *mot.* headlight; *thea.* spotlight.

Scheit [ʃait] *n* (-[e]s/-e) log, billet.

Scheitel ['ʃaitəl] *m* (-s/-) crown *or* top of the head; *hair:* parting; summit, peak; *esp.* Ⓐ vertex; '2n *v/t.* (ge-, h) part (*hair*).

Scheiterhaufen ['ʃaitər-] *m* (funeral) pile; stake.

'scheitern *v/i.* (ge-, sein) ⚓ run aground, be wrecked; *fig.* fail, miscarry.   [box on the ear.]

Schelle ['ʃɛlə] *f* (-/-n) (little) bell;
'Schellfisch *ichth. m* haddock.

Schelm [ʃɛlm] *m* (-[e]s/-e) rogue; '~enstreich *m* roguish trick; '2isch *adj.* roguish, arch.

Schelte ['ʃɛltə] *f* (-/-n) scolding; '2n (*irr.,* ge-, h) **1.** *v/t.* scold, rebuke; **2.** *v/i.* scold.

Schema ['ʃe:ma] *n* (-s/-s, -ta, Schemen) scheme; model, pattern; arrangement; 2tisch *adj.* [ʃe'ma:tiʃ] schematic.

Schemel ['ʃe:məl] *m* (-s/-) stool.

Schemen ['ʃe:mən] *m* (-s/-) phantom, shadow; '2haft *adj.* shadowy.

Schenke ['ʃɛŋkə] *f* (-/-n) public house, F pub; tavern, inn.

Schenkel ['ʃɛŋkəl] *m* (-s/-) *anat.* thigh; *anat.* shank; *triangle, etc.*: leg; Ⓐ *angle:* side.

schenken ['ʃɛŋkən] *v/t.* (ge-, h) give; remit (*penalty, etc.*); j-m et. ~ give s.o. s.th., present s.o. with s.th., make s.o. a present of s.th.

'Schenkung ♂ *f* (-/-en) donation; ~surkunde ♂ ['ʃɛŋkuŋsʔ-] *f* deed of gift.

Scherbe ['ʃɛrbə] *f* (-/-n), '~n *m* (-s/-) (broken) piece, fragment.

Schere ['ʃe:rə] *f* (-/-n) (e-e a pair of) scissors *pl.*; *zo.* crab, *etc.*: claw; '2n *v/t.* **1.** (*irr.,* ge-, h) shear (*a. sheep*), clip; shave (*beard*); cut (*hair*); clip, prune (*hedge*); **2.** (ge-, h): *sich um et.* ~ trouble about s.th.; '~nschleifer *m* (-s/-) knife-grinder; ~rei [~'rai] *f* (-/-en) trouble, bother.

Scherz [ʃɛrts] *m* (-es/-e) jest, joke; ~ *beiseite* joking apart; *im* ~, *zum* ~ in jest *or* joke; '~ *treiben mit* make fun of; '2en *v/i.* (ge-, h) jest, joke; '2haft *adj.* joking, sportive.

scheu [ʃɔy] **1.** *adj.* shy, bashful, timid; *horse:* skittish; ~ *machen* frighten; **2.** 2 *f* (-/*no pl.*) shyness, timidity; aversion (*vor dat.* to).

scheuchen ['ʃɔyçən] *v/t.* (ge-, h) scare, frighten (away).

'scheuen (ge-, h) **1.** *v/i.* shy (*vor dat.* at), take fright (at); **2.** *v/t.* shun, avoid; fear; *sich* ~ *vor* (*dat.*) shy at, be afraid of.

Scheuer|lappen ['ʃɔyər-] *m* scouring-cloth, floor-cloth; '~leiste *f* skirting-board; '2n (ge-, h) **1.** *v/t.* scour, scrub; chafe; **2.** *v/i.* chafe.

'Scheuklappe *f* blinker, *Am.* a. blinder.

Scheune ['ʃɔynə] *f* (-/-n) barn.

Scheusal ['ʃɔyza:l] *n* (-[e]s/-e) monster.

scheußlich *adj.* ['ʃɔyslɪç] hideous, atrocious (F *a. fig.*), abominable (F *a. fig.*); '2keit *f* **1.** (-/*no pl.*) hideousness; **2.** (-/-en) abomination; atrocity.

Schi [ʃi:] *m* (-s/-er) *etc.* s. Ski, *etc.*

Schicht [ʃiçt] *f* (-/-en) layer; *geol.* stratum (*a. fig.*); *at work:* shift; (social) class, rank, walk of life; '2en *v/t.* (ge-, h) arrange *or* put in layers, pile up; classify; '2weise *adv.* in layers; *work:* in shifts.

Schick [ʃik] **1.** *m* (-[e]s/*no pl.*) chic, elegance, style; **2.** 2 *adj.* chic, stylish, fashionable.

schicken ['ʃikən] *v/t.* (ge-, h) send

(*nach, zu* to); remit (*money*); nach j-m ~ send for s.o.; sich ~ für become, suit, befit *s.o.*; sich ~ in put up with, resign o.s. to *s.th.*

'**schicklich** *adj.* becoming, proper, seemly; '2keit *f* (-/*no pl.*) propriety, seemliness.

'**Schicksal** *n* (-[e]s/-e) fate, destiny.

Schiebe|dach *mot.* ['ʃiːbə-] *n* sliding roof; '**.fenster** *n* sash-window; '2n (*irr.*, ge-, h) 1. *v/t.* push, shove; shift (*blame*) (auf *acc.* on to); F *fig.* sell on the black market; 2. F *fig. v/i.* profiteer; '**.r** *m* (-s/-) bolt (*of door*); ⊕ slide; *fig.* profiteer, black marketeer, *sl.* spiv; '**.tür** *f* sliding door.

'**Schiebung** *fig. f* (-/-en) black marketeering, profiteering; put-up job.

schied [ʃiːt] *pret. of* scheiden.

Schieds|gericht ['ʃiːts-] *n* court of arbitration, arbitration committee; '**.richter** *m* arbitrator; *tennis, etc.:* umpire; *football, etc.:* referee; '2richterlich *adj.* arbitral; '**.spruch** *m* award, arbitration.

schief [ʃiːf] 1. *adj.* sloping, slanting, oblique; *face, mouth:* wry; *fig.* false, wrong; **.e** Ebene A inclined plane; 2. *adv.:* j-n ~ ansehen look askance at s.o.

Schiefer ['ʃiːfər] *m* (-s/-) slate; splinter; '**.stift** *m* slate-pencil; '**.tafel** *f* slate.

'**schiefgehen** *v/i.* (*irr. gehen, sep.,* -ge-, sein) go wrong or awry.

schielen ['ʃiːlən] *v/i.* (ge-, h) squint, be cross-eyed; ~ auf (*acc.*) squint at; leer at.

schien [ʃiːn] *pret. of* scheinen.

Schienbein ['ʃiːn-] *n* shin(-bone), tibia.

Schiene ['ʃiːnə] *f* (-/-n) ⛟, *etc.:* rail; ⚕ splint; '2n *v/t.* (ge-, h) splint.

schießen ['ʃiːsən] (*irr.*, ge-) 1. *v/t.* (h) shoot; tot ~ shoot dead; *ein Tor* ~ score (a goal); *Salut* ~ fire a salute; 2. *v/i.* (h): auf j-n ~ shoot or fire at; gut ~ be a good shot; 3. *v/i.* (sein) shoot, dart, rush.

'**Schieß|pulver** *n* gunpowder; '**.scharte** *f* loop-hole, embrasure; '**.scheibe** *f* target; '**.stand** *m* shooting-gallery *or* -range.

Schiff [ʃif] *n* (-[e]s/-e) ⛵ ship, vessel; △ *church:* nave.

Schiffahrt ['ʃifaːrt] *f* (-/-en) navigation.

'**schiff|bar** *adj.* navigable; '2bau *m* shipbuilding; '2bauer *m* (-s/-) shipbuilder; '2bruch *m* shipwreck (*a. fig.*); ~ erleiden be shipwrecked; *fig.* make *or* suffer shipwreck; '**.brüchig** *adj.* shipwrecked; '2brücke *f* pontoon-bridge; '**.en** *v/i.* (ge-, sein) navigate, sail; '2er

15*

m (-s/-) sailor; boatman; navigator; skipper.

'**Schiffs|junge** *m* cabin-boy; '**.kapitän** *m* (sea-)captain; '**.ladung** *f* shipload; cargo; '**.makler** *m* shipbroker; '**.mannschaft** *f* crew; '**.raum** *m* hold; tonnage; '**.werft** *f* shipyard, *esp.* ⚓ dockyard, *Am. a.* navy yard.

Schikan|e [ʃiˈkaːnə] *f* (-/-n) vexation, nasty trick; '2ieren [.kaˈniːrən] *v/t.* (*no* -ge-, h) vex, ride.

Schild [ʃilt] 1. ⚔ *m* (-[e]s/-e) shield, buckler; 2. *n* (-[e]s/-er) shop, *etc.:* sign(board), facia; name-plate; *traffic:* signpost; label; *cap:* peak; '**.drüse** *anat. f* thyroid gland.

'**Schilder|haus** ⚔ *n* sentry-box; '**.maler** *m* sign-painter; '2n *v/t.* (ge-, h) describe, delineate; '**.ung** *f* (-/-en) description, delineation.

'**Schild|kröte** *zo. f* tortoise; turtle; '**.wache** ⚔ *f* sentinel, sentry.

Schilf ♣ [ʃilf] *n* (-[e]s/-e) reed; '2ig *adj.* reedy; '**.rohr** *n* reed.

schillern ['ʃilərn] *v/i.* (ge-, h) show changing colo(u)rs; be iridescent.

Schimmel ['ʃiməl] *m* 1. *zo.* (-s/-) white horse; 2. ♣ (-s/*no pl.*) mo(u)ld, mildew; '2ig *adj.* mo(u)ldy, musty; '2n *v/i.* (ge-, h) become mo(u)ldy, *Am. a.* mo(u)ld.

Schimmer ['ʃimər] *m* (-s/*no pl.*) glimmer, gleam (*a. fig.*); '2n *v/i.* (ge-, h) glimmer, gleam.

Schimpanse *zo.* [ʃimˈpanzə] *m* (-n/-n) chimpanzee.

Schimpf [ʃimpf] *m* (-[e]s/-e) insult; disgrace; mit ~ und Schande ignominiously; '2en (ge-, h) 1. *v/i.* rail (*über acc., auf acc.* at, against); 2. *v/t.* scold; j-n e-n Lügner ~ call s.o. a liar; '2lich *adj.* disgraceful (*für* to), ignominious (to); '**.name** *m* abusive name; '**.wort** *n* term of abuse; ~ *pl. a.* invectives *pl.*

Schindel ['ʃindəl] *f* (-/-n) shingle.

schinden ['ʃindən] *v/t.* (*irr.*, ge-, h) flay, skin (*rabbit, etc.*); sweat (*worker*); sich ~ drudge, slave, sweat.

'**Schinder** *m* (-s/-) knacker; *fig.* sweater, slave-driver; '**.ei** *fig.* [.'raı] *f* (-/-en) sweating; drudgery, grind.

Schinken ['ʃiŋkən] *m* (-s/-) ham.

Schippe ['ʃipə] *f* (-/-n) shovel; '2n *v/t.* (ge-, h) shovel.

Schirm [ʃirm] *m* (-[e]s/-e) umbrella, parasol, sunshade; *wind, television, etc.:* screen; *lamp:* shade; *cap:* peak, visor; '**.futteral** *n* umbrella-case; '**.herr** *m* protector; patron; '**.herrschaft** *f* protectorate; patronage; *unter der ~ von event:* under the auspices of; '**.mütze** *f* peaked cap; '**.ständer** *m* umbrella-stand.

Schlacht ⚔ [ʃlaxt] *f* (-/-en) battle (*bei* of); '**.bank** *f* shambles; '2en *v/t.* (ge-, h) slaughter, butcher.

Schlächter ['ʃlɛçtər] m (-s/-) butcher.

'Schlacht|feld ✕ n battle-field; '~haus n, '~hof m slaughter-house, abattoir; '~kreuzer ⚓ m battle-cruiser; '~plan m ✕ plan of action (a. fig.); '~schiff ⚓ n battleship; '~vieh n slaughter cattle.

Schlack|e ['ʃlakə] f (-/-n) wood, coal: cinder; metall. dross (a. fig.), slag; geol. scoria; '2ig adj. drossy, slaggy; F weather: slushy.

Schlaf [ʃlaːf] m (-[e]s/no pl.) sleep; im ~(e) in one's sleep; e-n leichten (festen) ~ haben be a light (sound) sleeper; in tiefem ~e liegen be fast asleep; '~abteil ⚓ n sleeping-compartment; '~anzug m (ein a pair of) pyjamas pl. or Am. pajamas pl.

Schläfchen ['ʃlɛːfçən] n (-s/-) doze, nap, F forty winks pl.; ein ~ machen take a nap, F have one's forty winks.

'Schlafdecke f blanket.

Schläfe ['ʃlɛːfə] f (-/-n) temple.

'schlafen v/i. (irr., ge-, h) sleep; ~ gehen, sich ~ legen go to bed.

schlaff adj. [ʃlaf] slack, loose; muscles, etc.: flabby, flaccid; plant, etc.: limp; discipline, morals, etc.: lax; '2heit f (-/no pl.) slackness; flabbiness; limpness; fig. laxity.

'Schlaf|gelegenheit f sleeping accommodation; '~kammer f bedroom; '~krankheit ⚕ f sleeping-sickness; '~lied n lullaby; '2los adj. sleepless; '~losigkeit f (-/no pl.) sleeplessness; ~ insomnia; '~mittel ⚕ n soporific; '~mütze f nightcap; fig. sleepyhead.

schläfrig adj. ['ʃlɛːfriç] sleepy, drowsy; '2keit f (-/no pl.) sleepiness, drowsiness.

'Schlaf|rock m dressing-gown, Am. a. robe; '~saal m dormitory; '~sack m sleeping-bag; '~stelle f sleeping-place; night's lodging; '~tablette ⚕ f sleeping-tablet; '2trunken adj. very drowsy; '~wagen ⚘ m sleeping-car(riage), Am. a. sleeper; ~wandler ['~vandlər] m (-s/-) sleep-walker, somnambulist; '~zimmer n bedroom.

Schlag [ʃlaːk] m (-[e]s/~e) blow (a. fig.); stroke (of clock, piston) (a. tennis, etc.); slap (with palm of hand); punch (with fist); kick (of horse's hoof); ⚡ shock; beat (of heart or pulse); clap (of thunder); warbling (of bird); door (of carriage); ⚕ apoplexy; fig. race, kind, sort; breed (esp. of animals); Schläge bekommen get a beating; ~ sechs Uhr on the stroke of six; '~ader anat. f artery; '~anfall ⚕ m (stroke of) apoplexy, stroke; '2artig 1. adj. sudden, abrupt; 2. adv. all of a sudden; '~baum m turnpike.

schlagen ['ʃlaːgən] (irr., ge-, h) 1. v/t. strike, beat, hit; punch; slap; beat, defeat; fell (trees); fight (battle); Alarm ~ sound the alarm; zu Boden ~ knock down; in den Wind ~ cast or fling to the winds; sich ~ (have a) fight; sich et. aus dem Kopf or Sinn ~ put s.th. out of one's mind, dismiss s.th. from one's mind; 2. v/i. strike, beat; heart, pulse: beat, throb; clock: strike; bird: warble; das schlägt nicht in mein Fach that is not in my line; um sich ~ lay about one; '~d fig. adj. striking.

Schlager ['ʃlaːgər] m (-s/-) ♪ song hit; thea. hit, draw, box-office success; book: best seller.

Schläger ['ʃlɛːgər] m (-s/-) rowdy, hooligan; cricket, etc.: batsman; horse: kicker; cricket, etc.: bat; golf: club; tennis, etc.: racket; hockey, etc.: stick; ~ei [~'raɪ] f (-/-en) tussle, fight.

'schlag|fertig fig. adj. quick at repartee; ~ен Antwort repartee; '2fertigkeit fig. f (-/no pl.) quickness at repartee; '2instrument ♪ n percussion instrument; '2kraft f (-/no pl.) striking power (a. ✕); '2loch n pot-hole; '2mann m rowing: stroke; '2ring m knuckleduster, Am. a. brass knuckles pl.; '2sahne f whipped cream; '2schatten m cast shadow; '2seite ⚓ f list; ~ haben ⚓ list; F fig. be half-seas-over; '2uhr f striking clock; '2werk n clock: striking mechanism; '2wort n catchword, slogan; '2zeile f headline; banner headline, Am. banner; '2zeug ♪ n in orchestra: percussion instruments pl.; in band: drums pl., percussion; '2zeuger ♪ m (-s/-) in orchestra: percussionist; in band: drummer.

schlaksig adj. ['ʃlaːkzɪç] gawky.

Schlamm [ʃlam] m (-[e]s/✎ -e, ✎e) mud, mire; '~bad n mud-bath; '2ig adj. muddy, miry.

Schlämmkreide ['ʃlɛm-] f (-/no pl.) whit(en)ing.

Schlampe ['ʃlampə] f (-/-n) slut, slattern; '2ig adj. slovenly, slipshod.

schlang [ʃlaŋ] pret. of schlingen.

Schlange ['ʃlaŋə] f (-/-n) zo. snake, rhet. serpent (a. fig.); fig.: snake in the grass; queue, Am. a. line; ~ stehen queue up (um for), Am. line up (for).

schlängeln ['ʃlɛŋəln] v/refl. (ge-, h): sich ~ durch person: worm one's way or o.s. through; path, river, etc.: wind (one's way) through, meander through.

'Schlangenlinie f serpentine line.

schlank adj. [ʃlaŋk] slender, slim; '2heit f (-/no pl.) slenderness, slimness; '2heitskur f: e-e ~ machen slim.

schlapp F adj. [ʃlap] tired, exhausted,

worn out; '2e F f (-/-n) reverse, setback; defeat; '~machen F v/i. (sep., -ge-, h) break down, faint.

schlau adj. [ʃlaʊ] sly, cunning; crafty, clever, F cute.

Schlauch [ʃlaʊx] m (-[e]s/ᵉe) tube; hose; car, etc.: inner tube; '~boot n rubber dinghy, pneumatic boat.

Schlaufe ['ʃlaʊfə] f (-/-n) loop.

schlecht [ʃlɛçt] 1. adj. bad; wicked; poor; temper: ill; quality: inferior; ~e Laune haben be in a bad temper; ~e Aussichten poor prospects; ~e Zeiten hard times; mir ist ~ I feel sick; 2. adv. badly, ill; ~erdings adv. ['~ʔər'dɪŋs] absolutely, downright, utterly; ~gelaunt adj. ['~gə-laʊnt] ill-humo(u)red, in a bad temper; '~'hin adv. plainly, simply; '2igkeit f (-/-en) badness, wickedness; ~en pl. base acts pl., mean tricks pl.; '~machen v/t. (sep., -ge-, h) run down, backbite; '~weg adv. ['~vɛk] plainly, simply.

schleich|en ['ʃlaɪçən] v/i. (irr., ge-, sein) creep (a. fig.); sneak, steal; '2er m (-s/-) creeper; fig. sneak; '2handel m illicit trade; smuggling, contraband; '2händler m smuggler, contrabandist; black marketeer; '2weg m secret path.

Schleier ['ʃlaɪər] m (-s/-) veil (a. fig.); mist: a. haze; den ~ nehmen take the veil; '2haft fig. adj. mysterious, inexplicable.

Schleife ['ʃlaɪfə] f (-/-n) loop (a. ℀); slip-knot; bow; wreath: streamer; loop, horse-shoe bend.

'schleif|en 1. v/t. (irr., ge-, h) whet (knife, etc.); cut (glass, precious stones); polish (a. fig.); 2. v/t. (ge-, h) ✗ slur; drag, trail; ✗ raze (fortress, etc.); 3. v/i. (ge-, h) drag, trail; '2stein m grindstone, whetstone.

Schleim [ʃlaɪm] m (-[e]s/-e) slime; ✗ mucus, phlegm; '~haut anat. f mucous membrane; '2ig adj. slimy (a. fig.); ~ mucous.

schlemm|en ['ʃlɛmən] v/i. (ge-, h) feast, gormandize; '2er m (-s/-) glutton, gormandizer; 2erei [~'raɪ] f (-/-en) feasting; gluttony.

schlen|dern ['ʃlɛndərn] v/i. (ge-, sein) stroll, saunter; 2drian ['~dria:n] m (-[e]s/no pl.) jogtrot; beaten track.

schlenkern ['ʃlɛŋkərn] (ge-, h) 1. v/t. dangle, swing; 2. v/i.: mit den Armen ~ swing one's arms.

Schlepp|dampfer ['ʃlɛp-] m steam tug, tug(boat); '~e f (-/-n) train (of woman's dress); '2en (ge-, h) 1. v/t. carry with difficulty, haul, Am. a. tote; ⊥, ℀, mot. tow, haul; ✝ tout (customers); sich ~ drag o.s.; 2. v/i. dress: drag, trail; '2end adj. speech: drawling; gait: shuffling; style: heavy; con-

versation, etc.: tedious; '~er ⊥ m (-s/-) steam tug, tug(boat); '~tau n tow(ing)-rope; ins ~ nehmen take in or on tow (a. fig.).

Schleuder ['ʃlɔʏdər] f (-/-n) sling, catapult (a. ℀), Am. a. slingshot; spin drier; 2n (ge-, h) 1. v/t. fling, hurl (a. fig.); sling, catapult (a. ℀); spin-dry (washing); 2. mot. v/i. skid; '~preis ✝ m ruinous or give-away price; zu ~en dirt-cheap.

schleunig adj. ['ʃlɔʏnɪç] prompt, speedy, quick.

Schleuse ['ʃlɔʏzə] f (-/-n) lock, sluice; 2n v/t. (ge-, h) lock (boat) (up or down); fig. manœuvre, Am. maneuver.

schlich [ʃlɪç] pret. of schleichen.

schlicht adj. [ʃlɪçt] plain, simple; modest, unpretentious; hair: smooth, sleek; '~en fig. v/t. (ge-, h) settle, adjust; settle by arbitration; '2er fig. m (-s/-) mediator; arbitrator.

schlief [ʃli:f] pret. of schlafen.

schließ|en ['ʃli:sən] (irr., ge-, h) 1. v/t. shut, close; shut down (factory, etc.), shut up (shop); contract (marriage); conclude (treaty, speech, etc.); parl. close (debate); in die Arme ~ clasp in one's arms; in sich ~ comprise, include; Freundschaft ~ make friends (mit with); 2. v/i. shut, close; school: break up; aus et. ~ auf (acc.) infer or conclude s.th. from s.th.; '2fach ☒ n post-office box; '~lich adv. finally, eventually; at last; after all.

Schliff [ʃlɪf] 1. m (-[e]s/-e) polish (a. fig.); precious stones, glass: cut; 2. 2 pret. of schleifen 1.

schlimm [ʃlɪm] 1. adj. bad; evil, wicked, nasty, serious; F ✗ bad, sore; ~er worse; am ~sten, das 2ste the worst; es wird immer ~er things are going from bad to worse; 2. adv.: ~ daran sein be badly off; '~sten'falls adv. at (the) worst.

Schling|e ['ʃlɪŋə] f (-/-n) loop, sling (a. ✗); noose; coil (of wire or rope); hunt. snare (a. fig.); den Kopf in die ~ stecken put one's head in the noose; '~el m (-s/-) rascal, naughty boy; '2en v/t. (irr., ge-, h) wind, twist; plait; die Arme ~ um (acc.) fling one's arms round; sich um et. ~ wind round; '~pflanze ♀ f creeper, climber.

Schlips [ʃlɪps] m (-es/-e) (neck)tie.

Schlitten ['ʃlɪtən] m (-s/-) sled(ge); sleigh; sports: toboggan.

'Schlittschuh m skate; ~ laufen skate; '~läufer m skater.

Schlitz [ʃlɪts] m (-es/-e) slit, slash; slot; '2en v/t. (ge-, h) slit, slash.

Schloß [ʃlɔs] 1. n (Schlosses/Schlösser) lock (of door, gun, etc.); castle; palace; ins ~ fallen door: snap to;

hinter ~ und *Riegel* behind prison bars; 2. ♀ *pret. of* schließen.

Schlosser ['ʃlɔsər] *m* (-s/-) locksmith; mechanic, fitter.

Schlot [ʃloːt] *m* (-[e]s/-e, "e) chimney; flue; ♃, 🏭 funnel; '~feger *m* (-s/-) chimney-sweep(er).

schlotter|ig *adj.* ['ʃlɔtəriç] shaky, tottery, loose; '~n *v/i.* (ge-, *h*) *garment:* hang loosely; *p.* shake, tremble (*both: vor dat.* with).

Schlucht [ʃluxt] *f* (-/-en) gorge, mountain cleft; ravine, *Am. a.* gulch.

schluchzen ['ʃluxtsən] *v/i.* (ge-, *h*) sob.

Schluck [ʃluk] *m* (-[e]s/-e, "e) draught, swallow; mouthful, sip; '~auf *m* (-s/*no pl.*) hiccup(s *pl.*).

'schlucken 1. *v/t. and v/i.* (ge-, *h*) swallow (*a. fig.*); 2. ♀ *m* (-s/*no pl.*) hiccup(s *pl.*).

schlug [ʃluːk] *pret. of* schlagen.

Schlummer ['ʃlumər] *m* (-s/*no pl.*) slumber; '~n *v/i.* (ge-, *h*) slumber.

Schlund [ʃlunt] *m* (-[e]s/"e) *anat.* pharynx; *fig.* abyss, chasm, gulf.

schlüpf|en ['ʃlʏpfən] *v/i.* (ge-, *sein*) slip, slide; *in die Kleider* ~ slip on one's clothes; *aus den Kleidern* ~ slip out of *or* slip off one's clothes; '2er *m* (-s/-) (*ein a pair of*) knickers *pl. or* drawers *pl. Am. F* panties *pl.*; briefs *pl.*

Schlupfloch ['ʃlupf-] *n* loop-hole.

'schlüpfrig *adj.* slippery; *fig.* lascivious.

'Schlupfwinkel *m* hiding-place.

schlurfen ['ʃlurfən] *v/i.* (ge-, *sein*) shuffle, drag one's feet.

schlürfen ['ʃlʏrfən] *v/t. and v/i.* (ge-, *h*) drink *or* eat noisily; sip.

Schluß [ʃlus] *m* (*Schlusses/Schlüsse*) close, end; conclusion; *parl.* closing (*of debate*).

Schlüssel ['ʃlʏsəl] *m* (-s/-) key (*zu* of; *fig.* to); ♪ clef; *fig.:* code; quota; '~bart *m* key-bit; '~bein *anat. n* collar-bone, clavicle; '~bund *m, n* (-[e]s/-e) bunch of keys; '~industrie *fig. f* key industry; '~loch *n* keyhole; '~ring *m* key-ring.

'Schlußfolgerung *f* conclusion, inference; '~formel *f in letter:* complimentary close.

schlüssig *adj.* ['ʃlʏsiç] *evidence:* conclusive; *sich* ~ *werden* make up one's mind (*über acc.* about).

'Schlußlicht *n* ⊕, *mot.,* etc.: taillight; *sports:* last runner; bottom club; '~runde *f sports:* final; '~schein † *m* contract-note.

Schmach [ʃmaːx] *f* (-/*no pl.*) disgrace; insult; humiliation.

schmachten ['ʃmaxtən] *v/i.* (ge-, *h*) languish (*nach* for); pine (for).

schmächtig *adj.* ['ʃmɛçtiç] slender, slim; *ein* ~er *Junge* a (mere) slip of a boy.

'schmachvoll *adj.* disgraceful; humiliating.

schmackhaft *adj.* ['ʃmakhaft] palatable, savo(u)ry.

schmäh|en ['ʃmɛːən] *v/t.* (ge-, *h*) abuse, revile; decry, disparage; slander, defame; '~lich *adj.* ignominious, disgraceful; '2schrift *f* libel, lampoon; '2ung *f* (-/-en) abuse; slander, defamation.

schmal *adj.* [ʃmaːl] narrow; *figure:* slender, slim; *face:* thin; *fig.* poor, scanty.

schmäler|n ['ʃmɛːlərn] *v/t.* (ge-, *h*) curtail; impair; belittle; '2ung *f* (-/-en) curtailment; impairment; detraction.

'Schmal|film *phot. m* substandard film; '~spur 🚂 *f* narrow ga(u)ge; '~spurbahn 🚂 *f* narrow-ga(u)ge railway; '2spurig ⊕ *adj.* narrow-ga(u)ge.

Schmalz [ʃmalts] *n* (-es/-e) grease; lard; '2ig *adj.* greasy; lardy; F *fig.* soppy, sentimental.

schmarotz|en [ʃma'rɔtsən] *v/i.* (*no* -ge-, *h*) sponge (*bei* on); 2er *m* (-s/-) ♀, *zo.* parasite; *fig. a.* sponge.

Schmarre F ['ʃmarə] *f* (-/-n) slash, cut; scar.

Schmatz [ʃmats] *m* (-es/-e) smack, loud kiss; '2en *v/i.* (ge-, *h*) smack (*mit den Lippen* one's lips); eat noisily.

Schmaus [ʃmaus] *m* (-es/"e) feast, banquet; *fig.* treat; 2en ['~zən] *v/i.* (ge-, *h*) feast, banquet.

schmecken ['ʃmɛkən] (ge-, *h*) **1.** *v/t.* taste, sample; 2. *v/i.:* ~ *nach* taste *or* smack of (*both a. fig.*); *dieser Wein schmeckt mir* I like *or* enjoy this wine.

Schmeichel|ei [ʃmaiçə'lai] *f* (-/-en) flattery; cajolery; '2haft *adj.* flattering; '2n *v/i.* (ge-, *h*): *j-m* ~ flatter s.o.; cajole s.o.

Schmeichler ['ʃmaiçlər] *m* (-s/-) flatterer; '2isch *adj.* flattering, cajoling.

schmeiß|en F ['ʃmaisən] (*irr.,* ge-, *h*) **1.** *v/t.* throw, fling, hurl; slam, bang (*door*); **2.** *v/i.:* *mit Geld um sich* ~ squander one's money; '2fliege *zo. f* blowfly, bluebottle.

Schmelz [ʃmɛlts] *m* **1.** -es/-e) enamel; **2.** *fig.* (-es/*no pl.*) bloom; ♪ sweetness, mellowness; '2en (*irr.,* ge-) **1.** *v/i.* (*sein*) melt (*a. fig.*); liquefy; *fig.* melt away, dwindle; **2.** *v/t.* (*h*) melt; smelt, fuse (*ore, etc.*); liquefy; ~erei [~'rai] *f* (-/-en), '~hütte *f* foundry; '~ofen *m* smelting furnace; '~tiegel *m* melting-pot, crucible.

Schmerbauch F ['ʃmeːr-] *m* paunch, pot-belly, F corporation, *Am. sl. a.* bay window.

Schmerz [ʃmɛrts] *m* (-es/-en) pain (*a. fig.*); ache; *fig.* grief, sorrow;

'Ωen (ge-, h) 1. v/i. pain (a. fig.), hurt; ache; 2. v/t. pain (a. fig.); hurt; fig. grieve, afflict; '2haft adj. painful; '2lich adj. painful, grievous; '2lindernd adj. soothing; '2los adj. painless.

Schmetter|ling zo. ['ʃmetərlɪŋ] m (-s/-e) butterfly; '2n (ge-, h) 1. v/t. dash (zu Boden to the ground; in Stücke to pieces); 2. v/i. crash; trumpet, etc.: bray, blare; bird: warble.

Schmied [ʃmiːt] m (-[e]s/-e) (black-)smith; ⁓e ['⁓də] f (-/-n) forge, smithy; ⁓eeisen ['⁓dəʔ-] n wrought iron; '⁓ehammer m sledge(-hammer); 2en ['⁓dən] v/t. (ge-, h) forge; make, devise, hatch (plans).

schmiegen ['ʃmiːgən] v/refl. (ge-, h) nestle (an acc. to).

schmiegsam adj. ['ʃmiːkzaːm] pliant, flexible; supple (a. fig.); '2keit f (-/no pl.) pliancy, flexibility; suppleness (a. fig.).

Schmier|e ['ʃmiːrə] f (-/-n) grease; thea. contp. troop of strolling players, sl. penny gaff; '2en v/t. (ge-, h) smear; ⊕ grease, oil, lubricate; butter (bread); spread (butter, etc.); scrawl, scribble; painter: daub; ⁓enkomödiant ['⁓kɔmødjant] m (-en/-en) strolling actor, barnstormer, sl. ham (actor); ⁓erei [⁓'raɪ] f (-/-en) scrawl; paint. daub; '2ig adj. greasy; dirty; fig.: filthy; F smarmy; '⁓mittel ⊕ n lubricant.

Schminke ['ʃmɪŋkə] f (-/-n) make-up (a. thea.), paint; rouge; thea. grease-paint; '2n v/t. and v/refl. (ge-, h) paint, make up; rouge (o.s.); put on lipstick.

Schmirgel ['ʃmɪrgəl] m (-s/no pl.) emery; '2n v/t. (ge-, h) (rub with) emery; '⁓papier n emery-paper.

Schmiß [ʃmɪs] 1. m (Schmisses/Schmisse) gash, cut; (duelling-)scar; 2. F m (Schmisses/no pl.) verve, go, Am. sl. a. pep; 3. 2 pret. of schmeißen.

schmoll|en ['ʃmɔlən] v/i. (ge-, h) sulk, pout; '2winkel m sulking-corner.

schmolz [ʃmɔlts] pret. of schmelzen.

Schmor|braten ['ʃmoːr-] m stewed meat; '2en v/t. and v/i. (ge-, h) stew (a. fig.).

Schmuck [ʃmuk] 1. m (-[e]s/⁓-e) ornament; decoration; jewel(le)ry, jewels pl.; 2. 2 adj. neat, smart, spruce, trim.

schmücken ['ʃmykən] v/t. (ge-, h) adorn, trim; decorate.

'schmuck|los adj. unadorned; plain; '2sachen f/pl. jewel(le)ry, jewels pl.

Schmuggel ['ʃmugəl] m (-s/no pl.), ⁓ei [⁓'laɪ] f (-/-en) smuggling; '2n v/t. and v/i. (ge-, h) smuggle; '⁓ware f contraband, smuggled goods pl.

Schmuggler ['ʃmuglər] m (-s/-) smuggler.

schmunzeln ['ʃmuntsəln] v/i. (ge-, h) smile amusedly.

Schmutz [ʃmuts] m (-es/no pl.) dirt; filth; fig. a. smut; '2en v/i. (ge-, h) soil, get dirty; '⁓fink fig. m mudlark; '⁓fleck m smudge, stain; fig. blemish; '2ig adj. dirty; filthy; fig. a. mean, shabby.

Schnabel ['ʃnaːbəl] m (-s/⁼) bill, esp. bird of prey: beak.

Schnalle ['ʃnalə] f (-/-n) buckle; '2n v/t. (ge-, h) buckle; strap.

schnalzen ['ʃnaltsən] v/i. (ge-, h): mit den Fingern ⁓ snap one's fingers; mit der Zunge ⁓ click one's tongue.

schnappen ['ʃnapən] (ge-, h) 1. v/i. lid, spring, etc.: snap; lock: catch; nach et. ⁓ snap or snatch at; nach Luft ⁓ gasp for breath; 2. F v/t. catch, sl. nab (criminal).

'Schnapp|messer n flick-knife; '⁓schloß n spring-lock; '⁓schuß phot. m snapshot.

Schnaps [ʃnaps] m (-es/⁼e) strong liquor, Am. hard liquor; brandy; ein (Glas) ⁓ a dram.

schnarch|en ['ʃnarçən] v/i. (ge-, h) snore; '2er m (-s/-) snorer.

schnarren ['ʃnarən] v/i. (ge-, h) rattle; jar.

schnattern ['ʃnatərn] v/i. (ge-, h) cackle; fig. a. chatter, gabble.

schnauben ['ʃnaubən] (ge-, h) 1. v/i. snort; vor Wut ⁓ foam with rage; 2. v/t.: sich die Nase ⁓ blow one's nose.

schnaufen ['ʃnaufən] v/i. (ge-, h) pant, puff, blow; wheeze.

Schnauz|bart ['ʃnauts-] m m(o)ustache; '⁓e f (-/-n) snout, muzzle; ⊕ nozzle; teapot, etc.: spout; sl. fig. potato-trap; '2en F v/i. (ge-, h) jaw.

Schnecke zo. ['ʃnɛkə] f (-/-n) snail; slug; '⁓nhaus n snail's shell; '⁓n-tempo n: im ⁓ at a snail's pace.

Schnee [ʃne:] m (-s/no pl.) snow; '⁓ball m snowball; '⁓ballschlacht f pelting-match with snowballs; 2bedeckt adj. ['⁓bədɛkt] snow-covered, mountain-top: snow-capped; '2blind adj. snow-blind; '⁓blindheit f snow-blindness; '⁓brille f (e-e a pair of) snow-goggles pl.; '⁓fall m snow-fall; '⁓flocke f snow-flake; '⁓gestöber n (-s/-) snow-storm; ⁓glöckchen ⁊ ['⁓glœkçən] n (-s/-) snowdrop; '⁓grenze f snow-line; '⁓mann m snow man; '⁓pflug m snow-plough, Am. snowplow; '⁓schuh m snow-shoe; '⁓sturm m snow-storm, blizzard; '⁓wehe f (-/-n) snow-drift; '2weiß adj. snow-white.

Schneid F [ʃnaɪt] m (-[e]s/no pl.) pluck, dash, sl. guts pl.

Schneide ['ʃnaɪdə] f (-/-n) edge; '⁓mühle f sawmill; '2n (irr., ge-, h)

1. *v/t.* cut; carve (*meat*); pare, clip (*finger-nails*, etc.); 2. *v/i.* cut.
'Schneider *m* (-s/-) tailor; ～ei [～'raɪ] *f* 1. (-/no *pl.*) tailoring; dressmaking; 2. (-/-en) tailor's shop; dressmaker's shop; ～in *f* (-/-nen) dressmaker; ～meister *m* master tailor; '2n (ge-, h) 1. *v/i.* tailor; do tailoring; do dressmaking; 2. *v/t.* make, tailor.
'Schneidezahn *m* incisor.
'schneidig *fig. adj.* plucky; dashing, keen; smart, *Am. sl. a.* nifty.
schneien ['ʃnaɪən] *v/i.* (ge-, h) snow.
schnell [ʃnɛl] 1. *adj.* quick, fast; rapid; swift, speedy; *reply*, etc.: prompt; sudden; 2. *adv.:* ～ fahren drive fast; ～ handeln act promptly or without delay; (mach) ～! be quick!, hurry up!
Schnelläufer ['ʃnɛlɔʏfər] *m* sprinter; speed skater.
'schnell|en (ge-) *v/t.* (h) and *v/i.* (sein) jerk; '2feuer ⚔ *n* rapid fire; '2hefter *m* (-s/-) folder.
'Schnelligkeit *f* (-/no *pl.*) quickness, fastness; rapidity; swiftness; promptness; speed, velocity.
'Schnell|imbiß *m* snack (bar); '～imbißstube *f* snack bar; '～kraft *f* (-/no *pl.*) elasticity; '～verfahren *n* ⚖ summary proceeding; ⊕ high-speed process; '～zug 🚂 *m* fast train, express (train).
schneuzen ['ʃnɔʏtsən] *v/refl.* (ge-, h) blow one's nose.
schniegeln ['ʃniːgəln] *v/refl.* (ge-, h) dress or smarten or spruce (o.s.) up.
Schnipp|chen ['ʃnɪpçən] *n: ～* *f-m* ein ～ schlagen outwit or overreach s.o.; '2isch *adj.* pert, snappish, *Am. F a.* snippy.
Schnitt [ʃnɪt] 1. *m* (-[e]s/-e) cut; *dress*, etc.: cut, make, style; pattern; *book:* edge; ⅄ (inter)section; *fig.:* average; F profit; 2. *pret. of* schneiden; '～blumen *f/pl.* cut flowers *pl.*; '～e *f* (-/-n) slice; '～er *m* (-s/-) reaper, mower; '～fläche ⅄ *f* section(al plane); '2ig *adj.* streamline(d); '～muster *n* pattern; '～punkt *m* (point of) intersection; '～wunde *f* cut, gash.
Schnitzel ['ʃnɪtsəl] 1. *n* (-s/-) schnitzel; 2. F *n, m* (-s/-) chip; *paper:* scrap; ～ *pl.* ⊕ parings *pl.*, shavings *pl.*; *paper: a.* clippings *pl.*; '2n *v/t.* (ge-, h) chip, shred, whittle.
schnitzen ['ʃnɪtsən] *v/t.* (ge-, h) carve, cut (in wood).
'Schnitzer *m* (-s/-) carver; F *fig.* blunder, *Am. sl. a.* boner; '～ei [～'raɪ] *f* 1. (-/-en) carving, carved work; 2. (-/no *pl.*) carving.
schnöde *adj.* ['ʃnøːdə] contemptuous; disgraceful; base, vile; ～r Mammon filthy lucre.

Schnörkel ['ʃnœrkəl] *m* (-s/-) flourish (*a. fig.*), scroll (*a.* ⚗).
schnorr|en F ['ʃnɔrən] *v/t. and v/i.* (ge-, h) cadge; '2er *m* (-s/-) cadger.
schnüff|eln ['ʃnʏfəln] *v/i.* (ge-, h) sniff, nose (*both: an dat.* at); *fig.* nose about, *Am.* F *a.* snoop around; '2ler *fig. m* (-s/-) spy, *Am.* F *a.* snoop; F sleuth(-hound).
Schnuller ['ʃnʊlər] *m* (-s/-) dummy, comforter.
Schnulze F ['ʃnʊltsə] *f* (-/-n) sentimental song or film or play, F tearjerker.
Schnupf|en ['ʃnʊpfən] 1. *m* (-s/-) cold, catarrh; 2. 2 *v/i.* (ge-, h) take snuff; '～er *m* (-s/-) snuff-taker; '～tabak *m* snuff.
schnuppe F *adj.* ['ʃnʊpə]: *das ist mir ～* I don't care (F a damn); '～rn *v/i.* (ge-, h) sniff, nose (*both: an dat.* at).
Schnur [ʃnuːr] *f* (-/⁀e, ⚓-en) cord; string, twine; line; ≨ flex.
Schnür|band ['ʃnyːr-] *n* lace; '～chen ['～çən] *n* (-s/-): *wie am ～ like* clockwork; '2en *v/t.* (ge-, h) lace (up); (bind with) cord, tie up.
'schnurgerade *adj.* dead straight.
Schnurr|bart ['ʃnur-] *m* m(o)ustache; '2en (ge-, h) 1. *v/i.* wheel, etc.: whir(r); *cat:* purr (*a. fig.*); F *fig.* cadge; 2. F *fig. v/t.* cadge.
Schnür|senkel ['ʃnyːrzɛŋkəl] *m* (-s/-) shoe-lace, shoe-string; '～stiefel *m* lace-boot.
schnurstracks *adv.* ['ʃnuːr'ʃtraks] direct, straight; on the spot, at once, *sl.* straight away.
schob [ʃoːp] *pret. of* schieben.
Schober ['ʃoːbər] *m* (-s/-) rick, stack.
Schock [ʃɔk] 1. *n* (-[e]s/-e) three-score; 2. 🗲 *m* (-[e]s/-s, ⚓-e) shock; 2ieren [～'kiːrən] *v/t.* (no -ge-, h) shock, scandalize.
Schokolade [ʃokoˈlaːdə] *f* (-/-n) chocolate.
scholl [ʃɔl] *pret. of* schallen.
Scholle ['ʃɔlə] *f* (-/-n) clod (*of earth*), *poet.* glebe; floe (*of ice*); *ichth.* plaice.
schon *adv.* [ʃoːn] already; ～ lange for a long time; ～ gut! all right!; ～ der Gedanke the very idea; ～ der Name the bare name; hast du ～ einmal ...? have you ever ...?; mußt du ～ gehen? need you go yet?; ～ um 8 Uhr as early as 8 o'clock.
schön [ʃøːn] 1. *adj.* beautiful; *man:* handsome (*a. fig.*); *weather:* fair, fine (*a. iro.*); *das ～e Geschlecht* the fair sex; *die ～en Künste* the fine arts; *～e Literatur* belles-lettres *pl.*; 2. *adv.:* ～ warm nice and warm; *du hast mich ～ erschreckt* you gave me quite a start.
schonen ['ʃoːnən] *v/t.* (ge-, h) spare (*j-n s.o.*); *j-s Leben* s.o.'s life); take

care of; husband (*strength, etc.*); sich ~ take care of o.s., look after o.s.

'**Schönheit** f 1. (-/no pl.) beauty; of woman: a. pulchritude; 2. (-/-en) beauty; beautiful woman, belle; '~spflege f beauty treatment.

'**schöntun** v/i. (irr. tun, sep., -ge-, h) flatter (j-m s.o.); flirt (dat. with).

'**Schonung** f 1. (-/no pl.) mercy; sparing, forbearance; careful treatment; 2. (-/-en) tree-nursery; '2slos adj. unsparing, merciless, relentless.

Schopf [ʃɔpf] m (-[e]s/=e) tuft; orn. a. crest.

schöpfen ['ʃœpfən] v/t. (ge-, h) scoop, ladle; draw (*water at well*); draw, take (*breath*); take (*courage*); neue Hoffnung ~ gather fresh hope; Verdacht ~ become suspicious.

'**Schöpf|er** m (-s/-) creator; '2erisch adj. creative; '~ung f (-/-en) creation.

schor [ʃoːr] pret. of scheren.

Schorf [ʃɔrf] m (-[e]s/-e) scurf; scab, crust; '2ig adj. scurfy; scabby.

Schornstein ['ʃɔrn-] m chimney; ⚓, 🚂 funnel; '~feger m (-s/-) chimney-sweep(er).

Schoß 1. [ʃoːs] m (-es/=e) lap; womb; coat: tail; 2. 2 [ʃos] pret. of schießen.

Schote ♀ ['ʃoːtə] f (-/-n) pod, husk.

Schott|e ['ʃɔtə] m (-n/-n) Scot, Scotchman, Scotsman; die ~n pl. the Scotch pl.; '~er m (-s/-) gravel; (road-)metal; '2isch adj. Scotch, Scottish.

schräg [ʃrɛːk] 1. adj. oblique, slanting; sloping; 2. adv.: ~ gegenüber diagonally across (von from).

schrak [ʃraːk] pret. of schrecken 2.

Schramme ['ʃramə] f (-/-n) scratch; skin: a. abrasion; '2n v/t. (ge-, h) scratch; graze, abrade (skin).

Schrank [ʃraŋk] m (-[e]s/=e) cupboard, esp. Am. closet; wardrobe.

'**Schranke** f (-/-n) barrier (a. fig.); 🚂 a. (railway-)gate; 🚃 bar; ~n pl. fig. bounds pl., limits pl.; '2nlos fig. adj. boundless; unbridled; '~nwärter 🚂 m gate-keeper.

'**Schrankkoffer** m wardrobe trunk.

Schraube ['ʃraubə] f (-/-n) ⊕ screw; ⚓ screw(-propeller); '2n v/t. (ge-, h) screw.

'**Schrauben|dampfer** ⚓ m screw (steamer); '~mutter ⊕ f nut; '~schlüssel ⊕ m spanner, wrench; '~zieher ⊕ m screwdriver.

Schraubstock ⊕ ['ʃraup-] m vice, Am. vise.

Schrebergarten ['ʃreːbər-] m allotment garden.

Schreck [ʃrek] m (-[e]s/-e) fright, terror; consternation; '~bild n bugbear; '~en m (-s/-) fright, terror, consternation; '2en (ge-) 1. v/t. (h) frighten, scare; 2. v/i. (irr., sein);

only in compounds; '~ensbotschaft f alarming or terrible news; '~ensherrschaft f reign of terror; '2haft adj. fearful, timid; '2lich adj. terrible, dreadful (both a. F fig.); '~schuß m scare shot; fig. warning shot.

Schrei [ʃraɪ] m (-[e]s/-e) cry; shout; scream.

schreiben ['ʃraɪbən] 1. v/t. and v/i. (irr., ge-, h) write (j-m to s.o.; über acc. on); mit der Maschine ~ type(write); 2. v/t. (irr., ge-, h) spell; 3. 2 n (-s/-) letter.

'**Schreiber** m (-s/-) writer; secretary, clerk.

schreib|faul adj. ['ʃraɪp-] lazy in writing; '2feder f pen; '2fehler m mistake in writing or spelling, slip of the pen; '2heft n exercise-book; '2mappe f writing-case; '2maschine f typewriter; (mit der) ~ schreiben type(write); '2material n writing-materials pl., stationery; '2papier n writing-paper; '2schrift typ. f script; '2tisch m (writing-)desk; '2ung f (-/-en) spelling; '2unterlage f desk pad; '2waren f/pl. writing-materials pl., stationery; '2warenhändler m stationer; '2zeug n writing-materials pl.

'**schreien** (irr., ge-, h) 1. v/t. shout; scream; 2. v/i. cry (out) (vor dat. with pain, etc.); nach for bread, etc.); shout (vor with); scream (with); '~d adj. colour: loud; injustice: flagrant.

schreiten ['ʃraɪtən] v/i. (irr., ge-, sein) step, stride (über acc. across); fig. proceed (zu to).

schrie [ʃriː] pret. of schreien.

schrieb [ʃriːp] pret. of schreiben.

Schrift [ʃrɪft] f (-/-en) (hand-)writing, hand; typ. type; character, letter; writing; publication; die Heilige ~ the (Holy) Scriptures pl.; '~art f type; '2deutsch adj. literary German; '~führer m secretary; '~leiter m editor; '2lich 1. adj. written, in writing; 2. adv. in writing; '~satz m ⚖ pleadings pl.; typ. composition, type-setting; '~setzer m compositor, type-setter; '~sprache f literary language; '~steller m (-s/-) author, writer; '~stück n piece of writing, paper, document; '~tum n (-s/no pl.) literature; '~wechsel m exchange of letters, correspondence; '~zeichen n character, letter.

schrill adj. [ʃrɪl] shrill, piercing.

Schritt [ʃrɪt] m (-[e]s/-e) step (a. fig.); pace (a. fig.); ~e unternehmen take steps; 2. 2 pret. of schreiten; '~macher m (-s/-) sports: pace-maker; '2weise 1. adj. gradual; 2. adv. a. step by step.

schroff adj. [ʃrɔf] rugged, jagged;

steep, precipitous; *fig.* harsh, gruff; ~er *Widerspruch* glaring contradiction.

schröpfen ['ʃrœpfən] *v/t.* (ge-, h) 🜍 cup; *fig.* milk, fleece.

Schrot [ʃroːt] *m, n* (-[e]s/-e) crushed grain; small shot; '~brot *n* wholemeal bread; '~flinte *f* shotgun.

Schrott [ʃrɔt] *m* (-[e]s/-e) scrap (-iron *or* -metal).

schrubben ['ʃrubən] *v/t.* (ge-, h) scrub.

Schrulle ['ʃrulə] *f* (-/-n) whim, fad.

schrumpf|en ['ʃrumpfən] *v/i.* (ge-, sein) shrink (*a.* ⊕, 🜍, *fig.*); '2ung *f* (-/-en) shrinking; shrinkage.

Schub [ʃuːp] *m* (-[e]s/~e) push, shove; *phys.*, ⊕ thrust; *bread, people, etc.*: batch; '~fach *n* drawer; '~karren *m* wheelbarrow; '~kasten *m* drawer; '~kraft *phys.*, ⊕ *f* thrust; '~lade *f* (-/-n) drawer.

Schubs F [ʃups] *m* (-es/-e) push; '2en F *v/t.* (ge-, h) push.

schüchtern *adj.* ['ʃʏçtərn] shy, bashful, timid; *girl*: coy; '2heit *f* (-/no *pl.*) shyness, bashfulness, timidity; coyness (*of girl*).

schuf [ʃuːf] *pret. of* schaffen 1.

Schuft [ʃuft] *m* (-[e]s/-e) scoundrel, rascal; cad; '2en F *v/i.* (ge-, h) drudge, slave, plod; '2ig *adj.* scoundrelly, rascally; caddish.

Schuh [ʃuː] *m* (-[e]s/-e) shoe; *j-m et. in die ~e schieben* put the blame for s.th. on s.o.; *wissen, wo der ~ drückt* know where the shoe pinches; '~anzieher *m* (-s/-) shoehorn; '~band *n* shoe-lace *or* -string; '~creme *f* shoe-cream, shoepolish; '~geschäft *n* shoe-shop; '~löffel *m* shoehorn; '~macher *m* (-s/-) shoemaker; '~putzer *m* (-s/-) shoeblack, *Am. a.* shoeshine; '~sohle *f* sole; '~spanner *m* (-s/-) shoetree; '~werk *n*, '~zeug F *n* foot-wear, boots and shoes *pl.*

'**Schul|amt** *n* school-board; '~arbeit *f* homework; '~bank *f* (school-)desk; '~beispiel *n* test-case, typical example; '~besuch *m* (-[e]s/no *pl.*) attendance at school; '~bildung *f* education; *höhere ~* secondary education; '~buch *n* school-book.

Schuld [ʃult] *f* 1. (-/no *pl.*) guilt; fault, blame; *es ist s-e ~* it is his fault, he is to blame for it; 2. (-/-en) debt; ~en *machen* contract *or* incur debts; '2bewußt *adj.* conscious of one's guilt; 2en ['~dən] *v/t.* (ge-, h): *j-m et. ~* owe s.o. s.th.; *j-m Dank ~* be indebted to s.o. (*für* for); 2haft *adj.* ['~thaft] culpable.

'**Schuldiener** *m* school attendant *or* porter.

schuldig *adj.* ['ʃuldɪç] guilty (*e-r Sache* of s.th.); *respect, etc.*: due; *j-m et. ~ sein* owe s.o. s.th.; *Dank ~ sein* be indebted *to* s.o. (*für* for);

für ~ befinden 🜩 find guilty; 2e ['~gə] *m, f* (-/-n) guilty person; culprit; '2keit *f* (-/no *pl.*) duty, obligation.

'**Schuldirektor** *m* headmaster, *Am. a.* principal.

'**schuld|los** *adj.* guiltless, innocent; '2losigkeit *f* (-/no *pl.*) guiltlessness, innocence; 2ner ['~dnər] *m* (-s/-) debtor; '2schein *m* evidence of debt, certificate of indebtedness, IOU (= I owe you); '2verschreibung *f* bond, debt certificate.

Schule ['ʃuːlə] *f* (-/-n) school; *höhere ~* secondary school, *Am. a.* high school; *auf or in der ~* at school; *in die ~ gehen* go to school; '2n *v/t.* (ge-, h) train, school; *pol.* indoctrinate.

Schüler ['ʃyːlər] *m* (-s/-) schoolboy, pupil; *phls., etc.*: disciple; '~austausch *m* exchange of pupils; '~in *f* (-/-nen) schoolgirl.

'**Schul|ferien** *pl.* holidays *pl.*, vacation; '~fernsehen *n* educational TV; '~funk *m* educational broadcast; '~gebäude *n* school(house); '~geld *n* school fee(s *pl.*), tuition; '~hof *m* playground, *Am. a.* schoolyard; '~kamerad *m* schoolfellow; '~lehrer *m* schoolmaster, teacher; '~mappe *f* satchel; '2meistern *v/t.* (ge-, h) censure pedantically; '~ordnung *f* school regulations *pl.*; '2pflichtig *adj.* schoolable; '~rat *m* supervisor of schools, school inspector; '~schiff *n* training-ship; '~schluß *m* end of school; end of term; '~schwänzer *m* (-s/-) truant; '~stunde *f* lesson.

Schulter ['ʃultər] *f* (-/-n) shoulder; '~blatt *anat. n* shoulder-blade; '2n *v/t.* (ge-, h) shoulder.

'**Schul|unterricht** *m* school, lessons *pl.*; school instruction; '~versäumnis *f* (-/no *pl.*) absence from school; '~wesen *n* educational system; '~zeugnis *n* report.

schummeln F ['ʃuməln] *v/i.* (ge-, h) cheat, *Am.* F *a.* chisel.

Schund [ʃunt] 1. *m* (-[e]s/no *pl.*) trash, rubbish (*both a. fig.*); 2. 2 *pret. of* schinden; '~literatur *f* trashy literature; '~roman *m* trashy novel, *Am. a.* dime novel.

Schupp|e ['ʃupə] *f* (-/-n) scale; ~n *pl. on head*: dandruff; '~en *m* (-s/-) shed; *mot.* garage; ✈ hangar; 2. 2 *v/t.* (ge-, h) scale (*fish*); *sich ~ skin*: scale off; '2ig *adj.* scaly.

Schür|eisen ['ʃyːr'-] *n* poker; '2en *v/t.* (ge-, h) poke; stoke; *fig.* fan, foment.

schürfen ['ʃʏrfən] (ge-, h) 1. ⚒ *v/i.* prospect (*nach* for); 2. *v/t.* ⚒ prospect for; *sich den Arm ~* graze one's arm.

Schurk|e ['ʃurkə] *m* (-n/-n) scoundrel, knave; ~erei [~'raɪ] *f* (-/-en) rascality, knavish trick; '**∼isch** *adj.* scoundrelly, knavish.

Schürze ['ʃyrtsə] *f* (-/-n) apron; *children*: pinafore; '**∼n** *v/t.* (ge-, *h*) tuck up (*skirt*); tie (*knot*); purse (*lips*); '**∼njäger** *m* skirt-chaser, *Am. sl.* wolf.

Schuß [ʃus] *m* (Schusses/Schüsse) shot (*a. sports*); *ammunition*: round; *sound*: report; charge; *wine, etc.*: dash (*a. fig.*); *in ∼ sein* be in full swing, be in full working order.

Schüssel ['ʃysəl] *f* (-/-n) basin (*for water, etc.*); bowl, dish, tureen (*for soup, vegetables, etc.*).

'**Schuß|waffe** *f* fire-arm; '**∼weite** *f* range; '**∼wunde** *f* gunshot wound.

Schuster ['ʃu:stər] *m* (-s/-) shoemaker; '**∼n** *fig. v/i.* (ge-, *h*) *s. pfuschen.*

Schutt [ʃut] *m* (-[e]s/*no pl.*) rubbish, refuse; rubble, debris.

Schüttel|frost ⚕ ['ʃytəl-] *m* shivering-fit; '**∼n** *v/t.* (ge-, *h*) shake; *den Kopf ∼* shake one's head; *j-m die Hand ∼* shake hands with s.o.

schütten ['ʃytən] (ge-, *h*) **1.** *v/t.* pour; spill (*auf acc.* on); **2.** *v/i.*: *es schüttet* it is pouring with rain.

Schutz [ʃuts] *m* (-es/*no pl.*) protection (*gegen, vor dat.* against), defen|ce, *Am.* -se (against, from); shelter (from); safeguard; cover; '**∼brille** *f* (e-e a pair of) goggles *pl.*

Schütze ['ʃytsə] *m* (-n/-n) marksman, shot; ⚔ rifleman; '**∼n** *v/t.* (ge-, *h*) protect (*gegen, vor dat.* against, from), defend (against, from), guard (against, from); shelter (from); safeguard (*rights, etc.*).

Schutzengel ['ʃuts?-] *m* guardian angel.

'**Schützen|graben** ⚔ *m* trench; '**∼könig** *m* champion shot.

'**Schutz|haft** ⚖ *f* protective custody; '**∼heilige** *m* patron saint; '**∼herr** *m* patron, protector; '**∼impfung** ⚕ *f* protective inoculation; *smallpox*: vaccination.

Schützling ['ʃytsliŋ] *m* (-s/-e) protégé, *female*: protégée.

'**schutz|los** *adj.* unprotected; defen|celess, *Am.* -seless; '**∼mann** *m* (-[e]s/¨er, Schutzleute) policeman, (police) constable, *sl.* bobby, *sl.* cop; '**∼marke** *f* trade mark, brand; '**∼mittel** *n* preservative; ⚕ prophylactic; '**∼patron** *m* patron saint; '**∼umschlag** *m* (dust-)jacket, wrapper; '**∼zoll** *m* protective duty.

Schwabe ['ʃva:bə] *m* (-n/-n) Swabian.

schwäbisch *adj.* ['ʃvε:biʃ] Swabian.

schwach *adj.* [ʃvax] *resistance, team, knees* (*a. fig.*), *eyes, heart, voice, character, tea, gr. verb,* ✝ *demand, etc.*: weak; *person, etc.*: infirm; *person, recollection, etc.*: feeble; *sound, light, hope, idea, etc.*: faint; *consolation, attendance, etc.*: poor; *light, recollection, etc.*: dim; *resemblance*: remote; *das ∼e Geschlecht* the weaker sex; *∼e Seite* weak point or side.

Schwäche ['ʃvεçə] *f* (-/-n) weakness (*a. fig.*); infirmity; *fig.* foible; *e-e ∼ haben für* have a weakness for; '**∼n** *v/t.* (ge-, *h*) weaken (*a. fig.*); impair (*health*).

'**Schwach|heit** *f* (-/-en) weakness; *fig. a.* frailty; '**∼kopf** *m* simpleton, soft(y), *Am.* F *a.* sap(head); **∼köpfig** *adj.* ['∼kœpfiç] weak-headed, soft, *Am. sl. a.* sappy.

schwäch|lich *adj.* ['ʃvεçliç] weakly, feeble; delicate, frail; '**∼ling** *m* (-s/-e) weakling (*a. fig.*).

'**schwach|sinnig** *adj.* weak- or feeble-minded; '**∼strom** ⚡ *m* (-[e]s/*no pl.*) weak current.

Schwadron ⚔ [ʃva'dro:n] *f* (-/-en) squadron; **∼ieren** [∼o'ni:rən] *v/t.* (*no* -ge-, *h*) swagger, vapo(u)r.

Schwager ['ʃva:gər] *m* (-s/¨) brother-in-law.

Schwägerin ['ʃvε:gərin] *f* (-/-nen) sister-in-law.

Schwalbe *orn.* ['ʃvalbə] *f* (-/-n) swallow.

Schwall [ʃval] *m* (-[e]s/-e) swell, flood; *words*: torrent.

Schwamm [ʃvam] **1.** *m* (-[e]s/¨e) sponge; ♀ fungus; ♀ dry-rot; **2.** **∼** *pret. of schwimmen*; '**∼ig** *adj.* spongy; *face, etc.*: bloated.

Schwan *orn.* [ʃva:n] *m* (-[e]s/¨e) swan.

schwand [ʃvant] *pret. of schwinden.*

schwang [ʃvaŋ] *pret. of schwingen.*

schwanger *adj.* ['ʃvaŋər] pregnant, with child, in the family way.

schwängern ['ʃvεŋərn] *v/t.* (ge-, *h*) get with child, impregnate (*a. fig.*).

'**Schwangerschaft** *f* (-/-en) pregnancy.

schwanken ['ʃvaŋkən] *v/i.* (ge-) **1.** (*h*) *earth, etc.*: shake, rock; ✝ *prices*: fluctuate; *branches, etc.*: sway; *fig.* waver, oscillate, vacillate; **2.** (*sein*) stagger, totter.

Schwanz [ʃvants] *m* (-es/¨e) tail (*a.* ✈, *ast.*); *fig.* train.

schwänz|eln ['ʃvεntsəln] *v/i.* (ge-, *h*) wag one's tail; *fig.* fawn (*um* [up]on); '**∼en** *v/t.* (ge-, *h*) cut (*lecture, etc.*); *die Schule ∼* play truant, *Am. a.* play hooky.

Schwarm [ʃvarm] *m* (-[e]s/¨e) *bees, etc.*: swarm; *birds*: *a.* flight, flock; *fish*: school, schoal; *birds, girls, etc.*: bevy; F *fig.* fancy, craze; *p.*: idol, hero; flame.

schwärmen ['ʃvεrmən] *v/i.* (ge-, *h*) *bees, etc.*: swarm; *fig.*: revel; rave (*von* about, of), gush (over); *∼ für* be wild about, adore *s.o.*

'**Schwärmer** *m* (-s/-) enthusiast; *esp. eccl.* fanatic; visionary; *fireworks*: cracker, squib; *zo.* hawkmoth; ~**ei** [~'raɪ] *f* (-/-*en*) enthusiasm (*für* for); idolization; ecstasy; *esp. eccl.* fanaticism; '**&isch** *adj.* enthusiastic; gushing, raving; adoring; *esp. eccl.* fanatic(al).

Schwarte ['ʃvartə] *f* (-/-*n*) *bacon*: rind; F *fig.* old book.

schwarz *adj.* [ʃvarts] black (*a. fig.*); dark; dirty; ~*es Brett* notice-board, *Am.* bulletin board; ~*es Brot* brown bread; ~*er Mann* bog(e)y; ~*er Markt* black market; ~ *auf weiß* in black and white; *auf die* ~*e Liste setzen* blacklist; '**&arbeit** *f* illicit work; '**&brot** *n* brown bread; '**&e** *m, f* (-*n*/-*n*) black.

Schwärze ['ʃvɛrtsə] *f* (-/*no pl.*) blackness (*a. fig.*); darkness; '**&n** *v/t.* (ge-, *h*) blacken.

'**schwarz|fahren** F *v/i.* (*irr. fahren, sep.*, -ge-, *sein*) travel without a ticket; *mot.* drive without a licence; '**&fahrer** *m* fare-dodger; *mot.* person driving without a licence; '**&fahrt** *f* ride without a ticket; *mot.* drive without a licence; '**&handel** *m* illicit trade, black marketeering; '**&händler** *m* black marketeer; '**&hörer** *m* listener without a licence.

'**schwärzlich** *adj.* blackish.

'**Schwarz|markt** *m* black market; '~**seher** *m* pessimist; *TV*: viewer without a licence; '~**sender** *m* pirate broadcasting station; ~'**weißfilm** *m* black-and-white film.

schwatzen ['ʃvatsən] *v/i.* (ge-, *h*) chat; chatter, tattle.

schwätz|en ['ʃvɛtsən] *v/i.* (ge-, *h*) *s. schwatzen*; '**&er** *m* (-*s*/-) chatterbox; tattler, prattler; gossip.

'**schwatzhaft** *adj.* talkative, garrulous.

Schwebe *fig.* ['ʃve:bə] *f* (-/*no pl.*): *in der* ~ *sein* be in suspense; *law, rule, etc.*: be in abeyance; '~**bahn** *f* aerial railway *or* ropeway; '**&n** *v/i.* (ge-, *h*) be suspended; *bird*: hover (*a. fig.*); glide; *fig.* be pending (*a.* ⚖); *in Gefahr* ~ be in danger.

Schwed|e ['ʃve:də] *m* (-*n*/-*n*) Swede; '**&isch** *adj.* Swedish.

Schwefel ⚗ ['ʃve:fəl] *m* (-*s*/*no pl.*) sulphur, *Am. a.* sulfur; '~**säure** ⚗ *f* (-/*no pl.*) sulphuric acid, *Am. a.* sulfuric acid.

Schweif [ʃvaɪf] *m* (-[e]*s*/-e) tail (*a. ast.*); *fig.* train; '**&en** (ge-) **1.** *v/i.* (*sein*) rove, ramble; **2.** ⊕ *v/t.* (*h*) curve; scallop.

schweigen ['ʃvaɪgən] **1.** *v/i.* (*irr.*, ge-, *h*) be silent; **2.** & *n* (-*s*/*no pl.*) silence; '~**d** *adj.* silent.

schweigsam *adj.* ['ʃvaɪkza:m] taciturn; '**&keit** *f* (-/*no pl.*) taciturnity.

Schwein [ʃvaɪn] *n* **1.** (-[e]*s*/-e) *zo.* pig, hog, swine (*all a. contp. fig.*); **2.** F (-[e]*s*/*no pl.*): ~ *haben* be lucky.

'**Schweine|braten** *m* roast pork; '~**fleisch** *n* pork; '~**hund** F *contp. m* swine; ~**rei** [~'raɪ] *f* (-/-en) mess; dirty trick; smut(ty story); '~**stall** *m* pigsty (*a. fig.*).

'**schweinisch** *fig. adj.* swinish; smutty.

'**Schweinsleder** *n* pigskin.

Schweiß [ʃvaɪs] *m* (-es/-e) sweat, perspiration; '**&en** ⊕ *v/t.* (ge-, *h*) weld; '~**er** ⊕ *m* (-*s*/-) welder; '~**fuß** *m* perspiring foot; '**&ig** *adj.* sweaty, damp with sweat.

Schweizer ['ʃvaɪtsər] *m* (-*s*/-) Swiss; *on farm*: dairyman.

schwelen ['ʃve:lən] *v/i.* (ge-, *h*) smo(u)lder (*a. fig.*).

schwelg|en ['ʃvɛlgən] *v/i.* (ge-, *h*) lead a luxurious life; revel; *fig.* revel (*in dat.* in); '**&er** *m* (-*s*/-) revel(l)er; epicure; **&erei** [~'raɪ] *f* (-/-en) revel(ry), feasting; '~**erisch** *adj.* luxurious; revel(l)ing.

Schwell|e ['ʃvɛlə] *f* (-/-*n*) sill, threshold (*a. fig.*); 🚂 sleeper, *Am.* tie; '**&en 1.** *v/i.* (*irr.*, ge-, *sein*) swell (out); **2.** *v/t.* (ge-, *h*) swell; '~**ung** *f* (-/-en) swelling.

Schwemme ['ʃvɛmə] *f* (-/-*n*) watering-place; horse-pond; *at tavern, etc.*: taproom; ✝ glut (*of fruit, etc.*).

Schwengel ['ʃvɛŋəl] *m* (-*s*/-) clapper (*of bell*); handle (*of pump*).

schwenk|en ['ʃvɛŋkən] (ge-) **1.** *v/t.* (*h*) swing; wave (*hat, etc.*); brandish (*stick, etc.*); rinse (*washing*); **2.** *v/i.* (*sein*) turn, wheel; '**&ung** *f* (-/-en) turn; *fig.* change of mind.

schwer [ʃve:r] **1.** *adj.* heavy; *problem, etc.*: hard, difficult; *illness, mistake, etc.*: serious; *punishment, etc.*: severe; *fault, etc.*: grave; *wine, cigar, etc.*: strong; ~*e Zeiten* hard times; *2 Pfund* ~ *sein* weigh two pounds; **2.** *adv.*: ~ *arbeiten* work hard; ~ *hören* be hard of hearing; '**&e** *f* (-/*no pl.*) heaviness; *phys.* gravity (*a. fig.*); severity; '~**fällig** *adj.* heavy, slow; clumsy; '**&gewicht** *n sports*: heavy-weight; *fig.* main emphasis; '**&gewichtler** *m* (-*s*/-) *sports*: heavy-weight; '~**hörig** *adj.* hard of hearing; '**&industrie** *f* heavy industry; '**&kraft** *phys. f* (-/*no pl.*) gravity; '~**lich** *adv.* hardly, scarcely; '**&mut** *f* (-/*no pl.*) melancholy; ~**mütig** *adj.* ['~my:tiç] melancholy; '**&punkt** *m* centre of gravity, *Am.* center of gravity; *fig.*: crucial point; emphasis.

Schwert [ʃve:rt] *n* (-[e]*s*/-er) sword.

'**Schwer|verbrecher** *m* felon; '**&verdaulich** *adj.* indigestible, heavy; '**&verständlich** *adj.* difficult *or* hard to understand; '**&verwundet** *adj.* seriously wounded; '**&wiegend** *fig. adj.* weighty, momentous.

Schwester ['ʃvɛstər] f (-/-n) sister; nurse.

schwieg [ʃviːk] pret. of schweigen.

Schwieger|eltern ['ʃviːgər-] pl. parents-in-law pl.; **'~mutter** f mother-in-law; **'~sohn** m son-in-law; **'~tochter** f daughter-in-law; **'~vater** m father-in-law.

Schwiel|e ['ʃviːlə] f (-/-n) callosity; **'2ig** adj. callous.

schwierig adj. ['ʃviːriç] difficult, hard; **'2keit** f (-/-en) difficulty, trouble.

Schwimm|bad ['ʃvim-] n swimming-bath, Am. swimming pool; **'2en** v/i. (irr., ge-) **1.** (sein) swim; thing: float; ich bin über den Fluß geschwommen I swam across the river; in Geld ~ be rolling in money; **2.** (h) swim; ich habe lange unter Wasser geschwommen I swam under water for a long time; **'~gürtel** m swimming-belt; lifebelt; **'~haut** f web; **'~lehrer** m swimming-instructor; **'~weste** f life-jacket.

Schwindel ['ʃvindəl] m (-s/no pl.) vertigo, giddiness, dizziness; F fig.: swindle, humbug, sl. swindle; cheat, fraud; **'~anfall** ⊹ m fit of dizziness; **'2erregend** adj. dizzy (a. fig.); **'~firma** ⊹ f long firm, Am. wildcat firm; **'2n** v/i. (ge-, h) cheat, humbug, swindle.

schwinden ['ʃvindən] v/i. (irr., ge-, sein) dwindle, grow less; strength, colour, etc.: fade.

'Schwindl|er m (-s/-) swindler, cheat, humbug; liar; **'2ig** adj. giddy, dizzy.

Schwind|sucht ⁂ ['ʃvint-] f (-/no pl.) consumption; **'2süchtig** ⁂ adj. consumptive.

Schwing|e ['ʃviŋə] f (-/-n) wing, poet. pinion; swingle; **'2en** (irr., ge-, h) **1.** v/t. swing; brandish (weapon); swingle (flax); **2.** v/i. swing; ⊕ oscillate; sound, etc.: vibrate; **'~ung** f (-/-en) oscillation; vibration.

Schwips F [ʃvips] m (-es/-e): e-n ~ haben be tipsy, have had a drop too much.

schwirren ['ʃvirən] v/i. (ge-) **1.** (sein) whir(r); arrow, etc.: whiz(z); insects: buzz; rumours, etc.: buzz, circulate; **2.** (h): mir schwirrt der Kopf my head is buzzing.

'Schwitz|bad n sweating-bath, hot-air bath, vapo(u)r bath; **'2en** (ge-, h) **1.** v/i. sweat, perspire; **2.** F fig. v/t.: Blut und Wasser ~ be in great anxiety.

schwoll [ʃvɔl] pret. of schwellen.

schwor [ʃvoːr] pret. of schwören.

schwören ['ʃvøːrən] (irr., ge-, h) **1.** v/t. swear; e-n Meineid ~ commit perjury; j-m Rache ~ vow vengeance against s.o.; **2.** v/i. swear (bei by);

~ auf (acc.) have great belief in, F swear by.

schwül adj. [ʃvyːl] sultry, oppressively hot; **'2e** f (-/no pl.) sultriness.

Schwulst [ʃvulst] m (-es/⁺e) bombast.

schwülstig adj. ['ʃvylstiç] bombastic, turgid.

Schwund [ʃvunt] m (-[e]s/no pl.) dwindling; wireless, etc.: fading; ⁂ atrophy.

Schwung [ʃvuŋ] m (-[e]s/⁺e) swing; fig. verve, go; flight (of imagination); buoyancy; **'2haft** ⊹ adj. flourishing, brisk; **'~rad** ⊕ n flywheel; watch, clock: balance-wheel; **'2voll** adj. full of energy or verve; attack, translation, etc.: spirited; style, etc.: racy.

Schwur [ʃvuːr] m (-[e]s/⁺e) oath; **'~gericht** ⁑⁑ n England, Wales: appr. court of assize.

sechs [zɛks] **1.** adj. six; **2.** 2 f (-/-en) six; **'2eck** n (-[e]s/-e) hexagon; **'~eckig** adj. hexagonal; **'~fach** adj. sixfold, sextuple; **'~mal** adv. six times; **'~monatig** adj. lasting or of six months, six-months ...; **'~monatlich 1.** adj. six-monthly; **2.** adv. every six months; **~stündig** adj. [-ʃtyndiç] lasting or of six hours, six-hour ...; **2'tagerennen** n cycling: six-day race; **~tägig** adj. ['-tɛːgiç] lasting or of six days.

sechs|te adj. ['zɛkstə] sixth; **'2tel** n (-s/-) sixth (part); **'~tens** adv. sixthly, in the sixth place.

sech|zehn(te) adj. ['zɛç-] sixteen(th); **~zig** adj. ['-tsiç] sixty; **'~zigste** adj. sixtieth.

See [zeː] **1.** m (-s/-n) lake; **2.** f (-/no pl.) sea; an die ~ gehen go to the seaside; in ~ gehen or stechen put to sea; auf ~ at sea; auf hoher ~ on the high seas; zur ~ gehen go to sea; **3.** f (-/-n) sea, billow; **'~bad** n seaside resort; **'~fahrer** m sailor, navigator; **'~fahrt** f navigation; voyage; **'2fest** adj. seaworthy; ~ sein be a good sailor; **'~gang** m (motion of the) sea; **'~hafen** m seaport; **'~handel** ⊹ m maritime trade; **'~herrschaft** f naval supremacy; **'~hund** zo. m seal; **'2krank** adj. seasick; **'~krankheit** f (-/no pl.) seasickness; **'~krieg** m naval war(fare).

Seele ['zeːlə] f (-/-n) soul (a. fig.); mit or von ganzer ~ with all one's heart.

'Seelen|größe f (-/no pl.) greatness of soul or mind; **'~heil** n salvation, spiritual welfare; **'2los** adj. soulless; **'~qual** f anguish of mind, (mental) agony; **'~ruhe** f peace of mind; coolness.

'seelisch adj. psychic(al), mental.

'Seelsorge f (-/no pl.) cure of souls;

ministerial work; '∼r m (-s/-) pastor, minister.

'See|macht f naval power; '∼mann m (-[e]s/Seeleute) seaman, sailor; '∼meile f nautical mile; '∼not f (-/no pl.) distress (at sea); '∼räuber m pirate; ∼räuberei [∼'raɪ] f (-/-en) piracy; '∼recht n maritime law; '∼reise f voyage; '∼schiff n sea-going ship; '∼schlacht f naval battle; '∼schlange f sea serpent; '∼sieg m naval victory; '∼stadt f seaside town; '∼streitkräfte f/pl. naval forces pl.; '2tüchtig adj. seaworthy; '∼warte f naval observatory; '∼weg m sea-route; auf dem ∼ by sea; '∼wesen n (-s/no pl.) maritime or naval affairs pl.

Segel ['zeːgəl] n (-s/-) sail; unter ∼ gehen set sail; '∼boot n sailing-boat, Am. sailboat; sports: yacht; '∼fliegen n (-s/no pl.) gliding, soaring; '∼flug m gliding flight, glide; '∼flugzeug n glider; '2n (ge-) 1. v/i. (h, sein) sail; sports: yacht; 2. v/t. (h) sail; '∼schiff n sailing-ship, sailing-vessel; '∼sport m yachting; '∼tuch n (-[e]s/-e) sail-cloth, canvas.

Segen ['zeːgən] m (-s/-) blessing (a. fig.), esp. eccl. benediction; '2s-reich adj. blessed.

Segler ['zeːglər] m (-s/-) sailing-vessel, sailing-ship; fast, good, etc. sailer; yachtsman.

segn|en ['zeːgnən] v/t. (ge-, h) bless; '2ung f (-/-en) s. Segen.

sehen ['zeːən] (irr., ge-, h) 1. v/i. see; gut ∼ have good eyes; ∼ auf (acc.) look at; be particular about; ∼ nach look for; look after; 2. v/t. see; notice; watch, observe; '∼swert adj. worth seeing; '2swürdigkeit f (-/-en) object of interest, curiosity, ∼en pl. sights pl. (of a place).

Seher ['zeːər] m (-s/-) seer, prophet; '∼blick m (-[e]s/no pl.) prophetic vision; '∼gabe f (-/no pl.) gift of prophecy.

'Seh|fehler m visual defect; '∼kraft f vision, eyesight.

Sehne ['zeːnə] f (-/-n) anat. sinew, tendon; string (of bow); ⚓ chord.

'sehnen v/refl. (ge-, h) long (nach for), yearn (for, after); sich danach ∼ zu inf. be longing to inf.

'Sehnerv anat. m visual or optic nerve.

'sehnig adj. sinewy (a. fig.), stringy.

'sehn|lich adj. longing; ardent; passionate; '2sucht f longing, yearning; '∼süchtig adj., '∼suchtsvoll adj. longing, yearning; eyes, etc.: a. wistful.

sehr adv. [zeːr] before adj. and adv.: very, most; with vb.: (very) much, greatly.

'Seh|rohr ⚓ n periscope; '∼weite f

range of sight, visual range; in ∼ within eyeshot or sight.

seicht adj. [zaɪçt] shallow; fig. a. superficial.

Seide ['zaɪdə] f (-/-n) silk.

'seiden adj. silk, silken (a. fig.); '2flor m silk gauze; '2glanz m silky lust|re, Am. -er; '2händler m mercer; '2papier n tissue(-paper); '2raupe zo. f silkworm; '2spinnerei f silk-spinning mill; '2stoff m silk cloth or fabric.

'seidig adj. silky.

Seife ['zaɪfə] f (-/-n) soap.

'Seifen|blase f soap-bubble; '∼kistenrennen n soap-box derby; '∼lauge f (soap-)suds pl.; '∼pulver n soap-powder; '∼schale f soapdish; '∼schaum m lather.

'seifig adj. soapy.

seih|en ['zaɪən] v/t. (ge-, h) strain, filter; '2er m (-s/-) strainer, colander.

Seil [zaɪl] n (-[e]s/-e) rope; '∼bahn f funicular or cable railway; '∼er m (-s/-) rope-maker; '∼tänzer m rope-dancer.

sein[1] [zaɪn] 1. v/i. (irr., ge-, sein) be; exist; 2. 2 n (-s/no pl.) being; existence.

sein[2] poss. pron. [∼] his, her, its (in accordance with gender of possessor); der (die, das) ∼e his, hers, its; ∼ Glück machen make one's fortune; die Seinen pl. his family or people.

'seiner|'seits adv. for his part; '∼zeit adv. then, at that time; in those days.

'seines|'gleichen pron. his equal(s pl.); j-n wie ∼ behandeln treat s.o. as one's equal; er hat nicht ∼ he has no equal; there is no one like him.

seit [zaɪt] 1. prp. (dat.): ∼ 1945 since 1945; ∼ drei Wochen for three weeks; 2. cj. since; es ist ein Jahr her, ∼ ... it is a year now since ...; '∼dem [∼'deːm] 1. adv. since or from that time, ever since; 2. cj. since.

Seite ['zaɪtə] f (-/-n) side (a. fig.); flank (a. ✕, △); page (of book).

'Seiten|ansicht f profile, side-view; '∼blick m side-glance; '∼flügel △ m wing; '∼hieb fig. m innuendo, sarcastic remark; '2s prp. (gen.) on the part of; by; '∼schiff △ n church: aisle; '∼sprung fig. m extra-marital adventure; '∼straße f bystreet; '∼stück fig. n counterpart (zu of); '∼weg m by-way.

seit'her adv. since (then, that time).

'seit|lich adj. lateral; ∼wärts adv. ['∼vɛrts] sideways; aside.

Sekret|är [zekre'tɛːr] m (-s/-e) secretary; bureau; ∼ariat [∼'ari'aːt] n (-[e]s/-e) secretary's office; secretariat(e); ∼ärin f (-/-nen) secretary.

Sekt [zɛkt] *m* (-[e]s/-e) champagne.

Sekt|e ['zɛktə] *f* (-/-n) sect; **~ierer** [~'tiːrər] *m* (-s/-) sectarian.

Sektor ['zɛktɔr] *m* (-s/-en) Å, ✕, *pol.* sector; *fig.* field, branch.

Sekunde [ze'kundə] *f* (-/-n) second; **~nbruchteil** *m* split second; **~nzeiger** *m* second-hand.

selb *adj.* [zɛlp] same; **~er** F *pron.* ['~bər] *s. selbst 1.*

selbst [zɛlpst] 1. *pron.* self; personally; *ich* ~ I myself; *von* ~ *p.* of one's own accord; *thing:* by itself, automatically; 2. *adv.* even; 3. ♀ *n* (-/no *pl.*) (one's own) self; ego.

selbständig *adj.* ['zɛlpʃtɛndiç] independent; *sich* ~ *machen* set up for o.s.; '♀keit *f* (-/no *pl.*) independence.

'Selbst|anlasser *mot. m* self-starter; '**~anschluß** *teleph. m* automatic connection; '**~bedienungsladen** *m* self-service shop; '**~beherrschung** *f* self-command, self-control; '**~bestimmung** *f* self-determination; '**~betrug** *m* self-deception; '♀bewußt *adj.* self-confident, self-reliant; '**~bewußtsein** *n* self-confidence, self-reliance; '**~binder** *m* (-s/-) tie; '**~erhaltung** *f* self-preservation; '**~erkenntnis** *f* self-knowledge; '**~erniedrigung** *f* self-abasement; '♀gefällig *adj.* (self-)complacent; '**~gefälligkeit** *f* (-/no *pl.*) (self-)complacency; '**~gefühl** *n* (-[e]s/no *pl.*) self-reliance; '♀gemacht *adj.* ['~gəmaxt] homemade; '♀gerecht *adj.* self-righteous; '**~gespräch** *n* soliloquy, monolog(ue); '♀herrlich 1. *adj.* high-handed, autocratic(al); 2. *adv.* with a high hand; '**~hilfe** *f* self-help; '**~kostenpreis** ♱ *m* cost price; '**~laut** *gr. m* vowel; '♀los *adj.* unselfish, disinterested; '**~mord** *m* suicide; '**~mörder** *m* suicide; '♀mörderisch *adj.* suicidal; '♀sicher *adj.* self-confident, self-assured; '**~sucht** *f* (-/no *pl.*) selfishness, ego(t)ism; '♀süchtig *adj.* selfish, ego(t)istic(al); '♀tätig ⊕ *adj.* self-acting, automatic; '**~täuschung** *f* self-deception; '**~überwindung** *f* (-/no *pl.*) self-conquest; '**~unterricht** *m* self-instruction; '**~verleugnung** *f* self-denial; '**~versorger** *m* (-s/-) self-supporter; '♀verständlich 1. *adj.* self-evident, obvious; 2. *adv.* of course, naturally; ~*l a.* by all means!; '**~verständlichkeit** *f* 1. (-/-en) matter of course; 2. (-/no *pl.*) matter-offactness; '**~verteidigung** *f* self-defen|ce, *Am.* -se; '**~vertrauen** *n* self-confidence, self-reliance; '**~verwaltung** *f* self-government, autonomy; '♀zufrieden *adj.* self-satisfied; '**~zufriedenheit** *f* self-

satisfaction; '**~zweck** *m* (-[e]s/no *pl.*) end in itself.

selig *adj.* ['zeːliç] *eccl.* blessed; late, deceased; *fig.* blissful, overjoyed; '♀keit *fig. f* (-/-en) bliss, very great joy.

Sellerie ♀ ['zɛləriː] *m* (-s/-[s]), *f* (-/-) celery.

selten ['zɛltən] 1. *adj.* rare; scarce; 2. *adv.* rarely, seldom; '♀heit *f* (-/-en) rarity, scarcity; rarity, curio(sity); '♀heitswert *m* (-[e]s/no *pl.*) scarcity value.

Selterswasser ['zɛltərs-] *n* (-s/~) seltzer (water), soda-water.

seltsam *adj.* ['zɛltzaːm] strange, odd.

Semester *univ.* [ze'mɛstər] *n* (-s/-) term.

Semikolon *gr.* [zemi'koːlən] *n* (-s/-s, *Semikola*) semicolon.

Seminar [zemi'naːr] *n* (-s/-e) *univ.* seminar; seminary (*for priests*).

Senat [ze'naːt] *m* (-[e]s/-e) senate; *parl.* Senate.

send|en ['zɛndən] *v/t.* 1. (*irr.*, ge-, *h*) send; forward; 2. (ge-, *h*) transmit; broadcast, *Am. a.* radio(broadcast); telecast; '♀er *m* (-s/-) transmitter; broadcasting station.

'Sende|raum *m* (broadcasting) studio; '**~zeichen** *n* interval signal.

'Sendung *f* (-/-en) ♱ consignment, shipment; broadcast; telecast; *fig.* mission. [♀.)

Senf [zɛnf] *m* (-[e]s/-e) mustard (*a.*)

sengen ['zɛŋən] *v/t.* (ge-, *h*) singe, scorch; '**~d** *adj. heat:* parching.

senil *adj.* [ze'niːl] senile; ♀ität [~ili'tɛːt] *f* (-/no *pl.*) senility.

senior *adj.* ['zeːniɔr] senior.

Senk|blei ['zɛŋk-] *n* △ plumb, plummet; ⚓ *a.* sounding-lead; '♀e *geogr. f* (-/-n) depression, hollow; '♀en *v/t.* (ge-, *h*) lower; sink (*a. voice*); let down; bow (*head*); cut (*prices, etc.*); *sich* ~ *land, buildings, etc.:* sink, subside; *ceiling, etc.:* sag; '**~fuß** ⚕ *m* flat-foot; '**~fußeinlage** *f* arch support; '**~grube** *f* cesspool; '♀recht *adj.* vertical, *esp.* Å perpendicular; '**~ung** *f* (-/-en) *geogr.* depression, hollow; lowering, reduction (*of prices*); ⚒ sedimentation.

Sensation [zɛnza'tsjoːn] *f* (-/-en) sensation; ♀ell *adj.* [~o'nɛl] sensational; **~slust** *f* (-/no *pl.*) sensationalism; **~spresse** *f* yellow press.

Sense ['zɛnzə] *f* (-/-n) scythe.

sensi|bel *adj.* [zɛn'ziːbəl] sensitive; ♀bilität [~ibili'tɛːt] *f* (-/no *pl.*) sensitiveness.

sentimental *adj.* [zɛntimɛn'taːl] sentimental; ♀ität [~ali'tɛːt] *f* (-/-en) sentimentality.

September [zɛp'tɛmbər] *m* (-[s]/-) September.

Serenade ♪ [zereˈnɑːdə] f (-/-n) serenade.

Serie [ˈzeːrjə] f (-/-n) series; set; *billiards*: break; 'Onmäßig **1.** adj. standard; **2.** adv.: ~ herstellen produce in mass; '~nproduktion f mass production.

seriös adj. [zeˈrjøːs] serious; trustworthy, reliable.

Serum [ˈzeːrum] n (-s/Seren, Sera) serum.

Service¹ [zɛrˈviːs] n (-s/-) service, set.

Service² [ˈzœːrvis] m, n (-/-s) service.

servier|en [zɛrˈviːrən] v/t. (no -ge-, h) serve; Owagen m trolley(-table).

Serviette [zɛrˈvjɛtə] f (-/-n) (table-)napkin.

Sessel [ˈzɛsəl] m (-s/-) armchair, easy chair; '~lift m chair-lift.

seßhaft adj. [ˈzɛshaft] settled, established; resident.

Setzei [ˈzɛtsʔ-] n fried egg.

'**setzen** (ge-) **1.** v/t. (h) set, place, put; *typ.* compose; ♂ plant; erect, raise (*monument*); stake (*money*) (auf acc. on); sich ~ sit down, take a seat; *bird*: perch; *foundations of house, sediment, etc.*: settle; **2.** v/i. (h): ~ auf (acc.) back (*horse, etc.*); **3.** v/i. (sein): ~ über (acc.) leap (*wall, etc.*); clear (*hurdle, etc.*); take (*ditch, etc.*).

'**Setzer** typ. m (-s/-) compositor, type-setter; ~ei typ. [~ˈraɪ] f (-/-en) composing-room.

Seuche [ˈzɔʏçə] f (-/-n) epidemic (disease).

seufz|en [ˈzɔʏftsən] v/i. (ge-, h) sigh; '2er m (-s/-) sigh.

sexuell adj. [zɛksuˈɛl] sexual.

sezieren [zeˈtsiːrən] v/t. (no -ge-, h) dissect (a. fig.).

sich refl. pron. [ziç] oneself; sg. himself, herself, itself; pl. themselves; sg. yourself, pl. yourselves; each other, one another; sie blickte ~ um she looked about her.

Sichel [ˈziçəl] f (-/-n) sickle; s. Mondsichel.

sicher [ˈziçər] **1.** adj. secure (vor dat. from), safe (from); proof (against); hand: steady; certain, sure; positive; aus ~er Quelle from a reliable source; e-r Sache ~ sein be sure of s.th.; **2.** adv. s. sicherlich; um ~ zu gehen to be on the safe side, to make sure.

'**Sicherheit** f (-/-en) security; safety; surety, certainty; positiveness; assurance (of manner); in ~ bringen place in safety; '~snadel f safety-pin; '~sschloß n safety-lock.

'**sicher|lich** adv. surely, certainly; undoubtedly; er wird ~ kommen he is sure to come; '~n v/t. (ge-, h) secure (a. ✕, ⊕); guarantee (a. ✝); protect, safeguard; sich et. ~ secure

(*prize, seat, etc.*); '~stellen v/t. (sep., -ge-, h) secure; 'Oung f (-/-en) securing; safeguard(ing); ⊕ security, guaranty; ⊕ safety device; ⚡ fuse.

Sicht [ziçt] f (-/no pl.) visibility; view; in ~ kommen come in(to) view or sight; auf lange ~ in the long run; auf or bei ~ ✝ at sight; '2bar adj. visible; '2en v/t. (ge-, h) ⚓ sight; fig. sift; '2lich adv. visibly; '~vermerk m visé, visa (on passport).

sickern [ˈzikərn] v/i. (ge-, sein) trickle, ooze, seep.

sie pers. pron. [ziː] nom.: sg. she, pl. they; acc.: sg. her, pl. them; Sie nom. and acc.: sg. and pl. you.

Sieb [ziːp] n (-[e]s/-e) sieve; riddle (for soil, gravel, etc.).

sieben¹ [ˈziːbən] v/t. (ge-, h) sieve, sift; riddle.

sieben² [~] **1.** adj. seven; **2.** ♀ f (-/-) (number) seven; böse ~ shrew, vixen; '~fach adj. sevenfold; '~mal adj. seven times; '2'sachen F f/pl. belongings pl., F traps pl.; '~te adj. seventh; '2tel n (-s/-) seventh (part); '~tens adv. seventhly, in the seventh place.

sieb|zehn(te) adj. [ˈziːp-] seventeen(th); ~zig adj. [ˈ~tsiç] seventy; '~zigste adj. seventieth.

siech adj. [ziːç] sickly; '2tum n (-s/no pl.) sickliness, lingering illness.

Siedehitze [ˈziːdə-] f boiling-heat.

siedeln [ˈziːdəln] v/i. (ge-, h) settle; Am. a. homestead.

siede|n [ˈziːdən] v/t. and v/i. ([irr.,] ge-, h) boil, simmer; '2punkt m boiling-point (a. fig.).

Siedler [ˈziːdlər] m (-s/-) settler; Am. a. homesteader; '~stelle f settler's holding; Am. a. homestead.

'**Siedlung** f (-/-en) settlement; housing estate.

Sieg [ziːk] m (-[e]s/-e) victory (über acc. over); sports: a. win; den ~ davontragen win the day, be victorious.

Siegel [ˈziːgəl] n (-s/-) seal (a. fig.); signet; '~lack m sealing-wax; '2n v/t. (ge-, h) seal; '~ring m signet-ring.

sieg|en [ˈziːgən] v/i. (ge-, h) be victorious (über acc. over), conquer s.o.; sports: win; '2er m (-s/-) conqueror, rhet. victor; sports: winner. **Siegeszeichen** [ˈziːgəs-] n trophy. '**siegreich** adj. victorious, triumphant.

Signal [ziˈgnɑːl] n (-s/-e) signal; 2isieren [~aliˈziːrən] v/t. (no -ge-, h) signal.

Silbe [ˈzilbə] f (-/-n) syllable; '~ntrennung f syllabi(fi)cation.

Silber [ˈzilbər] n (-s/no pl.) silver; s. Tafelsilber; '2n adj. (of) silver;

'**zeug** F *n* silver plate, *Am. a.* silverware.

Silhouette [zilu'ɛtə] *f* (-/-n) silhouette; skyline.

Silvester [zil'vɛstər] *n* (-s/-), **~abend** *m* new-year's eve.

simpel ['zimpəl] 1. *adj.* plain, simple; stupid, silly; 2. 2 *m* (-s/-) simpleton.

Sims [zims] *m, n* (-es/-e) ledge; sill (*of window*); mantelshelf (*of fireplace*); shelf; △ cornice.

Simul|ant [zimu'lant] *m* (-en/-en) *esp.* ✕, ⚓ malingerer; **~ieren** (*no -ge-, h*) 1. *v/t.* sham, feign, simulate (*illness, etc.*); 2. *v/i.* sham, feign; *esp.* ✕, ⚓ malinger.

Sinfonie ♪ [zinfo'ni:] *f* (-/-n) symphony.

sing|en ['ziŋən] *v/t. and v/i.* (*irr., ge-, h*) sing; *vom Blatt* **~** sing at sight; *nach Noten* **~** sing from music; '2**sang** F *m* (-[e]s/*no pl.*) singsong; '2**spiel** *n* musical comedy; '2**stimme** ♪ *f* vocal part.

Singular *gr.* ['ziŋgula:r] *m* (-s/-e) singular (number).

'**Singvogel** *m* song-bird, songster.

sinken ['ziŋkən] *v/i.* (*irr., ge-, sein*) sink; *ship:* a. founder, go down; ✝ *prices:* fall, drop, go down; *den Mut* **~** lose courage.

Sinn [zin] *m* (-[e]s/-e) sense; taste (*für* for); tendency; sense, meaning; *von* **~en** *sein* be out of one's senses; *im* **~** *haben* have in mind; *in gewissem* **~e** in a sense; '**~bild** *n* symbol, emblem; '2**bildlich** *adj.* symbolic(al), emblematic; '2**en** *v/i.* (*irr., ge-, h*): *auf Rache* **~** meditate revenge.

'**Sinnen|lust** *f* sensuality; '**~mensch** *m* sensualist; '**~rausch** *m* intoxication of the senses.

sinnentstellend *adj.* ['zin?-] garbling, distorting. [world.]

'**Sinnenwelt** *f* (-/*no pl.*) material)

'**Sinnes|änderung** *f* change of mind; '**~art** *f* disposition, mentality; '**~organ** *n* sense-organ; '**~täuschung** *f* illusion, hallucination.

'**sinn|lich** *adj.* sensual; material; '2**lichkeit** *f* (-/*no pl.*) sensuality; '**~los** *adj.* senseless; futile, useless; '2**losigkeit** *f* (-/-en) senselessness; futility, uselessness; '**~reich** *adj.* ingenious; '**~verwandt** *adj.* synonymous.

Sipp|e ['zipə] *f* (-/-n) tribe; (blood-)relations *pl.*; family; '**~schaft** *contp. f* (-/-en) relations *pl.*; *fig.* clan, clique; *die ganze* **~** the whole lot.

Sirene [zi're:nə] *f* (-/-n) siren.

Sirup ['zi:rup] *m* (-s/-e) syrup, *Am.* sirup; treacle, molasses *sg.*

Sitte ['zitə] *f* (-/-n) custom; habit; usage; **~n** *pl.* morals *pl.*; manners *pl.*

'**Sitten|bild** *n*, '**~gemälde** *n* genre (-painting); *fig.* picture of manners and morals; '**~gesetz** *n* moral law; '**~lehre** *f* ethics *pl.*; '2**los** *adj.* immoral; '**~losigkeit** *f* (-/-en) immorality; '**~polizei** *f* *appr.* vice squad; '**~prediger** *m* moralizer; '**~richter** *fig. m* censor, moralizer; '2**streng** *adj.* puritanic(al).

'**sittlich** *adj.* moral; '2**keit** *f* (-/*no pl.*) morality; '2**keitsverbrechen** *n* sexual crime.

'**sittsam** *adj.* modest; '2**keit** *f* (-/*no pl.*) modesty.

Situation [zitua'tsjo:n] *f* (-/-en) situation.

Sitz [zits] *m* (-es/-e) seat (*a. fig.*); fit (*of dress, etc.*).

'**sitzen** *v/i.* (*irr., ge-, h*) sit, be seated; *dress, etc.*: fit; *blow, etc.*: tell; F *fig.* do time; **~** *bleiben* remain seated, keep one's seat; '**~bleiben** *v/i.* (*irr. bleiben, sep., -ge-, sein*) *girl at dance:* F be a wallflower; *girl:* be left on the shelf; *at school:* not to get one's remove; **~** *auf* (*dat.*) be left with (*goods*) on one's hands; '**~d** *adj.*: **~e** *Tätigkeit* sedentary work; '**~lassen** *v/t.* (*irr. lassen, sep., [no] -ge-, h*) leave *s.o.* in the lurch, let *s.o.* down; *girl:* jilt (*lover*); leave (*girl*) high and dry; *auf sich* **~** pocket (*insult, etc.*).

'**Sitz|gelegenheit** *f* seating accommodation, seat(s *pl.*); **~** *bieten für* seat; '**~platz** *m* seat; '**~streik** *m* sit-down *or* stay-in strike.

'**Sitzung** *f* (-/-en) sitting (*a. parl., paint.*); meeting, conference; '**~speriode** *f* session.

Skala ['ska:la] *f* (-/Skalen, Skalas) scale (*a.* ♪); dial (*of radio set*); *fig.* gamut; *gleitende* **~** sliding scale.

Skandal [skan'da:l] *m* (-s/-e) scandal; row, riot; 2**ös** *adj.* [~a'lø:s] scandalous.

Skelett [ske'lɛt] *n* (-[e]s/-e) skeleton.

Skep|sis ['skɛpsis] *f* (-/*no pl.*) scepticism, *Am. a.* skepticism; **~tiker** ['~tikər] *m* (-s/-) sceptic, *Am. a.* skeptic; 2**tisch** *adj.* sceptical, *Am. a.* skeptical.

Ski [ʃi:] *m* (-s/-er, ✎-) ski; **~** *laufen or fahren* ski; '**~fahrer** *m*, '**~läufer** *m* skier; '**~lift** *m* ski-lift; '**~sport** *m* (-[e]s/*no pl.*) skiing.

Skizz|e ['skitsə] *f* (-/-n) sketch (*a. fig.*); 2**ieren** [~'tsi:rən] *v/t.* (*no -ge-, h*) sketch, outline (*both a. fig.*).

Sklav|e ['skla:və] *m* (-n/-n) slave (*a. fig.*); '**~enhandel** *m* slave-trade; '**~enhändler** *m* slave-trader; 2**e'rei** *f* (-/-en) slavery; '2**isch** *adj.* slavish.

Skonto ✝ ['skɔnto] *m, n* (-s/-s, ✎ Skonti) discount.

Skrupel ['skru:pəl] *m* (-s/-) scruple; '2**los** *adj.* unscrupulous.

Skulptur [skulp'tu:r] *f* (-/-en) sculpture.

Slalom ['slɑːləm] *m* (-s/-s) *skiing, etc.*: slalom.

Slaw|e ['slɑːvə] *m* (-n/-n) Slav; **'ℒisch** *adj.* Slav(onic).

Smaragd [sma'rakt] *m* (-[e]s/-e) emerald; **ℒgrün** *adj.* emerald.

Smoking ['smoːkiŋ] *m* (-s/-s) dinner-jacket, *Am. a.* tuxedo, F tux.

so [zoː] 1. *adv.* so, thus; like this *or* that; as; ~ ein such a; ~ ... wie as ... as; nicht ~ ... wie not so ... as; ~ oder ~ by hook or by crook; 2. *cj.* so, therefore, consequently; ~ daß so that; **~bald** *cj.* [zo'-]: ~ (als) as soon as.

Socke ['zɔkə] *f* (-/-n) sock; **'~l** *m* (-s/-) △ pedestal, socle; socket (*of lamp*); **'~n** *m* (-s/-) sock; **'~nhalter** *m*/*pl.* suspenders *pl.*, *Am.* garters *pl.*

Sodawasser ['zoːda-] *n* (-s/⁼) soda(-water).

Sodbrennen ♔ ['zoːt-] *n* (-s/*no pl.*) heartburn.

soeben *adv.* [zo'-] just (now).

Sofa ['zoːfa] *n* (-s/-s) sofa.

sofern *cj.* [zo'-] if, provided that; ~ nicht unless.

soff [zɔf] *pret. of* saufen.

sofort *adv.* [zo'-] at once, immediately, directly, right *or* straight away; **~ig** *adj.* immediate, prompt.

Sog [zoːk] 1. *m* (-[e]s/-e) suction; ⚓ wake (*a. fig.*), undertow; 2. ♀ *pret. of* saugen.

so|gar *adv.* [zo'-] even; **~genannt** *adj.* ['zoː-] so-called; **~gleich** *adv.* [zo'-] *s.* sofort.

Sohle ['zoːlə] *f* (-/-n) sole; bottom (*of valley, etc.*); ⚒ floor.

Sohn [zoːn] *m* (-[e]s/⁼e) son.

solange *cj.* [zo'-]: ~ (als) so *or* as long as.   [such.)

solch *pron.* [zɔlç] such; *als* ~e(r) as)

Sold ⚔ [zɔlt] *m* (-[e]s/-e) pay.

Soldat [zɔl'daːt] *m* (-en/-en) soldier; der unbekannte ~ the Unknown Warrior *or* Soldier.

Söldner ['zœldnər] *m* (-s/-) mercenary.

Sole ['zoːlə] *f* (-/-n) brine, salt water.

solid *adj.* [zo'liːt] solid (*a. fig.*); basis, *etc.*: sound; † firm, *etc.*: sound, solvent; *prices*: reasonable, fair; *p.* steady, staid, respectable.

solidarisch *adj.* [zoli'daːriʃ]: sich ~ erklären mit declare one's solidarity with.

solide *adj.* [zo'liːdə] *s.* solid.

Solist [zo'list] *m* (-en/-en) soloist.

Soll † [zɔl] *n* (-[s]/-[s]) debit; (output) target.

sollen (h) 1. *v/i.* (ge-): ich sollte (eigentlich) I ought to; 2. *v/aux.* (irr., no -ge-): er soll he shall; he is to; he is said to; ich sollte I should; er sollte (eigentlich) zu Hause sein he ought to be at home; er sollte seinen Vater niemals wiedersehen he was never to see his father again.

Solo ['zoːlo] *n* (-s/-s, Soli) solo.

somit *cj.* [zo'-] thus; consequently.

Sommer ['zɔmər] *m* (-s/-) summer; **'~frische** *f* (-/-n) summer-holidays *pl.*; summer-resort; **'ℒlich** *adj.* summer-like, summer(l)y; **'~sprosse** *f* freckle; **'ℒsprossig** *adj.* freckled; **'~wohnung** *f* summer residence, *Am.* cottage, summer house; **'~zeit** *f* 1. (-/-en) *season*: summertime; 2. (-/*no pl.*) summer time, *Am.* daylight-saving time.

Sonate ♪ [zo'naːtə] *f* (-/-n) sonata.

Sonde ['zɔndə] *f* (-/-n) probe.

Sonder|angebot ['zɔndər-] *n* special offer; **~ausgabe** *f* special (edition); **'ℒbar** *adj.* strange, odd; **~beilage** *f* inset, supplement (*of newspaper*); **'~berichterstatter** *m* special correspondent; **'ℒlich** 1. *adj.* special, peculiar; 2. *adv.*: nicht ~ not particularly; **'~ling** *m* (-s/-e) crank, odd person; **'ℒn** 1. *cj.* but; nicht nur, ~ auch not only, but (also); 2. *v/t.* (ge-, h): die Spreu vom Weizen ~ sift the chaff from the wheat; **'~recht** *n* privilege; **'~zug** 🚂 *m* special (train).

sondieren [zɔn'diːrən] (*no* -ge-, h) 1. *v/t.* ⚕ probe (*a. fig.*); 2. *fig. v/i.* make tentative inquiries.

Sonn|abend ['zɔn?-] *m* (-s/-e) Saturday; **'~e** *f* (-/-n) sun; **'ℒen** *v/t.* (ge-, h) (expose to the) sun; sich ~ sun o.s. (*a. fig. in dat.* in), bask in the sun.

'Sonnen|aufgang *m* sunrise; **'~bad** *n* sun-bath; **'~brand** *m* sunburn; **'~bräune** *f* sunburn, tan, *Am.* (sun) tan; **'~brille** *f* (e-e a pair of) sunglasses *pl.*; **'~finsternis** *f* solar eclipse; **'~fleck** *m* sun-spot; **'ℒklar** *fig. adj.* (as) clear as daylight; **'~licht** *n* (-[e]s/*no pl.*) sunlight; **'~schein** *m* (-[e]s/*no pl.*) sunshine; **'~schirm** *m* sunshade, parasol; **'~segel** *n* awning; **'~seite** *f* sunny side (*a. fig.*); **'~stich** ⚕ *m* sunstroke; **'~strahl** *m* sunbeam; **'~uhr** *f* sun-dial; **'~untergang** *m* sunset, sundown; **'ℒverbrannt** *adj.* sunburnt, tanned; **'~wende** *f* solstice.

'sonnig *adj.* sunny (*a. fig.*).

'Sonntag *m* Sunday.

'Sonntags|anzug *m* Sunday suit *or* best; **'~fahrer** *mot. contp. m* Sunday driver; **'~kind** *n* person born on a Sunday; *fig.* person born under a lucky star; **'~rückfahrkarte** 🚂 *f* week-end ticket; **'~ruhe** *f* Sunday rest; **'~staat** F *co. m* (-[e]s/*no pl.*) Sunday go-to-meeting clothes *pl.*

sonor *adj.* [zo'noːr] sonorous.

sonst [zɔnst] 1. *adv.* otherwise, with *pron.* else; usually, normally; wer ~? who else?; wie ~ as usual; ~ nichts nothing else; 2. *cj.* otherwise, or else; **'~ig** *adj.* other; **'~wie** *adv.*

in some other way; '₋wo adv. elsewhere, somewhere else.

Sopran ♪ [zo'prɑːn] m (-s/-e) soprano; sopranist; ₋istin [₋a'nistin] f (-/-nen) soprano, sopranist.

Sorge ['zɔrgə] f (-/-n) care; sorrow; uneasiness, anxiety; ~ tragen für take care of; sich ₋n machen um be anxious or worried about; mach dir keine ₋n don't worry.

'**sorgen** (ge-, h) 1. v/i.: ~ für care for, provide for; take care of, attend to; dafür ₋, daß take care that; 2. v/refl.: sich ₋ um be anxious or worried about; '₋frei adj., '₋los adj. carefree, free from care; '₋voll adj. full of cares; face: worried, troubled.

Sorg|falt ['zɔrkfalt] f (-/no pl.) care(fulness); ꝗfältig adj. ['₋fɛltiç] careful; 'ꝗlich adj. careful, anxious; 'ꝗlos adj. carefree; thoughtless; negligent; careless; 'ꝗsam adj. careful.

Sort|e ['zɔrtə] f (-/-n) sort, kind, species, Am. a. stripe; ꝗieren [₋'tiːrən] v/t. (no -ge-, h) (as)sort; arrange; ₋iment [₋i'ment] n (-[e]s/-e) assortment.

Soße ['zoːsə] f (-/-n) sauce; gravy.

sott [zɔt] pret. of sieden.

Souffl|eurkasten thea. [su'fløːr-] m prompt-box, promter's box; ₋euse thea. [₋zə] f (-/-n) prompter; ꝗieren thea. (no -ge-, h) 1. v/i. prompt (j-m s.o.); 2. v/t. prompt.

Souverän [suvə'rɛːn] 1. m (-s/-e) sovereign; 2. ꝗ adj. sovereign; fig. superior; ₋ität [₋eni'tɛːt] f (-/no pl.) sovereignty.

so|viel [zo'-] 1. cj. so or as far as; ₋ ich weiß so far as I know; 2. adv.: doppelt ~ twice as much; ₋'weit 1. cj.: ~ es mich betrifft in so far as it concerns me, so far as I am concerned; 2. adv.: ~ ganz gut not bad (for a start); ₋'wieso adv. [zovi'zoː] in any case, anyhow, anyway.

Sowjet [zɔ'vjɛt] m (-s/-s) Soviet; ꝗisch adj. Soviet.

sowohl cj. [zo'-]: ~ ... als (auch) ... both ... and ..., ... as well as ...

sozial adj. [zo'tsjaːl] social; ꝗdemokrat m social democrat; ₋isieren [₋ali'ziːrən] v/t. (no -ge-, h) socialize; ꝗisierung [₋ali'ziːruŋ] f (-/-en) socialization; ꝗist [₋a'list] m (-en/-en) socialist; ₋istisch adj. [₋a'listiʃ] socialist.

Sozius ['zoːtsjus] m (-/-se) ♀ partner; mot. pillion-rider; '₋sitz mot. m pillion.

sozusagen adv. [zotsu'zaːgən] so to speak, as it were.

Spachtel ['ʃpaxtəl] m (-s/-), f (-/-n) spatula.

spähe|n ['ʃpɛːən] v/i. (ge-, h) look out (nach for); peer; '₋r m (-s/-) look-out; ✕ scout.

Spalier [ʃpa'liːr] n (-s/-e) trellis, espalier; fig. lane; ~ bilden form a lane.

Spalt [ʃpalt] m (-[e]s/-e) crack, split, rift, crevice, fissure; '₋e f (-/-n) s. Spalt; typ. column; 'ꝗen v/t. ([irr.,] ge-, h) split (a. fig. hairs), cleave (block of wood, etc.); sich ~ split (up); '₋ung f (-/-en) splitting, cleavage; fig. split; eccl. schism.

Span [ʃpaːn] m (-[e]s/ꝗe) chip, shaving, splinter.

Spange ['ʃpaŋə] f (-/-n) clasp; buckle; clip; slide (in hair); strap (of shoes); bracelet.

Span|ier ['ʃpaːnjər] m (-s/-) Spaniard; ꝗisch adj. Spanish.

Spann [ʃpan] 1. m (-[e]s/-e) instep; 2. ♀ pret. of spinnen; '₋e f (-/-n) span; orn. spread (of wings); ✝ margin; 'ꝗen (ge-, h) 1. v/t. stretch (rope, muscles, etc.); cock (rifle); bend (bow, etc.); tighten (spring, etc.); vor den Wagen ~ harness to the carriage; s. gespannt; 2. v/i. be (too) tight; 'ꝗend adj. exciting, thrilling, gripping; '₋kraft f (-/no pl.) elasticity; fig. energy; '₋ung f (-/-en) tension (a. fig.); ⊕ voltage; ⊕ strain, stress; ⚠ span; fig. close attention.

Spar|büchse ['ʃpaːr-] f money-box; 'ꝗen (ge-, h) 1. v/t. save (money, strength, etc.); put by; 2. v/i. save; economize, cut down expenses; ~ mit be chary of (praise, etc.); '₋er m (-s/-) saver.

Spargel ♀ ['ʃpargəl] m (-s/-) asparagus.

'**Spar|kasse** f savings-bank; '₋konto n savings-account.

spärlich adj. ['ʃpɛːrliç] crop, dress, etc.: scanty; population, etc.: sparse; hair: thin.

Sparren ['ʃparən] m (-s/-) rafter, spar.

'**sparsam** 1. adj. saving, economical (mit of); 2. adv.: ~ leben lead a frugal life, economize; ~ umgehen mit use sparingly, be frugal of; 'ꝗkeit f (-/no pl.) economy, frugality.

Spaß [ʃpaːs] m (-es/ꝗe) joke, jest; fun, lark; amusement; aus or im or zum ~ in fun; ~ beiseite joking apart; er hat nur ~ gemacht he was only joking; 'ꝗen v/i. (ge-, h) joke, jest, make fun; damit ist nicht zu ~ that is no joking matter; 'ꝗhaft adj., 'ꝗig adj. facetious, waggish; funny; '₋macher m (-s/-), '₋vogel m wag, joker.

spät [ʃpɛː] 1. adj. late; advanced; zu ~ too late; am ~en Nachmittag late in the afternoon; wie ~ ist es? what time is it?; 2. adv. late; er kommt 5 Minuten zu ~ he is five minutes late (zu for); ~ in der Nacht late at night.

Spaten ['ʃpaːtən] m (-s/-) spade.

'späte|r 1. adj. later; 2. adv. later on; afterward(s); früher oder ~ sooner or later; **_stens** adv. ['_stəns] at the latest.

Spatz orn. [ʃpats] m (-en, -es/-en) sparrow.

spazieren [ʃpa'tsiːrən] v/i. (no -ge-, sein) walk, stroll; **_fahren** (irr. fahren, sep., -ge-) 1. v/i. (sein) go for a drive; 2. v/t. (h) take for a drive; take (baby) out (in pram); **_gehen** v/i. (irr. gehen, sep., -ge-, sein) go for a walk.

Spa'zier|fahrt f drive, ride; **_gang** m walk, stroll; e-n ~ machen go for a walk; **_gänger** [_gɛŋər] m (-s/-) walker, stroller; **_weg** m walk.

Speck [ʃpɛk] m (-[e]s/-e) bacon.

Spedi|teur [ʃpedi'tøːr] m (-s/-e) forwarding agent; (furniture) remover; **_tion** [_'tsjoːn] f (-/-en) forwarding agent or agency.

Speer [ʃpeːr] m (-[e]s/-e) spear; sports: javelin; **_werfen** n (-s/no pl.) javelin-throw(ing); **_werfer** m (-s/-) javelin-thrower.

Speiche ['ʃpaɪçə] f (-/-n) spoke.

Speichel ['ʃpaɪçəl] m (-s/no pl.) saliva; **_lecker** fig. m (-s/-) lickspittle, toady.

Speicher ['ʃpaɪçər] m (-s/-) granary; warehouse; garret, attic.

speien ['ʃpaɪən] (irr., ge-, h) 1. v/t. spit out (blood, etc.); volcano, etc.: belch (fire, etc.); 2. v/i. spit; vomit, be sick.

Speise ['ʃpaɪzə] f (-/-n) food, nourishment; meal; dish; **_eis** n ice-cream; **_kammer** f larder, pantry; **_karte** f bill of fare, menu; **'2n** (ge-, h) 1. v/t.: s. essen 1; at restaurants: take one's meals; 2. v/t. feed; ⊕, ⚡ a. supply (mit with); **_nfolge** f menu; **_röhre** anat. f gullet, (o)esophagus; **_saal** m dining-hall; **_schrank** m (meat-) safe; **_wagen** m dining-car, diner; **_zimmer** n dining-room.

Spektakel F [ʃpɛk'taːkəl] m (-s/-) noise, din.

Spekul|ant [ʃpeku'lant] m (-en/-en) speculator; **_ation** [_a'tsjoːn] f (-/-en) speculation; ✝ a. venture; **2ieren** [_'liːrən] v/i. (no -ge-, h) speculate (auf acc. on).

Spelunke [ʃpe'luŋkə] f (-/-n) den, drinking-den, Am. F a. dive.

Spende ['ʃpɛndə] f (-/-n) gift; alms pl.; contribution; **'2n** v/t. (ge-, h) give; donate (money to charity, blood, etc.); eccl. administer (sacraments); bestow (praise) (dat. on); **'_r** m (-s/-) giver; donor.

spen'dieren v/t. (no -ge-, h): j-m et. ~ treat s.o. to s.th., stand s.o. s.th.

Sperling orn. ['ʃpɛrliŋ] m (-s/-e) sparrow.

Sperr|e ['ʃpɛrə] f (-/-n) barrier; 🚇 barrier, Am. gate; toll-bar; ⊕ lock(ing device), detent; barricade; ✝, ⚓ embargo; ✕ blockade; sports: suspension; **'2en** (ge-, h) 1. v/t. close; ✝, ⚓ embargo; cut off (gas supply, electricity, etc.); stop (cheque, etc.); sports: suspend; 2. v/i. jam, be stuck; **_holz** n plywood; **_konto** ✝ n blocked account; **_kreis** ⚡ m wave-trap; **_sitz** thea. m stalls pl., Am. orchestra; **_ung** f (-/-en) closing; stoppage (of cheque, etc.); ✝, ⚓ embargo; ✕ blockade; **_zone** f prohibited area.

Spesen ['ʃpeːzən] pl. expenses pl., charges pl.

Spezial|ausbildung [ʃpe'tsjaːl?-] f special training; **_fach** n special(i)ty; **_geschäft** ✝ n one-line shop, Am. specialty store; **2isieren** [_ali'ziːrən] v/refl. (no -ge-, h) specialize (auf acc. in); **_ist** [_a'ist] m (-en/-en) specialist; **_ität** [_ali'tɛːt] f (-/-en) special(i)ty.

speziell adj. [ʃpe'tsjɛl] specific, special, particular.

spezifisch adj. [ʃpe'tsiːfiʃ]: ~es Gewicht specific gravity.

Sphäre ['sfɛːrə] f (-/-n) sphere (a. fig.).

Spick|aal ['ʃpik-] m smoked eel; **'2en** (ge-, h) 1. v/t. lard; fig. (inter-) lard (mit with); F: j-n ~ grease s.o.'s palm; 2. F fig. v/i. crib.

spie [ʃpiː] pret. of speien.

Spiegel ['ʃpiːgəl] m (-s/-) mirror (a. fig.), looking-glass; '2bild n reflected image; '2blank adj. mirror-like; **_ei** ['ʃpiːgəl?-] n fried egg; '2glatt adj. water: glassy, unrippled; road, etc.: very slippery; '2n (ge-, h) 1. v/i. shine; 2. v/refl. be reflected; **_schrift** f mirror-writing.

Spieg(e)lung ['ʃpiːg(ə)luŋ] f (-/-en) reflection, reflexion; mirage.

Spiel [ʃpiːl] n (-[e]s/-e) play (a. fig.); game (a. fig.); match; ✝ playing; ein ~ Karten a pack of playing-cards, Am. a. a deck; auf dem ~ stehen be at stake; aufs ~ setzen jeopardize, stake; **_art** ⚡, zo. f variety; **_ball** m tennis: game ball; billiards: red ball; fig. plaything, sport; **_bank** f (-/-en) gaming-house; '2en (ge-, h) 1. v/i. play; gamble; ~ mit play with; fig. a. toy with; 2. v/t. play (tennis, violin, etc.); thea. act, play (part); mit j-m Schach ~ play s.o. at chess; den Höflichen ~ do the polite; '2end fig. adv. easily; '_er m (-s/-) player; gambler; **_e'rei** f (-/-en) pastime; child's amusement; **_ergebnis** n sports: result, score; **_feld** n sports: (playing-)field; pitch; **_film** m feature film or picture; '~gefährte m playfellow, playmate; '~karte f playing-card; '~leiter m thea. stage manager; cinematography: director; sports: referee; '~marke f counter, sl. chip; '~plan m thea., etc.: pro-gram(me); repertory; '~platz m playground; '~raum fig. m play, scope; '~regel f rule (of the game); '~sachen f/pl. playthings pl., toys pl.; '~schuld f gambling-debt; '~schule f infant-school, kinder-garten; '~tisch m card-table; gambling-table; '~uhr f musical box, Am. music box; '~verderber m (-s/-) spoil-sport, killjoy, wet blanket; '~waren f/pl. playthings pl., toys pl.; '~zeit f thea. season; sports: time of play; '~zeug n toy(s pl.), plaything(s pl.).

Spieß [ʃpiːs] m (-es/-e) spear, pike; spit; den ~ umdrehen turn the tables; '~bürger m bourgeois, Philistine, Am. a. Babbit; '2bür-gerlich adj. bourgeois, Philistine; '~er m (-s/-) s. Spießbürger; '~ge-selle m accomplice; '~ruten f/pl.: ~ laufen run the gauntlet (a. fig.).

spinal adj. [ʃpiˈnaːl]: ~e Kinder-lähmung ✠ infantile paralysis, poliomyelitis, F polio.

Spinat ⚘ [ʃpiˈnaːt] m (-[e]s/-e) spinach.

Spind [ʃpint] n, m (-[e]s/-e) ward-robe, cupboard; ✕, sports, etc.: locker.

Spindel ['ʃpindəl] f (-/-n) spindle; '2dürr adj. (as) thin as a lath.

Spinn|e zo. ['ʃpinə] f (-/-n) spider; '2en (irr., ge-, h) 1. v/t. spin (a. fig.); hatch (plot, etc.); 2. v/i. cat: purr; F fig. be crazy, sl. be nuts; '~engewebe n cobweb; '~er m (-s/-) spinner; F fig. silly; ~e'rei f (-/-en) spinning; spinning-mill; '~maschine f spinning-machine; '~webe f (-/-n) cobweb.

Spion [ʃpiˈoːn] m (-s/-e) spy, intel-ligencer; fig. judas; '~age [~oˈnaːʒə] f (-/no pl.) espionage; 2ieren [~oˈniːrən] v/i. (no -ge-, h) (play the) spy.

Spiral|e [ʃpiˈraːlə] f (-/-n) spiral (a. ✠), helix; 2förmig adj. [~fœr-miç] spiral, helical.

Spirituosen [ʃpirituˈoːzən] pl. spir-its pl.

Spiritus ['ʃpiːritus] m (-/-se) spirit, alcohol; '~kocher m (-s/-) spirit stove.

Spital [ʃpiˈtaːl] n (-s/⸚er) hospital; alms-house; home for the aged.

spitz [ʃpits] 1. adj. pointed (a. fig.); ✠ angle: acute; fig. poignant; ~e Zunge sharp tongue; 2. adv.: ~ zu-laufen taper (off); '2bube m thief; rogue, rascal (both a. co.); 2büberei [~byːbəˈraɪ] f (-/-en) roguery, ras-

cality (both a. co.); ~bübisch adj. [~byːbiʃ] eyes, smile, etc.: roguish.

'Spitz|e f (-/-n) point (of pencil, weapon, jaw, etc.); tip (of nose, finger, etc.); nib (of tool, etc.); spire; head (of enterprise, etc.); lace; an der ~ liegen sports: be in the lead; j-m die ~ bieten make head against s.o.; auf die ~ treiben carry to an extreme; '~el m (-s/-) (common) informer; '2en v/t. (ge-, h) point, sharpen; den Mund ~ purse (up) one's lips; die Ohren ~ prick up one's ears (a. fig.).

'Spitzen|leistung f top perform-ance; ⊕ maximum capacity; '~lohn m top wages pl.

'spitz|findig adj. subtle, captious; '2findigkeit f (-/-en) subtlety, captiousness; '2hacke f pickax(e), pick; '~ig adj. pointed; fig. a. poignant; '2marke typ. f head(ing); '2name m nickname.

Splitter ['ʃplitər] m (-s/-) splinter, shiver; chip; '2frei adj. glass: shatterproof; '2ig adj. splintery; '2n v/i. (ge-, h, sein) splinter, shiver; '2nackt F adj. stark naked, Am. a. mother-naked; '~partei pol. f splinter party.

spontan adj. [ʃpɔnˈtaːn] spontane-ous.

sporadisch adj. [ʃpoˈraːdiʃ] sporad-ic.

Sporn [ʃpɔrn] m (-[e]s/Sporen) spur; die Sporen geben put or set spurs to (horse); sich die Sporen verdienen win one's spurs; '2en v/t. (ge-, h) spur.

Sport [ʃpɔrt] m (-[e]s/⚘-e) sport; fig. hobby; ~ treiben go in for sports; '~ausrüstung f sports equipment; '~geschäft n sporting-goods shop; '~kleidung f sport clothes pl., sportswear; '~lehrer m games-master; '2lich adj. sporting, sportsmanlike; figure: athletic; '~nachrichten f/pl. sports news sg., pl.; '~platz m sports field; stadium.

Spott [ʃpɔt] m (-[e]s/no pl.) mockery; derision; scorn; (sin mit ~ treiben mit make sport of; '2billig F adj. dirt-cheap.

Spötte|lei [ʃpœtəˈlaɪ] f (-/-en) raillery, sneer, jeer; '2ln v/i. (ge-, h) sneer (über acc. at), jeer (at).

'spotten v/i. (ge-, h) mock (über acc. at); jeer (at); jeder Beschreibung ~ beggar description.

Spötter ['ʃpœtər] m (-s/-) mocker, scoffer; ~ei [~ˈraɪ] f (-/-en) mockery.

'spöttisch adj. mocking; sneering; ironical.

'Spott|name m nickname; '~preis m ridiculous price; für e-n ~ for a mere song; '~schrift f lampoon, satire.

sprach [ʃpraːx] pret. of sprechen.

'Sprache f (-/-n) speech; language

(*a. fig.*); diction; *zur ~ bringen* bring up, broach; *zur ~ kommen* come up (for discussion).

'**Sprach|eigentümlichkeit** *f* idiom; '**~fehler** *m* impediment (in one's speech); '**~führer** *m* language guide; '**~gebrauch** *m* usage; '**~gefühl** *n* (-[e]s/*no pl.*) linguistic instinct; 2**kundig** *adj.* ['~kundiç] versed in languages; '**~lehre** *f* grammar; '**~lehrer** *m* teacher of languages; 2**lich** *adj.* linguistic; grammatical; 2**los** *adj.* speechless; '**~rohr** *n* speaking-trumpet, megaphone; *fig.*: mouthpiece; organ; '**~schatz** *m* vocabulary; '**~störung** *f* impediment (in one's speech); '**~wissenschaft** *f* philology, science of language; linguistics *pl.*; '**~wissenschaftler** *m* philologist; linguist; 2**wissenschaftlich** *adj.* philological; linguistic.

sprang [ʃpraŋ] *pret. of* springen.

Sprech|chor ['ʃpreç-] *m* speaking chorus; 2**en** (*irr.*, ge-, h) **1.** *v/t.* speak (*language, truth, etc.*); pronounce (*judgement*); say (*prayer*); *j-n zu ~ wünschen* wish to see s.o.; *j-n schuldig ~* pronounce s.o. guilty; F *Bände ~* speak volumes (*für for*); **2.** *v/i.* speak; talk (*both: mit* to, with; *über acc., von, of, about*); *er ist nicht zu ~* you cannot see him; '**~er** *m* (-s/-) speaker; *radio:* announcer; spokesman; '**~fehler** *m* slip of the tongue; '**~stunde** *f* consulting-hours *pl.*; '**~übung** *f* exercise in speaking; '**~zimmer** *n* consulting-room, surgery.

spreizen ['ʃpraitsən] *v/t.* (ge-, h) spread (out); *a.* straddle (*legs*); *sich ~* pretend to be unwilling.

Spreng|bombe ⚔ ['ʃpreŋ-] *f* high-explosive bomb, demolition bomb; '**~el** *eccl.* *m* (-s/-) diocese, see; parish; 2**en** (ge-) **1.** *v/t.* (h) sprinkle, water (*road, lawn, etc.*); blow up, blast (*bridge, rocks, etc.*); burst open (*door, etc.*); spring (*mine, etc.*); *gambling:* break (*bank*); break up (*meeting, etc.*); **2.** *v/i.* (sein) gallop; '**~stoff** *m* explosive; '**~ung** *f* (-/-en) blowing-up, blasting; explosion; '**~wagen** *m* water(ing)-cart.

Sprenkel ['ʃprɛŋkəl] *m* (-s/-) speckle, spot; 2**n** *v/t.* (ge-, h) speckle, spot.

Spreu [ʃprɔy] *f* (-/*no pl.*) chaff; *s. sondern* 2.

Sprich|wort ['ʃpriç-] *n* (-[e]s/=er) proverb, adage; 2**wörtlich** *adj.* proverbial (*a. fig.*).

sprießen ['ʃpriːsən] *v/i.* (*irr.*, ge-, sein) sprout; germinate.

Spring|brunnen ['ʃpriŋ-] *m* fountain; 2**en** *v/i.* (*irr.*, ge-, sein) jump, leap; *ball, etc.*: bounce; *swimming:* dive; burst, crack, break; *in die Augen ~* strike the eye; *~ über* (*acc.*)

jump (over), leap, clear; '**~er** *m* (-s/-) jumper; *swimming:* diver; *chess:* knight; '**~flut** *f* spring tide.

Sprit [ʃprit] *m* (-[e]s/-e) spirit, alcohol; F *mot.* fuel, petrol, *sl.* juice, *Am.* gasoline, F gas.

Spritz|e ['ʃpritsə] *f* (-/-n) syringe (*a.* ⚕), squirt; ⊕ fire-engine; *j-m e-e ~ geben* ⚕ give s.o. an injection; 2**en** (ge-) **1.** *v/t.* (h) sprinkle, water (*road, lawn, etc.*); splash (*water, etc.*) (*über acc.* on, over); **2.** *v/t.* (h) splash; *pen:* splutter; **3.** *v/i.* (sein) F *fig.* dash, flit; *~ aus blood, etc.:* spurt or spout from (*wound, etc.*); '**~er** *m* (-s/-) splash; '**~tour** F *f:* *e-e ~ machen* go for a spin.

spröde *adj.* ['ʃprøːdə] *glass, etc.:* brittle; *skin:* chapped, chappy; *esp. girl:* prudish, prim, coy.

Sproß [ʃprɔs] **1.** *m* (Sprosses/Sprosse) ⚘ shoot, sprout, scion (*a. fig.*); *fig.* offspring; **2.** ♀ *pret. of* sprießen.

Sprosse ['ʃprɔsə] *f* (-/-n) rung, round, step.

Sprößling ['ʃprœslɪŋ] *m* (-s/-e) ♂ *s.* Sproß 1.; *co.* son.

Spruch [ʃprux] *m* (-[e]s/=e) saying; dictum; ⚖ sentence; ⚖ verdict; '**~band** *n* banner; 2**reif** *adj.* ripe for decision.

Sprudel ['ʃpruːdəl] *m* (-s/-) mineral water; 2**n** *v/i.* (ge-) **1.** (h) bubble, effervesce; **2.** (sein): *~ aus or von* gush from.

sprüh|en ['ʃpryːən] (ge-) **1.** *v/t.* (h) spray, sprinkle (*liquid*); throw off (*sparks*); *Feuer ~ eyes:* flash fire; **2.** *v/i.* (h): *~ vor* sparkle with (*wit, etc.*); *es sprüht* it is drizzling; **3.** *v/i.* (sein) *sparks:* fly; '**2regen** *m* drizzle.

Sprung [ʃpruŋ] *m* (-[e]s/=e) jump, leap, bound; *swimming:* dive; crack, fissure; '**~brett** *n sports:* springboard; *fig.* stepping-stone; '**~feder** *f* spiral spring.

Spuck|e F ['ʃpukə] *f* (-/*no pl.*) spit(tle); 2**en** (ge-, h) **1.** *v/t.* spit (out) (*blood, etc.*); **2.** *v/i.* spit; *engine:* splutter; '**~napf** *m* spittoon, *Am. a.* cuspidor.

Spuk [ʃpuːk] *m* (-[e]s/-e) apparition, ghost, *co.* spook; F *fig.* noise; 2**en** *v/i.* (ge-, h): *~ in* (*dat.*) haunt (*a place*); *hier spukt es* this place is haunted.

Spule ['ʃpuːlə] *f* (-/-n) spool, reel; bobbin; ⚡ coil; 2**n** *v/t.* (ge-, h) spool, reel.

spülen ['ʃpyːlən] (ge-, h) **1.** *v/t.* rinse (*clothes, mouth, cup, etc.*); wash up (*dishes, etc.*); *an Land ~* wash ashore; **2.** *v/i.* flush the toilet.

Spund [ʃpunt] *m* (-[e]s/=e) bung; plug; '**~loch** *n* bunghole.

Spur [ʃpuːr] *f* (-/-en) trace (*a. fig.*); track (*a. fig.*); print (*a. fig.*); rut (*of wheels*); *j-m auf der ~ sein* be on s.o.'s track.

spür|en ['ʃpyːrən] v/t. (ge-, h) feel; sense; perceive; '⍛sinn m (-[e]s/no pl.) scent; fig. a. flair (für for).

Spurweite ⚙ f ga(u)ge.

sputen ['ʃpuːtən] v/refl. (ge-, h) make haste, hurry up.

Staat [ʃtaːt] m 1. F (-[e]s/no pl.) pomp, state; finery; ~ machen mit make a parade of; 2. (-[e]s/-en) state; government; '⍛enbund m (-[e]s/⍛e) confederacy, confederation; '⍛enlos adj. stateless; '⍛lich adj. state; national; political; public.

'Staats|angehörige m, f (-n/-n) national, citizen, esp. Brt. subject; '⍛angehörigkeit f (-/no pl.) nationality, citizenship; '⍛anwalt ⚖ m public prosecutor, Am. prosecuting attorney; '⍛beamte m Civil Servant, Am. a. public servant; '⍛begräbnis n state or national funeral; '⍛besuch m official or state visit; national; public; '⍛bürgerkunde f (-/no pl.) civics sg.; '⍛bürgerschaft f (-/-en) citizenship; '⍛dienst m Civil Service; '⍛eigen adj. state-owned; '⍛feind m public enemy; '⍛feindlich adj. subversive; '⍛gewalt f (-/no pl.) supreme power; '⍛haushalt m budget; '⍛hoheit f (-/no pl.) sovereignty; '⍛kasse f treasury, Brt. exchequer; '⍛klugheit f political wisdom; '⍛kunst f (-/no pl.) statesmanship; '⍛mann m statesman; ⍛männisch adj. ['⍛meniʃ] statesmanlike; '⍛oberhaupt n head of (the) state; '⍛papiere n/pl. Government securities pl.; '⍛rat m Privy Council; '⍛recht n public law; '⍛schatz m s. Staatskasse; '⍛schulden f/pl. national debt; '⍛sekretär m under-secretary of state; '⍛streich m coup d'état; '⍛trauer f national mourning; '⍛vertrag m treaty; '⍛wesen n polity; '⍛wirtschaft f public sector of the economy; '⍛wissenschaft f political science; '⍛wohl n public weal.

Stab [ʃtaːp] m (-[e]s/⍛e) staff (a. fig.); bar (of metal, wood); crosier, staff (of bishop); wand (of magician); relay-race, ♪ conducting: baton; pole-vaulting: pole.

stabil adj. [ʃtaˈbiːl] stable (a. ✝); health: robust.

stabilisier|en [ʃtabiliˈziːrən] v/t. (no -ge-, h) stabilize (a. ✝); ⍛ung f (-/-en) stabilization (a. ✝).

stach [ʃtaːx] pret. of stechen.

Stachel ['ʃtaxəl] m (-s/-n) prickle (of plant, hedgehog, etc.); sting (of bee, etc.); tongue (of buckle); spike (of sports shoe); fig.: sting; goad; '⍛beere ♀ f gooseberry; '⍛draht m barbed wire; '⍛ig adj. prickly, thorny.

'stachlig adj. s. stachelig.

Stadi|on ['ʃtaːdjɔn] n (-s/Stadien) stadium; ⍛um ['⍛um] n (-s/Stadien) stage, phase.

Stadt [ʃtat] f (-/⍛e) town; city.

Städt|chen ['ʃtɛːtçən] n (-s/-) small town; '⍛ebau m (-[e]s/no pl.) town-planning; '⍛er m (-s/-) townsman; ~ pl. townspeople pl.

'Stadt|gebiet n urban area; '⍛gespräch n teleph. local call; fig. town talk, talk of the town; '⍛haus n town house.

städtisch adj. ['ʃtɛːtiʃ] municipal.

'Stadt|plan m city map; plan (of a town); '⍛planung f town-planning; '⍛rand m outskirts pl. (of a town); '⍛rat m (-[e]s/⍛e) town council; town council(l)or; '⍛teil m, '⍛viertel n quarter.

Staffel ['ʃtafəl] f (-/-n) relay; relay-race; ⍛ei paint. [⍛ˈlaɪ] f (-/-en) easel; '⍛lauf m relay-race; '⍛n v/t. (ge-, h) graduate (taxes, etc.); stagger (hours of work, etc.).

Stahl[1] [ʃtaːl] m (-[e]s/⍛e, -e) steel.

stahl[2] [⍛] pret. of stehlen.

stählen ['ʃtɛːlən] v/t. (ge-, h) ⊕ harden (a. fig.), temper.

'Stahl|feder f steel pen; steel spring; '⍛kammer f strong-room; '⍛stich m steel engraving.

stak [ʃtaːk] pret. of stecken 2.

Stall [ʃtal] m (-[e]s/⍛e) stable (a. fig.); cow-house, cowshed; pigsty, Am. a. pigpen; shed; '⍛knecht m stableman; '⍛ung f (-/-en) stabling; ⍛en pl. stables pl.

Stamm [ʃtam] m (-[e]s/⍛e) ⚘ stem (a. gr.), trunk; fig.: race; stock; family; tribe; '⍛aktie ✝ f ordinary share, Am. common stock; '⍛baum m family or genealogical tree, pedigree (a. zo.); '⍛buch n album; book that contains the births, deaths, and marriages in a family; zo. studbook; '⍛eln ['⍛e) v/t. (ge-) 1. v/t. stammer (out); 2. v/i. stammer; '⍛eltern pl. ancestors pl., first parents pl.; '⍛en v/i. (ge-, sein): ~ von or aus come from (town, etc.), Am. a. hail from; date from (certain time); gr. be derived from; aus gutem Haus ~ be of good family; '⍛gast m regular customer or guest, F regular.

stämmig adj. ['ʃtɛmiç] stocky; thickset, squat(ty).

'Stamm|kapital ✝ n share capital, Am. capital stock; '⍛kneipe F f one's favo(u)rite pub, local; '⍛kunde m regular customer, patron; '⍛tisch m table reserved for regular guests; ⍛utter ['ʃtammutər] f (-/⍛) ancestress; '⍛vater m ancestor; ⍛verwandt adj. cognate, kindred; pred. of the same race.

stampfen ['ʃtampfən] (ge-) 1. v/t. (h) mash (potatoes, etc.); aus dem Boden ~ conjure up; 2. v/i. (h) stamp (one's foot); horse: paw;

3. *v/i.* (sein): ~ *durch* plod through; ⚓ pitch through.

Stand [ʃtant] **1.** *m* (-[e]s/*e) stand (-ing), standing *or* upright position; footing, foothold; *s. Standplatz*; stall; *fig.*: level; state; station, rank, status; class; profession; reading (*of thermometer, etc.*); *ast.* position; *sports*: score; *auf den neuesten ~ bringen* bring up to date; *e-n schweren ~ haben* have a hard time (of it); **2.** ⚥ *pret. of* stehen.

Standarte [ʃtan'dartə] *f* (-/-n) standard, banner.

'Standbild *n* statue.

Ständchen ['ʃtentçən] *n* (-s/-) serenade; *j-m ein ~ bringen* serenade s.o.

Ständer ['ʃtendər] *m* (-s/-) stand; post, pillar, standard.

'Standes|amt *n* registry (office), register office; '2amtlich *adj.*: ~e *Trauung* civil marriage; '~beamte *m* registrar; '2gemäß *adj.*, '2mäßig *adj.* in accordance with one's rank; '~person *f* person of rank *or* position; '~unterschied *m* social difference.

'standhaft *adj.* steadfast; firm; constant; ~ *bleiben* stand pat; resist temptation; '2igkeit *f* (-/no *pl.*) steadfastness; firmness.

'standhalten *v/i.* (irr. halten, sep., -ge-, h) hold one's ground; *j-m or e-r Sache ~* resist s.o. *or* s.th.

ständig *adj.* ['ʃtendiç] permanent; constant; *income, etc.*: fixed.

'Stand|ort *m* position (*of ship, etc.*); ✕ garrison, post; '~platz *m* stand; '~punkt *fig. m* point of view, standpoint, angle, *Am. a.* slant; '~quartier ✕ *n* fixed quarters *pl.*; '~recht ✕ *n* martial law; '~uhr *f* grandfather's clock.

Stange ['ʃtaŋə] *f* (-/-n) pole; rod, bar (*of iron, etc.*); staff (*of flag*); *Anzug or Kleid von der ~ sl.* reach-me-down, *Am.* F hand-me-down.

stank [ʃtaŋk] *pret. of* stinken.

Stänker|(er) *contp.* ['ʃteŋkər(ər)] *m* (-s/-) mischief-maker, quarrel(l)er; '2n F *v/i.* (ge-, h) make mischief.

Stanniol [ʃta'njoːl] *n* (-s/-e) tin foil.

Stanze ['ʃtantsə] *f* (-/-n) stanza; ⊕ punch, stamp, die; '2n ⊕ *v/t.* (ge-, h) punch, stamp.

Stapel ['ʃtaːpəl] *m* (-s/-) pile, stack, ⚓ stocks *pl.*; *vom or von ~ lassen* ⚓ launch; *vom or von ~ laufen* ⚓ be launched; '~lauf ⚓ *m* launch; '2n *v/t.* (ge-, h) pile (up), stack; '~platz *m* dump; emporium.

stapfen ['ʃtapfən] *v/i.* (ge-, sein) plod (durch through).

Star **1.** [ʃtaːr] *m* (-[e]s/-e) *orn.* starling; *cataract*; *j-m den ~ stechen* open s.o.'s eyes; **2.** [staːr] *m* (-s/-s) *thea., etc.*: star.

starb [ʃtarp] *pret. of* sterben.

stark [ʃtark] **1.** *adj.* strong (*a. fig.*); stout, corpulent; *fig.*: intense; large; ~e *Erkältung* bad cold; ~er *Raucher* heavy smoker; ~e *Seite* strong point, forte; **2.** *adv.* very much; ~ *erkältet sein* have a bad cold; ~ *übertrieben* grossly exaggerated.

Stärke ['ʃterkə] *f* (-/-n) strength (*a. fig.*); stoutness, corpulence; *fig.*: intensity; largeness; strong point, forte; 🜋 starch; '2n *v/t.* (ge-, h) strengthen (*a. fig.*); starch (*linen, etc.*); *sich ~* take some refreshment(s).

'Starkstrom ⚡ *m* heavy current.

'Stärkung *f* (-/-en) strengthening; *fig. a.* refreshment; '~smittel *n* restorative; 🜋 *a.* tonic.

starr [ʃtar] **1.** *adj.* rigid (*a. fig.*), stiff; *gaze*: fixed; ~ *vor* (*dat.*) numb with (*cold, etc.*); transfixed with (*horror, etc.*); dumbfounded with (*amazement, etc.*); **2.** *adv.*: *j-n an-sehen* stare at s.o.; '~en *v/i.* (ge-, h) stare (*auf acc.* at); *vor Schmutz ~* be covered with dirt; '2heit *f* (-/no *pl.*) rigidity (*a. fig.*), stiffness; '2kopf *m* stubborn *or* obstinate fellow; '~köpfig *adj.* ['~kœpfiç] stubborn, obstinate; '2krampf 🜋 *m* (-[e]s/no *pl.*) tetanus; '2sinn *m* (-[e]s/no *pl.*) stubbornness, obstinacy; '~sinnig *adj.* stubborn, obstinate.

Start [ʃtart] *m* (-[e]s/-s, ✈ -e) start (*a. fig.*); ✈ take-off; '~bahn ✈ *f* runway; '2bereit *adj.* ready to start; ✈ ready to take off; '2en (ge-) **1.** *v/i.* (sein) start; ✈ take off; **2.** *v/t.* (h) start; *fig. a.* launch; '~er *m* (-s/-) *sports*: starter; '~platz *m* starting-place.

Station [ʃta'tsjoːn] *f* (-/-en) station; ward (*of hospital*); (*gegen*) *freie ~* board and lodging (found); ~ *machen* break one's journey; '~svorsteher 🚂 *m* station-master, *Am. a.* station agent.

Statist [ʃta'tist] *m* (-en/-en) *thea.* supernumerary (actor), F super; *film*: extra; ~ik *f* (-/-en) statistics *pl., sg.*; '~iker *m* (-s/-) statistician; 2isch *adj.* statistic(al).

Stativ [ʃta'tiːf] *n* (-s/-e) tripod.

Statt [ʃtat] **1.** *f* (-/no *pl.*): *an Eides ~* in lieu of an oath; *an Kindes ~ annehmen* adopt; **2.** ⚥ *prp.* (*gen.*) instead of; ~ *zu inf.* instead of *ger.*; ~ *meiner* in my place.

Stätte ['ʃtetə] *f* (-/-n) place, spot; scene (*of events*).

'statt|finden *v/i.* (irr. finden, sep., -ge-, h) take place, happen; '~haft *adj.* admissible, allowable; legal.

'Statthalter *m* (-s/-) governor.

'stattlich *adj.* stately; impressive; *sum of money, etc.*: considerable.

Statue ['ʃtaːtuə] *f* (-/-n) statue.

statuieren [ʃtatuˈiːrən] *v/t.* (no -ge-,

h): ein Exempel ~ make an example (an dat. of).

Statur [ʃtaˈtuːr] f (-/-en) stature, size.

Statut [ʃtaˈtuːt] n (-[e]s/-en) statute; ~en pl. regulations pl.; ✝ articles pl. of association.

Staub [ʃtaup] m (-[e]s/⊕ -e, ~e) dust; powder.

Staubecken [ˈʃtauʔ-] n reservoir.

stauben [ˈʃtaubən] v/i. (ge-, h) give off dust, make or raise a dust.

stäuben [ˈʃtɔybən] (ge-, h) 1. v/t. dust; 2. v/i. spray.

'**Staub|faden** ♀ m filament; ♀ig adj. [ˈ~bɪç] dusty; ~sauger [ˈ~p-] m (-s/-) vacuum cleaner; ~tuch [ˈ~p-] n (-[e]s/~er) duster.

stauchen ⊕ [ˈʃtauxən] v/t. (ge-, h) upset, jolt.

'**Staudamm** m dam.

Staude ♀ [ˈʃtaudə] f (-/-n) perennial (plant); head (of lettuce).

stau|en [ˈʃtauən] v/t. (ge-, h) dam (up) (river, etc.); ⚓ stow; sich ~ waters, etc.: be dammed (up); vehicles: be jammed (up); ♀er ⚓ m (-s/-) stevedore.

staunen [ˈʃtaunən] 1. v/i. (ge-, h) be astonished (über acc. at); 2. ♀ n (-s/no pl.) astonishment; ~swert adj. astonishing. [temper.]

Staupe vet. [ˈʃtaupə] f (-/-n) dis-]

'**Stau|see** m reservoir; '~ung f (-/-en) damming (up) (of water); stoppage; ⚕ congestion (a. of traffic); jam; ⚓ stowage.

stechen [ˈʃteçən] (irr., ge-, h) 1. v/t. prick; insect, etc.: sting; flea, mosquito, etc.: bite; card: take, trump (other card); ⊕ engrave (in or auf acc. on); cut (lawn, etc.); sich in den Finger ~ prick one's finger; 2. v/i. prick; stab (nach at); insect, etc.: sting; flea, mosquito, etc.: bite; sun: burn; j-m in die Augen ~ strike s.o.'s eye; '~d adj. pain, look, etc.: piercing; pain: stabbing.

Steck|brief ⚖ m warrant of apprehension; '♀brieflich ⚖ adv.: er wird ~ gesucht a warrant is out against him; '~dose ⚡ f (wall) socket; '♀en 1. v/t. (ge-, h) put; esp. ⊕ insert (in acc. into); F stick; pin (an acc. to, on); ⚘ set, plant; 2. v/i. ([irr.,] ge-, h) be; stick, be stuck; tief in Schulden ~ be deeply in debt; '~en m (-s/-) stick; '♀enbleiben v/i. (irr. bleiben, sep., -ge-, sein) get stuck; speaker, etc.: break down; '~enpferd n hobby-horse; fig. hobby; '~er ⚡ m (-s/-) plug; '~kontakt ⚡ m s. Steckdose; '~nadel f pin.

Steg [ʃteːk] m (-[e]s/-e) foot-bridge; ⚓ landing-stage; '~reif m (-[e]s/-e): aus dem ~ extemporize, offhand (both a. attr.); aus dem ~ sprechen extemporize, F ad-lib.

stehen [ˈʃteːən] v/i. (irr., ge-, h) stand; be; be written; dress: suit, become (j-m s.o.); ~ vor be faced with; gut ~ mit be on good terms with; es kam ihm or ihn teuer zu ~ it cost him dearly; wie steht's mit ...? what about ...?; wie steht das Spiel? what's the score?; ~ bleiben remain standing; '~bleiben v/i. (irr. bleiben, sep., -ge-, sein) stand (still), stop; leave off reading, etc.; '~lassen v/t. (irr. lassen, sep., [no] -ge-, h) turn one's back (up)on; leave (meal) untouched; leave (behind), forget; leave alone.

'**Steher** m (-s/-) sports: stayer.

'**Steh|kragen** m stand-up collar; '~lampe f standard lamp; '~leiter f (e-e a pair of) steps pl., step-ladder.

stehlen [ˈʃteːlən] (irr., ge-, h) 1. v/t. steal; j-m Geld ~ steal s.o.'s money; 2. v/i. steal.

'**Stehplatz** m standing-room; '~inhaber m Am. F standee; in bus, etc.: straphanger.

steif adj. [ʃtaif] stiff (a. fig.); numb (vor Kälte with cold); '~halten v/t. (irr. halten, sep. -ge-, h) F die Ohren ~ keep a stiff upper lip.

Steig [ʃtaik] m (-[e]s/-e) steep path; '~bügel m stirrup.

steigen [ˈʃtaigən] 1. v/i. (irr., ge-, sein) flood, barometer, spirits, prices, etc.: rise; mists, etc.: ascend; blood, tension, etc.: mount; prices, etc.: increase; auf e-n Baum ~ climb a tree; 2. ♀ n (-s/no pl.) rise; fig. a. increase.

steigern [ˈʃtaigərn] v/t. (ge-, h) raise; increase; enhance; gr. compare.

'**Steigerung** f (-/-en) raising; increase; enhancement; gr. comparison; '~sstufe gr. f degree of comparison.

Steigung [ˈʃtaiguŋ] f (-/-en) rise, gradient, ascent, grade.

steil adj. [ʃtail] steep; precipitous.

Stein [ʃtain] m (-[e]s/-e) stone (a. ♀, ♞), Am. F a. rock; s. Edel♀; '♀alt F adj. (as) old as the hills; '~bruch m quarry; '~druck m 1. (-[e]s/no pl.) lithography; 2. (-[e]s/-e) lithograph; '~drucker m lithographer; '♀ern adj. stone-..., of stone; fig. stony; '~gut n (-[e]s/-e) crockery, stoneware, earthenware; '♀ig adj. stony; '♀igen [ˈ~gən] v/t. (ge-, h) stone; '~igung [ˈ~guŋ] f (-/-en) stoning; '~kohle f mineral coal; pit-coal; '~metz [ˈ~mets] m (-en/-en) stonemason; '~obst n stone-fruit; '♀reich F adj. immensely rich; '~salz n (-es/no pl.) rock-salt; '~setzer m (-s/-) pavio(u)r; '~wurf m throwing of a stone; fig. stone's throw; '~zeit f (-/no pl.) stone age.

Steiß [ʃtais] m (-es/-e) buttocks pl., rump; '~bein anat. n coccyx.

Stelldichein co. ['ʃtɛldiçʔaın] n (-[s]/-[s]) meeting, appointment, rendezvous, Am. F a. date.

Stelle ['ʃtɛlə] f (-/-n) place; spot; point; employment, situation, post, place, F job; agency, authority; passage (of book, etc.); freie ~ vacancy; an deiner ~ in your place, if I were you; auf der ~ on the spot; zur ~ sein be present.

'stellen v/t. (ge-, h) put, place, set, stand; regulate (watch, etc.); set (watch, trap, task, etc.); stop (thief, etc.); hunt down (criminal); furnish, supply, provide; Bedingungen ~ make conditions; e-e Falle ~ a. lay a snare; sich ~ give o.s. up (to the police); stand, place o.s. (somewhere); sich krank ~ feign or pretend to be ill.

'Stellen|angebot n position offered, vacancy; **'~gesuch** n application for a post; **'2weise** adv. here and there, sporadically.

'Stellung f (-/-en) position, posture; position, situation, (place of) employment; position, rank, status; arrangement (a. gr.); ⚔ position; ~ nehmen give one's opinion (zu on), comment (upon); **~nahme** ['~nɑːmə] f (-/-n) attitude (zu to[wards]); opinion (on); comment (on); **2slos** adj. unemployed.

'stellvertret|end adj. vicarious, representative; acting, deputy; **~er** Vorsitzender vice-chairman, deputy chairman; **2er** m representative; deputy; proxy; **2ung** f representation; substitution; proxy.

Stelz|bein contp. ['ʃtɛlts-] n wooden leg; **~e** f (-/-n) stilt; **2en** mst iro. v/i. (ge-, sein) stalk.

stemmen ['ʃtɛmən] v/t. (ge-, h) lift (weight); sich ~ press (gegen against); fig. resist or oppose s.th.

Stempel ['ʃtɛmpəl] m (-s/-) stamp; ⊕ piston; ♀ pistil; **'~geld** F n the dole; **'~kissen** n ink-pad; **'2n** (ge-, h) **1.** v/t. stamp; hallmark (gold, silver); **2.** v/i. F: ~ gehen be on the dole.

Stengel ♀ ['ʃtɛŋəl] m (-s/-) stalk, stem.

Steno F ['ʃtɛno] f (-/no pl.) s. Stenographie, **~'gramm** n (-s/-e) stenograph; **~graph** [~'grɑːf] m (-en/-en) stenographer; **~graphie** [~a'fiː] f (-/-n) stenography, shorthand; **2graphieren** [~a'fiːrən] (no -ge-, h) **1.** v/t. take down in shorthand; **2.** v/i. know shorthand; **2graphisch** [~'grɑːfiʃ] **1.** adj. shorthand, stenographic; **2.** adv. in shorthand; **~typistin** [~ty'pistin] f (-/-nen) shorthand-typist.

Stepp|decke ['ʃtɛp-] f quilt, Am. a. comforter; **2en** (ge-, h) **1.** v/t. quilt; stitch; **2.** v/i. tap-dance.

Sterbe|bett ['ʃtɛrbə-] n deathbed;

'~fall m (case of) death; **'~kasse** f burial-fund.

'sterben 1. v/i. (irr., ge-, sein) die (a. fig.) (an dat. of); esp. ⚕ decease; **2.** ⚕ n (-s/no pl.): im ~ liegen be dying.

sterblich ['ʃtɛrplıç] **1.** adj. mortal; **2.** adv.: ~ verliebt sein be desperately in love (in acc. with); **2keit** f (-/no pl.) mortality; **2keitsziffer** f death-rate, mortality.

stereotyp adj. [stereo'tyːp] typ. stereotyped (a. fig.); **~ieren** typ. [~y'piːrən] v/t. (no -ge-, h) stereotype.

steril adj. [ʃte'riːl] sterile; **~isieren** [~ili'ziːrən] v/t. (no -ge-, h) sterilize.

Stern [ʃtɛrn] m (-[e]s/-e) star (a. fig.); **'~bild** ast. n constellation; **'~deuter** m (-s/-) astrologer; **'~deutung** f astrology; **'~enbanner** n Star-Spangled Banner, Stars and Stripes pl., Old Glory; **'~fahrt** mot. f motor rally; **'~gucker** F m (-s/-) star-gazer; **'2hell** adj. starry, starlit; **'~himmel** m (-s/no pl.) starry sky; **'~kunde** f (-/no pl.) astronomy; **'~schnuppe** f (-/-n) shooting star; **'~warte** f observatory.

stet adj. [ʃteːt], **'~ig** adj. continual, constant; steady; **2igkeit** f (-/no pl.) constancy, continuity; steadiness; **~s** adv. always; constantly.

Steuer ['ʃtɔyər] **1.** n (-s/-) ⚓ helm, rudder; steering-wheel; **2.** f (-/-n) tax; duty; rate, local tax; **'~amt** n s. Finanzamt; **'~beamte** m revenue officer; **'~berater** m (-s/-) tax adviser; **'~bord** ⚓ n (-[e]s/-e) starboard; **'~erhebung** f levy of taxes; **'~erklärung** f tax-return; **'~ermäßigung** f tax allowance; **'2frei** adj. tax-free; goods: duty-free; **'~freiheit** f (-/no pl.) exemption from taxes; **'~hinterziehung** f tax-evasion; **'~jahr** n fiscal year; **'~klasse** f tax-bracket; **'~knüppel** ✈ m control lever or stick; **'~mann** m (-[e]s/-er, Steuerleute) ⚓ helmsman, steersman, Am. a. wheelsman; coxwain (a. rowing); **'2n** (ge-) **1.** v/t. (h) ⚓, ✈ steer, navigate, pilot; ⊕ control; fig. direct, control; **2.** v/i. (h) check s.th.; **3.** v/i. (sein): ~ in (acc.) ⚓ enter (harbour, etc.); ~ nach ⚓ be bound for; **'2pflichtig** adj. taxable; goods: dutiable; **'~rad** n steering-wheel; **'~ruder** ⚓ n helm, rudder; **'~satz** m rate of assessment; **'~ung** f (-/-en) ⚓, ✈ steering; ⊕, ✈ control (a. fig.); ✈ controls pl.; **'~veranlagung** f tax assessment; **'~zahler** m (-s/-) taxpayer; ratepayer.

Steven ⚓ ['ʃteːvən] m (-s/-) stem; stern-post.

Stich [ʃtıç] m (-[e]s/-e) prick (of needle, etc.); sting (of insect, etc.);

stab (of knife, etc.); sewing: stitch; cards: trick; ⊕ engraving; ⚟ stab; ~ halten hold water; im ~ lassen abandon, desert, forsake.

Stichel|ei fig. [ʃtiçə'laɪ] f (-/-en) gibe, jeer; 'ℒn fig. v/i. (ge-, h) gibe (gegen at), jeer (at).

'Stich|flamme f flash; **'ℒhaltig** adj. valid, sound; ~ sein hold water; '~probe f random test or sample, Am. a. spot check; '~tag m fixed day; '~wahl f second ballot; '~wort n 1. typ. (-[e]s/-er) headword; 2. thea. (-[e]s/-e) cue; '~wunde f stab.

sticken ['ʃtikən] v/t. and v/i. (ge-, h) embroider.

'Stick|garn n embroidery floss; '~husten ⚕ m (w)hooping cough; 'ℒig adj. stuffy, close; '~stoff 🜅 m (-[e]s/no pl.) nitrogen.

stieben ['ʃtiːbən] v/i. ([irr.,] ge-, h, sein) sparks, etc.: fly about.

Stief... ['ʃtiːf-] step...

Stiefel ['ʃtiːfəl] m (-s/-) boot; '~knecht m bootjack; '~schaft m leg of a boot.

'Stief|mutter f (-/=) stepmother; '~mütterchen ♀ ['~mytərçən] n (-s/-) pansy; '~vater m stepfather.

stieg [ʃtiːk] pret. of steigen.

Stiel [ʃtiːl] m (-[e]s/-e) handle; helve (of weapon, tool); haft (of axe); stick (of broom); ♀ stalk.

Stier [ʃtiːr] 1. zo. m (-[e]s/-e) bull; 2. ℒ adj. staring; 'ℒen v/i. (ge-, h) stare (auf acc. at); '~kampf m bullfight.

stieß [ʃtiːs] pret. of stoßen.

Stift [ʃtift] 1. m (-[e]s/-e) pin; peg; tack; pencil, crayon; F fig.: youngster; apprentice; 2. n (-[e]s/-e, -er) charitable institution; 'ℒen v/t. (ge-, h) endow, give, Am. a. donate; found; fig. cause; make (mischief, peace); '~er m (-s/-) donor; founder; fig. author; '~ung f (-/-en) (charitable) endowment, donation; foundation.

Stil [ʃtiːl] m (-[e]s/-e) style (a. fig.); 'ℒgerecht adj. stylish; ℒisieren [ʃtili'ziːrən] v/t. (no -ge-, h) stylize; ℒistisch adj. [ʃti'listiʃ] stylistic.

still adj. [ʃtil] still, quiet; silent; ✝ dull, slack; secret; ~! silence!; im ~en secretly; ~er Gesellschafter ✝ sleeping or silent partner; der ℒe Ozean the Pacific (Ocean); 'ℒe f (-/no pl.) stillness, quiet(ness); silence; in aller ~ quietly, silently; privately; 'ℒeben paint. ['ʃtilɛːbən] n (-s/-) still life; '~legen ['ʃtile:gən] v/t. (sep., -ge-, h) shut down (factory, etc.); stop (traffic); '~en v/t. (ge-, h) soothe (pain); appease (appetite); quench (thirst); sta(u)nch (blood); nurse (baby); '~halten v/i. (irr. halten, sep., -ge-, h) keep still; '~liegen ['ʃtili:gən] v/i.

(irr. liegen, sep., -ge-, h) factory, etc.: be shut down; traffic: be suspended; machines, etc.: be idle.

stillos adj. ['ʃtiːlloːs] without style.

'stillschweigen 1. v/i. (irr. schweigen, sep., -ge-, h) be silent; '~ zu et. ignore s.th.; 2. ℒ n (-s/no pl.) silence; secrecy; '~ bewahren observe secrecy; et. mit ~ übergehen pass s.th. over in silence; '~d adj. silent; agreement, etc.: tacit.

'Still|stand m (-[e]s/no pl.) standstill; fig.: stagnation (a. ✝); deadlock; 'ℒstehen v/i. (irr. stehen, sep., -ge-, h) stop; be at a standstill; stillgestanden! ✕ attention!

'Stil|möbel n/pl. period furniture; 'ℒvoll adj. stylish.

Stimm|band anat. ['ʃtim-] n (-[e]s/=er) vocal c(h)ord; 'ℒberechtigt adj. entitled to vote; '~e f (-/-en) voice (a. ♪, fig.); vote; comment; ♪ part; 'ℒen (ge-, h) 1. v/t. tune (piano, etc.); j-n fröhlich ~ put s.o. in a merry mood; 2. v/i. be true or right; sum, etc.: be correct; ~ für vote for; '~enmehrheit f majority or plurality of votes; '~enthaltung f abstention; '~enzählung f counting of votes; '~gabel ♪ f tuning-fork; '~recht n right to vote; pol. franchise; '~ung f (-/-en) ♪ tune; fig. mood, humo(u)r; 'ℒungsvoll adj. impressive; '~zettel m ballot, voting-paper.

stinken ['ʃtiŋkən] v/i. (irr., ge-, h) stink (nach of); F fig. be fishy.

Stipendium univ. [ʃti'pɛndjum] n (-s/Stipendien) scholarship; exhibition.

stipp|en ['ʃtipən] v/t. (ge-, h) dip, steep; 'ℒvisite F f flying visit.

Stirn [ʃtirn] f (-/-en) forehead, brow; fig. face, cheek; j-m die ~ bieten make head against s.o.; s. runzeln; '~runzeln n (-s/no pl.) frown(ing).

stob [ʃtoːp] pret. of stieben.

stöbern F ['ʃtøːbərn] v/i. (ge-, h) rummage (about) (in dat. in).

stochern ['ʃtɔxərn] v/i. (ge-, h): ~ in (dat.) poke (fire); pick (teeth).

Stock [ʃtɔk] m 1. (-[e]s/=e) stick; cane; ♪ baton; beehive; ✠ stock; 2. (-[e]s/-) stor(e)y, floor; im ersten ~ on the first floor, Am. on the second floor; 'ℒbe'trunken F adj. dead drunk; 'ℒ'blind F adj. stone-blind; 'ℒ'dunkel F adj. pitch-dark.

Stöckelschuh ['ʃtœkəl-] m high-heeled shoe.

'stocken v/i. (ge-, h) stop; liquid: stagnate (a. fig.); speaker: break down; voice: falter; traffic: be blocked; ihm stockte das Blut his blood curdled.

'Stock|'engländer F m thorough or true-born Englishman; 'ℒ'finster F adj. pitch-dark; '~fleck m spot of mildew; '⑂(fleck)ig adj. foxy, mildewy; '⑂'nüchtern F adj. (as) sober as a judge; '‿schnupfen ✗ m chronic rhinitis; '⑂'taub F adj. stone-deaf; '‿ung f (-/-en) stop (-page); stagnation (of liquid) (a. fig.); block (of traffic); '‿werk n stor(e)y, floor.

Stoff [ʃtɔf] m (-[e]s/-e) matter, substance; material, fabric, textile, material, stuff; fig.: subject(-matter); food; '⑂lich adj. material.

stöhnen ['ʃtøːnən] v/i. (ge-, h) groan, moan.

Stolle ['ʃtɔlə] f (-/-n) loaf-shaped Christmas cake; '‿n m (-s/-) s. Stolle; ⚒ tunnel, gallery (a. ⚒).

stolpern ['ʃtɔlpərn] v/i. (ge-, sein) stumble (über acc. over), trip (over) (both a. fig.).

stolz [ʃtɔlts] 1. adj. proud (auf acc. of) (a. fig.); haughty; 2. ⑂ m (-es/no pl.) pride (auf acc. in); haughtiness; ‿ieren [‿'tsiːrən] v/i. (no -ge-, sein) strut, flaunt.

stopfen ['ʃtɔpfən] (ge-, h) 1. v/t. stuff; fill (pipe); cram (poultry, etc.); darn (sock, etc.); j-m den Mund ‿ stop s.o.'s mouth; 2. ✗ v/i. cause constipation.

'Stopf|garn n darning-yarn; '‿nadel f darning-needle.

Stoppel ['ʃtɔpəl] f (-/-n) stubble; '‿bart F m stubbly beard; '⑂ig adj. stubbly.

stopp|en ['ʃtɔpən] (ge-, h) 1. v/t. stop; time, F clock; 2. v/i. stop; '⑂licht mot. n stop-light; '⑂uhr f stop-watch.

Stöpsel ['ʃtœpsəl] m (-s/-) stopper, cork; plug (a. ⚡); F fig. whippersnapper; '⑂n v/t. (ge-, h) stopper, cork; plug (up).

Storch orn. [ʃtɔrç] m (-[e]s/⁼e) stork.

stören ['ʃtøːrən] (ge-, h) 1. v/t. disturb; trouble; radio: jam (reception); lassen Sie sich nicht ‿! don't let me disturb you!; darf ich Sie kurz ‿? may I trouble you for a minute?; 2. v/i. be intruding; be in the way; ⑂fried ['‿friːt] m (-[e]s/-e) troublemaker; intruder.

störr|ig adj. ['ʃtœrɪç], '‿isch adj. stubborn, obstinate; a. horse: restive.

'Störung f (-/-en) disturbance; trouble (a. ⊕); breakdown; radio: jamming, interference.

Stoß [ʃtoːs] m (-es/⁼e) push, shove; thrust (a. fencing); kick; butt; shock; knock, strike; blow; swimming, billiards: stroke; jolt (of car, etc.); pile, stock, heap; '‿dämpfer mot. m shock-absorber; '⑂en (irr., ge-) 1. v/t. (h) push, shove; thrust (weapon, etc.); knock; butt; knock, strike; pound (pepper, etc.); sich ‿ an (dat.) strike or knock against; fig. take offence at; 2. v/i. (h) thrust

(nach at); kick (at); butt (at); goat, etc.: butt; car: jolt; ‿ an (acc.) adjoin, border on; 3. v/i. (sein): F ‿ auf (acc.) come across; meet with (opposition, etc.); ‿ gegen or an (acc.) knock or strike against.

'Stoß|seufzer m ejaculation; '‿stange mot. f bumper; '⑂weise adv. by jerks; by fits and starts; '‿zahn m tusk.

stottern ['ʃtɔtərn] (ge-, h) 1. v/t. stutter (out); stammer; 2. v/i. stutter; stammer; F mot. conk (out).

Straf|anstalt ['ʃtraːfˀ-] f penal institution; prison; Am. penitentiary; '‿arbeit f imposition, F impo(t); '⑂bar adj. punishable, penal; '‿e f (-/-n) punishment; ½, ⚓, sports, fig. penalty; fine; bei ‿ von on or under pain of; zur ‿ as a punishment; '⑂en v/t. (ge-, h) punish.

straff adj. [ʃtraf] tight; rope: a. taut; fig. strict, rigid.

'straf|fällig adj. liable to prosecution; '⑂gesetz n penal law; '⑂gesetzbuch n penal code.

sträf|lich adj. ['ʃtrɛːflɪç] culpable; reprehensible; inexcusable; ⑂ling ['‿lɪŋ] m (-s/-e) convict, Am. sl. a. lag.

'straf|los adj. unpunished; '⑂losigkeit f (-/no pl.) impunity; '⑂porto n surcharge; '⑂predigt f severe lecture; j-m e-e ‿ halten lecture s.o. severely; '⑂prozeß m criminal action; '⑂raum m football: penalty area; '⑂stoß m football: penalty kick; '⑂verfahren n criminal proceedings pl.

Strahl [ʃtraːl] m (-[e]s/-en) ray (a. fig.); beam; flash (of lightning, etc.); jet (of water, etc.); '⑂en v/i. (ge-, h) radiate; shine (vor dat. with); fig. beam (vor dat. with), shine (with); '‿ung f (-/-en) radiation, rays pl.

Strähne ['ʃtrɛːnə] f (-/-n) lock, strand (of hair); skein, hank (of yarn); fig. stretch.

stramm adj. [ʃtram] tight; rope: a. taut; stalwart; soldier: smart.

strampeln ['ʃtrampəln] v/i. (ge-, h) kick.

Strand [ʃtrant] m (-[e]s/⁑-e, ⁼e) beach; '‿anzug m beach-suit; ⑂en ['‿dən] v/i. (ge-, sein) ⚓ strand, run ashore; fig. fail, founder; '‿gut n stranded goods pl.; fig. wreckage; '‿korb m roofed wicker chair for use on the beach; ‿promenade ['‿promənɑːdə] f (-/-n) promenade, Am. boardwalk.

Strang [ʃtraŋ] m (-[e]s/⁼e) cord (a. anat.); rope; halter (for hanging s.o.); trace (of harness); ⚒ track; über die Stränge schlagen kick over the traces.

Strapaz|e [ʃtraˈpaːtsə] f (-/-n) fatigue; toil; ⑂ieren [‿aˈtsiːrən] v/t.

(no -ge-, h) fatigue, strain (a. fig.); wear out (fabric, etc.); **2ierfähig** adj. [⸚a'tsi:r-] long-lasting; **2iös** adj. [⸚a'tsjø:s] fatiguing.

Straße ['ʃtra:sə] f (-/-n) road, highway; street (of town, etc.); strait; auf der ∼ on the road; in the street. **'Straßen|anzug** m lounge-suit, Am. business suit; **'∼bahn** f tram(way), tram-line, Am. street railway, streetcar line; s. Straßenbahnwagen; **'∼bahnhaltestelle** f tram stop, Am. streetcar stop; **'∼bahnwagen** m tram(-car), Am. streetcar; **'∼beleuchtung** f street lighting; **'∼damm** m roadway; **'∼händler** m hawker; **'∼junge** m street arab, Am. street Arab; **'∼kehrer** m (-s/-) scavenger, street orderly; **'∼kreuzung** f crossing, cross roads; **'∼reinigung** f street-cleaning, scavenging; **'∼rennen** n road-race.

strategisch adj. [ʃtra'te:giʃ] strategic(al).

sträuben ['ʃtrɔybən] v/t. (ge-, h) ruffle up (its feathers, etc.); sich ∼ hair: stand on end; sich ∼ gegen kick against or at.

Strauch [ʃtraux] m (-[e]s/ᵗer) shrub; bush.

straucheln ['ʃtrauxəln] v/i. (ge-, sein) stumble (über acc. over, at), trip (over) (both a. fig.).

Strauß [ʃtraus] m 1. orn. (-es/-e) ostrich; 2. (-es/ᵗe) bunch (of flowers); bouquet; strife, combat.

Strebe ['ʃtre:bə] f (-/-n) strut, support, brace.

'streben 1. v/i. (ge-, h): ∼ nach strive for or after, aspire to or after; **2.** 2 n (-s/no pl.) striving (nach for, after), aspiration (for, after); effort, endeavo(u)r.

'Streber m (-s/-) pusher, careerist; at school: sl. swot.

strebsam adj. ['ʃtre:pza:m] assiduous; ambitious; **2keit** f (-/no pl.) assiduity; ambition.

Strecke ['ʃtrɛkə] f (-/-n) stretch; route; tract, extent; distance (a. sports); course; 🐗, etc.: section, line; hunt. bag; zur ∼ bringen hunt. bag, hunt down (a. fig.); **'2n** v/t. (ge-, h) stretch, extend; dilute (fluid); sich ∼ stretch (o.s.); die Waffen ∼ lay down one's arms; fig. a. give in.

Streich [ʃtraiç] m (-[e]s/-e) stroke; blow; fig. trick, prank; j-m e-n ∼ spielen play a trick on s.o.; **2eln** ['⸚əln] v/t. (ge-, h) stroke; caress; pat; **'2en** (irr., ge-) **1.** v/t. (h) rub; spread (butter, etc.); paint; strike out, delete, cancel (a. fig.); strike, lower (flag, sail); **2.** v/i. (sein) prowl (um round); **3.** v/i.(h): mit der Hand über et. ∼ pass one's hand over s.th.; **'∼holz** n match; **'∼instrument** ♪ n stringed instrument;

'∼orchester n string band; **'∼riemen** m strop.

Streif [ʃtraif] m (-[e]s/-e) s. Streifen; **'∼band** n (-[e]s/ᵗer) wrapper; **'∼e** f (-/-n) patrol; patrolman; raid.

'streifen (ge-) **1.** v/t. (h) stripe, streak; graze, touch lightly in passing, brush; touch (up)on (subject); **2.** v/i. (sein): ∼ durch rove, wander through; **3.** v/i. (h): ∼ an (acc.) graze, brush; fig. border or verge on; **4.** 2 m (-s/-) strip; stripe; streak. **'streif|ig** adj. striped; **'2licht** n sidelight; **'2schuß** ✗ m grazing shot; **'2zug** m ramble; ✗ raid.

Streik [ʃtraik] m (-[e]s/-s) strike, Am. F a. walkout; in den ∼ treten go on strike, Am. F a. walk out; **'∼brecher** m (-s/-) strike-breaker, blackleg, scab; **'2en** v/i. (ge-, h) (be on) strike; go on strike, Am. F a. walk out; **∼ende** ['⸚əndə] m, f (-/-n) striker; **'∼posten** m picket.

Streit [ʃtrait] m (-[e]s/-e) quarrel; dispute; conflict; ⚖ litigation; **'2bar** adj. pugnacious; **'2en** v/i. and v/refl. (irr., ge-, h) quarrel (mit with; wegen for; über acc. about); **'∼frage** f controversy, (point of) issue; **'2ig** adj. debatable, controversial; j-m et. ∼ machen dispute s.o.'s right to s.th.; **'∼igkeiten** f/pl. quarrels pl.; disputes pl.; **'∼kräfte** ✗ ['⸚krɛftə] f/pl. (military or armed) forces pl.; **'2lustig** adj. pugnacious, aggressive; **'2süchtig** adj. quarrelsome; pugnacious.

streng [ʃtrɛŋ] **1.** adj. severe; stern; strict; austere; discipline, etc.: rigorous; weather, climate: inclement; examination: stiff; **2.** adv.: ∼ vertraulich in strict confidence; **'2e** f (-/no pl.) s. streng 1: severity; sternness; strictness; austerity; rigo(u)r; inclemency; stiffness; **'∼genommen** adv. strictly speaking; **'∼gläubig** adj. orthodox.

Streu [ʃtrɔy] f (-/-en) litter; **'2en** v/t. (ge-, h) strew, scatter; **'∼zucker** m castor sugar.

Strich [ʃtriç] **1.** m (-[e]s/-e) stroke; line; dash; tract (of land); j-m e-n ∼ durch die Rechnung machen queer s.o.'s pitch; **2.** 2 pret. of streichen; **'∼regen** m local shower; **'2weise** adv. here and there.

Strick [ʃtrik] m (-[e]s/-e) cord; rope; halter, rope (for hanging s.o.); F fig. (young) rascal; **'2en** v/t. and v/i. (ge-, h) knit; **'∼garn** n knitting-yarn; **'∼jacke** f cardigan, jersey; **'∼leiter** f rope-ladder; **'∼nadel** f knitting-needle; **'∼waren** f/pl. knit-wear; **'∼zeug** n knitting(-things pl.).

Striemen ['ʃtri:mən] m (-s/-) weal, wale.

Strippe F ['ʃtripə] f (-/-n) band; string; shoe-lace; an der ∼ hängen be on the phone.

stritt [ʃtrit] *pret. of* streiten; '~**ig** *adj.* debatable, controversial; ~**er** Punkt (point of) issue.

Stroh [ʃtroː] *n* (-[e]s/*no pl.*) straw; thatch; '~**dach** *n* thatch(ed roof); '~**halm** *m* straw; *nach e-m* ~ *greifen* catch at a straw; '~**hut** *m* straw hat; '~**mann** *m* man of straw; scarecrow; *fig.* dummy; '~**sack** *m* straw mattress; '~**witwe** F *f* grass widow.

Strolch [ʃtrɔlç] *m* (-[e]s/-e) scamp, F vagabond; '**2en** *v/i.* (ge-, sein); ~ *durch* rove.

Strom [ʃtroːm] *m* (-[e]s/=e) stream (*a. fig.*); (large) river; ⚡ current (*a. fig.*); *es regnet in Strömen* it is pouring with rain; **2'ab(wärts)** *adv.* down-stream; **2'auf(wärts)** *adv.* up-stream.

strömen [ʃtrøːmən] *v/i.* (ge-, sein) stream; flow, run; *rain:* pour; *people:* stream, pour (*aus* out of; *in acc.* into).

'**Strom|kreis** ⚡ *m* circuit; '~**linien-form** *f* (-/*no pl.*) streamline shape; '**2linienförmig** *adj.* streamline(d); '~**schnelle** *f* (-/-n) rapid, *Am. a.* riffle; '~**sperre** ⚡ *f* stoppage of current.

'**Strömung** *f* (-/-en) current; *fig. a.* trend, tendency.

'**Stromzähler** ⚡ *m* electric meter.

Strophe [ʃtroːfə] *f* (-/-n) stanza, verse.

strotzen [ʃtrɔtsən] *v/i.* (ge-, h): ~ *von* abound in; teem with (*blunders, etc.*); burst with (*health, etc.*).

Strudel [ʃtruːdəl] *m* (-s/-) eddy, whirlpool; *fig.* whirl; '**2n** *v/i.* (ge-, h) swirl, whirl. [ture.]

Struktur [ʃtrukˈtuːr] *f* (-/-en) struc-

Strumpf [ʃtrumpf] *m* (-[e]s/=e) stocking; **2band** *n* (-[e]s/=er) garter; '~**halter** *m* (-s/-) suspender; *Am.* garter; '~**waren** *f/pl.* hosiery.

struppig *adj.* [ʃtrupiç] *hair:* rough, shaggy; *dog, etc.:* shaggy.

Stube [ʃtuːbə] *f* (-/-n) room.

'**Stuben|hocker** *fig. m* (-s/-) stay-at-home; '~**mädchen** *n* chambermaid; '**2rein** *adj.* house-trained.

Stück [ʃtyk] *n* (-[e]s/-e) piece (*a.* ♪); fragment; head (*of cattle*); lump (*of sugar*); *thea.* play; *aus freien ~en* of one's own accord; *in ~e gehen or schlagen* break to pieces; '~**arbeit** *f* piece-work; '**2weise** *adv.* piece by piece; (by) piecemeal; ✝ by the piece; '~**werk** *fig. n* patchwork.

Student [ʃtuˈdɛnt] *m* (-en/-en), ~**in** *f* (-/-nen) student, undergraduate.

Studie [ʃtuːdjə] *f* (-/-n) study (*über acc., zu* of, in) (*a. art, literature*); *paint, etc.:* sketch; '~**nrat** *m* (-[e]s/=e) *appr.* secondary-school teacher; '~**nreise** *f* study trip.

studier|en [ʃtuˈdiːrən] (*no* -ge-, h) **1.** *v/t.* study, read (*law, etc.*); **2.** *v/i.*

study; be a student; **2zimmer** *n* study.

Studium [ʃtuːdjum] *n* (-s/*Studien*) study (*a. fig.*); studies *pl.*

Stufe [ʃtuːfə] *f* (-/-n) step; *fig.:* degree; grade; stage.

'**Stufen|folge** *fig. f* gradation; '~**leiter** *f* step-ladder; *fig.* scale; '**2weise 1.** *adj.* gradual; **2.** *adv.* gradually, by degrees.

Stuhl [ʃtuːl] *m* (-[e]s/=e) chair, seat; *in a church:* pew; *weaving:* loom; ♨ *s.* Stuhlgang; '~**gang** ♨ *m* (-[e]s/*no pl.*) stool; motion; '~**lehne** *f* back of a chair.

stülpen [ʃtylpən] *v/t.* (ge-, h) put (*über acc.* over); clap (*hat*) (*auf acc.* on).

stumm *adj.* [ʃtum] dumb, mute; *fig. a.* silent; *gr.* silent, mute.

Stummel [ʃtuməl] *m* (-s/-) stump; stub.

'**Stummfilm** *m* silent film.

Stümper F [ʃtympər] *m* (-s/-) bungler; ~**ei** F [~ˈraɪ] *f* (-/-en) bungling; bungle; '**2haft** *adj.* bungling; '**2n** F *v/i.* (ge-, h) bungle, botch.

stumpf [ʃtumpf] **1.** *adj.* blunt; ⅄ *angle:* obtuse; *senses:* dull, obtuse; apathetic; **2.** ⚥ *m* (-[e]s/=e) stump, stub; *mit* ~ *und Stiel* root and branch; '**2sinn** *m* (-[e]s/*no pl.*) stupidity, dul(l)ness; '~**sinnig** *adj.* stupid, dull.

Stunde [ʃtundə] *f* (-/-n) hour; lesson, *Am. a.* period; '**2n** *v/t.* (ge-, h) grant respite for.

'**Stunden|kilometer** *m* kilometre per hour, *Am.* kilometer per hour; '**2lang 1.** *adj.:* *nach ~em Warten* after hours of waiting; **2.** *adv.* for hours (and hours); '~**lohn** *m* hourly wage; '~**plan** *m* timetable, *Am.* schedule; '**2weise 1.** *adj.:* ~ *Beschäftigung* part-time employment; **2.** *adv.* by the hour; '~**zeiger** *m* hour-hand.

stündlich [ʃtyntliç] **1.** *adj.* hourly; **2.** *adv.* hourly, every hour; at any hour.

'**Stundung** *f* (-/-en) respite.

stur F *adj.* [ʃtuːr] *gaze:* fixed, staring; *p.* pigheaded, mulish.

Sturm [ʃturm] *m* (-[e]s/=e) storm (*a. fig.*); ⚓ gale.

stürm|en [ʃtyrmən] (ge-) **1.** *v/t.* (h) ⚔ storm (*a. fig.*); **2.** *v/i.* (h) *wind:* storm, rage; *es stürmt* it is stormy weather; **3.** *v/i.* (sein) rush; '**2er** *m* (-s/-) *football, etc.:* forward; '~**isch** *adj.* stormy; *fig.:* impetuous; tumultuous.

'**Sturm|schritt** ⚔ *m* double-quick step; '~**trupp** ⚔ *m* storming-party; '~**wind** *m* storm-wind.

Sturz [ʃturts] *m* (-es/=e) fall, tumble; overthrow (*of government, etc.*);

fig. ruin; ✝ slump; '**⏜bach** *m* torrent.

stürzen ['ʃtyrtsən] (ge-) **1.** *v/i.* (*sein*) (have a) fall, tumble; *fig.* rush, plunge (*in acc.* into); **2.** *v/t.* (h) throw; overthrow (*government, etc.*); *fig.* plunge (*in acc.* into), precipitate (into); *j-n ins Unglück* ⏜ ruin s.o.; *sich in Schulden* ⏜ plunge into debt.

'**Sturz|flug** ≯ *m* (nose)dive; '**⏜helm** *m* crash-helmet.

Stute *zo.* ['ʃtuːtə] *f* (-/-n) mare.

Stütze ['ʃtytsə] *f* (-/-n) support, prop, stay (*all a. fig.*).

stutzen ['ʃtutsən] (ge-, h) **1.** *v/t.* cut (*hedge*); crop (*ears, tail, hair*); clip (*hedge, wing*); trim (*hair, beard, hedge*); dock (*tail*); lop (*tree*); **2.** *v/i.* start (*bei* at); stop dead *or* short.

'**stützen** *v/t.* (ge-, h) support, prop, stay (*all a. fig.*); ⏜ *auf* (*acc.*) base *or* found on; *sich* ⏜ *auf* (*acc.*) lean on; *fig.* rely (up)on; *argument, etc.*: be based on.

'**Stutz|er** *m* (-s/-) dandy, fop, *Am. a.* dude; '**⏝ig** *adj.* suspicious; ⏜ *machen* make suspicious.

'**Stütz|pfeiler** △ *m* abutment; '**⏜punkt** *m phys.* fulcrum; ⚔ base.

Subjekt [zup'jɛkt] *n* (-[e]s/-e) *gr.* subject; *contp.* individual; ⏁**iv** *adj.* [⏜'tiːf] subjective; ⏁**ivität** [⏜ivi'tɛːt] *f* (-/*no pl.*) subjectivity.

Substantiv *gr.* ['zupstanti:f] *n* (-s/-e) noun, substantive; ⏁**isch** *gr. adj.* ['⏜viʃ] substantival.

Substanz [zup'stants] *f* (-/-en) substance (*a. fig.*).

subtra|hieren ⅋ [zuptra'hiːrən] *v/t.* (*no* -ge-, h) subtract; ⏁**ktion** ⅋ [⏜k'tsjoːn] *f* (-/-en) subtraction.

Such|dienst ['zuːx-] *m* tracing service; '**⏜e** *f* (-/*no pl.*) search (*nach* for); *auf der* ⏜ *nach* in search of; '⏁**en** (ge-) **1.** *v/t.* seek (*advice, etc.*); search for; look for; *Sie haben hier nichts zu* ⏜ you have no business to be here; **2.** *v/i.*: ⏜ *nach* seek for *or* after; search for; look for; '**⏜er** *phot.* *m* (-s/-) view-finder.

Sucht [zuxt] *f* (-/⏜e) mania (*nach* for), rage (for), addiction (to).

süchtig ['zyçtiç] having a mania (*nach* for); ⏜ *sein* be a drug addict; ⏁**e** ['⏜ɡə] *m, f* (-n/-n) drug addict *or* fiend.

Süd *geogr.* [zyːt], ⏜**en** ['⏜dən] *m* (-s/*no pl.*) south; **⏜früchte** ['zyːtfryçtə] *f/pl.* fruits from the south; '⏁**lich 1.** *adj.* south(ern); southerly; **2.** *adv.*: ⏜ *von* (to the) south of; ⏜'ost *geogr.*, ⏜'osten *m* (-s/*no pl.*) south-east; ⏁'östlich *adj.* south-east(ern); '⏜pol *geogr. m* (-s/*no pl.*) South Pole; ⏁**wärts** *adv.* ['⏜vɛrts] southward(s); ⏜'west *geogr.*, ⏜'westen *m* (-s/*no pl.*) south-west;

⏁'westlich *adj.* south-west(ern); '⏜wind *m* south wind.

süffig F *adj.* ['zyfiç] palatable, tasty.

suggerieren [zugeˈriːrən] *v/t.* (*no* -ge-, h) suggest.

suggestiv *adj.* [zuɡɛsˈtiːf] suggestive.

Sühne ['zyːnə] *f* (-/-n) expiation, atonement; '⏁**n** *v/t.* (ge-, h) expiate, atone for.

Sülze ['zyltsə] *f* (-/-n) jellied meat.

summ|arisch *adj.* [zuˈmaːriʃ] summary (*a.* ⚖); '⏁**e** *f* (-/-n) sum (*a. fig.*); (sum) total; amount.

'**summen** (ge-, h) **1.** *v/i.* bees, *etc.*: buzz, hum; **2.** *v/t.* hum (*song, etc.*).

sum'mieren *v/t.* (*no* -ge-, h) sum *or* add up; *sich* ⏜ run up.

Sumpf [zumpf] *m* (-[e]s/⏜e) swamp, bog, marsh; '⏁**ig** *adj.* swampy, boggy, marshy.

Sünd|e ['zyndə] *f* (-/-n) sin (*a. fig.*); '**⏜enbock** F *m* scapegoat; '**⏜er** *m* (-s/-) sinner; ⏁**haft** ['⏜t-] **1.** *adj.* sinful; **2.** *adv.*: F ⏜ *teuer* awfully expensive; ⏁**ig** ['⏜diç] *adj.* sinful; ⏁**igen** ['⏜diɡən] *v/i.* (ge-, h) (commit *a*) sin.

Superlativ ['zuːperlatiːf] *m* (-s/-e) *gr.* superlative degree; *in* ⏜*en sprechen* speak in superlatives.

Suppe ['zupə] *f* (-/-n) soup; broth.

'**Suppen|löffel** *m* soup-spoon; '**⏜schöpfer** *m* soup ladle; '**⏜schüssel** *f* tureen; '**⏜teller** *m* soup-plate.

surren ['zurən] *v/i.* (ge-, h) whir(r); insects: buzz.

Surrogat [zuroˈɡaːt] *n* (-[e]s/-e) substitute.

suspendieren [zuspɛnˈdiːrən] *v/t.* (*no* -ge-, h) suspend.

süß *adj.* [zyːs] sweet (*a. fig.*); ⏁**e** *f* (-/*no pl.*) sweetness; '⏜**en** *v/t.* (ge-, h) sweeten; ⏁**igkeiten** *pl.* sweets *pl.*, sweetmeats *pl.*, *Am. a.* candy; '⏜**lich** *adj.* sweetish; mawkish (*a. fig.*); ⏁**stoff** *m* saccharin(e); ⏁'wasser *n* (-s/-) fresh water.

Symbol [zymˈboːl] *n* (-s/-e) symbol; **⏜ik** *f* (-/*no pl.*) symbolism; ⏁**isch** *adj.* symbolic(al).

Symmetr|ie [zymeˈtriː] *f* (-/-n) symmetry; ⏁**isch** *adj.* [⏜'meːtriʃ] symmetric(al).

Sympath|ie [zympaˈtiː] *f* (-/-n) liking; ⏁**isch** *adj.* [⏜'paːtiʃ] likable; *er ist mir* ⏜ I like him; ⏁**isieren** [⏜iˈziːrən] *v/i.* (*no* -ge-, h) sympathize (*mit* with).

Symphonie ♪ [zymfoˈniː] *f* (-/-n) symphony; **⏜orchester** *n* symphony orchestra.

Symptom [zympˈtoːm] *n* (-s/-e) symptom; ⏁**atisch** *adj.* [⏜oˈmaːtiʃ] symptomatic (*für* of).

Synagoge [zynaˈɡoːɡə] *f* (-/-n) synagogue.

synchronisieren [zynkroniˈziːrən] *v/t.* (*no* -ge-, h) synchronize; dub.

Syndik|at [zyndi'kɑːt] *n* (-[e]s/-e) syndicate; **~us** ['zyndikus] *m* (-/-se, *Syndizi*) syndic.

Synkope ♪ [zyn'koːpə] *f* (-/-n) syncope.

synonym [zyno'nyːm] **1.** *adj.* synonymous; 2. ♫ *n* (-s/-e) synonym.

Syntax *gr.* ['zyntaks] *f* (-/-en) syntax.

synthetisch *adj.* [zyn'teːtiʃ] synthetic.

System [zys'teːm] *n* (-s/-e) system; scheme; **~atisch** [~e'mɑːtiʃ] *adj.* [~e'mɑːtiʃ] systematic(al), methodic(al).

Szene ['stseːnə] *f* (-/-n) scene (*a. fig.*); *in* ~ *setzen* stage; **~rie** [stsenə'riː] *f* (-/-n) scenery.

T

Tabak ['tɑːbak, 'tabak, ta'bak] *m* (-s/-e) tobacco; (')**~händler** *m* tobacconist; (')**~sbeutel** *m* tobacco-pouch; (')**~sdose** *f* snuff-box; (')**~waren** *pl.* tobacco products *pl.*, F smokes *pl.*

tabellarisch [tabe'lɑːriʃ] **1.** *adj.* tabular; 2. *adv.* in tabular form.

Tabelle [ta'belə] *f* (-/-n) table; schedule.

Tablett [ta'blet] *n* (-[e]s/-e, -s) tray; *of metal*: salver; **~e** *pharm. f* (-/-n) tablet; lozenge.

Tachometer [taxo'-] *n, m* (-s/-) ⊕ tachometer; *mot. a.* speedometer.

Tadel ['tɑːdəl] *m* (-s/-) blame; censure; reprimand, rebuke, reproof; reproach; *at school*: bad mark; **'2los** *adj.* faultless, blameless; excellent, splendid; **'2n** *v/t.* (ge-, h) blame (*wegen for*); censure; reprimand, rebuke, reprove; scold; find fault with.

Tafel ['tɑːfəl] *f* (-/-n) table; plate (*a. book illustration*); slab; *on houses, etc.*: tablet, plaque; slate; blackboard; signboard, notice-board, *Am.* billboard; cake, bar (*of chocolate, etc.*); dinner-table; dinner; **2förmig** *adj.* ['~fœrmiç] tabular; **'~geschirr** *n* dinner-service, dinner-set; **'~land** *n* tableland, plateau; **'2n** *v/i.* (ge-, h) dine; feast, banquet; **'~service** *n s. Tafelgeschirr*; **'~silber** *n* silver plate, *Am.* silverware.

Täf(e)lung ['teːf(ə)luŋ] *f* (-/-en) wainscot, panelling.

Taft [taft] *m* (-[e]s/-e) taffeta.

Tag [tɑːk] *m* (-[e]s/-e) day; *officially*: *a.* date; *am or bei ~e* by day; *e-s ~es* one day; *den ganzen ~* all day long; *~ für ~* day by day; *über ~e* ✕ aboveground; *unter ~e* ✕ underground; *heute vor acht ~en* a week ago; *heute in acht (vierzehn) ~en* today *or* this day week (fortnight), a week (fortnight) today; *denkwürdiger or freudiger ~* red-letter day; *freier ~* day off; *guten ~!* how do you do?; good morning!; good afternoon!; F hallo!, hullo!, *Am.* hello!; *am hellichten ~e* in broad daylight; *es wird ~* it dawns; *an den*

~ bringen (kommen) bring (come) to light; *bis auf den heutigen ~* to this day; 2'*aus adv.*: ~, *tagein* day in, day out.

Tage|blatt ['tɑːgə-] *n* daily (paper); **'~buch** *n* journal, diary.

tagein *adv.* [tɑːk'aɪn] *s. tagaus.*

tage|lang *adv.* ['tɑːgə-] day after day, for days together; '2lohn *m* day's *or* daily wages *pl.*; 2löhner ['~løːnər] *m* (-s/-) day-labo(u)rer; **~n** *v/i.* (ge-, h) dawn; hold a meeting, meet, sit; ⅌ be in session; '2reise *f* day's journey.

Tages|anbruch ['tɑːgəs?-] *m* daybreak, dawn; *bei* ~ *at* daybreak *or* dawn; '~befehl ✕ *m* order of the day; '~bericht *m* daily report, bulletin; '~einnahme *f* receipts *pl. or* takings *pl.* of the day; '~gespräch *n* topic of the day; '~kasse *f thea.* box-office, booking-office; *s. Tageseinnahme*; '~kurs ♱ *m* current rate; *stock exchange*: quotation of the day; '~licht *n* daylight; '~ordnung *f* order of the day, agenda; *das ist an der ~ that* is the order of the day, that is quite common; '~presse *f* daily press; '~zeit *f* time of day; daytime; *zu jeder ~* at any hour, at any time of the day; '~zeitung *f* daily (paper).

tage|weise *adv.* ['tɑːgə-] by the day; '2werk *n* day's work; man-day.

täglich *adj.* ['teːkliç] daily.

tags *adv.* [tɑːks]: ~ *darauf* the following day, the day after; ~ *zuvor* (on) the previous day, the day before.

'Tagschicht *f* day shift.

tagsüber *adv.* ['tɑːks?-] during the day, in the day-time.

Tagung ['tɑːguŋ] *f* (-/-en) meeting.

Taille ['taljə] *f* (-/-n) waist; bodice (*of dress*).

Takel ♱ ['tɑːkəl] *n* (-s/-) tackle; **~age** ♱ [takə'lɑːʒə] *f* (-/-n) rigging, tackle; '2n ♱ *v/t.* (ge-, h) rig (*ship*); '~werk ♱ *n s. Takelage.*

Takt [takt] *m* **1.** (-[e]s/-e) ♪ time, measure; bar; *mot.* stroke; *den ~ halten* ♪ keep time; *den ~ schlagen* ♪ beat time; 2. (-[e]s/*no pl.*) tact; '2fest *adj.* steady in keeping time;

fig. firm; '.**ik** ✕ *f* (-/-*en*) tactics
pl. and *sg.* (*a. fig.*); '.**iker** *m* (-*s*/-)
tactician; '**2isch** *adj.* tactical; '**2los**
adj. tactless; '.**stock** *m* baton;
'.**strich** ♪ *m* bar; '**2voll** *adj.* tact-
ful.

Tal [ta:l] *n* (-[*e*]*s*/ᵘ*er*) valley, *poet. a.*
dale; *enges* ~ glen.

Talar [ta'la:r] *m* (-*s*/-*e*) ⅟₂, *eccl.*,
univ. gown; ⅟₂ robe.

Talent [ta'lɛnt] *n* (-[*e*]*s*/-*e*) talent,
gift, aptitude, ability; **2iert** *adj.*
[.ᵛti:rt] talented, gifted.

'**Talfahrt** *f* downhill journey; ⚓
passage downstream.

Talg [talk] *m* (-[*e*]*s*/-*e*) suet; *melted*:
tallow; '.**drüse** *anat.* *f* sebaceous
gland; **2ig** *adj.* ['.ᵍiç] suety; tallow-
ish, tallowy; '.**licht** *n* tallow
candle.

Talisman ['ta:lisman] *m* (-*s*/-*e*)
talisman, (good-luck) charm.

'**Talsperre** *f* barrage, dam.

Tampon [tã'põ:, 'tampon] *m*
(-*s*/-*s*) tampon, plug.

Tang ♣ [taŋ] *m* (-[*e*]*s*/-*e*) seaweed.

Tank [taŋk] *m* (-[*e*]*s*/-*s*, -*e*) tank;
'**2en** *v/i.* (ge-, *h*) get (some) petrol,
Am. get (some) gasoline; '.**er** ⚓ *m*
(-*s*/-) tanker; '.**stelle** *f* petrol station, *Am.* gas *or* filling station;
'.**wagen** *m mot.* tank truck, *Am.*
a. gasoline truck, tank trailer; 🚂
tank-car; '.**wart** ['.ᵛvart] *m* (-[*e*]*s*/-*e*)
pump attendant.

Tanne 🌲 ['tanə] *f* (-/-*n*) fir(-tree).

'**Tannen**|**baum** *m* fir-tree; '.**nadel**
f fir-needle; '.**zapfen** *m* fir-cone.

Tante ['tantə] *f* (-/-*n*) aunt.

Tantieme [tã'tjɛ:mə] *f* (-/-*n*) roy-
alty, percentage, share in profits.

Tanz [tants] *m* (-*es*/-*e*) dance.

tänzeln ['tɛntsəln] *v/i.* (ge-, *h*, *sein*)
dance, trip, frisk.

'**tanzen** (ge-) *v/i.* (*h*, *sein*) and *v/t.*
(*h*) dance.

Tänzer ['tɛntsər] *m* (-*s*/-), '.**in** *f*
(-/-*nen*) dancer; *thea.* ballet-dancer;
partner.

'**Tanz**|**lehrer** *m* dancing-master;
'.**musik** *f* dance-music; '.**saal** *m*
dancing-room, ball-room, dance-
hall; '.**schule** *f* dancing-school;
'.**stunde** *f* dancing-lesson.

Tapete [ta'pe:tə] *f* (-/-*n*) wallpaper,
paper-hangings *pl.*

tapezier|**en** [tape'tsi:rən] *v/t.* (*no*
-ge-, *h*) paper; **2er** *m* (-*s*/-) paper-
hanger; upholsterer.

tapfer *adj.* ['tapfər] brave; valiant,
heroic; courageous; '**2keit** *f* (-/*no*
pl.) bravery, valo(u)r; heroism;
courage.

tappen ['tapən] *v/i.* (ge-, *sein*) grope
(about), fumble.   [awkward.\

täppisch *adj.* ['tɛpiʃ] clumsy,\

tapsen F ['tapsən] *v/i.* (ge-, *sein*)
walk clumsily.

Tara ✝ ['ta:ra] *f* (-/-*Taren*) tare.

Tarif [ta'ri:f] *m* (-*s*/-*e*) tariff, (table
of) rates *pl.*, price-list; **2lich** *adv.*
according to tariff; **2lohn** *m*
standard wage(s *pl.*); .**vertrag** *m*
collective *or* wage agreement.

tarn|**en** ['tarnən] *v/t.* (ge-, *h*) cam-
ouflage; *esp. fig.* disguise; '**2ung** *f*
(-/-*en*) camouflage.

Tasche ['taʃə] *f* (-/-*n*) pocket (*of
garment*); (hand)bag; pouch; *s.*
Aktentasche, Schultasche.

'**Taschen**|**buch** *n* pocket-book;
'.**dieb** *m* pickpocket, *Am. sl.* dip;
'.**geld** *n* pocket-money; *monthly*:
allowance; '.**lampe** *f* (electric)
torch, *esp. Am.* flashlight; '.**messer**
n pocket-knife; '.**spielerei** *f* jug-
gle(ry); '.**tuch** *n* (pocket) handkerchief; '.**uhr** *f* (pocket-)watch;
'.**wörterbuch** *n* pocket dictionary.

Tasse ['tasə] *f* (-/-*n*) cup.

Tastatur [tasta'tu:r] *f* (-/-*en*) keyboard, keys *pl.*

Tast|**e** ['tastə] *f* (-/-*n*) key; '**2en**
(ge-, *h*) **1.** *v/i.* touch; grope (*nach*
for, *after*), fumble (for); **2.** *v/t.*
touch, feel; *sich* ~ feel *or* grope
one's way; '.**sinn** *m* (-[*e*]*s*/*no pl.*)
sense of touch.

Tat [ta:t] **1.** *f* (-/-*en*) action, act,
deed; offen|ce, *Am.* -se, crime; *in
der* ~ indeed, in fact, as a matter of
fact, really; *auf frischer* ~ *ertappen*
catch *s.o.* red-handed; *zur* ~ *schreiten* proceed to action; *in die* ~ *umsetzen* implement, carry into effect;
2. **2** *pret. of* tun; '.**bestand** ⅟₂ *m*
facts *pl.* of the case; '**2enlos** *adj.*
inactive, idle.

Täter ['tɛ:tər] *m* (-*s*/-) perpetrator,
offender, culprit.

tätig *adj.* ['tɛ:tiç] active; busy; ~
sein bei work at; be employed with;
.**en** 🕂 ['.ᵍən] *v/t.* (ge-, *h*) effect,
transact; conclude; '**2keit** *f* (-/-*en*)
activity; occupation, business, job;
profession.

'**Tatkraft** *f* (-/*no pl.*) energy;
enterprise; '**2kräftig** *adj.* energetic,
active.

tätlich *adj.* ['tɛ:tliç] violent; ~ *werden gegen* assault; '**2keiten** *f/pl.*
(acts *pl.* of) violence; ⅟₂ assault (and
battery).

Tatort ⅟₂ ['ta:tʔ-] *m* (-[*e*]*s*/-*e*) place
or scene of a crime.

tätowieren [teto'vi:rən] *v/t.* (*no*
-ge-, *h*) tattoo.

'**Tat**|**sache** *f* (matter of) fact; '.~
sachenbericht *m* factual *or* documentary report, matter-of-fact
account; '**2sächlich** *adj.* actual,
real.   [pat.\

tätscheln ['tɛtʃəln] *v/t.* (ge-, *h*) pet,\

Tatze ['tatsə] *f* (-/-*n*) paw, claw.

Tau¹ [tau] *n* (-[*e*]*s*/-*e*) rope, cable.

Tau² [.] *m* (-[*e*]*s*/*no pl.*) dew.

taub *adj.* [taup] deaf (*fig.*: *gegen* to);
fingers, etc.: benumbed, numb; *nut*:

deaf, empty; *rock*: dead; ~es Ei addle egg; *auf e-m Ohr* ~ *sein* be deaf of or in one ear.

Taube orn. ['taubə] f (-/-n) pigeon; '~nschlag m pigeon-house.

'Taub|heit f (-/no pl.) deafness; numbness; '2stumm adj. deaf and dumb; '~stumme m, f (-n/-n) deaf mute.

tauch|en ['tauxən] (ge-) **1.** v/t. (h) dip, plunge; **2.** v/i. (h, sein) dive, plunge; dip; *submarine*: submerge; '2er m (-s/-) diver; '2sieder m (-s/-) immersion heater.

tauen ['tauən] v/i. (ge-) **1.** (h, sein): *der Schnee or es taut* the snow or it is thawing; *der Schnee ist von den Dächern getaut* the snow has melted off the roofs; **2.** (h): *es taut* dew is falling.

Taufe ['taufə] f (-/-n) baptism, christening; '2n v/t. (ge-, h) baptize, christen.

Täufling ['tɔyfliŋ] m (-s/-e) child or person to be baptized.

'Tauf|name m Christian name, *Am. a.* given name; '~pate **1.** m godfather; **2.** f godmother; '~patin f godmother; '~schein m certificate of baptism.

taug|en ['taugən] v/i. (ge-, h) be good, be fit, be of use (*all*: zu for); (zu) *nichts* ~ be good for nothing, be no good, be of no use; '2enichts m (-, -es/-e) good-for-nothing, *Am. sl.* dead beat; '~lich adj. ['tauk-] good, fit, useful (*all*: für, zu for, to *inf.*); able; ✂, ⚓ able-bodied.

Taumel ['tauməl] m (-s/no pl.) giddiness; rapture, ecstasy; '2ig adj. reeling; giddy; '2n v/i. (ge-, sein) reel, stagger; be giddy.

Tausch [tauʃ] m (-es/-e) exchange; barter; '2en v/t. (ge-, h) exchange; barter (*gegen* for).

täuschen ['tɔyʃən] v/t. (ge-, h) deceive, delude, mislead (on purpose); cheat; *sich* ~ deceive o.s.; be mistaken; *sich* ~ *lassen* let o.s. be deceived; '~d adj. deceptive, delusive; *resemblance*: striking.

'Tauschhandel m barter.

'Täuschung f (-/-en) deception, delusion.

tausend adj. ['tauzənt] a thousand; '~fach adj. thousandfold; '2fuß zo. m, 2füß(l)er zo. ['~fy:s(l)ər] m (-s/-) millepede, milliped(e), *Am. a.* wireworm; '~st adj. thousandth; '2stel n (-s/-) thousandth (part).

'Tau|tropfen m dew-drop; '~wetter n thaw.

Taxameter [taksa'-] m taximeter.

Taxe ['taksə] f (-/-n) rate; fee; estimate; *s. Taxi.*

Taxi ['taksi] n (-[s]/-[s]) taxi(-cab), cab, *Am. a.* hack.

ta'xieren v/t. (no -ge-, h) rate, estimate; *officially*: value, appraise.

'Taxistand m cabstand.

Technik ['tɛçnik] f **1.** (-/no pl.) technology; engineering; **2.** (-/-en) skill, workmanship; technique, practice; ♪ execution; '~er m (-s/-) (technical) engineer; technician; ~um ['~um] n (-s/Technika, Techniken) technical school.

'technisch adj. technical; ~e *Hochschule* school of technology.

Tee [te:] m (-s/-s) tea; '~büchse f tea-caddy; '~gebäck n scones pl., biscuits pl., *Am. a.* cookies pl.; '~kanne f teapot; '~kessel m tea-kettle; '~löffel m tea-spoon.

Teer [te:r] m (-[e]s/-e) tar; '2en v/t. (ge-, h) tar.

'Tee|rose ⚘ f tea-rose; '~sieb n tea-strainer; '~tasse f teacup; '~wärmer m (-s/-) tea-cosy.

Teich [taiç] m (-[e]s/-e) pool, pond.

Teig [taik] m (-[e]s/-e) dough, paste; 2ig adj. ['~giç] doughy, pasty; '~waren f/pl. farinaceous food; noodles pl.

Teil [tail] m, n (-[e]s/-e) part; portion, share; component; ½ party; *zum* ~ partly, in part; *für mein* ~ ... for my part I ...; '2bar adj. divisible; '~chen n (-s/-) particle; '2en v/t. (ge-, h) divide; *fig.* share; '2haben v/i. (irr. haben, sep., -ge-, h) participate, (have a) share (*both*: *an dat.* in); '~haber ⚱ m (-s/-) partner; ~nahme ['~na:mə] f (-/no pl.) participation (*an dat.* in); *fig.*: interest (in); sympathy (with); 2nahmslos adj. ['~na:mslo:s] indifferent, unconcerned; passive; apathetic; '~nahmslosigkeit f (-/no pl.) indifference; passiveness; apathy; 2nehmen v/i. (irr. nehmen, sep., -ge-, h): ~ *an* (dat.) take part or participate in; join in; be present at, attend at; *fig.* sympathize with; '~nehmer m (-s/-) participant; member; *univ., etc.*: student; contestant; *sports*: competitor; *teleph.* subscriber; 2s adv. [~s] partly; '~strecke f section; stage, leg; ~ fare stage; '~ung f (-/-en) division; 2weise adv. partly, partially, in part; '~zahlung f (payment by) instal(l)ments.

Teint [tɛ̃:] m (-s/-s) complexion.

Tele|fon [tele'fo:n] n (-s/-e) etc. s. *Telephon, etc.*; ~graf [~'gra:f] m (-en/-en) etc. s. *Telegraph, etc.*; ~gramm [~'gram] n (-s/-e) telegram, wire; *overseas*: cable(gram).

Telegraph [tele'gra:f] m (-en/-en) telegraph; ~enamt [~gra:fən-] n telegraph office; 2ieren [~a'fi:rən] v/t. and v/i. (no -ge-, h) telegraph, wire; *overseas*: cable; 2isch [~gra'fiʃ] **1.** adj. telegraphic; **2.** adv. by telegram, by wire; by cable; ~ist [~a'fist] m (-en/-en), ~istin f (-/-nen) telegraph operator, telegrapher; telegraphist.

Teleobjektiv *phot.* ['te:le-] *n* telephoto lens.

Telephon [tele'fo:n] *n* (-s/-e) telephone, F phone; *am* ~ on the (tele)phone; *ans* ~ *gehen* answer the (tele)phone; ~ *haben* be on the (tele)phone; **~anschluß** *m* telephone connexion *or* connection; **~buch** *n* telephone directory; **~gespräch** *n* (tele)phone call; conversation *or* chat over the (tele)phone; **~hörer** *m* (telephone) receiver, handset; **2ieren** [~o'ni:rən] *v/i.* (no -ge-, h) telephone, F phone; *mit j-m* ~ ring s.o. up, *Am.* call s.o. up; **2isch** *adv.* [~'fo:niʃ] by (tele)phone, over the (tele)phone; **~ist** [~o'nist] *m* (-en/-en), **~istin** *f* (-/-nen) (telephone) operator, telephonist; **~vermittlung** *f s. Telephonzentrale*; **~zelle** *f* telephone kiosk *or* box, call-box, *Am.* telephone booth; **~zentrale** *f* (telephone) exchange.

Teleskop *opt.* [tele'sko:p] *n* (-s/-e) telescope.

Teller ['tɛlər] *m* (-s/-) plate.

Tempel ['tɛmpəl] *m* (-s/-) temple.

Temperament [tɛmpəra'mɛnt] *n* (-[e]s/-e) temper(ament); *fig.* spirit(s *pl.*); **2los** *adj.* spiritless; **2voll** *adj.* (high-)spirited.

Temperatur [tɛmpəra'tu:r] *f* (-/-en) temperature; *j-s* ~ *messen* take s.o.'s temperature.

Tempo ['tɛmpo] *n* (-s/-s, *Tempi*) time; pace; speed; rate.

Tendenz [tɛn'dɛnts] *f* (-/-en) tendency; trend; **2iös** *adj.* [~'tsjø:s] tendentious.

Tennis ['tɛnis] *n* (-/no *pl.*) (lawn) tennis; **~ball** *m* tennis-ball; **~platz** *m* tennis-court; **~schläger** *m* (tennis-)racket; **~spieler** *m* tennis player; **~turnier** *n* tennis tournament.

Tenor ♪ [te'no:r] *m* (-s/*≈e) tenor.

Teppich ['tɛpiç] *m* (-s/-e) carpet; **~kehrmaschine** *f* carpet-sweeper.

Termin [tɛr'mi:n] *m* (-s/-e) appointed time *or* day; ㅝㅑ, † date, term; *sports*: fixture; *äußerster* ~ final date, dead(-)line; **~geschäfte** † *n/pl.* futures *pl.*; **~kalender** *m* appointment book *or* pad; ㅝㅑ causelist, *Am.* calendar; **~liste** ㅝㅑ *f* causelist, *Am.* calendar.

Terpentin [tɛrpən'ti:n] *n* (-s/-e) turpentine.

Terrain [tɛ'rɛ̃:] *n* (-s/-s) ground; plot; building site.

Terrasse [tɛ'rasə] *f* (-/-n) terrace; **2nförmig** *adj.* [~nfœrmiç] terraced, in terraces.

Terrine [tɛ'ri:nə] *f* (-/-n) tureen.

Territorium [tɛri'to:rjum] *n* (-s/*Territorien*) territory.

Terror ['tɛrɔr] *m* (-s/no *pl.*) terror; **2isieren** [~ori'zi:rən] *v/t.* (no -ge-, h) terrorize.

Terz ♪ [tɛrts] *f* (-/-en) third; **~ett** ♪ [~'tsɛt] *n* (-[e]s/-e) trio.

Testament [tɛsta'mɛnt] *n* (-[e]s/-e) (last) will, (*often:* last will and) testament; *eccl.* Testament; **2arisch** [~'ta:riʃ] *1. adj.* testamentary; *2. adv.* by will; **~svollstrecker** *m* (-s/-) executor; *officially:* administrator.

testen ['tɛstən] *v/t.* (ge-, h) test.

teuer *adj.* ['tɔyər] dear (*a. fig.*), expensive; *wie* ~ *ist es?* how much is it?

Teufel ['tɔyfəl] *m* (-s/-) devil; *der* ~ the Devil, Satan; *zum* ~! F dickens!, hang it!; *wer zum* ~? F who the devil *or* deuce?; *der* ~ *ist los* the fat's in the fire; *scher dich zum* ~! F go to hell!, go to blazes!; **~ei** [~'lai] *f* (-/-en) devilment, mischief, devilry, *Am.* deviltry; **'~skerl** F *m* devil of a fellow.

'teuflisch *adj.* devilish, diabolic(al).

Text [tɛkst] *m* (-es/-e) text; words *pl.* (*of song*); book, libretto (*of opera*); **'~buch** *n* book; libretto.

Textil|ien [tɛks'ti:ljən] *pl.*, **~waren** *pl.* textile fabrics *pl.*, textiles *pl.*

'textlich *adv.* concerning the text.

Theater [te'a:tər] *n 1.* (-s/-) theat|re, *Am.* -er; stage; *2.* F (-s/no *pl.*) playacting; **~besucher** *m* playgoer; **~karte** *f* theatre ticket; **~kasse** *f* box-office; **~stück** *n* play; **~vorstellung** *f* theatrical performance; **~zettel** *m* playbill.

theatralisch *adj.* [tea'tra:liʃ] theatrical, stagy.

Theke ['te:kə] *f* (-/-n) *at inn:* bar, *Am. a.* counter; *at shop:* counter.

Thema ['te:ma] *n* (-s/*Themen, Themata*) theme, subject; topic (*of discussion*).

Theolog|e [teo'lo:gə] *m* (-n/-n) theologian, divine; **~ie** [~o'gi:] *f* (-/-n) theology.

Theoret|iker [teo're:tikər] *m* (-s/-) theorist; **2isch** *adj.* theoretic(al).

Theorie [teo'ri:] *f* (-/-n) theory.

Therapie ⚕ [tera'pi:] *f* (-/-n) therapy. [spa.\

Thermalbad [tɛr'ma:l-] *n* thermal⎰

Thermometer [tɛrmo'-] *n* (-s/-) thermometer; **~stand** *m* (thermometer) reading.

Thermosflasche ['tɛrmɔs-] *f* vacuum bottle *or* flask, thermos (flask).

These ['te:zə] *f* (-/-n) thesis.

Thrombose ⚕ [trɔm'bo:zə] *f* (-/-n) thrombosis.

Thron [tro:n] *m* (-[e]s/-e) throne; **~besteigung** *f* accession to the throne; **~erbe** *m* heir to the throne, heir apparent; **~folge** *f* succession to the throne; **'~folger** *m* (-s/-) successor to the throne; **'~rede** *parl.* *f* Queen's *or* King's Speech.

17*

Thunfisch *ichth.* ['tuːn-] *m* tunny, tuna.

Tick F [tik] *m* (-[e]s/-s, -e) crotchet, fancy, kink; e-n ~ haben have a bee in one's bonnet.

ticken ['tikən] *v/i.* (ge-, h) tick.

tief [tiːf] **1.** *adj.* deep (*a. fig.*); *fig.*: profound; low; im ~sten Winter in the dead *or* depth of winter; **2.** *adv.*: bis ~ in die Nacht far into the night; das läßt ~ blicken that speaks volumes; zu ~ singen sing flat; **3.** ♀ *meteor.* n (-[e]s/-s) depression, low(-pressure area); '~bau *m* civil *or* underground engineering; '♀-druckgebiet *meteor.* n s. Tief; '♀e *f* (-/-n) depth (*a. fig.*); *fig.* profundity; '♀ebene *f* low plain, lowland; '♀enschärfe *phot.* *f* depth of focus; '♀flug *m* low-level flight; '~gang ♣ *m* draught, *Am.* draft; '~gebeugt *fig. adj.* ['~gəbɔʏkt] deeply afflicted, bowed down; '~gekühlt *adj.* deep-frozen; '~greifend *adj.* fundamental, radical; '♀land n lowland(s *pl.*); '~liegend *adj. eyes*: sunken; *fig.* deep-seated; '♀schlag *m boxing*: low hit; '~schürfend *fig. adj.* profound; thorough; '♀see *f* deep sea; '~sinnig *adj.* thoughtful, pensive; F melancholy; '♀stand *m* (-[e]s/*no pl.*) low level.

Tiegel ['tiːgəl] *m* (-s/-) saucepan, stew-pan; ⊕ crucible.

Tier [tiːr] *n* (-[e]s/-e) animal; beast; brute; großes ~ *fig. sl.* bigwig, big bug, *Am.* big shot; '~arzt *m* veterinary (surgeon), F vet, *Am. a.* veterinarian; '~garten *m* zoological gardens *pl.*, zoo; '~heilkunde *f* veterinary medicine; '♀isch *adj.* animal; *fig.* bestial, brutish, savage; '~kreis *ast. m* zodiac; '~quälerei [~kvɛːləˈraɪ] *f* (-/-en) cruelty to animals; '~reich *n* (-[e]s/*no pl.*) animal kingdom; '~schutzverein *m* Society for the Prevention of Cruelty to Animals.

Tiger zo. ['tiːgər] *m* (-s/-) tiger; '~in zo. *f* (-/-nen) tigress.

tilg|en ['tilgən] *v/t.* (ge-, h) extinguish; efface; wipe *or* blot out, erase; *fig.* obliterate; annul, cancel; discharge, pay (*debt*); redeem (*mortgage*, *etc.*); '♀ung *f* (-/-en) extinction; extermination; cancel(l)ing; discharge, payment; redemption.

Tinktur [tiŋkˈtuːr] *f* (-/-en) tincture. [*sitzen* F be in a scrape.]

Tinte ['tintə] *f* (-/-n) ink; in der ~]

'Tinten|faß *n* ink-pot, desk: inkwell; '~fisch *ichth. m* cuttle-fish; '~fleck *m*, '~klecks *m* (ink-)blot; '~stift *m* indelible pencil.

Tip [tip] *m* (-s/-s) hint, tip; '♀pen (ge-, h) **1.** *v/i.* F type; *fig.* guess; j-m auf die Schulter ~ tap s.o. on his shoulder. **2.** *v/t.* tip; foretell, predict; F type.

Tiroler [tiˈroːlər] **1.** *m* (-s/-) Tyrolese; **2.** *adj.* Tyrolese.

Tisch [tiʃ] *m* (-es/-e) table; bei ~ at table; den ~ decken lay the table *or* cloth, set the table; reinen ~ machen make a clean sweep (*damit* of it); zu ~ bitten invite *or* ask to dinner *or* supper; bitte zu ~! dinner is ready!; '~decke *f* table-cloth; '♀fertig *adj. food*: ready-prepared; '~gast *m* guest; '~gebet n: das ~ sprechen say grace; '~gesellschaft *f* dinner-party; '~gespräch n table-talk; '~lampe *f* table-lamp; desk lamp.

Tischler ['tiʃlər] *m* (-s/-) joiner; carpenter; cabinet-maker; '~ei [~ˈraɪ] *f* (-/-en) joinery; joiner's workshop.

'Tisch|platte *f* top (of a table), table top; leaf (of *extending table*); '~rede *f* toast, after-dinner speech; '~tennis n table tennis, ping-pong; '~tuch n table-cloth; '~zeit *f* dinner-time.

Titan [tiˈtaːn] *m* (-en/-en) Titan; ♀isch *adj.* titanic.

Titel ['tiːtəl] *m* (-s/-) title; e-n ~ (inne)haben *sports*: hold a title; '~bild n frontispiece; cover picture (of *magazine*, *etc.*); '~blatt n title-page; cover (of *magazine*); '~halter *m* (-s/-) *sports*: title-holder; '~kampf *m boxing*: title fight; '~rolle *thea. f* title-role.

titulieren [tituˈliːrən] *v/t.* (no -ge-, h) style, call, address as.

Toast [toːst] *m* (-es/-e, -s) toast (*a. fig.*).

tob|en ['toːbən] *v/i.* (ge-, h) rage, rave, storm, bluster; *children*: romp; ♀sucht ⋆ ['toːp-] *f* (-/*no pl.*) raving madness, frenzy; '~süchtig *adj.* ['toːp-] raving mad, frantic.

Tochter ['tɔxtər] *f* (-/⸚) daughter; '~gesellschaft ♀ *f* subsidiary company.

Tod [toːt] *m* (-[e]s/⸚, -e) death; ☆ decease.

Todes|angst ['toːdəs⁹-] *f* mortal agony; *fig.* mortal fear; Todesängste ausstehen be scared to death, be frightened out of one's wits; '~anzeige *f* obituary (notice); '~fall *m* (case of) death; Todesfälle *pl.* deaths *pl.*, ✗ casualties *pl.*; '~kampf *m* death throes *pl.*, mortal agony; '~strafe *f* capital punishment, death penalty; bei ~ verboten forbidden on *or* under pain *or* penalty of death; '~ursache *f* cause of death; '~urteil n death *or* capital sentence, death-warrant.

'Tod|feind *m* deadly *or* mortal enemy; '♀krank *adj.* dangerously ill.

tödlich *adj.* ['tøːtliç] deadly; fatal; wound: *a.* mortal.

'tod|müde *adj.* dead tired; '~

'schick F *adj.* dashing, gorgeous;
'~sicher F *adj.* cock-sure; '2sünde
f deadly *or* mortal sin.

Toilette [toa'lɛtə] *f* (-/-n) dress(ing):
toilet; lavatory, gentlemen's *or*
ladies' room, *esp. Am.* toilet.

Toi'letten|artikel *m*/*pl.* toilet ar-
ticles *pl., Am. a.* toiletry; ~papier
n toilet-paper; ~tisch *m* toilet
(-table), dressing-table, *Am. a.*
dresser.

toleran|t *adj.* [tole'rant] tolerant
(gegen of); 2z [~ts] *f* 1. (-/*no pl.*)
tolerance, toleration (*esp. eccl.*);
2. ⊕ (-/-en) tolerance, allowance.

toll [tɔl] 1. *adj.* (raving) mad, frantic;
mad, crazy, wild (*all a. fig.*);
fantastic; *noise, etc.*: frightful, F
awful; *das ist ja* ~ F that's (just)
great; 2. *adv.*: es ~ treiben carry on
like mad; es zu ~ treiben go too far;
'~en *v/i.* (ge-, h, sein) *children*:
romp; '2haus *fig. n* bedlam; '2heit
f (-/-en) madness; mad trick;
'~kühn *adj.* foolhardy, rash; '2wut
vet. f rabies.

Tolpatsch F ['tɔlpatʃ] *m* (-es/-e)
awkward *or* clumsy fellow; '2ig F
adj. awkward, clumsy.

Tölpel F ['tœlpəl] *m* (-s/-) awkward
or clumsy fellow; boob(y).

Tomate ⚓ [to'ma:tə] *f* (-/-n) tomato.

Ton¹ [to:n] *m* (-[e]s/-e) clay.

Ton² [~] *m* (-[e]s/-e) sound; ♪ tone
(*a. of language*); ♪ single: note; accent, stress; *fig.* tone; paint. tone,
tint, shade; *guter* ~ good form; *den*
~ *angeben* set the fashion; *zum*
guten ~ *gehören* be the fashion;
große Töne reden or F *spucken* F
talk big, boast; '~abnehmer *m*
pick-up; '2angebend *adj.* setting
the fashion, leading; '~arm *m*
pick-up arm (*of record-player*); '~-
art ♪ *f* key; '~band *n* recording
tape; '2bandgerät *n* tape recorder.

tönen ['tø:nən] (ge-, h) 1. *v/i.* sound,
ring; 2. *v/t.* tint, tone, shade.

tönern *adj.* ['tø:nərn] (of) clay,
earthen.

'Ton|fall *m in speaking*: intonation,
accent; '~film *m* sound film; '~lage
f pitch; '~leiter ♪ *f* scale, gamut;
'2los *adj.* soundless; *fig.* toneless;
'~meister *m* sound engineer.

Tonne ['tɔnə] *f* (-/-n) large: tun;
smaller: barrel, cask; ⚓ *measure of*
weight: ton.

Tonsilbe *gr. f* accented syllable.

Tonsur [tɔn'zu:r] *f* (-/-en) tonsure.

Tönung *paint. f* (-/-en) tint, tinge,
shade.

'Tonwaren *f*/*pl. s.* Töpferware.

Topf [tɔpf] *m* (-[e]s/=e) pot.

Töpfer ['tœpfər] *m* (-s/-) potter;
stove-fitter; '~ei [~'raı] *f* (-/-en)
pottery; '~ware *f* pottery, earthenware, crockery.

topp¹ *int.* [tɔp] done!, agreed!

Topp² ⚓ [~] *m* (-s/-e, -s) top, mast-
head.

Tor¹ [to:r] *n* (-[e]s/-e) gate; gate-
way (*a. fig.*); *football*: goal; *skiing*:
gate.

Tor² [~] *m* (-en/-en) fool.

Torf [tɔrf] *m* (-[e]s/*no pl.*) peat.

Torheit ['to:rhaıt] *f* (-/-en) folly.

'Torhüter *m* gate-keeper; *sports*:
goalkeeper.

töricht *adj.* ['tø:rıçt] foolish, silly.

Törin ['tø:rın] *f* (-/-nen) fool(ish
woman).

torkeln ['tɔrkəln] *v/i.* (ge-, h, sein)
reel, stagger, totter.

'Tor|latte *f sports*: cross-bar; '~lauf
m skiing: slalom; '~linie *f sports*:
goal-line.

Tornister [tɔr'nıstər] *m* (-s/-) knapsack; satchel.

torpedieren [tɔrpe'di:rən] *v/t.* (no
-ge-, h) torpedo (*a. fig.*).

Torpedo [tɔr'pe:do] *m* (-s/-s)
torpedo; ~boot *n* torpedo-boat.

'Tor|pfosten *m* gate-post; *sports*:
goal-post; '~schuß *m* shot at the
goal; '~schütze *m sports*: scorer.

Torte ['tɔrtə] *f* (-/-n) fancy cake,
Am. layer cake; tart, *Am.* pie.

Tortur [tɔr'tu:r] *f* (-/-en) torture;
fig. ordeal.

'Tor|wart ['to:rvart] *m* (-[e]s/-e)
sports: goalkeeper; '~weg *m* gate-
way.

tosen ['to:zən] *v/i.* (ge-, h, sein) roar,
rage; '~d *adj. applause*: thunderous.

tot *adj.* [to:t] dead (*a. fig.*); deceased;
~er Punkt ⊕ dead cent|re, *Am.* -er;
fig.: deadlock; fatigue; ~es Rennen
sports: dead heat.

total *adj.* [to'ta:l] total, complete.

'tot|arbeiten *v/refl.* (*sep.*, -ge-, h)
work o.s. to death; '2e (-n/-n) 1. *m*
dead man; (dead) body, corpse; *die*
~n *pl.* the dead *pl.*, the deceased
pl. or departed *pl.*; ✗ casualties *pl.*;
2. *f* dead woman.

töten ['tø:tən] *v/t.* (ge-, h) kill;
destroy; murder; deaden (*nerve*,
etc.).

'Toten|bett *n* deathbed; '2blaß
adj. deadly *or* deathly pale; '~
blässe *f* deadly paleness *or* pallor;
'2bleich *adj. s.* totenblaß; '~gräber
['~grɛ:bər] *m* (-s/-) grave-digger
(*a. zo.*); '~hemd *n* shroud; '~kopf
m death's-head (*a. zo.*); *emblem of*
death: a. skull and cross-bones;
'~liste *f* death-roll (*a.* ✗), *esp.* ✗
casualty list; '~maske *f* death-
mask; '~messe *eccl. f* mass for the
dead, requiem; '~schädel *m*
death's-head, skull; '~schein *m*
death certificate; '2still *adj.* (as)
still as the grave; '~stille *f* dead(ly)
silence, deathly stillness.

'tot|geboren *adj.* still-born; '2ge-
burt *f* still birth; '~lachen *v/refl.*
(*sep.*, -ge-, h) die of laughing.

Toto ['to:to] *m*, F *a. n* (-*s*/-*s*) football pools *pl.*

'tot|schießen *v/t.* (*irr. schießen, sep., -ge-, h*) shoot dead, kill; **'~schlag** ⚔ *m* manslaughter, homicide; **'~schlagen** *v/t.* (*irr. schlagen, sep., -ge-, h*) kill (*a. time*), slay; **'~schweigen** *v/t.* (*irr. schweigen, sep., -ge-, h*) hush up; **'~stechen** *v/t.* (*irr. stechen, sep., -ge-, h*) stab to death; **'~stellen** *v/refl.* (*sep., -ge-, h*) feign death.

'Tötung *f* (-/-en) killing, slaying; ⚔ homicide; *fahrlässige ~* ⚔ manslaughter.

Tour [tu:r] *f* (-/-en) tour; excursion, trip; ⊕ turn, revolution; *auf ~en kommen mot.* pick up speed; **'~enwagen** *mot. m* touring car.

Tourist [tu'rist] *m* (-en/-en), **~in** *f* (-/-nen) tourist.

Tournee [tur'ne:] *f* (-/-s, -n) tour.

Trab [tra:p] *m* (-[e]s/*no pl.*) trot.

Trabant [tra'bant] *m* (-en/-en) satellite.

trab|en ['tra:bən] *v/i.* (ge-, *h, sein*) trot; **2rennen** ['tra:p-] *n* trotting race.

Tracht [traxt] *f* (-/-en) dress, costume; uniform; fashion; load; *e-e (gehörige) ~ Prügel* a (sound) thrashing; **2en** *v/i.* (ge-, *h*): *~ nach et.* strive for; *j-m nach dem Leben ~* seek s.o.'s life.

trächtig *adj.* ['trɛçtiç] (big) with young, pregnant. [tradition.]

Tradition [tradi'tsjo:n] *f* (-/-en)

traf [tra:f] *pret. of* treffen.

Trag|bahre ['tra:k-] *f* stretcher, litter; **2bar** *adj.* portable; *dress:* wearable; *fig.:* bearable; reasonable; **~e** ['~gə] *f* (-/-n) hand-barrow; *s. Tragbahre.*

träge *adj.* ['trɛ:gə] lazy, indolent; *phys.* inert (*a. fig.*).

tragen ['tra:gən] (*irr., ge-, h*) **1.** *v/t.* carry; bear (*costs, name, responsibility, etc.*); bear, endure; support; bear, yield (*fruit, ⊤ interest, etc.*); wear (*dress, etc.*); *bei sich ~* have about one; *sich gut ~ material:* wear well; *zur Schau ~* show off; **2.** *v/i. tree:* bear, yield; *gun, voice:* carry; *ice:* bear.

Träger ['trɛ:gər] *m* (-s/-) carrier; porter (*of luggage*); holder, bearer (*of name, licence, etc.*); wearer (*of dress*); (shoulder-)strap (*of slip, etc.*); ⊕ support; ▲ girder.

Trag|fähigkeit ['tra:k-] *f* carrying or load capacity; ⬩ tonnage; **~fläche** ⬩ *f*, **~flügel** ⬩ *m* wing, plane.

Trägheit ['trɛ:khaɪt] *f* (-/*no pl.*) laziness, indolence; *phys.* inertia (*a. fig.*).

tragisch *adj.* ['tra:giʃ] tragic (*a. fig.*); *fig.* tragical.

Tragödie [tra'gø:djə] *f* (-/-n) tragedy.

Trag|riemen ['tra:k-] *m* (carrying) strap; sling (*of gun*); **~tier** *n* pack animal; **'~tüte** *f* carrier-bag; **'~weite** *f* range; *fig.* import(ance), consequences *pl.*; *von großer ~* of great moment.

Train|er ['trɛ:nər] *m* (-s/-) trainer; coach; **2ieren** ['~ni:rən] (*no -ge-, h*) **1.** *v/t.* train; coach; **2.** *v/i.* train; **~ing** ['~iŋ] *n* (-s/-s) training; **'~ingsanzug** *m sports:* track suit.

traktieren [trak'ti:rən] *v/t.* (*no -ge-, h*) treat (badly).

Traktor ⊕ ['traktɔr] *m* (-s/-en) tractor.

trällern ['trɛlərn] *v/t. and v/i.* (ge-, *h*) troll.

trampeln ['trampəln] *v/i.* (ge-, *h*) trample, stamp; **2pfad** *m* beaten track.

Tran [tra:n] *m* (-[e]s/-e) train-oil, whale-oil.

Träne ['trɛ:nə] *f* (-/-n) tear; *in ~n ausbrechen* burst into tears; **2n** *v/i.* (ge-, *h*) water; **'~ngas** *n* tear-gas.

Trank [traŋk] **1.** *m* (-[e]s/=e) drink, beverage; ⬨ potion; **2.** *2 pret. of* trinken.

Tränke ['trɛŋkə] *f* (-/-n) watering-place; **2n** *v/t.* (ge-, *h*) water (*animals*); soak, impregnate (*material*).

Trans|formator ⚡ [transfɔr'ma:tɔr] *m* (-s/-en) transformer; **~fusion** ⬨ [~u'zjo:n] *f* (-/-en) transfusion.

Transistorradio [tran'zistɔr-] *n* transistor radio *or* set.

transitiv *gr. adj.* ['tranziti:f] transitive.

transparent [transpa'rɛnt] **1.** *adj.* transparent; **2.** *2 n* (-[e]s/-e) transparency; *in political processions, etc.*: banner.

transpirieren [transpi'ri:rən] *v/i.* (*no -ge-, h*) perspire.

Transplantation ⬨ [transplanta'tsjo:n] *f* transplant (operation).

Transport [trans'pɔrt] *m* (-[e]s/-e) transport(ation), conveyance, carriage; **2abel** *adj.* [~'ta:bəl] (trans-)portable; **~er** *m* (-s/-) ⬩, ✈ (troop-)transport; ✈ transport (aircraft *or* plane); **2fähig** *adj.* transportable, *sick person:* a. transferable; **2ieren** [~'ti:rən] *v/t.* (*no -ge-, h*) transport, convey, carry; **~unternehmen** *n* carrier.

Trapez [tra'pe:ts] *n* (-es/-e) ⒜ trapezium, *Am.* trapezoid; *gymnastics:* trapeze.

trappeln ['trapəln] *v/i.* (ge-, *sein*) *horse:* clatter; *children, etc.*: patter.

Trass|ant ⊤ [tra'sant] *m* (-en/-en) drawer; **~at** ⊤ [~'sa:t] *m* (-en/-en) drawee; **~e** ⊕ *f* (-/-n) line; **2ieren** [~'si:rən] *v/t.* (*no -ge-, h*) ⊕ lay *or* trace out; *~ auf (acc.)* ⊤ draw on.

trat [traːt] *pret. of* treten.

Tratte ♱ ['tratə] *f* (-/-n) draft.

Traube ['traubə] *f* (-/-n) bunch of grapes; grape; cluster; '**~nsaft** *m* grape-juice; '**~nzucker** *m* grape-sugar, glucose.

trauen ['trauən] (ge-, h) **1.** *v/t.* marry; *sich ~ lassen* get married; **2.** *v/i.* trust (*j-m* s.o.), confide (*dat.* in); *ich traute meinen Ohren nicht* I could not believe my ears.

Trauer ['trauər] *f* (-/no pl.) sorrow, affliction; *for dead person:* mourning; '**~botschaft** *f* sad news; '**~fall** *m* death; '**~feier** *f* funeral ceremonies *pl.*, obsequies *pl.*; '**~flor** *m* mourning-crape; '**~geleit** *n* funeral procession; '**~gottesdienst** *m* funeral service; '**~kleid** *n* mourning (-dress); '**~marsch** *m* funeral march; '**2n** *v/i.* (ge-, h) mourn (*um* for); be in mourning; '**~spiel** *n* tragedy; '**~weide** ♀ *f* weeping willow; '**~zug** *m* funeral procession.

Traufe ['traufə] *f* (-/-n) eaves *pl.*; gutter; *s. Regen.*

träufeln ['trɔyfəln] *v/t.* (ge-, h) drop, drip, trickle. [cosy, snug.]

traulich *adj.* ['trauliç] intimate;)

Traum [traum] *m* (-[e]s/~e) dream (*a. fig.*); reverie; *das fällt mir nicht im ~ ein!* I would not dream of (doing) it!; '**~bild** *n* vision; '**~deuter** *m* (-s/-) dream-reader.

träum|en ['trɔymən] *v/i. and v/t.* (ge-, h) dream; '**2er** *m* (-s/-) dreamer (*a. fig.*); **2erei** [~'rai] *f* (-/-en) dreaming; *fig. a.* reverie (*a. ♪*), day-dream, musing; '**~erisch** *adj.* dreamy; musing.

traurig *adj.* ['trauriç] sad (*über acc.* at), *Am.* F blue; wretched.

'**Trau|ring** *m* wedding-ring; '**~schein** *m* marriage certificate *or* lines *pl.*; '**~ung** *f* (-/-en) marriage, wedding; '**~zeuge** *m* witness to a marriage.

Trecker ⊕ ['trekər] *m* (-s/-) tractor.

Treff [trɛf] *n* (-s/-s) *cards:* club(s *pl.*).

treffen ['trɛfən] (*irr.*, ge-) **1.** *v/t.* (h) hit (*a. fig.*), strike; concern, *disadvantageously:* affect; meet; *nicht ~ miss;* *e-e Entscheidung ~* come to a decision; *Maßnahmen ~* take measures *or* steps; *Vorkehrungen ~* take precautions *or* measures; *sich ~* happen; meet; gather, assemble; *a.* have an appointment (*mit* with), F have a date (with); *das trifft sich gut!* that's lucky!, how fortunate!; *sich getroffen fühlen* feel hurt; *wen trifft die Schuld?* who is to blame?; *das Los traf ihn* the lot fell on him; *du bist gut getroffen* *paint.*, *phot.* this is a good likeness of you; *vom Blitz getroffen* struck by lightning; **2.** *v/i.* (h) hit; **3.** *v/i.* (sein): *~ auf* (*acc.*) meet with; encounter (*a. ⚔*).

Treffen² [~] *n* (-s/-) meeting; rally; gathering; ⚔ encounter; '**2d** *adj.* *remark:* appropriate, to the point.

'**Treff|er** *m* (-s/-) hit (*a. fig.*); prize; '**~punkt** *m* meeting-place.

Treibeis ['traip9-] *n* drift-ice.

treiben¹ ['traibən] (*irr.*, ge-) **1.** *v/t.* (h) drive; ⊕ put in motion, propel; drift (*smoke, snow*); put forth (*leaves*); force (*plants*); *fig.* impel, urge, press (*j-n zu inf.* s.o. to *inf.*); carry on (*business, trade*); *Musik (Sport) ~* go in for music (sports); *Sprachen ~* study languages; *es zu weit ~* go too far; *wenn er es weiterhin so treibt* if he carries *or* goes on like that; *was treibst du da?* what are you doing there?; **2.** *v/i.* (sein) drive; float, drift; **3.** *v/i.* (h) ♀ shoot; *dough:* ferment, work.

Treiben² [~] *n* (-s/no pl.) driving; doings *pl.*, goings-on *pl.*; *geschäftiges ~* bustle; '**2d** *adj.*: *~e Kraft* driving force.

Treib|haus ['traip-] *n* hothouse; '**~holz** *n* drift-wood; '**~jagd** *f* battue; '**~riemen** *m* driving-belt; '**~stoff** *m* fuel; propell|ant, -ent (*of rocket*).

trenn|en ['trɛnən] *v/t.* (ge-, h) separate, sever; rip (*seam*); *teleph.*, ⚡ cut off, disconnect; isolate, segregate; *sich ~* separate (*von* from), part (*from or* with *s.o.*; with *s.th.*); '**2schärfe** *f* radio: selectivity; '**2ung** *f* (-/-en) separation; disconne|xion, -ction; segregation (*of races, etc.*); '**2(ungs)wand** *f* partition (wall). [(-bit).]

Trense ['trɛnzə] *f* (-/-n) snaffle)

Treppe ['trɛpə] *f* (-/-n) staircase, stairway, (e-e a flight *or* pair of) stairs *pl.*; *zwei ~n hoch* on the second floor, *Am.* on the third floor.

'**Treppen|absatz** *m* landing; '**~geländer** *n* banisters *pl.*; '**~haus** *n* staircase; '**~stufe** *f* stair, step.

Tresor [tre'zoːr] *m* (-s/-e) safe; *bank:* strong-room, vault.

treten ['treːtən] (*irr.*) **1.** *v/i.* (h) tread, step (*j-n or j-m auf die Zehen* on s.o.'s toes); **2.** *v/i.* (sein) tread, step (*j-m auf die Zehen* on s.o.'s toes); walk; *ins Haus ~* enter the house; *j-m unter die Augen ~* appear before s.o., face s.o.; *j-m zu nahe ~* offend s.o.; *zu j-m ~* step *or* walk up to s.o.; *über die Ufer ~* overflow its banks; **3.** *v/t.* (h) tread; kick; *mit Füßen ~* trample upon.

treu *adj.* [trɔy] faithful, loyal; '**2bruch** *m* breach of faith, perfidy; '**2e** *f* (-/no pl.) fidelity, faith(ful-ness), loyalty; **2händer** ['~hɛndər] *m* (-s/-) trustee; '**~herzig** *adj.* guileless; ingenuous, simple-minded; '**~los** *adj.* faithless (*gegen* to), disloyal (to); perfidious.

Tribüne [tri'by:nə] *f* (-/-n) platform; *sports, etc.*: (grand) stand.
Tribut [tri'bu:t] *m* (-[e]s/-e) tribute.
Trichter ['trɪçtər] *m* (-s/-) funnel; *made by bomb, shell, etc.*: crater; horn (*of wind instruments, etc.*).
Trick [trɪk] *m* (-s/-e, -s) trick; '~film *m* animation, animated cartoon.
Trieb [tri:p] 1. *m* (-[e]s/-e) ⚘ sprout, (new) shoot; driving force; impulse; instinct; (sexual) urge; desire; 2. ♀ *pret. of* treiben; '~feder *f* main-spring; *fig.* driving force, motive; '~kraft *f* motive power; *fig.* driving force, motive; '~wagen 🚃 *m* rail-car, rail-motor; '~werk ⊕ *n* gear (drive), (driving) mechanism, transmission; engine.
triefen ['tri:fən] *v/i.* (*[irr.,] ge-, h*) drip (*von* with); *eye*: run.
triftig *adj.* ['trɪftɪç] valid.
Trigonometrie ꜝ [trigonome'tri:] *f* (-/no *pl.*) trigonometry.
Trikot [tri'ko:] (-s/-s) 1. *m* stockinet; 2. *n* tights *pl.*; vest; ~**agen** [~o'ta:-ʒən] *f/pl.* hosiery.
Triller ♪ ['trɪlər] *m* (-s/-) trill, shake, quaver; '~**n** ♪ *v/i. and v/t.* (ge-, h) trill, shake, quaver; *bird*: a. warble.
trink|**bar** *adj.* ['trɪŋkbaːr] drinkable; '~**becher** *m* drinking-cup; '~**en** (*irr.*, ge-, h) 1. *v/t.* drink; take, have (*tea, etc.*); 2. *v/i.* drink; ~ *auf* (*acc.*) drink to, toast; '~**er** *m* (-s/-) drinker; drunkard; '~**gelage** *n* drinking-bout; '~**geld** *n* tip, gratuity; *j-m e-e Mark* ~ geben tip s.o. one mark; '~**glas** *n* drinking-glass; '~**halle** *f at spa*: pump-room; '~**kur** *f*: *e-e* ~ *machen* drink the waters; '~**spruch** *m* toast; '~**wasser** *n* (-s/no *pl.*) drinking-water.
Trio ['tri:o] *n* (-s/-s) trio (*a.* ♪).
trippeln ['trɪpəln] *v/i.* (ge-, sein) trip.
Tritt [trɪt] *m* (-[e]s/-e) tread, step; footprint; *noise*: footfall, (foot)step; kick; ⊕ treadle; *s.* Trittbrett, Trittleiter; *im (falschen)* ~ in (out of) step; ~ *halten* keep step; '~**brett** *n* step, footboard; *mot.* running-board; '~**leiter** *f* stepladder, (*e-e* a pair *or* set of) steps *pl.*
Triumph [tri'umf] *m* (-[e]s/-e) triumph; ♀**al** *adj.* [~'fa:l] triumphant; ♀**bogen** *m* triumphal arch; ♀**ieren** [~'fi:rən] *v/i.* (no -ge-, h) triumph (*über acc.* over).
trocken *adj.* ['trɔkən] dry (*a. fig.*); *soil, land*: arid; '♀**dock** ⚓ *n* dry dock; '♀**haube** *f* (hood of) hair-drier; '♀**heit** *f* (-/no *pl.*) dryness; drought, aridity; '~**legen** *v/t.* (*sep.*, -ge-, h) dry up; drain (*land*); change the napkins of (*baby*), *Am.* change the diapers of (*baby*); '♀**obst** *n* dried fruit.

trocknen ['trɔknən] (ge-) 1. *v/i.* (sein) dry; 2. *v/t.* (h) dry.
Troddel ['trɔdəl] *f* (-/-n) tassel.
Trödel F ['trø:dəl] *m* (-s/no *pl.*) second-hand articles *pl.*; lumber, *Am.* junk; rubbish; '♀**n** F *fig. v/i.* (ge-, h) dawdle, loiter.
Trödler ['trø:dlər] *m* (-s/-) second-hand dealer, *Am.* junk dealer, junkman; *fig.* dawdler, loiterer.
troff [trɔf] *pret. of* triefen.
Trog[1] [tro:k] *m* (-[e]s/-̈e) trough.
trog[2] [~] *pret. of* trügen.
Trommel ['trɔməl] *f* (-/-n) drum; ⊕ *a.* cylinder, barrel; '~**fell** *n* drumskin; *anat.* ear-drum; '♀**n** *v/i. and v/t.* (ge-, h) drum.
Trommler ['trɔmlər] *m* (-s/-) drummer.
Trompete [trɔm'pe:tə] *f* (-/-n) trumpet; ♀**n** *v/i. and v/t.* (no -ge-, h) trumpet; ~**r** *m* (-s/-) trumpeter.
Tropen ['tro:pən]: *die* ~ *pl.* the tropics *pl.*
Tropf F [trɔpf] *m* (-[e]s/-̈e) simpleton; *armer* ~ poor wretch.
tröpfeln ['trœpfəln] (ge-) 1. *v/i.* drop, drip, trickle; *tap*: a. leak; *es tröpfelt rain*: a few drops are falling; 2. *v/i.* (sein): ~ *aus or von* trickle or drip from; 3. *v/t.* (h) drop, drip.
tropfen[1] ['trɔpfən] (ge-) 1. *v/i.* drop, drip, trickle; *tap*: a. leak; *candle*: gutter; 2. *v/i.* (sein): ~ *aus or von* trickle or drip from; 3. *v/t.* (h) drop, drip.
Tropfen[2] [~] *m* (-s/-) drop; *ein* ~ *auf den heißen Stein* a drop in the ocean *or* bucket; ♀**förmig** *adj.* ['~fœrmɪç] drop-shaped; ♀**weise** *adv.* drop by drop, by drops.
Trophäe [tro'fɛ:ə] *f* (-/-n) trophy.
tropisch *adj.* ['tro:pɪʃ] tropical.
Trosse ['trɔsə] *f* (-/-n) cable; ⚓ *a.* hawser.
Trost [tro:st] *m* (-es/no *pl.*) comfort, consolation; *das ist ein schlechter* ~ that is cold comfort; *du bist wohl nicht (recht) bei* ~! F you must be out of your mind!
tröst|**en** ['trø:stən] *v/t.* (ge-, h) console, comfort; *sich* ~ console o.s. (*mit* with); ~ *Sie sich!* be of good comfort!, cheer up!; '~**lich** *adj.* comforting.
'**trost**|**los** *adj.* disconsolate, inconsolable; *land, etc.*: desolate; *fig.* wretched; '♀**losigkeit** *f* (-/no *pl.*) desolation; *fig.* wretchedness; '♀**preis** *m* consolation prize, booby prize; '~**reich** *adj.* consolatory, comforting.
Trott [trɔt] *m* (-[e]s/-e) trot; F *fig.* jogtrot, routine; '~**el** F *m* (-s/-) idiot, fool, ninny; '♀**en** *v/i.* (ge-, sein) trot.
trotz [trɔts] 1. *prp.* (*gen.*) in spite of, despite; ~ *alledem* for all that; 2. ♀ *m* (-es/no *pl.*) defiance; obsti-

nacy; ~dem *cj.* ['~de:m] nevertheless; (al)though; '~en *v/i.* (ge-, h) (*dat.*) defy, dare; brave (*danger*); be obstinate; sulk; '~ig *adj.* defiant; obstinate; sulky.

trüb *adj.* [try:p], ~e *adj.* ['~bə] *liquid:* muddy, turbid, thick; *mind, thinking:* confused, muddy, turbid; *eyes, etc.:* dim, dull; *weather:* dull, cloudy, dreary (*all a. fig.*); *experiences:* sad.

Trubel ['tru:bəl] *m* (-s/no *pl.*) bustle.

trüben ['try:bən] *v/t.* (ge-, h) make thick *or* turbid *or* muddy; dim; darken; spoil (*pleasures, etc.*); blur (*view*); dull (*mind*); *sich* ~ *liquid:* become thick *or* turbid *or* muddy; dim, darken; *relations:* become strained.

Trüb|sal ['try:pza:l] *f* (-/~e): ~ blasen mope, F be in the dumps, have the blues; '2selig *adj.* sad, gloomy, melancholy; wretched, miserable; dreary; '~sinn *m* (-[e]s/ no *pl.*) melancholy, sadness, gloom; '2sinnig *adj.* melancholy, gloomy, sad; '~ung *f* (-/-en) *liquid:* muddiness, turbidity (*both a. fig.*); dimming, darkening.

Trüffel ♣ ['tryfəl] *f* (-/-n), F *m* (-s/-) truffle.

Trug[1] [tru:k] *m* (-[e]s/no *pl.*) deceit, fraud; delusion (*of senses*).

trug[2] [~] *pret. of* tragen.

'Trugbild *n* phantom; illusion.

trüg|en ['try:ɡən] (*irr.*, ge-, h) 1. *v/t.* deceive; 2. *v/i.* be deceptive; '~erisch *adj.* deceptive, delusive; treacherous.

'Trugschluß *m* fallacy, false conclusion.

Truhe ['tru:ə] *f* (-/-n) chest, trunk; *radio, etc.:* cabinet; console.

Trümmer ['trymər] *pl.* ruins *pl.*; rubble, debris; ♣, ⚓ wreckage; '~haufen *m* heap of ruins *or* rubble.

Trumpf [trumpf] *m* (-[e]s/~e) *cards:* trump (card) (*a. fig.*); s-n ~ ausspielen play one's trump card.

Trunk [truŋk] *m* (-[e]s/~e) drink; draught; drinking; '2en *adj.* drunken; *pred.* drunk (*a. fig. von, vor* with); intoxicated; ~enbold *contp.* ['~bolt] *m* (-[e]s/-e) drunkard, sot; '~enheit *f* (-/no *pl.*) drunkenness, intoxication; ~ am Steuer ⚖ drunken driving, drunkenness at the wheel; '~sucht *f* alcoholism, dipsomania; '2süchtig *adj.* addicted to drink, given to drinking.

Trupp [trup] *m* (-s/-s) troop, band, gang; ⚔ detachment.

'Truppe *f* (-/-n) ⚔ troop, body; ⚔ unit; *thea.* company, troupe; ~n *pl.* ⚔ troops *pl.*, forces *pl.*; die ~n *pl.* ⚔ the (fighting) services *pl.*, the armed forces *pl.*

'Truppen|gattung *f* arm, branch, division; '~schau *f* military review;

'~transporter ♣, ⚔ *m* (troop-) transport; '~übungsplatz *m* training area.

Truthahn *orn.* ['tru:t-] *m* turkey (-cock).

Tschech|e ['tʃɛçə] *m* (-n/-n), '~in *f* (-/-nen) Czech; '2isch *adj.* Czech.

Tube ['tu:bə] *f* (-/-n) tube.

tuberkul|ös ♣ *adj.* [tuberku'lø:s] tuberculous, tubercular; '2ose ♣ [~o:zə] *f* (-/-n) tuberculosis.

Tuch [tu:x] *n* 1. (-[e]s/-e) cloth; fabric; 2. (-[e]s/~er) head covering: kerchief; shawl, scarf; *round neck:* neckerchief; duster; rag; '~fühlung *f* (-/no *pl.*) close touch.

tüchtig ['tyçtiç] 1. *adj.* able, fit; clever; proficient; efficient; excellent; good; thorough; 2. *adv.* vigorously; thoroughly; F awfully; '2keit *f* (-/no *pl.*) ability, fitness; cleverness; proficiency; efficiency; excellency.

'Tuchwaren *f/pl.* drapery, cloths *pl.*

Tück|e ['tykə] *f* (-/-n) malice, spite; '2isch *adj.* malicious, spiteful; treacherous.

tüfteln ['tyftəln] *v/i.* (ge-, h) puzzle (*an dat.* over).

Tugend ['tu:ɡənt] *f* (-/-en) virtue; ~bold ['~bolt] *m* (-[e]s/-e) paragon of virtue; '2haft *adj.* virtuous.

Tüll [tyl] *m* (-s/-e) tulle.

Tulpe ♣ ['tulpə] *f* (-/-n) tulip.

tummel|n ['tuməln] *v/refl.* (ge-, h) *children:* romp; hurry; bestir o.s.; '2platz *m* playground; *fig.* arena.

Tümmler ['tymlər] *m* (-s/-) *orn.* tumbler; *zo.* porpoise.

Tumor ♣ ['tu:mɔr] *m* (-s/-en) tumo(u)r.

Tümpel ['tympəl] *m* (-s/-) pool.

Tumult [tu'mult] *m* (-[e]s/-e) tumult; riot, turmoil, uproar; row.

tun [tu:n] 1. *v/t.* (*irr.*, ge-, h) do; make; put (*to school, into the bag, etc.*); dazu ~ add to it; contribute; ich kann nichts dazu ~ I cannot help it; es ist mir darum zu ~ I am anxious about (it); zu ~ haben have to do; be busy; es tut nichts it doesn't matter; 2. *v/i.* (*irr.*, ge-, h) do; make; so ~ als ob make as if; pretend to *inf.*; das tut gut! that is a comfort!; that's good!; 3. ♀ *n* (-s/no *pl.*) doings *pl.*; proceedings *pl.*; action; ~ und Treiben ways and doings *pl.*

Tünche ['tynçə] *f* (-/-n) whitewash (*a. fig.*); '2n *v/t.* (ge-, h) whitewash.

Tunichtgut ['tu:niçtɡu:t] *m* (-, -[e]s/-e) ne'er-do-well, good-for-nothing.

Tunke ['tuŋkə] *f* (-/-n) sauce; '2n *v/t.* (ge-, h) dip, steep.

tunlichst *adv.* ['tu:nliçst] if possible.

Tunnel ['tunəl] *m* (-s/-, -s) tunnel; subway.

Tüpfel ['typfəl] *m, n* (-s/-) dot, spot; '**Qn** *v/t.* (ge-, *h*) dot, spot.

tupfen ['tupfən] **1.** *v/t.* (ge-, *h*) dab; dot, spot; **2.** **Q** *m* (-s/-) dot, spot.

Tür [ty:r] *f* (-/-en) door; *mit der ~ ins Haus fallen* blurt (things) out; *j-n vor die ~ setzen* turn s.o. out; *vor der ~ stehen* be near *or* close at hand; *zwischen ~ und Angel* in passing; '**~angel** *f* (door-)hinge.

Turbine ⊕ [tur'bi:nə] *f* (-/-n) turbine; **~nflugzeug** *n* turbo-jet.

Turbo-Prop-Flugzeug ['turbo-'prɔp-] *n* turbo-prop.

'**Tür|flügel** *m* leaf (of a door); '**~füllung** *f* (door-)panel; '**~griff** *m* door-handle.

Türk|e ['tyrkə] *m* (-n/-n) Turk; '**~in** *f* (-/-nen) Turk(ish woman); **~is** *min.* [~'ki:s] *m* (-es/-e) turquoise; '**Qisch** *adj.* Turkish.

'**Türklinke** *f* door-handle; latch.

Turm [turm] *m* (-[e]s/⁀e) tower; *a.* steeple (*of church*); *chess:* castle, rook.

Türm|chen ['tyrmçən] *n* (-s/-) turret; '**Qen** (ge-) **1.** *v/t.* (*h*) pile up; *sich ~* tower; **2.** F *v/i.* (sein) bolt, F skedaddle, *Am. sl. a.* skiddoo.

'**turm|hoch** *adv.: j-m ~ überlegen sein* stand head and shoulders above s.o.; '**Qspitze** *f* spire; '**Q-springen** *n* (-s/no *pl.*) swimming: high diving; '**Quhr** *f* tower-clock, church-clock.

turnen ['turnən] **1.** *v/i.* (ge-, *h*) do gymnastics; **2.** **Q** *n* (-s/no *pl.*) gymnastics *pl.*

'**Turn|er** *m* (-s/-), '**~erin** *f* (-/-nen) gymnast; '**~gerät** *n* gymnastic apparatus; '**~halle** *f* gym(nasium); '**~hemd** *n* (gym-)shirt; '**~hose** *f* shorts *pl.*

Turnier [tur'ni:r] *n* (-s/-e) tournament.

'**Turn|lehrer** *m* gym master; '**~lehrerin** *f* gym mistress; '**~schuh** *m* gym-shoe; '**~stunde** *f* gym lesson; '**~unterricht** *m* instruction in gymnastics; '**~verein** *m* gymnastic *or* athletic club.

'**Tür|pfosten** *m* door-post; '**~rahmen** *m* door-case, door-frame; '**~schild** *n* door-plate.

Tusche ['tuʃə] *f* (-/-n) India(n) *or* Chinese ink; '**Qn** *v/i.* (ge-, *h*) whisper; '**Qn** *v/t.* (ge-, *h*) draw in India(n) ink.

Tüte ['ty:tə] *f* (-/-n) paper-bag.

tuten ['tu:tən] *v/i.* (ge-, *h*) toot(le); *mot.* honk, blow one's horn.

Typ [ty:p] *m* (-s/-en) type; ⊕ *a.* model; '**~e** *f* (-/-n) *typ.* type; F *fig.* (queer) character.

Typhus ✠ ['ty:fus] *m* (-/no *pl.*) typhoid (fever).

'**typisch** *adj.* typical (*für* of).

Tyrann [ty'ran] *m* (-en/-en) tyrant; **~ei** [~'naɪ] *f* (-/no *pl.*) tyranny; **Qisch** *adj.* [ty'raniʃ] tyrannical; **Qisieren** [~i'zi:rən] *v/t.* (no -ge-, *h*) tyrannize (over) s.o., oppress, bully.

U

U-Bahn ['u:-] *f s. Untergrundbahn.*

übel ['y:bəl] **1.** *adj.* evil, bad; *nicht ~* not bad, pretty good; *mir ist ~* I am *or* feel sick; **2.** *adv.* ill; *~ gelaunt sein* be in a bad mood; *es gefällt mir nicht ~* I rather like it; **3.** **Q** *n* (-s/-) evil; *s. Übelstand; das kleinere ~ wählen* choose the lesser evil; '**~gelaunt** *adj.* ill-humo(u)red; '**Qkeit** *f* (-/-en) sickness, nausea; '**~nehmen** *v/t.* (*irr. nehmen, sep.*, -ge-, *h*) take *s.th.* ill *or* amiss; '**Q-stand** *m* grievance; '**Qtäter** *m* evil-doer, wrongdoer.

'**übelwollen 1.** *v/i.* (sep., -ge-, *h*): *j-m ~* wish s.o. ill; *be ill-disposed towards s.o.*; **2.** **Q** *n* (-s/no *pl.*) ill will, malevolence; '**~d** *adj.* malevolent.

üben ['y:bən] (ge-, *h*) **1.** *v/t.* exercise; practi|se, *Am. a.* -ce; *Geduld ~* exercise patience; *Klavier ~* practise the piano; **2.** *v/i.* exercise; practi|se, *Am. a.* -ce.

über ['y:bər] **1.** *prp.* (*dat.; acc.*) over, above; across (*river, etc.*); via,

by way of (*Munich, etc.*); *sprechen ~* (*acc.*) talk about *or* of; *~ Politik sprechen* talk politics; *nachdenken ~* (*acc.*) think about *or* of; *ein Buch schreiben ~* (*acc.*) write a book on; *~ Nacht bleiben bei* stay overnight at; *~ s-e Verhältnisse leben* live beyond one's income; *~ kurz oder lang* sooner *or* later; **2.** *adv.: die ganze Zeit ~* all along; *j-m in et. ~ sein* excel s.o. in s.th.

über'all *adv.* everywhere, anywhere, *Am. a.* all over.

über|'anstrengen *v/t.* (no -ge-, *h*) overstrain; *sich ~* overstrain o.s.; **~'arbeiten** *v/t.* (no -ge-, *h*) retouch (*painting, etc.*); revise (*book, etc.*); *sich ~* overwork o.s.

überaus *adv.* ['y:bər⁹-] exceedingly, extremely.

'**überbelichten** *phot. v/t.* (no -ge-, *h*) over-expose.

über'bieten *v/t.* (*irr. bieten, no* -ge-, *h*) *at auction:* outbid; *fig.:* beat; surpass.

Überbleibsel ['y:bərblaɪpsəl] *n*

(-s/-) remnant, *Am.* F *a.* holdover; ~ *pl. a.* remains *pl.*
'Überblick *fig. m* survey, general view (*both*: über acc. of).
über|'blicken *v/t.* (*no -ge-, h*) overlook; *fig.* survey, have a general view of; ~'bringen *v/t.* (*irr. bringen, no -ge-, h*) deliver; 2'bringer *m* (-s/-) bearer; ~'brücken *v/t.* (*no -ge-, h*) bridge; *fig.* bridge over *s.th.*; ~'dachen *v/t.* (*no -ge-, h*) roof over; ~'dauern *v/t.* (*no -ge-, h*) outlast, outlive; ~'denken *v/t.* (*irr. denken, no -ge-, h*) think *s.th.* over.
über'dies *adv.* besides, moreover.
über'drehen *v/t.* (*no -ge-, h*) overwind (*watch, etc.*); strip (*screw*).
'Überdruck *m* 1. (-[e]s/-e) overprint; ✞ *a.* surcharge; 2. ⊕ (-[e]s/~e) overpressure.
Über|'druß ['y:bərdrus] *m* (Überdrusses/*no pl.*) satiety; *bis zum ~ to* satiety; 2'drüssig *adj.* (*gen.*) ['~y-siç] disgusted with, weary *or* sick of.
Überreif|er ['y:bər²-] *m* over-zeal; 2rig *adj.* ['~ər²-] over-zealous.
über'eil|en *v/t.* (*no -ge-, h*) precipitate, rush; *sich ~* hurry too much; ~t *adj.* precipitate, rash.
übereinander *adv.* [y:bər²aɪ'nandər] one upon the other; ~schlagen *v/t.* (*irr. schlagen, sep., -ge-, h*) cross (*one's legs*).
über'ein|kommen *v/i.* (*irr. kommen, sep., -ge-, sein*) agree; 2kommen *n* (-s/-), 2kunft [~kunft] *f* (-/~e) agreement; ~stimmen *v/i.* (*sep., -ge-, h*) p. agree (*mit* with); *thing:* correspond (with; to); 2stimmung *f* agreement; correspondence; *in ~ mit* in agreement *or* accordance with.
über'fahr|en 1. ['~faːrən] *v/i.* (*irr. fahren, sep., -ge-, sein*) cross; 2. [~'faːrən] *v/t.* (*irr. fahren, no -ge-, h*) run over; disregard (*traffic sign, etc.*); 2fahrt *f* passage; crossing.
'Überfall *m* ✕ surprise; ✕ invasion (*auf acc.* of); ✕ raid; hold-up; assault (*[up]on*).
über'fallen *v/t.* (*irr. fallen, no -ge-, h*) ✕ surprise; ✕ invade; ✕ raid; hold up; assault.
'über|fällig *adj.* overdue; 2fallkommando *n* flying squad, *Am.* riot squad.
über'fliegen *v/t.* (*irr. fliegen, no -ge-, h*) fly over *or* across; *fig.* glance over, skim (through); *den Atlantik ~* fly (across) the Atlantic.
'überfließen *v/i.* (*irr. fließen, sep., -ge-, sein*) overflow.
über'flügeln *v/t.* (*no -ge-, h*) ✕ outflank; *fig.* outstrip, surpass.
'Über|fluß *m* (Überflusses/*no pl.*) abundance (*an dat.* of); superfluity (of); *~ haben an* (*dat.*) abound in;

'2flüssig *adj.* superfluous; redundant.
über'fluten *v/t.* (*no -ge-, h*) overflow, flood (*a. fig.*).
'Überfracht *f* excess freight.
über|führen *v/t.* 1. ['~fyːrən] (*sep., -ge-, h*) convey (*dead body*); 2. [~'fyːrən] (*no -ge-, h*) *s.* 1; ⓣⓣ convict (*gen.* of); 2führung *f* (-/-en) conveyance (*of dead body*); bridge, *Am.* overpass; ⓣⓣ conviction (*gen.* of) [*dat.* of).]
'Überfülle *f* superabundance (*an*)
über|'füllen *v/t.* (*no -ge-, h*) overfill; cram; overcrowd; *sich den Magen ~* glut o.s.; ~'füttern *v/t.* (*no -ge-, h*) overfeed.
'Übergabe *f* delivery; handing over; surrender (*a.* ✕).
'Übergang *m* bridge; 🚋 crossing; *fig.* transition (*a.* ♪); *esp.* ⓣⓣ devolution; ~sstadium *n* transition stage.
über|'geben *v/t.* (*irr. geben, no -ge-, h*) deliver up; hand over; surrender (*a.* ✕); *sich ~* vomit, be sick; ~'gehen 1. ['~geːən] *v/i.* (*irr. gehen, sep., -ge-, sein*) pass over; *work, duties:* devolve (*auf acc.* [up]on); *~ in* (*acc.*) pass into; *~ zu et.* proceed to *s.th.*; 2. [~'geːən] *v/t.* (*irr. gehen, no -ge-, h*) pass over, ignore.
'Übergewicht *n* (-[e]s/*no pl.*) overweight; *fig. a.* preponderance (*über acc.* over).
über'gießen *v/t.* (*irr. gießen, no -ge-, h*): *mit Wasser ~* pour water over *s.th.*; *mit Fett ~* baste (*roasting meat*).
'über|greifen *v/i.* (*irr. greifen, sep., -ge-, h*): *~ auf* (*acc.*) encroach (up)on (*s.o.'s rights*); *fire, epidemic, etc.*: spread to; 2griff *m* encroachment (*auf acc.* [up]on), inroad (on); '~haben F *v/t.* (*irr. haben, sep., -ge-, h*) have (*coat, etc.*) on; *fig.* have enough of, *sl.* be fed up with.
über'handnehmen *v/i.* (*irr. nehmen, sep., -ge-, h*) be rampant, grow *or* wax rife.
'überhängen 1. *v/i.* (*irr. hängen, sep., -ge-, h*) overhang; 2. *v/t.* (*sep., -ge-, h*) put (*coat, etc.*) round one's shoulders; sling (*rifle*) over one's shoulder.
über'häufen *v/t.* (*no -ge-, h*): *~ mit* swamp with (*letters, work, etc.*); overwhelm with (*inquiries, etc.*).
über'haupt *adv.*: *wer will denn ~, daß er kommt?* who wants him to come anyhow?; *wenn ~* if at all; *~ nicht* not at all; *~ kein* no ... whatever.
überheblich *adj.* [y:bər'heːplɪç] presumptuous, arrogant; 2keit *f* (-/~-en) presumption, arrogance.
über|'hitzen *v/t.* (*no -ge-, h*) overheat (*a.* ✞); ⊕ superheat; ~'holen *v/t.* (*no -ge-, h*) overtake (*a. mot.*);

esp. sports: outstrip (*a. fig.*); over-haul, *esp. Am. a.* service; ~'holt *adj.* outmoded; *pred. a.* out of date; ~'hören *v/t.* (*no -ge-, h*) fail to hear, miss; ignore.

'**überirdisch** *adj.* supernatural; un-earthly.

'**überkippen** *v/i.* (*sep., -ge-, sein*) *p.* overbalance, lose one's balance.

über'kleben *v/t.* (*no -ge-, h*) paste over.

'**Überkleidung** *f* outer garments *pl.*

'**überklug** *adj.* would-be wise, sapient.

'**überkochen** *v/i.* (*sep., -ge-, sein*) boil over; F *leicht* ~ be very irritable.

über'|kommen *v/t.* (*irr. kommen, no -ge-, h*): *Furcht überkam ihn* he was seized with fear; ~'laden *v/t.* (*irr. laden, no -ge-, h*) overload; overcharge (*battery, picture, etc.*).

'**Überland|flug** *m* cross-country flight; '~zentrale *≠ f* long-distance power-station.

über'|lassen *v/t.* (*irr. lassen, no -ge-, h*): *j-m et.* ~ let s.o. have s.th.; *fig.* leave s.th. to s.o.; *j-n sich selbst* ~ leave to himself; *j-n s-m Schicksal* ~ leave *or* abandon s.o. to his fate; ~'lasten *v/t.* (*no -ge-, h*) overload; *fig.* overburden.

über|laufen 1. ['~laufən] *v/i.* (*irr. laufen, sep., -ge-, sein*) run over; boil over; ✗ desert (*zu* to); **2.** [~'laufən] *v/t.* (*irr. laufen, no -ge-, h*): *es überlief mich kalt* a shudder passed over me; *überlaufen werden von doctor, etc.*: be besieged by (*patients, etc.*); **3.** *adj.* [~'laufən] place, profession, *etc.*: overcrowded; '2läufer *m* ✗ deserter; *pol.* renegade, turncoat.

'**überlaut** *adj.* too loud.

über'leben (*no -ge-, h*) **1.** *v/t.* survive, outlive; **2.** *v/i.* survive; 2de *m, f* (*-n/-n*) survivor.

'**überlebensgroß** *adj.* bigger than life-size(d).

überlebt *adj.* [y:bər'le:pt] outmod-ed, disused, out of date.

'**überlegen**[1] F *v/t.* (*sep., -ge-, h*) give (*child*) a spanking.

über'leg|en[2] **1.** *v/t. and v/refl.* (*no -ge-, h*) consider, reflect upon, think about; *ich will es mir* ~ I will think it over; *es sich anders* ~ change one's mind; **2.** *v/i.* (*no -ge-, h*): *er überlegt noch* he hasn't made up his mind yet; **3.** *adj.* superior (*dat.* to; *an dat.* in); 2enheit *f* (*-/no pl.*) superiority; preponderance; ~t *adj.* [~kt] deliberate; prudent; 2ung [~guŋ] *f* (*-/-en*) consideration, reflection; *nach reiflicher* ~ after mature deliberation.

über'lesen *v/t.* (*irr. lesen, no -ge-, h*) read *s.th.* through quickly, run over *s.th.*; overlook.

über'liefer|n *v/t.* (*no -ge-, h*) hand down *or* on (*dat.* to); 2ung *f* tradition.

über'listen *v/t.* (*no -ge-, h*) outwit, F outsmart.

'**Über|macht** *f* (*-/no pl.*) superiority; *esp.* ✗ superior forces *pl.*; *in der* ~ *sein* be superior in numbers; '2mächtig *adj.* superior.

über'|malen *v/t.* (*no -ge-, h*) paint out; ~'mannen *v/t.* (*no -ge-, h*) overpower, overcome, overwhelm (*all. a. fig.*).

'**Über|maß** *n* (*-es/no pl.*) excess (*an dat.* of); '2mäßig **1.** *adj.* excessive; immoderate; **2.** *adv.* excessively, *Am. a.* overly; ~ *trinken* drink to excess.

'**Übermensch** *m* superman; '2lich *adj.* superhuman.

über'mitt|eln *v/t.* (*no -ge-, h*) transmit; convey; 2lung *f* (*-/-en*) transmission; conveyance.

'**übermorgen** *adv.* the day after tomorrow.

über'müd|et *adj.* overtired; 2ung *f* (*-/✗-en*) overfatigue.

'**Über|mut** *m* wantonness; frolicsomeness; '2mütig *adj.* ['~my:tiç] wanton; frolicsome.

'**übernächst** *adj. the* next but one; ~*e* Woche the week after next.

über'nacht|en *v/i.* (*no -ge-, h*) stay overnight (*bei at a friend's* [*house*], with *friends*), spend the night (at, with); 2ung *f* (*-/-en*) spending the night; ~ *und Frühstück* bed and breakfast.

Übernahme ['y:bərna:mə] *f* (*-/-n*) field of application *s.* übernehmen **1**: taking over; undertaking; assumption; adoption.

'**übernatürlich** *adj.* supernatural.

übernehmen *v/t.* **1.** [~'ne:mən] *irr. nehmen, no -ge-, h*) take over (*business, etc.*); undertake (*responsibility, etc.*); take (*lead, risk, etc.*); assume (*direction of business, office, etc.*); adopt (*idea, custom, etc.*); *sich* ~ overreach o.s.; **2.** ✗ ['~ne:mən] (*irr. nehmen, sep., -ge-, h*) slope, shoulder (*arms*).

'**über|ordnen** *v/t.* (*sep., -ge-, h*): *j-n j-m* ~ set s.o. over s.o.; '~parteilich *adj.* non-partisan; '2produktion *f* over-production.

über'prüf|en *v/t.* (*no -ge-, h*) reconsider; verify; check; review; screen *s.o.*; 2ung *f* reconsideration; checking; review.

über'|queren *v/t.* (*no -ge-, h*) cross; ~'ragen *v/t.* (*no -ge-, h*) tower above (*a. fig.*), overtop; *fig.* surpass.

überrasch|en [y:bər'raʃən] *v/t.* (*no -ge-, h*) surprise; catch (*bei at, in*); 2ung *f* (*-/-en*) surprise.

über'red|en *v/t.* (*no -ge-, h*) persuade (*zu inf.* to *inf., into ger.*);

talk (into *ger.*); Ωung *f* (-/&-en) persuasion.

über'reich|en *v/t.* (*no* -ge-, *h*) present; Ωung *f* (-/&-en) presentation.

über|'reizen *v/t.* (*no* -ge-, *h*) overexcite; ~'reizt *adj.* overstrung; ~'rennen *v/t.* (*irr.* rennen, *no* -ge-, *h*) overrun.

'Überrest *m* remainder; ~e *pl.* remains *pl.*; sterbliche ~e *pl.* mortal remains *pl.*

über'rump|eln *v/t.* (*no* -ge-, *h*) (take by) surprise; Ω(e)lung *f* (-/&-en) surprise.

über'rund|en *v/t.* (*no* -ge-, *h*) *sports*: lap; *fig.* surpass; Ωung *f* (-/-en) lapping.

übersät *adj.* [y:bər'zɛ:t] studded, dotted.

über'sättig|en *v/t.* (*no* -ge-, *h*) surfeit (*a. fig.*); ⚗ supersaturate; Ωung *f* (-/-en) surfeit (*a. fig.*); ⚗ supersaturation.

'Überschallgeschwindigkeit *f* supersonic speed.

über|'schatten *v/t.* (*no* -ge-, *h*) overshadow (*a. fig.*); ~'schätzen *v/t.* (*no* -ge-, *h*) overrate, overestimate.

'Überschlag *m* *gymnastics*: somersault; ⚡ loop; ⚡ flashover; *fig.* estimate, approximate calculation; Ωen (*irr.* schlagen) 1. [-'ʃlaːɡən] *v/t.* (*sep.*, -ge-, *sein*) cross (*one's legs*); 2. ['-ʃlaːɡən] *v/i.* (*sep.*, -ge-, *sein*) *voice*: become high-pitched; 3. [~'ʃlaːɡən] *v/t.* (*no* -ge-, *h*) skip (*page*, *etc.*); make a rough estimate of (*cost*, *etc.*); sich ~ fall head over heels; *car*, *etc.*: (be) turn(ed) over; ⚡ loop the loop; *voice*: become high-pitched; sich ~ vor (*dat.*) outdo (*one's friendliness*, *etc.*); 4. *adj.* [~'ʃlaːɡən] lukewarm, tepid.

'überschnappen *v/i.* (*sep.*, -ge-, *sein*) *voice*: become high-pitched; F *p.* go mad, turn crazy.

über|'schneiden *v/refl.* (*irr.* schneiden, *no* -ge-, *h*) overlap; intersect; ~'schreiben *v/t.* (*irr.* schreiben, *no* -ge-, *h*) superscribe, entitle; make *s.th.* over (*dat.* to); ~'schreiten *v/t.* (*irr.* schreiten, *no* -ge-, *h*) cross; transgress (*limit*, *bound*); infringe (*rule*, *etc.*); exceed (*speed limit*, *one's instructions*, *etc.*); sie hat die 40 bereits überschritten she is on the wrong side of 40.

'Über|schrift *f* heading; title; headline; '~schuh *m* overshoe.

'Über|schuß *m* surplus, excess; profit; Ωschüssig *adj.* ['-ʃysiç] surplus, excess.

über'schütten *v/t.* (*no* -ge-, *h*): ~ mit pour (*water*, *etc.*) on; *fig.*: overwhelm with (*inquiries*, *etc.*); shower (*gifts*, *etc.*) upon.

überschwemm|en [y:bər'ʃvɛmən]

v/t. (*no* -ge-, *h*) inundate, flood (*both a. fig.*); Ωung *f* (-/-en) inundation, flood(ing).

überschwenglich *adj.* ['y:bər-ʃvɛnliç] effusive, gushy.

'Übersee: nach ~ gehen go overseas; '~dampfer ⚓ *m* transoceanic steamer; '~handel *m* (-s/*no pl.*) oversea(s) trade.

über'sehen *v/t.* (*irr.* sehen, *no* -ge-, *h*) survey; overlook (*printer's error, etc.*); *fig.* ignore, disregard.

über'send|en *v/t.* ([*irr.* senden,] *no* -ge-, *h*) send, transmit; consign; Ωung *f* sending, transmission; ☩ consignment.

'übersetzen[1] (*sep.*, -ge-) 1. *v/i.* (*sein*) cross; 2. *v/t.* (*h*) ferry.

über'setz|en[2] *v/t.* (*no* -ge-, *h*) translate (*in acc.* into), render (into); ⊕ gear; Ωer *m* (-s/-) translator; Ωung *f* (-/-en) translation (*aus* from; *in acc.* into); rendering; ⊕ gear(ing), transmission.

'Übersicht *f* (-/-en) survey (*über acc.* of); summary; Ωlich *adj.* clear(ly arranged).

über|siedeln ['y:bərziːdəln] *v/i.* (*sep.*, -ge-, *sein*) and [~'ziːdəln] *v/i.* (*no* -ge-, *sein*) remove (*nach* to); Ωsiedelung [~'ziːdəluŋ] *f* (-/-en), Ωsiedlung [~'ziːdluŋ] *f* (-/-en) removal (*nach* to).

'übersinnlich *adj.* transcendental; *forces*: psychic.

über'spann|en *v/t.* (*no* -ge-, *h*) cover (*mit* with); den Bogen ~ go too far; ~t *adj.* extravagant; *p.* eccentric; *claims*, *etc.*: exaggerated; Ωtheit *f* (-/&-en) extravagance; eccentricity.

über'spitzt *adj.* oversubtle; exaggerated.

überspringen 1. ['-ʃpriŋən] *v/i.* (*irr.* springen, *sep.*, -ge-, *sein*) ⚡ spark: jump; *in a speech*, *etc.*: ~ von ... zu ... jump or skip from (*one subject*) to (*another*); 2. [~'ʃpriŋən] *v/t.* (*irr.* springen, *no* -ge-, *h*) jump, clear; skip (*page*, *etc.*); jump (*class*).

überstehen (*irr.* stehen) 1. ['-ʃteːən] *v/i.* (*sep.*, -ge-, *h*) jut (*out or forth*), project; 2. [~'ʃteːən] *v/t.* (*no* -ge-, *h*) survive (*misfortune*, *etc.*); weather (*crisis*); get over (*illness*).

über|'steigen *v/t.* (*irr.* steigen, *no* -ge-, *h*) climb over; *fig.* exceed; ~'stimmen *v/t.* (*no* -ge-, *h*) outvote, vote down.

'überstreifen *v/t.* (*sep.*, -ge-, *h*) slip *s.th.* over.

überströmen 1. ['-ʃtrøːmən] *v/i.* (*sep.*, -ge-, *sein*) overflow (*vor dat.* with); 2. [~'ʃtrøːmən] *v/t.* (*no* -ge-, *h*) flood, inundate.

'Überstunden *f/pl.* overtime; ~ machen work overtime.

über'stürz|en *v/t.* (*no* -ge-, *h*) rush, hurry (up *or* on); sich ~ act rashly; *events*: follow in rapid succession; ~t *adj.* precipitate, rash; 2ung *f* (-/~ -en) precipitancy.

über|'teuern *v/t.* (*no* -ge-, *h*) overcharge; ~'**tölpeln** *v/t.* (*no* -ge-, *h*) dupe, take in; ~'**tönen** *v/t.* (*no* -ge-, *h*) drown.

Übertrag † ['y:bərtra:k] *m* (-[e]s/ ~e) carrying forward; sum carried forward.

über'trag|bar *adj.* transferable; † negotiable; ℱ communicable; ~en [~gən] 1. *v/t.* (*irr.* tragen, *no* -ge-, *h*) † carry forward; make over (*property*) (*auf acc.* to); ℱ transfuse (*blood*); delegate (*rights, etc.*) (*dat.* to); render (*book, etc.*) (*in acc.* into); transcribe (*s.th. written in shorthand*); ℱ, ⊕, *phys., radio:* transmit; *radio:* a. broadcast; *im Fernsehen* ~ televise; *ihm wurde eine wichtige Mission* ~ he was charged with an important mission; 2. *adj.* figurative; 2ung [~guŋ] *f* (-/-en) *field of application s.* übertragen 1: carrying forward; making over; transfusion; delegation; rendering, free translation; transcription; transmission; broadcast; ~ *im Fernsehen* telecast.

über'treffen *v/t.* (*irr.* treffen, *no* -ge-, *h*) excel *s.o.* (*an dat.* in; *in dat.* in, at); surpass (*in*), exceed (*in*).

über'treib|en (*irr.* treiben, *no* -ge-, *h*) 1. *v/t.* overdo; exaggerate, overstate; 2. *v/i.* exaggerate, draw the long bow; 2ung *f* (-/-en) exaggeration, overstatement.

'**übertreten**[1] *v/i.* (*irr.* treten, *sep.,* -ge-, *sein*) *sports:* cross the take-off line; *fig.* go over (*zu* to); *zum Katholizismus* ~ turn Roman Catholic.

über'tret|en[2] *v/t.* (*irr.* treten, *no* -ge-, *h*) transgress, violate, infringe (*law, etc.*); *sich den Fuß* ~ sprain one's ankle; 2ung *f* (-/-en) transgression, violation, infringement.

'**Übertritt** *m* going over (*zu* to); *eccl.* conversion (to).

übervölker|n [y:bər'fœlkərn] *v/t.* (*no* -ge-, *h*) over-populate; 2ung *f* (-/~ -en) over-population.

über'vorteilen *v/t.* (*no* -ge-, *h*) overreach, F do.

über'wach|en *v/t.* (*no* -ge-, *h*) supervise, superintend; control; *police:* keep under surveillance, shadow; 2ung *f* (-/~ -en) supervision, superintendence; control; surveillance.

überwältigen [y:bər'vɛltigən] *v/t.* (*no* -ge-, *h*) overcome, overpower, overwhelm (*all a. fig.*); ~d *fig. adj.* overwhelming.

über'weis|en *v/t.* (*irr.* weisen, *no* -ge-, *h*) remit (*money*) (*dat. or an acc.* to); (*zur Entscheidung etc.*) ~ refer (to); 2ung *f* (-/-en) remittance;

reference (*an acc.* to); *parl.* devolution.

überwerfen (*irr.* werfen) 1. ['~vɛrfən] *v/t.* (*sep.,* -ge-, *h*) slip (*coat*) on; 2. [~'vɛrfən] *v/refl.* (*no* -ge-, *h*) fall out (*mit* with).

über|'wiegen (*irr.* wiegen, *no* -ge-, *h*) 1. *v/t.* outweigh; 2. *v/i.* preponderate; predominate; ~'**wiegend** *adj.* preponderant; predominant; ~ '**winden** *v/t.* (*irr.* winden, *no* -ge-, *h*) overcome (*a. fig.*), subdue; *sich* ~ *zu inf.* bring o.s. to *inf.*; ~'**wintern** *v/i.* (*no* -ge-, *h*) (pass the) winter.

'**Über|wurf** *m* wrap; '~**zahl** *f* (-/~ -en) numerical superiority; *in der* ~ superior in numbers; 2**zählig** *adj.* ['~tsɛ:liç] supernumerary; surplus.

über'zeug|en *v/t.* (*no* -ge-, *h*) convince (*von* of); satisfy (of); 2ung *f* (-/-en) conviction.

überziehe|n *v/t.* (*irr.* ziehen) 1. ['~tsi:ən] (*sep.,* -ge-, *h*) put on; 2. [~'tsi:ən] (*no* -ge-, *h*) cover; put clean sheets on (*bed*); † overdraw (*account*); *sich* ~ *sky:* become overcast; '2r *m* (-s/-) overcoat, topcoat.

'**Überzug** *m* cover; case, tick; ⊕ coat(ing). [ary; normal.}

üblich *adj.* ['y:pliç] usual, custom-}

U-Boot ⚓, ✕ [~] *n* submarine, *in Germany: a.* U-boat.

übrig *adj.* ['y:briç] left, remaining; *die* ~*e Welt* the rest of the world; *die* ~*en pl.* the others *pl.,* the rest; *im* ~*en* for the rest; by the way; ~ *haben* have *s.th.* left; *keine Zeit* ~ *haben* have no time to spare; *etwas* ~ *haben für* care for, have a soft spot for; *ein* ~*es tun* go out of one's way; '~**bleiben** *v/i.* (*irr.* bleiben, *sep.,* -ge-, *sein*) be left; remain; *es blieb ihm nichts anderes übrig* he had no (other) alternative (*als* but); ~**ens** *adv.* ['~gəns] by the way; ~**lassen** ['~] *v/t.* (*irr.* lassen, *sep.,* -ge-, *h*) leave; *viel zu wünschen* ~ leave much to be desired.

'**Übung** *f* (-/-en) exercise; practice; drill; '~**shang** *m skiing:* nursery slope.

Ufer ['u:fər] *n* (-s/-) shore (*of sea, lake*); bank (*of river, etc.*).

Uhr [u:r] *f* (-/-en) clock; watch; *um vier* ~ at four o'clock; '~**armband** *n* (-[e]s/~er) watch-strap; '~**feder** *f* watch-spring; '~**macher** *m* (-s/-) watch-maker; '~**werk** *n* clockwork; watch-work; '~**zeiger** *m* hand (*of clock or watch*); '~**zeigersinn** *m* (-[e]s/*no pl.*): *im* ~ clockwise; *entgegen dem* ~ counter-clockwise.

Uhu *orn.* ['u:hu:] *m* (-s/-s) eagle-owl.

Ulk [ulk] *m* (-[e]s/-e) fun, lark; 2**en** *v/i.* (ge-, *h*) (sky)lark, joke; 2**ig** *adj.* funny.

Ulme ♀ ['ulmə] *f* (-/-n) elm.

Ultimatum [ulti'ma:tum] *n* (-s/*Ul-*

timaten, *-s*) ultimatum; *j-m ein* ~ *stellen* deliver an ultimatum to s.o.

Ultimo † ['ultimo] *m* (-s/-s) last day of the month.

Ultrakurzwelle *phys.* [ultra'-] *f* ultra-short wave, very-high-frequency wave.

um [um] **1.** *prp.* (*acc.*) round, about; ~ *vier Uhr* at four o'clock; ~ *sein Leben laufen* run for one's life; *et.* ~ *einen Meter verfehlen* miss s.th. by a metre; *et.* ~ *zwei Mark verkaufen* sell s.th. at two marks; **2.** *prp.* (*gen.*): ~ *seinetwillen* for his sake; **3.** *cj.:* ~ *so besser* all the better, so much the better; ~ *so mehr* (*weniger*) all the more (less); ~ *zu* (in order) to; **4.** *adv.:* *er drehte sich* ~ he turned round.

um|ändern ['um?-] *v/t.* (*sep.*, *-ge-*, *h*) change, alter; **~arbeiten** ['um?-] *v/t.* (*sep.*, *-ge-*, *h*) make over (*coat*, *etc.*); revise (*book*, *etc.*); ~ *zu* make into.

um'arm|en *v/t.* (*no* -ge-, *h*) hug, embrace; *sich* ~ embrace; **2ung** *f* (-/-en) embrace, hug.

'Umbau *m* (-[e]s/-e, -ten) rebuilding; reconstruction; **2en** *v/t.* (*sep.*, *-ge-*, *h*) rebuild; reconstruct.

'umbiegen *v/t.* (*irr.* biegen, *sep.*, *-ge-*, *h*) bend; turn up *or* down.

'umbild|en *v/t.* (*sep.*, *-ge-*, *h*) remodel, reconstruct; reorganize, reform; reshuffle (*cabinet*); **2ung** *f* (-/-en) remodel(l)ing, reconstruction; reorganization, *pol.* reshuffle.

'um|binden *v/t.* (*irr.* binden, *sep.*, *-ge-*, *h*) put on (*apron*, *etc.*); **~blättern** (*sep.*, *-ge-*, *h*) **1.** *v/t.* turn over; **2.** *v/i.* turn over the page; **~brechen** *v/t.* (*irr.* brechen) **1.** ~ ['~brɛçən] (*sep.*, *-ge-*, *h*) dig, break up (*ground*); **2.** *typ.* [~'brɛçən] (*no* -ge-, *h*) make up; **~bringen** *v/t.* (*irr.* bringen, *sep.*, *-ge-*, *h*) kill; *sich* ~ kill o.s.; **'2bruch** *m* *typ.* make-up; *fig.:* upheaval; radical change; **~buchen** *v/t.* (*sep.*, *-ge-*, *h*) † transfer *or* switch to another account; book for another date; **~disponieren** *v/i.* (*sep.*, *no* -ge-, *h*) change one's plans.

'umdreh|en *v/t.* (*sep.*, *-ge-*, *h*) turn; *s.* Spieß; *sich* ~ turn round; **2ung** [um'-] *f* (-/-en) turn; *phys.*, ⊕ rotation, revolution.

um|fahren (*irr.* fahren) **1.** ['~fa:rən] *v/t.* (*sep.*, *-ge-*, *h*) run down; **2.** [~'fa:rən] *v/i.* (*sep.*, *-ge-*, *sein*) go a roundabout way; **3.** [~'fa:rən] *v/t.* (*no* -ge-, *h*) drive round; ⚓ sail round; ⚓ double (*cape*); **~fallen** *v/i.* (*irr.* fallen, *sep.*, *-ge-*, *sein*) fall; collapse; *tot* ~ drop dead.

'Umfang *m* (-[e]s/*no pl.*) circumference, circuit; perimeter; girth (*of body*, *tree*, *etc.*); *fig.:* extent; volume; *in großem* ~ on a large

scale; **'2reich** *adj.* extensive; voluminous; spacious.

um'fassen *v/t.* (*no* -ge-, *h*) clasp; embrace (*a. fig.*); ✗ envelop; *fig.* comprise, cover, comprehend; **~d** *adj.* comprehensive, extensive; sweeping, drastic.

'umform|en *v/t.* (*sep.*, *-ge-*, *h*) remodel, recast, transform (*a. ⚡*); ⚡ convert; **'2er** ⚡ *m* (-s/-) transformer; converter.

'Umfrage *f* poll; *öffentliche* ~ public opinion poll.

'Umgang *m* **1.** (-[e]s/ᵘe) △ gallery, ambulatory; *eccl.* procession (*round the fields*, *etc.*); **2.** (-[e]s/*no pl.*) intercourse (*mit* with); company; ~ *haben mit* associate with.

umgänglich *adj.* ['umgɛnliç] sociable, companionable, affable.

'Umgangs|formen *f/pl.* manners *pl.*; **~sprache** *f* colloquial usage; *in der deutschen* ~ in colloquial German.

um'garnen *v/t.* (*no* -ge-, *h*) ensnare.

um'geb|en **1.** *v/t.* (*irr.* geben, *no* -ge-, *h*) surround; *mit e-r Mauer* ~ wall in; **2.** *adj.* surrounded (*von* with, by) (*a. fig.*); **2ung** *f* (-/-en) environs *pl.* (*of town*, *etc.*); surroundings *pl.*, environment (*of place*, *person*, *etc.*).

umgeh|en (*irr.* gehen) **1.** ['~ge:ən] *v/i.* (*sep.*, *-ge-*, *sein*) make a detour; *rumour*, *etc.:* go about, be afloat; *ghost:* walk; ~ *mit use* s.th.; deal with *s.o.*; keep company with; *ein Gespenst soll im Schlosse* ~ the castle is said to be haunted; **2.** [~'ge:ən] *v/t.* (*no* -ge-, *h*) go round; ✗ flank; bypass (*town*, *etc.*); *fig.* avoid, evade; circumvent, elude (*law*, *etc.*); **~end** *adj.* immediate; **2ungsstraße** [um'ge:uŋs-] *f* bypass.

umgekehrt ['umgəke:rt] **1.** *adj.* reverse; inverse, inverted; *in ~er Reihenfolge* in reverse order; *im ~en Verhältnis zu* in inverse proportion to; **2.** *adv.* vice versa.

'umgraben *v/t.* (*irr.* graben, *sep.*, *-ge-*, *h*) dig (up).

um'grenzen *v/t.* (*no* -ge-, *h*) encircle; enclose; *fig.* circumscribe, limit.

'umgruppier|en *v/t.* (*sep.*, *no* -ge-, *h*) regroup; **2ung** *f* (-/-en) regrouping.

'um|haben F *v/t.* (*irr.* haben, *sep.*, *-ge-*, *h*) have (*coat*, *etc.*) on; **'2hang** *m* wrap; cape; **'~hängen** *v/t.* (*sep.*, *-ge-*, *h*) rehang (*pictures*); sling (*rifle*) over one's shoulder; *sich den Mantel* ~ put one's coat round one's shoulders; **'~hauen** *v/t.* (*irr.* hauen, *sep.*, *-ge-*, *h*) fell, cut down; F: *die Nachricht hat mich umgehauen* I was bowled over by the news.

um'her|blicken v/i. (sep., -ge-, h) look about (one); ~streifen v/i. (sep., -ge-, sein) rove.

um'hinkönnen v/i. (irr. können, sep., -ge-, h): ich kann nicht umhin, zu sagen I cannot help saying.

um'hüll|en v/t. (no -ge-, h) wrap up (mit in), envelop (in); 2ung f (-/-en) wrapping, wrapper, envelopment.

Umkehr ['umke:r] f (-/no pl.) return; 2en (sep., -ge-) 1. v/i. (sein) return, turn back; 2. v/t. (h) turn out (one's pocket, etc.); invert (a. ♩); reverse (a. ♂, ♫); '~ung f (-/-en) reversal; inversion.

'umkippen (sep., -ge-) 1. v/t. (h) upset, tilt; 2. v/i. (sein) upset, tilt (over); F faint.

um'klammer|n v/t. (no -ge-, h) clasp; boxing: clinch; 2ung f (-/-en) clasp; boxing: clinch.

'umkleid|en v/refl. (sep., -ge-, h) change (one's clothes); 2eraum m dressing-room.

'umkommen v/i. (irr. kommen, sep., -ge-, sein) be killed (bei in), die (in), perish (in); vor Langeweile ~ die of boredom.

'Umkreis m (-es/no pl.) ♫ circumscribed circle; im ~ von within a radius of. [round.]

um'kreisen v/t. (no -ge-, h) circle)

um'krempeln v/t. (sep., -ge-, h) tuck up (shirt-sleeves, etc.); change (plan, etc.); (völlig) ~ turn s.th. inside out; '~laden v/t. (irr. laden, sep., -ge-, h) reload; ♥, ♣ tranship.

'Umlauf m circulation; phys., ⊕ rotation; circular (letter); in ~ setzen or bringen circulate, put into circulation; im ~ sein circulate, be in circulation; rumours: a. be afloat; außer ~ setzen withdraw from circulation; '~bahn f orbit; 2en (irr. laufen) 1. ['~laufen] v/t. (sep., -ge-, h) knock over; 2. ['~laufen] v/i. (sep., -ge-, sein) circulate; make a detour; 3. [~'laufen] v/t. (no -ge-, h) run round.

'Umlege|kragen m turn-down collar; '2n v/t. (sep., -ge-, h) lay down; ⊕ throw (lever); storm, etc.: beat down (wheat, etc.); re-lay (cable, etc.); put (coat, etc.) round one's shoulders; apportion (costs, etc.); fig. sl. do s.o. in.

'umleit|en v/t. (sep., -ge-, h) divert; 2ung f diversion, detour.

'umliegend adj. surrounding; circumjacent.

um'nacht|et adj.: geistig ~ mentally deranged; 2ung f (-/↖-en); geistige ~ mental derangement.

'um|packen v/t. (sep., -ge-, h) repack; ~pflanzen v/t. 1. ['~pflantsən] (sep., -ge-, h) transplant; 2. [~'pflantsən] (no -ge-, h): ~ mit

plant s.th. round with; '~pflügen v/t. (sep., -ge-, h) plough, Am. plow.

um'rahmen v/t. (no -ge-, h) frame; musikalisch ~ put into a musical setting.

umrand|en [um'randən] v/t. (no -ge-, h) edge, border; 2ung f (-/-en) edge, border.

um'ranken v/t. (no -ge-, h) twine (mit with).

'umrechn|en v/t. (sep., -ge-, h) convert (in acc. into); 2ung f (-/no pl.) conversion; '2ungskurs m rate of exchange.

umreißen v/t. (irr. reißen) 1. ['~raisən] (sep., -ge-, h) pull down; knock s.o. over; 2. [~'raisən] (no -ge-, h) outline. [round (a. fig.).)

um'ringen v/t. (no -ge-, h) sur-)

'Um|riß m outline (a. fig.), contour; '2rühren v/t. (sep., -ge-, h) stir; '2satteln (sep., -ge-, h) 1. v/t. resaddle; 2. F fig. v/i. change one's studies or occupation; ~ von ... auf (acc.) change from ... to ...; '~satz ♠ m turnover; sales pl.; return(s pl.); stock exchange: business done.

'umschalt|en (sep., -ge-, h) 1. v/t. ⊕ change over; ≴ commutate; ⊕ switch; 2. ≴, ⊕ v/i. switch over; '2er m ⊕ change-over switch; ≴ commutator; 2ung f (-/-en) ⊕ change-over; ≴ commutation.

'Umschau f (-/no pl.): ~ halten nach look out for, be on the look-out for; '2en v/refl. (sep., -ge-, h) look round (nach for); look about (for) (a. fig.), look about one.

'umschicht|en v/t. (sep., -ge-, h) pile afresh; fig. regroup (a. ♥); '~ig adv. by or in turns; 2ung fig. f (-/-en) regrouping; soziale ~en pl. social upheavals pl.

um'schiff|en v/t. (no -ge-, h) circumnavigate; double (cape); 2ung f (-/↖-en) circumnavigation; doubling.

'Umschlag m envelope; cover, wrapper; jacket; turn-up, Am. a. cuff (of trousers); ♫ compress; ♫ poultice; trans-shipment (of goods); fig. change, turn; '2en (irr. schlagen, sep., -ge-) 1. v/t. (h) knock s.o. down; cut down, fell (tree); turn (leaf); turn up (sleeves, etc.); turn down (collar); trans-ship (goods); 2. v/i. (sein) turn over, upset; ♫ capsize, upset; wine, etc.: turn sour; fig. turn (in acc. into); '~hafen m port of trans-shipment.

um'schließen v/t. (irr. schließen, no -ge-, h) embrace, surround (a. ✕), enclose; ✕ invest; 'schlingen v/t. (irr. schlingen, no -ge-, h) embrace.

'umschmeißen F v/t. (irr. schmeißen, sep., -ge-, h) s. umstoßen; '~-

schnallen v/t. (sep., -ge-, h) buckle on.

umschreib|en v/t. (irr. schreiben) 1. ['~ʃraibən] (sep., -ge-, h) rewrite; transfer (property, etc.) (auf acc. to); 2. [~ʃraibən] (no -ge-, h) ⅋ circumscribe; paraphrase; 2ung f (-/-en) 1. ['~ʃraibuŋ] rewriting; transfer (auf acc. to); 2. [~ʃraibuŋ] ⅋ circumscription; paraphrase.

'Umschrift f circumscription; phonetics: transcription.

'umschütten v/t. (sep., -ge-, h) pour into another vessel; spill.

'Um|schweife pl.: ~ machen beat about the bush; ohne ~ point-blank; '2schwenken fig. v/i. (sep., -ge-, sein) veer or turn round; '~schwung fig. m revolution; reversion (of public feeling, etc.); change (in the weather, etc.); reversal (of opinion, etc.).

um'seg|eln v/t. (no -ge-, h) sail round; double (cape); circumnavigate (globe, world); 2(e)lung f (-/-en) sailing round (world, etc.); doubling; circumnavigation.

'um|sehen v/refl. (irr. sehen, sep., -ge-, h) look round (nach for); look about (for) (a. fig.), look about one; '~sein F v/i. (irr. sein, sep., -ge-, sein) time: be up; holidays, etc.: be over; '~setzen v/t. (sep., -ge-, h) transpose (a. ♪); ✓ transplant; ✝ turn over; spend (money) (in acc. on books, etc.); in die Tat ~ realize, convert into fact.

'Umsicht f (-/no pl.) circumspection; '2ig adj. circumspect.

'umsied|eln (sep., -ge-) 1. v/t. (h) resettle; 2. v/i. (sein) (re)move (nach, in acc. to); '2lung f(-/-en) resettlement; evacuation; removal.

um'sonst adv. gratis, free of charge; in vain; to no purpose; nicht ~ not without good reason.

umspann|en v/t. 1. ['~ʃpanən] (sep., -ge-, h) change (horses); ⚡ transform; 2. [~ʃpanən] (no -ge-, h) span; fig. a. embrace; '2er ⚡ m (-s/-) transformer.

'umspringen v/i. (irr. springen, sep., -ge-, sein) shift, veer (round); ~ mit treat badly, etc.

'Umstand m circumstance; fact, detail; unter diesen Umständen in or under the circumstances; unter keinen Umständen in or under no circumstances, on no account; unter Umständen possibly; ohne Umstände without ceremony; in anderen Umständen sein in the family way.

umständlich adj. ['umʃtentliç] story, etc.: long-winded; method, etc.: roundabout; p. fussy; das ist (mir) viel zu ~ that is far too much trouble (for me); '2keit f (-/~-en) long-windedness; fussiness.

'Umstands|kleid n maternity robe; '~wort gr. n (-[e]s/~er) adverb.

'umstehend 1. adj.: auf der ~en Seite overleaf; 2. adv. overleaf; 2en ['~dən] pl. the bystanders pl.

'Umsteige|karte f transfer; '2n v/i. (irr. steigen, sep., -ge-, sein) change (nach for); 🚋 a. change trains (for). Umsteigkarte ['umʃtaik-] f s. Umsteigekarte.

umstell|en v/t. 1. ['~ʃtelən] (sep., -ge-, h) transpose (a. gr.); shift (furniture) about or round; convert (currency, production) (auf acc. to); sich ~ change one's attitude; accommodate o.s. to new conditions; adapt o.s. (auf acc. to); 2. [~ʃtelən] (no -ge-, h) surround; 2ung ['~ʃtelung] f transposition; fig.: conversion; adaptation; change.

'um|stimmen v/t. (sep., -ge-, h) ♪ tune to another pitch; j-n ~ change s.o.'s mind, bring s.o. round; '~stoßen v/t. (irr. stoßen, sep., -ge-, h) knock over; upset; fig. annul; ⅌ overrule, reverse; upset (plan).

um|'stricken fig. v/t. (no -ge-, h) ensnare; ~stritten adj. [~ʃtritən] disputed, contested; controversial.

'Um|sturz m subversion, overturn; '2stürzen (sep., -ge-) 1. v/t. (h) upset, overturn (a. fig.); fig. subvert; 2. v/i. (sein) upset, overturn; fall down; 2stürzlerisch adj. ['~ləriʃ] subversive.

'Umtausch m (-es/~-e) exchange; ✝ conversion (of currency, etc.); '2en v/t. (sep., -ge-, h) exchange (gegen for); ✝ convert.

'umtun F v/t. (irr. tun, sep., -ge-, h) put (coat, etc.) round one's shoulders; sich ~ nach look about for.

'umwälz|en v/t. (sep., -ge-, h) roll round; fig. revolutionize; '~end adj. revolutionary; '2ung fig. f (-/-en) revolution, upheaval.

'umwand|eln v/t. (sep., -ge-, h) transform (in acc. into); ⚡, ✝ convert (into); ⅌ commute (into); '2lung f transformation; ⚡, ✝ conversion; ⅌ commutation.

'um|wechseln v/t. (sep., -ge-, h) change; '2weg m roundabout way or route; detour; auf ~en in a roundabout way; '~wehen v/t. (sep., -ge-, h) blow down or over; '2welt f (-/~-en) environment; '~wenden 1. v/t. (sep., -ge-, h) turn over; 2. v/refl. (irr. wenden] sep., -ge-, h) look round (nach for).

um'werben v/t. (irr. werben, no -ge-, h) court, woo.

'umwerfen v/t. (irr. werfen, sep., -ge-, h) upset (a. fig.), overturn; sich e-n Mantel ~ throw a coat round one's shoulders.

um|'wickeln v/t. (no -ge-, h): et. mit Draht ~ wind wire round s.th.;

~wölken [ˌ~'vœlkən] *v/refl.* (*no* -ge-, *h*) cloud over (*a. fig.*); **~zäu-nen** [ˌ~'tsɔʏnən] *v/t.* (*no* -ge-, *h*) fence (in).

umziehen (*irr. ziehen*) **1.** [ˈ~tsiːən] *v/i.* (*sep.*, -ge-, *sein*) (re)move (*nach* to); move house; **2.** [ˈ~tsiːən] *v/refl.* (*sep.*, -ge-, *h*) change (one's clothes); **3.** [ˌ~'tsiːən] *v/refl.* (*no* -ge-, *h*) cloud over.

umzingeln [um'tsiŋəln] *v/t.* (*no* -ge-, *h*) surround, encircle.

'Umzug *m* procession; move (*nach* to), removal (to); change of residence.

unab|änderlich *adj.* [unˀap'ˀɛndərliç] unalterable; **~hängig** [ˈ~hɛŋiç] **1.** *adj.* independent (*von* of); **2.** *adv.*: ~ *von* irrespective of; **'2hängigkeit** *f* (-/*no pl.*) independence (*von* of); **~kömmlich** *adj.* [ˈ~kœmliç]: *er ist im Moment* ~ we cannot spare him at the moment, we cannot do without him at the moment; **~'lässig** *adj.* incessant, unremitting; **~sehbar** *adj.* [ˌ~'zeːbaːr] incalculable; *in ~er Ferne* in a distant future; **'~sichtlich** *adj.* unintentional; inadvertent; **~wendbar** *adj.* [ˌ~'vɛntbaːr] inevitable, inescapable.

unachtsam *adj.* [ˈunˀ-] careless, heedless; **'2keit** *f* (-/~-en) carelessness, heedlessness.

unähnlich *adj.* [ˈunˀ-] unlike, dissimilar (*dat.* to).

unan|fechtbar *adj.* [unˀan'-] unimpeachable, unchallengeable, incontestable; **'~gebracht** *adj.* inappropriate; *pred. a.* out of place; **'~gefochten** **1.** *adj.* undisputed; unchallenged; **2.** *adv.* without any hindrance; **~gemessen** *adj.* unsuitable; improper; inadequate; **'~genehm** *adj.* disagreeable, unpleasant; awkward; troublesome; **~'nehmbar** *adj.* unacceptable (*für* to); **'2nehmlichkeit** *f* (-/-en) unpleasantness; awkwardness; troublesomeness; **~en** *pl.* trouble, inconvenience; **'~sehnlich** *adj.* unsightly; plain; **'~ständig** *adj.* indecent; obscene; **'2ständigkeit** *f* (-/-en) indecency; obscenity; **~'tastbar** *adj.* unimpeachable; inviolable.

unappetitlich *adj.* [ˈunˀ-] *food, etc.*: unappetizing; *sight, etc.*: distasteful, ugly.

Unart [ˈunˀ-] **1.** *f* bad habit; **2.** *m* (-[e]s/-e) naughty child; **'2ig** *adj.* naughty; **'~igkeit** *f* (-/-en) naughty behavio(u)r, naughtiness.

unauf|dringlich *adj.* [ˈunˀauf-] unobtrusive; unostentatious; **'~fällig** *adj.* inconspicuous; unobtrusive; **~findbar** *adj.* [ˌ~'fintbaːr] undiscoverable, untraceable; **~gefordert** [ˈ~gəfɔrdərt] **1.** *adj.* un-

asked; **2.** *adv.* without being asked, of one's own accord; **~'hörlich** *adj.* incessant, continuous, uninterrupted; **~merksam** *adj.* inattentive; **'2merksamkeit** *f* (-/-en) inattention, inattentiveness; **'~richtig** *adj.* insincere; **'2richtigkeit** *f* (-/-en) insincerity; **~schiebbar** *adj.* [ˌ~'ʃiːpbaːr] urgent; ~ *sein* brook no delay.

unaus|bleiblich *adj.* [unˀaus'blaɪpliç] inevitable; *das war* ~ that was bound to happen; **~'führbar** *adj.* impracticable; **~geglichen** *adj.* [ˈ~gəgliçən] unbalanced (*a.* †); **~'löschlich** *adj.* indelible; *fig. a.* inextinguishable; **~'sprechlich** *adj.* unutterable; unspeakable; inexpressible; **~'stehlich** *adj.* unbearable, insupportable.

'unbarmherzig *adj.* merciless, unmerciful; **'2keit** *f* (-/*no pl.*) mercilessness, unmercifulness.

unbe|absichtigt *adj.* [ˈunbəˀapziçtiçt] unintentional, undesigned; **'~achtet** *adj.* unnoticed; **~anstandet** *adj.* [ˈunbəˀ-] unopposed, not objected to; **'~baut** *adj.* untilled; land: undeveloped; **'~dacht** *adj.* inconsiderate; imprudent; **~denklich** **1.** *adj.* unobjectionable; **2.** *adv.* without hesitation; **~deutend** *adj.* insignificant; slight; **~dingt** **1.** *adj.* unconditional; *obedience, etc.*: implicit; **2.** *adv.* by all means; under any circumstances; **~'fahrbar** *adj.* impracticable, impassable; **~'fangen** *adj.* unprejudiced, unbias(s)ed; ingenuous; unembarrassed; **~'friedigend** *adj.* unsatisfactory; **~friedigt** *adj.* [ˈ~çt] dissatisfied; disappointed; **~'fugt** *adj.* unauthorized; incompetent; **'2fugte** *m* (-n/-n) unauthorized person; ~*n ist der Zutritt verboten!* no trespassing!; **'~gabt** *adj.* untalented; **~'greiflich** *adj.* inconceivable, incomprehensible; **~'grenzt** *adj.* unlimited; boundless; **'~gründet** *adj.* unfounded; **'2hagen** *n* uneasiness; discomfort; **'~haglich** *adj.* uneasy; uncomfortable; **~'helligt** *adj.* [ˌ~'hɛliçt] unmolested; **~herrscht** *adj.* lacking self-control; **'2herrschtheit** *f* (-/*no pl.*) lack of self-control; **'~hindert** *adj.* unhindered, free; **~'holfen** *adj.* [ˌ~'bɔhɔlfən] clumsy, awkward; **'2holfenheit** *f* (-/*no pl.*) clumsiness, awkwardness; **~'irrt** *adj.* unswerving; **'~kannt** *adj.* unknown; ~*e Größe* ♃ unknown quantity (*a. fig.*); **~'kümmert** *adj.* unconcerned (*um, wegen* about), careless (*of, about*); **'~lebt** *adj.* inanimate; *street, etc.*: unfrequented; **~'lehrbar** *adj.*: ~ *sein* take no advice; **~'liebt** *adj.* unpopular; *sich* ~ *machen* get o.s. disliked; **'~mannt** *adj.* unmanned;

'∼merkt adj. unnoticed; '∼mittelt adj. impecunious, without means; ∼nommen adj. [∼'nɔmən]: es bleibt ihm ∼ zu inf. he is at liberty to inf.; '∼nutzt adj. unused; '∼quem adj. uncomfortable; inconvenient; '2quemlichkeit f lack of comfort; inconvenience; '∼rechtigt adj. unauthorized; unjustified; ∼schadet prp. (gen.) [∼'ʃaːdət] without prejudice to; ∼schädigt adj. ['∼çt] uninjured, undamaged; ∼scheiden adj. immodest; ∼scholten adj. ['∼ʃɔltən] blameless, irreproachable; '∼schränkt adj. unrestricted; absolute; ∼schreiblich adj. [∼'ʃraɪpliç] indescribable; ∼'sehen adv. unseen; without inspection; '∼setzt adj. unoccupied; vacant; ∼siegbar adj. [∼'ziːkbaːr] invincible; '∼sonnen adj. thoughtless, imprudent; rash; '2sonnenheit f (-/-en) thoughtlessness; rashness; ∼'ständig adj. inconstant; unsteady; weather: changeable, unsettled (a. ♁); p. erratic; '2ständigkeit f (-/no pl.) inconstancy; changeability; ∼stätig adj. ['∼çt] unconfirmed; letter, etc.: unacknowledged; ∼'stechlich adj. incorruptible, unbribable; 2'stechlichkeit f (-/no pl.) incorruptibility; '∼stimmt adj. indeterminate (a. ♌); indefinite (a. gr.); uncertain; feeling, etc.: vague; '2stimmtheit f (-/no pl.) indeterminateness, indetermination; indefiniteness; uncertainty; vagueness; ∼'streitbar adj. incontestable; indisputable; ∼'stritten adj. uncontested, undisputed; '∼teiligt adj. unconcerned (an dat. in); indifferent; ∼'trächtlich adj. inconsiderable, insignificant. [flexible.]

unbeugsam adj. [un'bɔykzaːm] in-]

'unbe|wacht adj. unwatched, unguarded (a. fig.); '∼waffnet adj. unarmed; eye: naked; '∼weglich adj. immovable; motionless; '∼wiesen adj. unproven; '∼wohnt adj. uninhabited; unoccupied, vacant; '∼wußt adj. unconscious; ∼'zähmbar adj. indomitable.

'Un|bilden pl.: ∼ der Witterung inclemency of the weather; '∼bildung f lack of education.

'un|billig adj. unfair; '∼blutig 1. adj. bloodless; 2. adv. without bloodshed.

unbotmäßig adj. ['unboːt-] insubordinate; '2keit f (-/-en) insubordination.

'un|brauchbar adj. useless; '∼christlich adj. unchristian.

und cj. [unt] and; F: na ∼? so what?

'Undank m ingratitude; '2bar adj. ungrateful (gegen to); task, etc.: thankless; '∼barkeit f ingratitude, ungratefulness; fig. thanklessness.

un|'denkbar adj. unthinkable; inconceivable; ∼'denklich adj.: seit ∼en Zeiten from time immemorial; '∼deutlich adj. indistinct; speech: a. inarticulate; fig. vague, indistinct; '∼deutsch adj. un-German; '∼dicht adj. leaky; '2ding n: es wäre ein ∼, zu behaupten, daß ... it would be absurd to claim that ... '∼duldsam adj. intolerant; '2keit f intolerance.

un|durch|'dringlich adj. impenetrable; countenance: impassive; ∼'führbar adj. impracticable; '∼lässig adj. impervious, impermeable; '∼sichtig adj. opaque; fig. mysterious.

uneben adj. ['un ʔ-] ground: uneven, broken; way, etc.: bumpy; '2heit f 1. (-/no pl.) unevenness; 2. (-/-en) bump.

un|echt adj. ['un ʔ-] jewellery, etc.: imitation; hair, teeth, etc.: false; money, jewellery, etc.: counterfeit; picture, etc.: fake; ⅍ fraction: improper; '∼ehelich adj. illegitimate. **Unehr|e** ['un ʔ-] f dishono(u)r; j-m ∼ machen discredit s.o.; '2enhaft adj. dishono(u)rable; '2lich adj. dishonest; '∼lichkeit f dishonesty.

uneigennützig adj. ['un ʔ-] disinterested, unselfish.

uneinig adj. ['un ʔ-]: ∼ sein be at variance (mit with); disagree (über acc. on); '2keit f variance, disagreement.

un|ein|'nehmbar adj. impregnable; '∼empfänglich adj. insusceptible (für of, to).

unempfindlich adj. ['un ʔ-] insensitive (gegen to); '2keit f insensitiveness (gegen to).

un|'endlich 1. adj. endless, infinite (both a. fig.); 2. adv. infinitely (a. fig.); ∼ lang endless; ∼ viel no end of (money, etc.); 2keit f (-/no pl.) endlessness, infinitude, infinity (all a. fig.).

unent|'behrlich adj. ['un ʔent'beːrliç] indispensable; ∼'geltlich 1. adj. gratuitous, gratis; 2. adv. gratis, free of charge; ∼'rinnbar adj. ineluctable; '∼schieden 1. adj. undecided; ∼ enden game: end in a draw or tie; 2. 2 n (-s/-) draw, tie; '∼schlossen adj. irresolute; '2-schlossenheit f irresoluteness, irresolution; ∼'schuldbar adj. [∼'ʃultbaːr] inexcusable; ∼wegt adv. [∼'veːkt] untiringly; continuously; ∼'wirrbar adj. inextricable.

uner|'bittlich adj. ['un ʔer'bitliç] inexorable; fact: stubborn; '∼fahren adj. inexperienced; ∼'findlich adj. [∼'fintliç] incomprehensible; ∼'forschlich adj. inscrutable; '∼freulich adj. unpleasant; ∼'füllbar adj. unrealizable; '∼giebig adj. unproductive (an dat. of); '∼heb-

lich *adj.* irrelevant (*für* to); inconsiderable; **~hört** *adj.* **1.** ['~hø:rt] unheard; **2.** [~'hø:rt] unheard-of; outrageous; **~kannt** *adj.* unrecognized; **~klärlich** *adj.* inexplicable; **~läßlich** *adj.* [~'lesliç] indispensable (*für* to, for); **~laubt** *adj.* ['~laupt] unauthorized; illegal, illicit; **~e** *Handlung* ## tort; **~ledigt** *adj.* ['~le:diçt] unsettled (*a.* ✝); **~meßlich** *adj.* [~'mesliç] immeasurable, immense; **~müdlich** *adj.* [~'my:t-liç] *p.* indefatigable, untiring; *efforts, etc.*: untiring, unremitting; **~quicklich** *adj.* unpleasant, unedifying; **~reichbar** *adj.* inattainable; inaccessible; *pred. a.* above *or* beyond *or* out of reach; **~reicht** *adj.* unrival(l)ed, unequal(l)ed; **~sättlich** *adj.* [~'zetliç] insatiable, insatiate; **~schöpflich** *adj.* inexhaustible.

unerschrocken *adj.* ['un~⁹-] intrepid, fearless; **Qheit** *f* (-/*no pl.*) intrepidity, fearlessness.

uner|schütterlich *adj.* [un⁹er'fy-tərliç] unshakable; **~schwinglich** *adj.* *price*: prohibitive; *pred. a.* above *or* beyond *or* out of reach (*für* of); **~setzlich** *adj.* irreplaceable; *loss, etc.*: irreparable; **~träglich** *adj.* intolerable, unbearable; **~wartet** *adj.* unexpected; **~wünscht** *adj.* undesirable, undesired.

'unfähig *adj.* incapable (*zu inf.* of *ger.*); unable (*to inf.*); inefficient; **Qkeit** *f* incapability (*zu inf.* of *ger.*); inability (*to inf.*); inefficiency.

'Unfall *m* accident; *e-n* **~** *haben* meet with *or* have an accident; **~station** *f* emergency ward; **~versicherung** *f* accident insurance.

un'faßlich *adj.* incomprehensible, inconceivable; *das ist mir* **~** that is beyond me.

un'fehlbar 1. *adj.* infallible (*a. eccl.*); *decision, etc.*: unimpeachable; *instinct, etc.*: unfailing; **2.** *adv.* without fail; inevitably; **Qkeit** *f* (-/*no pl.*) infallibility.

'un|fein *adj.* indelicate; *pred. a.* lacking in refinement; **~fern** *prp.* (*gen. or von*) not far from; **~fertig** *adj.* unfinished; *fig. a.* half-baked; **~flätig** *adj.* ['~fle:tiç] dirty, filthy.

unfolgsam *adj.* disobedient; **Q-keit** *f* disobedience.

un|förmig *adj.* ['unfœrmiç] misshapen; shapeless; **~frankiert** *adj.* unstamped; **~frei** *adj.* not free; ✍ unstamped; **~freiwillig** *adj.* involuntary; *humour*: unconscious; **~freundlich** *adj.* unfriendly (*zu* with), unkind (*to*); *climate, weather*: inclement; *room, day*: cheerless; **Qfriede(n)** *m* discord.

'unfruchtbar *adj.* unfruitful; ster-

ile; **Qkeit** *f* (-/*no pl.*) unfruitfulness; sterility.

Unfug ['unfu:k] *m* (-[e]s/*no pl.*) mischief.

Ungar ['uŋgar] *m* (-n/-n) Hungarian; **Qisch** *adj.* Hungarian.

'ungastlich *adj.* inhospitable.

unge|achtet *prp.* (*gen.*) ['uŋgə⁹ax-tət] regardless of; despite; **~ahnt** *adj.* ['uŋgə⁹-] undreamt-of; unexpected; **~bärdig** *adj.* ['~bɛ:rdiç] unruly; **~beten** *adj.* uninvited, unasked; **~er** *Gast* intruder, *sl.* gate-crasher; **~bildet** *adj.* uneducated; **~bräuchlich** *adj.* unusual; **~braucht** *adj.* unused; **~bührlich** *adj.* improper, undue, unseemly; **~bunden** *adj.* *book*: unbound; *fig.*: free; single; **~deckt** *adj.* *table*: unlaid; *sports,* ✗, ✝: uncovered; *paper currency*: fiduciary.

'Ungeduld *f* impatience; **Qig** *adj.* impatient.

'ungeeignet *adj.* unfit (*für* for *s.th.*, *to do s.th.*); *p. a.* unqualified; *moment*: inopportune.

ungefähr ['uŋgəfɛ:r] **1.** *adj.* approximate, rough; **2.** *adv.* approximately, roughly, about, *Am.* F *a.* around; *von* **~** by chance; **~det** *adj.* unendangered, safe; **~lich** *adj.* harmless; *pred. a.* not dangerous.

unge|fällig *adj.* disobliging; **~halten** *adj.* displeased (*über acc.* at); **~hemmt 1.** *adj.* unchecked; **2.** *adv.* without restraint; **~heuchelt** *adj.* unfeigned.

ungeheuer ['uŋgəhɔʏər] **1.** *adj.* vast, huge, enormous; **2.** ♀ *n* (-s/-) monster; **~lich** *adj.* [~'hɔʏərliç] monstrous.

'ungehobelt *adj.* not planed; *fig.* uncouth, rough.

'ungehörig *adj.* undue, improper; **Qkeit** *f* (-/-, -en) impropriety.

'ungehorsam 1. *adj.* disobedient; **2.** ♀ *m* disobedience.

'unge|künstelt *adj.* unaffected; **~kürzt** *adj.* unabridged.

'ungelegen *adj.* inconvenient, inopportune; **Qheiten** *f/pl.* inconvenience; trouble; *j-m* **~** *machen* put s.o. to inconvenience.

'unge|lehrig *adj.* indocile; **~lenk** *adj.* awkward, clumsy; **~lernt** *adj.* unskilled; **~mütlich** *adj.* uncomfortable; *room*: *a.* cheerless; *p.* nasty; **~nannt** *adj.* unnamed; *p.* anonymous.

'ungenau *adj.* inaccurate, inexact; **Qigkeit** *f* inaccuracy, inexactness.

'ungeniert *adj.* free and easy, unceremonious; undisturbed.

unge|nießbar *adj.* ['uŋgəni:sba:r] uneatable; undrinkable; F *p.* unbearable, *pred. a.* in a bad humo(u)r; **~nügend** *adj.* insufficient; **~pflegt** *adj.* unkempt; **~rade** *adj.* odd; **~raten** *adj.* spoilt, undutiful.

'**ungerecht** *adj.* unjust (*gegen* to); '$\mathcal{Q}$**igkeit** *f* (*-/-en*) injustice.

'**un|gern** *adv.* unwillingly, grudgingly; reluctantly; '$\sim$**geschehen** *adj.*: $\sim$ *machen* undo *s.th.*

'**Ungeschick** *n* (*-[e]s/no pl.*), '$\sim$**lichkeit** *f* awkwardness, clumsiness, maladroitness; '$\mathcal{Q}$**t** *adj.* awkward, clumsy, maladroit.

unge|schlacht *adj.* ['ungəʃlaxt] hulking; uncouth; '$\sim$**schliffen** *adj.* unpolished, rough (*both a. fig.*); '$\sim$**schminkt** *adj.* not made up; *fig.* unvarnished.

'**ungesetzlich** *adj.* illegal, unlawful, illicit; '$\mathcal{Q}$**keit** *f* (*-/-en*) illegality, unlawfulness.

'**unge|sittet** *adj.* uncivilized; unmannerly; '$\sim$**stört** *adj.* undisturbed, uninterrupted; '$\sim$**straft 1.** *adj.* unpunished; **2.** *adv.* with impunity; $\sim$ *davonkommen* get off *or* escape scot-free.

ungestüm ['ungəʃty:m] **1.** *adj.* impetuous; violent; **2.** $\mathcal{Q}$ *n* (*-[e]s/no pl.*) impetuosity; violence.

'**unge|sund** *adj. climate:* unhealthy; *appearance: a.* unwholesome; *food:* unwholesome; '$\sim$**teilt** *adj.* undivided (*a. fig.*); '$\sim$**trübt** *adj.* ['$\sim$try:pt] untroubled; unmixed; $\mathcal{Q}$**tüm** ['$\sim$ty:m] *n* (*-[e]s/-e*) monster; $\sim$**übt** *adj.* ['$\sim$?y:pt] untrained; inexperienced; '$\sim$**waschen** *adj.* unwashed.

'**ungewiß** *adj.* uncertain; *j-n im ungewissen lassen* keep s.o. in suspense; '$\mathcal{Q}$**heit** *f* (*-/$\sim$-en*) uncertainty; suspense.

'**unge|wöhnlich** *adj.* unusual, uncommon; '$\sim$**wohnt** *adj.* unaccustomed; unusual; '$\sim$**zählt** *adj.* numberless, countless; $\mathcal{Q}$**ziefer** ['$\sim$tsi:fər] *n* (*-s/-*) vermin; '$\sim$**ziemend** *adj.* improper, unseemly; '$\sim$**zogen** *adj.* ill-bred, rude, uncivil; *child:* naughty; '$\sim$**zügelt** *adj.* unbridled.

'**ungezwungen** *adj.* unaffected, easy; '$\mathcal{Q}$**heit** *f* (*-/$\sim$-en*) unaffectedness, ease, easiness.

'**Unglaube(n)** *m* unbelief, disbelief.

'**ungläubig** *adj.* incredulous, unbelieving (*a. eccl.*); infidel; '$\mathcal{Q}$**e** *m, f* unbeliever; infidel.

unglaub|lich *adj.* [un'glaupliç] incredible; '$\sim$**würdig** *adj. p.* untrustworthy; *thing:* incredible; $\sim$**e** *Geschichte* cock-and-bull story.

'**ungleich 1.** *adj.* unequal, different; uneven; unlike; **2.** *adv.* (by) far, much; '$\sim$**artig** *adj.* heterogeneous; '$\mathcal{Q}$**heit** *f* difference, inequality; unevenness; unlikeness; '$\sim$**mäßig** *adj.* uneven; irregular.

'**Unglück** *n* (*-[e]s/$\sim$-e*) misfortune; bad *or* ill luck; accident; calamity, disaster; misery; '$\mathcal{Q}$**lich** *adj.* unfortunate, unlucky; unhappy; $\mathcal{Q}$**licher'weise** *adv.* unfortunately,

unluckily; '$\mathcal{Q}$**selig** *adj.* unfortunate; disastrous.

'**Unglücks|fall** *m* misadventure; accident; '$\sim$**rabe** F *m* unlucky fellow.

'**Un|gnade** *f* (*-/no pl.*) disgrace, disfavo(u)r; *in $\sim$ fallen bei* fall into disgrace with, incur *s.o.'s* disfavo(u)r; '$\mathcal{Q}$**gnädig** *adj.* ungracious, unkind.

'**ungültig** *adj.* invalid; *ticket:* not available; *money:* not current; $\overset{\text{t}}{\text{z}\text{t}}$ (null and) void; '$\mathcal{Q}$**keit** *f* invalidity; $\overset{\text{t}}{\text{z}\text{t}}$ *a.* voidness.

'**Un|gunst** *f* disfavo(u)r; inclemency (*of weather*); *zu meinen $\sim$en* to my disadvantage; '$\mathcal{Q}$**günstig** *adj.* unfavo(u)rable; disadvantageous.

'**un|gut** *adj.*: $\sim$*es Gefühl* misgiving; *nichts für $\sim$!* no offen|ce, *Am.* -se!; '$\sim$**haltbar** *adj. shot:* unstoppable; *theory, etc.*: untenable; '$\sim$**handlich** *adj.* unwieldy, bulky.

'**Unheil** *n* mischief; disaster, calamity; '$\mathcal{Q}$**bar** *adj.* incurable; '$\mathcal{Q}$**voll** *adj.* sinister, ominous.

'**unheimlich 1.** *adj.* uncanny (*a. fig.*), weird; sinister; F *fig.* tremendous, terrific; **2.** F *fig. adv.*: $\sim$ *viel* heaps of, an awful lot of.

'**unhöflich** *adj.* impolite, uncivil; '$\mathcal{Q}$**keit** *f* impoliteness, incivility.

Unhold ['unhɔlt] *m* (*-[e]s/-e*) fiend.

'**un|hörbar** *adj.* inaudible; '$\sim$**hygienisch** *adj.* unsanitary, insanitary.

Uni ['uni] *f* (*-/-s*) F varsity.

Uniform [uni'fɔrm] *f* (*-/-en*) uniform.

Unikum ['u:nikum] *n* (*-s/Unika, -s*) unique (thing); queer fellow.

uninteress|ant *adj.* ['unʔ-] uninteresting, boring; '$\sim$**iert** *adj.* uninterested (*an dat.* in).

Universität [univerzi'tɛ:t] *f* (*-/-en*) university.

Universum [uni'vɛrzum] *n* (*-s/no pl.*) universe.

Unke ['uŋkə] *f* (*-/-n*) *zo.* fire-bellied toad; F *fig.* croaker; '$\mathcal{Q}$**n** F *v/i.* (*ge-, h*) croak.

'**unkennt|lich** *adj.* unrecognizable; '$\mathcal{Q}$**lichkeit** *f* (*-/no pl.*): *bis zur $\sim$* past all recognition; '$\mathcal{Q}$**nis** *f* (*-/no pl.*) ignorance.

'**unklar** *adj.* not clear; *meaning, etc.*: obscure; *answer, etc.*: vague; *im $\sim$en sein* be in the dark (*über acc.* about); '$\mathcal{Q}$**heit** *f* want of clearness; vagueness; obscurity.

'**unklug** *adj.* imprudent, unwise.

'**Unkosten** *pl.* cost(*s pl.*), expenses *pl.*; *sich in (große) $\sim$ stürzen* go to great expense.

'**Unkraut** *n* weed.

un|kündbar *adj.* ['unkyntba:r] *loan, etc.*: irredeemable; *employment:* permanent; $\sim$**kundig** *adj.* ['$\sim$kundiç] ignorant (*gen.* of); '$\sim$**längst**

adv. lately, recently, the other day; **'~lauter** *adj.* competition: unfair; **'~leidlich** *adj.* intolerable, insufferable; **'~leserlich** *adj.* illegible; **~leugbar** *adj.* ['~lɔykbaːr] undeniable; **'~logisch** *adj.* illogical; **'~lösbar** *adj.* unsolvable, insoluble. **'Unlust** *f* (-/no pl.) reluctance (zu inf. to inf.); **'Qig** *adj.* reluctant.

'un|manierlich *adj.* unmannerly; **'~männlich** *adj.* unmanly; **~maßgeblich** *adj.* ['~ge:pliç]: nach m-r ~en Meinung in my humble opinion; **'~mäßig** *adj.* immoderate; intemperate; **'Qmenge** *f* enormous or vast quantity or number.

'Unmensch *m* monster, brute; **'Q~lich** *adj.* inhuman, brutal; **'~lichkeit** *f* inhumanity, brutality.

'un|mißverständlich *adj.* unmistakable; **'~mittelbar** *adj.* immediate, direct; **'~möbliert** *adj.* unfurnished; **'~modern** *adj.* unfashionable, outmoded.

'unmöglich *adj.* impossible; **'Qkeit** *f* impossibility.

'Unmoral *f* immorality; **'Qisch** *adj.* immoral.

'unmündig *adj.* under age.

'un|musikalisch *adj.* unmusical; **'Qmut** *m* (-[e]s/no pl.) displeasure (über acc. at, over); **'~nachahmlich** *adj.* inimitable; **'~nachgiebig** *adj.* unyielding; **'~nachsichtig** *adj.* strict, severe; inexorable; **~nahbar** *adj.* inaccessible, unapproachable; **'~natürlich** *adj.* unnatural; affected; **'~nötig** *adj.* unnecessary, needless; **'~nütz** *adj.* useless; **~ordentlich** *adj.* ['un'~] untidy; room, etc.: a. disorderly; **Qordnung** ['un'~] *f* disorder, mess.

'unpartei|isch *adj.* impartial, unbias(s)ed; **'Qische** *m* (-n/-n) referee; umpire; **'Qlichkeit** *f* impartiality.

'un|passend *adj.* unsuitable; improper; inappropriate; **'~passierbar** *adj.* impassable.

unpäßlich *adj.* ['unpesliç] indisposed, unwell; **'Qkeit** *f* (-/-en) indisposition.

'un|persönlich *adj.* impersonal (a. gr.); **'~politisch** *adj.* unpolitical; **~praktisch** *adj.* unpractical, Am. a. impractical; **'Qrat** *m* (-[e]s/no pl.) filth; rubbish; **~ wittern** smell a rat.

'unrecht **1.** *adj.* wrong; **~ haben** be wrong; j-m **~** tun wrong s.o.; **2.** **Q** *n* (-[e]s/no pl.): mit or zu **~** wrongly; ihm ist **~** geschehen he has been wronged; **'~mäßig** *adj.* unlawful; **'Qmäßigkeit** *f* unlawfulness.

'unreell *adj.* dishonest; unfair.

'unregelmäßig *adj.* irregular (a. gr.); **'Qkeit** *f* (-/-en) irregularity.

'unreif *adj.* unripe, immature (both a. fig.); **'Qe** *f* unripeness, immaturity (both a. fig.).

'un|rein *adj.* impure (a. eccl.); unclean (a. fig.); **'~reinlich** *adj.* uncleanly; **~'rettbar** *adv.:* ~ verloren irretrievably lost; **'~richtig** *adj.* incorrect, wrong.

Unruh ['unruː] *f* (-/-en) balance (-wheel); **'Q~e** *f* (-/-n) restlessness, unrest (a. pol.); uneasiness, disquiet(ude); flurry; alarm; **~n** *pl.* disturbances *pl.*, riots *pl.*; **'Qig** *adj.* restless; uneasy; sea: rough, choppy.

'unrühmlich *adj.* inglorious.

uns *pers. pron.* [uns] us; *dat.:* a. to us; ~ (selbst) ourselves, after prp.: us; ein Freund von ~ a friend of ours.

'un|sachgemäß *adj.* inexpert; **'~sachlich** *adj.* not objective; personal; **~säglich** *adj.* [~'ze:kliç] unspeakable; untold; **'~sanft** *adj.* ungentle; **'~sauber** *adj.* dirty; fig. a. unfair (a. sports); **'~schädlich** *adj.* innocuous, harmless; **'~scharf** *adj.* blurred; pred. a. out of focus; **~'schätzbar** *adj.* inestimable, invaluable; **'~scheinbar** *adj.* plain, Am. a. homely.

'unschicklich *adj.* improper, indecent; **'Qkeit** *f* (-/-en) impropriety, indecency.

unschlüssig *adj.* ['unʃlysiç] irresolute; **'Qkeit** *f* (-/no pl.) irresoluteness, irresolution.

'un|schmackhaft *adj.* insipid; unpalatable, unsavo(u)ry; **'~schön** *adj.* unlovely, unsightly; fig. unpleasant.

'Unschuld *f* (-/no pl.) innocence; **'Qig** *adj.* innocent (an dat. of).

'unselbständig *adj.* dependent (on others); **'Qkeit** *f* (lack of in)dependence.

unser ['unzɔr] **1.** poss. pron. our; der (die, das) ~e ours; die ~en pl. our relations pl.; **2.** pers. pron. of us; wir waren ~ drei there were three of us.

'unsicher *adj.* unsteady; unsafe, insecure; uncertain; **'Qheit** *f* unsteadiness; insecurity, unsafeness; uncertainty.

'unsichtbar *adj.* invisible.

'Unsinn *m* (-[e]s/no pl.) nonsense; **'Qig** *adj.* nonsensical.

'Unsitt|e *f* bad habit; abuse; **'Qlich** *adj.* immoral; indecent (a. ½⅛); **'~lichkeit** *f* (-/-en) immorality.

'un|solid(e) *adj.* p. easy-going; life: dissipated; ✝ unreliable; **'~sozial** *adj.* unsocial, antisocial; **'~sportlich** *adj.* unsportsmanlike; unfair (gegenüber to).

'unstatthaft *adj.* inadmissible.

'unsterblich *adj.* immortal.

Un'sterblichkeit *f* immortality.

'un|stet *adj.* unsteady; character, life: unsettled; **Qstimmigkeit** ['~ʃtimiçkait] *f* (-/-en) discrepancy; dissension; **'~sträflich** *adj.* blameless; '~streitig adj. incontestable; '~sympathisch adj. disagreeable; er ist mir ~ I don't like him; '~tätig adj. inactive; idle.

'untauglich adj. unfit (a. ✗); unsuitable; '2keit f (-/no pl.) unfitness (a. ✗).

un'teilbar adj. indivisible.

unten adv. ['untən] below; downstairs; von oben bis ~ from top to bottom.

unter ['untər] 1. prp. (dat.; acc.) below, under; among; ~ anderem among other things; ~ zehn Mark (for) less than ten marks; ~ Null below zero; ~ aller Kritik beneath contempt; ~ diesem Gesichtspunkt from this point of view; 2. adj. lower; inferior; die ~en Räume the downstair(s) rooms.

Unter|abteilung ['untər?-] f subdivision; ~arm ['untər?-] m forearm; '~bau m (-[e]s/-ten) ∆ substructure (a. 🏠), foundation.

unter|'bieten v/t. (irr. bieten, no -ge-, h) underbid; ✝ undercut, undersell (competitor); lower (record); ~'binden v/t. (irr. binden, no -ge-, h) ligature; fig. stop; ~'bleiben v/i. (irr. bleiben, no -ge-, sein) remain undone; not to take place.

unter'brech|en v/t. (irr. brechen, no -ge-, h) interrupt (a. 𝄞); break, Am. a. stop over; ✂ break (circuit); 2ung f (-/-en) interruption; break, Am. a. stopover. [mit.)

unter'breiten v/t. (no -ge-, h) sub-)

'unterbring|en v/t. (irr. bringen, sep., -ge-, h) place (a. ✝); accommodate, lodge; '2ung f (-/-en) accommodation; ✝ placement.

unterdessen adv. [untər'desən] (in the) meantime, meanwhile.

unter'drück|en v/t. (no -ge-, h) oppress (subjects, etc.); repress (revolt, sneeze, etc.); suppress (rising, truth, yawn, etc.); put down (rebellion, etc.); 2ung f (-/-en) oppression; repression; suppression; putting down.

unterernähr|t adj. ['untər?-] underfed, undernourished; '2ung f (-/no pl.) underfeeding, malnutrition.

Unter'führung f subway, Am. underpass.

'Untergang m (-[e]s/⚹⚺e) ast. setting; ⚓ sinking; fig. ruin.

Unter'gebene m (-n/-n) inferior, subordinate; contp. underling.

'untergehen v/i. (irr. gehen, sep., -ge-, sein) ast. set; ⚓ sink, founder; fig. be ruined.

untergeordnet adj. ['untərgə?ördnət] subordinate; importance: secondary.

'Untergewicht n (-[e]s/no pl.) underweight.

unter'graben fig. v/t. (irr. graben, no -ge-, h) undermine.

'Untergrund m (-[e]s/no pl.) subsoil; '~bahn f underground (railway), in London: tube; Am. subway; '~bewegung f underground movement.

'unterhalb prp. (gen.) below, underneath.

'Unterhalt m (-[e]s/no pl.) support, subsistence, livelihood; maintenance.

unter'halt|en v/t. (irr. halten, no -ge-, h) maintain; support; entertain, amuse; sich ~ converse (mit with; über acc. on, about), talk (with; on, about); sich gut ~ enjoy o.s.; 2ung f maintenance, upkeep; conversation, talk; entertainment.

'Unterhändler m negotiator; ✗ Parlementaire.

'Unter|haus parl. n (-es/no pl.) House of Commons; '~hemd n vest, undershirt; '~holz n (-es/no pl.) underwood, brushwood; '~hose f (e-e a pair of) drawers pl., pants pl.; '2irdisch adj. subterranean, underground (both a. fig.).

unter'joch|en v/t. (no -ge-, h) subjugate, subdue; 2ung f (-/-en) subjugation.

'Unter|kiefer m lower jaw; '~kleid n slip; '~kleidung f underclothes pl., underclothing, underwear.

'unterkommen 1. v/i. (irr. kommen, sep., -ge-, sein) find accommodation; find employment; 2. 2 n (-s/✗ -) accommodation; employment, situation.

'unter|kriegen F v/t. (sep., -ge-, h) bring to heel; sich nicht ~ lassen not to knuckle down or under; 2kunft ['~kunft] f (-/⚹⚺e) accommodation, lodging; ✗ quarters pl.; '2lage f base; pad; fig.: voucher; ~n pl. documents pl.; data pl.

unter'lass|en v/t. (irr. lassen, no -ge-, h) omit (zu tun doing, to do); neglect (to do, doing); fail (to do); 2ung f (-/-en) omission; neglect; failure; 2ungssünde f sin of omission.

'unterlegen[1] v/t. (sep., -ge-, h) lay or put under; give (another meaning).

unter'legen[2] adj. inferior (dat. to); 2e m (-n/-n) loser; underdog; 2heit f (-/no pl.) inferiority.

'Unterleib m abdomen, belly.

unter'liegen v/i. (irr. liegen, no -ge-, sein) be overcome (dat. by); be defeated (by), sports: a. lose (to); fig.: be subject to; be liable to; es unterliegt keinem Zweifel, daß ... there is no doubt that ...

'Unter|lippe f lower lip; '~mieter m subtenant, lodger, Am. a. roomer.

unter'nehmen 1. v/t. (irr. nehmen, no -ge-, h) undertake; take (steps);

2. ⚥ n (-s/-) enterprise; ✝ a. business; ✖ operation.

unter'nehm|end adj. enterprising; ⚥er ✝ m (-s/-) entrepreneur; contractor; employer; ⚥ung f (-/-en) enterprise, undertaking; ✖ operation; **ungslustig** adj. enterprising.

'Unter|offizier ✖ m non-commissioned officer; **'ordnen** v/t. (sep., -ge-, h) subordinate (dat. to); sich ~ submit (to).

Unter'redung f (-/-en) conversation, conference.

Unterricht ['untərriçt] m (-[e]s/✖ -e) instruction, lessons pl.

unter'richten v/t. (no -ge-, h): ~ in (dat.) instruct in, teach (English, etc.); ~ von inform s.o. of.

'Unterrichts|ministerium n ministry of education; **'stunde** f lesson, (teaching) period; **'wesen** n (-s/no pl.) education; teaching.

'Unterrock m slip.

unter'sagen v/t. (no -ge-, h) forbid (j-m et. s.o. to do s.th.).

'Untersatz m stand; saucer.

unter'schätzen v/t. (no -ge-, h) undervalue; underestimate, underrate.

unter'scheid|en v/t. and v/i. (irr. scheiden, no -ge-, h) distinguish (zwischen between; von from); sich ~ differ (von from); **⚥ung** f distinction.

'Unterschenkel m shank.

'unterschieb|en v/t. (irr. schieben, sep., -ge-, h) push under; fig.: attribute (dat. to); substitute (statt for); **⚥ung** f substitution.

Unterschied ['untərʃiːt] m (-[e]s/-e) difference; distinction; zum ~ von in distinction from or to; **⚥lich** adj. different; differential; variable, varying; **⚥slos** adj. indiscriminate; undiscriminating.

unter'schlag|en v/t. (irr. schlagen, no -ge-, h) embezzle; suppress (truth, etc.); **⚥ung** f (-/-en) embezzlement; suppression.

'Unterschlupf m (-[e]s/ᵘe, -e) shelter, refuge.

unter'schreiben v/t. and v/i. (irr. schreiben, no -ge-, h) sign.

'Unterschrift f signature.

'Untersee|boot ⚓, ✖ n s. U-Boot; **'kabel** n submarine cable.

unter'setzt adj. thick-set, squat.

unterst adj. ['untərst] lowest, undermost.

'Unterstand ✖ m shelter, dug-out.

unter'stehen (irr. stehen, no -ge-, h) 1. v/i. (dat.) be subordinate to; be subject to (law, etc.); 2. v/refl. dare; untersteh dich! don't you dare!; **stellen** v/t. 1. ['ʃtelən] (sep., -ge-, h) put or place under; garage (car); sich ~ take shelter (vor dat. from); 2. [~'ʃtelən] (no -ge-, h) (pre)suppose, assume; impute (dat.

to); j-m ~ ✖ put (troops, etc.) under s.o.'s command; **⚥'stellung** f (-/-en) assumption, supposition; imputation; **'streichen** v/t. (irr. streichen, no -ge-, h) underline, underscore (both a. fig.).

unter'stütz|en v/t. (no -ge-, h) support; back up; **⚥ung** f (-/-en) support (a. ✖); assistance, aid; relief.

unter'such|en v/t. (no -ge-, h) examine (a. ♋); inquire into, investigate (a. ♋); ✖ try; analy|se, Am. -ze (a. ♋); **⚥ung** f (-/-en) examination (a. ♋); inquiry (gen. into), investigation (a. 👓); exploration; analysis (a. 👓).

Unter'suchungs|gefangene m prisoner on remand; **gefängnis** n remand prison; **haft** f detention on remand; **richter** m investigating judge.

Untertan ['untərtaːn] m (-s, -en/ -en) subject.

untertänig adj. ['untərtɛːniç] submissive.

'Unter|tasse f saucer; **'tauchen** (sep., -ge-) 1. v/i. (sein) dive, dip; duck; fig. disappear; 2. v/t. (h) duck.

'Unterteil n, m lower part.

unter'teil|en v/t. (no -ge-, h) subdivide; **⚥ung** f subdivision.

'Unter|titel m subheading; subtitle; a. caption (of film); **'ton** m undertone; **'vermieten** v/t. (no -ge-, h) sublet.

unter'wander|n pol. v/t. (no -ge-, h) infiltrate; **⚥ung** pol. f infiltration.

'Unterwäsche f s. Unterkleidung.

unterwegs adv. [untər've:ks] on the or one's way.

unter'weis|en v/t. (irr. weisen, no -ge-, h) instruct (in dat. in); **⚥ung** f instruction.

'Unterwelt f underworld (a. fig.).

unter'werf|en v/t. (irr. werfen, no -ge-, h) subdue (dat. to), subjugate (to); subject (to); submit (to); sich ~ submit (to); **⚥ung** f (-/-en) subjugation, subjection; submission (unter acc. to).

unterworfen adj. [untər'vɔrfən] subject (dat. to).

unterwürfig adj. [untər'vyrfiç] submissive; subservient; **⚥keit** f (-/no pl.) submissiveness; subservience.

unter'zeichn|en v/t. (no -ge-, h) sign; **⚥er** m signer, the undersigned; subscriber (gen. to); signatory (gen. to treaty); **⚥erstaat** m signatory state; **⚥ete** m, f (-n/-n) the undersigned; **⚥ung** f signature, signing.

unterziehen v/t. (irr. ziehen) 1. ['~tsiːən] (sep., -ge-, h) put on underneath; 2. [~'tsiːən] (no -ge-, h) subject (dat. to); sich e-r Operation ~ undergo an operation; sich e-r Prüfung ~ go in or sit for an examination; sich der Mühe ~ zu inf. take the trouble to inf.

'**Untiefe** *f* shallow, shoal.
'**Untier** *n* monster (*a. fig.*).
un|tilgbar *adj.* [un'tilkbɑːr] indelible; † *government annuities*: irredeemable; ‿'**tragbar** *adj.* unbearable, intolerable; *costs*: prohibitive; ‿'**trennbar** *adj.* inseparable.
'**untreu** *adj.* untrue (*dat.* to), disloyal (to); *husband, wife*: unfaithful (to); '‿e *f* disloyalty; unfaithfulness, infidelity.
un|'tröstlich *adj.* inconsolable, disconsolate; ‿**trüglich** *adj.* [‿'tryːkliç] infallible, unerring.
'**Untugend** *f* vice, bad habit.
un|über|legt *adj.* ['un‿yːbər-] inconsiderate, thoughtless; '‿**sichtlich** *adj.* badly arranged; difficult to survey; involved; *mot. corner*: blind; ‿'**trefflich** *adj.* unsurpassable; ‿**windlich** *adj.* [‿'vintliç] invincible; *fortress*: impregnable; *obstacle, etc.*: insurmountable; *difficulties, etc.*: insuperable.
unum|gänglich *adj.* [un‿um'gɛŋliç] absolutely necessary; ‿**schränkt** *adj.* [‿'ʃrɛŋkt] absolute; ‿**stößlich** *adj.* [‿'ʃtøːsliç] irrefutable; incontestable; irrevocable; ‿**wunden** *adj.* ['‿vundən] frank, plain.
ununterbrochen *adj.* ['un‿untərbrɔxən] uninterrupted; incessant.
unver|'änderlich *adj.* unchangeable; invariable; ‿'**antwortlich** *adj.* irresponsible; inexcusable; ‿'**besserlich** *adj.* incorrigible; '‿**bindlich** *adj.* not binding *or* obligatory; *answer, etc.*: non-committal; ‿**blümt** *adj.* [‿'blyːmt] plain, blunt; ‿**bürgt** *adj.* [‿'byrkt] unwarranted; *news*: unconfirmed; '‿**dächtig** *adj.* unsuspected; '‿**daulich** *adj.* indigestible (*a. fig.*); '‿**dient** *adj.* undeserved; '‿**dorben** *adj.* unspoiled, unspoilt; *fig.*: uncorrupted; pure, innocent; '‿**drossen** *adj.* indefatigable, unflagging; '‿**dünnt** *adj.* undiluted, *Am.* a. straight; ‿'**einbar** *adj.* incompatible; '‿**fälscht** *adj.* unadulterated; *fig.* genuine; ‿**fänglich** *adj.* ['‿fɛŋliç] not captious; ‿**froren** *adj.* ['‿froːrən] unabashed, impudent; '**⊆frorenheit** *f* (-/-en) impudence, F cheek; '‿**gänglich** *adj.* imperishable; ‿'**geßlich** *adj.* unforgettable; ‿'**gleichlich** *adj.* incomparable; '‿**hältnismäßig** *adj.* disproportionate; '‿**heiratet** *adj.* unmarried, single; '‿**hofft** *adj.* unhoped-for, unexpected; '‿**hohlen** *adj.* unconcealed; '‿**käuflich** *adj.* unsal(e)able; not for sale; ‿'**kennbar** *adj.* unmistakable; ‿'**letzbar** *adj.* invulnerable; *fig. a.* inviolable; ‿**meidlich** *adj.* [‿'martliç] inevitable; '‿**mindert** *adj.* undiminished; '‿**mittelt** *adj.* abrupt.

'**Unvermögen** *n* (-s/*no pl.*) inability; impotence; '**⊆d** *adj.* impecunious, without means.
'**unvermutet** *adj.* unexpected.
'**Unver|nunft** *f* unreasonableness, absurdity; '**⊆nünftig** *adj.* unreasonable, absurd; '**⊆richteterdinge** *adv.* without having achieved one's object.
'**unverschämt** *adj.* impudent, impertinent; '**⊆heit** *f* (-/-en) impudence, impertinence.
'**unver|schuldet** *adj.* not in debt; through no fault of mine, *etc.*; '‿**sehens** *adv.* unawares, suddenly, all of a sudden; '‿**sehrt** *adj.* ['‿zeːrt] uninjured; '‿**söhnlich** *adj.* implacable, irreconcilable; '‿**sorgt** *adj.* unprovided for; '**⊆stand** *m* injudiciousness; folly, stupidity; '‿**ständig** *adj.* injudicious; foolish; '‿**ständlich** *adj.* unintelligible; incomprehensible; *das ist mir* ‿ *that is beyond me*; '‿**sucht** *adj.: nichts* ‿ *lassen* leave nothing undone; '‿**träglich** *adj.* unsociable; quarrelsome; '‿**wandt** *adj.* steadfast; ‿**wundbar** *adj.* [‿'vuntbɑːr] invulnerable; ‿**wüstlich** *adj.* [‿'vyːstliç] indestructible; *fig.* irrepressible; ‿**zagt** *adj.* ['‿tsaːkt] intrepid, undaunted; ‿'**zeihlich** *adj.* unpardonable; ‿'**zinslich** *adj.* bearing no interest; non-interest-bearing; ‿**züglich** *adj.* [‿'tsyːkliç] immediate, instant.
'**unvollendet** *adj.* unfinished.
'**unvollkommen** *adj.* imperfect; '**⊆heit** *f* imperfection.
'**unvollständig** *adj.* incomplete; '**⊆keit** *f* (-/*no pl.*) incompleteness.
'**unvorbereitet** *adj.* unprepared; extempore.
'**unvoreingenommen** *adj.* unbias(s)ed, unprejudiced; '**⊆heit** *f* freedom from prejudice.
'**unvor|hergesehen** *adj.* unforeseen; ‿**schriftsmäßig** *adj.* irregular.
'**unvorsichtig** *adj.* incautious; imprudent; '**⊆keit** *f* incautiousness; imprudence.
unvor|'stellbar *adj.* unimaginable; '‿**teilhaft** *adj.* unprofitable; *dress, etc.*: unbecoming.
'**unwahr** *adj.* untrue; '**⊆heit** *f* untruth.
'**unwahrscheinlich** *adj.* improbable, unlikely; '**⊆keit** *f* (-/-en) improbability, unlikelihood.
'**un|wegsam** *adj.* pathless, impassable; '‿**weit** *prp.* (*gen. or von*) not far from; '**⊆wesen** *n* (-s/*no pl.*) nuisance; *sein* ‿ *treiben* be up to one's tricks; '‿**wesentlich** *adj.* unessential, immaterial (*für* to); '**⊆wetter** *n* thunderstorm; '‿**wichtig** *adj.* unimportant, insignificant.
unwider|legbar *adj.* [unviːdər'leːk-

ba:r] irrefutable; **~'ruflich** adj. irrevocable (a. ✝).

unwider'stehlich adj. irresistible; **2keit** f (-/no pl.) irresistibility.

unwieder'bringlich adj. irretrievable.

'Unwill|e m (-ns/no pl.), **'~en** m (-s/no pl.) indignation (*über* acc. at), displeasure (at, over); **2ig** adj. indignant (*über* acc. at), displeased (at, with); unwilling; **2kürlich** adj. involuntary.

'unwirklich adj. unreal.

'unwirksam adj. ineffective, inefficient; *laws, rules, etc.*: inoperative; 🔁 inactive; **2keit** f (-/no pl.) ineffectiveness, inefficiency; 🔁 inactivity.

unwirsch adj. ['unvirʃ] testy.

'unwirt|lich adj. inhospitable, desolate; **'~schaftlich** adj. uneconomic(al).

'unwissen|d adj. ignorant; **'2heit** f (-/no pl.) ignorance; **'~tlich** adj. unwitting, unknowning.

'unwohl adj. unwell, indisposed; **2sein** n (-s/no pl.) indisposition.

'unwürdig adj. unworthy (*gen.* of).

un|zählig adj. ['un'tse:liç] innumerable; **'2zart** adj. indelicate.

Unze ['untsə] f (-/-n) ounce.

'Unzeit f: *zur ~* inopportunely; **'2-gemäß** adj. old-fashioned; inopportune; **'2ig** adj. untimely; unseasonable; *fruit*: unripe.

unzer|'brechlich adj. unbreakable; **~'reißbar** adj. untearable; **~'stör-bar** adj. indestructible; **~'trenn-lich** adj. inseparable.

'un|ziemlich adj. unseemly; **'2-zucht** f (-/no pl.) lewdness; 🟦 sexual offen|ce, *Am.* -se; **'~züchtig** adj. lewd; obscene.

'unzufrieden adj. discontented (*mit* with), dissatisfied (with, at); **'2heit** f discontent, dissatisfaction.

'unzugänglich adj. inaccessible.

unzulänglich adj. ['untsulɛŋliç] insufficient; **'2keit** f (-/-en) insufficiency; shortcoming.

'unzulässig adj. inadmissible; *esp.* 🟦 *influence*: undue.

'unzurechnungsfähig adj. irresponsible; **'2keit** f irresponsibility.

'unzu|reichend adj. insufficient; **'~sammenhängend** adj. incoherent; **'~träglich** adj. unwholesome; **'~treffend** adj. incorrect; inapplicable (*auf* acc. to).

'unzuverlässig adj. unreliable, untrustworthy; *friend*: a. uncertain; **'2keit** f unreliability, untrustworthiness.

'unzweckmäßig adj. inexpedient; **'2keit** f inexpediency.

'un|zweideutig adj. unequivocal; unambiguous; **'~zweifelhaft 1.** adj. undoubted, undubitable; **2.** adv doubtless.

üppig adj. ['ypiç] ♀ luxuriant, exuberant, opulent; *food*: luxurious opulent; *figure*: voluptuous; **2keit** f (-/~-en) luxuriance, luxuriancy, exuberance; voluptuousness.

ur|alt adj. ['u:r'alt] very old; (as) old as the hills; **2aufführung** ['u:r'-] f world première.

Uran [u'ra:n] n (-s/no pl.) uranium.

urbar adj. ['u:rba:r] arable, cultivable; *~ machen* reclaim; **'2ma-chung** f (-/-en) reclamation.

'Ur|bevölkerung f aborigines pl.; **'~bild** n original, prototype; **'2-eigen** adj. one's very own; **'~enkel** m great-grandson; **'~großeltern** pl. great-grandparents pl.; **'~groß-mutter** f great-grandmother; **'~großvater** m great-grandfather.

'Urheber m (-s/-) author; **'~rech** n copyright (*an* dat. in); **'~schaft** (-/no pl.) authorship.

Urin [u'ri:n] m (-s/-e) urine; **2ieren** [~i'ni:rən] v/i. (no -ge-, h) urinate

'Urkund|e f document; deed; **'~en-fälschung** f forgery of documents **2lich** adj. ['~ntliç] documentary.

Urlaub ['u:rlaup] m (-[e]s/-e) leave (of absence) (a. 🟦); holiday(s pl.) esp. *Am.* vacation; **~er** ['~bər] m (-s/-) holiday-maker, *esp. Am* vacationist, vacationer.

Urne ['urnə] f (-/-n) urn; ballot-box.

'ur|plötzlich 1. adj. very sudden abrupt; **2.** adv. all of a sudden **'2sache** f cause; reason; *keine ~* don't mention it, *Am. a.* you are welcome; **'~sächlich** adj. causal **'2schrift** f original (text); **'2-sprung** m origin, source; **'~sprünglich** adj. ['~ʃpryŋliç] original; **'2stoff** m primary matter.

Urteil ['urtail] n (-s/-e) judg(e) ment; 🟦 a. sentence; *meinem ~ nach* in my judg(e)ment; *sich ei ~ bilden* form a judg(e)ment (*übe* acc. of, on); **'2en** v/i. (ge-, h) judg (*über* acc. of; *nach* by, from); **'2s-kraft** f (-/🔁-e) discernment.

'Ur|text m original (text); **'~wald** m primeval *or* virgin forest; **2 wüchsig** adj. ['~vy:ksiç] original *fig.*: natural; rough; **'~zeit** f primi tive times pl.

Utensilien [uten'zi:ljən] pl. uten sils pl.

Utop|ie [uto'pi:] f (-/-n) Utopia **2isch** adj. [u'to:piʃ] Utopian utopian.

V

Vagabund [vaga'bunt] m (-en/-en) vagabond, vagrant, tramp, Am. hobo, F bum.

Vakuum ['vɑːkuʸum] n (-s/Vakua, Vakuen) vacuum.

Valuta † [va'luːta] f (-/Valuten) value; currency.

Vanille [va'niljə] f (-/no pl.) vanilla.

variabel adj. [vari'ɑːbəl] variable.

Varia|nte [vari'antə] f (-/-n) variant; ~tion [~'tsjoːn] f (-/-en) variation.

Varieté [varie'teː] n (-s/-s), ~theater n variety theatre, music-hall, Am. vaudeville theater.

variieren [vari'iːrən] v/i. and v/t. (no -ge-, h) vary.

Vase ['vɑːzə] f (-/-n) vase.

Vater ['fɑːtər] m (-s/ⁿ) father; '~land n native country or land, mother country; '~landsliebe f patriotism.

väterlich adj. ['fɛːtərliç] fatherly, paternal.

'Vater|schaft f (-/no pl.) paternity, fatherhood; '~unser eccl. n (-s/-) Lord's Prayer.

Vati ['fɑːti] m (-s/-s) dad(dy).

Veget|arier [vege'tɑːrjər] m (-s/-) vegetarian; ~arisch adj. vegetarian; ~ation [~a'tsjoːn] f (-/-en) vegetation; ~ieren [~'tiːrən] v/i. (no -ge-, h) vegetate.

Veilchen ♀ ['faɪlçən] n (-s/-) violet.

Vene anat. ['veːnə] f (-/-n) vein.

Ventil [vɛn'tiːl] n (-s/-e) valve (a. ♪); ♪ stop (of organ); fig. vent, outlet; ~ation [~ila'tsjoːn] f (-/-en) ventilation; ~ator [~i'lɑːtər] m (-s/-en) ventilator, fan.

verab|folgen [fɛr'ap-] v/t. (no -ge-, h) deliver; give; ⚕ administer (medicine); ~reden v/t. (no -ge-, h) agree upon, arrange; appoint, fix (time, place); sich ~ make an appointment, Am. F (have a) date; ꝙredung f (-/-en) agreement; arrangement; appointment, Am. F date; ~reichen v/t. (no -ge-, h) s. verabfolgen; ~scheuen v/t. (no -ge-, h) abhor, detest, loathe; ~schieden [~'ʃiːdən] v/t. (no -ge-, h) dismiss; retire (officer); ✕ discharge (troops); parl. pass (bill); sich ~ take leave (von of), say goodbye (to); ꝙschiedung f (-/-en) dismissal; discharge; passing.

ver|'achten v/t. (no -ge-, h) despise; ~ächtlich adj. [~'ɛçtliç] contemptuous; contemptible; ꝙ'achtung f contempt; ~allgemeinern [~ʸalgə'maɪnərn] v/t. (no -ge-, h) generalize; ~'altet adj. antiquated, obsolete, out of date.

Veranda [ve'randa] f (-/Veranden) veranda(h), Am. a. porch.

veränder|lich adj. [fɛr'ɛndərliç] changeable; variable (a. ♈, gr.); ~n v/t. and v/refl. (no -ge-, h) alter, change; vary; ꝙung f change, alteration (in dat. in; an dat. to); variation.

verängstigt adj. [fɛr'ɛŋstiçt] intimidated, scared.

ver'anlag|en v/t. (no -ge-, h) of taxation: assess; ~t adj. [~kt] talented; ꝙung [~gʊŋ] f (-/-en) assessment; fig. talent(s pl.); ⚕ predisposition.

ver'anlass|en v/t. (no -ge-, h) cause, occasion; arrange; ꝙung f (-/-en) occasion, cause; auf m-e ~ at my request or suggestion.

ver|'anschaulichen v/t. (no -ge-, h) illustrate; ~'anschlagen v/t. (no -ge-, h) rate, value, estimate (all: auf acc. at).

ver'anstalt|en v/t. (no -ge-, h) arrange, organize; give (concert, ball, etc.); ꝙung f (-/-en) arrangement; event; sports: event, meeting, Am. meet.

ver'antwort|en v/t. (no -ge-, h) take the responsibility for; account for; ~lich adj. responsible; j-n ~ machen für hold s.o. responsible for.

Ver'antwortung f (-/-en) responsibility; die ~ tragen be responsible; zur ~ ziehen call to account; ꝙslos adj. irresponsible.

ver|'arbeiten v/t. (no -ge-, h) work up; ⊕ process, manufacture (both: zu into); digest (food) (a. fig.); ~'ärgern v/t. (no -ge-, h) vex, annoy.

ver'arm|en v/i. (no -ge-, sein) become poor; ~t adj. impoverished.

ver|'ausgaben v/t. (no -ge-, h) spend (money); sich ~ run short of money; fig. spend o.s.; ~'äußern v/t. (no -ge-, h) sell; alienate.

Verb gr. [vɛrp] n (-s/-en) verb.

Ver'band m (-[e]s/ⁿe) ⚕ dressing, bandage; association, union; ✕ formation, unit; ~(s)kasten m first-aid box; ~(s)zeug n dressing (material).

ver'bann|en v/t. (no -ge-, h) banish (a. fig.), exile; ꝙung f (-/-en) banishment, exile.

ver|barrikadieren [fɛrbarika'diːrən] v/t. (no -ge-, h) barricade; block (street, etc.); ~'bergen v/t. (irr. bergen, no -ge-, h) conceal, hide.

ver'besser|n v/t. (no -ge-, h) improve; correct; ꝙung f improvement; correction.

ver'beug|en v/refl. (no -ge-, h) bow (vor dat. to); ꝙung f bow.

ver|'biegen v/t. (irr. biegen, no

-ge-, h) bend, twist, distort; ~'**bieten** v/t. (irr. bieten, no -ge-, h) forbid, prohibit; ~'**billigen** v/t. (no -ge-, h) reduce in price, cheapen.

ver'**bind|en** v/t. (irr. binden, no -ge-, h) ⚕ dress; tie (together); bind (up); link (mit to); join, unite, combine; connect (a. teleph.); teleph. put s.o. through (mit to); j-m die Augen ~ blindfold s.o.; sich ~ join, unite, combine (a. 🜚); ich bin Ihnen sehr verbunden I am greatly obliged to you; falsch verbunden! teleph. wrong number!; ~lich adj. [~tlic] obligatory; obliging; 2lichkeit f (-/-en) obligation, liability; obligingness, civility.

Ver'**bindung** f union; alliance; combination; association (of ideas); connexion, (Am. only) connection (a. teleph., 🜚, 🜚, ⊕); relation; communication (a. teleph.); 🜚 compound; geschäftliche ~ business relations pl.; teleph.: ~ bekommen (haben) get (be) through; die ~ verlieren mit lose touch with; in ~ bleiben (treten) keep (get) in touch (mit with); sich in ~ setzen mit communicate with, esp. Am. contact s.o.; ~sstraße f communication road, feeder road; ~stür f communication door.

ver'**bissen** adj. [fɛr'bisən] dogged; crabbed; ~'**bitten** v/refl. (irr. bitten, no -ge-, h): das verbitte ich mir! I won't suffer or stand that!

ver'**bitter|n** v/t. (no -ge-, h) embitter; 2ung f (-/%-en) bitterness (of heart).

verblassen [fɛr'blasən] v/i. (no -ge-, sein) fade (a. fig.).

Verbleib [fɛr'blaip] m (-[e]s/no pl.) whereabouts sg., pl.; 2en [~bən] v/i. (irr. bleiben, no -ge-, sein) be left, remain.

ver'**blend|en** v/t. (no -ge-, h) △ face (wall, etc.); fig. blind, delude; 2ung f (-/%-en) △ facing; fig. blindness, delusion. [faded.]

verblichen adj. [fɛr'bliçən] colour:|

verblüff|en [fɛr'blyfən] v/t. (no -ge-, h) amaze; perplex; puzzle; dumbfound; 2ung f (-/%-en) amazement, perplexity.

ver'**blühen** v/i. (no -ge-, sein) fade, wither; ~'**bluten** v/i. (no -ge-, sein) bleed to death.

ver'**borgen** adj. hidden; secret; 2heit f (-/no pl.) concealment; secrecy.

Verbot [fɛr'bo:t] n (-[e]s/-e) prohibition; 2en adj. forbidden, prohibited; Rauchen ~ no smoking.

Ver'**brauch** m (-[e]s/% -e) consumption (an dat. of); 2en v/t. (no -ge-, h) consume, use up; wear out; ~er m (-s/-) consumer; 2t adj. air: stale; p. worn out.

ver'**brechen** 1. v/t. (irr. brechen, no -ge-, h) commit; was hat er verbrochen? what is his offen|ce, Am. -se?, what has he done?; 2. 2 n (-s/-) crime, offen|ce, Am. -se.

Ver'**brecher** m (-s/-) criminal; 2isch adj. criminal; ~tum n (-s/no pl.) criminality.

ver'**breit|en** v/t. (no -ge-, h) spread, diffuse; shed (light, warmth, happiness); sich ~ spread; sich ~ über (acc.) enlarge (up)on (theme); ~ern v/t. and v/refl. (no -ge-, h) widen, broaden; 2ung f (-/%-en) spread (-ing), diffusion.

ver'**brenn|en** (irr. brennen, no -ge-) 1. v/i. (sein) burn; 2. v/t. (h) burn (up); cremate (corpse); 2ung f (-/-en) burning, combustion; cremation (of corpse); wound: burn.

ver'**bringen** v/t. (irr. bringen, no -ge-, h) spend, pass.

verbrüder|n [fɛr'bry:dərn] v/refl. (no -ge-, h) fraternize; 2ung f (-/-en) fraternization.

ver|'**brühen** v/t. (no -ge-, h) scald; sich ~ scald o.s.; ~'**buchen** v/t. (no -ge-, h) book.

Verbum gr. ['vɛrbum] n (-s/Verba) verb.

verbünden [fɛr'byndən] v/refl. (no -ge-, h) ally o.s. (mit to, with).

Verbundenheit [fɛr'bundənhait] f (-/no pl.) bonds pl., ties pl.; solidarity; affection.

Ver'**bündete** m, f (-n/-n) ally, confederate; die ~n pl. the allies pl.

ver|'**bürgen** v/t. (no -ge-, h) guarantee, warrant; sich ~ für answer or vouch for; ~'**büßen** v/t. (no -ge-, h): e-e Strafe ~ serve a sentence, serve (one's) time.

Verdacht [fɛr'daxt] m (-[e]s/no pl.) suspicion; in ~ haben suspect.

verdächtig adj. [fɛr'dɛçtiç] suspected (gen. of); pred. suspect; suspicious; ~en [~gən] v/t. (no -ge-, h) suspect s.o. (gen. of); cast suspicion on; 2ung f (-/-en) suspicion; insinuation.

verdamm|en [fɛr'damən] v/t. (no -ge-, h) condemn, damn (a. eccl.); 2nis f (-/no pl.) damnation; ~t 1. adj. damned; F: ~! (damn (it)!, confound it!; 2. F adv.: ~ kalt beastly cold; 2ung f (-/%-en) condemnation, damnation.

ver|'**dampfen** (no -ge-) v/t. (h) and v/i. (sein) evaporate; ~'**danken** v/t. (no -ge-, h): j-m et. ~ owe s.th. to s.o.

verdarb [fɛr'darp] pret. of verderben.

verdau|en [fɛr'dauən] v/t. (no -ge-, h) digest; ~lich adj. digestible; leicht ~ easy to digest, light; 2ung f (-/no pl.) digestion; 2ungsstörung f indigestion.

Ver'**deck** n (-[e]s/-e) 🜚 deck;

hood (*of carriage, car, etc.*); top (*of vehicle*); **~en** *v/t.* (*no -ge-, h*) cover; conceal, hide.

ver'denken *v/t.* (*irr.* denken, *no -ge-, h*): *ich kann es ihm nicht* **~,** *daß I* cannot blame him for *ger.*

Verderb [fɛr'dɛrp] *m* (*-[e]s/no pl.*) ruin; **~en** [**~**bən] **1.** *v/i.* (*irr., no -ge-, sein*) spoil (*a. fig.*); rot; *meat, etc.*: go bad; *fig.* perish; **2.** *v/t.* (*irr., no -ge-, h*) spoil; *fig. a.*: corrupt; ruin; *er will es mit niemandem* **~** he tries to please everybody; *sich den Magen* **~** upset one's stomach; **~en** [**~**bən] *n* (*-s/no pl.*) ruin; **Qlich** *adj.* [**~**plɪç] pernicious; *food*: perishable; **~nis** [**~**pnɪs] *f* (*-/**~**-se*) corruption; depravity; **Qt** *adj.* [**~**pt] corrupted, depraved.

ver'|deutlichen *v/t.* (*no -ge-, h*) make plain or clear; **~'dichten** *v/t.* (*no -ge-, h*) condense; *sich* **~** condense; *suspicion*: grow stronger; **~'dicken** *v/t. and v/refl.* (*no -ge-, h*) thicken; **~'dienen** *v/t.* (*no -ge-, h*) merit, deserve; earn (*money*).

Ver'dienst (*-es/-e*) **1.** *m* gain, profit; earnings *pl.*; **2.** *n* merit; *es ist sein* **~,** *daß* it is owing to him that; **Qvoll** *adj.* meritorious, deserving; **~spanne** † *f* profit margin.

ver'|dient *adj. p.* of merit; (well-) deserved; *sich* **~** *gemacht haben um* deserve well of; **~'dolmetschen** *v/t.* (*no -ge-, h*) interpret (*a. fig.*); **~'doppeln** *v/t. and v/refl.* (*no -ge-, h*) double.

verdorben [fɛr'dɔrbən] **1.** *p.p.* of verderben; **2.** *adj. meat*: tainted; *stomach*: disordered, upset; *fig.* corrupt, depraved.

ver|dorren [fɛr'dɔrən] *v/i.* (*no -ge-, sein*) wither (up); **~'drängen** *v/t.* (*no -ge-, h*) push away, thrust aside; *fig.* displace; *psych.* repress; **~'drehen** *v/t.* (*no -ge-, h*) distort, twist (*both a. fig.*); roll (*eyes*); *fig.* pervert; *j-m den Kopf* **~** turn s.o.'s head; **~'dreht** F *fig. adj.* crazy; **~'dreifachen** *v/t. and v/refl.* (*no -ge-, h*) triple.

verdrieß|en [fɛr'dri:sən] *v/t.* (*irr., no -ge-, h*) vex, annoy; **~lich** *adj.* vexed, annoyed, sulky; *thing*: annoying.

ver|droß [fɛr'drɔs] *pret.* of verdrießen; **~drossen** [**~**'drɔsən] **1.** *p.p.* of verdrießen; **2.** *adj.* sulky; listless.

ver'drucken *typ. v/t.* (*no -ge-, h*) misprint.

Verdruß [fɛr'drus] *m* (Verdrusses/**~** Verdrusse) vexation, annoyance.

ver'dummen (*no -ge-*) **1.** *v/t.* (*h*) make stupid; **2.** *v/i.* (*sein*) become stupid.

ver'dunk|eln *v/t.* (*no -ge-, h*) darken, obscure (*both a. fig.*); black out (*window*); *sich* **~** darken;

Q(e)lung *f* (*-/**~**-en*) darkening; obscuration; black-out; **⚖** collusion.

ver'|dünnen *v/t.* (*no -ge-, h*) thin; dilute (*liquid*); **~'dunsten** *v/i.* (*no -ge-, sein*) volatilize, evaporate; **~'dursten** *v/i.* (*no -ge-, sein*) die of thirst; **~dutzt** *adj.* [**~**'dutst] nonplussed.

ver'ed|eln *v/t.* (*no -ge-, h*) ennoble; refine; improve; **♀** graft; process (*raw materials*); **Q(e)lung** *f* (*-/**~**-en*) refinement; improvement; processing.

ver'ehr|en *v/t.* (*no -ge-, h*) revere, venerate; worship; admire, adore; **Qer** *m* (*-s/-*) worship(p)er; admirer, adorer; **Qung** *f* (*-/**~**-en*) reverence, veneration; worship; adoration.

vereidigen [fɛr'aɪdɪgən] *v/t.* (*no -ge-, h*) swear (*witness*); *at entrance into office*: swear *s.o.* in.

Verein [fɛr'aɪn] *m* (*-[e]s/-e*) union; society, association; club.

ver'einbar *adj.* compatible (*mit* with), consistent (*with*); **~en** *v/t.* (*no -ge-, h*) agree upon, arrange; **Qung** *f* (*-/-en*) agreement, arrangement.

ver'einen *v/t.* (*no -ge-, h*) s. vereinigen.

ver'einfach|en *v/t.* (*no -ge-, h*) simplify; **Qung** *f* (*-/-en*) simplification.

ver'einheitlichen *v/t.* (*no -ge-, h*) unify, standardize.

ver'einig|en *v/t.* (*no -ge-, h*) unite, join; associate; *sich* **~** unite, join; associate o.s.; **Qung** *f* **1.** (*-/**~**-en*) union; **2.** (*-/-en*) union; society, association.

ver'ein|samen *v/i.* (*no -ge-, sein*) grow lonely or solitary; **~zelt** *adj.* isolated; sporadic.

ver|'eiteln *v/t.* (*no -ge-, h*) frustrate; **~'ekeln** *v/t.* (*no -ge-, h*): *er hat mir das Essen verekelt* he spoilt my appetite; **~'enden** *v/i.* (*no -ge-, sein*) *animals*: die, perish; **~enge(r)n** [**~**'ɛŋə(r)n] *v/t. and v/refl.* (*no -ge-, h*) narrow.

ver'erb|en *v/t.* (*no -ge-, h*) leave, bequeath; *biol.* transmit; *sich* **~** be hereditary; *sich* **~** *auf* (*acc.*) descend (up)on; **Qung** *f* (*-/**~**-en*) *biol.* transmission; *physiol.* heredity; **Qungslehre** *f* genetics.

verewig|en [fɛr'e:vɪgən] *v/t.* (*no -ge-, h*) perpetuate; **~t** *adj.* [**~**çt] deceased, late.

ver'fahren 1. *v/i.* (*irr.* fahren, *no -ge-, sein*) proceed; **~** *mit* deal with; **2.** *v/t.* (*irr.* fahren, *no -ge-, h*) mismanage, muddle, bungle; *sich* **~** miss one's way; **3.** **♀** *n* (*-s/-*) procedure; proceeding(s *pl.* ⚖); **⊕** process.

Ver'fall *m* (*-[e]s/no pl.*) decay, decline; dilapidation (*of house, etc.*);

$\natural\natural$ forfeiture; expiration; maturity (*of bill of exchange*); 2en **1.** v/i. (*irr.* fallen, *no* -ge-, sein) decay; *house*: dilapidate; *document, etc.*: expire; *pawn*: become forfeited; *right*: lapse; *bill of exchange*: fall due; *sick person*: waste away; ~ auf (*acc.*) hit upon (*idea, etc.*); ~ in (*acc.*) fall into; j-m ~ become s.o.'s slave; **2.** *adj.* ruinous; addicted (*dat.* to *drugs, etc.*); ~serscheinung [fer'fals⁹-] f symptom of decline; ~tag m day of payment.

ver|'fälschen v/t. (*no* -ge-, h) falsify; adulterate (*wine, etc.*); ~fänglich *adj.* [~'fɛŋlɪç] *question*: captious, insidious; risky; embarrassing; ~'färben v/refl. (*no* -ge-, h) change colo(u)r.

ver'fass|en v/t. (*no* -ge-, h) compose, write; 2er m (-s/-) author. Ver'fassung f state, condition; *pol.* constitution; disposition (*of mind*); 2smäßig *adj.* constitutional; 2swidrig *adj.* unconstitutional.

ver|'faulen v/i. (*no* -ge-, sein) rot, decay; ~'fechten v/t. (*irr.* fechten, *no* -ge-, h) defend, advocate. ver'fehl|en v/t. (*no* -ge-, h) miss; 2ung f (-/-en) offen|ce, *Am.* -se.

ver|feinden [fer'faɪndən] v/refl. (*no* -ge-, h) make enemies of; sich ~ mit make an enemy of; ~feinern [~'faɪnərn] v/t. *and* v/refl. (*no* -ge-, h) refine; ~fertigen [~'fɛrtɪgən] v/t. (*no* -ge-, h) make, manufacture; compose.

ver'film|en v/t. (*no* -ge-, h) film, screen; 2ung f (-/-en) filmversion.

ver|'finstern v/t. (*no* -ge-, h) darken, obscure; sich ~ darken; ~'flachen (*no* -ge-) v/i. (sein) *and* v/refl. (h) (become) shallow (a. fig.); ~'flechten v/t. (*irr.* flechten, *no* -ge-, h) interlace; *fig.* involve; ~'fliegen (*irr.* fliegen, *no* -ge-) **1.** v/i. (sein) evaporate; *time*: fly; *fig.* vanish; **2.** v/refl. (h) *bird*: stray; ✈ lose one's bearings, get lost; ~'fließen v/i. (*irr.* fließen, *no* -ge-, sein) *colours*: blend; *time*: elapse; ~flossen *adj.* [~'flɔsən] *time*: past; F ein ~er Freund a late friend, an ex-friend.

ver|'fluch|en v/t. (*no* -ge-, h) curse, *Am.* F cuss; ~t *adj.* damned; ~! damn (it)!, confound it!

ver|flüchtigen [fer'flyçtɪgən] v/t. (*no* -ge-, h) volatilize; sich ~ evaporate (a. fig.); F fig. vanish; ~flüssigen [~'flysɪgən] v/t. *and* v/refl. (*no* -ge-, h) liquefy.

ver'folg|en v/t. (*no* -ge-, h) pursue; persecute; follow (*tracks*); trace; *thoughts, dream*: haunt; gerichtlich ~ prosecute; 2er m (-s/-) pursuer; persecutor; 2ung f (-/-en) pursuit; persecution; pursuance; gericht-

liche ~ prosecution; 2ungswahn $\natural$ m persecution mania.

ver|frachten [fer'fraxtən] v/t. (*no* -ge-, h) freight, *Am. a.* ship (*goods*); ⚓ ship; F j-n ~ in (*acc.*) bundle s.o. in(to) (*train, etc.*); ~'froren *adj.* chilled through; ~'früht *adj.* premature.

verfüg|bar *adj.* [fer'fy:kba:r] available; ~en [~gən] (*no* -ge-, h) **1.** v/t. decree, order; **2.** v/i.: ~ über (*acc.*) have at one's disposal; dispose of; 2ung [~guŋ] f (-/-en) decree, order; disposal; j-m zur ~ stehen (stellen) be (place) at s.o.'s disposal.

ver'führ|en v/t. (*no* -ge-, h) seduce; 2er m (-s/-) seducer; ~erisch *adj.* seductive; enticing, tempting; 2ung f seduction.

vergangen *adj.* [fer'gaŋən] gone, past; im ~en Jahr last year; 2heit f (-/-en) past; gr. past tense.

vergänglich *adj.* [fer'gɛŋlɪç] transient, transitory.

vergas|en [fer'ga:zən] v/t. (*no* -ge-, h) gasify; gas s.o.; 2er mot. m (-s/-) carburet(t)or.

vergaß [fer'ga:s] pret. of vergessen.

ver'geb|en v/t. (*irr.* geben, *no* -ge-, h) give away (*an* j-n to s.o.); confer (on), bestow (on); place (*order*); forgive; sich et. ~ compromise one's dignity; ~ens *adv.* [~s] in vain; ~lich [~plɪç] **1.** *adj.* vain; **2.** *adv.* in vain; 2ung [~buŋ] f (-/⅔-en) bestowal, conferment (*both: an* acc. *on*); forgiveness, pardon.

vergegenwärtigen [fergɛgən'vɛrtigən] v/t. (*no* -ge-, h) represent; sich et. ~ visualize s.th.

ver'gehen **1.** v/i. (*irr.* gehen, *no* -ge-, sein) pass (away); fade (away); ~ vor (*dat.*) die of; **2.** v/refl. (*irr.* gehen, *no* -ge-, h): sich an j-m ~ assault s.o.; violate s.o.; sich gegen das Gesetz ~ offend against *or* violate the law; **3.** 2 n (-s/-) offen|ce, *Am.* -se.

ver'gelt|en v/t. (*irr.* gelten, *no* -ge-, h) repay, requite; reward; retaliate; 2ung f (-/-en) requital; retaliation, retribution.

vergessen [fer'gɛsən] **1.** v/t. (*irr.*, *no* -ge-, h) forget; leave; **2.** *p.p.* of 1; 2heit f (-/*no pl.*): in ~ geraten sink *or* fall into oblivion.

vergeßlich *adj.* [fer'gɛslɪç] forgetful.

vergeud|en [fer'gɔydən] v/t. (*no* -ge-, h) dissipate, squander, waste (*time, money*); 2ung f (-/⅔-en) waste.

vergewaltig|en [fergə'valtigən] v/t. (*no* -ge-, h) violate; rape; 2ung f (-/-en) violation; rape.

ver|gewissern [fergə'visərn] v/refl. (*no* -ge-, h) make sure (e-r Sache of s.th.); ‿'gießen v/t. (irr. gießen, no -ge-, h) shed (tears, blood); spill (liquid).

ver'gift|en v/t. (no -ge-, h) poison (a. fig.); sich ‿ take poison; ⚬ung f (-/-en) poisoning.

Vergißmeinnicht ♀ [fɛr'gismaɪn-nɪçt] n (-[e]s-[-e]) forget-me-not.

vergittern [fɛr'gɪtərn] v/t. (no -ge-, h) grate.

Vergleich [fɛr'glaɪç] m (-[e]s/-e) comparison; ⚥: agreement; compromise, composition; ⚬bar adj. comparable (mit to); ⚬en v/t. (irr. gleichen, no -ge-, h) compare (mit with, to); sich ‿ mit ⚥ come to terms with; verglichen mit as against, compared to; ⚬sweise adv. comparatively.

vergnügen [fɛr'gny:gən] 1. v/t. (no -ge-, h) amuse; sich ‿ enjoy o.s.; 2. ⚬ n (-s/-) pleasure, enjoyment; entertainment; ‿ finden an (dat.) take pleasure in; viel ‿! have a good time!   [gay.|

vergnügt adj. [fɛr'gny:kt] merry,|

Ver'gnügung f (-/-en) pleasure, amusement, entertainment; ‿s-reise f pleasure-trip, tour; ⚬s-süchtig adj. pleasure-seeking.

ver'golden [fɛr'gɔldən] v/t. (no -ge-, h) gild; ‿göttern fig. [‿'gœ-tərn] v/t. (no -ge-, h) idolize, adore; ‿'graben v/t. (irr. graben, no -ge-, h) bury (a. fig.); sich ‿ bury o.s.; ‿'greifen v/refl. (irr. greifen, no -ge-, h) sprain (one's hand, etc.); sich ‿ an (dat.) lay (violent) hands on, attack, assault; embezzle (money); encroach upon (s.o.'s property); ‿griffen adj. [‿'grɪfən] goods: sold out; book: out of print.

vergrößer|n [fɛr'grø:sərn] v/t. (no -ge-, h) enlarge (a. phot.); opt. magnify; sich ‿ enlarge; ⚬ung f 1. (-/-en) phot. enlargement; opt. magnification; 2. (-/‿-en) enlargement; increase; extension; ⚬ungs-glas n magnifying glass.

Vergünstigung [fɛr'gynstɪguŋ] f (-/-en) privilege.

vergüt|en [fɛr'gy:tən] v/t. (no -ge-, h) compensate (j-m et. s.o. for s.th.); reimburse (money spent); ⚬ung f (-/-en) compensation; reimbursement.

ver'haft|en v/t. (no -ge-, h) arrest; ⚬ung f (-/-en) arrest.

ver'halten 1. v/i. (irr. halten, no -ge-, h) keep back; catch or hold (one's breath); suppress, check; sich ‿ thing: be; p. behave; sich ruhig ‿ keep quiet; 2. ⚬ n (-s/no pl.) behavio(u)r, conduct.

Verhältnis [fɛr'hɛltnɪs] n (-ses/-se) proportion, rate; relation(s pl.) (zu with); F liaison, love-affair; F mistress; ‿se pl. conditions pl., circumstances pl.; means pl.; ⚬mäßig

adv. in proportion; comparatively; ‿wort gr. n (-[e]s/‿er) preposition.

Ver'haltungsmaßregeln f/pl. instructions pl.

ver'hand|eln (no -ge-, h) 1. v/i. negotiate, treat (über acc., wegen for); ⚥ try (über et. s.th.); 2. v/t. discuss; ⚬ung f negotiation; discussion; ⚥ trial, proceedings pl.

ver'häng|en v/t. (no -ge-, h) cover (over), hang; inflict (punishment) (über acc. upon); ⚬nis n (-ses/-se) fate; ‿nisvoll adj. fatal; disastrous.

ver'härmt adj. [fɛr'hɛrmt] careworn; ‿harren [‿'harən] v/i. (no -ge-, h, sein) persist (auf dat., bei, in dat. in), stick (to); ‿'härten v/t. and v/refl. (no -ge-, h) harden; ‿haßt adj. [‿'hast] hated; hateful, odious; ‿'hätscheln v/t. (no -ge-, h) coddle, pamper, spoil; ‿'hauen v/t. (irr. hauen, no -ge-, h) thrash.

verheer|en [fɛr'he:rən] v/t. (no -ge-, h) devastate, ravage, lay waste; ‿end fig. adj. disastrous; ⚬ung f (-/-en) devastation.

ver'hehlen [fɛr'he:lən] v/t. (no -ge-, h) s. verheimlichen; ‿'heilen v/i. (no -ge-, sein) heal (up).

ver'heimlich|en v/t. (no -ge-, h) hide, conceal; ⚬ung f (-/‿-en) concealment.

ver'heirat|en v/t. (no -ge-, h) marry (mit to); sich ‿ marry; ⚬ung f (-/‿-en) marriage.

ver'heiß|en v/t. (irr. heißen, no -ge-, h) promise; ⚬ung f (-/-en) promise; ‿ungsvoll adj. promising.

ver'helfen v/i. (irr. helfen, no -ge-, h): j-m zu et. ‿ help s.o. to s.th.

ver'herrlich|en v/t. (no -ge-, h) glorify; ⚬ung f (-/‿-en) glorification.

ver|'hetzen v/t. (no -ge-, h) instigate; ‿'hexen v/t. (no -ge-, h) bewitch.

ver'hinder|n v/t. (no -ge-, h) prevent; ⚬ung f (-/‿-en) prevention.

ver'höhn|en v/t. (no -ge-, h) deride, mock (at), taunt; ⚬ung f (-/-en) derision, mockery.

Verhör ⚥ [fɛr'hø:r] n (-[e]s/-e) interrogation, questioning (of prisoners, etc.); examination; ⚬en v/t. (no -ge-, h) examine, hear; interrogate; sich ‿ hear it wrong.

ver|'hüllen v/t. (no -ge-, h) cover, veil; ‿'hungern v/i. (no -ge-, sein) starve; ‿'hüten v/t. (no -ge-, h) prevent.

ver'irr|en v/refl. (no -ge-, h) go astray, loose one's way; ⚥ adj.: ‿es Schaf stray sheep; ⚬ung fig. f (-/-en) aberration; error.

ver'jagen v/t. (no -ge-, h) drive away.

verjähr|en ⚥ [fɛr'jɛ:rən] v/i. (no -ge-, sein) become prescriptive;

2ung f (-/-en) limitation, (negative) prescription.

verjüngen [fɛr'jyŋən] v/t. (no -ge-, h) make young again, rejuvenate; reduce (*scale*); *sich* ~ grow young again, rejuvenate; taper off.

Ver'kauf m sale; **2en** v/t. (no -ge-, h) sell; *zu* ~ for sale; *sich gut* ~ sell well.

Ver'käuf|er m seller; vendor; shop-assistant, salesman, *Am. a.* (sales-)clerk; **~erin** f (-/-nen) seller; vendor; shop-assistant, saleswoman, shop girl, *Am. a.* (sales)clerk; **2lich** *adj.* sal(e)able; for sale.

Ver'kaufs|automat m slot-machine, vending machine; **~schlager** m best seller.

Verkehr [fɛr'ke:r] m (-[e]s/~ -e) traffic; transport(ation); communication; correspondence; ⚓, 🚂, ✈, *etc.*: service; commerce, trade; intercourse (*a. sexually*); *aus dem* ~ *ziehen* withdraw from service; withdraw (*money*) from circulation; **2en** (no -ge-, h) **1.** v/t. convert (*in acc.* into), turn (into); **2.** v/i. ship, bus, *etc.*: run, ply (*zwischen dat.* between); *bei j-m* ~ go to or visit s.o.'s house; ~ *in* (*dat.*) frequent (*public house, etc.*); ~ *mit* associate or mix with; have (sexual) intercourse with.

Ver'kehrs|ader f arterial road; **~ampel** f traffic lights *pl.*, traffic signal; **~büro** n tourist bureau; **~flugzeug** n air liner; **~insel** f refuge, island; **~minister** m minister of transport; **~mittel** n (means of) conveyance or transport, *Am.* transportation; **~polizist** m traffic policeman or constable, *sl.* traffic cop; **2reich** *adj.* congested with traffic, busy; **~schild** n traffic sign; **~schutzmann** m *s.* Verkehrspolizist; **~stauung** f, **~stockung** f traffic block, traffic jam; **~störung** f interruption of traffic; 🚂, *etc.*: breakdown; **~straße** f thoroughfare; **~teilnehmer** m road user; **~unfall** m traffic accident; **~verein** m tourist agency; **~verhältnisse** *pl.* traffic conditions *pl.*; **~vorschrift** f traffic regulation; **~wesen** n (-s/no *pl.*) traffic; **~zeichen** n traffic sign.

ver'|kehrt *adj.* inverted, upside down; *fig.* wrong; **~'kennen** v/t. (*irr.* kennen, no -ge-, h) mistake; misunderstand, misjudge.

Ver'kettung f (-/-en) concatenation (*a. fig.*).

ver'|klagen ⚖ v/t. (no -ge-, h) sue (*auf acc., wegen* for); bring an action against *s.o.*; **~'kleben** v/t. (no -ge-, h) paste *s.t.h.* up.

ver'kleid|en v/t. (no -ge-, h) disguise; ⊕: line; face; wainscot; encase; *sich* ~ disguise o.s.; **2ung** f

(-/-en) disguise; ⊕: lining; facing; panel(l)ing, wainscot(t)ing.

verkleiner|n [fɛr'klaɪnərn] v/t. (no -ge-, h) make smaller, reduce, diminish; *fig.* belittle, derogate; **2ung** f (-/-en) reduction, diminution; *fig.* derogation.

ver'|klingen v/i. (*irr.* klingen, no -ge-, sein) die away; **~knöchern** [~'knœçərn] (no -ge-) **1.** v/t. (h) ossify; **2.** v/i. (sein) ossify; *fig. a.* fossilize; **~knoten** v/t. (no -ge-, h) knot; **~'knüpfen** v/t. (no -ge-, h) knot or tie (together); *fig.* connect, combine; **~'kohlen** (no -ge-) **1.** v/t. (h) carbonize; char; F: *j-n* ~ pull s.o.'s leg; **2.** v/i. (sein) char; **~'kommen 1.** v/i. (*irr.* kommen, no -ge-, sein) decay; *p.:* go downhill or to the dogs; become demoralized; **2.** *adj.* decayed; depraved, corrupt; **~'korken** v/t. (no -ge-, h) cork (up).

ver'körper|n v/t. (no -ge-, h) personify, embody; represent; *esp. thea.* impersonate; **2ung** f (-/-en) personification, embodiment; impersonation.

ver'|krachen F v/refl. (no -ge-, h) fall out (*mit* with); **~'krampft** *adj.* cramped; **~'kriechen** v/refl. (*irr.* kriechen, no -ge-, h) hide; **~'krümmt** *adj.* crooked; **~'krüppelt** *adj.* [~'krYpəlt] crippled; stunted; **~krustet** *adj.* [~'krʊstət] (en)crusted; caked; **~'kühlen** v/refl. (no -ge-, h) catch (a) cold.

ver'kümmer|n v/i. (no -ge-, sein) ❀, 🐾 become stunted; 🐾 atrophy; *fig.* waste away; **~t** *adj.* stunted; atrophied; rudimentary (*a. biol.*).

verkünd|en [fɛr'kYndən] v/t. (no -ge-, h), **~igen** v/t. (no -ge-, h) announce; publish, proclaim; pronounce (*judgement*); **2igung** f, **2ung** f (-/-en) announcement; proclamation; pronouncement.

ver'|kuppeln v/t. (no -ge-, h) ⊕ couple; *fig.* pander; **~'kürzen** v/t. (no -ge-, h) shorten; abridge; beguile (*time, etc.*); **~'lachen** v/t. (no -ge-, h) laugh at; **~'laden** v/t. (*irr.* laden, no -ge-, h) load, ship; 🚂 entrain (*esp. troops*).

Verlag [fɛr'la:k] m (-[e]s/-e) publishing house, *the* publishers *pl.*; *im* ~ *von* published by.

ver'lagern v/t. (no -ge-, h) displace, shift; *sich* ~ shift.

Ver'lags|buchhändler m publisher; **~buchhandlung** f publishing house; **~recht** n copyright.

ver'langen 1. v/t. (no -ge-, h) demand; require; desire; **2.** v/i. (no -ge-, h): ~ *nach* ask for; long for; **3.** 2 n (-s/~ -) desire; longing (*nach* for); demand, request; *auf* ~ by request, ✝ on demand; *auf* ~ *von* at the request of, at *s.o.'s* request.

verlänger|n [fɛr'lɛŋərn] v/t. (no

-ge-, h) lengthen; prolong, extend; Qung f (-/-en) lengthening; prolongation, extension.

ver'langsamen v/t. (no -ge-, h) slacken, slow down.

ver'lassen v/t. (irr. lassen, no -ge-, h) leave; forsake, abandon, desert; sich ~ auf (acc.) rely on; Qheit f (-/no pl.) abandonment; loneliness.

verläßlich adj. [fer'lɛslic] reliable.

Ver'lauf m lapse, course (of time); progress, development (of matter); course (of disease, etc.); im ~ (gen.) or von in the course of; e-n schlimmen ~ nehmen take a bad turn; Qen (irr. laufen, no -ge-) 1. v/i. (sein) time: pass, elapse; matter: take its course; turn out, develop; road, etc.: run, extend; 2. v/refl. (h) lose one's way, go astray; crowd: disperse; water: subside.

ver'lauten v/i. (no -ge-, sein): ~ lassen give to understand, hint; wie verlautet as reported.

ver'leb|en v/t. (no -ge-, h) spend, pass; ~t adj. [~pt] worn out.

ver'leg|en 1. v/t. (no -ge-, h) mislay; transfer, shift, remove; ⊕ lay (cable, etc.); bar (road); put off, postpone; publish (book); sich ~ auf (acc.) apply o.s. to; 2. adj. embarrassed; at a loss (um for answer, etc.); Qenheit f (-/-en) embarrassment; difficulty; predicament; Qer m (-s/-) publisher; Qung (-/-en) transfer, removal; ⊕ laying; time: postponement.

ver'leiden v/t. (no -ge-, h) s. verekeln.

ver'leih|en v/t. (irr. leihen, no -ge-, h) lend, Am. a. loan; hire or let out; bestow (right, etc.) (j-m on s.o.); award (price); Qung f (-/-en) lending, loan; bestowal.

ver'leiten v/t. (no -ge-, h) mislead; induce; seduce; ⟨♫ suborn; ~'lernen v/t. (no -ge-, h) unlearn, forget; ~'lesen v/t. (irr. lesen, no -ge-, h) read out; call (names) over; pick (vegetables, etc.); sich ~ read wrong.

verletz|en [fɛr'lɛtsən] v/t. (no -ge-, h) hurt, injure; fig. a.: offend; violate; ~end adj. offensive; Qte [~tə] m, f (-n/-n) injured person; die ~n pl. the injured pl.; Qung f (-/-en) hurt, injury, wound; fig. violation.

ver'leugn|en v/t. (no -ge-, h) deny; disown; renounce (belief, principle, etc.); sich ~ lassen have o.s. denied (vor j-m to s.o.); Qung f (-/-en) denial; renunciation.

verleumd|en [fɛr'lɔymdən] v/t. (no -ge-, h) slander, defame; ~erisch adj. slanderous; Qung f (-/-en) slander, defamation, in writing: libel.

ver'lieb|en v/refl. (no -ge-, h): sich ~ in (acc.) fall in love with; ~t adj.

[~pt] in love (in acc. with); amorous; Qtheit f (-/~-en) amorousness.

verlieren [fɛr'li:rən] (irr., no -ge-, h) 1. v/t. lose (leaves, etc.); sich ~ lose o.s.; disappear; 2. v/i. lose.

ver'lob|en v/t. (no -ge-, h) engage (mit to); sich ~ become engaged; Qte [~ptə] (-n/-n) 1. m fiancé; die ~n pl. the engaged couple sg.; 2. f fiancée; Qung f (-/-en) engagement.

ver'lock|en v/t. (no -ge-, h) allure, entice; tempt; ~end adj. tempting; Qung f (-/-en) allurement, enticement.

verlogen adj. [fɛr'lo:gən] mendacious; Qheit f (-/~-en) mendacity.

verlor [fɛr'lo:r] pret. of verlieren; ~en 1. p.p. of verlieren; 2. adj. lost; fig. forlorn; ~e Eier poached eggs; ~engehen v/i. (irr. gehen, sep., -ge-, sein) be lost.

ver'los|en v/t. (no -ge-, h) raffle; Qung f (-/-en) lottery, raffle.

ver'löten v/t. (no -ge-, h) solder.

Verlust [fɛr'lust] m (-es/-e) loss; ~e pl. ⚔ casualties pl.

ver'machen v/t. (no -ge-, h) bequeath, leave s.th. (dat. to).

Vermächtnis [fɛr'mɛçtnis] n (-ses/-se) will; legacy, bequest.

vermähl|en [fɛr'mɛ:lən] v/t. (no -ge-, h) marry (mit to); sich ~ (mit) marry (s.o.); Qung f (-/-en) wedding, marriage.

ver'mehr|en v/t. (no -ge-, h) increase (um by), augment; multiply; add to; durch Zucht ~ propagate; breed; sich ~ increase, augment; multiply (a. biol.); propagate (itself), zo. breed; Qung f (-/~-en) increase; addition (gen. to); propagation.

ver'meid|en v/t. (irr. meiden, no -ge-, h) avoid; Qung f (-/~-en) avoidance.

ver'meintlich adj. [fɛr'maintliç] supposed; ~'mengen v/t. (no -ge-, h) mix, mingle, blend.

Vermerk [fɛr'mɛrk] m (-[e]s/-e) note, entry; Qen v/t. (no -ge-, h) note down, record.

ver'mess|en 1. v/t. (irr. messen, no -ge-, h) measure; survey (land); 2. adj. presumptuous; Qenheit f (-/~-en) presumption; Qung f (-/-en) measurement; survey (of land).

ver'miete|n v/t. (no -ge-, h) let, esp. Am. rent; hire (out); lease; zu ~ on or for hire; Haus zu ~ house to (be) let; Qr m landlord, ♫♫ lessor; letter, hirer.

ver'mindern v/t. (no -ge-, h) diminish, lessen; reduce, cut.

ver'misch|en v/t. (no -ge-, h) mix, mingle, blend; ~t adj. mixed; news, *etc.*: miscellaneous; 2ung *f* (-/&-en) mixture.

ver'mi|ssen *v/t.* (*no* -ge-, *h*) miss; ~ßt *adj.* [~'mist] missing; 2ßte *m, f* (-n/-n) missing person; *die* ~n *pl.* the missing *pl.*

vermitt|eln [fɛr'mitəln] (*no* -ge-, *h*) 1. *v/t.* mediate (*settlement, peace*); procure, get; give (*impression, etc.*); impart (*knowledge*) (*j-m* to *s.o.*); 2. *v/i.* mediate (*zwischen dat.* between); intercede (*bei* with, *für* for), intervene; 2ler *m* mediator; go-between; † agent; 2lung *f* (-/-en) mediation; intercession, intervention; *teleph.* (telephone) exchange.

ver'modern *v/i.* (*no* -ge-, *sein*) mo(u)lder, decay, rot.

ver'mögen 1. *v/t.* (*irr.* mögen, *no* -ge-, *h*): ~ *zu inf.* be able to *inf.*; et. ~ *bei j-m* have influence with *s.o.*; 2. 2 *n* (-s/-) ability, power; property; fortune; means *pl.*, ½½ assets *pl.*; ~d *adj.* wealthy; *pred.* well off; 2sverhältnisse *pl.* pecuniary circumstances *pl.*

vermut|en [fɛr'mu:tən] *v/t.* (*no* -ge-, *h*) suppose, presume, *Am. a.* guess; conjecture, surmise; ~lich 1. *adj.* presumable; 2. *adv.* presumably; I suppose; 2ung *f* (-/-en) supposition, presumption; conjecture, surmise.

vernachlässig|en [fɛr'nɑ:xlɛsigən] *v/t.* (*no* -ge-, *h*) neglect; 2ung *f* (-/&-en) neglect(ing).

ver'narben *v/i.* (*no* -ge-, *sein*) cicatrize, scar over. [with.]

ver'narrt *adj.*: ~ *in* (*acc.*) infatuated]

ver'nehm|en [fɛr'ne:mən] *v/t.* (*no* -ge-, *h*) hear, learn; examine, interrogate; ~lich *adj.* audible, distinct; 2ung ½½ *f* (-/-en) interrogation; questioning; examination.

ver'neig|en *v/refl.* (*no* -ge-, *h*) bow (*vor dat.* to); 2ung *f* bow.

vernein|en [fɛr'naɪnən] (*no* -ge-, *h*) 1. *v/t.* answer in the negative; deny; 2. *v/i.* answer in the negative; ~end *adj.* negative; 2ung *f* (-/-en) negation; denial; *gr.* negative.

vernicht|en [fɛr'niçtən] *v/t.* (*no* -ge-, *h*) annihilate; destroy; dash (*hopes*); ~end *adj.* destructive (*a. fig.*); *look*: withering; *criticism*: scathing; *defeat, reply*: crushing; 2ung *f* (-/&-en) annihilation; destruction.

ver|nickeln [fɛr'nikəln] *v/t.* (*no* -ge-, *h*) nickel(-plate); ~'nieten *v/t.* (*no* -ge-, *h*) rivet.

Vernunft [fɛr'nunft] *f* (-/*no pl.*) reason; ~ *annehmen* listen to *or* hear reason; *j-n zur* ~ *bringen* bring *s.o.* to reason *or* to his senses.

vernünftig *adj.* [fɛr'nynftiç] rational; reasonable; sensible.

ver'öden (*no* -ge-) 1. *v/t.* (*h*) make

desolate; 2. *v/i.* (*sein*) become desolate.

ver'öffentlich|en *v/t.* (*no* -ge-, *h*) publish; 2ung *f* (-/-en) publication.

ver'ordn|en *v/t.* (*no* -ge-, *h*) decree; order (*a.* ﷼); ﷼ prescribe (*j-m* to *or* for *s.o.*); 2ung *f* decree, order; ﷼ prescription.

ver'pachten *v/t.* (*no* -ge-, *h*) rent, ½½ lease (*building, land*).

Ver'pächter *m* landlord, ½½ lessor.

ver'pack|en *v/t.* (*no* -ge-, *h*) pack (up); wrap up; 2ung *f* packing (material); wrapping.

ver|'passen *v/t.* (*no* -ge-, *h*) miss (*train, opportunity, etc.*); ~patzen F [~'patsən] *v/t.* (*no* -ge-, *h*) *s.* verpfuschen; ~'pesten *v/t.* (*no* -ge-, *h*) *fumes*: contaminate (*the air*); ~'pfänden *v/t.* (*no* -ge-, *h*) pawn, pledge (*a. fig.*); mortgage.

ver'pflanz|en *v/t.* (*no* -ge-, *h*) transplant (*a.* ﷼); 2ung *f* transplantation; ﷼ *a.* transplant.

ver'pfleg|en *v/t.* (*no* -ge-, *h*) board; supply with food, victual; 2ung *f* (-/&-en) board; food-supply; provisions *pl.*

ver'pflicht|en *v/t.* (*no* -ge-, *h*) oblige; engage; 2ung *f* (-/-en) obligation, duty; †, ½½ liability; engagement, commitment.

ver'pfusch|en F *v/t.* (*no* -ge-, *h*) bungle, botch; make a mess of; ~t *adj. life*: ruined, wrecked.

ver|pönt *adj.* [fɛr'pø:nt] taboo; ~'prügeln F *v/t.* (*no* -ge-, *h*) thrash, flog, F wallop; ~'puffen *fig. v/i.* (*no* -ge-, *h*) fizzle out.

Ver'putz △ *m* (-es/&-e) plaster; 2en △ *v/t.* (*no* -ge-, *h*) plaster.

ver|'quicken [fɛr'kvikən] *v/t.* (*no* -ge-, *h*) mix up; ~'quollen *adj. wood*: warped; *face*: bloated; *eyes*: swollen; ~'rammeln [~'raməln] *v/t.* (*no* -ge-, *h*) bar(ricade).

Verrat [fɛr'ra:t] *m* (-[e]s/*no pl.*) betrayal (*an dat.* of); treachery (to); ½½ treason (to); 2en *v/t.* (*irr.* raten, *no* -ge-, *h*) betray, give *s.o.* away; give away (*secret*); *sich* ~ betray *o.s.*, give *o.s.* away.

Verräter [fɛr'rɛ:tər] *m* (-s/-) traitor (*an dat.* to); 2isch *adj.* treacherous; *fig.* telltale.

ver'rechn|en *v/t.* (*no* -ge-, *h*) reckon up; charge; settle; set off (*mit* against); account for; ~ *mit* offset against; *sich* ~ miscalculate, make a mistake (*a. fig.*); *fig.* be mistaken; *sich um e-e Mark* ~ be one mark out; 2ung *f* settlement; clearing; booking *or* charging (*to account*); 2ungsscheck *m* collection-only cheque *or* Am. check.

ver'regnet *adj.* rainy, rain-spoilt.

ver'reis|en *v/i.* (*no* -ge-, *sein*) go on a journey; ~t *adj.* out of town; (*geschäftlich*) ~ away (on business).

verrenk|en [fɛr'rɛŋkən] v/t. (no -ge-, h) ⚕: wrench; dislocate, luxate; sich et. ⚕ dislocate or luxate s.th.; sich den Hals ~ crane one's neck; ⚥ung ⚕ f (-/-en) dislocation, luxation.

ver|'richten v/t. (no -ge-, h) do, perform; execute; sein Gebet ~ say one's prayer(s); ~'riegeln v/t. (no -ge-, h) bolt, bar.

verringer|n [fɛr'rɪŋərn] v/t. (no -ge-, h) diminish, lessen; reduce, cut; sich ~ diminish, lessen; ⚥ung f (-/-en) diminution; reduction, cut.

ver|'rosten v/i. (no -ge-, sein) rust; ~rotten [~'rɔtən] v/i. (no -ge-, sein) rot.

ver|'rück|en v/t. (no -ge-, h) displace, (re)move, shift; ~t adj. mad, crazy (both a. fig.: nach about); wie ~ like mad; j-n ~ machen drive s.o. mad; ⚥te (-n/-n) 1. m lunatic, madman; 2. f lunatic, madwoman; ⚥theit f (-/-en) madness; foolish action; craze.

Ver|'ruf m (-[e]s/no pl.): in ~ bringen bring discredit (up)on; in ~ kommen get into discredit; ⚥en adj. ill-reputed, ill-famed.

ver|'rutsch|en v/i. (no -ge-, sein) slip; ~t adj. not straight.

Vers [fɛrs] m (-es/-e) verse.

ver|'sagen 1. v/t. (no -ge-, h) refuse, deny (j-m et. s.o. s.th.); sich et. ~ deny o.s. s.th.; **2.** v/i. (no -ge-, h) fail, break down; gun: misfire; **3.** ⚥ n (-s/no pl.) failure. [ure.]

Ver|'sager m (-s/-) misfire; p. fail-)

ver|'salzen v/t. (irr. salzen, no -ge-, h) oversalt; F fig. spoil.

ver|'samm|eln v/t. (no -ge-, h) assemble; sich ~ assemble, meet; ⚥lung f assembly, meeting.

Versand [fɛr'zant] m (-[e]s/no pl.) dispatch, Am. a. shipment; mailing; ~ ins Ausland a. export(ation); ~abteilung f forwarding department; ~geschäft n, ~haus n mailorder business or firm or house.

ver|'säum|en v/t. (no -ge-, h) neglect (one's duty, etc.); miss (opportunity, etc.); lose (time); ~ zu inf. fail or omit to inf.; ⚥nis n (-ses/-se) neglect, omission, failure.

ver|'schachern F v/t. (no -ge-, h) barter (away); ~'schaffen v/t. (no -ge-, h) procure, get; sich ~ obtain, get; raise (money); sich Respekt ~ make o.s. respected; ~'schämt adj. bashful; ~'schanzen v/refl. (no -ge-, h) entrench o.s.; sich ~ hinter (dat.) (take) shelter behind; ~'schärfen v/t. (no -ge-, h) heighten, intensify; aggravate; sich ~ get worse; ~'scheiden v/i. (irr. scheiden, no -ge-, sein) pass away; ~'schenken v/t. (no -ge-, h) give s.th. away; make a present of; ~'scherzen v/t. and v/refl. (no

-ge-, h) forfeit; ~'scheuchen v/t. (no -ge-, h) frighten or scare away; fig. banish; ~'schicken v/t. (no -ge-, h) send (away), dispatch, forward.

ver|'schieb|en v/t. (irr. schieben, no -ge-, h) displace, shift, (re)move; 🚂 shunt; put off, postpone; F fig. † sell underhand; sich ~ shift; ⚥ung f shift(ing); postponement.

verschieden adj. [fɛr'ʃiːdən] different (von from); dissimilar, unlike; aus ~en Gründen for various or several reasons; Verschiedenes various things pl., esp. † sundries pl.; ~artig adj. of a different kind, various; ⚥heit f (-/-en) difference; diversity, variety; ~tlich adv. repeatedly; at times.

ver|'schiff|en v/t. (no -ge-, h) ship; ⚥ung f (-/⚒-en) shipment.

ver|'schimmeln v/i. (no -ge-, sein) get mo(u)ldy, Am. mo(u)ld; ~'schlafen 1. v/t. (irr. schlafen, no -ge-, h) miss by sleeping; sleep off (afternoon, etc.) away; sleep off (headache, etc.); 2. v/i. (irr. schlafen, no -ge-, h) oversleep (o.s.); 3. adj. sleepy, drowsy.

Ver|'schlag m shed; box; crate; ⚥en [~gən] 1. v/t. (irr. schlagen, no -ge-, h) board up; nail up; es verschlug ihm die Sprache it dum(b)founded him; 2. adj. cunning; eyes: a. shifty; ~enheit f (-/no pl.) cunning.

verschlechter|n [fɛr'ʃlɛçtərn] v/t. (no -ge-, h) deteriorate, make worse; sich ~ deteriorate, get worse; ⚥ung f (-/⚒-en) deterioration; change for the worse.

ver|'schleiern v/t. (no -ge-, h) veil (a. fig.).

Verschleiß [fɛr'ʃlaɪs] m (-es/⚒-e) wear (and tear); ⚥en v/t. ([irr.,] no -ge-, h) wear out.

ver|'schleppen v/t. (no -ge-, h) carry off; pol. displace (person); abduct, kidnap; delay, protract; neglect (disease); ~'schleudern v/t. (no -ge-, h) dissipate, waste; † sell at a loss, sell dirt-cheap; ~'schließen v/t. (irr. schließen, no -ge-, h) shut, close; lock (door); lock up (house).

verschlimmern [fɛr'ʃlɪmərn] v/t. (no -ge-, h) make worse, aggravate; sich ~ get worse.

ver|'schlingen v/t. (irr. schlingen, no -ge-, h) devour; wolf (down) (one's food); intertwine, entwine, interlace; sich ~ intertwine, entwine, interlace.

verschli|ß [fɛr'ʃlɪs] pret. of verschleißen; ~ssen [~sən] p.p. of verschleißen.

verschlossen adj. [fɛr'ʃlɔsən] closed, shut; fig. reserved; ⚥heit f (-/no pl.) reserve.

ver'schlucken v/t. (no -ge-, h) swallow (up); **sich ~** swallow the wrong way.

Ver'schluß m lock; clasp; lid; plug; stopper (of bottle); seal; fastener, fastening; phot. shutter; **unter ~** under lock and key.

ver|'schmachten v/i. (no -ge-, sein) languish, pine away; **vor Durst ~** die or be dying of thirst, be parched with thirst; **~'schmähen** v/t. (no -ge-, h) disdain, scorn.

ver'schmelz|en (irr. schmelzen, no -ge-) v/t. (h) and v/i. (sein) melt, fuse (a. fig.); blend; fig.: amalgamate; merge (mit in, into); **2ung** f (-/-en) fusion; ✝ merger; fig. amalgamation.

ver|'schmerzen v/t. (no -ge-, h) get over (the loss of); **~'schmieren** v/t. (no -ge-, h) smear (over); blur; **~schmitzt** adj. ['~∫mitst] cunning; roguish; arch; **~'schmutzen** (no -ge-) 1. v/t. (h) soil, dirty; pollute (water); 2. v/i. (sein) get dirty; **~'schnaufen** F v/i. and v/refl. (no -ge-, h) stop for breath; **~'schneiden** v/t. (irr. schneiden, no -ge-, h) cut badly; blend (wine, etc.); geld, castrate; **~'schneit** adj. covered with snow; mountains: a. snow-capped; roofs: a. snow-covered.

Ver'schnitt m (-[e]s/no pl.) blend.

ver'schnupf|en F fig. v/t. (no -ge-, h) nettle, pique; ~t ✱ adj.: **~ sein** have a cold.

ver|'schnüren v/t. (no -ge-, h) tie up, cord; **~schollen** adj. [~'∫ɔlən] not heard of again; missing; ⚖ presumed dead; **~'schonen** v/t. (no -ge-, h) spare; **j-n mit et. ~** spare s.o. s.th.

verschöne|(r)n [fɛr'∫ø:nə(r)n] v/t. (no -ge-, h) embellish, beautify; **2rung** f (-/-en) embellishment.

ver|schossen adj. [fɛr'∫ɔsən] colour: faded; F **~ sein** in (acc.) be madly in love with; **~schränken** [~'∫rɛŋkən] v/t. (no -ge-, h) cross, fold (one's arms).

ver|schreib|en v/t. (irr. schreiben, no -ge-, h) use up (in writing); 🕮 prescribe (j-m for s.o.); ⚖ assign (j-m to s.o.); **sich ~** make a slip of the pen; **sich e-r Sache ~** devote o.s. to s.th.; **2ung** f (-/-en) assignment; prescription.

ver|schroben adj. [fɛr'∫ro:bən] eccentric, queer, odd; **~'schrotten** v/t. (no -ge-, h) scrap; **~schüchtert** adj. [~'∫yçtərt] intimidated.

ver'schulden 1. v/t. (no -ge-, h) be guilty of; be the cause of; **2. 2** n (-s/no pl.) fault.

ver|'schuldet adj. indebted, in debt; **~'schütten** v/t. (no -ge-, h) spill (liquid); block (up) (road); bury s.o. alive; **~schwägert** adj. [~'∫vɛ:gərt] related by marriage;

~'schweigen v/t. (irr. schweigen, no -ge-, h) conceal (j-m et. s.th. from s.o.).

verschwend|en [fɛr'∫vendən] v/t. (no -ge-, h) waste, squander (an acc. on); lavish (on); **2er** m (-s/-) spendthrift, prodigal; **~erisch** adj. prodigal, lavish (both: mit of); wasteful; **2ung** f (-/⚹-en) waste; extravagance.

ver|'schwiegen adj. discreet; place: secret, secluded; **2heit** f (-/no pl.) discretion; secrecy.

ver|'schwimmen v/i. (irr. schwimmen, no -ge-, sein) become indistinct or blurred; **~'schwinden** v/i. (irr. schwinden, no -ge-, sein) disappear, vanish; F verschwinde! go away!, sl. beat it!; **2'schwinden** n (-s/no pl.) disappearance; **~schwommen** adj. [~'∫vɔmən] vague (a. fig.); blurred; fig. woolly.

ver|'schwör|en v/refl. (irr. schwören, no -ge-, h) conspire; **2er** m (-s/-) conspirator; **2ung** f (-/-en) conspiracy, plot.

ver'sehen 1. v/t. (irr. sehen, no -ge-, h) fill (an office); look after (house, etc.); **mit et. ~** furnish or supply with; **sich ~** make a mistake; **ehe man sich's versieht** all of a sudden; **2. 2** n (-s/-) oversight, mistake, slip; **aus ~ = ~tlich** adv. by mistake; inadvertently.

Versehrte [fɛr'ze:rtə] m (-n/-n) disabled person.

ver'send|en v/t. ([irr. senden,] no -ge-, h) send, dispatch, forward, Am. ship; by water: ship; **ins Ausland ~** a. export; **2ung** f (-/⚹-en) dispatch, shipment, forwarding.

ver|'sengen v/t. (no -ge-, h) singe, scorch; **~'senken** v/t. (no -ge-, h) sink; **sich ~ in** (acc.) immerse o.s. in; **~sessen** adj. [~'zesən]: **~ auf** (acc.) bent on, mad after.

ver'setz|en v/t. (no -ge-, h) displace, remove; transfer (officer); at school: remove, move up, Am. promote; transplant (tree, etc.); pawn, pledge; F fig. stand (lover, etc.) up; **~ in** (acc.) put or place into (situation, condition); **j-m e-n Schlag ~** give or deal s.o. a blow; **in Angst ~** frighten or terrify s.o.; **in den Ruhestand ~** pension s.o. off, retire s.o.; **versetzt werden** be transferred; at school: go up; **~ Sie sich in meine Lage** put or place yourself in my position; **Wein mit Wasser ~** mix wine with water, add water to wine; **et. ~** reply s.th.; **2ung** f (-/-en) removal; transfer; at school: remove, Am. promotion.

ver'seuch|en v/t. (no -ge-, h) infect; contaminate; **2ung** f (-/⚹-en) infection; contamination.

ver'sicher|n v/t. (no -ge-, h) assure

(*a. one's life*); protest, affirm; insure (*one's property or life*); *sich ~* insure *or* assure o.s.; *sich ~* (*, daß*) make sure (that); 2te *m*, *f* (*-n*/*-n*) insurant, the insured *or* assured, policy-holder; 2ung *f* assurance, affirmation; insurance; (life-)assurance; insurance company.

Ver'sicherungs|gesellschaft *f* insurance company; ~**police** *f*, ~**schein** *m* policy of assurance, insurance policy.

ver'|sickern *v/i.* (*no -ge-, sein*) trickle away; ~**siegeln** *v/t.* (*no -ge-, h*) seal (up); ~**siegen** *v/i.* (*no -ge-, sein*) dry up, run dry; ~**silbern** *v/t.* (*no -ge-, h*) silver; F *fig.* realize, convert into cash; ~**'sinken** *v/i.* (*irr. sinken, no -ge-, sein*) sink; *s.* versunken; *s.* **sinnbildlichen** *v/t.* (*no -ge-, h*) symbolize.

Version [vɛr'zjoːn] *f* (*-/-en*) version.
'Versmaß *n* met|re, *Am.* -er.
versöhn|en [fɛr'zøːnən] *v/t.* (*no -ge-, h*) reconcile (*mit* to, with); *sich* (*wieder*) ~ become reconciled; ~**lich** *adj.* conciliatory; 2ung *f* (*-/-*~ *-en*) reconciliation.

ver'sorg|en *v/t.* (*no -ge-, h*) provide (*mit* with), supply (with); take care of, look after; ~**t** *adj.* [~kt] provided for; 2ung [~guŋ] *f* (*-/-en*) providing (*mit* with), supplying (with); supply, provision.

ver'spät|en *v/refl.* (*no -ge-, h*) be late; ~**et** *adj.* belated, late, *Am.* tardy; 2ung *f* (*-/-en*) lateness, *Am.* tardiness; ~ *haben* be late; *mit* 2 *Stunden* ~ two hours behind schedule.

ver'|speisen *v/t.* (*no -ge-, h*) eat (up); ~**'sperren** *v/t.* (*no -ge-, h*) lock (up); bar, block (up), obstruct (*a. view*); ~**'spielen** *v/t.* (*no -ge-, h*) *at cards, etc.*: lose (*money*); ~**'spielt** *adj.* playful; ~**'spotten** *v/t.* (*no -ge-, h*) scoff at, mock (at), deride, ridicule; ~**'sprechen** *v/t.* (*irr. sprechen, no -ge-, h*) promise; *sich* ~ make a mistake in speaking; *sich viel ~ von* expect much of; 2**'sprechen** *n* (*-s/*~*-*) promise; ~**'sprühen** *v/t.* (*no -ge-, h*) spray; ~**'spüren** *v/t.* (*no -ge-, h*) feel; perceive, be conscious of.

ver'staatlich|en *v/t.* (*no -ge-, h*) nationalize; 2ung *f* (*-/*~*-en*) nationalization.

Verstand [fɛr'ʃtant] *m* (*-[e]s/no pl.*) understanding; intelligence, intellect, brains *pl.*; mind, wits *pl.*; reason; (common) sense.

Verstandes|kraft [fɛr'ʃtandəs-] *f* intellectual power *or* faculty; 2**mäßig** *adj.* rational; intellectual; ~**mensch** *m* matter-of-fact person.

verständ|ig *adj.* [fɛr'ʃtɛndɪç] intelligent; reasonable, sensible; judi-

cious; ~**igen** [~gən] *v/t.* (*no -ge-, h*) inform (*von* of), notify (of); *sich mit j-m* ~ make o.s. understood to s.o.; come to an understanding with s.o.; 2**igung** [~guŋ] *f* (*-/*~*-en*) information; understanding, agreement; *teleph.* communication; ~**lich** *adj.* [~tlɪç] intelligible; understandable; *j-m et.* ~ *machen* make s.th. clear to s.o.; *sich* ~ *machen* make o.s. understood.

Verständnis [fɛr'ʃtɛntnɪs] *n* (*-ses/*~ *-se*) comprehension, understanding; insight; appreciation (*für* of); ~ *haben für* appreciate; 2**los** *adj.* uncomprehending; *look, etc.*: blank; unappreciative; 2**voll** *adj.* understanding; appreciative; sympathetic; *look*: knowing.

ver'stärk|en *v/t.* (*no -ge-, h*) strengthen, reinforce (*a.* ⊕, ✕); amplify (*radio signals, etc.*); intensify; 2**er** *m* (*-s/-*) *in radio, etc.*: amplifier; 2**ung** *f* (*-/*~*-en*) strengthening, reinforcement (*a.* ✕); amplification; intensification.

ver'staub|en *v/i.* (*no -ge-, sein*) get dusty; ~**t** *adj.* [~pt] dusty.

ver'stauch|en *v/t.* (*no -ge-, h*) sprain; *sich den Fuß* ~ sprain one's foot; 2**ung** ✆ *f* (*-/-en*) sprain.

ver'stauen *v/t.* (*no -ge-, h*) stow away.

Versteck [fɛr'ʃtɛk] *n* (*-[e]s/-e*) hiding-place; *for gangsters, etc.*: *Am.* F *a.* hide-out; ~ *spielen* play at hide-and-seek; 2**en** *v/t.* (*no -ge-, h*) hide, conceal; *sich* ~ hide.

ver'stehen *v/t.* (*irr. stehen, no -ge-, h*) understand, see, F get; comprehend; realize; know (*language*); *es* ~ *zu inf.* know how to *inf.*; *Spaß* ~ take a joke; *zu* ~ *geben* intimate; ~ *Sie?* do you see?; *ich* ~! I see!; *verstanden?* (do you) understood?, F (do you) get me?; *falsch* ~ misunderstand; ~ *Sie mich recht!* don't misunderstand me!; *was* ~ *Sie unter* (*dat.*)? what do you mean *or* understand by ...?; *er versteht et. davon* he knows a thing or two about it; *sich* ~ understand one another; *sich* ~ *auf* (*acc.*) know well, be an expert at *or* in; *sich mit j-m gut* ~ get on well with s.o.; *es versteht sich von selbst* it goes without saying.

ver'steifen *v/t.* (*no -ge-, h*) ⊕ strut, brace; stiffen; *sich* ~ stiffen; *sich* ~ *auf* (*acc.*) make a point of, insist on.

ver'steiger|n *v/t.* (*no -ge-, h*) (sell by *or Am.* at) auction; 2**ung** *f* (sale by *or Am.* at) auction, auction-sale.

ver'steinern (*no -ge-*) *v/t.* (*h*) *and v/i.* (*sein*) turn into stone, petrify (*both a. fig.*).

ver'stell|bar *adj.* adjustable; ~**en** *v/t.* (*no -ge-, h*) shift; adjust; disarrange; bar, block (up), obstruct; disguise (*voice*, *etc.*); *sich* ~ play *or* act a part; dissemble, feign; 2ung *f* (-/~-en) disguise; dissimulation.

ver'|steuern *v/t.* (*no* -ge-, *h*) pay duty *or* tax on; ~stiegen *fig. adj.* [~'fti:gǝn] eccentric.

ver'stimm|en *v/t.* (*no* -ge-, *h*) put out of tune; *fig.* put out of humo(u)r; ~t *adj.* out of tune; *fig.* out of humo(u)r, F cross; 2ung *f* ill humo(u)r; disagreement; ill feeling.

ver'stockt *adj.* stubborn, obdurate; 2heit *f* (-/*no pl.*) obduracy.

verstohlen *adj.* [fɛr'fto:lǝn] furtive.

ver'stopf|en *v/t.* (*no* -ge-, *h*) stop (up); clog, block (up), obstruct; jam, block (*passage*, *street*); ✚ constipate; 2ung *f* ✚ (-/~-en) constipation.

verstorben *adj.* [fɛr'ftɔrbǝn] late, deceased; 2e *m*, *f* (-n/-n) the deceased, *Am.* ✚ *a.* decedent; die ~n *pl.* the deceased *pl.*, the departed *pl.*

ver'stört *adj.* scared; distracted, bewildered; 2heit *f* (-/*no pl.*) distraction, bewilderment.

Ver'stoß *m* offen|ce, *Am.* -se; contravention (*gegen* of *law*); infringement (on *trade name*, *etc.*); blunder; 2en (*irr.* stoßen, *no* -ge-, *h*) 1. *v/t.* expel (*aus* from); repudiate, disown (*wife*, *child*, *etc.*); 2. *v/i.*: ~ *gegen* offend against; contravene (*law*); infringe (*rule*, *etc.*).

ver'|streichen (*irr.* streichen, *no* -ge-) 1. *v/i.* (*sein*) *time*: pass, elapse; expire; 2. *v/t.* (*h*) spread (*butter*, *etc.*); ~'streuen *v/t.* (*no* -ge-, *h*) scatter.

verstümmel|n [fɛr'ftymǝln] *v/t.* (*no* -ge-, *h*) mutilate; garble (*text*, *etc.*); 2ung *f* (-/-en) mutilation.

ver'stummen *v/i.* (*no* -ge-, *sein*) grow silent *or* dumb.

Verstümmlung [fɛr'ftymluŋ] *f* (-/-en) mutilation.

Versuch [fɛr'zu:x] *m* (-[e]s/-e) attempt, trial; *phys.*, *etc.*: experiment; e-n ~ *machen mit* give *s.o.* or *s.th.* a trial; try one's hand at *s.th.*, have a go at *s.th.*; 2en *v/t.* (*no* -ge-, *h*) try, attempt; taste; *j-n* ~ tempt *s.o.*; *es* ~ *mit* give *s.o.* or *s.th.* a trial.

Ver'suchs|anstalt *f* research institute; ~kaninchen *fig. n* guinea-pig; 2weise *adv.* by way of trial *or* (an) experiment; on trial; ~zweck *m*: *zu* ~en *pl.* for experimental purposes *pl.*

Ver'suchung *f* (-/-en) temptation; *j-n in* ~ *bringen* tempt *s.o.*; *in* ~ *sein* be tempted.

ver'|sündigen *v/refl.* (*no* -ge-, *h*) sin (*an dat.* against); ~sunken *fig. adj.* [~'zuŋkǝn]: ~ *in* (acc.) absorbed

or lost in; ~'süßen *v/t.* (*no* -ge-, *h*) sweeten.

ver'tag|en *v/t.* (*no* -ge-, *h*) adjourn; *parl.* prorogue; *sich* ~ adjourn, *Am. a.* recess; 2ung *f* adjournment; *parl.* prorogation.

ver'tauschen *v/t.* (*no* -ge-, *h*) exchange (*mit* for).

verteidig|en [fɛr'taidigǝn] *v/t.* (*no* -ge-, *h*) defend; *sich* ~ defend *o.s.*; 2er *m* (-s/-) defender; ⚖, *fig.* advocate; ⚖ counsel for the defen|ce, *Am.* -se, *Am.* attorney for the defendant *or* defense; *football*: fullback; 2ung *f* (-/~-en) defen|ce, *Am.* -se.

Ver'teidigungs|bündnis *n* defensive alliance; ~minister *m* minister of defence; *Brt.* Minister of Defence, *Am.* Secretary of Defense; ~ministerium *n* ministry of defence; *Brt.* Ministry of Defence, *Am.* Department of Defense.

ver'teil|en *v/t.* (*no* -ge-, *h*) distribute; spread (*colour*, *etc.*); 2er *m* (-s/-) distributor; 2ung *f* (-/~-en) distribution.

ver'teuern *v/t.* (*no* -ge-, *h*) raise *or* increase the price of.

ver'tief|en *v/t.* (*no* -ge-, *h*) deepen (*a. fig.*); *sich* ~ deepen; *sich* ~ *in* (acc.) plunge in(to); become absorbed in; 2ung *f* (-/-en) hollow, cavity; recess.

vertikal *adj.* [vɛrti'ka:l] vertical.

ver'tilg|en *v/t.* (*no* -ge-, *h*) exterminate; F consume, eat (up) (*food*); 2ung *f* (-/~-en) extermination.

ver'tonen ♪ *v/t.* (*no* -ge-, *h*) set to music.

Vertrag [fɛr'tra:k] *m* (-[e]s/~e) agreement, contract; *pol.* treaty; 2en [~gǝn] *v/t.* (*irr.* tragen, *no* -ge-, *h*) endure, bear, stand; *diese Speise kann ich nicht* ~ this food does not agree with me; *sich* ~ *things*: be compatible *or* consistent; *colours*: harmonize; *p.*: agree; get on with one another; *sich wieder* ~ be reconciled, make it up; 2lich [~kliç] 1. *adj.* contractual, stipulated; 2. *adv.* as stipulated; ~ *verpflichtet sein* be bound by contract; *sich* ~ *verpflichten* contract (*zu* for *s.th.*; *zu inf.* to *inf.*).

verträglich *adj.* [fɛr'trɛ:kliç] sociable.

Ver'trags|bruch *m* breach of contract; 2brüchig *adj.*: ~ *werden* commit a breach of contract; ~entwurf *m* draft agreement; ~partner *m* party to a contract.

ver'trauen 1. *v/i.* (*no* -ge-, *h*) trust (*j-m s.o.*); ~ *auf* (acc.) trust *or* confide in; 2. 2 *n* (-s/*no pl.*) confidence, trust; *im* ~ confidentially, between you and me; ~erweckend *adj.* inspiring confidence; promising.

Ver'trauens|bruch *m* breach *or*

betrayal of trust; ~frage *parl. f*: die ~ *stellen* put the question of confidence; ~mann *m* (-[e]s/~er, Vertrauensleute) spokesman; shop-steward; confidential agent; ~sache *f*: *das ist* ~ that is a matter of confidence; ~stellung *f* position of trust; 2voll *adj.* trustful, trust-ing; ~votum *parl. n* vote of confidence; 2würdig *adj.* trustworthy, reliable.

ver'traulich *adj.* confidential, in confidence; intimate, familiar; 2-keit *f* (-/-en) confidence; intimacy, familiarity.

ver'traut *adj.* intimate, familiar; 2e (-n/-n) 1. *m* confidant, intimate friend; 2. *f* confidante, intimate friend; 2heit *f* (-/~-en) familiarity.

ver'treib|en *v/t.* (*irr. treiben, no* -ge-, *h*) drive away; expel (*aus* from); turn out; ✝ sell, distribute (*goods*); *sich die Zeit* ~ pass one's time, kill time; 2ung *f* (-/~-en) expulsion.

ver'tret|en *v/t.* (*irr. treten, no* -ge-, *h*) represent (*s.o.*, *firm*, *etc.*); sub-stitute for *s.o.*; attend to, look after (*s.o.'s interests*); hold (*view*); *parl.* sit for (*borough*); answer for *s.th.*; *j-s Sache* ~ ⚖ plead *s.o.'s* case *or* cause; *sich den Fuß* ~ sprain one's foot; F *sich die Beine* ~ stretch one's legs; 2er *m* (-s/-) representa-tive; ✝ *a.* agent; proxy, agent; substitute, deputy; exponent; (sales) representative; door-to-door sales-man; commercial travel(l)er, *esp. Am.* travel(l)ing salesman; 2ung *f* (-/-en) representation (*a. pol.*); ✝ agency; *in office*: substitution; *in* ~ by proxy; *gen.*: acting for.

Vertrieb ✝ [fer'tri:p] *m* (-[e]s/-e) sale; distribution; ~ene [~bənə] *m,f* (-n/-n) expellee.

ver'trocknen *v/i.* (*no* -ge-, *sein*) dry up; ~'trödeln F *v/t.* (*no* -ge-, *h*) dawdle away, waste (*time*); ~'trö-sten *v/t.* (*no* -ge-, *h*) put off; ~'tu-schen F *v/t.* (*no* -ge-, *h*) hush up; ~'übeln *v/t.* (*no* -ge-, *h*) take *s.th.* amiss; ~'üben *v/t.* (*no* -ge-, *h*) com-mit, perpetrate.

ver'unglück|en *v/i.* (*no* -ge-, *sein*) meet with *or* have an accident; F *fig.* fail, go wrong; *tödlich* ~ be killed in an accident; 2te *m, f* (-n/-n) casualty.

verun|reinigen [fer'unrainigən] *v/t.* (*no* -ge-, *h*) soil, dirty; defile; contaminate (*air*); pollute (*water*); ~stalten [~ʃtaltən] *v/t.* (*no* -ge-, *h*) disfigure.

ver'untreu|en *v/t.* (*no* -ge-, *h*) em-bezzle; 2ung *f* (-/-en) embezzle-ment.

ver'ursachen *v/t.* (*no* -ge-, *h*) cause.

ver'urteil|en *v/t.* (*no* -ge-, *h*) con-demn (*zu* to) (*a. fig.*), sentence (to);

convict (*wegen* of); 2te *m, f* (-n/-n) convict; 2ung *f* (-/-en) condemna-tion (*a. fig.*), conviction.

ver|vielfältigen [fer'fi:lfɛltigən] *v/t.* (*no* -ge-, *h*) manifold; ~vollkomm-nen [~'fɔlkɔmnən] *v/t.* (*no* -ge-, *h*) perfect; *sich* ~ perfect o.s.

vervollständig|en [fer'fɔlʃtɛndigən] *v/t.* (*no* -ge-, *h*) complete; 2ung *f* (-/~-en) completion.

ver|'wachsen 1. *v/i.* (*irr. wachsen*, *no* -ge-, *sein*): *miteinander* ~ grow together; 2. *adj.* deformed; 🦴 humpbacked, hunchbacked; ~'wackeln *phot. v/t.* (*no* -ge-, *h*) blur.

ver'wahr|en *v/t.* (*no* -ge-, *h*) keep; *sich* ~ *gegen* protest against; ~lost *adj.* [~lo:st] *child, garden, etc.*: uncared-for, neglected; degenerate; 2ung *f* keeping; charge; custody; *fig.* protest; *j-m et. in* ~ *geben* give *s.th.* into *s.o.'s* charge; *in* ~ *nehmen* take charge of.

verwaist *adj.* [fer'vaist] orphan(ed); *fig.* deserted.

ver'walt|en *v/t.* (*no* -ge-, *h*) ad-minister, manage; 2er *m* (-s/-) ad-ministrator, manager; steward (*of estate*); 2ung *f* (-/-en) administra-tion; management.

ver'wand|eln *v/t.* (*no* -ge-, *h*) change, turn, transform; *sich* ~ change (*all: in acc.* into); 2lung *f* (-/-en) change; transformation.

verwandt *adj.* [fer'vant] related (*mit* to); languages, tribes, *etc.*: kindred; languages, sciences: cog-nate (with); *pred.* akin (to) (*a. fig.*); 2e *m, f* (-n/-n) relative, relation; 2schaft *f* (-/-en) relationship; re-lations *pl.*; *geistige* ~ congeniality.

ver'warn|en *v/t.* (*no* -ge-, *h*) cau-tion; 2ung *f* caution.

ver'wässern *v/t.* (*no* -ge-, *h*) water (down), dilute; *fig.* water down, dilute.

ver'wechs|eln *v/t.* (*no* -ge-, *h*) mistake (*mit* for); confound, mix up, confuse (*all: mit* with); 2(e)-lung *f* (-/-en) mistake; confusion.

verwegen *adj.* [fer've:gən] daring, bold, audacious; 2heit *f* (-/~-en) boldness, audacity, daring.

ver|'wehren *v/t.* (*no* -ge-, *h*): *j-m et.* ~ (de)bar *s.o.* from (doing) *s.th.*; *den Zutritt* ~ deny *or* refuse admit-tance (*zu* to); ~'weichlicht *adj.* ef-feminate, soft.

ver'weiger|n *v/t.* (*no* -ge-, *h*) deny, refuse; disobey (*order*); 2ung *f* denial, refusal.

ver'weilen *v/i.* (*no* -ge-, *h*) stay, linger; *bei et.* ~ dwell (up)on *s.th.*

Verweis [fer'vais] *m* (-es/-e) repri-mand; rebuke, reproof; reference (*auf acc.* to); 2en [~zən] *v/t.* (*irr. weisen, no* -ge-, *h*): *j-n des Landes* ~ expel *s.o.* from Germany, *etc.*;

j-m et. ~ reprimand s.o. for s.th.; j-n ~ *auf* (*acc.*) or an (*acc.*) refer s.o. to.

ver|'welken *v/i.* (*no -ge-, sein*) fade, wither (up).

ver'wend|en *v/t.* ([*irr.* wenden,] *no -ge-, h*) employ, use; apply (*für* for); spend (*time, etc.*) (*auf acc.* on); *sich bei j-m ~ für* intercede with s.o. for; 2ung *f* (-/~-en) use, employment; application; *keine ~ haben* have no use for.

ver'werf|en *v/t.* (*irr.* werfen, *no -ge-, h*) reject; ⁜ quash (*verdict*); ~lich *adj.* abominable.

ver'werten *v/t.* (*no -ge-, h*) turn to account, utilize.

verwes|en [fɛr'veːzən] *v/i.* (*no -ge-, sein*) rot, decay; 2ung *f* (-/~-en) decay.

ver'wick|eln *v/t.* (*no -ge-, h*) entangle (*in acc.* in); *sich ~* entangle o.s. (in) (*a. fig.*); ~elt *fig. adj.* complicated; 2(e)lung *f* (-/-en) entanglement; *fig. a.* complication.

ver'wilder|n *v/i.* (*no -ge-, sein*) run wild; ~t *adj.* garden, *etc.*: uncultivated, weed-grown; *fig.* wild, unruly.

ver'winden *v/t.* (*irr.* winden, *no -ge-, h*) get over *s.th.*

ver'wirklich|en *v/t.* (*no -ge-, h*) realize; *sich ~ be* realized, *esp. Am.* materialize; come true; 2ung *f* (-/~-en) realization.

ver'wirr|en *v/t.* (*no -ge-, h*) entangle; *j-n ~* confuse s.o.; embarrass s.o.; ~t *fig. adj.* confused; embarrassed; 2ung *fig. f* (-/-en) confusion.

ver'wischen *v/t.* (*no -ge-, h*) wipe *or* blot out; efface (*a. fig.*); blur, obscure; cover up (*one's tracks*).

ver'witter|n *geol. v/i.* (*no -ge-, sein*) weather; ~t *adj. geol.* weathered; weather-beaten (*a. fig.*).

ver'witwet *adj.* widowed.

verwöhn|en [fɛr'vøːnən] *v/t.* (*no -ge-, h*) spoil; ~t *adj.* fastidious, particular.

verworren *adj.* [fɛr'vɔrən] *ideas, etc.*: confused; *situation, plot*: intricate.

verwund|bar *adj.* [fɛr'vʊntbɑːr] vulnerable (*a. fig.*); 2en [~dən] *v/t.* (*no -ge-, h*) wound.

ver'wunder|lich *adj.* astonishing; 2ung *f* (-/~-en) astonishment.

Ver'wund|ete ⚔ *m* (-n/-n) wounded (soldier), casualty; ~ung *f* (-/-en) wound, injury.

ver'wünsch|en *v/t.* (*no -ge-, h*) curse; 2ung *f* (-/-en) curse.

ver'wüst|en *v/t.* (*no -ge-, h*) lay waste, devastate, ravage (*a. fig.*); 2ung *f* (-/-en) devastation, ravage.

verzag|en [fɛr'tsɑːgən] *v/i.* (*no -ge-, h*) despond (*an dat.* of); ~t *adj.* [~kt] despondent; 2theit [~kt-] *f* (-/*no pl.*) desponden|ce, -cy.

ver|'zählen *v/refl.* (*no -ge-, h*) miscount; ~zärteln [~'tsɛːrtəln] *v/t.* (*no -ge-, h*) coddle, pamper; ~'zaubern *v/t.* (*no -ge-, h*) bewitch, enchant, charm; ~'zehren *v/t.* (*no -ge-, h*) consume (*a. fig.*).

ver'zeichn|en *v/t.* (*no -ge-, h*) note down; record; list; *fig.* distort; *können, zu ~ haben* score (*success, etc.*); ~et *paint. adj.* out of drawing; 2is *n* (-ses/-se) list, catalog(ue); register; inventory; index (*of book*); table, schedule.

verzeih|en [fɛr'tsaɪən] (*irr., no -ge-, h*) **1.** *v/i.* pardon, forgive; ~ Sie! I beg your pardon!; excuse me!; sorry!; **2.** *v/t.* pardon, forgive (*j-m et.* s.o. s.th.); ~lich *adj.* pardonable; 2ung *f* (-/*no pl.*) pardon; ~! I beg your pardon!, sorry!

ver'zerr|en *v/t.* (*no -ge-, h*) distort; *sich ~* become distorted; 2ung *f* distortion.

ver'zetteln *v/t.* (*no -ge-, h*) enter on cards; *sich ~* fritter away one's energies.

Verzicht [fɛr'tsɪçt] *m* (-[e]s/-e) renunciation (*auf acc.* of); 2en *v/i.* (*no -ge-, h*) renounce (*auf et.* s.th.); do without (*s.th.*).

verzieh [fɛr'tsiː] *pret.* of verzeihen.

ver'ziehen¹ (*irr.* ziehen, *no -ge-*) **1.** *v/i.* (*sein*) (re)move (*nach* to); **2.** *v/t.* (*h*) spoil (*child*); distort; *das Gesicht ~* make a wry face, screw up one's face, grimace; *ohne e-e Miene zu ~* without betraying the least emotion; *sich ~ wood*: warp; *crowd, clouds*: disperse; *storm, clouds*: blow over; F disappear.

ver'ziehen² *p.p.* of verzeihen.

ver'zier|en *v/t.* (*no -ge-, h*) adorn, decorate; 2ung *f* (-/-ęn) decoration; ornament.

verzins|en [fɛr'tsɪnzən] *v/t.* (*no -ge-, h*) pay interest on; *sich ~* yield interest; 2ung *f* (-/~-en) interest.

ver'zöger|n *v/t.* (*no -ge-, h*) delay, retard; *sich ~ be* delayed; 2ung *f* (-/-en) delay, retardation.

ver'zollen *v/t.* (*no -ge-, h*) pay duty on; *haben Sie et. zu ~?* have you anything to declare?

verzück|t *adj.* [fɛr'tsʏkt] ecstatic, enraptured; 2ung *f* (-/~-en) ecstasy, rapture; *in ~ geraten* go into ecstasies (*wegen* over).

Ver'zug *m* (-[e]s/*no pl.*) delay; ⚖ default; *in ~ geraten* ⚖ come in default; *im ~ sein* (be in) default.

ver'zweif|eln *v/i.* (*no -ge-, h, sein*) despair (*an dat.* of); *es ist zum Verzweifeln* it is enough to drive one mad; ~elt *adj.* hopeless; desperate; 2lung [~luŋ] *f* (-/-en) despair; *j-n zur ~ bringen* drive s.o. to despair.

verzweig|en [fɛr'tsvaɪgən] *v/refl.* (*no -ge-, h*) ramify; *trees*: branch (out); *road*: branch; *business firm*, *etc.*: branch out; **~ung** *f* (-/-en) ramification; branching.

verzwickt *adj.* [fer'tsvikt] intricate, complicated.

Veteran [vete'ra:n] *m* (-en/-en) ✕ veteran (*a. fig.*), ex-serviceman.

Veterinär [veteri'nɛ:r] *m* (-s/-e) veterinary (surgeon), F vet.

Veto ['ve:to] *n* (-s/-s) veto; *ein* ~ *einlegen gegen* put a veto on, veto *s.th.*

Vetter ['fɛtər] *m* (-s/-n) cousin; **~nwirtschaft** *f* (-/no pl.) nepotism.

vibrieren [vi'bri:rən] *v/i.* (no -ge-, h) vibrate.

Vieh [fi:] *n* (-[e]s/no pl.) livestock, cattle; animal, brute, beast; F *fig.* brute, beast; **'~bestand** *m* livestock; **'~händler** *m* cattle-dealer; **'~hof** *m* stockyard; **'2isch** *adj.* bestial, beastly, brutal; **'~wagen** 🚃 *m* stock-car; **'~weide** *f* pasture; **'~zucht** *f* stock-farming, cattle-breeding; **'~züchter** *m* stock-breeder, stock-farmer, cattle-breeder, *Am. a.* rancher.

viel [fi:l] 1. *adj.* much; **~e** *pl.* many; a lot (of), lots of; plenty of (*cake, money, room, time, etc.*); *das* ~ *Geld* all that money; *seine* ~*en Geschäfte pl.* his numerous affairs *pl.*; *sehr* ~*e pl.* a great many *pl.*; *ziemlich* ~ a good deal of; *ziemlich* ~*e pl.* a good many *pl.*; ~ *zuviel* far too much; *sehr* ~ a great or good deal; 2. *adv.* much; ~ *besser* much or a good deal or a lot better; et. ~ *lieber tun* prefer to do s.th.

viel|beschäftigt *adj.* ['fi:lbəʃɛftiçt] very busy; **'~deutig** *adj.* ambiguous; **~erlei** *adj.* ['~ər'laɪ] of many kinds, many kinds of; multifarious; **~fach** ['~fax] 1. *adj.* multiple; 2. *adv.* in many cases, frequently; **~fältig** *adj.* ['~fɛltiç] multiple, manifold, multifarious; **~'leicht** *adv.* perhaps, maybe; **~mals** *adv.* ['~ma:ls]: *ich danke Ihnen* ~ many thanks, thank you very much; *sie läßt (dich)* ~ *grüßen* she sends you her kind regards; *ich bitte* ~ *um Entschuldigung* I am very sorry, I do beg your pardon; **~'mehr** *cj.* rather; **'~sagend** *adj.* significant, suggestive; **~seitig** *adj.* ['~zaitiç] many-sided, versatile; **'~versprechend** *adj.* (very) promising.

vier *adj.* [fi:r] four; *zu* ~*t* four of us *or* them; *auf allen* ~*en* on all fours; *unter* ~ *Augen* confidentially, privately; *um halb* ~ at half past three; **'~beinig** *adj.* four-legged; **'2eck** *n* square, quadrangle; **'~eckig** *adj.* square, quadrangular; **~erlei** *adj.* ['~ər'laɪ] of four different kinds, four kinds of; **'~fach** *adj.* ['~fax] fourfold; ~*e Ausfertigung* four copies; **2füßer** *zo.* ['~fy:sər] *m* (-s/-) quadruped; **~füßig** *adj.* ['~fy:siç]

four-footed; *zo.* quadruped; **2füßler** *zo.* ['~fy:slər] *m* (-s/-) quadruped; **~händig** ♩ *adv.* ['~hɛndiç]: ~ *spielen* play a duet; **~jährig** *adj.* ['~jɛ:riç] four-year-old, of four; **2linge** ['~liŋə] *m/pl.* quadruplets *pl.*, F quads *pl.*; **~mal** *adv.* four times; **~schrötig** *adj.* ['~ʃrø:tiç] square-built, thickset; **~seitig** *adj.* ['~zaitiç] four-sided; ⅋ quadrilateral; **2sitzer** *esp. mot. m* (-s/-) four-seater; **~stöckig** *adj.* ['~ʃtœkiç] four-storeyed, four-storied; **2takt-motor** *mot. m* four-stroke engine; **~te** *adj.* fourth; **~teilen** *v/t.* (ge-, h) quarter.

Viertel ['firtəl] *n* (-s/-) fourth (part); quarter; ~ *fünf* (*ein*) ~ *nach vier* a quarter past four; *drei* ~ *vier* a quarter to four; **~jahr** *n* three months *pl.*, quarter (of a year); **2jährlich, 2'jährlich** 1. *adj.* quarterly, 2. *adv.* every three months, quarterly; **~note** ♩ *f* crotchet, *Am. a.* quarter note; **'~pfund** *n*, **~'pfund** *n* quarter of a pound; **~stunde** *f* quarter of an hour, *Am.* quarter hour.

vier|tens *adv.* ['fi:rtəns] fourthly; **2'vierteltakt** ♩ *m* common time.

vierzehn *adj.* ['firtse:n] fourteen; ~ *Tage pl.* a fortnight, *Am.* two weeks *pl.*; **'~te** *adj.* fourteenth.

vierzig *adj.* ['firtsiç] forty; **'~ste** *adj.* fortieth.

Vikar *eccl.* [vi'ka:r] *m* (-s/-e) curate; vicar.

Villa ['vila] *f* (-/Villen) villa.

violett *adj.* [vio'lɛt] violet.

Violine ♩ [vio'li:nə] *f* (-/-n) violin.

Viper *zo.* ['vi:pər] *f* (-/-n) viper.

virtuos *adj.* [virtu'o:s] masterly; **2e** [~zə] *m* (-n/-n), **2in** [~zin] *f* (-/-nen) virtuoso; **2ität** [~ozi'tɛ:t] *f* (-/no pl.) virtuosity.

Virus 🐍 ['vi:rus] *n, m* (-/Viren) virus.

Vision [vi'zjo:n] *f* (-/-en) vision.

Visitation [vizita'tsjo:n] *f* (-/-en) search; inspection.

Visite 🐍 [vi'zi:tə] *f* (-/-n) visit; **~nkarte** *f* visiting-card, *Am.* calling card.

Visum ['vi:zum] *n* (-s/Visa, Visen) visa, visé.

Vitalität [vitali'tɛ:t] *f* (-/no pl.) vitality. [min.⟩

Vitamin [vita'mi:n] *n* (-s/-e) vita-⟩

Vize|kanzler ['fi:tsə-] *m* vice-chancellor; **'~könig** *m* viceroy; **'~konsul** *m* vice-consul; **~präsident** *m* vice-president.

Vogel ['fo:gəl] *m* (-s/~) bird; F *e-n* ~ *haben* have a bee in one's bonnet, *sl.* have bats in the belfry; *den* ~ *abschießen* carry off the prize, *Am. sl.* take the cake; **'~bauer** *n, m* (-s/-) bird-cage; **'~flinte** *f* fowling-piece; **'2frei** *adj.* outlawed; **'~futter** *n* food for birds, bird-seed; **'~kunde**

f (-/no *pl.*) ornithology; '~**liebhaber** *m* bird-fancier; '~**nest** *n* bird's nest, bird-nest; '~**perspektive** *f* (-/no *pl.*), '~**schau** *f* (-/no *pl.*) bird's-eye view; '~**scheuche** *f* (-/-*n*) scarecrow (*a. fig.*); ~'**Straußpolitik** *f* ostrich policy; ~ *betreiben* hide one's head in the sand (like an ostrich); '~**warte** *f* ornithological station; '~**zug** *m* passage *or* migration of birds.

Vokab|el [vo'ka:bəl] *f* (-/-*n*) word; ~**ular** [~abu'la:r] *n* (-*s*/-*e*) vocabulary.

Vokal *ling.* [vo'ka:l] *m* (-*s*/-*e*) vowel.

Volk [fɔlk] *n* 1. (-[*e*]*s*/~er) people; nation; swarm (*of bees*); covey (*of partridges*); 2. (-[*e*]*s*/no *pl.*) populace, *the* common people; *contp. the* common *or* vulgar herd; *der Mann aus dem* ~*e* the man in the street *or Am.* on the street.

Völker|bund ['fœlkər-] *m* (-[*e*]*s*/no *pl.*) League of Nations; '~**kunde** *f* (-/no *pl.*) ethnology; '~**recht** *n* (-[*e*]*s*/no *pl.*) international law, law of nations; '~**wanderung** *f* age of national migrations.

'**Volks|abstimmung** *pol. f* plebiscite; '~**ausgabe** *f* popular edition (*of book*); '~**bücherei** *f* free *or* public library; '~**charakter** *m* national character; '~**dichter** *m* popular *or* national poet; ~**entscheid** *pol.* ['~ɛntʃaɪt] *m* (-[*e*]*s*/-*e*) referendum; plebiscite; '~**fest** *n* fun fair, amusement park *or* grounds *pl.*; public merry-making; national festival; '~**gunst** *f* popularity; '~**herrschaft** *f* democracy; '~**hochschule** *f* adult education (courses *pl.*); '~**lied** *n* folk-song; '~**menge** *f* crowd (of people), multitude; '~**partei** *f* people's party; '~**republik** *f* people's republic; '~**schule** *f* elementary *or* primary school, *Am. a.* grade school; '~**schullehrer** *m* elementary *or* primary teacher, *Am.* grade teacher; '~**sprache** *f* vernacular; '~**stamm** *m* tribe, race; '~**stück** *thea. n* folk-play; '~**tanz** *m* folk-dance; '~**tracht** *f* national costume; **2tümlich** *adj.* ['~ty:mlɪç] national; popular; '~**versammlung** *f* public meeting; '~**vertreter** *parl. m* deputy, representative; member of parliament; *Brt.* Member of Parliament, *Am.* Representative; '~**vertretung** *parl. f* representation of the people; parliament; '~**wirt** *m* (political) economist; '~**wirtschaft** *f* economics, political economy; ~**wirtschaftler** ['~tlər] *m* (-*s*/-) *s.* Volkswirt; '~**zählung** *f* census.

voll [fɔl] 1. *adj.* full; filled; whole, complete, entire; *figure, face*: full, round; *figure*: buxom; ~*er Knospen* full of buds; *aus* ~*em Halse* at the

top of one's voice; *aus* ~*em Herzen* from the bottom of one's heart; *in* ~*er Blüte* in full blossom; *in* ~*er Fahrt* at full speed; *mit* ~*en Händen* lavishly, liberally; *mit* ~*em Recht* with perfect right; *um das Unglück* ~*zumachen* to make things worse; 2. *adv.* fully, in full; ~ *und ganz* fully, entirely; *j-n nicht für* ~ *ansehen or nehmen* have a poor opinion of s.o., think little of s.o.

'**voll|auf** *adv.*, ~'**auf** *adv.* abundantly, amply, F plenty; '~**automatisch** *adj.* fully automatic; **2bad** *n* bath; **2bart** *m* beard; **2beschäftigung** *f* full employment; **2besitz** *m* full possession; **2blut(pferd)** *zo. n* thoroughbred (horse); ~'**bringen** *v/t.* (*irr. bringen, no* -ge-, *h*) accomplish, achieve; perform; **2dampf** *m* full steam; F: *mit* ~ at *or* in full blast; ~'**enden** *v/t.* (*no* -ge-, *h*) finish, complete; ~'**endet** *adj.* perfect; ~*ends* *adv.* ['~ɛnts] entirely, wholly, altogether; **2endung** *f* (-/~-*en*) finishing, completion; *fig.* perfection.

Völlerei [fœlə'raɪ] *f* (-/~-*en*) gluttony.

voll|'führen *v/t.* (*no* -ge-, *h*) execute, carry out; ~'**füllen** *v/t.* (*sep.*, -ge-, *h*) fill (up); **2gas** *mot. n*: ~ *geben* open the throttle; *mit* ~ with the throttle full open; at full speed; ~**gepfropft** *adj.* ['~gəpfrɔpft] crammed, packed; '~**gießen** *v/t.* (*irr. gießen, sep.*, -ge-, *h*) fill (up); **2gummi** *n, m* solid rubber.

völlig *adj.* ['fœlɪç] entire, complete; *silence, calm, etc.*: dead.

voll|jährig *adj.* ['fɔljɛ:rɪç]: ~ *sein* be of age; ~ *werden* come of age; **2jährigkeit** *f* (-/no *pl.*) majority; ~'**kommen** *adj.* perfect; **2'kommenheit** *f* (-/~-*en*) perfection; '**2kornbrot** *n* whole-meal bread; '~**machen** *v/t.* (*sep.*, -ge-, *h*) fill (up); F soil, dirty; *um das Unglück vollzumachen* to make things worse; '**2macht** *f* (-/-*en*) full power, authority; ⊞ power of attorney; ~ *haben* be authorized; '**2matrose** ⊕ *m* able-bodied seaman; '**2milch** *f* whole milk; '**2mond** *m* full moon; '~**packen** *v/t.* (*sep.*, -ge-, *h*) stuff, cram; '**2pension** *f* (-/-*en*) full board; '~**schenken** *v/t.* (*sep.*, -ge-, *h*) fill (up); '~**schlank** *adj.* stout, corpulent; '~**ständig** *adj.* complete; '~**stopfen** *v/t.* (*sep.*, -ge-, *h*) stuff, cram; *sich* ~ stuff o.s.; *sich die Taschen* ~ stuff one's pockets; ~'**strecken** *v/t.* (*no* -ge-, *h*) execute; **2'streckung** *f* (-/-*en*) execution; '~**tönend** *adj.* sonorous, rich; '**2treffer** *m* direct hit; '**2versammlung** *f* plenary meeting *or* assembly; General Assembly (*of the United Nations*); '~**wertig** *adj.* equivalent,

equal in value; full; '⸱zählig adj.
complete; ⸱'ziehen v/t. (irr. ziehen,
no -ge-, h) execute; consummate
(marriage); sich ⸱ -⸗ take place;
2'ziehung f (-/⸢ -en), 2'zug m
(-[e]s/no pl.) execution.

Volontär[volɔn'tɛ:r]m(-s/-e) unpaid
assistant.

Volt ≵ [vɔlt] n (-, -[e]s/-) volt.

Volumen [vo'lu:mən] n (-s/-, Vo-
lumina) volume.

vom prp. [fɔm] = von dem

von prp. (dat.) [fɔn] space, time:
from; instead of gen.: of; passive:
by; ⸱ Hamburg from Hamburg;
⸱ nun an from now on; ⸱ morgen an
from tomorrow (on), beginning
tomorrow; ein Freund ⸱ mir a
friend of mine; die Einrichtung ⸱
Schulen the erection of schools; ⸱
dem or vom Apfel essen eat (some)
of the apple; der Herzog ⸱ Edinburgh the Duke of Edinburgh; ein
Gedicht ⸱ Schiller a poem by
Schiller; ⸱ selbst by itself; ⸱ selbst,
⸱ sich aus by oneself; ⸱ drei Meter
Länge three metres long; ein Betrag
⸱ 300 Mark a sum of 300 marks;
e-e Stadt ⸱ 10 000 Einwohnern a
town of 10,000 inhabitants; reden ⸱
talk of or about s.th.; speak on
(scientific subject); ⸱ mir aus as far
as I am concerned; I don't mind,
for all I care; das ist nett ⸱ ihm that
is nice of him; ich habe ⸱ ihm gehört I have heard of him; ⸱statten
adv. [⸱'ʃtatən]: gut ⸱ gehen go well.

vor prp. (dat.; acc.) [fo:r] space: in
front of, before; time: before; ⸱
langer Zeit a long time ago; ⸱ einigen Tagen a few days ago; (heute) ⸱
acht Tagen a week ago (today); am
Tage ⸱ (on) the day before, on the
eve of; 5 Minuten ⸱ 12 five minutes
to twelve; Am. five minutes of
twelve; fig. at the eleventh hour;
⸱ der Tür stehen be imminent,
be close at hand; ⸱ e-m Hintergrund
against a background; ⸱ Zeugen in
the presence of witnesses; ⸱ allen
Dingen above all; (dicht) ⸱ dem
Untergang stehen be on the brink
or verge of ruin; ⸱ Hunger sterben
die of hunger; ⸱ Kälte zittern
tremble with cold; schützen (verstecken) ⸱ protect (hide) from or
against; ⸱ sich gehen take place, pass
off; ⸱ sich hin lächeln smile to o.s.;
sich fürchten ⸱ be afraid of, fear.

Vor|abend['fo:r⸢-]m eve;'⸱ahnung
f presentiment, foreboding.

voran adv. [fo'ran] at the head (dat.
of), in front (of), before; Kopf ⸱
head first; ⸱gehen v/i. (irr. gehen,
sep., -ge-, sein) lead the way;
precede; ⸱kommen v/i. (irr. kommen, sep., -ge-, sein) make progress; fig. get on (in life).

Voran|schlag ['fo:r⸢an-] m (rough)

estimate; '⸱zeige f advance notice;
film: trailer.

vorarbeite|n ['fo:r⸢-] v/t. and v/i.
(sep., -ge-, h) work in advance;
'2r m foreman.

voraus adv. [fo'raus] in front (dat.
of), ahead (of); im ⸱ in advance,
beforehand; ⸱bestellen v/t. (sep.,
no -ge-, h) s. vorbestellen; ⸱bezah-
len v/t. (sep., no -ge-, h) pay in
advance, prepay; ⸱gehen v/i. (irr.
gehen, sep., -ge-, sein) go on before;
s. vorangehen; 2sage f prediction;
prophecy; forecast (of weather);
⸱sagen v/t. (sep., -ge-, h) foretell,
predict; prophesy; forecast (weather,
etc.); ⸱schicken v/t. (sep., -ge-, h)
send on in advance; fig. mention
beforehand, premise; ⸱sehen v/t.
(irr. sehen, sep., -ge-, h) foresee;
setzen v/t. (sep., -ge-, h) (pre)sup-
pose, presume, assume; voraus-
setzt, daß provided that; 2setzung
f (-/-en) (pre)supposition, assumption; prerequisite; 2sicht f fore-
sight; aller ⸱ nach in all probability;
⸱sichtlich adj. presumable, prob-
able, likely; 2zahlung f advance
payment or instal(l)ment.

'Vor|bedacht 1. m (-[e]s/no pl.): mit
⸱ deliberately, on purpose; 2. 2 adj.
premeditated; '⸱bedeutung f foreboding, omen, portent; '⸱bedin-
gung f prerequisite.

Vorbehalt ['fo:rbəhalt] m (-[e]s/-e)
reservation, reserve; 2en 1. v/t.
(irr. halten, sep., no -ge-, h): sich
⸱ reserve (right, etc.); 2. adj.: Än-
derungen ⸱ subject to change (without notice); 2los adj. unreserved,
unconditional.

vorbei adv. [fɔr'baɪ] space: along,
by, past (all: an dat. s.o., s.th.); time:
over, gone; 3 Uhr ⸱ past three
(o'clock); ⸱fahren v/i. (irr. fahren,
sep., -ge-, sein) drive past; ⸱gehen
v/i. (irr. gehen, sep., -ge-, sein) pass,
go by; pain: pass (off); storm:
blow over; ⸱ an (dat.) pass; im
Vorbeigehen in passing; ⸱kommen
v/i. (irr. kommen, sep., -ge-, sein)
pass by; F drop in; F ⸱ an (dat.)
get past (obstacle, etc.); ⸱lassen v/t.
(irr. lassen, sep., -ge-, h) let
pass.

'Vorbemerkung f preliminary remark or note.

'vorbereit|en v/t. (sep., no -ge-, h)
prepare (für, auf acc. for); '2ung f
preparation (für, auf acc. for).

'Vorbesprechung f preliminary discussion or talk.

'vor|bestellen v/t. (sep., no -ge-, h)
order in advance; book (room, etc.);
'⸱bestraft adj. previously con-
victed.

'vorbeug|en (sep., -ge-, h) 1. v/i.
prevent (e-r Sache s.th.); 2. v/t.
and v/refl. bend forward; '⸱end

adj. preventive; $\mathscr{F}$ *a.* prophylactic; **'_ung** *f* prevention.

'Vorbild *n* model; pattern; example; prototype; **'_lich** *adj.* exemplary; **_ung** ['_duŋ] *f* preparatory training.

'vor|bringen *v/t.* (*irr. bringen, sep.,* -ge-, *h*) bring forward, produce; advance (*opinion*); $\frac{1}{2}\frac{1}{4}$ prefer (*charge*); utter, say, state; **'_datieren** *v/t.* (*sep., no* -ge-, *h*) post-date.

vorder *adj.* ['fɔrdər] front, fore.

'Vorder|achse *f* front axle; **'_ansicht** *f* front view; **'_bein** *n* foreleg; **'_fuß** *m* forefoot; **'_grund** *m* foreground (*a. fig.*); **'_haus** *n* front building; **'_mann** *m* man in front (*of s.o.*); **'_rad** *n* front wheel; **_radantrieb** *mot.* ['fɔrdərɑːt?-] *m* front-wheel drive; **'_seite** *f* front (side); obverse (*of coin*); **'_sitz** *m* front seat; **'_2st** *adj.* foremost; **'_teil** *n, m* front (part); **'_tür** *f* front door; **'_zahn** *m* front tooth; **'_zimmer** *n* front room.

'vordrängen *v/refl.* (*sep.,* -ge-, *h*) press *or* push forward.

'vordring|en *v/i.* (*irr. dringen, sep.,* -ge-, *sein*) advance; **'_lich** *adj.* urgent. [blank.]

'Vordruck *m* (-[e]s/-e) form, *Am. a.*)

voreilig *adj.* ['foːr?-] hasty, rash, precipitate; **_e** *Schlüsse ziehen* jump to conclusions.

voreingenommen *adj.* ['foːr?-] prejudiced, bias(s)ed; **'2heit** *f* (-/no *pl.*) prejudice, bias.

vor|enthalten ['foːr?-] *v/t.* (*irr. halten, sep., no* -ge-, *h*) keep back, withhold (*j-m et. s.th. from s.o.*); **2entscheidung** ['foːr?-] *f* preliminary decision; **_erst** *adv.* ['foːr?-] for the present, for the time being.

Vorfahr ['foːrfɑːr] *m* (-en/-en) ancestor.

'vorfahr|en *v/i.* (*irr. fahren, sep.,* -ge-, *sein*) drive up; pass; *den Wagen _ lassen* order the car; **'2t(srecht** *n*) *f* right of way, priority.

'Vorfall *m* incident, occurrence, event; **'2en** *v/i.* (*irr. fallen, sep.,* -ge-, *sein*) happen, occur.

'vorfinden *v/t.* (*irr. finden, sep.,* -ge-, *h*) find.

'Vorfreude *f* anticipated joy.

'vorführ|en *v/t.* (*sep.,* -ge-, *h*) bring forward, produce; bring (*dat. before*); show, display, exhibit; demonstrate (*use of s.th.*); show, present (*film*); **'2er** *m* projectionist (*in cinema theatre*); **'2ung** *f* presentation, showing; $\oplus$ demonstration; $\frac{1}{2}\frac{1}{4}$ production (*of prisoner*); *thea., film:* performance.

'Vor|gabe *f sports:* handicap; *athletics:* stagger; *golf, etc.:* odds *pl.*; **'_gang** *m* incident, occurrence, event; facts *pl.*; file, record(s *pl.*); *biol.,* $\oplus$ process; **_gänger** ['_gɛŋər]

m (-s/-), **'_gängerin** *f* (-/-nen) predecessor; **'_garten** *m* front garden.

'vorgeben *v/t.* (*irr. geben, sep.,* -ge-, *h*) *sports:* give (*j-m s.o.*); *fig.* pretend, allege.

'Vor|gebirge *n* promontory, cape, headland; foot-hills *pl.*; **'_gefühl** *n* presentiment, foreboding.

'vorgehen 1. *v/i.* (*irr. gehen, sep.,* -ge-, *sein*) $\times$ advance; F lead the way; go on before; *watch, clock:* be fast, gain (*fünf Minuten five minutes*); take precedence (*dat. of, over*), be more important (*than*); take action, act; proceed (*a.* $\frac{1}{2}\frac{1}{4}$; *gegen against*); go on, happen, take place; 2. 2 *n* (-*s/no pl.*) action, proceeding.

'Vor|geschmack *m* (-[e]s/no *pl.*) foretaste; **_gesetzte** ['_gəzetstə] *m* (-*n*/-*n*) superior; *esp. Am.* F boss; **'2gestern** *adv.* the day before yesterday; **'2greifen** *v/i.* (*irr. greifen, sep.,* -ge-, *h*) anticipate (*j-m or e-r Sache s.o. or s.th.*).

'vorhaben 1. *v/t.* (*irr. haben, sep.,* -ge-, *h*) intend, mean; be going to *do s.th.*; *nichts _* be at a loose end; *haben Sie heute abend et. vor?* have you anything on tonight?; *was hat er jetzt wieder vor?* what is he up to now?; *was hast du mit ihm vor?* what are you going to *do with him?*; 2. 2 *n* (-*s*/-) intention, purpose, $\frac{1}{2}\frac{1}{4}$ intent; plan; project.

'Vorhalle *f* vestibule, (entrance-) hall; lobby; porch.

'vorhalt|en (*irr. halten, sep.,* -ge-, *h*) 1. *v/t.: j-m et. _* hold s.th. before s.o.; *fig.* reproach s.o. with s.th.; 2. *v/i.* last; **'2ung** *f* remonstrance; *j-m _en machen* remonstrate with s.o. (*wegen on*).

vorhanden *adj.* [for'handən] at hand, present; available (*a.* $\dagger$); $\dagger$ on hand, in stock; *_ sein* exist; **2sein** *n* presence, existence.

'Vor|hang *m* curtain; **'_hängeschloß** *n* padlock.

'vorher *adv.* before, previously; in advance, beforehand.

vor'her|bestellen *v/t.* (*sep., no* -ge-, *h*) *s.* vorbestellen; **_bestimmen** *v/t.* (*sep., no* -ge-, *h*) determine beforehand, predetermine; **_gehen** *v/i.* (*irr. gehen, sep.,* -ge-, *sein*) precede; **_ig** *adj.* preceding, previous.

'Vorherr|schaft *f* predominance; **'2schen** *v/i.* (*sep.,* -ge-, *h*) predominate, prevail; **'2schend** *adj.* predominant, prevailing.

vor'her|sage *f s.* Voraussage, **_sagen** *v/t.* (*sep.,* -ge-, *h*) *s.* voraussagen; **2sehen** *v/t.* (*irr. sehen, sep.,* -ge-, *h*) foresee; **2wissen** *v/t.* (*irr. wissen, sep.,* -ge-, *h*) know beforehand, foreknow.

'vor|hin adv., ~'hin adv. a short while ago, just now.

'Vor|hof m outer court, forecourt; anat. auricle (of heart); '~hut ⚔ f vanguard.

'vor|ig adj. last; ~jährig adj. ['~je:riç] of last year, last year's.

'Vor|kämpfer m champion, pioneer; '~kehrung f (-/-en) precaution; ~en treffen take precautions; '~kenntnisse f/pl. preliminary or basic knowledge (in dat. of); mit guten ~n in (dat.) well grounded in.

'vorkommen 1. v/i. (irr. kommen, sep., -ge-, sein) be found; occur, happen; es kommt mir vor it seems to me; 2. ♀ n (-s/-) occurrence.

'Vor|kommnis n (-ses/-se) occurrence; event; '~kriegszeit f pre-war times pl.

'vorlad|en ⚖ v/t. (irr. laden, sep., -ge-, h) summon; '♀ung ⚖ f summons.

'Vorlage f copy; pattern; parl. bill; presentation; production (of document); football: pass.

'vorlassen v/t. (irr. lassen, sep., -ge-, h) let s.o. pass, allow s.o. to pass; admit.

'Vorläuf|er m, '~erin f (-/-nen) forerunner; '♀ig 1. adj. provisional, temporary; 2. adv. provisionally, temporarily; for the present, for the time being.

'vorlaut adj. forward, pert.

'Vorleben n past (life), antecedents pl.

'vorlege|n v/t. (sep., -ge-, h) put (lock) on; produce (document); submit (plans, etc. for discussion, etc.); propose (plan, etc.); present (bill, etc.); j-m et. ~ lay or place or put s.th. before s.o.; show s.o. s.th.; at table: help s.o. to s.th.; j-m e-e Frage ~ put a question to s.o.; sich ~ lean forward; '♀r m (-s/-) rug.

'vorles|en v/t. (irr. lesen, sep., -ge-, h) read aloud; j-m et. ~ read (out) s.th. to s.o.; '♀ung f lecture (über acc. on; vor dat. to); e-e ~ halten (give) a lecture.

'vorletzt adj. last but one; ~e Nacht the night before last.

'Vorlieb|e f (-/no pl.) predilection, preference; ♀nehmen ['~li:p-] v/i. (irr. nehmen, sep., -ge-, h) be satisfied (mit with); ~ mit dem, was da ist at meals: take pot luck.

'vorliegen v/i. (irr. liegen, sep., -ge-, h) lie before s.o.; be there, exist; da muß ein Irrtum ~ there must be a mistake; was liegt gegen ihn vor? what is the charge against him?; '~d adj. present, in question.

'vor|lügen v/t. (irr. lügen, sep., -ge-, h): j-m et. ~ tell s.o. lies; '~machen v/t. (sep., -ge-, h): j-m et. ~ show s.o. how to do s.th.; fig. impose upon s.o.; sich (selbst) et. ~ fool o.s.

'Vormacht f (-/⚔ ~e), '~stellung f predominance; supremacy; hegemony.

'Vormarsch ⚔ m advance.

'vormerken v/t. (sep., -ge-, h) note down, make a note of; reserve; sich ~ lassen für put one's name down for.

'Vormittag m morning, forenoon; '♀s adv. in the morning.

'Vormund m (-[e]s/-e, ~er) guardian; '~schaft f (-/-en) guardianship.

vorn adv. [forn] in front; nach ~ forward; von ~ from the front; ich sah sie von ~ I saw her face; von ~ anfangen begin at the beginning; noch einmal von ~ anfangen begin anew, make a new start.

'Vorname m Christian name, first name, Am. a. given name.

vornehm ['fo:rne:m] 1. adj. of (superior) rank, distinguished; aristocratic; noble; fashioanble; ~e Gesinnung high character; 2. adv.: ~ tun give o.s. airs; '~en v/t. (irr. nehmen, sep., -ge-, h) take s.th. in hand; deal with; make (changes, etc.); take up (book); F sich j-n ~ take s.o. to task (wegen for, about); sich ~ resolve (up)on s.th.; resolve (zu inf. to inf.), make up one's mind (to inf.); sich vorgenommen haben a. be determined (zu inf. to inf.); '♀heit f (-/no pl.) refinement; elegance; high-mindedness.

'vorn|herein adv., ~he'rein adv.: von ~ from the first or start or beginning.

Vorort ['fo:r⁹-] m (-[e]s/-e) suburb; '~(s)verkehr m suburban traffic; '~(s)zug m local (train).

'Vor|posten m outpost (a. ⚔); '~rang m (-[e]s/no pl.) precedence (vor dat. of, over), priority (over); '~rat m store, stock (an dat. of); Vorräte pl. a. provisions pl., supplies pl.; ♀rätig adj. ['~rɛ:tiç] available; ~ a. on hand, in stock; '♀rechnen v/t. (sep., -ge-, h) reckon up (j-m to s.o.); '~recht n privilege; '~rede f preface, introduction; '~redner m previous speaker; '~richtung ⊕ f contrivance, device; '♀rücken (sep., -ge-) 1. v/t. (h) move (chair, etc.) forward; 2. v/i. (sein) advance; '~runde f sports: preliminary round; '♀sagen v/i. (sep., -ge-, h): j-m ~ prompt s.o.; '~saison f off or dead season; '~satz m intention, purpose, design; ♀sätzlich adj. ['~zɛtsliç] intentional, deliberate; '~er Mord ⚖ wil(l)ful murder; '~schein m: zum ~ bringen bring forward, produce; zum ~ kommen appear, turn up; '♀schieben v/t. (irr. schieben, sep., -ge-, h) push s.th. forward; slip (bolt); s. vorschützen; '♀schießen *v/t.* (*irr.* schießen, *sep.*, -ge-, *h*) advance (*money*).

'**Vorschlag** *m* proposition, proposal; suggestion; offer; 2en ['~gən] *v/t.* (*irr.* schlagen, *sep.*, -ge-, *h*) propose; suggest; offer.

'**Vor|schlußrunde** *f sports:* semifinal; '2schnell *adj.* hasty, rash; '2schreiben *v/t.* (*irr.* schreiben, *sep.*, -ge-, *h*): j-m et. ~ write s.th. out for s.o.; *fig.* prescribe.

'**Vorschrift** *f* direction, instruction; prescription (*esp.* 🅰); order (*a.* 🅰); regulation(s *pl.*); '2smäßig *adj.* according to regulations; ~e *Kleidung* regulation dress; '2swidrig *adj.* and *adv.* contrary to regulations.

'**Vor|schub** *m:* ~ leisten (*dat.*) countenance (*fraud, etc.*); further, encourage; 🆃🆃 aid and abet; '~schule *f* preparatory school; '~schuß *m* advance; *for barrister:* retaining fee, retainer; '2schützen *v/t.* (*sep.*, -ge-, *h*) pretend, plead (*sickness, etc. as excuse*); '2schweben *v/i.* (*sep.*, -ge-, *h*): mir schwebt et. vor I have s.th. in mind.

'**vorseh|en** *v/t.* (*irr.* sehen, *sep.*, -ge-, *h*) plan; design; 🆃🆃 provide; sich ~ take care, be careful; sich ~ vor (*dat.*) guard against; '2ung *f* (-/~-en) providence.

'**vorsetzen** *v/t.* (*sep.*, -ge-, *h*) put forward; place or put or set before, offer.

'**Vorsicht** *f* caution; care; ~! caution!, danger!; look out!, be careful!; ~, *Glas!* Glass, with care!; ~, *Stufe!* mind the step!; '2ig *adj.* cautious; careful; ~! F steady!

'**vorsichts|halber** *adv.* as a precaution; '2maßnahme *f*, '2maßregel *f* precaution(ary measure); ~n treffen take precautions.

'**Vorsilbe** *gr. f* prefix.

'**vorsingen** *v/t.* (*irr.* singen, *sep.*, -ge-, *h*): j-m et. ~ sing s.th. to s.o.

'**Vorsitz** *m* (-es/*no pl.*) chair, presidency; den ~ führen or haben be in the chair, preside (*bei* over; *at*); den ~ übernehmen take the chair; ~ende ['~ondə] (-n/-n) 1. *m* chairman, president; 2. *f* chairwoman.

'**Vorsorg|e** *f* (-/*no pl.*) provision, providence; precaution; ~ treffen make provision; '2en *v/i.* (*sep.*, -ge-, *h*) provide; 2lich ['~kliç] 1. *adj.* precautionary; 2. *adv.* as a precaution.

'**Vorspeise** *f* appetizer, hors d'œuvre.

'**vorspieg|eln** *v/t.* (*sep.*, -ge-, *h*) pretend; j-m et. ~ delude s.o. (with false hopes, *etc.*); '2(e)lung *f* preten|ce, *Am.* -se.

'**Vorspiel** *n* prelude; '2en *v/t.* (*sep.*, -ge-, *h*): j-m et. ~ play s.th. to s.o.

'**vor|sprechen** (*irr.* sprechen, *sep.*, -ge-, *h*) 1. *v/t.* pronounce (j-m et.

s.th. to or for s.o.); 2. *v/i.* call (*bei* on *s.o.*; *at an office*); *thea.* audition; '~springen *v/i.* (*irr.* springen, *sep.*, -ge-, *sein*) jump forward; project; '2sprung *m* 🔺 projection; *sports:* lead; *fig.* start, advantage (*vor dat.* of); '2stadt *f* suburb; '~städtisch *adj.* suburban; '2stand *m* board of directors, managing directors *pl.*

'**vorsteh|en** *v/i.* (*irr.* stehen, *sep.*, -ge-, *h*) project, protrude; *fig.:* direct; manage (*both:* e-r Sache s.th.); '2er *m* director, manager; head, chief.

'**vorstell|en** *v/t.* (*sep.*, -ge-, *h*) put forward; put (*clock*) on; introduce (j-n j-m s.o. to s.o.); mean, stand for; represent; sich ~ *bei* have an interview with; sich et. ~ imagine or fancy s.th.; '2ung *f* introduction; presentation; interview (*of applicant for post*); *thea.* performance; *fig.:* remonstrance; idea, conception; imagination; 2ungsvermögen *n* imagination.

'**Vor|stoß** ⚔ *m* thrust, advance; '~strafe *f* previous conviction; '2strecken *v/t.* (*sep.*, -ge-, *h*) thrust out, stretch forward; advance (*money*); '~stufe *f* first step or stage; '2täuschen *v/t.* (*sep.*, -ge-, *h*) feign, pretend.

Vorteil ['fɔrtaɪl] *m* advantage (*a. sports*); profit; *tennis:* (ad)vantage; '2haft *adj.* advantageous (*für* to), profitable (to).

Vortrag ['fo:rtraːk] *m* (-[e]s/-̈e) performance; execution (*esp.* ♪); recitation (*of poem*); ♪ recital; lecture; report; ♱ balance carried forward; e-n ~ halten (give a) lecture (*über acc.* on); 2en ['~gən] *v/t.* (*irr.* tragen, *sep.*, -ge-, *h*) ♱ carry forward; report on; recite (*poem*); perform, *esp.* ♪ execute; lecture on; state, express (*opinion*); ~ende ['~gəndə] *m* (-n/-n) performer; lecturer; speaker.

vor|trefflich *adj.* ['fo:r'treflɪç] excellent; '~treten *v/i.* (*irr.* treten, *sep.*, -ge-, *sein*) step forward; *fig.* project, protrude, stick out; '2tritt *m* (-[e]s/*no pl.*) precedence.

vorüber *adv.* ['fo'ryːbər] *space:* by, past; *time:* gone by, over; ~gehen *v/i.* (*irr.* gehen, *sep.*, -ge-, *sein*) pass, go by; ~gehend *adj.* passing; temporary; 2gehende [.də] *m* (-n/-n) passer-by; ~ziehen *v/i.* (*irr.* ziehen, *sep.*, -ge-, *sein*) march past, pass by; *storm:* blow over.

Vor|übung ['fo:rʔ-] *f* preliminary practice; ~untersuchung 🆃🆃 ['fo:rʔ-] *f* preliminary inquiry.

Vorurteil ['fo:rʔ-] *n* prejudice; '2slos *adj.* unprejudiced, unbias(s)ed.

'**Vor|verkauf** *thea. m* booking in advance; *im* ~ bookable (*bei* at);

'Qverlegen v/t. (sep., no -ge-, h)
advance; '⌣wand m (-[e]s/⌣e) pre-
text, preten|ce, Am. -se.
vorwärts adv. ['fo:rverts] forward,
onward, on; ⌣! go ahead!; '⌣kom-
men v/i. (irr. kommen, sep., -ge-,
sein) (make) progress; fig. make
one's way, get on (in life).
vorweg adv. [for'vek] beforehand;
⌣nehmen v/t. (irr. nehmen, sep.,
-ge-, h) anticipate.
vor|weisen v/t. (irr. weisen, sep.,
-ge-, h) produce, show; '⌣werfen
v/t. (irr. werfen, sep., -ge-, h) throw
or cast before; j-m et. ⌣ reproach
s.o. with s.th.; '⌣wiegend 1. adj.
predominant, preponderant; 2. adv.
predominantly, chiefly, mainly,
mostly; '⌣witzig adj. forward, pert;
inquisitive.
'Vorwort n (-[e]s/-e) preface (by
author); foreword.
'Vorwurf m reproach; subject (of
drama, etc.); j-m e-n ⌣ or Vorwürfe
machen reproach s.o. (wegen with);
'Qsvoll adj. reproachful.
'vor|zählen v/t. (sep., -ge-, h) enu-

merate, count out (both: j-m to
s.o.); 'Qzeichen n omen; '⌣zeich-
nen v/t. (sep., -ge-, h): j-m et. ⌣
draw or sketch s.th. for s.o.; show
s.o. how to draw s.th.; fig. mark
out, destine; '⌣zeigen v/t. (sep.,
-ge-, h) produce, show.
'Vorzeit f antiquity; in literature
often: times of old, days of yore;
'Qig adj. premature.
'vor|ziehen v/t. (irr. ziehen, sep.,
-ge-, h) draw forth; draw (curtains);
fig. prefer; 'Qzimmer n antecham-
ber, anteroom; waiting-room; 'Q-
zug fig. m preference; advantage;
merit; priority; ⌣züglich adj. [⌣-
'tsy:kliç] excellent, superior, exquisite.
'Vorzugs|aktie f preference share
or stock, Am. preferred stock; '⌣-
preis m special price; 'Qweise adv.
preferably; chiefly.
Votum ['vo:tum] n (-s/Voten, Vota)
vote.
vulgär adj. [vul'gɛ:r] vulgar.
Vulkan [vul'ka:n] m (-s/-e) volcano;
Qisch adj. volcanic.

W

Waag|e ['va:gə] f (-/-n) balance,
(e-e a pair of) scales pl.; die ⌣ halten (dat.) counterbalance; 'Qerecht
adj., Qrecht adj. ['va:k-] horizontal, level; ⌣schale ['va:k-] f scale.
Wabe ['va:bə] f (-/-n) honeycomb.
wach adj. [vax] awake; hell⌣ wide
awake; ⌣ werden awake, wake up;
'Qe f (-/-n) watch; guard; guard-
house, guardroom; police-station;
sentry, sentinel; ⌣ haben be on
guard; ⌣ halten keep watch; '⌣en
v/i. (ge-, h) (keep) watch (über acc.
over); sit up (bei with); 'Qhund m
watch-dog.
Wacholder ϙ [va'xɔldər] m (-s/-)
juniper.
'wach|rufen v/t. (irr. rufen, sep.,
-ge-, h) rouse, evoke; '⌣rütteln v/t.
(sep., -ge-, h) rouse (up); fig. rouse,
shake up.
Wachs [vaks] n (-es/-e) wax.
'wachsam adj. watchful, vigilant;
'Qkeit f (-/no pl.) watchfulness,
vigilance.
wachsen¹ ['vaksən] v/i. (irr., ge-,
sein) grow; fig. increase.
wachsen² [⌣] v/t. (ge-, h) wax.
wächsern adj. ['vɛksərn] wax; fig.
waxen, waxy.
'Wachs|kerze f, '⌣licht n wax
candle; '⌣tuch n waxcloth, oil-
cloth.
Wachstum ['vakstu:m] n (-s/no
pl.) growth; fig. increase.

Wächte mount. ['vɛçtə] f (-/-n)
cornice.
Wachtel orn. ['vaxtəl] f (-/-n) quail.
Wächter ['vɛçtər] m (-s/-) watcher,
guard(ian); watchman.
'Wacht|meister m sergeant; '⌣-
turm m watch-tower.
wackel|ig adj. ['vakəliç] shaky (a.
fig.), tottery; furniture, etc.: rickety;
tooth, etc.: loose; 'Qkontakt ⨍ m
loose connexion or (Am. only) connection; '⌣n v/i. (ge-, h) shake;
table, etc.: wobble; tooth, etc.: be
loose; tail, etc.: wag; ⌣ mit wag
s.th.
wacker adj. ['vakər] honest, upright; brave, gallant.
wacklig adj. ['vakliç] s. wackelig.
Wade ['va:də] f (-/-n) calf; '⌣nbein
anat. n fibula.
Waffe ['vafə] f (-/-n) weapon (a.
fig.); ⌣n pl. a. arms pl.
Waffel ['vafəl] f (-/-n) waffle;
wafer.
'Waffen|fabrik f armaments fac-
tory, Am. a. armory; '⌣gattung f
arm; '⌣gewalt f (-/no pl.): mit ⌣
by force of arms; 'Qlos adj. weapon-
less, unarmed; '⌣schein m firearm
certificate, Am. gun license; '⌣still-
stand m armistice (a. fig.), truce.
Wage|hals ['va:gəhals] m dare-
devil; 'Qhalsig adj. daring, foolhardy; attr. a. daredevil; '⌣mut m
daring

wagen[1] ['va:gən] v/t. (ge-, h) venture; risk, dare; sich ~ venture (an acc. [up]on).

Wagen[2] [~] m (-s/-, ¨) carriage (a. Am. 🚂 car; 🚂 coach); wag(g)on; cart; car; lorry, truck; van.

wägen ['vɛ:gən] v/t. ([irr.,] ge-, h) weigh (a. fig.).

'Wagen|heber m (-s/-) (lifting) jack; '~park m (-[e]s/no pl.) fleet of vehicles; '~schmiere f grease; '~spur f rut.

Waggon 🚂 [va'gõ:] m (-s/-s) (railway) carriage, Am. (railroad) car.

wag|halsig adj. ['va:khalsiç] s. wagehalsig; '2nis n (-ses/-se) venture, risk.

Wahl [va:l] f (-/-en) choice; alternative; selection; pol. election; e-e ~ treffen make a choice; s-e ~ treffen take one's choice; ich hatte keine ~ I had no choice.

wählbar adj. ['vɛ:lba:r] eligible; '2keit f (-/no pl.) eligibility.

wahl|berechtigt adj. ['va:lbərɛçtiçt] entitled to vote; '2beteiligung f percentage of voting, F turn-out; '2bezirk m constituency.

'wählen (ge-, h) 1. v/t. choose; pol. elect; teleph. dial; 2. v/i. choose, take one's choice; teleph. dial (the number).

'Wahlergebnis n election return.

'Wähler m (-s/-) elector, voter; '2isch adj. particular (in dat. in, about, as to), nice (about), fastidious, F choosy; '~schaft f (-/-en) constituency, electorate.

'Wahl|fach n optional subject, Am. a. elective; '2fähig adj. having a vote; eligible; '~gang m ballot; '~kampf m election campaign; '~kreis m constituency; '~lokal n polling station; '2los adj. indiscriminate; '~recht n (-[e]s/no pl.) franchise; '~rede f electoral speech; **'Wählscheibe** teleph. f dial.

'Wahl|spruch m device, motto; '~stimme f vote; '~urne f ballot-box; '~versammlung f electoral rally; '~zelle f polling-booth; '~zettel m ballot, voting-paper.

Wahn [va:n] m (-[e]s/no pl.) delusion, illusion; mania; '~sinn m (-[e]s/no pl.) insanity, madness (both a. fig.); '2sinnig adj. insane, mad (vor dat. with) (both a. fig.); ~sinnige ['~gə] m (-n/-n) madman, lunatic; '~vorstellung f delusion, hallucination; '~witz m (-es/no pl.) madness, insanity; '2witzig adj. mad, insane.

wahr adj. [va:r] true; real; genuine; ~en v/t. (ge-, h) safeguard (interests, etc.); maintain (one's dignity); den Schein ~ keep up or save appearances.

währen ['vɛ:rən] v/i. (ge-, h) last, continue.

'während 1. prp. (gen.) during; pending; 2. cj. while, whilst; while, whereas.

'wahrhaft adv. really, truly, indeed; ~ig ['~haftiç] 1. adj. truthful, veracious; 2. adv. really, truly, indeed.

'Wahrheit f (-/-en) truth; in ~ in truth; j-m die ~ sagen give s.o. a piece of one's mind; '2sgetreu adj. true, faithful; '~sliebe f (-/no pl.) truthfulness, veracity; '2sliebend adj. truthful, veracious.

'wahr|lich adv. truly, really; '~nehmbar adj. perceivable, perceptible; '~nehmen v/t. (irr. nehmen, sep.-, -ge-, h) perceive, notice; avail o.s. of (opportunity); safeguard (interests); '2nehmung f (-/-en) perception, observation; '~sagen v/i. (sep., -ge-, h) tell or read fortunes; sich ~ lassen have one's fortune told; '2sagerin f (-/-nen) fortuneteller; ~'scheinlich 1. adj. probable; likely; 2. adv.: ich werde ~ gehen I am likely to go; 2'scheinlichkeit f (-/~-en) probability, likelihood; aller ~ nach in all probability or likelihood.

'Wahrung f (-/no pl.) maintenance; safeguarding.

Währung ['vɛ:ruŋ] f (-/-en) currency; standard; '~sreform f currency or monetary reform.

'Wahrzeichen n landmark.

Waise ['vaizə] f (-/-n) orphan; '~nhaus n orphanage.

Wal zo. [va:l] m (-[e]s/-e) whale.

Wald [valt] m (-[e]s/¨er) wood, forest; '~brand m forest fire; 2ig adj. ['~diç] wooded, woody; 2reich adj. ['~r-] rich in forests; ~ung ['~duŋ] f (-/-en) forest.

Walfänger ['va:lfɛŋər] m (-s/-) whaler.

walken ['valkən] v/t. (ge-, h) full (cloth); mill (cloth, leather).

Wall [val] m (-[e]s/¨e) 🗡 rampart (a. fig.); dam; mound.

Wallach ['valax] m (-[e]s/-e) gelding.

wallen ['valən] v/i. (ge-, h, sein) hair, articles of dress, etc.: flow; simmer; boil (a. fig.).

wall|fahren ['valfa:rən] v/i. (ge-, sein) (go on a) pilgrimage; '2fahrer m pilgrim; '2fahrt f pilgrimage; '~fahrten v/i. (ge-, sein) (go on a) pilgrimage.

'Wallung f (-/-en) ebullition; 🩸 congestion; (Blut) in ~ bringen make s.o.'s blood boil, enrage.

Walnuß ['val-] f walnut; '~baum 🌳 m walnut(-tree).

Walroß zo. ['val-] n walrus.

walten ['valtən] v/i. (ge-, h): s-s Amtes ~ attend to one's duties; Gnade ~ lassen show mercy.

Walze ['valtsə] f (-/-n) roller, cylinder; ⊕ *a.* roll; ⊕, ♪ barrel; '⊊n *v/t.* (ge-, h) roll (*a.* ⊕).

wälzen ['vɛltsən] *v/t.* (ge-, h) roll; roll (*problem*) round in one's mind; shift (*blame*) (*auf acc.* [up]on); *sich* ⁓ roll; wallow (*in mud, etc.*); welter (*in blood, etc.*).

Walzer ♪ ['valtsər] *m* (-s/-) waltz.

Wand [vant] 1. *f* (-/⁓e) wall; partition; 2. ⊋ *pret. of* winden.

Wandel ['vandəl] *m* (-s/*no pl.*) change; '⊊bar *adj.* changeable; variable; '⁓gang *m*, '⁓halle *f* lobby; '⊊n (ge-) 1. *v/i.* (sein) walk; 2. *v/refl.* (h) change.

Wander|er ['vandərər] *m* (-s/-) wanderer; hiker; '⁓leben *n* (-s/*no pl.*) vagrant life; '⊊n *v/i.* (ge-, sein) wander; hike; '⁓niere 𝒔 *f* floating kidney; '⁓prediger *m* itinerant preacher; '⁓preis *m* challenge trophy; '⁓schaft *f* (-/*no pl.*) wanderings *pl.*; *auf (der)* ⁓ on the tramp; '⁓ung *f* (-/-en) walking-tour; hike.

'Wand|gemälde *n* mural (painting); '⁓kalender *m* wall-calendar; '⁓karte *f* wall-map.

Wandlung ['vandluŋ] *f* (-/-en) change, transformation; *eccl.* transubstantiation; 𝔱𝔱 redhibition.

'Wand|schirm *m* folding-screen; '⁓schrank *m* wall-cupboard; '⁓spiegel *m* wall-mirror; '⁓tafel *f* blackboard; '⁓teppich *m* tapestry; '⁓uhr *f* wall-clock.

wandte ['vantə] *pret. of* wenden 2.

Wange ['vaŋə] *f* (-/-n) cheek.

Wankel|mut ['vaŋkəlmuːt] *m* fickleness, inconstancy; ⊋mütig *adj.* ['⁓myːtiç] fickle, inconstant.

wanken ['vaŋkən] *v/i.* (ge-, h, sein) totter, stagger (*a. fig.*); house, *etc.*: rock; *fig.* waver.

wann *adv.* [van] when; *s. dann*; *seit* ⁓? how long?, since when?

Wanne ['vanə] *f* (-/-n) tub; bath (-tub), F tub; '⁓nbad *n* bath, F tub.

Wanze *zo.* ['vantsə] *f* (-/-n) bug, *Am. a.* bedbug.

Wappen ['vapən] *n* (-s/-) (coat of) arms *pl.*; '⁓kunde *f* (-/*no pl.*) heraldry; '⁓schild *m*, *n* escutcheon; '⁓tier *n* heraldic animal.

wappnen *fig.* ['vapnən] *v/refl.* (ge-, h): *sich* ⁓ *gegen* be prepared for; *sich mit Geduld* ⁓ have patience.

war [vaːr] *pret. of* sein[1].

warb [varp] *pret. of* werben.

Ware ['vaːrə] *f* (-/-n) commodity, article of trade; ⁓n *pl. a.* goods *pl.*, merchandise, wares *pl.*

'Waren|aufzug *m* hoist; '⁓bestand *m* stock (on hand); '⁓haus *n* department store; '⁓lager *n* stock; warehouse, *Am. a.* stock room; '⁓probe *f* sample; '⁓zeichen *n* trade mark.

warf [varf] *pret. of* werfen.

warm *adj.* [varm] warm (*a. fig.*); *meal*: hot; *schön* ⁓ nice and warm.

Wärme ['vɛrmə] *f* (-/⁓-n) warmth; *phys.* heat; '⁓grad *m* degree of heat; '⊊n *v/t.* (ge-, h) warm; *sich die Füße* ⁓ warm one's feet.

'Wärmflasche *f* hot-water bottle.

'warmherzig *adj.* warm-hearted.

Warm'wasser|heizung *f* hot-water heating; '⁓versorgung *f* hot-water supply.

warn|en ['varnən] *v/t.* (ge-, h) warn (*vor dat.* of, against), caution (against); '⊊signal *n* danger-signal (*a. fig.*); '⊊streik *m* token strike; '⁓ung *f* (-/-en) warning, caution; **ungstafel** ['varnuŋs-] *f* noticeboard.

Warte *fig.* ['vartə] *f* (-/-n) point of view.

warten ['vartən] *v/i.* (ge-, h) wait (*auf acc.* for); be in store (for *s.o.*); *j-n* ⁓ *lassen* keep *s.o.* waiting.

Wärter ['vertər] *m* (-s/-) attendant; keeper; (male) nurse.

'Warte|saal *m*, '⁓zimmer *n* waiting-room.

Wartung ⊕ ['vartuŋ] *f* (-/⁓-en) maintenance.

warum *adv.* [va'rum] why.

Warze ['vartsə] *f* (-/-n) wart; nipple.

was [vas] 1. *interr. pron.* what; ⁓ *kostet das Buch?* how much is this book?; F ⁓ *rennst du denn so* (*schnell*)? why are you running like this?; ⁓ *für* (*ein*) ...! what a(n) ...!; ⁓ *für ein* ...? what ...?; 2. *rel. pron.* what; ⁓ (*auch immer*), *alles* ⁓ what(so)ever; ..., ⁓ *ihn völlig kalt ließ* ... which left him quite cold; 3. F *indef. pron.* something; *ich will dir mal* ⁓ *sagen* I'll tell you what.

wasch|bar *adj.* ['vaʃbaːr] washable; '⊊becken *n* wash-basin, *Am.* washbowl.

Wäsche ['vɛʃə] *f* (-/-n) wash(ing); laundry; linen (*a. fig.*); underwear; *in der* ⁓ *sein* be at the wash; *sie hat heute große* ⁓ she has a large wash today.

waschecht *adj.* ['vaʃʔ-] washable; *colour*: *a.* fast; *fig.* dyed-in-the-wool.

'Wäsche|klammer *f* clothes-peg, clothes-pin; '⁓leine *f* clothes-line.

'waschen *v/t.* (*irr.*, ge-, h) wash; *sich* ⁓ (have a) wash; *sich das Haar or den Kopf* ⁓ wash *or* shampoo one's hair *or* head; *sich gut* ⁓ (*lassen*) wash well.

Wäscher|ei [vɛʃə'rai] *f* (-/-en) laundry; '⁓in *f* (-/-nen) washerwoman, laundress.

'Waschschrank *m* linen closet.

'Wasch|frau *f s.* Wäscherin; '⁓haus *n* wash-house; '⁓kessel *m* copper; '⁓korb *m* clothes-basket;

'~küche f wash-house; '~lappen m face-cloth, Am. washrag, wash-cloth; '~maschine f washing machine, washer; '~pulver n washing powder; '~raum m lavatory, Am. a. washroom; '~schüssel f wash-basin; '~tag m wash(ing)-day; '~ung f (-/-en) ❋ wash; ablution; '~weib contp. n gossip; '~wanne f wash-tub.

Wasser ['vasər] n (-s/-, ⁼) water; ~ lassen make water; zu ~ und zu Land(e) by sea and land; '~ball m 1. beach-ball; water-polo ball; 2. (-[e]s/no pl.) water-polo; '~ball-spiel n 1. (-[e]s/no pl.) water-polo; 2. water-polo match; '~behälter m reservoir, water-tank; '~blase ❋ f water-blister; '~dampf m steam; '2dicht adj. waterproof; water-tight; '~eimer m water-pail, bucket; '~fall m waterfall, cascade; cataract; '~farbe f water-colo(u)r; '~flugzeug n waterplane, seaplane; '~glas n 1. tumbler; 2. ❋ (-es/no pl.) water-glass; '~graben m ditch; '~hahn m tap, Am. a. faucet; '~hose f waterspout.

wässerig adj. ['vɛsəriç] watery; washy (a. fig.); j-m den Mund ~ machen make s.o.'s mouth water. 'Wasser|kanne f water-jug, ewer; '~kessel m kettle; '~klosett n water-closet, W.C.; '~kraft f water-power; '~kraftwerk n hydroelectric power station or plant, water-power station; '~krug m water-jug, ewer; '~kur f water-cure, hydropathy; '~lauf m water-course; '~leitung f water-supply; '~leitungsrohr n water-pipe; '~mangel m shortage of water; '2n v/i. (ge-, h) alight on water; splash down. [(salted herring, etc.).\
wässern ['vɛsərn] v/t. (ge-, h) soak∫ 'Wasser|pflanze f aquatic plant; '~rinne f gutter; '~rohr n water-pipe; '~schaden m damage caused by water; '~scheide f watershed, Am. a. divide; '2scheu adj. afraid of water; '~schlauch m water-hose; '~spiegel m water-level; '~sport m aquatic sports pl.; '~spülung f (-/-en) flushing (system); '~stand m water-level; '~standsanzeiger ['vasərʃtants⁹-] m water-gauge; '~stiefel m/pl. waders pl.; '~stoff ❋ m (-[e]s/no pl.) hydrogen; '~stoff-bombe f hydrogen bomb, H-bomb; '~strahl m jet of water; '~straße f waterway; '~tier n aquatic animal; '~verdrängung f (-/-en) displacement; '~versorgung f water-supply; '~waage f spirit-level, water-level; '~weg m waterway; auf dem ~ by water; '~welle f water-wave; '~werk n waterworks sg., pl.; '~zeichen n watermark.

wäßrig adj. ['vɛsriç] s. wässerig.
waten ['va:tən] v/i. (ge-, sein) wade.
watscheln ['va:tʃəln] v/i. (ge-, sein, h) waddle.
Watt ❢ [vat] n (-s/-) watt.
Watt|e ['vatə] f (-/-n) cotton-wool; surgical cotton; wadding; '~e-bausch m wad; 2ieren [~'ti:rən] v/t. wad, pad.
weben ['ve:bən] v/t. and v/i. ([irr.,] ge-, h) weave.
'Weber m (-s/-) weaver; ~ei [~'raɪ] f 1. (-/no pl.) weaving; 2. (-/-en) weaving-mill.
Webstuhl ['ve:pʃtu:l] m loom.
Wechsel ['vɛksəl] m (-s/-) change; allowance; ❢ bill (of exchange); hunt. runway; eigener ~ ❢ promissory note; '~beziehung f correlation; '~fälle ['~fɛlə] pl. vicissitudes pl.; '~fieber ❋ n (-s/no pl.) intermittent fever; malaria; '~frist ❢ f usance; '~geld n change; '~kurs m rate of exchange; '~makler ❢ m bill-broker; '2n (ge-, h) 1. v/t. change; vary; exchange (words, etc.); den Besitzer ~ change hands; die Kleider ~ change (one's clothes); 2. v/i. change; vary; alternate; '~nehmer ❢ m (-s/-) payee; '2seitig adj. ['~zaitiç] mutual, reciprocal; '~strom ❢ m alternating current; '~stube f exchange office; '2weise adv. alternately, by or in turns; '~wirkung f interaction.
wecke|n ['vɛkən] v/t. (ge-, h) wake (up), waken; arouse (a. fig.); '2r m (-s/-) alarm-clock.
wedeln ['ve:dəln] v/i. (ge-, h): ~ mit wag (tail).
weder cj. ['ve:dər]: ~ ... noch neither ... nor.
Weg¹ [ve:k] m (-[e]s/-e) way (a. fig.); road (a. fig.); path; route; walk; auf halbem ~ half-way; am ~e by the roadside; aus dem ~e gehen steer clear of; aus dem ~e räumen remove (a. fig.); in die ~e leiten set on foot, initiate.
weg² adv. [vɛk] away, off; gone; geh ~! be off (with you)!; ~ mit ihm! off with him!; Hände ~! hands off!; F ich muß ~ I must be off; F ganz ~ sein be quite beside o.s.; '~bleiben F v/i. (irr. bleiben, sep., -ge-, sein) stay away; be omitted; '~bringen v/t. (irr. bringen, sep., -ge-, h) take away; a. remove (things).
wegen prp. (gen.) ['ve:gən] because of, on account of, owing to.
weg|fahren ['vɛk-] (irr. fahren, sep., -ge-) 1. v/t. (h) remove; cart away; 2. v/i. (sein) leave; '~fallen v/i. (irr. fallen, sep., -ge-, sein) be omitted; be abolished; '2gang m (-[e]s/no pl.) going away, departure; '~gehen v/i. (irr. gehen, sep., -ge-, sein) go away or off; merchandise:

sell; '~haben F v/t. (irr. haben, sep., -ge-, h): e-n ~ be tight; have a screw loose; er hat noch nicht weg, wie man es machen muß he hasn't got the knack of it yet; '~jagen v/t. (sep., -ge-, h) drive away; '~kommen F v/i. (irr. kommen, sep., -ge-, sein) get away; be missing; gut (schlecht) ~ come off well (badly); mach, daß du wegkommst! be off (with you)!; '~lassen v/t. (irr. lassen, sep., -ge-, h) let s.o. go; leave out, omit; '~laufen v/i. (irr. laufen, sep., -ge-, sein) run away; '~legen v/t. (sep., -ge-, h) put away; '~machen F v/t. (sep., -ge-, h) remove; a. take out (stains); '~müssen F v/i. (irr. müssen 1, sep., -ge-, h): ich muß weg I must be off; 2nahme ['~na:mə] f (-/-n) taking (away); '~nehmen v/t. (irr. nehmen, sep., -ge-, h) take up, occupy (time, space); j-m et. ~ take s.th. away from s.o.; '~raffen fig. v/t. (sep., -ge-, h) carry off.

Wegrand ['ve:k-] m wayside.

weg|räumen ['vɛk-] v/t. (sep., -ge-, h) clear away, remove; '~schaffen v/t. (sep., -ge-, h) remove; '~schicken v/t. (sep., -ge-, h) send away or off; '~sehen v/i. (irr. sehen, sep., -ge-, h) look away; ~ über (acc.) overlook, shut one's eyes to; '~setzen v/t. (sep., -ge-, h) put away; sich ~ über (acc.) disregard, ignore; '~streichen v/t. (irr. streichen, sep., -ge-, h) strike off or out; '~tun v/t. (irr. tun, sep., -ge-, h) put away or aside.

Wegweiser ['ve:kvaizər] m (-s/-) signpost, finger-post; fig. guide.

weg|wenden ['vɛk-] v/t. (irr. wenden,] sep., -ge-, h) turn away, avert (one's eyes); sich ~ turn away; '~werfen v/t. (irr. werfen, sep., -ge-, h) throw away; '~werfend adj. disparaging; '~wischen v/t. (sep., -ge-, h) wipe off; '~ziehen (irr. ziehen, sep., -ge-) 1. v/t. (h) pull or draw away; 2. v/i. (sein) (re)move.

weh [ve:] 1. adj. sore; 2. adv.: ~ tun ache, hurt; j-m ~ tun pain or hurt s.o.; fig. a. grieve s.o.; sich ~ tun hurt o.s.; mir tut der Finger ~ my finger hurts.

Wehen¹ ♀ ['ve:ən] f/pl. labo(u)r, travail.

wehen² [~] (ge-, h) 1. v/t. blow; 2. v/i. blow; es weht ein starker Wind it is blowing hard.

'weh|klagen v/i. (ge-, h) lament (um for, over); '~leidig adj. snivel(l)ing; voice: plaintive; '2mut f (-/no pl.) wistfulness; ~mütig adj. ['~my:-tiç] wistful.

Wehr [ve:r] 1. f (-/-en): sich zur ~ setzen offer resistance (gegen to), show fight; 2. n (-[e]s/-e) weir;

'~dienst ✕ m military service; '2en v/refl. (ge-, h) defend o.s.; offer resistance (gegen to); '2fähig ✕ adj. able-bodied; '2los adj. defenceless, Am. defenseless; '~pflicht ✕ f (-/no pl.) compulsory military service, conscription; '2-pflichtig ✕ adj. liable to military service.

Weib [vaip] n (-[e]s/-er) woman; wife; '~chen zo. n (-s/-) female.

Weiber|feind ['vaibər-] m womanhater; '~held contp. m ladies' man; '~volk F n (-[e]s/no pl.) womenfolk.

weib|isch adj. ['vaibiʃ] womanish, effeminate; '~lich adj. ['~p-] female; gr. feminine; womanly, feminine.

weich adj. [vaiç] soft (a. fig.); meat, etc.: tender; egg: soft-boiled; ~ werden soften; fig. relent.

Weiche¹ ▥ ['vaiçə] f (-/-n) switch; ~n pl. points pl.

Weiche² anat. [~] f (-/-n) flank, side.

weichen¹ ['vaiçən] v/i. (irr., ge-, sein) give way, yield (dat. to); nicht von der Stelle ~ not to budge an inch; j-m nicht von der Seite ~ stick to s.o.

weichen² [~] v/i. (ge-, h, sein) soak.

'Weichensteller ▥ m (-s/-) pointsman, switch-man.

'weich|herzig adj. soft-hearted, tender-hearted; '~lich adj. somewhat soft; fig. effeminate; '2ling ['~liŋ] m (-s/-e) weakling, milksop, molly(-coddle), sl. sissy; '2tier n mollusc.

Weide¹ ♀ ['vaidə] f (-/-n) willow.

Weide² ⚶ [~] f (-/-n) pasture; auf der ~ out at grass; '~land n pasture(-land); '2n (ge-, h) 1. v/t. feed, pasture, graze; sich ~ an (dat.) gloat over; feast on; 2. v/i. pasture, graze.

'Weiden|korb m wicker basket, osier basket; '~rute f osier switch.

weidmännisch hunt. adj. ['vaitmeniʃ] sportsmanlike.

weiger|n ['vaigərn] v/refl. (ge-, h) refuse, decline; '2ung f (-/-en) refusal.

Weihe eccl. ['vaiə] f (-/-n) consecration; ordination; '2n eccl. v/t. (ge-, h) consecrate; j-n zum Priester ~ ordain s.o. priest.

Weiher ['vaiər] m (-s/-) pond.

'weihevoll adj. solemn.

Weihnachten ['vainaxtən] n (-s/no pl.) Christmas, Xmas.

'Weihnachts|abend m Christmas eve; '~baum m Christmas-tree; '~ferien pl. Christmas holidays pl.; '~fest n Christmas; '~geschenk n Christmas present; '~gratifikation f Christmas bonus; '~karte f Christmas card; '~lied n carol, Christmas hymn; '~mann m Father Christmas, Santa Claus; '~markt m Christmas fair; '~zeit f

(-/no pl.) Christmas(-tide) (in Germany beginning on the first Advent Sunday).

'Weih|rauch eccl. m incense; '~wasser eccl. n (-s/no pl.) holy water.

weil cj. because, since, as.

Weil|chen ['vaɪlçən] n (-s/-): ein ~ a little while, a spell; '~e f (-/no pl.): e-e ~ a while.

Wein [vaɪn] m (-[e]s/-e) wine; ♀ vine; wilder ~ ♀ Virginia creeper; '~bau m (-[e]s/no pl.) vine-growing, viticulture; '~beere f grape; '~berg m vineyard; '~blatt n vine-leaf.

wein|en ['vaɪnən] v/i. (ge-, h) weep (um, vor dat. for), cry (vor dat. for joy, etc., with hunger, etc.); '~erlich adj. tearful, lachrymose; whining.

'Wein|ernte f vintage; '~essig m vinegar; '~faß n wine-cask; '~flasche f wine-bottle; '~geist m (-[e]s/-e) spirit(s pl.) of wine; '~glas n wineglass; '~handlung f wine-merchant's shop; '~karte f wine-list; '~keller m wine-vault; '~kelter f winepress; '~kenner m connoisseur of or in wines.

'Weinkrampf ✗ m paroxysm of weeping.

'Wein|kühler m wine-cooler; '~lese f vintage; '~presse f winepress; '~ranke f vine-tendril; '~rebe f vine; '2rot adj. claret-colo(u)red; '~stock m vine; '~traube f grape, bunch of grapes.

weise¹ ['vaɪzə] 1. adj. wise; sage; 2. ⚥ m (-n/-n) wise man, sage.

Weise² [~] f (-/-n) ♪ melody, tune; fig. manner, way; auf diese ~ in this way.

weisen ['vaɪzən] (irr., ge-, h) 1. v/t.: j-m die Tür ~ show s.o. the door; von der Schule ~ expel from school; von sich ~ reject (idea, etc.); deny (charge, etc.); 2. v/i.: ~ auf (acc.) point at or to.

Weis|heit ['vaɪshaɪt] f (-/✗-en) wisdom; am Ende s-r ~ sein be at one's wit's end; '~heitszahn m wisdom-tooth; '2machen v/t. (sep., -ge-, h): j-m et. ~ make s.o. believe s.th.

weiß adj. [vaɪs] white; '2blech n tin(-plate); '2brot n white bread; '2e m (-n/-n) white (man); '~en v/t. (ge-, h) whitewash; '~glühend adj. white-hot, incandescent; '2kohl m white cabbage; '~lich adj. whitish; '2waren pl. linen goods pl.; '2wein m white wine.

Weisung ['vaɪzuŋ] f (-/-en) direction, directive.

weit [vaɪt] 1. adj. distant (von from); world, garment: wide; area, etc.: vast; conscience: elastic; 2. adv.: ~ entfernt far away; ~ entfernt von a. a long distance from; fig. far from;

~ und breit far and wide; ~ über sechzig (Jahre alt) well over sixty; bei ~em (by) far; von ~em from a distance.

weit|ab adv. ['vaɪt'-] far away (von from); '~aus adv. (by) far, much; '2blick m (-[e]s/no pl.) far-sightedness; '~blickend adj. far-sighted, far-seeing; '~en v/t. and v/refl. (ge-, h) widen.

'weiter 1. adj. particulars, etc.: further; charges, etc.: additional, extra; ~e fünf Wochen another five weeks; bis auf ~es until further notice; ohne ~es without any hesitation; off-hand; 2. adv. furthermore, moreover; ~! go on!; nichts ~ nothing more; und so ~ and so on; bis hierher und nicht ~ so far and no farther; '2e n (-n/no pl.) the rest; further details pl.

'weiter|befördern v/t. (sep., no -ge-, h) forward; '~bestehen v/i. (irr. stehen, sep., no -ge-, h) continue to exist, survive; '~bilden v/t. (sep., -ge-, h) give s.o. further education; sich ~ improve one's knowledge; continue one's education; '~geben v/t. (irr. geben, sep., -ge-, h) pass (dat., an acc. to); '~gehen v/i. (irr. gehen, sep., -ge-, sein) pass or move on, walk along; fig. continue; go on; '~'hin adv. in (the) future; furthermore; et. ~ tun continue doing or to do s.th.; '~kommen v/i. (irr. kommen, sep., -ge-, sein) get on; '~können v/i. (irr. können, sep., -ge-, h) be able to go on; '~leben v/i. (sep., -ge-, h) live on, survive (a. fig.); '~machen v/t. and v/i. (sep., -ge-, h) carry on.

'weit|gehend adj. powers: large; support: generous; '~gereist adj. travel(l)ed; '~greifend adj. far-reaching; '~herzig adj. broad-minded; '~'hin adv. far off; '~läufig ['~lɔyfiç] 1. adj. house, etc.: spacious; story, etc.: detailed; relative: distant; 2. adv.: ~ erzählen (tell in) detail; er ist ~ verwandt mit mir he is a distant relative of mine; '~reichend adj. far-reaching; '~schweifig adj. diffuse, prolix; '~sichtig adj. ✗ far-sighted; fig. a. far-seeing; '2sichtigkeit ✗ f (-/✗-en) far-sightedness; '2sprung m (-[e]s/no pl.) long jump, Am. broad jump; '~tragend adj. ✗ long-range; fig. far-reaching; '~verbreitet adj. widespread.

Weizen ♀ ['vaɪtsən] m (-s/-) wheat; '~brot n wheaten bread; '~mehl n wheaten flour.

welch [vɛlç] 1. interr. pron. what; which; ~er? which one?; ~er von beiden? which of the two?; 2. rel. pron. who, that; which, that; 3. F indef. pron.: es gibt ~e, die sagen, daß ... there are some who say that ...; *es sollen viele Ausländer hier sein, hast du schon ~e gesehen?* many foreigners are said to be here, have you seen any yet?

welk *adj.* [vɛlk] faded, withered; *skin:* flabby, flaccid; '**~en** *v/i.* (ge-, *sein*) fade, wither.

Wellblech ['vɛlblɛç] *n* corrugated iron.

Welle ['vɛlə] *f* (-/-n) wave (*a. fig.*); ⊕ shaft.

'**wellen** *v/t. and v/refl.* (ge-, *h*) wave; '**2bereich** ≨ *m* wave-range; **~förmig** *adj.* ['~fœrmiç] undulating, undulatory; '**2länge** ≨ *f* wavelength; '**2linie** *f* wavy line; '**2reiten** *n* (-s/*no pl.*) surf-riding.

'**wellig** *adj.* wavy.

'**Wellpappe** *f* corrugated cardboard *or* paper.

Welt [vɛlt] *f* (-/-en) world; *die ganze* ~ the whole world, all the world; *auf der* ~ in the world, *auf der ganzen* ~ all over the world; *zur* ~ *bringen* give birth to, bring into the world.

'**Welt|all** *n* universe, cosmos; '**~anschauung** *f* Weltanschauung; '**~ausstellung** *f* world fair; '**2bekannt** *adj.* known all over the world; '**2berühmt** *adj.* worldfamous; '**2bürger** *m* cosmopolite; '**2erschütternd** *adj.* world-shaking; '**2fremd** *adj.* wordly innocent; '**~friede(n)** *m* universal peace; '**~geschichte** *f* (-/*no pl.*) universal history; '**2gewandt** *adj.* knowing the ways of the world; '**~handel** ✝ *m* (-s/*no pl.*) world trade; '**~karte** *f* map of the world; '**2klug** *adj.* wordly-wise; '**~krieg** *m* world war; *der zweite* ~ World War II; '**~lage** *f* international situation; '**~lauf** *m* course of the world; '**2lich 1.** *adj.* wordly, secular, temporal; **2.** *adv.*: ~ *gesinnt* wordly-minded; '**~literatur** *f* world literature; '**~macht** *f* world-power; **2männisch** *adj.* ['~mɛniʃ] man-of-the-world; '**~markt** *m* (-[e]s/*no pl.*) world market; '**~meer** *n* ocean; '**~meister** *m* world champion; '**~meisterschaft** *f* world championship; '**~raum** *m* (-[e]s/*no pl.*) (outer) space; '**~reich** *n* universal empire; *das Britische* ~ the British Empire; '**~reise** *f* journey round the world; '**~rekord** *m* world record; '**~ruf** *m* (-[e]s/*no pl.*) world-wide reputation; '**~schmerz** *m* Weltschmerz; '**~sprache** *f* world *or* universal language; '**~stadt** *f* metropolis; '**2weit** *adj.* world-wide; '**~wunder** *n* wonder of the world.

Wende ['vɛndə] *f* (-/-n) turn (*a. swimming*); *fig. a.* turning-point; '**~kreis** *m geogr.* tropic; *mot.* turning-circle.

Wendeltreppe ['vɛndəl-] *f* winding staircase, (*e-e* a flight of) winding stairs *pl.*, spiral staircase.

'**Wende|marke** *f sports:* turning-point; '**2n 1.** *v/t.* (ge-, *h*) turn (*coat, etc.*); turn (*hay*) about; **2.** *v/refl.* ([irr.,] ge-, *h*): *sich* ~ *an* (*acc.*) turn to; address o.s. to; apply to (*wegen* for); **3.** *v/i.* (ge-, *h*) ⚓, *mot.* turn; *bitte* ~*!* please turn over!; '**~punkt** *m* turning-point.

'**wend|ig** *adj.* nimble, agile (*both a. fig.*); *mot.,* ⚓ easily steerable; *mot.* flexible; '**2ung** *f* (-/-en) turn (*a. fig.*); ✕ facing; *fig.:* change; expression; idiom.

wenig ['ve:niç] **1.** *adj.* little; ~*e pl.* few *pl.*; ~*er* less; ~*er* fewer; *ein klein* ~ *Geduld* a little bit of patience; *das* ~*e* the little; **2.** *adv.* little; ~*er* less; ☆ *a.* minus; *am* ~*sten* least (of all); '**2keit** *f* (-/-en): *meine* ~ my humble self; '**~stens** *adv.* ['~stəns] at least.

wenn *cj.* [vɛn] when; if; ~ ... *nicht* if ... not, unless; ~ *auch* (al)though, even though; ~ *auch noch so* however; *und* ~ *nun* ...? what if ...?; *wie wäre es,* ~ *wir jetzt heimgingen?* what about going home now?

wer [ve:r] **1.** *interr. pron.* who; which; ~ *von euch?* which of you?; **2.** *rel. pron.* who; ~ *auch* (*immer*) who(so)ever; **3.** F *indef. pron.* somebody; anybody; *ist schon* ~ *gekommen?* has anybody come yet?

Werbe|abteilung ['vɛrbə-] *f* advertising *or* publicity department; '**~film** *m* advertising film.

'**werb|en** (*irr.,* ge-, *h*) **1.** *v/t.* canvass (*votes, subscribers, etc.*); ✕ recruit, enlist; **2.** *v/i.*: ~ *für* advertise, *Am. a.* advertize; make propaganda for; canvass for; '**2ung** *f* (-/-en) advertising, publicity, *Am. a.* advertizing; propaganda; canvassing; ✕ enlistment, recruiting.

Werdegang ['ve:rdə-] *m* career; ⊕ process of manufacture.

'**werden 1.** *v/i.* (*irr.,* ge-, *sein*) become, get; grow; turn (*pale, sour, etc.*); *was ist aus ihm geworden?* what has become of him?; *was will er (einmal)* ~*?* what is he going to be?; **2.** ♀ *n* (-s/*no pl.*): *noch im* ~ *sein* be in embryo.

werfen ['vɛrfən] (*irr.,* ge-, *h*) **1.** *v/t.* throw (*nach at*); *zo.* throw (*young*); cast (*shadow, glance, etc.*); *Falten* ~ fall in folds; set badly; **2.** *v/i.* throw; *zo.* litter; ~ *mit* throw (*auf acc., nach* at).

Werft ⚓ [vɛrft] *f* (-/-en) shipyard, dockyard.

Werk [vɛrk] *n* (-[e]s/-e) work; act; ⊕ works *pl.*; works *sg., pl.,* factory; *das* ~ *e-s Augenblicks* the work of a moment; *zu* ~*e gehen* proceed; '**~bank** ⊕ *f* work-bench; '**~meister** *m* foreman; **~statt** ['~ʃtat] *f*

(-/ᵘen) workshop; '**_tag** *m* work-day; '**\²tätig** *adj.* working; '**_zeug** *n* tool; implement; instrument.

Wermut ['ve:rmu:t] *m* (-[e]s/*no pl.*) ♀ wormwood; verm(o)uth.

wert [ve:rt] **1.** *adj.* worth; worthy (*gen.* of); **_, getan zu werden** worth doing; **2.** ♀ *m* (-[e]s/-e) value (*a.* ♫, ♬, *phys.*, *fig.*); worth (*a. fig.*); Brief-marken im **_ von 2 Schilling** 2 shil-lings' worth of stamps; *großen* **_** *legen auf* (*acc.*) set a high value (up)on.

'**Wert|brief** *m* money-letter; '**\²en** *v/t.* (ge-, *h*) value; appraise; '**_ge-genstand** *m* article of value; '**\²los** *adj.* worthless, valueless; '**_pa-piere** *n/pl.* securities *pl.*; '**_sachen** *pl.* valuables *pl.*; '**_ung** *f* (-/-en) valuation; appraisal; *sports:* score; '**\²voll** *adj.* valuable, precious.

Wesen ['ve:zən] *n* **1.** (-s/*no pl.*) entity, essence; nature, character; *viel* **_s machen** um make a fuss of; **2.** (-s/-) being; creature; '**\²los** *adj.* unreal; '**\²tlich** *adj.* essential, sub-stantial.

weshalb [ves'halp] **1.** *interr. pron.* why; **2.** *cj.* that's why.

Wespe *zo.* ['vespə] *f* (-/-n) wasp.

West *geogr.* [vɛst] west; '**_en** *m* (-s/*no pl.*) west; the West.

Weste ['vɛstə] *f* (-/-n) waistcoat, ♀ *and Am.* vest; *e-e reine* **_** *haben* have a clean slate.

'**west|lich** *adj.* west; westerly; western; '**\²wind** *m* west(erly) wind.

Wett|bewerb ['vɛtbəvɛrp] *m* (-[e]s/-e) competition (*a.* ♀); '**_büro** *n* betting office; '**_e** *f* (-/-n) wager, bet; *e-e* **_** *eingehen* lay *or* make a bet; '**_eifer** *m* emulation, rivalry; '**\²eifern** *v/i.* (ge-, *h*) vie (*mit* with; *in dat.* in; *um* for); '**\²en** (ge-, *h*) **1.** *v/t.* wager, bet; **2.** *v/i.:* *mit j-m um et.* **_** wager *or* bet s.o. s.th.; **_** *auf* (*acc.*) wager *or* bet on, back.

Wetter¹ ['vɛtər] *n* (-s/-) weather.

Wetter² [_] *m* (-s/-) bettor.

'**Wetter|bericht** *m* weather-fore-cast; '**\²fest** *adj.* weather-proof; '**_karte** *f* weather-chart; '**_lage** *f* weather-conditions *pl.*; '**_leuchten** *n* (-s/*no pl.*) sheet-lightning; '**_vor-hersage** *f* (-/-n) weather-forecast; '**_warte** *f* weather-station.

'**Wett|kampf** *m* contest, competi-tion; '**_kämpfer** *m* contestant; '**_lauf** *m* race; '**_läufer** *m* racer, runner; '**\²machen** *v/t.* (sep., -ge-, *h*) make up for; '**_rennen** *n* race; '**_rüsten** *n* (-s/*no pl.*) armament race; '**_spiel** *n* match, game; '**_streit** *m* contest. [sharpen.)

wetzen ['vɛtsən] *v/t.* (ge-, *h*) whet,)

wich [viç] *pret. of* **weichen¹**.

Wichse ['viksə] *f* **1.** (-/-n) blacking; polish; **2.** F *fig.* (-/*no pl.*) thrashing; '**\²n** *v/t.* (ge-, *h*) black; polish.

---

wichtig *adj.* ['viçtiç] important; *sich* **_** *machen* show off; '**\²keit** *f* (-/**_**-en) importance; **\²tuer** ['**_**tu:-ər] *m* (-s/-) pompous fellow; '**_tue-risch** *adj.* pompous.

Wickel ['vikəl] *m* (-s/-) roll(er); ⚙: compress; packing; '**\²n** *v/t.* (ge-, *h*) wind; swaddle (*baby*); wrap.

Widder *zo.* ['vidər] *m* (-s/-) ram.

wider *prp.* (*acc.*) ['vi:dər] against, contrary to; '**_borstig** *adj.* cross-grained; **_'fahren** *v/i.* (*irr.* fahren, *no* -ge-, *sein*) happen (*dat.* to); '**²haken** *m* barb; **²hall** ['**_**hal] *m* (-[e]s/-e) echo, reverberation; *fig.* response; **_'hallen** *v/i.* (sep., -ge-, *h*) (re-)echo (*von* with), resound (with); **_'legen** *v/t.* (*no* -ge-, *h*) refute, disprove; '**_lich** *adj.* repug-nant, repulsive; disgusting; '**_na-türlich** *adj.* unnatural; '**_recht-lich** *adj.* illegal, unlawful; '**²rede** *f* contradiction; '**²ruf** *m* ♫ revoca-tion; retraction; **_'rufen** *v/t.* (*irr.* rufen, *no* -ge-, *h*) revoke; retract (*a.* ♫); '**_ruflich** *adj.* revocable; **²sa-cher** ['**_**zaxər] *m* (-s/-) adversary; '**²schein** *m* reflection; **_'setzen** *v/refl.* (*no* -ge-, *h*): *sich e-r Sache* **_** oppose *or* resist s.th.; **_'setzlich** *adj.* refractory; insubordinate; '**_sinnig** *adj.* absurd; **_spenstig** *adj.* ['**_**ʃpɛnstiç] refractory; **²spenstig-keit** *f* (-/**_**-en) refractoriness; '**_spiegeln** *v/t.* (sep., -ge-, *h*) reflect (*a. fig.*); *sich* **_** *in* (*dat.*) be reflected in; **_'sprechen** *v/i.* (*irr.* sprechen, *no* -ge-, *h*): *j-m* **_** con-tradict s.o.; '**²spruch** *m* contradic-tion; opposition; *im* **_** *zu* in con-tradiction to; '**_sprüchlich** *adj.* ['**_**ʃpry:çliç] contradictory; '**_spruchslos** **1.** *adj.* uncontradicted; **2.** *adv.* without contradiction; '**²stand** *m* resistance (*a.* ⚡); op-position; **_** *leisten* offer resistance (*dat.* to); *auf heftigen* **_** *stoßen* meet with stiff opposition; '**_stands-fähig** *adj.* resistant (*a.* ⊕); **_'ste-hen** *v/i.* (*irr.* stehen, *no* -ge-, *h*) resist (*e-r Sache* s.th.); **_'streben** *v/i.* (*no* -ge-, *h*): *es widerstrebt mir, dies zu tun* I hate doing *or* to do that, I am reluctant to do that; **_'strebend** *adv.* reluctantly; '**²-streit** *m* (-[e]s/**_**-e) antagonism; *fig.* conflict; **_wärtig** *adj.* ['**_**vɛrtiç] unpleasant, disagreeable; disgust-ing; '**²wille** *m* aversion (*gegen* to, for, from); dislike (to, of, for); disgust (at, for); reluctance, un-willingness; '**_willig** *adj.* reluctant, unwilling.

widm|en ['vitmən] *v/t.* (ge-, *h*) dedicate; '**²ung** *f* (-/-en) dedica-tion.

widrig *adj.* ['vi:driç] adverse; **_en-falls** *adv.* ['**_**gən-] failing which, in default of which.

wie [vi:] **1.** *adv.* how; ~ *alt ist er?* what is his age?; ~ *spät ist es?* what is the time?; **2.** *cj.*: *ein Mann ~ er* a man such as he, a man like him; ~ *er dies hörte* hearing this; *ich hörte, ~ er es sagte* I heard him saying so.

wieder *adv.* ['vi:dər] again, anew; *immer ~* again and again; '²aufbau *m* (-[e]s/*no pl.*) reconstruction; rebuilding; ',aufbauen *v/t.* (*sep.*, -ge-, h) reconstruct; ',aufleben *v/i.* (*sep.*, -ge-, sein) revive; '²aufleben *n* (-s/*no pl.*) revival; '²aufnahme *f* resumption; ',aufnehmen *v/t.* (*irr.* nehmen, *sep.*, -ge-, h) resume; '²beginn *m* recommencement; re-opening; ',bekommen *v/t.* (*irr.* kommen, *sep.*, no -ge-, h) get back; ',beleben *v/t.* (*sep.*, no -ge-, h) resurrect; '²belebung *f* (-/-en) revival; *fig. a.* resurrection; '²belebungsversuch *m* attempt at resuscitation; ',bringen *v/t.* (*irr.* bringen, *sep.*, -ge-, h) bring back; restore, give back; ',einsetzen *v/t.* (*sep.*, -ge-, h) restore; ',einstellen *v/t.* (*sep.*, -ge-, h) re-engage; '²ergreifung *f* reseizure; ',erkennen *v/t.* (*irr.* kennen, *sep.*, no -ge-, h) recognize (*an dat.* by); ',erstatten *v/t.* (*sep.*, no -ge-, h) restore; reimburse, refund (*money*); ',geben *v/t.* (*irr.* geben, *sep.*, -ge-, h) give back, return; render, reproduce; ',gutmachen *v/t.* (*sep.*, -ge-, h) make up for; '²gutmachung *f* (-/-en) reparation; ',herstellen *v/t.* (*sep.*, -ge-, h) restore; ',holen *v/t.* (h) **1.** [',ho:lən] (*no* -ge-) repeat; **2.** [',ho:lən] (*sep.*, -ge-) fetch back; '²holung *f* (-/-en) repetition; ',käuen ['kɔyən] (*sep.*, -ge-, h) **1.** *v/i.* ruminate, chew the cud; **2.** F *fig. v/t.* repeat over and over; '²kehr ['ke:r] *f* (-/*no pl.*) return; recurrence; ',kehren *v/i.* (*sep.*, -ge-, sein) return; recur; ',kommen *v/i.* (*irr.* kommen, *sep.*, -ge-, sein) come back; return; ',sehen *v/t. and v/refl.* (*irr.* sehen, *sep.*, -ge-, h) see *or* meet again; '²sehen *n* (-s/*no pl.*) meeting again; *auf ~!* good-bye!; ',tun *v/t.* (*irr.* tun, *sep.*, -ge-, h) do again, repeat; ',um *adv.* again, anew; ',vereinigen *v/t.* (*sep.*, no -ge-, h) reunite; '²vereinigung *f* reunion; *pol.* reunification; '²verheiratung *f* remarriage; '²verkäufer *m* reseller; retailer; '²wahl *f* re-election; ',wählen *v/t.* (*sep.*, -ge-, h) re-elect; '²zulassung *f* readmission.

Wiege ['vi:gə] *f* (-/-n) cradle.

wiegen¹ ['vi:gən] *v/t. and v/i.* (*irr.*, -ge-, h) weigh.

wiegen² [~] *v/t.* (-ge-, h) rock; *in Sicherheit ~* rock in security, lull into (a false sense of) security.

'Wiegenlied *n* lullaby.

wiehern ['vi:ərn] *v/i.* (-ge-, h) neigh.

Wiener ['vi:nər] *m* (-s/-) Viennese; '²isch *adj.* Viennese.

wies [vi:s] *pret. of* weisen.

Wiese ['vi:zə] *f* (-/-n) meadow.

wie'**so** *interr. pron.* why; why so.

wie'**viel** *adv.* how much; ~ *pl.* how many *pl.*; ~**te** *adv.* [~tə]: *den ~ten haben wir heute?* what's the date today?

wild [vilt] **1.** *adj.* wild; savage; ~*es Fleisch* ⚕ proud flesh; ~*e Ehe* concubinage; ~*er Streik* ⚒ wildcat strike; **2.** ⚲ *n* (-[e]s/*no pl.*) game.

'Wild|**bach** *m* torrent; ',bret [',brɛt] *n* (-s/*no pl.*) game; venison.

Wilde ['vildə] *m* (-n/-n) savage.

Wilder|**er** ['vildərər] *m* (-s/-) poacher; '²n *v/i.* (-ge-, h) poach.

'Wild|**fleisch** *n s.* Wildbret; '²fremd F *adj.* quite strange; ',hüter *m* gamekeeper; ',leder *n* buckskin; '²ledern *adj.* buckskin; doeskin; ',nis *f* (-/-se) wilderness, wild (*a. fig.*); ',schwein *n* wild-boar.

Wille ['vilə] *m* (-ns/⚬-n) will; *s-n ~n durchsetzen* have one's way; *gegen s-n ~n* against one's will; *j-m s-n ~n lassen* let s.o. have his (own) way; '²nlos *adj.* lacking will-power.

'Willens|**freiheit** *f* (-/*no pl.*) freedom of (the) will; ',kraft *f* (-/*no pl.*) will-power; ',schwäche *f* (-/*no pl.*) weak will; '²stark *adj.* strong-willed; ',stärke *f* (-/*no pl.*) strong will, will-power.

'will|**ig** *adj.* willing, ready; ',kommen *adj.* welcome; ',kür ['ky:r] *f* (-/*no pl.*) arbitrariness; ',kürlich *adj.* arbitrary.

wimmeln ['viməln] *v/i.* (-ge-, h) swarm (*von* with), teem (with).

wimmern ['vimərn] *v/i.* (-ge-, h) whimper, whine.

Wimpel ['vimpəl] *m* (-s/-) pennant, pennon, streamer.

Wimper ['vimpər] *f* (-/-n) eyelash.

Wind [vint] *m* (-[e]s/-e) wind; ',beutel *m* cream-puff; F *fig.* windbag.

Winde ['vində] *f* (-/-n) windlass, reel.

Windel ['vindəl] *f* (-/-n) diaper, (baby's) napkin; ',n *pl. a.* swaddling-clothes *pl.*

'winden *v/t.* (*irr.*, -ge-, h) wind; twist, twirl; make, bind (*wreath*); *sich ~ vor* (*dat.*) writhe with.

'Wind|**hose** *f* whirlwind, tornado; ',hund *m* greyhound; '²ig *adj.* [',diç] windy; F *fig. excuse:* thin, lame; ',mühle *f* windmill; ',pokken ⚕ *pl.* chicken-pox; ',richtung *f* direction of the wind; ',rose ⚓ *f* compass card; ',schutzscheibe *f* wind-screen, *Am.* windshield; ',stärke *f* wind veloc-

ity; '2still adj. calm; '~stille f
calm; '~stoß m blast of wind, gust.
'Windung f (-/-en) winding, turn;
bend (of way, etc.); coil (of snake,
etc.).
Wink [viŋk] m (-[e]s/-e) sign; wave;
wink; fig.: hint; tip.
Winkel ['viŋkəl] m (-s/-) ⚔ angle;
corner, nook; '2ig adj. angular;
street: crooked; '~zug m subterfuge,
trick, shift.
'winken v/i. (ge-, h) make a sign;
beckon; mit dem Taschentuch ~
wave one's handkerchief.
winklig adj. ['viŋkliç] s. winkelig.
winseln ['vinzəln] v/i. (ge-, h)
whimper, whine.
Winter ['vintər] m (-s/-) winter; im
~ in winter; '2lich adj. wintry;
'~schlaf m hibernation; '~sport m
winter sports pl.
Winzer ['vintsər] m (-s/-) vine-
dresser; vine-grower; vintager.
winzig adj. ['vintsiç] tiny, diminu-
tive.
Wipfel ['vipfəl] m (-s/-) top.
Wippe ['vipə] f (-/-n) seesaw; '2n
v/i. (ge-, h) seesaw.
wir pers. pron. [vi:r] we; ~ drei the
three of us.
Wirbel ['virbəl] m (-s/-) whirl,
swirl; eddy; flurry (of blows, etc.);
anat. vertebra; '2ig adj. giddy,
vertiginous; wild; '2n v/i. (ge-, h)
whirl; drums: roll; '~säule anat. f
spinal or vertebral column; '~
sturm m cyclone, tornado, Am. a.
twister; '~tier n vertebrate; '~wind
m whirlwind (a. fig.).
wirk|en ['virkən] (ge-, h) 1. v/t.
knit, weave; work (wonders); 2.
v/i.: ~ als act or function as; ~ auf
(acc.) produce an impression on;
beruhigend ~ have a soothing effect;
'~lich adj. real, actual; true, genuine; '2lichkeit f (-/-en) reality; in ~
in reality; '~sam adj. effective,
efficacious; '2samkeit f (-/~-en)
effectiveness, efficacy; '2ung f
(-/-en) effect.
'Wirkungs|kreis m sphere or field
of activity; '2los adj. ineffective,
inefficacious; '~losigkeit f (-/no pl.)
ineffectiveness, inefficacy; '2voll
adj. s. wirksam.
wirr adj. [vir] confused; speech:
incoherent; hair: dishevel(l)ed;
'2en pl. disorders pl.; troubles pl.;
2warr ['~var] m (-s/no pl.) confusion, muddle.
Wirsingkohl ['virziŋ-] m (-[e]s/no
pl.) savoy.
Wirt [virt] m (-[e]s/-e) host; landlord; innkeeper.
'Wirtschaft f (-/-en) housekeeping;
economy; trade and industry;
economics pl.; s. Wirtshaus; F mess;
'2en v/i. (ge-, h) keep house;
economize; F bustle (about); '~erin

f (-/-nen) housekeeper; '2lich adj.
economic; economical.
'Wirtschafts|geld n housekeeping
money; '~jahr n financial year;
'~krise f economic crisis; '~politik
f economic policy; '~prüfer m
(-s/-) chartered accountant, Am.
certified public accountant.
'Wirtshaus n public house, F pub.
Wisch [viʃ] m (-es/-e) wisp (of straw,
etc.); contp. scrap of paper; '2en
v/t. (ge-, h) wipe.
wispern ['vispərn] v/t. and v/i. (ge-,
h) whisper.
Wiß|begierde ['vis-] f (-/no pl.)
thirst for knowledge; '2begierig
adj. eager for knowledge.
wissen ['visən] 1. v/t. (irr., ge-, h)
know; man kann nie ~ you never
know, you never can tell; 2. 2 n
(-s/no pl.) knowledge; meines ~s
to my knowledge, as far as I know.
'Wissenschaft f (-/-en) science;
knowledge; '~ler m (-s/-) scholar;
scientist; researcher; '2lich adj.
scientific.
'Wissens|drang m (-[e]s/no pl.)
urge or thirst for knowledge; '2-
wert adj. worth knowing.
'wissentlich adj. knowing, conscious.
wittern ['vitərn] v/t. (ge-, h) scent,
smell; fig. a. suspect.
'Witterung f (-/~-en) weather;
hunt. scent; '~sverhältnisse ['~sfer-
heltnisə] pl. meteorological conditions pl.   [m (-s/-) widower.]
Witwe ['vitvə] f (-/-n) widow; '~r)
Witz [vits] m 1. (-es/no pl.) wit;
2.(-es/-e) joke; ~e reißen crack jokes;
'~blatt n comic paper; '2ig adj.
witty; funny.
wo [vo:] 1. adv. where?; 2. cj.: F
ach ~! nonsense!
wob [vo:p] pret. of weben.
wo'bei adv. at what?; at which; in
doing so.
Woche ['vɔxə] f (-/-n) week; heute
in e-r ~ today week.
'Wochen|bett n childbed; '~blatt
n weekly (paper); '~ende n week-
end; '2lang 1. adj.: nach ~em Warten after (many) weeks of waiting;
2. adv. for weeks; '2lohn m weekly
pay or wages pl.; '~markt m weekly
market; '~schau f news-reel; '~tag
m week-day.
wöchentlich ['vœçəntliç] 1. adj.
weekly; 2. adv. weekly, every week;
einmal ~ once a week.
Wöchnerin ['vœçnərin] f (-/-nen)
woman in childbed.
wo|'durch adv. by what?, how?; by
which, whereby; ~'für adv. for
what?, what ... for?; (in return)
for which.   [gen¹.]
wog [vo:k] pret. of wägen and wie-)
Woge ['vo:gə] f (-/-n) wave (a. fig.),
billow; die ~n glätten pour oil on

troubled waters; '2n v/i. (ge-, h) surge (a. fig.), billow; wheat: a. wave; heave.

wo|'her adv. from where?, where ... from?; ~ wissen Sie das? how do you (come to) know that?; ~'hin adv. where (... to)?

wohl [vo:l] 1. adv. well; sich nicht ~ fühlen be unwell; ~ oder übel willy-nilly; leben Sie ~! farewell!; er wird ~ reich sein he is rich, I suppose; 2. 2 n (-[e]s/no pl.): ~ und Wehe weal and woe; auf Ihr ~! your health!, here is to you!

'Wohl|befinden n well-being; good health; '~behagen n comfort, ease; '2behalten adv. safe; '2bekannt adj. well-known; '~ergehen n (-s/no pl.) welfare, prosperity; 2er-zogen adj. ['~ʔertso:gən] well-bred, well-behaved; '~fahrt f (-/no pl.) welfare; public assistance; '~ge-fallen n (-s/no pl.) pleasure; sein ~ haben an (dat.) take delight in; '2gemeint adj. well-meant, well-intentioned; 2gemut adj. ['~gə-mu:t] cheerful; 2genährt adj. well-fed; '~geruch m scent, perfume; '2gesinnt adj. well-disposed (j-m towards s.o.); '2habend adj. well-to-do; '2ig adj. comfortable; cosy, snug; '~klang m (-[e]s/no pl.) melodious sound, harmony; '2-klingend adj. melodious, harmoni-ous; '~laut m s. Wohlklang; '~leben n (-s/no pl.) luxury; '2riechend adj. fragrant; 2schmeckend adj. savo(u)ry; '~sein n well-being; good health; '~stand m (-[e]s/no pl.) prosperity, wealth; '~tat f kindness, charity; fig. comfort, treat; '~täter m benefactor; '2tätig adj. charitable, beneficent; '~tä-tigkeit f charity; 2tuend adj. ['~tu:-ənt] pleasant, comfortable; 2tun v/i. (irr. tun, sep., -ge-, h) do good; '2verdient adj. well-deserved; p. of great merit; '~wollen n (-s/no pl.) goodwill; benevolence; favo(u)r; '2wollen v/i. (sep., -ge-, h) be well-disposed (j-m towards s.o.).

wohn|en ['vo:nən] v/i. (ge-, h) live (in dat. in, at; bei j-m with s.o.); reside (in, at; with); '2haus n dwelling-house; block of flats, Am. apartment house; '~haft adj. resident, living; '2lich adj. comfort-able; cosy, snug; '2ort m dwelling-place, residence; esp. ₰₰ domicile; '2sitz m residence; mit ~ in resident in or at; ohne festen ~ without fixed abode; '2ung f (-/-en) dwell-ing, habitation; flat, Am. apartment.

'Wohnungs|amt n housing office; '~not f housing shortage; '~pro-blem n housing problem.

'Wohn|wagen m caravan, trailer; '~zimmer n sitting-room, esp. Am. living room.

wölb|en ['vœlbən] v/t. (ge-, h) vault; arch; sich ~ arch; '2ung f (-/-en) vault, arch; curvature.

Wolf zo. [vɔlf] m (-[e]s/⁅e) wolf.

Wolke ['vɔlkə] f (-/-n) cloud.

'Wolken|bruch m cloud-burst; '~kratzer m (-s/-) skyscraper; '2los adj. cloudless.

'wolkig adj. cloudy, clouded.

Woll|decke ['vɔl-] f blanket; '~e f (-/-n) wool.

wollen[1] ['vɔlən] (h) 1. v/t. (ge-) wish, desire; want; lieber ~ prefer; nicht ~ refuse; er weiß, was er will he knows his mind; 2. v/i. (ge-): ich will schon, aber ... I want to, but ...; 3. v/aux. (no -ge-) be willing; intend, be going to; be about to; lieber ~ prefer; nicht ~ refuse; er hat nicht gehen ~ he refused to go.

woll|en[2] adj. [~] wool(l)en; '~ig adj. wool(l)y; '2stoff m wool(l)en.

Woll|lust ['vɔlust] f (-/⁅e) volupt-uousness; 2lüstig adj. ['~lystiç] voluptuous.

'Wollwaren pl. wool(l)en goods pl.

wo|'mit adv. with what?, what ... with?; with which; ~'möglich adv. perhaps, maybe.

Wonn|e ['vɔnə] f (-/-n) delight, bliss; '2ig adj. delightful, blissful.

wo|ran adv. [vo:'ran]: ~ denkst du? what are you thinking of?; ich weiß nicht, ~ ich mit ihm bin I don't know what to make of him; ~ liegt es, daß ...? how is it that ...?; ~'rauf adv. on what?, what ... on?; where-upon, after which; ~ wartest du? what are you waiting for?; ~'raus adv. from what?, what ... of?; from which; ~rin adv. [~'rin] in what?; in which.

Wort [vɔrt] n 1. (-[e]s/⁅er) word; er kann seine Wörter noch nicht he hasn't learnt his words yet; 2. (-[e]s/-e) word; term, expression; ums ~ bitten ask permission to speak; das ~ ergreifen begin to speak; parl. rise to speak, address the House, esp. Am. take the floor; das ~ führen be the spokesman; ~ halten keep one's word; '2brüchig adj.: er ist ~ geworden he has broken his word.

Wörter|buch ['vœrtər-] n diction-ary; '~verzeichnis n vocabulary, list of words.

'Wort|führer m spokesman; '2ge-treu adj. literal; 2karg adj. taci-turn; ~klauberei [~klaubə'raɪ] f (-/-en) word-splitting; '~laut m (-[e]s/no pl.) wording; text. [eral.)

wörtlich adj. ['vœrtliç] verbal, lit-)

'Wort|schatz m (-es/no pl.) vocabu-lary; '~schwall m (-[e]s/no pl.) verbiage; '~spiel n pun (über acc., mit [up]on), play upon words; '~stellung gr. f word order, order of words; '~stamm ling. m stem; '~streit m, '~wechsel m dispute.

wo|rüber adv. [vo:'ry:bər] over or upon what?, what ... over or about or on?; over or upon which, about which; **~rum** adv. [~'rum] about what?, what ... about?; about or for which; ~ handelt es sich? what is it about?; **~runter** adv. [~'run-tər] under or among what?, what ... under?; under or among which; **~'von** adv. of or from what?, what ... from or of?; about what?, what ... about?; of or from which; **~'vor** adv. of what?, what ... of?; of which; **~'zu** adv. for what?, what ... for?; for which.

Wrack [vrak] n (-[e]s/-e, -s) ⚓ wreck (a. fig.).

wrang [vraŋ] pret. of wringen.

wring|en ['vriŋən] v/t. (irr., ge-, h) wring; **'~maschine** f wringing-machine.

Wucher ['vu:xər] m (-s/no pl.) usury; ~ treiben practise usury; **'~er** m (-s/-) usurer; **'~gewinn** m excess profit; **'2isch** adj. usurious; **'2n** v/i. (ge-, h) grow exuberantly; **'~ung** f (-/-en) ⚕ exuberant growth; 🌿 growth; **'~zinsen** m/pl. usurious interest.

Wuchs [vu:ks] 1. m (-es/⁼e) growth; figure, shape; stature; 2. ♀ pret. of wachsen.

Wucht [vuxt] f (-/♀-en) weight; force; **'2ig** adj. heavy.

Wühl|arbeit fig. ['vy:l-] f insidious agitation, subversive activity; **'2en** v/i. (ge-, h) dig; pig: root; fig. agitate; ~ in (dat.) rummage (about) in; **'~er** m (-s/-) agitator.

Wulst [vulst] m (-es/⁼e), f (-/⁼e) pad; bulge; ▲ roll(-mo[u]lding); ⊕ bead; **'2ig** adj. lips: thick.

wund adj. [vunt] sore; ~e Stelle sore; ~er Punkt tender spot; **2e** ['~də] f (-/-n) wound; alte ~n wieder auf-reißen reopen old sores.

Wunder ['vundər] n (-s/-) miracle; fig. a. wonder, marvel; ~ wirken pills, etc.: work marvels; kein ~, wenn man bedenkt ... no wonder, considering ...; **'2bar** adj. miraculous; fig. a. wonderful, marvel-(l)ous; **'~kind** n infant prodigy; **'2lich** adj. queer, odd; **'2n** v/t. (ge-, h) surprise, astonish; sich ~ be surprised or astonished (über acc. at); **'2schön** adj. very beautiful; **'~tat** f wonder, miracle; **'~täter** m wonder-worker; **'2tätig** adj. wonder-working; **'2voll** adj. wonderful; **'~werk** n marvel, wonder.

'Wund|fieber 🌿 n wound-fever; **'~starrkrampf** 🌿 m tetanus.

Wunsch [vunʃ] m (-es/⁼e) wish, desire; request; auf ~ by or on request; je desired; nach ~ as desired; mit den besten Wünschen zum Fest with the compliments of the season.

Wünschelrute ['vynʃəl-] f divin-

ing-rod, dowsing-rod; **~ngänger** ['~geŋər] m (-s/-) diviner, dowser.

wünschen ['vynʃən] v/t. (ge-, h) wish, desire; wie Sie ~ as you wish; was ~ Sie? what can I do for you?; **'~swert** adj. desirable.

'wunsch|gemäß adv. as requested or desired, according to one's wishes; **'2zettel** m list of wishes.

wurde ['vurdə] pret. of werden.

Würde ['vyrdə] f (-/-n) dignity; unter seiner ~ beneath one's dignity; **'2los** adj. undignified; **'~n-träger** m dignitary; **'2voll** adj. dignified; grave.

'würdig adj. worthy (gen. of); dignified; grave; **~en** ['~gən] v/t. (ge-, h) appreciate, value; mention hono(u)rably; laud, praise; j-n keines Blickes ~ ignore s.o. completely; **2ung** ['~guŋ] f (-/-en) appreciation, valuation.

Wurf [vurf] m (-[e]s/⁼e) throw, cast; zo. litter.

Würfel ['vyrfəl] m (-s/-) die; cube (a. ℞); **'~becher** m dice-box; **'2n** v/i. (ge-, h) (play) dice; **'~spiel** n game of dice; **'~zucker** m lump sugar. [tile.]

'Wurfgeschoß n missile, project-/

würgen ['vyrgən] (ge-, h) 1. v/t. choke, strangle; 2. v/i. choke; retch.

Wurm zo. [vurm] m (-[e]s/⁼er) worm; **'2en** F v/t. (ge-, h) vex; rankle (j-n in s.o.'s mind); **'2-stichig** adj. worm-eaten.

Wurst [vurst] f (-/⁼e) sausage; F das ist mir ganz ~ I don't care a rap.

Würstchen ['vyrstçən] n (-s/-) sausage; heißes ~ hot sausage, Am. hot dog.

Würze ['vyrtsə] f (-/-n) seasoning, flavo(u)r; spice, condiment; fig. salt.

Wurzel ['vurtsəl] f (-/-n) root (a. gr., ℞); ~ schlagen strike or take root (a. fig.); **'2n** v/i. (ge-, h) (strike or take) root; ~ in (dat.) take one's root in, be rooted in.

'würz|en v/t. (ge-, h) spice, season, flavo(u)r; **'~ig** adj. spicy, well-seasoned, aromatic.

wusch [vu:ʃ] pret. of waschen.

wußte ['vustə] pret. of wissen.

Wust F [vu:st] m (-es/no pl.) tangled mass; rubbish; mess.

wüst adj. [vy:st] desert, waste; confused; wild, dissolute; rude; **'2e** f (-/-n) desert, waste; **2ling** ['~liŋ] m (-s/-e) debauchee, libertine, rake.

Wut [vu:t] f (-/no pl.) rage, fury; in ~ in a rage; **'~anfall** m fit of rage.

wüten ['vy:tən] v/i. (ge-, h) rage (a. fig.); **'~d** adj. furious, enraged (über acc. at; auf acc. with), esp. Am. F a. mad (über acc., auf acc. at).

Wüterich ['vy:tərıç] m (-[e]s/-e) berserker; bloodthirsty man.

'wutschnaubend adj. foaming with rage.

X, Y

X-Beine ['iks-] *n/pl.* knock-knees *pl.*; **'X-beinig** *adj.* knock-kneed.

x-beliebig *adj.* [iksbə'li:biç] any (... you please); *jede(r, -s)* ~e ... any ...

x-mal *adv.* ['iks-] many times, *sl.* umpteen times.

X-Strahlen ['iks-] *m/pl.* X-rays *pl.*

x-te *adj.* ['ikstə]: *zum* ~n *Male* for the umpteenth time.

Xylophon ♪ [ksylo'fo:n] *n* (-s/-e) xylophone.

Yacht ⚓ [jaxt] *f* (-/-en) yacht.

Z

Zacke ['tsakə] *f* (-/-n) *s.* Zacken.

'Zacken 1. *m* (-s/-) (sharp) point; prong; tooth (*of comb, saw, rake*); jag (*of rock*); **2.** ⚓ *v/t.* (ge-, h) indent, notch; jag.

'zackig *adj.* indented, notched; *rock:* jagged; pointed; ⚔ F *fig.* smart.

zaghaft *adj.* ['tsɑ:khaft] timid; **'Zigkeit** *f* (-/*no pl.*) timidity.

zäh *adj.* [tsɛ:] tough, tenacious (*both a. fig.*); *liquid:* viscid, viscous; *fig.* dogged; **'~flüssig** *adj.* viscid, viscous, sticky; **'Zigkeit** *f* (-/*no pl.*) toughness, tenacity (*both a. fig.*); viscosity; *fig.* doggedness.

Zahl [tsɑ:l] *f* (-/-en) number; figure, cipher; **'Zbar** *adj.* payable.

'zählbar *adj.* countable.

zahlen ['tsɑ:lən] (ge-, h) **1.** *v/i.* pay; *at restaurant:* ~ (, bitte)! the bill, please!, *Am.* the check, please!; **2.** *v/t.* pay.

zählen ['tsɛ:lən] (ge-, h) **1.** *v/t.* count, number; ~ *zu* count *or* number among; **2.** *v/i.* count; ~ *auf* (*acc.*) count (up)on, rely (up)on.

'Zahlen|lotto *n s.* Lotto; **'Zmäßig 1.** *adj.* numerical; **2.** *adv.:* j-m ~ *überlegen sein* outnumber s.o.

'Zähler *m* (-s/-) counter; ♣ numerator; *for gas, etc.:* meter.

'Zahl|karte *f* money-order form (*for paying direct into the postal cheque account*); **'Zlos** *adj.* numberless, innumerable, countless; **'~meister** ⚔ *m* paymaster; **'Zreich 1.** *adj.* numerous; **2.** *adv.* in great number; **'~tag** *m* pay-day; **'~ung** *f* (-/-en) payment.

'Zahlung *f* (-/-en) counting.

'Zahlungs|anweisung *f* order to pay; **'~aufforderung** *f* request for payment; **'~bedingungen** *f/pl.* terms *pl.* of payment; **'~befehl** *m* order to pay; **'~einstellung** *f* suspension of payment; **'Zfähig** *adj.* solvent; **'Zfähigkeit** *f* solvency; **'~frist** *f* term for payment; **'~mittel** *n* currency; *gesetzliches* ~ legal tender; **'~schwierigkeiten** *f/pl.* financial *or* pecuniary difficulties

pl.; **'~termin** *m* date of payment; **'Zunfähig** *adj.* insolvent; **'~unfähigkeit** *f* insolvency.

'Zahlwort *gr.* *n* (-[e]s/~er) numeral.

zahm *adj.* [tsɑ:m] tame (*a. fig.*), domestic(ated).

zähm|en ['tsɛ:mən] *v/t.* (ge-, h) tame (*a. fig.*), domesticate; **'Zung** *f* (-/-⚔-en) taming (*a. fig.*), domestication.

Zahn [tsɑ:n] *m* (-[e]s/~e) tooth; ⊕ tooth, cog; *Zähne bekommen* cut one's teeth; **'~arzt** *m* dentist, dental surgeon; **'~bürste** *f* toothbrush; **'~creme** *f* tooth-paste; **'Zen** *v/i.* (ge-, h) teethe, cut one's teeth; **'~ersatz** *m* denture; **'~fäule** ⚕ ['⚕fɔylə] *f* (-/*no pl.*) dental caries; **'~fleisch** *n* gums *pl.*; **'~füllung** *f* filling, stopping; **'~geschwür** ⚕ *n* gumboil; **'~heilkunde** *f* dentistry; **'Zlos** *adj.* toothless; **'~lücke** *f* gap between the teeth; **'~pasta** [~pasta] *f* (-/*Zahnpasten*), **'~paste** *f* toothpaste; **'~rad** ⊕ *n* cog-wheel; **'~radbahn** *f* rack-railway; **'~schmerzen** *m/pl.* toothache; **'~stocher** *m* (-s/-) toothpick.

Zange ['tsaŋə] *f* (-/-n) (e-e *a* pair of) tongs *pl.* *or* pliers *pl.* *or* pincers *pl.*; ⚔, *zo.* forceps *sg.*; *pl.*

Zank [tsaŋk] *m* (-[e]s/*no pl.*) quarrel, F row; **'~apfel** *m* bone of contention; **'Zen** (ge-, h) **1.** *v/i.* scold (*mit* j-m s.o.); **2.** *v/refl.* quarrel, wrangle.

zänkisch *adj.* ['tsɛŋkiʃ] quarrelsome.

Zäpfchen ['tsɛpfçən] *n* (-s/-) small peg; *anat.* uvula.

Zapfen ['tsapfən] **1.** *m* (-s/-) plug; peg, pin; bung (*of barrel*); pivot; ♀ cone; **2.** ⚓ *v/t.* (ge-, h) tap; **'~streich** ⚔ *m* tattoo, retreat, *Am. a.* taps *pl.*

'Zapf|hahn *m* tap, *Am.* faucet; **'~säule** *mot.* *f* petrol pump.

zappel|ig *adj.* ['tsapəliç] fidgety; **'~n** *v/i.* (ge-, h) struggle; fidget.

zart *adj.* [tsɑ:rt] tender; soft; gentle; delicate; **'~fühlend** *adj.* delicate; **'Zgefühl** *n* (-[e]s/*no pl.*) delicacy (of feeling).

zärtlich adj. ['tsɛːrtliç] tender; fond, loving; '2keit f 1. (-/no pl.) tenderness; fondness; 2. (-/-en) caress.

Zauber ['tsaubər] m (-s/-) spell, charm, magic (all a. fig.); fig.: enchantment; glamo(u)r; **~ei** [~'rai] f (-/-en) magic, sorcery; witchcraft; conjuring; **~er** m (-s/-) sorcerer, magician; conjurer; '**~flöte** f magic flute; '**~formel** f spell; '2-**haft** adj. magic(al); fig. enchanting; '**~in** f (-/-nen) sorceress, witch; fig. enchantress; '**~kraft** f magic power; '**~kunststück** n conjuring trick; '2n (ge-, h) 1. v/i. practise magic or witchcraft; do conjuring tricks; 2. v/t. conjure; '**~spruch** m spell; '**~stab** m (magic) wand; '**~wort** n (-[e]s/-e) magic word, spell.

zaudern ['tsaudərn] v/i. (ge-, h) hesitate; linger, delay.

Zaum [tsaum] m (-[e]s/⸚e) bridle; im ~ halten keep in check.

zäumen ['tsɔymən] v/t. (ge-, h) bridle.

'**Zaumzeug** n bridle.

Zaun [tsaun] m (-[e]s/⸚e) fence; '**~gast** m deadhead; '**~könig** orn. m wren; '**~pfahl** m pale.

Zebra zo. ['tseːbra] n (-s/-s) zebra; '**~streifen** m zebra crossing.

Zech|e ['tsɛçə] f (-/-n) score, reckoning, bill; ⚒ mine; coal-pit, colliery; F die ~ bezahlen foot the bill, F stand treat; '2en v/i. (ge-, h) carouse, tipple; '**~gelage** n carousal, carouse; '**~preller** m (-s/-) bilk(er).

Zeh [tseː] m (-[e]s/-en), '**~e** f (-/-n) toe; '**~enspitze** f point or tip of the toe; auf ~n on tiptoe.

zehn adj. [tseːn] ten; '2er m (-s/-) ten; coin: F ten-pfennig piece; **~fach** adj. ['~fax] tenfold; **~jährig** adj. ['~jɛːriç] ten-year-old, of ten (years); '2**kampf** m sports: decathlon; '**~mal** adv. ten times; **~te** ['~tə] 1. adj. tenth; 2. ♀ † m (-n/-n) tithe; 2**tel** ['~tɔl] n (-s/-) tenth (part); '**~tens** adv. ['~təns] tenthly.

zehren ['tseːrən] v/i. (ge-, h) make thin; ~ von live on s.th.; fig. live off (the capital); ~ an prey (up)on (one's mind); undermine (one's health).

Zeichen ['tsaiçən] n (-s/-) sign; token; mark; indication, symptom; signal; zum ~ (gen.) in sign of, as a sign of; '**~block** m drawing-block; '**~brett** n drawing-board; '**~lehrer** m drawing-master; '**~papier** n drawing-paper; '**~setzung** gr. f (-/no pl.) punctuation; '**~sprache** f sign-language; '**~stift** m pencil, crayon; '**~trickfilm** m animation, animated cartoon; '**~unterricht** m drawing-lessons pl.

zeichn|en ['tsaiçnən] (ge-, h) 1. v/t.

draw (plan, etc.); design (pattern); mark; sign; subscribe (sum of money) (zu to); subscribe for (shares); 2. v/i. draw; sie zeichnet gut she draws well; '2er m (-s/-) draftsman, draughtsman; designer; subscriber (gen. for shares); '2**ung** f (-/-en) drawing; design; illustration; zo. marking (of skin, etc.); subscription.

Zeige|finger ['tsaigə-] m forefinger, index (finger); '2n (ge-, h) 1. v/t. show; point out; indicate; demonstrate; sich ~ appear; 2. v/i.: ~ auf (acc.) point at; ~ nach point to; '**~r** m (-s/-) hand (of clock, etc.); pointer (of dial, etc.); '**~stock** m pointer.

Zeile ['tsailə] f (-/-n) line; row; j-m ein paar ~n schreiben drop s.o. a line or a few lines.   [siskin.]

Zeisig orn. ['tsaiziç] m (-[e]s/-e)

Zeit [tsait] f (-/-en) time; epoch, era, age; period, space (of time); term; freie ~ spare time; mit der ~ in the course of time; von ~ zu ~ from time to time; vor langer ~ long ago, a long time ago; zur ~ (gen.) in the time of; at (the) present; zu meiner ~ in my time; zu s-r ~ in due course (of time); das hat ~ there is plenty of time for that; es ist höchste ~ it is high time; j-m ~ lassen give s.o. time; laß dir ~! take your time!; sich die ~ vertreiben pass the time, kill time.

'**Zeit|abschnitt** m epoch, period; '**~alter** n age; '**~angabe** f exact date and hour; date; '**~aufnahme** phot. f time-exposure; '**~dauer** f length of time, period (of time); '**~enfolge** gr. f sequence of tenses; '**~geist** m (-es/no pl.) spirit of the time(s), zeitgeist; '2**gemäß** adj. modern, up-to-date; '2**genosse** m contemporary; 2**genössisch** adj. ['~gənœsiʃ] contemporary; '**~geschichte** f contemporary history; '**~gewinn** m gain of time; '2**ig** 1. adj. early; 2. adv. on time; '**~karte** f season-ticket, Am. commutation ticket; '**~lang** f: e-e ~ for some time, for a while; 2'**lebens** adv. for life, all one's life; '2**lich** 1. adj. temporal; 2. adv. as to time; ~ zusammenfallen coincide; '2**los** adj. timeless; '**~lupe** phot. f slow motion; '**~lupenaufnahme** phot.f slow-motion picture; '2**nah** adj. current, up-to-date; '**~ordnung** f chronological order; '**~punkt** m moment; time; date; '**~rafferaufnahme** phot. f time-lapse photography; '2**raubend** adj. time-consuming; pred. a. taking up much time; '**~raum** m space (of time), period; '**~rechnung** f chronology; era; '**~schrift** f journal, periodical, magazine; review; '**~tafel** f chronological table.

'Zeitung f (-/-en) (news)paper, journal.
'Zeitungs|abonnement n subscription to a paper; '~artikel m newspaper article; '~ausschnitt m (press or newspaper) cutting, (Am. only) (newspaper) clipping; ~kiosk ['~kiɔsk] m (-[e]s/-e) news-stand; '~notiz f press item; '~papier n newsprint; '~verkäufer m newsvendor; news-boy, news-man; '~wesen n journalism, the press.
'Zeit|verlust m loss of time; '~verschwendung f waste of time; ~vertreib ['~fɛrtraɪp] m (-[e]s/-e) pastime; zum ~ to pass the time; 2weilig adj. ['~vaɪlɪç] temporary; '2weise adv. for a time; at times, occasionally; '~wort gr. n (-[e]s/~er) verb; '~zeichen n time-signal.
Zell|e ['tsɛlə] f (-/-n) cell; '~stoff m, ~ulose ⊕ [~u'lo:zə] f (-/-n) cellulose.
Zelt [tsɛlt] n (-[e]s/-e) tent; '2en v/i. (ge-, h) camp; '~leinwand f canvas; '~platz m camping-ground.
Zement [tse'mɛnt] m (-[e]s/-e) cement; 2ieren [~'ti:rən] v/t. (no -ge-, h) cement.
Zenit [tse'ni:t] m (-[e]s/no pl.) zenith (a. fig.).
zens|ieren [tsɛn'zi:rən] v/t. (no -ge-, h) censor (book, etc.); at school: mark, Am. a. grade; 2or ['~ɔr] m (-s/-en) censor; 2ur [~'zu:r] f 1. (-/no pl.) censorship; 2. (-/-en) at school: mark, Am. a. grade; (school) report, Am. report card.
Zentimeter [tsɛnti'-] n, m centimet|re, Am. -er.
Zentner ['tsɛntnər] m (-s/-) (Brt. appr.) hundredweight.
zentral [tsɛn'tra:l] central; 2ef (-/-n) central office; teleph. (telephone) exchange, Am. a. central; 2heizung f central heating.
Zentrum ['tsɛntrum] n (-s/Zentren) cent|re, Am. -er.　　[Am. -er.]
Zepter ['tsɛptər] n (-s/-) scept|re, |
zer|beißen [tsɛr'-] v/t. (irr. beißen, no -ge-, h) bite to pieces; ~'bersten v/i. (irr. bersten, no -ge-, sein) burst asunder.
zer'brech|en (irr. brechen, no -ge-) 1. v/t. (h) break (to pieces); sich den Kopf ~ rack one's brains; 2. v/i. (sein) break; ~lich adj. breakable, fragile.
zer|'bröckeln v/t. (h) and v/i. (sein) (no -ge-) crumble; ~'drücken v/t. (no -ge-, h) crush; crease (dress).
Zeremon|ie [tseremo'ni:, ~'mo:njə] f (-/-n) ceremony; 2iell [~'njɛl] adj. [~o'njɛl] n (-s/-e) ceremonial; ~iell [~o'njɛl] n (-s/-e) ceremonial.
zer'fahren adj. road: rutted; p.: flighty, giddy; scatter-brained; absent-minded.
Zer'fall m (-[e]s/no pl.) ruin, decay,

disintegration; 2en v/i. (irr. fallen, no -ge-, sein) fall to pieces, decay; disintegrate; in mehrere Teile ~ fall into several parts.
zer|'fetzen v/t. (no -ge-, h) tear in or to pieces; ~'fleischen v/t. (no -ge-, h) mangle; lacerate; ~'fließen v/i. (irr. fließen, no -ge-, sein) melt (away); ink, etc.: run; ~'fressen v/t. (irr. fressen, no -ge-, h) eat away; ⊕ corrode; ~'gehen v/i. (irr. gehen, no -ge-, sein) melt, dissolve; ~'gliedern v/t. (no -ge-, h) dismember; anat. dissect; fig. analy|se, Am. -ze; ~'hacken v/t. (no -ge-, h) cut (in)to pieces; mince; chop (up) (wood, meat); ~'kauen v/t. (no -ge-, h) chew; ~'kleinern v/t. (no -ge-, h) mince (meat); chop up (wood); grind.
zer'knirsch|t adj. contrite; 2ung f (-/~-en) contrition.
zer|'knittern v/t. (no -ge-, h) (c)rumple, wrinkle, crease; ~'knüllen v/t. (no -ge-, h) crumple up (sheet of paper); ~'kratzen v/t. (no -ge-, h) scratch; ~'krümeln v/t. (no -ge-, h) crumble; ~'lassen v/t. (irr. lassen, no -ge-, h) melt; ~'legen v/t. (no -ge-, h) take apart or to pieces; carve (joint); ⊕, gr., fig. analy|se, Am. -ze; ~'lumpt adj. ragged, tattered; ~'mahlen v/t. (irr. mahlen, no -ge-, h) grind; ~'malmen [~'malmən] v/t. (no -ge-, h) crush; crunch; ~'mürben v/t. (no -ge-, h) wear down or out; ~'platzen v/i. (no -ge-, sein) burst; explode; ~'quetschen v/t. (no -ge-, h) crush, squash; mash (esp. potatoes).
Zerrbild ['tsɛr-] n caricature.
zer|'reiben v/t. (irr. reiben, no -ge-, h) rub to powder, grind down, pulverize; ~'reißen (irr. reißen, no -ge-) 1. v/t. (h) tear, rip up; in Stücke ~ tear to pieces; 2. v/i. (sein) tear; rope, string: break.
zerren ['tsɛrən] (ge-, h) 1. v/t. tug, pull; drag; ✗ strain; 2. v/i.: ~ an (dat.) pull at.
zer'rinnen v/i. (irr. rinnen, no -ge-, sein) melt away; fig. vanish.
'Zerrung ✗ f (-/-en) strain.
zer|'rütten [tsɛr'rytən] v/t. (no -ge-, h) derange, unsettle; disorganize; ruin, shatter (one's health or nerves); wreck (marriage); ~'sägen v/t. (no -ge-, h) saw up; ~'schellen [~'ʃɛlən] v/i. (no -ge-, sein) be dashed or smashed; ⊕ be wrecked; ✗ crash; ~'schlagen 1. v/t. (irr. schlagen, no -ge-, h) break or smash (to pieces); sich ~ come to nothing; 2. adj. battered; fig. knocked up; ~'schmettern v/t. (no -ge-, h) smash, dash, shatter; ~'schneiden v/t. (irr. schneiden, no -ge-, h) cut in two; cut up, cut to pieces.

zer'setz|en v/t. and v/refl. (no -ge-, h) decompose; **2ung** f (-/⊸-en) decomposition.

zer'|spalten v/t. ([irr. spalten,] no -ge-, h) cleave, split; **⊸'splittern** (no -ge-) **1.** v/t. (h) split (up), splinter; fritter away (one's energy, etc.); **2.** v/i. (sein) split (up), splinter; **⊸'sprengen** v/t. (no -ge-, h) burst (asunder); disperse (crowd); **⊸'springen** v/i. (irr. springen, no -ge-, sein) burst; glass: crack; mein Kopf zerspringt mir I've got a splitting headache; **⊸'stampfen** v/t. (no -ge-, h) crush; pound.

zer'stäub|en v/t. (no -ge-, h) spray; **2er** m (-s/-) sprayer, atomizer.

zer'stör|en v/t. (no -ge-, h) destroy; **2er** m (-s/-) destroyer (a. ⚓); **2ung** f destruction.

zer'streu|en v/t. (no -ge-, h) disperse, scatter; dissipate (doubt, etc.); fig. divert; sich ⊸ disperse, scatter; fig. amuse o.s.; **⊸t** fig. adj. absent(-minded); **2theit** f (-/⊸-en) absent-mindedness; **2ung** f **1.** (-/-en) dispersion; diversion, amusement; **2.** phys. (-/no pl.) dispersion (of light).

zerstückeln [tsɛr'ʃtykəln] v/t. (no -ge-, h) cut up, cut (in)to pieces; dismember (body, etc.).

zer'teilen v/t. and v/refl. (no -ge-, h) divide (in acc. into); **⊸'trennen** v/t. (no -ge-, h) rip (up) (dress); **⊸'treten** v/t. (irr. treten, no -ge-, h) tread down; crush; tread or stamp out (fire); **⊸'trümmern** v/t. (no -ge-, h) smash.

Zerwürfnis [tsɛr'vyrfnis] n (-ses/-se) dissension, discord.

Zettel ['tsetəl] m (-s/-) slip (of paper), scrap of paper; note; ticket; label, sticker; tag; s. An- schlagzettel; s. Theaterzettel; '⊸- kartei f, '⊸kasten m card index.

Zeug [tsɔʏk] n (-[e]s/-e) stuff (a. fig. contp.), material; cloth; tools pl.; things pl.

Zeuge ['tsɔʏgə] m (-n/-n) witness; '**2n** (ge-, h) **1.** v/i. witness; ⚖ give evidence; für (gegen, von) et. ⊸ testify for (against, of) s.th.; ⊸ von be evidence of, bespeak (courage, etc.); **2.** v/t. beget.

'**Zeugen|aussage** ⚖ f testimony, evidence; '⊸bank f (-/⊸e) witness- box, Am. witness stand.

Zeugin ['tsɔʏgin] f (-/-nen) (female) witness.

Zeugnis ['tsɔʏknis] n (-ses/-se) ⚖ testimony, evidence; certificate; (school) report, Am. report card.

Zeugung ['tsɔʏgun] f (-/-en) pro- creation; **2sfähig** adj. capable of begetting; '⊸skraft f generative power; **2sunfähig** adj. ['tsɔʏ- guns?-] impotent.

Zick|lein zo. ['tsiklain] n (-s/-) kid;

⊸zack ['⊸tsak] m (-[e]s/-e) zigzag; im ⊸ fahren etc. zigzag.

Ziege zo. ['tsi:gə] f (-/-n) (she-)goat, nanny(-goat).

Ziegel ['tsi:gəl] m (-s/-) brick; tile (of roof); '⊸dach n tiled roof; '⊸ei [⊸'lai] f (-/-en) brickworks sg., pl., brickyard; '⊸stein m brick.

'**Ziegen|bock** zo. m he-goat; '⊸fell n goatskin; '⊸hirt m goatherd; '⊸- leder n kid(-leather); '⊸peter ⚕ m (-s/-) mumps.

Ziehbrunnen ['tsi:-] m draw-well.

ziehen ['tsi:ən] (irr., ge-) **1.** v/t. (h) pull, draw; draw (line, weapon, lots, conclusion, etc.); drag; ♣ cultivate; zo. breed; take off (hat); dig (ditch); draw, extract (tooth); A extract (root of number); Blasen ⊸ ⚕ raise blisters; e-n Vergleich ⊸ draw or make a comparison; j-n ins Ver- trauen ⊸ take s.o. into one's confi- dence; in Erwägung ⊸ take into con- sideration; in die Länge ⊸ draw out; fig. protract; Nutzen ⊸ aus derive profit or benefit from; an sich ⊸ draw to one; Aufmerksamkeit etc. auf sich ⊸ attract attention, etc.; et. nach sich ⊸ entail or involve s.th.; **2.** v/i. (h) pull (on dat. at); chimney, cigar, etc.: draw; puff (an e-r Zigarre at a cigar); tea: infuse, draw; play: draw (large audiences); F ♣ goods: draw (customers), take; es zieht there is a draught, Am. there is a draft; **3.** v/i. (sein) move, go; march; (re)move (nach to); birds: migrate; **4.** v/refl. (h) extend, stretch, run; wood: warp; sich in die Länge ⊸ drag on.

'**Zieh|harmonika** ♪ f accordion; '⊸ung f (-/-en) drawing (of lots).

Ziel [tsi:l] n (-[e]s/-e) aim (a. fig.); mark; sports: winning-post, goal (a. fig.); target; ⊠ objective; des- tination (of voyage); fig. end, pur- pose, target, object(ive); term; sein ⊸ erreichen gain one's end(s pl.); über das ⊸ hinausschießen overshoot the mark; zum ⊸e führen succeed, be successful; sich zum ⊸ setzen zu inf. aim at ger., Am. aim to inf.; '⊸band n sports: tape; '2- bewußt adj. purposeful; '2en v/i. (ge-, h) (take) aim (auf acc. at); '⊸fernrohr n telescopic sight; '2- los adj. aimless, purposeless; '⊸- scheibe f target, butt; ⊸ des Spot- tes butt or target (of derision); '2- strebig adj. purposive.

ziemlich ['tsi:mliç] **1.** adj. fair, tolerable; considerable; **2.** adv. pretty, fairly, tolerably, rather; about.

Zier [tsi:r] f (-/no pl.), ⊸de ['⊸də] f (-/-n) ornament; fig. a. hono(u)r (für to); '2en v/t. (ge-, h) orna- ment, adorn; decorate; sich ⊸ be affected; esp. of woman: be prudish; refuse; **'Qlich** adj. delicate; neat; graceful, elegant; **'_lichkeit** f (-/~-en) delicacy; neatness; gracefulness, elegance; **_pflanze** f ornamental plant.

Ziffer ['tsifər] f (-/-n) figure, digit; **'_blatt** n dial(-plate), face.

Zigarette [tsiga'rɛtə] f (-/-n) cigaret(te); **_nautomat** [_n?-] m cigarette slot-machine; **_netui** [_n?-] n cigarette-case; **_nspitze** f cigarette-holder; **_nstummel** m stub, Am. a. butt.

Zigarre [tsi'garə] f (-/-n) cigar.

Zigeuner [tsi'gɔʏnər] m (-s/-), **_inf** (-/-nen) gipsy, gypsy.

Zimmer ['tsimər] n (-s/-) room; apartment; **'_antenne** f radio, etc.: indoor aerial, Am. a. indoor antenna; **'_einrichtung** f furniture; **'_flucht** f suite (of rooms); **'_mädchen** n chamber-maid; **'_mann** m (-[e]s/Zimmerleute) carpenter; **'Qn** (ge-, h) 1. v/t. carpenter; fig. frame; 2. v/i. carpenter; **'_pflanze** f indoor plant; **'_vermieterin** f (-/-nen) landlady.

zimperlich adj. ['tsimpərliç] prim; prudish; affected.

Zimt [tsimt] m (-[e]s/-e) cinnamon.

Zink [tsiŋk] n (-[e]s/no pl.) zinc; **'_blech** n sheet zinc.

Zinke ['tsiŋkə] f (-/-n) prong; tooth (of comb or fork); **'_n** m (-s/-) s. Zinke.

Zinn [tsin] n (-[e]s/no pl.) tin.

Zinne ['tsinə] f (-/-n) △ pinnacle; ⚔ battlement.

Zinnober [tsi'no:bər] m (-s/-) cinnabar; **Qrot** adj. vermilion.

Zins [tsins] m (-es/-en) rent; tribute; mst _en pl. interest; _en tragen yield or bear interest; **'Qbringend** adj. bearing interest; **_eszins** ['_zɔs-] m compound interest; **'Qfrei** adj. rent-free; free of interest; **'_fuß** m, **'_satz** m rate of interest.

Zipf|el ['tsipfəl] m (-s/-) tip, point, end; corner (of handkerchief, etc.); lappet (of garment); **'Qelig** adj. having points or ends; **'_elmütze** f jelly-bag cap; nightcap.

Zirkel ['tsirkəl] m (-s/-) circle (a. fig.); △ (ein a pair of) compasses pl. or dividers pl.

zirkulieren [tsirku'li:rən] v/i. (no -ge-, h) circulate.

Zirkus ['tsirkus] m (-/-se) circus.

zirpen ['tsirpən] v/i. (ge-, h) chirp, cheep.

zisch|eln ['tsiʃəln] v/t. and v/i. (ge-, h) whisper; **'_en** v/i. (ge-, h) hiss; whiz(z).

ziselieren [tsize'li:rən] v/t. (no -ge-, h) chase.

Zit|at [tsi'ta:t] n (-[e]s/-e) quotation; **Qieren** [_'ti:rən] v/t. (no -ge-, h) summon; quote.

Zitrone [tsi'tro:nə] f (-/-n) lemon;

_nlimonade f lemonade; lemon squash; **_npresse** f lemon-squeezer; **_nsaft** m lemon juice.

zittern ['tsitərn] v/i. (ge-, h) tremble, shake (vor dat. with).

zivil [tsi'vi:l] 1. adj. civil; civilian; price: reasonable; 2. **Ქ** n (-s/no pl.) civilians pl.; s. Zivilkleidung; **Qbevölkerung** f civilian population, civilians pl.; **Qisation** [_iliza'tsjo:n] f (-/-en) civilization; **_isieren** [_ili'zi:rən] v/t. (no -ge-, h) civilize; **Qist** [_'i:list] m (-en/-en) civilian; **Qkleidung** f civilian or plain clothes pl.

Zofe ['tso:fə] f (-/-n) lady's maid.

zog [tso:k] pret. of ziehen.

zögern ['tsø:gərn] 1. v/i. (ge-, h) hesitate; linger; delay; 2. **Ქ** n (-s/no pl.) hesitation; delay.

Zögling ['tsø:kliŋ] m (-s/-e) pupil.

Zoll [tsɔl] m 1. (-[e]s/-) inch; 2. (-[e]s/ᵘe) customs pl., duty; the Customs pl.; **'_abfertigung** f customs clearance; **'_amt** n customhouse; **'_beamte** m customs officer; **'_behörde** f the Customs pl.; **'_erklärung** f customs declaration; **'Qfrei** adj. duty-free; **'_kontrolle** f customs examination; **'Qpflichtig** adj. liable to duty; **'_stock** m footrule; **'_tarif** m tariff.

Zone ['tso:nə] f (-/-n) zone.

Zoo [tso:] m (-[s]/-s) zoo.

Zoolog|e [tso?o'lo:gə] m (-n/-n) zoologist; **_ie** [_o'gi:] f (-/no pl.) zoology; **Qisch** adj. [_'lo:giʃ] zoological.

Zopf [tsɔpf] m (-[e]s/ᵘe) plait, tress; pigtail; alter ~ antiquated ways pl. or custom.

Zorn [tsɔrn] m (-[e]s/no pl.) anger; **'Qig** adj. angry (auf j-n with s.o.; auf et. at s.th.).

Zote ['tso:tə] f (-/-n) filthy or smutty joke, obscenity.

Zott|el ['tsɔtəl] f (-/-n) tuft (of hair); tassel; **'Q(e)lig** adj. shaggy.

zu [tsu:] 1. prp. (dat.) direction: to, towards, up to; at, in; on; in addition to, along with; purpose: for; ~ Beginn at the beginning or outset; ~ Weihnachten at Christmas; zum ersten Mal for the first time; ~ e-m ... Preise at a ... price; ~ meinem Erstaunen to my surprise; ~ Tausenden by thousands; ~ Wasser by water; ~ zweien by twos; zum Beispiel for example; 2. adv. too; direction: towards, to; F closed, shut; with inf.: to; ich habe ~ arbeiten I have to work.

'zubauen v/t. (sep., -ge-, h) build up or in; block.

Zubehör ['tsu:bəhø:r] n, m (-[e]s/-e) appurtenances pl., fittings pl., Am. F fixings pl.; esp. ⊕ accessories pl.

'zubereit|en v/t. (sep., no -ge-, h) prepare; **'Qung** f preparation.

'zu|billigen v/t. (sep., -ge-, h) grant; '~binden v/t. (irr. binden, sep., -ge-, h) tie up; '~blinzeln v/i. (sep., -ge-, h) wink at s.o.; '~bringen v/t. (irr. bringen, sep., -ge-, h) pass, spend (time).

Zucht [tsuxt] f 1. (-/no pl.) discipline; breeding, rearing; rearing of bees, etc.: culture; ♀ cultivation; 2. (-/-en) breed, race; '~bulle zo. m bull (for breeding).

zücht|en ['tsyçtən] v/t. (ge-, h) breed (animals); grow, cultivate (plants); '2er m (-s/-) breeder (of animals); grower (of plants).

'Zucht|haus n penitentiary; punishment: penal servitude; '~häusler ['~hɔyslər] m (-s/-) convict; '~hengst zo. m stud-horse, stallion.

züchtig adj. ['tsyçtiç] chaste, modest; '~en ['~gən] v/t. (ge-, h) flog.

'zucht|los adj. undisciplined; '2losigkeit f (-/♀ -en) want of discipline; '2stute zo. f brood-mare.

zucken ['tsukən] v/i. (ge-, h) jerk; move convulsively, twitch (all: mit et. s.th.); with pain: wince; lightning: flash.

zücken ['tsykən] v/t. (ge-, h) draw (sword); F pull out (purse, pencil).

Zucker ['tsukər] m (-s/no pl.) sugar; '~dose f sugar-basin, Am. sugar bowl; '~erbse ♀ f green pea; '~guß m icing, frosting; '~hut m sugar-loaf; '2ig adj. sugary; '2krank adj. diabetic; '2n v/t. (ge-, h) sugar; '~rohr ♀ n sugar-cane; '~rübe ♀ f sugar-beet; '2'süß adj. (as) sweet as sugar; '~wasser n sugared water; '~zange f (e-e a pair of) sugar-tongs pl.

zuckrig adj. ['tsukriç] sugary.

'Zuckung ⚕ f (-/-en) convulsion.

'zudecken v/t. (sep., -ge-, h) cover (up).

zudem adv. [tsu'de:m] besides, moreover.

'zu|drehen v/t. (sep., -ge-, h) turn off (tap); j-m den Rücken ~ turn one's back on s.o.; '~dringlich adj. importunate, obtrusive; '~drücken v/t. (sep., -ge-, h) close, shut; '~erkennen v/t. (irr. kennen, sep., no -ge-, h) award (a. ⚖); adjudge (dat. to) (a. ⚖).

zuerst adv. [tsu'-] first (of all); at first; er kam ~ an he was the first to arrive.

'zufahr|en v/i. (irr. fahren, sep., -ge-, sein) drive on; ~ auf (acc.) drive to (-wards); fig. rush at s.o.; '2t f approach; drive, Am. driveway; '2tstraße f approach (road).

'Zufall m chance, accident; durch ~ by chance, by accident; '2en v/i. (irr. fallen, sep., -ge-, sein) eyes: be closing (with sleep); door: shut (of) itself; j-m ~ fall to s.o.('s share).

'zufällig 1. adj. accidental; attr.

chance; casual; 2. adv. accidentally, by chance.

'zufassen v/i. (sep., -ge-, h) seize (hold of) s.th.; (mit) ~ lend or give a hand.

'Zuflucht f (-/♀ ̈e) refuge, shelter, resort; s-e ~ nehmen zu have recourse to s.th., take refuge in s.th.

'Zufluß m afflux; influx (a. ✝); affluent, tributary (of river); ✝ supply.

'zuflüstern v/t. (sep., -ge-, h): j-m et. ~ whisper s.th. to s.o.

zufolge prp. (gen.; dat.) [tsu'fɔlgə] according to.

zufrieden adj. [tsu'-] content(ed), satisfied; 2heit f (-/no pl.) contentment, satisfaction; ~lassen v/t. (irr. lassen, sep., -ge-, h) let s.o. alone; ~stellen v/t. (sep., -ge-, h) satisfy; ~stellend adj. satisfactory.

'zu|frieren v/i. (irr. frieren, sep., -ge-, sein) freeze up or over; '~fügen v/t. (sep., -ge-, h) add; do, cause; inflict (wound, etc.) (j-m [up]on s.o.); 2fuhr f ['~fu:r] f (-/-en) supply; supplies pl.; influx; '~führen v/t. (sep., -ge-, h) carry, lead, bring; ⊕ feed; supply (a. ⊕).

Zug [tsu:k] m (-[e]s/♀ ̈e) draw(ing), pull(ing); ⊕ traction; ✕ expedition, campaign; procession; migration (of birds); drift (of clouds); range (of mountains); ⊞ train; feature, trait (of character); bent, tendency, trend; draught, Am. draft (of air); at chess: move; drinking: draught, Am. draft; at cigarette, etc.: puff.

'Zu|gabe f addition; extra; thea. encore; '~gang m entrance; access; approach; 2gänglich adj. ['~gɛnliç] accessible (für to); '2geben v/t. (irr. geben, sep., -ge-, h) add; fig.: allow; confess; admit.

zugegen adj. [tsu'-] present (bei at.).

'zugehen v/i. (irr. gehen, sep., -ge-, sein) door, etc.: close, shut; p. move on, walk faster; happen; auf j-n ~ go up to s.o., move or walk towards s.o.

'Zugehörigkeit f (-/no pl.) membership (zu to) (society, etc.); belonging (to).

Zügel ['tsy:gəl] m (-s/-) rein; bridle (a. fig.); '2los adj. unbridled; fig.: unrestrained; licentious; '2n v/t. (ge-, h) rein (in); fig. bridle, check (a. fig.).

'Zuge|ständnis n concession; '2stehen v/t. (irr. stehen, sep., -ge-, h) concede.

'zugetan adj. attached (dat. to).

'Zugführer ⊞ m guard, Am. conductor. [-ge-, h) add.]

'zugießen v/t. (irr. gießen, sep.,'

zug|ig adj. ['tsu:giç] draughty, Am. drafty; 2kraft ['~k-] f ⊕ traction; fig. attraction, draw, appeal; '~kräftig adj. ['~k-]: ~ sein be a draw-

zugleich adv. [tsu'-] at the same time; together.

'**Zug|luft** f (-/no pl.) draught, Am. draft; '**~maschine** f traction-engine, tractor; '**~pflaster** ✴ n blister.

'**zu|greifen** v/i. (irr. greifen, sep., -ge-, h) grasp or grab at s.th.; at table: help o.s.; lend a hand; '**2griff** m grip, clutch.

zugrunde adv. [tsu'grundə]: **~ gehen** perish; **~ richten** ruin.

'**Zugtier** n draught animal, Am. draft animal.

zu|gunsten prp. (gen.) [tsu'gunstən] in favo(u)r of; **~gute** adv.: j-m et. **~ halten** give s.o. credit for s.th.; **~ kommen** be for the benefit (dat. of).

'**Zugvogel** m bird of passage.

'**zuhalten** v/i. (irr. halten, sep., -ge-, h) hold (door) to; sich die Ohren **~** stop one's ears. [home.\

Zuhause [tsu'hauzə] n (-/no pl.)\

'**zu|heilen** v/i. (sep., -ge-, sein) heal up, skin over; '**~hören** v/i. (sep., -ge-, h) listen (dat. to).

'**Zuhörer** m hearer, listener; **~** pl. audience; '**~schaft** f (-/✴-en) audience.

'**zu|jubeln** v/i. (sep., -ge-, h) cheer; '**~kleben** v/t. (sep., -ge-, h) paste or glue up; gum (letter) down; '**~knallen** v/t. (sep., -ge-, h) bang, slam (door, etc.); '**~knöpfen** v/t. (sep., -ge-, h) button (up); '**~kommen** v/i. (irr. kommen, sep., -ge-, sein): auf j-n **~** come up to s.o.; j-m et. **~** be due to s.o.; j-m et. **~ lassen** let s.o. have s.th.; send s.o. s.th.; '**~korken** v/t. (sep., -ge-, h) cork (up).

Zu|kunft ['tsu:kunft] f (-/no pl.) future; gr. future (tense); '**2künftig** 1. adj. future; **~er** Vater father-to-be; 2. adv. in future.

'**zu|lächeln** v/i. (sep., -ge-, h) smile at or (up)on; '**2lage** f extra pay, increase; rise, Am. raise (in salary or wages); '**~langen** v/i. (sep., -ge-, h) at table: help o.s.; '**~lassen** v/t. (irr. lassen, sep., -ge-, h) leave (door) shut; keep closed; fig.: admit s.o.; license; allow, suffer; admit of (only one interpretation, etc.); '**~lässig** adj. admissible, allowable; '**2lassung** f (-/-en) admission; permission; licen|ce, Am. -se.

'**zulegen** v/t. (sep., -ge-, h) add; F sich et. **~** get o.s. s.th.

zuleide adv. [tsu'laidə]: j-m et. **~ tun** do s.o. harm, harm or hurt s.o.

'**zuleiten** v/t. (sep., -ge-, h) let in (water, etc.); conduct to; pass on to s.o.

zu|letzt adv. [tsu'-] finally, at last; er kam **~** an he was the last to arrive; **~'liebe** adv.: j-m **~** for s.o.'s sake.

zum prp. [tsum] = zu dem.

'**zumachen** v/t. (sep., -ge-, h) close, shut; button (up) (coat); fasten.

zumal cj. [tsu'-] especially, particularly. [up.\

'**zumauern** v/t. (sep., -ge-, h) wall\

zumut|en ['tsu:mu:tən] v/t. (sep., -ge-): j-m et. **~** expect s.th. of s.o.; sich zuviel **~** overtask o.s., overtax one's strength, etc.; '**2ung** f (-/-en) exacting demand, exaction; fig. impudence.

zunächst [tsu'-] 1. prp. (dat.) next to; 2. adv. first of all; for the present.

'**zu|nageln** v/t. (sep., -ge-, h) nail up; '**~nähen** v/t. (sep., -ge-, h) sew up; '**2nahme** ['**~**na:mə] f (-/-n) increase, growth; '**2name** m surname.

zünden ['tsyndən] v/i. (ge-, h) kindle; esp. mot. ignite; fig. arouse enthusiasm.

Zünd|holz ['tsynt-] n match; '**~ker-ze** mot. f spark(ing)-plug, Am. spark plug; '**~schlüssel** mot. m ignition key; '**~schnur** f fuse; '**~stoff** fig. m fuel; '**~ung** mot. ['**~**duŋ] f (-/-en) ignition.

'**zunehmen** v/i. (irr. nehmen, sep., -ge-, h) increase (an dat. in); grow; put on weight; moon: wax; days: grow longer.

'**zuneig|en** (sep., -ge-, h) 1. v/i. incline to(wards); 2. v/refl. incline to(wards); dem Ende **~** draw to a close; '**2ung** f (-/✴-en) affection.

Zunft [tsunft] f (-/ᵘe) guild, corporation.

Zunge ['tsuŋə] f (-/-n) tongue.

züngeln ['tsyŋəln] v/i. (ge-, h) play with its tongue; flame: lick.

'**zungen|fertig** adj. voluble; '**2fer-tigkeit** f (-/no pl.) volubility; '**2spitze** f tip of the tongue.

zunichte adv. [tsu'niçtə]: **~ machen** or werden bring or come to nothing.

'**zunicken** v/i. (sep., -ge-, h) nod to.

zu|nutze adv. [tsu'nutsə]: sich et. **~ machen** turn s.th. to account, utilize s.th.; '**~oberst** adv. at the top, uppermost.

zupfen ['tsupfən] (ge-, h) 1. v/t. pull, tug, twitch; 2. v/i. pull, tug, twitch (all: an dat. at).

zur prp. [tsu:r] = zu der.

'**zurechnungsfähig** adj. of sound mind; '**2keit** 🏛 f (-/no pl.) responsibility.

zurecht|finden [tsu'-] v/refl. (irr. finden, sep., -ge-, h) find one's way; '**~kommen** v/i. (irr. kommen, sep., -ge-, sein) arrive in time; **~** (mit) get on (well) (with); manage s.th.; '**~legen** v/t. (sep., -ge-, h) arrange; sich e-e Sache **~** think s.th. out; '**~machen** F v/t. (sep., -ge-, h) get ready, prepare, Am. F fix; adapt (für to, for purpose); sich **~** of

woman: make (o.s.) up; **~weisen**
v/t. (irr. weisen, sep., -ge-, h)
reprimand; **2weisung** f reprimand.
'**zu|reden** v/i. (sep., -ge-, h): j-m ~
try to persuade s.o.; encourage s.o.;
'**~reiten** v/t. (irr. reiten, sep., -ge-,
h) break in; '**~riegeln** v/t. (sep.,
-ge-, h) bolt (up).
zürnen ['tsyrnən] v/i. (ge-, h) be
angry (j-m with s.o.).
zurück adv. [tsu'ryk] back; back-
ward(s); behind; **~behalten** v/t.
(irr. halten, sep., no -ge-, h) keep
back, retain; **~bekommen** v/t.
(irr. kommen, sep., no -ge-, h) get
back; **~bleiben** v/i. (irr. bleiben,
sep., -ge-, sein) remain or stay
behind; fall behind, lag; **~blicken**
v/i. (sep., -ge-, h) look back; **~brin-
gen** v/t. (irr. bringen, sep., -ge-, h)
bring back; **~datieren** v/t. (sep., no
-ge-, h) date back, antedate; **~drän-
gen** v/t. (sep., -ge-, h) push back;
fig. repress; **~erobern** v/t. (sep., no
-ge-, h) reconquer; **~erstatten** v/t.
(sep., no -ge-, h) restore, return;
refund (expenses); **~fahren** (irr.
fahren, sep., -ge-) **1.** v/i. (sein)
drive back; fig. start; **2.** v/t. (h)
drive back; **~fordern** v/t. (sep.,
-ge-, h) reclaim; **~führen** v/t. (sep.,
-ge-, h) lead back; ~ auf (acc.)
reduce to (rule, etc.); refer to (cause,
etc.); **~geben** v/t. (irr. geben, sep.,
-ge-, h) give back, return, restore;
~gehen v/i. (irr. gehen, sep., -ge-,
sein) go back; return; **~gezogen**
adj. retired; **~greifen** fig. v/i. (irr.
greifen, sep., -ge-, h): ~ auf (acc.)
fall back (up)on; **~halten** (irr.
halten, sep., -ge-, h) **1.** v/t. hold
back; **2.** v/i.: ~ mit keep back;
~haltend adj. reserved; **2haltung**
f (-/%-en) reserve; **~kehren** v/i.
(sep., -ge-, sein) return; **~kommen**
v/i. (irr. kommen, sep., -ge-, sein)
come back; return (fig. auf acc. to);
~lassen v/t. (irr. lassen, sep., -ge-,
h) leave (behind); **~legen** v/t. (sep.,
-ge-, h) lay aside; cover (distance,
way); **~nehmen** v/t. (irr. nehmen,
sep., -ge-, h) take back, withdraw,
retract (words, etc.); **~prallen** v/i.
(sep., -ge-, sein) rebound; start; ~
rufen v/t. (irr. rufen, sep., -ge-, h)
call back; sich ins Gedächtnis ~ recall;
~schicken v/t. (sep., -ge-, h) send
back; **~schlagen** (irr. schlagen,
sep., -ge-, h) **1.** v/t. drive (ball) back;
repel (enemy); turn down (blanket);
2. v/i. strike back; **~schrecken** v/i.
(sep., -ge-, sein) **1.** (irr. schrecken)
shrink back (vor dat. from spectacle,
etc.); **2.** shrink (vor dat. from
work, etc.); **~setzen** v/t. (sep., -ge-,
h) put back; fig. slight, neglect;
~stellen v/t. (sep., -ge-, h) put
back (a. clock); fig. defer, postpone;
~strahlen v/t. (sep., -ge-, h) reflect;

~streifen v/t. (sep., -ge-, h) turn or
tuck up (sleeve); **~treten** v/i. (irr.
treten, sep., -ge-, sein) step or stand
back; fig.: recede; resign; withdraw; **~weichen** v/i. (irr. weichen,
sep., -ge-, sein) fall back; recede (a.
fig.); **~weisen** v/t. (irr. weisen, sep.,
-ge-, h) decline, reject; repel (attack); **~zahlen** v/t. (sep., -ge-, h)
pay back (a. fig.); **~ziehen** (irr.
ziehen, sep., -ge-) **1.** v/t. (h) draw
back; fig. withdraw; sich ~ retire,
withdraw; ✕ retreat; **2.** v/i. (sein)
move or march back.
'**Zuruf** m call; '**2en** v/t. (irr. rufen,
sep., -ge-, h) call (out), shout (j-m
et. s.th. to s.o.).
'**Zusage** f promise; assent; '**2n**
(sep., -ge-) **1.** v/t. promise; **2.** v/i.
promise to come; j-m ~ food, etc.:
agree with s.o.; accept s.o.'s invitation; suit s.o
zusammen adv. [tsu'zamən] together; at the same time; alles ~
(all) in all; ~ betragen amount to,
total (up to); **2arbeit** f (-/no pl.)
co-operation; team-work; **~arbei-
ten** v/i. (sep., -ge-, h) work together;
co-operate; **~beißen** v/t. (irr. beißen, sep., -ge-, h): die Zähne ~ set
one's teeth; **~brechen** v/i. (irr.
brechen, sep., -ge-, sein) break
down; collapse; **2bruch** m breakdown; collapse; **~drücken** v/t.
(sep., -ge-, h) compress, press together; **~fahren** fig. v/i. (irr. fahren,
sep., -ge-, sein) start (bei at; vor dat.
with); **~fallen** v/i. (irr. fallen, sep.,
-ge-, sein) fall in, collapse; coincide;
~falten v/t. (sep., -ge-, h) fold up;
~fassen v/t. (sep., -ge-, h) sum-
marize, sum up; **2fassung** f (-/-en)
summary; **~fügen** v/t. (sep., -ge-, h)
join (together); **~halten** (irr. halten, sep., -ge-, h) **1.** v/t. hold together; **2.** v/i. hold together;
friends: F stick together; **2hang** m
coherence, coherency, connection;
context; **~hängen** (sep., -ge-, h)
1. v/i. (irr. hängen) cohere; fig. be
connected; **2.** v/t. hang together;
~klappen v/t. (sep., -ge-, h) fold
up; close (clasp-knife); **~kommen**
v/i. (irr. kommen, sep., -ge-, sein)
meet; **2kunft** [~kunft] f (-/⸚e) meeting; **~laufen** v/i. (irr. laufen, sep.,
-ge-, sein) run or crowd together;
A converge; milk: curdle; **~legen**
v/t. (sep., -ge-, h) lay together; fold
up; club (money) (together); **~neh-
men** fig. v/t. (irr. nehmen, sep.,
-ge-, h) collect (one's wits); sich ~
be on one's good behavio(u)r; pull
o.s. together; **~packen** v/t. (sep.,
-ge-, h) pack up; **~passen** v/i. (sep.,
-ge-, h) match, harmonize; **~rech-
nen** v/t. (sep., -ge-, h) add up;
~reißen F v/refl. (irr. reißen, sep.,
-ge-, h) pull o.s. together; **~rollen**

v/t. and *v/refl.* (*sep.*, ~ge~, *h*) coil (up); ~rotten *v/refl.* (*sep.*, ~ge~, *h*) band together; ~rücken (*sep.*, ~ge~) 1. *v/t.* (*h*) move together; 2. *v/i.* (*sein*) close up; ~schlagen (*irr. schlagen, sep.*, ~ge~) 1. *v/t.* (*h*) clap (*hands*) (together); F smash to pieces; beat *s.o.* up; 2. *v/i.* (*sein*): ~ über (*dat.*) close over; ~schließen *v/refl.* (*irr. schließen, sep.*, ~ge~, *h*) join; unite; ~schluß *m* union; ~schrumpfen *v/i.* (*sep.*, ~ge~, *sein*) shrivel (up), shrink; ~setzen *v/t.* (*sep.*, ~ge~, *h*) put together; compose; compound (*a.* ~, *word*); ⊕ assemble; *sich* ~ *aus* consist of; 2setzung *f* (-/-*en*) composition; compound; ⊕ assembly; ~stellen *v/t.* (*sep.*, ~ge~, *h*) put together; compile; combine; 2stoß *m* collision (*a. fig.*); ⚔ encounter; *fig.* clash; ~stoßen *v/i.* (*irr. stoßen, sep.*, ~ge~, *sein*) collide (*a. fig.*); adjoin; *fig.* clash; ~ *mit* knock (*heads, etc.*) together; ~stürzen *v/i.* (*sep.*, ~ge~, *sein*) collapse; house, *etc.*: fall in; ~tragen *v/t.* (*irr. tragen, sep.*, ~ge~, *h*) collect; compile (*notes*); ~treffen *v/i.* (*irr. treffen, sep.*, ~ge~, *h*) meet; coincide; 2treffen *n* (-*s*/*no pl.*) meeting; encounter (*of enemies*); coincidence; ~treten *v/i.* (*irr. treten, sep.*, ~ge~, *sein*) meet; *parl. a.* convene; ~wirken *v/i.* (*sep.*, ~ge~, *h*) co-operate; 2wirken *n* (-*s*/*no pl.*) co-operation; ~zählen *v/t.* (*sep.*, ~ge~, *h*) add up, count up; ~ziehen *v/t.* (*irr. ziehen, sep.*, ~ge~, *h*) draw together; contract; concentrate (*troops*); *sich* ~ contract.

'Zusatz *m* addition; admixture, *metall.* alloy; supplement.

zusätzlich *adj.* ['tsu:zetslɪç] additional.

'zuschau|en *v/i.* (*sep.*, ~ge~, *h*) look on (e-r *Sache* at s.th.); *j-m* ~ watch s.o. (*bei* s. doing s.th.); 2er *m* (-*s*/-) spectator, looker-on, onlooker; 2erraum *thea. m* auditorium.

'zuschicken *v/t.* (*sep.*, ~ge~, *h*) send (*dat.* to); mail; consign (*goods*).

'Zuschlag *m* addition; extra charge; excess fare; ⚬ surcharge; *at auction*: knocking down; 2en ['~gən] (*irr. schlagen, sep.*, ~ge~) 1. *v/t.* (*h*) strike; 2. *v/i.* (*sein*) door: slam (to); 3. *v/t.* (*h*) bang, slam (*door*) (to); *at auction*: knock down (*dat.* to).

'zu|schließen *v/t.* (*irr. schließen, sep.*, ~ge~, *h*) lock (up); ~schnallen *v/t.* (*sep.*, ~ge~, *h*) buckle (up); ~schnappen (*sep.*, ~ge~) 1. *v/i.* (*h*) dog: snap; 2. *v/i.* (*sein*) door: snap to; ~schneiden *v/t.* (*irr. schneiden, sep.*, ~ge~, *h*) cut up; cut (*suit*) (to size); 2schnitt *m* (-[*e*]*s*/⚔ -*e*) cut; style; ~schnüren *v/t.* (*sep.*, ~ge~, *h*) lace up; cord up; ~schrauben *v/t.*

(*sep.*, ~ge~, *h*) screw up *or* tight; ~schreiben *v/t.* (*irr. schreiben, sep.*, ~ge~, *h*): *j-m et.* ~ ascribe *or* attribute s.th. to s.o.; 2schrift *f* letter.

zuschulden *adv.* [tsu'-]: *sich et.* ~ *kommen lassen* make o.s. guilty of s.th.

'Zu|schuß *m* allowance; subsidy, grant (*of government*); 2schütten *v/t.* (*sep.*, ~ge~, *h*) fill up (*ditch*); F add; 2sehen *v/i.* (*irr. sehen, sep.*, ~ge~, *h*) s. *zuschauen*; ~, *daß* see (to it) that; 2sehends *adv.* ['~ts] visibly; 2senden *v/t.* ([*irr. senden,*] *sep.*, ~ge~, *h*) s. *zuschicken*; 2setzen (*sep.*, ~ge~, *h*) 1. *v/t.* add; lose (*money*); 2. *v/i.* lose money; *j-m* ~ press s.o. hard.

'zusicher|n *v/t.* (*sep.*, ~ge~, *h*): *j-m et.* ~ assure s.o. of s.th.; promise s.o. s.th.; 2ung *f* promise, assurance.

'zu|spielen *v/t.* (*sep.*, ~ge~, *h*) *sports*: pass (*ball*) (*dat.* to); ~spitzen *v/t.* (*sep.*, ~ge~, *h*) point; *sich* ~ taper (off); *fig.* come to a crisis; 2spruch *m* (-[*e*]*s*/*no pl.*) encouragement; consolation; † custom; 2stand *m* condition, state; *in gutem* ~ *house*: in good repair.

zustande *adv.* [tsu'ʃtandə]: ~ *bringen* bring about; ~ *kommen* come about; *nicht* ~ *kommen* not to come off.

'zuständig *adj.* competent; 2keit *f* (-/-*en*) competence.

zustatten *adv.* [tsu'ʃtatən]: *j-m* ~ *kommen* be useful to s.o.

'zustehen *v/i.* (*irr. stehen, sep.*, ~ge~, *h*) be due (*dat.* to).

'zustell|en *v/t.* (*sep.*, ~ge~, *h*) deliver (*a.* ⚬); ⚖ serve (*j-m on* s.o.); 2ung *f* delivery; ⚖ service.

'zustimm|en *v/i.* (*sep.*, ~ge~, *h*) agree (*dat.*: to *s.th.*; with *s.o.*); consent (*to* s.th.); 2ung *f* consent.

'zustoßen *fig. v/i.* (*irr. stoßen, sep.*, ~ge~, *sein*): *j-m* ~ happen to s.o.

zutage *adv.* [tsu'ta:gə]: ~ *treten* come to light.

Zutaten ['tsu:ta:tən] *f/pl.* ingredients *pl.* (*of food*); trimmings *pl.* (*of dress*). {fall to s.o.'s share.}

zuteil *adv.* [tsu'taɪl]: *j-m* ~ *werden*{
'zuteil|en *v/t.* (*sep.*, ~ge~, *h*) allot, apportion; 2ung *f* allotment, apportionment; ration.

'zutragen *v/refl.* (*irr. tragen, sep.*, ~ge~, *h*) happen.

'zutrauen 1. *v/t.* (*sep.*, ~ge~, *h*): *j-m et.* ~ credit s.o. with s.th.; *sich zuviel* ~ overrate o.s.; 2. 2 *n* (-*s*/*no pl.*) confidence (*zu* in).

'zutraulich *adj.* confiding, trustful, trusting; *animal*: friendly, tame.

'zutreffen *v/i.* (*irr. treffen, sep.*, ~ge~, *h*) be right, be true; ~ *auf* (*acc.*) be true of; ~d *adj.* right, correct; applicable.

'zutrinken v/i. (irr. trinken, sep., -ge-, h): j-m ~ drink to s.o.

'Zutritt m (-[e]s/no pl.) access; admission; ~ verboten! no admittance! [bottom.]

zuunterst adv. [tsu'-] right at the]

zuverlässig adj. ['tsu:ferlɛsiç] reliable; certain; **2keit** f (-/no pl.) reliability; certainty.

Zuversicht ['tsu:ferziçt] f (-/no pl.) confidence; **2lich** adj. confident.

zuviel adv. [tsu'-] too much; e-r ~ one too many.

zuvor adv. [tsu'-] before, previously; first; **~kommen** v/i. (irr. kommen, sep., -ge-, sein): j-m ~ anticipate s.o.; e-r Sache ~ anticipate or prevent s.th.; **~kommend** adj. obliging; courteous.

Zuwachs ['tsu:vaks] m (-es/no pl.) increase; **2en** v/i. (irr. wachsen, sep., -ge-, sein) become overgrown; wound: close.

zu|wege adv. [tsu've:gə]: ~ bringen bring about; **~'weilen** adv. sometimes.

'zu|weisen v/t. (irr. weisen, sep., -ge-, h) assign; **~wenden** v/t. ([irr. wenden,] sep., -ge-, h) (dat.) turn to(wards), fig.: give; bestow on; sich ~ (dat.) turn to(wards).

zuwenig adv. [tsu'-] too little.

'zuwerfen v/t. (irr. werfen, sep., -ge-, h) fill up (pit); slam (door) (to); j-m ~ throw (ball, etc.) to s.o.; cast (look) at s.o.

zuwider prp. (dat.) [tsu'-] contrary to, against; repugnant, distasteful; **~handeln** v/i. (sep., -ge-, h) (dat.) act contrary or in opposition to; esp. ⊕ contravene; **2handlung** ⊕ f contravention.

'zu|winken v/i. (sep., -ge-, h) (dat.) wave to; beckon to; **~zahlen** v/t. (sep., -ge-, h) pay extra; **~zählen** v/t. (sep., -ge-, h) add; **~ziehen** (irr. ziehen, sep., -ge-) 1. v/t. (h) draw together; draw (curtains); consult (doctor, etc.); sich ~ incur (s.o.'s displeasure, etc.); ⊕ catch (disease); 2. v/i. (sein) move in; **~züglich** prp. (gen.) ['~tsy:k-] plus.

Zwang [tsvaŋ] 1. m (-[e]s/⊕~e) compulsion, coercion; constraint; ⊕ duress(e); force; sich ~ antun check or restrain o.s.; 2. ⊕ pret. of zwingen.

zwängen ['tsvɛŋən] v/t. (ge-, h) press, force.

'zwanglos fig. adj. free and easy, informal; **2igkeit** f (-/-en) ease, informality.

'Zwangs|arbeit f hard labo(u)r; **~jacke** f strait waistcoat or jacket; **~lage** f embarrassing situation; **2läufig** fig. adj. ['~ləyfiç] necessary; **~maßnahme** f coercive measure; **~vollstreckung** ⊕ f distraint, execution; **~vorstellung** ⊕ f

obsession, hallucination; **2weise** adv. by force; **~wirtschaft** f (-/⊕~-en) controlled economy.

zwanzig adj. ['tsvantsiç] twenty; **~ste** adj. ['~stə] twentieth.

zwar cj. [tsva:r] indeed, it is true; und ~ and that, that is.

Zweck [tsvɛk] m (-[e]s/-e) aim, end, object, purpose; design; keinen ~ haben be of no use; s-n ~ erfüllen answer its purpose; zu dem ~ (gen.) for the purpose of; **2dienlich** adj. serviceable, useful, expedient.

Zwecke ['tsvɛkə] f (-/-n) tack; drawing-pin, Am. thumbtack.

'zweck|los adj. aimless, purposeless; useless; **~mäßig** adj. expedient, suitable; **2mäßigkeit** f (-/no pl.) expediency.

zwei adj. [tsvaɪ] two; **~beinig** adj. two-legged; **2bettzimmer** n double (bedroom); **~deutig** adj. ['~dɔy-tiç] ambiguous; suggestive; **~erlei** adj. ['~ər'laɪ] of two kinds, two kinds of; **~fach** adj. ['~fax] double, twofold.

Zweifel ['tsvaɪfəl] m (-s/-) doubt; **2haft** adj. doubtful, dubious; **2los** adj. doubtless; **2n** v/i. (ge-, h) doubt (an e-r Sache s.th.; an j-m s.o.).

Zweig [tsvaɪk] m (-[e]s/-e) branch (a. fig.); kleiner ~ twig; **~geschäft** n, **~niederlassung** f, **~stelle** f branch.

zwei|jährig adj. ['tsvaɪjɛ:riç] two-year-old, of two (years); **2kampf** m duel, single combat; **~mal** adv. twice; **~malig** adj. (twice) repeated; **~motorig** adj. ['~moto:riç] two- or twin-engined; **~reihig** adj. having two rows; suit: double-breasted; **~schneidig** adj. double- or two-edged (both a. fig.); **~seitig** adj. two-sided; contract, etc.: bilateral; fabric: reversible; **2sitzer** esp. mot. m (-s/-) two-seater; **~sprachig** adj. bilingual; **~stimmig** adj. for two voices; **~stöckig** adj. ['~ʃtœkiç] two-stor|eyed, -ied; **~stufig** ⊕ adj. two-stage; **~stündig** adj. ['~ʃtyndiç] of or lasting two hours, two-hour.

zweit adj. [tsvaɪt] second; ein ~er another; aus ~er Hand second-hand; zu ~ by twos; wir sind zu ~ there are two of us. [engine.]

'Zweitaktmotor mot. m two-stroke]

'zweit'best adj. second-best.

'zweiteilig adj. garment: two-piece.

zweitens adv. ['tsvaɪtəns] secondly.

'zweitklassig adj. second-class, second-rate.

Zwerchfell anat. ['tsvɛrç-] n diaphragm.

Zwerg [tsvɛrk] m (-[e]s/-e) dwarf; **2enhaft** adj. ['~gən-] dwarfish.

Zwetsch(g)e ['tsvɛtʃ(g)ə] f (-/-n) plum.

Zwick|el ['tsvikəl] *m* (-s/-) *sewing*: gusset; '**~en** *v/t. and v/i.* (ge-, h) pinch, nip; '**~er** *m* (-s/-) (*ein a pair of*) eye-glasses *pl.*, pince-nez; '**~mühle** *fig. f* dilemma, quandary, fix.

Zwieback ['tsvi:bak] *m* (-[e]s/ⁿe, -e) rusk, zwieback.

Zwiebel ['tsvi:bəl] *f* (-/-n) onion; bulb (*of flowers, etc.*).

Zwie|gespräch ['tsvi:-] *n* dialog(ue); '**~licht** *n* (-[e]s/*no pl.*) twilight; '**~spalt** *m* (-[e]s/-e, ⁿe) disunion; conflict; **⚬spältig** *adj.* ['~ʃpeltiç] disunited; *emotions*: conflicting; '**~tracht** *f* (-/*no pl.*) discord.

Zwilling|e ['tsviliŋə] *m/pl.* twins *pl.*; '**~sbruder** *m* twin brother; '**~sschwester** *f* twin sister.

Zwinge ['tsviŋə] *f* (-/-n) ferrule (*of stick, etc.*); ⊕ clamp; '**⚬n** *v/t.* (*irr.*, ge-, h) compel, constrain; force; **⚬nd** *adj.* forcible; *arguments*: cogent, compelling; imperative; '**~r** *m* (-s/-) outer court; kennel(s *pl.*); bear-pit.

zwinkern ['tsviŋkərn] *v/i.* (ge-, h) wink, blink.

Zwirn [tsvirn] *m* (-[e]s/-e) thread, cotton; '**~sfaden** *m* thread.

zwischen *prp.* (*dat.; acc.*) ['tsviʃən] between (*two*); among (*several*); '**⚬bilanz** † *f* interim balance; '**⚬deck** ⚓ *n* steerage; '**~durch** F *adv.* in between; for a change; '**⚬ergebnis** *n* provisional result; '**⚬fall** *m* incident; '**⚬händler** † *m* middleman; '**⚬landung** ✈ *f* intermediate landing, stop, *Am. a.* stopover; (*Flug*) ohne ~ non-stop (flight);

'**⚬pause** *f* interval, intermission; '**⚬prüfung** *f* intermediate examination; '**⚬raum** *m* space, interval; '**⚬ruf** *m* (loud) interruption; '**⚬spiel** *n* interlude; '**~staatlich** *adj.* international; *Am. between States*: interstate; '**⚬station** *f* intermediate station; '**⚬stecker** ∮ *m* adapter; '**⚬stück** *n* intermediate piece, connexion, (*Am. only*) connection; '**⚬stufe** *f* intermediate stage; '**⚬wand** *f* partition (wall); '**⚬zeit** *f* interval; *in der* ~ in the meantime.

Zwist [tsvist] *m* (-es/-e), '**~igkeit** *f* (-/-en) discord; disunion; quarrel.

zwitschern ['tsvitʃərn] *v/i.* (ge-, h) twitter, chirp.

Zwitter ['tsvitər] *m* (-s/-) hermaphrodite.

zwölf *adj.* [tsvœlf] twelve; *um* ~ (*Uhr*) at twelve (o'clock); (*um*) ~ *Uhr mittags* (at) noon; (*um*) ~ *Uhr nachts* (at) midnight; '**⚬fingerdarm** *anat. m* duodenum; **~te** *adj.* ['~tə] twelfth.

Zyankali [tsyan'kɑːli] *n* (-s/*no pl.*) potassium cyanide.

Zyklus ['tsyːklus, 'tsyk-] *m* (-/Zyklen) cycle; course, set (*of lectures, etc.*).

Zylind|er [tsi'lindər, tsy'-] *m* (-s/-) ∆, ⊕ cylinder; chimney (*of lamp*); top hat; **⚬risch** *adj.* [~driʃ] cylindrical.

Zyni|ker ['tsyːnikər] *m* (-s/-) cynic; **⚬sch** *adj.* cynical; **~smus** [tsy-'nismus] *m* (-/Zynismen) cynicism.

Zypresse ♦ [tsy'prɛsə] *f* (-/-n) cypress.

Zyste ✷ ['tsystə] *f* (-/-n) cyst.

PART II

ENGLISH-GERMAN
DICTIONARY

A

a [ei, ə] *Artikel:* ein(e); per, pro, je; *all of a size* alle gleich groß; *twice a week* zweimal wöchentlich.

A 1 F [ei'wʌn] Ia, prima.

aback [ə'bæk] rückwärts; *taken ~ fig.* überrascht, verblüfft, bestürzt.

abandon [ə'bændən] auf-, preisgeben; verlassen; überlassen; **~ed** verworfen; **~ment** [ˌnmənt] Auf-, Preisgabe *f;* Unbeherrschtheit *f.*

abase [ə'beis] erniedrigen, demütigen; **~ment** [ˌsmənt] Erniedrigung *f.*

abash [ə'bæʃ] beschämen, verlegen machen; **~ment** [ˌʃmənt] Verlegenheit *f.*

abate [ə'beit] *v/t.* verringern; *Mißstand* abstellen; *v/i.* abnehmen, nachlassen; **~ment** [ˌtmənt] Verminderung *f;* Abschaffung *f.*

abattoir ['æbətwaː] Schlachthaus *n.*

abb|ess ['æbis] Äbtissin *f;* **~ey** ['æbi] Abtei *f;* **~ot** ['æbət] Abt *m.*

abbreviat|e [ə'briːvieit] (ab)kürzen; **~ion** [əbriːvi'eiʃən] Abkürzung *f.*

ABC ['eibiː'siː] Abc *n,* Alphabet *n.*

ABC weapons *pl.* ABC-Waffen *f/pl.*

abdicat|e ['æbdikeit] entsagen *(dat.);* abdanken; **~ion** [æbdi-'keiʃən] Verzicht *m;* Abdankung *f.*

abdomen ['æbdəmen] Unterleib *m,* Bauch *m.*

abduct [æb'dʌkt] entführen.

aberration [æbə'reiʃən] Abweichung *f; fig.* Verirrung *f.*

abet [ə'bet] aufhetzen; anstiften; unterstützen; **~tor** [ˌtə] Anstifter *m;* (Helfers)Helfer *m.*

abeyance [ə'beiəns] Unentschiedenheit *f; in ~* ⚖ in der Schwebe.

abhor [əb'hɔː] verabscheuen; **~rence** [əb'hɔrəns] Abscheu *m* (*of* vor *dat.*); **~rent** □ [ˌnt] zuwider (*to dat.*); abstoßend.

abide [ə'baid] [*irr.*] *v/i.* bleiben (*by* bei); *v/t.* erwarten; (v)ertragen.

ability [ə'biliti] Fähigkeit *f.*

abject □ ['æbdʒekt] verächtlich, gemein.

abjure [əb'dʒuə] abschwören; entsagen *(dat.).*

able □ ['eibl] fähig, geschickt; *be ~* imstande sein, können; **~-bodied** kräftig.

abnegat|e ['æbnigeit] ableugnen; verzichten auf *(acc.);* **~ion** [æbni-'geiʃən] Ableugnung *f;* Verzicht *m.*

abnormal □ [æb'nɔːməl] abnorm.

aboard [ə'bɔːd] ⚓ an Bord (*gen.*); *all ~!* Am. ⚙ *etc.* einsteigen!

abode [ə'boud] 1. *pret. u. p.p. von abide;* 2. Aufenthalt *m;* Wohnung *f.*

aboli|sh [ə'bɔliʃ] abschaffen, aufheben; **~tion** [æbə'liʃən] Abschaffung *f,* Aufhebung *f;* **~tionist** [ˌnist] Gegner *m* der Sklaverei.

A-bomb ['eibɔm] = *atomic bomb.*

abomina|ble □ [ə'bɔminəbl] abscheulich; **~te** [ˌneit] verabscheuen; **~tion** [əbɔmi'neiʃən] Abscheu *m.*

aboriginal □ [æbə'ridʒənl] einheimisch; Ur...

abortion ⚕ [ə'bɔːʃən] Fehlgeburt *f;* Abtreibung *f.*

abortive □ [ə'bɔːtiv] vorzeitig; erfolglos, fehlgeschlagen; verkümmert.

abound [ə'baund] reichlich vorhanden sein; Überfluß haben (*in* an *dat.*).

about [ə'baut] 1. *prp.* um(...herum); bei; im Begriff; über *(acc.); I had no money ~* me ich hatte kein Geld bei mir; *what are you ~?* was macht ihr da?; 2. *adv.* herum, umher; in der Nähe; etwa; ungefähr um, gegen; *bring ~* zustande bringen.

above [ə'bʌv] 1. *prp.* über; *fig.* erhaben über; *~ all* vor allem; *~ ground fig.* am Leben; 2. *adv.* oben; darüber; 3. *adj.* obig.

abreact [æbri'ækt] abreagieren.

abreast [ə'brest] nebeneinander.

abridg|e [ə'bridʒ] (ver)kürzen; **~(e)ment** [ˌdʒmənt] (Ver)Kürzung *f;* Auszug *m.*

abroad [ə'brɔːd] im (ins) Ausland; überall(hin); *there is a report ~* es geht das Gerücht; *all ~* ganz im Irrtum.

abrogate ['æbrougeit] aufheben.

abrupt □ [ə'brʌpt] jäh; zs.-hanglos; schroff.

abscess ⚕ ['æbsis] Geschwür *n.*

abscond [əb'skɔnd] sich davonmachen.

absence ['æbsəns] Abwesenheit *f;* Mangel *m;* *~ of mind* Zerstreutheit *f.*

absent 1. □ ['æbsənt] abwesend; nicht vorhanden; 2. [æb'sent]: *~ o.s.* fernbleiben; **~-minded** □ ['æbsənt'maindid] zerstreut, geistesabwesend.

absolut|e □ ['æbsəluːt] absolut; unumschränkt; vollkommen; unvermischt; unbedingt; **~ion** [æbsə-'luːʃən] Lossprechung *f.*

absolve [əb'zɔlv] frei-, lossprechen.

absorb [əb'sɔːb] aufsaugen; *fig.* ganz in Anspruch nehmen.

absorption [əb'sɔːpʃən] Aufsaugung *f; fig.* Vertieftsein *n.*

abstain [əb'stein] sich enthalten.

abstemious □ [æb'sti:mjəs] enthaltsam; mäßig.

abstention [æb'stenʃən] Enthaltung f.

abstinen|ce ['æbstinəns] Enthaltsamkeit f; ⹀t □ [⹀nt] enthaltsam.

abstract 1. □ ['æbstrækt] abstrakt; **2.** [⹀] Auszug m; gr. Abstraktum n; **3.** [æb'strækt] abstrahieren; ablenken; entwenden; Inhalt kurz zs.-fassen; ⹀ed □ zerstreut; ⹀ion [⹀kʃən] Abstraktion f; (abstrakter) Begriff.

abstruse □ [æb'stru:s] fig. dunkel, schwer verständlich; tiefgründig.

absurd □ [əb'sə:d] absurd, sinnwidrig; lächerlich.

abundan|ce [ə'bʌndəns] Überfluß m; Fülle f; Überschwang m; ⹀t □ [⹀nt] reich(lich).

abus|e 1. [ə'bju:s] Mißbrauch m; Beschimpfung f; **2.** [⹀u:z] mißbrauchen; beschimpfen; ⹀ive □ [⹀u:siv] schimpfend; Schimpf...

abut [ə'bʌt] (an)grenzen (upon an).

abyss [ə'bis] Abgrund m.

academic|(al □) [ækə'demik(əl)] akademisch; ⹀ian [əkædə'miʃən] Akademiemitglied n.

academy [ə'kædəmi] Akademie f.

accede [æk'si:d]: ⹀ to beitreten (dat.); Amt antreten; Thron besteigen.

accelerat|e [æk'seləreit] beschleunigen; fig. ankurbeln; ⹀or [æk'seləreitə] Gaspedal n.

accent 1. ['æksənt] Akzent m (a. gr.); **2.** [æk'sent] v/t. akzentuieren, betonen; ⹀uate [⹀tjueit] akzentuieren, betonen.

accept [ək'sept] annehmen; ✝ akzeptieren; hinnehmen; ⹀able □ [⹀təbl] annehmbar; ⹀ance [⹀əns] Annahme f; ✝ Akzept n.

access ['ækses] Zugang m; ✝ Anfall m; easy of ⹀ zugänglich; ⹀ road Zufahrtsstraße f; ⹀ary [æk'sesəri] Mitwisser(in), Mitschuldige(r m) f; = accessory 2; ⹀ible □ [⹀səbl] zugänglich; ⹀ion [ək'seʃən] Antritt m (to gen.); Eintritt m (to in acc.); ⹀ to the throne Thronbesteigung f.

accessory [æk'sesəri] **1.** □ zusätzlich; **2.** Zubehörteil n.

accident ['æksidənt] Zufall m; Un-(glücks)fall m; ⹀al □ [æksi'dentl] zufällig; nebensächlich.

acclaim [ə'kleim] j-m zujubeln.

acclamation [æklə'meiʃən] Zuruf m.

acclimatize [ə'klaimətaiz] akklimatisieren, eingewöhnen.

acclivity [ə'kliviti] Steigung f; Böschung f.

accommodat|e [ə'kɔmədeit] anpassen; unterbringen; Streit schlichten; versorgen; j-m aushelfen (with mit Geld); ⹀ion [əkɔmə'deiʃən] Anpassung f; Aushilfe f; Bequemlich-

keit f; Unterkunft f; Beilegung f; seating ⹀ Sitzgelegenheit f; ⹀ train Am. Personenzug m.

accompan|iment [ə'kʌmpənimənt] Begleitung f; ⹀y [ə'kʌmpəni] begleiten; accompanied with verbunden mit.

accomplice [ə'kɔmplis] Komplice m.

accomplish [ə'kɔmpliʃ] vollenden; ausführen; ⹀ed vollendet, perfekt; ⹀ment [⹀mənt] Vollendung f; Ausführung f; Tat f, Leistung f; Talent n.

accord [ə'kɔ:d] **1.** Übereinstimmung f; with one ⹀ einstimmig; **2.** v/i. übereinstimmen; v/t. gewähren; ⹀ance [⹀dəns] Übereinstimmung f; ⹀ant □ [⹀ənt] übereinstimmend; ⹀ing [⹀diŋ]: ⹀ to gemäß (dat.); ⹀ingly [⹀ŋli] demgemäß.

accost [ə'kɔst] j-n bsd. auf der Straße ansprechen.

account [ə'kaunt] **1.** Rechnung f; Berechnung f; ✝ Konto n; Rechenschaft f; Bericht m; of no ⹀ ohne Bedeutung; on no ⹀ auf keinen Fall; on ⹀ of wegen; take into ⹀ in Betracht ziehen, berücksichtigen; turn to ⹀ ausnutzen; keep ⹀s die Bücher führen; call to ⹀ zur Rechenschaft ziehen; give a good ⹀ of o.s. sich bewähren; make ⹀ of Wert auf et. (acc.) legen; **2.** v/i.: ⹀ for Rechenschaft über et. (acc.) ablegen; (sich) erklären; be much ⹀ed of hoch geachtet sein; v/t. ansehen als; ⹀able □ [⹀təbl] verantwortlich; erklärlich; ⹀ant [⹀ənt] Buchhalter m; chartered ⹀, Am. certified public ⹀ vereidigter Bücherrevisor; ⹀ing [⹀tiŋ] Buchführung f.

accredit [ə'kredit] beglaubigen.

accrue [ə'kru:] erwachsen (from aus).

accumulat|e [ə'kju:mjuleit] (sich) (an)häufen; ansammeln; ⹀ion [əkju:mju'leiʃən] Anhäufung f.

accura|cy ['ækjurəsi] Genauigkeit f; ⹀te □ [⹀rit] genau; richtig.

accurs|ed [ə'kə:sid], ⹀t [⹀st] verflucht, verwünscht.

accus|ation [ækju:(:)'zeiʃən] Anklage f, Beschuldigung f; ⹀ative gr. [ə'kju:zətiv] a. ⹀ case Akkusativ m; ⹀e [ə'kju:z] anklagen, beschuldigen; ⹀er [⹀zə] Kläger(in).

accustom [ə'kʌstəm] gewöhnen (to an acc.); ⹀ed gewohnt, üblich; gewöhnt (to an acc., zu inf.).

ace [eis] As n (a. fig.); ⹀ in the hole Am. F fig. Trumpf m in Reserve; within an ⹀ um ein Haar.

acerbity [ə'sə:biti] Herbheit f.

acet|ic [ə'si:tik] essigsauer; ⹀ify [ə'setifai] säuern.

ache [eik] **1.** schmerzen; sich sehnen (for nach; to do zu tun); **2.** anhaltende Schmerzen m/pl.

achieve [ə'tʃi:v] ausführen; erreichen; ~ment [~vmənt] Ausführung f; Leistung f.

acid ['æsid] 1. sauer; 2. Säure f; ~ity [ə'siditi] Säure f.

acknowledg|e [ək'nɔlidʒ] anerkennen; zugeben; † bestätigen; ~(e)ment [~dʒmənt] Anerkennung f; Bestätigung f; Eingeständnis n.

acme ['ækmi] Gipfel m; ♂ Krisis f.

acorn ♀ ['eikɔ:n] Eichel f.

acoustics [ə'ku:stiks] pl. Akustik f.

acquaint [ə'kweint] bekannt machen; j-m mitteilen; be ~ed with kennen; ~ance [~təns] Bekanntschaft f; Bekannte(r m) f.

acquiesce [ækwi'es] (in) hinnehmen (acc.); einwilligen (in acc.).

acquire [ə'kwaiə] erwerben; ~ment [~əmənt] Fertigkeit f.

acquisition [ækwi'ziʃən] Erwerbung f; Errungenschaft f.

acquit [ə'kwit] freisprechen; ~ o.s. of Pflicht erfüllen; ~ o.s. well s-e Sache gut machen; ~tal [~tl] Freisprechung f, Freispruch m; ~tance [~təns] Tilgung f.

acre ['eikə] Morgen m (4047 qm).

acrid ['ækrid] scharf, beißend.

across [ə'krɔs] 1. adv. hin-, herüber; (quer) drüben; überkreuz; 2. prp. (quer) über (acc.); jenseits (gen.), über (dat.); come ~, run ~ stoßen auf (acc.).

act [ækt] 1. v/i. handeln; sich benehmen; wirken; funktionieren; thea. spielen; v/t. thea. spielen; 2. Handlung f, Tat f; thea. Akt m; Gesetz n; Beschluß m; Urkunde f, Vertrag m; ~ing ['æktiŋ] 1. Handeln n; thea. Spiel(en) n; 2. tätig, amtierend.

action ['ækʃən] Handlung f (a. thea.); Tätigkeit f; Tat f; Wirkung f; Klage f, Prozeß m; Gang m (Pferd etc.); Gefecht n; Mechanismus m; take ~ Schritte unternehmen.

activ|e □ ['æktiv] aktiv; tätig; rührig, wirksam; † lebhaft; ~ity [æk'tiviti] Tätigkeit f; Betriebsamkeit f; bsd. † Lebhaftigkeit f.

act|or ['æktə] Schauspieler m; ~ress ['æktris] Schauspielerin f.

actual □ ['æktjuəl] wirklich, tatsächlich, eigentlich.

actuate ['æktjueit] in Gang bringen.

acute [ə'kju:t] spitz; scharf(sinnig); brennend (Frage); ♂ akut.

ad F [æd] = advertisement.

adamant fig. ['ædəmənt] unerbittlich.

adapt [ə'dæpt] anpassen (to, for dat.); Text bearbeiten (from nach); zurechtmachen; ~ation [ædæp-'teiʃən] Anpassung f, Bearbeitung f.

add [æd] v/t. hinzufügen; addieren; v/i.: ~ to vermehren; hinzukommen zu.

addict ['ædikt] Süchtige(r m) f; ~ed [ə'diktid] ergeben (to dat.); ~ to e-m Laster verfallen.

addition [ə'diʃən] Hinzufügen n; Zusatz m; An-, Ausbau m; Addition f; in ~ außerdem; in ~ to außer, zu; ~al □ [~nl] zusätzlich.

address [ə'dres] 1. Worte richten (to an acc.); sprechen zu; 2. Adresse f; Anschrift f; Ansprache f; Anstand m, Manieren f/pl.; pay one's ~es to a lady e-r Dame den Hof machen; ~ee [ædre'si:] Adressat m, Empfänger m.

adept ['ædept] 1. erfahren; geschickt; 2. Eingeweihte(r m) f; Kenner m.

adequa|cy ['ædikwəsi] Angemessenheit f; ~te □ [~kwit] angemessen.

adhere [əd'hiə] (to) haften (an dat.); fig. festhalten (an dat.); ~nce [~rəns] Anhaften n, Festhalten n; ~nt [~nt] Anhänger(in).

adhesion [əd'hi:ʒən] = adherence; fig. Einwilligung f.

adhesive [əd'hi:siv] 1. □ klebend; ~ plaster, ~ tape Heftpflaster n; 2. Klebstoff m.

adjacent □ [ə'dʒeisənt] (to) anliegend (dat.); anstoßend (an acc.); benachbart.

adjective gr. ['ædʒiktiv] Adjektiv n, Eigenschaftswort n.

adjoin [ə'dʒɔin] angrenzen an (acc.).

adjourn [ə'dʒə:n] aufschieben; (v/i. sich) vertagen; ~ment [~nmənt] Aufschub m; Vertagung f.

adjudge [ə'dʒʌdʒ] zuerkennen; verurteilen.

adjust [ə'dʒʌst] in Ordnung bringen; anpassen; Streit schlichten; Mechanismus u. fig. einstellen (to auf acc.); ~ment [~tmənt] Anordnung f; Einstellung f; Schlichtung f.

administ|er [əd'ministə] verwalten; spenden; † verabfolgen; ~ justice Recht sprechen; ~ration [ədminis-'treiʃən] Verwaltung f; Regierung f; bsd. Am. Amtsperiode f e-s Präsidenten; ~rative [əd'ministrətiv] Verwaltungs...; ~rator [~reitə] Verwalter m.

admir|able □ ['ædmərəbl] bewundernswert; (vor)trefflich; ~ation [ædmə'reiʃən] Bewunderung f; ~e [əd'maiə] bewundern; verehren.

admiss|ible □ [əd'misəbl] zulässig; ~ion [~ʃən] Zulassung f; F Eintritt(sgeld n) m; Eingeständnis n.

admit [əd'mit] v/t. (her)einlassen (to, into in acc.), eintreten lassen; zulassen (to zu); zugeben; ~tance [~təns] Einlaß m; Zutritt m.

admixture [əd'mikstʃə] Beimischung f, Zusatz m.

admon|ish [əd'mɔniʃ] ermahnen; warnen (of, against vor dat.); ~ition [ædmə'niʃən] Ermahnung f; Warnung f.

ado [ə'du:] Getue n; Lärm m; Mühe f.

adolescen|ce [ædou'lesns] Adoleszenz f, Reifezeit f; ~t [_nt] 1. jugendlich, heranwachsend; 2. Jugendliche(r m) f.

adopt [ə'dɔpt] adoptieren; sich aneignen; ~ion [_pʃən] Annahme f.

ador|able □ [ə'dɔːrəbl] verehrungswürdig; ~ation [ædɔː'reiʃən] Anbetung f; ~e [ə'dɔː] anbeten.

adorn [ə'dɔːn] schmücken, zieren; ~ment [_nmənt] Schmuck m.

adroit [ə'drɔit] gewandt.

adult ['ædʌlt] 1. erwachsen; 2. Erwachsene(r m) f.

adulter|ate [ə'dʌltəreit] (ver)fälschen; ~er [_rə] Ehebrecher m; ~ess [_ris] Ehebrecherin f; ~ous □ [_rəs] ehebrecherisch; ~y [_ri] Ehebruch m.

advance [əd'vɑːns] 1. v/i. vorrücken, vorgehen; steigen; Fortschritte machen; v/t. vorrücken, vorbringen; vorausbezahlen; vorschießen; (be)fördern; Preis erhöhen; beschleunigen; 2. Vorrücken n; Fortschritt m; Angebot n; Vorschuß m; Erhöhung f; in ~ im voraus; ~d vor-, fortgeschritten; ~ in years im vorgerücktem Alter; ~ment [_smənt] Förderung f; Fortschritt m.

advantage [əd'vɑːntidʒ] Vorteil m; Überlegenheit f; Gewinn m; take ~ of ausnutzen; ~ous □ [ædvən'teidʒəs] vorteilhaft.

adventur|e [əd'ventʃə] Abenteuern, Wagnis n; Spekulation f; ~er [_rə] Abenteurer m; Spekulant m; ~ous □ [_rəs] abenteuerlich; wagemutig.

adverb gr. ['ædvəːb] Adverb n, Umstandswort n.

advers|ary ['ædvəsəri] Gegner m, Feind m; ~e □ ['ædvəːs] widrig; feindlich; ungünstig, nachteilig (to für); ~ity [əd'vəːsiti] Unglück n.

advertis|e ['ædvətaiz] ankündigen; inserieren; Reklame machen (für); ~ement [əd'vəːtismənt] Ankündigung f, Inserat n; Reklame f; ~ing ['ædvətaiziŋ] Reklame f, Werbung f; ~ agency Annoncenbüro n; ~ designer Reklamezeichner m; ~ film Reklamefilm m; screen ~ Filmreklame f.

advice [əd'vais] Rat(schlag) m; (mst pl.) Nachricht f, Meldung f; take medical ~ e-n Arzt zu Rate ziehen.

advis|able □ [əd'vaizəbl] ratsam; ~e [əd'vaiz] v/t. j-n beraten; j-m raten; † benachrichtigen, avisieren; v/i. (sich) beraten; ~er [_zə] Ratgeber(in).

advocate 1. ['ædvəkit] Anwalt m; Fürsprecher m; 2. [_keit] verteidigen, befürworten.

aerial ['ɛəriəl] 1. □ luftig; Luft...;

~ view Luftaufnahme f; 2. Radio, Fernsehen: Antenne f.

aero|... ['ɛərou] Luft...; ~cab Am. F ['ɛərəkæb] Lufttaxi n (Hubschrauber als Zubringer); ~drome [_ədroum] Flugplatz m; ~naut [_ənɔːt] Luftschiffer m; ~nautics [ɛərɔː'nɔːtiks] pl. Luftfahrt f; ~plane ['ɛərəplein] Flugzeug n; ~stat ['ɛəroustæt] Luftballon m.

aesthetic [iːs'θetik] ästhetisch; ~s sg. Ästhetik f.

afar [ə'fɑː] fern, weit (weg).

affable □ ['æfəbl] leutselig.

affair [ə'fɛə] Geschäft n; Angelegenheit f; Sache f; F Ding n; Liebschaft f.

affect [ə'fekt] (ein- od. sich aus-) wirken auf (acc.); (be)rühren; Gesundheit angreifen; gern mögen; vortäuschen, nachahmen; ~ation [æfek'teiʃən] Vorliebe f; Ziererei f; Verstellung f; ~ed □ gerührt; befallen (von Krankheit); angegriffen (Augen etc.); geziert, affektiert; ~ion [_kʃən] Gemütszustand m; (Zu)Neigung f; Erkrankung f; ~ionate □ [_ʃnit] liebevoll.

affidavit [æfi'deivit] schriftliche beeidigte Erklärung.

affiliate [ə'filieit] als Mitglied aufnehmen; angliedern; ~d company Tochtergesellschaft f.

affinity [ə'finiti] fig. (geistige) Verwandtschaft; ♎ Affinität f.

affirm [ə'fəːm] bejahen; behaupten; bestätigen; ~ation [æfə:'meiʃən] Behauptung f; Bestätigung f; ~ative [ə'fəːmətiv] 1. □ bejahend; 2.: answer in the ~ bejahen.

affix [ə'fiks] (to) anheften (an acc.); befestigen (an dat.); Siegel aufdrücken (dat.); bei-, zufügen (dat.).

afflict [ə'flikt] betrüben; plagen; ~ion [_kʃən] Betrübnis f; Leiden n.

affluen|ce ['æfluəns] Überfluß m; Wohlstand m; ~t [_nt] 1. □ reich (-lich); ~ society Wohlstandsgesellschaft f; 2. Nebenfluß m.

afford [ə'fɔːd] liefern; erschwingen; I can ~ it ich kann es mir leisten.

affront [ə'frʌnt] 1. beleidigen; trotzen (dat.); 2. Beleidigung f.

afield [ə'fiːld] im Felde; (weit) weg.

afloat [ə'flout] ♾ u. fig. flott; schwimmend; auf See; umlaufend; set ~ flottmachen; fig. in Umlauf setzen.

afraid [ə'freid] bange; be ~ of sich fürchten od. Angst haben vor (dat.).

afresh [ə'freʃ] von neuem.

African ['æfrikən] 1. afrikanisch; 2. Afrikaner(in). Am. a. Neger(in).

after ['ɑːftə] 1. adv. hinterher; nachher; 2. prp. nach; hinter (... her); ~ all schließlich (doch); 3. cj. nachdem; 4. adj. später; Nach...; ~crop Nachernte f; ~glow Abendrot n; ~math [_məθ]

Nachwirkung(en *pl.*) *f*, Folgen *f/pl.*; **~noon** [,ə'nu:n] Nachmittag *m*; **~season** Nachsaison *f*; **~taste** Nachgeschmack *m*; **~thought** nachträglicher Einfall; **~wards** [,ɔwədz] nachher; später.

again [ə'gen] wieder(um); ferner; dagegen; **~ and ~**, **time and ~** immer wieder; *as much ~* noch einmal soviel.

against [ə'genst] gegen; *räumlich*: gegen; an, vor (*dat. od. acc.*); *fig.* in Erwartung (*gen.*), für; *as ~* verglichen mit.

age [eidʒ] **1.** (Lebens)Alter *n*; Zeit (-alter *n*) *f*; Menschenalter *n*; (*old*) **~** Greisenalter *f*; *of ~* mündig; *over ~* zu alt; *under ~* unmündig; *wait for ~s* F e-e Ewigkeit warten; **2.** alt werden *od.* machen; **~d** ['eidʒid] alt; [eidʒd]: **~** *twenty* 20 Jahre alt.

agency ['eidʒənsi] Tätigkeit *f*; Vermittlung *f*; Agentur *f*, Büro *n*.

agenda [ə'dʒendə] Tagesordnung *f*.

agent ['eidʒənt] Handelnde(r *m*) *f*; Agent *m*; wirkende Kraft, Agens *n*.

age-worn ['eidʒwɔ:n] altersschwach.

agglomerate [ə'glɔməreit] (sich) zs.-ballen; (sich) (an)häufen.

agglutinate [ə'glu:tineit] zs.-, an-, verkleben.

aggrandize [ə'grændaiz] vergrößern; erhöhen.

aggravate ['ægrəveit] erschweren; verschlimmern; F ärgern.

aggregate 1. ['ægrigeit] (sich) anhäufen; vereinigen (*to* mit); sich belaufen auf (*acc.*); **2.** □ [~git] gehäuft; gesamt; **3.** [~] Anhäufung *f*; Aggregat *n*.

aggress|ion [ə'greʃən] Angriff *m*; **~or** [~esə] Angreifer *m*.

aggrieve [ə'gri:v] kränken; schädigen. [setzt.|

aghast [ə'gɑ:st] entgeistert, ent-|

agil|e □ ['ædʒail] flink, behend; **~ity** [ə'dʒiliti] Behendigkeit *f*.

agitat|e ['ædʒiteit] *v/t.* bewegen, schütteln; *fig.* erregen; erörtern; *v/i.* agitieren; **~ion** [ædʒi'teiʃən] Bewegung *f*, Erschütterung *f*; Aufregung *f*; Agitation *f*; **~or** ['ædʒiteitə] Agitator *m*, Aufwiegler *m*.

ago [ə'gou]: *a year ~* vor e-m Jahr.

agonize ['ægənaiz] (sich) quälen.

agony ['ægəni] Qual *f*, Pein *f*; Ringen *n*; Todeskampf *m*.

agree [ə'gri:] *v/i.* übereinstimmen; sich vertragen; einig werden (*on*, *upon* über *acc.*); übereinkommen; **~ to** zustimmen (*dat.*); einverstanden sein mit (*dat.*); **~able** □ [ə'griəbl] (*to*) angenehm (für); übereinstimmend (mit); **~ment** [ə'gri:mənt] Übereinstimmung *f*; Vereinbarung *f*, Abkommen *n*; Vertrag *m*.

agricultur|al [ægri'kʌltʃərəl] land-

wirtschaftlich; **~e** ['ægrikʌltʃə] Landwirtschaft *f*; **~ist** [ægri'kʌltʃərist] Landwirt *m*.

aground ⚓ [ə'graund] gestrandet; *run ~* stranden, auflaufen.

ague ⚕ ['eigju:] Wechselfieber *n*; Schüttelfrost *m*.

ahead [ə'hed] vorwärts; voraus; vorn; *straight ~* geradeaus.

aid [eid] **1.** helfen (*dat.*; *in* bei *et.*); fördern; **2.** Hilfe *f*, Unterstützung *f*.

ail [eil] *v/i.* kränkeln; *v/t.* schmerzen, weh(e) tun (*dat.*); *what ~s him?* was fehlt ihm?; **~ing** ['eiliŋ] leidend; **~ment** ['eilmənt] Leiden *n*.

aim [eim] **1.** *v/i.* zielen (*at auf acc.*); **~ at** *fig.* streben nach; **~ to do** *bsd. Am.* beabsichtigen *od.* versuchen zu tun, tun wollen; *v/t.* **~ at** *Waffe etc.* richten auf *od.* gegen (*acc.*); **2.** Ziel *n*; Absicht *f*; **~less** □ ['eimlis] ziellos.

air¹ [ɛə] **1.** Luft *f*; Luftzug *m*; *by ~* auf dem Luftwege; *in the open ~* im Freien; *be in the ~* *fig.* in der Luft liegen; ungewiß sein; *on the ~* im Rundfunk (*senden*); *be on (off) the ~* in (außer) Betrieb sein (*Sender*); *put on the ~* im Rundfunk (*Sender*); **2.** (aus)lüften; *fig.* an die Öffentlichkeit bringen; erörtern.

air² [~] Miene *f*; Aussehen *n*; *give o.s. ~s* vornehm tun.

air³ ♪ [~] Arie *f*, Weise *f*, Melodie *f*.

air|-base ✈ ['ɛəbeis] Luftstützpunkt *m*; **~bed** Luftmatratze *f*; **~borne** ✈ in der Luft (*Flugzeug*); ✈ Luftlande...; **~brake** Druckluftbremse *f*; **~conditioned** mit Klimaanlage; **~craft** Flugzeug (-e *pl.*) *n*; **~field** ✈ Flugplatz *m*; **~ force** ✈ Luftwaffe *f*; **~ hostess** ✈ Stewardess *f*; **~jacket** Schwimmweste *f*; **~lift** Luftbrücke *f*; **~ liner** ✈ Verkehrsflugzeug *n*; **~ mail** Luftpost *f*; **~man** ['ɛəmæn] Flieger *m*; **~plane** *Am.* Flugzeug *n*; **~pocket** ✈ Luftloch *n*; **~port** ✈ Flughafen *m*; **~ raid** ✈ Luftangriff *m*; **~raid precautions** *pl.* Luftschutz *m*; **~raid shelter** Luftschutzraum *m*; **~route** ✈ Luftweg *m*; **~tight** luftdicht; **~ case** *sl.* todsicherer Fall; **~tube** Luftschlauch *m*; **~ umbrella** ✈ Luftsicherung *f*; **~way** ✈ Luftverkehrslinie *f*.

airy □ ['ɛəri] luftig; leicht(fertig).

aisle ▲ [ail] Seitenschiff *n*; Gang *m*.

ajar [ə'dʒɑ:] halb offen, angelehnt.

akin [ə'kin] verwandt (*to* mit).

alacrity [ə'lækriti] Munterkeit *f*; Bereitwilligkeit *f*, Eifer *m*.

alarm [ə'lɑ:m] **1.** Alarm(zeichen *n*) *m*; Angst *f*; **2.** alarmieren; beunruhigen; **~clock** Wecker *m*.

albuminous [æl'bju:minəs] eiweißartig, -haltig.

alcohol ['ælkəhɔl] Alkohol *m*; **~ic**

[ælkə'həlik] alkoholisch; ~ism ['æl-kəhəlizəm] Alkoholvergiftung f.

alcove ['ælkouv] Nische f; Laube f.

alderman ['ɔːldəmən] Stadtrat m.

ale [eil] Ale n (Art engl. Bier).

alert [ə'ləːt] 1. □ wachsam; munter; 2. Alarm(bereitschaft f) m; on the ~ auf der Hut; in Alarmbereitschaft.

alibi ['ælibai] Alibi n; Am. F Entschuldigung f; Ausrede f.

alien ['eiljən] 1. fremd, ausländisch; 2. Ausländer(in); ~able [~nəbl] veräußerlich; ~ate [~neit] veräußern; fig. entfremden (from dat.); ~ist [~nist] Irrenarzt m, Psychiater m.

alight [ə'lait] 1. brennend; erhellt; 2. ab-, aussteigen; ✈ niedergehen, landen; sich niederlassen.

align [ə'lain] (sich) ausrichten (with nach); surv. abstecken; ~ o.s. with sich anschließen an (acc.).

alike [ə'laik] 1. adj. gleich, ähnlich; 2. adv. gleich; ebenso.

aliment ['ælimənt] Nahrung f; ~ary [æli'mentəri] nahrhaft; ~ canal Verdauungskanal m.

alimony 𝔤𝔤 ['æliməni] Unterhalt m.

alive [ə'laiv] lebendig; in Kraft, gültig; empfänglich (to für); lebhaft; belebt (with von).

all [ɔːl] 1. adj. all; ganz; jede(r, -s); for ~ that dessenungeachtet, trotzdem; 2. pron. alles; alle pl.; at ~ gar, überhaupt; not at ~ durchaus nicht; for ~ (that) I care meinetwegen; for ~ I know soviel ich weiß; 3. adv. ganz, völlig; ~ at once auf einmal; ~ the better desto besser; ~ but beinahe, fast; ~ in Am. F fertig, ganz erledigt; ~ right (alles) in Ordnung.

all-American [ɔːlə'merikən] rein amerikanisch; die ganzen USA vertretend.

allay [ə'lei] beruhigen; lindern.

alleg|ation [æle'geiʃən] unerwiesene Behauptung; ~e [ə'ledʒ] behaupten; ~ed angeblich.

allegiance [ə'liːdʒəns] Lehnspflicht f; (Untertanen)Treue f.

alleviate [ə'liːvieit] erleichtern, lindern.

alley ['æli] Allee f; Gäßchen n; Gang m; bsd. Am. schmale Zufahrtsstraße.

alliance [ə'laiəns] Bündnis n.

allocat|e ['æləkeit] zuteilen, anweisen; ~ion [ælə'keiʃən] Zuteilung f.

allot [ə'lɔt] zuweisen; ~ment [~t-mənt] Zuteilung f; Los n; Parzelle f.

allow [ə'lau] erlauben, bewilligen, gewähren; zugeben; ab-, anrechnen; vergüten; ~ for berücksichtigen; ~able □ [ə'lauəbl] erlaubt, zulässig; ~ance [~əns] Erlaubnis f; Bewilligung f; Taschengeld n, Zuschuß m; Vergütung f; Nachsicht f;

make ~ for s.th. et. in Betracht ziehen.

alloy 1. ['æbi] Legierung f; 2. [ə'lɔi] legieren; fig. verunedeln.

all-red ['ɔːl'red] rein britisch.

all-round ['ɔːl'raund] zu allem brauchbar; vielseitig.

all-star Am. ['ɔːl'stɑː] Sport u. thea.: aus den besten (Schau)Spielern bestehend.

allude [ə'luːd] anspielen (to auf acc.).

allure [ə'ljuə] (an-, ver)locken; ~ment [~əmənt] Verlockung f.

allusion [ə'luːʒən] Anspielung f.

ally 1. [ə'lai] (sich) vereinigen, verbünden (to, with mit); 2. ['ælai] Verbündete(r m) f, Bundesgenosse m; the Allies pl. die Alliierten pl.

almanac ['ɔːlmənæk] Almanach m.

almighty [ɔːl'maiti] 1. □ allmächtig; 2. ♀ Allmächtige(r) m.

almond ♀ ['ɑːmənd] Mandel f.

almoner ['ɑːmənə] Krankenhausfürsorger(in).

almost ['ɔːlmoust] fast, beinahe.

alms [ɑːmz] sg. u. pl. Almosen n; ~-house ['ɑːmzhaus] Armenhaus n.

aloft [ə'lɔft] (hoch) (dr)oben.

alone [ə'loun] allein; let od. leave ~ in Ruhe od. bleiben lassen; let ~ ... abgesehen von ...

along [ə'lɔŋ] 1. adv. weiter, vorwärts, her; mit, bei (sich); all ~ die ganze Zeit; ~ with zs. mit; get ~ with you! F scher dich weg!; 2. prp. entlang, längs; ~side [~ŋ'said] Seite an Seite; neben.

aloof [ə'luːf] fern; weitab; stand ~ abseits stehen.

aloud [ə'laud] laut; hörbar.

alp [ælp] Alp(e) f; ♀s pl. Alpen pl.

already [ɔːl'redi] bereits, schon.

also ['ɔːlsou] auch; ferner.

altar ['ɔːltə] Altar m.

alter ['ɔːltə] (sich) (ver)ändern; ab-, umändern; ~ation [ɔːltə'reiʃən] Änderung f (to an dat.).

alternat|e 1. ['ɔːltəneit] abwechseln (lassen); alternating current ⚡ Wechselstrom m; 2. □ [ɔːl'təːnit] abwechselnd; 3. [~] Am. Stellvertreter m; ~ion [ɔːltə'neiʃən] Abwechslung f; Wechsel m; ~ive [ɔːl'təːnə-tiv] 1. □ nur eine Wahl zwischen zwei Möglichkeiten lassend; 2. Alternative f; Wahl f; Möglichkeit f.

although [ɔːl'ðou] obgleich.

altitude ['æltitjuːd] Höhe f.

altogether [ɔːltə'geðə] im ganzen (genommen), alles in allem; gänzlich.

aluminium [ælju'minjəm] Aluminium n.

aluminum Am. [ə'luːminəm] = aluminium.

always ['ɔːlwəz] immer, stets.

am [æm; im Satz əm] 1. sg. pres. von be.

amalgamate [ə'mælgəmeit] amalgamieren; (sich) verschmelzen.

amass [ə'mæs] (an-, auf)häufen.

amateur ['æmətə:] Amateur *m*; Liebhaber *m*; Dilettant *m*.

amaz|e [ə'meiz] in Staunen setzen, verblüffen; **~ement** [~zmənt] Staunen *n*, Verblüffung *f*; **~ing** □ [~ziŋ] erstaunlich, verblüffend.

ambassador [æm'bæsədə] Botschafter *m*, Gesandte(r) *m*.

amber ['æmbə] Bernstein *m*.

ambigu|ity [æmbi'gju(:)iti] Zwei-, Vieldeutigkeit *f*; **~ous** □ [æm-'bigjuəs] zwei-, vieldeutig; doppelsinnig.

ambitio|n [æm'biʃən] Ehrgeiz *m*; Streben *n* (*of* nach); **~us** □ [~ʃəs] ehrgeizig; begierig (*of*, *for* nach).

amble ['æmbl] 1. Paßgang *m*; 2. im Paßgang gehen *od*. reiten; schlendern.

ambulance ['æmbjuləns] Feldlazarett *n*; Krankenwagen *m*; **~ station** Sanitätswache *f*, Unfallstation *f*.

ambus|cade [æmbəs'keid], **~h** ['æmbuʃ] 1. Hinterhalt *m*; *be od*. *lie in ambush for s.o.* j-m auflauern; 2. auflauern (*dat*.); überfallen.

ameliorate [ə'mi:ljəreit] *v/t*. verbessern; *v/i*. besser werden.

amend [ə'mend] (sich) (ver)bessern; berichtigen; *Gesetz* (ab)ändern; **~ment** [~dmənt] Besserung *f*; *šɨ* Berichtigung *f*; *parl*. Änderungsantrag *m*; *Am*. Zusatzartikel *m* zur Verfassung der USA; **~s** *sg*. (Schaden)Ersatz *m*.

amenity [ə'mi:niti] Annehmlichkeit *f*; Anmut *f*; *amenities pl*. angenehmes Wesen.

American [ə'merikən] 1. amerikanisch; **~** *cloth* Wachstuch *n*; **~** *plan* Hotelzimmervermietung *mit voller Verpflegung*; 2. Amerikaner(in); **~ism** [~nizəm] Amerikanismus *m*; **~ize** [~naiz] (sich) amerikanisieren.

amiable □ ['eimjəbl] liebenswürdig, freundlich.

amicable □ ['æmikəbl] freundschaftlich; gütlich.

amid(st) [ə'mid(st)] inmitten (*gen*.); (mitten) unter; mitten in (*dat*.).

amiss [ə'mis] verkehrt; übel; ungelegen; *take* **~** übelnehmen.

amity ['æmiti] Freundschaft *f*.

ammonia [ə'mounjə] Ammoniak *n*.

ammunition [æmju'niʃən] Munition *f*.

amnesty ['æmnesti] 1. Amnestie *f* (*Straferlaß*); 2. begnadigen.

among(st) [ə'mʌŋ(st)] (mitten) unter, zwischen. [in *acc*.).

amorous □ ['æmərəs] verliebt (*of*

amount [ə'maunt] 1. (*to*) sich belaufen (auf *acc*.); hinauslaufen (auf *acc*.); 2. Betrag *m*, (Gesamt-)

Summe *f*; Menge *f*; Bedeutung *f*, Wert *m*.

amour [ə'muə] Liebschaft *f*; **~propre** Selbstachtung *f*; Eitelkeit *f*.

ample □ ['æmpl] weit, groß; geräumig; reichlich.

ampli|fication [æmplifi'keiʃən] Erweiterung *f*; *rhet*. weitere Ausführung; *phys*. Verstärkung *f*; **~fier** ['æmplifaiə] *Radio*: Verstärker *m*; **~fy** [~fai] erweitern; verstärken; weiter ausführen; **~tude** [~itju:d] Umfang *m*, Weite *f*, Fülle *f*.

amputate ['æmpjuteit] amputieren.

amuse [ə'mju:z] amüsieren; unterhalten; belustigen; **~ment** [~zmənt] Unterhaltung *f*; Zeitvertreib *m*.

an [æn, ən] *Artikel*: ein(e).

an(a)emia [ə'ni:mjə] Blutarmut *f*.

an(a)esthetic [ænis'θetik] 1. betäubend, Narkose...; 2. Betäubungsmittel *n*.

analog|ous □ [ə'næləgəs] analog, ähnlich; **~y** [~ədʒi] Ähnlichkeit *f*, Analogie *f*.

analys|e [ə'nælaiz] analysieren; zerlegen; **~is** [ə'næləsis] Analyse *f*.

anarchy ['ænəki] Anarchie *f*, Gesetzlosigkeit *f*; Zügellosigkeit *f*.

anatom|ize [ə'nætəmaiz] zergliedern; **~y** [~mi] Anatomie *f*; Zergliederung *f*, Analyse *f*.

ancest|or ['ænsistə] Vorfahr *m*, Ahn *m*; **~ral** [æn'sestrəl] angestammt; **~ress** ['ænsistris] Ahne *f*; **~ry** [~ri] Abstammung *f*; Ahnen *m/pl*.

anchor ['æŋkə] 1. Anker *m*; *at* **~** vor Anker; 2. (ver)ankern; **~age** [~əridʒ] Ankerplatz *m*.

anchovy ['æntʃəvi] Sardelle *f*.

ancient ['einʃənt] 1. alt, antik; uralt; 2. *the* **~s** *pl. hist*. die Alten, die antiken Klassiker.

and [ænd, ənd] und.

anew [ə'nju:] von neuem.

angel ['eindʒəl] Engel *m*; **~ic(al** □) [æn'dʒelik(əl)] engelgleich.

anger ['æŋgə] 1. Zorn *m*, Ärger *m* (*at* über *acc*.); 2. erzürnen, ärgern.

angina *š* [æn'dʒainə] Angina *f*, Halsentzündung *f*.

angle ['æŋgl] 1. Winkel *m*; *fig*. Standpunkt *m*; 2. angeln (*for* nach).

Anglican ['æŋglikən] 1. anglikanisch; *Am. a*. englisch; 2. Anglikaner(in).

Anglo-Saxon ['æŋglou'sæksən] 1. Angelsachse *m*; 2. angelsächsisch.

angry ['æŋgri] zornig, böse (*a. š*) (*with s.o.*, *at s.th*. über, auf *acc*.).

anguish ['æŋgwiʃ] Pein *f*, (Seelen-) Qual *f*, Schmerz *m*.

angular □ ['æŋgjulə] winkelig; Winkel...; *fig*. eckig.

animadver|sion [ænimæd'və:ʃən]

Verweis *m*, Tadel *m*; ~t [~ə:t] tadeln, kritisieren.

animal ['ænəməl] **1.** Tier *n*; **2.** tierisch.

animat|e ['ænimeit] beleben; beseelen; aufmuntern; ~ion [æni-'meiʃən] Leben *n* (und Treiben *n*), Lebhaftigkeit *f*, Munterkeit *f*.

animosity [æni'mɔsiti] Feindseligkeit *f*.

ankle ['æŋkl] Fußknöchel *m*.

annals ['ænlz] *pl.* Jahrbücher *n/pl.*

annex 1. [ə'neks] anhängen; annektieren; **2.** ['æneks] Anhang *m*; Anbau *m*; ~ation [ænek'seiʃən] Annexion *f*, Aneignung *f*; Einverleibung *f*.

annihilate [ə'naiəleit] vernichten; = annul.

anniversary [æni'və:səri] Jahrestag *m*; Jahresfeier *f*.

annotat|e ['ænouteit] mit Anmerkungen versehen; kommentieren; ~ion [ænou'teiʃən] Kommentieren *n*; Anmerkung *f*.

announce [ə'nauns] ankündigen; ansagen; ~ment [~smənt] Ankündigung *f*; Ansage *f*; *Radio*: Durchsage *f*; Anzeige *f*; ~r [~sə] *Radio*: Ansager *m*.

annoy [ə'nɔi] ärgern; belästigen; ~ance [ə'nɔiəns] Störung *f*; Plage *f*; Ärgernis *n*.

annual ['ænjuəl] **1.** □ jährlich; Jahres...; **2.** einjährige Pflanze; Jahrbuch *n*. [Rente *f*.}

annuity [ə'nju(:)iti] (Jahres-)}

annul [ə'nʌl] für ungültig erklären, annullieren; ~ment [~lmənt] Aufhebung *f*.

anodyne ❀ ['ænoudain] **1.** schmerzstillend; **2.** schmerzstillendes Mittel.

anoint [ə'nɔint] salben.

anomalous □ [ə'nɔmələs] anomal, unregelmäßig, regelwidrig.

anonymous □ [ə'nɔniməs] anonym, ungenannt.

another [ə'nʌðə] ein anderer; ein zweiter; noch ein.

answer ['ɑ:nsə] **1.** *v/t. et.* beantworten; *j-m* antworten; entsprechen (*dat.*); *Zweck* erfüllen; *dem Steuer* gehorchen; *e-r Vorladung* Folge leisten; ~ *the bell od. door* (die Haustür) aufmachen; *v/i.* antworten (*to s.o.* j-m; *to a question* auf e-e Frage); entsprechen (*to dat.*); Erfolg haben; sich lohnen; ~ *for* einstehen für; bürgen für; **2.** Antwort *f* (*to auf acc.*); ~able □ [~ərəbl] verantwortlich.

ant [ænt] Ameise *f*.

antagonis|m [æn'tægənizəm] Widerstreit *m*; Widerstand *m*; Feindschaft *f*; ~t [~ist] Gegner(in).

antagonize [æn'tægənaiz] ankämpfen gegen; sich *j-n* zum Feind machen.

antecedent [ænti'si:dənt] **1.** □ vor-

hergehend; früher (*to* als); **2.** Vorhergehende(s) *n*.

anterior [æn'tiəriə] vorhergehend; früher (*to* als); vorder.

ante-room ['æntirum] Vorzimmer *n*.

anthem ['ænθəm] Hymne *f*.

anti|... ['ænti] Gegen...; gegen ... eingestellt *od.* wirkend; ~aircraft Fliegerabwehr...; ~biotic [~ibai-'ɔtik] Antibiotikum *n*.

antic ['æntik] Posse *f*; ~s *pl.* Mätzchen *n/pl.*; (tolle) Sprünge *m/pl.*

anticipat|e [æn'tisipeit] vorwegnehmen; zuvorkommen (*dat.*); voraussehen, ahnen; erwarten; ~ion [æntisi'peiʃən] Vorwegnahme *f*; Zuvorkommen *n*; Voraussicht *f*; Erwartung *f*; *in* ~ im voraus.

antidote ['æntidout] Gegengift *n*.

antipathy [æn'tipəθi] Abneigung *f*.

antiqua|ry ['æntikwəri] Altertumsforscher *m*; Antiquitätensammler *m*, -händler *m*; ~ted [~kweitid] veraltet, überlebt.

antiqu|e [æn'ti:k] **1.** □ antik, alt (-modisch); **2.** alter Kunstgegenstand; ~ity [æn'tikwiti] Altertum *n*; Vorzeit *f*.

antiseptic [ænti'septik] **1.** antiseptisch; **2.** antiseptisches Mittel.

antlers ['æntləz] *pl.* Geweih *n*.

anvil ['ænvil] Amboß *m*.

anxiety [æŋ'zaiəti] Angst *f*; *fig.* Sorge *f* (*for* um); ❀ Beklemmung *f*.

anxious □ ['æŋkʃəs] ängstlich, besorgt (*about* um, wegen); begierig, gespannt (*for* auf *acc.*); bemüht (*for* um).

any ['eni] **1.** *pron.* (irgend)einer; einige *pl.*; (irgend)welcher; (irgend) etwas; jeder (beliebige); *not* ~ keiner; **2.** *adv.* irgend(wie); ~body (irgend) jemand; jeder; ~how irgendwie; jedenfalls; ~one = anybody; ~thing (irgend) etwas, alles; ~ *but* alles andere als; ~way = anyhow; ohnehin; ~where irgendwo(hin); überall.

apart [ə'pɑ:t] einzeln; getrennt; für sich; beiseite; ~ *from* abgesehen von.

apartheid *pol.* [ə'pɑ:theit] Apartheid *f*, Rassentrennung(spolitik) *f*.

apartment [ə'pɑ:tmənt] Zimmer *n*, *Am. a.* Wohnung *f*; ~s *pl.* Wohnung *f*; ~ *house Am.* Mietshaus *n*.

apathetic [æpə'θetik] apathisch, gleichgültig.

ape [eip] **1.** Affe *m*; **2.** nachäffen.

aperient [ə'piəriənt] Abführmittel *n*.

aperture ['æpətjuə] Öffnung *f*.

apiary ['eipiəri] Bienenhaus *n*.

apiculture ['eipikʌltʃə] Bienenzucht *f*.

apiece [ə'pi:s] (für) das Stück; je.

apish □ ['eipiʃ] affig; äffisch.

apolog|etic [əpɔlə'dʒetik] (~ally) verteidigend; rechtfertigend; entschuldigend; ~ize [ə'pɔlədʒaiz] sich entschuldigen (*for* wegen; *to* bei); **~y** [~dʒi] Entschuldigung *f*; Rechtfertigung *f*; F Notbehelf *m*.

apoplexy ['æpəpleksi] Schlag(anfall) *m*.

apostate [ə'pɔstit] Abtrünnige(r*m*)*f*.

apostle [ə'pɔsl] Apostel *m*.

apostroph|e [ə'pɔstrəfi] Anrede *f*; Apostroph *m*; **~ize** [~faiz] anreden, sich wenden an (*acc.*).

appal [ə'pɔːl] erschrecken.

apparatus [æpə'reitəs] Apparat *m*, Vorrichtung *f*, Gerät *n*.

apparel [ə'pærəl] 1. Kleidung *f*; 2. (be)kleiden.

appar|ent □ [ə'pærənt] anscheinend; offenbar; **~ition** [æpə'riʃən] Erscheinung *f*; Gespenst *n*.

appeal [ə'piːl] 1. (*to*) ⚖ appellieren (an *acc.*); sich berufen (auf *e-n Zeugen*); sich wenden (an *acc.*); wirken (auf *acc.*); Anklang finden (bei); **~ to the country** *parl.* Neuwahlen ausschreiben; 2. ⚖ Revision *f*, Berufung(sklage) *f*; ⚖ Rechtsmittel *n*; *fig.* Appell *m* (*to* an *acc.*); Wirkung *f*, Reiz *m*; **~ for mercy** ⚖ Gnadengesuch *n*; **~ing** □ [~liŋ] flehend; ansprechend.

appear [ə'piə] (er)scheinen; sich zeigen; *öffentlich* auftreten; **~ance** [~rəns] Erscheinen *n*, Auftreten *n*; Äußere(s) *n*, Erscheinung *f*; Anschein *m*; **~s** *pl.* äußerer Schein; **to od. by all ~s** allem Anschein nach.

appease [ə'piːz] beruhigen; beschwichtigen; stillen; mildern; beilegen.

appellant [ə'pelənt] 1. appellierend; 2. Appelant(in), Berufungskläger (-in).

append [ə'pend] anhängen; hinzubeifügen; **~age** [~didʒ] Anhang *m*; Anhängsel *n*; Zubehör *n*, *m*; **~icitis** [əpendi'saitis] Blinddarmentzündung *f*; **~ix** [ə'pendiks] Anhang *m*; *a. vermiform* **~** ⚕ Wurmfortsatz *m*, Blinddarm *m*.

appertain [æpə'tein] gehören (*to* zu).

appetite ['æpitait] (*for*) Appetit *m* (auf *acc.*); *fig.* Verlangen *n* (nach).

appetizing ['æpitaiziŋ] appetitanregend.

applaud [ə'plɔːd] applaudieren, Beifall spenden; loben.

applause [ə'plɔːz] Applaus *m*, Beifall *m*.

apple ['æpl] Apfel *m*; **~-cart** Apfelkarren *m*; *upset s.o.'s* **~** F j-s Pläne über den Haufen werfen; **~-pie** gedeckter Apfelkuchen; *in* **~** *order* F in schönster Ordnung; **~-sauce** Apfelmus *n*; *Am. sl.* Schmus *m*, Quatsch *m*.

appliance [ə'plaiəns] Vorrichtung *f*; Gerät *n*; Mittel *n*.

applica|ble ['æplikəbl] anwendbar

(*to* auf *acc.*); **~nt** [~ənt] Bittsteller (-in); Bewerber(in) (*for* um); **~tion** [æpli'keiʃən] (*to*) Auf-, Anlegung *f* (auf *acc.*); Anwendung *f* (auf *acc.*); Bedeutung *f* (für); Gesuch *n* (*for* um); Bewerbung *f*.

apply [ə'plai] *v/t.* (*to*) (auf)legen (auf *acc.*); anwenden (auf *acc.*); verwenden (für); **~ o.s. to** sich widmen (*dat.*); *v/i.* (*to*) passen, sich anwenden lassen (auf *acc.*); gelten (für); sich wenden (an *acc.*); (*for*) sich bewerben (um); nachsuchen (um).

appoint [ə'pɔint] bestimmen; festsetzen; verabreden; ernennen (*s.o. governor* j-n zum ...); berufen (*to* auf *e-n Posten*); *well* **~ed** gut eingerichtet; **~ment** [~tmənt] Bestimmung *f*; Stelldichein *n*; Verabredung *f*; Ernennung *f*, Berufung *f*; Stelle *f*; **~s** *pl.* Ausstattung *f*, Einrichtung *f*.

apportion [ə'pɔːʃən] ver-, zuteilen; **~ment** [~nmənt] Verteilung *f*.

apprais|al [ə'preizl] Abschätzung *f*; **~e** [ə'preiz] abschätzen, taxieren.

apprecia|ble □ [ə'priːʃəbl] (ab-)schätzbar; merkbar; **~te** [~ʃieit] *v/t.* schätzen; würdigen; dankbar sein für; *v/i.* im Werte steigen; **~tion** [əpriːʃi'eiʃən] Schätzung *f*, Würdigung *f*; Verständnis *n* (*of* für); Einsicht *f*; Dankbarkeit *f*; Aufwertung *f*.

apprehen|d [æpri'hend] ergreifen; fassen; begreifen; befürchten; **~sion** [~nʃən] Ergreifung *f*, Festnahme *f*; Fassungskraft *f*, Auffassung *f*; Besorgnis *f*; **~sive** □ [~nsiv] schnell begreifend (*of acc.*); ängstlich; besorgt (*of*, *for* um, wegen; *that* daß).

apprentice [ə'prentis] 1. Lehrling *m*; 2. in die Lehre geben (*to dat.*); **~ship** [~iʃip] Lehrzeit *f*; Lehre *f*.

approach [ə'prəutʃ] 1. *v/i.* näherkommen, sich nähern; *v/t.* sich nähern (*dat.*), herangehen *od.* herantreten an (*acc.*); 2. Annäherung *f*; *fig.* Herangehen *n*; Methode *f*; Zutritt *m*; Auffahrt *f*.

approbation [æprə'beiʃən] Billigung *f*, Beifall *m*.

appropriat|e 1. [ə'prouprieit] sich aneignen; verwenden; *parl.* bewilligen; 2. □ [~iit] (*to*) angemessen (*dat.*); passend (für); eigen (*dat.*); **~ion** [əproupri'eiʃən] Aneignung *f*; Verwendung *f*.

approv|al [ə'pruːvəl] Billigung *f*, Beifall *m*; **~e** [~v] billigen, anerkennen; (**~** *o.s.* sich) erweisen als; **~ed** □ bewährt.

approximate 1. [ə'prɔksimeit] sich nähern; 2. □ [~mit] annähernd; ungefähr; nahe.

apricot ['eiprikɔt] Aprikose *f*.

April ['eiprəl] April *m*.

apron ['eiprən] Schürze *f*; **~-string** Schürzenband *n*; *be tied to one's wife's (mother's)* **~s** *fig.* unterm Pantoffel stehen (der Mutter am Rockzipfel hängen).

apt □ [æpt] geeignet, passend; begabt; **~** *to* geneigt zu; **~itude** ['æptitju:d], **~ness** ['æptnis] Neigung *f* (*to* zu); Befähigung *f*.

aquatic [ə'kwætik] Wasserpflanze *f*; **~s** *pl.* Wassersport *m*.

aque|duct ['ækwidʌkt] Aquädukt *m*, Wasserleitung *f*; **~ous** □ ['eikwiəs] wässerig.

aquiline ['ækwilain] Adler...; gebogen; **~** *nose* Adlernase *f*.

Arab ['ærəb] Araber(in); **~ic** [~bik] **1.** arabisch; **2.** Arabisch *n*.

arable ['ærəbl] pflügbar; Acker...

arbit|er ['a:bitə] Schiedsrichter *m*; *fig.* Gebieter *m*; **~rariness** [~trərinis] Willkür *f*; **~rary** □ [~trəri] willkürlich; eigenmächtig; **~rate** [~reit] entscheiden, schlichten; **~ration** [a:bi'treifən] Schiedsspruch *m*; Entscheidung *f*; **~rator** ⚖ ['a:bitreitə] Schiedsrichter *m*.

arbo(u)r ['a:bə] Laube *f*.

arc *ast.*, Å *etc.* [a:k] (⚡ Licht-) Bogen *f*; **~ade** [a:'keid] Arkade *f*; Bogen-, Laubengang *m*.

arch¹ [a:tʃ] **1.** Bogen *m*; Gewölbe *n*; **2.** (sich) wölben; überwölben.

arch² [~] erst; schlimmst; Haupt...; Erz...

arch³ □ [~] schelmisch.

archaic [a:'keiik] (~ally) veraltet.

archangel ['a:keindʒəl] Erzengel *m*.

archbishop ['a:tʃ'bifəp] Erzbischof *m*.

archer ['a:tʃə] Bogenschütze *m*; **~y** [~əri] Bogenschießen *n*.

architect ['a:kitekt] Architekt *m*; Urheber(in), Schöpfer(in); **~onic** [a:kitek'tonik] (~ally) architektonisch; *fig.* aufbauend; **~ure** ['a:kitektʃə] Architektur *f*, Baukunst *f*.

archives ['a:kaivz] *pl.* Archiv *n*.

archway ['a:tʃwei] Bogengang *m*.

arc|-lamp ['a:klæmp], **~-light** ⚡ Bogenlampe *f*.

arctic ['a:ktik] **1.** arktisch, nördlich; Nord..., Polar...; **2.** *Am.* wasserdichter Überschuh.

arden|cy ['a:dənsi] Hitze *f*, Glut *f*; Innigkeit *f*; **~t** □ [~nt] *mst fig.* heiß, glühend; *fig.* feurig; eifrig.

ardo(u)r ['a:də] *fig.* Glut *f*; Eifer *m*.

arduous □ ['a:djuəs] mühsam; zäh.

are [a:; *im Satz ə*] *pres. pl. u. 2. sg. von* be.

area ['ɛəriə] Areal *n*; (Boden-) Fläche *f*; Flächenraum *m*; Gegend *f*; Gebiet *n*; Bereich *m*.

Argentine ['a:dʒəntain] **1.** argentinisch; **2.** Argentinier(in); *the* **~** Argentinien *n*.

argue ['a:gju:] *v/t.* erörtern; beweisen; begründen; einwenden; **~**

s.o. into j-n zu *et.* bereden; *v/i.* streiten; Einwendungen machen.

argument ['a:gjumənt] Beweis (-grund) *m*; Streit(frage *f*) *m*; Erörterung *f*; Thema *n*; **~ation** [a:gjumen'teifən] Beweisführung *f*.

arid ['ærid] dürr, trocken (*a. fig.*).

arise [ə'raiz] [*irr.*] sich erheben (*a. fig.*); ent-, erstehen (*from* aus); **~n** [ə'rizn] *p.p von* arise.

aristocra|cy [æris'tokrəsi] Aristokratie *f* (*a. fig.*), Adel *m*; **~t** ['æristəkræt] Aristokrat(in); **~tic(al** □) [æristə'krætik(əl)] aristokratisch.

arithmetic [ə'riθmətik] Rechnen *n*.

ark [a:k] Arche *f*.

arm¹ [a:m] Arm *m*; Armlehne *f*; *keep s.o. at* **~'s** *length* sich j-n vom Leibe halten; *infant in* **~s** Säugling *m*.

arm² [~] **1.** Waffe *f* (*mst pl.*); Waffengattung *f*; *be* (*all*) *up in* **~s** in vollem Aufruhr sein; in Harnisch geraten; **2.** (sich) (be)waffnen; (aus)rüsten; ⊕ armieren.

armada [a:'ma:də] Kriegsflotte *f*.

arma|ment ['a:məmənt] (Kriegsaus)Rüstung *f*; Kriegsmacht *f*; **~race** Wettrüsten *n*; **~ture** [a:'mətjuə] Rüstung *f*; ⚡, *phys.* Armatur *f*.

armchair ['a:m'tʃɛə] Lehnstuhl *m*, Sessel *m*.

armistice ['a:mistis] Waffenstillstand *m* (*a. fig.*).

armo(u)r ['a:mə] **1.** ⚔ Rüstung *f*, Panzer *m* (*a. fig.*, *zo.*); **2.** panzern; **~ed car** Panzerwagen *m*; **~y** [a:'məri] Rüstkammer *f* (*a. fig.*); *Am.* Rüstungsbetrieb *m*, Waffenfabrik *f*.

armpit ['a:mpit] Achselhöhle *f*.

army ['a:mi] Heer *n*, Armee *f*; *fig.* Menge *f*; **~ chaplain** Militärgeistliche(r) *m*.

arose [ə'rouz] *pret. von* arise.

around [ə'raund] **1.** *adv.* rund-(her)um; *Am.* F hier herum; **2.** *prp.* um ... her(um); *bsd. Am.* F ungefähr, etwa (*bei Zahlenangaben*).

arouse [ə'rauz] aufwecken; *fig.* aufrütteln; erregen.

arraign [ə'rein] vor Gericht stellen, anklagen; *fig.* rügen.

arrange [ə'reindʒ] (an)ordnen, *bsd.* ♪ einrichten; festsetzen; *Streit* schlichten; vereinbaren; erledigen; **~ment** [~dʒmənt] Anordnung *f*; Disposition *f*; Übereinkommen *n*; Vorkehrung *f*; ♪ Arrangement *n*.

array [ə'rei] **1.** (Schlacht)Ordnung *f*; *fig.* Aufgebot *n*; **2.** ordnen, aufstellen; aufbieten; kleiden, putzen.

arrear [ə'riə] *mst pl.* Rückstand *m*, *bsd.* Schulden *f/pl.*

arrest [ə'rest] **1.** Verhaftung *f*; Haft *f*; Beschlagnahme *f*; **2.** verhaften; beschlagnahmen; anhalten, hemmen.

arriv|al [ə'raivəl] Ankunft *f*; Auftreten *n*; Ankömmling *m*; **~s** *pl.* angekommene Personen *f/pl.*; Züge *m/pl.*, Schiffe *n/pl.*; ~e [ə'raiv] (an-) kommen, eintreffen; erscheinen; eintreten (*Ereignis*); ~ *at* erreichen (*acc.*).

arroga|nce ['ærəgəns] Anmaßung *f*; Überheblichkeit *f*; ~nt □ [~nt] anmaßend; überheblich; ~te ['ærougeit] sich *et.* anmaßen.

arrow ['ærou] Pfeil *m*; ~head Pfeilspitze *f*; ~y ['æroui] pfeilartig.

arsenal ꬵ ['ɑːsinl] Zeughaus *n.*

arsenic ['ɑːsnik] Arsen(ik) *n.*

arson ꬵ ['ɑːsn] Brandstiftung *f.*

art [ɑːt] Kunst *f*, *fig.* List *f*; Kniff *m*; ~s *pl.* Geisteswissenschaften *f/pl.*; Faculty of ~s philosophische Fakultät *f.*

arter|ial [ɑː'tiəriəl] Pulsader...; ~ road Hauptstraße *f*; ~y ['ɑːtəri] Arterie *f*, Pulsader *f*; *fig.* Verkehrsader *f.*   [schmitzt.]

artful □ ['ɑːtful] schlau, verzarticle ['ɑːtikl] Artikel *m*; *fig.* Punkt *m*; ~d to in die Lehre bei.

articulat|e 1. [ɑː'tikjuleit] deutlich (aus)sprechen; *Knochen* zs.-fügen; 2. □ [~lit] deutlich; gegliedert; ~ion [ɑːtikju'leiʃən] deutliche Aussprache; *anat.* Gelenkfügung *f.*

artific|e ['ɑːtifis] Kunstgriff *m*, List *f*; ~ial □ [ɑː'tifiʃəl] künstlich; *Kunst...*; ~ person ꬵꬵ juristische Person.

artillery [ɑː'tiləri] Artillerie *f*; ~man Artillerist *m.*

artisan [ɑːti'zæn] Handwerker *m.*

artist ['ɑːtist] Künstler(in); ~e [ɑː'tiːst] Artist(in); ~ic(al) □ [ɑː-'tistik(əl)] künstlerisch; *Kunst...*

artless □ ['ɑːtlis] ungekünstelt, schlicht; arglos.

as [æz, əz] 1. *adv.* so; (ebenso) wie; (*in der Eigenschaft*) als; ~ big ~ so groß wie; ~ well ebensogut; auch; ~ well ~ sowohl ... als auch; 2. *cj.* (so-) wie; ebenso; (*zu der Zeit*) als, während; da, weil, indem; sofern; ~ it were sozusagen; such ~ to etwa; daß; ~ for, ~ to was (an)betrifft; ~ from von ... an.

ascend [ə'send] *v/i.* (auf-, empor-, hinauf)steigen; *zeitlich*: zurückgehen (*to* bis zu); *v/t.* be-, ersteigen; hinaufsteigen; *Fluß etc.* hinauffahren; ~ancy, ~ency [~dənsi] Überlegenheit *f*, Einfluß *m*; Herrschaft *f.*

ascension [ə'senʃən] Aufsteigen *n* (*bsd. ast.*); *Am. a.* Aufstieg *m* (*e-s Ballons etc.*); ♎ (*Day*) Himmelfahrt(stag *m*) *f.*

ascent [ə'sent] Aufstieg *m*; Besteigung *f*; Steigung *f*; Aufgang *m.*

ascertain [æsə'tein] ermitteln.

ascetic [ə'setik] (~ally) asketisch.

ascribe [əs'kraib] zuschreiben.

aseptic ꬵ [æ'septik] 1. aseptisch; 2. aseptisches Mittel.

---

ash[1] [æʃ] ♄ Esche *f*; Eschenholz *n.*

ash[2] (~), *mst. pl.* ~es ['æʃiz] Asche *f*; Ash Wednesday Aschermittwoch *m.*

ashamed [ə'ʃeimd] beschämt; be ~ of sich e-r *Sache* od. *j-s* schämen.

ash can *Am.* ['æʃkæn] = dust-bin.

ashen ['æʃn] Aschen...; aschfahl.

ashore [ə'ʃɔː] am *od.* ans Ufer *od.* Land; run ~ be driven ~ stranden.

ash|-pan ['æʃpæn] Asch(en)kasten *m*; ~tray Asch(en)becher *m.*

ashy ['æʃi] aschig; aschgrau.

Asiatic [eiʃi'ætik] 1. asiatisch; 2. Asiat(in).

aside [ə'said] 1. beiseite (*a. thea.*); abseits; seitwärts; ~ from *Am.* abgesehen von; 2. *thea.* Aparte *n.*

ask [ɑːsk] *v/t.* fragen (*s.th.* nach et.); verlangen (*of, from s.o.* von j-m); bitten (*s.o.* [for] *s.th.* j. um et.; that darum, daß); erbitten; ~ (*s.o.*) a question (j-m) e-e Frage stellen; *v/i.*: ~ for bitten um, fragen nach; he ~ed for it *od.* for trouble er wollte es ja so haben; to be had for the ~ing umsonst zu haben.

askance [əs'kæns], askew [əs'kjuː] von der Seite, seitwärts; schief.

asleep [ə'sliːp] schlafend; in den Schlaf; eingeschlafen, be ~ schlafen; fall ~ einschlafen.

asparagus ♄ [əs'pærəgəs] Spargel *m.*

aspect ['æspekt] Äußere *n*; Aussicht *f*, Lage *f*; Aspekt *m*, Seite *f*, Gesichtspunkt *m.*

asperity [æs'periti] Rauheit *f*; Unebenheit *f*; *fig.* Schroffheit *f.*

asphalt ['æsfælt] 1. Asphalt *m*; 2. asphaltieren.

aspic ['æspik] Aspik *m*, Sülze *f.*

aspir|ant [əs'paiərənt] Bewerber (-in); ~ate *ling.* ['æspəreit] aspirieren; ~ation [æspə'reiʃən] Aspiration *f*; Bestrebung *f*; ~e [əs'paiə] streben, trachten (to, after, at nach).

ass [æs] Esel *m.*

assail [ə'seil] angreifen, überfallen (*a. fig.*); befallen (*Zweifel etc.*); ~ant [~lənt] Angreifer(in).

assassin [ə'sæsin] (Meuchel)Mörder(in); ~ate [~neit] (meuchlings) ermorden; ~ation [əsæsi'neiʃən] Meuchelmord *m.*

assault [ə'sɔːlt] 1. Angriff *m* (*a. fig.*); 2. anfallen; ꬵꬵ tätlich angreifen *od.* beleidigen; ⚔ bestürmen (*a. fig.*).

assay [ə'sei] 1. (Erz-, Metall-) Probe *f*; 2. *v/t.* untersuchen; *v/i. Am.* Edelmetall enthalten.

assembl|age [ə'semblidʒ] (An-) Sammlung *f*; ⊕ Montage *f*; ~e [ə'sembl] (sich) versammeln; *j-s* berufen; ⊕ montieren; ~y [~li] Versammlung *f*; Gesellschaft *f*; ⊕ Montage *f*; ~ line ⊕ Fließband *n*; ~ man *pol.* Abgeordnete(r) *m.*

assent [ə'sent] **1.** Zustimmung *f*; **2.** (*to*) zustimmen (*dat.*); billigen.

assert [ə'sə:t] (sich) behaupten; **~ion** [ə'sə:ʃən] Behauptung *f*; Erklärung *f*; Geltendmachung *f*.

assess [ə'ses] besteuern; zur Steuer veranlagen (*at* mit); **~able** □ [~əbl] steuerpflichtig; **~ment** [~smənt] (Steuer)Veranlagung *f*; Steuer *f*.

asset ['æset] † Aktivposten *m*; *fig.* Gut *n*, Gewinn *m*; **~s** *pl.* Vermögen *n*; † Aktiva *pl.*; ‡‡ Konkursmasse *f*.

asseverate [ə'sevəreit] beteuern.

assiduous □ [ə'sidjuəs] emsig, fleißig; aufmerksam.

assign [ə'sain] an-, zuweisen; bestimmen; zuschreiben; **~ation** [æsig'neiʃən] Verabredung *f*, Stelldichein *n*; = **~ment** [ə'sainmənt] An-, Zuweisung *f*; *bsd. Am.* Auftrag *m*; ‡‡ Übertragung *f*.

assimilat|e [ə'simileit] (sich) angleichen (*to*, *with dat.*); **~ion** [əsimi'leiʃən] Assimilation *f*, Angleichung *f*.

assist [ə'sist] *j-m* beistehen, helfen; unterstützen; **~ance** [~təns] Beistand *m*; Hilfe *f*; **~ant** [~nt] **1.** behilflich; **2.** Assistent(in).

assize ‡‡ [ə'saiz] (Schwur)Gerichtssitzung *f*; **~s** *pl. periodisches* Geschworenengericht.

associa|te 1. [ə'souʃieit] (sich) zugesellen (*with dat.*), (sich) vereinigen; Umgang haben (*with* mit); **2.** [~ʃiit] verbunden; **3.** [~] (Amts)Genosse *m*; Teilhaber *m*; **~tion** [əsousi'eiʃən] Vereinigung *f*, Verbindung *f*; *Handels- etc.* Gesellschaft *f*; Genossenschaft *f*; Verein *m*.

assort [ə'sɔ:t] *v/t.* sortieren, zs.-stellen; *v/i.* passen (*with* zu); **~ment** [~tmənt] Sortieren *n*; † Sortiment *n*, Auswahl *f*.

assum|e [ə'sju:m] annehmen; vorgeben; übernehmen; **~ption** [ə'sʌmpʃən] Annahme *f*; Übernahme *f*; *eccl.* ♀ (*Day*) Mariä Himmelfahrt *f*.

assur|ance [ə'ʃuərəns] Zu-, Versicherung *f*; Zuversicht *f*; Sicherheit *f*, Gewißheit *f*; Selbstsicherheit *f*; Dreistigkeit *f*; **~e** [ə'ʃuə] (*Leben* usw/*sichern*; *sicherstellen*; **~ed 1.** (*adv.* **~edly** [~əridli]) sicher; dreist; **2.** Versicherte(r *m*) *f*.

asthma ['æsmə] Asthma *n*.

astir [ə'stə:] auf (den Beinen); in Bewegung, rege.

astonish [əs'tɔniʃ] in Erstaunen setzen; verwundern; befremden; *be* **~ed** erstaunt sein (*at* über *acc.*); **~ing** □ [~ʃiŋ] erstaunlich; **~ment** [~ʃmənt] (Er)Staunen *n*; Verwunderung *f*.

astound [əs'taund] verblüffen.

astray [əs'trei] vom (rechten) Wege ab (*a. fig.*); irre; *go* **~** sich verlaufen, fehlgehen.

astride [əs'traid] mit gespreizten Beinen; rittlings (*of* auf *dat.*).

astringent ⚕ [əs'trindʒənt] **1.** □ zs.-ziehend; **2.** zs.-ziehendes Mittel.

astro|logy [əs'trɔlədʒi] Astrologie *f*; **~naut** ['æstrənɔ:t] Astronaut *m*, Raumfahrer *m*; **~nomer** [əs'trɔnəmə] Astronom *m*; **~nomy** [~mi] Astronomie *f*.

astute □ [əs'tju:t] scharfsinnig; schlau; **~ness** [~tnis] Scharfsinn *m*.

asunder [ə'sʌndə] auseinander; entzwei.

asylum [ə'sailəm] Asyl *n*.

at [æt; *unbetont* ət] *prp.* an; auf; aus; bei; für; in; mit; nach; über; um; von; vor; zu; **~** *school* in der Schule; **~** *the age of* im Alter von.

ate [et] *pret. von* eat **1**.

atheism ['eiθiizəm] Atheismus *m*.

athlet|e ['æθli:t] (*bsd. Leicht-*) Athlet *m*; **~ic** [æθ'letik(əl)] athletisch; **~ics** *pl.* (*bsd. Leicht-*)Athletik *f*.

Atlantic [ət'læntik] **1.** atlantisch; **2.** *a.* **~** *Ocean* Atlantik *m*.

atmospher|e ['ætməsfiə] Atmosphäre *f* (*a. fig.*); **~ic(al** □) [ætməs'ferik(əl)] atmosphärisch.

atom ⚛ ['ætəm] Atom *n* (*a. fig.*); **~ic** [ə'tɔmik] atomartig, Atom...; atomistisch; **~** *age* Atomzeitalter *n*; **~** (*a. atom*) *bomb* Atombombe *f*; **~** *pile* Atomreaktor *m*; **~ic-powered** durch Atomkraft betrieben; **~ize** ['ætəmaiz] in Atome auflösen; atomisieren; **~izer** [~zə] Zerstäuber *m*.

atone [ə'toun]: **~** *for* büßen für *acc.*; **~ment** [~nmənt] Buße *f*; Sühne *f*.

atroci|ous □ [ə'trouʃəs] scheußlich, gräßlich; grausam; **~ty** [ə'trɔsiti] Scheußlichkeit *f*, Gräßlichkeit *f*; Grausamkeit *f*.

attach [ə'tætʃ] *v/t.* (*to*) anheften (an, *acc.*), befestigen (an *dat.*); *Wert, Wichtigkeit etc.* beilegen (*dat.*); ‡‡ *j-n* verhaften; *et.* beschlagnahmen; **~** *o.s. to* sich anschließen an (*acc.*); **~ed:** **~** *to* gehörig zu; *j-m* zugetan, ergeben; **~ment** [~ʃmənt] Befestigung *f*; Bindung *f* (*to*, *for* an *acc.*); Anhänglichkeit *f* (an *acc.*), Neigung *f* (zu); Anhängsel *n* (*to* an); ‡‡ Verhaftung *f*; Beschlagnahme *f*.

attack [ə'tæk] **1.** angreifen (*a. fig.*); befallen (*Krankheit*); *Arbeit* in Angriff nehmen; **2.** Angriff *m*; ⚕ Anfall *m*; Inangriffnahme *f*.

attain [ə'tein] *v/t.* Ziel erreichen; *v/i.* **~** *to* gelangen zu; **~ment** [~nmənt] Erreichung *f*; *fig.* Aneignung *f*; **~s** *pl.* Kenntnisse *f/pl.*; Fertigkeiten *f/pl.*

attempt [ə'tempt] **1.** versuchen; **2.** Versuch *m*; Attentat *n*.

attend [ə'tend] *v/t.* begleiten; bedienen; pflegen; ✗ behandeln; *j-m* aufwarten; beiwohnen (*dat.*); *Vorlesung etc.* besuchen; *v/i.* achten, hören (*to auf acc.*); anwesend sein (*at* bei); ~ to erledigen; **~ance** [~dəns] Begleitung *f*; Aufwartung *f*; Pflege *f*; ✗ Behandlung *f*; Gefolge *n*; Anwesenheit *f* (*at* bei); Besuch *m* (*der Schule etc.*); Besucher(zahl *f*) *m/pl.*; Publikum *n*; *be in* ~ zu Diensten stehen; **~ant** [~nt] **1.** begleitend (*on, upon acc.*); anwesend (*at* bei); **2.** Diener(in) Begleiter(in); Wärter(in); Besucher(in) (*at gen.*); ⊕ Bedienungsmann *m*; **~s** *pl.* Dienerschaft *f*.

attent|ion [ə'tenʃən] Aufmerksamkeit *f* (*a. fig.*); **~!** ✗ Achtung!; **~ive** □ [~ntiv] aufmerksam.

attest ['test] bezeugen; beglaubigen; *bsd.* ✗ vereidigen.

attic ['ætik] Dachstube *f*. [dung *f*.]

attire [ə'taiə] **1.** kleiden; **2.** Kleif

attitude ['ætitju:d] (Ein)Stellung *f*; Haltung *f*; *fig.* Stellungnahme *f*.

attorney [ə'tə:ni] Bevollmächtigte(r) *m*; *Am.* Rechtsanwalt *m*; *power of* ~ Vollmacht *f*; ♀ *General* Generalstaats- *od.* Kronanwalt *m*, *Am.* Justizminister *m*.

attract [ə'trækt] anziehen, *Aufmerksamkeit* erregen; *fig.* reizen; **~ion** [~kʃən] Anziehung(skraft) *f*; *fig.* Reiz *m*; Zugartikel *m*; *thea.* Zugstück *n*; **~ive** □ [~ktiv] anziehend; reizvoll; zugkräftig; **~iveness** [~vnis] Reiz *m*.

attribute 1. [ə'tribju(:)t] beimessen, zuschreiben; zurückführen (*to auf acc.*); **2.** ['ætribju:t] Attribut *n* (*a. gr.*), Eigenschaft *f*, Merkmal *n*.

attune [ə'tju:n] (ab)stimmen.

auburn ['ɔ:bən] kastanienbraun.

auction ['ɔ:kʃən] **1.** Auktion *f*; *sell by* ~, *put up for* ~ verauktionieren; **2.** *mst* ~ *off* versteigern; **~eer** [ɔ:kʃə'niə] Auktionator *m*.

audaci|ous □ [ɔ:'deiʃəs] kühn; unverschämt; **~ty** [ɔ:'dæsiti] Kühnheit *f*; Unverschämtheit *f*.

audible □ ['ɔ:dəbl] hörbar; Hör...

audience ['ɔ:djəns] Publikum *n*, Zuhörerschaft *f*; Leserkreis *m*; Audienz *f*; Gehör *n*; *give* ~ *to* Gehör schenken (*dat.*).

audit ['ɔ:dit] **1.** Rechnungsprüfung *f*; **2.** *Rechnungen* prüfen; **~or** [~tə] Hörer *m*; Rechnungs-, Buchprüfer *m*; **~orium** [ɔ:di'tɔ:riəm] Hörsaal *m*; *Am.* Vortrags-, Konzertsaal *m*.

auger ⊕ ['ɔ:gə] *großer Bohrer*.

aught [ɔ:t] (irgend) etwas; *for* ~ *I care* meinetwegen; *for* ~ *I know* soviel ich weiß.

augment [ɔ:g'ment] vergrößern; **~ation** [ɔ:gmen'teiʃən] Vermehrung *f*, Vergrößerung *f*; Zusatz *m*.

augur ['ɔ:gə] **1.** Augur *m*; **2.** weissagen, voraussagen (*well Gutes, ill*

Übles); **~y** ['ɔ:gjuri] Prophezeiung *f*; An-, Vorzeichen *n*; Vorahnung *f*.

August¹ ['ɔ:gəst] *Monat* August *m*.

august² □ [ɔ:'gʌst] erhaben.

aunt [ɑ:nt] Tante *f*.

auspic|e ['ɔ:spis] Vorzeichen *n*; **~s** *pl.* Auspizien *pl.*; Schirmherrschaft *f*; **~ious** □ [ɔ:s'piʃəs] günstig.

auster|e □ [ɔs'tiə] streng; herb; hart; einfach; **~ity** [ɔs'teriti] Strenge *f*; Härte *f*; Einfachheit *f*.

Australian [ɔs'treiljən] **1.** australisch; **2.** Australier(in).

Austrian ['ɔstriən] **1.** österreichisch; **2.** Österreicher(in).

authentic [ɔ:'θentik] (*~ally*) authentisch; zuverlässig; echt.

author ['ɔ:θə] Urheber(in); Autor (-in); Verfasser(in); **~itative** □ [ɔ:'θɔritətiv] maßgebend; gebieterisch; zuverlässig; **~ity** [ɔ:'θɔriti] Autorität *f*; (Amts)Gewalt *f*, Vollmacht *f*; Einfluß *m* (*over auf acc.*); Ansehen *n*; Glaubwürdigkeit *f*; Quelle *f*; Fachmann *m*; Behörde *f* (*mst pl.*); *on the* ~ *of* auf *j-s* Zeugnis hin; **~ize** [ɔ:'θəraiz] *j-n* autorisieren, bevollmächtigen; *et.* gutheißen; **~ship** [ɔ:'θəʃip] Urheberschaft *f*.

autocar ['ɔ:touka:] Kraftwagen *m*.

autocra|cy [ɔ:'tɔkrəsi] Autokratie *f*; **~tic(al** □) [ɔ:tə'krætik(əl)] autokratisch, despotisch.

autogiro ✈ ['ɔ:tou'dʒaiərou] Autogiro *n*, Tragschrauber *m*.

autograph ['ɔ:təgra:f] Autogramm *n*. [Restaurant *n*.]

automat ['ɔ:təmæt] Automaten-f

automat|ic [ɔ:tə'mætik] (*~ally*) **1.** automatisch; ~ *machine* (Verkaufs)Automat *m*; **2.** *Am.* Selbstladepistole *f*, -gewehr *n*; **~ion** [~'meiʃən] Automation *f*; **~on** *fig.* [ɔ:'tɔmətən] Roboter *m*.

automobile *bsd. Am.* ['ɔ:təməbi:l] Automobil *n*.

autonomy [ɔ:'tɔnəmi] Autonomie *f*.

autumn ['ɔ:təm] Herbst *m*; **~al** □ [ɔ:'tʌmnəl] herbstlich; Herbst...

auxiliary [ɔ:g'ziljəri] helfend; Hilfs...

avail [ə'veil] **1.** nützen, helfen; ~ *o.s. of* sich *e-r* ✗ bedienen; **2.** Nutzen *m*; *of no* ~ nutzlos; **~able** □ [~ləbl] benutzbar; verfügbar; *pred.* erhältlich, vorhanden; gültig.

avalanche ['ævəla:nʃ] Lawine *f*.

avaric|e ['ævəris] Geiz *m*; Habsucht *f*; **~ious** □ [ævə'riʃəs] geizig; habgierig.

avenge [ə'vendʒ] rächen, *et.* ahnden; **~r** [~dʒə] Rächer(in).

avenue ['ævinju:] Allee *f*; Prachtstraße *f*; *fig.* Weg *m*, Straße *f*.

aver [ə'və:] behaupten.

average ['ævəridʒ] **1.** Durchschnitt *m*; ⚓ Havarie *f*; **2.** □ durchschnittlich; Durchschnitts...; **3.** durchschnittlich schätzen (*at* auf *acc.*); durchschnittlich betragen *od.* arbeiten *etc.*

avers|e □ [ə'vəːs] abgeneigt (*to*, *from dat.*); widerwillig; **~ion** [ə'vəːʃən] Widerwille *m.*

avert [ə'vəːt] abwenden (*a. fig.*).

aviat|ion ≶ [eivi'eiʃən] Fliegen *n*; Flugwesen *n*; Luftfahrt *f*; **~or** ['eivieitə] Flieger *m.*

avid □ ['ævid] gierig (*of* nach; *for* auf *acc.*).

avoid [ə'vɔid] (ver)meiden; *j-m* ausweichen; ₫ᵗₐ anfechten; ungültig machen; **~ance** [**~**dəns] Vermeidung *f.*

avouch [ə'vautʃ] verbürgen, bestätigen; = avow.

avow [ə'vau] bekennen, (ein)gestehen; anerkennen; **~al** [ə'vauəl] Bekenntnis *n*, (Ein)Geständnis *n*; **~edly** [ə'vauidli] eingestandenermaßen.

await [ə'weit] erwarten (*a. fig.*).

awake [ə'weik] 1. wach, munter; *be* **~** *to* sich *e-r* S. bewußt sein; 2. [*irr.*] *v/t.* (*mst* **~n** [**~**kən]) (er-)wecken; *v/i.* erwachen; gewahr werden (*to s.th.* et.).

award [ə'wɔːd] 1. Urteil *n*, Spruch

m; Belohnung *f*; Preis *m*; 2. zuerkennen, *Orden etc.* verleihen.

aware [ə'wɛə]: *be* **~** wissen (*of von od. acc.*), sich bewußt sein (*of gen.*); *become* **~** *of et.* gewahr werden, merken.

away [ə'wei] (hin)weg; fort; immer weiter, darauflos; **~** *back Am.* F (schon) damals, weit zurück.

awe [ɔː] 1. Ehrfurcht *f*, Scheu *f* (*of* vor *dat.*); 2. (Ehr)Furcht einflößen (*dat.*).

awful □ ['ɔːful] ehrfurchtgebietend; furchtbar; F *fig.* schrecklich.

awhile [ə'wail] e-e Weile.

awkward □ ['ɔːkwəd] ungeschickt, unbeholfen; linkisch; unangenehm; dumm, ungünstig, unpraktisch.

awl [ɔːl] Ahle *f*, Pfriem *m.*

awning ['ɔːniŋ] Plane *f*; Markise *f.*

awoke [ə'wouk] *pret. u. p.p. von* awake 2.

awry [ə'rai] schief; *fig.* verkehrt.

ax(e) [æks] Axt *f*, Beil *n.*

axis ['æksis], *pl.* **axes** ['æksiːz] Achse *f.*

axle ⊕ ['æksl] *a.* **~-tree** (Rad-) Achse *f*, Welle *f.*

ay(e) [ai] Ja *n*; *parl.* Jastimme *f*; *the* **~**s *have it* die Mehrheit ist dafür.

azure ['æʒə] azurn, azurblau.

B

babble ['bæbl] 1. stammeln; (nach-) plappern; schwatzen; plätschern (*Bach*); 2. Geplapper *n*; Geschwätz *n.*

baboon *zo.* [bə'buːn] Pavian *m.*

baby ['beibi] 1. Säugling *m*, kleines Kind, Baby *n*; *Am. sl.* Süße *f* (*Mädchen*); 2. Baby...; Kinder...; klein; **~hood** [**~**ihud] frühe Kindheit.

bachelor ['bætʃələ] Junggeselle *m*; *univ.* Bakkalaureus *m* (*Grad*).

back [bæk] 1. Rücken *m*; Rückseite *f*; Rücklehne *f*; Hinterende *n*; *Fußball*: Verteidiger *m*; 2. *adj.* Hinter..., Rück...; hinter; rückwärtig; entlegen; rückläufig; rückständig; 3. *adv.* zurück; 4. *v/t.* mit e-m Rücken versehen; unterstützen; hinten anstoßen an (*acc.*); zurückbewegen; wetten *od.* setzen auf (*acc.*); ✝ indossieren; *v/i.* sich rückwärts bewegen, zurückgehen *od.* zurückfahren; **~** *alley Am.* finstere Seitengasse; **~bite** ['bækbait] [*irr.* (*bite*)] verleumden; **~bone** Rückgrat *n*; **~er** ['bækə] Unterstützer (-in); ✝ Indossierer *m*; Wetter(in); **~fire** *mot.* Frühzündung *f*; **~ground** Hintergrund *m*; **~ number** alte Nummer (*e-r Zeitung*); **~**

pedal rückwärtstreten (*Radfahren*); **~ling** *brake* Rücktrittbremse *f*; **~side** Hinter-, Rückseite *f*; **~slapper** *Am.* [**~**slæpə] plump vertraulicher Mensch; **~slide** [*irr.* (*slide*)] rückfällig werden; **~stairs** Hintertreppe *f*; **~stop** *Am. Baseball*: Gitter *n hinter dem Fänger*; *Schießstand*: Kugelfang *m*; **~stroke** Rückenschwimmen *n*; **~talk** *Am.* freche Antworten; **~track** *Am.* F *fig.* e-n Rückzieher machen; **~ward** ['bækwəd] 1. *adj.* Rück(wärts)...; langsam; zurückgeblieben, rückständig; zurückhaltend; 2. *adv.* (*a.* **~wards** [**~**dz]) rückwärts, zurück; **~water** Stauwasser *n*; **~woods** *pl.* weit abgelegene Waldgebiete; *fig.* Provinz *f*; **~woodsman** Hinterwäldler *m.*

bacon ['beikən] Speck *m.*

bacteri|ologist [bæktiəri'ɔlədʒist] Bakteriologe *m*; **~um** [bæk'tiəriəm], *pl.* **~a** [**~**iə] Bakterie *f.*

bad □ [bæd] schlecht, böse, schlimm; falsch (*Münze*); faul (*Schuld*); *he is* **~***ly off* er ist übel dran; **~***ly want* schwerwundet; *want* **~***ly* F dringend brauchen; *be in* **~** *with Am.* F in Ungnade bei.

bade [beid] *pret. von* bid 1.

badge [bædʒ] Ab-, Kennzeichen *n*.

badger ['bædʒə] 1. *zo*. Dachs *m*; 2. hetzen, plagen, quälen.

badlands *Am*. ['bædlændz] *pl*. Ödland *n*.

badness ['bædnis] schlechte Beschaffenheit; Schlechtigkeit *f*.

baffle ['bæfl] *j-n* verwirren; *Plan etc.* vereiteln, durchkreuzen.

bag [bæg] 1. Beutel *m*, Sack *m*; Tüte *f*; Tasche *f*; ~ *and baggage* mit Sack und Pack; 2. in e-n Beutel *etc.* tun, einsacken; *hunt.* zur Strecke bringen; (sich) bauschen.

baggage *Am*. ['bægidʒ] (Reise-) Gepäck *n*; ~ **car** *Am*. ☒ Gepäckwagen *m*; ~ **check** *Am*. Gepäckschein *m*.

bagpipe ['bægpaip] Dudelsack *m*.

bail [beil] 1. Bürge *m*; Bürgschaft *f*; Kaution *f*; *admit to* ~ *t/z* gegen Bürgschaft freilassen; 2. bürgen für; ~ *out j-n* freibürgen; ☒ mit dem Fallschirm abspringen.

bailiff ['beilif] Gerichtsdiener *m*; (Guts)Verwalter *m*; Amtmann *m*.

bait [beit] 1. Köder *m*; *fig.* Lockung *f*; 2. *v/t. Falle etc.* beködern; *hunt.* hetzen; *fig.* quälen; reizen; *v/i.* rasten; einkehren.

bak|e [beik] 1. backen; braten; *Ziegel* brennen; (aus)dörren; 2. *Am.* gesellige Zusammenkunft; ~**er** ['beikə] Bäcker *m*; ~**ery** [ˌəri] Bäckerei *f*; ~**ing-powder** [ˌkiŋpaudə] Backpulver *n*.

balance ['bæləns] 1. Waage *f*; Gleichgewicht *n* (*a. fig.*); Harmonie *f*; † Bilanz *f*, Saldo *m*, Überschuß *m*; Restbetrag *m*; F Rest *m*; *a.* ~ *wheel* Unruh(e) *f der Uhr*; ~ *of power pol.* Kräftegleichgewicht *n*; ~ *of trade* (Außen-) Handelsbilanz *f*; 2. *v/t.* (ab-er)wägen; im Gleichgewicht halten; ausgleichen; † bilanzieren; saldieren; *v/i.* balancieren; sich ausgleichen.

balcony ['bælkəni] Balkon *m*.

bald [bɔːld] kahl; *fig.* nackt; dürftig.

bale † [beil] Ballen *m*.

baleful □ ['beilful] verderblich; unheilvoll.

balk [bɔːk] 1. (Furchen)Rain *m*; Balken *m*; Hemmnis *n*; 2. *v/t.* (ver-)hindern; enttäuschen; vereiteln; *v/i.* stutzen, scheuen.

ball[1] [bɔːl] 1. Ball *m*; Kugel *f*; (Hand-, Fuß)Ballen *m*; Knäuel *m*, *n*; Kloß *m*; *Sport:* Wurf *m*; *keep the* ~ *rolling* das Gespräch in Gang halten; *play* ~ *Am.* F mitmachen; 2. (sich) (zs.-)ballen.

ball[2] [ˌ] Ball *m*, Tanzgesellschaft *f*.

ballad ['bæləd] Ballade *f*; Lied *n*.

ballast ['bæləst] 1. Ballast *m*; ☒ Schotter *m*, Bettung *f*; 2. mit Ballast beladen; ☒ beschottern, betten.

ball-bearing(s *pl*.) ⊕ ['bɔːl-'bɛəriŋ(z)] Kugellager *n*.

ballet ['bælei] Ballett *n*.

balloon [bə'luːn] 1. Ballon *m*; 2. im Ballon aufsteigen; sich blähen; ~**ist** [ˌnist] Ballonfahrer *m*.

ballot ['bælət] 1. Wahlzettel *m*; (geheime) Wahl; 2. (geheim) abstimmen; ~ *for losen um*; ~**box** Wahlurne *f*.

ball(-point) pen ['bɔːl(pɔint)pen] Kugelschreiber *m*.

ball-room ['bɔːlrum] Ballsaal *m*.

balm [bɑːm] Balsam *m*; *fig.* Trost *m*.

balmy □ ['bɑːmi] balsamisch (*a. fig.*).

baloney *Am. sl.* [bə'louni] Quatsch *m*.

balsam ['bɔːlsəm] Balsam *m*.

balustrade [bæləs'treid] Balustrade *f*, Brüstung *f*; Geländer *n*.

bamboo [bæm'buː] Bambus *m*.

bamboozle F [bæm'buːzl] beschwindeln.

ban [bæn] 1. Bann *m*; Acht *f*; (amtliches) Verbot; 2. verbieten.

banal [bə'nɑːl] banal, abgedroschen.

banana [bə'nɑːnə] Banane *f*.

band [bænd] 1. Band *n*; Streifen *m*; Schar *f*; ♪ Kapelle *f*; 2. zs.-binden; ~ *o.s.* sich zs.-tun *od*. zs.-rotten.

bandage ['bændidʒ] 1. Binde *f*; Verband *m*; 2. bandagieren; verbinden.

bandbox ['bændbɔks] Hutschachtel *f*.

bandit ['bændit] Bandit *m*.

band|-master ['bændmɑːstə] Kapellmeister *m*; ~**stand** Musikpavillon *m*; ~ **wagon** *Am.* Wagen *m* mit Musikkapelle; *jump on the* ~ sich der erfolgversprechenden Sache anschließen.

bandy ['bændi] *Worte etc.* wechseln; ~**legged** säbelbeinig.

bane [bein] Ruin *m*; ~**ful** □ ['beinful] verderblich.

bang [bæŋ] 1. Knall *m*; Ponyfrisur *f*; 2. dröhnend (zu)schlagen; ~**up** *Am. sl.* ['bæŋʌp] Klasse, prima.

banish ['bæniʃ] verbannen; ~**ment** [ˌʃmənt] Verbannung *f*.

banisters ['bænistəz] *pl*. Treppengeländer *n*.

bank [bæŋk] 1. Damm *m*; Ufer *n*; (Spiel-, Sand-, Wolken- *etc.*)Bank *f*; ~ *of issue* Notenbank *f*; 2. *v/t.* eindämmen; † *Geld* auf die Bank legen; ☒ in die Kurve bringen; *v/i.* Bankgeschäfte machen; ein Bankkonto haben; ☒ in die Kurve gehen; ~ *on* sich verlassen auf (*acc.*); ~**bill** ['bæŋkbil] Bankwechsel *m*; *Am. s.* banknote; ~**er** [ˌkə] Bankier *m*; ~**ing** [ˌkiŋ] Bankgeschäft *n*; Bankwesen *n*; *attr.* Bank...; ~**note** Banknote *f*; Kassenschein *m*; ~

rate Diskontsatz *m*; ~rupt [~krəpt]
1. Bankrotteur *m*; 2. bankrott;
3. bankrott machen; ~ruptcy
[~tsi] Bankrott *m*, Konkurs *m*.
banner ['bænə] Banner *n*; Fahne *f*.
banns [bænz] *pl.* Aufgebot *n*.
banquet ['bæŋkwit] 1. Festmahl *n*;
2. *v/t.* festlich bewirten; *v/i.* tafeln.
banter ['bæntə] necken, hänseln.
baptism ['bæptizəm] Taufe *f*.
baptist ['bæptist] Täufer *m*.
baptize [bæp'taiz] taufen.
bar [baː] 1. Stange *f*; Stab *m*;
Barren *m*; Riegel *m*; Schranke *f*;
Sandbank *f*; *fig.* Hindernis *n*; ✗
Spange *f*; ♪ Takt(strich) *m*; (Gerichts)Schranke *f*; *fig.* Urteil *n*;
Anwaltschaft *f*; Bar *f im Hotel etc.*;
2. verriegeln; (ver-, ab)sperren;
verwehren; einsperren; (ver)hin-
dern; ausschließen.
barb [baːb] Widerhaken *m*; ~ed
wire Stacheldraht *m*.
barbar|ian [baː'bɛəriən] 1. bar-
barisch; 2. Barbar(in); ~ous [,]
['baːbərəs] barbarisch; roh; grausam.
barbecue ['baːbikjuː] 1. großer
Bratrost; *Am.* Essen *n* (*im Freien*),
bei dem Tiere ganz gebraten
werden; 2. im ganzen braten.
barber ['baːbə] (Herren)Friseur *m*.
bare [bɛə] 1. nackt, bloß; kahl; bar,
leer; arm, entblößt; 2. entblößen;
~faced □ ['bɛəfeist] frech; ~foot,
~footed barfuß; ~headed bar-
häuptig; ~ly ['bɛəli] kaum.
bargain ['baːgin] 1. Geschäft *n*;
Handel *m*, Kauf *m*; vorteilhafter
Kauf; *a (dead)* ~ spottbillig; *it's a* ~!
F abgemacht!; *into the* ~ obendrein;
2. handeln, übereinkommen.
barge [baːdʒ] Flußboot *m*, Lastkahn
m; Hausboot *n*; ~man ['baːdʒmən]
Kahnführer *m*.
bark¹ [baːk] 1. Borke *f*, Rinde *f*;
2. abrinden; *Haut* abschürfen.
bark² [,] 1. bellen; 2. Bellen *n*.
bar-keeper ['baːkiːpə] Barbesitzer
m; Barkellner *m*.
barley ['baːli] Gerste *f*; Graupe *f*.
barn [baːn] Scheune *f*; *bsd. Am.*
(Vieh)Stall *m*; ~storm *Am. pol.*
['baːnstɔːm] herumreisen u.(Wahl-)
Reden halten.
barometer [bə'rɔmitə] Barometer *n*.
baron ['bærən] Baron *m*, Freiherr
m; ~ess [,nis] Baronin *f*.
barrack(s *pl.*) ['bærək(s)] (Miets-)
Kaserne *f*.
barrage ['bæraːʒ] Staudamm *m*.
barrel ['bærəl] 1. Faß *n*, Tonne *f*;
Gewehr~ etc. Lauf *m*; ⊕ Trommel
f; Walze *f*; 2. in Fässer füllen;
~organ ♪ Drehorgel *f*.
barren □ ['bærən] unfruchtbar;
dürr, trocken; tot (*Kapital*).
barricade [bæri'keid] 1. Barrikade
f; 2. verbarrikadieren; sperren.

barrier ['bæriə] Schranke *f* (*a. fig.*);
Barriere *f*, Sperre *f*; Hindernis
n.
barrister ['bæristə] (plädierender)
Rechtsanwalt, Barrister *m*.
barrow¹ ['bærou] Trage *f*; Karre *f*.
barrow² [,] Hügelgrab *n*, Tumulus
m.
barter ['baːtə] 1. Tausch(handel)
m; 2. tauschen (*for* gegen); F
schachern.
base¹ □ [beis] gemein; unecht.
base² □ [,] 1. Basis *f*; Grundlage *f*;
Fundament *n*; Fuß *m*; ✗ Base *f*;
Stützpunkt *m*; 2. gründen, stützen.
base|ball ['beisbɔːl] Baseball *m*;
~born von niedriger Abkunft;
unehelich; ~less ['beislis] grundlos;
~ment ['beismənt] Fundament *n*;
Kellergeschoß *n*.
baseness ['beisnis] Gemeinheit *f*.
bashful □ ['bæʃful] schüchtern.
basic ['beisik] (~ally) grundlegend;
Grund...; ✗ basisch.
basin ['beisn] Becken *n*; Schüssel *f*;
Tal-, Wasser-, Hafenbecken *n*.
bas|is ['beisis], *pl.* ~es ['beisiːz]
Basis *f*, Grundlage *f*; ✗, ⚓ Stützpunkt *m*.
bask [baːsk] sich sonnen (*a. fig.*).
basket ['baːskit] Korb *m*; ~ball
Korbball(spiel *n*) *m*; ~ dinner, ~
supper *Am.* Picknick *n*.
bass ♪ [beis] Baß *m*.
basso ♪ ['bæsou] Baß(sänger) *m*.
bastard ['bæstəd] 1. □ unehelich;
unecht; Bastard...; 2. Bastard *m*.
baste¹ [beist] *Braten* begießen;
durchprügeln.
baste² [,] lose nähen, (an)heften.
bat¹ [bæt] Fledermaus *f*; *as blind
as a* ~ stockblind.
bat² [,] *Sport:* 1. Schlagholz *n*;
Schläger *m*; 2. *den Ball* schlagen.
batch [bætʃ] Schub *m Brote* (*a. fig.*);
Stoß *m Briefe etc.* (*a. fig.*).
bate [beit] verringern; vermindern.
bath [baːθ] 1. Bad *n*; ♀ *chair* Rollstuhl *m*; 2. baden.
bathe [beið] baden.
bathing ['beiðiŋ] Baden *n*, Bad *n*;
attr. Bade...; ~suit Badeanzug *m*.
bath|robe *Am.* ['baːθroub] Bade-
mantel *m*; ~room Badezimmer *n*;
~sheet Badelaken *n*; ~towel
Badetuch *n*; ~tub Badewanne *f*.
batiste ✝ [bæ'tiːst] Batist *m*.
baton ['bætən] Stab *m*; Taktstock
m.
battalion ✗ [bə'tæljən] Bataillon *n*.
batten ['bætn] 1. Latte *f*; 2. sich
mästen.
batter ['bætə] 1. *Sport:* Schläger *m*;
Rührteig *m*; 2. heftig schlagen;
verbeulen; ~ *down od. in* Tür einschlagen; ~y [,əri] Schlägerei *f*;
Batterie *f*; ⚡ Akku *m*; *fig.* Satz *m*;
assault and ~ ⚖ tätlicher Angriff.
battle ['bætl] 1. Schlacht *f* (*of* bei);

2. streiten, kämpfen; **~ax(e)** Streitaxt *f*; F Xanthippe *f*; **~field** Schlachtfeld *n*; **~ments** [~lmənts] *pl.* Zinnen *f*/*pl.*; **~plane** ✕ Kriegsflugzeug *n*; **~ship** ✕ Schlachtschiff *n*.

Bavarian [bə'vɛəriən] **1.** bay(e)-risch; **2.** Bayer(in).

bawdy ['bɔːdi] unzüchtig.

bawl [bɔːl] brüllen; johlen, grölen; **~ out** auf-, losbrüllen.

bay¹ [bei] **1.** rotbraun; **2.** Braune(r) *m* (*Pferd*).

bay² [~] Bai *f*, Bucht *f*; Erker *m*.

bay³ [~] Lorbeer *m*.

bay⁴ [~] **1.** bellen, anschlagen; **2.** stand at **~** sich verzweifelt wehren; bring to **~** Wild etc. stellen.

bayonet ✕ ['beiənit] **1.** Bajonett *n*; **2.** mit dem Bajonett niederstoßen.

bayou Am. ['baiu] sumpfiger Nebenarm.

bay window ['bei'windou] Erkerfenster *n*; Am. sl. Vorbau *m* (*Bauch*).

baza(a)r [bə'zɑː] Basar *m*.

be [biː, bi] [irr.] **1.** v/i. sein; there is od. are es gibt; here you are again! da haben wir's wieder!; **~** about beschäftigt sein mit; **~** at s.th. et. vorhaben; **~** off aus sein; sich fortmachen; **2.** v/aux.: **~** reading beim Lesen sein, gerade lesen; I am to inform you ich soll Ihnen mitteilen; **3.** v/aux. mit p.p. zur Bildung des Passivs: werden.

beach [biːtʃ] **1.** Strand *m*; **2.** ⚓ auf den Strand setzen od. ziehen; **~comber** ['biːtʃkoumə] fig. Nichtstuer *m*.

beacon ['biːkən] Blinklicht *n*; Leuchtfeuer *n*, Leuchtturm *m*.

bead [biːd] Perle *f*; Tropfen *m*; Visier-Korn *n*; **~s** pl. a. Rosenkranz *m*.

beak [biːk] Schnabel *m*; Tülle *f*.

beaker ['biːkə] Becher(glas *n*) *m*.

beam [biːm] **1.** Balken *m*; Waagebalken *m*; Strahl *m*; Glanz *m*; Radio: Richtstrahl *m*; **2.** (aus-)strahlen.

bean [biːn] Bohne *f*; Am. sl. Birne *f* (*Kopf*); full of **~s** F lebensprühend.

bear¹ [bɛə] Bär *m*; † sl. Baissier *m*.

bear² [~] [irr.] v/t. tragen; hervorbringen, gebären; Liebe etc. hegen; ertragen; **~** down überwältigen; **~** out unterstützen; bestätigen; v/i. tragen; fruchtbar od. trächtig sein; leiden, dulden; **~** up standhalten, fest bleiben; **~** (up)on einwirken auf (acc.); bring to **~** zur Anwendung bringen, einwirken lassen, Druck etc. ausüben.

beard [biəd] **1.** Bart *m*; ♀ Granne *f*; **2.** v/t. j-m entgegentreten, trotzen.

bearer ['bɛərə] Träger(in); Überbringer(in), Wechsel-Inhaber(in).

bearing ['bɛəriŋ] (Er)Tragen *n*;

Betragen *n*; Beziehung *f*; Richtung *f*.

beast [biːst] Vieh *n*, Tier *n*; Bestie *f*; **~ly** ['biːstli] viehisch; scheußlich.

beat [biːt] **1.** [irr.] v/t. schlagen; prügeln; besiegen; Am. F j-m zuvorkommen; übertreffen; Am. F betrügen; **~** it! Am. sl. hau ab!; **~** the band Am. F wichtig od. großartig sein; **~** a retreat den Rückzug antreten; **~** one's way Am. F sich durchschlagen; **~** up auftreiben; v/i. schlagen; **~** about the bush wie die Katze um den heißen Brei herumgehen; **2.** Schlag *m*; ♩ Takt(schlag) *m*; Pulsschlag *m*; Runde *f*, Revier *n* e-s Schutzmannes etc.; Am. sensationelle Erstmeldung e-r Zeitung; **3.** F baff, verblüfft; **~en** ['biːtn] p.p. von beat 1; (aus)getreten (Weg).

beatitude [biː(ː)'ætitjuːd] (Glück-)Seligkeit *f*.

beatnik ['biːtnik] Beatnik *m*, junger Antikonformist und Bohemien.

beau [bou] Stutzer *m*; Anbeter *m*.

beautiful □ ['bjuːtəful] schön.

beautify ['bjuːtifai] verschönern.

beauty ['bjuːti] Schönheit *f*; Sleeping ♀ Dornrös-chen *n*; **~** parlo(u)r, **~** shop Schönheitssalon *m*.

beaver ['biːvə] Biber *m*; Biberpelz *m*.

becalm [bi'kɑːm] beruhigen.

became [bi'keim] pret. von become.

because [bi'kɔz] weil; **~** of wegen.

beckon ['bekən] (j-m zu)winken.

becom|e [bi'kʌm] [irr.] v/i. werden (of aus); v/t. anstehen, ziemen (dat.); sich schicken für; kleiden (Hut etc.); **~ing** □ [~miŋ] passend; schicklich; kleidsam.

bed [bed] **1.** Bett *n*; Lager *n* e-s Tieres; ✓ Beet *n*; Unterlage *f*; **2.** betten.

bed-clothes ['bedklouðz] pl. Bettwäsche *f*.

bedding ['bediŋ] Bettzeug *n*; Streu *f*.

bedevil [bi'devl] behexen; quälen.

bedlam ['bedləm] Tollhaus *n*.

bed|rid(den) ['bedrid(n)] bettlägerig; **~room** Schlafzimmer *n*; **~spread** Bett-, Tagesdecke *f*; **~stead** Bettstelle *f*; **~time** Schlafenszeit *f*.

bee [biː] zo. Biene *f*; Am. nachbarliches Treffen; Wettbewerb *m*; have a **~** in one's bonnet F e-e fixe Idee haben.

beech ♀ [biːtʃ] Buche *f*; **~nut** Bucheckar *f*.

beef [biːf] **1.** Rindfleisch *n*; **2.** Am. F nörgeln; **~** tea Fleischbrühe *f*; **~y** ['biːfi] fleischig; kräftig.

bee|hive ['biːhaiv] Bienenkorb *m*, -stock *m*; **~keeper** Bienenzüchter *m*; **~line** kürzester Weg; make a **~** for Am. schnurstracks losgehen auf (acc.).

been [biːn, bin] *p.p. von* be.

beer [biə] Bier *n*; *small* ~ Dünnbier *n*. [Bete *f*.]

beet ♀ [biːt] (Runkel)Rübe *f*.

beetle¹ ['biːtl] Käfer *m*.

beetle² [~] 1. überhängend; buschig (*Brauen*); 2. *v/i.* überhängen.

beetroot ['biːtruːt] rote Rübe.

befall [bi'fɔːl] [*irr. (fall)*] *v/t.* zustoßen (*dat.*); *v/i.* sich ereignen.

befit [bi'fit] sich schicken für.

before [bi'fɔː] 1. *adv. Raum:* vorn; voran; *Zeit:* vorher, früher; schon (früher); 2. *cj.* bevor, ehe, bis; 3. *prp.* vor; ~hand vorher, zuvor; voraus (*with dat.*).

befriend [bi'frend] sich *j-m* freundlich erweisen.

beg [beg] *v/t. et.* erbetteln; erbitten (*of von*); *j-n* bitten; ~ *the question* um den Kern der Frage herumgehen; *v/i.* betteln; bitten; betteln gehen; sich gestatten.

began [bi'gæn] *pret. von* begin.

beget [bi'get] [*irr. (get)*] (er)zeugen.

beggar ['begə] 1. Bettler(in) *f*; F Kerl *m*; 2. zum Bettler machen; *fig.* übertreffen; it ~s *all description* es spottet jeder Beschreibung.

begin [bi'gin] [*irr.*] beginnen (*at* bei, mit); *anfangen (at* bei, mit); ~ner [~nə] Anfänger(in); ~ning [~niŋ] Beginn *m*, Anfang *m*.

begone [bi'gɔn] fort!, F pack dich!

begot [bi'gɔt] *pret. von* beget; ~ten [~tn] 1. *p.p. von* beget; 2. *adj.* erzeugt.

begrudge [bi'grʌdʒ] mißgönnen.

beguile [bi'gail] täuschen; betrügen (*of, out of* um); *Zeit* vertreiben.

begun [bi'gʌn] *p.p. von* begin.

behalf [bi'hɑːf]: *on od. in* ~ *of* im Namen von; um ... (*gen.*) willen.

behav|e [bi'heiv] sich benehmen; ~io(u)r [~vjə] Benehmen *n*, Betragen *n*.

behead [bi'hed] enthaupten.

behind [bi'haind] 1. *adv.* hinten; dahinter; zurück; 2. *prp.* hinter; ~hand zurück, im Rückstand.

behold [bi'hould] [*irr. (hold)*] 1. erblicken; 2. siehe (da)!; ~en [~dən] verpflichtet, verbunden.

behoof [bi'huːf]: *to (for, on) (the)* ~ *of* in *j-s* Interesse, um *j-s* willen.

behoove *Am.* [bi'huːv] = behove.

behove [bi'houv]: *it* ~ *s.o. to inf.* es ist *j-s* Pflicht, zu *inf.*

being ['biːiŋ] (Da)Sein *n*; Wesen *n*; *in* ~ lebend; wirklich (vorhanden).

belabo(u)r F [bi'leibə] verbleuen.

belated [bi'leitid] verspätet.

belch [beltʃ] 1. rülpsen; ausspeien; 2. Rülpsen *n*; Ausbruch *m*.

beleaguer [bi'liːgə] belagern.

belfry ['belfri] Glockenturm *m*, -stuhl *m*. [2. Belgier(in).]

Belgian ['beldʒən] 1. belgisch;}

belie [bi'lai] Lügen strafen.

belief [bi'liːf] Glaube *m* (*in an acc.*).

believable [bi'liːvəbl] glaubhaft.

believe [bi'liːv] glauben (*in an acc.*); ~r [~və] Gläubige(r *m*) *f*.

belittle *fig.* [bi'litl] verkleinern.

bell [bel] Glocke *f*; Klingel *f*; ~boy *Am.* ['belbɔi] Hotelpage *m*.

belle [bel] Schöne *f*, Schönheit *f*.

belles-lettres ['bel'letr] *pl.* Belletristik *f*, schöne Literatur.

bellhop *Am. sl.* ['belhɔp] Hotelpage *m*.

bellied ['belid] bauchig.

belligerent [bi'lidʒərənt] 1. kriegführend; 2. kriegführendes Land.

bellow ['belou] 1. brüllen; 2. Gebrüll *n*; ~s *pl.* Blasebalg *m*.

belly ['beli] 1. Bauch *m*; 2. (sich) bauchen; (an)schwellen.

belong [bi'lɔŋ] (an)gehören; ~ *to* gehören *dat. od.* zu; sich gehören für; *j-m* gebühren; ~ings [~iŋz] *pl.* Habseligkeiten *f/pl.*

beloved [bi'lʌvd] 1. geliebt; 2. Geliebte(r *m*) *f*.

below [bi'lou] 1. *adv.* unten; 2. *prp.* unter.

belt [belt] 1. Gürtel *m*; ✗ Koppel *n*; Zone *f*, Bezirk *m*; ⊕ Treibriemen *m*; 2. umgürten; ~ *out Am.* herausschmettern, loslegen (*singen*).

bemoan [bi'moun] betrauern, beklagen.

bench [bentʃ] Bank *f*; Richterbank *f*; Gerichtshof *m*; Arbeitstisch *m*.

bend [bend] 1. Biegung *f*, Kurve *f*; ⚓ Seemannsknoten *m*; 2. [*irr.*] (sich) biegen; *Geist etc.* richten (*to, on* auf *acc.*); (sich) beugen; sich neigen (*to* vor *dat.*).

beneath [bi'niːθ] = below.

benediction [beni'dikʃən] Segen *m*.

benefact|ion [beni'fækʃən] Wohltat *f*; ~or ['benifæktə] Wohltäter *m*.

beneficen|ce [bi'nefisəns] Wohltätigkeit *f*; ~t □ [~nt] wohltätig.

beneficial □ [beni'fiʃəl] wohltuend; zuträglich; nützlich.

benefit ['benifit] 1. Wohltat *f*; Nutzen *m*, Vorteil *m*; Wohltätigkeitsveranstaltung *f*; (Wohlfahrts-) Unterstützung *f*; 2. nützen; begünstigen; Nutzen ziehen.

benevolen|ce [bi'nevələns] Wohlwollen *n*; ~t □ [~nt] wohlwollend; gütig, mildherzig.

benign □ [bi'nain] freundlich, gütig; zuträglich; ✗ gutartig.

bent [bent] 1. *pret. u. p.p. von* bend 2; ~ *on* versessen auf (*acc.*); 2. Hang *m*; Neigung *f*.

benzene ⚗ ['benziːn] Benzol *n*.

benzine ⚗ ['benziːn] Benzin *n*.

bequeath [bi'kwiːð] vermachen.

bequest [bi'kwest] Vermächtnis *n*.

bereave [bi'riːv] [*irr.*] berauben.

bereft [bi'reft] *pret. u. p.p. von* bereave.

beret ['berei] Baskenmütze *f*.

berry ['beri] Beere f.

berth [bəːθ] 1. ⚓ Ankergrund m; Koje f; fig. (gute) Stelle; 2. vor Anker gehen.

beseech [bi'siːtʃ] [irr.] ersuchen; bitten; um et. bitten; flehen.

beset [bi'set] [irr. (set)] umgeben; bedrängen; verfolgen.

beside prp. [bi'said] neben; weitab von; ~ o.s. außer sich (with vor); ~ the point, ~ the question nicht zur Sache gehörig; ~s [~dz] 1. adv. außerdem; 2. prp. abgesehen von, außer.

besiege [bi'siːdʒ] belagern.

besmear [bi'smiə] beschmieren.

besom ['biːzəm] (Reisig)Besen m.

besought [bi'sɔːt] pret. u. p.p. von beseech.

bespatter [bi'spætə] (be)spritzen.

bespeak [bi'spiːk] [irr. (speak)] vorbestellen; verraten, (an)zeigen; bespoke tailor Maßschneider m.

best [best] 1. adj. best; höchst; größt, meist; ~ man Brautführer m; 2. adv. am besten, aufs beste; 3. Beste(r m, -s n) f, Besten pl.; to the ~ of ... nach bestem ...; make the ~ of tun, was man kann, mit; at ~ im besten Falle.

bestial □ ['bestjəl] tierisch, viehisch.

bestow [bi'stou] geben, schenken, verleihen (on, upon dat.).

bet [bet] 1. Wette f; 2. [irr.] wetten; you ~ F sicherlich.

betake [bi'teik] [irr. (take)]: ~ o.s. to sich begeben nach; fig. s-e Zuflucht nehmen zu.

bethink [bi'θiŋk] [irr. (think)]: ~ o.s. sich besinnen (of auf acc.); ~ o.s. to inf. sich in den Kopf setzen zu inf.

betimes [bi'taimz] beizeiten.

betray [bi'trei] verraten (a. fig.); verleiten; ~er [~eiə] Verräter(in).

betrothal [bi'trouðəl] Verlobung f.

better ['betə] 1. adj. besser; he is ~ es geht ihm besser; 1. Bessere(s) n; ~s pl. Höherstehenden pl., Vorgesetzten pl.; get the ~ of die Oberhand gewinnen über (acc.); überwinden; 3. adv. besser; mehr; so much the ~ desto besser; you had ~ go es wäre besser, wenn du gingest; 4. v/t. (ver)bessern; v/i. sich bessern; ~ment [~əmənt] Verbesserung f.

between [bi'twiːn] (a. betwixt [bi'twikst]) 1. adv. dazwischen; 2. prp. zwischen, unter.

bevel ['bevəl] schräg, schief.

beverage ['bevəridʒ] Getränk n.

bevy ['bevi] Schwarm m; Schar f.

bewail [bi'weil] be-, wehklagen.

beware [bi'wεə] sich hüten (of vor).

bewilder [bi'wildə] irremachen; verwirren; bestürzt machen; ~ment [~əmənt] Verwirrung f; Bestürzung f.

bewitch [bi'witʃ] bezaubern, behexen.

beyond [bi'jɔnd] 1. adv. darüber hinaus; 2. prp. jenseits, über (... hinaus); mehr als; außer.

bi... [bai] zwei ...

bias ['baiəs] 1. adj. u. adv. schief, schräg; 2. Neigung f; Vorurteil n; 3. beeinflussen; ~sed befangen.

bib [bib] (Sabber)Lätzchen n.

Bible ['baibl] Bibel f.

biblical □ ['biblikəl] biblisch; Bibel...

bibliography [bibli'ɔgrəfi] Bibliographie f.

bicarbonate 🜹 [bai'kɑːbənit] doppeltkohlensaures Natron.

biceps ['baiseps] Bizeps m.

bicker ['bikə] (sich) zanken; flakkern; plätschern; prasseln.

bicycle ['baisikl] 1. Fahrrad n; 2. radfahren, radeln.

bid [bid] 1. [irr.] gebieten, befehlen; (ent)bieten; Karten: reizen; ~ fair versprechen; ~ farewell Lebewohl sagen; 2. Gebot n, Angebot n; ~den ['bidn] p.p. von bid 1.

bide [baid] [irr.]: ~ one's time den rechten Augenblick abwarten.

biennial [bai'eniəl] zweijährig.

bier [biə] (Toten)Bahre f.

big [big] groß; erwachsen; schwanger; F wichtig(tuerisch); ~ business Großunternehmertum n; ~ shot F hohes Tier; ~ stick Am. Macht (-entfaltung) f; talk ~ den Mund vollnehmen.

bigamy ['bigəmi] Doppelehe f.

bigot ['bigət] Frömmler(in); blinder Anhänger; ~ry [~tri] Frömmelei f.

bigwig F ['bigwig] hohes Tier (P.).

bike F [baik] (Fahr)Rad n.

bilateral □ ['bai'lætərəl] zweiseitig.

bile [bail] Galle f (a. fig.).

bilious □ ['biljəs] gallig (a. fig.).

bill¹ [bil] Schnabel m; Spitze f.

bill² [~] 1. Gesetzentwurf m; Klage-, Rechtsschrift f; a. ~ of exchange Wechsel m; Zettel m; Am. Banknote f; ~ of fare Speisekarte f; ~ of lading Seefrachtbrief m, Konnossement n; ~ of sale Kaufvertrag m; ♀ of Rights englische Freiheitsurkunde (1689); Am. die ersten 10 Zusatzartikel zur Verfassung der USA; 2. (durch Anschlag) ankündigen.

billboard Am. ['bil'bɔːd] Anschlagbrett n.

billfold Am. ['bilfould] Brieftasche f für Papiergeld.

billiards ['biljədz] pl. od. sg. Billiard(spiel) n.

billion ['biljən] Billion f; Am. Milliarde f.

billow ['bilou] 1. Woge f (a. fig.); 2. wogen; ~y [~oui] wogend.

billy Am. ['bili] (Gummi)Knüppel m.

bin [bin] Kasten *m*, Behälter *m*.

bind [baind] [*irr.*] *v/t.* (an-, ein-, um-, auf-, fest-, ver)binden; verpflichten; *Handel* abschließen; *Saum* einfassen; *v/i.* binden; **~er** ['baində] Binder *m*; Binde *f*; **~ing** [~diŋ] **1.** bindend; **2.** Binden *n*; Einband *m*; Einfassung *f*.

binocular [bi'nɔkjulə] *mst* **~s** *pl.* Feldstecher *m*, Fern-, Opernglas *n*.

biography [bai'ɔgrəfi] Biographie *f*.

biology [bai'ɔlədʒi] Biologie *f*.

biped *zo.* ['baiped] Zweifüßer *m*.

birch [bəːtʃ] **1.** ♀ Birke *f*; (Birken-) Rute *f*; **2.** mit der Rute züchtigen.

bird [bəːd] Vogel *m*; **~'s-eye** ['bəːdzai]: **~** *view* Vogelperspektive *f*.

birth [bəːθ] Geburt *f*; Ursprung *m*; Entstehung *f*; Herkunft *f*; *bring to* **~** entstehen lassen, veranlassen; *give* **~** *to* gebären, zur Welt bringen; **~control** Geburtenregelung *f*; **~day** ['bəːθdei] Geburtstag *m*; **~place** Geburtsort *m*.

biscuit ['biskit] Zwieback *m*; Keks *m, n*; Biskuit *n* (*Porzellan*).

bishop ['biʃəp] Bischof *m*; Läufer *m im Schach*; **~ric** [~prik] Bistum *n*.

bison *zo.* ['baisn] Wisent *m*.

bit [bit] **1.** Bißchen *n*, Stückchen *n*; Gebiß *n am Zaum*; Schlüssel-Bart *m*; *a (little)* **~** ein (kleines) bißchen; **2.** zäumen; zügeln; **3.** *pret. von bite* 2.

bitch [bitʃ] Hündin *f*; V Hure *f*.

bite [bait] **1.** Beißen *n*; Biß *m*; Bissen *m*; ⊕ Fassen *n*; **2.** [*irr.*] (an)beißen; brennen (*Pfeffer*); schneiden (*Kälte*); ⊕ fassen; *fig.* verletzen.

bitten ['bitn] *p.p. von bite* 2.

bitter ['bitə] **1.** ☐ bitter; streng; *fig.* verbittert; **2.** **~s** *pl.* Magenbitter *m*.

biz F [biz] Geschäft *n*.

blab F [blæb] (aus)schwatzen.

black [blæk] **1.** ☐ schwarz; dunkel; finster; **~** *eye* blaues Auge; **2.** schwärzen; wichsen; **~** *out* verdunkeln; **3.** Schwarz *n*; Schwärze *f*; Schwarze(r *m*) *f* (*Neger*); **~amoor** ['blækəmuə] Neger *m*; **~berry** Brombeere *f*; **~bird** Amsel *f*; **~board** Wandtafel *f*; **~en** [~kən] *v/t.* schwärzen; *fig.* anschwärzen; *v/i.* schwarz werden; **~guard** ['blægaːd] **1.** Lump *m*, Schuft *m*; **2.** ☐ schuftig; **~head** ❀ Mitesser *m*; **~ing** [~kiŋ] Schuhwichse *f*; **~ish** ☐ [~iʃ] schwärzlich; **~jack 1.** *bsd. Am.* Totschläger *m* (*Instrument*); **2.** niederknüppeln; *leg* Betrüger *m*; **~letter** *typ.* Fraktur *f*; **~mail 1.** Erpressung *f*; **2.** *j-n* erpressen; **~ market** schwarzer Markt; **~ness** [~knis] Schwärze *f*; **~out** Verdunkelung *f*; **~ pudding** Blutwurst *f*; **~smith** Grobschmied *m*.

bladder *anat.* ['blædə] Blase *f*.

blade [bleid] Blatt *n*, ♀ Halm *m*; *Säge-, Schulter- etc.* Blatt *n*; Propellerflügel *m*; Klinge *f*.

blame [bleim] **1.** Tadel *m*; Schuld *f*; **2.** tadeln; *be to* **~** *for* schuld sein an (*dat.*); **~ful** ['bleimful] tadelnswert; **~less** ☐ [~mlis] tadellos.

blanch [blaːntʃ] bleichen; erbleichen (lassen); **~** *over* beschönigen.

bland ☐ [blænd] mild, sanft.

blank [blæŋk] **1.** ☐ blank; leer; unausgefüllt; unbeschrieben; ✝ Blanko...; verdutzt; **~** *cartridge* ✗ Platzpatrone *f*; **2.** Weiße *n*; Leere *f*; leerer Raum; Lücke *f*; unbeschriebenes Blatt, Formular *n*; Niete *f*.

blanket ['blæŋkit] **1.** Wolldecke *f*; *wet* **~** *fig.* Dämpfer *m*; Spielverderber *m*; **2.** (mit e-r Wolldecke) zudecken; **3.** *Am.* umfassend, Gesamt...

blare [blɛə] schmettern; grölen.

blasphem|e [blæs'fiːm] lästern (*against* über *acc.*); **~y** ['blæsfimi] Gotteslästerung *f*.

blast [blaːst] **1.** Windstoß *m*; Ton *m e-s Blasinstruments*; ⊕ Gebläse (-luft *f*) *n*; Luftdruck *m e-r Explosion*; ♀ Meltau *m*; **2.** (in die Luft) sprengen; zerstören (*a. fig.*); **~** (*it*)! verdammt; **~-furnace** ⊕ ['blaːstfəːnis] Hochofen *m*.

blatant ☐ ['bleitənt] lärmend.

blather *Am.* ['blæðə] schwätzen.

blaze [bleiz] **1.** Flamme(n *pl.*) *f*; Feuer *n*; **~s** *pl. sl.* Teufel *m*, Hölle *f*; heller Schein; *fig.* Ausbruch *m*; *go to* **~s!** zum Teufel mit dir!; **2.** *v/i.* brennen, flammen, lodern; leuchten; *v/t.*: **~** *abroad* ausposaunen; **~r** ['bleizə] Blazer *m*.

blazon ['bleizn] Wappen(kunde *f*) *n*.

bleach [bliːtʃ] bleichen; **~er** ['bliːtʃə] Bleicher(in); *mst* **~s** *pl. Am.* nichtüberdachte Zuschauerplätze.

bleak ☐ [bliːk] öde, kahl; rauh; *fig.* trüb, freudlos, finster.

blear [bliə] **1.** trüb; **2.** trüben; **~-eyed** ['bliəraid] triefäugig.

bleat [bliːt] **1.** Blöken *n*; **2.** blöken.

bleb [bleb] Bläs-chen *n*, Pustel *f*.

bled [bled] *pret. u. p.p. von bleed.*

bleed [bliːd] [*irr.*] *v/i.* bluten; *v/t.* zur Ader lassen; ⚕ schröpfen; **~ing** ['bliːdiŋ] **1.** Bluten *n*; Aderlaß *m*; **2.** *sl.* verflixt.

blemish ['blemiʃ] **1.** Fehler *m*; Makel *m*, Schande *f*; **2.** verunstalten; brandmarken.

blench [blentʃ] *v/i.* zurückschrecken; *v/t.* die Augen schließen vor.

blend [blend] **1.** (sich) (ver-)mischen; *Wein etc.* verschneiden; **2.** Mischung *f*; ✝ verschnitt...

blent [blent] *pret. u. p.p. von blend* 1.

bless [bles] segnen; preisen; be-

glücken; ~ me! herrje!; ~ed □
[pret. u. p.p. blest]; adj. 'blesid]
glückselig; gesegnet; ~ing [~siŋ]
Segen m.

blew [blu:] pret. von blow² u. blow³1.

blight [blait] 1. ♀ Mehltau m; fig.
Gifthauch m; 2. vernichten.

blind □ [blaind] 1. blind (fig. to
gegen); geheim; nicht erkennbar;
~ alley Sackgasse f; ~ly fig. blindlings; 2. Blende f; Fenster-Vor-
hang m, Jalousie f; Am. Versteck
n; Vorwand m; 3. blenden; ver-
blenden (to gegen); abblenden;
~fold ['blaindfould] 1. blindlings;
2. j-m die Augen verbinden;
~worm Blindschleiche f.

blink [bliŋk] 1. Blinzeln n; Schimmer m; 2. v/i. blinzeln; blinken;
schimmern; v/t. absichtlich übersehen; ~er ['bliŋkə] Scheuklappe f.

bliss [blis] Seligkeit f, Wonne f.

blister ['blistə] 1. Blase f (auf der
Haut, im Lack); Zugpflaster n;
2. Blasen bekommen od. ziehen
(auf dat.).

blithe □ mst poet. [blaið] lustig.

blizzard ['blizəd] Schneesturm m.

bloat [blout] aufblasen; aufschwel-
len; ~er ['bloutə] Bückling m.

block [blɔk] 1. (Häuser-, Schreib-
etc.)Block m; Klotz m; Druckstock
m; Verstopfung f, Stockung f;
2. formen; verhindern; ~ in entwerfen, skizzieren; mst ~ up (ab-, ver-)
sperren; blockieren.

blockade [blɔ'keid] 1. Blockade f;
2. blockieren.

block|head ['blɔkhed] Dummkopf
m; ~ letters Druckschrift f.

blond(e f) [blɔnd] 1. blond;
2. Blondine f.

blood [blʌd] Blut n; fig. Blut n;
Abstammung f; in cold ~ kalten
Blutes, kaltblütig; ~-curdling
['blʌdkə:dliŋ] haarsträubend; ~-
horse Vollblutpferd n; ~shed Blut-
vergießen n; ~shot blutunterlaufen;
~thirsty blutdürstig; ~vessel
Blutgefäß n; ~y □ ['blʌdi] blutig;
blutdürstig.

bloom [blu:m] 1. Blüte f; Reif m auf
Früchten; fig. Schmelz m; 2. (er-)
blühen (a. fig.).

blossom ['blɔsəm] 1. Blüte f;
2. blühen.

blot [blɔt] 1. Klecks m; fig. Makel m;
2. v/t. beklecksen, beflecken; (ab-)
löschen; ausstreichen; v/i. klecksen.

blotch [blɔtʃ] Pustel f; Fleck m.

blotter ['blɔtə] Löscher m; Am.
Protokollbuch n. [Löschpapier n.]

blotting-paper ['blɔtiŋpeipə]

blouse [blauz] Bluse f.

blow¹ [blou] Schlag m, Stoß m.

blow² [~] [irr.] blühen.

blow³ [~] 1. [irr.] v/i. blasen; wehen;
~ up in die Luft fliegen; ♂
v/t. (weg- etc.)blasen; wehen; ♂

durchbrennen; ~ one's nose sich die
Nase putzen; ~ up sprengen;
2. Blasen n, Wehen n; ~er ['blouə]
Bläser m.

blown [bloun] p.p. von blow² und
blow³ 1.

blow|-out mot. ['blouaut] Reifen-
panne f; ~pipe Gebläsebrenner m.

bludgeon ['blʌdʒən] Knüppel m.

blue [blu:] 1. □ blau; F trüb,
schwermütig; 2. Blau n; 3. blau
färben; blauen; ~bird ['blu:bə:d]
amerikanische Singdrossel; ~ laws
Am. strenge (puritanische) Gesetze;
~s [blu:z] pl. Trübsinn m; ♪
Blues m.

bluff [blʌf] 1. □ schroff; steil; derb;
2. Steilufer n; Irreführung f;
3. bluffen, irreführen.

bluish ['blu:iʃ] bläulich.

blunder ['blʌndə] 1. Fehler m,
Schnitzer m; 2. e-n Fehler machen;
stolpern; stümpern; verpfuschen.

blunt [blʌnt] 1. □ stumpf (a. fig.);
plump, grob, derb; 2. abstumpfen.

blur [blə:] 1. Fleck(en) m; fig. Ver-
schwommenheit f; 2. v/t. beflecken;
verwischen; Sinn trüben.

blush [blʌʃ] 1. Schamröte f; Erröten n; flüchtiger Blick; 2. erröten; (sich) röten.

bluster ['blʌstə] 1. Brausen n, Getöse n; Prahlerei f; 2. brausen;
prahlen.

boar [bɔ:] Eber m; hunt. Keiler m.

board [bɔ:d] 1. (Anschlag)Brett n;
Konferenztisch m; Ausschuß m;
Gremium n; Behörde f; Verpflegung f; Pappe f; on ~ a train Am.
in e-m Zug; ♀ of Trade Handels-
ministerium n; 2. v/t. dielen, verschalen; beköstigen; an Bord gehen; ♣ entern; bsd. Am. einsteigen
in (ein Fahr- od. Flugzeug); v/i. in
Kost sein; ~er ['bɔ:də] Kost-
gänger(in); Internatsschüler(in);
~ing-house ['bɔ:diŋhaus] Pension
f; ~ing-school ['bɔ:diŋsku:l] Internatsschule f; ~walk bsd. Am.
Strandpromenade f.

boast [boust] 1. Prahlerei f; 2. (of,
about) sich rühmen (gen.), prahlen
(mit); ~ful □ ['boustful] prahlerisch.

boat [bout] Boot n; Schiff n; ~ing
['boutiŋ] Bootfahrt f.

bob [bɔb] 1. Quaste f; Ruck m;
Knicks m; sl. Schilling
m; 2. v/t. Haar stutzen; ~bed hair
Bubikopf m; v/i. springen, tanzen;
knicksen.

bobbin ['bɔbin] Spule f (a. ⚡).

bobble Am. [F 'bɔbl] Fehler m.

bobby sl. ['bɔbi] Schupo m, Polizist
m.

bobsleigh ['bɔbslei] Bob(sleigh) m
(Rennschlitten).

bode¹ [boud] prophezeien.

bode² [~] pret. von bide.

bodice ['bɔdis] Mieder n; Taille f.

bodily ['bɔdili] körperlich.

body ['bɔdi] Körper m, Leib m; Leichnam m; Körperschaft f; Hauptteil m; mot. Karosserie f; ✗ Truppenkörper m; **~-guard** Leibwache f.

Boer ['bouə] Bure m; attr. Buren...

bog [bɔg] 1. Sumpf m, Moor n; 2. im Schlamm versenken.

boggle ['bɔgl] stutzen; pfuschen.

bogus ['bougəs] falsch; Schwindel...

boil [bɔil] 1. kochen, sieden; (sich) kondensieren; 2. Sieden n; Beule f, Geschwür n; **~er** ['bɔilə] (Dampf-) Kessel m.

boisterous □ ['bɔistərəs] ungestüm; heftig, laut; lärmend.

bold □ [bould] kühn; keck, dreist; steil; typ. fett; make ~ sich erkühnen; **~ness** ['bouldnis] Kühnheit f; Keckheit f, Dreistigkeit f.

bolster ['boulstə] 1. Kopfkeil m; Unterlage f; 2. polstern; (unter-) stützen.

bolt [boult] 1. Bolzen m; Riegel m; Blitz(strahl) m; Ausreißen n; 2. adv. ~ upright kerzengerade; 3. v/t. verriegeln; F hinunterschlingen; sieben; v/i. eilen; durchgehen (Pferd); Am. pol. abtrünnig werden; **~er** ['boultə] Ausreißer(in).

bomb [bɔm] 1. Bombe f; 2. mit Bomben belegen.

bombard [bɔm'ba:d] bombardieren.

bombastic [bɔm'bæstik] schwülstig.

bomb-proof ['bɔmpru:f] bombensicher.

bond [bɔnd] Band n; Fessel f; Bündnis n; Schuldschein m; ✝ Obligation f; in ~ ✝ unter Zollverschluß; **~age** ['bɔndidʒ] Hörigkeit f; Knechtschaft f; **~(s)man** [~d(z)mən] Leibeigene(r) m.

bone [boun] Knochen m; Gräte f; ~s pl. a. Gebeine n/pl.; ~ of contention Zankapfel m; make no ~s about F nicht lange fackeln mit; 2. die Knochen auslösen (aus); aus-, entgräten.

bonfire ['bɔnfaiə] Freudenfeuer n.

bonnet ['bɔnit] Haube f, Schute(nhut m) f; ⊕ (Motor)Haube f.

bonus ✝ ['bounəs] Prämie f; Gratifikation f; Zulage f.

bony ['bouni] knöchern; knochig.

boob Am. [bu:b] Dummkopf m.

booby ['bu:bi] Tölpel m.

book [buk] 1. Buch n; Heft n; Liste f; Bloc m; 2. buchen; eintragen; Fahrkarte etc. lösen; e-n Platz etc. bestellen; Gepäck aufgeben; **~burner** Am. F [bukbə:nə] intoleranter Mensch; **~case** Bücherschrank m; **~ing-clerk** F [buk-kla:k] Schalterbeamt|e(r) m, -in f; **~ing-office** ['bukiŋɔfis] Fahrkartenausgabe f, -schalter m; thea.

Kasse f; **~ish** □ [~iʃ] gelehrt; **~keeping** Buchführung f; **~let** ['buklit] Büchlein n; Broschüre f; **~seller** Buchhändler m.

boom¹ [bu:m] 1. ✝ Aufschwung m, Hochkonjunktur f, Hausse f; Reklamerummel m; 2. in die Höhe treiben od. gehen; für et. Reklame machen.

boom² [~] brummen; dröhnen.

boon¹ [bu:n] Segen m, Wohltat f.

boon² [~] freundlich, munter.

boor fig. [buə] Bauer m, Lümmel m; **~ish** □ ['buəriʃ] bäuerisch, lümmel-, flegelhaft.

boost [bu:st] heben; verstärken (a. ∮); Reklame machen.

boot¹ [bu:t]: to ~ obendrein.

boot² [~] Stiefel m; Kofferraum m; **~black** Am. ['bu:tblæk] = shoeblack; **~ee** ['bu:ti:] Damen-Halbstiefel m.

booth [bu:ð] (Markt- etc.)Bude f; Wahlzelle f; Am. Fernsprechzelle f.

boot|lace ['bu:tleis] Schnürsenkel m; **~legger** Am. [~legə] Alkoholschmuggler m.

booty ['bu:ti] Beute f, Raub m.

border ['bɔ:də] 1. Rand m, Saum m; Grenze f; Einfassung f; Rabatte f; 2. einfassen; grenzen (upon an acc.).

bore¹ [bɔ:] 1. Bohrloch n; Kaliber n; fig. langweiliger Mensch; Plage f; 2. bohren; langweilen; belästigen.

bore² [~] pret. von bear².

born [bɔ:n] p.p. von bear² gebären.

borne [bɔ:n] p.p. von bear² tragen.

borough ['bʌrə] Stadt(teil m) f; Am. a. Wahlbezirk m von New York City; municipal ~ Stadtgemeinde f.

borrow ['bɔrou] borgen, entleihen.

bosom ['buzəm] Busen m; fig. Schoß m.

boss F [bɔs] 1. Boss m, Chef m; bsd. Am. pol. (Partei)Bonze m; 2. leiten; **~y** Am. F ['bɔsi] tyrannisch, herrisch.

botany ['bɔtəni] Botanik f.

botch [bɔtʃ] 1. Flicken m; Flickwerk n; 2. flicken; verpfuschen.

both [bouθ] beide(s); ~ ... and sowohl ... als (auch).

bother F ['bɔðə] 1. Plage f; 2. (sich) plagen, (sich) quälen.

bottle ['bɔtl] 1. Flasche f; 2. auf Flaschen ziehen.

bottom ['bɔtəm] 1. Boden m, Grund m; Grundfläche f, Fuß m, Ende n; F Hintern m; fig. Wesen n, Kern m; at the ~ ganz unten; fig. im Grunde; 2. grundlegend, Grund...

bough [bau] Ast m, Zweig m.

bought [bɔ:t] pret. u. p.p von buy.

boulder ['bouldə] Geröllblock m.

bounce [bauns] 1. Sprung m, Rückprall m; F Aufschneiderei f; Auftrieb m; 2. (hoch)springen; F aufschneiden; **~r** ['baunsə] F Mordskerl m; Am. sl. Rausschmeißer m.

bound¹ [baund] 1. *pret. u. p.p von* bind; 2. *adj.* verpflichtet; bestimmt, unterwegs (*for* nach).

bound² [~] 1. Grenze *f*, Schranke *f*; 2. begrenzen; beschränken.

bound³ [~] 1. Sprung *m*; 2. (hoch-) springen; an-, abprallen.

boundary ['baundəri] Grenze *f*.

boundless □ ['baundlis] grenzenlos.

bount|eous □ ['bauntiəs], **~iful** □ [~iful] freigebig; reichlich.

bounty ['baunti] Freigebigkeit *f*; Spende *f*; ✝ Prämie *f*.

bouquet ['bukei] Bukett *n*, Strauß *m*; Blume *f des Weines*.

bout [baut] Fecht-Gang *m*; Tanz-Tour *f*; ✗ Anfall *m*; Kraftprobe *f*.

bow¹ [bau] 1. Verbeugung *f*; 2. *v/i*. sich (ver)beugen; *v/t*. biegen; beugen.

bow² ⚓ [~] Bug *m*.

bow³ [bou] 1. Bogen *m*; Schleife *f*; 2. geigen.

bowdlerize ['baudləraiz] *Text* von anstößigen Stellen reinigen.

bowels ['bauəlz] *pl.* Eingeweide *n*; *das Innere*, *fig.* Herz *n*.

bower ['bauə] Laube *f*.

bowl¹ [boul] Schale *f*, Schüssel *f*; *Pfeifen*-Kopf *m*.

bowl² [~] 1. Kugel *f*; ~s *pl*. Bowling *n*; 2. *v/t*. *Ball etc.* werfen; *v/i*. rollen; kegeln.

box¹ [bɔks] Buchsbaum *m*; Büchse *f*, Schachtel *f*, Kasten *m*; Koffer *m*; ⊕ Gehäuse *n*; *thea.* Loge *f*; Abteilung *f*; 2. in Kästen *etc.* tun.

box² [~] 1. boxen; 2.: ~ *on the ear* Ohrfeige *f*.

Boxing-Day ['bɔksiŋdei] zweiter Weihnachtsfeiertag.

box|-keeper ['bɔkski:pə] Logenschließer(in); **~-office** Theaterkasse *f*.

boy [bɔi] Junge *m*, junger Mann; Bursche *m* (a. *Diener*); **~friend** Freund *m*; ~ *scout* Pfadfinder *m*; **~hood** □ ['bɔihud] Knabenalter *n*; **~ish** □ ['bɔiiʃ] knabenhaft; kindisch.

brace [breis] 1. ⊕ Strebe *f*; Stützbalken *m*; Klammer *f*; Paar *n* (*Wild, Geflügel*); ~s *pl.* Hosenträger *m/pl.*; 2. absteifen; verankern; (an)spannen; *fig.* stärken.

bracelet ['breislit] Armband *n*.

bracket ['brækit] 1. △ Konsole *f*; Winkelstütze *f*; *typ.* Klammer *f*; *Leuchter*-Arm *m*; *lower income* ~ niedrige Einkommensstufe; 2. einklammern; *fig.* gleichstellen.

brackish ['brækiʃ] brackig, salzig.

brag [bræg] 1. Prahlerei *f*; 2. prahlen. [2. □ prahlerisch.\]

braggart ['brægət] 1. Prahler *m*;\

braid [breid] 1. *Haar*-Flechte *f*; Borte *f*; Tresse *f*; 2. flechten; mit Borte besetzen.

brain [brein] 1. Gehirn *n*; Kopf *m*

(*fig. mst* ~s = *Verstand*); 2. *j-m* den Schädel einschlagen; **~-pan** ['breinpæn] Hirnschale *f*; **~(s) trust** *Am.* [~n(z)trʌst] Expertenrat *m* (*mst pol.*); **~-wave** F Geistesblitz *m*.

brake [breik] 1. ⊕ Bremse *f*; 2. bremsen; **~(s)man** 🚂 ['breik(s)mən] Bremser *m*; *Am.* Schaffner *m*.

bramble ['bræmbl] Brombeerstrauch *m*.

bran [bræn] Kleie *f*.

branch [brɑ:ntʃ] 1. Zweig *m*; Fach *n*; Linie *f des Stammbaumes*; Zweigstelle *f*; 2. sich ver-, abzweigen.

brand [brænd] 1. (*Feuer*)Brand *m*; Brandmal *n*; Marke *f*; Sorte *f*; 2. einbrennen; brandmarken.

brandish ['brændiʃ] schwingen.

bran(d)-new ['bræn(d)'nju:] nagelneu.

brandy ['brændi] Kognak *m*; Weinbrand *m*.

brass [brɑ:s] Messing *n*; F Unverschämtheit *f*; ~ *band* Blechblaskapelle *f*; ~ *knuckles pl. Am.* Schlagring *m*.

brassière ['bræsiə] Büstenhalter *m*.

brave [breiv] 1. tapfer; prächtig; 2. trotzen; mutig begegnen (*dat.*); **~ry** ['breivəri] Tapferkeit *f*; Pracht *f*.

brawl [brɔ:l] 1. Krakeel *m*, Krawall *m*; 2. krakeelen, Krawall machen.

brawny ['brɔ:ni] muskulös.

bray¹ [brei] 1. Eselsschrei *m*; 2. schreien; schmettern; dröhnen.

bray² [~] (zer)stoßen, zerreiben.

brazen □ ['breizn] bronzen; metallisch; *a.* **~-faced** unverschämt.

Brazilian [brə'ziljən] 1. brasilianisch; 2. Brasilianer(in).

breach [bri:tʃ] 1. Bruch *m*; ✗ Verletzung *f*; ✗ Bresche *f*; 2. e-e Bresche schlagen in (*acc.*).

bread [bred] Brot *n*; *know which side one's ~ is buttered* s-n Vorteil (er)kennen.

breadth [bredθ] Breite *f*, Weite *f*, Größe *f des Geistes*; *Tuch*-Bahn *f*.

break [breik] 1. Bruch *m*; Lücke *f*; Pause *f*; Absatz *m*; ✝ *Am.* (Preis-)Rückgang *m*; *Tages*-Anbruch *m*; *a bad* ~ F e-e Dummheit; Pech *n*; *a lucky* ~ Glück *n*; 2. [*irr.*] *v/t.* (zer)brechen; unterbrechen; übertreten; *Tier* abrichten; *Bank* sprengen; *Brief* erbrechen; *Tür* aufbrechen; abbrechen; *Vorrat* anbrechen; *Nachricht* schonend mitteilen; ruinieren; ~ *up* aufbrechen; auflösen; *v/i.* (zer)brechen; aus-, los-, an-, auf-, hervorbrechen; umschlagen (*Wetter*); ~ *away* sich losreißen; ~ *down* zs.-brechen; steckenbleiben; versagen; **~able** ['breikəbl] zerbrechlich; **~age** [~kidʒ] (*a.* ✝ *Waren*)Bruch *m*; **~down** Zs.-bruch *m*; Maschinenschaden *m; mot.* Panne *f;* ~fast ['brekfəst] **1.** Frühstück *n;* **2.** frühstücken; ~up ['breik'ʌp] Verfall *m;* Auflösung *f;* Schulschluß *m;* ~water ['~kwɔːtə] Wellenbrecher *m.*

breast [brest] Brust *f;* Busen *m;* Herz *n; make a clean ~ of s.th.* et. offen gestehen; ~stroke ['breststrouk] Brustschwimmen *n.*

breath [breθ] Atem(zug) *m;* Hauch *m; waste one's ~* s-e Worte verschwenden; ~e [briːð] *v/i.* atmen; *fig.* leben; *v/t.* (aus-, ein)atmen; hauchen; flüstern; ~less □ ['breθlis] atemlos.

bred [bred] *pret. u. p.p. von breed* 2.

breeches ['britʃiz] *pl.* Knie-, Reithosen *f/pl.*

breed [briːd] **1.** Zucht *f;* Rasse *f;* Herkunft *f; Am.* Mischling *m bsd. weiß-indianisch;* **2.** [*irr.*] *v/t.* erzeugen; auf-, erziehen; züchten; *v/i.* sich fortpflanzen; ~er ['briːdə] Erzeuger(in); Züchter(in); ~ing [~diŋ] Erziehung *f;* Bildung *f;* (Tier-) Zucht *f.*

breez|e [briːz] Brise *f;* ~y ['briːzi] windig, luftig; frisch, flott.

brethren ['breðrin] *pl.* Brüder *m/pl.*

brevity ['breviti] Kürze *f.*

brew [bruː] **1.** *v/t. u. v/i.* brauen; zubereiten; *fig.* anzetteln; **2.** Gebräu *n;* ~ery ['bruəri] Brauerei *f.*

briar ['braiə] = *brier.*

brib|e [braib] **1.** Bestechung(sgeld *n,* -sgeschenk *n*) *f;* **2.** bestechen; ~ery ['braibəri] Bestechung *f.*

brick [brik] **1.** Ziegel(stein) *m; drop a ~ sl.* ins Fettnäpfchen treten; **2.** mauern; ~layer ['brikleiə] Maurer *m;* ~works *sg.* Ziegelei *f.*

bridal □ ['braidl] bräutlich; Braut-...; ~ procession Brautzug *m.*

bride [braid] Braut *f,* Neuvermählte *f;* ~groom ['braidgrum] Bräutigam *m,* Neuvermählte(r) *m;* ~smaid [~dzmeid] Brautjungfer *f.*

bridge [bridʒ] **1.** Brücke *f;* **2.** e-e Brücke schlagen über (*acc.*); *fig.* überbrücken.

bridle ['braidl] **1.** Zaum *m;* Zügel *m;* **2.** *v/t.* (auf)zäumen; zügeln; *v/i. a.* ~ up den Kopf zurückwerfen; ~path, ~road Reitweg *m.*

brief [briːf] **1.** □ kurz, bündig; **2.** ⚖ schriftliche Instruktion; *hold a ~ for* einstehen für; ~case ['briːfkeis] Aktenmappe *f.*

brier ⚘ ['braiə] Dorn-, Hagebuttenstrauch *m,* wilde Rose.

brigade ✕ [bri'geid] Brigade *f.*

bright □ [brait] hell, glänzend, klar; lebhaft; gescheit; ~en ['braitn] *v/t.* auf-, erhellen; polieren; aufheitern; *v/i.* sich aufhellen; ~ness [~nis] Helligkeit *f;* Glanz *m;* Klarheit *f;* Heiterkeit *f;* Aufgewecktheit *f.*

brillian|ce, ~cy ['briljəns, ~si] Glanz *m;* ~t [~nt] **1.** □ glänzend; prächtig; **2.** Brillant *m.*

brim [brim] **1.** Rand *m;* Krempe *f;* **2.** bis zum Rande füllen *od.* voll sein; ~full, ~ful ['brim'ful] ganz voll; ~stone † ['brimstən] Schwefel *m.*

brindle(d) ['brindl(d)] scheckig.

brine [brain] Salzwasser *n,* Sole *f.*

bring [briŋ] [*irr.*] bringen; *j.* veranlassen; *Klage* erheben; *Grund etc.* vorbringen; ~ *about, ~ to pass* zustande bringen; ~ *down Preis* herabsetzen; ~ *forth* hervorbringen; gebären; ~ *home to j.* überzeugen; ~ *round* wieder zu sich bringen; ~ *up* auf-, erziehen.

brink [briŋk] Rand *m.*

brisk □ [brisk] lebhaft, munter; frisch; flink; belebend.

bristl|e ['brisl] **1.** Borste *f;* **2.** (sich) sträuben; hochfahren, zornig werden; ~ *with fig.* starren von; ~ed, ~y [~li] gesträubt; struppig.

British ['britiʃ] britisch; *the ~ pl.* die Briten *pl.;* ~er *bsd. Am.* [~ʃə] Einwohner(in) Großbritanniens.

brittle ['britl] zerbrechlich, spröde.

broach [broutʃ] *Faß* anzapfen; vorbringen; *Thema* anschneiden.

broad □ [brɔːd] breit; weit; hell (*Tag*); deutlich (*Wink etc.*); derb (*Witz*); allgemein; weitherzig, liberal; ~cast ['brɔːdkɑːst] **1.** weitverbreitet; **2.** [*irr.* (cast)] weit verbreiten; *Radio:* senden; **3.** Rundfunk (-sendung *f*) *m;* ~cloth feiner Wollstoff; ~minded großzügig.

brocade † [brə'keid] Brokat *m.*

broil [brɔil] **1.** Lärm *m,* Streit *m;* **2.** auf dem Rost braten; *fig.* schmoren.

broke [brouk] **1.** *pret. von break* 2; **2.** *sl.* pleite, ohne e-n Pfennig; ~n ['broukən] **1.** *p.p. von break* 2; **2.:** ~ *health* zerrüttete Gesundheit.

broker ['broukə] Altwarenhändler *m;* Zwangsversteigerer *m;* Makler *m.*

bronc(h)o *Am.* ['brɔŋkou] (halb-) wildes Pferd; ~buster [~oubʌstə] Zureiter *m.*

bronze [brɔnz] **1.** Bronze *f;* **2.** bronzen, Bronze...; **3.** bronzieren.

brooch [broutʃ] Brosche *f;* Spange *f.*

brood [bruːd] **1.** Brut *f; attr.* Zucht...; **2.** brüten (*a. fig.*); ~er *Am.* ['bruːdə] Brutkasten *m.*

brook [bruk] Bach *m.*

broom [brum] Besen *m;* ~stick ['brumstik] Besenstiel *m.*

broth [brɔθ] Fleischbrühe *f.*

brothel ['brɔθl] Bordell *n.*

brother ['brʌðə] Bruder *m;* ~(s) *and sister(s)* Geschwister *pl.;* ~hood [~hud] Bruderschaft *f;* ~in-law [~ərinlɔː] Schwager *m;* ~ly [~əli] brüderlich.

brought [brɔːt] *pret. u. p.p. von* bring.

brow [brau] (Augen)Braue *f*; Stirn *f*; Rand *m e-s Steilhanges*; **~beat** ['braubiːt] [*irr.* (*beat*)] einschüchtern; tyrannisieren.

brown [braun] 1. braun; 2. Braun *n*; 3. (sich) bräunen.

browse [brauz] 1. Grasen *n*; *fig.* Schmökern *n*; 2. grasen, weiden; *fig.* schmökern.

bruise [bruːz] 1. Quetschung *f*; 2. (zer)quetschen.

brunt [brʌnt] Hauptstoß *m*, (volle) Wucht; *das* Schwerste.

brush [brʌʃ] 1. Bürste *f*; Pinsel *m*; *Fuchs*-Rute *f*; Scharmützel *n*; Unterholz *n*; 2. *v/t.* (ab-, aus)bürsten; streifen; *j.* abbürsten; **~ up** wieder aufbürsten, *fig.* auffrischen; *v/i.* bürsten; (davon)stürzen; **~ against** *s.o.* j. streifen; **~wood** ['brʌʃwud] Gestrüpp *n*, Unterholz *n*.

brusque □ [brusk] brüsk, barsch.

Brussels sprouts ♀ ['brʌsl'sprauts] *pl.* Rosenkohl *m*.

brut|al □ ['bruːtl] viehisch; roh, gemein; **~ality** [bruːˈtæliti] Brutalität *f*, Roheit *f*; **~e** [bruːt] 1. tierisch; unvernünftig; gefühllos; 2. Vieh *n*; F Untier *n*, Scheusal *n*.

bubble ['bʌbl] 1. Blase *f*; Schwindel *m*; 2. sieden; sprudeln.

buccaneer [bʌkəˈniə] Seeräuber *m*.

buck [bʌk] 1. *zo.* Bock *m*; Stutzer *m*; *Am. sl.* Dollar *m*; 2. *v/i.* bocken; **~ for** *Am.* sich bemühen um; **~ up** F sich zs.-reißen; *v/t. Am.* F sich stemmen gegen; *Am.* F die Oberhand gewinnen wollen über *et.*

bucket ['bʌkit] Eimer *m*, Kübel *m*.

buckle ['bʌkl] 1. Schnalle *f*; 2. *v/t.* (an-, auf-, um-, zu)schnallen; *v/i.* ⊕ sich (ver)biegen; **~ to a task** sich ernsthaft an eine Aufgabe machen.

buck|shot *hunt.* ['bʌkʃɔt] Rehposten *m*; **~skin** Wildleder *n*.

bud [bʌd] 1. Knospe *f*; *fig.* Keim *m*; 2. *v/t.* ✗ veredeln; *v/i.* knospen.

buddy *Am.* F ['bʌdi] Kamerad *m*.

budge [bʌdʒ] (sich) bewegen.

budget ['bʌdʒit] Vorrat *m*; Staatshaushalt *m*; *draft*~ Haushaltsplan *m*.

buff [bʌf] 1. Ochsenleder *n*; Lederfarbe *f*; 2. lederfarben.

buffalo *zo.* ['bʌfələu] Büffel *m*.

buffer ⚙ ['bʌfə] Puffer *m*; Prellbock *m*.

buffet[1] ['bʌfit] 1. Puff *m*, Stoß *m*, Schlag *m*; 2. puffen, schlagen; kämpfen.

buffet[2] [~] Büfett *n*; Anrichte *f*.

buffet[3] ['bufei] Büfett *n*, Theke *f*; Tisch *m* mit Speisen u. Getränken; Erfrischungsraum *m*.

buffoon [bʌˈfuːn] Possenreißer *m*.

bug [bʌg] Wanze *f*; *Am.* Insekt *n*, Käfer *m*; *Am. sl.* Defekt *m*, Fehler *m*; *big* **~** *sl.* hohes Tier.

bugle ['bjuːgl] Wald-, Signalhorn *n*.

build [bild] 1. [*irr.*] bauen; errichten; 2. Bauart *f*; Schnitt *m*; **~er** ['bildə] Erbauer *m*, Baumeister *m*; **~ing** [~diŋ] Erbauen *n*; Bau *m*, Gebäude *n*; *attr.* Bau...

built [bilt] *pret. u. p.p. von* build 1.

bulb [bʌlb] ♀ Zwiebel *f*, Knolle *f*; (Glüh)Birne *f*.

bulge [bʌldʒ] 1. (Aus)Bauchung *f*; Anschwellung *f*; 2. sich (aus)bauchen; (an)schwellen; hervorquellen.

bulk [bʌlk] Umfang *m*; Masse *f*; Hauptteil *m*; ⚓ Ladung *f*; *in* **~** lose; *in großer Menge*; **~y** ['bʌlki] umfangreich; unhandlich; ☙ sperrig.

bull[1] [bul] 1. Bulle *m*, Stier *m*; ✝ *sl.* Haussier *m*; 2. ✝ *die Kurse* treiben.

bull[2] [~] *päpstliche* Bulle.

bulldog ['buldɔg] Bulldogge *f*.

bulldoze *Am.* F ['buldouz] terrorisieren; **~r** ⊕ [~zə] Bulldozer *m*, Planierraupe *f*.

bullet ['bulit] Kugel *f*, Geschoß *n*.

bulletin ['bulitin] Tagesbericht *m*; **~ board** *Am.* Schwarzes Brett.

bullion ['buljən] Gold-, Silberbarren *m*; Gold-, Silberlitze *f*.

bully ['buli] 1. Maulheld *m*; Tyrann *m*; 2. prahlerisch; *Am.* F prima; 3. einschüchtern; tyrannisieren.

bulwark *mst fig.* ['bulwək] Bollwerk *n*.

bum *Am.* F [bʌm] 1. Nichtstuer *m*, Vagabund *m*; 2. *v/t.* nassauern.

bumble-bee ['bʌmblbiː] Hummel *f*.

bump [bʌmp] 1. Schlag *m*; Beule *f*; *fig.* Sinn *m* (of für); 2. (zs.-)stoßen; holpern; *Rudern:* überholen.

bumper ['bʌmpə] volles Glas (*Wein*); F *et.* Riesiges; *mot.* Stoßstange *f*; **~ crop** Rekordernte *f*; **~ house** *thea.* volles Haus.

bun [bʌn] Rosinenbrötchen *n*; *Haar*-Knoten *m*.

bunch [bʌntʃ] 1. Bund *n*; Büschel *n*; Haufen *m*; **~ of grapes** Weintraube *f*; 2. (zs.-)bündeln; bauschen.

bundle ['bʌndl] 1. Bündel *n*, Bund *n*; 2. *v/t. a.* **~ up** (zs.-)bündeln.

bung [bʌŋ] Spund *m*.

bungalow ['bʌŋgəlou] Bungalow *m* (*einstöckiges Haus*).

bungle ['bʌŋgl] 1. Pfuscherei *f*; 2. (ver)pfuschen.

bunion ✗ ['bʌnjən] entzündeter Fußballen.

bunk[1] *Am. sl.* [bʌŋk] Quatsch *m*.

bunk[2] [~] Schlafkoje *f*.

bunny ['bʌni] Kaninchen *n*.

buoy ⚓ [bɔi] 1. Boje *f*; 2. *Fahrwasser* betonnen; *mst* **~ up** *fig.* aufrechterhalten; **~ant** □ ['bɔiənt] schwimmfähig; hebend; spannkräftig; *fig.* heiter.

burden ['bəːdn] 1. Last *f*; Bürde *f*; ⚓ Ladung *f*; ⚓ Tragfähigkeit *f*;

2. beladen; belasten; **~some** [~n-som] lästig; drückend.

bureau [bjuə'rou] Büro *n*, Geschäftszimmer *n*; Schreibpult *n*; *Am.* Kommode *f*; **~cracy** [~'rɔkrəsi] Bürokratie *f*.

burg F [bə:g] Stadt *f*.

burgess ['bə:dʒis] Bürger *m*.

burglar ['bə:glə] Einbrecher *m*; **~y** [~əri] Einbruch(sdiebstahl) *m*.

burial ['beriəl] Begräbnis *n*.

burlesque [bə:'lesk] **1.** possenhaft; **2.** Burleske *f*, Posse *f*; **3.** parodieren.

burly ['bə:li] stämmig, kräftig.

burn [bə:n] **1.** Brandwunde *f*; Brandmal *n*; **2.** [*irr.*] (ver-, an-) brennen; **~er** ['bə:nə] Brenner *m*.

burnish ['bə:niʃ] polieren, glätten.

burnt [bə:nt] *pret. u. p.p. von* burn 2.

burrow ['bʌrou] **1.** Höhle *f*, Bau *m*; **2.** (sich ein-, ver)graben.

burst [bə:st] **1.** Bersten *n*; Krach *m*; Riß *m*; Ausbruch *m*; **2.** [*irr.*] *v/i.* bersten, platzen; zerspringen; explodieren; **~** *from* sich losreißen von; **~** *forth*, **~** *out* hervorbrechen; **~** *into tears* in Tränen ausbrechen; *v/t.* (zer)sprengen.

bury ['beri] be-, vergraben; beerdigen; verbergen.

bus F [bʌs] (Omni)Bus *m*; **~** *boy Am.* Kellnergehilfe *m*.

bush [buʃ] Busch *m*; Gebüsch *n*.

bushel ['buʃl] Scheffel *m* (*36,37 Liter*).

bushy ['buʃi] buschig.

business ['biznis] Geschäft *n*; Beschäftigung *f*; Beruf *m*; Angelegenheit *f*; Aufgabe *f*; **✝** Handel *m*; **~** *of the day* Tagesordnung *f*; on **~** geschäftlich; *have no* **~** *to inf.* nicht befugt sein zu *inf.*; *mind one's own* **~** sich um s-e eigenen Angelegenheiten kümmern; **~** *hours pl.* Geschäftszeit *f*; **~like** geschäftsmäßig; sachlich; **~man** Geschäftsmann *m*; **~** *tour*, **~** *trip* Geschäftsreise *f*.

bust[1] [bʌst] Büste *f*.

bust[2] *Am.* F [~] Bankrott *m*.

bustle ['bʌsl] **1.** Geschäftigkeit *f*; geschäftiges Treiben; **2.** *v/i.* (umher)wirtschaften; hasten; *v/t.* hetzen, jagen.

busy □ ['bizi] **1.** beschäftigt; geschäftig; fleißig (*at* bei, *an dat.*); lebhaft; *Am. teleph.* besetzt; **2.** (*mst* **~** *o.s.* sich) beschäftigen (*with*, *in*, *at*, *about*, *ger.* mit).

but [bʌt, bət] **1.** *cj.* aber, jedoch, sondern; *a.* **~** *that* wenn nicht, indessen; **2.** *prp.* außer; *the last* **~** *one* der vorletzte; *the next* **~** *one* der übernächste; **~** *for* wenn nicht ... gewesen wäre; ohne; **3.** *nach Negation:* der (die od. das) nicht; *there is*

no one **~** *knows* es gibt niemand, der nicht wüßte; **4.** *adv.* nur; **~** *just* soeben, eben erst; **~** *now* erst jetzt; *all* **~** fast, nahe daran; *nothing* **~** nur; *I cannot* **~** *inf.* ich kann nur *inf.*

butcher ['butʃə] **1.** Schlächter *m*, Fleischer *m*, Metzger *m*; *fig.* Mörder *m*; **2.** (*fig.* ab-, hin)schlachten; **~y** [~əri] Schlächterei *f*; Schlachthaus *n*.

butler ['bʌtlə] Butler *m*; Kellermeister *m*.

butt [bʌt] **1.** Stoß *m*; *a.* **~** *end* (dikkes) Ende *e-s Baumes etc.*; Stummel *m*, Kippe *f*; *Gewehr-*Kolben *m*; Schießstand *m*; (End)Ziel *n*; *fig.* Zielscheibe *f*; **2.** (mit dem Kopf) stoßen.

butter ['bʌtə] **1.** Butter *f*; F Schmeichelei *f*; **2.** mit Butter bestreichen; **~cup** Butterblume *f*; **~-fingered** tolpatschig; **~fly** Schmetterling *m*; **~y** [~əri] **1.** butter(art)ig; Butter...; **2.** Speisekammer *f*.

buttocks ['bʌtəks] *pl.* Gesäß *n*.

button ['bʌtn] **1.** Knopf *m*; Knospe *f*; **2.** an-, zuknöpfen.

buttress ['bʌtris] **1.** Strebepfeiler *m*; *fig.* Stütze *f*; **2.** (unter)stützen.

buxom ['bʌksəm] drall, stramm.

buy [bai] [*irr.*] *v/t.* (an-, ein)kaufen (*from* bei); **~er** ['baiə] (Ein)Käufer (-in).

buzz [bʌz] **1.** Gesumm *n*; Geflüster *n*; **~** *saw Am.* Kreissäge *f*; **2.** *v/i.* summen; surren; **~** *about* herumschwirren, herumeilen.

buzzard ['bʌzəd] Bussard *m*.

by [bai] **1.** *prp. Raum:* bei; an, neben; *Richtung:* durch, über; an (*dat.*) entlang *od.* vorbei; *Zeit:* an, bei; spätestens bis, bis zu; *Urheber, Ursache:* von, durch (*bsd. beim pass.*); *Mittel, Werkzeug:* durch, mit; *Art u. Weise:* bei; *Schwur:* bei; *Maß:* um, bei; *Richtschnur:* gemäß, bei; **~** *the dozen* dutzendweise; **~** *o.s.* allein; **~** *land* zu Lande; **~** *rail* per Bahn; *day* **~** *day* Tag für Tag; **~** *twos* zu zweien; **2.** *adv.* dabei; vorbei; beiseite; **~** *and* **~** nächstens, bald; nach und nach; **~** *the* **~** nebenbei bemerkt; **~** *and large Am.* im großen und ganzen; **3.** *adj.* Neben...; Seiten...; **~-election** ['baiilekʃən] Nachwahl *f*; **~-gone** vergangen; **~-law** Ortsstatut *n*; **~s** *pl.* Satzung *f*, Statuten *n/pl.*; **~-line** *Am.* Verfasserangabe *f* *zu e-m Artikel*; **~-name** Bei-, Spitzname *m*; **~-pass** Umgehungsstraße *f*; **~-path** Seitenpfad *m*; **~-product** Nebenprodukt *n*; **~-road** Seitenweg *m*; **~-stander** Zuschauer *m*; **~-street** Neben-, Seitenstraße *f*; **~-way** Seitenweg *m*; **~-word** Sprichwort *n*; Inbegriff *m*; *be a* **~** *of* sprichwörtlich bekannt sein wegen.

C

cab [kæb] Droschke f, Mietwagen m, Taxi n; ⛴ Führerstand m.
cabbage ♀ ['kæbidʒ] Kohl m.
cabin ['kæbin] 1. Hütte f; ⚓ Kabine f, Kajüte f; Kammer f; 2. einpferchen; ~-boy Schiffsjunge m; ~ cruiser ⚓ Kabinenkreuzer m.
cabinet ['kæbinit] Kabinett n, Ministerrat m; Schrank m, Vitrine f; (Radio)Gehäuse n; ~ council Kabinettssitzung f; ~-maker Kunsttischler m.
cable ['keibl] 1. Kabel n; ⚓ Ankertau n; 2. tel. kabeln; ~-car Kabine f, Gondel f; Drahtseilbahn f; ~gram [⸱lgræm] Kabeltelegramm n.
cabman ['kæbmən] Droschkenkutscher m, Taxifahrer m.
caboose [kə'bu:s] ⚓ Kombüse f; Am. 🚂 Eisenbahnerwagen m am Güterzug.
cab-stand ['kæbstænd] Taxi-, Droschkenstand m.
cacao ♀ [kə'ka:ou] Kakaobaum m, -bohne f.
cackle ['kækl] 1. Gegacker n, Geschnatter n; 2. gackern, schnattern.
cad F [kæd] Prolet m; Kerl m.
cadaverous □ [kə'dævərəs] leichenhaft; leichenblaß.
cadence ♪ ['keidəns] Kadenz f; Tonfall m; Rhythmus m.
cadet [kə'det] Kadett m.
café ['kæfei] Café n.
cafeteria bsd. Am. [kæfi'tiəriə] Restaurant n mit Selbstbedienung.
cage [keidʒ] 1. Käfig m; Kriegsgefangenenlager n; ✗ Förderkorb m; 2. einsperren.
cagey □ bsd. Am. F ['keidʒi] gerissen, raffiniert.
cajole [kə'dʒoul] j-m schmeicheln; j-n beschwatzen.
cake [keik] 1. Kuchen m; Tafel f Schokolade, Riegel m Seife etc.; 2. zs.-backen.
calami|tous □ [kə'læmitəs] elend; katastrophal; ~ty [⸱ti] Elend n, Unglück n; Katastrophe f.
calcify ['kælsifai] (sich) verkalken.
calculat|e ['kælkjuleit] v/t. kalkulieren; be-, aus-, errechnen; v/i. rechnen (on, upon auf acc.); Am. F vermuten; ~ion [kælkju'leiʃən] Kalkulation f, Berechnung f; Voranschlag m; Überlegung f.
caldron ['kɔ:ldrən] Kessel m.
calendar ['kælində] 1. Kalender m; Liste f; 2. registrieren.
calf [ka:f], pl. calves [ka:vz] Kalb n; Wade f; a. ~-leather ['ka:fleðə] Kalbleder n; ~-skin Kalbfell n.
calibre ['kælibə] Kaliber n.
calico ✝ ['kælikou] Kaliko m.
call [kɔ:l] 1. Ruf m; teleph. Anruf m,

Gespräch n; fig. Berufung f (to in ein Amt; auf e-n Lehrstuhl); Aufruf m; Aufforderung f; Signal n; Forderung f; Besuch m; Nachfrage f (for nach); Kündigung f v. Geldern; on ~ ✝ auf Abruf; 2. v/t. (herbei-)rufen; (an)rufen; (ein)berufen; Am. Baseball: Spiel abbrechen; fig. berufen (to in ein Amt); nennen; wecken; Aufmerksamkeit lenken (to auf acc.); be ~ed heißen; ~ s.o. names j. beschimpfen, beleidigen; ~ down bsd. Am. F anpfeifen; ~ in Geld kündigen; ~ over Namen verlesen; ~ up aufrufen; teleph. anrufen; v/i. rufen; teleph. anrufen; vorsprechen (at an e-m Ort; on s.o. bei j-m); ~ at a port e-n Hafen anlaufen; ~ for rufen nach; et. fordern; abholen; to be (left till) ~ed for postlagernd; ~ on sich an j. wenden (for wegen); j. berufen, auffordern (to inf. zu); ~-box ['kɔ:lbɔks] Fernsprechzelle f; ~er ['kɔ:lə] teleph. Anrufer(in); Besucher(in).
calling ['kɔ:liŋ] Rufen n; Berufung f; Beruf m; ~ card Am. Visitenkarte f.
call-office ['kɔ:lɔfis] Fernsprechstelle f.
callous □ ['kæləs] schwielig; fig. dickfellig; herzlos.
callow ['kælou] nackt (ungefiedert); fig. unerfahren.
calm [ka:m] 1. □ still, ruhig; 2. (Wind)Stille f, Ruhe f; 3. (~ down sich) beruhigen; besänftigen.
calori|c phys. [kə'lɔrik] Wärme f; ~e phys. ['kælɔri] Wärmeeinheit f.
column|iate [kə'lʌmnieit] verleumden; ~iation [kəlʌmni'eiʃən], ~y ['kæləmni] Verleumdung f.
calve [ka:v] kalben; ~s [ka:vz] pl. von calf.
cambric ✝ ['keimbrik] Batist m.
came [keim] pret. von come.
camel zo., ⚓ ['kæməl] Kamel n.
camera ['kæmərə] Kamera f; in ~ ⚖ unter Ausschluß der Öffentlichkeit.
camomile ♀ ['kæməmail] Kamille f.
camouflage ✗ ['kæmufla:ʒ] 1. Tarnung f; 2. tarnen.
camp [kæmp] 1. Lager n; ✗ Feldlager n; ~ bed Feldbett n; 2. lagern; ~ out zelten.
campaign [kæm'pein] 1. Feldzug m; 2. e-n Feldzug mitmachen od. führen.
camphor ['kæmfə] Kampfer m.
campus Am. ['kæmpəs] Universitätsgelände n.
can¹ [kæn] [irr.] v/aux. können, fähig sein zu; dürfen.
can² [~] 1. Kanne f; Am. Büchse f; 2. Am. in Büchsen konservieren.

Canadian [kə'neidjən] **1.** kanadisch; **2.** Kanadier(in).

canal [kə'næl] Kanal m (a. 🐾).

canard [kæ'nɑːd] (Zeitungs)Ente f.

canary [kə'nɛəri] Kanarienvogel m.

cancel ['kænsəl] (durch)streichen; entwerten; absagen; a. ~ out fig. aufheben; be ~led ausfallen.

cancer ast., 🐾 ['kænsə] Krebs m; ~ous [~ərəs] krebsartig.

candid □ ['kændid] aufrichtig, offen.

candidate ['kændidit] Kandidat m (for für), Bewerber m (for um).

candied ['kændid] kandiert.

candle ['kændl] Licht n, Kerze f; burn the ~ at both ends mit s-n Kräften Raubbau treiben; ~stick Leuchter m.

cando(u)r ['kændə] Aufrichtigkeit f.

candy ['kændi] **1.** Kandis(zucker) m; Am. Süßigkeiten f/pl.; **2.** v/t. kandieren.

cane [kein] **1.** 🐾 Rohr n; (Rohr-) Stock m; **2.** prügeln.

canine ['keinain] Hunde...

canker ['kæŋkə] 🐾 Mundkrebs m; 🐾 Brand m.

canned Am. [kænd] Büchsen...

cannery Am. ['kænəri] Konservenfabrik f.

cannibal ['kænibəl] Kannibale m.

cannon ['kænən] Kanone f.

cannot ['kænət] nicht können etc.; s. can[1].

canoe [kə'nuː] Kanu n; Paddelboot n.

canon ['kænən] Kanon m; Regel f; Richtschnur f; ~ize [~naiz] heiligsprechen.

canopy ['kænəpi] Baldachin m; fig. Dach m; 🔺 Überdachung f.

cant[1] [kænt] **1.** Schrägung f; Stoß m; **2.** kippen; kanten.

cant[2] [~] **1.** Zunftsprache f; Gewäsch f; scheinheiliges Gerede f; **2.** zunftmäßig od. scheinheilig reden.

can't F [kɑːnt] = cannot.

cantankerous F □ [kən'tæŋkərəs] zänkisch, mürrisch.

canteen [kæn'tiːn] 🗙 Feldflasche f; Kantine f; 🗙 Kochgeschirr n; Besteckkasten m.

canton ['kæntən] Bezirk m; **2.** 🗙 [kən'tuːn] (sich) einquartieren.

canvas ['kænvəs] Segeltuch n; Zelt (-e pl.) n; Zeltbahn f; Segel n/pl.; paint. Leinwand f; Gemälde n.

canvass [~] **1.** (Stimmen)Werbung f; Am. a. Wahlnachprüfung f; **2.** v/t. erörtern; v/i. (Stimmen, a. Kunden) werben.

caoutchouc ['kautʃuk] Kautschuk m.

cap [kæp] **1.** Kappe f; Mütze f; Haube f; ⊕ Aufsatz m; Zündhütchen n; set one's ~ at sich e-n Mann

angeln (Frau); **2.** mit e-r Kappe etc. bedecken; fig. krönen; F übertreffen; die Mütze abnehmen.

capab|ility [keipə'biliti] Fähigkeit f; ~le □ ['keipəbl] fähig (of zu).

capaci|ous □ [kə'peiʃəs] geräumig; ~ty [kə'pæsiti] Inhalt m; Aufnahmefähigkeit f; geistige (od. ⊕ Leistungs)Fähigkeit f (for ger. zu inf.); Stellung f; in my ~ as in meiner Eigenschaft als.

cape[1] [keip] Kap n, Vorgebirge n.

cape[2] [~] Cape n, Umhang m.

caper ['keipə] **1.** Kapriole f, Luftsprung m; cut ~s = **2.** Kapriolen od. Sprünge machen.

capital ['kæpitl] **1.** □ Kapital...; todeswürdig, Todes...; hauptsächlich, Haupt...; vortrefflich; ~ crime Kapitalverbrechen n; ~ punishment Todesstrafe f; **2.** Hauptstadt f; Kapital n; mst ~ letter Großbuchstabe m; ~ism [~təlizəm] Kapitalismus m; ~ize [kə'pitəlaiz] kapitalisieren.

capitulate [kə'pitjuleit] kapitulieren (to vor dat.).

capric|e [kə'priːs] Laune f; ~ious □ [~iʃəs] kapriziös, launisch.

Capricorn ast. ['kæprikɔːn] Steinbock m.

capsize [kæp'saiz] v/i. kentern; v/t. zum Kentern bringen.

capsule ['kæpsjuːl] Kapsel f.

captain ['kæptin] Führer m; Feldherr m; 🚢 Kapitän m; 🗙 Hauptmann m.

caption ['kæpʃən] **1.** Überschrift f; Titel m; Film: Untertitel m; **2.** v/t. Am. mit Überschrift etc. versehen.

captious □ ['kæpʃəs] spitzfindig.

captiv|ate ['kæptiveit] fig. gefangennehmen, fesseln; ~e ['kæptiv] **1.** gefangen, gefesselt; **2.** Gefangene(r m) f; ~ity [kæp'tiviti] Gefangenschaft f.

capture ['kæptʃə] **1.** Eroberung f; Gefangennahme f; **2.** (ein)fangen; erobern; erbeuten; 🚢 kapern.

car [kɑː] Auto n; (Eisenbahn-, Straßenbahn)Wagen m; Ballonkorb m; Luftschiff-Gondel f; Kabine f e-s Aufzugs.

caramel ['kærəmel] Karamel m; Karamelle f.

caravan ['kærəvæn] Karawane f; Wohnwagen m.

caraway 🐾 ['kærəwei] Kümmel m.

carbine ['kɑːbain] Karabiner m.

carbohydrate 🐾 ['kɑːbou'haidreit] Kohle(n)hydrat m.

carbon ['kɑːbən] 🐾 Kohlenstoff m; ~ copy Brief-Durchschlag m; ~ paper Kohlepapier n.

carburet(t)or mot. ['kɑːbjuretə] Vergaser m.

car|case, mst ~cass ['kɑːkəs] (Tier-) Kadaver m; Fleischerei: Rumpf m.

card [kɑːd] Karte f; have a ~ up

one's s/eeve et. in petto haben;
~board ['kɑːbɔːd] Kartonpapier
n; Pappe f; ~ **box** Pappkarton m.
cardigan ['kɑːdigən] Wolljacke f.
cardinal □ ['kɑːdinl] 1. Haupt...;
hochrot; ~ **number** Grundzahl f; 2.
Kardinal m.
card-index ['kɑːdindeks] Kartei f.
card-sharper ['kɑːdʃɑːpə] Falsch-
spieler m.
care [kɛə] 1. Sorge f; Sorgfalt f,
Obhut f, Pflege f; medical ~ ärztliche Behandlung; ~ of (abbr. c/o) ...
per Adresse, bei ...; take ~ of
acht(geb)en auf (acc.); with ~! Vorsicht!; 2. Lust haben (to inf. zu);
~ for sorgen für; sich kümmern um;
sich etwas machen aus; I don't ~!
F meinetwegen!; I couldn't ~ less F
es ist mir völlig egal; well ~d-for
gepflegt. (bahn f; 2. rasen.)
career [kəˈriə] 1. Karriere f; Lauf-
carefree ['kɛəfriː] sorgenfrei.
careful □ ['kɛəful] besorgt (for um),
achtsam (of auf acc.); vorsichtig;
sorgfältig; **~ness** [~lnis] Sorgsam-
keit f; Vorsicht f; Sorgfalt f.
careless □ ['kɛəlis] sorglos; nachlässig; unachtsam; leichtsinnig;
~ness [~snis] Sorglosigkeit f; Nachlässigkeit f.
caress [kəˈres] 1. Liebkosung f;
2. liebkosen; fig. schmeicheln.
caretaker ['kɛəteikə] Wärter(in);
(Haus)Verwalter(in).
care-worn ['kɛəwɔːn] abgehärmt.
carfare Am. ['kɑːfɛə] Fahrgeld n.
cargo ⊕ ['kɑːgou] Ladung f.
caricature [ˌkærikəˈtjuə] 1. Karikatur f; 2. karikieren.
carmine ['kɑːmain] Karmin(rot) n.
carn|al □ ['kɑːnl] fleischlich; sinn-
lich; **~ation** [kɑːˈneiʃən] 1. Fleisch-
ton m; ⚘ Nelke f; 2. liebrot.
carnival ['kɑːnivl] Karneval m.
carnivorous [kɑːˈnivərəs] fleisch-
fressend.
carol ['kærəl] 1. Weihnachtslied n;
2. Weihnachtslieder singen.
carous|e [kəˈrauz] 1. a. **~al** [~zəl]
(Trink)Gelage n; 2. zechen.
carp [kɑːp] Karpfen m.
carpent|er ['kɑːpintə] · Zimmer-
mann m; **~ry** [~tri] Zimmerhand-
werk n; Zimmermannsarbeit f.
carpet ['kɑːpit] 1. Teppich m;
bring on the ~ aufs Tapet bringen;
2. mit e-m Teppich belegen; **~bag**
Reisetasche f; **~bagger** [~tbægə]
politischer Abenteurer.
carriage ['kæridʒ] Beförderung f,
Transport m; Fracht f; Wagen m;
Fuhr-, Frachtlohn m; Haltung f;
Benehmen n; **~drive** Anfahrt f
(vor e-m Hause); **~-free**, **~paid**
frachtfrei; **~way** Fahrbahn f.
carrier ['kæriə] Fuhrmann m;
Spediteur m; Träger m; Gepäckträger m; **~-pigeon** Brieftaube f.

carrion ['kæriən] Aas n; attr. Aas...
carrot ['kærət] Mohrrübe f.
carry ['kæri] 1. v/t. wohin bringen,
führen, tragen (a. v/i.), fahren, befördern; (bei sich) haben; Ansicht
durchsetzen; Gewinn, Preis davontragen; Zahlen übertragen; Ernte,
Zinsen tragen; Mauer etc. weiter-
führen; Benehmen fortsetzen; Antrag, Kandidaten durchbringen; ✕
erobern; be carried angenommen
werden (Antrag); durchkommen
(Kandidat); ~ the day den Sieg
davontragen; ~ forward od. over ✝
übertragen; ~ on fortsetzen, weiter-
führen; Geschäft etc. betreiben; ~
out od. through durchführen; 2.
Trag-, Schußweite f.
cart [kɑːt] 1. Karren m; Wagen m;
put the ~ before the horse fig. das
Pferd beim Schwanz aufzäumen;
2. karren, fahren; **~age** ['kɑːtidʒ]
Fahren n; Fuhrlohn m.
carter ['kɑːtə] Fuhrmann m.
cartilage ['kɑːtilidʒ] Knorpel m.
carton ['kɑːtən] Karton m.
cartoon [kɑːˈtuːn] paint. Karton m;
⊕ Musterzeichnung f; Karikatur f;
Zeichentrickfilm m; **~ist** [~nist]
Karikaturist m.
cartridge ['kɑːtridʒ] Patrone f;
~paper Zeichenpapier n.
cart-wheel ['kɑːtwiːl] Wagenrad n;
Am. Silberdollar m; turn ~s rad-
schlagen.
carve [kɑːv] Fleisch vorschneiden,
zerlegen; schnitzen; meißeln; **~r**
['kɑːvə] (Bild)Schnitzer m; Vor-
schneider m; Vorlegemesser n.
carving ['kɑːviŋ] Schnitzerei f.
cascade [kæsˈkeid] Wasserfall m.
case¹ [keis] m Behälter m; Kiste f;
Etui n; Gehäuse n; Schachtel f;
Fach n; typ. Setzkasten m; 2. (ein-)
stecken; ver-, umkleiden.
case² [~] Fall m (a. gr., ✻, ✝); gr.
Kasus m; ✻ a. Kranke(r m) f; Am.
F komischer Kauz; ✝ Schriftsatz
m; Hauptargument n; Sache f, Angelegenheit f.
case-harden ⊕ ['keishɑːdn] hart-
gießen; **~ed** fig. hartgesotten.
case-history ['keishistəri] Vor-
geschichte f; Krankengeschichte f.
casement ['keismənt] Fensterflügel
m; ~ window Flügelfenster n.
cash [kæʃ] 1. Bargeld n, Kasse f;
~ down, for ~ gegen bar; ~ on delivery Lieferung f gegen bar; (per)
Nachnahme f; ~ register Registrierkasse f; 2. einkassieren, einlösen; **~book** ['kæʃbuk] Kassa-
buch n; **~ier** [kæˈʃiə] Kassierer(in).
casing ['keisiŋ] Überzug m, Gehäuse n, Futteral n; △ Verkleidung f.
cask [kɑːsk] Faß n.
casket ['kɑːskit] Kassette f; Am.
Sarg m.

casserole ['kæsəroul] Kasserolle f.
cassock eccl. ['kæsək] Soutane f.
cast [kɑːst] 1. Wurf m; ⊕ Guß
(-form f) m; Abguß m, Abdruck m;
Schattierung f, Anflug m; Form f,
Art f; ⚓ Auswerfen n von Senkblei
etc.; thea. (Rollen)Besetzung f;
2. [irr.] v/t. (ab-, aus-, hin-, um-,
weg)werfen; zo. Haut etc. abwerfen; Zähne etc. verlieren; verwerfen; gestalten; ⊕ gießen; a.
~ up aus-, zs.-rechnen; thea. Rolle
besetzen; Rolle übertragen (to
dat.); be ~ in a lawsuit ⚖ e-n
Prozeß verlieren; ~ lots losen (for
um); ~ in one's lot with s.o. j-s Los
teilen; be ~ down niedergeschlagen
sein; v/i. sich gießen lassen; ⊕
sich (ver)werfen; ~ about for sinnen
auf (acc.); sich et. überlegen.
castanet [kæstə'net] Kastagnette f.
castaway ['kɑːstəwei] 1. verworfen,
⚓ schiffbrüchig; 2. Verworfene(r
m) f; Schiffbrüchige(r m) f.
caste [kɑːst] Kaste f (a. fig.).
castigate ['kæstigeit] züchtigen;
fig. geißeln.
cast iron ['kɑːst'aiən] Gußeisen n;
cast-iron gußeisern.
castle ['kɑːsl] Burg f, Schloß n;
Schach: Turm m.
castor[1] ['kɑːstə]: ~ oil Rizinusöl n.
castor[2] [⌐] Laufrolle f unter Möbeln;
(Salz-, Zucker- etc.) Streuer m.
castrate ['kæstreit] kastrieren.
cast steel ['kɑːst'stiːl] Gußstahl m;
cast-steel aus Gußstahl.
casual □ ['kæʒjuəl] zufällig; gelegentlich; F lässig; ~ty [⌐lti] Unfall m; ✕ Verlust m.
cat [kæt] Katze f; ~ burglar Fas-
sadenkletterer m.
catalo|gue, Am. ~g ['kætələg] 1. Ka-
talog m; Am. univ. Vorlesungs-
verzeichnis n; 2. katalogisieren.
catapult ['kætəpʌlt] Schleuder f;
✈ Katapult m, n.
cataract ['kætərækt] Katarakt m,
Wasserfall m; ⚕ grauer Star.
catarrh [kə'tɑː] Katarrh m; Schnupfen m.
catastrophe [kə'tæstrəfi] Kata-
strophe f.
catch [kætʃ] 1. Fang m; Beute f,
fig. Vorteil m; ♪ Rundgesang m;
Kniff m; ⊕ Haken m, Griff m,
Klinke f; 2. [irr.] v/t. fassen, F
kriegen; fangen, ergreifen; ertappen; Blick etc. auffangen; Zug
etc. erreichen; bekommen; sich
Krankheit zuziehen, holen; fig. erfassen; ~ (a) cold sich erkälten; ~
s.o.'s eye j-m ins Auge fallen; ~ up
auffangen; F j. unterbrechen; einholen; 3. v/i. sich verfangen, hängenbleiben; fassen, einschnappen
(Schloß etc.); ~ on F Anklang
finden; Am. F kapieren; ~ up with
✝. einholen; ~all ['kætʃɔːl] Am.

Platz m od. Behälter m für alles
mögliche (a. fig. u. attr.); ~er [⌐ʃə]
Fänger(in); ~ing [⌐ʃiŋ] packend; ✗
ansteckend; ~-line Schlagzeile f;
~word Schlagwort n; Stichwort n.
catechism ['kætikizəm] Katechismus m.
categor|ical □ [kæti'gɔrikəl] kate-
gorisch; ~y ['kætigəri] Kategorie f.
cater ['keitə]: ~ for Lebensmittel
liefern für; fig. sorgen für; ~ing
[⌐əriŋ] Verpflegung f.
caterpillar ['kætəpilə] zo. Raupe f;
⊕ Raupe(nschlepper m) f.
catgut ['kætgʌt] Darmsaite f.
cathedral [kə'θiːdrəl] Dom m,
Kathedrale f.
Catholic ['kæθəlik] 1. katholisch;
2. Katholik(in).
catkin ♀ ['kætkin] Kätzchen n.
cattish fig. ['kætiʃ] falsch.
cattle ['kætl] Vieh n; ~-breeding
Viehzucht f; ~-plague vet. Rinder-
pest f.   [catch 2.]
caught [kɔːt] pret. u. p.p. von⌐
ca(u)ldron ['kɔːldrən] Kessel m.
cauliflower ♀ ['kɔliflauə] Blumen-
kohl m.
caulk ⚓ [kɔːk] kalfatern (abdichten).
caus|al □ ['kɔːzəl] ursächlich; ~e
[kɔːz] 1. Ursache f, Grund m; ⚖
Klage(grund m) f; Prozeß m; Angelegenheit f, Sache f; 2. verursachen, veranlassen; ~eless □
['kɔːzlis] grundlos.
causeway ['kɔːzwei] Damm m.
caustic [U ['kɔːstik] (~ally) ätzend;
fig. beißend, scharf.
caution ['kɔːʃən] 1. Vorsicht f;
Warnung f; Verwarnung f; ~
money Kaution f; 2. warnen; verwarnen.
cautious □ ['kɔːʃəs] behutsam, vorsichtig; ~ness [⌐snis] Behutsam-
keit f, Vorsicht f.
cavalry ✕ ['kævəlri] Reiterei f.
cave [keiv] 1. Höhle f; 2. v/i. ~ in
einstürzen; klein beigeben.
cavern ['kævən] Höhle f; ~ous fig.
[⌐nəs] hohl.
cavil ['kævil] 1. Krittelei f; 2. kritteln (at, about an dat.).
cavity ['kæviti] Höhle f; Loch n.
cavort Am. F [kə'vɔːt] sich auf-
bäumen, umherspringen.
caw [kɔː] 1. krächzen; 2. Krächzen n.
cayuse Am. F ['kaijuːs] kleines
(Indianer)Pferd.
cease [siːs] v/i. (from) aufhören
(mit), ablassen (von); v/t. aufhören
mit; ~less □ ['siːslis] unaufhörlich.
cede [siːd] abtreten, überlassen.
ceiling ['siːliŋ] Zimmer-Decke f; fig.
Höchstgrenze f; ~ price Höchst-
preis m.
celebrat|e ['selibreit] feiern; ~ed
gefeiert, berühmt (for wegen);
~ion [seli'breiʃən] Feier f.

celebrity [si'lebriti] Berühmtheit f.

celerity [si'leriti] Geschwindigkeit f.

celery ♀ ['seləri] Sellerie m, f.

celestial □ [si'lestjəl] himmlisch.

celibacy ['selibəsi] Ehelosigkeit f.

cell [sel] allg. Zelle f; ⚡ Element n.

cellar ['selə] Keller m.

cement [si'ment] 1. Zement m; Kitt m; 2. zementieren; (ver)kitten.

cemetery ['semitri] Friedhof m.

censor ['sensə] 1. Zensor m; 2. zensieren; ~ious □ [sen'sɔːriəs] kritisch; kritt(e)lig; ~ship ['sensəʃip] Zensur f; Zensoramt n.

censure ['senʃə] 1. Tadel m; Verweis m; 2. tadeln.

census ['sensəs] Volkszählung f.

cent [sent] Hundert n; Am. Cent m = ¹/₁₀₀ Dollar; per ~ Prozent n.

centenary [sen'tiːnəri] Hundertjahrfeier f.

centennial [sen'tenjəl] 1. hundertjährig; 2. hundertjähriges Jubiläum.

centi|grade ['sentigreid]: 10 degrees ~ 10 Grad Celsius; ~metre, Am. ~meter Zentimeter n; m; ~pede zo. [~ipiːd] Hundertfüßer m.

central □ ['sentrəl] zentral; ~ heating Zentralheizung f; ~ office, ⚡ ~ station Zentrale f; ~ize [~laiz] zentralisieren.

cent|re, Am. ~er ['sentə] 1. Zentrum n, Mittelpunkt m; 2. zentral; 3. (sich) konzentrieren; zentralisieren; zentrieren.

century ['sentʃuri] Jahrhundert n.

cereal ['siəriəl] 1. Getreide...; 2. Getreide(pflanze f) n; Hafer-, Weizenflocken f/pl.; Corn-flakes pl.

cerebral anat. ['seribrəl] Gehirn...

ceremon|ial [seri'mounjəl] 1. □ a. ~ious □ [~jəs] zeremoniell; förmlich; 2. Zeremoniell n; ~y ['seriməni] Zeremonie f; Feierlichkeit f; Förmlichkeit(en pl.) f.

certain □ ['səːtn] sicher, gewiß; zuverlässig; bestimmt; gewisse(r, -s); ~ty [~nti] Sicherheit f, Gewißheit f; Zuverlässigkeit f.

certi|ficate 1. [sə'tifikit] Zeugnis n, Schein m; ~ of birth Geburtsurkunde f; medical ~ ärztliches Attest; 2. [~keit] bescheinigen; ~fication [səːtifi'keiʃən] Bescheinigung f; ~fy ['səːtifai] et. bescheinigen; bezeugen; ~tude [~itjuːd] Gewißheit f.

cessation [se'seiʃən] Aufhören n.

cession ['seʃən] Abtretung f.

cesspool ['sespuːl] Senkgrube f.

chafe [tʃeif] v/t. reiben; wundreiben; erzürnen; v/i. sich scheuern; sich wundreiben; toben.

chaff [tʃaːf] 1. Spreu f; Häcksel n; F Neckerei f; 2. zu Häcksel schneiden; F necken.

chaffer ['tʃæfə] feilschen.

chaffinch ['tʃæfintʃ] Buchfink m.

chagrin ['ʃægrin] 1. Ärger m; 2. ärgern.

chain [tʃein] 1. Kette f; fig. Fessel f; ~ store bsd. Am. Kettenladen m, Zweiggeschäft n; 2. (an)ketten; fig. fesseln.

chair [tʃeə] Stuhl m; Lehrstuhl m; Vorsitz m; be in the ~ den Vorsitz führen; ~man ['tʃeəmən] Vorsitzende(r) m; Präsident m.

chalice ['tʃælis] Kelch m.

chalk [tʃɔːk] 1. Kreide f; 2. mit Kreide (be)zeichnen; mst ~ up ankreiden; ~ out entwerfen.

challenge ['tʃælindʒ] 1. Herausforderung f; ✕ Anruf m; bsd. ⚖ Ablehnung f; 2. herausfordern; anrufen; ablehnen; anzweifeln.

chamber ['tʃeimbə] parl., zo., ♀, ⊕, Am. Kammer f; ~s pl. Geschäftsräume m/pl.; ~maid Zimmermädchen n.

chamois ['ʃæmwaː] 1. Gemse f; a. ~-leather [oft a. 'ʃæmileðə] Wildleder n; 2. chamois (gelbbraun).

champagne [ʃæm'pein] Champagner m.

champion ['tʃæmpjən] 1. Vorkämpfer m, Verfechter m; Verteidiger m; Sport: Meister m; 2. verteidigen; kämpfen für; fig. stützen; 3. großartig; ~ship Meisterschaft f.

chance [tʃaːns] 1. Zufall m; Schicksal n; Glück(sfall m) n; Chance f; Aussicht f (of auf acc.); (günstige) Gelegenheit; Möglichkeit f; by ~ zufällig; take a ~, take one's ~ es darauf ankommen lassen; 2. zufällig; gelegentlich; 3. v/i. geschehen; sich ereignen; ~ upon stoßen auf (acc.); v/t. F wagen.

chancellor ['tʃaːnsələ] Kanzler m.

chancery ['tʃaːnsəri] Kanzleigericht n; fig. in ~ in der Klemme.

chandelier [ʃændi'liə] Lüster m.

chandler ['tʃaːndlə] Krämer m.

change [tʃeindʒ] 1. Veränderung f, Wechsel m, Abwechs(e)lung f; Tausch m; Wechselgeld n; Kleingeld n; 2. v/t. (ver)ändern; (aus)wechseln, (aus-, ver)tauschen (for gegen); ~ trains umsteigen; v/i. sich ändern, wechseln; sich umziehen; ~able □ ['tʃeindʒəbl] veränderlich; ~less □ [~dʒlis] unveränderlich; ~ling [~liŋ] Wechselbalg m; ~ over Umstellung f.

channel ['tʃænl] 1. Kanal m; Flußbett n; Rinne f; fig. Weg m; 2. furchen; aushöhlen.

chant [tʃaːnt] 1. (Kirchen)Gesang m; fig. Singsang m; 2. singen.

chaos ['keiɔs] Chaos n.

chap¹ [tʃæp] 1. Riß m, Sprung m; 2. rissig machen od. werden.

chap² F [~] Bursche m, Kerl m, Junge m.

chap³ [␣] Kinnbacken *m*; ␣s *pl.* Maul *n*; ⊕ Backen *f/pl.*

chapel ['tʃæpəl] Kapelle *f*; Gottesdienst *m*.

chaplain ['tʃæplin] Kaplan *m*.

chapter ['tʃæptə] Kapitel *n*; *Am.* Orts-, Untergruppe *f e-r Vereinigung.*

char [tʃɑː] verkohlen.

character ['kæriktə] Charakter *m*; Merkmal *n*; Schrift(zeichen *n*) *f*; Sinnesart *f*; Persönlichkeit *f*; Original *n*; *thea., Roman:* Person *f*; Rang *m*, Würde *f*; (*bsd.* guter) Ruf; Zeugnis *n*; ␣istic [kæriktə'ristik] 1. (␣ally) charakteristisch (*of für*); 2. Kennzeichen, ␣ize ['kæriktəraiz] charakterisieren.

charcoal ['tʃɑːkoul] Holzkohle *f*.

charge [tʃɑːdʒ] 1. Ladung *f*; *fig.* Last *f* (*on für*); Verwahrung *f*, Obhut *f*; Schützling *m*; Mündel *m, f, n*; Amt *n*, Stelle *f*; Auftrag *m*, Befehl *m*; Angriff *m*; Ermahnung *f*; Beschuldigung *f*, Anklage *f*; Preis *m*, Forderung *f*; ␣s *pl.* ✝ Kosten *pl.*; be in ␣ of *et.* in Verwahrung haben; mit *et.* beauftragt sein; für *et.* sorgen; 2. *v/t.* laden; beladen, belasten; beauftragen; *j-m et.* einschärfen, befehlen; ermahnen; beschuldigen, anklagen (*with gen.*); zuschreiben (*on, upon dat.*); fordern, verlangen; an-, berechnen, in Rechnung stellen (*to dat.*); angreifen (*a. v/i.*); behaupten.

chariot *poet. od. hist.* ['tʃæriət] Streit-, Triumphwagen *m*.

charitable □ ['tʃæritəbl] mild(tätig), wohltätig.

charity ['tʃæriti] Nächstenliebe *f*; Wohltätigkeit *f*; Güte *f*; Nachsicht *f*; milde Gabe.

charlatan ['ʃɑːlətən] Marktschreier *m*.

charm [tʃɑːm] 1. Zauber *m*; *fig.* Reiz *m*; 2. bezaubern; *fig.* entzücken; ␣ing □ ['tʃɑːmiŋ] bezaubernd.

chart [tʃɑːt] 1. ⚓ Seekarte *f*; Tabelle *f*; 2. auf e-r Karte einzeichnen.

charter ['tʃɑːtə] 1. Urkunde *f*; Freibrief *m*; Patent *n*; Frachtvertrag *m*; 2. privilegieren; ⚓, ✈ chartern, mieten.

charwoman ['tʃɑːwumən] Putz-, Reinemachefrau *f*.

chary ['tʃɛəri] vorsichtig.

chase [tʃeis] 1. Jagd *f*; Verfolgung *f*; gejagtes Wild; 2. jagen, hetzen; Jagd machen auf (*acc.*).

chasm ['kæzəm] Kluft *f* (*a. fig.*); Lücke *f*.

chaste □ [tʃeist] rein, keusch, unschuldig; schlicht (*Stil*).

chastise [tʃæs'taiz] züchtigen.

chastity ['tʃæstiti] Keuschheit *f*.

chat [tʃæt] 1. Geplauder *n*, Plauderei *f*; 2. plaudern.

chattels ['tʃætlz] *pl. mst* goods and ␣ Hab *n* und Gut *n*; Vermögen *n*.

chatter ['tʃætə] 1. plappern; schnattern; klappern; 2. Geplapper *n*; ␣box F Plaudertasche *f*; ␣er [␣ərə] Schwätzer(in).

chatty ['tʃæti] gesprächig.

chauffeur ['ʃoufə] Chauffeur *m*.

chaw *sl.* [tʃɔː] kauen; ␣ up *Am. mst fig.* fix und fertig machen.

cheap □ [tʃiːp] billig; *fig.* gemein; ␣en ['tʃiːpən] (sich) verbilligen; *fig.* herabsetzen.

cheat [tʃiːt] 1. Betrug *m*, Schwindel *m*; Betrüger(in); 2. betrügen.

check [tʃek] 1. Schach(stellung *f*) *n*; Hemmnis *n* (*on für*); Zwang *m*, Aufsicht *f*; Kontrolle *f* (*on gen.*); Kontrollmarke *f*; *Am.* (Gepäck-) Schein *m*; *Am.* ✝ = cheque; *Am.* Rechnung *f im Restaurant*; karierter Stoff; 2. *v/i.* an-, innehalten; *Am.* e-n Scheck ausstellen; ␣ in *Am.* (in e-m Hotel) absteigen; ␣ out *Am.* das Hotel (*nach Bezahlung der Rechnung*) verlassen; *v/t.* hemmen; kontrollieren; nachprüfen; *Kleider* in der Garderobe abgeben; *Am. Gepäck* aufgeben; ␣er ['tʃekə] Aufsichtsbeamte(r) *m*; ␣s *pl. Am.* Damespiel *n*; ␣ing-room [␣kiŋrum] *Am.* Gepäckaufbewahrung *f*; ␣mate 1. Schachmatt *n*; 2. matt setzen; ␣up *Am.* scharfe Kontrolle.

cheek [tʃiːk] Backe *f*, Wange *f*; Unverschämtheit *f*; cheeky F ['tʃiːki] frech.

cheer [tʃiə] 1. Stimmung *f*, Fröhlichkeit *f*; Hoch(ruf *m*) *n*; Beifall(sruf) *m*; Speisen *f/pl.*, Mahl *n*; three ␣s! dreimal hoch!; 2. *v/t. a.* ␣ up aufheitern; mit Beifall begrüßen; *a.* ␣ on anspornen; *v/i.* hoch rufen; jauchzen; *a.* ␣ up Mut fassen; ␣ful □ ['tʃiəful] heiter; ␣io F [␣əri'ou] mach's gut!, tschüs!; prosit!; ␣less □ [␣əlis] freudlos; ␣y □ [␣əri] heiter, froh.

cheese [tʃiːz] Käse *m*.

chef [ʃef] Küchenchef *m*.

chemical ['kemikəl] 1. □ chemisch; 2. ␣s *pl.* Chemikalien *pl*.

chemise [ʃi'miːz] (Frauen)Hemd *n*.

chemist ['kemist] Chemiker(in); Apotheker *m*; Drogist *m*; ␣ry [␣tri] Chemie *f*.

cheque ✝ [tʃek] Scheck *m*; crossed ␣ Verrechnungsscheck *m*.

chequer ['tʃekə] 1. *mst* ␣s *pl.* Karomuster *n*; 2. karieren; ␣ed gewürfelt; *fig.* bunt.

cherish ['tʃeriʃ] hegen, pflegen.

cherry ['tʃeri] Kirsche *f*.

chess [tʃes] Schach(spiel) *n*; ␣board ['tʃesbɔːd] Schachbrett *n*; ␣man Schachfigur *f*.

chest [tʃest] Kiste *f*, Lade *f*; *anat.* Brustkasten *m*; ␣ of drawers Kommode *f*.

chestnut ['tʃesnʌt] 1. ⚘ Kastanie f;
F alter Witz; 2. kastanienbraun.

chevy F ['tʃevi] 1. Hetzjagd f;
Barlaufspiel n; 2. hetzen, jagen.

chew [tʃu:] kauen; sinnen; ~ the
fact od. rag Am. sl. die Sache
durchkauen; ~ing-gum ['tʃu(:)iŋ-
gʌm] Kaugummi m.

chicane [ʃi'kein] 1. Schikane f;
2. schikanieren.

chicken ['tʃikin] Hühnchen n, Küken n; ~-hearted furchtsam, feige;
~-pox [~pɒks] Windpocken
f/pl.

chid [tʃid] pret. u. p.p. von chide;
~den ['tʃidn] p.p. von chide.

chide lit. [tʃaid] [irr.] schelten.

chief [tʃi:f] 1. □ oberst; Ober...,
Haupt...; hauptsächlich; ~ clerk
Bürovorsteher m; 2. Oberhaupt n,
Chef m; Häuptling m; ...-in-~
Ober...; ~tain ['tʃi:ftən] Häuptling
m.

chilblain ['tʃilblein] Frostbeule f.

child [tʃaild] Kind n; from a ~ von
Kindheit an; with ~ schwanger;
~birth ['tʃaildbə:θ] Niederkunft f;
~hood [~dhud] Kindheit f; ~ish □
[~diʃ] kindlich; kindisch; ~like
kindlich; ~ren ['tʃildrən] pl. v. child.

chill [tʃil] 1. eisig, frostig; 2. Frost
m, Kälte f; ⚕ Fieberfrost m; Erkältung f; 3. v/t. erkalten lassen;
abkühlen; v/i. erkalten; erstarren;
~y ['tʃili] kalt, frostig.

chime [tʃaim] 1. Glockenspiel n;
Geläut n; fig. Einklang m; 2. läuten;
fig. harmonieren, übereinstimmen.

chimney ['tʃimni] Schornstein m;
Rauchfang m; Lampen-Zylinder m;
~-sweep(er) Schornsteinfeger m.

chin [tʃin] 1. Kinn n; take it on the ~
Am. F es standhaft ertragen; 2.: ~
o.s. Am. e-n Klimmzug machen.

china ['tʃainə] Porzellan n.

Chinese ['tʃai'ni:z] 1. chinesisch;
2. Chinese(n pl.) m, Chinesin f.

chink [tʃiŋk] Ritz m, Spalt m.

chip [tʃip] 1. Schnitzel n, Stückchen
n; Span m; Glas- etc. Splitter m;
Spielmarke f; have a ~ on one's
shoulder Am. F aggressiv sein; ~s pl.
Pommes frites pl.; 2. v/t. schnitzeln; an-, abschlagen; v/i. ab-
bröckeln; ~muck ['tʃipmʌk], ~
munk [~ʌŋk] nordamerikanisches
gestreiftes Eichhörnchen.

chirp [tʃə:p] 1. zirpen; zwitschern;
2. Gezirp n.

chisel ['tʃizl] 1. Meißel m; 2. meißeln; sl. (be)mogeln.

chit-chat ['tʃittʃæt] Geplauder n.

chivalr|ous □ ['ʃivəlrəs] ritterlich;
~y [~ri] Ritterschaft f, Rittertum n;
Ritterlichkeit f.

chive ⚘ [tʃaiv] Schnittlauch m.

chlor|ine ['klɔ:ri:n] Chlor n; ~o-
form ['klɔrəfɔ:m] 1. Chloroform n;
2. chloroformieren.

chocolate ['tʃɔkəlit] Schokolade f.

choice [tʃɔis] 1. Wahl f; Auswahl f;
2. □ auserlesen, vorzüglich.

choir ['kwaiə] Chor m.

choke [tʃouk] 1. v/t. (er)würgen,
(a. v/i.) ersticken; ≠ (ab)drosseln;
(ver)stopfen; mst ~ down hinunter-
würgen; 2. Erstickungsanfall m; ⊕
Würgung f; mot. Choke m, Starter-
klappe f.

choose [tʃu:z] [irr.] (aus)wählen;
~ to inf. vorziehen zu inf.

chop [tʃɔp] 1. Hieb m; Kotelett n;
~s pl. Maul n, Rachen m; ⊕
Backen f/pl.; 2. v/t. hauen, hacken;
zerhacken; austauschen; v/i. wechseln; ~per ['tʃɔpə] Hackmesser n;
~py [~pi] unstet; unruhig (See);
böig (Wind).

choral ['kɔ:rəl] chormäßig;
Chor...; ~(e) ♪ [kɔ'ra:l] Choral m.

chord [kɔ:d] Saite f; Akkord m.

chore Am. [tʃɔ:] Hausarbeit f (mst
pl.).

chorus ['kɔrəs] 1. Chor m; Kehrreim m; 2. im Chor singen od.
sprechen.

chose [tʃouz] pret. von choose; ~n
['tʃouzn] p.p. von choose.

chow Am. sl. [tʃau] Essen n.

Christ [kraist] Christus m.

christen ['krisn] taufen; ~ing
[~niŋ] Taufe f; attr. Tauf...

Christian ['kristjən] 1. □ christ-
lich; ~ name Vor-, Taufname m;
2. Christ(in); ~ity [kristi'æniti]
Christentum n.

Christmas ['krisməs] Weihnachten n.

chromium ['kroumjəm] Chrom n
(Metall); ~-plated verchromt.

chronic ['krɔnik] (~ally) chronisch
(mst ⚕), dauernd; sl. ekelhaft; ~le
[~kl] 1. Chronik f; 2. aufzeichnen.

chronolog|ical □ [krɔnə'lɔdʒikəl]
chronologisch; ~y [krɔ'nɔlədʒi]
Zeitrechnung f; Zeitfolge f.

chubby F ['tʃʌbi] rundlich; paus-
bäckig; plump (a. fig.).

chuck¹ [tʃʌk] 1. Glucken n; my ~!
mein Täubchen!; 2. glucken.

chuck² F [~] 1. schmeißen; 2. (Hinaus)Wurf m.

chuckle ['tʃʌkl] kichern, glucksen.

chum F [tʃʌm] 1. (Stuben)Kame-
rad m; 2. zs.-wohnen.

chump F [tʃʌmp] Holzklotz m.

chunk F [tʃʌnk] Klotz m.

church [tʃə:tʃ] Kirche f; attr.
Kirch(en)...; ~ service Gottesdienst
m; ~warden ['tʃə:tʃ'wɔ:dn] Kir-
chenvorsteher m; ~yard Kirchhof
m.

churl [tʃə:l] Grobian m; Flegel m;
~ish □ ['tʃə:liʃ] grob, flegelhaft.

churn [tʃə:n] 1. Butterfaß n; 2. but-
tern; aufwühlen.

chute [ʃu:t] Stromschnelle f; Gleit-,
Rutschbahn f; Fallschirm m.

cider ['saidə] Apfelmost *m*.

cigar [si'gɑː] Zigarre *f*.

cigarette [sigə'ret] Zigarette *f*; **~-case** Zigarettenetui *n*.

cigar-holder [si'gɑːhouldə] Zigarrenspitze *f*.

cilia ['siliə] *pl*. (Augen)Wimpern *f/pl*.

cinch *Am. sl.* [sintʃ] sichere Sache.

cincture ['siŋktʃə] Gürtel *m*, Gurt *m*.

cinder ['sində] Schlacke *f*; **~s** *pl*. Asche *f*; **♀ella** [sində'relə] Aschenbrödel *n*; **~-path** *Sport*: Aschenbahn *f*.

cine-camera ['sini'kæmərə] Filmkamera *f*.

cinema ['sinəmə] Kino *n*; Film *m*.

cinnamon ['sinəmən] Zimt *m*.

cipher ['saifə] 1. Ziffer *f*; Null *f* (*a. fig.*); Geheimschrift *f*, Chiffre *f*; 2. chiffrieren; (aus)rechnen.

circle ['səːkl] 1. Kreis *m*; Bekannten- *etc.* Kreis *m*; Kreislauf *m*; *thea.* Rang *m*; Ring *m*; 2. (um)kreisen.

circuit ['səːkit] Kreislauf *m*; ⚡ Stromkreis *m*; Rundreise *f*; Gerichtsbezirk *m*; ⚡ Rundflug *m*; **short** ~ ⚡ Kurzschluß *m*; **~ous** □ [sə(:)'kju(:)itəs] weitschweifig; Um...

circular ['səːkjulə] 1. □ kreisförmig; Kreis...; **~** *letter* Rundschreiben *n*; **~** *note* ♁ Kreditbrief *m*; 2. Rundschreiben *n*; Laufzettel *m*.

circulat|e ['səːkjuleit] *v/i.* umlaufen, zirkulieren; *v/t.* in Umlauf setzen; *~ing* [~tiŋ]: ~ *library* Leihbücherei *f*; **~ion** [səːkju'leiʃən] Zirkulation *f*, Kreislauf *m*; *fig.* Umlauf *m*; Verbreitung *f*; Zeitungs-Auflage *f*.

circum|... ['səːkəm] (her)um; **~ference** [se'kʌmfərəns] (Kreis-)Umfang *m*, Peripherie *f*; **~jacent** [səːkəm'dʒeisənt] umliegend; **~locution** [~mlə'kjuːʃən] Umständlichkeit *f*; Weitschweifigkeit *f*; **~navigate** [~m'nævigeit] umschiffen; **~scribe** ['səːkəmskraib] ♁ umschreiben; *fig.* begrenzen; **~spect** □ [~spekt] um-, vorsichtig; **~stance** [~stəns] Umstand *m* (~s *pl. a.* Verhältnisse *n/pl.*); Einzelheit *f*; Umständlichkeit *f*; **~stantial** □ [səːkəm'stænʃəl] umständlich; ~ *evidence* ♁ Indizienbeweis *m*; **~vent** [~m'vent] überlisten; vereiteln.

circus ['səːkəs] Zirkus *m*; (runder) Platz.

cistern ['sistən] Wasserbehälter *m*.

cit|ation [sai'teiʃən] **Vorladung** *f*; Anführung *f*, Zitat *n*; *Am. öffentliche* Ehrung; **~e** [sait] ♁ vorladen; anführen; zitieren.

citizen ['sitizn] (Staats)Bürger(in); Städter(in); **~ship** [~nʃip] Bürgerrecht *n*, Staatsangehörigkeit *f*.

citron ['sitrən] Zitrone *f*.

city ['siti] 1. Stadt *f*; *the* ♀ die City, das Geschäftsviertel; 2. städtisch, Stadt...; ♀ *article* Börsen-, Handelsbericht *m*; ~ *editor Am.* Lokalredakteur *m*; ~ *hall Am.* Rathaus *n*; ~ *manager Am.* Oberstadtdirektor *m*.

civic ['sivik] (staats)bürgerlich; städtisch; **~s** *sg.* Staatsbürgerkunde *f*.

civil □ ['sivl] bürgerlich, Bürger...; zivil; ♁ zivilrechtlich; höflich; ♀ *Servant* Verwaltungsbeamt|e(r) *m*, -in *f*; ♀ *Service* Staatsdienst *m*; **~ian** ✗ [si'viljən] Zivilist *m*; **~ity** [~liti] Höflichkeit *f*; **~ization** [sivilai'zeiʃən] Zivilisation *f*, Kultur *f*; **~ize** [si'vilaiz] zivilisieren.

clad [klæd] 1. *pret. u. p.p. von clothe*; 2. *adj.* gekleidet.

claim [kleim] 1. Anspruch *m*; Anrecht *n* (*to* auf *acc.*); Forderung *f*; *Am.* Parzelle *f*; 2. beanspruchen; fordern; sich berufen auf (*acc.*); ~ *to be* sich ausgeben für; **~ant** ['kleimənt] Beanspruchende(r *m*) *f*; ♁ Kläger *m*.

clairvoyant(e) [klɛə'vɔiənt] Hellseher(in).

clamber ['klæmbə] klettern.

clammy □ ['klæmi] feuchtkalt, klamm.

clamo(u)r ['klæmə] 1. Geschrei *n*, Lärm *m*; 2. schreien (*for* nach).

clamp ⊕ [klæmp] 1. Klammer *f*; 2. verklammern; befestigen.

clan [klæn] Clan *m*, Sippe *f* (*a. fig.*).

clandestine □ [klæn'destin] heimlich; Geheim...

clang [klæŋ] 1. Klang *m*, Geklirr *n*; 2. schallen; klirren (lassen).

clank [klæŋk] 1. Gerassel *n*, Geklirr *n*; 2. rasseln, klirren (mit).

clap [klæp] 1. Klatschen *n*; Schlag *m*, Klaps *m*; 2. schlagen (mit); klatschen; **~board** *Am.* ['klæpbɔːd] Schaltbrett *n*; **~trap** Effekthascherei *f*.

claret ['klærət] roter Bordeaux; *allg.* Rotwein *m*; Weinrot *n*; *sl.* Blut *n*.

clarify ['klærifai] *v/t.* (ab)klären; *fig.* klären; *v/i.* sich klären.

clarity ['klæriti] Klarheit *f*.

clash [klæʃ] 1. Geklirr *n*; Zs.-stoß *m*; Widerstreit *m*; 2. klirren (mit); zs.-stoßen.

clasp [klɑːsp] 1. Haken *m*, Klammer *f*; Schnalle *f*; Spange *f*; *fig.* Umklammerung *f*; Umarmung *f*; 2. *v/t.* an-, zuhaken; *fig.* umklammern; umfassen; *v/i.* festhalten; **~-knife** ['klɑːsp'naif] Taschenmesser *n*.

class [klɑːs] 1. Klasse *f*; Stand *m*; (Unterrichts)Stunde *f*; Kurs *m*; *Am. univ.* Jahrgang *m*; 2. (in Klassen) einteilen, einordnen.

classic ['klæsik] Klassiker *m*; **~s**

pl. die alten Sprachen; ~(al □) [~k(əl)] klassisch.

classi|fication [klæsifi'keiʃən] Klassifizierung *f*, Einteilung *f*; ~fy ['klæsifai] klassifizieren, einstufen.

clatter ['klætə] 1. Geklapper *n*; 2. klappern (mit); *fig.* schwatzen.

clause [klɔ:z] Klausel *f*, Bestimmung *f*; *gr.* (Neben)Satz *m*.

claw [klɔ:] 1. Klaue *f*, Kralle *f*, Pfote *f*; *Krebs*-Schere *f*; 2. (zer)-kratzen; (um)krallen.

clay [klei] Ton *m*; *fig.* Erde *f*.

clean [kli:n] 1. *adj.* □ rein; sauber; 2. *adv.* rein, völlig; 3. reinigen (*of* von); sich waschen lassen (*Stoff etc.*); ~ up aufräumen; ~er ['kli:nə] Reiniger *m*; *mst* ~s *pl.* (chemische) Reinigung; ~ing [~niŋ] Reinigung *f*; ~liness ['klenlinis] Reinlichkeit *f*; ~ly 1. *adv.* ['kli:nli] rein; sauber; 2. *adj.* ['klenli] reinlich; ~se [klenz] reinigen; säubern.

clear [kliə] 1. □ klar; hell, rein; *fig.* rein (*from* von); frei (*of* von); ganz, voll; ✝ rein, netto; 2. *v/t.* er-, aufhellen; (auf)klären; reinigen (*of, from* von); *Wald* lichten, roden; wegräumen (*a.* ~ *away od. off*); *Hindernis* nehmen; *Rechnung* bezahlen; ✝ (aus)klarieren, verzollen; ✝ freisprechen; befreien; rechtfertigen (*from* von); *v/i. a.* ~ *up* sich aufhellen; sich verziehen; ~ance ['kliərəns] Aufklärung *f*; Freilegung *f*; Räumung *f*; ✝ Abrechnung *f*; ✝, ✝ Verzollung *f*; ~ing [~riŋ] Aufklärung *f*; Lichtung *f*, Rodung *f*; ✝ Ab-, Verrechnung *f*; 2 *House* Ab-, Verrechnungsstelle *f*.

cleave[1] [kli:v] [*irr.*] (sich) spalten; *Wasser*, *Luft* (zer)teilen.

cleave[2] [~] *fig.* festhalten (*to an dat.*); treu bleiben (*dat.*).

cleaver ['kli:və] Hackmesser *n*.

clef ♪ [klef] Schlüssel *m*.

cleft [kleft] 1. Spalte *f*; Sprung *m*, Riß *m*; 2. *pret. u. p.p. von* cleave[1].

clemen|cy ['klemənsi] Milde *f*; ~t □ [~nt] mild.

clench [klentʃ] *Lippen etc.* fest zs.-pressen; *Zähne* zs.-beißen; *Faust* ballen; festhalten.

clergy ['klə:dʒi] Geistlichkeit *f*; ~man Geistliche(r) *m*.

clerical ['klerikəl] 1. □ geistlich; Schreib(er)...; 2. Geistliche(r) *m*.

clerk [kla:k] Schreiber(in); Büroangestellte(r *m*) *f*; Sekretär(in); ✝ kaufmännische(r) Angestellte(r); *Am.* Verkäufer(in); Küster *m*.

clever ['klevə] geschickt; gescheit.

clew [klu:] Knäuel *m*, *n*; = clue.

click [klik] 1. Knacken *n*; ⊕ Sperrhaken *m*, -klinke *f*; 2. knacken; zu-, einschnappen; klappen.

client ['klaiənt] Klient(in); Kund|e

m, -in *f*; ~ele [kli:ã:n'teil] Kundschaft *f*.

cliff [klif] Klippe *f*; Felsen *m*.

climate ['klaimit] Klima *n*.

climax ['klaimæks] 1. *rhet.* Steigerung *f*; Gipfel *m*, Höhepunkt *m*; 2. (sich) steigern.

climb [klaim] (er)klettern, (er)klimmen, (er)steigen; ~er ['klaimə] Kletterer *m*, Bergsteiger(in); *fig.* Streber(in); ♀ Kletterpflanze *f*; ~ing [~miŋ] Klettern *n*; *attr.* Kletter...

clinch [klintʃ] 1. ⊕ Vernietung *f*; Festhalten *n*; *Boxen*: Umklammerung *f*; 2. *v/t.* vernieten; festmachen; *s. clench*; *v/i.* festhalten.

cling [kliŋ] [*irr.*] (to) festhalten (an *dat.*), sich klammern (an *acc.*); sich (an)schmiegen (an *acc.*); *j-m* anhängen.

clinic ['klinik] Klinik *f*; klinisches Praktikum; ~al □ [~kəl] klinisch.

clink [kliŋk] 1. Geklirr *n*; 2. klingen, klirren (lassen); klimpern mit; ~er ['kliŋkə] Klinker(stein) *m*.

clip[1] [klip] 1. Schur *f*; *at one* ~ *Am.* F auf einmal; 2. ab-, aus-, beschneiden; *Schafe etc.* scheren.

clip[2] [~] Klammer *f*; Spange *f*.

clipp|er ['klipə]: (*a. pair of*) ~s *pl.* Haarschneide-, Schermaschine *f*; Klipper *m*; ⊕ Schnellsegler *m*; ⚡ Verkehrsflugzeug *n*; ~ings [~piŋz] *pl.* Abfälle *m/pl.*; Zeitungs- *etc.* Ausschnitte *m/pl.*

cloak [klouk] 1. Mantel *m*; 2. *fig.* bemänteln, verhüllen; ~-room ['kloukrum] Garderobe(nraum *m*) *f*; Toilette *f*; ⚙ Gepäckabgabe *f*.

clock [klɔk] Schlag-, Wand-Uhr *f*; ~wise ['klɔkwaiz] im Uhrzeigersinn; ~work Uhrwerk *n*; *like* ~ wie am Schnürchen.

clod [klɔd] Erdklumpen *m*; *a.* ~-hopper (Bauern)Tölpel *m*.

clog [klɔg] 1. Klotz *m*; Holzschuh *m*, Pantine *f*; 2. belasten; hemmen; (sich) verstopfen.

cloister ['klɔistə] Kreuzgang *m*; Kloster *n*.

close 1. □ [klous] geschlossen; verborgen; verschwiegen; knapp, eng; begrenzt; nah, eng; bündig; dicht; gedrängt; schwül; knickerig; genau; fest (*Griff*); ~ *by*, ~ *to* dicht bei; ~ *fight*, ~ *quarters pl.* Handgemenge *n*, Nahkampf *m*; ~(ed) *season*, ~ *time hunt.* Schonzeit *f*; *sail* ~ *to the wind fig.* sich hart an der Grenze des Erlaubten bewegen; 2. [klouz] Schluß *m*; Abschluß *m*; [klous] Einfriedung *f*; Hof *m*; 3. [klouz] *v/t.* (ab-, ein-, ver-)schließen; beschließen; *v/i.* (sich) schließen; abschließen; handgemein werden; ~ *in* hereinbrechen (*Nacht*); kürzer werden (*Tage*); ~ *on* (*prp.*) sich schließen um, umfassen; **~ness** ['klousnis] Genauig-keit *f*, Geschlossenheit *f*.

closet ['klɔzit] **1.** Kabinett *n*; (Wand)Schrank *m*; = *water-~*; **2.**: *be ~ed with* mit *j-m* e-e geheime Beratung haben. [nahme *f*.]

close-up ['klousʌp] *Film*: Großauf-]

closure ['klouʒə] Verschluß *m*; *parl.* (Antrag *m* auf) Schluß *m* e-r *De-batte*.

clot [klɔt] **1.** Klümpchen *n*; **2.** zu Klümpchen gerinnen (lassen).

cloth [klɔθ] Stoff *m*, Tuch *n*; Tisch-tuch *n*; Kleidung *f*, *Amts*-Tracht *f*; *the ~* F der geistliche Stand; *lay the ~* den Tisch decken; **~binding** Leineneinband *m*; **~bound** in Lei-nen gebunden.

clothe [klouð] [*irr.*] (an-, be)kleiden; einkleiden.

clothes [klouðz] *pl.* Kleider *n/pl.*; Kleidung *f*; Anzug *m*; Wäsche *f*; **~basket** ['klouðzbɑ:skit] Wäsche-korb *m*; **~line** Wäscheleine *f*; **~peg** Kleiderhaken *m*; Wäsche-klammer *f*; **~pin** *bsd. Am.* Wäsche-klammer *f*; **~press** Kleider-, Wäscheschrank *m*.

clothier ['klouðiə] Tuch-, Kleider-händler *m*.

clothing ['klouðiŋ] Kleidung *f*.

cloud [klaud] **1.** Wolke *f* (*a. fig.*); Trübung *f*; Schatten *m*; **2.** (sich) be-, umwölken (*a. fig.*); **~burst** ['klaudbə:st] Wolkenbruch *m*; **~less** [‿dlis] wolkenlos; **~y** [‿di] wolkig; Wolken...; trüb; unklar.

clout [klaut] Lappen *m*; F Kopf-nuß *f*.

clove¹ [klouv] (Gewürz)Nelke *f*.

clove² [‿] *pret. von cleave¹*; **~n** ['klouvn] **1.** *p.p. von cleave¹*; **2.** *adj.* gespalten.

clover ❧ ['klouvə] Klee *m*.

clown [klaun] Hanswurst *m*; Tölpel *m*; **~ish** □ ['klauniʃ] bäurisch; plump; clownhaft.

cloy [klɔi] übersättigen, überladen.

club [klʌb] **1.** Keule *f*; (Gummi-) Knüppel *m*; Klub *m*; ~*s pl. Karten*: Kreuz *n*; **2.** *v/t.* mit e-r Keule schlagen; *v/i.* sich zs.-tun; **~foot** ['klʌb'fut] Klumpfuß *m*.

clue [klu:] Anhaltspunkt *m*, Finger-zeig *m*.

clump [klʌmp] **1.** Klumpen *m*; *Baum*-Gruppe *f*; **2.** trampeln; zs.-drängen.

clumsy □ ['klʌmzi] unbeholfen, un-geschickt; plump.

clung [klʌŋ] *pret. u. p.p. von cling.*

cluster ['klʌstə] **1.** Traube *f*; Büschel *n*; Haufen *m*; **2.** büschel-weise wachsen; (sich) zs.-drängen.

clutch [klʌtʃ] **1.** Griff *m*; ⊕ Kupp-lung *f*; Klaue *f*; **2.** (er)greifen.

clutter ['klʌtə] **1.** Wirrwarr *m*; **2.** durch-ea.-rennen; durch-ea.-bringen.

coach [koutʃ] **1.** Kutsche *f*; 🚃 Wagen *m*; Reisebus *m*; Einpauker *m*; Trainer *m*; **2.** in e-r Kutsche fahren; (ein)pauken; trainieren; **~man** ['koutʃmən] Kutscher *m*.

coagulate [kou'ægjuleit] gerinnen (lassen).

coal [koul] **1.** (Stein)Kohle *f*; *carry ~s to Newcastle* Eulen nach Athen tragen; **2.** ⚓ (be)kohlen.

coalesce [kouə'les] zs.-wachsen; sich vereinigen.

coalition [kouə'liʃən] Verbindung *f*; Bund *m*, Koalition *f*.

coal-pit ['koulpit] Kohlengrube *f*.

coarse □ [kɔ:s] grob; ungeschliffen.

coast [koust] **1.** Küste *f*; *bsd. Am.* Rodelbahn *f*; **2.** die Küste entlang-fahren; im Freilauf fahren; rodeln; **~er** ['koustə] *Am.* Rodelschlitten *m*; ⚓ Küstenfahrer *m*.

coat [kout] **1.** Jackett *n*, Jacke *f*, Rock *m*; Mantel *m*; Pelz *m*, Ge-fieder *n*; Überzug *m*; ~ *of arms* Wappen(schild *m*, *n*) *n*; **2.** über-ziehen; anstreichen; **~hanger** ['kouthæŋə] Kleiderbügel *m*; **~ing** ['koutiŋ] Überzug *m*; Anstrich *m*; Mantelstoff *m*.

coax [kouks] schmeicheln (*dat.*); be-schwatzen (*into* zu).

cob [kɔb] kleines starkes Pferd; Schwan *m*; *Am.* Maiskolben *m*.

cobbler ['kɔblə] Schuhmacher *m*; Stümper *m*.

cobweb ['kɔbweb] Spinn(en)ge-webe *n*.

cock [kɔk] **1.** Hahn *m*; Anführer *m*; Heuhaufen *m*; **2.** *a.* ~ *up* aufrichten; Gewehrhahn spannen.

cockade [kɔ'keid] Kokarde *f*.

cockatoo [kɔkə'tu:] Kakadu *m*.

cockboat ⚓ ['kɔkbout] Jolle *f*.

cockchafer ['kɔktʃeifə] Maikäfer *m*.

cock|-eyed *sl.* ['kɔkaid] schieläugig; *Am.* blau (*betrunken*); **~horse** Steckenpferd *n*.

cockney ['kɔkni] waschechter Lon-doner.

cockpit ['kɔkpit] Kampfplatz *m* für Hähne; ⚓ Raumdeck *n*; ✈ Führer-raum *m*, Kanzel *f*.

cockroach *zo.* ['kɔkroutʃ] Schabe *f*.

cock|sure F ['kɔk'ʃuə] absolut sicher; überheblich; **~tail** Cocktail *m*; **~y** □ F ['kɔki] selbstbewußt; frech.

coco ['koukou] Kokospalme *f*.

cocoa ['koukou] Kakao *m*.

coco-nut ['koukənʌt] Kokosnuß *f*.

cocoon [kə'ku:n] *Seiden*-Kokon *m*.

cod [kɔd] Kabeljau *m*.

coddle ['kɔdl] verhätscheln.

code [koud] **1.** Gesetzbuch *n*; Kodex *m*; *Telegramm*-, *Signal*-Schlüssel *m*; **2.** chiffrieren.

codger F ['kɔdʒə] komischer Kauz.

cod-liver ['kɔdlivə]: ~ *oil* Lebertran *m*.

co-ed *Am.* F ['kou'ed] Schülerin *f* e-r Koedukationsschule, *allg.* Studentin *f*.

coerc|e [kou'ə:s] (er)zwingen; **~ion** [kou'ə:ʃən] Zwang *m*.

coeval [kou'i:vəl] gleichzeitig; gleichalt(e)rig.

coexist ['kouig'zist] gleichzeitig bestehen.

coffee ['kɔfi] Kaffee *m*; **~pot** Kaffeekanne *f*; **~room** Speisesaal *m e-s Hotels*; **~set** Kaffeeservice *n*.

coffer ['kɔfə] (Geld)Kasten *m*.

coffin ['kɔfin] Sarg *m*.

cogent □ ['koudʒənt] zwingend.

cogitate ['kɔdʒiteit] *v/i.* nachdenken; *v/t.* (er)sinnen.

cognate ['kɔgneit] verwandt.

cognition [kɔg'niʃən] Erkenntnis *f*.

cognizable ['kɔgnizəbl] erkennbar.

coheir ['kou'ɛə] Miterbe *m*.

coheren|ce [kou'hiərəns] Zs.-hang *m*; **~t** □ [**~**nt] zs.-hängend.

cohesi|on [kou'hi:ʒən] Kohäsion *f*; **~ve** [**~**isiv] (fest) zs.-hängend.

coiff|eur [kwa:'fə:] Friseur *m*; **~ure** [**~**'fjuə] Frisur *f*.

coil [kɔil] **1.** *a.* **~ up** aufwickeln; (sich) zs.-rollen; **2.** Rolle *f*, Spirale *f*; Wicklung *f*; ⚡ Spule *f*; Windung *f*; ⊕ (Rohr)Schlange *f*.

coin [kɔin] **1.** Münze *f*; **2.** prägen (*a. fig.*); münzen; **~age** ['kɔinidʒ] Prägung *f*; Geld *n*, Münze *f*.

coincide [kouin'said] zs.-treffen; übereinstimmen; **~nce** [kou'insidəns] Zs.-treffen *n*; *fig.* Übereinstimmung *f*.

coke [kouk] Koks *m* (*a. sl.* = *Kokain*); *Am.* F Coca-Cola *n, f*.

cold [kould] **1.** □ kalt; **2.** Kälte *f*, Frost *m*; Erkältung *f*; **~ness** ['kouldnis] Kälte *f*.

coleslaw *Am.* ['koulslɔ:] Krautsalat *m*.

colic ⅏ ['kɔlik] Kolik *f*.

collaborat|e [kə'læbəreit] zs.-arbeiten; **~ion** [kəlæbə'reiʃən] Zs.-, Mitarbeit *f*; *in* **~** gemeinsam.

collaps|e [kə'læps] **1.** zs.-, einfallen; zs.-brechen; **2.** Zs.-bruch *m*; **~ible** [**~**səbl] zs.-klappbar.

collar ['kɔlə] **1.** Kragen *m*; Halsband *n*; Kum(me)t *n*; ⊕ Lager *n*; **2.** beim Kragen packen; *Fleisch* zs.-rollen; **~bone** Schlüsselbein *n*; **~stud** Kragenknopf *m*.

collate [kɔ'leit] *Texte* vergleichen.

collateral [kɔ'lætərəl] **1.** □ parallel laufend; Seiten..., Neben...; indirekt; **2.** Seitenverwandte(r *m*) *f*.

colleague ['kɔli:g] Kolleg|e *m*, -in *f*.

collect 1. *eccl.* ['kɔlekt] Kollekte *f*; **2.** *v/t.* [kə'lekt] (ein)sammeln; *Gedanken etc.* sammeln; einkassieren; abholen; *v/i.* sich (ver)sammeln; **~ed** □ *fig.* gefaßt; **~ion** [**~**kʃən] Sammlung *f*; Einziehung *f*; **~ive** [**~**ktiv] gesammelt; Sammel...; **~**

bargaining Tarifverhandlungen *f/pl.*; **~ively** [**~**vli] insgesamt; zs.-fassend; **~or** [**~**tə] Sammler *m*; Steuereinnehmer *m*; 🚋 Fahrkartenabnehmer *m*; ⚡ Stromabnehmer *m*.

college ['kɔlidʒ] College *n* (*Teil e-r Universität*); höhere Schule *od.* Lehranstalt *f*; Hochschule *f*; Akademie *f*; Kollegium *n*.

collide [kə'laid] zs.-stoßen.

collie ['kɔli] Collie *m*, schottischer Schäferhund.

collier ['kɔliə] Bergmann *m*; ⚓ Kohlenschiff *n*; **~y** ['kɔljəri] Kohlengrube *f*.

collision [kə'liʒən] Zs.-stoß *m*.

colloquial □ [kə'loukwiəl] umgangssprachlich, familiär.

colloquy ['kɔləkwi] Gespräch *n*.

colon *typ.* ['koulən] Doppelpunkt *m*.

colonel ⚔ ['kə:nl] Oberst *m*.

coloni|al [kə'lounjəl] Kolonial...; **~alism** *pol.* [**~**lizəm] Kolonialismus *m*; **~ze** ['kɔlənaiz] kolonisieren; (sich) ansiedeln; besiedeln.

colony ['kɔləni] Kolonie *f*; Siedlung *f*.

colossal □ [kə'lɔsl] kolossal.

colo(u)r ['kʌlə] **1.** Farbe *f*; *fig.* Färbung *f*; Anschein *m*; Vorwand *m*; **~s** *pl.* ⚔ Fahne *f*, Flagge *f*; **2.** *v/t.* färben; anstreichen; *fig.* beschönigen; *v/i.* sich (ver)färben; erröten; **~bar** Rassenschranke *f*; **~ed** gefärbt, farbig; **~ man** Farbige(r) *m*; **~ful** [**~**əful] farbenreich, -freudig; lebhaft; **~ing** [**~**əriŋ] Färbung *f*; Farbton *m*; *fig.* Beschönigung *f*; **~less** □ [**~**əlis] farblos; **~ line** *bsd. Am.* Rassenschranke *f*.

colt [koult] Hengstfüllen *n*; *fig.* Neuling *m*.

column ['kɔləm] Säule *f*; *typ.* Spalte *f*; ⚔ Kolonne *f*; **~ist** *Am.* [**~**mnist] Kolumnist *m*.

comb [koum] **1.** Kamm *m*; ⊕ Hechel *f*; **2.** *v/t.* kämmen; striegeln; *Flachs* hecheln.

combat ['kɔmbət] **1.** Kampf *m*; single **~** Zweikampf *m*; **2.** (be-)kämpfen; **~ant** [**~**tənt] Kämpfer *m*.

combin|ation [kɔmbi'neiʃən] Verbindung *f*; *mst* **~s** *pl.* Hemdhose *f*; **~e** [kəm'bain] (sich) verbinden, vereinigen.

combust|ible [kəm'bʌstəbl] **1.** brennbar; **2.** **~s** *pl.* Brennmaterial *n*; *mot.* Betriebsstoff *m*; **~ion** [**~**tʃən] Verbrennung *f*.

come [kʌm] [*irr.*] kommen; *to* **~** künftig, kommend; **~** *about* sich zutragen; **~** *across* *auf et.* stoßen; **~** *at* erreichen; **~** *by* vorbeikommen; zu *et.* kommen; **~** *down* herunterkommen (*a. fig.*); *Am.* F erkranken (*with an dat.*); **~** *for* abholen; **~** *off* davonkommen; losgehen (*Knopf*), ausfallen (*Haare etc.*); stattfinden;

~ round vorbeikommen (*bsd. zu Besuch*); wiederkehren; F zu sich kommen; *fig.* einlenken; **~ to** *adv.* dazukommen; ♣ beidrehen; *prp.* betragen; **~ up to** entsprechen (*dat.*); es *j-m* gleichtun; *Stand, Maß* erreichen; **~-back** ['kʌmbæk] Wiederkehr *f*, Comeback *n*; *Am. sl.* schlagfertige Antwort.

comedian [kə'mi:djən] Schauspieler(in); Komiker(in); Lustspieldichter *m*.

comedy ['kɔmidi] Lustspiel *n*.

comeliness ['kʌmlinis] Anmut *f*.

comfort ['kʌmfət] 1. Bequemlichkeit *f*; Behaglichkeit *f*; Trost *m*; *fig.* Beistand *m*; Erquickung *f*; 2. trösten; erquicken, beleben; **~able** □ [~təbl] behaglich; bequem; tröstlich; **~er** [~tə] Tröster *m*; *fig.* wollenes Halstuch; Schnuller *m*; *Am.* Steppdecke *f*; **~less** □ [~tlis] unbehaglich; trostlos; **~ station** *m*. Bedürfnisanstalt *f*.

comic(al □) ['kɔmik(əl)] komisch; lustig, drollig.

coming ['kʌmiŋ] 1. kommend; künftig; 2. Kommen *n*.

comma ['kɔmə] Komma *n*.

command [kə'mɑːnd] 1. Herrschaft *f*, Beherrschung *f* (*a. fig.*); Befehl *m*; ⚔ Kommando *n*; be (*have*) **at ~** zur Verfügung stehen (haben); 2. befehlen; ⚔ kommandieren; verfügen über (*acc.*); beherrschen; **~er** [~də] Kommandeur *m*, Befehlshaber *m*; ♣ Fregattenkapitän *m*; **~er-in-chief** [~ərin-'tʃiːf] Oberbefehlshaber *m*; **~ment** [~dmənt] Gebot *f*.

commemorat|e [kə'meməreit] gedenken (*gen.*), feiern; **~ion** [kəme-mə'reiʃən] Gedächtnisfeier *f*.

commence [kə'mens] anfangen, beginnen; **~ment** [~smənt] Anfang *m*.

commend [kə'mend] empfehlen; **commensurable** □ [kə'menʃərəbl] vergleichbar (**with**, **to** mit).

comment ['kɔment] 1. Kommentar *m*; Erläuterung *f*; An-, Bemerkung *f*; 2. (**upon**) erläutern (*acc.*); sich auslassen (über *acc.*); **~ary** ['kɔ-məntəri] Kommentar *m*; **~ator** ['kɔmenteitə] Kommentator *m*; *Radio*: Berichterstatter *m*.

commerc|e ['kɔmə(:)s] Handel *m*; Verkehr *m*; **~ial** □ [kə'mə:ʃəl] 1. kaufmännisch; Handels..., Geschäfts...; gewerbsmäßig; **~ traveller** Handlungsreisende(r) *m*; 2. *bsd. Am. Radio, Fernsehen*: kommerzielle (Werbe)Sendung.

commiseration [kəmizə'reiʃən] Mitleid *n* (**for** mit).

commissary ['kɔmisəri] Kommissar *m*; ⚔ Intendanturbeamte(r) *m*.

commission [kə'miʃən] 1. Auftrag *m*; Übertragung *f* von *Macht etc.*;

Begehung *f e-s Verbrechens*; Provision *f*; Kommission *f*; (Offiziers-) Patent *n*; 2. beauftragen; bevollmächtigen; ⚔ bestallen; ♣ in Dienst stellen; **~er** [~nə] Bevollmächtigte(r *m*) *f*; Kommissar *m*.

commit [kə'mit] anvertrauen; übergeben, überweisen; *Tat* begehen; bloßstellen; **~** (**o.s.** sich) verpflichten; **~** (**to prison**) in Untersuchungshaft nehmen; **~ment** [~tmənt], **~tal** [~tl] Überweisung *f*; Verpflichtung *f*; Verübung *f*; **~tee** [~ti] Ausschuß *m*, Komitee *n*.

commodity [kə'mɔditi] Ware *f* (*mst pl.*), Gebrauchsartikel *m*.

common [kɔmən] 1. □ (all)gemein; gewöhnlich; gemeinschaftlich; öffentlich; gemein (*niedrig*); ♀ *Council* Gemeinderat *m*; 2. Gemeindewiese *f*; **in ~** gemeinsam; **in ~ with** *fig.* genau wie; **~er** [~nə] Bürger *m*, Gemeine(r) *m*; Mitglied *n* des Unterhauses; **~ law** Gewohnheitsrecht *n*; ♀ **Market** Gemeinsamer Markt; **~place** 1. Gemeinplatz *m*; 2. gewöhnlich, F abgedroschen; **~s** *pl.* das gemeine Volk; Gemeinschaftsverpflegung *f*; (*mst House of*) ♀ Unterhaus *n*; **~ sense** gesunder Menschenverstand; **~wealth** [~nwelθ] Gemeinwesen *n*, Staat *m*; *bsd.* Republik *f*; **the British** ♀ das Commonwealth.

commotion [kə'mouʃən] Erschütterung *f*; Aufruhr *m*; Aufregung *f*.

communal □ ['kɔmjunl] gemeinschaftlich; Gemeinde...

commune 1. [kə'mjuːn] sich vertraulich besprechen; 2. ['kɔmjuːn] Gemeinde *f*.

communicat|e [kə'mjuːnikeit] *v/t.* mitteilen; *v/i.* das Abendmahl nehmen, kommunizieren; in Verbindung stehen; **~ion** [kəmjuːni'kei-ʃən] Mitteilung *f*; Verbindung *f*; **~ive** [kə'mjuːnikətiv] gesprächig.

communion [kə'mjuːnjən] Gemeinschaft *f*; *eccl.* Kommunion *f*, Abendmahl *n*.

communis|m ['kɔmjunizəm] Kommunismus *m*; **~t** [~ist] 1. Kommunist(in); 2. kommunistisch.

community [kə'mjuːniti] Gemeinschaft *f*; Gemeinde *f*; Staat *m*.

commut|ation [kɔmju(:)'teiʃən] Vertauschung *f*; Umwandlung *f*; Ablösung *f*; Strafmilderung *f*; **~ ticket** *Am.* Zeitkarte *f*; **~e** [kə'mjuːt] ablösen; Strafe (mildernd) umwandeln; *Am.* pendeln *im Arbeitsverkehr*.

compact 1. ['kɔmpækt] Vertrag *m*; 2. [kəm'pækt] *adj.* dicht, fest; knapp, bündig; *v/t.* fest verbinden.

companion [kəm'pænjən] Gefährt|e *m*, -in *f*; Gesellschafter(in); **~able** [~nəbl] gesellig; **~ship** [~nʃip] Gesellschaft *f*.

company ['kʌmpəni] Gesellschaft f; Kompanie f; Handelsgesellschaft f; Genossenschaft f; ⚓ Mannschaft f; thea. Truppe f; have ~ Gäste haben; keep ~ with verkehren mit.

compar|able □ ['kɔmpərəbl] vergleichbar; **~ative** [kəm'pærətiv] 1. □ vergleichend; verhältnismäßig; 2. a. ~ degree gr. Komparativ m; ~e [~'pɛə] 1.: beyond ~, without ~, past ~ unvergleichlich; 2. v/t. vergleichen; gleichstellen (to mit); v/i. sich vergleichen (lassen); **~ison** [~'pærisn] Vergleich(ung f) m.

compartment [kəm'pɑːtmənt] Abteilung f; △ Fach n; 🚃 Abteil n.

compass ['kʌmpəs] 1. Bereich m; ♪ Umfang m; Kompaß m; oft pair of ~es pl. Zirkel m; 2. herumgehen um; einschließen; erreichen; planen.

compassion [kəm'pæʃən] Mitleid n; **~ate** □ [~nit] mitleidig.

compatible □ [kəm'pætəbl] vereinbar, verträglich; schicklich.

compatriot [kəm'pætriət] Landsmann m.

compel [kəm'pel] (er)zwingen.

compensat|e ['kɔmpenseit] j-n entschädigen; et. ersetzen; ausgleichen; **~ion** [kɔmpen'seiʃən] Ersatz m; Ausgleich(ung f) m; Entschädigung f; Am. Vergütung f (Gehalt).

compère ['kɔmpɛə] 1. Conférencier m; 2. ansagen (bei).

compete [kəm'piːt] sich mitbewerben (for um); konkurrieren.

competen|ce, **~cy** ['kɔmpitəns, ~si] Befugnis f, Zuständigkeit f; Auskommen n; **~t** □ [~nt] hinreichend; (leistungs)fähig; fachkundig; berechtigt, zuständig.

competit|ion [kɔmpi'tiʃən] Mitbewerbung f; Wettbewerb m; ♣ Konkurrenz f; **~ive** [kəm'petitiv] wetteifernd; **~or** [~tə] Mitbewerber(-in) f; Konkurrent(in).

compile [kəm'pail] zs.-tragen, zs.-stellen (from aus); sammeln.

complacen|ce, **~cy** ['kɔm'pleisns, ~si] Selbstzufriedenheit f.

complain [kəm'plein] (sich be-)klagen; ~ant [~nənt] Kläger(in); **~t** [~nt] Klage f, Beschwerde f; 𝔐 Leiden n.

complaisan|ce [kəm'pleizəns] Gefälligkeit f; Entgegenkommen n; **~t** □ [~nt] gefällig; entgegenkommend.

complement ['kɔmplimənt] Ergänzung f; volle Anzahl f; 2. [~ment] ergänzen.

complet|e [kəm'pliːt] 1. □ vollständig, ganz; vollkommen; 2. vervollständigen; vervollkommnen; abschließen; **~ion** [~i:ʃən] Vervollständigung f; Abschluß m; Erfüllung f.

complex ['kɔmpleks] 1. □ zs.-gesetzt; fig. kompliziert; 2. Gesamtheit f, Komplex m; **~ion** [kəm'plekʃən] Aussehen n; Charakter m, Zug m; Gesichtsfarbe f, Teint m; **~ity** [~ksiti] Kompliziertheit f.

complian|ce [kəm'plaiəns] Einwilligung f; Einverständnis n; in ~ with gemäß; **~t** □ [~nt] gefällig.

complicate ['kɔmplikeit] komplizieren, erschweren.

complicity [kəm'plisiti] Mitschuld f (in an dat.).

compliment 1. ['kɔmplimənt] Kompliment n; Schmeichelei f; Gruß m; 2. [~ment] v/t. (on) beglückwünschen (zu); j-m Komplimente machen (über acc.); **~ary** [kɔmpli'mentəri] höflich.

comply [kəm'plai] sich fügen; nachkommen, entsprechen (with dat.).

component [kəm'pounənt] 1. Bestandteil m; 2. zs.-setzend.

compos|e [kəm'pouz] zs.-setzen; komponieren, verfassen; ordnen; beruhigen; typ. setzen; **~ed** □ ruhig, gesetzt; **~er** [~zə] Komponist(in); Verfasser(in); **~ition** [kɔmpə'ziʃən] Zs.-setzung f; Abfassung f; Komposition f (Schrift-)Satz m; Aufsatz m; ⚔ Vergleich m; **~t** ['kɔmpost] Kompost m; **~ure** [kəm'pouʒə] Fassung f, Gemütsruhe f.

compound 1. ['kɔmpaund] zs.-gesetzt; ~ interest Zinseszinsen m/pl.; 2. Zs.-setzung f, Verbindung f; 3. [kəm'paund] v/t. zs.-setzen; Streit beilegen; v/i. sich einigen.

comprehend [kɔmpri'hend] umfassen; begreifen, verstehen.

comprehen|sible □ [kɔmpri'hensəbl] verständlich; **~sion** [~nʃən] Verständnis n; Fassungskraft f; Umfang m; **~sive** □ [~nsiv] umfassend.

compress [kəm'pres] zs.-drücken; ~ed air Druckluft f; **~ion** [~eʃən] phys. Verdichtung f; ⊕ Druck m.

comprise [kəm'praiz] in sich fassen, einschließen, enthalten.

compromise ['kɔmprəmaiz] 1. Kompromiß m, n; 2. v/t. Streit beilegen; bloßstellen; v/i. e-n Kompromiß schließen.

compuls|ion [kəm'pʌlʃən] Zwang m; **~ory** [~lsəri] obligatorisch; Zwangs...; Pflicht...

compunction [kəm'pʌŋkʃən] Gewissensbisse m/pl.; Reue f; Bedenken n.

comput|ation [kɔmpju(ː)'teiʃən] (Be)Rechnung f; **~e** [kəm'pjuːt] (be-, er)rechnen; schätzen; **~er** [~tə] Computer m.

comrade ['kɔmrid] Kamerad m.

con[1] abbr. [kɔn] = contra.

con² *Am. sl.* [~] **1.**: ~ *man* = confidence man; **2.** 'reinlegen (*betrügen*).

conceal [kən'si:l] verbergen; *fig.*
verhehlen, verheimlichen, ver-
schweigen.

concede [kən'si:d] zugestehen; ein-
räumen; gewähren, nachgeben.

conceit [kən'si:t] Einbildung *f*;
spitzfindiger Gedanke; übertriebe-
nes sprachliches Bild; ~ed □ eingebildet (*of auf acc.*).

conceiv|able □ [kən'si:vəbl] denk-
bar; begreiflich; ~e [kən'si:v] *v/i.*
empfangen (*schwanger werden*);
sich denken (*of acc.*); *v/t. Kind
empfangen*; sich denken; aussinnen.

concentrate ['kɔnsentreit] (sich)
zs.-ziehen, (sich) konzentrieren.

conception [kən'sepʃən] Begreifen
n; Vorstellung *f*, Begriff *m*, Idee *f*;
biol. Empfängnis *f*.

concern [kən'sə:n] **1.** Angelegenheit
f; Interesse *n*; Sorge *f*; Beziehung *f*
(*with zu*); † Geschäft *n*, (in-
dustrielles) Unternehmen; **2.** betreffen, angehen, interessieren; ~
o.s. about od. for sich kümmern um;
be ~ed in Betracht kommen; ~ed □
interessiert, beteiligt (*in an dat.*);
bekümmert; ~ing *prp.* [~niŋ] betreffend, über, wegen, hinsichtlich.

concert 1. ['kɔnsət] Konzert *n*;
2. [~sə(:)t] Einverständnis *n*;
3. [kən'sə:t] sich einigen, verabreden; ~ed gemeinsam; ♪ mehr-
stimmig.

concession [kən'seʃən] Zugeständ-
nis *n*; Erlaubnis *f*. [räumend.]

concessive □ [kən'sesiv] ein-

conciliat|e [kən'silieit] aus-, ver-
söhnen; ausgleichen; ~or [~tə]
Vermittler *m*; ~ory [~iətəri] versöhnlich, vermittelnd.

concise □ [kən'sais] kurz, bündig,
knapp; ~ness [~snis] Kürze *f*.

conclude [kən'klu:d] schließen, beschließen; abschließen; folgern;
sich entscheiden; *to be ~d Schluß
folgt*.

conclusi|on [kən'klu:ʒən] Schluß *m*,
Ende *n*; Abschluß *m*; Folgerung *f*;
Beschluß *m*; ~ve □ [~u:siv]
schlüssig; endgültig.

concoct [kən'kɔkt] zs.-brauen; *fig.*
aussinnen; ~ion [~kʃən] Gebräu *n*;
fig. Erfindung *f*.

concord ['kɔŋkɔ:d] Eintracht *f*;
Übereinstimmung *f* (*a. gr.*); ♪
Harmonie *f*; ~ant □ [kən'kɔ:dənt]
übereinstimmend; einstimmig; ♪
harmonisch.

concourse ['kɔŋkɔ:s] Zusammen-,
Auflauf *m*; Menge *f*; *Am.* Bahn-
hofs-, Schalterhalle *f*.

concrete 1. ['kɔnkri:t] konkret; Beton...; **2.** [~] Beton *m*; **3.** [kən'kri:t]
zu e-r Masse verbinden; ['kɔnkri:t]
betonieren.

concur [kən'kə:] zs.-treffen, zs.-wir-
ken; übereinstimmen; ~rence [~
'kʌrəns] Zusammentreffen *n*; Übereinstimmung *f*; Mitwirkung *f*.

concussion [kən'kʌʃən]: ~ *of the
brain* Gehirnerschütterung *f*.

condemn [kən'dem] verdammen;
verurteilen; verwerfen; *Kranke*
aufgeben; beschlagnahmen; ~a-
tion [kɔndem'neiʃən] Verurtei-
lung *f*; Verdammung *f*; Verwerfung *f*.

condens|ation [kɔnden'seiʃən] Ver-
dichtung *f*; ~e [kən'dens] (sich)
verdichten; ⊕ kondensieren; zs.-
drängen; ~er [~sə] ⊕ Konden-
sator *m*.

condescen|d [kɔndi'send] sich herab-
lassen; geruhen; ~sion [~nʃən]
Herablassung *f*.

condiment ['kɔndimənt] Würze *f*.

condition [kən'diʃən] **1.** Zustand *m*,
Stand *m*; Stellung *f*, Bedingung *f*;
~s *pl.* Verhältnisse *n/pl.*; **2.** bedingen; in e-n bestimmten Zustand
bringen; ~al □ [~nl] bedingt (*on,
upon durch*); Bedingungs...; ~
clause gr. Bedingungssatz *m*; ~
mood gr. Konditional *m*.

condol|e [kən'doul] kondolieren
(*with dat.*); ~ence [~ləns] Beileid *n*.

conduc|e [kən'dju:s] führen, dienen;
~ive [~siv] dienlich, förderlich.

conduct 1. ['kɔndəkt] Führung *f*;
Verhalten *n*, Betragen *n*; **2.** [kən-
'dʌkt] führen; ♪ dirigieren; ~ion
[~kʃən] Leitung *f*; ~or [~ktə]
Führer *m*; Leiter *m*; Schaffner *m*;
♪ Dirigent *m*; ∉ Blitzableiter *m*.

conduit ['kɔndit] (Leitungs-)
Röhre *f*.

cone [koun] Kegel *m*; ⚲ Zapfen *m*.

confabulation [kɔnfæbju'leiʃən]
Plauderei *f*.

confection [kən'fekʃən] Konfekt *n*;
~er [~ʃnə] Konditor *m*; ~ery
[~əri] Konfekt *n*; Konditorei *f*;
bsd. Am. Süßwarengeschäft *n*.

confedera|cy [kən'fedərəsi] Bünd-
nis *n*; *the* ⚲ *bsd. Am.* die 11 Südstaaten *bei der Sezession 1860—61*;
~te **1.** [~rit] verbündet; **2.** [~] Bundesgenosse *m*; **3.** [~reit] (sich) ver-
bünden; ~tion [~'reiʃən] Bund *m*, Bündnis *n*; *the* ⚲ *bsd. Am.*
die Staatenkonföderation *f* von
1781—1789.

confer [kən'fə:] *v/t.* übertragen, verleihen; *v/i.* sich besprechen; ~
ence ['kɔnfərəns] Konferenz *f*.

confess [kən'fes] bekennen, gestehen; beichten; ~ion [~eʃən] Ge-
ständnis *n*; Bekenntnis *n*; Beichte
f; ~ional [~nl] Beichtstuhl *m*; ~or
[~esə] Bekenner *m*; Beichtvater *m*.

confide [kən'faid] *v/t.* anvertrauen;
v/i. vertrauen (*in auf acc.*); ~nce
['kɔnfidəns] Vertrauen *n*; Zuversicht *f*; ~nce man Schwindler *m*.

Hochstapler *m*; ~nce trick Bauern-
fängerei *f*; ~nt □ [~nt] vertrauend;
zuversichtlich; ~ntial □ [kɔnfi-
'denʃəl] vertraulich.

confine [kən'fain] begrenzen; beschränken; einsperren; be ~d
niederkommen (of mit); be ~d to
bed das Bett hüten müssen; ~ment
[~nmənt] Haft *f*; Beschränkung *f*;
Entbindung *f*.

confirm [kən'fəːm] (be)kräftigen;
bestätigen; konfirmieren; firmen;
~ation [kɔnfə'meiʃən] Bestätigung
f; *eccl.* Konfirmation *f*; *eccl.* Fir-
mung *f*.

confiscat|e ['kɔnfiskeit] beschlag-
nahmen; ~ion [kɔnfis'keiʃən] Beschlagnahme *f*.   [ßer Brand.\
conflagration [kɔnflə'greiʃən] gro-
conflict 1. ['kɔnflikt] Konflikt *m*;
2. [kən'flikt] im Konflikt stehen.
conflu|ence ['kɔnfluəns], ~x [~ʌks]
Zs.-fluß *m*; Auflauf *m*; ~ent [~luənt]
1. zs.-fließend, zs.-laufend; 2. Zu-,
Nebenfluß *m*.

conform [kən'fɔːm] (sich) anpassen; ~able □ [~məbl] (to) übereinstimmen (mit); entsprechend
(*dat.*); nachgiebig (gegen); ~ity [~
miti] Übereinstimmung *f*.

confound [kən'faund] vermengen;
verwechseln; *j-n* verwirren; ~ it! F
verdammt!; ~ed □ F verdammt.

confront [kən'frʌnt] gegenüberstellen; entgegentreten (*dat.*).

confus|e [kən'fjuːz] verwechseln;
verwirren; ~ion [~uːʒən] Verwirrung *f*; Verwechs(e)lung *f*.

confut|ation [kɔnfjuː'teiʃən] Wider-
legung *f*; ~e [kən'fjuːt] widerlegen.

congeal [kən'dʒiːl] erstarren (lassen); gerinnen (lassen).

congenial □ [kən'dʒiːnjəl] (geistes-)
verwandt (*with dat.*); zusagend.

congenital □ [kən'dʒenitl] angeboren.

congestion [kən'dʒestʃən] (Blut-)
Andrang *m*; Stauung *f*; *traffic* ~
Verkehrsstockung *f*.

conglomeration [kɔnglɔmə'reiʃən]
Anhäufung *f*; Konglomerat *n*.

congratulat|e [kən'grætjuleit] be-
glückwünschen; *j-m* gratulieren;
~ion [kɔngrætju'leiʃən] Glück-
wunsch *m*.

congregat|e ['kɔngrigeit] (sich)
(ver)sammeln; ~ion [kɔngri'geiʃən]
Versammlung *f*; *eccl.* Gemeinde *f*.

congress ['kɔngres] Kongreß *m*;
♀ Kongreß *m*, *gesetzgebende Körperschaft der USA*; ♀man, ♀woman
Am. pol. Mitglied *n* des Repräsen-
tantenhauses.

congruous □ ['kɔngruəs] angemessen (to für); übereinstimmend;
folgerichtig.

conifer ['kounifə] Nadelholzbaum
m.

conjecture [kən'dʒektʃə] 1. Mut-
maßung *f*; 2. mutmaßen.

conjoin [kən'dʒɔin] (sich) verbinden; ~t ['kɔndʒɔint] verbunden.

conjugal □ ['kɔndʒugəl] ehelich.

conjugat|e *gr.* ['kɔndʒugeit] kon-
jugieren, beugen; ~ion *gr.* [kɔndʒu-
'geiʃən] Konjugation *f*, Beugung *f*.

conjunction [kən'dʒʌŋkʃən] Verbindung *f*; Zs.-treffen *n*; *gr.* Konjunktion *f*.

conjunctivitis [kəndʒʌŋkti'vaitis]
Bindehautentzündung *f*.

conjure[1] [kən'dʒuə] beschwören,
inständig bitten.

conjur|e[2] ['kʌndʒə] *v/t.* beschwö-
ren; *et. wohin* zaubern; *v/i.* zaubern;
~er [~ərə] Zauber|er *m*, -in *f*;
Taschenspieler(in); ~ing-trick
[~ɾiŋtrik] Zauberkunststück *n*; ~or
[~ɾə] = conjurer.

connect [kə'nekt] (sich) verbinden;
≠ schalten; ~ed □ verbunden;
zs.-hängend (*Rede etc.*); be ~ with
in Verbindung stehen mit *j-m*;
~ion [~kʃən] = connexion.

connexion [kə'nekʃən] Verbindung
f; ≠ Schaltung *f*; Anschluß *m* (*a.*
♀, ♂); Zs.-hang *m*; Verwandtschaft
f.

connive [kə'naiv]: ~ at ein Auge zudrücken bei.

connoisseur [kɔni'səː] Kenner(in).

connubial □ [kə'njuːbjəl] ehelich.

conquer ['kɔŋkə] erobern; (be)sie-
gen; ~or [~ərə] Eroberer *m*; Sieger
m.

conquest ['kɔŋkwest] Eroberung *f*;
Errungenschaft *f*; Sieg *m*.

conscience ['kɔnʃəns] Gewissen *n*.

conscientious □ [kɔnʃi'enʃəs] gewissenhaft; Gewissens...; ~ *objector*
Kriegsdienstverweigerer *m* aus
Überzeugung; ~ness [~snis] Ge-
wissenhaftigkeit *f*.

conscious □ ['kɔnʃəs] bewußt; be ~
of sich bewußt sein (*gen.*); ~ness
[~snis] Bewußtsein *n*.

conscript ⚔ ['kɔnskript] Wehr-
pflichtige(r) *m*; ~ion ⚔ [kən'skrip-
ʃən] Einberufung *f*.

consecrat|e ['kɔnsikreit] weihen,
einsegnen; heiligen; widmen; ~ion
[kɔnsi'kreiʃən] Weihung *f*, Ein-
segnung *f*; Heiligung *f*.

consecutive □ [kən'sekjutiv] auf-
ea.-folgend; fortlaufend.

consent [kən'sent] 1. Zustimmung *f*;
2. einwilligen, zustimmen (*dat.*).

consequen|ce ['kɔnsikwəns] (to)
Folge *f*, Konsequenz *f* (für); ~ [Wir-
kung *f*, Einfluß *m* (auf *acc.*); Bedeutung *f* (für); ~t [~t] 1. folgend;
2. Folge(rung) *f*; ~tial □ [kɔnsi-
'kwenʃəl] sich ergebend (*on* aus);
folgerichtig; wichtigtuerisch; ~tly
['kɔnsikwəntli] folglich, daher.

conserv|ation [kɔnsə(ː)'veiʃən] Er-
haltung *f*; ~ative □ [kən'səːvətiv]
1. erhaltend (*of acc.*); konservativ;
vorsichtig; 2. Konservative(r) *m*;

~atory [kɔn'sɔ:vətri] Treib-, Gewächshaus n; ♪ Konservatorium n; ~e [kɔn'sɔ:v] erhalten.

consider [kən'sidə] v/t. betrachten; erwägen; überlegen; in Betracht ziehen; berücksichtigen; meinen, glauben; v/i. überlegen; all things ~ed wenn man alles in Betracht zieht; ~able □ [~ərəbl] ansehnlich, beträchtlich; ~ably [~li] bedeutend, ziemlich, (sehr) viel; ~ate □ [~rit] rücksichtsvoll; ~ation [kɔn-sidə'reiʃən] Betrachtung f, Erwägung f, Überlegung f; Rücksicht f; Wichtigkeit f; Entschädigung f; Entgelt n; be under ~ erwogen werden; in Betracht kommen; on no ~ unter keinen Umständen; ~ing □ [kən'sidəriŋ] 1. prp. in Anbetracht (gen.); 2. F adv. den Umständen entsprechend.

consign [kən'sain] übergeben, überliefern; anvertrauen; † konsignieren; ~ment † [~nmənt] Übersendung f; Konsignation f.

consist [kən'sist] bestehen (of aus); in Einklang stehen (with mit); ~ence, ~ency [~təns, ~si] Festigkeit(sgrad m) f; Übereinstimmung f; Konsequenz f; ~ent [~nt] fest; übereinstimmend, vereinbar (with mit); konsequent.

consol|ation [kɔnsə'leiʃən] Trost m; ~e [kɔn'soul] trösten.

consolidate [kən'sɔlideit] festigen; fig. vereinigen; zs.-legen.

consonan|ce [kɔnsənəns] Konsonanz f; Übereinstimmung f; ~t [~nt] 1. □ übereinstimmend; 2. gr. Konsonant m, Mitlaut m.

consort ['kɔnsɔ:t] Gemahl(in); ♣ Geleitschiff n.

conspicuous □ [kən'spikjuəs] sichtbar; auffallend; hervorragend; make o.s.~ sich auffällig benehmen.

conspir|acy [kən'spirəsi] Verschwörung f; ~ator [~tə] Verschwörer m; ~e [~'spaiə] sich verschwören.

constab|le ['kʌnstəbl] Polizist m; Schutzmann m; ~ulary [kən-'stæbjuləri] Polizei(truppe) f.

constan|cy ['kɔnstənsi] Standhaftigkeit f; Beständigkeit f; ~t □ [~nt] beständig, fest; unveränderlich; treu.

consternation [kɔnstə(:)'neiʃən] Bestürzung f.

constipation ♫ [kɔnsti'peiʃən] Verstopfung f.

constituen|cy [kən'stitjuənsi] Wählerschaft f; Wahlkreis m; ~t [~nt] 1. wesentlich; Grund..., Bestand...; konstituierend; 2. wesentlicher Bestandteil; Wähler m.

constitut|e ['kɔnstitju:t] ein-, errichten; ernennen; bilden, ausmachen; ~ion [kɔnsti'tju:ʃən] Ein-, Errichtung f; Bildung f; Körper-

bau m; Verfassung f; ~ional □ [~nl] konstitutionell; natürlich; verfassungsmäßig.

constrain [kən'strein] zwingen; et. erzwingen; ~t [~nt] Zwang m.

constrict [kən'strikt] zs.-ziehen; ~ion [~kʃən] Zs.-ziehung f.

constringent [kən'strindʒənt] zs.-ziehend.

construct [kən'strʌkt] bauen, errichten; fig. bilden; ~ion [~kʃən] Konstruktion f; Bau m; Auslegung f; ~ive [~ktiv] aufbauend, schöpferisch, konstruktiv, positiv; Bau...; ~or [~tə] Erbauer m, Konstrukteur m.

construe [kən'stru:] gr. konstruieren; auslegen, auffassen; übersetzen.

consul ['kɔnsəl] Konsul m; ~-general Generalkonsul m; ~ate [~sjulit] Konsulat n (a. Gebäude).

consult [kən'sʌlt] v/t. konsultieren, um Rat fragen; in e-m Buch nachschlagen; v/i. sich beraten; ~ation [kɔnsəl'teiʃən] Konsultation f, Beratung f; Rücksprache f; ~ hour Sprechstunde f; ~ative [kən'sʌl-tətiv] beratend.

consume [kən'sju:m] v/t. verzehren; verbrauchen; vergeuden; ~r [~mə] Verbraucher m; Abnehmer m.

consummate 1. □ [kən'sʌmit] vollendet; 2. ['kɔnsʌmeit] vollenden.

consumpti|on [kən'sʌmpʃən] Verbrauch m; ♫ Schwindsucht f; ~ve □ [~ptiv] verzehrend; ♫ schwindsüchtig.

contact 1. ['kɔntækt] Berührung f; Kontakt m; ~ lenses pl. Haft-, Kontaktschalen f/pl.; 2. [kən'tækt] Fühlung nehmen mit.

contagi|on ♫ [kən'teidʒən] Ansteckung f; Verseuchung f; Seuche f; ~ous □ [~əs] ansteckend.

contain [kən'tein] (ent)halten, (um)fassen; ~ o.s. an sich halten; ~er [~nə] Behälter m; Großbehälter m (im Frachtverkehr).

contaminat|e [kən'tæmineit] verunreinigen; fig. anstecken, vergiften; verseuchen; ~ion [kɔntæmi-'neiʃən] Verunreinigung f; (radioaktive) Verseuchung f.

contemplat|e fig. ['kɔntempleit] betrachten; beabsichtigen; ~ion [kɔntəm'pleiʃən] Betrachtung f; Nachsinnen n; ~ive □ ['kɔntem-pleitiv] nachdenklich; [kən'tem-plətiv] beschaulich.

contempora|neous □ [kəntempə-'reinjəs] gleichzeitig; ~ry [kən-'tempərəri] 1. zeitgenössisch; gleichzeitig; 2. Zeitgenoss|e m,-in f.

contempt [kən'tempt] Verachtung f; ~ible □ [~təbl] verachtenswert; ~uous □ [~tjuəs] geringschätzig (of gegen); verächtlich.

contend [kən'tend] *v/i.* streiten, ringen (*for* um); *v/t.* behaupten.

content [kən'tent] **1.** zufrieden; **2.** befriedigen; ~ *o.s.* sich begnügen; **3.** Zufriedenheit *f*; *to one's heart's* ~ nach Herzenslust; ['kɔntent] Umfang *m*; Gehalt *m*; ~*s pl. stofflicher* Inhalt; ~**ed** □ [kən'tentid] zufrieden; genügsam.

contention [kən'tenʃən] (Wort-)Streit *m*; Wetteifer *m*.

contentment [kən'tentmənt] Zufriedenheit *f*, Genügsamkeit *f*.

contest 1. ['kɔntest] Streit *m*; Wettkampf *m*; **2.** [kən'test] (be)streiten; anfechten; *um et.* streiten. [*m.*]

context ['kɔntekst] Zusammenhang]

contiguous □ [kən'tigjuəs] anstoßend (*to an acc.*); benachbart.

continent ['kɔntinənt] **1.** □ enthaltsam; mäßig; **2.** Kontinent *m*, Erdteil *m*; Festland *n*; ~**al** [kɔnti'nentl] **1.** □ kontinental; Kontinental...; **2.** Kontinentaleuropäer(in).

contingen|cy [kən'tindʒənsi] Zufälligkeit *f*; Zufall *m*; Möglichkeit *f*; ~**t** [~nt] **1.** □ zufällig; möglich (to bei); **2.** ⚔ Kontingent *n*.

continu|al □ [kən'tinjuəl] fortwährend, unaufhörlich; ~**ance** [~əns] (Fort)Dauer *f*; ~**ation** [kəntinju'eiʃən] Fortsetzung *f*; Fortdauer *f*; ~ *school* Fortbildungsschule *f*; ~**e** [kən'tinju(:)] *v/t.* fortsetzen; beibehalten; to be ~**d** Fortsetzung folgt; *v/i.* fortdauern; fortfahren; ~**ity** [kɔnti'nju(:)iti] Kontinuität *f*; *Film*: Drehbuch *n*; *Radio*: verbindende Worte; ~ *girl* Skriptgirl *n*; ~**ous** □ [kən'tinjuəs] ununterbrochen.

contort [kən'tɔːt] verdrehen; verzerren; ~**ion** [~ɔːʃən] Verdrehung *f*; Verzerrung *f*.

contour ['kɔntuə] Umriß *m*.

contra ['kɔntrə] wider.

contraband ['kɔntrəbænd] Schmuggelware *f*; Schleichhandel *m*; *attr.* Schmuggel...

contraceptive [kɔntrə'septiv] **1.** empfängnisverhütend; **2.** empfängnisverhütendes Mittel.

contract 1. [kən'trækt] *v/t.* zs.-ziehen; sich *et.* zuziehen; *Schulden* machen; *Heirat etc.* (ab)schließen; *v/i.* einschrumpfen; e-n Vertrag schließen; sich verpflichten; **2.** ['kɔntrækt] Kontrakt *m*, Vertrag *m*; ~**ion** [kən'trækʃən] Zs.-ziehung *f*; *gr.* Kurzform *f*; ~**or** [~ktə] Unternehmer *m*; Lieferant *m*.

contradict [kɔntrə'dikt] widersprechen (*dat.*); ~**ion** [~kʃən] Widerspruch *m*; ~**ory** □ [~ktəri] (sich) widersprechend.

contrar|iety [kɔntrə'raiəti] Widerspruch *m*; Widrigkeit *f*; ~**y** ['kɔntrəri] **1.** entgegengesetzt; widrig; ~ *to* zuwider (*dat.*); gegen; **2.** Gegenteil *n*; *on the* ~ im Gegenteil.

contrast 1. ['kɔntrɑːst] Gegensatz *m*; **2.** [kən'trɑːst] *v/t.* gegenüberstellen; vergleichen; *v/i.* sich unterscheiden, abstechen (*with* von).

contribut|e [kən'tribju(:)t] beitragen, beisteuern; ~**ion** [kɔntri'bju(:)ʃən] Beitrag *m*; ~**or** [kən'tribjutə] Beitragende(r *m*) *f*; Mitarbeiter(in) *an e-r Zeitung*; ~**ory** [~əri] beitragend.

contrit|e □ ['kɔntrait] reuevoll; ~**ion** [kən'triʃən] Zerknirschung *f*.

contriv|ance [kən'traivəns] Erfindung *f*; Plan *m*; Vorrichtung *f*; Kunstgriff *m*; Scharfsinn *m*; ~**e** [kən'traiv] *v/t.* ersinnen; planen; zuwegebringen; *v/i.* es fertig bringen (*to inf.* zu *inf.*); ~**er** [~və] Erfinder(in).

control [kən'troul] **1.** Kontrolle *f*, Aufsicht *f*; Befehl *m*; Zwang *m*; Gewalt *f*; Zwangswirtschaft *f*; Kontrollvorrichtung *f*; Steuerung *f*; ~ *board* ⊕ Schaltbrett *n*; **2.** einbeschränken; kontrollieren; beaufsichtigen, überwachen; beherrschen; (nach)prüfen; bewirtschaften; regeln; ⚙ steuern (*a. fig. dat.*); ~**ler** [~lə] Kontrolleur *m*, Aufseher *m*; Leiter *m*; Rechnungsprüfer *m*.

controver|sial □ [kɔntrə'vəːʃəl] umstritten; streitsüchtig; ~**sy** ['kɔntrəvəːsi] Streit(frage *f*) *m*; ~**t** [~əːt] bestreiten.

contumacious □ [kɔntju(:)'meiʃəs] widerspenstig; ⚖ ungehorsam.

contumely ['kɔntju(:)mli] Beschimpfung *f*; Schmach *f*.

contuse ⚕ [kən'tjuːz] quetschen.

convalesce [kɔnvə'les] genesen; ~**nce** [~sns] Genesung *f*; ~**nt** [~nt] **1.** □ genesend; **2.** Genesende(r *m*) *f*.

convene [kən'viːn] (sich) versammeln; zs.-rufen; ⚖ vorladen.

convenien|ce [kən'viːnjəns] Bequemlichkeit *f*; Angemessenheit *f*; Vorteil *m*; Klosett *n*; *at your earliest* ~ möglichst bald; ~**t** □ [~nt] bequem; passend; brauchbar.

convent ['kɔnvənt] (Nonnen)Kloster *n*; ~**ion** [kən'venʃən] Versammlung *f*; Konvention *f*, Übereinkommen *n*, Vertrag *m*; Herkommen *n*; ~**ional** [~nl] vertraglich; herkömmlich, konventionell.

converge [kən'vəːdʒ] konvergieren, zs.-laufen (lassen).

convers|ant [kən'vəːsənt] vertraut; ~**ation** [kɔnvə'seiʃən] Gespräch *n*, Unterhaltung *f*; ~**ational** [~nl] Unterhaltungs...; umgangssprachlich; ~**e 1.** □ ['kɔnvəːs] umgekehrt; **2.** [kən'vəːs] sich unterhalten; ~**ion** [~ɔːʃən] Um-, Verwandlung *f*, ⊕ Umformung *f*; *eccl.* Bekehrung *f*; *pol.* Meinungswechsel *m*, Übertritt *m*; ✝ Konvertierung *f*; Umstellung *f* *e-r Währung etc.*

convert 1. ['kɔnvəːt] Bekehrte(r *m*) *f*, Konvertit *m*; **2.** [kən'vəːt] (sich) um-, verwandeln; ⊕, ⚡ umformen; *eccl.* bekehren; † konvertieren; *Währung etc.* umstellen; **~er** ⊕, ⚡ [~tə] Umformer *m*; **~ible 1.** □ [~təbl] um-, verwandelbar; † konvertierbar; **2.** *mot.* Kabrio(lett) *n*.

convey [kən'vei] befördern, bringen, schaffen; übermitteln; mitteilen; ausdrücken; übertragen; **~ance** [~ʃəns] Beförderung *f*; † Spedition *f*; Übermittlung *f*; Verkehrsmittel *n*; Fuhrwerk *n*; Übertragung *f*; **~er**, **~or** ⊕ [~ʃə] *a*. **~ belt** Förderband *n*.

convict 1. ['kɔnvikt] Sträfling *m*; **2.** [kən'vikt] *j-n* überführen; **~ion** [~kʃən] ⚡ Überführung *f*; Überzeugung *f* (*of* von).

convince [kən'vins] überzeugen.

convivial □ [kən'viviəl] festlich; gesellig.

convocation [kɔnvə'keiʃən] Einberufung *f*; Versammlung *f*.

convoke [kən'vouk] einberufen.

convoy ['kɔnvɔi] **1.** Geleit *n*; Geleitzug *m*; (Geleit)Schutz *m*; **2.** geleiten.

convuls|ion [kən'vʌlʃən] Zuckung *f*, Krampf *m*; **~ive** □ [~lsiv] krampfhaft, -artig, konvulsiv.

coo [kuː] girren, gurren.

cook [kuk] **1.** Koch *m*; Köchin *f*; **2.** kochen; *Bericht etc.* frisieren; **~book** *Am.* ['kukbuk] Kochbuch *n*; **~ery** ['kukəri] Kochen *n*; Kochkunst *f*; **~ie** *Am.* ['kuki] Plätzchen *n*; **~ing** [~iŋ] Küche *f* (*Kochweise*); **~y** *Am.* ['kuki] = *cookie*.

cool [kuːl] **1.** □ kühl; *fig.* kaltblütig, gelassen; unverfroren; **2.** Kühle *f*; **3.** (sich) abkühlen.

coolness ['kuːlnis] Kühle *f* (*a. fig.*); Kaltblütigkeit *f*.

coon *Am.* F [kuːn] *zo.* Waschbär *m*; Neger *m*; (schlauer) Bursche.

coop [kuːp] **1.** Hühnerkorb *m*; **2. ~ up** *od.* *in* einsperren.

co-op F [kou'ɔp] = *co-operative* (*store*).

cooper ['kuːpə] Böttcher *m*, Küfer *m*.

co(-)operat|e [kou'ɔpəreit] mitwirken; zs.-arbeiten; **~ion** [kouɔpə-'reiʃən] Mitwirkung *f*; Zs.-arbeit *f*; **~ive** [kou'ɔpərətiv] zs.-wirkend; **~ society** Konsumverein *m*; **~ store** Konsum(vereinsladen) *m*; **~or** [~reitə] Mitarbeiter *m*.

co-ordinat|e **1.** □ [kou'ɔːdnit] gleichgeordnet; **2.** [~dineit] koordinieren, gleichordnen; auf-ea. einstellen; **~ion** [kouɔːdi'neiʃən] Gleichordnung *f*, -schaltung *f*.

copartner ['kou'paːtnə] Teilhaber *m*.

cope [koup]: **~ with** sich messen mit, fertig werden mit.

copious □ ['koupjəs] reich(lich); weitschweifig; **~ness** [~snis] Fülle *f*.

copper¹ ['kɔpə] **1.** Kupfer *n*; Kupfermünze *f*; **2.** kupfern; Kupfer...

copper² ['kɔpə] *sl.* [~] Polyp *m* (*Polizist*).

coppice, copse ['kɔpis, kɔps] Unterholz *n*, Dickicht *n*.

copy ['kɔpi] **1.** Kopie *f*; Nachbildung *f*; Abschrift *f*; Durchschlag *m*; Muster *n*; Exemplar *n e-s Buches*; Zeitungs-Nummer *f*; druckfertiges Manuskript; *fair od.* clean **~** Reinschrift *f*; **2.** kopieren; abschreiben; nachbilden, nachahmen; **~book** Schreibheft *n*; **~ing** [~iiŋ] Kopier...; **~ist** [~ist] Abschreiber *m*; Nachahmer *m*; **~right** Verlagsrecht *n*, Copyright *n*.

coral ['kɔrəl] Koralle *f*.

cord [kɔːd] **1.** Schnur *f*, Strick *m*; *anat.* Strang *m*; **2.** (zu)schnüren, binden; **~ed** ['kɔːdid] gerippt.

cordial □ ['kɔːdjəl] **1.** □ herzlich; herzstärkend; **2.** (Magen)Likör *m*; **~ity** [kɔːdi'æliti] Herzlichkeit *f*.

cordon ['kɔːdn] **1.** Postenkette *f*; **2. ~ off** abriegeln, absperren.

corduroy ['kɔːdərɔi] Kord *m*; **~s** *pl.* Kordhosen *f/pl.*; **~ road** Knüppeldamm *m*.

core [kɔː] **1.** Kerngehäuse *n*; *fig.* Herz *n*; Kern *m*; **2.** entkernen.

cork [kɔːk] **1.** Kork *m*; **2.** (ver)korken; **~ing** *Am.* F ['kɔːkiŋ] fabelhaft, prima; **~jacket** Schwimmweste *f*; **~screw** Kork(en)zieher *m*.

corn [kɔːn] **1.** Korn *n*; Getreide *n*; *a. Indian ~* Am. Mais *m*; ⚡ Hühnerauge *n*; **2.** einpökeln.

corner ['kɔːnə] **1.** Ecke *f*, Winkel *m*; Kurve *f*; *fig.* Enge *f*; † Aufkäufer-Ring *m*; **2.** Eck...; **3.** in die Ecke (*fig.* Enge) treiben; † aufkaufen; **~ed** ...eckig.

cornet ♩ ['kɔːnit] (kleines) Horn.

cornice △ ['kɔːnis] Gesims *n*.

corn|-juice *Am.* *sl.* ['kɔːndʒuːs] Maisschnaps *m*; **~ pone** *Am.* ['kɔːnpoun] Maisbrot *n*; **~stalk** Getreidehalm *m*; *Am.* Maisstengel *m*; **~starch** *Am.* Maisstärke *f*.

coron|ation [kɔrə'neiʃən] Krönung *f*; **~er** ['kɔrənə] Leichenbeschauer *m*; **~et** [~nit] Adelskrone *f*.

corpor|al ['kɔːpərəl] **1.** □ körperlich; **2.** ✗ Korporal *m*; **~ation** [kɔːpə'reiʃən] Körperschaft *f*, Innung *f*, Zunft *f*; Stadtverwaltung *f*; *Am.* Aktiengesellschaft *f*.

corpse [kɔːps] Leichnam *m*.

corpulen|ce, **~cy** ['kɔːpjuləns, ~si] Beleibtheit *f*; **~t** [~nt] beleibt.

corral *Am.* [kɔː'raːl] **1.** Einzäunung *f*; **2.** zs.-pferchen, einsperren.

correct [kə'rekt] **1.** *adj.* □ korrekt, richtig; **2.** *v/t.* korrigieren; zurechtweisen; strafen; **~ion** [~kʃən] Berichtigung *f*; Verweis *m*; Strafe *f*;

Korrektur f; house of ~ Besserungsanstalt f.

correlate ['korileit] in Wechselbeziehung stehen od. bringen.

correspond [koris'pond] entsprechen (with, to dat.); korrespondieren; ~ence [~dəns] Übereinstimmung f; Briefwechsel m; ~ent [~nt] 1. □ entsprechend; 2. Briefschreiber(in); Korrespondent(in).

corridor ['koridɔ:] Korridor m; Gang m; ~ train D-Zug m.

corrigible □ ['koridʒəbl] verbesserlich; zu verbessern(d).

corroborate [kə'robəreit] stärken; bestätigen.

corro|de [kə'roud] zerfressen; wegätzen; ~sion [~ouʒən] Ätzen n, Zerfressen n; ⊕ Korrosion f; Rost m; ~sive [~ousiv] 1. □ zerfressend, ätzend; 2. Ätzmittel n.

corrugate ['korugeit] runzeln; ⊕ riefen; ~d iron Wellblech n.

corrupt [kə'rapt] 1. □ verdorben; verderbt; bestechlich; 2. v/t. verderben; bestechen; anstecken; v/i. (ver)faulen, verderben; ~ible □ [~təbl] verderblich; bestechlich; ~ion [~pʃən] Verderbnis f, Verdorbenheit f; Fäulnis f; Bestechung f.

corsage [kɔ:'sa:ʒ] Taille f, Mieder n; Am. Ansteckblume(n pl.) f.

corset ['kɔ:sit] Korsett n.

coruscate ['korəskeit] funkeln.

co-signatory ['kou'signətəri] 1. mitunterzeichnend; 2. Mitunterzeichner m.

cosmetic [koz'metik] 1. kosmetisch; 2. Schönheitsmittel n; Kosmetik f; ~ian [kozme'tiʃən] Kosmetiker(in).

cosmonaut [kozmə'nɔ:t] Kosmonaut m, Weltraumfahrer m.

cosmopolit|an [kozmə'politən], ~e [koz'mopəlait] 1. kosmopolitisch; 2. Weltbürger(in).

cost [kost] 1. Preis m; Kosten pl.; Schaden m; first od. prime ~ Ansch.ffungskosten pl.; 2. [irr.] kosten.

cost||iness ['kostlinis] Kostbarkeit f; ~y ['kostli] kostbar; kostspielig.

costume ['kostju:m] Kostüm n; Kleidung f; Tracht f.

cosy ['kouzi] 1. □ behaglich, gemütlich; 2. = tea-cosy.

cot [kot] Feldbett n; ⚓ Hängematte f mit Rahmen, Koje f; Kinderbettn.

cottage ['kotidʒ] Hütte f; kleines Landhaus, Sommerhaus n; ~ cheese Am. Quark(käse) m; ~ piano Pianino n; ~r [~dʒə] Häusler m; Hüttenbewohner m; Am. Sommergast m.

cotton ['kotn] 1. Baumwolle f; ✝ Kattun m; Näh-Garn n; 2. baumwollen; Baumwoll...; ~ wool Watte f; ✝ sich vertragen; sich anschließen; ~-wood ⚘ e-e amerikanische Pappel.

couch [kautʃ] 1. Lager n; Couch f, Sofa n, Liege f; Schicht f; 2. v/t. Meinung etc. ausdrücken; Schriftsatz etc. abfassen; ⚔ Star stechen; v/i. sich (nieder)legen; versteckt liegen; kauern.

cough [kof] 1. Husten m; 2. husten.

could [kud] pret. von can[1].

coulee Am. ['ku:li] (trockenes) Bachbett.

council ['kaunsl] Rat(sversammlung f) m; ~(l)or [~silə] Ratsmitglied n, Stadtrat m.

counsel ['kaunsəl] 1. Beratung f; Rat(schlag) m; ⚖ Anwalt m; ~ for the defense Verteidiger m; ~ for the prosecution Anklagevertreter m; 2. j-n beraten; j-m raten; ~(l)or [~slə] Ratgeber(in); Anwalt m; Am. Rechtsbeistand m.

count[1] [kaunt] 1. Rechnung f; Zahl f; ⚖ Anklagepunkt m; 2. v/t. zählen; rechnen; dazurechnen; fig. halten für; v/i. zählen; rechnen; gelten (for little wenig).

count[2] [~] nichtbritischer Graf.

count-down ['kauntdaun] Countdown m, n, Startzählung f (beim Raketenstart).

countenance ['kauntinəns] 1. Gesicht n; Fassung f; Unterstützung f; 2. begünstigen, unterstützen.

counter[1] ['kauntə] Zähler m, Zählapparat m; Spielmarke f; Zahlpfennig m; Ladentisch m; Schalter m.

counter[2] [~] 1. entgegen, zuwider (to dat.); Gegen...; 2. Gegenschlag m; 3. Gegenmaßnahmen treffen.

counteract [kauntə'rækt] zuwiderhandeln (dat.).

counterbalance 1. [kauntə'bæləns] Gegengewicht n; 2. [kauntə'bæləns] aufwiegen; ✝ ausgleichen.

counter-espionage ['kauntər'espiəna:ʒ] Spionageabwehr f.

counterfeit ['kauntəfit] 1. □ nachgemacht; falsch, unecht; 2. Nachahmung f; Fälschung f; Falschgeld n; 3. nachmachen; fälschen; heucheln.

counterfoil ['kauntəfɔil] Kontrollabschnitt m.

countermand [kauntə'ma:nd] 1. Gegenbefehl m; Widerruf m; 2. widerrufen; abbestellen.

counter-move fig. ['kauntəmu:v] Gegenzug m, -maßnahme f.

counterpane ['kauntəpein] Bettdecke f.

counterpart ['kauntəpɑ:t] Gegenstück n.

counterpoise ['kauntəpɔiz] 1. Gegengewicht n; 2. das Gleichgewicht halten (dat.) (a. fig.), ausbalancieren.

countersign ['kauntəsain] 1. Gegenzeichen n; ⚔ Losung(swort n) f; 2. gegenzeichnen.

countervail ['kauntəveil] aufwiegen.

countess ['kauntis] Gräfin f.

counting-house ['kauntiŋhaus] Kontor n.

countless ['kauntlis] zahllos.

countrified ['kʌntrifaid] ländlich; bäurisch.

country ['kʌntri] **1.** Land n; Gegend f; Heimatland n; **2.** Land(s)..., ländlich; **~man** Landmann m (*Bauer*); Landsmann m; **~side** Gegend f; Land(bevölkerung f) n.

county ['kaunti] Grafschaft f, Kreis m; **~ seat** Am. = **~ town** Kreisstadt f.

coup [ku:] Schlag m, Streich m.

couple ['kʌpl] **1.** Paar n; Koppel f; **2.** (ver)koppeln; ⊕ kuppeln; (sich) paaren; **~r** [~lə] Radio: Koppler m.

coupling ['kʌpliŋ] Kupplung f; Radio: Kopplung f; attr. Kupplungs...

coupon ['ku:pɔn] Abschnitt m.

courage ['kʌridʒ] Mut m; **~ous** □ [kə'reidʒəs] mutig, beherzt.

courier ['kuriə] Kurier m, Eilbote m; Reiseführer m.

course [kɔ:s] **1.** Lauf m, Gang m; Weg m; ♣, fig. Kurs m; Rennbahn f; Gang m (Speisen); Kursus m; univ. Vorlesung f; Ordnung f, Folge f; of **~** selbstverständlich; **2.** v/t. hetzen; jagen; v/i. rennen.

court [kɔ:t] **1.** Hof m; Hofgesellschaft f; Gericht(shof m) n; General ♀ Am. gesetzgebende Versammlung; pay (one's) **~** to j-m den Hof machen; **2.** j-m den Hof machen; werben um; **~-day** ['kɔ:tdei] Gerichtstag m; **~eous** □ ['kɔ:tjəs] höflich; **~esy** ['kɔ:tisi] Höflichkeit f; Gefälligkeit f; **~-house** ['kɔ:t-'haus] Gerichtsgebäude n; Am. a. Amtshaus n e-s Kreises; **~ier** ['kɔ:tjə] Höfling m; **~ly** ['kɔ:tli] höfisch; höflich; **~-martial** ⚔ Kriegs-, Militärgericht n; **~-martial** ⚔ ['kɔ:t'ma:ʃəl] vor ein Kriegs- od. Militärgericht stellen; **~ room** Gerichtssaal m; **~ship** ['kɔ:tʃip] Werbung f; **~yard** Hof m.

cousin ['kʌzn] Vetter m; Base f.

cove [kouv] **1.** Bucht f; fig. Obdach n.

covenant ['kʌvinənt] **1.** ⚖ Vertrag m; Bund m; **2.** v/t. geloben; v/i. übereinkommen.

cover ['kʌvə] **1.** Decke f; Deckel m; Umschlag m; Hülle f; Deckung f; Schutz m; Dickicht n; Deckmantel m; Decke f, Mantel m (Bereifung); **2.** (be-, zu)decken; einschlagen; einwickeln; verbergen, verdecken; schützen; Weg zurücklegen; ✝ decken; mit e-r Schußwaffe zielen nach; ⚔ Gelände bestreichen; umfassen; fig. erfassen; Zeitung: berichten über (acc.); **~age** [~əridʒ]

Berichterstattung f (of über acc.); **~ing** [~riŋ] Decke f; Bett-Bezug m; Überzug m; Bekleidung f; Bedachung f.

covert 1. □ ['kʌvət] heimlich, versteckt; **2.** ['kʌvə] Schutz m; Versteck n; Dickicht n.

covet ['kʌvit] begehren; **~ous** □ [~təs] (be)gierig; habsüchtig.

cow¹ [kau] Kuh f.

cow² [~] einschüchtern, ducken.

coward ['kauəd] **1.** □ feig; **2.** Feigling m; **~ice** [~dis] Feigheit f; **~ly** [~dli] feig(e).

cow|boy ['kaubɔi] Cowboy m (berittener Rinderhirt); **~-catcher** Am. 🚂 Schienenräumer m.

cower ['kauə] kauern; sich ducken.

cow|herd ['kauhə:d] Kuhhirt m; **~hide 1.** Rind(s)leder n; **2.** peitschen; **~-house** Kuhstall m.

cowl [kaul] Mönchskutte f; Kapuze f; Schornsteinkappe f.

cow|man ['kaumən] Melker m; Am. Viehzüchter m; **~-puncher** Am. F ['kaupʌntʃə] Rinderhirt m; **~shed** Kuhstall m; **~slip** ♀ Schlüsselblume f; Am. Sumpfdotterblume f.

coxcomb ['kɔkskoum] Geck m.

coxswain ['kɔkswein, ♣ mst 'kɔksn] Bootsführer m; Steuermann m.

coy □ [kɔi] schüchtern; spröde.

crab [kræb] Krabbe f, Taschenkrebs m; ⊕ Winde f; F Querkopf m.

crab-louse ['kræblaus] Filzlaus f.

crack [kræk] **1.** Krach m; Riß m, Sprung m; F derber Schlag; Versuch m; Witz m; **2.** F erstklassig; **3.** v/t. (zer)sprengen; knallen mit et.; (auf)knacken; **~ a joke** e-n Witz reißen; v/i. platzen, springen; knallen; umschlagen (Stimme); **~ed** geborsten; F verdreht; **~er** ['krækə] Knallbonbon m, n; Schwärmer m; Am. Keks m (ungesüßt); **~le** [~kl] knattern, knistern; **~-up** Zs.-stoß m; ⚔ Bruchlandung f.

cradle ['kreidl] **1.** Wiege f; Kindheit f (a. fig.); **2.** (ein)wiegen.

craft [kra:ft] Handwerk n, Gewerbe n; Schiff(e pl.) n; Gerissenheit f; **~sman** ['kra:ftsmən] (Kunst)Handwerker m; ✝ ['kra:fti] gerissen, raffiniert.

crag [kræg] Klippe f, Felsspitze f.

cram [kræm] (voll)stopfen; nudeln, mästen; F (ein)pauken.

cramp [kræmp] **1.** Krampf m; ⊕ Klammer f; fig. Fessel f; **2.** verkrampfen; einengen, hemmen.

cranberry ['krænbəri] Preiselbeere f.

crane [krein] **1.** Kranich m; ⊕ Kran m; **2.** (den Hals) recken; **~-fly** zo. ['kreinflai] Schnake f.

crank [kræŋk] **1.** Kurbel f; Schwengel m; Wortspiel n; Schrulle f; komischer Kauz; fixe Idee; **2.** (an-)kurbeln; **~-shaft** ⊕ ['kræŋkʃa:ft]

Kurbelwelle f; ~y [~ki] wacklig; launisch; verschroben.

cranny ['kræni] Riß m, Ritze f.

crape [kreip] Krepp m, Flor m.

craps Am. [kræps] pl. Würfelspiel.

crash [kræʃ] 1. Krach m (a. ✝); ⚔ Absturz m; 2. v/i. krachen; einstürzen; ⚔ abstürzen; mot. zs.-stoßen; fahren, fliegen, stürzen (into in, auf acc.); v/t. zerschmettern; 3. Am. F blitzschnell ausgeführt; ~helmet ['kræʃhelmit] Sturzhelm m; ~landing Bruchlandung f.

crate [kreit] Lattenkiste f.

crater ['kreitə] Krater m; Trichter m.

crave [kreiv] v/t. dringend bitten od. flehen um; v/i. sich sehnen.

craven ['kreivən] feig.

crawfish ['krɔːfiʃ] 1. Krebs m; 2. Am. F sich drücken.

crawl [krɔːl] 1. Kriechen n; 2. kriechen; schleichen; wimmeln; kribbeln; Schwimmen: kraulen; it makes one's flesh ~ man bekommt e-e Gänsehaut davon.

crayfish ['kreifiʃ] Flußkrebs m.

crayon ['kreiən] Zeichenstift m, bsd. Pastellstift m; Pastell(gemälde) n.

craz|e [kreiz] Verrücktheit f; F Fimmel m; be the ~ Mode sein; ~y □ ['kreizi] baufällig; verrückt (for, about nach).

creak [kriːk] knarren.

cream [kriːm] 1. Rahm m, Sahne f; Creme f; Auslese f; das Beste; 2. den Rahm abschöpfen; ~ery ['kriːməri] Molkerei f; Milchgeschäft n; ~y □ [~mi] sahnig.

crease [kriːs] 1. (Bügel)Falte f; 2. (sich) kniffen, (sich) falten.

creat|e [kri(ː)'eit] (er)schaffen; thea. e-e Rolle gestalten; verursachen; erzeugen; ernennen; ~ion [~'eiʃən] Schöpfung f; Ernennung f; ~ive [~'eitiv] schöpferisch; ~or [~tə] Schöpfer m; ~ure ['kriːtʃə] Geschöpf n; Kreatur f.

creden|ce ['kriːdəns] Glaube m; ~tials [kri'denʃəlz] pl. Beglaubigungsschreiben n; Unterlagen f/pl.

credible □ ['kredəbl] glaubwürdig; glaubhaft.

credit ['kredit] 1. Glaube(n) m; Ruf m, Ansehen n; Guthaben n; ✝ Kredit m; ✝ Kredit m; Einfluß m; Verdienst n, Ehre f; Am. Schule: (Anrechnungs)Punkt m; 2. j-m glauben; j-m trauen; ✝ gutschreiben; ~ s.o. with s.th. j-m et. zutrauen; ~able □ [~təbl] achtbar; ehrenvoll (to für); ~or [~tə] Gläubiger m.

credulous □ ['kredjuləs] leichtgläubig.

creed [kriːd] Glaubensbekenntnis n.

creek [kriːk] Bucht f; Am. Bach m.

creel [kriːl] Fischkorb m.

creep [kriːp] [irr.] kriechen; fig. (sich ein)schleichen; kribbeln; it makes my flesh ~ ich bekomme e-e Gänsehaut davon; ~er ['kriːpə] Kriecher(in); Kletterpflanze f.

cremator|ium [kremə'tɔːriəm], bsd. Am. ~y ['kremətəri] Krematorium n.

crept [krept] pret. u. p.p. von creep.

crescent ['kresnt] 1. zunehmend; halbmondförmig; 2. Halbmond m; ♀ City Am. New Orleans.

cress ♀ [kres] Kresse f.

crest [krest] Hahnen-, Berg- etc. Kamm m; Mähne f; Federbusch m; Heraldik: family ~ Familienwappen n; ~fallen ['krestfɔːlən] niedergeschlagen.

crevasse [kri'væs] (Gletscher)Spalte f; Am. Deichbruch m.

crevice ['krevis] Riß m, Spalte f.

crew¹ [kruː] Schar f; ⚓, ⚔ Mannschaft f.

crew² [~] pret. von crow 2.

crib [krib] 1. Krippe f; Kinderbett (-stelle f) n; F Schule: Klatsche f; bsd. Am. Behälter m; 2. einsperren; F mausen; F abschreiben.

crick [krik] Krampf m; ~ in the neck steifer Hals.

cricket ['krikit] zo. Grille f; Sport: Kricket n; not ~ F nicht fair.

crime [kraim] Verbrechen n.

criminal ['kriminl] 1. verbrecherisch; Kriminal..., Straf...; 2. Verbrecher(in); ~ity [krimi'næliti] Strafbarkeit f; Verbrechertum n.

crimp [krimp] kräuseln.

crimson ['krimzn] karmesin(rot).

cringe [krindʒ] sich ducken.

crinkle ['krinkl] 1. Windung f; Falte f; 2. (sich) winden; (sich) kräuseln.

cripple ['kripl] 1. Krüppel m; Lahme(r m) f; 2. verkrüppeln; fig. lähmen.

cris|is ['kraisis], pl. ~es [~siːz] Krisis f, Krise f, Wende-, Höhepunkt m.

crisp [krisp] 1. kraus; knusperig; frisch; klar; steif; 2. (sich) kräuseln; knusperig machen od. werden; 3. ~s pl., a. potato ~s pl. Kartoffelchips pl.

criss-cross ['kriskrɔs] 1. Kreuzzeichen n; 2. (durch)kreuzen.

criteri|on [krai'tiəriən], pl. ~a [~riə] Kennzeichen n, Prüfstein m.

criti|c ['kritik] Kritiker(in); ~cal □ [~kəl] kritisch; bedenklich; ~cism [~isizəm] Kritik f (of an dat.); ~cize [~saiz] kritisieren; beurteilen; tadeln; ~que [kri'tiːk] kritischer Essay; die Kritik.

croak [krouk] krächzen; quaken.

crochet ['krouʃei] 1. Häkelei f; 2. häkeln.

crock [krɔk] irdener Topf; **~ery** ['krɔkəri] Töpferware f.

crocodile zo. ['krɔkədail] Krokodil n.

crone F [kroun] altes Weib.

crony F ['krouni] alter Freund.

crook [kruk] **1.** Krümmung f; Haken m; Hirtenstab m; sl. Gauner m; **2.** (sich) krümmen; (sich) (ver)biegen; **~ed** ['krukid] krumm; bucklig; unehrlich; [krukt] Krück...

croon [kru:n] schmalzig singen; summen; **~er** ['kru:nə] Schnulzensänger m.

crop [krɔp] **1.** Kropf m; Peitschenstiel m; Reitpeitsche f; Ernte f; kurzer Haarschnitt; **2.** (ab-, be-) schneiden; (ab)ernten; Acker bebauen; **~ up** fig. auftauchen.

cross [krɔs] **1.** Kreuz n (a. fig. Leiden); Kreuzung f; **2.** □ sich kreuzend; quer (liegend, laufend etc.); ärgerlich, verdrießlich; entgegengesetzt; Kreuz..., Quer...; **3.** v/t. kreuzen(durchstreichen); fig. durchkreuzen; überqueren; in den Weg kommen (dat.); ~ o.s. sich bekreuzigen; keep one's fingers ~ed den Daumen halten; v/i. sich kreuzen; **~bar** ['krɔsba:] Fußball: Torlatte f; **~breed** (Rassen)Kreuzung f; **~country** querfeldein; **~examination** Kreuzverhör n; **~eyed** schieläugig; **~ing** ['krɔsin] Kreuzung f; Übergang m; -fahrt f; **~road** Querstraße f, **~roads** pl. od. sg. Kreuzweg m; **~section** Querschnitt m; **~wise** kreuzweise; **~word (puzzle)** Kreuzworträtsel n.

crotchet ['krɔtʃit] Haken m; ♪ Viertelnote f; wunderlicher Einfall.

crouch [krautʃ] **1.** sich ducken; **2.** Hockstellung f.

crow [krou] **1.** Krähe f; Krähen n; eat ~ Am. F zu Kreuze kriechen; **2.** [irr.] krähen; triumphieren; **~bar** ['krouba:] Brecheisen n.

crowd [kraud] **1.** Haufen m, Menge f; Gedränge n; F Bande f; **2.** (sich) drängen; (über)füllen; wimmeln.

crown [kraun] **1.** Krone f; Kranz m; Gipfel m; Scheitel m; **2.** krönen; Zahn überkronen; to ~ all zu guter Letzt, zu allem Überfluß.

cruci|al □ ['kru:ʃəl] entscheidend; kritisch; **~ble** ['kru:sibl] Schmelztiegel m; **~fixion** [kru:si'fikʃən] Kreuzigung f; **~fy** ['kru:sifai] kreuzigen.

crude □ [kru:d] roh; unfertig; unreif; unfein; grob; Roh...; grell.

cruel □ ['kruəl] grausam; hart; fig. blutig; **~ty** [~lti] Grausamkeit f.

cruet ['kru:(:)it] (Essig-, Öl)Fläschchen n.

cruise ♫ [kru:z] **1.** Kreuzfahrt f, Seereise f; **2.** kreuzen; **~r** ['kru:zə]

♫ Kreuzer m; Jacht f; Am. Funkstreifenwagen m.

crumb [krʌm] **1.** Krume f; Brocken m; **2.** panieren; zerkrümeln; **~le** ['krʌmbl] (zer)bröckeln; fig. zugrunde gehen.

crumple ['krʌmpl] v/t. zerknittern; fig. vernichten; v/i. (sich) knüllen.

crunch [krʌntʃ] (zer)kauen; zermalmen; knirschen.

crusade [kru:'seid] Kreuzzug m (a. fig.); **~r** [~də] Kreuzfahrer m.

crush [krʌʃ] **1.** Druck m; Gedränge n; (Frucht)Saft m; Am. sl. Schwarm m; have a ~ on s.o. in j-n verliebt od. verschossen sein; **2.** v/t. (zer-, aus)quetschen; zermalmen; fig. vernichten; v/i. sich drängen; **~ barrier** ['krʌʃbæriə] Absperrgitter n.

crust [krʌst] **1.** Kruste f, Rinde f; Am. sl. Frechheit f; **2.** (sich) be-, überkrusten, verharschen; **~y** □ ['krʌsti] krustig; fig. mürrisch.

crutch [krʌtʃ] Krücke f.

cry [krai] **1.** Schrei m; Geschrei n; Ruf m; Weinen n; Gebell n; **2.** schreien; (aus)rufen; weinen; ~ for verlangen nach.

crypt [kript] Gruft f; **~ic** ['kriptik] verborgen, geheim.

crystal ['kristl] Kristall m, n; Am. Uhrglas n; **~line** [~təlain] kristallen; **~lize** [~aiz] kristallisieren.

cub [kʌb] **1.** Junge(s) n; Flegel m; Anfänger m; **2.** (Junge) werfen.

cub|e ♣ [kju:b] Würfel m; Kubikzahl f; ~ root Kubikwurzel f; **~ic(al** □) ['kju:bik(əl)] würfelförmig; kubisch; Kubik...

cuckoo ['kuku:] Kuckuck m.

cucumber ['kju:kəmbə] Gurke f; as cool as a ~ fig. eiskalt, gelassen.

cud [kʌd] wiedergekäutes Futter; chew the ~ wiederkäuen; fig. überlegen.

cuddle ['kʌdl] v/t. (ver)hätscheln.

cudgel ['kʌdʒəl] **1.** Knüttel m; **2.** (ver)prügeln.

cue [kju:] Billard-Queue n; Stichwort n; Wink m.

cuff [kaf] **1.** Manschette f; Handschelle f; (Ärmel-, Am. a. Hosen-) Aufschlag m; Faust-Schlag m; **2.** puffen, schlagen.

cuisine [kwi(:)'zi:n] Küche f (Art zu kochen).

culminate ['kʌlmineit] gipfeln.

culpable □ ['kʌlpəbl] strafbar.

culprit ['kʌlprit] Angeklagte(r m) f; Schuldige(r m) f, Missetäter(in).

cultivat|e ['kʌltiveit] kultivieren; an-, bebauen; ausbilden; pflegen; **~ion** [kʌlti'veiʃən] (An-, Acker)Bau m; Ausbildung f; Pflege f, Zucht f; **~or** ['kʌltiveitə] Landwirt m; Züchter m; ♪ Kultivator m (Maschine).

cultural □ ['kʌltʃərəl] kulturell.

culture ['kʌltʃə] Kultur f; Pflege f; Zucht f; ~d kultiviert.

cumb|er ['kʌmbə] überladen; belasten; ~ersome [~əsəm], ~rous □ [~brəs] lästig; schwerfällig.

cumulative □ ['kju:mjulətiv] (an-, auf)häufend; Zusatz...

cunning ['kʌniŋ] **1.** □ schlau, listig; geschickt; *Am.* reizend; **2.** List f, Schlauheit f; Geschicklichkeit f.

cup [kʌp] Becher m, Schale f, Tasse f; Kelch m; *Sport:* Pokal m; ~board ['kʌbəd] (Speise- *etc.*)Schrank m.

cupidity [kju(:)'piditi] Habgier f.

cupola ['kju:pələ] Kuppel f.

cur [kə:] Köter m; Schurke m, Halunke m.

curable ['kjuərəbl] heilbar.

curate ['kjuərit] Hilfsgeistliche(r) m.

curb [kə:b] **1.** Kinnkette f; Kandare f (a. fig.); a. ~stone ['kə:bstoun] Bordschwelle f; **2.** an die Kandare nehmen (a. fig.); fig. zügeln; ~market *Am. Börse:* Freiverkehr m; ~roof Mansardendach n.

curd [kə:d] **1.** Quark m; **2.** (mst ~le ['kə:dl]) gerinnen (lassen).

cure [kjuə] **1.** Kur f; Heilmittel n; Seelsorge f; Pfarre f; **2.** heilen; pökeln; räuchern; trocknen.

curfew ['kə:fju:] Abendglocke f; *pol.* Ausgehverbot n; ~bell Abendglocke f.

curio ['kjuəriou] Rarität f; ~sity [kjuəri'ositi] Neugier f; Rarität f; ~us □ ['kjuəriəs] neugierig; genau; seltsam, merkwürdig.

curl [kə:l] **1.** Locke f; **2.** (sich) kräuseln; (sich) locken; (sich) ringeln; ~y ['kə:li] gekräuselt; lockig.

currant ['kʌrənt] Johannisbeere f; a. dried ~ Korinthe f.

curren|cy ['kʌrənsi] Umlauf m; ♦ Lauffrist f; Kurs m, Währung f; ~t [~nt] **1.** □ umlaufend; ♦ kursierend (*Geld*); allgemein (bekannt); laufend (*Jahr etc.*); **2.** Strom m (a. ♂); Strömung f (a. fig.); Luftzug m.

curricul|um [kə'rikjuləm], pl. ~a [~lə] Lehr-, Stundenplan m; ~um vitae [~əm'vaiti:] Lebenslauf m.

curry¹ ['kʌri] Curry m, n.

curry² [~] *Leder* zurichten; *Pferd* striegeln.

curse [kə:s] **1.** Fluch m; **2.** (ver)fluchen; strafen; ~d □ ['kə:sid] verflucht.

curt □ [kə:t] kurz; knapp; barsch.

curtail [kə:'teil] beschneiden; fig. beschränken; kürzen (of um).

curtain ['kə:tn] **1.** Vorhang m; Gardine f; **2.** verhängen, verschleiern; ~lecture F Gardinenpredigt f.

curts(e)y ['kə:tsi] **1.** Knicks m; **2.** knicksen (*to* vor).

curvature ['kə:vətʃə] (Ver)Krümmung f.

curve [kə:v] **1.** Kurve f; Krümmung f; **2.** (sich) krümmen; (sich) biegen.

cushion ['kuʃən] **1.** Kissen n; Polster n; *Billard-*Bande f; **2.** polstern.

cuss *Am.* F [kʌs] **1.** Nichtsnutz m; **2.** fluchen.

custody ['kʌstədi] Haft f; (Ob)Hut f.

custom ['kʌstəm] Gewohnheit f, Brauch m; Sitte f; Kundschaft f; ~s pl. Zoll m; ~ary □ [~məri] gewöhnlich, üblich; ~er [~mə] Kund|e m, -in f; F Bursche m; ~house Zollamt n; ~made *Am.* maßgearbeitet.

cut [kʌt] **1.** Schnitt m; Hieb m; Stich m; (Schnitt)Wunde f; Einschnitt m; Graben m; Kürzung f; Ausschnitt m; Wegabkürzung f (mst short-~); *Holz-*Schnitt m; *Kupfer-*Stich m; Schliff m; Schnitte f, Scheibe f; *Karten-*Abheben n; *Küche:* cold ~s pl. Aufschnitt m; give s.o. the ~ (direct) F j. schneiden; **2.** [irr.] v/t. schneiden; schnitzen; gravieren; ab-, an-, auf-, aus-, be-, durch-, zer-, zuschneiden; *Edelstein etc.* schleifen; *Karten* abheben; j. beim Begegnen schneiden; ~ teeth zahnen; ~ short j. unterbrechen; ~ back einschränken; ~ down fällen; mähen; beschneiden; *Preis* drücken; ~ out ausschneiden; *Am.* Vieh aussondern *aus der Herde*; fig. j. ausstechen; ♂ ausschalten; be ~ out for das Zeug zu e-r S. haben; v/i. ~ in sich einschneiden; s. cut 2. **3.** adj. geschnitten *etc.*, s. cut 2.

cute □ F [kju:t] schlau; *Am.* reizend.

cuticle ['kju:tikl] Oberhaut f; ~ scissors pl. Hautschere f.

cutlery ['kʌtləri] Messerschmiedearbeit f; Stahlwaren f/pl.; Bestecke n/pl.

cutlet ['kʌtlit] Kotelett n; Schnitzel n.

cut|-off *Am.* ['kʌtɔ:f] Abkürzung f (*Straße, Weg*); ~out *mot.* Auspuffklappe f; ♂ Sicherung f; Ausschalter m; *Am.* Ausschneidebogen m, -bild n; ~purse Taschendieb m; ~ter ['kʌtə] Schneidende(r m) f; Schnitzer m; Zuschneider(in); *Film:* Cutter m; ⊕ Schneidezeug n, -maschine f; ♣ Kutter m; *Am.* leichter Schlitten; ~throat Halsabschneider m; Meuchelmörder m; ~ting ['kʌtiŋ] **1.** □ schneidend; scharf; ♀ Schneid..., Fräs...; **2.** Schneiden n; ♀ etc. Einschnitt m; ♀ Steckling m; *Zeitungs-*Ausschnitt m; ~s pl. Schnipsel m, n/pl.; ⊕ Späne m/pl.

cycl|e ['saikl] **1.** Zyklus m; Kreis (-lauf) m; Periode f; ⊕ Arbeitsgang *m*; Fahrrad *n*; **2.** radfahren; ~ist [~list] Radfahrer(in).

cyclone ['saikloun] Wirbelsturm *m*.

cylinder ['silində] Zylinder *m*, Walze *f*; ⊕ Trommel *f*.

cymbal ♪ ['simbəl] Becken *n*.

cynic ['sinik] **1.** *a.* ~al □ [~kəl] zynisch; **2.** Zyniker *m*.

cypress ♀ ['saipris] Zypresse *f*.

cyst ⚕ [sist] Blase *f*; Sackgeschwulst *f*; ~itis ⚕ [sis'taitis] Blasenentzündung *f*.

Czech [tʃek] **1.** Tschech|e *m*, -in *f*; **2.** tschechisch.

Czechoslovak ['tʃekou'slouvæk] **1.** Tschechoslowak|e *m*, -in *f*; **2.** tschechoslowakisch.

D

dab [dæb] **1.** Klaps *m*; Tupf(en) *m*, Klecks *m*; **2.** klapsen; (be)tupfen.

dabble ['dæbl] bespritzen; plätschern; (hinein)pfuschen.

dad F [dæd], ~dy F ['dædi] Papa *m*.

daddy-longlegs F *zo.* ['dædi'lɔŋlegz] Schnake *f*; *Am.* Weberknecht *m*.

daffodil ♀ ['dæfədil] gelbe Narzisse.

daft F [dɑ:ft] blöde, doof.

dagger ['dægə] Dolch *m*; *be at* ~*s drawn fig.* auf Kriegsfuß stehen.

dago *Am. sl.* ['deigou] *contp. für Spanier, Portugiese, mst Italiener.*

daily ['deili] **1.** täglich; **2.** Tageszeitung *f*.

dainty ['deinti] **1.** □ lecker; zart, fein; wählerisch; **2.** Leckerei *f*.

dairy ['dɛəri] Molkerei *f*, Milchwirtschaft *f*; Milchgeschäft *n*; ~ **cattle** Milchvieh *n*; ~**man** Milchhändler *m*.

daisy ♀ ['deizi] Gänseblümchen *n*.

dale [deil] Tal *n*.

dall|iance ['dæliəns] Trödelei *f*; Liebelei *f*; ~y ['dæli] vertrödeln; schäkern.

dam [dæm] **1.** Mutter *f von Tieren*; Deich *m*, Damm *m*; **2.** (ab)dämmen.

damage ['dæmidʒ] **1.** Schaden *m*; ~*s pl.* ⚖ Schadenersatz *m*; **2.** (be-)schädigen.

damask ['dæməsk] Damast *m*.

dame [deim] Dame *f*; *sl.* Weib *n*.

damn [dæm] verdammen; verurteilen; ~**ation** [dæm'neiʃən] Verdammung *f*.

damp [dæmp] **1.** feucht, dunstig; **2.** Feuchtigkeit *f*, Dunst *m*; Gedrücktheit *f*; **3.** *a.* ~**en** ['dæmpən] anfeuchten; dämpfen; niederdrücken; ~**er** [~pə] Dämpfer *m*.

danc|e [dɑ:ns] **1.** Tanz *m*; Ball *m*; **2.** tanzen (lassen); ~**er** ['dɑ:nsə] Tänzer(in) *f*; ~**ing** [~siŋ] Tanzen *n*; *attr.* Tanz ... [zahn *m*.]

dandelion ♀ ['dændilaiən] Löwen-]

dandle *sl.* ['dændl] wiegen, schaukeln.

dandruff ['dændrəf] (Kopf)Schuppen *f/pl.*

dandy ['dændi] **1.** Stutzer *m*; F erstklassige Sache; **2.** *Am.* F prima.

Dane [dein] Dän|e *m*, -in *f*.

danger ['deindʒə] Gefahr *f*; ~**ous** □ [~dʒrəs] gefährlich; ~**signal** 🚩 Notsignal *n*.

dangle ['dæŋgl] baumeln (lassen); schlenkern (mit); *fig.* schwanken.

Danish ['deiniʃ] dänisch.

dank [dæŋk] dunstig, feucht.

Danubian [dæ'nju:bjən] Donau...

dapper □ F ['dæpə] nett; behend.

dapple ['dæpl] sprenkeln; ~**d** scheckig; ~**-grey** Apfelschimmel *m*.

dar|e [dɛə] *v/i.* es wagen; *v/t. et.* wagen; *j-n* herausfordern; *j-m* trotzen; ~**e-devil** ['dɛədevl] Draufgänger *m*; ~**ing** □ ['dɛəriŋ] **1.** verwegen; **2.** Verwegenheit *f*.

dark [dɑ:k] **1.** □ dunkel; brünett; schwerverständlich; geheim(nisvoll); trüb(selig); **2.** Dunkel(heit *f*) *n*; *before (after)* ~ vor (nach) Einbruch der Dunkelheit; *2 Ages pl. das* frühe Mittelalter; ~**en** ['dɑ:kən] (sich) (ver)dunkeln; (sich) verfinstern; ~**ness** ['dɑ:knis] Dunkelheit *f*, Finsternis *f*; ~**y** F ['dɑ:ki] Schwarze(r *m*) *f*.

darling ['dɑ:liŋ] **1.** Liebling *m*; **2.** Lieblings...; geliebt.

darn [dɑːn] stopfen; ausbessern.

dart [dɑːt] **1.** Wurfspieß *m*; Wurfpfeil *m*; Sprung *m*, Satz *m*; ~*s pl.* Wurfpfeilspiel *n*; **2.** *v/t.* schleudern; *v/i. fig.* schießen, (sich) stürzen.

dash [dæʃ] **1.** Schlag *m*, (Zs.-)Stoß *m*; Klatschen *n*; Schwung *m*; Ansturm *m*; *fig.* Anflug *m*; Prise *f*; Schuß *m* Rum *etc.*; Feder-Strich *m*; Gedankenstrich *m*; **2.** *v/t.* schlagen, werfen, schleudern; zerschmettern; vernichten; (be)spritzen; vermengen; verwirren; *v/i.* stoßen, schlagen; stürzen; stürmen; jagen; ~**board** *mot.* ['dæʃbɔːd] Armaturenbrett *n*; ~**ing** □ ['dæʃiŋ] schneidig, forsch; flott, F fesch.

dastardly ['dæstədli] heimtückisch; feig.

data ['deitə] *pl.*, *Am. a. sg.* Angaben

f/pl.; Tatsachen f/pl.; Unterlagen f/pl.; Daten pl.

date [deit] 1. ♀ Dattel f; Datum n; Zeit f; Termin m; Am. F Verabredung f; Freund(in); out of ~ veraltet, unmodern; up to ~ zeitgemäß, modern; auf dem laufenden; 2. datieren; Am. F sich verabreden.

dative gr. ['deitiv] a. ~ case Dativ m.

daub [dɔ:b] (be)schmieren; (be-)klecksen.

daughter ['dɔ:tə] Tochter f; ~-in-law [~ɔrinlɔ:] Schwiegertochter f.

daunt [dɔ:nt] entmutigen; ~less ['dɔ:ntlis] furchtlos, unerschrocken.

daw orn. [dɔ:] Dohle f.

dawdle F ['dɔ:dl] (ver)trödeln.

dawn [dɔ:n] 1. Dämmerung f; fig. Morgenrot n; 2. dämmern, tagen; it ~ed upon him fig. es wurde ihm langsam klar.

day [dei] Tag m; oft ~s pl. (Lebens-)Zeit f; ~ off dienst-freier Tag; carry od. win the ~ den Sieg davontragen; the other ~ neulich; this ~ week heute in einer Woche; heute vor einer Woche; let's call it a ~ machen wir Schluß für heute; ~break ['deibreik] Tagesanbruch m; ~-labo(u)rer Tagelöhner m; ~-star Morgenstern m.

daze [deiz] blenden; betäuben.

dazzle ['dæzl] blenden; ♣ tarnen.

dead [ded] 1. tot; unempfindlich (to für); matt (Farbe etc.); blind (Fenster etc.); erloschen (Feuer); schal (Getränk); tief (Schlaf); ✝ tot (Kapital etc.); ~ bargain Spottpreis m; ~ letter unzustellbarer Brief; ~ loss Totalverlust m; a ~ shot ein Meisterschütze; ~ wall blinde Mauer; ~ wood Reisig n; Am. Plunder m; 2. adv. gänzlich, völlig, total; durchaus; genau, (haar)scharf; ~ against gerade od. ganz und gar (ent)gegen; 3. the ~ der Tote; die Toten pl.; Totenstille f; in the ~ of winter im tiefsten Winter; in the ~ of night mitten in der Nacht; ~en ['dedn] abstumpfen; dämpfen; (ab)schwächen; ~end Sackgasse f (a. fig.); ~line Am. Sperrlinie f im Gefängnis; Schlußtermin m; Stichtag m; ~lock Stockung f; fig. toter Punkt; ~ly [~li] tödlich.

deaf □ [def] taub; ~en ['defn] taub machen; betäuben.

deal [di:l] 1. Teil m; Menge f; Kartengeben n; F Geschäft n; Abmachung f; a good ~ ziemlich viel; a great ~ sehr viel; 2. [irr.] v/t. (aus-, ver-, zu)teilen; Karten geben; e-n Schlag versetzen; v/i. handeln (in mit e-r Ware); verfahren, verkehren; ~ with sich befassen mit, behandeln; ~er ['di:lə] Händler m; Kartengeber m; ~ing ['di:liŋ] mst

~s pl. Handlungsweise f; Verfahren n; Verkehr m; ~t [delt] pret. u p.p. von deal 2.

dean [di:n] Dekan m.

dear [diə] 1. □ teuer; lieb; 2. Liebling m; herziges Geschöpf; 3. o(h) ~!, ~ me! F du liebe Zeit!; ach herrje!

death [deθ] Tod m; Todesfall m; ~-bed ['deθbed] Sterbebett n; ~-duty Erbschaftsteuer f; ~less ['deθlis] unsterblich; ~ly [~li] tödlich; ~-rate Sterblichkeitsziffer f; ~-warrant Todesurteil n.

debar [di'ba:] ausschließen; hindern.

debarkation [di:ba:'keiʃən] Ausschiffung f.

debase [di'beis] verschlechtern; erniedrigen; verfälschen.

debat|able □ [di'beitəbl] strittig; umstritten; ~e [di'beit] 1. Debatte f; 2. debattieren; erörtern; überlegen.

debauch [di'bɔ:tʃ] 1. Ausschweifung f; 2. verderben; verführen.

debilitate [di'biliteit] schwächen.

debit ✝ ['debit] 1. Debet n, Schuld f; 2. j-n belasten; debitieren.

debris ['debri:] Trümmer pl.

debt [det] Schuld f; ~or ['detə] Schuldner(in).

debunk ['di:'bʌŋk] den Nimbus nehmen (dat.).

début ['deibu:] Debüt n.

decade ['dekeid] Jahrzehnt n.

decadence ['dekədəns] Verfall m.

decamp [di'kæmp] aufbrechen; ausreißen; ~ment [~pmənt] Aufbruch m.

decant [di'kænt] abgießen; umfüllen; ~er [~tə] Karaffe f.

decapitate [di'kæpiteit] enthaupten; Am. F fig. absägen (entlassen).

decay [di'kei] 1. Verfall m; Fäulnis f; 2. verfallen; (ver)faulen.

decease bsd. ✝✝ [di'si:s] 1. Ableben n; 2. sterben.

deceit [di'si:t] Täuschung f; Betrug m; ~ful □ [~tful] (be)trügerisch.

deceive [di'si:v] betrügen; täuschen; verleiten; ~r [~və] Betrüger(in).

December [di'sembə] Dezember m.

decen|cy ['di:snsi] Anstand m; ~t □ [~nt] anständig; F annehmbar, nett.

deception [di'sepʃən] Täuschung f.

decide [di'said] (sich) entscheiden; bestimmen; ~d □ entschieden; bestimmt; entschlossen.

decimal ['desiməl] Dezimalbruch m; attr. Dezimal...

decipher [di'saifə] entziffern.

decisi|on [di'siʒən] Entscheidung f; ✝✝ Urteil n; Entschluß m; Entschlossenheit f; ~ve □ [di'saisiv] entscheidend; entschieden.

deck [dek] **1.** ♣ Deck *n*; *Am.* Pack *m* Spielkarten; on ~ *Am.* F da(bei), bereit; **2.** *rhet.* schmücken; **~-chair** ['dek'tʃɛə] Liegestuhl *m*.

declaim [di'kleim] vortragen; (sich er)eifern.

declar|able [di'klɛərəbl] steuer-, zollpflichtig; **~ation** [deklə'reiʃən] Erklärung *f*; *Zoll*-Deklaration *f*; **~e** [di'klɛə] (sich) erklären; behaupten; deklarieren.

declension [di'klenʃən] Abfall *m* (*Neigung*); Verfall *m*; *gr.* Deklination *f*.

declin|ation [dekli'neiʃən] Neigung *f*; Abweichung *f*; **~e** [di'klain] **1.** Abnahme *f*; Niedergang *m*; Verfall *m*; **2.** *v/t.* neigen, biegen; *gr.* deklinieren; ablehnen; *v/i.* sich neigen; abnehmen; verfallen.

declivity [di'kliviti] Abhang *m*.

declutch *mot.* ['di:'klʌtʃ] auskuppeln.

decode *tel.* ['di:'koud] entschlüsseln.

decompose [di:kəm'pouz] zerlegen; (sich) zersetzen; verwesen.

decontrol ['di:kən'troul] *Waren, Handel* freigeben.

decorat|e ['dekəreit] (ver)zieren; schmücken; **~ion** [dekə'reiʃən] Verzierung *f*; Schmuck *m*; Orden(sauszeichnung *f*) *m*; ♀ Day *Am.* Heldengedenktag *m*; **~ive** ['dekərətiv] dekorativ; Zier...; **~or** [~reitə] Dekorateur *m*, Maler *m*.

decor|ous □ ['dekərəs] anständig; **~um** [di'kɔːrəm] Anstand *m*.

decoy [di'kɔi] **1.** Lockvogel *m* (*a. fig.*); Köder *m*; **2.** ködern; locken.

decrease 1. ['di:kri:s] Abnahme *f*; **2.** [di:'kri:s] (sich) vermindern.

decree [di'kri:] **1.** Dekret *n*, Verordnung *f*, Erlaß *m*; ⚖ Entscheid *m*; **2.** beschließen; verordnen, verfügen.

decrepit [di'krepit] altersschwach.

decry [di'krai] in Verruf bringen.

dedicat|e ['dedikeit] widmen; **~ion** [dedi'keiʃən] Widmung *f*.

deduce [di'djuːs] ableiten; folgern.

deduct [di'dʌkt] abziehen; **~ion** [~kʃən] Abzug *m*; ✝ Rabatt *m*; Schlußfolgerung *f*.

deed [di:d] **1.** Tat *f*; Heldentat *f*; Urkunde *f*; **2.** *Am.* urkundlich übertragen (to auf *acc.*).

deem [di:m] *v/t.* halten für; *v/i.* denken, urteilen (of über *acc.*).

deep [di:p] **1.** □ tief; gründlich; schlau; vertieft; dunkel (*a. fig.*); verborgen; **2.** Tiefe *f*; *poet.* Meer *n*; **~en** ['di:pən] (sich) vertiefen; (sich) verstärken; **~-freeze 1.** tiefkühlen; **2.** Tiefkühlfach *n*, -truhe *f*; **~ness** ['di:pnis] Tiefe *f*.

deer [diə] Rotwild *n*; Hirsch *m*.

deface [di'feis] entstellen; unkenntlich machen; ausstreichen.

defalcation [di:fæl'keiʃən] Unterschlagung *f*.

defam|ation [defə'meiʃən] Verleumdung *f*; **~e** [di'feim] verleumden; verunglimpfen.

default [di'fɔːlt] **1.** Nichterscheinen *n vor Gericht*; Säumigkeit *f*; Verzug *m*; in ~ of which widrigenfalls; **2.** *s-n etc.* Verbindlichkeiten nicht nachkommen.

defeat [di'fi:t] **1.** Niederlage *f*; Besiegung *f*; Vereitelung *f*; **2.** ✕ besiegen; vereiteln; vernichten.

defect [di'fekt] Mangel *m*; Fehler *m*; **~ive** □ [~tiv] mangelhaft; unvollständig; fehlerhaft.

defen|ce, *Am.* **~se** [di'fens] Verteidigung *f*; Schutzmaßnahme *f*; witness for the ~ Entlastungszeuge *m*; **~celess,** *Am.* **~seless** [~slis] schutzlos, wehrlos.

defend [di'fend] verteidigen; schützen (*from vor dat.*); **~ant** [~dənt] Angeklagte(r *m*) *f*; Beklagte(r *m*) *f*; **~er** [~də] Verteidiger(in).

defensive [di'fensiv] Defensive *f*; *attr.* Verteidigungs...

defer [di'fəː] auf-, verschieben, *Am.* ✕ zurückstellen; sich fügen; nachgeben; *payment* ~*red terms* Ratenzahlung *f*; **~ence** ['defərəns] Ehrerbietung *f*; Nachgiebigkeit *f*; **~ential** □ [defə'renʃəl] ehrerbietig.

defian|ce [di'faiəns] Herausforderung *f*; Trotz *m*; **~t** □ [~nt] herausfordernd; trotzig.

deficien|cy [di'fiʃənsi] Unzulänglichkeit *f*; Mangel *m*; = *deficit*; **~t** [~nt] mangelhaft; unzureichend.

deficit ['defisit] Fehlbetrag *m*.

defile 1. ['di:fail] Engpaß *m*; **2.** [di'fail] *v/i.* vorbeiziehen; *v/t.* beflecken; schänden.

defin|e [di'fain] definieren; erklären; genau bestimmen; **~ite** □ ['definit] bestimmt; deutlich; genau; **~ition** [defi'niʃən] (Begriffs-)Bestimmung *f*; Erklärung *f*; **~itive** □ [di'finitiv] bestimmt; entscheidend; endgültig.

deflect [di'flekt] ablenken; abweichen.

deform [di'fɔːm] entstellen, verunstalten; **~ed** verwachsen; **~ity** [~miti] Unförmigkeit *f*; Mißgestalt *f*.

defraud [di'frɔːd] betrügen (of um).

defray [di'frei] *Kosten* bestreiten.

defroster *mot.* [di:'frɔstə] Entfroster *m*.

deft □ [deft] gewandt, flink.

defunct [di'fʌŋkt] verstorben.

defy [di'fai] herausfordern; trotzen.

degenerate 1. [di'dʒenəreit] entarten; **2.** □ [~rit] entartet.

degrad|ation [degrə'deiʃən] Absetzung *f*; **~e** [di'greid] *v/t.* absetzen; erniedrigen; demütigen.

degree [di'gri:] Grad *m*; *fig.* Stufe *f*,

Schritt *m*; Rang *m*, Stand *m*; *by* ~*s* allmählich; *in no* ~ in keiner Weise; *in some* ~ einigermaßen; *take one's* ~ sein Abschlußexamen machen.

dehydrated [di:'haidreitid] Trokken...

deify ['di:ifai] vergöttern; vergöttlichen.

deign [dein] geruhen; gewähren.

deity ['di:iti] Gottheit *f*.

deject [di'dʒekt] entmutigen; ~**ed** □ niedergeschlagen; ~**ion** [~kʃən] Niedergeschlagenheit *f*.

delay [di'lei] 1. Aufschub *m*; Verzögerung *f*; 2. *v/t.* aufschieben; verzögern; *v/i.* zögern; trödeln.

delega|te 1. ['deligeit] abordnen; übertragen; 2. [~git] Abgeordnete(*r m*) *f*; ~**tion** [deli'geiʃən] Abordnung *f*; *Am. parl. die* Kongreßabgeordneten *m/pl. e-s Staates.*

deliberat|e 1. [di'libəreit] *v/t.* überlegen, erwägen; *v/i.* nachdenken; beraten; 2. □ [~rit] bedachtsam; wohlüberlegt; vorsätzlich; ~**ion** [dilibə'reiʃən] Überlegung *f*; Beratung *f*; Bedächtigkeit *f*.

delica|cy ['delikəsi] Wohlgeschmack *m*; Leckerbissen *m*; Zartheit *f*; Schwächlichkeit *f*; Feinfühligkeit *f*; ~**te** [~kit] schmackhaft; lecker; zart; fein; schwach; heikel; empfindlich; feinfühlig; wählerisch; ~**tessen** [delikə'tesn] Feinkost(geschäft *n*) *f*.

delicious [di'liʃəs] köstlich.

delight [di'lait] 1. Lust *f*, Freude *f*, Wonne *f*; 2. entzücken; (sich) erfreuen (*in an dat.*); ~ *to inf.* Freude daran finden, zu *inf.*; ~**ful** □ [~tful] entzückend. [schildern.)

delineate [di'linieit] entwerfen;)

delinquen|cy [di'liŋkwənsi] Vergehen *n*; Kriminalität *f*; Pflichtvergessenheit *f*; ~**t** [~nt] 1. straffällig; pflichtvergessen; 2. Verbrecher(in).

deliri|ous □ [di'liriəs] wahnsinnig; ~**um** [~iəm] Fieberwahn *m*.

deliver [di'livə] befreien; über-, aus-, abliefern; *Botschaft* ausrichten; äußern; *Rede etc.* vortragen, halten; ❀ entbinden; *Schlag* führen; werfen; ~**ance** [~ərəns] Befreiung *f*; (Meinungs)Äußerung *f*; ~**er** [~rə] Befreier(in); Überbringer(in); ~**y** [~ri] ❀ Entbindung *f*; (Ab)Lieferung *f*; ❀ Zustellung *f*; Übergabe *f*; Vortrag *m*; Wurf *m*; *special* ~ Lieferung *f* durch Eilboten; ~**y-truck**, ~**y-van** Lieferwagen *m*.

dell [del] kleines Tal.

delude [di'lu:d] täuschen; verleiten.

deluge ['delju:dʒ] 1. Überschwemmung *f*; 2. überschwemmen.

delus|ion [di'lu:ʒən] Täuschung *f*, Verblendung *f*; Wahn *m*; ~**ive** □ [~u:siv] (be)trügerisch; täuschend.

demand [di'ma:nd] 1. Verlangen *n*; Forderung *f*; Bedarf *m*; ♦ Nachfrage *f*; ⅌⅌ Rechtsanspruch *m*; 2. verlangen, fordern; fragen (nach).

demean [di'mi:n] ~ *o.s.* sich benehmen; sich erniedrigen; ~**o(u)r** [~nə] Benehmen *n*.

demented [di'mentid] wahnsinnig.

demerit [di:'merit] Fehler *m*.

demesne [di'mein] Besitz *m*.

demi... ['demi] Halb..., halb...

demijohn ['demidʒɔn] große Korbflasche, Glasballon *m*.

demilitarize ['di:'militəraiz] entmilitarisieren.

demise [di'maiz] 1. Ableben *n*; 2. vermachen.

demobilize [di:'moubilaiz] demobilisieren.

democra|cy [di'mɔkrəsi] Demokratie *f*; ~**t** ['deməkræt] Demokrat(in); ~**tic(al** □) [demə'krætik(əl)] demokratisch.

demolish [di'mɔliʃ] nieder-, abreißen; zerstören.

demon ['di:mən] Dämon *m*; Teufel *m*.

demonstrat|e ['demənstreit] anschaulich darstellen; beweisen; demonstrieren; ~**ion** [deməns'treiʃən] Demonstration *f*; anschauliche Darstellung; Beweis *m*; (Gefühls-)Äußerung *f*; ~**ive** □ [di'mɔnstrətiv] überzeugend; demonstrativ; ausdrucksvoll; auffällig, überschwenglich.

demote [di:'mout] degradieren.

demur [di'mə:] 1. Einwendung *f*; 2. Einwendungen erheben.

demure □ [di'mjuə] ernst; prüde.

den [den] Höhle *f*; Grube *f*; *sl.* Bude *f*.

denial [di'naiəl] Leugnen *n*; Verneinung *f*; abschlägige Antwort.

denizen ['denizn] Bewohner *m*.

denominat|e [di'nɔmineit] (be-) nennen; ~**ion** [dinɔmi'neiʃən] Benennung *f*; Klasse *f*; Sekte *f*, Konfession *f*.

denote [di'nout] bezeichnen; bedeuten.

denounce [di'nauns] anzeigen; brandmarken; *Vertrag* kündigen.

dens|e □ [dens] dicht, dick (*Nebel*); beschränkt; ~**ity** ['densiti] Dichte *f*; Dichtigkeit *f*.

dent [dent] 1. Kerbe *f*; Beule *f*; 2. ver-, einbeulen.

dent|al ['dentl] Zahn...; ~ *surgeon* Zahnarzt *m*; ~**ist** [~tist] Zahnarzt *m*.

denunciat|ion [dinʌnsi'eiʃən] Anzeige *f*; Kündigung *f*; ~**or** [di'nʌnsieitə] Denunziant *m*.

deny [di'nai] verleugnen; verweigern, abschlagen; *j-n* abweisen.

depart [di'pa:t] *v/i.* abreisen, abfahren; abstehen, (ab)weichen;

verscheiden; **~ment** [~tmənt] Abteilung *f*; Bezirk *m*; ♱ Branche *f*; *Am.* Ministerium *n*; *State* ♀ *Am.* Außenministerium *n*; **~** *store* Warenhaus *n*; **~ure** [~tʃə] Abreise *f*, 🚂, ⚓ Abfahrt *f*; Abweichung *f*.

depend [di'pend]: **~** (*up*)*on* abhängen von; angewiesen sein auf (*acc.*); sich verlassen auf (*acc.*); **it ~s F** es kommt (ganz) darauf an; **~able** [~dəbl] zuverlässig; **~ant** [~ənt] Abhängige(r *m*) *f*; Angehörige(r *m*) *f*; **~ence** [~dəns] Abhängigkeit *f*; Vertrauen *n*; **~ency** [~si] Schutzgebiet *n*; **~ent** [~nt] 1. □ (*on*) abhängig (von); angewiesen (auf *acc.*); 2. *Am.* = dependant.

depict [di'pikt] darstellen; schildern.

deplete [di'pliːt] (ent)leeren; *fig.* erschöpfen.

deplor|able □ [di'plɔːrəbl] beklagenswert; kläglich; jämmerlich; **~e** [di'plɔː] beklagen, bedauern.

deponent ⚖ [di'pounənt] vereidigter Zeuge. [entvölkern.|

depopulate [diː'pɔpjuleit] (sich)|

deport [di'pɔːt] *Ausländer* abschieben; verbannen; **~** *o.s.* sich benehmen; **~ment** [~tmənt] Benehmen *n*.

depose [di'pouz] absetzen; ⚖ (eidlich) aussagen.

deposit [di'pozit] 1. Ablagerung *f*; Lager *n*; ♱ Depot *n*; *Bank-*Einlage *f*; Pfand *n*; Hinterlegung *f*; 2. (nieder-, ab-, hin)legen; *Geld* einlegen, einzahlen; hinterlegen; (sich) ablagern; **~ion** [depə'ziʃən] Ablagerung *f*; eidliche Zeugenaussage; Absetzung *f*; **~or** [di'pozitə] Hinterleger *m*, Einzahler *m*; Kontoinhaber *m*.

depot [di'depou] Depot *n*; Lagerhaus *n*; *Am.* Bahnhof *m*.

deprave [di'preiv] *sittlich* verderben.

deprecate ['deprikeit] ablehnen.

depreciate [di'priːʃieit] herabsetzen; geringschätzen; entwerten.

depredation [depri'deiʃən] Plünderung *f*.

depress [di'pres] niederdrücken; *Preise etc.* senken, drücken; bedrücken; **~ed** *fig.* niedergeschlagen; **~ion** [~eʃən] Senkung *f*; Niedergeschlagenheit *f*; ♱ Flaute *f*, Wirtschaftskrise *f*; ⚡ Schwäche *f*; Sinken *n*.

deprive [di'praiv] berauben; entziehen; ausschließen (of von).

depth [depθ] Tiefe *f*; *attr.* Tiefen...

deput|ation [depju(ː)'teiʃən] Abordnung *f*; **~e** [di'pjuːt] abordnen; **~y** ['depjuti] Abgeordnete(r *m*) *f*; Stellvertreter *m*, Beauftragte(r) *m*.

derail 🚂 [di'reil] *v/i.* entgleisen; *v/t.* zum Entgleisen bringen.

derange [di'reindʒ] in Unordnung bringen; stören; zerrütten; (*mentally*) **~d** geistesgestört; *a* **~d** *stomach* eine Magenverstimmung.

derelict ['derilikt] 1. verlassen; *bsd. Am.* nachlässig; 2. herrenloses Gut; Wrack *n*; **~ion** [deri'likʃən] Verlassen *n*; Vernachlässigung *f*.

deri|de [di'raid] verlachen, verspotten; **~sion** [di'riʒən] Verspottung *f*; **~sive** □ [di'raisiv] spöttisch.

deriv|ation [deri'veiʃən] Ableitung *f*; Herkunft *f*; **~e** [di'raiv] herleiten; *Nutzen etc.* ziehen (*from* aus).

derogat|e ['derogeit] schmälern (*from acc.*); **~ion** [derə'geiʃən] Beeinträchtigung *f*; Herabwürdigung *f*; **~ory** □ [di'rogətəri] (*to*) nachteilig (*dat.*, für); herabwürdigend.

derrick ['derik] ⊕ Drehkran *m*; ⚓ Ladebaum *m*; ♱ Bohrturm *m*.

descend [di'send] (her-, hin)absteigen, herabkommen; sinken; ♱ niedergehen; **~** (*up*)*on* herfallen über (*acc.*); einfallen in (*acc.*); (ab)stammen; **~ant** [~dənt] Nachkomme *m*.

descent [di'sent] Herabsteigen *n*; Abstieg *m*; Sinken *n*; Gefälle *n*; feindlicher Einfall; Landung *f*; Abstammung *f*; Abhang *m*.

describe [dis'kraib] beschreiben.

description [dis'kripʃən] Beschreibung *f*, Schilderung *f*; F Art *f*.

descry [dis'krai] wahrnehmen.

desecrate ['desikreit] entweihen.

desegregate *Am.* [diː'segrigeit] die Rassentrennung aufheben in (*dat.*).

desert[1] ['dezət] 1. verlassen; wüst, öde; Wüsten...; 2. Wüste *f*.

desert[2] [di'zəːt] *v/t.* verlassen; *v/i.* ausreißen; desertieren.

desert[3] [di'zəːt] Verdienst *n*.

desert|er [di'zəːtə] Fahnenflüchtige(r) *m*; **~ion** [~ʃən] Verlassen *n*; Fahnenflucht *f*.

deserv|e [di'zəːv] verdienen; sich verdient machen (of um); **~ing** [~viŋ] würdig (of *gen.*); verdienstvoll.

design [di'zain] 1. Plan *m*; Entwurf *m*; Vorhaben *n*, Absicht *f*; Zeichnung *f*, Muster *n*; 2. ersinnen; zeichnen, entwerfen; planen; bestimmen.

designat|e ['dezigneit] bezeichnen; ernennen, bestimmen; **~ion** [dezig'neiʃən] Bezeichnung *f*; Bestimmung *f*, Ernennung *f*.

designer [di'zainə] (Muster)Zeichner(in) *f*; Konstrukteur *m*.

desir|able □ [di'zaiərəbl] wünschenswert; angenehm; **~e** [di'zaiə] 1. Wunsch *m*; Verlangen *n*; 2. verlangen, wünschen; **~ous** □ [~rəs] begierig.

desist [di'zist] abstehen, ablassen.

desk [desk] Pult *n*; Schreibtisch *m*.

desolat|e 1. ['desəleit] verwüsten; 2. □ [~lit] einsam; verlassen; öde; **~ion** [desə'leiʃən] Verwüstung *f*; Einöde *f*; Verlassenheit *f*.

despair [dis'pɛə] 1. Verzweiflung *f*;

2. verzweifeln (of an dat.); ~ing
□ [~əriŋ] verzweifelt.
despatch [dis'pætʃ] = dispatch.
desperat|e adj. □ ['despərit] ver-
zweifelt; hoffnungslos; F schrecklich; ~ion [despə'reiʃən] Verzweiflung f; Raserei f.
despicable □ ['despikəbl] verächtlich.
despise [dis'paiz] verachten.
despite [dis'pait] 1. Verachtung f;
Trotz m; Bosheit f; in ~ of zum
Trotz, trotz; 2. prp. a. ~ of trotz.
despoil [dis'pɔil] berauben (of gen.).
despond [dis'pɔnd] verzagen, verzweifeln; ~ency [~dənsi] Verzagt-
heit f; ~ent □ [~nt] verzagt.
despot ['despɔt] Despot m, Tyrann
m; ~ism [~pətizəm] Despotismus
m.
dessert [di'zə:t] Nachtisch m, Dessert m; Am. Süßspeise f.
destin|ation [desti'neiʃən] Be-
stimmung(sort m) f; ~e ['destin]
bestimmen; ~y [~ni] Schicksal n.
destitute □ ['destitju:t] mittellos,
notleidend; entblößt (of von).
destroy [dis'trɔi] zerstören, vernichten; töten; unschädlich machen; ~er [~ɔiə] Zerstörer(in).
destruct|ion [dis'trʌkʃən] Zerstö-
rung f; Tötung f; ~ive □ [~ktiv]
zerstörend; vernichtend (of, to
acc.); ~or [~tə] (Müll)Verbren-
nungsofen m.
desultory □ ['desəltəri] unstet;
planlos; oberflächlich.
detach [di'tætʃ] losmachen, (ab-)
lösen; absondern; ⚔ (ab)komman-
dieren; ~ed abgesondert (stehend); unbeeinflußt; ~ment [~mənt] Los-
lösung f; Trennung f; ⚔ Abteilung f.
detail ['di:teil] 1. Einzelheit f; ein-
gehende Darstellung; ⚔ Kom-
mando n; in ~ ausführlich; 2. genau
schildern; ⚔ abkommandieren.
detain [di'tein] zurück-, auf-, abhalten; j-n in Haft behalten.
detect [di'tekt] entdecken; (auf-)
finden; ~ion [~kʃən] Entdeckung f;
~ive [~ktiv] Detektiv m; ~ story, ~
novel Kriminalroman m.
detention [di'tenʃən] Vorenthal-
tung f; Zurück-, Abhaltung f;
Haft f. [von).\
deter [di'tə:] abschrecken (from)
detergent [di'tə:dʒənt] 1. reini-
gend; 2. Reinigungsmittel n.
deteriorat|e [di'tiəriəreit] (sich)
verschlechtern; entarten; ~ion
[ditiəriə'reiʃən] Verschlechterung f.
determin|ation [detə:mi'neiʃən]
Bestimmung f; Entschlossenheit f;
Entscheidung f; Entschluß m; ~e
[di'tə:min] v/t. bestimmen; entscheiden; veranlassen; Strafe festsetzen; beendigen; v/i. sich entschließen; ~ed entschlossen.

deterrent [di'terənt] 1. abschrek-
kend; 2. Abschreckungsmittel n;
nuclear ~ pol. atomare Abschrek-
kung.
detest [di'test] verabscheuen; ~able
□ [~təbl] abscheulich; ~ation [di:-
tes'teiʃən] Abscheu m.
dethrone [di'θroun] entthronen.
detonate ['detouneit] explodieren
(lassen).
detour, détour ['deituə] 1. Umweg m; Umleitung f; 2. e-n Umweg machen.
detract [di'trækt]: ~ from s.th. et.
beeinträchtigen, schmälern; ~ion
[~kʃən] Verleumdung f; Herabset-
zung f.
detriment ['detrimənt] Schaden m.
deuce [dju:s] Zwei f im Spiel;
Tennis: Einstand m; F Teufel m;
the ~! zum Teufel!
devalu|ation [di:vælju'eiʃən] Ab-
wertung f; ~e ['di:'vælju:] abwer-
ten.
devastat|e ['devəsteit] verwüsten;
~ion [devəs'teiʃən] Verwüstung f.
develop [di'veləp] (sich) entwickeln;
(sich) entfalten; (sich) erweitern;
Gelände erschließen; ausbauen;
Am. (sich) zeigen; ~ment [~pmənt]
Entwicklung f, Entfaltung f; Erweiterung f; Ausbau m.
deviat|e ['di:vieit] abweichen; ~ion
[di:vi'eiʃən] Abweichung f.
device [di'vais] Plan m; Kniff m;
Erfindung f; Vorrichtung f; Muster n; Wahlspruch m; leave s.o. to
his own ~s j. sich selbst überlassen.
devil ['devl] 1. Teufel m (a. fig.);
🕇🕇 Hilfsanwalt m; Laufbursche m;
2. v/t. Gericht stark pfeffern; Am.
plagen, quälen; ~ish □ [~liʃ] teuflisch; ~(t)ry [~l(t)ri] Teufelei f.
devious □ ['di:vjəs] abwegig.
devise [di'vaiz] 1. 🕇🕇 Vermachen n;
Vermächtnis n; 2. ersinnen; 🕇🕇 vermachen.
devoid [di'vɔid] ~ of bar (gen.), ohne.
devot|e [di'vout] weihen, widmen;
~ed □ ergeben; zärtlich; ~ion
[~ouʃən] Ergebenheit f; Hingebung
f; Frömmigkeit f; ~s pl. Andacht f.
devour [di'vauə] verschlingen.
devout □ [di'vaut] andächtig,
fromm; innig.
dew [dju:] 1. Tau m; 2. tauen; ~y
['dju:i] betaut; taufrisch.
dexter|ity [deks'teriti] Gewandtheit
f; ~ous □ ['dekstərəs] gewandt.
diabolic(al □) [daiə'bɔlik(əl)] teuflisch.
diagnose ['daiəgnouz] diagnosti-
zieren, erkennen.
diagram ['daiəgræm] graphische
Darstellung; Schema n, Plan m.
dial ['daiəl] 1. Sonnenuhr f; Zifferblatt n; teleph. Wähl(er)scheibe f;
Radio: Skala f; 2. teleph. wählen.
dialect ['daiəlekt] Mundart f.

dialo|gue, *Am. a.* **~g** ['daɪəlɔg] Dialog *m*, Gespräch *n*.
dial-tone *teleph.* ['daɪəltoun] Amtszeichen *n*.
diameter [daɪ'æmitə] Durchmesser *m*.
diamond ['daɪəmənd] Diamant *m*; Rhombus *m*; *Am. Baseball:* Spielfeld *n*; *Karten:* Karo *n*.
diaper ['daɪəpə] 1. Windel *f*; 2. *Am. Baby* trockenlegen, wickeln.
diaphragm ['daɪəfræm] Zwerchfell *n*; *opt.* Blende *f*; *teleph.* Membran(e) *f*.
diarrh(o)ea ♂ [daɪə'riə] Durchfall *m*.
diary ['daɪəri] Tagebuch *n*.
dice [daɪs] 1. *pl. von* die²; 2. würfeln; **~-box** ['daɪsbɔks] Würfelbecher *m*.
dick *Am. sl.* [dik] Detektiv *m*.
dicker *Am.* F ['dikə] (ver)schachern.
dick(e)y ['diki] 1. *sl.* schlecht, schlimm; 2. F Notsitz *m*; Hemdenbrust *f*; *a.* **~-bird** Piepvögelchen *n*.
dictat|e 1. ['dikteit] Diktat *n*, Vorschrift *f*; Gebot *n*; 2. [dik'teit] diktieren; *fig.* vorschreiben; **~ion** [~ʃən] Diktat *n*; Vorschrift *f*; **~orship** [~eitəʃip] Diktatur *f*.
diction ['dikʃən] Ausdruck(sweise *f*) *m*, Stil *m*; **~ary** [~nri] Wörterbuch *n*.
did [did] *pret. von* do.
die¹ [daɪ] sterben, umkommen; untergehen; absterben; F schmachten; **~** *away* ersterben; verhallen (*Ton*); sich verlieren (*Farbe*); verlöschen (*Licht*); **~** *down* hinsiechen; (dahin)schwinden; erlöschen.
die² [~], *pl.* **dice** [daɪs] Würfel *m*; *pl.* **dies** [daɪz] ⊕ Preßform *f*; *Münz-Stempel m*; *lower* **~** Matrize *f*.
die-hard ['daɪhɑːd] Reaktionär *m*.
diet ['daɪət] 1. Diät *f*; Nahrung *f*, Kost *f*; Landtag *m*; 2. *v/t.* Diät vorschreiben; beköstigen; *v/i.* diät leben.
differ ['difə] sich unterscheiden; anderer Meinung sein (*with, from* als); abweichen; **~ence** ['difrəns] Unterschied *m*; Å, ✝ Differenz *f*; Meinungsverschiedenheit *f*; **~ent** □ [~nt] verschieden; anders, andere(r, -s) (*from* als); **~entiate** [difə'renʃieit] (sich) unterscheiden.
difficult □ ['difikəlt] schwierig; **~y** [~ti] Schwierigkeit *f*.
diffiden|ce ['difidəns] Schüchternheit *f*; **~t** □ [~nt] schüchtern.
diffuse 1. *fig.* [di'fjuːz] verbreiten; 2. □ [~uːs] weitverbreitet, zerstreut (*bsd. Licht*); weitschweifig; **~ion** [~uːʒən] Verbreitung *f*.
dig [dig] 1. [*irr.*] (um-, aus)graben; wühlen (*in* in *dat.*); 2. (Aus)Grabung(sstelle) *f*; **~s** *pl.* F Bude *f*, Einzelzimmer *n*; F Stoß *m*, Puff *m*.
digest 1. [di'dʒest] *v/t.* ordnen; verdauen (*a. fig. = überdenken; verwinden*); *v/i.* verdaut werden;

2. ['daidʒest] Abriß *m*; Auslese *f*, Auswahl *f*; ⅛ Gesetzsammlung *f*; **~ible** [di'dʒestəbl] verdaulich; **~ion** [~tʃən] Verdauung *f*; **~ive** [~tiv] Verdauungsmittel *n*.
digg|er ['digə] (*bsd.* Gold)Gräber *m*; *sl.* Australier *m*; **~ings** F ['diginz] *pl.* Bude *f* (*Wohnung*); *Am.* Goldmine(n *pl.*) *f*.
dignif|ied □ ['dignifaid] würdevoll; würdig; **~y** [~fai] Würde verleihen (*dat.*); (be)ehren; *fig.* adeln.
dignit|ary ['dignitəri] Würdenträger *m*; **~y** [~ti] Würde *f*.
digress [daɪ'gres] abschweifen.
dike [daɪk] 1. Deich *m*; Damm *m*; Graben *m*; 2. eindeichen; eindämmen. [(lassen).]
dilapidate [di'læpideit] verfallen.
dilat|e [daɪ'leit] (sich) ausdehnen; *Augen* weit öffnen; **~ory** □ ['dilətəri] aufschiebend; saumselig.
diligen|ce ['dilidʒəns] Fleiß *m*; **~t** □ [~nt] fleißig, emsig.
dilute [daɪ'ljuːt] 1. verdünnen; verwässern; 2. verdünnt.
dim [dim] 1. □ trüb; dunkel; matt; 2. (sich) verdunkeln; abblenden; (sich) trüben; matt werden.
dime *Am.* [daɪm] Zehncentstück *n*.
dimension [di'menʃən] Abmessung *f*; **~s** *pl. a.* Ausmaß *n*.
dimin|ish [di'miniʃ] (sich) vermindern; abnehmen; **~ution** [dimi'njuːʃən] Verminderung *f*; Abnahme *f*; **~utive** □ [di'minjutiv] winzig.
dimple ['dimpl] 1. Grübchen *n*; 2. Grübchen bekommen.
din [din] Getöse *n*, Lärm *m*.
dine [daɪn] (zu Mittag) speisen; bewirten; **~r** ['daɪnə] Speisende(r *m*) *f*; (Mittags)Gast *m*; ₲ *bsd. Am.* Speisewagen *m*; *Am.* Restaurant *n*.
dingle ['dingl] Waldschlucht *f*.
dingy □ ['dindʒi] schmutzig.
dining|-car ₲ ['daiɳkɑː] Speisewagen *m*; **~-room** Speisezimmer *n*.
dinner ['dinə] (Mittag-, Abend-) Essen *n*; Festessen *n*; **~-jacket** Smoking *m*; **~-pail** *Am.* Essenträger *m* (*Gerät*); **~-party** Tischgesellschaft *f*; **~-service**, **~-set** Tafelgeschirr *n*.
dint [dint] 1. Beule *f*; *by* **~** *of* kraft, vermöge (*gen.*); 2. ver-, einbeulen.
dip [dip] 1. *v/t.* (ein)tauchen; senken; schöpfen; abblenden; *v/i.* (unter)tauchen, untersinken; sich neigen; sich senken; 2. Eintauchen *n*; F kurzes Bad; Senkung *f*, Neigung *f*. [rie *f*.]
diphtheria ♂ [dif'θiəriə] Diphthe-
diploma [di'ploumə] Diplom *n*; **~cy** [~əsi] Diplomatie *f*; **~tic(al** □) [diplə'mætik(əl)] diplomatisch; **~tist** [di'ploumətist] Diplomat(in).
dipper ['dipə] Schöpfkelle *f*; *Am. Great od. Big ♀ ast. der* Große Bär.

dire ['daiə] gräßlich, schrecklich.

direct [di'rekt] **1.** □ direkt; gerade; unmittelbar; offen, aufrichtig; deutlich; ~ current & Gleichstrom m; ~ train durchgehender Zug; **2.** adv. geradeswegs; = ~ly **3.** richten; lenken, steuern; leiten; anordnen; j-n (an)weisen; Brief adressieren; ~ion [~kʃən] Richtung f; Gegend f; Leitung f; Anordnung f; Adresse f; Vorstand m; ~ion-finder [~nfaində] Radio: (Funk)Peiler m; Peil-(funk)empfänger m; ~ion-indicator mot. Fahrtrichtungsanzeiger m; ⚡ Kursweiser m; ~ive [~ktiv] richtungweisend; leitend; ~ly [~tli] **1.** adv. sofort; **2.** cj. sobald, als.

director [di'rektə] Direktor m; Film: Regisseur m; board of ~s Aufsichtsrat m; ~ate [~ərit] Direktion f; ~y [~ri] Adreßbuch n; telephone ~ Telephonbuch f.

dirge [də:dʒ] Klage(lied n) f.

dirigible ['diridʒəbl] **1.** lenkbar; **2.** lenkbares Luftschiff.

dirt [də:t] Schmutz m; (lockere) Erde; ~-cheap F ['də:t'tʃi:p] spottbillig; ~y ['də:ti] **1.** □ schmutzig (a. fig.); **2.** beschmutzen; besudeln.

disability [disə'biliti] Unfähigkeit f.

disable [dis'eibl] (dienst-, kampf-) unfähig machen; ~d dienst-, kampfunfähig; körperbehindert; kriegsbeschädigt.

disabuse [disə'bju:z] e-s Besseren belehren (of über acc.).

disadvantage [disəd'va:ntidʒ] Nachteil m; Schaden m; ~ous [disædvə:n'teidʒəs] nachteilig, ungünstig.

disagree [disə'gri:] nicht übereinstimmen; uneinig sein; nicht bekommen (with s.o. j-m); ~able □ [~riəbl] unangenehm; ~ment [~ri:mənt] Verschiedenheit f; Unstimmigkeit f; Meinungsverschiedenheit f.

disappear [disə'piə] verschwinden; ~ance [~ərəns] Verschwinden n.

disappoint [disə'point] enttäuschen; vereiteln; j-n im Stich lassen; ~ment [~tmənt] Enttäuschung f; Vereitelung f. [Mißbilligung f.]

disapprobation [disæprou'beiʃən]

disapprov|al [disə'pru:vəl] Mißbilligung f; ~e ['disə'pru:v] mißbilligen (of et.).

disarm [dis'a:m] v/t. entwaffnen (a. fig.); v/i. abrüsten; ~ament [~məmənt] Entwaffnung f; Abrüstung f.

disarrange ['disə'reindʒ] in Unordnung bringen, verwirren.

disarray ['disə'rei] **1.** Unordnung f; **2.** in Unordnung bringen.

disast|er [di'za:stə] Unglück(sfall m) n, Katastrophe f; ~rous □ [~trəs] unheilvoll; katastrophal.

disband [dis'bænd] entlassen; auflösen.

disbelieve ['disbi'li:v] nicht glauben.

disburse [dis'bə:s] auszahlen.

disc [disk] = disk.

discard 1. [dis'ka:d] Karten, Kleid etc. ablegen; entlassen; **2.** ['diska:d] Karten: Abwerfen n; bsd. Am. Abfall(haufen) m.

discern [di'sə:n] unterscheiden; erkennen; beurteilen; ~ing □ [~niŋ] kritisch, scharfsichtig; ~ment [~nmənt] Einsicht f; Scharfsinn m.

discharge [dis'tʃa:dʒ] **1.** v/t. ent-, ab-, ausladen; entlasten, entbinden; abfeuern; Flüssigkeit absondern; Amt versehen; Pflicht etc. erfüllen; Zorn etc. auslassen (on an dat.); Schuld tilgen; quittieren; Wechsel einlösen; entlassen; freisprechen; v/i. sich entladen; eitern; **2.** Entladung f; Abfeuern n; Ausströmen n; Ausfluß m, Eiter(ung f) m; Entlassung f; Entlastung f; Bezahlung f; Quittung f; Erfüllung f e-r Pflicht.

disciple [di'saipl] Schüler m; Jünger m.

discipline ['disiplin] **1.** Disziplin f, Zucht f; Erziehung f; Züchtigung f; **2.** erziehen; schulen; bestrafen.

disclaim [dis'kleim] (ab)leugnen; ablehnen; verzichten auf (acc.).

disclose [dis'klouz] aufdecken; erschließen, offenbaren, enthüllen.

discolo(u)r [dis'kʌlə] (sich) verfärben.

discomfiture [dis'kʌmfitʃə] Niederlage f; Verwirrung f; Vereitelung f.

discomfort [dis'kʌmfət] **1.** Unbehagen n; **2.** j-m Unbehagen verursachen.

discompose [diskəm'pouz] beunruhigen.

disconcert [diskən'sə:t] außer Fassung bringen; vereiteln.

disconnect ['diskə'nekt] trennen (a. &); ⊕ auskuppeln; ⚡ ab-, ausschalten; ~ed □ zs.-hanglos.

disconsolate □ [dis'kɔnsəlit] trostlos.

discontent ['diskən'tent] Unzufriedenheit f; ~ed □ mißvergnügt, unzufrieden.

discontinue ['diskən'tinju(:)] aufgeben, aufhören mit; unterbrechen.

discord ['diskɔ:d], ~ance [dis'kɔ:dəns] Uneinigkeit f; ♪ Mißklang m.

discount ['diskaunt] **1.** ✝ Diskont m; Abzug m, Rabatt m; **2.** ✝ diskontieren; abrechnen; fig. absehen von; Nachricht mit Vorsicht aufnehmen; beeinträchtigen; ~enance [dis'kauntinəns] mißbilligen; entmutigen.

discourage [dis'kʌridʒ] entmutigen;

abschrecken; ~ment [~dʒmənt] Entmutigung f; Schwierigkeit f.

discourse [dis'kɔːs] 1. Rede f; Abhandlung f; Predigt f; 2. reden, sprechen; e-n Vortrag halten.

discourte|ous □ [dis'kɔːtjəs] unhöflich; ~sy [~tisi] Unhöflichkeit f.

discover [dis'kʌvə] entdecken; ausfindig machen; ~y [~əri] Entdeckung f.

discredit [dis'kredit] 1. schlechter Ruf; Unglaubwürdigkeit f; 2. nicht glauben; in Mißkredit bringen.

discreet □ [dis'kriːt] besonnen, vorsichtig; klug; verschwiegen.

discrepancy [dis'krepənsi] Widerspruch m; Unstimmigkeit f.

discretion [dis'kreʃən] Besonnenheit f, Klugheit f; Takt m; Verschwiegenheit f; Belieben n; age (od. years) of ~ Strafmündigkeit f (14 Jahre); surrender at ~ sich auf Gnade und Ungnade ergeben.

discriminat|e [dis'krimineit] unterscheiden; ~ against benachteiligen; ~ing [~tiŋ] unterscheidend; scharfsinnig; urteilsfähig; ~ion [diskrimi'neiʃən] Unterscheidung f; unterschiedliche (bsd. nachteilige) Behandlung; Urteilskraft f.

discuss [dis'kʌs] erörtern, besprechen; ~ion [~ʌʃən] Erörterung f.

disdain [dis'dein] 1. Verachtung f; 2. geringschätzen, verachten; verschmähen.

disease [di'ziːz] Krankheit f; ~d krank.

disembark ['disim'bɑːk] v/t. ausschiffen; v/i. landen, an Land gehen.

disengage ['disin'geidʒ] (sich) freimachen, (sich) lösen; ⊕ loskuppeln.

disentangle ['disin'tæŋgl] entwirren; fig. freimachen (from von).

disfavo(u)r ['dis'feivə] 1. Mißfallen n, Ungnade f; 2. nicht mögen.

disfigure [dis'figə] entstellen.

disgorge [dis'gɔːdʒ] ausspeien.

disgrace [dis'greis] 1. Ungnade f; Schande f; 2. in Ungnade fallen lassen; j-n entehren; ~ful □ [~sful] schimpflich.

disguise [dis'gaiz] 1. verkleiden; Stimme verstellen; verhehlen; 2. Verkleidung f; Verstellung f; Maske f.

disgust [dis'gʌst] 1. Ekel m; 2. anekeln; ~ing □ [~tiŋ] ekelhaft.

dish [diʃ] 1. Schüssel f, Platte f; Gericht n (Speise); the ~es das Geschirr; 2. anrichten; mst ~ up auftischen; ~-cloth ['diʃklɔθ] Geschirrspültuch n.

dishearten [dis'hɑːtn] entmutigen.

dishevel(l)ed [di'ʃevəld] zerzaust.

dishonest □ [dis'ɔnist] unehrlich, unredlich; ~y [~ti] Unredlichkeit f.

dishono(u)r [dis'ɔnə] 1. Unehre f,

Schande f; 2. entehren; schänden; Wechsel nicht honorieren; ~able □ [~ərəbl] entehrend; ehrlos.

dish|-pan Am. ['diʃpæn] Spülschüssel f; ~rag = dish-cloth; ~-water Spülwasser n.

disillusion [disi'luːʒən] 1. Ernüchterung f, Enttäuschung f; 2. ernüchtern, enttäuschen.

disinclined ['disin'klaind] abgeneigt.

disinfect [disin'fekt] desinfizieren; ~ant [~tənt] Desinfektionsmittel n.

disintegrate [dis'intigreit] (sich) auflösen; (sich) zersetzen.

disinterested □ [dis'intristid] uneigennützig, selbstlos.

disk [disk] Scheibe f; Platte f; Schallplatte f; ~ brake mot. Scheibenbremse f; ~ jockey Ansager m e-r Schallplattensendung.

dislike [dis'laik] 1. Abneigung f; Widerwille m; 2. nicht mögen.

dislocate ['disləkeit] aus den Fugen bringen; verrenken; verlagern.

dislodge [dis'lɔdʒ] vertreiben, verjagen; umquartieren.

disloyal □ ['dis'lɔiəl] treulos.

dismal □ ['dizməl] trüb(selig); öde; trostlos, elend.

dismantl|e [dis'mæntl] abbrechen; niederreißen; ⚓ abtakeln; ⊕ demontieren; ~ing [~liŋ] Demontage f.

dismay [dis'mei] 1. Schrecken m; Bestürzung f; 2. v/t. erschrecken.

dismember [dis'membə] zerstückeln.

dismiss [dis'mis] v/t. entlassen, wegschicken; ablehnen; Thema etc. fallen lassen; ⛫ abweisen; ~al [~səl] Entlassung f; Aufgabe f; ⛫ Abweichung f.

dismount ['dis'maunt] v/t. aus dem Sattel werfen; demontieren; ⊕ aus-ea.-nehmen; v/i. absteigen.

disobedien|ce [disə'biːdjəns] Ungehorsam m; ~t □ [~nt] ungehorsam.

disobey ['disə'bei] ungehorsam sein.

disoblige ['disə'blaidʒ] ungefällig sein gegen; kränken.

disorder [dis'ɔːdə] 1. Unordnung f; Aufruhr m; ⚕ Störung f; 2. in Unordnung bringen; stören; zerrütten; ~ly [~əli] unordentlich; ordnungswidrig; unruhig; aufrührerisch.

disorganize [dis'ɔːgənaiz] zerrütten.

disown [dis'oun] nicht anerkennen, verleugnen; ablehnen.

disparage [dis'pæridʒ] verächtlich machen, herabsetzen.

disparity [dis'pæriti] Ungleichheit f.

dispassionate □ [dis'pæʃnit] leidenschaftslos; unparteiisch.

dispatch [dis'pætʃ] 1. (schnelle) Erledigung; (schnelle) Absendung; Abfertigung f; Eile f; Depesche f; 2. (schnell) abmachen, erledigen (a. fig. = töten); abfertigen; (eilig) absenden.

dispel [dis'pel] vertreiben, zerstreuen.

dispensa|ble [dis'pensəbl] entbehrlich; ~ry [~əri] Apotheke f; ~tion [dispen'seiʃən] Austeilung f; Befreiung f (with von); göttliche Fügung.

dispense [dis'pens] v/t. austeilen; Gesetze handhaben; Arzneien anfertigen und ausgeben; befreien.

disperse [dis'pə:s] (sich) zerstreuen; auseinandergehen.

dispirit [dis'spirit] entmutigen.

displace [dis'pleis] verschieben; absetzen; ersetzen; verdrängen.

display [dis'plei] 1. Entfaltung f; Aufwand m; Schaustellung f; Schaufenster-Auslage f; 2. entfalten; zur Schau stellen; zeigen.

displeas|e [dis'pli:z] j-m mißfallen; ~ed unwillig; ~ure [~leʒə] Mißfallen n; Verdruß m.

dispos|al [dis'pouzəl] Anordnung f; Verfügung f (recht n) f; Beseitigung f; Veräußerung f; Übergabe f; ~e [~ouz] v/t. (an)ordnen, einrichten; geneigt machen, veranlassen; v/i. ~ of verfügen über (acc.); erledigen; verwenden; veräußern; unterbringen; beseitigen; ~ed geneigt; ...gesinnt; ~ition [dispə'ziʃən] Disposition f; Anordnung f; Neigung f; Sinnesart f; Verfügung f.

dispossess [dispə'zes] (of) vertreiben (aus od. von); berauben (gen.).

dispraise [dis'preiz] tadeln.

disproof ['dis'pru:f] Widerlegung f.

disproportionate □ [disprə'pɔ:ʃnit] unverhältnismäßig.

disprove ['dis'pru:v] widerlegen.

dispute [dis'pju:t] 1. Streit(igkeit f) m; Rechtsstreit m; beyond (all) ~, past ~ zweifellos; 2. (be)streiten.

disqualify [dis'kwɔlifai] unfähig od. untauglich machen; für untauglich erklären.

disquiet [dis'kwaiət] beunruhigen.

disregard ['disri'ga:d] 1. Nicht(be)achtung f; 2. unbeachtet lassen.

disreput|able □ [dis'repjutəbl] schimpflich; verrufen; ~e ['disri'pju:t] übler Ruf; Schande f.

disrespect ['disris'pekt] Nichtachtung f; Respektlosigkeit f; ~ful □ [~tful] respektlos; unhöflich.

disroot [dis'ru:t] entwurzeln.

disrupt [dis'rʌpt] zerreißen; spalten.

dissatis|faction ['dissætis'fækʃən] Unzufriedenheit f; ~factory [~ktəri] unbefriedigend; ~fy ['dis'sætisfai] nicht befriedigen; j-m mißfallen.

dissect [di'sekt] zerlegen; zergliedern.

dissemble [di'sembl] v/t. verhehlen; v/i. sich verstellen, heucheln.

dissen|sion [di'senʃən] Zwietracht f, Streit m; Uneinigkeit f; ~t [~nt] 1. abweichende Meinung; Nichtzugehörigkeit f zur Staatskirche; 2. andrer Meinung sein (from als).

dissimilar □ ['di'similə] (to) unähnlich (dat.); verschieden (von).

dissimulation [disimju'leiʃən] Verstellung f, Heuchelei f.

dissipat|e ['disipeit] (sich) zerstreuen; verschwenden; ~ion [disi'peiʃən] Zerstreuung f; Verschwendung f; ausschweifendes Leben.

dissociate [di'souʃieit] trennen; ~ o.s. sich distanzieren, abrücken.

dissoluble [di'sɔljubl] (auf)lösbar.

dissolut|e □ ['disəlu:t] liederlich, ausschweifend; ~ion [disə'lu:ʃən] Auflösung f; Zerstörung f; Tod m.

dissolve [di'zɔlv] v/t. (auf)lösen; schmelzen; v/i. sich auflösen; vergehen.

dissonant ['disənənt] ♪ mißtönend; abweichend; uneinig.

dissuade [di'sweid] j-m abraten.

distan|ce ['distəns] 1. Abstand m, Entfernung f; Ferne f; Strecke f; Zurückhaltung f; at a ~ von weitem; in e-r gewissen Entfernung; weit weg; keep s.o. at a ~ j-m gegenüber reserviert sein (~t [~nt] entfernt; fern; zurückhaltend; Fern...; ~ control Fernsteuerung f.

distaste [dis'teist] Widerwille m; Abneigung f; ~ful [~tful] widerwärtig; ärgerlich.

distemper [dis'tempə] Krankheit f (bsd. von Tieren); (Hunde)Staupe f.

distend [dis'tend] (sich) ausdehnen; (auf)blähen; (sich) weiten.

distil [dis'til] herabtröpfeln (lassen); ⌐, destillieren; ~lery [~ləri] Branntweinbrennerei f.

distinct □ [dis'tiŋkt] verschieden; getrennt; deutlich, klar; ~ion [~kʃən] Unterscheidung f; Unterschied m; Auszeichnung f; Rang m; ~ive □ [~ktiv] unterscheidend; apart; kennzeichnend; bezeichnend.

distinguish [dis'tiŋgwiʃ] unterscheiden; auszeichnen; ~ed berühmt, ausgezeichnet; vornehm.

distort [dis'tɔ:t] verdrehen; verzerren.

distract [dis'trækt] ablenken, zerstreuen; beunruhigen; verwirren; verrückt machen; ~ion [~kʃən] Zerstreutheit f; Verwirrung f; Wahnsinn m; Zerstreuung f.

distraught [dis'trɔ:t] verwirrt, bestürzt.

distress [dis'tres] 1. Qual f; Elend n, Not f; Erschöpfung f; 2. in Not bringing; quälen; erschöpfen; **~ed** in Not befindlich; bekümmert; **~** *area* Notstandsgebiet *n*.

distribut|e [dis'tribju(:)t] verteilen; einteilen; verbreiten; **~ion** [distri-'bju:ʃən] Verteilung *f*; *Film*-Verleih *m*; Verbreitung *f*; Einteilung *f*.

district ['distrikt] Bezirk *m*; Gegend *f*.

distrust [dis'trʌst] 1. Mißtrauen *n*; 2. mißtrauen (*dat.*); **~ful** □ [~tful] mißtrauisch; **~** (*of o.s.*) schüchtern.

disturb [dis'tə:b] beunruhigen; stören; **~ance** [~bəns] Störung *f*; Unruhe *f*; Aufruhr *m*; **~** *of the peace* ₤₤ öffentliche Ruhestörung; **~er** [~bə] Störenfried *m*, Unruhestifter *m*.

disunite ['disju:'nait] (sich) trennen.

disuse ['dis'ju:z] nicht mehr gebrauchen.

ditch [ditʃ] Graben *m*.

ditto ['ditou] dito, desgleichen.

divan [di'væn] Diwan *m*; **~-bed** [*oft* 'daivænbed] Bettcouch *f*, Liege *f*.

dive [daiv] 1. (unter)tauchen; *vom Sprungbrett* springen; e-n Sturzflug machen; eindringen in (*acc.*); 2. *Schwimmen*: Springen *n*; (Kopf-) Sprung *m*; Sturzflug *m*; Kellerlokal *n*; *Am.* F Kaschemme *f*; **~r** ['daivə] Taucher *m*.

diverge [dai'və:dʒ] aus-ea.-laufen; abweichen; **~nce** [~dʒəns] Abweichung *f*; **~nt** □ [~nt] (von-ea.-)abweichend.

divers ['daivə(:)z] mehrere.

divers|e □ [dai'və:s] verschieden; mannigfaltig; **~ion** [~ə:ʃən] Ablenkung *f*; Zeitvertreib *m*; **~ity** [~ə:siti] Verschiedenheit *f*; Mannigfaltigkeit *f*.

divert [dai'və:t] ablenken; *j-n* zerstreuen; unterhalten; *Verkehr* umleiten.

divest [dai'vest] entkleiden (*a.fig.*).

divid|e [di'vaid] 1. *v/t.* teilen; trennen; einteilen; ℞ dividieren (*by* durch); *v/i.* sich teilen; zerfallen; ℞ aufgehen; sich trennen *od.* auflösen; 2. Wasserscheide *f*; **~end** ['dividend] Dividende *f*.

divine [di'vain] 1. □ göttlich; **~** *service* Gottesdienst *m*; 2. Geistliche(r) *m*; 3. weissagen; ahnen.

diving ['daiviŋ] Kunstspringen *n*; *attr.* Taucher...

divinity [di'viniti] Gottheit *f*; Göttlichkeit *f*; Theologie *f*.

divis|ible □ [di'vizəbl] teilbar; **~ion** [~iʒən] Teilung *f*; Trennung *f*; Abteilung *f*; ✕, ℞ Division *f*.

divorce [di'vɔ:s] 1. (Ehe)Scheidung *f*; 2. *Ehe* scheiden; sich scheiden lassen.

divulge [dai'vʌldʒ] ausplaudern; verbreiten; bekanntmachen.

dixie ✕ *sl.* ['diksi] Kochgeschirr *n*;

Feldkessel *m*; ♀ *Am.* die Südstaaten *pl.*; **♀crat** *Am. pol.* opponierender Südstaatendemokrat.

dizz|iness ['dizinis] Schwindel *m*; **~y** □ ['dizi] schwind(e)lig.

do [du:] [*irr.*] *v/t.* tun; machen; (zu)bereiten; *Rolle, Stück* spielen; **~** *London sl.* London besichtigen; *have done reading* fertig sein mit Lesen; **~** in F um die Ecke bringen; **~** *into* übersetzen in; **~** *over* überstreifen, -ziehen; **~** *up* instand setzen; einpacken; *v/i.* tun; handeln; sich benehmen; sich befinden; genügen; *that will* **~** das genügt; *how* **~** *you* **~**? guten Tag!, Wie geht's?; **~** *well* s-e Sache gut machen; gute Geschäfte machen; **~** *away with* weg-, abschaffen; *I could* **~** *with* ... ich könnte ... brauchen *od.* vertragen; **~** *without* fertig werden ohne; **~** *be quick* beeile dich doch; **~** *you like London?* — *I* **~** gefällt Ihnen London? — Ja.

docil|e ['dousail] gelehrig; fügsam; **~ity** [dou'siliti] Gelehrigkeit *f*.

dock¹ [dɔk] stutzen; *fig.* kürzen.

dock² [~] 1. ♣ Dock *n*; *bsd. Am.* Kai *m*, Pier *m*; ₤₤ Anklagebank *f*; 2. ♣ docken.

dockyard ['dɔkjɑ:d] Werft *f*.

doctor ['dɔktə] 1. Doktor *m*; Arzt *m*; 2. Fverarzten; F *fig.* (ver)fälschen.

doctrine ['dɔktrin] Lehre *f*; Dogma *n*.

document 1. ['dɔkjumənt] Urkunde *f*; 2. [~ment] beurkunden.

dodge [dɔdʒ] 1. Seitensprung *m*; Kniff *m*, Winkelzug *m*; 2. *fig.* irreführen; ausweichen; Winkelzüge machen; **~r** ['dɔdʒə] Schieber(in); *Am.* Hand-, Reklamezettel *m*; *Am.* Maisbrot *n*, -kuchen *m*.

doe [dou] Hirschkuh *f*; Reh *n*; Häsin *f*.

dog [dɔg] 1. Hund *m*; Haken *m*, Klammer *f*; 2. nachspüren (*dat.*).

dogged □ ['dɔgid] verbissen.

dogma ['dɔgmə] Dogma *n*; Glaubenslehre *f*; **~tic(al** □) [dɔg'mæ-tik(əl)] dogmatisch; bestimmt; **~tism** ['dɔgmətizəm] Selbstherrlichkeit *f*.

dog's-ear F ['dɔgziə] Eselsohr *n im Buch*.

dog-tired F['dɔg'taiəd]hundemüde.

doings ['du:(i)ŋz] *pl.* Dinge *n/pl.*; Begebenheiten *f/pl.*; Treiben *n*; Betragen *n*.

dole [doul] 1. Spende *f*; F Erwerbslosenunterstützung *f*; 2. verteilen.

doleful □ ['doulful] trübselig.

doll [dɔl] Puppe *f*.

dollar ['dɔlə] Dollar *m*.

dolly ['dɔli] Püppchen *n*.

dolorous ['dɔlərəs] schmerzhaft; traurig.

dolphin ['dɔlfin] Delphin *m*.

dolt [doult] Tölpel *m*.

domain [də'mein] Domäne *f*; *fig.*
Gebiet *n*; Bereich *m*.
dome [doum] Kuppel *f*; ⊕ Haube
f; **.d** gewölbt.
Domesday Book ['du:mzdei'buk]
Reichsgrundbuch *n Englands*.
domestic [də'mestik] 1. (*.ally*)
häuslich; inländisch; einheimisch;
zahm; **~** *animal* Haustier *n*; 2.
Dienstbote *m*; **~s** *pl.* Haushalts-
artikel *m/pl.*; **~ate** [.keit] zähmen;
domicile ['dɔmisail] Wohnsitz *m*;
.d wohnhaft.
domin|ant ['dɔminənt] (vor)herr-
schend; **~ate** [.neit] (be)herrschen;
~ation [dɔmi'neiʃən] Herrschaft *f*;
~eer [.'niə] (despotisch) herrschen;
~eering [.'əriŋ] herrisch, tyrannisch; überheblich.
dominion [də'minjən] Herrschaft *f*;
Gebiet *n*; ♀ Dominion *n* (*im Brt.
Commonwealth*).
don [dɔn] anziehen; *Hut* aufsetzen.
donat|e *Am.* [dou'neit] schenken;
stiften; **~ion** [.eiʃən] Schenkung *f*.
done [dʌn] 1. *p.p. von do*; 2. *adj.*
abgemacht; fertig; gar *gekocht*.
donkey ['dɔŋki] *zo.* Esel *m*; *attr.*
Hilfs...
donor ['dounə] (♀ Blut)Spender *m*.
doom [du:m] 1. Schicksal *n*, Verhängnis *n*; 2. verurteilen, verdammen.
door [dɔ:] Tür *f*, Tor *n*; *next ~*
nebenan; **~-handle** ['dɔ:hændl]
Türgriff *m*; **~-keeper**, *Am.* **~man**
Pförtner *m*; Portier *m*; **~way** Tür-
öffnung *f*; Torweg *m*; **~yard** *Am.*
Vorhof *m*, Vorgarten *m*.
dope [doup] 1. Schmiere *f*; *bsd.* ⚡
Lack *m*; Aufputschmittel *n*;
Rauschgift *n*; *Am. sl.* Geheimtip *m*;
2. lackieren; *sl.* betäuben; auf-
pulvern; *Am. sl.* herauskriegen.
dormant *mst fig.* ['dɔ:mənt] schlafend, ruhend; unbenutzt; ♱ tot.
dormer(-window) ['dɔ:mə('win-
dou)] Dachfenster *n*.
dormitory ['dɔ:mitri] Schlafsaal *m*;
bsd. Am. Studenten(wohn)heim *n*.
dose [dous] 1. Dosis *f*, Portion *f*;
2. *j-m* e-e Medizin geben.
dot [dɔt] 1. Punkt *m*, Fleck *m*; 2.
punktieren, tüpfeln; *fig.* verstreuen.
dot|e [dout]: **~** (*up*)*on* vernarrt sein
in (*acc.*); **~ing** ['doutiŋ] vernarrt.
double □ ['dʌbl] 1. doppelt; zu
zweien; gekrümmt; zweideutig; 2.
Doppelte(s) *n*; Doppelgänger(in) *f*;
Tennis: Doppel(spiel) *n*; 3. *v/t.* verdoppeln; *a.* **~** *up* zs.-legen; *et.*
umfahren, umsegeln; **.d** *up* zs.-
gekrümmt; *v/i.* sich verdoppeln;
a. **~** *back* e-n Haken schlagen
(*Hase*); **~-breasted** zweireihig
(*Jackett*); **~-cross** *sl. Partner* betrügen; **~-dealing** Doppelzüngig-
keit *f*; **~-edged** zweischneidig;
~-entry doppelte Buchführung;

~-feature *Am.* Doppelprogramm *n*
im Kino; **~-header** *Am. Baseball*:
Doppelspiel *n*; **~-park** *Am. verboten* in zweiter Reihe parken.
doubt [daut] 1. *v/i.* zweifeln; *v/t.*
bezweifeln; mißtrauen (*dat.*); 2.
Zweifel *m*; *no ~* ohne Zweifel; **~ful**
□ ['dautful] zweifelhaft; **~fulness**
[.lnis] Zweifelhaftigkeit *f*; **~less**
['dautlis] ohne Zweifel.
douche [du:ʃ] 1. Dusche *f*; Irriga-
tor *m*; 2. duschen; spülen.
dough [dou] Teig *m*; **~boy** *Am.* F
['doubɔi] Landser *m*; **~nut** *Schmalz-
gebackenes*.
dove [dʌv] Taube *f*; *fig.* Täubchen *n*.
dowel ⊕ ['dauəl] Dübel *m*.
down[1] [daun] Daune *f*; Flaum *m*;
Düne *f*; **~s** *pl.* Höhenrücken *m*.
down[2] [.] 1. *adv.* nieder; her-, hinunter, ab; abwärts; unten; *be ~
upon* F über *j-n* herfallen; 2. *prp.*
herab, hinab, her-, hinunter; **~** *the
river* flußabwärts; 3. *adj.* nach unten gerichtet; **~** *platform* Abfahrts-
bahnsteig *m* (*London*); **~** *train* Zug
m von London (fort); 4. *v/t.* niederwerfen; herunterholen; **~cast**
['daunkɑ:st] niedergeschlagen; **~**
easter Am. Neuengländer *m bsd.
von Maine*; **~fall** Fall *m*, Sturz *m*;
Verfall *m*; **~-hearted** niedergeschlagen; **~hill** bergab; **~pour**
Regenguß *m*; **~right** □ 1. *adv.*
geradezu, durchaus; völlig; 2. *adj.*
ehrlich; plump (*Benehmen*); richtig, glatt (*Lüge etc.*); **~stairs** die
Treppe hinunter, (nach) unten;
~stream stromabwärts; **~town**
bsd. Am. Hauptgeschäftsviertel *n*;
~ward(s) ['daunwəd(z)] abwärts
(gerichtet).
downy ['dauni] flaumig; *sl.* gerissen.
dowry ['dauəri] Mitgift *f* (*a. fig.*).
doze [douz] 1. dösen; 2. Schläfchen *n*.
dozen ['dʌzn] Dutzend *n*.
drab [dræb] gelblichgrau; eintönig.
draft [drɑ:ft] 1. Entwurf *m*; ♱
Tratte *f*; Abhebung *f*; ✕ (Sonder-)
Kommando *n*; Einberufung *f*; =
draught; 2. entwerfen; aufsetzen;
✕ abkommandieren; *Am.* einziehen; **~ee** *Am.* ✕ [.f'ti:] Dienst-
pflichtige(r) *m*; **~sman** ['drɑ:fts-
mən] (technischer) Zeichner; Verfasser *m*, Entwerfer *m*.
drag [dræg] 1. Schleppnetz *n*;
Schleife *f für Lasten*; Egge *f*; 2. *v/t.*
schleppen, ziehen; *v/i.* (sich) schleppen, schleifen; (mit e-m Schleppnetz) fischen; [Libelle *f*.]
dragon ['drægən] Drache *m*; **~-fly**]
drain [drein] 1. Abfluß(graben *m*,
-rohr *n*) *m*; F Schnaps *m*; 2. *v/t.*
entwässern; *Glas* leeren; *a.* **~** *off*
abziehen; verzehren; *v/i.* ablaufen;
~age ['dreinidʒ] Abfluß *m*; Ent-
wässerung(sanlage) *f*.

drake [dreik] Enterich *m*.

dram [dræm] Schluck *m*; *fig.* Schnaps *m*.

drama ['drɑːmə] Drama *n*; **~tic** [drə'mætik] (**~ally**) dramatisch; **~tist** ['dræmətist] Dramatiker *m*; **~tize** [~taiz] dramatisieren.

drank [dræŋk] *pret. von* drink 2.

drape [dreip] 1. drapieren; in Falten legen; 2. *mst* **~s** *pl.* Vorhänge *m/pl.*; **~ry** ['dreipəri] Tuchhandel *m*; Tuchwaren *f/pl.*; Faltenwurf *m*.

drastic ['dræstik] (**~ally**) drastisch.

draught [drɑːft] Zug *m* (*Ziehen*; *Fischzug*; *Zugluft*; *Schluck*); ♪ Tiefgang *m*; **~s** *pl.* Damespiel *n*; *s.* draft; **~ beer** Faßbier *n*; **~horse** ['drɑːfthɔːs] Zugpferd *n*; **~sman** [~tsmən] Damestein *m*; = drafts- man; **~y** [~ti] zugig.

draw [drɔː] 1. [*irr.*] ziehen; an-, auf-, ein-, zuziehen; (sich) zs.- ziehen; in die Länge ziehen; deh- nen; herausziehen, herauslocken; entnehmen; *Geld* abheben; an- locken, anziehen; abzapfen; aus- fischen; *Geflügel* ausnehmen; zeich- nen; entwerfen; *Urkunde* abfassen; unentschieden spielen; *Luft* schöp- fen; **~ near** heranrücken; **~ out** in die Länge ziehen; **~ up ab-, ver-** fassen; **~ (up)on ✝** (e-n Wechsel) ziehen auf (*acc.*); *fig.* in Anspruch nehmen; 2. Zug *m* (*Ziehen*); *Lot- terie*: Ziehung *f*; Los *n*; *Sport*: un- entschiedenes Spiel; F Zugstück *n*, -artikel *m*; **~back** ['drɔːbæk] Nach- teil *m*; Hindernis *n*; **✝** Rückzoll *m*; *Am.* Rückzahlung *f*; **~er** ['drɔːə] Ziehende(r *m*) *f*; Zeichner *m*; ✝ Aussteller *m*, Trassant *m*; [drɔː] Schublade *f*; (*a pair of*) **~s** *pl.* (eine) Unterhose; (ein) Schlüpfer *m*; *mst chest of* **~s** Kommode *f*.

drawing ['drɔːiŋ] Ziehen *n*; Zeich- nen *n*; Zeichnung *f*; **~account** Girokonto *n*; **~board** Reißbrett *n*; **~room** Gesellschaftszimmer *n*.

drawn [drɔːn] 1. *p.p. von* draw 1; 2. *adj.* unentschieden; verzerrt.

dread [dred] 1. Furcht *f*; Schrecken *m*; 2. (sich) fürchten; **~ful** ☐ ['dredful] schrecklich; furchtbar.

dream [driːm] 1. Traum *m*; 2. [*irr.*] träumen; **~er** ['driːmə] Träumer (-in) *m*; **~t** [dremt] *pret. u. p.p. von* dream 2; **~y** ☐ ['driːmi] träume- risch; verträumt.

dreary ☐ ['driəri] traurig; öde.

dredge [dredʒ] 1. Schleppnetz *n*; Bagger(maschine *f*) *m*; 2. (aus-) baggern.

dregs [dregz] *pl.* Bodensatz *m*, Hefe *f*.

drench [drentʃ] 1. (Regen)Guß *m*; 2. durchnässen; *fig.* baden.

dress [dres] 1. Anzug *m*; Kleidung *f*; Kleid *n*; 2. an-, ein-, zurichten; ✗ (sich) richten; zurechtmachen;

(sich) ankleiden; putzen; ✗ ver- binden; frisieren; **~circle** *thea.* ['dres'səːkl] erster Rang; **~er** [~sə] Anrichte *f*; *Am.* Frisiertoilette *f*.

dressing ['dresiŋ] An-, Zurichten *n*; Ankleiden *n*; Verband *m*; Appretur *f*; *Küche*: Soße *f*; Füllung *f*; **~s** *pl.* ✗ Verbandzeug *n*; **~ down** Stand- pauke *f*; **~gown** Morgenrock *m*; **~table** Frisiertisch *m*.

dress|maker ['dresmeikə] Schnei- derin *f*; **~parade** Modenschau *f*.

drew ['druː] *pret. von* draw 1.

dribble ['dribl] tröpfeln, träufeln (lassen); geifern; *Fußball*: drib- beln.

dried [draid] getrocknet; Dörr...

drift [drift] 1. (Dahin)Treiben *n*; *fig.* Lauf *m*; *fig.* Hang *m*; Zweck *m*; (Schnee-, Sand)Wehe *f*; 2. *v/t.* (zs.-)treiben, (zs.-)wehen; *v/i.* (da- hin)treiben; sich anhäufen.

drill [dril] 1. Drillbohrer *m*; Furche *f*; ✗ Drill-, Sämaschine *f*; ✗ Exer- zieren *n* (*a. fig.*); 2. bohren; ✗ (ein)exerzieren (*a. fig.*).

drink [driŋk] 1. Trunk *m*; (geistiges) Getränk *n*; 2. [*irr.*] trinken.

drip [drip] 1. Tröpfeln *n*; Traufe *f*; 2. tröpfeln (lassen); triefen; **~dry shirt** ['drip'drai ʃəːt] bügelfreies Hemd; **~ping** [~piŋ] Bratenfett *n*.

drive [draiv] 1. (Spazier)Fahrt *f*; Auffahrt *f*, Fahrweg *m*; ⊕ Antrieb *m*; *fig.* (Auf)Trieb *m*; Drang *m*; Unternehmen *n*, Feldzug *m*; *Am.* Sammelaktion *f*; 2. [*irr.*] *v/t.* (an-) ein)treiben; *Geschäft* betreiben; fahren; lenken; zwingen; vertrei- ben; *v/i.* treiben; fahren; **~ at** hin- zielen auf.

drive-in *Am.* ['draiv'in] 1. *mst attr.* Auto...; **~ cinema** Autokino *n*; 2. Autokino *n*; Autorestaurant *n*.

drivel ['drivl] 1. geifern; faseln; 2. Geifer *m*; Faselei *f*.

driven ['drivn] *p.p. von* drive 2.

driver ['draivə] Treiber *m*; *mot.* Fahrer *m*, Chauffeur *m*; 🚂 Führer *m*.

driving| licence ['draiviŋ laisəns] Führerschein *m*; **~ school** Fahr- schule *f*.

drizzle ['drizl] 1. Sprühregen *m*; 2. sprühen, nieseln.

drone [droun] 1. *zo.* Drohne *f*; *fig.* Faulenzer *m*; 2. summen; dröhnen.

droop [druːp] *v/t.* sinken lassen; *v/i.* schlaff niederhängen; den Kopf hängen lassen; (ver)welken; schwin- den.

drop [drɔp] 1. Tropfen *m*; Frucht- bonbon *m*, *n*; Fall *m*; Falltür *f*; *thea.* Vorhang *m*; *get* (*have*) *the* **~** *on Am.* F zuvorkommen; 2. *v/t.* tropfen (lassen); niederlassen; fal- len lassen; *Brief* einwerfen; *Fahr- gast* absetzen; senken; **~ s.o. a few lines** *pl.* j-m ein paar Zeilen schreiben; *v/i.* tropfen; (herab)fallen; um-, hinsinken; ~ *in* unerwartet kommen.

dropsy ['drɒpsi] Wassersucht *f.*

drought [draut], **drouth** [drauθ] Trockenheit *f*, Dürre *f.*

drove [drouv] 1. Trift *f* Rinder; Herde *f* (*a. fig.*); 2. *pret. von* drive 2.

drown [draun] *v/t.* ertränken; überschwemmen; *fig.* übertäuben; übertönen; *v/i.* ertrinken.

drows|e [drauz] schlummern, schläfrig sein od. machen; ~**y** ['drauzi] schläfrig; einschläfernd.

drudge [drʌdʒ] 1. *fig.* Sklave *m*, Packesel *m*, Kuli *m*; 2. sich (ab-) placken.

drug [drʌg] 1. Droge *f*, Arzneiware *f*; Rauschgift *n*; unverkäufliche Ware; 2. mit (schädlichen) Zutaten versetzen; Arznei *od.* Rauschgift geben (*dat.*) *od.* nehmen; ~**gist** ['drʌgist] Drogist *m*; Apotheker *m*; ~**store** *Am.* Drugstore *m.*

drum [drʌm] 1. Trommel *f*; Trommelfell *n*; 2. trommeln; ~**mer** ['drʌmə] Trommler *m*; *bsd. Am.* F Vertreter *m.*

drunk [drʌŋk] 1. *p.p. von* drink 2; 2. *adj.* (be)trunken; get ~ sich betrinken; ~**ard** ['drʌŋkəd] Trinker *m*, Säufer *m*; ~**en** *adj.* [~kən] (be-) trunken.

dry [drai] 1. ☐ trocken; herb (*Wein*); F durstig; F antialkoholisch; ~ goods *pl. Am.* F Kurzwaren *f/pl.*; 2. *Am.* F Alkoholgegner *m*; 3. trocknen; dörren; ~ *up* austrocknen; verdunsten; ~**clean** ['drai'kli:n] chemisch reinigen; ~**nurse** Kinderfrau *f.*

dual ☐ ['dju(:)əl] doppelt; Doppel...

dubious ☐ ['dju:bjəs] zweifelhaft.

duchess ['dʌtʃis] Herzogin *f.*

duck [dʌk] 1. *zo.* Ente *f*; *Am. sl.* Kerl *m*; Verbeugung *f*; Ducken *n*; (Segel)Leinen *n*; F Liebling *m*; 2. (unter)tauchen; (sich) ducken; *Am. j-m* ausweichen.

duckling ['dʌkliŋ] Entchen *n.*

dude *Am.* [dju:d] Geck *m*; ~ *ranch Am.* Vergnügungsfarm *f.*

dudgeon ['dʌdʒən] Groll *m.*

due [dju:] 1. schuldig; gebührend; gehörig; fällig; in ~ time zur rechten Zeit; be ~ to *j-m* gebühren; herrühren *od.* kommen von; be ~ to *inf.* sollen, müssen; *Am.* im Begriff sein zu; 2. *adv.* ⊕ gerade; genau; 3. Schuldigkeit *f*; Recht *n*, Anspruch *m*; Lohn *m*; *mst* ~*s pl.* Abgabe(n *pl.*) *f*, Gebühr(en *pl.*) *f*; Beitrag *m.* 2. sich duellieren.

duel ['dju(:)əl] 1. Zweikampf *m*; ~

dug [dʌg] *pret. u. p.p. von* dig 1.

duke [dju:k] Herzog *m*; ~**dom** ['dju:kdəm] Herzogtum *n*; Herzogswürde *f.*

dull [dʌl] 1. ☐ dumm; träge;

schwerfällig; stumpf(sinnig); matt (*Auge etc.*); schwach (*Gehör*); langweilig; teilnahmslos; dumpf; trüb; † flau; 2. stumpf machen; *fig.* abstumpfen; (sich) trüben; ~**ness** ['dʌlnis] Stumpfsinn *m*; Dummheit *f*; Schwerfälligkeit *f*; Mattheit *f*; Langweiligkeit *f*; Teilnahmslosigkeit *f*; Trübheit *f*; Flauheit *f.*

duly *adv.* ['dju:li] gehörig; richtig.

dumb ☐ [dʌm] stumm; sprachlos; *Am.* F doof, blöd; ~**founded** [dʌm'faundid] sprachlos; ~**waiter** ['dʌm'weitə] Drehtisch *m*; *Am.* Speisenaufzug *m.*

dummy ['dʌmi] Attrappe *f*; Schein *m*, Schwindel *m*; *fig.* Strohmann *m*; Statist *m*; *attr.* Schein...; Schwindel...

dump [dʌmp] 1. *v/t.* auskippen; *Schutt etc.* abladen; *Waren* zu Schleuderpreisen ausführen; *v/i.* hinplumpsen; 2. Klumpen *m*; Plumps *m*; Schuttabladestelle *f*; ✕ Munitionslager *n*; ~**ing** † ['dʌmpiŋ] Schleuderausfuhr *f*; ~*s pl.*: (down) *in the* ~ F niedergeschlagen.

dun [dʌn] mahnen, drängen.

dunce [dʌns] Dummkopf *m.*

dune [dju:n] Düne *f.*

dung [dʌŋ] 1. Dung *m*; 2. düngen.

dungeon ['dʌndʒən] Kerker *m.*

dunk *Am.* F [dʌŋk] (ein)tunken.

dupe [dju:p] anführen, täuschen.

duplex ⊕ ['dju:pleks] *attr.* Doppel...; *Am.* Zweifamilienhaus *n.*

duplic|ate 1. ['dju:plikit] doppelt; 2. [~] Duplikat *n*; 3. [~keit] doppelt ausfertigen; ~**ity** [dju(:)'plisiti] Doppelzüngigkeit *f.*

dura|ble ☐ ['djuərəbl] dauerhaft; ~**tion** [djuə'reiʃən] Dauer *f.*

duress(e) [djuə'res] Zwang *m.*

during *prp.* ['djuəriŋ] während.

dusk [dʌsk] Halbdunkel *n*, Dämmerung *f*; ~**y** ☐ ['dʌski] dämmerig, düster (*a. fig.*); schwärzlich.

dust [dʌst] 1. Staub *m*; 2. abstauben; bestreuen; ~**bin** ['dʌstbin] Mülleimer *m*; ~ **bowl** *Am.* Sandstaub-u. Dürregebiet *n im Westen der USA*; ~**cart** Müllwagen *m*; ~**er** [~tə] Staublappen *m*, -wedel *m*; *Am.* Staubmantel *m*; ~**jacket** *Am.* Schutzumschlag *m e-s Buches*; ~**man** Müllabfuhrmann *m*; ~**y** ☐ [~ti] staubig.

Dutch [dʌtʃ] 1. holländisch; ~ treat *Am.* F getrennte Rechnung; 2. Holländisch *n*; the ~ die Holländer *pl.*

duty ['dju:ti] Pflicht *f*; Ehrerbietung *f*; Abgabe *f*, Zoll *m*; Dienst *m*; off ~ dienstfrei; ~**free** zollfrei.

dwarf [dwɔ:f] 1. Zwerg *m*; 2. in der Entwicklung hindern; verkleinern.

dwell [dwel] [*irr.*] wohnen; verweilen (*on, upon* bei); ~ (*up*)*on* bestehen auf (*acc.*); ~**ing** ['dweliŋ] Wohnung *f.*

dwelt [dwelt] *pret. u. p.p. von dwell*.
dwindle ['dwindl] (dahin)schwinden, abnehmen; (herab)sinken.
dye [dai] 1. Farbe *f; of deepest ~ fig.* schlimmster Art; 2. färben.
dying ['daiiŋ] 1. ☐ sterbend; Sterbe...; 2. Sterben *n*.

dynam|ic [dai'næmik] dynamisch, kraftgeladen; **~ics** [~ks] *mst sg.* Dynamik *f;* **~ite** ['dainəmait] 1. Dynamit *n;* 2. mit Dynamit sprengen.
dysentery ['disntri] Ruhr *f*.
dyspepsia [dis'pepsiə] Verdauungsstörung *f*.

E

each [iːtʃ] jede(r, -s); *~ other* einander, sich.
eager ☐ ['iːgə] (be)gierig; eifrig; **~ness** ['iːgənis] Begierde *f;* Eifer *m*.
eagle ['iːgl] Adler *m; Am.* Zehndollarstück *n;* **~eyed** scharfsichtig.
ear [iə] Ähre *f;* Ohr *n;* Öhr *n,* Henkel *m; keep an ~ to the ground bsd. Am.* aufpassen, was die Leute sagen *od.* denken; **~drum** ['iədrʌm] Trommelfell *n*.
earl [əːl] *englischer* Graf.
early ['əːli] früh; Früh...; Anfangs...; erst; bald(ig); *as ~ as* schon in *(dat.);* [nen.]
ear-mark ['iəmaːk] (kenn)zeich-|
earn [əːn] verdienen; einbringen.
earnest ['əːnist] 1. ☐ ernst(lich, -haft); ernstgemeint; 2. Ernst *m*.
earnings ['əːniŋz] Einkommen *n*.
ear|piece *teleph.* ['iəpiːs] Hörmuschel *f;* **~shot** Hörweite *f*.
earth [əːθ] 1. Erde *f;* Land *n;* 2. *v/t. ∮* erden; **~en** ['əːθən] irden; **~enware** [~nwɛə] 1. Töpferware *f;* Steingut *n;* 2. irden; **~ing** *∮* ['əːθiŋ] Erdung *f;* **~ly** ['əːθli] irdisch; **~quake** Erdbeben *n;* **~worm** Regenwurm *m*.
ease [iːz] 1. Bequemlichkeit *f,* Behagen *n;* Ruhe *f;* Ungezwungenheit *f;* Leichtigkeit *f; at ~* bequem, behaglich; 2. *v/t.* erleichtern; lindern; beruhigen; bequem(er) machen; *v/i.* sich entspannen *(Lage).*
easel ['iːzl] Staffelei *f*.
easiness ['iːzinis] = *ease 1*.
east [iːst] 1. Ost(en *m*); Orient *m; the 2 Am.* die Oststaaten *der USA;* 2. Ost...; östlich; ostwärts.
Easter ['iːstə] Ostern *n; attr.* Oster...
easter|ly ['iːstəli] östlich; Ost...; nach Osten; **~n** [~ən] = *easterly;* orientalisch; **~ner** [~nə] Ostländer (-in); Orientale *m,* -in *f; 2 Am.* Oststaatler(in).
eastward(s) ['iːstwəd(z)] ostwärts.
easy ['iːzi] ☐ leicht; bequem; frei von Schmerzen; ruhig; willig; ungezwungen; *in ~ circumstances* wohlhabend; *on ~ street Am.* in guten Verhältnissen; *take it ~!* immer mit der Ruhe!; **~ chair** Klubsessel *m;* **~-going** *fig.* bequem.

eat [iːt] 1. [*irr.*] essen; (zer)fressen; 2. **~s** *pl. Am. sl.* Essen *n,* Eßwaren *f/pl.;* **~ables** ['iːtəblz] Eßwaren *f/pl.;* **~en** ['iːtn] *p.p. von eat 1.*
eaves [iːvz] *pl.* Dachrinne *f,* Traufe *f;* **~drop** ['iːvzdrɔp] (er)lauschen; horchen.
ebb [eb] 1. Ebbe *f; fig.* Abnahme *f;* Verfall *m;* 2. verebben; *fig.* abnehmen, sinken; **~tide** ['eb'taid] Ebbe *f*.
ebony ['ebəni] Ebenholz *n*.
ebullition [ebə'liʃən] Überschäumen *n;* Aufbrausen *n*.
eccentric [ik'sentrik] 1. exzentrisch; *fig.* überspannt; 2. Sonderling *m*.
ecclesiastic [ikliːzi'æstik] Geistliche(r) *m;* **~al** ☐ [~kəl] geistlich, kirchlich.
echo ['ekou] 1. Echo *n;* 2. widerhallen; *fig.* echoen, nachsprechen.
eclipse [i'klips] 1. Finsternis *f;* 2. (sich) verfinstern, verdunkeln.
econom|ical (☐) [iːkə'nɔmik(əl)] haushälterisch; wirtschaftlich; Wirtschafts...; **~ics** [~ks] *sg.* Volkswirtschaft(slehre) *f;* **~ist** [i(ː)'kɔnəmist] Volkswirt *m;* **~ize** [~maiz] sparsam wirtschaften (mit); **~y** [~mi] Wirtschaft *f;* Wirtschaftlichkeit *f;* Einsparung *f; political ~* Volkswirtschaft(slehre) *f*.
ecsta|sy ['ekstəsi] Ekstase *f,* Verzückung *f;* **~tic** [eks'tætik] (~ally) verzückt.
eddy ['edi] 1. Wirbel *m;* 2. wirbeln.
edge [edʒ] 1. Schneide *f;* Schärfe *f;* Rand *m;* Kante *f;* Tisch-Ecke *f; be on ~* nervös sein; *have the ~ on s.o. bsd. Am.* F j-m über sein; 2. schärfen; (um)säumen; (sich) drängen; **~ways, ~wise** ['edʒweiz, 'edʒwaiz] seitwärts; von der Seite.
edging ['edʒiŋ] Einfassung *f;* Rand|
edgy ['edʒi] scharf; F nervös. *[m.]*
edible ['edibl] eßbar.
edict ['iːdikt] Edikt *n*.
edifice ['edifis] Gebäude *n*.
edifying ☐ ['edifaiiŋ] erbaulich.
edit ['edit] *Text* herausgeben, redigieren; *Zeitung* als Herausgeber leiten; **~ion** [i'diʃən] Buch-Ausgabe *f;* Auflage *f;* **~or** ['editə] Herausgeber *m;* Redakteur *m;* **~orial**

[edi'tɔ:riəl] Leitartikel m; attr. Redaktions...; ~orship ['editəʃip] Schriftleitung f, Redaktion f.

educat|e ['edju(:)keit] erziehen; unterrichten; ~ion [edju(:)'keiʃən] Erziehung f; (Aus)Bildung f; Erziehungs-, Schulwesen n; Ministry of ♀ Unterrichtsministerium n; ~ional □ [~nl] erzieherisch; Erziehungs...; Bildungs...; ~or ['edju:keitə] Erzieher m.

eel [i:l] Aal m.

efface [i'feis] auslöschen; fig. tilgen.

effect [i'fekt] 1. Wirkung f; Folge f; ⊕ Leistung f; ~s pl. Effekten pl. Habseligkeiten f/pl.; be of ~ Wirkung haben; take ~ in Kraft treten; in ~ in der Tat; to the ~ des Inhalts; 2. bewirken, ausführen; ~ive □ [~tiv] wirkend; wirksam; eindrucksvoll; wirklich vorhanden; ⊕ nutzbar; ~ date Tag m des Inkrafttretens; ~ual □ [~tjuəl] wirksam, kräftig.

effeminate □ [i'feminit] verweichlicht; weibisch.

effervesce [efə'ves] (auf)brausen; ~nt [~snt] sprudelnd, schäumend.

effete [e'fi:t] verbraucht; entkräftet.

efficacy ['efikəsi] Wirksamkeit f, Kraft f.

efficien|cy [i'fiʃənsi] Leistung(sfähigkeit) f; ~ expert Am. Rationalisierungsfachmann m; ~t □ [~nt] wirksam; leistungsfähig; tüchtig.

efflorescence [əflɔ:'resns] Blütezeit f; ♣ Beschlag m.

effluence ['efluəns] Ausfluß m.

effort ['efət] Anstrengung f, Bemühung f (at um) Mühe f.

effrontery [e'frʌntəri] Frechheit f.

effulgent □ [e'fʌldʒənt] glänzend.

effus|ion [i'fju:ʒən] Erguß m; ~ive □ [~u:siv] überschwenglich.

egg[1] [eg] mst ~ on aufreizen.

egg[2] [~] Ei n; put all one's ~s in one basket alles auf eine Karte setzen; as sure as ~s is ~s F todsicher; ~-cup ['egkʌp] Eierbecher m; ~head Am. sl. Intellektuelle(r) m.

egotism ['egoutizəm] Selbstgefälligkeit f.

egregious iro. □ [i'gri:dʒəs] ungeheuer.

egress ['i:gres] Ausgang m; Ausweg m.

Egyptian [i'dʒipʃən] 1. ägyptisch; 2. Ägypter(in).

eider ['aidə]: ~ down Eiderdaunen f/pl.; Daunendecke f.

eight [eit] 1. acht; 2. Acht f; behind the ~ ball Am. in der (die) Klemme; ~een ['ei'ti:n] achtzehn; ~eenth [~nθ] achtzehnt; ~fold ['eitfould] achtfach; ~h [eitθ] 1. achte(r, -s); 2. Achtel n; ~hly ['eitθli] achtens; ~ieth ['eitiiθ] achtzigste(r, -s); ~y ['eiti] achtzig.

either ['aiðə] 1. adj. u. pron. einer

von beiden; beide; 2. cj. ~ ... or entweder ... oder; not (...) ~ auch nicht.

ejaculate [i'dʒækjuleit] Worte, Flüssigkeit ausstoßen.

eject [i(:)'dʒekt] ausstoßen; vertreiben, ausweisen; entsetzen (e-s Amtes).

eke [i:k]: ~ out ergänzen; verlängern; sich mit et. durchhelfen.

el Am. F [el] = elevated railroad.

elaborat|e 1. □ [i'læbərit] sorgfältig ausgearbeitet; kompliziert; 2. [~reit] sorgfältig ausarbeiten; ~eness [~ritnis], ~ion [ilæbə'reiʃən] sorgfältige Ausarbeitung.

elapse [i'læps] verfließen, verstreichen.

elastic [i'læstik] 1. (~ally) dehnbar; spannkräftig; 2. Gummiband n; ~ity [elæs'tisiti] Elastizität f, Dehnbarkeit f; Spannkraft f.

elate [i'leit] (er)heben, ermutigen, froh erregen; stolz machen; ~d in gehobener Stimmung, freudig erregt (at über acc.; with durch).

elbow ['elbou] 1. Ellbogen m; Biegung f; ♣ Knie n; at one's ~ nahe, bei der Hand; out at ~s fig. heruntergekommen; 2. mit dem Ellbogen (weg)stoßen; ~ out verdrängen; ~grease F Armschmalz n (Kraftanstrengung).

elder ['eldə] 1. älter; 2. der, die Ältere; (Kirchen)Älteste(r) m; ♀ Holunder m; ~ly [~əli] ältlich.

eldest ['eldist] älteste(r, -s).

elect [i'lekt] 1. (aus)gewählt; 2. (auser)wählen; ~ion [~kʃən] Wahl f; ~ive □ [~ktiv] 1. □ wählend; gewählt; Wahl...; Am. fakultativ; 2. Am. Wahlfach n; ~or [~tə] Wähler m; Am. Wahlmann m; Kurfürst m; ~oral [~ərəl] Wahl..., Wähler...; ~ college Am. Wahlmänner m/pl.; ~orate [~rit] Wähler(schaft f) m/pl.

electric|(al □) [i'lektrik(əl)] elektrisch; Elektro...; fig. faszinierend; ~al engineer Elektrotechniker m; ~ blue stahlblau; ~ chair elektrischer Stuhl; ~ian [ilek'triʃən] Elektriker m; ~ity [~isiti] Elektrizität f.

electri|fy [i'lektrifai], ~ze [~raiz] elektrifizieren; elektrisieren.

electro|cute [i'lektrəkju:t] auf dem elektrischen Stuhl hinrichten; durch elektrischen Strom töten; ~metallurgy Elektrometallurgie f.

electron [i'lektrən] Elektron n; ~ray tube magisches Auge.

electro|plate [i'lektroupleit] galvanisch versilbern; ~type galvanischer Druck; Galvano n.

elegan|ce ['eligəns] Eleganz f; Anmut f; ~t □ [~nt] elegant; geschmackvoll; Am. erstklassig.

element ['elimənt] Element n; Urstoff m; (Grund)Bestandteil m; ~s pl. Anfangsgründe m/pl.; ~al □

[eli'mentl] elementar; wesentlich; ~ary [~təri] 1. □ elementar; Anfangs...; ~ school Volks-, Grundschule f; 2. elementaries pl. Anfangsgründe m/pl.

elephant ['elifənt] Elefant m.

elevat|e ['eliveit] erhöhen; fig. erheben; ~ed erhaben; ~ (railroad) Am. Hochbahn f; ~ion [eli'veiʃən] Erhebung f, Erhöhung f; Höhe f; Erhabenheit f; ~or ⊕ ['eliveitə] Aufzug m; Am. Fahrstuhl m; ⚓ Höhenruder n; (grain) ~ Am. Getreidespeicher m.

eleven [i'levn] 1. elf; 2. Elf f; ~th [~nθ] elfte(r, -s).

elf [elf] Elf(e f) m, Kobold m; Zwerg m.

elicit [i'lisit] hervorlocken, herausholen.

eligible □ ['elidʒəbl] geeignet, annehmbar; passend.

eliminat|e [i'limineit] aussondern, ausscheiden; ausmerzen; ~ion [ilimi'neiʃən] Aussonderung f; Ausscheidung f.

élite [ei'liːt] Elite f; Auslese f.

elk zo. [elk] Elch m.

ellipse ♫ [i'lips] Ellipse f.

elm ♀ [elm] Ulme f, Rüster f.

elocution [elə'kjuːʃən] Vortrag(skunst, -sweise f) m.

elongate ['iːlɔŋgeit] verlängern.

elope [i'loup] entlaufen, durchgehen.

eloquen|ce ['eləkwəns] Beredsamkeit f; ~t □ [~nt] beredt.

else [els] sonst, andere(r, -s), weiter; ~where ['elsweə] anderswo(hin).

elucidat|e [i'luːsideit] erläutern; ~ion [iluːsi'deiʃən] Aufklärung f.

elude [i'luːd] geschickt umgehen; ausweichen, sich entziehen (dat.).

elus|ive [i'luːsiv] schwer faßbar; ~ory [~səri] trügerisch.

emaciate [i'meiʃieit] abzehren, ausmergeln.

emanat|e ['eməneit] ausströmen; ausgehen (from von); ~ion [emə'neiʃən] Ausströmen n; fig. Ausstrahlung f.

emancipat|e [i'mænsipeit] emanzipieren, befreien; ~ion [imænsi'peiʃən] Emanzipation f; Befreiung f.

embalm [im'baːm] (ein)balsamieren; be ~ed in fortleben in (dat.).

embankment [im'bæŋkmənt] Eindämmung f; Deich m; (Bahn-)Damm m; Uferstraße f, Kai m.

embargo [em'baːgou] (Hafen-, Handels)Sperre f, Beschlagnahme f.

embark [im'baːk] (sich) einschiffen (for nach); Geld anlegen; sich einlassen (in, on, upon in, auf acc.).

embarrass [im'bærəs] (be)hindern; verwirren; in (Geld)Verlegenheit bringen; verwickeln; ~ing □ [~siŋ] unangenehm; unbequem; ~ment [~smənt] (Geld)Verlegenheit f; Schwierigkeit f.

embassy ['embəsi] Botschaft f; Gesandtschaft f.

embed [im'bed] (ein)betten, lagern.

embellish [im'beliʃ] verschönern; ausschmücken. [(Asche.)

embers ['embəz] pl. glühende]

embezzle [im'bezl] unterschlagen; ~ment [~mənt] Unterschlagung f.

embitter [im'bitə] verbittern.

emblazon [im'bleizən] mit e-m Wappenbild bemalen; fig. verherrlichen.

emblem ['embləm] Sinnbild n; Wahrzeichen n.

embody [im'bɔdi] verkörpern; vereinigen; einverleiben (in dat.).

embolden [im'bouldən] ermutigen.

embolism ⚕ ['embəlizəm] Embolie f.

embosom [im'buzəm] ins Herz schließen; ~ed with umgeben von.

emboss [im'bɔs] bossieren; mit dem Hammer treiben.

embrace [im'breis] 1. (sich) umarmen; umfassen; Beruf etc. ergreifen; Angebot annehmen; 2. Umarmung f.

embroider [im'brɔidə] sticken; ausschmücken; ~y [~əri] Stickerei f.

embroil [im'brɔil] (in Streit) verwickeln; verwirren.

emendation [iːmen'deiʃən] Verbesserung f.

emerald ['emərəld] Smaragd m.

emerge [i'məːdʒ] auftauchen; hervorgehen; sich erheben; sich zeigen; ~ncy [~dʒənsi] unerwartetes Ereignis; Notfall m; attr. Not...; ~ brake Notbremse f; ~ call Notruf m; ~ exit Notausgang m; ~ man Sport: Ersatzmann m; ~nt [~nt] auftauchend, entstehend; ~ countries Entwicklungsländer n/pl.

emersion [i(ː)'məːʃən] Auftauchen n.

emigra|nt ['emigrənt] 1. auswandernd; 2. Auswanderer m; ~te [~reit] auswandern; ~tion [emi'greiʃən] Auswanderung f.

eminen|ce ['eminəns] (An)Höhe f; Auszeichnung f; hohe Stellung; Eminenz f (Titel); ~t □ [~nt] fig. ausgezeichnet, hervorragend; ~tly [~tli] ganz besonders.

emissary ['emisəri] Emissär m.

emit [i'mit] von sich geben; aussenden, ausströmen; ✝ ausgeben.

emolument [i'mɔljumənt] Vergütung f; ~s pl. Einkünfte pl.

emotion [i'mouʃən] (Gemüts)Bewegung f; Gefühl(sregung f) n; Rührung f; ~al □ [~nl] gefühlsmäßig; gefühlvoll; gefühlsbetont; ~less [~nlis] gefühllos, kühl.

emperor ['empərə] Kaiser m.

empha|sis ['emfəsis] Nachdruck *m*; **~size** [~saiz] nachdrücklich betonen; **~tic** [im'fætik] (~ally) nachdrücklich; ausgesprochen.

empire ['empaiə] (Kaiser)Reich *n*; Herrschaft *f*; the British 2 das britische Weltreich.

empirical □ [em'pirikəl] erfahrungsgemäß.

employ [im'plɔi] **1.** beschäftigen, anstellen; an-, verwenden, gebrauchen; **2.** Beschäftigung *f*; in the ~ of angestellt bei; **~ee** [emplɔi'iː] Angestellte(r *m*) *f*; Arbeitnehmer(in); **~er** [im'plɔiə] Arbeitgeber *m*; † Auftraggeber *m*; **~ment** [~imənt] Beschäftigung *f*; Arbeit *f*; ~ agency Stellenvermittlungsbüro *n*; 2 Exchange Arbeitsamt *n*.

empower [im'pauə] ermächtigen; befähigen.

empress ['empris] Kaiserin *f*.

empt|iness ['emptinis] Leere *f*; Hohlheit *f*; **~y** □ ['empti] **1.** leer; *fig.* hohl; **2.** (sich) (aus-, ent)leeren.

emul|ate ['emjuleit] wetteifern mit; nacheifern, es gleichtun (*dat.*); **~ation** [emju'leiʃən] Wetteifer *m*.

enable [i'neibl] befähigen, es *j-m* ermöglichen; ermächtigen.

enact [i'nækt] verfügen, verordnen; Gesetz erlassen; *thea.* spielen.

enamel [i'næməl] **1.** Email(le *f*) *n*, (Zahn)Schmelz *m*; Glasur *f*; Lack *m*; **2.** emaillieren; glasieren.

enamo(u)r [i'næmə] verliebt machen; **~ed of** verliebt in.

encamp ⚔ [in'kæmp] (sich) lagern.

encase [in'keis] einschließen.

enchain [in'tʃein] anketten; fesseln.

enchant [in'tʃɑːnt] bezaubern; **~ment** [~tmənt] Bezauberung *f*; Zauber *m*; **~ress** [~tris] Zauberin *f*.

encircle [in'səːkl] einkreisen.

enclos|e [in'klouz] einzäunen; einschließen; beifügen; **~ure** [~ouʒə] Einzäunung *f*; eingehegtes Grundstück; Bei-, Anlage *f* zu e-m Brief.

encompass [in'kʌmpəs] umgeben.

encore *thea.* [ɔŋ'kɔː] **1.** um e-e Zugabe bitten; **2.** Zugabe *f*.

encounter [in'kauntə] **1.** Begegnung *f*; Gefecht *n*; **2.** begegnen (*dat.*); auf *Schwierigkeiten etc.* stoßen; mit *j-m* zs.-stoßen.

encourage [in'kʌridʒ] ermutigen; fördern; **~ment** [~dʒmənt] Ermutigung *f*; Unterstützung *f*.

encroach [in'kroutʃ] (on, upon) eingreifen, eindringen (in *acc.*); beschränken (*acc.*); mißbrauchen (*acc.*); **~ment** [~ʃmənt] Ein-, Übergriff *m*.

encumb|er [in'kʌmbə] belasten; (be)hindern; **~rance** [~brəns] Last *f*; *fig.* Hindernis *n*; Schuldenlast *f*; without ~ ohne (Familien)Anhang;

encyclop(a)edia [ensaiklou'piːdjə]
Enzyklopädie *f*, Konversationslexikon *n*.

end [end] **1.** Ende *n*; Ziel *n*, Zweck *m*; no ~ of unendlich viel(e), unzählige; in the ~ am Ende, auf die Dauer; on ~ aufrecht; stand on ~ zu Berge stehen; to no ~ vergebens; go off the deep ~ *fig.* in die Luft gehen; make both ~s meet gerade auskommen; **2.** enden, beend(ig)en.

endanger [in'deindʒə] gefährden.

endear [in'diə] teuer machen; **~ment** [~əmənt] Liebkosung *f*, Zärtlichkeit *f*.

endeavo(u)r [in'devə] **1.** Bestreben *n*, Bemühung *f*; **2.** sich bemühen.

end|ing ['endiŋ] Ende *n*; Schluß *m*; *gr.* Endung *f*; **~less** □ ['endlis] endlos, unendlich; ⊕ ohne Ende.

endorse [in'dɔːs] † indossieren; *et.* vermerken (on auf der Rückseite e-r Urkunde); gutheißen; **~ment** [~smənt] Aufschrift *f*; † Indossament *n*.

endow [in'dau] ausstatten; **~ment** [~aumənt] Ausstattung *f*; Stiftung *f*.

endue *fig.* [in'djuː] (be)kleiden.

endur|ance [in'djuərəns] (Aus-)Dauer *f*; Ertragen *n*; **~e** [in'djuə] (aus)dauern; ertragen.

enema ⚕ ['enimə] Klistier(spritze *f*) *n*.

enemy ['enimi] **1.** Feind *m*; the 2 der Teufel; **2.** feindlich.

energ|etic [enə'dʒetik] (~ally) energisch; **~y** ['enədʒi] Energie *f*.

enervate ['enəːveit] entnerven.

enfeeble [in'fiːbl] schwächen.

enfold [in'fould] einhüllen; umfassen.

enforce [in'fɔːs] erzwingen; aufzwingen (upon *dat.*); bestehen auf (*dat.*); durchführen; **~ment** [~smənt] Erzwingung *f*; Geltendmachung *f*; Durchführung *f*.

enfranchise [in'fræntʃaiz] das Wahlrecht verleihen (*dat.*); Sklaven befreien.

engage [in'geidʒ] *v/t.* anstellen; verpflichten; mieten; in Anspruch nehmen; ⚔ angreifen; be ~d verlobt sein (to mit); beschäftigt sein (in mit); besetzt sein; ~ the clutch einkuppeln; *v/i.* sich verpflichten, versprechen, garantieren; sich beschäftigen (in mit); ⚔ angreifen; ⊕ greifen (Zahnräder); **~ment** [~dʒmənt] Verpflichtung *f*; Verlobung *f*; Verabredung *f*; Beschäftigung *f*; ⚔ Gefecht *n*; Einrücken *n* e-s Ganges etc.

engaging □ [in'geidʒiŋ] einnehmend.

engender *fig.* [in'dʒendə] erzeugen.

engine ['endʒin] Maschine *f*, Motor *m*; 🚂 Lokomotive *f*; **~-driver** Lokomotivführer *m*.

engineer [endʒi'niə] **1.** Ingenieur *m*,

Techniker *m*; Maschinist *m*; *Am.* Lokomotivführer *m*; ⚒ Pionier *m*; **2.** Ingenieur sein; bauen; **~ing** [~əriŋ] **1.** Maschinenbau *m*; Ingenieurwesen *n*; **2.** technisch; Ingenieur...

English ['iŋgliʃ] **1.** englisch; **2.** Englisch *n*; the ~ *pl.* die Engländer *pl.*; *in plain ~ fig.* unverblümt; **~man** Engländer *m*.

engrav|e [in'greiv] gravieren, stechen; *fig.* einprägen; **~er** [~və] Graveur *m*; **~ing** [~viŋ] (Kupfer-, Stahl)Stich *m*; Holzschnitt *m*.

engross [in'grous] an sich ziehen; ganz in Anspruch nehmen.

engulf *fig.* [in'gʌlf] verschlingen.

enhance [in'hɑ:ns] erhöhen.

enigma [i'nigmə] Rätsel *n*; **~tic(al** □) [enig'mætik(əl)] rätselhaft.

enjoin [in'dʒɔin] auferlegen (*on j-m*).

enjoy [in'dʒɔi] sich erfreuen an (*dat.*); genießen; *did you ~ it?* hat es Ihnen gefallen?; *~ o.s.* sich amüsieren; *I ~ my dinner* es schmeckt mir; **~able** [~ɔiəbl] genußreich, erfreulich; **~ment** [~ɔimənt] Genuß *m*, Freude *f*.

enlarge [in'lɑ:dʒ] (sich) erweitern, ausdehnen; vergrößern; **~ment** [~dʒmənt] Erweiterung *f*; Vergrößerung *f*.

enlighten [in'laitn] *fig.* erleuchten; *j-n* aufklären; **~ment** [~nmənt] Aufklärung *f*.

enlist [in'list] *v/t.* ⚒ anwerben; gewinnen; **~ed men** *pl. Am.* ⚒ Unteroffiziere *pl.* und Mannschaften *pl.*; *v/i.* sich freiwillig melden.

enliven [in'laivn] beleben.

enmity ['enmiti] Feindschaft *f*.

ennoble [i'noubl] adeln; veredeln.

enorm|ity [i'nɔːmiti] Ungeheuerlichkeit *f*; **~ous** □ [~məs] ungeheuer.

enough [i'nʌf] genug.

enquire [in'kwaiə] = *inquire.*

enrage [in'reidʒ] wütend machen; **~d** wütend (*at* über *acc.*).

enrapture [in'ræptʃə] entzücken.

enrich [in'ritʃ] be-, anreichern.

enrol(l) [in'roul] *in e-e Liste* eintragen; ⚒ anwerben; aufnehmen; **~ment** [~lmənt] Eintragung *f*; *bsd.* ⚒ Anwerbung *f*, Einstellung *f*; Aufnahme *f*; Verzeichnis *n*; Schüler-, Studenten-, Teilnehmerzahl *f*.

ensign ['ensain] Fahne *f*; Flagge *f*; Abzeichen *n*; ⚓ *Am.* ['ensn] Leutnant *m* zur See.

enslave [in'sleiv] versklaven; **~ment** [~vmənt] Versklavung *f*.

ensnare *fig.* [in'snɛə] verführen.

ensue [in'sjuː] folgen; sich ergeben.

ensure [in'ʃuə] sichern.

entail [in'teil] **1.** zur Folge haben; als unveräußerliches Gut vererben; **2.** (Übertragung *f* als) unveräußerliches Gut.

entangle [in'tæŋgl] verwickeln; **~ment** [~lmənt] Verwicklung *f*; ⚒ Draht-Verhau *m*.

enter ['entə] *v/t.* (ein)treten in (*acc.*); betreten; einsteigen, einfahren *etc.* in (*acc.*); eindringen in (*acc.*); eintragen, † buchen; *Protest* einbringen; aufnehmen; melden; *~ s.o. at school* j-n zur Schule anmelden; *v/i.* eintreten; sich einschreiben; *Sport:* sich melden; aufgenommen werden; *~ into fig.* eingehen auf (*acc.*); *~* (*up*)*on Amt etc.* antreten; sich einlassen auf (*acc.*).

enterpris|e ['entəpraiz] Unternehmen *n*; Unternehmungslust *f*; **~ing** □ [~ziŋ] unternehmungslustig.

entertain [entə'tein] unterhalten; bewirten; in Erwägung ziehen; *Meinung etc.* hegen; **~er** [~ə] Gastgeber *m*; Unterhaltungskünstler *m*; **~ment** [~mənt] Unterhaltung *f*; Bewirtung *f*; Fest *n*, Gesellschaft *f*.

enthral(l) *fig.* [in'θrɔːl] bezaubern.

enthrone [in'θroun] auf den Thron setzen.

enthusias|m [in'θjuːziæzəm] Begeisterung *f*; **~t** [~æst] Schwärmer (-in); **~tic** [inθjuːzi'æstik] (~ally) begeistert (*at, about* von).

entice [in'tais] (ver)locken; **~ment** [~smənt] Verlockung *f*, Reiz *m*.

entire □ [in'taiə] ganz; vollständig; ungeteilt; **~ly** [~li] völlig, lediglich; **~ty** [~ti] Gesamtheit *f*.

entitle [in'taitl] betiteln; berechtigen.

entity ['entiti] Wesen *n*; Dasein *n*.

entrails ['entreilz] *pl.* Eingeweide *n/pl.*; Innere(s) *n*.

entrance ['entrəns] Ein-, Zutritt *m*; Einfahrt *f*, Eingang *m*; Einlaß *m*.

entrap [in'træp] (ein)fangen; verleiten.

entreat [in'triːt] bitten, ersuchen; *et.* erbitten; **~y** [~ti] Bitte *f*, Gesuch *n*.

entrench ⚒ [in'trentʃ] (mit *od.* in Gräben) verschanzen.

entrust [in'trʌst] anvertrauen (*s. th. to s.o.* j-m *et.*); betrauen.

entry ['entri] Eintritt *m*; Eingang *m*; ⚖ Besitzantritt *m* (*on, upon gen.*); Eintragung *f*; *Sport:* Meldung *f*; *~ permit* Einreisegenehmigung *f*; *book-keeping by double* (*single*) *~* doppelte (einfache) Buchführung.

enumerate [i'njuːməreit] aufzählen.

enunciate [i'nʌnsieit] verkünden; *Lehrsatz* aufstellen; aussprechen.

envelop [in'veləp] einhüllen; einwickeln; umgeben; ⚒ einkreisen; **~e** ['enviloup] Briefumschlag *m*; **~ment** [in'veləpmənt] Umhüllung *f*.

envi|able □ ['enviəbl] beneidenswert; **~ous** □ [~iəs] neidisch.

environ [in'vaiərən] umgeben; ~ment [͵nmənt] Umgebung f e-r Person; ~s ['envirənz] pl. Umgebung f e-r Stadt.

envisage [in'vizidʒ] sich et. vorstellen.

envoy ['envɔi] Gesandte(r) m; Bote m.

envy ['envi] 1. Neid m; 2. beneiden.

epic ['epik] 1. episch; 2. Epos n.

epicure ['epikjuə] Feinschmecker m.

epidemic [epi'demik] 1. (~ally) seuchenartig; ~ disease = 2. Seuche f.

epidermis [epi'də:mis] Oberhaut f.

epilepsy ['epilepsi] Epilepsie f.

epilogue ['epilɔg] Nachwort n.

episcopa|cy [i'piskəpəsi] bischöfliche Verfassung; ~l [͵ɔl] bischöflich; ~te [͵pit] Bischofswürde f; Bistum n.

epist|le [i'pisl] Epistel f; ~olary [͵stələri] brieflich; Brief...

epitaph ['epitɑ:f] Grabschrift f.

epitome [i'pitəmi] Auszug m, Abriß m.

epoch ['i:pɔk] Epoche f.

equable ['ekwəbl] gleichförmig, gleichmäßig; fig. gleichmütig.

equal [i:kwəl] 1. gleich, gleichmäßig; ~ to fig. gewachsen (dat.); 2. Gleiche(r m) f; 3. gleichen (dat.); ~ity [i(:)'kwɔliti] Gleichheit f; ~iza-tion [i:kwəlai'zeiʃən] Gleichstellung f; Ausgleich m; ~ize [i:kwə-laiz] gleichmachen, gleichstellen; ausgleichen.

equanimity [i:kwə'nimiti] Gleichmut m.

equat|ion [i'kweiʃən] Ausgleich m; ⚖ Gleichung f; ~or [͵eitə] Äquator m.

equestrian [i'kwestriən] Reiter m.

equilibrium [i:kwi'libriəm] Gleichgewicht n; Ausgleich m.

equip [i'kwip] ausrüsten; ~ment [͵pmənt] Ausrüstung f; Einrichtung f.

equipoise ['ekwipɔiz] Gleichgewicht n; Gegengewicht n.

equity ['ekwiti] Billigkeit f; equities pl. ✝ Aktien f/pl.

equivalent [i'kwivələnt] 1. gleichwertig; gleichbedeutend (to mit); 2. Äquivalent n, Gegenwert m.

equivoca|l [i'kwivəkəl] zweideutig, zweifelhaft; ~te [͵keit] zweideutig reden.

era ['iərə] Zeitrechnung f; -alter n.

eradicate [i'rædikeit] ausrotten.

eras|e [i'reiz] ausradieren, ausstreichen; auslöschen; ~er [͵zə] Radiergummi m; ~ure [i'reizə] Ausradieren n; radierte Stelle.

ere [εə] 1. cj. ehe, bevor; 2. prp. vor.

erect [i'rekt] 1. □ aufrecht; 2. aufrichten; Denkmal etc. errichten; aufstellen; ~ion [͵kʃən] Auf-, Errichtung f; Gebäude n.

eremite ['erimait] Einsiedler m.

ermine zo. ['ə:min] Hermelin n.

erosion [i'rouʒən] Zerfressen n; Auswaschung f.

erotic [i'rɔtik] 1. erotisch; 2. erotisches Gedicht; ~ism [͵isizəm] Erotik f.

err [ə:] (sich) irren; fehlen, sündigen.

errand ['erənd] Botengang m, Auftrag m; ~boy Laufbursche m.

errant □ ['erənt] (umher)irrend.

errat|ic [i'rætik] (~ally) wandernd; unberechenbar; ~um [e'rɑ:təm], pl. ~a [͵tə] Druckfehler m.

erroneous □ [i'rounjəs] irrig.

error ['erə] Irrtum m, Fehler m; ~s excepted Irrtümer vorbehalten.

erudit|e □ ['eru(:)dait] gelehrt; ~ion [eru(:)'diʃən] Gelehrsamkeit f.

erupt [i'rʌpt] ausbrechen (Vulkan); durchbrechen (Zähne); ~ion [͵pʃən] Vulkan-Ausbruch m; ⚕ Hautausschlag m.

escalat|ion [eskə'leiʃən] Eskalation f (stufenweise Steigerung); ~or ['eskəleitə] Rolltreppe f.

escap|ade [eskə'peid] toller Streich; ~e [is'keip] 1. entschlüpfen, entgehen; entkommen, entrinnen; entweichen; j-m entfallen; 2. Entrinnen n; Entweichen n; Flucht f.

eschew [is'tʃu:] (ver)meiden.

escort 1. ['eskɔ:t] Eskorte f; Geleit n; 2. [is'kɔ:t] eskortieren, geleiten.

escutcheon [is'kʌtʃən] Wappenschild m, n; Namensschild n.

especial [is'peʃəl] besonder; vorzüglich; ~ly [͵li] besonders.

espionage [espi'nɑ:ʒ] Spionage f.

espresso [is'presou] Espresso m (Kaffee); ~ bar, ~ café Espressobar f.

espy [is'pai] erspähen.

esquire [is'kwaiə] Landedelmann m, Gutsbesitzer m; auf Briefen: John Smith Esq. Herrn J. S.

essay 1. [e'sei] versuchen; probieren; 2. ['esei] Versuch m; Aufsatz m, kurze Abhandlung, Essay m, n.

essen|ce ['esns] Wesen n e-r Sache; Extrakt m; Essenz f; ~tial [i'senʃəl] 1. □ (to für) wesentlich; wichtig; 2. Wesentliche(s) n.

establish [is'tæbliʃ] festsetzen; errichten, gründen; einrichten; einsetzen; ~ o.s. sich niederlassen; ⚓ed Church Staatskirche f; ~ment [͵mənt] Festsetzung f; Gründung f; Er-, Einrichtung f; (bsd. großer) Haushalt; Anstalt f; Firma f.

estate [is'teit] Grundstück n; Grundbesitz m, Gut n; Besitz m; (Konkurs)Masse f, Nachlaß m; Stand m; real ~ Liegenschaften pl.; housing ~ Wohnsiedlung f; ~ agent Grundstücksmakler m; ~ car Kombiwagen m; ~ duty Nachlaßsteuer f.

esteem [is'ti:m] 1. Achtung f, Ansehen n (with bei); 2. (hoch)achten, (hoch)schätzen; erachten für.

estimable ['estiməbl] schätzenswert.

estimat|e 1. ['estimeit] (ab)schätzen; veranschlagen; **2.** [ˌmit] Schätzung f; (Vor)Anschlag m; **~ion** [esti'meiʃən] Schätzung f; Meinung f; Achtung f.

estrange [is'treindʒ] entfremden.

estuary ['estjuəri] (den Gezeiten ausgesetzte) weite Flußmündung.

etch [etʃ] ätzen, radieren.

etern|al [i(:)'təːnl] immerwährend, ewig; **~ity** [ˌniti] Ewigkeit f.

ether ['iːθə] Äther m; **~eal** [i(:)'θiəriəl] ätherisch (a. fig.).

ethic|al [ˈeθikəl] sittlich, ethisch; **~s** [ˌks] sg. Sittenlehre f, Ethik f.

etiquette [eti'ket] Etikette f.

etymology [eti'mɔlədʒi] Etymologie f, Wortableitung f.

Eucharist ['juːkərist] Abendmahl n.

euphemism ['juːfimizəm] beschönigender Ausdruck.

European [juərə'pi(:)ən] **1.** europäisch; **2.** Europäer(in).

evacuate [i'vækjueit] entleeren; evakuieren; Land etc. räumen.

evade [i'veid] (geschickt) ausweichen (dat.); umgehen.

evaluate [i'væljueit] zahlenmäßig bestimmen, auswerten; berechnen.

evanescent [iːvə'nesnt] (ver)schwindend. [evangelisch.]

evangelic(al □) [iːvæn'dʒelik(əl)]

evaporat|e [i'væpəreit] verdunsten, verdampfen (lassen); **~ion** [ivæpə-'reiʃən] Verdunstung f, Verdampfung f.

evasi|on [i'veiʒən] Umgehung f; Ausflucht f; **~ve** □ [ˌveisiv] ausweichend; be ~ ausweichen.

eve [iːv] Vorabend m; Vortag m; on the ~ of unmittelbar vor (dat.), am Vorabend (gen.).

even ['iːvən] **1.** adj. □ eben, gleich; gleichmäßig; ausgeglichen; glatt; gerade (Zahl); unparteiisch; get ~ with s.o. fig. mit j-m abrechnen; **2.** adv. selbst, sogar, auch; not ~ nicht einmal; ~ though, ~ if wenn auch; **3.** ebnen, glätten; gleichstellen; **~handed** unparteiisch.

evening ['iːvniŋ] Abend m; ~ dress Gesellschaftsanzug m; Frack m, Smoking m; Abendkleid n.

evenness ['iːvənnis] Ebenheit f; Geradheit f; Gleichmäßigkeit f; Unparteilichkeit f; Seelenruhe f.

evensong ['iːvənsɔŋ] Abendgottesdienst m.

event [i'vent] Ereignis n; Vorfall m; fig. Ausgang m; (sportliche Veranstaltung; athletic ~s pl. Leichtathletikwettkämpfe m/pl.; at all ~s auf alle Fälle; in the ~ of im Falle (gen.); **~ful** [ˌtful] ereignisreich.

eventual □ [i'ventjuəl] etwaig, möglich; schließlich; **~ly** am Ende; im Laufe der Zeit; gegebenenfalls.

ever ['evə] je, jemals; immer; ~ so noch so. (sehr); as soon as ~ I can sobald ich nur irgend kann; ~ after, ~ since von der Zeit an; ~ and anon von Zeit zu Zeit; for ~ für immer, auf ewig; Briefschluß: yours ~ stets Dein ...; **~glade** Am. Sumpfsteppe f; **~green 1.** immergrün; **2.** immergrüne Pflanze; **~lasting** □ [evə-'laːstiŋ] ewig; dauerhaft; **~more** ['evə'mɔː] immerfort.

every ['evri] jede(r, -s); alle(s); ~ now and then dann und wann; ~ one of them jeder von ihnen; ~ other day einen Tag um den anderen, jeden zweiten Tag; **~body** jeder (-mann); **~day** Alltags...; **~one** jeder(mann); **~thing** alles; **~where** überall.

evict [i(:)'vikt] exmittieren; ausweisen.

eviden|ce ['evidəns] **1.** Beweis(material n) m; ⅍ Zeugnis n; Zeuge m; in ~ als Beweis; deutlich sichtbar; **2.** beweisen; **~t** □ [ˌnt] augenscheinlich, offenbar, klar.

evil ['iːvl] **1.** □ übel, schlimm, böse; the ⚹ One der Böse (Teufel); **2.** Übel n, Böse(s) n; **~-minded** ['iːvl'maindid] übelgesinnt, boshaft.

evince [i'vins] zeigen, bekunden.

evoke [i'vouk] (herauf)beschwören.

evolution [iːvə'luːʃən] Entwicklung f; ⚔ Entfaltung f e-r Formation.

evolve [i'vɔlv] (sich) entwickeln.

ewe [juː] Mutterschaf n.

ex [eks] prp. ✝ ab Fabrik etc.; Börse: ohne; aus.

ex-... [ˌ] früher, früher.

exact [ig'zækt] **1.** □ genau; pünktlich; **2.** Zahlung eintreiben; fordern; **~ing** [ˌtiŋ] streng, genau; **~itude** [ˌitjuːd], **~ness** [ˌtnis] Genauigkeit f; Pünktlichkeit f.

exaggerate [ig'zædʒəreit] übertreiben.

exalt [ig'zɔːlt] erhöhen, erheben; verherrlichen; **~ation** [egzɔːl'teiʃən] Erhöhung f, Erhebung f; Höhe f; Verzückung f.

exam Schul-sl. [ig'zæm] Examen n.

examin|ation [igzæmi'neiʃən] Examen n, Prüfung f; Untersuchung f; Vernehmung f; **~e** [ig'zæmin] untersuchen; prüfen, verhören.

example [ig'zaːmpl] Beispiel n; Vorbild n, Muster n; for ~ zum Beispiel.

exasperate [ig'zaːspəreit] erbittern; ärgern; verschlimmern.

excavate ['ekskəveit] ausgraben, ausheben, ausschachten.

exceed [ik'siːd] überschreiten; übertreffen; zu weit gehen; **~ing** □ [ˌdiŋ] übermäßig, **~ingly** [ˌŋli] außerordentlich, überaus.

excel [ik'sel] *v/t.* übertreffen; *v/i.* sich auszeichnen; **~lence** ['eksə-ləns] Vortrefflichkeit *f*; hervorragende Leistung; Vorzug *m*; **~lency** [~si] Exzellenz *f*; **~lent** □ [~nt] vortrefflich.

except [ik'sept] **1.** ausnehmen; *et.* einwenden; **2.** *prp.* ausgenommen, außer; **~ for** abgesehen von; **~ing** *prp.* [~tiŋ] ausgenommen; **~ion** [~pʃən] Ausnahme *f*; Einwendung *f* (*to* gegen); *by way of* **~** ausnahmsweise; *take* **~** *to* Anstoß nehmen an (*dat.*); **~ional** [~nl] außergewöhnlich; **~ionally** [~ʃnəli] un-, außergewöhnlich.

excerpt ['eksə:pt] Auszug *m*.

excess [ik'ses] Übermaß *n*; Überschuß *m*; Ausschweifung *f*; *attr.* Mehr...; **~** *fare* Zuschlag *m*; **~** *luggage* Übergewicht *n* (*Gepäck*); **~** *postage* Nachgebühr *f*; **~ive** □ [~siv] übermäßig, übertrieben.

exchange [iks'tʃeindʒ] **1.** (aus-, einum)tauschen (*for* gegen); wechseln; **2.** (Aus-, Um)Tausch *m*; (*bsd.* Geld)Wechsel *m*; *a. bill of* **~** Wechsel *m*; *a.* ♀ Börse *f*; Fernsprechamt *n*; *foreign* **~**(*s pl.*) Devisen *f/pl.*; (*rate of*) **~** Wechselkurs *m*.

exchequer [iks'tʃekə] Schatzamt *n*; Staatskasse *f*; *Chancellor of the* ♀ (britischer) Schatzkanzler, Finanzminister *m*.

excise[1] [ek'saiz] indirekte Steuer; Verbrauchssteuer *f*.

excise[2] [~] (her)ausschneiden.

excit|able [ik'saitəbl] reizbar; **~e** [ik'sait] er-, anregen; reizen; **~ement** [~tmənt] Auf-, Erregung *f*; Reizung *f*; **~ing** [~tiŋ] erregend.

exclaim [iks'kleim] ausrufen; eifern.

exclamation [eksklə'meiʃən] Ausruf(ung *f*) *m*; **~s** *pl.* Geschrei *n*; *note of* **~**, *point of* **~**, **~** *mark* Ausrufezeichen *n*.

exclude [iks'klu:d] ausschließen.

exclusi|on [iks'klu:ʒən] Ausschließung *f*, Ausschluß *m*; **~ve** □ [~u:siv] ausschließlich; sich abschließend; **~** *of* abgesehen von, ohne.

excommunicat|e [ekskə'mju:nikeit] exkommunizieren; **~ion** ['eks-kəmju:ni'keiʃən] Kirchenbann *m*.

excrement ['ekskrimənt] Kot *m*.

excrete [eks'kri:t] ausscheiden.

excruciat|e [iks'kru:ʃieit] martern; **~ing** □ [~tiŋ] qualvoll.

exculpate ['ekskʌlpeit] entschuldigen; rechtfertigen; freisprechen (*from* von).

excursion [iks'kə:ʃən] Ausflug *m*; Abstecher *m*.

excursive □ [eks'kə:siv] abschweifend.

excus|able □ [iks'kju:zəbl] entschuldbar; **~e 1.** [iks'kju:z] ent-

schuldigen; **~** *s.o. s.th.* j-m et. erlassen; **2.** [~u:s] Entschuldigung *f*.

exeat ['eksiæt] *Schule etc.*: Urlaub *m*.

execra|ble □ ['eksikrəbl] abscheulich; **~te** ['eksikreit] verwünschen.

execut|e ['eksikju:t] ausführen; vollziehen; ♪ vortragen; hinrichten; *Testament* vollstrecken; **~ion** [eksi-'kju:ʃən] Ausführung *f*; Vollziehung *f*; (Zwangs)Vollstreckung *f*; Hinrichtung *f*; ♪ Vortrag *m*; *put od.* *carry a plan into* **~** e-n Plan ausführen *od.* verwirklichen; **~ioner** [~ʃnə] Scharfrichter *m*; **~ive** [ig-'zekjutiv] **1.** □ vollziehend; **~** *committee* Vorstand *m*; **2.** vollziehende Gewalt; *Am.* Staats-Präsident *m*; ♀ Geschäftsführer *m*; **~or** [~tə] (Testaments)Vollstrecker *m*.

exemplary [ig'zempləri] vorbildlich.

exemplify [ig'zemplifai] durch Beispiele belegen; veranschaulichen.

exempt [ig'zempt] **1.** befreit, frei; **2.** ausnehmen, befreien.

exercise ['eksəsaiz] **1.** Übung *f*; Ausübung *f*; *Schule:* Übungsarbeit *f*; Leibesübung *f*; *take* **~** sich Bewegung machen; *Am.* **~s** *pl.* Feierlichkeit(en *pl.*) *f*; ✗ Manöver *n*; **2.** üben; ausüben; (sich) Bewegung machen; exerzieren.

exert [ig'zə:t] *Einfluß etc.* ausüben; **~** *o.s.* sich anstrengen *od.* bemühen; **~ion** [~ə:ʃən] Ausübung *f etc.*

exhale [eks'heil] ausdünsten, ausatmen; aushauchen; *Gefühlen* Luft machen.

exhaust [ig'zɔ:st] **1.** erschöpfen; entleeren; auspumpen; **2.** ⊕ Abgas *n*, Abdampf *m*; **~** *box* Auspufftopf *m*; **~** *pipe* Auspuffrohr *n*; **~ed** erschöpft (*a. fig.*); vergriffen (*Auflage*); **~ion** [~tʃən] Erschöpfung *f*; **~ive** □ [~tiv] erschöpfend.

exhibit [ig'zibit] **1.** ausstellen; zeigen, darlegen; aufweisen; **2.** Ausstellungsstück *n*; Beweisstück *n*; **~ion** [eksi'biʃən] Ausstellung *f*; Darlegung *f*; Zurschaustellung *f*; Stipendium *n*.

exhilarate [ig'ziləreit] erheitern.

exhort [ig'zɔ:t] ermahnen.

exigen|ce, -cy ['eksidʒəns, ~si] dringende Not; Erfordernis *n*; **~t** [~nt] dringlich; anspruchsvoll.

exile ['eksail] **1.** Verbannung *f*, Exil *n*; Verbannte(r *m*) *f*; **2.** verbannen.

exist [ig'zist] existieren, vorhanden sein; leben; **~ence** [~təns] Existenz *f*, Dasein *n*, Vorhandensein *n*; Leben *n*; *in* **~** vorhanden; **~ent** [~nt] vorhanden.

exit ['eksit] **1.** Abgang *m*; Tod *m*; Ausgang *m*; **2.** *thea.* (geht) ab.

exodus ['eksədəs] Auszug *m*.

exonerate [ig'zɔnəreit] *fig.* entlasten, entbinden, befreien; rechtfertigen.

exorbitant □ [ig'zɔ:bitənt] maßlos, übermäßig.

exorci|se, ~**ze** ['eksɔ:saiz] *Geister* beschwören, austreiben (*from* aus); befreien (*of* von).

exotic [eg'zɔtik] ausländisch, exotisch; fremdländisch.

expan|d [iks'pænd] (sich) ausbreiten; (sich) ausdehnen; (sich) erweitern; *Abkürzungen* (voll) ausschreiben; freundlich *od.* heiter werden; ~**se** [~ns], ~**sion** [~nʃən] Ausdehnung *f;* Weite *f;* Breite *f;* ~**sive** □ [~nsiv] ausdehnungsfähig; ausgedehnt, weit; *fig.* mitteilsam.

expatiate [eks'peiʃieit] sich weitläufig auslassen (*on* über *acc.*).

expatriate [eks'pætrieit] ausbürgern.

expect [iks'pekt] erwarten; F annehmen; *be* ~**ing** ein Kind erwarten; ~**ant** [~tənt] **1.** erwartend (*of acc.*); ~ mother werdende Mutter; **2.** Anwärter *m;* ~**ation** [ekspek'teiʃən] Erwartung *f;* Aussicht *f.*

expectorate [eks'pektəreit] *Schleim etc.* aushusten, auswerfen.

expedi|ent [iks'pi:djənt] **1.** □ zweckmäßig; berechnend; **2.** Mittel *n;* (Not)Behelf *m;* ~**tion** [ekspi'diʃən] Eile *f;* ✕ Feldzug *m;* (Forschungs)Reise *f;* ~**tious** □ [~ʃəs] schnell, eilig, flink.

expel [iks'pel] (hin)ausstoßen; vertreiben, verjagen; ausschließen.

expen|d [iks'pend] *Geld* ausgeben; aufwenden; verbrauchen; ~**diture** [~ditʃə] Ausgabe *f;* Aufwand *m;* ~**se** [iks'pens] Ausgabe *f;* Kosten *pl.;* ~**s** *pl.* Unkosten *pl.;* Auslagen *f/pl.; at the* ~ *of* auf Kosten (*gen.*); *at any* ~ um jeden Preis; *go to the* ~ *of* Geld ausgeben für; ~**se account** Spesenrechnung *f;* ~**sive** □ [~siv] kostspielig, teuer.

experience [iks'piəriəns] **1.** Erfahrung *f;* Erlebnis *n;* **2.** erfahren, erleben; ~**d** erfahren.

experiment 1. [iks'perimənt] Versuch *m;* **2.** [~iment] experimentieren; ~**al** □ [eksperi'mentl] Versuchs...; erfahrungsmäßig.

expert [iks'pɔ:t] **1.** □ [*pred.* eks'pɔ:t] erfahren, geschickt; fachmännisch; **2.** Fachmann *m;* Sachverständige(r *m*) *f.*

expiate ['ekspieit] büßen, sühnen.

expir|ation [ekspai'reiʃən] Ausatmung *f;* Ablauf *m,* Ende *n;* ~**e** [iks'paiə] ausatmen; verscheiden; ablaufen; ✝ verfallen; erlöschen.

explain [iks'plein] erklären, erläutern; *Gründe* auseinandersetzen; ~ *away* wegdiskutieren.

explanat|ion [eksplə'neiʃən] Erklärung *f;* Erläuterung *f;* ~**ory** □ [iks'plænətəri] erklärend.

explicable ['eksplikəbl] erklärlich.

explicit □ [iks'plisit] deutlich.

explode [iks'ploud] explodieren (lassen); ausbrechen; platzen (*with* vor).

exploit 1. ['eksplɔit] Heldentat *f;* **2.** [iks'plɔit] ausbeuten; ~**ation** [eksplɔi'teiʃən] Ausbeutung *f.*

explor|ation [eksplɔ:'reiʃən] Erforschung *f;* ~**e** [iks'plɔ:] erforschen; ~**er** [~:rə] (Er)Forscher *m;* Forschungsreisende(r) *m.*

explosi|on [iks'plouʒən] Explosion *f;* Ausbruch *m;* ~**ve** [~ousiv] **1.** □ explosiv; **2.** Sprengstoff *m.*

exponent [eks'pounənt] Exponent *m;* Vertreter *m.*

export 1. [eks'pɔ:t] ausführen; **2.** ['ekspɔ:t] Ausfuhr(artikel *m*) *f;* ~**ation** [ekspɔ:'teiʃən] Ausfuhr *f.*

expos|e [iks'pouz] aussetzen; *phot.* belichten; ausstellen; entlarven; bloßstellen; ~**ition** [ekspə'ziʃən] Ausstellung *f;* Erklärung *f.*

expostulate [iks'pɔstjuleit] protestieren; ~ *with j-m* Vorhaltungen machen.

exposure [iks'pouʒə] Aussetzen *n;* Ausgesetztsein *n;* Aufdeckung *f;* Enthüllung *f,* Entlarvung *f; phot.* Belichtung *f;* Bild *n;* Lage *f e-s Hauses;* ~ *meter* Belichtungsmesser *m.* [legen.]

expound [iks'paund] erklären, aus-]

express [iks'pres] **1.** □ ausdrücklich, deutlich; Expreß..., Eil...; ~ *company Am.* Transportfirma *f;* ~ *highway* Schnellverkehrsstraße *f;* **2.** Eilbote *m; a.* ~ *train* Schnellzug *m; by* ~ = **3.** *adv.* durch Eilboten; als Eilgut; **4.** äußern, ausdrücken; auspressen; ~**ion** [~ʃən] Ausdruck *m;* ~**ive** □ [~esiv] ausdrückend (*of acc.*); ausdrucksvoll; ~**ly** [~sli] ausdrücklich, eigens; ~**way** *Am.* Autobahn *f.* [eignen.]

expropriate [eks'prouprieit] ent-]

expulsi|on [iks'pʌlʃən] Vertreibung *f;* ~**ve** [~lsiv] (aus)treibend.

expunge [eks'pʌndʒ] streichen.

expurgate ['ekspə:geit] säubern.

exquisite □ ['ekskwizit] auserlesen, vorzüglich; fein; heftig, scharf.

extant [eks'tænt] (noch) vorhanden.

extempor|aneous □ [ekstempə'reinjəs], ~**ary** [iks'tempərəri], ~**e** [eks'tempəri] aus dem Stegreif (vorgetragen).

extend [iks'tend] *v/t.* ausdehnen; ausstrecken; erweitern; verlängern; *Gunst etc.* erweisen; ✕ (aus)schwärmen lassen; *v/i.* sich erstrecken.

extensi|on [iks'tenʃən] Ausdehnung *f;* Erweiterung *f;* Verlängerung *f;* Aus-, Anbau *m; teleph.* Nebenanschluß *m;* ~ *cord* ≠ Verlängerungsschnur *f; University* ☿ Volkshochschule *f;* ~**ve** □ [~nsiv] ausgedehnt, umfassend.

extent [iks'tent] Ausdehnung *f*, Weite *f*, Größe *f*, Umfang *m*; Grad *m*; to the ~ of bis zum Betrage von; to some ~ einigermaßen.

extenuate [eks'tenjueit] abschwächen, mildern, beschönigen.

exterior [eks'tiəriə] 1. äußerlich; Außen...; außerhalb; 2. Äußere(s) *n*; *Film*: Außenaufnahme *f*.

exterminate [eks'tə:mineit] ausrotten, vertilgen.

external [eks'tə:nl] 1. □ äußere(r, -s), äußerlich; Außen...; 2. ~s *pl.* Äußere(s) *n*; *fig.* Äußerlichkeiten *f/pl.*

extinct [iks'tiŋkt] erloschen; ausgestorben.

extinguish [iks'tiŋgwiʃ] (aus)löschen; vernichten.

extirpate ['ekstə:peit] ausrotten; ♣ *Organ etc.* entfernen.

extol [iks'tɔl] erheben, preisen.

extort [iks'tɔ:t] erpressen; abnötigen (*from dat.*); ~ion [~ɔ:ʃən] Erpressung *f*.

extra ['ekstrə] 1. Extra...; außer...; Neben...; Sonder...; ~ *pay* Zulage *f*; 2. *adv.* besonders; außerdem; 3. *et.* Zusätzliches; Zuschlag *m*; Extrablatt *n*; *thea.*, *Film*: Statist(in).

extract 1. ['ekstrækt] Auszug *m*; 2. [iks'trækt] (heraus)ziehen; herauslocken; ab-, herleiten; ~ion [~kʃən] (Heraus)Ziehen *n*; Herkunft *f*.

extradit|e ['ekstrədait] *Verbrecher* ausliefern (lassen); ~ion [ekstrə-'diʃən] Auslieferung *f*.

extraordinary □ [iks'trɔ:dnri]

außerordentlich; Extra...; ungewöhnlich; *envoy* ~ außerordentlicher Gesandter.

extra student ['ekstrə'stju:dənt] Gasthörer(in).

extravagan|ce [iks'trævigəns] Übertriebenheit *f*; Überspanntheit *f*; Verschwendung *f*, Extravaganz *f*; ~t □ [~nt] übertrieben, überspannt; verschwenderisch; extravagant.

extrem|e [iks'tri:m] 1. □ äußerst, größt, höchst; sehr streng; außergewöhnlich; 2. Äußerste(s) *n*; Extrem *n*; höchster Grad; ~ity [~remiti] Äußerste(s) *n*; höchste Not; äußerste Maßnahme; extremities *pl.* Gliedmaßen *pl.*

extricate ['ekstrikeit] herauswinden, herausziehen; befreien; ♣ entwickeln.

extrude [eks'tru:d] ausstoßen.

exuberan|ce [ig'zju:bərəns] Überfluß *m*; Überschwenglichkeit *f*; ~t □ [~nt] reichlich; üppig; überschwenglich.

exult [ig'zʌlt] frohlocken.

eye [ai] 1. Auge *n*; Blick *m*; Öhr *n*; Öse *f*; up to the ~s in work bis über die Ohren in Arbeit; with an ~ to mit Rücksicht auf (*acc.*); mit der Absicht zu; 2. ansehen; mustern; ~ball ['aibɔ:l] Augapfel *m*; ~brow Augenbraue *f*; ~d ...äugig; ~glass Augenglas *n*; (a pair of) ~es *pl.* (ein) Kneifer; (e-e) Brille; ~lash Augenwimper *f*; ~lid Augenlid *n*; ~sight Augen(licht *n*) *pl.*; Sehkraft *f*; ~witness Augenzeug|e *m*, -in *f*.

F

fable ['feibl] Fabel *f*; Mythen *pl.*, Legenden *pl.*; fabulieren.

fabric ['fæbrik] Bau *m*, Gebäude *n*; Struktur *f*; Gewebe *n*, Stoff *m*; ~ate [~keit] fabrizieren (*mst fig.* = erdichten, fälschen).

fabulous □ ['fæbjuləs] legendär; sagen-, fabelhaft.

façade △ [fə'sa:d] Fassade *f*.

face [feis] 1. Gesicht *n*; Anblick *m*; *fig.* Stirn *f*, Unverschämtheit *f*; (Ober)Fläche *f*; Vorderseite *f*; Zifferblatt *n*; ~ to ~ with Auge in Auge mit; save one's ~ das Gesicht wahren; in the ~ of it auf den ersten Blick; set one's ~ against sich gegen *et.* stemmen; 2. *v/t.* ansehen; gegenüberstehen (*dat.*); (hinaus)gehen auf (*acc.*); die Stirn bieten (*dat.*); einfassen; △ bekleiden; *v/i.* ~ about sich umdrehen; ~cloth ['feisklɔθ] Waschlappen *m*.

facetious □ [fə'si:ʃəs] witzig.

facil|e ['fæsail] leicht; gewandt; ~itate [fə'siliteit] erleichtern; ~ity [~ti] Leichtigkeit *f*; Gewandtheit *f*; *mst facilities pl.* Erleichterung(en *pl.*) *f*, Möglichkeit(en *pl.*) *f*, Gelegenheit(en *pl.*) *f*.

facing ['feisiŋ] ⊕ Verkleidung *f*; ~s *pl. Schneiderei*: Besatz *m*.

fact [fækt] Tatsache *f*; Wirklichkeit *f*; Wahrheit *f*; Tat *f*; [keit *f*.]

faction ['fækʃən] Partei *f*; Uneinig-

factitious □ [fæk'tiʃəs] künstlich.

factor ['fæktə] *fig.* Umstand *m*, Moment *n*, Faktor *m*; Agent *m*; Verwalter *m*; ~y [~əri] Fabrik *f*.

faculty ['fækəlti] Fähigkeit *f*; Kraft *f*; *fig.* Gabe *f*; *univ.* Fakultät *f*.

fad F *fig.* Steckenpferd *n*.

fade [feid] (ver)welken (lassen), verblassen; schwinden; *Radio*: ~ in einblenden.

fag F [fæg] v/i. sich placken; v/t. erschöpfen, mürbe machen.

fail [feil] 1. v/i. versagen, mißlingen, fehlschlagen; versäumen; versiegen; nachlassen; Bankrott machen; durchfallen (*Kandidat*); he ~ed to do es mißlang ihm zu tun; he cannot ~ to er muß (einfach); v/t. im Stich lassen, verlassen; versäumen; 2. without ~ unfehlbar; ~ing ['feiliŋ] Fehler m, Schwäche f; ~ure [~ljə] Fehlen n; Ausbleiben n; Fehlschlag m; Mißerfolg m; Verfall m; Versäumnis n; Bankrott m; Versager m (P.).

faint [feint] 1. □ schwach, matt; 2. schwach werden; in Ohnmacht fallen (with vor); 3. Ohnmacht f; ~-hearted □ ['feint'ha:tid] verzagt.

fair[1] [fɛə] 1. adj. gerecht, ehrlich, anständig, fair; ordentlich; schön (*Wetter*), günstig (*Wind*); reichlich; blond; hellhäutig; freundlich; sauber, in Reinschrift; schön (*Frau*); 2. adv. gerecht, ehrlich, anständig, fair; in Reinschrift; direkt.

fair[2] [~] (Jahr)Markt m, Messe f.

fair|ly ['fɛəli] ziemlich; völlig; ~ness ['fɛənis] Schönheit f; Blondheit f; Gerechtigkeit f; Redlichkeit f; Billigkeit f; ~way ✠ Fahrwasser n.

fairy ['fɛəri] Fee f; Zauberin f; Elf(e) f) m; ♀land Feen-, Märchenland n; ~tale Märchen n.

faith [feiθ] Glaube m; Vertrauen n; Treue f; ~ful □ ['feiθful] treu; ehrlich; yours ~ly Ihr ergebener; ~less □ ['feiθlis] treulos; ungläubig.

fake sl. [feik] 1. Schwindel m; Fälschung f; Schwindler m; 2. a. ~ up fälschen.

falcon ['fɔ:lkən] Falke m.

fall [fɔ:l] 1. Fall(en n) m; Sturz m; Verfall m; Einsturz m; Am. Herbst m; Sinken n der Preise etc.; Fällen n; Wasserfall m (mst pl.); Senkung f, Abhang m; 2. [irr.] fallen; ab-, einfallen; sinken; sich legen (*Wind*); in e-n Zustand verfallen; ~ back zurückweichen; ~ back (up)on zurückkommen auf; ~ ill od. sick krank werden; ~ in love with sich verlieben in (acc.); ~ out sich entzweien; sich zutragen; ~ short knapp werden (of an dat.); ~ short of zurückbleiben hinter (dat.); ~ to sich machen an (acc.).

fallacious □ [fə'leiʃəs] trügerisch.

fallacy ['fæləsi] Täuschung f.

fallen □ ['fɔ:lən] p.p. von fall 2.

fall guy Am. sl. ['fɔ:l'gai] der Lackierte, der Dumme.

fallible □ ['fæləbl] fehlbar.

falling ['fɔ:liŋ] Fallen n; ~ sickness

Fallsucht f; ~ star Sternschnuppe f.

fallow ['fælou] zo. falb; ⚹ brach (-liegend).

false □ [fɔ:ls] falsch; ~hood ['fɔ:lshud], ~ness [~snis] Falschheit f.

falsi|fication ['fɔ:lsifi'keiʃən] (Ver-) Fälschung f; ~fy ['fɔ:lsifai] (ver-) fälschen; ~ty [~iti] Falschheit f.

falter ['fɔ:ltə] schwanken; stocken (*Stimme*); stammeln; fig. zaudern.

fame [feim] Ruf m, Ruhm m; ~d [~md] berühmt (for wegen).

familiar [fə'miljə] 1. □ vertraut; gewohnt; familiär; 2. Vertraute(r m) f; ~ity [fəmili'æriti] Vertrautheit f; (plumpe) Vertraulichkeit; ~ize [fə'miljəraiz] vertraut machen.

family ['fæmili] 1. Familie f; 2. Familien..., Haus...; in the ~ way in anderen Umständen; ~ allowance Kinderzulage f; ~ tree Stammbaum m.

fami|ne ['fæmin] Hungersnot f; Mangel m (of an dat.); ~sh [~iʃ] (aus-, ver)hungern.

famous □ ['feiməs] berühmt.

fan[1] [fæn] 1. Fächer m; Ventilator m; 2. (an)fächeln; an-, fig. entfachen.

fan[2] F [~] Sport- etc. Fanatiker m; Liebhaber m; Radio: Bastler m; ...narr m, ...fex m.

fanatic [fə'nætik] 1. a. ~al □ [~kəl] fanatisch; 2. Fanatiker(in).

fanciful □ ['fænsiful] phantastisch.

fancy ['fænsi] 1. Phantasie f; Einbildung(skraft) f; Schrulle f; Vorliebe f; Liebhaberei f; 2. Phantasie...; Liebhaber...; Luxus...; Mode...; ~ ball Maskenball m; ~ goods pl. Modewaren f/pl.; 3. sich einbilden; Gefallen finden an (dat.); just ~! denken Sie nur!; ~work feine Handarbeit, Stickerei f.

fang [fæŋ] Fangzahn m; Giftzahn m.

fantas|tic [fæn'tæstik] (~ally) phantastisch; ~y ['fæntəsi] Phantasie f.

far [fɑ:] 1. adj. fern, entfernt; weit; 2. adv. fern; weit; (sehr) viel; as ~ as bis; in so ~ as insofern als; ~-away ['fɑ:rəwei] weit entfernt.

fare [fɛə] 1. Fahrgeld n; Fahrgast m; Verpflegung f, Kost f; 2. gut leben; he ~d well es (er)ging ihm gut; ~well ['fɛə'wel] 1. lebe(n Sie) wohl!; 2. Abschied m, Lebewohl n.

far|-fetched fig. ['fɑ:'fetʃt] weit hergeholt, gesucht; ~ gone F fertig (todkrank, betrunken etc.).

farm [fɑ:m] 1. Bauernhof m, -gut m; Gehöft n, Farm f; Züchterei f; chicken ~ Hühnerfarm f; 2. (ver-) pachten; Land bewirtschaften; ~er ['fɑ:mə] Landwirt m; Pächter m; ~hand Landarbeiter(in); ~house Bauern-, Gutshaus n; ~ing ['fɑ:mi-

1. Acker...; landwirtschaftlich;
2. Landwirtschaft f; ~stead Gehöft n; ~yard Wirtschaftshof m e-s
Bauernguts.

far-off ['fɑːɔːf] entfernt, fern; ~-
sighted fig. weitblickend.

farthe|r ['fɑːðə] comp. von far; ~st
['fɑːðist] sup. von far.

fascinat|e ['fæsineit] bezaubern;
~ion [fæsi'neiʃən] Zauber m, Reiz
m.

fashion ['fæʃən] Mode f; Art f;
feine Lebensart; Form f; Schnitt
m; in (out of) ~ (un)modern; 2. gestalten; Kleid machen; ~able □
['fæʃnəbl] modern, elegant.

fast¹ [fɑːst] schnell; fest; treu; waschecht; flott; be ~ vorgehen (Uhr).

fast² [~] 1. Fasten n; 2. fasten.

fasten ['fɑːsn] v/t. befestigen; anheften; fest (zu)machen; zubinden;
Augen etc. heften (on, upon auf
acc.); v/i. schließen (Tür); ~ upon
fig. sich klammern an (acc.); ~er
[~nə] Verschluß m; Klammer f.

fastidious □ ['fæs'tidiəs] anspruchs-
voll, heikel, wählerisch, verwöhnt.

fat [fæt] 1. □ fett; dick; fettig;
2. Fett n; 3. fett machen od. werden; mästen.

fatal □ ['feitl] verhängnisvoll (to
für); Schicksals...; tödlich; ~ity
[fə'tæliti] Verhängnis n; Unglücks-,
Todesfall m; Todesopfer n.

fate [feit] Schicksal n; Verhängnis n.

father ['fɑːðə] 1. Vater m; 2. der
Urheber sein von; ~hood [~hud]
Vaterschaft f; ~-in-law [~ərinlɔː]
Schwiegervater m; ~less [~əlis]
vaterlos; ~ly [~li] väterlich.

fathom ['fæðəm] 1. Klafter f (Maß);
⏚ Faden m; 2. ⏚ loten; fig. ergründen; ~less [~mlis] unergründlich.

fatigue [fə'tiːg] 1. Ermüdung f;
Strapaze f; 2. ermüden; strapa-
zieren.

fat|ness ['fætnis] Fettigkeit f; Fett-
heit f; ~ten ['fætn] fett machen
od. werden; mästen; Boden düngen.

fatuous □ ['fætjuəs] albern.

faucet Am. ['fɔːsit] (Zapf)Hahn m.

fault [fɔːlt] Fehler m; Defekt m;
Schuld f; find ~ with et. aus-
zusetzen haben an (dat.); be at ~ auf falscher
Fährte sein; ~-finder ['fɔːltfaində]
Nörgler m; ~less [~lis] fehler-
frei, tadellos; ~y □ [~ti] mangelhaft.

favo(u)r ['feivə] 1. Gunst(bezei-
gung) f; Gefallen m; Begünstigung
f; in ~ of zugunsten von od. gen.;
do s.o. a ~ j-m e-n Gefallen tun;
2. begünstigen; beehren; ~able □
[~ərəbl] günstig; ~ite [~rit] Günstling m; Liebling m; Sport: Favorit
m; attr. Lieblings...

fawn¹ [fɔːn] 1. zo. (Dam)Kitz n;
Rehbraun n; 2. (Kitze) setzen.

fawn² [~] schwänzeln (Hund);
kriechen (upon vor).

faze bsd. Am. F [feiz] durcheinanderbringen.

fear [fiə] 1. Furcht f (of vor dat.);
Befürchtung f; Angst f; 2. (befürchten; sich fürchten vor (dat.);
~ful □ ['fiəful] furchtsam; furchtbar; ~less □ ['fiəlis] furchtlos.

feasible □ ['fiːzəbl] ausführbar.

feast [fiːst] 1. Fest n; Feiertag m;
Festmahl n, Schmaus m; 2. v/t.
festlich bewirten; v/i. sich ergöt-
zen; schmausen.   [stück n.]

feat [fiːt] (Helden)Tat f; Kunst-

feather ['feðə] 1. Feder f; a. ~s
Gefieder n; show the white ~ F
sich feige zeigen; in high ~ in gehobener Stimmung; 2. mit Federn
schmücken; ~-bed n; 1. Feder-Un-
terbett n; 2. verwöhnen; ~brained,
~-headed unbesonnen; albern;
~ed be-, gefiedert; ~y [~əri] feder-
(art)ig.

feature ['fiːtʃə] 1. (Gesichts-,
Grund-, Haupt-, Charakter)Zug
m; (charakteristisches) Merkmal;
Radio: Feature n; Am. Bericht m,
Artikel m; ~s pl. Gesicht n; Charakter m; 2. kennzeichnen; sich auszeichnen durch; groß aufziehen;
Film: in der Hauptrolle zeigen;
~ film Haupt-, Spielfilm m.

February ['februəri] Februar m.

fecund ['fiːkənd] fruchtbar.

fed [fed] pret. u. p.p. von feed 2.

federa|l □ ['fedərəl] Bundes...;
~lize [~laiz] (sich) verbünden; ~tion
[fedə'reiʃən] Staatenbund m; Vereinigung f; Verband m.

fee [fiː] 1. Gebühr f; Honorar n;
Trinkgeld n; 2. bezahlen.

feeble □ ['fiːbl] schwach.

feed [fiːd] 1. Futter n; Nahrung f;
Fütterung f; ⊕ Zuführung f, Spei-
sung f; 2. [irr.] v/t. füttern; speisen
(a. ⊕), nähren; weiden; Material
etc. zuführen; be fed up with et. od.
j-n satt haben; well fed wohlgenährt;
v/i. (fr)essen; sich nähren; ~er
['fiːdə] Fütterer m; Am. Viehmä-
ster m; Esser(in); ~er road Zu-
bringer(straße f) m; ~ing-bottle
['fiːdiŋbɔtl] Saugflasche f.

feel [fiːl] 1. [irr.] (sich) fühlen; be-
fühlen; empfinden; sich anfühlen;
I ~ like doing ich möchte am liebsten
tun; 2. Gefühl n; Empfindung f;
~er ['fiːlə] Fühler m; ~ing ['fiːliŋ]
1. □ (mit)fühlend; gefühlvoll;
2. Gefühl n; Meinung f.

feet [fiːt] pl. von foot 1.

feign [fein] heucheln; vorgeben.

feint [feint] Verstellung f; Finte f.

felicit|ate [fi'lisiteit] beglückwün-
schen; ~ous □ [~təs] glücklich; ~y
[~ti] Glück(seligkeit f) n.

fell [fel] 1. pret. von fall 2; 2. niederschlagen; fällen.

felloe ['felou] (Rad)Felge f.

fellow ['felou] Gefährt|e m, -in f, Kamerad(in); Gleiche(r, -s); Gegenstück n; univ. Fellow m, Mitglied n e-s College; Bursche m, Mensch m; attr. Mit...; old ~ F alter Junge; the ~ of a glove der andere Handschuh; **~countryman** Landsmann m; **~ship** [~ouʃip] Gemeinschaft f; Kameradschaft f; Mitgliedschaft f.

felly ['feli] (Rad)Felge f.

felon ['felən] Verbrecher m; **~y** [~ni] Kapitalverbrechen n.

felt¹ [felt] pret. u. p.p. von feel 1.

felt² [~] 1. Filz m; 2. (be)filzen.

female ['fi:meil] 1. weiblich; 2. Weib n; zo. Weibchen n.

feminine ☐ ['feminin] weiblich; weibisch.

fen [fen] Fenn n, Moor n; Marsch f.

fence [fens] 1. Zaun m; Fechtkunst f; sl. Hehler(nest n) m; sit on the ~ abwarten; 2. v/t. a. ~ in ein-, umzäunen; schützen; v/i. fechten; sl. hehlen.

fencing ['fensiŋ] Einfriedung f; Fechten n; attr. Fecht...

fend [fend]: ~ off abwehren; **~er** ['fendə] Schutzvorrichtung f; Schutzblech n; Kamingitter n, -vorsetzer m; Stoßfänger m.

fennel ♣ ['fenl] Fenchel m.

ferment 1. ['fə:ment] Ferment n; Gärung f; 2. [fə(:)'ment] gären (lassen); **~ation** [fə:men'teiʃən] Gärung f.

fern ♣ [fə:n] Farn(kraut n) m.

feroci|ous ☐ [fə'rouʃəs] wild; grausam; **~ty** [fə'rɔsiti] Wildheit f.

ferret ['ferit] 1. zo. Frettchen n; fig. Spürhund m; 2. (umher)stöbern; ~ out aufstöbern.

ferry ['feri] 1. Fähre f; 2. übersetzen; **~boat** Fährboot n, Fähre f; **~man** Fährmann m.

fertil|e ☐ ['fə:tail] fruchtbar; reich (of, in an dat.); **~ity** [fə:'tiliti] Fruchtbarkeit f (a. fig.); **~ize** ['fə:tilaiz] fruchtbar machen; befruchten; düngen; **~izer** [~zə] Düngemittel n.

ferven|cy ['fə:vənsi] Glut f; Inbrunst f; **~t** ☐ [~nt] heiß; inbrünstig, glühend; leidenschaftlich.

fervo(u)r ['fə:və] Glut f; Inbrunst f.

festal ☐ ['festl] festlich.

fester ['festə] eitern; verfaulen.

festiv|al ['festəvəl] Fest n; Feier f; Festspiele n/pl.; **~e** ☐ [~tiv] festlich; **~ity** [fes'tiviti] Festlichkeit f.

festoon [fes'tu:n] Girlande f.

fetch [fetʃ] holen; Preis erzielen; Seufzer ausstoßen; **~ing** ☐ F ['fetʃiŋ] reizend.

fetid ☐ ['fetid] stinkend.

fetter ['fetə] 1. Fessel f; 2. fesseln.

feud [fju:d] Fehde f; Leh(e)n n;

~al ☐ ['fju:dl] lehnbar; Lehns...; **~alism** [~dəlizm] Lehnswesen n.

fever ['fi:və] Fieber n; **~ish** ☐ [~əriʃ] fieb(e)rig; fig. fieberhaft.

few [fju:] wenige; a ~ ein paar; quite a ~, a good ~ eine ganze Menge.

fiancé [fi'ã:nsei] Verlobte(r) m; **~e** [~] Verlobte f.

fiat ['faiæt] Befehl m; ~ money Am. Papiergeld n (ohne Deckung).

fib F [fib] 1. Flunkerei f, Schwindelei f; 2. schwindeln, flunkern.

fib|re, Am. **~er** ☐ [faibə] Faser f; Charakter m; **~rous** ☐ ['faibrəs] faserig.

fickle ['fikl] wankelmütig; unbeständig; **~ness** [~lnis] Wankelmut m.

fiction ['fikʃən] Erfindung f; Roman-, Unterhaltungsliteratur f; **~al** ☐ [~nl] erdichtet; Roman...

fictitious ☐ [fik'tiʃəs] erfunden.

fiddle F ['fidl] 1. Geige f, Fiedel f; 2. fiedeln; tändeln; **~r** [~lə] Geiger (-in); **~stick** Fiedelbogen m; **~s!** fig. dummes Zeug!

fidelity [fi'deliti] Treue f; Genauigkeit f.

fidget F ['fidʒit] 1. nervöse Unruhe f; 2. nervös machen od. sein; **~y** [~ti] nervös.

fie [fai] pfui! [kribbelig.]

field [fi:ld] Feld n; (Spiel)Platz m; Arbeitsfeld n; Gebiet n; Bereich m; hold the ~ das Feld behaupten; **~day** ['fi:lddei] ✕ Felddienstübung f; Parade f; fig. großer Tag; Am. (Schul)Sportfest n; Am. Exkursionstag m; **~events** pl. Sport: Sprung- u. Wurfwettkämpfe m/pl.; **~glass(es)** Feldstecher m; **~officer** Stabsoffizier m; **~sports** pl. Jagen n u. Fischen n.

fiend [fi:nd] böser Feind, Teufel m; **~ish** ☐ ['fi:ndiʃ] teuflisch, boshaft.

fierce ☐ [fiəs] wild; grimmig; **~ness** [~fiəsnis] Wildheit f; Grimm m.

fiery ☐ ['faiəri] feurig; hitzig.

fif|teen ['fif'ti:n] fünfzehn; **~teenth** [~nθ] fünfzehnte(r, -s); **~th** [fifθ] 1. fünfte(r, -s). 2. Fünftel n; **~thly** ['fifθli] fünftens; **~tieth** ['fiftiiθ] fünfzigste(r, -s); **~ty** [~ti] fünfzig; **~ty-fifty** F halb und halb.

fig [fig] Feige f; F Zustand m.

fight [fait] 1. Kampf m; Kampflust f; show ~ sich zur Wehr setzen; 2. [irr.] v/t. bekämpfen; erkämpfen; v/i. kämpfen, sich schlagen; **~er** ['faitə] Kämpfer m, Streiter m; ✕ Jagdflugzeug n; **~ing** ['faitiŋ] Kampf m.

figurative ☐ ['figjurətiv] bildlich.

figure ['figə] 1. Figur f; Gestalt f; Ziffer f; Preis m; be good at ~s gut im Rechnen sein; 2. v/t. abbilden; darstellen; sich vorstellen; beziffern; ~ up od. out berechnen; v/i. erscheinen; e-e Rolle spielen as) als); ~ on *Am. et.* überdenken; ~-skating [~əskeitiŋ] Eiskunstlauf *m.*

filament ['filəmənt] Faden *m*, Faser *f*; ⚓ Staubfaden *m*; ⚡ Glüh-, Heizfaden *m.*

filbert ⚓ ['filbə(:)t] Haselnuß *f.*

filch [filtʃ] stibitzen (*from dat.*).

file[1] [fail] 1. Akte *f*, Ordner *m*; Ablage *f*; Reihe *f*; ✕ Rotte *f*; on ~ bei den Akten; 2. *v/t.* aufreihen; *Briefe etc.* einordnen; ablegen; einreichen; *v/i.* hinter-ea. marschieren.

file[2] [~] 1. Feile *f*; 2. feilen.

filial □ ['filjəl] kindlich, Kindes...

filibuster ['filibəstə] 1. *Am.* Obstruktion(spolitiker *m*) *f*; 2. *Am.* Obstruktion treiben.

fill [fil] 1. (sich) füllen; an-, aus-, erfüllen; *Am. Auftrag* ausführen; ~ *in Formular* ausfüllen; 2. Fülle *f*, Genüge *f*; Füllung *f.*

fillet ['filit] Haarband *n*; Lendenbraten *m*; Roulade *f*; *bsd.* ⚓ Band *n.*

filling ['filiŋ] Füllung *f*; ~ station *Am.* Tankstelle *f.*

fillip ['filip] Nasenstüber *m.*

filly ['fili] (Stuten)Füllen *n*; *fig.* wilde Hummel.

film [film] 1. Häutchen *n*; Membran(e) *f*; Film *m*; Trübung *f des Auges*; Nebelschleier *m*; *take od.* shoot a ~ e-n Film drehen; 2. (sich) verschleiern; (ver)filmen.

filter ['filtə] 1. Filter *m*; 2. filtern.

filth [filθ] Schmutz *m*; ~y □ ['filθi] schmutzig; *fig.* unflätig.

filtrate ['filtreit] filtrieren.

fin [fin] Flosse *f* (*a. sl.* = Hand).

final ['fainl] 1. □ letzte(r, -s); endlich; schließlich; End...; endgültig; 2. Schlußprüfung *f*; *Sport:* Schlußrunde *f*, Endspiel *n.*

financ|e [fai'næns] 1. Finanzwesen *n*; ~s *pl.* Finanzen *pl.*; 2. *v/t.* finanzieren; *v/i.* Geldgeschäfte machen; ~ial □ [~nʃəl] finanziell; ~ier [~nsiə] Finanzmann *m*; Geldgeber *m.*

finch *orn.* [fintʃ] Fink *m.*

find [faind] 1. [*irr.*] finden; (an-)treffen; auf-, herausfinden; *schuldig etc.* befinden; beschaffen; versorgen; *all found* freie Station; 2. Fund *m*; ~ings ['faindiŋz] *pl.* Befund *m*; Urteil *n.*

fine[1] □ [fain] 1. schön; fein; verfeinert; rein; spitz, dünn, scharf; geziert; vornehm; 2. *adv.* gut, bestens.

fine[2] [~] 1. Geldstrafe *f*; 2. zu e-r Geldstrafe verurteilen.

fineness ['fainnis] Fein-, Zartheit, Schönheit *f*, Eleganz *f*; Genauigkeit *f.*

finery ['fainəri] Glanz *m*; Putz *m*; Staat *m.*

finger ['fiŋgə] 1. Finger *m*; 2. betasten, (herum)fingern an (*dat.*);

~-language Zeichensprache *f*; ~-nail Fingernagel *m*; ~-print Fingerabdruck *m.*

fini|cal □ ['finikəl], ~cking [~kiŋ], ~kin [~in] geziert; wählerisch.

finish ['finiʃ] 1. *v/t.* beenden, vollenden; fertigstellen; abschließen; vervollkommnen; erledigen; *v/i.* enden; 2. Vollendung *f*, letzter Schliff (*a. fig.*); Schluß *m.*

finite □ ['fainait] endlich, begrenzt.

fink *Am. sl.* [fiŋk] Streikbrecher *m.*

Finn [fin] Finn|e *m*, -in *f*; ~ish ['finiʃ] finnisch.

fir [fə:] (Weiß)Tanne *f*; Fichte *f*; ~-cone ['fə:koun] Tannenzapfen *m.*

fire ['faiə] 1. Feuer *n*; on ~ in Brand, in Flammen; 2. *v/t.* an-, entzünden; *fig.* anfeuern; abfeuern; *Ziegel etc.* brennen; F 'rausschmeißen (*entlassen*); heizen; *v/i.* Feuer fangen (*a. fig.*); feuern; ~-alarm ['faiərəla:m] Feuermelder *m*; ~-brigade Feuerwehr *f*; ~-bug *Am.* F Brandstifter *m*; ~-cracker Frosch *m* (*Feuerwerkskörper*); ~ department *Am.* Feuerwehr *f*; ~-engine ['faiərendʒin] (Feuer)Spritze *f*; ~-escape [~riskeip] Rettungsgerät *n*; Nottreppe *f*; ~-extinguisher [~rikstiŋwiʃə] Feuerlöscher *m*; ~man Feuerwehrmann *m*; Heizer *m*; ~-place Herd *m*; Kamin *m*; ~-plug Hydrant *m*; ~-proof feuerfest; ~-screen Ofenschirm *m*; ~-side Herd *m*; Kamin *m*; ~-station Feuerwache *f*; ~-wood Brennholz *n*; ~-works *pl.* Feuerwerk *n.*

firing ['faiəriŋ] Heizung *f*; Feuerung *f.*

firm [fə:m] 1. □ fest; derb; standhaft; 2. Firma *f*; ~ness ['fə:mnis] Festigkeit *f.*

first [fə:st] 1. *adj.* erste(r, -s); beste(r, -s); 2. *adv.* erstens; zuerst; ~ of all an erster Stelle; zu allererst; 3. Erste(r, -s); ~ of exchange † Primawechsel *m*; at ~ zuerst, anfangs; *from the* ~ von Anfang an; ~-born ['fə:stbɔ:n] erstgeboren; ~ class 1. Klasse (*e-s Verkehrsmittels*); ~-class erstklassig; ~ly [~tli] erstlich; erstens; ~ name Vorname *m*; Beiname *f*; ~ papers *Am.* vorläufige Einbürgerungspapiere; ~-rate ersten Ranges; erstklassig.

firth [fə:θ] Förde *f*; (Flut)Mündung *f.*

fish [fiʃ] 1. Fisch(e *pl.*) *m*; F Kerl *m*; 2. fischen, angeln; haschen; ~-bone ['fiʃboun] Gräte *f.*

fisher ['fiʃə], ~man Fischer *m*; ~y [~əri] Fischerei *f.*

fishing ['fiʃiŋ] Fischen *n*; ~-line Angelschnur *f*; ~-tackle Angelgerät *n*.   [händler *m.*]

fishmonger ['fiʃmʌŋgə] Fisch-[

fiss|ion ⚛ ['fiʃən] Spaltung *f*; ~ure ['fiʃə] Spalt *m*; Riß *m.*

fist [fist] Faust *f*; F Klaue *f*; **~cuffs** ['fistikʌfs] *pl.* Faustschläge *m/pl.*

fit¹ [fit] 1. □ geeignet, passend; tauglich; *Sport:* in (guter) Form; bereit; 2. *v/t.* passen für *od. dat.*; anpassen, passend machen; befähigen; geeignet machen (*for, to* für, zu); *a.* ~ *on* anprobieren; ausstatten; ~ *out* ausrüsten; ~ *up* einrichten; montieren; *v/i.* passen; sich schikken; sitzen (*Kleid*); 3. Sitz *m* (*Kleid*).

fit² [~] Anfall *m*; ⚕ Ausbruch *m*; Anwandlung *f*; *by* ~*s and starts* ruckweise; *give s.o. a* ~ j-n hochbringen; j-m e-n Schock versetzen.

fit|ful □ ['fitful] ruckartig; *fig.* unstet; **~ness** ['fitnis] Schicklichkeit *f*; Tauglichkeit *f*; **~ter** ['fitə] Monteur *m*; Installateur *m*; **~ting** ['fitiŋ] 1. passend; 2. Montage *f*; Anprobe *f*; ~*s pl.* Einrichtung *f*; Armaturen *f/pl.*

five [faiv] 1. fünf; 2. Fünf *f*.

fix [fiks] 1. *v/t.* befestigen, anheften; fixieren; *Augen etc.* heften, richten; fesseln; aufstellen; bestimmen, festsetzen; *bsd. Am.* machen, *Bett etc.* machen; ~ *o.s.* sich niederlassen; ~ *up* in Ordnung bringen, arrangieren; *v/i.* fest werden; ~ *on* sich entschließen für; 2. F Klemme *f*; *Am.* Zustand *m*; **~ed** fest; bestimmt; starr; **~ing** ['fiksiŋ] Befestigen *n*; Instandsetzen *n*; Fixieren *n*; Aufstellen *n*, Montieren *n*; Besatz *m*, Versteifung *f*; *Am.* ~*s pl.* Zubehör *n*, Extraausrüstung *f*; **~ture** [~stʃə] fest angebrachtes Zubehörteil, feste Anlage; Inventarstück *n*; *lighting* ~ Beleuchtungskörper *m*.

fizz [fiz] 1. zischen, sprudeln; 2. Zischen *n*; F Schampus *m* (*Sekt*).

flabbergast F ['flæbəgɑːst] verblüffen; *be* ~*ed* baff *od.* platt sein.

flabby □ ['flæbi] schlaff, schlapp.

flag [flæg] 1. Flagge *f*; Fahne *f*; Fliese *f*; Schwertlilie *f*; 2. beflaggen; durch Flaggen signalisieren; mit Fliesen belegen; ermatten; mutlos werden; **~-day** ['flægdei] Opfertag *m*; *Flag Day Am.* Tag *m* des Sternenbanners (*14. Juni*).

flagitious □ [fla'dʒiʃəs] schändlich.

flagrant □ ['fleigrənt] abscheulich; berüchtigt; offenkundig.

flag|staff ['flægstɑːf] Fahnenstange *f*; **~stone** Fliese *f*.

flair [flɛə] Spürsinn *m*, feine Nase.

flake [fleik] 1. Flocke *f*; Schicht *f*; 2. (sich) flocken; abblättern.

flame [fleim] 1. Flamme *f*, Feuer *n*; *fig.* Hitze *f*; 2. flammen, lodern.

flank [flæŋk] 1. Flanke *f*; Weiche *f* der *Tiere*; 2. flankieren.

flannel ['flænl] Flanell *m*; Waschlappen *m*; ~*s pl.* Flanellhose *f*.

flap [flæp] 1. (Ohr)Läppchen *n*;

Rockschoß *m*; *Hut*-Krempe *f*; Klappe *f*; Klaps *m*; (Flügel)Schlag *m*; 2. *v/t.* klatschen(d schlagen); *v/i.* lose herabhängen; flattern.

flare [flɛə] 1. flackern; sich nach außen erweitern, sich bauschen; ~ *up* aufflammen; *fig.* aufbrausen; 2. flackerndes Licht; Lichtsignal *n*.

flash [flæʃ] 1. aufgedonnert; unecht; Gauner...; 2. Blitz *m*; *fig.* Aufblitzen *n*; *bsd. Am. Zeitung:* kurze Meldung; *in a* ~ im Nu; ~ *of wit* Geistesblitz *m*; 3. (auf)blitzen; auflodern (lassen); *Blick etc.* werfen; flitzen; funken, telegraphieren; *it* ~*ed on me* mir kam plötzlich der Gedanke; **~back** ['flæʃbæk] *Film:* Rückblende *f*; **~-light** *phot.* Blitzlicht *n*; Blinklicht *n*; Taschenlampe *f*; **~y** □ [~ʃi] auffallend.

flask [flɑːsk] Taschen-, Reiseflasche *f*.

flat [flæt] 1. □ flach, platt; schal; ♩ flau; klar; glatt; ♪ um e-n halben Ton erniedrigt; ~ *price* Einheitspreis *m*; 2. *adv.* glatt; völlig; *fall* ~ danebenneben; *sing* ~ zu tief singen; 3. Fläche *f*, Ebene *f*; Flachland *n*; Untiefe *f*; (Miet)Wohnung *f*; ♪ B *n*; F Simpel *m*; *mot. sl.* Plattfuß *m*; **~-foot** ['flætfut] Plattfuß *m*; *Am. sl.* Polyp *m* (*Polizist*); **~-footed** plattfüßig; *Am.* F *fig.* stur, eisern; **~-iron** Plätteisen *n*; **~ness** [~tnis] Flachheit *f*; Plattheit *f*; ♩ Flauheit *f*; **~ten** [~tn] (sich) ab-, verflachen.

flatter ['flætə] schmeicheln (*dat.*); **~er** [~ərə] Schmeichler(in); **~y** [~ri] Schmeichelei *f*.

flavo(u)r ['fleivə] 1. Geschmack *m*; Aroma *n*; Blume *f* (*Wein*); *fig.* Beigeschmack *m*; Würze *f*; 2. würzen; **~less** [~əlis] geschmacklos, fad.

flaw [flɔː] 1. Sprung *m*, Riß *m*; Fehler *m*; ♧ Bö *f*; 2. zerbrechen; beschädigen; **~less** □ ['flɔːlis] fehlerlos.

flax ♣ [flæks] Flachs *m*, Lein *m*.

flay [flei] die Haut abziehen (*dat.*).

flea [fliː] Floh *m*.

fled [fled] *pret. u. p.p. von* flee.

fledg|e [fledʒ] *v/i.* flügge werden; *v/t.* befiedern; **~(e)ling** ['fledʒliŋ] Küken *n* (*a. fig.*); Grünschnabel *m*.

flee [fliː] [*irr.*] fliehen; meiden.

fleec|e [fliːs] 1. Vlies *n*; 2. scheren; prellen; **~y** ['fliːsi] wollig.

fleer [fliə] höhnen (*at* über *acc.*).

fleet [fliːt] 1. □ schnell; 2. Flotte *f*; ♀ *Street* die (Londoner) Presse.

flesh [fleʃ] 1. *lebendiges* Fleisch; *fig.* Fleisch(eslust *f*) *n*; 2. *hunt.* Blut kosten lassen; **~ly** ['fleʃli] fleischlich; irdisch; **~y** [~ʃi] fleischig; fett.

flew [fluː] *pret. von* fly 2.

flexib|ility [fleksə'biliti] Biegsamkeit *f*; **~le** □ ['fleksəbl] flexibel, biegsam; *fig.* anpassungsfähig.

flick [flik] schnippen; schnellen.

flicker ['flikə] 1. flackern; flattern; flimmern; 2. Flackern *n*, Flimmern *n*; Flattern *n*; *Am.* Buntspecht *m*.

flier ['flaiə] = flyer.

flight [flait] Flucht *f*; Flug *m* (*a. fig.*); Schwarm *m*; ⚓, ⚔ Kette *f*; (~ of stairs Treppen)Flucht *f*; put to ~ in die Flucht schlagen; ~y □ ['flaiti] flüchtig; leichtsinnig.

flimsy ['flimzi] dünn, locker; schwach; *fig.* fadenscheinig.

flinch [flintʃ] zurückweichen; zukken.

fling [fliŋ] 1. Wurf *m*; Schlag *m*; have one's ~ sich austoben; 2. [*irr.*] *v/i.* eilen; ausschlagen (*Pferd*); *fig.* toben; *v/t.* werfen, schleudern; ~ o.s. sich stürzen; ~ open aufreißen.

flint [flint] Kiesel *m*; Feuerstein *m*.

flip [flip] 1. Klaps *m*; Ruck *m*; 2. schnippen; klapsen; (umher-) flitzen.

flippan|cy ['flipənsi] Leichtfertigkeit *f*; ~t □ [~nt] leichtfertig; vorlaut.

flirt [flə:t] 1. Kokette *f*; Weiberheld *m*; 2. flirten, kokettieren; = flip 2; ~ation [flə:'teiʃən] Flirt *m*.

flit [flit] flitzen; wandern; umziehen.

flivver *Am. sl.* ['flivə] 1. Nuckelpinne *f* (*billiges Auto*); 2. mißlingen.

float [flout] 1. Schwimmer *m*; Floß *n*; Plattformwagen *m*; 2. *v/t.* überfluten; flößen; tragen (*Wasser*); ⚓ flott machen; *fig.* in Gang bringen; † gründen; verbreiten; *v/i.* schwimmen, treiben; schweben; umlaufen.

flock [flɔk] 1. Herde *f* (*a. fig.*); Schar *f*; 2. sich scharen; zs.-strömen.

floe [flou] (treibende) Eisscholle.

flog [flɔg] peitschen; prügeln.

flood [flʌd] 1. *a.* ~-tide Flut *f*; Überschwemmung *f*; 2. überfluten, überschwemmen; ~gate ['flʌdgeit] Schleusentor *n*; ~light ⚡ Flutlicht *n*.

floor [flɔ:] 1. Fußboden *m*; Stock (-werk *n*) *m*; ⚓ Tenne *f*; ~ leader *Am.* Fraktionsvorsitzende(r) *m*; ~ show Nachtklubvorstellung *f*; take the ~ das Wort ergreifen; 2. dielen; zu Boden schlagen; verblüffen; ~-cloth ['flɔ:klɔθ] Putzlappen *m*; ~ing ['flɔ:riŋ] Dielung *f*; Fußboden *m*; ~-lamp Stehlampe *f*; ~walker *Am.* ['flɔ:wɔ:kə] = shopwalker.

flop [flɔp] 1. schlagen; flattern; (hin)plumpsen (lassen); *Am.* versagen; 2. Plumps *m*; Versager *m*; ~house *Am. sl.* Penne *f*.

florid □ ['flɔrid] blühend.

florin ['flɔrin] Zweischillingstück *n*.

florist ['flɔrist] Blumenhändler *m*.

floss [lɔs] Florettseide *f*.

flounce[1] [flauns] Volant *m*.

flounce[2] [~] stürzen; zappeln.

flounder[1] *ichth.* ['flaundə] Flunder *f*.

flounder[2] [~] sich (ab)mühen.

flour ['flauə] (feines) Mehl.

flourish ['flʌriʃ] 1. Schnörkel *m*; Schwingen *n*; ♪ Tusch *m*; 2. *v/i.* blühen, gedeihen; *v/t.* schwingen.

flout [flaut] (ver)spotten.

flow [flou] 1. Fluß *m*; Flut *f*; 2. fließen, fluten; wallen.

flower ['flauə] 1. Blume *f*; Blüte *f* (*a. fig.*); Zierde *f*; 2. blühen; ~pot Blumentopf *m*; ~y [~əri] blumig.

flown [floun] *p.p. von fly* 2.

flubdub *Am. sl.* ['flʌbdʌb] Geschwätz *n*.

fluctuat|e ['flʌktjueit] schwanken; ~ion [flʌktju'eiʃən] Schwankung *f*.

flue[1] ⚓ F [flu:] = influenza.

flue[2] [flu:] Kaminrohr *n*; Heizrohr *n*.

fluen|cy *fig.* ['flu(:)ənsi] Fluß *m*; ~t □ [~nt] fließend, geläufig (*Rede*).

fluff [flʌf] 1. Flaum *m*; Flocke *f*; *fig.* Schnitzer *m*; 2. Kissen aufschütteln; Federn aufplustern (*Vogel*); ~y [~'flʌfi] flaumig; flockig.

fluid ['flu(:)id] 1. flüssig; 2. Flüssigkeit *f*.

flung [flʌŋ] *pret. u. p.p. von fling* 2.

flunk *Am.* F *fig.* [flʌŋk] durchfallen (lassen).

flunk(e)y ['flʌŋki] Lakai *m*.

fluorescent [fluə'resnt] fluoreszierend.

flurry ['flʌri] Nervosität *f*; Bö *f*; *Am. a.* (Regen)Schauer *m*; Schneegestöber *n*.

flush [flʌʃ] 1. ⊕ in gleicher Ebene; reichlich; (über)voll; 2. Erröten *n*; Übermut *m*; Fülle *f*; Wachstum *n*; *fig.* Blüte *f*; Spülung *f*; *Karten*: Flöte *f*; 3. über-, durchfluten; (aus)spülen; strömen; sprießen (lassen); erröten (machen); übermütig machen; aufjagen.

fluster ['flʌstə] 1. Aufregung *f*; 2. *v/t.* aufregen.

flute [flu:t] 1. ♪ Flöte *f*; Falte *f*; 2. (auf der) Flöte spielen; riefeln; fälteln.

flutter ['flʌtə] 1. Geflatter *n*; Erregung *f*; F Spekulation *f*; 2. *v/t.* aufregen; *v/i.* flattern.

flux [flʌks] *fig.* Fluß *m*; ⚕ Ausfluß *m*.

fly [flai] 1. *zo.* Fliege *f*; Flug *m*; *Am. Baseball*: hochgeschlagener Ball; Droschke *f*; 2. [*irr.*] (*a. fig.*) fliegen (lassen); entfliehen (*Zeit*); ⚔ führen; *Flagge* hissen; fliehen; ⚔ überfliegen; ~ at herfallen über; ~ into a passion *od.* rage in Zorn geraten.

flyer ['flaiə] Flieger *m*; Renner *m*; take a ~ *Am.* F Vermögen riskieren.

fly-flap ['flaiflæp] Fliegenklatsche *f*.

flying ['flaiiŋ] fliegend; Flug...; ~ squad Überfallkommando *n*.

fly|-over ['flaiouvə] (Straßen)Überführung *f*; ~-weight Boxen: Flie-

gengewicht *n*; ~-wheel Schwung-
rad *n*.
foal [foul] 1. Fohlen *n*; 2. fohlen.
foam [foum] 1. Schaum *m*; 2.
schäumen; ~y ['foumi] schaumig.
focus ['foukəs] 1. Brennpunkt *m*;
2. (sich) im Brennpunkt vereinigen;
opt. einstellen (*a. fig.*); konzentrieren.
fodder ['fodə] (Trocken)Futter *n*.
foe *poet.* [fou] Feind *m*, Gegner *m*.
fog [fog] 1. (dichter) Nebel; *fig.*
nebelung *f*; *phot.* Schleier *m*; 2. *mst*
fig. umnebeln; *phot.* verschleiern.
fogey F ['fougi]: old ~ komischer
alter Kauz.
foggy □ ['fogi] neb(e)lig; *fig.* nebelhaft.
fogy *Am.* ['fougi] = fogey.
foible *fig.* ['foibl] Schwäche *f*.
foil¹ [foil] Folie *f*; Hintergrund *m*.
foil² [~] 1. vereiteln; 2. Florett *n*.
fold¹ [fould] 1. Schafhürde *f*; *fig.*
Herde *f*; 2. einpferchen.
fold² [~] 1. Falte *f*; Falz *m*; 2. ...fach,
...fältig; 3. *v/t.* falten; falzen; *Arme*
kreuzen; ~ (up) einwickeln; *v/i.*
sich falten; *Am.* F eingehen; ~er
['fouldə] Mappe *f*, Schnellhefter *m*;
Faltprospekt *m*.
folding   ['foulding] zs.-legbar;
Klapp...; ~-bed Feldbett *n*; ~boat
Faltboot *n*; ~-door(s *pl.*) Flügeltür
f; ~-screen spanische Wand;
~-seat Klappsitz *m*.
foliage ['fouliidʒ] Laub(werk) *n*.
folk [fouk] *pl.* Leute *pl.*; ~s *pl.* Leute
pl. (F *a. Angehörige*); ~lore ['fouk-
lɔː] Volkskunde *f*; Volkssagen *f/pl.*;
~song Volkslied *n*.
follow ['folou] folgen (*dat.*); folgen
auf (*acc.*); be~, verfolgen; *s-m Be-*
ruf nachgehen; ~er [~ouə]
Nachfolger(in); Verfolger(in); An-
hänger(in); ~ing [~ouin] Anhänger-
schaft *f*, Gefolge *n*.
folly ['foli] Torheit *f*; Narrheit *f*.
foment [fou'ment] *j-m* warme Um-
schläge machen; *Unruhe* stiften.
fond □ [fond] zärtlich; vernarrt (*of*
in acc.); be ~ of gern haben, lieben;
~le ['fondl] liebkosen; streicheln;
(ver)hätscheln; ~ness [~dnis] Zärtlichkeit *f*; Vorliebe *f*.
font [font] Taufstein *m*; *Am.* Quelle
f.
food [fuːd] Speise *f*, Nahrung *f*;
Futter *n*; Lebensmittel *n/pl.*; ~-
stuff ['fuːdstaf] Nahrungsmittel *n*.
fool [fuːl] 1. Narr *m*, Tor *m*; Hanswurst *m*; make a ~ of s.o. j-n zum
Narren halten; make a ~ of o.s. sich
lächerlich machen; 2. *Am.* F närrisch, dumm; 3. *v/t.* narren; prellen (*out of* um *et.*); ~ away F vertrödeln; *v/i.* albern; (herum)spie-
len; ~ (a)round *bsd. Am.* Zeit vertrödeln.
fool|ery ['fuːləri] Torheit *f*; ~hardy

□ ['fuːlhɑːdi] tollkühn; ~ish □
['fuːlif] töricht; ~ishness [~ʃnis]
Torheit *f*; ~-proof kinderleicht.
foot [fut] 1. *pl.* feet [fiːt] Fuß *m*
(*a. Maß*); ~s Fußende *n*; ✕ Infanterie
f; on ~ zu Fuß; im Gange, in Gang;
2. *v/t. mst* ~ up addieren; ~ the bill
F die Rechnung bezahlen; *v/i.* ~ it
zu Fuß gehen; ~board ['futbɔːd]
Trittbrett *n*; ~boy Page *m*; ~fall
Tritt *m*, Schritt *m*; ~gear Schuh-
werk *n*; ~hold fester Stand; *fig.*
Halt *m*.
footing ['futing] Halt *m*, Stand *m*;
Grundlage *f*, Basis *f*; Stellung *f*;
fester Fuß; Verhältnis *n*; ✕ Zustand *m*; Endsumme *f*; be on a
friendly ~ with s.o. ein gutes Verhältnis zu j-m haben; lose one's ~
ausgleiten.
foot|lights *thea.* ['futlaits] *pl.* Ram-
penlicht(er *pl.*) *n*; Bühne *f*; ~man
Diener *m*; ~-passenger Fußgänger
(-in); ~-path Fußpfad *m*; ~print
Fußstapfe *f*, -spur *f*; ~sore fuß-
krank; ~step Fußstapfe *f*, Spur *f*;
~stool Fußbank *f*; ~wear = footgear.
fop [fop] Geck *m*, Fatzke *m*.
for [fɔː, fɔr, fə] 1. *prp. mst* für; *Zweck,*
Ziel, Richtung: zu; nach; *warten,*
hoffen etc. auf (*acc.*); *sich sehnen etc.*
nach; *Grund, Anlaß:* aus, vor (*dat.*),
wegen; *Zeitdauer:* ~ three days drei
Tage (lang); seit drei Tagen; *Ent-*
fernung: I walked ~ a mile ich ging
eine Meile (weit); *Austausch:* (an-)
statt; *in der Eigenschaft* als; I ~ one
ich zum Beispiel; ~ sure sicher!, gewiß!; 2. *cj.* denn.
forage ['foridʒ] 1. Futter *n*; 2. (nach
Futter) suchen.
foray ['forei] räuberischer Einfall.
forbear¹ [fɔː'bɛə] [*irr.* (*bear*)] *v/t.*
unterlassen; *v/i.* sich enthalten
(*from gen.*); Geduld haben.
forbear² ['fɔːbɛə] Vorfahr *m*.
forbid [fə'bid] [*irr.* (*bid*)] verbieten;
hindern; ~ding □ [~din] absto-
ßend.
force [fɔːs] 1. *mst* Kraft *f*, Gewalt *f*;
Nachdruck *m*; Zwang *m*; Heer *n*;
Streitmacht *f*; the ~ die Polizei;
armed ~s *pl.* Streitkräfte *f/pl.*;
come (put) in ~ in Kraft treten
(setzen); 2. zwingen, nötigen; erzwingen; aufzwingen; *Gewalt* antun (*dat.*); beschleunigen; aufbrechen; künstlich reif machen; ~ open
aufbrechen; ~d: ~ landing Notlan-
dung *f*; ~ loan Zwangsanleihe *f*; ~
march Eilmarsch *m*; ~ful □ ['fɔːs-
ful] kräftig; eindringlich.
forceps ✵ ['fɔːseps] Zange *f*.
forcible □ ['fɔːsəbl] gewaltsam;
Zwangs...; eindringlich; wirksam.
ford [fɔːd] 1. Furt *f*; 2. durchwaten.
fore [fɔː] 1. *adv.* vorn; 2. Vorderteil
m, *n*; bring (come) to the ~ zum

Vorschein bringen (kommen); **3.** *adj.* vorder; Vorder...; **~bode** [fɔː'boud] vorhersagen; ahnen; **~boding** [~diŋ] (böses) Vorzeichen; Ahnung *f*; **~cast** ['fɔːkɑːst] **1.** Vorhersage *f*; **2.** [*irr.* (*cast*)] vorhersehen; voraussagen; **~father** Vorfahr *m*; **~finger** Zeigefinger *m*; **~foot** Vorderfuß *m*; **~go** [fɔː'gou] [*irr.* (*go*)] vorangehen; **~gone** [fɔː'gɔn, *adj.* 'fɔːgɔn] von vornherein feststehend; **~** *conclusion* Selbstverständlichkeit *f*; **~ground** Vordergrund *m*; **~head** ['fɔrid] Stirn *f*.

foreign ['fɔrin] fremd; ausländisch; auswärtig; **~er** [~nə] Ausländer(in), Fremde(r *m*) *f*; ♀ Office Außenministerium *n*; **~** policy Außenpolitik *f*; **~** trade Außenhandel *m*.

fore|knowledge ['fɔː'nɔlidʒ] Vorherwissen *n*; **~leg** ['fɔːleg] Vorderbein *n*; **~lock** Stirnhaar *n*; *fig.* Schopf *m*; **~man** ♀ Obmann *m*; Vorarbeiter *m*, (Werk)Meister *m*; ⚒ Steiger *m*; **~most** vorderst, erst; **~name** Vorname *m*; **~noon** Vormittag *m*; **~runner** Vorläufer *m*, Vorbote *m*; **~see** [fɔː'siː] [*irr.* (*see*)] vorhersehen; **~shadow** ankündigen; **~sight** ['fɔːsait] Voraussicht *f*; Vorsorge *f*.

forest ['fɔrist] **1.** Wald *m* (*a. fig.*), Forst *m*; **2.** aufforsten.

forestall [fɔː'stɔːl] *et.* vereiteln; *j-m* zuvorkommen.

forest|er ['fɔristə] Förster *m*; Waldarbeiter *m*; **~ry** [~tri] Forstwirtschaft *f*; Waldgebiet *n*.

fore|taste ['fɔːteist] Vorgeschmack *m*; **~tell** [fɔː'tel] [*irr.* (*tell*)] vorhersagen; vorbedeuten; **~thought** ['fɔːθɔːt] Vorbedacht *m*; Aufseherin *f*; Vorarbeiterin *f*; **~word** Vorwort *n*.

forfeit ['fɔːfit] **1.** Verwirkung *f*; Strafe *f*; Pfand *n*; **2.** verwirken; einbüßen; **~able** [~təbl] verwirkbar.

forge¹ [fɔːdʒ] *mst* **~** ahead sich vor(wärts)arbeiten.

forge² [~] **1.** Schmiede *f*; **2.** schmieden (*fig. ersinnen*); fälschen; **~ry** ['fɔːdʒəri] Fälschung *f*.

forget [fə'get] [*irr.*] vergessen; **~ful** ☐ [~tful] vergeßlich; **~-me-not** ♀ Vergißmeinnicht *n*.

forgiv|e [fə'giv] [*irr.* (*give*)] vergeben, verzeihen; *Schuld* erlassen; **~eness** [~vnis] Verzeihung *f*; **~ing** ☐ [~viŋ] versöhnlich; nachsichtig.

forgo [fɔː'gou] [*irr.* (*go*)] verzichten auf (*acc.*); aufgeben.

forgot [fə'gɔt] *pret. von* forget; **~ten** [~tn] *p.p. von* forget.

fork [fɔːk] **1.** Gabel *f*; **2.** (sich) gabeln; **~-lift** ['fɔːklift] Gabelstapler *m*.

forlorn [fə'lɔːn] verloren, verlassen.

form [fɔːm] **1.** Form *f*; Gestalt *f*; Formalität *f*; Formular *n*; (Schul-)Bank *f*; *Schul-*Klasse *f*; Kondition

f; geistige Verfassung; **2.** (sich) formen, (sich) bilden, gestalten; ⚒ (sich) aufstellen.

formal ☐ ['fɔːməl] förmlich; formell; äußerlich; **~ity** [fɔː'mæliti] Förmlichkeit *f*, Formalität *f*.

formati|on [fɔː'meiʃən] Bildung *f*; **~ve** ['fɔːmətiv] bildend; gestaltend; **~** years *pl.* Entwicklungsjahre *n/pl.*

former ['fɔːmə] vorig, früher; ehemalig, vergangen; erstere(r, -s); jene(r, -s); **~ly** [~li] ehemals, früher.

formidable ☐ ['fɔːmidəbl] furchtbar, schrecklich; ungeheuer.

formula ['fɔːmjulə] Formel *f*; ⚕ Rezept *n*; **~te** [~leit] formulieren.

forsake [fə'seik] [*irr.*] aufgeben; verlassen; **~n** [~kən] *p.p. von* forsake.

forsook [fə'suk] *pret. von* forsake.

forsooth *iro.* [fə'suːθ] wahrlich.

forswear [fɔː'swɛə] [*irr.* (*swear*)] abschwören. [werk *n*) *f*.\

fort ⚔ [fɔːt] Fort *n*, Festungs-)\

forth [fɔːθ] vor(wärts), voran; heraus, hinaus, hervor; weiter, fort(an); **~-coming** [fɔː'θ'kamiŋ] erscheinend; bereit; bevorstehend; F entgegenkommend; **~-with** ['fɔː'θ'wiθ] sogleich.

fortieth ['fɔːtiiθ] **1.** vierzigste(r, -s); **2.** Vierzigstel *n*.

forti|fication [fɔːtifi'keiʃən] Befestigung *f*; **~fy** ['fɔːtifai] ⚔ befestigen; *fig.* (ver)stärken; **~tude** [~itjuːd] Seelenstärke *f*; Tapferkeit *f*.

fortnight ['fɔːtnait] vierzehn Tage.

fortress ['fɔːtris] Festung *f*.

fortuitous ☐ [fɔː'tju(ː)itəs] zufällig.

fortunate ['fɔːtʃnit] glücklich; **~ly** [~tli] glücklicherweise.

fortune ['fɔːtʃən] Glück *n*; Schicksal *n*; Zufall *m*; Vermögen *n*; **~-teller** Wahrsager(in).

forty ['fɔːti] **1.** vierzig; **~-niner** *Am. kalifornischer Goldsucher von 1849*; **~** winks *pl.* F Nickerchen *n*; **2.** Vierzig *f*.

forward ['fɔːwəd] **1.** *adj.* vorder; bereit(willig); fortschrittlich; vorwitzig, keck; **2.** *adv.* vor(wärts); **3.** *Fußball:* Stürmer *m*; **4.** (be)fördern; (ab-, ver)senden.

forwarding-agent ['fɔːwədiŋeidʒənt] Spediteur *m*.

foster ['fɔstə] **1.** *fig.* nähren, pflegen; **~** up aufziehen; **2.** Pflege...

fought [fɔːt] *pret. u. p.p. von* fight **2.**

foul [faul] **1.** ☐ widerwärtig; schmutzig (*a. fig.*); unehrlich; regelwidrig; übelriechend; faul, verdorben; widrig; schlecht (*Wetter*); *fall ~ of* mit *dem Gesetz* in Konflikt kommen; **2.** Zs.-stoß *m*; *Sport:* regelwidriges Spiel; *through fair and ~* durch dick und dünn; **3.** be-, verschmutzen; (sich) verwickeln.

found [faund] **1.** *pret. u. p.p. von* find 1; **2.** (be)gründen; stiften; ⊕ gießen.

foundation [faun'deiʃən] Gründung *f*; Stiftung *f*; Fundament *n*.

founder ['faundə] **1.** (Be)Gründer (-in), Stifter(in); Gießer *m*; **2.** *v/i.* scheitern; lahmen.

foundling ['faundliŋ] Findling *m*.

foundry ⊕ ['faundri] Gießerei *f*.

fountain ['fauntin] Quelle *f*; Springbrunnen *m*; **~-pen** Füllfederhalter *m*.

four [fɔː] **1.** vier; **2.** Vier *f*; *Sport*: Vierer *m*; **~-flusher** *Am. sl.* ['fɔː-'flʌʃə] Hochstapler *m*; **~-square** viereckig; *fig.* unerschütterlich; **~-stroke** *mot.* Viertakt...; **~teen** ['fɔː'tiːn] vierzehn; **~teenth** [~nθ] vierzehnte(r, -s); **~th** [fɔːθ] **1.** vierte(r, -s); **2.** Viertel *n*; **~thly** ['fɔːθli] viertens.

fowl [faul] Geflügel *n*; Huhn *n*; Vogel *m*; **~ing-piece** ['fauliŋpiːs] Vogelflinte *f*.

fox [fɔks] **1.** Fuchs *m*; **2.** überlisten; **~-glove** ['fɔksglʌv] Fingerhut *m*; **~y** ['fɔksi] fuchsartig; schlau.

fraction ['frækʃən] Bruch(teil) *m*.

fracture ['fræktʃə] **1.** *(bsd.* Knochen)Bruch *m*; **2.** brechen.

fragile ['frædʒail] zerbrechlich.

fragment ['frægmənt] Bruchstück *n*.

fragran|ce ['freigrəns] Wohlgeruch *m*, Duft *m*; **~t** □ [~nt] wohlriechend.

frail □ [freil] ge-, zerbrechlich; schwach; **~ty** *fig.* ['freilti] Schwäche *f*.

frame [freim] **1.** Rahmen *m*; Gerippe *n*; Gerüst *n*; (Brillen)Gestell *n*; Körper *m*; (An)Ordnung *f*; *phot.* (Einzel)Bild *n*; ⊕ Frühbeetkasten *m*; **~ of mind** Gemütsverfassung *f*; **2.** bilden, formen, bauen; entwerfen; (ein)rahmen; sich entwickeln; **~-house** ['freimhaus] Holzhaus *n*; **~-up** *bsd. Am.* F abgekartetes Spiel; **~-work** ⊕ Gerippe *n*; Rahmen *m*; *fig.* Bau *m*.

franchise ⚖ ['fræntʃaiz] Wahlrecht *n*; Bürgerrecht *n*; *bsd. Am.* Konzession *f*.

frank [fræŋk] **1.** □ frei(mütig), offen; **2.** *Brief* maschinell frankieren.

frankfurter ['fræŋkfətə] Frankfurter Würstchen *n*.

frankness ['fræŋknis] Offenheit *f*.

frantic ['fræntik] (~ally) wahnsinnig.

fratern|al □ [frə'təːnl] brüderlich; **~ity** [~niti] Brüderlichkeit *f*; Brüderschaft *f*; *Am. univ.* Verbindung *f*.

fraud [frɔːd] Betrug *m*; F Schwindel *m*; **~ulent** □ ['frɔːdjulənt] betrügerisch.

fray [frei] **1.** (sich) abnutzen; (sich) durchscheuern; **2.** Schlägerei *f*.

frazzle *bsd. Am.* F ['fræzl] **1.** Fetzen *m/pl.*; **2.** zerfetzen.

freak [friːk] Einfall *m*, Laune *f*.

freckle ['frekl] Sommersprosse *f*.

free [friː] **1.** □ *allg.* frei; freigebig (*of* mit); freiwillig; *he is ~ to inf.* es steht ihm frei, zu *inf.*; ~ *and easy* zwanglos; sorglos; *make* ~ sich Freiheiten erlauben; *set* ~ freilassen; **2.** befreien; freilassen, *et.* freimachen; **~-booter** ['friːbuːtə] Freibeuter *m*; **~dom** ['friːdəm] Freiheit *f*; freie Benutzung; Offenheit *f*; Zwanglosigkeit *f*; (plumpe) Vertraulichkeit; ~ *of a city* (Ehren-) Bürgerrecht *n*; **~-holder** Grundeigentümer *m*; **~-man** freier Mann; Vollbürger *m*; **~-mason** Freimaurer *m*; **~-wheel** Freilauf *m*.

freez|e [friːz] *[irr.]* *v/i.* (ge)frieren; erstarren; *v/t.* gefrieren lassen; **~e** ['friːz] Eismaschine *f*; Gefriermaschine *f*; Gefriertruhe *f*; **~ing** □ [~ziŋ] eisig; ~ *point* Gefrierpunkt *m*.

freight [freit] **1.** Fracht(geld *n*) *f*; *attr. Am.* Güter...; **2.** be-, verfrachten; **~-car** *Am.* 🚃 ['freitkɑː] Güterwagen *m*; ~ *train* *Am.* Güterzug *m*.

French [frentʃ] **1.** französisch; *take ~ leave* heimlich weggehen; ~ *window* Balkon-, Verandatür *f*; **2.** Französisch *n*; *the ~ pl.* die Franzosen *pl.*; **~-man** ['frentʃmən] Franzose *m*.

frenz|ied ['frenzid] wahnsinnig; **~y** [~zi] Wahnsinn *m*.

frequen|cy ['friːkwənsi] Häufigkeit *f*; ⚡ Frequenz *f*; **~t 1.** □ [~nt] häufig; **2.** [fri'kwent] (oft) besuchen.

fresh [freʃ] frisch; neu; unerfahren; *Am.* F frech; ~ *water* Süßwasser *n*; **~en** ['freʃn] frisch machen *od.* werden; **~et** [~ʃit] Hochwasser *n*; *fig.* Flut *f*; **~man** *univ.* Student *m* im ersten Jahr; **~ness** [~ʃnis] Frische *f*; Neuheit *f*; Unerfahrenheit *f*; **~water** Süßwasser...; ~ *college Am.* drittrangiges College.

fret [fret] **1.** Aufregung *f*; Ärger *m*; ♪ Bund *m*, Griffleiste *f*; **2.** zerfressen; (sich) ärgern; (sich) grämen; ~ *away*, ~ *out* aufreiben.

fretful □ ['fretful] ärgerlich.

fret-saw ['fretsɔː] Laubsäge *f*.

fretwork ['fretwəːk] (geschnitztes) Gitterwerk; Laubsägearbeit *f*.

friar ['fraiə] Mönch *m*.

friction ['frikʃn] Reibung *f* (*a. fig.*).

Friday ['fraidi] Freitag *m*.

fridge F [fridʒ] Kühlschrank *m*.

friend [frend] Freund(in); Bekannte(r *m*) *f*; **~ly** ['frendli] freund(schaft)lich; **~ship** [~dʃip] Freundschaft *f*.

frigate ⚓ ['frigit] Fregatte *f*.

frig(e) F [fridʒ] = *fridge*.

fright [frait] Schreck(en) *m*; *fig.*
Vogelscheuche *f*; ~en ['fraitn] erschrecken; ~ed *at* od. *of* bange vor
(*dat.*); ~ful □ [~tful] schrecklich.
frigid □ ['fridʒid] kalt, frostig.
frill [fril] Krause *f*, Rüsche *f*.
fringe [frindʒ] 1. Franse *f*; Rand *m*;
a. ~s *pl.* Ponyfrisur *f*; 2. mit Fran-
sen besetzen.
frippery ['fripəri] Flitterkram *m*.
Frisian ['friziən] friesisch.
frisk [frisk] 1. Luftsprung *m*;
2. hüpfen; *sl. nach Waffen etc.* durchsuchen; ~y □ ['friski] munter.
fritter ['fritə] 1. Pfannkuchén *m*,
Krapfen *m*; 2.: ~ *away* verzetteln.
frivol|ity [fri'vɔliti] Frivolität *f*,
Leichtfertigkeit *f*; ~ous □ ['fri-
vələs] nichtig; leichtfertig.
frizzle ['frizl] *a.* ~ *up* (sich) kräuseln; *Küche:* brutzeln.
fro [frou]: *to and* ~ hin und her.
frock [frɔk] Kutte *f*; *Frauen-*Kleid
n; Kittel *m*; Gehrock *m*.
frog [frɔg] Frosch *m*.
frolic ['frɔlik] 1. Fröhlichkeit *f*;
Scherz *m*; 2. scherzen, spaßen;
~some □ [~ksəm] lustig, fröhlich.
from [frɔm, frəm] von; aus,
von ... her; von ... (an); aus, vor,
wegen; nach, gemäß; *defend* ~
schützen vor (*dat.*); ~ *amidst* mitten aus.
front [frʌnt] 1. Stirn *f*; Vorderseite
f; ✗ Front *f*; Hemdbrust *f*; Strandpromenade *f*; Kühnheit *f*, Frechheit *f*; *in* ~ vorn; *in* ~ *of* räumlich
vor; 2. Vorder...; 3. *a.* ~ *on*, ~
towards die Front haben nach;
gegenüberstehen, gegenübertreten
(*dat.*); ~al ['frʌntl] Stirn..., Front-
...; ~ *door* Haustür *f*; ~ier
[~tjə] Grenze *f*, *bsd. Am. hist.*
Grenze zum Wilden Westen; *attr.*
Grenz...; ~iersman [~ɔzmən]
Grenzbewohner *m*; *fig.* Pionier *m*;
~ispiece [~tispi:s] ⚓ Vorderseite *f*;
typ. Titelblatt *p*; ~ *man fig.* Aus-
hängeschild *n*; ~-page *Zeitung*:
Titelseite *f*; ~-wheel drive *mot.*
Vorderradantrieb *m*.
frost [frɔst] 1. Frost *m*; *a. hoar* ~,
white ~ Reif *m*; 2. (mit Zucker)
bestreuen; glasieren; mattieren;
~ed glass Milchglas *n*; ~-bite 🏵
['frɔstbait] Erfrierung *f*; ~y □
[~ti] frostig; bereift.
froth [frɔθ] 1. Schaum *m*; 2. schäumen; zu Schaum schlagen; ~y □
['frɔθi] schaumig; *fig.* seicht.
frown [fraun] 1. Stirnrunzeln *n*;
finsterer Blick; 2. *v/i.* die Stirn
runzeln; finster blicken.
frow|sty □ ['frausti], ~zy ['frauzi]
moderig; schlampig.
froze [frouz] *pret. von* freeze; ~n
['frouzn] 1. *p.p. von* freeze; 2. *adj.*
(eis)kalt; (ein)gefroren.
frugal □ ['fru:gəl] mäßig; sparsam.

fruit [fru:t] 1. Frucht *f*; Früchte *pl.*;
Obst *n*; 2. Frucht tragen; ~erer
['fru:tərə] Obsthändler *m*; ~ful □
[~tful] fruchtbar; ~less □ [~tlis]
unfruchtbar.
frustrat|e [frʌs'treit] vereiteln;
enttäuschen; ~ion [~eiʃən] Vereitelung *f*; Enttäuschung *f*.
fry [frai] 1. Gebratene(s) *n*; Fisch-
brut *f*; 2. braten, backen; ~ing-pan
['fraiiŋpæn] Bratpfanne *f*.
fuchsia ⚘ ['fju:ʃə] Fuchsie *f*.
fudge [fʌdʒ] 1. F zurechtpfuschen;
2. Unsinn *m*; Weichkaramelle *f*.
fuel [fjuəl] 1. Brennmaterial *n*;
Betriebs-, *mot.* Kraftstoff *m*; 2. *mot.*
tanken.
fugitive ['fju:dʒitiv] 1. flüchtig
(*a. fig.*); 2. Flüchtling *m*.
fulfil(l) [ful'fil] erfüllen; vollziehen;
~ment [~lmənt] Erfüllung *f*.
full [ful] 1. □ *allg.* voll; Voll...;
vollständig, völlig; reichlich; ausführlich; *of* ~ *age* volljährig; 2. *adv.*
völlig, ganz; genau; 3. Ganze(s) *n*;
Höhepunkt *m*; *in* ~ völlig; ausführlich; *to the* ~ vollständig; ~-
blooded ['ful'blʌdid] vollblütig;
kräftig; reinrassig; ~ dress Gesellschaftsanzug *m*; ~-dress ['fuldres]
formell, Gala...; *Am.* ausführlich;
~-fledged ['ful'fledʒd] flügge; voll
ausgewachsen; ~ stop Punkt *m*.
ful(l)ness ['fulnis] Fülle *f*.
full-time ['fultaim] vollbeschäftigt;
Voll...
fulminate ['fʌlmineit] wettern.
fumble ['fʌmbl] tasten; fummeln.
fume [fju:m] 1. Dunst *m*, Dampf *m*;
2. rauchen; aufgebracht sein.
fumigate ['fju:migeit] ausräuchern,
desinfizieren.
fun [fʌn] Scherz *m*, Spaß *m*; *make* ~
of sich lustig machen über (*acc.*).
function ['fʌŋkʃən] 1. Funktion *f*;
Beruf *m*; Tätigkeit *f*; Aufgabe *f*;
Feierlichkeit *f*; 2. funktionieren;
~ary [~ʃnəri] Beamte(r) *m*; Funk-
tionär *m*.
fund [fʌnd] 1. Fonds *m*; ~s *pl.*
Staatspapiere *n/pl.*; Geld(mittel
n/pl.) *n*; Vorrat *m*; 2. *Schuld* fun-
dieren; *Geld* anlegen.
fundamental □ [fʌndə'mentl]
1. grundlegend; Grund...; 2. ~s *pl.*
Grundlage *f*, -züge *m/pl.*, -begriffe
m/pl.
funer|al ['fju:nərəl] Beerdigung *f*;
attr. Trauer..., Begräbnis...; ~eal □
[fju(:)'niəriəl] traurig, düster.
fun-fair ['fʌnfeə] Rummelplatz
m.
funicular [fju(:)'nikjulə] 1. Seil...;
2. *a.* ~ *railway* (Draht)Seilbahn *f*.
funnel ['fʌnl] Trichter *m*; Rauchfang *m*; ⚓, 🚂 Schornstein *m*.
funnies *Am.* ['fʌniz] *pl.* Comics *pl.*
(*primitive Bildserien*).
funny □ ['fʌni] spaßig, komisch.

fur [fə:] 1. Pelz *m*; Belag *m der Zunge*; Kesselstein *m*; *~s pl*. Pelzwaren *pl*.; 2. mit Pelz besetzen *od*. füttern.

furbish ['fə:biʃ] putzen, polieren.

furious □ ['fjuəriəs] wütend; wild.

furl [fə:l] zs.-rollen; zs.-klappen.

furlough ✕ ['fə:lou] Urlaub *m*.

furnace ['fə:nis] Schmelz-, Hochofen *m*; (Heiz)Kessel *m*; Feuerung *f*.

furnish ['fə:niʃ] versehen (*with* mit); *et*. liefern; möblieren; ausstatten.

furniture ['fə:nitʃə] Möbel *pl*., Einrichtung *f*; Ausstattung *f*; *sectional ~* Anbaumöbel *pl*.

furrier ['fʌriə] Kürschner *m*.

furrow ['fʌrou] 1. Furche *f*; 2. furchen.

further ['fə:ðə] 1. *adj. u. adv.* ferner, weiter; 2. fördern; *~ance* [~ərəns] Förderung *f*; *~more* [~ɔ:mɔ:] ferner, überdies; *~most* [~ɔmoust] weitest.

furthest ['fə:ðist] = *furthermost*.

furtive □ ['fə:tiv] verstohlen.

fury ['fjuəri] Raserei *f*, Wut *f*; Furie *f*.

fuse [fju:z] 1. (ver)schmelzen; *≠* durchbrennen; ausgehen (*Licht*); ✕ mit Zünder versehen; 2. *≠* (Schmelz)Sicherung *f*; ✕ Zünder *m*.

fuselage ['fju:zila:ʒ] (Flugzeug-) Rumpf *m*.

fusion ['fju:ʒən] Schmelzen *n*; Verschmelzung *f*, Fusion *f*; *~ bomb* ✕ Wasserstoffbombe *f*.

fuss F [fʌs] 1. Lärm *m*; Wesen *n*, Getue *n*; 2. viel Aufhebens machen (*about* um, von); (sich) aufregen.

fusty ['fʌsti] muffig; *fig.* verstaubt.

futile ['fju:tail] nutzlos, nichtig.

future ['fju:tʃə] 1. (zu)künftig; 2. Zukunft *f*; *gr*. Futur *n*, Zukunft *f*; *~s pl*. *†* Termingeschäfte *n/pl*.

fuzz [fʌz] 1. feiner Flaum; Fussel *f*; 2. fusseln, (zer)fasern.

G

gab F [gæb] Geschwätz *n*; *the gift of the ~* ein gutes Mundwerk.

gabardine ['gæbədi:n] Gabardine *m* (*Wollstoff*).

gabble ['gæbl] 1. Geschnatter *n*, Geschwätz *n*; 2. schnattern, schwatzen.

gaberdine ['gæbədi:n] Kaftan *m*; = *gabardine*.

gable ['geibl] Giebel *m*.

gad F [gæd]: *~ about* sich herumtreiben.

gadfly *zo*. ['gædflai] Bremse *f*.

gadget *sl*. ['gædʒit] Dings *n*, Apparat *m*; Kniff *m*, Pfiff *m*.

gag [gæg] 1. Knebel *m*; Witz *m*; 2. knebeln; *pol*. mundtot machen.

gage¹ [geidʒ] Pfand *m*.

gage² [~] = *gauge*.

gaiety ['geiəti] Fröhlichkeit *f*.

gaily ['geili] *adv. von* gay.

gain [gein] 1. Gewinn *m*; Vorteil *m*; 2. *v/t*. gewinnen; erreichen; bekommen; *v/i*. vorgehen (*Uhr*); *~ in* zunehmen an (*acc*.); *~ful* □ ['geinful] einträglich.

gait [geit] Gang(art *f*) *m*; Schritt *m*.

gaiter ['geitə] Gamasche *f*.

gal *Am. sl.* [gæl] Mädel *n*.

gale [geil] Sturm *m*; steife Brise.

gall [gɔ:l] 1. Galle *f*; *≉* Wolf *m*; Pein *f*; *bsd. Am. sl.* Frechheit *f*; 2. wundreiben; ärgern.

gallant ['gælənt] 1. □ stattlich; tapfer, galant, höflich; 2. Kavalier *m*; 3. galant sein; *~ry* [~tri] Tapferkeit *f*; Galanterie *f*.

gallery ['gæləri] Galerie *f*; Empore *f*.

galley ['gæli] *⚓* Galeere *f*; *⚓* Kombüse *f*; *~-proof* Korrekturfahne *f*.

gallon ['gælən] Gallone *f* (*4,54 Liter*, *Am. 3,78 Liter*).

gallop ['gæləp] 1. Galopp *m*; 2. galoppieren (lassen).

gallows ['gælouz] *sg*. Galgen *m*.

galore [gə'lɔ:] in Menge.

gamble ['gæmbl] (um Geld) spielen; 2. F Glücksspiel *n*; *~r* [~ə] Spieler(in).

gambol ['gæmbəl] 1. Luftsprung *m*; 2. (fröhlich) hüpfen, tanzen.

game [geim] 1. Spiel *n*; Scherz *m*; Wild *n*; 2. F entschlossen; furchtlos; 3. spielen; *~keeper* ['geimki:pə] Wildhüter *m*; *~-licence* Jagdschein *m*; *~ster* ['geimstə] Spieler(in).

gander ['gændə] Gänserich *m*.

gang [gæŋ] 1. Trupp *m*; Bande *f*; 2. *~ up* sich zs.-rotten *od*. zs.-tun; *~-board* *⚓* ['gæŋbɔ:d] Laufplanke *f*.

gangster *Am.* ['gæŋstə] Gangster *m*.

gangway ['gæŋwei] (Durch)Gang *m*; *⚓* Fallreep *n*; *⚓* Laufplanke *f*.

gaol [dʒeil], *~-bird* ['dʒeilbə:d], *~er* ['dʒeilə] *s. jail etc.*

gap [gæp] Lücke *f*; Kluft *f*; Spalte *f*.

gape [geip] gähnen; klaffen; gaffen.

garage ['gæra:ʒ] 1. Garage *f*; Autowerkstatt *f*; 2. Auto einstellen.

garb [gɑ:b] Gewand *n*, Tracht *f*.

garbage ['gɑ:bidʒ] Abfall *m*;

Schund *m*; ~ *can Am.* Mülltonne *f*;
~ *pail* Mülleimer *m*.

garden ['gɑ:dn] **1.** Garten *m*;
2. Gartenbau treiben; ~**er** [~nə]
Gärtner(in); ~**ing** [~niŋ] Garten-
arbeit *f*.

gargle ['gɑ:gl] **1.** gurgeln; **2.** Gur-
gelwasser *n*.

garish □ ['gɛəriʃ] grell, auffallend.

garland ['gɑ:lənd] Girlande *f*.

garlic ⚕ ['gɑ:lik] Knoblauch *m*.

garment ['gɑ:mənt] Gewand *n*.

garnish ['gɑ:niʃ] garnieren; zieren.

garret ['gærət] Dachstube *f*.

garrison ✕ ['gærisn] **1.** Besatzung
f; Garnison *f*; **2.** mit e-r Besatzung
belegen.   [haft.]

garrulous □ ['gæruləs] schwatz-

garter ['gɑ:tə] Strumpfband *n*; *Am.*
Socken-, Strumpfhalter *m*.

gas [gæs] **1.** Gas *n*; *Am.* = *gasoline*;
2. *v/t.* vergasen; *v/i.* F faseln; ~**eous**
['geizjəs] gasförmig.

gash [gæʃ] **1.** klaffende Wunde;
Hieb *m*; Riß *m*; **2.** tief (ein)schnei-
den in (*acc.*).

gas|-light ['gæslait] Gasbeleuch-
tung *f*; ~**-meter** Gasuhr *f*; ~**o-**
lene, ~**oline** *Am. mot.* ['gæsəli:n]
Benzin *n*.

gasp [gɑ:sp] **1.** Keuchen *n*; **2.** keuchen; nach Luft schnappen.

gas|sed [gæst] gasvergiftet; ~**stove**
['gæs'stouv] Gasofen *m*, -herd *m*;
~**works** ['gæswə:ks] *sg.* Gaswerk
n, -anstalt *f*.

gat *Am. sl.* [gæt] Revolver *m*.

gate [geit] Tor *n*; Pforte *f*; Sperre *f*;
~**man** 🚇 ['geitmən] Schranken-
wärter *m*; ~**way** Tor(weg *m*) *n*,
Einfahrt *f*.

gather ['gæðə] **1.** *v/t.* (ein-, ver-)
sammeln; ernten; pflücken; schließen (*from* aus); zu-...ziehen; kräuseln; ~ *speed* schneller werden; *v/i.*
sich (ver)sammeln; sich vergrö-
ßern; 𝕤 *u. fig.* reifen; **2.** Falte *f*;
~**ing** [~əriŋ] Versammlung *f*; Zs.-
kunft *f*.

gaudy □ ['gɔ:di] grell; protzig.

gauge [geidʒ] **1.** (Normal)Maß *n*;
Maßstab *m*; ⊕ Lehre *f*; 🚂 Spurweite *f*; Meßgerät *n*; **2.** eichen;
(aus)messen; *fig.* abschätzen.

gaunt [gɔ:nt] hager; finster.

gauntlet ['gɔ:ntlit] *fig.* Fehde-
handschuh *m*; *run the* ~ Spieß-
ruten laufen.

gauze [gɔ:z] Gaze *f*.

gave [geiv] *pret. von* give.

gavel *Am.* ['gævl] Hammer *m des
Versammlungsleiters od. Auktiona-
tors.*

gawk F [gɔ:k] Tölpel *m*; ~**y** [gɔ:'ki]
tölpisch.

gay □ [gei] lustig, heiter; bunt, lebhaft, glänzend.

gaze [geiz] **1.** starrer *od.* aufmerk-
samer Blick; **2.** starren.

gazette [gə'zet] **1.** Amtsblatt *n*;
2. amtlich bekanntgeben.

gear [giə] **1.** ⊕ Getriebe *n*; *mot.*
Gang *m*; Mechanismus *m*; Gerät *n*;
in ~ mit eingelegtem Gang; in Betrieb; *out of* ~ im Leerlauf; außer
Betrieb; *landing* ~ ✈ Fahrgestell *n*;
steering ~ ⚓ Ruderanlage *f*; *mot.*
Lenkung *f*; **2.** einschalten; ⊕
greifen; ~**ing** ['giəriŋ] (Zahnrad-)
Getriebe *n*; Übersetzung *f*; ~**-**
lever, *bsd. Am.* ~**-shift** Schalthebel
m.

gee [dʒi:] **1.** *Kindersprache:* Hottehü
n (*Pferd*); **2.** *Fuhrmannsruf:* hü!
hott!; *Am.* nanu!, so was!

geese [gi:s] *pl. von* goose.

gem [dʒem] Edelstein *m*; Gemme *f*;
fig. Glanzstück *n*.

gender *gr.* ['dʒendə] Genus *n*,
Geschlecht *n*.

general ['dʒenərəl] **1.** □ allgemein;
gewöhnlich; Haupt..., General...;
~ *election* allgemeine Wahlen; **2.** ✕
General *m*; Feldherr *m*; ~**ity**
[dʒenə'ræliti] Allgemeinheit *f*; *die
große Masse*; ~**ize** ['dʒenərəlaiz]
verallgemeinern; ~**ly** [~li] im allgemeinen, überhaupt; gewöhnlich.

generat|e ['dʒenəreit] erzeugen;
~**ion** [dʒenə'reiʃən] (Er)Zeugung *f*;
Generation *f*; Menschenalter *n*;
~**or** ['dʒenəreitə] Erzeuger *m*; ⊕
Generator *m*; *bsd. Am. mot.* Licht-
maschine *f*.

gener|osity [dʒenə'rɔsiti] Großmut
f; Großzügigkeit *f*; ~**ous** □
['dʒenərəs] großmütig, großzügig.

genial □ ['dʒi:njəl] freundlich; anregend; gemütlich (*Person*); heiter.

genitive *gr.* ['dʒenitiv] *a.* ~ *case*
Genitiv *m*.

genius ['dʒi:njəs] Geist *m*; Genie *n*.

gent F [dʒent] Herr *m*.

genteel □ [dʒen'ti:l] vornehm; elegant.

gentile ['dʒentail] **1.** heidnisch,
nichtjüdisch; **2.** Heid|e *m*, -in *f*.

gentle □ ['dʒentl] sanft, mild;
zahm; leise, sacht; vornehm; ~**man**
Herr *m*; Gentleman *m*; ~**manlike**,
~**manly** [~li] gebildet; vornehm;
~**ness** [~lnis] Sanftheit *f*; Milde *f*,
Güte *f*, Sanftmut *f*.

gentry ['dʒentri] niederer Adel;
gebildete Stände *m/pl.*

genuine □ ['dʒenjuin] echt; aufrichtig.

geography [dʒi'ɔgrəfi] Geographie
f.

geology [dʒi'ɔlədʒi] Geologie *f*.

geometry [dʒi'ɔmitri] Geometrie *f*.

germ [dʒə:m] **1.** Keim *m*; **2.** keimen.

German[1] ['dʒə:mən] **1.** deutsch;
2. Deutsche(r *m*) *f*; Deutsch *n*.

german[2] [~] *brother* ~ leiblicher
Bruder; ~ (to) [dʒə:'mein] (*to*) verwandt (mit); entsprechend (*dat.*).

germinate ['dʒə:mineit] keimen.

gesticulat|e [dʒes'tikjuleit] gestikulieren; ~ion [dʒestikju'leiʃən] Gebärdenspiel n.

gesture ['dʒestʃə] Geste f, Gebärde f.

get [get] [irr.] v/t. erhalten, bekommen, F kriegen; besorgen; holen; bringen; erwerben; verdienen; ergreifen, fassen; (veran)lassen; mit adv. mst bringen, machen; have got haben; ~ one's hair cut sich das Haar schneiden lassen; ~ by heart auswendig lernen; v/i. gelangen, geraten, kommen; gehen; werden; ~ ready sich fertig machen; ~ about auf den Beinen sein; ~ abroad bekannt werden; ~ ahead vorwärtskommen; ~ at (heran)kommen an ... (acc.); zu et. kommen; ~ away wegkommen; sich fortmachen; ~ in einsteigen; ~ on with s.o. mit j-m auskommen; ~ out aussteigen; ~ to hear (know, learn) erfahren; ~ up aufstehen; ~-up ['getʌp] Aufmachung f; Am. F Unternehmungsgeist m.

ghastly [gɑːstli] gräßlich; schrecklich; (toten)bleich; gespenstisch.

gherkin ['gəːkin] Gewürzgurke f.

ghost [goust] Geist m, Gespenst n; fig. Spur f; ~like ['goustlaik], ~ly [~li] geisterhaft.

giant ['dʒaiənt] 1. riesig; 2.Riese m.

gibber ['dʒibə] kauderwelschen; ~ish ['gibəriʃ] Kauderwelsch n.

gibbet ['dʒibit] 1. Galgen m; 2. hängen.

gibe [dʒaib] verspotten, aufziehen.

giblets ['dʒiblits] pl. Gänseklein n.

gidd|iness ['gidinis] ⚓ Schwindel m; Unbeständigkeit f; Leichtsinn m; ~y □ ['gidi] schwind(e)lig; leichtfertig; unbeständig; albern.

gift [gift] Gabe f; Geschenk n; Talent n; ~ed ['giftid] begabt.

gigantic [dʒai'gæntik] (~ally) riesenhaft, riesig, gigantisch.

giggle ['gigl] 1. kichern; 2. Gekicher n.

gild [gild] [irr.] vergolden; verschönen; ~ed youth Jeunesse f dorée.

gill [gil] ichth. Kieme f; ♀ Lamelle f.

gilt [gilt] 1. pret. u. p.p. von gild; 2. Vergoldung f.

gimmick Am. sl. ['gimik] Trick m.

gin [dʒin] Gin m (Wacholderschnaps); Schlinge f; ⊕ Entkörnungsmaschine f.

ginger ['dʒindʒə] 1. Ingwer m; Lebhaftigkeit f; 2. ~ up in Schwung bringen; 3. hellrot, rötlich-gelb; ~bread Pfefferkuchen m; ~ly [~ʤli] zimperlich; sachte.

gipsy ['dʒipsi] Zigeuner(in).

gird [gəːd] sticheln; [irr.] (um)gürten; umgeben.

girder ⊕ ['gəːdə] Tragbalken m.

girdle ['gəːdl] 1. Gürtel m; Hüfthalter m, -gürtel m; 2. umgürten.

girl [gəːl] Mädchen n; ♀ Guide ['gəːlgaid] Pfadfinderin f; ~hood ['gəːlhud] Mädchenzeit f; Mädchenjahre n/pl.; ~ish □ ['gəːliʃ] mädchenhaft; ~y Am. F ['gəːli] mit spärlich bekleideten Mädchen (Magazin, Varieté etc.).

girt [gəːt] pret. u. p.p. von gird.

girth [gəːθ] (Sattel)Gurt m; Umfang m.

gist [dʒist] das Wesentliche.

give [giv] [irr.] v/t. geben; abübergeben; her-, hingeben; überlassen; zum besten geben; schenken; gewähren; von sich geben; ergeben; ~ birth to zur Welt bringen; ~ away verschenken; F verraten; ~ forth von sich geben; herausgeben; ~ in einreichen; ~ up Geschäft etc. aufgeben; j-n ausliefern; v/i. mst ~ in nachgeben; weichen; ~ into, ~ (up)on hinausgehen auf (acc.) (Fenster etc.); ~ out aufhören; versagen; ~ and take [givən'teik] (Meinungs)Austausch m; Kompromiß m, n; ~away Preisgabe f; ~ show od. program bsd. Am. Radio, Fernsehen: öffentliches Preisraten; ~n □ ['givn] 1. p.p. von give; 2. ~ to ergeben (dat.).

glaci|al □ [gleisjəl] eisig; Eis...; Gletscher...; ~er ['glæsjə] Gletscher m.

glad □ [glæd] froh, erfreut; erfreulich; ~ly gern; ~den ['glædn] erfreuen.

glade [gleid] Lichtung f; Am. sumpfige Niederung.

gladness ['glædnis] Freude f.

glair [glεə] Eiweiß n.

glamo|rous ['glæmərəs] bezaubernd; ~(u)r ['glæmə] 1. Zauber m, Glanz m, Reiz m; 2. bezaubern.

glance [glɑːns] 1. Schimmer m, Blitz m; flüchtiger Blick; 2. hinweggleiten; mst ~ off abprallen; blitzen; glänzen; ~ at flüchtig ansehen; anspielen auf (acc.).

gland anat. [glænd] Drüse f.

glare [glεə] 1. grelles Licht; wilder, starrer Blick; 2. grell leuchten; wild blicken; ~ (at an)starren.

glass [glɑːs] 1. Glas n; Spiegel m; Opern-, Fernglas n; Barometer n; (a pair of) ~es pl. (eine) Brille; 2. gläsern; Glas...; 3. verglasen; ~case ['glɑːskeis] Vitrine f; Schaukasten m; ~house Treibhaus m; × sl. Bau m; ~y [~si] gläsern; glasig.

glaz|e [gleiz] 1. Glasur f; 2. v/t. verglasen; glasieren; polieren; v/i. trüb(e) od. glasig werden (Auge); ~ier ['gleizjə] Glaser m.

gleam [gliːm] 1. Schimmer m, Schein m; 2. schimmern.

glean [gli:n] v/t. sammeln; v/i. Ähren lesen.

glee [gli:] Fröhlichkeit f; mehrstimmiges Lied; ~ club Gesangverein m.

glen [glen] Bergschlucht f.

glib □ [glib] glatt, zungenfertig.

glid|e [glaid] 1. Gleiten n; ✈ Gleitflug m; 2. (dahin)gleiten (lassen); e-n Gleitflug machen; ~er ['glaidə] Segelflugzeug n.

glimmer ['glimə] 1. Schimmer m; min. Glimmer m; 2. schimmern.

glimpse [glimps] 1. flüchtiger Blick (of auf acc.); Schimmer m; flüchtiger Eindruck; 2. flüchtig (er)blicken.

glint [glint] 1. blitzen, glitzern; 2. Lichtschein m.

glisten ['glisn], **glitter** ['glitə] glitzern, glänzen.

gloat [glout]: ~ (up)on od. over sich weiden an (dat.).

globe [gloub] (Erd)Kugel f; Globus m.

gloom [glu:m], ~iness ['glu:minis] Düsterkeit f, Dunkelheit f; Schwermut f; ~y □ ['glu:mi] dunkel, düster; schwermütig; verdrießlich.

glori|fy ['glɔ:rifai] verherrlichen; ~ous □ [~iəs] herrlich, glorreich.

glory ['glɔ:ri] 1. Ruhm m; Herrlichkeit f, Pracht f; Glorienschein m; 2. frohlocken; stolz sein.

gloss [glɔs] 1. Glosse f, Bemerkung f; Glanz m; 2. Glossen machen (zu); Glanz geben (dat.); ~ over beschönigen.

glossary ['glɔsəri] Wörterverzeichnis n.

glossy □ ['glɔsi] glänzend, blank.

glove [glʌv] Handschuh m.

glow [glou] 1. Glühen n; Glut f; 2. glühen.

glower ['glauə] finster blicken.

glow-worm ['glouwə:m] Glühwürmchen n.

glucose ['glu:kous] Traubenzucker m.

glue [glu:] 1. Leim m; 2. leimen.

glum □ [glʌm] mürrisch.

glut [glʌt] überfüllen.

glutinous □ ['glu:tinəs] klebrig.

glutton ['glʌtn] Unersättliche(r m) f; Vielfraß m; ~ous □ [~nəs] gefräßig; ~y [~ni] Gefräßigkeit f.

G-man Am. F ['dʒi:mæn] FBI-Agent m.

gnarl [nɑ:l] Knorren m, Ast m.

gnash [næʃ] knirschen (mit).

gnat [næt] (Stech)Mücke f.

gnaw [nɔ:] (zer)nagen; (zer)fressen.

gnome [noum] Erdgeist m, Gnom m.

go [gou] 1. [irr.] allg. gehen, fahren; vergehen (Zeit); werden; führen (to nach); sich wenden (to an); funktionieren, arbeiten; passen; kaputtgehen; let ~ loslassen; ~

shares teilen; ~ to od. and see besuchen; ~ at losgehen auf (acc.); ~ between vermitteln (zwischen); ~ by sich richten nach; ~ for gehen nach, holen; ~ for a walk, etc. einen Spaziergang etc. machen; ~ in for an examination e-e Prüfung machen; ~ on weitergehen; fortfahren; ~ through durchgehen; durchmachen; ~ without sich behelfen ohne; 2. F Mode f; Schwung m, Schneid m; on the ~ auf den Beinen; im Gange; it is no ~ es geht nicht; in one ~ auf Anhieb; have a ~ at es versuchen mit.

goad [goud] 1. Stachelstock m; fig. Ansporn m; 2. fig. anstacheln.

go-ahead F ['gouəhed] 1. zielstrebig; unternehmungslustig; 2. bsd. Am. F Erlaubnis f zum Weitermachen.

goal [goul] Mal n; Ziel n; Fußball: Tor n; ~keeper ['goulki:pə] Torwart m.

goat [gout] Ziege f, Geiß f.

gob [gɔb] V Schleimklumpen m; F Maul n; Am. F Blaujacke f (Matrose).

gobble ['gɔbl] gierig verschlingen; ~dygook Am. sl. [~ldiguk] Amts-, Berufsjargon m; Geschwafel n; ~r [~lə] Vielfraß m; Truthahn m.

go-between ['goubitwi:n] Vermittler(in).

goblet ['gɔblit] Kelchglas n; Pokal m.

goblin ['gɔblin] Kobold m, Gnom m.

god, eccl. ♀ [gɔd] Gott m; fig. Abgott m; ~child ['gɔdtʃaild] Patenkind n; ~dess ['gɔdis] Göttin f; ~father Pate m; ~head Gottheit f; ~less ['gɔdlis] gottlos; ~like göttähnlich; göttlich; ~ly [~li] gottesfürchtig; fromm; ~mother Patin f.

go-getter Am. sl. ['gou'getə] Draufgänger m.

goggle ['gɔgl] 1. glotzen; 2. ~s pl. Schutzbrille f.

going ['gouiŋ] 1. gehend; im Gange (befindlich); be ~ to inf. im Begriff sein zu inf., gleich zun wollen od. werden; 2. Gehen n; Vorwärtskommen n; Straßenzustand m; Geschwindigkeit f, Leistung f; ~s-on F [~ŋz'ɔn] pl. Treiben n.

gold [gould] 1. Gold n; 2. golden; ~digger Am. ['goulddigə] Goldgräber m; ~en mst fig. [~dən] golden, goldgelb; ~finch zo. Stieglitz m; ~smith Goldschmied m.

golf [gɔlf] 1. Golf(spiel) n; 2. Golf spielen; ~course ['gɔlfkɔːs]; ~links pl. Golfplatz m.

gondola ['gɔndələ] Gondel f.

gone [gɔn] 1. p.p. von go 1; 2. adj. fort; F futsch; vergangen; tot; F hoffnungslos.

good [gud] 1. allg. gut; artig; gütig;

† zahlungsfähig; gründlich; ~ at geschickt in (dat.); 2. Gute(s) n; Wohl n, Beste(s) n; ~s pl. Waren f/pl.; Güter n/pl.; that's no ~ das nützt nichts; for ~ für immer; ~by(e) 1. [gud'bai] Lebewohl n; 2. ['gud'bai] (auf) Wiedersehen!; ♀ Friday Karfreitag m; ~ly ['gudli] anmutig, hübsch; fig. ansehnlich; ~natured gutmütig; ~ness [~nis] Güte f; das Beste; thank ~! Gott sei Dank!; ~will Wohlwollen n; † Kundschaft f; † Firmenwert m.

goody ['gudi] Bonbon m, n.

goon Am. sl. [gu:n] bestellter Schläger bsd. für Streik; Dummkopf m.

goose [gu:s], pl. geese [gi:s] Gans f (a. fig.); Bügeleisen n.

gooseberry ['guzbəri] Stachelbeere f.

goose|-flesh ['gu:sfleʃ], Am. ~ pimples pl. fig. Gänsehaut f.

gopher bsd. Am. ['goufə] Erdeichhörnchen n.

gore [gɔː] 1. (geronnenes) Blut; Schneiderei: Keil m; 2. durchbohren, aufspießen.

gorge [gɔːdʒ] 1. Kehle f, Schlund m; enge (Fels)Schlucht; 2. (ver-)schlingen; (sich) vollstopfen.

gorgeous □ ['gɔːdʒəs] prächtig.

gory □ ['gɔːri] blutig.

gospel ['gospəl] Evangelium n.

gossip ['gosip] 1. Geschwätz n; Klatschbase f; 2. schwatzen.

got [got] pret. u. p.p. von get.

Gothic ['goθik] gotisch; fig. barbarisch.

gotten Am. ['gotn] p.p. von get.

gouge [gaudʒ] 1. ⊕ Hohlmeißel m; 2. ausmeißeln; Am. F betrügen.

gourd [guəd] Kürbis m.

gout ⚕ [gaut] Gicht f.

govern ['gʌvən] v/t. regieren, beherrschen; lenken; leiten v/i. herrschen; ~ess [~nis] Erzieherin f; ~ment ['gʌvənmənt] Regierung(s-form) f; Leitung f; Herrschaft f (of über acc.); Ministerium n; Statthalterschaft f; attr. Staats...; ~mental [gʌvən'mentl] Regierungs...; ~or ['gʌvənə] Gouverneur m; Direktor m, Präsident m; F Alte(r) m (Vater, Chef).

gown [gaun] 1. (Frauen)Kleid n; Robe f, Talar m; 2. kleiden.

grab F [græb] 1. grapsen; an sich reißen, packen; 2. plötzlicher Griff; ⊕ Greifer m; ~-bag bsd. Am. Glückstopf m.

grace [greis] 1. Gnade f; Gunst f; (Gnaden)Frist f; Grazie f, Anmut f; Anstand m; Zier(de) f; Reiz m; Tischgebet n; Your ♀ Euer Gnaden; 2. zieren, schmücken; begünstigen, auszeichnen; ~ful □ ['greisful] anmutig; ~fulness [~nis] Anmut f.

gracious □ ['greiʃəs] gnädig.

gradation [grə'deiʃən] Abstufung f.

grade [greid] 1. Grad m, Rang m; Stufe f; Qualität f; bsd. Am. = gradient; Am. Schule: Klasse f, Note f; make the ~ Am. Erfolg haben; ~ crossing bsd. Am. schienengleicher Bahnübergang; ~(d) school bsd. Am. Grundschule f; 2. abstufen; einstufen; ⊕ planieren.

gradient ⚙ etc. ['greidjənt] Steigung f.

gradua|l □ ['grædjuəl] stufenweise, allmählich; ~te 1. [~weit] graduieren; (sich) abstufen; die Abschlußprüfung machen; promovieren; 2. univ. [~uit] Graduierte(r m) f; ~tion [grædju'eiʃən] Gradeinteilung f; Abschlußprüfung f; Promotion f.

graft [grɑːft] 1. ✿ Pfropfreis n; Am. Schiebung f; 2. ✿ pfropfen; ⚘ verpflanzen; Am. fig. schieben.

grain [grein] (Samen)Korn n; Getreide n; Gefüge n; fig. Natur f; Gran n (Gewicht).

gram [græm] = gramme.

gramma|r ['græmə] Grammatik f; ~r-school höhere Schule, Gymnasium n; Am. a. Mittelschule f; ~tical □ [grə'mætikəl] grammati(kali)sch.

gramme [græm] Gramm n.

granary ['grænəri] Kornspeicher m.

grand □ [grænd] 1. fig. großartig; erhaben; groß; Groß..., Haupt...; ♀ Old Party Am. Republikanische Partei; ~ stand Sport: (Haupt-)Tribüne f; 2. ♪ a. ~ piano Flügel m; Am. sl. tausend Dollar pl.; ~child ['græntʃaild] Enkel(in); ~eur [~dʒə] Größe f, Hoheit f; Erhabenheit f; ~father Großvater m.

grandiose □ ['grændious] großartig.

grand|mother ['grænmʌðə] Großmutter f; ~parents [~npeərənts] pl. Großeltern pl.

grange [greindʒ] Gehöft n; Gut n; Am. Name für Farmerorganisation f.

granny F ['græni] Oma f.

grant [grɑːnt] 1. Gewährung f; Unterstützung f; Stipendium n; 2. gewähren; bewilligen; verleihen; zugestehen; ⚖ übertragen; take for ~ed als selbstverständlich annehmen.

granul|ate ['grænjuleit] (sich) körnen; ~e [~ju:l] Körnchen n.

grape [greip] Weinbeere f, -traube f; ~fruit ♀ ['greipfru:t] Pampelmuse f.

graph [græf] graphische Darstellung; ~ic(al □) ['græfik(əl)] graphisch; anschaulich; graphic arts pl. Graphik f; ~ite min. [~fait] Graphit m.

grapple ['græpl] entern; packen; ringen.

grasp [grɑːsp] 1. Griff *m*; Bereich *m*; Beherrschung *f*; Fassungskraft *f*; 2. (er)greifen, packen; begreifen.

grass [grɑːs] Gras *n*; Rasen *m*; *send to* ~ auf die Weide schicken; **~hopper** ['grɑːshɔpə] Heuschrecke *f*; ~ **roots** *pl. Am. pol. die* landwirtschaftlichen Bezirke, *die* Landbevölkerung; **~widow(er)** F Strohwitwe(r *m*) *f*; **~y** [~si] grasig; Gras...

grate [greit] 1. (Kamin)Gitter *n*; (Feuer)Rost *m*; 2. (zer)reiben; mit *et.* knirschen; *fig.* verletzen.

grateful □ ['greitful] dankbar.

grater ['greitə] Reibeisen *n*.

grati|fication [grætifi'keiʃən] Befriedigung *f*; Freude *f*; **~fy** ['grætifai] erfreuen; befriedigen.

grating ['greitiŋ] 1. □ schrill; unangenehm; 2. Gitter(werk) *n*.

gratitude ['grætitjuːd] Dankbarkeit *f*.

gratuit|ous □ [grə'tjuː(ː)itəs] unentgeltlich; freiwillig; **~y** [~ti] Abfindung *f*; Gratifikation *f*; Trinkgeld *n*.

grave [greiv] 1. □ ernst; (ge)wichtig; gemessen; 2. Grab *n*; 3. [*irr.*] *mst* *fig.* (ein)graben; **~digger** ['greivdigə] Totengräber *m*.

gravel ['grævəl] 1. Kies *m*; ♂ Harngrieß *m*; 2. mit Kies bedecken.

graven ['greivən] *p.p. von* **grave** 3.

graveyard ['greivjɑːd] Kirchhof *m*.

gravitation [grævi'teiʃən] Schwerkraft *f*; *fig.* Hang *m*.

gravity ['græviti] Schwere *f*; Wichtigkeit *f*; Ernst *m*; Schwerkraft *f*.

gravy ['greivi] Fleischsaft *m*, Bratensoße *f*.

gray *bsd. Am.* [grei] grau.

graze [greiz] (ab)weiden; (ab)grasen; streifen, schrammen.

grease 1. [griːs] Fett *n*; Schmiere *f*; 2. [griːz] (be)schmieren.

greasy □ ['griːzi] fettig; schmierig.

great □ [greit] *allg.* groß; Groß...; F großartig; **~coat** [greit'kout] Überzieher *m*; **~grandchild** Urenkel(in); **~grandfather** Urgroßvater *m*; **~ly** [~tli] sehr; **~ness** [~tnis] Größe *f*; Stärke *f*.

greed [griːd] Gier *f*; **~y** □ ['griːdi] (be)gierig (*of, for* nach); habgierig.

Greek [griːk] 1. griechisch; 2. Grieche *m*, -in *f*; Griechisch *n*.

green [griːn] 1. □ grün (*a. fig.*); frisch (*Fisch etc.*); neu; Grün...; 2. Grün *n*; Rasen *m*; Wiese *f*; **~s** *pl.* frisches Gemüse; **~back** *Am.* ['griːnbæk] Dollarnote *f*; **~grocer** Gemüsehändler(in); **~grocery** Gemüsehandlung *f*; **~horn** Grünschnabel *m*; **~house** Gewächshaus *n*; **~ish** [~niʃ] grünlich; **~sickness** Bleichsucht *f*.

greet [griːt] (be)grüßen; **~ing** ['griːtiŋ] Begrüßung *f*; Gruß *m*.

grenade ✗ [gri'neid] Granate *f*.

grew [gruː] *pret. von* **grow**.

grey [grei] 1. □ grau; 2. Grau *n*; 3. grau machen *od.* werden; **~hound** ['greihaund] Windhund *m*.

grid [grid] Gitter *n*; ⊞, ⚡ Netz *n*; *Am. Fußball:* Spielfeld *n*; **~iron** ['gridaiən] (Brat)Rost *m*.

grief [griːf] Gram *m*, Kummer *m*; *come to* ~ zu Schaden kommen.

griev|ance ['griːvəns] Beschwerde *f*; Mißstand *m*; **~e** [griːv] kränken; (sich) grämen; **~ous** □ ['griːvəs] kränkend, schmerzlich; schlimm.

grill [gril] 1. grillen; braten (*a. fig.*); 2. Bratrost *m*, Grill *m*; gegrilltes Fleisch; *a.* **~room** Grillroom *m*.

grim □ [grim] grimmig; schrecklich.

grimace [gri'meis] 1. Fratze *f*, Grimasse *f*; 2. Grimassen schneiden.

grim|e [graim] Schmutz *m*; Ruß *m*; **~y** □ ['graimi] schmutzig; rußig.

grin [grin] 1. Grinsen *n*; 2. grinsen.

grind [graind] 1. [*irr.*] (zer)reiben; mahlen; schleifen; *Leierkasten etc.* drehen; *fig.* schinden; mit *den Zähnen* knirschen; 2. Schinderei *f*; **~stone** ['graindstoun] Schleif-, Mühlstein *m*.

grip [grip] 1. packen, fassen (*a. fig.*); 2. Griff *m*; Gewalt *f*; Herrschaft *f*; *Am.* = **gripsack**.

gripe [graip] Griff *m*; **~s** *pl.* Kolik *f*; *bsd. Am.* Beschwerden *f/pl.*

gripsack *Am.* ['gripsæk] Handtasche *f*, -köfferchen *n*.

grisly ['grizli] gräßlich, schrecklich.

gristle ['grisl] Knorpel *m*.

grit [grit] 1. Kies *m*; Sand(stein) *m*; *fig.* Mut *m*; 2. knirschen (mit).

grizzly ['grizli] 1. grau; 2. Graubär *m*.

groan [groun] seufzen, stöhnen.

grocer ['grousə] Lebensmittelhändler *m*; **~ies** [~əriz] *pl.* Lebensmittel *n/pl.*; **~y** [~ri] Lebensmittelgeschäft *n*.

groceteria *Am.* [grousi'tiəriə] Selbstbedienungsladen *m*.

groggy ['grɔgi] taumelig; schwankend.

groin *anat.* [grɔin] Leistengegend *f*.

groom [grum] 1. Reit-, Stallknecht *m*; Bräutigam *m*; 2. pflegen; *Am. pol. Kandidaten* lancieren.

groove [gruːv] 1. Rinne *f*, Nut *f*; *fig.* Gewohnheit *f*; 2. nuten, falzen.

grope [group] (be)tasten, tappen.

gross [grous] 1. □ dick; grob; derb; ♥ Brutto...; 2. Gros *n* (*12 Dutzend*); *in the* ~ im ganzen.

grotto ['grɔtou] Grotte *f*.

grouch *Am.* F [grautʃ] 1. quengeln, meckern; 2. Griesgram *m*; schlechte Laune; **~y** ['grautʃi] quenglig.

ground¹ [graund] 1. *pret. u. p.p. von* grind 1; 2. ~ glass Mattglas *n.*

ground² [graund] 1. *mst* Grund *m*; Boden *m*; Gebiet *n*; Spiel- *etc.* Platz *m*; Beweg- *etc.* Grund *m*; ℰ Erde *f*; ~s *pl.* Grundstück *n*, Park(s *pl.*) *m*, Gärten *m/pl.*; Kaffee-Satz *m*; on the ~(s) of auf Grund (*gen.*); stand od. hold od. keep one's ~ sich behaupten; 2. niederlegen; (be)gründen; *j-m* die Anfangs-gründe beibringen; ℰ erden; ~floor ['graund'flɔ:] Erdgeschoß *n*; ~hog [ˌdhɔg] *bsd. Am.* Murmel-tier *n*; ~less □ [ˌdlis] grundlos; ~staff ℀ Bodenpersonal *n*; ~work Grundlage *f.*

group [gru:p] 1. Gruppe *f*; 2. (sich) gruppieren.

grove [grouv] Hain *m*; Gehölz *n.*

grovel *mst fig.* ['grɔvl] kriechen.

grow [grou] [*irr.*] *v/i.* wachsen; werden; *v/t.* ♀ anpflanzen, an-bauen; ~er ['grouə] Bauer *m*, Züchter *m.*

growl [graul] knurren, brummen; ~er ['graulə] *fig.* Brummbär *m*; *Am. sl.* Bierkrug *m.*

grow|n [groun] 1. *p.p. von* grow; 2. *adj.* erwachsen; bewachsen; ~n-up ['grounʌp] 1. erwachsen; 2. Erwachsene(r *m*) *f*; ~th [grouθ] Wachstum *n*; (An)Wachsen *n*; Ent-wicklung *f*; Wuchs *m*; Gewächs *n*, Erzeugnis *n.*

grub [grʌb] 1. Raupe *f*, Larve *f*, Made *f*; *contp.* Prolet *m*; 2. graben; sich abmühen; ~by ['grʌbi] schmie-rig.

grudge [grʌdʒ] 1. Groll *m*; 2. miß-gönnen; ungern geben *od.* tun *etc.*

gruel [gruəl] Haferschleim *m.*

gruff □ [grʌf] grob, schroff, barsch.

grumble ['grʌmbl] murren; (g)rol-len; ~r *fig.* [ˌlə] Brummbär *m.*

grunt [grʌnt] grunzen.

guarant|ee [gærən'ti:] 1. Bürge *m*; = guaranty; 2. bürgen für; ~or [ˌ'tɔ:] Bürge *m*; ~y ['gærənti] Bürg-schaft *f*, Garantie *f*; Gewähr *f.*

guard [ga:d] 1. Wacht *f*; ⚔ Wache *f*; Wächter *m*, Wärter *m*; 🚂 Schaffner *m*; Schutz(vorrichtung *f*) *m*; ⚡s *pl.* Garde *f*; be on (off) one's ~ (nicht) auf der Hut sein; 2. *v/t.* bewachen, (be)schützen (from *vor dat.*); *v/i.* sich hüten (against *vor dat.*); ~ian ['ga:djən] Hüter *m*, Wächter *m*; ⚖ Vormund *m*; *attr.* Schutz...; ~ianship [ˌnʃip] Obhut *f*; Vor-mundschaft *f.*

guess [ges] 1. Vermutung *f*; 2. ver-muten; (er)raten; *Am.* denken.

guest [gest] Gast *m*; ~house ['gesthaus] (Hotel)Pension *f*, Fremden-heim *n*; ~room Gast-, Fremden-zimmer *n.*

guffaw [gʌ'fɔ:] schallendes Ge-lächter.

guidance ['gaidəns] Führung *f*; (An)Leitung *f.*

guide [gaid] 1. Führer *m*; ⊕ Füh-rung *f*; *attr.* Führungs...; 2. leiten; führen; lenken; ~book ['gaidbuk] Reiseführer *m*; ~post Wegweiser *m.*

guild [gild] Gilde *f*, Innung *f*; ℨhall ['gild'hɔ:l] Rathaus *n* (*in Lon-don*).

guile [gail] Arglist *f*; ~ful □ ['gailful] arglistig; ~less □ ['gaillis] arglos.

guilt [gilt] Schuld *f*; Strafbarkeit *f*; ~less □ ['giltlis] schuldlos; un-kundig; ~y □ [ˌti] schuldig; straf-bar.

guinea ['gini] Guinee *f* (21 Schil-ling); ~pig Meerschweinchen *n.*

guise [gaiz] Erscheinung *f*, Gestalt *f*; Maske *f.*

guitar ♪ [gi'ta:] Gitarre *f.*

gulch *Am.* [gʌlʃ] tiefe Schlucht.

gulf [gʌlf] Meerbusen *m*, Golf *m*; Abgrund *m*; Strudel *m.*

gull [gʌl] 1. Möwe *f*; Tölpel *m*; 2. übertölpeln; verleiten (into zu).

gullet ['gʌlit] Speiseröhre *f*; Gur-gel *f.*

gulp [gʌlp] Schluck *m*; Schlucken *n.*

gum [gʌm] 1. *a.* ~s *pl.* Zahnfleisch *n*; Gummi *n*; Klebstoff *m*; ~s *pl. Am.* Gummischuhe *m/pl.*; 2. gummie-ren; zukleben.

gun [gʌn] 1. Gewehr *n*; Flinte *f*; Geschütz *n*, Kanone *f*; *Am.* Re-volver *m*; big ~ *F fig.* hohes Tier; 2. *Am.* auf die Jagd gehen; ~boat ['gʌnbout] Kanonenboot *n*; ~licence Waffenschein *m*; ~man *Am.* Gangster *m*; ~ner ⚔, ⚓ ['gʌnə] Kanonier *m*; ~powder Schießpulver *n*; ~smith Büchsen-macher *m.*

gurgle ['gə:gl] gluckern, gur-geln.

gush [gʌʃ] 1. Guß *m*; *fig.* Erguß *m*; 2. (sich) ergießen, schießen (from aus); *fig.* schwärmen; ~er ['gʌʃə] *fig.* Schwärmer(in); Ölquelle *f.*

gust [gʌst] Windstoß *m*, Bö *f.*

gut [gʌt] Darm *m*; ♪ Darmsaite *f*; ~s *pl.* Eingeweide *n/pl.*; *das* In-nere; *fig.* Mut *m.*

gutter ['gʌtə] Dachrinne *f*; Gosse *f* (*a. fig.*), Rinnstein *m.*

guy [gai] 1. Halteseil *n*; F Vogel-scheuche *f*; *Am.* F Kerl *m*; 2. ver-ulken.

guzzle ['gʌzl] saufen; fressen.

gymnas|ium [dʒim'neizjəm] Turn-halle *f*, -platz *m*; ~tics [ˌ'næstiks] *pl.* Turnen *n*; Gymnastik *f.*

gypsy *bsd. Am.* ['dʒipsi] = gipsy.

gyrate [dʒaiə'reit] kreisen; wir-beln.

gyroplane ['dʒaiərəplein] Hub-schrauber *m.*

H

haberdasher ['hæbədæʃə] Kurz-warenhändler *m*; *Am.* Herrenarti-kelhändler *m*; ~y [~əri] Kurzwaren (-geschäft *n*) *f*/*pl.*; *Am.* Herren-artikel *m*/*pl.*

habit ['hæbit] 1. (An)Gewohnheit *f*; Verfassung *f*; Kleid(ung *f*) *n*; *fall od. get into bad* ~s schlechte Gewohnheiten annehmen; 2. (an-) kleiden; ~able [~təbl] bewohnbar; ~ation [hæbi'teiʃən] Wohnung *f*.

habitual ☐ [hə'bitjuəl] gewohnt, gewöhnlich; Gewohnheits...

hack [hæk] 1. Hieb *m*; Einkerbung *f*; Miet-, Arbeitspferd *n* (*a. fig.*); *a.* ~ *writer* literarischer Lohn-schreiber *m*; 2. (zer)hacken.

hackneyed *fig.* ['hæknid] abge-droschen.

had [hæd] *pret. u. p.p. von* have.

haddock ['hædək] Schellfisch *m*.

h(a)emorrhage ⚕ ['heməridʒ] Blut-sturz *m*.

hag [hæg] (*mst fig.* alte) Hexe.

haggard ☐ ['hægəd] verstört; ha-ger.

haggle ['hægl] feilschen, schachern.

hail [heil] 1. Hagel *m*; Anruf *m*; 2. (nieder)hageln (lassen); anrufen; (be)grüßen; ~ *from* stammen aus; ~stone ['heilstoun] Hagelkorn *n*; ~storm Hagelschauer *m*.

hair [hɛə] Haar *n*; ~-breadth ['hɛəbredθ] Haaresbreite *f*; ~cut Haarschnitt *m*; ~do *Am.* Frisur *f*; ~dresser (*bsd.* Damen)Friseur *m*; ~drier [~draiə] Trockenhaube *f*; Fön *m*; ~less ['hɛəlis] ohne Haare, kahl; ~pin Haarnadel *f*; ~raising ['hɛəreiziŋ] haarsträubend; ~split-ting Haarspalterei *f*; ~y ['hɛəri] haarig.

hale [heil] gesund, frisch, rüstig.

half [hɑːf] 1. *pl.* **halves** [hɑːvz] Hälfte *f*; *by halves* nur halb; *go halves* halbpart machen, teilen 2. halb; ~ *a crown* eine halbe Krone; ~back ['hɑːf'bæk] *Fuß-ball:* Läufer *m*; ~breed ['hɑːf-briːd] Halbblut *n*; ~caste Halb-blut *n*; ~hearted ☐ ['hɑːf'hɑːtid] lustlos, lau; ~length Brustbild *n*; ~penny ['heipni] halber Penny; ~time ['hɑːf'taim] *Sport:* Halb-zeit *f*; ~way halbwegs; ~witted einfältig, idiotisch.

halibut *ichth.* ['hælibət] Heilbutt *m*.

hall [hɔːl] Halle *f*; Saal *m*; Vorraum *m*; Flur *m*; Diele *f*; Herren-, Guts-haus *n*; *univ.* Speisesaal *m*; ~ *of residence* Studentenwohnheim *n*.

halloo [hə'luː] (hallo) rufen.

hallow ['hælou] heiligen, weihen; 2mas [~ouməs] Allerheiligenfest *n*.

halo ['heilou] *ast.* Hof *m*; Heiligen-schein *m*.

halt [hɔːlt] 1. Halt(estelle *f*) *m*; Stillstand *m*; 2. (an)halten; *mst fig.* hinken; schwanken.

halter ['hɔːltə] Halfter *f*; Strick *m*.

halve [hɑːv] halbieren; ~s [hɑːvz] *pl. von* half 1.

ham [hæm] Schenkel *m*; Schinken *m*.

hamburger *Am.* ['hæmbəːgə] Fri-kadelle *f*; mit Frikadelle belegtes Brötchen.

hamlet ['hæmlit] Weiler *m*.

hammer ['hæmə] 1. Hammer *m*; 2. (be)hämmern.

hammock ['hæmək] Hängematte *f*.

hamper ['hæmpə] 1. Geschenk-, Eßkorb *m*; 2. verstricken; behin-dern.

hamster *zo.* ['hæmstə] Hamster *m*.

hand [hænd] 1. Hand *f* (*a. fig.*); Handschrift *f*; Handbreite *f*; (Uhr)Zeiger *m*; Mann *m*, Arbeiter *m*; *Karten:* Blatt *n*; *at* ~ bei der Hand; *nahe bevorstehend*; *at first* ~ aus erster Hand; *a good (poor)* ~ *at* (un)geschickt in (*dat.*); ~ *and glove* ein Herz und eine Seele; *change* ~s den Besitzer wechseln; *lend a* ~ (mit) anfassen; *off* ~ aus dem Hand-gelenk *od.* Stegreif; *on* ~ ✝ vor-rätig, auf Lager; *bsd. Am.* zur Stelle, bereit; *on one's* ~s auf dem Halse; *on the one* ~ einerseits; *on the other* ~ andererseits; ~ *to* ~ Mann gegen Mann; *come to* ~ sich bieten; einlaufen (*Briefe*) 2. reichen; ~ *about* herumreichen; ~ *down* vererben; ~ *in* einhändigen; einreichen; ~ *over* aushändigen; ~bag ['hændbæg] Handtasche *f*; ~bill Hand-, Reklamezettel *m*; ~brake ⊕ Handbremse *f*; ~cuff Handfessel *f*; ~ful [~dful] Hand-voll *f*; F Plage *f*; ~glass Hand-spiegel *m*; Leselupe *f*.

handicap ['hændikæp] 1. Handikap *n*; Vorgaberennen *n*, Vorgabespiel *n*; (Extra)Belastung *f*; 2. (extra) belasten; beeinträchtigen.

handi|craft ['hændikrɑːft] Hand-werk *n*; Handfertigkeit *f*; ~crafts-man Handwerker *m*; ~work Hand-arbeit *f*; Werk *n*.

handkerchief ['hæŋkətʃi(ː)f] Ta-schentuch *n*; Halstuch *n*.

handle ['hændl] 1. Griff *m*; Stiel *m*; Henkel *m*; *Pumpen- etc.* Schwengel *m*; *fig.* Handhabe *f*; *fly off the* ~ F platzen vor Wut; 2. anfassen; hand-haben; behandeln; ~bar Lenk-stange *f* *e-s Fahrrades*.

hand|-luggage ['hændlʌgidʒ] Handgepäck *n*; ~made handge-arbeitet; ~me-downs *Am.* F *pl.* Fertigkleidung *f*; getragene Kleider *pl.*; ~rail Geländer *n*; ~shake Händedruck *m*; ~some □ ['hænsəm] ansehnlich; hübsch; anständig; ~work Handarbeit *f*; ~writing Handschrift *f*; ~y □ ['hændi] geschickt; handlich; zur Hand.

hang [hæŋ] **1.** [*irr.*] *v/t.* hängen; auf-, einhängen; verhängen; (*pret. u. p.p. mst* ~ed) (er)hängen; hängen lassen; *Tapete* ankleben; *v/i.* hängen; schweben; sich neigen; ~ *about* (*Am. around*) herumlungern; sich an *j-n* hängen; ~ *back* sich zurückhalten; ~ *on* sich klammern an (*acc.*); *fig.* hängen an (*dat.*); **2.** Hang *m*; Fall *m* e-*r Gardine etc.*; F Wesen *n*; F *fig.* Kniff *m*; Dreh *m*.

hangar ['hæŋə] Flugzeughalle *f*.

hang-dog ['hæŋdɔg] Armesünder...

hanger ['hæŋə] Aufhänger *m*; Hirschfänger *m*; ~on *fig.* [~ər'ɔn] Klette *f*.

hanging ['hæŋiŋ] **1.** Hänge...; **2.** ~s *pl.* Behang *m*; Tapeten *f/pl.*

hangman ['hæŋmən] Henker *m*.

hang-nail ⚓ ['hæŋneil] Niednagel *m*.

hang-over *sl.* ['hæŋouvə] Katzenjammer *m*, Kater *m*.

hanker ['hæŋkə] sich sehnen.

hap|hazard ['hæp'hæzəd] **1.** Zufall *m*; *at* ~ aufs Geratewohl; **2.** zufällig; ~less □ ['hæplis] unglücklich.

happen ['hæpən] sich ereignen, geschehen; *he* ~ed *to be at home or* war zufällig zu Hause; ~ (*up)on* zufällig treffen auf (*acc.*); ~ *in Am.* F hereinschneien; ~ing ['hæpniŋ] Ereignis *n*.

happi|ly ['hæpili] glücklicherweise; ~ness [~inis] Glück(seligkeit *f*) *n*.

happy □ ['hæpi] *allg.* glücklich; beglückt; erfreut; erfreulich; geschickt; treffend; F angeheitert; ~-go-lucky F unbekümmert.

harangue [hə'ræŋ] **1.** Ansprache *f*, Rede *f*; **2.** *v/t.* feierlich anreden.

harass ['hærəs] belästigen, quälen.

harbo(u)r ['ha:bə] **1.** Hafen *m*; Zufluchtsort *m*; **2.** (be)herbergen; *Rache etc.* hegen; ankern; ~age [~ɔridʒ] Herberge *f*; Zuflucht *f*.

hard [ha:d] **1.** *adj. allg.* hart; schwer; mühselig; streng; ausdauernd; fleißig; heftig; *Am.* stark (*Spirituosen*); ~ *of hearing* schwerhörig; **2.** *adv.* stark; tüchtig; mit Mühe; ~ *by* nahe bei; ~ *up* in Not; ~-boiled ['ha:d'bɔild] hartgesotten; *Am.* gerissen; ~ *cash* Bargeld *n*; klingende Münze; ~en ['ha:dn] härten; hart machen *od.* werden; (sich) abhärten; *fig.* (sich) verhärten; † sich festigen (*Preise*); ~headed nüchtern denkend; ~hearted □ hartherzig; ~ihood ['ha:dihud] Kühnheit *f*; ~iness [~inis] Widerstandsfähigkeit *f*, Härte *f*; ~ly ['ha:dli] kaum; streng;

mit Mühe; ~ness ['ha:dnis] Härte *f*; Schwierigkeit *f*; Not *f*; ~pan *Am.* harter Boden, *fig.* Grundlage *f*; ~ship ['ha:dʃip] Bedrängnis *f*, Not *f*; Härte *f*; ~ware Eisenwaren *f/pl.*; ~y □ ['ha:di] kühn; widerstandsfähig, hart; abgehärtet; winterfest (*Pflanze*).

hare [hɛə] Hase *m*; ~bell ♀ ['hɛəbəl] Glockenblume *f*; ~brained zerfahren; ~lip *anat.* ['hɛə'lip] Hasenscharte *f*.

hark [ha:k] horchen (*to* auf *acc.*).

harlot ['ha:lət] Hure *f*.

harm [ha:m] **1.** Schaden *m*; Unrecht *n*, Böse(s) *n*; **2.** beschädigen, verletzen; schaden, Leid zufügen (*dat.*); ~ful □ ['ha:mful] schädlich; ~less □ ['ha:mlis] harmlos; unschädlich.

harmon|ic [ha:'mɔnik] (~*ally*), ~ious □ [ha:'mounjəs] harmonisch; ~ize ['ha:mənaiz] *v/t.* in Einklang bringen; *v/i.* harmonieren; ~y [~ni] Harmonie *f*.

harness ['ha:nis] **1.** Harnisch *m*; Zug-Geschirr *n*; *die in* ~ in den Sielen sterben; **2.** anschirren; bändigen; *Wasserkraft* nutzbar machen.

harp [ha:p] **1.** Harfe *f*; **2.** Harfe spielen; ~ (*up)on* herumreiten auf (*dat.*). [**2.** herumpausieren.)

harpoon [ha:'pu:n] **1.** Harpune *f*;)

harrow ♫ ['hærou] **1.** Egge *f*; **2.** eggen; *fig.* quälen, martern.

harry ['hæri] plündern; quälen.

harsh □ [ha:ʃ] rauh; herb; grell; streng; schroff; barsch.

hart *zo.* [ha:t] Hirsch *m*.

harvest ['ha:vist] **1.** Ernte(zeit) *f*; Ertrag *m*; **2.** ernten; einbringen.

has [hæz] *3. sg. pres. von* have.

hash [hæʃ] **1.** gehacktes Fleisch; *Am.* F Essen *n*, Fraß *m*; *fig.* Mischmasch *m*; **2.** (zer)hacken.

hast|e [heist] Eile *f*; Hast *f*; *make* ~ (sich) be)eilen; ~en ['heisn] (sich be)eilen; *j-n* antreiben; *et.* beschleunigen; ~y □ ['heisti] (vor)eilig; hastig; hitzig, heftig.

hat [hæt] Hut *m*.

hatch [hætʃ] **1.** Brut *f*, Hecke *f*; ⚓, 🐟 Luke *f*; *serving* ~ Durchreiche *f*; **2.** (aus)brüten (*a. fig.*).

hatchet ['hætʃit] Beil *n*.

hatchway ⚓ ['hætʃwei] Luke *f*.

hat|e [heit] **1.** Haß *m*; **2.** hassen; ~eful □ ['heitful] verhaßt; abscheulich; ~red ['heitrid] Haß *m*.

haught|iness ['hɔ:tinis] Stolz *m*; Hochmut *m*; ~y □ ['hɔ:ti] stolz; hochmütig.

haul [hɔ:l] **1.** Ziehen *n*; (Fisch-)Zug *m*; *Am.* Transport(weg) *m*; **2.** ziehen; schleppen; transportieren; ⚒ fördern; ⚓ abdrehen; ~ *down one's flag* die Flagge streichen; *fig.* sich geschlagen geben.

haunch [hɔːntʃ] Hüfte *f*; Keule *f von Wild*.

haunt [hɔːnt] **1.** Aufenthaltsort *m*; Schlupfwinkel *m*; **2.** oft besuchen; heimsuchen; verfolgen; spuken in (*dat.*).

have [hæv] [*irr.*] *v/t.* haben; bekommen; *Mahlzeit* einnehmen; lassen; ~ *to* du tun müssen; *I ~ my hair cut* ich lasse mir das Haar schneiden; *he will ~ it that ...* er behauptet, daß ...; *I had better go* es wäre besser, wenn ich ginge; *I had rather go* ich möchte lieber gehen; ~ *about one* bei *od.* an sich haben; ~ *on* anhaben; ~ *it out with* sich auseinandersetzen mit; *v/aux.* haben; *bei v/i.* oft sein; ~ *come gekommen sein*.

haven ['heivn] Hafen *m* (*a. fig.*).

havoc ['hævək] Verwüstung *f*; *make ~ of, play ~ with od.* among verwüsten; übel zurichten.

haw ♀ [hɔː] Hagebutte *f*.

Hawaiian [hɑːˈwaiiən] **1.** hawaiisch; **2.** Hawaiier(in).

hawk [hɔːk] **1.** Habicht *m*; Falke *m*; **2.** sich räuspern; hausieren mit.

hawthorn ♀ ['hɔːθɔːn] Weißdorn *m*.

hay [hei] **1.** Heu *n*; **2.** heuen; ~**cock** ['heikɔk] Heuhaufen *m*; ~**fever** Heuschnupfen *m*; ~**loft** Heuboden *m*; ~**maker** *bsd.* Am. K.o.-Schlag *m*; ~**rick** = *haycock*; ~**seed** *bsd. Am.* F Bauerntölpel *m*; ~**stack** = *haycock*.

hazard ['hæzəd] **1.** Zufall *m*; Gefahr *f*, Wagnis *n*; Hasard(spiel) *n*; **2.** wagen; ~**ous** [˗dəs] gewagt.

haze [heiz] **1.** Dunst *m*; **2.** ⚓ *u. Am.* schinden; F schurigeln.

hazel ['heizl] **1.** ♀ Hasel(staude) *f*; **2.** nußbraun; ~**nut** Haselnuß *f*.

hazy □ ['heizi] dunstig; *fig.* unklar.

H-bomb ⚔ ['eitʃbɔm] H-Bombe *f*, Wasserstoffbombe *f*.

he [hiː] **1.** er; ~ *who* derjenige, welcher; **2.** Mann *m*; *zo.* Männchen *n*; **3.** *adj. in Zssgn:* männlich, ...männchen *n*; ~**goat** Ziegenbock *m*.

head [hed] **1.** *allg.* Kopf *m* (*a. fig.*); Haupt *n* (*a. fig.*); *nach Zahlwort:* Mann *m* (*a. pl.*); Stück *n* (*a. pl.*); Leiter(in); Chef *m*; Kopfende *n e-s Bettes etc.*; Kopfseite *f e-r Münze*; Gipfel *m*; Quelle *f*; *Schiffs-*Vorderteil *n*; Hauptpunkt *m*, Abschnitt *m*; Überschrift *f*; *come to a ~* eitern (*Geschwür*); *fig.* sich zuspitzen, zur Entscheidung kommen; *get it into one's ~ that ...* es sich in den Kopf setzen, daß; ~ *over heels* Hals über Kopf; **2.** erst; Ober...; Haupt...; **3.** *v/t.* (an)führen; an der Spitze von *et.* stehen; vorausgehen (*dat.*); mit e-r Überschrift versehen; ~ *off* ablenken; *v/i.* ⚓ zusteuern (*for auf acc.*); *Am.* entspringen (*Fluß*); ~**ache** ['hedeik] Kopfweh *n*; ~

dress Kopfputz *m*; Frisur *f*; ~**gear** Kopfbedeckung *f*; Zaumzeug *n*; ~**ing** ['hediŋ] Brief-, Titelkopf *m*, Rubrik *f*; Überschrift *f*, Titel *m*; *Sport:* Kopfball *m*; ~**land** ['hedlənd] Vorgebirge *n*; ~**light** *mot.* Scheinwerfer(licht *n*) *m*; ~**line** Überschrift *f*; Schlagzeile *f*; ~s *pl.* Radio: *das* Wichtigste in Kürze; ~**long 1.** *adj.* ungestüm; **2.** *adv.* kopfüber; ~**master** Direktor *m e-r Schule*; ~**phone** Radio: Kopfhörer *m*; ~**quarters** *pl.* ⚔ Hauptquartier *n*; Zentral(stell)e *f*; ~**strong** halsstarrig; ~**waters** *pl.* Quellgebiet *n*; ~**way** Fortschritt(e *pl.*) *m*; *make ~* vorwärtskommen; ~**word** Stichwort *n e-s Wörterbuchs*; ~**y** □ ['hedi] ungestüm; voreilig; zu Kopfe steigend.

heal [hiːl] heilen; ~ *up* zuheilen.

health [helθ] Gesundheit *f*; ~**ful** □ ['helθful] gesund; heilsam; ~**resort** Kurort *m*; ~**y** □ ['helθi] gesund.

heap [hiːp] **1.** Haufe(n) *m*; **2.** *a.* ~ *up* (auf)häufen; überhäufen.

hear [hiə] [*irr.*] hören; erfahren; anhören; *j-m* zuhören; erhören; *Zeugen* verhören; *Lektion* abhören; ~**d** [həːd] *pret. u. p.p. von hear*; ~**er** ['hiərə] (Zu)Hörer(in); ~**ing** [˗riŋ] Gehör *n*; Audienz *f*; ⚖ Verhör *n*; Hörweite *f*; ~**say** Hörensagen *n*.

hearse [həːs] Leichenwagen *m*.

heart [hɑːt] *allg.* Herz *n* (*a. fig.*); Innere(s) *n*; Kern *m*; *fig.* Schatz *m*; *by ~* auswendig; *out of ~* mutlos; *lay to ~* sich zu Herzen nehmen; *lose ~* den Mut verlieren; *take ~* sich ein Herz fassen; ~**ache** ['hɑːteik] Kummer *m*; ~**break** Herzeleid *n*; ~**breaking** [˗kiŋ] herzzerbrechend; ~**broken** gebrochenen Herzens; ~**burn** Sodbrennen *n*; ~**en** ['hɑːtn] ermutigen; ~**failure** ⚕ Herzversagen *n*; ~**felt** innig, tief empfunden.

hearth [hɑːθ] Herd *m* (*a. fig.*).

heart|less □ ['hɑːtlis] herzlos; ~**rending** ['hɑːtrendiŋ] herzzerreißend; ~ *transplant* Herzverpflanzung *f*; ~**y** □ ['hɑːti] □ herzlich; aufrichtig; gesund; herzhaft.

heat [hiːt] **1.** *allg.* Hitze *f*; Wärme *f*; Eifer *m*; *Sport:* Gang *m*, einzelner Lauf; *zo.* Läufigkeit *f*; **2.** heizen; (sich) erhitzen (*a. fig.*); ~**er** ['hiːtə] Erhitzer *m*; Ofen *m*.

heath [hiːθ] Heide *f*; ♀ Heidekraut *n*.

heathen ['hiːðən] **1.** Heid|e *m*, -in *f*; **2.** heidnisch.

heather ♀ ['heðə] Heide(kraut *n*) *f*.

heat|ing ['hiːtiŋ] Heizung *f*; *attr.* Heiz...; ~ *lightning Am.* Wetterleuchten *n*.

heave [hiːv] **1.** Heben *n*; Übelkeit *f*;

2. [*irr.*] *v/t.* heben; schwellen; *Seufzer* ausstoßen; *Anker* lichten; *v/i.* sich heben, wogen, schwellen.
heaven ['hevn] Himmel *m*; ~ly [~nli] himmlisch.
heaviness ['hevinis] Schwere *f*, Druck *m*; Schwerfälligkeit *f*; Schwermut *f*.
heavy □ ['hevi] *allg.* schwer; schwermütig; schwerfällig; trüb; drückend; heftig (*Regen etc.*); unwegsam (*Straße*); Schwer...; ~ **current** ⚡ Starkstrom *m*; ~-**handed** ungeschickt; ~-**hearted** niedergeschlagen; ~-**weight** *Boxen:* Schwergewicht *n*.
heckle ['hekl] durch Zwischenfragen in die Enge treiben.
hectic 🐾 ['hektik] hektisch (*auszehrend; sl.* fieberhaft erregt).
hedge [hed3] **1.** Hecke *f*; **2.** *v/t.* einhegen, einzäunen; umgeben; ~ *up* sperren; *v/i.* sich decken; sich nicht festlegen; ~**hog** *zo.* ['hed3hog] Igel *m*; *Am.* Stachelschwein *n*; ~**row** Hecke *f*.
heed [hi:d] **1.** Beachtung *f*, Aufmerksamkeit *f*; *take* ~ *of*, *give od.* *pay* ~ *to* achtgeben auf (*acc.*), beachten; **2.** beachten, achten auf (*acc.*); ~**less** □ ['hi:dlis] unachtsam; unbekümmert (*of* um).
heel [hi:l] **1.** Ferse *f*; Absatz *m*; *Am. sl.* Lump *m*; *head over* ~*s* Hals über Kopf; *down at* ~ mit schiefen Absätzen; *fig.* abgerissen; schlampig; **2.** mit e-m Absatz versehen; ~**ed** *Am. F* finanzstark; ~**er** *Am. sl. pol.* ['hi:lə] Befehlsempfänger *m*.
heft [heft] Gewicht *n*; *Am. F* Hauptteil *m*.
heifer ['hefə] Färse *f* (*junge Kuh*).
height [hait] Höhe *f*; Höhepunkt *m*; ~**en** ['haitn] erhöhen; vergrößern.
heinous □ ['heinəs] abscheulich.
heir [ɛə] Erbe *m*; ~ *apparent* rechtmäßiger Erbe; ~**ess** ['ɛəris] Erbin *f*; ~**loom** ['ɛəlu:m] Erbstück *n*.
held [held] *pret. u. p.p. von hold* 2.
helibus *Am. F* ['helibʌs] Lufttaxi *n*.
helicopter ✈ ['helikɒptə] Hubschrauber *m*.
hell [hel] Hölle *f*; *attr.* Höllen...; *what the* ~ ...? *F* was zum Teufel ...?; *raise* ~ Krach machen; ~-**bent** ['helbent] *Am. sl.* unweigerlich entschlossen; ~**ish** □ ['heliʃ] höllisch.
hello ['he'lou] hallo!
helm ⚓ [helm] (Steuer)Ruder *n*.
helmet ['helmit] Helm *m*.
helmsman ⚓ ['helmzmən] Steuermann *m*.
help [help] **1.** *allg.* Hilfe *f*; (Hilfs-)Mittel *n*; (Dienst)Mädchen *n*; **2.** *v/t.* (ab)helfen (*dat.*); unterlassen; *bei Tisch* geben, reichen;

~ *o.s.* sich bedienen, zulangen; *I could not* ~ *laughing* ich konnte nicht umhin zu lachen; *v/i.* helfen, dienen; ~**er** ['helpə] Helfer(in), Gehilf|e *m*, -in *f*; ~**ful** □ [~pful] hilfreich; nützlich; ~**ing** [~piŋ] Portion *f*; ~**less** □ [~plis] hilflos; ~**lessness** [~snis] Hilflosigkeit *f*; ~**mate**, ~**meet** Gehilf|e *m*, -in *f*; Gattin *f*.
helter-skelter ['heltə'skeltə] holterdiepolter.
helve [helv] Stiel *m*, Griff *m*.
Helvetian [hel'vi:ʃjən] Helvetier (-in); *attr.* Schweizer...
hem [hem] **1.** Saum *m*; **2.** *v/t.* säumen; ~ *in* einschließen; *v/i.* sich räuspern.
hemisphere ['hemisfiə] Halbkugel *f*.
hem-line ['hemlain] *Kleid:* Saum *m*.
hemlock ♣ ['hemlɒk] Schierling *m*; ~-**tree** Schierlingstanne *f*.
hemp [hemp] Hanf *m*.
hemstitch ['hemstitʃ] Hohlsaum *m*.
hen [hen] Henne *f*; *Vogel-*Weibchen *n*.
hence [hens] weg; hieraus; daher; von jetzt an; *a year* ~ heute übers Jahr; ~**forth** ['hens'fɔ:θ], ~-**forward** [~'wəd] von nun an.
hen|-coop ['henku:p] Hühnerstall *m*; ~-**pecked** unter dem Pantoffel (stehend).
hep *Am. sl.* [hep]: *to be* ~ *to* kennen; ~**cat** *Am. sl.* ['hepkæt] Eingeweihte(r *m*) *f*; Jazzfanatiker(in).
her [hə:, hə] sie; ihr; ihr(e).
herald ['herəld] **1.** Herold *m*; **2.** (sich) ankündigen; ~ *in* einführen; ~**ry** [~dri] Wappenkunde *f*, Heraldik *f*.
herb [hə:b] Kraut *n*; ~**age** [~bid3] Gras *n*; Weide *f*; ~**ivorous** [hə:-'bivərəs] pflanzenfressend.
herd [hə:d] **1.** Herde *f* (*a. fig.*); **2.** *v/t.* Vieh hüten; *v/i. a.* ~ *together* in e-r Herde leben; zs.-hausen; ~**er** ['hə:də], ~**sman** ['hə:dzmən] Hirt *m*.
here [hiə] hier; hierher; ~*'s to* ...! auf das Wohl von ...!
here|after [hiər'ɑ:ftə] **1.** künftig; **2.** Zukunft *f*; ~**by** ['hiə'bai] hierdurch.
heredit|ary [hi'reditəri] erblich; Erb...; ~**y** [~ti] Erblichkeit *f*.
here|in ['hiər'in] hierin; ~**of** [hiər-'ɔv] hiervon.
heresy ['herəsi] Ketzerei *f*.
heretic ['herətik] Ketzer(in).
here|tofore ['hiətu'fɔ:] bis jetzt; ehemals; ~**upon** ['hiərə'pɒn] hierauf; ~**with** hiermit.
heritage ['heritid3] Erbschaft *f*.
hermit ['hə:mit] Einsiedler *m*.
hero ['hiərou] Held *m*; ~**ic(al** □) [hi'rouik(əl)] heroisch; heldenhaft;

Helden...; ~ine ['herouin] Heldin f; ~ism [~izəm] Heldenmut m, -tum n.

heron zo. ['herən] Reiher m.

herring ichth. ['heriŋ] Hering m.

hers [hə:z] der (die, das) ihrige; ihr.

herself [hə:'self] (sie, ihr, sich) selbst; sich; of ~ von selbst; by ~ allein.

hesitat|e ['heziteit] zögern, unschlüssig sein; Bedenken tragen; ~ion [hezi'teiʃən] Zögern n; Unschlüssigkeit f; Bedenken n.

hew [hju:] [irr.] hauen, hacken; ~n [hju:n] p.p. von hew.

hey [hei] ei!; hei!; he!, heda!

heyday ['heidei] 1. heisa!; oho!; 2. fig. Höhepunkt m, Blüte f.

hi [hai] he!, heda!; hallo!

hicc|ough, ~up ['hikʌp] 1 Schlukken m; 2. schlucken; den Schlukken haben.

hid [hid] pret. u. p.p. von hide 2; ~den ['hidn] p.p. von hide 2.

hide [haid] 1. Haut f; 2. [irr.] (sich) verbergen, verstecken; ~-and-seek ['haidənd'si:k] Versteckspiel n.

hidebound fig. ['haidbaund] engherzig.

hideous □ ['hidiəs] scheußlich.

hiding ['haidiŋ] F Tracht f Prügel; Verbergen n; ~-place Versteck n.

hi-fi Am. ['hai'fai] = high-fidelity.

high [hai] 1. adj. □ allg. hoch; vornehm; gut, edel (Charakter); stolz; hochtrabend; angegangen (Fleisch); extrem; stark; üppig, flott (Leben); Hoch...; Ober...; with a ~ hand arrogant, anmaßend; in ~ spirits in gehobener Stimmung, guter Laune; ~ life die vornehme Welt; ~ time höchste Zeit; ~ words heftige Worte; 2. meteor. Hoch n; bsd. Am. für Zssgn wie high school, etc.; 3. adv. hoch; sehr, mächtig; ~ball Am. ['haibɔ:l] Whisky m mit Soda; ~bred vornehm erzogen; ~brow F 1. Intellektuelle(r m) f; 2. betont intellektuell; ~class erstklassig; ~fidelity mit höchster Wiedergabetreue, Hi-Fi; ~grade hochwertig; ~handed anmaßend; ~land ['hailənd] Hochland n; ~lights pl. fig. Höhepunkte m/pl.; ~ly ['haili] hoch; sehr; speak ~ of s.o. j-n loben; ~minded hochherzig; ~ness ['hainis] Höhe f; fig. Hoheit f; ~pitched schrill (Ton); steil (Dach); ~power: ~ station Großkraftwerk n; ~road Landstraße f; ~school höhere Schule; ~strung überempfindlich; ~ tea frühes Abendessen mit Tee u. Fleisch etc.; ~water Hochwasser n; ~way Landstraße f; fig. Weg m; ~ code Straßenverkehrsordnung f; ~wayman Straßenräuber m.

hike F [haik] 1. wandern; 2. Wan-

derung f; bsd. Am. F Erhöhung f (Preis etc.); ~r ['haikə] Wanderer m.

hilarious □ [hi'lɛəriəs] ausgelassen.

hill [hil] Hügel m, Berg m; ~billy Am. F ['hilbili] Hinterwäldler m; ~ock ['hilək] kleiner Hügel; ~side ['hil'said] Hang m; ~y ['hili] hügelig.

hilt [hilt] Griff m (bsd. am Degen).

him [him] ihn; ihm; den, dem(jenigen); ~self [him'self] (er, ihm, ihn, sich) selbst; sich; of ~ von selbst; by ~ allein.

hind¹ zo. [haind] Hirschkuh f.

hind² [~] Hinter...; ~er 1. ['haində] hintere(r, -s); Hinter...; 2. ['hində] v/t. hindern (from an dat.); hemmen; ~most ['haindmoust] hinterst, letzt.

hindrance ['hindrəns] Hindernis n.

hinge [hindʒ] 1. Türangel f; Scharnier n; fig. Angelpunkt m; 2. ~ upon fig. abhängen von.

hint [hint] 1. Wink m; Anspielung f; 2. andeuten; anspielen (at auf acc.).

hinterland ['hintəlænd] Hinterland n. [butte f.\

hip [hip] anat. Hüfte f; ♀ Hage-\

hippopotamus zo. [hipə'potəməs] Flußpferd n.

hire ['haiə] 1. Miete f; Entgelt m, n, Lohn m; 2. mieten; j-n anstellen; ~ out vermieten.

his [hiz] sein(e); der (die, das) seinige.

hiss [his] v/i. zischen; zischeln; v/t. a. ~ off auszischen, auspfeifen.

histor|ian [his'tɔ:riən] Historiker m; ~ic(al □) [his'tɔrik(əl)] historisch, geschichtlich; Geschichts...; ~y ['histəri] Geschichte f.

hit [hit] 1. Schlag m, Stoß m; fig. (Seiten)Hieb m; (Glücks)Treffer m; thea., ♪ Schlager m; 2. [irr.] schlagen, stoßen; treffen; auf et. stoßen; Am. F eintreffen in (dat.) ~ s.o. a blow j-m e-n Schlag versetzen; ~ it off with F sich vertragen mit; ~ (up)on (zufällig) kommen od. stoßen od. verfallen auf (acc.).

hitch [hitʃ] 1. Ruck m; ♫ Knoten m; fig. Haken m, Hindernis n; 2. rükken; (sich) festmachen, festhaken; hängenbleiben; rutschen; ~hike F ['hitʃhaik] per Anhalter fahren.

hither lit. ['hiðə] hierher; ~to bisher.

hive [haiv] 1. Bienenstock m; Bienenschwarm m; fig. Schwarm m; 2. ~ up aufspeichern; zs.-wohnen.

hoard [hɔ:d] 1. Vorrat m, Schatz m; 2. a. ~ up aufhäufen; horten.

hoarfrost ['hɔ:'frɔst] (Rauh)Reif m.

hoarse □ [hɔ:s] heiser, rauh.

hoary ['hɔ:ri] (alters)grau.

hoax [houks] 1. Täuschung f; Falschmeldung f; 2. foppen.

hob [hɔb] = hobgoblin; raise ~ bsd. Am. F Krach schlagen.

hobble ['hɔbl] **1.** Hinken *n*, Humpeln *n*; F Klemme *f*, Patsche *f*; **2.** *v/i.* humpeln, hinken (a. *fig.*); *v/t.* an den Füßen fesseln.

hobby ['hɔbi] *fig.* Steckenpferd *n*, Hobby *n*; ~**horse** Steckenpferd *n*; Schaukelpferd *n*.

hobgoblin ['hɔbgɔblin] Kobold *m*.

hobo *Am. sl.* ['houbou] Landstreicher *m*.

hock¹ [hɔk] Rheinwein *m*.

hock² *zo.* [~] Sprunggelenk *n*.

hod [hɔd] Mörteltrog *m*.

hoe ⚴ [hou] **1.** Hacke *f*; **2.** hacken.

hog [hɔg] **1.** Schwein *n* (a. *fig.*); **2.** *Mähne* stutzen; *mot.* drauflos rasen; ~**gish** □ ['hɔgiʃ] schweinisch; gefräßig.

hoist [hɔist] **1.** Aufzug *m*; **2.** hochziehen, hissen.

hokum *sl.* ['houkəm] Mätzchen *n/pl.*; Kitsch *m*; Humbug *m*.

hold [hould] **1.** Halten *n*; Halt *m*, Griff *m*; Gewalt *f*, Einfluß *m*; ⚓ Lade-, Frachtraum *m*; *catch* (*od. get, lay, take, seize*) ~ *of* erfassen, ergreifen; sich aneignen; *keep* ~ *of* festhalten; **2.** [*irr.*] *v/t.* allg. halten; fest-, aufhalten; enthalten; *fig.* behalten; *Versammlung etc.* abhalten; (inne)haben; *Ansicht* vertreten; *Gedanken etc.* hegen; halten für; glauben; behaupten; ~ *one's ground*, ~ *one's own* sich behaupten; ~ *the line* teleph. am Apparat bleiben; ~ *on et.* (an s-m Platz fest)halten; ~ *over* aufschieben; ~ *up* aufrecht halten; (unter-)stützen; aufhalten; (räuberisch) überfallen; *v/i.* (fest)halten; gelten; sich bewähren; standhalten; ~ *forth* Reden halten; ~ *good od. true* gelten; sich bestätigen; ~ *off* sich fernhalten; ~ *on* ausharren; fortdauern; sich festhalten; *teleph.* am Apparat bleiben; ~ *to* festhalten an (*dat.*); ~ *up* sich (aufrecht) halten; ~**er** ['houldə] Pächter *m*; Halter *m* (*Gerät*); Inhaber(in) (*bsd.* ✝); ~**ing** [~diŋ] Halten *n*; Halt *m*; Pachtgut *n*; Besitz *m*; ~ *company* Dachgesellschaft *f*; ~**over** *Am.* Rest *m*; ~**up** Raubüberfall *m*; Stauung *f*, Stockung *f*.

hole [houl] **1.** Loch *n*; Höhle *f*; F *fig.* Klemme *f*; *pick* ~*s in* bekritteln; **2.** aushöhlen; durchlöchern.

holiday ['hɔlədi] Feiertag *m*; freier Tag; ~*s pl.* Ferien *pl.*, Urlaub *m*; ~**maker** Urlauber(in).

holler *Am.* F ['hɔlə] laut rufen.

hollow ['hɔlou] **1.** □ hohl; leer; falsch; **2.** Höhle *f*, (Aus)Höhlung *f*; *Land*-Senke *f*; **3.** aushöhlen.

holly ⚘ ['hɔli] Stechpalme *f*.

holster ['houlstə] Pistolentasche *f*.

holy ['houli] heilig; ♀ *Thursday* Gründonnerstag *m*; ~ *water* Weihwasser *n*; ♀ *Week* Karwoche *f*.

homage ['hɔmidʒ] Huldigung *f*; *do od. pay od. render* ~ huldigen (*to dat.*).

home [houm] **1.** Heim *n*; Haus *n*, Wohnung *f*; Heimat *f*; Mal *n*; *at* ~ zu Hause; **2.** *adj.* (ein)heimisch, inländisch; wirkungsvoll; tüchtig (*Schlag etc.*); ♀ *Office* Innenministerium *n*; ~ *rule* Selbstregierung *f*; ♀ *Secretary* Innenminister *m*; ~ *trade* Binnenhandel *m*; **3.** *adv.* heim, nach Hause; an die richtige Stelle; gründlich; *hit od. strike* ~ den rechten Fleck treffen; ♀ *Counties* die Grafschaften um London; ~ *economics Am.* Hauswirtschaftslehre *f*; ~**felt** ['houmfelt] tief empfunden; ~**less** ['houmlis] heimatlos; ~**like** anheimelnd, gemütlich; ~**ly** [~li] anheimelnd, häuslich; *fig.* hausbacken; schlicht; anspruchslos; reizlos; ~**made** selbstgemacht; Hausmacher...; ~**sickness** Heimweh *n*; ~**stead** Anwesen *n*; ~ *team Sport:* Gastgeber *m/pl.*; ~**ward(s)** ['houmwəd(z)] heimwärts (gerichtet); Heim...; ~**work** Hausaufgabe(n *pl.*) *f*, Schularbeiten *f/pl.*

homicide ['hɔmisaid] Totschlag *m*; Mord *m*; Totschläger(in).

homogeneous □ [hɔmə'dʒiːnjəs] homogen, gleichartig.

hone ⊕ [houn] **1.** Abziehstein *m*; **2.** *Rasiermesser* abziehen.

honest □ ['ɔnist] ehrlich, rechtschaffen; aufrichtig; echt; ~**y** [~ti] Ehrlichkeit *f*, Rechtschaffenheit *f*; Aufrichtigkeit *f*.

honey ['hʌni] Honig *m*; *fig.* Liebling *m*; ~**comb** [~ikoum] (Honig-)Wabe *f*; ~**ed** ['hʌnid] honigsüß; ~**moon 1.** Flitterwochen *f/pl.*; **2.** die Flitterwochen verleben.

honk *mot.* [hɔŋk] hupen, tuten.

honky-tonk *Am. sl.* ['hɔŋkitɔŋk] Spelunke *f*.

honorary ['ɔnərəri] Ehren...; ehrenamtlich.

hono(u)r ['ɔnə] **1.** Ehre *f*; Achtung *f*; Würde *f*; *fig.* Zierde *f*; *Your* ♀ *Euer Gnaden*; **2.** (be)ehren; ✝ honorieren; ~**able** □ ['ɔnərəbl] ehrenvoll; redlich; ehrbar; ehrenwert.

hood [hud] **1.** Kapuze *f*; *mot.* Verdeck *n*; *Am.* (Motor)Haube *f*; ⊕ Kappe *f*; **2.** mit e-r Kappe *etc.* bekleiden; ein-, verhüllen.

hoodlum *Am.* F ['huːdləm] Strolch *m*.

hoodoo *bsd. Am.* ['huːduː] Unglücksbringer *m*; Pech *n* (*Unglück*).

hoodwink ['hudwiŋk] täuschen.

hooey *Am. sl.* ['huːi] Quatsch *m*.

hoof [huːf] Huf *m*; Klaue *f*.

hook [huk] **1.** (*bsd.* Angel)Haken *m*; Sichel *f*; *by* ~ *or by crook* so oder so;

2. (sich) (zu-, fest)haken; angeln (a. fig.); ~y ['huki] **1.** hakig; **2.:** play ~ Am. sl. (die Schule) schwänzen.

hoop [hu:p] **1.** Faß- etc. Reif(en) m; ⊕ Ring m; **2.** Fässer binden.

hooping-cough ♬ ['hu:piŋkɔf] Keuchhusten m.

hoot [hu:t] **1.** Geschrei n; **2.** v/i. heulen; johlen; mot. hupen; v/t. auspfeifen, auszischen.

Hoover ['hu:və] **1.** Staubsauger m; **2.** (mit e-m Staubsauger) saugen.

hop [hɔp] **1.** ♀ Hopfen m; Sprung m; F Tanzerei f; **2.** hüpfen, springen (über acc.).

hope [houp] **1.** Hoffnung f; **2.** hoffen (for auf acc.); ~ in vertrauen auf (acc.); ~ful □ ['houpful] hoffnungsvoll; ~less □ ['houplis] hoffnungslos; verzweifelt.

horde [hɔ:d] Horde f.

horizon [hə'raizn] Horizont m.

horn [hɔ:n] Horn n; Schalltrichter m; mot. Hupe f; ~s pl. Geweih n; ~ of plenty Füllhorn n.

hornet zo. ['hɔ:nit] Hornisse f.

horn|swoggle Am. sl. ['hɔ:nswɔgl] j-n 'reinlegen; ~y ['hɔ:ni] hornig; schwielig.

horr|ible □ ['hɔrəbl] entsetzlich; scheußlich; ~id □ ['hɔrid] gräßlich, abscheulich; schrecklich; ~ify ['~ifai] erschrecken; entsetzen; ~or ['hɔrə] Entsetzen n, Schauder m; Schrecken m; Greuel m.

horse [hɔ:s] zo. Pferd n; Reiterei f; Bock m, Gestell n; ~back ['hɔ:sbæk]: on ~ zu Pferde; ~hair Roßhaar n; ~laugh F wieherndes Lachen; ~man Reiter m; ~manship [~nʃip] Reitkunst f; ~ opera Am. drittklassiger Wildwestfilm; ~power Pferdestärke f; ~radish Meerrettich m; ~shoe Hufeisen n.

horticulture ['hɔ:tikʌltʃə] Gartenbau m.

hose [houz] Schlauch m; Strumpfhose f; coll. Strümpfe m/pl.

hosiery ['houʒəri] Strumpfwaren f/pl.

hospitable □ ['hɔspitəbl] gastfrei.

hospital ['hɔspitl] Krankenhaus n; ✕ Lazarett n; ~ity [hɔspi'tæliti] Gastfreundschaft f, Gastlichkeit f.

host [houst] Wirt m; Gastgeber m; Gastwirt m; fig. Heer n; Schwarm m; eccl. Hostie f.

hostage ['hɔstidʒ] Geisel m, f.

hostel ['hɔstəl] Herberge f; univ. Studenten(w)heim n.

hostess ['houstis] Wirtin f; Gastgeberin f; = air ~.

hostil|e □ ['hɔstail] feindlich (gesinnt); ~ity [hɔs'tiliti] Feindseligkeit f (to gegen).

hot [hɔt] heiß; scharf; beißend; hitzig, heftig; eifrig; warm (Speise, Fährte); Am. sl. falsch (Scheck); gestohlen; radioaktiv; ~bed ['hɔtbed] Mistbeet n; fig. Brutstätte f.

hotchpotch ['hɔtʃpɔtʃ] Mischmasch m; Gemüsesuppe f. [chen.)

hot dog F ['hɔt 'dɔg] heißes Würst-)

hotel [hou'tel] Hotel n.

hot|head ['hɔthed] Hitzkopf m; ~house Treibhaus n; ~pot Irish Stew n; ~ rod Am. sl. mot. frisiertes altes Auto; ~spur Hitzkopf m.

hound [haund] **1.** Jagd-, Spürhund m; fig. Hund m; **2.** jagen, hetzen.

hour ['auə] Stunde f; Zeit f, Uhr f; ~ly ['auəli] stündlich.

house 1. [haus] allg. Haus n; the ♀ das Unterhaus; die Börse; **2.** [hauz] v/t. unterbringen; v/i. hausen; ~agent ['hauseidʒənt] Häusermakler m; ~breaker ['hausbreikə] Abbrucharbeiter m; ~hold Haushalt m; attr. Haushalts...; Haus...; ~holder Hausherr m; ~keeper Haushälterin f; ~keeping Haushaltung f; ~maid Hausmädchen n; ~warming ['hauswɔ:miŋ] Einzugsfeier f; ~wife ['hauswaif] Hausfrau f; ['hʌzif] Nähtäschchen n; ~wifery ['hauswifəri] Haushaltung f; ~work Haus(halts)arbeit f/pl.

housing ['hauziŋ] Unterbringung f; Wohnung f; ~ estate Wohnsiedlung f.

hove [houv] pret. u. p.p. von heave 2.

hovel ['hɔvəl] Schuppen m; Hütte f.

hover ['hɔvə] schweben; lungern; fig. schwanken; ~craft Luftkissenfahrzeug n.

how [hau] wie; ~ do you do? Begrüßungsformel bei der Vorstellung; ~ about ...? wie steht's mit ...? ~ever [hau'evə] **1.** adv. wie auch (immer); wenn auch noch so ...; **2.** cj. jedoch.

howl [haul] **1.** heulen, brüllen; **2.** Geheul n; ~er ['haulə] Heuler m; sl. grober Fehler.

hub [hʌb] (Rad)Nabe f; fig. Mittel-, Angelpunkt m.

hubbub ['hʌbʌb] Tumult m, Lärm m.

hub(by) F ['hʌb(i)] (Ehe)Mann m.

huckleberry ♀ ['hʌklberi] amerikanische Heidelbeere f.

huckster ['hʌkstə] Hausierer(in).

huddle ['hʌdl] **1.** a. ~ together (sich) zs.-drängen, zs.-pressen; ~ (o.s.) up sich zs.-kauern; **2.** Gewirr n, Wirrwarr m. [cry Zetergeschrei n.)

hue [hju:] Farbe f; Hetze f; ~ and)

huff [hʌf] **1.** üble Laune; **2.** v/t. grob anfahren; beleidigen; v/i. wütend werden; schmollen.

hug [hʌg] **1.** Umarmung f; **2.** an sich drücken, umarmen; fig. festhalten an (dat.); sich dicht am Weg etc. halten.

huge □ [hju:dʒ] ungeheuer, riesig; ~ness ['hju:dʒnis] ungeheure Größe.

hulk fig. [hʌlk] Klotz m.

hull [hʌl] **1.** ♀ Schale *f*; Hülse *f*; ⚓ Rumpf *m*; **2.** enthülsen; schälen.
hullabaloo [hʌləbə'lu:] Lärm *m*.
hullo ['hʌ'lou] hallo (*bsd. teleph.*).
hum [hʌm] summen; brumme(l)n; *make things* ~ F Schwung in die Sache bringen.
human ['hju:mən] **1.** ☐ menschlich; ~ly nach menschlichem Ermessen; **2.** F Mensch *m*; ~e ☐ [hju(:)'mein] human, menschenfreundlich; ~i~ tarian [hju(:)'mæni'teəriən] **1.** Menschenfreund *m*; **2.** menschenfreundlich; ~ity [hju(:)'mæniti] menschliche Natur; Menschheit *f*; Humanität *f*; ~kind ['hju:mən'kaind] Menschengeschlecht *n*.
humble ['hʌmbl] **1.** ☐ demütig; bescheiden; **2.** erniedrigen; demütigen.
humble-bee ['hʌmblbi:] Hummel *f*.
humbleness ['hʌmblnis] Demut *f*.
humbug ['hʌmbʌg] **1.** (be)schwindeln; **2.** Schwindel *m*.
humdinger *Am. sl.* [hʌm'diŋə] Mordskerl *m*, -sache *f*.
humdrum ['hʌmdrʌm] eintönig.
humid ['hju:mid] feucht, naß; ~ity [hju(:)'miditi] Feuchtigkeit *f*.
humiliat|e [hju(:)'milieit] erniedrigen, demütigen; ~ion [hju(:)milii'eiʃən] Erniedrigung *f*, Demütigung *f*.
humility [hju(:)'militi] Demut *f*.
humming F ['hʌmiŋ] mächtig, gewaltig; ~bird *zo.* Kolibri *m*.
humorous ☐ ['hju:mərəs] humoristisch, humorvoll; spaßig.
humo(u)r ['hju:mə] **1.** Laune *f*, Stimmung *f*; Humor *m*; *das* Spaßige; ⚕ *hist.* Körpersaft *m*; *out of* ~ schlecht gelaunt; *j-m* ~ *in* Willen lassen; eingehen auf (*acc.*).
hump [hʌmp] **1.** Höcker *m*, Buckel *m*; **2.** krümmen; ärgern, verdrießen; ~ *o.s. Am. sl.* sich daranhalten; ~back ['hʌmpbæk] = hunchback.
hunch [hʌntʃ] **1.** Höcker *m*; großes Stück; *Am.* F Ahnung *f*; **2.** a. ~ *out*, ~ *up* krümmen; ~back ['hʌntʃbæk] Bucklige(r *m*) *f*.
hundred ['hʌndrəd] **1.** hundert; **2.** Hundert *n*; ~th [~dθ] **1.** hundertste; **2.** Hundertstel *n*; ~weight englischer Zentner (*50,8 kg*).
hung [hʌŋ] *1. pret. u. p.p. von* hang 1; *2. adj.* abgehangen (*Fleisch*).
Hungarian [hʌŋ'geəriən] **1.** ungarisch; **2.** Ungar(in); Ungarisch *n*.
hunger ['hʌŋgə] **1.** Hunger *m* (*a. fig.*; for nach); **2.** *v/i.* hungern (for, after nach); *v/t.* durch Hunger zwingen (*into* zu).
hungry ☐ ['hʌŋgri] hungrig.
hunk F [hʌŋk] dickes Stück.
hunt [hʌnt] **1.** Jagd *f* (for nach); Jagd(revier *n*) *f*; Jagd(gesellschaft) *f*; **2.** jagen; *Revier* bejagen; hetzen; ~ *out od.* up aufspüren; ~ *for*, ~ *after*

Jagd machen auf (*acc.*); ~er ['hʌntə] Jäger *m*; Jagdpferd *n*; ~ing [~tiŋ] Jagen *n*; Verfolgung *f*; *attr.* Jagd...; ~ing-ground Jagdrevier *n*; ~sman [~tsmən] Jäger *m*; Rüdemann *m* (*Meutenführer*).
hurdle ['hə:dl] Hürde *f* (*a. fig.*); ~r [~lə] Hürdenläufer(in); ~-race Hürdenrennen *n*.
hurl [hə:l] **1.** Schleudern *n*; **2.** schleudern; *Worte* ausstoßen.
hurricane ['hʌrikən] Orkan *m*.
hurried ☐ ['hʌrid] eilig; übereilt.
hurry ['hʌri] **1.** (große) Eile, Hast *f*; *be in a* ~ es eilig haben; *not ... in a* ~ F nicht so bald, nicht so leicht; **2.** *v/t.* (an)treiben; drängen; *et.* beschleunigen; eilig schicken *od.* bringen; *v/i.* eilen, hasten; ~ *up* sich beeilen.
hurt [hə:t] **1.** Verletzung *f*; Schaden *m*; **2.** [*irr.*] verletzen (*a. fig.*); weh tun (*dat.*); schaden (*dat.*).
husband ['hʌzbənd] **1.** (Ehe)Mann *m*; **2.** haushalten mit; verwalten; ~man Landwirt *m*; ~ry [~dri] Landwirtschaft *f*, Ackerbau *m*.
hush [hʌʃ] **1.** still! **2.** Stille *f*; **3.** *v/t.* zum Schweigen bringen; beruhigen; *Stimme* dämpfen; ~ *up* vertuschen; *v/i.* still sein; ~-money ['hʌʃmʌni] Schweigegeld *n*.
husk [hʌsk] **1.** ♀ Hülse *f*, Schote *f*; Schale *f* (*a. fig.*); **2.** enthülsen; ~y ['hʌski] ☐ hülsig; trocken; heiser; F stramm, stämmig; **2.** F stämmiger Kerl.
hussy ['hʌsi] Flittchen *n*; Range *f*.
hustle ['hʌsl] **1.** *v/t.* (an)rempeln; stoßen; drängen; *v/i.* (sich) drängen; *bsd. Am.* mit Hochdruck arbeiten; **2.** Hochbetrieb *m*; Rührigkeit *f*; ~ *and bustle* Gedränge und Gehetze *n*.
hut [hʌt] Hütte *f*; ✂ Baracke *f*.
hutch [hʌtʃ] Kasten *m*; *bsd. Kaninchen*-Stall *m* (*a. fig.*); Trog *m*.
hyacinth ♀ ['haiəsinθ] Hyazinthe *f*.
hyaena *zo.* [hai'i:nə] Hyäne *f*.
hybrid Ⓠ ['haibrid] Bastard *m*, Mischling *m*; Kreuzung *f*; *attr.* Bastard...; Zwitter...; ~ize [~daiz] kreuzen.
hydrant ['haidrənt] Hydrant *m*.
hydro|... Ⓠ ['haidrou] Wasser...; ~carbon Kohlenwasserstoff *m*; ~chloric acid [~ə'klɔrikæsid] Salzsäure *f*; ~gen [~ridʒən] Wasserstoff *m*; ~gen bomb Wasserstoffbombe *f*; ~pathy [hai'drɔpəθi] Wasserheilkunde *f*; Wasserkur *f*; ~phobia [haidrə'foubjə] Wasserscheu *f*; ✝ Tollwut *f*; ~plane ['haidrouplein] Wasserflugzeug *n*; (Motor)Gleitboot *n*, Rennboot *n*.
hyena *zo.* [hai'i:nə] Hyäne *f*.
hygiene ['haidʒi:n] Hygiene *f*.
hymn [him] **1.** Hymne *f*; Lobgesang *m*; Kirchenlied *n*; **2.** preisen.

hyphen ['haifən] 1. Bindestrich *m*; 2. mit Bindestrich schreiben *od.* verbinden; ~ated [~neitid] mit Bindestrich geschrieben; ~ *Americans pl.* Halb-Amerikaner *m/pl.* (*z. B. German-Americans*). [ren.]
hypnotize ['hipnətaiz] hypnotisie-|
hypo|chondriac [haipou'kɔndriæk] Hypochonder *m*; ~crisy [hi'pɔ-

krəsi] Heuchelei *f*; ~crite ['hipə-krit] Heuchler(in); Scheinheilige(r *m*) *f*; ~critical □ [hipə'kritikəl] heuchlerisch; ~thesis [hai'pɔθisis] Hypothese *f*.
hyster|ia ⚕ [his'tiəriə] Hysterie *f*; ~ical □ [~'terikəl] hysterisch; ~ics [~ks] *pl.* hysterischer Anfall; *go into* ~ hysterisch werden.

I

I [ai] ich.
ice [ais] 1. Eis *n*; 2. gefrieren lassen; *a.* ~ *up* vereisen; *Kuchen* mit Zuk-kerguß überziehen; in Eis kühlen; ~-age ['aiseidʒ] Eiszeit *f*; ~berg ['aisbə:g] Eisberg *m* (*a. fig.*); ~-bound eingefroren; ~-box Eis-schrank *m*; *Am. a.* Kühlschrank *m*; ~-cream Speiseeis *n*; ~-floe Eis-scholle *f*.
icicle ['aisikl] Eiszapfen *m*.
icing ['aisiŋ] Zuckerguß *m*; Ver-eisung *f*.
icy □ ['aisi] eisig (*a. fig.*); vereist.
idea [ai'diə] Idee *f*; Begriff *m*; Vorstellung *f*; Gedanke *m*; Mei-nung *f*; Ahnung *f*; Plan *m*; ~l [~əl] 1. □ ideell; eingebildet; ideal; 2. Ideal *n*.
identi|cal □ [ai'dentikəl] identisch, gleich(bedeutend); ~fication [aidentifi'keiʃən] Identifizierung *f*; Ausweis *m*; ~fy [ai'dentifai] identi-fizieren; ausweisen; erkennen; ~ty [~iti] Identität *f*; Persönlichkeit *f*, Eigenart *f*; ~ *card* Personalaus-weis *m*, Kennkarte *f*; ~ *disk* ⚔ Er-kennungsmarke *f*.
ideological □ [aidiə'lɔdʒikəl] ideo-logisch.
idiom ['idiəm] Idiom *n*; Mundart *f*; Redewendung *f*.
idiot ['idiət] Idiot(in), Schwach-sinnige(r *m*) *f*; ~ic [idi'ɔtik] (~ally) blödsinnig.
idle ['aidl] 1. □ müßig, untätig; träg, faul; unnütz; nichtig; ~ *hours pl.* Mußestunden *f/pl.*; 2. *v/t. mst* ~ *away* vertrödeln; *v/i.* faulenzen; ⊕ leer laufen; ~ness ['aidlnis] Muße *f*; Trägheit *f*; Nichtigkeit *f*; ~r ['aidlə] Müßiggänger(in).
idol ['aidl] Idol *n*, Götzenbild *n*; *fig.* Abgott *m*; ~atrous □ [ai'dɔlə-trəs] abgöttisch; ~atry [~ri] Ab-götterei *f*; Vergötterung *f*; ~ize ['aidəlaiz] vergöttern.
dyl(1) ['idil] Idyll(e *f*) *n*.
if [if] 1. wenn, falls; ob; 2. Wenn *n*; ~fy *Am.* F ['ifi] zweifelhaft.
ignit|e [ig'nait] (sich) entzünden; zünden; ~ion [ig'niʃən] 🔧 Entzün-dung *f*; *mot.* Zündung *f*.

ignoble □ [ig'noubl] unedel; niedrig, gemein.
ignominious □ [ignə'miniəs] schändlich, schimpflich.
ignor|ance ['ignərəns] Unwissen-heit *f*; ~ant [~nt] unwissend; un-kundig; ~e [ig'nɔ:] ignorieren, nicht beachten; ⛪ verwerfen.
ill [il] 1. *adj. u. adv.* übel, böse; schlimm, schlecht; krank; *adv.* kaum; *fall* ~, *be taken* ~ krank wer-den; 2. Übel *n*; Üble(s) *n*, Böse(s)*n*.
ill-advised □ ['iləd'vaizd] schlecht beraten; unbesonnen, unklug; ~-bred ungebildet, ungezogen; ~ *breeding* schlechtes Benehmen.
illegal □ [i'li:gəl] ungesetzlich.
illegible □ [i'ledʒəbl] unleserlich.
illegitimate □ [ili'dʒitimit] illegi-tim; unrechtmäßig; unehelich.
ill-|favo(u)red □ [il'feivəd] häßlich; ~-humo(u)red übellaunig.
illiberal □ [i'libərəl] engstirnig; intolerant; knauserig.
illicit □ [i'lisit] unerlaubt.
illiterate □ [i'litərit] 1. ungelehrt, ungebildet; 2. Analphabet(in).
ill-|judged ['il'dʒʌdʒd] unklug, un-vernünftig; ~-mannered unge-zogen; mit schlechten Umgangs-formen; ~-natured □ boshaft, bös-artig.
illness ['ilnis] Krankheit *f*.
illogical □ [i'lɔdʒikəl] unlogisch.
ill-|starred ['il'stɑ:d] unglücklich; ~-tempered schlecht gelaunt; ~-timed ungelegen; ~-treat miß-handeln.
illuminat|e [i'lju:mineit] be-, er-leuchten (*a. fig.*); erläutern; auf-klären; ~ing □ *fig.* Leucht...; *fig.* aufschlußreich; ~ion [ilju:mi'nei-ʃən] Er-, Beleuchtung *f*; Erläute-rung *f*; Aufklärung *f*.
ill-use ['il'ju:z] mißhandeln.
illus|ion [i'lu:ʒən] Illusion *f*, Täu-schung *f*; ~ive [i'lu:siv], ~ory □ [~səri] illusorisch, täuschend.
illustrat|e ['iləstreit] illustrieren; erläutern; bebildern; ~ion [iləs-'treiʃən] Erläuterung *f*; Illustra-tion *f*; ~ive □ ['iləstreitiv] erläu-ternd.

illustrious □ [i'lʌstriəs] berühmt.
ill will ['il'wil] Feindschaft f.
image ['imidʒ] Bild n; Standbild n; Ebenbild n; Vorstellung f; ~ry [~dʒəri] Bilder n/pl.; Bildersprache f, Metaphorik f.
imagin|able □ [i'mædʒinəbl] denkbar; ~ary [~əri] eingebildet; ~ation [imædʒi'neiʃən] Einbildung(skraft) f; ~ative □ [i'mædʒinətiv] ideenreich; ~e [i'mædʒin] sich et. einbilden od. vorstellen od. denken.
imbecile □ ['imbisi:l] 1. geistesschwach; 2. Schwachsinnige(r m) f.
imbibe [im'baib] einsaugen; fig. sich zu eigen machen.
imbue [im'bju:] (durch)tränken; tief färben; fig. erfüllen.
imitat|e ['imiteit] nachahmen; imitieren; ~ion [imi'teiʃən] 1. Nachahmung f; 2. künstlich, Kunst...
immaculate □ [i'mækjulit] unbefleckt, rein; fehlerlos.
immaterial □ [imə'tiəriəl] unkörperlich; unwesentlich (to für).
immature [imə'tjuə] unreif.
immeasurable □ [i'meʒərəbl] unermeßlich.
immediate □ [i'mi:djət] unmittelbar; unverzüglich, sofortig; ~ly [~tli] 1. adv. sofort; 2. cj. gleich nachdem.
immense □ [i'mens] ungeheuer.
immerse [i'mə:s] (ein-, unter)tauchen; fig. ~ o.s. in sich versenken od. vertiefen in (acc.).
immigra|nt ['imigrənt] Einwanderer(in); ~te [~greit] v/i. einwandern; v/t. ansiedeln (into in dat.); ~tion [imi'greiʃən] Einwanderung f.
imminent □ ['iminənt] bevorstehend, drohend.
immobile [i'moubail] unbeweglich.
immoderate □ [i'mɔdərit] maßlos.
immodest □ [i'mɔdist] unbescheiden; unanständig.
immoral □ [i'mɔrəl] unmoralisch.
immortal [i'mɔ:tl] 1. □ unsterblich; 2. Unsterbliche(r m) f; ~ity [imɔ:'tæliti] Unsterblichkeit f.
immovable [i'mu:vəbl] 1. □ unbeweglich; unerschütterlich; 2. ~s pl. Immobilien pl.
immun|e [i'mju:n] immun, gefeit (from gegen); ~ity [~niti] Immunität f, Freiheit f (from von); Unempfänglichkeit f (für).
immutable □ [i'mju:təbl] unveränderlich.
imp [imp] Teufelchen n; Schelm m.
impact ['impækt] (Zs.-)Stoß m; Anprall m; Einwirkung f.
impair [im'pɛə] schwächen; (ver-)mindern; beeinträchtigen.
impart [im'pɑ:t] verleihen; weitergeben.
impartial [im'pɑ:ʃəl] unparteiisch; ~ity ['impɑ:ʃi'æliti] Unparteilichkeit f, Objektivität f.

impassable □ [im'pɑ:səbl] ungangbar, unpassierbar.
impassible □ [im'pæsibl] unempfindlich; gefühllos (to gegen).
impassioned [im'pæʃənd] leidenschaftlich.
impassive □ [im'pæsiv] unempfindlich; teilnahmslos; heiter.
impatien|ce [im'peiʃəns] Ungeduld f; ~t □ [~nt] ungeduldig.
impeach [im'pi:tʃ] anklagen (of, with gen.); anfechten, anzweifeln.
impeccable □ [im'pekəbl] sündlos; makellos, einwandfrei.
impede [im'pi:d] (ver)hindern.
impediment [im'pedimənt] Hindernis n.
impel [im'pel] (an)treiben.
impend [im'pend] hängen, schweben; bevorstehen, drohen.
impenetrable □ [im'penitrəbl] undurchdringlich; fig. unergründlich; fig. unzugänglich (to dat.).
impenitent □ [im'penitənt] unbußfertig, verstockt.
imperative [im'perətiv] 1. □ notwendig, dringend, unbedingt erforderlich; befehlend; gebieterisch; gr. imperativisch; 2. Befehl m; a. ~ mood gr. Imperativ m, Befehlsform f. [unmerklich.]
imperceptible □ [impə'septəbl]
imperfect [im'pə:fikt] 1. □ unvollkommen; unvollendet; 2. a. ~ tense gr. Imperfekt n.
imperial [im'piəriəl] kaiserlich; Reichs...; majestätisch; großartig; ~ism [~lizəm] Imperialismus m, Weltmachtpolitik f.
imperil [im'peril] gefährden.
imperious □ [im'piəriəs] gebieterisch, anmaßend; dringend.
imperishable □ [im'periʃəbl] unvergänglich.
impermeable □ [im'pə:mjəbl] undurchdringlich, undurchlässig.
impersonal □ [im'pə:snl] unpersönlich.
impersonate [im'pə:səneit] verkörpern; thea. darstellen.
impertinen|ce [im'pə:tinəns] Unverschämtheit f; Nebensächlichkeit f; ~t □ [~nt] unverschämt; ungehörig; nebensächlich.
imperturbable □ [impə(:)'tə:bəbl] unerschütterlich.
impervious □ [im'pə:vjəs] unzugänglich (to für); undurchlässig.
impetu|ous □ [im'petjuəs] ungestüm, heftig; ~s ['impitəs] Antrieb m.
impiety [im'paiəti] Gottlosigkeit f.
impinge [im'pindʒ] v/i. (ver)stoßen (on, upon, against gegen).
impious □ ['impiəs] gottlos; pietätlos; frevelhaft.
implacable □ [im'plækəbl] unversöhnlich, unerbittlich.
implant [im'plɑ:nt] einpflanzen.

implement 1. ['implimənt] Werkzeug *n*; Gerät *n*; **2.** [ˌiment] ausführen.

implicat|e ['implikeit] verwickeln; in sich schließen; ~ion [impli'keiʃən] Verwick(e)lung *f*; Folgerung *f*.

implicit □ [im'plisit] mit eingeschlossen; blind (*Glaube etc.*).

implore [im'plɔ:] (an-, er)flehen.

imply [im'plai] mit einbegreifen, enthalten; bedeuten; andeuten.

impolite □ [impə'lait] unhöflich.

impolitic □ [im'pɔlitik] unklug.

import 1. ['impɔ:t] Bedeutung *f*; Wichtigkeit *f*; Einfuhr *f*; ~s *pl*. Einfuhrwaren *f/pl.*; **2.** [im'pɔ:t] einführen; bedeuten; ~ance [ˌtəns] Wichtigkeit *f*; ~ant □ [ˌnt] wichtig; wichtigtuerisch; ~ation [impɔ:'teiʃən] Einfuhr(waren *f/pl.*) *f*.

importun|ate □ [im'pɔ:tjunit] lästig; zudringlich; ~e [im'pɔ:tju:n] dringend bitten; belästigen.

impos|e [im'pouz] *v/t.* auf(er)legen, aufbürden (*on, upon dat.*); *v/i.* ~ *upon j-m* imponieren; *j-n* täuschen; ~ition [impə'ziʃən] Auf(er)legung *f*; Steuer *f*; Strafarbeit *f*; Betrügerei *f*.

impossib|ility [impɔsə'biliti] Unmöglichkeit *f*; ~le □ [im'pɔsəbl] unmöglich.

impost|or [im'pɔstə] Betrüger *m*; ~ure [ˌtʃə] Betrug *m*.

impoten|ce ['impətəns] Unfähigkeit *f*; Machtlosigkeit *f*; ~t □ [ˌnt] unvermögend, machtlos, schwach.

impoverish [im'pɔvəriʃ] arm machen; *Boden* auslaugen.

impracticable □ [im'præktikəbl] undurchführbar; unwegsam.

impractical [im'præktikəl] unpraktisch; theoretisch; unnütz.

imprecate ['imprikeit] *Böses* herabwünschen (*upon* auf *acc.*).

impregn|able □ [im'pregnəbl] uneinnehmbar; unüberwindlich; ~ate ['impregneit] schwängern; ⚔ sättigen; ⊕ imprägnieren.

impress 1. ['impres] (Ab-, Ein-)Druck *m*; *fig.* Stempel *m*; **2.** [im'pres] eindrücken, prägen; *Kraft etc.* übertragen; *Gedanken etc.* einprägen (*on dat.*); *j-n* beeindrucken; *j-n mit et.* erfüllen; ~ion [ˌeʃən] Eindruck *m*; *typ.* Abdruck *m*; Abzug *m*; Auflage *f*; *be under the ~ that* den Eindruck haben, daß; ~ive □ [ˌesiv] eindrucksvoll.

imprint 1. [im'print] aufdrücken, prägen; *fig.* einprägen (*on, in dat.*); **2.** ['imprint] Eindruck *m*; Stempel *m* (*a. fig.*); *typ.* Druckvermerk *m*.

imprison [im'prizn] inhaftieren; ~ment [ˌnment] Haft *f*; Gefängnis (-strafe *f*) *n*.

improbable □ [im'prɔbəbl] unwahrscheinlich.

improper □ [im'prɔpə] ungeeignet, unpassend; falsch; unanständig.

impropriety [imprə'praiəti] Ungehörigkeit *f*; Unanständigkeit *f*.

improve [im'pru:v] *v/t.* verbessern; veredeln; aus-, benutzen; *v/i.* sich (ver)bessern; ~ *upon* vervollkommnen; ~ment [ˌvmənt] Verbesserung *f*, Vervollkommnung *f*; Fortschritt *m* (*on, upon* gegenüber *dat.*).

improvise ['imprəvaiz] improvisieren.

imprudent □ [im'pru:dənt] unklug.

impuden|ce ['impjudəns] Unverschämtheit *f*, Frechheit *f*; ~t □ [ˌnt] unverschämt, frech.

impuls|e ['impʌls], ~ion [im'pʌlʃən] Impuls *m*, (An)Stoß *m*; *fig.* (An)Trieb *m*; ~ive □ [ˌlsiv] (an-) treibend; *fig.* impulsiv; rasch (handelnd).

impunity [im'pju:niti] Straflosigkeit *f*; *with* ~ ungestraft.

impure □ [im'pjuə] unrein (*a. fig.*); unkeusch.

imput|ation [impju(:)'teiʃən] Beschuldigung *f*; ~e [im'pju:t] zurechnen, beimessen; zur Last legen.

in [in] **1.** *prp. allg.* in (*dat.*); *engS.*: (~ *the morning*, ~ *number*, ~ *itself*, *professor* ~ *the university*) an (*dat.*); (~ *the street*, ~ *English*) auf (*dat.*); (~ *this manner*) auf (*acc.*); (~ *velvet*) aus; (~ *Shakespeare*, ~ *the daytime*, ~ *crossing the road*) bei; (*engaged* ~ *reading*, ~ *a word*) mit; (~ *my opinion*) nach; (*rejoice* ~ *s.th.*) über (*acc.*); (~ *the circumstances*, ~ *the reign of*, *one* ~ *ten*) unter (*dat.*); (*cry out* ~ *alarm*) vor (*dat.*); (*grouped* ~ *tens*, *speak* ~ *reply*, ~ *excuse*, ~ *honour of*) zu; ~ *1949* im Jahre 1949; ~ *that* ... *insofern als*, weil; **2.** *adv.* drin(nen); herein; hinein; *be* ~ *for et.* zu erwarten haben; *e-e Prüfung etc.* vor sich haben; F *be well* ~ *with* sich gut mit *j-m* stehen; **3.** *adj.* hereinkommend; Innen...

inability [inə'biliti] Unfähigkeit *f*.

inaccessible □ [inæk'sesəbl] unzugänglich. [unrichtig.]

inaccurate □ [in'ækjurit] ungenau;]

inactiv|e □ [in'æktiv] untätig, ♀ lustlos; ⚙ unwirksam; ~ity [inæk'tiviti] Untätig-, Lustlosigkeit *f*.

inadequate □ [in'ædikwit] unangemessen; unzulänglich.

inadmissible □ [inəd'misəbl] unzulässig.

inadvertent □ [inəd'və:tənt] unachtsam; unbeabsichtigt, versehentlich.

inalienable □ [in'eiljənəbl] unveräußerlich.

inane □ [i'nein] *fig.* leer; albern.

inanimate □ [in'ænimit] leblos; *fig.* unbelebt; geistlos, langweilig.

inapproachable [inə'proutʃəbl] unnahbar, unzugänglich.

inappropriate □ [inə'proupriit] unangebracht, unpassend.

inapt □ [in'æpt] ungeeignet, untauglich; ungeschickt; unpassend.

inarticulate □ [inɑː'tikjulit] undeutlich; schwer zu verstehen(d); undeutlich sprechend.

inasmuch [inəz'mʌtʃ]: ~ *as* insofern als. [merksam.]

inattentive □ [inə'tentiv] unauf-)

inaudible □ [in'ɔːdəbl] unhörbar.

inaugura|l [i'nɔːgjurəl] Antrittsrede *f*; *attr.* Antritts...; **~te** [~reit] (feierlich) einführen, einweihen; beginnen; **~tion** [inɔːgju'reiʃən] Einführung *f*, Einweihung *f*; ♀ *Day Am.* Amtseinführung *f* des neugewählten Präsidenten der USA.

inborn ['in'bɔːn] angeboren.

incalculable □ [in'kælkjuləbl] unberechenbar; unzählig.

incandescent [inkæn'desnt] weiß glühend; Glüh...

incapa|ble □ [in'keipəbl] unfähig, ungeeignet (*of* zu); **~citate** [inkə'pæsiteit] unfähig machen; **~city** [~ti] Unfähigkeit *f*.

incarnate [in'kɑːnit] Fleisch geworden; *fig.* verkörpert.

incautious □ [in'kɔːʃəs] unvorsichtig.

incendiary [in'sendjəri] **1.** brandstifterisch; *fig.* aufwieglerisch; **2.** Brandstifter *m*; Aufwiegler *m*.

incense[1] ['insens] Weihrauch *m*.

incense[2] [in'sens] in Wut bringen.

incentive [in'sentiv] Antrieb *m*.

incessant □ [in'sesnt] unaufhörlich.

incest ['insest] Blutschande *f*.

inch [intʃ] Zoll *m* (2,54 cm); *fig. ein* bißchen; by **~es** allmählich; *every ~* ganz (u. gar).

inciden|ce ['insidəns] Vorkommen *n*; Wirkung *f*; **~t** [~nt] **1.** (*to*) vorkommend (bei), eigen (*dat.*); **2.** Zu-, Vor-, Zwischenfall *m*; Nebenumstand *m*; **~tal** □ [insi'dentl] zufällig, gelegentlich; Neben...; *be ~ to* gehören zu; **~ly** nebenbei.

incinerate [in'sinəreit] einäschern; Müll verbrennen.

incis|e [in'saiz] einschneiden; **~ion** [in'siʒən] Einschnitt *m*; **~ive** □ [in'saisiv] (ein)schneidend, scharf; **~or** [~aizə] Schneidezahn *m*.

incite [in'sait] anspornen, anregen, anstiften; **~ment** [~tmənt] Anregung *f*; Ansporn *m*; Anstiftung *f*.

inclement [in'klemənt] rauh.

inclin|ation [inkli'neiʃən] Neigung *f* (*a. fig.*); **~e** [in'klain] **1.** *v/i.* sich neigen (*a. fig.*); ~ *to fig.* zu et. neigen; *v/t.* neigen; geneigt machen; **2.** Neigung *f*, Abhang *m*.

inclos|e [in'klouz], **~ure** [~ouʒə] *s.* enclose, enclosure.

inclu|de [in'kluːd] einschließen; enthalten; **~sive** □ [~uːsiv] einschließlich; alles einbegriffen; *be ~ of* einschließen; ~ *terms pl.* Pauschalpreis *m*.

incoheren|ce, ~cy [inkou'hiərəns, ~si] Zs.-hangslosigkeit *f*; Inkonsequenz *f*; **~t** □ [~nt] unzs.-hängend; inkonsequent.

income ['inkəm] Einkommen *n*; **~-tax** Einkommensteuer *f*.

incommode [inkə'moud] belästigen.

incommunica|do *bsd. Am.* [inkəmjuːni'kɑːdou] ohne Verbindung mit der Außenwelt; **~tive** □ [in-kə'mjuːnikətiv] nicht mitteilsam, verschlossen.

incomparable □ [in'kɔmpərəbl] unvergleichlich.

incompatible □ [inkəm'pætəbl] unvereinbar; unverträglich.

incompetent [in'kɔmpitənt] unfähig; unzuständig, unbefugt.

incomplete □ [inkəm'pliːt] unvollständig; unvollkommen.

incomprehensible □ [inkəmpri-'hensəbl] unbegreiflich.

inconceivable □ [inkən'siːvəbl] unbegreiflich, unfaßbar.

incongruous □ [in'kɔŋgruəs] nicht übereinstimmend; unpassend.

inconsequent [in'kɔnsikwənt] inkonsequent, folgewidrig; **~ial** [inkɔnsi'kwenʃəl] unbedeutend; = *inconsequent*.

inconsidera|ble □ [inkən'sidərəbl] unbedeutend; **~te** □ [~rit] unüberlegt; rücksichtslos.

inconsisten|cy [inkən'sistənsi] Unvereinbarkeit *f*; Inkonsequenz *f*; **~t** □ [~nt] unvereinbar; widerspruchsvoll; inkonsequent.

inconsolable □ [inkən'souləbl] untröstlich.

inconstant □ [in'kɔnstənt] unbeständig; veränderlich.

incontinent □ [in'kɔntinənt] unmäßig; ausschweifend.

inconvenien|ce [inkən'viːnjəns] **1.** Unbequemlichkeit *f*; Unannehmlichkeit *f*; **2.** belästigen; **~t** □ [~nt] unbequem; ungelegen; lästig.

incorporate[1.] [in'kɔːpəreit] einverleiben (*into dat.*); (sich) vereinigen; *als Mitglied* aufnehmen; ⚖ī *als Körperschaft* eintragen; **2.** [~rit] einverleibt; vereinigt; **~ed** (amtlich) eingetragen; **~ion** [inkɔːpə'reiʃən] Einverleibung *f*; Verbindung *f*; [fehlerhaft; ungehörig.]

incorrect □ [inkə'rekt] unrichtig;)

incorrigible □ [in'kɔridʒəbl] unverbesserlich.

increas|e 1. [in'kriːs] *v/i.* zunehmen; sich vergrößern od. vermehren; *v/t.* vermehren, vergrößern; erhöhen; **2.** ['inkriːs] Zunahme *f*; Vergrößerung *f*; Zuwachs *m*; **~ingly** [in'kriːsiŋli] zunehmend, immer (*mit folgendem comp.*); ~ *difficult* immer schwieriger.

incredible □ [in'kredəbl] unglaublich.

incredul|ity [inkri'dju:liti] Unglaube *m*; ~ous □ [in'kredjuləs] ungläubig, skeptisch.

incriminate [in'krimineit] beschuldigen; belasten.

incrustation [inkrʌs'teiʃən] Verkrustung *f*; Kruste *f*; ⊕ Belag *m*.

incub|ate ['inkjubeit] (aus)brüten; ~ator [~tə] Brutapparat *m*.

inculcate ['inkʌlkeit] einschärfen (*upon dat.*).

incumbent [in'kʌmbənt] obliegend; *be ~ on s.o.* j-m obliegen.

incur [in'kə:] sich *et.* zuziehen; geraten in (*acc.*); *Verpflichtung* eingehen; *Verlust* erleiden.

incurable [in'kjuərəbl] 1. □ unheilbar; 2. Unheilbare(r *m*) *f*.

incurious □ [in'kjuəriəs] gleichgültig, uninteressiert.

incursion [in'kə:ʃən] *feindlicher* Einfall.

indebted [in'detid] verschuldet; *fig.* (zu Dank) verpflichtet.

indecen|cy [in'di:snsi] Unanständigkeit *f*; ~t □ [~nt] unanständig.

indecisi|on [indi'siʒən] Unentschlossenheit *f*; ~ve □ [~'saisiv] nicht entscheidend; unbestimmt.

indecorous □ [in'dekərəs] unpassend; ungehörig.

indeed [in'di:d] 1. *adv.* in der Tat, tatsächlich; wirklich; allerdings; 2. *int.* so?; nicht möglich!

indefatigable □ [indi'fætigəbl] unermüdlich.

indefensible □ [indi'fensəbl] unhaltbar.

indefinite □ [in'definit] unbestimmt; unbeschränkt; ungenau.

indelible □ [in'delibl] untilgbar.

indelicate [in'delikit] unfein; taktlos.

indemni|fy [in'demnifai] sicherstellen; *j-m* Straflosigkeit zusichern; entschädigen; ~ty [~iti] Sicherstellung *f*; Straflosigkeit *f*; Entschädigung *f*.

indent 1. [in'dent] einkerben, auszacken; eindrücken; ᵗᵇᵏ *Vertrag* mit Doppel ausfertigen; ~ *upon s.o. for s.th.* ✝ et. bei j-m bestellen; 2. ['indent] Kerbe *f*; Vertiefung *f*; ✝ Auslandsauftrag *m*; = *indenture*; ~ation [inden'teiʃən] Einkerbung *f*; Einschnitt *m*; ~ure [in'dentʃə] 1. Vertrag *m*; Lehrbrief *m*; 2. vertraglich verpflichten.

independen|ce [indi'pendəns] Unabhängigkeit *f*; Selbständigkeit *f*; Auskommen *n*; ♀ *Day Am.* Unabhängigkeitstag *m* (4. *Juli*); ~t □ [~nt] unabhängig; selbständig.

indescribable □ [indis'kraibəbl] unbeschreiblich.

indestructible □ [indis'trʌktəbl] unzerstörbar.

indeterminate □ [indi'tə:minit] unbestimmt.

index ['indeks] 1. (An)Zeiger *m*; Anzeichen *n*; Zeigefinger *m*; Index *m*; (Inhalts-, Namen-, Sach)Verzeichnis *n*; 2. *Buch* mit e-m Index versehen.

Indian ['indjən] 1. indisch; indianisch; 2. Inder(in); *a.* Red ~ Indianer(in); ~ *corn* Mais *m*; ~ *file: in* ~ im Gänsemarsch; ~ *pudding Am.* Maismehlpudding *m*; ~ *summer* Altweiber-, Nachsommer *m*.

Indiarubber ['indjə'rʌbə] Radiergummi *m*.

indicat|e ['indikeit] (an)zeigen; hinweisen auf (*acc.*); andeuten; ~ion [indi'keiʃən] Anzeige *f*; Anzeichen *n*; Andeutung *f*; ~ive [in'dikətiv] *a.* ~ *mood gr.* Indikativ *m*; ~or ['indikeitə] Anzeiger *m* (*a.* ⊕); *mot.* Blinker *m*.

indict [in'dait] anklagen (*for* wegen); ~ment [~tmənt] Anklage *f*.

indifferen|ce [in'difrəns] Gleichgültigkeit *f*; ~t □ [~nt] gleichgültig (*to* gegen); unparteiisch; (nur) mäßig; unwesentlich; unbedeutend.

indigenous [in'didʒinəs] eingeboren, einheimisch.

indigent □ ['indidʒənt] arm.

indigest|ible □ [indi'dʒestəbl] unverdaulich; ~ion [~tʃən] Verdauungsstörung *f*, Magenverstimmung *f*.

indign|ant □ [in'dignənt] entrüstet, empört, ungehalten; ~ation [indig'neiʃən] Entrüstung *f*; ~ity [in'digniti] Beleidigung *f*.

indirect □ [indi'rekt] indirekt; nicht direkt; *gr. a.* abhängig.

indiscre|et □ [indis'kri:t] unbesonnen; unachtsam; indiskret; ~tion [~reʃən] Unachtsamkeit *f*; Unbesonnenheit *f*; Indiskretion *f*.

indiscriminate □ [indis'kriminit] unterschieds-, wahllos.

indispensable □ [indis'pensəbl] unentbehrlich, unerläßlich.

indispos|ed [indis'pouzd] unpäßlich; abgeneigt; ~ition [indispə-'ziʃən] Abneigung *f* (*to* gegen); Unpäßlichkeit *f*.

indisputable □ [indis'pju:təbl] unbestreitbar, unstreitig.

indistinct □ [indis'tiŋkt] undeutlich; unklar.

indistinguishable □ [indis'tiŋgwiʃəbl] nicht zu unterscheiden(d).

indite [in'dait] ab-, verfassen.

individual [indi'vidjuəl] 1. □ persönlich, individuell; besondere(r, -s); einzeln; Einzel...; 2. Individuum *n*; ~ism [~lizəm] Individualismus *m*; ~ist [~ist] Individualist *m*; ~ity [individju'æliti] Individualität *f*.

indivisible □ [indi'vizəbl] unteilbar.

indolen|ce ['indələns] Trägheit *f*;

~t □ [~nt] indolent, träge, lässig; ~
schmerzlos.

indomitable □ [in'dɔmitəbl] unbezähmbar.

indoor ['indɔ:] im Hause (befindlich); Haus..., Zimmer..., *Sport:*
Hallen...; ~s ['in'dɔ:z] zu Hause;
im *od.* ins Haus.

indorse [in'dɔ:s] = *endorse etc.*

induce [in'dju:s] veranlassen;
~ment [~smənt] Anlaß *m,* Antrieb
m.

induct [in'dʌkt] einführen; ~ion
[~kʃən] Einführung *f,* Einsetzung *f*
in Amt, Pfründe; ⚡ Induktion *f.*

indulge [in'dʌldʒ] nachsichtig sein
gegen *j-n;* *j-m* nachgeben; ~ with
j-n erfreuen mit; ~ (*o.s.*) *in s.th.* sich
et. gönnen; sich *e-r* S. hin- *od.* ergeben; ~nce [~dʒəns] Nachsicht *f;*
Nachgiebigkeit *f;* Sichgehenlassen
n; Vergünstigung *f;* ~nt □ [~nt]
nachsichtig.

industri|al □ [in'dʌstriəl] gewerbe-
treibend, gewerblich; industriell;
Gewerbe...; Industrie...; ~ area
Industriebezirk *m;* ~ estate In-
striegebiet *n e-r Stadt;* ~ school
Gewerbeschule *f;* ~alist [~list]
Industrielle(r) *m;* ~alize [~laiz]
industrialisieren; ~ous □ [~iəs]
fleißig.

industry ['indəstri] Fleiß *m;* Gewerbe *n;* Industrie *f.*

inebriate 1. [i'ni:brieit] betrunken
machen; 2. [~iit] Trunkenbold *m.*

ineffable □ [in'efəbl] unaussprechlich.

ineffect|ive [ini'fektiv], ~ual □
[~tjuəl] unwirksam, fruchtlos.

inefficient □ [ini'fiʃənt] wirkungs-
los; (leistungs)unfähig.

inelegant □ [in'eligənt] unelegant,
geschmacklos.

ineligible □ [in'elidʒəbl] nicht
wählbar; ungeeignet; *bsd.* ✗ untauglich.

inept □ [i'nept] unpassend; albern.

inequality [ini(:)'kwɔliti] Ungleichheit *f;* Ungleichmäßigkeit *f;* Unebenheit *f.*

inequitable [in'ekwitəbl] unbillig.

inert □ [i'nə:t] träge; ~ia [i'nə:ʃjə],
~ness [i'nə:tnis] Trägheit *f.*

inescapable [inis'keipəbl] unent-
rinnbar.

inessential [ini'senʃəl] unwesentlich (*to* für).

inestimable □ [in'estiməbl] unschätzbar.

inevitab|le □ [in'evitəbl] unver-
meidlich; ~ly [~li] unweigerlich.

inexact □ [inig'zækt] ungenau.

inexcusable □ [iniks'kju:zəbl] un-
entschuldbar.

inexhaustible □ [inig'zɔ:stəbl] unerschöpflich; unermüdlich.

inexorable □ [in'eksərəbl] unerbittlich.

inexpedient □ [iniks'pi:djənt] unzweckmäßig, unpassend.

inexpensive □ [iniks'pensiv] nicht
teuer, billig, preiswert.

inexperience [iniks'piəriəns] Unerfahrenheit *f,* ~d [~st] unerfahren.

inexpert □ [ineks'pə:t] unerfahren.

inexplicable □ [in'eksplikəbl] unerklärlich.

inexpressi|ble □ [iniks'presəbl]
unaussprechlich; ~ve [~siv] aus-
druckslos.

inextinguishable □ [iniks'tiŋgwi-
ʃəbl] unauslöschlich.

inextricable □ [in'ekstrikəbl] un-
entwirrbar.

infallible □ [in'fæləbl] unfehlbar.

infam|ous □ ['infəməs] ehrlos;
schändlich; verrufen; ~y [~mi] Ehr-
losigkeit *f;* Schande *f;* Nieder-
tracht *f.*

infan|cy ['infənsi] Kindheit *f;* ⚖️
Minderjährigkeit *f;* ~t [~nt] Säugling *m;* (kleines) Kind; Minder-
jährige(r *m*) *f.*

infanti|le ['infəntail], ~ne [~ain]
kindlich; Kindes..., Kinder...; kindisch.

infantry ✗ ['infəntri] Infanterie *f.*

infatuate [in'fætjueit] betören; ~d
vernarrt (*with in acc.*).

infect [in'fekt] anstecken (*a. fig.*);
infizieren, verseuchen, verpesten;
~ion [~kʃən] Ansteckung *f;* ~ious
□ [~ʃəs], ~ive [~ktiv] ansteckend;
Ansteckungs...

infer [in'fə:] folgern, schließen;
~ence [~infərəns] Folgerung *f.*

inferior [in'fiəriə] 1. untere(r, -s);
minderwertig; zu niedriger *od.*
geringer als; untergeordnet (*dat.*);
unterlegen (*dat.*); 2. Geringere(r *m*)
f; Untergebene(r *m*) *f;* ~ity [infiəri-
'ɔriti] geringerer Wert *od.* Stand;
Unterlegenheit *f;* Minderwertig-
keit *f.*

infern|al □ [in'fə:nl] höllisch; ~o
[~nou] Inferno *n,* Hölle *f.*

infertile [in'fə:tail] unfruchtbar.

infest [in'fest] heimsuchen; verseuchen; *fig.* überschwemmen.

infidelity [infi'deliti] Unglaube *m;*
Untreue *f* (*to* gegen).

infiltrate [in'filtreit] *v/t.* durchdringen; *v/i.* durchsickern, eindringen.

infinite □ ['infinit] unendlich.

infinitive [in'finitiv] *a.* ~ mood *gr.*
Infinitiv *m,* Nennform *f.*

infinity [in'finiti] Unendlichkeit *f.*

infirm □ [in'fə:m] kraftlos, schwach;
~ary [~məri] Krankenhaus *n;* ~ity
[~miti] Schwäche *f* (*a. fig.*); Ge-
brechen *n.*

inflame [in'fleim] entflammen (*mst
fig.*); (sich) entzünden (*a. fig. u.* ⚕️).

inflamma|ble □ [in'flæməbl] ent-
zündlich; feuergefährlich; ~tion
[inflə'meiʃən] Entzündung *f;* ~tory

[in'flæmətəri] entzündlich; *fig.* aufrührerisch; hetzerisch; Hetz...

inflat|e [in'fleit] aufblasen, aufblähen (*a. fig.*); **~ion** [~eiʃən] Aufblähung *f*; ✝ Inflation *f*; *fig.* Aufgeblasenheit *f*.

inflect [in'flekt] biegen; *gr.* flektieren, beugen.

inflexi|ble □ [in'fleksəbl] unbiegsam; *fig.* unbeugsam; **~on** [~kʃən] Biegung *f*; *gr.* Flexion *f*, Beugung *f*; Modulation *f*.

inflict [in'flikt] auferlegen; zufügen; *Hieb* versetzen; *Strafe* verhängen; **~ion** [~kʃən] Auferlegung *f*; Zufügung *f*; Plage *f*.

influen|ce ['influəns] 1. Einfluß *m*; 2. beeinflussen; **~tial** □ [influ-'enʃəl] einflußreich.

influenza [influ'enzə] Grippe *f*.

influx ['inflʌks] Einströmen *n*; *fig.* Zufluß *m*, (Zu)Strom *m*.

inform [in'fɔːm] *v/t.* benachrichtigen, unterrichten (*of* von); *v/i.* anzeigen (*against* s.o. j.); **~al** □ [~ml] formlos, zwanglos; **~ality** [infɔː-'mæliti] Formlosigkeit *f*; Formfehler *m*; **~ation** [infə'meiʃən] Auskunft *f*; Nachricht *f*, Information *f*; **~ative** [in'fɔːmətiv] informatorisch; lehrreich; mitteilsam; **~er** [in'fɔːmə] Denunziant *m*; Spitzel *m*.

infrequent [in'friːkwənt] selten.

infringe [in'frindʒ] *a.* **~ upon** *Vertrag etc.* verletzen; übertreten.

infuriate [in'fjuərieit] wütend machen.

infuse [in'fjuːz] einflößen; aufgießen.

ingen|ious □ [in'dʒiːnjəs] geist-, sinnreich; erfinderisch; raffiniert; genial; **~uity** [indʒi'njuː(:)iti] Genialität *f*; **~uous** □ [in'dʒenjuəs] freimütig; unbefangen, naiv.

ingot ['ingət] Gold- *etc.* Barren *m*.

ingrati|ate [in'greiʃieit]: **~ o.s.** sich beliebt machen (*with* bei); **~tude** [~rætitjuːd] Undankbarkeit *f*.

ingredient [in'griːdjənt] Bestandteil *m*.

ingrowing ['ingrouiŋ] nach innen wachsend; eingewachsen.

inhabit [in'hæbit] bewohnen; **~able** [~təbl] bewohnbar; **~ant** [~ənt] Bewohner(in), Einwohner(in).

inhal|ation [inhə'leiʃən] Einatmung *f*; **~e** [in'heil] einatmen.

inherent □ [in'hiərənt] anhaftend; innewohnend, angeboren (*in dat.*).

inherit [in'herit] (er)erben; **~ance** [~təns] Erbteil *n*, Erbe *n*; Erbschaft *f*; *biol.* Vererbung *f*.

inhibit [in'hibit] (ver)hindern; verbieten; zurückhalten; **~ion** [inhi-'biʃən] Hemmung *f*; Verbot *n*.

inhospitable □ [in'hɔspitəbl] ungastlich, unwirtlich.

inhuman □ [in'hjuːmən] unmenschlich.

inimical □ [i'nimikəl] feindlich; schädlich.

inimitable □ [i'nimitəbl] unnachahmlich.

iniquity [i'nikwiti] Ungerechtigkeit *f*; Schlechtigkeit *f*.

initia|l [i'niʃəl] 1. □ Anfangs...; anfänglich; 2. Anfangsbuchstabe *m*; **~te 1.** [~ʃiit] Eingeweihte(r *m*) *f*; 2. [~ʃieit] beginnen; anbahnen; einführen, einweihen; **~tion** [iniʃi'eiʃən] Einleitung *f*; Einführung *f*, Einweihung *f*; **~ fee** *bsd. Am.* Aufnahmegebühr *f* (*Vereinigung*); **~tive** [i'niʃiətiv] Initiative *f*; einleitender Schritt; Entschlußkraft *f*; Unternehmungsgeist *m*; Volksbegehren *n*; **~tor** [~ieitə] Initiator *m*, Urheber *m*.

inject [in'dʒekt] einspritzen; **~ion** [~kʃən] Injektion *f*, Spritze *f*.

injudicious □ [indʒuː'diʃəs] unverständig, unklug, unüberlegt.

injunction [in'dʒʌŋkʃən] gerichtliche Verfügung; ausdrücklicher Befehl.

injur|e ['indʒə] (be)schädigen; schaden (*dat.*); verletzen; beleidigen; **~ious** [in'dʒuəriəs] schädlich; ungerecht; beleidigend; **~y** ['indʒəri] Unrecht *n*; Schaden *m*; Verletzung *f*; Beleidigung *f*.

injustice [in'dʒʌstis] Ungerechtigkeit *f*; Unrecht *n*.

ink [iŋk] 1. Tinte *f*; *mst printer's* **~** Druckerschwärze *f*; *attr.* Tinten...; 2. (mit Tinte) schwärzen; beklecksen.

inkling ['iŋkliŋ] Andeutung *f*; dunkle *od.* leise Ahnung.

ink|pot ['iŋkpɔt] Tintenfaß *n*; **~stand** Schreibzeug *n*; **~y** ['iŋki] tintig; Tinten...; tintenschwarz.

inland 1. ['inlənd] inländisch; Binnen...; 2. [~] Landesinnere(s) *n*, Binnenland *n*; 3. [in'lænd] landeinwärts.

inlay 1. ['in'lei] [*irr.* (*lay*)] einlegen; 2. ['inlei] Einlage *f*; Einlegearbeit *f*.

inlet ['inlet] Bucht *f*; Einlaß *m*.

inmate ['inmeit] Insass|e *m*, -in *f*; Hausgenoss|e *m*, -in *f*.

inmost ['inmoust] innerst.

inn [in] Gasthof *m*, Wirtshaus *n*.

innate □ ['i'neit] angeboren.

inner ['inə] inner, inwendig; geheim; **~most** innerst; geheimst.

innervate ['inəːveit] Nervenkraft geben (*dat.*); kräftigen.

innings ['iniŋz] *Sport:* Dransein *n*.

innkeeper ['inkiːpə] Gastwirt(in).

innocen|ce ['inəsns] Unschuld *f*; Harmlosigkeit *f*; Einfalt *f*; **~t** [~nt] 1. □ unschuldig; harmlos; 2. Unschuldige(r *m*) *f*; Einfältige(r *m*) *f*.

innocuous □ [i'nɔkjuəs] harmlos.

innovation [inou'veiʃən] Neuerung *f*.

innoxious □ [i'nɔkʃəs] unschädlich.

innuendo [inju(ː)'endou] Andeutung *f*.

innumerable □ [i'njuːmərəbl] unzählbar, unzählig.

inoccupation ['inɔkjuˈpeiʃən] Beschäftigungslosigkeit *f*.

inoculate [i'nɔkjuleit] (ein)impfen.

inoffensive [inəˈfensiv] harmlos.

inofficial [inəˈfiʃəl] inoffiziell.

inoperative [in'ɔpərətiv] unwirksam.

inopportune □ [in'ɔpətjuːn] unangebracht, zur Unzeit.

inordinate □ [i'nɔːdinit] unmäßig.

in-patient ['inpeiʃənt] Krankenhauspatient *m*, stationärer Patient.

inquest ᵰᵵᵴ ['inkwest] Untersuchung *f*; coroner's ~ Leichenschau *f*.

inquir|e [in'kwaiə] fragen, sich erkundigen (*of* bei *j-m*); ~ *into* untersuchen; ~ing □ [.əriŋ] forschend; ~y [.əri] Erkundigung *f*, Nachfrage *f*; Untersuchung *f*; Ermittlung *f*.

inquisit|ion [inkwi'ziʃən] Untersuchung *f*; ~ive □ [in'kwizitiv] neugierig; wißbegierig.

inroad ['inroud] *feindlicher* Einfall; Ein-, Übergriff *m*.

insan|e □ [in'sein] wahnsinnig; ~ity [in'sæniti] Wahnsinn *m*.

insatia|ble □ [in'seiʃjəbl], ~te [.ʃiit] unersättlich (*of* nach).

inscribe [in'skraib] ein-, auf-, beschreiben; beschriften; *fig.* einprägen (*in, on dat.*); *Buch* widmen.

inscription [in'skripʃən] In-, Aufschrift *f*; ✝ Eintragung *f*.

inscrutable □ [in'skruːtəbl] unerforschlich, unergründlich.

insect ['insekt] Insekt *n*; ~icide [in'sektisaid] Insektengift *n*.

insecure □ [insi'kjuə] unsicher.

insens|ate [in'senseit] gefühllos; unvernünftig; ~ible □ [.səbl] unempfindlich; bewußtlos; unmerklich; gleichgültig; ~itive [.sitiv] unempfindlich.

inseparable □ [in'sepərəbl] untrennbar; unzertrennlich.

insert 1. [in'səːt] einsetzen, einschalten, einfügen; (hinein)stecken; *Münze* einwerfen; inserieren; **2.** ['insəːt] Bei-, Einlage *f*; ~ion [in'səːʃən] Einsetzung *f*, Einfügung *f*, Eintragung *f*; Einwurf *m* e-r *Münze*; Anzeige *f*, Inserat *n*.

inshore ⚓ ['in'ʃɔː] an *od.* nahe der Küste (befindlich); Küsten...

inside [in'said] **1.** Innenseite *f*; Innere(s) *n*; turn ~ out umkrempeln; auf den Kopf stellen; **2.** *adj.* inner, inwendig; Innen...; **3.** *adv.* im Innern; **4.** *prp.* innerhalb.

insidious □ [in'sidiəs] heimtückisch.

insight ['insait] Einsicht *f*, Einblick *m*.

insignia [in'signiə] *pl.* Abzeichen *n/pl.*, Insignien *pl.*

insignificant [insig'nifikənt] bedeutungslos; unbedeutend.

insincere □ [insin'siə] unaufrichtig.

insinuat|e [in'sinjueit] unbemerkt hineinbringen; zu verstehen geben; andeuten; ~ion [insinju'eiʃən] Einschmeichelung *f*; Anspielung *f*, Andeutung *f*; Wink *m*.

insipid [in'sipid] geschmacklos, fad.

insist [in'sist]: ~ (*up*)*on* bestehen auf (*dat.*); dringen auf (*acc.*); ~ence [.təns] Bestehen *n*; Beharrlichkeit *f*; Drängen *n*; ~ent □ [.nt] beharrlich; eindringlich.

insolent □ ['insələnt] unverschämt.

insoluble □ [in'sɔljubl] unlöslich.

insolvent [in'sɔlvənt] zahlungsunfähig. [keit *f*.)

insomnia [in'sɔmniə] Schlaflosig-)

insomuch [insou'mʌtʃ]: ~ *that* dermaßen *od.* so sehr, daß.

inspect [in'spekt] untersuchen, prüfen, nachsehen; ~ion [.kʃən] Prüfung *f*, Untersuchung *f*, Inspektion *f*; ~or [.ktə] Aufsichtsbeamte(r) *m*.

inspir|ation [inspə'reiʃən] Einatmung *f*; Eingebung *f*; Begeisterung *f*; ~e [in'spaiə] einatmen; *fig.* eingeben, erfüllen; *j-n* begeistern.

install [in'stɔːl] einsetzen; (sich) niederlassen; ⊕ installieren; ~ation [instə'leiʃən] Einsetzung *f*; ⊕ Installation *f*, Einrichtung *f*; ⚡ etc. Anlage *f*.

instal(l)ment [in'stɔːlmənt] Rate *f*; Teil-, Ratenzahlung *f*; (Teil)Lieferung *f*; Fortsetzung *f*.

instance ['instəns] Ersuchen *n*; Beispiel *n*; (besonderer) Fall; ᵰᵵᵴ Instanz *f*; for ~ zum Beispiel.

instant □ [in'stænt] **1.** dringend; sofortig; *on the 10th* ~ am 10. dieses Monats; **2.** Augenblick *m*; ~aneous □ [instən'teinjəs] augenblicklich; Moment...; ~ly ['instəntli] sogleich.

instead [in'sted] dafür; ~ *of* anstatt.

instep ['instep] Spann *m*.

instigat|e ['instigeit] anstiften; aufhetzen; ~or [.tə] Anstifter *m*, Hetzer *m*.

instil(l) [in'stil] einträufeln; *fig.* einflößen (*into dat.*).

instinct ['instiŋkt] Instinkt *m*; ~ive □ [in'stiŋktiv] instinktiv.

institut|e ['institjuːt] **1.** Institut *n*; **2.** einsetzen, stiften, einrichten; an-, verordnen; ~ion [insti'tjuːʃən] Einsetzung *f*, Einrichtung *f*; An-, Verordnung *f*; Satzung *f*; Institut(ion *f*) *n*; Gesellschaft *f*; Anstalt *f*; ~ional □ [.nl] Instituts..., Anstalts...

instruct [in'strʌkt] unterrichten; belehren; *j-n* anweisen; ~ion [.kʃən] Vorschrift *f*; Unterweisung *f*; Anweisung *f*; ~ive □ [.ktiv] lehrreich; ~or [.tə] Lehrer *m*; Ausbilder *m*; *Am. univ.* Dozent *m*.

instrument ['instrumənt] Instrument *n*, Werkzeug *n* (*a. fig.*); ‡̃ Urkunde *f*; **~al** □ [instru'mentl] als Werkzeug dienend; dienlich; ♩ Instrumental...; **~ality** [instrumen-'tæliti] Mitwirkung *f*, Mittel *n*.

insubordinat|e [insə'bɔ:dnit] aufsässig; **~ion** ['insəbɔ:di'neiʃən] Auflehnung *f*.

insubstantial [insəb'stænʃəl] unwirklich; gebrechlich.

insufferable □ [in'sʌfərəbl] unerträglich, unausstehlich.

insufficient □ [insə'fiʃənt] unzulänglich, ungenügend.

insula|r □ ['insjulə] Insel...; *fig.* engstirnig; **~te** [~leit] isolieren; **~tion** [insju'leiʃən] Isolierung *f*.

insult 1. ['insʌlt] Beleidigung *f*; **2.** [in'sʌlt] beleidigen.

insupportable □ [insə'pɔ:təbl] unerträglich, unausstehlich.

insur|ance [in'ʃuərəns] Versicherung *f*; *attr.* Versicherungs...; **~ance policy** Versicherungspolice *f*, -schein *m*; **~e** [in'ʃuə] versichern.

insurgent [in'sɔ:dʒənt] **1.** aufrührerisch; **2.** Aufrührer *m*.

insurmountable □ [insə(:)'mauntəbl] unübersteigbar, *fig.* unüberwindlich.

insurrection [insə'rekʃən] Aufstand *m*, Empörung *f*.

intact [in'tækt] unberührt; unversehrt.

intangible □ [in'tændʒəbl] unfühlbar; unfaßbar; unantastbar.

integ|ral □ ['intigrəl] ganz, vollständig; wesentlich; **~rate** [~reit] ergänzen; zs.-tun; einfügen; **~rity** [in'tegriti] Vollständigkeit *f*; Redlichkeit *f*, Integrität *f*.

intellect ['intilekt] Verstand *m*; *konkr. die* Intelligenz; **~ual** [inti-'lektjuəl] **1.** □ intellektuell; Verstandes...; geistig; verständig; **2.** Intellektuelle(r *m*) *f*.

intelligence [in'telidʒəns] Intelligenz *f*; Verstand *m*; Verständnis *n*; Nachricht *f*, Auskunft *f*; **~ department** Nachrichtendienst *m*.

intellig|ent [in'telidʒənt] intelligent; klug; **~ible** □ [~dʒəbl] verständlich (*to* für).

intempera|nce [in'tempərəns] Unmäßigkeit *f*; Trunksucht *f*; **~te** □ [~rit] unmäßig; zügellos; unbeherrscht; trunksüchtig.

intend [in'tend] beabsichtigen, wollen; **~** *for* bestimmen für *od.* zu; **~ed 1.** absichtlich; beabsichtigt, *a.* zukünftig; **2.** F Verlobte(r *m*) *f*.

intense □ [in'tens] intensiv; angestrengt; heftig; kräftig (*Farbe*).

intensify [in'tensifai] (sich) verstärken *od.* steigern.

intensity [in'tensiti] Intensität *f*.

intent [in'tent] **1.** □ gespannt; bedacht; beschäftigt (*on* mit); **2.** Absicht *f*; Vorhaben *n*; *to all* **~s** *and*

purposes in jeder Hinsicht; **~ion** [~nʃən] Absicht *f*; Zweck *m*; **~ional** □ [~nl] absichtlich; **~ness** [~ntnis] gespannte Aufmerksamkeit; Eifer *m*.

inter [in'tə:] beerdigen, begraben.

inter... ['intə(:)] zwischen; Zwischen...; gegenseitig, einander.

interact [intər'ækt] sich gegenseitig beeinflussen.

intercede [intə(:)'si:d] vermitteln.

intercept [intə(:)'sept] ab-, auffangen; abhören; aufhalten; unterbrechen; **~ion** [~pʃən] Ab-, Auffangen *n*; Ab-, Mithören *n*; Unterbrechung *f*; Aufhalten *n*.

intercess|ion [intə'seʃən] Fürbitte *f*; **~or** [~esə] Fürsprecher *m*.

interchange 1. [intə(:)'tʃeindʒ] *v/t.* austauschen, auswechseln; *v/i.* abwechseln; **2.** ['intə(:)'tʃeindʒ] Austausch *m*; Abwechs(e)lung *f*.

intercourse ['intə(:)kɔ:s] Verkehr *m*.

interdict 1. [intə(:)'dikt] untersagen, verbieten (*s.th. to s.o.* j-m et.; *s.o. from doing* j-n zu tun); **2.** ['intə(:)-dikt], **~ion** [intə(:)'dikʃən] Verbot *n*; Interdikt *n*.

interest ['intrist] **1.** Interesse *n*; Anziehungskraft *f*; Bedeutung *f*; Nutzen *m*; † Anteil *m*, Beteiligung *f*, Kapital *n*; Zins(en *pl.*) *m*; **~s** *pl.* Interessenten *m/pl.*, Kreise *m/pl.*; *take an* **~** *in* sich interessieren für; *return a blow with* **~** noch heftiger zurückschlagen; *banking* **~s** *pl.* Bankkreise *m/pl.*; **2.** *allg.* interessieren (*in* für et.); **~ing** □ [~tiŋ] interessant.

interfere [intə'fiə] sich einmischen (*with* in *acc.*); vermitteln; (ea.) stören; **~nce** [~ərəns] Einmischung *f*; Beeinträchtigung *f*; Störung *f*.

interim ['intərim] **1.** Zwischenzeit *f*; **2.** vorläufig; Interims...

interior [in'tiəriə] **1.** □ inner; innerlich; Innen...; **~** *decorator* Innenarchitekt *m*; Maler *m*, Tapezierer *m*; **2.** Innere(s) *n*; Interieur *n*; *pol.* innere Angelegenheiten; *Department of the* ♀ *Am.* Innenministerium *n*.

interjection [intə(:)'dʒekʃən] Ausruf *m*.

interlace [intə(:)'leis] *v/t.* durchflechten, -weben; *v/i.* sich kreuzen.

interlock [intə(:)'lɔk] in-ea.-greifen; in-ea.-schlingen; in-ea.-haken.

interlocut|ion [intə(:)lou'kju:ʃən] Unterredung *f*; **~or** [~ɔ(:)'lɔkjutə] Gesprächspartner *m*.

interlope [intə(:)'loup] sich eindrängen; **~r** ['intə(:)loupə] Eindringling *m*.

interlude ['intə(:)lu:d] Zwischenspiel *n*; Zwischenzeit *f*; **~s** *of bright weather* zeitweilig schön.

intermarriage [intə(:)'mæridʒ] Mischehe *f*.

intermeddle [intə(:)'medl] sich einmischen (with, in in acc.).

intermedia|ry [intə(:)'mi:djəri] 1. = intermediate; vermittelnd; 2. Vermittler m; ~te □ [~ət] in der Mitte liegend; Mittel..., Zwischen...; ~range ballistic missile Mittelstreckenrakete f; ~ school Am. Mittelschule f.

interment [in'tə:mənt] Beerdigung f.

interminable □ [in'tə:minəbl] endlos, unendlich.

intermingle [intə(:)'miŋgl] (sich) vermischen.

intermission [intə(:)'miʃən] Aussetzen n, Unterbrechung f; Pause f.

intermit [intə(:)'mit] unterbrechen, aussetzen; ~tent □ [~tənt] aussetzend; ~ fever ⚕ Wechselfieber n.

intermix [intə(:)'miks] (sich) vermischen.

intern¹ [in'tə:n] internieren.

intern² ['in'tə:n] Assistenzarzt m.

internal □ [in'tə:nl] inner(lich); inländisch.

international □ [intə(:)'næʃənl] international; ~ law Völkerrecht n.

interphone ['intəfoun] Haustelephon n; Am. ⚓ Bordsprechanlage f.

interpolate [in'tə:pouleit] einschieben.

interpose [intə(:)'pouz] v/t. Veto einlegen; Wort einwerfen; v/i. dazwischentreten; vermitteln.

interpret [in'tə:prit] auslegen, erklären, interpretieren; (ver)dolmetschen; darstellen; ~ation [intə:pri'teiʃən] Auslegung f; Darstellung f; ~er [in'tə:pritə] Ausleger (-in); Dolmetscher(in); Interpret (-in).

interrogat|e [in'terəgeit] (be-, aus)fragen; verhören; ~ion [interə'geiʃən] (Be-, Aus)Fragen n, Verhör(en) n; Frage f; note od. mark od. point of ~ Fragezeichen n; ~ive □ [intə'rɔgətiv] fragend; Frage...

interrupt [intə'rʌpt] unterbrechen; ~ion [~pʃən] Unterbrechung f.

intersect [intə(:)'sekt] (sich) schneiden; ~ion [~kʃən] Durchschnitt m; Schnittpunkt m; Straßen- etc. Kreuzung f.

intersperse [intə(:)'spə:s] einstreuen; untermengen, durchsetzen.

interstate Am. [intə(:)'steit] zwischenstaatlich.

intertwine [intə(:)'twain] verflechten.

interval ['intəvəl] Zwischenraum m; Pause f; (Zeit)Abstand m.

interven|e [intə(:)'vi:n] dazwischenkommen; sich einmischen; einschreiten; dazwischenliegen; ~tion [~'venʃən] Dazwischenkommen n; Einmischung f; Vermitt(e)lung f.

interview ['intəvju:] 1. Zusammenkunft f, Unterredung f; Interview n; 2. interviewen.

intestine [in'testin] 1. inner; 2. Darm m; ~s pl. Eingeweide n/pl.

intima|cy ['intiməsi] Intimität f, Vertraulichkeit f; ~te 1. [~meit] bekanntgeben; zu verstehen geben; 2. □ [~mit] intim; 3. [~] Vertraute(r m) f; ~tion [inti'meiʃən] Andeutung f, Wink m; Ankündigung f.

intimidate [in'timideit] einschüchtern.

into prp. ['intu, vor Konsonant 'intə] in (acc.), in ... hinein.

intolera|ble □ [in'tɔlərəbl] unerträglich; ~nt □ [~ənt] unduldsam, intolerant.

intonation [intou'neiʃən] Anstimmen n; gr. Intonation f, Tonfall m.

intoxica|nt [in'tɔksikənt] 1. berauschend; 2. berauschendes Getränk; ~te [~keit] berauschen (a. fig.); ~tion [intɔksi'keiʃən] Rausch m (a. fig.).

intractable □ [in'træktəbl] unlenksam, störrisch; schwer zu bändigen(d).

intransitive □ gr. [in'trænsitiv] intransitiv.

intrastate Am. [intrə'steit] innerstaatlich.

intrench [in'trentʃ] = entrench.

intrepid [in'trepid] unerschrocken.

intricate □ [in'trikit] verwickelt.

intrigue [in'tri:g] 1. Ränkespiel n, Intrige f; (Liebes)Verhältnis n; 2. v/i. Ränke schmieden, intrigieren; ein (Liebes)Verhältnis haben; v/t. neugierig machen; ~r [~gə] Intrigant(in).

intrinsic(al □) [in'trinsik(əl)] inner(lich); wirklich, wahr.

introduc|e [intrə'dju:s] einführen (a. fig.); bekannt machen (to mit), vorstellen (to j-m); einleiten; ~tion [~'dʌkʃən] Einführung f; Einleitung f; Vorstellung f; letter of ~ Empfehlungsschreiben n; ~tory [~ktəri] einleitend, einführend.

introspection [introu'spekʃən] Selbstprüfung f; Selbstbetrachtung f.

introvert 1. [introu'və:t] einwärtskehren; 2. psych. ['introuvə:t] nach innen gekehrter Mensch.

intru|de [in'tru:d] hineinzwängen; (sich) ein- od. aufdrängen; ~der [~də] Eindringling m; ~sion [~u:ʒən] Eindringen n; Auf-, Zudringlichkeit f; ~sive □ [~u:siv] zudringlich.

intrust [in'trʌst] = entrust.

intuition [intju(:)'iʃən] unmittelbare Erkenntnis, Intuition f.

inundate ['inʌndeit] überschwemmen.

inure [i'njuə] gewöhnen (to an acc.).

invade [in'veid] eindringen in, ein-

fallen in (acc.); fig. befallen; ~r [~də] Angreifer m; Eindringling m.
invalid¹ ['invəli:d] 1. dienstunfähig; kränklich; 2. Invalide m.
invalid² [in'vælid] (rechts)ungültig; ~ate [~deit] entkräften; ⚡ ungültig machen. [schätzbar.\
invaluable □ [in'væljuəbl] un-\
invariab|le □ [in'vɛəriəbl] unveränderlich; ~ly [~li] ausnahmslos.
invasion [in'veiʒən] Einfall m, Angriff m, Invasion f; Eingriff m; ⚡ Anfall m.
invective [in'vektiv] Schmähung f, Schimpfrede f, Schimpfwort n.
inveigh [in'vei] schimpfen (against über, auf acc.).
inveigle [in'vi:gl] verleiten.
invent [in'vent] erfinden; ~ion [~nʃən] Erfindung(sgabe) f; ~ive □ [~ntiv] erfinderisch; ~or [~tə] Erfinder(in); ~ory ['invəntri] 1. Inventar n; Inventur f; 2. inventarisieren.
invers|e □ ['in'və:s] umgekehrt; ~ion [in'və:ʃən] Umkehrung f; gr. Inversion f.
invert [in'və:t] umkehren; umstellen; ~ed commas pl. Anführungszeichen n/pl.
invest [in'vest] investieren, anlegen; bekleiden; ausstatten; umgeben (with von); ✠ belagern.
investigat|e [in'vestigeit] erforschen; untersuchen; nachforschen; ~ion [investi'geiʃən] Erforschung f; Untersuchung f; Nachforschung f; ~or [in'vestigeitə] Untersuchende(r m) f.
invest|ment ✝ [in'vestmənt] Kapitalanlage f; Investition f; ~or [~tə] Geldgeber m.
inveterate □ [in'vetərit] eingewurzelt.
invidious □ [in'vidiəs] verhaßt; gehässig; beneidenswert.
invigorate [in'vigəreit] kräftigen.
invincible □ [in'vinsəbl] unbesiegbar; unüberwindlich.
inviola|ble □ [in'vaiələbl] unverletzlich; ~te [~lit] unverletzt.
invisible □ [in'vizəbl] unsichtbar.
invit|ation [invi'teiʃən] Einladung f, Aufforderung f; ~e [in'vait] einladen; auffordern; (an)locken.
invoice ✝ [in'vois] Faktura f, Warenrechnung f.
invoke [in'vouk] anrufen; zu Hilfe rufen (acc.); sich berufen auf (acc.); Geist heraufbeschwören.
involuntary □ [in'vɔləntəri] unfreiwillig; unwillkürlich.
involve [in'vɔlv] verwickeln, hineinziehen; in sich schließen, enthalten; mit sich bringen; ~ment [~vmənt] Verwicklung f; (bsd. Geld)Schwierigkeit f.
invulnerable □ [in'vʌlnərəbl] unverwundbar; fig. unanfechtbar.

inward ['inwəd] 1. □ inner(lich); 2. adv. mst ~s einwärts; nach innen; 3. ~s pl. Eingeweide n/pl.
iodine ['aiədi:n] Jod n.
IOU ['aiou'ju:] (= I owe you) Schuldschein m.
irascible □ [i'ræsibl] jähzornig.
irate [ai'reit] zornig, wütend.
iridescent [iri'desnt] schillernd.
iris ['aiəris] anat. Regenbogenhaut f, Iris f; ⚘ Schwertlilie f.
Irish ['aiəriʃ] 1. irisch; 2. Irisch n; the ~ pl. die Iren pl.; ~man Ire m.
irksome □ ['ə:ksəm] lästig, ermüdend.
iron ['aiən] 1. Eisen n; a. flat-~ Bügeleisen n; ~s pl. Fesseln f/pl.; strike while the ~ is hot fig. das Eisen schmieden, solange es heiß ist; 2. eisern (a. fig.); Eisen...; 3. bügeln; in Eisen legen; ~bound eisenbeschlagen; felsig; unbeugsam; ~clad 1. gepanzert; 2. Panzerschiff n; ~curtain pol. eiserner Vorhang; ~hearted fig. hartherzig.
ironic(al □) [ai'rɔnik(əl)] ironisch, spöttisch.
iron|ing ['aiəniŋ] Plätten n, Bügeln n; attr. Plätt..., Bügel...; ~lung ⚕ eiserne Lunge; ~monger Eisenhändler m; ~mongery [~ɔri] Eisenwaren f/pl.; ~mo(u)ld Rostfleck m; ~work eisenschmiedeeiserne Arbeit; ~works mst sg. Eisenhütte f.
irony¹ ['aiəni] eisenartig, -haltig.
irony² ['aiərəni] Ironie f.
irradiant [i'reidjənt] strahlend (with vor Freude etc.).
irradiate [i'reidieit] bestrahlen (a. ⚕); fig. aufklären; strahlen lassen.
irrational [i'ræʃnl] unvernünftig.
irreclaimable □ [iri'kleiməbl] unverbesserlich.
irrecognizable □ [i'rekəgnaizəbl] nicht (wieder)erkennbar.
irreconcilable □ [i'rekənsailəbl] unversöhnlich; unvereinbar.
irrecoverable □ [iri'kʌvərəbl] unersetzlich; unwiederbringlich.
irredeemable □ [iri'di:məbl] unkündbar; nicht einlösbar; unersetzlich.
irrefutable □ [i'refjutəbl] unwiderleglich, unwiderlegbar.
irregular □ [i'regjulə] unregelmäßig, regelwidrig; ungleichmäßig.
irrelevant □ [i'relivənt] nicht zur Sache gehörig; unzutreffend; unerheblich, belanglos (to für).
irreligious □ [iri'lidʒəs] gottlos.
irremediable □ [iri'mi:djəbl] unheilbar; unersetzlich.
irremovable □ [iri'mu:vəbl] nicht entfernbar; unabsetzbar.
irreparable □ [i'repərəbl] nicht wieder gutzumachen(d).
irreplaceable [iri'pleisəbl] unersetzlich.
irrepressible □ [iri'presəbl] ununterdrückbar; unbezähmbar.

irreproachable □ [iri'prəutʃəbl] einwandfrei, untadelig.

irresistible □ [iri'zistəbl] unwiderstehlich.

irresolute □ [i'rezəlu:t] unentschlossen.

irrespective □ [iris'pektiv] (*of*) rücksichtslos (gegen); ohne Rücksicht (auf *acc.*); unabhängig (von).

irresponsible □ [iris'pɔnsəbl] unverantwortlich; verantwortungslos.

irretrievable □ [iri'tri:vəbl] unwiederbringlich, unersetzlich; nicht wieder gutzumachen(d).

irreverent □ [i'revərənt] respektlos, ehrfurchtslos.

irrevocable □ [i'revəkəbl] unwiderruflich; unabänderlich, endgültig.

irrigate ['irigeit] bewässern.

irrita|ble □ [iritəbl] reizbar; **~nt** [~ənt] Reizmittel *n*; **~te** [~teit] reizen; ärgern; **~ting** □ [~tiŋ] aufreizend; ärgerlich (*Sache*); **~tion** [iri'teiʃən] Reizung *f*; Gereiztheit *f*, Ärger *m*.

irrupt|ion [i'rʌpʃən] Einbruch *m* (*mst fig.*); **~ive** [~ptiv] (her)einbrechend.

is [iz] 3. sg. pres. von be.

island ['ailənd] Insel *f*; Verkehrsinsel *f*; **~er** [~də] Inselbewohner(in).

isle [ail] Insel *f*; **~t** ['ailit] Inselchen *n*.

isolat|e ['aisəleit] absondern; isolieren; **~ed** abgeschieden; **~ion** [aisə'leiʃən] Isolierung *f*, Absonderung *f*; **~ ward** ⚕ Isolierstation *f*; **~ionist** *Am. pol.* [~ʃnist] Isolationist *m*.

issue ['isju:, *Am.* 'iʃu:] 1. Herauskommen *n*, Herausfließen *n*; Abfluß *m*; Ausgang *m*; Nachkommen (-schaft *f*) *m/pl.*; *fig.* Ausgang *m*, Ergebnis *n*; Streitfrage *f*; Ausgabe *f* *v. Material etc.*, Erlaß *m v. Befehlen*; Ausgabe *f*, Exemplar *n*; Nummer *f e-r Zeitung*; **~** *in law* Rechtsfrage *f*; be at **~** uneinig sein; *point* at **~** strittiger Punkt; 2. *v/i.* herauskommen; herkommen, entspringen; endigen (*in in acc.*); *v/t.* von sich geben; *Material etc.* ausgeben; *Befehl* erlassen; *Buch* herausgeben.

isthmus ['isməs] Landenge *f*.

it [it] 1. es; *nach prp.* da... (*z.B. by* **~** dadurch; *for* **~** dafür); 2. das gewisse Etwas.

Italian [i'tæljən] 1. italienisch; 2. Italiener(in); Italienisch *n*.

italics *typ.* [i'tæliks] Kursivschrift *f*.

itch [itʃ] 1. ⚕ Krätze *f*; Jucken *n*; Verlangen *n*; 2. jucken; *be* **~ing** *to inf.* darauf brennen, zu *inf.*; *have an* **~ing** *palm* raffgierig sein; **~ing** ['itʃiŋ] Jucken *n*; *fig.* Gelüste *n*.

item ['aitem] 1. desgleichen; 2. Einzelheit *f*, Punkt *m*; Posten *m*; (Zeitungs)Artikel *m*; **~ize** [~maiz] einzeln angeben *od.* aufführen.

iterate ['itəreit] wiederholen.

itiner|ant □ [i'tinərənt] reisend; umherziehend; Reise...; **~ary** [ai'tinərəri] Reiseroute *f*, -plan *m*; Reisebericht *m*; *attr.* Reise...

its [its] sein(e); dessen, deren.

itself [it'self] (es, sich) selbst; sich; *of* **~** von selbst; *in* **~** in sich, an sich; *by* **~** für sich allein, besonders.

ivory ['aivəri] Elfenbein *n*.

ivy ⚘ ['aivi] Efeu *m*.

J

jab F [dʒæb] 1. stechen; stoßen; 2. Stich *m*, Stoß *m*.

jabber ['dʒæbə] plappern.

jack [dʒæk] 1. Hebevorrichtung *f*, *bsd.* Wagenheber *m*; Malkugel *f* *beim Bowlspiel*; ⚓ Gösch *f*, kleine Flagge; *Karten:* Bube *m*; 2. *a.* **~** *up* aufbocken. [Handlanger *m.*]

jackal ['dʒækɔ:l] *zo.* Schakal *m*; *fig.*)

jack|ass ['dʒækæs] Esel *m* (*a. fig.*); **~boots** Reitstiefel *m/pl.*; hohe Wasserstiefel *m/pl.*; **~daw** *orn.* Dohle *f*.

jacket ['dʒækit] Jacke *f*; ⊕ Mantel *m*; Schutzumschlag *m e-s Buches.*

jack|-knife ['dʒæknaif] (großes) Klappmesser *n*; **♀ of all trades** Hansdampf in allen Gassen; **♀ of all work** Faktotum *n*; **~pot** *Poker:* Einsatz *m*; *hit the* **~** *Am.* F großes Glück haben.

jade [dʒeid] (Schind)Mähre *f*, Klepper *m*; *contp.* Frauenzimmer *n*.

jag [dʒæg] Zacken *m*; *sl.* Sauferei *f*; **~ged** ['dʒægid] zackig; gekerbt; *bsd. Am. sl.* voll (*betrunken*).

jaguar *zo.* ['dʒægjuə] Jaguar *m*.

jail [dʒeil] 1. Kerker *m*; 2. einkerkern; **~bird** ['dʒeilbə:d] F Knastbruder *m*; Galgenvogel *m*; **~er** ['dʒeilə] Kerkermeister *m*.

jalop(p)y *bsd. Am.* F *mot.*, ✈ [dʒə'lɔpi] Kiste *f*.

jam¹ [dʒæm] Marmelade *f*.

jam² [~] 1. Gedränge *n*; ⊕ Hemmung *f*; *Radio:* Störung *f*; *traffic* **~** Verkehrsstockung *f*; *be in a* **~** *sl.* in der Klemme sein; 2. (sich) (fest-, ver)klemmen; pressen, quetschen; versperren; *Radio:* stören; **~** *the brakes* mit aller Kraft bremsen.

jamboree [dʒæmbə'ri:] (*bsd.* Pfadfinder)Treffen *n*; *sl.* Vergnügen *n*, Fez *m*.

jangle ['dʒæŋgl] schrillen (lassen); laut streiten, keifen.

janitor ['dʒænitə] Portier m.

January ['dʒænjuəri] Januar m.

Japanese [dʒæpə'ni:z] 1. japanisch; 2. Japaner(in); Japanisch n; the ~ pl. die Japaner pl.

jar [dʒɑ:] 1. Krug m; Topf m; Glas n; Knarren n, Mißton m; Streit m; mißliche Lage; 2. knarren; unangenehm berühren; erzittern (lassen); streiten.

jaundice ♂ ['dʒɔ:ndis] Gelbsucht f; ~d [~st] ♂ gelbsüchtig; fig. neidisch.

jaunt [dʒɔ:nt] 1. Ausflug m, Spritztour f; 2. e-n Ausflug machen; ~y □ ['dʒɔ:nti] munter; flott.

javelin ['dʒævlin] Wurfspeer m.

jaw [dʒɔ:] Kinnbacken m, Kiefer m; ~s pl. Rachen m; Maul n; Schlund m; ⊕ Backen f/pl.; ~bone ['dʒɔ:boun] Kieferknochen m.

jay orn. [dʒei] Eichelhäher m; ~walker Am. F ['dʒeiwɔ:kə] achtlos die Straße überquerender Fußgänger.

jazz [dʒæz] 1. Jazz m; 2. F grell.

jealous □ ['dʒeləs] eifersüchtig; besorgt (of um); neidisch; ~y [~si] Eifersucht f; Neid m.

jeans [dʒi:nz] pl. Jeans pl., Niet(en)-hose f.

jeep [dʒi:p] Jeep m.

jeer [dʒiə] Spott m, Spötterei f; 2. spotten (at über acc.); (ver-)höhnen.

jejune □ [dʒi'dʒu:n] nüchtern, fad.

jelly ['dʒeli] 1. Gallert(e f) n; Gelee n; 2. gelieren; ~fish zo. Qualle f.

jeopardize ['dʒepədaiz] gefährden.

jerk [dʒə:k] 1. Ruck m; (Muskel-)Krampf m; 2. rucken od. zerren (an dat.); schnellen; schleudern; ~water Am. ['dʒə:kwɔ:tə] 1. 🚂 Nebenbahn f; 2. F klein, unbedeutend; ~y ['dʒə:ki] 1. □ ruckartig; holperig; 2. Am. luftgetrocknetes Rindfleisch.

jersey ['dʒə:zi] Wollpullover m; wollenes Unterhemd.

jest [dʒest] 1. Spaß m; 2. scherzen; ~er ['dʒestə] Spaßmacher m.

jet [dʒet] 1. (Wasser-, Gas)Strahl m; Strahlrohr n; ⊕ Düse f; Düsenflugzeug n; Düsenmotor m; 2. hervorsprudeln; ~propelled ['dʒetprəpeld] mit Düsenantrieb.

jetty ⚓ ['dʒeti] Mole f; Pier m.

Jew [dʒu:] Jude m; attr. Juden...

jewel ['dʒu:əl] Juwel n, m; ~(l)er [~lə] Juwelier m; ~(le)ry [~lri] Juwelen pl., Schmuck m.

Jew|ess ['dʒu(:)is] Jüdin f; ~ish ['dʒu(:)iʃ] jüdisch.

jib ⚓ [dʒib] Klüver m.

jibe Am. F [dʒaib] zustimmen.

jiffy F ['dʒifi] Augenblick m.

jig-saw ['dʒigsɔ:] Laubsägema-schine f; ~ puzzle Zusammensetzspiel n.

jilt [dʒilt] 1. Kokette f; 2. Liebhaber versetzen.

Jim [dʒim]: ~ Crow Am. Neger m; Am. Rassentrennung f.

jingle ['dʒiŋgl] 1. Geklingel n; 2. klingeln, klimpern (mit).

jitney Am. sl. ['dʒitni] 5-Cent-Stück n; billiger Omnibus.

jive Am. sl. [dʒaiv] heiße Jazzmusik; Jazzjargon m.

job [dʒɔb] 1. (Stück n) Arbeit f; Sache f, Aufgabe f; Beruf m; Stellung f; by the ~ stückweise; im Akkord; ~ lot F Ramschware f; ~ work Akkordarbeit f; 2. v/t. Pferd etc. (ver)mieten; ♦ vermitteln; v/i. im Akkord arbeiten; Maklergeschäfte machen; ~ber ['dʒɔbə] Akkordarbeiter m; Makler m; Schieber m.

jockey ['dʒɔki] 1. Jockei m; 2. prellen.

jocose □ [dʒə'kous] scherzhaft, spaßig.

jocular □ ['dʒɔkjulə] lustig; spaßig.

jocund □ ['dʒɔkənd] lustig, fröhlich.

jog [dʒɔg] 1. Stoß(en n) m; Rütteln n; Trott m; 2. v/t. (an)stoßen, (auf-)rütteln; v/i. mst ~ along, ~ on dahintrotten, dahinschlendern.

John [dʒɔn]: ~ Bull John Bull (der Engländer); ~ Hancock Am. F Friedrich Wilhelm m (Unterschrift).

join [dʒɔin] 1. v/t. verbinden, zs.-fügen (to mit); sich vereinigen mit, sich gesellen zu; eintreten in (acc.); ~ battle den Kampf beginnen; ~ hands die Hände falten; sich die Hände reichen (a. fig.); v/i. sich verbinden, sich vereinigen; ~ in mitmachen bei; ~ up Soldat werden; 2. Verbindung(sstelle) f.

joiner ['dʒɔinə] Tischler m; ~y [~əri] Tischlerhandwerk n; Tischlerarbeit f.

joint [dʒɔint] 1. Verbindung(sstelle) f; Scharnier n; anat. Gelenk n; ♀ Knoten m; Braten m; Am. sl. Spelunke f; put out of ~ verrenken; 2. □ gemeinsam; Mit...; ~ heir Miterbe m; ~ stock ♦ Aktienkapital n; 3. zs.-fügen; zerlegen; ~ed ['dʒɔintid] gegliedert; Glieder...; ~stock ♦ Aktien...; ~ company Aktiengesellschaft f.

jok|e [dʒouk] 1. Scherz m, Spaß m; practical ~ Streich m; 2. v/i. scherzen; schäkern; v/t. necken (about mit); ~er ['dʒoukə] Spaßvogel m; Karten: Joker m; Am. versteckte Klausel; ~y □ ['dʒouki] spaßig.

jolly ['dʒɔli] lustig, fidel; F nett.

jolt [dʒoult] 1. stoßen, rütteln; holpern; 2. Stoß m; Rütteln n.

Jonathan ['dʒɔnəθən]: Brother ~ der Amerikaner.

josh *Am. sl.* [dʒɔʃ] **1.** Ulk *m*; **2.** aufziehen, auf die Schippe nehmen.

jostle ['dʒɔsl] **1.** anrennen; zs.-stoßen; **2.** Stoß *m*; Zs.-Stoß *m*.

jot [dʒɔt] **1.** Jota *n*, Pünktchen *n*; **2.** ~ *down* notieren.

journal ['dʒɔːnl] Journal *n*; Tagebuch *n*; Tageszeitung *f*; Zeitschrift *f*; ⊕ Wellenzapfen *m*; ~**ism** ['dʒɔːnəlizəm] Journalismus *m*.

journey ['dʒɔːni] **1.** Reise *f*; Fahrt *f*; **2.** reisen; ~**man** Geselle *m*.

jovial □ ['dʒouvjəl] heiter; gemütlich.

joy [dʒɔi] Freude *f*; Fröhlichkeit *f*; ~**ful** □ ['dʒɔiful] freudig; erfreut; fröhlich; ~**less** □ ['dʒɔilis] freudlos; unerfreulich; ~**ous** □ ['dʒɔiəs] freudig, fröhlich.

jubil|ant ['dʒuːbilənt] jubilierend, frohlockend; ~**ate** [~leit] jubeln; ~**ee** [~liː] Jubiläum *n*.

judge [dʒʌdʒ] **1.** Richter *m*; Schiedsrichter *m*; Beurteiler(in), Kenner(in); **2.** *v/i.* urteilen (*of* über *acc.*); *v/t.* richten; aburteilen; beurteilen (*by* nach); ansehen als.

judg(e)ment ['dʒʌdʒmənt] Urteil *n*; Urteilsspruch *m*; Urteilskraft *f*; Einsicht *f*; Meinung *f*; *göttliches* (Straf)Gericht; *Day of* ♉, ♉ *Day* Jüngstes Gericht.

judicature ['dʒuːdikətʃə] Gerichtshof *m*; Rechtspflege *f*.

judicial □ [dʒuː(ː)'diʃəl] gerichtlich; Gerichts...; kritisch; unparteiisch.

judicious □ [dʒuː(ː)'diʃəs] verständig, klug; ~**ness** [~snis] Einsicht *f*.

jug [dʒʌg] Krug *m*, Kanne *f*.

juggle ['dʒʌgl] **1.** Trick *m*; Schwindel *m*; **2.** jonglieren (*a. fig.*); verfälschen; betrügen; ~**r** [~lə] Jongleur *m*; Taschenspieler(in).

Jugoslav ['juːgou'slɑːv] **1.** Jugoslaw|e *m*, -in *f*; **2.** jugoslawisch.

juic|e [dʒuːs] Saft *m*; *sl. mot.* Sprit *m*, Gas *n*; ~**y** □ ['dʒuːsi] saftig; F interessant. [sikautomat *m*.]

juke-box *Am.* F ['dʒuːkbɔks] Mu-]

julep ['dʒuːlep] *süßes* (Arznei)Getränk; *bsd. Am. alkoholisches* Eisgetränk.

July [dʒuː(ː)'lai] Juli *m*.

jumble ['dʒʌmbl] **1.** Durcheinander *n*; **2.** *v/t.* durch-ea.-werfen; ~**sale** Wohltätigkeitsbasar *m*.

jump [dʒʌmp] **1.** Sprung *m*; ~*s pl.*

nervöses Zs.-fahren; *high* (*long*) ~ Hoch- (Weit)Sprung *m*; *get* (*have*) *the* ~ *on Am.* F zuvorkommen; **2.** *v/i.* (auf)springen; ~ *at* sich stürzen auf (*acc.*); ~ *to conclusions* übereilte Schlüsse ziehen; *v/t.* hinwegspringen über (*acc.*); überspringen; springen lassen; ~**er** ['dʒʌmpə] Springer *m*; Jumper *m*; ~**y** [~pi] nervös.

junct|ion ['dʒʌŋkʃən] Verbindung *f*; Kreuzung *f*; ⚏ Knotenpunkt *m*; ~**ure** [~ktʃə] Verbindungspunkt *m*, -stelle *f*; (kritischer) Zeitpunkt; *at this* ~ bei diesem Stand der Dinge.

June [dʒuːn] Juni *m*.

jungle ['dʒʌŋgl] Dschungel *m*, *n*, *f*.

junior ['dʒuːnjə] **1.** jünger (*to* als); *Am. univ.* der Unterstufe (angehörend); ~ *high school Am.* Oberschule *f* mit Klassen 7, 8, 9; **2.** Jüngere(r *m*) *f*; *Am.* (Ober)Schüler *m od.* Student *m* im 3. Jahr; *F* Kleine(r) *m*.

junk [dʒʌŋk] ⚓ Dschunke *f*; Plunder *m*, alter Kram.

junket ['dʒʌŋkit] Quarkspeise *f*; *Am.* Party *f*; Vergnügungsfahrt *f*.

juris|diction [dʒuəris'dikʃən] Rechtsprechung *f*; Gerichtsbarkeit *f*; Gerichtsbezirk *m*; ~**prudence** ['djuərispruːdəns] Rechtswissenschaft *f*.

juror ['dʒuərə] Geschworene(r) *m*.

jury ['dʒuəri] *die* Geschworenen *pl.*; Jury *f*, Preisgericht *n*; ~**man** Geschworene(r) *m*.

just □ [dʒʌst] **1.** *adj.* gerecht; rechtschaffen; **2.** *adv.* richtig; genau; (so)eben; nur; ~ *now* eben od. gerade jetzt.

justice ['dʒʌstis] Gerechtigkeit *f*; Richter *m*; Recht *n*; Rechtsverfahren *n*; *court of* ~ Gericht(shof *m*) *n*.

justification [dʒʌstifi'keiʃən] Rechtfertigung *f*.

justify ['dʒʌstifai] rechtfertigen.

justly ['dʒʌstli] mit Recht.

justness ['dʒʌstnis] Gerechtigkeit *f*, Billigkeit *f*; Rechtmäßigkeit *f*; Richtigkeit *f*.

jut [dʒʌt] *a.* ~ *out* hervorragen.

juvenile ['dʒuːvinail] **1.** jung, jugendlich; Jugend...; **2.** junger Mensch.

K

kale [keil] (*bsd.* Kraus-, Grün)Kohl *m*; *Am. sl.* Moos *n* (*Geld*).

kangaroo [kæŋgə'ru:] Känguruh *n*.

keel ⚓ [ki:l] 1. Kiel *m*; 2. ~ *over* kieloben *legen od.* liegen; umschlagen.

keen □ [ki:n] scharf (*a. fig.*); eifrig, heftig; stark, groß (*Appetit etc.*); ~ *on* F scharf *od.* erpicht auf *acc.*; *be* ~ *on hunting* ein leidenschaftlicher Jäger sein; ~**-edged** ['ki:ned3d] scharfgeschliffen; ~**ness** ['ki:nnis] Schärfe *f*; Heftigkeit *f*; Scharfsinn *m*.

keep [ki:p] 1. (Lebens)Unterhalt *m*; *for* ~*s* F für immer; 2. [*irr.*] *v/t. allg.* halten; behalten; unterhalten; (er-)halten; einhalten; (ab)halten; *Buch, Ware etc.* führen; *Bett etc.* hüten; fest-, aufhalten; (bei)behalten; (auf)bewahren; ~ *s.o. company* j-m Gesellschaft leisten; ~ *company with* verkehren mit; ~ *one's temper* sich beherrschen; ~ *time* richtig gehen (*Uhr*); ♪, ✕ Takt, Schritt halten; ~ *s.o. waiting* j-n warten lassen; ~ *away* fernhalten; ~ *s.th. from s.o.* j-m *et.* vorenthalten; ~ *in* zurückhalten; *Schüler* nachsitzen lassen; ~ *on Kleid* anbehalten, *Hut* aufbehalten; ~ *up* aufrechterhalten; (*Mut*) bewahren; in Ordnung halten; hindern, zu Bett zu gehen; aufbleiben lassen; ~ *it up* (es) durchhalten; *v/i.* sich halten, bleiben; F sich aufhalten; sich immer wieder tun; ~ *away* sich fernhalten; ~ *from* sich enthalten (*gen.*); ~ *off* sich fernhalten; ~ *on talking* fortfahren zu sprechen; ~ *to* sich halten an (*acc.*); ~ *up* sich aufrecht halten; sich aufrechterhalten; ~ *up with* Schritt halten mit; ~ *up with the Joneses* es den Nachbarn gleichtun.

keep|er ['ki:pə] Wärter *m*, Wächter *m*, Aufseher *m*; Verwalter *m*; Inhaber *m*; ~**ing** ['ki:piŋ] Verwahrung *f*; Obhut *f*; Gewahrsam *m*, *n*; Unterhalt *m*; *be in* (*out of*) ~ *with* ... (nicht) übereinstimmen mit ...; ~**sake** ['ki:pseik] Andenken *n*.

keg [keg] Fäßchen *n*.

kennel ['kenl] Gosse *f*, Rinnstein *m*; Hundehütte *f*, -zwinger *m*.

kept [kept] *pret. u. p.p. von keep* 2.

kerb [kə:b], ~**stone** ['kə:bstoun] = curb *etc.*

kerchief ['kə:tʃif] (Kopf)Tuch *n*.

kernel ['kə:nl] Kern *m* (*a. fig.*); Hafer-, Mais- *etc.* Korn *n*.

kettle ['ketl] Kessel *m*; ~**drum** ♪ Kesselpauke *f*.

key [ki:] 1. Schlüssel *m* (*a. fig.*); ⚒ Keil *m*; ⊕ Keil *m*; Schraubenschlüssel *m*; *Klavier- etc.* Taste *f*; ⚡ Taste *f*, Druck-

knopf *m*; ♪ Tonart *f*; *fig.* Ton *m*; 2. ~ *up* ♪ stimmen; erhöhen; *fig.* in erhöhte Spannung versetzen; ~**board** ['ki:bɔ:d] Klaviatur *f*, Tastatur *f*; ~**hole** Schlüsselloch *n*; ~**man** Schlüsselfigur *f*; ~ **money** Ablösung *f* (*für e-e Wohnung*); ~**note** ♪ Grundton *m*; *fig.* Grundlage *f*; ~**stone** Schlußstein *m*; *fig.* Grundlage *f*.

kibitzer *Am.* F ['kibitsə] Kiebitz *m*, Besserwisser *m*.

kick [kik] 1. (Fuß)Tritt *m*; Stoß *m*; Schwung *m*; F Nervenkitzel *m*; *get a* ~ *out of* F Spaß finden an (*dat.*); 2. *v/t.* (mit dem Fuß) stoßen *od.* treten; *Fußball:* schießen; ~ *out* F hinauswerfen; *v/i.* (hinten) ausschlagen; stoßen (*Gewehr*); sich auflehnen; ~ *in with Am. sl.* Geld 'reinbuttern; ~ *off Fußball:* anstoßen; ~**back** *bsd. Am.* F ['kikbæk] Rückzahlung *f*; ~**er** ['kikə] Fußballspieler *m*.

kid [kid] 1. Zicklein *n*; *sl.* Kind *n*; Ziegenleder *n*; 2. *sl.* foppen; ~**dy** *sl.* ['kidi] Kind *n*; ~ *glove* Glacéhandschuh *m* (*a. fig.*); ~**-glove** sanft, zart.

kidnap ['kidnæp] entführen; ~(**p**)**er** [~pə] Kindesentführer *m*, Kidnapper *m*.

kidney ['kidni] *anat.* Niere *f*; F Art *f*; ~ *bean* ♣ weiße Bohne.

kill [kil] 1. töten (*a. fig.*); *fig.* vernichten; *parl.* zu Fall bringen; ~ *off* abschlachten; ~ *time* die Zeit totschlagen; 2. Tötung *f*; Jagdbeute *f*; ~**er** ['kilə] Totschläger *m*; ~**ing** ['kiliŋ] 1. □ mörderisch; F komisch; 2. *Am.* F finanzieller Volltreffer.

kiln [kiln] Brenn-, Darrofen *m*.

kilo|gram(me) ['kiləgræm] Kilogramm *n*; ~**metre**, *Am.* ~**meter** Kilometer *m*.

kilt [kilt] Kilt *m*, Schottenrock *m*.

kin [kin] (Bluts)Verwandtschaft *f*.

kind [kaind] 1. □ gütig, freundlich; 2. Art *f*, Gattung *f*, Geschlecht *n*; Art und Weise *f*; *pay in* ~ in Naturalien zahlen; *fig.* mit gleicher Münze heimzahlen.

kindergarten ['kindəga:tn] Kindergarten *m*.

kind-hearted ['kaind'ha:tid] gütig.

kindle ['kindl] anzünden; (sich) entzünden (*a. fig.*).

kindling ['kindliŋ] Kleinholz *n*.

kind|ly ['kaindli] freundlich; günstig; ~**ness** [~dnis] Güte *f*, Freundlichkeit *f*; Gefälligkeit *f*.

kindred ['kindrid] 1. verwandt, gleichartig; 2. Verwandtschaft *f*.

king [kiŋ] König *m* (*a. fig. u. Schach, Kartenspiel*); ~**dom** [~dəm] Königreich *n*; *bsd.* ♣, *zo.* Reich *n*, Gebiet *n*; *eccl.* Reich *n* Gottes; ~**like**

['kiŋlaik], ~ly [~li] königlich; ~-size F ['kiŋsaiz] überlang, übergroß.

kink [kiŋk] Schlinge f, Knoten m; fig. Schrulle f, Fimmel m.

kin|ship ['kinʃip] Verwandtschaft f; ~sman ['kinzmən] Verwandte(r) m.

kipper ['kipə] Räucherhering m Bückling m; sl. Kerl m.

kiss [kis] 1. Kuß m; 2. (sich) küssen.

kit [kit] Ausrüstung f (a. ✕ u. Sport); Handwerkszeug n, Werkzeug n; ~-bag ['kitbæg] ✕ Tornister m; Seesack m; Reisetasche f.

kitchen ['kitʃin] Küche f; ~ette [kitʃi'net] Kochnische f; ~-garden ['kitʃin'ga:dn] Gemüsegarten m.

kite [kait] Papier-Drachen m.

kitten ['kitn] Kätzchen n.

Klan Am. [klæn] Ku-Klux-Klan m; ~sman ['klænzmən] Mitglied n des Ku-Klux-Klan.

knack [næk] Kniff m, Dreh m; Geschicklichkeit f.   [Rucksack m.\

knapsack ['næpsæk] Tornister m;\

knave [neiv] Schurke m; Kartenspiel: Bube m; ~ry ['neivəri] Gaunerei f.

knead [ni:d] kneten; massieren.

knee [ni:] Knie n; ⊕ Kniestück n; ~-cap ['ni:kæp] Kniescheibe f; ~-deep bis an die Knie (reichend); ~-joint Kniegelenk n; ~l [ni:l] [irr.] knien (to vor dat.).

knell [nel] Totenglocke f.

knelt [nelt] pret. u. p.p. von kneel.

knew [nju:] pret. von know.

knicker|bockers ['nikəbɔkəz] pl. Knickerbocker pl., Kniehosen f/pl.; ~s F ['nikəz] pl. Schlüpfer m; = knickerbockers.

knick-knack ['niknæk] Spielerei f; Nippsache f.

knife [naif] 1. pl. knives [naivz] Messer n; 2. schneiden; (er)stechen.

knight [nait] 1. Ritter m; Springer m im Schach; 2. zum Ritter schlagen; ~-errant ['nait'erənt] fahrender Ritter; ~hood ['naithud] Rittertum n; Ritterschaft f; ~ly ['naitli] ritterlich.

knit [nit] [irr.] stricken; (ver)knüpfen; (sich) eng verbinden; ~ the brows die Stirn runzeln; ~ting ['nitiŋ] Stricken n; Strickzeug n; attr. Strick...

knives [naivz] pl. von knife 1.

knob [nɔb] Knopf m; Buckel m; Brocken m.

knock [nɔk] 1. Schlag m; Anklopfen n; mot. Klopfen n; 2. v/i. klopfen; pochen; stoßen; schlagen; ~ about F sich herumtreiben; v/t. klopfen, stoßen, schlagen; Am. sl. bekritteln, schlechtmachen; ~ about herumstoßen, übel zurichten; ~ down niederschlagen; Auktion: zuschlagen; ⊕ aus-ea.-nehmen; be ~ed down überfahren werden; ~ off aufhören mit; F zs.-hauen (schnell erledigen); Summe abziehen; ~ out Boxen: k.o. schlagen; ~er ['nɔkə] Klopfende(r) m; Türklopfer m; Am. sl. Kritikaster m; ~-kneed ['nɔk-ni:d] x-beinig; fig. hinkend; ~-out Boxen: Knockout m, K.o. m; sl. tolle Sache od. Person.

knoll¹ [noul] kleiner Erdhügel.

knoll² [~] (bsd. zu Grabe) läuten.

knot [nɔt] 1. Knoten m; Knorren m; Seemeile f; Schleife f, Band n (a. fig.); Schwierigkeit f; 2. (ver)knoten, (ver)knüpfen (a. fig.); Stirn runzeln; verwickeln; ~ty ['nɔti] knotig; knorrig; fig. verwickelt.

know [nou] [irr.] wissen; (er)kennen; erfahren; ~ French Französisch können; come to ~ erfahren; get to ~ kennenlernen; ~ one's business, ~ the ropes, ~ a thing or two, ~ what's what sich auskennen, Erfahrung haben; you ~ (am Ende des Satzes) nämlich; ~ing □ ['nouiŋ] erfahren; klug; schlau; verständnisvoll; wissentlich; ~ledge ['nɔlidʒ] Kenntnis(se pl.) f; Wissen n; to my ~ meines Wissens; ~n [noun] p.p. von know; come to be ~ bekannt werden; make ~ bekanntmachen.

knuckle ['nʌkl] 1. Knöchel m; 2. ~ down, ~ under nachgeben.

Kremlin ['kremlin] der Kreml.

Ku-Klux-Klan Am. ['kju:klʌks-'klæn] Geheimbund in den USA.

L

label ['leibl] 1. Zettel m, Etikett n; Aufschrift f; Schildchen n; Bezeichnung f; 2. etikettieren, beschriften; fig. abstempeln (as als).

laboratory [lə'bɔrətəri] Laboratorium n; ~ assistant Laborant(in).

laborious □ [lə'bɔːriəs] mühsam; arbeitsam; schwerfällig (Stil).

labo(u)r ['leibə] 1. Arbeit f; Mühe

f; (Geburts)Wehen f/pl.; Arbeiter m/pl.; Ministry of ♀ Arbeitsministerium n; hard ~ Zwangsarbeit f; ♀ Arbeiter...; Arbeits...; 3. v/i. arbeiten; sich abmühen; ~ under leiden unter (dat.), zu kämpfen haben mit; v/t. ausarbeiten; ~ed schwerfällig (Stil); mühsam (Atem etc.); ~er [~ərə] ungelernter Arbeiter; ♀ Exchange Arbeitsamt n; Labour

Party *pol.* Labour Party *f*; **labor union** *Am.* Gewerkschaft *f*.

lace [leis] **1.** Spitze *f*; Borte *f*; Schnur *f*; **2.** (zu)schnüren; mit Spitze *etc.* besetzen; *Schnur* durch-, einziehen; ~ (*into*) *s.o.* j-n verprügeln.

lacerate ['læsəreit] zerreißen; *fig.* quälen.

lack [læk] **1.** Fehlen *n*, Mangel *m*; **2.** *v/t.* ermangeln (*gen.*); *he* ~*s money* es fehlt ihm an Geld; *v/i.* *be* ~*ing* fehlen, mangeln; ~**lustre** ['læklʌstə] glanzlos, matt.

laconic [lə'kɔnik] (~*ally*) lakonisch, wortkarg, kurz und prägnant.

lacquer ['lækə] **1.** Lack *m*; **2.** lakkieren.

lad [læd] Bursche *m*, Junge *m*.

ladder ['lædə] Leiter *f*; Laufmasche *f*; ~**proof** maschenfest (*Strumpf etc.*).

laden ['leidn] beladen.

lading ['leidiŋ] Ladung *f*, Fracht *f*.

ladle ['leidl] **1.** Schöpflöffel *m*, Kelle *f*; **2.** ~ *out* Suppe austeilen.

lady ['leidi] Dame *f*, Lady *f*; Herrin *f*; ~ *doctor* Ärztin *f*; ~**bird** Marienkäfer *m*; ~**like** damenhaft; ~**love** Geliebte *f*; ~**ship** [~ʃip]: *her* ~ die gnädige Frau; *Your* 2 gnädige Frau, Euer Gnaden.

lag [læg] **1.** zögern; *a.* ~ *behind* zurückbleiben; **2.** Verzögerung *f*.

lager (beer) ['lɑːgə(biə)] Lagerbier *n*.

laggard ['lægəd] Nachzügler *m*.

lagoon [lə'guːn] Lagune *f*.

laid [leid] *pret. u. p.p. von* lay[3] 2; ~ *up* bettlägerig (with mit, wegen).

lain [lein] *p.p. von* lie[2] 2.

lair [lεə] Lager *n e-s wilden Tieres*.

laity ['leiiti] Laien *m/pl*.

lake [leik] See *m*; rote Pigmentfarbe.

lamb [læm] **1.** Lamm *n*; **2.** lammen.

lambent ['læmbənt] leckend; züngelnd (*Flamme*); funkelnd.

lamb|kin ['læmkin] Lämmchen *n*; ~**like** lammfromm.

lame [leim] **1.** □ lahm (*a. fig.* = *mangelhaft*); **2.** lähmen.

lament [lə'ment] **1.** Wehklage *f*; **2.** (be)klagen; trauern; ~**able** □ ['læməntəbl] beklagenswert; kläglich; ~**ation** [læmən'teiʃən] Wehklage *f*.

lamp [læmp] Lampe *f*; *fig.* Leuchte *f*.

lampoon [læm'puːn] **1.** Schmähschrift *f*; **2.** schmähen.

lamp-post ['læmppoust] Laternenpfahl *m*.

lampshade ['læmpʃeid] Lampenschirm *m*.

lance [lɑːns] **1.** Lanze *f*; Speer *m*; **2.** ✄ aufschneiden; ~**corporal** ✗ ['lɑːns'kɔːpərəl] Gefreite(r) *m*.

land [lænd] **1.** Land *n*; Grundstück *n*; *by* ~ auf dem Landweg; ~*s pl.*

Ländereien *f/pl.*; **2.** landen; ⚓ löschen; *Preis* gewinnen; ~**agent** ['lændeidʒənt] Grundstücksmakler *m*; Gutsverwalter *m*; ~**ed** grundbesitzend; Land..., Grund...; ~**holder** Grundbesitzer(in).

landing ['lændiŋ] Landung *f*; Treppenabsatz *m*; Anlegestelle *f*; ~**field** ✄ Landebahn *f*; ~**gear** Fahrgestell *n*; ~**stage** Landungsbrücke *f*.

land|lady ['lænleidi] Vermieterin *f*, Wirtin *f*; ~**lord** [~lɔːd] Vermieter *m*; Wirt *m*; Haus-, Grundbesitzer *m*; ~**lubber** ⚓ *contp.* Landratte *f*; ~**mark** Grenz-, Markstein *m* (*a. fig.*); Wahrzeichen *n*; ~**owner** Grundbesitzer(in); ~**scape** ['lænskeip] Landschaft *f*; ~**slide** Erdrutsch *m* (*a. pol.*); *a Democratic* ~ ein Erdrutsch zugunsten der Demokraten; ~**slip** *konkr.* Erdrutsch *m*.

lane [lein] Feldweg *m*; Gasse *f*; Spalier *n*; *mot.* Fahrbahn *f*, Spur *f*.

language ['læŋgwidʒ] Sprache *f*; *strong* ~ Kraftausdrücke *m/pl*.

languid □ ['læŋgwid] matt; träg.

languish ['læŋgwiʃ] matt werden; schmachten; dahinsiechen.

languor ['læŋgə] Mattigkeit *f*; Schmachten *n*; Stille *f*.

lank □ [læŋk] schmächtig, dünn; schlicht; ~**y** □ ['læŋki] schlaksig.

lantern ['læntən] Laterne *f*; ~**slide** Dia(positiv) *n*, Lichtbild *n*.

lap [læp] **1.** Schoß *m*; ⊕ Vorstoß *m*; Runde *f*; **2.** über-ea.-legen; (ein)hüllen; (auf)lecken; schlürfen; plätschern (gegen) (*Wellen*).

lapel [lə'pel] Aufschlag *m am Rock*.

lapse [læps] **1.** Verlauf *m der Zeit*; Verfallen *n*; Versehen *n*; **2.** (ver)fallen; verfließen; fehlen.

larceny ⚖ ['lɑːsni] Diebstahl *m*.

larch ♀ [lɑːtʃ] Lärche *f*.

lard [lɑːd] **1.** (Schweine)Schmalz *n*; **2.** spicken (*a. fig.*); ~**er** ['lɑːdə] Speisekammer *f*.

large □ [lɑːdʒ] groß; weit; reichlich; weitherzig; flott; Groß...; *at* ~ auf freiem Fuß; ausführlich; *als Ganzes*; ~**ly** ['lɑːdʒli] zum großen Teil, weitgehend; ~**minded** weitherzig; ~**ness** ['lɑːdʒnis] Größe *f*; Weite *f*; ~**sized** groß(formatig).

lariat *Am.* ['læriət] Lasso *n*, *m*.

lark [lɑːk] *orn.* Lerche *f*; *fig.* Streich *m*.

larkspur ♀ ['lɑːkspəː] Rittersporn *m*.

larva *zo.* ['lɑːvə] Larve *f*, Puppe *f*.

larynx *anat.* ['læriŋks] Kehlkopf *m*.

lascivious □ [lə'siviəs] lüstern.

lash [læʃ] **1.** Peitsche(nschnur) *f*; Hieb *m*; Wimper *f*; **2.** peitschen; *fig.* geißeln; schlagen; anbinden.

lass, ~ie [læs, 'læsi] Mädchen *n*.

lassitude ['læsitjuːd] Mattigkeit *f*, Abgespanntheit *f*; Desinteresse *n*.

last¹ [lɑːst] **1.** *adj.* letzt; vorig; äußerst; geringst; ~ but one vorletzt; ~ night gestern abend; **2.** Letzte(r *m*, -s *n*) *f*; Ende *n*; at ~ zuletzt, endlich; **3.** *adv.* zuletzt; ~, but not least nicht zuletzt.

last² [~] dauern; halten (*Farbe*); ausreichen; ausdauern.

last³ [~] (Schuhmacher)Leisten *m*.

lasting □ ['lɑːstiŋ] dauerhaft; beständig.

lastly ['lɑːstli] zuletzt, schließlich.

latch [lætʃ] **1.** Klinke *f*, Drücker *m*; Druckschloß *n*; **2.** ein-, zuklinken.

late [leit] spät; (kürzlich)verstorben; ehemalig; jüngst; at (the) ~st spätestens; as ~ as noch (in *dat.*); of ~ letzthin; ~r on später; be ~ (zu) spät kommen; ~ly ['leitli] kürzlich.

latent □ ['leitənt] verborgen, latent; gebunden (*Wärme etc.*).

lateral □ ['lætərəl] seitlich; Seiten...

lath [lɑːθ] **1.** Latte *f*; **2.** belatten.

lathe ⊕ [leið] Drehbank *f*; Lade *f*.

lather ['lɑːðə] **1.** (Seifen)Schaum *m*; **2.** *v/t.* einseifen; *v/i.* schäumen.

Latin ['lætin] **1.** lateinisch; **2.** Latein *n*.

latitude ['lætitjuːd] Breite *f*; *fig.* Umfang *m*, Weite *f*; Spielraum *m*.

latter ['lætə] neuer; *der* (*die, das*) letztere; ~ly [~əli] neuerdings.

lattice ['lætis] *a.* ~-work Gitter *n*.

laud [lɔːd] loben, preisen; ~able □ ['lɔːdəbl] lobenswert, löblich.

laugh [lɑːf] **1.** Gelächter *n*, Lachen *n*; **2.** lachen; ~ at j-n auslachen; he ~s best who ~s last wer zuletzt lacht, lacht am besten; ~able □ ['lɑːfəbl] lächerlich; ~ter ['lɑːftə] Gelächter *n*, Lachen *n*.

launch [lɔːntʃ] **1.** ⚓ Stapellauf *m*; Barkasse *f*; **2.** vom Stapel laufen lassen; *Boot* aussetzen; schleudern (*a. fig.*); *Schläge* versetzen; *Rakete* starten, abschießen; *fig.* in Gang bringen; ~ing-pad ['lɔːntʃiŋpæd] (Raketen)Abschußrampe *f*.

launderette [lɔːndə'ret] Selbstbedienungswaschsalon *m*.

laund|ress ['lɔːndris] Wäscherin *f*; ~ry [~ri] Waschanstalt *f*; Wäsche *f*.

laurel ⚘ ['lɔrəl] Lorbeer *m* (*a. fig.*).

lavatory ['lævətəri] Waschraum *m*; Toilette *f*; public ~ Bedürfnisanstalt *f*.

lavender ⚘ ['lævində] Lavendel *m*.

lavish ['læviʃ] **1.** □ freigebig, verschwenderisch; **2.** verschwenden.

law [lɔː] Gesetz *n*; (Spiel)Regel *f*; Recht(swissenschaft *f*) *n*; Gericht(sverfahren *n*); go to ~ vor Gericht gehen; lay down the ~ den Ton angeben; ~-abiding ['lɔːəbaidiŋ] friedlich; ~-court Gericht(shof *m*) *n*; ~ful □ ['lɔːful] gesetzlich; gültig; ~less □ ['lɔːlis] gesetzlos; ungesetzlich; zügellos.

lawn [lɔːn] Rasen(platz) *m*; Batist *m*

law|suit ['lɔːsjuːt] Prozeß *m*; ~yer ['lɔːjə] Jurist *m*; (Rechts)Anwalt *m*

lax □ [læks] locker; schlaff (*a. fig.*) lasch; ~ative ⚕ ['læksətiv] **1.** abführend; **2.** Abführmittel *n*.

lay¹ [lei] *pret. von* lie² 2.

lay² [~] weltlich; Laien...

lay³ [~] **1.** Lage *f*, Richtung *f*; 2 [*irr.*] *v/t.* legen; umlegen; *Plan etc* ersinnen; stellen, setzen; *Tisch* decken; lindern; besänftigen; auf erlegen; *Summe* wetten; ~ befor s.o. j-m vorlegen; ~ in einlagern sich eindecken mit; ~ low niederwerfen; ~ open darlegen; ~ out aus legen; *Garten etc.* anlegen; ~ u Vorräte hinlegen, sammeln; be lai up ans Bett gefesselt sein; ~ wit belegen mit; *v/i.* (Eier) legen; *a.* ~ wager wetten.

lay-by ['leibai] Park-, Rastplatz *n* an e-r Fernstraße.

layer ['leiə] Lage *f*, Schicht *f*.

layman ['leimən] Laie *m*.

lay|off ['leiɔf] Arbeitsunterbre chung *f*; ~out Anlage *f*; Plan *m*

lazy □ ['leizi] faul.

lead¹ [led] Blei *n*; ⚓ Lot *n*, Senk blei *n*; *typ.* Durchschuß *m*.

lead² [liːd] **1.** Führung *f*; Leitung *f* Beispiel *n*; *thea.* Hauptrolle *f*; *Kar tenspiel:* Vorhand *f*; ≠ Leitung *f* *Hunde-*Leine *f*; **2.** [*irr.*] *v/t.* (anführen, leiten; bewegen (to zu) *Karte* ausspielen; ~ on (ver)locken *v/i.* vorangehen; ~ off den Anfan machen; ~ up to überleiten zu.

leaden ['ledn] bleiern (*a. fig.*) Blei...

leader ['liːdə] (An)Führer(in), Lei ter(in); Erste(r) *m*; Leitartikel *m* ~ship [~əʃip] Führerschaft *f*.

leading ['liːdiŋ] **1.** leitend; Leit... Haupt...; **2.** Leitung *f*, Führung

leaf [liːf] *pl.* leaves [liːvz] Blatt *n Tür-* etc. Flügel *m*; *Tisch-*Platte *f* ~let ['liːflit] Blättchen *n*; Flug Merkblatt *n*; ~y ['liːfi] belaubt.

league [liːg] **1.** Liga *f* (*a. hist. u Sport*); Bund *m*; *mst poet.* Meile *f* **2.** (sich) verbünden.

leak [liːk] **1.** Leck *n*; **2.** leck sein tropfen; ~ out durchsickern; ~ag ['liːkidʒ] Lecken *n*; ⚓ Leckage *f* Verlust *m* (*a. fig.*), Schwund *n* Durchsickern *n*; ~y ['liːki] leck; un dicht.

lean [liːn] **1.** [*irr.*] (sich) (an)lehne (sich) stützen; (sich) (hin)neige **2.** mager; **3.** mageres Fleisch.

leant [lent] *pret. u. p.p. von* lean

leap [liːp] **1.** Sprung *m*; **2.** [*irr* (über)springen; ~t [lept] *pret. p.p. von* leap 2; ~-year ['liːpjə Schaltjahr *n*.

learn [lɜːn] [*irr.*] lernen; erfahre hören; ~ from ersehen aus; ~ ['lɜːnid] gelehrt; ~er ['lɜːnə] An fänger(in); ~ing ['lə:niŋ] Lernen n; Gelehrsamkeit f; ~t [lə:nt] pret. u. p.p. von learn.

lease [li:s] 1. Verpachtung f, Vermietung f; Pacht f, Miete f; Pacht-, Mietvertrag m; 2. (ver-) pachten, (ver)mieten.

leash [li:ʃ] 1. Koppelleine f; Koppel f (3 Hunde etc.); 2. koppeln.

least [li:st] 1. adj. kleinst, geringst; wenigst, mindest; 2. adv. a. ~ of all am wenigsten; at ~ wenigstens; 3. das Mindeste, das Wenigste; to say the ~ gelinde gesagt.

leather ['leðə] 1. Leder n (fig.Haut); 2. a. ~n ledern; Leder...

leave [li:v] 1. Erlaubnis f; a. ~ of absence Urlaub m; Abschied m; 2. [irr.] v/t. (ver)lassen; zurück-, hinterlassen; übriglassen; überlassen; ~ off aufhören (mit); Kleid ablegen; v/i. ablassen; weggehen, abreisen (for nach).

leaven ['levn] Sauerteig m; Hefe f.

leaves [li:vz] pl. von leaf; Laub n.

leavings ['li:viŋz] pl. Überbleibsel n/pl.

lecherous ['letʃərəs] wollüstig.

lecture ['lektʃə] 1. Vorlesung f, Vortrag m; Strafpredigt f; 2. v/i. Vorlesungen od. Vorträge halten; v/t. abkanzeln; ~r [~ərə] Vortragende(r m) f; univ. Dozent(in).

led [led] pret. u. p.p. von lead² 2.

ledge [ledʒ] Leiste f; Sims m, n; Riff n.

ledger † ['ledʒə] Hauptbuch n.

leech [li:tʃ] zo. Blutegel m; fig. Schmarotzer m.

leek ♀ [li:k] Lauch m, Porree m.

leer [liə] 1. (lüsterner od. finsterer) Seitenblick; 2. schielen (at nach).

lees [li:z] pl. Bodensatz m, Hefe f.

lee|ward ⚓ ['li:wəd] leewärts; ~way ['li:wei] ⚓ Abtrift f; make up ~ fig. Versäumtes nachholen.

left¹ [left] pret. u. p.p. von leave 2.

left² [~] 1. link(s); 2. Linke f; ~-handed □ ['left'hændid] linkshändig; linkisch.

left|-luggage office ['left'lʌgidʒ-ɔfis] Gepäckaufbewahrung(sstelle) f; ~overs pl. Speisereste m/pl.

leg [leg] Bein n; Keule f; (Stiefel-) Schaft m; & Schenkel m; pull s.o.'s ~j-n auf den Arm nehmen (hänseln).

legacy ['legəsi] Vermächtnis n.

legal □ ['li:gəl] gesetzlich; rechtsgültig; juristisch; Rechts...; ~ize [~laiz] rechtskräftig machen; beurkunden.

legation [li'geiʃən] Gesandtschaft f.

legend ['ledʒənd] Legende f; ~ary [~dəri] legendär, sagenhaft.

leggings ['legiŋz] pl. Gamaschen f/pl.

legible □ ['ledʒəbl] leserlich.

legionary ['li:dʒənəri] Legionär m.

legislat|ion [ledʒis'leiʃən] Gesetz-

gebung f; ~ive ['ledʒislətiv] gesetzgebend; ~or [~leitə] Gesetzgeber m.

legitima|cy [li'dʒitiməsi] Rechtmäßigkeit f; ~te [~meit] legitimieren; 2. [~mit] rechtmäßig.

leisure ['leʒə] Muße f; at your ~ wenn es Ihnen paßt; ~ly [~əli] gemächlich.

lemon ['lemən] Zitrone f; ~ade [lemə'neid] Limonade f; ~ squash Zitronenwasser n.

lend [lend] [irr.] (ver-, aus)leihen; Hilfe leisten, gewähren.

length [leŋθ] Länge f; Strecke f; (Zeit)Dauer f; at ~ endlich, zuletzt; go all ~s aufs Ganze gehen; ~en ['leŋθən] (sich) verlängern, (sich) ausdehnen; ~wise [~θwaiz] der Länge nach; ~y □ [~θi] sehr lang.

lenient □ ['li:njənt] mild, nachsichtig.

lens opt. [lenz] Linse f.

lent¹ [lent] pret. u. p.p. von lend.

Lent² [~] Fasten pl., Fastenzeit f.

leopard ['lepəd] Leopard m.

lepr|osy ♂ ['leprəsi] Aussatz m, Lepra f; ~ous [~əs] aussätzig.

less [les] 1. adj. u. adv. kleiner, geringer; weniger; 2. prp. minus.

lessen ['lesn] v/t. vermindern, schmälern; v/i. abnehmen.

lesser ['lesə] kleiner; geringer.

lesson ['lesn] Lektion f; Aufgabe f; (Unterrichts)Stunde f; Lehre f; ~s pl. Unterricht m.

lest [lest] damit nicht, daß nicht.

let [let] [irr.] lassen; vermieten, verpachten; ~ alone in Ruhe lassen; geschweige denn; ~ down j-n im Stich lassen; ~ go loslassen; ~ into einweihen in (acc.); ~ off abschießen; j-n laufen lassen; ~ out hinauslassen; ausplaudern; vermieten; ~ up aufhören.

lethal □ ['li:θəl] tödlich; Todes...

lethargy ['leθədʒi] Lethargie f.

letter ['letə] 1. Buchstabe m; Type f; Brief m; ~s pl. Literatur f, Wissenschaft f; attr. Brief...; to the ~ buchstäblich; 2. beschriften, betiteln; ~-box Briefkasten m; ~-card Kartenbrief m; ~-carrier Am. Briefträger m; ~-case Brieftasche f; ~-cover Briefumschlag m; ~ed (literarisch) gebildet; ~-file Briefordner m; ~ing [~əriŋ] Beschriftung f; ~-press Kopierpresse f.

lettuce ♀ ['letis] Lattich m, Salat m.

leuk(a)emia ♂ [lju:'ki:miə] Leukämie f.

levee¹ ['levi] Morgenempfang m.

levee² Am. [~] Uferdamm m.

level ['levl] 1. waag(e)recht, eben; gleich; ausgeglichen; my ~ best mein möglichstes; ~ crossing ⚓ schienengleicher Übergang m; 2. ebene Fläche; (gleiche) Höhe, Niveau n, Stand m; fig. Maßstab m; Wasserwaage f; sea ~ Meeresspiegel m; on the ~ F offen, aufrichtig; 3. v/t. gleichmachen, ebnen; fig. anpassen; richten, zielen mit; ~ up erhöhen; v/i. ~ at, against zielen auf (acc.); ~-headed vernünftig, nüchtern.

lever ['li:və] Hebel m; Hebestange f; ~age [~əridʒ] Hebelkraft f.

levity ['leviti] Leichtfertigkeit f.

levy ['levi] 1. Erhebung f von Steuern; ⚔ Aushebung f; Aufgebot n; 2. Steuern erheben; ⚔ ausheben.

lewd □ [lu:d] liederlich, unzüchtig.

liability [laiə'biliti] Verantwortlichkeit f; ⚖ Haftpflicht f; Verpflichtung f; fig. Hang m; liabilities pl. Verbindlichkeiten f/pl., † Passiva pl.

liable □ ['laiəbl] verantwortlich; haftpflichtig; verpflichtet; ausgesetzt (to dat.); be ~ to neigen zu.

liar ['laiə] Lügner(in).

libel ['laibəl] 1. Schmähschrift f; Verleumdung f; 2. schmähen; verunglimpfen.

liberal ['libərəl] 1. □ liberal (a. pol.); freigebig; reichlich; freisinnig; 2. Liberale(r) m; ~ity [libə-'reliti] Freigebigkeit f; Freisinnigkeit f.

liberat|e ['libəreit] befreien; freilassen; ~ion [libə'reiʃən] Befreiung f; ~or ['libəreitə] Befreier m.

libertine ['libə(:)tain] Wüstling m.

liberty ['libəti] Freiheit f; take liberties sich Freiheiten erlauben; be at ~ frei sein.

librar|ian [lai'brɛəriən] Bibliothekar(in); ~y ['laibrəri] Bibliothek f.

lice [lais] pl. von louse.

licen|ce, Am. **~se** ['laisəns] 1. Lizenz f; Erlaubnis f; Konzession f; Freiheit f; Zügellosigkeit f; driving ~ Führerschein m; 2. lizenzieren, berechtigen; et. genehmigen; ~see [laisən'si:] Lizenznehmer m.

licentious □ [lai'senʃəs] unzüchtig; ausschweifend.

lichen ♀, ⚕ ['laikən] Flechte f.

lick [lik] 1. Lecken n; Salzlecke f; F Schlag m; 2. (be)lecken; F verdreschen; übertreffen; ~ the dust im Staub kriechen; fallen; geschlagen werden; ~ into shape zurechtstutzen.

licorice ['likəris] Lakritze f.

lid [lid] Deckel m; (Augen)Lid n.

lie¹ [lai] 1. Lüge f; give s.o. the ~ j-n Lügen strafen; 2. lügen.

lie² [~] 1. Lage f; 2. [irr.] liegen; ~ by still-, brachliegen; ~ down sich niederlegen; ~ in wait for j-m auflauern; let sleeping dogs ~ fig. daran rühren wir lieber nicht; ~-down [lai'daun] Nickerchen n; ~-in: have a ~ sich gründlich ausschlafen.

lien ⚖ ['liən] Pfandrecht n.

lieu [lju:]: in ~ of (an)statt.

lieutenant [lef'tenənt; ⚓ le'tenənt; Am. lu:'tenənt] Leutnant m; Statthalter m; ~-commander ⚓ Korvettenkapitän m.

life [laif], pl. **lives** [laivz] Leben n; Menschenleben n; Lebensbeschreibung f; for ~ auf Lebenszeit; for one's ~, for dear ~ ums (liebe) Leben; to the ~ naturgetreu; ~ sentence lebenslängliche Zuchthausstrafe; ~ assurance Lebensversicherung f; ~belt ['laifbelt] Rettungsgürtel m; ~boat Rettungsboot n; ~guard Leibwache f; Bademärter m am Strand; ~ insurance Lebensversicherung f; ~jacket ✕ Schwimmweste f; ~less □ ['laiflis] leblos; matt (a. fig.); ~like lebenswahr; ~long lebenslänglich; ~preserver Am. ['laifprizə:və] Schwimmgürtel m; Totschläger m (Stock mit Bleikopf); ~time Lebenszeit f.

lift [lift] 1. Heben n; phys., ✈ Auftrieb m; fig. Erhebung f; Fahrstuhl m; give s.o. a ~ j-m helfen; j-n (im Auto) mitnehmen; 2. v/t. (auf)heben; erheben; beseitigen; sl. klauen, stehlen; v/i. sich heben.

ligature ['ligətʃuə] Binde f; ⚕ Verband m.

light¹ [lait] 1. Licht n (a. fig.); Fenster n; Aspekt m, Gesichtspunkt m; Feuer n; Glanz m; fig. Leuchte f; ~s pl. Fähigkeiten f/pl.; will you give me a ~ darf ich Sie um Feuer bitten; put a ~ to anzünden; 2. licht, hell; blond; 3. [irr.] v/t. oft ~ up be-, erleuchten; anzünden; v/i. mst ~ up aufleuchten; ~ out Am. sl. schnell losziehen, abhauen.

light² [~] 1. adj. □ u. adv. leicht (a. fig.); ~ current ⚡ Schwachstrom m; make ~ of et. leicht nehmen; 2. ~ (up)on stoßen od. fallen auf (acc.), geraten an (acc.); sich niederlassen auf (dat.).

lighten ['laitn] blitzen; (sich) erhellen; leichter machen; (sich) erleichtern.

lighter ['laitə] Anzünder m; (Taschen)Feuerzeug n; ⚓ L(e)ichter m.

light|-headed ['lait'hedid] wirr im Kopf, irr; ~-hearted □ [~'ha:tid] leichtherzig; fröhlich; ~house ['laithaus] Leuchtturm m.

lighting ['laitiŋ] Beleuchtung f; Anzünden n.

light|-minded ['lait'maindid] leichtsinnig; ~ness ['laitnis] Leichtigkeit f; Leichtsinn m.

lightning ['laitniŋ] Blitz m; ~ bug Am. zo. Leuchtkäfer m; ~-conductor, ~-rod ⚡ Blitzableiter m.

light-weight ['laitweit] Sport: Leichtgewicht n.

like [laik] 1. gleich; ähnlich; wie; such ~ dergleichen; feel ~ F sich aufgelegt fühlen zu et.; ~ that so; what is he ~? wie sieht er aus?; wie ist er?; 2. Gleiche m, f, n; ~s pl. Neigungen f/pl.; his ~ seinesgleichen; the ~ der-, desgleichen; 3. mögen, gern haben; how do you ~ London? wie gefällt Ihnen L.?; I should ~ to know ich möchte wissen.

like|lihood ['laiklihud] Wahrscheinlichkeit f; ~ly ['laikli] wahrscheinlich; geeignet; he is ~ to die er wird wahrscheinlich sterben.

like|n ['laikən] vergleichen (to mit); ~ness ['laiknis] Ähnlichkeit f; (Ab-)Bild n; Gestalt f; ~wise ['laikwaiz] gleich-, ebenfalls.

liking ['laikiŋ] (for) Neigung f (für, zu), Gefallen n (an dat.).

lilac ['lailək] 1. lila; 2. ♀ Flieder m.

lily ♀ ['lili] Lilie f; ~ of the valley Maiglöckchen n; ~-white schneeweiß.

limb [lim] Körper-Glied n; Ast m.

limber ['limbə] 1. biegsam, geschmeidig; 2.: ~ up (sich) lockern.

lime [laim] Kalk m; Vogelleim m; ♀ Limone f; ♀ Linde f; ~light ['laimlait] Kalklicht n; thea. Scheinwerfer(licht n) m; fig. Mittelpunkt m des öffentlichen Interesses.

limit ['limit] 1. Grenze f; in (off) ~s Zutritt gestattet (verboten) (to für); that is the ~! F das ist der Gipfel!; das ist (doch) die Höhe!; go the ~ Am. F bis zum Äußersten gehen; 2. begrenzen; beschränken (to auf acc.); ~ation [limi'teiʃən] Begrenzung f, Beschränkung f; fig. Grenze f; tt Verjährung f; ~ed: ~ (liability) company Gesellschaft f mit beschränkter Haftung; ~ in time befristet; ~less □ [~tlis] grenzenlos.

limp [limp] 1. hinken; 2. Hinken n; 3. schlaff; weich.

limpid □ ['limpid] klar, durchsichtig.

line [lain] 1. Linie f; Reihe f; Zeile f; Vers m; Strich m; Falte f; Furche f; (Menschen)Schlange f; Folge f; Verkehrsgesellschaft f; Eisenbahnlinie f; Strecke f; tel. Leitung f; Branche f, Fach n; Leine f, Schnur f; Äquator m; Richtung f; ✗ Linie(ntruppe) f; Front f; ~s pl. Richtlinien f/pl.; Grundlage f; ~ of conduct Lebensweise f; hard ~s pl. hartes Los, Pech n; in ~ with in Übereinstimmung mit; stand in ~ Schlange stehen; draw the ~ fig. nicht mehr mitmachen; hold the ~ teleph. am Apparat bleiben; 2. v/t. liniieren; aufstellen; Weg etc. säumen, einfassen; Kleid füttern; ~ out entwerfen; v/i. ~ up sich auf-, anstellen.

linea|ge ['liniidʒ] Abstammung f; Familie f; Stammbaum m; ~l □ [~iəl] gerade, direkt (Nachkomme

etc.); ~ment [~əmənt] (Gesichts-)Zug m; ~r ['liniə] geradlinig.

linen ['linin] 1. Leinen n, Leinwand f; Wäsche f; 2. leinen; ~-closet, ~-cupboard Wäscheschrank m; ~-draper [~ndreipə] Weißwarenhändler m, Wäschegeschäft n.

liner ['lainə] Linienschiff n, Passagierdampfer m; Verkehrsflugzeug n.

linger ['liŋgə] zögern; (ver)weilen; sich aufhalten; sich hinziehen; dahinsiechen; ~ at, ~ about sich herumdrücken an od. bei (dat.).

lingerie ['lɛ̃:nʒəri:] Damenunterwäsche f.   [Einreibemittel n.)

liniment ♣ ['linimənt] Liniment n.)

lining ['lainiŋ] Kleider- etc. Futter n; Besatz m; ⊕ Verkleidung f.

link [liŋk] 1. Ketten-Glied n, Gelenk n; Manschettenknopf m; fig. Bindeglied n; 2. (sich) verbinden.

links [liŋks] pl. Dünen f/pl.; a. golf-~ Golf(spiel)platz m.

linseed ['linsi:d] Leinsame(n) m; ~ oil Leinöl n.

lion ['laiən] Löwe m; fig. Größe f, Berühmtheit f; ~ess [~nis] Löwin f.

lip [lip] Lippe f; Rand m; sl. Unverschämtheit f; ~-stick ['lipstik] Lippenstift m.

liquefy ['likwifai] schmelzen.

liquid ['likwid] 1. flüssig; ♣ liquid; klar (Luft etc.); 2. Flüssigkeit f.

liquidat|e ['likwideit] ♣ liquidieren; bezahlen; ~ion [likwi'deiʃən] Abwicklung f, Liquidation f.

liquor ['likə] Flüssigkeit f; Alkohol m, alkoholisches Getränk.

liquorice ['likəris] Lakritze f.

lisp [lisp] 1. Lispeln n; 2. lispeln.

list [list] 1. Liste f, Verzeichnis n; Leiste f; Webkante f; 2. (in e-e Liste) eintragen; verzeichnen.

listen ['lisn] (to) lauschen, horchen (auf acc.); anhören (acc.), zuhören (dat.); hören (auf acc.); ~ in teleph., Radio: (mit)hören (to acc.); ~er [~nə] Zuhörer(in); a. ~-in (Rundfunk)Hörer(in).

listless ['listlis] gleichgültig; lustlos.

lists [lists] pl. Schranken f/pl.

lit [lit] pret. u. p.p. von light[1] 3.

literal □ ['litərəl] buchstäblich; am Buchstaben klebend; wörtlich.

litera|ry □ ['litərəri] literarisch; Literatur...; Schrift...; ~ture [~ritʃə] Literatur f.

lithe [laið] geschmeidig, wendig.

lithography [li'θɔgrəfi] Lithographie f, Steindruck m.

litigation [liti'geiʃən] Prozeß m.

lit|re, Am. ~er ['li:tə] Liter n, m.

litter ['litə] 1. Sänfte f; Tragbahre f; Streu f; Abfall m; Unordnung f; Wurf m junger Tiere; 2. ~ down mit Streu versehen; ~ up in Unordnung bringen; Junge werfen; ~-basket, ~-bin Abfallkorb m.

little ['litl] **1.** *adj.* klein; gering(fügig); wenig; *a* ~ *one* ein Kleines (*Kind*); **2.** *adv.* wenig; **3.** Kleinigkeit *f*; *a* ~ ein bißchen; ~ *by* ~ nach und nach; *not a* ~ nicht wenig.

live 1. [liv] *allg.* leben; wohnen; ~ *to see* erleben; ~ *s.th.* down et. durch guten Lebenswandel vergessen machen; ~ *through* durchmachen, durchstehen, überleben; ~ *up to s-m Ruf* gerecht werden, *s-n Grundsätzen* gemäß leben; *Versprechen* halten; **2.** [laiv] lebendig; richtig; aktuell; glühend; ✕ scharf (*Munition*); ⚡ stromführend; *Radio*: Direkt..., Original...; **~lihood** ['laivlihud] Unterhalt *m*; **~liness** [~inis] Lebhaftigkeit *f*; **~ly** ['laivli] lebhaft; lebendig; aufregend; schnell; bewegt.

liver *anat.* ['livə] Leber *f*.

livery ['livəri] Livree *f*; (Amts-) Tracht *f*; *at* ~ *in* Futter (*stehen etc.*).

live|s [laivz] *pl. von* life; **~stock** ['laivstɔk] Vieh(bestand *m*) *n*.

livid ['livid] bläulich; fahl; F wild.

living ['liviŋ] **1.** ☐ lebend(ig); the ~ *image of* das genaue Ebenbild *gen.*; **2.** Leben *n*; Lebensweise *f*; Lebensunterhalt *m*; *eccl.* Pfründe *f*; **~room** Wohnzimmer *n*.

lizard *zo.* ['lizəd] Eidechse *f*.

load [loud] **1.** Last *f*; Ladung *f*; **2.** (be)laden; *fig.* überhäufen; überladen; **~ing** ['loudiŋ] Laden *n*; Ladung *f*, Fracht *f*; *attr.* Lade...

loaf [louf] **1.** *pl.* **loaves** [louvz] *Brot*-Laib *m*; (Zucker)Hut *m*; **2.** herumlungern.

loafer ['loufə] Bummler *m*.

loam [loum] Lehm *m*, Ackerkrume *f*.

loan [loun] **1.** Anleihe *f*, Darlehen *n*; Leihen *s*; Leihgabe *f*; *on* ~ leihweise; **2.** *bsd. Am.* ausleihen.

loath ☐ [louθ] abgeneigt; **~e** [louð] sich ekeln vor (*dat.*); verabscheuen; **~ing** ['louðiŋ] Ekel *m*; **~some** ☐ ['louðsəm] ekelhaft; verhaßt.

loaves [louvz] *pl. von* loaf 1.

lobby ['lɔbi] **1.** Vorhalle *f*; *parl.* Wandelgang *m*; *thea.* Foyer *n*; **2.** *parl.* s-n Einfluß geltend machen.

lobe *anat.*, ⚘ [loub] Lappen *m*.

lobster ['lɔbstə] Hummer *m*.

local ☐ ['loukəl] **1.** örtlich; Orts...; lokal; ~ *government* Gemeindeverwaltung *f*; **2.** *Zeitung*: Lokalnachricht *f*; 🚃 ⊕ ~ *train* Vorortzug *m*; F Wirtshaus *n* (am Ort); **~ity** [lou'kæliti] Örtlichkeit *f*; Lage *f*; **~ize** ['loukəlaiz] lokalisieren.

locat|e [lou'keit] *v/t.* versetzen, verlegen, unterbringen; ausfindig machen; *Am.* an-, festlegen; *be* ~*d* gelegen sein; wohnen; *v/i.* sich niederlassen; **~ion** [~eiʃən] Lage *f*; Niederlassung *f*; *Am.* Anweisung *f* von Land; angewiesenes Land; Ort

m; *Film*: Gelände *n* für Außenaufnahmen.

loch *schott.* [lɔk] See *m*; Bucht *f*.

lock [lɔk] **1.** Tür-, Gewehr- *etc.* Schloß *n*; Schleuse(nkammer) *f*; ⊕ Sperrvorrichtung *f*; Stauung *f*; Locke *f*; Wollflocke *f*; **2.** (ver)schließen (*a. fig.*), absperren; sich verschließen lassen; ⊕ blockieren, sperren, greifen; umschließen; ~ *s.o. in* j-n einsperren; ~ *up* wegschließen; abschließen; einsperren; *Geld* fest anlegen.

lock|er ['lɔkə] Schrank *m*, Kasten *m*; **~et** ['lɔkit] Medaillon *n*; **~out** Aussperrung *f* von *Arbeitern*; **~smith** Schlosser *m*; **~up** **1.** Haftzelle *f*; ✝ zinslose Kapitalanlage; **2.** verschließbar.

loco *Am. sl.* ['loukou] verrückt.

locomot|ion [loukə'mouʃən] Fortbewegung(sfähigkeit) *f*; **~ive** ['loukəmoutiv] **1.** sich fortbewegend; bewegend; **2.** *a.* ~ *engine* Lokomotive *f*.

locust ['loukəst] *zo.* Heuschrecke *f*; ⚘ unechte Akazie.

lode|star ['loudstɑː] Leitstern *m* (*a. fig.*); **~stone** Magnet(eisenstein) *m*.

lodg|e [lɔdʒ] **1.** Häus-chen *n*; (Forst-, Park-, Pförtner)Haus *n*; Portierloge *f*; Freimaurer-Loge *f*; **2.** *v/t.* beherbergen, aufnehmen; *Geld* hinterlegen; *Klage* einreichen; *Hieb* versetzen; *v/i.* (*bsd. zur Miete*) wohnen; logieren; **~er** [~ə] (Unter)Mieter(in); **~ing** ['lɔdʒiŋ] Unterkunft *f*; **~s** *pl.* möbliertes Zimmer; Wohnung *f*.

loft [lɔːft] (Dach)Boden *m*; Empore *f*; **~y** ☐ ['lɔːfti] hoch; erhaben; stolz.

log [lɔg] Klotz *m*; Block *m*; gefällter Baumstamm; ⚓ Log *n*; **~cabin** ['lɔgkæbin] Blockhaus *n*; **~gerhead** ['lɔgəhed]: *be at* ~*s* sich in den Haaren liegen; **~house**, **~hut** Blockhaus *n*.

logic ['lɔdʒik] Logik *f*; **~al** ☐ [~kəl] logisch.

logroll *bsd. Am. pol.* ['lɔgroul] (sich gegenseitig) in die Hände arbeiten.

loin [lɔin] Lende(nstück *n*) *f*.

loiter ['lɔitə] trödeln, schlendern.

loll [lɔl] (sich) strecken; (sich) rekeln; ~ *about* herumlungern.

lone|liness ['lounlinis] Einsamkeit *f*; **~ly** ☐ ['lounli], **~some** ☐ ['lounsəm] einsam.

long¹ [lɔŋ] **1.** Länge *f*; *before* ~ binnen kurzem; *for* ~ lange; *take* ~ lange brauchen *od.* dauern; **2.** *adj.* lang; langfristig; langsam; *in the* ~ *run* am Ende; auf die Dauer; *be* ~ lange dauern *od.* brauchen; **3.** *adv.* lang(e); *so* ~! bis dann! (*auf Wiedersehen*); (*no*) ~*er* (nicht) länger *od.* mehr.

long² [~] sich sehnen (for nach).

long|-distance['lɔŋ'distəns]Fern..., Weit...; ~evity [lɔn'dʒeviti] Langlebigkeit f; langes Leben; ~hand ['lɔŋhænd] Langschrift f.

longing ['lɔŋiŋ] 1. □ sehnsüchtig; 2. Sehnsucht f; Verlangen n.

longitude geogr. ['lɔndʒitjuːd] Länge f.

long|-shore-man ['lɔŋʃɔːmən] Hafenarbeiterm;~sighted['lɔŋ'saitid] weitsichtig; ~standing seit langer Zeit bestehend, alt; ~suffering 1. langmütig; 2. Langmut f; ~term ['lɔŋtəːm] langfristig; ~winded □ ['lɔŋ'windid] langatmig.

look [luk] 1. Blick m; Anblick m; oft ~s pl. Aussehen n; have a ~ at s.th. sich et. ansehen; I don't like the ~ of it es gefällt mir nicht; 2. v/i. sehen, blicken (at, on auf acc., nach); zusehen, daß od. wie ...; nachsehen, wer etc. ...; krank etc. aussehen; nach e-r Richtung liegen; ~ after sehen nach, sich kümmern um; versorgen; nachsehen, nachblicken (dat.); ~ at ansehen; ~ for erwarten; suchen; ~ forward to sich freuen auf (acc.); ~ in als Besucher hereinschauen (on bei); ~ into prüfen; erforschen; ~ on zuschauen (dat.); betrachten (as als); liegen zu, gehen auf (acc.) (Fenster); ~ out vorsehen; ~ (up)on fig. ansehen (as als); v/t. ~ disdain verächtlich blicken; ~ over et. durchsehen; j-n mustern; ~ up et. nachschlagen.

looker-on ['lukər'ɔn]Zuschauer(in).

looking-glass ['lukiŋglɑːs] Spiegel m.

look-out ['luk'aut] Ausguck m, Ausblick m, Aussicht f (a. fig.); that is my ~ F das ist meine Sache.

loom [luːm] 1. Webstuhl m; 2. undeutlich zu sehen sein, sich abzeichnen.

loop [luːp] 1. Schlinge f, Schleife f, Öse f; 2. v/t. in Schleifen legen; schlingen; v/i. e-e Schleife machen; sich winden; ~hole ['luːphoul] Guck-, Schlupfloch n; ⚔ Schießscharte f.

loose [luːs] 1. □ allg. lose, locker; schlaff; weit; frei; un-zs.-hängend; ungenau; liederlich; 2. lösen; aufbinden; lockern; ~n ['luːsn] (sich) lösen, (sich) lockern.

loot [luːt] 1. plündern; 2. Beute f.

lop [lɔp] Baum beschneiden; stutzen; schlaff herunterhängen (lassen); ~sided ['lɔp'saidid] schief; einseitig.

loquacious □ [lou'kweiʃəs] geschwätzig.

lord [lɔːd] Herr m; Gebieter m; Magnat m; Lord m; the 2 der Herr (Gott); my ~ [mi'lɔːd] Mylord, Euer Gnaden; the 2's Prayer das Vaterunser; the 2's Supper das

Abendmahl; ~ly ['lɔːdli] vornehm, edel; großartig; hochmütig; ~ship ['lɔːdʃip] Lordschaft f (Titel).

lore [lɔː] Lehre f, Kunde f.

lorry ['lɔri] Last(kraft)wagen m, LKW m; 🚂 Lore f.

lose [luːz] [irr.] v/t. verlieren; vergeuden; verpassen; abnehmen; ~ o.s. sich verirren; v/i. verlieren; nachgehen (Uhr).

loss [lɔs] Verlust m; Schaden m; at a ~ in Verlegenheit; außerstande.

lost [lɔst] pret. u. p.p. von lose; be ~ verlorengehen; verschwunden sein; fig. versunken sein; ~property office Fundbüro n.

lot [lɔt] Los n (a. fig.); Anteil m; ⚓ Partie f; Posten m; F Menge f; Parzelle f; Am. Film: Ateliergelände n; a ~ of people F eine Menge Leute; draw ~s losen; fall to s.o.'s ~ j-m zufallen.

loth □ [louθ] s. loath.

lotion ['louʃən] (Haut)Wasser n.

lottery ['lɔtəri] Lotterie f.

loud □ [laud] laut (a. adv.); fig. schreiend, grell; ~speaker ['laud'spiːkə] Lautsprecher m.

lounge [laundʒ] 1. sich rekeln; faulenzen; 2. Bummel m; Wohnzimmer n, ~diele f; Gesellschaftsraum m e-s Hotels; thea. Foyer n; Chaiselongue f; ~chair ['laundʒ'tʃeə] Klubsessel m; ~suit Straßenanzug m.

lour ['lauə] finster blicken od. aussehen; die Stirn runzeln.

lous|e [laus], pl. lice [lais] Laus f; ~y ['lauzi] verlaust; lausig; Lause...

lout [laut] Tölpel m, Lümmel m.

lovable □ ['lʌvəbl] liebenswürdig, liebenswert.

love [lʌv] 1. Liebe f (of, a. for, to, towards zu); Liebschaft f; Angebetete f; Liebling m (als Anrede); liebeGrüßem/pl.; Sport: nichts,null; attr. Liebes...; give od. send one's ~ to s.o. j-n freundlichst grüßen (lassen); in ~ with verliebt in (acc.); fall in ~ with sich verlieben in (acc.); make ~ to werben um; 2. lieben; gern haben; ~ to do gern tun; ~affair ['lʌvəfeə] Liebschaft f; ~ly ['lʌvli] lieblich; entzückend, reizend; ~r ['lʌvə] Liebhaber m; fig. Verehrer(in), Liebhaber(in).

loving □ ['lʌviŋ] liebevoll.

low¹ [lou] 1. niedrig; tief; gering; leise; fig. niedergeschlagen; schwach; gemein; ~est bid Mindestgebot n; 2. meteor. Tief(druckgebiet) n; bsd. Am. Tiefstand m, -punkt m.

low² [~] brüllen, muhen (Rind).

low-brow F ['loubrau] 1. geistig anspruchslos, spießig; 2. Spießer m, Banause m.

lower¹ ['louə] 1. niedriger; tiefer; geringer; leiser; untere(r, -s); Unter...; 2. v/t. nieder-, herunterlassen; senken; erniedrigen; abschwächen; *Preis etc.* herabsetzen; v/i. fallen, sinken.

lower² ['lauə] s. *lour.*

low|land ['loulənd] Tiefland *n*; **~liness** ['loulinis] Demut *f*; **~ly** ['louli] demütig; bescheiden; **~-necked** (tief) ausgeschnitten (*Kleid*); **~-spirited** niedergeschlagen. [Treue *f*.]

loyal □ ['lɔiəl] treu; **~ty** [‿lti]]

lozenge ['lɔzindʒ] Pastille *f*.

lubber ['lʌbə] Tölpel *m*, Stoffel *m*.

lubric|ant ['lu:brikənt] Schmiermittel *n*; **~ate** [‿keit] schmieren; **~ation** [lu:bri'keiʃən] Schmieren *n*, ⊕ Ölung *f*.

lucid □ ['lu:sid] leuchtend, klar.

luck [lʌk] Glück(sfall *m*) *n*; Geschick *n*; *good* **~** Glück *n*; *bad* **~**, *hard* **~**, *ill* **~** Unglück *n*, Pech *n*; *worse* **~** unglücklicherweise, **~ily** ['lʌkili] glücklicherweise, zum Glück; **~y** □ ['lʌki] glücklich; *Glücks...*; *be* **~** Glück haben.

lucr|ative □ ['lu:krətiv] einträglich; **~e** ['lu:kə] Gewinn(sucht *f*) *m*.

ludicrous □ ['lu:dikrəs] lächerlich.

lug [lʌg] zerren, schleppen.

luge [lu:ʒ] 1. Rodelschlitten *m*; 2. rodeln.

luggage ['lʌgidʒ] Gepäck *n*; **~-carrier** Gepäckträger *m am Fahrrad*; **~-office** 🚉 Gepäckschalter *m*; **~-rack** Gepäcknetz *n*; **~-ticket** Gepäckschein *m*.

lugubrious □ [lu:'gju:briəs] traurig.

lukewarm ['lu:kwɔ:m] lau (*a. fig.*).

lull [lʌl] 1. einlullen; (sich) beruhigen; 2. (Wind)Stille *f*; Ruhepause *f*.

lullaby ['lʌləbai] Wiegenlied *n*.

lumbago ♨ [lʌm'beigou] Hexenschuß *m*.

lumber ['lʌmbə] 1. Bau-, Nutzholz *n*; Gerümpel *n*; 2. v/t. *a.* **~** *up* vollstopfen; v/i. rumpeln, poltern; sich (dahin)schleppen; **~er** [‿ərə], **~jack**, **~man** Holzfäller *m*, -arbeiter *m*; **~mill** Sägewerk *n*; **~room** Rumpelkammer *f*; **~yard** Holzplatz *m*, -lager *n*.

lumin|ary ['lu:minəri] Himmelskörper *m*; Leuchtkörper *m*; *fig.* Leuchte *f*; **~ous** □ [‿nəs] leuchtend; Licht...; Leucht...; *fig.* lichtvoll.

lump [lʌmp] 1. Klumpen *m*; *fig.* Klotz *m*; Beule *f*; Stück *n Zucker etc.*; *in the* **~** in Bausch und Bogen; **~** *sugar* Würfelzucker *m*; **~** *sum*

Pauschalsumme *f*; 2. v/t. zs.-werfen, zs.-fassen; v/i. Klumpen bilden; **~ish** ['lʌmpiʃ] schwerfällig; **~y** □ [‿pi] klumpig.

lunacy ['lu:nəsi] Wahnsinn *m*.

lunar ['lu:nə] Mond...

lunatic ['lu:nətik] 1. irr-, wahnsinnig; 2. Irre(r *m*) *f*; Wahnsinnige(r *m*) *f*; Geistesgestörte(r *m m*) *f*; **~** *asylum* Irrenhaus *n*, -anstalt *f*.

lunch [lʌntʃ], (**eon**) ['lʌntʃ, 'lʌntʃ*ə*n] 1. Lunch *m*, Mittagessen *n*; zweites Frühstück; 2. zu Mittag essen; *j-m* ein Mittagessen geben; **~-hour** Mittagzeit *f*, -pause *f*.

lung *anat.* [lʌŋ] Lunge(nflügel *m*) *f*; *the* **~s** *pl.* die Lunge.

lunge [lʌndʒ] 1. *Fechten:* Ausfall *m*; 2. v/i. ausfallen (*at gegen*); (dahin)stürmen; v/t. stoßen.

lupin(e) ⚘ ['lu:pin] Lupine *f*.

lurch [lə:tʃ] 1. taumeln, torkeln; 2.: *leave in the* **~** im Stich lassen.

lure [ljuə] 1. Köder *m*; *fig.* Lockung *f*; 2. ködern, (an)locken.

lurid □ ['ljuərid] unheimlich; erschreckend, schockierend; düster, finster.

lurk [lə:k] lauern; versteckt liegen.

luscious □ ['lʌʃəs] köstlich; üppig; süß(lich), widerlich.

lust [lʌst] (sinnliche) Begierde; *fig.* Gier *f*, Sucht *f*.

lust|re, *Am.* **~er** ['lʌstə] Glanz *m*; Kronleuchter *m*; **~rous** □ [‿trəs] glänzend.

lusty □ ['lʌsti] rüstig; *fig.* lebhaft, kräftig.

lute¹ ♪ [lu:t] Laute *f*.

lute² [‿] 1. Kitt *m*; 2. (ver)kitten.

Lutheran ['lu:θərən] lutherisch.

luxate ♨ ['lʌkseit] verrenken.

luxur|iant □ [lʌg'zjuəriənt] üppig; **~ious** □ [‿iəs] luxuriös, üppig; **~y** ['lʌkʃəri] Luxus *m*, Üppigkeit *f*; Luxusartikel *m*; Genußmittel *n*.

lyceum [lai'siəm] Vortragsraum *m*; *bsd. Am.* Volkshochschule *f*.

lye [lai] Lauge *f*.

lying ['laiiŋ] 1. *p.pr. von* lie¹ 2 *u.* lie² 2; 2. *adj.* lügnerisch; **~-in** [‿ŋ'in] Wochenbett *n*; **~** *hospital* Entbindungsheim *n*.

lymph ♨ [limf] Lymphe *f*.

lynch [lintʃ] lynchen; **~-law** ['lintʃlɔ:] Lynchjustiz *f*.

lynx *zo.* [liŋks] Luchs *m*.

lyric ['lirik] 1. lyrisch; 2. lyrisches Gedicht; **~s** *pl.* (Lied)Text *m* (*bsd. e-s Musicals*); Lyrik *f*; **~al** □ [‿kəl] lyrisch, gefühlvoll; schwärmerisch, begeistert.

M

ma'am [mæm] Majestät *f* (*Anrede für die Königin*); Hoheit *f* (*Anrede für Prinzessinnen*); F [mɔm] gnä' Frau *f* (*von Dienstboten verwendete Anrede*).

macaroni [mækə'rouni] Makkaroni *pl.*

macaroon [mækə'ru:n] Makrone *f.*

machin|ation [mæki'neiʃən] Anschlag *m*; ~s *pl.* Ränke *pl.*; ~e [mə'ʃi:n] 1. Maschine *f*; Mechanismus *m* (*a. fig.*); 2. maschinell herstellen *od.* (be)arbeiten; ~e-made maschinell hergestellt; ~ery [~nəri] Maschinen *f/pl.*; Maschinerie *f*; ~ist [~nist] Maschinist *m*; Maschinennäherin *f.*

mackerel *ichth.* ['mækrəl] Makrele *f.*

mackinow *Am.* ['mækinɔ:] Stutzer *m* (*Kleidungsstück*).

mackintosh ['mækintɔʃ] Regenmantel *m.*

mad □ [mæd] wahnsinnig; toll (-wütig); *fig.* wild; F wütend; go ~ verrückt werden; *drive* ~ verrückt machen.

madam ['mædəm] gnädige Frau, gnädiges Fräulein (*Anrede*).

mad|cap ['mædkæp] 1. toll; 2. Tollkopf *m*; Wildfang *m*; ~den ['mædn] toll *od.* rasend machen.

made [meid] *pret. u. p.p. von* **make** 1.

made-up ['meid'ʌp] zurechtgemacht; erfunden; fertig; ~ *clothes pl.* Konfektion *f.*

mad|house ['mædhaus] Irrenhaus *n*; ~man Wahnsinnige(r) *m*; ~ness ['mædnis] Wahnsinn *m*; (Toll)Wut *f.*

magazine [mægə'zi:n] Magazin *n*; (Munitions)Lager *n*; Zeitschrift *f.*

maggot *zo.* ['mægət] Made *f.*

magic ['mædʒik] 1. *a.* ~al □ [~kəl] magisch; Zauber...; 2. Zauberei *f*; *fig.* Zauber *m*; ~ian [me'dʒiʃən] Zauberer *m.*

magistra|cy ['mædʒistrəsi] Richteramt *n*; *die* Richter *m/pl.*; ~te [~rit] (Polizei-, Friedens)Richter *m.*

magnanimous □ [mæg'næniməs] großmütig.

magnet ['mægnit] Magnet *m*; ~ic [mæg'netik] (~ally) magnetisch.

magni|ficence [mæg'nifisns] Pracht *f*, Herrlichkeit *f*; ~ficent [~nt] prächtig, herrlich; ~fy ['mægnifai] vergrößern; ~tude [~itju:d] Größe *f*, Wichtigkeit *f.*

magpie *orn.* ['mægpai] Elster *f.*

mahagony [mə'hɔgəni] Mahagoni (-holz) *n.*

maid [meid] *lit.* Mädchen *n*; (Dienst)Mädchen *n*; *old* ~ alte

Jungfer; ~ *of all work* Mädchen *n* für alles; ~ *of honour* Ehren-, Hofdame *f.*

maiden ['meidn] 1. = *maid*; 2. jungfräulich; unverheiratet; *fig.* Jungfern..., Erstlings...; ~ *name* Mädchenname *m e-r* Frau; ~head Jungfräulichkeit *f*; ~hood [~hud] Mädchenjahre *n/pl.*; ~ly [~nli] jungfräulich, mädchenhaft.

mail¹ [meil] (Ketten)Panzer *m.*

mail² [~] 1. Post(dienst *m*) *f*; Post(sendung) *f*; 2. *Am.* mit der Post schicken, aufgeben; ~able *Am.* ['meiləbl] postversandfähig; ~bag Briefträger-, Posttasche *f*; Postsack *m*; ~box *bsd. Am.* Briefkasten *m*; ~ *carrier Am.* Briefträger *m*; ~man *Am.* Briefträger *m*; ~-order firm, *bsd. Am.* ~-order house (Post)Versandgeschäft *n.*

maim [meim] verstümmeln.

main [mein] 1. Haupt..., hauptsächlich; *by* ~ *force* mit voller Kraft; 2. Hauptrohr *n*, -leitung *f*; ~s *pl.* ⚡ (Strom)Netz *n*; *in the* ~ in der Hauptsache, im wesentlichen; ~land ['meinlənd] Festland *n*; ~ly [~li] hauptsächlich; ~spring Uhrfeder *f*; *fig.* Haupttriebfeder *f*; ~stay ⚓ Großstag *n*; *fig.* Hauptstütze *f* ♀ *Street Am.* Hauptstraße *f*; ♀ *Streeter Am.* Kleinstadtbewohner *m.*

maintain [men'tein] (aufrecht)erhalten; beibehalten; (unter)stützen; unterhalten; behaupten.

maintenance ['meintinəns] Erhaltung *f*; Unterhalt *m*; ⊕ Wartung *f.*

maize ♀ [meiz] Mais *m.*

majest|ic [mə'dʒestik] (~ally) majestätisch; ~y ['mædʒisti] Majestät *f*; Würde *f*, Hoheit *f.*

major ['meidʒə] 1. größer; wichtig(er); mündig; ♪ Dur *n*; ~ *key* Dur-Tonart *f*; ~ *league Am.* Baseball: Oberliga *f*; 2. ⚔ Major *m*; Mündige(r *m*) *f*; *Am. univ.* Hauptfach *n*; ~general ⚔ Generalmajor *m*; ~ity [mə'dʒɔriti] Mehrheit *f*; Mündigkeit *f*; Majorsrang *m.*

make [meik] 1. [*irr.*] *v/t. allg.* machen; verfertigen, fabrizieren; bilden; (aus)machen; ergeben; (veran)lassen; gewinnen, verdienen; sich erweisen als, abgeben; *Regel etc.* aufstellen; *Frieden etc.* schließen; *e-e Rede* halten; ~ *good* wieder gutmachen; *war* machen; *do you* ~ *one of us?* machen Sie mit?; ~ *port* ⚓ den Hafen anlaufen; ~ *way* vorwärtskommen; ~ *into* verarbeiten zu; ~ *out* ausfindig machen; erkennen; verstehen; entziffern; *Rechnung etc.* ausstellen; ~ *over* übertragen; ~ *up* ergänzen; vervollständigen; zs.-stellen; bilden, ausmachen; *Streit* beilegen; zurechtmachen, schminken; = ~ *up for* (v/i.); ~ *up one's mind* sich entschließen; v/i. sich begeben; gehen; ~ *away with* beseitigen; *Geld* vertun; ~ *for* zugehen auf (acc.); sich aufmachen nach; ~ *off* sich fortmachen; ~ *up* sich zurechtmachen; sich schminken; ~ *up for* nach-, aufholen; für *et.* entschädigen; 2. Mach-, Bauart *f*; Bau *m des Körpers*; Form *f*; Fabrikat *n*, Erzeugnis *n*; **~believe** ['meikbili:v] Schein *m*, Vorwand *m*, Verstellung *f*; **~r** ['meikə] Hersteller *m*; ♀ Schöpfer *m* (*Gott*); **~shift** 1. Notbehelf *m*; 2. behelfsmäßig; **~up** *typ.* Umbruch *m*; *fig.* Charakter *m*; Schminke *f*, Make-up *n*.

maladjustment ['mælə'dʒʌstmənt] mangelhafte Anpassung.

maladministration ['mælədminis'treiʃən] schlechte Verwaltung.

malady ['mælədi] Krankheit *f*.

malcontent ['mælkəntent] 1. unzufrieden; 2. Unzufriedene(r) *m*.

male [meil] 1. männlich; 2. Mann *m*; *zo.* Männchen *n*.

malediction [mæli'dikʃən] Fluch *m*.

malefactor ['mælifæktə] Übeltäter *m*.

malevolen|ce [mə'levələns] Böswilligkeit *f*; **~t** □ [~nt] böswillig.

malice ['mælis] Bosheit *f*; Groll *m*.

malicious [mə'liʃəs] boshaft; böswillig; **~ness** [~snis] Bosheit *f*.

malign [mə'lain] 1. □ schädlich; 2. verleumden; **~ant** □ [mə'lignənt] böswillig; ♀ bösartig; **~ity** [~niti] Bosheit *f*; Schadenfreude *f*; *bsd.* ♀ Bösartigkeit *f*.

malleable ['mæliəbl] hämmerbar; *fig.* geschmeidig.

mallet ['mælit] Schlegel *m*.

malnutrition ['mælnju(:)'triʃən] Unterernährung *f*.

malodorous □ [mæ'loudərəs] übelriechend.

malpractice ['mæl'præktis] Übeltat *f*; ♠ falsche Behandlung.

malt [mɔ:lt] Malz *n*.

maltreat [mæl'tri:t] schlecht behandeln; mißhandeln.

mam(m)a [mə'ma:] Mama *f*.

mammal ['mæməl] Säugetier *n*.

mammoth ['mæməθ] riesig.

mammy F ['mæmi] Mami *f*; *Am.* farbiges Kindermädchen.

man [mæn, *in Zssgn* ...mən] 1. *pl.* **men** [men] Mann *m*; Mensch(en *pl.*) *m*; Menschheit *f*; Diener *m*; *Schach:* Figur *f*; Damestein *m*; 2. männlich; 3. ✕, ♠ bemannen; ~ *o.s.* sich ermannen.

manage ['mænidʒ] v/t. handhaben; verwalten, leiten; *Menschen, Tiere* lenken; mit *j-m* fertig werden; *et.*

fertigbringen; ~ *to inf.* es fertigbringen, zu *inf.*; v/i. die Aufsicht haben, die Geschäfte führen; auskommen; F es schaffen; **~able** □ [~dʒəbl] handlich; lenksam; **~ment** [~dʒmənt] Verwaltung *f*, Leitung *f*, Direktion *f*, Geschäftsführung *f*; geschickte Behandlung; **~r** [~dʒə] Leiter *m*, Direktor *m*; Regisseur *m*; Manager *m*; **~ress** [~ə res] Leiterin *f*, Direktorin *f*.

managing ['mænidʒiŋ] geschäftsführend; Betriebs...; ~ *clerk* Geschäftsführer *m*, Prokurist *m*.

mandat|e ['mændeit] Mandat *n*; Befehl *m*; Auftrag *m*; Vollmacht *f*; **~ory** [~dətəri] befehlend.

mane [mein] Mähne *f*.

maneuver [mə'nu:və] = manoeuvre.

manful □ ['mænful] mannhaft.

mange *vet.* [meindʒ] Räude *f*.

manger ['meindʒə] Krippe *f*.

mangle ['mæŋgl] 1. Wringmaschine *f*; Wäschemangel *f*; 2. mangeln; wringen; zerstückeln; *fig.* verstümmeln.

mangy ['meindʒi] räudig; *fig.* schäbig.

manhood ['mænhud] Mannesalter *n*; Männlichkeit *f*; die Männer *m/pl.*

mania ['meinjə] Wahnsinn *m*; Sucht *f*, Manie *f*; **~c** ['meiniæk] 1. Wahnsinnige(r *m*) *f*; 2. wahnsinnig.

manicure ['mænikjuə] 1. Maniküre *f*; 2. maniküren.

manifest ['mænifest] 1. □ offenbar; 2. ♠ Ladungsverzeichnis *n*; 3. v/t. offenbaren; kundtun; **~ation** [mænifes'teiʃən] Offenbarung *f*; Kundgebung *f*; **~o** [mæni'festou] Manifest *n*.

manifold □ ['mænifould] 1. mannigfaltig; 2. vervielfältigen.

manipulat|e [mə'nipjuleit] (geschickt) handhaben; **~ion** [mənipju'leiʃən] Handhabung *f*, Behandlung *f*, Verfahren *n*; Kniff *m*.

man|kind [mæn'kaind] die Menschheit; ['mænkaind] die Männer *pl.*; **~ly** ['mænli] männlich; mannhaft.

manner ['mænə] Art *f*, Weise *f*; Stil(art *f*) *m*; Manier *f*; **~s** *pl.* Manieren *f/pl.*, Sitten *f/pl.*; *in a* ~ gewissermaßen; **~ed** [~əd] ...geartet; gekünstelt; **~ly** [~əli] manierlich, gesittet.

manoeuvre, *Am. a.* **maneuver** [mə'nu:və] 1. Manöver *n* (*a. fig.*); 2. manövrieren (lassen).

man-of-war ♠ ['mænəv'wɔ:] Kriegsschiff *n*.

manor ['mænə] Rittergut *n*; *lord of the* ~ Gutsherr *m*; **~-house** Herrschaftshaus *n*, Herrensitz *m*; Schloß *n*.

manpower ['mænpauə] Menschenpotential *n*; Arbeitskräfte *f/pl.*

man-servant ['mænsə:vənt] Diener *m*.

mansion ['mænʃən] (herrschaftliches) Wohnhaus.

manslaughter ['mænslɔ:tə] Totschlag *m*, fahrlässige Tötung.

mantel|piece ['mæntlpi:s], **~shelf** Kaminsims *m*, -platte *f*.

mantle ['mæntl] 1. Mantel *m*; *fig.* Hülle *f*; Glühstrumpf *m*; 2. *v/t.* verhüllen; *v/i.* sich röten (*Gesicht*).

manual ['mænjuəl] 1. □ Hand...; mit der Hand (gemacht); 2. Handbuch *n*.   [brik *f*.\

manufactory [mænju'fæktəri] Fa-/

manufactur|e [mænju'fæktʃə] 1. Fabrikation *f*; Fabrikat *n*; 2. fabrizieren; verarbeiten; **~er** [~ərə] Fabrikant *m*; **~ing** [~riŋ] Fabrik...; Gewerbe...; Industrie...

manure [mə'njuə] 1. Dünger *m*; 2. düngen.

manuscript ['mænjuskript] Manuskript *n*; Handschrift *f*.

many ['meni] 1. viele; ~ *a* manche(r, -s); *be one too ~ for s.o.* j-m überlegen sein; 2. Menge *f*; *a good* ~, *a great* ~ ziemlich viele, sehr viele.

map [mæp] 1. (Land)Karte *f*; 2. aufzeichnen; ~ *out* planen; einteilen.

maple ♀ ['meipl] Ahorn *m*.

mar [mɑ:] schädigen; verderben.

maraud [mə'rɔ:d] plündern.

marble ['mɑ:bl] 1. Marmor *m*; Murmel *f*; 2. marmorn.

March¹ [mɑ:tʃ] März *m*.

march² [~] 1. Marsch *m*; Fortschritt *m*; Gang *m der Ereignisse etc.*; 2. marschieren (lassen); *fig.* vorwärtsschreiten.

marchioness ['mɑ:ʃənis] Marquise *f*.

mare [mɛə] Stute *f*; ~*'s nest fig.* Schwindel *m*; (Zeitungs)Ente *f*.

marg|arine [mɑ:dʒə'ri:n], *a.* ~**e** F [mɑ:dʒ] Margarine *f*.

margin ['mɑ:dʒin] Rand *m*; Grenze *f*; Spielraum *m*; Verdienst-, Gewinn-, Handelsspanne *f*; ~**al** □ [~nl] am Rande (befindlich); Rand...; ~ *note* Randbemerkung *f*.

marine [mə'ri:n] Marineinfanterist *m*; Marine *f*; *paint.* Seestück *n*; *attr.* See...; Marine...; Schiffs...; ~**r** ['mærinə] Seemann *m*.

marital □ ['mæritl] ehelich, Ehe...

maritime ['mæritaim] an der See liegend *od.* lebend; See...; Küsten...; Schiffahrt(s)...

mark¹ [mɑ:k] Mark *f* (*Geldstück*).

mark² [~] 1. Marke *f*, Merkmal *n*, Zeichen *n*; ♀ Preiszettel *m*; Fabrik-, Schutzmarke *f* (Körper)Mal *n*; Norm *f*; *Schule:* Zensur *f*, Note *f*, Punkt *m*; *Sport:* Startlinie *f*; Ziel *n*; *a man of* ~ ein Mann von Bedeutung; *fig. up to the* ~ auf der Höhe;

beside the ~, *wide of the* ~ den Kern der Sache verfehlend; unrichtig; 2. *v/t.* (be)zeichnen, markieren; *Sport:* anschreiben; kennzeichnen; be(ob)achten; sich *et.* merken; ~ *off* abtrennen; ~ *out* bezeichnen; abstecken; ~ *time* auf der Stelle treten; *v/i.* achtgeben; ~**ed** □ auffallend; merklich; ausgeprägt.

market ['mɑ:kit] 1. Markt(platz) *m*; Handel *m*; ♀ Absatz *m*; *in the* ~ auf dem Markt; *play the* ~ *Am. sl.* an der Börse spekulieren; 2. *v/t.* auf den Markt bringen, verkaufen; *v/i.* einkaufen gehen; ~**able** □ [~təbl] marktfähig, -gängig; ~**ing** [~tiŋ] ♀ Marketing *n*, Absatzpolitik *f*; Marktbesuch *m*.

marksman ['mɑ:ksmən] (guter) Schütze.

marmalade ['mɑ:məleid] Orangenmarmelade *f*.

maroon [mə'ru:n] 1. kastanienbraun; 2. *auf e-r einsamen Insel* aussetzen; 3. Leuchtrakete *f*.

marquee [mɑ:'ki] (großes) Zelt.

marquis ['mɑ:kwis] Marquis *m*.

marriage ['mæridʒ] Heirat *f*, Ehe (-stand *m*) *f*; Hochzeit *f*; *civil* ~ standesamtliche Trauung; ~**able** [~dʒəbl] heiratsfähig; ~ **articles** *pl.* Ehevertrag *m*; ~ **lines** *pl.* Trauschein *m*; ~ **portion** Mitgift *f*.

married ['mærid] verheiratet; ehelich; Ehe...; ~ *couple* Ehepaar *n*.

marrow ['mærou] Mark *n*; *fig.* Kern *m*, Beste(s) *n*; ~**y** [~oui] markig.

marry ['mæri] *v/t.* (ver)heiraten; *eccl.* trauen; *v/i.* sich ver)heiraten.

marsh [mɑ:ʃ] Sumpf *m*, Morast *m*.

marshal ['mɑ:ʃəl] 1. Marschall *m*; *hist.* Hofmarschall *m*; Zeremonienmeister *m*; *Am.* Bezirkspolizeichef *m*; Leiter *m* der Feuerwehr; 2. ordnen; führen; zs.-stellen.

marshy ['mɑ:ʃi] sumpfig.

mart [mɑ:t] Markt *m*; Auktionsraum *m*.

marten *zo.* ['mɑ:tin] Marder *m*.

martial □ ['mɑ:ʃəl] kriegerisch; Kriegs...; ~ *law* Stand-, Kriegsrecht *n*.

martyr ['mɑ:tə] 1. Märtyrer(in) (*to gen.*); 2. (zu Tode) martern.

marvel ['mɑ:vel] 1. Wunder *n*; 2. sich wundern; ~**lous** □ ['mɑ:viləs] wunderbar, erstaunlich.

mascot ['mæskət] Maskottchen *n*.

masculine ['mɑ:skjulin] männlich.

mash [mæʃ] 1. Gemisch *n*; Maische *f*; Mengfutter *n*; 2. mischen; zerdrücken; (ein)maischen; ~*ed potatoes pl.* Kartoffelbrei *m*.

mask [mɑ:sk] 1. Maske *f*; 2. maskieren; *fig.* verbergen; tarnen; ~**ed**: ~ *ball* Maskenball *m*.

mason ['meisn] Steinmetz *m*; Maurer *m*; Freimaurer *m*; ~**ry** [~nri] Mauerwerk *n*.

masque [mɑːsk] Maskenspiel *n*.

masquerade [mæskə'reid] 1. Maskenball *m*; Verkleidung *f*; 2. *fig.* sich maskieren.

mass [mæs] 1. *eccl.* Messe *f*; Masse *f*; Menge *f*; ~ *meeting* Massenversammlung *f*; 2. (sich) (an)sammeln.

massacre ['mæsəkə] 1. Blutbad *n*; 2. niedermetzeln.

massage ['mæsɑːʒ] 1. Massage *f*; 2. massieren.

massif ['mæsiːf] (Gebirgs)Massiv *n*.

massive ['mæsiv] massiv; schwer.

mast ⚓ [mɑːst] Mast *m*.

master ['mɑːstə] 1. Meister *m*; Herr *m* (*a. fig.*); Gebieter *m*; Lehrer *m*; Kapitän *m* e-s *Handelsschiffs*; *Anrede*: (junger) Herr; *univ.* Rektor *m* e-s *College*; ♀ of *Arts* Magister *m* Artium; ♀ of *Ceremonies* Conférencier *m*; 2. Meister...; *fig.* führend; 3. Herr sein *od.* werden über (*acc.*); *Sprache etc.* meistern, beherrschen; **~-builder** Baumeister *m*; **~ful** □ [~əful] herrisch; meisterhaft; **~key** Hauptschlüssel *f*; **~ly** [~əli] meisterhaft; **~piece** Meisterstück *n*; **~ship** [~əʃip] Meisterschaft *f*; Herrschaft *f*; Lehramt *n*; **~y** [~əri] Herrschaft *f*; Vorrang *m*; Oberhand *f*; Meisterschaft *f*; Beherrschung *f*.

masticate ['mæstikeit] kauen.

mastiff ['mæstif] englische Dogge.

mat [mæt] 1. Matte *f*; Deckchen *n*; Unterlage *f*; 2. *fig.* bedecken; (sich) verflechten; 3. mattieren, matt.

match¹ [mætʃ] Streichholz *n*.

match² [~] 1. Gleiche(r *m*, -s *n*) *f*; Partie *f*; Wettspiel *n*, -kampf *m*; Heirat *f*; *be a* ~ *for j-m* gewachsen sein; *meet one's* ~ s-n Meister finden; 2. *v/t.* anpassen; passen zu; et. Passendes finden *od.* geben zu; es aufnehmen mit; verheiraten; *well* ~*ed* zs.-passend; *v/i.* zs.-passen; *to* ~ dazu passend; **~less** □ ['mætʃlis] unvergleichlich, ohnegleichen; **~maker** Ehestifter(in).

mate¹ [meit] *Schach*: matt (setzen).

mate² [~] 1. Gefährt|e *m*, -in *f*; Kamerad(in); Gatt|e *m*, -in *f*; Männchen *n*, Weibchen *n* *von Tieren*; Gehilf|e *m*, -in *f*; ⚓ Maat *m*; 2. (sich) verheiraten; (sich) paaren.

material □ [mə'tiəriəl] 1. materiell; körperlich; materialistisch; wesentlich; 2. Material *n*, Stoff *m*; Werkstoff *m*; *writing* ~*s pl.* Schreibmaterial(ien *pl.*) *n*.

matern|al □ [mə'təːnl] mütterlich; Mutter...; mütterlicherseits; **~ity** [~niti] Mutterschaft *f*; Mütterlichkeit *f*; *mst* ~ *hospital* Entbindungsanstalt *f*.

mathematic|ian [mæθimə'tiʃən] Mathematiker *m*; **~s** [~'mætiks] *mst sg.* Mathematik *f*.

matriculate [mə'trikjuleit] (sich) immatrikulieren (lassen).

matrimon|ial □ [mætri'mounjəl] ehelich; Ehe...; **~y** ['mætriməni] Ehe(stand *m*) *f*.

matrix ['meitriks] Matrize *f*.

matron ['meitrən] Matrone *f*; Hausmutter *f*; Oberin *f*.

matter ['mætə] 1. Materie *f*, Stoff *m*; ☞ Eiter *m*; Gegenstand *m*; Ursache *f*; Sache *f*; Angelegenheit *f*, Geschäft *n*; *printed* ~ ⊗ Drucksache *f*; *what's the* ~? was gibt es?; *what's the* ~ *with you?* was fehlt Ihnen?; *no* ~ es hat nichts zu sagen; *no* ~ *who* gleichgültig wer; ~ *of course* Selbstverständlichkeit *f*; *for that* ~, *for the* ~ *of that* was dies betrifft; ~ *of fact* Tatsache *f*; 2. von Bedeutung sein; *it does not* ~ es macht nichts; ~*-of-fact* tatsächlich; sachlich.

mattress ['mætris] Matratze *f*.

matur|e [mə'tjuə] 1. □ reif; reiflich; ✝ fällig; 2. reifen; zur Reife bringen; ✝ fällig werden; **~ity** [~əriti] Reife *f*; ✝ Fälligkeit *f*.

maudlin □ ['mɔːdlin] rührselig.

maul [mɔːl] beschädigen; *fig.* heruntermachen; roh umgehen mit.

Maundy Thursday *eccl.* ['mɔːndi 'θəːzdi] Gründonnerstag *m*.

mauve [mouv] 1. Malvenfarbe *f*; 2. hellviolett.

maw [mɔː] *Tier*-Magen *m*; Rachen *m*.

mawkish □ ['mɔːkiʃ] rührselig, sentimental.

maxim ['mæksim] Grundsatz *m*; **~um** [~məm] Höchstmaß *n*, -stand *m*, -betrag *m*; *attr.* Höchst...

May¹ [mei] Mai *m*.

may² [~] (*irr.*) mag, kann, darf.

maybe *Am.* ['meibi] vielleicht.

may|-beetle *zo.* ['meibiːtl], **~bug** Maikäfer *m*.

May Day ['meidei] der 1. Mai.

mayor [mɛə] Bürgermeister *m*.

maypole ['meipoul] Maibaum *m*.

maz|e [meiz] Irrgarten *m*, Labyrinth *n*; *fig.* Wirrnis *f*; *in a* ~ = **~ed** [meizd] bestürzt, verwirrt; **~y** □ ['meizi] labyrinthisch; wirr.

me [miː, mi] mich; mir; F ich.

mead [miːd] Met *m*; *poet.* = *meadow*.

meadow ['medou] Wiese *f*.

meag|re, *Am.* **~er** □ ['miːgə] mager, dürr; dürftig.

meal [miːl] Mahl(zeit *f*) *n*; Mehl *n*.

mean¹ [miːn] gemein, niedrig, gering; armselig; knauserig.

mean² [~] 1. mittler, mittelmäßig; Durchschnitts...; *in the* ~ *time* inzwischen; 2. Mitte *f*; *fig.* (Geld-) Mittel *n*/*pl.*; (*a. sg.*) Mittel *n*; *by all* ~*s* jedenfalls; *by* ~*s* of mittels; *by no* ~*s* keineswegs; *by* ~*s of* mittels (*gen.*).

mean³ [~] (*irr.*) meinen; beabsich-

tigen; bestimmen; bedeuten; ~ well (ill) es gut (schlecht) meinen.
meaning ['mi:niŋ] 1. □ bedeutsam; 2. Sinn *m*, Bedeutung *f*; ~less [~lis] bedeutungslos; sinnlos.
meant [ment] *pret. u. p.p. von* mean³.
mean|time ['mi:n'taim], ~while mittlerweile, inzwischen.
measles ['mi:zlz] *sg.* Masern *pl.*
measure ['meʒə] 1. Maß *n*; ♪ Takt *m*; Maßregel *f*; ~ of capacity Hohlmaß *n*; beyond ~ über alle Maßen; in a great ~ großenteils; made to ~ nach Maß gemacht; 2. (ab-, aus-, ver)messen; j-m Maß nehmen; ~ up Am. heranreichen; ~less [~lis] unermeßlich; ~ment Messung *f*; Maß *n*.
meat [mi:t] Fleisch *n*; fig. Gehalt *m*; ~ tea frühes Abendessen mit Tee; ~y ['mi:ti] fleischig; fig. gehaltvoll.
mechanic [mi'kænik] Handwerker *m*; Mechaniker *m*; ~al □ [~kəl] mechanisch; Maschinen...; ~ian [mekə'niʃən] Mechaniker *m*; ~s [mi'kæniks] *mst sg.* Mechanik *f*.
mechan|ism ['mekənizəm] Mechanismus *m*; ~ize [~naiz] mechanisieren; ⚙ motorisieren.
medal ['medl] Medaille *f*; Orden *m*.
meddle ['medl] sich einmischen (with, in in acc.); ~some [~lsəm] zu-, aufdringlich.
mediaeval □ [medi'i:vəl] mittelalterlich.
media|l □ ['mi:djəl], ~n [~ən] Mittel..., in der Mitte (befindlich).
mediat|e ['mi:dieit] vermitteln; ~ion [mi:di'eiʃən] Vermittlung *f*; ~or ['mi:dieitə] Vermittler *m*.
medical □ ['medikəl] medizinisch, ärztlich; ~ certificate Krankenschein *m*, Attest *n*; ~ evidence ärztliches Gutachten; ~ man Arzt *m*, Mediziner *m*; ~ supervision ärztliche Aufsicht.
medicate ['medikeit] medizinisch behandeln; mit Arzneistoff versehen; ~d bath medizinisches Bad.
medicin|al □ [me'disinl] medizinisch; heilend, heilsam; ~e ['medsin] Medizin *f*.
medieval □ [medi'i:vəl] = mediaeval.
mediocre ['mi:dioukə] mittelmäßig.
meditat|e ['mediteit] v/i. nachdenken, überlegen; v/t. sinnen auf (acc.); erwägen; ~ion [medi'teiʃən] Nachdenken *n*; innere Betrachtung; ~ive □ ['meditətiv] nachdenklich, meditativ.
Mediterranean [meditə'reinjən] Mittelmeer *n*; attr. Mittelmeer...
medium ['mi:djəm] 1. Mitte *f*; Mittel *n*; Vermittlung *f*; Medium *n*; Lebens-Element *n*; 2. mittler; Mittel..., Durchschnitts...

medley ['medli] Gemisch *n*; ♪ Potpourri *n*.
meek □ [mi:k] sanft-, demütig; ~ness ['mi:knis] Sanft-, Demut *f*.
meerschaum ['miəʃəm] Meerschaum(pfeife *f*) *m*.
meet¹ [mi:t] passend; schicklich.
meet² [~] [irr.] v/t. treffen; begegnen (dat.); abholen; stoßen auf den Gegner; Wunsch etc. befriedigen; e-r Verpflichtung nachkommen; Am. j-m vorgestellt werden; go to ~ s.o. j-m entgegengehen; v/i. sich treffen; zs.-stoßen; sich versammeln; ~ with stoßen auf (acc.); erleiden; ~ing ['mi:tiŋ] Begegnung *f*; (Zs.-)Treffen *n*, Versammlung *f*; Tagung *f*.
melancholy ['melənkəli] 1. Schwermut *f*; 2. melancholisch.
meliorate ['mi:ljəreit] (sich) verbessern.
mellow ['melou] 1. □ mürbe; reif; weich; mild; 2. reifen (lassen); weich machen od. werden; (sich) mildern.
melo|dious □ [mi'loudjəs] melodisch; ~dramatic [meloudrə'mætik] melodramatisch; ~dy ['melədi] Melodie *f*; Lied *n*.
melon ♀ ['melən] Melone *f*.
melt [melt] (zer)schmelzen; fig. zerfließen; Gefühl erweichen.
member ['membə] (Mit)Glied *n*; parl. Abgeordnete(r *m*) *f*; ~ship [~əʃip] Mitgliedschaft *f*; Mitgliederzahl *f*.
membrane ['membrein] Membran(e) *f*, Häutchen *n*. [*n*.]
memento [mi'mentou] Andenken [
memo ['mi:mou] = memorandum.
memoir ['memwɑ:] Denkschrift *f*; ~s pl. Memoiren pl.
memorable □ ['memərəbl] denkwürdig.
memorandum [memə'rændəm] Notiz *f*; pol. Note *f*; Schriftsatz *m*.
memorial [mi'mɔ:riəl] Denkmal *n*; Gedenkzeichen *n*; Denkschrift *f*, Eingabe *f*; attr. Gedächtnis..., Gedenk...
memorize ['meməraiz] auswendig lernen, memorieren.
memory ['meməri] Gedächtnis *n*; Erinnerung *f*; Andenken *n*; commit to ~ dem Gedächtnis einprägen; in ~ of zum Andenken an (acc.).
men [men] pl. von man 1; Mannschaft *f*.
menace ['menəs] 1. (be)drohen; 2. Gefahr *f*; Drohung *f*.
mend [mend] 1. v/t. (ver)bessern; ausbessern, flicken, besser machen; ~ one's ways v/i. sich bessern; 2. Flicken *m*; on the ~ auf dem Wege der Besserung.
mendacious □ [men'deiʃəs] lügnerisch, verlogen.
mendicant ['mendikənt] 1. bet-

telnd; Bettel...; 2. Bettler *m*; Bettelmönch *m*.

menial *contp.* ['mi:njəl] **1.** □ knechtisch; niedrig; 2. Knecht *m*; Lakai *m*.

meningitis ❀ [menin'dʒaitis] Hirnhautentzündung *f*, Meningitis *f*.

mental □ ['mentl] geistig; Geistes...; ~ arithmetic Kopfrechnen *n*; ~ity [men'tæliti] Mentalität *f*.

mention ['menʃən] **1.** Erwähnung *f*; 2. erwähnen; *don't ~ it!* bitte!

menu ['menju] Speisenfolge *f*, Menü *n*; Speisekarte *f*.

mercantile ['mə:kəntail] kaufmännisch; Handels...

mercenary ['mə:sinəri] **1.** □ feil, käuflich; gedungen; gewinnsüchtig; 2. ✕ Söldner *m*.

mercer ['mə:sə] Seidenwaren-, Stoffhändler *m*.

merchandise ['mə:tʃəndaiz] Ware(n *pl.*) *f*.

merchant ['mə:tʃənt] **1.** Kaufmann *m*; *Am.* (Klein)Händler *m*; 2. Handels..., Kaufmanns...; *law ~* Handelsrecht *n*; ~man Handelsschiff *n*.

merci|ful □ ['mə:siful] barmherzig; ~less □ [~ilis] unbarmherzig.

mercury ['mə:kjuri] Quecksilber *n*.

mercy ['mə:si] Barmherzigkeit *f*; Gnade *f*; *be at s.o.'s ~* in j-s Gewalt sein.

mere □ [miə] rein, lauter; bloß; ~ly ['miəli] bloß, lediglich, allein.

meretricious □ [meri'triʃəs] aufdringlich; kitschig.

merge [mə:dʒ] verschmelzen (*in* mit); ~r ['mə:dʒə] Verschmelzung *f*.

meridian [mə'ridiən] *geogr.* Meridian *m*; *fig.* Gipfel *m*; *attr.* Mittags...

merit ['merit] **1.** Verdienst *n*; Wert *m*; Vorzug *m*; *bsd.* ~*s pl.* Hauptpunkte *m/pl.*, Wesen *n* e-r *Sache*; *make a ~ of* als Verdienst ansehen; 2. *fig.* verdienen; ~orious □ [meri'tɔ:riəs] verdienstvoll.

mermaid ['mə:meid] Nixe *f*.

merriment ['merimənt] Lustigkeit *f*; Belustigung *f*.

merry □ ['meri] lustig, fröhlich; *make ~* lustig sein; ~ andrew Hanswurst *m*; ~go-round Karussell *n*; ~making [~imeikin] Lustbarkeit *f*.

mesh [meʃ] **1.** Masche *f*; *fig.* oft ~es *pl.* Netz *n*; *be in ~* ⊕ (inea.-)greifen; 2. in e-m Netz fangen.

mess¹ [mes] **1.** Unordnung *f*; Schmutz *m*, F Schweinerei *f*; F Patsche *f*; *make a ~ of* verpfuschen; 2. *v/t.* in Unordnung bringen; verpfuschen; *v/i. ~ about* F herummurksen.

mess² [~] Kasino *n*, Messe *f*.

message ['mesidʒ] Botschaft *f*; *go on a ~* e-e Besorgung machen.

messenger ['mesindʒə] Bote *m*.

Messieurs, *mst* **Messrs.** ['mesəz] (die) Herren *m/pl.*; Firma *f*.

met [met] *pret. u. p.p. von* meet².

metal ['metl] **1.** Metall *n*; Schotter *m*; 2. beschottern; ~lic [mi'tælik] (~ally) metallisch; Metall...; ~lurgy [me'tælədʒi] Hüttenkunde *f*.

metamorphose [metə'mɔ:fouz] verwandeln, umgestalten.

metaphor ['metəfə] Metapher *f*.

meteor ['mi:tjə] Meteor *m* (*a. fig.*); ~ology [mi:tjə'rɔlədʒi] Meteorologie *f*, Wetterkunde *f*.

meter ['mi:tə] Messer *m*, Zähler *m*; *Am.* = metre.

methinks † [mi'θinks] mich dünkt.

method ['meθəd] Methode *f*; Art u. Weise *f*; Verfahren *n*; Ordnung *f*, System *n*; ~ic(al □) [mi'θɔdik(əl)] methodisch.

methought [mi'θɔ:t] *pret. von* methinks.

meticulous □ [mi'tikjuləs] peinlich genau.

met|re, *Am.* ~er ['mi:tə] Meter *n*, *m*; Versmaß *n*.

metric ['metrik] (~ally) metrisch; ~ system Dezimalsystem *n*.

metropoli|s [mi'trɔpəlis] Hauptstadt *f*, Metropole *f*; ~tan [metrə'pɔlitən] hauptstädtisch.

mettle ['metl] Feuereifer *m*, Mut *m*; *be on one's ~* sein Bestes tun.

mews [mju:z] Stallung *f*; *daraus entstandene* Garagen *f/pl. od.* Wohnhäuser *n/pl.*

Mexican ['meksikən] **1.** mexikanisch; 2. Mexikaner(in).

miaow [mi(:)'au] miauen; mauzen.

mice [mais] *pl. von* mouse.

Michaelmas ['miklməs] Michaelis (-tag *m*) *n* (29. *September*).

micro... ['maikrou] klein..., Klein...

micro|phone ['maikrəfoun] Mikrophon *n*; ~scope Mikroskop *n*.

mid [mid] mittler; Mitt(el)...; *in ~ air* mitten in der Luft; *in ~ winter* mitten im Winter; ~day ['middei] **1.** Mittag *m*; 2. mittägig; Mittags...

middle ['midl] **1.** Mitte *f*; Hüften *f/pl.*; 2. mittler; Mittel...; ♀ Ages *pl.* Mittelalter *n*; ~aged von mittlerem Alter; ~class Mittelstands...; ~ class(es *pl.*) Mittelstand *m*; ~man Mittelsmann *m*; ~name zweiter Vorname *m*; ~sized mittelgroß; ~weight *Boxen:* Mittelgewicht *n*.

middling ['midlin] mittelmäßig; leidlich; Mittel...

middy F ['midi] = midshipman.

midge [midʒ] Mücke *f*; ~t ['midʒit] Zwerg *m*, Knirps *m*.

mid|land ['midlənd] **1.** binnenländisch; 2. *the* ♀s *pl.* Mittelengland *n*; ~most mittelste(r, -s); ~night Mitternacht *f*; ~riff ['midrif] Zwerchfell *n*; ~shipman Leutnant *m* zur See; *Am.* Oberfähnrich *m* zur See; ~st [midst] Mitte *f*; *in the ~ of* inmitten (*gen.*); ~summer

Sommersonnenwende *f*; Hochsommer *m*; **~way** 1. halber Weg; *Am.* Schaubudenstraße *f*; 2. *adj.* in der Mitte befindlich; 3. *adv.* auf halbem Wege; **~wife** Hebamme *f*; **~wifery** ['midwifəri] Geburtshilfe *f*; **~winter** Wintersonnenwende *f*; Mitte *f* des Winters.

mien [mi:n] Miene *f*.

might [mait] 1. Macht *f*, Gewalt *f*, Kraft *f*; **with ~ and main** mit aller Gewalt; 2. *pret. von* may²; **~y** □ ['maiti] mächtig, gewaltig.

migrat|e [mai'greit] (aus)wandern; **~ion** [~eiʃən] Wanderung *f*; **~ory** ['maigrətəri] wandernd; Zug...

mild □ [maild] mild, sanft; gelind.

mildew ♀ ['mildju:] Mehltau *m*.

mildness ['maildnis] Milde *f*.

mile [mail] Meile *f* (1609.33 m).

mil(e)age ['mailidʒ] Laufzeit *f in Meilen*, Meilenstand *m e-s Autos*; Kilometergeld *n*.

milestone ['mailstoun] Meilenstein *m*.

milit|ary ['militəri] 1. □ militärisch; Kriegs...; ♀ *Government* Militärregierung *f*; 2. *das* Militär; **~ia** [mi'liʃə] Land-, Bürgerwehr *f*.

milk [milk] 1. Milch *f*; *it's no use crying over spilt ~* geschehen ist geschehen; 2. *v/t.* melken; *v/i.* Milch geben; **~maid** ['milkmeid] Melkerin *f*; Milchmädchen *n*; **~man** Milchmann *m*; **~-powder** Milchpulver *n*; **~-shake** Milchmischgetränk *n*; **~sop** Weichling *m*; **~y** ['milki] milchig; Milch...; ♀ *Way* Milchstraße *f*.

mill¹ [mil] 1. Mühle *f*; Fabrik *f*, Spinnerei *f*; 2. mahlen; ⊕ fräsen; *Geld* prägen; *Münze* rändeln.

mill² *Am.* [~] ¹/₁₀₀₀ Dollar *m*.

millepede *zo.* ['milipi:d] Tausendfüß(l)er *m*.

miller ['milə] Müller *m*; ⊕ Fräsmaschine *f*.

millet ♀ ['milit] Hirse *f*.

milliner ['milinə] Putzmacherin *f*, Modistin *f*; **~y** [~əri] Putz-, Modewaren(geschäft *n*) *pl.*

million ['miljən] Million *f*; **~aire** [miljə'nɛə] Millionär(in); **~th** ['miljənθ] 1. millionste(r, ~s); 2. Millionstel *n*.

mill|-pond ['milpɔnd] Mühlteich *m*; **~stone** Mühlstein *m*.

milt [milt] Milch *f der Fische*.

mimic ['mimik] 1. mimisch; Schein...; 2. Mime *m*; 3. nachahmen, nachäffen; **~ry** [~kri] Nachahmung *f*; *zo.* Angleichung *f*.

mince [mins] 1. *v/t.* zerhacken; *he does not ~ matters* er nimmt kein Blatt vor den Mund; *v/i.* sich zieren; 2. *a.* **~d meat** Hackfleisch *n*; **~meat** [minsi:t] *e-e* Tortenfüllung; **~pie** Torte *f* aus mincemeat; **~r** [~sə] Fleischwolf *m*.

mincing-machine ['minsiŋməʃi:n] = mincer.

mind [maind] 1. Sinn *m*, Gemüt *n*; Geist *m*, Verstand *m*; Meinung *f*; Absicht *f*; Neigung *f*, Lust *f*; Gedächtnis *n*; Sorge *f*; *to my ~* meiner Ansicht nach; *out of one's ~*, *not in one's right ~* von Sinnen; *change one's ~* sich anders besinnen; *bear s.th. in ~* (immer) an et. denken; *have (half) a ~ to* (beinahe) Lust haben zu; *have s.th. on one's ~* et. auf dem Herzen haben; *make up one's ~* sich entschließen; 2. merken *od.* achten auf (*acc.*); sich kümmern um; etwas (einzuwenden) haben gegen; *~! gib acht!; never ~!* macht nichts!; *~ the step!* Achtung, Stufe!; *I don't ~ (it)* ich habe nichts dagegen; *do you ~ if I smoke?* stört es Sie, wenn ich rauche?; *would you ~ taking off your hat?* würden Sie bitte den Hut abnehmen?; *~ your own business!* kümmern Sie sich um Ihre Angelegenheiten!; **~ful** □ ['maindful] (*of*) eingedenk (*gen.*); achtsam (auf *acc.*).

mine¹ [main] 1. der (die, das) meinige; mein; 2. die Mein(ig)en *pl.*

mine² [~] 1. Bergwerk *n*, Grube *f*; *fig.* Fundgrube *f*; ✕ Mine *f*; 2. *v/i.* graben, minieren; *v/t.* graben; ✕ fördern; ✕ unterminieren; ✕ verminen; **~r** ['mainə] Bergmann *m*.

mineral ['minərəl] 1. Mineral *n*; **~s** *pl.* Mineralwasser *n*; 2. mineralisch.

mingle ['miŋgl] (ver)mischen; sich mischen *od.* mengen (*with* unter).

miniature ['minjətʃə] 1. Miniatur (-gemälde *n*) *f*; 2. in Miniatur; Miniatur...; Klein...; **~ camera** Kleinbildkamera *f*.

minikin ['minikin] 1. winzig; geziert; 2. Knirps *m*.

minim|ize ['minimaiz] möglichst klein machen; *fig.* verringern; **~um** [~məm] Minimum *n*; Mindestmaß *n*; Mindestbetrag *m*; *attr.* Mindest...

mining ['mainiŋ] Bergbau *m*; *attr.* Berg(bau)...; Gruben...

minion ['minjən] Günstling *m*; *fig.* Lakai *m*.

miniskirt ['miniskə:t] Minirock *m*.

minister ['ministə] 1. Diener *m*; *fig.* Werkzeug *n*; Geistliche(r) *m*; Minister *m*; Gesandte(r) *m*; 2. *v/t.* darreichen; *v/i.* dienen; Gottesdienst halten.

ministry ['ministri] geistliches Amt; Ministerium *n*; Regierung *f*.

mink *zo.* [miŋk] Nerz *m*.

minor ['mainə] 1. kleiner, geringer, weniger bedeutend; ♪ Moll; A ~ A-moll *n*; 2. Minderjährige(r *m*) *f*; *Am. univ.* Nebenfach *n*; **~ity** [mai'nɔriti] Minderheit *f*; Unmündigkeit *f*.

minster ['minstə] Münster *n*.

minstrel ['minstrəl] Minnesänger m; ~s pl. Negersänger m/pl.

mint [mint] 1. ♀ Minze f; Münze f; fig. Goldgrube f; a ~ of money e-e Menge Geld; 2. münzen, prägen.

minuet ♪ [minju'et] Menuett n.

minus ['mainəs] 1. prp. weniger; F ohne; 2. adj. negativ.

minute 1. □ [mai'nju:t] sehr klein, winzig; unbedeutend; sehr genau; 2. ['minit] Minute f; Augenblick m; ~s pl. Protokoll n; ~ness [mai-'nju:tnis] Kleinheit f; Genauigkeit f.

mirac|le ['mirəkl] Wunder n; ~ulous □ [mi'rækjuləs] wunderbar.

mirage ['mira:ʒ] Luftspiegelung f.

mire ['maiə] 1. Sumpf m; Kot m, Schlamm m; 2. mit Schlamm od. Schmutz bedecken.

mirror ['mirə] 1. Spiegel m; 2. (wider)spiegeln (a. fig.).

mirth [mə:θ] Fröhlichkeit f; ~ful □ ['mə:θful] fröhlich; ~less □ ['mə:θlis] freudlos.

miry ['maiəri] kotig.

mis... [mis] miß..., übel, falsch.

misadventure ['misəd'ventʃə] Mißgeschick n, Unfall m.

misanthrop|e ['mizənθroup], ~ist ['mi'zænθrəpist] Menschenfeind m.

misapply ['misə'plai] falsch anwenden. [mißverstehen.]

misapprehend ['misæpri'hend])

misappropriate ['misə'prouprieit] unterschlagen, veruntreuen.

misbehave ['misbi'heiv] sich schlecht benehmen.

misbelief ['misbi'li:f] Irrglaube m.

miscalculate ['miskælkjuleit] falsch (be)rechnen.

miscarr|iage [mis'kæridʒ] Mißlingen n; Verlust m v. Briefen; Fehlgeburt f; ~ of justice Fehlspruch m; ~y [~ri] mißlingen; verlorengehen (Brief); fehlgebären.

miscellan|eous □ [misi'leinjəs] ge~, vermischt; vielseitig; ~y [mi-'seləni] Gemisch n; Sammelband m.

mischief ['mistʃif] Schaden m, Unfug m; Mutwille m, Übermut m; ~-maker Unheilstifter(in).

mischievous □ ['mistʃivəs] schädlich; boshaft, mutwillig.

misconceive ['miskən'si:v] falsch auffassen od. verstehen.

misconduct 1. [mis'kɔndəkt] schlechtes Benehmen; Ehebruch m; schlechte Verwaltung; 2. ['miskən-'dʌkt] schlecht verwalten; ~ o.s. sich schlecht benehmen; e-n Fehltritt begehen.

misconstrue ['miskən'stru:] mißdeuten.

miscreant ['miskriənt] Schurke m.

misdeed ['mis'di:d] Missetat f.

misdemeano(u)r ⚖ [misdi'mi:nə] Vergehen n.

misdirect ['misdi'rekt] irreleiten; an die falsche Adresse richten.

misdoing ['misdu(:)iŋ] Vergehen n (mst pl.).

mise en scène thea. ['mi:zã:n'sein] Inszenierung f.

miser ['maizə] Geizhals m.

miserable □ ['mizərəbl] elend; unglücklich, erbärmlich.

miserly ['maizəli] geizig, filzig.

misery ['mizəri] Elend n, Not f.

misfit ['misfit] schlecht passendes Stück (Kleid, Stiefel etc.); Einzelgänger m, Eigenbrötler m.

misfortune [mis'fɔ:tʃən] Unglück(sfall m) n; Mißgeschick n.

misgiving [mis'giviŋ] böse Ahnung, Befürchtung f.

misguide ['mis'gaid] irreleiten.

mishap ['mishæp] Unfall m; mot. Panne f.

misinform ['misin'fɔ:m] falsch unterrichten. [deuten.]

misinterpret ['misin'tə:prit] falsch)

mislay [mis'lei] irr. (lay) verlegen.

mislead [mis'li:d] irr. (lead) irreführen; verleiten.

mismanage ['mis'mænidʒ] schlecht verwalten.

misplace ['mis'pleis] falsch stellen, verstellen; verlegen; falsch anbringen.

misprint 1. [mis'print] verdrucken; 2. ['mis'print] Druckfehler m.

misread ['mis'ri:d] irr. (read) falsch lesen od. deuten.

misrepresent['misrepri'zent]falsch darstellen, verdrehen.

miss¹ [mis] mst ♀ Fräulein n.

miss² [~] 1. Verlust m; Fehlschuß m, -stoß m, -wurf m; 2. v/t. (ver)missen; verfehlen; verpassen; auslassen; übersehen; überhören; v/i. fehlen (nicht treffen); fehlgehen.

misshapen ['mis'ʃeipən] verunstaltet; mißgestaltet.

missile ['misail] (Wurf)Geschoß n; Rakete f.

missing ['misiŋ] fehlend; ✗ vermißt; be ~ fehlen; vermißt werden.

mission ['miʃən] Sendung f; Auftrag m; Berufung f, Lebensziel n; Gesandtschaft f; eccl., pol. Mission f; ~ary ['miʃnəri] Missionar m; attr. Missions...

missive ['misiv] Sendschreiben n.

mis-spell ['mis'spel] irr. (spell) falsch buchstabieren od. schreiben.

mis-spend ['mis'spend] irr. (spend)] falsch verwenden; vergeuden.

mist [mist] 1. Nebel m; 2. (um)nebeln; sich trüben; beschlagen.

mistake [mis'teik] 1. irr. (take) sich irren in (dat.), verkennen; mißverstehen; verwechseln (for mit); be ~n sich irren; 2. Irrtum m; Versehen n; Fehler m; ~n □ [~kən] irrig, falsch (verstanden).

mister ['mistə] Herr *m* (*abbr.* **Mr.**).

mistletoe ♀ ['misltou] Mistel *f.*

mistress ['mistris] Herrin *f*; Hausfrau *f*; Lehrerin *f*; Geliebte *f*; Meisterin *f.*

mistrust ['mis'trʌst] **1.** mißtrauen (*dat.*); **2.** Mißtrauen *n*; **ful** □ [ʌtful] mißtrauisch.

misty □ ['misti] neb(e)lig; unklar.

misunderstand ['misʌndə'stænd] [*irr.* (*stand*)] mißverstehen; **ing** [ʌdiŋ] Mißverständnis *n.*

misus|age [mis'ju:zidʒ] Mißbrauch *m*; Mißhandlung *f*; **e 1.** ['mis'ju:z] mißbrauchen, mißhandeln; **2.** [ʌu:s] Mißbrauch *m.*

mite [mait] *zo.* Milbe *f*; Heller *m*; *fig.* Scherflein *n*; Knirps *m.*

mitigate ['mitigeit] mildern, lindern (*a. fig.*).

mit|re, *Am.* **er** ['maitə] Bischofsmütze *f.*

mitt [mit] *Baseball*-Handschuh *m*; F Boxhandschuh *m*; = **mitten.**

mitten ['mitn] Fausthandschuh *m*; Halbhandschuh *m* (*ohne Finger*); *Am. sl.* Tatze *f* (*Hand*).

mix [miks] (sich) (ver)mischen; verkehren (*with* mit); **ed** gemischt; *fig.* zweifelhaft; **~** *up* durch-ea.bringen; *be* **~***ed up with* in e-e S. verwickelt sein; **ture** ['mikstʃə] Mischung *f.*

moan [moun] **1.** Stöhnen *n*; **2.** stöhnen.

moat [mout] Burg-, Stadtgraben *m.*

mob [mɔb] **1.** Pöbel *m*; **2.** anpöbeln.

mobil|e ['moubail] beweglich; ✕ mobil; **ization**✕ [moubilai'zeiʃən] Mobilmachung *f*; **ize** ✕ ['moubilaiz] mobil machen.

moccasin ['mɔkəsin] weiches Leder; Mokassin *m* (*Schuh*).

mock [mɔk] **1.** Spott *m*; **2.** Schein...; falsch, nachgemacht; **3.** *v/t.* verspotten; nachmachen; täuschen; *v/i.* spotten (*at* über *acc.*); **ery** ['mɔkəri] Spötterei *f*, Gespött *n*; Äfferei *f.*

mocking-bird *orn.* ['mɔkiŋbə:d] Spottdrossel *f.*

mode [moud] Art und Weise *f*; (Erscheinungs)Form *f*; Sitte *f*, Mode *f.*

model ['mɔdl] **1.** Modell *n*; Muster *n*; *fig.* Vorbild *n*; Vorführdame *f*; *attr.* Muster...; **2.** modellieren; (ab)formen; *fig.* modeln, bilden.

moderat|e 1. □ ['mɔdərit] (mittel-)mäßig; **2.** [ʌreit] (sich) mäßigen; **ion** [mɔdə'reiʃən] Mäßigung *f*; Mäßigkeit *f.*

modern ['mɔdən] modern, neu; **ize** [ʌ(:)naiz] (sich) modernisieren.

modest □ ['mɔdist] bescheiden; anständig; **y** [ʌti] Bescheidenheit *f.*

modi|fication [mɔdifi'keiʃən] Ab-,

Veränderung *f*; Einschränkung *f*; **fy** ['mɔdifai] (ab)ändern; mildern.

mods [mɔdz] *pl.* Halbstarke *m/pl.*

modulate ['mɔdjuleit] modulieren.

moiety ['mɔiəti] Hälfte *f*; Teil *m.*

moist [mɔist] feucht, naß; **en** ['mɔisn] be-, anfeuchten; **ure** ['mɔistʃə] Feuchtigkeit *f.*

molar ['moulə] Backenzahn *m.*

molasses [mə'læsiz] Melasse *f*; Sirup *m.*

mole[1] *zo.* [moul] Maulwurf *m.*

mole[2] [ʌ] Muttermal *n.*

mole[3] [ʌ] Mole *f*, Hafendamm *m.*

molecule ['mɔlikju:l] Molekül *n.*

molehill ['moulhil] Maulwurfshügel *m*; *make a mountain out of a* **~** aus e-r Mücke e-n Elefanten machen.

molest [mou'lest] belästigen.

mollify ['mɔlifai] besänftigen.

mollycoddle ['mɔlikɔdl] **1.** Weichling *m*, Muttersöhnchen *n*; **2.** verzärteln.

molten ['moultən] geschmolzen.

moment ['moumənt] Augenblick *m*; Bedeutung *f*; = *momentum*; **ary** □ [ʌtəri] augenblicklich; vorübergehend; **ous** □ [mou'mentəs] (ge)wichtig, bedeutend; **um** *phys.* [ʌtəm] Moment *n*; Triebkraft *f.*

monarch ['mɔnək] Monarch(in); **y** [ʌki] Monarchie *f.*

monastery ['mɔnəstəri] (Mönchs-) Kloster *n.*

Monday ['mʌndi] Montag *m.*

monetary ['mʌnitəri] Geld...

money ['mʌni] Geld *n*; *ready* **~** Bargeld *n*; **box** Sparbüchse *f*; **changer** [ʌtʃeindʒə] (Geld-) Wechsler *m*; **order** Postanweisung *f.*

monger ['mʌŋgə] ...händler *m*, ...krämer *m.*

mongrel ['mʌŋgrəl] Mischling *m*, Bastard *m*; *attr.* Bastard...

monitor ['mɔnitə] ⊕ Monitor *m*; (Klassen)Ordner *m.*

monk [mʌŋk] Mönch *m.*

monkey ['mʌŋki] **1.** *zo.* Affe *m* (*a. fig.*); ⊕ Rammblock *m*; *put s.o.'s* **~** *up* F j-n auf die Palme bringen; **~** *business Am. sl.* fauler Zauber; **2.** F (herum)albern; **~** *with* herummurksen an (*dat.*); **wrench** ⊕ Engländer *m* (*Schraubenschlüssel*); *throw a* **~** *in s.th. Am. sl.* et. über den Haufen werfen.

monkish ['mʌŋkiʃ] mönchisch.

mono|... ['mɔnou] ein(fach)...; **cle** ['mɔnɔkl] Monokel *n*; **gamy** [mɔ'nɔgəmi] Einehe *f*; **logue**, *Am. a.* **log** ['mɔnɔlɔg] Monolog *m*; **polist** [mə'nɔpəlist] Monopolist *m*; **polize** [ʌlaiz] monopolisieren; *fig.* an sich reißen; **poly** [ʌli] Monopol *n* (*of auf acc.*); **tonous** □ [ʌtnəs] monoton, eintönig; **tony** [ʌni] Monotonie *f.*

monsoon ['mɔn'su:n] Monsun *m*.

monster ['mɔnstə] Ungeheuer *n* (*a. fig.*); Monstrum *n*; *attr.* Riesen...

monstro|sity [mɔns'trɔsiti] Ungeheuer(lichkeit *f*) *n*; ~us □ ['mɔnstrəs] ungeheuer(lich); gräßlich.

month [mʌnθ] Monat *m*; *this day* ~ heute in e-m Monat; ~ly ['mʌnθli] 1. monatlich; Monats...; 2. Monatsschrift *f*.

monument ['mɔnjumənt] Denkmal *n*; ~al □ [mɔnju'mentl] monumental; Gedenk...; großartig.

mood [mu:d] Stimmung *f*, Laune *f*; ~y □ ['mu:di] launisch; schwermütig; übellaunig.

moon [mu:n] 1. Mond *m*; *once in a blue* ~ F alle Jubeljahre einmal; 2. *mst* ~ *about* F herumdösen; ~light ['mu:nlait] Mondlicht *n*, -schein *m*; ~lit mondhell; ~struck mondsüchtig.

Moor[1] [muə] Maure *m*; Mohr *m*.

moor[2] [~] Ödland *n*, Heideland *n*.

moor[3] ♃ [~] (sich) vertäuen; ~ings ♃ *pl.* Vertäuungen *f/pl.*

moose *zo.* [mu:z] *a.* ~-deer amerikanischer Elch.

moot [mu:t]: ~ *point* Streitpunkt *m*.

mop [mɔp] 1. Mop *m*; (Haar)Wust *m*; 2. auf-, abwischen.

mope [moup] den Kopf hängen lassen.

moral ['mɔrəl] 1. □ Moral...; moralisch; 2. Moral *f*; Nutzanwendung *f*; ~s *pl.* Sitten *f/pl.*; ~e [mɔ'ra:l] *bsd.* ✕ Moral *f*, Haltung *f*; ~ity [mə'ræliti] Moralität *f*; Sittlichkeit *f*, Moral *f*; ~ize ['mɔrəlaiz] moralisieren.

morass [mə'ræs] Morast *m*, Sumpf *m*.

morbid □ ['mɔ:bid] krankhaft.

more [mɔ:] mehr; *once* ~ noch einmal, wieder; *so much od. all the* ~ um so mehr; *no* ~ nicht mehr.

morel ♀ [mɔ'rel] Morchel *f*.

moreover [mɔ:'rouvə] überdies, weiter, ferner.

morgue [mɔ:g] Leichenschauhaus *n*; Archiv *n*.

moribund ['mɔribʌnd] im Sterben (liegend), dem Tode geweiht.

morning ['mɔ:niŋ] Morgen *m*; Vormittag *m*; *tomorrow* ~ morgen früh; ~ *dress* Tagesgesellschaftsanzug *m*; [(*m*) *f.*\]

moron ['mɔ:rɔn] Schwachsinnige(r)

morose □ [mə'rous] mürrisch.

morph|ia ['mɔ:fjə], ~ine ['mɔ:fi:n] Morphium *n*.

morsel ['mɔ:səl] Bissen *m*; Stückchen *n*, *das* bißchen.

mortal ['mɔ:tl] 1. □ sterblich; tödlich; Tod(es)...; 2. Sterbliche(r *m*) *f*; ~ity [mɔ:'tæliti] Sterblichkeit *f*.

mortar ['mɔ:tə] Mörser *m*; Mörtel *m*.

mortgag|e ['mɔ:gidʒ] 1. Pfandgut *n*; Hypothek *f*; 2. verpfänden; ~ee [mɔ:gə'dʒi:] Hypothekengläubiger *m*; ~er ['mɔ:gidʒə], ~or [mɔ:gə'dʒɔ:] Hypothekenschuldner *m*.

mortician *Am.* [mɔ:'tiʃən] Leichenbestatter *m*.

morti|fication [mɔ:tifi'keiʃən] Kasteiung *f*; Kränkung *f*; ~fy ['mɔ:tifai] kasteien; kränken.

morti|se, ~ce ⊕ ['mɔ:tis] Zapfenloch *n*.

mortuary ['mɔ:tjuəri] Leichenhalle *f*.

mosaic [mə'zeiik] Mosaik *n*.

mosque [mɔsk] Moschee *f*.

mosquito *zo.* [məs'ki:tou] Moskito *m*. [moosig.\]

moss [mɔs] Moos *n*; ~y ['mɔsi]\]

most [moust] 1. *adj.* □ meist; 2. *adv.* meist, am meisten; höchst; 3. das meiste; die meisten; Höchste(s) *n*; *at* (*the*) ~ höchstens; *make the* ~ *of* möglichst ausnutzen; ~ly ['moustli] meistens.

moth [mɔθ] Motte *f*; ~-eaten ['mɔθi:tn] mottenzerfressen.

mother ['mʌðə] 1. Mutter *f*; 2. bemuttern; ~ *country* Vaterland *n*; Mutterland *n*; ~hood [~hud] Mutterschaft *f*; ~-in-law [~ɔrinlɔ:] Schwiegermutter *f*; ~ly [~əli] mütterlich; ~-of-pearl [~ərəv'pə:l] Perlmutter *f*; ~-tongue Muttersprache *f*.

motif [mou'ti:f] (Leit)Motiv *n*.

motion ['mouʃən] 1. Bewegung *f*; Gang *m* (*a.* ⊕); *parl.* Antrag *m*; 2. *v/t.* durch Gebärden auffordern *od.* andeuten; *v/i.* winken; ~less [~nlis] bewegungslos; ~ *picture* Film *m*.

motivate ['moutiveit] motivieren, begründen.

motive ['moutiv] 1. bewegend; 2. Motiv *n*, Beweggrund *m*; 3. veranlassen; ~less [~vlis] grundlos.

motley ['mɔtli] (bunt)scheckig.

motor ['moutə] 1. Motor *m*; treibende Kraft; Automobil *n*; ⚕ Muskel *m*; 2. motorisch, bewegend; Motor...; Kraft...; Auto...; 3. (im) Auto fahren; ~-assisted [~ərə'sistid] mit Hilfsmotor; ~ *bicycle*, ~bike = *motor cycle*; ~ *boat* Motorboot *m*; ~ *bus* Autobus *m*; ~cade *Am.* [~əkeid] Autokolonne *f*; ~-car Auto(mobil) *n*; ~ *coach* Reisebus *m*; ~ *cycle* Motorrad *n*; ~ing [~əriŋ] Autofahren *n*; ~ist [~rist] Kraftfahrer(in); ~ize [~raiz] motorisieren; ~ *launch* Motorbarkasse *f*; ~-road, ~way Autobahn *f*.

mottled ['mɔtld] gefleckt.

mo(u)ld [mould] 1. Gartenerde *f*; Schimmel *m*, Moder *m* (Guß-) Form *f* (*a. fig.*); Abdruck *m*; Art *f*; 2. formen, gießen (*on*, *upon* nach).

mo(u)lder ['mouldə] zerfallen.

mo(u)lding △ ['mouldiŋ] Fries m.

mo(u)ldy ['mouldi] schimm(e)lig, dumpfig, mod(e)rig.

mo(u)lt [moult] (fig. sich) mausern.

mound [maund] Erdhügel m, -wall m.

mount [maunt] 1. Berg m; Reitpferd n; 2. v/i. (empor)steigen; aufsteigen (Reiter); v/t. be-, ersteigen; beritten machen; montieren; aufziehen, aufkleben; Edelstein fassen.

mountain ['mauntin] 1. Berg m; ~s pl. Gebirge n; 2. Berg..., Gebirgs...; ~eer [maunti'niə] Bergbewohner(in); Bergsteiger(in); ~ous ['mauntinəs] bergig, gebirgig.

mountebank ['mauntibæŋk]Marktschreier m, Scharlatan m.

mourn [mɔːn] (be)trauern; ~er ['mɔːnə] Leidtragende(r m) f; ~ful □ ['mɔːnful] Trauer...; traurig; ~ing ['mɔːniŋ] Trauer f; attr. Trauer... [Maus f.]

mouse [maus], pl. mice [mais]

moustache [məs'taːʃ] Schnurrbart m.

mouth [mauθ], pl. ~s [mauðz]Mund m; Maul n; Mündung f; Öffnung f; ~ful ['mauθful] Mundvoll m; ~organ Mundharmonika f; ~piece Mundstück n; fig. Sprachrohr n.

move [muːv] 1. v/t. allg. bewegen; in Bewegung setzen; (weg)rücken; (an)treiben; Leidenschaft erregen; seelisch rühren; beantragen; ~ heaven and earth Himmel und Hölle in Bewegung setzen; v/i. sich (fort)bewegen; sich rühren; Schach: ziehen; (um)ziehen (Mieter); ~ for s.th. et. beantragen; ~ in einziehen; ~ on weitergehen; ~ out ausziehen; 2. Bewegung f; Schach: Zug m; fig. Schritt m; on the ~ in Bewegung; make a ~ die Tafel aufheben; ~ment ['muːvmənt] Bewegung f; ♩ Tempo n; ♩ Satz m; ⊕ (Geh-)Werk n.

movies ['muːviz] pl. Kino n.

moving □ ['muːviŋ] bewegend; beweglich; ~ staircase Rolltreppe f.

mow [mou] [irr.] mähen; ~er ['mouə] Mäher(in); Mähmaschine f; ~ing-machine ['mouiŋməʃiːn] Mähmaschine f; ~n [moun] p.p. von mow.

much [mʌtʃ] 1. adj. viel; 2. adv. sehr; viel; bei weitem; fast; ~ as I would like so gern ich möchte; I thought as ~ das dachte ich mir; make ~ of viel Wesens machen von; I am not ~ of a dancer ich bin kein großer Tänzer.

muck [mʌk] Mist m (F a. fig.); ~rake ['mʌkreik] 1. Mistgabel f; = ~r; 2. im Schmutz wühlen; ~raker [~kə] Am. Korruptionsschnüffler m.

mucus ['mjuːkəs] (Nasen)Schleim m.

mud [mʌd] Schlamm m; Kot m; ~dle ['mʌdl] 1. v/t. verwirren; a. ~ up, ~ together durcheinanderbringen; F benebeln; v/i. stümpern; ~ through F sich durchwursteln; 2. Wirrwarr m; F Unordnung f; ~dy ['mʌdi] schlammig; trüb; ~guard Kotflügel m.

muff [mʌf] Muff m.

muffin ['mʌfin] Muffin n (heißes Teegebäck).

muffle ['mʌfl] oft ~ up ein-, umhüllen, umwickeln; Stimme etc. dämpfen; ~r [~lə] Halstuch n; Boxhandschuh m; mot. Auspufftopf m.

mug [mʌg] Krug m; Becher m.

muggy ['mʌgi] schwül.

mugwump Am. iro. ['mʌgwʌmp] großes Tier (Person); pol. Unabhängige(r) m.

mulatto [mju(ː)'lætou] Mulatt|e m, -in f.

mulberry ['mʌlbəri] Maulbeere f.

mule [mjuːl] Maultier n, -esel m; störrischer Mensch; ~teer [mjuːli'tiə] Maultiertreiber m.

mull¹ [mʌl] Mull m.

mull² [~]: ~ over überdenken.

mulled [mʌld]: ~ wine Glühwein m.

mulligan Am. F ['mʌligən] Eintopf m aus Resten.

mullion ['mʌliən]Fensterpfosten m.

multi|farious □ [mʌlti'fɛəriəs] mannigfaltig; ~form ['mʌltifɔːm] vielförmig; ~ple [~ipl] 1. vielfach; 2. Vielfache(s) n; ~plication [mʌltipli'keiʃən] Vervielfältigung f, Vermehrung f; Multiplikation f; compound (simple) ~ Großes (Kleines) Einmaleins n; ~ table Einmaleins n; ~plicity [~i'plisiti] Vielfalt f; ~ply ['mʌltiplai] (sich) vervielfältigen; multiplizieren; ~tude [~itjuːd] Vielheit f, Menge f; ~tudinous [mʌlti-'tjuːdinəs] zahlreich.

mum [mʌm] still.

mumble ['mʌmbl] murmeln, nuscheln; mummeln (mühsam essen).

mummery contp. ['mʌməri] Mummenschanz m.

mummify ['mʌmifai] mumifizieren.

mummy¹ ['mʌmi] Mumie f.

mummy² F [~] Mami f, Mutti f.

mumps ♣ [mʌmps] sg. Ziegenpeter m, Mumps m.

munch [mʌntʃ] mit vollen Backen (fr)essen, mampfen.

mundane □ ['mʌndein] weltlich.

municipal □ [mju(ː)'nisipəl] städtisch, Gemeinde..., Stadt...; ~ity [mju(ː)nisi'pæliti] Stadtbezirk m; Stadtverwaltung f.

munificen|ce [mju(ː)'nifisns] Freigebigkeit f; ~t [~nt] freigebig.

munitions [mju(ː)'niʃənz] pl. Munition f.

mural ['mjuərəl] Mauer...

murder ['məːdə] 1. Mord m; 2. (er-)

morden; *fig.* verhunzen; **~er** [~ərə] Mörder *m*; **~ess** [~ris] Mörderin *f*; **~ous** □ [~rəs] mörderisch.

murky □ ['mə:ki] dunkel, finster.

murmur ['mə:mə] 1. Gemurmel *n*; Murren *n*; 2. murmeln; murren.

murrain ['mʌrin] Viehseuche *f*.

musc|le ['mʌsl] 1. Muskel *m*; 2. ~ *in Am. sl.* sich rücksichtslos eindrängen; **~le-bound** mit Muskelkater; be ~ Muskelkater haben; **~ular** ['mʌskjulə] Muskel...; muskulös.

Muse¹ [mju:z] Muse *f*.

muse² [~] (nach)sinnen, grübeln.

museum [mju(:)'ziəm] Museum *n*.

mush [mʌʃ] Brei *m*, Mus *n*; *Am.* Polenta *f*, Maisbrei *m*.

mushroom ['mʌʃrum] 1. Pilz *m*, *bsd.* Champignon *m*; 2. rasch wachsen; ~ *up* in die Höhe schießen.

music ['mju:zik] Musik *f*; Musikstück *n*; Noten *f/pl.*; set to ~ vertonen; **~al** □ [~kəl] musikalisch; Musik...; wohlklingend; ~ *box* Spieldose *f*; **~ box** *Am.* Spieldose *f*; **~-hall** Varieté(theater) *n*; **~ian** [mju(:)'ziʃən] Musiker(in); **~-stand** Notenständer *m*; **~-stool** Klavierstuhl *m*.

musk [mʌsk] Moschus *m*, Bisam *m*; **~-deer** *zo.* ['mʌsk'diə] Moschustier *n*.

musket ['mʌskit] Muskete *f*.

musk-rat *zo.* ['mʌskræt] Bisamratte *f*.

muslin ['mʌzlin] Musselin *m*.

musquash ['mʌskwɔʃ] Bisamratte *f*; Bisampelz *m*.

muss *bsd. Am.* F [mʌs] Durcheinander *n*.

mussel ['mʌsl] (Mies)Muschel *f*.

must¹ [mʌst] 1. muß(te); darf; durfte; *I* ~ *not* ich darf nicht; 2. Muß *n*.

must² [~] Schimmel *m*, Moder *m*.

must³ [~] Most *m*.

mustach|e *Am.* [məs'tæʃ], **~io** *Am.* [məs'ta:ʃou] = *moustache*.

mustard ['mʌstəd] Senf *m*.

muster ['mʌstə] 1. ✕ Musterung *f*; *fig.* Heerschau *f*; 2. ✕ mustern; aufbieten, aufbringen.

musty ['mʌsti] mod(e)rig, muffig.

muta|ble □ ['mju:təbl] veränderlich; wankelmütig; **~tion** [mju(:)-'teiʃn] Veränderung *f*.

mute [mju:t] 1. □ stumm; 2. Stumme(r *m*) *f*; 3. dämpfen.

mutilate ['mju:tileit] verstümmeln.

mutin|eer [mju:ti'niə] Meuterer *m*; **~ous** □ ['mju:tinəs] meuterisch; **~y** [~ni] 1. Meuterei *f*; 2. meutern.

mutter ['mʌtə] 1. Gemurmel *n*; Gemurre *n*; 2. murmeln; murren.

mutton ['mʌtn] Hammelfleisch *n*; leg of ~ Hammelkeule *f*; ~ **chop** Hammelkotelett *n*.

mutual □ ['mju:tjuəl] gegenseitig, gemeinsam.

muzzle ['mʌzl] 1. Maul *n*, Schnauze *f*; Mündung *f* e-r *Feuerwaffe*; Maulkorb *m*; 2. e-n Maulkorb anlegen (*dat.*); *fig.* den Mund stopfen (*dat.*).

my [mai] mein(e).

myrrh ♣ [mə:] Myrrhe *f*.

myrtle ♣ ['mə:tl] Myrte *f*.

myself [mai'self] (ich) selbst; mir; mich; by ~ allein.

myster|ious □ [mis'tiəriəs] geheimnisvoll, mysteriös; **~y** ['mistəri] Mysterium *n*; Geheimnis *n*; Rätsel *n*.

mysti|c ['mistik] 1. *a.* **~cal** □ [~kəl] mystisch, geheimnisvoll; 2. Mystiker *m*; **~fy** [~ifai] mystifizieren, täuschen.

myth [miθ] Mythe *f*, Mythos *m*, Sage *f*.

N

nab *sl.* [næb] schnappen, erwischen.

nacre ['neikə] Perlmutter *f*.

nadir ['neidiə] *ast.* Nadir *m* (*Fußpunkt*); *fig.* tiefster Stand.

nag [næg] 1. F Klepper *m*; 2. *v/i.* nörgeln, quengeln; *v/t.* bekritteln.

nail [neil] 1. (Finger-, Zehen)Nagel *m*; ⊕ Nagel *m*; *zo.* Kralle *f*, Klaue *f*; 2. (an-, fest)nageln; *Augen etc.* heften (*to* auf *acc.*); **~-scissors** ['neilsizəz] *pl.* Nagelschere *f*; **~-varnish** Nagellack *m*.

naïve □ [na:'i:v], **naive** □ [neiv] naiv; ungekünstelt.

naked □ ['neikid] nackt, bloß; kahl; *fig.* unverhüllt; *poet.* schutzlos;

~ness [~dnis] Nacktheit *f*, Blöße *f*; Kahlheit *f*; Schutzlosigkeit *f*; *fig.* Unverhülltheit *f*.

name [neim] 1. Name *m*; Ruf *m*; of ~ by the ~ of ... namens ...; call *s.o.* ~s j-n beschimpfen; 2. (be-) nennen; erwähnen; ernennen; **~less** □ ['neimlis] namenlos; unbekannt; **~ly** [~li] nämlich; **~plate** Namens-, Tür-, Firmenschild *n*; **~sake** ['neimseik] Namensvetter *m*.

nanny ['næni] Kindermädchen *n*; **~-goat** Ziege *f*.

nap [næp] 1. *Tuch-*Noppe *f*; Schläfchen *n*; have *od.* take a ~ ein Nickerchen machen; 2. schlummern.

nape [neip] *mst* ~ *of the neck* Genick *n.*

nap|kin ['næpkin] Serviette *f;* Windel *f;* *mst sanitary* ~ *Am.* Monatsbinde *f;* ~**py** F ['næpi] Windel *f.*

narcosis ♂ [nɑː'kousis] Narkose *f.*

narcotic [nɑː'kɔtik] **1.** (~*ally*) narkotisch; **2.** Betäubungsmittel *n.*

narrat|e [næ'reit] erzählen; ~**ion** [~eiʃən] Erzählung *f;* ~**ive** ['nærətiv] **1.** □ erzählend; **2.** Erzählung *f;* ~**or** [næ'reitə] Erzähler *m.*

narrow ['nærou] **1.** eng, schmal; beschränkt; knapp (*Mehrheit, Entkommen*); engherzig; **2.** ~**s** *pl.* Engpaß *m;* Meerenge *f;* **3.** (sich) verengen; beschränken; einengen; *Maschen* abnehmen; ~**chested** schmalbrüstig; ~**minded** □ engherzig; ~**ness** [~ounis] Enge *f;* Beschränktheit *f (a. fig.);* Engherzigkeit *f.*

nary *Am.* F ['nɛəri] kein.

nasal □ ['neizəl] nasal; Nasen...

nasty □ ['nɑːsti] schmutzig; garstig; eklig, widerlich; häßlich; unflätig; ungemütlich.

natal ['neitl] Geburts...

nation ['neiʃən] Nation *f,* Volk *n.*

national ['næʃənl] **1.** □ national; Volks..., Staats...; **2.** Staatsangehörige(r *m*) *f;* ~**ity** [næʃə'næliti] Nationalität *f;* ~**ize** ['næʃnəlaiz] naturalisieren, einbürgern; verstaatlichen.

nation-wide ['neiʃənwaid] die ganze Nation umfassend.

native ['neitiv] **1.** □ angeboren; heimatlich, Heimat...; eingeboren; einheimisch; ~ *language* Muttersprache *f;* **2.** Eingeborene(r *m*) *f;* ~**born** (im Lande) geboren, einheimisch.

nativity [nə'tiviti] Geburt *f.*

natter F ['nætə] plaudern.

natural □ ['nætʃrəl] natürlich; *engS.:* angeboren; ungezwungen; unehelich (*Kind*); ~ *science* Naturwissenschaft *f;* ~**ist** [~list] Naturalist *m;* Naturforscher *m;* Tierhändler *m;* ~**ize** [~laiz] einbürgern; ~**ness** [~nis] Natürlichkeit *f.*

nature ['neitʃə] Natur *f.*

naught [nɔːt] Null *f;* *set at* ~ für nichts achten; ~**y** ['nɔːti] unartig.

nause|a ['nɔːsjə] Übelkeit *f;* Ekel *m;* ~**ate** ['nɔːsieit] *v/i.* Ekel empfinden; *v/t.* verabscheuen; *be* ~*d* sich ekeln; ~**ous** ['nɔːsjəs] ekelhaft.

nautical ['nɔːtikəl] nautisch; See...

naval ✕ ['neivəl] See..., Marine...; ~ *base* Flottenstützpunkt *m.*

nave[1] ▲ [neiv] (Kirchen)Schiff *n.*

nave[2] [~] Rad-Nabe *f.*

navel ['neivəl] Nabel *m;* Mitte *f.*

naviga|ble □ ['nævigəbl] schiffbar; fahrbar; lenkbar; ~**te** [~geit] *v/i.* schiffen, fahren; *v/t.* See *etc.* befahren; steuern; ~**tion** [nævi'geiʃən]

Schiffahrt *f;* Navigation *f;* ~**tor** ['nævigeitə] Seefahrer *m.*

navy ['neivi] (Kriegs)Marine *f.*

nay † [nei] nein; nein vielmehr.

near [niə] **1.** *adj.* nahe; gerade (*Weg*); nahe verwandt; verwandt; vertraut; genau; knapp; knauserig; ~ *at hand* dicht dabei; **2.** *adv.* nahe; 3. *prp.* nahe (*dat.*), nahe bei *od.* an; **4.** sich nähern (*dat.*); ~**by** ['niəbai] in der Nähe (gelegen); nah; ~**ly** ['niəli] nahe; fast, beinahe; genau; ~**ness** ['niənis] Nähe *f;* ~**sighted** kurzsichtig.

neat □ [niːt] nett; niedlich; geschickt; ordentlich; sauber; rein; ~**ness** ['niːtnis] Nettigkeit *f;* Sauberkeit *f;* Zierlichkeit *f.*

nebulous □ ['nebjuləs] neblig.

necess|ary □ ['nesisəri] **1.** notwendig; unvermeidlich; **2.** *mst necessaries pl.* Bedürfnisse *n/pl.;* ~**itate** [ni'sesiteit] *et.* erfordern; zwingen; ~**ity** [~ti] Notwendigkeit *f;* Zwang *m;* Not *f.*

neck [nek] **1.** (*a. Flaschen*)Hals *m;* Nacken *m,* Genick *n;* Ausschnitt *m* (*Kleid*); ~ *and* ~ Kopf an Kopf; ~ *or nothing* F alles oder nichts; **2.** *sl.* sich abknutschen; ~**band** ['nekbænd] Halsbund *m;* ~**erchief** ['nekətʃif] Halstuch *m;* ~**lace** ['neklis], ~**let** [~lit] Halskette *f;* ~**tie** ~ Krawatte *f.*

necromancy ['nekroumænsi] Zauberei *f.*

née [nei] *bei Frauennamen:* geborene.

need [niːd] **1.** Not *f;* Notwendigkeit *f;* Bedürfnis *n;* Mangel *m,* Bedarf *m; be od. stand in* ~ *of* brauchen; **2.** nötig haben, brauchen; bedürfen (*gen.*); müssen; ~**ful** ['niːdful] notwendig.

needle ['niːdl] **1.** Nadel *f;* Zeiger *m;* **2.** nähen; *bsd. Am.* irritieren; anstacheln.

needless □ ['niːdlis] unnötig.

needle|woman ['niːdlwumən] Näherin *f;* ~**work** Handarbeit *f.*

needy □ ['niːdi] bedürftig, arm.

nefarious □ [ni'fɛəriəs] schändlich.

negat|e [ni'geit] verneinen; ~**ion** [~eiʃən] Verneinung *f;* Nichts *n;* ~**ive** ['negətiv] **1.** □ negativ; verneinend; **2.** Verneinung *f; phot.* Negativ *n;* **3.** ablehnen.

neglect [ni'glekt] **1.** Vernachlässigung *f;* Nachlässigkeit *f;* **2.** vernachlässigen; ~**ful** [~tful] nachlässig.

negligen|ce ['neglidʒəns] Nachlässigkeit *f;* ~**t** □ [~nt] nachlässig.

negligible □ ['neglidʒəbl] nebensächlich; unbedeutend.

negotia|te [ni'gouʃieit] verhandeln (über *acc.*); zustande bringen; bewältigen; *Wechsel* begeben; ~**tion** [nigouʃi'eiʃən] Begebung *f e-s Wechsels etc.;* Ver-, Unterhandlung *f*; Bewältigung *f*; ~tor [ni'gouʃieitə] Unterhändler *m*.

negr|ess ['ni:gris] Negerin *f*; ~o [~rou], *pl.* ~oes Neger *m*.

neigh [nei] 1. Wiehern *n*; 2. wiehern.

neighbo(u)r ['neibə] Nachbar(in); Nächste(r *m*) *f*; ~hood [~hud] Nachbarschaft *f*; ~ing [~əriŋ] benachbart; ~ly [~əli] nachbarlich, freundlich; ~ship [~əʃip] Nachbarschaft *f*.

neither ['naiðə] 1. keiner (von beiden); 2. ~ ... nor ... weder ... noch ...; *not* ... ~ auch nicht.

nephew ['nevju(:)] Neffe *m*.

nerve [nə:v] 1. Nerv *m*; Sehne *f*; *Blatt*-Rippe *f*; Kraft *f*, Mut *m*; Dreistigkeit *f*; *get on one's* ~*s* e-m auf die Nerven gehen; 2. kräftigen; ermutigen; ~less □ ['nə:vlis] kraftlos.

nervous □ ['nə:vəs] Nerven...; nervig, kräftig; nervös; ~ness [~snis] Nervigkeit *f*; Nervosität *f*.

nest [nest] 1. Nest *n* (*a. fig.*); 2. nisten; ~le ['nesl] *v/i.* (sich ein)nisten; sich (an)schmiegen; *v/t.* schmiegen.

net¹ [net] 1. Netz *n*; 2. mit e-m Netz fangen *od.* umgeben.

net² [~] 1. netto; Rein...; 2. netto einbringen.

nether ['neðə] nieder; Unter...

nettle ['netl] 1. ♀ Nessel *f*; 2. ärgern.

network ['netwə:k] (Straßen-, Kanal- *etc.*)Netz *n*; Sendergruppe *f*.

neurosis ✻ [njuə'rousis] Neurose *f*.

neuter ['nju:tə] 1. geschlechtslos; 2. geschlechtsloses Tier; *gr.* Neutrum *n*.

neutral ['nju:trəl] 1. neutral; unparteiisch; 2. Neutrale(r *m*) *f*; Null(punkt *m*) *f*; Leerlauf(stellung *f*) *m*; ~ity [nju(:)'træliti] Neutralität *f*; ~ize ['nju:trəlaiz] neutralisieren.

neutron *phys.* ['nju:trɔn] Neutron *n*.

never ['nevə] nie(mals); gar nicht; ~more [~ə'mɔ:] nie wieder; ~theless [nevəðə'les] nichtsdestoweniger.

new [nju:] neu; frisch; unerfahren; ~comer ['nju:'kʌmə] Ankömmling *m*; ~ly ['nju:li] neulich; neu.

news [nju:z] *mst. sg.* Neuigkeit(en *pl.*) *f*, Nachricht(en *pl.*) *f*; ~agent ['nju:zeidʒənt] Zeitungshändler *m*; ~boy Zeitungsausträger *m*; ~butcher *Am. sl.* Zeitungsverkäufer *m*; ~cast *Radio*: Nachrichten *f/pl.*; ~monger Neuigkeitskrämer *m*; ~paper Zeitung *f*; *attr.* Zeitungs...; ~print Zeitungspapier *n*; ~reel *Film*: Wochenschau *f*; ~room Lesezimmer *n*; *Am. Zeitung*: Nachrichtenredaktion *f*; ~stall, *Am.* ~stand Zeitungskiosk *m*.

new year ['nju:'jə:] *das* neue Jahr; *New Year's Day* Neujahr(stag *m*) *n*; *New Year's Eve* Silvester *m*.

next [nekst] 1. *adj.* nächst; ~ *but one der* übernächste; ~ *door* to fig. beinahe; ~ *to* nächst (*dat.*); 2. *adv.* zunächst, gleich darauf; nächstens.

nibble ['nibl] *v/t.* knabbern an (*dat.*); *v/i.* ~ *at* nagen *od.* knabbern an (*dat.*); (herum)kritteln an (*dat.*).

nice □ [nais] fein; wählerisch; peinlich (genau); heikel; nett; niedlich; hübsch; ~ly ['naisli] F (sehr) gut; ~ty ['naisiti] Feinheit *f*; Genauigkeit *f*; Spitzfindigkeit *f*.

niche [nitʃ] Nische *f*.

nick [nik] 1. Kerbe *f*; *in the* ~ *of time* gerade zur rechten Zeit; 2. (ein)kerben; *sl. j-n* schnappen.

nickel ['nikl] 1. *min.* Nickel *m* (*Am. a. Fünfcentstück*); 2. vernickeln.

nick-nack ['niknæk] = *knick-knack*.

nickname ['nikneim] 1. Spitzname *m*; 2. e-n Spitznamen geben (*dat.*).

niece [ni:s] Nichte *f*.

nifty *Am. sl.* ['nifti] elegant; stinkend.

niggard ['nigəd] Geizhals *m*; ~ly [~dli] geizig, knauserig; karg.

nigger F *mst contp.* ['nigə] Nigger *m* (*Neger*); ~ *in the woodpile Am. sl.* der Haken an der Sache.

night [nait] Nacht *f*; Abend *m*; *by* ~ *in the* ~, *at* ~ nachts; ~cap ['naitkæp] Nachtmütze *f*; Nachttrunk *m*; ~club Nachtlokal *n*; ~dress (Damen)Nachthemd *n*; ~fall Einbruch *m* der Nacht; ~gown = *night-dress*; ~ingale *orn.*['naitiŋgeil] Nachtigall *f*; ~ly ['naitli] nächtlich; jede Nacht; ~mare Alptraum *m*; ~shirt (Herren)Nachthemd *n*; ~spot *Am.* Nachtlokal *n*; ~y ['naiti] F(Damen-*od.*Kinder)Nachthemd *n*.

nil [nil] *bsd. Sport*: nichts, null.

nimble □ ['nimbl] flink, behend.

nimbus ['nimbəs] Nimbus *m*, Heiligenschein *m*; Regenwolke *f*.

nine [nain] 1. neun; 2. Neun *f*; ~pins ['nainpinz] *pl.* Kegel(spiel *n*) *m/pl.*; ~teen ['nain'ti:n] neunzehn; ~ty ['nainti] neunzig.

ninny F ['nini] Dummkopf *m*.

ninth [nainθ] 1. neunte(r, -s); 2. Neuntel *n*; ~ly ['nainθli] neuntens.

nip [nip] 1. Kniff *m*; scharfer Frost; Schlückchen *n*; 2. zwicken; schneiden (*Kälte*); *sl.* flitzen; nippen; ~ *in the bud* im Keime ersticken.

nipper ['nipə] Krebsschere *f*; (*a pair of*) ~s *pl.* (eine) (Kneif)Zange.

nipple ['nipl] Brustwarze *f*.

Nisei *Am.* ['ni:'sei] (*a. pl.*) Japaner *m*, geboren in *den USA*.

nit|re, *Am.* ~er ⚗ ['naitə] Salpeter *m*.

nitrogen ['naitridʒən] Stickstoff *m*.

no [nou] 1. *adj.* kein; *in ~ time* im Nu; *~ one* keiner; 2. *adv.* nein; nicht; 3. Nein *n.*

nobility [nou'biliti] Adel *m (a. fig.).*

noble ['noubl] 1. □ adlig; edel, vornehm; vortrefflich; 2. Adlige(r *m) f;* ~**man** Adlige(r) *m;* ~**minded** edelmütig; ~**ness** [~lnis] Adel *m;* Würde *f.*

nobody ['noubədi] niemand.

nocturnal [nɔk'təːnl] Nacht...

nod [nɔd] 1. nicken; schlafen; (sich) neigen; ~*ding acquaintance* oberflächliche Bekanntschaft; 2. Nicken *n;* Wink *m.*

node [noud] Knoten *m (a. & u. ast.);* ⚕ Überbein *n.*

noise [nɔiz] 1. Lärm *m;* Geräusch *n;* Geschrei *n; big ~ bsd. Am.* F großes Tier (*Person*); 2. ~ *abroad* ausschreien; ~**less** □ ['nɔizlis] geräuschlos.

noisome ['nɔisəm] schädlich; widerlich.

noisy □ ['nɔizi] geräuschvoll, lärmend; aufdringlich (*Farbe*).

nomin|al □ ['nɔminl] nominell; (nur) dem Namen nach (vorhanden); namentlich; ~ *value* Nennwert *m;* ~**ate** [~neit] ernennen; zur Wahl vorschlagen; ~**ation** [nɔmi-'neiʃən] Ernennung *f;* Vorschlagsrecht *n.*

nominative ['nɔminətiv] *a. ~ case gr.* Nominativ *m.*

non [nɔn] *in Zssgn:* nicht, un..., Nicht...

nonage ['nounidʒ] Minderjährigkeit *f.*

non-alcoholic ['nɔnælkə'hɔlik] alkoholfrei.

nonce [nɔns]: *for the ~* nur für diesen Fall.

non-commissioned ['nɔnkə'miʃənd] nicht bevollmächtigt; ~ *officer* ✕ Unteroffizier *m.*

non-committal ['nɔnkə'mitl] unverbindlich.

non-compliance ['nɔnkəm'plaiəns] Zuwiderhandlung *f,* Verstoß *m.*

non-conductor ⚡ ['nɔnkəndʌktə] Nichtleiter *m.*

nonconformist ['nɔnkən'fɔːmist] Dissident(in), Freikirchler(in).

nondescript ['nɔndiskript] unbestimmbar; schwer zu beschreiben(d).

none [nʌn] 1. keine(r, -s); nichts; 2. keineswegs, gar nicht; ~ *the less* nichtsdestoweniger.

nonentity [nɔ'nentiti] Nichtsein *n;* Unding *n;* Nichts *n; fig.* Null *f.*

non-existence ['nɔnig'zistəns] Nicht(da)sein *n.*

non-fiction ['nɔn'fikʃən] Sachbücher *n/pl.*

nonpareil ['nɔnpərəl] Unvergleichliche(r *m,* -s *n) f.*

non-party ['nɔn'pɑːti] parteilos.

non-performance ⚖ ['nɔnpə-'fɔːməns] Nichterfüllung *f.*

nonplus ['nɔn'plʌs] 1. Verlegenheit *f;* 2. in Verlegenheit bringen.

non-resident ['nɔn'rezidənt] nicht im Haus *od.* am Ort wohnend.

nonsens|e ['nɔnsəns] Unsinn *m;* ~**ical** □ [nɔn'sensikəl] unsinnig.

non-skid ['nɔn'skid] rutschfest.

non-smoker ['nɔn'smoukə] Nichtraucher *m.*

non-stop 🚆, ✈ ['nɔn'stɔp] durchgehend; Ohnehalt...

non-union ['nɔn'juːnjən] nicht organisiert (*Arbeiter*).

non-violence ['nɔn'vaiələns] (Politik *f* der) Gewaltlosigkeit *f.*

noodle ['nuːdl] Nudel *f.*

nook [nuk] Ecke *f,* Winkel *m.*

noon [nuːn] Mittag *m; attr.* Mittags...; ~**day** ['nuːndei], ~**tide**, ~**time** = *noon.*

noose [nuːs] 1. Schlinge *f;* 2. (mit der Schlinge) fangen; schlingen.

nope *Am.* F ['noup] nein.

nor [nɔː] noch; auch nicht.

norm [nɔːm] Norm *f,* Regel *f;* Muster *n;* Maßstab *m;* ~**al** □ ['nɔːməl] normal; ~**alize** [~laiz] normalisieren; normen.

north [nɔːθ] 1. Nord(en *m); 2.* nördlich; Nord...; ~**east** ['~'iːst] 1. Nordost *m;* 2. *a.* ~**eastern** [~tən] nordöstlich; ~**erly** ['nɔːðəli], ~**ern** [~ən] nördlich; Nord...; ~**erner** [~nə] Nordländer(in); *Am.* ♀ Nordstaatler(in); ~**ward(s)** ['nɔːθwəd(z)] *adv.* nördlich; nordwärts; ~**west** ['nɔːθ'west] 1. Nordwest *m;* 2. *a.* ~**western** [~tən] nordwestlich.

Norwegian [nɔː'wiːdʒən] 1. norwegisch; 2. Norweger(in); Norwegisch *n.*

nose [nouz] 1. Nase *f;* Spitze *f;* Schnauze *f;* 2. *v/t.* riechen; ~ *one's way* vorsichtig fahren; *v/i.* schnüffeln; ~**dive** ✈ ['nouzdaiv] Sturzflug *m;* ~**gay** ['nouzgei] Blumenstrauß *m.*

nostalgia [nɔs'tældʒiə] Heimweh *n,* Sehnsucht *f.*

nostril ['nɔstril] Nasenloch *n,* Nüster *f.*

nostrum ['nɔstrəm] Geheimmittel *n;* Patentlösung *f.*

nosy F ['nouzi] neugierig.

not [nɔt] nicht.

notable ['noutəbl] 1. □ bemerkenswert; 2. angesehene Person.

notary ['noutəri] *oft ~ public* Notar *m.*   [*f.*\

notation [nou'teiʃən] Bezeichnung *f.*

notch [nɔtʃ] 1. Kerbe *f,* Einschnitt *m;* Scharte *f; Am.* Engpaß *m,* Hohlweg *m;* 2. einkerben.

note [nout] 1. Zeichen *n;* Notiz *f;* Anmerkung *f;* Briefchen *n; (bsd.* Schuld)Schein *m;* Note *f;* Ton *m;* Ruf *m;* Beachtung *f; take ~s* sich

Notizen machen; 2. be(ob)achten; besonders erwähnen; *a.* ~ **down** notieren; mit Anmerkungen versehen; ~**book** ['noutbuk] Notizbuch *n*; ~**d** bekannt; berüchtigt; ~**paper** Briefpapier *n*; ~**worthy** beachtenswert.

nothing ['nʌθiŋ] 1. nichts; 2. Nichts *n*; Null *f*; *for* ~ umsonst; *good for* ~ untauglich; *bring* (*come*) *to* ~ zunichte machen (werden).

notice ['noutis] 1. Notiz *f*; Nachricht *f*, Bekanntmachung *f*; Kündigung *f*; Warnung *f*; Beachtung *f*; *at short* ~ kurzfristig; *give* ~ *that* bekanntgeben, daß; *give a week's* ~ acht Tage vorher kündigen; *take* ~ *of* Notiz nehmen von; *without* ~ fristlos; 2. bemerken; be(ob)achten; ~**able** □ [~səbl] wahrnehmbar; bemerkenswert.

noti|fication [noutifi'keiʃən] Anzeige *f*; Meldung *f*; Bekanntmachung *f*; ~**fy** ['noutifai] *et.* anzeigen, melden; bekanntmachen.

notion ['nouʃən] Begriff *m*, Vorstellung *f*; Absicht *f*; ~**s** *pl. Am.* Kurzwaren *f/pl.*

notorious □ [nou'tɔːriəs] all-, weltbekannt; notorisch; berüchtigt.

notwithstanding *prp.* [nɔtwiθ-'stændiŋ] ungeachtet, trotz (*gen.*).

nought [nɔːt] Null *f*, Nichts *n.*

noun *gr.* [naun] Hauptwort *n.*

nourish ['nʌriʃ] (er)nähren; *fig.* hegen; ~**ing** [~ʃiŋ] nahrhaft; ~**ment** [~ʃmənt] Nahrung(smittel *n*) *f.*

novel ['nɔvəl] 1. neu; ungewöhnlich; 2. Roman *m*; ~**ist** [~list] Romanschriftsteller(in), Romancier *m*; ~**ty** [~lti] Neuheit *f.*

November [nou'vembə] November *m.*

novice ['nɔvis] Neuling *m*; *eccl.* Novize *m*, *f.*

now [nau] 1. nun, jetzt; eben; *just* ~ soeben; ~ *and again od. then* dann u. wann; 2. *cj. a.* ~ *that* nun da.

nowadays ['nauədeiz] heutzutage.

nowhere ['nouwɛə] nirgends.

noxious □ ['nɔkʃəs] schädlich.

nozzle ['nɔzl] ⊕ Düse *f*; Tülle *f.*

nuance [nju(ː)'ãːns] Nuance *f*, Schattierung *f.*

nub [nʌb] Knubbe(n *m*) *f*; *Am.* F springender Punkt *in e-r Sache.*

nucle|ar ['njuːkliə] Kern...; ~ *reactor* Kernreaktor *m*; ~ *research* (Atom-)Kernforschung *f*; ~**us** [~iəs] Kern *m.*

nude [njuːd] 1. nackt; 2. *paint.* Akt *m.*

nudge F [nʌdʒ] 1. *j-n* heimlich anstoßen; 2. Rippenstoß *m.*

nugget ['nʌgit] (*bsd.* Gold)Klumpen *m.*

nuisance ['njuːsns] Mißstand *m*;

Ärgernis *n*; Unfug *m*; *fig.* Plage *f*; *what a* ~! wie ärgerlich!; *make o.s. od. be a* ~ lästig fallen.

null [nʌl] nichtig; nichtssagend; ~ *and void* null u. nichtig; ~**ify** ['nʌlifai] zunichte machen; aufheben, ungültig machen; ~**ity** [~iti] Nichtigkeit *f*, Ungültigkeit *f.*

numb [nʌm] 1. starr; taub (*empfindungslos*); 2. starr *od.* taub machen; ~*ed* erstarrt.

number ['nʌmbə] 1. Nummer *f*; (An)Zahl *f*; Heft *n*, Lieferung *f*, Nummer *f e-s Werkes*; *without* ~ zahllos; *in* ~ an der Zahl; 2. zählen; numerieren; ~**less** [~əlis] zahllos; ~**plate** *mot.* Nummernschild *n.*

numera|l ['njuːmərəl] 1. Zahl...; 2. Ziffer *f*; ~**tion** [njuːmə'reiʃən] Zählung *f*; Numerierung *f.*

numerical □ [njuː'merikəl] zahlenmäßig; Zahl...

numerous □ ['njuːmərəs] zahlreich.

numskull F ['nʌmskʌl] Dummkopf *m.*

nun [nʌn] Nonne *f*; *orn.* Blaumeise *f.*

nunnery ['nʌnəri] Nonnenkloster *n.*

nuptial ['nʌpʃəl] 1. Hochzeits...; Ehe...; 2. ~**s** *pl.* Hochzeit *f.*

nurse [nəːs] 1. Kindermädchen *n*, Säuglingsschwester *f*; *a.* *wet*-~ Amme *f*; (Kranken)Pflegerin *f*, (Kranken)Schwester *f*; *at* ~ in Pflege; *put out to* ~ in Pflege geben; 2. stillen, nähren; großziehen; pflegen; hätscheln; ~**ling** ['nəːsliŋ] Säugling *m*; Pflegling *m*; ~**maid** ['nəːsmeid] Kindermädchen *n*; ~**ry** ['nəːsri] Kinderzimmer *n*; ✔ Pflanzschule *f*; ~ *rhymes pl.* Kinderlieder *n/pl.*, -reime *m/pl.*; ~ *school* Kindergarten *m*; ~ *slopes pl.* Ski: Idiotenhügel *m/pl.*

nursing ['nəːsiŋ] Stillen *n*; (Kranken)Pflege *f*; ~ *bottle* Saugflasche *f*; ~ *home* Privatklinik *f.*

nursling ['nəːsliŋ] = *nurseling.*

nurture ['nəːtʃə] 1. Pflege *f*; Erziehung *f*; 2. aufziehen; nähren

nut [nʌt] Nuß *f*; ⊕ (Schrauben-) Mutter *f*; *sl.* verrückter Kerl; ~**s** *pl* Nußkohle *f*; ~**cracker** [nʌtkrækə] Nußknacker *m*; ~**meg** ['nʌtmeg] Muskatnuß *f.*

nutriment ['njuːtrimənt] Nahrung *f.*

nutri|tion [njuː(ː)'triʃən] Ernährung *f*; Nahrung *f*; ~**tious** [~əs], ~**tive** □ ['njuːtritiv] nahrhaft; Ernährungs...

nut|shell ['nʌtʃel] Nußschale *f*; *in a* ~ in aller Kürze; ~**ty** ['nʌti] nußreich; nußartig; *sl.* verrückt.

nylon ['nailɔn] Nylon *n*; ~**s** *pl* Nylonstrümpfe *m/pl.*

nymph [nimf] Nymphe *f.*

O

o [ou] 1. oh!; ach!; 2. (in Telefonnummern) Null f.

oaf [ouf] Dummkopf m; Tölpel m.

oak [ouk] Eiche f.

oar [ɔː] 1. Ruder n; 2. rudern; ~sman ['ɔːsmən] Ruderer m.

oas|is [ou'eisis], pl. ~es [ou'eisiːz] Oase f (a. fig.).

oat [out] mst ~s pl. Hafer m; feel one's ~s Am. F groß in Form sein; sich wichtig vorkommen; sow one's wild ~s sich austoben.

oath [ouθ], pl. ~s [ouðz] Eid m; Schwur m; Fluch m; take (make, swear) an ~ e-n Eid leisten, schwören.

oatmeal ['outmiːl] Haferflocken f/pl.

obdurate □ ['ɔbdjurit] verstockt.

obedien|ce [ə'biːdjəns] Gehorsam m; ~t □ [~nt] gehorsam.

obeisance [ou'beisəns] Ehrerbietung f; Verbeugung f; do ~ huldigen.

obesity [ou'biːsiti] Fettleibigkeit f.

obey [ə'bei] gehorchen (dat.); Befehl etc. befolgen, Folge leisten (dat.).

obituary [ə'bitjuəri] Totenliste f; Todesanzeige f; Nachruf m; attr. Todes..., Toten...

object 1. ['ɔbdʒikt] Gegenstand m; Ziel n, fig. Zweck m; Objekt n (a. gr.); 2. [əb'dʒekt] v/t. einwenden (to gegen); v/i. et. dagegen haben (to ger. daß).

objection [əb'dʒekʃən] Einwand m; ~able □ [~ʃnəbl] nicht einwandfrei; unangenehm.

objective [əb'dʒektiv] 1. □ objektiv, sachlich; 2. ⚔ Ziel n.

object-lens opt. ['ɔbdʒiktlenz] Objektiv n.

obligat|ion [ɔbli'geiʃən] Verpflichtung f; ✝ Schuldverschreibung f; be under (an) ~ to s.o. j-m zu Dank verpflichtet sein; be under ~ to inf. die Verpflichtung haben, zu inf.; ~ory ['ɔ'bligətəri] verpflichtend; verbindlich.

oblig|e [ə'blaidʒ] (zu Dank) verpflichten; nötigen; ~ s.o. j-m e-n Gefallen tun; much ~d sehr verbunden; danke bestens; ~ing □ [~dʒiŋ] verbindlich, hilfsbereit, gefällig.

oblique □ [ə'bliːk] schief, schräg.

obliterate [ə'blitəreit] auslöschen, tilgen (a. fig.); Schrift ausstreichen; Briefmarken entwerten.

oblivi|on [ə'bliviən] Vergessen(heit f) n; ~ous □ [~iəs] vergeßlich.

oblong ['ɔblɔŋ] länglich; rechteckig.

obnoxious □ [əb'nɔkʃəs] anstößig; widerwärtig, verhaßt.

obscene □ [ɔb'siːn] unanständig.

obscur|e [əb'skjuə] 1. □ dunkel (a. fig.); unbekannt; 2. verdunkeln; ~ity [~ɔriti] Dunkelheit f (a. fig.); Unbekanntheit f; Niedrigkeit f der Geburt.

obsequies ['ɔbsikwiz] pl. Leichenbegängnis n, Trauerfeier f.

obsequious □ [əb'siːkwiəs] unterwürfig (to gegen).

observ|able □ [əb'zəːvəbl] bemerkbar; bemerkenswert; ~ance [~əns] Befolgung f; Brauch m; ~ant □ [~nt] beobachtend; achtsam; ~ation [ɔbzə(ː)'veiʃən] Beobachtung f; Bemerkung f; attr. Beobachtungs...; Aussichts...; ~atory [əb'zəːvətri] Sternwarte f; ~e [əb'zəːv] v/t. be(ob)achten; acht(geb)en auf (acc.); bemerken; v/i. sich äußern.

obsess [əb'ses] heimsuchen, quälen; ~ed by od. with besessen von; ~ion [~eʃən] Besessenheit f.

obsolete ['ɔbsəlit] veraltet.

obstacle ['ɔbstəkl] Hindernis n.

obstina|cy ['ɔbstinəsi] Hartnäckigkeit f; ~te □ [~nit] halsstarrig; eigensinnig; hartnäckig.

obstruct [əb'strʌkt] verstopfen, versperren; hindern; ~ion [~kʃən] Verstopfung f; Hemmung f; Hindernis n; ~ive □ [~ktiv] hinderlich.

obtain [əb'tein] v/t. erlangen, erhalten, erreichen, bekommen; v/i. sich erhalten (haben); ~able ✝ [~nəbl] erhältlich.

obtru|de [əb'truːd] (sich) aufdrängen (on dat.); ~sive □ [~uːsiv] aufdringlich; [schwerfällig.]

obtuse □ [əb'tjuːs] stumpf(sinnig).

obviate ['ɔbvieit] vorbeugen (dat.).

obvious □ ['ɔbviəs] offensichtlich, augenfällig, einleuchtend.

occasion [ə'keiʒən] 1. Gelegenheit f; Anlaß m; Veranlassung f; F (festliches) Ereignis n; on the ~ of anläßlich (gen.); 2. veranlassen; ~al □ [~nl] gelegentlich; Gelegenheits...

occident ['ɔksidənt] Westen m; Okzident m, Abendland n; ~al □ [ɔksi'dentl] abendländisch, westlich.

occult □ [ɔ'kʌlt] geheim, verborgen; magisch, okkult.

occup|ant ['ɔkjupənt] Besitzergreifer(in); Bewohner(in); ~ation[ɔkju'peiʃən] Besitz(ergreifung f) m; ⚔ Besetzung f; Beruf m; Beschäftigung f; ~y ['ɔkjupai] einnehmen, in Besitz nehmen, ⚔ besetzen; besitzen; innehaben; in Anspruch nehmen; beschäftigen.

occur [ə'kəː] vorkommen; sich ereignen; it ~red to me es fiel mir ein; ~rence [ə'kʌrəns] Vorkommen n; Vorfall m, Ereignis n.

ocean ['oufən] Ozean m, Meer n.

o'clock [ə'klɔk] Uhr (bei Zeitangaben); five ~ fünf Uhr.

October [ɔk'toubə] Oktober m.

ocul|ar □ ['ɔkjulə] Augen...; **~ist** [~list] Augenarzt m.

odd □ [ɔd] ungerade (Zahl); einzeln; und einige od. etwas darüber; überzählig; gelegentlich; sonderbar, merkwürdig; **~ity** ['ɔditi] Seltsamkeit f; **~s** [ɔdz] of sg. (Gewinn)Chancen f/pl.; Wahrscheinlichkeit f; Vorteil m; Vorgabe f, Handikap n; Verschiedenheit f; Unterschied m; Streit m; be at ~ with s.o. mit j-m im Streit sein; nicht übereinstimmen mit j-m; ~ and ends Reste m/pl.; Krimskrams m.

ode [oud] Ode f (Gedicht).

odious □ ['oudjəs] verhaßt; ekelhaft.

odo(u)r ['oudə] Geruch m; Duft m.

of prp. [ɔv, əv] allg. von; Ort: bei (the battle ~ Quebec); um (cheat s.o. ~ s.th.); aus (~ charity); vor (dat.) (afraid ~); auf (acc.) (proud ~); über (acc.) (ashamed ~); nach (smell ~ roses; desirous ~); an (acc.) (think ~ s.th.); nimble ~ foot leichtfüßig.

off [ɔːf, ɔf] 1. adv. weg; ab; herunter; aus (vorbei); Zeit: hin (3 months ~); ~ and on ab und an; hin und her; be ~ fort sein; weg sein; engS.: (weg)gehen; zu sein (Hahn etc.); aus sein; well etc. ~ gut etc. daran; 2. prp. von ... (weg, ab, herunter); frei von, ohne; unweit (gen.), neben; ⊕ auf der Höhe von; 3. adj. entfernt(er); abseitsliegend; Neben...; arbeits-, dienstfrei; † ~ shade Fehlfarbe f; 4. int. weg!, fort!, raus!

offal ['ɔfəl] Abfall m; Schund m; **~s** pl. Fleischerei: Innereien f/pl.

offen|ce, Am. **~se** [ə'fens] Angriff m; Beleidigung f, Kränkung f; Ärgernis n, Anstoß m; Vergehen n.

offend [ə'fend] v/t. beleidigen, verletzen; ärgern; v/i. sich vergehen; **~er** [~də] Übel-, Missetäter(in); Straffällige(r m) f; first ~ noch nicht Vorbestrafte(r m) f.

offensive [ə'fensiv] 1. □ beleidigend; anstößig; ekelhaft; Offensiv..., Angriffs...; 2. Offensive f.

offer ['ɔfə] 1. Angebot n, Anerbieten n; ~ of marriage Heiratsantrag m; 2. v/t. anbieten; Preis, Möglichkeit etc. bieten; Gebet, Opfer darbringen; versuchen; zeigen; Widerstand leisten; v/i. sich bieten; **~ing** ['ɔfəriŋ] Opfer n; Anerbieten n, Angebot n.

off-hand ['ɔːf'hænd] aus dem Handgelenk od. Stegreif, unvorbereitet; ungezwungen, frei.

office ['ɔfis] Büro n; Geschäftsstelle

f; Ministerium n; Amt n, Pflicht f; **~s** pl. Hilfe f; booking-~ Schalter m; box-~ (Theater- etc.)Kasse f; Divine ♀ Gottesdienst m; **~r** [~ə] Beamt|e(r) m, -in f; ✗ Offizier m.

official [ə'fiʃəl] 1. □ offiziell, amtlich; Amts...; 2. Beamte(r) m.

officiate [ə'fiʃieit] amtieren.

officious □ [ə'fiʃəs] aufdringlich, übereifrig; offiziös, halbamtlich.

off|-licence ['ɔːflaisəns] Schankrecht n über die Straße; **~-print** Sonderdruck m; **~set** ausgleichen; **~shoot** Sproß m; Ausläufer m; **~side** ['ɔːf'said] Sport: abseits; **~spring** ['ɔːfspriŋ] Nachkomme(nschaft f) m; Ergebnis n.

often ['ɔːfn] oft(mals), häufig.

ogle ['ougl] liebäugeln (mit).

ogre ['ougə] Menschenfresser m.

oh [ou] oh!; ach!

oil [ɔil] 1. Öl n; Erdöl n, Petroleum n; 2. ölen; (a. fig.) schmieren; **~cloth** ['ɔilklɔθ] Wachstuch n; **~skin** Ölleinwand f; **~s** pl. Ölzeug n; **~y** □ ['ɔili] ölig (a. fig.); fettig; schmierig (a. fig.).

ointment ['ɔintmənt] Salbe f.

O.K., okay F ['ou'kei] 1. richtig, stimmt!; gut, in Ordnung; 2. annehmen, gutheißen.

old [ould] alt; altbekannt; althergebracht; erfahren; ~ age (das) Alter; days of ~ alte Zeiten f/pl.; **~-age** ['ouldeidʒ] Alters...; **~-fashioned** ['ould'fæʃənd] altmodisch; altväterlich; ♀ Glory Sternenbanner n; **~ish** ['ouldiʃ] ältlich.

olfactory anat. [ɔl'fæktəri] Geruchs...

olive ['ɔliv] ♀ Olive f; Olivgrün n.

Olympic Games [ou'limpik 'geimz] Olympische Spiele pl.

ominous □ ['ɔminəs] unheilvoll.

omission [ou'miʃən] Unterlassung f; Auslassung f.

omit [ou'mit] unterlassen; auslassen.

omnipoten|ce [ɔm'nipətəns] Allmacht f; **~t** □ [~nt] allmächtig.

omniscient □ [ɔm'nisiənt] allwissend.

on [ɔn] 1. prp. mst auf; engS.: an (~ the wall, ~ the Thames); auf ... (los), an ... (hin) (march ~ London); auf ... (hin) (~ his authority); Zeit: an (~ the 1st of April); (gleich) nach, bei (~ his arrival); über (acc.) (talk ~ a subject); nach (~ this model); get ~ a train bsd. Am. in e-n Zug einsteigen; ~ hearing it als ich etc. es hörte; 2. adv. darauf; auf (keep one's hat ~), an (have a coat ~); voraus, vorwärts; weiter (and so ~); be ~ im Gange sein; auf sein (Hahn etc.); an sein (Licht etc.); 3. int. drauf!, ran!

once [wʌns] 1. adv. einmal; einst (-mals); at ~ (so)gleich; sofort; zu-

gleich; ~ *for all* ein für allemal; ~ *in a while* dann und wann; *this* ~ dieses eine Mal; 2. *cj. a.* ~ *that* sobald.

one [wʌn] 1. ein; einzig; eine(r), ein; eins; man; ~ *day* eines Tages; 2. Eine(r) m; Eins f; *the little* ~s *pl.* die Kleinen *pl.;* ~ *another* einander; *at* ~ einig; ~ *by* ~ einzeln; *I for* ~ ich für meinen Teil.

onerous □ ['ɔnərəs] lästig.

one|self [wʌn'self] (man) selbst, sich; ~-**sided** □ ['wʌn'saidid] einseitig; ~-**way** [~'wʌnwei]: ~ *street* Einbahnstraße f.

onion ['ʌnjən] Zwiebel f.

onlooker ['ɔnlukə] Zuschauer(in).

only ['ounli] 1. *adj.* einzig; 2. *adv.* nur; bloß; erst; ~ *yesterday* erst gestern; 3. *cj.* ~ (*that*) nur daß.

onrush ['ɔnrʌʃ] Ansturm m.

onset ['ɔnset], **onslaught** ['ɔnslɔːt] Angriff m; *bsd. fig.* Anfall m; Anfang m.

onward ['ɔnwəd] 1. *adj.* fortschreitend; 2. *a.* ~s *adv.* vorwärts, weiter.

ooze [uːz] 1. Schlamm m; 2. *v/i.* (durch)sickern; ~ *away* schwinden; *v/t.* ausströmen, ausschwitzen.

opaque □ [ou'peik] undurchsichtig.

open ['oupən] 1. □ *allg.* offen; geöffnet, auf; frei (*Feld etc.*); öffentlich; offenstehend, unentschieden; aufrichtig; zugänglich (*to dat.*); aufgeschlossen (*to gegenüber*); mild (*Wetter*); 2. *in the* ~ (*air*) im Freien; *come out into the* ~ *fig.* an die Öffentlichkeit treten; 3. *v/t.* öffnen; eröffnen (*a. fig.*); *v/i.* (sich) öffnen; anfangen; ~ *into* führen in (*acc.*) (*Tür etc.*); ~ *on to* hinausgehen auf (*acc.*) (*Fenster etc.*); ~ *out* sich ausbreiten; ~-**air** ['oupn'ɛə] im Freien (stattfindend), Freilicht..., Frei-(luft)...; ~-**armed** ['oupn'ɑːmd] herzlich, warm; ~-**er** ['oupnə] (Er-)Öffner(in); (Dosen)Öffner m; ~-**eyed** ['oupn'aid] wach; mit offenen Augen; aufmerksam; ~-**handed** ['oupn'hændid] freigebig, großzügig; ~-**hearted** ['oupnhɑːtid] offen(herzig), aufrichtig; ~**ing** ['oupniŋ] (Er)Öffnung f; Gelegenheit f; *attr.* Eröffnungs...; ~-**minded** *fig.* ['oupn'maindid] aufgeschlossen. [*pl.*) Opernglas n.|

opera ['ɔpərə] Oper f; ~-**glass(es**

operat|e ['ɔpəreit] *v/t.* 💉 operieren; *bsd. Am.* in Gang bringen; *Maschine* bedienen; *Unternehmen* leiten; *v/i.* (ein)wirken; sich auswirken; arbeiten; 📈, ✗ operieren; ~**ion** [ɔpə-'reiʃən] Wirkung f; Tätigkeit f; 📈, ✗; ⚔ Operation f; *be in* ~ in Betrieb sein; in Kraft sein; ~**ive** ['ɔpərətiv] 1. □ wirksam, tätig; praktisch; ✗ operativ; 2. Arbeiter m; ~**or** [~reitə] Operateur m; Telephonist(in); ⊕ Maschinist m.

opin|e [ou'pain] meinen; ~**ion** [ə'pinjən] Meinung f; Ansicht f; Stellungnahme f; Gutachten n; *in my* ~ meines Erachtens.

opponent [ə'pounənt] Gegner m.

opportun|e □ ['ɔpətjuːn] passend; rechtzeitig; günstig; ~**ity** [ɔpə'tjuːniti] (günstige) Gelegenheit.

oppos|e [ə'pouz] entgegen-, gegenüberstellen; bekämpfen; ~**ed** entgegengesetzt; *be* ~ *to* gegen ... sein; ~**ite** ['ɔpəzit] 1. □ gegenüberliegend; entgegengesetzt; 2. *prp. u. adv.* gegenüber; 3. Gegenteil n; ~**ition** [ɔpə'ziʃən] Gegenüberstehen n; Widerstand m; Gegensatz m; Widerspruch m, -streit m; ⚔ Konkurrenz f; Opposition f.

oppress [ə'pres] be-, unterdrücken; ~**ion** [~eʃən] Unterdrückung f; Druck m; Bedrängnis f; Bedrücktheit f; ~**ive** □ [~esiv] (be)drückend; gewaltsam.

optic ['ɔptik] Augen..., Seh...; = ~**al** □ [~kəl] optisch; ~**ian** [ɔp'tiʃən] Optiker m.

optimism ['ɔptimizəm] Optimismus m.

option ['ɔpʃən] Wahl(freiheit) f; ⚔ Vorkaufsrecht n, Option f; ~**al** □ [~nl] freigestellt, wahlfrei.

opulence ['ɔpjuləns] Reichtum m.

or [ɔː] oder; ~ *else* sonst, wo nicht.

oracular □ [ɔ'rækjulə] orakelhaft.

oral □ ['ɔːrəl] mündlich; Mund...

orange ['ɔrindʒ] 1. Orange(farbe) f; Apfelsine f; 2. orangefarben; ~**ade** ['ɔrindʒ'eid] Orangenlimonade f.

orat|ion [ɔ'reiʃən] Rede f; ~**or** ['ɔrətə] Redner m; ~**ory** [~əri] Redekunst f, Rhetorik f; Kapelle f.

orb [ɔːb] Ball m; *fig.* Himmelskörper m; *poet.* Augapfel m; ~**it** ['ɔːbit] 1. Planetenbahn f; Kreis-, Umlaufbahn f; Auge(nhöhle f) n; 2. sich in e-r Umlaufbahn bewegen.

orchard ['ɔːtʃəd] Obstgarten m.

orchestra ♩ ['ɔːkistrə] Orchester n.

orchid ⚘ ['ɔːkid] Orchidee f.

ordain [ɔː'dein] an-, verordnen; bestimmen; *Priester* ordinieren.

ordeal *fig.* [ɔː'diːl] schwere Prüfung.

order ['ɔːdə] 1. Ordnung f; Anordnung f; Befehl m; Regel f; ⚔ Auftrag m; Zahlungsanweisung f; Klasse f, Rang m; Orden m (*a. eccl.*); *take* (*holy*) ~s in den geistlichen Stand treten; *in* ~ *to inf.* um zu *inf.*; *in* ~ *that* damit; *make to* ~ auf Bestellung anfertigen; *standing* ~s *pl. parl.* Geschäftsordnung f; 2. (an)ordnen; befehlen; ⚔ bestellen; *j-n* beordern; ~**ly** ['ɔːdəli] 1. ordentlich; ruhig; regelmäßig; 2. ✗ Ordonnanz f; ✗ Bursche m; Krankenpfleger m.

ordinal ['ɔːdinl] 1. Ordnungs...; 2. *a.* ~ *number* Ordnungszahl f.

ordinance ['ɔːdinəns] Verordnung f.

ordinary □ ['ɔːdnri] gewöhnlich.

ordnance ✕, ⚓ ['ɔːdnəns] Artillerie *f*, Geschütze *n/pl.*; Feldzeugwesen *n*.

ordure ['ɔːdjuə] Kot *m*, Schmutz *m*.

ore [ɔː] Erz *n*.

organ ['ɔːgən] ♪ Orgel *f*; Organ *n*; ~grinder [~ŋgraində] Leierkastenmann *m*; ~ic [ɔːˈgænik] (~ally) organisch; ~ization [ɔːgənaiˈzeiʃən] Organisation *f*; ~ize ['ɔːgənaiz] organisieren; ~izer [~zə] Organisator(in).

orgy ['ɔːdʒi] Ausschweifung *f*.

orient ['ɔːrient] 1. Osten *m*; Orient *m*, Morgenland *n*; 2. orientieren; ~al [ɔːriˈentl] 1. □ östlich; orientalisch; 2. Oriental|e *m*, -in *f*; ~ate ['ɔːrienteit] orientieren.

orifice ['ɔrifis] Mündung *f*; Öffnung *f*.

origin ['ɔridʒin] Ursprung *m*; Anfang *m*; Herkunft *f*.

original [əˈridʒənl] 1. □ ursprünglich; originell; Original...; ♱ Stamm...; 2. Original *n*; ~ity [əridʒiˈnæliti] Originalität *f*; ~ly [əˈridʒnəli] originell; ursprünglich; zuerst, anfangs, anfänglich.

originat|e [əˈridʒineit] *v/t.* hervorbringen, schaffen; *v/i.* entstehen; ~or [~tə] Urheber *m*.

ornament 1. ['ɔːnəmənt] Verzierung *f*; *fig.* Zierde *f*; 2. [~ment] verzieren; schmücken; ~al [ɔːnəˈmentl] zierend; schmückend.

ornate □ [ɔːˈneit] reich verziert; überladen.

orphan □ ['ɔːfən] 1. Waise *f*; 2. *a.* ~ed verwaist; ~age [~nidʒ] Waisenhaus *n*.

orthodox □ ['ɔːθədɔks] rechtgläubig; üblich; anerkannt.

oscillate ['ɔsileit] schwingen; *fig.* schwanken.

osier ♀ ['ouʒə] Korbweide *f*.

osprey *orn.* ['ɔspri] Fischadler *m*.

ossify ['ɔsifai] verknöchern.

ostensible □ [ɔsˈtensəbl] angeblich.

ostentatio|n [ɔstənˈteiʃən] Zurschaustellung *f*; Protzerei *f*; ~us □ [~ʃəs] prahlend, prahlerisch.

ostler ['ɔslə] Stallknecht *m*.

ostracize ['ɔstrəsaiz] verbannen; ächten.

ostrich *orn.* ['ɔstritʃ] Strauß *m*.

other ['ʌðə] andere(r, -s); the ~ day neulich; the ~ morning neulich morgens; every ~ day einen Tag um den anderen, jeden zweiten Tag; ~wise [~ˈʌðəwaiz] anders; sonst.

otter *zo.* ['ɔtə] Otter(pelz) *m*.

ought [ɔːt] sollte; you ~ to have done it Sie hätten es tun sollen.

ounce [auns] Unze *f* (= 28,35 g).

our ['auə] unser; ~s ['auəz] der (die, das) unsrige; unsere(r, -s); *pred.* unser; ~selves [auəˈselvz] wir selbst; uns (selbst).

oust [aust] verdrängen, vertreiben, hinauswerfen; *e-s Amtes* entheben.

out [aut] 1. *adv.* aus; hinaus, heraus; draußen; außerhalb; (bis) zu Ende; be ~ with böse sein mit; ~ and ~ durch und durch; ~ and about wieder auf den Beinen; way ~ Ausgang *m*; 2. *Am.* F Ausweg *m*; the ~s *pl. parl.* die Opposition; 3. ♱ übernormal, Über... (*Größe*); 4. *prp.* ~ of aus, aus ... heraus; außerhalb; außer; aus, von.

out|balance [autˈbæləns] schwerer wiegen als; ~bid [~ˈbid] [*irr.* (*bid*)] überbieten; ~board ['autbɔːd] *Am.* Außenbord...; ~break [~breik] Ausbruch *m*; ~building [~bildiŋ] Nebengebäude *n*; ~burst [~bəːst] Ausbruch *m*; ~cast [~kaːst] 1. ausgestoßen; 2. Ausgestoßene(r *m*) *f*; ~come [~kʌm] Ergebnis *n*; ~cry [~krai] Aufschrei *m*, Schrei *m* der Entrüstung; ~dated [autˈdeitid] zeitlich überholt; ~distance [~ˈdistəns] überholen; ~do [~ˈduː] [*irr.* (*do*)] übertreffen; ~door *adj.* ['autdɔː], ~doors *adv.* [~ˈdɔːz] Außen...; draußen, außer dem Hause; im Freien.

outer ['autə] äußer; Außen...; ~most ['autəmoust] äußerst.

out|fit ['autfit] Ausrüstung *f*, Ausstattung *f*; *Am.* Haufen *m*, Trupp *m*, (Arbeits)Gruppe *f*; ~going [~gouiŋ] 1. weg-, abgehend; 2. Ausgehen *n*; ~s *pl.* Ausgaben *f/pl.*; ~grow [autˈgrou] [*irr.* (*grow*)] herauswachsen aus; hinauswachsen über (*acc.*); ~house ['authaus] Nebengebäude *n*; *Am.* Außenabort *m*.

outing ['autiŋ] Ausflug *m*, Tour *f*.

out|last [autˈlaːst] überdauern; ~law ['autlɔː] 1. Geächtete(r *m*) *f*; 2. ächten; ~lay [~lei] Geld-Auslage(n *pl.*) *f*; ~let [~let] Auslaß *m*; Ausgang *m*; Abfluß *m*; ~line [~lain] 1. Umriß *m*; Überblick *m*; Skizze *f*; 2. umreißen; skizzieren; ~live [autˈliv] überleben; ~look ['autluk] Ausblick *m* (*a. fig.*); Auffassung *f*; ~lying [~laiiŋ] entlegen; ~match [autˈmætʃ] weit übertreffen; ~number [~ˈnʌmbə] an Zahl übertreffen; ~patient ⚕ ['autpeiʃənt] ambulanter Patient; ~post [~poust] Vorposten *m*; ~pouring [~pɔːriŋ] Erguß *m* (*a. fig.*); ~put [~put] Produktion *f*, Ertrag *m*.

outrage [autˈreidʒ] 1. Gewalttätigkeit *f*; Attentat *n*; Beleidigung *f*; 2. gröblich verletzen; Gewalt antun (*dat.*); ~ous [autˈreidʒəs] abscheulich; empörend; gewalttätig.

out|reach [autˈriːtʃ] weiter reichen als; ~right [*adj.* 'autrait, *adv.* aut'rait] gerade heraus; völlig; ~run [~ˈrʌn] [*irr.* (*run*)] schneller laufen als; hinausgehen über (*acc.*); ~set ['autset] Anfang m; Aufbruch m; ~shine [aut'ʃain] [irr. (shine)] überstrahlen; ~side ['aut'said] 1. Außenseite f; fig. Äußerste(s) n; at the ~ höchstens; 2. Außen...; außenstehend; äußerst (Preis); 3. (nach) (dr)außen; 4. prp. außerhalb; ~sider [~də] Außenseiter(in), -stehende(r m) f; ~size [~saiz] Übergröße f; ~skirts [~skə:ts] pl. Außenbezirke m/pl., (Stadt)Rand m; ~smart Am. F [aut'smɑːt] übervorteilen; ~spoken [~'spoukən] freimütig; ~spread ['aut'spred] ausgestreckt, ausgebreitet; ~standing [aut'stændiŋ] hervorragend (a. fig.); ausstehend (Schuld); offenstehend (Frage); ~stretched ['autstretʃt] = outspread; ~strip [aut'strip] überholen (a. fig.).

outward ['autwəd] 1. äußer(lich); nach (dr)außen gerichtet; 2. adv. mst ~s auswärts, nach (dr)außen; ~ly [~dli] äußerlich; an der Oberfläche.

out|weigh [aut'wei] überwiegen; ~wit [~'wit] überlisten; ~worn ['autwɔːn] erschöpft; fig. abgegriffen; überholt.

oval ['ouvəl] 1. oval; 2. Oval n.

oven ['ʌvn] Backofen m.

over ['ouvə] 1. adv. über; hin-, herüber; drüben; vorbei; übermäßig; darüber; von Anfang bis zu Ende; noch einmal; ~ and above neben, zusätzlich zu; (all) ~ again noch einmal (von vorn); ~ against gegenüber (dat.); all ~ ganz und gar; ~ and ~ again immer wieder; read ~ durchlesen; 2. prp. über; all ~ the town durch die ganze od. in der ganzen Stadt.

over|act ['ouvər'ækt] übertreiben; ~all [~rɔːl] 1. Arbeitsanzug m, -kittel m; Kittel(schürze f) m; 2. gesamt, Gesamt...; ~awe [ouvər'ɔː] einschüchtern; ~balance [ouvə'bæləns] 1. Übergewicht n; 2. umkippen; überwiegen; ~bearing □ [~'bɛəriŋ] anmaßend; ~board ⚓ ['ouvəbɔːd] über Bord; ~cast [~kɑːst] bewölkt; ~charge [~'tʃɑːdʒ] 1. überladen; überfordern; 2. Überladung f; Überforderung f; ~coat [~kout] Mantel m; ~come [ouvə'kʌm][irr.(come)]überwinden; überwältigen; ~crowd [~'kraud] überfüllen; ~do [~'duː] [irr. (do)] zu viel tun; übertreiben; zu sehr kochen; überanstrengen; ~draw [~'drɔː] [irr. (draw)] übertreiben; † Konto überziehen; ~dress [~'dres] (sich) übertrieben anziehen; ~due [~'djuː] überfällig; ~eat [~'iːt] [irr. (eat)]: ~ o.s. sich überessen; ~flow 1. [ouvə'flou] [irr. (flow)] v/t. überfluten; v/i. überfließen; 2.['ouvəflou] Überschwemmung f; Überfüllung f; ~grow

[~'grou] [irr. (grow)] v/t. überwuchern; v/i. zu sehr wachsen; ~hang 1. [~'hæŋ] [irr. (hang)] v/t. über (acc.) hängen; v/i. überhängen; 2. [~hæŋ] Überhang m; ~haul [ouvə'hɔːl] überholen; ~head 1. adv. ['ouvə'hed] (dr)oben; 2. adj. [~hed] Ober...; † allgemein (Unkosten); 3. ~s pl. † allgemeine Unkosten pl.; ~hear [ouvə'hiə] [irr. (hear)] belauschen; ~joyed [~'dʒɔid] überglücklich; ~lap [~'læp] v/t. übergreifen auf (acc.); überschneiden; v/i. ineinandergreifen, überlappen; ~lay [~'lei] [irr. (lay)] belegen; ⊕ überlagern; ~leaf [ouvə'liːf] umseitig; ~load [~'loud] überladen; ~look [ouvə'luk] übersehen; beaufsichtigen; ~master [~'mɑːstə] überwältigen; ~much ['ouvə'mʌtʃ] zu viel; ~night [~'nait] 1. am Vorabend; über Nacht; 2. Nacht...; nächtlich; Übernachtungs...; ~pay [~'pei] [irr. (pay)] zu viel bezahlen für; ~peopled [ouvə'piːpld] übervölkert; ~plus ['ouvəplʌs] Überschuß m; ~power [ouvə'pauə] überwältigen; ~rate ['ouvə'reit] überschätzen; ~reach [ouvə'riːtʃ] übervorteilen; ~ o.s. sich übernehmen; ~ride fig. [~'raid] [irr. (ride)] sich hinwegsetzen über (acc.); umstoßen; ~rule [~'ruːl] überstimmen; ♫♫ verwerfen; ~run [~'rʌn] [irr. (run)] überrennen; überziehen; überlaufen; bedecken; ~sea ['ouvə'siː] 1. a. ~s überseeisch; Übersee...; 2. ~s in od. nach Übersee; ~see [~'siː] [irr. (see)] beaufsichtigen; ~seer [~'siə] Aufseher m; ~shadow [ouvə'ʃædou] überschatten; ~sight ['ouvəsait] Versehen n; ~sleep [~'sliːp] [irr. (sleep)] verschlafen; ~state [~'steit] übertreiben; ~statement [~'tmənt] Übertreibung f; ~strain [~'strein] (sich) überanstrengen; fig. übertreiben; 2. [~strein] Überanstrengung f.

overt ['ouvəːt] offen(kundig).

over|take [ouvə'teik] [irr. (take)] einholen; j-n überraschen; ~tax ['ouvə'tæks] zu hoch besteuern; fig. überschätzen; übermäßig in Anspruch nehmen; ~throw 1. [ouvə'θrou] [irr. (throw)] (um)stürzen (a. fig.); vernichten; 2. ['ouvəθrou] Sturz m; Vernichtung f; ~time [~taim] Überstunden f/pl.

overture ['ouvətjuə] ♪ Ouvertüre f; Vorspiel n; Vorschlag m, Antrag m.

over|turn [ouvə'təːn] (um)stürzen; ~value ['ouvə'væljuː] zu hoch einschätzen; ~weening [ouvə'wiːniŋ] eingebildet; ~weight ['ouvəweit] Übergewicht n; ~whelm [ouvə'welm] überschütten (a. fig.); überwältigen; ~work ['ouvə'wəːk] 1.

Überarbeitung f; 2. [irr. (work)] sich überarbeiten; **~wrought** [~'rɔːt] überarbeitet; überreizt.

owe [ou] Geld, Dank etc. schulden, schuldig sein; verdanken.

owing ['ouiŋ] schuldig; **~ to** infolge.

owl orn. [aul] Eule f.

own [oun] 1. eigen; richtig; einzig, innig geliebt; 2. my ~ mein Eigentum; a house of one's ~ ein eigenes Haus; hold one's ~ standhalten;

3. besitzen; zugeben; anerkennen; sich bekennen (to zu).

owner ['ounə] Eigentümer(in); **~ship** ['ounəʃip] Eigentum(srecht) n.

ox [ɔks], pl. **oxen** ['ɔksən] Ochse m; Rind n.

oxid|ation [ɔksi'deiʃən] Oxydation f, Oxydierung f; **~e** ['ɔksaid] Oxyd n; **~ize** ['ɔksidaiz] oxydieren.

oxygen [ˈɔksidʒən] Sauerstoff m.

oyster ['ɔistə] Auster f.

ozone ʔ ['ouzoun] Ozon n.

P

pace [peis] 1. Schritt m; Gang m; Tempo n; 2. v/t. abschreiten; v/i. (einher)schreiten; (im) Paß gehen.

pacific [pə'sifik] (~ally) friedlich; the 2 (Ocean) der Pazifik, der Pazifische od. Stille Ozean; **~ation** [pæsifi'keiʃən] Beruhigung f.

pacify ['pæsifai] beruhigen.

pack [pæk] 1. Pack(en) m; Paket n; Ballen m; Spiel n Karten; Meute f; Rotte f, Bande f; Packung f; 2. v/t. oft ~ up (zs.-, ver-, ein)packen; a. ~ off fortjagen; Am. F (bei sich) tragen (als Gepäck etc.); bepacken, vollstopfen; ⊕ dichten; v/i. oft ~ up packen; sich packen (lassen); **~age** ['pækidʒ] Pack m, Ballen m; bsd. Am. Paket n; Packung f; Frachtstück n; **~er** ['pækə] Packer(in); Am. Konservenfabrikant m; **~et** ['pækit] Paket n; Päckchen n; a. **~boat** Postschiff n.

packing ['pækiŋ] Packen n; Verpackung f; **~ house** Am. (bsd. Fleisch)Konservenfabrik f.

packthread ['pækθred] Bindfaden m.

pact [pækt] Vertrag m, Pakt m.

pad [pæd] 1. Polster n; Sport: Beinschutz m; Schreibblock m; Stempelkissen n; (Abschuß)Rampe f; 2. (aus)polstern; **~ding** ['pædiŋ] Polsterung f; fig. Lückenbüßer m.

paddle ['pædl] 1. Paddel(ruder) n; ⚓ (Rad)Schaufel f; 2. paddeln; planschen; **~wheel** Schaufelrad n.

paddock ['pædək] (Pferde)Koppel f; Sport: Sattelplatz m.

padlock ['pædlɔk] Vorhängeschloß n.

pagan ['peigən] 1. heidnisch; 2. Heid|e m, -in f.

page¹ [peidʒ] 1. Buch-Seite f; fig. Buch n; 2. paginieren.

page² [~] 1. (Hotel)Page m; Am. Amtsdiener m; 2. Am. (durch e-n Pagen) holen lassen.

pageant ['pædʒənt] historisches Festspiel; festlicher Umzug.

paid [peid] pret. u. p.p. von pay 2.

pail [peil] Eimer m.

pain [pein] 1. Pein f, Schmerz m; Strafe f; **~s** pl. Leiden n/pl.; Mühe f; on od. under ~ of death bei Todesstrafe; be in ~ leiden; take ~ sich Mühe geben; 2. j-m weh tun; **~ful** □ ['peinful] schmerzhaft, schmerzlich; peinlich; mühevoll; **~less** □ ['peinlis] schmerzlos; **~staking** □ ['peinzteikiŋ] fleißig.

paint [peint] 1. Farbe f; Schminke f; Anstrich m; 2. (be)malen; anstreichen; (sich) schminken; **~brush** ['peintbrʌʃ] Malerpinsel m; **~er** [~tə] Maler(in); **~ing** [~tiŋ] Malen n; Malerei f; Gemälde n.

pair [pɛə] 1. Paar n; a ~ of scissors eine Schere; 2. (sich) paaren; zs.-passen; a. ~ off paarweise weggehen.

pal sl. [pæl] Kumpel m, Kamerad m.

palace ['pælis] Palast m.

palatable □ ['pælətəbl] schmackhaft. [schmack m (a. fig.).)

palate ['pælit] Gaumen m; Geschmack m (a. fig.).

pale¹ [peil] 1. □ blaß, bleich; fahl; ~ ale helles Bier; 2. (er)bleichen.

pale² [~] Pfahl m; fig. Grenzen f/pl.

paleness ['peilnis] Blässe f.

palisade [pæli'seid] 1. Palisade f; Staket n; **~s** pl. Am. Steilufer n; 2. umpfählen.

pall [pɔːl] schal werden; ~ (up)on j-n langweilen.

pallet ['pælit] Strohsack m.

palliat|e ['pælieit] bemänteln; lindern; **~ive** [~iətiv] Linderungsmittel n.

pall|id □ ['pælid] blaß; **~idness** [~dnis], **~or** ['pælə] Blässe f.

palm [pɑːm] 1. Handfläche f; ♀ Palme f; 2. in der Hand verbergen; ~ s.th. off upon s.o. j-m et. andrehen; **~-tree** ['pɑːmtriː] Palme f.

palpable □ ['pælpəbl] fühlbar; fig. handgreiflich, klar, eindeutig.

palpitat|e ['pælpiteit] klopfen (Herz); **~ion** [pælpi'teiʃən] Herzklopfen n.

palsy ['pɔːlzi] 1. Lähmung f; fig. Ohnmacht f; 2. fig. lähmen.

palter ['pɔːltə] sein Spiel treiben.

paltry □ ['pɔːltri] erbärmlich.

pamper ['pæmpə] verzärteln.

pamphlet ['pæmflit] Flugschrift f.

pan [pæn] Pfanne f; Tiegel m.

pan... [ˌ] all..., gesamt...; pan..., Pan...

panacea [pænə'siə] Allheilmittel n.

pancake ['pænkeik] Pfannkuchen m; ~ landing ✈ Bumslandung f.

pandemonium fig. [pændi'mounjəm] Hölle(nlärm m) f.

pander ['pændə] 1. Vorschub leisten (to dat.); kuppeln; 2. Kuppler m.

pane [pein] (Fenster)Scheibe f.

panegyric [pæni'dʒirik] Lobrede f.

panel ['pænl] 1. △ Fach n; Tür-Füllung f; ⚖ Geschworenen(liste f) m/pl.; Diskussionsteilnehmer m/pl.; Kassenarztliste f; 2. täfeln.

pang [pæŋ] plötzlicher Schmerz, Weh n; fig. Angst f, Qual f.

panhandle ['pænhændl] 1. Pfannenstiel m; Am. schmaler Fortsatz e-s Staatsgebiets; 2. Am. F betteln.

panic ['pænik] 1. panisch; 2. Panik f.

pansy ♀ ['pænzi] Stiefmütterchen n.

pant [pænt] nach Luft schnappen; keuchen; klopfen (Herz); lechzen (for, after nach).

panther zo. ['pænθə] Panther m.

panties F ['pæntiz] (Damen)Schlüpfer m; (Kinder)Hös-chen n.

pantry ['pæntri] Vorratskammer f.

pants [pænts] pl. Hose f; ✝ lange) pap [pæp] Brei m.   [Unterhose.

papa [pə'paː] Papa m.

papal □ ['peipəl] päpstlich.

paper ['peipə] 1. Papier n; Zeitung f; Prüfungsaufgabe f; Vortrag m, Aufsatz m; ~s pl. (Ausweis)Papiere n/pl.; 2. tapezieren; ~back Taschenbuch n, Paperback n; ~bag Tüte f; ~-clip Büroklammer f; ~-fastener Musterklammer f; ~-hanger Tapezierer m; ~-mill Papierfabrik f; ~-weight Briefbeschwerer m.

pappy ['pæpi] breiig.

par [paː] ✝ Nennwert m, Pari n; at ~ zum Nennwert; be on a ~ with gleich od. ebenbürtig sein (dat.).

parable ['pærəbl] Gleichnis n.

parachut|e ['pærəʃuːt] Fallschirm m; ~ist [ˌtist] Fallschirmspringer(in).

parade [pə'reid] 1. ✕ (Truppen-) Parade f; Zurschaustellung f; Promenade f; (Um)Zug m; programme ~ Radio: Programmvorschau f; make a ~ of et. zur Schau stellen; 2. ✕ antreten (lassen); ✕ vorbeimarschieren (lassen); zur Schau stellen; ~-ground ✕ Exerzier-, Paradeplatz m.

paradise ['pærədais] Paradies n.

paragon ['pærəgən] Vorbild n; Muster n.

paragraph ['pærəgraːf] Absatz m; Paragraph(zeichen n) m; kurze Zeitungsnotiz.

parallel ['pærəlel] 1. parallel; 2. Parallele f (a. fig.); Gegenstück n; Vergleich m; without (a) ~ ohnegleichen; 3. vergleichen; entsprechen; gleichen; parallel laufen (mit).

paraly|se ['pærəlaiz] lähmen; fig. unwirksam machen; ~sis ⚕ [pə'rælisis] Paralyse f, Lähmung f.

paramount ['pærəmaunt] oberst, höchst, hervorragend; größer, höher stehend (to als).

parapet ['pærəpit] ✕ Brustwehr f; Brüstung f; Geländer n.

paraphernalia [pærəfə'neiljə] pl. Ausrüstung f; Zubehör n, m.

parasite ['pærəsait] Schmarotzer m.

parasol ['pærəsɔl] Sonnenschirm m.

paratroops ✕ ['pærətruːps] Luftlandetruppen f/pl.

parboil ['paːbɔil] ankochen.

parcel ['paːsl] 1. Paket n; Parzelle f; 2. ~ out aus-, aufteilen.

parch [paːtʃ] rösten, (aus)dörren.

parchment ['paːtʃmənt] Pergament n.

pard Am. sl. [paːd] Partner m.

pardon ['paːdn] 1. Verzeihung f; ⚖ Begnadigung f; 2. verzeihen; f. begnadigen; ~able □ [ˌnəbl] verzeihlich.

pare [pɛə] (be)schneiden (a. fig.); schälen.

parent ['pɛərənt] Vater m, Mutter f; fig. Ursache f; ~s pl. Eltern pl.; ~age [ˌtidʒ] Herkunft f; ~al [pə'rentl] elterlich.

parenthe|sis [pə'renθisis], pl. ~ses [ˌsiːz] Einschaltung f; typ. (runde) Klammer.

paring ['pɛəriŋ] Schälen n, Abschneiden n; ~s pl. Schalen f/pl.; Schnipsel m/pl.

parish ['pæriʃ] 1. Kirchspiel n, Gemeinde f; 2. Pfarr...; Gemeinde...; ~ council Gemeinderat m; ~ioner [pə'riʃənə] Pfarrkind n, Gemeindemitglied n.

parity ['pæriti] Gleichheit f.

park [paːk] 1. Park m, Anlagen f/pl.; Naturschutzgebiet n; ✕ car-... Parkplatz m; 2. mot. parken; ~ing mot. ['paːkiŋ] Parken n; ~ing lot Parkplatz m; ~ing meter Parkuhr f.

parlance ['paːləns] Ausdrucksweise f.

parley ['paːli] 1. Unterhandlung f; 2. unterhandeln; sich besprechen.

parliament ['paːləmənt] Parlament n; ~arian [paːləmen'tɛəriən] Parlamentarier(in); ~ary □ [paːlə'mentəri] parlamentarisch; Parlaments...

parlo(u)r ['pɑ:lə] Wohnzimmer *n*; Empfangs-, Sprechzimmer *n*; *beauty* ~ *bsd. Am.* Schönheitssalon *m*; ~ *car* 🚗 *Am.* Salonwagen *m*; **~maid** Stubenmädchen *n*.

parochial □ [pə'roukjəl] Pfarr...; Gemeinde...; *fig.* engstirnig, beschränkt.

parole [pə'roul] **1.** 📝 mündlich; **2.** ✕ Parole *f*; Ehrenwort *n*; *put on* ~ = **3.** 📝 *bsd. Am.* bedingt freilassen.

parquet [pɑ:'kei] Parkett(fußboden *m*) *n*; *Am. thea.* Parkett *n*.

parrot ['pærət] **1.** *orn.* Papagei *m* (*a. fig.*); **2.** (nach)plappern.

parry ['pæri] abwehren, parieren.

parsimonious □ [pɑ:si'mounjəs] sparsam, karg; knauserig.

parsley ♀ ['pɑ:sli] Petersilie *f*.

parson ['pɑ:sn] Pfarrer *m*; **~age** [~nidʒ] Pfarrei *f*; Pfarrhaus *n*.

part [pɑ:t] **1.** Teil *m*; Anteil *m*; Partei *f*; *thea.*, *fig.* Rolle *f*; ♪ *Einzel*-Stimme *f*; Gegend *f*; *a man of* ~ *s* ein fähiger Mensch; *take* ~ *in s.th.* an e-r Sache teilnehmen; *take in good (bad)* ~ gut (übel) aufnehmen; *for my (own)* ~ meinerseits; *in* ~ teilweise; *on the* ~ *of* von seiten (*gen.*); *on my* ~ meinerseits; *for my* ~ meinerseits; **2.** *adv.* teils; **3.** *v/t.* (ab-, ein-, zer)teilen; *Haar* scheiteln; ~ *company* sich trennen (*with von*); *v/i.* sich trennen (*with von*); scheiden.

partake [pɑ:'teik] [*irr.* (*take*)] teilnehmen, teilhaben; ~ *of Mahlzeit* einnehmen; grenzen an (*acc.*).

partial □ ['pɑ:ʃəl] Teil...; teilweise; partiell; parteiisch; eingenommen (*to von, für*); **~ity** [pɑ:ʃi'æliti] Parteilichkeit *f*; Vorliebe *f*.

particip|ant [pɑ:'tisipənt] Teilnehmer(in); **~ate** [~peit] teilnehmen; **~ation** [pɑ:tisi'peiʃən] Teilnahme *f*.

participle *gr.* ['pɑ:tsipl] Partizip *n*, Mittelwort *n*.

particle ['pɑ:tikl] Teilchen *n*.

particular [pə'tikjulə] **1.** □ *mst* besonder; einzeln; Sonder...; genau; eigen; wählerisch; **2.** Einzelheit *f*; Umstand *m*; *in* ~ insbesondere; **~ity** [pətikju'læriti] Besonderheit *f*; Ausführlichkeit *f*; Eigenheit *f*; **~ly** [pə'tikjuləli] besonders.

parting ['pɑ:tiŋ] **1.** Trennung *f*; Teilung *f*; Abschied *m*; *Haar*-Scheitel *m*; ~ *of the ways bsd. fig.* Scheideweg *m*; **2.** Abschieds...

partisan [pɑ:ti'zæn] Parteigänger (-in); ✕ Partisan *m*; *attr.* Partei...

partition [pɑ:'tiʃən] **1.** Teilung *f*; Scheidewand *f*; Verschlag *m*, Fach *n*; **2.** *mst* ~ *off* (ab)teilen.

partly ['pɑ:tli] teilweise, zum Teil.

partner ['pɑ:tnə] **1.** Partner(in); **2.** (sich) zs.-tun mit, zs.-arbeiten mit; **~ship** [~əʃip] Teilhaber-, Part-nerschaft *f*; ♻ Handelsgesellschaft *f*.

part-owner ['pɑ:tounə] Miteigentümer(in).

partridge *orn.* ['pɑ:tridʒ] Rebhuhn *n*.

part-time ['pɑ:ttaim] **1.** *adj.* Teilzeit..., Halbtags...; **2.** *adv.* halbtags.

party ['pɑ:ti] Partei *f*; ✕ Trupp *m*, Kommando *n*; Party *f*, Gesellschaft *f*; Beteiligte(r) *m*; *co.* Type *f*, Individuum *n*; ~ *line pol.* Parteilinie *f*, -direktive *f*.

pass [pɑ:s] **1.** Paß *m*, Ausweis *m*; Passierschein *m*; Bestehen *n* e-s *Examens*; *univ.* gewöhnlicher Grad; (kritische) Lage; *Fußball*: Paß *m*; Bestreichung *f*, Strich *m*; (*Gebirgs*-)Paß *m*, Durchgang *m*; *Karten*: Passen *n*; *free* ~ Freikarte *f*; **2.** *v/i.* passieren, geschehen; hingenommen werden; *Karten*: passen; (vorbei)gehen, (vorbei)kommen, (vorbei)fahren; vergehen (*Zeit*); sich verwandeln; angenommen werden (*Banknoten*); bekannt sein; durchgehen; aussterben; *a.* ~ *away* vergehen; durchkommen (*Gesetz*; *Prüfling*); ~ *for* gelten als; ~ *off* vonstatten gehen; ~ *out* F ohnmächtig werden; *come to* ~ geschehen; *bring to* ~ bewirken; *v/t.* vorbeigehen *od.* vorbeikommen *od.* vorbeifahren an (*dat.*); passieren; kommen *od.* fahren durch; verbringen, reichen, geben; *Bemerkung* machen, von sich geben; *Banknoten* in Umlauf bringen; *Gesetz* durchbringen, annehmen; *Prüfling* durchkommen lassen; *Prüfung* bestehen; (hinaus-) gehen über (*acc.*); *Urteil* abgeben; *Meinung* äußern; bewegen; streichen mit; *Ball* zuspielen; *Truppen* vorbeimaschieren lassen; **~able** □ ['pɑ:səbl] passierbar; gangbar, gültig (*Geld*); leidlich.

passage ['pæsidʒ] Durchgang *m*, Durchfahrt *f*; Überfahrt *f*; Durchreise *f*; Korridor *m*, Gang *m*; Weg *m*; Annahme *f* e-s *Gesetzes*; ♪ Passage *f*; *Text*-Stelle *f*; *bird of* ~ Zugvogel *m*.

passbook ♻ ['pɑ:sbuk] Sparbuch *n*.

passenger ['pæsindʒə] Passagier *m*, Fahr-, Fluggast *m*, Reisende(r *m*) *f*.

passer-by ['pɑ:sə'bai] Vorübergehende(r *m*) *f*, Passant(in).

passion ['pæʃən] Leidenschaft *f*; (Gefühls)Ausbruch *m*; Zorn *m*; ♀ *eccl.* Passion *f*; *be in a* ~ zornig sein; *in* ~ 📝 im Affekt; ♀ *Week eccl.* Karwoche *f*; **~ate** □ [~nit] leidenschaftlich.

passive □ ['pæsiv] passiv (*a. gr.*); teilnahmslos; untätig.

passport ['pɑ:spɔ:t] (Reise)Paß *m*.

password ✕ ['pɑ:swɔ:d] Losung *f*.

past [pɑ:st] **1.** *adj.* vergangen; *gr.* Vergangenheits...; früher; *for some*

time ~ seit einiger Zeit; ~ tense gr.
Vergangenheit f; **2.** adv. vorbei;
3. prp. nach, über; über ... (acc.)
hinaus; an ... (dat.) vorbei; half ~
two halb drei; ~ endurance unerträglich; ~ hope hoffnungslos;
4. Vergangenheit f (a. gr.).
paste [peist] **1.** Teig m; Kleister m;
Paste f; **2.** (be)kleben; ~board
['peistbɔ:d] Pappe f; attr. Papp...
pastel [pæs'tel] Pastell(bild) n.
pasteurize ['pæstəraiz] pasteurisie-
ren, keimfrei machen.
pastime ['pɑ:staim] Zeitvertreib m.
pastor ['pɑ:stə] Pastor m; Seel-
sorger m; ~al □ [~ərəl] Hirten...;
pastoral.
pastry ['peistri] Tortengebäck n,
Konditorwaren f/pl.; Pasteten f/pl.;
~cook Pastetenbäcker m, Konditor m.
pasture ['pɑ:stʃə] **1.** Vieh-Weide f;
Futter n; **2.** (ab)weiden.
pat [pæt] **1.** Klaps m; Portion f
Butter; **2.** tätscheln; klopfen; **3.** gelegen, gerade recht; bereit.
patch [pætʃ] **1.** Fleck m; Flicken m;
Stück n Land; ✗ Pflaster n; **2.** flik-
ken; ~work ['pætʃwə:k] Flickwerk
n.
pate F [peit] Schädel m.
patent ['peitənt, Am. 'pætənt] **1.** offenkundig; patentiert; Patent...;
letters ~ ['pætənt] pl. Freibrief m;
~ leather Lackleder n; **2.** Patent n;
Privileg n, Freibrief m; ~ agent
Patentanwalt m; **3.** patentieren;
~ee [peitən'ti:] Patentinhaber m.
patern|al □ [pə'tə:nl] väterlich;
~ity [~niti] Vaterschaft f.
path [pɑ:θ], pl. ~s [pɑ:ðz] Pfad m;
Weg m.
pathetic [pə'θetik] (~ally) pathe-
tisch; rührend, ergreifend.
pathos ['peiθɔs] Pathos m.
patien|ce ['peiʃəns] Geduld f; Aus-
dauer f; Patience f (Kartenspiel);
~t [~nt] **1.** □ geduldig; **2.** Pa-
tient(in).
patio Am. ['pætiou] Innenhof m,
Patio m.
patrimony ['pætriməni] väterliches
Erbteil.
patriot ['peitriət] Patriot(in).
patrol ✗ [pə'troul] **1.** Patrouille f,
Streife f; ~ wagon Am. Polizei-
gefangenenwagen m; **2.** (ab)pa-
trouillieren; ~man [~lmæn] pa-
trouillierender Polizist; Pannen-
helfer m e-s Automobilclubs.
patron ['peitrən] (Schutz)Patron m;
Gönner m; Kunde m; ~age ['pætrə-
nidʒ] Gönnerschaft f; Kundschaft f;
Schutz m; ~ize [~naiz] beschützen;
begünstigen; ~ Kunde sein bei; gön-
nerhaft behandeln.
patter ['pætə] v/i. platschen; trappeln; v/t. (her)plappern.
pattern ['pætən] **1.** Muster n (a.

fig.); Modell n; **2.** formen (after, on
nach).
paunch ['pɔ:ntʃ] Wanst m.
pauper ['pɔ:pə] Fürsorgeempfän-
ger(in); ~ize [~əraiz] arm machen.
pause [pɔ:z] **1.** Pause f; **2.** pausie-
ren.
pave [peiv] pflastern; fig. Weg bahnen; ~ment ['peivmənt] Bürgersteig m, Gehweg m; Pflaster n.
paw [pɔ:] **1.** Pfote f, Tatze f; **2.** scharren; F befingern; rauh behandeln.
pawn [pɔ:n] **1.** Bauer m im Schach;
Pfand n; in od. at ~ verpfändet; **2.**
verpfänden; ~broker ['pɔ:nbroukə]
Pfandleiher m; ~shop Leihhaus n.
pay [pei] **1.** (Be)Zahlung f; Sold m,
Lohn m; **2.** [irr.] v/t. (be)zahlen;
(be)lohnen; sich lohnen für; Ehre
etc. erweisen; Besuch abstatten; ~
attention od. heed to achtgeben auf
(acc.); ~ down bar bezahlen; ~ off v/i.
bezahlen u. entlassen; j-n voll
auszahlen; v/i. zahlen; sich lohnen;
~ for (für) et. bezahlen; ~able
['peiəbl] zahlbar; fällig; ~day
Zahltag m; ~ee ✝ [pei'i:] Zahlungs-
empfänger m; ~ing ['peiiŋ] loh-
nend; ~master Zahlmeister m;
~ment ['peimənt] (Be)Zahlung f;
Lohn m, Sold m; ~off Abrechnung
f (a. fig.); Am. F Höhepunkt m;
~roll Lohnliste f.
pea ✿ [pi:] Erbse f.
peace [pi:s] Frieden m, Ruhe f; at ~
friedlich; ~able □ ['pi:səbl] fried-
liebend, friedlich; ~ful □ ['pi:sful]
friedlich; ~maker Friedensstif-
ter(in).
peach ✿ [pi:tʃ] Pfirsich(baum) m.
pea|cock orn. ['pi:kɔk] Pfau(hahn)
m; ~hen orn. ['pi:hen] Pfauhenne f.
peak [pi:k] Spitze f; Gipfel m;
Mützen-Schirm m; attr. Spitzen...,
Höchst...; ~ed [pi:kt] spitz.
peal [pi:l] **1.** Geläut n; Glockenspiel n; Dröhnen n; ~s of laughter
dröhnendes Gelächter; **2.** erschallen (lassen); laut verkünden; dröhnen.
peanut ['pi:nʌt] Erdnuß f.
pear ✿ [pεə] Birne f.
pearl [pə:l] **1.** Perle f (a. fig.); attr.
Perl(en)...; **2.** tropfen, perlen; ~y
['pə:li] perlenartig.
peasant ['pezənt] **1.** Bauer m;
2. bäuerlich; ~ry [~tri] Landvolk n.
peat [pi:t] Torf m.
pebble ['pebl] Kiesel(stein) m.
peck [pek] **1.** Viertelscheffel m
(9,087 Liter); fig. Menge f; **2.** pik-
ken, hacken (at nach).
peculate ['pekjuleit] unterschlagen.
peculiar □ [pi'kju:ljə] eigen(tümlich); besonder; seltsam; ~ity
[pikju:li'æriti] Eigenheit f; Eigentümlichkeit f.
pecuniary [pi'kju:njəri] Geld...
pedagog|ics [pedə'gɔdʒiks] mst sg.

Pädagogik *f*; ~ue ['pedəgɔg] Pädagoge *m*; Lehrer *m*.

pedal ['pedl] **1.** Pedal *n*; **2.** Fuß...; **3.** *Radfahren*: fahren, treten.

pedantic [pi'dæntik] (~ally) pedantisch.

peddle ['pedl] hausieren (mit); ~r *Am.* [~lə] = *pedlar.*

pedestal ['pedistl] Sockel *m* (*a. fig.*).

pedestrian [pi'destriən] **1.** zu Fuß; nüchtern; **2.** Fußgänger(in); ~ *crossing* Fußgängerübergang *m.*

pedigree ['pedigri:] Stammbaum *m.*

pedlar ['pedlə] Hausierer *m.*

peek [pi:k] **1.** spähen, gucken, lugen; **2.** flüchtiger Blick.

peel [pi:l] **1.** Schale *f*; Rinde *f*; **2.** *a.* ~ *off v/t.* (ab)schälen; *Kleid* abstreifen; *v/i.* sich (ab)schälen.

peep [pi:p] **1.** verstohlener Blick; Piepen *n*; **2.** (verstohlen) gucken; *a.* ~ *out* (hervor(gucken (*a. fig.*); piepen; ~-**hole** ['pi:phoul] Guckloch *n.*

peer [piə] **1.** spähen, lugen; ~ *at* angucken; **2.** Gleiche(r *m*) *f*; Pair *m*; ~**less** □ ['piəlis] unvergleichlich.

peevish □ ['pi:viʃ] verdrießlich.

peg [peg] **1.** Stöpsel *m*, Dübel *m*, Pflock *m*; *Kleider*-Haken *m*; ♩ Wirbel *m*; *Wäsche*-Klammer *f*; *fig.* Aufhänger *m*; *take s.o. down a* ~ *or two j-n* demütigen; **2.** festpflöcken; ~ *away od. along* F darauflosarbeiten; ~-**top** ['pegtɔp] Kreisel *m.*

pelican *orn.* ['pelikən] Pelikan *m.*

pellet ['pelit] Kügelchen *n*; Pille *f*; Schrotkorn *n.*

pell-mell ['pel'mel] durcheinander.

pelt [pelt] **1.** Fell *n*; ✝ *rohe* Haut; **2.** *v/t.* bewerfen; *v/i.* niederprasseln.

pelvis *anat.* ['pelvis] Becken *n.*

pen [pen] **1.** (Schreib)Feder *f*; Hürde *f*; **2.** schreiben; [*irr.*] einpferchen.

penal □ ['pi:nl] Straf...; strafbar; ~ *code* Strafgesetzbuch *n*; ~ *servitude* Zuchthausstrafe *f*; ~**ize** ['pi:nəlaiz] bestrafen; ~**ty** ['penlti] Strafe *f*; *Sport*: Strafpunkt *m*; ~ *area Fußball*: Strafraum *m*; ~ *kick Fußball*: Freistoß *m.*

penance ['penəns] Buße *f.*

pence [pens] *pl. von* penny.

pencil ['pensl] **1.** Bleistift *m*; **2.** zeichnen; (mit Bleistift) anzeichnen *od.* anstreichen; *Augenbrauen* nachziehen; ~-**sharpener** Bleistiftspitzer *m.*

pendant ['pendənt] Anhänger *m.*

pending ['pendiŋ] **1.** ⚖ schwebend; **2.** *prp.* während; bis zu.

pendulum ['pendjuləm] Pendel *n.*

penetra|ble □ ['penitrəbl] durchdringbar; ~**te** [~reit] durchdringen; ergründen; eindringen (in *acc.*); vordringen (*to* bis zu); ~**tion** [peni-

'treiʃən] Durch-, Eindringen *n*; Scharfsinn *m*; ~**tive** □ ['penitrətiv] durchdringend (*a. fig.*); eindringlich; scharfsinnig.

pen-friend ['penfrend] Brieffreund (-in).

penguin *orn.* ['peŋgwin] Pinguin *m.*

penholder ['penhouldə] Federhalter *m.*

peninsula [pi'ninsjulə] Halbinsel *f.*

peniten|ce ['penitəns] Buße *f*, Reue *f*; ~**t 1.** □ reuig, bußfertig; **2.** Büßer(in); ~**tiary** [peni'tenʃəri] Besserungsanstalt *f*; *Am.* Zuchthaus *n.*

pen|knife ['pennaif] Taschenmesser *n*; ~**man** Schönschreiber *m*; Schriftsteller *m*; ~-**name** Schriftstellername *m*, Pseudonym *n.*

pennant ⚓ ['penənt] Wimpel *m.*

penniless □ ['penilis] ohne Geld.

penny ['peni], *pl. mst* **pence** [pens] (englischer) Penny (1/12 *Schilling*); *Am.* Cent *m*; Kleinigkeit *f*; ~**weight** *englisches* Pennygewicht (1½ *Gramm*).

pension ['penʃən] **1.** Pension *f*, Ruhegehalt *n*; **2.** *oft* ~ *off* pensionieren; ~**ary**, ~**er** [~nəri, ~nə] Pensionär(in).

pensive □ ['pensiv] gedankenvoll.

pent [pent] *pret. u. p.p. von* pen 2; ~-*up* aufgestaut (*Zorn etc.*).

Pentecost ['pentikɔst] Pfingsten *n.*

penthouse ['penthaus] Schutzdach *n*; Dachwohnung *f auf e-m Hochhaus.*

penu|rious □ [pi'njuəriəs] geizig; ~**ry** ['penjuri] Armut *f*; Mangel *m.*

people ['pi:pl] **1.** Volk *n*, Nation *f*; *coll.* die Leute *pl.*; man; **2.** bevölkern.

pepper ['pepə] **1.** Pfeffer *m*; **2.** pfeffern; ~**mint** ♀ Pfefferminze *f*; ~**y** □ [~əri] pfefferig; *fig.* hitzig.

per [pə:] per, durch, für; laut; je.

perambulat|e [pə'ræmbjuleit] (durch)wandern; bereisen; ~**or** ['præmbjuleitə] Kinderwagen *m.*

perceive [pə'si:v] (be)merken, wahrnehmen; empfinden; erkennen.

per cent [pə'sent] Prozent *n.*

percentage [pə'sentidʒ] Prozentsatz *m*; Prozente *n/pl.*; *fig.* Teil *m.*

percept|ible □ [pə'septəbl] wahrnehmbar; ~**ion** [~pʃən] Wahrnehmung(svermögen *n*) *f*; Erkenntnis *f*; Auffassung(skraft) *f.*

perch [pə:tʃ] **1.** *ichth.* Barsch *m*; Rute *f* (5,029 *m*); (Sitz)Stange *f für Vögel*; **2.** (sich) setzen; sitzen.

perchance [pə'tʃɑ:ns] zufällig; vielleicht.

percolate ['pə:kəleit] durchtropfen, durchsickern (lassen); sickern.

percussion [pə:'kʌʃən] Schlag *m*; Erschütterung *f*; ⚕ Abklopfen *n.*

perdition [pə:'diʃən] Verderben *n.*

peregrination [perigri'neiʃən] Wanderschaft *f*; Wanderung *f.*

peremptory ☐ [pə'remptəri] bestimmt; zwingend; rechthaberisch.
perennial ☐ [pə'renjəl] dauernd;
immerwährend; ♀ perennierend.
perfect 1. ['pə:fikt] ☐ vollkommen;
vollendet; gänzlich, völlig; **2.** [~] a.
~ tense gr. Perfekt n; **3.** [pə-
'fekt] vervollkommnen; vollenden;
~ion [~kʃən] Vollendung f; Vollkommenheit f; fig. Gipfel m.
perfidious ☐ [pə:'fidiəs] treulos (to
gegen), verräterisch.
perfidy ['pə:fidi] Treulosigkeit f.
perforate ['pə:fəreit] durchlöchern.
perforce [pə'fɔ:s] notgedrungen.
perform [pə'fɔ:m] verrichten; ausführen; tun; Pflicht etc. erfüllen;
thea., ♪ aufführen, spielen, vortragen (a. v/i.); ~ance [~məns] Verrichtung f; thea. Aufführung f;
Vortrag m; Leistung f; ~er [~mə]
Vortragende(r m) f.
perfume 1. ['pə:fju:m] Wohlgeruch
m; Parfüm n; **2.** [pə'fju:m] parfümieren; ~ry [~məri] Parfümerie(n
pl.) f.
perfunctory ☐ [pə'fʌŋktəri] mechanisch; oberflächlich.
perhaps [pə'hæps, præps] vielleicht.
peril ['peril] **1.** Gefahr f; **2.** gefährden; ~ous ☐ [~ləs] gefährlich.
period ['piəriəd] Periode f; Zeitraum m; gr. Punkt m; langer Satz;
(Unterrichts)Stunde f; mst ~s pl. ♂
Periode f; ~ic [piəri'ɔdik] periodisch; ~ical [~kəl] **1.** ☐ periodisch;
2. Zeitschrift f.
perish ['periʃ] umkommen, zugrunde gehen; ~able ☐ [~ʃəbl] vergänglich; leicht verderblich; ~ing
☐ [~ʃiŋ] vernichtend, tödlich.
periwig ['periwig] Perücke f.
perjur|e ['pə:dʒə] ~ o.s. falsch
schwören; ~y [~əri] Meineid m.
perk [pə:k] v/i. mst ~ up selbst-
bewußt auftreten; sich wieder erholen; v/t. recken; ~ o.s. (up) sich
putzen.
perky ☐ ['pə:ki] keck, dreist; flott.
perm F [pə:m] **1.** Dauerwelle f;
2. j-m Dauerwellen machen.
permanen|ce ['pə:mənəns] Dauer
f; ~t ☐ [~nt] dauernd, ständig;
dauerhaft; Dauer...; ~ wave Dauerwelle f.
permea|ble ☐ ['pə:mjəbl] durch-
lässig; ~te ['pə:mieit] durchdringen; eindringen.
permissi|ble ☐ [pə'misəbl] zuläs-
sig; ~on [~iʃən] Erlaubnis f.
permit 1. [pə'mit] erlauben, gestatten; **2.** ['pə:mit] Erlaubnis f,
Genehmigung f; Passierschein m.
pernicious ☐ [pə:'niʃəs] verderblich; ♂ bösartig.
perpendicular ☐ [pə:pən'dikjulə]
senkrecht; aufrecht; steil.
perpetrate ['pə:pitreit] verüben.
perpetu|al ☐ [pə'petjuəl] fort-

während, ewig; ~ate [~ueit] ver-
ewigen.
perplex [pə'pleks] verwirren; ~ity
[~siti] Verwirrung f.
perquisites ['pə:kwizits] pl. Neben-
einkünfte pl.
persecut|e ['pə:sikju:t] verfolgen;
~ion [pə:si'kju:ʃən] Verfolgung f;
~or ['pə:sikju:tə] Verfolger m.
persever|ance [pə:si'viərəns] Be-
harrlichkeit f, Ausdauer f; ~e [pə:-
si'viə] beharren; aushalten.
persist [pə'sist] beharren (in auf
dat.); ~ence, ~ency [~təns, ~si]
Beharrlichkeit f; ~ent ☐ [~nt] beharrlich.
person ['pə:sn] Person f (a. gr.);
Persönlichkeit f; thea. Rolle f;
~age [~nidʒ] Persönlichkeit f; thea.
Charakter m; ~al ☐ [~nl] persönlich (a. gr.); attr. Personal...; Pri-
vat...; eigen; ~ality [pə:sə'næliti]
Persönlichkeit f; personalities pl.
persönliche Bemerkungen f/pl.;
~ate ['pə:səneit] darstellen; sich
ausgeben für; ~ify [pə:'sɔnifai] verkörpern; ~nel [pə:sə'nel] Personal
n.
perspective [pə'spektiv] Perspektive
f; Ausblick m, Fernsicht f.
perspex ['pə:speks] Plexiglas n.
perspicuous ☐ [pə'spikjuəs] klar.
perspir|ation [pə:spə'reiʃən]
Schwitzen n; Schweiß m; ~e [pəs-
'paiə] (aus)schwitzen.
persua|de [pə'sweid] überreden;
überzeugen; ~sion [~eiʒən] Über-
redung f; Überzeugung f; Glaube
m; ~sive ☐ [~eisiv] überredend,
überzeugend. [weis.)
pert ☐ [pə:t] keck, vorlaut, nase-)
pertain [pə:'tein] (to) gehören (dat.
od. zu); betreffen (acc.).
pertinacious ☐ [pə:ti'neiʃəs] hartnäckig, zäh.
pertinent ☐ ['pə:tinənt] sachdienlich, -gemäß; zur Sache gehörig.
perturb [pə'tə:b] beunruhigen,
stören.
perus|al [pə'ru:zəl] sorgfältige
Durchsicht; ~e [~u:z] durchlesen;
prüfen.
pervade [pə:'veid] durchdringen.
pervers|e ☐ [pə'və:s] verkehrt; ♂
pervers; eigensinnig; vertrackt
(Sache); ~ion [~ə:ʃən] Verdrehung
f; Abkehr f; ~ity [~siti] Verkehrt-
heit f; ♂ Perversität f; Eigensinn m.
pervert 1. [pə'və:t] verdrehen; verführen; **2.** ♂ ['pə:və:t] perverser
Mensch.
pessimism ['pesimizəm] Pessimis-
mus m.
pest [pest] Pest f; Plage f; Schäd-
ling m; ~er ['pestə] belästigen.
pesti|ferous ☐ [pes'tifərəs] krank-
heiterregend; ~lence ['pestiləns]
Seuche f, bsd. Pest f; ~lent ☐ [~nt]
gefährlich; co. verdammt; ~lential

☐ [pestiˈlenʃəl] pestartig; verder-benbringend.

pet [pet] 1. üble Laune; zahmes Tier; Liebling *m*; 2. Lieblings...; ~ *dog* Schoßhund *m*; ~ *name* Kosename *m*; 3. (ver)hätscheln; knutschen.

petal ♀ [ˈpetl] Blütenblatt *n*.

petition [piˈtiʃən] 1. Bitte *f*; Bittschrift *f*, Eingabe *f*; 2. bitten, ersuchen; e-e Eingabe machen.

petrify [ˈpetrifai] versteinern.

petrol [ˈpetrəl] Benzin *n*; ~ *station* Tankstelle *f*.

petticoat [ˈpetikout] Unterrock *m*.

pettish [ˈpetiʃ] launisch.

petty ☐ [ˈpeti] klein, geringfügig.

petulant [ˈpetjulənt] gereizt.

pew [pju:] Kirchensitz *m*, -bank *f*.

pewter [ˈpju:tə] Zinn(gefäße *n*/*pl*.) *n*.

phantasm [ˈfæntæzəm] Trugbild *n*.

phantom [ˈfæntəm] Phantom *n*, Trugbild *n*; Gespenst *n*.

Pharisee [ˈfærisi:] Pharisäer *m*.

pharmacy [ˈfɑ:məsi] Pharmazie *f*; Apotheke *f*. [Phasen.\
phase [feiz] Phase *f*; ~*d* [feizd] in]

pheasant *orn*. [ˈfeznt] Fasan *m*.

phenomen|on [fiˈnɔminən], *pl.* ~**a** [~nə] Phänomen *n*, Erscheinung *f*.

phial [ˈfaiəl] Phiole *f*, Fläschchen *n*.

philander [fiˈlændə] flirten.

philanthropist [fiˈlænθrəpist] Menschenfreund(in).

philolog|ist [fiˈlɔlədʒist] Philolog|e *m*, -in *f*; ~**y** [~dʒi] Philologie *f*.

philosoph|er [fiˈlɔsəfə] Philosoph *m*; ~**ize** [~faiz] philosophieren; ~**y** [~fi] Philosophie *f*.

phlegm [flem] Schleim *m*; Phlegma *n*.

phone F [foun] *s.* telephone.

phonetics [fouˈnetiks] *pl.* Phonetik *f*, Lautbildungslehre *f*.

phon(e)y *Am. sl.* [ˈfouni] 1. Fälschung *f*; Schwindler *m*; 2. unecht.

phosphorus [ˈfɔsfərəs] Phosphor *m*.

photograph [ˈfoutəgrɑ:f] 1. Photographie *f* (*Bild*); 2. photographieren; ~**er** [fəˈtɔgrəf] Photograph (-in); ~**y** [~fi] Photographie *f*.

phrase [freiz] 1. (Rede)Wendung *f*, Redensart *f*, Ausdruck *m*; 2. ausdrücken.

physic|al ☐ [ˈfizikl] physisch; körperlich; physikalisch; ~ *education*, ~ *training* Leibeserziehung *f*; ~**ian** [fiˈziʃən] Arzt *m*; ~**ist** [ˈfizisist] Physiker *m*; ~**s** [~iks] *sg.* Physik *f*.

physique [fiˈzi:k] Körperbau *m*.

piano [ˈpjænou] Klavier *n*.

piazza [piˈætsə] Piazza *f*, (Markt-)Platz *m*; *Am.* große Veranda.

pick [pik] Auswahl *f*; = *pickaxe*; 2. auf-, aufnehmen; pflücken; (herum)stochern; *in der Nase* bohren; abnagen; *Schloß* knacken; *Streit* suchen; auswählen; (auf-)picken; bestehlen; ~ *out* auswählen;

heraussuchen; ~ *up* aufreißen, aufbrechen; aufnehmen, auflesen; sich *e-e Fremdsprache* aneignen; erfassen; (*im Auto*) mitnehmen, abholen; *Täter* ergreifen; gesund werden; ~**-a-back** [ˈpikəbæk] huckepack; ~**axe** Spitzhacke *f*.

picket [ˈpikit] 1. Pfahl *m*; ✕ Feldwache *f*; Streikposten *m*; 2. einpfählen; an e-n Pfahl binden; mit Streikposten besetzen.

picking [ˈpikiŋ] Picken *n*, Pflücken *n*; Abfall *m*; *mst* ~*s pl*. Nebengewinn *m*.

pickle [ˈpikl] 1. Pökel *m*; Eingepökelte(s) *n*, Pickles *pl*.; F mißliche Lage; 2. (ein)pökeln; ~*d herring* Salzhering *m*.

pick|lock [ˈpiklɔk] Dietrich *m*; ~**pocket** Taschendieb *m*; ~**up** Ansteigen *n*; Tonabnehmer *m*; Kleinlieferwagen *m*; *sl.* Straßenbekanntschaft *f*.

picnic [ˈpiknik] Picknick *n*.

pictorial [pikˈtɔ:riəl] 1. ☐ malerisch; illustriert; 2. Illustrierte *f*.

picture [ˈpiktʃə] 1. Bild *n*, Gemälde *n*; *et*. Bildschönes; ~*s pl*. F Kino *n*; *attr*. Bilder...; *put s.o. in the* ~ j-n ins Bild setzen, j. informieren; 2. (aus-)malen; sich *et*. ausmalen; 2. (aus-)**postcard** Ansichtskarte *f*; ~**sque** [piktʃəˈresk] malerisch.

pie [pai] Pastete *f*; Obsttorte *f*.

piebald [ˈpaibɔ:ld] (bunt)scheckig.

piece [pi:s] 1. Stück *n*; Geschütz *n*; Gewehr *n*; Teil *n* e-*s Services*; *Schach- etc.* Figur *f*; *a* ~ *of advice* ein Rat; *a* ~ *of news* e-e Neuigkeit; *of a* ~ gleichmäßig; *give s.o. a* ~ *of one's mind* j-m gründlich die Meinung sagen; *take to* ~*s* zerlegen; 2. *a.* ~ *up* flicken, ausbessern; ~ *together* zs.-stellen, -setzen, -stücken, -flicken; ~ *out* ausfüllen; ~**meal** [ˈpi:smi:l] stückweise; ~**work** Akkordarbeit *f*.

pieplant *Am.* [ˈpaiplɑ:nt] Rhabarber *m*.

pier [piə] Pfeiler *m*; Wellenbrecher *m*; Pier *m*, *f*, Hafendamm *m*, Mole *f*, Landungsbrücke *f*.

pierce [piəs] durchbohren; durchdringen; eindringen (in *acc*.).

piety [ˈpaiəti] Frömmigkeit *f*; Pietät *f*.

pig [pig] Ferkel *n*; Schwein *n*.

pigeon [ˈpidʒin] Taube *f*; ~**hole** 1. Fach *n*; 2. in ein Fach legen.

pig|headed [ˈpigˈhedid] dickköpfig; ~**iron** [ˈpigaiən] Roheisen *n*; ~**skin** Schweinsleder *n*; ~**sty** Schweinestall *m*; ~**tail** (Haar)Zopf *m*.

pike [paik] ✕ Pike *f*; Spitze *f*; *ichth*. Hecht *m*; Schlagbaum *m*; gebührenpflichtige Straße.

pile [pail] 1. (Scheiter)Haufen *m*; Stoß *m* (*Holz*); großes Gebäude; ⚡ Batterie *f*; Pfahl *m*; Haar *n*;

Noppe *f*; ~s *pl.* ♣ Hämorrhoiden *f*/*pl.*; (*atomic*) ~ *phys.* Atommeiler *m*, Reaktor *m*; 2. *oft* ~ *up*, ~ *on* auf-, anhäufen; aufschichten.

pilfer ['pilfə] mausen, stibitzen.

pilgrim ['pilgrim] Pilger *m*; ~age [~midʒ] Pilgerfahrt *f*.

pill [pil] Pille *f*.

pillage ['pilidʒ] 1. Plünderung *f*; 2. plündern.

pillar ['pilə] Pfeiler *m*, Ständer *m*; Säule *f*; ~box Briefkasten *m*.

pillion *mot.* ['piljən] Soziussitz *m*.

pillory ['piləri] 1. Pranger *m*; 2. an den Pranger stellen; anprangern.

pillow ['pilou] (Kopf)Kissen *n*; ~case, ~slip (Kissen)Bezug *m*, ~case *m*.

pilot ['pailət] 1. ✈ Pilot *m*; ♣ Lotse *m*; *fig.* Führer *m*; 2. lotsen, steuern; ~balloon Versuchsballon *m*.

pimp [pimp] 1. Kuppler(in); 2. kuppeln.

pin [pin] 1. (Steck-, Krawatten-, Hut- *etc.*)Nadel *f*; Reißnagel *m*; Pflock *m*; ♪ Wirbel *m*; Kegel *m*; 2. (an)heften; befestigen; *fig.* festnageln.

pinafore ['pinəfɔ:] Schürze *f*.

pincers ['pinsəz] *pl.* Kneifzange *f*.

pinch [pintʃ] 1. Kniff *m*; Prise *f* (*Tabak etc.*); Druck *m*, Not *f*; 2. *v/t.* kneifen, zwicken; F klauen; *v/i.* drücken; in Not sein; knausern.

pinch-hit *Am.* ['pintʃhit] einspringen (*for* für).

pincushion ['pinkuʃin] Nadelkissen *n*.

pine [pain] 1. ♀ Kiefer *f*, Föhre *f*; 2. sich abhärmen; sich sehnen, schmachten; ~apple ♀ ['painæpl] Ananas *f*; ~cone Kiefernzapfen *m*.

pinion ['pinjən] 1. Flügel(spitze *f*) *m*; Schwungfeder *f*; ⊕ Ritzel *n* (*Antriebsrad*); 2. die Flügel beschneiden (*dat.*); *fig.* fesseln.

pink [piŋk] 1. ♀ Nelke *f*; Rosa *n*; *fig.* Gipfel *m*; 2. rosa(farben).

pin-money ['pinmʌni] Nadelgeld *n*.

pinnacle ['pinəkl] △ Zinne *f*, Spitztürmchen *n*; (Berg)Spitze *f*; *fig.* Gipfel *m*.

pint [paint] Pinte *f* (*0,57 od. Am. 0,47 Liter*).

pioneer [paiə'niə] 1. Pionier *m* (*a.* ✕); 2. den Weg bahnen (für).

pious □ ['paiəs] fromm, religiös; pflichtgetreu.

pip [pip] *vet.* Pips *m*; *sl.* miese Laune; Obstkern *m*; Auge *n* auf Würfeln *etc.*; ✕ Stern *m* (*Rangabzeichen*).

pipe [paip] 1. Rohr *n*, Röhre *f*; Pfeife *f* (*a. ♪*); Flöte *f*; Lied *n es Vogels*; Luftröhre *f*; Pipe *f* (*Weinfaß = 477,3 Liter*); 2. pfeifen; quieken; ~layer ['paipleiə] Rohrleger *m*; *Am. pol.* Drahtzieher *m*;

~line Ölleitung *f*, Pipeline *f*; ~r ['paipə] Pfeifer *m*.

piping ['paipiŋ] 1. pfeifend; schrill (*Stimme*); ~ hot siedend heiß; 2. Rohrnetz *n*; *Schneiderei:* Paspel *f*.

piquant □ ['pi:kənt] pikant.

pique [pi:k] 1. Groll *m*; 2. *j-n* reizen; ~ *o.s. on* sich brüsten mit.

pira|cy ['paiərəsi] Seeräuberei *f*; Raubdruck *m von Büchern*; ~te [~rit] 1. Seeräuber(schiff *n*) *m*; Raubdrucker *m*; 2. unerlaubt nachdrucken.

pistol ['pistl] Pistole *f*.

piston ⊕ ['pistən] Kolben *m*; ~rod Kolbenstange *f*; ~stroke Kolbenhub *m*.

pit [pit] 1. Grube *f* (*a.* ✕*, anat.*); ✗ Miete *f*; *thea.* Parterre *n*; Pockennarbe *f*; (Tier)Falle *f*; *Am. Börse:* Maklerstand *m*; *Am. Obst-*Stein *m*; 2. ✗ einmieten; mit Narben bedecken.

pitch [pitʃ] 1. Pech *n*; Stand(platz) *m*; Tonhöhe *f*; Grad *m*, Stufe *f*; Steigung *f*, Neigung *f*; Wurf *m*; ♣ Stampfen *n*; 2. *v/t.* werfen; schleudern; Zelt *etc.* aufschlagen; ♪ stimmen (*a. fig.*); ~ *too high fig.* Ziel *etc.* zu hoch stecken; *v/i.* ✕ (sich) lagern; fallen; ♣ stampfen; ~ *into* F herfallen über (*acc.*).

pitcher ['pitʃə] Krug *m*.

pitchfork ['pitʃfɔ:k] Heu-, Mistgabel *f*; ♪ Stimmgabel *f*.

piteous □ ['pitiəs] kläglich.

pitfall ['pitfɔ:l] Fallgrube *f*, Falle *f*.

pith [piθ] Mark *n*; *fig.* Kern *m*; Kraft *f*; ~y □ ['piθi] markig, kernig.

pitiable □ ['pitiəbl] erbärmlich.

pitiful □ ['pitiful] mitleidig; erbärmlich, jämmerlich (*a. contp.*).

pitiless □ ['pitilis] unbarmherzig.

pittance ['pitəns] Hungerlohn *m*.

pity ['piti] 1. Mitleid *n* (*on* mit); *it is a* ~ es ist schade; 2. bemitleiden.

pivot ['pivət] 1. ⊕ Zapfen *m*; (Tür-) Angel *f*; *fig.* Drehpunkt *m*; 2. sich drehen (*on, upon* um). [verrückt.╲

pixilated *Am.* F ['piksileitid] leicht╱

placable □ ['plækəbl] versöhnlich.

placard ['plæka:d] 1. Plakat *n*; 2. anschlagen; mit e-m Plakat bekleben.

place [pleis] 1. Platz *m*; Ort *m*; Stadt *f*; Stelle *f*; Stätte *f*; Stellung *f*; Aufgabe *f*; Anwesen *n*, Haus *n*, Wohnung *f*; ~ *of delivery* ✝ Erfüllungsort *m*; *give* ~ *to j-m* Platz machen; *in* ~ *of* an Stelle (*gen.*); *out of* ~ fehl am Platz; 2. stellen, legen, setzen; *j-n* anstellen; *Auftrag* erteilen; *I can't place him fig.* ich weiß nicht, wo ich ihn hintun soll (*identifizieren*).

placid □ ['plæsid] sanft; ruhig.

plagiar|ism ['pleidʒjərizəm] Plagiat *n*; ~ize [~raiz] abschreiben.

plague [pleig] **1.** Plage *f*; Seuche *f*; Pest *f*; **2.** plagen, quälen.

plaice *ichth.* [pleis] Scholle *f*.

plaid [plæd] *schottisches* Plaid.

plain [plein] **1.** □ flach, eben; klar; deutlich; rein; einfach, schlicht; unscheinbar; offen, ehrlich; einfarbig; **2.** *adv.* klar, deutlich; **3.** Ebene *f*, Fläche *f*; *bsd. Am.* Prärie *f*; ~**-clothes man** ['plein-klouðz mən] Geheimpolizist *m*; ~ **dealing** ehrliche Handlungsweise; ~**dealing** ehrlich.

plainsman ['pleinzmən] Flachlandbewohner *m*; *Am.* Präriebewohner *m*.

plaint|iff ꜰꜱ ['pleintif] Kläger(in); ~**ive** □ [~iv] traurig, klagend.

plait [plæt, *Am.* pleit] **1.** Haar- *etc.* Flechte *f*; Zopf *m*; **2.** flechten.

plan [plæn] **1.** Plan *m*; **2.** e-n Plan machen von *od.* zu; *fig.* planen.

plane [plein] **1.** flach, eben; **2.** Ebene *f*, Fläche *f*; ⚔ Tragfläche *f*; Flugzeug *n*; *fig.* Stufe *f*; ⊕ Hobel *m*; **3.** ebnen; (ab)hobeln; ⚔ fliegen.

plank [plæŋk] **1.** Planke *f*, Bohle *f*, Diele *f*; *Am. pol.* Programmpunkt *m*; **2.** dielen; verschalen; ~ **down** *sl.*, *Am.* F Geld auf den Tisch legen.

plant [plɑːnt] **1.** Pflanze *f*; ⊕ Anlage *f*; Fabrik *f*; **2.** (an-, ein)pflanzen (*a. fig.*); (auf)stellen; anlegen; *Schlag* verpassen; bepflanzen; besiedeln; ~**ation** [plæn'teiʃən] Pflanzung *f* (*a. fig.*); Plantage *f*; Besiedelung *f*; ~**er** ['plɑːntə] Pflanzer *m*.

plaque [plɑːk] Platte *f*; Gedenktafel *f*.

plash [plæʃ] platschen.

plaster ['plɑːstə] **1.** *pharm.* Pflaster *n*; ⊕ Putz *m*; *mst* ~ of Paris Gips *m*, Stuck *m*; **2.** bepflastern; verputzen.

plastic ['plæstik] **1.** (~ally) plastisch; Plastik...; **2.** *oft* ~s *pl.* Plastik(material) *n*, Kunststoff *m*.

plat [plæt] *s.* plait; *s.* plot **1.**

plate [pleit] **1.** *allg.* Platte *f*; *Bild*-Tafel *f*; Schild *n*; *Kupfer*-Stich *m*; Tafelsilber *n*; Teller *m*; *Am. Baseball*: (Schlag)Mal *n*; ⊕ Grobblech *n*; **2.** plattieren; ✂, ⚓ panzern.

platform ['plætfɔːm] Plattform *f*; *geogr.* Hochebene *f*; ⛟ Bahnsteig *m*; *Am. bsd.* Plattform *f am Wagen-ende*; Rednerbühne *f*; *pol.* Parteiprogramm *n*; *bsd. Am. pol.* Aktionsprogramm *n im Wahlkampf*.

platinum *min.* ['plætinəm] Platin *n*.

platitude *fig.* ['plætitjuːd] Plattheit *f*.

platoon ✗ [plə'tuːn] Zug *m*.

plat(t)en ['plætən] (Schreibmaschinen)Walze *f*.

platter ['plætə] (Servier)Platte *f*.

plaudit ['plɔːdit] Beifall *m*.

plausible □ ['plɔːzəbl] glaubhaft.

play [plei] **1.** Spiel *n*; Schauspiel *n*; ⊕ Spiel *n*, Gang *m*; Spielraum *m*; **2.** spielen; ⊕ laufen; ~ upon einwirken auf (*acc.*); ~ off *fig.* ausspielen (*against* gegen); ~**ed out** erledigt; ~**bill** ['pleibil] Theaterzettel *m*; ~**book** *thea.* Textbuch *n*; ~**boy** Playboy *m*; ~**er** [pleiə] (Schau)Spieler(in); ~**piano** elektrisches Klavier; ~**fellow** Spielgefährt|e *m*, -in *f*; ~**ful** □ [~ful] spielerisch; scherzhaft; ~**goer** ['pleigouə] Theaterbesucher(in); ~**ground** Spielplatz *m*; Schulhof *m*; ~**house** Schauspielhaus *n*; *Am.* Miniaturhaus *n für Kinder*; ~**mate** *s.* playfellow; ~**thing** Spielzeug *n*; ~**wright** Bühnenautor *m*, Dramatiker *m*.

plea [pliː] ꜰꜱ Einspruch *m*; Ausrede *f*; Gesuch *n*; on the ~ of *od.* that unter dem Vorwand (*gen.*) *od.* daß.

plead [pliːd] *v/i.* plädieren; ~ for für *j-n* sprechen; sich einsetzen für; ~ guilty sich schuldig bekennen; *v/t.* Sache vertreten; als Beweis anführen; ~**er** *f*ꜱ ['pliːdə] Vertreidiger *m*; ~**ing** ꜰꜱ [~diŋ] Schriftsatz *m*.

pleasant □ ['pleznt] angenehm; erfreulich; ~**ry** [~tri] Scherz *m*, Spaß *m*.

please [pliːz] *v/i.* gefallen; belieben; if you ~ *iro.* stellen Sie sich vor; ~ come in! bitte, treten Sie ein!; *v/t.* *j-m* gefallen, angenehm sein; befriedigen; ~ yourself tun Sie, was Ihnen gefällt; be ~d to *od.* et. gerne tun; be ~d with Vergnügen haben an (*dat.*); ~d erfreut; zufrieden.

pleasing □ ['pliːziŋ] angenehm.

pleasure ['pleʒə] Vergnügen *n*, Freude *f*; Belieben *n*; *attr.* Vergnügungs...; at ~ nach Belieben; ~**-ground** (Vergnügungs)Park *m*.

pleat [pliːt] **1.** (Plissee)Falte *f*; **2.** fälteln, plissieren.

pledge [pledʒ] **1.** Pfand *n*; Zutrinken *n*; Gelöbnis *n*; **2.** verpfänden; *j-m* zutrinken; he ~d himself er gelobte.

plenary ['pliːnəri] Voll...

plenipotentiary [plenipə'tenʃəri] Bevollmächtigte(r *m*) *f* [reichlich.]

plenteous □ *poet.* ['plentjəs] voll,]

plentiful □ ['plentiful] reichlich.

plenty ['plenti] **1.** Fülle *f*, Überfluß *m*; ~ of reichlich; **2.** F reichlich.

pliable □ ['plaiəbl] biegsam; *fig.* geschmeidig, nachgiebig.

pliancy ['plaiənsi] Biegsamkeit *f*.

pliers ['plaiəz] *pl.* (a pair of ~ pl. eine) (Draht-, Kombi)Zange.

plight [plait] **1.** Ehre, Wort verpfänden; verloben; **2.** Gelöbnis *n*; Zustand *m*, (Not)Lage *f*.

plod [plɔd] *a.* ~ along, ~ on sich dahinschleppen; sich plagen, schuften.

plot [plɔt] 1. Platz *m*; Parzelle *f*; Plan *m*; Komplott *n*, Anschlag *m*; Intrige *f*; Handlung *f e-s Dramas etc.*; 2. *v/t.* aufzeichnen; planen, anzetteln; *v/i.* intrigieren.

plough, *Am. mst.* **plow** [plau] 1. Pflug *m*; 2. pflügen; (*a. fig.*) furchen; **~man** ['plaumən] Pflüger *m*; **~share** ['plauʃɛə] Pflugschar *f*.

pluck [plʌk] 1. Mut *m*, Schneid *m*, *f*; Innereien *f/pl.*; Zug *m*, Ruck *m*; 2. pflücken; *Vogel* rupfen (*a. fig.*); reißen; **~** *at* zerren an; **~** *up courage* Mut fassen; **~y** F □ ['plʌki] mutig.

plug [plʌg] 1. Pflock *m*; Dübel *m*; Stöpsel *m*; ⚡ Stecker *m*; Zahn-Plombe *f*; Priem *m* (*Tabak*); *Am. Radio:* Reklamehinweis *m*; alter Gaul; **~** *socket* Steckdose *f*; 2. *v/t.* zu-, verstopfen; *Zahn* plombieren; stöpseln; *Am.* F *im Rundfunk etc.* Reklame machen für *et.*

plum [plʌm] Pflaume *f*; Rosine *f* (*a. fig.*).

plumage ['plu:midʒ] Gefieder *n*.

plumb [plʌm] 1. lotrecht; gerade; richtig; 2. (Blei)Lot *m*; 3. *v/t.* lotrecht machen; loten; sondieren (*a. fig.*); F *Wasser- od.* Gasleitungen legen in; *v/i.* F als Rohrleger arbeiten; **~er** ['plʌmə] Klempner *m*, Installateur *m*; **~ing** [‿miŋ] Klempnerarbeit *f*; Rohrleitungen *f/pl.*

plume [plu:m] 1. Feder *f*; Federbusch *m*; 2. *mit Federn* schmücken; *die Federn* putzen; **~** *o.s.* on sich brüsten mit.

plummet ['plʌmit] Senkblei *n*.

plump [plʌmp] 1. *adj.* drall, prall, mollig; F □ glatt (*Absage etc.*); 2. (hin)plumpsen (lassen); 3. Plumps *m*; 4. F *adv.* geradeswegs.

plum pudding ['plʌm'pudiŋ] Plumpudding *m*.

plunder ['plʌndə] 1. Plünderung *f*; Raub *m*, Beute *f*; 2. plündern.

plunge [plʌndʒ] 1. (Unter)Tauchen *n*; (Kopf)Sprung *m*; Sturz *m*; *make a ~ take* the **~** *den entscheidenden Schritt tun*; 2. (unter-)tauchen; (sich) stürzen (*into in acc.*); *Schwert etc.* stoßen; ⚓ stampfen.

plunk [plʌŋk] *v/t. Saite* zupfen; *et.* hinplumpsen lassen, hinwerfen; *v/i.* (hin)plumpsen, fallen.

pluperfect *gr.* ['plu:'pə:fikt] Plusquamperfekt *n*.

plural *gr.* ['pluərəl] Plural *m*, Mehrzahl *f*; **~ity** ['pluə'ræliti] Vielheit *f*, Mehrheit *f*; Mehrzahl *f*.

plus [plʌs] 1. *prp.* plus; 2. *adj.* positiv; 3. Plus *n*; Mehr *n*.

plush [plʌʃ] Plüsch *m*.

ply [plai] 1. Lage *f Tuch etc.*; Strähne *f*; *fig.* Neigung *f*; 2. *v/t.* fleißig anwenden; *j-m* zusetzen, *j-n* überhäufen; *v/i.* regelmäßig fahren; **~wood** ['plaiwud] Sperrholz *n*.

pneumatic [nju(:)'mætik] 1. (‿ally) Luft...; pneumatisch; 2. Luftreifen *m*.

pneumonia ✠ [nju(:)'mounjə] Lungenentzündung *f*.

poach [poutʃ] wildern; *Erde* zertreten; **~ed** *eggs pl.* verlorene Eier *n/pl.*

poacher ['poutʃə] Wilddieb *m*.

pock ✠ [pɔk] Pocke *f*, Blatter *f*.

pocket ['pɔkit] 1. Tasche *f*; ✠ *Luft-*Loch *n*; 2. einstecken (*a. fig.*); *Am. pol. Gesetzesvorlage* nicht unterschreiben; *Gefühl* unterdrücken; 3. Taschen...; **~book** Notizbuch *n*; Brieftasche *f*; *Am.* Geldbeutel *m*; Taschenbuch *n*.

pod ♉ [pɔd] Hülse *f*, Schale *f*, Schote *f*.

poem ['pouim] Gedicht *n*.

poet ['pouit] Dichter *m*; **~ess** [‿tis] Dichterin *f*; **~ic(al** □) [pou'etik(əl)] dichterisch; *as* [‿ks] *sg.* Poetik *f*; **~ry** ['pouitri] Dichtkunst *f*; Dichtung *f*, *coll.* Dichtungen *f/pl.*

poignan|cy ['pɔinənsi] Schärfe *f*; **~t** [‿nt] scharf; *fig.* eindringlich.

point [pɔint] 1. Spitze *f*; Pointe *f*; Landspitze *f*; ⭐, *phys. etc.* Punkt *m*; Fleck *m*, Stelle *f*; ⚓ Kompaßstrich *m*; Auge *n auf Karten etc.*; Grad *m*; (springender) Punkt; Zweck *m*; *fig.* Eigenschaft *f*; **~s** *pl.* ⚙ Weichen *f/pl.*; **~** *of view* Stand-, Gesichtspunkt *m*; *the* **~** *is that* ... die Sache ist die, daß ...; *make a* **~** *of s.th.* auf et. bestehen; *in* **~** *of* in Hinsicht auf (*acc.*); *off od. beside the* **~** nicht zur Sache (gehörig); *on the* **~** *of ger.* im Begriff zu *inf.*; *win on* **~s** nach Punkten siegen; *to the* **~** zur Sache (gehörig); 2. *v/t.* (zu)spitzen; *oft* **~** *out* zeigen, hinweisen auf (*acc.*); punktieren; *at Waffe etc.* richten auf (*acc.*); *v/i.* **~** *at* weisen auf (*acc.*); **~** *to* nach *e-r Richtung* weisen; **~ed** □ ['pointid] spitz(ig), Spitz...; *fig.* scharf; **~er** [‿tə] Zeiger *m*; Zeigestock *m*; Hühnerhund *m*; **~less** [‿tlis] stumpf; witzlos; zwecklos.

poise [pɔiz] 1. Gleichgewicht *n*; Haltung *f*; 2. *v/t.* im Gleichgewicht erhalten; *Kopf etc.* tragen, halten; *v/i.* schweben.

poison ['pɔizn] 1. Gift *n*; 2. vergiften; **~ous** □ [‿nəs] giftig (*a. fig.*).

poke [pouk] 1. Stoß *m*, Puff *m*; 2. *v/t.* stoßen; schüren; *Nase etc. in et.* stecken; **~** *fun at* sich über *j-n* lustig machen; *v/i.* stoßen; stochern.

poker ['poukə] Feuerhaken *m*.

poky ['pouki] eng; schäbig; erbärmlich; [*m.*\]

polar ['poulə] polar; **~** *bear* Eisbär

Pole¹ [poul] Pole *m*, Polin *f*.

pole² [‿] Pol *m*; Stange *f*, Mast *m*; Deichsel *f*; (Sprung)Stab *m*.

polecat zo. ['poulkæt] Iltis m; Am. Skunk m.
polemic [po'lemik], a. **~al** □ [~kəl] polemisch; feindselig.
pole-star ['poulsta:] Polarstern m; fig. Leitstern m.
police [po'li:s] 1. Polizei f; 2. überwachen; **~man** Polizist m; **~-office** Polizeipräsidium n; **~-officer** Polizeibeamte(r) m, Polizist m; **~-station** Polizeiwache f.
policy ['polisi] Politik f; (Welt-) Klugheit f; Police f; Am. Zahlenlotto n.
polio(myelitis) ☞ ['pouliou(maiə'laitis)] spinale Kinderlähmung.
Polish¹ ['poulif] polnisch.
polish² ['polif] 1. Politur f; fig. Schliff m; 2. polieren; fig. verfeinern.
polite □ [po'lait] artig, höflich; fein; **~ness** [~tnis] Höflichkeit f.
politic □ ['politik] politisch; schlau; **~al** [po'litikəl] politisch; staatlich; Staats..; **~ian** [poli'tifən] Politiker m; **~s** ['politiks] oft sg. Staatswissenschaft f, Politik f.
polka ['polkə] Polka f; **~ dot** Am. Punktmuster n auf Stoff.
poll [poul] 1. Wählerliste f; Stimmenzählung f; Wahl f; Stimmenzahl f; Umfrage f; co. Kopf m; 2. v/t. Stimmen erhalten; v/i. wählen; **~-book** ['poulbuk] Wählerliste f.
pollen ☞ ['polin] Blütenstaub m.
polling-district ['poulindistrikt] Wahlbezirk m.
poll-tax ['poultæks] Kopfsteuer f.
pollute [po'lu:t] beschmutzen, beflecken; entweihen.
polyp(e) zo. ['polip], **~us** ☞ [~pəs] Polyp m.
pommel ['pʌml] 1. Degen-, Sattel-Knopf m; 2. knuffen, schlagen.
pomp [pomp] Pomp m, Gepränge n.
pompous □ ['pompəs] prunkvoll; hochtrabend; pompös.
pond [pond] Teich m, Weiher m.
ponder ['pondə] v/t. erwägen; v/i. nachdenken; **~able** [~ərəbl] wägbar; **~ous** □ [~rəs] schwer(fällig).
pontiff ['pontif] Hohepriester m; Papst m.
pontoon ✗ [pon'tu:n] Ponton m; **~-bridge** Schiffsbrücke f.
pony ['pouni] Pony n, Pferdchen n.
poodle ['pu:dl] Pudel m.
pool [pu:l] 1. Teich m; Pfütze f, Lache f; (Schwimm)Becken n; (Spiel)Einsatz m; ✝ Ring m, Kartell n; **~ room** Am. Billardspielhalle f; Wettannahmestelle f; 2. ✝ zu e-m Ring vereinigen; Gelder zs.-werfen.
poop ⚓ [pu:p] Heck n; Achterhütte f.
poor □ [puə] arm(selig); dürftig; schlecht; **~-house** ['puəhaus] Armenhaus n; **~-law** ⚖ Armenrecht

n; **~ly** [~li] 1. adj. unpäßlich; 2. adv. dürftig; **~ness** ['puənis] Armut f.
pop¹ [pop] 1. Knall m; F Sprudel m; F Schampus m; 2. v/t. knallen lassen; Am. Mais rösten; schnell wohin tun, stecken; v/i. puffen, knallen; mit adv. huschen; **~ in** hereinplatzen.
pop² F [~] 1. populär, beliebt; 2. Schlager m; volkstümliche Musik.
pop³ Am. F [~] Papa m, alter Herr.
popcorn Am. ['popko:n] Puffmais m.
pope [poup] Papst m.
poplar ☞ ['poplə] Pappel f.
poppy ☞ ['popi] Mohn m; **~cock** Am. F Quatsch m.
popu|lace ['popjuləs] Pöbel m; **~lar** □ [~lə] Volks..; volkstümlich; populär; **~larity** [popju'læriti] Popularität f.
populat|e ['popjuleit] bevölkern; **~ion** [popju'leifən] Bevölkerung f.
populous □ ['popjuləs] volkreich.
porcelain ['po:slin] Porzellan n.
porch [po:tf] Vorhalle f, Portal n; Am. Veranda f.
porcupine zo. ['po:kjupain] Stachelschwein n.
pore [po:] 1. Pore f; 2. fig. brüten.
pork [po:k] Schweinefleisch n; **~ barrel** Am. sl. ['po:kbærəl] politisch berechnete Geldzuwendung der Regierung; **~y** F ['po:ki] 1. fett, dick; 2. Am. = porcupine.
porous □ ['po:rəs] porös.
porpoise ichth. ['po:pəs] Tümmler m.
porridge ['poridʒ] Haferbrei m.
port [po:t] 1. Hafen m; ⚓ (Pfort-, Lade)Luke f; ⚓ Backbord n; Portwein m; 2. ⚓ das Ruder nach der Backbordseite umlegen.
portable ['po:təbl] transportabel.
portal ['po:tl] Portal n, Tor n.
portend [po:'tend] vorbedeuten.
portent ['po:tent] (bsd. üble) Vorbedeutung; Wunder n; **~ous** □ [po:'tentəs] unheilvoll; wunderbar.
porter ['po:tə] Pförtner m; (Gepäck)Träger m; Porterbier n.
portion ['po:fən] 1. (An)Teil m; Portion f Essen; Erbteil n; Aussteuer f; fig. Los n; 2. teilen; ausstatten.
portly ['po:tli] stattlich.
portmanteau [po:t'mæntou] Handkoffer m. [nis n.]
portrait ['po:trit] Porträt n, Bild-]
portray [po:'trei] (ab)malen, porträtieren; schildern; **~al** [~eiəl] Porträtieren n; Schilderung f.
pose [pouz] 1. Pose f; 2. (sich) in Positur setzen; F sich hinstellen (as als); Frage aufwerfen.
posh sl. [pof] schick, erstklassig.
position [po'zifən] Lage f, Stellung f (a. fig.); Stand m; fig. Standpunkt m.

positive ['pɔzətiv] **1.** □ bestimmt, ausdrücklich; feststehend, sicher; unbedingt; positiv; überzeugt; rechthaberisch; **2.** *das* Bestimmte; *gr.* Positiv *m*; *phot.* Positiv *n*.

possess [pə'zes] besitzen; beherrschen; *fig.* erfüllen; ~ *o.s. of et.* in Besitz nehmen; ~ed besessen; ~ion [~eʃən] Besitz *m*; *fig.* Besessenheit *f*; ~ive *gr.* [~esiv] **1.** □ besitzanzeigend; ~ *case* Genitiv *m*; **2.** Possessivpronomen *n*, besitzanzeigendes Fürwort; Genitiv *m*; ~or [~sə] Besitzer *m*.

possib|ility [pɔsə'biliti] Möglichkeit *f*; ~le ['pɔsəbl] möglich; ~ly [~li] möglicherweise, vielleicht; *if I* ~ *can* wenn ich irgend kann.

post [poust] **1.** Pfosten *m*; Posten *m*; Stelle *f*, Amt *n*; Post *f*; ~ *exchange Am.* ✕ Einkaufsstelle *f*; **2.** *v/t.* Plakat *etc.* anschlagen; postieren; eintragen; zur Post geben; per Post senden; ~ *up j-n* informieren; *v/i.* (dahin)eilen.

postage ['poustidʒ] Porto *n*; ~ **stamp** Briefmarke *f*.

postal □ ['poustəl] **1.** postalisch; Post...; ~ *order* Postanweisung *f*; **2.** *a.* ~ **card** *Am.* Postkarte *f*.

postcard ['poustka:d] Postkarte *f*.

poster ['poustə] Plakat *n*, Anschlag *m*.

posterior [pɔs'tiəriə] **1.** □ später (*to als*); hinter; **2.** Hinterteil *n*.

posterity [pɔs'teriti] Nachwelt *f*; Nachkommenschaft *f*.

post-free ['poust'fri:] portofrei.

post-graduate ['poust'grædjuit] **1.** nach beendigter Studienzeit; **2.** Doktorand *m*.

post-haste ['poust'heist] eilig(st).

posthumous □ ['pɔstjuməs] nachgeboren; hinterlassen.

post|man ['poustmən] Briefträger *m*; ~**mark 1.** Poststempel *m*; **2.** abstempeln; ~**master** Postamtsvorsteher *m*.

post-mortem ['poust'mɔːtem] **1.** nach dem Tode; **2.** Leichenschau *f*.

post|(-)office ['poustɔfis] Postamt *n*; ~ *box* Post(schließ)fach *n*; ~ *paid* frankiert.

postpone [poust'poun] ver-, aufschieben; ~**ment** [~nmənt] Aufschub *m*. [tum *n*.]

postscript ['pousskript] Postskrip-/

postulate 1. ['pɔstjulit] Forderung *f*; **2.** [~leit] fordern; (als gegeben) voraussetzen.

posture ['pɔstʃə] **1.** Stellung *f*, Haltung *f des Körpers*; **2.** (sich) zurechtstellen; posieren.

post-war ['poust'wɔː] Nachkriegs...

posy ['pouzi] Blumenstrauß *m*.

pot [pɔt] **1.** Topf *m*; Kanne *f*; Tiegel *m*; **2.** in e-n Topf tun; einlegen.

potation [pou'teiʃən] *mst* ~*s pl.* Trinken *n*, Zecherei *f*; Trunk *m*.

potato [pə'teitou], *pl.* ~es Kartoffel *f*.

pot-belly ['pɔtbeli] Schmerbauch *m*.

poten|cy ['poutənsi] Macht *f*; Stärke *f*; ~t [~nt] mächtig; stark; ~tial [pə'tenʃəl] **1.** potentiell; möglich; **2.** Leistungsfähigkeit *f*.

pother ['pɔðə] Aufregung *f*.

pot|-herb ['pɔthɔːb] Küchenkraut *n*; ~-**house** Kneipe *f*.

potion ['pouʃən] (Arznei)Trank *m*.

potter[1] ['pɔtə]: ~ *about* herumwerkeln.

potter[2] [~] Töpfer *m*; ~y [~əri] Töpferei *f*; Töpferware(n *pl.*) *f*.

pouch [pautʃ] **1.** Tasche *f*; Beutel *m*; **2.** einstecken; (sich) beuteln.

poulterer ['poultərə] Geflügelhändler *m*.

poultice ✍ ['poultis] Packung *f*.

poultry ['poultri] Geflügel *n*.

pounce [pauns] **1.** Stoß *m*, Sprung *m*; **2.** sich stürzen (*on, upon auf acc.*).

pound [paund] **1.** Pfund *n*; ~ (*sterling*) Pfund *n* Sterling (*abbr.* £ = *20 shillings*); Pfandstall *m*; Tierasyl *n*; **2.** (zer)stoßen; stampfen; schlagen.

pounder ['paundə] ...pfünder *m*.

pour [pɔː] *v/t.* gießen, schütten; ~ *out Getränk* eingießen; *v/i.* sich ergießen, strömen; *it never rains but it* ~*s fig.* ein Unglück kommt selten allein.

pout [paut] **1.** Schmollen *n*; **2.** *v/t.* *Lippen* aufwerfen; *v/i.* schmollen.

poverty ['pɔvəti] Armut *f*.

powder ['paudə] **1.** Pulver *n*; Puder *m*; **2.** pulverisieren; (sich) pudern; bestreuen; ~-**box** Puderdose *f*.

power ['pauə] Kraft *f*; Macht *f*, Gewalt *f*; ✴ Vollmacht *f*; ♃ Potenz *f*; *in* ~ an der Macht, im Amt; ~-**current** Starkstrom *m*; ~**ful** □ ['pauəful] mächtig, kräftig; wirksam; ~**less** ['pauəlis] macht-, kraftlos; ~**plant** *s.* power-station; ~**station** Kraftwerk *n*.

politics *oft sg.* Machtpolitik *f*; ~-**station** Kraftwerk *n*.

powwow ['pauwau] Medizinmann *m*; *Am.* F Versammlung *f*.

practica|ble □ ['præktikəbl] ausführbar; gangbar (*Weg*); brauchbar; ~l [~l] praktisch; tatsächlich; eigentlich; sachlich; ~ *joke* Schabernack *m*; ~**lly** [~li] so gut wie.

practice ['præktis] **1.** Praxis *f*; Übung *f*; Gewohnheit *f*; Brauch *m*; Praktik *f*; *put into* ~ in die Praxis umsetzen; **2.** *Am.* = *practise*.

practise [~] *v/t.* in die Praxis umsetzen; ausüben; betreiben; üben; *v/i.* üben; praktizieren; ~ *upon j-s Schwäche* ausnutzen; ~**d** geübt (*P.*).

practitioner [præk'tiʃnə] a. general ~ praktischer Arzt; Rechtsanwalt m.

prairie Am. ['prɛəri] Grasebene f; Prärie f; ~-schooner Am. Planwagen m.

praise [preiz] 1. Preis m, Lob n; 2. loben, preisen.

praiseworthy □ ['preizwə:ði] lobenswert.

pram F [præm] Kinderwagen m.

prance [prɑːns] sich bäumen; paradieren; einherstolzieren.

prank [præŋk] Possen m, Streich m.

prate [preit] 1. Geschwätz n; 2. schwatzen, plappern.

prattle ['prætl] s. prate.

pray [prei] beten; (er)bitten; bitte!

prayer [prɛə] Gebet n; Bitte f; oft ~s pl. Andacht f; Lord's ♀ Vaterunser n; ~-book ['prɛəbuk] Gebetbuch n.

pre... [priː; pri] vor(her)...; Vor...; früher.

preach [priːtʃ] predigen; ~er ['priːtʃə] Prediger(in).

preamble [priː'æmbl] Einleitung f.

precarious □ [pri'kɛəriəs] unsicher.

precaution [pri'kɔːʃən] Vorsicht(smaßregel) f; ~ary [~ʃnəri] vorbeugend.

precede [priː'siːd] voraus-, vorangehen (dat.); ~nce, ~ncy [~dəns, ~si] Vortritt m, Vorrang m; ~nt ['presidənt] Präzedenzfall m.

precept ['priːsept] Vorschrift f, Regel f; ~or [pri'septə] Lehrer m.

precinct ['priːsiŋkt] Bezirk m, bsd. Am. Wahlbezirk m, -kreis m; ~s pl. Umgebung f; Bereich m; Grenze f; pedestrian ~ Fußgängerzone f.

precious ['preʃəs] 1. □ kostbar; edel; F arg, gewaltig, schön; 2. F adv. recht, äußerst.

precipi|ce ['presipis] Abgrund m; ~tate 1. [pri'sipiteit] (hinab)stürzen; ⚗ fällen; überstürzen; 2. □ [~tit] übereilt, hastig; 3. [~] ⚗ Niederschlag m; ~tation [prisipi-'teiʃən] Sturz m; Überstürzung f, Hast f; ⚗ Niederschlag(en n) m; ~tous □ [pri'sipitəs] steil, jäh.

précis ['preisiː] gedrängte Übersicht, Zs.-fassung f.

precis|e □ [pri'sais] genau; ~ion [~'siʒən] Genauigkeit f; Präzision f.

preclude [pri'kluːd] ausschließen; vorbeugen (dat.); j-n hindern.

precocious □ [pri'kouʃəs] frühreif; altklug.

preconceive ['priːkən'siːv] vorher ausdenken; ~d vorgefaßt (Meinung).

preconception ['priːkən'sepʃən] vorgefaßte Meinung. [m.]

precursor [priː(ː)'kəːsə] Vorläufer/

predatory ['predətəri] räuberisch.

predecessor ['priːdisesə] Vorgänger m.

predestin|ate [pri(ː)'destineit]

vorherbestimmen; ~ed [~nd] auserkoren.

predetermine ['priːdi'təːmin] vorher festsetzen; vorherbestimmen.

predicament [pri'dikəmənt] (mißliche) Lage.

predicate 1. ['predikeit] aussagen; 2. gr. [~kit] Prädikat n, Satzaussage f.

predict [pri'dikt] vorhersagen; ~ion [~kʃən] Prophezeiung f.

predilection [priːdi'lekʃən] Vorliebe f.

predispos|e ['priːdis'pouz] vorher geneigt od. empfänglich machen (to für); ~ition [~spə'ziʃən] Geneigtheit f; bsd. ⚕ Anfälligkeit f (to für).

predomina|nce [pri'dɔminəns] Vorherrschaft f; Übergewicht n; Vormacht(stellung) f; ~nt □ [~nt] vorherrschend; ~te [~neit] die Oberhand haben; vorherrschen.

pre-eminent □ [pri(ː)'eminənt] hervorragend.

pre-emption [pri(ː)'empʃən] Vorkauf(srecht n) m.

pre-exist [pri(ː)ig'zist] vorher dasein.

prefabricate ['priː'fæbrikeit] vorfabrizieren.

preface ['prefis] 1. Vorrede f, Vorwort n, Einleitung f; 2. einleiten.

prefect ['priːfekt] Präfekt m; Schule: Vertrauensschüler m, Klassensprecher m.

prefer [pri'fəː] vorziehen; Gesuch etc. vorbringen; Klage einreichen; befördern; ~able □ ['prefərəbl] (to) vorzuziehen(d) (dat.); vorzüglicher (als); ~ably [~li] vorzugsweise; besser; ~ence [~rəns] Vorliebe f; Vorzug m; ~ential □ [prefə'renʃəl] bevorzugt; Vorzugs-...; ~ment [pri'fəːmənt] Beförderung f.

prefix ['priːfiks] Präfix n, Vorsilbe f.

pregnan|cy ['pregnənsi] Schwangerschaft f; fig. Fruchtbarkeit f; Bedeutungsreichtum m; ~t □ [~nt] schwanger; fig. fruchtbar, inhaltsvoll.

prejud|ge ['priː'dʒʌdʒ] vorher (ver-)urteilen; ~ice ['predʒudis] 1. Voreingenommenheit f; Vorurteil n; Schaden m; 2. voreinnehmen; benachteiligen; e-r S. Abbruch tun; ~d (vor)eingenommen; ~icial □ [predʒu'diʃəl] nachteilig.

prelate ['prelit] Prälat m.

preliminary [pri'liminəri] 1. □ vorläufig; einleitend; Vor...; 2. Einleitung f.

prelude ♪ ['prelju:d] Vorspiel n.

premature □ ['premə'tjuə] fig. frühreif; vorzeitig; vorschnell.

premeditat|e [pri(ː)'mediteit] vorher überlegen; ~ion [pri(ː)medi-'teiʃən] Vorbedacht m.

premier ['premjə] 1. erst; 2. Premierminister m.

premises ['premisiz] pl. (Gebäude pl. mit) Grundstück n, Anwesen n; Lokal n.

premium ['pri:mjəm] Prämie f; Anzahlung f; ✝ Agio n; Versicherungsprämie f; Lehrgeld n; at a ~ über pari; sehr gesucht.

premonition [pri:mə'niʃən] Warnung f; (Vor)Ahnung f.

preoccup|ied [pri(:)'ɔkjupaid] in Gedanken verloren; ~y (~pai) vorher in Besitz nehmen; ausschließlich beschäftigen; in Anspruch nehmen.

prep F [prep] = preparation, preparatory school.

preparat|ion [prepə'reiʃən] Vorbereitung f; Zubereitung f; ~ory □ [pri'pærətəri] vorbereitend; ~ (school) Vorschule f.

prepare [pri'pɛə] v/t. vorbereiten; zurechtmachen; (zu)bereiten; (aus)rüsten; v/i. sich vorbereiten; sich anschicken; ~d □ bereit.

prepay ['pri:'pei] [irr. (pay)] vorausbezahlen; frankieren.

prepondera|nce [pri'pɔndərəns] Übergewicht n; ~nt □ [~nt] überwiegend; ~te [~reit] überwiegen.

preposition gr. [prepə'ziʃən] Präposition f, Verhältniswort n.

prepossess [pri:pə'zes] günstig stimmen; ~ing □ [~siŋ] einnehmend.

preposterous [pri'pɔstərəs] widersinnig, albern; grotesk.

prerequisite ['pri:'rekwizit] Vorbedingung f, Voraussetzung f.

prerogative [pri'rɔgətiv] Vorrecht n.

presage ['presidʒ] 1. Vorbedeutung f; Ahnung f; 2. vorbedeuten; ahnen; prophezeien.

prescribe [pris'kraib] vorschreiben; ✂ verschreiben.

prescription [pris'kripʃən] Vorschrift f, Verordnung f; ✂ Rezept n.

presence ['prezns] Gegenwart f; Anwesenheit f; Erscheinung f; ~ of mind Geistesgegenwart f.

present[1] ['preznt] 1. □ gegenwärtig; anwesend, vorhanden; jetzig; laufend (Jahr etc.); vorliegend (Fall etc.); ~ tense gr. Präsens n; 2. Gegenwart f, gr. a. Präsens n; Geschenk n; at ~ jetzt; for the ~ einstweilen.

present[2] [pri'zent] präsentieren; (dar)bieten; (vor)zeigen; j-n vorstellen; vorschlagen; (über)reichen; (be)schenken.

presentation [prezen'teiʃən] Darstellung f, Vorstellung f; Ein-, Überreichung f; Schenkung f; Vorzeigen n, Vorlage f.

presentiment [pri'zentimənt] Vorgefühl n, Ahnung f.

presently ['prezntli] sogleich, bald (darauf), alsbald; Am. zur Zeit.

preservati|on [prezə(:)'veiʃən] Bewahrung f, Erhaltung f; ~ve [pri-'zə:vətiv] 1. bewahrend; 2. Schutz-, Konservierungsmittel n.

preserve [pri'zə:v] 1. bewahren, behüten; erhalten; einmachen; Wild hegen; 2. hunt. Gehege n (a. fig.); mst ~s pl. Eingemachte(s) n. [ren (over bei).)

preside [pri'zaid] den Vorsitz füh-]

presiden|cy ['prezidənsi] Vorsitz m; Präsidentschaft f; ~t [~nt] Präsident m, Vorsitzende(r) m; Am. ✝ Direktor m.

press [pres] 1. Druck m der Hand; (Wein- etc.)Presse f; die Presse (Zeitungen); Druckerei f; Verlag m; Druck(en n) m; a. printing-~ Druckerpresse f; Menge f; fig. Druck m, Last f, Andrang m; Schrank m; 2. v/t. (aus)pressen; drücken; lasten auf (dat.); (be)drängen; dringen auf (acc.); aufdrängen (on dat.); bügeln; be ~ed for time es eilig haben; v/i. drücken; (sich) drängen; ~ for sich eifrig bemühen um; ~ on weitereilen; ~ (up)on eindringen auf (acc.); ~ agency Nachrichtenbüro n; ~ agent Reklameagent m; ~ button Druckknopf m; ~ing □ ['presiŋ] dringend; ~ure ['preʃə] Druck m (a. fig.); Drang(sal f) m.

prestige [pres'ti:ʒ] Prestige n.

presum|able □ [pri'zju:məbl] vermutlich; ~e [pri'zju:m] v/t. annehmen; vermuten; voraussetzen; v/i. vermuten; sich erdreisten; anmaßend sein; ~ (up)on pochen auf (acc.); ausnutzen, mißbrauchen.

presumpt|ion [pri'zʌmpʃən] Mutmaßung f; Wahrscheinlichkeit f; Anmaßung f; ~ive □ [~ptiv] mutmaßlich; ~uous □ [~tjuəs] überheblich; vermessen.

presuppos|e [pri:sə'pouz] voraussetzen; ~ition [pri:sʌpə'ziʃən] Voraussetzung f.

preten|ce, Am. ~se [pri'tens] Vortäuschung f; Vorwand m; Schein m, Verstellung f.

pretend [pri'tend] vorgeben; vortäuschen; heucheln; Anspruch erheben (to auf acc.); ~ed □ angeblich.

pretension [pri'tenʃən] Anspruch m (to auf acc.); Anmaßung f.

preterit(e) gr. [pri'terit] Präteritum n, Vergangenheitsform f.

pretext ['pri:tekst] Vorwand m.

pretty ['priti] 1. □ hübsch, niedlich; nett; 2. adv. ziemlich.

prevail [pri'veil] die Oberhand haben od. gewinnen; (vor)herrschen; maßgebend sein; ausschlaggebend sein; ~ (up)on s.o. j-n dazu bewegen, et. zu tun; ~ing □ [~liŋ] (vor)herrschend.

prevalent □ ['prevələnt] vorherr-schend, weit verbreitet.

prevaricate [pri'værikeit] Aus-flüchte machen.

prevent [pri'vent] verhüten, *e-r S.* vorbeugen; *j-n* hindern; **~ion** [**~**n-Jən] Verhinderung *f*; Verhütung *f*; **~ive** [**~**ntiv] **1.** □ vorbeugend; **2.** Schutzmittel *n*.

preview [pri:'vju:] Vorschau *f*; Vorbesichtigung *f*.

previous □ ['pri:vjəs] vorherge-hend; vorläufig; Vor...; **~** *to* vor (*dat.*); **~ly** [**~**sli] vorher, früher.

pre-war ['pri:'wɔ:] Vorkriegs...

prey [prei] **1.** Raub *m*, Beute *f*; *beast of* **~** Raubtier *n*; *bird of* **~** Raub-vogel *m*; *be a* **~** *to* geplagt werden von; **2.** **~** (*up*)*on* rauben, plündern; fressen; *fig.* nagen an (*dat.*).

price [prais] **1.** Preis *m*; Lohn *m*; **2.** *Waren* auszeichnen; *die Preise* festsetzen für; (ab)schätzen; **~less** ['praislis] unschätzbar; unbezahl-bar.

prick [prik] **1.** Stich *m*; Stachel *m* (*a. fig.*); **2.** *v/t.* (durch)stechen; *fig.* peinigen; *a.* **~** *out Muster* punktie-ren; **~** *up one's ears* die Ohren spitzen; *v/i.* stechen; **~le** ['prikl] Stachel *m*, Dorn *m*; **~ly** [**~**li] stache-lig.

pride [praid] **1.** Stolz *m*; Hochmut *m*; *take* **~** *in* stolz sein auf (*acc.*); **2.** **~** *o.s.* sich brüsten (*on, upon* mit).

priest [pri:st] Priester *m*.

prig [prig] Tugendbold *m*, selbst-gerechter Mensch; Pedant *m*.

prim □ [prim] steif; zimperlich.

prima|**cy** ['praiməsi] Vorrang *m*; **~rily** [**~**ərili] in erster Linie; **~ry** □ [**~**ri] **1.** ursprünglich; hauptsäch-lich; Ur..., Anfangs..., Haupt...; Elementar...; höchst; ♂, ♂ Pri-mär...; **2.** *a.* **~** *meeting Am.* Wahl-versammlung *f*; **~ry school** Ele-mentar-, Grundschule *f*.

prime [praim] **1.** □ erst; wichtigst; Haupt...; vorzüglich(st); **~** *cost* †Selbstkosten *pl.*; **~** *minister* Mini-sterpräsident *m*; **~** *number* Prim-zahl *f*; **2.** *fig.* Blüte(zeit) *f*; Beste(s) *n*; höchste Vollkommenheit; **3.** *v/t.* vorbereiten; *Pumpe* anlassen; in-struieren; F vollaufen lassen (*be-trunken machen*); *paint.* grundieren.

primer ['praimə] Fibel *f*, Elementar-tarbuch *n*. [lich; Ur...]

primeval [prai'mi:vəl] uranfäng-

primitive ['primitiv] **1.** □ erst, ur-sprünglich; Stamm...; primitiv; **2.** *gr.* Stammwort *n*.

primrose ♀ ['primrouz] Primel *f*.

prince [prins] Fürst *m*; Prinz *m*; **~ss** [prin'ses, *vor npr.* 'prinses] Fürstin *f*; Prinzessin *f*.

principal ['prinsəpəl] **1.** □ erst, hauptsächlich(st); Haupt...; **~** *parts pl. gr.* Stammformen *f/pl. des vb.*;

2. Hauptperson *f*; Vorsteher *m*; *bsd. Am.* (Schul)Direktor *m*, Rektor *m*; ✝ Chef *m*; ♊ Hauptschuldige(r) *m*; ✝ Kapital *n*; **~ity** [prinsi'pæliti] Fürstentum *n*.

principle ['prinsəpl] Prinzip *n*; Grund(satz) *m*; Ursprung *m*; *on* **~** grundsätzlich, aus Prinzip.

print [print] **1.** Druck *m*; (Finger-*etc.*)Abdruck *m*; bedruckter Kat-tun, Druckstoff *m*; Stich *m*; *phot.* Abzug *m*; *Am.* Zeitungsdrucksache *f*; *out of* **~** vergriffen; **2.** (ab-, auf-, be)drucken; *phot.* kopieren; *fig.* einprägen (*on dat.*); in Druckbuch-staben schreiben; **~er** ['printə] (Buch)Drucker *m*.

printing ['printiŋ] Druck *m*; Drucken *n*; *phot.* Abziehen *n*, Ko-pieren *n*; **~-ink** Druckerschwärze *f*; **~-office** (Buch)Druckerei *f*; **~-press** Druckerpresse *f*.

prior ['praiə] **1.** früher, älter (*to* als); **2.** *adv.* **~** *to* vor (*dat.*); **3.** *eccl.* Prior *m*; **~ity** [prai'ɔriti] Priorität *f*; Vorrang *m*; Vorfahrtsrecht *n*.

prism ['prizəm] Prisma *n*.

prison ['prizn] Gefängnis *n*; **~er** [**~**nə] Gefangene(r *m*) *f*, Häftling *m*; *take s.o.* **~** j-n gefangennehmen.

privacy ['praivəsi] Zurückgezogen-heit *f*; Geheimhaltung *f*.

private ['praivit] **1.** □ privat; Pri-vat...; persönlich; vertraulich; ge-heim; ✗ (gewöhnlicher) Soldat; *in* **~** privatim; im geheimen.

privation [prai'veiʃən] Mangel *m*, Entbehrung *f*.

privilege [privilidʒ] **1.** Privileg *n*; Vorrecht *n*; **2.** bevorrechten.

privy ['privi] **1.** □ **~** *to* eingeweiht in (*acc.*); **2** *Council* Staatsrat *m*; **2** *Councillor* Geheimer Rat; **2** *Seal* Geheimsiegel *n*; **2**, ♊ Mitinteres-sent *m* (*to an dat.*); Abort *m*.

prize [praiz] **1.** Preis *m*, Prämie *f*; ⚓ Beute *f*; (Lotterie)Gewinn *m*; **2.** preisgekrönt, Preis...; **3.** (hoch-)schätzen; aufbrechen (*öffnen*); **~-fighter** ['praizfaitə] Berufsboxer *m*.

pro [prou] für.

probab|**ility** [prɔbə'biliti] Wahr-scheinlichkeit *f*; **~le** □ ['prɔbəbl] wahrscheinlich.

probation [prə'beiʃən] Probe *f*, Probezeit *f*; ♊ Bewährungsfrist *f*; **~** *officer* Bewährungshelfer *m*.

probe [proub] **1.** ♂ Sonde *f*; *fig.* Untersuchung *f*; *lunar* **~** Mond-sonde *f*; **2.** *a.* **~** *into* sondieren; untersuchen.

probity ['proubiti] Redlichkeit *f*.

problem ['prɔbləm] Problem *n*; ♊ Aufgabe *f*; **~atic(al** □) [prɔbli-'mætik(əl)] problematisch, zweifel-haft. [*n*; Handlungsweise *f*.]

procedure [prə'si:dʒə] Verfahren

proceed [prə'si:d] weitergehen; fortfahren; vor sich gehen; vorgehen; *univ.* promovieren; ~ *from* von *od.* aus *et.* kommen; ausgehen von; ~ *to* zu *et.* übergehen; ~ing [~diŋ] Vorgehen *n*; Handlung *f*; ~s *pl.* t̶z̶ Verfahren *n*; Verhandlungen *f/pl.*, (Tätigkeits)Bericht *m*; ~s ['prousi:dz] *pl.* Ertrag *m*, Gewinn *m*.

process ['prouses] **1.** Fortschreiten *n*, Fortgang *m*; Vorgang *m*; Verlauf *m der Zeit*; Prozeß *m*, Verfahren *n*; *in* ~ im Gange; *in* ~ *of construction* im Bau (befindlich); **2.** gerichtlich belangen; ⊕ bearbeiten; ~ion [prə'seʃən] Prozession *f*.

proclaim [prə'kleim] proklamieren; erklären; ausrufen.

proclamation [prɔklə'meiʃən] Proklamation *f*; Bekanntmachung *f*; Erklärung *f*.

proclivity [prə'kliviti] Neigung *f*.

procrastinate [prou'kræstineit] zaudern.

procreate ['proukrieit] (er)zeugen.

procurat|ion [prɔkjuə'reiʃən] Vollmacht *f*; ✝ Prokura *f*; ~or [prɔ-kjuəreitə] Bevollmächtigte(r) *m*.

procure [prə'kjuə] *v/t.* be-, verschaffen; *v/i.* Kuppelei treiben.

prod [prɔd] **1.** Stich *m*; Stoß *m*; *fig.* Ansporn *m*; **2.** stechen; stoßen; *fig.* anstacheln.

prodigal ['prɔdigəl] **1.** ☐verschwenderisch; *the* ~ *son* der verlorene Sohn; **2.** Verschwender(in).

prodig|ious ☐ [prə'didʒəs] erstaunlich, ungeheuer; ~y ['prɔdidʒi] Wunder *n* (*a. fig.*); Ungeheuer *n*; *oft infant* ~ Wunderkind *n*.

produce 1. [prə'dju:s] vorbringen, vorführen, vorlegen; beibringen; hervorbringen; produzieren, erzeugen; *Zinsen etc.* (ein)bringen; ⅄ verlängern; *Film etc.* herausbringen; **2.** ['prɔdju:s] (Natur)Erzeugnis(se *pl.*) *n*, Produkt *n*; Ertrag *m*; ~r [prə'dju:sə] Erzeuger *m*, Hersteller *m*; *Film:* Produzent *m*; *thea.* Regisseur *m*.

product ['prɔdəkt] Produkt *n*, Erzeugnis *n*; ~ion [prə'dʌkʃən] Hervorbringung *f*; Vorlegung *f*, Beibringung *f*; Produktion *f*, Erzeugung *f*; *thea.* Herausbringen *n*; Erzeugnis *n*; ~ive [~ktiv] schöpferisch; produktiv, erzeugend; ertragreich; fruchtbar; ~iveness [~vnis], ~ivity [prɔdʌk'tiviti] Produktivität *f*.

prof *Am.* F [prɔf] Professor *m*.

profan|ation [prɔfə'neiʃən] Entweihung *f*; ~e [prə'fein] **1.** ☐ profan; weltlich; uneingeweiht; gottlos; **2.** entweihen; ~ity [~'fæniti] Gottlosigkeit *f*; Fluchen *n*.

profess [prə'fes] (sich) bekennen (zu); erklären; *Reue etc.* bekunden; *Beruf* ausüben; lehren; ~ed ☐ erklärt; angeblich; Berufs...; ~ion

[~eʃən] Bekenntnis *n*; Erklärung *f*; Beruf *m*; ~ional [~nl] **1.** ☐ Berufs...; Amts...; berufsmäßig; freiberuflich; ~ *men* Akademiker *m/pl.*; **2.** Fachmann *m*; *Sport:* Berufsspieler *m*; Berufskünstler *m*; ~or [~esə] Professor *m*.

proffer ['prɔfə] **1.** anbieten; **2.** Anerbieten *n*.

proficien|cy [prə'fiʃənsi] Tüchtigkeit *f*; ~t [~nt] **1.** ☐ tüchtig; bewandert; **2.** Meister *m*.

profile ['proufail] Profil *n*.

profit ['prɔfit] **1.** Vorteil *m*, Nutzen *m*, Gewinn *m*; **2.** *v/t. j-m* Nutzen bringen; *v/i.* ~ *by* Nutzen ziehen aus; ausnutzen; ~able ☐ [~təbl] nützlich, vorteilhaft, einträglich; ~eer [prɔfi'tiə] **1.** Schiebergeschäfte machen; **2.** Profitmacher *m*, Schieber *m*; ~-sharing ['prɔfitʃeəriŋ] Gewinnbeteiligung *f*.

profligate ['prɔfligit] **1.** ☐ liederlich; **2.** liederlicher Mensch.

profound ☐ [prə'faund] tief; tiefgründig; gründlich; *fig.* dunkel.

profundity [prə'fʌnditi] Tiefe *f*.

profus|e ☐ [prə'fju:s] verschwenderisch; übermäßig, überreich; ~ion *fig.* [~u:ʒən] Überfluß *m*.

progen|itor [prou'dʒenitə] Vorfahr *m*, Ahn *m*; ~y ['prɔdʒini] Nachkommen(schaft *f*) *m/pl.*; Brut *f*.

prognos|is ⚕ [prɔg'nousis], *pl.* ~es [~si:z] Prognose *f*.

prognostication [prəgnɔsti'keiʃən] Vorhersage *f*.

program(me) ['prougræm] Programm *n*.

progress 1. ['prougres] Fortschritt(e *pl.*) *m*; Vorrücken *n* (*a.* ⚔); Fortgang *m*; *in* ~ im Gang; **2.** [prə'gres] fortschreiten; ~ion [prə-'greʃən] Fortschreiten *n*; ⅄ Reihe *f*; ~ive [~esiv] **1.** ☐ fortschreitend; fortschrittlich; **2.** *pol.* Fortschrittler *m*.

prohibit [prə'hibit] verbieten; verhindern; ~ion [proui'biʃən] Verbot *n*; Prohibition *f*; ~ionist [~ʃnist] *bsd. Am.* Prohibitionist *m*; ~ive ☐ [prə'hibitiv] verbietend; Sperr...; unerschwinglich.

project 1. ['prɔdʒekt] Projekt *n*; Vorhaben *n*, Plan *m*; **2.** [prə'dʒekt] *v/t.* planen; (ent)werfen; ⅄ projizieren; *v/i.* vorspringen; ~ile ['prɔdʒiktail] Projektil *n*, Geschoß *n*; ~ion [prə'dʒekʃən] Werfen *n*; Entwurf *m*; Vorsprung *m*; ⅄, *ast.*, *phot.* Projektion *f*; ~or [~ktə] ✝ Gründer *m*; *opt.* Projektor *m*.

proletarian [proule'teəriən] **1.** proletarisch; **2.** Proletarier(in).

prolific [prə'lifik] (~ally) fruchtbar.

prolix ☐ ['prouliks] weitschweifig.

prolo|gue, *Am. a.* ~g ['proulɔg] Prolog *m*.

prolong [prə'lɔŋ] verlängern.

promenade [prɔmi'nɑːd] **1.** Promenade *f*; **2.** promenieren.

prominent □ ['prɔminənt] hervorragend (*a. fig.*); *fig.* prominent.

promiscuous □ [prə'miskjuəs] unordentlich, verworren; gemeinsam; unterschiedslos.

promis|e ['prɔmis] **1.** Versprechen *n*; *fig.* Aussicht *f*; **2.** versprechend; **~ing** □ [~siŋ] vielversprechend; **~sory** [~səri] versprechend; **~ note** ✝ Eigenwechsel *m*.

promontory ['prɔməntri] Vorgebirge *n*.

promot|e [prə'mout] *et.* fördern; *j-n* befördern; *bsd. Am. Schule:* versetzen; *parl.* unterstützen; ✝ gründen; *bsd. Am. Verkauf durch Werbung* steigern; **~ion** [~ouʃən] Förderung *f*; Beförderung *f*; ✝ Gründung *f*.

prompt [prɔmpt] **1.** □ schnell; bereit(willig); sofortig; pünktlich; **2.** *j-n* veranlassen; *Gedanken* eingeben; *j-m* vorsagen, soufflieren; **~er** ['prɔmptə] Souffleu|r *m*, -se *f*; **~ness** [~tnis] Schnelligkeit *f*; Bereitschaft *f*.

promulgate ['prɔmʌlgeit] verkünden, verbreiten.

prone □ [proun] mit dem Gesicht nach unten (liegend); hingestreckt; **~ to** *fig.* geneigt *od.* neigend zu.

prong [prɔŋ] Zinke *f*; Spitze *f*.

pronoun *gr.* ['prounaun] Pronomen *n*, Fürwort *n*.

pronounce [prə'nauns] aussprechen; verkünden; erklären (für).

pronto *Am.* F ['prɔntou] sofort.

pronunciation [prənʌnsi'eiʃən] Aussprache *f*.

proof [pruːf] **1.** Beweis *m*; Probe *f*; Versuch *m*; *typ.* Korrekturbogen *m*; *typ., phot.* Probeabzug *m*; **2.** fest; *in Zssgn:* ...fest, ...dicht, ...sicher; **~-reader** *typ.* ['pruːfriːdə] Korrektor *m*.

prop [prɔp] **1.** Stütze *f* (*a. fig.*); **2.** *a.* **~ up** (unter)stützen.

propaga|te ['prɔpəgeit] (sich) fortpflanzen; verbreiten; **~tion** [prɔpə'geiʃən] Fortpflanzung *f*; Verbreitung *f*.

propel [prə'pel] (vorwärts-, an-)treiben; **~ler** [~lə] Propeller *m*, (Schiffs-, Luft)Schraube *f*.

propensity [prə'pensiti] Neigung *f*.

proper □ ['prɔpə] eigen(tümlich); eigentlich; passend, richtig; anständig; **~ty** [~əti] Eigentum *n*, Besitz *m*; Vermögen *n*; Eigenschaft *f*.

prophe|cy ['prɔfisi] Prophezeiung *f*; **~sy** [~sai] prophezeien.

prophet ['prɔfit] Prophet *m*.

propi|tiate [prə'piʃieit] günstig stimmen, versöhnen; **~tious** □ [~ʃəs] gnädig; günstig.

proportion [prə'pɔːʃən] **1.** Verhältnis *n*; Gleichmaß *n*; (An)Teil *m*;

~s *pl.* (Aus)Maße *n/pl.*; **2.** in ein Verhältnis bringen; **~al** □ [~nl] im Verhältnis (*to* zu); **~ate** □ [~ʃnit] angemessen.

propos|al [prə'pouzəl] Vorschlag *m*, (*a.* Heirats)Antrag *m*; Angebot *n*; Plan *m*; **~e** [~ouz] *v/t.* vorschlagen; e-n Toast ausbringen auf (*acc.*); **~ to o.s.** sich vornehmen; *v/i.* beabsichtigen; anhalten (*to* um); **~ition** [prɔpə'ziʃən] Vorschlag *m*, Antrag *m*; Behauptung *f*; Problem *n*.

propound [prə'paund] *Frage etc.* vorlegen; vorschlagen.

propriet|ary [prə'praiətəri] Eigentümer...; Eigentums...; Besitz(er)...; gesetzlich geschützt (*bsd. Arzneimittel*); **~or** [~tə] Eigentümer *m*; **~y** [~ti] Richtigkeit *f*; Schicklichkeit *f*; *the proprieties pl.* die Anstandsformen *f/pl.* [*m.*]

propulsion ⊕ [prə'pʌlʃən] Antrieb]

prorate *Am.* [prou'reit] anteilmäßig verteilen.

prosaic [prou'zeiik] (**~ally**) *fig.* prosaisch (*nüchtern, trocken*).

proscribe [prous'kraib] ächten.

proscription [prous'kripʃən] Achtung *f*; Acht *f*; Verbannung *f*.

prose [prouz] **1.** Prosa *f*; **2.** prosaisch.

prosecut|e ['prɔsikjuːt] (*a.* gerichtlich) verfolgen; *Gewerbe etc.* betreiben; verklagen; **~ion** [prɔsi'kjuːʃən] Verfolgung *f* e-s *Plans etc.*; Betreiben *n* e-s *Gewerbes etc.*; gerichtliche Verfolgung; **~or** ✝ [~tə] Kläger *m*; Anklagevertreter *m*; *public* ~ Staatsanwalt *m*.

prospect 1. ['prɔspekt] Aussicht *f* (*a. fig.*); Anblick *m*; ✝ Interessent *m*; **2.** [prəs'pekt] ☒ schürfen; bohren (*for* nach *Öl*); **~ive** □ [~tiv] vorausblickend; voraussichtlich; **~us** [~təs] (Werbe)Prospekt *m*.

prosper ['prɔspə] *v/i.* Erfolg haben, gedeihen, blühen; *v/t.* begünstigen, segnen; **~ity** [prɔs'periti] Gedeihen *n*; Wohlstand *m*; Glück *n*; *fig.* Blüte *f*; **~ous** □ ['prɔspərəs] glücklich, gedeihlich; *fig.* blühend; günstig.

prostitute ['prɔstitjuːt] **1.** Dirne *f*; **2.** zur Dirne machen; (der Schande) preisgeben, feilbieten (*a. fig.*).

prostrat|e 1. ['prɔstreit] hingestreckt; erschöpft; daniederliegend; demütig; gebrochen; **2.** [prɔs'treit] niederwerfen; *fig.* niederschmettern; entkräften; **~ion** [~eiʃən] Niederwerfung *f*; Fußfall *m*; *fig.* Demütigung *f*; Entkräftung *f*.

prosy *fig.* ['prouzi] prosaisch; langweilig.

protagonist [prou'tægənist] *thea.* Hauptfigur *f*; *fig.* Vorkämpfer(in).

protect [prə'tekt] (be)schützen; **~ion** [~kʃən] Schutz *m*; Wirtschaftsschutz *m*, Schutzzoll *m*; **~ive**

[⸤ktiv] schützend; Schutz...; ~ duty Schutzzoll m; ~or [⸤tə] (Be)Schützer m; ~ Schutz-, Schirmherr m; ~orate [⸤ərit] Protektorat n.

protest 1. ['proutest] Protest m; Einspruch m; 2. [prə'test] beteuern; protestieren; reklamieren.

Protestant ['protistənt] 1. protestantisch; 2. Protestant(in).

protestation [proutes'teiʃən] Beteuerung f; Verwahrung f.

protocol ['proutəkɔl] 1. Protokoll n; 2. protokollieren.

prototype ['proutətaip] Urbild n; Prototyp m, Modell n.

protract [prə'trækt] in die Länge ziehen, hinziehen.

protru|de [prə'tru:d] (sich) (her-)vorstrecken; (her)vorstehen, (her)vortreten (lassen); ~sion [~u:ʒən] Vorstrecken n; (Her)Vorstehen n, (Her)Vortreten n.

protuberance [prə'tju:bərəns] Hervortreten n; Auswuchs m, Höcker m.

proud □ [praud] stolz (of auf acc.).

prove [pru:v] v/t. be-, er-, nachweisen; prüfen; erleben, erfahren; v/i. sich herausstellen od. erweisen (als); ausfallen; ~n ['pru:vən] erwiesen; bewährt.

provenance ['provinəns] Herkunft f.

provender ['provində] Futter n.

proverb ['provə:b] Sprichwort n.

provide [prə'vaid] v/t. besorgen, beschaffen, liefern; bereitstellen; versehen, versorgen; żż vorsehen, festsetzen; v/i. (vor)sorgen; ~d (that) vorausgesetzt, daß; sofern.

providen|ce ['providəns] Vorsehung f; Voraussicht f; Vorsorge f; ~t □ [~nt] vorausblickend; vorsorglich; haushälterisch; ~tial □ [provi'denʃəl] durch die göttliche Vorsehung bewirkt; glücklich.

provider [prə'vaidə] Ernährer m der Familie; Lieferant m.

provinc|e ['provins] Provinz f; fig. Gebiet n; Aufgabe f; ~ial [prə'vinʃəl] 1. provinziell; kleinstädtisch; 2. Provinzbewohner(in).

provision [prə'viʒən] Beschaffung f; Vorsorge f; żż Bestimmung f; Vorkehrung f, Maßnahme f; Vorrat m; ~s pl. Proviant m, Lebensmittel pl.; ~al □ [~nl] provisorisch.

proviso [prə'vaizou] Vorbehalt m.

provocat|ion [provə'keiʃən] Herausforderung f; ~ive [prə'vɔkətiv] herausfordernd; (auf)reizend.

provoke [prə'vouk] auf-, anreizen; herausfordern.

provost ['provəst] Leiter m e-s College; schott. Bürgermeister m; ✕ [prə'vou]: ~ marshal Kommandeur m der Militärpolizei.

prow ⚓ [prau] Bug m, Vorschiff n.

prowess ['prauis] Tapferkeit f.

prowl [praul] 1. v/i. umherstreifen; v/t. durchstreifen; 2. Umherstreifen n; ~ car Am. ['praulka:] Streifenwagen m der Polizei.

proximity [prɔk'simiti] Nähe f.

proxy ['prɔksi] Stellvertreter m; Stellvertretung f; Vollmacht f; by ~ in Vertretung.

prude [pru:d] Prüde f, Spröde f; Zimperliese f.

pruden|ce ['pru:dəns] Klugheit f, Vorsicht f; ~t □ [~nt] klug, vorsichtig.

prud|ery ['pru:dəri] Prüderie f, Sprödigkeit f; Zimperlichkeit f; ~ish □ [~diʃ] prüde, zimperlich, spröde.

prune [pru:n] 1. Backpflaume f; 2. ⸝ beschneiden (a. fig.); a. ~ away, ~ off wegschneiden.

prurient □ ['pruəriənt] geil, lüstern.

pry [prai] 1. neugierig gucken; ~ into s-e Nase stecken in (acc.); ~ open aufbrechen; ~ up hochheben; 2. Hebel(bewegung f) m.

psalm [sɑːm] Psalm m.

pseudo|... ['psju:dou] Pseudo..., falsch; ~nym [~dənim] Deckname m.

psychiatr|ist [sai'kaiətrist] Psychiater m (Nervenarzt); ~y [~ri] Psychiatrie f.

psychic(al) □ ['saikik(əl)] psychisch, seelisch.

psycholog|ical □ [saikə'lɔdʒikəl] psychologisch; ~ist [sai'kɔlədʒist] Psychologe m, -in f; ~y [~dʒi] Psychologie f (Seelenkunde).

pub F [pʌb] Kneipe f, Wirtschaft f.

puberty ['pju:bəti] Pubertät f.

public ['pʌblik] 1. □ öffentlich; staatlich, Staats...; allbekannt; ~ spirit Gemeinsinn m; 2. Publikum n; Öffentlichkeit f; ~an [~kən] Gastwirt m; ~ation [pʌbli'keiʃən] Bekanntmachung f; Veröffentlichung f; Verlagswerk n; monthly ~ Monatsschrift f; ~ house Wirtshaus n; ~ity [pʌb'lisiti] Öffentlichkeit f; Propaganda f, Reklame f, Werbung f; ~ library Volksbücherei f; ~ relations pl. Verhältnis n zur Öffentlichkeit; Public Relations pl.; ~ school Public School f, Internatsschule f.

publish ['pʌbliʃ] bekanntmachen, veröffentlichen; Buch etc. herausgeben, verlegen; ~ing house Verlag m; ~er [~ʃə] Herausgeber m, Verleger m; ~s pl. Verlag(sanstalt f) m.

pucker ['pʌkə] 1. Falte f; 2. falten; Falten werfen; runzeln.

pudding ['pudiŋ] Pudding m; Süßspeise f; Auflauf m; Wurst f; black ~ Blutwurst f.

puddle ['pʌdl] Pfütze f.

pudent ['pju:dənt] verschämt.

puerile □ ['pjuərail] kindisch.

puff [pʌf] 1. Hauch m; Zug m beim

Rauchen; (Dampf-, Rauch)Wölkchen *n;* Puderquaste *f;* (aufdringliche) Reklame; 2. *v/t.* (auf)blasen, pusten; paffen; anpreisen; ~ out sich (auf)blähen; ~ up *Preise* hochtreiben; ~ed up *fig.* aufgeblasen; ~ed eyes geschwollene Augen; *v/i.* paffen; pusten; ~-paste ['pʌfpeist] Blätterteig *m;* ~y ['pʌfi] böig; kurzatmig; geschwollen; dick; bauschig.

pug [pʌg], ~-dog ['pʌgdɔg] Mops *m.*

pugnacious [pʌg'neiʃəs] kämpferisch; kampflustig; streitsüchtig.

pug-nose ['pʌgnouz] Stupsnase *f.*

puissant ['pju(:)isnt] mächtig.

puke [pju:k] (sich) erbrechen.

pull [pul] 1. Zug *m;* Ruck *m; typ.* Abzug *m;* Ruderpartie *f;* Griff *m;* Vorteil *m;* 2. ziehen; zerren; reißen; zupfen; pflücken; rudern; ~ *about* hin- u. herzerren; ~ *down* niederreißen; ~ *in* einfahren (*Zug*); ~ *off* zustande bringen; *Preis* erringen; ~ *out* heraus-, hinausfahren; ausscheren; ~ *round* wiederherstellen; ~ *through j-n* durchbringen; ~ *o.s. together* sich zs.-nehmen; ~ *up Wagen* anhalten; halten; ~ *up with*, ~ *up* to einholen.

pulley ⊕ ['puli] Rolle *f;* Flaschenzug *m;* Riemenscheibe *f.*

pull|-over ['pulouvə] Pullover *m;* ~-up Halteplatz *m,* Raststätte *f.*

pulp [pʌlp] Brei *m;* Frucht-, Zahn-Mark *n;* ⊕ Papierbrei *m; a.* ~ *magazine Am.* Schundillustrierte *f.*

pulpit ['pulpit] Kanzel *f.*

pulpy □ ['pʌlpi] breiig; fleischig.

puls|ate [pʌl'seit] pulsieren; schlagen; ~e [pʌls] Puls(schlag) *m.*

pulverize ['pʌlvəraiz] *v/t.* pulverisieren; *v/i.* zu Staub werden.

pumice ['pʌmis] Bimsstein *m.*

pump [pʌmp] 1. Pumpe *f;* Pumps *m;* 2. pumpen; F *j-n* aushorchen.

pumpkin ♀ ['pʌmpkin] Kürbis *m.*

pun [pʌn] 1. Wortspiel *n;* 2. ein Wortspiel machen.

Punch¹ [pʌntʃ] Kasperle *n, m.*

punch² [~] 1. ⊕ Punze(n *m*) *f,* Locheisen *n,* Locher *m;* Lochzange *f;* (Faust)Schlag *m;* Punsch *m;* 2. punzen, durchbohren; lochen; knuffen, puffen; *Am.* Vieh treiben, hüten.

puncher ['pʌntʃə] Locheisen *n;* Locher *m;* F Schläger *m; Am.* Cowboy *m.*

punctilious [pʌŋk'tiliəs] peinlich (genau), spitzfindig; förmlich.

punctual □ ['pʌŋktjuəl] pünktlich; ~ity ['pʌŋktju'æliti] Pünktlichkeit *f.*

punctuat|e ['pʌŋktjueit] (inter-)punktieren; *fig.* unterbrechen; ~ion *gr.* [pʌŋktju'eiʃən] Interpunktion *f.*

puncture ['pʌŋktʃə] 1. Punktur *f,*

Stich *m;* Reifenpanne *f;* 2. (durch-)stechen; platzen (*Luftreifen*).

pungen|cy ['pʌndʒənsi] Schärfe *f;* ~t [~nt] stechend, beißend, scharf.

punish ['pʌniʃ] (be)strafen; ~able □ [~ʃəbl] strafbar; ~ment [~ʃmənt] Strafe *f,* Bestrafung *f.*

punk *Am.* [pʌŋk] Zunderholz *n;* Zündmasse *f;* F *fig.* Mist *m,* Käse *m.*

puny □ ['pju:ni] winzig; schwächlich.

pupa *zo.* ['pju:pə] Puppe *f.*

pupil ['pju:pl] *anat.* Pupille *f;* Schüler(in); Mündel *m, n.*

puppet ['pʌpit] Marionette *f (a.fig.);* ~-show Puppenspiel *n.*

pup(py) [pʌp, 'pʌpi] Welpe *m,* junger Hund; *fig.* Laffe *m,* Schnösel *m.*

purchase ['pə:tʃəs] 1. (An-, Ein-)Kauf *m;* Erwerb(ung *f) m;* Anschaffung *f;* ⊕ Hebevorrichtung *f; fig.* Ansatzpunkt *m; make* ~s Einkäufe machen; 2. kaufen; *fig.* erkaufen; anschaffen; ⊕ aufwinden; ~r [~sə] Käufer(in).

pure □ [pjuə] *allg.* rein; *engS.:* lauter; echt; gediegen; theoretisch; ~bred *Am.* ['pjuəbred] reinrassig.

purgat|ive ♂ ['pə:gətiv] 1. abführend; 2. Abführmittel *n;* ~ory [~təri] Fegefeuer *n.*

purge [pə:dʒ] 1. ♂ Abführmittel *n; pol.* Säuberung *f;* 2. *mst fig.* reinigen; *pol.* säubern; ⊕ abführen.

purify ['pjuərifai] reinigen; läutern.

Puritan ['pjuəritn] 1. Puritaner (-in); 2. puritanisch.

purity ['pjuəriti] Reinheit *f (a.fig.).*

purl [pə:l] murmeln (*Bach*).

purlieus ['pə:lju:z] *pl.* Umgebung *f.*

purloin [pə:'lɔin] entwenden.

purple ['pə:pl] 1. purpurn, purpurrot; 2. Purpur *m;* 3. (sich) purpurn färben.

purport ['pə:pət] 1. Sinn *m;* Inhalt *m;* 2. besagen; beabsichtigen; vorgeben.

purpose ['pə:pəs] 1. Vorsatz *m;* Absicht *f,* Zweck *m;* Entschlußkraft *f; for the* ~ *of ger.* um zu *inf.; on* ~ absichtlich; *to no* ~ zwecksdienlich; *to no* ~ vergebens; 2. vorhaben, bezwecken; ~ful □ [~sful] zweckmäßig; absichtlich; zielbewußt; ~less □ [~slis] zwecklos; ziellos; ~ly [~li] vorsätzlich.

purr [pə:] schnurren (*Katze*).

purse [pə:s] 1. Börse *f,* Geldbeutel *m;* Geld(preis *m) n; public* ~ Staatssäckel *m;* 2. *oft* ~ *up* Mund spitzen; *Stirn* runzeln; *Augen* zs.-kneifen.

pursuan|ce [pə'sju(:)əns] Verfolgung *f;* in ~ of zufolge (*dat.*); ~t □ [~nt]: ~ to zufolge, gemäß, entsprechend (*dat.*).

pursu|e [pə'sju:] verfolgen (*a. fig.*); streben nach; *e-m Beruf etc.* nachgehen; fortsetzen, fortfahren; ~er

[~ju(:)ə] Verfolger(in); ~it [~ju:t] Verfolgung f; mst ~s pl. Beschäftigung f.

purvey [pə:'vei] Lebensmittel liefern; ~or [~ʿeiə] Lieferant m.

pus [pʌs] Eiter m.

push [puʃ] 1. (An-, Vor)Stoß m; Schub m; Druck m; Notfall m; Energie f; 2. Unternehmungsgeist m; Elan m; 2. stoßen; schieben; drängen; Knopf drücken; (an)treiben; a. ~ through durchführen; Anspruch etc. durchdrücken; ~ s.th. on s.o. j-m et. aufdrängen; ~ one's way sich durch- od. vordrängen; ~ along, ~ on, ~ forward weitermachen, -gehen, -fahren etc.; ~-button ⚡ ['puʃbʌtn] Druckknopf m; ~-over Am. fig. Kinderspiel n; leicht zu beeinflussender Mensch.

pusillanimous □ [pju:si'læniməs] kleinmütig.

puss [pus] Kätzchen n, Katze f (a. fig. = Mädchen); ~y ['pusi], a. ~-cat Mieze f, Kätzchen n; ~yfoot Am. F leisetreten, sich zurückhalten.

put [put] (irr.) v/t. setzen, legen, stellen, stecken, tun, machen; Frage stellen, vorlegen; werfen; ausdrücken, sagen; ~ about Gerüchte etc. verbreiten; ♣ wenden; ~ across sl. drehen, schaukeln; ~ back zurückstellen; ~ by Geld zurücklegen; ~ down niederlegen, -setzen, -werfen; aussteigen lassen; notieren; zuschreiben (to dat.); unterdrücken; ~ forth Kräfte aufbieten; Knospen etc. treiben; ~ forward Meinung etc. vorbringen; ~ o.s. forward sich hervortun; ~ in hinein-, hereinlegen; Anspruch erheben; Gesuch einreichen; Urkunde vorlegen; anstellen; ~ off auf-, verschieben; vertrösten; abbringen; hindern; fig. ablegen; ~ on Kleid anziehen, Hut aufsetzen; fig. annehmen; an-, einschalten;

vergrößern; ~ on airs sich aufspielen; ~ on weight zunehmen; ~ out ausmachen, (aus)löschen; verrenken; (her)ausstrecken; verwirren; j-m Ungelegenheiten bereiten; Kraft aufbieten; Geld ausleihen; ~ right in Ordnung bringen; ~ through teleph. verbinden (to mit); ~ to hinzufügen; ~ to death hinrichten; ~ to the rack od. torture auf die Folter spannen; ~ up aufstellen etc.; errichten, bauen; Waren anbieten; Miete erhöhen; ver-, wegpacken; Widerstand leisten; Kampf liefern; Gäste unterbringen; Bekanntmachung anschlagen; v/i. ~ off, ~ out, ~ to sea ♣ auslaufen; ~ in ♣ einlaufen; ~ up at einkehren od. absteigen in (dat.); ~ up for sich bewerben um; ~ up with sich gefallen lassen; sich abfinden mit.

putrefy ['pju:trifai] (ver)faulen.

putrid □ ['pju:trid] faul, verdorben; sl. scheußlich, saumäßig, ~ity [pju:'triditi] Fäulnis f.

putty ['pʌti] 1. Kitt m; 2. kitten.

puzzle ['pʌzl] 1. schwierige Aufgabe, Rätsel n; Verwirrung f; Geduldspiel n; 2. v/t. irremachen; j-m Kopfzerbrechen machen; ~ out austüfteln; v/i. sich den Kopf zerbrechen; ~-headed konfus.

pygm|(a)ean [pig'mi:ən] zwerghaft; ~y ['pigmi] Zwerg m; attr. zwerghaft.

pyjamas [pə'dʒɑ:məz] pl. Schlafanzug m.

pyramid ['pirəmid] Pyramide f; ~al □ [pi'ræmidl] pyramidal.

pyre ['paiə] Scheiterhaufen m.

pyrotechnic|(al □)] [pairou'teknik(əl)] pyrotechnisch, Feuerwerks...; ~s pl. Feuerwerk n (a. fig.).

Pythagorean [paiθægə'ri(:)ən] 1. pythagoreisch; 2. Pythagoreer m.

pyx eccl. [piks] Monstranz f.

Q

quack [kwæk] 1. Quaken n; Scharlatan m; Quacksalber m, Kurpfuscher m; Marktschreier m; 2. quacksalberisch; 3. quaken; quacksalbern (an dat.); ~ery ['kwækəri] Quacksalberei f.

quadrangle ['kwɔdrængl] Viereck n; Innenhof m e-s College.

quadrennial □ [kwɔ'dreniəl] vierjährig; vierjährlich.

quadru|ped ['kwɔdruped] Vierfüßer m; ~ple [~pl] 1. □ vierfach; 2. (sich) vervierfachen; ~plets [~lits] pl. Vierlinge m/pl.

quagmire ['kwægmaiə] Sumpf (-land n) m, Moor n.

quail[1] orn. [kweil] Wachtel f.

quail[2] [~] verzagen; beben.

quaint □ [kweint] anheimelnd, malerisch; putzig; seltsam.

quake [kweik] 1. beben, zittern (with, for vor dat.); 2. Erdbeben n.

Quaker ['kweikə] Quäker m.

quali|fication [kwɔlifi'keiʃən] (erforderliche) Befähigung; Einschränkung f; gr. nähere Bestimmung; ~fy ['kwɔlifai] v/t. befähigen; (be-) nennen; gr. näher bestimmen; ein-

schränken, mäßigen; mildern; v/i.
seine Befähigung nachweisen; ~ty
[~iti] Eigenschaft f, Beschaffenheit
f; ✝ Qualität f; vornehmer Stand.

qualm [kwɔːm] plötzliche Übelkeit;
Zweifel m; Bedenken n.

quandary ['kwɔndəri] verzwickte
Lage, Verlegenheit f.

quantity ['kwɔntiti] Quantität f,
Menge f; großer Teil.

quantum ['kwɔntəm] Menge f,
Größe f, Quantum n; Anteil m.

quarantine ['kwɔrəntiːn] 1. Quarantäne f; 2. unter Quarantäne
stellen.

quarrel ['kwɔrəl] 1. Zank m, Streit
m; 2. (sich) zanken, streiten; ~-
some □ [~ləsm] zänkisch; streitsüchtig.

quarry ['kwɔri] 1. Steinbruch m;
fig. Fundgrube f; (Jagd)Beute f;
2. Steine brechen; fig. stöbern.

quart [kwɔːt] Quart n (1,136 l).

quarter ['kwɔːtə] 1. Viertel n, vierter Teil m; bsd. Viertelstunde f; Vier-
teljahr n, Quartal n; Viertelzentner
m; Am. 25 Cent; Keule f, Viertel n
e-s geschlachteten Tieres; Stadtvier-
tel n; (Himmels)Richtung f, Gegend f; ✕ Gnade f, Pardon m; ~s
pl. Quartier n (a. ✕), Unterkunft f;
fig. Kreise m/pl.; live in close ~s
beengt wohnen; at close ~s dicht
aufeinander; come to close ~s handgemein werden; 2. vierteln, vier-
teilen; beherbergen; ✕ einquartieren; ~back Am. Sport: Abwehr-
spieler m; ~day Quartalstag m;
~deck Achterdeck n; ~ly [~li]
1. vierteljährlich; 2. Vierteljahres-
schrift f; ~master ✕ Quartiermei-
ster m. [n.]

quartet(te) ♪ [kwɔːˈtet] Quartett n.

quarto ['kwɔːtou] Quart(format) n.

quash ✝ [kwɔʃ] aufheben, verwerfen; unterdrücken.

quasi ['kwɑːzi(ː)] gleichsam, sozusagen; Quasi..., Schein...

quaver ['kweivə] 1. Zittern n; ♪
Triller m; 2. mit zitternder Stimme
sprechen od. singen; trillern.

quay [kiː] Kai m; Uferstraße f.

queasy □ ['kwiːzi] empfindlich
(Magen, Gewissen); heikel, mäkelig; ekelhaft.

queen [kwiːn] 1. Königin f; ~ bee
Bienenkönigin f; ~like ['kwiːnlaik],
~ly [~li] wie eine Königin, königlich.

queer [kwiə] sonderbar, seltsam;
wunderlich; komisch; homo-
sexuell.

quench [kwentʃ] fig. Durst etc. löschen, stillen; kühlen; Aufruhr
unterdrücken.

querulous □ ['kwerələs] quengelig,
mürrisch, verdrossen.

query ['kwiəri] 1. Frage(zeichen n)
f; 2. (be)fragen; (be-, an)zweifeln.

quest [kwest] 1. Suche(n n) f, Nach-
forschen n; 2. suchen, forschen.

question ['kwestʃən] 1. Frage f;
Problem n; Untersuchung f; Streitfrage f; Zweifel m; Sache f, Angelegenheit f; beyond (all) ~ ohne
Frage; in ~ fraglich; call in ~ anzweifeln; that is out of the ~ das
steht außer od. kommt nicht in
Frage; 2. befragen; bezweifeln;
~able □ [~nəbl] fraglich; fragwürdig; ~er [~nə] Fragende(r m) f;
~mark Fragezeichen n; ~naire
[kwestiəˈnɛə] Fragebogen m.

queue [kjuː] 1. Reihe f v. Personen
etc., Schlange f; Zopf m; 2. mst ~
up (in e-r Reihe) anstehen, Schlange
stehen.

quibble ['kwibl] 1. Wortspiel n;
Spitzfindigkeit f; Ausflucht f; 2. fig.
ausweichen; witzeln.

quick [kwik] 1. schnell, rasch; voreilig; lebhaft; gescheit; beweglich;
lebendig; scharf (Gehör etc.); 2. lebendes Fleisch; the ~ die Leben-
den; to the ~ (bis) ins Fleisch; fig.
(bis) ins Herz, tief; cut s.o. to the ~
j-n aufs empfindlichste kränken; ~en
['kwikən] v/t. beleben; beschleunigen; v/i. aufleben; sich regen; ~ly
[~kli] schnell, rasch; ~ness [~knis]
Lebhaftigkeit f; Schnelligkeit f;
Voreiligkeit f; Schärfe f des Verstandes etc.; ~sand Triebsand m;
~set f; a. ~ hedge lebende Hecke;
~sighted scharfsichtig; ~silver min.
Quecksilber n; ~witted schlag-
fertig.

quid¹ [kwid] Priem m (Kautabak).

quid² sl. [~] Pfund n Sterling.

quiescen|ce [kwaiˈesns] Ruhe f,
Stille f; ~t □ [~nt] ruhend; fig.
ruhig, still.

quiet ['kwaiət] 1. □ ruhig, still;
2. Ruhe f; on the ~ (sl. on the q.t.)
unter der Hand, im stillen; 3. a. ~
down (sich) beruhigen; ~ness
[~tnis], ~ude [ˈkwaiitjuːd] Ruhe f,
Stille f.

quill [kwil] 1. Federkiel m; fig. Feder f; Stachel m des Igels etc.;
2. rund fälteln; ~ing ['kwiliŋ]
Rüsche f, Krause f; ~pen Gänse-
feder f zum Schreiben.

quilt [kwilt] 1. Steppdecke f;
2. steppen; wattieren.

quince ♀ [kwins] Quitte f.

quinine pharm. [kwiˈniːn, Am.
ˈkwainain] Chinin n.

quinquennial □ [kwiŋˈkweniəl]
fünfjährig; fünfjährlich.

quinsy ✝ ['kwinzi] Mandelentzündung f.

quintal ['kwintl] (Doppel)Zentner
m.

quintessence [kwinˈtesns] Quint-
essenz f, Kern m, Inbegriff m.

quintuple ['kwintjupl] 1. □ fünf-

fach; 2. (sich) verfünffachen; **~ts**
[.lits] *pl.* Fünflinge *m/pl.*

quip [kwip] Stich(elei *f*) *m*; Witz
(-wort *n*) *m*; Spitzfindigkeit *f.*

quirk [kwə:k] Spitzfindigkeit *f*;
Witz(elei *f*) *m*; Kniff *m*; Schnörkel
m; Eigentümlichkeit *f*; △ Hohl-
kehle *f.*

quisling ['kwizliŋ] Quisling *m*, Kol-
laborateur *m.*

quit [kwit] 1. *v/t.* verlassen; aufgeben; *Am.* aufhören (mit); vergelten;
Schuld tilgen; *v/i.* aufhören; ausziehen (*Mieter*); *give notice to* ~
kündigen; 2. quitt; frei, los.

quite [kwait] ganz, gänzlich; recht;
durchaus; ~ *a hero* ein wirklicher
Held; ~ (so)*!*, ~ *that!* ganz recht;
~ *the thing* F große Mode.

quittance ['kwitəns] Quittung *f.*

quitter *Am.* F ['kwitə] Drückeberger *m.*

quiver[1] ['kwivə] zittern, beben.

quiver[2] [.~] Köcher *m.*

quiz [kwiz] 1. Prüfung *f*, Test *m*;
Quiz *n*; belustigter Blick; 2. (aus-)
fragen; prüfen; necken, foppen;
anstarren, beäugen; **~zical** □
['kwizikəl] spöttisch; komisch.

quoit [kɔit] Wurfring *m*; **~s** *pl.*
Wurfringspiel *n.*

Quonset *Am.* ['kwɔnsit] *a.* ~ *hut*
Wellblechbaracke *f.*

quorum *parl.* ['kwɔːrəm] beschluß-
fähige Mitgliederzahl.

quota ['kwoutə] Quote *f*, Anteil *m*,
Kontingent *n.*

quotation [kwou'teiʃən] Anführung
f, Zitat *n*; ✝ Preisnotierung *f*;
Kostenvoranschlag *m*; **~-marks** *pl.*
Anführungszeichen *n/pl.*

quote [kwout] anführen, zitieren;
✝ berechnen, notieren (*at* mit).

quotient Å ['kwouʃənt] Quotient
m.

quoth † [kwouθ]: ~ *I* sagte ich; ~
he sagte er.

quotidian [kwɔ'tidiən] (all)täglich.

R

rabbi ['ræbai] Rabbiner *m.*

rabbit ['ræbit] Kaninchen *n.*

rabble ['ræbl] Pöbel(haufen) *m.*

rabid □ ['ræbid] tollwütig (*Tier*);
fig. wild, wütend.

rabies *vet.* ['reibiːz] Tollwut *f.*

raccoon [rə'kuːn] = racoon.

race [reis] 1. Geschlecht *n*, Stamm
m; Rasse *f*, Schlag *m*; Lauf *m* (*a.
fig.*); Wettrennen *n*; Strömung *f*;
~s *pl.* Pferderennen *n*; 2. rennen;
rasen; um die Wette laufen (mit);
⊕ leer laufen; **~course** ['reiskɔːs]
Rennbahn *f*, -strecke *f*; **~horse**
Rennpferd *n*; **~r** [*'reisə*] Rennpferd *n*; Rennwagen *m*; Rennwagen]

racial □ ['reiʃəl] Rassen... [*m.*]

racing ['reisiŋ] Rennsport *m*; *attr.*
Renn...

rack [ræk] 1. Gestell *n*; Kleider-
ständer *m*; Gepäcknetz *n*; Raufe *f*,
Futtergestell *n*; Folter(bank) *f*;
go to ~ *and ruin* völlig zugrunde
gehen; 2. strecken; foltern, quälen
(*a. fig.*); ~ *one's brains* sich den
Kopf zermartern.

racket ['rækit] 1. *Tennis*-Schläger *m*;
Lärm *m*; Trubel *m*; *Am.* F Schwin-
del(geschäft *n*) *m*; Strapaze *f*;
2. lärmen; sich amüsieren; **~eer**
Am. [ræki'tiə] Erpresser *m*; **~eering**
Am. [.~əriŋ] Erpresserwesen *n*; **~y**
['rækiti] ausgelassen.

racoon *zo.* [rə'kuːn] Waschbär *m.*

racy □ ['reisi] kraftvoll, lebendig;
stark; würzig; urwüchsig.

radar ['reidə] Radar(gerät) *n.*

radian|ce, ~cy ['reidjəns, ~si]
Strahlen *n*; **~t** □ [.~nt] strahlend,
leuchtend.

radiat|e ['reidieit] (aus)strahlen;
strahlenförmig ausgehen; **~ion** [rei-
di'eiʃən] (Aus)Strahlung *f*; **~or**
['reidieitə] Heizkörper *m*; *mot.*
Kühler *m.*

radical ['rædikəl] 1. □ Wurzel...,
Grund...; gründlich; eingewurzelt;
pol. radikal; 2. *pol.* Radikale(r *m*) *f.*

radio ['reidiou] 1. Radio *n*; Funk
(-spruch) *m*; ~ *drama*, ~ *play* Hör-
spiel *n*; ~ *set* Radiogerät *n*; 2. funken; **~(-)active** radioaktiv; **~graph**
[.~ougraːf] 1. Röntgenbild *n*; 2. ein
Röntgenbild machen von; **~-tele-
gram** Funktelegramm *n*; **~-thera-
py** Strahlen-, Röntgentherapie *f.*

radish ♀ ['rædiʃ] Rettich *m*; (red) ~
Radieschen *n.*

radius ['reidjəs] Radius *m.*

raffle ['ræfl] 1. Tombola *f*, Verlo-
sung *f*; 2. verlosen.

raft [rɑːft] 1. Floß *n*; 2. flößen; **~er**
['rɑːftə] ⊕ (Dach)Sparren *m.*

rag[1] [ræg] Lumpen *m*; Fetzen *m*;
Lappen *m.*

rag[2] *sl.* [.~] 1. Unfug *m*; Radau *m*;
2. Unfug treiben (mit); *j-n* aufziehen; *j-n* beschimpfen; herum-
tollen, Radau machen.

ragamuffin ['rægəmafin] Lumpen-
kerl *m*; Gassenjunge *m.*

rage [reidʒ] 1. Wut *f*, Zorn *m*,
Raserei *f*; Sucht *f*, Gier *f* (*for*
nach); Manie *f*; Ekstase *f*; *it is all
the* ~ es ist allgemein Mode;
2. wüten, rasen.

rag-fair ['rægfɛə] Trödelmarkt m.

ragged □ ['rægid] rauh; zottig; zackig; zerlumpt.

ragman ['rægmən] Lumpensammler m.

raid [reid] 1. (feindlicher) Überfall, Streifzug m; (Luft)Angriff m; Razzia f; 2. einbrechen in (acc.); überfallen.

rail¹ [reil] schimpfen.

rail² [~] 1. Geländer n; Stange f; 🚂 Schiene f; off the ~s entgleist; fig. in Unordnung; by ~ per Bahn; 2. a. ~ in, ~ off mit e-m Geländer umgeben.

railing ['reiliŋ], a. ~s pl. Geländer n; Staket n.

raillery ['reiləri] Spötterei f.

railroad Am. ['reilroud] Eisenbahn f. [~man Eisenbahner m.]

railway ['reilwei] Eisenbahn f.]

rain [rein] 1. Regen m; 2. regnen; ~bow ['reinbou] Regenbogen m; ~coat Regenmantel m; ~fall Regenmenge f; ~proof 1. regendicht; 2. Regenmantel m; ~y □ ['reini] regnerisch; Regen...; a ~ day fig. Notzeiten f/pl.

raise [reiz] oft ~ up heben; (oft fig.) erheben; errichten; erhöhen (a. fig.); Geld etc. aufbringen; Anleihe aufnehmen; verursachen; fig. erwecken; anstiften; züchten, ziehen; Belagerung etc. aufheben.

raisin ['reizn] Rosine f.

rake [reik] 1. Rechen m, Harke f; Wüstling m; Lebemann m; 2. v/t (zs.-)harken; ~s-scharren; fig. (durch)stöbern; ~off Am. sl. ['reikɔːf] Schwindelprofit m.

rakish □ ['reikiʃ] schnittig; liederlich, ausschweifend; verwegen; salopp.

rally ['ræli] 1. Sammeln n; Treffen n; Am. Massenversammlung f; Erholung f; mot. Rallye f; 2. (sich ver)sammeln; sich erholen; necken.

ram [ræm] 1. zo., ast. Widder m; ⊕, ⚓ Ramme f; 2. (fest)rammen; ⚓ rammen.

rambl|e ['ræmbl] 1. Streifzug m; 2. umherstreifen; abschweifen; ~er [~lə] Wanderer m; ⚓ Kletterrose f; ~ing [~liŋ] weitläufig.

ramify ['ræmifai] (sich) verzweigen.

ramp [ræmp] Rampe f; ~ant □ ['ræmpənt] wuchernd; fig. zügellos.

rampart ['ræmpɑːt] Wall m.

ramshackle ['ræmʃækl] wack(e)lig.

ran [ræn] pret. von run 1.

ranch [rɑːntʃ, Am. ræntʃ] Ranch f, Viehfarm f; ~er [~ə, Am. rɑːntʃə, Am. 'ræntʃə], ~man Rancher m, Viehzüchter m; Farmer m.

rancid □ ['rænsid] ranzig.

ranco(u)r ['ræŋkə] Groll m, Haß m.

random ['rændəm] 1. at ~ aufs Geratewohl, blindlings; 2. ziellos; wahllos; zufällig.

rang [ræŋ] pret. von ring 2.

range [reindʒ] 1. Reihe f; (Berg-) Kette f; ✝ Kollektion f, Sortiment n; Herd m; Raum m; Umfang m, Bereich m; Reichweite f; Schußweite f; (ausgedehnte) Fläche; Schießstand m; 2. v/t. (ein)reihen, ordnen; Gebiet etc. durchstreifen; ⚓ längs et. fahren; v/i. in e-r Reihe od. Linie stehen; (umher-) streifen; sich erstrecken, reichen; ~r ['reindʒə] Förster m; Aufseher m e-s Parks; Am. Förster m; ✕ Nahkampfspezialist m.

rank [ræŋk] 1. Reihe f, Linie f; ✕ Glied n; Klasse f; Rang m, Stand m; the ~s pl., the ~ and file die Mannschaften f/pl.; fig. die große Masse; 2. v/t. (ein)reihen, (ein-) ordnen; v/i. sich reihen, sich ordnen; gehören (with zu); e-e Stelle einnehmen (above über dat.); ~ as gelten als; 3. üppig; ranzig; stinkend.

rankle fig. ['ræŋkl] nagen.

ransack ['rænsæk] durchwühlen, durchstöbern, durchsuchen; ausrauben.

ransom ['rænsəm] 1. Lösegeld n; Auslösung f; 2. loskaufen; erlösen.

rant [rænt] 1. Schwulst m; 2. Phrasen dreschen; mit Pathos vortragen.

rap [ræp] 1. Klaps m; Klopfen n; fig. Heller m; 2. schlagen, klopfen.

rapaci|ous □ [rə'peiʃəs] raubgierig; ~ty [rə'pæsiti] Raubgier f.

rape [reip] 1. Raub m; Entführung f; Notzucht f, Vergewaltigung f; ⚘ Raps m; 2. rauben; vergewaltigen.

rapid ['ræpid] 1. □ schnell, reißend, rapid(e); steil; 2. ~s pl. Stromschnelle(n pl.) f; ~ity [rə'piditi] Schnelligkeit f.

rapprochement pol. ['ræ'prɔʃmɑ̃ːŋ] Wiederannäherung f.

rapt [ræpt] entzückt; versunken; ~ure ['ræptʃə] Entzücken n; go into ~s in Entzücken geraten.

rare [rɛə] selten; phys. dünn.

rarebit ['rɛəbit]: Welsh ~ geröstete Käseschnitte.

rarefy ['rɛərifai] (sich) verdünnen.

rarity ['rɛəriti] Seltenheit f; Dünnheit f.

rascal ['rɑːskəl] Schuft m; co. Gauner m; ~ity [rɑːsˈkæliti] Schurkerei f; ~ly [rɑːskəli] schuftig; erbärmlich.

rash¹ □ [ræʃ] hastig, vorschnell; übereilt; unbesonnen; waghalsig.

rash² 🕮 [~] Hautausschlag m.

rasher ['ræʃə] Speckschnitte f.

rasp [rɑːsp] 1. Raspel f; 2. raspeln; j-m weh(e) tun; kratzen; krächzen.

raspberry ['rɑːzbəri] Himbeere f.

rat [ræt] zo. Ratte f; pol. Überläufer m; smell a ~ Lunte od. den Braten riechen; ~s! Quatsch!

rate [reit] 1. Verhältnis n, Maß n,

Satz *m*; Rate *f*; Preis *m*, Gebühr *f*; Taxe *f*; (Gemeinde)Abgabe *f*, Steuer *f*; Grad *m*, Rang *m*; *bsd.* ⚓ Klasse *f*; Geschwindigkeit *f*; *at any ~* auf jeden Fall; *~ of exchange* (Umrechnungs)Kurs *m*; *~ of interest* Zinsfuß *m*; 2. (ein)schätzen; besteuern; ~ *among* rechnen, zählen zu (*dat.*); ~ ausschelten.

rather ['rɑːðə] eher, lieber; vielmehr; besser gesagt; eigentlich; *~! F* und ob!; *I had od. would ~ do* ich möchte lieber tun.

ratify ['rætifai] ratifizieren.

rating ['reitiŋ] Schätzung *f*; Steuersatz *m*; ⚓ Dienstgrad *m*; ⚓ (Segel-) Klasse *f*; Matrose *m*; Schelte(n *n*) *f*.

ratio ⚗ etc. ['reiʃiou] Verhältnis *n*.

ration ['ræʃən] 1. Ration *f*, Zuteilung *f*; 2. rationieren.

rational □ ['ræʃənl] vernunftgemäß; vernünftig, (*a.* ⚗) rational; **~ity** [ræʃə'næliti] Vernunft(mäßigkeit) *f*; **~ize** ['ræʃnəlaiz] rationalisieren; wirtschaftlich gestalten.

rat race ['ræt 'reis] sinnlose Hetze; rücksichtsloses Aufstiegsstreben.

ratten ['rætn] sabotieren.

rattle ['rætl] 1. Gerassel *n*; Geklapper *n*; Geplapper *n*; Klapper *f*; (Todes)Röcheln *n*; 2. rasseln (mit); klappern; plappern; röcheln; ~ *off* herunterrasseln; **~-brain**, **~-pate** Hohl-, Wirrkopf *m*; **~snake** Klapperschlange *f*; **~trap** *fig.* Klapperkasten *m* (*Fahrzeug*).

rattling ['rætliŋ] 1. *adj.* rasselnd; *fig.* scharf (*Tempo*); 2. *adv.* sehr, äußerst.

raucous □ ['rɔːkəs] heiser, rauh.

ravage ['rævidʒ] 1. Verwüstung *f*; 2. verwüsten; plündern.

rave [reiv] rasen, toben; schwärmen (*about, of* von).

ravel ['rævəl] *v/t.* verwickeln; ~ (*out*) auftrennen; *fig.* entwirren; *v/i. a.* ~ *out* ausfasern, aufgehen.

raven *orn.* ['reivn] Rabe *m*.

raven|ing ['rævniŋ], **~ous** □ ['rævinəs] gefräßig; heißhungrig; raubgierig.

ravine [rə'viːn] Hohlweg *m*; Schlucht *f*.

ravings ['reiviŋz] *pl.* Delirien *n/pl.*

ravish ['ræviʃ] entzücken; vergewaltigen; rauben; **~ing** □ [~ʃiŋ] hinreißend, entzückend; **~ment** [~ʃmənt] Schändung *f*; Entzücken *n*.

raw □ [rɔː] roh; Roh...; wund; rauh (*Wetter*); ungeübt, unerfahren; **~-boned** ['rɔː'bound] knochig, hager; **~ hide** Rohleder *n*.

ray [rei] Strahl *m*; *fig.* Schimmer *m*.

rayon ['reiɔn] Kunstseide *f*.

raze [reiz] *Haus etc.* abreißen; *Festung* schleifen; tilgen.

razor ['reizə] Rasiermesser *n*; Rasierapparat *m*; **~-blade** Rasierklinge *f*; **~-edge** *fig. des Messers* Schneide *f*, kritische Lage.

razz *Am. sl.* [ræz] aufziehen.

re... [riː] wieder...; zurück...; neu...; um...

reach [riːtʃ] 1. Ausstrecken *n*; Griff *m*; Reichweite *f*; Fassungskraft *f*, Horizont *m*; Flußstrecke *f*; *beyond ~, out of ~* unerreichbar; *within easy ~* leicht erreichbar; 2. *v/i.* reichen; langen, greifen; sich erstrecken; *v/t.* (hin-, her)reichen, (hin-, her)langen; ausstrecken; erreichen.

react [riː'ækt] reagieren (*to* auf *acc.*); (ein)wirken (*on, upon* auf *acc.*); sich auflehnen (*against* gegen).

reaction [riː'ækʃən] Reaktion *f* (*a. pol.*); **~ary** [~ʃnəri] 1. reaktionär; 2. Reaktionär(in).

reactor *phys.* [riː'æktə] Reaktor *m*.

read 1. [riːd] [*irr.*] lesen; deuten; (an)zeigen (*Thermometer*); studieren; sich *gut etc.* lesen; lauten; ~ *to s.o.* j-m vorlesen; 2. [red] *pret. u. p.p. von* 1; 3. [~] *adj.* belesen; **~able** □ ['riːdəbl] lesbar; leserlich; lesenswert; **~er** ['riːdə] (Vor)Leser(in); *typ.* Korrektor *m*; Lektor *m*; *univ.* Dozent *m*; Lesebuch *n*.

readi|ly ['redili] *adv.* gleich, leicht; gern; **~ness** [~inis] Bereitschaft *f*; Bereitwilligkeit *f*; Schnelligkeit *f*.

reading ['riːdiŋ] Lesen *n*; Lesung *f* (*a. parl.*); Stand *m des Thermometers*; Belesenheit *f*; Lektüre *f*; Lesart *f*; Auffassung *f*; *attr.* Lese...

readjust ['riːə'dʒʌst] wieder in Ordnung bringen; wieder anpassen; **~ment** [~tmənt] Wiederanpassung *f*; Neuordnung *f*.

ready □ ['redi] bereit, fertig; bereitwillig; im Begriff (*to do zu* tun); schnell; gewandt; leicht; zur Hand; † bar; ~ *for use* gebrauchsfertig; *make od. get ~* (sich) fertig machen; **~-made** fertig, Konfektions...

reagent ⚗ [riː'eidʒənt] Reagens *n*.

real □ [riəl] wirklich, tatsächlich, real; echt; ~ *estate* Grundbesitz *m*, Immobilien *pl.*; **~ism** ['riəlizəm] Realismus *m*; **~istic** [riə'listik] (~*ally*) realistisch; sachlich, wirklichkeitsnah; **~ity** [riː(ː)'æliti] Wirklichkeit *f*; **~ization** [riəlai'zeiʃən] Verwirklichung *f*; Erkenntnis *f*; † Realisierung *f*; **~ize** ['riəlaiz] sich klarmachen; erkennen; verwirklichen; realisieren, zu Geld machen; **~ly** [~li] wirklich, in der Tat.

realm [relm] Königreich *n*; Reich *n*.

realt|or *Am.* ['riəltə] Grundstücksmakler *m*; **~y** ⚖ [~ti] Grundeigentum *n*.

reap [riːp] *Korn* schneiden; Feld

mähen; *fig.* ernten; **~er** ['ri:pə] Schnitter(in); Mähmaschine *f.*

reappear ['ri:ə'piə] wieder erscheinen.

rear [riə] 1. *v/t.* auf-, großziehen; züchten; *v/i.* sich aufrichten; 2. Rück-, Hinterseite *f*; *mot.*, ⚓ Heck *n*; ⚔ Nachhut *f*; *at the ~ of, in* (*the*) *~ of* hinter (*dat.*); 3. Hinter..., Nach...; *~ wheel drive* Hinterradantrieb *m*; **~-admiral** ['riə-'ædmərəl] Konteradmiral *m*; **~-guard** ⚔ Nachhut *f*; **~-lamp** *mot.* Schlußlicht *n.*

rearm ['ri:'ɑ:m] (wieder)aufrüsten; **~ament** [~'mɑ:mənt] Aufrüstung *f.*

rearmost ['riəmoust] hinterst.

rearward ['riəwəd] 1. *adj.* rückwärtig; 2. *adv. a.* **~s** rückwärts.

reason ['ri:zn] 1. Vernunft *f*; Verstand *m*; Recht *n*, Billigkeit *f*; Ursache *f*, Grund *m*; *by ~ of* wegen; *for this ~* aus diesem Grund; *listen to ~* Vernunft annehmen; *it stands to ~ that* es leuchtet ein, daß; 2. *v/i.* vernünftig denken; schließen; urteilen; argumentieren; *v/t. a. ~ out* durchdenken; *~ away* fortdisputieren; *~ s.o. into* (*out of*) *s.th.* j-m et. ein- (aus)reden; **~able** □ [~nəbl] vernünftig; billig; angemessen; leidlich.

reassure [riə'ʃuə] wieder versichern; (wieder) beruhigen.

rebate ['ri:beit] † Rabatt *m*, Abzug *m*; Rückzahlung *f.*

rebel 1. ['rebl] Rebell *m*; Aufrührer *m*; 2. [~] rebellisch; 3. [ri'bel] sich auflehnen; **~lion** [~ljən] Empörung *f*; **~lious** [~jəs] = *rebel* 2.

rebirth ['ri:'bə:θ] Wiedergeburt *f.*

rebound [ri'baund] 1. zurückprallen; 2. Rückprall *m*, Rückschlag *m.*

rebuff [ri'bʌf] 1. Zurück-, Abweisung *f*; 2. zurück-, abweisen.

rebuild ['ri:'bild] (*irr.* (*build*)) wieder(auf)bauen.

rebuke [ri'bju:k] 1. Tadel *m*; 2. tadeln.

rebut [ri'bʌt] zurückweisen.

recall [ri'kɔ:l] 1. Zurückrufung *f*; Abberufung *f*; Widerruf *m*; *beyond ~, past ~* unwiderruflich; 2. zurückrufen; ab(be)rufen; (sich) erinnern an (*acc.*); widerrufen; † *Kapital* kündigen.

recapitulate [ri:kə'pitjuleit] kurz wiederholen, zs.-fassen.

recapture ['ri:'kæptʃə] wieder (gefangen)nehmen; ⚔ zurückerobern.

recast ['ri:'kɑ:st] *irr.* (*cast*)) ⊕ umgießen; umformen, neu gestalten.

recede [ri(:)'si:d] zurücktreten.

receipt [ri'si:t] 1. Empfang *m*; Eingang *m v. Waren*; Quittung *f*; (Koch)Rezept *n*; **~s** *pl.* Einnahmen *f/pl.*; 2. quittieren.

receiv|able [ri'si:vəbl] annehmbar; † noch zu fordern(d), ausstehend; **~e** [ri'si:v] empfangen; erhalten, bekommen; aufnehmen; annehmen; anerkennen; **~ed** anerkannt; **~er** [~və] Empfänger *m*; *teleph.* Hörer *m*; Hehler *m*; *Steuer- etc.* Einnehmer *m*; *official ~* ⚖ Masseverwalter *m.*

recent □ ['ri:snt] neu; frisch; modern; *~ events pl. die* jüngsten Ereignisse *n/pl.*; **~ly** [~tli] neulich, vor kurzem.

receptacle [ri'septəkl] Behälter *m.*

reception [ri'sepʃən] Aufnahme *f* (*a. fig.*), (*a.* Radio)Empfang *m*; Annahme *f*; **~ist** [~nist] Empfangsdame *f*, -herr *m*; **~-room** Empfangszimmer *n.*

receptive □ [ri'septiv] empfänglich, aufnahmefähig (*of* für).

recess [ri'ses] Pause *f*; *bsd. parl.* Ferien *pl.*; (entlegener) Winkel; Nische *f*; **~es** *pl. fig.* Tiefe(n *pl.*); **~ion** [~eʃən] Zurückziehen *n*, Zurücktreten *n*; † Konjunkturrückgang *m*, rückläufige Bewegung.

recipe ['resipi] Rezept *n.*

recipient [ri'sipiənt] Empfänger(in).

reciproc|al □ [ri'siprəkəl] wechsel-, gegenseitig; **~ate** [~keit] *v/i.* sich erkenntlich zeigen; ⊕ sich hin- und herbewegen; *v/t. Glückwünsche etc.* erwidern; **~ity** [resi'prɔsiti] Gegenseitigkeit *f.*

recit|al [ri'saitl] Bericht *m*; Erzählung *f*; ♪ (Solo)Vortrag *m*, Konzert *n*; **~ation** [resi'teiʃən] Hersagen *n*; Vortrag *m*; **~e** [ri'sait] vortragen; aufsagen; berichten.

reckless □ ['reklis] unbekümmert; rücksichtslos; leichtsinnig.

reckon ['rekən] *v/t.* rechnen; *a. ~ for, ~ as* schätzen als, halten für; *~ up* zs.-zählen; *v/i.* rechnen; denken, vermuten; *~ (up)on* sich verlassen auf (*acc.*); **~ing** [ri'rekniŋ] Rechnen *n*; (Ab-, Be)Rechnung *f.*

reclaim [ri'kleim] wiedergewinnen; *j-n* bessern; zivilisieren; urbar machen.

recline [ri'klain] (sich) (zurück)lehnen; *~ upon fig.* sich stützen auf.

recluse [ri'klu:s] Einsiedler(in).

recogni|tion [rekəg'niʃən] Anerkennung *f*; Wiedererkennen *n*; **~ze** ['rekəgnaiz] anerkennen; (wieder)erkennen.

recoil [ri'kɔil] 1. zurückprallen; 2. Rückstoß *m*, -lauf *m.*

recollect[1] [rekə'lekt] sich erinnern an (*acc.*).

re-collect[2] ['ri:kə'lekt] wieder sammeln; *~ o.s.* sich fassen.

recollection [rekə'lekʃən] Erinnerung *f* (*of an acc.*); Gedächtnis *n.*

recommend [rekə'mend] empfehlen; **~ation** [rekəmen'deiʃən] Empfehlung *f*; Vorschlag *m.*

recompense ['rekəmpens] 1. Belohnung *f*, Vergeltung *f*; Ersatz *m*;

2. belohnen, vergelten; entschädigen; ersetzen.

reconcil|e ['rekənsail] aus-, versöhnen; in Einklang bringen; schlichten; **~iation** [rekənsili'eiʃən] Ver-, Aussöhnung f.

recondition ['ri:kən'diʃən] wieder herrichten; ⊕ überholen.

reconn|aissance ✕ [ri'kɔnisəns] Aufklärung f, Erkundung f; fig. Übersicht f; **~oitre**, Am. **~oiter** [rekə'nɔitə] erkunden, auskundschaften.

reconsider ['ri:kən'sidə] wieder erwägen; nochmals überlegen.

reconstitute ['ri:'kɔnstitju:t] wiederherstellen.

reconstruct ['ri:kəns'trʌkt] wiederaufbauen; **~ion** [~kʃən] Wiederaufbau m, Wiederherstellung f.

reconvert ['ri:kən'və:t] umstellen.

record 1. ['rekɔ:d] Aufzeichnung f; ⚖ Protokoll n; schriftlicher Bericht; Ruf m, Leumund m; Wiedergabe f; Schallplatte f; Sport: Rekord m; place on ~ schriftlich niederlegen; ⚘ Office Staatsarchiv n; off the ~ Am. inoffiziell; 2. [ri'kɔ:d] auf-, verzeichnen; auf Schallplatte etc. aufnehmen; **~er** [~də] Registrator m; Stadtrichter m; Aufnahmegerät n, bsd. Tonbandgerät n; ♪ Blockflöte f; **~ing** [~diŋ] Radio: Aufzeichnung f, Aufnahme f; **~player** Plattenspieler m.

recount [ri'kaunt] erzählen.

recoup [ri'ku:p] j-n entschädigen (for für); et. wieder einbringen.

recourse [ri'kɔ:s] Zuflucht f; have ~ to s-e Zuflucht nehmen zu.

recover [ri'kʌvə] v/t. wiedererlangen, wiederfinden; wieder einbringen, wiedergutmachen; Schulden etc. eintreiben; be ~ed wiederhergestellt sein; v/i. sich erholen; genesen; **~y** [~əri] Wiedererlangung f; Wiederherstellung f; Genesung f; Erholung f.

recreat|e ['rekrieit] v/t. erfrischen; v/i. a. ~ o.s. sich erholen; **~ion** [rekri'eiʃən] Erholung(spause) f.

recrimination [rikrimi'neiʃən] Gegenbeschuldigung f; Gegenklage f.

recruit [ri'kru:t] 1. Rekrut m; fig. Neuling m; 2. erneuern, ergänzen; Truppe rekrutieren; ✕ Rekruten ausheben; sich erholen.

rectangle ⟀ ['rektæŋgl] Rechteck n.

recti|fy ['rektifai] berichtigen; verbessern; ⨀, Radio: gleichrichten; **~tude** [~itju:d] Geradheit f.

rector ['rektə] Pfarrer m; Rektor m; **~y** [~əri] Pfarre(i) f; Pfarrhaus n.

recumbent □ [ri'kʌmbənt] liegend.

recuperate [ri'kju:pəreit] wiederherstellen; sich erholen.

recur [ri'kə:] zurück-, wiederkehren (to zu), zurückkommen (to auf acc.); ~ to j-m wieder einfallen; **~rence**

[ri'kʌrəns] Wieder-, Rückkehr f; **~rent** □ [~nt] wiederkehrend.

red [red] 1. rot; ~ heat Rotglut f; ~ herring Bückling m; ~ tape Amtsschimmel m; 2. Rot n; (bsd. pol.) Rote(r m) f; be in the ~ Am. F in Schulden stecken.

red|breast ['redbrest] a. robin ~ Rotkehlchen n; **~cap** Militärpolizist m; Am. Gepäckträger m; **~den** ['redn] (sich) röten; erröten; **~dish** ['rediʃ] rötlich.

redecorate ['ri:'dekəreit] Zimmer renovieren (lassen).

redeem [ri'di:m] zurück-, loskaufen; ablösen; Versprechen einlösen; büßen; entschädigen für; erlösen; **2er** eccl. [~mə] Erlöser m, Heiland m.

redemption [ri'dempʃən] Rückkauf m; Auslösung f; Erlösung f.

red|-handed ['red'hændid]: catch od. take s.o. ~ j-n auf frischer Tat ertappen; **~head** Rotschopf m; Hitzkopf m; **~-headed** rothaarig; **~-hot** rotglühend; fig. hitzig; ⚘ Indian Indianer(in); **~-letter day** Festtag m; fig. Freuden-, Glückstag m; **~ness** ['rednis] Röte f.

redolent ['redoulənt] duftend.

redouble [ri'dʌbl] (sich) verdoppeln.

redoubt ✕ [ri'daut] Redoute f; **~able** rhet. [~təbl] fürchterlich.

redound [ri'daund]: ~ to beitragen od. gereichen zu, führen zu.

redress [ri'dres] 1. Abhilfe f; Wiedergutmachung f; ⚖ Entschädigung f; 2. abhelfen (dat.); wiedergutmachen.

red|-tapism ['red'teipizəm] Bürokratismus m; **~tapist** [~ist] Bürokrat m.

reduc|e [ri'dju:s] fig. zurückführen, bringen (to auf, in acc., zu); verwandeln (to in acc.); verringern, vermindern; einschränken; Preise herabsetzen; (be)zwingen; ♫, ⚘ reduzieren; ⚕ einrenken; ~ to writing schriftlich niederlegen; **~tion** [ri'dakʃən] Reduktion f; Verwandlung f; Herabsetzung f, (Preis)Nachlaß m, Rabatt m; Verminderung f; Verkleinerung f; ⚙ Einrenkung f.

redundant □ [ri'dʌndənt] überflüssig; übermäßig; weitschweifig.

reed [ri:d] Schilfrohr n; Rohrflöte f.

re-education ['ri:edju(:)'keiʃən] Umschulung f, Umerziehung f.

reef [ri:f] (Felsen)Riff n; ♠ Reff n.

reefer ['ri:fə] Seemannsjacke f; Am. sl. Marihuana-Zigarette f.

reek [ri:k] 1. Rauch m, Dampf m; Dunst m; 2. rauchen, dampfen (with von); unangenehm riechen.

reel [ri:l] 1. Haspel f; (Garn-, Film)Rolle f, Spule f; 2. v/t. haspeln; wickeln, spulen; v/i. wirbeln; schwanken; taumeln.

re-elect ['ri:i'lekt] wiederwählen.
re-enter [ri:'entə] wieder eintreten (in *acc.*).
re-establish ['ri:is'tæbliʃ] wiederherstellen.
refection [ri'fekʃən] Erfrischung *f.*
refer [ri'fə:]: ~ to ver-, überweisen an (*acc.*); sich beziehen auf (*acc.*); erwähnen (*acc.*); zuordnen (*dat.*); befragen (*acc.*), nachschlagen in (*dat.*); zurückführen auf (*acc.*), zuschreiben (*dat.*); ~ee [refə'ri:] Schiedsrichter *m*; *Boxen:* Ringrichter *m*; ~ence ['refrəns] Referenz *f*, Empfehlung *f*, Zeugnis *n*; Verweisung *f*; Bezugnahme *f*; Anspielung *f*; Beziehung *f*; Auskunft (-geber *m*) *f*; *in od.* with ~ to in betreff (*gen.*), in bezug auf (*acc.*); ~ book Nachschlagewerk *n*; ~ library Handbibliothek *f*; ~ number Aktenzeichen *n*; make ~ to et. erwähnen.
referendum [refə'rendəm] Volksentscheid *m.*
refill 1. ['ri:fil] Nachfüllung *f*; Ersatzfüllung *f*; **2.** ['ri:'fil] (sich) wieder füllen, auffüllen.
refine [ri'fain] (sich) verfeinern *od.* veredeln *f* ⊕ raffinieren; (sich) läutern (*a. fig.*); klügeln; ~ (*up*)*on* et. verfeinern, verbessern; ~ment [~nmənt] Verfeinerung *f*, Veredelung *f*; Läuterung *f*; Feinheit *f*, Bildung *f*; Spitzfindigkeit *f*; ~ry [~nəri] ⊕ Raffinerie *f*; *metall.* (Eisen)Hütte *f.*
refit ⚓ ['ri:'fit] *v/t.* ausbessern; neu ausrüsten; *v/i.* ausgebessert werden.
reflect [ri'flekt] *v/t.* zurückwerfen, reflektieren; zurückstrahlen, widerspiegeln (*a. fig.*); zum Ausdruck bringen; *v/i.* ~ (*up*)*on* nachdenken über (*acc.*); sich abfällig äußern über (*acc.*); ein schlechtes Licht werfen auf (*acc.*); ~ion [~kʃən] Zurückstrahlung *f*, Widerspiegelung *f*; Reflex *m*; Spiegelbild *n*; Überlegung *f*; Gedanke *m*; abfällige Bemerkung *f*; Makel *m*; ~ive □ [~ktiv] zurückstrahlend; nachdenklich.
reflex ['ri:fleks] **1.** Reflex...; **2.** Widerschein *m*, Reflex *m* (*a. physiol.*).
reflexive □ [ri'fleksiv] zurückwirkend; *gr.* reflexiv, rückbezüglich.
reforest ['ri:'fɔrist] aufforsten.
reform[1] [ri'fɔ:m] **1.** Verbesserung *f*, Reform *f*; **2.** verbessern, reformieren; (sich) bessern.
re-form[2] ['ri:'fɔ:m] (sich) neu bilden; ⚔ sich wieder formieren.
reform|ation [refə'meiʃən] Umgestaltung *f*; Besserung *f*; *eccl.* ♀ Reformation *f*; ~atory [~'fɔ:mətəri] **1.** bessernd; **2.** Besserungsanstalt *f*; ~er [ri'fɔ:mə] *eccl.* Reformator *m*; *bsd. pol.* Reformer *m.*

refract|ion [ri'frækʃən] Strahlenbrechung *f*; ~ory □ [~ktəri] widerspenstig; hartnäckig; ⊕ feuerfest.
refrain [ri'frein] **1.** sich enthalten (*from gen.*), unterlassen (*from acc.*); **2.** Kehrreim *m*, Refrain *m.*
refresh [ri'freʃ] (sich) erfrischen; auffrischen; ~ment [~ʃmənt] Erfrischung *f* (*a. Getränk etc.*).
refrigerat|e [ri'fridʒəreit] kühlen; ~or [~tə] Kühlschrank *m*, -raum *m*; ~ car Kühlwagen *m.*
refuel ['ri:'fjuəl] tanken.
refuge ['refju:dʒ] Zuflucht(sstätte) *f*; *a.* street~ Verkehrsinsel *f*; ~e [refju:(')dʒi:] Flüchtling *m*; ~ camp Flüchtlingslager *n.*
refulgent □ [ri'fʌldʒənt] strahlend.
refund [ri:'fʌnd] zurückzahlen.
refurbish ['ri:'fə:biʃ] aufpolieren.
refusal [ri'fju:zəl] abschlägige Antwort; (Ver)Weigerung *f*; Vorkaufsrecht *n* (*of auf acc.*).
refuse[1] [ri'fju:z] *v/t.* verweigern; abweisen, ablehnen; scheuen vor (*dat.*); *v/i.* sich weigern; scheuen (*Pferd*).   [fall *m*, Müll *m.*]
refuse[2] ['refju:s] Ausschuß *m*; Ab-
refute [ri'fju:t] widerlegen.
regain [ri'gein] wiedergewinnen.
regal □ ['ri:gəl] königlich; Königs...
regale [ri'geil] *v/t.* festlich bewirten; *v/i.* schwelgen (*in in dat.*).
regard [ri'gɑ:d] **1.** *fester* Blick; (Hoch)Achtung *f*, Rücksicht *f*; Beziehung *f*; with ~ to im Hinblick auf (*acc.*); kind ~s herzliche Grüße; **2.** ansehen; (be)achten; betrachten; betreffen; as ~s ... was ... anbetrifft; ~ing □ [~diŋ] hinsichtlich (*gen.*); ~less □ [~dlis]: ~ of ohne Rücksicht auf (*acc.*).
regenerate 1. [ri'dʒenəreit] (sich) erneuern; (sich) regenerieren; (sich) neu bilden; **2.** [~rit] wiedergeboren.
regent ['ri:dʒənt] **1.** herrschend; **2.** Regent *m.*
regiment ⚔ ['redʒimənt] **1.** Regiment *n*; **2.** [~mənt] organisieren; ~als ⚔ [redʒi'mentlz] *pl.* Uniform*f.*
region ['ri:dʒən] Gegend *f*, Gebiet *n*; *fig.* Bereich *m*; ~al □ [~nl] örtlich; Orts...
register ['redʒistə] **1.** Register *n*, Verzeichnis *n*; ⊕ Schieber *m*, Ventil *n*; ♪ Register *n*; Zählwerk *n*; cash ~ Registrierkasse *f*; **2.** registrieren *od.* eintragen (lassen); (an-) zeigen, auf-, verzeichnen; *Postsache* einschreiben (lassen), Gepäck aufgeben; sich *polizeilich* melden.
registr|ar [redʒis'trɑ:] Registrator *m*; Standesbeamte(r) *m*; ~ation [~reiʃən] Eintragung *f*; Fee Anmeldegebühr *f*; ~y ['redʒistri] Eintragung *f*; Registratur *f*; Register *n*; ~ office Standesamt *n.*
regress, ~ion ['ri:gres, ri'greʃən] Rückkehr *f*; *fig.* Rückgang *m.*

regret [ri'gret] **1.** Bedauern *n*; Schmerz *m*; **2.** bedauern; *Verlust* beklagen; **~ful** □ [~tful] bedauernd; **~fully** [~li] mit Bedauern; **~table** □ [~təbl] bedauerlich.

regular □ ['regjulə] regelmäßig; regelrecht, richtig; ordentlich; pünktlich; ✕ regulär; **~ity** [regju'læriti] Regelmäßigkeit *f*; Richtigkeit *f*, Ordnung *f*.

regulat|e ['regjuleit] regeln, ordnen; regulieren; **~ion** [regju'leiʃən] **1.** Regulierung *f*; Vorschrift *f*, Bestimmung *f*; **2.** vorschriftsmäßig.

rehash *fig.* ['ri:'hæʃ] **1.** wieder durchkauen *od.* aufwärmen; **2.** Aufguß *m*.

rehears|al [ri'hə:səl] *thea.*, *♪* Probe *f*; Wiederholung *f*; **~e** [ri'hə:s] *thea.* proben; wiederholen; aufsagen.

reign [rein] **1.** Regierung *f*; *fig.* Herrschaft *f*; **2.** herrschen, regieren.

reimburse [ri:im'bə:s] *j-n* entschädigen; *Kosten* wiedererstatten.

rein [rein] **1.** Zügel *m*; **2.** zügeln.

reindeer *zo.* ['reindiə] Ren(tier)*n*.

reinforce [ri:in'fɔ:s] verstärken; **~ment** [~smənt] Verstärkung *f*.

reinstate ['ri:in'steit] wieder einsetzen; wieder instand setzen.

reinsure ['ri:in'ʃuə] rückversichern.

reiterate [ri:'itəreit] (dauernd) wiederholen.

reject [ri'dʒekt] ver-, wegwerfen; ablehnen, ausschlagen; zurückweisen; **~ion** [~kʃən] Verwerfung *f*; Ablehnung *f*; Zurückweisung *f*.

rejoic|e [ri'dʒɔis] *v/t.* erfreuen; *v/i.* sich freuen (*at*, *in* über *acc.*); **~ing** [~siŋ] **1.** □ freudig; **2.** *oft* **~s** *pl.* Freude(nfest *n*) *f*.

rejoin ['ri:'dʒɔin] (sich) wieder vereinigen (mit); wieder zurückkehren zu; [ri'dʒɔin] erwidern.

rejuvenate [ri'dʒu:vineit] verjüngen. [entzünden.]

rekindle ['ri:'kindl] (sich) wieder)

relapse [ri'læps] **1.** Rückfall *m*; **2.** zurückfallen, rückfällig werden.

relate [ri'leit] *v/t.* erzählen; in Beziehung bringen; *v/i.* sich beziehen (*to* auf *acc.*); **~d** verwandt (*to* mit).

relation [ri'leiʃən] Erzählung *f*; Beziehung *f*; Verhältnis *n*; Verwandtschaft *f*; Verwandte(r *m*) *f*; *in* **~** *to* in bezug auf (*acc.*); **~ship** [~ʃip] Verwandtschaft *f*; Beziehung *f*.

relative ['relətiv] **1.** □ bezüglich (*to gen.*); *gr.* relativ; verhältnismäßig; entsprechend; **2.** *gr.* Relativpronomen *n*; Verwandte(r *m*) *f*.

relax [ri'læks] (sich) lockern; mildern; nachlassen (in *dat.*); (sich) entspannen, ausspannen; milder **~ation** [ri:læk'seiʃən] Lockerung *f*; Nachlassen *n*; Entspannung *f*, Erholung *f*.

relay¹ [ri'lei] frisches Gespann; Ablösung *f*; ['ri:'lei] *⚡* Relais *n*; *Radio:* Übertragung *f*; **2.** [~] *Radio:* übertragen.

re-lay² ['ri:'lei] *Kabel etc.* neu verlegen.

relay-race ['ri:leireis] *Sport:* Staffellauf *m*.

release [ri'li:s] **1.** Freilassung *f*; *fig.* Befreiung *f*; Freigabe *f*; *Film:* oft first **~** Uraufführung *f*; ⊕, *phot.* Auslöser *m*; **2.** freilassen; erlösen; freigeben; *Recht* aufgeben, übertragen; *Film* uraufführen; ⊕ auslösen.

relegate ['religeit] verbannen; verweisen (*to an acc.*).

relent [ri'lent] sich erweichen lassen; **~less** □ [~tlis] unbarmherzig.

relevant ['relivənt] sachdienlich; zutreffend; wichtig, erheblich.

reliab|ility [rilaiə'biliti] Zuverlässigkeit *f*; **~le** □ [ri'laiəbl] zuverlässig.

reliance [ri'laiəns] Ver-, Zutrauen *n*; Verlaß *m*.

relic ['relik] Überrest *m*; Reliquie *f*; **~t** [~kt] Witwe *f*.

relief [ri'li:f] Erleichterung *f*; (angenehme) Unterbrechung; Unterstützung *f*; ✕ Ablösung *f*; Entsatz *m*; Hilfe *f*; △ *etc.* Relief *n*; **~ works** *pl.* Notstandsarbeiten *f/pl.*

relieve [ri'li:v] erleichtern; mildern, lindern; *Arme etc.* unterstützen; ✕ ablösen; ⚡ entsetzen; *♪♪* (ab)helfen (*dat.*); befreien; hervortreten lassen; (angenehm) unterbrechen.

religion [ri'lidʒən] Religion *f*; Ordensleben *n*; *fig.* Ehrensache *f*.

religious □ [ri'lidʒəs] Religions...; religiös; *eccl.* Ordens...; gewissenhaft.

relinquish [ri'liŋkwiʃ] aufgeben; verzichten auf (*acc.*); loslassen.

relish ['reliʃ] **1.** (Bei)Geschmack *m*; Würze *f*; Genuß *m*; **2.** gern essen; Geschmack finden an (*dat.*); schmackhaft machen.

reluctan|ce [ri'lʌktəns] Widerstreben *n*; *bsd. phys.* Widerstand *m*; **~t** □ [~nt] widerstrebend, widerwillig.

rely [ri'lai] **~** (*up*)*on* sich verlassen (auf *acc.*), bauen auf (*acc.*).

remain [ri'mein] **1.** (ver)bleiben; übrigbleiben; **2.** **~s** *pl.* Überbleibsel *n/pl.*, Überreste *m/pl.*; sterbliche Reste *m/pl.*; **~der** [~ndə] Rest *m*.

remand [ri'mɑ:nd] **1.** *♪♪* in die Untersuchungshaft) zurückschicken; **2.** (Zurücksendung *f* in die) Untersuchungshaft *f*; *prisoner on* **~** Untersuchungsgefangene(r *m*) *f*; **~ home** Jugendstrafanstalt *f*.

remark [ri'mɑ:k] **1.** Beachtung *f*; Bemerkung *f*; **2.** *v/t.* bemerken; *v/i.* sich äußern; **~able** □ [~kəbl] bemerkenswert; merkwürdig.

remedy ['remidi] 1. (Heil-, Hilfs-, Gegen-, Rechts)Mittel *n*; (Ab-)Hilfe *f*; 2. heilen; abhelfen (*dat.*).

rememb|er [ri'membə] sich erinnern an (*acc.*); denken an (*acc.*); beherzigen; ~ me to her grüße sie von mir; ~rance [~brəns] Erinnerung *f*; Gedächtnis *n*; Andenken *n*; ~s *pl.* Empfehlungen *f/pl.*, Grüße *m/pl.*

remind [ri'maind] erinnern (*of* an *acc.*); ~er [~də] Mahnung *f*.

reminiscen|ce [remi'nisns] Erinnerung *f*; ~t □ [~nt] (sich) erinnernd.

remiss □ [ri'mis] schlaff, (nach-)lässig; ~ion [~ʃən] *Sünden*-Vergebung *f*; Erlassung *f* v. *Strafe etc.*; Nachlassen *n*.

remit [ri'mit] *Sünden* vergeben; *Schuld etc.* erlassen; nachlassen in (*dat.*); überweisen; ~tance [~təns] (Geld)Sendung *f*; ✝ Rimesse *f*.

remnant ['remnənt] (Über)Rest *m*.

remodel [ri'mɔdl] umbilden.

remonstra|nce [ri'mɔnstrəns] Vorstellung *f*, Einwendung *f*; ~te [~treit] Vorstellungen machen (*on* über *acc.*; *with s.o.* j-m); einwenden.

remorse [ri'mɔːs] Gewissensbisse *m/pl.*; ~less □ [~slis] hart(herzig).

remote □ [ri'mout] entfernt, entlegen; ~ness [~nis] Entfernung *f*.

remov|al [ri'muːvəl] Entfernen *n*; Beseitigung *f*; Umzug *m*; Entlassung *f*; ~ van Möbelwagen *m*; ~e [~uːv] 1. *v/t.* entfernen; wegräumen, wegrücken; beseitigen; entlassen; *v/i.* (aus-, um-, ver)ziehen; 2. Entfernung *f*; Grad *m*; *Schule*: Versetzung *f*; Abteilung *f* e-r *Klasse*; ~er [~və] (Möbel)Spediteur *m*.

remunerat|e [ri'mjuːnəreit] (be-)lohnen; *Dank* abstatten; entschädigen; ~ive □ [~rətiv] lohnend.

Renaissance [rə'neisəns] Renaissance *f*.

renascen|ce [ri'næsns] Wiedergeburt *f*; Renaissance *f*; ~t [~nt] wieder wachsend.

rend [rend] [*irr.*] (zer)reißen.

render ['rendə] wieder-, zurückgeben; *Dienst etc.* leisten; *Ehre etc.* erweisen; *Dank* abstatten; übersetzen; ♪ vortragen; darstellen; interpretieren; *Grund* angeben; ✝ *Rechnung* überreichen; übergeben; machen (zu); *Fett* auslassen; ~ing [~əriŋ] Wiedergabe *f*; Interpretation *f*; Übersetzung *f*, Wiedergabe *f*; △ Rohbewurf *m*.

rendition [ren'diʃən] Wiedergabe *f*.

renegade ['renigeid] Abtrünnige(r *m*) *f*.

renew [ri'njuː] erneuern; ~al [~u(ː)əl] Erneuerung *f*.

renounce [ri'nauns] entsagen (*dat.*); verzichten auf (*acc.*); verleugnen.

renovate ['renouveit] erneuern.

renown [ri'naun] Ruhm *m*, Ansehen *n*; ~ed [~nd] berühmt, namhaft.

rent[1] [rent] 1. *pret. u. p.p. von* rend; 2. Riß *m*; Spalte *f*.

rent[2] [~] 1. Miete *f*; Pacht *f*; 2. (ver)mieten, (ver)pachten; ~al ['rentl] (Einkommen *n* aus) Miete *f* *od.* Pacht *f*.

renunciation [rinʌnsi'eiʃən] Entsagung *f*; Verzicht *m* (*of* auf *acc.*).

repair[1] [ri'pɛə] 1. Ausbesserung *f*, Reparatur *f*; ~s *pl.* Instandsetzungsarbeiten *f/pl.*; ~ shop Reparaturwerkstatt *f*; *in good* ~ in gutem (baulichen) Zustand, gut erhalten; *out of* ~ baufällig; 2. reparieren, ausbessern; erneuern; wiedergutmachen.

repair[2] [~]: ~ *to* sich begeben nach.

reparation [repə'reiʃən] Ersatz *m*; Entschädigung *f*; *make* ~s *pol.* Reparationen leisten.

repartee [repɑː'tiː] schlagfertige Antwort; Schlagfertigkeit *f*.

repast [ri'pɑːst] Mahl(zeit *f*) *n*.

repay [riː'pei] [*irr.* (*pay*)] *et.* zurückzahlen; *fig.* erwidern; *et.* vergelten; *j-n* entschädigen; ~ment [~eimənt] Rückzahlung *f*.

repeal [ri'piːl] 1. Aufhebung *f* von *Gesetzen*; 2. aufheben, widerrufen.

repeat [ri'piːt] 1. (sich) wiederholen; aufsagen; nachliefern; aufstoßen (*Essen*); 2. Wiederholung *f*; *oft* ~ *order* Nachbestellung *f*; ♪ Wiederholungszeichen *n*.

repel [ri'pel] zurückstoßen, zurücktreiben, zurückweisen; *fig.* abstoßen.

repent [ri'pent] bereuen; ~ance [~təns] Reue *f*; ~ant [~nt] reuig.

repercussion [riːpəː'kʌʃən] Rückprall *m*; *fig.* Rückwirkung *f*.

repertory ['repətəri] *thea.* Repertoire *n*; *fig.* Fundgrube *f*.

repetition [repi'tiʃən] Wiederholung *f*; Aufsagen *n*; Nachbildung *f*.

replace [ri'pleis] wieder hinstellen *od.* einsetzen; ersetzen; an *j-s* Stelle treten; ~ment [~smənt] Ersatz *m*.

replant ['riː'plɑːnt] umpflanzen.

replenish [ri'pleniʃ] wieder auffüllen; ~ment [~ʃmənt] Auffüllung *f*; Ergänzung *f*.

replete [ri'pliːt] angefüllt, voll.

replica ['replikə] Nachbildung *f*.

reply [ri'plai] 1. antworten, erwidern (*to* auf *acc.*); 2. Erwiderung *f*.

report [ri'pɔːt] 1. Bericht *m*; Gerücht *n*; *guter* Ruf; Knall *m*; *school* ~ (Schul)Zeugnis *n*; 2. berichten (*über acc.*); (sich) melden; anzeigen; ~er [~tə] Berichterstatter(in).

repos|e [ri'pouz] 1. *allg.* Ruhe *f*; 2. *v/t.* ausruhen; (aus)ruhen lassen; ~ *trust etc. in* Vertrauen *etc.* setzen auf (*acc.*); *v/i. a.* ~ *o.s.* (sich) ausruhen; ruhen; beruhen (*on* auf *dat.*); **~itory** [ri'pɔzitəri] Verwahrungsort *m*; Warenlager *n*; *fig.* Fundgrube *f*.

reprehend [repri'hend] tadeln.

represent [repri'zent] darstellen; verkörpern; *thea.* aufführen; schildern; bezeichnen (*as* als); vertreten; **~ation** [reprizən'teiʃən] Darstellung *f*; *thea.* Aufführung *f*; Vorstellung *f*; Vertretung *f*; **~ative** □ [repri'zentətiv] **1.** dar-, vorstellend (*of acc.*); vorbildlich; (stell)vertretend; *parl.* repräsentativ; typisch; **2.** Vertreter(in); *House of ~s Am. parl.* Repräsentantenhaus *n*.

repress [ri'pres] unterdrücken; **~ion** [~eʃən] Unterdrückung *f*.

reprieve [ri'pri:v] **1.** (Gnaden)Frist *f*; Aufschub *m*; **2.** *j-m* Aufschub *od.* eine Gnadenfrist gewähren.

reprimand ['reprima:nd] **1.** Verweis *m*; **2.** *j-m* e-n Verweis geben.

reprisal [ri'praizəl] Repressalie *f*.

reproach [ri'prouʧ] **1.** Vorwurf *m*; Schande *f*; **2.** vorwerfen (*s.o. with s.th.* j-m et.); Vorwürfe machen; **~ful** □ [~ʃful] vorwurfsvoll.

reprobate ['reproubeit] **1.** verkommen, verderbt; **2.** verkommenes Subjekt; **3.** mißbilligen; verdammen.

reproduc|e [ri:prə'dju:s] wiedererzeugen; (sich) fortpflanzen; wiedergeben, reproduzieren; **~tion** [~'dʌkʃən] Wiedererzeugung *f*; Fortpflanzung *f*; Reproduktion *f*.

reproof [ri'pru:f] Vorwurf *m*, Tadel *m*.

reprov|al [ri'pru:vəl] Tadel *m*, Rüge *f*; **~e** [~u:v] tadeln, rügen.

reptile *zo.* ['reptail] Reptil *n*.

republic [ri'pʌblik] Republik *f*; **~an** [~kən] **1.** republikanisch; **2.** Republikaner(in).

repudiate [ri'pju:dieit] nicht anerkennen; ab-, zurückweisen.

repugnan|ce [ri'pʌgnəns] Abneigung *f*, Widerwille *m*; **~t** □ [~nt] abstoßend; widerwärtig.

repuls|e [ri'pʌls] **1.** Zurück-, Abweisung *f*; **2.** zurück-, abweisen; **~ive** □ [~siv] abstoßend; widerwärtig.

reput|able □ ['repjutəbl] achtbar; ehrbar, anständig; **~ation** [repju(:)'teiʃən] (*bsd.* guter) Ruf, Ansehen *n*; **~e** [ri'pju:t] **1.** Ruf *m*; **2.** halten für; **~ed** vermeintlich; angeblich.

request [ri'kwest] **1.** Gesuch *n*, Bitte *f*; Ersuchen *n*; ✝ Nachfrage*f*; *by ~, on ~* auf Wunsch; *in (great) ~* (sehr) gesucht, begehrt; *~ stop* Bedarfshaltestelle *f*; **2.** um et. bitten *od.* ersuchen; *j-n* bitten; et. erbitten.

require [ri'kwaiə] verlangen, fordern; brauchen, erfordern; **~d** er-

forderlich; **~ment** [~əmənt] (An-) Forderung *f*; Erfordernis *n*.

requisit|e ['rekwizit] **1.** erforderlich; **2.** Erfordernis *n*; Bedarfs-, Gebrauchsartikel *m*; *toilet ~s pl.* Toilettenartikel *m/pl.*; **~ion** [rekwi'ziʃən] **1.** Anforderung *f*; ✕ Requisition *f*; **2.** anfordern; ✕ requirieren.

requital [ri'kwaitl] Vergeltung *f*.

requite [ri'kwait] *j-m et.* vergelten.

rescind [ri'sind] aufheben.

rescission [ri'siʒən] Aufhebung *f*.

rescue ['reskju:] **1.** Rettung *f*; (✝ gewaltsame) Befreiung; **2.** retten; (✝ gewaltsam) befreien.

research [ri'sə:ʧ] Forschung *f*; Untersuchung *f*; Nachforschung *f*; **~er** [~ʃə] Forscher *m*.

resembl|ance [ri'zembləns] Ähnlichkeit *f* (*to* mit); **~e** [ri'zembl] gleichen, ähnlich sein (*dat.*).

resent [ri'zent] übelnehmen; **~ful** □ [~tful] übelnehmerisch; ärgerlich; **~ment** [~tmənt] Ärger *m*; Groll *m*.

reservation [rezə'veiʃən] Vorbehalt *m*; *Am.* Indianerreservation *f*; Vorbestellung *f von Zimmern etc.*

reserve [ri'zə:v] **1.** Vorrat *m*; ♦ Rücklage *f*; Reserve *f* (*a. fig.*, ✕); Zurückhaltung *f*, Verschlossenheit *f*; Vorsicht *f*; Vorbehalt *f*; *Sport:* Ersatzmann *m*; **2.** aufbewahren, aufsparen; vorbehalten; zurücklegen; *Platz etc.* reservieren; **~d** □ *fig.* zurückhaltend, reserviert.

reservoir ['rezəvwa:] Behälter *m für Wasser etc.*; Sammel-, Staubecken *n*; *fig.* Reservoir *n*.

reside [ri'zaid] wohnen; (orts)ansässig sein; *~ in* innewohnen (*dat.*); **~nce** ['rezidəns] Wohnen *n*; Ortsansässigkeit *f*; (Wohn)Sitz *m*; Residenz *f*; *~ permit* Aufenthaltsgenehmigung *f*; **~nt** [~nt] **1.** wohnhaft; ortsansässig; **2.** Ortsansässige(r *m*) *f*, Einwohner(in).

residu|al [ri'zidjuəl] übrigbleibend; **~e** ['rezidju:] Rest *m*; Rückstand *m*; ✝✝ Reinnachlaß *m*.

resign [ri'zain] *v/t.* aufgeben; *Amt* niederlegen; überlassen; *~ o.s. to* sich ergeben in (*acc.*), sich abfinden mit; *v/i.* zurücktreten; **~ation** [rezig'neiʃən] Rücktritt *m*; Ergebung *f*; Entlassungsgesuch *n*; **~ed** □ ergeben, resigniert.

resilien|ce [ri'ziliəns] Elastizität *f*; **~t** [~nt] elastisch, *fig.* spannkräftig.

resin ['rezin] **1.** Harz *n*; **2.** harzen.

resist [ri'zist] widerstehen (*dat.*); sich widersetzen (*dat.*); **~ance** [~təns] Widerstand *m*; *attr.* Widerstands...; *line of least ~* Weg *m* des geringsten Widerstands; **~ant** [~nt] widerstehend; widerstandsfähig.

resolut|e □ ['rezəlu:t] entschlossen; **~ion** [rezə'lu:ʃən] (Auf)Lösung *f*;

Entschluß *m*; Entschlossenheit *f*; Resolution *f*.

resolve [ri'zɔlv] **1.** *v/t.* auflösen; *fig.* lösen; *Zweifel etc.* beheben; entscheiden; *v/i. a.* ~ o.s. sich auflösen; beschließen; ~ (*up*)*on* sich entschließen zu; **2.** Entschluß *m*; *Am.* Beschluß *m*; ~d □ entschlossen.

resonan|ce ['reznəns] Resonanz *f*; ~t □ [~nt] nach-, widerhallend.

resort [ri'zɔːt] **1.** Zuflucht *f*; Besuch *m*; Aufenthalt(sort) *m*; Erholungsort *m*; *health* ~ Kurort *m*; *seaside* ~ Seebad *n*; *summer* ~ Sommerfrische *f*; **2.** ~ *to* oft besuchen; seine Zuflucht nehmen zu. [sen).|

resound [ri'zaund] widerhallen(las-|

resource [ri'sɔːs] *natürlicher* Reichtum; Hilfsquelle *f*, -mittel *n*; Zuflucht *f*; Findigkeit *f*; Zeitvertreib *m*, Entspannung *f*; ~ful □ [~sful] findig.

respect [ris'pekt] **1.** Rücksicht *f* (*to*, *of* auf *acc.*); Beziehung *f*; Achtung *f*; ~s *pl.* Empfehlungen *f/pl.*; **2.** *v/t.* (hoch)achten; Rücksicht nehmen auf (*acc.*); betreffen; ~able □ [~təbl] achtbar; ansehnlich; anständig; *bsd.* ✝ solid; ~ful □ [~tful] ehrerbietig; *yours* ~*ly* hochachtungsvoll; ~ing [~tiŋ] hinsichtlich (*gen.*); ~ive □ [~iv] jeweilig; we went to our ~ *places* wir gingen jeder an seinen Platz; ~ively [~vli] beziehungsweise; je.

respirat|ion [respə'reiʃən] Atmen *n*; Atemzug *m*; ~or ['respəreitə] Atemfilter *m*; ✠ Atemgerät *n*; Gasmaske *f*.

respire [ris'paiə] atmen; aufatmen.

respite ['respait] Frist *f*; Stundung *f*.

resplendent □ [ris'plendənt] glänzend.

respond [ris'pɔnd] antworten, erwidern; ~ *to* reagieren auf (*acc.*).

response [ris'pɔns] Antwort *f*, Erwiderung *f*; *fig.* Reaktion *f*.

responsi|bility [rispɔnsə'biliti] Verantwortlichkeit *f*; Verantwortung *f*; ✝ Zahlungsfähigkeit *f*; ~ble [ris'pɔnsəbl] verantwortlich; verantwortungsvoll; ✝ zahlungsfähig.

rest [rest] **1.** Rest *m*; Ruhe *f*; Rast *f*; Schlaf *m*; *fig.* Tod *m*; Stütze *f*; Pause *f*; **2.** *v/i.* ruhen; rasten; schlafen; (sich) lehnen, sich stützen (*on* auf *acc.*); ~ (*up*)*on fig.* beruhen auf (*dat.*); *in e-m Zustand* bleiben; *v/t.* (aus)ruhen lassen; stützen.

restaurant ['restərɔ̃ːŋ, ~rɔnt] Gaststätte *f*.

rest-cure ✠ ['restkjuə] Liegekur *f*.

restful ['restful] ruhig, geruhsam.

resting-place ['restiŋpleis] Ruheplatz *m*, -stätte *f*.

restitution [resti'tjuːʃən] Wiederherstellung *f*; Rückerstattung *f*.

restive □ ['restiv] widerspenstig.

restless ['restlis] ruhelos; rastlos; unruhig; ~ness [~snis] Ruhelosigkeit *f*; Rastlosigkeit *f*; Unruhe *f*.

restorat|ion [restə'reiʃən] Wiederherstellung *f*; Wiedereinsetzung *f*; Rekonstruktion *f*, Nachbildung *f*; ~ive [ris'tɔrətiv] **1.** stärkend; **2.** Stärkungsmittel *n*.

restore [ris'tɔː] wiederherstellen; wiedereinsetzen (*to in acc.*); wiedergeben; ~ *to health* wieder gesund machen.

restrain [ris'trein] zurückhalten (*from* von); in Schranken halten; unterdrücken; einsperren; ~t [~nt] Zurückhaltung *f*; Beschränkung *f*, Zwang *m*; Zwangshaft *f*.

restrict [ris'trikt] be-, einschränken; ~ion [~kʃən] Be-, Einschränkung *f*; Vorbehalt *m*.

result [ri'zʌlt] **1.** Ergebnis *n*, Folge *f*, Resultat *n*; **2.** folgen, sich ergeben (*from* aus); ~ *in* hinauslaufen auf (*acc.*), zur Folge haben.

resum|e [ri'zjuːm] wiedernehmen, -erlangen; wiederaufnehmen; zs.-fassen; ~ption [ri'zʌmpʃən] Zurücknahme *f*; Wiederaufnahme *f*.

resurgent [ri'səːdʒənt] sich wiedererhebend, wieder aufkommend.

resurrection [rezə'rekʃən] Wiederaufleben *n*; ⚥ *eccl.* (Wieder)Auferstehung *f*.

resuscitate [ri'sʌsiteit] wiedererwecken, wiederbeleben.

retail 1. ['riːteil] Einzelhandel *m*; *by* ~ im Einzelverkauf; **2.** [~] Einzelhandels...; *Detail...*; **3.** [riː'teil] im kleinen verkaufen; ~er [~lə] Einzelhändler(in).

retain [ri'tein] behalten (*a. fig.*); zurück-, festhalten; beibehalten [*Anwalt* nehmen.

retaliat|e [ri'tælieit] *v/t. Unrecht* vergelten; *v/i.* sich rächen; ~ion [ritæli'eiʃən] Vergeltung *f*.

retard [ri'tɑːd] verzögern; aufhalten; verspäten.

retention [ri'tenʃən] Zurück-, Behalten *n*; Beibehaltung *f*.

reticent ['retisənt] verschwiegen; schweigsam; zurückhaltend.

retinue ['retinjuː] Gefolge *n*.

retir|e [ri'taiə] *v/t.* zurückziehen; pensionieren; *v/i.* sich zurückziehen; zurück-, abtreten; in den Ruhestand treten; ~ed □ zurückgezogen; im Ruhestand (lebend) entlegen; ~ *pay* Pension *f*; ~ement [~əmənt] Sichzurückziehen *n*; Ausrücktritt *m*; Ruhestand *m*; Zurückgezogenheit *f*; ~ing [~əriŋ] zurückhaltend; schüchtern; ~ *pension* Ruhegehalt *n*.

retort [ri'tɔːt] **1.** Erwiderung *f*; ✍ Retorte *f*; **2.** erwidern.

retouch ['riː'tʌtʃ] *et.* überarbeiten; *phot.* retuschieren.

retrace [ri'treis] zurückverfolgen; ~ one's steps zurückgehen.

retract [ri'trækt] (sich) zurückziehen; ⊕ einziehen; widerrufen.

retread [ri'tred] 1. *Reifen* runderneuern; 2. runderneuerter Reifen.

retreat [ri'tri:t] 1. Rückzug m; Zurückgezogenheit f; Zuflucht(sort m) f; ✕ Zapfenstreich m; beat a ~ fig. es aufgeben; 2. sich zurückziehen; fig. zurücktreten.

retrench [ri'trentʃ] (sich) einschränken; kürzen; *Wort etc.* streichen; ✕ verschanzen.

retribution [retri'bju:ʃən] Vergeltung f.

retrieve [ri'tri:v] wiederbekommen; wiederherstellen; wiedergutmachen; *hunt.* apportieren.

retro|... ['retrou] (zu)rück...; ~active [retrou'æktiv] rückwirkend; ~grade ['retrougreid] 1. rückläufig; 2. zurückgehen; ~gression [retrou'greʃən] Rück-, Niedergang m; ~spect ['retrouspekt] Rückblick m; ~spective □ [retrou'spektiv] zurückblickend; rückwirkend.

retry ᵗᵗₜ ['ri:'trai] *Prozeß* wiederaufnehmen.

return [ri'tə:n] 1. Rückkehr f; Wiederkehr f; *parl.* Wiederwahl f; oft ~s pl. ✝ Gewinn m, Ertrag m; Umsatz m; ♣ Rückfall m; Rückgabe f, Rückzahlung f; Vergeltung f; Erwiderung f; Gegenleistung f; Dank m; *amtlicher* Bericht; Wahlergebnis n; Steuererklärung f; F Rückfahrkarte f; *attr.* Rück...; *many happy* ~s of the day herzliche Glückwünsche zum Geburtstag; in ~ dafür; als Ersatz (for für); by ~ (of post) postwendend; ~ ticket Rückfahrkarte f; 2. v/i. zurückkehren; wiederkehren; v/t. zurückgeben; zurücktun; zurückzahlen; zurücksenden; *Dank* abstatten; erwidern; berichten, angeben; *parl.* wählen; *Gewinn* abwerfen.

reunification *pol.* ['ri:ju:nifi'keiʃən] Wiedervereinigung f.

reunion ['ri:'ju:njən] Wiedervereinigung f; Treffen n, Zs.-kunft f.

reval|orization ✝ [ri:vælərai'zeiʃən] Aufwertung f; ~uation [ˌri:ˈvælju'eiʃən] Neubewertung f.

revamp ⊕ ['ri:'væmp] vorschuhen; *Am.* F aufmöbeln; erneuern.

reveal [ri'vi:l] enthüllen; offenbaren; ~ing [ˌiŋ] aufschlußreich.

revel ['revl] 1. Lustbarkeit f; Gelage n; 2. ausgelassen sein; schwelgen; zechen.

revelation [revi'leiʃən] Enthüllung f; Offenbarung f.

revel(l)er ['revlə] Feiernde(r m) f; Zecher m; ~ry [ˌlri] Gelage n; Lustbarkeit f, Rummel m; Orgie f.

revenge [ri'vendʒ] 1. Rache f; Sport: Revanche f; 2. rächen; ~ful □ [ˌdʒful] rachsüchtig; ~r [ˌdʒə] Rächer(in).

revenue ['revinju:] Einkommen n; ~s pl. Einkünfte pl.; ~ board, ~ office Finanzamt n.

reverberate [ri'və:bəreit] zurückwerfen; zurückstrahlen; widerhallen.

revere [ri'viə] (ver)ehren; ~nce ['revərəns] 1. Verehrung f; Ehrfurcht f; 2. (ver)ehren; ~nd [ˌnd] 1. ehrwürdig; 2. Geistliche(r) m.

reverent(ial) □ ['revərənt, revə'renʃəl] ehrerbietig, ehrfurchtsvoll.

reverie ['revəri] Träumerei f.

revers|al [ri'və:səl] Umkehrung f; Umschwung m; ᵗᵗₜ Umstoßung f; ⊕ Umsteuerung f; ~e [ˌə:s] 1. Gegenteil n; Kehrseite f; Rückschlag m; 2. □ umgekehrt; Rück(wärts)...; ~ (gear) mot. Rückwärtsgang m; ~ side linke *Stoff*-Seite; 3. umkehren, umdrehen; *Urteil* umstoßen; ⊕ umsteuern; ~ion [ˌə:ʃən] Umkehrung f; Rückkehr f; ᵗᵗₜ Heimfall m; *biol.* Rückartung f.

revert [ri'və:t] um-, zurückkehren; *biol.* zurückarten; *Blick* wenden.

review [ri'vju:] 1. Nachprüfung f; ᵗᵗₜ Revision f; ✕, ♣ Parade f; Rückblick m; Überblick m; Rezension f; Zeitschrift f; *pass s.th. in* ~ et. Revue passieren lassen; 2. (über-, nach)prüfen; zurückblicken auf (acc.); überblicken; ✕, ♣ besichtigen; rezensieren; ~er [ˌu(:)ə] Rezensent m. [fen.]

revile [ri'vail] schmähen, beschimp-}

revis|e [ri'vaiz] überarbeiten, durchsehen, revidieren; ~ion [ri'viʒən] Revision f; Überarbeitung f.

reviv|al [ri'vaivəl] Wiederbelebung f; Wiederaufleben n, Wiederaufblühen n; Erneuerung f; fig. Erweckung f; ~e [ˌaiv] wiederbeleben; wieder aufleben (lassen); erneuern; wieder aufblühen.

revocation [revə'keiʃən] Widerruf m; Aufhebung f.

revoke [ri'vouk] v/t. widerrufen; v/i. *Karten:* nicht bedienen.

revolt [ri'voult] 1. Revolte f, Empörung f, Aufruhr m; 2. v/i. sich empören; abfallen; v/t. fig. abstoßen.

revolution [revə'lu:ʃən] Umwälzung f, Umdrehung f; pol. Revolution f; ~ary [ˌʃnəri] 1. revolutionär; 2. a. ~ist [ˌʃnist] Revolutionär(in); ~ize [ˌʃnaiz] aufwiegeln; umgestalten.

revolv|e [ri'vɔlv] v/i. sich drehen (about, round um); v/t. umdrehen; fig. erwägen; ~ing [ˌviŋ] sich drehend; Dreh...

revue *thea.* [ri'vju:] Revue f; **Kabarett** n.

revulsion [ri'vʌlʃən] fig. **Umschwung** m; ♣ Ableitung f.

reward [ri'wɔːd] **1.** Belohnung *f*; Vergeltung *f*; **2.** belohnen; vergelten.

rewrite ['riː'rait] [*irr. (write)*] neu (*od.* um)schreiben.

rhapsody ['ræpsədi] Rhapsodie *f*; *fig.* Schwärmerei *f*; Wortschwall *m*.

rhetoric ['retərik] Rhetorik *f*.

rheumatism ♒ ['ruːmətizəm] Rheumatismus *m*.

rhubarb ♧ ['ruːbɑːb] Rhabarber *m*.

rhyme [raim] **1.** Reim *m* (to auf *acc.*); Vers *m*; *without* ~ *or reason* ohne Sinn u. Verstand; **2.** (sich) reimen.

rhythm ['riðəm] Rhythmus *m*; **~ic(al** □) ['riðmik(əl)] rhythmisch.

Rialto *Am.* [ri'æltou] Theaterviertel *n e-r Stadt, bsd. in New York.*

rib [rib] **1.** Rippe *f*; **2.** rippen; *sl.* aufziehen, necken.

ribald ['ribəld] lästerlich; unflätig; **~ry** [~dri] Zoten *f/pl.*; derbe Späße *m/pl.*

ribbon ['ribən] Band *n*; Streifen *m*; **~s** *pl.* Fetzen *m/pl.*; Zügel *m/pl.*; ~ *building*, ~ *development* Reihenbau *m*.

rice [rais] Reis *m*.

rich □ [ritʃ] reich (*in an dat.*); reichlich; prächtig, kostbar, ergiebig, fruchtbar; voll (*Ton*); schwer (*Speise, Wein, Duft*); satt (*Farbe*); **~es** ['ritʃiz] *pl.* Reichtum *m*, Reichtümer *m/pl.*; **~ness** [~nis] Reichtum *m*; Fülle *f*.

rick [rik] (Heu)Schober *m*.

ricket|s ♒ ['rikits] *sg. od. pl.* Rachitis *f*; **~y** [~ti] rachitisch; wack(e)lig (*Möbel*).

rid [rid] [*irr.*] befreien, frei machen (*of* von); *get* ~ *of* loswerden.

ridden ['ridn] **1.** *p.p. von* ride 2; **2.** *in Zssgn:* bedrückt *od.* geplagt von ...

riddle ['ridl] **1.** Rätsel *n*; grobes Sieb; **2.** sieben; durchlöchern.

ride [raid] **1.** Ritt *m*; Fahrt *f*; Reitweg *m*; **2.** [*irr.*] *v/i.* reiten; rittlings sitzen; fahren; treiben; schweben; liegen; *v/t. Pferd etc.* reiten; *Land* durchreiten; **~r** ['raidə] Reiter(in); Fahrende(r *m*) *f*.

ridge [ridʒ] **1.** (Gebirgs)Kamm *m*, Grat *m*; △ First *m*; ✓ Rain *m*; **2.** (sich) furchen.

ridicul|e ['ridikjuːl] **1.** Hohn *m*, Spott *m*; **2.** lächerlich machen; **~ous** □ [ri'dikjuləs] lächerlich.

riding ['raidiŋ] Reiten *n*; *attr.* Reit... (~ *with* voll von.)

rife [raif] häufig; vorherrschend;

riff-raff ['rifræf] Gesindel *n*.

rifle ['raifl] **1.** Gewehr *n*; **2.** (aus)plündern; **~man** ⚔ Schütze *m*.

rift [rift] Riß *m*, Sprung *m*; Spalte *f*.

rig¹ [rig] **1.** Markt *etc.* manipulieren; **2.** Schwindelmanöver *n*.

rig² [~] **1.** ♣ Takelung *f*; F Aufma-

chung *f*; **2.** auftakeln; ~ *s.o. out* j-n versorgen *od.* ausrüsten; j-n herausputzen *od.* herrichten; **~ging** ♣ ['rigiŋ] Takelage *f*.

right [rait] **1.** □ recht; richtig; recht (*Ggs. left*); *be* ~ recht haben; *all* ~! alles in Ordnung!; ganz recht!; *put od. set* ~ in Ordnung bringen; berichtigen; **2.** *adv.* recht, richtig; gerade; direkt; ganz (und gar); ~ *away* sogleich; ~ *on* geradeaus; **3.** Recht *n*; Rechte *f*, rechte Seite *u.* Hand; *the* ~s *and wrongs* der wahre Sachverhalt; *by* ~ *of* auf Grund (*gen.*); *on od. to the* ~ rechts; ~ *of way* Wegerecht *n*; Vorfahrt(s-recht *n*) *f*; **4.** *j-m* Recht verschaffen; *et.* in Ordnung bringen; ♣ (sich) aufrichten; **~-down** ['rait'daun] regelrecht, ausgemacht; wirklich; **~eous** □ ['raitʃəs] rechtschaffen; **~ful** □ ['raitful] recht(mäßig); gerecht.

rigid □ ['ridʒid] starr; *fig. a.* streng, hart; **~ity** [ri'dʒiditi] Starrheit *f*; Strenge *f*, Härte *f*.

rigmarole ['rigməroul] Geschwätz *n*.

rigor ♒ ['raigə:] Fieberfrost *m*.

rigo(u)r ['rigə] Strenge *f*, Härte *f*.

rigorous □ ['rigərəs] streng, rigoros.

rim [rim] **1.** Felge *f*; Radkranz *m*; Rand *m*; **2.** rändern; einfassen.

rime [raim] Reim *m*; Rauhreif *m*.

rind [raind] Rinde *f*, Schale *f*; *Speck*-Schwarte *f*.

ring¹ [riŋ] **1.** Klang *m*; Geläut(e) *n*; Klingeln *n*; Rufzeichen *n*; Anruf *m*; *give s.o. a* ~ j-n anrufen; **2.** [*irr.*] läuten; klingen (lassen); erschallen (*with* von); ~ *again* widerhallen; ~ *off teleph.* das Gespräch beenden; ~ *the bell* klingeln; ~ *s.o. up* j-n *od.* bei j-m anrufen.

ring² [~] **1.** Ring *m*; Kreis *m*; **2.** beringen; *mst* ~ *in*, ~ *round*, ~ *about* umringen; **~leader** ['riŋliːdə] Rädelsführer *m*; **~let** [~lit] (Ringel)Locke *f*.

rink [riŋk] Eisbahn *f*; Rollschuhbahn *f*.

rinse [rins] *oft* ~ *out* (aus)spülen.

riot ['raiət] **1.** Tumult *m*; Aufruhr *m*; Orgie *f* (*a. fig.*); *run* ~ durchgehen; (sich aus)toben; **2.** Krawall machen, im Aufruhr sein; toben; schwelgen; **~er** [~tə] Aufrührer(in); Randalierer *m*; **~ous** □ [~təs] aufrührerisch; lärmend; liederlich (*Leben*).

rip [rip] **1.** Riß *m*; **2.** (auf)trennen; (auf-, zer)reißen; (dahin)sausen.

ripe □ [raip] reif; ~**n** ['raipən] reifen; **~ness** ['raipnis] Reife *f*.

ripple ['ripl] **1.** kleine Welle; Kräuselung *f*; Geriesel *n*; **2.** (sich) kräuseln; rieseln.

rise [raiz] **1.** (An-, Auf)Steigen *n*;

Anschwellen *n*; (Preis-, Gehalts-) Erhöhung *f*; *fig.* Aufstieg *m*; Steigung *f*; Anhöhe *f*; Ursprung *m*; take (one's) ~ entstehen; entspringen; 2. [*irr.*] sich erheben, aufstehen; die Sitzung schließen; steigen; aufsteigen (*a. fig.*); auferstehen; aufgehen (*Sonne, Samen*); anschwellen; sich empören; entspringen (*Fluß*); ~ to sich e-r Lage gewachsen zeigen; ~ in ['rizn] *p.p. von* rise 2; ~r ['raizə]: early ~ Frühaufsteher(in).

rising ['raiziŋ] 1. (Auf)Steigen *n*; Steigung *f*; *ast.* Aufgang *m*; Aufstand *m*; 2. heranwachsend (*Generation*).

risk [risk] 1. Gefahr *f*, Wagnis *n*; † Risiko *n*; run the ~ Gefahr laufen; 2. wagen, riskieren; ~y □ ['riski] gefährlich, gewagt.

rit|e [rait] Ritus *m*, Brauch *m*; ~ual ['ritjuəl] 1. rituell; 2. Ritual *n*.

rival ['raivəl] 1. Nebenbuhler(in); Rivale *m*; 2. rivalisierend; † Konkurrenz...; 3. wetteifern (mit); ~ry [~lri] Rivalität *f*; Wetteifer *m*.

rive [raiv] [*irr.*] (sich) spalten; ~n ['rivən] *p.p. von* rive.

river ['rivə] Fluß *m*; Strom *m* (*a. fig.*); ~side 1. Flußufer *n*; 2. am Wasser (gelegen).

rivet ['rivit] 1. ⊕ Niet(e *f*) *m*; 2. (ver)nieten; *fig.* heften (to an *acc.*; on, upon auf *acc.*); fesseln.

rivulet ['rivjulit] Bach *m*, Flüßchen *n*.

road [roud] Straße *f* (*a. fig.*), Weg *m*; *Am.* = railroad; mst ~s *pl.* ⊕ Reede *f*; ~stead ⊕ ['roudsted] Reede *f*; ~ster [~tə] Roadster *m*, offener Sportwagen; ~way Fahrbahn *f*.

roam [roum] *v/i.* umherstreifen, wandern; *v/t.* durchstreifen.

roar [rɔː] 1. brüllen; brausen, tosen, donnern; 2. Gebrüll *n*; Brausen *n*; Krachen *n*; Getöse *n*; brüllendes Gelächter.

roast [roust] 1. rösten, braten; 2. geröstet; gebraten; ~ meat Braten *m*.

rob [rɔb] (be)rauben; ~ber ['rɔbə] Räuber *m*; ~bery [~əri] Raub (-überfall) *m*; Räuberei *f*.

robe [roub] (Amts)Robe *f*, Talar *m*; (Staats)Kleid *n*; *Am.* Morgenrock *m*.

robin *orn.* ['rɔbin] Rotkehlchen *n*.

robust □ [rə'bʌst] robust, kräftig.

rock [rɔk] 1. Felsen *m*; Klippe *f*; Gestein *n*; Zuckerstange *f*; ~ crystal Bergkristall *m*; 2. schaukeln; (ein)wiegen.

rocker ['rɔkə] Kufe *f*; *Am.* Schaukelstuhl *m*; Rocker *m*, Halbstarke(r) *m*.

rocket ['rɔkit] Rakete *f*; *attr.* Ra-

keten...; ~-powered mit Raketenantrieb; ~ry [~tri] Raketentechnik*f*.

rocking-chair ['rɔkiŋtʃɛə] Schaukelstuhl *m*.

rocky ['rɔki] felsig; Felsen...

rod [rɔd] Rute *f*; Stab *m*; ⊕ Stange *f*; Meßrute *f* (5½ yards); *Am. sl.* Pistole *f*.

rode [roud] *pret. von* ride 2.

rodent ['roudənt] Nagetier *n*.

rodeo [rou'deiou] Rodeo *m*; Zusammentreiben *n*; Cowboyturnier *n*.

roe[1] [rou] Reh *n*.

roe[2] *ichth.* [~] *a.* hard ~ Rogen *m*; soft ~ Milch *f*.

rogu|e [roug] Schurke *m*; Schelm *m*; ~ish ['rougiʃ] schurkisch; schelmisch.

roister ['rɔistə] krakeelen.

role, rôle *thea.* [roul] Rolle *f* (*a.fig.*).

roll [roul] 1. Rolle *f*; ⊕ Walze *f*; Brötchen *n*, Semmel *f*; Verzeichnis *n*; Urkunde *f*; (Donner)Rollen *n*; (Trommel)Wirbel *m*; ⊕ Schlingern *n*; 2. *v/t.* rollen; wälzen; walzen; *Zigarette* drehen; ~ up zs.-rollen; einwickeln; *v/i.* rollen; sich wälzen; wirbeln (*Trommel*); ⊕ schlingern; ~-call ⊠ ['roulkɔːl] Appell *m*; ~er ['roulə] Rolle *f*, Walze *f*; Sturzwelle *f*; ~ coaster *Am.* Achterbahn *f*; ~ skate Rollschuh *m*.

rolliking ['rɔlikiŋ] übermütig.

rolling ['rouliŋ] rollend; Roll..., Walz...; ~ mill ⊕ Walzwerk *n*.

Roman ['roumən] 1. römisch; 2. Römer(in); mst ♀ *typ.* Antiqua *f*.

romance[1] [rə'mæns] 1. (Ritter-, Vers)Roman *m*; Abenteuer-, Liebesroman *m*; Romanze *f* (*a. fig.*); *fig.* Märchen *n*; Romantik *f*; 2. *fig.* aufschneiden.

Romance[2] *ling.* [~]: ~ languages romanische Sprachen *f/pl.*

romancer [rə'mænsə] Romanschreiber(in); Aufschneider(in).

Romanesque [roumə'nesk] 1. romanisch; 2. romanischer Baustil.

romantic [rə'mæntik] (~ally) romantisch; ~ism [~isizəm] Romantik *f*; ~ist [~ist] Romantiker(in).

romp [rɔmp] 1. Range *f*, Wildfang *m*; Balgerei *f*; 2. sich balgen, toben; ~er(s) ['rɔmpə(z)] Spielanzug *m*.

rood [ruːd] Kruzifix *n*; Viertelmorgen *m* (10,117 Ar).

roof [ruːf] 1. Dach *n*; ~ of the mouth Gaumen *m*; 2. *a.* ~ over überdachen; ~ing ['ruːfiŋ] 1. Bedachung*f*; 2. Dach...; ~ felt Dachpappe *f*.

rook [ruk] 1. *Schach:* Turm *m*; *fig.* Gauner *m*; *orn.* Saatkrähe *f*; 2. betrügen.

room [rum] 1. Raum *m*; Platz *m*; Zimmer *n*; Möglichkeit *f*; ~s *pl.* Wohnung *f*; in my ~ an meiner Stelle; 2. *Am.* wohnen; ~er ['rumə] *bsd. Am.* Untermieter(in); **~ing-house** ['rumiŋhaus] *bsd. Am.* Miets-, Logierhaus *n*; **~mate** Stubenkamerad *m*; **~y** □ ['rumi] geräumig.

roost [ru:st] 1. Schlafplatz *m e-s Vogels*; Hühnerstange *f*; Hühnerstall *m*; 2. sich (zum Schlaf) niederhocken; *fig.* übernachten; **~er** ['ru:stə] Haushahn *m*.

root [ru:t] 1. Wurzel *f*; 2. (ein)wurzeln; (auf)wühlen; **~** *for Am. sl.* Stimmung machen für; **~** *out* ausrotten; **~** *out od.* up ausgraben; **~ed** ['ru:tid] eingewurzelt; **~er** *Am. sl.* ['ru:tə] Fanatiker *m für et.*

rope [roup] 1. Tau *n*, Seil *n*; Strick *m*; Schnur *f Perlen etc.*; *be at the end of one's ~* F mit s-m Latein zu Ende sein; *know the ~s* sich auskennen; 2. mit e-m Seil befestigen *od.* (*mst ~ in od.* off *od.* out) absperren; anseilen; **~way** ['roupwei] Seilbahn *f.*

ropy ['roupi] klebrig, zähflüssig.

rosary *eccl.* ['rouzəri] Rosenkranz *m.*

rose[1] [rouz] & Rose *f*; (Gießkannen)Brause *f*; Rosenrot *n.*

rose[2] [~] *pret. von* rise 2.

rosebud ['rouzbʌd] Rosenknospe *f*; *Am.* hübsches Mädchen; Debütantin *f.*

rosin ['rɔzin] (Geigen)Harz *n.*

rostrum ['rɔstrəm] Rednertribüne *f.*

rosy □ ['rouzi] rosig.

rot [rɔt] 1. Fäulnis *f*; *sl.* Quatsch *m*; 2. *v/t.* faulen lassen; Quatsch machen mit *j-m*; *v/i.* verfaulen, vermodern.

rota|ry ['routəri] drehend; Rotations...; **~te** [rou'teit] (sich) drehen, (ab)wechseln; **~tion** [~'eiʃən] Umdrehung *f*; Kreislauf *m*; Abwechs(e)lung *f*; **~tory** ['routətəri] *s. rotary*; abwechselnd.

rote [rout]: *by ~* auswendig.

rotten □ ['rɔtn] verfault, faul(ig); mod(e)rig; morsch (*alle a. fig.*); *sl.* saumäßig, dreckig.

rotund □ ['rou'tʌnd] rund; voll (*Stimme*); hochtrabend.

rouge [ru:ʒ] 1. Rouge *n*; Silberputzmittel *n*; 2. Rouge auflegen (auf *acc.*).

rough [rʌf] 1. □ rauh; roh; grob; *fig.* ungehobelt; ungefähr (*Schätzung*); **~** *and ready* grob (gearbeitet); *Not...,* Behelfs...; **~** *copy* roher Entwurf; 2. Rauhe *n*, Grobe *n*; Lümmel *m*; 3. (an-, auf)rauhen; **~** *it* sich mühsam durchschlagen; **~cast** ['rʌfkɑ:st] 1. ⊕ Rohputz *m*; 2. unfertig; 3. ⊕ roh verputzen; roh entwerfen; **~en** ['rʌfən] rauh machen *od.* werden; **~neck** *Am. sl.* Rabauke *m*; **~ness** [~nis] Rauheit *f*; Roheit *f*; Grobheit *f*; **~shod**: *ride ~ over* rücksichtslos behandeln.

round [raund] 1. □ rund; voll (*Stimme etc.*); flott (*Gangart*); abgerundet (*Stil*); unverblümt; **~** *game* Gesellschaftsspiel *n*; **~** *trip* Rundreise *f*; 2. *adv.* rund-, ringsum(her); *a.* **~** *about* in der Runde; *all* **~** ringsum; *fig.* ohne Unterschied; *all the year* **~** das ganze Jahr hindurch; 3. *prp.* um ... herum; 4. Rund *n*, Kreis *m*; Runde *f*; Kreislauf *m*; (Leiter)Sprosse *f*; Rundgesang *m*; *Lach- etc.*Salve *f*; *100 ~s* ✕ 100 Schuß *m*; 5. *v/t.* runden; herumgehen *od.* herumfahren um; **~** *off* abrunden; **~** *up* einkreisen; *v/i.* sich runden; sich umdrehen; **~about** ['raundəbaut] 1. umschweifig; 2. Umweg *m*; Karussell *n*; Kreisverkehr *m*; Kreis [~diʃ] rundlich; **~up** Einkreisung *f*; Razzia *f.*

rous|e [rauz] *v/t.* wecken; ermuntern; aufjagen; (auf)reizen; **~** *o.s.* sich aufraffen; *v/i.* aufwachen; **~ing** ['rauziŋ] brausend (*Beifall etc.*).

roustabout *Am.* ['raustəbaut] ungelernter (*mst* Hafen)Arbeiter.

rout [raut] 1. Rotte *f*; wilde Flucht; *a. put to* **~** vernichtend schlagen; 2. aufwühlen.

route [ru:t, ✕ *a.* raut] Weg *m*; ✕ Marschroute *f.*

routine [ru:'ti:n] 1. Routine *f*; 2. üblich; Routine...

rove [rouv] umherstreifen, umherwandern.

row[1] [rou] 1. Reihe *f*; Ruderfahrt *f*; 2. rudern.

row[2] F [rau] 1. Spektakel *m*; Krach *m*; Schlägerei *f*; 2. ausschimpfen.

row-boat ['roubout] Ruderboot *n.*

rower ['rouə] Ruder|er *m*, -in *f.*

royal □ ['rɔiəl] königlich; prächtig; **~ty** [~lti] Königtum *n*, -reich *n*; Königswürde *f*; königliche Persönlichkeit; Tantieme *f.*

rub [rʌb] 1. Reiben *n*; Schwierigkeit *f*; *fig.* Stichelei *f*; Unannehmlichkeit *f*; 2. *v/t.* reiben; (ab)wischen; (wund)scheuern; schleifen; **~** *down* abreiben; **~** *in* einreiben; *fig.* betonen; **~** *off* abreiben; **~** *out* auslöschen; **~** *up* auffrischen; verreiben; *v/i.* sich reiben; *fig.* **~** *along od.* on *od.* through sich durchschlagen.

rubber ['rʌbə] 1. Gummi *n*, *m*; Radiergummi *m*; Masseur *m*; Wischtuch *n*; *Whist:* Robber *m*; **~** *spl. Am.* Gummischuhe *m/pl.*; 2. Gummi...; **~** *check Am. sl.* geplatzter Scheck; **~neck** *Am. sl.* 1. Gaffer(in); 2. sich den Hals verrenken; mithören; **~** *stamp* Gummistempel *m*; *Am.* F *fig.* Nachbeter *m*; **~-stamp** automatisch gutheißen.

rubbish ['rʌbiʃ] Schutt *m*; Abfall *m*; Kehricht *m*; *fig.* Schund *m*; Unsinn *m.*

rubble ['rʌbl] Schutt *m.*

rube *Am.sl.* ['ru:b] Bauernlümmel *m*.

ruby ['ru:bi] Rubin(rot *n*) *m*.

rucksack ['ruksæk] Rucksack *m*.

rudder ['rʌdə] ⏚ (Steuer)Ruder *n*; ✺ Seitenruder *n*.

rudd|iness ['rʌdinis] Röte *f*; ~y ['rʌdi] rot; rotbäckig.

rude □ [ru:d] unhöflich; unanständig; heftig, unsanft; ungebildet; einfach, kunstlos; robust; roh.

rudiment *biol.* ['ru:dimənt] Ansatz *m*; ~s *pl.* Anfangsgründe *m/pl.*

rueful □ ['ru:ful] reuig; traurig.

ruff [rʌf] Halskrause *f*.

ruffian ['rʌfjən] Rohling *m*; Raufbold *m*; Schurke *m*.

ruffle ['rʌfl] 1. Krause *f*, Rüsche *f*; Kräuseln *n*; *fig.* Unruhe *f*; 2. kräuseln; zerdrücken; zerknüllen; *fig.* aus der Ruhe bringen; stören.

rug [rʌg] (Reise-, Woll)Decke *f*; Vorleger *m*, Brücke *f*; ~ged □ ['rʌgid] rauh (*a. fig.*); uneben; gefurcht.

ruin [ruin] 1. Ruin *m*, Zs.-bruch *m*; Untergang *m*; *mst* ~s *pl.* Ruine(n *pl.*) *f*, Trümmer *pl.*; 2. ruinieren; zugrunde richten; zerstören; verderben; ~ous □ ['ruinəs] ruinenhaft; verfallen; verderblich; ruinös.

rul|e [ru:l] 1. Regel *f*; Vorschrift *f*; Ordnung *f*; Satzung *f*; Herrschaft *f*; Lineal *n*; *as a* ~ in der Regel; ~(s) *of the road* Straßenverkehrsordnung *f*; 2. *v/t.* regeln; leiten; beherrschen; verfügen; liniieren; ~ *out* ausschließen; *v/i.* herrschen; ~er ['ru:lə] Herrscher(in) *f*; Lineal *n*.

rum [rʌm] Rum *m*; *Am.* Alkohol *m*.

Rumanian [ru(:)'meinjən] 1. rumänisch; 2. Rumän|e *m*, -in *f*; Rumänisch *n*.

rumble ['rʌmbl] 1. Rumpeln *n*; *a.* ~-seat *Am. mot.* Notsitz *m*; *Am.* F Fehde *f* zwischen Gangsterbanden); 2. rumpeln, rasseln; grollen (*Donner*).

rumina|nt ['ru:minənt] 1. wiederkäuend; 2. Wiederkäuer *m*; ~te [~neit] wiederkäuen; *fig.* nachsinnen.

rummage ['rʌmidʒ] 1. Durchsuchung *f*; Ramsch *m*, Restwaren *f/pl.*; 2. *v/t.* durchsuchen, durchstöbern, durchwühlen; *v/i.* wühlen.

rumo(u)r ['ru:mə] 1. Gerücht *n*; 2. (als Gerücht) verbreiten; *it is* ~ed es geht das Gerücht. [*m.*\

rump *anat.* ['rʌmp] Steiß *m*; Rumpf\

rumple ['rʌmpl] zerknittern; zerren, (zer)zausen.

rum-runner *Am.* ['rʌmrʌnə] Alkoholschmuggler *m*.

run [rʌn] 1. *irr.*] *v/i. allg.* laufen; rennen (*Mensch, Tier*); eilen; zerlaufen (*Farbe etc.*); umgehen (*Gerücht etc.*); lauten (*Text*); gehen (*Melodie*); ✝ sich stellen (*Preis*); ~ *across s.o.* j-m in die Arme laufen;

~ *away* davonlaufen; ~ *down* ⓐblaufen (*Uhr etc.*); *fig.* herunterkommen; ~ *dry* aus~, vertrocknen; ~ *for parl.* kandidieren für; ~ *into* geraten in (*acc.*); werden zu; *j-m* in die Arme laufen; ~ *low* zur Neige gehen; ~ *mad* verrückt werden; ~ *off* weglaufen; ~ *on* fortfahren; ~ *out*, ~ *short* zu Ende gehen; ~ *through* durchmachen; durchlesen; ~ *to* sich belaufen auf (*acc.*); sich entwickeln zu; ~ *up to* sich belaufen auf (*acc.*); *v/t.* Strecke durchlaufen; *Weg* einschlagen; laufen lassen; *Hand etc.* gleiten lassen; stecken, stoßen; transportieren; *Flut* ergießen; *Geschäft* betreiben, leiten; *hunt.* verfolgen, hetzen; um die Wette rennen mit; schmuggeln; heften; ~ *the blockade* die Blockade brechen; ~ *down* umrennen; zur Strecke bringen; *fig.* schlecht machen; herunterwirtschaften; *be* ~ *down* abgearbeitet sein; ~ *errands* Botengänge machen; ~ *in mot.* einfahren; F *Verbrecher* einbuchten; ~ *off* ablaufen lassen; ~ *out* hinausjagen; ~ *over* überfahren; *Text* überfliegen; ~ *s.o. through* j-n durchbohren; ~ *up Preis, Neubau etc.* emportreiben; *Rechnung etc.* auflaufen lassen; 2. Laufen *n*, Rennen *n*, Lauf *m*; Verlauf *m*; Fahrt *f e-s Schiffes*; Reihe *f*; Folge *f*; Serie *f*; Reise *f*, Ausflug *m*; ✝ Andrang *m*; Ansturm *m*; *Am.* Bach *m*; *Am.* Laufmasche *f*; *Vieh-Trift f*; freie Benutzung; Art *f*, Schlag *m*; the *common* ~ die große Masse; *have a* ~ *of 20 nights thea.* 20mal nacheinander gegeben werden; *in the long* ~ auf die Dauer, am Ende; *in the short* ~ fürs nächste.

run|about mot. ['rʌnəbaut] kleiner (Sport)Wagen; ~away Ausreißer *m*.

rune [ru:n] Rune *f*.

rung¹ [rʌŋ] *p.p. von* ring 2.

rung² [~] (Leiter)Sprosse *f* (*a. fig.*).

run-in ['rʌn'in] *Sport:* Einlauf *m*; *Am.* F Krach *m*, Zs.-stoß *m* (*Streit*).

run|let ['rʌnlit], ~nel ['rʌnl] Rinnsal *n*; Rinnstein *m*.

runner ['rʌnə] Läufer *m*; Bote *m*; (Schlitten)Kufe *f*; Schieber *m am Schirm*; ⅋ Ausläufer *m*; ~-up [~ər'ʌp] *Sport:* Zweitbeste(r *m*) *f*, Zweite(r *m*) *f*.

running ['rʌniŋ] 1. laufend; *two days* ~ zwei Tage nacheinander; ~ *hand* Kurrentschrift *f*; 2. Rennen *n*; ~-board Trittbrett *n*.

runt [rʌnt] *zo.* Zwergrind *n*; *fig.* Zwerg *m*; *attr.* Zwerg...

runway ['rʌnwei] ≽ Rollbahn *f*; *hunt.* Wechsel *m*; Holzrutsche *f*; ~ *watching* Ansitzjagd *f*.

rupture ['rʌptʃə] 1. Bruch *m* (*a. ⚕*); 2. brechen; sprengen.

rural □ ['ruərəl] ländlich; Land...

ruse [ru:z] List *f*, Kniff *m*.
rush [rʌʃ] 1. ♀ Binse *f*; Jagen *n*, Hetzen *n*, Stürmen *n*; (An)Sturm *m*; Andrang *m*; ⚓ stürmische Nachfrage; ~ *hour(s pl.)* Hauptverkehrszeit *f*; 2. *v/i.* stürzen, jagen, hetzen, stürmen; ~ at sich stürzen auf (*acc.*); ~ *into print et.* überstürzt veröffentlichen; *v/t.* jagen, hetzen; drängen; ✗ *u. fig.* stürmen; *sl.* neppen.
russet [ˈrʌsit] braunrot; grob.
Russian [ˈrʌʃən] 1. russisch; 2. Russ|e *m*, -in *f*; Russisch *n*.
rust [rʌst] 1. Rost *m*; 2. (ver-, ein)rosten (lassen) (*a. fig.*).

rustic [ˈrʌstik] 1. (~ally) ländlich; bäurisch; Bauern...; 2. Bauer *m*.
rustle [ˈrʌsl] 1. rascheln (mit *od.* in *dat.*); rauschen; *Am.* F sich ranhalten; *Vieh* stehlen; 2. Rascheln *n*.
rust|less [ˈrʌstlis] rostfrei; ~y [~ti] rostig; eingerostet (*a. fig.*); verschossen (*Stoff*); rostfarben.
ruthless ☐ [ˈru:θlis] unbarmherzig; rücksichts-, skrupellos.
rutted [ˈrʌtid] ausgefahren (*Weg*).
rutty [ˈrʌti] ausgefahren (*Weg*).
rye ♀ [rai] Roggen *m*.

S

sable [ˈseibl] Zobel(pelz) *m*; Schwarz *n*. [2. sabotieren.]
sabotage [ˈsæbətɑ:ʒ] 1. Sabotage *f*;
sabre [ˈseibə] Säbel *m*.
sack [sæk] 1. Plünderung *f*; Sack *m*; *Am.* Tüte *f*; Sackkleid *n*; Sakko *m*, *n*; *give (get) the ~* F entlassen (werden); den Laufpaß geben (bekommen); 2. plündern; einsacken; F rausschmeißen; *j-m* den Laufpaß geben; ~cloth [ˈsækklɔθ], ~ing [ˈsækiŋ] Sackleinwand *f*.
sacrament *eccl.* [ˈsækrəmənt] Sakrament *n*.
sacred ☐ [ˈseikrid] heilig; geistlich.
sacrifice [ˈsækrifais] 1. Opfer *n*; at *a* ~ ✝ mit Verlust; 2. opfern; ✝ mit Verlust verkaufen.
sacrileg|e [ˈsækrilidʒ] Kirchenraub *m*, -schändung *f*; Sakrileg *n*; ~ious ☐ [sækriˈlidʒəs] frevelhaft.
sad ☐ [sæd] traurig; jämmerlich, kläglich; schlimm, arg; dunkel.
sadden [ˈsædn] (sich) betrüben.
saddle [ˈsædl] 1. Sattel *m*; 2. satteln; *fig.* belasten; ~r [~lə] Sattler *m*.
sadism [ˈsædizəm] Sadismus *m*.
sadness [ˈsædnis] Traurigkeit *f*, Trauer *f*, Schwermut *f*.
safe [seif] 1. ☐ *allg.* sicher; unversehrt; zuverlässig; 2. Safe *m*, *n*, Geldschrank *m*; Speiseschrank *m*; ~blower *Am.* [ˈseifblouə] Geldschrankknacker *m*; ~ conduct freies Geleit; Geleitbrief *m*; ~guard 1. Schutz *m*; 2. sichern, schützen.
safety [ˈseifti] Sicherheit *f*; ~belt *mot.* Sicherheitsgurt *m*; ~ island Verkehrsinsel *f*; ~lock Sicherheitsschloß *n*; ~pin Sicherheitsnadel *f*; ~ razor Rasierapparat *m*.
saffron [ˈsæfrən] Safran(gelb *n*) *m*.
sag [sæg] durchsacken; ⊕ durchhängen; ⚓ (ab)sacken (*a. fig.*).

sagaci|ous ☐ [səˈgeiʃəs] scharfsinnig; ~ty [səˈgæsiti] Scharfsinn *m*.
sage [seidʒ] 1. ☐ klug, weise; 2. Weise(r) *m*; ♀ Salbei *m*, *f*.
said [sed] *pret. u. p.p. von* say 1.
sail [seil] 1. Segel *n*; Fahrt *f*; Windmühlenflügel *m*; (Segel-)Schiff(e *pl.*) *n*; set ~ in See stechen; 2. *v/i.* (ab)segeln, fahren; *fig.* schweben; *v/t.* befahren; *Schiff* führen; ~boat *Am.* [ˈseilbout] Segelboot *n*; ~er [ˈseilə] Segler *m* (*Schiff*); ~ing-ship [ˈseiliŋʃip], ~ing-vessel [~ŋvesl] Segelschiff *n*; ~or [ˈseilə] Seemann *m*, Matrose *m*; *be a good (bad)* ~ (nicht) seefest sein; ~plane Segelflugzeug *n*.
saint [seint] 1. Heilige(r *m*) *f*; [*vor npr.* snt] Sankt...; 2. heiligsprechen; ~ly [ˈseintli] *adj.* heilig, fromm.
saith ✝ *od. poet.* [seθ] 3. *sg. pres. von* say 1.
sake [seik]: *for the* ~ of um ... (*gen.*) willen; *for my* ~ meinetwegen; *for God's* ~ um Gottes willen.
salad [ˈsæləd] Salat *m*.
salary [ˈsæləri] 1. Besoldung *f*; Gehalt *n*; 2. besolden; ~earner [~iə:nə] Gehaltsempfänger(in).
sale [seil] (Aus)Verkauf *m*; Absatz *m*; Auktion *f*; for ~, on ~ zum Verkauf, zu verkaufen, verkäuflich.
sal(e)able [ˈseiləbl] verkäuflich.
sales|man [ˈseilzmən] Verkäufer *m*; ~woman Verkäuferin *f*.
salient ☐ [ˈseiljənt] vorspringend; *fig.* hervorragend, hervortretend; Haupt...
saline [ˈseilain] salzig; Salz...
saliva [səˈlaivə] Speichel *m*.
sallow [ˈsælou] blaß; gelblich.
sally [ˈsæli] 1. ✗ Ausbruch *m*; witziger Einfall; 2. *a.* ~ out sich ausbrechen; ~ forth, ~ out sich aufmachen.
salmon *ichth.* [ˈsæmən] Lachs *m*, Salm *m*.

saloon [sə'lu:n] Salon *m*; (Gesellschafts)Saal *m*; erste Klasse *auf Schiffen*; *Am.* Kneipe *f.*

salt [sɔ:lt] **1.** Salz *n*; *fig.* Würze *f*; *old* ~ alter Seebär; **2.** salzig; gesalzen; Salz...; Pökel...; **3.** (ein)salzen; pökeln; ~-cellar ['sɔ:ltselə] Salzfäßchen *n*; ~petre, *Am.* ~peter [ˌtpi:tə] Salpeter *m*; ~-water Salzwasser...; ~y [ˌti] salzig.

salubrious □ [sə'lu:briəs], **salutary** □ ['sæljutəri] heilsam, gesund.

salut|ation [sælju(:)'teiʃən] Gruß *m*, Begrüßung *f*; Anrede *f*; ~e [sə-'lu:t] **1.** Gruß *m*; *co.* Kuß *m*; ⚔ Salut *m*; **2.** (be)grüßen; ⚔ salutieren.

salvage ['sælvidʒ] **1.** Bergung(sgut *n*) *f*; Bergegeld *n*; **2.** bergen.

salvation [sæl'veiʃən] Erlösung *f*; (Seelen)Heil *n*; *fig.* Rettung *f*; ⚔ S̲ Army Heilsarmee *f.*

salve[1] [sælv] retten, bergen.

salve[2] [sɑːv] **1.** Salbe *f*; *fig.* Balsam *m*; **2.** *mst fig.* (ein)salben; beruhigen.

salvo ['sælvou] Vorbehalt *m*; ⚔ Salve *f* (*fig.* Beifall).

same [seim]: the ~ der-, die-, dasselbe; *all the* ~ trotzdem; *it is all the* ~ *to me* es ist mir (ganz) gleich.

samp *Am.* [sæmp] grobgemahlener Mais.

sample ['sɑ:mpl] **1.** Probe *f*, Muster *n*; **2.** bemustern; (aus)probieren.

sanatorium [sænə'tɔ:riəm] (*bsd.* Lungen)Sanatorium *n*; Luftkurort *m.*

sanct|ify ['sæŋktifai] heiligen, weihen; ~imonious □ [sæŋkti'mounjəs] scheinheilig; ~ion ['sæŋkʃən] **1.** Sanktion *f*; Bestätigung *f*; Genehmigung *f*; Zwangsmaßnahme *f*; **2.** bestätigen, genehmigen; ~ity [ˌktiti] Heiligkeit *f*; ~uary [ˌtjuəri] Heiligtum *n*; *das* Allerheiligste; Asyl *n*, Freistätte *f.*

sand [sænd] **1.** Sand *m*; ~s *pl.* Sand (-massen *f/pl.*) *m*; Sandwüste *f*; Sandbank *f*; **2.** mit Sand bestreuen.

sandal ['sændl] Sandale *f.*

sand|-glass ['sændglɑ:s] Sanduhr*f*; ~-hill Sanddüne *f*; ~piper *orn.* Flußuferläufer *m.*

sandwich ['sænwidʒ] **1.** Sandwich *n*; **2.** *a.* ~ *in* einlegen, einklemmen.

sandy ['sændi] sandig; sandfarben.

sane [sein] geistig gesund; vernünftig (*Antwort etc.*).

sang [sæŋ] *pret. von* sing.

sanguin|ary ['sæŋgwinəri] blutdürstig; blutig; ~e [ˌwin] leichtblütig; zuversichtlich; vollblütig.

sanitarium *Am.* [sæni'tɛəriəm] = sanatorium.

sanitary □ ['sænitəri] Gesundheits...; gesundheitlich; ⊕ Sanitär...; ~ towel Damenbinde *f.*

sanit|ation [sæni'teiʃən] Gesund-

heitspflege *f*; sanitäre Einrichtung; ~y ['sæniti] gesunder Verstand.

sank [sæŋk] *pret. von* sink 1.

Santa Claus [sæntə'klɔ:z] Nikolaus *m.*

sap [sæp] **1.** ⚘ Saft *m*; *fig.* Lebenskraft *f*; ⚔ Sappe *f*; **2.** untergraben (*a. fig.*); *sl.* büffeln; ~less ['sæplis] saft-, kraftlos; ~ling [ˌliŋ] junger Baum; *fig.* Grünschnabel *m.*

sapphire *min.* ['sæfaiə] Saphir *m.*

sappy ['sæpi] saftig; *fig.* kraftvoll.

sarcasm ['sɑ:kæzm] bitterer Spott.

sardine *ichth.* [sɑ:'di:n] Sardine *f.*

sash [sæʃ] Schärpe *f*; Fensterrahmen *m*. [befenster *n*.\]

sash-window ['sæʃwindou] Schie-|

sat [sæt] *pret. u. p.p. von* sit.

Satan ['seitən] Satan *m.*

satchel ['sætʃəl] Schulmappe *f.*

sate [seit] (über)sättigen.

sateen [sæ'ti:n] Satin *m.*

satellite ['sætəlait] Satellit(enstaat) *m.*

satiate ['seiʃieit] (über)sättigen.

satin ['sætin] Seidensatin *m.*

satir|e ['sætaiə] Satire *f*; ~ist ['sætərist] Satiriker *m*; ~ize [ˌraiz] verspotten.

satisfaction [sætis'fækʃən] Befriedigung *f*; Genugtuung *f*; Zufriedenheit *f*; Sühne *f*; Gewißheit *f.*

satisfactory □ [sætis'fæktəri] befriedigend, zufriedenstellend.

satisfy ['sætisfai] befriedigen; genügen (*dat.*); zufriedenstellen; überzeugen; *Zweifel* beheben.

saturate ⚗ *u. fig.* ['sætʃəreit] sättigen.

Saturday ['sætədi] Sonnabend *m*, Samstag *m.*

saturnine ['sætə:nain] düster, finster.

sauce [sɔ:s] **1.** (*oft kalte*) Soße; *Am.* Kompott *n*; *fig.* Würze *f*; F Frechheit *f*; **2.** würzen; F frech werden zu *j-m*; ~-boat ['sɔ:sbout] Soßenschüssel *f*; ~pan Kochtopf *m*; Kasserolle *f*; ~r ['sɔ:sə] Untertasse *f.*

saucy □ F ['sɔ:si] frech; dreist.

saunter ['sɔ:ntə] **1.** Schlendern *n*; Bummel *m*; **2.** (umher)schlendern; bummeln.

sausage ['sɔsidʒ] Wurst *f.*

savage ['sævidʒ] **1.** □ wild; roh, grausam; **2.** Wilde(r *m*) *f*; *fig.* Barbar *m*; ~ry [ˌdʒəri] Wildheit *f*; Barbarei *f.*

savant ['sævənt] Gelehrte(r) *m.*

save [seiv] **1.** retten; erlösen; bewahren; (er)sparen; schonen; **2.** *rhet. prp. u. cj.* außer; ~ *for* bis auf (*acc.*); ~ *that* nur daß.

saver ['seivə] Retter(in); Sparer(in).

saving ['seiviŋ] **1.** □ sparsam; **2.** Rettung *f*; ~s *pl.* Ersparnisse*f/pl.*

savings|-bank ['seiviŋzbæŋk] Sparkasse *f*; ~-deposit Spareinlage *f.*

savio(u)r ['seivjə] Retter *m*; *Saviour eccl.* Heiland *m*.

savo(u)r ['seivə] 1. Geschmack *m*; *fig.* Beigeschmack *m*; 2. *fig.* schmecken, riechen (*of* nach).

savo(u)ry[^1] □ ['seivəri] schmackhaft; appetitlich; pikant.

savo(u)ry[^2] ♀ [♫] Bohnenkraut *n*.

saw[^1] [sɔː] *pret. von* see.

saw[^2] [♫] Spruch *m*.

saw[^3] [♫] 1. [*irr.*] sägen; 2. Säge *f*; **~dust** ['sɔːdʌst] Sägespäne *m/pl.*; **~mill** Sägewerk *n*; **~n** [sɔːn] *p.p. von saw*[^3] 1.

Saxon ['sæksn] 1. sächsisch; *ling. oft* germanisch; 2. Sachse *m*, Sächsin *f*.

say [sei] 1. [*irr.*] sagen; hersagen; berichten; *~ grace* das Tischgebet sprechen; *that is to ~* das heißt; *you don't ~!* was Sie nicht sagen!; *I ~* sag(en Sie) mal; ich muß schon sagen; *he is said to be ... er soll ... sein*; *no sooner said than done* gesagt, getan; 2. Rede *f*, Wort *n*; *it is my ~ now* jetzt ist die Reihe zu reden an mir; *have a od. some (no) ~ in s.th. et.* (nichts) zu sagen haben bei et.; **~ing** ['seiiŋ] Rede *f*; Redensart *f*; Ausspruch *m*; *it goes without ~* es versteht sich von selbst.

scab [skæb] ♂, ♀ Schorf *m*; *vet.* Räude *f*; *sl.* Streikbrecher *m*.

scabbard ['skæbəd] Säbel-Scheide *f*.

scabrous ['skeibrəs] heikel.

scaffold ['skæfəld] (Bau)Gerüst *n*; Schafott *n*; **~ing** [♫diŋ] (Bau)Gerüst *n*.

scald [skɔːld] 1. Verbrühung *f*; 2. verbrühen; *Milch* abkochen.

scale[^1] [skeil] 1. Schuppe *f*; Kesselstein *m*; ♂ Zahnstein *m*; Waagschale *f*; (*a pair of*) *~s pl.* (eine) Waage; 2. (sich) abschuppen, ablösen; ⊕ *Kesselstein* abklopfen; ♂ *Zähne* vom Zahnstein reinigen; wiegen.

scale[^2] [♫] 1. Stufenleiter *f*; ♪ Tonleiter *f*; Skala *f*; Maßstab *m*; *fig.* Ausmaß *n*; 2. ersteigen; *~ up* (*down*) maßstabsgetreu vergrößern (verkleinern).

scallop ['skɔləp] 1. *zo.* Kammuschel *f*; ⊕ Langette *f*; 2. ausbogen.

scalp [skælp] 1. Kopfhaut *f*; Skalp *m*; 2. skalpieren.

scaly ['skeili] schuppig; voll Kesselstein.

scamp [skæmp] 1. Taugenichts *m*; 2. pfuschen; **~er** ['skæmpə] 1. (umher)tollen; hetzen; 2. *fig.* Hetzjagd *f*.

scan [skæn] *Verse* skandieren; absuchen; *fig.* überfliegen.

scandal ['skændl] Skandal *m*; Ärgernis *n*; Schande *f*; Klatsch *m*; **~ize** [♫dəlaiz] Anstoß erregen bei *j-m*; **~ous** □ [♫ləs] skandalös, anstößig; schimpflich; klatschhaft.

Scandinavian [skændi'neivjən]

1. skandinavisch; 2. Skandinavier (-in).

scant *lit.* [skænt] 1. knapp, kärglich; 2. knausern mit, sparen an (*dat.*); **~y** □ ['skænti] knapp, spärlich, kärglich, dürftig.

scape|goat ['skeipgout] Sündenbock *m*; **~grace** [♫greis] Taugenichts *m*.

scar [skɑː] 1. Narbe *f*; *fig.* (Schand-) Fleck *m*, Makel *m*; Klippe *f*; 2. *v/t.* schrammen; *v/i.* vernarben.

scarc|e [skɛəs] knapp; rar; selten; **~ely** ['skɛəsli] kaum; **~ity** [♫siti] Mangel *m*; Knappheit *f*; Teuerung *f*.

scare [skɛə] 1. er-, aufschrecken; verscheuchen; **~d** verstört; ängstlich; 2. Panik *f*; **~crow** ['skɛəkrou] Vogelscheuche *f* (*a. fig.*); **~head** (**~ing**) Riesenschlagzeile *f*.

scarf [skɑːf], *pl.* **~s**, **scarves** [♫fs, skɑːvz] Schal *m*; Hals-, Kopftuch *n*; Krawatte *f*; ⚒ Schärpe *f*.

scarlet ['skɑːlit] 1. Scharlach(rot *n*) *m*; 2. scharlachrot; **~ fever** ♂ Scharlach *m*; *~ runner* ♀ Feuerbohne *f*.

scarred [skɑːd] narbig.

scarves [skɑːvz] *pl. von scarf.*

scathing *fig.* ['skeiðiŋ] vernichtend.

scatter ['skætə] (sich) zerstreuen; aus-, verstreuen; (sich) verbreiten.

scavenger ['skævindʒə] Straßenkehrer *m*.

scenario [si'nɑːriou] *Film:* Drehbuch *n*.

scene [siːn] Szene *f*; Bühne(nbild *n*) *f*; Schauplatz *m*; **~s** *pl.* Kulissen *f/pl.*; **~ry** ['siːnəri] Szenerie *f*; Bühnenausstattung *f*; Landschaft *f*.

scent [sent] 1. (Wohl)Geruch *m*; Duft *m*; Parfüm *n*; *hunt.* Witterung(svermögen *n*) *f*; Fährte *f*; 2. wittern; parfümieren; **~less** ['sentlis] geruchlos.

sceptic ['skeptik] Skeptiker(in); **~al** □ [♫kəl] skeptisch.

scept|re, *Am.* **~er** ['septə] Zepter *n*.

schedule ['ʃedjuːl, *Am.* 'skedjuːl] 1. Verzeichnis *n*; Tabelle *f*; *Am.* Fahrplan *m*; *on ~* fahrplanmäßig; 2. auf-, verzeichnen; festsetzen.

scheme [skiːm] 1. Schema *n*; Zusammenstellung *f*; Plan *m*; 2. *v/t.* planen; *v/i.* Pläne machen; Ränke schmieden.

schism ['sizm] (Kirchen)Spaltung *f*.

scholar ['skɔlə] Gelehrte(r) *m*; *univ.* Stipendiat *m*; † Schüler(in); **~ly** *adj.* [♫əli] gelehrt; **~ship** [♫əʃip] Gelehrsamkeit *f*; Wissenschaftlichkeit *f*; *univ.* Stipendium *n*.

scholastic [skə'læstik] 1. (**~ally**) *phls.* scholastisch; schulmäßig; Schul...; 2. *phls.* Scholastiker *m*.

school [skuːl] 1. Schwarm *m*; Schule *f* (*a. fig.*); *univ.* Fakultät *f*;

Diszplin *f*; Hochschule *f*; *at* ~ *auf od.* in der Schule; 2. schulen, erziehen; ~**boy** ['sku:lbɔi] Schüler *m*; ~**fellow** Mitschüler(in); ~**girl** Schülerin *f*; ~**ing** [~liŋ] (Schul-) Ausbildung *f*; ~**master** Lehrer *m* (*bsd. e-r höheren Schule*); ~**mate** Mitschüler(in); ~**mistress** Lehrerin *f* (*bsd. e-r höheren Schule*); ~**teacher** (*bsd.* Volksschul)Lehrer (-in).

schooner ['sku:nə] ♣ Schoner *m*; *Am.* großes Bierglas; = *prairie-schooner*.

science ['saiəns] Wissenschaft *f*; Naturwissenschaft(en *pl.*) *f*; Technik *f*.

scientific [saiən'tifik] (~*ally*) (*engS.* natur)wissenschaftlich; kunstgerecht.

scientist ['saiəntist] (*bsd.* Natur-) Wissenschaftler *m*.

scintillate ['sintileit] funkeln.

scion ['saiən] Sproß *m*, Sprößling *m*.

scissors ['sizəz] *pl.* (*a pair of* ~ *pl.* eine) Schere.

scoff [skɔf] 1. Spott *m*; 2. spotten.

scold [skould] 1. zänkisches Weib; 2. (aus)schelten, schimpfen.

scon(e) [skɔn] weiches Teegebäck.

scoop [sku:p] 1. Schaufel *f*, Schippe *f*; Schöpfeimer *m*, -kelle *f*; F Coup *m*, gutes Geschäft; F Exklusivmeldung *f*; 2. (aus)schaufeln; einscheffeln.

scooter ['sku:tə] (Kinder)Roller *m*; Motorroller *m*.

scope [skoup] Bereich *m*; geistiger Gesichtskreis; Spielraum *m*.

scorch [skɔ:tʃ] *v/t.* versengen, verbrennen; *v/i.* F (dahin)rasen.

score [skɔ:] 1. Kerbe *f*; Zeche *f*, Rechnung *f*; 20 Stück; *Sport:* Punktzahl *f*; (Tor)Stand *m*; Grund *m*; ♪ Partitur *f*; ~*s of* viele; *four* ~ achtzig; *run up* ~*s* Schulden machen; *on the* ~ *of* wegen (*gen.*); 2. (ein)kerben; anschreiben; *Sport:* (Punkte) machen; *Fußball:* ein Tor schießen; gewinnen; instrumentieren; *Am.* F scharfe Kritik üben an (*dat.*).

scorn [skɔ:n] 1. Verachtung *f*; Spott *m*; 2. verachten; verschmähen; ~**ful** □ ['skɔ:nful] verächtlich.

Scotch [skɔtʃ] 1.schottisch; 2.Schottisch *n*; *the* ~ die Schotten *pl.*; ~**man** ['skɔtʃmən] Schotte *m*.

scot-free ['skɔt'fri:] straflos.

Scots [skɔts], ~**man** ['skɔtsmən] = *Scotch(man).*

scoundrel ['skaundrəl] Schurke *m*.

scour ['skauə] *v/t.* scheuern; reinigen; durchstreifen, absuchen; *v/i.* eilen.

scourge [skə:dʒ] 1. Geißel *f*; 2. geißeln.

scout [skaut] 1. Späher *m*, Kundschafter *m*; ♣ Aufklärungsfahrzeug

---

n; ✈ Aufklärer *m*; *mot.* Mitglied *n* der Straßenwacht; (*Boy*) ♀ Pfadfinder *m*; ~ *party* ✕ Spähtrupp *m*; 2. (aus)kundschaften, spähen; verächtlich zurückweisen.

scowl [skaul] 1. finsteres Gesicht; 2. finster blicken.

scrabble ['skræbl] (be)kritzeln; scharren; krabbeln.

scrag *fig.* [skræg] Gerippe *n* (*dürrer Mensch etc.*).

scramble ['skræmbl] 1. klettern; sich balgen (*for* um); ~*d eggs pl.* Rührei *n*; 2. Kletterei *f*; Balgerei *f*.

scrap [skræp] 1. Stückchen *n*; (Zeitungs)Ausschnitt *m*, Bild *n* *zum Einkleben*; Altmaterial *n*; Schrott *m*; ~*s pl.* Reste *m/pl.*; 2. ausrangieren; verschrotten; ~**book** ['skræpbuk] Sammelalbum *n*.

scrap|e [skreip] 1. Kratzen *n*, Scharren *n*; Kratzfuß *m*; Not *f*, Klemme *f*; 2. schrap(p)en; (ab)schaben; (ab)kratzen; scharren; (entlang)streifen; ~**er** ['skreipə] Kratzeisen *n*.

scrap|-heap ['skræphi:p] Abfall *f*, Schrotthaufen *m*; ~-**iron** Alteisen *n*, Schrott *m*.

scratch [skrætʃ] 1. Schramme *f*; *Sport:* Startlinie *f*; 2. zs.-gewürfelt; Zufalls...; *Sport:* ohne Vorgabe; 3. (zer)kratzen; (zer)schrammen; *parl. u. Sport:* streichen; ~ *out* ausstreichen.

scrawl [skrɔ:l] 1. kritzeln; 2. Gekritzel *n*.

scrawny *Am.* F ['skrɔ:ni] dürr.

scream [skri:m] 1. Schrei *m*; Gekreisch *n*; *he is a* ~ F er ist zum Schreien komisch; 2. schreien, kreischen.

screech [skri:tʃ] *s.* scream; ~**owl** *orn.* ['skri:tʃaul] Käuzchen *n*.

screen [skri:n] 1. Wand-, Ofen-, Schutzschirm *m*; *fig.* Schleier *m*; (Film)Leinwand *f*; *der* Film; Sandsieb *n*; (Fliegen)Gitter *n*; 2. (ab)schirmen; (be)schützen; ✕ tarnen; auf die Leinwand zeigen; verfilmen; (durch)sieben; ~ *play* Drehbuch *n*; Fernsehfilm *m*.

screw [skru:] 1. Schraube *f*; ✈ Propeller *m*; 2. (fest)schrauben; *fig.* bedrängen; ver-, umdrehen; ~ *up* festschrauben; ~ *up one's courage* Mut fassen; ~**ball** *Am. sl.* ['skru:bɔ:l] komischer Kauz; ~**driver** Schraubenzieher *m*; ~**jack** Wagenheber *m*; ~**propeller** Schiffs-, Flugzeugschraube *f*.

scribble ['skribl] 1. Gekritzel *n*; 2. kritzeln. [*skimp etc.*]

scrimp [skrimp], ~**y** ['skrimpi] =]

scrip † [skrip] Interimsschein(e *pl.*) *m*.

script [skript] Schrift *f*; Schreibschrift *f*; Manuskript *n*; *Film:* Drehbuch *n*.

Scripture ['skriptʃə] *mst the Holy ~s pl.* die Heilige Schrift.

scroll [skroul] Schriftrolle *f*, Liste*f*; ⚔ Schnecke *f*; Schnörkel *m*.

scrub [skrʌb] 1. Gestrüpp *n*; Zwerg *m*; *Am. Sport:* zweite (Spieler-) Garnitur; 2. schrubben, scheuern.

scrubby ['skrʌbi] struppig; schäbig.

scrup|le ['skru:pl] 1. Skrupel *m*, Zweifel *m*, Bedenken *n*; 2. Bedenken haben; **~ulous** □ [~pjuləs] (allzu) bedenklich; gewissenhaft; ängstlich.

scrutin|ize ['skru:tinaiz] (genau) prüfen; **~y** [~ni] forschender Blick; genaue (*bsd.* Wahl)Prüfung.

scud [skʌd] 1. (Dahin)Jagen *n*; (dahintreibende) Wolkenfetzen *m/pl.*; Bö *f*; 2. eilen, jagen; gleiten.

scuff [skʌf] schlurfen, schlorren.

scuffle ['skʌfl] 1. Balgerei *f*, Rauferei *f*; 2. sich balgen, raufen.

scull ⚓ [skʌl] 1. kurzes Ruder; 2. rudern, skullen.

scullery ['skʌləri] Spülküche *f*.

sculptor ['skʌlptə] Bildhauer *m*.

sculpture ['skʌlptʃə] 1. Plastik *f*; Bildhauerkunst *f*, Skulptur *f*; 2. (heraus)meißeln, formen.

scum *fig.* [skʌm] (Ab)Schaum *m*.

scurf [skə:f] (Haut)Schuppen *f/pl.*

scurrilous ['skʌriləs] gemein.

scurry ['skʌri] hasten, rennen.

scurvy[1] 🛥 ['skə:vi] Skorbut *m*.

scurvy[2] [~] (hunds)gemein.

scuttle ['skʌtl] 1. Kohlenbehälter *m*; 2. eilen; *fig.* sich drücken.

scythe ⚘ [saið] Sense *f*.

sea [si:] See *f*, Meer *n* (*a. fig.*); hohe Welle; *at* ~ auf See; *fig.* ratlos; **~board** ['si:bɔ:d] Küste(ngebiet *n*) *f*; **~coast** Küste *f*; **~faring** ['si:fɛəriŋ] seefahrend; **~food** eßbare Seefische *m/pl.*; Meeresfrüchte *pl.*; **~going** Hochsee...; **~gull** (See)Möwe *f*.

seal [si:l] 1. *zo.* Seehund *m*, Robbe *f*; Siegel *n*; Stempel *m*; Bestätigung *f*; 2. versiegeln; *fig.* besiegeln; ~ *up* (fest) verschließen; ⊕ abdichten.

sea-level ['si:levl] Meeresspiegel *m*.

sealing-wax ['si:liŋwæks] Siegellack *m*.

seam [si:m] 1. Saum *m*; (*a.* ⊕) Naht *f*; ⊕ Fuge *f*; *geol.* Flöz *n*; Narbe *f*; 2. schrammen; furchen.

seaman ['si:mən] Seemann *m*, Matrose *m*.

seamstress ['semstris] Näherin *f*.

sea|-plane ['si:plein] Wasserflugzeug *n*; **~power** Seemacht *f*.

sear [siə] 1. dürr, welk; 2. austrocknen, versengen; 🖋 brennen; *fig.* verhärten.

search [sə:tʃ] 1. Suchen *n*, Forschen *n*; Unter-, Durchsuchung *f*; *in* ~ *of* auf der Suche nach; 2. *v/t.* durch-, untersuchen; 🖋 sondieren; erfor-

schen; durchdringen; *v/i.* suchen, forschen (*for* nach); ~ *into* ergründen; **~ing** □ ['sə:tʃiŋ] forschend, prüfend; eingehend (*Prüfung etc.*); **~light** (Such)Scheinwerfer *m*; **~warrant** ⚖ Haussuchungsbefehl *m*.

sea|-shore ['si:'ʃɔ:] Seeküste *f*; **~sick** seekrank; **~side** Strand *m*, Küste *f*; ~ *place*, ~ *resort* Seebad *n*; *go to the* ~ an die See gehen.

season ['si:zn] 1. Jahreszeit *f*; (rechte) Zeit; Saison *f*; F *für* **~ticket:** *cherries are in* ~ jetzt ist Kirschenzeit; *out of* ~ zur Unzeit; *with the compliments of the* ~ mit den besten Wünschen zum Fest; 2. *v/t.* reifen (lassen); würzen; abhärten (*to* gegen); *v/i.* ablagern; **~able** □ [~nəbl] zeitgemäß; rechtzeitig; **~al** □ ['si:zənl] Saison...; periodisch; **~ing** ['si:zniŋ] Würze *f*; **~ticket** ⚖ Zeitkarte *f*; *thea.* Abonnement *n*.

seat [si:t] 1. Sitz *m* (*a. fig.*); Sessel *m*, Stuhl *m*, Bank *f*; (Sitz)Platz *m*; Landsitz *m*; Gesäß *n*; Schauplatz *m*; 2. (hin)setzen; e-n Hosenboden einsetzen in (*acc.*); fassen, Sitzplätze haben für; **~ed** sitzend; ...sitzig; *be* ~*ed* sitzen; sich setzen; **~belt** ⚖ ['si:tbelt] Sicherheitsgurt *m*.

sea|-urchin *zo.* ['si:'ə:tʃin] Seeigel *m*; **~ward** ['si:wəd] 1. *adj.* seewärts gerichtet; 2. *adv. a.* ~*s* seewärts; **~weed** ⚘ (See)Tang *m*; **~worthy** seetüchtig.

secede [si:si:d] sich trennen.

secession [si:seʃən] Lossagung *f*; Abfall *m*; **~ist** [~ʃnist] Abtrünnige(r *m*) *f*.

seclu|de [si:klu:d] abschließen, absondern; **~ded** einsam; zurückgezogen; abgelegen; **~sion** [~u:ʒən] Abgeschlossen-, Abgeschiedenheit *f*.

second ['sekənd] 1. □ zweite(r, -s); nächste(r, -s); geringer (*to* als); *on* ~ *thoughts* bei genauerer Überlegung; 2. Zweite(r, -s) Sekundant *m*; Beistand *m*; Sekunde *f*; ~*s pl.* Waren *pl.* zweiter Wahl; 3. sekundieren (*dat.*); unterstützen; **~ary** □ [~dəri] sekundär; untergeordnet; Neben...; Hilfs...; Sekundär...; **~ary school** höhere Schule; weiterführende Schule; **~hand** aus zweiter Hand; gebraucht; antiquarisch; **~ly** [~dli] zweitens; **~rate** zweiten Ranges; zweitklassig.

secre|cy ['si:krisi] Heimlichkeit *f*; Verschwiegenheit *f*; **~t** [~it] 1. □ geheim; Geheim...; verschwiegen; verborgen; 2. Geheimnis *n*; *in* ~ insgeheim; *be in the* ~, *be taken into the* ~ eingeweiht sein.

secretary ['sekrətri] Schriftführer *m*; Sekretär(in); ⚖ *of State* Staatssekretär *m*, Minister *m*; *Am.* Außenminister *m*.

secret|e [si'kri:t] verbergen; absondern; ~ion [~i:ʃən] Absonderung *f*; ~ive [~i:tiv] *fig.* verschlossen; geheimtuerisch.

section ['sekʃən] ⚓ Sektion *f*; (Durch)Schnitt *m*; Teil *m*; Abschnitt *m*, Paragraph *m*; *typ.* Absatz *m*; Abteilung *f*; Gruppe *f*.

secular □ ['sekjulə] weltlich.

secur|e [si'kjuə] 1. □ sicher; 2. (sich et.) sichern; schützen; festmachen; ~ity [~riti] Sicherheit *f*; Sorglosigkeit *f*; Gewißheit *f*; Schutz *m*; Kaution *f*; securities *pl.* Wertpapiere *n/pl.*

sedan [si'dæn] Limousine *f*; *a.* ~-chair Sänfte *f*.

sedate □ [si'deit] gesetzt; ruhig.

sedative *mst* ⚕ ['sedətiv] 1. beruhigend; 2. Beruhigungsmittel *n*.

sedentary □ ['sedntəri] sitzend; seßhaft.

sediment ['sedimənt] (Boden)Satz *m*; *geol.* Ablagerung *f*.

sediti|on [si'diʃən] Aufruhr *m*; ~ous □ [~ʃəs] aufrührerisch.

seduc|e [si'dju:s] verführen; ~tion [si'dʌkʃən] Verführung *f*; ~tive □ [~ktiv] verführerisch.

sedulous □ ['sedjuləs] emsig.

see¹ [si:] *irr.* *v/i.* sehen; *fig.* einsehen; *I* ~ ich verstehe; ~ *about* s.th. sich um et. kümmern; ~ *through* s.o. *od.* s.th. j-n *od.* et. durchschauen; ~ *to* achten auf (*acc.*); *v/t.* sehen; beobachten; einsehen; sorgen (*daß* et. *geschieht*); besuchen; *Arzt* aufsuchen; ~ *s.o. home* j-n nach Hause begleiten; ~ *off Besuch etc.* wegbringen; ~ *out Besuch* hinausbegleiten; *et.* zu Ende erleben; ~ *s.th. through* et. durchhalten; ~ *s.o. through* j-m durchhelfen; *live to* ~ erleben.

see² [~] (erz)bischöflicher Stuhl.

seed [si:d] 1. Same(n) *m*, Saat(gut *n*) *f*; (Obst)Kern *m*; Keim *m* (*a. fig.*); *go od.* run *to* ~ in Samen schießen; *fig.* herunterkommen; 2. *v/t.* (be-)säen; entkernen; *v/i.* in Samen schießen; ~less ['si:dlis] kernlos (*Obst*); ~ling ✐ [~liŋ] Sämling *m*; ~y ['si:di] schäbig; F elend.

seek [si:k] [*irr.*] suchen (nach) begehren; trachten nach.

seem [si:m] (er)scheinen; ~ing □ ['si:miŋ] anscheinend; scheinbar; ~ly ['si:mli] schicklich.

seen [si:n] *p.p. von* see¹.

seep [si:p] durchsickern, tropfen.

seer ['si(:)ə] Seher(in), Prophet(in).

seesaw ['si:sɔ:] 1. Wippen *n*; Wippe *f*, Wippschaukel *f*; 2. wippen; *fig.* schwanken.

seethe [si:ð] sieden, kochen.

segment ['segmənt] Abschnitt *m*.

segregat|e ['segrigeit] absondern,

trennen; ~ion [segri'geiʃən] Absonderung *f*; Rassentrennung *f*.

seiz|e [si:z] ergreifen, fassen; mit Beschlag belegen; *fig.* erfassen; *a.* ~ *upon* sich e-r S. *od.* j-s bemächtigen; ~ure ['si:ʒə] Ergreifung *f*; ⚖ Beschlagnahme *f*; ⚕ plötzlicher Anfall.

seldom *adv.* ['seldəm] selten.

select [si'lekt] 1. auswählen, auslesen, aussuchen; 2. auserwählt; erlesen; exklusiv; ~ion [~kʃən] Auswahl *f*, Auslese *f*; ~man *Am.* Stadtrat *m in den Neuenglandstaaten.*

self [self] 1. *pl.* selves [selvz] Selbst *n*, Ich *n*; Persönlichkeit *f*; 2. *pron.* selbst; ✝ *od.* F = myself *etc.*; 3. *adj.* ⚘ einfarbig; ~-centered ['self-'sentəd] egozentrisch; ~-command Selbstbeherrschung *f*; ~-conceit Eigendünkel *m*; ~-conceited dünkelhaft; ~-confidence Selbstvertrauen *n*; ~-conscious befangen, gehemmt; ~-contained (in sich) abgeschlossen; *fig.* verschlossen; ~-control Selbstbeherrschung *f*; ~-defence, *Am.* ~-defense Selbstverteidigung *f*; in ~ in (der) Notwehr; ~-denial Selbstverleugnung *f*; ~-employed selbständig (*Handwerker etc.*); ~-evident selbstverständlich; ~-government Selbstverwaltung *f*, Autonomie *f*; ~-indulgent bequem; zügellos; ~-interest Eigennutz *m*; ~ish □ [~fiʃ] selbstsüchtig; ~-possession Selbstbeherrschung *f*; ~-reliant [~fri-'laiənt] selbstsicher; ~-righteous selbstgerecht; ~-seeking [~f'si:kiŋ] eigennützig; ~-willed eigenwillig.

sell [sel] [*irr.*] *v/t.* verkaufen (*a. fig.*); *Am.* aufschwatzen; *v/i.* handeln; gehen (*Ware*); ~ *off*, ~ *out* ~ ausverkaufen; ~er ['selə] Verkäufer *m*; good *etc.* ~ ✝ gut *etc.* gehende Ware.

selves [selvz] *pl. von* self 1.

semblance ['sembləns] Anschein *m*; Gestalt *f*.

semi... ['semi] halb...; Halb...; ~colon Strichpunkt *m*; ~-detached house Doppelhaus(hälfte *f*) *n*); ~-final *Sport*: Vorschlußrunde *f*.

seminary ['seminəri] (Priester)Seminar *n*; *fig.* Schule *f*.

sempstress ['sempstris] Näherin *f*.

senate ['senit] Senat *m*.

senator ['senətə] Senator *m*.

send [send] [*irr.*] senden, schicken; (*mit adj. od. p.pr.*) machen; ~ *for* kommen lassen, holen (lassen); ~ *forth* aussenden; veröffentlichen; ~ *in* einsenden; einreichen; ~ *up* in die Höhe treiben; ~ *word* mitteilen.

senile ['si:nail] greisenhaft, senil; ~ity [si'niliti] Greisenalter *n*.

senior ['si:njə] 1. älter; dienstälter; Ober...; ~ *partner* ✝ Chef *m*; 2. Ältere(r) *m*; Dienstältere(r) *m*;

Senior *m*; *he is my ~ by a year* er ist ein Jahr älter als ich; **~ity** [si:ni-'ɔriti] höheres Alter *od.* Dienstalter.

sensation [sen'seiʃən] (Sinnes-) Empfindung *f*, Gefühl *n*; Eindruck *m*; Sensation *f*; **~al** □ [~nl] Empfindungs...; sensationell.

sense [sens] **1.** *allg.* Sinn *m* (of für); Empfindung *f*, Gefühl *n*; Verstand *m*; Bedeutung *f*; Ansicht *f*; *in (out of) one's ~s* bei (von) Sinnen; *bring s.o. to his ~s* j-n zur Vernunft bringen; *make ~* Sinn haben (*S.*); *talk ~* vernünftig reden; **2.** spüren.

senseless □ ['senslis] sinnlos; bewußtlos; gefühllos; **~ness** [~snis] Sinnlosigkeit *f*; Bewußt-, Gefühllosigkeit *f*.

sensibility [sensi'biliti] Sensibilität *f*, Empfindungsvermögen *n*; Empfindlichkeit *f*; **sensibilities** *pl.* Empfindsamkeit *f*, Zartgefühl *n*.

sensible □ ['sensəbl] verständig, vernünftig; empfänglich (*of* für); fühlbar; *be ~ of sich e-r S.* bewußt sein; *et.* empfinden.

sensitiv|e □ ['sensitiv] empfindlich (*to* für); Empfindungs...; feinfühlig; **~eness** [~vnis], **~ity** [sensi-'tiviti] Empfindlichkeit *f* (*to* für).

sensual □ ['sensjuəl] sinnlich.

sensuous □ ['sensjuəs] sinnlich; Sinnes...; sinnenfreudig.

sent [sent] *pret. u. p.p. von* send.

sentence ['sentəns] **1.** ⚖ Urteil *n*; *gr.* Satz *m*; *serve one's ~* s-e Strafe absitzen; **2.** verurteilen.

sententious □ [sen'tenʃəs] sentenziös; salbungsvoll; salbaderisch.

sentient ['senʃənt] empfindend.

sentiment ['sentimənt] (seelische) Empfindung, Gefühl *n*; Meinung *f*; *s. sentimentality*; **~al** □ [senti'mentl] empfindsam; sentimental; **~ality** [sentimen'tæliti] Sentimentalität *f*.

sent|inel ⚔ ['sentinl], **~ry** ⚔ [~tri] Schildwache *f*, Posten *m*.

separa|ble □ ['sepərəbl] trennbar; **~te 1.** □ ['seprit] (ab)getrennt, gesondert, besonder, separat, für sich; **2.** ['sepəreit] (sich) trennen; (sich) absondern; (sich) scheiden; **~tion** [sepə'reiʃən] Trennung *f*, Scheidung *f*.

sepsis ✚ ['sepsis] Sepsis *f*, Blutvergiftung *f*. [*m.*]

September [səp'tembə] September)

septic ✚ ['septik] septisch.

sepul|chral [si'pʌlkrəl] Grab...; Toten...; *fig.* düster; **~chre, ~m. ~cher** ['sepəlkə] Grab(stätte *f*) *n*; **~ture** [~ltʃə] Begräbnis *n*.

sequel ['si:kwəl] Folge *f*; Nachspiel *n*; (Roman)Fortsetzung *f*.

sequen|ce ['si:kwəns] Aufeinander-, Reihenfolge *f*; Film: Szene *f*; *~ of tenses gr.* Zeitenfolge *f*; **~t** [~nt] aufeinanderfolgend.

sequestrate ⚖ [si'kwestreit] *Eigentum* einziehen; beschlagnahmen.

serenade [seri'neid] **1.** ♪ Serenade *f*, Ständchen *n*; **2.** *j-m* ein Ständchen bringen.

seren|e □ [si'ri:n] klar, heiter; ruhig; **~ity** [si'reniti] Heiterkeit *f*; Ruhe *f*.

serf [sə:f] Leibeigene(r *m*) *f*, Hörige(r *m*) *f*; *fig.* Sklave *m*.

sergeant ['sɑ:dʒənt] ⚔ Feldwebel *m*, Wachtmeister *m*; (Polizei)Wachtmeister *m*.

serial □ ['siəriəl] **1.** fortlaufend, reihenweise, Serien...; Fortsetzungs...; **2.** Fortsetzungsroman *m*.

series ['siəri:z] *sg. u. pl.* Reihe *f*; Serie *f*; Folge *f*; *biol.* Gruppe *f*.

serious □ ['siəriəs] *allg.* ernst; ernsthaft, ernstlich; *be ~* es im Ernst meinen; **~ness** [~snis] Ernst (-haftigkeit *f*) *m*.

sermon ['sə:mən] (*iro.* Straf)Predigt *f*.

serpent ['sə:pənt] Schlange *f*; **~ine** [~tain] schlangengleich, -förmig; Serpentinen...

serum ['siərəm] Serum *n*.

servant ['sə:vənt] Diener(in); *a.* domestic ~ Dienstbote *m*, Bedienstete(r *m*) *f*; Dienstmädchen *n*.

serve [sə:v] **1.** *v/t.* dienen (*dat.*); *Zeit* abdienen; bedienen; *Speisen* reichen; *Speisen* auftragen; behandeln; nützen, dienlich sein (*dat.*); *Zweck* erfüllen; *Tennis:* angeben; (*it*) *~s him right* (das) geschieht ihm recht; *s. sentence*; *~ out et.* austeilen; *v/i.* dienen (*a.* ⚔; *as,* für als, zu); bedienen; nützen, zweckmäßig sein; *~ at table* servieren; **2.** *Tennis:* Aufschlag *m.*

service ['sə:vis] **1.** Dienst *m*; Bedienung *f*; Gefälligkeit *f*; *a.* divine ~ Gottesdienst *m*; Betrieb *m*; Verkehr *m*; Nutzen *m*; Gang *m von Speisen*; Service *n*; ⚖ Zustellung *f*; *Tennis:* Aufschlag *m*; *be at s.o.'s ~* j-m zu Diensten stehen; **2.** ⊕ warten, pflegen; **~able** □ [~səbl] dienlich, nützlich; benutzbar; strapazierfähig; *~ station* Tankstelle *f*; Werkstatt *f*.

servil|e □ ['sə:vail] sklavisch (*a. fig.*); unterwürfig; kriecherisch; **~ity** [sə:'viliti] Unterwürfigkeit *f*, Kriecherei *f*.

serving ['sə:viŋ] Portion *f*.

servitude ['sə:vitju:d] Knechtschaft *f*; Sklaverei *f*.

session ['seʃən] (*a.* Gerichts)Sitzung *f*; *be in ~* tagen.

set [set] **1.** [*irr.*] *v/t.* setzen; stellen; legen; zurechtstellen, (ein)richten; ordnen; *Aufgabe, Wecker* stellen; *Messer* abziehen; *Edelstein* fassen; festsetzen; erstarren lassen; *Haar* legen; ✚ *Knochenbruch* einrichten; *~ s.o. laughing* j-n zum Lachen

bringen; ~ an example ein Beispiel
geben; ~ sail Segel setzen; ~ one's
teeth die Zähne zs.-beißen; ~ aside
beiseite stellen od. legen; fig. verwerfen; ~ at ease beruhigen; ~ at
rest beruhigen; Frage entscheiden;
~ store by Wert legen auf (acc.); ~
forth darlegen; ~ off hervorheben;
anrechnen; ~ up auf-, er-, einrichten; aufstellen; j-n etablieren; v/i.
ast. untergehen; gerinnen, fest
werden; lassen (Flut etc.); sitzen
(Kleid etc.); ~ about s.th. sich an et.
machen; ~ about s.o. F über j-n
herfallen; ~ forth aufbrechen; ~
off aufbrechen; ~ (up)on anfangen;
angreifen; ~ out aufbrechen; ~ to
sich daran machen; ~ up sich niederlassen; ~ up for sich aufspielen
als; 2. fest; starr; festgesetzt, bestimmt; vorgeschrieben; ~ (up)on
versessen auf (acc.); ~ with besetzt
mit; Barometer: ~ fair beständig;
hard ~ in großer Not; ~ speech
wohlüberlegte Rede; 3. Reihe f,
Folge f, Serie f, Sammlung f, Satz
m; Garnitur f; Service n; Radio-
Gerät n; ♣ Kollektion f; Gesellschaft f; Sippschaft f; ♪ Setzling
m; Tennis: Satz m; Neigung f;
Richtung f; Sitz m e-s Kleides etc.;
poet. Untergang m der Sonne; thea.
Bühnenausstattung f.
set|-back ['setbæk] fig. Rückschlag
m; ~-down fig. Dämpfer m; ~-off
Kontrast m; fig. Ausgleich m.
settee [se'tiː] kleines Sofa.
setting ['setiŋ] Setzen n; Einrichten
n; Fassung f e-s Edelsteins; Lage f;
Schauplatz m; Umgebung f; thea.
Ausstattung f; fig. Umrahmung f;
♪ Komposition f; (Sonnen- etc.)
Untergang m; ⊕ Einstellung f.
settle ['setl] 1. Sitzbank f; 2. v/t.
(fest)setzen; Kind etc. versorgen,
ausstatten; j-n etablieren; regeln;
Geschäft abschließen, abmachen,
erledigen; Frage entscheiden; Rechnung begleichen; ordnen; beruhigen; Streit beilegen; Rente aussetzen; ansiedeln; Land besiedeln;
v/i. sich senken (Haus); oft ~ down
sich niederlassen; a. ~ in sich einrichten; sich legen (Wut etc.);
beständig werden (Wetter); sich
entschließen; ~ down to sich widmen (dat.); ~d fest; beständig;
auf Rechnungen: bezahlt; ~ment
[~lmant] Erledigung f; Überein-
kunft f; (Be)Siedlung f; ⚖ (Eigen-
tums)Übertragung f; ~r [~lə]
Siedler m.
set|-to F ['set'tuː] Kampf m; Schlä-
gerei f; ~-up F Aufbau m; Am. sl.
abgekartete Sache.
seven ['sevn] 1. sieben; 2. Sieben f;
~teen(th) [~n'tiːn(θ)] siebzehn
(-te[r, -s]); ~th [~nθ] 1. □ sieben(en)-
te(r, -s); 2. Sieb(en)tel n; ~thly

[~θli] sieb(en)tens; ~tieth [~ntiiθ]
siebzigste(r, -s); ~ty [~ti] 1. siebzig;
2. Siebzig f.
sever ['sevə] (sich) trennen; (auf-)
lösen; zerreißen.
several □ ['sevrəl] mehrere, verschiedene; einige; einzeln; besonder; getrennt; ~ly [~li] besonders,
einzeln.
severance ['sevərəns] Trennung f.
sever|e □ [si'viə] streng; rauh
(Wetter); hart (Winter); scharf
(Tadel); ernst (Mühe); heftig
(Schmerz etc.); schlimm, schwer
(Unfall etc.); ~ity [si'veriti] Strenge
f, Härte f; Schwere f; Ernst m.
sew [sou] [irr.] nähen; heften.
sewage ['sjuː(i)dʒ] Abwasser n.
sewer¹ ['souə] Näherin f.
sewer² ['sjuə] Abwasserkanal m;
~age [~əridʒ] Kanalisation f.
sew|ing ['souiŋ] Nähen n; Nähe-
rei f; attr. Näh...; ~n [soun] p.p.
von sew.
sex [seks] Geschlecht n.
sexton ['sekstən] Küster m, Totengräber m.
sexual □ ['seksjuəl] geschlechtlich;
Geschlechts...; sexuell; Sexual...
shabby □ ['ʃæbi] schäbig; gemein.
shack Am. [ʃæk] Hütte f, Bude f.
shackle ['ʃækl] 1. Fessel f (fig. mst
pl.); 2. fesseln.
shade [ʃeid] 1. Schatten m, Dunkel n
(a. fig.); Lampen- etc. Schirm m;
Schattierung f; Am. Rouleau n;
fig. Spur f, Kleinigkeit f; 2. beschatten; verdunkeln (a. fig.); ab-
schirmen; schützen; schattieren; ~
away, ~ off allmählich übergehen
(lassen) (into in acc.).
shadow ['ʃædou] 1. Schatten m (a.
fig.); Phantom n; Spur f, Kleinigkeit f; 2. beschatten; (mst ~ forth
od. out) andeuten; versinnbildlichen;
j-n beschatten, überwachen; ~y
[~oui] schattig, dunkel; schatten-
haft; wesenlos.
shady □ ['ʃeidi] schattenspendend;
schattig; dunkel; F zweifelhaft.
shaft [ʃɑːft] Schaft m; Stiel m;
Pfeil m (a. fig.); poet. Strahl m; ⊕
Welle f; Deichsel f; ⚒ Schacht m.
shaggy □ ['ʃægi] zottig.
shake [ʃeik] 1. [irr.] v/t. schütteln,
rütteln; erschüttern; ~ down her-
unterschütteln; Stroh etc. hin-
schütten; ~ hands sich die Hände
geben od. schütteln; ~ up Bett aufschütteln; fig. aufrütteln; v/i. zittern, beben, wackeln, wanken (with
vor dat.); ♪ trillern; 2. Schütteln n;
Erschütterung f; Beben n; ♪ Triller m; ~down ['ʃeik'daun] 1. Not-
lager n; Am. sl. Erpressung f; 2.
adj.: ~ cruise ♣ Probefahrt f;
~-hands pl. Händedruck m; ~n
['ʃeikən] 1. p.p. von shake 1; 2. adj.
erschüttert.

shaky □ ['ʃeiki] wack(e)lig (*a. fig.*); (sch)wankend; zitternd, zitterig.

shall [ʃæl] [*irr.*] *v/aux.* soll; werde.

shallow ['ʃælou] 1. seicht; flach; *fig.* oberflächlich; 2. Untiefe *f*; 3. (sich) verflachen.

sham [ʃæm] 1. falsch; Schein...; 2. Trug *m*; Täuschung *f*; Schwindler(in); 3. *v/t.* vortäuschen; *v/i.* sich verstellen; simulieren; ~ ill (-ness) sich krank stellen.

shamble ['ʃæmbl] watscheln; ~s *pl. od. sg.* Schlachthaus *n*; *fig.* Schlachtfeld *n*.

shame [ʃeim] 1. Scham *f*; Schande *f*; for ~!, ~ on you! pfui!, schäm dich!; put to ~ beschämen; 2. beschämen; *j-m* Schande machen; ~faced □ ['ʃeimfeist] schamhaft, schüchtern; ~ful □ [~ful] schändlich, beschämend; ~less □ [~ʃeimlis] schamlos.

shampoo [ʃæm'puː] 1. Shampoo *n*; Haarwäsche *f*; 2. *Haare* waschen.

shamrock ['ʃæmrɔk] Kleeblatt *n*.

shank [ʃæŋk] (Unter)Schenkel *m*; ⚓ Stiel *m*; (⚓ Anker)Schaft *m*.

shanty ['ʃænti] Hütte *f*, Bude *f*.

shape [ʃeip] 1. Gestalt *f*, Form *f* (*a. fig.*); Art *f*; 2. *v/t.* gestalten, formen, bilden; anpassen (to *dat.*); *v/i.* sich entwickeln; ~d ...förmig; ~less ['ʃeiplis] formlos; ~ly [~li] wohlgestaltet.

share [ʃɛə] 1. (An)Teil *m*; Beitrag *m*; † Aktie *f*; ✕ Kux *m*; have a ~ in teilhaben an (*dat.*); go ~s teilen; 2. *v/t.* teilen; *v/i.* teilhaben (in an *dat.*); ~cropper *Am.* ['ʃɛəkrɔpə] *kleiner* Farmpächter; ~holder † Aktionär(in).

shark [ʃɑːk] *ichth.* Hai(fisch) *m*; Gauner *m*; *Am. sl.* Kanone *f* (*Experte*).

sharp [ʃɑːp] 1. □ *allg.* scharf (*a. fig.*); spitz; schneidend, stechend; schrill; hitzig; schnell; pfiffig, schlau, gerissen; C ~ ♪ Cis *n*; 2. *adv.* ♪ zu hoch; F pünktlich; look ~! (mach) schnell!; 3. ♪ Kreuz *n*; durch ein Kreuz erhöhte Note; F Gauner *m*; ~en ['ʃɑːpən] (ver-) schärfen; spitzen; ~ener ['ʃɑːpnə] *Messer*-Schärfer *m*; *Bleistift*-Spitzer *m*; ~er ['ʃɑːpə] Gauner *m*; ~ness ['ʃɑːpnis] Schärfe *f* (*a. fig.*); ~set ['ʃɑːp'set] hungrig; erpicht; ~sighted scharfsichtig; ~witted scharfsinnig.

shatter ['ʃætə] zerschmettern, zerschlagen; *Nerven etc.* zerrütten.

shave [ʃeiv] 1. [*irr.*] (sich) rasieren; (ab)schälen; haarscharf vorbeigehen *od.* vorbeifahren *od.* vorbeikommen an (*dat.*); 2. Rasieren *n*, Rasur *f*; have a ~ sich rasieren (lassen); a close ~ ein Entkommen mit knapper Not; ~n ['ʃeivn] *p.p. von* shave 1.

shaving ['ʃeiviŋ] 1. Rasieren *n*; ~s *pl.* (*bsd.* Hobel)Späne *m/pl.*; 2. Rasier...

shawl [ʃɔːl] Schal *m*, Kopftuch *n*.

she [ʃiː] 1. sie; 2. Sie *f*; *zo.* Weibchen *n*; 3. *adj. in Zssgn*: weiblich, ...weibchen *n*, ~dog Hündin *f*.

sheaf [ʃiːf], *pl.* **sheaves** [ʃiːvz] Garbe *f*; Bündel *n*.

shear [ʃiə] 1. [*irr.*] scheren; *fig.* rupfen; 2. ~s *pl.* große Schere.

sheath [ʃiːθ] Scheide *f*; ~e [ʃiːð] (in die Scheide) stecken; einhüllen; ⊕ bekleiden, beschlagen.

sheaves [ʃiːvz] *pl. von* sheaf.

shebang *Am. sl.* [ʃə'bæŋ] Bude *f*, Laden *m*.

shed[1] [ʃed] [*irr.*] aus-, vergießen; verbreiten; *Blätter etc.* abwerfen.

shed[2] [~] Schuppen *m*; Stall *m*.

sheen [ʃiːn] Glanz *m* (*bsd. Stoff*).

sheep [ʃiːp] Schaf(e) *pl.*; Schafleder *n*; ~-cot ['ʃiːpkɔt] = sheepfold; ~dog Schäferhund *m*; ~fold Schafhürde *f*; ~ish □ ['ʃiːpiʃ] blöd(e), einfältig; ~man *Am.* Schafzüchter *m*; ~skin Schaffell *n*; Schafleder *n*; F Diplom *n*.

sheer [ʃiə] rein; glatt; *Am.* hauchdünn; steil; senkrecht; direkt.

sheet [ʃiːt] Bett-, Leintuch *n*, Laken *n*; (*Glas- etc.*)Platte *f*; ⊕ ...blech *n*; Blatt *n*, Bogen *m Papier*; weite Fläche (*Wasser etc.*); ⚓ Schot(e) *f*; the rain came down in ~s es regnete in Strömen; ~ iron Eisenblech *n*; ~ lightning ['ʃiːtlaitniŋ] Wetterleuchten *n*.

shelf [ʃelf], *pl.* **shelves** [ʃelvz] Brett *n*, Regal *n*, Fach *n*; Riff *n*; on the ~ *fig.* ausrangiert.

shell [ʃel] 1. Schale *f*, Hülse *f*, Muschel *f*; Gehäuse *n*; Gerippe *n* e-s *Hauses*; ✕ Granate *f*; 2. schälen, enthülsen; ✕ bombardieren; ~fire ['ʃelfaiə] Granatfeuer *n*; ~fish *zo.* Schalentier *n*; ~proof bombensicher.

shelter ['ʃeltə] 1. Schuppen *m*; Schutz-, Obdach *n*; *fig.* Schutz *m*; Schirm *m*; 2. *v/t.* (be)schützen; (be)schirmen; Zuflucht gewähren (*dat.*); *v/i. a.* take ~ Schutz suchen.

shelve [ʃelv] mit Brettern *od.* Regalen versehen; auf ein Brett stellen; *fig.* zu den Akten legen; *fig.* beiseite legen; sich allmählich neigen.

shelves [ʃelvz] *pl. von* shelf.

shenanigan *Am.* F [ʃi'nænigən] Gaunerei *f*; Humbug *m*.

shepherd ['ʃepəd] 1. Schäfer *m*, Hirt *m*; 2. (be)hüten; leiten.

sherbet ['ʃəːbət] Brauselimonade *f*; (*Art*) (Speise)Eis *n*.

shield [ʃiːld] 1. (Schutz)Schild *m*; Wappenschild *m*; 2. (be)schirmen (*from vor dat.*, gegen).

shift [ʃift] 1. Veränderung *f*, Verschiebung f, Wechsel m; Notbehelf m; List f, Kniff m; Ausflucht f; (Arbeits)Schicht f; make ~ es möglich machen (to inf. zu inf.); sich behelfen; sich durchschlagen; 2. v/t. (ver-, weg)schieben; (ab)wechseln; verändern; Platz, Szene verlegen, verlagern; v/i. wechseln; sich verlagern; sich behelfen; ~ for o.s. sich selbst helfen; ~less □ ['ʃiftlis] hilflos; faul; ~y □ [~ti] fig. gerissen; unzuverlässig.

shilling ['ʃiliŋ] englischer Schilling.
shin [ʃin] 1. a. ~bone Schienbein n; 2. ~ up hinaufklettern.
shine [ʃain] 1. Schein m; Glanz m; 2. [irr.] v/i. scheinen; leuchten; fig. glänzen, strahlen; v/t. blank putzen.
shingle ['ʃiŋgl] Schindel f; Am. F (Aushänge)Schild n; Strandkiesel m/pl.; ~s pl. ✍ Gürtelrose f.
shiny □ ['ʃaini] blank, glänzend.
ship [ʃip] 1. Schiff n; Am. F Flugzeug n; 2. an Bord nehmen od. bringen; verschiffen, versenden; ⚓ heuern; ~board ['ʃipbɔːd]: on ~ ⚓ an Bord; ~ment ['ʃipmənt] Verschiffung f; Versand m; Schiffsladung f; ~owner Reeder m; ~ping ['ʃipiŋ] Verschiffung f; Schiffe n/pl., Flotte f; attr. Schiffs...; Verschiffungs..., Verlade...; ~wreck 1. Schiffbruch m; 2. scheitern (lassen); ~wrecked schiffbrüchig; ~yard Schiffswerft f. [schaft f.]
shire ['ʃaiə, in Zssgn ...ʃiə] Graf-]
shirk [ʃəːk] sich drücken (um et.); ~er ['ʃəːkə] Drückeberger m.
shirt [ʃəːt] Herrenhemd n; ~waist Am. Hemdbluse f; ~sleeve ['ʃəːtsliːv] 1. Hemdsärmel m; 2. hemdsärmelig; informell; ~ diplomacy bsd. Am. offene Diplomatie.
shiver ['ʃivə] 1. Splitter m; Schauer m; 2. zersplittern; schau(d)ern; (er)zittern; frösteln; ~y [~əri] fröstelnd.
shoal [ʃoul] 1. Schwarm m, Schar f; Untiefe f; 2. flacher werden; 3. seicht.
shock [ʃɔk] 1. Garbenhaufen m; (Haar)Schopf m; Stoß m; Anstoß m; Erschütterung f, Schlag m; ✍ (Nerven)Schock m; 2. fig. verletzen; empören, Anstoß erregen bei; erschüttern; ~ing □ ['ʃɔkiŋ] anstößig; empörend; haarsträubend.
shod [ʃɔd] pret. u. p.p. von shoe 2.
shoddy ['ʃɔdi] 1. Reißwolle f; fig. Schund m; Am. Protz m; 2. falsch; minderwertig; Am. protzig.
shoe [ʃuː] 1. Schuh m; Hufeisen n; 2. [irr.] beschuhen; beschlagen; ~black ['ʃuːblæk] Schuhputzer m; ~blacking Schuhwichse f; ~horn Schuhanzieher m; ~lace Schnürsenkel m; ~maker Schuhmacher m; ~string Schnürsenkel m.

shone [ʃɔn] pret. u. p.p. von shine 2.
shook [ʃuk] pret. von shake 1.
shoot [ʃuːt] 1. fig. Schuß m; ♀ Schößling m; 2. [irr.] v/t. (ab-) schießen; erschießen; werfen, stoßen; Film aufnehmen, drehen; fig. unter e-r Brücke etc. hindurchschießen, über et. hinwegschießen; ♀ treiben; ✍ (ein)spritzen; v/i. schießen; stechen (Schmerz); daherschießen; stürzen; a. ~ forth ♀ ausschlagen; ~ ahead vorwärtsschießen; ~er ['ʃuːtə] Schütze m.
shooting ['ʃuːtiŋ] 1. Schießen n; Schießerei f; Jagd f; Film: Dreharbeiten f/pl.; 2. stechend (Schmerz); ~gallery Schießstand m, -bude f; ~range Schießplatz m; ~ star Sternschnuppe f.
shop [ʃɔp] 1. Laden m, Geschäft n; Werkstatt f, Betrieb m; talk ~ fachsimpeln; 2. mst go ~ping einkaufen gehen; ~assistant ['ʃɔpəsistənt] Verkäufer(in); ~keeper Ladeninhaber(in); ~lifter ['ʃɔpliftə] Ladendieb m; ~man Ladengehilfe m; ~per ['ʃɔpə] Käufer(in); ~ping ['ʃɔpiŋ] Einkaufen n; attr. Einkaufs...; ~ centre Einkaufszentrum n; ~steward Betriebsrat m; ~walker ['ʃɔpwɔːkə] Aufsichtsherr m, -dame f; ~window Schaufenster n.
shore [ʃɔː] 1. Küste f, Ufer n; Strand m; Stütze f; on ~ an Land; 2. ~ up abstützen.
shorn [ʃɔːn] p.p. von shear 1.
short [ʃɔːt] 1. adj. kurz (a. fig.); klein; knapp; mürbe (Gebäck); wortkarg; in ~ kurz(um); ~ of knapp an (dat.); 2. adv. ~ of abgesehen von; come od. fall ~ of et. nicht erreichen; cut ~ plötzlich unterbrechen; run ~ (of) ausgehen (Vorräte); stop ~ of zurückschrecken vor (dat.); ~age ['ʃɔːtidʒ] Fehlbetrag m; Gewichtsverlust m; Knappheit f; ~coming Unzulänglichkeit f; Fehler m; Mangel m; ~ cut Abkürzungsweg m; ~dated ♀ auf kurze Sicht; ~en ['ʃɔːtn] v/t. ab-, verkürzen; v/i. kürzer werden; ~ening [~niŋ] Backfett n; ~hand Kurzschrift f; ~ typist Stenotypistin f; ~ly ['ʃɔːtli] adv. kurz; bald; ~ness ['ʃɔːtnis] Kürze f; Mangel m; ~sighted kurzsichtig; ~term kurzfristig; ~winded kurzatmig.
shot [ʃɔt] 1. pret. u. p.p. von shoot 2; 2. Schuß m; Geschoß n, Kugel f; Schrot(korn) m; Schußweite f; Schütze m; Sport: Stoß m, Schlag m, Wurf m; phot., Film: Aufnahme f; ♀ Spritze f; have a ~ at et. versuchen; not by a long ~ F noch lange nicht; big ~ F großes Tier; ~gun ['ʃɔtgʌn] Schrotflinte f; ~ marriage Am. F Mußheirat f.
should [ʃud, ʃəd] pret. von shall.

shoulder ['ʃouldə] 1. Schulter f (a. v. Tieren; fig. Vorsprung); Achsel f; 2. auf die Schulter od. fig. auf sich nehmen; ⚔ schultern; drängen; **~blade** anat. Schulterblatt n; **~strap** Träger m am Kleid; ⚔ Schulter-, Achselstück n.

shout [ʃaut] 1. lauter Schrei od. Ruf; Geschrei n; 2. laut schreien.

shove [ʃʌv] 1. Schub m, Stoß m; 2. schieben, stoßen.

shovel ['ʃʌvl] 1. Schaufel f; 2. schaufeln.

show [ʃou] 1. [irr.] v/t. zeigen; ausstellen; erweisen; beweisen; ~ in hereinführen; ~ off zur Geltung bringen; ~ out hinausgeleiten; ~ round herumführen; ~ up hinaufführen; entlarven; v/i. a. ~ up sich zeigen; zu sehen sein; ~ off angeben, prahlen, sich aufspielen; 2. Schau(stellung) f; Ausstellung f; Auf-, Vorführung f; Anschein m; on ~ zu besichtigen; **~ business** ['ʃoubiznis] Unterhaltungsindustrie f; Schaugeschäft n; **~case** Schaukasten m, Vitrine f; **~down** Aufdecken n der Karten (bsd. Am. a. fig.); fig. Kraftprobe f.

shower ['ʃauə] 1. (Regen)Schauer m; Dusche f; fig. Fülle f; 2. v/t. herabschütten (a. fig.); überschütten; v/i. sich ergießen; **~y** ['ʃauəri] regnerisch.

show|n [ʃoun] p.p. von show 1; **~room** ['ʃourum] Ausstellungsraum m; **~window** Schaufenster n; **~y** □ ['ʃoui] prächtig; protzig.

shrank [ʃræŋk] pret. von shrink.

shred [ʃred] 1. Stückchen n; Schnitz(el n) m; Fetzen m (a. fig.); 2. [irr.] (zer)schnitzeln; zerfetzen.

shrew [ʃru:] zänkisches Weib.

shrewd □ [ʃru:d] scharfsinnig schlau.

shriek [ʃri:k] 1. (Angst)Schrei m; Gekreisch n; 2. kreischen, schreien.

shrill [ʃril] 1. □ schrill, gellend; 2. schrillen, gellen; schreien.

shrimp [ʃrimp] zo. Krabbe f; fig. Knirps m. [m.]

shrine [ʃrain] Schrein m; Altar]

shrink [ʃriŋk] [irr.] (ein-, zs.-) schrumpfen (lassen); einlaufen; sich zurückziehen; zurückschrekken (from, at vor dat.); **~age** ['ʃriŋkidʒ] Einlaufen n, Zs.-schrumpfen n; Schrumpfung f; fig. Verminderung f.

shrivel ['ʃrivl] einschrumpfen (lassen).

shroud [ʃraud] 1. Leichentuch n; fig. Gewand n; 2. in ein Leichentuch einhüllen; fig. hüllen.

Shrove|tide ['ʃrouvtaid] Fastnachtszeit f; **~ Tuesday** Fastnachtsdienstag m.

shrub [ʃrʌb] Strauch m; Busch m; **~bery** ['ʃrʌbəri] Gebüsch n.

shrug [ʃrʌg] 1. (die Achseln) zucken; 2. Achselzucken n.

shrunk [ʃrʌŋk] p.p. von shrink; **~en** ['ʃrʌŋkən] adj. (ein)geschrumpft.

shuck bsd. Am. [ʃʌk] 1. Hülse f, Schote f; **~s!** F Quatsch!; 2. enthülsen.

shudder ['ʃʌdə] 1. schaudern; (er-) beben; 2. Schauder m.

shuffle ['ʃʌfl] 1. schieben; Karten: mischen; schlurfen; Ausflüchte machen; ~ off von sich schieben; abstreifen; 2. Schieben n; Mischen n; Schlurfen n; Ausflucht f; Schiebung f.

shun [ʃʌn] (ver)meiden.

shunt [ʃʌnt] 🚂 1. Rangieren n; ⊕ Weiche f; ⚡ Nebenschluß m; 2. 🚂 rangieren; ⚡ nebenschließen; fig. verschieben.

shut [ʃʌt] [irr.] (sich) schließen; zumachen; ~ down Betrieb schließen; ~ up ein-, verschließen; einsperren; ~ up! F halt den Mund!; **~ter** ['ʃʌtə] Fensterladen m; phot. Verschluß m.

shuttle ['ʃʌtl] 1. ⊕ Schiffchen n; Pendelverkehr m; 2. pendeln.

shy [ʃai] 1. □ scheu; schüchtern; 2. (zurück)scheuen (at vor dat.).

shyness ['ʃainis] Schüchternheit f; Scheu f.

shyster sl., bsd. Am. ['ʃaistə] gerissener Kerl; Winkeladvokat m.

Siberian [sai'biəriən] 1. sibirisch; 2. Sibirier(in).

sick [sik] krank (of an dat.; with vor dat.); übel; überdrüssig; be ~ for sich sehnen nach; be ~ of genug haben von; go ~ report sich krank melden; **~benefit** [~benifit] Krankengeld n; **~en** ['sikn] v/i. krank werden; kränkeln; ~ at sich ekeln vor (dat.); v/t. krank machen; anekeln.

sickle ['sikl] Sichel f.

sick|-leave ['sikli:v] Krankheitsurlaub m; **~ly** [~li] kränklich; schwächlich; bleich, blaß; ungesund (Klima); ekelhaft; matt (Lächeln); **~ness** ['siknis] Krankheit f; Übelkeit f.

side [said] 1. allg. Seite f; ~ by ~ Seite an Seite; take ~ with Partei ergreifen für; 2. Seiten...; Neben...; 3. Partei ergreifen (with für); **~board** ['saidbɔ:d] Anrichte(tisch m) f, Sideboard n; **~car** mot. Beiwagen m; **~d** ...seitig; **~light** Streiflicht n; **~long** 1. adv. seitwärts; 2. adj. seitlich; Seiten...; **~stroke** Seitenschwimmen n; **~track** 1. 🚂 Nebengleis n; 2. auf ein Nebengleis schieben; bsd. Am. fig. aufschieben; beiseite schieben; **~walk** bsd. Am. Bürgersteig m; **~ward(s)** [~wəd(z)], **~ways** seitlich; seitwärts.

siding 🚂 ['saidiŋ] Nebengleis n.

sidle ['saidl] seitwärts gehen.
siege [si:dʒ] Belagerung f; lay ~ to belagern.
sieve [siv] 1. Sieb n; 2. (durch-)sieben.
sift [sift] sieben; fig. sichten; prüfen.
sigh [sai] 1. Seufzer m; 2. seufzen; sich sehnen (after, for nach).
sight [sait] 1. Sehvermögen n, Sehkraft f; fig. Auge n; Anblick m; Visier n; Sicht f; ~s pl. Sehenswürdigkeiten f/pl.; at ~, a. on ~ beim Anblick; ♪ vom Blatt; † nach Sicht; catch ~ of erblicken, zu Gesicht bekommen; lose ~ of aus den Augen verlieren; within ~ in Sicht; know by ~ vom Sehen kennen; 2. sichten; (an)visieren; ~ed ['saitid] ...sichtig; ~ly ['saitli] ansehnlich, stattlich; ~seeing ['saitsi:iŋ] Besichtigung f von Sehenswürdigkeiten; ~seer Tourist(in).
sign [sain] 1. Zeichen n; Wink m; Schild n; in ~ of zum Zeichen (gen.); 2. v/i. winken, Zeichen geben; v/t. (unter)zeichnen, unterschreiben.
signal ['signl] 1. Signal n; Zeichen n; 2. □ bemerkenswert, außerordentlich; 3. signalisieren; ~ize [~nəlaiz] auszeichnen; = signal 3.
signat|ory ['signətəri] 1. Unterzeichner m; 2. unterzeichnend; ~ powers pl. Signatarmächte f/pl.; ~ure [~nitʃə] Signatur f; Unterschrift f; ~ tune Radio: Kennmelodie f.
sign|board ['sainbɔ:d] (Aushänge-)Schild n; ~er ['sainə] Unterzeichner(in).
signet ['signit] Siegel n.
signific|ance [sig'nifikəns] Bedeutung f; ~ant □ [~nt] bedeutsam; bezeichnend (of für); ~ation [signifi'keiʃən] Bedeutung f.
signify ['signifai] bezeichnen, andeuten; kundgeben; bedeuten.
signpost ['sainpoust] Wegweiser m.
silence ['sailəns] 1. (Still)Schweigen n; Stille f, Ruhe f; ~! Ruhe! put od. reduce to ~ = 2. zum Schweigen bringen; ~r [~sə] ⊕ Schalldämpfer m; mot. Auspufftopf m.
silent ['sailənt] still; schweigend; schweigsam; stumm; ~ partner † stiller Teilhaber.
silk [silk] Seide f; attr. Seiden...; ~en □ ['silkən] seiden; ~stocking Am. vornehm; ~worm Seidenraupe f; ~y □ [~ki] seid(enart)ig.
sill [sil] Schwelle f; Fensterbrett n.
silly □ ['sili] albern, töricht.
silt [silt] 1. Schlamm m; 2. mst ~ up verschlammen.
silver ['silvə] 1. Silber n; 2. silbern; Silber...; 3. versilbern; silberig od. silberweiß werden (lassen); ~ware Am. Tafelsilber n; ~y [~əri] silberglänzend; silberhell.

similar □ ['similə] ähnlich, gleich; ~ity [simi'læriti] Ähnlichkeit f.
simile ['simili] Gleichnis n.
similitude [si'militju:d] Gestalt f; Ebenbild n; Gleichnis n.
simmer ['simə] sieden od. brodeln (lassen); fig. kochen, gären (Gefühl, Aufstand); ~ down ruhig(er) werden.
simper ['simpə] 1. einfältiges Lächeln; 2. einfältig lächeln.
simple □ ['simpl] einfach; schlicht; einfältig; arglos; ~hearted, ~minded arglos, naiv; ~ton [~ltən] Einfaltspinsel m.
simpli|city [sim'plisiti] Einfachheit f; Klarheit f; Schlichtheit f; Einfalt f; ~fication [simplifi'keiʃən] Vereinfachung f; ~fy [~fai] vereinfachen.
simply ['simpli] einfach; bloß.
simulate ['simjuleit] vortäuschen; (er)heucheln; sich tarnen als.
simultaneous □ [siməl'teinjəs] gleichzeitig.
sin [sin] 1. Sünde f; 2. sündigen.
since [sins] 1. prp. seit; 2. adv. seitdem; 3. cj. seit(dem); da (ja).
sincer|e □ [sin'siə] aufrichtig; Yours ~ly Ihr ergebener; ~ity [~'seriti] Aufrichtigkeit f.
sinew ['sinju:] Sehne f; fig. mst. ~s pl. Nerven(kraft f) m/pl.; Seele f; ~y [~ju(:)i] sehnig; nervig, stark.
sinful □ ['sinful] sündig, sündhaft, böse.
sing [siŋ] [irr.] singen; besingen; ~ to s.o. j-m vorsingen.
singe [sindʒ] (ver)sengen.
singer ['siŋə] Sänger(in).
singing ['siŋiŋ] Gesang m, Singen n; ~ bird Singvogel m.
single ['siŋgl] 1. □ einzig; einzeln; Einzel...; einfach; ledig, unverheiratet; book-keeping by ~ entry einfache Buchführung; ~ file Gänsemarsch m; 2. einfache Fahrkarte; mst ~s sg. Tennis: Einzel n; 3. ~ out auswählen, aussuchen; ~breasted einreihig (Jacke etc.); ~engined ✈ einmotorig; ~handed eigenhändig, allein; ~hearted □, ~minded □ aufrichtig; zielstrebig; ~t [~lit] Unterhemd n; ~track eingleisig.
singular ['siŋgjulə] 1. □ einzigartig; eigenartig; sonderbar; 2. a. ~ number gr. Singular m, Einzahl f; ~ity [siŋgju'læriti] Einzigartigkeit f; Sonderbarkeit f.
sinister □ ['sinistə] unheilvoll; böse.
sink [siŋk] 1. [irr.] v/i. sinken; nieder-, unter-, versinken; sich senken; eindringen; erliegen; v/t. (ver)senken; Brunnen bohren; Geld festlegen; Namen etc. aufgeben; 2. Ausguß m; ~ing ['siŋkiŋ] (Ver-)Sinken n; Versenken n; ✿ Schwäche(gefühl n) f; Senkung f; †

Tilgung *f*; ~ fund (Schulden)Tilgungsfonds *m*.

sinless ['sinlis] sündenlos, -frei.

sinner ['sinə] Sünder(in).

sinuous □ ['sinjuəs] gewunden.

sip [sip] 1. Schlückchen *n*; 2. schlürfen; nippen; langsam trinken.

sir [sə:] Herr *m*; ♀ Sir (*Titel*).

sire ['saiə] *mst poet*. Vater *m*; Vorfahr *m*; *zo.* Vater(tier *n*) *m*.

siren ['saiərin] Sirene *f*.

sirloin ['sə:lɔin] Lendenstück *n*.

sissy *Am.* ['sisi] Weichling *m*.

sister ['sistə] (*a.* Ordens-, Ober-) Schwester *f*; ~**hood** [~hud] Schwesternschaft *f*; ~**in-law** [~ərinlɔ:] Schwägerin *f*; ~**ly** [~əli] schwesterlich.

sit [sit] (*irr.*) *v/i.* sitzen; Sitzung halten, tagen; *fig.* liegen; ~ **down** sich setzen; ~ **up** aufrecht sitzen; aufbleiben; *v/t.* setzen; sitzen auf (*dat.*).

site [sait] Lage *f*; (Bau)Platz *m*.

sitting ['sitin] Sitzung *f*; ~**room** Wohnzimmer *n*.

situat|ed ['sitjueitid] gelegen; be ~ liegen, gelegen sein; ~**ion** [sitju-'eiʃən] Lage *f*; Stellung *f*.

six [siks] 1. sechs; 2. Sechs *f*; ~**teen** ['siks'ti:n] sechzehn; ~**teenth** [~θ] sechzehnte(r, -s); ~**th** [siksθ] 1. sechste(r, -s); 2. Sechstel *n*; ~**thly** ['siksθli] sechstens; ~**tieth** [~stiiθ] sechzigste(r, -s); ~**ty** [~ti] 1. sechzig; 2. Sechzig *f*.

size [saiz] 1. Größe *f*; Format *n*; 2. nach der Größe ordnen; ~ **up** F *j-n* abschätzen; ~**d** von ... Größe.

siz(e)able □ ['saizəbl] ziemlich groß.

sizzle ['sizl] zischen; knistern; brutzeln; *sizzling hot* glühend heiß.

skat|e [skeit] 1. Schlittschuh *m*; roller-~ Rollschuh *m*; 2. Schlittschuh- *od.* Rollschuh laufen; ~**er** ['skeitə] Schlittschuh-, Rollschuhläufer(in).

skedaddle F ['ski'dædl] abhauen.

skeesicks *Am.* F ['ski:ziks] Nichtsnutz *m*.

skein [skein] Strähne *f*, Docke *f*.

skeleton ['skelitn] Skelett *n*; Gerippe *n*; Gestell *n*; *attr.* Skelett...; ✕ Stamm...; ~ **key** Nachschlüssel *m*.

skeptic ['skeptik] *s.* **sceptic**.

sketch [sketʃ] 1. Skizze *f*; Entwurf *m*; Umriß *m*; 2. skizzieren, entwerfen.

ski [ski:] 1. *pl. a.* **ski** Schi *m*, Ski *m*; 2. Schi *od.* Ski laufen.

skid [skid] 1. Hemmschuh *m*, Bremsklotz *m*; ✕ (Gleit)Kufe *f*; Rutschen *n*; *mot.* Schleudern *n*; 2. *v/t.* hemmen; *v/i.* (aus)rutschen.

skiddoo *Am. sl.* [ski'du:] abhauen.

ski|er ['ski:ə] Schi-, Skiläufer(in); ~**ing** [ski:in] Schi-, Skilauf(en *n*) *m*.

skilful □ ['skilful] geschickt; kundig.

skill [skil] Geschicklichkeit *f*, Fertigkeit *f*; ~**ed** [skild] geschickt; gelernt; ~ **worker** Facharbeiter *m*.

skillful *Am.* ['skilful] *s.* **skilful**.

skim [skim] 1. abschöpfen; abrahmen; dahingleiten über (*acc.*); *Buch* überfliegen; ~ **through** durchblättern; 2. ~ **milk** Magermilch *f*.

skimp [skimp] *j-n* knapp halten; sparen (*mit et.*); ~**y** □ ['skimpi] knapp, dürftig.

skin [skin] 1. Haut *f*; Fell *n*; Schale *f*; 2. *v/t.* (ent)häuten; abbalgen; schälen; ~ **off** F abstreifen; *v/i. a.* ~ **over** zuheilen; ~**deep** ['skin'di:p] (nur) oberflächlich; ~**flint** Knicker *m*; ~**ny** [~ni] mager.

skip [skip] 1. Sprung *m*; 2. *v/i.* hüpfen, springen; seilhüpfen; *v/t.* überspringen.

skipper ['skipə] ♫ Schiffer *m*; ♫, ✕, *Sport:* Kapitän *m*.

skirmish ['skə:miʃ] 1. ✕ Scharmützel *n*; 2. plänkeln.

skirt [skə:t] 1. (Damen)Rock *m*; (Rock)Schoß *m*; *oft* ~**s** *pl.* Rand *m*, Saum *m*; 2. umsäumen; (sich) entlangziehen (an *dat.*); entlangfahren; ~**ing-board** ['skə:tinbɔ:d] Scheuerleiste *f*.

skit [skit] Stichelei *f*; Satire *f*; ~**tish** □ ['skitiʃ] ungebärdig.

skittle ['skitl] Kegel *m*; *play (at)* ~**s** Kegel schieben; ~**alley** Kegelbahn *f*. [Gemeinheit *f*.]

skulduggery *Am.* F [skʌl'dʌgəri]

skulk [skʌlk] schleichen; sich verstecken; lauern; sich drücken; ~**er** ['skʌlkə] Drückeberger *m*.

skull [skʌl] Schädel *m*.

sky [skai] *oft* **skies** *pl.* Himmel *m*; ~**lark** ['skaila:k] 1. *orn.* Feldlerche *f*; 2. Ulk treiben; ~**light** Oberlicht *n*; Dachfenster *n*; ~**line** Horizont *m*; Silhouette *f*; ~**rocket** F emporschnellen; ~**scraper** Wolkenkratzer *m*; ~**ward(s)** ['skaiwəd(z)] himmelwärts.

slab [slæb] Platte *f*; Scheibe *f*; Fliese *f*.

slack [slæk] 1. schlaff; locker; (nach)lässig; ♫ flau; 2. ♫ Lose *n* (*loses Tauende*); ♫ Flaute *f*; Kohlengrus *m*; 3. = **slacken**; = **slake**; ~**en** [slækən] schlaff machen *od.* werden; verringern; nachlassen; (sich) lockern; (sich) entspannen; (sich) verlangsamen; ~**s** *pl.* (lange) Hose.

slag [slæg] Schlacke *f*.

slain [slein] *p.p. von* **slay**.

slake [sleik] *Durst*, *Kalk* löschen; *fig.* stillen.

slam [slæm] 1. Zuschlagen *n*; Knall *m*; 2. *Tür etc.* zuschlagen, zuknallen; *et. auf den Tisch etc.* knallen.

slander ['sla:ndə] 1. Verleumdung *f*; 2. verleumden; ~**ous** □ [~ərəs] verleumderisch.

slang [slæŋ] 1. Slang *m*; Berufs-sprache *f*; lässige Umgangssprache; 2. *j-n* wüst beschimpfen.

slant [slɑːnt] 1. schräge Fläche; Abhang *m*; Neigung *f*; *Am.* Standpunkt *m*; 2. schräg legen *od.* liegen; sich neigen; ~ing *adj.*, □ ['slɑːntiŋ], ~wise *adv.* [~twaiz] schief, schräg.

slap [slæp] 1. Klaps *m*, Schlag *m*; 2. klapsen; schlagen; klatschen; ~jack *Am.* ['slæpdʒæk] *Art* Pfannkuchen *m*; ~stick (Narren)Pritsche *f*; *a.* ~ comedy *thea.* Posse *f*, Burleske *f*.

slash [slæʃ] 1. Hieb *m*; Schnitt *m*; Schlitz *m*; 2. (auf)schlitzen; schlagen, hauen; verreißen (*Kritiker*).

slate [sleit] 1. Schiefer *m*; Schiefertafel *f*; *bsd. Am.* Kandidatenliste *f*; 2. mit Schiefer decken; heftig kritisieren; *Am. für e-n Posten* vorschlagen; ~pencil ['sleit'pensl] Griffel *m*.

slattern ['slætə(ː)n] Schlampe *f*.

slaughter ['slɔːtə] 1. Schlachten *n*; Gemetzel *n*; 2. schlachten; niedermetzeln; ~house Schlachthaus *n*.

Slav [slɑːv] 1. Slaw|e *m*, -in *f*; 2. slawisch.

slave [sleiv] 1. Sklav|e *m*, -in *f* (*a. fig.*); 2. *F* sich placken, schuften.

slaver ['slævə] 1. Geifer *m*, Sabber *m*; 2. (be)geifern, *F* (be)sabbern.

slav|ery ['sleivəri] Sklaverei *f*; *F* Plackerei *f*; ~ish □ [~viʃ] sklavisch.

slay *rhet.* [slei] [*irr.*] erschlagen; töten.

sled [sled] = *sledge 1.*

sledge¹ [sledʒ] 1. Schlitten *m*; 2. Schlitten fahren.

sledge² [~] *a.* ~hammer Schmiedehammer *m*.

sleek [sliːk] 1. □ glatt, geschmeidig; 2. glätten; ~ness ['sliːknis] Glätte *f*.

sleep [sliːp] 1. [*irr.*] *v/i.* schlafen; ~ (up)on *od.* over *et.* beschlafen; *v/t. j-n* für die Nacht unterbringen; ~ away Zeit verschlafen; 2. Schlaf *m*; go to ~ einschlafen; ~er ['sliːpə] Schläfer(in); ⚒ Schwelle *f*; Schlafwagen *m*; ~ing [~piŋ] schlafend; Schlaf...; ꭥing Beauty Dornröschen *n*; ~ing-car(riage) ⚒ Schlafwagen *m*; ꭥing partner ꭕ stiller Teilhaber; ~less □ [~plis] schlaflos; ~walker Schlafwandler(in); ~y □ [~pi] schläfrig; verschlafen.

sleet [sliːt] 1. Graupelregen *m*; 2. graupeln; ~y ['sliːti] graupelig.

sleeve [sliːv] Ärmel *m*; ⊕ Muffe *f*; ~link ['sliːvliŋk] Manschettenknopf *m*.

sleigh [slei] 1. (*bsd.* Pferde)Schlitten *m*; 2. (im) Schlitten fahren.

sleight [slait]: ~of-hand Taschenspielerei *f*; Kunststück *n*.

slender □ ['slendə] schlank; schmächtig; schwach; dürftig.

slept [slept] *pret. u. p.p. von sleep 1.*

sleuth [sluːθ], ~hound ['sluːθ-haund] Blut-, Spürhund *m* (*a. fig.*).

slew [sluː] *pret. von slay.*

slice [slais] 1. Schnitte *f*, Scheibe *f*, Stück *n*; Teil *m*, *n*; 2. (in) Scheiben schneiden; aufschneiden.

slick *F* [slik] 1. *adj.* glatt; *fig.* raffiniert; 2. *adv.* direkt; 3. *a.* ~ paper *Am. sl.* vornehme Zeitschrift; ~er *Am. F* ['slikə] Regenmantel *m*; gerissener Kerl.

slid [slid] *pret. u. p.p. von slide 1.*

slide [slaid] 1. [*irr.*] gleiten (lassen); rutschen; schlittern; ausgleiten; geraten (*into in acc.*); let things ~ die Dinge laufen lassen; 2. Gleiten *n*; Rutsche *f*; ⊕ Schieber *m*; Diapositiv *n*; *a. land*~ Erdrutsch *m*; ~rule ['slaidruːl] Rechenschieber *m*.

slight [slait] 1. □ schmächtig; schwach; gering, unbedeutend; 2. Geringschätzung *f*; 3. geringschätzig behandeln; unbeachtet lassen.

slim [slim] 1. □ schlank; dünn; schmächtig; dürftig; *sl.* schlau, gerissen; 2. e-e Schlankheitskur machen.

slim|e [slaim] Schlamm *m*; Schleim *m*; ~y ['slaimi] schlammig; schleimig.

sling [sliŋ] 1. Schleuder *f*; Tragriemen *m*; ꭗ Schlinge *f*, Binde *f*; Wurf *m*; 2. [*irr.*] schleudern; auf-, umhängen; *a.* ~ up hochziehen.

slink [sliŋk] [*irr.*] schleichen.

slip [slip] 1. [*irr.*] *v/i.* schlüpfen, gleiten, rutschen; ausgleiten; ausrutschen; *oft* ~ away entschlüpfen; sich versehen; *v/t.* schlüpfen *od.* gleiten lassen; loslassen; entschlüpfen, entgleiten (*dat.*); ~ in Bemerkung dazwischenwerfen; ~ into hineinstecken *od.* hineinschieben in (*acc.*); ~ on (off) *Kleid* über-, (ab)streifen; have ~ped s.o.'s memory *j-m* entfallen sein; 2. (Aus)Gleiten *n*; Fehltritt *m* (*a. fig.*); Versehen *n*; (Flüchtigkeits)Fehler *m*; Verstoß *m*; Streifen *m*; Zettel *m*; Unterkleid *n*; *a.* ~way ⚓ Helling *f*; (Kissen)Überzug *m*; ~s *pl.* Badehose *f*; give s.o. the ~ *j-m* entwischen; ~per ['slipə] Pantoffel *m*, Hausschuh *m*; ~pery □ [~əri] schlüpfrig; ~shod [~ʃɔd] schlampig, nachlässig; ~t [slipt] *pret. u. p.p. von slip 1.*

slit [slit] 1. Schlitz *m*; Spalte *f*; 2. [*irr.*] (auf-, zer)schlitzen.

sliver ['slivə] Splitter *m*.

slobber ['slɔbə] 1. Sabber *m*; Gesabber *n*; 2. *F* (be)sabbern.

slogan ['slougən] Schlagwort *n*, Losung *f*; (Werbe)Slogan *m*.

sloop ⚓ [sluːp] Schaluppe *f*.

slop [slɔp] 1. Pfütze *f*; ~s *pl.* Spül-, Schmutzwasser *n*; Krankenspeise *f*; 2. *v/t.* verschütten; *v/i.* überlaufen.

slope [sloup] 1. (Ab)Hang *m*; Neigung *f*; 2. schräg legen; ⊕ abschrägen; abfallen; schräg verlaufen; (sich) neigen.

sloppy □ ['slɔpi] naß, schmutzig; schlampig; F labb(e)rig; rührselig.

slops [slɔps] *pl.* billige Konfektionskleidung; ♣ Kleidung *f* u. Bettzeug *n*.

slot [slɔt] Schlitz *m*.

sloth [slouθ] Faulheit *f*; *zo.* Faultier *n*.

slot-machine ['slɔtməʃiːn] (Warenod. Spiel)Automat *m*.

slouch [slautʃ] 1. faul herumhängen; F herumlatschen; 2. schlaffe Haltung; ~ hat Schlapphut *m*.

slough¹ [slau] Sumpf(loch *n*) *m*.

slough² [slʌf] *Haut* abwerfen.

sloven ['slʌvn] unordentlicher Mensch; F Schlampe *f*; ~ly [~nli] liederlich.

slow [slou] 1. □ langsam (*of* in *dat.*); schwerfällig; lässig; *be* ~ nachgehen (*Uhr*); 2. *adv.* langsam; 3. *oft* ~ *down od.* up *od.* off *v/t.* verlangsamen; *v/i.* langsam(er) werden *od.* gehen *od.* fahren; ~coach ['sloukoutʃ] Langweiler *m*; altmodischer Mensch; ~-motion picture Zeitlupenaufnahme *f*; ~-worm *zo.* Blindschleiche *f*.

sludge [slʌdʒ] Schlamm *m*; Matsch *m*.

slug [slʌg] 1. Stück *n* Rohmetall; *zo.* Wegschnecke *f*; *Am.* F (Faust-)Schlag *m*; 2. *Am.* F hauen.

slugg|ard ['slʌɡəd] Faulenzer(in); ~ish □ [~ɡiʃ] träge, faul.

sluice [sluːs] 1. Schleuse *f*; 2. ausströmen (lassen); ausspülen; waschen.

slum [slʌm] schmutzige Gasse; ~s *pl.* Elendsviertel *n*, Slums *pl.*

slumber ['slʌmbə] 1. *a.* ~s *pl.* Schlummer *m*; 2. schlummern.

slump [slʌmp] *Börse:* 1. fallen, stürzen; 2. (Kurs-, Preis)Sturz *m*.

slung [slʌŋ] *pret. u. p.p. von* sling.

slunk [slʌŋk] *pret. u. p.p. von* slink.

slur [sləː] 1. Fleck *m*; *fig.* Tadel *m*; ♪ Bindebogen *m*; 2. *v/t.* oft ~ *over* übergehen; ♪ *Töne* binden.

slush [slʌʃ] Schlamm *m*; Matsch *m*; F Kitsch *m*.

slut [slʌt] F Schlampe *f*; Nutte *f*.

sly □ [slai] schlau, verschmitzt; hinterlistig; *on the* ~ heimlich.

smack [smæk] 1. (Bei)Geschmack *m*; Prise *f* Salz *etc.*; *fig.* Spur *f*; Schmatz *m*; Schlag *m*, Klatsch *m*, Klaps *m*; 2. schmecken (*of* nach); e-n Beigeschmack haben; klatschen, knallen (mit); schmatzen (mit); *j-m* e-n Klaps geben.

small [smɔːl] 1. *allg.* klein; unbe-

deutend; *fig.* kleinlich; niedrig; wenig; *feel* ~, *look* ~ sich gedemütigt fühlen; *the* ~ *hours* die frühen Morgenstunden *f/pl.*; *in a* ~ *way* bescheiden; 2. dünner Teil; ~s *pl.* F Leibwäsche *f*; ~ *of the back* anat. Kreuz *n*; ~-arms ['smɑːlɑːmz] *pl.* Handfeuerwaffen *f/pl.*; ~ change Kleingeld *n*; *fig.* triviale Bemerkungen *f/pl.*; ~ish [~liʃ] ziemlich klein; ~pox ✗ [~lpɔks] Pocken *f/pl.*; ~ talk Plauderei *f*; ~-time *Am.* F unbedeutend.

smart [smɑːt] 1. □ scharf; gewandt; geschickt; gescheit; gerissen; schmuck, elegant, adrett; forsch; ~ aleck *Am.* F Neunmalkluge(r) *m*; 2. Schmerz *m*; 3. schmerzen; leiden; ~-money ['smɑːtmʌni] Schmerzensgeld *n*; ~ness [~tnis] Klugheit *f*; Schärfe *f*; Gewandtheit *f*; Gerissenheit *f*; Eleganz *f*.

smash [smæʃ] 1. *v/t.* zertrümmern; *fig.* vernichten; (zer)schmettern; *v/i.* zerschellen; zs.-stoßen; *fig.* zs.-brechen; 2. Zerschmettern *n*; Krach *m*; Zs.-bruch *m* (*a.* ✝); *Tennis:* Schmetterball *m*; ~-up ['smæʃʌp] Zs.-stoß *m*; Zs.-bruch *m*.

smattering ['smætəriŋ] oberflächliche Kenntnis.

smear [smiə] 1. (be)schmieren; *fig.* beschmutzen; 2. Schmiere *f*; Fleck *m*.

smell [smel] 1. Geruch *m*; 2. [*irr.*] riechen (*of* nach *et.*); *a.* ~ *at* riechen an (*dat.*); ~y ['smeli] übelriechend.

smelt¹ [smelt] *pret. u. p.p. von* smell 2.

smelt² [~] schmelzen.

smile [smail] 1. Lächeln *n*; 2. lächeln.

smirch [sməːtʃ] besudeln.

smirk [sməːk] grinsen.

smite [smait] [*irr.*] schlagen; heimsuchen; *schwer* treffen; quälen.

smith [smiθ] Schmied *m*.

smithereens ['smiðə'riːnz] *pl.* Stücke *n/pl.*, Splitter *m/pl*, Fetzen *m/pl.*

smithy ['smiði] Schmiede *f*.

smitten ['smitn] 1. *p.p. von* smite; 2. *adj.* ergriffen; betroffen; *fig.* hingerissen (*with* von).

smock [smɔk] 1. fälteln; 2. Kittel *m*; ~frock ['smɔk'frɔk] Bauernkittel *m*.

smog [smɔg] Smog *m*, Gemisch *n* von Nebel und Rauch.

smoke [smouk] 1. Rauch *m*; *have a* ~ (eine) rauchen; 2. rauchen; dampfen; (aus)räuchern; ~-dried ['smoukdraid] geräuchert; ~r [~kə] Raucher *m*; 🚬 F Raucherwagen *m*, -abteil *n*; ~-stack 🚬, ♣ Schornstein *m*.

smoking ['smoukiŋ] Rauchen *n*; *attr.* Rauch(er)...; ~-compartment 🚬 Raucherabteil *n*.

smoky □ ['smouki] rauchig; verräuchert. [der.)

smolder Am. ['smouldə] = smoul-)

smooth [smu:ð] **1.** □ glatt; fig. fließend; mild; schmeichlerisch; **2.** glätten; ebnen (a. fig.); plätten; mildern; a. ~ over, ~ away fig. wegräumen; **~ness** ['smu:ðnis] Glätte f.

smote [smout] pret. von smite.

smother ['smʌðə] ersticken.

smoulder ['smouldə] schwelen.

smudge [smʌdʒ] **1.** (be)schmutzen; (be)schmieren; **2.** Schmutzfleck m.

smug [smʌg] selbstzufrieden.

smuggle ['smʌgl] schmuggeln; **~r** [Jə] Schmuggler(in).

smut [smʌt] Schmutz m; Ruß(fleck) m; Zoten f/pl.; **2.** beschmutzen.

smutty □ ['smʌti] schmutzig.

snack [snæk] Imbiß m; **~-bar** ['snækbɑ:], **~-counter** Snackbar f, Imbißstube f.

snaffle ['snæfl] Trense f.

snag [snæg] (Ast-, Zahn)Stumpf m; fig. Haken m; Am. Baumstumpf m (bsd. unter Wasser).

snail zo. [sneil] Schnecke f.

snake zo. [sneik] Schlange f.

snap [snæp] **1.** Schnappen n, Biß m; Knack(s) m; Knall m; fig. Schwung m, Schmiß m; Schnappschloß n; phot. Schnappschuß m; cold ~ Kältewelle f; **2.** v/i. schnappen (at nach); zuschnappen (Schloß); krachen; knacken; (zer)brechen; knallen; schnauzen; ~ at s.o. j-n anschnauzen; ~ into it! Am. sl. mach schnell!, Tempo!; ~ out of it! Am. sl. hör auf damit! ; komm, komm!; v/t. (er)schnappen; (zu)schnappen lassen; phot. knipsen; zerbrechen; ~ out Wort hervorstoßen; ~ up wegschnappen; **~-fastener** ['snæpfɑ:snə] Druckknopf m; **~-pish** □ [Jpiʃ] bissig; schnippisch; **~py** [Jpi] bissig; F flott; **~-shot** Schnappschuß m, Photo n, Momentaufnahme f.

snare [snɛə] **1.** Schlinge f; **2.** fangen; fig. umgarnen.

snarl [snɑ:l] **1.** knurren; murren; **2.** Knurren n; Gewirr n.

snatch [snætʃ] **1.** schneller Griff; Ruck m; Stückchen n; **2.** schnappen; ergreifen; an sich reißen; nehmen; ~ at greifen nach.

sneak [sni:k] **1.** v/i. schleichen; F petzen; v/t. F stibitzen; **2.** Schleicher m; F Petzer m; **~ers** ['sni:kəz] pl. F leichte Segeltuchschuhe m/pl.

sneer [sniə] **1.** Hohnlächeln n; Spott m; **2.** hohnlächeln; spotten; spötteln.

sneeze [sni:z] **1.** niesen; **2.** Niesen n.

snicker ['snikə] kichern; wiehern.

sniff [snif] schnüffeln, schnuppern; riechen; die Nase rümpfen.

snigger ['snigə] kichern.

snip [snip] **1.** Schnitt m; Schnipsel m, n; **2.** schnippeln, schnipseln; knipsen.

snipe [snaip] **1.** orn. (Sumpf-) Schnepfe f; **2.** ✗ aus dem Hinterhalt (ab)schießen; **~r** ✗ ['snaipə] Scharf-, Heckenschütze m.

snivel ['snivl] schniefen; schluchzen; plärren.

snob [snɔb] Großtuer m; Snob m; **~bish** □ ['snɔbiʃ] snobistisch.

snoop Am. [snu:p] **1.** fig. (herum-) schnüffeln; **2.** Schnüffler(in).

snooze F [snu:z] **1.** Schläfchen n; **2.** dösen.

snore [snɔ:] schnarchen.

snort [snɔ:t] schnauben, schnaufen.

snout [snaut] Schnauze f; Rüssel m.

snow [snou] **1.** Schnee m; **2.** (be-) schneien; be ~ed under fig. erdrückt werden; **~bound** ['snoubaund] eingeschneit; **~capped**, **~clad**, **~covered** schneebedeckt; **~drift** Schneewehe f; **~drop** ♀ Schneeglöckchen n; **~y** □ ['snoui] schneeig; schneebedeckt, verschneit; schneeweiß.

snub [snʌb] **1.** schelten, anfahren; **2.** Verweis m; **~-nosed** ['snʌbnouzd] stupsnasig.

snuff [snʌf] **1.** Schnuppe f e-r Kerze; Schnupftabak m; **2.** a. take ~ schnupfen; Licht putzen; **~le** ['snʌfl] schnüffeln; näseln.

snug □ [snʌg] geborgen; behaglich; eng anliegend; **~gle** ['snʌgl] (sich) schmiegen od. kuscheln (to an acc.).

so [sou] so; deshalb; also; I hope ~ ich hoffe es; are you tired? ~ I am bist du müde? Ja; are you tired, ~ am I du bist müde, ich auch; ~ far bisher.

soak [souk] v/t. einweichen; durchnässen; (durch)tränken; auf-, einsaugen; v/i. weichen; durchsickern.

soap [soup] **1.** Seife f; soft ~ Schmierseife f; **2.** (ein)seifen; **~box** ['soupbɔks] Seifenkiste f; improvisierte Rednertribüne; **~y** □ ['soupi] seifig; fig. unterwürfig.

soar [sɔ:] sich erheben, sich aufschwingen; schweben; ✈ segelfliegen.

sob [sɔb] **1.** Schluchzen n; **2.** schluchzen.

sober ['soubə] **1.** □ nüchtern; **2.** (sich) ernüchtern; **~ness** [Jnis], **sobriety** [sou'braiəti] Nüchternheit f.

so-called ['sou'kɔ:ld] sogenannt.

soccer F ['sɔkə] (Verbands)Fußball m (Spiel).

sociable ['souʃəbl] **1.** □ gesellig; gemütlich; **2.** geselliges Beisammensein.

social ['souʃəl] **1.** □ gesellschaftlich; gesellig; sozial(istisch), Sozial...; ~ insurance Sozialversicherung f; ~ services pl. Sozialeinrichtungen f/pl.; **2.** geselliges Beisammensein;

~ism [~lizəm] Sozialismus *m*; **~ist** [~ist] **1.** Sozialist(in); **2.** *a.* **~istic** [souʃə'listik] (*~ally*) sozialistisch; **~ize** ['souʃəlaiz] sozialisieren; verstaatlichen.

society [sə'saiəti] Gesellschaft *f*; Verein *m*, Klub *m*.

sociology [sousi'ɔlədʒi] Sozialwissenschaft *f*.

sock [sɔk] Socke *f*; Einlegesohle *f*.

socket ['sɔkit] (Augen-, Zahn)Höhle *f*; (Gelenk)Pfanne *f*; ⊕ Muffe *f*; ⚡ Fassung *f*; ⚡ Steckdose *f*.

sod [sɔd] **1.** Grasnarbe *f*; Rasen (-stück *n*) *m*; **2.** mit Rasen bedecken.

soda ['soudə] Soda *f*, *n*; **~-fountain** Siphon *m*; *Am.* Erfrischungshalle *f*, Eisdiele *f*.

sodden ['sɔdn] durchweicht; teigig.

soft [sɔft] **1.** □ *allg.* weich; *engS.*: mild; sanft; sacht, leise; zart, zärtlich; weichlich; F einfältig; **~ drink** F alkoholfreies Getränk; **2.** *adv.* weich; **3.** F Trottel *m*; **~en** ['sɔfn] weich machen; (sich) erweichen; mildern; **~-headed** schwachsinnig; **~-hearted** gutmütig.

soggy ['sɔgi] durchnäßt; feucht.

soil [sɔil] **1.** Boden *m*, Erde *f*; Fleck *m*; Schmutz *m*; **2.** (be)schmutzen; beflecken.

sojourn ['sɔdʒə:n] **1.** Aufenthalt *m*; **2.** sich aufhalten.

solace ['sɔləs] **1.** Trost *m*; **2.** trösten.

solar ['soulə] Sonnen...

sold [sould] *pret. u. p.p. von* **sell**.

solder ['sɔldə] **1.** Lot *n*; **2.** löten.

soldier ['souldʒə] Soldat *m*; **~like**, **~ly** [~li] soldatisch; **~y** [~əri] Militär *n*.

sole[1] □ [soul] alleinig, einzig; **~ agent** Alleinvertreter *m*.

sole[2] [~] **1.** Sohle *f*; **2.** besohlen.

solemn ['sɔləm] feierlich; ernst; **~ity** [sə'lemniti] Feierlichkeit *f*; Steifheit *f*; **~ize** ['sɔləmnaiz] feiern; feierlich vollziehen.

solicit [sə'lisit] (dringend) bitten; ansprechen, belästigen; **~ation** [səlisi'teiʃən] dringende Bitte; **~or** [sə'lisitə] ⅌ Anwalt *m*; *Am.* Agent *m*, Werber *m*; **~ous** □ [~təs] besorgt; **~ of** begierig nach; **~ to** *inf.* bestrebt zu *inf.*; **~ude** [~tju:d] Sorge *f*, Besorgnis *f*; Bemühung *f*.

solid ['sɔlid] **1.** □ fest; dauerhaft, haltbar; derb; massiv; ⅌ körperlich, Raum...; *fig.* gediegen; solid; triftig; solidarisch; *a* **~ hour** *e* volle Stunde; **2.** (fester) Körper; **~arity** [sɔli'dæriti] Solidarität *f*; **~ify** [sə'lidifai] (sich) verdichten; **~ity** [~iti] Solidität *f*; Gediegenheit *f*.

soliloquy [sə'liləkwi] Selbstgespräch *n*, Monolog *m*.

solit|ary □ ['sɔlitəri] einsam; einzeln; einsiedlerisch; **~ude** [~tju:d]

Einsamkeit *f*; Verlassenheit *f*; Öde *f*.

solo ['soulou] Solo *n*; ⚞ Alleinflug *m*; **~ist** [~ouist] Solist(in).

solu|ble ['sɔljubl] löslich; (auf)lösbar; **~tion** [sə'lu:ʃən] (Auf)Lösung *f*; ⊕ Gummilösung *f*.

solve [sɔlv] lösen; **~nt** ['sɔlvənt] **1.** (auf)lösend; ⅌ zahlungsfähig; **2.** Lösungsmittel *n*.

somb|re, *Am.* **~er** □ ['sɔmbə] düster.

some [sʌm, səm] irgendein; etwas; einige, manche *pl.*; *Am.* F prima; **~ 20 miles** etwa 20 Meilen; in **~ degree**, to **~ extent** einigermaßen; **~body** ['sʌmbədi] jemand; **~ day** eines Tages; **~how** irgendwie; **~ or other** so oder so; **~one** jemand.

somersault ['sʌməːsɔːlt] Salto *m*; Rolle *f*, Purzelbaum *m*; **turn a ~** e-n Purzelbaum schlagen.

some|thing ['sʌmθiŋ] (irgend) etwas; **~ like** so etwas wie, so ungefähr; **~time 1.** einmal, dereinst; **2.** ehemalig; **~times** manchmal; **~what** etwas, ziemlich; **~where** irgendwo(hin).

somniferous □ [sɔm'nifərəs] einschläfernd.

son [sʌn] Sohn *m*.

song [sɔŋ] Gesang *m*; Lied *n*; Gedicht *n*; *for a mere od.* **an old ~** für e-n Pappenstiel; **~-bird** ['sɔŋbəːd] Singvogel *m*; **~ster** ['sɔŋstə] Singvogel *m*; Sänger *m*.

sonic ['sɔnik] Schall...

son-in-law ['sʌninlɔː] Schwiegersohn *m*.

sonnet ['sɔnit] Sonett *n*.

sonorous □ [sə'nɔːrəs] klangvoll.

soon [suːn] bald; früh; gern; *as od.* **so ~ as** sobald als *od.* wie; **~er** ['suːnə] eher; früher; lieber; *no* **~ ... than kaum ... als**; *no* **~ said than done** gesagt, getan.

soot [sut] **1.** Ruß *m*; **2.** verrußen.

sooth [suːθ]: **in ~** in Wahrheit, fürwahr; **~e** [suːð] beruhigen; mildern; **~sayer** ['suːθseiə] Wahrsager(in).

sooty □ ['suti] rußig.

sop [sɔp] **1.** eingeweichter Brocken; *fig.* Bestechung *f*; **2.** eintunken.

sophist|icate [sə'fistikeit] verdrehen; verfälschen; **~icated** kultiviert, raffiniert; intellektuell; blasiert; hochentwickelt, kompliziert; **~ry** ['sɔfistri] Spitzfindigkeit *f*.

sophomore *Am.* ['sɔfəmɔː] Student *m* im zweiten Jahr.

soporific [soupə'rifik] **1.** (*~ally*) einschläfernd; **2.** Schlafmittel *n*.

sorcer|er ['sɔːsərə] Zauberer *m*; **~ess** [~ris] Zauberin *f*; Hexe *f*; **~y** [~ri] Zauberei *f*.

sordid □ ['sɔːdid] schmutzig, schäbig (*bsd. fig.*).

sore [sɔː] **1.** □ schlimm, entzündet;

wund; weh; empfindlich; ~ throat Halsweh n; 2. wunde Stelle; ~head Am. F ['sɔːhed] 1. mürrischer Mensch; 2. enttäuscht.

sorrel ['sɔrəl] 1. rötlichbraun (bsd. Pferd); 2. Fuchs m (Pferd).

sorrow ['sɔrou] 1. Sorge f; Kummer m, Leid n; Trauer f; 2. trauern; sich grämen; ~ful □ ['sɔrəful] traurig, betrübt; elend.

sorry □ ['sɔri] betrübt, bekümmert; traurig; (I am) (so) ~! es tut mir (sehr) leid; Verzeihung!; I am ~ for him er tut mir leid; we are ~ to say wir müssen leider sagen.

sort [sɔːt] 1. Sorte f, Art f; what ~ of was für; of a ~, of ~s F so was wie; ~ of F gewissermaßen; out of ~s F unpäßlich; verdrießlich; 2. sortieren; ~ out (aus)sondern.

sot [sɔt] Trunkenbold m.

sough [sau] 1. Sausen n; 2. rauschen.

sought [sɔːt] pret. u. p.p. von seek.

soul [soul] Seele f (a. fig.).

sound [saund] 1. □ allg. gesund; ganz; vernünftig; gründlich; fest; ✝ sicher; ⚓ gültig; 2. Ton m, Schall m, Laut m, Klang m; ⚓ Sonde f; Meerenge f; Fischblase f; 3. (er)tönen, (er)klingen; erschallen (lassen); sich gut etc. anhören; sondieren; ⚓ loten; ⚓ abhorchen; ~film ['saundfilm] Tonfilm m; ~ing ⚓ [~diŋ] Lotung f; ~s pl. lotbare Wassertiefe; ~less □ [~dlis] lautlos; ~ness [~dnis] Gesundheit f; ~proof schalldicht; ~track Film: Tonspur f; ~wave Schallwelle f.

soup[1] [suːp] Suppe f.

soup[2] Am. sl. mot. [~] 1. Stärke f; 2. ~ up Motor frisieren.

sour ['sauə] 1. □ sauer; fig. bitter; mürrisch; 2. v/t. säuern; fig. ver-, erbittern; v/i. sauer (fig. bitter) werden.

source [sɔːs] Quelle f; Ursprung m.

sour|ish □ ['sauəriʃ] säuerlich; ~ness ['sauənis] Säure f; fig. Bitterkeit f.

souse [saus] eintauchen; (mit Wasser) begießen; Fisch etc. einlegen, einpökeln.

south [sauθ] 1. Süd(en m); 2. Süd...; südlich; ~east [sauθ'iːst] 1. Südosten m; 2. a. ~eastern [sauθ'iːstən] südöstlich.

souther|ly ['sʌðəli], ~n [~ən] südlich; Süd...; ~ner [~nə] Südländer(in), m. Am. Südstaatler(in).

southernmost ['sʌðənmoust] südlichst.

southpaw Am. ['sauθpɔː] Baseball: Linkshänder m.

southward(s) adv. ['sauθwəd(z)] südwärts, nach Süden.

south|-west [sauθ'west] 1. Südwesten m; 2. südwestlich; ~wester [sauθ'westə] Südwestwind

m; ⚓ Südwester m; ~westerly, ~western südwestlich.

souvenir ['suːvəniə] Andenken n.

sovereign ['sɔvrin] 1. □ höchst; unübertrefflich; unumschränkt; 2. Herrscher(in); Sovereign m (20-Schilling-Stück); ~ty [~rənti] Oberherrschaft f, Landeshoheit f.

soviet ['souviet] Sowjet m; attr. Sowjet...

sow[1] [sau] zo. Sau f, (Mutter-) Schwein n; ⊕ Sau f, Massel f.

sow[2] [sou] [irr.] (aus)säen, ausstreuen; besäen; ~n [soun] p.p. von sow[2].

spa [spaː] Heilbad n; Kurort m.

space [speis] 1. (Welt)Raum m; Zwischenraum m; Zeitraum m; 2. typ. sperren; ~craft ['speiskraːft], ~ship Raumschiff n; ~suit Raumanzug m.

spacious □ ['speiʃəs] geräumig; weit, umfassend.

spade [speid] Spaten m; Kartenspiel: Pik n.

span[1] [spæn] 1. Spanne f; Spannweite f; Am. Gespann n; 2. (um-, über)spannen; (aus)messen.

span[2] [~] pret. von spin 1.

spangle ['spæŋgl] 1. Flitter m; 2. (mit Flitter) besetzen; fig. übersäen.

Spaniard ['spænjəd] Spanier(in).

Spanish ['spæniʃ] 1. spanisch; 2. Spanisch n.

spank F [spæŋk] 1. verhauen; 2. Klaps m; ~ing ['spæŋkiŋ] 1. □ schnell, scharf; 2. F Haue f, Tracht f Prügel.

spanner ⊕ ['spænə] Schraubenschlüssel m.

spar [spaː] 1. ⚓ Spiere f; ≱ Holm m; 2. boxen; fig. sich streiten.

spare [spɛə] 1. □ spärlich, sparsam; mager; überzählig; überschüssig; Ersatz...; Reserve...; ~ hours Mußestunden f/pl.; ~ room Gastzimmer n; ~ time Freizeit f; 2. ⊕ Ersatzteil m, n; 3. (ver)schonen; erübrigen; entbehren; (übrig) haben für; (er)sparen; sparen mit.

sparing □ ['spɛəriŋ] sparsam.

spark [spaːk] 1. Funke(n) m; fig. flotter Kerl; Galan m; 2. Funken sprühen; ~(ing)-plug mot. ['spaːk-(iŋ)plʌg] Zündkerze f.

sparkle ['spaːkl] 1. Funke(n) m; Funkeln n; fig. sprühendes Wesen; 2. funkeln; blitzen; schäumen; sparkling wine Schaumwein m.

sparrow orn. ['spærou] Sperling m, Spatz m; ~hawk orn. Sperber m.

sparse □ [spaːs] spärlich, dünn.

spasm ['spæzəm] Krampf m; ~odic(al) □ [spæz'mɔdik(əl)] krampfhaft, ~artig; fig. sprunghaft.

spat[1] [spæt] (Schuh)Gamasche f.

spat[2] [~] pret. u. p.p. von spit[2].

spatter ['spætə] (be)spritzen.

spawn [spɔ:n] 1. Laich *m*; *fig.*
contp. Brut *f*; 2. laichen; *fig.* aus-
hecken.
speak [spi:k] [*irr.*] *v/i.* sprechen;
reden; ~ out, ~ up laut sprechen;
offen reden; ~ to *j-n od.* mit *j-m*
sprechen; *v/t.* (aus)sprechen; äußern; ~-easy *Am. sl.* ['spi:ki:zi]
Flüsterkneipe *f* (*ohne Konzession*);
~er [⌣kə] Sprecher(in), Redner(in);
parl. Vorsitzende(r) *m*; ~ing-
trumpet [⌣kintrʌmpit] Sprachrohr *n*.
spear [spiə] 1. Speer *m*, Spieß *m*;
Lanze *f*; 2. (auf)spießen.
special ['speʃəl] 1. □ besonder;
Sonder...; speziell; Spezial...;
2. Hilfspolizist *m*; Sonderausgabe *f*;
Sonderzug *m*; *Am.* Sonderangebot
n; *Am.* (Tages)Spezialität *f*; ~ist
[⌣list] Spezialist *m*; ~ity [speʃi'eliti]
Besonderheit *f*; Spezialfach *n*; ✝
Spezialität *f*; ~ize ['speʃəlaiz] besonders anführen; (sich) speziali-
sieren; ~ty [⌣lti] *s. speciality.*
specie ['spi:ʃi:] Metall-, Hartgeld *n*;
~s [⌣i:z] *pl. u. sg.* Art *f*, Spezies *f*.
speci|fic [spi'sifik] (~ally) spezi-
fisch; besonder; bestimmt; ~fy
['spesifai] spezifizieren, einzeln angeben; ~men [⌣imin] Probe *f*,
Exemplar *n*.
specious □ ['spi:ʃəs] blendend, be-
stechend; trügerisch; Schein...
speck [spek] 1. Fleck *m*; Stückchen
n; 2. flecken; ~le [⌣spekl] 1. Fleck-
chen *n*; 2. flecken, sprenkeln.
spectacle ['spektəkl] Schauspiel *n*;
Anblick *m*; (*a pair of*) ~s *pl.* (eine)
Brille.
spectacular [spek'tækjulə] 1. □
eindrucksvoll; auffallend, spekta-
kulär; 2. *Am.* ✝ Galarevue *f*.
spectator [spek'teitə] Zuschauer *m*.
spect|ral □ ['spektrəl] gespenstisch;
~re, *Am.* ~er [⌣tə] Gespenst *n*.
speculat|e ['spekjuleit] grübeln,
nachsinnen; ✝ spekulieren; ~ion
[spekju'leiʃən] theoretische Betrachtung; Grübelei *f*; ✝ Spekulation *f*; ~ive □ ['spekjulətiv] grüb-
lerisch; theoretisch; ✝ spekulie-
rend; ~or [⌣leitə] Denker *m*; ✝
Spekulant *m*.
sped [sped] *pret. u. p.p. von* speed 2.
speech [spi:tʃ] Sprache *f*; Rede *f*,
Ansprache *f*; *make a* ~ e-e Rede
halten; ~day ['spi:tʃdei] *Schule:*
(Jahres)Schlußfeier *f*; ~less □
[⌣ʃlis] sprachlos.
speed [spi:d] 1. Geschwindigkeit *f*;
Schnelligkeit *f*; Eile *f*; ⊕ Drehzahl
f; 2. [*irr.*] *v/i.* schnell fahren, rasen;
~ up (*pret. u. p.p.* ~ed) die Geschwindigkeit erhöhen; *v/t. j-m*
Glück verleihen; befördern; ~ up
(*pret. u. p.p.* ~ed) beschleunigen;
~-limit ['spi:dlimit] Geschwindig-
keitsbegrenzung *f*; ~ometer *mot.*

[spi'dɔmitə] Geschwindigkeitsmes-
ser *m*, Tachometer *n*; ~way Motor-
radrennbahn *f*; *bsd. Am.* Schnell-
straße *f*; ~y □ [⌣di] schnell.
spell [spel] 1. (Arbeits)Zeit *f*, ⊕
Schicht *f*; Weilchen *n*; Zauber
(-spruch) *m*; 2. abwechseln mit *j-m*;
[*irr.*] buchstabieren; richtig schreiben; bedeuten; ~binder *Am.*
['spelbaində] fesselnder Redner;
~bound *fig.* (fest)gebannt; ~er
bsd. Am. [⌣lə] Fibel *f*; ~ing [⌣liŋ]
Rechtschreibung *f*; ~ing-book
Fibel *f*.
spelt [spelt] *pret. u. p.p. von*
spell 2.
spend [spend] [*irr.*] verwenden;
(*Geld*) ausgeben; verbrauchen;
verschwenden; verbringen; ~ *o.s.*
sich erschöpfen; ~thrift ['spend-
θrift] Verschwender *m*.
spent [spent] 1. *pret. u. p.p. von*
spend; 2. *adj.* erschöpft, matt.
sperm [spɔ:m] Same(n) *m*.
spher|e [sfiə] Kugel *f*; Erd-, Him-
melskugel *f*; *fig.* Sphäre *f*; (Wir-
kungs)Kreis *m*; Bereich *m*; *fig.*
Gebiet *n*; ~ical □ ['sferikəl] sphä-
risch; kugelförmig.
spice [spais] 1. Gewürz(e *pl.*) *n*; *fig.*
Würze *f*; Anflug *m*; 2. würzen.
spick and span ['spikən'spæn]
frisch u. sauber; schmuck; funkel-
nagelneu.
spicy □ ['spaisi] würzig, pikant.
spider *zo.* ['spaidə] Spinne *f*.
spiel *Am. sl.* [spi:l] Gequassel *n*.
spigot ['spigət] (Faß)Zapfen *m*.
spike [spaik] 1. Stift *m*; Spitze *f*;
Dorn *m*; Stachel *m*; *Sport:* Lauf-
dorn *m*; *mot.* Spike *m*; ♀ Ähre *f*;
2. festnageln; mit *eisernen* Stacheln
versehen.
spill [spil] 1. [*irr.*] *v/t.* verschütten;
vergießen; F *Reiter etc.* abwerfen;
schleudern; *v/i.* überlaufen; 2. F
Sturz *m*.
spilt [spilt] *pret. u. p.p. von* spill 1;
cry over ~ *milk* über et. jammern,
was doch nicht zu ändern ist.
spin [spin] 1. [*irr.*] spinnen (*a. fig.*);
wirbeln; sich drehen; *Münze* hochwerfen; sich et. ausdenken; erzählen; ✈ trudeln; ~ *along* dahinsau-
sen; ~ *s.th. out* et. in die Länge
ziehen; 2. Drehung *f*; Spritztour *f*;
✈ Trudeln *n*.
spinach ♀ ['spinidʒ] Spinat *m*.
spinal *anat.* ['spainl] Rückgrat...; ~
column Wirbelsäule *f*; ~ cord, ~
marrow Rückenmark *n*.
spindle ['spindl] Spindel *f*.
spin-drier ['spindraiə] Wäsche-
schleuder *f*.
spine [spain] *anat.* Rückgrat *n*;
Dorn *m*; (Gebirgs)Grat *m*; (Buch-)
Rücken *m*.
spinning|-mill ['spiniŋmil] Spin-
nerei *f*; ~-wheel Spinnrad *n*.

spinster ['spinstə] unverheiratete Frau; (alte) Jungfer.

spiny ['spaini] dornig.

spiral ['spaiərəl] **1.** □ spiralig; ~ staircase Wendeltreppe f; **2.** Spirale f; fig. Wirbel m.

spire ['spaiə] Turm-, Berg- etc. Spitze f; Kirchturm(spitze f) m.

spirit ['spirit] **1.** allg. Geist m; Sinn m; Temperament n, Leben n; Mut m; Gesinnung f; Spiritus m; Sprit m, Benzin n; ~s pl. Spirituosen pl.; high (low) ~s pl. gehobene (gedrückte) Stimmung; **2.** ~ away od. off wegzaubern; ~ed □ geistvoll; temperamentvoll; mutig; ~less □ [~tlis] geistlos; temperamentlos; mutlos.

spiritual □ ['spiritjuəl] geistig; geistlich; geistvoll; ~ism [~lizəm] Spiritismus m.

spirituous ['spiritjuəs] alkoholisch.

spirt [spə:t] (hervor)spritzen.

spit¹ [spit] **1.** Bratspieß m; Landzunge f; **2.** aufspießen.

spit² [~] **1.** Speichel m; F Ebenbild n; **2.** [irr.] (aus)spucken; fauchen; sprühen (fein regnen).

spite [spait] **1.** Bosheit f; Groll m; in ~ of trotz (gen.); **2.** ärgern; kränken; ~ful □ ['spaitful] boshaft, gehässig.

spitfire ['spitfaiə] Hitzkopf m.

spittle ['spitl] Speichel m, Spucke f.

spittoon [spi'tu:n] Spucknapf m.

splash [splæʃ] **1.** Spritzfleck m; P(l)atschen n; **2.** (be)spritzen; p(l)atschen; planschen; (hin)klecksen.

splay [splei] **1.** Ausschrägung f; **2.** auswärts gebogen; **3.** v/t. ausschrägen; v/i. ausgeschrägt sein; ~foot ['spleifut] Spreizfuß m.

spleen [spli:n] anat. Milz f; üble Laune, Ärger m.

splend|id □ ['splendid] glänzend, prächtig, herrlich; ~o(u)r [~də] Glanz m, Pracht f, Herrlichkeit f.

splice [splais] (ver)spleißen.

splint [splint] **1.** Schiene f; **2.** schienen; ~er ['splintə] **1.** Splitter m; **2.** (zer)splittern.

split [split] **1.** Spalt m, Riß m; fig. Spaltung f; **2.** gespalten; **3.** [irr.] v/t. (zer)spalten; zerreißen; (sich) et. teilen; ~ hairs Haarspalterei treiben; ~ one's sides with laughter sich totlachen; v/i. sich spalten; platzen; ~ting ['spliting] heftig, rasend (Kopfschmerz).

splutter ['splʌtə] s. sputter.

spoil [spɔil] **1.** oft ~s pl. Beute f, Raub m; fig. Ausbeute f; Schutt m; ~s pl. pol. bsd. Am. Futterkrippe f; **2.** [irr.] (be)rauben; plündern; verderben; verwöhnen; Kind verziehen; ~sman Am. pol. ['spɔilzmən] Postenjäger m; ~-sport Spielver-

derber(in); ~s system Am. pol. Futterkrippensystem n.

spoilt [spɔilt] pret. u. p.p. von spoil 2.

spoke [spouk] **1.** pret. von speak; **2.** Speiche f; (Leiter)Sprosse f; ~n ['spoukən] p.p. von speak; ~sman [~ksmən] Wortführer m.

sponge [spʌndʒ] **1.** Schwamm m; **2.** v/t. mit e-m Schwamm (ab)wischen; ~ up aufsaugen; v/i. schmarotzen; ~-cake ['spʌndʒ'keik] Biskuitkuchen m; ~r f fig. [~dʒə] Schmarotzer(in).

spongy ['spʌndʒi] schwammig.

sponsor ['spɔnsə] **1.** Pate m; Bürge m; Förderer m; Auftraggeber m für Werbesendungen; **2.** Pate stehen bei; fördern; ~ship [~əʃip] Paten-, Gönnerschaft f.

spontane|ity [spɔntə'ni:iti] Freiwilligkeit f; eigener Antrieb; ~ous □ [spɔn'teinjəs] freiwillig, von selbst (entstanden); Selbst...; spontan; unwillkürlich; unvermittelt.

spook [spu:k] Spuk m; ~y ['spu:ki] geisterhaft, Spuk...

spool [spu:l] **1.** Spule f; **2.** spulen.

spoon [spu:n] **1.** Löffel m; **2.** löffeln; ~ful ['spu:nful] Löffelvoll m.

sporadic [spə'rædik] (~ally) sporadisch, verstreut.

spore ♀ [spɔ:] Spore f, Keimkorn n.

sport [spɔ:t] **1.** Sport m; Spiel n; fig. Spielball m; Scherz m; sl. feiner Kerl; ~s pl. allg. Sport m; Sportfest n; **2.** v/i. sich belustigen; spielen; v/t. F protzen mit; ~ive □ ['spɔ:tiv] lustig; scherzhaft; ~sman [~tsmən] Sportler m.

spot [spɔt] **1.** allg. Fleck m; Tupfen m; Makel m; Stelle f; ♀ Leberfleck m; ♀ Pickel m; Tropfen m; a ~ of F etwas; on the ~ auf der Stelle; sofort; **2.** sofort liefer- od. zahlbar; **3.** (be)flecken; ausfindig machen; erkennen; ~less □ ['spɔtlis] fleckenlos; ~light thea. Scheinwerfer (-licht n) m; ~ter [~tə] Beobachter m; Am. Kontrolleur m; ~ty [~ti] fleckig.

spouse [spauz] Gatte m; Gattin f.

spout [spaut] **1.** Tülle f; Strahlrohr n; (Wasser)Strahl m; **2.** (aus)spritzen; F salbadern.

sprain ♀ [sprein] **1.** Verstauchung f; **2.** verstauchen.

sprang [spræŋ] pret. von spring 2.

sprat ichth. [spræt] Sprotte f.

sprawl [sprɔ:l] sich rekeln, ausgestreckt daliegen; ♀ wuchern.

spray [sprei] **1.** zerstäubte Flüssigkeit; Sprühregen m; Gischt m; Spray m, n; = sprayer; **2.** zerstäuben; et. besprühen; ~er ['spreiə] Zerstäuber m.

spread [spred] **1.** [irr.] v/t. a. ~ out ausbreiten; (aus)dehnen; verbreiten; belegen; Butter etc. aufstreichen; Brot etc. bestreichen; ~ the *table* den Tisch decken; *v/i.* sich aus- *od.* verbreiten; 2. Aus-, Verbreitung *f*; Spannweite *f*; Fläche *f*; *Am.* Bett- *etc.* Decke *f*; Brot-Aufstrich *m*; F Festschmaus *m.*

spree F [spriː] Spaß *m*, Jux *m*; Zechgelage *n*; Orgie *f*; *Kauf- etc.* Welle *f.*

sprig [sprig] Sproß *m*, Reis *n* (*a. fig.*); ⊕ Zwecke *f*, Stift *m.*

sprightly ['spraitli] lebhaft, munter.

spring [spriŋ] 1. Sprung *m*, Satz *m*; (Sprung)Feder *f*; Federkraft *f*, Elastizität *f*; Triebfeder *f*; Quelle *f*; *fig.* Ursprung *m*; Frühling *m*; 2. [*irr.*] *v/t.* springen lassen; (zer-)sprengen; *Wild* aufjagen; ~ *a leak* ⚓ leck werden; ~ *a surprise on s.o.* j-n überraschen; *v/i.* springen; entspringen; ♃ sprießen; ~ *up* aufkommen (*Ideen etc.*); ~**board** ['spriŋbɔːd] Sprungbrett *n*; ~ *tide* Springflut *f*; ~**tide**, ~**time** Frühling(szeit *f*) *m*; ~**y** □ [~li] federnd.

sprinkl|e ['spriŋkl] (be)streuen; (be)sprengen; ~**er** [~lə] Berieselungsanlage *f*; Rasensprenger *m*; ~**ing** [~liŋ] Sprühregen *m*; *a* ~ *of* ein wenig, ein paar.

sprint [sprint] *Sport:* 1. sprinten; spurten; 2. Sprint *m*; Kurzstreckenlauf *m*; Endspurt *m*; ~**er** ['sprintə] Sprinter *m*, Kurzstreckenläufer *m.*

sprite [sprait] Geist *m*, Kobold *m.*

sprout [spraut] 1. sprießen, wachsen (lassen); 2. ♃ Sproß *m*; (*Brussels*) ~*s pl.* Rosenkohl *m.*

spruce[1] □ [spruːs] schmuck, nett.

spruce[2] ♃ [~] *a.* ~ *fir* Fichte *f*, Rottanne *f.*

sprung [sprʌŋ] *pret.* (♘) *u. p.p.* *von* spring 2.

spry [sprai] munter, flink.

spun [spʌn] *pret. u. p.p. von* spin 1.

spur [spɜː] 1. Sporn *m* (*a. zo.*, ♃); *fig.* Ansporn *m*; Vorsprung *m*, Ausläufer *m* e-s Berges; *on the* ~ *of the moment* der Eingebung des Augenblicks folgend; spornstreichs; 2. (an)spornen.

spurious □ ['spjuəriəs] unecht, gefälscht.

spurn [spɜːn] verschmähen, verächtlich zurückweisen.

spurt [spɜːt] 1. alle s-e Kräfte zs.-nehmen; *Sport:* spurten; *s. spirt*; 2. plötzliche Anstrengung, Ruck *m*; *Sport:* Spurt *m.*

sputter ['spʌtə] 1. Gesprudel *n*; 2. (hervor)sprudeln; spritzen.

spy [spai] 1. Späher(in), Spion(in); 2. (er)spähen; erblicken; spionieren; ~**glass** ['spaiglɑːs] Fernglas *n*; ~**hole** Guckloch *n.*

squabble ['skwɔbl] 1. Zank *m*, Kabbelei *f*; 2. (sich) zanken.

squad [skwɔd] Rotte *f*, Trupp *m*; ~**ron** ['skwɔdrən] ✕ Schwadron *f*; 🏵 Staffel *f*; ♃ Geschwader *n.*

squalid □ ['skwɔlid] schmutzig, armselig.

squall [skwɔːl] 1. ⚓ Bö *f*; Schrei *m*; ~*s pl.* Geschrei *n*; 2. schreien.

squalor ['skwɔlə] Schmutz *m.*

squander ['skwɔndə] verschwenden.

square [skwɛə] 1. □ viereckig; quadratisch; rechtwinklig; eckig; passend, stimmend; in Ordnung; direkt; quitt, gleich; ehrlich, offen; F altmodisch, spießig; ~ *measure* Flächenmaß *n*; ~ *mile* Quadratmeile *f*; 2. Quadrat *n*; Viereck *n*; *Schach-Feld n*; öffentlicher Platz; Winkelmaß *n*; F altmodischer Spießer; 3. *v/t.* viereckig machen; einrichten (*with* nach), anpassen (*dat.*); ⊕ be-, ausgleichen; *v/i.* passen (*with* zu); übereinstimmen; ~**built** ['skwɛə'bilt] vierschrötig; ~ *dance* Quadrille *f*; ~**toes** *sg.* F Pedant *m.*

squash[1] [skwɔʃ] 1. Gedränge *n*; Fruchtsaft *m*; Platsch(en *n*) *m*; Rakettspiel *n*; 2. (zer-, zs.-)quetschen; drücken.

squash[2] [~] Kürbis *m.*

squat [skwɔt] 1. kauernd; untersetzt; 2. hocken, kauern; ~**ter** ['skwɔtə] *Am.* Schwarzsiedler *m*; *Australien:* Schafzüchter *m.*

squawk [skwɔːk] 1. kreischen, schreien; 2. Gekreisch *n*, Geschrei *n.*

squeak [skwiːk] quieken, quietschen.

squeal [skwiːl] quäken; gell schreien; quieken.

squeamish □ ['skwiːmiʃ] empfindlich; mäkelig; heikel; penibel.

squeeze [skwiːz] 1. (sich) drücken, (sich) quetschen; auspressen; *fig.* (be)drängen; 2. Druck *m*; Gedränge *n*; ~**r** ['skwiːzə] Presse *f.*

squelch [skweltʃ] zermalmen.

squid *zo.* [skwid] Tintenfisch *m.*

squint [skwint] schielen; blinzeln.

squire ['skwaiə] 1. Gutsbesitzer *m*; (Land)Junker *m*; *Am.* F (Friedens-)Richter *m*; 2. e-e *Dame* begleiten.

squirm F [skwɜːm] sich winden.

squirrel *zo.* ['skwirəl, *Am.* 'skwɜːrəl] Eichhörnchen *n.*

squirt [skwɜːt] 1. Spritze *f*; Strahl *m*; F Wichtigtuer *m*; 2. spritzen.

stab [stæb] 1. Stich *m*; 2. *v/t.* (er-)stechen; *v/i.* stechen (*at* nach).

stabili|ty [stə'biliti] Stabilität *f*; Standfestig-, Beständigkeit *f*; ~**ze** ['steibilaiz] stabilisieren (*a.* ✈).

stable[1] □ ['steibl] stabil, fest.

stable[2] [~] 1. Stall *m*; 2. einstallen.

stack [stæk] 1. ✎ (Heu-, Stroh-, Getreide)Schober *m*; Stapel *m*; Schornstein(reihe *f*) *m*; Regal *n*; ~*s pl. Am.* Hauptmagazin *n* e-r

Bibliothek; F Haufen *m;* 2. aufstapeln.

stadium ['steidjəm] *Sport:* Stadion *n,* Sportplatz *m,* Kampfbahn *f.*

staff [sta:f] 1. Stab *m (a.* ⚕), Stock *m;* Stütze *f;* ♩ Notensystem *n;* Personal *n;* Belegschaft *f;* Beamten-, Lehrkörper *m;* 2. (mit Personal, Beamten *od.* Lehrern) besetzen.

stag *zo.* [stæg] Hirsch *m.*

stage [steidʒ] 1. Bühne *f,* Theater *n; fig.* Schauplatz *m;* Stufe *f,* Stadium *n;* Teilstrecke *f,* Etappe *f;* Haltestelle *f;* Gerüst *n,* Gestell *n;* 2. inszenieren; **~coach** ['steidʒkoutʃ] Postkutsche *f;* **~craft** dramatisches Talent; Theatererfahrung *f;* **~ direction** Bühnenanweisung *f;* **~ fright** Lampenfieber *n;* **~ manager** Regisseur *m.*

stagger ['stægə] 1. *v/i.* (sch)wanken, taumeln; *fig.* stutzen; *v/t.* ins Wanken bringen; staffeln; 2. Schwanken *n;* Staffelung *f.*

sta̱gna|nt □ ['stægnənt] stehend (*Wasser*); stagnierend; stockend; träg; ♱ still; **~te** [~neit] stocken.

staid □ [steid] gesetzt, ruhig.

stain [stein] 1. Fleck(en) *m (a. fig.);* Beize *f;* 2. fleckig machen; *fig.* beflecken; beizen, färben; **~ed glass** buntes Glas; **~less** □ ['steinlis] ungefleckt; *fig.* fleckenlos; rostfrei.

stair [stɛə] Stufe *f;* **~s** *pl.* Treppe *f,* Stiege *f;* **~case** ['stɛəkeis], **~way** Treppe(nhaus *n) f.*

stake [steik] 1. Pfahl *m;* Marterpfahl *m;* (Spiel)Einsatz *m (a. fig.);* **~s** *pl.* Pferderennen: Preis *m;* Rennen *n; pull up* **~s** *Am.* F abhauen; *be at* **~** auf dem Spiel stehen; 2. (um)pfählen; aufs Spiel setzen; **~ out,** **~ off** abstecken.

stale □ [steil] alt; schal, abgestanden; verbraucht (*Luft*); fad.

stalk [stɔ:k] 1. Stengel *m,* Stiel *m;* Halm *m; hunt.* Pirsch *f;* 2. *v/i.* einherstolzieren; heranschleichen; *hunt.* pirschen; *v/t.* beschleichen.

stall [stɔ:l] 1. (Pferde)Box *f;* (Verkaufs)Stand *m,* Marktbude *f; thea.* Sperrsitz *m;* 2. *v/t.* einstallen; *Motor* abwürgen; *v/i. mot.* aussetzen.

stallion ['stæljən] Hengst *m.*

stalwart □ ['stɔ:lwət] stramm, stark.

stamina ['stæminə] Ausdauer *f.*

stammer ['stæmə] 1. stottern, stammeln; 2. Stottern *n.*

stamp [stæmp] 1. (Auf)Stampfen *n;* ⊕ Stampfe(r *m) f;* Stempel *m (a. fig.);* (Brief)Marke *f;* Gepräge *n;* Art *f;* 2. (auf)stampfen; prägen; stanzen; (ab)stempeln *(a. fig.);* frankieren.

stampede [stæm'pi:d] 1. Panik *f,* wilde Flucht; 2. *v/i.* durchgehen; *v/t.* in Panik versetzen.

stanch [sta:ntʃ] 1. hemmen; stillen; 2. □ fest; zuverlässig; treu.

stand [stænd] 1. [*irr.*] *v/i. allg.* stehen; sich befinden; beharren; *mst* **~ still** stillstehen, stehenbleiben; bestehen (bleiben); **~** *against j-m* widerstehen; **~ aside** beiseite treten; **~ back** zurücktreten; **~** *by* dabeistehen; *fig.* (fest) stehen zu; helfen; bereitstehen; **~** *for* kandidieren für; bedeuten; eintreten für; F sich *et.* gefallen lassen; **~** *in* einspringen; **~** *in with* sich gut stehen mit; **~ off** zurücktreten (von); **~ off!** weg da! **~** *on (fig.* be)stehen auf; **~ out** hervorstehen; sich abheben (*against* gegen); standhalten (*dat.*); **~** *over* stehen *od.* liegen bleiben; **~** *pat Am.* F stur bleiben; **~** *to* bleiben bei; **~** *up* aufstehen; sich erheben; **~** *up for* eintreten für; **~** *up to* sich zur Wehr setzen gegen; standhalten (*dat.*); **~** *upon (fig.* be)stehen auf (*dat.*); *v/t.* (hin)stellen; aushalten, (v)ertragen; über sich ergehen lassen; F spendieren; 2. Stand *m;* Standplatz *m;* Bude *f;* Standpunkt *m;* Stillstand *m;* Ständer *m;* Tribüne *f; bsd. Am.* Zeugenstand *m; make a od.* one's **~** *against* standhalten (*dat.*).

standard ['stændəd] 1. Standarte *f,* Fahne *f;* Standard *m,* Norm *f;* Regel *f;* Maßstab *m;* Niveau *n;* Stufe *f;* Münzfuß *m;* Währung *f;* Ständer *m,* Mast *m;* 2. maßgebend; Normal...; **~ize** [~daiz] norm(ier)en.

stand-by ['stændbai] Beistand *m.*

standee [stæn'di:] Stehende(r) *m; Am.* Stehplatzinhaber *m.*

standing ['stændiŋ] 1. □ stehend; fest; (be)ständig; **~** *orders pl. parl.* Geschäftsordnung *f;* 2. Stellung *f,* Rang *m,* Ruf *m;* Dauer *f; of long* **~** alt; **~room** Stehplatz *m.*

stand|off *Am.* ['stændɔ:f] Unentschieden *n;* Dünkel *m;* **~offish** [~'dɔ:fiʃ] zurückhaltend; **~patter** *Am. pol.* [stænd'pætə] sturer Konservativer; **~point** ['stændpoint] Standpunkt *m;* **~still** Stillstand *m;* **~up:** **~** *collar* Stehkragen *m.*

stank [stæŋk] *pret. von* stink 2.

stanza ['stænzə] Stanze *f;* Strophe *f.*

staple¹ ['steipl] Hauptterzeugnis *n;* Hauptgegenstand *m; attr.* Haupt...

staple² [~] Krampe *f;* Heftklammer *f.*

star [sta:] 1. Stern *m; thea.* Star *m;* **~s** *and Stripes pl. Am.* Sternenbanner *n;* 2. mit Sternen schmücken; *thea., fig.* die Hauptrolle spielen.

starboard ⚓ ['sta:bəd] 1. Steuerbord *n;* 2. *Ruder* steuerbord legen.

starch [sta:tʃ] 1. (Wäsche)Stärke *f; fig.* Steifheit *f;* 2. stärken.

stare [stɛə] 1. Starren *n;* Staunen *n;* starrer Blick; 2. starren, staunen.

stark [stɑːk] **1.** *adj.* starr; bar, völlig (*Unsinn*); **2.** *adv.* völlig.

starlight ['stɑːlait] Sternenlicht *n.*

starling *orn.* ['stɑːliŋ] Star *m.*

starlit ['stɑːlit] sternenklar.

star|ry ['stɑːri] Stern(en)...; gestirnt; **~-spangled** ['stɑːspæŋgld] sternenbesät; ♀ *Banner Am.* Sternenbanner *n.*

start [stɑːt] **1.** Auffahren *n*, Stutzen *n*; Ruck *m*; *Sport*: Start *m*; Aufbruch *m*; Anfang *m*; *fig.* Vorsprung *m*; *get the ~ of s.o.* j-m zuvorkommen; **2.** *v/i.* aufspringen, auffahren; stutzen; *Sport*: starten; abfahren; aufbrechen; *mot.* anspringen; anfangen (*on* mit; *doing* zu tun); *v/t.* in Gang bringen; *mot.* anlassen; *Sport*: starten (lassen); aufjagen; *fig.* anfangen; veranlassen (*doing* zu tun); **~er** ['stɑːtə] *Sport*: Starter *m*; Läufer *m*; *mot.* Anlasser *m.*

startl|e ['stɑːtl] (er-, auf)schrecken; **~ing** [~liŋ] bestürzend, überraschend, aufsehenerregend.

starv|ation [stɑː'veiʃən] (Ver)Hungern *n*, Hungertod *m*; *attr.* Hunger...; **~e** [stɑːv] verhungern (lassen); *fig.* verkümmern (lassen).

state [steit] **1.** Zustand *m*; Stand *m*; Staat *m*; *pol. mst* ♀ Staat *m*; *attr.* Staats...; *in ~* feierlich; **2.** angeben; darlegen, darstellen; feststellen; melden; *Regel etc.* aufstellen; ♀ **Department** *Am. pol.* Außenministerium *n*; **~ly** ['steitli] stattlich; würdevoll; erhaben; **~ment** [~tmənt] Angabe *f*; Aussage *f*; Darstellung *f*; Feststellung *f*; Aufstellung *f*; † (*~ of account* Konto-) Auszug *m*; **~room** Staatszimmer *n*; ♣ Einzelkabine *f*; **~side** *Am.* F **1.** *adj.* USA-..., Heimat...; **2.** *adv.*: *go ~* heimkehren; **~man** [~smən] Staatsmann *m.*

static ['stætik] statisch, Ruhe...

station ['steiʃən] **1.** Stand(ort) *m*; Stelle *f*; Stellung *f*; ✕, ♣, 🚆 Station *f*; Bahnhof *m*; Rang *m*, Stand *m*; **2.** aufstellen, postieren, stationieren; **~ary** [~ʃnəri] stillstehend; feststehend; **~ery** [~] Schreibwaren *f/pl.*; **~-master** 🚆 Stationsvorsteher *m*; **~ wagon** *Am. mot.* Kombiwagen *m.*

statistics [stə'tistiks] *pl.* Statistik *f.*

statu|ary ['stætjuəri] Bildhauer(-kunst *f*) *m*; **~e** [~ju] Standbild *n*, Plastik *f*, Statue *f.*

stature ['stætʃə] Statur *f*, Wuchs *m.*

status ['steitəs] Zustand *m*; Stand *m.*

statute ['stætjuːt] Statut *n*, Satzung *f*; (Landes)Gesetz *n.*

staunch [stɔːntʃ] *s.* stanch.

stave [steiv] **1.** Faßdaube *f*; Strophe *f*; **2.** [*irr.*] *mst ~ in* ein Loch schlagen in (*acc.*); *~ off* abwehren.

stay [stei] **1.** ♣ Stag *n*; ⊕ Strebe *f*;

Stütze *f*; Aufschub *m*; Aufenthalt *m*; *~s pl.* Korsett *n*; **2.** bleiben; wohnen; (sich) aufhalten; Ausdauer haben; hemmen; aufschieben; *Hunger* vorläufig stillen; stützen; **~er** ['steiə] *Sport*: Steher *m.*

stead [sted] Stelle *f*, Statt *f*; **~fast** □ ['stedfəst] fest, unerschütterlich; standhaft; unverwandt (*Blick*).

steady ['stedi] **1.** □ (be)ständig; stetig; sicher; fest; ruhig; gleichmäßig; unerschütterlich; zuverlässig; **2.** stetig *od.* sicher machen *od.* werden; (sich) festigen; stützen; (sich) beruhigen; **3.** *Am.* F feste Freundin, fester Freund.

steal [stiːl] **1.** [*irr.*] *v/t.* stehlen (*a. fig.*); *v/i.* sich stehlen *od.* schleichen; **2.** *Am.* Diebstahl *m.*

stealth [stelθ] Heimlichkeit *f*; *by ~* heimlich; **~y** □ ['stelθi] verstohlen.

steam [stiːm] **1.** Dampf *m*; Dunst *m*; *attr.* Dampf...; **2.** *v/i.* dampfen; *~ up* beschlagen (*Glas*); *v/t.* ausdünsten; dämpfen; **~er** ♣ ['stiːmə] Dampfer *m*; **~y** □ [~mi] dampfig; dampfend; dunstig.

steel [stiːl] **1.** Stahl *m*; **2.** stählern; Stahl...; **3.** (ver)stählen.

steep [stiːp] **1.** steil, jäh; F toll; **2.** einweichen; einlegen; eintauchen; tränken; *fig.* versenken.

steeple ['stiːpl] Kirchturm *m*; **~-chase** *Sport*: Hindernisrennen *n.*

steer[1] [stiə] junger Ochse.

steer[2] [~] steuern; **~age** ♣ ['stiəridʒ] Steuerung *f*; Zwischendeck *n*; **~ing-wheel** [~riŋwiːl] Steuerrad *n*; *mot.* Lenkrad *n*; **~sman** ♣ [~əzmən] Rudergänger *m.*

stem [stem] **1.** (Baum-, Wort-) Stamm *m*; Stiel *m*; Stengel *m*; ♣ Vordersteven *m*; **2.** *Am.* (ab)stammen (*from* von); sich stemmen gegen, ankämpfen gegen.

stench [stentʃ] Gestank *m.*

stencil ['stensl] Schablone *f*; *typ.* Matrize *f*. [graph(in).\

stenographer [ste'nɔgrəfə] Steno-/

step[1] [step] **1.** Schritt *m*, Tritt *m*; *fig.* Strecke *f*; Fußstapfe *f*; (Treppen)Stufe *f*; Trittbrett *n*; *~s pl.* Trittleiter *f*; **2.** *v/i.* schreiten; treten, gehen; *~ out* ausschreiten; *v/t.* *~ off*, *~ out* abschreiten; *~ up* ankurbeln.

step[2] [~] *in Zssgn* Stief...; **~father** ['stepfɑːðə] Stiefvater *m*; **~mother** Stiefmutter *f.*

steppe [step] Steppe *f.*

stepping-stone *fig.* ['stepiŋstoun] Sprungbrett *n.*

steril|e ['sterail] unfruchtbar; steril; **~ity** [ste'riliti] Sterilität *f*; **~ize** ['sterilaiz] sterilisieren.

sterling ['stəːliŋ] vollwertig, echt; gediegen; † Sterling *m* (*Währung*).

stern [stəːn] **1.** □ ernst; finster, streng, hart; **2.** ♣ Heck *n*; **~ness**

['stə:nnis] Ernst *m*; Strenge *f*;
~-post ⚓ Hintersteven *m*.

stevedore ⚓ ['sti:vidɔ:] Stauer *m*.

stew [stju:] 1. schmoren, dämpfen;
2. Schmorgericht *n*; F Aufregung *f*.

steward [stjuəd] Verwalter *m*; ⚓,
✠ Steward *m*; (Fest)Ordner *m*;
~ess ⚓, ✠ ['stjuədis] Stewardeß *f*.

stick [stik] 1. Stock *m*; Stecken *m*;
Stab *m*; (Besen- *etc.*)Stiel *m*; Stange
f; F Klotz *m* (*unbeholfener Mensch*);
~s *pl.* Kleinholz *n*; the ~s *pl. Am.* F
die hinterste Provinz; 2. [*irr.*] *v/i.*
stecken (bleiben); haften; kleben
(to an *dat.*); ~ at nothing vor nichts
zurückscheuen; ~ out, ~ up hervorstehen; F standhalten; ~ to bleiben
bei; *v/t.* (ab)stechen; (an)stecken,
(an)heften; (an)kleben; F ertragen;
~ing-plaster ['stikinpla:stə] Heftpflaster *n*.

sticky □ ['stiki] kleb(e)rig; zäh.

stiff □ [stif] steif; starr; hart; fest;
mühsam; stark (*Getränk*); be bored
~ F zu Tode gelangweilt sein; keep
a ~ upper lip die Ohren steifhalten;
~en ['stifn] (sich) (ver)steifen;
~-necked [~'nekt] halsstarrig.

stifle ['staifl] ersticken (*a. fig.*).

stigma ['stigmə] (Brand-, Schand-)
Mal *n*; Stigma *n*; ~tize [~ətaiz]
brandmarken.

stile [stail] Zauntritt *m*, Zaunüber-
gang *m*.

still [stil] 1. *adj.* still; 2. *adv.* noch
(immer); 3. *cj.* doch, dennoch;
4. stillen; beruhigen; 5. Destillier-
apparat *m*; ~-born ['stilbɔ:n] tot-
geboren; ~life Stilleben *n*; ~ness
Stille *f*, Ruhe *f*.

stilt [stilt] Stelze *f*; ~ed ['stiltid]
gespreizt, hochtrabend, geschraubt.

stimul|ant ['stimjulənt] 1. ✠ stimu-
lierend; 2. ✠ Reizmittel *n*; Genuß-
mittel *n*; Anreiz *m*; ~ate [~leit]
(an)reizen; anregen; ~ation [stimju-
'leiʃən] Reizung *f*, Antrieb *m*; ~us
['stimjuləs] Antrieb *m*; Reizmittel *n*.

sting [stiŋ] 1. Stachel *m*; Stich *m*,
Biß *m*; *fig.* Schärfe *f*; Antrieb *m*;
2. [*irr.*] stechen; brennen; schmerzen; (an)treiben.

sting|iness ['stindʒinis] Geiz *m*; ~y
□ ['stindʒi] geizig; knapp, karg.

stink [stiŋk] 1. Gestank *m*; 2. [*irr.*]
v/i. stinken; *v/t.* verstänkern.

stint [stint] 1. Einschränkung *f*;
Arbeit *f*; 2. knausern mit; einschränken; *j-n* knapp halten.

stipend ['staipend] Gehalt *n*.

stipulat|e ['stipjuleit] *a.* ~ for aus-
bedingen, ausmachen, vereinbaren;
~ion [stipju'leiʃən] Abmachung *f*;
Klausel *f*, Bedingung *f*.

stir [stə:] 1. Regung *f*; Bewegung *f*;
Rühren *n*; Aufregung *f*; Aufsehen
n; 2. (sich) rühren; umrühren, bewegen; aufregen; ~ up aufrühren;
aufrütteln.

34*

stirrup ['stirəp] Steigbügel *m*.

stitch [stitʃ] 1. Stich *m*; Masche *f*;
Seitenstechen *n*; 2. nähen; heften.

stock [stɔk] 1. (Baum)Strunk *m*;
Pfropfunterlage *f*; Griff *m*, Kolben
m e-s Gewehrs; Stamm *m*, Herkunft *f*; Rohstoff *m*; (Fleisch-,
Gemüse)Brühe *f*; Vorrat *m*, (Waren)Lager *n*; (Wissens)Schatz *m*;
a. live~ Vieh(bestand *m*) *n*; ✠
Stammkapital *n*; Anleihekapital *n*; ~s
pl. Effekten *pl.*; Aktien *f/pl.*; Staatspapiere *n/pl.*; ~s *pl.* ✠ Stapel *m*; in
(out of) ~ (nicht) vorrätig; take ~ ✠
Inventur machen; take ~ of *fig.* sich
klarwerden über (*acc.*); 2. vorrätig;
ständig; gängig; Standard...; 3. versorgen; *Waren* führen; ✠ vorrätig
haben.

stockade [stɔ'keid] Staket *n*.

stock|-breeder ['stɔkbri:də] Vieh-
züchter *m*; ~broker ✠ Börsen-
makler *m*; ~ exchange ✠ Börse *f*;
~farmer Viehzüchter *m*; ~holder
✠ Aktionär(in).

stockinet [stɔki'net] Trikot *n*.

stocking ['stɔkiŋ] Strumpf *m*.

stock|jobber ✠ ['stɔkdʒɔbə] Börsen-
makler *m*; ~market ✠ Börse *f*;
~still unbeweglich; ~taking Inventur *f*; ~y ['stɔki] stämmig.

stog|ie, ~y *Am.* ['stougi] billige
Zigarre.

stoic ['stouik] 1. stoisch; 2. Stoiker
m.

stoker ['stoukə] Heizer *m*.

stole [stoul] *pret. von steal* 1; ~n
['stouln] *p.p. von steal* 1.

stolid □ ['stɔlid] schwerfällig;
gleichmütig; stur.

stomach ['stʌmək] 1. Magen *m*;
Leib *m*, Bauch *m*; *fig.* Lust *f*; 2. verdauen, vertragen; *fig.* ertragen.

stomp *Am.* [stɔmp] (auf)stampfen.

stone [stoun] 1. Stein *m*; (Obst-)
Kern *m*; *Gewichtseinheit von 6,35 kg*;
2. steinern; Stein...; 3. steinigen;
entsteinen; ~blind ['stoun'blaind]
stockblind; ~dead mausetot;
~ware [~nwɛə] Steingut *n*.

stony ['stouni] steinig; *fig.* steinern.

stood [stud] *pret. u. p.p. von stand* 1.

stool [stu:l] Schemel *m*; ✠ Stuhlgang *m*; ~pigeon *Am.* ['stu:l-
pidʒin] Lockvogel *m*; Spitzel *m*.

stoop [stu:p] 1. *v/i.* sich bücken;
sich erniedrigen *od.* herablassen;
krumm gehen; *v/t.* neigen; 2. ge-
beugte Haltung; *Am.* Veranda *f*.

stop [stɔp] 1. *v/t.* anhalten; hindern;
aufhören; *a.* ~ up (ver)stopfen;
Zahn plombieren; (ver)sperren;
Zahlung einstellen; *Lohn* einbehal-
ten; *v/i.* stehenbleiben; aufhören;
halten; F bleiben; ~ dead, ~ short
plötzlich anhalten; ~ over halt-
machen; 2. (Ein)Halt *m*; Pause *f*;
Hemmung *f*; ⊕ Anschlag *m*; Aufhören *n*, Ende *n*; Haltestelle *f*; *mst*

full ~ *gr.* Punkt *m*; ~**gap** ['stɔpgæp] Notbehelf *m*; ~**page** [~pidʒ] Verstopfung *f*; (Zahlungs- *etc.*)Einstellung *f*; Sperrung *f*; (Lohn)Abzug *m*; Aufenthalt *m*; ⊕ Hemmung *f*; Betriebsstörung *f*; (Verkehrs-) Stockung *f*; ~**per** [~pə] Stöpsel *m*; ~**ping** ⚓ [~piŋ] Plombe *f*.

storage ['stɔ:ridʒ] Lagerung *f*, Aufbewahrung *f*; Lagergeld *n*.

store [stɔ:] 1. Vorrat *m*; *fig.* Fülle *f*; Lagerhaus *n*; *Am.* Laden *m*; ~*s pl.* Kauf-, Warenhaus *n*; *in* ~ vorrätig, auf Lager; 2. *a.* ~ *up* (auf)speichern; (ein)lagern; versorgen; ~**house** Lagerhaus *n*; *fig.* Schatzkammer *f*; ~**keeper** Lagerverwalter *m*; *Am.* Ladenbesitzer *m*.

stor(e)y ['stɔ:ri] Stock(werk *n*) *m*.

storeyed ['stɔ:rid] mit ... Stockwerken, ...stöckig.

storied [~] *s.* storeyed.

stork [stɔ:k] Storch *m*.

storm [stɔ:m] 1. Sturm *m*; Gewitter *n*; 2. stürmen; toben; ~**y** ['stɔ:mi] stürmisch.

story ['stɔ:ri] Geschichte *f*; Erzählung *f*; Märchen *n*; *thea.* Handlung *f*; F Lüge *f*; *short* ~ Kurzgeschichte *f*.

stout [staut] 1. □ stark, kräftig; derb; dick; tapfer; 2. Starkbier *n*.

stove [stouv] 1. Ofen *m*; Herd *m*; 2. *pret. u. p.p. von* stave 2.

stow [stou] (ver)stauen, packen; ~**away** ⚓ ['stouəwei] blinder Passagier.

straddle ['strædl] (die Beine) spreizen; rittlings sitzen auf (*dat.*); *Am. fig.* es mit beiden Parteien halten; schwanken.

straggl|e ['strægl] verstreut *od.* einzeln liegen; umherstreifen; bummeln; *fig.* abschweifen; ⚘ wuchern; ~**ing** □ [~.liŋ] weitläufig, lose.

straight [streit] 1. *adj.* gerade; *fig.* aufrichtig, ehrlich; glatt (*Haar*); *Am.* pur, unverdünnt; *Am. pol.* hundertprozentig; *put* ~ in Ordnung bringen; 2. *adv.* gerade(wegs); geradeaus; direkt; sofort; ~ *away* sofort; ~ *out* rundheraus; ~**en** ['streitn] gerade machen *od.* werden; ~ *out* in Ordnung bringen; ~**forward** □ [streit'fɔ:wəd] gerade; ehrlich, redlich.

strain [strein] 1. Abstammung *f*; Art *f*; ⊕ Spannung *f*; (Über)Anstrengung *f*; starke Inanspruchnahme (*on gen.*); Druck *m*; ♂ Zerrung *f*; Ton *m*; *mst* ~*s pl.* ♪ Weise *f*; Hang *m* (*of zu*); 2. *v/t.* (an)spannen; (über)anstrengen; überspannen; ⊕ beanspruchen; ♂ zerren; durchseihen; *v/i.* sich spannen; sich anstrengen; sich abmühen (*after um*); zerren (*at an dat.*); ~**er** ['streinə] Durchschlag *m*; Filter *m*; Sieb *n*.

strait [streit] (*in Eigennamen* ♀*s pl.*)

Meerenge *f*, Straße *f*; ~*s pl.* Not (-lage) *f*; ~ *jacket* Zwangsjacke *f*; ~**ened** ['streitnd] dürftig; in Not.

strand [strænd] 1. Strand *m*; Strähne *f* (*a. fig.*); 2. auf den Strand setzen; *fig.* stranden (lassen).

strange □ [streindʒ] fremd (*a. fig.*); seltsam; ~**r** ['streindʒə] Fremde(r) *m*.

strangle ['stræŋgl] erwürgen.

strap [stræp] 1. Riemen *m*; Gurt *m*; Band *n*; 2. an-, festschnallen; mit Riemen peitschen. [List *f.*]

stratagem ['strætidʒəm] (Kriegs-)]

strateg|ic [strə'ti:dʒik] (~*ally*) strategisch; ~**y** ['strætidʒi] Kriegskunst *f*, Strategie *f*.

strat|um *geol.* ['stra:təm], *pl.* ~**a** [~tə] Schicht *f* (*a. fig.*), Lage *f*.

straw [strɔ:] 1. Stroh(halm *m*) *n*; 2. Stroh...; ~ *vote Am.* Probeabstimmung *f*; ~**berry** ['strɔ:bəri] Erdbeere *f*.

stray [strei] 1. irregehen; sich verirren; abirren; umherschweifen; 2. *a.* ~*ed* verirrt; vereinzelt; 3. verirrtes Tier.

streak [stri:k] 1. Strich *m*, Streifen *m*; *fig.* Ader *f*, Spur *f*; kurze Periode; ~ *of lightning* Blitzstrahl *m*; 2. streifen; jagen, F flitzen.

stream [stri:m] 1. Bach *m*; Strom *m*; Strömung *f*; 2. *v/i.* strömen; triefen; flattern; *v/t.* strömen lassen; ausströmen; ~**er** ['stri:mə] Wimpel *m*; (fliegendes) Band; Lichtstrahl *m*; *typ.* Schlagzeile *f*.

street [stri:t] Straße *f*; ~**car** *Am.* ['stri:tka:] Straßenbahn(wagen *m*) *f*.

strength [streŋθ] Stärke *f*, Kraft *f*; *on the* ~ *of* auf ... hin, auf Grund (*gen.*); ~**en** ['streŋθən] *v/t.* stärken, kräftigen; bestärken; *v/i.* erstarken.

strenuous □ ['strenjuəs] rührig, emsig; eifrig; anstrengend.

stress [stres] 1. Druck *m*; Nachdruck *m*; Betonung *f* (*a. gr.*); *fig.* Schwergewicht *n*; Ton *m*; *psych.* Stress *m*; 2. betonen.

stretch [stretʃ] 1. *v/t.* strecken; (aus)dehnen; *mst* ~ *out* ausstrecken; (an)spannen; *fig.* überspannen; *Gesetz* zu weit auslegen; *v/i.* sich (er)strecken; sich dehnen (lassen); 2. Strecken *n*; Dehnung *f*; (An-)Spannung *f*; Überdehnung *f*, Überschreitung *f*; Strecke *f*, Fläche *f*; ~**er** ['stretʃə] Tragbahre *f*; Streckvorrichtung *f*.

strew [stru:] [*irr.*] (be)streuen; ~**n** [~u:n] *p.p. von* strew.

stricken ['strikən] 1. *p.p. von* strike 2; 2. *adj.* ge-, betroffen.

strict [strikt] streng; genau; ~*ly speaking* strenggenommen; ~**ness** ['striktnis] Genauigkeit *f*; Strenge *f*.

stridden ['stridn] *p.p. von* stride 1.

stride [straid] 1. [*irr.*] *v/t.* über-, durchschreiten; 2. (weiter) Schritt.

strident □ ['straidnt] kreischend.

strife [straif] Streit m, Hader m.

strike [straik] **1.** Streik m; (Öl-, Erz)Fund m; fig. Treffer m; ✗ (Luft)Angriff m auf ein Einzelziel; Am. Baseball: Verlustpunkt m; be on ~ streiken; **2.** [irr.] v/t. treffen, stoßen, schlagen; gegen od. auf (acc.) schlagen od. stoßen; stoßen od. treffen auf (acc.); Flagge etc. streichen; Ton anschlagen; auffallen (dat.); ergreifen; Handel abschließen; Streichholz, Licht anzünden; Wurzel schlagen; Pose annehmen; Bilanz ziehen; ~ up ♪ anstimmen; Freundschaft schließen; v/i. schlagen; ⚓ auf Grund stoßen; streiken; ~ home (richtig) treffen; ~r ['straikə] Streikende(r) m.

striking □ ['straikiŋ] Schlag...; auffallend; eindrucksvoll; treffend.

string [striŋ] **1.** Schnur f; Bindfaden m; Band n; Am. F Bedingung f; (Bogen)Sehne f; ♀ Faser f; ♪ Saite f; Reihe f, Kette f; ~s pl. ♪ Saiteninstrumente n/pl., Streicher m/pl.; pull the ~s der Drahtzieher sein; **2.** [irr.] spannen; aufreihen; besaiten (a. fig.), bespannen; (ver-, zu)schnüren; Bohnen abziehen; Am. sl. j-n verkohlen; be strung up angespannt od. erregt sein; ~band♪ ['strinbænd] Streichorchester n.

stringent □ ['strindʒənt] streng, scharf; bindend, zwingend; knapp.

stringy ['striŋi] faserig; zäh.

strip [strip] **1.** entkleiden (a. fig.); (sich) ausziehen; abziehen; fig. entblößen, berauben; ⊕ auseinandernehmen; ⚓ abtakeln; a. ~ off ausziehen, abstreifen; **2.** Streifen m.

stripe [straip] Streifen m; ✗ Tresse f.

stripling ['striplin] Bürschchen n.

strive [straiv] [irr.] streben; sich bemühen; ringen (for um); ~n ['strivn] p.p. von strive.

strode [stroud] pret. von stride 1.

stroke [strouk] **1.** Schlag m (a. ♣); Streich m; Stoß m; Strich m; ~ of luck Glücksfall m; **2.** streiche(l)n.

stroll [stroul] **1.** schlendern; umherziehen; **2.** Bummel m; Spaziergang m; ~er ['stroulə] Bummler(in), Spaziergänger(in); Am. (Falt)Sportwagen m.

strong □ [strɔŋ] allg. stark; kräftig; energisch, eifrig; fest; schwer (Speise etc.); ~box ['strɔŋbɔks] Stahlkassette f; ~hold Festung f; fig. Bollwerk n; ~room Stahlkammer f; ~willed eigenwillig.

strop [strɔp] **1.** Streichriemen m; **2.** Messer abziehen.

strove [strouv] pret. von strive.

struck [strʌk] pret. u. p.p. von strike 2.

structure ['strʌktʃə] Bau(werk n) m; Struktur f, Gefüge n; Gebilde n.

struggle ['strʌgl] **1.** sich (ab)mühen; kämpfen, ringen; sich sträuben; **2.** Kampf m; Ringen n; Anstrengung f.

strung [strʌŋ] pret. u. p.p. von string 2.

strut [strʌt] **1.** v/i. stolzieren; v/t. ⊕ abstützen; **2.** Stolzieren n; ⊕ Strebe(balken n) m; Stütze f.

stub [stʌb] **1.** (Baum)Stumpf m; Stummel m; Am. Kontrollabschnitt m; **2.** (aus)roden; sich den Fuß stoßen.

stubble ['stʌbl] Stoppel(n pl.) f.

stubborn □ ['stʌbən] eigensinnig; widerspenstig; störrig; hartnäckig.

stuck [stʌk] pret. u. p.p. von stick 2; ~up ['stʌk'ʌp] F hochnäsig.

stud [stʌd] **1.** (Wand)Pfosten m; Ziernagel m; Knauf m; Manschetten-, Kragenknopf m; Gestüt n; **2.** beschlagen; besetzen; ~book ['stʌdbuk] Gestütbuch n.

student ['stju:dənt] Student(in).

studied □ ['stʌdid] einstudiert; gesucht; gewollt.

studio ['stju:diou] Atelier n; Studio n; Radio: Aufnahme-, Senderaum m.

studious □ ['stju:djəs] fleißig; bedacht; bemüht; geflissentlich.

study ['stʌdi] **1.** Studium n; Studier-, Arbeitszimmer n; paint. etc. Studie f; be in a brown ~ versunken sein; **2.** (ein)studieren; sich et. genau ansehen; sich bemühen um.

stuff [stʌf] **1.** Stoff m; Zeug n; fig. Unsinn m; **2.** v/t. (voll-, aus)stopfen; ~ed shirt Am. sl. Fatzke m; v/i. sich vollstopfen; ~ing ['stʌfin] Füllung f; ~y □ [~fi] dumpf(ig), muffig; stickig; fig. verärgert.

stultify ['stʌltifai] lächerlich machen, blamieren; et. hinfällig machen.

stumble ['stʌmbl] **1.** Stolpern n; Fehltritt m; **2.** stolpern; straucheln; ~ upon stoßen auf (acc.).

stump [stʌmp] **1.** Stumpf m, Stummel m; **2.** v/t. F verblüffen; Am. F herausfordern; ~ the country als Wahlredner im Land umherziehen; v/i. (daher)stapfen; ~y □ ['stʌmpi] gedrungen; plump.

stun [stʌn] betäuben (a. fig.).

stung [stʌŋ] pret. u. p.p. von sting 2.

stunk [stʌŋk] pret. u. p.p. von stink 2.

stunning □ F ['stʌniŋ] toll, famos.

stunt[1] F [stʌnt] Kraft-, Kunststück n; (Reklame)Trick m; Sensation f.

stunt[2] [~] im Wachstum hindern; ~ed ['stʌntid] verkümmert.

stup|efy ['stju:pifai] fig. betäuben; verblüffen; verdummen; ~endous □ [stju:'pendəs] erstaunlich; ~id □ ['stju:pid] dumm, einfältig, stumpfsinnig; blöd; ~idity [stju:'piditi] Dummheit f; Stumpfsinn m; ~or ['stju:pə] Erstarrung f, Betäubung f.

sturdy ['stɜːdi] derb, kräftig, stark; stämmig; stramm; handfest.

stutter ['stʌtə] 1. stottern; 2. Stottern n.

sty[1] [stai] Schweinestall m, Koben m.

sty[2], **stye** ﹐ [~] Gerstenkorn n am Auge.

style [stail] 1. Stil m; Mode f; Betitelung f; 2. (be)nennen, betiteln.

stylish □ ['stailiʃ] stilvoll; elegant; **~ness** [~nis] Eleganz f.

stylo F ['stailou], **~graph** [~ləgrɑːf] Tintenkuli m.

suave □ [swɑːv] verbindlich; mild.

sub... [sʌb] mst Unter..., unter...; Neben...; Hilfs...; fast ...

subdeb Am. F [sʌb'deb] Backfisch m, junges Mädchen.

subdivision ['sʌbdiviʒən] Unterteilung f; Unterabteilung f.

subdue [səb'djuː] unterwerfen; bezwingen; bändigen; unterdrücken; verdrängen; dämpfen.

subject ['sʌbdʒikt] 1. unterworfen; untergeben, abhängig; untertan; unterliegend (to dat.); be ~ to neigen zu; 2. adv. ~ to vorbehaltlich (gen.); 3. Untertan m, Staatsangehörige(r m) f; phls., gr. Subjekt n; a. ~ matter Thema n, Gegenstand m; 4. [səb'dʒekt] unterwerfen; fig. aussetzen; **~ion** [~kʃən] Unterwerfung f. [chen.]

subjugate ['sʌbdʒugeit] unterjo-

subjunctive gr. [səb'dʒʌnktiv] a. ~ mood Konjunktiv m.

sub|lease ['sʌb'liːs], **~let** [irr. (let)] untervermieten.

sublime □ [sə'blaim] erhaben.

submachine-gun ['sʌbmə'ʃiːngʌn] Maschinenpistole f.

submarine ['sʌbməriːn] 1. unterseeisch; 2. ⚓ Unterseeboot n.

submerge [səb'mɜːdʒ] untertauchen; überschwemmen.

submiss|ion [səb'miʃən] Unterwerfung f; Unterbreitung f; **~ive** □ [~isiv] unterwürfig.

submit [səb'mit] (sich) unterwerfen; anheimstellen; unterbreiten; einreichen; fig. sich fügen od. ergeben (to in acc.).

subordinate 1. □ [sə'bɔːdnit] untergeordnet; untergeben; ~ clause gr. Nebensatz m; 2. [~] Untergebene(r m) f; 3. [~dineit] unterordnen.

suborn ﹐ [sʌ'bɔːn] verleiten.

subscribe [səb'skraib] v/t. Geld stiften (to für); Summe zeichnen; s-n Namen setzen (to unter acc.); unterschreiben mit; v/i. ~ to Zeitung etc. abonnieren; e-r Meinung zustimmen, et. unterschreiben; **~r** [~bə] (Unter)Zeichner(in); Abonnent(in); teleph. Teilnehmer(in).

subscription [səb'skripʃən] (Unter-)Zeichnung f; Abonnement n.

subsequent □ ['sʌbsikwent] folgend; später; **~ly** hinterher.

subservient □ [səb'sɜːvjənt] dienlich; dienstbar; unterwürfig.

subsid|e [səb'said] sinken, sich senken; sich setzen; sich legen (Wind); ~ into verfallen in (acc.); **~iary** [~'sidjəri] 1. □ Hilfs...; Neben...; untergeordnet; 2. Tochtergesellschaft f; Filiale f; **~ize** ['sʌbsidaiz] mit Geld unterstützen, subventionieren; **~y** [~di] Beihilfe f; Subvention f.

subsist [səb'sist] bestehen; leben (on, by von); **~ence** [~təns] Dasein n; (Lebens)Unterhalt m.

substance ['sʌbstəns] Substanz f; Wesen n; fig. Hauptsache f; Inhalt m; Wirklichkeit f; Vermögen n.

substantial □ [səb'stænʃəl] wesentlich; wirklich; kräftig; stark; solid; vermögend; namhaft (Summe).

substantiate [səb'stænʃieit] beweisen, begründen, dartun.

substantive gr. ['sʌbstəntiv] Substantiv n, Hauptwort n.

substitut|e ['sʌbstitjuːt] 1. an die Stelle setzen od. treten (for von); unterschieben (for statt); 2. Stellvertreter m; Ersatz m; **~ion** [sʌbsti-'tjuːʃən] Stellvertretung f; Ersatz m.

subterfuge ['sʌbtəfjuːdʒ] Ausflucht f.

subterranean □ [sʌbtə'reinjən] unterirdisch.

sub-title ['sʌbtaitl] Untertitel m.

subtle □ ['sʌtl] fein(sinnig); subtil; spitzfindig; **~ty** [~lti] Feinheit f.

subtract ⅍ [səb'trækt] abziehen, subtrahieren.

subtropical ['sʌb'trɒpikəl] subtropisch.

suburb ['sʌbɜːb] Vorstadt f, Vorort m; **~an** [sə'bɜːbən] vorstädtisch.

subvention [səb'venʃən] 1. Subvention f; 2. subventionieren.

subver|sion [sʌb'vɜːʃən] Umsturz m; **~sive** [~siv] zerstörend (of acc.); subversiv; **~t** [~ɜːt] (um)stürzen; untergraben.

subway ['sʌbwei] (bsd. Fußgänger-) Unterführung f; Am. Untergrundbahn f.

succeed [sək'siːd] Erfolg haben; glücken, gelingen; (nach)folgen (dat.); ~ to übernehmen; erben.

success [sək'ses] Erfolg m; **~ful** □ [~sful] erfolgreich; **~ion** [~eʃən] (Nach-, Erb-, Reihen)Folge f; Nachkommenschaft f; in ~ nacheinander; **~ive** [~esiv] aufeinanderfolgend; **~or** [~sə] Nachfolger(in). [fen.]

succo(u)r ['sʌkə] 1. Hilfe f; 2. hel-

succulent □ ['sʌkjulənt] saftig.

succumb [sə'kʌm] unter-, erliegen.

such [sʌtʃ] solch(er, -e, -es); derartig; so groß; ~ a man ein solcher Mann; ~ as die, welche.

suck [sʌk] **1.** (ein)saugen; saugen an (*dat.*); aussaugen; lutschen; **2.** Saugen *n*; ～er ['sʌkə] Saugorgan *n*; ♀ Wurzelsproß *m*; *Am.* Einfaltspinsel *m*; ～le ['sʌkl] säugen, stillen; ～ling [～liŋ] Säugling *m*.

suction ['sʌkʃən] (An)Saugen *n*; Sog *m*; *attr.* Saug...

sudden □ ['sʌdn] plötzlich; *all of a* ～ ganz plötzlich.

suds [sʌdz] *pl.* Seifenlauge *f*; Seifenschaum *m*; ～y *Am.* ['sʌdzi] schaumig, seifig.

sue [sjuː] *v/t.* verklagen; ～ *out* erwirken; *v/i.* nachsuchen (*for um*); klagen.

suède [sweid] (feines) Wildleder.

suet [sjuit] Nierenfett *n*; Talg *m*.

suffer ['sʌfə] *v/i.* leiden (*from an dat.*); *v/t.* erleiden, erdulden, (zu-)lassen; ～ance [～ərəns] Duldung *f*; ～er [～rə] Leidende(r *m*) *f*; Dulder(in); ～ing [～riŋ] Leiden *n*.

suffice [sə'fais] genügen; ～ *it to say* es sei nur gesagt.

sufficien|cy [sə'fiʃənsi] genügende Menge; Auskommen *n*; ～t [～nt] genügend, ausreichend.

suffix *gr.* ['sʌfiks] **1.** anhängen; **2.** Nachsilbe *f*, Suffix *n*.

suffocate ['sʌfəkeit] ersticken.

suffrage ['sʌfridʒ] (Wahl)Stimme *f*; Wahl-, Stimmrecht *n*.

suffuse [sə'fjuːz] übergießen; überziehen.

sugar ['ʃugə] **1.** Zucker *m*; **2.** zukkern; ～-basin, *Am.* ～-bowl Zuckerdose *f*; ～-cane ♀ Zuckerrohr *n*; ～-coat überzuckern, versüßen; ～y [～əri] zuckerig; zuckersüß.

suggest [sə'dʒest] vorschlagen, anregen; nahelegen; vorbringen; *Gedanken* eingeben; andeuten; denken lassen an (*acc.*); ～ion [～tʃən] Anregung *f*; Rat *m*, Vorschlag *m*; Suggestion *f*; Eingebung *f*; Andeutung *f*; ～ive [～tiv] anregend; andeutend (*of acc.*); gehaltvoll; zweideutig.

suicide ['sjuisaid] **1.** Selbstmord *m*; Selbstmörder(in); **2.** *Am.* Selbstmord begehen.

suit [sjuːt] **1.** (Herren)Anzug *m*; (Damen)Kostüm *n*; Anliegen *n*; (Heirats)Antrag *m*; *Karten:* Farbe *f*; ♄♄ Prozeß *m*; **2.** *v/t. j-m* passen, zusagen, bekommen; *j-n* kleiden, *j-m* stehen, passen zu (*Kleidungsstück etc.*); ～ *oneself* tun, was e-m beliebt; ～ *s.th. to et.* anpassen (*dat.*); *be* ～*ed* geeignet sein (*for für*), passen (*to* ♔u); *v/i.* **p**assen; ～**able** □ ['sjuːtəbl] passend, geeignet; entsprechend; ～**case** (Hand)Koffer *m*; ～**e** [swiːt] Gefolge *n*; (Reihen)Folge *f*; ♪ Suite *f*; *a.* ～ *of rooms* Zimmerflucht *f*; Garnitur *f*, (Zimmer)Einrichtung *f*; ～**or** ['sjuːtə] Freier *m*; ♄♄ Kläger(in).

sulk [sʌlk] schmollen, bocken; ～**i- ness** ['sʌlkinis] üble Laune; ～**s** *pl.* = *sulkiness*; ～**y** ['sʌlki] **1.** verdrießlich; launisch; schmollend; **2.** *Sport:* Trabrerwagen *m*, Sulky *n*.

sullen □ ['sʌlən] verdrossen, mürrisch.

sully ['sʌli] *mst fig.* beflecken.

sulphur ♔ ['sʌlfə] Schwefel *m*; ～**ic** [sʌl'fjuərik] Schwefel...

sultriness ['sʌltrinis] Schwüle *f*.

sultry □ ['sʌltri] schwül; *fig.* heftig, hitzig.

sum [sʌm] **1.** Summe *f*; Betrag *m*; *fig.* Inbegriff *m*, Inhalt *m*; Rechenaufgabe *f*; *do* ～*s* rechnen; **2.** *mst* ～ *up* zs.-rechnen; zs.-fassen.

summar|ize ['sʌməraiz] (kurz) zs.-fassen; ～**y** [～ri] **1.** □ kurz (zs.-gefaßt); ♄♄ Schnell...; **2.** (kurze) Inhaltsangabe, Auszug *m*.

summer ['sʌmə] Sommer *m*; ～ *resort* Sommerfrische *f*; ～ *school* Ferienkurs *m*; ～**ly** [～əli], ～**y** [～əri] sommerlich.

summit ['sʌmit] Gipfel *m* (*a. fig.*).

summon ['sʌmən] auffordern; (be-)rufen; ♄♄ vorladen; *Mut etc.* aufbieten; ～**s** Aufforderung *f*; ♄♄ Vorladung *f*.

sumptuous □ ['sʌmptjuəs] kostbar.

sun [sʌn] **1.** Sonne *f*; *attr.* Sonnen...; **2.** (sich) sonnen; ～**bath** ['sʌnbɑːθ] Sonnenbad *n*; ～**beam** Sonnenstrahl *m*; ～**burn** Sonnenbräune *f*; Sonnenbrand *m*.

Sunday ['sʌndi] Sonntag *m*.

sun|-dial ['sʌndaiəl] Sonnenuhr *f*; ～**down** Sonnenuntergang *m*.

sundr|ies ['sʌndriz] *pl. bsd.* ♔ Verschiedene(s) *n*; Extraausgaben *f/pl.*; ～**y** [～ri] verschiedene.

sung [sʌŋ] *pret. u. p.p. von sing.*

sun-glasses ['sʌnglɑːsiz] *pl.* (*a pair of* ～ *pl.* eine) Sonnenbrille *f*.

sunk [sʌŋk] *pret. u. p.p. von sink* 1.

sunken ['sʌŋkən] **1.** *p.p. von sink* 1; **2.** *adj.* versunken; *fig.* eingefallen.

sun|ny □ ['sʌni] sonnig; ～**rise** Sonnenaufgang *m*; ～**set** Sonnenuntergang *m*; ～**shade** Sonnenschirm *m*; ～**shine** Sonnenschein *m*; ～**stroke** ♔ Sonnenstich *m*.

sup [sʌp] zu Abend essen.

super F ['sjuːpə] erstklassig, prima, super.

super|... ['sjuːpə] Über..., über...; Ober..., ober...; Groß...; ～**abundant** [sjuːpərə'bʌndənt] überreichlich; überschwenglich; ～**annuate** [～ə'rænjueit] pensionieren; ～**d** ausgedient; veraltet (*S.*).

superb □ [sjuː(ː)'pəːb] prächtig; herrlich.

super|charger *mot.* ['sjuːpətʃɑːdʒə] Kompressor *m*; ～**cilious** [sjuːpə-

'siljəs] hochmütig; **~ficial** □ [**~o'fi-ʃəl**] oberflächlich; **~fine** ['sju:pə-'fain] extrafein; **~fluity** [sju:pə-flu(:)iti] Überfluß *m*; **~fluous** □ [sju(:)'pə:fluəs] überflüssig; **~heat** ⊕ [sju:pə'hi:t] überhitzen; **~human** □ [~'hju:mən] übermenschlich; **~impose** ['sju:pərim'pouz] darauf-, darüberlegen; **~induce** [~rin'dju:s] noch hinzufügen; **~intend** [sju:prin'tend] die Oberaufsicht haben über (*acc.*); überwachen; **~intendent** [~dənt] **1.** Leiter *m*, Direktor *m*; (Ober)Aufseher *m*, Inspektor *m*; **2.** aufsichtführend.

superior [sju(:)'piəriə] **1.** □ ober; höher(stehend); vorgesetzt; besser, hochwertiger; überlegen (*to dat.*); vorzüglich; **2.** Höherstehende(r *m*) *f*, *bsd.* Vorgesetzte(r *m*) *f*; *eccl.* Obere(r) *m*; *mst* Lady ♀, Mother ♀ *eccl.* Oberin *f*; **~ity** [sju(:)piəri'ɔriti] Überlegenheit *f*.

super|lative [sju(:)'pə:lətiv] **1.** □ höchst; überragend; **2.** *a.* **~ degree** *gr.* Superlativ *m*; **~market** Supermarkt *m*; **~natural** □ [sju:pə'nætʃrəl] übernatürlich; **~numerary** [~'nju:mərəri] **1.** überzählig; **2.** Überzählige(r *m*) *f*; *thea.* Statist (-in); **~scription** [~ə'skripʃən] Über-, Aufschrift *f*; **~sede** [~'si:d] ersetzen; verdrängen; absetzen; *fig.* überholen; **~sonic** *phys.* ['sju:-pə'sɔnik] Überschall...; **~stition** [sju:pə'stiʃən] Aberglaube *m*; **~stitious** □ [~ʃəs] abergläubisch; **~vene** [~'vi:n] noch hinzukommen; unerwartet eintreten; **~vise** ['sju:pəvaiz] beaufsichtigen, überwachen; **~vision** [sju:pə'viʒən] (Ober)Aufsicht *f*; Beaufsichtigung *f*; **~visor** ['sju:pəvaizə] Aufseher *m*, Inspektor *m*.

supper ['sʌpə] Abendessen *n*; the (Lord's) ♀ das Heilige Abendmahl.

supplant [sə'plɑ:nt] verdrängen.

supple ['sʌpl] geschmeidig (machen).

supplement 1. ['sʌplimənt] Ergänzung *f*; Nachtrag *m*; (Zeitungs-etc.)Beilage *f*; **2.** [~ment] ergänzen; **~al** □ [sʌpli'mentl], **~ary** [~təri] Ergänzungs...; nachträglich; Nachtrags...

suppliant ['sʌpliənt] **1.** □ demütig bittend, flehend; **2.** Bittsteller(in).

supplicat|e ['sʌplikeit] demütig bitten, anflehen; **~ion** [sʌpli'keiʃən] demütige Bitte.

supplier [sə'plaiə] Lieferant(in).

supply [sə'plai] **1.** liefern; *e-m Mangel* abhelfen; *e-e Stelle* ausfüllen; vertreten; ausstatten, versorgen; ergänzen; **2.** Lieferung *f*; Versorgung *f*; Zufuhr *f*; Vorrat *m*; Bedarf *m*; Angebot *n*; (Stell)Vertretung *f*; *mst* supplies *pl. parl.* Etat *m*.

support [sə'pɔ:t] **1.** Stütze *f*; Hilfe *f*; ⊕ Träger *m*; Unterstützung *f*; Lebensunterhalt *m*; **2.** (unter)stützen; unterhalten, sorgen für (*Familie etc.*); aufrechterhalten; (v)ertragen.

suppose [sə'pouz] annehmen; voraussetzen; vermuten; he is ~d to do er soll tun; ~ we go gehen wir; wie wär's, wenn wir gingen.

supposed □ [sə'pouzd] vermeintlich; **~ly** [~zidli] vermutlich.

supposition [sʌpə'ziʃən] Voraussetzung *f*; Annahme *f*; Vermutung *f*.

suppress [sə'pres] unterdrücken; **~ion** [~eʃən] Unterdrückung *f*.

suppurate ['sʌpjuəreit] eitern.

suprem|acy [sju'preməsi] Oberhoheit *f*; Vorherrschaft *f*; Überlegenheit *f*; Vorrang *m*; **~e** □ [sju(:)'pri:m] höchst; oberst; Ober...; größt.

surcharge [sə:'tʃɑ:dʒ] **1.** überladen; Zuschlag *od.* Nachgebühr erheben von *j-m*; **2.** ['sə:tʃɑ:dʒ] Überladung *f*; (Straf)Zuschlag *m*; Nachgebühr *f*; Überdruck *m auf Briefmarken*.

sure □ [ʃuə] *allg.* sicher; to be ~!, ~ enough!, *Am.* ~! F sicher(lich)!; **~ly** ['ʃuəli] sicherlich; **~ty** ['ʃuəti] Bürge *m*.

surf [sə:f] Brandung *f*.

surface ['sə:fis] **1.** (Ober)Fläche *f*; ✕ Tragfläche *f*; **2.** ⚓ auftauchen (*U-Boot*).

surf|-board ['sə:fbɔ:d] Wellenreiterbrett *n*; **~-boat** Brandungsboot *n*.

surfeit ['sə:fit] **1.** Übersättigung *f*; Ekel *m*; **2.** (sich) überladen.

surf-riding ['sə:fraidiŋ] *Sport:* Wellenreiten *n*.

surge [sə:dʒ] **1.** Woge *f*; **2.** wogen.

surg|eon ['sə:dʒən] Chirurg *m*; **~ery** [~əri] Chirurgie *f*; Sprechzimmer *n*; ~ hours *pl.* Sprechstunde(n *pl.*) *f*.

surgical □ ['sə:dʒikəl] chirurgisch.

surly □ ['sə:li] mürrisch; grob.

surmise 1. ['sə:maiz] Vermutung *f*; Argwohn *m*; **2.** [sə:'maiz] vermuten; argwöhnen.

surmount [sə:'maunt] übersteigen; überragen; *fig.* überwinden.

surname ['sə:neim] Zu-, Nachname *m*.

surpass *fig.* [sə:'pɑ:s] übersteigen; übertreffen; **~ing** [~siŋ] überragend.

surplus ['sə:pləs] **1.** Überschuß *m*, Mehr *n*; **2.** überschüssig; Über...

surprise [sə'praiz] **1.** Überraschung *f*; ✕ Überrump(e)lung *f*; **2.** überraschen; ✕ überrumpeln.

surrender [sə'rendə] **1.** Übergabe *f*, Ergebung *f*; Kapitulation *f*; Aufgeben *n*; **2.** *v/t.* übergeben; aufgeben; *v/i. a.* ~ *o.s.* sich ergeben.

surround [sə'raund] umgeben; ✕

umzingeln; ~ing [~diŋ] umliegend; ~ings pl. Umgebung f.

surtax ['sɜːtæks] Steuerzuschlag m.

survey 1. [sɜː'vei] überblicken; mustern; begutachten; surv. vermessen; 2. ['sɜːvei] Überblick m (a. fig.); Besichtigung f; Gutachten n; surv. Vermessung f; ~or [sɜ(:)-'veiə] Land-, Feldmesser m.

surviv|al [sə'vaivəl] Über-, Fortleben n; Überbleibsel n; ~e [~aiv] überleben; noch leben; fortleben; am Leben bleiben; bestehen bleiben; ~or [~və] Überlebende(r m) f.

suscept|ible □ [sə'septəbl], ~ive [~tiv] empfänglich (of, to für); empfindlich (gegen); be ~ of et. zulassen.

suspect 1. [səs'pekt] (be)argwöhnen; in Verdacht haben, verdächtigen; vermuten, befürchten; 2. ['sʌspekt] Verdächtige(r m) f; 3. [~] = ~ed [səs'pektid] verdächtig.

suspend [səs'pend] (auf)hängen; aufschieben; in der Schwebe lassen; Zahlung einstellen; aussetzen; suspendieren, sperren; ~ed schwebend; ~er [~də] Strumpf-, Sockenhalter m; ~s pl. Am. Hosenträger m/pl.

suspens|e [səs'pens] Ungewißheit f; Unentschiedenheit f; Spannung f; ~ion [~nʃən] Aufhängung f; Aufschub m; Einstellung f; Suspendierung f, Amtsenthebung f; Sperre f; ~ion bridge Hängebrücke f; ~ive □ [~nsiv] aufschiebend.

suspici|on [səs'piʃən] Verdacht m; Argwohn m; fig. Spur f; ~ous □ [~ʃəs] argwöhnisch; verdächtig.

sustain [səs'tein] stützen; fig. aufrechterhalten; aushalten; erleiden; t's anerkennen; ~ed anhaltend; ununterbrochen.

sustenance ['sʌstinəns] (Lebens-) Unterhalt m; Nahrung f.

svelte [svelt] schlank (Frau).

swab [swɔb] 1. Aufwischmop m; ☸ Tupfer m; ☸ Abstrich m; 2. aufwischen.

swaddl|e ['swɔdl] Baby wickeln; ~ing-clothes mst fig. [~liŋklouðz] pl. Windeln f/pl.

swagger ['swægə] 1. stolzieren; prahlen, renommieren; 2. F elegant.

swale Am. [sweil] Mulde f, Niederung f.

swallow ['swɔlou] 1. orn. Schwalbe f; Schlund m; Schluck m; 2. (hinunter-, ver)schlucken; fig. Ansicht etc. begierig aufnehmen.

swam [swæm] pret. von swim 1.

swamp [swɔmp] 1. Sumpf m; 2. überschwemmen (a. fig.); versenken; ~y ['swɔmpi] sumpfig.

swan [swɔn] Schwan m.

swank sl. [swæŋk] 1. Angabe f,

Protzerei f; 2. angeben, protzen; ~y ['swæŋki] protzig, angeberisch.

swap F ['swɔp] 1. Tausch m; 2. (ver-, aus)tauschen.

sward [swɔːd] Rasen m.

swarm [swɔːm] 1. Schwarm m; Haufe(n) m, Gewimmel n; 2. schwärmen; wimmeln (with von).

swarthy □ ['swɔːði] dunkelfarbig.

swash [swɔʃ] plan(t)schen.

swat [swɔt] Fliege klatschen.

swath ✎ [swɔːθ] Schwade(n m) f.

swathe [sweið] (ein)wickeln.

sway [swei] 1. Schaukeln n; Einfluß m; Herrschaft f; 2. schaukeln; beeinflussen; beherrschen.

swear [swɛə] [irr.] (be)schwören; fluchen; ~ s.o. in j-n vereidigen.

sweat [swet] 1. Schweiß m; by the ~ of one's brow im Schweiße seines Angesichts; all of a ~ F in Schweiß gebadet (a. fig.); 2. [irr.] v/i. schwitzen; v/t. (aus)schwitzen; in Schweiß bringen; Arbeiter ausbeuten; ~er ['swetə] Sweater m, Pullover m; Trainingsjacke f; fig. Ausbeuter m; ~y [~ti] schweißig; verschwitzt.

Swede [swiːd] Schwed|e m, -in f.

Swedish ['swiːdiʃ] 1. schwedisch; 2. Schwedisch n.

sweep [swiːp] 1. [irr.] fegen (a.fig.), kehren; fig. streifen; bestreichen (a. ✕); (majestätisch) (dahin)rauschen; 2. (fig. Dahin)Fegen n; Kehren n; Schwung m; Biegung f; Spielraum m, Bereich m; Schornsteinfeger m; make a clean ~ reinen Tisch machen (of mit); ~er ['swiːpə] (Straßen)Feger m; Kehrmaschine f; ~ing □ [~piŋ] weitgehend; schwungvoll; ~ings pl. Kehricht m, Müll m.

sweet [swiːt] 1. □ süß; lieblich; freundlich; frisch; duftend; have a ~ tooth ein Leckermaul sein; 2. Liebling m; Süßigkeit f, Bonbon m, n; Nachtisch m; ~en ['swiːtn] (ver)süßen; ~heart Liebling m, Liebste(r m) f; ~ish [~tiʃ] süßlich; ~meat Bonbon m, n; kandierte Frucht; ~ness [~tnis] Süßigkeit f; Lieblichkeit f; ~ pea ♀ Gartenwicke f.

swell [swel] 1. [irr.] v/i. (an)schwellen; sich blähen; sich (aus)bauchen; v/t. anschwellen lassen; aufblähen; 2. F fein; sl. prima; 3. Anschwellen n; Schwellung f; ♪ Dünung f; F feiner Herr; ~ing ['sweliŋ] Geschwulst f.

swelter ['sweltə] vor Hitze umkommen.

swept [swept] pret. u. p.p. von sweep 1.

swerve [swɜːv] 1. (plötzlich) abbiegen; 2. (plötzliche) Wendung f.

swift □ [swift] schnell, eilig, flink; ~ness ['swiftnis] Schnelligkeit f.

swill [swil] 1. Spülicht n; Schweine-trank m; 2. spülen; saufen.

swim [swim] 1. [irr.] (durch-)schwimmen; schweben; my head ~s mir schwindelt; 2. Schwimmen n; be in the ~ auf dem laufenden sein; ~ming ['swimiŋ] 1. Schwim-men n; 2. Schwimm...; ~-bath (bsd. Hallen)Schwimmbad n; ~-pool Schwimmbecken n; ~-suit Bade-anzug m.

swindle ['swindl] 1. (be)schwin-deln; 2. Schwindel m.

swine [swain] Schwein(e pl.) n.

swing [swiŋ] 1. [irr.] schwingen, schwanken; F baumeln; (sich) schaukeln; schwenken; sich drehen; 2. Schwingen n; Schwung m; Schaukel f; Spielraum m; in full ~ in vollem Gange; ~-door ['swiŋdɔ:] Drehtür f.

swinish □ ['swainiʃ] schweinisch.

swipe [swaip] 1. aus vollem Arm schlagen; 2. starker Schlag.

swirl [swə:l] 1. (herum)wirbeln, strudeln; 2. Wirbel m, Strudel m.

Swiss [swis] 1. schweizerisch, Schweizer...; 2. Schweizer(in); the ~ pl. die Schweizer m/pl.

switch [switʃ] 1. Gerte f; ⚙ Weiche f; ∲ Schalter m; falscher Zopf; 2. peitschen; ⚙ rangieren; ∲ (um-)schalten; fig. wechseln, überleiten; ~ on (off) ∲ ein- (aus)schalten; ~-board ∲ ['switʃbɔ:d] Schaltbrett n, -tafel f.

swivel ⊕ ['swivl] Drehring m; attr. Dreh...

swollen ['swoulən] p.p. von swell 1.

swoon [swu:n] 1. Ohnmacht f; 2. in Ohnmacht fallen.

swoop [swu:p] 1. ~ down on od. upon (herab)stoßen auf (acc.) (Raub-vogel); überfallen; 2. Stoß m.

swop F [swɔp] s. swap.

sword [sɔ:d] Schwert n, Degen m.

swordsman ['sɔ:dzmən] Fechter m.

swore [swɔ:] pret. von swear.

sworn [swɔ:n] p.p. von swear.

swum [swʌm] p.p. von swim 1.

swung [swʌŋ] pret. u. p.p. von swing 1.

sycamore ['sikəmɔ:] Bergahorn m; Am. Platane f.

sycophant ['sikəfənt] Kriecher m.

syllable ['siləbl] Silbe f.

syllabus ['siləbəs] (bsd. Vorlesungs-)Verzeichnis n; (bsd. Lehr)Plan m.

sylvan ['silvən] waldig, Wald...

symbol ['simbəl] Symbol n, Sinn-bild n; ~ic(al □) [sim'bɔlik(əl)] sinnbildlich; ~ism ['simbəlizəm] Symbolik f.

symmetr|ical □ [si'metrikəl] eben-mäßig; ~y [simitri] Ebenmaß n.

sympath|etic [simpə'θetik] (~ally) mitfühlend; sympathisch; ~ strike Sympathiestreik m; ~ize ['sim-pəθaiz] sympathisieren, mitfühlen; ~y [~θi] Sympathie f, Mitgefühl n.

symphony ♪ ['simfəni] Symphonie f.

symptom ['simptəm] Symptom n.

synchron|ize ['siŋkrənaiz] v/i. gleichzeitig sein; v/t. als gleichzeitig zs.-stellen; Uhren auf-ea. abstim-men; Tonfilm: synchronisieren; ~ous □ [~nəs] gleichzeitig.

syndicate 1. ['sindikit] Syndikat n; 2. [~keit] zu e-m Syndikat verbin-den.

synonym ['sinənim] Synonym n; ~ous □ [si'nɔniməs] sinnverwandt.

synop|sis [si'nɔpsis], pl. ~ses [~si:z] zs.-fassende Übersicht.

syntax gr. ['sintæks] Syntax f.

synthe|sis ['sinθisis], pl. ~ses [~si:z] Synthese f, Verbindung f; ~tic(al □) [sin'θetik(əl)] synthetisch.

syringe ['sirindʒ] 1. Spritze f; 2. (be-, ein-, aus)spritzen.

syrup ['sirəp] Sirup m.

system ['sistim] System n; Organis-mus m, Körper m; Plan m, Ord-nung f; ~atic [sisti'mætik] (~ally) systematisch.

T

tab [tæb] Streifen m; Schildchen n; Anhänger m; Schlaufe f, Aufhänger m; F Rechnung f, Konto n.

table ['teibl] 1. Tisch m, Tafel f; Tisch-, Tafelrunde f; Tabelle f, Verzeichnis n; Bibel: Gesetzestafel f; ⚬. ~-land; at ~ bei Tisch; turn the ~s den Spieß umdrehen (on gegen); 2. auf den Tisch legen; tabellarisch anordnen.

tableau ['tæblou], pl. ~x [~ouz] lebendes Bild.

table|-cloth ['teiblklɔθ] Tischtuch n; ~-land Tafelland n, Plateau n,

Hochebene f; ~-linen Tisch-wäsche f; ~-spoon Eßlöffel m.

tablet ['tæblit] Täfelchen n; (Ge-denk)Tafel f; (Schreib- etc.)Block m; Stück n Seife; Tablette f.

table-top ['teibltɔp] Tischplatte f.

taboo [tə'bu:] 1. tabu, unantastbar; verboten; 2. Tabu n; Verbot n; 3. verbieten.

tabulate ['tæbjuleit] tabellarisch ordnen.

tacit □ ['tæsit] stillschweigend; ~urn □ ['tæsitə:n] schweigsam.

tack [tæk] 1. Stift m, Zwecke f;

Heftstich m; ⚓ Halse f; ⚓ Gang m
beim Lavieren; fig. Weg m; 2. v/t.
(an)heften; fig. (an)hängen; v/i. ⚓
wenden; fig. lavieren.
tackle ['tækl] 1. Gerät n; ⚓ Takel-,
Tauwerk n; ⊕ Flaschenzug m;
2. (an)packen; in Angriff nehmen;
fertig werden mit; j-n angehen (for
um).
tacky ['tæki] klebrig; Am. F schäbig.
tact [tækt] Takt m, Feingefühl n;
~**ful** □ ['tæktful] taktvoll.
tactics ['tæktiks] Taktik f.
tactless □ ['tæktlis] taktlos.
tadpole zo. ['tædpoul] Kaulquappe f.
taffeta ['tæfitə] Taft m.
taffy Am. ['tæfi] = toffee; F Schmus
m, Schmeichelei f.
tag [tæg] 1. (Schnürsenkel)Stift m;
Schildchen n, Etikett n; Redensart
f, Zitat n; Zusatz m; loses Ende;
Fangen n (Kinderspiel); 2. etikettieren, auszeichnen; anhängen (to,
onto an acc.); ~ after herlaufen hinter (dat.); ~ together an-ea.-reihen.
tail [teil] 1. Schwanz m; Schweif m;
hinteres Ende, Schluß m; ~s pl.
Rückseite f e-r Münze; F Frack m;
turn ~ davonlaufen; ~s up in Hoch-
stimmung; 2. ~ after s.o. j-m nach-
laufen; ~ s.o. Am. j-n beschatten; ~
away, ~ off abflauen, sich verlieren;
zögernd enden; ~-**coat** ['teil'kout]
Frack m; ~-**light** mot. etc. ['teillait]
Rück-, Schlußlicht n.
tailor ['teilə] 1. Schneider m;
2. schneidern; ~-**made** Schneider..., Maß...
taint [teint] 1. Flecken m, Makel m;
⚕ Ansteckung f; fig. krankhafter
Zug; Verderbnis f; 2. beflecken;
verderben; ⚕ anstecken.
take [teik] 1. [irr.] v/t. nehmen; an-,
ab-, auf-, ein-, fest-, hin-, wegnehmen; (weg)bringen; Speise (zu
sich) nehmen; Maßnahme, Gelegenheit ergreifen; Eid, Gelübde, Examen ablegen; phot. aufnehmen; et.
gut etc. aufnehmen; Beleidigung
hinnehmen; fassen, ergreifen; fangen; fig. fesseln; sich e-e Krankheit
holen; erfordern; brauchen; Zeit
dauern; auffassen; halten, ansehen
(for für); I ~ it that ich nehme an,
daß; ~ breath verschnaufen; ~ comfort sich trösten; ~ compassion on
Mitleid empfinden mit; sich erbarmen (gen.); ~ counsel beraten; ~ a
drive e-e Fahrt machen; ~ fire Feuer
fangen; ~ in hand unternehmen; ~
hold of ergreifen; ~ pity on Mitleid
haben mit; ~ place stattfinden;
spielen (Handlung); ~ a seat Platz
nehmen; ~ a walk e-n Spaziergang
machen; ~ my word for it verlaß
dich drauf; ~ about herumführen;
~ along mitnehmen; ~ down her-
unternehmen; notieren; ~ for halten für; ~ from j-m wegnehmen;

abziehen von; ~ in enger machen;
Zeitung halten; aufnehmen (als
Gast etc.); einschließen; verstehen;
erfassen; F j-n reinlegen; ~ off ab-,
wegnehmen; Kleid ausziehen, Hut
abnehmen; ~ on an-, übernehmen;
Arbeiter etc. einstellen; Fahrgäste
zusteigen lassen; ~ out heraus-, entnehmen; Fleck entfernen; j-n ausführen; Versicherung abschließen;
~ to pieces auseinandernehmen; ~
up aufnehmen; sich e-r S. annehm-
men; Raum, Zeit in Anspruch nehmen; v/i. wirken, ein-, anschlagen;
gefallen, ziehen; ~ after j-m nachschlagen; ~ off abspringen; ✈ aufsteigen, starten; ~ on F Anklang
finden; ~ over die Amtsgewalt übernehmen; ~ to liebgewinnen; fig.
sich verlegen auf (acc.); Zuflucht
nehmen zu; sich ergeben (dat.); ~
up F sich bessern (Wetter); ~ up
with sich anfreunden mit; that
won't ~ with me das verfängt bei
mir nicht; 2. Fang m; Geld-Ein-
nahme f; Film: Szene(naufnahme)
f; ~-**in** F ['teik'in] Reinfall m; ~-**n**
['teikən] p.p. von take 1; be ~ besetzt sein; be ~ with entzückt sein
von; be ~ ill krank werden; ~-**off**
['teiko:f] Karikatur f; Absprung m;
✈ Start m.
taking ['teikin] 1. □ F anziehend,
fesselnd, einnehmend; ansteckend;
2. (An-, Ab-, Auf-, Ein-, Ent-,
Hin-, Weg- etc.)Nehmen n; Inbe-
sitznahme f; ✗ Einnahme f; F Aufregung f; ~s pl. ✝ Einnahmen f/pl.
tale [teil] Erzählung f, Geschichte f;
Märchen n, Sage f; it tells its own ~
es spricht für sich selbst; ~-**bearer**
['teilbeərə] Zuträger(in).
talent ['tælənt] Talent n, Begabung
f, Anlage f; ~**ed** [~tid] talentvoll,
begabt.
talk [tɔ:k] 1. Gespräch n; Unterredung f; Plauderei f; Vortrag m;
Geschwätz n; 2. sprechen, reden
(von et.); plaudern; ~**ative** □ ['tɔ:-
kətiv] gesprächig, geschwätzig; ~**er**
['tɔ:kə] Schwätzer(in); Sprechen-
de(r m) f.
tall [tɔ:l] groß, lang, hoch; F übertrieben, unglaublich; that's a ~
order F das ist ein bißchen viel
verlangt.
tallow ['tælou] ausgelassener Talg.
tally ['tæli] 1. Kerbholz n; Gegenstück n (of zu); Kennzeichen n;
2. übereinstimmen.
talon orn. ['tælən] Kralle f, Klaue
f.
tame [teim] 1. □ zahm; folgsam;
harmlos; lahm, fad(e); 2. (be)zäh-
men, bändigen.
Tammany Am. ['tæməni] New
Yorker Demokraten-Vereinigung.
tamper ['tæmpə]: ~ with sich (unbefugt) zu schaffen machen mit;

j-n zu bestechen suchen; *Urkunde* fälschen.

tan [tæn] **1.** Lohe *f*; Lohfarbe *f*; (Sonnen)Bräune *f*; **2.** lohfarben; **3.** gerben; bräunen.

tang [tæŋ] Beigeschmack *m*; *scharfer* Klang; ♀ Seetang *m*.

tangent ['tændʒənt] Å Tangente *f*; *fly od.* go off at a ~ vom Gegenstand abspringen.

tangerine ♀ [tændʒə'ri:n] Mandarine *f*.

tangible □ ['tændʒəbl] fühlbar, greifbar (*a. fig.*); klar.

tangle ['tæŋgl] **1.** Gewirr *n*; Verwicklung *f*; **2.** (sich) verwirren, verwickeln.

tank [tæŋk] **1.** Zisterne *f*, Wasserbehälter *m*; ⊕, ✗ Tank *m*; **2.** tanken. [(Bier)Krug *m*.]

tankard ['tæŋkəd] Kanne *f*, *bsd.*)

tanner ['tænə] Gerber *m*; ~y [~əri] Gerberei *f*.

tantalize ['tæntəlaiz] quälen.

tantamount ['tæntəmaunt] gleichbedeutend (mit).

tantrum F ['tæntrəm] Koller *m*.

tap [tæp] **1.** leichtes Klopfen; (Wasser-, Gas-, Zapf)Hahn *m*; Zapfen *m*; Schankstube *f*; F Sorte *f*; ~s *pl. Am.* ✗ Zapfenstreich *m*; **2.** pochen, klopfen, tippen (auf, an, gegen *acc.*); an-, abzapfen; ~dance ['tæpdɑ:ns] Stepptanz *m*.

tape [teip] schmales Band; *Sport:* Zielband *n*; *tel.* Papierstreifen *m*; Tonband *n*; red ~ Bürokratismus *m*; ~measure ['teipmeʒə] Bandmaß *n*.

taper ['teipə] **1.** dünne Wachskerze; **2.** *adj.* spitz (zulaufend); schlank; **3.** *v/i.* spitz zulaufen; *v/t.* zuspitzen.

tape| recorder ['teiprikɔ:də] Tonbandgerät *n*; ~ **recording** Tonbandaufnahme *f*.

tapestry ['tæpistri] Gobelin *m*.

tapeworm ['teipwə:m] Bandwurm *m*.

tap-room ['tæprum] Schankstube *f*.

tar [tɑ:] **1.** Teer *m*; **2.** teeren.

tardy □ ['tɑ:di] langsam; spät.

tare ♀ [tɛə] Tara *f*.

target ['tɑ:git] (Schieß)Scheibe *f*; *fig.* Ziel(scheibe *f*) *n*; Ziel(leistung *f*) *n*; Soll *n*; ~ *practice* Scheibenschießen *n*.

tariff ['tærif] (*bsd.* Zoll)Tarif *m*.

tarnish ['tɑ:niʃ] **1.** *v/t.* ⊕ trüb *od.* blind machen; *fig.* trüben; *v/i.* trüb werden, anlaufen; **2.** Trübung *f*; Belag *m*.

tarry¹ *lit.* ['tæri] säumen, zögern; verweilen.

tarry² ['tɑ:ri] teerig.

tart [tɑ:t] **1.** □ sauer, herb; *fig.* scharf, schroff; **2.** (Obst)Torte *f*; *sl.* Dirne *f*.

tartan ['tɑ:tən] Tartan *m*; Schottentuch *n*; Schottenmuster *n*.

task [tɑ:sk] **1.** Aufgabe *f*; Arbeit *f*; *take to* ~ zur Rede stellen; **2.** beschäftigen; in Anspruch nehmen.

tassel ['tæsəl] Troddel *f*, Quaste *f*.

taste [teist] **1.** Geschmack *m*; (Kost)Probe *f*; Lust *f* (for zu); **2.** kosten, schmecken; versuchen; genießen; ~ful □ ['teistful] geschmackvoll; ~less □ [~tlis] geschmacklos.

tasty □ F ['teisti] schmackhaft.

ta-ta ['tæ'tɑ:] auf Wiedersehen!

tatter ['tætə] **1.** zerfetzen; **2.** ~s *pl.* Fetzen *m/pl.*

tattle ['tætl] **1.** schwatzen; tratschen; **2.** Geschwätz *n*; Tratsch *m*.

tattoo [tə'tu:] **1.** ✗ Zapfenstreich *m*; Tätowierung *f*; **2.** *fig.* trommeln; tätowieren.

taught [tɔ:t] *pret. u. p.p. von teach.*

taunt [tɔ:nt] **1.** Stichelei *f*, Spott *m*; **2.** verhöhnen, verspotten.

taut ⊕ [tɔ:t] steif, straff; schmuck.

tavern ['tævən] Schenke *f*.

tawdry □ ['tɔ:dri] billig; kitschig.

tawny ['tɔ:ni] lohfarben.

tax [tæks] **1.** Steuer *f*, Abgabe *f*; *fig.* Inanspruchnahme *f* (on, upon *gen.*); **2.** besteuern; *fig.* stark in Anspruch nehmen; ⚖ *Kosten* schätzen; auf e-e harte Probe stellen; *j-n* zur Rede stellen; ~ *s.o.* with *s.th.* j-n e-r S. beschuldigen; ~ation [tæk'seiʃən] Besteuerung *f*; Steuer(n *pl.*) *f*; *bsd.* ⚖ Schätzung *f*.

taxi F ['tæksi] **1.** = ~cab; **2.** mit e-m Taxi fahren; ⤤ rollen; ~cab Taxi *n*, (Auto)Droschke *f*.

taxpayer ['tækspeiə] Steuerzahler *m*.

tea [ti:] Tee *m*; high ~, meat ~ frühes Abendbrot mit Tee.

teach [ti:tʃ] [*irr.*] lehren, unterrichten, *j-m et.* beibringen; ~able □ ['ti:tʃəbl] gelehrig; lehrbar; ~er [~ʃə] Lehrer(in); ~-in [~ʃ'in] (politische) Diskussion *als Großveranstaltung.*

tea|-cosy ['ti:kouzi] Teewärmer *m*; ~cup Teetasse *f*; storm in a ~ *fig.* Sturm *m* im Wasserglas; ~kettle Wasserkessel *m*.

team [ti:m] Team *n*, Arbeitsgruppe *f*; Gespann *n*; *bsd. Sport:* Mannschaft *f*; ~ster ['ti:mstə] Gespannführer *m*; *Am.* LKW-Fahrer *m*; ~work Zusammenarbeit *f*, Teamwork *n*; Zusammenspiel *n*.

teapot ['ti:pɔt] Teekanne *f*.

tear¹ [tɛə] **1.** [*irr.*] zerren, (zer)reißen; rasen, stürmen; **2.** Riß *m*.

tear² [tiə] Träne *f*.

tearful □ ['tiəful] tränenreich.

tea-room ['ti:rum] Tearoom *m*. Teestube *f*, Café *n*.

tease [ti:z] **1.** necken, hänseln; quälen; **2.** Necker *m*; Quälgeist *m*.

teat [ti:t] Zitze *f*; Brustwarze *f*; (Gummi)Sauger *m*.

technic|al □ ['teknikəl] technisch; gewerblich, Gewerbe...; fachlich, Fach...; ~ality [tekni'kæliti] technische Eigentümlichkeit *od.* Einzelheit; Fachausdruck *m*; ~ian [tek'niʃən] Techniker(in).

technique [tek'ni:k] Technik *f*, Verfahren *n*.

technology [tek'nɔlədʒi] Gewerbekunde *f*; *school of* ~ Technische Hochschule.

teddy boy F ['tedibɔi] Halbstarke(r) *m.*

tedious □ ['ti:djəs] langweilig, ermüdend; weitschweifig.

tee [ti:] *Sport:* Mal *n*, Ziel *n*; *Golf:* Abschlagmal *n.*

teem [ti:m] wimmeln, strotzen (*with* von).

teens [ti:nz] *pl.* Lebensjahre *n/pl.* von 13—19.

teeny F ['ti:ni] winzig.

teeth [ti:θ] *pl. von* tooth; ~e [ti:ð] zahnen.

teetotal(l)er [ti:'toutlə] Abstinenzler(in).

telecast ['telikɑ:st] 1. Fernsehsendung *f*; 2. [*irr.* (cast)] im Fernsehen übertragen.

telecourse *Am.* F ['telikɔ:s] Fernsehlehrgang *m.*

telegram ['teligræm] Telegramm *n.*

telegraph ['teligrɑ:f] 1. Telegraph *m*; 2. Telegraphen...; 3. telegraphieren; ~ic [teli'græfik] (~ally) telegraphisch; telegrammäßig (*Stil*); ~y [ti'legrəfi] Telegraphie *f.*

telephon|e ['telifoun] 1. Telephon *n*, Fernsprecher *m*; 2. telephonieren; anrufen; ~e booth Telephonzelle *f*; ~ic [teli'fonik] (~ally) telephonisch; ~y [ti'lefəni] Fernsprechwesen *n.*

telephoto *phot.* ['teli'foutou] *a.* ~ lens Teleobjektiv *n.*

teleprinter ['teliprintə] Fernschreiber *m.*

telescope ['teliskoup] 1. *opt.* Fernrohr *n*; 2. (sich) ineinanderschieben.

teletype ['telitaip] Fernschreiber *m.*

televis|e ['telivaiz] im Fernsehen übertragen; ~ion [ˌteli'viʒən] Fernsehen *n*; *watch* ~ fernsehen; ~ion set, ~or [ˌteli'vaizə] Fernsehapparat *m.*

tell [tel] [*irr.*] *v/t.* zählen; sagen, erzählen; erkennen; ~ s.o. to do s.th. j-m sagen, er solle et. tun; ~ off abzählen; auswählen; F abkanzeln; *v/i.* erzählen (*of, about* von); (aus)plaudern; sich auswirken; sitzen (*Hieb etc.*); ~er ['telə] (Er)Zähler *m*; ~ing ['teliŋ] wirkungsvoll; ~tale ['telteil] 1. Klatschbase *f*; ⊕ Anzeiger *m*; 2. *fig.* verräterisch.

temerity [ti'meriti] Unbesonnenheit *f*, Verwegenheit *f.*

temper ['tempə] 1. mäßigen, mildern; *Kalk etc.* anrühren; *Stahl* anlassen; 2. ⊕ Härte(grad *m*) *f*;

(Gemüts)Ruhe *f*, Gleichmut *m*; Temperament *n*, Wesen *n*; Stimmung *f*; Wut *f*; *lose one's* ~ in Wut geraten; ~ament [ˌ~ərəmənt] Temperament *n*; ~amental □ [tempərə'mentl] anlagebedingt; launisch; ~ance ['tempərəns] Mäßigkeit *f*; Enthaltsamkeit *f*; ~ate □ [ˌ~rit] gemäßigt; zurückhaltend; maßvoll; mäßig; ~ature [ˌ~pritʃə] Temperatur *f.*

tempest ['tempist] Sturm *m*; Gewitter *n*; ~uous □ [tem'pestjəs] stürmisch; ungestüm.

temple ['templ] Tempel *m*; *anat.* Schläfe *f.*

tempor|al □ ['tempərəl] zeitlich; weltlich; ~ary □ [ˌ~əri] zeitweilig; vorläufig; vorübergehend; Not..., (Aus)Hilfs..., Behelfs...; ~ize ['ˌ~raiz] Zeit zu gewinnen suchen.

tempt [tempt] *j-n* versuchen; verleiten; verlocken; ~ation [temp'teiʃən] Versuchung *f*; Reiz *m*; ~ing □ ['temptiŋ] verführerisch.

ten [ten] 1. zehn; 2. Zehn *f.*

tenable ['tenəbl] haltbar (*Theorie etc.*); verliehen (*Amt*).

tenaci|ous □ [ti'neiʃəs] zäh; festhaltend (*of an dat.*); gut (*Gedächtnis*); ~ty [ti'næsiti] Zähigkeit *f*; Festhalten *n*; Verläßlichkeit *f des Gedächtnisses.*

tenant ['tenənt] Pächter *m*; Mieter *m.*

tend [tend] *v/i.* (*to*) gerichtet sein (auf *acc.*); hinstreben (zu); abzielen (auf *acc.*); neigen (zu); *v/t.* pflegen; hüten; ⊕ bedienen; ~ance ['tendəns] Pflege *f*; Bedienung *f*; ~ency [ˌ~si] Richtung *f*; Neigung *f*; Zweck *m.*

tender ['tendə] 1. □ zart; weich; empfindlich; heikel (*Thema*); zärtlich; 2. Angebot *n*; Kostenanschlag *m*; ⎘, ♨ Tender *m*; *legal* ~ gesetzliches Zahlungsmittel; 3. anbieten; *Entlassung* einreichen; ~foot *Am.* F Neuling *m*, Anfänger *m*; ~loin *bsd. Am.* Filet *n*; *Am.* berüchtigtes Viertel; ~ness [ˌ~nis] Zartheit *f*; Zärtlichkeit *f.*

tendon *anat.* ['tendən] Sehne *f.*

tendril ♣ ['tendril] Ranke *f.*

tenement ['tenimənt] Wohnhaus *n*; (*bsd.* Miet)Wohnung *f*; ~ house Mietshaus *n.*

tennis ['tenis] Tennis(spiel) *n*; ~ court Tennisplatz *m.*

tenor ['tenə] Fortgang *m*, Verlauf *m*; Inhalt *m*; ♪ Tenor *m.*

tens|e [tens] 1. *gr.* Zeit(form) *f*, Tempus *n*; 2. □ gespannt (*a. fig.*); straff; ~ion ['tenʃən] Spannung *f.*

tent [tent] 1. Zelt *n*; 2. zelten.

tentacle *zo.* ['tentəkl] Fühler *m*; Fangarm *m e-s Polypen.*

tentative □ ['tentətiv] versuchend; Versuchs...; ~ly versuchsweise.

tenth [tenθ] **1.** zehnte(r, -s); **2.** Zehntel *n*; **ly** ['tenθli] zehntens.

tenuous □ ['tenjuǝs] dünn; zart, fein; dürftig.

tenure ['tenjuǝ] Besitz(art *f*, -dauer *f*) *m*.

tepid □ ['tepid] lau(warm).

term [tǝ:m] **1.** (bestimmte) Zeit, Frist *f*, Termin *m*; Zahltag *m*; Amtszeit *f*; ♪ Sitzungsperiode *f*; Semester *n*, Quartal *n*, Trimester *n*, Tertial *n*; Ⱥ, *phls.* Glied *n*; (Fach-) Ausdruck *m*, Wort *n*, Bezeichnung *f*; Begriff *m*; **s** *pl.* Bedingungen *f*/*pl.*; Beziehungen *f*/*pl.*; *be on good (bad)* **s** *with* gut (schlecht) stehen mit; *come to* **s**, *make* **s** sich einigen; **2.** (be)nennen; bezeichnen (als).

termagant ['tǝ:mǝgǝnt] **1.** □ zanksüchtig; **2.** Zankteufel *m* (*Weib*).

termina|l ['tǝ:minl] **1.** □ End...; letzt; **ly** terminweise; **2.** Endstück *n*; ∮ Pol *m*; *Am.* 🚗 Endstation *f*; **te** [_neit] begrenzen; (be)endigen; **tion** [tǝ:mi'neiʃǝn] Beendigung *f*; Ende *n*; *gr.* Endung *f*.

terminus ['tǝ:minǝs] Endstation *f*.

terrace ['terǝs] Terrasse *f*; Häuserreihe *f*; **house** Reihenhaus *n*; **d** [_st] terrassenförmig.

terrestrial □ [ti'restriǝl] irdisch; Erd...; *bsd. zo.*, ♀ Land...

terrible □ ['terǝbl] schrecklich.

terri|fic [tǝ'rifik] (**ally**) fürchterlich, schrecklich, F ungeheuer, großartig; **fy** ['terifai] *v*/*t.* erschrecken.

territor|ial [teri'tɔ:riǝl] **1.** □ territorial; Land...; Bezirks...; ♀ Army, ♀ Force Territorialarmee *f*; **2.** 🗡 Angehörige(r) *m* der Territorialarmee; **y** ['teritǝri] Territorium *n*, (Hoheits-, Staats)Gebiet *n*.

terror ['terǝ] Schrecken *m*, Entsetzen *n*; **ize** [_ɔraiz] terrorisieren.

terse □ [tǝ:s] knapp; kurz u. bündig.

test [test] **1.** Probe *f*; Untersuchung *f*; (Eignungs)Prüfung *f*; Test *m*; 🜹 Reagens *n*; **2.** probieren, prüfen, testen.

testament ['testǝmǝnt] Testament *n*.

testicle *anat.* ['testikl] Hode(n *m*) [*m*, *f*.

testify ['testifai] (be)zeugen; (als Zeuge) aussagen (*on* über *acc.*).

testimon|ial [testi'mounjǝl] (Führungs)Zeugnis *n*; Zeichen *n* der Anerkennung; **y** ['testimǝni] Zeugnis *n*; Beweis *m*.

test-tube 🜹 ['testtju:b] Reagenzglas *n*.

testy □ ['testi] reizbar, kribbelig.

tether ['teðǝ] **1.** Haltestrick *m*; *fig.* Spielraum *m*; *at the end of one's* **~** *fig.* am Ende s-r Kraft; **2.** anbinden.

text [tekst] Text *m*; Bibelstelle *f*;

book ['tekstbuk] Leitfaden *m*, Lehrbuch *n*.

textile ['tekstail] **1.** Textil..., Web...; **2.** **s** *pl.* Webwaren *f*/*pl.*, Textilien *pl.*

texture ['tekstʃǝ] Gewebe *n*; Gefüge *n*.

than [ðæn, ðǝn] als.

thank [θæŋk] **1.** danken (*dat.*); **~** *you, bei Ablehnung* no, **~** *you* danke; **2.** **s** *pl.* Dank *m*; **s!** vielen Dank!; danke (schön)!; **s** *to* dank (*dat.*); **ful** □ ['θæŋkful] dankbar; **less** □ [_klis] undankbar; **sgiving** [_ksgiviŋ] Danksagung *f*; Dankfest *n*; ♀ (*Day*) *bsd. Am.* (Ernte)Dankfest *n*.

that [ðæt, ðǝt] **1.** *pl.* those [ðouz] *pron.* jene(r, -s); der, die, das; der-, die-, das(jenige); welche(r, -s) **2.** *cj.* daß; damit.

thatch [θætʃ] **1.** Dachstroh *n*; Strohdach *n*; **2.** mit Stroh decken.

thaw [θɔ:] **1.** Tauwetter *n*; (Auf-) Tauen *n*; **2.** auf/tauen.

the [ði:; *vor Vokalen* ði; *vor Konsonanten* ðǝ] **1.** *art.* der, die, das; **2.** *adv.* desto, um so; **~** ... **~** ... je ... desto ...

theat|re, *Am.* **er** ['θiǝtǝ] Theater *n*; *fig.* (Kriegs)Schauplatz *m*; **ric(al** □) [θi'ætrik(ǝl)] Theater...; theatralisch.

thee *Bibel, poet.* [ði:] dich; dir.

theft [θeft] Diebstahl *m*.

their [ðεǝ] ihr(e); **s** [_z] der (die, das) ihrige *od.* ihre.

them [ðem, ðǝm] sie (*acc. pl.*); ihnen.

theme [θi:m] Thema *n*; Aufgabe *f*.

themselves [ðem'selvz] sie (*acc. pl.*) selbst; sich selbst.

then [ðen] **1.** *adv.* dann; damals; da; *by* **~** bis dahin; inzwischen; *every now and* **~** alle Augenblicke; *there and* **~** sogleich; *now* **~** nun denn; **2.** *cj.* denn, also, folglich; **3.** *adj.* damalig.

thence *lit.* [ðens] daher; von da.

theolog|ian [θiǝ'loudʒǝn] Theologe *m*; **y** [θi'ɔlǝdʒi] Theologie *f*.

theor|etic(al □) [θiǝ'retik(ǝl)] theoretisch; **ist** ['θiǝrist] Theoretiker *m*; **y** [_ri] Theorie *f*.

therap|eutic [θerǝ'pju:tik] **1.** (**ally**) therapeutisch; **2.** **s** *mst. sg.* Therapeutik *f*; **y** ['θerǝpi] Therapie *f*, Heilbehandlung *f*.

there [ðεǝ] da, dort; darin; dorthin; na!; **~** *is*, **~** *are* es gibt, es ist, es sind; **about(s)** ['θεǝrǝbaut(s)] da herum; so ungefähr ...; **after** [θεǝr'a:ftǝ] danach; **by** ['ðεǝ'bai] dadurch, damit; **fore** ['ðεǝfɔ:] darum, deswegen; deshalb, daher; **upon** ['θεǝrǝ'pɔn] darauf(hin); **with** [ðεǝ'wið] damit.

thermal ['θǝ:mǝl] **1.** □ Thermal...; *phys.* Wärme...; **2.** Aufwind *m*.

thermo|meter [θəˈmɔmitə] Thermometer *n*; 2s ['θəːmɔs] *a.* ~ **flask**, ~ **bottle** Thermosflasche *f.*

these [ðiːz] *pl. von* this.

thes|is ['θiːsis], *pl.* ~**es** ['θiːsiːz] These *f*; Dissertation *f.*

they [ðei] sie (*pl.*).

thick [θik] 1. □ *allg.* dick; dicht; trüb; legiert (*Suppe*); heiser; dumm; *pred.* F dick befreundet; ~ **with** dicht besetzt mit; 2. dickster Teil; *fig.* Brennpunkt *m; in the* ~ **of** mitten in (*dat.*); ~**en** ['θikən] (sich) verdicken; (sich) verstärken; legieren; (sich) verdichten; ~**et** ['θikit] Dickicht *n;* ~**headed** dumm; ~**ness** ['θiknis] Dicke *f,* Stärke *f*; Dichte *f*; Schicht *f*; ~**set** dicht (gepflanzt); untersetzt; ~**skinned** *fig.* dickfellig.

thief [θiːf], *pl.* **thieves** [θiːvz] Dieb(in); **thieve** [θiːv] stehlen.

thigh [θai] (Ober)Schenkel *m.*

thimble ['θimbl] Fingerhut *m.*

thin [θin] 1. □ *allg.* dünn; leicht; mager; spärlich, dürftig; schwach; fadenscheinig (*bsd. fig.*); 2. verdünnen; (sich) lichten; abnehmen.

thine *Bibel, poet.* [ðain] dein; der (die, das) deinige *od.* deine.

thing [θiŋ] Ding *n*; Sache *f*; Geschöpf *n;* ~**s** *pl.* Sachen *f/pl.*; die Dinge *n/pl.* (*Umstände*); *the* ~ F das Richtige; richtig; die Hauptsache; ~**s are going better** es geht jetzt besser.

think [θiŋk] [*irr.*] *v/i.* denken (*of* an *acc.*); nachdenken; sich besinnen; meinen, glauben; gedenken (*to inf.* zu *inf.*); *v/t.* (sich) *et.* denken; halten für; ~ **much** *etc.* **of** viel *etc.* halten von; ~ **s.th. over** (sich) *et.* überlegen, über *et.* nachdenken.

third [θəːd] 1. dritte(r, -s); 2. Drittel *n*; ~**ly** ['θəːdli] drittens; ~**rate** ['θəːd'reit] drittklassig.

thirst [θəːst] 1. Durst *m*; 2. dürsten; ~**y** □ ['θəːsti] durstig; dürr (*Boden*).

thirt|een ['θəː'tiːn] dreizehn; ~**eenth** [~nθ] dreizehnte(r, -s); ~**ieth** ['θəːtiiθ] dreißigste(r, -s), ~**y** ['θəːti] dreißig.

this [ðis], *pl.* **these** [ðiːz] diese(r, -s); ~ **morning** heute morgen.

thistle ♣ ['θisl] Distel *f.*

thong [θɔŋ] (Leder-, Peitschen-) Riemen *m.*

thorn ♣ [θɔːn] Dorn *m*; ~**y** ['θɔːni] dornig, stach(e)lig; beschwerlich.

thorough □ ['θʌrə] vollkommen; vollständig; vollendet; gründlich; ~**ly** *a.* durchaus; ~**bred** Vollblüter *m*; *attr.* Vollblut...; ~**fare** Durchgang *m*, Durchfahrt *f*; Hauptverkehrsstraße *f*; ~**going** gründlich; tatkräftig.

those [ðouz] *pl. von* that 1.

thou *Bibel, poet.* [ðau] du.

though [ðou] obgleich, obwohl,

wenn auch; zwar; aber, doch; freilich; *as* ~ als ob.

thought [θɔːt] 1. *pret. u. p.p. von* **think**; 2. Gedanke *m*; (Nach)Denken *n; on second* ~**s** nach nochmaliger Überlegung; ~**ful** □ ['θɔːtful] gedankenvoll, nachdenklich; rücksichtsvoll (*of* gegen); ~**less** □ ['θɔːtlis] gedankenlos; unbesonnen; rücksichtslos (*of* gegen).

thousand ['θauzənd] 1. tausend; 2. Tausend *n*; **a** ~ tausend; **two** ~ zweitausend; ~**th** [~ntθ] 1. tausendste(r, -s); 2. Tausendstel *n.*

thrash [θræʃ] (ver)dreschen, (ver)prügeln; (hin und her) schlagen; *s.* thresh; ~**ing** ['θræʃiŋ] Dresche *f,* Tracht *f* Prügel; *s.* threshing.

thread [θred] 1. Faden *m* (*a. fig.*); Zwirn *m*, Garn *n*; ⊕ (Schrauben-) Gewinde *n*; 2. einfädeln; sich durchwinden (durch); durchziehen; ~**bare** ['θredbeə] fadenscheinig.

threat [θret] Drohung *f*; ~**en** ['θretn] (be-, an)drohen; ~**ening** [~niŋ] bedrohlich.

three [θriː] 1. drei; 2. Drei *f*; ~**fold** ['θriːfould] dreifach; ~**pence** ['θrepəns] Dreipence(stück *n*) *m/pl.*; ~**score** ['θriː'skɔː] sechzig.

thresh [θreʃ] ✔ (aus)dreschen; *s.* thrash; ~ **out** *fig.* durchdreschen; ~**er** ['θreʃə] Drescher *m*; Dreschmaschine *f*; ~**ing** [~ʃiŋ] Dreschen *n*; ~**ing-machine** Dreschmaschine *f.*

threshold ['θreʃhould] Schwelle *f.*

threw [θruː] *pret. von* throw 1.

thrice [θrais] dreimal.

thrift [θrift] Sparsamkeit *f,* Wirtschaftlichkeit *f*; ~**less** □ ['θriftlis] verschwenderisch; ~**y** □ [~ti] sparsam; *poet.* gedeihend.

thrill [θril] 1. *v/t.* durchdringen, durchschauern; *fig.* packen, aufwühlen; aufregen; *v/i.* (er)beben; 2. Schauer *m*; Beben *n*; aufregendes Erlebnis; Sensation *f*; ~**er** F ['θrilə] Reißer *m*, Thriller *m*, Schauerroman *m*, Schauerstück *n*; ~**ing** [~iŋ] spannend.

thrive [θraiv] [*irr.*] gedeihen; *fig.* blühen; Glück haben; ~**n** ['θrivn] *p.p. von* thrive.

throat [θrout] Kehle *f*; Hals *m*; Gurgel *f*; Schlund *m*; *clear one's* ~ sich räuspern.

throb [θrɔb] 1. pochen, klopfen, schlagen; pulsieren; 2. Pochen *n*; Schlagen *n*; Pulsschlag *m.*

throes [θrouz] *pl.* Geburtswehen *f/pl.* [Thrombose *f.*]
thrombosis ✘ [θrɔmˈbousis]}
throne [θroun] Thron *m.*

throng [θrɔŋ] 1. Gedränge *n*; Menge *f*, Schar *f*; 2. sich drängen (in *dat.*); anfüllen mit.

throstle *orn.* ['θrɔsl] Drossel *f.*

throttle ['θrɔtl] 1. erdrosseln; ⊕ (ab)drosseln; 2. ⊕ Drosselklappe *f.*

through [θru:] 1. durch; 2. Durch-
gangs...; durchgehend; **~out**
[θru(:)'aut] 1. *prp.* überall in (*dat.*);
2. *adv.* durch u. durch, ganz und
gar, durchweg.

throve [θrouv] *pret. von* thrive.

throw [θrou] 1. [*irr.*] (ab)werfen,
schleudern; *Am.* F *Wettkampf etc.*
betrügerisch verlieren; würfeln; ⊕
schalten; ~ *off* (die Jagd) beginnen;
~ *over* aufgeben; ~ *up* in die Höhe
werfen; erbrechen; *fig.* hinwerfen;
2. Wurf *m*; **~n** [θroun] *p.p. von*
throw 1.

thru *Am.* [θru:] = through.

thrum [θrʌm] klimpern (auf *dat.*).

thrush *orn.* [θrʌʃ] Drossel *f*.

thrust [θrʌst] 1. Stoß *m*; Vorstoß
m; ⊕ Druck *m*, Schub *m*; 2. [*irr.*]
stoßen; ~ *o.s. into* sich drängen in
(*acc.*); ~ *upon s.o.* j-m aufdrängen.

thud [θʌd] 1. dumpf aufschlagen,
F bumsen; 2. dumpfer (Auf)Schlag,
F Bums *m*.

thug [θʌg] Strolch *m*.

thumb [θʌm] 1. Daumen *m*; Tom ♀
Däumling *m im Märchen*; 2. *Buch
etc.* abgreifen; ~ *a lift* per Anhalter
fahren; **~tack** *Am.* ['θʌmtæk]
Reißzwecke *f*.

thump [θʌmp] 1. F Bums *m*; F Puff
m; 2. *v/t.* F bumsen *od.* pochen auf
(*acc.*) *od.* gegen; F knuffen, puffen;
v/i. F (auf)bumsen.

thunder ['θʌndə] 1. Donner *m*;
2. donnern; **~bolt** Blitz *m* (*u.* Donner *m*); **~clap** Donnerschlag *m*;
~ous □ [~ərəs] donnernd; **~storm**
Gewitter *n*; **~struck** wie vom
Donner gerührt.

Thursday ['θə:zdi] Donnerstag *m*.

thus [ðʌs] so; also, somit.

thwart [θwɔ:t] 1. durchkreuzen;
hintertreiben; 2. Ruderbank *f*.

thy *Bibel, poet.* [ðai] dein(e).

tick[1] *zo.* [tik] Zecke *f*.

tick[2] [~] 1. Ticken *n*; (Vermerk-)
Häkchen *n*; 2. *v/i.* ticken; *v/t.* an-
haken; ~ *off* abhaken.

tick[3] [~] Inlett *n*; Matratzenbezug *m*.

ticket ['tikit] 1. Fahrkarte *f*, -schein
m; Flugkarte *f*; Eintrittskarte *f*;
(Straf)Zettel *m*; (Preis- *etc.*)Schild-
chen *n*; *pol.* (Wahl-, Kandidaten-)
Liste *f*; 2. etikettieren, *Ware* auszeichnen; **~machine** Fahrkarten-
automat *m*; ~ **office**, ~ **window**
bsd. Am. Fahrkartenschalter *m*.

tick|**le** ['tikl] kitzeln (*a. fig.*); **~ish**
□ [~liʃ] kitzlig; heikel.

tidal ['taidl]: ~ *wave* Flutwelle *f*.

tide [taid] 1. Gezeit(en *pl.*) *f*; Ebbe *f*
und Flut *f*; *fig.* Strom *m*, Flut *f*; *in
Zssgn*: *rechte* Zeit; *high* ~ Flut *f*;
low ~ Ebbe *f*; 2. ~ *over fig.* hinweg-
kommen *od. j-m* hinweghelfen über
(*acc.*).

tidings ['taidiŋz] *pl. od. sg.* Neuig-
keiten *f/pl.*, Nachrichten *f/pl.*

tidy ['taidi] 1. ordentlich, sauber,
reinlich; F ganz schön, beträchtlich
(*Summe*); 2. Behälter *m*; Abfallkorb
m; 3. *a.* ~ *up* zurechtmachen; ordnen; aufräumen.

tie [tai] 1. Band *n* (*a. fig.*); Schleife *f*;
Krawatte *f*, Schlips *m*; Bindung *f*;
fig. Fessel *f*, Verpflichtung *f*; *Sport*:
Punkt-, *parl.* Stimmengleichheit *f*;
Sport: Entscheidungsspiel *n*; ⬚
Am. Schwelle *f*; 2. *v/t.* (ver)binden;
~ *down fig.* binden (*to an acc.*); ~
up zu-, an-, ver-, zs.-binden; *v/i.*
Sport: punktgleich sein.

tier [tiə] Reihe *f*; Rang *m*.

tie-up ['taiʌp] (Ver)Bindung *f*; ✝
Fusion *f*; Stockung *f*; *bsd. Am.*
Streik *m*.

tiffin ['tifin] Mittagessen *n*.

tiger ['taigə] *zo.* Tiger *m*; *Am.* F
Beifallsgebrüll *n*.

tight [tait] 1. □ dicht; fest; eng;
knapp (sitzend); straff, prall;
knapp; F beschwipst; *be in a* ~
place od. corner F in der Klemme
sein; 2. *adv.* fest; *hold* ~ festhalten;
~en ['taitn] *a.* ~ *up* (sich) zs.-ziehen;
Gürtel enger schnallen; **~fisted**
knick(e)rig; **~ness** ['taitnis] Festigkeit *f*, Dichtigkeit *f*; Straffheit *f*;
Knappheit *f*; Enge *f*; Geiz *m*; **~s**
[taits] *pl.* Trikot *n*.

tigress ['taigris] Tigerin *f*.

tile [tail] 1. (Dach)Ziegel *m*; Kachel
f; Fliese *f*; 2. mit Ziegeln *etc.*
decken; kacheln; fliesen.

till[1] [til] Laden(tisch)kasse *f*.

till[2] [~] 1. *prp.* bis (zu); 2. *cj.* bis.

till[3] ✓ [~] 1. bestellen, bebauen; **~age**
['tilidʒ] (Land)Bestellung *f*; Ackerbau *m*; Ackerland *n*.

tilt [tilt] 1. Plane *f*; Neigung *f*,
Kippe *f*; Stoß *m*; Lanzenbrechen *n*
(*a. fig.*); 2. kippen; ~ *against* anrennen gegen.

timber ['timbə] 1. (Bau-, Nutz-)
Holz *n*; Balken *m*; Baumbestand
m, Bäume *m/pl.*; 2. zimmern.

time [taim] 1. Zeit *f*; Mal *n*; Takt
m; Tempo *n*; ~ *and again* immer
wieder; *at a* ~ zugleich; *for the* ~
being einstweilen; *have a good* ~
es gut haben; sich amüsieren; *in*
~, *on* ~ zur rechten Zeit, rechtzeitig; 2. zeitlich festsetzen; zeitlich abpassen; die Zeitdauer messen; **~hono(u)red** ['taimɔnəd] alt-
ehrwürdig; **~ly** ['taimli] (recht)zei-
tig; **~piece** Uhr *f*; **~sheet** An-
wesenheitsliste *f*; **~table** Termin-
kalender *m*; Fahr-, Stundenplan *m*.

tim|**id** □ ['timid], **~orous** □ ['ti-
mərəs] furchtsam; schüchtern.

tin [tin] 1. Zinn *n*; Weißblech *n*;
(Konserven)Büchse *f*; 2. verzinnen;
in Büchsen einmachen, eindosen.

tincture ['tiŋktʃə] 1. Farbe *f*; Tinktur *f*; *fig.* Anstrich *m*; 2. färben.

tinfoil ['tin'fɔil] Stanniol *n*.

tinge [tindʒ] 1. Färbung f; fig. Anflug m, Spur f; 2. färben; fig. e-n Anstrich geben (dat.).

tingle ['tiŋgl] klingen; prickeln.

tinker ['tiŋkə] basteln (at an dat.).

tinkle ['tiŋkl] klingeln (mit).

tin|-opener ['tinoupnə] Dosenöffner m; **~-plate** Weißblech n.

tinsel ['tinsəl] Flitter(werk n) m; Lametta n.

tin-smith ['tinsmiθ] Klempner m.

tint [tint] 1. Farbe f; (Farb)Ton m, Schattierung f; 2. färben; (ab-)tönen.

tiny ['taini] winzig, klein.

tip [tip] 1. Spitze f; Mundstück n; Trinkgeld n; Tip m, Wink m; leichter Stoß; Schuttabladeplatz m; 2. mit e-r Spitze versehen; (um-)kippen; j-m ein Trinkgeld geben; a. ~ off j-m e-n Wink geben.

tipple ['tipl] zechen, picheln.

tipsy ['tipsi] angeheitert.

tiptoe ['tiptou] 1. auf Zehenspitzen gehen; 2. on ~ auf Zehenspitzen.

tire¹ ['taiə] (Rad-, Auto)Reifen m.

tire² [~] ermüden, müde machen od. werden; **~d** □ müde; **~less** □ ['taiəlis] unermüdlich; **~some** □ ['taiəsəm] ermüdend; lästig.

tiro ['taiərou] Anfänger m.

tissue ['tisju:; Am. 'tiʃu:] Gewebe n; **~-paper** Seidenpapier n.

tit¹ [tit] = teat.

tit² orn. [~] Meise f.

titbit ['titbit] Leckerbissen m.

titillate ['titileit] kitzeln.

title ['taitl] 1. (Buch-, Ehren)Titel m; Überschrift f; ↄↄ Anspruch m; 2. betiteln; **~d** bsd. ad(e)lig.

titmouse orn. ['titmaus] Meise f.

titter ['titə] 1. kichern; 2. Kichern n.

tittle ['titl] Pünktchen n; fig. Tütelchen n; **~-tattle** [~lætl] Schnickschnack m.

to [tu:; tu, tə] prp. zu (a. adv.); gegen, nach, an, in, auf; bis zu, bis an (acc.); um zu; für; ~ me etc. mir etc.; I weep ~ think of it ich weine, wenn ich daran denke; here's ~ you! auf Ihr Wohl!, Prosit!

toad zo. [toud] Kröte f; **~stool** ['toudstu:l] (größerer Blätter)Pilz; Giftpilz m; **~y** ['toudi] 1. Speichellecker m; 2. fig. vor j-m kriechen.

toast [toust] 1. Toast m, geröstetes Brot; Trinkspruch m; 2. toasten, rösten; fig. wärmen; trinken auf (acc.).

tobacco [tə'bækou] Tabak m; **~nist** [~kənist] Tabakhändler m.

toboggan [tə'bɔgən] 1. Toboggan m; Rodelschlitten m; 2. rodeln.

today [tə'dei] heute.   [teln.]

toddle ['tɔdl] unsicher gehen; zot-]

toddy ['tɔdi] Art Grog m.

to-do F [tə'du:] Lärm m, Aufheben n.

toe [tou] 1. Zehe f; Spitze f; 2. mit den Zehen berühren.

toff|ee, ~y ['tɔfi] Sahnebonbon m, n, Toffee n.

together [tə'geðə] zusammen; zugleich; nacheinander.

toil [tɔil] 1. schwere Arbeit; Mühe f, F Plackerei f; 2. sich plagen.

toilet ['tɔilit] Toilette f; **~-paper** Toilettenpapier n; **~-table** Frisiertoilette f.   [n.]

toils [tɔilz] pl. Schlingen f/pl., Netz]

toilsome □ ['tɔilsəm] mühsam.

token ['toukən] Zeichen n; Andenken n, Geschenk n; ~ money Notgeld n; in ~ of zum Zeichen (gen.).

told [tould] pret. u. p.p. von tell.

tolera|ble □ ['tɔlərəbl] erträglich; **~nce** [~əns] Duldsamkeit f; **~nt** □ [~nt] duldsam (of gegen); **~te** [~reit] dulden; ertragen; **~tion** [tɔlə'reiʃən] Duldung f.

toll [toul] 1. Zoll m (a. fig.); Wege-, Brücken-, Marktgeld n; fig. Tribut m; ~ of the road die Verkehrsopfer n/pl.; 2. läuten; **~-bar** ['toulbɑ:], **~-gate** Schlagbaum m.

tomato ↄ [tə'mɑ:tou, Am. tə'meitou], pl. **~es** Tomate f.

tomb [tu:m] Grab(mal) n.

tomboy ['tɔmbɔi] Range f.

tombstone ['tu:mstoun] Grabstein m.

tom-cat ['tɔm'kæt] Kater m.

tomfool ['tɔm'fu:l] Hansnarr m.

tomorrow [tə'mɔrou] morgen.

ton [tʌn] Tonne f (Gewichtseinheit).

tone [toun] 1. Ton m; Klang m; Laut m; out of ~ verstimmt; 2. e-n Ton geben (dat.); stimmen; paint. abtönen; ~ down (sich) abschwächen, mildern.

tongs [tɔŋz] pl. (a pair of ~ pl. eine) Zange.

tongue [tʌŋ] Zunge f; Sprache f; Landzunge f; (Schuh)Lasche f; hold one's ~ den Mund halten; **~-tied** ['tʌŋtaid] sprachlos; schweigsam; stumm.

tonic ['tɔnik] 1. (~ally) tonisch; ↄↄ stärkend; 2. ♪ Grundton m; ↄↄ Stärkungsmittel n, Tonikum n.

tonight [tə'nait] heute abend od. nacht.

tonnage ↄↄ ['tʌnidʒ] Tonnengehalt m; Lastigkeit f; Tonnengeld n.

tonsil anat. ['tɔnsl] Mandel f; **~litis** ↄↄ [tɔnsi'laitis] Mandelentzündung f.

too [tu:] zu, allzu; auch, noch dazu.

took [tuk] pret. von take 1.

tool [tu:l] Werkzeug n, Gerät n; **~-bag** ['tu:lbæg], **~-kit** Werkzeugtasche f.

toot [tu:t] 1. blasen, tuten; 2. Tuten n.

tooth [tu:θ] pl. teeth [ti:θ] Zahn m; **~ache** ['tu:θeik] Zahnschmerzen pl. **~-brush** Zahnbürste f; **~less** □

['tu:θlis] zahnlos; ~-paste Zahn-
pasta f; ~pick Zahnstocher m;
~some □ ['tu:θsəm] schmackhaft.

top [tɔp] 1. oberstes Ende; Ober-
teil n; Gipfel m (a. fig.); Wipfel m;
Kopf m e-r Seite; mot. Am. Verdeck n; fig. Haupt n, Erste(r) m;
Stiefel-Stulpe f; Kreisel m; at the
~ of one's voice aus voller Kehle;
on ~ obenauf; obendrein; 2. ober(er,
-e, -es); oberst; höchst; 3. oben
bedecken; fig. überragen; vorangehen in (dat.); als erste(r) stehen
auf e-r Liste; ~boots ['tɔp'bu:ts]
pl. Stulpenstiefel m/pl.

toper ['toupə] Zecher m.

tophat F ['tɔp'hæt] Zylinderhut m.

topic ['tɔpik] Gegenstand m, Thema
n; ~al □ [~kəl] lokal; aktuell.

topmost ['tɔpmoust] höchst, oberst.

topple ['tɔpl] (um)kippen.

topsyturvy □ ['tɔpsi'tə:vi] auf den
Kopf gestellt; das Oberste zuunterst; drunter und drüber.

torch [tɔ:tʃ] Fackel f; electric ~
Taschenlampe f; ~light ['tɔ:tʃlait]
Fackelschein m; ~ procession Fak-
kelzug m.

tore [tɔ:] pret. von tear[1]1.

torment 1. ['tɔ:ment] Qual f,
Marter f; 2. [tɔ:'ment] martern,
quälen.

torn [tɔ:n] p.p. von tear[1] 1.

tornado [tɔ:'neidou], pl. ~es Wirbelsturm m, Tornado m.

torpedo [tɔ:'pi:dou], pl. ~es 1. Torpedo m; 2. ✠ torpedieren (a. fig.).

torp|id □ ['tɔ:pid] starr; apathisch;
träg; ~idity [tɔ:'piditi], ~or ['tɔ:pə]
Erstarrung f, Betäubung f.

torrent ['tɔrənt] Sturz~, Gießbach m; (reißender) Strom; ~ial □
[tɔ'renʃəl] gießbachartig; strömend;
fig. ungestüm.

torrid ['tɔrid] brennend heiß.

tortoise zo. ['tɔ:təs] Schildkröte f.

tortuous □ ['tɔ:tjuəs] gewunden.

torture ['tɔ:tʃə] 1. Folter f, Marter f,
Tortur f; 2. foltern, martern.

toss [tɔs] 1. Werfen n, Wurf m;
Zurückwerfen n (Kopf); 2. a.
~ about (sich) hin und her werfen;
schütteln (mit adv.) werfen; a. ~
up hochwerfen; ~ off Getränk hin-
unterstürzen; Arbeit hinhauen; a.
~ up losen (for um); ~-up ['tɔsʌp]
Losen n; fig. etwas Zweifelhaftes.

tot F [tɔt] Knirps m (kleines Kind).

total ['toutl] 1. □ ganz, gänzlich;
total; gesamt; 2. Gesamtbetrag m;
3. sich belaufen auf (acc.); sum-
mieren; ~itarian [toutæli'tɛəriən]
totalitär; ~ity [tou'tæliti] Gesamtheit f.

totter ['tɔtə] wanken, wackeln.

touch [tʌtʃ] 1. (sich) berühren; anrühren, anfassen; stoßen an (acc.);
betreffen; fig. rühren; erreichen; ♪
anschlagen; a bit ~ed fig. ein biß-

chen verrückt; ~ at ✠ anlegen in
(dat.); ~ up auffrischen; retuschieren; 2. Berührung f; Gefühl(s-
sinn m) n; Anflug m, Zug m; Fertigkeit f; ♪ Anschlag m; (Pinsel-)
Strich m; ~-and-go ['tʌtʃən'gou]
gewagte Sache; it is ~ es steht auf
des Messers Schneide; ~ing [~ʃiŋ]
rührend; ~stone Prüfstein m;
~y [~ʃi] empfindlich; heikel.

tough [tʌf] zäh (a. fig.); schwer,
hart; grob, brutal, übel; ~en ['tʌfn]
zäh machen od. werden; ~ness
[~nis] Zähigkeit f.

tour [tuə] 1. (Rund)Reise f, Tour
(-nee) f; conducted ~ Führung f;
Gesellschaftsreise f; 2. (be)reisen;
~ist ['tuərist] Tourist(in); ~ agency,
~ bureau, ~ office Reisebüro n; ~
season Reisezeit f.   [n.]

tournament ['tuənəmənt] Turnier

tousle ['tauzl] (zer)zausen.

tow [tou] 1. Schleppen n; take in
~ ins Schlepptau nehmen; 2. (ab-)
schleppen; treideln; ziehen.

toward(s) [tə'wɔ:d(z)] gegen; nach
... zu, auf ... (acc.) zu; (als Beitrag)
zu.

towel ['tauəl] 1. Handtuch n; 2. abreiben; ~-rack Handtuchhalter m.

tower ['tauə] 1. Turm m; fig. Hort
m, Bollwerk n; 2. sich erheben;
~ing □ ['tauəriŋ] (turm)hoch; rasend (Wut).

town [taun] 1. Stadt f; 2. Stadt...;
städtisch; ~ clerk Stadtsyndikus m;
~ council Stadtrat m (Versammlung); ~ councillor Stadtrat m
(Person); ~ hall Rathaus n; ~sfolk
['taunzfouk] pl. Städter pl.; ~ship
['taunʃip] Stadtgemeinde f; Stadt-
gebiet n; ~sman ['taunzmən]
(Mit)Bürger m; ~speople [~zpi:pl]
pl. = townsfolk.

toxi|c(al □) ['tɔksik(əl)] giftig;
Gift...; ~n [~in] Giftstoff m.

toy [tɔi] 1. Spielzeug n; Tand m;
~s pl. Spielwaren f/pl.; 2. Spiel-
(zeug)...; Miniatur...; Zwerg...;
3. spielen; ~book ['tɔibuk] Bilder-
buch n.

trace [treis] 1. Spur f (a. fig.);
Strang m; 2. nachspüren (dat.); fig.
verfolgen; herausfinden; (auf-)
zeichnen; (durch)pausen.

tracing ['treisiŋ] Pauszeichnung f.

track [træk] 1. Spur f; Sport: Bahn
f; Rennstrecke f; Pfad m; Gleis
n; ~ events pl. Laufdisziplinen f/pl.;
2. nachspüren (dat.); verfolgen; ~
down, ~ out aufspüren.

tract [trækt] Fläche f, Strecke f,
Gegend f; Traktat n, Abhandlung f.

tractable □ ['træktəbl] lenk-, füg-
sam.

tract|ion ['trækʃən] Ziehen n, Zug
m; ~ engine Zugmaschine f; ~or ⊕
[~ktə] Trecker m, Traktor m.

trade [treid] 1. Handel *m*; Gewerbe *n*; Handwerk *n*; *Am.* Kompensationsgeschäft *n*; 2. Handel treiben; handeln; ~ on ausnutzen; ~ **mark** ⚓ Warenzeichen *n*, Schutzmarke *f*; ~ **price** Händlerpreis *m*; ~**r** ['treidə] Händler *m*; ~**sman** [⹁dzmən] Geschäftsmann *m*; ~ **union** Gewerkschaft *f*; ~ **wind** ⚓ Passatwind *m*.

tradition [trə'diʃən] Tradition *f*, Überlieferung *f*; ~**al** □ [⹁nl] traditionell.

traffic ['træfik] 1. Verkehr *m*; Handel *m*; 2. handeln (*in* mit); ~ **jam** Verkehrsstauung *f*; ~ **light** Verkehrsampel *f*.

traged|ian [trə'dʒi:djən] Tragiker *m*; *thea.* Tragöd|e *m*, -in *f*; ~**y** ['trædʒidi] Tragödie *f*.

tragic(al □) ['trædʒik(əl)] tragisch.

trail [treil] 1. *fig.* Schweif *m*; Schleppe *f*; Spur *f*; Pfad *m*; 2. *v/t.* hinter sich (her)ziehen; verfolgen; *v/i.* (sich) schleppen; ⚓ kriechen; ~ **blazer** *Am.* Bahnbrecher *m*; ~**er** ['treilə] (Wohnwagen)Anhänger *m*; ⚓ Kriechpflanze *f*; *Film:* Vorschau *f*.

train [trein] 1. (Eisenbahn)Zug *m*; *allg.* Zug *m*; Gefolge *n*; Reihe *f*, Folge *f*, Kette *f*; Schleppe *f* am *Kleid*; 2. erziehen; schulen; abrichten; ausbilden; trainieren; (sich) üben; ~**ee** [trei'ni:] in der Ausbildung Begriffene(r) *m*; ~**er** ['treinə] Ausbilder *m*; Trainer *m*.

trait [trei] (Charakter)Zug *m*.

traitor ['treitə] Verräter *m*.

tram [træm] *s.* ~*-car*, ~*way*; ~**-car** ['træmka:] Straßenbahnwagen *m*.

tramp [træmp] 1. Getrampel *n*; Wanderung *f*; Tramp *m*, Landstreicher *m*; 2. trampeln, treten; (durch)wandern; ~**le** ['træmpl] (zer)trampeln.

tramway ['træmwei] Straßenbahn *f*.

trance [trɑ:ns] Trance *f*.

tranquil □ ['træŋkwil] ruhig; gelassen; ~**(l)ity** [træŋ'kwiliti] Ruhe *f*; Gelassenheit *f*; ~**(l)ize** ['træŋkwilaiz] beruhigen; ~**(l)izer** [⹁zə] Beruhigungsmittel *n*.

transact [træn'zækt] abwickeln, abmachen; ~**ion** [⹁kʃən] Verrichtung *f*; Geschäft *n*, Transaktion *f*; ~**s** *pl.* (Tätigkeits)Bericht(e *pl.*) *m*.

transalpine ['trænz'ælpain] transalpin(isch).

transatlantic ['trænzət'læntik] transatlantisch, Transatlantik...

transcend [træn'send] überschreiten, übertreffen; hinausgehen über (*acc.*); ~**ence**, ~**ency** [⹁dəns, ⹁si] Überlegenheit *f*; *phls.* Transzendenz *f*.

transcribe [træns'kraib] abschreiben; *Kurzschrift* übertragen.

transcript ['trænskript], ~**ion**

[træns'kripʃən] Abschrift *f*; Umschrift *f*.

transfer 1. [træns'fə:] *v/t.* übertragen; versetzen, verlegen; *v/i.* übertreten; *Am.* umsteigen; 2. ['trænsfə(:)] Übertragung *f*; ⚓ Transfer *m*; Versetzung *f*, Verlegung *f*; *Am.* Umsteigefahrschein *m*; ~**able** [træns'fə:rəbl] übertragbar.

transfigure [træns'figə] umgestalten; verklären.

transfix [træns'fiks] durchstechen; ~**ed** *fig.* versteinert, starr (*with* vor *dat.*).

transform [træns'fɔ:m] umformen; um-, verwandeln; ~**ation** [trænsfə'meiʃən] Umformung *f*; Um-, Verwandlung *f*.

transfus|e [træns'fju:z] ⚕ *Blut etc.* übertragen; *fig.* einflößen; *fig.* durchtränken; ~**ion** [⹁u:ʒən] (*bsd.* ⚕ Blut)Übertragung *f*, Transfusion *f*.

transgress [træns'gres] *v/t.* überschreiten; übertreten, verletzen; *v/i.* sich vergehen; ~**ion** [⹁eʃən] Überschreitung *f*; Übertretung *f*; Vergehen *n*; ~**or** [⹁esə] Übertreter *m*.

transient ['trænziənt] 1. = *transitory*; 2. *Am.* Durchreisende(r *m*) *f*.

transit ['trænsit] Durchgang *m*; Durchgangsverkehr *m*.

transition [træn'siʒən] Übergang *m*.

transitive □ *gr.* ['trænsitiv] transitiv.

transitory □ ['trænsitəri] vorübergehend; vergänglich, flüchtig.

translat|e [træns'leit] übersetzen, übertragen; überführen; *fig.* umsetzen; ~**ion** [⹁eiʃən] Übersetzung *f*, Übertragung *f*; *fig.* Auslegung *f*; ~**or** [⹁eitə] Übersetzer(in).

translucent [trænz'lu:snt] durchscheinend; *fig.* hell.

transmigration [trænzmai'greiʃən] (Aus)Wanderung *f*; Seelenwanderung *f*.

transmission [trænz'miʃən] Übermittlung *f*; *biol.* Vererbung *f*; *phys.* Fortpflanzung *f*; *mot.* Getriebe *n*; *Radio:* Sendung *f*.

transmit [trænz'mit] übermitteln, übersenden; übertragen; senden; *biol.* vererben; *phys.* fortpflanzen; ~**ter** [⹁tə] Übermittler(in); *tel. etc.* Sender *m*.

transmute [trænz'mju:t] um-, verwandeln.

transparent □ [træns'pɛərənt] durchsichtig (*a. fig.*).

transpire [træns'paiə] ausdünsten, ausschwitzen; *fig.* durchsickern.

transplant [træns'plɑ:nt] um-, verpflanzen; ~**ation** [trænsplɑ:n'teiʃən] Verpflanzung *f*.

transport 1. [træns'pɔ:t] fortschaffen, befördern, transportieren; *fig.* hinreißen; 2. ['trænspɔ:t] Fortschaffen n; Beförderung f; Transport m; Verkehr m; Beförderungsmittel n; Transportschiff n; Verzückung f; be in ~s außer sich sein; **~ation** [trænspɔ:'teiʃən] Beförderung f, Transport m.

transpose [træns'pouz] versetzen, umstellen; ♪ transponieren.

transverse □ ['trænzvɔ:s] quer laufend; Quer...

trap [træp] 1. Falle f (a. fig.); Klappe f; 2. (in e-r Falle) fangen, in die Falle locken; fig. ertappen; **~door** ['træpdɔ:] Falltür f; thea. Versenkung f.

trapeze [trə'pi:z] Zirkus: Trapez n.

trapper ['træpə] Trapper m, Fallensteller m, Pelzjäger m.

trappings fig. ['træpiŋz] pl. Schmuck m, Putz m.

traps F [træps] pl. Siebensachen pl.

trash [træʃ] Abfall m; fig. Plunder m; Unsinn m, F Blech n; Kitsch m; **~y** □ ['træʃi] wertlos, kitschig.

travel ['trævl] 1. v/i. reisen; sich bewegen; wandern; v/t. bereisen; 2. das Reisen; ⊕ Lauf m; **~s** pl. Reisen f/pl.; **~(l)er** [~lə] Reisende(r) m; **~'s cheque** (Am. check) Reisescheck m.

traverse ['trævə(:)s] 1. Durchquerung f; 2. (über)queren; durchqueren; fig. durchkreuzen.

travesty ['trævisti] 1. Travestie f, Karikatur f; 2. travestieren; verulken.

trawl [trɔ:l] 1. (Grund)Schleppnetz n; 2. mit dem Schleppnetz fischen; **~er** ['trɔ:lə] Trawler m.

tray [trei] (Servier)Brett n, Tablett n; Ablage f; pen~ Federschale f.

treacherous □ ['tretʃərəs] verräterisch, treulos; (heim)tückisch, trügerisch; **~y** [~ri] Verrat m, Verräterei f, Treulosigkeit f; Tücke f.

treacle ['tri:kl] Sirup m.

tread [tred] 1. [irr.] treten; schreiten; 2. Tritt m, Schritt m; Lauffläche f; **~le** ['tredl] Pedal n; Tritt m; **~mill** Tretmühle f.

treason ['tri:zn] Verrat m; **~able** □ [~nəbl] verräterisch.

treasure ['treʒə] 1. Schatz m, Reichtum m; ~ trove Schatzfund m; 2. Schätze sammeln, aufhäufen; **~r** [~ərə] Schatzmeister m, Kassenwart m.

treasury ['treʒəri] Schatzkammer f; (bsd. Staats)Schatz m; ♀ **Bench** parl. Ministerbank f; ♀ **Board**, Am. ♀ **Department** Finanzministerium n.

treat [tri:t] 1. v/t. behandeln; betrachten; ~ s.o. to s.th. j-m et. spendieren; v/i. ~ of handeln von; ~ with unterhandeln mit; 2. Vergnügen n; school ~ Schulausflug m; it is my ~ F es geht auf meine Rechnung; **~ise** ['tri:tiz] Abhandlung f;

~ment [~tmənt] Behandlung f, ⚕ Kur f; follow-up ~ ⚕ Nachkur f; **~y** [~ti] Vertrag m.

treble ['trebl] 1. □ dreifach; 2. Dreifache(s) n; ♪ Diskant m, Sopran m; 3. (sich) verdreifachen.

tree [tri:] Baum m.

trefoil ♣ ['trefɔil] Klee m.

trellis ['trelis] 1. ✗ Spalier n; 2. vergittern; ✗ am Spalier ziehen.

tremble ['trembl] zittern.

tremendous □ [tri'mendəs] schrecklich, furchtbar; F kolossal, riesig.

tremor ['tremə] Zittern n, Beben n.

tremulous □ ['tremjuləs] zitternd, bebend.

trench [trentʃ] 1. (Schützen)Graben m; Furche f; 2. v/t. mit Gräben durchziehen; ✗ umgraben; ~ (up)on eingreifen in (acc.); **~ant** □ ['trentʃənt] scharf.

trend [trend] 1. Richtung f; fig. Lauf m; fig. Strömung f; Tendenz f; 2. sich erstrecken, laufen.

trepidation [trepi'deiʃən] Zittern n, Beben n; Bestürzung f.

trespass ['trespəs] 1. Übertretung f; 2. unbefugt eindringen (on, upon in acc.); über Gebühr in Anspruch nehmen; **~er** ⚖ [~sə] Rechtsverletzer m; Unbefugte(r m) f.

tress [tres] Haarlocke f, -flechte f.

trestle ['tresl] Gestell n, Bock m.

trial ['traiəl] Versuch m; Probe f, Prüfung f (a. fig.); Plage f; ⚖ Verhandlung f, Prozeß m; on ~ auf Probe; vor Gericht; give s.o. a ~ es mit j-m versuchen; **~ run** Probefahrt f.

triangle ['traiæŋgl] Dreieck n; **~ular** □ [trai'æŋgjulə] dreieckig.

tribe [traib] Stamm m; Geschlecht n; contp. Sippe f; ♀, zo. Klasse f.

tribunal [trai'bju:nl] Richterstuhl m; Gericht(shof m) n; **~e** [~'tribju:n] Tribun m; Tribüne f.

tributary ['tribjutəri] 1. □ zinspflichtig; fig. helfend; Neben...; 2. Nebenfluß m; **~e** [~ju:t] Tribut m (a. fig.), Zins m; Anerkennung f.

trice [trais]: in a ~ im Nu.

trick [trik] 1. Kniff m, List f, Trick m; Kunstgriff m, -stück n; Streich m; Eigenheit f; 2. betrügen; herausputzen; **~ery** ['trikəri] Betrügerei f.

trickle ['trikl] tröpfeln, rieseln.

trickster ['trikstə] Gauner m; **~y** □ [~ki] verschlagen; F heikel; verzwickt, verwickelt, schwierig.

tricycle ['traisikl] Dreirad n.

trident ['traidənt] Dreizack m.

trifle ['traifl] 1. Kleinigkeit f; Lappalie f; a ~ ein bißchen, ein wenig, etwas; 2. v/i. spielen, spaßen; v/t. ~ away verschwenden; **~ing** □ [~liŋ] geringfügig; unbedeutend.

trig [trig] 1. hemmen; 2. schmuck.

trigger ['trigə] Abzug *m am Gewehr*; *phot.* Auslöser *m*.

trill [tril] 1. Triller *m*; gerolltes R; 2. trillern; *bsd.* das R rollen.

trillion ['triljən] Trillion *f*; *Am.* Billion *f*.

trim [trim] 1. □ ordentlich; schmuck; gepflegt; 2. (richtiger) Zustand; Ordnung *f*; 3. zurechtmachen; (~ *up* aus)putzen, schmükken; besetzen; stutzen; beschneiden; ⚓, ⚒ trimmen; **~ming** ['trimiŋ] *mst* **~s** *pl.* Besatz *m*, Garnierung *f*.

Trinity *eccl.* ['triniti] Dreieinigkeit *f*.

trinket ['triŋkit] wertloses Schmuckstück; **~s** *pl.* F Kinkerlitzchen *pl.*

trip [trip] 1. Reise *f*, Fahrt *f*; Ausflug *m*, Spriztour *f*; Stolpern *n*, Fallen *n*; Fehltritt *m* (*a. fig.*); *fig.* Versehen *n*, Fehler *m*; 2. *v/i.* trippeln; stolpern; e-n Fehltritt tun (*a. fig.*); *fig.* e-n Fehler machen; *v/t.* *a.* ~ *up* j-m ein Bein stellen (*a. fig.*).

tripartite ['trai'pa:tait] dreiteilig.

tripe [traip] Kaldaunen *f/pl.*

triple □ ['tripl] dreifach; **~ts** [~lits] *pl.* Drillinge *m/pl.*

triplicate 1. ['triplikit] dreifach; 2. [~keit] verdreifachen.

tripod ['traipɔd] Dreifuß *m*; *phot.* Stativ *n*.

tripper F ['tripə] Ausflügler(in).

trite □ [trait] abgedroschen, platt.

triturate ['tritjureit] zerreiben.

triumph ['traiəmf] 1. Triumph *m*, Sieg *m*; 2. triumphieren; **~al** [trai'amfəl] Sieges..., Triumph...; **~ant** □ [~ənt] triumphierend.

trivial □ ['triviəl] bedeutungslos; unbedeutend; trivial; alltäglich.

trod [trɔd] *pret. von* tread 1; **~den** ['trɔdn] *p.p. von* tread 1.

troll [troul] (vor sich hin)trällern.

troll(e)y ['trɔli] Karren *m*; Draisine *f*; Servierwagen *m*; ⚡ Kontaktrolle *f* *e-s Oberleitungsfahrzeugs*; *Am.* Straßenbahnwagen *m*; **~bus** O(berleitungs)bus *m*. [Hure *f*.]

trollop ['trɔləp] F Schlampe *f*.

trombone ♪ [trɔm'boun] Posaune *f*.

troop [tru:p] 1. Truppe *f*; Schar *f*; ✕ (Reiter)Zug *m*; 2. sich scharen, sich sammeln; ~ *away*, ~ *off* abziehen; ~*ing the colour(s)* ✕ Fahnenparade *f*; **~er** ✕ ['tru:pə] Kavallerist *m*.

trophy ['troufi] Trophäe *f*.

tropic ['trɔpik] Wendekreis *m*; **~s** *pl.* Tropen *pl.*; **~al** □ [~k(ə)l] tropisch.

trot [trɔt] 1. Trott *m*, Trab *m*; 2. traben (lassen).

trouble ['trʌbl] 1. Unruhe *f*; Störung *f*; Kummer *m*, Not *f*; Mühe *f*; Plage *f*; Unannehmlichkeiten *f/pl.*; *ask od.* look for ~ sich (selbst) Schwierigkeiten machen; das Schicksal herausfordern; *take* (*the*) ~ sich (die) Mühe machen; 2. stören, beunruhigen, belästigen; quälen, plagen; Mühe machen (*dat.*); (sich) bemühen; ~ *s.o. for* j-n bemühen um; **~man**, **~shooter** *Am.* F Störungssucher *m*; **~some** □ [~lsəm] beschwerlich, lästig.

trough [trɔf] (Futter)Trog *m*; Backtrog *m*, Mulde *f*.

trounce F [trauns] j-n verhauen.

troupe *thea.* [tru:p] Truppe *f*.

trousers ['trauzəz] *pl.* (*a pair of* ~ *pl.* eine) (lange) Hose; Hosen *f/pl.*

trousseau ['tru:sou] Aussteuer *f*.

trout *ichth.* [traut] Forelle(n *pl.*) *f*.

trowel ['trauəl] Maurerkelle *f*.

truant ['tru(:)ənt] 1. müßig; 2. Schulschwänzer *m*; *fig.* Bummler *m*.

truce [tru:s] Waffenstillstand *m*.

truck [trʌk] 1. (offener) Güterwagen; Last(kraft)wagen *m*, Lkw *m*; Transportkarren *m*; Tausch (-handel) *m*; Verkehr *m*; Naturallohnsystem *n*; *Am.* Gemüse *n*; 2. (ver)tauschen; **~farm** *Am.* ['trʌkfa:m] Gemüsegärtnerei *f*.

truckle ['trʌkl] zu Kreuze kriechen.

truculent □ ['trʌkjulənt] wild, roh.

trudge [trʌdʒ] wandern; sich (dahin)schleppen, mühsam gehen.

true [tru:] wahr; echt, wirklich; treu; genau; richtig; *it is* ~ gewiß, freilich, zwar; *come* ~ sich bewahrheiten; in Erfüllung gehen; ~ *to nature* naturgetreu.

truism ['tru(:)izəm] Binsenwahrheit *f*.

truly ['tru:li] wirklich; wahrhaft; aufrichtig; genau; treu; *Yours* ~ Hochachtungsvoll.

trump [trʌmp] 1. Trumpf *m*; 2. (über)trumpfen; ~ *up* erdichten; **~ery** ['trʌmpəri] Plunder *m*.

trumpet ['trʌmpit] 1. Trompete *f*; 2. trompeten; *fig.* ausposaunen.

truncheon ['trʌntʃən] (Polizei-) Knüppel *m*; Kommandostab *m*.

trundle ['trʌndl] rollen.

trunk [trʌŋk] (Baum)Stamm *m*; Rumpf *m*; Rüssel *m*; *großer* Koffer; **~call** *teleph.* ['trʌŋkkɔ:l] Ferngespräch *n*; **~exchange** *teleph.* Fernamt *n*; **~line** ⚡ Hauptlinie *f*; *teleph.* Fernleitung *f*; **~s** [trʌŋks] *pl.* Turnhose *f*; Badehose *f*; Herrenunterhose *f*.

trunnion ⊕ ['trʌnjən] Zapfen *m*.

truss [trʌs] 1. Bündel *n*, Bund *n*; ⚕ Bruchband *n*; △ Binder *m*, Gerüst *n*; 2. (zs.-)binden; △ stützen.

trust [trʌst] 1. Vertrauen *n*; Glaube *m*; Kredit *m*; Pfand *n*; Verwahrung *f*; ⚖ Treuhand *f*; ✝ Ring *m*, Trust *m*; **~company** Treuhandgesellschaft *f*; *in* ~ zu treuen Händen; 2. *v/t.* (ver)trauen (*dat.*); anvertrauen, übergeben (*s.o. with s.th.*, *s.th. to s.o.* j-m et.); zuversichtlich hoffen;

v/i. vertrauen (*in,* to auf *acc.*); **~ee** [trʌs'tiː] Sach-, Verwalter *m*; ‡‡ Treuhänder *m*; **~ful** □ ['trʌstful], **~ing** □ [~tiŋ] vertrauensvoll; **~worthy** [~twɔːði] vertrauenswürdig; zuverlässig.

truth [truːθ], *pl.* **~s** [truːðz] Wahrheit *f*; Wirklichkeit *f*; Wahrhaftigkeit *f*; Genauigkeit *f*; **~ful** □ ['truːθful] wahrhaft(ig).

try [trai] 1. versuchen; probieren; prüfen; ‡‡ verhandeln über *et. od.* gegen *j-n*; vor Gericht stellen; aburteilen; *die Augen etc.* angreifen; sich bemühen *od.* bewerben; **~** on *Kleid* anprobieren; 2. Versuch *m*; **~ing** □ ['traiiŋ] anstrengend; kritisch.

Tsar [zɑː] Zar *m*.

T-shirt ['tiːʃəːt] kurzärmeliges Sporthemd.

tub [tʌb] 1. Faß *n*, Zuber *m*; Kübel *m*; Badewanne *f*; F (Wannen)Bad *n*.

tube [tjuːb] Rohr *n*; (*Am. bsd.* Radio)Röhre *f*; Tube *f*; (Luft-) Schlauch *m*; Tunnel *m*; F (Londoner) Untergrundbahn *f*.

tuber ♀ ['tjuːbə] Knolle *f*; **~culosis** [tju(ː)bəːkjuˈlousis] Tuberkulose *f*.

tubular □ ['tjuːbjulə] röhrenförmig.

tuck [tʌk] 1. Falte *f*; Abnäher *m*; 2. ab-, aufnähen; packen, stecken; **~** *up* hochschürzen, aufkrempeln; *in e-e Decke etc.* einwickeln.

Tuesday ['tjuːzdi] Dienstag *m*.

tuft [tʌft] Büschel *n*, Busch *m*; (Haar)Schopf *m*.

tug [tʌg] 1. Zug *m*, Ruck *m*; ⚓ Schlepper *m*; *fig.* Anstrengung *f*; 2. ziehen, zerren; ⚓ schleppen; sich mühen.

tuition [tju(ː)ˈiʃən] Unterricht *m*; Schulgeld *n*.

tulip ♀ ['tjuːlip] Tulpe *f*.

tumble ['tʌmbl] 1. *v/i.* fallen, purzeln; taumeln; sich wälzen; *v/t.* werfen; zerknüllen; 2. Sturz *m*; Wirrwarr *m*; **~down** baufällig; **~r** [~lə] Becher *m*; *orn.* Tümmler *m*.

tumid □ ['tjuːmid] geschwollen.

tummy F ['tʌmi] Bäuchlein *n*, Magen *m*.

tumo(u)r ♀ ['tjuːmə] Tumor *m*.

tumult ['tjuːmʌlt] Tumult *m*; **~uous** □ [tju(ː)ˈmʌltjuəs] stürmisch.

tun [tʌn] Tonne *f*, Faß *n*.

tuna *ichth.* ['tuːnə] Thunfisch *m*.

tune [tjuːn] 1. Melodie *f*, Weise *f*; ♩ Stimmung *f* (*a. fig.*); *in* **~** (gut-) gestimmt; *out of* **~** verstimmt; 2. stimmen (*a. fig.*); **~** *in Radio:* einstellen; **~** *out Radio:* ausschalten; **~** *up* die Instrumente stimmen; *fig. Befinden etc.* heben; *mot.* die Leistung erhöhen; **~ful** □ ['tjuːnful] melodisch; **~less** □ [~nlis] unmelodisch.

tunnel ['tʌnl] 1. Tunnel *m*; ⚒

Stollen *m*; 2. e-n Tunnel bohren (durch).

tunny *ichth.* ['tʌni] Thunfisch *m*.

turbid ['təːbid] trüb; dick.

turb|ine ⊕ ['təːbin] Turbine *f*; **~o-jet** ['təːbouˈdʒet] Strahlturbine *f*; **~o-prop** [~ouˈprɔp] Propellerturbine *f*.

turbot *ichth.* ['təːbət] Steinbutt *m*.

turbulent □ ['təːbjulənt] unruhig; ungestüm; stürmisch, turbulent.

tureen [təˈriːn] Terrine *f*.

turf [təːf] 1. Rasen *m*; Torf *m*; Rennbahn *f*; Rennsport *m*; 2. mit Rasen bedecken; **~y** ['təːfi] rasenbedeckt.

turgid □ ['təːdʒid] geschwollen.

Turk [təːk] Türk|e *m*, -in *f*.

turkey ['təːki] *orn.* Truthahn *m*, -henne *f*, Pute(r *m*) *f*; *Am. sl. thea.: Film:* Pleite *f*, Versager *m*.

Turkish ['təːkiʃ] türkisch.

turmoil ['təːmɔil] Aufruhr *m*, Unruhe *f*; Durcheinander *n*.

turn [təːn] 1. *v/t.* drehen; (um)wenden, umkehren; lenken; verwandeln; abbringen; abwehren; übertragen; bilden; drechseln; verrückt machen; **~** *a corner* um eine Ecke biegen; **~** *s.o. against* j-n aufhetzen gegen; **~** *aside* abwenden; **~** *away* abwenden; abweisen; **~** *down* biegen; *Gas etc.* kleinstellen; *Decke etc.* zurückschlagen; ablehnen; **~** *off* (on) ab-/andrehen, ab- (ein)schalten; **~** *out* hinauswerfen; *Fabrikat* herausbringen; *Gas etc.* ausdrehen; **~** *over* umwenden; *fig.* übertragen; ✝ umsetzen; überlegen; **~** *up* nach oben richten; hochklappen; umwenden; *Hose etc.* auf-, umschlagen; *Gas etc.* aufdrehen; *v/i.* sich (um)drehen; sich wenden; sich verwandeln; umschlagen (*Wetter etc.*); *Christ, grau etc.* werden; *a.* **~** *sour* sauer werden (*Milch*); **~** *about* sich umdrehen; ⚔ kehrtmachen; **~** *back* zurückkehren; **~** *in* einkehren; F zu Bett gehen; **~** *off* abbiegen; **~** *on* sich drehen um; **~** *out* ausfallen; ausgehen; sich herausstellen als; **~** *to* sich zuwenden (*dat.*), sich wenden an (*acc.*); werden zu; **~** *up* auftauchen; **~** *upon* sich wenden gegen; 2. (Um)Drehung *f*; Biegung *f*; Wendung *f*; Neigung *f*; Wechsel *m*; Gestalt *f*, Form *f*; Spaziergang *m*; Reihe(nfolge) *f*; Dienst(leistung *f*) *m*; F Schreck *m*; *at every* **~** auf Schritt und Tritt; *by od. in* **~s** der Reihe nach, abwechselnd; *it is my* **~** ich bin an der Reihe; *take* **~s** mit-ea. abwechseln; *does it serve your* **~?** entspricht das Ihren Zwecken?; **~coat** ['təːnkout] Abtrünnige(r) *m*; **~er** ['təːnə] Drechsler *m*; ~ery [~əri] Drechslerei *f*; Drechslerarbeit *f*.

turning ['tə:niŋ] Drechseln *n*; Wendung *f*; Biegung *f*; Straßenecke *f*; (Weg)Abzweigung *f*; Querstraße *f*; ~-point *fig.* Wendepunkt *m*.

turnip ♀ ['tə:nip] (*bsd.* weiße) Rübe.

turn|key ['tə:nki:] Schließer *m*; ~out ['tə:n'aut] Ausstaffierung *f*; Arbeitseinstellung *f*; † Gesamtproduktion *f*; ~over ['tə:nouvə] † Umsatz *m*; Verschiebung *f*; ~pike Schlagbaum *m*; (gebührenpflichtige) Schnellstraße; ~stile Drehkreuz *n*. [pentin *n*.]

turpentine 🜋 ['tə:pəntain] Ter-/

turpitude ['tə:pitju:d] Schändlichkeit *f*.

turret ['tʌrit] Türmchen *n*; ✂ ⚓ Panzerturm *m*; ⚔ Kanzel *f*.

turtle ['tə:tl] *zo.* Schildkröte *f*; *orn.* *mst* ~-dove Turteltaube *f*.

tusk [tʌsk] Fangzahn *m*; Stoßzahn *m*; Hauer *m*.

tussie ['tʌsl] 1. Rauferei *f*, Balgerei *f*; 2. raufen, sich balgen.

tussock ['tʌsək] Büschel *n*.

tut [tʌt] ach was!; Unsinn!

tutelage ['tju:tilidʒ] ⚖ Vormundschaft *f*; Bevormundung *f*.

tutor ['tju:tə] 1. (Privat-, Haus-) Lehrer *m*; *univ.* Tutor *m*; *Am.univ.* Assistent *m* mit Lehrauftrag; ⚖ Vormund *m*; 2. unterrichten; schulen, erziehen; *fig.* beherrschen; ~ial [tju(:)'tɔ:riəl] *univ.* Unterrichtsstunde *f* e-s Tutors; *attr.* Lehrer...; Tutoren...

tuxedo *Am.* [tʌk'si:dou] Smoking *m*.

TV ['ti:'vi:] Fernsehen *n*; Fernsehapparat *m*; *attr.* Fernseh...

twaddle ['twɔdl] 1. Geschwätz *n*; 2. schwatzen, quatschen.

twang [twæŋ] 1. Schwirren *n*; *mst nasal* ~ näselnde Aussprache; 2. schwirren (lassen); klimpern; näseln.

tweak [twi:k] zwicken.

tweet [twi:t] zwitschern.

tweezers ['twi:zəz] *pl.* (*a pair of* ~ *pl.* eine) Pinzette.

twelfth [twelfθ] 1. zwölfte(r, -s); 2. Zwölftel *n*; Ջ-night ['twelfθnait] Dreikönigsabend *m*.

twelve [twelv] zwölf.

twent|ieth ['twentiiθ] 1. zwanzigste(r, -s); 2. Zwanzigstel *n*; ~y [~ti] zwanzig.

twice [twais] zweimal.

twiddle ['twidl] (sich) drehen; mit *et.* spielen.

twig [twig] Zweig *m*, Rute *f*.

twilight ['twailait] Zwielicht *n*; Dämmerung *f* (*a. fig.*).

twin [twin] 1. Zwillings...; doppelt; 2. Zwilling *m*; ~-engined ⚔ ['twinendʒind] zweimotorig.

twine [twain] 1. Bindfaden *m*,

Schnur *f*; Zwirn *m*; 2. zs.-drehen; verflechten; (sich) schlingen *od.* winden; umschlingen, umranken.

twinge [twindʒ] Zwicken *n*; Stich *m*; bohrender Schmerz.

twinkle ['twiŋkl] 1. funkeln, blitzen; huschen; zwinkern; 2. Funkeln *n*, Blitzen *n*; (Augen)Zwinkern *n*, Blinzeln *n*.

twirl [twə:l] 1. Wirbel *m*; 2. wirbeln.

twist [twist] 1. Drehung *f*; Windung *f*; Verdrehung *f*; Verdrehtheit *f*; Neigung *f*; (Gesichts)Verzerrung *f*; Garn *n*; Kringel *m*, Zopf *m* (*Backwaren*); 2. (sich) drehen *od.* winden; zs.-drehen; verdrehen, verzerren.

twit *fig.* [twit] *j-n* aufziehen.

twitch [twitʃ] 1. zupfen (an *dat.*); zucken; 2. Zupfen *n*; Zuckung *f*.

twitter ['twitə] 1. zwitschern; 2. Gezwitscher *n*; be in *a* ~ zittern.

two [tu:] 1. zwei; in ~ entzwei; *put* ~ *and* ~ *together* sich et. zs.-reimen; 2. Zwei *f*; in ~s zu zweien; ~bit *Am.* F ['tu:'bit] 25-Cent...; *fig.* unbedeutend, Klein...; ~edged ['tu:'edʒd] zweischneidig; ~fold ['tu:fould] zweifach; ~pence ['tʌpəns] zwei Pence; ~penny ['tʌpni] zwei Pence wert; ~piece ['tu:pi:s] zweiteilig; ~seater *mot.* ['tu:'si:tə] Zweisitzer *m*; ~storey ['tu:stɔ:ri], ~storied zweistöckig; ~stroke *mot.* Zweitakt...; ~way Doppel...; ~ *adapter* ⚡ Doppelstecker *m*; ~ *traffic* Gegenverkehr *m*.

tycoon *Am.* F [tai'ku:n] Industriekapitän *m*, Industriemagnat *m*.

tyke [taik] Köter *m*; Kerl *m*.

type [taip] Typ *m*; Urbild *n*; Vorbild *n*; Muster *n*; Art *f*; Sinnbild *n*; *typ.* Type *f*, Buchstabe *m*; *true to* ~ artecht; *set in* ~ setzen; ~write ['taiprait] [*irr.* (write)] (mit der) Schreibmaschine schreiben; ~writer Schreibmaschine *f*; ~ *ribbon* Farbband *n*.

typhoid ['taifoid] 1. typhös; ~ *fever* = 2. (Unterleibs)Typhus *m*.

typhoon [tai'fu:n] Taifun *m*.

typhus ⚕ ['taifəs] Flecktyphus *m*.

typi|cal □ ['tipikəl] typisch; richtig; bezeichnend, kennzeichnend; ~fy [~ifai] typisch sein für; versinnbildlichen; ~st ['taipist] *a.* shorthand ~ Stenotypistin *f*.

tyrann|ic(al □) [ti'rænik(əl)] tyrannisch; ~ize ['tirənaiz] tyrannisieren; ~y [~ni] Tyrannei *f*.

tyrant ['taiərənt] Tyrann(in).

tyre ['taiə] s. tire 1.

tyro ['taiərou] s. tiro.

Tyrolese [tirə'li:z] 1. Tiroler(in); 2. tirolisch, Tiroler...

Tzar [za:] Zar *m*...

U

ubiquitous □ [ju(:)'bikwitəs] allgegenwärtig, überall zu finden(d).

udder ['Adə] Euter *n*.

ugly □ ['Agli] häßlich; schlimm.

ulcer ⚕ ['Alsə] Geschwür *n*; (Eiter-)Beule *f*; ~ate ⚕ [~reit] eitern (lassen); ~ous ⚕ [~rəs] geschwürig.

ulterior □ [Al'tiəriə] jenseitig; *fig.* weiter; tiefer liegend, versteckt.

ultimate □ ['Altimit] letzt; endlich; End...; ~ly [~tli] zu guter Letzt.

ultimat|um [Alti'meitəm], *pl. a.* ~a [~tə] Ultimatum *n*.

ultimo † ['Altimou] vorigen Monats.

ultra ['Altrə] übermäßig; Ultra..., ultra...; ~fashionable ['Altrə'fæʃənəbl] hypermodern; ~modern hypermodern.

umbel ♀ ['Ambəl] Dolde *f*.

umbrage ['Ambridʒ] Anstoß *m* (*Ärger*); Schatten *m*.

umbrella [Am'brelə] Regenschirm *m*; *fig.* Schirm *m*, Schutz *m*; ✕ Abschirmung *f*.

umpire ['Ampaiə] 1. Schiedsrichter *m*; 2. Schiedsrichter sein.

un... [An] un...; Un...; ent...; nicht...

unabashed ['Anə'bæʃt] unverfroren; unerschrocken.

unabated ['Anə'beitid] unvermindert.   [stande.)

unable ['An'eibl] unfähig, außer-)

unaccommodating ['Anə'kɔmədeitiŋ] unnachgiebig.

unaccountable □ ['Anə'kauntəbl] unerklärlich; seltsam; nicht zur Rechenschaft verpflichtet.

unaccustomed ['Anə'kʌstəmd] ungewohnt; ungewöhnlich.

unacquainted ['Anə'kweintid]: ~ with unbekannt mit; *e-r S* unkundig.

unadvised □ ['Anəd'vaizd] unbedacht; unberaten.

unaffected □ ['Anə'fektid] unberührt; ungerührt; ungekünstelt.

unaided ['An'eidid] ohne Unterstützung; (ganz) allein; bloß (*Auge*).

unalter|able □ [An'ɔ:ltərəbl] unveränderlich; ~ed ['An'ɔ:ltəd] unverändert.

unanim|ity [ju:nə'nimiti] Einmütigkeit *f*; ~ous □ [ju(:)'næniməs] einmütig, einstimmig.

unanswer|able □ [An'ɑ:nsərəbl] unwiderleglich; ~ed ['An'ɑ:nsəd] unbeantwortet.

unapproachable □ [Anə'proutʃəbl] unzugänglich.

unapt □ [An'æpt] ungeeignet.

unashamed □ ['Anə'ʃeimd] schamlos.

unasked ['An'ɑ:skt] unverlangt; ungebeten.

unassisted □ ['Anə'sistid] ohne Hilfe *od.* Unterstützung.

unassuming □ ['Anə'sju:miŋ] anspruchslos, bescheiden.

unattached ['Anə'tætʃt] nicht gebunden; ungebunden, ledig, frei.

unattractive □ ['Anə'træktiv] wenig anziehend, reizlos, uninteressant.

unauthorized ['An'ɔ:θəraizd] unberechtigt, unbefugt.

unavail|able ['Anə'veiləbl] nicht verfügbar; ~ing [~liŋ] vergeblich.

unavoidable □ [Anə'vɔidəbl] unvermeidlich.

unaware ['Anə'wɛə] ohne Kenntnis; *be ~ of et.* nicht merken; ~s [~ɛəz] unversehens, unvermutet; versehentlich.

unbacked ['An'bækt] ohne Unterstützung; ungedeckt (*Scheck*).

unbag ['An'bæg] aus dem Sack holen *od.* lassen.

unbalanced ['An'bælənst] nicht im Gleichgewicht befindlich; unausgeglichen; geistesgestört.

unbearable □ [An'bɛərəbl] unerträglich.

unbeaten ['An'bi:tn] ungeschlagen; unbetreten (*Weg*).

unbecoming □ ['Anbi'kʌmiŋ] unkleidsam; unpassend, unschicklich.

unbeknown F ['Anbi'noun] unbekannt.

unbelie|f ['Anbi'li:f] Unglaube *m*; ~vable □ [Anbi'li:vəbl] unglaublich; ~ving □ ['Anbi'li:viŋ] ungläubig.

unbend ['An'bend] [*irr. (bend)*] (sich) entspannen; freundlich werden, auftauen; ~ing □ [~diŋ] unbiegsam; *fig.* unbeugsam.

unbias(s)ed □ ['An'baiəst] vorurteilsfrei, unbefangen, unbeeinflußt.

unbid(den) ['An'bid(n)] ungeheißen, unaufgefordert; ungebeten.

unbind ['An'baind] [*irr. (bind)*] losbinden, befreien; lösen.

unblushing □ [An'blʌʃiŋ] schamlos.   [boren.)

unborn ['An'bɔ:n] (noch) unge-)

unbosom [An'buzəm] offenbaren.

unbounded □ [An'baundid] unbegrenzt; schrankenlos.

unbroken □ ['An'broukən] ungebrochen; unversehrt; ununterbrochen.

unbutton ['An'bAtn] aufknöpfen.

uncalled-for [An'kɔ:ldfɔ:] ungerufen; unverlangt (*S.*); unpassend.

uncanny □ [An'kæni] unheimlich.

uncared-for ['An'kɛədfɔ:] unbeachtet, vernachlässigt.

unceasing □ [An'si:siŋ] unaufhörlich.

unceremonious □ ['Anseri'mounjəs] ungezwungen; formlos.

uncertain □ [ʌn'sə:tn] unsicher; ungewiß; unbestimmt; unzuverlässig; **~ty** [~nti] Unsicherheit f.

unchallenged ['ʌn'tʃælindʒd] unangefochten.

unchang|eable □ [ʌn'tʃeindʒəbl] unveränderlich, unwandelbar; **~ed** ['ʌn'tʃeindʒd] unverändert; **~ing** □ [ʌn'tʃeindʒiŋ] unveränderlich.

uncharitable □ ['ʌn'tʃæritəbl] lieblos; unbarmherzig; unfreundlich.

unchecked ['ʌn'tʃekt] ungehindert.

uncivil □ ['ʌn'sivl] unhöflich; **~ized** [~vilaizd] unzivilisiert.

unclaimed ['ʌn'kleimd] nicht beansprucht; unzustellbar (bsd. Brief).

unclasp ['ʌn'kla:sp] auf-, loshaken, auf-, losschnallen; aufmachen.

uncle ['ʌŋkl] Onkel m.

unclean □ ['ʌn'kli:n] unrein.

unclose ['ʌn'klouz] (sich) öffnen.

uncomely ['ʌn'kʌmli] reizlos; unpassend.

uncomfortable □ [ʌn'kʌmfətəbl] unbehaglich, ungemütlich; unangenehm.

uncommon □ [ʌn'kɔmən] ungewöhnlich.

uncommunicative □ ['ʌnkə'mju:nikətiv] wortkarg, schweigsam.

uncomplaining □ ['ʌnkəm'pleiniŋ] klaglos; ohne Murren; geduldig.

uncompromising ['ʌn'kɔmprəmaiziŋ] kompromißlos.

unconcern ['ʌnkən'sə:n] Unbekümmertheit f; Gleichgültigkeit f; **~ed** □ [~nd] unbekümmert; unbeteiligt.

unconditional □ ['ʌnkən'diʃənl] unbedingt; bedingungslos.

unconfirmed ['ʌnkən'fə:md] unbestätigt; eccl. nicht konfirmiert.

unconnected □ ['ʌnkə'nektid] unverbunden.

unconquer|able □ [ʌn'kɔŋkərəbl] unüberwindlich; **~ed** ['ʌn'kɔŋkəd] unbesiegt.

unconscionable □ [ʌn'kɔnʃnəbl] gewissenlos; F unverschämt, übermäßig.

unconscious □ [ʌn'kɔnʃəs] unbewußt; bewußtlos; **~ness** [~snis] Bewußtlosigkeit f.

unconstitutional □ ['ʌnkɔnsti'tju:ʃənl] verfassungswidrig.

uncontroll|able □ [ʌnkən'trouləbl] unkontrollierbar; unbändig; **~ed** ['ʌnkən'trould] unbeaufsichtigt; fig. unbeherrscht.

unconventional □ ['ʌnkən'venʃənl] unkonventionell; ungezwungen.

unconvinc|ed ['ʌnkən'vinst] nicht überzeugt; **~ing** [~siŋ] nicht überzeugend.

uncork ['ʌn'kɔ:k] entkorken.

uncount|able ['ʌn'kauntəbl] unzählbar; **~ed** [~tid] ungezählt.

uncouple ['ʌn'kʌpl] loskoppeln.

uncouth □ [ʌn'ku:θ] ungeschlacht.

uncover [ʌn'kʌvə] aufdecken, freilegen; entblößen.

unct|ion ['ʌŋkʃən] Salbung f (a. fig.); Salbe f; **~uous** □ ['ʌŋktjuəs] fettig, ölig; fig. salbungsvoll.

uncult|ivated ['ʌn'kʌltiveitid], **~ured** [~tʃəd] unkultiviert.

undamaged ['ʌn'dæmidʒd] unbeschädigt.

undaunted □ [ʌn'dɔ:ntid] unerschrocken.

undeceive ['ʌndi'si:v] j-n aufklären.

undecided □ ['ʌndi'saidid] unentschieden; unentschlossen.

undefined □ ['ʌndi'faind] unbestimmt; unbegrenzt.

undemonstrative □ ['ʌndi'mɔnstrətiv] zurückhaltend.

undeniable □ [ʌndi'naiəbl] unleugbar; unbestreitbar.

under ['ʌndə] **1.** adv. unten; darunter; **2.** prp. unter; **3.** adj. unter; in Zssgn: unter...; Unter...; mangelhaft ...; **~bid** [~'bid] [irr. (bid)] unterbieten; **~brush** [~brʌʃ] Unterholz n; **~carriage** ⚓ (Flugzeug)Fahrwerk n; mot. Fahrgestell n; **~clothes**, **~clothing** Unterkleidung f, Unterwäsche f; **~cut** [~'kʌt] Preise unterbieten; **~dog** [~dɔg] Unterlegene(r) m; Unterdrückte(r) m; **~done** [~'dʌn] nicht gar; **~estimate** [~r'estimeit] unterschätzen; **~fed** [~ə'fed] unterernährt; **~go** [ʌndə'gou] [irr. (go)] erdulden; sich unterziehen (dat.); **~graduate** [~'grædjuit] Student (-in); **~ground** ['ʌndəgraund] **1.** unterirdisch; Untergrund...; **2.** Untergrundbahn f; **~growth** Unterholz n; **~hand** unter der Hand; heimlich; **~lie** [ʌndə'lai] [irr. (lie)] zugrunde liegen (dat.); **~line** [~'lain] unterstreichen; **~ling** ['ʌndəliŋ] Untergeordnete(r) m; **~mine** [ʌndə'main] unterminieren; fig. untergraben; schwächen; **~most** ['ʌndəmoust] unterst; **~neath** [ʌndə'ni:θ] **1.** prp. unter (-halb); **2.** adv. unten; darunter; **~pin** [~'pin] untermauern; **~plot** ['ʌndəplɔt] Nebenhandlung f; **~privileged** [~'privilidʒd] benachteiligt; **~rate** [ʌndə'reit] unterschätzen; **~-secretary** ['ʌndə'sekrətəri] Unterstaatssekretär m; **~sell** ⚓ [~'sel] [irr. (sell)] j-n unterbieten; Ware verschleudern; **~signed** [~'saind] Unterzeichnete(r) m; **~sized** [~'saizd] zu klein; **~staffed** [ʌndə'sta:ft] unterbesetzt; **~stand** [~'stænd] [irr. (stand)] allg. verstehen; sich verstehen auf (acc.); (als sicher) annehmen; auffassen; (sinngemäß) ergänzen; make o.s. understood sich verständlich machen; an understood thing e-e abgemachte Sache; **~standable** [~dəbl] verständlich; **~standing** [~diŋ]

Verstand *m*; Einvernehmen *n*; Verständigung *f*; Abmachung *f*; Voraussetzung *f*; ˷state ['ʌndə'steit] zu gering angeben; abschwächen; ˷statement Unterbewertung *f*; Understatement *n*, Untertreibung *f*; ˷take [ʌndə'teik] *irr.* (*take*)] unternehmen; übernehmen; sich verpflichten; ˷taker ['ʌndəteikə] Bestattungsinstitut *n*; ˷taking [ʌndə'teikiŋ] Unternehmung *f*; Verpflichtung *f*; ['ʌndəteikiŋ] Leichenbestattung *f*; ˷tone leiser Ton; ˷value [˷'vælju:] unterschätzen; ˷wear [˷wɛə] Unterkleidung *f*, Unterwäsche *f*; ˷wood Unterholz *n*; ˷write [*irr.* (*write*)] *Versicherung* abschließen; ˷writer Versicherer *m*.

undeserv|ed □ ['ʌndi'zə:vd] unverdient; ˷ing [˷viŋ] unwürdig.

undesigned □ ['ʌndi'zaind] unbeabsichtigt, absichtlos.

undesirable ['ʌndi'zairəbl] **1.** □ unerwünscht; **2.** unerwünschte Person.

undeviating □ [ʌn'di:vieitiŋ] unentwegt.

undignified □ [ʌn'dignifaid] würdelos.

undisciplined [ʌn'disiplind] zuchtlos, undiszipliniert; ungeschult.

undisguised □ ['ʌndis'gaizd] unverkleidet; unverhohlen.

undisputed □ ['ʌndis'pju:tid] unbestritten.

undo ['ʌn'du:] [*irr.* (*do*)] aufmachen; (auf)lösen; ungeschehen machen, aufheben; vernichten; ˷ing [˷u(:)iŋ] Aufmachen *n*; Ungeschehenmachen *n*; Vernichtung *f*; Verderben *n*; ˷ne ['ʌn'dʌn] erledigt, vernichtet.

undoubted □ [ʌn'dautid] unzweifelhaft, zweifellos.

undreamt [ʌn'dremt]: ˷of ungeahnt.

undress ['ʌn'dres] **1.** (sich) entkleiden *od.* ausziehen; **2.** Hauskleid *n*; ˷ed unbekleidet; unangezogen; nicht zurechtgemacht.

undue □ ['ʌn'dju:] ungebührlich; übermäßig; † noch nicht fällig.

undulat|e ['ʌndjuleit] wogen; wallen; wellig sein; ˷ion [ʌndju'leiʃən] wellenförmige Bewegung.

undutiful □ ['ʌn'dju:tiful] ungehorsam, pflichtvergessen.

unearth ['ʌn'ə:θ] ausgraben; *fig.* aufstöbern; ˷ly [ʌn'ə:θli] überirdisch.

uneas|iness [ʌn'i:zinis] Unruhe *f*; Unbehagen *n*; ˷y □ [ʌn'i:zi] unbehaglich; unruhig; unsicher.

uneducated ['ʌn'edjukeitid] unerzogen; ungebildet.

unemotional □ ['ʌni'mouʃənl] leidenschaftslos; passiv; nüchtern.

unemploy|ed ['ʌnim'plɔid] **1.** un-

beschäftigt; arbeitslos; unbenutzt; **2.:** the ˷ *pl.* die Arbeitslosen *pl.*; ˷ment [˷'ɔimənt] Arbeitslosigkeit *f*.

unending □ [ʌn'endiŋ] endlos.

unendurable □ ['ʌnin'djuərəbl] unerträglich.

unengaged ['ʌnin'geidʒd] frei.

unequal □ ['ʌn'i:kwəl] ungleich; nicht gewachsen (*to dat.*); ˷(l)ed [˷ld] unvergleichlich, unerreicht.

unerring □ ['ʌn'ə:riŋ] unfehlbar.

unessential □ ['ʌni'senʃəl] unwesentlich, unwichtig (*to für*).

uneven □ ['ʌn'i:vən] uneben; ungleich(mäßig); ungerade (*Zahl*).

uneventful □ ['ʌni'ventful] ereignislos; ohne Zwischenfälle.

unexampled [ʌnig'za:mpld] beispiellos.

unexceptionable □ [ʌnik'sepʃnəbl] untadelig; einwandfrei.

unexpected □ ['ʌniks'pektid] unerwartet.

unexplained ['ʌniks'pleind] unerklärt.

unfading □ [ʌn'feidiŋ] nicht welkend; unvergänglich; echt (*Farbe*).

unfailing □ [ʌn'feiliŋ] unfehlbar; nie versagend; unerschöpflich; *fig.* treu.

unfair □ ['ʌn'fɛə] unehrlich; unfair; ungerecht.

unfaithful □ ['ʌn'feiθful] un(ge)treu, treulos; nicht wortgetreu.

unfamiliar ['ʌnfə'miljə] unbekannt; ungewohnt.

unfasten ['ʌn'fa:sn] aufmachen; lösen; ˷ed unbefestigt, lose.

unfathomable □ [ʌn'fæðəməbl] unergründlich.

unfavo(u)rable □ ['ʌn'feivərəbl] ungünstig.

unfeeling □ [ʌn'fi:liŋ] gefühllos.

unfilial □ ['ʌn'filjəl] respektlos, pflichtvergessen (*Kind*).

unfinished ['ʌn'finiʃt] unvollendet; unfertig.

unfit 1. □ ['ʌn'fit] ungeeignet, unpassend; **2.** [ʌn'fit] untauglich machen.

unfix ['ʌn'fiks] losmachen, lösen.

unfledged ['ʌn'fledʒd] ungefiedert; (noch) nicht flügge; *fig.* unreif.

unflinching □ [ʌn'flintʃiŋ] fest entschlossen, unnachgiebig.

unfold ['ʌn'fould] (sich) entfalten *od.* öffnen; [ʌn'fould] klarlegen; enthüllen.

unforced □ ['ʌn'fɔ:st] ungezwungen.

unforeseen ['ʌnfɔ:'si:n] unvorhergesehen.

unforgettable □ ['ʌnfə'getəbl] unvergeßlich.

unforgiving ['ʌnfə'giviŋ] unversöhnlich.

unforgotten ['ʌnfə'gɔtn] unvergessen.

unfortunate [ʌn'fɔ:tʃnit] **1.** □ un-

glücklich; 2. Unglückliche(r *m*) *f*;
~ly [~tli] unglücklicherweise, leider.
unfounded □ ['ʌn'faundid] unbe-
gründet; grundlos.
unfriendly □ ['ʌn'frendli] unfreundlich; ungünstig.
unfurl [ʌn'fə:l] entfalten, aufrollen.
unfurnished ['ʌn'fə:niʃt] unmö-
bliert.
ungainly [ʌn'geinli] unbeholfen,
plump.
ungenerous □ ['ʌn'dʒenərəs] un-
edelmütig; nicht freigebig.
ungentle □ ['ʌn'dʒentl] unsanft.
ungodly □ ['ʌn'gɔdli] gottlos.
ungovernable □ [ʌn'gʌvənəbl] unlenksam; zügellos, unbändig.
ungraceful □ ['ʌn'greisful] ungra-
ziös, ohne Anmut; unbeholfen.
ungracious □ ['ʌn'greiʃəs] ungnä-
dig; unfreundlich.
ungrateful □ [ʌn'greitful] undankbar.
unguarded □ ['ʌn'gɑ:did] unbewacht; unvorsichtig; ungeschützt.
unguent ['ʌŋgwənt] Salbe *f*.
unhampered ['ʌn'hæmpəd] ungehindert.   [schön.}
unhandsome □ [ʌn'hænsəm] un-)
unhandy □ [ʌn'hændi] unhandlich;
ungeschickt; unbeholfen.
unhappy □ [ʌn'hæpi] unglücklich.
unharmed ['ʌn'hɑ:md] unversehrt.
unhealthy □ [ʌn'helθi] ungesund.
unheard-of [ʌn'hə:dɔv] unerhört.
unheeded ['ʌn'hi:did] unbeachtet,
unbewacht; ~ing [~diŋ] sorglos.
unhesitating □ [ʌn'heziteitiŋ] ohne
Zögern; unbedenklich.
unholy □ ['ʌn'houli] unheilig; gottlos.
unhono(u)red ['ʌn'ɔnəd] ungeehrt;
uneingelöst (*Pfand, Scheck*).
unhook ['ʌn'huk] auf-, aushaken.
unhoped-for [ʌn'houptfɔ:] unver-
hofft.
unhurt ['ʌn'hə:t] unverletzt.
unicorn ['ju:nikɔ:n] Einhorn *n*.
unification [ju:nifi'keiʃən] Vereinigung *f*; Vereinheitlichung *f*.
uniform ['ju:nifɔ:m] **1.** □ gleichförmig, gleichmäßig; einheitlich;
2. Dienstkleidung *f*; Uniform *f*;
3. uniformieren; ~ity [ju:ni'fɔ:miti]
Gleichförmigkeit *f*, Gleichmäßigkeit *f*.
unify ['ju:nifai] verein(ig)en; ver-
einheitlichen.
unilateral □ ['ju:ni'lætərəl] einseitig.
unimagina|ble □ [ʌni'mædʒinəbl]
undenkbar; ~tive □ ['ʌni'mædʒi-
nətiv] einfallslos.
unimportant □ ['ʌnim'pɔ:tənt]
unwichtig.
unimproved ['ʌnim'pru:vd] nicht
kultiviert, unbebaut (*Land*); unver-
bessert.
uninformed ['ʌnin'fɔ:md] nicht
unterrichtet.

uninhabit|able ['ʌnin'hæbitəbl] un-
bewohnbar; ~ed [~tid] unbewohnt.
uninjured ['ʌn'indʒəd] unbeschädigt, unverletzt.
unintelligible □ ['ʌnin'telidʒəbl]
unverständlich.
unintentional □ ['ʌnin'tenʃənl] un-
absichtlich.
uninteresting □ ['ʌn'intristiŋ] uninteressant.
uninterrupted □ ['ʌnintə'rʌptid]
ununterbrochen.
union ['ju:njən] Vereinigung *f*; Verbindung *f*; Union *f*, Verband *m*;
Einigung *f*; Einigkeit *f*; Verein *m*,
Bund *m*; *univ.* (Debattier)Klub *m*;
Gewerkschaft *f*; ~ist [~nist] Ge-
werkschaftler *m*; ♀ **Jack** Union
Jack *m* (*britische Nationalflagge*) ~
suit *Am.* Hemdhose *f*.
unique □ [ju:'ni:k] einzigartig, ein-
malig.
unison ♪ *u. fig.* ['ju:nizn] Einklang
m.
unit ['ju:nit] Einheit *f*; ♀ Einer *m*;
~e [ju:'nait] (sich) vereinigen, verbinden; sich vereinigt, vereint; ~y
['ju:niti] Einheit *f*; Einigkeit *f*.
univers|al □ [ju:ni'və:səl] allge-
mein; allumfassend; Universal...,
Welt...; ~ality [ju:nivə:'sæliti] Allgemeinheit *f*; umfassende Bildung,
Vielseitigkeit *f*; ~e ['ju:nivə:s]
Weltall *n*, Universum *n*; ~ity [ju:-
ni'və:siti] Universität *f*.
unjust □ ['ʌn'dʒʌst] ungerecht; ~i-
fiable □ [ʌn'dʒʌstifaiəbl] nicht zu
rechtfertigen(d), unverantwortlich.
unkempt [ʌn'kempt] ungepflegt.
unkind □ [ʌn'kaind] unfreundlich.
unknow|ing □ ['ʌn'nouiŋ] unwis-
send; unbewußt; ~n *n* [~oun] **1.** unbekannt; unbewußt; ~ to me ohne
mein Wissen; **2.** Unbekannte(r *m*,
~s *n*) *f*.
unlace ['ʌn'leis] aufschnüren.
unlatch ['ʌn'lætʃ] aufklinken.
unlawful □ ['ʌn'lɔ:ful] ungesetzlich; *weitS.* unrechtmäßig.
unlearn ['ʌn'lə:n] (*irr.* (learn)) ver-
lernen.
unless [ən'les] wenn nicht, außer
wenn; es sei denn, daß.
unlike ['ʌn'laik] **1.** *adj.* □ ungleich;
2. *prp.* anders als; ~ly [ʌn'laikli]
unwahrscheinlich.
unlimited [ʌn'limitid] unbegrenzt.
unload ['ʌn'loud] ent-, ab-, ausladen; *Ladung* löschen.
unlock ['ʌn'lɔk] aufschließen; *Waffe*
entsichern; ~ed unverschlossen.
unlooked-for [ʌn'luktfɔ:] unerwartet.
unloose, ~n ['ʌn'lu:s, ʌn'lu:sn] lösen, losmachen.
unlov|ely ['ʌn'lʌvli] reizlos, un-
schön; ~ing □ [~viŋ] lieblos.
unlucky □ [ʌn'lʌki] unglücklich.

unmake ['ʌn'meik] [irr. (make)] vernichten; rückgängig machen; umbilden; Herrscher absetzen.

unman ['ʌn'mæn] entmannen.

unmanageable □ [ʌn'mænidʒəbl] unlenksam, widerspenstig.

unmarried ['ʌn'mærid] unverheiratet, ledig.

unmask ['ʌn'mɑːsk] (sich) demaskieren; fig. entlarven.

unmatched ['ʌn'mætʃt] unerreicht; unvergleichlich.

unmeaning □ [ʌn'miːniŋ] nichtssagend.

unmeasured [ʌn'meʒəd] ungemessen; unermeßlich.

unmeet ['ʌn'miːt] ungeeignet.

unmentionable [ʌn'menʃnəbl] nicht zu erwähnen(d), unnennbar.

unmerited ['ʌn'meritid] unverdient.

unmindful □ [ʌn'maindful] unbedacht; sorglos; ohne Rücksicht.

unmistakable □ ['ʌnmis'teikəbl] unverkennbar; unmißverständlich.

unmitigated [ʌn'mitigeitid] ungemildert; richtig; fig. Erz...

unmolested ['ʌnmou'lestid] unbelästigt.

unmounted ['ʌn'mauntid] unberitten; nicht gefaßt (Stein); unaufgezogen (Bild); unmontiert.

unmoved □ ['ʌn'muːvd] unbewegt, ungerührt.

unnamed ['ʌn'neimd] ungenannt.

unnatural □ [ʌn'nætʃrəl] unnatürlich. [nötig.]

unnecessary □ [ʌn'nesisəri] un-]

unneighbo(u)rly ['ʌn'neibəli] nicht gutnachbarlich.

unnerve ['ʌn'nɔːv] entnerven.

unnoticed ['ʌn'noutist] unbemerkt.

unobjectionable □ ['ʌnəb'dʒekʃnəbl] einwandfrei.

unobserv|ant □ ['ʌnəb'zɔːvənt] unachtsam; ~ed □ [~vd] unbemerkt.

unobtainable ['ʌnəb'teinəbl] unerreichbar.

unobtrusive □ ['ʌnəb'truːsiv] unaufdringlich, bescheiden.

unoccupied ['ʌn'ɔkjupaid] unbesetzt; unbewohnt; unbeschäftigt.

unoffending ['ʌnə'fendiŋ] harmlos.

unofficial □ ['ʌnə'fiʃəl] nichtamtlich, inoffiziell.

unopposed ['ʌnə'pouzd] ungehindert.

unostentatious □ ['ʌnɔstən'teiʃəs] anspruchslos; unauffällig; schlicht.

unowned ['ʌn'ound] herrenlos.

unpack ['ʌn'pæk] auspacken.

unpaid ['ʌn'peid] unbezahlt; unbelohnt; & unfrankiert.

unparalleled [ʌn'pærəleld] beispiellos, ohnegleichen.

unperceived □ ['ʌnpə'siːvd] unbemerkt.

unperturbed ['ʌnpə(ː)'tɔːbd] ruhig, gelassen.

unpleasant □ [ʌn'plezənt] unangenehm; unerfreulich; ~ness [~tnis] Unannehmlichkeit f.

unpolished ['ʌn'pɔliʃt] unpoliert; fig. ungebildet.

unpolluted ['ʌnpə'luːtid] unbefleckt.

unpopular □ ['ʌn'pɔpjulə] unpopulär, unbeliebt; ~ity ['ʌnpɔpju'læriti] Unbeliebtheit f.

unpracti|cal □ ['ʌn'præktikəl] unpraktisch; ~sed, Am. ~ced [ʌn'præktist] ungeübt.

unprecedented □ [ʌn'presidəntid] beispiellos; noch nie dagewesen.

unprejudiced □ [ʌn'predʒudist] unbefangen, unvoreingenommen.

unpremeditated □ ['ʌnpri'mediteitid] unbeabsichtigt.

unprepared □ ['ʌnpri'pɛəd] unvorbereitet.

unpreten|ding □ ['ʌnpri'tendiŋ], ~tious □ [~ʃəs] anspruchslos.

unprincipled [ʌn'prinsəpld] ohne Grundsätze; gewissenlos.

unprivileged [ʌn'privilidʒd] sozial benachteiligt; arm.

unprofitable □ [ʌn'prɔfitəbl] unnütz.

unproved ['ʌn'pruːvd] unerwiesen.

unprovided ['ʌnprə'vaidid] nicht versehen (with mit); ~ for unversorgt, mittellos.

unprovoked ['ʌnprə'voukt] ohne Grund.

unqualified ['ʌn'kwɔlifaid] ungeeignet; unberechtigt; [ʌn'kwɔlifaid] unbeschränkt.

unquestion|able [ʌn'kwestʃənəbl] unzweifelhaft, fraglos; ~ed [~nd] ungefragt; unbestritten.

unquote ['ʌn'kwout] Zitat beenden.

unravel [ʌn'rævəl] (sich) entwirren; enträtseln.

unready □ ['ʌn'redi] nicht bereit od. fertig; unlustig, zögernd.

unreal □ ['ʌn'riəl] unwirklich; ~istic ['ʌnriə'listik] (~ally) wirklichkeitsfremd, unrealistisch.

unreasonable □ [ʌn'riːznəbl] unvernünftig; grundlos; unmäßig.

unrecognizable □ [ʌn'rekəgnaizəbl] nicht wiederzuerkennen(d).

unredeemed □ ['ʌnri'diːmd] unerlöst; uneingelöst; ungemildert.

unrefined ['ʌnri'faind] ungeläutert; fig. ungebildet. [dankenlos.]

unreflecting □ ['ʌnri'flektiŋ] ge-]

unregarded ['ʌnri'gɑːdid] unbeachtet; unberücksichtigt.

unrelated ['ʌnri'leitid] ohne Beziehung (to zu).

unrelenting □ ['ʌnri'lentiŋ] erbarmungslos; unerbittlich.

unreliable ['ʌnri'laiəbl] unzuverlässig.

unrelieved □ ['ʌnri'liːvd] ungelindert; ununterbrochen.

unremitting □ [ʌnri'mitiŋ] unablässig, unaufhörlich; unermüdlich.

unrepining □ ['ʌnri'painiŋ] klaglos; unverdrossen.

unrequited □ ['ʌnri'kwaitid] unerwidert; unbelohnt.

unreserved □ ['ʌnri'zəːvd] rückhaltlos; unbeschränkt; ohne Vorbehalt.

unresisting □ ['ʌnri'zistiŋ] widerstandslos.

unresponsive ['ʌnris'pɔnsiv] unempfänglich (*to* für).

unrest ['ʌn'rest] Unruhe *f*.

unrestrained □ ['ʌnris'treind] ungehemmt; unbeschränkt.

unrestricted □ ['ʌnris'triktid] uneingeschränkt.

unriddle ['ʌn'ridl] enträtseln.

unrighteous □ ['ʌn'raitʃəs] ungerecht; unredlich.

unripe ['ʌn'raip] unreif.

unrival(l)ed [ʌn'raivəld] unvergleichlich, unerreicht, einzigartig.

unroll ['ʌn'roul] ent-, aufrollen.

unruffled ['ʌn'rʌfld] glatt; ruhig.

unruly [ʌn'ruːli] ungebärdig.

unsafe □ ['ʌn'seif] unsicher.

unsal(e)able ['ʌn'seiləbl] unverkäuflich.

unsanitary ['ʌn'sænitəri] unhygienisch.

unsatisf|actory □ ['ʌnsætis'fæktəri] unbefriedigend; unzulänglich; **ied** ['ʌn'sætisfaid] unbefriedigt; **ying** □ [ˌ̃aiiŋ] = *unsatisfactory*.

unsavo(u)ry □ ['ʌn'seivəri] unappetitlich (*a. fig.*), widerwärtig.

unsay ['ʌn'sei] [*irr*. (*say*)] zurücknehmen, widerrufen.

unscathed ['ʌn'skeiðd] unversehrt.

unschooled ['ʌn'skuːld] ungeschult; unverbildet.

unscrew ['ʌn'skruː] *v/t.* ab-, los-, aufschrauben; *v/i.* sich abschrauben lassen.

unscrupulous □ [ʌn'skruːpjuləs] bedenkenlos; gewissenlos; skrupellos.

unsearchable □ [ʌn'sɔːtʃəbl] unerforschlich; unergründlich.

unseason|able □ [ʌn'siːznəbl] unzeitig; *fig.* ungelegen; **ed** ['ʌn'siznd] nicht abgelagert (*Holz*); *fig.* nicht abgehärtet; ungewürzt.

unseat ['ʌn'siːt] des Amtes entheben; abwerfen.

unseemly [ʌn'siːmli] unziemlich.

unseen ['ʌn'siːn] ungesehen; unsichtbar.

unselfish □ ['ʌn'selfiʃ] selbstlos, uneigennützig; **ness** [ˌ̃ʃnis] Selbstlosigkeit *f*.

unsettle ['ʌn'setl] in Unordnung

bringen; verwirren; erschüttern; **d** nicht festgesetzt; unbeständig; † unbezahlt; unerledigt; ohne festen Wohnsitz; unbesiedelt.

unshaken ['ʌn'ʃeikən] unerschüttert; unerschütterlich.

unshaven ['ʌn'ʃeivn] unrasiert.

unship ['ʌn'ʃip] ausschiffen.

unshrink|able ['ʌn'ʃriŋkəbl] nicht einlaufend (*Stoff*); **ing** □ [ʌn'ʃriŋkiŋ] unverzagt.

unsightly [ʌn'saitli] häßlich.

unskil|(l)ful □ ['ʌn'skilful] ungeschickt; **led** [ˌ̃ld] ungelernt.

unsoci|able [ʌn'souʃəbl] ungesellig; **al** [ˌ̃əl] ungesellig; unsozial.

unsolder ['ʌn'sɔldə] los-, ablösten.

unsolicited ['ʌnsə'lisitid] nicht gefragt (*S.*); unaufgefordert (*P.*).

unsolv|able ['ʌn'sɔlvəbl] unlösbar; **ed** [ˌ̃vd] ungelöst.

unsophisticated ['ʌnsə'fistikeitid] unverfälscht; ungekünstelt; unverdorben, unverbildet.

unsound □ ['ʌn'saund] ungesund; verdorben; wurmstichig; morsch; nicht stichhaltig (*Beweis*); verkehrt.

unsparing □ [ʌn'spɛəriŋ] freigebig; schonungslos, unbarmherzig.

unspeakable □ [ʌn'spiːkəbl] unsagbar; unsäglich.

unspent ['ʌn'spent] unverbraucht; unerschöpft.

unspoil|ed, ~t ['ʌn'spɔilt] unverdorben; unbeschädigt; nicht verzogen (*Kind*).

unspoken ['ʌn'spoukən] ungesagt; **of** unerwähnt.

unstable □ ['ʌn'steibl] nicht (stand)fest; unbeständig; unstet(ig); labil.

unsteady □ ['ʌn'stedi] unstet(ig), unsicher; schwankend; unbeständig; unsolid; unregelmäßig.

unstrained ['ʌn'streind] unfiltriert; *fig.* ungezwungen.

unstrap ['ʌn'stræp] los-, abschnallen.

unstressed ['ʌn'strest] unbetont.

unstring ['ʌn'striŋ] [*irr*. (*string*)] *Saite* entspannen.

unstudied ['ʌn'stʌdid] ungesucht, ungekünstelt, natürlich.

unsubstantial □ ['ʌnsəb'stænʃəl] wesenlos; gegenstandslos; inhaltlos; gehaltlos; dürftig.

unsuccessful □ ['ʌnsək'sesful] erfolglos, ohne Erfolg.

unsuitable □ ['ʌn'sjuːtəbl] unpassend; unangemessen.

unsurpassed ['ʌnsə(ː)'pɑːst] unübertroffen.

unsuspect|ed □ ['ʌnsəs'pektid] unverdächtig; unvermutet; **ing** [ˌ̃tiŋ] nichts ahnend; arglos.

unsuspicious □ ['ʌnsəs'piʃəs] nicht argwöhnisch, arglos.

unswerving □ [ʌn'swəːviŋ] unentwegt.

untangle ['ʌn'tæŋgl] entwirren.

untarnished ['ʌn'taːniʃt] unbefleckt; ungetrübt.

unteachable ['ʌn'tiːtʃəbl] unbelehrbar (P.); unlehrbar (S.).

untenanted ['ʌn'tənəntid] unvermietet, unbewohnt.

unthankful □ ['ʌn'θæŋkful] undankbar.

unthink|able [ʌn'θiŋkəbl] undenkbar; ~ing □ ['ʌn'θiŋkiŋ] gedankenlos.

unthought ['ʌn'θɔːt] unbedacht; ~of unvermutet.

unthrifty □ ['ʌn'θrifti] verschwenderisch; nicht gedeihend.

untidy □ [ʌn'taidi] unordentlich.

untie ['ʌn'tai] aufbinden, aufknüpfen; *Knoten etc.* lösen; *j-n* losbinden.

until [ən'til] 1. *prp.* bis; 2. *cj.* bis (daß); *not ~* erst wenn *od.* als.

untimely [ʌn'taimli] unzeitig; vorzeitig; ungelegen. [lich.)

untiring □ [ʌn'taiəriŋ] unermüd-)

unto ['ʌntu] = to.

untold ['ʌn'tould] unerzählt; ungezählt; unermeßlich, unsäglich.

untouched ['ʌn'tʌtʃt] unberührt; *fig.* ungerührt; *phot.* unretuschiert.

untried ['ʌn'traid] unversucht; unerprobt; ₰ noch nicht verhört.

untrod ['ʌn'trɔd, ~dn] unbetreten.

untroubled ['ʌn'trʌbld] ungestört.

untrue □ ['ʌn'truː] unwahr; untreu.

untrustworthy □ ['ʌn'trʌstwəːði] unzuverlässig, nicht vertrauenswürdig.

unus|ed ['ʌn'juːzd] ungebraucht; [~ːst] nicht gewöhnt (*to an acc.*; *zu inf.*); ~ual □ [ʌn'juːʒuəl] ungewöhnlich; ungewohnt.

unutterable □ [ʌn'ʌtərəbl] unaussprechlich.

unvarnished *fig.* ['ʌn'vaːniʃt] ungeschminkt.

unvarying □ [ʌn'veəriiŋ] unveränderlich.

unveil [ʌn'veil] entschleiern, enthüllen.

unversed ['ʌn'vəːst] unbewandert, unerfahren (*in in dat.*).

unvouched ['ʌn'vautʃt] *a.* ~*for* unverbürgt, unbezeugt.

unwanted ['ʌn'wɔntid] unerwünscht.

unwarrant|able □ [ʌn'wɔrəntəbl] unverantwortlich, ~ed [~tid] unberechtigt; ['ʌn'wɔrəntid] unverbürgt.

unwary □ [ʌn'weəri] unbedachtsam.

unwelcome [ʌn'welkəm] unwillkommen.

unwholesome ['ʌn'houlsəm] ungesund; schädlich.

unwieldy □ [ʌn'wiːldi] unhandlich; ungefüge; sperrig.

unwilling □ ['ʌn'wiliŋ] un-, widerwillig, abgeneigt.

unwind ['ʌn'waind] [*irr.* (*wind*)] auf-, loswickeln; (sich) abwickeln.

unwise □ ['ʌn'waiz] unklug.

unwitting □ [ʌn'witiŋ] unwissentlich; unbeabsichtigt.

unworkable ['ʌn'wəːkəbl] undurchführbar; ⊕ nicht betriebsfähig.

unworthy □ [ʌn'wəːði] unwürdig.

unwrap ['ʌn'ræp] auswickeln, auspacken, aufwickeln.

unwrought ['ʌn'rɔːt] unbearbeitet; roh; Roh...

unyielding □ [ʌn'jiːldiŋ] unnachgiebig.

up [ʌp] 1. *adv.* (her-, hin)auf; aufwärts, empor; oben; auf(gestanden); aufgegangen (*Sonne*); hoch; abgelaufen, um (*Zeit*); *Am. Baseball*: am Schlag; ~ *and about* wieder auf den Beinen; *be hard* ~ in Geldschwierigkeiten sein; ~ *against a task* e-r Aufgabe gegenüber; ~ *to* bis (zu); *it is* ~ *to me to do es ist* an mir, zu tun; *what are you* ~ *to there?* was macht ihr da? *what's* ~? *sl.* was ist los? 2. *prp.* hinauf; ~ *the river* flußaufwärts; ~ *train* Zug *m* nach der Stadt; 3. *adj.*: ~ *the* ~*s and downs* das Auf und Ab, die Höhen und Tiefen *des Lebens*; 5. F (sich) erheben; hochfahren; hochtreiben.

up|-and-coming *Am.* F ['ʌpən'kʌmiŋ] unternehmungslustig; ~**braid** [ʌp'breid] schelten; ~**bringing** ['ʌpbriŋiŋ] Erziehung *f*; ~**country** ['ʌp'kʌntri] landeinwärts (gelegen); ~**heaval** [ʌp'hiːvəl] Umbruch *m*; ~**hill** ['ʌp'hil] bergan; mühsam; ~**hold** [ʌp'hould] [*irr.* (*hold*)] aufrecht(er)halten; stützen; ~**holster** [~lstə] *Möbel* (auf)polstern; *Zimmer* dekorieren; ~**holsterer** [~ərə] Tapezierer *m*, Dekorateur *m*, Polsterer *m*; ~**holstery** [~ri] Polstermöbel *n/pl.*; Möbelstoffe *m/pl.*; Tapezierarbeit *f*.

up|keep ['ʌpkiːp] Instandhaltung(skosten *pl.*) *f*; Unterhalt *m*; ~**land** ['ʌplənd] Hoch-, Oberland *n*; ~**lift** 1. [ʌp'lift] (empor-, er)heben; 2. ['ʌplift] Erhebung *f*; *fig.* Aufschwung *m*.

upon [ə'pɔn] = on.

upper ['ʌpə] ober; Ober...; ~**most** oberst, höchst.

up|raise [ʌp'reiz] erheben; ~**rear** [ʌp'riə] aufrichten; ~**right** 1. □ ['ʌp'rait] aufrecht; ~ *piano* ♪ Klavier *n*; *fig.* ['ʌprait] rechtschaffen; 2. Pfosten *m*; Ständer *m*; ~**rising** [ʌp'raiziŋ] Erhebung *f*, Aufstand *m*.

uproar ['ʌprɔː] Aufruhr *m*; ~**ious** □ [ʌp'rɔːriəs] tobend; tosend.

up|root [ʌp'ruːt] entwurzeln; (her-)ausreißen; **~set** [ʌp'set] [*irr.* (set)] umwerfen; (um)stürzen; außer Fassung *od.* in Unordnung bringen; stören; verwirren; *be ~* außer sich sein; **~shot** ['ʌpʃɔt] Ausgang *m;* **~side** ['ʌpsaid] *adv.:* ~ *down* das Oberste zuunterst; verkehrt; **~stairs** [ʌp'stɛəz] die Treppe hinauf, (nach) oben; **~start** ['ʌpstɑːt] Emporkömmling *m;* **~state** [ʌp'steit] Hinterland *n e-s Staates;* **~stream** ['ʌp'striːm] fluß-, stromaufwärts; **~-to-date** ['ʌptə'deit] modern, neuzeitlich; **~town** ['ʌp'taun] im *od.* in den oberen Stadtteil; *Am.* im Wohn- *od.* Villenviertel; **~turn** [ʌp'tɜːn] nach oben kehren; **~ward(s)** ['ʌpwəd(z)] aufwärts (gerichtet).

uranium ⚗ [juə'reinjəm] Uran *n.*

urban ['ɜːbən] städtisch; Stadt...; **~e** □ [ɜː'bein] höflich; gebildet.

urchin ['ɜːtʃin] Bengel *m.*

urge [ɜːdʒ] **1.** *oft ~ on j-n* drängen, (an)treiben; dringen in *j-n;* dringen auf *et.; Recht* geltend machen; **2.** Drang *m;* **~ncy** ['ɜːdʒənsi] Dringlichkeit *f;* Drängen *n;* **~nt** □ [~nt] dringend; dringlich; eilig.

urin|al ['juərinl] Harnglas *n;* Bedürfnisanstalt *f;* **~ate** [~neit] urinieren; **~e** [~in] Urin *m,* Harn *m.*

urn [ɜːn] Urne *f;* Tee- *etc.* Maschine *f.*

us [ʌs, əs] uns; *of ~* unser.

usage ['juːzidʒ] Brauch *m,* Gepflogenheit *f;* Sprachgebrauch *m;* Behandlung *f,* Verwendung *f,* Gebrauch *m.*

usance † ['juːzəns] Wechselfrist *f.*

use 1. [juːs] Gebrauch *m;* Benutzung *f;* Verwendung *f;* Gewohnheit *f,* Übung *f;* Brauch *m;* Nutzen *m;* (*of*) *no ~* unnütz, zwecklos; *have no ~ for* keine Verwendung haben

für; *Am.* F nicht mögen; **2.** [juːz] gebrauchen; benutzen, ver-, anwenden; behandeln; *~ up* ver-, aufbrauchen; *I ~d to do* ich pflegte zu tun, früher tat ich; **~d** [juːzd] gebraucht; [juːst] gewöhnt (*to* an *acc.*); gewohnt (*to* zu *od. acc.*); **~ful** □ ['juːsful] brauchbar; nützlich; Nutz...; **~less** □ ['juːslis] nutz-, zwecklos, unnütz.

usher ['ʌʃə] **1.** Türhüter *m,* Pförtner *m;* Gerichtsdiener *m;* Platzanweiser *m;* **2.** *mst.* ~ *in* (hin)einführen, anmelden; **~ette** [ʌʃə'ret] Platzanweiserin *f.*

usual □ ['juːʒuəl] gewöhnlich; üblich; gebräuchlich.

usurer ['juːʒərə] Wucherer *m.*

usurp [juː'zɜːp] sich *et.* widerrechtlich aneignen, an sich reißen; **~er** [~ə] Usurpator *m.*

usury ['juːʒuri] Wucher(zinsen *pl.*) *m.*

utensil [juː(ː)'tensl] Gerät *n;* Geschirr *n.*

uterus *anat.* ['juːtərəs] Gebärmutter *f.*

utility [juː(ː)'tiliti] **1.** Nützlichkeit *f,* Nutzen *m; public ~* öffentlicher Versorgungsbetrieb; **2.** Gebrauchs..., Einheits...

utiliz|ation [juːtilai'zeiʃən] Nutzbarmachung *f;* Nutzanwendung *f;* **~e** ['juːtilaiz] sich *et.* zunutze machen.

utmost ['ʌtmoust] äußerst.

Utopian [juː'toupjən] **1.** utopisch; **2.** Utopist(in), Schwärmer(in).

utter ['ʌtə] **1.** *fig.* äußerst; völlig, gänzlich; **2.** äußern; *Seufzer etc.* ausstoßen, von sich geben; *Falschgeld etc.* in Umlauf setzen; **~ance** ['ʌtərəns] Äußerung *f,* Ausdruck *m;* Aussprache *f;* **~most** ['ʌtəmoust] äußerst.

uvula *anat.* ['juːvjulə] Zäpfchen *n.*

V

vacan|cy ['veikənsi] Leere *f;* leerer *od.* freier Platz; Lücke *f;* offene Stelle; **~t** □ [~nt] leer (*a. fig.*); frei (*Zeit, Zimmer*); offen (*Stelle*); unbesetzt, vakant (*Amt*).

vacat|e [və'keit, *Am.* 'veikeit] räumen; *Stelle* aufgeben, aus *e-m Amt* scheiden; **~ion** [və'keiʃən, *Am.* vei'keiʃən] **1.** (Schul)Ferien *pl.; bsd. Am.* Urlaub *m;* Räumung *f;* Niederlegung *f e-s Amtes;* **2.** *Am.* Urlaub machen; **~ionist** *Am.* [~nist] Ferienreisende(r *m*) *f.*

vaccin|ate ['væksineit] impfen;

~ation [væksi'neiʃən] Impfung *f;* **~e** ['væksiːn] Impfstoff *m.*

vacillate ['væsileit] schwanken.

vacu|ous □ ['vækjuəs] *fig.* leer, geistlos; **~um** *phys.* [~uəm] Vakuum *n;* ~ *cleaner* Staubsauger *m;* ~ *flask,* ~ *bottle* Thermosflasche *f.*

vagabond ['vægəbɔnd] **1.** vagabundierend; **2.** Landstreicher *m.*

vagary ['veigəri] wunderlicher Einfall, Laune *f,* Schrulle *f.*

vagrant ['veigrənt] **1.** wandernd; *fig.* unstet; **2.** Landstreicher *m,* Vagabund *m;* Strolch *m.*

vague □ [veig] unbestimmt; unklar.

vain □ [vein] eitel, eingebildet; leer; nichtig; vergeblich; *in* ~ vergebens, umsonst; ~glorious □ [vein'glɔːriəs] prahlerisch.

vale [veil] *poet. od. in Namen:* Tal *n.*

valediction [væli'dikʃən] Abschied(sworte *n/pl.*) *m.*

valentine ['væləntain] Valentinsschatz *m,* -gruß *m (am Valentinstag, 14. Februar, erwählt, gesandt.).*

valerian ♣ [və'liəriən] Baldrian *m.*

valet ['vælit] 1. (Kammer)Diener *m;* 2. Diener sein bei *j-m; j-n* bedienen.

valetudinarian ['vælitjuːdi'nɛəriən] 1. kränklich; 2. kränklicher Mensch; Hypochonder *m.*

valiant □ ['væljənt] tapfer.

valid □ ['vælid] triftig, richtig, stichhaltig; (rechts)gültig; *be* ~ gelten; ~ity [və'liditi] Gültigkeit *f;* Triftig-, Richtigkeit *f.*

valise [və'liːz] Reisetasche *f;* ✕ Tornister *m.*

valley ['væli] Tal *n.*

valo(u)r ['vælə] Tapferkeit *f.*

valuable ['væljuəbl] 1. □ wertvoll; 2. ~s *pl.* Wertsachen *f/pl.*

valuation [vælju'eiʃən] Abschätzung *f;* Taxwert *m.*

value ['væljuː] 1. Wert *m;* Währung *f; give (get) good* ~ *(for one's money)* ⊤ reell bedienen (bedient werden); 2. (ab)schätzen; *fig.* schätzen; ~less [~julis] wertlos.

valve [vælv] Klappe *f;* Ventil *n; Radio:* Röhre *f.*

vamoose *Am. sl.* [və'muːs] *v/i.* abhauen; *v/t.* räumen *(verlassen).*

vamp F [væmp] 1. Vamp *m (verführerische Frau);* 2. neppen.

vampire ['væmpaiə] Vampir *m.*

van [væn] Möbelwagen *m;* Lieferwagen *m;* ⊞ Pack-, Güterwagen *m;* ✕ Vorhut *f.*

vane [vein] Wetterfahne *f;* (Windmühlen-, Propeller)Flügel *m.*

vanguard ✕ ['vænɡɑːd] Vorhut *f.*

vanilla ♣ [və'nilə] Vanille *f.*

vanish ['væniʃ] (ver)schwinden.

vanity ['væniti] Eitelkeit *f,* Einbildung *f;* Nichtigkeit *f;* ~ bag Kosmetiktäschchen *n.*

vanquish ['væŋkwiʃ] besiegen.

vantage ['vɑːntidʒ] *Tennis:* Vorteil *m;* ~-ground günstige Stellung.

vapid □ ['væpid] schal; fad(e).

vapor Am. ['veipəraiz] verdampfen, verdunsten (lassen); ~ous □ [~rəs] dunstig; nebelhaft.

vapo(u)r ['veipə] Dunst *m;* Dampf *m.*

varia|ble □ ['vɛəriəbl] veränderlich; ~nce [~əns] Veränderung *f;* Uneinigkeit *f; be at* ~ uneinig sein; (sich) widersprechen; *set at* ~ entzweien; ~nt [~ənt] 1. abweichend; 2. Variante *f;* ~tion [vɛəri'eiʃən]

Abänderung *f;* Schwankung *f;* Abweichung *f;* ♪ Variation *f.*

varicose ♂ ['værikous] Krampfader(n)...; ~ vein Krampfader *f.*

varie|d □ ['vɛərid] verschieden, verändert, mannigfaltig; ~gate [~igeit] bunt gestalten; ~ty [və'raiəti] Mannigfaltigkeit *f,* Vielzahl *f; biol.* Abart *f;* ♂ Auswahl *f;* Menge *f;* ~ show Varietévorstellung *f;* ~ theatre Varieté(theater) *n.*

various □ ['vɛəriəs] verschiedene, mehrere; mannigfaltig; verschiedenartig. [Racker.]

varmint *sl.* ['vɑːmint] *kleiner*]

varnish ['vɑːniʃ] 1. Firnis *m,* Lack *m; fig.* (äußerer) Anstrich; 2. firnissen, lackieren; *fig.* beschönigen.

vary ['vɛəri] (sich) (ver)ändern; wechseln (mit *et.*); abweichen.

vase [vɑːz] Vase *f.*

vassal ['væsəl] Vasall *m; attr.* Vasallen...

vast □ [vɑːst] ungeheuer, gewaltig, riesig, umfassend, weit.

vat [væt] Faß *n;* Bottich *m;* Kufe *f.*

vaudeville *Am.* ['voudəvil] Varieté *n.*

vault [vɔːlt] 1. Gewölbe *n;* Wölbung *f;* Stahlkammer *f;* Gruft *f; bsd. Sport:* Sprung *m;* wine-Weinkeller *m;* 2. (über)wölben; *bsd. Sport:* springen (über *acc.*).

vaulting-horse ['vɔːltiŋhɔːs] *Turnen:* Pferd *n.*

vaunt *lit.* [vɔːnt] (sich) rühmen.

veal [viːl] Kalbfleisch *n; roast* ~ Kalbsbraten *m.*

veer [viə] (sich) drehen.

vegeta|ble ['vedʒitəbl] 1. Pflanzen..., pflanzlich; 2. Pflanze *f; mst* ~s *pl.* Gemüse *n;* ~rian [vedʒi'tɛəriən] 1. Vegetarier(in); 2. vegetarisch; ~te ['vedʒiteit] vegetieren; ~tive □ [~tətiv] vegetativ; wachstumfördernd.

vehemen|ce ['viːiməns] Heftigkeit *f;* Gewalt *f;* ~t □ [~nt] heftig; ungestüm.

vehicle ['viːikl] Fahrzeug *n,* Beförderungsmittel *n; fig.* Vermittler *m,* Träger *m;* Ausdrucksmittel *n.*

veil [veil] 1. Schleier *m;* Hülle *f;* 2. (sich) verschleiern *(a. fig.).*

vein [vein] Ader *f (a. fig.);* Anlage *f;* Neigung *f;* Stimmung *f.*

velocipede [vi'losipiːd] *Am.* (Kinder)Dreirad *n; hist.* Veloziped *n.*

velocity [vi'lositi] Geschwindigkeit *f.*

velvet ['velvit] 1. Samt *m; hunt.* Bast *m;* 2. Samt...; samten; ~y [~ti] samtig.

venal ['viːnl] käuflich, feil.

vend [vend] verkaufen; ~er, ~or ['vendə, ~dɔː] Verkäufer *m,* Händler *m.*

veneer [vi'niə] 1. Furnier *n;* 2. furnieren; *fig.* bemänteln.

venera|ble □ ['venərəbl] ehrwürdig; ~te [~reit] (ver)ehren; ~tion [venə'reifən] Verehrung f.

venereal [vi'niəriəl] Geschlechts...

Venetian [vi'ni:ʃən] 1. venetianisch; ~ blind (Stab)Jalousie f; 2. Venetianer(in).

vengeance ['vendʒəns] Rache f; with a ~ F und wie, ganz gehörig.

venial ['vi:njəl] verzeihlich.

venison ['venzn] Wildbret n.

venom ['venəm] (bsd. Schlangen-) Gift n; fig. Gift n; Gehässigkeit f; ~ous □ [~məs] giftig.

venous ['vi:nəs] Venen...; venös.

vent [vent] 1. Öffnung f; Luft-, Spundloch n; Auslaß m; Schlitz m; give ~ to s-m Zorn etc. Luft machen; 2. fig. Luft machen (dat.).

ventilat|e ['ventileit] ventilieren, (be-, ent-, durch)lüften; fig. erörtern; ~ion [venti'leiʃn] Ventilation f, Lüftung f; fig. Erörterung f; ~or ['ventileitə] Ventilator m.

ventral anat. ['ventrəl] Bauch...

ventriloquist [ven'triləkwist] Bauchredner m.

ventur|e ['ventʃə] 1. Wagnis n; Risiko n; Abenteuer n; Spekulation f; at a ~ auf gut Glück; 2. (sich) wagen; riskieren; ~esome □ [~əsəm], ~ous □ [~rəs] verwegen, kühn.

veracious □ [ve'reiʃəs] wahrhaft.

verb gr. [və:b] Verb(um) n, Zeitwort n; ~al □ ['və:bəl] wörtlich; mündlich; ~iage ['və:biidʒ] Wortschwall m; ~ose □ [və:'bous] wortreich. [reif.\

verdant □ ['və:dənt] grün; fig. un-\

verdict ['və:dikt] ⚖ (Urteils-) Spruch m der Geschworenen; fig. Urteil n; bring in od. return a ~ of guilty auf schuldig erkennen.

verdigris ['və:digris] Grünspan m.

verdure ['və:dʒə] Grün n.

verge [və:dʒ] 1. Rand m, Grenze f; on the ~ of am Rande (gen.); dicht vor (dat.); 2. sich (hin)neigen; ~ (up)on grenzen an (acc.).

veri|fy ['verifai] (nach)prüfen; beweisen; bestätigen; ~similitude [verisi'militju:d] Wahrscheinlichkeit f; ~table □ ['veritəbl] wahr (-haftig).

vermi|celli [və:mi'seli] Fadennudeln f/pl.; ~ular [və:'mikjulə] wurmartig.

vermilion [və'miljən] 1. Zinnoberrot n; 2. zinnoberrot.

vermin ['və:min] Ungeziefer n; hunt. Raubzeug n; fig. Gesindel n; ~ous □ [~nəs] voller Ungeziefer.

vernacular [və'nækjulə] 1. □ einheimisch; Volks...; 2. Landes-, Muttersprache f; Jargon m.

versatile □ ['və:sətail] wendig.

verse [və:s] Vers(e pl.) m; Strophe f; Dichtung f; ~d [və:st] bewandert.

versify ['və:sifai] v/t. in Verse bringen; v/i. Verse machen.

version ['və:ʃən] Übersetzung f; Fassung f, Darstellung f; Lesart f.

versus bsd. ⚖ ['və:səs] gegen.

vertebra anat. ['və:tibrə], pl. ~e [~ri:] Wirbel m.

vertical □ ['və:tikəl] vertikal, senkrecht.

vertig|inous □ [və:'tidʒinəs] schwindlig; schwindelnd (Höhe); ~o ['və:tigou] Schwindel(anfall) m.

verve [veəv] Schwung m, Verve f.

very ['veri] 1. adv. sehr; the ~ best das allerbeste; 2. adj. wirklich; eben; bloß; the ~ same ebenderselbe; in the ~ act auf frischer Tat; gerade dabei; the ~ thing gerade das; the ~ thought der bloße Gedanke; the ~ stones sogar die Steine; the veriest rascal der größte Schuft.

vesicle ['vesikl] Bläschen n.

vessel ['vesl] Gefäß n (a. anat., ⚕, fig.); ⚓ Fahrzeug n, Schiff n.

vest [vest] 1. Unterhemd n; Weste f; 2. v/t. bekleiden (with mit); j-n einsetzen (in in acc.); et. übertragen (in s.o. j-m); v/i. verliehen werden.

vestibule ['vestibju:l] Vorhof m (a. anat.); Vorhalle f; Hausflur m; bsd. Am. ⚙ Korridor m zwischen zwei D-Zug-Wagen; ~ train D-Zug m.

vestige ['vestidʒ] Spur f.

vestment ['vestmənt] Gewand n.

vestry ['vestri] eccl. Sakristei f; Gemeindevertretung f; Gemeindesaal m; ~man Gemeindevertreter m.

vet F [vet] 1. Tierarzt m; Am. ✗ Veteran m; 2. co. verarzten; gründlich prüfen.

veteran ['vetərən] 1. ausgedient; erfahren; 2. Veteran m.

veterinary ['vetərinəri] 1. tierärztlich; 2. a. ~ surgeon Tierarzt m.

veto ['vi:tou] 1. pl. ~es Veto n; 2. sein Veto einlegen gegen.

vex [veks] ärgern; schikanieren; ~ation [vek'seiʃən] Verdruß m; Ärger(nis n) m; ~atious [~ʃəs] ärgerlich.

via [vaiə] über, via.

viaduct ['vaiədʌkt] Viadukt m, Überführung f.

vial ['vaiəl] Phiole f, Fläschchen n.

viand ['vaiənd] mst. ~s pl. Lebensmittel n/pl.

vibrat|e [vai'breit] vibrieren, zittern; ~ion [~eiʃən] Schwingung f, Zittern n, Vibrieren n, Erschütterung f.

vicar eccl. ['vikə] Vikar m; ~age [~əridʒ] Pfarrhaus n.

vice¹ [vais] Laster n; Fehler m; Unart f; ⊕ Schraubstock m.

vice² prp. ['vaisi] an Stelle von.

vice³ [vais] F Stellvertreter m; attr. Vize..., Unter...; ~roy ['vaisrɔi] Vizekönig m.

vice versa ['vaisi'vəːsə] umgekehrt.

vicinity [vi'siniti] Nachbarschaft *f*; Nähe *f*.

vicious □ ['viʃəs] lasterhaft; bösartig; boshaft; fehlerhaft.

vicissitude [vi'sisitjuːd] Wandel *m*, Wechsel *m*; ~s *pl.* Wechselfälle *m/pl.*

victim ['viktim] Opfer *n*; ~ize [~maiz] (hin)opfern; *fig. j-n* hereinlegen.

victor ['viktə] Sieger *m*; ♀ian *hist.* [vik'tɔːriən] Viktorianisch; ~ious □ [~iəs] siegreich; Sieges...; ~y ['viktəri] Sieg *m*.

victual ['vitl] 1. (sich) verpflegen *od.* verproviantieren; 2. *mst* ~s *pl.* Lebensmittel *n/pl.*, Proviant *m*; ~(l)er [~lə] Lebensmittellieferant*m*.

video ['vidiou] Fernseh...

vie [vai] wetteifern.

Viennese [viə'niːz] 1. Wiener(in); 2. Wiener..., wienerisch.

view [vjuː] 1. Sicht *f*, Blick *m*; Besichtigung *f*; Aussicht *f* (of auf *acc.*); Anblick *m*; Ansicht *f* (*a.fig.*); Absicht *f*; *at first* ~ auf den ersten Blick; *in* ~ sichtbar, zu sehen; *in* ~ *of* im Hinblick auf (*acc.*); *fig.* angesichts (*gen.*); *on* ~ zu besichtigen; *with a* ~ *to inf. od. of ger.* in der Absicht zu *inf.*; *have* (keep) *in* ~ im Auge haben (behalten); 2. ansehen, besichtigen; *fig.* betrachten; ~er ['vjuːə] Betrachter(in), Zuschauer (-in); ~less ['vjuːlis] ohne eigene Meinung; *poet.* unsichtbar; ~point Gesichts-, Standpunkt *m*.

vigil ['vidʒil] Nachtwache *f*; ~ance [~ləns] Wachsamkeit *f*; ~ant □ [~nt] wachsam.

vigo|rous □ ['vigərəs] kräftig; energisch; nachdrücklich; ~(u)r ['vigə] Kraft *f*; Vitalität *f*; Nachdruck *m*.

viking ['vaikiŋ] 1. Wiking(er) *m*; 2. wikingisch, Wikinger...

vile □ [vail] gemein; abscheulich.

vilify ['vilifai] verunglimpfen.

village ['vilidʒ] Dorf *n*; ~ **green** Dorfanger *m*, -wiese *f*; ~r [~dʒə] Dorfbewohner(in).

villain ['vilən] Schurke *m*, Schuft *m*, Bösewicht *m*; ~ous □ [~nəs] schurkisch; F scheußlich; ~y [~ni] Schurkerei *f*.

vim F [vim] Schwung *m*, Schneid *m*.

vindicat|e ['vindikeit] rechtfertigen (*from* gegen); verteidigen; ~ion [vindi'keiʃən] Rechtfertigung *f*.

vindictive □ [vin'diktiv] rachsüchtig.

vine ♀ [vain] Wein(stock) *m*, Rebe *f*; ~gar ['vinigə] (Wein)Essig *m*; ~growing ['vaingrouiŋ] Weinbau *m*; ~yard ['vinjəd] Weinberg *m*.

vintage ['vintidʒ] 1. Weinlese *f*; (Wein)Jahrgang *m*; 2. klassisch; erlesen; altmodisch; ~ *car mot.* Veteran *m*; ~r [~dʒə] Winzer *m*.

viola ♪ [vi'oulə] Bratsche *f*.

violat|e ['vaiəleit] verletzen; *Eid etc.* brechen; vergewaltigen, schänden; ~ion [vaiə'leiʃən] Verletzung *f*; (Eid- *etc.*)Bruch *m*; Vergewaltigung *f*, Schändung *f*.

violen|ce ['vaiələns] Gewalt(samkeit, -tätigkeit) *f*; Heftigkeit *f*; ~t □ [~nt] gewaltsam; gewalttätig; heftig.

violet ♀ ['vaiəlit] Veilchen *n*.

violin ♪ [vaiə'lin] Violine *f*, Geige *f*.

V.I.P., VIP ['viːai'piː] F hohes Tier.

viper *zo.* ['vaipə] Viper *f*, Natter *f*.

virago [vi'rɑːgou] Zankteufel *m*.

virgin ['vəːdʒin] 1. Jungfrau *f*; 2. *a.* ~al □ [~nl] jungfräulich; Jungfern...; ~ity [vəː'dʒiniti] Jungfräulichkeit *f*.

viril|e ['virail] männlich; Mannes...; ~ity [vi'riliti] Männlichkeit *f*.

virtu [vəː'tuː]: *article of* ~ Kunstgegenstand *m*; ~al □ ['vəːtjuəl] eigentlich; ~ally [~li] praktisch; ~e ['vəːtjuː] Tugend *f*; Wirksamkeit *f*; Vorzug *m*, Wert *m*; *in od. by* ~ *of* kraft, vermöge (*gen.*); *make a* ~ *of necessity* aus der Not e-e Tugend machen; ~osity [vəːtju'ɔsiti] Virtuosität *f*; ~ous □ ['vəːtjuəs] tugendhaft.

virulent □ ['virulənt] giftig; ♂ virulent; *fig.* bösartig.

virus ['vaiərəs] Virus *n*; *fig.* Gift *n*.

visa ['viːzə] Visum *n*, Sichtvermerk *m*; ~ed [~əd] mit e-m Sichtvermerk *od.* Visum versehen.

viscose ⚗ ['viskous] Viskose *f*; ~ *silk* Zellstoffseide *f*.

viscount ['vaikaunt] Vicomte *m*; ~ess [~tis] Vicomtesse *f*.

viscous □ ['viskəs] zähflüssig.

vise *Am.* [vais] Schraubstock *m*.

visé ['viːzei] = *visa*.

visib|ility [vizi'biliti] Sichtbarkeit *f*; Sichtweite *f*; ~le □ ['vizəbl] sichtbar; *fig.* (er)sichtlich; *pred.* zu sehen (*S.*); zu sprechen (*P.*).

vision ['viʒən] Sehvermögen *n*, Sehkraft *f*; *fig.* Seherblick *m*; Vision *f*, Erscheinung *f*; ~ary ['viʒnəri] 1. phantastisch; 2. Geisterseher(in); Phantast(in).

visit ['vizit] 1. *v/t.* besuchen; besichtigen; *fig.* heimsuchen; *et.* vergelten, *v/i.* Besuche machen; *Am.* sich unterhalten, plaudern (*with* mit); 2. Besuch *m*; ~ation [vizi'teiʃən] Besuch *m*; Besichtigung *f*; *fig.* Heimsuchung *f*; ~or ['vizitə] Besucher(in), Gast *m*; Inspektor *m*.

vista ['vistə] Durchblick *m*; Rückod. Ausblick *m*.

visual □ ['vizjuəl] Seh...; Gesichts...; ~ize [~aiz] (sich) vor Augen stellen, sich ein Bild machen von.

vital □ ['vaitl] 1. Lebens...; lebenswichtig, wesentlich; lebensgefähr-

lich; ~ parts pl. = 2. ~s pl. lebens-
wichtige Organe n/pl.; edle Teile
m/pl.; ~ity [vai'tæliti] Lebenskraft
f; Vitalität f; ~ize ['vaitəlaiz] beleben.

vitamin(e) ['vitəmin] Vitamin n.

vitiate ['viʃieit] verderben; beeinträchtigen; hinfällig (st unültig)
machen.

vitreous □ ['vitriəs] Glas...; gläsern.

vituperate [vi'tju:pəreit] schelten;
schmähen, beschimpfen.

vivaci|ous □ [vi'veiʃəs] lebhaft; ~ty
[vi'væsiti] Lebhaftigkeit f.

vivid □ ['vivid] lebhaft, lebendig.

vivify ['vivifai] (sich) beleben.

vixen ['viksn] Füchsin f; zänkisches
Weib.

vocabulary [və'kæbjuləri] Wörterverzeichnis n; Wortschatz m.

vocal □ ['voukəl] stimmlich;
Stimm...; gesprochen; laut; ♪ Vokal..., Gesang...; klingend; gr.
stimmhaft; ~ist [~list] Sänger(in);
~ize [~laiz] (gr. stimmhaft) aussprechen; singen.

vocation [vou'keiʃən] Berufung f;
Beruf m; ~al □ [~nl] beruflich;
Berufs...

vociferate [vou'sifəreit] schreien.

vogue [voug] Beliebtheit f; Mode f.

voice [vɔis] 1. Stimme f; active
(passive) ~ gr. Aktiv n (Passiv n);
give ~ to Ausdruck geben (dat.);
2. äußern, ausdrücken; gr. stimmhaft aussprechen.

void [vɔid] 1. leer; st ungültig; ~
of frei von; arm an (dat.); ohne;
2. Leere f; Lücke f; 3. entleeren;
ungültig machen, aufheben.

volatile ['vɔlətail] ✺ flüchtig (a.
fig.); flatterhaft.

volcano [vɔl'keinou] pl. ~es Vulkan m.

volition [vou'liʃən] Wollen n; Wil-
le(nskraft f) m.

volley ['vɔli] 1. Salve f; (Geschoß-
etc.)Hagel m; fig. Schwall m; Tennis: Flugball m; 2. mst ~ out e-n
Schwall von Worten etc. von sich
geben; Salven abgeben; fig. hageln;
dröhnen; ~-ball Sport: Volleyball
m, Flugball m.

volt ⚡ [voult] Volt n; ~age ⚡
['voultidʒ] Spannung f; ~meter ⚡
Volt-, Spannungsmesser m.

volub|ility [vɔlju'biliti] Redege-
wandtheit f; ~le □ ['vɔljubl] (rede-)
gewandt.

volum|e ['vɔljum] Band m e-s
Buches; Volumen n; fig. Masse f;

große Menge; (bsd. Stimm)Umfang
m; ~ of sound Radio: Lautstärke f;
~inous □ [və'lju:minəs] vielbän-
dig; umfangreich, voluminös.

volunt|ary □ ['vɔləntəri] freiwillig;
willkürlich; ~eer [vɔlən'tiə] 1. Frei-
willige(r m) f; attr. Freiwilligen...;
2. v/i. freiwillig dienen; sich freiwillig melden; sich erbieten; v/t.
anbieten; sich e-e Bemerkung erlauben.

voluptu|ary [və'lʌptjuəri] Woll-
lüstling m; ~ous □ [~əs] woll-
lüstig; üppig.

vomit ['vɔmit] 1. (sich) erbrechen;
fig. (aus)speien, ausstoßen; 2. Er-
brochene(s) n; Erbrechen n.

voraci|ous □ [və'reiʃəs] gefräßig;
gierig; ~ty [vɔ'ræsiti] Gefräßigkeit f; Gier f.

vort|ex ['vɔ:teks], pl. mst ~ices
['vɔ:tisi:z] Wirbel m, Strudel m
(mst fig.).

vote [vout] 1. (Wahl)Stimme f; Abstimmung f; Stimmrecht n; Beschluß m, Votum n; ~ of no confidence Mißtrauensvotum n; cast a ~
(s)eine Stimme abgeben; take a ~
on s.th. über et. abstimmen; 2. v/t.
stimmen für; v/i. (ab)stimmen;
wählen; ~ for stimmen für; F für
et. sein; et. vorschlagen; ~r ['voutə]
Wähler(in).

voting ['voutiŋ] Abstimmung f; attr.
Wahl...; ~ machine Stimmenzähl-
maschine f; ~-paper Stimmzettel
m; ~-power Stimmrecht n.

vouch [vautʃ] verbürgen; ~ for bürgen für; ~er ['vautʃə] Beleg m,
Unterlage f; Gutschein m; Zeuge
m; ~safe [vautʃ'seif] gewähren; geruhen.

vow [vau] 1. Gelübde n; (Treu-)
Schwur m; 2. v/t. geloben.

vowel gr. ['vauəl] Vokal m, Selbst-
laut m.

voyage [vɔidʒ] 1. längere (See-,
Flug)Reise; 2. reisen, fahren; ~r
['vɔiədʒə] (See)Reisende(r m) f.

vulgar ['vʌlgə] 1. □ gewöhnlich,
gemein, vulgär, pöbelhaft; ~ tongue
Volkssprache f; 2.: the ~ der Pöbel;
~ism [~ərizəm] vulgärer Ausdruck;
~ity [vʌl'gæriti] Gemeinheit f; ~ize
['vʌlgəraiz] gemein machen; erniedrigen; populär machen.

vulnerable □ ['vʌlnərəbl] ver-
wundbar; fig. angreifbar.

vulpine ['vʌlpain] Fuchs...; fuchsartig; schlau, listig.

vulture orn. ['vʌltʃə] Geier m.

vying ['vaiiŋ] wetteifernd.

W

wacky *Am. sl.* ['wæki] verrückt.
wad [wɔd] **1.** (Watte)Bausch *m*; Polster *n*; Pfropf(en) *m*; Banknotenbündel *n*; **2.** wattieren; polstern; zs.-pressen; zustopfen; ~**ding** ['wɔdiŋ] Wattierung *f*; Watte *f*.
waddle ['wɔdl] watscheln, wackeln.
wade [weid] *v/i.* waten; *fig.* sich hindurcharbeiten; *v/t.* durchwaten.
wafer ['weifə] Waffel *f*; Oblate *f*; *eccl.* Hostie *f*.
waffle ['wɔfl] **1.** Waffel *f*; **2.** F quasseln.
waft [wɑ:ft] **1.** wehen, tragen; **2.** Hauch *m*.
wag [wæg] **1.** wackeln (mit); wedeln (mit); **2.** Schütteln *n*; Wedeln *n*; Spaßvogel *m*.
wage¹ [weidʒ] *Krieg* führen.
wage² [~] *mst* ~**s** *pl.* Lohn *m*; ~**earner** ['weidʒə:nə] Lohnempfänger *m*.
wager ['weidʒə] **1.** Wette *f*; **2.** wetten.
waggish □ ['wægiʃ] schelmisch.
waggle F ['wægl] wackeln (mit).
wag(g)on ['wægən] (Roll-, Güter-)Wagen *m*; ~**er** [~nə] Fuhrmann *m*.
wagtail *orn.* ['wægteil] Bachstelze *f*.
waif [weif] herrenloses Gut; Strandgut *n*; Heimatlose(r *m*) *f*.
wail [weil] **1.** (Weh)Klagen *n*; **2.** (weh)klagen.
wainscot ['weinskət] (Holz)Täfelung *f*.
waist [weist] Taille *f*; schmalste Stelle; ♣ Mitteldeck *n*; ~**coat** ['weiskout] Weste *f*; ~**line** ['weistlain] *Schneiderei:* Taille *f*.
wait [weit] **1.** *v/i.* warten (*for* auf *acc.*); *a.* ~ *at* (*Am.* on) table bedienen, servieren; ~ (up)on *j-n* bedienen; *j-n* besuchen; ~ *and see* abwarten; *v/t.* abwarten; mit *dem Essen* warten (*for* auf *j-n*); **2.** Warten *n*, Aufenthalt *m*; *lie in* ~ *for s.o.* j-m auflauern; ~**er** ['weitə] Kellner *m*; Tablett *n*.
waiting ['weitiŋ] Warten *n*; Dienst *m*; *in* ~ dienstuend; ~**room** Wartezimmer *n*; ➅ *etc.* Wartesaal *m*.
waitress ['weitris] Kellnerin *f*.
waive [weiv] verzichten auf (*acc.*), aufgeben; ~**r** ⚖ ['weivə] Verzicht *m*.
wake [weik] **1.** ♣ Kielwasser *n* (*a. fig.*); Totenwache *f*; Kirmes *f*; **2.** [*irr.*] *v/i. a.* ~ *up* aufwachen; *v/t. a.* ~ *up* (auf)wecken; erwecken; *fig.* wachrufen; ~**ful** □ ['weikful] wachsam; schlaflos; ~**n** ['weikən] *s.* wake 2.
wale *bsd. Am.* [weil] Strieme *f*.
walk [wɔ:k] **1.** *v/i.* (zu Fuß) gehen; spazierengehen; wandern; Schritt gehen; ~ *out* F streiken; ~ *out on sl.*

im Stich lassen; *v/t.* führen; *Pferd* Schritt gehen lassen; begleiten; (durch)wandern; umhergehen auf *od.* in (*dat.*); **2.** (Spazier)Gang *m*; Spazierweg *m*; ~ *of life* Lebensstellung *f*, Beruf *m*; ~**er** ['wɔ:kə] Fuß-, Spaziergänger(in).
walkie-talkie ⚔ ['wɔ:kitɔ:ki] tragbares Sprechfunkgerät.
walking ['wɔ:kiŋ] Spazierengehen *n*, Wandern *n*; *attr.* Spazier...; Wander...; ~ *papers pl. Am.* F Entlassung(spapiere *n/pl.*) *f*; Laufpaß *m*; ~**stick** Spazierstock *m*; ~**tour** (Fuß)Wanderung *f*.
walk|out *Am.* ['wɔ:kaut] Ausstand *m*; ~**over** Kinderspiel *n*, leichter Sieg.
wall [wɔ:l] **1.** Wand *f*; Mauer *f*; **2.** mit Mauern umgeben; ~ *up* zumauern.
wallet ['wɔlit] Ränzel *n*; Brieftasche *f*.
wallflower *fig.* ['wɔ:lflauə] Mauerblümchen *n*.
wallop F ['wɔləp] *j-n* verdreschen.
wallow ['wɔlou] sich wälzen.
wall|-paper ['wɔ:lpeipə] Tapete *f*; ~**socket** ⚡ Steckdose *f*.
walnut ♀ ['wɔ:lnʌt] Walnuß(baum *m*) *f*.
walrus *zo.* ['wɔ:lrəs] Walroß *n*.
waltz [wɔ:ls] **1.** Walzer *m*; **2.** Walzer tanzen.
wan □ [wɔn] blaß, bleich, fahl.
wand [wɔnd] (Zauber)Stab *m*.
wander ['wɔndə] wandern; umherschweifen, umherwandern; *fig.* abschweifen; irregehen; phantasieren.
wane [wein] **1.** abnehmen (*Mond*); *fig.* schwinden; **2.** Abnehmen *n*.
wangle *sl.* ['wæŋgl] *v/t.* deichseln, hinkriegen; *v/i.* mogeln.
want [wɔnt] **1.** Mangel *m* (of an *dat.*); Bedürfnis *n*; Not *f*; **2.** *v/i.*: be ~*ing* fehlen; es fehlen lassen (in an *dat.*); unzulänglich sein; ~ *for* Not leiden an (*dat.*); *it* ~*s of* es fehlt an (*dat.*); *v/t.* bedürfen (*gen.*); brauchen; nicht haben; wünschen, (haben) wollen; *it* ~*s s.th.* es fehlt an et. (*dat.*); *he* ~*s energy* es fehlt ihm an Energie; ~*ed* gesucht; ~**ad** F ['wɔntæd] Kleinanzeige *f*; Stellenangebot *n*, -gesuch *n*.
wanton ['wɔntən] **1.** □ geil; üppig; mutwillig; **2.** Dirne *f*; **3.** umhertollen.
war [wɔ:] **1.** Krieg *m*; *attr.* Kriegs...; *make* ~ Krieg führen (*upon gegen*); **2.** (ea. wider)streiten.
warble ['wɔ:bl] trillern; singen.
ward [wɔ:d] **1.** Gewahrsam *m*; Vormundschaft *f*; Mündel *n*; Schützling *m*; Gefängniszelle *f*; Abteilung *f*, Station *f*, Krankenzimmer *n*;

(Stadt)Bezirk *m*; ⊕ Einschnitt *m im Schlüsselbart*; 2. ~ off abwehren; ~en ['wɔːdn] Aufseher *m*; (Luftschutz)Wart *m*; *univ.* Rektor *m*; ~er ['wɔːdə] (Gefangenen)Wärter *m*; ~robe ['wɔːdroub] Garderobe *f*; Kleiderschrank *m*; ~ trunk Schrankkoffer *m*.

ware [weə] Ware *f*; Geschirr *n*.

warehouse 1. ['weəhaus] (Waren-) Lager *n*; Speicher *m*; 2. [~auz] auf Lager bringen, einlagern.

war|fare ['wɔːfeə] Krieg(führung*f*) *m*; ~head ⚔ Sprengkopf *m e-r Rakete etc.*

wariness ['weərinis] Vorsicht *f*.

warlike ['wɔːlaik] kriegerisch.

warm [wɔːm] 1. □ warm (*a. fig.*); heiß; *fig.* hitzig; 2. F Erwärmung*f*; 3. *v/t. a.* ~ up (auf-, an-, er)wärmen; *v/i. a.* ~ up warm werden, sich erwärmen; ~th [wɔːmθ] Wärme *f*.

warn [wɔːn] warnen (*of, against* vor *dat.*); verwarnen; ermahnen; verständigen; ~ing ['wɔːniŋ] (Ver-)Warnung *f*; Mahnung *f*; Kündigung *f*.

warp [wɔːp] *v/i.* sich verziehen (*Holz*); *v/t. fig.* verdrehen, verzerren; beeinflussen; *j-n* abbringen (*from* von).

warrant ['wɔrənt] 1. Vollmacht *f*; Rechtfertigung *f*; Berechtigung *f*; ⚄ (Vollziehungs)Befehl *m*; Berechtigungsschein *m*; ~ *of arrest* ⚄ Haftbefehl *m*; 2. bevollmächtigen; *j-n* berechtigen; *et.* rechtfertigen; verbürgen; † garantieren; ~y [~ti] Garantie *f*; Berechtigung *f*.

warrior ['wɔriə] Krieger *m*.

wart [wɔːt] Warze *f*; Auswuchs *m*.

wary □ ['weəri] vorsichtig, behutsam; wachsam.

was [wɔz, wəz] 1. *und* 3. *sg. pret.* von be; *pret. pass.* von be; he ~ to have come er hätte kommen sollen.

wash [wɔʃ] 1. *v/t.* waschen; (um-)spülen; ~ up abwaschen, spülen; *v/i.* sich waschen (lassen); waschecht sein (*a. fig.*); spülen, schlagen (*Wellen*); 2. Waschen *n*; Wäsche *f*; Wellenschlag *m*; Spülwasser *n*; *contp.* Gewäsch *n*; *mouth-*~ Mundwasser *n*; ~able ['wɔʃəbl] waschbar; ~-basin Waschbecken *n*; ~cloth Waschlappen *m*; ~er ['wɔʃə] Wäscherin *f*; Waschmaschine *f*; ⊕ Unterlagscheibe *f*; ~erwoman Waschfrau *f*; ~ing ['wɔʃiŋ] 1. Waschen *n*; Wäsche *f*; ~ *s pl.* Spülicht *n*; 2. Wasch...; ~ing-up Abwaschen *n*; ~rag *bsd. Am.* Waschlappen *m*; ~y ['wɔʃi] wässerig.

wasp [wɔsp] Wespe *f*.

wastage ['weistidʒ] Abgang *m*, Verlust *m*; Vergeudung *f*.

waste [weist] 1. wüst, öde; unbebaut; überflüssig; Abfall...; *lay* ~ verwüsten; ~ *paper* Altpapier *n*;

2. Verschwendung*f*, Vergeudung*f*; Abfall *m*; Einöde *f*, Wüste *f*; 3. *v/t.* verwüsten; verschwenden; verzehren; *v/i.* verschwendet werden; ~ful □ ['weistful] verschwenderisch; ~paper-basket [weist'peipəbɑːskit] Papierkorb *m*; ~pipe ['weistpaip] Abflußrohr *n*.

watch [wɔtʃ] 1. Wache *f*; Taschenuhr *f*; 2. *v/i.* wachen; ~ *for* warten auf (*acc.*); ~ *out* F aufpassen; *v/t.* bewachen; beobachten; achtgeben auf (*acc.*); *Gelegenheit* abwarten; ~dog ['wɔtʃdɔg] Wachhund *m*; ~ful □ [~ful] wachsam, achtsam; ~maker Uhrmacher *m*; ~man (Nacht)Wächter *m*; ~word Losung *f*.

water ['wɔːtə] 1. Wasser *n*; Gewässer *n*; *drink the* ~s Brunnen trinken; 2. *v/t.* bewässern; (be-)sprengen; (be)gießen; mit Wasser versorgen; verdünnen; verwässern (*a. fig.*); *v/i.* wässern (*Mund*); tränen (*Augen*); Wasser einnehmen; ~closet (Wasser)Klosett *n*; ~colo(u)r Aquarell(malerei *f*) *n*; ~course Wasserlauf *m*; ~cress ♣ Brunnenkresse *f*; ~fall Wasserfall *m*; ~front Ufer *n, bsd. Am. städtisches* Hafengebiet; ~ga(u)ge ⊕ Wasserstands(an)zeiger *m*; Pegel *m*.

watering ['wɔːtəriŋ] ~can Gießkanne *f*; ~place Wasserloch *n*; Tränke *f*; Bad(eort *m*) *n*; Seebad *n*; ~pot Gießkanne *f*.

water|-level ['wɔːtəlevl] Wasserspiegel *m*; Wasserstand(slinie *f*) *m*; ⊕ Wasserwaage *f*; ~man Fährmann *m*; Bootsführer *m*; Ruderer *m*; ~proof 1. wasserdicht; 2. Regenmantel *m*; 3. imprägnieren; ~shed Wasserscheide *f*; Stromgebiet *n*; ~side 1. Fluß-, Seeufer *n*; 2. am Wasser (gelegen); ~tight wasserdicht; *fig.* unangreifbar; ~way Wasserstraße *f*; ~works *oft sg.* Wasserwerk *n*; ~y [~əri] wässerig.

watt ⚡ [wɔt] Watt *n*.

wattle ['wɔtl] 1. Flechtwerk *n*; 2. aus Flechtwerk herstellen.

wave [weiv] 1. Welle *f*; Woge *f*; Winken *n*; 2. *v/t.* wellig machen, wellen; schwingen; schwenken; ~ *s.o. aside* j-n beiseite winken; *v/i.* wogen; wehen, flattern; winken; ~length *phys.* ['weivleŋθ] Wellenlänge *f*.

waver ['weivə] (sch)wanken; flakkern.

wavy ['weivi] wellig, wogend.

wax¹ [wæks] 1. Wachs *n*; Siegellack *m*; Ohrenschmalz *n*; 2. wachsen; bohnern.

wax² [~] [*irr.*] zunehmen (*Mond*).

wax|en *fig.* ['wæksən] wächsern; ~y □ [~si] wachsartig; weich.

way [wei] 1. *mst* Weg *m*; Straße *f*;

Art u. Weise f; *eigene* Art; Strecke f; Richtung f; F Gegend f; ♁ Fahrt f; *fig.* Hinsicht f; Zustand m; ♁ Helling f; ~ in Eingang m; ~ out Ausgang m; *fig.* Ausweg m; *right of* ~ ♁ Wegerecht n; *bsd. mot.* Vorfahrt(srecht n) f; *this* ~ hierher, hier entlang; *by the* ~ übrigens; *by* ~ *of* durch; *on the* ~, *on one's* ~ unterwegs; *out of the* ~ ungewöhnlich; *under* ~ in Fahrt; *give* ~ zurückgehen; *mot.* die Vorfahrt lassen (*to dat.*); nachgeben; abgelöst werden (*to* von); sich hingeben (*to dat.*); *have one's* ~ s-n Willen haben; *lead the* ~ vorangehen; 2. *adv.* weit; ~bill ['weibil] Frachtbrief m; ~farer ['weifeərə] Wanderer m; ~lay [wei'lei] *[irr.* (lay)] j-m auflauern; ~side 1. Wegrand m; 2. am Wege; ~ station *Am.* Zwischenstation f; ~ train *Am.* Bummelzug m; ~ward □ ['weiwəd] starrköpfig, eigensinnig.

we [wi:, wi] wir.

weak [wi:k] schwach; schwächlich; dünn (*Getränk*); ~en ['wi:kən] *v/t.* schwächen; *v/i.* schwach werden; ~ling ['wi:kliŋ] Schwächling m; ~ly [~li] schwächlich; ~minded ['wi:k'maindid] schwachsinnig; ~ness ['wi:knis] Schwäche f.

weal [wi:l] Wohl n; Strieme f.

wealth [welθ] Wohlstand m; Reichtum m; *fig.* Fülle f; ~y □ ['welθi] reich; wohlhabend.

wean [wi:n] entwöhnen; ~ *s.o. from s.th.* j-m et. abgewöhnen.

weapon ['wepən] Waffe f.

wear [wɛə] 1. *[irr.] v/t. am Körper* tragen; zur Schau tragen; *a.* ~ *away*, ~ *down*, ~ *off*, ~ *out* abnutzen, abtragen, verbrauchen; erschöpfen; ermüden; zermürben; *v/i.* sich *gut etc.* tragen *od.* halten; *a.* ~ *off od.* ~ *out* sich abnutzen *od.* abtragen; *fig.* sich verlieren; ~ *on* vergehen; 2. Tragen n; (Be)Kleidung f; Abnutzung f; *for hard* ~ strapazierfähig; *the worse for* ~ abgetragen; ~ *and tear* Verschleiß m.

wear|iness ['wiərinis] Müdigkeit f; Ermüdung f; *fig.* Überdruß m; ~some □ [~isəm] ermüdend; langweilig; ~y ['wiəri] 1. □ müde; *fig.* überdrüssig; ermüdend; anstrengend; 2. ermüden.

weasel *zo.* ['wi:zl] Wiesel n.

weather ['weðə] 1. Wetter n, Witterung f; 2. *v/t.* dem Wetter aussetzen; ♁ *Sturm* abwettern; *fig.* überstehen; *v/i.* verwittern; ~beaten vom Wetter mitgenommen; ~bureau Wetteramt n; ~chart Wetterkarte f; ~forecast Wetterbericht m, -vorhersage f; ~worn verwittert.

weav|e ['wi:v] *[irr.]* weben; wirken; flechten; *fig.* ersinnen, erfinden;

sich schlängeln; ~er ['wi:və] Weber m.

weazen ['wi:zn] verhutzelt.

web [web] Gewebe n; *orn.* Schwimmhaut f; ~bing ['webiŋ] Gurtband n.

wed [wed] heiraten; *fig.* verbinden (*to* mit); ~ding ['wediŋ] 1. Hochzeit f; 2. Hochzeits...; Braut...; Trau...; ~ring Ehe-, Trauring m.

wedge [wedʒ] 1. Keil m; 2. (ver)keilen; *a.* ~ *in* (hin)einzwängen.

wedlock ['wedlɔk] Ehe f.

Wednesday ['wenzdi] Mittwoch m.

wee [wi:] klein, winzig; *a* ~ *bit* ein klein wenig.

weed [wi:d] 1. Unkraut n; 2. jäten; säubern (*of* von); ~ *out* ausmerzen; ~killer ['wi:dkilə] Unkrautvertilgungsmittel n; ~s *pl. mst widow's* Witwenkleidung f; ~y ['wi:di] voll Unkraut, verkrautet; *fig.* lang aufgeschossen.

week [wi:k] Woche f; *this day* ~ heute in *od.* vor e-r Woche; ~day ['wi:kdei] Wochentag m; ~end ['wi:k'end] Wochenende n; ~ly ['wi:kli] 1. wöchentlich; 2. *a.* ~ *paper* Wochenblatt n, Wochen(zeit)schrift f.

weep [wi:p] *[irr.]* weinen; tropfen; ~ing ['wi:piŋ] Trauer...; ~ *willow* ♁ Trauerweide f.

weigh [wei] *v/t.* (ab)wiegen, *fig.* ab-, erwägen; ~ *anchor* ♁ den Anker lichten; ~ed down niedergebeugt; *v/i.* wiegen (*a. fig.*); ausschlaggebend sein; ~ (*up*)on lasten auf (*dat.*).

weight [weit] 1. Gewicht n (*a. fig.*); Last f (*a. fig.*); *fig.* Bedeutung f; Wucht f; 2. beschweren; *fig.* belasten; ~y □ ['weiti] (ge)wichtig; wuchtig.

weir [wiə] Wehr n; Fischreuse f.

weird [wiəd] Schicksals...; unheimlich; F sonderbar, seltsam.

welcome ['welkəm] 1. willkommen; *you are* ~ *to inf.* es steht Ihnen frei, zu *inf.*; (*you are*) ~*!* gern geschehen!, bitte sehr!; 2. Willkomm(en n) m; 3. willkommen heißen; *fig.* begrüßen.

weld ⊕ [weld] (zs.-)schweißen.

welfare ['welfɛə] Wohlfahrt f; ~ centre Fürsorgeamt n; ~ state Wohlfahrtsstaat m; ~ work Fürsorge f, Wohlfahrtspflege f; ~ worker Fürsorger(in).

well[1] [wel] 1. Brunnen m; *fig.* Quelle f; ⊕ Bohrloch n; Treppen-, Aufzugs-, Licht-, Luftschacht m; 2. quellen.

well[2] [~] 1. wohl; gut; ordentlich, gründlich; gesund; ~ *off* in guten Verhältnissen, wohlhabend; *I am not* ~ mir ist nicht wohl; 2. *int.* nun!, F na!; ~being n; ~being ['wel'bi:iŋ] Wohl(sein) n; ~born von guter

Herkunft; ~bred wohlerzogen; ~defined deutlich, klar umrissen; ~favo(u)red gut aussehend; ~intentioned wohlmeinend; gut gemeint; ~ known, ~known bekannt; ~mannered mit guten Manieren; ~nigh ['welnai] beinahe; ~ timed rechtzeitig; ~to-do ['welt∂'du:] wohlhabend; ~wisher Gönner m, Freund m; ~worn abgetragen; fig. abgedroschen.

Welsh [welʃ] 1. walisisch; 2. Walisisch n; the ~ pl. die Waliser pl.; ~ rabbit überbackene Käseschnitte.

welt [welt] ⊕ Rahmen m, Schuh-Rahmen m; Einfassung f; Strieme f.

welter ['welt∂] 1. rollen, sich wälzen; 2. Wirrwarr m, Durcheinander n.

wench [wentʃ] Mädchen n; Dirne f.

went [went] pret. von go 1.

wept [wept] pret. u. p.p. von weep.

were [w∂:, w∂] 1. pret. pl. u. 2. sg. von be; 2. pret. pass. von be; 3. subj. pret. von be.

west [west] 1. West(en m); 2. West...; westlich; westwärts; ~erly ['west∂li], ~ern [~∂n] westlich; ~erner [~n∂] Am. Weststaatler(in); ~ward(s) [~tw∂d(z)] westwärts.

wet [wet] 1. naß, feucht; Am. den Alkoholhandel gestattend; 2. Nässe f; Feuchtigkeit f; 3. [irr.] naß machen, anfeuchten.

wetback Am. sl. ['wetbæk] illegaler Einwanderer aus Mexiko.

wether ['weð∂] Hammel m.

wet-nurse ['wetn∂:s] Amme f.

whack F [wæk] 1. verhauen; 2. Hieb m.

whale [weil] Wal m; ~bone ['weilboun] Fischbein n; ~oil Tran m; ~r ['weil∂] Walfischfänger m.

whaling ['weiliŋ] Walfischfang m.

wharf [wɔ:f], pl. a. wharves [wɔ:vz] Kai m, Anlegeplatz m.

what [wɔt] 1. was; das, was; know ~'s Bescheid wissen; 2. was?; wie?; wieviel?; welch(er, -e, -es)?; was für ein(e)?; ~ about ...? wie steht's mit ...?; ~ for? wozu?; ~ of it? was ist denn dabei?; ~ next? was sonst noch?; iro. was denn noch alles?; ~ a blessing! was für ein Segen!; 3. ~ with ... ~ with ... teils durch ... teils durch ...; ~(so)ever [wɔt(sou)'ev∂] was od. welcher auch (immer).

wheat ⊘ [wi:t] Weizen m.

wheedle ['wi:dl] beschwatzen; ~ s.th. out of s.o. j-m et. abschwatzen.

wheel [wi:l] 1. Rad n; Steuer n; bsd. Am. F Fahrrad n; Töpferscheibe f; Drehung f; ⚔ Schwenkung f; 2. rollen, fahren, schieben; sich drehen; sich umwenden; ⚔ schwenken; F radeln; ~barrow

['wi:lbærou] Schubkarren m; ~ chair Rollstuhl m; ~ed mit Rädern; fahrbar; ...räd(e)rig.

wheeze [wi:z] schnaufen, keuchen.

whelp [welp] 1. zo. Welpe m; allg. Junge(s) n; F Balg m, n (ungezogenes Kind); 2. (Junge) werfen.

when [wen] 1. wann?; 2. wenn; als; während od. da doch; und da.

whence [wens] woher, von wo.

when(so)ever [wen(sou)'ev∂] immer od. jedesmal wenn; sooft (als).

where [wε∂] wo; wohin; ~about(s) 1. ['wε∂r∂'bauts] wo herum; 2. [~'ræz]... ∂bauts] Aufenthalt m; ~as [~'ræz] wohingegen, während (doch); ~at [~'æt] wobei, worüber, worauf; ~by [wε∂'bai] wodurch; ~fore ['wε∂fɔ:] weshalb; ~in [wε∂r'in] worin; ~of [~r'ɔv] wovon; ~upon [~r∂'pɔn] worauf(hin); ~ver [~r'ev∂] wo(hin) (auch) immer; ~withal ['wε∂wiðɔ:l] Erforderliche(s) n; Mittel n/pl.

whet [wet] wetzen, schärfen; anstacheln.

whether ['weð∂] ob; ~ or no so oder so.

whetstone ['wetstoun] Schleifstein m.

whey [wei] Molke f.

which [witʃ] 1. welche(r, -s)?; 2. der, die, das; was; ~ever [~ʃ'ev∂] welche(r, -s) (auch) immer.

whiff [wif] 1. Hauch m; Zug m beim Rauchen; Zigarillo n; 2. paffen.

while [wail] 1. Weile f; Zeit f; for a ~ e-e Zeitlang; worth ~ der Mühe wert; 2. mst ~ away Zeit verbringen; 3. a. whilst [wailst] während.

whim [wim] Schrulle f, Laune f.

whimper ['wimp∂] wimmern.

whim|sical □ ['wimzik∂l] wunderlich; ~sy ['wimzi] Grille f, Laune f.

whine [wain] winseln; wimmern.

whinny ['wini] wiehern.

whip [wip] 1. v/t. peitschen; geißeln (a. fig.); j-n verprügeln; schlagen (F a. fig.); umschnüren; werfen; reißen; ~ in parl. zs.-trommeln; ~ on Kleidungsstück überwerfen; ~ up antreiben; aufraffen; v/i. springen, flitzen; 2. Peitsche f; Geißel f.

whippet zo. ['wipit] Whippet m (kleiner englischer Rennhund).

whipping ['wipiŋ] Prügel pl.; ~top Kreisel m.

whippoorwill orn. ['wippu∂wil] Ziegenmelker m.

whirl [w∂:l] 1. wirbeln; (sich) drehen; 2. Wirbel m, Strudel m; ~pool [~'lpu:l] Strudel m; ~wind Wirbelwind m.

whir(r) [w∂:] schwirren.

whisk [wisk] 1. Wisch m; Staubwedel m; Küche: Schneebesen m; Schwung m; 2. v/t. (ab-, weg)wischen, (ab-, weg)fegen; wirbeln (mit); schlagen; v/i. huschen, flitzen; ~er ['wiskə] Barthaar n; mst ~s pl. Backenbart m.

whisper ['wispə] 1. flüstern; 2. Geflüster n.

whistle ['wisl] 1. pfeifen; 2. Pfeife f; Pfiff m; F Kehle f; ~stop Am. 🏥 Haltepunkt m; fig. Kaff n; pol. kurzes Auftreten e-s Kandidaten im Wahlkampf.

Whit [wit] in Zssgn: Pfingst...

white [wait] 1. allg. weiß; rein; F anständig; Weiß...; 2. Weiß(e) n; Weiße(r m) f (Rasse); ~collar ['wait'kɔlə] geistig, Kopf..., Büro...; ~ workers pl. Angestellte pl.; ~ heat Weißglut f; ~ lie fromme Lüge; ~n ['waitn] weiß machen od. werden; bleichen; ~ness [~nis] Weiße f; Blässe f; ~wash 1. Tünche f; 2. weißen; fig. rein waschen.

whither lit. ['wiðə] wohin.

whitish ['waitiʃ] weißlich.

Whitsun ['witsn] Pfingst...; ~tide Pfingsten pl.

whittle ['witl] schnitze(l)n; ~ away verkleinern, schwächen.

whiz(z) [wiz] zischen, sausen.

who [hu:, hu] 1. welche(r, -s); der, die, das; 2. wer?

whodun(n)it sl. [hu:'dʌnit] Krimi (-nalroman, -nalfilm) m.

whoever [hu(:)'evə] wer auch immer.

whole [houl] 1. □ ganz; heil, unversehrt; made out of ~ cloth Am. F frei erfunden; 2. Ganze(s) n; (up)on the ~ im ganzen; in allgemeinen; ~hearted □ ['houl'hɑː-tid] aufrichtig; ~-meal bread ['houlmi:l bred] Vollkorn-, Schrotbrot n; ~sale 1. mst ~ trade Großhandel m; 2. Großhandels...; Engros...; fig. Massen...; ~ dealer = ~saler [~lə] Großhändler m; ~some □ [~səm] gesund.

wholly adv. ['houli] ganz, gänzlich.

whom [hu:m, hum] acc. von who.

whoop [hu:p] 1. Schrei m, Geschrei n; 2. laut schreien; ~ it up Am. sl. laut feiern; ~ee Am. F ['wupi:] Freudenfest n; make ~ auf die Pauke hauen; ~ing-cough 🏥 ['hu:-piŋkɔf] Keuchhusten m.

whore [hɔ:] Hure f.

whose [hu:z] gen. von who.

why [wai] 1. warum, weshalb; ~ so? wieso?; 2. ei!, ja!; (je) nun.

wick [wik] Docht m.

wicked □ ['wikid] moralisch böse, schlimm; ~ness [~dnis] Bosheit f.

wicker ['wikə] aus Weide geflochten; Weiden...; Korb...; ~ basket Weidenkorb m; ~ chair Korbstuhl m.

wicket ['wikit] Pförtchen n; Kricket: Dreistab m, Tor n; ~-keeper Torhüter m.

wide [waid] a. □ u. adv. weit; ausgedehnt; weitgehend; großzügig;

breit; weitab; ~ awake völlig (od. hell)wach; aufgeweckt (schlau); 3 feet ~ 3 Fuß breit; ~n ['waidn] (sich) erweitern; ~open ['waid'oupən] weit geöffnet; Am. sl. großzügig in der Gesetzesdurchführung; ~spread weitverbreitet, ausgedehnt.

widow ['widou] Witwe f; attr. Witwen...; ~er [~ouə] Witwer m.

width [widθ] Breite f, Weite f.

wield lit. [wi:ld] handhaben.

wife [waif], pl. wives [waivz] (Ehe-) Frau f; Gattin f; Weib n; ~ly ['waifli] fraulich.

wig [wig] Perücke f.

wigging F ['wigiŋ] Schelte f.

wild [waild] 1. □ wild; toll; unbändig; abenteuerlich; planlos; run ~ wild (auf)wachsen; talk ~ (wild) darauflos reden; ~ for od. about (ganz) verrückt nach; 2. mst ~s pl. Wildnis f; ~cat ['waildkæt] 1. zo. Wildkatze f; Am. Schwindelunternehmen n; bsd. Am. wilde Ölbohrung; 2. wild (Streik); Schwindel...; ~erness ['wildənis] Wildnis f, Wüste f; Einöde f; ~fire: like ~ wie ein Lauffeuer.

wile [wail] List f; mst ~s pl. Tücke f.

wil(l)ful □ ['wilful] eigensinnig; vorsätzlich.

will [wil] 1. Wille m; Wunsch m; Testament n; of one's own free ~ aus freien Stücken; 2. [irr.] v/aux.: he ~ come er wird kommen; er kommt gewöhnlich; I ~ do it ich will es tun; 3. wollen; durch Willenskraft zwingen; entscheiden; ⚖ vermachen.

willing □ ['wiliŋ] willig, bereit (-willig); pred. gewillt (to inf. zu); ~ness [~nis] (Bereit)Willigkeit f.

will-o'-the-wisp ['wiləðwisp] Irrlicht n.

willow ♀ ['wilou] Weide f.

willy-nilly ['wili'nili] wohl oder übel.

wilt [wilt] (ver)welken.

wily □ ['waili] schlau, verschmitzt.

win [win] 1. [irr.] v/t. gewinnen; erringen; erlangen, erreichen; j-n dazu bringen (to do zu tun); ~ s.o. over j-n für sich gewinnen; v/i. gewinnen; siegen; 2. Sport: Sieg m.

wince [wins] (zs.-)zucken.

winch [wintʃ] Winde f; Kurbel f.

wind¹ [wind, poet. a. waind] 1. Wind m; Atem m, Luft f; ♪ Blähung f; ♪ Blasinstrumente n/pl.; 2. wittern; außer Atem bringen; verschnaufen lassen.

wind² [waind] [irr.] v/t. winden; wickeln; Horn blasen; ~ up Uhr aufziehen; Geschäft abwickeln; ✝ liquidieren; v/i. sich winden; sich schlängeln.

wind|bag ['windbæg] Schwätzer m; ~fall Fallobst n; Glücksfall m.

winding ['waindiŋ] 1. Windung *f*;
2. □ sich windend; ~ *stairs pl.*
Wendeltreppe *f*; ~-**sheet** Leichentuch *n*.

wind-instrument ♪ ['windinstru-
mənt] Blasinstrument *n*.

windlass ⊕ ['windləs] Winde *f*.

windmill ['winmil] Windmühle *f*.

window ['windou] Fenster *n*;
Schaufenster *n*; ~-**dressing** Schau-
fensterdekoration *f*; *fig.* Aufmachung *f*, Mache *f*; ~-**shade** *Am.*
Rouleau *n*; ~-**shopping** Schau-
fensterbummel *m*.

wind|pipe ['windpaip] Luftröhre *f*;
~-**screen**, *Am.* ~-**shield** *mot.*
Windschutzscheibe *f*; ~ **wiper**
Scheibenwischer *m*.

windy □ ['windi] windig (*a. fig.
inhaltlos*); geschwätzig.

wine [wain] Wein *m*; ~**press**
['wainpres] Kelter *f*.

wing [wiŋ] 1. Flügel *m* (*a.* ✕ *u.* ⚙);
Schwinge *f*; F *co.* Arm *m*; *mot.*
Kotflügel *m*; ✈ Tragfläche *f*; ✕,
✕ Geschwader *n*; ~*s pl.* Kulissen
f/pl.; take ~ weg-, auffliegen; on
the ~ im Fluge; 2. *fig.* beflügeln;
fliegen.

wink [wiŋk] 1. Blinzeln *n*, Zwinkern
n; not get a ~ of sleep kein Auge
zutun; *s.* **forty**; 2. blinzeln, zwinkern (mit); ~ at ein Auge zudrücken bei *et.*; *j-m* zublinzeln.

winn|er ['winə] Gewinner(in); Sie-
ger(in); ~**ing** ['winiŋ] 1. □ einnehmend, gewinnend; 2. ~*s pl.*
Gewinn *m*.

winsome ['winsəm] gefällig, einnehmend.

wint|er ['wintə] 1. Winter *m*;
2. überwintern; ~**ry** ['wintri] winter-
lich; *fig.* frostig.

wipe [waip] (ab-, auf)wischen; reinigen; (ab)trocknen; ~ out weg-
wischen; (aus)löschen; *fig.* vernichten; tilgen.

wire ['waiə] 1. Draht *m*; Leitung *f*;
F Telegramm *n*; pull the ~s der
Drahtzieher sein; s-e Beziehungen
spielen lassen; 2. (ver)drahten; telegraphieren; ~**drawn** ['waiədrɔ:n]
spitzfindig; ~**less** ['waiəlis] 1. □
drahtlos; Funk...; 2. *a.* ~ set Radio
(-apparat *m*) *n*; on the ~ im Rundfunk; 3. funken; ~-**netting** ['waiə-
'netiŋ] Drahtgeflecht *n*.

wiry □ ['waiəri] drahtig, sehnig.

wisdom ['wizdəm] Weisheit *f*;
Klugheit *f*; ~ **tooth** Weisheitszahn
m.

wise [waiz] 1. □ weise, verständig;
klug; erfahren; ~ *guy Am. sl.*
Schlauberger *m*; 2. Weise *f*, Art *f*.

wise-crack F ['waizkræk] 1. witzige
Bemerkung; 2. witzeln.

wish [wiʃ] 1. wünschen; wollen; ~
for (sich) *et.* wünschen; ~ well (ill)
wohl- (übel)wollen; 2. Wunsch *m*;

~**ful** □ ['wiʃful] sehnsüchtig; ~
thinking Wunschdenken *n*.

wisp [wisp] Wisch *m*; Strähne *f*.

wistful □ ['wistful] sehnsüchtig.

wit [wit] 1. Witz *m*; *a.* ~*s pl.* Verstand *m*; witziger Kopf; be at one's
~'s end mit s-r Weisheit zu Ende
sein; keep one's ~s about one e-n
klaren Kopf behalten; 2.: to ~ nämlich, das heißt.

witch [witʃ] Hexe *f*, Zauberin *f*;
~**craft** ['witʃkra:ft], ~**ery** [~ʃəri]
Hexerei *f*; ~-**hunt** *pol.* Hexenjagd
f (*Verfolgung politisch verdächtiger
Personen*).

with [wið] mit; nebst; bei; von;
durch; vor (*dat.*); ~ it *sl.* schwer
auf der Höhe.

withdraw [wið'drɔ:] [*irr.* (draw)]
v/t. ab-, ent-, zurückziehen; zurücknehmen; Geld abheben; *v/i.*
sich zurückziehen; abtreten; ~**al**
[~əl] Zurückziehung *f*; Rückzug
m.

wither ['wiðə] *v/i.* (ver)welken;
verdorren; austrocknen; *v/t.* welk
machen.

with|hold [wið'hould] [*irr.* (hold)]
zurückhalten; *et.* vorenthalten; ~**in**
[wi'ðin] 1. *adv. lit.* im Innern,
drin(nen); zu Hause; 2. *prp.* in(ner-
halb); ~ doors im Hause; ~ call in
Rufweite; ~**out** [wi'ðaut] 1. *adv. lit.*
(dr)außen; äußerlich; 2. *prp.* ohne;
lit. außerhalb; zuvor; ~**stand**
[*irr.* (stand)] widerstehen (*dat.*).

witness ['witnis] 1. Zeug|e *m*, -in *f*;
bear ~ Zeugnis ablegen (to für; of
von); in ~ of zum Zeugnis (*gen.*);
2. (be)zeugen; Zeuge sein von *et.*;
~-**box**, *Am.* ~ **stand** Zeugenstand
m.

wit|ticism ['witisizəm] Witz *m*;
~**ty** □ ['witi] witzig; geistreich.

wives [waivz] *pl. von* **wife**.

wiz *Am. sl.* [wiz] Genie *n*; ~**ard**
['wizəd] Zauberer *m*; Genie *n*.

wizen(ed) ['wizn(d)] schrump(e)lig.

wobble ['wɔbl] schwanken; wackeln.

woe [wou] Weh *n*, Leid *n*; ~ is me!
wehe mir!; ~**begone** ['woubigɔn]
jammervoll; ~**ful** □ ['wouful]
jammervoll, traurig, elend.

woke [wouk] *pret. u. p.p. von* **wake** 2;
~**n** ['woukən] *p.p. von* **wake** 2.

wold [would] (hügeliges) Heideland.

wolf [wulf] 1. *zo. pl.* **wolves**
[wulvz] Wolf *m*; 2. verschlingen;
~**ish** □ ['wulfiʃ] wölfisch; Wolfs...

woman ['wumən], *pl.* **women** ['wi-
min] 1. Frau *f*; Weib *n*; 2. weiblich;
~ doctor Ärztin *f*; ~ student Studentin *f*; ~**hood** [~nhud] die
Frauen *f/pl.*; Weiblichkeit *f*; ~**ish**
□ [~niʃ] weibisch; ~**kind** [~n-
'kaind] Frauen(welt *f*) *f/pl.*; ~**like**
[~nlaik] fraulich; ~**ly** [~li] weiblich.

womb [wu:m] *anat.* Gebärmutter *f*;
Mutterleib *m*; *fig.* Schoß *m*.

women ['wimin] *pl. von* **woman**; **~folk(s)**, **~kind** die Frauen *f/pl.*; F Weibervolk *n*.

won [wʌn] *pret. u. p.p. von* **win** 1.

wonder ['wʌndə] 1. Wunder *n*; Verwunderung *f*; 2. sich wundern; gern wissen mögen, sich fragen; **~ful** □ [~əful] wunderbar, -voll; **~ing** □ [~əriŋ] staunend, verwundert.

won't [wount] = **will not**.

wont [~] 1. *pred.* gewohnt; *be ~ to inf.* pflegen zu *inf.*; 2. Gewohnheit *f*; **~ed** ['wountid] gewohnt.

woo [wu:] werben um; locken.

wood [wud] Wald *m*, Gehölz *n*; Holz *n*; Faß *n*; ♪ Holzblasinstrument (-e *pl.*) *n*; *touch ~!* unberufen!; **~chuck** *zo.* ['wudtʃʌk] Waldmurmeltier *n*; **~cut** Holzschnitt *m*; **~cutter** Holzfäller *m*; *Kunst*: Holzschneider *m*; **~ed** ['wudid] bewaldet; **~en** ['wudn] hölzern (*a. fig.*); **Holz...**; **~man** Förster *m*; Holzfäller *m*; **~pecker** *orn.* ['wudpekə] Specht *m*; **~sman** ['wudzmən] *s.* **woodman**; **~wind** ♪ Holzblasinstrument *n*; *oft* **~s** *pl.* ♪ Holzbläser *m/pl.*; **~work** Holzwerk *n*; **~y** ['wudi] waldig; holzig.

wool [wul] Wolle *f*; **~-gathering** ['wulɡæðəriŋ] Geistesabwesenheit *f*; **~(l)en** ['wulin] 1. wollen; Woll...; 2. **~s** *pl.* Wollsachen *f/pl.*; **~(l)y** ['wuli] 1. wollig; Woll...; belegt (*Stimme*); verschwommen; 2. **woollies** *pl.* F Wollsachen *f/pl.*

word [wə:d] 1. *mst* Wort *n*; *engS.*: Vokabel *f*; Nachricht *f*; ✗ Losung(swort *n*) *f*; Versprechen *n*; Befehl *m*; Spruch *m*; **~s** *pl.* Wörter *n/pl.*; Worte *n/pl.*; *fig.* Wortwechsel *m*; Text *e-s Liedes*; *have a ~ with mit j-m* sprechen; 2. (in Worten) ausdrücken, (ab-)fassen; **~ing** ['wə:diŋ] Wortlaut *m*, Fassung *f*; **~-splitting** Wortklauberei *f*.

wordy □ ['wə:di] wortreich; Wort...

wore [wɔ:] *pret. von* **wear** 1.

work [wə:k] 1. Arbeit *f*; Werk *n*; *attr.* Arbeits...; **~s** *pl.* ⊕ (Uhr-, Feder)Werk *n*; ⊕ Befestigungen *pl.*; **~s** *sg.* Werk *n*, Fabrik *f*; **~ of art** Kunstwerk *n*; *at ~* bei der Arbeit; *be in ~* Arbeit haben; *be out of ~* arbeitslos sein; *set to ~*, *set od. go about one's ~* an die Arbeit gehen; **~s council** Betriebsrat *m*; 2. [*a. irr.*] *v/i.* arbeiten (*a. fig.*); wirken; gären; sich *hindurch- etc.* arbeiten; *~ at* arbeiten an (*dat.*); *~ out* herauskommen (*Summe*); *v/t.* (be)arbeiten; arbeiten lassen; betreiben; *Maschine etc.* bedienen; (be)wirken; ausrechnen, *Aufgabe* lösen; *~ one's way* sich durcharbeiten; *~ off* abarbeiten; *Gefühl* abreagieren; ♣ abstoßen; *~ out* ausarbeiten; lösen;

ausrechnen; *~ up* hochbringen; aufregen; verarbeiten (*into* zu).

work|able □ ['wə:kəbl] bearbeitungs-, betriebsfähig; ausführbar; **~aday** [~ədei] Alltags...; **~day** Werktag *m*; **~er** ['wə:kə] Arbeiter (-in); **~house** Armenhaus *n*; *Am.* Besserungsanstalt *f*, Arbeitshaus *n*.

working ['wə:kiŋ] 1. Bergwerk *n*; Steinbruch *m*; Arbeits-, Wirkungsweise *f*; 2. arbeitend; Arbeits...; Betriebs...; **~class** Arbeiter...; **~day** Werk-, Arbeitstag *m*; **~ hours** *pl.* Arbeitszeit *f*.

workman ['wə:kmən] Arbeiter *m*; Handwerker *m*; **~like** [~nlaik] kunstgerecht; **~ship** [~nʃip] Kunstfertigkeit *f*.

work|out *Am.* F ['wə:kaut] *mst Sport:* (Konditions)Training *n*; Erprobung *f*; **~shop** Werkstatt *f*; **~woman** Arbeiterin *f*.

world [wə:ld] *allg.* Welt *f*; *a ~ of* e-e Unmenge (von); *bring* (*come*) *into the ~* zur Welt bringen (kommen); *think the ~ of* alles halten von; **~ling** ['wə:ldliŋ] Weltkind *n*.

worldly ['wə:ldli] weltlich; Welt...; **~-wise** [~i'waiz] weltklug.

world|-power *pol.* ['wə:ldpauə] Weltmacht *f*; **~-wide** weltweit; weltumspannend; Welt...

worm [wə:m] 1. Wurm *m* (*a. fig.*); 2. *ein Geheimnis* entlocken (*out of dat.*); *~ o.s.* sich schlängeln; *fig.* sich einschleichen (*into* in *acc.*); **~-eaten** ['wə:mi:tn] wurmstichig.

worn [wɔ:n] *p.p. von* **wear** 1; **~-out** ['wɔ:n'aut] abgenutzt; abgetragen; verbraucht (*a. fig.*); müde, erschöpft; gealtert; verhärmt.

worry ['wʌri] 1. (sich) beunruhigen, (sich) ärgern; sich sorgen; sich aufregen; bedrücken; zerren, (ab-)würgen; plagen, quälen; 2. Unruhe *f*; Sorge *f*; Ärger *m*; Qual *f*, Plage *f*; Quälgeist *m*.

worse [wə:s] schlechter; schlimmer; *~ luck!* leider!; um so schlimmer!; *from bad to ~* vom Regen in die Traufe; **~n** ['wə:sn] (sich) verschlechtern.

worship ['wə:ʃip] 1. Verehrung *f*; Gottesdienst *m*; Kult *m*; 2. verehren; anbeten; den Gottesdienst besuchen; **~(p)er** [~pə] Verehrer (-in); Kirchgänger(in).

worst [wə:st] 1. schlechtest; ärgst; schlimmst; 2. überwältigen.

worsted ['wustid] Kammgarn *n*.

worth [wə:θ] 1. wert; *~ reading* lesenswert; 2. Wert *m*; Würde *f*; **~less** □ ['wə:θlis] wertlos; unwürdig; **~while** ['wə:θ'wail] der Mühe wert; **~y** □ ['wə:ði] würdig.

would [wud] [*pret. von* **will** 1] wollte; würde, möchte; pflegte; **~be** ['wudbi:] angeblich, soge-

nannt; möglich, potentiell; Pseu-
do...

wound¹ [wu:nd] 1. Wunde *f*, Ver-
wundung *f*, Verletzung *f*; *fig.*
Kränkung *f*; 2. verwunden, verletzen (*a. fig.*).

wound² [waund] *pret. u. p.p. von*
wind 2.

wove [wouv] *pret. von* weave; **~n**
['wouvən] *p.p. von* weave.

wow *Am.* [wau] 1. *int.* Mensch!;
toll!; 2. *sl.* Bombenerfolg *m*.

wrangle ['ræŋgl] 1. streiten, (sich)
zanken; 2. Streit *m*, Zank *m*.

wrap [ræp] 1. *v/t.* (ein)wickeln; *fig.*
einhüllen; *be* **~**ped up *in* gehüllt sein
in (*acc.*); ganz aufgehen in (*dat.*);
v/i. **~** up sich einhüllen; 2. Hülle *f*;
engS.: Decke *f*; Schal *m*; Mantel
m; **~per** ['ræpə] Hülle *f*, Umschlag
m; *a. postal* **~** Streifband *n*; **~ping**
['ræpiŋ] Verpackung *f*.

wrath *lit.* [rɔ:θ] Zorn *m*, Grimm *m*.

wreak [ri:k] *Rache* üben, *Zorn* auslassen (*upon* an *j-m*).

wreath [ri:θ], *pl.* **~s** [ri:ðz] (Blu-
men)Gewinde *n*; Kranz *m*; Girlande *f*; Ring *m*, Kreis *m*; Schneewehe *f*; **~e** [ri:ð] [*irr.*] *v/t.* (um-)
winden; *v/i.* sich ringeln.

wreck [rek] 1. ♣ Wrack *n*; Trümmer *pl.*; Schiffbruch *m*; *fig.* Untergang *m*; 2. zum Scheitern (🚂 Entgleisen) bringen; zertrümmern;
vernichten; *be* **~ed** ♣ scheitern;
Schiffbruch erleiden; **~age** ['rekidʒ]
Trümmer *pl.*; Wrackteile *n/pl.*; **~ed**
schiffbrüchig; ruiniert; **~er** ['rekə]
♣ Bergungsschiff *n*, -arbeiter *m*;
Strandräuber *m*; Abbrucharbeiter
m; *Am. mot.* Abschleppwagen *m*;
~ing ['rekiŋ] Strandraub *m*; **~** company *Am.* Abbruchfirma *f*; **~** service *Am. mot.* Abschlepp-, Hilfs-
dienst *m*.

wren *orn.* [ren] Zaunkönig *m*.

wrench [rentʃ] 1. drehen; reißen;
entwinden (*from s.o.* j-m); verdrehen (*a. fig.*); verrenken; **~** open auf-
reißen; 2. Ruck *m*; Verrenkung *f*;
fig. Schmerz *m*; ⊕ Schraubenschlüssel *m*.

wrest [rest] reißen; verdrehen; ent-
reißen; **~le** ['resl] ringen (mit);
~ling [‚liŋ] Ringkampf *m*, Ringen
n.

wretch [retʃ] Elende(r *m*) *f*; Kerl *m*.

wretched ☐ ['retʃid] elend.

wriggle ['rigl] sich winden *od.*
schlängeln; **~** out of sich drücken
von *et.*

wright [rait]...macher *m*,...bauer *m*.

wring [riŋ] [*irr.*] *Hände* ringen;
(aus)wringen; pressen; *Hals* umdrehen; abringen (*from s.o.* j-m);
~ *s.o.'s heart* j-m zu Herzen gehen.

wrinkle ['riŋkl] 1. Runzel *f*; Falte *f*;
Wink *m*; Trick *m*; 2. (sich) runzeln.

wrist [rist] Handgelenk *n*; **~watch**
Armbanduhr *f*; **~band** ['ristbænd]
Bündchen *n*, (Hemd)Manschette *f*.

writ [rit] Erlaß *m*; (gerichtlicher)
Befehl; *Holy* ♀ Heilige Schrift.

write [rait] [*irr.*] schreiben; **~** down
auf-, niederschreiben; ausarbeiten;
hervorheben; **~r** ['raitə] Schreiber
(-in); Verfasser(in); Schriftsteller
(-in).

writhe [raið] sich krümmen.

writing ['raitiŋ] Schreiben *n*; Aufsatz *m*; Werk *n*; Schrift *f*; Schrift-
stück *n*; Urkunde *f*; Stil *m*; *attr.*
Schreib...; *in* **~** schriftlich; **~case**
Schreibmappe *f*; **~desk** Schreibtisch *m*; **~paper** Schreibpapier *n*.

written ['ritn] 1. *p.p. von* write;
2. *adj.* schriftlich.

wrong [rɔŋ] 1. ☐ unrecht; verkehrt;
falsch; *be* **~** unrecht haben; in Unordnung sein; falsch gehen (*Uhr*);
go **~** schiefgehen; *on the* **~** *side of
sixty* über die 60 hinaus; 2. Un-
recht *n*; Beleidigung *f*; 3. unrecht
tun (*dat.*); ungerecht behandeln;
~doer ['rɔŋ'du:ə] Übeltäter(in); **~-
ful** ☐ ['rɔŋful] ungerecht; unrechtmäßig.

wrote [rout] *pret. von* write.

wrought [rɔ:t] *pret. u. p.p. von*
work 2; **~ iron** Schmiedeeisen *n*;
~-iron ['rɔ:t'aiən] schmiedeeisern;
~-up erregt.

wrung [rʌŋ] *pret. u. p.p. von* wring.

wry ☐ [rai] schief, krumm, verzerrt.

X, Y

Xmas ['krisməs] = *Christmas*.

X-ray ['eks'rei] 1. **~s** *pl.* Röntgen-
strahlen *m/pl.*; 2. Röntgen...;
3. durchleuchten, röntgen.

xylophone ♪ ['zailəfoun] Xylophon
n.

yacht ♣ [jɔt] 1. (Motor)Jacht *f*;
Segelboot *n*; 2. auf e-r Jacht fah-

ren; segeln; **~club** ['jɔtklʌb]
Segel-, Jachtklub *m*; **~ing** ['jɔtiŋ]
Segelsport *m*; *attr.* Segel...

Yankee F ['jæŋki] Yankee *m* (*Amerikaner, bsd. der Nordstaaten*).

yap [jæp] kläffen; F quasseln.

yard [jɑ:d] Yard *n*, *englische Elle*
(= 0,914 *m*); ♣ Rah(e) *f*; Hof *m*;
(Bau-, Stapel)Platz *m*; *Am.* Garten
m (*um das Haus*); **~measure**

['jɑ:dmeʒə], **~stick** Yardstock *m*, -maß *n*.

yarn [jɑ:n] **1.** Garn *n*; F Seemannsgarn *n*; abenteuerliche Geschichte; **2.** F erzählen.

yawl ⚓ [jɔ:l] Jolle *f*.

yawn [jɔ:n] **1.** gähnen; **2.** Gähnen *n*.

ye †, *poet.*, *co.* [ji:] ihr.

yea †, *prov.* [jei] **1.** ja; **2.** Ja *n*.

year [jɔ:] Jahr *n*; **~ly** ['jɔ:li] jährlich.

yearn [jɔ:n] sich sehnen, verlangen; **~ing** ['jɔ:niŋ] **1.** Sehnen *n*, Sehnsucht *f*; **2.** □ sehnsüchtig.

yeast [ji:st] Hefe *f*; Schaum *m*.

yegg(man) *Am.* *sl.* ['jeg(mən)] Stromer *m*; Einbrecher *m*.

yell [jel] **1.** (gellend) schreien; aufschreien; **2.** (gellender) Schrei; anfeuernder Ruf.

yellow ['jelou] **1.** gelb; F hasenfüßig (*feig*); Sensations...; Hetz...; **2.** Gelb *n*; **3.** (sich) gelb färben; **~ed** vergilbt; **~ fever** ⚕ Gelbfieber *n*; **~ish** [⁓ouiʃ] gelblich.

yelp [jelp] **1.** Gekläff *n*; **2.** kläffen.

yen *Am.* *sl.* [jen] brennendes Verlangen.

yeoman ['joumən] freier Bauer.

yep *Am.* F [jep] ja.

yes [jes] **1.** ja; doch; **2.** Ja *n*.

yesterday ['jestədi] gestern.

yet [jet] **1.** *adv.* noch; bis jetzt; schon; sogar; *as ~* bis jetzt; *not ~* noch nicht; **2.** *cj.* (je)doch, dennoch, trotzdem.

yew ♣ [ju:] Eibe *f*, Taxus *m*.

yield [ji:ld] **1.** *v/t.* hervorbringen, liefern; ergeben; *Gewinn* (ein)bringen; gewähren; übergeben; zugestehen; *v/i.* ↗ tragen; sich fügen; nachgeben; **2.** Ertrag *m*; **~ing** □ ['ji:ldiŋ] nachgebend; *fig.* nachgiebig.

yip *Am.* F [jip] jaulen.

yod|el, ~le ['joudl] **1.** Jodler *m*; **2.** jodeln.

yoke [jouk] **1.** Joch *n* (*a. fig.*); Paar *n* (Ochsen); Schultertrage *f*; **2.** anzs.-spannen; *fig.* paaren (*to* mit).

yolk [jouk] (Ei)Dotter *m*, *n*, Eigelb *n*.

yon [jɔn], **~der** *lit.* ['jɔndə] **1.** jene(r, -s); jenseitig; **2.** dort drüben.

yore [jɔ:]: *of ~* ehemals, ehedem.

you [ju:, ju] Ihr; du, Sie; man.

young [jʌŋ] **1.** jung; *von Kindern a.* klein; **2.** (Tier)Junge(s) *n*; (Tier)Junge *pl.*; *with ~* trächtig; **~ster** ['jʌŋstə] Junge *m*.

your [jɔ:] euer(e); dein(e), Ihr(e); **~s** [jɔːz] der (die, das) eurige, deinige, Ihrige; euer; dein, Ihr; **~self** [jɔː'self], *pl.* **~selves** [⁓lvz] (du, ihr, Sie) selbst; dich, euch, Sie (selbst), sich (selbst); *by ~* allein.

youth [ju:θ], *pl.* **~s** [ju:ðz] Jugend *f*; Jüngling *m*; **~ hostel** Jugendherberge *f*; **~ful** □ ['ju:θful] jugendlich.

yule *lit.* [ju:l] Weihnacht *f*.

Z

zeal [zi:l] Eifer *m*; **~ot** ['zelət] Eiferer *m*; **~ous** □ [⁓əs] eifrig; eifrig bedacht (*for* auf *acc.*); innig, heiß.

zebra *zo.* ['zi:brə] Zebra *n*; **~ crossing** Fußgängerüberweg *m*.

zenith ['zeniθ] Zenit *m*; *fig.* Höhepunkt *m*.

zero ['ziərou] Null *f*; Nullpunkt *m*.

zest [zest] **1.** Würze *f* (*a. fig.*); Lust *f*, Freude *f*; Genuß *m*; **2.** würzen.

zigzag ['zigzæg] Zickzack *m*.

zinc [ziŋk] **1.** *min.* Zink *n*; **2.** verzinken.

zip [zip] Schwirren *n*; F Schwung *m*; **~fastener** ['zipfɑːsnə], **~per** ['zipə] Reißverschluß *m*.

zodiac *ast.* ['zoudiæk] Tierkreis *m*.

zone [zoun] Zone *f*; *fig.* Gebiet *n*.

Zoo F [zu:] Zoo *m*.

zoolog|ical □ [zouə'lɔdʒikəl] zoologisch; **~y** [zou'ɔlədʒi] Zoologie *f*.

Alphabetical List of the German Irregular Verbs

Infinitive — Preterite — Past Participle

backen - backte (buk) - gebacken
bedingen - bedang (bedingte) - bedungen (*conditional*: bedingt)
befehlen - befahl - befohlen
beginnen - begann - begonnen
beißen - biß - gebissen
bergen - barg - geborgen
bersten - barst - geborsten
bewegen - bewog - bewogen
biegen - bog - gebogen
bieten - bot - geboten
binden - band - gebunden
bitten - bat - gebeten
blasen - blies - geblasen
bleiben - blieb - geblieben
bleichen - blich - geblichen
braten - briet - gebraten
brauchen - brauchte - gebraucht (*v/aux.* brauchen)
brechen - brach - gebrochen
brennen - brannte - gebrannt
bringen - brachte - gebracht
denken - dachte - gedacht
dreschen - drosch - gedroschen
dringen - drang - gedrungen
dürfen - durfte - gedurft (*v/aux.* dürfen)
empfehlen - empfahl - empfohlen
erlöschen - erlosch - erloschen
erschrecken - erschrak - erschrocken
essen - aß - gegessen
fahren - fuhr - gefahren
fallen - fiel - gefallen
fangen - fing - gefangen
fechten - focht - gefochten
finden - fand - gefunden
flechten - flocht - geflochten
fliegen - flog - geflogen
fliehen - floh - geflohen
fließen - floß - geflossen
fressen - fraß - gefressen
frieren - fror - gefroren
gären - gor (*esp. fig.* gärte) - gegoren (*esp. fig.* gegärt)
gebären - gebar - geboren
geben - gab - gegeben
gedeihen - gedieh - gediehen
gehen - ging - gegangen
gelingen - gelang - gelungen
gelten - galt - gegolten
genesen - genas - genesen
genießen - genoß - genossen
geschehen - geschah - geschehen
gewinnen - gewann - gewonnen

gießen - goß - gegossen
gleichen - glich - geglichen
gleiten - glitt - geglitten
glimmen - glomm - geglommen
graben - grub - gegraben
greifen - griff - gegriffen
haben - hatte - gehabt
halten - hielt - gehalten
hängen - hing - gehangen
hauen - haute (hieb) - gehauen
heben - hob - gehoben
heißen - hieß - geheißen
helfen - half - geholfen
kennen - kannte - gekannt
klingen - klang - geklungen
kneifen - kniff - gekniffen
kommen - kam - gekommen
können - konnte - gekonnt (*v/aux.* können)
kriechen - kroch - gekrochen
laden - lud - geladen
lassen - ließ - gelassen (*v/aux.* lassen)
laufen - lief - gelaufen
leiden - litt - gelitten
leihen - lieh - geliehen
lesen - las - gelesen
liegen - lag - gelegen
lügen - log - gelogen
mahlen - mahlte - gemahlen
meiden - mied - gemieden
melken - melkte (molk) - gemolken (gemelkt)
messen - maß - gemessen
mißlingen - mißlang - mißlungen
mögen - mochte - gemocht (*v/aux.* mögen)
müssen - mußte - gemußt (*v/aux.* müssen)
nehmen - nahm - genommen
nennen - nannte - genannt
pfeifen - pfiff - gepfiffen
preisen - pries - gepriesen
quellen - quoll - gequollen
raten - riet - geraten
reiben - rieb - gerieben
reißen - riß - gerissen
reiten - ritt - geritten
rennen - rannte - gerannt
riechen - roch - gerochen
ringen - rang - gerungen
rinnen - rann - geronnen
rufen - rief - gerufen
salzen - salzte - gesalzen (gesalzt)
saufen - soff - gesoffen

saugen - sog - gesogen
schaffen - schuf - geschaffen
schallen - schallte (scholl) - ge-
schallt (*for erschallen a.* erschol-
len)
scheiden - schied - geschieden
scheinen - schien - geschienen
schelten - schalt - gescholten
scheren - schor - geschoren
schieben - schob - geschoben
schießen - schoß - geschossen
schinden - schund - geschunden
schlafen - schlief - geschlafen
schlagen - schlug - geschlagen
schleichen - schlich - geschlichen
schleifen - schliff - geschliffen
schließen - schloß - geschlossen
schlingen - schlang - geschlungen
schmeißen - schmiß - geschmissen
schmelzen - schmolz - geschmolzen
schneiden - schnitt - geschnitten
schrecken - schrak - † geschrocken
schreiben - schrieb - geschrieben
schreien - schrie - geschrie(e)n
schreiten - schritt - geschritten
schweigen - schwieg - geschwiegen
schwellen - schwoll - geschwollen
schwimmen - schwamm - ge-
schwommen
schwinden - schwand - geschwun-
den
schwingen - schwang - geschwun-
gen
schwören - schwor - geschworen
sehen - sah - gesehen
sein - war - gewesen
senden - sandte - gesandt
sieden - sott - gesotten
singen - sang - gesungen
sinken - sank - gesunken
sinnen - sann - gesonnen
sitzen - saß - gesessen
sollen - sollte - gesollt (*v/aux.* sollen)
spalten - spaltete - gespalten (ge-
spaltet)
speien - spie - gespie(e)n
spinnen - spann - gesponnen
sprechen - sprach - gesprochen

sprießen - sproß - gesprossen
springen - sprang - gesprungen
stechen - stach - gestochen
stecken - steckte (stak) - gesteckt
stehen - stand - gestanden
stehlen - stahl - gestohlen
steigen - stieg - gestiegen
sterben - starb - gestorben
stieben - stob - gestoben
stinken - stank - gestunken
stoßen - stieß - gestoßen
streichen - strich - gestrichen
streiten - stritt - gestritten
tragen - trug - getragen
treffen - traf - getroffen
treiben - trieb - getrieben
treten - trat - getreten
triefen - triefte (troff) - getrieft
trinken - trank - getrunken
trügen - trog - getrogen
tun - tat - getan
verderben - verdarb - verdorben
verdrießen - verdroß - verdrossen
vergessen - vergaß - vergessen
verlieren - verlor - verloren
verschleißen - verschliß - ver-
schlissen
verzeihen - verzieh - verziehen
wachsen - wuchs - gewachsen
wägen - wog (🎵 wägte) - gewogen
(🎵 gewägt)
waschen - wusch - gewaschen
weben - wob - gewoben
weichen - wich - gewichen
weisen - wies - gewiesen
wenden - wandte - gewandt
werben - warb - geworben
werden - wurde - geworden (wor-
den*)
werfen - warf - geworfen
wiegen - wog - gewogen
winden - wand - gewunden
wissen - wußte - gewußt
wollen - wollte - gewollt (*v/aux.*
wollen)
wringen - wrang -gewrungen
ziehen - zog - gezogen
zwingen - zwang - gezwungen

* only in connexion with the past participles of other verbs, *e.g. er ist gesehen
worden* he has been seen.

Alphabetical List of the English Irregular Verbs

Infinitive — Preterite — Past Participle

Irregular forms marked with asterisks (*) can be exchanged for the regular forms.

abide (*bleiben*) - abode* - abode*
arise (*sich erheben*) - arose - arisen
awake (*erwachen*) - awoke - awoke*
be (*sein*) - was - been
bear (*tragen; gebären*) - bore - getragen: borne - geboren: born
beat (*schlagen*) - beat - beat(en)
become (*werden*) - became - become
beget (*zeugen*) - begot - begotten
begin (*anfangen*) - began - begun
bend (*beugen*) - bent - bent
bereave (*berauben*) - bereft* - bereft* -
besought
beseech (*ersuchen*) - besought -
besought
bet (*wetten*) - bet* - bet*
bid (*[ge]bieten*) - bade, bid - bid(den)
bide (*abwarten*) - bode* - bided
bind (*binden*) - bound - bound
bite (*beißen*) - bit - bitten
bleed (*bluten*) - bled - bled
blend (*mischen*) - blent* - blent*
blow (*blasen; blühen*) - blew - blown
break (*brechen*) - broke - broken
breed (*aufziehen*) - bred - bred
bring (*bringen*) - brought - brought
build (*bauen*) - built - built
burn (*brennen*) - burnt* - burnt*
burst (*bersten*) - burst - burst
buy (*kaufen*) - bought - bought
cast (*werfen*) - cast - cast
catch (*fangen*) - caught - caught
chide (*schelten*) - chid - chid(den)*
choose (*wählen*) - chose - chosen
cleave (*[sich] spalten*) cleft, clove* -
cleft, cloven*
cling (*sich [an]klammern*) - clung -
clung
clothe (*[an-, be]kleiden*) - clad* -
clad*
come (*kommen*) - came - come
cost (*kosten*) - cost - cost
creep (*kriechen*) - crept - crept
crow (*krähen*) - crew* - crowed
cut (*schneiden*) - cut - cut
deal (*handeln*) - dealt - dealt
dig (*graben*) - dug - dug
do (*tun*) - did - done
draw (*ziehen*) - drew - drawn
dream (*träumen*) - dreamt* - dreamt*
drink (*trinken*) - drank - drunk
drive (*treiben; fahren*) - drove -
driven
dwell (*wohnen*) - dwelt - dwelt

eat (*essen*) - ate, eat - eaten
fall (*fallen*) - fell - fallen
feed (*füttern*) - fed - fed
feel (*fühlen*) - felt - felt
fight (*kämpfen*) - fought - fought
find (*finden*) - found - found
flee (*fliehen*) - fled - fled
fling (*schleudern*) - flung - flung
fly (*fliegen*) - flew - flown
forbid (*verbieten*) - forbade - forbidden
forget (*vergessen*) - forgot - forgotten
forsake (*aufgeben; verlassen*) - forsook - forsaken
freeze (*[ge]frieren*) - froze - frozen
get (*bekommen*) - got - got, *Am.*
gotten
gild (*vergolden*) - gilt* - gilt*
gird (*[um]gürten*) - girt* - girt*
give (*geben*) - gave - given
go (*gehen*) - went - gone
grave (*[ein]graben*) - graved - graven*
grind (*mahlen*) - ground - ground
grow (*wachsen*) - grew - grown
hang (*hängen*) - hung - hung
have (*haben*) - had - had
hear (*hören*) - heard - heard
heave (*heben*) - hove* - hove*
hew (*hauen, hacken*) - hewed - hewn*
hide (*verbergen*) - hid - hid(den)
hit (*treffen*) - hit - hit
hold (*halten*) - held - held
hurt (*verletzen*) - hurt - hurt
keep (*halten*) - kept - kept
kneel (*knien*) - knelt* - knelt*
knit (*stricken*) - knit* - knit*
know (*wissen*) - knew - known
lay (*legen*) - laid - laid
lead (*führen*) - led - led
lean (*[sich] [an]lehnen*) - leant* -
leant*
leap (*[über]springen*) - leapt* - leapt*
learn (*lernen*) - learnt* - learnt*
leave (*verlassen*) - left - left
lend (*leihen*) - lent - lent
let (*lassen*) - let - let
lie (*liegen*) - lay - lain
light (*anzünden*) - lit* - lit*
lose (*verlieren*) - lost - lost
make (*machen*) - made - made
mean (*meinen*) - meant - meant
meet (*begegnen*) - met - met
mow (*mähen*) - mowed - mown*

pay (*zahlen*) - paid - paid
pen (*einpferchen*) - pent - pent
put (*setzen, stellen*) - put - put
read (*lesen*) - read - read
rend ([*zer*]*reißen*) - rent - rent
rid (*befreien*) - rid* - rid*
ride (*reiten*) - rode - ridden
ring (*läuten*) - rang - rung
rise (*aufstehen*) - rose - risen
rive ([*sich*] *spalten*) - rived - riven*
run (*laufen*) - ran - run
saw (*sägen*) - sawed - sawn*
say (*sagen*) - said - said
see (*sehen*) - saw - seen
seek (*suchen*) - sought - sought
sell (*verkaufen*) - sold - sold
send (*senden*) - sent - sent
set (*setzen*) - set - set
sew (*nähen*) - sewed - sewn*
shake (*schütteln*) - shook - shaken
shave ([*sich*] *rasieren*) - shaved - shaven*
shear (*scheren*) - sheared - shorn
shed (*ausgießen*) - shed - shed
shine (*scheinen*) - shone - shone
shoe (*beschuhen*) - shod - shod
shoot (*schießen*) - shot - shot
show (*zeigen*) - showed - shown*
shred ([*zer*]*schnitzeln, zerfetzen*) - shred* - shred*
shrink (*einschrumpfen*) - shrank - shrunk
shut (*schließen*) - shut - shut
sing (*singen*) - sang - sung
sink (*sinken*) - sank - sunk
sit (*sitzen*) - sat - sat
slay (*erschlagen*) - slew - slain
sleep (*schlafen*) - slept - slept
slide (*gleiten*) - slid - slid
sling (*schleudern*) - slung - slung
slink (*schleichen*) - slunk - slunk
slip (*schlüpfen, gleiten*) - slipt* - slipt*
slit (*schlitzen*) - slit - slit
smell (*riechen*) - smelt* - smelt*
smite (*schlagen*) - smote - smitten, smote
sow ([*aus*]*säen*) - sowed - sown*
speak (*sprechen*) - spoke - spoken
speed (*eilen*) - sped* - sped*
spell (*buchstabieren*) - spelt* - spelt*
spend (*ausgeben*) - spent - spent

spill (*verschütten*) - spilt* - spilt*
spin (*spinnen*) - spun - spun
spit ([*aus*]*spucken*) - spat - spat
split (*spalten*) - split - split
spoil (*verderben*) - spoilt* - spoilt*
spread (*verbreiten*) - spread - spread
spring (*springen*) - sprang - sprung
stand (*stehen*) - stood - stood
stave (*den Boden einschlagen*) - stove* - stove*
steal (*stehlen*) - stole - stolen
stick (*stecken*) - stuck - stuck
sting (*stechen*) - stung - stung
stink (*stinken*) - stank - stunk
strew ([*be*]*streuen*) - strewed - strewn*
stride (*über-, durchschreiten*) - strode - stridden
strike (*schlagen*) - struck - struck
string (*spannen*) - strung - strung
strive (*streben*) - strove - striven
swear (*schwören*) - swore - sworn
sweat (*schwitzen*) - sweat* - sweat*
sweep (*fegen*) - swept - swept
swell ([*an*]*schwellen*) - swelled - swollen
swim (*schwimmen*) - swam - swum
swing (*schwingen*) - swung - swung
take (*nehmen*) - took - taken
teach (*lehren*) - taught - taught
tear (*ziehen*) - tore - torn
tell (*sagen*) - told - told
think (*denken*) - thought - thought
thrive (*gedeihen*) - throve* - thriven*
throw (*werfen*) - threw - thrown
thrust (*stoßen*) - thrust - thrust
tread (*treten*) - trod - trodden
wake (*wachen*) - woke* - woke(n)*
wax (*zunehmen*) - waxed - waxen*
wear ([*Kleider*] *tragen*) - wore - worn
weave (*weben*) - wove - woven
weep (*weinen*) - wept - wept
wet (*nässen*) - wet* - wet*
win (*gewinnen*) - won - won
wind (*winden*) - wound - wound
work (*arbeiten*) - wrought* - wrought*
wreathe ([*um*]*winden*) - wreathed - wreathen*
wring ([*aus*]*wringen*) - wrung - wrung
write (*schreiben*) - wrote - written

German Proper Names

Aachen ['ɑːxən] n Aachen, Aix-la-Chapelle.

Adenauer ['ɑːdənauər] first chancellor of the German Federal Republic.

Adler ['ɑːdlər] Austrian psychologist.

Adria ['ɑːdria] f Adriatic Sea.

Afrika ['ɑːfrika] n Africa.

Ägypten [ɛ'gyptən] n Egypt.

Albanien [al'bɑːnjən] n Albania.

Algerien [al'geːrjən] n Algeria.

Algier ['alʒiːr] f Algiers.

Allgäu ['algɔy] n Al(l)gäu (region of Bavaria).

Alpen ['alpən] pl. Alps pl.

Amerika [a'meːrika] n America.

Anden ['andən] pl. the Andes pl.

Antillen [an'tilən] f/pl. Antilles pl.

Antwerpen [ant'verpən] n Antwerp.

Apenninen [ape'niːnən] m/pl. the Apennines pl.

Argentinien [argen'tiːnjən] n Argentina, the Argentine.

Ärmelkanal ['ɛrməlkanɑːl] m English Channel.

Asien ['ɑːzjən] n Asia.

Athen [a'teːn] n Athens.

Äthiopien [ɛti'oːpjən] Ethiopia.

Atlantik [at'lantik] m Atlantic.

Australien [au'strɑːljən] n Australia.

Bach [bax] German composer.

Baden-Württemberg ['bɑːdən-'vyrtəmberk] n Land of the German Federal Republic.

Barlach ['barlax] German sculptor.

Basel ['bɑːzəl] n Bâle, Basle.

Bayern ['baɪərn] n Bavaria (Land of the German Federal Republic).

Becher ['beçər] German poet.

Beckmann ['bɛkman] German painter.

Beethoven ['beːthoːfən] German composer.

Belgien ['bɛlgjən] n Belgium.

Belgrad ['bɛlgrɑːt] n Belgrade.

Berg [berk] Austrian composer.

Berlin [bɛr'liːn] n Berlin.

Bermuda-Inseln [bɛr'muːdaʔinzəln] f/pl. Bermudas pl.

Bern [bern] n Bern(e).

Bismarck ['bismark] German statesman.

Bloch [blɔx] German philosopher.

Böcklin ['bœkliːn] German painter.

Bodensee ['boːdənzeː] m Lake of Constance.

Böhm [bøːm] Austrian conductor.

Böhmen ['bøːmən] n Bohemia.

Böll [bœl] German author.

Bonn [bɔn] n capital of the German Federal Republic.

Brahms [brɑːms] German composer.

Brandt [brant] German politician.

Brasilien [bra'ziːljən] n Brazil.

Braunschweig ['braunʃvaɪk] n Brunswick.

Brecht [brɛçt] German dramatist.

Bremen ['breːmən] n Land of the German Federal Republic.

Bruckner ['bruknər] Austrian composer.

Brüssel ['brysəl] n Brussels.

Budapest ['buːdapɛst] n Budapest.

Bukarest ['buːkarɛst] n Bucharest.

Bulgarien [bul'gɑːrjən] n Bulgaria.

Calais [ka'lɛː] n: Straße von ~ Straits of Dover.

Calvin [kal'viːn] Swiss religious reformer.

Chile ['tʃiːlə] n Chile.

China ['çiːna] n China.

Christus ['kristus] m Christ.

Daimler ['daɪmlər] German inventor.

Dänemark ['dɛːnəmark] n Denmark.

Deutschland ['dɔytʃlant] n Germany.

Diesel ['diːzəl] German inventor.

Döblin [dø'bliːn] German author.

Dolomiten [dolo'miːtən] pl. the Dolomites pl.

Donau ['doːnau] f Danube.

Dortmund ['dɔrtmunt] n industrial city in West Germany.

Dresden ['dreːsdən] n capital of Saxony.

Dublin ['dʌblin] n Dublin.

Dünkirchen ['dyːnkirçən] n Dunkirk.

Dürer ['dyːrər] German painter.

Dürrenmatt ['dyrənmat] Swiss dramatist.

Düsseldorf ['dysəldɔrf] n capital of North Rhine-Westphalia.

Ebert ['eːbərt] first president of the Weimar Republic.

Egk [ɛk] German composer.

Eichendorff ['aɪçəndɔrf] German poet.

Eiger ['aɪgər] Swiss mountain.

Einstein ['aɪnʃtaɪn] German physicist.

Elbe ['ɛlbə] f German river.

Elsaß ['ɛlzas] n Alsace.

Engels ['ɛŋəls] German philosopher.

England ['eŋlant] n England.
Essen ['esən] n industrial city in West Germany.
Europa [ɔy'ro:pa] n Europe.

Feldberg ['feltberk] German mountain.
Finnland ['finlant] n Finland.
Florenz [flo'rents] n Florence.
Fontane [fɔn'ta:nə] German author.
Franken ['fraŋkən] n Franconia.
Frankfurt ['fraŋkfurt] n Frankfort.
Frankreich ['fraŋkraiç] n France.
Freud [frɔyt] Austrian psychologist.
Frisch [friʃ] Swiss author.

Garmisch ['garmiʃ] n health resort in Bavaria.
Genf [genf] n Geneva; ~er See m Lake of Geneva.
Genua ['ge:nua] n Genoa.
Gibraltar [gi'braltar] n Gibraltar.
Goethe ['gø:tə] German poet.
Grass [gras] German author.
Graubünden [grau'byndən] n the Grisons.
Griechenland ['gri:çənlant] n Greece.
Grillparzer ['grilpartsər] Austrian dramatist.
Grönland ['grø:nlant] n Greenland.
Gropius ['gro:pjus] German architect. [Great Britain.]
Großbritannien[gro:sbri'tanjən]n)
Großglockner [gro:s'glɔknər] Austrian mountain.
Grünewald ['gry:nəvalt] German painter.

Haag [ha:k]: Den ~ The Hague.
Habsburg hist. ['ha:psburk] n Hapsburg (German dynasty).
Hahn [ha:n] German chemist.
Hamburg ['hamburk] n Land of the German Federal Republic.
Händel ['hendəl] Handel (German composer).
Hannover [ha'no:fər] n Hanover (capital of Lower Saxony).
Hartmann ['hartman] German composer.
Harz [ha:rts] m Harz Mountains pl.
Hauptmann ['hauptman] German dramatist.
Haydn ['haidən] Austrian composer.
Hegel ['he:gəl] German philosopher.
Heidegger ['haidegər] German philosopher.
Heidelberg ['haidəlberk] n university town in West Germany.
Heine ['hainə] German poet.
Heinemann ['hainəman] president of the German Federal Republic.
Heisenberg ['haizənberk] German physicist.
Heißenbüttel ['haisənbytəl] German poet.
Helgoland ['helgolant] n Heligoland.

Helsinki ['helziŋki] n Helsinki.
Henze ['hentsə] German composer.
Hesse ['hesə] German poet.
Hessen ['hesən] n Hesse (Land of the German Federal Republic).
Heuß [hɔys] first president of the German Federal Republic.
Hindemith ['hindəmit] German composer.
Hohenzollern hist. [ho:ən'tsɔlərn] n German dynasty.
Hölderlin ['hœldərli:n] German poet.
Holland ['hɔlant] n Holland.

Indien ['indjən] n India.
Inn [in] m affluent of the Danube.
Innsbruck ['insbruk] n capital of the Tyrol.
Irak [i'ra:k] m Iraq, a. Irak.
Irland ['irlant] n Ireland.
Island ['i:slant] n Iceland.
Israel ['israɛl] n Israel.
Italien [i'ta:ljən] n Italy.

Japan ['ja:pan] n Japan.
Jaspers ['jaspərs] German philosopher.
Jesus ['je:zus] m Jesus.
Jordanien [jɔr'da:njən] n Jordan.
Jugoslawien [jugo'sla:vjən] n Yugoslavia.
Jung [juŋ] Swiss psychologist.
Jungfrau ['juŋfrau] f Swiss mountain.

Kafka ['kafka] Czech poet.
Kanada ['kanada] n Canada.
Kant [kant] German philosopher.
Karajan ['ka:rajan] Austrian conductor.
Karlsruhe [karls'ru:ə] n city in South-Western Germany.
Kärnten ['kerntən] n Carinthia.
Kassel ['kasəl] n Cassel.
Kästner ['kestnər] German author.
Kiel [ki:l] n capital of Schleswig-Holstein.
Kiesinger ['ki:ziŋər] German politician.
Klee [kle:] German painter.
Kleist [klaist] German poet.
Klemperer ['klempərər] German conductor.
Koblenz ['ko:blents] n Coblenz, Koblenz.
Kokoschka [ko'kɔʃka] German painter.
Köln [kœln] n Cologne.
Kolumbien [ko'lumbjən] n Columbia.
Kolumbus [ko'lumbus] m Columbus.
Königsberg ['kø:niçsberk] n capital of East Prussia.
Konstanz ['kɔnstants] n Constance.
Kopenhagen [kopən'ha:gən] n Copenhagen.
Kordilleren [kɔrdil'je:rən] f/pl. the Cordilleras pl.

Kreml ['kreːməl] *m the* Kremlin.

Leibniz ['laıbnits] *German philosopher.*
Leipzig ['laıptsiç] *n* Leipsic.
Lessing ['lɛsiŋ] *German poet.*
Libanon ['liːbanɔn] *m* Lebanon.
Liebig ['liːbiç] *German chemist.*
Lissabon ['lisabɔn] *n* Lisbon.
London ['lɔndɔn] *n* London.
Lothringen ['loːtriŋən] *n* Lorraine.
Lübeck ['lyːbɛk] *n city in West Germany.*
Luther ['lutər] *German religious reformer.*
Luxemburg ['luksəmburk] *n* Luxemb(o)urg.
Luzern [luˈtsɛrn] *n* Lucerne.

Maas [maːs] *f* Meuse.
Madrid [maˈdrit] *n* Madrid.
Mahler ['maːlər] *Austrian composer.*
Mailand ['maılant] *n* Milan.
Main [maın] *m German river.*
Mainz [maınts] *n* Mayence (*capital of Rhineland-Palatinate*).
Mann [man] *name of three German authors.*
Marokko [maˈrɔko] *n* Morocco.
Marx [marks] *German philosopher.*
Matterhorn ['matərhɔrn] *Swiss mountain.*
Meißen ['maısən] *n* Meissen.
Meitner ['maıtnər] *German female physicist.*
Memel ['meːməl] *f frontier river in East Prussia.*
Menzel ['mɛntsəl] *German painter.*
Mexiko ['mɛksiko] *n* Mexico.
Mies van der Rohe ['miːsfandər-ˈroːə] *German architect.*
Mittelamerika ['mitəlʔaˈmeːrika] *n* Central America.
Mitteleuropa ['mitəlʔɔyˈroːpa] *n* Central Europe.
Mittelmeer ['mitəlmeːr] *n* Mediterranean (Sea).
Moldau ['mɔldau] *f Bohemian river.*
Mörike ['møːrikə] *German poet.*
Mosel ['moːzəl] *f* Moselle.
Mössbauer ['mœsbauər] *German physicist.*
Moskau ['mɔskau] *n* Moscow.
Mozart ['moːtsart] *Austrian composer.*
München ['mynçən] *n* Munich (*capital of Bavaria*).

Neapel [neˈaːpəl] *n* Naples.
Neisse [ˈnaısə] *f German river.*
Neufundland [nɔyˈfuntlant] *n* Newfoundland.
Neuseeland [nɔyˈzeːlant] *n* New Zealand.
Niederlande ['niːdərlandə] *n/pl. the* Netherlands *pl.*
Niedersachsen ['niːdərzaksən] *n* Lower Saxony (*Land of the German Federal Republic*).

Nietzsche ['niːtʃə] *German philosopher.*
Nil [niːl] *m* Nile.
Nordamerika ['nɔrtʔaˈmeːrika] *n* North America.
Nordrhein-Westfalen ['nɔrtraın-vestˈfaːlən] *n* North Rhine-Westphalia (*Land of the German Federal Republic*).
Nordsee ['nɔrtzeː] *f* German Ocean, North Sea.
Norwegen ['nɔrveːgən] *n* Norway.
Nürnberg ['nyrnbɛrk] *n* Nuremberg.

Oder ['oːdər] *f German river.*
Orff [ɔrf] *German composer.*
Oslo ['ɔslo] *n* Oslo.
Ostasien ['ɔstˈaːzjən] *n* Eastern Asia.
Ostende [ɔstˈɛndə] *n* Ostend.
Österreich ['øːstəraıç] *n* Austria.
Ostsee ['ɔstzeː] *f* Baltic.

Palästina [paleˈstiːna] *n* Palestine.
Paris [paˈriːs] *n* Paris.
Persien ['pɛrzjən] *n* Persia.
Pfalz [pfalts] *f* Palatinate.
Philippinen [filiˈpiːnən] *f/pl.* Philippines *pl.*, Philippine Islands *pl.*
Planck [plaŋk] *German physicist.*
Polen ['poːlən] *n* Poland.
Pommern ['pɔmərn] *n* Pomerania.
Portugal ['portugal] *n* Portugal.
Prag [praːg] *n* Prague.
Preußen *hist.* ['prɔysən] *n* Prussia.
Pyrenäen [pyreˈnɛːən] *pl.* Pyrenees *pl.*

Regensburg ['reːgənsburk] *n* Ratisbon.
Reykjavik ['raıkjaviːk] *n* Reykjavik.
Rhein [raın] *m* Rhine.
Rheinland-Pfalz ['raınlant'pfalts] *n* Rhineland-Palatinate (*Land of the German Federal Republic*).
Rilke ['rilkə] *Austrian poet.*
Rom [roːm] *n* Rome.
Röntgen ['rœntgən] *German physicist.*
Ruhr [ruːr] *f German river;* Ruhrgebiet ['ruːrgəbiːt] *n industrial centre of West Germany.*
Rumänien [ruˈmɛːnjən] *n* Ro(u)mania.
Rußland ['ruslant] *n* Russia.

Saale ['zaːlə] *f German river.*
Saar [zaːr] *f affluent of the Moselle;* Saarbrücken [zaːrˈbrykən] *n capital of the Saar;* Saarland ['zaːrlant] *n* Saar (*Land of the German Federal Republic*).
Sachsen ['zaksən] *n* Saxony.
Scherchen ['ʃɛrçən] *Swiss conductor.*
Schiller ['ʃilər] *German poet.*
Schlesien ['ʃleːzjən] *n* Silesia.
Schleswig-Holstein ['ʃleːsviçˈhɔl-

ʃtaın] n *Land of the German Federal Republic.*
Schönberg [ˈʃøːnbɛrk] *Austrian composer.*
Schottland [ˈʃɔtlant] n Scotland.
Schubert [ˈʃuːbərt] *Austrian composer.*
Schumann [ˈʃuːman] *German composer.*
Schwaben [ˈʃvaːbən] n Swabia.
Schwarzwald [ˈʃvartsvalt] m Black Forest.
Schweden [ˈʃveːdən] n Sweden.
Schweiz [ʃvaɪts] f: die ~ Switzerland.
Sibirien [ziˈbiːrjən] n Siberia.
Siemens [ˈziːməns] *German inventor.*
Sizilien [ziˈtsiːljən] n Sicily.
Skandinavien [skandiˈnaːvjən] n Scandinavia.
Sofia [ˈzɔfja] n Sofia.
Sowjetunion [zɔˈvjɛtʔunjoːn] f *the* Soviet Union.
Spanien [ˈʃpaːnjən] n Spain.
Spitzweg [ˈʃpitsveːk] *German painter.*
Spranger [ˈʃpraŋər] *German philosopher.*
Steiermark [ˈʃtaɪərmark] f Styria.
Stifter [ˈʃtiftər] *Austrian author.*
Stockholm [ˈʃtɔkhɔlm] n Stockholm.
Storm [ʃtɔrm] *German poet.*
Strauß [ʃtraus] *Austrian composer.*
Strauss [ʃtraus] *German composer.*
Stresemann [ˈʃtreːzəman] *German statesman.*
Stuttgart [ˈʃtutgart] n *capital of Baden-Württemberg.*
Südamerika [ˈzyːtʔaˈmeːrika] n South America.
Sudan [zuˈdaːn] m S(o)udan.
Syrien [ˈzyːrjən] n Syria.

Themse [ˈtɛmzə] f Thames.
Thoma [ˈtoːma] *German author.*
Thüringen [ˈtyːriŋən] n Thuringia.
Tirana [tiˈraːna] n Tirana.
Tirol [tiˈroːl] n the Tyrol.
Trakl [ˈtraːkəl] *Austrian poet.*
Tschechoslowakei [tʃɛçoslovaˈkaɪ] f: die ~ Czechoslovakia.
Türkei [tyrˈkaɪ] f: die ~ Turkey.

Ungarn [ˈuŋgarn] n Hungary.
Ural [uˈraːl] m Ural (Mountains pl.).

Vatikan [vatiˈkaːn] m the Vatican.
Venedig [veˈneːdiç] n Venice.
Vereinigte Staaten [vərˈainiçtə ˈʃtaːtən] m/pl. the United States pl.
Vierwaldstätter See [fiːrˈvaltʃtetər ˈzeː] m Lake of Lucerne.

Wagner [ˈvaːgnər] *German composer.*
Wankel [ˈvaŋkəl] *German inventor.*
Warschau [ˈvarʃau] n Warsaw.
Weichsel [ˈvaıksəl] f Vistula.
Weiß [vaıs] *German dramatist.*
Weizsäcker [ˈvaıtszɛkər] *German physicist.*
Werfel [ˈvɛrfəl] *Austrian author.*
Weser [ˈveːzər] f *German river.*
Westdeutschland pol. [ˈvestdɔytʃlant] n West Germany.
Wien [viːn] n Vienna.
Wiesbaden [ˈviːsbaːdən] n *capital of Hesse.*

Zeppelin [ˈtsɛpəliːn] *German inventor.*
Zuckmayer [ˈtsukmaıər] *German dramatist.*
Zweig [tsvaıg] *Austrian author.*
Zürich [ˈtsyːriç] n Zurich.
Zypern [ˈtsyːpərn] n Cyprus.

German Abbreviations

a. a. O. *am angeführten Ort* in the place cited, *abbr.* loc. cit., l. c.
Abb. *Abbildung* illustration.
Abf. *Abfahrt* departure, *abbr.* dep.
Abg. *Abgeordnete* Member of Parliament, *etc.*
Abk. *Abkürzung* abbreviation.
Abs. *Absatz* paragraph; *Absender* sender.
Abschn. *Abschnitt* paragraph, chapter. [dept.]
Abt. *Abteilung* department, *abbr.*
a. D. *außer Dienst* retired.
Adr. *Adresse* address.
AG *Aktiengesellschaft* joint-stock company, *Am.* (stock) corporation.
allg. *allgemein* general.
a. M. *am Main* on the Main.
Ank. *Ankunft* arrival.
Anm. *Anmerkung* note.
a. O. *an der Oder* on the Oder.
a. Rh. *am Rhein* on the Rhine.
Art. *Artikel* article.
atü *Atmosphärenüberdruck* atmospheric excess pressure.
Aufl. *Auflage* edition.

b. *bei* at; with; *with place names*: near, *abbr.* nr; care of, *abbr.* c/o.
Bd. *Band* volume, *abbr.* vol.; **Bde.** *Bände* volumes, *abbr.* vols.
beil. *beiliegend* enclosed.
Bem. *Bemerkung* note, comment, observation.
bes. *besonders* especially.
betr. *betreffend, betrifft, betreffs* concerning, respecting, regarding.
Betr. *Betreff, betrifft letter*: subject, re. [reference to.]
bez. *bezahlt* paid; *bezüglich* with
Bez. *Bezirk* district.
Bhf. *Bahnhof* station.
bisw. *bisweilen* sometimes, occasionally.
BIZ *Bank für Internationalen Zahlungsausgleich* Bank for International Settlements.
Bln. *Berlin* Berlin.
BRD *Bundesrepublik Deutschland* Federal Republic of Germany.
BRT *Bruttoregistertonnen* gross register tons.
b. w. *bitte wenden* please turn over, *abbr.* P.T.O.
bzw. *beziehungsweise* respectively.

C *Celsius* Celsius, *abbr.* C.
ca. *circa, ungefähr, etwa* about, approximately, *abbr.* c.
cbm *Kubikmeter* cubic met|re, *Am.* -er.

ccm *Kubikzentimeter* cubic centimet|re, *Am.* -er, *abbr.* c.c.
CDU *Christlich-Demokratische Union* Christian Democratic Union.
cm *Zentimeter* centimet|re, *Am.* -er.
Co. *Kompagnon* partner; *Kompanie* Company.
CSU *Christlich-Soziale Union* Christian Social Union.

d. Ä. *der Ältere* senior, *abbr.* sen.
DB *Deutsche Bundesbahn* German Federal Railway.
DDR *Deutsche Demokratische Republik* German Democratic Republic.
DGB *Deutscher Gewerkschaftsbund* Federation of German Trade Unions.
dgl. *dergleichen, desgleichen* the like.
d. Gr. *der Große* the Great.
d. h. *das heißt* that is, *abbr.* i. e.
d. i. *das ist* that is, *abbr.* i. e.
DIN, Din *Deutsche Industrie-Norm* (-en) German Industrial Standards.
Dipl. *Diplom* diploma.
d. J. *dieses Jahres* of this year; *der Jüngere* junior, *abbr.* jr, jun.
DM *Deutsche Mark* German Mark.
d. M. *dieses Monats* instant, *abbr.* inst.
do. *dito* ditto, *abbr.* do.
d. O. *der (die, das) Obige* the abovementioned.
dpa, DPA *Deutsche Presse-Agentur* German Press Agency.
Dr. *Doktor* Doctor, *abbr.* Dr; ~ **jur.** *Doktor der Rechte* Doctor of Laws (LL.D.); ~ **med.** *Doktor der Medizin* Doctor of Medicine (M.D.); ~ **phil.** *Doktor der Philosophie* Doctor of Philosophy (D. ph[il]., Ph. D.); ~ **theol.** *Doktor der Theologie* Doctor of Divinity (D. D.).
DRK *Deutsches Rotes Kreuz* German Red Cross.
dt(sch). *deutsch* German.
Dtz., Dtzd. *Dutzend* dozen.
d. Verf. *der Verfasser* the author.

ebd. *ebenda* in the same place.
ed. *edidit = hat (es) herausgegeben.*
eig., eigtl. *eigentlich* properly.
einschl. *einschließlich* including, inclusive, *abbr.* incl.
entspr. *entsprechend* corresponding.
Erl. *Erläuterung* explanation, (explanatory) note.
ev. *evangelisch* Protestant.
e. V. *eingetragener Verein* registered association, incorporated, *abbr.* inc.

evtl. *eventuell* perhaps, possibly.
EWG *Europäische Wirtschaftsgemeinschaft* European Economic Community, *abbr.* EEC.
exkl. *exklusive* except(ed), not included.
Expl. *Exemplar* copy.

Fa. *Firma* firm; *letter*: Messrs.
FDGB *Freier Deutscher Gewerkschaftsbund* Free Federation of German Trade Unions.
FDP *Freie Demokratische Partei* Liberal Democratic Party.
FD(-Zug) *Fernschnellzug* long-distance express.
ff. *sehr fein* extra fine; *folgende Seiten* following pages.
Forts. *Fortsetzung* continuation.
Fr. *Frau* Mrs.
frdl. *freundlich* kind.
Frl. *Fräulein* Miss.

g *Gramm* gram(me).
geb. *geboren* born; *geborene ...* née; *gebunden* bound.
Gebr. *Gebrüder* Brothers.
gef. *gefällig(st)* kind(ly).
gegr. *gegründet* founded.
geh. *geheftet* stitched.
gek. *gekürzt* abbreviated.
Ges. *Gesellschaft* association, company; society.   [registered.]
ges. gesch. *gesetzlich geschützt*
gest. *gestorben* deceased.
gez. *gezeichnet* signed, *abbr.* sgd.
GmbH *Gesellschaft mit beschränkter Haftung* limited liability company, *abbr.* Ltd., *Am.* closed corporation under German law.

ha *Hektar* hectare.
Hbf. *Hauptbahnhof* central *or* main station.
Hbg. *Hamburg* Hamburg.
h. c. *honoris causa* = ehrenhalber *academic title*: honorary.
Hr., Hrn. *Herr(n)* Mr.
hrsg. *herausgegeben* edited, *abbr.* ed.
Hrsg. *Herausgeber* editor, *abbr.* ed.

i. *im*, in *in*.
i. A. *im Auftrage* for, by order, under instruction.
i. allg. *im allgemeinen* in general, generally speaking.
i. Durchschn. *im Durchschnitt* on an average.
inkl. *inklusive, einschließlich* inclusive.
i. J. *im Jahre* in the year.
Ing. *Ingenieur* engineer.
Inh. *Inhaber* proprietor.
'Interpol *Internationale Kriminalpolizei-Kommission* International Criminal Police Commission, *abbr.* ICPC.
i. V. *in Vertretung* by proxy, as a substitute.

Jb. *Jahrbuch* annual.
jr., jun. *junior, der Jüngere* junior *abbr.* jr, jun.

Kap. *Kapitel* chapter.
kath. *katholisch* Catholic.
Kfm. *Kaufmann* merchant.
kfm. *kaufmännisch* commercial.
Kfz. *Kraftfahrzeug* motor vehicle.
kg *Kilogramm* kilogram(me).
KG *Kommanditgesellschaft* limited partnership.
Kl. *Klasse* class; *school*: form.
km *Kilometer* kilomet|re, *Am.* -er.
'Kripo *Kriminalpolizei* Criminal Investigation Department, *abbr.* CID.
Kto. *Konto* account, *abbr.* a/c.
kW *Kilowatt* kilowatt, *abbr.* kw.
kWh *Kilowattstunde* kilowatt hour.

l *Liter* lit|re, *Am.* -er.
LDP *Liberal-Demokratische Partei* Liberal Democratic Party.
lfd. *laufend* current, running.
lfde. Nr. *laufende Nummer* consecutive number.
Lfg., Lfrg. *Lieferung* delivery; instalment, part.
Lit. *Literatur* literature.
Lkw. *Lastkraftwagen* lorry, truck.
lt. *laut* according to.

m *Meter* met|re, *Am.* -er.
m. A. n. *meiner Ansicht nach* in my opinion.
M. d. B. *Mitglied des Bundestages* Member of the Bundestag.
m. E. *meines Erachtens* in my opinion.
MEZ *mitteleuropäische Zeit* Central European Time.
mg *Milligramm* milligram(me[s]), *abbr.* mg.
Mill. *Million(en)* million(s).
mm *Millimeter* millimet|re, *Am.* -er.
möbl. *möbliert* furnished.
MP *Militärpolizei* Military Police.
mtl. *monatlich* monthly.
m. W. *meines Wissens* as far as I know.

N *Nord(en)* north.
nachm. *nachmittags* in the afternoon, *abbr.* p. m.
n. Chr. *nach Christus* after Christ, *abbr.* A. D.
n. J. *nächsten Jahres* of next year.
n. M. *nächsten Monats* of next month.
No., Nr. *Numero, Nummer* number, *abbr.* N°.
NS *Nachschrift* postscript, *abbr.* P. S.

O *Ost(en)* east.
o. B. *ohne Befund* ⚕ without findings.
od. *oder* or.

OEZ *osteuropäische Zeit* time of the East European zone.

OHG *Offene Handelsgesellschaft* ordinary partnership.

o. J. *ohne Jahr* no date.

p. Adr. *per Adresse* care of, *abbr.* c/o.

Pf *Pfennig German coin:* pfennig.

Pfd. *Pfund German weight:* pound.

PKW, Pkw. *Personenkraftwagen* (motor) car.

P. P. *praemissis praemittendis* omitting titles, to whom it may concern.

p.p., p.pa., ppa. *per procura* per proxy, *abbr.* per pro.

Prof. *Professor* professor.

PS *Pferdestärke(n)* horse-power, *abbr.* H.P., h.p.; *postscriptum, Nachschrift* postscript, *abbr.* P.S.

qkm *Quadratkilometer* square kilomet|re, *Am.* -er. [*Am.* -er.]
qm *Quadratmeter* square met|re,}

Reg. Bez. *Regierungsbezirk* administrative district.

Rel. *Religion* religion.

resp. *respektive* respectively.

S *Süd(en)* south.

S. *Seite* page.

s. *siehe* see, *abbr.* v., vid. (= vide).

s. a. *siehe auch* see also.

Sa. *Summa, Summe* sum, total.

s. d. *siehe dies* see this.

SED *Sozialistische Einheitspartei Deutschlands* United Socialist Party of Germany.

sen. *senior, der Ältere* senior.

sm *Seemeile* nautical mile.

s. o. *siehe oben* see above.

sog. *sogenannt* so-called.

SPD *Sozialdemokratische Partei Deutschlands* Social Democratic Party of Germany.

St. *Stück* piece; *Sankt* Saint.

St(d)., Stde. *Stunde* hour, *abbr.* h.

Str. *Straße* street, *abbr.* St.

s. u. *siehe unten* see below.

s. Z. *seinerzeit* at that time.

t *Tonne* ton.

tägl. *täglich* daily, per day.

Tel. *Telephon* telephone; *Telegramm* wire, cable.

TH *Technische Hochschule* technical university *or* college.

u. *und* and.

u. a. *und andere(s)* and others; *unter anderem or anderen* among other things, inter alia.

u. ä. *und ähnliche(s)* and the like.

U.A.w.g. *Um Antwort wird gebeten* an answer is requested, *répondez s'il vous plait, abbr.* R.S.V.P.

u. dgl. (m.) *und dergleichen (mehr)* and the like.

u. d. M. *unter dem Meeresspiegel* below sea level; **ü. d. M.** *über dem Meeresspiegel* above sea level.

UdSSR *Union der Sozialistischen Sowjetrepubliken* Union of Soviet Socialist Republics.

u. E. *unseres Erachtens* in our opinion. [following.}

u. f., u. ff. *und folgende* and the}

UKW *Ultrakurzwelle* ultra-short wave, very high frequency, *abbr.* VHF.

U/min. *Umdrehungen in der Minute* revolutions per minute, *abbr.* r.p.m.

urspr. *ursprünglich* original(ly).

US(A) *Vereinigte Staaten (von Amerika)* United States (of America).

usw. *und so weiter* and so on, *abbr.* etc. [stances permitting.}

u. U. *unter Umständen* circum-}

v. *von, vom* of; from; by.

V *Volt* volt; *Volumen* volume.

V. *Vers* line, verse.

v. Chr. *vor Christus* before Christ, *abbr.* B. C.

VEB *Volkseigener Betrieb* People's Own Undertaking.

Verf., Vf. *Verfasser* author.

Verl. *Verlag* publishing firm; *Verleger* publisher.

vgl. *vergleiche* confer, *abbr.* cf.

v.g.u. *vorgelesen, genehmigt, unterschrieben* read, confirmed, signed.

v. H. *vom Hundert* per cent.

v. J. *vorigen Jahres* of last year.

v. M. *vorigen Monats* of last month.

vorm. *vormittags* in the morning, *abbr.* a. m.; *vormals* formerly.

Vors. *Vorsitzender* chairman.

v. T. *vom Tausend* per thousand.

VW *Volkswagen* Volkswagen, People's Car.

W *West(en)* west; *Watt* watt(s).

WE *Wärmeeinheit* thermal unit.

WEZ *westeuropäische Zeit* Western European time (Greenwich time).

WGB *Weltgewerkschaftsbund* World Federation of Trade Unions, *abbr.* WFTU.

Wwe. *Witwe* widow.

Z. *Zahl* number; *Zeile* line.

z. *zu, zum, zur* at; to.

z. B. *zum Beispiel* for instance, *abbr.* e. g.

z. H(d). *zu Händen* attention of, to be delivered to, care of, *abbr.* c/o.

z. S. *zur See* of the navy.

z. T. *zum Teil* partly.

Ztg. *Zeitung* newspaper.

Ztr. *Zentner* centner.

Ztschr. *Zeitschrift* periodical.

zus. *zusammen* together.

zw. *zwischen* between; among.

z. Z(t). *zur Zeit* at the time, at present, for the time being.

American and British Proper Names

Aberdeen [æbəˈdiːn] *Stadt in Schottland.*

Africa [ˈæfrikə] Afrika *n.* [*U.S.A.*]

Alabama [æləˈbæmə] *Staat der*

Alaska [əˈlæskə] *Staat der U.S.A.*

Albania [ælˈbeinjə] Albanien *n.*

Alberta [ælˈbəːtə] *Provinz in Kanada.* [*U.S.A.*]

Alleghany [ˈæligeini] *Gebirge in*

Alsace [ˈælsæs] Elsaß *n.*

America [əˈmerikə] Amerika *n.* [*U.S.A.*]

Antilles [ænˈtiliːz] *die Antillen.*

Appalachians [æpəˈleitʃjənz] *die* Appalachen (*Gebirge in U.S.A.*).

Arizona [æriˈzounə] *Staat der U.S.A.* [*U.S.A.*]

Arkansas [ˈɑːkənsɔː] *Staat der*

Arlington [ˈɑːliŋtən] *Nationalfriedhof bei Washington.*

Ascot [ˈæskət] *Stadt in England.*

Asia [ˈeiʃə] Asien *n.*

Athens [ˈæθinz] Athen *n.*

Australia [ɔsˈtreiljə] Australien *n.*

Austria [ˈɔstriə] Österreich *n.*

Avon [ˈeivən] *Fluß in England.*

Azores [əˈzɔːz] *die Azoren.*

Bacon [ˈbeikən] *engl. Philosoph.*

Bahamas [bəˈhɑːməz] *die Bahamainseln.*

Balmoral [bælˈmɔrəl] *Königsschloß in Schottland.*

Bedford(shire) [ˈbedfəd(ʃiə)] *Grafschaft in England.*

Belfast [belˈfɑːst] *Hauptstadt von Nordirland.*

Belgium [ˈbeldʒəm] Belgien *n.*

Belgrade [belˈgreid] Belgrad *n.*

Ben Nevis [benˈnevis] *höchster Berg in Großbritannien.*

Berkshire [ˈbɑːkʃiə] *Grafschaft in England.*

Bermudas [bəːˈmjuːdəz] *die Bermudainseln.*

Bern(e) [bəːn] Bern *n.*

Birmingham [ˈbəːmiŋəm] *Industriestadt in England* [Biskaya.]

Biscay [ˈbiskei] *Bay of* ~ *Golf m von*

Boston [ˈbɔstən] *Stadt in U.S.A.*

Bournemouth [ˈbɔːnməθ] *Seebad in England.*

Brighton [ˈbraitn] *Seebad in England.* [land.]

Bristol [ˈbristl] *Hafenstadt in Eng-*

Britten [ˈbritn] *engl. Komponist.*

Brooklyn [ˈbruklin] *Stadtteil von New York.*

Brussels [ˈbrʌslz] Brüssel *n.*

Bucharest [ˈbjuːkərest] Bukarest *n.*

Buckingham(shire) [ˈbʌkiŋəm(ʃiə)] *Grafschaft in England.*

Budapest [ˈbjuːdəˈpest] Budapest *n.*

Bulgaria [bʌlˈgeəriə] Bulgarien *n.*

Burns [bəːnz] *schott. Dichter.*

Byron [ˈbaiərən] *engl. Dichter.*

California [kæliˈfɔːnjə] Kalifornien *n* (*Staat der U.S.A.*).

Cambridge [ˈkeimbridʒ] *engl. Universitätsstadt; Stadt in U.S.A.; a.* ~shire [ˈ~ʃiə] *Grafschaft in England.*

Canada [ˈkænədə] Kanada *n.*

Canary Islands [kəˈneəri ˈailəndz] *die Kanarischen Inseln.*

Canberra [ˈkænbərə] *Hauptstadt von Australien.* [*England.*]

Canterbury [ˈkæntəbəri] *Stadt in*

Capetown [ˈkeiptaun] Kapstadt *n.*

Cardiff [ˈkɑːdif] *Hauptstadt von Wales.*

Carinthia [kəˈrinθiə] Kärnten *n.*

Carlyle [kɑːˈlail] *engl. Autor.*

Carolina [kærəˈlainə]: *North* ~ Nordkarolina *n* (*Staat der U.S.A.*); *South* ~ Südkarolina *n* (*Staat der U.S.A.*).

Ceylon [siˈlɔn] Ceylon *n.*

Chamberlain [ˈtʃeimbəlin, ~lein] *Name mehrerer brit. Staatsmänner.*

Cheshire [ˈtʃeʃə] *Grafschaft in England.*

Chicago [ʃiˈkɑːgou, *Am.* ʃiˈkɔːgou] *Industriestadt in U.S.A.*

China [ˈtʃainə] China *n.* [mann.]

Churchill [ˈtʃəːtʃil] *brit. Staats-*

Cleveland [ˈkliːvlənd] *Industrie- und Hafenstadt in U.S.A.*

Clyde [klaid] *Fluß in Schottland.*

Coleridge [ˈkoulridʒ] *engl. Dichter.*

Colorado [kɔləˈrɑːdou] *Staat der U.S.A.*

Columbia [kəˈlʌmbiə] *Fluß in U.S.A.; Bundesdistrikt der U.S.A.*

Connecticut [kəˈnetikət] *Staat der U.S.A.*

Constance [ˈkɔnstəns]: *Lake of* ~ Bodensee *m.*

Cooper [ˈkuːpə] *amer. Autor.*

Copenhagen [koupnˈheigən] Kopenhagen *n.* [dilleren.]

Cordilleras [kɔːdiˈljeərəz] *die Kor-*

Cornwall [ˈkɔːnwəl] *Grafschaft in England.*

Coventry [ˈkɔvəntri] *Industriestadt in England.* [mann.]

Cromwell [ˈkrɔmwəl] *engl. Staats-*

Cumberland [ˈkʌmbələnd] *Grafschaft in England.*

Cyprus [ˈsaiprəs] Zypern *n.*

Czecho-Slovakia [ˈtʃekouslouˈvækiə] *die Tschechoslowakei.*

Dakota [dəˈkoutə]: *North* ~ Norddakota *n* (*Staat der U.S.A.*); *South* ~ Süddakota *n* (*Staat der U.S.A.*).

Defoe [dəˈfou] *engl. Autor.*

Delaware [ˈdeləwɛə] *Staat der U.S.A.*

Denmark [ˈdenmaːk] Dänemark *n.*

Derby(shire) [ˈdaːbi(ʃə)] *Grafschaft in England.*

Detroit [dəˈtrɔit] *Industriestadt in U.S.A.*

Devon(shire) [ˈdevn(ʃiə)] *Grafschaft in England.*

Dickens [ˈdikinz] *engl. Autor.*

Dorset(shire) [ˈdɔːsit(ʃiə)] *Grafschaft in England.* [*land.*]

Dover [ˈdouvə] *Hafenstadt in Eng-*

Downing Street [ˈdauniŋ ˈstriːt] *Straße in London mit der Amtswohnung des Prime Minister.*

Dublin [ˈdʌblin] *Hauptstadt von Irland.*

Dunkirk [dʌnˈkəːk] Dünkirchen *n.*

Durham [ˈdʌrəm] *Grafschaft in England.*

Edinburgh [ˈedinbərə] Edinburg *n.*

Edison [ˈedisn] *amer. Erfinder.*

Egypt [ˈiːdʒipt] Ägypten *n.*

Eire [ˈɛərə] *Republik Irland.*

Eisenhower [ˈaizənhauə] *Präsident der U.S.A.*

Eliot [ˈeljət] *engl. Dichter.*

Emerson [ˈeməsn] *amer. Philosoph.*

England [ˈiŋglənd] England *n.*

Epsom [ˈepsəm] *Stadt in England.*

Erie [ˈiəri]: *Lake* ~ Eriesee *m.*

Essex [ˈesiks] *Grafschaft in England.*

Eton [ˈiːtn] *berühmte Public School.*

Europe [ˈjuərəp] Europa *n.*

Falkland Islands [ˈfɔːlklənd ˈailəndz] *die Falklandinseln.*

Faulkner [ˈfɔːknə] *amer. Autor.*

Finland [ˈfinlənd] Finnland *n.*

Florida [ˈflɔridə] *Staat der U.S.A.*

Flushing [ˈflʌʃiŋ] Vlissingen *n.*

France [fraːns] Frankreich *n.*

Franklin [ˈfræŋklin] *amer. Staatsmann und Physiker.*

Galsworthy [ˈgɔːlzwəːði] *engl. Autor.*

Geneva [dʒiˈniːvə] Genf *n*; *Lake of* ~ Genfer See *m.*

Georgia [ˈdʒɔːdʒə] *Staat der U.S.A.*

Germany [ˈdʒəːməni] Deutschland *n.* [*nist.*]

Gershwin [ˈgəːʃwin] *amer. Kompo-*

Gibraltar [dʒiˈbrɔːltə] Gibraltar *n.*

Glasgow [ˈglaːsgou] *Hafenstadt in Schottland.*

Gloucester [ˈglɔstə] *Stadt in England*; *a.* ~**shire** [ˈ_ʃiə] *Grafschaft in England.*

Great Britain [ˈgreit ˈbritn] Großbritannien *n.*

Greece [griːs] Griechenland *n.*

Greene [griːn] *engl. Autor.*

Greenland [ˈgriːnlənd] Grönland *n.*

Greenwich [ˈgrinidʒ] *Vorort von London.*

Guernsey [ˈgəːnzi] *Kanalinsel.*

Hague [heig]: *The* ~ Den Haag.

Hampshire [ˈhæmpʃiə] *Grafschaft in England.*

Harlem [ˈhaːlem] *Stadtteil von New York.*

Harrow [ˈhærou] *berühmte Public School.*

Harvard University [ˈhaːvəd juːniˈvəːsiti] *amer. Universität.*

Harwich [ˈhæridʒ] *Hafenstadt in England.*

Hawaii [haːˈwaiiː] *Staat der U.S.A.*

Hebrides [ˈhebridiːz] *die Hebriden.*

Helsinki [ˈhelsiŋki] Helsinki *n.*

Hemingway [ˈhemiŋwei] *amer. Autor.*

Hereford(shire) [ˈherifəd(ʃiə)] *Grafschaft in England.*

Hertford(shire) [ˈhaːtfəd(ʃiə)] *Grafschaft in England.*

Hollywood [ˈhɔliwud] *Filmstadt in Kalifornien, U.S.A.*

Houston [ˈjuːstən] *Stadt in U.S.A.*

Hudson [ˈhʌdsn] *Fluß in U.S.A.*

Hull [hʌl] *Hafenstadt in England.*

Hume [hjuːm] *engl. Philosoph.*

Hungary [ˈhʌŋgəri] Ungarn *n.*

Huntingdon(shire) [ˈhʌntiŋdən (-ʃiə)] *Grafschaft in England.* [*m.*]

Huron [ˈhjuərən]: *Lake* ~ Huronsee

Huxley [ˈhaksli] *engl. Autor.*

Iceland [ˈaislənd] Island *n.*

Idaho [ˈaidəhou] *Staat der U.S.A.*

Illinois [iliˈnɔi] *Staat der U.S.A.*

India [ˈindjə] Indien *n.*

Indiana [indiˈænə] *Staat der U.S.A.*

Iowa [ˈaiouə] *Staat der U.S.A.*

Irak, Iraq [iˈraːk] Irak *m.*

Iran [iˈraːn] Iran *m.*

Ireland [ˈaiələnd] Irland *n.*

Irving [ˈəːviŋ] *amer. Autor.*

Italy [ˈitəli] Italien *n.*

Jefferson [ˈdʒefəsn] *Präsident der U.S.A., Verfasser der Unabhängigkeitserklärung von 1776.*

Johnson [ˈdʒɔnsn] 1. *engl. Autor;* 2. *Präsident der U.S.A.*

Kansas [ˈkænzəs] *Staat der U.S.A.*

Kashmir [kæʃˈmiə] Kaschmir *n.*

Keats [kiːts] *engl. Dichter.*

Kennedy [ˈkenidi] *Präsident der U.S.A.;* ~ *Airport Flughafen von New York.*

Kent [kent] *Grafschaft in England.*

Kentucky [kenˈtʌki] *Staat der U.S.A.*

Kipling [ˈkipliŋ] *engl. Dichter.*

Klondike [ˈklɔndaik] *Fluß und Landschaft in Kanada und Alaska.*

Kremlin [ˈkremlin] *der Kreml.*

Labrador ['læbrədɔ:] *Halbinsel Nordamerikas.*

Lancashire ['læŋkəʃiə] *Grafschaft in England.*

Lancaster ['læŋkəstə] *Name zweier Städte in England und U.S.A.; s. Lancashire.* [*land.*\

Leeds [li:dz] *Industriestadt in Eng-*

Leicester ['lestə] *Stadt in England; a.* ~**shire** ['~ʃiə] *Grafschaft in England.*

Lincoln ['liŋkən] 1. *Präsident der U.S.A.*; 2. *a.* ~**shire** ['~ʃiə] *Grafschaft in England.*

Lisbon ['lizbən] *Lissabon n.*

Liverpool ['livəpu:l] *Hafen- und Industriestadt in England.*

Locke [lɔk] *engl. Philosoph.*

London ['lʌndən] *London n.*

Los Angeles [lɔs 'ændʒili:z] *Stadt in U.S.A.* [*U.S.A.*\

Louisiana [lu:izi'ænə] *Staat der*\

Lucerne [lu:'sə:n]: *Lake of* ~ *Vierwaldstätter See m.*

Luxemburg ['lʌksəmbə:g] *Luxemburg n.*

Madrid [mə'drid] *Madrid n.*

Maine [mein] *Staat der U.S.A.*

Malta ['mɔ:ltə] *Malta n.*

Manchester ['mæntʃistə] *Industriestadt in England.*

Manhattan [mæn'hætən] *Stadtteil von New York.* [*Kanada.*\

Manitoba [mæni'toubə] *Provinz in*\

Maryland ['mɛərilənd, *Am.* 'meriländ] *Staat der U.S.A.*

Massachusetts [mæsə'tʃu:sits] *Staat der U.S.A.*

Melbourne ['melbən] *Stadt in Australien.*

Miami [mai'æmi] *Badeort in Florida, U.S.A.*

Michigan ['miʃigən] *Staat der U.S.A.; Lake* ~ *Michigansee m.*

Middlesex ['midlseks] *Grafschaft in England.*

Miller ['milə] *amer. Dramatiker.*

Milton ['miltən] *engl. Dichter.*

Milwaukee [mil'wɔ:ki:] *Stadt in U.S.A.*

Minneapolis [mini'æpəlis] *Stadt in U.S.A.* [*U.S.A.*\

Minnesota [mini'soutə] *Staat der*\

Mississippi [misi'sipi] *Strom und Staat der U.S.A.*

Missouri [mi'zuəri] *Fluß und Staat der U.S.A.*

Monmouth(shire) ['mɔnməθ(ʃiə)] *Grafschaft in England.*

Monroe [mən'rou] *Präsident der U.S.A.* [*U.S.A.*\

Montana [mɔn'tænə] *Staat der*\

Montgomery [mənt'gɔməri] *brit. Feldmarschall.*

Montreal [mɔntri'ɔ:l] *Stadt in Kanada.*

Moore [muə] *engl. Bildhauer.*

Moscow ['mɔskou] *Moskau n.*

Nebraska [ni'bræskə] *Staat der U.S.A.*

Nelson ['nelsn] *engl. Admiral.*

Netherlands ['neðələndz] *die Niederlande.*

Nevada [ne'va:də] *Staat der U.S.A.*

New Brunswick [nju: 'brʌnzwik] *Provinz in Kanada.*

Newcastle ['nju:ka:sl] *Hafenstadt in England.* [*von Indien.*\

New Delhi [nju: 'deli] *Hauptstadt*\

New England [nju: 'iŋglənd] *Neuengland n.* [*Neufundland n.*\

Newfoundland [nju:fənd'lænd]\

New Hampshire [nju: 'hæmpʃiə] *Staat der U.S.A.*

New Jersey [nju: 'dʒə:si] *Staat der U.S.A.*

New Mexico [nju: 'meksikou] *Neumexiko n (Staat der U.S.A.).*

New Orleans [nju: 'ɔ:liənz] *Hafenstadt in U.S.A.*

Newton ['nju:tn] *engl. Physiker.*

New York ['nju: 'jɔ:k] *Stadt und Staat der U.S.A.*

New Zealand [nju: 'zi:lənd] *Neuseeland n.*

Niagara [nai'ægərə] *Niagara m.*

Nixon ['niksn] *Präsident der U.S.A.*

Norfolk ['nɔ:fək] *Grafschaft in England.*

Northampton [nɔ:'θæmptən] *Stadt in England; a.* ~**shire** ['~ʃiə] *Grafschaft in England.*

Northumberland [nɔ:'θʌmbələnd] *Grafschaft in England.*

Norway ['nɔ:wei] *Norwegen n.*

Nottingham ['nɔtiŋəm] *Stadt in England; a.* ~**shire** ['~ʃiə] *Grafschaft in England.*

Nova Scotia ['nouvə 'skouʃə] *Provinz in Kanada.*

Ohio [ou'haiou] *Staat der U.S.A.*

O'Neill [ou'ni:l] *amer. Dramatiker.*

Ontario [ɔn'tɛəriou] *Provinz in Kanada; Lake* ~ *Ontariosee m.*

Oregon ['ɔrigən] *Staat der U.S.A.*

Orkney Islands ['ɔ:kni 'ailəndz] *die Orkneyinseln.*

Osborne ['ɔzbən] *engl. Dramatiker.*

Oslo ['ɔzlou] *Oslo n.*

Ostend [ɔs'tend] *Ostende n.*

Ottawa ['ɔtəwə] *Hauptstadt von Kanada.*

Oxford ['ɔksfəd] *engl. Universitätsstadt; a.* ~**shire** ['~ʃiə] *Grafschaft in England.*

Pakistan [pa:kis'ta:n] *Pakistan n.*

Paris ['pæris] *Paris n.*

Pearl Harbour ['pə:l 'ha:bə] *Hafenstadt auf Hawaii.*

Pennsylvania [pensil'veinjə] *Pennsylvanien n (Staat der U.S.A.).*

Philadelphia [filə'delfjə] *Stadt in U.S.A.*

Philippines ['filipi:nz] *die Philippinen.*

Pittsburg(h) ['pitsbə:g] *Stadt in U.S.A.*

Plymouth ['pliməθ] *Hafenstadt in England.*

Poe [pou] *amer. Autor.*

Poland ['poulənd] Polen *n.*

Portsmouth ['pɔ:tsməθ] *Hafenstadt in England.*

Portugal ['pɔ:tjugəl] Portugal *n.*

Prague [prɑ:g] Prag *n.*

Purcell ['pə:sl] *engl. Komponist.*

Quebec [kwi'bek] *Provinz und Stadt in Kanada.*

Reykjavik ['reikjəvi:k] Reykjavik *n.*

Rhode Island [roud 'ailənd] *Staat der U.S.A.*

Rocky Mountains ['rɔki 'mauntinz] *Gebirge in U.S.A.*

Rome [roum] Rom *n.*

Roosevelt ['rouzəvelt] *Name zweier Präsidenten der U.S.A.* [School.)

Rugby ['rʌgbi] *berühmte Public)*

Rumania [ru:'meinjə] Rumänien *n.*

Russell ['rʌsl] *engl. Philosoph.*

Russia ['rʌʃə] Rußland *n.*

Rutland(shire) ['rʌtlənd(ʃiə)] *Grafschaft in England.*

San Francisco [sænfrən'siskou] *Hafenstadt in U.S.A.*

Saskatchewan [səs'kætʃiwən] *Provinz von Kanada.*

Scandinavia [skændi'neivjə] *Skandinavien n.*

Scotland ['skɔtlənd] Schottland *n.*

Shakespeare ['ʃeikspiə] *engl. Dichter.*

Shaw [ʃɔ:] *engl. Dramatiker.*

Shelley ['ʃeli] *engl. Dichter.*

Shetland Islands ['ʃetlənd 'ailəndz] *die* Shetlandinseln.

Shropshire ['ʃrɔpʃiə] *Grafschaft in England.*

Snowdon ['snoudn] *Berg in Wales.*

Sofia ['soufjə] Sofia *n.*

Somerset(shire) ['sʌməsit(ʃiə)] *Grafschaft in England.*

Southampton [sauθ'æmptən] *Hafenstadt in England.*

Spain [spein] Spanien *n.*

Stafford(shire) ['stæfəd(ʃiə)] *Grafschaft in England.*

Stevenson ['sti:vnsn] *engl. Autor.*

St. Lawrence [snt'lɔrəns] *der* St. Lorenz-Strom.

St. Louis [snt'luis] *Industriestadt in U.S.A.* [n.)

Stockholm ['stɔkhoum] Stockholm)

Stratford ['strætfəd]; ~on-Avon *Geburtsort Shakespeares.*

Suffolk ['sʌfək] *Grafschaft in England.* [rer See m.)

Superior [sju:'piəriə] : *Lake* ~ Obe-)

Surrey ['sʌri] *Grafschaft in England.*

Sussex ['sʌsiks] *Grafschaft in England.*

Sweden ['swi:dn] Schweden *n.*

Swift [swift] *engl. Autor.*

Switzerland ['switsələnd] *die* Schweiz. [tralien.)

Sydney ['sidni] *Hafenstadt in Aus-)*

Tennessee [tene'si] *Staat der U.S.A.*

Tennyson ['tenisn] *engl. Dichter.*

Texas ['teksəs] *Staat der U.S.A.*

Thackeray ['θækəri] *engl. Autor.*

Thames [temz] Themse *f.*

Tirana [ti'rɑ:nə] Tirana *n.* [nada.)

Toronto [tə'rɔntou] *Stadt in Ka-)*

Toynbee ['tɔinbi] *engl. Historiker.*

Trafalgar [trə'fælgə] *Vorgebirge bei Gibraltar.* [U.S.A.)

Truman ['tru:mən] *Präsident der)*

Turkey ['tə:ki] *die* Türkei.

Twain [twein] *amer. Autor.*

Tyrol ['tirəl] Tirol *n.*

United States of America [ju:'nai-tid 'steitsəvə'merikə] *die* Vereinigten Staaten von Amerika.

Utah ['ju:tɑ:] *Staat der U.S.A.*

Vancouver [væn'ku:və] *Stadt in Kanada.*

Vermont [və:'mɔnt] *Staat der)*

Vienna [vi'enə] Wien *n.* [U.S.A.)

Virginia [və'dʒinjə] Virginien *n (Staat der U.S.A.)*; West ~ *Staat der U.S.A.*

Wales [weilz] Wales *n.*

Warsaw ['wɔ:sɔ:] Warschau *n.*

Warwick(shire) ['wɔrik(ʃiə)] *Grafschaft in England.*

Washington ['wɔʃiŋtən] **1.** *Präsident der U.S.A.*; **2.** *Staat der U.S.A.*; **3.** *Bundeshauptstadt der U.S.A.*

Wellington ['weliŋtən] *Hauptstadt von Neuseeland.*

Westmoreland ['westmələnd] *Grafschaft in England.*

White House ['wait 'haus] *das* Weiße Haus.

Whitman ['witmən] *amer. Dichter.*

Wilson ['wilsn] **1.** *Präsident der U.S.A.*; **2.** *brit. Premier.*

Wiltshire ['wiltʃiə] *Grafschaft in England.*

Wimbledon ['wimbldən] *Vorort von London.* [Kanada.)

Winnipeg ['winipeg] *Stadt in)*

Wisconsin [wis'kɔnsin] *Staat der U.S.A.*

Worcester ['wustə] *Industriestadt in England*; *a.* ~shire ['~ʃiə] *Grafschaft in England.*

Wordsworth ['wə:dzwə:θ] *engl. Dichter.*

Yale University ['jeil ju:ni'və:siti] *amer. Universität.*

York [jɔ:k] *Stadt in England*; *a.* ~shire ['~ʃiə] *Grafschaft in England.*

Yugoslavia ['ju:gou'slɑ:vjə] Jugoslawien *n.*

American and British Abbreviations

abbr. *abbreviated* abgekürzt; *abbreviation* Abk., Abkürzung *f*.

A.B.C. *American Broadcasting Company* Amer. Rundfunkgesellschaft *f*.

A.C. *alternating current* Wechselstrom *m*.

A.E.C. *Atomic Energy Commission* Atomenergie-Kommission *f*.

AFL-CIO *American Federation of Labor & Congress of Industrial Organizations* (größter amer. Gewerkschaftsverband).

A.F.N. *American Forces Network* (Rundfunkanstalt der amer. Streitkräfte).

Ala. *Alabama*.

Alas. *Alaska*.

a.m. *ante meridiem* (*lateinisch = before noon*) vormittags.

A.P. *Associated Press* (amer. Nachrichtenbüro).

A.R.C. *American Red Cross* Amer. Rotes Kreuz.

Ariz. *Arizona*.

Ark. *Arkansas*.

arr. *arrival* Ank., Ankunft *f*.

B.A. *Bachelor of Arts* Bakkalaureus *m* der Philosophie.

B.B.C. *British Broadcasting Corporation* Brit. Rundfunkgesellschaft *f*.

B.E.A. *British European Airways* Brit.-Europäische Luftfahrtgesellschaft.

Beds. *Bedfordshire*.

Benelux *Belgium, Netherlands, Luxemburg* (Zollunion).

Berks. *Berkshire*.

B.F.N. *British Forces Network* (Sender der brit. Streitkräfte in Deutschland).

B.L. *Bachelor of Law* Bakkalaureus *m* des Rechts.

B.M. *Bachelor of Medicine* Bakkalaureus *m* der Medizin.

B.O.A.C. *British Overseas Airways Corporation* Brit. Übersee-Luftfahrtgesellschaft *f*.

B.R. *British Railways*.

Br(it). *Britain* Großbritannien *n*; *British* britisch.

B.S. *Bachelor of Science* Bakkalaureus *m* der Naturwissenschaften.

Bucks. *Buckinghamshire*.

C. *Celsius, centigrade*.

c. *cent(s)* Cent *m*; *circa* ca., ungefähr, zirka; *cubic* Kubik...

Cal(if). *California*.

Cambs. *Cambridgeshire*.

Can. *Canada* Kanada *n*; *Canadian* kanadisch.

cf. *confer* vgl., vergleiche.

Ches. *Cheshire*.

C.I.C. *Counter Intelligence Corps* (Spionageabwehrdienst der U.S.A.).

C.I.D. *Criminal Investigation Department* (brit. Kriminalpolizei).

Co. *Company* Gesellschaft *f*; *County* Grafschaft *f*, Kreis *m*.

c/o *care of* p.A., per Adresse, bei.

Col(o). *Colorado*.

Conn. *Connecticut*.

cp. *compare* vgl., vergleiche.

Cumb. *Cumberland*.

cwt. *hundredweight* (etwa 1) Zentner *m*.

d. *penny, pence*.

D.C. *direct current* Gleichstrom *m*; *District of Columbia* (mit der amer. Hauptstadt Washington).

Del. *Delaware*.

dep. *departure* Abf., Abfahrt *f*.

Dept. *Department* Abt., Abteilung *f*.

Derby. *Derbyshire*.

Devon. *Devonshire*.

Dors. *Dorsetshire*.

Dur(h). *Durham*.

dz. *dozen* Dutzend *n* od. *pl*.

E. *east* Ost(en *m*); *eastern* östlich; *English* englisch.

E.C. *East Central* (London) Mitte-Ost (Postbezirk).

ECOSOC *Economic and Social Council* Wirtschafts- und Sozialrat *m* (U.N.).

Ed., ed. *edition* Auflage *f*; *edited* hrsg., herausgegeben; *editor* Hrsg., Herausgeber *m*.

E.E.C. *European Economic Community* EWG, Europäische Wirtschaftsgemeinschaft.

E.F.T.A. *European Free Trade Association* EFTA, Europäische Freihandelsgemeinschaft od. -zone.

e.g. *exempli gratia* (lateinisch = for instance) z.B., zum Beispiel.

Enc. *enclosure(s)* Anlage(n *pl*.) *f*.

Ess. *Essex*.

F. *Fahrenheit*.

f. *fathom(s)* Faden *m*, Klafter *f, m, n*; *feminine* weiblich; *foot*, *pl.* feet Fuß *m* od. *pl*.; *following* folgend.

F.A.O. *Food and Agricultural Organization* Organisation *f* für Ernährung und Landwirtschaft (U.N.).

FBI *Federal Bureau of Investigation* (Bundeskriminalamt der U.S.A.).

fig. *figure(s)* Abb., Abbildung(en *pl*.) *f*.

Fla. *Florida*.

F.O. *Foreign Office* brit. Auswärtiges Amt.

fr. *franc(s)* Frank(en *pl*.) *m*.

ft. *foot*, *pl.* feet Fuß *m* od. *pl*.

g. *gramme* g, Gramm *n*; *guinea* Guinee *f* (*21 Schilling*).
Ga. *Georgia*.
gal. *gallon* Gallone *f*.
G.A.T.T. *General Agreement on Tariffs and Trade* Allgemeines Zoll- und Handelsabkommen.
G.B. *Great Britain* Großbritannien *n*.
G.I. *government issue* von der Regierung ausgegeben; Staatseigentum *n*; *fig. der* amer. Soldat.
Glos. *Gloucestershire*.
G.P.O. *General Post Office* Hauptpostamt *n.*
gr. *gross* brutto.
Gt.Br. *Great Britain* Großbritannien *n*.

h. *hour(s)* Std., Stunde(n *pl.*) *f*.
Hants. *Hampshire*.
H.C. *House of Commons* Unterhaus *n*.
Heref. *Herefordshire*.
Herts. *Hertfordshire*.
hf. *half* halb.
H.I. *Hawaiian Islands*.
H.L. *House of Lords* Oberhaus *n*.
H.M. *His (Her) Majesty* Seine (Ihre) Majestät.
H.M.S. *His (Her) Majesty's Service* Dienst *m*, & Dienstsache *f*; *His (Her) Majesty's Ship* Seiner (Ihrer) Majestät Schiff *n*.
H.O. *Home Office* brit. Innenministerium *n.* [stärke *f.*]
H.P., h.p. *horse-power* PS, Pferdestärke *f.*
H.Q., Hq. *Headquarters* Stab(squartier *n*) *m*, Hauptquartier *n*.
H.R. *House of Representatives* Repräsentantenhaus *n (der U.S.A.)*.
H.R.H. *His (Her) Royal Highness* Seine (Ihre) Königliche Hoheit *f*.
Hunts. *Huntingdonshire*.

Ia. *Iowa*.
I.C.B.M. *intercontinental ballistic missile* interkontinentaler ballistischer Flugkörper.
I.D. *Intelligence Department* Nachrichtenamt *n*.
Id(a). *Idaho.* [d.h., das heißt.]
i.e. *id est (lateinisch = that is to say)*
Ill. *Illinois*.
I.M.F. *International Monetary Fund* Weltwährungsfonds *m*.
in. *inch(es)* Zoll *m od. pl.* [gen.]
Inc. *Incorporated* (amtlich) eingetragen.
Ind. *Indiana*.
I.O.C. *International Olympic Committee* Internationales Olympisches Komitee.
Ir. *Ireland* Irland *n*; *Irish* irisch.
I.R.C. *International Red Cross* Internationales Rotes Kreuz.

J.P. *Justice of the Peace* Friedensrichter *m*.

Kan(s). *Kansas*.
k.o. *knock(ed) out* Boxen: k.o. (ge-) schlagen; *fig.* erledigen (erledigt).
Ky. *Kentucky*.

£ *pound sterling* Pfund *n* Sterling.
La. *Louisiana*.
Lancs. *Lancashire*. [*wicht*).]
lb. *pound(s)* Pfund *n od. pl. (Ge-)*
L.C. *letter of credit* Kreditbrief
Leics. *Leicestershire*. [*m.*]
Lincs. *Lincolnshire*.
LP *long-playing* Langspiel...(*Platte*).
L.P. *Labour Party* (*brit. Arbeiterpartei*). [tung.]
Ltd. *limited* mit beschränkter Haf-

m. *male* männlich; *metre* m, Meter *n*, *m*; *mile* Meile *f*; *minute* Min., Minute *f*. [Philosophie.]
M.A. *Master of Arts* Magister *m der*
Mass. *Massachusetts*.
M.D. *Medicinae Doctor (lateinisch = Doctor of Medicine)* Dr. med., Doktor *m* der Medizin.
Md. *Maryland*.
Me. *Maine*.
mi. *mile* Meile *f*.
Mich. *Michigan*.
Middx. *Middlesex*.
Minn. *Minnesota*.
Miss. *Mississippi*.
Mo. *Missouri*.
M.O. *money order* Postanweisung *f*.
Mon. *Monmouthshire*.
Mont. *Montana*.
MP, M.P. *Member of Parliament* Parlamentsabgeordnete *m*; *Military Police* Militärpolizei *f*.
m.p.h. *miles per hour* Stundenmeile *f.* [len *pl.*]
Mr *Mister* Herr *m*.
Mrs *Mistress* Frau *f*.
Mt. *Mount* Berg *n*.

N. *north* Nord(en *m*); *northern* nördlich.
n. *noon* Mittag *m*.
NASA *National Aeronautics and Space Administration (amer. Luftfahrt- und Raumforschungsbehörde)*.
NATO *North Atlantic Treaty Organization* Nordatlantikpakt-Organisation *f*.
N.C. *North Carolina*.
N.D(ak). *North Dakota*.
Neb(r). *Nebraska*.
Nev. *Nevada*.
N.H. *New Hampshire*.
N.H.S. *National Health Service* Nationaler Gesundheitsdienst (*brit. Krankenversicherung*).
N.J. *New Jersey*.
N.M(ex). *New Mexico*.
Norf. *Norfolk*.
Northants. *Northamptonshire*.
Northumb. *Northumberland*.
Notts. *Nottinghamshire*.
nt. *net* netto.
N.Y. *New York*. [York.]
N.Y.C. *New York City* Stadt *f* New

O. *Ohio*; *order* Auftrag *m*.
O.A.S. *Organization of American States* Organisation *f* amerikanischer Staaten.

O.E.E.C. *Organization of European Economic Co-operation* Organisation *f* für europäische wirtschaftliche Zusammenarbeit.

Okla. *Oklahoma.*

Ore(g). *Oregon.*

Oxon. *Oxfordshire.*

Pa. *Pennsylvania.*

P.A.A. *Pan-American Airways* Panamer. Luftfahrtgesellschaft *f.*

P.C. *police constable* Schutzmann *m.*

p.c. *per cent* %, Prozent *n od. pl.*

pd. *paid* bezahlt.

P.E.N., *mst* PEN Club *Poets, Playwrights, Editors, Essayists, and Novelists* Pen-Club *m, (Internationale Vereinigung von Dichtern, Dramatikern, Redakteuren, Essayisten und Romanschriftstellern).*

Penn(a). *Pennsylvania.*

Ph.D. *Philosophiae Doctor (lateinisch = Doctor of Philosophy)* Dr. phil., Doktor *m* der Philosophie.

p.m. *post meridiem (lateinisch = after noon)* nachmittags, abends.

P.O. *Post Office* Postamt *n; postal order* Postanweisung *f.*

P.O.B. *Post Office Box* Postschließfach *n.*

P.S. *Postscript* P.S., Nachschrift *f.*

P.T.O., p.t.o. *please turn over* b.w., bitte wenden.

PX *Post Exchange (Verkaufsläden der amer. Streitkräfte).*

R.A.F. *Royal Air Force* Königlich-Brit. Luftwaffe *f.*

Rd. *Road* Straße *f.*

ref(c). *(In) reference (to) (in)* Bezug *m* (auf); Empfehlung *f.*

regd. *registered* eingetragen; & eingeschrieben.   [tonne *f.*]

reg. tn. *register ton* RT, Register-

resp. *respective(ly)* bzw., beziehungsweise.

ret. *retired* i.R., im Ruhestand.

Rev. *Reverend* Ehrwürden.

R.I. *Rhode Island.*   Marine *f.*

R.N. *Royal Navy* Königlich-Brit.

R.R. *Railroad Am.* Eisenbahn *f.*

Rutland. *Rutlandshire.*

Ry. *Railway* Eisenbahn *f.*

S. *south* Süd(en *m*); *southern* südlich.

s. *second(s)* Sek., Sekunde(n *pl.*) *f; shilling(s)* Schilling *m od. pl.*

$ *dollar* Dollar *m.*

S.A. *South Africa* Südafrika *n; South America* Südamerika *n.*

Salop *Shropshire.*

S.C. *South Carolina; Security Council* Sicherheitsrat *m (U.N.).*

S.D(ak). *South Dakota.*

SEATO *South East Asia Treaty Organization* Südostasienpakt-Organisation *f.*

sh. *shilling(s)* Schilling *m od. pl.*

Soc. *society* Gesellschaft *f;* Verein *m.*

Som. *Somersetshire.*

Sq. *Square* Platz *m.*

sq. *square* ... Quadrat...

Staffs. *Staffordshire.*

St(.) *Saint* ... Sankt ...; *Station* Bahnhof *m; Street* Straße *f.*

Suff. *Suffolk.*

suppl. *supplement* Nachtrag *m.*

Sur. *Surrey.*

Suss. *Sussex.*

t. *ton(s)* Tonne(n *pl.*) *f.*

Tenn. *Tennessee.*

Tex. *Texas.*

T.M.O. *telegraph money order* telegraphische Geldanweisung.

T.O. *Telegraph (Telephone) Office* Telegraphen- (Fernsprech)amt *n*

T.U. *Trade(s) Union(s)* Gewerkschaft(en *pl.*) *f.*

T.U.C. *Trade(s) Union Congress brit.* Gewerkschaftsverband *m.*

U.K. *United Kingdom* Vereinigtes Königreich *(England, Schottland, Wales und Nordirland).*

U.N. *United Nations* Vereinte Nationen *pl.*

UNESCO *United Nations Educational, Scientific, and Cultural Organization* Organisation *f* der Vereinten Nationen für Wissenschaft, Erziehung und Kultur.

U.N.S.C. *United Nations Security Council* Sicherheitsrat *m* der Vereinten Nationen.

U.P.I. *United Press International (amer. Nachrichtenagentur).*

U.S.(A.) *United States (of America)* Vereinigte Staaten *pl.* (von America) Utah.   [rika.)]

Ut. *Utah.*   [rika.)]

Va. *Virginia.*

vol(s). *volume(s)* Band *m* (Bände)

Vt. *Vermont.*   [*pl.*).]

V.T.O.(L.) *vertical take-off (and landing) (aircraft)* Senkrechtstart(er) *m.*

W. *west* West(en *m*); *western* west-

War. *Warwickshire.*   [lich.]

Wash. *Washington.*

W.C. *West Central* (London) Mitte-West *(Postbezirk).*

W.F.T.U. *World Federation of Trade Unions* Weltgewerkschaftsbund *m.*

W.H.O. *World Health Organization* Weltgesundheitsorganisation *f (U.N.).*

W.I. *West Indies* Westindien *n.*

Wilts. *Wiltshire.*

Wis. *Wisconsin.*

Worcs. *Worcestershire.*

wt. *weight* Gewicht *n.*

W.Va. *West Virginia.*

Wyo. *Wyoming.*

yd. *yard(s)* Elle(n *pl.*) *f.*

Yorks. *Yorkshire.*

German Weights and Measures

I. Linear Measure

1 mm   *Millimeter* millimet|re, *Am.* -er = 0.039 inch

1 cm   *Zentimeter* centimet|re, *Am.* -er = 10 mm = 0.394 inch

1 m   *Meter* met|re, *Am.* -er = 100 cm = 1.094 yards = 3.281 feet

1 km   *Kilometer* kilomet|re, *Am.* -er = 1000 m = 0.621 mile

1 sm   *Seemeile* nautical mile = 1852 m

II. Square Measure

1 mm²   *Quadratmillimeter* square millimet|re, *Am.* -er = 0.002 square inch

1 cm²   *Quadratzentimeter* square centimet|re, *Am.* -er = 100 mm² = 0.155 square inch

1 m²   *Quadratmeter* square met|re, *Am.* -er = 10000 cm² = 1.196 square yards = 10.764 square feet

1 a   *Ar* are = 100 m² = 119.599 square yards

1 ha   *Hektar* hectare = 100 a = 2.471 acres

1 km²   *Quadratkilometer* square kilomet|re, *Am.* -er = 100 ha = 247.11 acres = 0.386 square mile

III. Cubic Measure

1 cm³   *Kubikzentimeter* cubic centimet|re, *Am.* -er = 1000 mm³ = 0.061 cubic inch

1 m³   *Kubikmeter* cubic met|re, *Am.* -er = 1000000 cm³ = 35.315 cubic feet = 1.308 cubic yards

1 RT   *Registertonne* register ton = 2,832 m³ = 100 cubic feet

IV. Measure of Capacity

1 l   *Liter* lit|re, *Am.* -er = 1.760 pints = *U.S.* 1.057 liquid quarts *or* 0.906 dry quart

1 hl   *Hektoliter* hectolit|re, *Am.* -er = 100 l = 2.75 bushels = *U.S.* 26.418 gallons

V. Weight

1 g   *Gramm* gram(me) = 15.432 grains

1 Pfd.   *Pfund* pound (German) = 500 g = 1.102 pounds avdp.

1 kg   *Kilogramm* kilogram(me) = 1000 g = 2.205 pounds avdp. = 2.679 pounds troy

1 Ztr.   *Zentner* centner = 100 Pfd. = 0.984 hundredweight = 1.102 *U.S.* hundredweights

1 dz   *Doppelzentner* = 100 kg = 1.968 hundredweights = 2.204 *U.S.* hundredweights

1 t   *Tonne* ton = 1000 kg = 0.984 long ton = *U.S.* 1.102 short tons

American and British Weights and Measures

1. Linear Measure

1 inch (in.) = 2,54 cm
1 foot (ft)
 = 12 inches = 30,48 cm
1 yard (yd)
 = 3 feet = 91,439 cm
1 perch (p.)
 = 5$\frac{1}{2}$ yards = 5,029 m
1 mile (m.)
 = 1,760 yards = 1,609 km

2. Nautical Measure

1 fathom (f., fm)
 = 6 feet = 1,829 m
1 nautical mile
 = 6,080 feet = 1853,18 m

3. Square Measure

1 square inch (sq. in.)
 = 6,452 cm²
1 square foot (sq. ft)
 = 144 square inches
 = 929,029 cm²
1 square yard (sq. yd)
 = 9 square feet = 8361,26 cm²
1 square perch (sq. p.)
 = 30$\frac{1}{4}$ square yards = 25,293 m²
1 rood
 = 40 square perches = 10,117 a
1 acre (a.) = 4 roods = 40,47 a
1 square mile
 = 640 acres = 258,998 ha

4. Cubic Measure

1 cubic inch (cu. in.)
 = 16,387 cm³
1 cubic foot (cu. ft)
 = 1,728 cubic inches = 0,028 m³
1 cubic yard (cu. yd)
 = 27 cubic feet = 0,765 m³
1 register ton (reg. ton)
 = 100 cubic feet = 2,832 m³

5. Measure of Capacity
Dry and Liquid Measure

1 British *or* **imperial gill (gl, gi.)**
 = 0,142 l
1 British *or* **imperial pint (pt)**
 = 4 gills = 0,568 l
1 British *or* **imperial quart (qt)**
 = 2 pints = 1,136 l
1 British *or* **imp. gallon (imp. gal.)**
 = 4 imperial quarts = 4,546 l

Dry Measure

1 British *or* **imperial peck (pk)**
 = 2 imperial gallons = 9,092 l
1 Brit. *or* **imp. bushel (bu., bus.)**
 = 8 imperial gallons = 36,366 l

1 Brit. *or* **imp. quarter (qr)**
 = 8 imperial bushels = 290,935 l

Liquid Measure

1 Brit. *or* **imp. barrel (bbl, bl)**
 = 36 imperial gallons = 163,656 l

★

1 U.S. dry pint = 0,551 l
1 U.S. dry quart
 = 2 dry pints = 1,101 l
1 U.S. dry gallon
 = 4 dry quarts = 4,405 l
1 U.S. peck
 = 2 dry gallons = 8,809 l
1 U.S. bushel
 = 8 dry gallons = 35,238 l
1 U.S. gill = 0,118 l
1 U.S. liquid pint
 = 4 gills = 0,473 l
1 U.S. liquid quart
 = 2 liquid pints = 0,946 l
1 U.S. liquid gallon
 = 8 liquid pints = 3,785 l
1 U.S. barrel
 = 31$\frac{1}{2}$ liquid gallons = 119,228 l
1 U.S. barrel petroleum
 = 42 liquid gallons = 158,97 l

6. Avoirdupois Weight

1 grain (gr.) = 0,065 g
1 dram (dr.)
 = 27.344 grains = 1,772 g
1 ounce (oz.)
 = 16 drams = 28,35 g
1 pound (lb.)
 = 16 ounces = 453,592 g
1 quarter (qr)
 = 28 pounds = 12,701 kg
 (*U.S.A.* 25 pounds
 = 11,339 kg)
1 hundredweight (cwt.)
 = 112 pounds
 = 50,802 kg (*U.S.A.* 100 pounds
 = 45,359 kg)
1 ton (t.)
 (*a.* long ton) = 20 hundredweights = 1016,05 kg (*U.S.A.*
 a. short ton, = 907,185 kg)
1 stone (st.) = 14 pounds = 6,35 kg

7. Troy Weight

1 grain = 0,065 g
1 pennyweight (dwt.)
 = 24 grains = 1,555 g
1 ounce
 = 20 pennyweights = 31,103 g
1 pound = 12 ounces = 373,242 g